THE ALMANAC

OF AMERICAN

POLITICS

2000

The Senators, the Representatives
and the Governors:
Their Records and Election Results,
Their States and Districts

Michael Barone and Grant Ujifusa
with Richard E. Cohen
and Charles E. Cook Jr.

National Journal

Washington, D.C.

NATIONAL JOURNAL GROUP INC.

Publishers of:

National Journal
Government Executive, CongressDaily, CongressDailyAM
The Hotline, Greenwire, and National Journal's Technology Daily
http://www.nationaljournal.com
also
The Capital Source, The Federal Technology Source and
National Journal Convention Daily, published every four years at the Democratic
and Republican National Conventions
and

The Almanac of American Politics®

Printed in the United States of America by United Book Press. Database design by
CDIS, Inc.; composition by Impressions Book and Journal Services Inc. Distributed to
the trade by Times Books, a division of Random House Inc.

Photographs by Richard A. Bloom, John Eisele, Liz Lynch and Bruce Reedy. For
information regarding photographs, contact: National Journal, 1501 M Street, N.W.,
Washington, D.C. 20005. 202-739-8400. All rights reserved.

ISBN 0-8129-3193-9 (cloth)
ISBN 0-8129-3194-7 (paper)

THE ALMANAC OF AMERICAN POLITICS 2000

Authors: Michael Barone, Grant Ujifusa

Editor: Eleanor Evans

Associate Editor & Research Director: Gideon Berger

Assistant Editor: Cherie Galyean

Research Associates: Jim Barnett, Chris M. Cillizza, Chris Donovan, Anne Keller, Rachel Kennedy

Contributing Editors: Richard E. Cohen, Charles E. Cook, Jr.

Contributing Writers: Jennifer E. Duffy, Louis Jacobson, Amy E. Walter

Editorial Assistant: Keri Weber

Photo Editors: Mari Dominguez, Liz Lynch, Bruce Reedy

Election Results & State Maps: Election Data Services Inc.

Presidential Election Results: NCEC Services Inc.

The Almanac staff would like to thank Amy Hession, Cathryn M. Newson and Troy Schneider for their assistance in the production of this edition.

TABLE OF CONTENTS

10   TABLE OF CONTENTS

12   TABLE OF CONTENTS

GUIDE TO USAGE

The *Almanac of American Politics* is designed to be self-explanatory. The following guide provides a brief description of each section and a list of sources from which information was derived, both of which serve as a road map to understanding the meaning behind the figures. In addition, buyers of the 2000 edition receive exclusive access to the Almanac Web edition where much of this data—including key votes of the 106th Congress and interest group ratings—will be frequently updated. For information on how to register, please see the first insert card bound into this book.

The People

Population. All population figures, excluding unemployment rates and voter registration, are from the Bureau of the Census, U.S. Department of Commerce, Washington D.C. 20230, 301-763-4040. Official April 1, 1990, Census figures are used as well as July 1, 1998, estimates for each state.

Race and Ethnic Origin. For the 1990 Census, the Census Bureau asked people what their race or ethnic origin was. Race, as defined by the Bureau of the Census, reflects the individual respondents' perception of his or her racial identity and does not reflect any biological or anthropological definition. The basic racial categories are: American Indian or Alaska Native; Asian or Pacific Islander; Black; and White. Hispanic origin is defined as an ethnicity, and includes those who classified themselves in one of three specific Hispanic categories on the census form (Cuban, Mexican, Puerto Rican) or as of "other Spanish/Hispanic origin"; *persons of Hispanic origin may be of any race.* The "Other" category was intended to include those persons who do not consider themselves to be in the basic racial or ethnic categories.

Households and Housing Information. A Household is defined as including all persons occupying a housing unit; a Married Couple Family is a household of persons related by marriage. Owner occupied housing units include only single-family houses on less than ten acres with no business or medical office on the property. The value of a housing unit is the respondent's estimate of how much the unit would sell for if it were for sale, and determines Median House Value. Monthly rent is defined as the per-month contract rent agreed to for a unit, regardless of any goods or services that may be included (e.g. utilities), and determines Median Monthly Rent.

Age. The Bureau of the Census defines age as based on the number of years a person completed as of April 1, 1990. This definition was used to determine the voting age population, the percentage of population over 65 years of age, and the median age. Many people, however, provided their age as of the date they completed the census form rather than the definition provided by the Bureau of the Census.

Education. The level of higher education is measured by the Census from persons over 25 years of age who have pursued vocational, public, or private forms of college education not necessarily leading to graduation.

Unemployment. All unemployment figures are from the Bureau of Labor Statistics, U.S. Department of Labor, Washington, D.C. 20210, 202-606-7828. These figures represent the average rate of unemployment for each state for 1998.

Registered Voters. Registered voter numbers are from the individual states' election bureaus or political parties, and represent the number of voters officially registered as close as possible to the November 1998 election. Some states have no voter registration.

Political Lineup. This block includes the names of top state officials as well as a breakdown by party of the state legislative bodies. The names of U.S. senators and a party breakdown of the state's congressional delegation are also provided.

Presidential Vote. The 1992 and 1996 presidential vote is included for each state and congressional district. Presidential vote by state and by congressional district was derived from state, county and precinct results as compiled by the staff of the National Committee for an Effective Congress (NCEC), 122 C Street, NW, Washington, DC 20001, 202-638-8300. The 1992 and 1996 presidential vote by congressional district was recalculated in eight states to reflect redistricting (remapping) changes. The eight states are: Florida, Georgia, Kentucky, Louisiana, New York, North Carolina, Texas and Virginia. Results of the presidential primaries were provided by the states and the FEC. Caucus results are not provided.

Biography. This section lists when each governor, senator and representative was elected or appointed, date and place of birth, home, college education and degrees obtained (if any), religion, marital status and, if applicable, spouse's name. Also listed is a brief outline of the politician's past elected offices, professional career and military service and his or her office addresses and telephone numbers. Committee and subcommittee assignments, as of June 15, 1999, are provided as well. (Note: On many committees, the chairman and ranking minority member are ex officio members of each subcommittee on which they do not hold a regular assignment.)

Ratings

Group Ratings. The congressional rating statistics of 11 interest groups provide an idea of a legislator's general ideology and the degree to which the legislator represents different groups' interests. Not just a record of liberal/conservative voting behavior, these ratings come from a range of groups concerned with everything from single issues (environmental concerns) to the political interests of a particular sector (e.g., businesses). The order of the groups is such that the more "liberal" groups are on the left and the more "conservative" are on the right. Five groups, ACLU, LCV, NFIB, NTLC and CHC provide one rating for the two-year congressional session. Following is a general description of each organization, its address and telephone number.

ADA   Americans for Democratic Action
1625 K St., N.W., #210, Washington, D.C. 20006, 202-785-5980.
Liberal: Since its founding in 1947, ADA members have pushed for legislation designed to reduce inequality, curtail rising defense spending, prevent encroachments on civil liberties and promote international human rights. The ADA uses a broad spectrum of issues for its vote analysis.

ACLU   American Civil Liberties Union
122 Maryland Ave., N.E., Washington, D.C. 20002, 202-544-1681.
Pro-individual liberties: ACLU seeks to protect individuals from legal, executive and congressional infringement on basic rights guaranteed by the Bill of Rights. The ACLU ratings are published for every Congress; the 1998 ratings include the years 1997 and 1998.

AFS   American Federation of State, County and Municipal Employees (AFSCME)
1625 L St., N.W., Washington, D.C. 20036, 202-429-1000.
Liberal Labor: As the nation's largest public employee and health care workers union, representing more than 1.3 million members, AFSCME is committed to achieving dignity and improving working conditions through collective bargaining. The AFSCME voting records are

based on a representative sample of roll call votes from the First and Second Sessions of the 105th Congress.

LCV   League of Conservation Voters
   1707 L St., N.W., #750, Washington, D.C. 20036, 202-785-8683.
   Environmental: Formed in 1970, LCV is the national, non-partisan arm of the environmental movement. LCV works to elect pro-environmental candidates to Congress. LCV ratings are based on key votes concerning energy, environment and natural resource issues, selected by leaders from major national environmental organizations.

CON   Concord Coalition
   1019 19th St., N.W., #810, Washington, D.C. 20036, 202-467-6222.
   Pro-Balanced Budget: The Concord Coalition is a nonpartisan, grassroots organization dedicated to eliminating the federal budget deficit and reforming entitlement programs. The Coalition, with members and active chapters in all 50 states, is determined to educate the American public about the dangers of the federal deficit.

NTU   National Taxpayers Union
   108 N. Alfred St., Alexandria, VA 22314, 703-683-5700.
   Pro-Taxpayer Rights: NTU is the nation's largest and oldest taxpayers' rights group, representing 300,000 members in all 50 states. NTU analyzes roll call votes taken during both sessions of Congress that significantly affect federal taxes, spending, debt or regulatory impact.

NFIB   National Federation of Independent Business
   600 Maryland Ave., S.W., #700, Washington, D.C. 20024, 202-554-9000.
   Pro-Small Business: The National Federation of Independent Business represents small and independent business owners—every kind and size of commerical enterprise; high-tech, family farmers, neighborhood retailers and service companies. Founded in 1943, NFIB gives small and independent business a voice in governmental decision making in Washington, D.C. and all 50 states.

COC   Chamber of Commerce of the United States
   1615 H Street, N.W., Washington, D.C. 20062, 202-659-6000.
   Pro-business: Founded in 1912 as a voice for organized business, COC represents local, regional and state chambers of commerce in addition to trade and professional organizations.

ACU   American Conservative Union
   1007 Cameron St., Alexandria, VA 22314, 703-836-8602.
   Conservative: Since 1971, ACU ratings have provided a means of gauging the conservatism of members of Congress. Foreign policy, social and budget issues are their primary concerns.

NTLC   National Tax-Limitation Committee
   151 North Sunrise Ave., #901, Roseville, CA 95661, 916-786-9400.
   Pro-tax limitation: NTLC was organized in 1975 to seek constitutional and other limits on taxes, spending and deficits at the state and federal levels. NTLC actively pursues a balanced budget/tax limitation amendment to the U.S. Constitution. These ratings are based on budget issue votes and bills which would have a major impact on long-term goverment taxing and spending programs.

CHC   Christian Coalition
   227 Massachusetts Avenue, N.E., #101, Washington, D.C. 20002, 202-547-3600.
   Conservative: Pro-family citizen organization and national lobby founded in 1989 working for family-friendly public policy on a local, state and national level with over 1.5 million members and activists.

National Journal Ratings. *National Journal*'s rating system establishes an objective method of analyzing congressional voting. A panel of *National Journal* editors and staff initially compiled a list of congressional roll call votes and classified them as either economic, social or foreign policy-related. The interrelationship of these votes was shown by a statistical procedure called "principal components analysis," which revealed which "yea" votes and which "nay" votes fit a liberal or a conservative pattern. The votes in each of the three subject areas were computer-weighted to reflect the degree they fit the common pattern. All members of Congress who participated in at least half of the votes in each area received ratings; those who missed more that half the votes were not scored (shown as *). Absences and abstentions were not counted.

Members of Congress were then ranked according to relative liberalism and conservatism. Finally, they were assigned percentiles showing their rank relative to others in their chamber. Percentile scores range from a minimum of 0 to a maximum of 99. Because some members voted liberal or conservative on every roll call, however, there are ties at the liberal and conservative ends of each scale. For that reason, the maximum percentiles often turn out to be less than 99.

Election Results

Election Results. Listed for each member of the House are results of the 1998 general, runoff and primary elections, as well as the 1996 general elections (results of any special elections are also listed). Gubernatorial and senatorial results are presented in a like manner. Votes and percentages are included, indicating the margin of victory (due to the process of rounding up and rounding down, some totals may equal more or less than 100%). Candidates receiving less than 4% of the total vote are grouped together and listed as "Other." Dollar amounts listed to the right of the vote totals are campaign expenditures as reported by the candidate to the Federal Election Commission. Election returns were provided by Election Data Services Inc., 1401 K Street, N.W., #500, Washington, D.C. 20005, 202-789-2004.

Campaign Finance

All data are derived from candidates' campaign finance reports and party reports available from the Federal Election Commission (FEC), 999 E St., NW, Washington, D.C. 20463, 202-694-1000 (toll free, 1-800-424-9530). The dollar figure, in parentheses to the right of the election results, represent the candidates net disbursements (expenditures) for the period beginning January 1, 1997, and ending December 31, 1998. *These figures may not include candidate loans which have been repaid, nor does it include any corrections or amendments filed with the FEC after May 1, 1999.*

Abbreviations

ABC	Americans for Better Childcare Act	AI	Alaska Independent Party
ACLU	American Civil Liberties Union	ANWR	Alaska National Wildlife Refuge
ACP	A Connecticut Party	AS	American Samoa
ACU	American Conservative Union	ASI	American Systems Independent Party (PA)
ADA	Americans for Democratic Action, Americans with Disabilities Act	BGH	Bovine Growth Hormone
		BVP	Brooklyn Voters Party (NY)
		C	Conservative Party (NY)
		CAB	Civil Aeronautics Board
AFDC	Aid to Families with Dependent Children	CAFE	Corporate Average Fuel Economy
AFS	American Federation of State, County & Municipal Employees (AFSCME)	CFA	Consumer Federation of America
		CCP	Change Congress Party

CHC	Christian Coalition
CHOB	Cannon House Office Building
CIA	Central Intelligence Agency
COC	Chamber of Commerce of the United States
COLA	Cost of Living Adjustment
CON	Concord Coalition
DCCC	Democratic Congressional Campaign Committee
DFL	Democratic-Farmer-Labor Party (MN)
DLC	Democratic Leadership Council
DNC	Democratic National Committee
DSCC	Democratic Senatorial Campaign Committee
DSOB	Dirksen Senate Office Building
EMILY	EMILY's List (Early Money is Like Yeast)
ERISA	Employee Retirement Income Security Act
FEC	Federal Election Commission
FR	Freedom Party (NY)
GATT	General Agreement on Tariffs & Trade
GREEN	Green Party
H	Capitol Bldg., House side
HMO	Stop HMO Abuses Party
HSOB	Hart Senate Office Building
I	Independent
IC	Independent Conservative
Ind	Independence Party
INF	Independent Fusion Party
INN	Independent Neighbors Party (NY)
IR	Independent-Republican Party (MN)
ISTEA	Intermodal Surface Transportation Efficiency Act
IVP	Independent Voters Party
JBS	Jobs Party (NY)
L	Liberal Party
LCV	League of Conservation Voters
LHOB	Longworth House Office Building
LIB	Libertarian Party
LIF	Long Island First Party (NY)
MFN	Most Favored Nation

NAFTA	North American Free Trade Agreement
NAP	New Alliance Party (MA)
NARAL	National Abortion Rights Action League
NEA	National Endowment for the Arts
NFIB	National Federation of Independent Business
NRCC	National Republican Congressional Committee
NRSC	National Republican Senatorial Committee
NTLC	National Tax-Limitation Committee
NTU	National Taxpayers Union
P&F	Peace & Freedom Party (CA)
PDP	Popular Democratic Party (PR)
POP	Populist Party
PR	Puerto Rico
PS	Protect Seniors Party (NY)
Ref	Reform Party
RHOB	Rayburn House Office Building
RLDS	Reorganized Church of the Latter Day Saints
RMM	Ranking Minority Member
RNC	Republican National Committee
RP	Republican Moderate Party (AK)
RSOB	Russell Senate Office Building
RTL	Right-to-Life Party
S	Capitol Bldg., Senate side
SDI	Strategic Defense Initiative
SIS	Staten Island Secession Party (NY)
SM	Save Medicare Party (NY)
SOC	Socialist Party
SOL	Solidarity Party (IL)
SWP	Socialist Workers Party (MN)
TFC	Twenty-First Century Party (NY)
TXB	Tax Break Party (NY)
UAW	United Auto Workers
VNS	Voter News Service
VRP	Voters Rights Party (NY)
WIC	Women and Infant Children

KEY VOTES OF THE 105TH CONGRESS

Key Votes. The Key Votes section attempts to illustrate a legislator's stance on important votes where he or she must vote *for* or *against* a national issue. The process grossly oversimplifies the legislative system where months of debate, amendment, pressure, persuasion, and compromise go into a final floor vote. However, the voting record remains the best indication of a member's general ideologies and position on specific issues.

Following is a list of key votes used. A member who was absent, voted present, or who was not in office at the time of a particular vote receives an asterisk. The votes were drawn from Legi-Slate, a computer system tracking legislation, voting attendance, committee schedules, etc. For information on Legi-Slate or their vote recording process, please contact: Legi-Slate, 10 G St., N.E., #500, Washington, D.C. 20002, 202-898-2300.

House Votes, 105th Congress:

1) **Clinton Budget Deal** (HR 2014) Approve budget reconciliation bill implementing tax cuts required by balanced budget agreement. June 26, 1997. Vote No. 245: Passed 253-179; (D: 27-177; R: 226-1).

2) **Education IRAs** (HR 2646) Expand individual retirement accounts to be spent on elementary and secondary education expenses. October 23, 1997. Vote No. 524: Passed 230-198; (D: 15-189; R: 215-8).

3) **Req. 2/3 to Raise Taxes** (HJR 111) Amend the Constitution to require two-thirds votes to raise taxes in the House and Senate. April 22, 1998. Vote No. 102: Failed two-thirds majority 238-186; (D: 25-173; R: 213-12).

4) **Fast-track Trade** (HR 2621) Permit negotiation of international trade-agreement under "fast-track" congressional authority. September 25, 1998. Vote No. 466: Failed 180-243; (D: 29-171; R: 151-71).

5) **Puerto Rico Sthood. Ref.** (HR 856) Schedule referendum on statehood in Puerto Rico. March 4, 1998. Vote No. 37: Passed 209-208; (D: 165-31; R: 43-177).

6) **End Highway Set-asides** (HR 2400) End federal highway program's minority set-aside funding benefits. April 1, 1998. Vote No. 93: Failed 194-225; (D: 3-195; R: 191-29).

7) **School Prayer Amend.** (HJR 78) Amend the Constitution to guarantee the right to prayer in school. June 4, 1998. Vote No. 201: Failed two-thirds majority 224-203; (D: 27-174; R: 197-28).

8) **Ovrd. Part. Birth Veto** (HR 1122) Override President Clinton's veto of ban on partial-birth abortions. July 23, 1998. Vote No. 325: Passed 296-132: (D: 77-123; R: 219-8).

9) **Cut $ for B-2 Bombers** (HR 1119) Cut funding for additional B-2 stealth bombers. June 23, 1997. Vote No. 228: Failed 209-216; (D: 148-53; R:60-163).

10) **Human Rights in China** (HR 1370) Require the Export-Import Bank to give preference, among U.S. firms doing business in China, to those that have adopted a code of conduct on human rights. September 30, 1997. Vote No. 472: Passed 241-182; (D: 181-19; R: 59-163).

11) **Withdraw Bosnia Troops** (HCR 227) Invoke the War Powers Resolution to require the withdrawal of U.S. military forces from Bosnia unless other action is taken. March 18, 1998. Vote No. 58: Failed 193-225; (D: 13-181; R: 180-43).

12) **End Cuban TV-Marti** (HR 4276) Strike funding for TV Marti television broadcasts to Cuba. August 4, 1998. Vote No. 382: Failed 172-251; (D: 142-56; R: 29-195).

Senate Votes, 105th Congress:

1) **Bal. Budget Amend.** (SJR 1) Amend the Constitution to require a balanced budget by 2002. March 4, 1997. Vote No. 24: Failed two-thirds majority 66-34; (D: 11-34; R: 55-0).

2) **Clinton Budget Deal** (S 947) Approve budget reconciliation bill implementing entitlement-spending cuts required by balanced budget agreement. June 25, 1997. Vote No. 130: Passed 73-27; (D: 21-24; R: 52-3).

3) **Cloture on Tobacco** (S 1415) Invoke cloture on the tobacco settlement. June 17, 1998. Vote No. 161: Failed required 60 votes 57-42; (D: 43-2; R: 14-40).

4) **Education IRAs** (HR 2646) Expand education savings accounts to cover private elementary and secondary school expenses. June 22, 1998. Vote No. 169: Passed 59-36; (D: 8-34; R: 51-2).

5) **Satcher for Surgeon Gen.** Confirmation of David Satcher to be U.S. Surgeon General. February 10, 1998. Vote No. 9: Passed 63-35; (D: 44-0; R: 19-35).

6) **Highway Set-asides** (S 1173) Table proposal to end federal highway program's minority set-aside funding benefits. March 6, 1998. Vote No. 23: Passed 58-37; (D: 43-1; R: 15-36).

7) **Table Child Gun locks** (S 2260) Table proposal requiring gun dealers to sell trigger and child safety locks with each handgun. July 21, 1998. Vote No. 216: Passed 61-39; (D: 9-36; R: 52-3).

8) **Ovrd. Part. Birth Veto** (HR 1122) Override President Clinton's veto of ban on partial-birth abortions. September 18, 1998. Vote No. 277: Failed two-thirds majority 64-36; (D: 13-32; R: 51-4).

9) **Chem. Weapons Treaty** (SRES 75) Ratify the treaty barring production, acquisition or use of chemical weapons. April 24, 1997. Vote No. 51: Passed 74-26; (D: 45-0; R: 29-26).

10) **Cuban Humanitarian Aid** (S 955) Provide humanitarian assistance to Cuban citizens. July 17, 1997. Vote No. 183: 38-61; (D: 33-12; R: 5-49).

11) **Table Bosnia Troops** (S 2057) Table proposal to require legislation for continued use of U.S. armed forces in Bosnia. June 24, 1998. Vote No. 171: Passed 65-31; (D: 40-2; R: 25-29).

12) **$ for Test-ban Treaty** (S 2334) Increase funding for expenses related to the nuclear test-ban treaty. September 1, 1998. Vote No. 254: Passed 49-44; (D: 42-0; R: 7-44).

IMPEACHMENT VOTE

The House of Representatives in 1998 debated the impeachment of a president for the first time since the Watergate scandal of 1974, when the Judiciary Committee's votes for three articles of impeachment led to President Richard Nixon's decision to resign. In the case of President Clinton, the House in September voted for a formal inquiry after Independent Counsel Kenneth Starr referred evidence of possible impeachable offenses resulting from Clinton's appearances in a civil deposition and before a federal grand jury. After the Judiciary Committee on December 11 and 12 voted four articles of impeachment, the House held two days of debate and then voted on each charge on December 19.

The first article accused Clinton of violating his constitutional oath by lying to the grand jury in his August 17, 1998, appearance during which he was questioned about his relationship with Monica Lewinsky. In this article, he also was accused of "corrupt efforts to influence the testimony of witnesses and to impede the discovery of evidence" in the Paula Jones civil-rights suit against him. In the second article, Clinton was accused of providing false testimony in his January 17, 1998, deposition in the Jones case. The third article charged Clinton with concealing the existence of evidence in the Jones case by encouraging Lewinsky to file a false affidavit in that case and providing a misleading account to his personal secretary Betty Currie of his activities in question. In the fourth article, the Judiciary Committee accused Clinton of failing to respond to inquiries and providing false and misleading sworn statements to the House of Representatives in its impeachment inquiry.

In voting to approve the first and third articles of impeachment, the House impeached a president for the first time since Andrew Johnson in 1868. Listed below are results of the four votes, plus the Republicans and Democrats who split from their party's majority.

HOUSE VOTE

Article 1
Passed: 228-206

For: 5 D, 223 R   Against: 201 D, 5 R

Reps. Against-5

Amo Houghton (NY-31)   Christopher Shays (CT-4)
Peter T. King (NY-3)   Mark Souder (IN-4)
Constance A. Morella (MD-8)

Dems. For-5

Virgil H. Goode (VA-5)   Charles W. Stenholm (TX-17)
Ralph M. Hall (TX-4)   Gene Taylor (MS-5)
Paul McHale (PA-15)

Article 2
Failed: 205-229

For: 5 D, 200 R

Against: 201 D, 28 R

Reps. Against-28

Richard Burr (NC-5)
Tom Campbell (CA-15)
Michael N. Castle (DE-AL)
Jay W. Dickey (AR-4)
Phil English (PA-21)
John Ensign (NV-1)
Mark Foley (FL-16)
Jim Gibbons (NV-2)
Benjamin A. Gilman (NY-20)
Lindsey Graham (SC-3)
Jim Greenwood (PA-8)
David Hobson (OH-7)
Amo Houghton (NY-31)
Sue W. Kelly (NY-19)

Jay C. Kim (CA-41)
Peter T. King (NY-3)
Scott L. Klug (WI-2)
Rick A. Lazio (NY-12)
Constance A. Morella (MD-8)
Bob Ney (OH-18)
Deborah Pryce (OH-15)
Jim Ramstad (MN-3)
Mark Sanford (SC-1)
Joe Scarborough (FL-1)
E. Clay Shaw Jr. (FL-22)
Christopher Shays (CT-4)
Bud Shuster (PA-9)
Mark Souder (IN-4)

Dems. For-5

Virgil H. Goode (VA-5)
Ralph M. Hall (TX-4)
Paul McHale (PA-15)

Charles W. Stenholm (TX-17)
Gene Taylor (MS-5)

Article 3
Passed: 221-212

For: 5 D, 216 R

Against: 200 D, 12 R

Reps. Against-12

Sherwood L. Boehlert (NY-23)
Michael N. Castle (DE-AL)
Phil English (PA-21)
Amo Houghton (NY-31)
Nancy L. Johnson (CT-6)
Jay C. Kim (CA-41)

Peter T. King (NY-3)
Jim Leach (IA-1)
John M. McHugh (NY-24)
Constance A. Morella (MD-8)
Ralph Regula (OH-16)
Christopher Shays (CT-4)

Dems. For-5

Virgil H. Goode (VA-5)
Ralph M. Hall (TX-4)
Paul McHale (PA-15)

Charles W. Stenholm (TX-17)
Gene Taylor (MS-5)

Article 4
Failed: 148-285

For: 1 D, 147 R

Against: 206 D, 79 R

Reps. Against-79

Charles Bass (NH-2)
Douglas K. Bereuter (NE-1)
Brian P. Bilbray (CA-49)
Sherwood L. Boehlert (NY-23)
Henry Bonilla (TX-23)
Richard Burr (NC-5)
Tom Campbell (CA-15)
Michael N. Castle (DE-AL)
Tom Davis (VA-11)
Jay W. Dickey (AR-4)
Robert L. Ehrlich (MD-2)
Jo Ann Emerson (MO-8)
Phil English (PA-21)
John Ensign (NV-1)
Harris W. Fawell (IL-13)
Mark Foley (FL-16)
Vito Fossella (NY-13)
Bob Franks (NJ-7)
Rodney Frelinghuysen (NJ-11)
Greg Ganske (IA-4)
Wayne T. Gilchrest (MD-1)
Paul E. Gillmor (OH-5)
Benjamin A. Gilman (NY-20)
Porter J. Goss (FL-14)
Kay Granger (TX-12)
Jim Greenwood (PA-8)
Joel Hefley (CO-5)
David Hobson (OH-7)
Amo Houghton (NY-31)
Kenny Hulshof (MO-9)
Bill Jenkins (TN-1)
Nancy L. Johnson (CT-6)
John R. Kasich (OH-12)
Sue W. Kelly (NY-19)
Jay C. Kim (CA-41)
Peter T. King (NY-3)
Scott L. Klug (WI-2)
Jim Kolbe (AR-5)
Steve Largent (OK-1)
Tom Latham (IA-5)

Steven C. LaTourette (OH-19)
Rick A. Lazio (NY-12)
Jim Leach (IA-1)
Frank A. LoBiondo (NJ-2)
Jim McCrery (LA-4)
John M. McHugh (NY-24)
Scott McInnis (CO-3)
David McIntosh (IN2)
Jerry Moran (KS-1)
Constance A. Morella (MD-8)
George Nethercutt (WA-5)
Bob Ney (OH-18)
Anne Northup (KY-3)
Mike Parker (MS-4)
John Edward Porter (IL-10)
Rob Portman (OH-2)
Deborah Pryce (OH-15)
Jack Quinn (NY-30)
Jim Ramstad (MN-3)
Ralph Regula (OH-16)
Frank Riggs (CA-1)
Harold Rogers (KY-5)
Jim Saxton (NJ-3)
Joe Scarborough (FL-1)
John Shadegg (AZ-4)
E. Clay Shaw Jr. (FL-22)
Christopher Shays (CT-4)
John M. Shimkus (IL-20)
Bud Shuster (PA-09)
Mark Souder (IN-4)
W.J. (Billy) Tauzin (LA-3)
Mac Thornberry (TX-13)
John Thune (SD-AL)
Fred Upton (MI-6)
James T. Walsh (NY-25)
Curt Weldon (PA-7)
Gerald C. (Jerry) Weller (IL-11)
Rick White (WA-1)
Edward Whitfield (KY-1)

Dem. For-1

Gene Taylor (MS-5)

Following a trial that began on January 7, 1999, and consumed 14 days of arguments by lawyers for the House and Clinton plus three days of closed-door debate among Senators, the Senate on February 12 rejected the two articles of impeachment from the House; the Constitution required a two-thirds vote to convict, and therefore the president was not removed from office. Listed below are Republicans who voted against the two articles; Democrats were unified in opposition.

SENATE VOTE

First Charge—Perjury
Not Guilty: 54-45

Not Guilty: 45 D, 9 R   Guilty: 0 D, 45 R

Republicans voting Not Guilty

John H. Chafee (R-RI)   Olympia Snowe (R-ME)
Susan Collins (R-ME)   Arlen Specter (R-PA)*
Slade Gorton (R-WA)   Ted Stevens (R-AK)
James M. Jeffords (R-VT)   Fred D. Thompson (R-TN)
Richard C. Shelby (R-AL)   John W. Warner (R-VA)

Second Charge—Obstruction of Justice
Not Guilty: 49-50

Not Guilty: 45 D, 4 R   Guilty: 0 D, 50 R

Republicans voting Not Guilty

John H. Chafee (R-RI)   Olympia Snowe (R-ME)
Susan Collins (R-ME)   Arlen Specter (R-PA)*
James M. Jeffords (R-VT)

* *Arlen Specter voted "Not Proven."*

INTRODUCTION

By Michael Barone

Comes the new millenium, and the temptation is to think a whole new era is about to begin. Since the middle 1980s, American politicians have been saying that the next election will determine the course of the next century; and in a trivial way this of course is always true. The 2000 Election may very well present Americans with a choice between a Republican government and a Democratic government, because the political balance between the two parties is close and American voters, while professing independence, have been voting straight tickets more often in the 1990s than in any decade since the 1940s. A Republican president will likely bring in a Republican House and a Democratic president will likely bring in a Democratic House; Republicans will likely retain control of the Senate, but it is highly unlikely that either party will have the 60 seats needed to stop filibusters and establish working control.

For one-party control, by either party, is unlikely to change the character of the society in the way one-party control shaped it in the 1860s, when the Republicans won the Civil War and freed the slaves, or the 1930s, when the Democrats created the makeshift American welfare state and asserted the primacy of the federal government in controlling the economy. The initiative in shaping public policy is leaching out of Washington, to the states, the localities, the private sector. Since about 1993 crime and welfare have been declining on as steep a curve as the one on which they increased in the awful decade from 1965 and 1975, when crime and welfare tripled. But this was not the work of Washington. The initiative was taken by others— on welfare, most prominently by Wisconsin's Governor Tommy Thompson; on crime, most prominently by New York's Mayor Rudolph Giuliani. Congress's passage and Bill Clinton's signing of the 1996 Welfare Reform Act simply enabled the states and cities to transform welfare more easily. The passage of federal crime laws has made only the most marginal contribution to the huge reduction in crime.

Nor has government done much to contribute to the vast increase in the wealth of ordinary Americans in the 1990s. The maintenance of low-inflation policies has of course contributed: Bill Clinton has had the good sense to follow Ronald Reagan here, and not Jimmy Carter (or, one might add, Richard Nixon). But Clinton can take little credit for the fact that stock ownership, in this decade of equity market growth, has increased from around 20% to around 50% of the American people. The primary cause has been the proliferation of defined contribution pension plans, a trend quietly encouraged by acts of Congress in the 1980s and reaching hurricane force in the 1990s. Indeed, by squelching proposals to include individual investment accounts in Social Security, Clinton (in his capacity as campaign manager for Al Gore) has delayed the public sector from catching up with the private sector here, as it has in other areas of American life.

Where the presidency can make a difference is in foreign policy. But it is hard to predict what that difference will be, and it depends very little on whether the president's party controls Congress. Few people predicted when Bill Clinton was running in 1992 that he would send military forces into or over Haiti, Bosnia, Iraq, Serbia and Somalia. Nor, in the 1990s at least, have many Americans cast their votes on foreign policy. Guesses can be hazarded of what foreign policy decisions various presidential candidates will make, and in some cases those guesses will be based on the candidates' past actions and experience. But it is a feature of the American system, which we take for granted but which arguably makes little sense, that men and women with the greatest foreign policy experience are generally considered ineligible to run. Only two of the dozen or so candidates have actually had experience making foreign policy in the executive branch, the two vice presidents, Al Gore and Dan Quayle. The others, for all their strengths, have never sat in those offices and affected the decisions being made.

So the odds are that, whoever wins in 2000, the basic conditions of American life will not be much changed. And the clear message from the elections of 1996 and 1998 is that most Americans do not want them vastly changed—at least not in ways that government can change them. The 1996 and 1998 elections were, above all, incumbent elections—and a vivid contrast to 1990, 1992 and 1994 in which incumbents in large numbers were eased to the door or booted out. The 1996 and 1998 House election results resembled each other more closely than any pair of House election results since 1976 and 1978, just as the 1992 and 1996 presidential election results resembled each other more closely than any pair since 1952 and 1956.

This left politicians of both parties deeply frustrated. In 1998 Democrats hoped to win a majority in the House, and Republicans hoped to increase their narrow majority. Both had some reason to expect they would succeed. Both failed. The failure of the Republicans was more dramatic, and led Speaker Newt Gingrich to announce his retirement three days later. Both parties had reason to hope that Bill Clinton would help them achieve their goal. Democrats hoped that the 70% job ratings he received after the Monica Lewinsky scandal surfaced on January 21 would help their candidates. It may have, but not enough. Republicans hoped that Clinton's admission August 17 that he lied to the American people would help their candidates. It may have, but after the Starr Report was made public September 11 Clinton's job rating went back up to 70% and many voters were visibly angry with Republicans. The response to the scandal and to impeachment was, among other things, proof of the strength of pro-incumbent fervor: Most Americans believed that things were going well, and did not want change.

And so they voted in November. Republican House candidates beat Democrats by 48.6%–47.7%, a narrow margin almost exactly the same as their 49.0%–48.5% popular vote margin in 1996. Only six incumbents were defeated, one Democrat and five Republicans. The Republican majority of House seats was slightly reduced, to a number perilously close to a minority but also very close to the results after the last two elections: 230 Republicans were elected in 1994 (their numbers went up to 235 by November 1996 because of party switches and special election victories), 227 Republicans were elected in 1996 (which went up to 228 by November 1998) and 223 Republicans were elected in 1998. A straight-line extrapolation of that pattern would give Republicans 218 seats in 2000, a one-vote majority. Of course it is true that the non-presidential party usually picks up seats in non-presidential years, and it has often (but by no means invariably) been the case that the non-presidential party makes major gains in the sixth year of a presidency. But the Republicans made their six-year pickup in Clinton's second year, after he had made the mistake presidents often make in landslide years—overinterpreting his mandate. Clinton, under the tutelage of pollsters Dick Morris and Mark Penn, was careful not to do that thereafter, and most voters liked the results.

Similar results were seen in the Senate races. Only one incumbent senator lost in 1996 and only three in 1998. Republicans had hoped to break even in 1996, and gained two seats; they hoped to make gains in 1998, and instead broke even. As for governorships, Republican incumbents had great victories in 1998, though the party had a net loss of one seat, not to a Democrat but to Reform Party candidate Jesse Ventura in Minnesota. After the elections Republicans held the governorships in seven of the eight largest states and in states with 64% of the nation's population (to 34% for Democrats and 2% for independents). But Democrat Gray Davis won a smashing 58%–38% victory in the largest state, California, and brought in a Democratic legislature and a Democratic near-sweep of top state offices.

The knife-edge margin between Republicans and Democrats in the House reflects the strength of most incumbents—and the weakness of both parties. Both are badly split—Republicans between economic and cultural conservatives, Democrats between New Democrats of the Democratic Leadership Council stripe and left Democrats more comfortable with the AFL-CIO. The Republican split is subjected to intensive scrutiny by a press corps whose members vote about 90% Democratic; the Democratic split, though it has more consequences for public policy—on Social Security and Medicare reform, most notably—is mostly ignored. But even apart from these splits, the parties have fundamental weaknesses, which can be summarized by saying that the Democrats are the fragile party and the Republicans the stupid party.

That the Democrats are the fragile party can easily be ignored, yet it is in line with the historic character of the party, the oldest continuing political party in the world. The Democrats tend to be a collection of out-people, of groups which are regarded by others and themselves as something a little different from ordinary people. At their best these out-people unite and become the in-party; at their worst, they are a fractious rabble. The Democrats are fragile, because their institutional base depends on factors that are contingent, that are here today but may not be tomorrow. One is Bill Clinton's popularity, greater in 1997 or 1998 than when he was running; Clinton, like Grover Cleveland, Woodrow Wilson and John Kennedy, was elected without ever winning an absolute majority of the vote. Clinton's 49.2% of the vote in 1996 was matched, but not exceeded, by House Democrats' 48.5% in 1996 and 47.7% in 1998.

Nor is it clear that Clinton's popularity can automatically be transferred to the vice president he is campaigning for as no president has ever campaigned for any vice president before. In late 1998 and early 1999, when Clinton's job approval hovered around 70%, Al Gore was consistently running behind George W. Bush in polls for 2000. The Clinton-Gore fundraising base—even shorn of the illegal foreign contributions the 1996 campaign gleefully raked in— is awesome and seems committed to Gore. But it is highly dependent on what some might call the Lincoln bedroom factor: the president as fundraiser. Democratic candidates in 1996 and 1998 were heavily dependent on Clinton and Gore to raise money; if Gore is not president in 2001, it is not clear that Democrats will be able to raise nearly as much. Also, without a Democratic veto pen in the White House, a Republican government could pass laws which would vastly reduce the fundraising ability of labor unions and trial lawyers—two major sources of Democratic contributions. Clinton has also done a superb job of raising money from new generations of Jewish contributors, but if the Republican Party presents a face less menacing to them than those of Newt Gingrich and the Christian right, their contributions might also be harder to come by. And, while the Democrats are strong in California, they are in disarray in other large states—New York, Pennsylvania, Ohio, Michigan, Illinois—where they are finding it hard to generate good candidates for higher office as well as raise money. The Democrats in the years after 2000, if they are not successful then, may find themselves in the institutionally weak position they were in in the 1920s and 1950s.

As for the Republicans, they often bring to mind Benjamin Disraeli's description of his fellow Conservatives as "the stupid party." The fact is that a disproportionate number of talented people interested in government and politics in this country are Democrats, presumably because smart Democrats like government and political careers and smart Republicans dislike government and prefer to stay in the private sector. The Democrats, the party of bureaucracy, tend to produce political entrepreneurs; the Republicans, the party of entrepreneurs, tend to produce political bureaucrats. So we have the Republican House leaders, in a time when voters are full of contentment, raise provocative issues and scheme to depose their own speaker. And when the advantages of incumbency are overwhelming and the Republicans hold even in open House races, more of their incumbents than the Democrats' manage to lose elections. In the 2000 presidential race, the Republican primary field is swelled by candidates with credentials no one has ever before found convincingly presidential and who are determined to raise provocative issues in a way which seems sure to antagonize contented voters. Democrats in the 1990s, unlike the 1980s, have managed to keep their obstreperous left-wingers mostly out of public view; many Republicans seem determined to thrust their obstreperous right-wingers into the spotlight, and the anti-Republican press is happy to help. The Democrats in the 20 years between 1974–94 often held their House and Senate majorities thanks only to the superior skills of political entrepreneurs who were able to carry states and districts which didn't much like Democratic policies. The Republicans in the 20 years starting in 1994 seem at risk of losing

House and Senate majorities because of the inferior skills of political bureaucrats who are unable to carry states and districts which don't mind Republican policies at all.

Still, a stupid party isn't necessarily doomed. Disraeli spent 22 years of his political career in opposition, but in the 130 years after he became prime minister in 1868, the Conservatives controlled the government for 90. American voters have been instructed by the press for the last third of the century to loath and despise the Republicans, but Republicans have held the presidency for 20 of the last 32 years and—despite negative polls, despite the personal unpopularity of Newt Gingrich, despite many weak candidates—voters have now elected Republican congressional majorities three times in a row, for the first time since the 1920s. Their margins have been too narrow for them to claim plausibly that they have a natural majority or, if they are sensible, to act as if they do. The Republican Congress, like the Reagan Presidency, is not a hideous and inexplicable accident, as many Democrats like to think; it has been voted in for reasons that are rational and explicable, and despite the party's many weaknesses.

1998: THE POLITICS OF SOGGINESS

How was the 1998 election different from all other elections? Not in party strength: Republicans and Democrats won almost exactly the same percentages of the vote and number of House seats as in 1996. Nor was there any great mandate for change: Only a handful of incumbents were defeated, and most were re-elected by wide margins. Not even in turnout: Apart from some local variations, the 36% turnout was within the same 36%–40% range of all off-year elections in the past quarter-century. What was different about this election was a fundamental change in mood. In 1998, Americans voted against what a classic 1988 editorial in *The Economist* called "crunchiness" and for what the magazine called "sogginess." What do these words mean? "Crunchy systems are those in which small changes have a big effect," *The Economist* editorialist declared. Crunchy choices are binary; the light switch is either off or on, with clearly distinct consequences. "Sogginess," the editorial continued, "is comfortable uncertainty." Soggy choices make no crisply defined differences; adjusting the dimmer makes only a marginal, perhaps imperceptible change.

According to *The Economist*'s theory, crunchiness and sogginess work in cyclical fashion, the one giving rise to the other. "Crunchiness brings wealth. Wealth leads to sogginess." But crunchiness and sogginess do not produce the same results in government, or in the life of a nation. Crunchiness prevents wars and wins them. Sogginess provokes and prolongs them. Personifying crunchiness are two great leaders who literally charged to greatness in 1898, just 100 years before the 1998 election, Theodore Roosevelt in the charge up San Juan Hill and Winston Churchill at the Battle of Omdurman. Two years later, in the first year of the new century, both first won national office, Churchill as a member of Parliament, Roosevelt as vice president. But at Versailles it was Woodrow Wilson, with his soggy ideas of internationalism and self-determination of peoples, who was in charge rather than the crunchy Roosevelt, and the great chance for a lasting peace was lost. In the interwar period, Prime Ministers Stanley Baldwin and Neville Chamberlain, believers in soggy appeasement, were no match for the crunchy totalitarians Hitler and Stalin. It took Churchill and the congenial but crunchy Franklin Roosevelt, who had closed the banks, defied the malefactors of great wealth and designed the great American war machine, to save Western civilization.

In the postwar years, presidents such as Harry Truman and Dwight Eisenhower set crunchy limits to Soviet expansion; they were set aside by soggy strategists who tried to fight half-a-war in Vietnam and allowed Soviet advances for the sake of detente. At home, the crunchy rules of civic morality of the 1950s produced a nation with low levels of crime and welfare, high levels of family stability and socially upward mobility; the soggy relativism of the Great Society years saw a tripling of crime and welfare and a skyrocketing rate of divorce. Crunchy economic rules barring budget deficits or dollar devaluation undergirded the growth and prosperity of a quarter-century; the soggy relativism of Keynesianism produced stagnant growth and nearly uncontrollable inflation—the stagflation of the 1970s.

In the early 1980s, Americans sensed their country was in trouble and called in the genially crunchy Ronald Reagan. In the prosperous, peaceful late 1990s, they have been comfortable with the incorrigibly soggy Bill Clinton. And they were deeply uncomfortable with the aggressive crunchiness of the most visible congressional Republican, Newt Gingrich. The results of the 1998 elections—and elections are always a crunchy process—produced no significantly different partisan balance. But they did produce very different outcomes for the two party leaders. For the soggy Clinton the result was soggy: It became less likely that he would be impeached, and unthinkable that he would be removed from office, though his personal popularity suffered to some unclear extent. For the crunchy Gingrich, the outcome was crunchy: he was forced to retire in just three days.

In 1998 voters were displeased with candidates who confronted them with stark (crunchy) choices and pleased with those who presented them with soothing (soggy) consensus. Not all of the latter were Democrats. Republican governors like George W. Bush and gubernatorial candidates like Jeb Bush in Florida were rewarded for presenting consensus-minded policies and visions of the future that are well to the right of Clinton's. In California, outgoing Governor Pete Wilson was considered a moderate, but he presented choices in a crunchy way: vote up or down for aid to illegal immigrants or racial quotas and preferences. Wilson was succeeded by Democrat Gray Davis, who said he would steer clear of such "wedge issues" and instead try to govern by consensus.

Sogginess comes naturally to a country that is fat and happy and optimistic, like America today. That is not at all apparent to many in Washington, focused as they were on the Clinton scandals and lamenting low voter turnout (as if the quality of the outcome would be improved by the input of the indifferent) and negative campaign ads (as if candidates for real offices, like candidates for second-grade president, are supposed to say only nice things about each other). But a quick look at the 1998 VNS exit poll shows an almost giddy sense of optimism. A solid 59% said the country is going in the right direction, while only 37% said it is off on the wrong track. That was the most positive response recorded around election time since Elmo Roper Jr. invented the question in 1973—even more positive than in 1984, when Ronald Reagan surged to re-election with ads proclaiming, "It's morning in America." That commercial, shot through gauze across the broad lawns of a small-town street, recalled an idealized past; later 1990s optimism, as in Bill Clinton's promise to "build a bridge to the 21st Century," was about a high-tech, multicultural, non-judgmental future. Sociologist Alan Wolfe described in his 1998 book, *One Nation, After All,* suburban middle-class Americans as not deeply divided on values, but ambivalent within themselves, tolerant sometimes to the point of indifference to principle. Underlying this attitude was not only good-heartedness toward one's fellow citizens but also a pervasive cheeriness about the country and its future. The 200 suburbanites whom Wolfe interviewed in depth cringed at crunchy choices and eagerly embraced soggy alternatives. Asked about affirmative action, one man said that it should apply to everybody. Or, as Bill Clinton put it in 1995, "Mend it, don't end it"—without ever defining what "mend it" meant.

The voters' optimism was reflected in the re-election of just about every visible incumbent. Only three incumbent senators were beaten: Democrat Carol Moseley-Braun of Illinois was felled by scandal, New York Republican Alfonse D'Amato lost in a Democratic state when he finally drew a strong opponent and 70-year-old Lauch Faircloth of North Carolina lost to a much smoother, heavy-spending trial lawyer. Two incumbent governors lost: Republican David Beasley of South Carolina was inundated by a tsunami of video poker money, and Republican Fob James of Alabama fell victim to his own zany behavior and lazy campaigning. Just seven House members lost, one in a primary, five Republicans and one Democrat in November—the lowest number of House members beaten in the last 50 years. For the first time in 50 years, incumbent House members of both parties raised their share of the vote: 78% of Republicans and 73% of Democrats won higher percentages in 1998 than in 1996, and a dozen of the rest had lower percentages in 1998 only because they had no major party opposition in 1996 but did in 1998. Usually when Republicans' percentages go up, Democrats' go down, and vice versa. Not so in 1998: both parties incumbents thrived. The Republican stand-pat strategy failed to win seats, because this year, as in the 1970s and 1980s, with few favorable open seats open, Republican challengers had to beat Democratic members who had the advantage of incumbents too.

The resulting close partisan balance in a country with a taste for sogginess rather than crunchiness leaves one with a soggy uncertainty about what comes next. "We won," said Dick Gephardt after the election—but he is still House Minority Leader. The election was a victory for Bill Clinton and a defeat for Newt Gingrich, but it was not a victory for either party. Both fell short of their goals: Republicans failed to make the gains they had, with some reason, expected to make; Democrats failed to win the majority that they wanted and that they argued plausibly in spring 1998 was within their grasp. Republicans may have lost the confidence that history was moving inexorably in their direction. But Democrats have no cause for confidence that it is moving inexorably in theirs.

The weakness of the parties can be seen in 1998's most striking gubernatorial result. This was not the victory of Gray Davis in Caliornia or that of George W. Bush in Texas, but that of Jesse Ventura in Minnesota. Suburban mayor, former professional wrestler, Reform party nominee, Ventura was trailing in every poll. But he beat Democrat-turned-Republican Norma Coleman, the reform mayor of St. Paul, and he beat Democratic-Farmer-Labor party heir and tobacco-wars-victor Skip Humphrey. In the only state Ronald Reagan never carried, Humphrey won only 28% of the vote, less than half the 60% his father won in his first Senate race 50 years before. Ventura's victory, plus Ross Perot's rise to the top of the polls in spring 1992 and Colin Powell's poll leads in fall 1995, are signs that voters are ready to abandon the major parties for a candidate who provides what they want. What they wanted in the crunchy early 1990s were crisply articulated choices. What they wanted in the soggy late 1990s was consensus-minded, can't-we-all-get-along leadership.

The country has gone from crunchy to soggy within the decade. In 1990, voters had a hearty appetite for crunchiness. After all, the still-fresh triumphs of the 1980s—the revival of the economy after the Reagan tax cuts, the American victory in the Cold War—seemed to be products of crunchy policies. Suddenly, with recession, times looked hard, and hard times elicit crunchiness: politicians of both parties had just raised taxes; the economy was sagging; housing prices—then the major source of personal wealth—were plunging in the Northeast and in California; American troops were being dispatched to the Persian Gulf. Voters responded in November 1990 by giving lower percentages to incumbents of both partes—the first time this had happened since World War II and the exact opposite of what happened in 1998. As one lobbyist said, "It's a tough year for the overdog." In 1992, voters again gave incumbents of both parties lower percentages, and the number of incumbents who retired or lost was the highest since 1948. The voters of 1992 ousted the incumbent president and seemed preprared for two months to elect an eccentric Texas billionaire. Then in 1994, they ousted Democrats from control of the Senate and—for the first time in 40 years—the House.

These were all victories for crunchiness. George Bush had won after a crunchy campaign, with its "Read my lips, no new taxes" pledge and its attack on Michael Dukakis for backing (as he had over 11 years) weekend furloughs for prisoners sentenced to life without parole. But Bush quickly became soggy, pledging a "kinder and gentler" administration and breaking the no-new-taxes pledge in June 1990. In contrast, Gingrich, just elected minority whip by 2 votes, opposed the tax increase. In 1992, Bush faced two crunchy challengers, first Patrick Buchanan and then Perot, and saw his support dwindle that spring well before Bill Clinton's began to rise. Clinton, with his pledge to "end welfare as we know it" and to address "the economy, stupid," seemed sufficiently crunchy during the campaign. But then his support of an ever-changing health care finance plan and his flower-child stands on cultural issues made him seem pretty soggy.

But soggy was not yet in fashion. The 1994 election turned out to be a triumph for Republican crunchiness. It was personified in Newt Gingrich's Contract with America, with its specific promises to bring 10 measures to a vote. (The Contract was imitated by the winning center-left Ulivo coalition in Italy in April 1996 and the victorious New Labour Party in Britain in May 1997.) Republicans crunchily pinned responsibility for the unpopular tax increase of 1993 on every Democrat who voted for it, since it passed both chambers by just one vote. And they were helped by other crunchy issues as well: gays in the military and gun control. The mood was apparent in culture as well as politics: Pop-culture critic Steven Stark has made the point that the two big film hits of 1994 were *Forrest Gump* and *The Lion King*, the first strongly anti-elite, the second pro-patriarchy—and both in tension with a president whose administration seemed permeated with elite feminism.

But the crunchy early 1990s gave way to the soggy late 1990s. Voters grew uncomfortable with the fierce rhetoric of revolutionary Republicans, and Clinton exploited the April 1995 Oklahoma City bombing by conflating the anger of critics of government with the rage of the bombers. Voters also deeply disliked the crunchy 1995–96 government shutdown, the Republicans' insistence that Clinton must sign their appropriations bills or have no government at all. More important, life in America was improving. Voters had been seeking reform—fiscal balance, welfare changes, crime control, better education—in a public sector that was not working well. A combination of the Clinton tax increase in 1993 and the Republicans' one-year standstill in federal spending in 1995 put the budget on the path to balance. The Republican-passed welfare reform, signed by Clinton after much hesitation in August 1996, freed up governors who were already reforming welfare and enabled them to cut the rolls by amazing percentages. Crime rates suddenly started falling with remarkable speed, as innovative mayors followed the lead of New York's Rudolph Giuliani. By 1998, even education reform was gaining steam, with charter schools, school choice, tougher standards and greater accountability.

Results were beginning to be perceptible by 1996. Americans were enjoying the benefits of low-inflation economic growth. And if incomes were rising not quite as vigorously as they had in the 1980s, wealth was rising more rapidly—not just the great wealth of entrepreneurs, but the wealth of ordinary people, as the percentage of Americans owning stocks doubled and the stock market zoomed upward. Crime and welfare were sharply declining, since 1993 on as steep a curve downward as they had risen upward in 1965–75. Then for nearly two decades crime and welfare plateaued, or changed slightly without much regard for the business cycle, and the idea grew among the elites that such high rates of crime and welfare were inevitable in a society as unequal and unfair as ours. Now suddenly, many things were getting very much better; it was not just "the economy, stupid" that accounted for voters' contentment.

In this atmosphere, the demand for crunchy solutions waned and the appetite for soggy rhetoric grew. Bill Clinton understood this better than the Republicans, and he won by a bigger margin in 1996 than House Republicans did. Governors of both parties also understood quite well what was happening: It was no accident that Republican governors associated with welfare reform and tough-on-crime policies were re-elected by very large marins in 1998 in big and often-Democratic states like Michigan, New York, Pennsylvania, Massachuetts and Wisconsin. Nor did the Lewinsky scandal change voters' attitudes. After it broke in January 1998, not only Clinton's job rating, but the job ratings of Clinton critics like Alfonse D'Amato rose sharply—as if voters, confronted with the possibility of the president's ouster, were saying, please, please, please don't let anything change. And don't hold anyone accountable either, at least in the opinion of Steven Stark, who has pointed out that the leading pop culture events of 1998 were the last *Seinfeld* episode and the movie *Titanic*. Both featured immature, self-absorbed people seeking personal gratificaton with little concern for anyone else. If the success of *Forrest Gump* and *The Lion King* showed that people were sick of Clinton in 1994, the success of *Seinfeld* and *Titanic* in 1998 showed that people wanted to keep Clinton, no matter what.

And so the move from confrontation to consensus, from arguments to agreement, from crunchiness to sogginess. The sogginess is personified by Clinton himself, a leader who tries to leave everyone more or less pleased, and who uses his charm and verbal skills, honed at governors' conferences and Democratic Leadership Council meetings, to proclaim a "third way," on which everyone can agree and be friends. A similar distaste for argument and confrontation became apparent in other democracies. In Britain, the crunchiness of Margaret Thatcher had given way to the sogginess of Tony Blair, who explained on election night in May 1997 that there was no reason for political argument anymore now that New Labour was in power. In Italy, the Ulivo coalition, in its final rally in April 1996 flew over Rome's Piazza del Popolo a banner reading, *"Un Italia, forte e serena"*—an Italy strong and calm. It was a meaningful contrast from the banner at the 1984 Republican National Convention in Dallas that read, "America—better, stronger, prouder": a crunchy nation seeks to be proud, a soggy nation to be calm.

Crunchiness is not necessarily conservative and sogginess is not necessarily liberal. George W. Bush in Texas defined his policies as "compassionate conservatism" and, after winning narrowly in 1994, built a consensus around positions notably to the right of Clinton's—tort reform, welfare reform including delivery of services through faith-based institutions, tougher penalties for crime, tax cuts, autonomy for local school districts. Some of these positions were originally crunchy, but by 1998 in Texas they were the essence of sogginess—just about everyone seemed to agree, and Bush was re-elected with 69% of the vote. Other Republicans achieved similar consensus after some controversy, and at points of varying distance to the right of Clinton—George Pataki and Rudolph Giuliani in New York, Tom Ridge in Pennsylvania, George Voinovich in Ohio, John Engler in Michigan, Tommy Thompson in Wisconsin.

At the same time, some Democrats sounded positively crunchy. In the 1998 campaign, Al Gore tried to draw sharp distinctions between Democrats and Republicans on Social Security, education and impeachment. This was partly a matter of falling into the traditional vice presidential role of attack dog, but it also reflected a genuine streak of strong partisanship. Gore speaks privately as well as publicly with sharp animosity toward Republicans, and he has never been much inclined to work across party lines; he showed his crunchiness as well in his book *Earth in the Balance* with its extreme environmentalism, and in debates in his losing performance against Dan Quayle in 1992 and his winning performances against Ross Perot in 1993 and Jack Kemp in 1996. In contrast, Bush speaks only respectfully about Democrats, and indeed worked so cooperatively with them in Austin that he was endorsed for re-election by the Democratic incumbent lieutenant governor. It is possible that in the 2000 presidential race the Republican will seem more soggy and the Democrat more crunchy—a reversal of 1996

In 1998 both parties failed to come up with a consensus-minded national message capable of capturing the voters' imaginations in 2000. The congressional Republicans' stand-pat message protected most of their incumbets, though not quite enough to prevent some losses, but it did nothing to help Republican challengers in that soggy year. The Democrats did not have much of a strategy either. The big government programs they advanced through the year mostly fizzled—campaign finance reform; the tobacco tax; and, only slightly more successful, HMO regulation. Their October mantra of saving Social Security and spending more on education was of only marginal help. And neither seems likely to be sustainable in 2000. In 1999 Clinton declined to advance a serious Social Security reform, while the number of seniors worried that their benefits won't be paid is declining and the number of baby boomers and generation Xers concerned that the current system will implode before they reach retirement is on the rise. And on education, the emphasis is shifting from spending to reform, on which a Democratic advantage is by no means guaranteed.

But what matters in the long run is not campaigning but governing. Sogginess can win an election, but ultimately it can't govern. "Crunchiness brings wealth. Wealth leads to sogginess," *The Economist* editorial begins. But there is more. "Sogginess brings poverty. Poverty creates crunchiness." But perhaps all is not as appears. Consider Bill Clinton. In many ways he is all sogginess. But at the same time, his soggy success owes much to a substratum of crunchiness. There is the crunchiness of hard money: Clinton, guided by Treasury Secretary Robert Rubin, has had the wisdom to understand that he must please Federal Reserve Board Chairman Alan Greenspan and the international marketplace by maintaining a strong dollar. No soggy inflation as in the Carter years. There is the crunchiness of military hegemony: Clinton has shown few traces of the neo-isolationism of George McGovern or the near-pacifism of Michael Dukakis. There is the crunchiness of Clinton's acceptance of the work requirements that have reformed welfare and the "no broken windows" police tactics that have cut crime. There is always the danger, though, of warm sogginess thawing the crunchy permafrost. From 1994 to 1997 the Clinton economic strategists undercut hard money when they urged devaluation on Mexico, Thailand, South Korea and Indonesia. But in 1998 they weren't urging it on China or Japan. Clinton's inclination to settle foreign crises with a soggy verbal formula has worked in some places, but may not continue to do so in the very crunchy cases of Iraq and North Korea. His March 1999 bombing of Serbia to "degrade" its military capacity plus his pledge not to use ground troops left him the option of a soggy exit but put crunchiness on the side of letting Milosevic pursue his ethnic cleansing of Kosovo.

How will the 2000 election be different from all other elections? It seems likely to be an election with no incumbent in a pro-incumbent time, an election that may match New Democrats and New Republicans at a time when the partisan balance is close to even: Clinton won with 49% in 1996 and House Republicans won with 49% in 1996 and 1998. Clinton's victories in 1992 and 1996 stand for the proposition that New Democrats beat Old Republicans, and the House Republicans' victories in 1994, 1996 and 1998 stand for the proposition that New Republicans beat Old Democrats. But we have little evidence for what will happen if New Democrats face New Republicans in 2000. Moreover, voters are likely to face a crunchy choice of a Republican government or a Democratic government. In the late 1990 they have been satisfied with the soggy choice of divided government, but they have also voted straight tickets more often. With the presidency open and the Senate and House narrowly divided, it is entirely possible that one party will take all three and quite likely that the same party will win the presidency and the House. Which leaves the last and most fateful open question, for 2001 and after: can the president's party, having won with a presumably soggy campaign in a soggy-minded country, maintain and strengthen the crunchy underpinnings that give this happy country the luxury of sogginess?

THE AMERICA OF THE EXIT POLLS
The America revealed in the presidential and congressional election results and the exit polls of the late 1990s is an America deeply divided, more along cultural than along economic lines, and increasingly along regional lines. Those who see economics as the motive force in political decisions will find only modest support in the results. The Voters' News Service 1998 exit poll showed the lowest income group (under $15,000) voting 57%–39% Democratic in House races, but that was only 8% of the electorate, and the next group ($15,000-$30,000) was only 53%–44% Democratic—not much of an aggrieved proletariat there. But neither were high-income groups heavily Republican. Half the voters reported incomes over $50,000, but they voted only 53%–45% Republican—not much of a plutocracy. And, despite all the talk of generational politics, there were no major differences by age. Interestingly, voters over 65 were 54%–43% Republican, an indication that the days are gone when the Social Security or Medicare issues could swing them to Democrats. Voters under 45 were even: an indication that neither party has yet inherited the future.

Differences are much greater along lines of race. Whites voted 55%–42% for Republicans, blacks 88%–11% for Democrats. Hispanics voted 59%–35% Democratic, much less than Clinton's 1996 margin of 73%–20%, and in fact closer to the percentages for whites than for blacks. But these national figures mask regional differences: California Latinos voted 78% for Democrat Gray Davis for governor, while Republican gubernatorial candidates won majorities or near-majorities of Hispanics in Florida and Texas. With 5% of the national vote and rising, and a disproportionate number of swing voters, Hispanics will be a major target for both parties in 2000. Asian-Americans, portrayed by some activists as a minority in need of special help from government, voted Democratic, but by only 54%–42%. That was a Democratic gain from 1996, when they were 48%–43% for Dole over Clinton; this trend reflects the good Democratic trend in California, where nearly 40% of Asian American voters live.

But the factor which divided voters more than anything else was religion. Definitions here are imprecise, and categories incommensurate between polls, but the chasm between groups is enormous. White voters who classified themselves as "religious right" (13% of the total) voted 73%–24% Republican—the most Republican demographic group in the VNS polls. Jews (3%) and those with no religion (9%) voted 78%–21% and 65%–32% Democratic. White Protestants gave Republicans a big margin, 64%–34%, and white Catholics a small one, 50%–47%. These numbers track closely with the 1996 exit polls.

Another factor that stands out in the results is education. From the New Deal up through the Reagan years, the pattern was clear: The least educated voters were the most Democratic, the most educated were the most Republican. But in the 1990s that has changed. In the 1998 VNS exit poll those who had not graduated from high school voted 57%–41% Democratic; but they were only 5% of the electorate, and are tilted heavily toward low-income seniors, still voting for (or less often, against) Franklin Roosevelt. The three middle groups, making up 69% of the electorate, were closely divided, with small increases for Republicans as incomes rise. High school graduates voted 49%–47% Democratic, those with some college 51%–45% Republican and college graduates 53%–44% Republican. But those with post-graduate degrees voted 52%–45% Democratic, and they were 18% of the electorate. Why? These graduate school degree holders are not just doctors and lawyers, but also teachers and social workers whose credentials earn them higher pay in government jobs under public employee union contracts; they reflect the liberal culture of the care-giving professions. They provided Democrats with less than half again as big a margin in popular votes than the party's former core constituency of non-high school graduates, and in states like New York are now the Democratic core constituency.

One of the most striking features of late 1990s elections is how voters in Democratic regions have become more Democratic, and voters in Republican regions have become more Republican. This is partly a result of local responses to national issues, but it is also a reflection in a country with enormous geographic and social mobility how people seem to be seeking their own kind. Many commentators in the national media have noted that Republicans have become a kind of endangered species in the Northeast, and point out accurately that there are only four Republican congressmen left in New England, arguably the historic heartland of the Republican Party. True enough, and significant. But the same commentators do not always notice that there are only five Democratic congressmen left in the Rocky Mountain states, arguably the heartland of William Jennings Bryan's Democratic Party but not the home base or college site of many of today's media elite. Since the Rocky Mountain states have grown more rapidly than New England, they have one more congressmen (and will have a bigger advantage after the 2000 Census); so the Democrats' 19–4 edge in New England is pretty much balanced off by the Republican's 19–5 edge in the Rocky Mountains. To which one might add the Great Plains states running north from Oklahoma to North Dakota, which elected 14 Republicans and one Democrat to the House in 1998.

The interesting point here is that both New England and the Rocky Mountain states have become much more monopartisan in the 1990s. As recently as 1992 they elected much more evenly divided delegations, New England 15–8 Democratic, and the Rocky Mountains 13–11 Republican. What we are looking at here is something reminiscent of the realignment in House elections in the 1930s. In 1932, when the economy was in collapse and Franklin Roosevelt was elected on an ambiguous platform, Democrats in House contests made uniform gains in all regions of the country, winning dozens of seats that never went Democratic before—and some that would never go Democratic again. In the 1934 election Democrats gained nine seats, winning seats in the industrial, factory districts which had gained population rapidly—a harbinger of the industrialized, unionized base of the Democratic Party for the next 30 years. In the three elections of 1994, 1996 and 1998, Republicans consolidated gains in House seats in areas where support for their policies was strong, and lost few enough in areas where opposition was strong to maintain their new majority. Which is not to say that they are guaranteed a majority for as long as the New Deal Democrats, but only that they represent a major force in public opinion, less visible in the precincts of the Washington-New York elite but as widely disseminated across the country as the New Deal majority of 1934.

REGION	PRESIDENT (R-D-I %)	HOUSE (R-D %)
United States 1998		**49-48**
Northeast Corridor		40-58
South Atlantic		54-42
Mississippi Valley		51-47
Interior		57-39
Pacific Rim		43-52
United States 1996	**41-49-8**	**49-49**
Northeast Corridor	31-59-8	41-58
South Atlantic	46-46-7	55-45
Mississippi Valley	41-49-9	49-48
Interior	48-42-8	56-41
Pacific Rim	38-51-8	45-51
United States 1994		**52-45**
Northeast Corridor		44-52
South Atlantic		58-41
Mississippi Valley		54-45
Interior		57-40
Pacific Rim		48-49
United States 1992	**37-43-19**	**46-51**
Northeast Corridor	33-49-17	43-52
South Atlantic	43-41-16	49-49
Mississippi Valley	38-43-18	46-51
Interior	40-36-23	48-49
Pacific Rim	33-45-21	41-55
United States 1990		**45-53**
Northeast Corridor		42-54
South Atlantic		44-55
Mississippi Valley		46-53
Interior		48-51
Pacific Rim		44-52
United States 1988	**53-46**	**45-54**
Northeast Corridor	49-51	42-54
South Atlantic	60-39	48-52
Mississippi Valley	53-46	46-54
Interior	57-42	49-50
Pacific Rim	50-48	43-55

To understand the contours of opinion across the country, let us examine the political responses in all regions of the country, divided along lines give meaning to the trends of the 1990s. Divide the country into five regions, four of which each include about one-sixth of the voters, the other about one-third. The first is New England and the Metroliner Corridor—the six states of New England and the New York, Philadelphia, Baltimore and Washington metropolitan areas down to the Potomac River. The second is the South Atlantic from Virginia south to Florida. The third is the Mississippi Valley—a bit more than one-third of the nation—from Upstate New York to Louisiana, from Minnesota to Alabama—the part of America which was settled from the 1770s to the 1850s and the great industrial base of the nation. The fourth region is the great Interior, the Great Plains and Rocky Mountain states from Texas to Idaho (and includes Alaska): the Great American Desert, as it was referred to in the years just before and after the Civil War. Finally there are the Pacific Rim states, California, Oregon, Washington and Hawaii, those far American outposts in the 19th Century and now our redoubts on the Pacific facing Asia. Each has its great economic capitals generating commerce and looking to the world beyond—New York, Atlanta, Chicago, Dallas, Los Angeles—and each has its own combinations of cultural attitudes and economic interests that send its politics in a different direction. Let us look at each region in turn.

New England/Metroliner Corridor. Throughout the late 1990s, reporters have been writing that voters were repelled by Republican revolutionaries and the religious right, that they supported Bill Clinton in overwhelming, if not always enthusiastic, majorities, that they were especially annoyed by opponents of abortion and supporters of impeachment and—while not interested in higher taxes—they were queasy about the prospect of dismantling government. This was an accurate picture—of one-sixth of the nation. The Northeast Corridor voted 59%–31% for Bill Clinton in 1996 and 58%–41% and 58%–40% for House Democrats in 1996 and 1998. This is the one region that moved toward the Democrats in the 1990s: in the three House elections of 1988–92 it produced an 11% Democratic margin; in the three House elections of 1994–98 it produced a 14% Democratic margin. In contrast the rest of the country moved from a 6% Democratic margin in 1988–92 to a 7% Republican margin in 1994–98.

The Northeast Corridor in the late 1990s voted more like post-Thatcher Britain than like the rest of the United States. Like Prime Ministers Margaret Thatcher and John Major, Northeast Corridor Governors William Weld, George Pataki, Christie Whitman and Tom Ridge have slashed spending and cut taxes; since the defeats of Neil Kinnock in Britain in 1992 and Jim Florio in New Jersey in 1993 it has become an article of faith that voters will not countenance a tax increase. But with the threat of tax increases removed, other issues come forward. Privatization has not gone as far in the Northeast Corridor as in Britain, and many people here, especially in and around New York, have got a government-connected niche which they are loath to give up. On cultural issues, the Northeast Corridor is not as secular or liberation-minded as Britain, but it's getting there. Nominal Catholics do not take the church's teaching on abortion or other issues seriously, and there are very few tradition-minded conservatives here. Nor is American exceptionalism—the idea that this country is special and different, a moral beacon for the world—very congenial in an area where many people think most people west of the Hudson wear sheets and hoods. Then there is style. The Northeast Corridor prizes articulateness and doesn't much mind corruption. The rancor of many Republicans and the earnestness of others turn Northeasterners off, while Bill Clinton's skill with words and off-and-on relationship with the truth play well.

But too much has been made of the Northeast Corridor's anti-Republican trend. The Corridor looms unnaturally large in the minds of the mostly New York- and Washington-headquartered media. In 1944 the region cast 24% of the nation's votes, with New York City by itself accounting for 7%; in 1996 and 1998 the same region cast 16% of the nation's votes, with New York City accounting for 2%. Democrats have already won almost every House seat they could hope to win here, and the Corridor casts only so many electoral votes—counting New York's but not Pennsylvania's, 99 in 2000 and probably 96 after the 2000 Census. The Northeast Corridor controls the nation's mind less than it thinks, and like Western Europe it is in demographic decline: Even in the prosperous 1990s, it has generated relatively few new jobs, and its population has grown only 2% in the 1990s, compared with 9% for the rest of the country. The Northeast Corridor cannot be ignored, but it is far from the whole story of America.

South Atlantic. A half century ago, there was not much to say about the South Atlantic states and their politics. They were America's backwater, economically far behind the rest of the nation, with low-wage Piedmont textile mills their only major industry, culturally bound by legally-enforced racial segregation, politically so heavily Democratic that few people bothered to pay their poll taxes and vote: they cast only 4% of the nation's votes in 1944. Now the surge of growth in the South Atlantic, accelerated after the dismantling of segregation, has grown even faster in the 1990s; the South Atlantic grew 10% from 1990–96 and in the latter year cast 15% of the nation's votes. (Its share of the vote declined in 1998 because Florida does not tabulate vote totals in races that are uncontested, as most Florida House races were.)

Yet the South Atlantic's politics are an outgrowth of deep traditions that go back in some cases to colonial days. Foremost among them is this area's Christian heritage. This is one of the most deeply religious places in any economically advanced country, with churches in every neighborhood and at country crossroads; if the tone of daily life in the Northeast Corridor is secular, in the South Atlantic it is religious. The prominence of the religious right in the Republican Party is an asset here, not a liability. Economically, the South Atlantic was within living memory a kind of underdeveloped country, desperate even for low-paying textile mills; politicians here have worked hard to attract industry, keeping taxes down and insisting on right-to-work laws: this is the least unionized part of America. The colonies along the South Atlantic had no large city, unless you count Charleston, and there remains a country atmosphere to life here today. Even in metropolitan Atlanta, in the big urban strips in Florida, in the Northern Virginia suburbs spilling out into the countryside, the look of the place is country: kudzu, swamps, trees and greenery of all kinds dominate the view, and the pleasant tone of southern life even infects migrants from the North.

Politically, the South Atlantic is one of the two most Republican regions (the other is the Interior). It cast off its Democratic heritage as early as 1952, when most states here went for Dwight Eisenhower; it began electing Republican congressmen in the 1950s, governors in the 1970s. By 1988 it was voting 60%–39% for George Bush; it has been closer since in presidential races, but still more Republican than the nation: 43%–41% for Bush in 1992, 46.4%–46.1% for Clinton in 1996. Clinton owes this carry to his intensive campaigning for Florida's 25 electoral votes; he lost the four other states, including Georgia, which he won in 1992. The underlying Republican trend is stronger. It shows up in House races: the South Atlantic voted 55%–44% Democratic in 1990, a last vestige of its old allegiance, then 49.0%–48.8% Republican in 1992, 58%–41% Republican in 1994, 55%–45% Republican in 1996, 54%–42% in 1998. Republican strength goes even further downballot: Republicans control four of the area's 10 state legislative chambers and have a tie in another.

The South Atlantic's traditions mixed well with 1990s Republicanism, indeed helped shape it: Newt Gingrich is from Georgia. But an offset is the support for lotteries and gambling by blacks and many downscale whites, which helped Democrats win gubernatorial elections in Georgia all through the decade and in South Carolina in 1998. Democratic as well as Republican governors here, aware of the need for high skills, have emphasized the need for tough education standards even as they have raised teacher pay. And no politician here sees a need to apologize for being tough on crime: The South Atlantic is ready to execute murderers and let law-abiding citizens carry concealed weapons. The major dissenters from this consensus are the South Atlantic's blacks—21% of the population, more than in any other region. Fresh from seeing desegregation imposed from Washington, they have regarded a large and interventionist federal government as their agent of change, even as their states have improved local schools and the booming private economy has brought new jobs. But most South Atlantic voters disagree and prefer their regional economic and moral order to that of liberal Washington.

Mississippi Valley. In 1682 the French explorer LaSalle sailed up the St. Lawrence, through the Great Lakes and down the Mississippi Valley: the first man to traverse the region we call the Mississippi Valley. This land between the Appalachian chains and the Great Plains is the center of America, the heartland, a place of great variety that is likely to be the central battleground in elections to come. It votes almost exactly like the nation as a whole: 49%–41% for Bill Clinton and 49%–48% for Republican House candidates in 1996; 54%–45% and 51%–47% for Republican House candidates in 1994 and 1998. When the Mississippi Valley does diverge from national patterns, it is worth inquiring the reasons. There is evidence of coattails and straight ticket voting in these results: House Democrats did significantly better in 1996 when Bill Clinton led the ticket than in 1994 or 1998 when popular Republican governors led their tickets in many of these states. Here as in the nation 1994 was a great divide: Democrats won the Mississippi Valley House vote in 1988–92 by 53%–46%; Republicans won it in 1994–98 by 51%–47%. The differences look small, but in the closely-divided balance of American politics they are large, and have had decisive consequences.

Historically, the Mississippi Valley was divided politically by the Old National Road, later U.S. 40 and Interstate 70, which runs through southwest Pennsylvania, Columbus, Indianapolis, St. Louis and Kansas City. North of the line people voted mostly Republican, south mostly Democratic. Then in the 1930s, with the CIO industrial unions organizing auto, steel and rubber factories, the big metropolitan areas of the Great Lakes became heavily Democratic. In the 1960s, white voters in the South shifted from Democrats toward Republicans, as did some blue-collar workers; blacks in both the South and the big cities of the north became heavily Democratic. All these shifts have left the Mississippi Valley pretty close to evenly divided between the parties.

The economy here is mostly industrial, until one gets to the southern reaches of the Mississippi River, and competition between the parties is also a contest between two visions of governance. The Democrats have been allied closely with the big industrial unions, and mostly see government as an instrument of economic redistribution. The constituency for that—blue-collar workers in big Great Lakes metro areas—seemed to die out in 1994, came faintly flickering back to life in 1996, then seemed to die down again in 1998. The Republicans, historically allied with big company management, have moved now toward market economics, trusting that lower taxes, less welfare and fewer regulations will invigorate their economies. And in fact manufacturing, in almost terminal condition in the early 1980s, is now thriving, with hundreds of thousands of jobs in small businesses quietly being created—many more than were noisily lost in big company plant closures and layoffs. In 1996 Clinton got some credit for this; in 1994 and 1998 Republicans did.

On cultural issues the Mississippi Valley, like America, is exceedingly diverse. Support for abortion rights seems to be an asset in Illinois and a liability in Louisiana; in other states there are large constituencies for both points of view. Neither of the core cultural constituencies of the two parties—the religious right and the feminist left—dominates the local political dialogue, as the former do in the South Atlantic and the latter in the Northeast Corridor and Pacific Rim.

Interior. As farmers moved west across the Great Plains, they came to land with less and less rainfall, until they reached the 100th parallel, which runs through North Dakota south to Texas and has long been considered the boundary between farm fields and grazing land. The land of most of this Interior region is brown and empty today, as farm counties have lost population because fewer hands are needed to harvest the crops. Except for its eastern edge, most of the Interior today is a place with large metropolitan areas rising from barren land, with small settlements—resorts, oil drilling towns, county seats—in the vast space in between. Even Kansas, Nebraska and the Dakotas are on their way to becoming city-states.

The original politics of these states revolved around Civil War loyalties and mining and farming interests: Texas voted for the Confederacy, Colorado for the union, Arizona for copper, North Dakota for wheat. But by the 1980s politics in all these states began revolving around the same theme: local interests versus federal control. Texans and Oklahomans were disgusted with federal oil and gas price controls; Nevadans were furious at being designated the nation's nuclear waste disposal site; Utah's Mormons and Colorado's new suburbanites disliked the cultural liberalism of Washington bureaucrats; Idahoans and New Mexicans rebelled at the ukases of federal land agencies. Even farm subsidies started to evoke not support but disdain: in 1996 and 1998 Kansas and Nebraska placidly accepted the phasing out of wheat and corn subsidies.

The result is that the Democratic Interior which cast 3% of the nation's votes in 1944 has been transformed into the Republican interior which cast 16% of the nation's votes in 1996 and 1998 and is now the most Republican region in the country. The Interior voted 48%–42% for native son Bob Dole over Bill Clinton, and 56%–41% for Republican House candidates in 1996; in 1998 it voted 57%–39% for Republican House candidates, almost exactly the same as in 1994. This was similar to the Interior's 57%–42% vote for George Bush in 1988. The changeover in congressional voting came in 1994; before that the Interior voted Democratic for the House, 50%–48% in 1988–92. Now Democratic congressmen are about as scarce here as Republican congressmen are in the Northeast Corridor. In the House the Interior is represented by 46 Republicans and 23 Democrats, of whom 17 come from Texas, with the cleverest Democratic redistricting plan of the 1990s. (In 1998 Texans voted 52%–44% Republican for House candidates, but elected 13 Republicans and 17 Democrats.) But Democrats will not control redistricting again here—George W. Bush won overwhelmingly here in 1998, Republican Rick Perry squeaked through in the lieutenant governor race; the state Senate is Republican and the state House, while Democratic, is not very partisan—and so Texas Republicans stand to make redistricting gains in 2002.

Pacific Rim. If the Interior is wide open, the Pacific Rim is densely packed: Most people here live in metropolitan areas filling up the narrow interstices between ocean and mountains. Houses are expensive, lots are small, offices are distant over clogged freeways (one reason why so many people work at home). This is the homeland of America's computer creativity and its connection with the economies of East Asia; it produced bounteous growth for decades, then foundered as California and Japan went through a deep recession in the early 1990s. California (but not Japan) has now recovered and is rapidly generating jobs and creating new goods and services; Washington and Oregon in the Pacific Northwest have beem booming; only tourism-dependent Hawaii is lagging. This is the part of America most affected by the vast flows of immigration from Latin America and East Asia. The Pacific Rim cast 10% of the nation's votes in 1944, 16% in 1996.

Ronald Reagan showed Republicans how to carry the Pacific Rim in the 1980s; Bill Clinton showed Democrats how to do so in the 1990s. George Bush won here in 1988 by only 50%–48%, but lost to Bill Clinton by a resounding 45%–33% in 1992. Clinton carried the Pacific Rim 51%–38% in 1996, while Democratic House candidates were prevailing 51%–45%. Even in 1994 Democrats won narrowly, 49%–48%; in 1998 Democrats won 52%–43%, an upswing from 1996 which was the result of their sweep in California. Reagan's success was based on his economic conservatism, his strong defense policy and sunny temperament; Clinton's success was based on his economic moderation, his careful attention to California and the Pacific Northwest and his personification (to an extreme, in his personal life) of the values of cultural liberation. The Pacific Rim is quite aware that its growth has come mainly from the private sector, with the important exception in the 1980s of defense, and from economic creativity and innovation. The economic interventionism which Democrats used to gain votes in the old industrial and farm belts was a liability here, from which Clinton has set his party free.

At the same time, cultural conservatism is affirmatively unpopular on the Pacific Rim. This is the most secular part of the nation, the place where people are least moored to old communities and folkways (as many still are in the slow-growth Northeast corridor). Exercise, environmentalism, New Age beliefs, gay identity, feminism—all have become religion substitutes for many Pacific Rimmers, and all correlate highly with political liberalism. Traditional religion does have some followers, notably in eastern Washington and Oregon and the Central Valley of California (which in many ways resemble the Interior, but are vastly outvoted by coastal counties in these states). Pacific Rim voters here tend to see the religious right as a rebuke and even a threat to their lifestyle. In the apolitical atmosphere here, so different from the blaring tabloid culture of the Northeast Corridor, voters have been willing to let highly skilled Democratic machine politicians control their legislatures; the California Assembly, briefly Republican, is now back in Democratic hands, as is the Senate. California Governor Gray Davis, elected by a huge 58%–38% margin, is a product of the political culture of the capital city of Sacramento; the governor of Oregon is a legislative veteran, the governor of Washington headed the liberal government in Seattle's King County, the governor of Hawaii, narrowly re-elected despite the state's economic decline, is a fixture of the Democratic machine which has held control of the governorship and the legislature without interruption since 1962. A possible countertrend: Oregon has elected a Republican legislature, perhaps to counterbalance liberal Democratic governors, perhaps because the values of its eastern regions are seeping west.

These regional differences help make some sense of the political trends of the 1990s. There is a seeming paradox here: Presidential voting became more Democratic while congressional voting became more Republican. But in fact Americans in the 1990s have been voting more straight tickets than at any time since the 1940s. In the 1970s and 1980s many voters stuck with their ancestral Democratic preference in House races, or voted for the smart young Democratic political entrepreneurs who were so numerous in those years, even while voting Republican for president. In the 1990s such behavior has stopped. In 1992, as a look at the table shows, voters in each region produced about the same margin for each party for president and for the House; this is what we should expect if Perot voters split their House votes evenly. In 1994, voters were plainly responding to national issues in general and Bill Clinton in particular. In 1996, the percentage for Clinton in each region is eerily similar to the Democratic percentage in House races; the 1998 results show the same eerie resemblance. In effect Clinton and Ross Perot got Americans to end their habit of voting Republican for president in 1992, while Clinton's actions in his first two years in office and Newt Gingrich's strategies got Americans to end their habit of voting Democratic for Congress in 1994. There, with minor corrections and qualifications, things stand in mid-1999.

But there is an important difference: Clinton's 49% in 1996 was contingent, while the House Republicans' 49% in 1996 and 1998 was fundamental. Clinton's victory owed much to superior skills and favorable circumstances not all of his making. Other Democrats are not guaranteed those advantages in the future. House Republicans' victories, on the other hand, occurred in unfavorable circumstances and despite the grave unpopularity of the most visible Republican leaders. Not all those disadvantages are guaranteed in the future. Much has been made of the unpopularity of House Republicans in the Northeast Corridor and, to a lesser extent, in the Pacific Rim. Less has been made about their affirmative strength in other regions. In 1990 none of these five regions voted for Republican House candidates. In 1992 only one did, by a fraction of a percentage point. But in 1994 Republican House candidates won 58% in the South Atlantic, 54% in the Mississippi Valley and 57% in the Interior. They held most of that vote and those pluralities in 1996 and 1998. It would be wrong to say that Republicans are bound to win future congressional elections; Democrats were confident in early 1999 that they would win the House elections in 2000, and certainly they could do so. But it is wrong to not acknowledge that the

Republican victories in 1994, 1996 and 1998 show that they represent a potential majority coalition capable of asserting itself in presidential as well as congressional contests.

Indeed, one could make the case that the Clinton Presidency has been disastrous for the Democratic Party. When Clinton was elected in November 1992 there were 57 Democratic senators. Now there are 45. In November 1992 there were 266 Democratic congressmen. In mid-1999 there were 211. When Clinton took office in January 1993 there were 28 Democratic governors. Now there are 17, in states with just 35% of the nation's population, only 23% outside California. Not all of these losses can be blamed on Bill Clinton, but many can. Some Democrats have successfully applied the New Democrat formula Clinton employed in 1992 and 1998: Governors Zell Miller and Roy Barnes of Georgia, Jim Hunt of North Carolina and Gray Davis of California, though Miller and Hunt were winning statewide races while Bill Clinton was just finishing law school. Davis's victory in 1998 is of national significance. But overall it is surprising how seldom a winning national formula has been applied in the states; it suggests that Old Democratic interest groups and activists still have decisive influence in most states' Democratic parties.

THE POLITICAL GOVERNMENT

In the ordinary course of things, incumbents who are re-elected to office emerge from the election more powerful and confident than when they went in. This is all the more true when the voting public is in a state of contentment with, and even enthusiasm for, things as they are. But federal officeholders have not responded with sureness and confidence since the election of 1996. The 49% president has been distracted by scandal and by foreign crises and conflicts he seems ill-prepared to handle. The 49% House Republicans have been distracted by something akin to a loss of nerve, a sense that history is no longer moving their way. Leaders of both parties said the election results in both years were a demand for bipartisan cooperation. But Democrats continued to resent the aggressive tactics Republicans used to win control of the House in 1994, and Republicans continued to be preoccupied by the Clinton scandals and seething with mistrust of an executive whose word is not good. Republicans had the sense that Clinton was somehow not legitimately the president, and Democrats had the sense that the Republicans were somehow not legitimately the House majority. The voters clearly were in a mood for tranquillity and were tired of what they regarded as bickering. But a free and representative government will have an adversarial politics, and it was the voters themselves who (as in five of the past seven presidential elections and seven of the last eight offyear elections) have chosen a president of one party and a House of the other.

Fortunately, in the late 1990s the state of the nation was good and the public agenda fairly clear. The United States was clearly the preeminent power around the world, at peace with other nations, at least until the bombing of Serbia in March 1999. The macroeconomy was performing well: steady economic growth, an outpouring of new jobs, low inflation. Indeed, the economy for some time has been performing better than most political rhetoric suggested: the Boskin Commission's conclusion in 1997 that the Consumer Price Index overstates inflation means that wages and incomes have been rising, not falling since 1973. The culture, it was generally conceded, was malfunctional in some ways, but crime rates were falling, welfare rolls were shrinking, the rate of divorce was declining—in very many ways things seemed to be moving in the right direction.

The agenda of officeholders in Washington was fairly clear. Congress needed to pass and the president needed to sign appropriations bills maintaining those parts of government that have been performing well while preserving the balanced budget achieved, well ahead of schedule, in 1998. In a post-industrial society where power has been devolving from the center to local communities, Congress needed to set terms and conditions under which government programs are devolved and commerce deregulated.

The looming major problem after the 1998 elections was what to do about the major entitlement programs, Medicare and Social Security. These creations of a now-gone industrial

America were proceeding on an unsustainable course: Pensions and health care cannot indefinitely be financed on a pay-as-you-go basis by a payroll tax in a country where there are, as there will be soon enough, only three workers for every two retirees. And since reform is unlikely without bipartisan backing, and since it seemed likely that the same party would control the presidency and the Congress after the 2000 election, the 106th Congress provided a window of opportunity. But in early 1999 no one seemed willing to take advantage of it. There were latent majorities for reform in both houses. Republicans have increasingly favored using part of the payroll tax for a system of individual accounts, to allow Social Security beneficiaries to build greater wealth from the market economy than can be obtained from future payroll taxes. Similar plans were supported in 1998 by serious Democrats like Daniel Patrick Moynihan, Bob Kerrey, John Breaux and Charles Stenholm. The bipartisan Medicare commission came up with a majority (though not the supermajority required for an official recommendation) for a "premium support" plan similar to federal employees' health care plan, sponsored by Breaux and Republican Bill Thomas.

But Bill Clinton quickly shot both initiatives down. His Social Security plan, offered in broad outline but not actual legislation, would have the government invest part of the payroll tax in the stock market—a proposal that would not have a majority even in a Democratic Congress. And almost without a comment he rejected premium support and called for coverage of prescription drugs—an expansion of a system already facing insolvency. After the 1996 election many expected Clinton to seek consensus solutions to these problems as a lasting legacy. But the legacy he seemed more interested in was the election in 2000 of Al Gore. His torpedoing of Social Security and Medicare reform can be seen as an attempt to preserve these issues for the Gore campaign in 2000 (although their efficacy has grown less as younger Americans come to believe the policies will implode before they become elderly) or, more charitably, to reserve the issues until a Democratic president and Congress can tackle them after 2000. In any case, the 106th Congress seemed more likely to be preoccupied with its quotidian tasks than with the major work of entitlement reform.

THE HOUSE OF REPRESENTATIVES

With the retirement of Newt Gingrich three days after the 1998 elections, the House of Representatives reverted to the workaday functions it has performed during most of our lifetimes, away from the agenda-setting function it has performed during most of the 1990s. The Framers had expected the House to be the prime institution of the federal government except in time of war: Article I of the Constitution is not about the president, it is about Congress, and the House of Representatives, not the Senate, comes first. The Framers took care to require that all tax laws originate in the House, and by custom appropriations bill originate there too. But in the 20th Century's decades of depression and World War, Cold War and welfare state, Congress became used to waiting for the president's program and then responding, usually with changes at the margins. Then, as the Cold War ended, Congress took on something of its old role. The Democratic Congress forced George Bush first to drop his capital gains tax cut in 1989 and then to break his "Read my lips" promise and support a major tax increase in 1990. The leaders of the Democratic Congress also pressed Bill Clinton in 1993 to increase taxes. Then in 1994 a Republican Congress was elected and Speaker Newt Gingrich, armed with the agenda of the Contract with America he had persuaded almost every Republican House candidate to sign in September 1994, passed a series of bills and set an agenda.

It is generally believed that Gingrich's showdown with Clinton over the budget in 1995–96 was a failure, and indeed it helped Clinton's ratings in the polls and hurt Gingrich's. But it also resulted in passage of a standstill, no-spending-increase budget which turned out to be an indispensable step toward the balanced budget the Republican House got Clinton to agree to in June 1995 and which became a reality three years later. The Republican House achieved a goal which would never have been reached with a Democratic Congress, and with political damage minimal enough that they retained their majorities, narrowly, in 1996 and 1998.

Then the Republicans lost their nerve. They were exhausted after their struggle to re-elect Gingrich speaker in 1997 despite the ethics charges he faced. In July 1997 Republican leaders plotted a coup to oust Gingrich, and failed. Beginning in January 1998, they were preoccupied with the Clinton scandals, and with their puzzlement over his rising popularity as his immoral behavior was exposed. Gingrich and other Republicans believed that their 1994 victory was the prelude to the election of a Republican president in 1996 and the enactment of a Republican program in 1998. When Clinton's triangulation and the voters' sense of contentment with incumbents enabled him to win re-election, Gingrich realized that Republicans would have to compromise with Clinton and mostly mark time until a breakthrough could be achieved in 2000—and that breakthrough looked to be, if still possible, far from certain in 1997 and 1998. The ouster of Gingrich and the installment of Dennis Hastert, then unknown outside the House, in January 1999, gave House Republicans a leader of the temperament and unloquaciousness capable of pursuing such a course. But it also meant that the House would be mostly reacting to events rather than setting a national agenda.

The House Republicans' continuing problem is that the House is a crunchy institution operating in a soggy time. The House by majority vote strictly limits the time for debate and the terms and conditions under which legislation is considered. These limits are set by the Rules Committee, on which the speaker's party has a 9–4 majority; and both parties' speakers have had iron control of Rules since the retirement in 1972 of Rules Chairman William Colmer, a conservative Southern Democrat, whose chief aide was a young man named Trent Lott. The House leadership expects that all party members, regardless of their views on the substantive issue, will support Rules on procedural votes, and they almost always have, with just occasional embarrassing exceptions, under Democratic Speakers Tip O'Neill, Jim Wright and Thomas Foley as well as under Gingrich. This makes for crunchy debate. The minority party will always have an incentive to argue that the rules are unfair, that the majority is framing the issue in a way that guarantees or at least enhances its chances for success on the floor; and of course that is often true.

But business in the House can be done in no other way. One consequence, however, is a heightening of partisan debate and dissension. Democrats' complaints about the majority's control of the impeachment debate, familiar to television viewers and persuasive to many, echo almost eerily Republicans' complaints, few seen by such large audiences, against hundreds of Democratic rules during their long ascendancy. The partisan atmosphere has been increased by the increasing homogeneity of the parties in the House. As the number of conservative Southern Democrats has fallen toward zero, the House Republican Conference has become more uniformly conservative and the House Democratic Caucus has become more uniformly liberal. There are exceptions in both groups, enough to make a big difference on votes in a closely-divided House. But Gingrich, like the Democratic speakers before him, spent much of his time holding together his party majority, and the House Republicans succeeded far more often in doing so than not. Managing the House is not an easy thing: Its rules are the most complex parliamentary rules in the world, not written down in any one source; its members represent a complex and variegated nation, and have geographical, economic, cultural and committee interests that are often in tension; holding together majorities large as well as small is not an easy thing to do. That Gingrich, Foley, Wright and O'Neill—all highly able, dedicated, politically sophisticated leaders—were able to do so as often as they did is what is remarkable, not that they sometimes failed.

On Speaker Dennis Hastert no final verdict can be pronounced. He is a professional legislator with nearly 20 years experience in Springfield, Illinois, and Washington; he was a high school history teacher and wrestling coach who managed to travel widely abroad and win a national championship. He worked against Gingrich in the race for minority whip which Gingrich won by two votes in March 1989; in November 1994 he supported Tom DeLay over Gingrich's choice for majority whip, and became DeLay's deputy. He is given to speaking briefly, with no flourishes or crescendos; he is known as a good listener, a fashioner of consensus, at least among Republicans, a frank negotiator who stands true to his word. (He was urged to run for majority leader in November 1998, and probably could have won, but declined to run because he had promised Dick Armey his vote.) In his first month he seemed to abandon the practice of speakers from O'Neill through Gingrich of trying to assemble majorities from the majority party only. The Republican majority was just too small, and the public hankering for consensus too great. Instead, he urged Republicans to seek agreement, and to give up ground to get them, with moderate and conservative Democrats. The result was some early successes: passage by wide margins of a missile defense resolution and an EdFlex bill, both considerable advances toward Republican positions. He also insisted on timeliness: Republicans won passage of the budget resolution by the often-ignored deadline of April 15, a step toward avoiding a highly-publicized confrontation over the budget.

Hastert is also more inclined to respect the autonomy of committee chairmen than Gingrich was. Gingrich, faced with a Republican delegation that had never served in the majority and with senior members that many regarded as deadwood, elevated relatively junior members to chairmanships they would not have got under strict seniority—John Kasich at Budget, Bob Livingston at Appropriations, Henry Hyde at Judiciary, Thomas Bliley at Commerce. He abolished some committees and imposed a three-term limit on committee chairmen. He worked to enforce leadership priorities on chairmen. All this produced considerable friction, but it was probably the best way to run a newly Republican House. Hastert, with committee chairmen in place, and many serving what is their third and presumably last term, seems sure to give them more autonomy.

What of House Democrats? They returned to the 106th Congress still in the minority but supremely confident that they will be in the majority after the 2000 elections. And they continued to show in the minority a degree of unity and good fellowship that they had by no means always showed when they were the majority party. But in a crunchy House it is usually easier for members of the minority party to achieve a soggy consensus: they have the luxury of knowing their positions will seldom prevail, so they do not have to live with the consequences, and they can pick and choose their issues to split the majority. Democrats did this shrewdly with the minimum wage in 1996 and campaign finance in 1998; and in the face of Clinton scandals, from the Banking Committee's hearings in July 1995 to the impeachment vote in December 1998, they enthusiastically defended Clinton against all charges, to the point of appearing at the White House with Clinton in a kind of campaign rally the day he was impeached—a spectacle the senior Democrat in Congress, Robert Byrd, called "an egregious display of shameless arrogance." That was not because House Democrats love Clinton or trust him very much—many cried out in dismay when he accepted the goal of a balanced budget in June 1995 and signed welfare reform in August 1996. But they seem to regard him as the main political force working in their favor: They can't have escaped noting that their 48.5% of the vote in 1996 and 48% in 1998 tracked closely with the 49% he won in 1996, with results uncannily close in dozens of districts, and that when he was in trouble in November 1994 their percentages were lower. They could not help but hope that the unity they showed in his behalf would be rewarded in 2000 with a share of the votes similar to the majority in polls opposed to impeachment.

But the unity the House Democrats have achieved only papers over cracks and differences which may become more apparent when they are in the majority again. After six years of the Clinton Presidency, there was clearly no Clinton Democratic Party in the House. The two top House Democrats, Minority Leader Richard Gephardt and Minority Whip David Bonior, take a different line on policy—economically less respectful of markets and free trade, culturally somewhat more tradition-minded. On Social Security and Medicare, some House Democrats are ready for reform, but Gephardt and Bonior most assuredly are not; Clinton's blocking of reform leaves those differences unexplored. Gephardt is a skillful caucus leader, a good listener with genuine good will for his colleagues, careful in his utterances and always uncomplainingly ready for more hard work. His hopes to be president have been destroyed by Bill Clinton's historically unprecedented campaign to install his vice president in his place; Clinton and Gore made no discernible effort in 1996 to elect a Democratic House, and rallied to House Democrats only when the impeachment issue arose. But Gephardt has shown, and perhaps feels, no rancor for Clinton or Gore, and seems eager to soldier on steadily in their behalf.

His achievements are all the more impressive when one considers the heterogeneity of the Democratic Caucus. Nearly one-fifth of its members are in the Congressional Black Caucus, most of them far to the left on the issues, as are many of the party's Hispanics. The non-minority Democrats from big cities and heavily unionized districts are far fewer in number than they were in the Democratic majorities of the 1970s and 1980s. Yet seats crucial to any future Democratic majority are held, and not just in the South but in the Midwest and West as well, by moderates. Even they are disparate: the Blue Dog Democrats tend to be conservative on cultural issues and liberal on economics; the New Democrat Coalition tends to be conservative on economics and liberal on cultural issues. Both are wooable by Republicans on certain issues and House Democrats, from their days of large majorities, have less tradition of party unity than House Republicans. A small House Democratic majority in January 2001 might be even harder to hold together than the small Republican majority has been since January 1996.

Which party should be favored to win the House in 2000? Neither. The 1996 and 1998 elections were so close that a shift of 1% or 2% of the vote could change control. A district-by-district review of prospects in House seats in early 1999 could plausibly produce a prediction of 240 Republicans or 240 Democrats, or anything in between. Much will probably depend on the presidential contest, in an era when voters are increasingly voting straight tickets; but quirky results in a few out-of-the-way districts could make all the difference. What is likely is that the next House leadership, like this one, will have to struggle to provide soggy-looking leadership in what is quintessentially a crunchy institution.

A note on redistricting: It will not take effect until after the 2000 election, but it is very much on the minds of members and challengers in states with six or more seats. Population trends mean that states in the Southeast and West will pick up new seats, while the big industrial states and a few others will lose. On balance that should help Republicans, but not everywhere; certainly not in California, where Democratic Governor Gray Davis and, almost certainly, a Democratic legislature will draw the new lines for 53 or 54 districts. Offsetting California will be Texas, where Republicans will dominate the drawing of lines in the state that currently has the most partisan Democratic districting plan, and Florida, Pennsylvania, Michigan and Ohio, where Republicans need only hold their current legislative majorities to have total control. Some results are preordained: Massachusetts and Oklahoma are likely to lose a seat each, and their delegations respectively are all Democratic and all Republican.

THE SENATE

The Senate, first on the Sunday talk shows, comes second in the Constitution, after the House; its traditions are grand, but sometimes its performance seems less so. This is partly a matter of misplaced expectations. The Framers created the Senate as a balance wheel, a cooling saucer for hot coffee, a place where superior wisdom and experience could prevent unwise and rash mistakes. With only one-third of its members elected every two years, with a fair number of its members freed from political pressures because of their personal relationship with voters in small or one-party states, with its rules allowing even the politically weakest and personally least regarded of its members to stop the forward motion of legislation for some precious period of time, the Senate supplies some caution to the enthusiasms of the House. If the House disappoints a soggy nation by its crunchy character, the Senate disappoints an action-oriented nation by its plodding performance. No one could fail to be awed by the Senate's impeachment trial, with the chief justice on the podium and every senator in his seat, most listening intently. But much of this was rote performance; the moment the Senate acted together as a body was in the unprecedented session in the old Senate Chamber, which was closed to the public and press and for which no transcript presumably will ever be published.

Yet neither the pomp of the trial nor the candid interchange in the closed session is typical of the way the Senate actually works. For today's Senate is surely not "the greatest deliberative body in the world," as it likes to style itself; it is very seldom deliberative, and often scarcely a body at all. This is a legislature where it is every man and woman for him or herself, where the whole is equal to a fair lot less than the sum of its parts, where it is far easier to kill someone else's initiative than it is to sustain one's own. It is less a Senate than a collection of senators. Washington talk shows seem to assume that Majority Leader Trent Lott can run the Senate, but majority leader is a misleading title; its holder is often more of a coat-check attendant than a maitre d' or chef. The majority leadership is not a particularly historic office, like the speakership; it goes back to only 1911, and many of its holders have been obscure party wheelhorses. The notion that the position is powerful goes back to four years in the 1950s, when Lyndon Johnson exercised his extraordinary skills in a closely-divided Senate; when his Democrats gained 13 seats in 1958, Johnson's power was actually diminished because liberal Democrats insisted on pressing for measures that, under Senate rules, could not be passed. A better understanding of the position's power came from the man who held it longest, Mike Mansfield; in a speech intended to be delivered on the day that President Kennedy was murdered and which he only delivered in 1997 at the first Leader's Lecture, Mansfield argued that the majority leader should be the servant, not the master, of senators. So it must almost always be in a Senate which conducts most of its business under rules requiring unanimous consent for procedure, allows unlimited discussion and introduction of non-germane amendments at any time and requires a 60% supermajority for passage of strongly-opposed legislation.

Of course it still matters which party has a majority in—one should not use the word controls—the Senate. The partisan balance of the Senate, like the House, shifted sharply in the early 1990s and in the late 1990s has remained about the same. There were 57 Democratic senators when Bill Clinton was elected in 1992, not quite the 60 needed to stop a filibuster, but a strong Democratic position with a Democratic president. But Democrats lost two seats very quickly—one in the Georgia runoff three weeks after the election, the other in June 1993 when Kay Bailey Hutchison won Lloyd Bentsen's seat in Texas by a 2–1 margin. Democrats then proceeded to lose 10 seats, all six open seats plus two incumbents in 1994, and two more when Richard Shelby and Ben Nighthorse Campbell switched parties in November 1994 and March 1995. In January 1996 Republicans lost Bob Packwood's Oregon seat to Democrat Ron Wyden; in November 1996, Republicans won three open seats while losing one incumbent. In 1998, though Republicans seemed to have more targets, the result was stasis: Republicans won three open seats and beat one incumbent; Democrats won two open seats and beat two incumbents. And so the Senate stands: 55–45 Republican.

It is a more partisan, more conservative Senate than the Republican Senate of the 1980s. The 13 states of the South (leaving aside industrial West Virginia) now are represented by 18 Republicans and only 8 Democrats in the Senate. The eight Rocky Mountain states and Alaska are represented by 14 Republicans and only 4 Democrats. Almost all these Republicans are staunch conservatives, dedicated to reducing the power of the federal government and cutting spending and taxes, and so conservatives have a firm majority in the Republican Conference. Yet they do not in any sense control the Senate. Half a dozen or so Republicans disagree with conservative positions on many issues. And the 45 Democrats are more than enough to sustain a filibuster.

Harry McPherson, who worked for Lyndon Johnson in the 1950s, writes of a Senate made up of whales and minnows—a dozen or so men of large abilities and concerns, and then the rest who circled around waiting to follow. Today's Senate has very few whales and not so many minnows. Daniel Patrick Moynihan stands out, for the strength of his historic vision and his ability to spot issues before their time, but he is retiring in 2000. Most committee chairmen and ranking Democrats are competent, highly skilled and of admirable character in very many cases, but they are more workmanlike than inspirational. On the other hand, there are fewer minnows than there were in the 1950s, fewer weak senators who defer to the leadership of others. These are fair- and medium-sized fish in a small and sometimes turbulent pond.

Will the Republicans retain control in 2000? The easy answer is, probably, but not for sure. Retirements by May 1999 opened up seats which incumbents would probably easily have won: Democratic seats in New York, New Jersey and Nevada, Republican seats in Rhode Island and Florida. Democrat Charles Robb of Virginia, re-elected with a plurality in 1994, faces a tough challenger in former Governor George Allen. Republican John Ashcroft of Missouri, who seemed to be running for president in 1998, faces a tough challenger in Governor Mel Carnahan. Republican freshmen who are not well known face serious challenges in Michigan, Minnesota and Pennsylvania; Democrats have some hopes of beating veterans in Delaware, Vermont and Washington, but it was not clear in May 1999 that they would field strong challengers. Sweeps for the two parties would produce something like 59 Republicans or 54 Democrats—results that observers in May 1999 considered extremely unlikely. The more likely result, if the late 1990s pro-incumbent contentment continued, is a Senate pretty much like the one today.

THE PRESIDENCY

We have become accustomed to hearing that the president "runs the country." But as the 20th Century ends—as the private economy expands and reshapes the nation and power is devolved from Washington to states and localities and the private sector—the United States is not a country that any one person can run; the president is fortunate to run the government, or the parts of it he considers significant at a given time. This is not out of line with what the Framers intended. The words of the Constitution provide that in peacetime the president presides, does what Congress requires and little more. In wartime he has greater powers, unspecified, indeed unlikely to be challenged in the midst of great exigencies. And in cases of high crimes and misdemeanors, he can be impeached and removed from office.

This, one could argue, is how the Presidency has mostly worked in practice. In wartime the president has terrible powers: Lincoln suspended *habeas corpus* and expanded federal powers vastly. But 20 years later Woodrow Wilson, then a professor of political science, could argue that Congress runs the government and the president matters hardly at all. As a wartime president, Wilson himself exercised powers that would make us quail; yet when peace came, his grandest policy was frustrated when the Senate declined to ratify the peace treaties he had made. The power of the Presidency subsided again in the 1920s, only to be revived by Franklin D. Roosevelt in the frightening economic disorder of the 1930s. Then came the extended experience of war—World War II, the Cold War, Korea, Vietnam—in which the Presidency became the center of government—indeed, as a symbol of the whole country. We depended on presidents to preserve the nation, to prevent a world war; we were always aware that this one individual had the power to blow up the world. We spoke of "the Eisenhower era" and "the Johnson years"; a president's scandal could give its name to our times, "the Watergate era," or to a set of policies, "the Reagan revolution."

But after the American victories in the long Cold War in 1989 and the brief Gulf war in 1991, is the presidency as important anymore? One never hears people talking about "the Bush years" or "the Clinton era"; there is not even any convenient name for the Clinton scandals. When Bill Clinton started running for president, he like almost all Americans had no living memory of a time when presidents were not utterly central to our politics and government, when the office was swelled up to its wartime dimension. But now it seems to have shrunk back toward the size the Framers envisioned it would have in ordinary times. Clinton seems to understand this; at one point, several years before he launched the bombing of Serbia and Kosovo, he bemoaned that he did not have a real crisis like World War II on which to exercise his talents and win a large place in history. He has won some place in history: as the 15th president elected to a second term, and the first Democrat since Franklin Roosevelt to do so, and as the second president to be impeached for high crimes and misdemeanors but not removed from office.

The final verdict on Bill Clinton's Presidency cannot be written until January 2001 at the earliest. But in mid-1999 at least some things can be said. What is interesting at this point is that he leaves a legacy less of achievements than of accommodations, less of initiatives than of maneuvers, less of achieving honor than of evading, or trying to evade, dishonor. Some of this is the result less of the man than the times. Clinton has been the beneficiary, though he can also reasonably claim to be to some extent the maker, of the shifts in underlying political attitude in the 1990s. When he announced for president in October 1991, voters were in an anti-incumbent mood, full of discontent and anger with things as they were; when he was re-elected in 1996 and saved from removal from office in 1999, voters were in a pro-incumbent mood, full of contentment and a yearning for consensus and a desire to leave things as they were. As a candidate in a field none of whom had convinced people they were of presidential stature— a field winnowed of larger figures because so many leading Democrats had expressed an opposition to the Gulf war which seemed poor judgment when it was quickly won—Clinton's gifts of articulateness and divining public opinion enabled him to win a nomination which seemed worthless in March 1991 and proved to be worth very much indeed by July 1992. In this endeavor he was given invaluable assistance from Ross Perot, who as a billionaire and former military officer was able to, in the words of then deputy Democratic National Chairman Paul Tully, "departisanize" the critique of President George Bush in the spring of 1992 as no Democrat, including Clinton, then could. Perot's abrupt withdrawal from the race on July 16, 1992, and Clinton's acceptance speech that evening, enabled Clinton to rise more points in the polls in a 24-hour period than any candidate ever had before and than any candidate is likely to ever again. Perot—and the anti-incumbent mood of the voters and Clinton's own skills— handed Clinton the presidency.

At first he did not seem to know quite what to do with it. Unintentionally on some issues (gays in the military), intentionally on others (the stimulus package, taxes, health care), he presented Congress and the electorate with left-wing policy initiatives toward which most members and voters were dubious or hostile. Clinton is a man who tends to respond rather than to lead, and in 1993 and 1994 he responded to the desires and priorities of the Democrats on Capitol Hill, abandoning some projects when they disapproved, shaping other initiatives (like the budget and tax package and the crime bill) to suit their needs. All this was done in the confidence that Democrats would continue to hold their majorities in the House and Senate as they had mostly done for the previous 20 years, not so much by sticking closely to public opinion, but by using the advantages of incumbency and their candidates' superior political skills. But in an anti-incumbent time it didn't work. With Democrats in control of both the legislative and executive branches, Democratic candidates could no longer camouflage their views in anti-Democratic states and districts. Newt Gingrich's leadership enabled the Republicans for once to recruit a competitive number of politically competent candidates and in the Contract with America did the unusual thing of providing an articulate and unified basis for the out party's campaign. The result was the smashing Republican victory of 1994. It might be said that Clinton brought ruin to the Democratic majorities: since the eve of the 1992 election, they have gone from 57 senators to 45, from 266 House members to 211, from 28 governors to 17, from control of 37 state Houses to 26 and 32 state Senates to 26. But it also might be said that Democrats simply fell to their natural level, given the balance of opinion in the country, and that their previous majorities had been due to special factors and unusual circumstances which could be expected to vanish sooner or later.

So in 1995 Clinton took a different course and got a new seat of advisers including the pollster Dick Morris. With no Democratic majorities to respond to, he responded instead to the Republican initiatives of Newt Gingrich and others—sometimes confronting them when he sensed the voters would be with him, often accommodating them when he sensed that would suit the voters better. Morris has described the process as "triangulation," with Clinton taking a position between and, importantly to Morris, above both congressional Democrats and congressional Republicans. The major confrontation came in 1995–96 over the budget. Congress "shutting the government down" was how Clinton and the press styled the controversy, though technically it was Clinton who shut the government down; the Republicans had passed appropriations bills, and he had vetoed them. But Gingrich and the Republicans invited that characterization in the confidence that voters would rather like to see government shut down for a while. Clinton's numbers went up, the Republicans' numbers went down: a great Clinton victory, it seemed. Yet on substance the Republicans won a great victory of their own. For the budget that was finally adopted actually cut domestic discretionary spending for a year. Without that cut, the budget would never have been balanced in 1998, and spending today would be considerably higher. Similarly, on welfare reform Clinton let the Republicans prevail on substance. When they passed a free-standing welfare reform bill in August 1996, Clinton signed it—though, as Daniel Patrick Moynihan tartly noted, if it had come 14 weeks after the election instead of 14 before he would have vetoed it, as he had vetoed similar measures twice before. Clinton won with the voters, but by responding to and accommodating the Republican Congress.

This was good political strategy, because by 1995 and 1996 the voters had moved from an anti-incumbent mood to a pro-incumbent mood, from a zest for crunchiness to a yearning for sogginess. Clinton had hurried this along by his response to the April 1995 Oklahoma City bombing, in which he (aided by the news media) conflated the anger of many Gingrich Republicans with the presumed anger of the Oklahoma City bombers. Also aiding this mood was continuing low-inflation economic growth, which had started before Clinton's election and continued mostly smoothly through his first term and more than halfway into his second. To the extent Clinton was responsible for this, it was because he had learned from the experience of the Carter Administration that Americans would not tolerate inflation and from the Reagan years that economic markets, if left generally to themselves, would produce bountiful growth. But there is evidence that the economy was stimulated by the presence of a Republican Congress. Interest rates fell in Clinton's first year, then rose in 1994, then started to fall again when the Republicans won, and mostly stayed down after that. The Dow Jones average rose from 3223 to 3831 from Election Day November 1992 to November 1994, then rose to above 11,000 in May 1999. Another important trend, not stimulated by Clinton's policies but not retarded by them either, was a growth in wealth, not just the vast wealth of rentiers and entrepreneurs, but the wealth of ordinary citizens: Stock ownership rose from about 20% in the early 1990s to around 50% in 1997. Growth in wealth underlay continued exuberant consumer spending; it underlay a contentment that was not just a satisfaction with the economy at the moment, but a confidence in the long-run future; it underlay a desire to avoid confrontation and controversy that threatened to muck things up.

In industrial, big-unit America, where big government, big business and big labor seemed to run the country, decisions made by the president steered the major institutions of society and set the course of the lives of millions. In post-industrial, Tocquevillian America, where institutions are decentralized, power is devolved and markets are more powerful than bureaucracies, decisions made by the president make minor adjustments to existing trends and send sympathetic signals to various voters. This is the environment in which Clinton and Morris produced a poll-driven, photo-op, policy-gimmick Presidency, with breathless announcements of major initiatives like encouraging school uniforms (after lots of schools adopted them) and presidential vacation sites chosen by poll (rough-hewn Jackson Hole in election year 1996 rather than effete Martha's Vineyard). Though not quite fair to either past president, one could say that the Clinton strategy was to employ the rhetoric of Franklin Roosevelt and follow the policies of Calvin Coolidge.

The photo-op Presidency was also a way for Clinton to take credit for happy developments which were occurring with almost entirely no input from the federal government. Initiatives on crime and welfare in each case were being taken in states and localities, which were developing policies almost the opposite of those which the federal government in both Republican and Democratic administrations had urged. To this process Clinton and the Republican Congress have been interested and occasionally helpful spectators. But from the happy results they have profited at the polls.

For 1996 was, most of all, an incumbents' election—and so was the offyear election of 1998. Clinton was re-elected 49%–41%, a bit more than his 1992 margin of 43%–37%. The results of these two elections were more similar to each other than any two presidential elections since 1952 and 1956; in those the same two candidates ran against each other, while in the 1990s the elderly George Bush was replaced by the elderly Bob Dole, but otherwise the candidates were the same. Clinton increased his margins notably in some parts of the country— the Northeast Metroliner corridor and coastal California—but his margins shrunk or Republican margins increased in others—the Rocky Mountain basin, much of the South. At the same time, Clinton made virtually no effort to elect Democratic majorities to Congress: Clinton's and Al Gore's acceptance speeches at the Democratic Convention in Chicago each contained one sentence urging a Democratic Congress. Triangulation, after all, meant separating yourself from your party. In 1997 Clinton followed the same pattern in his dealings with the Congress. In May 1997 he and Republicans reached agreement on a balanced budget plan and, as the voters seemed to want, controversy seemed to subside.

It is against this background that the outcome of the Lewinsky scandal and the impeachment process makes sense. The issue struck suddenly in January 1998 when voters wanted anything but change. It confirmed what many suspected about Clinton—that he continued to be sexually promiscuous as president, that he was willing to parse words and lie to avoid political unpleasantness, that he was willing to use the perquisites of office ruthlessly to maintain his position. But voters wanted him to stay anyway. The late columnist Joseph Alsop used to say during the Watergate scandal that Americans regarded politicians like toilet fixtures: It was enough that they served their intended purpose, they need not be beautiful. That may not have been the case in 1974, but it was in 1998. Republicans mostly shied away from taking formal action against Clinton, until his admission of lying on August 17 forced them to the conclusion that he lied under oath—an obvious violation of the president's constitutional duty to take care that the laws be faithfully executed. Democrats mostly shied away from confronting the case at all, until the question of impeachment forced them to respond. The reaction on both sides could be attacked as partisan, though both could be defended: Republicans had available a strong argument that Clinton violated his constitutional duty; Democrats had available an argument, not perhaps as strong but not contemptible either, that the remedy was out of proportion to the offense. There is a natural human tendency to break ties in favor of the home team, and the strong feelings of party activists on both sides, and of Democratic fundraisers, gave added strength to the impulse to take one's party's side.

Neither party extracted great gain from the process. Republicans had hoped that the anti-Clinton faithful would turn out in droves in November 1998 but, after their disillusionment with the omnibus budget bill of October 1998, they didn't. Democrats hoped, more in retrospect after the returns were in than at the time, that their party faithful would turn out in great numbers to protect their president. But Democrats failed to gain the majority in the House that in the spring of 1998 they had hoped, with some reason, to gain. And Republicans failed to increase their majorities in Congress, and even lost five House seats, against the usual trend of opposition parties in offyears. Newt Gingrich was out as speaker in three days; but Dick Gephardt was not in, nor either, it turned out, was Speaker-designate Bob Livingston, who announced his retirement the morning of the impeachment vote. The new Speaker was Denny Hastert, formerly deputy whip, respected in the House but almost totally unknown outside.

The real winner of the impeachment crisis was Bill Clinton, who seemed sure to remain in office with a cowed congressional Republican majority and an energized Democratic minority who seemed confident of winning back the House in 2000 and to whose liberals Bill Clinton had shown increased deference ever since they emerged as his chief champions against removal. The question now was what Clinton would do. Conventional wisdom in Washington has had it since 1996 that Clinton, unable to run again, would seek a legacy of great bipartisan reform, and there were certainly issues—Social Security, Medicare—on which he was well positioned to do so. And when Clinton ordered the bombing of Serbia in March 1999, it seemed that he might be preoccupied by his duties as commander-in-chief during much of his remaining months in office.

But the role for which Clinton seems to have most relish is that of campaign-manager-in-chief. Bill Clinton has been running for public office since he was 27, and he was not about to stop just because he could no longer run for president. More than any other president in American history, he has been campaigning hard for his vice president to succeed him. Ronald Reagan did little for George Bush in 1988, and was conspicuously neutral during the primaries; Lyndon Johnson and Dwight Eisenhower made comments that undermined Hubert Humphrey in 1968 and Richard Nixon in 1960; many presidents—Richard Nixon, Harry Truman, Franklin Roosevelt, the list goes on and on—did not want their vice presidents to succeed them at all. Only two presidents have been succeeded by their vice presidents, Andrew Jackson in 1836 and Ronald Reagan in 1988, and in both cases those victories burnished their claims to have set the course of the nation for a generation. There is every reason to believe that Bill Clinton seeks similar validation for his presidency in the election of his vice president (and one wonders whether he will much mind if that successor fails to win the next term on his own, as Martin Van Buren did in 1840 and George Bush in 1992).

Clinton's priority was apparent even before the 1996 election, when he showcased Gore and humiliated Gephardt and other potential opponents at the Chicago convention. It was apparent in 1997 and 1998, as he and Gore worked to monopolize fundraiser and organizational support and eliminate other Democratic candidates from the 2000 race and mostly with success. In late 1997 and early 1998 one after another dropped out of the race: Paul Wellstone, Bob Kerrey, John Kerry, Dick Gephardt, Jesse Jackson. Only Bill Bradley remained, and Clinton and Gore made sure that party insiders in his home state of New Jersey were on the Gore team. This campaign required also that key Democratic constituencies, most of them on the left, be propitiated. Organized labor, miffed by Clinton-Gore support of NAFTA, was lavished with attention. In early 1999 Clinton purposively squelched the move to reform Social Security and Medicare. Serious reforms were advanced and were capable of winning bipartisan majorities in Congress—individual retirement accounts for Social Security were supported by Democrats like Daniel Patrick Moynihan, Bob Kerrey, John Breaux and Charles Stenholm; Breaux and Kerrey worked out a bipartisan premium support plan on the special Medicare commission chaired by Breaux. Clinton, while proclaiming that he wanted reform, effectively vetoed them both. And even as Gore posed as the great champion of the American high-tech industry, Clinton threatened the bipartisan Y2K liability legislation with a veto that would have been favored by the trial lawyers, the constituency for whom he suffered his one veto override in his first term.

Clinton's problem may be that he is trying too hard. The centrality of his role tends to increase the institutional tendency of the Vice Presidency to diminish the incumbent; when Clinton called Richard Berke of the *New York Times* in May 1999 to argue that Gore's campaign was not going all that badly, certainly not as badly as it had been a few months before, Gore and advisers were understandably furious. Plus, a Hillary Rodham Clinton Senate candidacy in New York, even if it is successful in that heavily Democratic state, will tend to associate Gore in other states with a figure who is polarizingly unpopular there and may diminish his candidacy as one part of a ploy to prolong Clinton power. Clinton's success in narrowing the Democratic field may have been too successful. Never has a party in which the incumbent has not been running had a candidate field as small as two, and this positions Bill Bradley, who cannot be dismissed as a fringe or frivolous candidate, to be a remainderman, the choice of all those voters who have any problem at all with Gore. Gore would probably be better off with a three- or four-candidate field, in which opposition would be split. He may lament the fact that it was only a bad back that kept Paul Wellstone out of the race.

THE 2000 FIELD

The 2000 election is only the fourth in the last three-quarters of a century in which it was clear from the outset that the incumbent was not running; the others were 1988 and 1960, when the incumbent was also barred by the 22d Amendment, and 1928, when Calvin Coolidge said "I do not choose to run." It is also peculiar for the fact that the size of the fields in the two parties is at odds with their basic character. The Democratic Party has always been fissiparous, a collection of out-people which at its best amounts to a diverse but fractious majority. But under Bill Clinton's tutelage, and now that it seems clear that the party can count on no natural majority, the Democrats had no contest for their nomination in 1996 (the first time that was true since 1944) and only two candidates running in mid-1999. The Republican Party, in contrast, has always been a party with a central faith and a clear sense of hierarchy and order, which has ended up deferring to seniority in its nominations, or staging battles labeled by one of their contestants Armageddon between two claimants to party orthodoxy (1976, 1952, 1912). But for 2000 no Republican starts out with a plausible claim to precedence, and mid-1999 a very large number, 11, were running or considering a run. To winnow among them, the Republicans must operate under a system of primaries and caucuses which was largely contrived by Democrats in response to, if not always turning out to be in harmony with, their perceived needs. The schedule has been refined and changed as various states scramble for the attention that early contests might bring, to the point that three-quarters of the delegates will have been chosen just a few weeks after the Iowa Caucus.

Let us turn now to look quickly at the strengths and weaknesses of the field of candidates as of May 1999, with the caveat that additional entries are always possible; Ross Perot didn't announce that he was thinking of running till February 1992.

DEMOCRATIC PRESIDENTIAL HOPEFULS:

Bill Bradley has been in the national spotlight on and off for a third of a century, first as an extraordinary basketball player for Princeton and the New York Knicks, then for 18 years as a senator from New Jersey. He grew up in Crystal City, Missouri, a small town 30 miles south of St. Louis, where he worked hard to develop high intellectual and academic skills. He has strong convictions on issues and has a penchant for studying them in depth, away from the spotlight, and then pushing for action. His signal success in the Senate was the 1986 tax reform which flattened tax rates and eliminated many tax preferences; many others in both parties contributed to the result, but Bradley more than anyone else put it on the national agenda and pushed it to passage. He is plainly a serious man and, while modest and unfond of grandiosity, a fierce competitor. Bradley is not, as is often noted, a great orator, but the stemwinder is not the persuasive form of political communication it was in the days of William Jennings Bryan and Franklin Roosevelt; on the more conversational medium of television, Bradley could turn out to be quite effective.

Bradley's greatest weakness as he begins his candidacy is that he is without institutional support. Almost every Democratic Party leader, even most in his own New Jersey, has been enlisted by the Clinton-Gore team; organized labor is just as unhappy with Bradley's free trade position as with Gore's (indeed, on that issue the big unions are closer to Patrick Buchanan); the feminist left, the biggest force at the 1992 and 1996 Democratic conventions, has been loyal to the Clinton-Gore team, as the reaction to the 1998 Lewinsky scandal showed, in the most trying of circumstances. Indeed, it was hard initially to see much difference on issues between the two candidates, which would seem to work against the lesser known. But Bradley has shown he is a good fundraiser, and he cannot be dismissed as a frivolous candidate; and he has the advantage of being the only alternative for whom any Democrat who for any reason does not want to vote for Gore.

Al Gore has had a long career in the federal government—eight years in the House, eight years in the Senate, going on eight years as vice president—and a family political heritage as well. His father Albert Gore was elected to the House in 1938 and the Senate in 1952 and served with distinction until he was narrowly defeated in 1970; Al Gore, who grew up mostly in Washington but also on the family's farm in Carthage, Tennessee, can remember rolling a bowling ball down the marble halls of the Russell Senate Office Building as a child. He remains on many issues a New Deal Democrat in the mold of his father—Social Security and Medicare foremost among them. But he developed on his own an interest in science and environmental issues; if he exaggerated when he claimed to be responsible for "creating" the Internet, he did much to promote it, and his belief in the theory of global warming set the course for the Clinton Administration's clean air standards (overturned in court in May 1999) and Kyoto treaty (not submitted to the Senate). He has been well acquainted with defense issues since the early 1980s. Gore is aggressive and often effective in debate, as he showed when he bested Jack Kemp in 1996 and Ross Perot in 1993, although his tendency to stick to his script can hurt, as it did when he was bested by Dan Quayle in 1992 (he never tried to refute Quayle's repeated charge that "Bill Clinton has trouble telling the truth"). He is well-disciplined and his personal life is by all accounts exemplary.

Gore begins with the institutional weakness that has bedeviled vice presidents even after Jimmy Carter and Walter Mondale gave substance to the job: the very faithfulness to a president's policies the voters demand makes the vice president seem somehow less than his own man, not the commanding figure voters want in the presidency. This can be overcome, as George Bush showed in 1988; but Clinton's close embrace of Gore and the major role he has taken in his campaign may make that more difficult this time. It is often said that Gore is wooden, and he chooses his words with evident care. But his greater problem could be that in a soggy era, when voters prize consensus, he is temperamentally crunchy, given to harshly condemning opponents in private as well as public, and with a bitterness that Bill Clinton (or George W. Bush) almost never sound. And finally there is Gore's involvement in the 1996 Clinton-Gore fundraising scandals. He was spared an independent counsel investigation by Attorney General Janet Reno, and his sins seem more venial than mortal. But if voters' distaste for scandal in 1998 worked for Bill Clinton, a similar distaste in 2000 may work against Al Gore.

REPUBLICAN PRESIDENTIAL HOPEFULS:
Among the 11 Republicans, two started off far ahead—first George W. Bush, then in second place Elizabeth Dole—seeming to squeeze the oxygen out of the rest of the field. But their greatest vulnerability will probably come in Iowa and New Hampshire, where voters expect to meet candidates personally and scrutinize them closely. The most valuable commodity in those contests is time, and Bush and Dole do not have the advantage in time that they seem likely to have in national fame, fundraising and support from party leaders. Setbacks in Iowa or New Hampshire for either could be explosive, and could supply a lot of oxygen for one or more of the candidates in the rest of the field. And since most other states will be voting in just a few weeks after Iowa and New Hampshire, the possibility of an upset cannot be ruled out. Consider the experience of the Democrats in 1984. Eight candidates went into Iowa, where Walter Mondale won about 50% of the vote. But Gary Hart, who had been trailing badly, came in second with 16%, and the headline was "Gary Hart surge." Hart proceeded to win New Hampshire and came very close to winning the nomination. Something like that could happen in 2000.

Lamar Alexander has been a serious political figure for more than a quarter-century. He grew up in Maryville in ancestrally Republican east Tennessee, the son of teachers; nothing suggested that he would become a major politician. But he rose quickly: He worked in the Nixon White House, went home to Tennessee to run for governor in 1974, at 34; he lost then, but then walked across the state in a plaid shirt and won in 1978, and was easily re-elected in 1982. He was the first governor to implement merit pay for teachers; he helped Tennessee become one of the economically fast-growing states in the South. He served as secretary of Education in the Bush Administration (1991–93). He has been running for president since 1993. He is hard-working, persistent, organized, disciplined: The morning after the November 1996 election, he held a 9:00 a.m. fundraising conference call. Alexander has changed his theme, though not his positions on issues, since his campaigning began. In the crunchy early 1990s his theme was "Cut their pay and send them home"; in the late 1990s it is helping parents raise children in a time of cultural turmoil.

It is a long time since Alexander was elected to office, and the press tends to dismiss this disciplined, now suit-clad candidate as a plaid-shirt automaton. But he has had a splendid fundraising organization, based in Nashville which has become a leading source of Republican money, and in 1996 he came within 7,625 votes of beating Bob Dole for second place in New Hampshire. If he had done that, Dole would probably have dropped out, and the race would have been between Alexander and Patrick Buchanan, and Alexander would almost certainly have won. Alexander's calm, moderate-sounding demeanor made him the Republican the Clinton-Gore team most feared in 1996 and seems well suited to the national mood going into 2000.

Gary Bauer has never won elective office; he was a domestic policy advisor in the Reagan White House, sometimes pushing successful projects, more often being frustrated by conventional political thinkers higher up on the staff. He grew up in a modest home in gambling-ridden Newport, Kentucky, and brings strong moral views to public policy: He is an especially fervent opponent of abortion, and is very much ready to say so. For ten years he headed the Family Research Council in Washington, and in 1997 founded the Campaign for Working Families PAC, which raised $7 million in two years. This fundraising success evidently sparked the idea, improbable to so many others, of running for president. In his appearances he is fluent, forthright and more polished than many expected; he talks fervently about the need to promote religious values.

Bauer's ability to raise money through direct mail is not in doubt and his capacity to mobilize Christian conservatives could turn out to be impressive. But his lack of experience in a job of the stature ordinarily considered necessary for a presidential candidate and the likelihood that opponents and the press will attack him as the candidate of a limited faction make it hard to imagine him winning the nomination.

Patrick Buchanan is one of America's most eloquent public figures, and one of its most intellectually honest and learned. He grew up in Washington, D.C., perhaps the only presidential candidate to have done so, in a large Catholic, feistily conservative family. But he has always seen himself as representing the little people beyond the Beltway who are overlooked and scorned by the capital's elite. He worked for Richard Nixon when he was making his political comeback in the middle 1960s, was a speechwriter in the Nixon and Reagan White Houses, and otherwise has made a good living as a columnist and television commentator—pugilist, really, on *The McLaughlin Group* and *Crossfire*. In December 1991 he launched a primary campaign against President George Bush. Initially, he seemed primarily interested in cultural issues—he has always been a strong and outspoken opponent of abortion—but when he encountered laid-off workers in New Hampshire, his focus turned to trade.

Trade has been Buchanan's focus ever since. He is convinced that American jobs are being lost to foreign countries, that the family-wage factory jobs which were once the economic sustenance of the patriotic working class are vanishing, to the benefit of the economic elite. In 1996 he ran for president again, won the New Hampshire primary, and fought—the word is carefully chosen: in Arizona he allowed himself to be videotaped in a black hat carrying a six-gun—unsuccessful primary battles against Bob Dole. In his 1998 book *The Great Betrayal* he argues for policies much like those of Republicans from Abraham Lincoln through William McKinley and after, with characteristically Buchananite turn of phrase and with a knowledge of history that few if any practicing politicians can match. In happy economic times, his thesis attracted less attention than Buchanan must have hoped. Buchanan is not a naif: After his two presidential races, he knows that even if he becomes one of the two surviving candidates in early primaries his high negatives make it very difficult for him to win the nomination. He knows that the biggest anti-free trade constituency is made up of the dwindling number of blue-collar union members who are strong Democrats. His candidacy can best be seen as an unselfish attempt to advance ideas which he believes are vitally needed to help ordinary Americans.

George W. Bush is the first son of a president to run for that office since Robert Taft and if elected would be the first to win since John Quincy Adams. He grew up in Midland and Houston, Texas—the twang is authentic, went off to school in the East, where he disliked trends on the elite campuses of the 1960s and 1970s, and returned to Texas to work in the oil business and to run for office—unsuccessfully for the House in 1978, successfully for governor in 1994 and 1998. Bush is focused and disciplined, likes to be prepared and dislikes improvisation; he studied Texas issues and communities hard before campaigning in 1993 and 1994 and has been taking tutorials in national and international issues in 1998 and 1999. He has prepared short agendas of serious reforms and mostly pushed them through, a sharply defined task since there is only one 90-day legislative session every two years. He has built a consensus around Texas issues—for tort reform, welfare reform including services by faith-based institutions, tough juvenile crime laws, limited tax cuts, friendly relations with Mexico—which is perceptibly more conservative than Bill Clinton's attempts at consensus, just as Texas is more conservative than the nation as a whole.

The question is whether he can duplicate his Texas success in the entire country. Bush's unwillingness to wing it on issues (so sharp a contrast with Clinton) will surely help him avoid mistakes, but can also make him look uncertain, as in his initial comments on the bombing of Serbia in March 1999. His ability to forge a consensus in Texas has been helped by the fact that the media environment there is heavily tilted to the left, as it is nationally. And his candidacy must pass through the chokepoint of Iowa and New Hampshire, where he will have no more time—indeed, given his concentration on Texas through June 1999, less time—to be in touch with voters than other candidates. Bush was well ahead in both primary and general election polls in the first half of 1999, but those results are not etched in stone, and represent more of a favorable first impression than a settled verdict.

Elizabeth Dole startled many people when she announced her retirement from the Red Cross in January 1999 and prepared to run for president. Her name had been mentioned before as a possible candidate, and she has had a career which entitles her to serious consideration. She grew up in North Carolina, went to Duke University and then was one of the few women in her class at Harvard Law School. A nominal Democrat (like most North Carolinians then), she made her way ahead in the Nixon Administration. In 1975 she married Bob Dole, then already a national figure as senator and Republican National Committee chairman. She was not noticed much as he ran for vice president in 1976 and president (winning very few votes) in 1980. Instead she held important office herself, as secretary of Transportation in the Reagan Administration and secretary of Labor under Bush. In 1991 she became head of the Red Cross, and by most accounts solved some serious problems there.

Dole is an accomplished speaker whose specialty is talking into a hand-held mike and walking amid the audience, repeating a memorized talk—not as easy as it looks. But she has had little experience in the hurlyburly of campaigning. Nor as of May 1999 had she staked out positions on some major issues. The thought is often advanced that she is running for vice president, and she certainly would be a plausible running mate. But it is also noteworthy that her candidacy is being taken seriously on its merits; the fact that she is a woman seems not to be an asset nor a liability. Without much notice, the Dole candidacy has moved America past a political milestone.

Steve Forbes was never considered a political, much less a presidential candidate, before he launched his candidacy in September 1995; he has hardly stopped running ever since. Forbes grew up in New Jersey, the son of *Forbes* publisher Malcolm Forbes; both Forbeses vastly increased the circulation and value of the magazine, and Steve Forbes has used some of his fortune to self-finance his campaigns. Forbes is brainy, well-learned in history and economics, with strong beliefs in free markets, hard money and flat taxes. His saturation ad campaigns, many of them directed at Bob Dole and others, made him a serious contender in several 1996 primaries, and the winner of some. But he stumbled in Iowa by criticizing the Christian right and in antitax New Hampshire ran poorly. In 1997 and 1998 he made amends with Christian conservatives, strongly backing the partial-birth abortion ban and calling for an effort to change public opinion so as to make abortion extinct.

Forbes's intellect and money make him a contender who cannot be ignored in 2000; strategists for Bush and others worry about him launching a barrage of negative attacks. But Forbes labors under certain handicaps. The flat tax may be a good message, but it is not clear that someone of Forbes's net worth is the best messenger. While Forbes has been successful in dulling the animosity and even attracting the affection of Christian right leaders, their setbacks in 1998—and the fact that almost every candidate has sought to meet their litmus tests—may have made them less inclined to flex their muscles in the Republican nominating process. Forbes's 1996 campaign was quintessentially crunchy, in the spirit of the early 1990s, condemning the political system and calling confrontationally for wholesale change—an appeal that seems out of sync with the soggier mood of the late 1990s.

John Kasich, the chairman of the House Budget Committee, grew up in a working-class suburb of Pittsburgh, the son of a mailman; he became a Republican partly because he disliked the bureaucratic restrictions he encountered as a student at Ohio State. Kasich's energy and enthusiasm propelled him to the Ohio Senate and the U.S. House, each at an early age and in Democratic years; his position as Budget chairman he owes to Newt Gingrich's decision in 1992 to elevate him over a more senior, more somber colleague. Kasich can take pride in playing a major part in achieving a balanced budget, and certainly has an in-depth knowledge of government; but some Republicans chafe at the compromises he has felt compelled to accept.

Kasich's greatest assets are his energy and enthusiasm; his backers hope he will shoot up out of the pack through "spontaneous combustion." His enthusiasm for the Grateful Dead and other rock musicians perhaps puts him in closer touch with younger Republican voters than any rival; some rivals say he is short on gravitas. He constantly proclaims his religious faith and has written a book, *Courage is Contagious*, profiling everyday Americans who have done extraordinary things to improve their communities or the lives of others. Kasich, more than any of the others, has an inspirational appeal. The question is whether there is enough oxygen in this crowded field to produce spontaneous combustion.

Alan Keyes is running a second time. He was born in New York City, but grew up on various military bases. He is a serious scholar, a Straussian who believes that the nation has strayed from the principles of the Declaration of Independence, especially in its abandonment of the respect for life which he sees in its elite's toleration of abortion and hostility toward family life. Keyes is a gifted speaker, energetic and articulate, who brings audiences full of cultural conservatives to their feet with cheering applause. He has won significant percentages in some straw polls in Iowa, New Hampshire and elsewhere.

Keyes served in the Reagan Administration's State Department, but has never had a job of the stature ordinarily considered necessary for a presidential candidate. That, and the likelihood that opponents and the press will attack him as the candidate of a limited faction, make it hard to imagine him winning the nomination.

John McCain is the son and grandson of admirals. He grew up in Navy posts, finished near the bottom of his class at Annapolis, was a Navy flier in Vietnam and was a prisoner of war for five and a half years: As he put it when he was attacked as a carpetbagger in his first Arizona House campaign, the longest place he had ever lived was Hanoi. In Vietnam he endured torture and refused offers of early release; he returned home in 1973. McCain served out his Navy duty as a liaison to the Senate; he moved to Arizona, his wife's home, and ran for and won an open House seat in 1982. In 1986 he was elected to Barry Goldwater's Senate seat. McCain has conventional conservative views on most issues, and expertise on military matters. He is ordinarily pleasant, but is gifted with a strong temper. Most of all, he seems motivated in Washington, as he was in Hanoi, by a sense of humor. This helps to explain his two departures from Republican orthodoxy, sponsorship of the McCain-Feingold campaign finance bill (a sort of atonement for his tangential involvement in the Keating Five affair) and of the tobacco bill that failed in 1998 (he was assigned the task by Trent Lott and carried it out).

McCain attracted attention in spring 1999 with his astringent criticism of Bill Clinton's strategy in Kosovo. With his usual spare eloquence, he argued that Clinton's ruling out of ground troops gave Slobodan Milosevic the opportunity to ethnically cleanse Kosovo. His poll ratings rose as he distinguished himself from the field and spotlighted his special credentials. Yet his stands, as on campaign finance and tobacco, can repel many Republican politicians and voters.

Dan Quayle is the only Republican candidate who has had what is arguably the experience a president most needs, of working in the White House and gauging how decisions made there work in the world beyond. He grew up in Arizona and Indiana, and beat strong incumbent Democrats to win election to the House in 1976 and the Senate in 1980. There he concentrated on military and job training issues. His selection as vice presidential nominee was a surprise and he responded maladroitly to questions then, and still suffers from the impression he made, and from a few subsequent gaffes heavily publicized by a hostile press. But Quayle, like Vice Presidents Mondale, Bush and Gore, was closely involved in making national policy, making contributions like selecting the NASA head who was kept in office by Al Gore, advising Bush to seek congressional approval of the Gulf war and besting Gore in the 1992 presidential debate.

Quayle's problem in 2000 is not just to exceed expectations, which are very low, but to demonstrate that he is up to the office. With more gray in his hair, he speaks more fluently and confidently than he did in 1988, and shows close acquaintance with major issues though he has been out of office since 1993. Quayle must make a breakthrough in Iowa and New Hampshire, or his candidacy will wilt; he hopes that if he can he will have changed public impression enough to be a competitive candidate in the fall. But he must convince many skeptical Republicans who fear that he is a sure loser.

Bob Smith, to the surprise of just about everyone, has decided to run for president in 2000. Smith grew up in New Jersey, served in Vietnam, then went into teaching and real estate in New Hampshire. With conservative support he won a seat in the House in 1984 and the Senate in 1990. He was narrowly re-elected in 1998; the VNS exit poll showed him losing. Smith is a pleasant, earnest man who gives an eloquent stump speech which energizes audiences at Republican cattle shows and caucuses.

But he has shown very little support in polls even in his own New Hampshire. Nor has he had great successes as a legislator; his efforts at Superfund reform had not borne fruit as of mid-1999. Smith has said that he will not continue his campaign if he does not make a good showing in Iowa, so it is not clear what impact he will have on New Hampshire if any.

THE GENERAL ELECTION

The fact is that in mid-1999 no one could be sure who—or which party—would win the 2000 election. Democrats could take comfort from Bill Clinton's victories in 1992 and 1996 and his high poll ratings during much of his second term, and believe that he has shown the formula for victory. But Clinton won only 43% and 49% of the vote in those two contests, and it is not clear that either Democratic candidate has the particular set of skills and appeals to duplicate those plurality showings, much less win a convincing absolute majority. Republicans could take comfort from their party's victories in three successive congressional elections, in which their House candidates won pluralities despite negative press coverage and the great unpopularity of their most conspicuous congressional leader. But if they won 52% of the votes in crunchy 1994, they won just 49% in soggy 1996 and 1998.

Past performances give both parties bragging rights, but give neither side any warrant for confidence they will win. Democrats can point to Bill Clinton's 70% job ratings in the second half of 1998; Republicans can point to George W. Bush's 20%-plus poll leads over Al Gore in the first half of 1999. But the odds are long that these numbers will not be translated into voting percentages in November 2000. It is more realistic to look at actual votes, and these tell a different story: Clinton's 49% in 1996, House Republicans' 49% in 1996 and 1998. Republicans can point to the success of their candidates for governor, but in doing so they must gaze at their debacle in California in 1998, and the brute fact is that even their successes have not been registered at the presidential level in the 1990s. Democrats can argue that Bill Clinton's New Democrat formula is a solid basis for success, but they can point to few candidates who won statewide with a similar formula: Gray Davis in California is the one shining example, Roy Barnes in Georgia may be another.

One way to gauge the electoral balance is to look at the different regions examined earlier, considering in each state not only the 1996 presidential vote but also the 1998 House vote. Four of the five look very one-sided for 2000. The New Engand/Metroliner by that measure is almost entirely Democratic; only New Hampshire and Delaware produce a Republican average, the latter because of the personal popularity of its single incumbent congressman. Score it 95–3 Democratic. Similarly, the four states of the Pacific Rim all lean Democratic by significant margins: 76–0. The South Atlantic states all lean Republican (if one adds to the reported figures the untabulated votes cast for unopposed Florida Republican House members): 73–0 Republican. The Great Interior is even more Republican; only New Mexico and North Dakota produce a Democratic average, the latter because of the personal popularity of its single congressman. Score the Great Interior 92–5 Republican. That leaves Democrats ahead by 176–168: pretty close.

The decision therefore is likely to be made in the Mississippi Valley. Two states there are solidly Democratic, West Virginia and Minnesota; add Al Gore's Tennessee and you get 26 electoral votes. Three states seem solidly Republican, Indiana, Alabama and Mississippi, with 28 electoral votes. This leaves the decision to 10 states. Five are from the industrial Great Lakes region: Pennsylvania, Ohio, Michigan, Wisconsin, Illinois. Five are from the Mississippi Valley, with varying degrees of southern accents: Kentucky, Iowa, Missouri, Arkansas and Louisiana. In an even race, the combined 1996–98 vote totals would yield 85 Republican and 51 Democratic electoral votes; that would mean a 281–253 Republican margin. But we are operating here well within the margin of error, overall and in many of these states. The focus of American politics has sometimes been on the two coasts, sometimes on the new and emerging South; in the 2000 general election it is likely to be on the Midwestern heartland.

WHAT A LONG STRANGE TRIP IT'S BEEN
How the Past Decade Has Transformed
the Face of American Politics

By Charlie Cook

Lost amid the hubbub about the coming millennium is the event of a truly remarkable decade in American politics coming to an end. Both the Democratic and Republican parties are in fundamentally different shape now than 10 years earlier. While no one knows where American politics is headed, it's imperative to see where we have been to fully understand where we are today.

The decade began with split party dominance of our political institutions. Republicans had won four of the five preceding presidential elections but Democrats dominated everything else. Democrats controlled the House for the past 40 years and for 58 of the 67 years since Franklin Roosevelt was elected in 1932. Only slightly less impressive, Democrats controlled the Senate for 34 out of the last 40 years and 52 of the 67 years since Roosevelt's election. Aside from brief surges when Republicans held a majority of the governorships in 1953–54 during the Eisenhower Administration and 1968–70 during the Nixon Administration, Republicans were largely shut out gubernatorially as well.

At the beginning of the decade, there seemed little reason to believe that this state of affairs would change. Historically Republicans had been unsuccessful in their attempts to seize control at the congressional and state level. A recession in 1958 foiled a Republican effort to leverage presidential successes for downballot offices. In 1973 and 1974, Watergate set back Republicans at a time when they could have reached parity below the presidential level, causing their only presidential loss during the two-decade stretch between 1968 and 1988. The 1982 recession similarly derailed the "Reagan Revolution," which had been threatening to end Democratic dominance.

Republican optimists argued that eventually an opportunity for Republican dominance would not be foiled by some weird twist of fortune, but others felt it was fated that Republicans would never reach parity. In late 1989 or 1990, during a cocktail party conversation I heard someone ask, "What do you think will happen first, Republicans elect a speaker or Democrats elect a president?" After a hearty round of guffaws, someone suggested that once one event transpired, the other would probably follow. That's exactly what happened.

While the champagne at 1992 Democratic victory parties was still bubbling, something far more ominous for the party was brewing. Congressional Democrats entered the 1990s with attitudes of arrogance about their power, particularly in the House, and the righteousness of their cause. These factors blinded them to a changing tide in public opinion. There was also a stream of scandals that actually began in 1989: the House Bank and Post Office, Keating Five, Jim Wright, Tony Coelho, David Durenberger and Brock Adams, to name a few. Not all, but most of the culprits were Democrats, bringing public opinion about Capitol Hill to a level of contempt and derision. The "time for a change" sentiment building around the country was palpable. What wasn't certain was whether it would be targeted generically at incumbents or be party specific.

These scandals began to take their toll about the same time that Bill Clinton won the presidency. Democrats were already starting to suffer some downballot losses, minor ones in the House and even a handful at the state legislative level. In 1992 Democrats lost 10 seats in the House even as Clinton won. The losses began to spread to the Senate in an early 1993 special

Senate election, where a Republican was chosen to replace Texan Lloyd Bentsen, who had been named secretary of Treasury. It was during those early months of 1993 that Clinton, who had run as a moderate "New Democrat," and his party took a hard pivot to the left. The rest is history. In the 1994 election, Democrats suffered devastating losses in the Senate, House and gubernatorial races and even all the way down to local-level offices. In just two elections in 1992 and 1994, the Republican share of the Senate grew from 44% to 53%, the House from 39% to 53%, governorships from 42% to 60% and state legislative seats nationwide from 39% to 48%.

In 1992 and 1994, Democrats lost a total of 50 House incumbents, excluding party switchers: 16 in 1992, 34 in 1994. Republicans lost only eight incumbents during those same elections. Thirty-three open Democratic seats fell to Republicans, while only 12 Republican seats fell to Democrats. In short, Democrats dropped from 61% of the House to 47%. The bottom didn't fall out of the Senate until 1994, when Democrats dropped two incumbents and six open seats, a net loss of 11 seats including the 1993 Texas special and subsequent party switches by Ben Nighthorse Campbell and Richard Shelby.

The story was much the same in the state Capitols. After the 1996 election, Democrats had only 17 governorships, precisely half of the 34 they had a decade earlier; in 1976 they had 36 and in 1966 33. Democrats lost full control of five state legislatures in the 1992 election. They lost six more after the 1994 wave. Not since 1948 had one party lost so many House seats as Democrats did in 1994. At the state legislative level, it was the worst defeat for either party since the Republican Watergate disaster in 1974 and the Goldwater debacle a decade earlier. The Democratic domination of American politics below the presidential level that began with Franklin Roosevelt in 1932 had officially ended.

Today we have parity—two evenly matched parties, with an electorate that doesn't trust either. Voters seem content to swing back and forth, punishing a party in one election, the other party in the next election, switching and splitting tickets almost on a whim. Republicans have a fairly comfortable 55–45 edge in the Senate, which gives them control but not really a working majority; they are still five seats short of a filibuster-proof Senate. Republicans still dominate the governorships, 31 to 17, but they lost the grand prize in 1998, California. Republicans hold onto the House by just six seats, 223 to 212, 51% to 49%.

Democrats have the upper hand in party identification, as well as in the state legislatures, albeit very narrowly. Gallup Organization polling of over 10,000 adults during the first quarter of 1999 indicated that 34% of Americans call themselves Democrats, 28% self-identify as Republicans while 38% call themselves independents. According to Gallup, since the beginning of the Clinton Administration, independents have consistently outpaced Democrats by three to four points while Democrats have usually run five to six points ahead of Republicans. In the state legislatures, Democrats control both chambers in 20 states, compared to 19 for Republicans, with split control in 10 states. Democrats also maintained a similarly narrow 1,016–913 edge in state Senate seats, and a 2,866–2,550 edge in state House seats, comprising a 52%–48% Democratic advantage in state legislative seats nationwide.

More than immediate political influence and bragging rights, the change from the early 1980s carries significance for the future. For many years, what helped perpetuate Democratic rule was their claim on a broader and deeper bench of elected office-holders than Republicans. All other things being equal, someone who has already won an election is more likely to win an election again. For years, Democrats dominated most state legislatures as well as municipal and county offices, and held the House to such a degree that Republicans often had to run candidates who had either never won an election or had never run. Sometimes it worked. Most of the time it didn't.

Now the Democratic edge is gone in the House and almost gone in the state legislatures, eliminating that Democratic seed-corn advantage. Now entrenched Republican incumbents need to be dislodged in governorships and Senate seats more often than ensconced Democrats.

What offers Democrats hope is that Republicans in 18 states pushed through term limitations for state legislators in 1995, which potentially puts Republican state legislative majorities in jeopardy in coming years. Term limits make the bodies more erratic, or more dynamic -- depending upon your perspective -- than ever before. Youthful and relatively inexperienced majority and minority leaders have now replaced the crusty, cigar-chomping pols of days gone by, but even these new faces will only be passing through, forced to seek other offices often after just six or eight years.

In short, the next decade in American politics will be dramatically different from the previous ones because of the fundamental changes that occurred during the 1990s. The Republican Party grew to be every bit the match of the Democrats, with term limitations almost insuring instability and change unless they are repealed.

THE 2000 ELECTIONS

Tip O'Neill only had it half right when he said "all politics is local." A more accurate characterization might be that "all politics is local, except when it isn't." In roughly two-thirds of our elections, local issues, individual candidates and specific circumstances are paramount. However, in another third, an invisible hand holds back the candidates of one party and pushes forward those of the other. Go tell a Republican candidate who lost or nearly lost during the recession of 1958, the Goldwater debacle of 1964, the Watergate election of 1974 or the recession of 1982 that all politics is local. Or tell a Democrat, who was pummeled in the 1966 recession, the 1980 Reagan landslide or the 1994 tsunami, the same. In all of these situations most of the candidates of one party started plunging in the polls while those of the other party began climbing for no rational, local reason. They were victims of a nationalized election.

More complicated are the "change-up" elections, when there is a sudden change in direction or momentum in the closing days of the campaign. This change almost instantaneously affects races from coast to coast without respect to circumstances. In 1996 for example, both national and district polls suggested that Democrats were headed for big gains, perhaps winning back the House. However, that momentum disappeared in the last two weeks of the campaign. Recall the 1990 election when Democrats seemed to be headed for fairly substantial gains after President Bush broke his "read my lips, no new taxes" pledge, but a last-minute focus on mounting tensions in the Persian Gulf shifted public attention enough to keep Republican losses minimal. More recently, Republicans seemed headed for modest gains in 1998 until a last minute anti-impeachment shift allowed the Democrats to hold their own in the Senate and pick up five seats in the House, confounding even the most optimistic of their own strategists.

The question on everyone's mind is whether that invisible hand will make an appearance in November 2000 and if so, where? Immediately after Bill Clinton's Senate impeachment trial had concluded, polling suggested that Republicans had suffered badly from the entire affair. Indeed, the generic Congressional ballot test measuring partisan preference gave Democrats a six- to 10-point advantage. An election at that point almost certainly would have resulted in Democrat's winning control of the House and perhaps substantial gains in the Senate. By May however, that Democratic advantage had disappeared, as had the probability, but not the possibility, that Democrats would recapture the House majority they lost in 1994 or make any huge Senate gains. In fact, the seat exposure for the two parties is almost perfectly symmetrical.

As of early June, each party had about a half dozen House seats in extreme jeopardy and about two dozen more that were either competitive or could easily become competitive. Democrats had three freshmen incumbents in real danger, Shelley Berkley (NV-01), Rush Holt (NJ-12) and Joe Hoeffel (PA-13), plus second-term Congressman Jim Maloney (CT-05) and an open seat in Michigan's 8th District where Debbie Stabenow is stepping down to run for the Senate.

Republicans should be most concerned with freshmen Robin Hayes (NC-08) and Don Sherwood (PA-10), who both barely won in 1998 and likely will face rematches in 2000; veteran Richard Baker (LA-06), who also faces a return engagement against a candidate who held him to just 51%, also warrants some concern. Jim Rogan (CA-27), who gained considerable national exposure as one of the most able and outspoken of the House managers prosecuting President

Clinton will face a strong opponent in a very marginal district. Rounding out the most vulnerable Republican list are two open seats, Oklahoma's 2d District, where Tom Coburn is retiring, and Washington's 2d District, where Jack Metcalf is also stepping down.

At this admittedly early stage in the 2000 campaign, there appears to be an unusually low number of competitive races, even lower than in 1990 and 1998, when the House playing field was exceedingly narrow. The final, pre-election issues of The Cook Political Report in 1992 showed 152 competitive races, a whopping 94 we listed as toss-ups. In 1994 there were 138 competitive races including 73 toss-ups, while in 1996 there were 119 competitive races, 57 of which were toss-ups. In 1998, the number of competitive races had dwindled to 62, with just 26 toss-ups, almost as low as in 1990 when there were 44 competitive contests, and 27 toss-ups.

There is no single reason for this decline in competition, though the rising cost of campaigns is certainly a major factor. There are also fewer Democrats sitting in what should be Republican seats, particularly in the southern and mountain states, just as there are fewer Republicans sitting in traditionally Democratic seats; most specifically in the Northeast but to a lesser extent in the Midwest. Both parties have consolidated in their strongest states and districts, providing fewer opportunities for takeovers. With the limits on party spending on individual candidates effectively removed, more party resources will likely be funneled into fewer races in 2000. This will concentrate the competition and create a small number of House races that will resemble smaller state Senate races in spending and sophistication. In the old days, national party committees ranked their target races from top to bottom; starting at the top of the list, they would "max out" by providing the maximum level of support for the top race. They would go down the list until they finally ran out of money somewhere near the middle. With the caps effectively removed, and with parties moving more into issue advocacy and independent expenditure advertising, more money will likely flow into the top races, meaning that funds will run out before the middle of the list.

The greatest focus in the House will be on open seats, as the incumbent re-election rate remains high, averaging 93.9% from 1980–98, ranging from a low of 88.3% in 1992 to a high of 98.3% in 1988 and the same in 1998. The greatest volatility in the House almost always comes in years with large numbers of open seats.

With few competitive races and open seats, the challenge for Democrats to score a net gain of six seats in the absence of some kind of momentum will be great. When elections are held on level playing fields, parties tend to suffer offsetting seat losses, making it difficult to accumulate big net gains. A net gain of six would be a far reach for 2000. Should Democrats develop some momentum, however, as they did at the close of the 1998 campaign, then gaining six would be highly possible, if not likely. The narrow playing field means Democrats have to win just over 60% of the 57 competitive races, which is certainly possible, but a tall order. Democrats don't need a major nationalization of the election, but they probably will need some boost of momentum, rather than individual race developments, to get them over the top.

Nothing in politics is ever impossible, giving Democrats some hope of recapturing control of the Senate, but it would take a major nationalization of the race in their favor to have any real chance. There are 19 Republican seats up for grabs in 2000, compared to only 14 for Democrats, who have four seats in immediate danger, compared to three for Republicans. Democrats need a lot of breaks to pick up the five seats if they hold the White House (a Democratic vice president can break the tie) or the six seats if they don't.

At the top of Democrats' target lists will be open Republican seats in Florida and Rhode Island, where Connie Mack and John Chafee are retiring. Next comes Missouri where Republican incumbent John Ashcroft is facing a stiff challenge from Democratic Governor Mel Carnahan in what is sure to be a very competitive race. In Michigan, freshman Republican Spence Abraham will face a very formidable adversary in Democratic Congresswoman Debbie Stabenow, the star recruit for Democrats so far this cycle. (Carnahan needed no recruiting.) Both Rod Grams in Minnesota and Rick Santorum in Pennsylvania appear to be very vulnerable but it's uncertain whether Democrats will nominate a top-tier candidate who will be up to the challenge in either race. In Washington, Slade Gorton always seems to face tough re-elections though Democrats have some unity problems at this writing. Democrats are anxiously awaiting decisions from Governor Tom Carper whether he will take on five-term Senator Bill Roth in Delaware and whether independent (but functionally a Democrat) Bernie Sanders will take on Jim Jeffords in Vermont. Both Carper and Sanders would be formidable challengers if they run, otherwise, the incumbent senators will be re-elected easily.

Republicans have their sights set on three Democratic open seats and one incumbent. First come the three "N's," Nevada where Dick Bryan is retiring, New Jersey where Frank Lautenberg is stepping down and New York, where the venerable Daniel Patrick Moynihan is not seeking a fifth-term. In Nevada, former Republican Congressman John Ensign, who came within 428 votes of unseating Senator Harry Reid in 1998, is almost certain to be the Republican nominee in 2000, while Democrats will likely field state Attorney General Frankie Sue Del Papa. Both are proven vote-getters and Nevada is increasingly becoming a competitive state though Del Papa has strained relations with organized labor, which undercut her chances somewhat. The Republican nod in New Jersey will be going to outgoing Governor Christie Todd Whitman, with the Democratic nomination still very much up in the air. Former Governor Jim Florio is running, seeking to avenge his 1991 re-election loss to Whitman, but Congressman Frank Pallone is also looking seriously at running, as is Jon Corzine, the very wealthy, former co-chairman of Goldman Sachs.

In New York, First Lady Hillary Rodham Clinton is edging closer to entering the race. New York City Mayor Rudy Giuliani seems all but announced to run on the Republican side. Late Spring polls show Clinton and Giuliani running roughly even when matched head-to-head. However, complicating matters for Giuliani, Republican Congressman Rick Lazio seems fairly determined to run, and is likely to both challenge Giuliani for the Republican nomination and seek the Conservative Party line. While Giuliani would certainly be favored to win the primary, Lazio could make it a race, given Giuliani's active campaigning for the much-hated (at least among Empire State Republicans) Mario Cuomo in 1994, his support for a New York City commuter tax and for partial-birth abortions. At the least, Lazio could soften Giuliani among Republicans. Many New York insiders say Lazio has the Conservative line all but wrapped up. The remaining question is whether Clinton could be beaten if Giuliani, carrying the Republican and possibly the Liberal Party lines, Lazio the Conservative line, and possibly a Right-to-Life candidate are in the race. Regardless, the presidential race is likely to share top billing with the New York Senate race.

Rounding out the list of vulnerable Democrats is Virginia's Charles Robb, who will face a very tough challenge from former Gov. George Allen. Early polls show Allen running well ahead but most observers expect the race to tighten once the fighting starts.

All-in-all, 2000 promises to be the most exciting election in recent memory: a "double-open" (no incumbent) presidential race, control of the House teetering on the edge and a complement of hotly-contested Senate races, which could include the Senate fight of the century in New York. Not a bad way to end an exciting decade and to begin a new millennium.

PRESIDENT

President William Jefferson (Bill) Clinton (D)

Elected 1992, term expires Jan. 2001; born, August 19, 1946, Hope, AR; home, Little Rock, AR; Georgetown U.; B.S. 1968; Rhodes Scholar, Oxford U., 1968–70; Yale U., J.D. 1973; Baptist; married (Hillary Rodham).

Elected Office: Dem. Nominee for U.S. House of Representatives, 1974; AR Atty. Gen., 1976–78; Gov. of AR, 1978–80, 1982–92.

Professional Career: Professor, U. of AR, 1974–76; Practicing atty., 1981–82.

Office: The White House, 1600 Pennsylvania Ave., NW, Washington, DC 20500, 202-456-1414; Web site: www.whitehouse.gov

VICE PRESIDENT

Vice President Albert (Al) Gore (D) Jr.

Elected 1992, term expires Jan. 2001; born, March 31, 1948, Washington, DC; home, Carthage, TN; Harvard, B.A. 1969; Vanderbilt School of Religion, 1971–72; Vanderbilt Law School, 1974–76; Baptist; married (Tipper).

Military Career: Army, 1969–71 (Vietnam).

Elected Office: U.S. House of Representatives, 1976–84; U.S. Senate, 1984–92.

Professional Career: Homebuilding business; Reporter, *Nashville Tennessean*, 1973–76.

Office: The White House, 1600 Pennsylvania Ave., NW, Washington, DC 20500, 202-456-1414; Web site: www.whitehouse.gov

1996 Presidential Vote		1992 Presidential Vote	
Clinton (D)	47,401,185 (49%)	Clinton (D)	44,908,233 (43%)
Dole (R)	39,197,469 (41%)	Bush (R)	39,102,282 (37%)
Perot (I)	8,085,294 (8%)	Perot (I)	19,741,048 (19%)

The People: Est. Pop. 1998: 270,298,524; Pop. 1990: 248,765,170, up 8.7% 1990–1998. 24.8& rural. Median age: 32.9 years. 12.6% 65 years and over. 75.6% White, 11.7% Black, 2.8% Asian, 1% American Indian; 9% Hispanic origin. Households: 55.1% married couple families; 25.6% married couple fams w. children; 45.3% college educ.; median household income: $30,056; per capita income: $14,420; 64.2% owner occupied housing; median house value: $79,100; median monthly rent: $374. 4.5% Unemployment. 1998 Voting age pop.: 200,927,000. 1998 Turnout: 72,454,276; 36% of VAP. Registered Voters (1998) (Est.): 149,845,904.

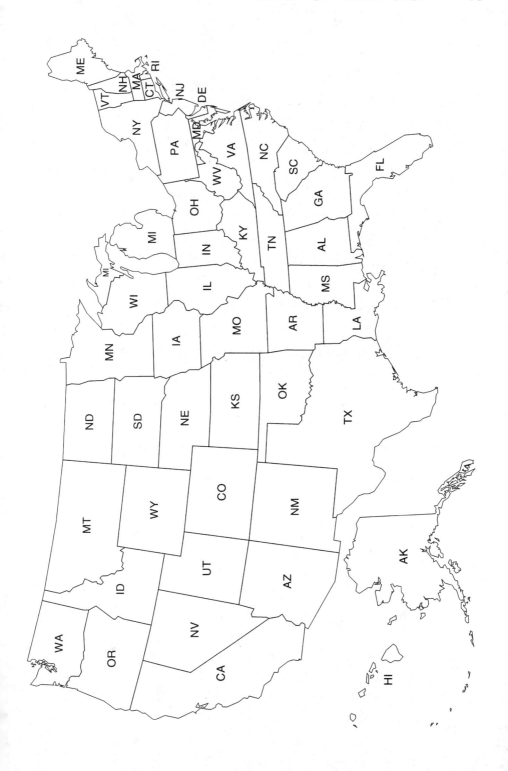

ALABAMA

The first capital of the Confederate States of America and the birthplace of the civil rights movement are both in Alabama, both in Montgomery. The restored Greek Revival Capitol stands on a hill overlooking downtown Montgomery where in February 1861 the Confederate Congress convened and Jefferson Davis took the oath of office as president of the Confederacy. Down the hill is the Dexter Avenue Baptist Church, where in December 1956 the 27-year-old Martin Luther King Jr. led the boycott that began when Rosa Parks refused to move to the back of the bus. The two buildings symbolize those two great movements that have done so much to set the civic tone of Alabama—the breakout of fiery defiance that led to the tragedy of the Civil War and the dignified resistance that produced the success of the civil rights revolution. Today both the Confederacy and the civil rights movement are celebrated, though as time goes on with less emphasis on the first and more on the latter: Maya Lin's circular Civil Rights Memorial in Montgomery, the Civil Rights Institute across the street from the 16th Street Baptist Church in Birmingham's Civil Rights District, the Pettus Bridge in Selma and the Dexter Avenue Baptist Church are among the many sites of civil rights and black history preserved and promoted by the state.

Yet for all the classic symmetry of the Capitol and the calm simplicity of the black churches, nature still seems untamed in Alabama, and the raw passions of the first settlers that gave life to these serene buildings often seem ready to break into anger and even violence. There has been a raucous tone to Alabama's history since the first Jacksonian farmers pushed the Indians west and plowed the steeply inclined red clay hills of northern Alabama, and the first plantation owners shipped in hundreds of slaves to grow cotton in the dark Black Belt soil. It was the violent reactions of white Alabamans that led to the greatest triumphs of civil rights: the police dogs and fire hoses of Birmingham in 1963 motivated President Kennedy to endorse what would become the Civil Rights Act of 1964, and the beatings on the bridge to Selma spurred President Johnson to propose the Voting Rights Act of 1965. Even in Alabama's peaceful economic development is evidence of the clang of metal on rock: miners hacking away in the 1880s at the solid-iron Red Mountain to feed newly cast steel mills glaring in the valley of Birmingham below; motorists of the 1990s speeding past exposed red earth of gouged-out hillsides towards the factories and Wal-Mart shopping centers that have sprouted up.

There is a similar rawness to Alabama's politics, as it has shifted from one of the nation's most Democratic to one of its more Republican states. In the 1930s and 1940s Alabama elected populist Democrats, crusaders against Wall Street and against the local economic potentates they called the "Big Mules": Hugo Black, a senator until he became a Supreme Court justice in 1937; Lister Hill and John Sparkman, who as senators sponsored landmark health and housing legislation; a House delegation that passed housing, health and public works bills. The dominant governor was Kissin' Jim Folsom, elected in 1946 and 1954, outsized in build and eloquence, whose career ended in 1962 when he appeared drunk in a late campaign appearance on the new medium of television; he lost the governor's race to his onetime protege, a young lawyer named George Wallace.

While Wallace was politicking, Martin Luther King was leading what turned out to be a civil rights revolution whose moral force he was among the first to comprehend. In the South of that day what King demanded seemed impossible, and in the short run it helped the politicians who most strongly proclaimed their opposition to desegregation. But in the long run it changed public life in America and in Alabama. But not before George Wallace made himself a national figure. Believing he had lost the 1958 governor's primary because he was "out-segged," he vowed that he never would be again. Elected governor in 1962, he pledged to stand in the

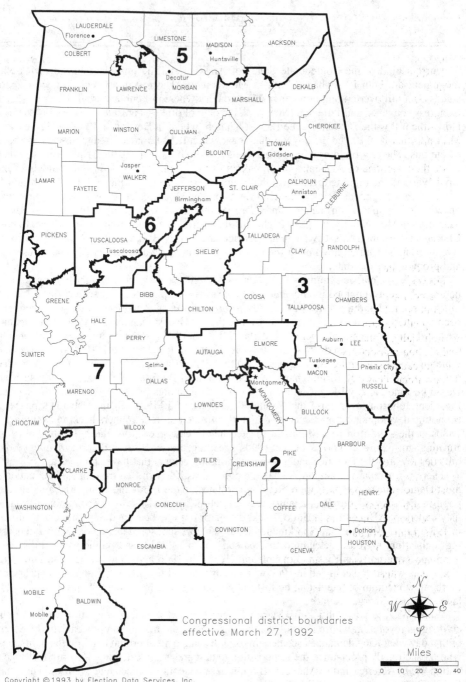

Congressional district boundaries effective March 27, 1992

Miles
0 10 20 30 40

schoolhouse door to prevent desegregation—a charade, but a dangerous one, for it encouraged violent resistance. It was the acts of Alabama officials—Birmingham Police Commissioner Bull Connor's police dogs and fire hoses in 1963, Sheriff Jim Clark's cordons in Selma in 1965—which, transmitted on evening newscasts, made civil rights a national issue. The North was no longer able to turn its eyes away from the South's legally imposed segregation, and most Americans decided it must end.

Despite his defeat, Wallace went national. With a shrewd sense of ordinary voters' resentment at elites' cultural liberalism, Wallace ran well in the 1964 and 1972 northern Democratic presidential primaries, and as a third-party candidate in the 1968 presidential race won 13.5% of the vote. He was partially paralyzed by a gunshot wound while campaigning in May 1972, and lost all force as a national politician when he lost to Jimmy Carter in the March 1976 Florida primary. But he remained the key figure in Alabama for a decade, retiring as governor in 1978 but returning to office in 1982 until his final retirement in 1986. He spent his last sad years apologizing for his acts, meeting with the grown-up student he tried to block in the schoolhouse door, and proclaiming, "The South has changed, and for the better," until his death in September 1998.

Unfortunately, in the Wallace years Alabama lost important ground. While Atlanta was peacefully desegregating and beginning three decades of vibrant white-collar growth, Birmingham was violently resisting the civil rights movement, only to see the shrinkage of its once substantial blue-collar base—the steel industry—and an outflow of talented people of all races. The state's economy, regarded as progressive when manufacturing was the leading edge of growth, seemed backward at the end of the Wallace era. The big steel mills of Birmingham turned cold as demand for steel fell; the shipyards of Mobile scrambled for work; the electric generators of TVA, once hailed as signs of progress, were condemned for burning dirty coal or allegedly hazardous nuclear fuel.

Politically, Wallace probably delayed for a generation the rise of the Republicans in Alabama and the non-metropolitan South. He gave cover to conservative Democratic candidates and pre-empted campaign money from Republicans. But since his retirement Alabama has moved toward Republicans. It voted for Republicans in five straight presidential elections, with Bob Dole carrying six of seven congressional districts. It has elected Republican governors in three of the last four contests, though one was forced from office and the other defeated for re-election. By the 1990s it was electing Republicans to downballot state offices. In 1996, when the last congressman elected as a Wallace Democrat retired after 30 years, the state's House delegation became 5–2 Republican.

The opposing political forces partly resemble those of 50 years ago. "Big Mules," angry at Alabama's ultraliberal tort law, are pro-Republican, but small business and tradition-minded Protestants are a bigger source of support; Republican enclaves are no longer confined to affluent urban precincts, but have spread out along the interstates to sprawling new subdivisions. The Democrats' institutional base is among teachers' unions and trial lawyers; their 1990 gubernatorial candidate had been a teacher and head of the Alabama Education Association, and their 1996 Senate candidate was a leading trial lawyer. The Republicans' base is larger, but more volatile: business conservatives on the one hand and religious conservatives on the other, determined to assert their beliefs in the public square.

In 1998, Governor Fob James was opposed for renomination by Winton Blount Jr., who argued that James had looked foolish promoting prayer in schools and allowed trial lawyers too much influence; former Governor Guy Hunt, freshly pardoned after an April 1993 conviction for misusing $200,000 in inaugural funds, stepped into the race as well. For the first time ever, more Alabamians voted in the Republican than the Democratic primary, 359,000 to 358,000—a sign of vitality perhaps for Republicans. But the Democrats were united in their support for Lieutenant Governor Don Siegelman, and when James eventually won a fractious runoff, Siegelman easily defeated him in November.

In the 1980s, Democrats fought each other for power; in the 1990s, it was Republicans who scrapped like dogs. Both parties paid a political price and now they are struggling against each other. Just days before he was set to take office, Siegelman made rule changes to limit the power of the lieutenant governor, who also serves as president of the state Senate, brandishing the power to appoint committees and direct the flow of legislation. This infuriated incoming Republican Lieutenant Governor Steve Windom and his coalition of 12 Republicans and five Democrats, who on the first day of the legislative session changed back the rules on a contested voice vote. The 18-Democrat majority boycotted sessions for nearly a month, until Siegelman called a special meeting that turned into a four-day session, during which Republicans filibustered and Windom felt compelled to urinate into a jug behind his podium for fear he would lose his powers if he left his post. The two groups finally reached an agreement under which both would share the power to appoint committee chairs and assign bills.

Governor. Don Siegelman was elected governor on his second try in 1998, after a political career lasting nearly 30 years. He grew up in Mobile, went to the University of Alabama and was elected student body president in 1968. While at Georgetown Law he worked as a Capitol policeman. He studied at Oxford and practiced law in Birmingham with Robert Vance, a federal judge who was later murdered. Siegelman became executive director of the state Democratic Party while Vance was chairman. He has been elected to statewide office five times now, as secretary of state in 1978 and 1982, attorney general in 1986 and lieutenant governor in 1994; he ran second in the Democratic primary for governor in 1990. As lieutenant governor, he ran the state Senate, and came out on the side of trial lawyers' in tort reform controversies. By 1998 he had no serious opposition in the primary for governor.

That was very much not the case for incumbent Republican Fob James. Elected governor as a Democrat in 1978, James was a familiar figure. In 1994 he ran as a Republican and won a come-from-behind victory over Acting Governor Jim Folsom Jr., who had been weakened by primary opposition. James made his biggest headlines on school prayer issues. He urged schools to defy court orders banning school prayer. When a county judge was ordered to remove a copy of the Ten Commandments posted in his courtroom, James threatened to call out the National Guard to protect him. When Attorney General Bill Pryor took the case to the Court of Appeals, James, with his son as his lawyer, filed an appeal in the U.S. Supreme Court, maintaining that federal courts could not apply the Bill of Rights to the states. This of course was the original understanding, but has been rejected by more than 50 years of settled precedent.

This was too much for many business conservatives. Winton Blount Jr., son of Richard Nixon's postmaster general (and donor of Alabama's Shakespeare theater) ran against James in the Republican primary. He said James had done little for economic development and had embarrassed the state. "A governor should be widely known for his achievements instead of his antics." For many, James's threat to call up the National Guard recalled George Wallace's standing in the schoolhouse door. "He's hurt our image," Blount said. Blount mentioned the day in 1995 when James appeared before the state Board of Education "walking across the stage like a monkey" to mock the theory of evolution. James, who called his opponent Win *TON*, responded, "I'm a monkey that's in good shape. I'm not a fat monkey. I'm not a monkey whose daddy has put $2.5 million in my campaign either." James led in the first primary 48%–41%; Guy Hunt's impulsive decision to run when he received his pardon deprived James of a majority. James won the runoff 56%–44%, carrying all but five counties but losing Birmingham, Huntsville, Montgomery and his original home town of Auburn.

Siegelman had two big advantages in the general election, his lottery-and-education plan and Fob James. As Siegelman put it, "Fob has done for me what I could never do for myself: divide the Republican Party and at the same time unite the Democratic Party." James also raised little money: in mid-September Siegelman had $3.6 million on hand and James $369,000, and James put ads up a month later than the challenger. Siegelman's lottery plan was modeled on the highly popular plan of former Georgia Governor Zell Miller, with lottery proceeds of $150 million to go to merit-based college scholarship, pre-kindergarten programs and computers for schools. James was against the lottery on moral grounds, and said a tax increase would be needed to pay for Siegelman's proposal. Siegelman, like Jim Hodges in South Carolina, argued that Alabamians were buying lottery tickets in Georgia and educating kids there. "We've already got a lottery. . . . I'm just saying we need to keep those hundreds of millions of dollars that are leaving Alabama." Siegelman's proposal was highly popular, and James was unable to change the subject—unless it was to defying courts on school prayer. But that hurt among upscale voters.

Thus in an election year that favored consensus over confrontation, the incumbent managed to sound confrontational and the challenger built a consensus. Siegelman won by an impressive 58%–42% margin, carrying all but 11 counties. He carried the big urban counties, usually Republican, by large margins. He cut into the upscale vote: James's percentage fell by only 4% among under-$30,000 voters, but by 18% among $30,000–75,000 voters. In 1994 James carried college graduates 53%–47%; in 1998 he lost them 59%–40%. James's percentage actually increased in 14 rural counties, but it was down 12% in the Birmingham area, 16% in Montgomery County, 15% in Huntsville, and 9% in Mobile. Siegelman certainly won a mandate for his lottery-plus-scholarship plans. But on the issue that dominated state politics before 1998, tort reform, trial lawyers lost ground as a Republican was elected lieutenant governor with 50.2% of the vote.

Senior Senator. Richard Shelby grew up in Birmingham, the son of a steelworker. After earning two degrees from the University of Alabama, he stayed in Tuscaloosa and went into law practice with Walter Flowers, later a conservative Democratic congressman; Shelby was well enough politically connected to be elected state senator in 1970, at 36. When Flowers ran for the Senate in 1978, and lost the Democratic primary to Howell Heflin, Shelby ran for his House seat. The critical contest was the Democratic runoff against Chris McNair, a black legislator whose daughter had been killed in the 1963 Birmingham church bombing. The district had the highest black percentage in Alabama at that time, and Shelby compiled a conservative voting record once in office, opposing the Voting Rights Act extension and the Martin Luther King Holiday. In the 1986 Senate race, he won the primary with 51% after getting a liberal to withdraw, then ran TV ads attacking incumbent Jeremiah Denton, a retired admiral who had been a prisoner of war in Vietnam, for voting to cut Social Security and owning two Mercedes (not a likely negative now, with the Mercedes plant in Tuscaloosa). Shelby won by 7,000 votes.

In the Senate Shelby was one of half a dozen or so conservative southern Democrats and attracted little notice. He voted for the confirmation of Clarence Thomas and for the Gulf war resolution. He voted against the campaign finance bill supported by almost all Democrats and he voted for the Strategic Defense Initiative. He was a major sponsor of a law to enforce court orders on fathers who default on child support payments. After a young Shelby aide was murdered a few blocks from the Capitol, Shelby pushed through a law requiring the District of Columbia to hold a referendum on capital punishment—it lost. In 1992 he beat Republican Richard Sellers easily, 65%–33%; this broke the political jinx on this seat which, before Shelby's election in 1986, had four occupants in 10 years.

Shelby's break with the Democratic Party came soon after Bill Clinton took office. In February 1993, angered by Shelby's criticism of the president's just-released economic plan—"the taxman cometh"—Clinton strategists ostentatiously decided to make an example of him and Shelby ostentatiously decided to make a display of his independence. At a meeting in which Vice President Al Gore tried to persuade Shelby to support the plan, Shelby turned to the 19 Alabama TV cameras there and, embarrassing Gore, further denounced the Clinton program as "high on taxes, low on spending cuts." As punishment, a multi-million dollar space facility was moved from Alabama to Texas. But, as Clinton's ratings slid downward, this only raised Shelby's popularity ratings to the highest level in the state, making a politician previously known more for his suppleness of maneuver now appear an embattled defender of principle. In retrospect this was a harbinger of the 1994 elections: a state long hungry for federal largess was willing to ease up pork in order to get a lower deficit. Relentlessly but without evident rancor, Shelby voted against the administration again and again and lined up with Republicans on almost every partisan issue, criticizing the Democrats' health care plan as "ill-conceived, unworkable and unwanted by the American people."

So it was not much of a surprise when, the day after Republicans regained control of the Senate in 1994, Shelby announced he was switching parties and increased the Republican majority to 53–47. Republicans happily allowed him to keep his seniority on the Banking Committee, ahead of those elected as Republicans in the same year, and gave him seats on Appropriations and its Defense Subcommittee and on Intelligence as well; he chaired the Treasury-Postal Appropriations Subcommittee, and in 1997 moved over to chair the Transportation Subcommittee. He became chairman of Intelligence in 1997 when Arlen Specter rotated off and Richard Lugar chose to remain chairman of Agriculture.

As a Republican, Shelby has maintained his conservative record and has sponsored many conservative measures: the balanced budget amendment, English as the official language, prohibiting takings of land without compensation under the Endangered Species and Wetlands Acts. He is the Senate sponsor of House Majority Leader Dick Armey's 17% flat tax. He sought to cut legal immigration to 350,000 annually. As Intelligence chairman, he criticized Anthony Lake's nomination as CIA director because of his role in allowing Iranian arms sales to Bosnian Muslims in 1994 and his involvement in Democratic fundraising efforts in 1996. Shelby presided over the less controversial confirmation of George Tenet in May 1997.

But Shelby is not a doctrinaire market conservative. Despite his party switch he has remained friendly with trial lawyers, who usually support Democrats in Alabama. He opposed his colleague Jeff Sessions's amendment to cap lawyers' fees in tobacco cases, and insists tort reform should be only a state issue. And, as an appropriator with jurisdiction over transportation, he supported enough projects to be named 1998 "King of Pork" by Citizens Against Government Waste. Projects totalling $80 million went to Huntsville (a missile and space intelligence center, advanced research center, battle integration center, software engineering complex) and to a tornado preparedness center in the town of Arab. The latter was attacked as pork by John McCain in July 1997 and line-item vetoed by Bill Clinton. But Shelby got it into an emergency spending bill—and had the satisfaction of seeing Clinton visit Alabama in May 1998 the week after a tornado. In October 1998 Shelby threatened to hold up the transportation authorization; to stop him Majority Leader Trent Lott promised another $100 million. Another Shelby cause: getting the Wright Amendment changed to allow direct flights from Alabama to Dallas's Love Field. Shelby was one of two votes in committee that held up the financial services bill in September 1998; he is concerned about expansion of the Community Reinvestment Act, and tried to get smaller banks exempted from it.

On Intelligence, Shelby found the Wye River Memorandum's use of CIA officers to monitor compliance "troubling," and promised to investigate the use of American-made satellites by the Chinese to gather military intelligence. He sought to allow CIA agents to disclose classified information to Congress related to violations of law or wrongdoing; the House and the administration stopped that. In 1999, charging that the Clinton Administration had done little to address Chinese spying at the Los Alamos National Laboratory, he introduced a measure that would curb visits to nuclear labs by foreign scientists. At Shelby's urging, the Senate Banking Committee in May 1999 began an investigation into suspicious ties between China and the Los Angeles-based Far East National Bank, which had received large deposits from the country.

Shelby's seat came up in 1998. He raised over $5 million, and no serious Democrat ran. The state AFL-CIO even discouraged Democrats to run, fearing Shelby would turn out Republican voters. The Democratic nominee, Clayton Suddith, a retired ironworker and former Franklin County commissioner, mortgaged his pickup truck to pay the $2,672 filing fee and was arrested for public intoxication at 11 a.m. one August morning. Shelby won 63%–37%, with most of the $5 million unspent.

Junior Senator. Alabama's junior senator, Jeff Sessions, had the satisfaction of being elected in 1996 to replace the Democrat who had blocked his nomination to a federal judgeship in 1986, Howell Heflin. Sessions grew up in Alabama's Black Belt, practiced law in a small town near the Tennessee Valley, became a federal prosecutor and then practiced law in Mobile. He was appointed U.S. Attorney in 1981, at 36, where he became known as a tough, aggressive prosecutor. In 1985 he was nominated for federal judge, but was attacked by some liberals for "gross insensitivity" in racial matters, and defended by conservatives; Heflin voted against him in the Judiciary Committee and his nomination never went to the floor. In 1994 Sessions ran against state Attorney General Jimmy Evans, who had successfully prosecuted Governor Guy Hunt the year before. Sessions won that race 57%–43% and, when Heflin announced his retirement in March 1995, Sessions immediately became the favorite to win the seat.

There were contests in both 1996 primaries, with 315,000 voting Democratic and 215,000 Republican; seven Republicans and four Democrats ran. Sessions started early, avoiding debates and controversy, and relying on his base in southern Alabama, territory that not long ago cast almost no Republican primary votes. The strongest competitor was long-distance carrier executive Sid McDonald, who ultimately spent more than $1 million, attacking Sessions for office-hopping, accepting a lenient plea bargain for a murderer, and improperly favoring tobacco and insurance companies. From Birmingham north, it was a close race: McDonald led Sessions there in the June 4 primary by 30%–29%. But in the rest of the state, Sessions led 48%–12%, for a 38%–22% statewide margin. In the runoff McDonald continued his attacks and Sessions ducked debates. McDonald extended his lead north from Birmingham, 54%–46%, but almost half the votes were cast to the south, and there Sessions led 73%–27%, for a 59%–41% win.

The Democrats also had a spirited contest, with an outcome different from historic precedent. In another era, the winner would probably have been Glen Browder, who had served three years as secretary of state and five years as congressman from the 3d District covering both the Birmingham and Montgomery media markets. But in this smaller primary electorate, the moderate Browder was outflanked and outcampaigned by candidates on his left. One was Natalie Davis, a Birmingham-Southern College political scientist and pollster who traveled around the state in a bus. Another was Roger Bedford, state Senator and trial lawyer, with the kind of dramatic past that seemed so resonant in campaign year 1996: in 1989, while running for attorney general, he was diagnosed with terminal cancer; he survived and nearly won the Democratic runoff. Bedford raised lots of money from trial lawyers and was endorsed by key public employee unions and black organizations—the heart of today's Alabama Democratic Party. Bedford won 45% in the June 4 primary, to 29% for Browder and 23% for Davis. In the June 25 runoff, Browder attacked Bedford for supporting NAFTA and gambling, and for being backed by trial lawyer. But Bedford had $400,000 to Browder's $75,000 coming out of the primary, and was the better campaigner as well. Bedford carried everything outside Browder's home district and won 62%–38%.

Bedford also proved the better campaigner in the general, was competitive in fundraising, and ran close in the polls. "The old liberal days of tax and spend are over," he insisted, and opposed abortion, gun control, and gays in the military. He accused Sessions of backing "the extreme Newt Gingrich agenda." Sessions avoided debates, at which Bedford excelled, and attacked the Democrat as a Ted Kennedy backer and for leading the battle against tort reform in the Alabama Senate in January 1996. He called government "a ball and chain on private enterprise" and signed the Americans for Tax Reform anti-tax pledge, while Bedford didn't. Sessions won 52%–45%, running best in the suburbanizing counties around Alabama's cities; Bedford carried the Black Belt and many rural counties in the north.

In the Senate, Sessions has a very conservative voting record. He has held up more than a few judicial nominations, to the point that Judiciary Chairman Orrin Hatch accused him of "playing politics with judges." Sessions sponsored a bill to replace the National Endowment for the Arts with block grants, which lost 62–37; then Majority Leader Trent Lott put him on the National Council of the Arts which oversees the NEA. He was one of the few to oppose the budget agreement of 1997 and one of 29 to oppose the final spending package for the 1999 budget. But he was undaunted by being on the short end of many votes. "Issues involving family and morality and excessive spending are very important to me, and I didn't come up here to be a potted plant." He passed an amendment limiting attorneys' fees in tobacco cases only to see it effectively overruled, 50–48.

Sessions's big project in 1998 was a juvenile justice bill, which would allow 14-year-olds to be tried as adults, allow juveniles and adults in the same prisons and ban automatic release of juveniles when they become adults. It was opposed by liberals as overly harsh, by gun control opponents for its weapons provisions and by Chief Justice William Rehnquist for fear it would over-expand federal jurisdiction. Sessions called Rehnquist and assured him he was "incorrect" and that only a few cases would be affected. In any case, it was never called up for consideration by the full Senate.

Presidential politics. Alabama is pretty firmly established as one of the most Republican states in presidential elections; it was a sign of Bill Clinton's confidence that he stopped there in the last days of the 1996 campaign. Alabama's presidential primary, held on Super Tuesday in the 1980s, was moved to June in 1992. About half of the 662,000 Democrats who turned out in 1996 were black; among the 211,000 Republicans who voted, Bob Dole led Pat Buchanan 76%–16%.

Congressional districting. The Voting Rights Act, as revised in 1982, was the engine that drove Alabama's congressional redistricting in 1992. The plan adopted was proposed by Republicans and ordered into effect by a federal court. The 68% black 7th District, stretching from central Birmingham through the Black Belt counties to downtown Montgomery, was the only Clinton district in 1992 and 1996. Republicans captured the 2d and 6th Districts in 1992 and the 3d and 4th in 1996, and now have a 5–2 edge in the delegation.

The People: Est. Pop. 1998: 4,351,999; Pop. 1990: 4,040,587, up 7.7% 1990–1998. 1.6% of U.S. total, 23d largest; 39.7% rural. Median age: 34.9 years. 13.5% 65 years and over. 73.6% White, 25.2% Black, 0.5% Asian, 0.5% Amer. Indian, 0.1% Other; 0.6% Hispanic Origin. Households: 57% married couple families; 27.7% married couple fams. w. children; 37.4% college educ.; median household income: $23,597; per capita income: $11,486; 70.5% owner occupied housing; median house value: $53,700; median monthly rent: $229. 4.2% Unemployment. 1998 Voting age pop.: 3,293,000. 1998 Turnout: 1,317,842; 40% of VAP. Registered voters (1998): 2,316,598; no party registration.

Political Lineup: Governor, Don Siegelman (D); Lt. Gov., Steve Windom (R); Secy. of State, Jim Bennett (R); Atty. Gen., Bill Pryor (R); Treasurer, Lucy Baxley (D); State Senate, 35 (23 D, 12 R); Majority Leader, Tom Butler (D); State Assembly, 105 (69 D, 36 R); House Speaker, Seth Hammett (D). Senators, Richard C. Shelby (R) and Jeff Sessions (R). Representatives, 7 (2 D, 5 R).

Elections Division: 334-242-7205; **Filing Deadline for U.S. Congress:** April 7, 2000.

1996 Presidential Vote

Dole (R)	768,826	(50%)
Clinton (D)	662,066	(43%)
Perot (I)	92,628	(6%)

1996 Republican Presidential Primary

Dole (R)	160,097	(76%)
Buchanan (R)	33,409	(16%)
Others	18,427	(8%)

1992 Presidential Vote

Bush (R)	804,283	(48%)
Clinton (D)	690,080	(41%)
Perot (I)	183,109	(11%)

GOVERNOR
Gov. Don Siegelman (D)

Elected 1998, term expires Jan. 2003; b. Feb. 24, 1946, Mobile; home, Montgomery; U. of AL, B.A. 1968, Georgetown U., J.D. 1972, Oxford U.1972–73; Catholic; married (Lori).

Military Career: Air Natl. Guard, 1968–69.

Elected Office: AL Secy. of State, 1978–86; AL Atty. Gen., 1986–90; AL Lt. Gov., 1994–98.

Professional Career: Practicing atty.; Capitol Hill Policeman, 1971; Law Clerk, U.S. Dept of Justice; Vestavia City Prosecutor; Exec. Dir, AL Dem. Party, 1973–78. .

Office: Alabama State Capitol, 11 S. Union St., Montgomery, 36130, 334-242-7150; Fax: 334-242-4407; Web site: www.state.al.us.

Election Results

1998 gen.	Don Siegelman (D)	....	760,155	(58%)
	Fob James Jr. (R)	....	554,746	(42%)
1998 prim.	Don Siegelman (D)	....	280,181	(78%)
	Lenora Pate (D)	....	59,300	(17%)
	Others	....	18,698	(5%)
1994 gen.	Fob James (R)	....	604,926	(50%)
	James Folsom Jr. (D)	....	594,169	(49%)

SENATORS
Sen. Richard C. Shelby (R)

Elected 1986, seat up 2004; b. May 6, 1934, Birmingham; home, Tuscaloosa; U. of AL, B.A. 1957, LL.B. 1963; Presbyterian; married (Annette).

Elected Office: AL Senate, 1970–78; U.S. House of Reps., 1978–86.

Professional Career: Practicing atty., 1963–78.

DC Office: 110 HSOB, 20510, 202-224-5744; Fax: 202-224-3416; Web site: www.senate.gov/~shelby.

State Offices: Birmingham, 205-731-1384; Huntsville, 205-772-0460; Mobile, 334-694-4164; Montgomery, 334-223-7303; Tuscaloosa, 205-759-5047.

Committees: *Aging (Special)* (5th of 11 R). *Appropriations* (9th of 15 R): Defense; Foreign Operations & Export Financing; Transportation (Chmn.); Treasury & General Government; VA, HUD & Independent Agencies. *Banking, Housing & Urban Affairs* (2d of 11 R): Financial Institutions; Housing & Transportation; Securities. *Intelligence* (Chmn. of 9 R).

Group Ratings

	ADA	ACLU	AFS	LCV	CON	NTU	NFIB	COC	ACU	NTLC	CHC
1998	5	14	11	0	2	64	89	78	92	85	100
1997	5	—	0	—	61	79	—	90	92	—	—

National Journal Ratings

	1997 LIB — 1997 CONS			1998 LIB — 1998 CONS	
Economic	44%	—	52%	18%	—	72%
Social	0%	—	83%	0%	—	88%
Foreign	0%	—	77%	29%	—	58%

Key Votes of the 105th Congress

1. Bal. Budget Amend.	Y	5. Satcher for Surgeon Gen.	N	9. Chem. Weapons Treaty	N
2. Clinton Budget Deal	Y	6. Highway Set-asides	N	10. Cuban Humanitarian Aid	N
3. Cloture on Tobacco	N	7. Table Child Gun locks	Y	11. Table Bosnia Troops	Y
4. Education IRAs	Y	8. Ovrd. Part. Birth Veto	Y	12. $ for Test-ban Treaty	N

Election Results

1998 general	Richard C. Shelby (R) 817,973	(63%)	($1,890,484)
	Clayton Suddith (D) 474,568	(37%)	($15,723)
1998 primary	Richard C. Shelby (R) .... unopposed		
1992 general	Richard C. Shelby (D) 1,022,698	(65%)	($2,807,764)
	Richard Sellers (R) 522,015	(33%)	($149,578)
	Others 31,811	(2%)	

Sen. Jeff Sessions (R)

Elected 1996, seat up 2002; b. Dec. 24, 1946, Hybert; home, Mobile; Huntingdon Col., B.A. 1969, U. of AL, J.D. 1973; Methodist; married (Mary).

Military Career: Army Reserves, 1973–86.

Elected Office: AL Atty. Gen., 1994–96.

Professional Career: Practicing atty., 1973–75, 1977–81, 1993–94; Asst. U.S. Atty., 1975–77; U.S. Atty., 1981–93.

DC Office: 495 RSOB, 20510, 202-224-4124; Fax: 202-224-3149; Web site: www.senate.gov/~sessions.

State Offices: Birmingham, 205-731-1500; Huntsville, 256-533-0979; Mobile, 334-690-3167; Montgomery, 334-265-9507.

Committees: *Armed Services* (11th of 11 R): Emerging Threats & Capabilities; Seapower; Strategic Forces. *Health, Education, Labor & Pensions* (10th of 10 R): Employment, Safety & Training; Public Health. *Judiciary* (9th of 10 R): Administrative Oversight & the Courts; Criminal Justice Oversight; Youth Violence (Chmn.). *Joint Economic Committee* (6th of 10 Sens.).

Group Ratings

	ADA	ACLU	AFS	LCV	CON	NTU	NFIB	COC	ACU	NTLC	CHC
1998	0	14	0	0	71	74	100	89	100	100	100
1997	0	—	0	—	47	85	—	70	100	—	—

National Journal Ratings

	1997 LIB — 1997 CONS			1998 LIB — 1998 CONS	
Economic	0%	—	89%	0%	—	88%
Social	0%	—	83%	0%	—	88%
Foreign	0%	—	77%	0%	—	88%

Key Votes of the 105th Congress

1. Bal. Budget Amend.	Y	5. Satcher for Surgeon Gen.	N	9. Chem. Weapons Treaty	N
2. Clinton Budget Deal	Y	6. Highway Set-asides	N	10. Cuban Humanitarian Aid	N
3. Cloture on Tobacco	N	7. Table Child Gun locks	Y	11. Table Bosnia Troops	N
4. Education IRAs	Y	8. Ovrd. Part. Birth Veto	Y	12. $ for Test-ban Treaty	N

Election Results

1996 general	Jeff Sessions (R)	786,436	(52%)	($3,862,359)
	Roger Bedford (D)	681,651	(45%)	($2,284,801)
	Others	31,306	(2%)	
1996 runoff	Jeff Sessions (R)	81,681	(59%)	
	Sid McDonald (R)	56,156	(41%)	
1996 primary	Jeff Sessions (R)	80,694	(38%)	
	Sid McDonald (R)	47,320	(22%)	
	Charles Woods (R)	23,796	(11%)	
	Frank McRight (R)	21,818	(10%)	
	Walter Clark (R)	18,513	(9%)	
	Jimmy Blake (R)	15,305	(7%)	
	Others	7,600	(4%)	
1990 general	Howell Heflin (D)	717,814	(61%)	($3,437,073)
	Bill Cabaniss (R)	467,190	(39%)	($1,853,869)

FIRST DISTRICT

Mobile, the port where the Tombigbee and Alabama rivers flow into the Gulf of Mexico, was long a key point on the American frontier. Spanish until after the Revolutionary War, it was wrested away by threats of war from Secretary of State John Quincy Adams. During the Civil War it was one of the major Confederate ports; here in 1864 Admiral David Farragut, while steaming into the harbor lashed to his mast, cried, "Damn the torpedoes! Full speed ahead." Today Mobile is full of graceful signs of its slightly exotic past: behind the docks and rail lines are downtown buildings and old houses with Spanish motifs, French accents, or tropical Art Deco lines. Further inland are neighborhoods with spacious houses, often with double porches, overhung by huge live oaks, graced with Spanish moss. Mobile is a Gulf Coast version of Charleston or a smaller, more comfortable New Orleans, with a taste for shellfish and spicy food and an even older Mardi Gras. As befits a frontier city with a martial past, Mobile is bristling with arms: one of the city's proudest possessions is the battleship *U.S.S. Alabama*, moored at the head of Mobile Bay, with its guns aimed out toward the Gulf. Mobile's economy was based originally on docks and shipyards, factories and terminals, but with a determination to impose touches of beauty on its hot, flat landscape. For years this southern seaboard of the Confederacy and the Union has been one of the most hawkish parts of America, and today it is solidly Republican in national elections. Its economy is thriving again; the shipyards and chemical plants have been busy and upriver new timber and paper mills are running.

Mobile is the focus of Alabama's 1st Congressional District, which extends north along the lazily flowing Tombigbee and Alabama rivers, near the old forts and mansions. This was the home of great writers—Harper Lee, whose *To Kill a Mockingbird* is set here, and her childhood playmate Truman Capote; and Winston Groom, author of *Forrest Gump*—and of old-fashioned southern traditions still lovingly maintained. Also here are surviving back-country settlements of blacks and Cajans (who may or may not be descended from Louisiana Cajuns) and Creek Indians. To the south, along the shores of the Gulf of Mexico, are fast-growing condominium communities; the glorious Gulf beaches are one of the South's best-kept secrets and this is one of the fastest-growing—and most Republican—parts of Alabama.

The congressman from the 1st District is Sonny Callahan, a Republican with a rags-to-riches biography, a party-switcher who now chairs one of the key subcommittees in the House. The oldest boy in a family of nine children whose father died young, Callahan went to work at the age of 12, during World War II; fortunately, the boss was his uncle, a warehouse company owner. He served in the Navy during Korea, then rose to become president of the company at 32 and expanded into real estate and insurance. Like so many go-getters, he ran for the state legislature and was elected at 38. As a Democrat, he lost the 1982 primary for lieutenant governor to liberal Bill Baxley. Then 1st District Republican Congressman Jack Edwards decided to retire in 1984 after 20 years and asked Callahan to run as a Republican; he did and won, with 61% in the primary and 51% in the general. For years he had a very conservative voting record; with the Republican majority pushing the House toward the right, he winds up as a bit moderate on economic and foreign policy.

From his modest beginnings and provincial political base, Callahan now occupies a key position in American foreign policy as chairman of the Appropriations Foreign Operations Subcommittee. For 10 years Callahan voted against all foreign aid bills; in 1995 he became chairman, and started writing them, as well as exerting influence just by talking. Bill Clinton has sought his advice; it was Callahan with whom Clinton was talking on the phone while he was busy with Monica Lewinsky in November 1995, though when the story came out in August 1998 Callahan said, "I can say unequivocally and without hesitation that I had no knowledge I was sharing the president's time or attention with anyone else." In October 1997 he threatened to cut off aid to Israel if they failed to extradite accused murderer Samuel Sheinbein; he withdrew the threat after then-Prime Minister Benjamin Netanyahu called him in Mobile. In his first year as chairman his budget was $2.4 billion less than the president's request; the next year it was $700 million less. It is no wonder that Secretary of State Madeleine Albright has taken time to deliver a speech in Mobile.

Callahan has insisted that voters are "sick of being asked to pay more, only to make government bigger, but not necessarily better," but he is not unwilling to steer some of that spending to south Alabama: a study of high-speed rail on the Gulf coast, the I-10 Mobile Causeway fog detection system, the Weeks Bay estuarine reserve. He has fought to preserve the Coastal Zone Management program and sought parity with Mississippi and Louisiana when the National Marine Fisheries Service said red snapper was overfished by commercial shrimp trawlers—an attempt to keep Mobile fishermen working.

Callahan was a supporter of fellow Gulf Coaster Bob Livingston for speaker; in return he was named one of three assistant speakers—but that was short-lived. He has been re-elected easily, in 1998 without opposition, but he has an exit plan: he lives on a houseboat in Washington which, he explains, he can take back to the 1st District when he retires.

Cook's Call. *Safe.* Though this Mobile-based district is not the most Republican in the state, Callahan has little reason for concern about re-election. While any Republican would have a huge advantage here, Callahan seems to have a lock on the seat for as long as he wants.

The People: Pop. 1990: 577,375; 34.1% rural; 13.1% age 65+; 69.8% White, 28.5% Black, 0.6% Asian, 1% Amer. Indian, 0.1% Other; 0.8% Hispanic Origin. Households: 56.3% married couple families; 28.4% married couple fams. w. children; 36.4% college educ.; median household income: $22,881; per capita income: $10,961; median house value: $53,000; median gross rent: $229.

1996 Presidential Vote			1992 Presidential Vote		
Dole (R)	112,999	(53%)	Bush (R)	118,420	(51%)
Clinton (D)	83,920	(39%)	Clinton (D)	84,193	(36%)
Perot (I)	14,660	(7%)	Perot (I)	26,749	(12%)

Rep. Sonny Callahan (R)

Elected 1984; b. Sept. 11, 1932, Mobile; home, Mobile; U. of AL, 1959–60; Catholic; married (Karen).

Military Career: Navy, 1952–54.

Elected Office: AL House of Reps., 1970–78; AL Senate, 1978–82.

Professional Career: Finch Cos. 1955–85, Pres., 1964–85.

DC Office: 2418 RHOB 20515, 202-225-4931; Fax: 202-225-0562; Web site: www.house.gov/callahan.

District Office: Mobile, 334-690-2811.

Committees: *Appropriations* (11th of 34 R): Energy & Water Development; Foreign Operations & Export Financing (Chmn.); Transportation.

Group Ratings

	ADA	ACLU	AFS	LCV	CON	NTU	NFIB	COC	ACU	NTLC	CHC
1998	0	7	0	8	8	50	92	100	96	100	100
1997	5	—	25	—	56	53	—	90	88	—	—

National Journal Ratings

	1997 LIB — 1997 CONS	1998 LIB — 1998 CONS
Economic	33% — 66%	0% — 88%
Social	10% — 82%	0% — 97%
Foreign	29% — 71%	43% — 53%

Key Votes of the 105th Congress

1. Clinton Budget Deal	Y	5. Puerto Rico Sthood. Ref.	N	9. Cut $ for B-2 Bombers	N
2. Education IRAs	Y	6. End Highway Set-asides	Y	10. Human Rights in China	N
3. Req. 2/3 to Raise Taxes	Y	7. School Prayer Amend.	Y	11. Withdraw Bosnia Troops	N
4. Fast-track Trade	Y	8. Ovrd. Part. Birth Veto	Y	12. End Cuban TV-Marti	N

Election Results

1998 general	Sonny Callahan (R) .... unopposed		($263,347)
1998 primary	Sonny Callahan (R) .... unopposed		
1996 general	Sonny Callahan (R) 132,206	(64%)	($402,128)
	Don Womack (D) 69,470	(34%)	($39,826)
	Others 3,741	(2%)	

SECOND DISTRICT

The thick green countryside is everywhere in southern Alabama. Even in Montgomery the stone and brick buildings that rise in the irregular downtown grid do not mask the contours of the hills or hide the lush foliage. You can look downhill from the restored Greek Revival Capitol toward Dexter Avenue Baptist Church where Martin Luther King Jr. was pastor, or out past the impressive theater where the Alabama Shakespeare Festival is held, toward new subdivisions and shopping malls, and easily imagine when this land was covered with pine trees and cotton fields. The atmosphere is even more rural in southeast Alabama's Wiregrass region, named for the stiff native grass, around the town of Dothan, past Daleville and the Army's Fort Rucker to Enterprise, site of the Boll Weevil Monument that commemorates the insect that destroyed two-thirds of the cotton crop here in 1915 and then spread throughout the South; in 1998 the statue was removed after someone hacked off the goddess's arms and stole the insect. Peanuts are now the main crop, with 25% of U.S. production within 75 miles of Dothan.

The 2d Congressional District covers most of the southeast corner of the state. An 80% black segment of Montgomery County is part of the black-majority 7th District, and the 2d includes 78% white Elmore and Autauga counties across the Alabama River. Without these adjustments, prompted by the Voting Rights Act, the 2d District would be closely split between the parties. But as now drawn, it is heavily Republican, for politics in southern Alabama remains racially polarized: blacks vote almost unanimously Democratic, whites vote very heavily (but not unanimously) Republican in national and statewide contests. It would be a mistake to see these preferences as purely racial, however. The civil rights laws of the 1960s have long since been accepted. Blacks here tend to support a larger and more generous government, and hence vote Democratic. Alabama whites tend to take a hard line on defense and crime, want government to promote traditional cultural values, and hence vote Republican.

The congressman from the 2d District is Terry Everett, a businessman from the Wiregrass first elected in 1992. He is a native son who served in Air Force Intelligence in Germany in the 1950s, learned Russian, worked as a sports and police beat reporter and circulation manager for southern Alabama newspapers. He bought some newspapers himself and sold them for far more, and ended up heading a S&L and owning a large farm and real estate development firm. In 1992, when he decided to run for the seat being vacated by embattled 28-year incumbent Republican Bill Dickinson, he was far from the favorite. But he beat two career politicians, a Montgomery legislator in the Republican primary by 58%–42%, then in the general state treasurer George Wallace Jr., son of the former governor. Everett spent $600,000 of his own money and, echoing an old George Wallace slogan, called on voters to "Send them a message, not a politician." Everett carried the Montgomery area and the Wiregrass and lost the Black Belt and rural counties in between. Redistricting made the difference: within the boundaries of the old district, the Democrat led 48%–46%. Since then, Everett has been re-elected easily.

In many ways, Everett resembles oldtime Democratic congressmen from the Deep South. His voting record is conservative on most issues, though he supports trade restrictions and voted against NAFTA. But he also shows a very practical-minded concern about local issues. One example is peanuts. In 1995 Everett formed a Peanut Caucus and on the Agriculture Committee held out against the Freedom to Farm Act until he got the peanut program continued, though with a 10% cut in the support price and a lower national quota. This was one of the prices Speaker Newt Gingrich and Chairman Pat Roberts had to pay to phase out most farm price supports in seven years. Since then Everett and the Peanut Caucus are nibbling back; in 1996 and 1997 the quotas were increased and Everett was working for a higher price for Segregation 3 peanuts (damaged peanuts). "Vigilance and hard work will continue to be necessary if we are to ensure the current and future profitability of the peanut program," he said.

Everett also serves on Armed Services and Veterans' Affairs. He usually supports the Republican leadership, but in 1997 sponsored an amendment that would essentially maintain the Clinton "privatization in place" plan to keep open McClellan and Kelly Air Force bases in California and Texas. Most Republicans were against it and became angry when an Everett spokeperson persuaded the *Montgomery Advertiser* to depict him as opposing the Clinton policy. Everett chairs the Veterans' Oversight Subcommittee that looked into Clinton waivers allowing burials of non-veterans in Arlington National Cemetery. The January 1998 report found no evidence of fraud except in the case of former Ambassador to Switzerland Larry Lawrence. More locally, Everett got an investigation of the Tuskegee Veterans' Hospital, which found examples of substandard treatment. Everett in October 1998 called for merger of the Tuskegee and Montgomery hospitals.

Cook's Call. *Safe.* The district is very conservative, highly dependent on both the military and agriculture, with Everett focusing his congressional energies on both. Don't look for any upset here in 2000.

The People: Pop. 1990: 577,203; 41.9% rural; 13.6% age 65 +; 74.8% White, 24.1% Black, 0.6% Asian, 0.3% Amer. Indian, 0.2% Other; 0.8% Hispanic Origin. Households: 57.7% married couple families; 28.3% married couple fams. w. children; 40% college educ.; median household income: $24,374; per capita income: $11,636; median house value: $54,200; median gross rent: $235.

1996 Presidential Vote			1992 Presidential Vote		
Dole (R)	121,306	(56%)	Bush (R)	123,856	(53%)
Clinton (D)	81,148	(37%)	Clinton (D)	82,656	(35%)
Perot (I)	12,691	(6%)	Perot (I)	27,319	(12%)

Rep. Terry Everett (R)

Elected 1992; b. Feb. 15, 1937, Dothan; home, Enterprise; Baptist; married (Barbara).

Military Career: Air Force, 1955–59.

Professional Career: Newspaper reporter, 1959–61, 1966–68; Businessman, 1961–64; Editor & Publisher, 1968–88; Real estate developer, 1988–92; Owner & Pres., *Union Springs Herald, 1988-present.*

DC Office: 208 CHOB 20515, 202-225-2901; Web site: www.house.gov/everett.

District Offices: Dothan, 334-794-9680; Montgomery, 334-277-9113; Opp, 334-493-9253.

Committees: *Agriculture* (9th of 27 R): Livestock & Horticulture; Risk Management, Research & Specialty Crops. *Armed Services* (14th of 32 R): Military Procurement; Military Readiness. *Veterans' Affairs* (5th of 17 R): Oversight & Investigations (Chmn.).

Group Ratings

	ADA	ACLU	AFS	LCV	CON	NTU	NFIB	COC	ACU	NTLC	CHC
1998	5	7	11	0	33	51	100	89	100	97	100
1997	0	—	13	—	42	57	—	80	96	—	—

National Journal Ratings

	1997 LIB — 1997 CONS			1998 LIB — 1998 CONS		
Economic	0%	—	90%	12%	—	85%
Social	10%	—	82%	0%	—	97%
Foreign	0%	—	88%	0%	—	93%

Key Votes of the 105th Congress

1. Clinton Budget Deal	Y	5. Puerto Rico Sthood. Ref.	N	9. Cut $ for B-2 Bombers	N
2. Education IRAs	Y	6. End Highway Set-asides	Y	10. Human Rights in China	N
3. Req. 2/3 to Raise Taxes	Y	7. School Prayer Amend.	Y	11. Withdraw Bosnia Troops	Y
4. Fast-track Trade	N	8. Ovrd. Part. Birth Veto	Y	12. End Cuban TV-Marti	N

Election Results

1998 general	Terry Everett (R)	131,428	(69%)	($567,408)
	Joe Fondren (D)	58,136	(31%)	($22,134)
1998 primary	Terry Everett (R)	unopposed		
1996 general	Terry Everett (R)	132,563	(63%)	($983,814)
	Bob E. Gaines (D)	74,317	(35%)	($171,208)

THIRD DISTRICT

Forty years ago, Lineville, Alabama, in the red hills of Clay County, was Ku Klux Klan country, with whites determined to resist race-mixing and blacks intimidated by threats of violence.

Today in Lineville, reports *The Washington Post*'s Eugene Robinson, integrated crowds cheer integrated high school teams, people of all races work amicably together, though they tend to pray separately on Sundays. Interracial dating is getting more common—though a high school principal in Wedowee made national headlines when he canceled the 1994 prom because of it—and Alabamans of both races are wondering how they will adjust to their new Hispanic neighbors. Lineville's progress is not complete, and perhaps it echoes that of America's most integrated institution, the military; for Lineville produced more men and women per capita for Operation Desert Storm than any other community in the nation.

The 3d Congressional District is centered geographically and perhaps spiritually in Lineville. There are other places of distinction: Horseshoe Bend, where Andrew Jackson won a climactic battle against the Indians; Tuskegee, home of Booker T. Washington's Tuskegee Institute; Auburn, home of Auburn University and its renowned sports teams and veterinary school; Talladega, home of the Alabama Institute for the Deaf and Blind, which is perhaps America's most user-friendly city for the disabled. From the red clay hills around the manufacturing town of Anniston south to the Black Belt around Tuskegee, this looks and feels like rural country. But few people here make a living off their farms; instead they ride in to work at Tysons Food or Wal-Mart or in dozens of textile mills and small- or medium-sized factories. Politically, this was long one of the heartlands of the Democratic Party, the home of populist white Democrats—patriotic supporters of the military, cautious supporters of some domestic programs—who won power so often in the House and Senate. But the towns where the interstates have brought in new businesses and new families—Auburn, Talladega, Pell City—have been trending Republican, and the 3d is now a Republican-held district.

The congressman from the 3d is Bob Riley, who grew up as a seventh-generation Clay County resident just down the road from Lineville. Riley was at the University of Alabama, watching when George Wallace stood in the schoolhouse door in 1963. Two years later he returned home with a business degree, and at 20 he and his brother started selling eggs door-to-door. That became a large egg-and-poultry company; he also ran a grocery store, airport, pharmacy, and sold real estate. He ended up with a car dealership (Midway Ford and Chrysler), a trucking company (Midway Transit), half a shopping center, and a cattle farm, and served on the city council in Ashland. In 1996, Glen Browder, the 3d District's moderate Democratic Congressman, ran for the Senate and lost to trial lawyer Roger Bedford in the primary; Riley ran for the House.

He was not the best-known candidate. Three state legislators ran in the Democratic primary, in which turnout was 53,000, compared to 20,000 for the Republicans. One of them, Braxton Bragg Comer, was the great-grandson of an Alabama governor. But Riley proved a strong and energetic campaigner, a supporter of school prayer, term limits, tax cuts, and a balanced budget amendment, and an opponent of abortion, gun control, and racial quotas. Comer carried only two counties, and Riley led 39%–20%; in the June 25 runoff Riley won 64%–36%. The leader in the Democratic primary was state Senator Ted Little, who opposed NAFTA, promised to "stand up to Newt Gingrich," and opposed cuts in Medicare and education. Little took 46% in the June 4 primary, and won the runoff 61%–39%.

In the general election, Riley pounded home his conservative views and assailed Little as a trial lawyer. Little said he would spend frugally and added, "It's my nature to stand up for the little people." Riley proclaimed, "The black community are very conservative people. We're going after the black vote and we're going after it big time." Both spent six-figures-plus of their own money. Little had more political experience but the tide was running Riley's way: the Alabama Farmers Federation withdrew its endorsement of Little and endorsed Riley at the end of October. Riley carried the northern half of the district, with big margins in suburbanizing St. Clair County east of Birmingham and his own Clay County. Little won large margins in the Black Belt. As Republicans Bob Dole and Jeff Sessions carried the 3d, so did Riley, 50%–47%. The victory left a couple of hangovers. Riley's campaign manager left his staff shortly after it was revealed he hadn't paid his taxes for years. And Democrats charged Riley with violating campaign finance laws because his son gave $3,500 to four PACs which promptly contributed $3,500 to Riley; but no violation was found.

In the House, Riley has a perfect conservative and near-perfect party-line voting record. In April 1997 he criticized Newt Gingrich for reaching out too much "to the more liberal, moderate side of our party." He said he came to Washington meaning to be bipartisan, but his first three months made him "become the most partisan person on the Hill," in his own words. Like many Southern conservatives he was not averse to federal spending in his district. He fought successfully to keep the Social Security office open in Talladega. He got Republican leaders to give him 90% of the highway money he sought, notably an Anniston Eastern Bypass to connect I-20 to Fort McClellan. Sometimes local issues have national implications. After Fort McClellan was included in the 1995 base closings, Riley fought to save the 3,600 jobs at the Anniston Army Depot. As a member of the Depot Caucus, Riley moved to stop the Clinton Administration's "privatization in place" of depots designed to save McClellan and Kelly Air Force bases in Sacramento and San Antonio. He was a prime mover in defeating an amendment brought forward by 2d District Congressman Terry Everett, which would have essentially upheld the Clinton plan. Riley's justification: "Alabama never received a second chance with Fort McClellan. I don't believe we should be treated as second class citizens simply because we don't have as many electoral votes as California and Texas." He added that the Clinton plan for two more base closings "is dead on arrival," as indeed it proved to be.

Democrats targeted the 3d District in 1998, and recruited Joe Turnham, son of a longtime legislator and state party chairman for three years, to run. He is an evangelical Christian with conservative views on many issues—a good profile for the district. But Riley raised money furiously and contributed $845,000 of his own. Turnham carried only two Black Belt counties, losing his home county, and Riley won 58%–42%.

Cook's Call. *Probably Safe.* Riley has become a very effective fundraiser (he outraised his 1998 opponent more than 4–1), and his affable style and attentiveness to the district make him a tough target. Though the district has a substantial black population (26%) and as recently as 1994 voters here were comfortably voting for moderate Democrats, it's unlikely that Riley—barring some self-inflicted wound—will be unseated.

The People: Pop. 1990: 577,116; 47% rural; 13.6% age 65 +; 73.1% White, 26% Black, 0.5% Asian, 0.2% Amer. Indian, 0.1% Other; 0.5% Hispanic Origin. Households: 56.6% married couple families; 27.6% married couple fams. w. children; 31.6% college educ.; median household income: $21,594; per capita income: $10,204; median house value: $47,400; median gross rent: $198.

1996 Presidential Vote		1992 Presidential Vote	
Dole (R)	97,798 (49%)	Bush (R)	104,928 (47%)
Clinton (D)	88,156 (44%)	Clinton (D)	91,983 (41%)
Perot (I)	13,112 (7%)	Perot (I)	23,733 (11%)

Rep. Bob Riley (R)

Elected 1996; b. Oct. 3, 1944, Ashland; home, Ashland; U. of AL, B.A. 1965; Baptist; married (Patsy).

Elected Office: Ashland City Cncl., 1972–76.

Professional Career: Owner, egg & poultry co.; Rancher; Owner, Midway Transit, 1965–present.

DC Office: 322 CHOB 20515, 202-225-3261; Fax: 202-225-5829; Web site: www.house.gov/riley.

District Offices: Anniston, 256-236-5655; Clanton, 205-755-1522; Opelika, 334-745-6222.

Committees: *Agriculture* (22d of 27 R): Livestock & Horticulture; Risk Management, Research & Specialty Crops. *Armed Services* (26th of 32 R): Military Readiness; Military Research & Development; Special Oversight Panel on Morale, Welfare and Recreation (Vice Chmn.). *Banking & Financial Services* (21st of 32 R): Capital Markets, Securities & Government Sponsored Enterprises; Financial Institutions & Consumer Credit.

Group Ratings

	ADA	ACLU	AFS	LCV	CON	NTU	NFIB	COC	ACU	NTLC	CHC
1998	5	6	11	0	13	49	100	89	100	100	100
1997	0	—	14	—	38	63	—	78	95	—	—

National Journal Ratings

	1997 LIB — 1997 CONS	1998 LIB — 1998 CONS
Economic	0% — 90%	28% — 70%
Social	0% — 90%	3% — 90%
Foreign	0% — 88%	0% — 93%

Key Votes of the 105th Congress

1. Clinton Budget Deal	Y	5. Puerto Rico Sthood. Ref.	N	9. Cut $ for B-2 Bombers	N
2. Education IRAs	Y	6. End Highway Set-asides	Y	10. Human Rights in China	N
3. Req. 2/3 to Raise Taxes	Y	7. School Prayer Amend.	Y	11. Withdraw Bosnia Troops	Y
4. Fast-track Trade	N	8. Ovrd. Part. Birth Veto	Y	12. End Cuban TV-Marti	N

Election Results

1998 general	Bob Riley (R)	101,731	(58%)	($1,985,984)
	Joe Turnham (D)	73,357	(42%)	($447,051)
1998 primary	Bob Riley (R)	unopposed		
1996 general	Bob Riley (R)	98,353	(50%)	($868,833)
	Ted Little (D)	92,325	(47%)	($799,043)
	Others	4,369	(2%)	

FOURTH DISTRICT

The Appalachians' corduroy ridges, dividing the Atlantic coast from the interior, are America's coal-and-steel industrial spine, from the black coal country of western Pennsylvania to the red hill country of northern Alabama. Here rose America's two premier steel cities, Pittsburgh and Birmingham; around both, and for many miles in between them, is the country settled by feisty Scotch-Irish farmers in the years between the Revolution and the Civil War. In valley land accessible to railroads are the great steel factories built in the 80 years after the Civil War and smaller factories that produce underwear and tires, glass and chemicals, socks and chickens. Politically, the two regions were separated by the Civil War: western Pennsylvania was overwhelmingly Republican until the 1930s, while northern Alabama was solidly Democratic through the 1950s. But they shared the same political impulses—populist on economics, conservative on culture—which made them both Democratic heartlands during the New Deal and in congressional politics for years afterwards. Now they seem to have traded partisan allegiances. Western Pennsylvania is Democratic, though less solidly so when the Democrats emphasize cultural liberalism, while northern Alabama has moved toward the Republicans, even though it has benefited from massive federal public works programs—the movement is most pronounced in counties close to Birmingham and along the interstates.

Alabama's 4th Congressional District crosses the state and the Appalachian ridges, from the Georgia line near the gritty factory town of Gadsden to the Mississippi line near lightly populated rural counties. It has the lowest black percentage of Alabama's congressional districts and, next to the black-majority 7th District, casts the highest Democratic percentages: it voted narrowly for George Bush in 1992 and Bill Clinton in 1996.

The congressman is Robert Aderholt, a Republican first elected in 1996 to replace 30-year Democrat Tom Bevill, a senior Appropriations member and benefactor of great federal projects—the Tennessee-Tombigbee Waterway project, the Jasper Bypass in the hills (its destination: the Tom Bevill industrial park) are just some. Aderholt is from Winston County, the one ancestrally Republican county in north Alabama, which opposed secession in the Civil War and declared itself the Free State of Winston. His father was a circuit judge for over 30 years; his wife's father was a state senator and state commissioner of Agriculture and Industry; Aderholt ran for the legislature in 1990, at 24, and came within 1% of winning. In 1992 he was appointed Haleyville municipal judge; in 1995 he became a top aide to Governor Fob James.

With that pedigree he decided to run for Congress when Bevill retired. Republican primary turnout was only 21,000, a vestige of old party loyalties, and in many counties few votes were cast. But 5,387 Republican ballots were cast in Winston County, and Aderholt won 87% of them, enough to account for just about all his 49%–27% lead; the runner-up decided not to seek a runoff. Some 63,000 votes were cast in the Democratic primary, split among four strong candidates. Billy Joe Camp, former press secretary to Governor George Wallace, led the first primary 32%–26% over state Senator Bob Wilson Jr. Wilson's base was Jasper, in Walker County, the home town of Congressman (1917–40) and House Speaker (1937–40) William Bankhead, one of four Alabama Bankheads to serve in Congress; Wilson's father was a state senator who nominated Wallace for president at the 1972 national convention. With a strong base in Walker County, he overtook Camp in the runoff, 52%–48%.

In the general, Wilson called himself a Democrat "in the Tom Bevill tradition" and said he supported family values. Aderholt recognized Bevill did a lot for the district, and said "I'm going to fight for what we ought to get in this district." To his proposed five-year moratorium on federal highway construction he made an exception for Corridor X, Bevill's idea for an interstate-quality road from Birmingham to Memphis. But in this culturally conservative district, he didn't hedge on cultural issues. Against abortion, gun control and same-sex marriage, and for school prayer, Aderholt said, "We want to go to Washington to deliver a message, and that is, don't mess with our traditional family values." He attacked Wilson for his support from unions and trial lawyers, and welcomed Newt Gingrich to come to the district. This was a nationally targeted race, seriously contested, and Aderholt won 50%–48%. Wilson carried Gadsden's Etowah County and Walker County, but Aderholt got 70% in Winston County and carried the faster-growing counties northeast from Birmingham on the interstate.

Everyone recognized that this would be a seriously contested district in 1998. Republican leaders put Aderholt on Appropriations and saw to it that he got more highway money than most Republicans. He raised large sums, spending more than $1 million. When Judge Roy Moore of Etowah County was ordered to take down a copy of the Ten Commandments from his court room, and when federal Judge Ira DeMent struck down DeKalb County's organized school prayer, Aderholt protested. In March 1997 he sponsored a resolution commending public display of the Ten Commandments in government buildings, including courthouses, and in early 1998 he sponsored a bill to that effect. He sponsored a Religious Freedom Amendment, which got a majority but not the required two-thirds.

Democrats worked hard to recruit a strong opponent. They were turned down by Martha Folsom, wife of former Governor Jim Folsom Jr., and by 1996 Senate nominee Roger Bedford (he made his decision at a stock car race). Finally they prevailed on Don Bevill, son of the former congressman, who beat 1996 nominee Bob Wilson 62%–38% in the primary.

Aderholt's just-about-perfect conservative voting record (though he does favor limiting steel imports) was not an attractive target, so Bevill talked of pushing public works; but unlike his father he had no seniority and no assurance of being in the majority party. In an optimistic, pro-incumbent year, Aderholt outspent the challenger by more than 2–1, and increased his percentage from 50% in 1996 to 56% in 1998. He was especially pleased to carry Etowah and Walker counties, and lost only three small counties at three edges of the district. This cannot be counted as an utterly safe seat, however; Bevill reserved the right to run again, and there are still some other strong Democrats in these hills.

Cook's Call. *Potentially Competitive.* If Republicans should be concerned about any of their five seats in Alabama, this is the one. A conservative and well-funded Democrat can still manage to make this race competitive, but Aderholt's seat on Appropriations and his moderate economic record make him a tough, expensive, and perhaps unattainable target.

The People: Pop. 1990: 577,058; 65.8% rural; 15.3% age 65 + ; 92.4% White, 6.6% Black, 0.2% Asian, 0.6% Amer. Indian, 0.1% Other; 0.4% Hispanic Origin. Households: 63.7% married couple families; 30.2% married couple fams. w. children; 26.4% college educ.; median household income: $20,877; per capita income: $10,170; median house value: $43,000; median gross rent: $168.

1996 Presidential Vote		
Dole (R)	101,636	(48%)
Clinton (D)	91,625	(43%)
Perot (I)	17,687	(8%)

1992 Presidential Vote		
Bush (R)	107,064	(44%)
Clinton (D)	104,526	(43%)
Perot (I)	28,558	(12%)

Rep. Robert Aderholt (R)

Elected 1996; b. July 22, 1965, Haleyville; home, Haleyville; Birmingham Southern U., B.A. 1987, Samford U., J.D. 1990; Congregationalist; married (Caroline).

Professional Career: Haleyville Municipal Judge, 1992–96; Asst. Legal Advisor, Gov. Fob James, 1995–96.

DC Office: 1007 LHOB 20515, 202-225-4876; Fax: 202-225-5587; Web site: www.house.gov/aderholt.

District Offices: Cullman, 256-734-6043; Gadsden, 256-546-0201; Jasper, 205-221-2310.

Committees: *Appropriations* (30th of 34 R): District of Columbia; Military Construction; Transportation.

Group Ratings

	ADA	ACLU	AFS	LCV	CON	NTU	NFIB	COC	ACU	NTLC	CHC
1998	10	6	33	0	13	46	93	83	96	97	100
1997	0	—	13	—	29	57	—	80	96	—	—

National Journal Ratings

	1997 LIB — 1997 CONS	1998 LIB — 1998 CONS
Economic	0% — 90%	42% — 58%
Social	0% — 90%	3% — 90%
Foreign	12% — 81%	0% — 93%

Key Votes of the 105th Congress

1. Clinton Budget Deal	Y	5. Puerto Rico Sthood. Ref.	N
2. Education IRAs	Y	6. End Highway Set-asides	Y
3. Req. 2/3 to Raise Taxes	Y	7. School Prayer Amend.	Y
4. Fast-track Trade	N	8. Ovrd. Part. Birth Veto	Y

9. Cut $ for B-2 Bombers	N
10. Human Rights in China	Y
11. Withdraw Bosnia Troops	Y
12. End Cuban TV-Marti	N

Election Results

1998 general	Robert Aderholt (R)	106,297	(56%)	($1,605,092)
	Donald Bevill (D)	82,065	(44%)	($662,224)
1998 primary	Robert Aderholt (R)	unopposed		
1996 general	Robert Aderholt (R)	102,741	(50%)	($763,117)
	Robert T. Wilson (D)	99,250	(48%)	($1,023,515)
	Others	3,926	(2%)	

FIFTH DISTRICT

Twice this century, the federal government has transformed the northern Alabama counties along the Tennessee River. The first time was when it created the Tennessee Valley Authority in 1933. Proposed by Nebraska Senator George Norris, a favorite of President Franklin Roosevelt, TVA took the World War I federal munitions plant at Muscle Shoals on the unnavigable Tennessee River, and built a series of dams to control flooding and produce cheap hydroelectric power. This was backwards country then: poor white farmers scratched a living out of hardscrabble land, were housed in shacks without electricity or running water, and lived off a diet that produced pellagra and rickets; and TVA was intended to be a showcase of what an enlightened, generous federal government could do. The second major federal project here was the space program. After the Soviets put up Sputnik in 1957, the Redstone Arsenal in Huntsville became the nation's major missile development center. NASA built its Marshall Space Flight Center nearby in the 1960s and the Huntsville-Decatur area achieved high-tech critical mass. In the middle-1990s northern Alabama has received $80 million in federal projects and $1.6 billion for a 400-employee Boeing research center here.

The 5th Congressional District of Alabama takes in most of the state's TVA and space counties. TVA and the space program were primarily Democratic projects, and for years most voters here were staunch New Deal Democrats, liberal on economics and not much interested in race, like the longtime Congressman (1937–46) and Senator (1946–79) John Sparkman, the party's V.P. nominee in 1952. But professional and technical people in the space business tend to combine high-tech and traditional values, and this has made much of northern Alabama marginal-to-Republican country in the 1990s. The 5th District has voted Republican for president since the departure of Jimmy Carter, and in the 1990s it has had seriously contested congressional elections.

The congressman from the 5th District is Bud Cramer Jr., a Democrat first elected in 1990. He was born in Huntsville, served as an Army tank officer after law school, beat the incumbent district attorney in 1980, at 33. In 1985 he set up the Child Advocacy Center, a child-friendly environment for abused children; as congressman, he set up a $5 million federal program to encourage such centers across the country. "We are the Mayo Clinic there in Huntsville of child abuse," he boasted. When Congressman Ronnie Flippo ran for governor, Cramer ran for Congress winning 44% in the Democratic primary; 60% in the runoff. He won the general 2–1.

In the House, Cramer got seats on the Transportation and Science committees and became a tireless booster of the beleaguered Space Station, which has been challenged 12 times in the past eight years. He won funding to start an Atlanta-Memphis highway. But in the TVA tradition he also supported the Democratic leadership on key issues. In July 1993 he voted for the Clinton budget and tax package and opposed the Penny-Kasich budget cuts. In August 1994 he supported the Clinton crime bill with its gun control provisions. These measures were unpopular locally, and were seized upon by Republican Wayne Parker, Huntsville native and son-in-law of Texas Congressman Bill Archer. Parker called for spending cuts, school choice, tougher sentences and put up billboards saying "Cramer, Clinton, Congress. We won't be fooled again! Vote Parker," when Clinton's job rating was 68% negative. With $288,000 from PACs, Cramer outspent Parker, and he had massive support from local media. But the issues worked against him, and he barely won, 50%–49%.

After that, Cramer avoided liberal votes on visible issues and, though he had once warned constituents that "a community like this is too tied to federal spending," worked to get federal dollars and contracts. He voted for the balanced budget amendment and joined the Blue Dog Democrats. He fought a National Weather Service decision to close its Huntsville office, ultimately unsuccessfully, and in October 1996 broke ground of a Next Generation radar station in northeast Alabama to track the area's frequent tornadoes. He strove to build an Atlanta-Memphis highway and the Keller Memorial Bridge in Decatur. In 1996 he was opposed again by Parker, who first had to win a tough primary fight. In November Cramer won 56%–42%, running ahead of Clinton and Democratic Senate candidate Roger Bedford, who did not carry the 5th District.

In October 1997, Cramer finally won the seat on Appropriations he had been seeking since 1991, becoming the first Blue Dog there. Alabama now has four members on House and Senate Appropriations, more than any other state except California; many of northern Alabama's projects came from Republican Senator Richard Shelby, granted a seat on Appropriations when he switched parties in November 1994. Cramer's overall voting record was middle of the House, but he voted conservative on key issues: he was one of 31 Democrats to vote for the Republicans' impeachment inquiry and one of 27 Democrats to vote for the religious freedom amendment, which would allow prayer in schools; he voted to ban partial-birth abortions and needle exchanges. But he also voted to allow abortions in military hospitals and against eliminating the National Endowment for the Arts. The League of Conservation Voters put Cramer on its "dirty dozen" list in June 1998, saying that his environmental record "has taken a nose dive" since 1994.

In 1998, Cramer's Republican opponent was Gil Aust, a Huntsville physician who was moved to run after his father was murdered tending his country store in 1996. Aust was accused in a press release signed with the misspelled name of his primary opponent Herb Dixon of being a Martian who crash-landed in a Louisiana swamp in the 1970s to infiltrate the Marshall Space Flight Center and steal American space secrets. Each accused the other of making this presumably untrue charge. Aust won the primary 69%–31% anyway. In late August Aust ran a TV ad calling for Clinton's resignation; he also accused Cramer of not doing enough to preserve federal spending in northern Alabama. In this pro-incumbent year, Cramer romped home 70%–30%.

Later that month, Cramer was elected administrative chairman of the Blue Dogs, whose ranks have swelled to 29 House Democrats—potentially a key bloc in a very narrowly Republican-controlled House.

Cook's Call. *Probably Safe.* Cramer continues to give national Republicans heartburn. The only white Democrat in the state and one of the few left in the South, he represents an increasingly conservative and suburban district, yet continues to elude defeat. Once he leaves though, Democrats will have their work cut out for them holding onto this one.

The People: Pop. 1990: 577,235; 38.9% rural; 11.7% age 65+; 83.5% White, 14.8% Black, 0.9% Asian, 0.7% Amer. Indian, 0.2% Other; 0.7% Hispanic Origin. Households: 61.1% married couple families; 29.2% married couple fams. w. children; 43.7% college educ.; median household income: $28,364; per capita income: $13,268; median house value: $63,500; median gross rent: $276.

1996 Presidential Vote			1992 Presidential Vote		
Dole (R)	111,652	(49%)	Bush (R)	110,268	(44%)
Clinton (D)	98,401	(43%)	Clinton (D)	102,130	(41%)
Perot (I)	18,403	(8%)	Perot (I)	36,921	(15%)

Rep. Bud Cramer, Jr. (D)

Elected 1990; b. Aug. 22, 1947, Huntsville; home, Huntsville; U. of AL, B.S. 1969, J.D. 1972; Methodist; widowed.

Military Career: Army, 1972; Army Reserves, 1976–78.

Professional Career: Instructor, U. of AL Law Schl., Dir., Clinical Studies Program, 1972–73; Madison Cnty. Asst. Dist. Atty., 1973–75; Practicing atty., 1975–80; Madison Cnty. Dist. Atty., 1981–90; Founder, Natl. Children's Advocacy Ctr., 1985.

DC Office: 2350 RHOB 20515, 202-225-4801; Fax: 202-225-4392; Web site: www.house.gov/cramer.

District Offices: Decatur, 205-355-9400; Huntsville, 205-551-0190; Muscle Shoals, 205-381-3450.

Committees: *Appropriations* (20th of 27 D): Interior; VA, HUD & Independent Agencies.

Group Ratings

	ADA	ACLU	AFS	LCV	CON	NTU	NFIB	COC	ACU	NTLC	CHC
1998	65	29	78	23	13	30	79	78	44	50	25
1997	45	—	50	—	29	39	—	80	48	—	—

National Journal Ratings

	1997 LIB	—	1997 CONS	1998 LIB	—	1998 CONS
Economic	54%	—	46%	54%	—	46%
Social	55%	—	44%	49%	—	51%
Foreign	46%	—	53%	56%	—	42%

Key Votes of the 105th Congress

1. Clinton Budget Deal	Y	5. Puerto Rico Sthood. Ref.	N	9. Cut $ for B-2 Bombers	N
2. Education IRAs	N	6. End Highway Set-asides	N	10. Human Rights in China	Y
3. Req. 2/3 to Raise Taxes	Y	7. School Prayer Amend.	Y	11. Withdraw Bosnia Troops	N
4. Fast-track Trade	N	8. Ovrd. Part. Birth Veto	Y	12. End Cuban TV-Marti	N

Election Results

1998 general	Bud Cramer Jr. (D)	134,819	(70%)	($1,122,250)
	Gil Aust (R)	58,536	(30%)	($819,992)
1998 primary	Bud Cramer Jr. (D)	unopposed		
1996 general	Bud Cramer Jr. (D)	126,702	(56%)	($1,006,341)
	Wayne Parker (R)	94,330	(42%)	($886,648)
	Others	4,708	(2%)	

SIXTH DISTRICT

Birmingham, once one of America's booming industrial cities, then the site of violence in the civil rights revolution, now has future prospects far more hopeful than seemed possible even a decade ago. This is a new city by southern standards: before the Civil War there was nothing here but a few creeks running below Red Mountain. But Red Mountain is almost pure iron ore, and by 1890 Birmingham had the South's largest steel mills. In the early 20th Century, as the statue of Vulcan, Roman god of fire and metalworking, looked out over the smokestack-rich valley, Birmingham seemed the most up-to-date and progressive city in the South. But the worldwide overcapacity in steel and technological obsolescence at home sent the American steel industry into long-term decline starting in the 1950s. Industrial Birmingham's political leaders plotted to avoid desegregation, and the city's violent reaction to civil rights—Police Commissioner Bull Connor set dogs and firehoses against peaceful demonstrators, and Ku Klux Klansmen bombed the 16th Street Baptist Church killing four young girls in 1963—made a vivid impression over the new medium of television news, spurring the Civil Rights Act of 1964, and created a reputation from which Birmingham still suffered a generation later.

But over the years, Birmingham developed a new economic base to generate growth and worked to improve race relations. Health care is one major industry: Birmingham has some of the largest and most advanced medical care centers in the South, and is especially renowned for its sports medicine facilities and specialists that have treated such greats as Bo Jackson and Michael Jordan. Banking is the other: while Atlanta's banks foundered and were acquired by outsiders, Birmingham became the largest southern banking center after Charlotte, North Carolina, with headquarters of SouthTrust, AmSouth Bancorp, First Alabama Bancshares and Central Bancshares of the South. In January 1998, a Birmingham abortion clinic was bombed, killing an off-duty police officer and critically wounding a nurse; the incident, believed to be the work of Eric Rudolph, launched the most intensive manhunt in U.S. history. There is still racial polarization here: most blacks live in Birmingham itself and the series of factory towns north of Red Mountain; this area is about two-thirds black. A new Birmingham has grown up along the freeways south of Red Mountain, starting with the old high-income suburb of Mountain Brook and spreading south into fast-growing Shelby County; this is over 90% white.

The 6th Congressional District, which once included all of Birmingham and most of its suburbs, is now, thanks to prevailing interpretations of the 1982 Voting Rights Act amendments, the white Birmingham-area district. It includes only a small part of the city, plus the high-income suburbs south of Red Mountain and in Shelby County and the middle-income suburbs north of Birmingham. It runs south to the white areas of the university town of Tuscaloosa. This is one of the most Republican districts in the nation, 2–1 for Bob Dole in 1996.

The congressman from the 6th District is Republican Spencer Bachus. A Birmingham native, he owned a sawmill company and practiced law, and boasted that he was a good enough trial lawyer to have produced four straight acquittals in murder trials. He was elected to the state legislature in 1982, at 35, and was an active legislator though one of very few Republicans. He ran for attorney general in 1990 and won 36% of the vote; he was Republican state chairman in 1991 and 1992. To win the new 6th District seat in 1992, he had to win a Republican primary and runoff, then take on incumbent Ben Erdreich, a moderate Democrat and one of the few prominent Birmingham whites who supported civil rights at a time when that was not only politically courageous but physically dangerous. Erdreich outspent Bachus nearly 2–1 and led in polls, but Bachus won 52%–45%. This is one seat Democrats lost to racial gerrymandering: Erdreich lost the 6th District portion of Jefferson County by 17,000 votes, but the rest of the county went Democratic by 57,000 votes in the adjacent 7th District race.

Bachus has a mostly, though not quite totally, conservative voting record and been an aggressive investigator. His legislation often has local angles. He wants to exempt from federal taxes Alabama's Prepaid Affordable College Tuition program. "To come back after people have done the responsible thing, to penalize them with a tax, makes no sense," he said. And, serving on the Transportation Committee, he was proud that Alabama highway spending was up 61% in the 1998 highway bill.

Bachus was the lead questioner of Treasury Secretary Lloyd Bentsen during the Banking Committee's Whitewater hearings. As chairman of the Banking Investigations Subcommittee, he spotlighted the threat of offshore counterfeiting of U.S. $100 bills and got more Secret Service agents abroad. In January 1997 he demanded Controller of the Currency Eugene Ludwig turn over papers of his meeting with leading bankers and Democratic fundraisers at a May 1996 White House "coffee." He accused Norman D'Amours, chairman of the National Credit Union Administration, of freezing out other board members and running a "dysfunctional agency." In May 1997 he honed in on the Community Development Financial Institutions Fund, which had given $11 million in loans to four banks with ties to Hillary Rodham Clinton without proper documentation—the two top CDFI officials resigned as a consequence. In October 1997 he demanded to know why the Treasury took no action against 7th District Congressman Earl Hilliard, who visited Libya despite U.S. sanctions; Hilliard called him a "racist," which Bachus said was "absurd."

Bachus has been re-elected three times with more than 70% of the vote. In July 1998, when Republican leaders asked members for contributions, he promptly handed over half his campaign treasury.

Cook's Call. *Safe.* As one of the dozen most Republican districts in the nation, Bachus is almost certainly never going to make it onto a Democratic target list. Only a substantial shift in lines could make this district playable for Democrats.

The People: Pop. 1990: 577,170; 22.7% rural; 12.7% age 65 + ; 89.7% White, 9.1% Black, 0.8% Asian, 0.3% Amer. Indian, 0.1% Other; 0.5% Hispanic Origin. Households: 59.6% married couple families; 28.3% married couple fams. w. children; 51.4% college educ.; median household income: $31,864; per capita income: $16,033; median house value: $73,100; median gross rent: $322.

1996 Presidential Vote		
Dole (R)	169,870	(68%)
Clinton (D)	68,545	(27%)
Perot (I)	10,995	(4%)

1992 Presidential Vote		
Bush (R)	183,127	(64%)
Clinton (D)	73,463	(26%)
Perot (I)	28,196	(10%)

Rep. Spencer Bachus (R)

Elected 1992; b. Dec. 28, 1947, Birmingham; home, Birmingham; Auburn U., B.A. 1969, U. of AL, J.D. 1972; Baptist; married (Linda).

Military Career: Natl. Guard, 1969–71.

Elected Office: AL Senate, 1983–84; AL House of Reps., 1984–87.

Professional Career: Owner, Lumber Co.; Practicing atty., 1972–92; AL Repub. Party Chmn., 1991–92.

DC Office: 442 CHOB 20515, 202-225-4921; Fax: 202-225-2082; Web site: www.house.gov/bachus.

District Offices: Birmingham, 205-969-2296; Northport, 205-333-9894.

Committees: *Banking & Financial Services* (7th of 32 R): Domestic & International Monetary Policy (Chmn.); General Oversight & Investigations. *Judiciary* (20th of 21 R): Commercial & Administrative Law; The Constitution. *Transportation & Infrastructure* (16th of 41 R): Aviation; Ground Transportation.

Group Ratings

	ADA	ACLU	AFS	LCV	CON	NTU	NFIB	COC	ACU	NTLC	CHC
1998	5	0	11	8	50	59	93	89	84	92	100
1997	0	—	25	—	56	57	—	90	96	—	—

National Journal Ratings

	1997 LIB — 1997 CONS		1998 LIB — 1998 CONS	
Economic	19%	— 76%	15%	— 81%
Social	10%	— 82%	26%	— 72%
Foreign	0%	— 88%	7%	— 83%

Key Votes of the 105th Congress

1. Clinton Budget Deal	Y	5. Puerto Rico Sthood. Ref.	N	9. Cut $ for B-2 Bombers	N
2. Education IRAs	Y	6. End Highway Set-asides	Y	10. Human Rights in China	N
3. Req. 2/3 to Raise Taxes	Y	7. School Prayer Amend.	Y	11. Withdraw Bosnia Troops	Y
4. Fast-track Trade	Y	8. Ovrd. Part. Birth Veto	Y	12. End Cuban TV-Marti	N

Election Results

1998 general	Spencer Bachus (R)	154,761	(72%)	($603,504)
	Donna Wesson Smalley (D)	60,657	(28%)	($27,860)
1998 primary	Spencer Bachus (R)	unopposed		
1996 general	Spencer Bachus (R)	181,336	(71%)	($511,226)
	Mary Lynn Bates (D)	70,081	(27%)	($36,522)
	Others	4,522	(2%)	

SEVENTH DISTRICT

Alabama celebrates its black heritage more than any other state, building striking memorials to the civil rights movement in Montgomery and Birmingham, promoting tourism to these and other black history sites, commemorating with dignified restraint a history that was full of raucous hatred and moving sacrifice. Blacks first came here as slaves; the last slave ship to the United States, the *Clotilde*, docked in Mobile in 1859, where its cargo was then set free. Blacks were part of the great migration into the cottonlands after the Jacksonians swept the Indians out of the Southeast and sent them on their Trail of Tears to what is now Oklahoma. Today, Alabama's rural blacks are still clustered in the Black Belt of fertile dark soil across the center of the state: around Montgomery, where Rosa Parks refused to move to the back of a city bus in 1955 and a young minister named Martin Luther King Jr. led a bus boycott; around Selma, founded by Alabama's one vice president, William Rufus King, and where Sheriff Jim Clark's troops beat up peaceful marchers on the Edmund Pettus Bridge in demonstrations that led to the march on Montgomery and the 1965 Voting Rights Act. All 10 of Alabama's majority-black counties are in the rich farm country of the Black Belt. But most Alabama blacks now live in urban areas, one-quarter in metropolitan Birmingham.

The 7th Congressional District, with its convoluted boundaries, was created as a black-majority district. Some 45% of its people live in the narrow valley of Birmingham and Jefferson County where the population is 75% black; another 13% are in an 80% black portion of west Montgomery County. The rest of the district includes Black Belt counties where the Alabama and Tombigbee Rivers flow past old plantations, plus part of Tuscaloosa, home of the University of Alabama, and nearby Vance, site of the much sought-after new Mercedes factory. It thus combines the remnants of Alabama's old cotton economy with neighborhoods built in the shadows of Birmingham's once booming steel mills. A 1997 lawsuit challenged the boundaries as racially motivated, but all parties agreed to drop the matter in March 1998.

The congressman from the 7th District is Earl Hilliard, the first black representative from Alabama since Republican Jeremiah Haralson retired in 1876. Hilliard grew up in segregated Birmingham and was educated in historically black schools—Morehouse, Howard, Atlanta University. In 1974, at 32, he was elected to the Alabama legislature, one of the first blacks there; 10 years later he became a committee chairman. He pushed for horse racing in Birmingham and sponsored tax abatement bills. In 1992 he outmaneuvered others and became the main Birmingham-based candidate for the new 7th District seat. The decisive Democratic primary was a "friends and neighbors" contest reminiscent of the old days of Southern white politics. Hilliard led in the primary with 31%, winning 58% in Jefferson County but running far behind elsewhere. The runoff was a contest with state Senator Hank Sanders, who won in his base, the Black Belt, and narrowly in Montgomery; but Hilliard's 71% in Jefferson County was enough for a 50.5%–49.5% victory.

In the House Hilliard has a largely liberal voting record. He voted for school prayer and flag amendments but against the religious freedom amendment and the Ten Commandments resolution in the 105th Congress. He pays much attention to local projects—establishing Enterprise Zones for Sumter and Greene counties and Smithfield-West End in Birmingham; reinstalling the Gee's Bend Ferry Boat in Wilcox County, which was closed in 1962; authorizing the Selma-to-Montgomery Historic Trail. In August 1997 Hilliard visited Libya, despite its designation as a terrorist state, and was soon sharply criticized by the 6th District's Spencer Bachus. But the Treasury ruled that he didn't engage in financial transactions and the House ethics committee noted that he did not stamp his passport, both declaring that he did not violate U.S. sanctions. Hilliard complained to the head of the Justice Department's Civil Rights division that racism is still rampant in Alabama, citing a Fob James flier, the number of blacks in state government and the Montgomery City Council redistricting. In May 1997 he called for a national commission to apologize for slavery and to decide on reparations: "It's often said that you can't fault the offspring of slaveholders. I would say that's incorrect because [some of] the offspring are still living off the wealth created by the labor of my ancestors. They are still benefiting from the work of my forefathers."

Hilliard has won re-election easily. In 1998 it was found that he got 90% of his campaign funds outside his district, the third highest of any congressional candidate. He was also criticized for failing to disclose ties to numerous corporate and non-profit organizations to which he gave more than $100,000, and because his office expenses, with large payments to temporary employees who are the children of local politicians or Hilliard staffers, were among the highest in the House.

Cook's Call. *Safe.* With a 67.5% black population, this is one of the 50 most Democratic districts in the country. The Voting Rights Act virtually precludes any changes making this district less Democratic.

The People: Pop. 1990: 577,430; 27.3% rural; 14.6% age 65 +; 32.1% White, 67.4% Black, 0.2% Asian, 0.1% Amer. Indian, 0.1% Other; 0.4% Hispanic Origin. Households: 42.8% married couple families; 21.7% married couple fams. w. children; 31.7% college educ.; median household income: $16,560; per capita income: $8,135; median house value: $40,700; median gross rent: $170.

1996 Presidential Vote

Clinton (D)	150,271	(72%)
Dole (R)	53,565	(26%)
Perot (I)	5,080	(2%)

1992 Presidential Vote

Clinton (D)	151,129	(69%)
Bush (R)	56,620	(26%)
Perot (I)	11,633	(5%)

Rep. Earl Hilliard (D)

Elected 1992; b. Apr. 9, 1942, Birmingham; home, Birmingham; Morehouse Col., B.A. 1964, Howard U., J.D. 1967, Atlanta U., M.B.A. 1970; Baptist; married (Mary).

Elected Office: AL House of Reps., 1974–80; AL Senate, 1980–92.

Professional Career: Practicing atty., 1972–92.

DC Office: 1314 LHOB 20515, 202-225-2665; Fax: 202-226-0772; Web site: www.house.gov/hilliard.

District Offices: Birmingham, 205-328-2841; Montgomery, 334-281-0531; Selma, 334-872-2684; Tuscaloosa, 205-752-3578.

Committees: *Agriculture* (8th of 24 D): Risk Management, Research & Specialty Crops. *International Relations* (13th of 23 D): International Economic Policy & Trade; International Operations and Human Rights.

Group Ratings

	ADA	ACLU	AFS	LCV	CON	NTU	NFIB	COC	ACU	NTLC	CHC
1998	100	87	100	69	55	15	7	28	8	17	0
1997	80	—	100	—	0	21	—	44	10	—	—

National Journal Ratings

	1997 LIB — 1997 CONS	1998 LIB — 1998 CONS
Economic	69% — 31%	79% — 0%
Social	80% — 20%	81% — 16%
Foreign	94% — 3%	90% — 5%

Key Votes of the 105th Congress

1. Clinton Budget Deal	N	5. Puerto Rico Sthood. Ref.	Y	9. Cut $ for B-2 Bombers	Y
2. Education IRAs	N	6. End Highway Set-asides	N	10. Human Rights in China	Y
3. Req. 2/3 to Raise Taxes	N	7. School Prayer Amend.	N	11. Withdraw Bosnia Troops	N
4. Fast-track Trade	N	8. Ovrd. Part. Birth Veto	N	12. End Cuban TV-Marti	Y

Election Results

1998 general	Earl Hilliard (D)	unopposed		($212,829)
1998 primary	Earl Hilliard (D)	unopposed		
1996 general	Earl Hilliard (D)	136,651	(71%)	($223,582)
	Joe Powell (R)	52,142	(27%)	($224,029)
	Others	3,320	(2%)	

ALASKA

Alaska is America in the Arctic, in the far northwest extension of North America, a state that was the creation of a federal government that it now often resents and an individualistic society that has responded to its unique situation in creative ways that commend themselves to the attention of what Alaskans call the Lower 48 or, more simply, the outside. Alaska would not be American at all but for the expansive dream of Secretary of State William Seward, who took advantage of a fleeting opportunity to create an American Pacific empire by purchasing it from Russia in 1867. The Alaska Territory owed most of its early growth to decisions made by the federal government. It started growing feverishly with the Klondike gold rush in 1897, just as William McKinley reaffirmed the gold standard. Anchorage, the major city here, had its beginnings in 1913 as the chief worksite of the federal government's Alaska Railroad. The Alcan Highway, connecting Alaska to the Lower 48, was built by the Army in the grim war days of 1942, when the Aleutian island of Attu was held by the Japanese, the only part of the United States occupied by a foreign enemy since the War of 1812. During the Cold War, Alaska was the only state abutting the Soviet Union, across the Bering Strait and over the North Pole. Even today Alaska remains militarily strategic, and the military remains a major presence, in Elmendorf Air Force Base near Anchorage and Fort Wainwright near Fairbanks. Alaska's giant size remains hard for Americans to comprehend: If superimposed on the Lower 48, it would stretch from Florida to southern California to Lake Superior. Yet only 620,000 of 270 million Americans live here, about half in the Anchorage area, the rest in Fairbanks in the interior and Juneau in the panhandle and scattered in a few small towns and Native settlements over millions of acres of stunning scenery.

Statehood was won in 1959, after a valiant campaign. But statehood did not end federal decision-making power over Alaska—or the widespread resentment of it. Alaska's economy at statehood depended on fishing, oil production in Cook Inlet around Anchorage and the military—all federally regulated or controlled. But less than a decade later Alaska's economy and public life were reshaped by the discovery of North Slope oil. It began suddenly, accidentally: On the day after Christmas 1967, at Prudhoe Bay on the Arctic coast, an undulating roar as loud as four jumbo jets directly overhead drew a crowd of 40 men, heavily clothed against the 30-below weather, to an oil rig. Suddenly a natural gas flare shot 30 feet straight up: This was the great 11 billion barrel North Slope oil field. Earlier oil companies had drilled seven dry wells on Prudhoe Bay, and ARCO chief executive Robert Anderson wouldn't have ordered this last try, except that he had a drilling rig nearby. This was the greatest oil strike ever in the United States and the beginning of much of today's Alaska.

Finding oil in Prudhoe Bay was something like finding it on the moon: It was not clear in 1967 who owned the oil or how it could be taken out. Ownership was in question because the Statehood Act of 1959 provided for the state to choose its own public lands, but only after settling Native land claims. Congress, not Alaska, settled such claims in the 1971 Alaska Native Claims Act which set up 12 regional and 220 village Native corporations, gave them $962 million and time to select their own 44 million acres, and ended the Interior Department's freeze that enabled the state to stake claims to mineral-rich acreage. The only feasible way to get the oil out—the Arctic Ocean ice only breaks up in late July for six weeks of the year—was a pipeline. But that was opposed by environmentalists for fear it would destroy the delicate permafrost and interfere with caribou migrations. Development-minded Alaskans got a pipeline bill through Congress in 1973, by just a one-vote margin in the Senate, but the pipeline had to be built on stilts and wasn't opened until 1977, and Congress banned oil exports to Japan and other obvious East Asian markets. Then in 1980, after brilliant lobbying by environmentalists,

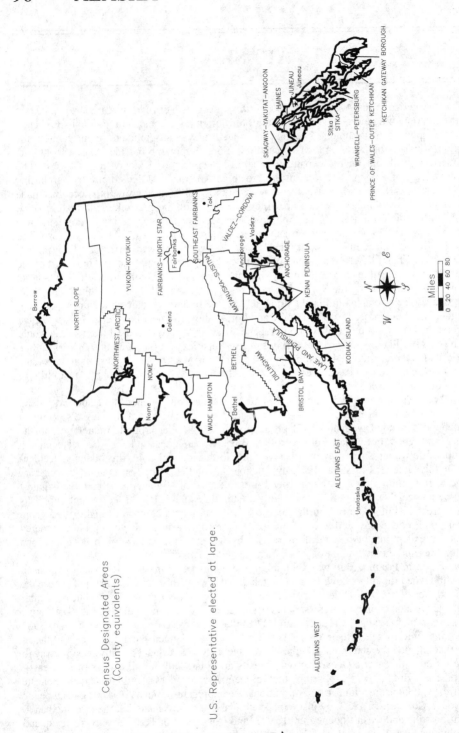

Census Designated Areas
(County equivalents)

U.S. Representative elected at large.

NORTH SLOPE

Barrow

YUKON–KOYUKUK

NORTHWEST ARCTIC

NOME

Nome

Galena

FAIRBANKS–NORTH STAR

Fairbanks

SOUTHEAST FAIRBANKS

Tok

MATANUSKA–SUSITNA

VALDEZ–CORDOVA

Valdez

Anchorage

ANCHORAGE

WADE HAMPTON

BETHEL

Bethel

DILLINGHAM

BRISTOL BAY

KENAI PENINSULA

LAKE AND PENINSULA

KODIAK ISLAND

ALEUTIANS EAST

Unalaska

ALEUTIANS WEST

SKAGWAY–YAKUTAT–ANGOON

HAINES

JUNEAU

Juneau

Sitka

SITKA

WRANGELL–PETERSBURG

PRINCE OF WALES–OUTER KETCHIKAN

KETCHIKAN GATEWAY BOROUGH

N
W   E
S

Miles

0 20 40 60 80

ALASKA 97

Congress passed, over the objections of Alaska's two senators and in the face of tears from its Congressman-at-Large Don Young, the Alaska Lands Act, which set aside 159 million acres as wilderness.

Much if not all of this was for the best. The pipeline came on line just as oil prices were approaching their peak, thus generating maximum revenues to the state, which gets 100% of the royalties; the environment was protected much better than it would have been without the environmentalists' goadings, and the caribou herd tripled statewide over a period of 20 years; the Natives got more autonomy than the non-Native majority of Alaskans would have given them. With oil providing more than 80% of its revenue, the state abolished its income tax in 1980 and created a low-tax regime which has helped Alaska to grow even as oil revenues and military spending declined.

Wisely, Alaska did not squander its windfall. In the 1970s, Governor Jay Hammond persuaded the legislature to establish a Permanent Fund for most of the oil revenues. Each year it presents every one-year resident with a dividend of 20% of the average of profits for the preceding five years—in 1998, $1,540. More important, most of the money is invested, so that in 1998, the Fund amounted to $24 billion, with most income coming from investments rather than oil. Some speculated that Alaska voters would pressure legislators for bigger payouts. But Alaskans have acted like investors: They want their dividend checks not just now but in the future. Politicians of both parties shudder when you suggest they dip into the Permanent Fund. As its current director Byron Mallot says, "No elected official looks at the Permanent Fund without the greatest caution."

Similarly, the 12 regional Native Corporations created by the Alaska Native Claims Act have proved to be successful, not just in providing income for Natives, but in helping them preserve their Native traditions and adapt to Alaska's market economy at the same time. On Indian reservations in the Lower 48, all land is held by the tribe and supervised by the government; elections held on the political model have produced a winner-take-all politics that is too often corrupt and incapable of pursuing long-range strategies. The corporate model allows the Alaska Native corporations' management more continuity in office—though some have made bad decisions and been thrown out. But the cumulative voting method, by which a minority can get a seat on the board, has produced management that is sensitive to all opinions. Huge windfalls are avoided because 70% of profits from mineral sales are shared by all corporations. But the corporation itself, not a distant federal bureaucracy, is left with the choice of how much ancestral land to retain and how much to exploit economically. Individual Natives can make the transition from their traditional communal economy, living on subsistence fishing and hunting, or make their way in the market economy in Anchorage or Fairbanks, as many have.

Not all is rosy here. Native villages in the bush have developed few enterprises (though many Natives work on the North Slope oil fields), and rates of alcoholism and suicide are agonizingly high. In the solemn mien so typical of Natives, one may be seeing the memory of great kill-offs by disease, which struck Native villages as recently as the 1920s. And the issue of subsistence hunting has been simmering in Alaska politics since a state Supreme Court ruling struck down the subsistence preference for fishing and hunting by rural residents. Under federal law, that would trigger a federal takeover of state game and fishing management—something almost no one in Alaska wants. Governor Tony Knowles and Senator Ted Stevens tried in 1997 and 1998 to get the legislature to pass a constitutional amendment to allow rural preference. But conservative legislators, who want a use-it-where-you-shoot-it requirement to prevent commercial sales and overfishing by Natives, resisted that and in October 1998 Stevens reluctantly got Congress to vote another one-year delay in federal management. The issue will be revisited in 1999, and perhaps beyond.

On the Tongass National Forest and Arctic National Wildlife Refuge, Alaska brought all it could hope for into the fray: its three-member delegation to Congress, all Republicans and in the majority since 1994, with 75 years of seniority going into the 106th Congress, and key committee positions. But they have been frustrated by accident and veto. Oil drilling in ANWR, just east of Prudhoe Bay, seemed about to be approved by Congress when the Exxon *Valdez* ran aground in Prince William Sound in March 1989. That disaster killed the proposal, and the delegation spent most of its efforts on oil-spill legislation. In the 1990s, environmentalists made ANWR one of their top issues, winning votes from Florida and East Coast Republicans eager to be known as champions of the environment. Stevens got ANWR drilling into the reconciliation bill in 1995, but Bill Clinton vetoed it, and everyone concedes it will not pass with a Democratic president, and may not with a Republican. The issue on the Tongass is how much logging should be allowed in this dense forest in the panhandle; its great champion is Senator Frank Murkowski, who grew up in the area. The Forest Service under Clinton cancelled an old contract to harvest timber and squelched attempts to revive it. In late September 1996, Murkowski held up the national parks bill, then gave in five days later, for a promise that the Forest Service would sell timber to the Ketchikan lumber mill for two years. Murkowski went along with a May 1997 Forest Service logging plan, and Tongass was not a major issue again until 1999, when the Clinton Administration introduced new restrictions on an additional 234,000 acres. But Alaska's delegation could intervene, and the courts could stop the plan.

As the 1990s have gone on, there seems to be a convergence of opinion in Alaska, and considerable progress, as the classic battles between Alaska's boomers and Washington's environmentalists have become less important and Alaska's successes—for some of which all sides can claim some credit—have become more apparent. In August 1998 Interior Secretary Bruce Babbitt approved oil-drilling in most of the 23-million acre National Petroleum Reserve-Alaska, just west of Prudhoe Bay, except for the bird-breeding swamps along Lake Teshekpuk. Oil companies wanted more drilling and some environmentalists wanted less; but Alaska environmentalists concede that today's drilling practices on the North Slope—with small "footprints" for wellheads and horizontal drilling to leave the surface mostly undisturbed—are acceptable. Similarly, environmentalists have endorsed, indeed helped prepare, the Yukon Pacific proposal to build a parallel pipeline to ship out the North Slope's currently unused natural gas. The Alaska Railroad, sold to the state by the federal government, is being run like a business and making a profit. The congressional delegation, with support from the Clinton Administration, repealed the economically mindless prohibition on exporting Alaskan oil to its obvious and lucrative markets in Japan and East Asia. And they revised the Magnuson Act to protect seafood stocks from being overfished. A 1996 Ninth Circuit Court of Appeals decision raised the threat that all Native territory would be classified as "Indian country," with the right to regulate and tax outsiders; this arose out of a case in which an Athabaskan Native village tried to tax a state contractor building a public school in the village of Venetie. But in February 1998 the U.S. Supreme Court, which routinely overturns Ninth Circuit decisions, unanimously ruled this contrary to the Native Claims Act, in which Natives relinquished all aboriginal rights in return for land grants and creation of the Native corporations.

In the middle 1990s there was uneasiness about Alaska's economy. The traditional mainstays seemed threatened—defense spending was down, oil prices were starting what by late 1998 looked like freefall, and fish prices were down as well. ANWR drilling was blocked and Tongass logging jobs threatened. Yet in population and jobs Alaska continued to grow. One reason is growth in tourism, with more than 1 million visitors a year, many on cruise ships and others headed to Denali National Park and Mount McKinley; Alaska is now trying to build winter tourism, with a ski resort in Girdwood near Anchorage, where winter temperatures are milder than in the Rockies. Another spur is the air freight business. Anchorage airport, near the top of the world, is seven hours from New York, Tokyo and London, and is a major transfer point for UPS and FedEx. More all-cargo, wide-bodied aircraft move through Anchorage International than any other U.S. airport. A third reason is that this is a low-tax, low-regulation state, which has been attracting independent-spirited, entrepreneurial-minded young families. Big institutions don't run things here: Unions, politically pivotal 20 years ago, aren't any more, and the oil companies, while not unpopular, weren't able to stop higher state oil taxes.

Politically, Alaska has become visibly even more Republican in the 1990s. In national politics it has been solidly Republican since the 1970s, because national Democrats seem to want to lock up natural resources. And no Democrat has been elected to Congress since 1974, though some contests have been close. Democrat Tony Knowles was elected governor in 1994 and 1998, but the first time by only 536 votes and the second with 51% after the Republican Party repudiated its nominee and launched a write-in candidacy against him. The legislature is not only solidly Republican, but conservative, pushing constantly for spending cuts and bucking Knowles and Senator Ted Stevens on subsistence. Referendums show Alaskans to be increasingly conservative, though with a libertarian tinge: In 1998 they voted for medical marijuana, English-only and a ban on same-sex marriage, but a ban on wolf snaring was defeated.

Some regional differences persist. Anchorage, with nearly half the population, is much like a prosperous Rocky Mountains' metropolis with longer summer days and winter nights; it is affluent and booming, with 70% of women in the work force, the highest in the country. Politically, it is solidly Republican. So are the smaller settlements in a 200-mile arc around Anchorage, which have been growing even more rapidly—the Matanuska Valley (one of the few places in Alaska where farming is possible), Seward, the Kenai peninsula and the little port of Valdez at the southern terminus of the pipeline. Fairbanks, Alaska's second largest city, is a pipeline and mineral service center deep in the interior, unprotected from Arctic winds in winter and crowds of mosquitoes in the brief but hot summer. It tends to vote Republican too.

The old Alaska, first settled by Russians, can be seen in the fishing towns of the Panhandle and in the capital of Juneau, located on an inlet of the Pacific up against a steep mountain; Alaskans voted to move the capital to a site near Anchorage in 1974 but defeated referendums to pay for it in 1978 and 1982, and Juneau prevailed in a 1994 referendum by 55%–45%. The Panhandle, historically Democratic, is now more evenly split. Mostly Democratic is the bush, the villages where Natives—Athabaskans, Aleuts, Yupiks, Inupiats—are the large majority. Natives make up 17% of Alaska's population and 50% in the vast lands north and west of Anchorage and Fairbanks. They are greatly outnumbered and outvoted on many issues, and yet are the object of awed respect for their achievement in building civilizations in such a forbidding environment.

Governor. Alaska has had a colorful array of governors in its four decades of statehood, from its first governor, Democrat William Egan, through bush pilot Jay Hammond, elected in 1974 and 1978, and Walter Hickel, an Anchorage developer, elected in 1966, appointed Richard Nixon's Interior secretary in 1969 (he resigned in 1970 in protest against the invasion of Cambodia) and elected again, as a member of the Alaska Independence Party, at 71, in 1990. None, incidentally, has won an absolute majority between Egan in 1970 and Tony Knowles in 1998; independent and third-party candidates have abounded.

The current governor is Tony Knowles, a Democrat elected in 1994 and 1998. Knowles was born in Oklahoma, served in the 82d Airborne in Vietnam, graduated from Yale, and came to Alaska in 1968 and worked as a roughneck. In 1969 he started his first Grizzly Burger, then added two more chains and opened the Downtown Deli; in the mode of local businessmen, he served on the council (the Anchorage Assembly) and as mayor from 1982–87. He boasts of building the Alaska Center for Performing Arts, the Egan Convention Center, and the 11-mile Tony Knowles Coastal Trail, used for cyclists and joggers, plus the most extensive cross-country ski trails of any city in the nation. In 1990 he ran for governor and lost to Hickel 39%–31%. In 1994 Knowles ran again, against Republican Jim Campbell and Lieutenant Governor Jack Coghill, who ran on Hickel's Alaska Independence ticket. Campbell started out with a big lead but squandered it with attacks on Knowles, who won by 536 votes, 41.1%–40.8%, with 13% for Coghill. Knowles had huge leads in the bush and Juneau, but ran behind in urban areas.

In office, Knowles has clashed repeatedly with the conservative Republican legislature, but reached some agreement on budgets, welfare reform and teacher tenure. He has stressed "jobs and families" issues, spotlighting child abuse and providing health care insurance for low-income families with children. He worked closely with the oil and tourism industries, pushing the Clinton Administration to approve oil drilling in the National Petroleum Reserve-Alaska, as it did in August 1998. He angered some Native leaders by appealing the Ninth Circuit *Venetie* decision declaring a Native village "Indian territory"; this was unanimously reversed by the U.S. Supreme Court. He did not support the congressional delegation on Tongass logging, but advanced his own initiatives to keep the Ketchikan pulp mill running. He unsuccessfully tried to get the legislature to put a constitutional amendment on subsistence fishing and hunting before the voters. He proposed the nation's highest taxes on tobacco and alcohol, but Republicans refused to allow a vote on his $1 cigarette tax. He went along with some Republican budget cuts as oil revenues declined.

In early 1998 it was not clear that Knowles would win a second term. No governor had been re-elected in 20 years, and the Democratic base in this increasingly Republican state is not large. But Senator Frank Murkowski, ahead in polls, decided not to run. The Republican field shook down to two conservatives, state Senator Robin Taylor and Anchorage lawyer Wayne Ross, and former University of Alaska Anchorage Chancellor and newspaper owner John Lindauer. Lindauer's record was not dazzling: He left the chancellor's office under criticism and his newspaper chain folded in 1992. But he had married a rich Chicago woman in 1995 and proceeded to spend $857,000 on his primary campaign. In Alaska's all-party primary, Knowles won just 36%; Lindauer's 23% was ahead of Taylor and Ross, who won 16% each. Lindauer's strategy was odd: He criticized Knowles for not backing "Indian country" status (which would undermine the Alaska Native Claims Act) and charged that Knowles was planning to dig into the Permanent Fund. But "Indian country" was highly unpopular with the non-Native majority and Knowles, like most sensible Alaska politicians, had shown no sign of designs on the Permanent Fund. Even fishier was Lindauer's residency and financing. Alaska requires seven years of residency for a governor, but for two years in the 1990s Lindauer had not applied for his Permanent Fund dividend. Then a citizen lawsuit questioned whether the campaign money Lindauer spent was his. In early October the *Anchorage Daily News* revealed that when it sued Lindauer on an old debt, he pleaded poverty and said he was supported by his wife. He admitted that his wife gave him the money he spent on the campaign. On October 20, the state Republican Party withdrew its support for Lindauer and backed Robin Taylor as a write-in candidate. Knowles, generally popular and flush with contributions from state and oil company employees, cruised to a 51% victory. Lindauer won only 18% of the vote, while Taylor took 20%.

Knowles names his second term priorities as the economy, education, subsistence and closing the fiscal gap. There are likely to be fights over spending (the Republicans want budget cuts) and subsistence.

Senior Senator. No other senator fills so central a place in his state's public and economic life as Ted Stevens of Alaska. "They sent me here," Stevens said in one impassioned debate, "to stand up for the state of Alaska." Stevens is now the second most senior Republican senator, the chairman of the Appropriations Committee and of its Defense Subcommittee; he has also been for two decades the leading public policymaker for and about Alaska. "We ask for special consideration," Stevens is not too shy to say, "because no one else is that far away, no one else has the problems that we have or the potential that we have, and no one else deals with the federal government day in and day out the way we do." Probably more than any other senator, Stevens has shaped the public institutions and private economy of his state.

He has had plenty of training. Stevens grew up in Indiana and California, served in World War II, graduated from UCLA and Harvard Law, then moved to Alaska in 1950. He was U.S. attorney there and worked in the Interior Department in Washington, served in the legislature in Juneau and was appointed to the Senate by Governor Walter Hickel in December 1968, at 45. He quickly gained a seat on Appropriations and worked on Alaska issues of all description. He has not been entirely successful. He could not stop the Alaska Lands Act in 1980 and could not get approval of Arctic National Wildlife Refuge oil drilling in 1991 or 1995. But he played a major role on the Native Claims Act in 1971 and got the oil pipeline through by one vote in

1973. In 1995 he finally secured the repeal of the 1977 law forbidding exports of Alaskan oil, thus opening up the obvious East Asian markets. He managed the oil spill bill of 1989 in response to the *Valdez* accident, requiring double hulls and compensating Alaska. He has worked on fishing legislation: to ban monofilament nets, to reauthorize the 200-mile limit and to revise the Magnuson Act to reduce bycatch and preserve fish stocks; in 1998, arguing that huge foreign-owned ships were wasting Alaskan fisheries, he succeeded in banning 165-foot-plus factory ships and requiring 75% U.S. ownership.

Although Alaska Natives usually vote Democratic and their positions on issues are often unpopular with most other Alaskans, Stevens has worked tirelessly with Native leaders, skillfully eliciting consensus when opinion is divided, getting more health and sanitation aid to bush villages and funding for health research on fetal alcohol syndrome and cancers common among Natives. He got funding for the Alaska Aviation Heritage Museum and the Alaskan Native Heritage Center, for Native cultural programs and for the American Russian Center and restoration of Russian Orthodox churches in Alaska. In 1998 he created the $20 million Denali Commission to push for rural infrastructure in central Alaska.

Stevens secured some $300 million for Alaska projects in 1998, including $50 million in disaster relief for fishermen in the Kuskokwim River and Bristol Bay, $28 million for an elevated Alaska Railroad station at Anchorage Airport to serve cruise ship tourists, $60 million for highways and ferries and, most notably, $37.7 million for an airport road, medical clinic and doctor and nurse for the tiny Aleutian village of King Cove. Stevens had been seeking only a land trade for a seven-mile road through the Izembeck National Wildlife Refuge so that King Cove residents could have better access to medical facilities; the Clinton Administration nixed that and offered three alternatives, and Stevens took all three. The Senate agreed, 59–38.

After Stevens succeeded Mark Hatfield as Appropriations chairman in 1997, he told colleagues, "Senator Hatfield had the patience of Job and the disposition of a saint. I don't. The watch has changed. I'm a mean, miserable SOB." But if he is terrible-tempered (or wants others to think so), he is also hard-working. As chairman of the Defense Appropriations Subcommittee, he has generally supported robust defense spending and favors a national missile defense that covers Alaska and Hawaii. But he opposed sending U.S. ground troops to Bosnia, and has required the Clinton Administration to periodically justify their presence there. He works hard to fund the National Guard, to raise military salaries and to keep troops in readiness. After surgery for prostate cancer in 1991, he pushed for more funding for breast, cervical and prostate cancer research, plus telemedicine projects to connect rural Alaskans to hospitals and specialists. His voting record overall is moderate. He supports the Corporation for Public Broadcasting: Alaska's public TV stations have the nation's largest audience shares. And, with the large government work force in high-cost Alaska, he supports increased salaries and benefits for federal workers and argues volubly for higher salaries for senators and Senate staffers.

Stevens's work on Alaska issues is widely respected and he has not received much serious opposition at home. In the August 1996 primary he was opposed by former state representative and millionaire banker David Cuddy, who spent $1.3 million of his own money charging that Stevens was insufficiently conservative on abortion, gun control, state control, and federal spending. Stevens won 59%–27%. The Democratic nominee, former Anchorage school board member Theresa Obermeyer, blamed Stevens for her husband's failure to pass the Alaska bar on 22 separate tries; she sometimes wore black-and-white prisoner stripes and a ball-and-chain to his public events. Democratic Governor Tony Knowles announced he was voting for Stevens, who won 77%, followed by Green Party candidate Jed Whittaker with 13%, and Obermeyer with 10%.

Junior Senator. Frank Murkowski stands as a major senator, chairman of the Energy and Natural Resources Committee and his party's point man on one of the stickiest foreign policy problems, North Korea. Murkowski grew up in Seattle and Ketchikan, served in the Coast Guard in Alaska, and became a banker in Fairbanks. A department head under Governor Walter Hickel in the 1960s, he ran for Congress and lost in 1970. He was elected to the Senate in

1980 by winning 54% against liberal Democrat Clark Gruening. He got a seat on Energy, which handles many Alaska issues, and has had many successes. They include a ban on drift net fishing in international waters, the Native Languages Preservation Act, initiating contacts between Alaska and Siberia, and the lifting of the ban on Alaskan oil exports, a 1977 policy that stayed on the books until November 1995.

He has been frustrated on the so-far unsuccessful fight for Arctic National Wildlife Refuge oil drilling and the only partially successful efforts to continue logging in the Tongass National Forest; on both he has faced Clinton vetoes. But on Tongass he has won a commitment for talks with the administration to provide a dependable timber supply plan for the Ketchikan pulp mill. He has worked for higher Medicaid funding and greater highway spending for Alaska, for unitization of any oil fields in the National Petroleum Reserve-Alaska, the Glacier Park ferry and many land exchanges. He sponsored bills to reduce IRS seizures of Alaska fishing permits and to allow adverse IRS decisions to be appealed in Alaska rather than Seattle. On many of these matters Murkowski worked harmoniously with Ted Stevens, sometimes with one taking the lead, sometimes the other, though they have differed on a few issues, notably on subsistence hunting and fishing, and on commercial fishing in Glacier Bay National Park.

On issues farther afield, Murkowski in April 1997 passed through the Senate a bill to allow the interim storage of high-level nuclear waste at the Nevada Test Site; a version passed the House, but the Senate vote, 65–34, was two short of the total needed to override a threatened veto by President Clinton. In 1996 he produced a parks bill, giving legal status to the Presidio Trust in San Francisco, Sterling Forest in New York and New Jersey, the Tallgrass Prairie Natural Preserve in Kansas, the New Bedford Whaling National Park, and the Selma-to-Montgomery National Historic Trail. He tried to hold it up in October 1996 to get concessions on the Tongass, then allowed it to go through. Murkowski has worked on East Asia issues, from Taiwan to North Korea, which he visited; in late 1994 he criticized the Clinton Administration's accord with North Korea, but declined to try to overturn it, and has said he is anxious to facilitate "meaningful dialogue" between North and South Korea.

Murkowski has been re-elected three times in contests that attracted little attention outside Alaska. In 1986 and 1992 Murkowski won by 54%–44% and 53%–38%. In 1998 he was in a stronger position. He was pressed to, but decided not to, run against Governor Tony Knowles. His Democratic opponent had run unsuccessfully for mayor of Juneau, state House and the U.S. Senate. Murkowski won 74%–20%.

Representative-At-Large. Alaska's Don Young, one-time tugboat captain on the Yukon and the only licensed mariner in Congress, in his words is, "not one of these smooth, namby-pamby politicians." He is a hot-tempered, salty-tongued true believer, given to malapropisms ("Pribilof's dog" and "bladderdash") and provocative insults (Republicans soft on the environment are "squishies"). Young grew up in rural California, served in the Army, then moved to Alaska where he became mayor of Fort Yukon. He was elected to the legislature in 1966 and ran for Congress in 1972; his opponent, incumbent Nick Begich, was killed in a plane crash, and Young won the March 1973 special election to succeed him. Young is not a free market conservative and casts many liberal economic votes; but he is a cultural and foreign policy conservative, and often an angry one. Some of that anger may have come from serving on the Resources Committee, where he was ranking minority member for 10 years before becoming chairman in 1995. For years this committee, which handles most Alaska issues, was packed with members, not all of them Democrats, tutored by environmentalist organizations on Alaska issues. Their numbers have been trimmed since the Republican victory of 1994, but environmental groups still have great sway on the floor of the House, where many Northeastern Republicans and many of the 20 Republicans from Florida and Arizona, two states Bill Clinton lost in 1992 and won in 1996, are eager to score high on the groups' scoresheets; that often comes at Alaska's, or Young's, expense. Alaska's two senators can use the Senate's dilatory rules to get their way; in the tightly controlled House, Young can be steamrollered, as he was often when in the minority—most notably when the Alaska Lands Act passed in 1980.

Even when he has prevailed in the House, Young has sometimes been stymied by Clinton vetoes. That was the case after the House finally approved oil drilling in the Arctic National Wildlife Refuge in 1995, and when Congress rallied to maintain logging in the Tongass National Forest. He was stymied in his efforts to rewrite the Endangered Species Act, on which his aggressive efforts in 1995 antagonized some other Republicans. He certainly does not steer away from the provocative. Of environmentalists, he once said, "They are Communists. They believe in communal ownership of all natural resources." And in 1998 he was criticized for asking whether Forest Service employees in the southwest regional office were members of environmental organizations that made deals with the office without notifying affected land-owners—a reasonable inquiry treated as a revival of the Inquisition.

Young's "I'm just going to ram it down their throats" attitude prompted Newt Gingrich in 1996 to prevent Young from naming all new Republican committee members; but Young did name three new development-minded Republicans from the West and created a Forests sub-committee for conservative Helen Chenoweth of Idaho. A move by the Wilderness Society to oust Young as chairman fell flat when New Yorker Sherwood Boehlert, a moderate on envi-ronmental issues, said he had worked well with Young and supported him. In the 106th Con-gress, under Republican term limits, Young is serving his last term as chairman.

But for all his stormy reputation, Young has also had his legislative successes, and has shown a capacity not only for hard work but for building consensus. Some of them are even endorsed by his environmental enemies. In 1997, he passed, by 419–1, the National Wildlife Improvement Act which sets new guidelines for the nation's 500-plus wildlife refuges. The bill, endorsed by Clinton and environmental groups, allows for recreational activities that are compatible with the refuges' conservation mission. He steered a reform of the 30-year-old ANWR Act to passage, with the help of its original sponsor John Dingell, by 388–37 in October 1995; but the Senate failed to act on it.

Very far afield from Alaska, he devoted much time and energy to the status of Puerto Rico. Young believes that "the status quo is no longer acceptable," and that Puerto Rico must move from its current commonwealth status toward either statehood or sovereignty. Where others have failed, he tried to draw up a bill authorizing a 1998 plebiscite with alternatives defined realistically and designed in a way to get Congress to accept them (something no one can guarantee). Undoubtedly one reason Young was attracted to this issue was his own memory of Alaska's struggle for statehood; and Speaker Newt Gingrich saw it as an opening to Hispanics for Republicans. They defeated an amendment by Gerald Solomon which would have made English the official language of a state of Puerto Rico, and mustered just enough votes, most of them from Democrats, to pass it 209–208 in March 1998. Senate Republicans had no interest in a bill that they thought would bring more Democrats to Congress; Majority Leader Trent Lott said the House had stepped into a "hornet's nest." So the bill died. The pro-statehood Puerto Rico government sponsored a referendum in December 1998, in which none-of-the-above beat statehood by 50%–46%; the Commonwealth Party thought the alternative presented on its behalf was unattractive and supported none-of-the-above. This issue will continue to be pursued in Puerto Rico, but it is unlikely that either Young or the House will have the energy to work on it, unless the Senate indicates some interest.

Another major issue for Young is missile defense. He has vigorously and persistently op-posed the 1995 Clinton National Intelligence Estimate that asked whether the U.S. would be safe from a hostile missile force for the next 15 years; Alaska and Hawaii, Young argues persuasively, are not excluded from the constitutional requirement that the federal government provide for the common defense. In fact, Alaska is now vulnerable to North Korean missiles, and Young wants a much more vigorous missile defense program than the Clinton Adminis-tration has been willing to consider.

Young has had his ups and downs with Alaska voters over the years, with significant op-position in 1978, 1984, 1986, 1990 and 1992. The *Anchorage Daily News*'s constant criticisms have sometimes hurt him in that usually Republican city, but his work for Native causes helped him run well ahead of party lines in the bush. More recently he seems safe: In 1998, against the state Senate Minority Leader Jim Duncan, a 24-year veteran from Juneau, he won by the impressive margin of 63%–35%—his best showing since 1982. For 2000, Young will have to step down as chairman of Resources, but he might become chairman of Transportation, on which he is now number two and on which Chairman Bud Shuster is term-limited.

Cook's Call. *Safe.* Young's controversial and colorful style over his 26 years in office has caused Democrats to consistently place this district on their target list through the '70s and '80s. With Young's appointment as chairman of the Resources Committee, any Democratic hopes of knocking him off probably evaporated. The voting patterns of the state in federal races are so Republican that, when Young eventually steps aside, only a Democrat with some extraordinary personal appeal would have a reasonable chance of picking up this seat.

Presidential politics. In presidential elections, Alaska votes Alaska issues, but this was not always so: In 1960 and 1968 its votes came eerily close to the national average. Since then, it has voted for development and against the national Democrats: In the year of the Alaska Lands Act, it gave only 26% of its votes to Jimmy Carter, who in some places ran behind Libertarian Ed Clark. In 1992, Ross Perot won 28% here, his second best showing in the country. In 1996, Bob Dole easily led Bill Clinton, 51%–33%, with 11% for Perot.

Alaska has no presidential primary. Party true-believers tend to dominate the caucuses. In the January 1996 straw poll or "beauty contest," Alaska Republicans voted 33% for Pat Buchanan, 31% for Steve Forbes, and 17% for Bob Dole. This gave Buchanan the confidence and verve he showed weeks later in Louisiana, where he beat Phil Gramm, and in other early contests climaxed by his win in New Hampshire on February 20.

The People: Est. Pop. 1998: 614,010; Pop. 1990: 550,043, up 11.6% 1990–1998. 0.2% of U.S. total, 48th largest; 32.6% rural. Median age: 31.9 years. 4.2% 65 years and over. 75.7% White, 4% Black, 3.5% Asian, 15.7% Amer. Indian, 1.1% Other; 3.3% Hispanic Origin. Households: 56.2% married couple families; 34.3% married couple fams. w. children; 57.9% college educ.; median household income: $41,408; per capita income: $17,610; 56.1% owner occupied housing; median house value: $94,400; median monthly rent: $503. 5.8% Unemployment. 1998 Voting age pop.: 437,000. 1998 Turnout: 227,156; 52% of VAP. Registered voters (1998): 453,332; 76,525 D (17%), 113,228 R (25%), 267,822 unaffiliated and minor parties (59%).

Political Lineup: Governor, Tony Knowles (D); Lt. Gov., Fran Ulmer (D); Atty. Gen., Bruce M. Botelho (D); Commissioner of Revenue, Wilson Condon (D); State Senate, 20 (5 D, 15 R); Majority Leader, Jerry Mackie (R); State House, 40 (14 D, 26 R); House Speaker, Brian Porter (R). Senators, Ted Stevens (R) and Frank Murkowski (R). Representative, 1 R at large.

Elections Division: 907-465-4611; **Filing Deadline for U.S. Congress:** June 1, 2000.

1996 Presidential Vote		
Dole (R)	122,746	(51%)
Clinton (D)	80,380	(33%)
Perot (I)	26,333	(11%)
Others	12,161	(5%)

1992 Presidential Vote		
Bush (R)	102,000	(40%)
Clinton (D)	78,294	(30%)
Perot (I)	73,481	(28%)

GOVERNOR

Gov. Tony Knowles (D)

Elected 1994, term expires Jan. 2003; b. Jan. 1, 1943, Tulsa, OK; home, Juneau; Yale U., B.A. 1968; Christian; married (Susan).

Military Career: Army, 1962–64 (Vietnam).

Elected Office: Anchorage Assembly, 1975–79; Anchorage Mayor, 1982–87.

Professional Career: Restaurant owner, 1968–present.

Office: P.O. Box 110001, Juneau, 99811, 907-465-3500; Fax: 907-465-3532; Web site: www.state.ak.us.

Election Results

1998 gen.	Tony Knowles (D)	112,879	(51%)
	Robin Taylor (write-in)	43,571	(20%)
	John Lindauer (R)	39,331	(18%)
	Ray Metcalfe (RP)	13,540	(6%)
	Others	10,856	(5%)
1998 prim.	Tony Knowles (D)	38,798	(36%)
	John Lindauer (R)	25,048	(23%)
	Robin Taylor (R)	17,671	(16%)
	Wayne Ross (R)	17,447	(16%)
	Others	10,062	(9%)
1994 gen.	Tony Knowles (D)	87,693	(41%)
	James O. (Jim) Campbell (R)	87,157	(41%)
	John B. (Jack) Coghill (I)	27,838	(13%)
	Jim Sykes (Green)	8,727	(4%)

SENATORS

Sen. Ted Stevens (R)

Appointed Dec. 1968, seat up 2002; b. Nov. 18, 1923, Indianapolis, IN; home, Girdwood; U.C.L.A., B.A. 1947, Harvard, LL.B. 1950; Episcopalian; married (Catherine).

Military Career: Army Air Corps, 1943–46 (WWII).

Elected Office: AK House of Reps., 1964–68.

Professional Career: Practicing atty., 1950–53, 1961–68; U.S. Atty., 1953–56; U.S. Dept. of Interior, Legis. Cnsl., 1956–58, Asst. to Secy., 1958–60, Solicitor, 1960–61.

DC Office: 522 HSOB, 20510, 202-224-3004; Fax: 202-224-2354; Web site: www.senate.gov/~stevens.

State Offices: Anchorage, 907-271-5915; Fairbanks, 907-456-0261; Juneau, 907-586-7400; Kenai, 907-283-5808; Ketchikan, 907-225-6880; Wasilla, 907-376-7665.

Committees: *Appropriations* (Chmn. of 15 R): Commerce, Justice, State & the Judiciary; Defense (Chmn.); Interior; Labor & HHS; Legislative Branch. *Commerce, Science & Transportation* (2d of 11 R): Aviation; Communications; Oceans & Fisheries; Science, Technology & Space; Surface Transportation & Merchant Marine. *Governmental Affairs* (3d of 9 R): International Security, Proliferation & Federal Services; Investigations (Permanent). *Rules & Administration* (3d of 9 R). *Joint Committee on the Library of Congress* (Chmn. of 5 Sens.).

Group Ratings

	ADA	ACLU	AFS	LCV	CON	NTU	NFIB	COC	ACU	NTLC	CHC
1998	20	43	11	0	67	54	89	94	56	71	73
1997	30	—	0	—	61	69	—	80	58	—	—

National Journal Ratings

	1997 LIB	—	1997 CONS	1998 LIB	—	1998 CONS
Economic	43%	—	56%	46%	—	52%
Social	55%	—	37%	52%	—	46%
Foreign	43%	—	50%	51%	—	36%

Key Votes of the 105th Congress

1. Bal. Budget Amend.	Y	5. Satcher for Surgeon Gen. Y
2. Clinton Budget Deal	Y	6. Highway Set-asides Y
3. Cloture on Tobacco	N	7. Table Child Gun locks Y
4. Education IRAs	Y	8. Ovrd. Part. Birth Veto Y

9. Chem. Weapons Treaty Y
10. Cuban Humanitarian Aid N
11. Table Bosnia Troops Y
12. $ for Test-ban Treaty Y

Election Results

1996 general	Ted Stevens (R) 177,893	(77%)	($2,711,710)
	Jed Whittaker (Green) 29,037	(13%)	
	Theresa Obermeyer (D) 23,977	(10%)	
1996 primary	Ted Stevens (R) 71,042	(59%)	
	Dave W. Cuddy (R) 32,994	(27%)	
	Others 16,640	(14%)	
1990 general	Ted Stevens (R) 125,806	(66%)	($1,618,098)
	Michael Beasley (D) 61,115	(32%)	($445)
	Others 2,999	(2%)	

Sen. Frank Murkowski (R)

Elected 1980, seat up 2004; b. Mar. 28, 1933, Seattle, WA; home, Fairbanks; U. of Santa Clara, Seattle U., B.A. 1955; Catholic; married (Nancy).

Military Career: Coast Guard, 1955–56.

Professional Career: Pacific Natl. Bank of Seattle, 1957–58; Natl. Bank of AK, 1959–67; Commissioner, AK Dept. of Econ. Devel., 1966–70; Pres., Natl. Bank of AK, 1971–80.

DC Office: 322 HSOB, 20510, 202-224-6665; Fax: 202-224-5301; Web site: www.senate.gov/~murkowski.

State Offices: Anchorage, 907-271-3735; Fairbanks, 907-456-0233; Juneau, 907-586-7400; Kenai, 907-283-5808; Ketchikan, 907-225-6880; Wasilla, 907-376-7665.

Committees: *Energy & Natural Resources* (Chmn. of 11 R). *Finance* (5th of 11 R): International Trade; Long-Term Growth & Debt Reduction (Chmn.); Taxation & IRS Oversight. *Indian Affairs* (2d of 8 R). *Veterans' Affairs* (2d of 7 R).

Group Ratings

	ADA	ACLU	AFS	LCV	CON	NTU	NFIB	COC	ACU	NTLC	CHC
1998	5	29	11	0	55	68	100	100	78	82	90
1997	10	—	0	—	66	70	—	100	68	—	—

National Journal Ratings

	1997 LIB — 1997 CONS			1998 LIB — 1998 CONS		
Economic	25%	—	67%	12%	—	85%
Social	28%	—	62%	31%	—	64%
Foreign	24%	—	72%	42%	—	56%

Key Votes of the 105th Congress

1. Bal. Budget Amend.	Y	5. Satcher for Surgeon Gen.	N	9. Chem. Weapons Treaty	Y
2. Clinton Budget Deal	Y	6. Highway Set-asides	Y	10. Cuban Humanitarian Aid	N
3. Cloture on Tobacco	N	7. Table Child Gun locks	Y	11. Table Bosnia Troops	Y
4. Education IRAs	Y	8. Ovrd. Part. Birth Veto	Y	12. $ for Test-ban Treaty	*

Election Results

1998 general	Frank Murkowski (R)	165,227	(74%)	($911,926)
	Joseph Sonneman (D)	43,743	(20%)	($26,091)
	Others	12,837	(6%)	
1998 primary	Frank Murkowski (R)	76,635	(72%)	
	Joseph Sonneman (D)	10,716	(10%)	
	Frank Vondersaar (D)	6,343	(6%)	
	William L. Hale (R)	6,312	(6%)	
	Jeffrey Gottlieb (Green)	4,793	(4%)	
	Others	1,986	(2%)	
1992 general	Frank Murkowski (R)	127,163	(53%)	($1,910,759)
	Tony Smith (D)	92,065	(38%)	($910,138)
	Mary Jordan (Green)	20,019	(8%)	($4,091)

REPRESENTATIVE

Rep. Don Young (R)

Elected Mar. 1973; b. June 9, 1933, Meridian, CA; home, Fort Yukon; Yuba Jr. Col., A.A. 1952, Chico St. Col., B.A. 1958; Episcopalian; married (Lu).

Military Career: Army, 1955–57

Elected Office: Fort Yukon City Cncl., 1960–64; Fort Yukon Mayor, 1964–68; AK House of Reps., 1966–70; AK Senate, 1970–73.

Professional Career: School teacher, Fort Yukon, 1960–68; Riverboat captain, 1960–68.

DC Office: 2111 RHOB, 20515, 202-225-5765; Fax: 202-225-0425; Web site: www.house.gov/donyoung.

District Offices: Anchorage, 907-271-5978; Fairbanks, 907-456-0210; Juneau, 907-586-7400; Kenai, 907-283-5808; Ketchikan, 907-225-6880; Mat-Su, 907-376-7665.

Committees: *Resources* (Chmn. of 28 R). *Transportation & Infrastructure* (2d of 41 R): Aviation; Coast Guard & Maritime Transportation; Water Resources & Environment.

Group Ratings

	ADA	ACLU	AFS	LCV	CON	NTU	NFIB	COC	ACU	NTLC	CHC
1998	20	20	44	0	2	48	85	78	84	83	100
1997	5	—	29	—	*	56	—	80	86	—	—

National Journal Ratings

	1997 LIB — 1997 CONS	1998 LIB — 1998 CONS
Economic	43% — 57%	47% — 53%
Social	0% — 90%	32% — 67%
Foreign	23% — 76%	27% — 68%

Key Votes of the 105th Congress

1. Clinton Budget Deal	Y	5. Puerto Rico Sthood. Ref.	Y	9. Cut $ for B-2 Bombers	N
2. Education IRAs	Y	6. End Highway Set-asides	Y	10. Human Rights in China	N
3. Req. 2/3 to Raise Taxes	Y	7. School Prayer Amend.	Y	11. Withdraw Bosnia Troops	N
4. Fast-track Trade	N	8. Ovrd. Part. Birth Veto	Y	12. End Cuban TV-Marti	N

Election Results

1998 general	Don Young (R)	139,676	(63%)	($1,385,073)
	Jim Duncan (D)	77,232	(35%)	($570,894)
	Others	6,392	(3%)	
1998 primary	Don Young (R)	65,972	(61%)	
	Jim Duncan (D)	27,670	(26%)	
	Jim Dore (R)	7,384	(7%)	
	Others	6,940	(6%)	
1996 general	Don Young (R)	138,834	(59%)	($1,176,954)
	Georgianna Lincoln (D)	85,114	(36%)	($245,941)
	Others	9,752	(4%)	

ARIZONA

Youth and age, new and old: Arizona is home to America's oldest continuous community and is one of America's fastest-growing and most rapidly changing states. The Hopi Indians, living as shepherds on plateaus east of the Grand Canyon, have not changed much in perhaps 500 years. In 1680 they killed the local Franciscan priests and burned their churches and have spurned Christianity since; more recently they have been involved in land disputes with the far more numerous Navajo. The Hopi are the oldest Arizonans; the newest are moving in every day, into subdivisions rising up out of the empty desert east, north, and west of Phoenix, hemmed in only by dry river beds, upcrops of mountains, and Indian reservation boundaries.

Politically, Arizona is also both old and young. The single year of 1998 saw the deaths of Arizona's two leading politicians, Republican Barry Goldwater and Democrat Morris Udall, whose political careers started 40-some years ago and whose fathers were prominent civic leaders in Arizona's early years of statehood—Baron Goldwater as owner of the owner of a large chain of department stores, Levi Udall as chief justice of the state Supreme Court. Barry Goldwater was elected to the Senate in 1952, just two years before Morris Udall's brother Stewart was elected to the House; when Stewart Udall became Interior secretary in 1961, Mo was elected to take his place. Morris Udall and Goldwater were both presidential candidates in their time—both unsuccessfully; both were well endowed with mordant frontier humor; and both saw within their lifetimes Arizona transformed from dusty frontier to glittering high tech.

For Arizona is one of the boom states of the 1990s, with some of the nation's fastest population growth, a state with an economy now sophisticated and decentralized enough that there is no easy explanation, as there once was, of how and why Arizona grows. The first explanation was copper: the dome of the state Capitol dome is encased in copper; one of Arizona's leading public figures was Lewis Douglas, copper heir and congressman, Franklin Roosevelt's first budget director and Harry Truman's ambassador to Britain. In those years Arizona depended heavily on the federal government, and on politicians like Carl Hayden, Democratic congressman from statehood in 1912 and senator from 1927–69, whose public works projects watered Arizona's cotton, citrus and cattle farms.

Then in the decades after World War II businessmen, lawyers, developers, and water companies, notably the Salt River Project, built an Arizona based on something like the opposite of New Deal principles: with minimal government and precious little regulation of business, a welcoming of new technological ideas and shunning of new cultural liberalism; like Disneyland, a more gleaming and spotless embodiment of old values than America had ever been. Their political champion was Barry Goldwater, city council member and senator and the nation's Mr. Conservative for much of the 1950s and 1960s. He helped to make Arizona Republican, the only state to vote Republican for president in every election from 1952–92.

This Arizona has grown phenomenally, from 700,000 people at the end of World War II to 3.6 million in 1990, and then to 4.6 million in 1998—an increase in eight years larger than its whole population in 1945. It is growth based on high-tech and low taxes, the one getting higher and the other lower every year. It is not growth based on an influx of elderly retirees—Arizona may have Sun City, but its proportion of people over 65 is near the national average; nor is it based on farming subsidized by cheap water, since thirsty cotton farms are being phased out for urban users who can easily outbid them. More than anything else, the engine of Arizona's growth has been technology: Phoenix has been attracting high-tech industries since Motorola built a research center for military electronics there in 1948, and big employers now include Motorola's semiconductor operation, Allied Signal, Honeywell flight systems, Intel and Tucson's Hughes Aircraft which merged with Raytheon in 1997. And landlocked Arizona is a major exporter—nearly $2 billion to Mexico and Japan in 1997, more than $1 billion to the Netherlands, Malaysia and Canada.

Arizona is a place where the private sector is expanding apace and the public sector, if not shriveling away, is yielding ground. Arizona has cut state taxes sharply in the 1990s. It has pioneered in providing choice in education, with America's largest proportion of charter schools (some 10% of the total) and the for-profit University of Phoenix, based here but with branches in many states, which leases space and hires working-age adults to teach job-related skills to working-age adults. Local choice prevails: the inaptly named Youngtown, near Phoenix, bars children from living there; so does Superstition Heights. Where government once used to allocate precious water, now "shadow governments" (Joel Garreau's term) like the Salt River District do so, heeding the market signals which say urban users will pay more than farmers; Interior Secretary (and Arizonan) Bruce Babbitt has proposed that Arizona can sell the surplus Colorado River water it stores in aquifers to even faster-growing and thirsty Las Vegas. In 1998 Arizona voters, desirous of preserving open space, authorized state government to buy it on the market rather than commandeer it. And on the same day Arizona became the first state to elect women to all of its top five statewide executive offices: Governor Jane Hull, Secretary of State Betsey Bayless, Attorney General Janet Napolitano, Treasurer Carol Springer, Superintendent of Public Instruction Lisa Graham Keegan; all but Napolitano are Republicans.

Governor. Arizona's governor is Jane Hull, who came to office when Fife Symington was convicted of financial fraud in September 1997. She was the fourth junior state official to succeed to the office in the last 20 years: Secretary of State Wesley Bolin became governor when Raul Castro resigned to become ambassador to Argentina in October 1977, Attorney General Bruce Babbitt became governor when Bolin died in March 1978 and Rose Mofford became governor when Evan Mecham was impeached and removed in April 1988. Hull grew up in Mission, Kansas, a suburb of Kansas City. She graduated from the University of Kansas, became a teacher, married and moved to the Navajo Reservation where her husband was a

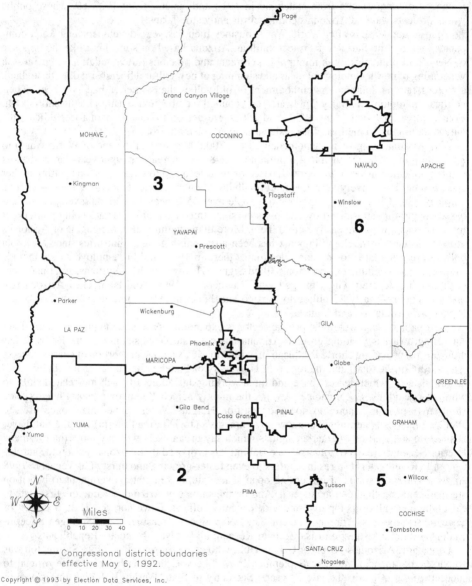

Congressional district boundaries
effective May 6, 1992.

Copyright © 1993 by Election Data Services, Inc.

doctor with the U.S. Public Health Service. They moved to Phoenix where he practiced medicine, she raised four children and—a Goldwater conservative since she saw him speak in Kansas—started volunteering in political campaigns. In 1978 she was elected to the state House, and in time became majority whip (1988–89) and speaker (1989–92). In that post she presided over the House during the AzScam scandal in which numerous legislators were charged with bribery. In 1993 she resigned to run for secretary of State and was elected in 1994.

In her early days in the legislature Hull was known as a strong conservative; later her stands on education, juvenile justice and abortion gained her the label of a moderate. But she supported Symington's relentless tax cutting. In her first year in office she kept most of Symington's staff and got through cuts in vehicle license income and business taxes of $140 million. But the state budget rose 13%, to $5.9 billion, mostly because of two Hull programs. One was a $150 million KidsCare program, to finance health care for low-income children, mostly with money from the tobacco tax and the federal government. Hull worked months and had to call a special session to get passage of a school funding law that would pass court muster; under her Students FIRST bill the state would spend $372 million to equalize funding, but still allow local districts to raise money by issuing bonds.

Hull started off her 1998 campaign well ahead in polls. In October 1997 Eddie Basha, the "chubby grocer" who was the Democratic nominee in 1994, decided not to run. In May 1998 conservative Congressman Matt Salmon bowed out of the race, while suggesting he might run in 2002. Hull's major opponent turned out to be Paul Johnson, successful entrepreneur and mayor of Phoenix from 1990–94. Johnson criticized Hull's conservative record as a legislator and her position on abortion. She had voted for abortion restrictions as a legislator, but as speaker kept them from coming to the floor; more recently, she has supported the partial-birth abortion ban, but says "there are times . . . when abortion is very definitely a decision between a woman, her physician and her spouse."

Hull raised $1.8 million and campaigned as an uncontroversial incumbent in a year in which people loved incumbents and hated controversy. Johnson put $500,000 of his own money into his campaign and in early October charged that Hull had made commitments to trade away Arizona water rights for campaign contributions during a Las Vegas fundraiser where she raised $31,000. But Johnson's claim fell flat when it was revealed that a planned Nevada subdivision Johnson had said could not be built without Arizona water was already under construction. The result was no surprise. Hull won 61%–36%. She carried Republican Maricopa County, where more than half the state's votes are cast, by 62%–34%; she also carried often Democratic Pima County (Tucson) 62%–35%, and prevailed in the rest of the state by 57%–39%; she lost the Hispanic vote by only 56%–40%.

Laws in Arizona are made not only by the governor and legislature but also by the voters. A campaign finance initiative, financed by a lobbyist fee, a voluntary tax checkoff and a surcharge on civil and criminal fines, which would produce public moneys for candidates who raised a certain amount and adhered to restrictions, was passed 51%–49%. On medical marijuana, voters reinstated the language of the initiative passed two years before, and overturned the legislature's attempt to repeal it. Voters by wide margins kept the lottery and outlawed cockfighting. Most interestingly, voters by 53%–47% approved Proposition 303, which authorized $220 million to preserve open land from development and barred the legislature from requiring local governments to maintain open space; this was supported by Hull and business interests and opposed by many environmental groups.

Senior Senator. John McCain is now Arizona's leading political figure, a possible presidential candidate and an important national policymaker whether he runs or not. His personal story is a dramatic one, told beautifully by Robert Timberg in *The Nightingale's Song*: he is the son and grandson of Navy admirals, a decorated Navy pilot himself who was shot down over Vietnam and who spent five years, most of it in pain and torture, in Communist prisoner of war camps; he refused to be let out ahead of those who had been in longer when he was offered release because of his father's rank. McCain returned to the United States in March

1973. His final assignment in the Navy was as Senate liaison. In 1980 he retired and moved to Arizona, his wife's home state; in 1982 he ran for an open House seat. Attacked as an outsider, he responded, "The longest place I ever lived in was Hanoi." He led 32%–26% in a four-way primary, and won the 1982 and 1984 general elections and then the 1986 Senate contest easily.

McCain is chairman of the Commerce Committee and a member of Armed Services, with a mostly conservative voting record. But on two important issues in the 105th Congress, campaign finance reform and the tobacco bill, McCain took stands opposed by almost all Republicans and supported by most Democrats. He was one of the lead sponsors of the line-item veto and has been an avid pork-buster, denouncing even defense and Arizona earmarks in the October 1998 budget. He has called for requiring a supermajority of 60 votes to raise taxes and for a biennial budget to reduce pork.

He has worked to ban small airplanes from flying over the Grand Canyon. Inspired by the plethora of lawsuits inspired by this issue, he worked for a $5.5 million grant for creating an office for mediation of environmental lawsuits at the Morris K. Udall Foundation he helped set up. McCain served as chairman of the Indian Affairs Committee in 1995–96. Arizona has one of the nation's largest percentages of Indians, and McCain, like Barry Goldwater and Morris Udall, obviously feels a sympathy for them. "Never deceive them," he says. "They have been deceived too many times in the last 200 years." Generally he has supported the tribal agenda. He cooperated with the vast expansion in the 1990s of Indian gambling. He has worked for Indian self-governance and sovereignty, but has also pushed laws on child abuse on reservations. On adoption issues, he backed limited changes in the law which allows tribes to control the adoptions even of children born off the reservation with low percentages of Indian blood.

On the Commerce Committee, McCain opposed the 1996 Telecommunications Act, passed after years of intense lobbying. "Every major telecommunications company was protected," he argued later, but cable and local telephone rates went up, and as of 1998 the local telephone companies were getting no effective competition from long distance servers and vice versa. Instead, the regional Bells were merging. McCain wanted an auction, not a giveaway, of the digital TV spectrum to the networks; later he charged that the networks were not resolving key standards for switching to digital and would not be able to return their analog frequencies in 2006, as they had promised in return for free digital frequencies. In 1997 McCain led key senators and congressmen to agree not to legislate for three years if the networks would come up with code letters for violence, sexual content and foul language in their programs. He favored requiring filtering technology on computers used in schools.

In the early 1990s McCain worked hard with Massachusetts's John Kerry on the special committee investigating charges that American POWs or MIAs remain in Vietnam; they found no evidence of any. With Kerry he supported ending the trade embargo on and initiating diplomatic relations with Vietnam, and has traveled there many times. He came to Bill Clinton's side when some veterans complained of the president's presence at military ceremonies. On other defense issues, McCain has called for more defense spending but has shown a professional military officer's caution about committing American troops without a clear end in sight, most notably in Bosnia, where he opposed the use of air power alone. He called the Clinton Administration's 1994 agreement with North Korea "appeasement" and said sanctions against North Korean nuclear proliferation should be backed by explicit threats of air strikes. He has been extremely vocal on Kosovo, pushing Clinton to either commit or get out; in May 1999 the Senate shelved McCain's proposal to authorize "all necessary force" including ground forces.

In 1997 and 1998 McCain took on two fights—campaign finance reform and the tobacco settlements—in which he was aligned mostly by Democrats and frustrated by his inability to win the 60 votes needed to end a filibuster. The opposition each time was led by a Republican senator, in one case a practical-minded senator citing idealistic reasons, in the other an idealistic senator pursuing practical political goals. One cause, campaign finance, he took on himself; the other, tobacco, was thrust on him. McCain's interest in campaign finance may have come from when he was one of the "Keating five" senators investigated for meeting in 1987 with regulators on behalf of Charles Keating's savings and loan. McCain was kept in the case by Democrats, though he had done nothing for Keating, because he was the one Republican involved and thus made the scandal bipartisan; he was cited for nothing more than bad judgment. Vindicated by reelection in 1992, in the majority after the election of 1994, he sought out Democrat Russ Feingold, whose campaign finance bill had gotten nowhere that year. The McCain-Feingold bills have gone through several transformations; the bill that came to the floor in 1998 purported to ban soft money contributions to political parties and to limit "issue ads" run by independent organizations within 60 days of an election. McCain hoped that Fred Thompson's hearings on the Clinton-Gore campaign finance shenanigans would convert Republicans, but it brought only a few. Meanwhile, Mitch McConnell, chairman of the Republicans' Senate campaign committee, argued to partisans that banning soft money would hurt Republicans and to wider audiences that McCain-Feingold would violate the First Amendment by limiting political speech. Majority Leader Trent Lott yanked the bill from the Senate floor in February 1998; it returned in September, after the House passed a similar bill, but could summon up no more than 52 votes and was killed.

The tobacco issue was thrust on McCain as Commerce Committee chairman: Lott told him to put together a bill with bipartisan support, and McCain's bill passed 19–1 in April 1998. It provided for closer regulation of tobacco advertising and marketing and stiffer penalties if the teenage smoking rate did not decline, plus a $1.10 cigarette tax; the cost was estimated at $516 billion, higher by opponents. At first it had little articulate opposition. But John Ashcroft, a non-smoker thinking of running for president, forthrightly opposed the tax. And the big tobacco companies, noting that the cost was well above the $368 billion in the settlement agreed to with state attorneys general in 1997, that the McCain bill did not protect them against lawsuits as that settlement did, and that the Finance Committee raised the tax to $1.50, decided to oppose it. They ran a huge ad campaign against the tobacco tax—naming McCain in, as he noted, Arizona, Iowa and New Hampshire. Although just about everyone in Washington seemed to favor McCain's bill, an NBC- *Wall Street Journal* poll showed that voter opinion was about evenly divided. McCain was obviously angered by the opposition. "Maybe we ought to remember the obligations that we incur when we govern America. Maybe we ought to remember the principles of the founders of our party. We might want to understand that our obligation first of all is to those who can't care for themselves in this society, and that includes our children." But the bill was dropped in June 1998 after only 57 senators voted to stop the filibuster. In November 1998, the attorneys general of 46 states reached a $206 billion settlement with the tobacco companies, which would restrict advertising and marketing but provide no protection against other lawsuits.

Many Republicans complained that McCain was acting against conservative principles on campaign finance and tobacco. But if, as Michael Lynch wrote in *Reason*, McCain is actuated less by abstract principle than by personal honor, his choices are readily explicable: he took the lead on campaign finance as a kind of atonement for the Keating Five, and he persevered on tobacco once he was given the mission of coming up with a conference bill in his committee.

McCain's political standing in Arizona is very strong. He won the Senate seat in 1986 by 60%–40%. In 1992 he was reelected 56%–32%, with 11% for conservative former Governor Evan Mecham. In 1998 he was opposed by Ed Ranger, an environmental lawyer in Arizona and Mexico who put 70,000 miles on a Harley Davidson and converted 1970s school bus traveling through the state. McCain raised more than $4 million, for fear of a tobacco assault, he said, and spent only about $2 million. He won by an impressive 69%–27%, carrying the heavily Navajo and Democratic Apache County 54%–42% and winning the Hispanic vote 52%–42%. He attributed that last not to his one $12,000 ad on Spanish-language radio, but to his longstanding positions on issues: "I favor bilingual education that works, I'm opposed to 'English only,' I favor legal immigration."

As president, McCain's great attraction is not his stands on issues (too conservative for many ticket-splitters, too apostate for many Republicans) or his scholarly credentials (though he is capable of a quiet eloquence, as in his speech nominating Bob Dole) but his forthrightness. In December 1998 he filed papers for an exploratory committee.

Junior Senator. Jon Kyl, Arizona's junior senator, is a Republican first elected in 1994. His father John Kyl was a Republican congressman from Iowa (1959–65, 1967–73), who eventually lost his seat in redistricting; Jon Kyl moved to a state that, in effect, was gaining the Republican seats Great Plains states like Iowa were losing. Kyl went to college and law school in Arizona, practiced law in Phoenix, worked on Republican campaigns and headed the Phoenix Chamber of Commerce; he won the heavily Republican 4th District seat in 1986 by beating 60%–28% former (1973–77) Congressman John Conlan, who had support from the religious right.

In the House, Kyl was a leader among Republicans on the Strategic Defense Initiative, the balanced budget amendment, and for disclosing the names of House members with overdrafts on the House bank—one of the causes that destabilized Democrats' control of the House in 1993 and 1994. But by that time Kyl was running for the Senate seat held for three terms by Democrat Dennis DeConcini, whose reputation was stained by his involvement in the Keating Five scandal. Kyl had no primary opposition and the further good fortune that one-term Congressman Sam Coppersmith won the September 13 primary by only 59 votes of 255,000 cast and after a two-week recount. Kyl, with far more money, ran ads with home movie texture showing him travelling through the desert countryside, dressed in jeans and working on ranches, while talking about how he and his wife first fell in love with the state. Coppersmith stressed his pro-choice stand on abortion and said he would welcome a campaign visit from President Clinton. Kyl won solidly, 54%–40%.

Kyl has had a solidly conservative record. He is perhaps the Senate's biggest champion of a missile defense system. He lead with Jesse Helms the losing fight against the Chemical Weapons Convention, convening a conference at the Arizona Biltmore featuring Margaret Thatcher, Henry Kissinger and George Shultz. He has criticized administration policy in the Middle East, arguing that it is false to equate new Jewish settlements with violent acts of terrorism. Kyl dropped his seat on Foreign Relations for 1999, and moved on to Appropriations.

Kyl serves on Judiciary and is sponsor, with Dianne Feinstein, of a constitutional amendment on victims' rights. It would give victims of crime a right to be informed, to be present and to be heard at critical stages in the judicial process; a right to speedy trial and final conclusion free from unreasonable delay; full restitution from the criminal; and protection from violence or intimidation. He has introduced bills outlawing identity theft and internet gambling and on-line casinos. He was a lead Senate sponsor of the bill to ban racial quotas and preferences. He has worked to beef up the Border Patrol and to track legal immigrants who overstay their visas. He supports cuts in legal immigration and new rules for family-based immigration—the kind of measures which have cost Republicans Hispanic votes.

On other issues, Kyl favors repeal of the estate tax, saying it would create up to 145,000 new jobs, and has backed bills to preserve Arizona's ponderosa pine forests and to crack down on bear poaching. He has been the Senate leader on the move to change the Clinton Administration's barring doctors who take Medicare patients from contracting with patients for more services or higher fees.

Kyl has said he does not expect to seek more than two terms. His seat is up in 2000, and he entered 1999 a heavy favorite.

Cook's Call. *Safe.* Kyl won this open seat in 1994 with 54% and is not expected to have any trouble securing a second term in 2000. Not a single first-tier Democrat is even contemplating giving him a challenge.

Presidential politics. In 1996 Arizona did two unlikely things: it staged one of the earliest presidential primaries in the nation in February, and then in November voted Democratic for president for the first time since 1948, breaking the longest such string in the nation. Arizona tried and failed to set its primary the same day as New Hampshire's; instead, it scheduled it a week later, February 27. The idea was to produce a victory for Phil Gramm, whom most leading

ARIZONA 115

Republicans were backing. But Gramm pulled out of the race even before New Hampshire, and Arizona was very much up for grabs.

Steve Forbes peppered the state with ads boosting his flat tax and attacking Washington politicians. But Pat Buchanan, urging followers to "mount up and ride" after his narrow victory in New Hampshire, hoped his opposition to illegal immigrants and support of property rights would boost him here. But Buchanan's truculence evidently rubbed some voters wrong. He finished third, with 27%, the end of any serious chance he had; Bob Dole, with Senator John McCain's support, finished second, with 30%; Steve Forbes, after all his ads, took 33% and all the delegates. For 2000, Arizona Republicans toyed with pushing the primary back to March—a move that would presumably help McCain, but the plan seemed to derail in early 1999.

Bill Clinton won all of Arizona's electoral votes in November, by a 47%–44% margin—the first Democrat to carry the state since Harry Truman. Clinton had come close to winning in 1992, losing to George Bush by only 38%–37%. Why was Clinton so competitive in a free enterprise state? Many speculated that elderly voters, fearing for their Medicare, went for him. But Arizona does not have a specially large elderly population, and the air seemed to go out of the Medicare issue in mid-October. More important was the environment issue. Arizona has a much lower percentage of rural and small town voters than other Rocky Mountain states: nearly 80% of Arizonans live in metro Phoenix and Tucson, and they want to preserve the environment that is so visibly being transformed by their own success. Clinton's staging of the announcement of a Utah land preserve at the Grand Canyon may have carried Arizona single-handedly (it may also have defeated the only Democratic congressman in Utah). Also, Hispanic voters went 10–1 for Clinton in 1996, perhaps out of anger at Republicans' attempts to deny government aid to legal as well as illegal immigrants and to reduce family-based immigration. Whether either of Arizona's 1996 unlikely developments will recur in 2000 is uncertain.

Congressional districting. Arizona gained one congressional district in each of the last four censuses, and, with the nation's fastest growth rate after Nevada, is expected to gain two in the 2000 count. A federal court drew the current plan, with a Phoenix-to-Tucson Hispanic majority district, which is solidly Democratic, and the other five districts Republican (two did elect Democrats in 1992). Arizona's Republican governor and presumably Republican legislature might try to stretch their party's lead to 7–1 in 2002. But that may be stretching it too far, and they might be forced to create one new Democratic and one new Republican seat.

The People: Est. Pop. 1998: 4,668,631; Pop. 1990: 3,665,228, up 27.4% 1990–1998. 1.7% of U.S. total, 21st largest; 12.5% rural. Median age: 34.4 years. 13.6% 65 years and over. 81% White, 3% Black, 1.5% Asian, 5.6% Amer. Indian, 9% Other; 18.6% Hispanic Origin. Households: 54.6% married couple families; 25.5% married couple fams. w. children; 52.5% college educ.; median household income: $27,540; per capita income: $13,461; 64.2% owner occupied housing; median house value: $80,100; median monthly rent: $370. 4.1% Unemployment. 1998 Voting age pop.: 3,547,000. 1998 Turnout: 1,037,550; 29% of VAP. Registered voters (1998): 2,264,301; 912,613 D (40%), 1,013,533 R (45%), 338,145 unaffiliated and minor parties (15%).

Political Lineup: Governor, Jane Dee Hull (R); Secy. of State, Betsey Bayless (R); Atty. Gen., Janet Napolitano (D); Treasurer, Carol Springer (R); State Senate, 30 (14 D, 16 R); Majority Leader, Russell Bowers (R); State House, 60 (22 D, 38 R); House Speaker, Jeff Groscost (R). Senators, John McCain (R) and Jon Kyl (R). Representatives, 6 (1 D, 5 R).

Elections Division: 602-542-8683; **Filing Deadline for U.S. Congress:** June 29, 2000.

1996 Presidential Vote

Clinton (D)	653,288	(47%)
Dole (R)	622,073	(44%)
Perot (I)	112,074	(8%)

1992 Presidential Vote

Bush (R)	572,086	(38%)
Clinton (D)	543,050	(37%)
Perot (I)	353,741	(24%)

1996 Republican Presidential Primary

Forbes (R)	115,962	(33%)
Dole (R)	102,980	(30%)
Buchanan (R)	95,742	(28%)
Alexander (R)	24,765	(7%)
Others	8,033	(2%)

GOVERNOR

Gov. Jane Dee Hull (R)

Assumed office Sept.1997, term expires Jan. 2003; b. Aug. 8, 1935, Kansas City, MO; home, Phoenix; U. of KS, B.S. 1957; AZ St. U., 1974–79; Josephson Ethics Inst., 1993; Catholic; married (Terry).

Elected Office: AZ House of Reps., 1978–93, Speaker, 1989–92; AZ Secy. of State., 1994–97.

Professional Career: Jr. High Teacher, 1957–63.

Office: 1700 W. Washington, Phoenix, 85007, 602-542-4331; Fax: 602-542-7601; Web site: www.state.az.us.

Election Results

1998 gen.	Jane Dee Hull (R)	620,188	(61%)
	Paul Johnson (D)	361,552	(36%)
	Others	35,876	(4%)
1998 prim.	Jane Dee Hull (R)	177,324	(77%)
	Jim Howl (R)	30,699	(13%)
	Charles Brown (R)	23,710	(10%)
1994 gen.	Fife Symington (R)	593,492	(53%)
	Eddie Basha (D)	500,702	(44%)
	Others	35,413	(3%)

SENATORS

Sen. John McCain (R)

Elected 1986, seat up 2004; b. Aug. 29, 1936, Panama Canal Zone; home, Phoenix; U.S. Naval Acad., B.S. 1958, Natl. War Col., 1973–74; Episcopalian; married (Cindy).

Military Career: Navy, 1958–80 (Vietnam).

Elected Office: U.S. House of Reps., 1982–1986.

Professional Career: Dir., Navy Senate Liaison Ofc., 1977–81.

DC Office: 241 RSOB, 20510, 202-224-2235; Fax: 202-228-2862; Web site: www.senate.gov/~mccain.

State Offices: Mesa, 602-491-4300; Phoenix, 602-952-2410; Tucson, 520-670-6334.

Committees: *Armed Services* (3d of 11 R): Personnel; Readiness & Management Support; Seapower. *Commerce, Science & Transportation* (Chmn. of 11 R). *Indian Affairs* (3d of 8 R).

Group Ratings

	ADA	ACLU	AFS	LCV	CON	NTU	NFIB	COC	ACU	NTLC	CHC
1998	20	14	33	0	93	73	100	76	68	96	73
1997	5	—	0	—	97	82	—	100	80	—	—

National Journal Ratings

	1997 LIB — 1997 CONS		1998 LIB — 1998 CONS	
Economic	24%	— 75%	29%	— 70%
Social	17%	— 72%	29%	— 69%
Foreign	34%	— 57%	29%	— 58%

Key Votes of the 105th Congress

1. Bal. Budget Amend.	Y	5. Satcher for Surgeon Gen.	Y	9. Chem. Weapons Treaty	Y
2. Clinton Budget Deal	Y	6. Highway Set-asides	Y	10. Cuban Humanitarian Aid	N
3. Cloture on Tobacco	Y	7. Table Child Gun locks	Y	11. Table Bosnia Troops	Y
4. Education IRAs	Y	8. Ovrd. Part. Birth Veto	Y	12. $ for Test-ban Treaty	N

Election Results

1998 general	John McCain (R)	696,577	(69%)	($2,461,900)
	Ed Ranger (D)	275,224	(27%)	($371,439)
	Others	41,479	(4%)	
1998 primary	John McCain (R)	unopposed		
1992 general	John McCain (R)	771,395	(56%)	($3,766,588)
	Claire Sargent (D)	436,321	(32%)	($287,682)
	Evan Mecham (I)	145,361	(11%)	($86,433)
	Others	28,974	(2%)	

Sen. Jon Kyl (R)

Elected 1994, seat up 2000; b. Apr. 25, 1942, Oakland, NE; home, Phoenix; U. of AZ, B.A. 1964, L.L.B. 1966; Presbyterian; married (Caryll).

Elected Office: U.S. House of Reps., 1986–94.

Professional Career: Practicing atty., 1966–86; Chmn., Phoenix Chamber of Commerce, 1984–85.

DC Office: 724 HSOB, 20510, 202-224-4521; Fax: 202-228-1239; Web site: www.senate.gov/~kyl.

State Offices: Phoenix, 602-840-1891; Tucson, 520-575-8633.

Committees: *Appropriations* (15th of 15 R): District of Columbia; Labor & HHS; Military Construction; Treasury & General Government; VA, HUD & Independent Agencies. *Intelligence* (5th of 9 R). *Judiciary* (5th of 10 R): Immigration; Technology, Terrorism & Government Information (Chmn.); Youth Violence.

Group Ratings

	ADA	ACLU	AFS	LCV	CON	NTU	NFIB	COC	ACU	NTLC	CHC
1998	0	14	0	0	95	88	88	76	96	100	100
1997	0	—	0	—	80	87	—	70	96	—	—

National Journal Ratings

	1997 LIB — 1997 CONS		1998 LIB — 1998 CONS	
Economic	0%	— 89%	0%	— 88%
Social	0%	— 83%	0%	— 88%
Foreign	0%	— 77%	29%	— 58%

Key Votes of the 105th Congress

1. Bal. Budget Amend.	Y	5. Satcher for Surgeon Gen.	N	9. Chem. Weapons Treaty	N
2. Clinton Budget Deal	Y	6. Highway Set-asides	N	10. Cuban Humanitarian Aid	N
3. Cloture on Tobacco	N	7. Table Child Gun locks	Y	11. Table Bosnia Troops	Y
4. Education IRAs	Y	8. Ovrd. Part. Birth Veto	Y	12. $ for Test-ban Treaty	N

Election Results

1994 general	Jon Kyl (R)	600,999	(54%)	($4,138,203)
	Sam Coppersmith (D)	442,510	(40%)	($1,577,556)
	Scott Grainger (Lib)	75,493	(7%)	
1994 primary	Jon Kyl (R)	unopposed		
1988 general	Dennis DeConcini (D)	660,403	(57%)	($2,640,650)
	Keith DeGreen (R)	478,060	(41%)	($238,369)

FIRST DISTRICT

The metropolis of Phoenix is exceedingly young—yet bears traces of a lost Indian civilization a millennium old. Barry Goldwater, born in 1909 and living on into 1998, grew up knowing men and women who remembered when the Valley of the Sun, as some call it today, was virtually empty, with a few parched settlements set above the dry river bed; eerily, this empty land was criss-crossed by more than 200 miles of irrigation channels built some 500 years ago by the Hohokam, who then mysteriously disappeared. Phoenix was founded in the years after the Civil War, near the Pueblo Grande Indian ruins and still functioning canals, as a haymarket for cavalry horses at Fort McDowell 40 miles away. On the usually-dry Salt River, Tempe was founded in 1871 as Hayden's Ferry, by the father of future Senator (1927–69) Carl Hayden; it was renamed in 1879 for an ancient Greek vale, and is now home of Arizona State University, founded in 1885, and the Fiesta Bowl. Further east is Mesa, founded by Mormons in 1878 on a square mile, laid out with broad streets with huge blocks holding just four homesites, using Indian canals built 1100 years before; a gleaming white Mormon Temple was built there in 1927, one of the few in the United States. North of the Salt River, directly east of Phoenix and in the shadows of Camelback Mountain, is Scottsdale, founded much more recently, with its trendy shops carefully decked out in Old West style.

For half a century this remained mostly empty land: As late as 1950 only 106,000 people lived in Phoenix and only 331,000 in all of Maricopa County. But in the years after World War II the air conditioner and military technology—in 1948 Motorola built an electronics research center here—transformed Phoenix, from a sleepy whistle-stop, where the small tufa stone turn-of-the-century Capitol was the most prominent building, to today's high-rise studded metropolis, with 1.2 million people in Phoenix and 2.7 million in Maricopa County. This is not, as some think, a giant retirement village; nor is it totally overrun with crooked land salesmen or fast-buck artists, though freewheeling Phoenix has attracted more than its share of both. The typical cactus-decorated desert-brown adobe tract house here is occupied by a growing family, living a more traditional life than many occupants of more traditional-looking houses back east.

The 1st District of Arizona includes much of the historic heart of Phoenix: Pueblo Grande and the old Indian School in Phoenix, Arizona State in Tempe and the Mormon Temple in Mesa and Old Town Scottsdale; it also goes south to include most of Chandler. Its boundaries are convoluted, designed to maximize the number of Hispanics in the 2d District and Indians (in the Salt River and Gilva River Reservations) in the 6th; geographically, it sits south of Camelback Mountain, west of the Superstition Mountains, east of South Mountain. It includes some high-income neighborhoods, but its cultural tone is resolutely middle class, hard-working, church-going; politically, it has been traditionally heavily Republican.

The congressman here is Matt Salmon, a Republican elected with the big freshman class of 1994. Salmon grew up in Utah, went to Arizona State, did Mormon missionary work in Taiwan from 1977–79, then finished school. He worked in public affairs for USWest in the 1980s and was elected to the Arizona Senate, a part-time job, in 1990, where he rose to assistant majority leader. In 1994, when one-term Democrat Sam Coppersmith ran for the Senate, Salmon ran for Congress. The real competition turned out to be in the Republican primary. There Salmon won 39% to 22% for cable TV lobbyist Susan Bitter Smith, 19% for attorney Linda Rawles, and 16% for educator Bev Hermon. Salmon was running on the Contract with America even before the Contract was signed, boosting the $500 dependent tax credit, term limits and a buydown of the national debt. He had spirited opposition from Democratic state Senator Chuck Blanchard, a former clerk for Supreme Court Justice Sandra Day O'Connor, who took some moderate stands. But Blanchard was the Arizona head of the 1992 Clinton campaign and defended the House Democrats' crime bill. Salmon won fairly easily, 56%–39%.

Salmon has turned out to be one of the leading rebels of his class—a rebel not only against 40 years of Democratic policies but, even more vociferously, against the leadership of Newt Gingrich. He was displeased to be passed over for a seat on the Commerce Committee and, self-limited to three terms, was displeased when his reforms were diluted. His proposal to require birthfathers to support offspring till they turn 18 did not make it into the welfare reform bill. His proposal to give victims the right to view executions did not make it into any crime bills. Nor does it seem likely Congress will pass his 1998 "no second chances" bill that would penalize states that free convicted murderers, rapists and child molesters with loss of federal funds if they later are convicted of similar offenses. Salmon favors building a light rail line from Phoenix to Tempe, but he irritated Transportation Chairman Bud Shuster by opposing an airline tax and the 1997 committee funding bill. In 1999 he introduced legislation to have Ronald Reagan's likeness added to Mt. Rushmore.

On the International Relations Committee, Salmon has taken a lead in two areas. As a fluent speaker of Mandarin Chinese, he has strongly criticized China's human rights violations, but opposed withdrawal of most favored nation status and other unilateral sanctions. "One thing we don't understand in our culture is the value of saving face and how important that is in their culture. None of this would be fixed if we disengage and withhold MFN." He has been a strong supporter of Israel: "I've read the Old Testament. I've read the New Testament. My faith has always talked about being supportive of Israel." In 1998 he took the lead in demanding that the Palestinian Authority turn over those who killed Americans in terrorist attacks. He sponsored a resolution calling on the U.S. to denounce any unilateral declaration of Palestinian statehood, which was put aside by Speaker Newt Gingrich in deference to Clinton Administration policy.

Salmon entered Congress a big fan of Gingrich but turned out to be the member who, more than anyone else, forced him out of the speakership. In early 1997 he was critical of Gingrich's ethics violations, and voted for him for speaker only after some hesitation. In April 1997 he was one of a group of 11 members who forced a meeting at which a contrite Gingrich promised a floor vote on tax cuts that year. In June 1997 he was one of the votes against the rule funding committees, which was beaten 213–210, and in July he was one of the supporters of the attempted "coup" against Gingrich. Immediately after the 1998 election Salmon said Gingrich had to go. Comparing the $8 per person Republican tax cut with the $20 billion in "emergency" spending the leadership supported, Salmon said, "This year we became the Seinfeld Congress, a Congress about nothing. We failed to put forth a clear agenda for America, instead opting to run out the clock." On *Larry King Live* he claimed that he and six other Republicans would not vote for him for speaker—enough to turn control of the House over to the Democrats. The following evening Gingrich announced he would quit. "My strategy worked," said Salmon. "I was the only one willing to put my neck on the line this time." He added, "The truth is that no one has damaged the ability of the Republican conference to carry forward a conservative agenda more than Newt Gingrich."

Rebirth or no, one reason Salmon was willing to put his House career on the line—indeed, one reason he was impatient to bring forward conservative issues—was that he had already promised to serve only three terms. Earlier in 1998 he had considered running against Governor Jane Hull; he was especially dismayed by her KidsCare program. But in May he bowed out, saying the timing was not right for his party or his family—and leaving wide open the possibility he would run in 2002, when Hull cannot run again.

Salmon's reelection in November was not in doubt. His 1996 opponent ran again, but had a stroke in August and died two days before the September primary. The Democratic Party organization was tied over a successor and, per state law, made the choice by game of chance, in this case a game of five-card stud: David Mendoza's ace high beat his opponent's jack of spades. But Salmon held the equivalent of a full house, and won 65%–35% in November. Possible candidates had he not run, and presumably possibilities in 2000, include Chandler state Senator John Huppenthal, former Scottsdale Councilwoman (and 1994 runner-up) Susan Bitter Smith, Phoenix Councilman Sal DiCiccio and Goldwater Institute Executive Director Jeffrey Flake—all Republicans.

Cook's Call. *Potentially Competitive.* Though not drawn to be quite as competitive as Jim Kolbe's 5th or J.D. Hayworth's 6th District, the 1st is only nominally Republican. With self-term limited Salmon stepping down in 2000, a reasonably strong Republican nominee should be able to take advantage of the 53% registration edge and hold this seat; only if a weak candidate or an unusually strong Democrat emerges would this seat come into play.

The People: Pop. 1990: 610,817; 0.4% rural; 9.7% age 65 + ; 87% White, 3.2% Black, 2.2% Asian, 1.8% Amer. Indian, 5.8% Other; 13% Hispanic Origin. Households: 48% married couple families; 23.9% married couple fams. w. children; 63.6% college educ.; median household income: $31,288; per capita income: $15,144; median house value: $88,700; median gross rent: $412.

1996 Presidential Vote			1992 Presidential Vote		
Dole (R)	109,137	(46%)	Bush (R)	105,784	(40%)
Clinton (D)	107,698	(45%)	Clinton (D)	88,247	(33%)
Perot (I)	17,048	(7%)	Perot (I)	68,143	(26%)

Rep. Matt Salmon (R)

Elected 1994; b. Jan. 21, 1958, Salt Lake City, UT; home, Mesa; AZ St. U., B.A. 1981, Brigham Young U., M.A. 1986; Mormon; married (Nancy).

Elected Office: AZ Senate, 1990–94; Asst. Majority Leader, 1993–94.

Professional Career: Public Affairs Mgr., U.S. West, 1981–94.

DC Office: 115 CHOB 20515, 202-225-2635; Fax: 202-225-3405; Web site: www.house.gov/salmon.

District Office: Scottsdale, 602-946-3600.

Committees: *Education & the Workforce* (23d of 27 R): Early Childhood, Youth & Families; Employer-Employee Relations. *International Relations* (17th of 26 R): Asia & the Pacific; International Operations and Human Rights.

Group Ratings

	ADA	ACLU	AFS	LCV	CON	NTU	NFIB	COC	ACU	NTLC	CHC
1998	5	6	0	8	92	82	93	83	96	95	100
1997	10	—	38	—	14	61	—	70	100	—	—

National Journal Ratings

	1997 LIB — 1997 CONS	1998 LIB — 1998 CONS
Economic	35% — 63%	15% — 81%
Social	20% — 71%	11% — 88%
Foreign	0% — 88%	19% — 75%

Key Votes of the 105th Congress

1. Clinton Budget Deal	Y	5. Puerto Rico Sthood. Ref.	N	9. Cut $ for B-2 Bombers	N
2. Education IRAs	Y	6. End Highway Set-asides	Y	10. Human Rights in China	N
3. Req. 2/3 to Raise Taxes	Y	7. School Prayer Amend.	Y	11. Withdraw Bosnia Troops	Y
4. Fast-track Trade	Y	8. Ovrd. Part. Birth Veto	Y	12. End Cuban TV-Marti	N

Election Results

1998 general	Matt Salmon (R)	98,840	(65%)	($362,374)
	David Mendoza (D)	54,108	(35%)	($4,058)
1998 primary	Matt Salmon (R)	unopposed		
1996 general	Matt Salmon (R)	135,634	(60%)	($456,089)
	John Cox (D)	89,738	(40%)	

SECOND DISTRICT

Southern Arizona, though technically part of Mexico for hundreds of years, was never a home to Hispanic civilization like northern New Mexico. Here the hot desert land was inhabited mainly by Indians who kept their native ways and language until English-speaking whites came in on cavalry horses, miners' wagons and railroad cars in the late 19th Century. Today's Hispanic Arizonans are mostly descendants of later immigrants from Mexico, some who came over the border in the sleepier days before World War II when it was scarcely patrolled and many more who came in the 1980s and 1990s to partake in the dazzling economic growth which has served as both an attraction and an example to so many *norteno* Mexicans.

The 2d District of Arizona was designed to be the state's Hispanic district; its population is 50% Hispanic and includes nearly two-thirds of the state's Hispanic population. On a map, it looks regularly-shaped, but in fact it is a collection of three distant communities connected by many acres of uninhabited desert. One center is central Phoenix, including the old downtown, the state Capitol to the west and the skyscraper districts on North Central Avenue out toward Camelback Road. The stereotypical Hispanic neighborhood here is a collection of 1940s and 1950s bungalows, spaced out by empty lots, not far from the railroad or Sky Harbor Airport or nestling within view of South Mountain. Actually this is a diverse area, with affluent and comfortable neighborhoods, where Hispanics have been moving in scatterings as well as clumps. The west side of Tucson, with about one-third of the people in the 2d, is similar. The 2d also includes Yuma, on a Colorado River crossing, in an irrigated agricultural valley, often the hottest place in the country, with a desalination plant to protect the farmlands. Across the desert, past the Luke Air Force Base shooting range, the Organ Pipe Cactus National Monument, and the Tohono O'odham Indian Reservation, is the Mexican border town of Nogales, 75% Hispanic and near many maquiladora plants, and the scene of many illegal crossings until the Border Patrol was beefed up. The 2d is the one solidly Democratic district in Arizona.

The congressman from the 2d is Ed Pastor, a Democrat who won a special election in September 1991 to replace Morris Udall, longtime chairman of the Interior Committee. Pastor grew up in Claypool, a mining town in Gila County, where his parents, he told fellow Democrats in 1996, "taught me the value of education, the need of tolerance and the responsibility of community service. But especially they taught me the reward of a hard day's work." Pastor has been a career politician: after teaching high school, he got a law degree at Arizona State, worked as an assistant to Governor Raul Castro in 1975, then was elected in 1976 to the

Maricopa County Board of Supervisors, where he served until elected to Congress. In the 1991 special he beat Republican Pat Connor 56%–44%.

Since 1994 Pastor has been the only Arizona Democrat in Congress; all along he has been a faithful follower of the Democratic leadership and has had a mostly liberal voting record. But he did support NAFTA, despite strong labor opposition. He vigorously opposed Arizona's English Only law and supports bilingual ballots, but says that "everyone acknowledges that English is the common language of our country." He strongly opposed the 1996 Immigration Act's limits on welfare for legal migrants and family unification preference for low-income households. He was proud of sponsoring the U.S.'s only current Hispanic U.S. Attorney.

Much of his work has been on the Appropriations Committee, on which he got a seat in his first full term but lost it for a while after Democrats lost control of the House. Now he sits on the Energy and Water Development and the Transportation Subcommittees, and brings home the bacon to southern Arizona—$2 million to restore the desert riparian habitat along the Salt River, $1.5 million for a Yuma wetlands project, $1.2 million for the Tres Rios Wetlands demonstration project, $800,000 for environmental improvements in Pima County, $400,000 for studies of the Gila and Santa Cruz River basins. Controversially, he wants to transfer the east end of the Baboquivari Peak Wilderness area to the Tohono O'odham nation; they want it because they believe it is the home of their creator I'itoi, while Republicans and environmentalists want it to remain wilderness to maintain its rock-climbing sites. With John McCain and Jim Kolbe, Pastor worked on creating the Institute for Environmental Conflict Resolution in the Morris K. Udall Foundation; the idea is to settle environmental arguments by arbitration rather than lawsuits.

Pastor has been easily reelected every two years, though in 1996 his Republican opponent carried Yuma County.

Cook's Call. *Safe.* The 2d District was designed to be a Democratic district, and has been reliably so for Pastor. With the state likely to pick up two new Congressional seats in 2002, there's a good chance that one more predominately Democratic seat will be added. In the remapping, if Republicans play their cards right and carefully pack every available Democratic voter into two districts, they should be able to draw five dependable Republican districts. For now, Pastor is very safe.

The People: Pop. 1990: 610,266; 9.7% rural; 10.1% age 65 + ; 60.2% White, 6.8% Black, 1.2% Asian, 4.6% Amer. Indian, 27.2% Other; 50.3% Hispanic Origin. Households: 50.8% married couple families; 28.9% married couple fams. w. children; 33.4% college educ.; median household income: $20,258; per capita income: $8,424; median house value: $54,900; median gross rent: $297.

1996 Presidential Vote			1992 Presidential Vote		
Clinton (D)	81,678	(63%)	Clinton (D)	74,588	(51%)
Dole (R)	36,584	(28%)	Bush (R)	41,757	(28%)
Perot (I)	9,292	(7%)	Perot (I)	28,767	(20%)

Rep. Ed Pastor (D)

Elected Sept. 1991; b. June 28, 1943, Claypool; home, Phoenix; AZ St. U., B.A. 1966, J.D. 1974; Catholic; married (Verma).

Elected Office: Maricopa Cnty. Bd. of Supervisors, 1976–91.

Professional Career: High schl. teacher, 1966–69; Asst., AZ Gov. Castro, 1975.

DC Office: 2465 RHOB 20515, 202-225-4065; Fax: 202-225-1655; Web site: www.house.gov/pastor.

District Offices: Phoenix, 602-256-0551; Tucson, 520-624-9986; Yuma, 520-726-2234.

Committees: *Chief Deputy Minority Whip. Appropriations* (16th of 27 D): Energy & Water Development; The Legislative Branch (RMM); Transportation. *Standards of Official Conduct* (3d of 5 D).

Group Ratings

	ADA	ACLU	AFS	LCV	CON	NTU	NFIB	COC	ACU	NTLC	CHC
1998	100	88	100	100	38	14	29	39	4	16	0
1997	95	—	88	—	37	21	—	50	8	—	—

National Journal Ratings

	1997 LIB	—	1997 CONS		1998 LIB	—	1998 CONS
Economic	79%	—	18%		79%	—	0%
Social	85%	—	0%		73%	—	25%
Foreign	69%	—	28%		78%	—	19%

Key Votes of the 105th Congress

1. Clinton Budget Deal	N	5. Puerto Rico Sthood. Ref.	Y	9. Cut $ for B-2 Bombers	Y
2. Education IRAs	N	6. End Highway Set-asides	N	10. Human Rights in China	Y
3. Req. 2/3 to Raise Taxes	N	7. School Prayer Amend.	N	11. Withdraw Bosnia Troops	N
4. Fast-track Trade	N	8. Ovrd. Part. Birth Veto	N	12. End Cuban TV-Marti	N

Election Results

1998 general	Ed Pastor (D)	57,178	(68%)	($418,113)
	Ed Barron (R)	23,628	(28%)	
	Others	3,557	(4%)	
1998 primary	Ed Pastor (D)	unopposed		
1996 general	Ed Pastor (D)	81,982	(65%)	($405,426)
	Jim Buster (R)	38,786	(31%)	($101,730)
	Alice Bangle (Lib)	5,333	(4%)	

THIRD DISTRICT

Most of Arizona's physical landscape, for all the vibrant metropolitan growth of Phoenix and Tucson, remains much as it was when white men first settled here. Beneath mountains and along mostly dry creek beds, they built towns that still have an Old West look, like Prescott, originally a gold mining camp, home since 1888 of America's oldest annual rodeo and now, to the distress of some, the home of many ex-Californians. The landscape retains a beauty that can overpower mere buildings and parking lots: think of the red rocks of Sedona, an esoteric resort between Prescott and Flagstaff, with its own film festival. Some landscape is intentionally preserved, like the sere uplands of the Hopi Indian Reservation. There are some abrupt juxta-positions of settlement and nature: the real London Bridge transplanted to Lake Havasu City, a retirement community on the Colorado River; or Bullhead City, one-third of whose people work in "family gambler" casinos in Laughlin, Nevada, just across the bridge over the rock-lined, piping-hot river.

All these areas are part of the 3d Congressional District, which stretches from the west side of Phoenix to cover most of the northwest quadrant of the state. Most of its people are clustered in its southeast corner, in metro Phoenix. Here, west of the Black Canyon Freeway, is the mushrooming suburb of Glendale, not so long ago just a crossroads but with 148,000 people in 1990; just west are Peoria, as Middle American as its namesake in Illinois, and the huge retirement community of Sun City, with a dozen or so golf courses and many dozens of shuf-fleboard courts. The 3d District also includes the fast-growing corridor along the westbound I-10 Papago Freeway, past Litchfield Park and its Wigwam resort to the once open spaces of Goodyear and Buckeye.

This is heavily Republican territory: the retirees here remember—and the upwardly-striving, family-oriented young migrants who have populated these new towns in the desert still try to live—the culturally conservative, Ozzie-and-Harriet lifestyle of the 1950s. Culture, more than affluence, which by national standards is not all that striking here, accounts for their political conservatism. Similarly Republican are the Colorado River new cities and Prescott, where Barry Goldwater used to end all his campaigns.

The 3d District's congressman is Bob Stump, a Republican who quietly and without much notice has become one of the more senior members of the House and is chairman of the Veterans' Affairs Committee. He grew up in Arizona, enlisted at 17 in the Navy during World War II, and took part in the bloody invasions of Luzon, Iwo Jima and Okinawa. After the war he grew cotton and grain, and was elected to the legislature in 1958. Like many older Arizonans, he was a "pinto" (conservative) Democrat, elected to Congress as a Democrat in 1976. In 1981, after voting for the Reagan budget and tax cuts, he switched parties, to reflect both his constituency and his convictions. It was a smooth switch: he won 64% as a Democrat in 1980 and 63% as a Republican in 1982. When Stump switched, Republicans gave him seats on the Armed Services and Veterans' Affairs Committees, whose conservatism was compatible with his own. Tight-lipped in public (he has no press secretary), he lets his voting record and style speak for him, as they do eloquently: he was one of the Republicans who called for the im-peachment of Bill Clinton in November 1997.

Stump became chairman of Veterans after the Republicans won control in 1994, but he has kept to the policies he supported when Mississippi Democrat Sonny Montgomery was chair-man. These include the innovative Montgomery G.I. veterans' benefits package of the 1980s and opposition to modernization of the troubled veterans' hospitals—aging facilities for aging beneficiaries. He combines his support of veterans' causes with thriftiness. He opposed full veterans' benefits for Filipino veterans of World War II, calling for "affordable proposals" instead; he agreed with the Clinton Administration and disagreed with the American Legion when he opposed benefits for veterans suffering from smoking-related illnesses—though he was angry that most of the money saved went not to veterans' programs but to the big trans-portation bill.

Stump made some headlines after it was found that Ambassador and big Democratic con-tributor Larry Lawrence had been buried in Arlington National Cemetery under false pretenses. With ranking Democrat Lane Evans, he sponsored a bill limiting burial in Arlington to veterans who were killed on active duty or who won major medals; it passed the House unanimously in March 1998 but went nowhere in the Senate. In August 1998 he kept true to his convictions and opposed the burial at Arlington of slain Capitol police officer John Gibson and of three U.S. embassy employees killed in the explosion in Nairobi.

Stump is also the second ranking Republican, behind South Carolina's Floyd Spence, on the Armed Services Committee, where he has been cautious about steep defense spending cuts.

On other issues, Stump has filed bills to bar states from taxing pension incomes of residents of other states and to repeal the Social Security earnings tax—popular causes in Sun City.

Stump eschews the common course of seeking pork-barrel projects for his district or backing publicity-worthy causes. Except for 1990, when his percentage dipped to 57%, he has been reelected easily in this strongly Republican district. In 1996 and 1998 he was reelected 67%–33%.

Cook's Call. *Safe.* With this part of the state growing at an incredible pace, redistricting will have a substantial impact on the lines of the 3d district. Stump has survived two previous map changes and it's unlikely that any new lines would change that. He is an overwhelming favorite for 2000.

The People: Pop. 1990: 610,424; 18.5% rural; 20.4% age 65 + ; 87.8% White, 1.9% Black, 1.1% Asian, 3.2% Amer. Indian, 6% Other; 11.6% Hispanic Origin. Households: 61.7% married couple families; 24.8% married couple fams. w. children; 48.7% college educ.; median household income: $27,627; per capita income: $13,185; median house value: $80,100; median gross rent: $376.

1996 Presidential Vote			1992 Presidential Vote		
Dole (R)	130,887	(48%)	Bush (R)	109,840	(40%)
Clinton (D)	113,635	(41%)	Clinton (D)	86,060	(31%)
Perot (I)	26,993	(10%)	Perot (I)	73,356	(27%)

Rep. Bob Stump (R)

Elected 1976; b. Apr. 4, 1927, Phoenix; home, Tolleson; AZ St. U., B.S. 1951; Seventh Day Adventist; divorced.

Military Career: Navy, 1943–46 (WWII).

Elected Office: AZ House of Reps., 1958–66; AZ Senate, 1966–76, Senate Pres., 1975–76.

Professional Career: Cotton & grain farmer.

DC Office: 211 CHOB 20515, 202-225-4576; Fax: 202-225-6328.

District Office: Phoenix, 602-379-6923.

Committees: *Armed Services* (Vice Chmn. of 32 R): Military Installations & Facilities; Military Procurement; Special Oversight Panel on Morale, Welfare and Recreation. *Veterans' Affairs* (Chmn. of 17 R): Oversight & Investigations.

Group Ratings

	ADA	ACLU	AFS	LCV	CON	NTU	NFIB	COC	ACU	NTLC	CHC
1998	0	13	0	0	60	79	100	78	96	100	100
1997	5	—	13	—	49	64	—	90	100	—	—

National Journal Ratings

	1997 LIB — 1997 CONS			1998 LIB — 1998 CONS		
Economic	0%	—	90%	0%	—	88%
Social	20%	—	71%	21%	—	76%
Foreign	0%	—	88%	19%	—	75%

Key Votes of the 105th Congress

1. Clinton Budget Deal	Y	5. Puerto Rico Sthood. Ref.	N	9. Cut $ for B-2 Bombers	N
2. Education IRAs	Y	6. End Highway Set-asides	Y	10. Human Rights in China	N
3. Req. 2/3 to Raise Taxes	Y	7. School Prayer Amend.	Y	11. Withdraw Bosnia Troops	Y
4. Fast-track Trade	Y	8. Ovrd. Part. Birth Veto	Y	12. End Cuban TV-Marti	N

126   ARIZONA

Election Results

1998 general	Bob Stump (R) 137,618	(67%)	($246,233)
	Stuart Marc Starky (D) 66,979	(33%)	($29,211)
1998 primary	Bob Stump (R) .... unopposed		
1996 general	Bob Stump (R) 175,231	(67%)	($233,997)
	Alexander (Big Al) Schneider (D) 88,214	(33%)	($23,567)

FOURTH DISTRICT

In May 1998 Barry Goldwater died at his home in the Phoenix suburb of Paradise Valley. His life spanned almost the whole history of Arizona. He was born on New Year's Day 1909, when Arizona was still a territory, and could remember when it was the "baby state," the fourth least populous in the nation, ahead of only Delaware, Wyoming and Nevada. When he returned from World War II, Paradise Valley was still empty land and Phoenix not much more than a small town, an outpost of American civilization in a sizzling desert. Now Arizona is 21st largest in population, and Phoenix is one of the major metropolises of the country, a diversified high-tech center, an example of how creativity and ingenuity can build a sophisticated city with relatively minimalist government and low taxes.

Today, from Camelback Mountain, 1800 feet above Phoenix and Paradise Valley, or from Frank Lloyd Wright's Taliesin West home and studio, you can with equal awe get a sense of what this land was originally like and an understanding of how impressively Phoenix has grown. South of Camelback, subdivisions were often built with grass and greenery; in the affluent areas north of Camelback and spreading out Scottsdale Road and the Black Canyon Freeway, the natural desert look is more common. Grass is discouraged, and often banned by subdivision covenant; planting anything but desert flora is frowned upon; the architecture of the houses tends toward unadorned stucco with picture windows facing away from the sun; the idea is to suggest that there is a horse corral over in the next lot and sometimes, especially in the northern edges of Phoenix, there is.

The 4th Congressional District of Arizona consists of this northern part of Phoenix, northern Scottsdale, Paradise Valley and part of Glendale, bounded approximately by Camelback Road on the south, Pima Road and the Salt River Indian Reservation on the east, Pinnacle Peak Road on the north and 47th and Grand Avenues on the west. For all its rustic and unplanned air, this is a highly affluent district, and usually a heavily Republican one, though Bill Clinton came close to carrying it in 1996.

The congressman from the 4th is John Shadegg, a freshman elected in 1994, with a fine Arizona Republican pedigree. His father, Stephen Shadegg, managed Barry Goldwater's first campaign for the Senate in 1952, when he upset Senate Majority Leader Ernest McFarland. John Shadegg helped deliver campaign press releases in those pre-fax days. He is a lawyer, served as special assistant in the state attorney general's office and a special counsel to the Arizona House Republican Caucus. When 4th District Congressman Jon Kyl ran for the Senate in 1994, Shadegg ran for the House seat and won 43% in the Republican primary, to 30% for a former aide to controversial Governor Evan Mecham, and 21% for a county supervisor. He won the general election easily, 60%–36%.

In the House Shadegg has been one of the firebrand 1994 Republican freshmen, a rebel against Democratic policies and often against his own party's leadership. He tried to insist on a three-fifths supermajority for tax increases in the balanced budget amendment; Speaker Newt Gingrich and Majority Leader Dick Armey disagreed and prevailed. Shadegg has pushed roll calls on his version, but has fallen well short of the two-thirds required. He has pushed to defund the National Endowment for the Arts, even when the leadership compromised in 1995 and 1997. He was one of 15 freshman to vote against a keep-the-government-open compromise in January 1996 and he voted against the Clinton-Gingrich budget deal in May 1997, saying its claims of budget balance and tax relief were "overblown and exaggerated." He tried to force a roll call vote on the congressional pay increase in September 1997. On the Budget Committee he proposed in April 1998 a budget with more domestic spending cuts, more defense increases and more tax cuts than chairman John Kasich's. In 1997 and 1998 on HMO reform he supported lawsuits against HMOs, though limited in amount and with losing litigants paying costs—a position arguably to the left of the leadership.

Shadegg's anti-leadership stands cost him a seat on Ways and Means in 1997 (it went to the 6th District's J.D. Hayworth instead). But he was entrusted with the leadership of GOPAC when Gingrich relinquished it in May 1995, and he was asked to help head recruitment by the House Republican campaign committee in September 1997 and was named one of six vice chairmen by Tom Davis in November 1998. He was named as one of five Republicans on the Census 2000 subcommittee in March 1998—to handle an issue Republican leaders regard as vital to their party. He skillfully grilled Attorney General Janet Reno in hearings on the Waco massacre and campaign finance charges against Al Gore. He and Senator Jon Kyl, inspired by an Arizonan couple who struggled to restore their credit rating after the husband's credit card and social security number was stolen, passed a law making the theft of a person's identity a crime. On the Resources Committee he opposed the June 1998 Park Service plan to manage as wilderness 94% of the Grand Canyon National Park's land, saying it would close roads, impact rafting and curb access by the disabled. He sponsored a bill to stop RICO suits against protestors who blockade abortion clinics.

Shadegg has won reelection easily. His 1996 opponent, Maria Milton, a follower of Lyndon LaRouche, ran ads saying he "wants to push your parents into the gas ovens of managed care," and "Congressman ValuJet . . . wants to send your Social Security crashing into the Everglades." Democratic leaders repudiated her and Shadegg won 67%–33%. In 1998 Milton lost the Democratic primary 57%–43%, but the general result was about the same, 65%–31%.

Cook's Call. *Safe.* The most conservative district in the state, the 4th district has sent Republicans to Congress for years. Shadegg appears to be a shoo-in for re-election in 2000.

The People: Pop. 1990: 610,708; 0.1% rural; 11.8% age 65 + ; 92.1% White, 1.9% Black, 1.8% Asian, 1.2% Amer. Indian, 2.9% Other; 7.6% Hispanic Origin. Households: 52.8% married couple families; 23.9% married couple fams. w. children; 62.1% college educ.; median household income: $33,681; per capita income: $18,331; median house value: $91,100; median gross rent: $401.

1996 Presidential Vote

Dole (R)	115,094	(48%)
Clinton (D)	103,878	(44%)
Perot (I)	16,547	(7%)

1992 Presidential Vote

Bush (R)	118,927	(43%)
Clinton (D)	86,922	(31%)
Perot (I)	70,682	(25%)

Rep. John Shadegg (R)

Elected 1994; b. Oct. 22, 1949, Phoenix; home, Phoenix; U. of AZ, B.A. 1972, J.D. 1975; Episcopalian; married (Shirley).

Military Career: Air Natl. Guard, 1969–75.

Professional Career: Practicing atty., 1975–94; US Spec. Asst. Atty. Gen., 1983–90; Spec. Cnsl., AZ House Republican Caucus, 1991–92; Cnsl., AZ Wildlife Conservation, 1992.

DC Office: 430 CHOB 20515, 202-225-3361; Fax: 202-225-3462; Web site: www.house.gov/shadegg.

District Office: Phoenix, 602-263-5300.

Committees: *Commerce* (24th of 29 R): Energy & Power; Finance & Hazardous Materials; Health and Environment.

Group Ratings

	ADA	ACLU	AFS	LCV	CON	NTU	NFIB	COC	ACU	NTLC	CHC
1998	0	20	0	0	70	76	93	89	100	97	100
1997	5	—	25	—	7	66	—	80	100	—	—

National Journal Ratings

	1997 LIB — 1997 CONS	1998 LIB — 1998 CONS
Economic	0% — 90%	0% — 88%
Social	41% — 57%	0% — 97%
Foreign	12% — 81%	0% — 93%

Key Votes of the 105th Congress

1. Clinton Budget Deal	Y	5. Puerto Rico Sthood. Ref.	N
2. Education IRAs	Y	6. End Highway Set-asides	Y
3. Req. 2/3 to Raise Taxes	Y	7. School Prayer Amend.	Y
4. Fast-track Trade	Y	8. Ovrd. Part. Birth Veto	Y

9. Cut $ for B-2 Bombers	N
10. Human Rights in China	N
11. Withdraw Bosnia Troops	Y
12. End Cuban TV-Marti	N

Election Results

1998 general	John Shadegg (R)	102,722	(65%)	($525,849)
	Eric Ehst (D)	49,538	(31%)	($14,206)
	Others	6,562	(4%)	
1998 primary	John Shadegg (R)	unopposed		
1996 general	John Shadegg (R)	150,486	(67%)	($512,249)
	Maria Elena Milton (D)	74,857	(33%)	($116,003)

FIFTH DISTRICT

Arizona's first frontier was just south of today's Tucson, where Franciscan friars built San Xavier del Bac mission in the 18th Century. To the east the late 19th Century mining towns of Tombstone and Bisbee sprang up on desert mountainsides, where miners dug up gold and silver and, for many years, much of America's copper; Cochise County, including those two towns, was the most populous county when Arizona became the 48th state in 1912. Here the white man last subdued the Indians, when the Apache leader Geronimo faced the U.S. Army in 1900. Southern Arizona remains pioneer country today: this was the site of the Biosphere II project, the greenhouse-like structure in the desert in which eight men and women lived more or less self-sufficiently from September 1991 until September 1993.

Biosphere has now joined Tombstone as a tourist attraction; both are within the orbit of Tucson, Arizona's second metropolis, much smaller, more rough-hewn and politically less conservative than Phoenix. Tucson is a high-tech city and home of the University of Arizona. For nearly 40 years, it was the political base of the brothers Udall: Stewart, congressman in the 1950s, Interior secretary in the 1960s, now an Arizona lawyer again; Morris, congressman for 30 years and Interior Committee chairman, who retired in 1991 because of Parkinson's disease and died in 1998.

The 5th Congressional District of Arizona includes most, but not all of Tucson and Pima County—the Latino west side of town is in the 2d District. The 5th also includes much southeastern Arizona desert real estate: all of Cochise County, including Tombstone and Bisbee and Sierra Vista near Fort Huachuca; and some small farming and mining towns in Pinal and Graham Counties. Politically, it is fairly evenly divided, voting Republican in state politics and twice for Bill Clinton.

The congressman from the 5th is Jim Kolbe, a Republican with a moderate record on many issues. He comes originally from Illinois, served in the Navy in Vietnam, became an assistant to Illinois's Republican Governor Richard Ogilvie in 1972, and moved to Arizona shortly thereafter and went into real estate. In 1976 he was elected to the Arizona Senate. In 1982 he ran in the new 5th District and lost to Democrat Jim McNulty 50%–48%. In 1984 he ran again and beat him 51%–48%.

Kolbe's voting record on economics has been mostly conservative; he ranks near the middle of the House on cultural and foreign issues. He voted for the balanced budget amendment and the line-item veto, but his greatest economic cause is free trade. He has long admired the maquiladora program, through which U.S.-made components shipped to Mexico for assembly can reenter the U.S. without paying full duty, and believes that more trade can boost the economies of both countries. He was one of the three Republicans who pushed their party to provide most of the votes to pass NAFTA in the House in November 1993, and has remained an enthusiast for it since. He was a strong supporter of GATT in November 1994. He was one of the Republican leaders in the fight for fast track in 1997, and again in 1998. It lost both times, but he hasn't given up; on visiting hurricane-torn Honduras in October 1998 he called for extending the NAFTA free-trade zone to all of Central America.

Another Kolbe cause is Social Security reform; he believes that America should move toward an individual account system. He served on the Center for Strategic and International Studies reform commission with Democrat Charles Stenholm and Senators John Breaux and Judd Gregg, and has sponsored their proposal which would raise the retirement age gradually, put 2% of the payroll tax into individual retirement accounts and guarantee a baseline pension.

Since 1997 Kolbe has been chairman of the Appropriations subcommittee with jurisdiction over the Treasury, the White House and Congress itself. He demanded an accounting in May 1997 of the cost of Bill Clinton's 938 overnight guests in the Lincoln bedroom. He angered many Republicans by supporting funding for the National Endowment for the Arts; a music buff, he says, "My dream in life is to come back as a conductor or concert pianist." He took a serious political risk in September 1997 by pushing to passage an appropriation without the usual language barring cost-of-living pay increases for members of Congress. He has used his Appropriations seat for Arizona causes—a $14 million Navajo-Hopi hospital, $4 million for land acquisition in the Saguaro National Park (East) just outside Tucson, $4 million for the Fort Apache Reservation. With John McCain and Ed Pastor, he got $5.5 million to establish an Institute for Environmental Conflict Resolution at the Morris K. Udall Foundation in Tucson.

Kolbe is pro-choice on abortion and voted for the 1994 crime bill with its gun control provisions. He voted for the Defense of Marriage Act and in July 1996, pressured by an impending article in *The Advocate*, announced that he is gay. This had little apparent impact on the 1996 election, in which he beat Morris Udall's chiropractor 69%–26%. But he has returned to the issue since. He told the Log Cabin Republicans in July 1997: "We gain acceptance and build our bridges, not by stressing that we are gay people who are Republicans, but that we are Republicans who happen to be gay or lesbian." He supported hate crimes legislation before the Matthew Shepard slaying and said afterward, "Thank God Wyoming has the death penalty." In July 1998 he opposed Joel Hefley's amendment to overturn Bill Clinton's order banning discrimination against homosexuals in federal employment. "It's a bad signal for Republicans to be sending, that we want to alienate this substantial group." Republican leaders got Hefley to agree not to offer his amendment to Kolbe's appropriation; when it came up later, Kolbe helped persuade 63 Republicans to vote against it.

In 1998 Kolbe had an unexpectedly close race for reelection. His opponent was Tom Volgy, University of Arizona political scientist, Tucson councilman for 10 years and mayor from 1987–91. Volgy called for allowing lawsuits against HMOs, more government spending on education and health care; he wanted Social Security taxes raised on high income-earners and said manufacturers of imports should be required to meet U.S. standards. His biggest issue was campaign finance: he limited his campaign to $250,000 and championed the plan he instituted in Tuscon which limits total contributions and bans PAC money. In October both candidates appeared before OUToberFEST'98 and opposed discrimination against gays. After Kolbe left, Volgy denounced those, without naming names, who did not speak out against Republican leaders making anti-gay remarks. Although Kolbe spent nearly three times as much money, he won by only 52%–45%, the closest congressional race in Arizona. Kolbe has continued to take political risks—on Social Security, on trade, on impeachment—and he may face a serious challenge again in 2000.

Cook's Call. *Competitive.* The biggest concern for Kolbe is how to position himself in this increasingly Democratic trending district: he can't move much more to the middle for fear of drawing a primary opponent, but can't move to the right because it would hurt his general election prospects. Kolbe should be able to hold the seat, but in a down year for Republicans, an upset is entirely possible.

The People: Pop. 1990: 611,128; 13.5% rural; 15.6% age 65 +; 88.2% White, 3% Black, 1.9% Asian, 0.9% Amer. Indian, 6.2% Other; 16.2% Hispanic Origin. Households: 54% married couple families; 23.4% married couple fams. w. children; 59.2% college educ.; median household income: $27,047; per capita income: $14,361; median house value: $81,200; median gross rent: $350.

1996 Presidential Vote			1992 Presidential Vote		
Clinton (D)	126,223	(47%)	Clinton (D)	116,226	(42%)
Dole (R)	116,965	(44%)	Bush (R)	104,509	(37%)
Perot (I)	20,732	(8%)	Perot (I)	56,516	(20%)

Rep. Jim Kolbe (R)

Elected 1984; b. June 28, 1942, Evanston, IL; home, Tucson; Northwestern U., B.A. 1965, Stanford U., M.B.A. 1967; United Methodist; divorced.

Military Career: Navy, 1968–69 (Vietnam), Naval Reserves, 1970–77.

Elected Office: AZ Senate, 1976–82.

Professional Career: Asst., IL Bldg. Authority Architect, 1970–72; Asst., IL Gov. Ogilvie, 1972–73; Vice Pres., land planning firm; Real estate consultant.

DC Office: 2266 RHOB 20515, 202-225-2542; Fax: 202-225-0378; Web site: www.house.gov/kolbe.

District Offices: Sierra Vista, 520-459-3115; Tucson, 520-881-3588.

Committees: *Appropriations* (9th of 34 R): Commerce, Justice, State & the Judiciary; Interior; Treasury, Postal Service & General Government (Chmn.).

Group Ratings

	ADA	ACLU	AFS	LCV	CON	NTU	NFIB	COC	ACU	NTLC	CHC
1998	15	44	11	23	65	63	100	89	72	82	58
1997	25	—	13	—	80	54	—	100	64	—	—

National Journal Ratings

	1997 LIB — 1997 CONS			1998 LIB — 1998 CONS		
Economic	24%	—	73%	28%	—	70%
Social	57%	—	42%	58%	—	42%
Foreign	56%	—	42%	78%	—	19%

Key Votes of the 105th Congress

1. Clinton Budget Deal	Y	5. Puerto Rico Sthood. Ref.	Y	9. Cut $ for B-2 Bombers	Y
2. Education IRAs	Y	6. End Highway Set-asides	Y	10. Human Rights in China	N
3. Req. 2/3 to Raise Taxes	Y	7. School Prayer Amend.	Y	11. Withdraw Bosnia Troops	N
4. Fast-track Trade	Y	8. Ovrd. Part. Birth Veto	N	12. End Cuban TV-Marti	Y

Election Results

1998 general	Jim Kolbe (R)	103,952	(52%)	($707,776)
	Tom Volgy (D)	91,030	(45%)	($257,651)
	Others	6,491	(3%)	
1998 primary	Jim Kolbe (R)	33,213	(77%)	
	Joseph Sweeney (R)	9,818	(23%)	
1996 general	Jim Kolbe (R)	179,349	(69%)	($415,550)
	Mort Nelson (D)	67,597	(26%)	
	Others	13,952	(5%)	

SIXTH DISTRICT

Arizona has one of the nation's largest and fastest-growing Indian populations. There are small, sparsely populated reservations across the state, but by far the largest Indian population is the Navajo, in the northeast corner of the state who form the majority in (oddly) Apache County and a large minority in Navajo County to the west. The Navajo have their own tribal politics, complete with fiercely contested elections for tribal chief; and, alas, considerable corruption. The political form of governance, with winner-take-all elections, seems not to have served the Navajo well: unemployment runs around 30% and nearly 30% live without running water and electricity. An alternative might be the corporate form that has worked much better for Alaska Natives.

The 6th Congressional District of Arizona covers nearly half the state, including the Navajo country and some of northern Phoenix and Scottsdale; household income levels in 1990 varied from $20,000 in the Indian country to $64,000 in Scottsdale. The 6th also takes in the old mining towns of Globe and Clifton; Flagstaff, south of the Grand Canyon, and Page, to the north, where townspeople making money off the recreational Lake Powell oppose the Sierra Club's proposal to get rid of the Glen Canyon Dam and the lake; the mountains of the Apache National Forest, where Mexican wolves were released in January 1998; and the sparsely-populated, wind-swept desert with seven Indian reservations in all (the erose boundaries exclude the Hopis, who have a long and angry boundary dispute with the Navajo). Closer to Phoenix, the 6th takes in the suburbs of Carefree and Cave Creek, rustic areas where the mile-square grids are far from filled in and the local stores are more likely to feature horse feed than designer clothes, and the Salt River and Gila Valley reservations, their edges now sprouting Wal-marts and Kmarts.

Politically, this is a sharply divided district. The Maricopa County portions, which cast 54% of the vote, are usually heavily Republican. Navajo County is recently, and the copper mining country has been historically, heavily Democratic; Flagstaff is moving that way. The Navajo vote heavily Democratic. The result is that the 6th District has been fiercely contested since it was created in 1992, and may be again in 2000.

The congressman from the 6th is J.D. Hayworth, a conservative Republican who grew up in North Carolina and made his way upward in the hierarchy of local TV stations as a sportscaster, from Raleigh to Greenville to Cincinnati and then, in 1987, to Phoenix. Hayworth is 6'5", weighs 290, speaks with a booming voice and has a certain resemblance—a help in some quarters, a hindrance in others—to Rush Limbaugh. Certainly he was well known when he entered the race in 1994. He won the five-way Republican primary with 45%. In the general he faced incumbent Democrat Karan English, who won the newly created seat in 1992 by 53%–41% over Doug Wead, a Reagan White House liaison to the religious right, who moved into the district to run. Wead's extreme conservative stands moved Barry Goldwater to endorse English, a state legislator from Flagstaff who supported the line-item veto and a balanced budget amendment. In 1994 Hayworth attacked English for voting for the Clinton tax increase and framed the race as "between a citizen who pays taxes and a career politician who raises them."

Hayworth issued his Action Plan for Arizona, full of denunciations of federal programs and praise for state and private initiatives, and enthusiastically signed the Contract with America. He carried Maricopa County 65%–32%, enough to easily overcome deficits on the Indian reservations and around Flagstaff, and won 55%–41%.

Hayworth became a strong voice and a solid vote in the new Republican majority. He seemed to irritate Democrats more than just about any other freshman. He got into shouting matches with Democrats, "cursing, and not backing off," *The Hill* reported. Veteran Democrat David Obey told him, "You are one of the most impolite members I have ever seen in my service in this House." Hayworth voted solidly with Gingrich and the Republican leadership, even as his 1994 Arizona colleagues Matt Salmon and John Shadegg were leading rebellion. He worked on some local issues and traveled around the district in a Subaru Outback specially designed for his large frame.

Early on Democrats targeted him. Steve Owens, an aide to then-Senator Al Gore in the 1980s and later Arizona Democratic chairman, returned to the district to run against Hayworth. Gore campaigned for him, and the AFL-CIO made Hayworth one of their top targets, spending some $2 million on ads charging him with Medicare "cuts." Through most of the fall the race was even in the polls. Owens called the race "a clear choice between the followers of Newt Gingrich on the extreme and all the rest of us in the mainstream." The Tribune chain, endorsing Owens, attacked "the bombastic Hayworth" and called him "an affront to his colleagues, an embarrassment for America." Hayworth called Owens a carpetbagger—a strange charge in a state where most people are from somewhere else—and ran ads pointing out that Owens had taken $5,000 from the Laborers' Union whose "bosses have admitted their connection to organized crime." Hayworth spent over $1 million, Owens some $750,000; labor's money was balanced by Republican National Committee ads. Hayworth won 48%–47%, one of the closest results in the country; he carried Maricopa County 56%–39% and trailed in the rest of the district 56%–38%.

In the House Hayworth continued his conservative rhetoric but also became an inside player. He reaped his reward for loyalty when Gingrich awarded him a seat on Ways and Means, and bypassed Shadegg. On that committee Hayworth organized a bipartisan coalition to defeat 22–16 a $1.9 billion proposed tax on Indian gambling. He was also a lead sponsor of the successful $500 per child tax credit. When Bill Clinton line-item vetoed funds for the experimental Case Grande copper mine, Hayworth got commitments for funds from Budget Director Jacob Lew and Interior Secretary Bruce Babbitt. The *Arizona Republic* still referred to his "infamous bluster," Matt Salmon called him "Foghorn Leghorn" and a *Washingtonian* survey named him number one in Congress in the "no rocket scientist" category and number two in "biggest windbag." (He objected to the latter, saying he should be number one.) But Hayworth proceeded to send out large amounts of franked mail and raise money for the 1998 election.

Steve Owens decided to run again. But, apparently stung by charges that he was the pawn of labor bosses, he asked the AFL-CIO to stay out of the race. Owens campaigned for a patient's bill of rights against "insurance company bureaucrats" and for the McCain-Feingold campaign finance reform bill. A Hayworth ad called Owens a "liberal opportunist," and accused him of keeping nuclear waste in Arizona (because he opposed a bill that would ship some of it to Nevada's Yucca Mountain) and supporting higher taxes on families. This time Hayworth spent more than in 1996, Owens about the same, but without the AFL-CIO money the balance was not the same. Hayworth won by the fairly comfortable margin of 53%–44%. He carried Maricopa County 61%–36% and lost the rest of the district 53%–44%. Whether this race will be seriously contested in 2000 is unclear: population growth in Maricopa County probably favors Hayworth, and he won by a larger percentage than Jim Kolbe in the 5th District.

Cook's Call. *Competitive.* For 1998, Hayworth toned down his blustery and flamboyant image that polarized the electorate in this district and almost cost him his seat in 1996. Still, while he has addressed his earlier problems enough to get by—maybe even enough to avoid drawing a serious challenger—this marginal district is still worth keeping an eye on.

The People: Pop. 1990: 611,885; 32.9% rural; 14% age 65 + ; 70.5% White, 1.3% Black, 0.6% Asian, 21.8% Amer. Indian, 5.8% Other; 12.9% Hispanic Origin. Households: 60.9% married couple families; 29.1% married couple fams. w. children; 45.4% college educ.; median household income: $25,710; per capita income: $11,322; median house value: $76,400; median gross rent: $349.

1996 Presidential Vote

Clinton (D) 120,176 (47%)
Dole (R) 113,406 (44%)
Perot (I) 21,462 (8%)

1992 Presidential Vote

Bush (R) 91,269 (38%)
Clinton (D) 91,007 (37%)
Perot (I) 56,277 (23%)

Rep. J. D. Hayworth (R)

Elected 1994; b. July 12, 1958, High Point, NC; home, Scottsdale; NC St. U., B.A. 1980; Baptist; married (Mary).

Professional Career: Sports Reporter/Anchor: WPTF-TV Raleigh, NC, 1980–81; WTFF-TV Greenville, SC, 1981–86; WLWT-TV, Cincinnati, OH, 1986–87; WKTSP-TV Phoenix, AZ, 1987–94; Insurance agent & PR consultant, 1994.

DC Office: 1023 LHOB 20515, 202-225-2190; Fax: 202-225-3263; Web site: www.house.gov/hayworth.

District Offices: Flagstaff, 520-556-8760; Mesa, 480-926-4151.

Committees: *Veterans' Affairs* (10th of 17 R): Benefits (Vice Chmn.). *Ways & Means* (18th of 23 R): Oversight; Social Security.

Group Ratings

	ADA	ACLU	AFS	LCV	CON	NTU	NFIB	COC	ACU	NTLC	CHC
1998	0	6	0	15	70	72	100	89	100	97	100
1997	5	—	13	—	70	61	—	90	96	—	—

National Journal Ratings

	1997 LIB	—	1997 CONS	1998 LIB	—	1998 CONS
Economic	10%	—	86%	0%	—	88%
Social	20%	—	71%	14%	—	81%
Foreign	12%	—	81%	27%	—	68%

Key Votes of the 105th Congress

1. Clinton Budget Deal	Y	5. Puerto Rico Sthood. Ref.	N	9. Cut $ for B-2 Bombers	N
2. Education IRAs	Y	6. End Highway Set-asides	Y	10. Human Rights in China	Y
3. Req. 2/3 to Raise Taxes	Y	7. School Prayer Amend.	Y	11. Withdraw Bosnia Troops	Y
4. Fast-track Trade	Y	8. Ovrd. Part. Birth Veto	Y	12. End Cuban TV-Marti	N

Election Results

1998 general	J.D. Hayworth (R) 106,891	(53%)	($1,839,460)
	Steve Owens (D) 88,001	(44%)	($836,074)
	Others 6,645	(3%)	
1998 primary	J.D. Hayworth (R) .... unopposed		
1996 general	J. D. Hayworth (R) 121,431	(48%)	($1,499,443)
	Steve Owens (D) 118,957	(47%)	($762,046)
	Robert Anderson (Lib) 14,899	(6%)	

ARKANSAS

When marketers in the travel business begin to design package trips for Arkansas, they might do well to set up two Bill Clinton tours. The pro-Clinton tour would include Hope, the gritty town where he was born; Hot Springs, the raffish gambling center where he grew up; Fayette-ville, where he taught law and in 1974 first ran for office, and lost; the red-brick Governor's Mansion in Little Rock, where he lived for 12 years and announced for president in October 1991; and the old State House, where he celebrated his victories in November 1992 and 1996. And, the anti-Clinton tour—presumably not many people would choose both—could include the failed Whitewater real estate development in Marion County; the Madison Guaranty and Trust savings and loan headquarters in downtown Little Rock; the Springdale brokerage in which Hillary Rodham Clinton made her $100,000 trading cattle futures; the Rose Law Firm, where she was a billing partner in the Whitewater case; and Little Rock's Excelsior Hotel, where in 1991 Bill Clinton spent time in a room alone with Paula Corbin Jones. Each Arkansas has been on display through much of the 1990s, even as Clinton has moved beyond Arkansas to the White House—and, in his leisure time, to Martha's Vineyard and Malibu—and as Re-publicans have been making surprising political headway back home. Which is the real Ar-kansas? This is like asking which Bill Clinton is authentic—the responsive New Democrat, the cynical insider, the caring campaigner, the indulger in fast food or the articulate intellectual? They are all real, depending on the time, place and circumstances.

Arkansas, like Clinton, began life without many advantages. In area, it's the smallest state between the Mississippi and the Pacific; in population, it's the smallest state in the South; it has not been blessed with any great natural resource or any growing major industry. Arkansas is the land left over when Louisiana and Missouri were carved out of the Louisiana Purchase and what is now Oklahoma was fenced off as Indian Territory. Settled by poor farmers with large families, few slaves, and little cash, it has had no Atlanta or Dallas or even Memphis to be a focus of growth. As Arkansas political scientist Diane Blair notes, Arkansas never had a power elite of great plantation owners or economic robber barons. That has left it a heritage without honored traditions or tight standards, but has also made Arkansas a land of great opportunities, where talented people can move up fast—like Blair and her husband, the house counsel at Tyson Foods, who guided Hillary Rodham Clinton's commodities trading that re-sulted in extraordinary profits.

This Arkansas produced old style politicians like John McClellan and William Fulbright, who represented Arkansas in the Senate for a total of 65 years from the 1940s to the 1970s, while chairing the Appropriations and Foreign Relations committees, and Wilbur Mills, chair-man of the House Ways and Means Committee from 1958–74; Governor Orval Faubus, who shamed Little Rock and Arkansas around the world by resisting integration at Central High School in 1957; and Governor Winthrop Rockefeller, who steered the state toward integration a decade later. More recently it produced moderate Democrats like Dale Bumpers and David Pryor, who each served as governor and in the Senate from the 1970s to the 1990s, and Jim Guy Tucker, whose career intersected several times with Clinton's until he was convicted in a Whitewater trial in 1996.

Arkansas has also produced men who have made huge fortunes by taking break-through ideas and making them work: Sam Walton believed that rural and small town America would support a chain of giant discount stores which, through tough bargaining with vendors and ultra-quick distribution, could undersell competitors, but through demanding management and employee profit-sharing could embody small town friendliness and service; Walton was the richest American when he died in April 1992. Jack Stephens and his late brother Witt started

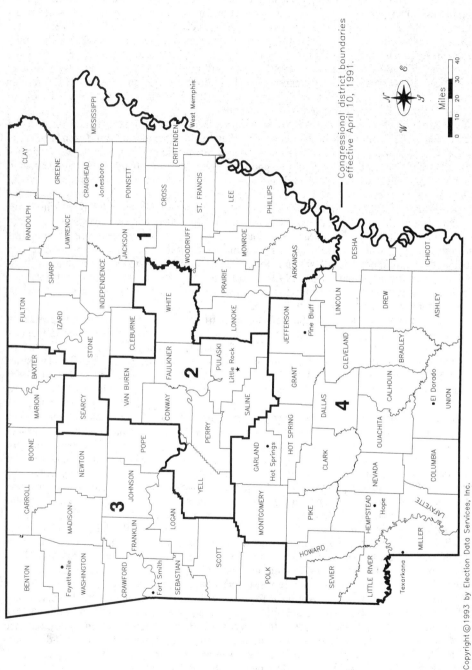

Congressional district boundaries effective April 10, 1991.

an investment banking house in Little Rock specializing in underwriting municipal bonds and investing in businesses that are a mix of private enterprise, government subsidies and public regulation; their success—and political connections in Arkansas and elsewhere—amassed a billion dollar fortune. Don Tyson took his father's chicken business and made it one of the biggest food producers in America. Other big Arkansas operations include TCBY (The Country's Best Yogurt) and J.B. Hunt's trucking empire. These business giants have cultivated a down-home, laid-back style. But they have also skillfully united their interests with those of the state's politicians, including—especially—Bill Clinton. Three-quarters of the $20 million needed to build the Tyson Center of Excellence for Poultry Science at the University of Arkansas came from the federal and state government.

A case can be made that Arkansas is America in the 1990s in exaggerated form. It has produced in Clinton and in businessmen like Walton, the Stephenses, and Tyson, leaders of unusual ability and outsized personality. At the same time the gulf between the very rich and the rest of Arkansas remains whole magnitudes larger than the oft-lamented (by Democrats until 1993, when most dropped the subject) growth in income disparity in the nation as a whole. Arkansas's economy has grown smartly in the 1990s. It leads the nation in growing rice and only recently ceded its first place status in producing chickens to Georgia. It has benefited from increased tourism and (if legal fees are gains) from independent counsel investigations.

Politically, Arkansas has resembled the nation in the 1990s, too. It has voted twice for Bill Clinton for president, and at the same time moved toward the Republican Party in races just below the top of the ticket in 1994 and 1996, and then moved a bit toward Democrats in 1998. Clinton's percentages here in the 1990s have been eerily similar: in 1990 he got 55% in a seriously contested primary race for governor and 57% in November; in 1992 he won the state's six electoral votes with 53%, in 1996 with 54%.

Underneath those totals were numbers signaling trouble for Democrats. Clinton's 1992 margin came primarily from voters over 45, who favored him 70%–26%; those under 45 went for Bush, 43%–41%. And northwest Arkansas, the fastest-growing part of the state, the home base of the Waltons and Tysons, has become heavily Republican: the 3d Congressional District, where Clinton ran his first race in 1974, voted for Clinton in 1992 but for Bob Dole in 1996. On election night 1992, Arkansas Democrats held the governorship and all lower state offices, both Senate seats, and three out of four House seats. In January 1999, Republicans held the governorship, one Senate seat, and two House seats; and, though still heavily outnumbered, they gained 10 seats in the legislature as well. Probably the most popular politician in the state is Governor Mike Huckabee, who was elected lieutenant governor in a 1993 special election and became governor when Jim Guy Tucker resigned in July 1996. Huckabee had been the favorite to win the Senate seat which David Pryor was vacating; his replacement as Republican nominee, 3d District Congressman Tim Hutchinson, won. Still, some statewide Democrats seem to have discovered the Clinton formula—Blanche Lincoln, elected to the Senate in 1998, and Mark Pryor, David Pryor's son, who was elected attorney general.

Governor. Mike Huckabee, who was not an elected official at all when Bill Clinton left Little Rock in January 1993, is now governor of Arkansas. Like Clinton, Huckabee was born in Hope; unlike Clinton, he grew up there. Clinton was elected governor of Arkansas Boys State in 1963, Huckabee in 1972. Clinton went off to Georgetown and Yale Law School; Huckabee graduated from Ouachita Baptist University at 19 and attended Southwestern Baptist Theological Seminary in Fort Worth for four years. He had a profound spiritual experience at 15, while on a two-week youth fellowship program at Cape Kennedy—the first time he had been outside Arkansas. In the 1980s Huckabee was a Baptist minister in Pine Bluff and then Texarkana; in both towns he started a 24-hour television station, where he produced documentaries and hosted a program called "Positive Alternatives." In 1989 he became president of the Arkansas Baptist Convention, with a membership of 490,000.

Huckabee's first effort was to run against Senator Dale Bumpers in 1992; he lost 60%–40%. Then, after Jim Guy Tucker replaced Bill Clinton as governor, Huckabee ran for lieutenant governor. It was July 1993, the Clinton tax plan and gays in the military had been in the headlines, and Huckabee beat pro-Clinton Democrat Nate Coulter 51%–49%; he was re-elected 59%–41% in November 1994. In October 1995, after David Pryor announced he was retiring from the Senate, Huckabee announced for the seat and was ahead in the polls. But in May 1996 Tucker was convicted on one count of arranging nearly $3 million in fraudulent loans from 1985–87 through Capital Management Services, a government-aided firm run by former municipal Judge David Hale. Tucker promised to resign July 15; on that day, claiming he had a good case on appeal, he hesitated, then finally in the early evening resigned. Huckabee, who had already bowed out of the Senate race, had insisted Tucker resign and handled the transition gracefully but firmly.

As governor, Huckabee promoted tourism, and backed a tiny (0.125%) tax increase to promote it; he presented this as an alternative to casino gambling, which was on the 1996 ballot and was defeated. Faced with a surplus, he proposed a $50 per person rebate of the sales tax on food. In the 1997 session, legislators overrode his veto on $140 million in capital improvements. And some chuckled when he refused to sign a disaster relief bill because it said tornadoes, floods, and earthquakes were "acts of God." But Huckabee had significant achievements. One was passage of a partial-birth abortion ban. Another was passage, five months before similar federal legislation, of an ARKids plan providing health insurance for uninsured children; some 30,000 qualified. Another Huckabee favorite was a $7.6 million Smart Start program for the first five grades, to teach "the basic skills of reading, math, and character."

Huckabee entered the election year of 1998 in a strong position. The Democratic nominee was Bill Bristow, an attorney representing state trooper Danny Ferguson in the case Paula Jones brought against Bill Clinton. He charged that Huckabee spent public funds at the Governor's Mansion on dry cleaning, pizza, and pantyhose, and called for a bond issue for road repairs similar to a Tucker bond issue that lost on the ballot 87%–13% in 1996. He criticized Huckabee for capitalizing on tragedy when he wrote a book called *Kids Who Kill*, and began it with an account of the two Jonesboro youths who turned guns on their schoolmates in March 1998. Bristow was outspent 3–1 and never had a serious chance. The big issue in fall 1998 was anti-property tax Amendment 4, until it was ruled off the ballot in mid-October. Huckabee and Bristow both opposed it, and Huckabee in response advanced a property taxpayers' bill of rights, freezing residential property taxes at age 65, limiting increases to 5% or inflation, and helping taxpayers appeal assessments. Huckabee won 60%–39%, carrying all but eight lightly-populated counties in eastern Arkansas.

For 1999, Huckabee promised to advance his property tax changes, to build on ARKids and do more for health care for children. He also proposed to eliminate the state capital gains tax and to provide a $1,500 tax credit to businessmen who hire welfare recipients. He took some risk by backing a highway program, a $1.8 billion bond issue, and an increase in the diesel fuel tax. In all, he is a Republican in his own mold, uncomfortable with criticism but uninterested in confrontational partisanship, faced with a still-heavily Democratic legislature but with half of its members newcomers in 1999 because the 1992 term-limits law takes effect. On Bill Clinton, he said early on, "We can attack his healthcare plan, gays in the military, his foreign policy or the lack of one, but we should not attack him personally. He is the embodiment of the American dream, a kid not of a prosperous family with a pedigree through inheritance. He got there the hard way. He gives a lot of people hope."

Senior Senator. Tim Hutchinson, elected in 1996, is the first Republican senator from Arkansas since 1879. Hutchinson grew up on a farm in northwest Arkansas, attended Bob Jones University and became a Baptist minister; he also owned and managed a radio station and was founder and administrator of a Christian school in Rogers. In 1984 he was elected to the Arkansas House, where Bill Clinton called him "No-Tax Tim." His brother Asa Hutchinson was the Republican nominee against Senator Dale Bumpers in 1986, later served as Republican state chairman, and ultimately succeeded Tim in the House. In 1992 Tim Hutchinson ran for Congress and won the three-candidate Republican primary impressively, 53%–32%, over a fellow state legislator. In the general, he backed term limits, the balanced budget amendment, the line-item veto—essentially the Contract with America two years early—and called for a base-closings-type commission to curb government spending. He called attacks on him as a religious extremist scare tactics reflecting a kind of intolerance. But Democrat John Van Winkle raised more money, Clinton carried the district, and Hutchinson won by just 50%–47%.

In the House, Hutchinson had a very conservative record, supporting NAFTA after watching U.S. exports sell in a Wal-Mart in Mexico City, and pushing for the $500 per child tax credit. He was re-elected with 68% and seemed headed for a third term when Governor Jim Guy Tucker was convicted of fraud in May 1996 and announced he would resign in July. That elevated Republican Lieutenant Governor Mike Huckabee, who was the Republican nominee for the Senate seat being vacated by Democrat David Pryor. Huckabee opted out of the Senate race May 30, and on June 3, Hutchinson said he would not run. But no other candidate seemed strong enough to win a seat Republicans had counted on as a sure gain, and on June 15, a Republican convention nominated Hutchinson. The winner of the Democratic primary was Attorney General Winston Bryant, a seasoned pol who had won seven statewide races for various offices. But he was held to a 40%–22% edge in the first primary over liberal state Senator Lu Hardin. Bryant promised to hold the line on taxes and hailed "rural values," and won the June 11 runoff 54%–46%.

Hutchinson started his general campaign with an ad showing John Kennedy and saying that his father voted for Kennedy while teaching Tim to have an open mind and open heart. Democrats squawked, and Bryant ran ads tying Hutchinson to Newt Gingrich and accusing him of government shut downs in 1995. But Hutchinson, one of four House Republicans to vote to release the outside counsel's report on Newt Gingrich, brushed aside the attacks saying, "The people of Arkansas are going to say, 'No, thumbs down, we don't want a senator who has nothing to offer but criticism.' " And Hutchinson protested Bryant's increased office budgets: "For 15 years Winston Bryant's been very liberal with your money." On election day, Hutchinson won 53%–47%. He carried all of Arkansas west and north of Little Rock and ran just about even in the capital. His brother Asa was elected to his old 3d District House seat, and the two became the second pair of congressional brothers. (The others are Democrats Sander and Carl Levin of Michigan.)

Hutchinson's voting record has been among the most conservative in the Senate, with emphasis on bolstering moral values and often in opposition to big business. His maiden speech was for the $500 per child tax credit. He passed an amendment denying U.S. visas to foreign officials involved in abortion, sterilization, genital mutilation, or religious persecution; this was originally aimed at China but, at Democrats' suggestion, broadened to include all countries. Hutchinson opposed normal trade status for China, though big Arkansas businesses like Wal-Mart and Tyson Foods are very much on the other side. He opposed the nomination of David Satcher as surgeon general because Satcher opposed the partial-birth abortion ban, and he called on J. Carter Brown to resign from the Commission on Fine Arts for calling the Marines' Iwo Jima Memorial "kitsch." He has served on Veterans' subcommittees in both houses, and attacked the VA for not stamping out sexual harassment. He opposed the EPA's and FDA's proposed ban on asthma inhalers, and wants to ban gambling on the Internet.

These may be small matters, but Hutchinson is also interested in big changes in public policy. He wants to block-grant federal aid to education and require that 95% of the money end up in the classroom. He led a move to scrap the entire Internal Revenue Code by the end of 2002 and saw it defeated by a 49–49 tie in July 1998, after it passed the House; the idea is to reform the tax law from the ground up, and it is strongly opposed by big business—and Finance Committee Chairman William Roth. Occasionally, Hutchinson has joined liberals, as on trade status for China, and when he backed his retiring colleague Dale Bumpers's eighth and last attempt to cut off funding for the Space Shuttle—"a barrel of pork in outer space," Hutchinson said. Very occasionally he seems to switch sides. He supported one effort to cut off the Republican filibuster of the McCain-Feingold campaign finance bill in 1997, then said two days later he was against the legislation, which his brother Asa has looked favorably on in the House. His seat comes up in 2002.

Junior Senator. Blanche Lincoln does not look like a standard Arkansas politician, but she has shown something close to perfect political pitch in her 1990s electoral career. Blanche Lambert (as she was until her marriage in August 1993) grew up in Helena, on the flat rice lands of eastern Arkansas, where her father and brother are the sixth and seventh generations running a farm raising rice, wheat, soybeans, and cotton, and where she stayed in public schools after they were integrated. Cheerful, active, endowed with good political sense, she lists her hobbies as duck hunting, fishing and yard sales. After college, in 1982, she worked as a staffer for 1st District Congressman Bill Alexander, then after two years worked as a lobbyist for, among others, Billy Broadhurst, Gary Hart's host on the "Monkey Business" cruise. In 1992 she moved back to Arkansas and ran against Alexander, sensing he was in trouble. He had lost a leadership race in 1986, was named in a lawsuit for a $308,000 debt, and had 487 overdrafts totaling $208,000 on the House bank. "I'll promise you one thing," the 31-year-old challenger said, "I can sure enough balance my checkbook." She won the primary 61%–39%, carrying 23 of 25 counties.

In the House, she compiled a moderate voting record, got a seat on the Commerce Committee, and was one of the lowest-spending Democrats. She saw Japan open its market to Arkansas rice and denounced the Supplemental Security Income program that provided disability checks to kids who act up in school. She supported much of the Contract with America in 1995. But when the moratorium on regulations threatened duck hunting season and national wildlife refuges were closed, she got laws changed to ensure it wouldn't happen again. Her reelection margin in 1994 was only 53%–47%, but she seemed well positioned to hold the seat when, in January 1996, she announced that she was pregnant with twin boys and would not run for re-election.

Then Senator Dale Bumpers, an eloquent liberal elected governor in 1970 and senator in 1974, who twice nearly ran for president in the 1980s, announced he would not run for re-election in 1998. Lincoln got into the race, and without much fuss about whether that was inconsistent with her decision to quit in 1996; evidently her fear then was that it would be impossible to campaign in a hot Arkansas summer during a difficult pregnancy. Lincoln used her maternal status as a plus, flashing snapshots of her twins, and running ads showing her overseeing mealtime, balancing one twin on her lap, bouncing the other on her knee, laying her head on her husband's shoulder. "Daughter, wife, mother, congresswoman . . . Living our rock-solid Arkansas values." On the issues, she was not terribly specific: she promised to work on children's and women's health issues; she wanted to improve education; she wanted to keep the budget balanced, and to use the surplus to replenish the Social Security trust fund and cut taxes. Though she has spent most of her adult life in Washington, she also showed she was in touch with Arkansas. "I was one of the few members of the Agriculture Committee," she told rice farmers, "that ever walked a rice levee."

In the primary she faced Winston Bryant, still attorney general and the Democratic nominee in the 1996 Senate race, and two other candidates. She led Bryant by an impressive 45%–27% in the May 19 primary. Nearly one-third of the votes were cast in Lincoln's old 1st District, where she took 64%; she also carried the Little Rock area solidly. In the runoff, Bryant called her a tool of national Democratic political interests and attacked her for taking PAC and tobacco money. Lincoln shrugged that off, and her strong fundraising enabled her to run positive, soft-focus ads. She won the runoff 62%–38%.

In the general election, Lincoln staunched the Republican tide that had been running since Bill Clinton left the state, and then some. The Republican nominee was Fay Boozman (pronounced in the Dutch manner, like Bozeman, Montana), an opthamologist from Rogers. Boozman attends the same church as Senator Tim Hutchinson, suggesting that statewide Republican talent is thin. He had a profound religious experience in 1992, sold his medical practice, ran for the state Senate; there he was the champion of the partial-birth abortion ban. Boozman seemed less gifted with political horse sense than Lincoln. He had no primary opposition and in June had as much cash-on-hand as Lincoln. But by November she had raised and spent more than double Boozman. He called on Clinton to resign—which would deprive Arkansas of its only president—and ran tough comparative ads on Lincoln. He said the Bible dictates his anti-tax philosophy—a bit of a stretch for some voters—and made a serious gaffe when he said it is rare for women to get pregnant by rape, because fear triggers a hormonal change that blocks conception. He denied calling this "God's little shield." But the broader point is that the cases for and against abortion in the case of rape do not depend for their seriousness on how frequently such pregnancies occur. Boozman signed off his speeches by pledging to be "a man of integrity who walks the talk and, with God's strength, who will make the difficult decisions that keep America great." Lincoln's affirmations of her religious faith had a more comforting demotic tone: "I've always had a personal relationship with Jesus Christ. When I talk to Him, it's pretty informal . . . I just lay it all out there, say it like it is."

Many expected Boozman to surge in the fall, but he never did. He carried only the northwest corner of the state and little else. Lambert won 55%–42%, a more solid win than Tim Hutchinson's in 1996. Her consensus-toned campaign seemed to have struck a chord. She explained, voters are "more anxious in seeing Washington devoting its resources and its time and energy to solving the problems of the people with everyday problems and hopefully to minimalize the political difference, the partisan difference." Lincoln's husband (he is a fertility specialist) joined a private practice in Fairfax County, Virginia. It seems quite possible that his wife can enjoy a long career in the Senate.

Presidential politics. Arkansas was Bill Clinton's strongest state in 1992. Not so in 1996, when he won higher percentages in Massachusetts, Rhode Island, New York, Hawaii, Maryland, Vermont and Illinois. Arkansas was long one of the least Republican of Southern states; now it seems to be moving heavily toward Republicans, and its 1996 showing was more a reflection of Clinton's personal home-state strength than of underlying Democratic allegiance. Al Gore, should he be the 2000 nominee, may have to strain hard to win here, as Clinton did in 1996 to win Gore's Tennessee.

The Arkansas presidential primary is now held in May, and attracts little attention. It didn't when it was held on Super Tuesday, in 1992, either. There is no party registration and Republican turnout has typically been very low; it will be interesting to see if that is still true in 2000.

Congressional districting. Arkansas made only minor changes in its district boundaries to meet the equal-population standard in the 1990s.

The People: Est. Pop. 1998: 2,538,303; Pop. 1990: 2,350,725, up 8% 1990–1998. 0.9% of U.S. total, 33d largest; 46.5% rural. Median age: 35.2 years. 15.5% 65 years and over. 82.7% White, 15.9% Black, 0.5% Asian, 0.6% Amer. Indian, 0.3% Other; 0.8% Hispanic Origin. Households: 59.2% married couple families; 27.8% married couple fams. w. children; 33.6% college educ.; median household income: $21,147; per capita income: $10,520; 69.6% owner occupied housing; median house value: $46,300; median monthly rent: $230. 5.5% Unemployment. 1998 Voting age pop.: 1,822,000. 1998 Turnout: 706,011; 39% of VAP. Registered voters (1998): 1,471,971; no party registration.

Political Lineup: Governor, Mike Huckabee (R); Lt. Gov., Winthrop P. Rockefeller (R); Secy. of State, Sharon Priest (D); Atty. Gen., Mark Pryor (D); Treasurer, Jimmie Lou Fisher (D); State Senate, 35 (29 D, 6 R); Majority Leader, Stanley Russ (D); State Assembly, 100 (75 D, 25 R); Assembly Speaker, Bob Johnson (D). Senators, Tim Hutchinson (R) and Blanche Lincoln (D). Representatives, 4 (2 D, 2 R).

Elections Division: 501-682-5070; **Filing Deadline for U.S. Congress:** April 4, 2000.

1996 Presidential Vote

Clinton (D)	475,171	(54%)
Dole (R)	325,416	(37%)
Perot (I)	69,884	(8%)
Others	13,791	(2%)

1992 Presidential Vote

Clinton (D)	505,823	(53%)
Bush (R)	337,324	(35%)
Perot (I)	99,132	(10%)

1996 Republican Presidential Primary

Dole (R)	32,759	(76%)
Buchanan (R)	10,067	(23%)

GOVERNOR

Gov. Mike Huckabee (R)

Assumed office, July 1996, term expires Jan. 2003; b. Aug. 24, 1955, Hope; home, Little Rock; Ouachita Baptist U., B.A. 1975, Southwestern Baptist Theological Seminary, 1976–80; Baptist; married (Janet).

Elected Office: AR Lt. Gov., 1993–96.

Professional Career: Advertising Dir., Focus, 1976–80; Baptist Minister, 1980–92; Pres., ACTS-TV, 1983–86; Pres., KBSC-TV, 1987–92; Pres., Cambridge Comm., 1992–96.

Office: State Capitol, #250, Little Rock, 72201, 501-682-2345; Fax: 501-682-3597; Web site: www.state.ar.us.

Election Results

1998 gen.	Mike Huckabee (R)	421,989	(60%)
	Bill Bristow (D)	272,923	(39%)
	Others	11,099	(2%)
1998 prim.	Mike Huckabee (R)	51,627	(90%)
	Gene McVay (R)	5,581	(10%)
1994 gen.	Jim Guy Tucker (D)	428,936	(60%)
	Sheffield Nelson (R)	287,904	(40%)

SENATORS

Sen. Tim Hutchinson (R)

Elected 1996, seat up 2002; b. Aug. 11, 1949, Gravette; home, Bentonville; Bob Jones U., B.A. 1979, U. of AR, M.A. 1990; Baptist; married (Donna King).

Elected Office: AR House of Reps., 1984–92; US House of Reps., 1992–96.

Professional Career: Baptist Minister; Founder & Admin., Benton Cnty. Christian Schl., 1975–85; Co-owner & Mgr., KBCV Radio, 1982–89; Prof., John Brown U., 1989–92.

DC Office: 245 DSOB, 20510, 202-224-2353; Web site: www.senate.gov/~hutchinson.

State Offices: El Dorado, 870-863-6406; Jonesboro, 870-935-5022; Little Rock, 501-324-6336.

Committees: *Aging (Special)* (11th of 11 R). *Armed Services* (10th of 11 R): Airland Forces; Readiness & Management Support; Strategic Forces. *Health, Education, Labor & Pensions* (6th of 10 R): Aging; Employment, Safety & Training. *Veterans' Affairs* (7th of 7 R).

Group Ratings

	ADA	ACLU	AFS	LCV	CON	NTU	NFIB	COC	ACU	NTLC	CHC
1998	5	14	0	0	65	70	100	89	100	100	100
1997	0	—	0	—	93	86	—	80	100	—	—

National Journal Ratings

	1997 LIB — 1997 CONS	1998 LIB — 1998 CONS
Economic	0% — 89%	0% — 88%
Social	0% — 83%	0% — 88%
Foreign	0% — 77%	0% — 88%

Key Votes of the 105th Congress

1. Bal. Budget Amend.	Y	5. Satcher for Surgeon Gen.	N	9. Chem. Weapons Treaty	N
2. Clinton Budget Deal	Y	6. Highway Set-asides	N	10. Cuban Humanitarian Aid	N
3. Cloture on Tobacco	N	7. Table Child Gun locks	Y	11. Table Bosnia Troops	N
4. Education IRAs	Y	8. Ovrd. Part. Birth Veto	Y	12. $ for Test-ban Treaty	N

Election Results

1996 general	Tim Hutchinson (R) 445,942	(53%)	($1,604,014)
	Winston Bryant (D) 400,241	(47%)	($1,577,838)
1996 primary	Tim Hutchinson (R) .... nominated by convention		
1990 general	David Pryor (D) .... unopposed		($622,479)

Sen. Blanche Lincoln (D)

Elected 1998, seat up 2004; b. Sept. 30, 1960, Helena; home, Horseshoe Lake; U. of AR, 1979–80, Randolph Macon Col., B.S. 1982; Episcopalian; married (Steve).

Elected Office: US House of Reps., 1992–96.

Professional Career: Staff Asst., U.S. Rep. Bill Alexander, 1982–84; Lobbyist & govt. affairs rep., 1985–91.

DC Office: 359 DSOB, 20510, 202-224-4843; Fax: 202-228-1371; Web site: www.senate.gov/~lincoln.

State Offices: Fort Smith, 501-646-7591; Jonesboro, 870-910-6896; Little Rock, 501-324-6286.

Committees: *Aging (Special)* (9th of 9 D). *Agriculture, Nutrition & Forestry* (8th of 8 D): Production & Price Competitiveness; Research, Nutrition & General Legislation. *Energy & Natural Resources* (9th of 9 D): Forests & Public Land Management; National Parks, Historic Preservation & Recreation; Water & Power.

Group Ratings and Key Votes: Newly Elected

Election Results

1998 general	Blanche Lincoln (D)	385,878	(55%)	($3,122,776)
	Fay Boozman (R)	292,906	(42%)	($1,093,007)
	Others	21,860	(3%)	
1998 runoff	Blanche Lincoln (D)	134,203	(62%)	
	Winston Bryant (D)	80,889	(38%)	
1998 primary	Blanche Lincoln (D)	145,009	(45%)	
	Winston Bryant (D)	87,183	(27%)	
	Scott Ferguson (D)	44,761	(14%)	
	Nate Coulter (D)	41,848	(13%)	
1992 general	Dale Bumpers (D)	553,635	(60%)	($2,016,112)
	Mike Huckabee (R)	366,373	(40%)	($910,212)

FIRST DISTRICT

The Mississippi Delta, the flat, mushy, river-crossed lowland on both sides of the great river, was some of the country's first industrial farmland. This land was uncultivated in the 19th Century, when plows were still pulled by mules and muddy flatlands were impassable. Then, a century ago, big landowners used machines to drain the marshlands and persuaded poor blacks to move here to tend fields of cotton, rice, and later, soybeans. The results were bountiful agriculture and impoverished people. Around 1940, the Delta began to change slowly: the first minimum wage and war industry jobs up north drew young people out of the Delta and mechanization forced many off the farms. But this land—stretching flat as far as the eye can see, past rows of telephone poles and ribbons of asphalt that shimmer in the heat—remains poor by national standards and the people are undereducated and underemployed.

The 1st Congressional District includes most of the Arkansas's Delta lands and stretches west to the cool green Ozarks. The Delta started off heavily Democratic, while some of the hill counties are ancestrally Republican. That changed as partisan preferences oscillated wildly just after the civil rights revolution, but the district returned to its historical norm by the late 1980s, and the Delta provided critical support for, perhaps saving the career of, Bill Clinton in 1990. In 1992, Delta counties voted from 58% to 69% for Clinton, some of his best county showings anywhere in the United States.

The congressman from the 1st District is Marion Berry, a Democrat and Clinton supporter who won this district, though only narrowly, in 1996. Berry grew up in Bayou Meto in Arkansas County in the Delta. He earned a pharmacy degree in Little Rock, then ran a pharmacy for two years, and has been a family farmer since 1968, with a net worth of $1 million or more. He is a hunter, who likes to serve coon at his town's annual supper. "He is the antithesis of cool and charisma," writes Michael Leahy of the *Arkansas Democrat-Gazette*. "He is quite satisfied to be the humble plodder appreciated by the people back home." Berry first met Clinton when he was running for attorney general in 1976, and was impressed with his fluency and knowledge: "You thought to yourself right then—even though you didn't know him—that this guy could be governor, even president, one day." Governor Clinton appointed him to the Arkansas Soil & Water Conservation Commission in 1986, and President Clinton appointed him White House liaison to the Agriculture Department in 1993. Berry returned to Arkansas in 1996, after Congresswoman Blanche Lincoln announced she would not run for re-election because she was pregnant with twins. The twins safely born, she ran for the Senate in 1998 and, with strong support from the 1st District and especially the Delta, won.

Berry turned out to have tough opposition for her seat. Republican Warren DuPwe, a former Jonesboro city attorney who had won 47% against Lincoln in 1994, was running again. And in the Democratic primary, Tom Donaldson, a 28-year-old deputy prosecutor in Crittenden County, spent little money but ran rural radio ads criticizing Berry for accepting farm subsidies. He held Berry to a 48%–30% lead in the May 21 primary. Lincoln endorsed Berry and he brought in Agriculture Secretary Dan Glickman to campaign for him. Yet he won the June 11 runoff by only 52%–48%. In the general, Berry repeatedly accused DuPwe of favoring Medicare cuts; DuPwe replied that he favored increasing Medicare spending more slowly. Both candidates opposed abortion rights and gun control and favored a balanced budget. Berry's Washington contacts proved more generous than DuPwe's; Berry outspent him nearly 2–1. Berry won 53%–44%.

Berry got seats on the Agriculture and Transportation committees—good spots for a constituency-oriented member. His voting record was moderate to liberal; a Blue Dog Democrat, he supported the balanced budget amendment and said he wanted to pay off the national debt and save Social Security and Medicare. He also said his primary goal was to avoid privatization of the Southwest Power Administration, which supplies electricity to city-owned utilities. He sponsored bills on rural health and fought a USDA and FDA investigation of dioxin spills which he said unwarrantedly threatened the local catfish and chicken industries. Unflashy but hard-working, he has worked to make this a safe district for re-election. Whether he has succeeded or not is unclear. Tommy Robinson, the tempestuous former (1984–1990) Democratic congressman from Little Rock, threatened to run here as a Republican in 1998, then suddenly withdrew; no one else ran, and Berry was unopposed in primary and general.

Cook's Call. *Probably Safe.* The fact that Berry, a freshman, was unopposed in 1998 was surprising given that the 1st District's performance for Democrats had declined rather precipitously in the two preceding elections. While Berry's moderate voting record and strong agricultural background may have solidified the district for him, it's pretty clear that this is no longer the yellow dog Democratic district that it once was. Republicans will probably take a hard look at this district in 2000 and beyond, but when Berry steps aside, watch for them to go all out here.

The People: Pop. 1990: 588,588; 52.8% rural; 15.8% age 65+; 81.4% White, 17.9% Black, 0.3% Asian, 0.3% Amer. Indian, 0.1% Other; 0.5% Hispanic Origin. Households: 59.4% married couple families; 28.5% married couple fams. w. children; 26.2% college educ.; median household income: $18,180; per capita income: $9,148; median house value: $40,100; median gross rent: $182.

1996 Presidential Vote			1992 Presidential Vote		
Clinton (D)	116,634	(58%)	Clinton (D)	131,585	(59%)
Dole (R)	65,707	(33%)	Bush (R)	71,160	(32%)
Perot (I)	16,269	(8%)	Perot (I)	20,116	(9%)

Rep. Marion Berry (D)

Elected 1996; b. Aug. 27, 1942, Bayou Meto; home, Gillett; U. of AR, B.S. 1965; Methodist; married (Carolyn).

Professional Career: Pharmacist, 1965–67; farmer, 1968–present; AR Soil & Water Conservation Comm., 1986–94, Chmn. 1992; Special Asst. to the Pres., Domestic Policy Cncl., White House, 1993–96.

DC Office: 1113 LHOB 20515, 202-225-4076; Fax: 202-225-5602; Web site: www.house.gov/berry.

District Office: Jonesboro, 870-972-4600.

Committees: *Agriculture* (14th of 24 D): Department Operations, Oversight, Nutrition & Forestry; Livestock & Horticulture. *Transportation & Infrastructure* (31st of 34 D): Aviation; Ground Transportation.

Group Ratings

	ADA	ACLU	AFS	LCV	CON	NTU	NFIB	COC	ACU	NTLC	CHC
1998	70	38	78	23	49	30	50	67	28	42	25
1997	75	—	88	—	15	34	—	60	44	—	—

National Journal Ratings

	1997 LIB — 1997 CONS		1998 LIB — 1998 CONS	
Economic	60%	— 40%	58%	— 41%
Social	57%	— 42%	47%	— 52%
Foreign	55%	— 44%	64%	— 31%

Key Votes of the 105th Congress

1. Clinton Budget Deal	N	5. Puerto Rico Sthood. Ref.	N	9. Cut $ for B-2 Bombers	Y
2. Education IRAs	N	6. End Highway Set-asides	N	10. Human Rights in China	N
3. Req. 2/3 to Raise Taxes	Y	7. School Prayer Amend.	Y	11. Withdraw Bosnia Troops	N
4. Fast-track Trade	Y	8. Ovrd. Part. Birth Veto	Y	12. End Cuban TV-Marti	Y

Election Results

1998 general	Marion Berry (D)	unopposed		($303,952)
1998 primary	Marion Berry (D)	unopposed		
1996 general	Marion Berry (D)	105,280	(53%)	($871,389)
	Warren DuPwe (R)	88,436	(44%)	($574,846)
	Others	5,734	(3%)	

SECOND DISTRICT

Little Rock has been the capital and largest city and central focus of Arkansas for more than a century. It is one of those capitals located at the geographical center of the state, and in a state that has no other metropolis, it stands out. For a long moment, Little Rock became internationally famous. That was in September 1957, when Governor Orval Faubus, eager for a third term, sent in the National Guard to block a desegregation order at Central High School. President Eisenhower sent in U.S. troops and federalized the Guard to enforce the order, and Little Rock became a synonym for bigotry around the world. Forty years later, the Little Rock nine who had integrated the high school returned for a 40th anniversary commemoration, and heard a speech by none other than Bill Clinton. "It was Little Rock that made racial equality a driving obsession in my life," he said, and added that American life was still in too many ways segregated. Also speaking was Governor Mike Huckabee, a Republican, who said, "Today we come to say once and for all that what happened here 40 years ago was simply wrong." Most impressive were the Little Rock nine themselves and what these graying and now 50-something adults had achieved, as suggested by their occupations—writer, managing director of an investment bank, real estate broker, chairman of a university psychology department, magazine publisher, financial specialist for the Department of Defense, teacher, public relations specialist and journalist. And Central High School today, about 60% black, gets academic prizes and Ivy League admissions: Little Rock has things to be proud of.

Little Rock is also the center of Arkansas not just geographically but politically. It sets the tone of the public life of its state as do only a few other state capitals—Boston, Providence, Atlanta, Denver, Honolulu. Little Rock is home to the *Arkansas Democrat-Gazette*, the feisty, conservative paper whose editor Paul Greenberg christened Clinton "Slick Willie." It is home to the state government, to Jack Stephens's investment banking firm, Worthen Bank, Dillards department stores, the TCBY yogurt chain, Excelsior Hotel, and the former home of now-defunct Madison Guaranty Savings & Loan. Little Rock may not be upscale by national standards, but it is in Arkansas.

The 2d Congressional District includes Little Rock, with its large black and affluent white neighborhoods, and North Little Rock, a kind of industrial suburb across the Arkansas River known informally for years as Dog Town. (At the turn of the century, Little Rock officials, peeved that North Little Rock was allowed to incorporate separately, dumped all their stray dogs there.) It also includes surrounding counties that have grown rapidly as people move farther out on the freeways, and a couple of small hill counties. Politically, Little Rock was long a progressive force in a state with widely divergent political tendencies; it provided key support to Clinton when he was in political trouble in the 1990 primary and general, and again in 1992. Yet like much of Arkansas, it has been trending Republican since he was elected; in 1996 the 2d District voted for Republican Senator Tim Hutchinson. Over the years its representation has varied widely. In 1958, after the Central High crisis, it elected a segregationist with write-in votes. From 1962–74 its congressman was Ways and Means Chairman Wilbur Mills. In 1976 it elected Jim Guy Tucker, who succeeded Clinton as governor; he was followed by three-term Republican Ed Bethune; then came Tommy Robinson, a nominal Democrat whose antics as sheriff earned him notoriety and popularity, who switched to the Republican Party in 1989; then for three terms Ray Thornton, once congressman from the 4th District, president of Arkansas State University and nephew of Jack Stephens.

The congressman now is Victor F. Snyder, a Democrat elected in 1996 when Thornton retired to run for the state Supreme Court. Snyder is an unusual politician, "an inveterately private man in a public profession, quite content to be all alone," as the *Arkansas Democrat-Gazette*'s Michael Leahy writes. He grew up fatherless in Medford, Oregon, dropped out of Willamette University, and at 20 signed up in the Marine Corps and served in Vietnam. Then he returned to Oregon for college and medical school and became a practicing physician, a general practitioner at the Columbia Family Clinic, and went on medical missions in Thailand, Honduras, Sierra Leone and Sudan. He got a law degree but never practiced law. In 1990 he was elected to the state Senate and made news when he called for repeal of Arkansas's anti-sodomy law and when he refused to accept a pension.

In 1996, Snyder, consulting no one, decided to run for Congress. He ran as a reformer, promising not to accept a congressional pension until the establishment of an equitable system for federal employees. His main Democratic opponents had more political backgrounds. The leader was Mark Stodola, the county prosecutor in Little Rock, a strong Clinton backer who said he would work to solve the root causes of crime. Also running was John Edwards, who handled casework for Senator David Pryor. Snyder cited his work as a doctor and legislator and pressed the attack: "If Stodola has solutions to juvenile crime, he should have introduced those ideas at the local level rather than campaigning on the theme that the current system is broken. He is the system." Stodola replied that "the laws Vic sponsors lets them out." Stodola led the May 21 primary with 48%, to 32% for Snyder and 20% for Edwards. Snyder won the June 11 runoff in an upset, 51%–49%. The Republican nominee, lawyer Bud Cummins, ran an aggressive campaign; Snyder continued to sound reform themes while outspending Cummins. Although Clinton carried his home district, the Little Rock area was moving toward Republicans lower on the ticket, and Snyder won by a narrow 52%–48% margin.

Snyder says he is non-ideological, but his voting record is consistently liberal. He voted against the partial-birth abortion ban and for needle exchanges; he was the single Democrat to vote against a resolution to urge an international tribunal to try Saddam Hussein for "crimes against humanity." Other Democrats urged him to vote yes, but he said, "As some old man said to me one time, 'We want you to be like a horse who stands on his hind legs when he has to'—even if I'm the only horse out there. . . . It just seemed to me like this was one of those times." He was also one of only two House members in March 1999 to vote against a bill to tighten burial restrictions at Arlington Cemetery. But Snyder has bragged of supporting more moderate measures—the balanced budget, tax cuts in 1997, a strong education system—and stressed his military record and service on the Armed Services and Veterans' Affairs Committees. In 1998 he was against tax cuts and increased spending, to save the budget surplus; but he said he would consider partial privatization of Social Security in 1999. He pushed to passage a law naming Central High School a National Historic Site.

The 1998 campaign came late to the 2d District. Snyder pledged to raise no money until 90 days before the May primary; his Republican opponent, Phil Wyrick, did not decide to run until March. Wyrick, a cattle farmer, served six years in the state House as a Democrat and then was elected as a Republican in January 1997 to replace Snyder in the state Senate. But for all his seeming naivete, Snyder was able to greatly out-raise Wyrick. Snyder carried Little Rock's Pulaski County with 62%, and though he was held to 50% in two suburbanizing counties, he won overall by 58%–42%.

Cook's Call. *Potentially Competitive.* Snyder's quirky nature and his penchant for taking on controversial issues certainly make him an enticing target. But he is well liked by voters here and his own personal appeal may be strong enough to overcome what should be a competitive district. Like so many Southern states, Arkansas is trending Republican, and as the rural pockets of this district continue to grow and suburbanize, the 2d District is no longer a reliable Democratic stronghold.

The People: Pop. 1990: 587,412; 31.5% rural; 12.9% age 65 +; 81.1% White, 17.6% Black, 0.6% Asian, 0.4% Amer. Indian, 0.3% Other; 0.9% Hispanic Origin. Households: 57% married couple families; 27.4% married couple fams. w. children; 43% college educ.; median household income: $25,142; per capita income: $12,334; median house value: $56,800; median gross rent: $280.

1996 Presidential Vote			1992 Presidential Vote		
Clinton (D)	124,545	(55%)	Clinton (D)	130,435	(55%)
Dole (R)	83,218	(37%)	Bush (R)	84,922	(36%)
Perot (I)	14,667	(6%)	Perot (I)	19,348	(8%)

Rep. Victor F. Snyder (D)

Elected 1996; b. Sept. 27, 1947, Medford, OR; home, Little Rock; Willamette U., B.A. 1975, U. of OR, M.D. 1979, U. of AR, J.D. 1988; Presbyterian; single.

Military Career: Marine Corps, 1967–69 (Vietnam).

Elected Office: AR Senate, 1990–96.

Professional Career: Practicing physician, 1982–present.

DC Office: 1319 LHOB 20515, 202-225-2506; Fax: 202-225-5903; Web site: www.house.gov/snyder.

District Office: Little Rock, 501-324-5941.

Committees: *Armed Services* (15th of 28 D): Military Installations & Facilities; Military Research & Development. *Veterans' Affairs* (9th of 14 D): Health.

Group Ratings

	ADA	ACLU	AFS	LCV	CON	NTU	NFIB	COC	ACU	NTLC	CHC
1998	85	81	89	85	91	17	43	61	16	18	0
1997	80	—	75	—	70	32	—	60	20	—	—

National Journal Ratings

	1997 LIB — 1997 CONS		1998 LIB — 1998 CONS	
Economic	64%	— 35%	66%	— 33%
Social	73%	— 24%	65%	— 35%
Foreign	64%	— 33%	61%	— 37%

Key Votes of the 105th Congress

1. Clinton Budget Deal	N	5. Puerto Rico Sthood. Ref.	Y	9. Cut $ for B-2 Bombers	Y
2. Education IRAs	N	6. End Highway Set-asides	N	10. Human Rights in China	N
3. Req. 2/3 to Raise Taxes	N	7. School Prayer Amend.	N	11. Withdraw Bosnia Troops	N
4. Fast-track Trade	Y	8. Ovrd. Part. Birth Veto	N	12. End Cuban TV-Marti	Y

Election Results

1998 general	Victor F. Snyder (D) 100,334	(58%)	($963,053)
	Phil Wyrick (R) 72,737	(42%)	($607,999)
1998 primary	Victor F. Snyder (D) .... unopposed		
1996 general	Victor F. Snyder (D) 114,841	(52%)	($798,145)
	Bud Cummins (R) 104,548	(48%)	($730,699)

THIRD DISTRICT

The northwest corner of Arkansas in the late 1990s has become one of America's boom areas, with tourist attractions and retirement developments, major corporate headquarters and dozens of small factories, some of America's richest families and growing numbers of hard-working Hispanic immigrants, the handsome University of Arkansas in Fayetteville and the mountain-bound resort town of Eureka Springs. This would have seemed most unlikely for most of this century, when these rounded green mountains and pleasant wide valleys, farmhouses and small towns seemed left behind. But the friendly atmosphere and strong religious faith of these communities have proved to be assets, not liabilities, conducive to economic creativity and personal serenity. There have also been touches of genius. Sam Walton, who opened his first Wal-Mart on the town square of Bentonville, had the inspiration of building a retail chain in tradition-minded small towns and rural areas using sophisticated computerized management; it made him the richest man in America, though he still drove a pickup truck and on the Wal-Mart headquarters building outside Bentonville some of the metal panels have fallen off. Don Tyson took his family chicken business and made Tyson Foods, in its sparkling headquarters outside Springdale, the nation's leading chicken producer and processor.

The 3d Congressional District covers northwest Arkansas, including Bentonville, Fayetteville and Springdale, plus Fort Smith on the Oklahoma line and several mountain and upcountry counties to the east and south. Some of these mountain counties have been Republican since the Civil War, for there were few slaves here and much suspicion of planters; others started leaning Republican in the 1950s, and a Republican congressman, John Paul Hammerschmidt, was elected here as long ago as 1966. He was strong enough even in Democratic 1974 to beat Bill Clinton, then 28, in his first election, though Clinton did get an impressive 48%. Lately this area has become even more Republican, as Christian conservatives have entered politics and new migrants and millionaires have voted heavily Republican. The 3d voted for Bill Clinton 43%–42% in 1992, but in 1996 it went 45%–44% for Bob Dole. The big companies may work with Democrats—Wal-Mart had Hillary Rodham Clinton on its board and Don Tyson's house counsel put her in the way of making unbelievable profits in commodities trades—but most voters here are staunchly Republican.

The congressman from the 3d District is Asa Hutchinson, a Republican elected in 1996 to replace his brother Tim, who was elected to the Senate. The Hutchinsons grew up on a farm in Gravette, the fifth and sixth children of a couple who started a Christian radio station and the Benton County Christian School. Both went to Bob Jones University, then came back to Arkansas—graduate school for Tim, law school for Asa. Asa entered the University of Arkansas Law School the year Bill Clinton started teaching there—not the first time their careers became intertwined. Hutchinson's first campaign work was for Democrat David Pryor in the 1972 Senate primary, but he soon became a strong Republican, and was Bentonville coordinator for Frank White, the Republican who beat one-term Governor Clinton in 1980. Recommended by

Hammerschmidt, Hutchinson became U.S. attorney in western Arkansas in 1981, the youngest U.S. attorney in the country. There he prosecuted a Republican sheriff for marijuana possession and Roger Clinton for cocaine possession; his signal achievement was the prosecution of a paramilitary group called the Covenant, the Sword, and the Arm of the Lord. In 1986 he ran for the Senate and lost to Dale Bumpers 62%–38%; in 1990 he ran for attorney general and lost to Democrat Winston Bryant. He practiced law in Fort Smith—taking a lot of civil rights and sex discrimination cases, "things you wouldn't think of a Republican lawyer doing"—and was state Republican chairman from 1990–95.

In early 1996, Asa Hutchinson wasn't running for Congress; indeed, neither party's ultimate nominees in this district even ran in their respective primaries. But after Governor Jim Guy Tucker was convicted of fraud and announced he would resign, Lieutenant Governor Mike Huckabee withdrew from the Senate race; Tim Hutchinson, after some hesitation, became the Republican candidate for Senate on June 15. That left the 3d District nomination open. Asa Hutchinson had opposition, but at the July 13 convention won 93–65. He seemed the clear favorite to win. But on September 4, the Democratic nominee dropped out, and the Democrats on September 14 nominated Ann Henry, a University of Arkansas business law professor and former Fayetteville councilwoman. She was a close friend of Bill and Hillary Rodham Clinton—they held their wedding reception at her house—and put $130,000 into her campaign and spent more than Hutchinson. She campaigned as a champion of the U.S. Department of Education and an opponent of "the Gingrich agenda." But Hutchinson's personal strength and party affiliation gave him a 56%–42% victory—better than Tim Hutchinson's 50%–47% four years before.

In the House, Hutchinson combined a very conservative voting record with an open and pleasant manner to become an important member in a short time. With seats on Transportation and Veterans, he also got a third committee assignment, on Judiciary. He got bipartisan support for a bill holding bounty hunters and bail bondsmen liable for civil rights violations and requiring them to report to law enforcement when they cross state lines. He sought to have the tranquilizer Rohypnol, used by rapists to quiet victims, made a Schedule 1 drug. With his brother, he protested China's human rights violations and "adopted" a Chinese "prisoner of conscience" and pledged to work for his release. He sought bipartisan agreement on incremental measures on health care finance and, most notably, campaign finance reform.

On that issue, he and freshman Democrat Tom Allen of Maine co-sponsored a so-called "freshman bill," which would ban soft money but not issue advocacy—though it did rouse some protest from Arkansas Right to Life. It would thus, Hutchinson argued, avoid constitutional issues. But most Democrats wanted to pass the Shays-Meehan bill, which did ban issue advocacy ads, within 60 days of an election, and in August 1998 the Hutchinson-Allen bill lost 147–226, with most Republicans voting for it but almost all Democrats voting against or present. Hutchinson responded to the defeat in typically upbeat manner: "What a great experience. I got an education worth three terms up here in the last six months. There's nothing like participating in debate to sharpen your parliamentary skills. I believe we had the right side. It doesn't get me down when I lose on something I believe in."

Hutchinson also played a mediating role on impeachment. Early on, as Democrats angrily turned the hearings partisan, he, Lindsey Graham and Ed Pease began meeting with Democrats William Delahunt and Howard Berman to see if they could reach some common ground. Not too much was found. But Hutchinson in his statements on the committee and on television struck a positive, open-minded, even friendly tone that was sharply in contrast with much of the discourse on the issue.

In the 1998 election, Hutchinson's only opponent was Ralph Forbes, former member of the American Nazi Party and the National Socialist White People's Party, who sued Arkansas Public Broadcasting for excluding him from a 1992 debate and, in a well-argued case, lost in the Supreme Court. Hutchinson won with 81% and seems to have a safe seat.

Cook's Call. *Safe.* Hutchinson's role as a House manager during the impeachment trial of

President Clinton has put this once low-profile member into the national spotlight and earned him the ire of national and local Democrats. Watch for Democrats to make a lot of noise here but don't expect a turnover, particularly without Clinton on the top of the ticket. What may be more important politically is that this is the fastest growing district in the state and is likely to become geographically smaller after the 2001 redistricting.

The People: Pop. 1990: 589,523; 49.4% rural; 16.3% age 65 +; 95.9% White, 1.6% Black, 1% Asian, 1.2% Amer. Indian, 0.4% Other; 1.1% Hispanic Origin. Households: 62.8% married couple families; 28.5% married couple fams. w. children; 35.7% college educ.; median household income: $21,903; per capita income: $10,876; median house value: $49,000; median gross rent: $248.

1996 Presidential Vote

Dole (R)	110,457	(45%)
Clinton (D)	107,096	(44%)
Perot (I)	22,976	(9%)
Others	4,419	(2%)

1992 Presidential Vote

Clinton (D)	109,111	(43%)
Bush (R)	107,351	(42%)
Perot (I)	35,991	(14%)

Rep. Asa Hutchinson (R)

Elected 1996; b. Dec. 3, 1950, Gravette; home, Fort Smith; Bob Jones U., B.S. 1972, U. of AR, J.D. 1975; Baptist; married (Susan).

Professional Career: U.S. Atty., AR Western Dist., 1982–85; Practicing atty., 1986–96; AR Repub. Party Chmn., 1990–95.

DC Office: 1535 LHOB 20515, 202-225-4301; Fax: 202-225-5713; Web site: www.house.gov/hutchinson.

District Offices: Fayetteville, 501-442-5258; Fort Smith, 501-782-7787; Harrison, 870-741-6900.

Committees: *Government Reform* (17th of 24 R): Civil Service (Vice Chmn.); Criminal Justice, Drug Policy & Human Resources. *Judiciary* (14th of 21 R): Crime; The Constitution. *Transportation & Infrastructure* (25th of 41 R): Aviation; Water Resources & Environment.

Group Ratings

	ADA	ACLU	AFS	LCV	CON	NTU	NFIB	COC	ACU	NTLC	CHC
1998	5	19	0	23	33	50	93	94	92	89	83
1997	10	—	14	—	45	58	—	90	88	—	—

National Journal Ratings

	1997 LIB — 1997 CONS			1998 LIB — 1998 CONS		
Economic	0%	—	90%	41%	—	59%
Social	36%	—	64%	13%	—	87%
Foreign	0%	—	88%	7%	—	83%

Key Votes of the 105th Congress

1. Clinton Budget Deal	Y	5. Puerto Rico Sthood. Ref.	N	9. Cut $ for B-2 Bombers	N
2. Education IRAs	Y	6. End Highway Set-asides	*	10. Human Rights in China	N
3. Req. 2/3 to Raise Taxes	Y	7. School Prayer Amend.	Y	11. Withdraw Bosnia Troops	Y
4. Fast-track Trade	*	8. Ovrd. Part. Birth Veto	Y	12. End Cuban TV-Marti	N

Election Results

1998 general	Asa Hutchinson (R)	154,780	(81%)	($296,736)
	Ralph Forbes (Ref)	36,917	(19%)	
1998 primary	Asa Hutchinson (R)	unopposed		
1996 general	Asa Hutchinson (R)	137,093	(56%)	($366,628)
	Ann Henry (D)	102,994	(42%)	($441,734)
	Others	6,045	(2%)	

FOURTH DISTRICT

West from the Delta flatlands along the Mississippi River, where the water-soaked fields produce America's largest rice crop, across small cities with antique pasts like Pine Bluff and El Dorado, southern Arkansas runs west to the Ouachita Mountains and the border town of Texarkana, where the main street divides two states and Texan Ross Perot grew up five blocks west of Arkansas. This is the northwestern corner of the Deep South. There is still a large black population here, a reminder that parts of southern Arkansas were once plantation country; there is also oil production, a reminder that this is the beginning of the Southwest. The broiler chicken industry looms large in these parts, and the accent is clearly Arkansan: El Dorado, Nevada and Lafayette are all pronounced with long As and penultimate syllable accents, and Ouachita is, with a bow to the original French, *waSHEEta*. The district also includes the little railroad-crossing, county seat town of Hope, where President Bill Clinton and his first White House Chief of Staff Mack McLarty were classmates at Miss Mary's kindergarten, and where Arkansas's Governor Mike Huckabee grew up a decade later, and Hot Springs, the spa resort and gambling haven where Bill Clinton's stepfather sold Buicks, his mother bet on the horses, and he excelled in high school as he began his climb from southern Arkansas to world eminence.

The 4th Congressional District occupies almost all of the southern geographical half of Arkansas, from the Mississippi River to the Ouachita Mountains, the Delta to Texarkana. It is historically a Democratic district, and one which for most of this century has elected a young man to the House and kept him there for years, to cut deals with the Democratic leadership and bring home the bacon. For a while in the 1990s it had a very different congressional politics: bipartisan, with rancorous debates on national issues followed by narrow election victories. But now it seems to have gone back to the old tradition, except now with a Republican.

The congressman from the 4th District is Jay W. Dickey, a Republican first elected in 1992. He replaced Beryl Anthony, head of the Democratic Congressional Campaign Committee and member of Ways and Means. Dickey is from Pine Bluff, where his uncle and grandfather were both state senators; he caught polio in 1960, but recovered and became a top college tennis player and runs 5K races today. Practicing law in Pine Bluff, Dickey represented the Arkansas Fox and Coon Hunters Association challenging state restrictions on running dogs; he won the case in the Arkansas Supreme Court and there are no restrictions on the running of dogs in Arkansas today. In the 1970s and 1980s, Dickey ran Baskin Robbins and Taco Bell franchises and formed an advertising sign company and a travel agency. He won the ordinarily worthless Republican nomination in 1992, then profited from a Democratic schism: Anthony, despite spending $1 million, lost the primary 51%–49% to Secretary of State Bill McCuen. Dickey attacked McCuen for a $324,000 no-bid contract on computers for his office; McCuen countered by charging that Dickey's pro-life views meant he condoned incest. Dickey won 52%–48%.

In the House, Dickey has a mostly conservative voting record and, with seats on Agriculture and Small Business, has worked on district projects. He sponsored a crime bill to allow flogging of prisoners and to remove color televisions and other "conveniences" from prisons. In 1994, he again faced a Democratic insider, state Senator Jay Bradford, who raised as much as Dickey. With majorities from the bigger towns, Dickey won again 52%–48%. In 1996, he had it easier. His opponent was Vincent Tolliver, a 28-year-old paralegal and poet recently returned from

California. In his opening statement in their first debate, Tolliver started by, in the words of *Roll Call*, chanting lines from the poem Maya Angelou wrote for the first Clinton inauguration, then added lines of his own, accusing Dickey of the "morals of a stray cat in a discarded alley," attacking "poorly-managed Taco Bells" he owned, and calling on him to resign. "That's the longest minute-and-a-half I've ever endured," Dickey replied. "I'm not going to resign." In fact he was re-elected 64%–36%, carrying every county.

Dickey moved to the Appropriations Committee in his second term, and seems to have devoted most of his considerable energies to getting federal projects for the disrict—$13 million for the National Center for Toxicological Research in Jefferson, $1.5 million from the Office of Minority Health for the University of Arkansas at Pine Bluff medicine and pharmacy programs. He complained when the Clinton Administration wouldn't accept the state Game and Fish Commission offer to keep national wildlife reserves open during the government shutdown for deer hunting and fishing. He is fighting to save 138 jobs at the Pine Bluff Arsenal threatened by the Pentagon's Quadrennial Defense Review.

His great project is building as much of I-69 as possible. The idea is to extend that highway, which now goes no farther south than Indianpolis, southwest through Kentucky, Tennessee, Mississippi, Arkansas, Louisiana, and Texas, to make it a Canada-to-Mexico freeway. Most of the areas it would serve are lightly populated; but every Southern politician knows that almost all growth in the region comes in counties with interstates. To put as much of I-69 as possible into Arkansas, Dickey proposed "the Dickey split"—one part of the road would cross the Mississippi at Memphis and another in the Mississippi Delta, to converge near the lucky town of Monticello. To this Senator Trent Lott of Mississippi asserts unovercomeable objections. Yet Dickey persisted. Getting one mile of I-69 in southeast Arkansas "is worth dying for, politically," he said. In May 1998, the Senate irrevocably rejected the Dickey split. The next day, Dickey went to Lott with a request for a $100 million interstate-quality spur from Monticello to Pine Bluff, where an existing interstate-quality highway heads to Little Rock. He also enlisted Transportation Secretary Rodney Slater, who hails from an eastern Arkansas town that would have been on the Dickey split. In October 1998, Lott capitulated and Dickey got his $100 million road.

Dickey has been a thorn in leadership's side in other ways. Newt Gingrich once cancelled a fundraiser for him when he refused to support a spending bill. He doesn't take PAC contributions. And he was the only Republican who voted for the Democrats' impeachment hearing resolution in October 1998: "I wanted so badly for us to have a bipartisan effort in this matter. I was surprised when I didn't see more of my colleagues join me."

Dickey has not had statewide ambitions, though for seven days in June 1996, when Senate candidate Mike Huckabee announced he was running for governor instead, he thought of running for the Senate. And he supported his former wife, Pine Bluff Prosecuting Attorney Betty Dickey, when she switched parties and ran for attorney general in 1998 (she lost to Democrat Mark Pryor). In 1998, he had stronger opposition than in 1996. State Representative Judy Smith ran a vigorous campaign, hitting Dickey for Medicare "cuts." She criticized Dickey for getting a $3 million study of beach erosion in Ludington, Michigan, where he owns a cottage; he moved to cancel the study the next day. Dickey ran ads featuring blacks and bragged of his support for a football stadium for the University of Arkansas at Pine Bluff. Dickey won 58%–42%. Smith carried the black-majority counties on the Mississippi River and ran about even in Pine Bluff and a circle of counties around Texarkana. But Dickey carried Hot Springs and El Dorado by 2–1 margins. Democrats may make a serious challenge in 2000, although they will have to take on the father of Arkansas's I-69.

Cook's Call. *Potentially Competitive.* This once was one of the more solidly Democratic districts in the South, but Democrats have come up short in each attempt to reclaim it since losing it in 1992. It is hard to gauge if Dickey has sunk deep political roots here given his lack of strong challengers over the past two elections. If Democrats do field a strong candidate (and avoid a messy primary) they could put this seat in play.

The People: Pop. 1990: 585,202; 52.2% rural; 17% age 65 + ; 72.4% White, 26.6% Black, 0.2% Asian, 0.4% Amer. Indian, 0.3% Other; 0.8% Hispanic Origin. Households: 57.4% married couple families; 26.9% married couple fams. w. children; 29.6% college educ.; median household income: $19,621; per capita income: $9,723; median house value: $40,400; median gross rent: $195.

1996 Presidential Vote			1992 Presidential Vote		
Clinton (D)	126,896	(60%)	Clinton (D)	134,692	(57%)
Dole (R)	66,034	(31%)	Bush (R)	73,891	(31%)
Perot (I)	15,972	(8%)	Perot (I)	23,677	(10%)

Rep. Jay W. Dickey (R)

Elected 1992; b. Dec. 14, 1939, Pine Bluff; home, Pine Bluff; Hendrix Col., 1958, U. of AR, B.A. 1961, J.D. 1963; Methodist; divorced.

Professional Career: Small business & franchise owner; Practicing atty., 1963–92; Pine Bluff City Atty., 1968–70.

DC Office: 2453 RHOB 20515, 202-225-3772; Fax: 202-225-1314; Web site: www.house.gov/dickey.

District Offices: Hot Springs, 501-623-5800; Pine Bluff, 870-536-3376.

Committees: *Appropriations* (19th of 34 R): Agriculture, Rural Development, & FDA; Defense; Labor, HHS & Education.

Group Ratings

	ADA	ACLU	AFS	LCV	CON	NTU	NFIB	COC	ACU	NTLC	CHC
1998	5	13	11	8	26	51	100	94	96	97	100
1997	5	—	25	—	9	53	—	80	88	—	—

National Journal Ratings

	1997 LIB — 1997 CONS		1998 LIB — 1998 CONS	
Economic	24% —	73%	0% —	88%
Social	10% —	82%	28% —	71%
Foreign	0% —	88%	7% —	83%

Key Votes of the 105th Congress

1. Clinton Budget Deal	Y	5. Puerto Rico Sthood. Ref.	N	9. Cut $ for B-2 Bombers	N
2. Education IRAs	Y	6. End Highway Set-asides	Y	10. Human Rights in China	N
3. Req. 2/3 to Raise Taxes	Y	7. School Prayer Amend.	Y	11. Withdraw Bosnia Troops	Y
4. Fast-track Trade	Y	8. Ovrd. Part. Birth Veto	Y	12. End Cuban TV-Marti	N

Election Results

1998 general	Jay W. Dickey (R)	92,346	(58%)	($842,243)
	Judy Smith (D)	68,194	(42%)	($316,927)
1998 primary	Jay W. Dickey (R)	unopposed		
1996 general	Jay W. Dickey (R)	125,956	(64%)	($452,572)
	Vincent Tolliver (D)	72,391	(36%)	

CALIFORNIA

California, long the great laboratory of America, the place where things—both good and bad—always seemed to happen first, is now moving off into uncharted territory of its own. Its leads the world in sophisticated high technology and it trails almost every other state in the nation in elementary and secondary education. It has generated an economy of enormous productivity but, as the recession of the early 1990s showed, not one impervious to shock. Its successful citizens by the hundreds of thousands have accumulated wealth beyond any historic predecent, and most of its people enjoy an impressive affluence; but only a few minutes ride away on the freeway are neighborhoods which closely resemble the Third World countries from which their residents recently came. Long proud of its efficient and incorruptible government, California has seen it grow larger and increasingly dysfunctional, as documented by California's greatest reporter, Lou Cannon, in his book *Official Negligence*, the definitive story of the Rodney King beating, the Los Angeles riot and the trials that followed. A country-sized state, with a larger percentage of the nation's population than any state since New York in the 1870s, California is optimistic about its own future, but is uncertain whether it is still the harbinger of the future it has been for most of the last half of the 20th Century.

California has recovered economically from the recession of the 1990s, but it has not re-covered its sense of confidence from the disasters of that period—the Loma Prieta earthquake in the San Francisco Bay area in October 1989, the Central Valley floods in early 1991, the Los Angeles riot following the acquittal of policemen accused of beating Rodney King in May 1992, the Malibu fires of September 1992, the Northridge earthquake of January 1994, the O.J. Simpson case, from the murder in June 1994 to the acquittal in October 1995. Less spectacu-larly, California lost many of its leading institutions in those years. The aerospace companies, which had done so much to produce America's victory in the Cold War, shut down factories and technical centers, and many were merged out of existence. California-based big businesses lost their identity through mergers with out-of-state firms—the department store chain Carter Hawley Hale, oil companies like Unocal and (proposed in early 1999) Arco, as well as defense contractors like Hughes and Lockheed. The big Los Angeles banks—Security Pacific, First Interstate—were sold to outsiders, so that the biggest Los Angeles area banks are owned by Japanese firms or ethnic Chinese; the Bank of America, whose branches are speckled all over California, saw its headquarters moved from California Street in San Francisco to Tryon Street in Charlotte, North Carolina. In the process California has lost much of its old Republican business elite. And the elites in the many relatively small firms of California's surging indus-tries, entertainment and computers, are almost uniformly cultural liberals who, heavily suspi-cious of the religious right and uncritical of Bill Clinton's transgressions, are largely Democrats, and generous Democratic contributors.

National media and the *Los Angeles Times* headlined California's troubles and said little about its recovery. Few of the small businesses that generated California's growth, except perhaps a few computer firms, got much notice nationally or at home. As a result, California has not recovered the national esteem it enjoyed from the 1940s through the 1980s, when the state was looked to as a national leader. Like President Clinton, whom most Californians sup-ported vehemently during the scandal stories and impeachment hearings of 1998–99, California is respected by the rest of the nation, but not admired.

And California itself was changing: From 1990–98 net outmigration from California to other states was 2 million; net inmigration into California from other countries was 2.1 million. In the 1980s, conservative-minded Anglos had been leaving the Los Angeles Basin and the San Francisco Bay Area for the Central Valley and the foothills of the Sierras, where population

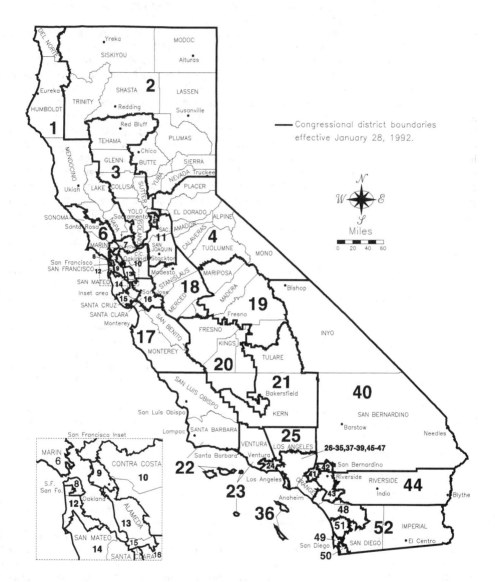

Congressional district boundaries
effective January 28, 1992.

grew rapidly and voting patterns became more Republican—one reason why Republicans won every gubernatorial race from 1982–94. But in the 1990s, the conservative-minded Anglos tended to leave California altogether, some for the Pacific Northwest, many more for the intermountain states of Nevada, Arizona, Colorado, Utah, Idaho and even Montana. All but two of those states had Democratic governors in 1990, and all have Republican governors now, while California in 1998 shifted in the opposite direction.

Meanwhile, as immigrants became citizens and moved into the voting stream, they veered toward the Democrats. Asians in 1992 and 1994 tended to vote Republican: a reaction perhaps to the Los Angeles riot and the fact that civic leaders seemed determined to propitiate blacks and seemed uninterested in helping the Koreans and other Asians who lost their life's work to the rioters. But in 1998, they voted more than 2–1 for Gray Davis for governor and even cast a majority against Matt Fong in the race for senator. The more numerous Hispanics moved heavily away from the Republicans. This is usually ascribed to Republican Governor Pete Wilson's support in 1994 for Proposition 187, which denied non-emergency state government aid to illegal aliens and their children. Others add that Latinos resented Republicans' support in 1996 for Proposition 209, which bans state government racial quotas and preferences, and in June 1998 for Proposition 227, which would have effectively ended bilingual education in California schools. But the issue is a little more complicated than that. One-third or more of Latinos voted for 187, 209 and 227, and Wilson was careful to underscore that it was aimed at illegal, not legal, immigrants—a distinction widely understood by Californians.

But Wilson's ads picturing Mexicans running across the border and proclaiming, "They just keep coming!" was taken as a slur, suggesting that all Latinos were more interested in welfare than work, which stung all the more because it is simply not true—Hispanic males have the highest work force participation rate of any measured group. And Republican firebrand Robert Dornan's challenge in 1997 of Loretta Sanchez's 984-vote victory over him in an Orange County congressional district, heavily publicized on Spanish-language television, was taken as a sign that Republicans did not want Latinos to vote, though Dornan insisted he was just challenging non-citizens' votes. The Latino vote increased from 10% of the vote in 1994 to 14% in 1998, and Gray Davis beat Republican Dan Lungren among Hispanics by 78%–16%— a huge drop for Republicans, since Wilson got almost 40% of the Latino vote in 1990.

Since more than 25% of California's residents, and more than 40% of its schoolchildren are Hispanic, the trend is auspicious for Democrats and ominous for Republicans. As Republican analyst Bernd Schwieren points out, these changes make a huge difference: if you take the 1988 presidential results, and use the same ethnic percentages for the candidates but adjust the results by the 1988–98 changes in ethnic participation, a 4% Republican victory turns into a 2% Republican defeat. California Republicans hope that George W. Bush, if nominated for president, can duplicate here in 2000 the appeal he showed in Texas where he won nearly half the Latino vote in 1998. Perhaps, but Republicans otherwise have few ideas on how to get themselves out of this hole they dug themselves.

These are important trends nationally, because California just by itself is important: it has 12% of the nation's population, 52 congressional districts and 54 electoral votes. If Republicans cannot carry California for president, as they did in every election but one from 1960 to 1988, they will have a hard time winning; if Democrats can count on California, as they have since 1960 on New York, they can concentrate time and resources on other more marginal states. But California is no longer typical of anywhere else. Two-thirds of America's Hispanics live in six states: in two of the other five, Texas and Florida, Republicans have competed successfully for their votes; in the three others, Illinois, New York and New Jersey, the Hispanic vote is not large enough to shift elections. No state has a public school system which has so spectacularly deteriorated, nor media which, with a very few exceptions, so totally ignore news of government and politics; a January 1999 survey by the Annenberg School of Communications found that only 0.31% of news time on local newscasts in all California markets covered the 1998 race for governor.

But if California is increasingly atypical of the country, there are also continuities with its past. For California has always been a place of economic vitality and personal creativity, settled by people from odd corners of the nation and the globe, who have transformed this once almost entirely empty land into arguably the most prosperous and creative place on earth, through hard work and intelligence and luck, sometimes helped by big government and big business. The Gold Rush of 1849 transformed San Francisco from nothing to a great city in just a year, and the Southern Pacific Railroad, the agribusinesses controlling vast chunks of the Central Valley and the architects of the great water engineering projects, created a framework in which individuals could work, innovate and prosper, inventing their own technologies and lifestyles. California grew from scratch to 7 million people by World War II, still an "island," as Carey McWilliams said, separated from the rest of the country. Then in World War II California became one of the great defense industry states, building ships and airplanes by the thousands. Millions of Americans came here and millions stayed. California's future was planned by the heads of the big units of government and business—Franklin Roosevelt and Henry J. Kaiser, who built vast shipyards and steel and aluminum factories, Governor Earl Warren, who husbanded tax monies to build schools and freeways in the years after the war, Robert Sproul and Clark Kerr, who built the University of California into what Kerr called "the multiversity," Governor Pat Brown, who completed the vast system of canals and aqueducts that brought water from the wet north to the thirsty south. But the real engine of growth was the little people who took advantage of this infrastructure and built a humming economy on it. When California's defense plants closed down after World War II, leaders imagined that hundreds of thousands would have to head back east. Instead, as urbanologist Jane Jacobs points out, one-eighth of all the new jobs in the nation in the late 1940s were created in metro Los Angeles. This small scale growth, multiplied thousands of times over, made California into the nation's most populous state by 1963.

Today there are 32.5 million Californians. Greater Los Angeles, with 15.5 million people, is the nation's second largest metropolitan area, not far behind New York's 17.3 million and well ahead of Chicago's 8.5 million; San Francisco, with 6.6 million, is fourth. And they owe their current preeminence not to natural advantage but to human ingenuity. Los Angeles, with no natural resources and no natural harbor, is the nation's leading manufacturer and port, as well as the world's entertainment center. San Francisco, which once lived by exporting food, is now the world's leader in computers and high-tech. California has grown not because it had to but because people wanted it to.

All the while California attracted newcomers—until 1965, almost all Americans; after 1965 slowly, at first invisibly, immigrants, mostly from Latin America and the Pacific Rim. California schools in the post-World War II years taught the basics and inculcated students in mainstream American culture, readying them for the rapidly growing network of universities and community colleges and for an expanding and increasingly high-skill private sector. But California's leaders in the years from the Watts riot of 1965 through the Los Angeles riot of 1992 have followed a different path. As affluent families withdrew their children into suburban enclaves or private schools, conservative elites were content to let school funding drop and liberal elites were content to turn over the education system to teachers' unions. "Multicultural" policies slotted newcomers into quota-fed monocultural enclaves in schools, universities, and big corporations. Public schools, with the pace set by teachers' unions, held students in "bilingual" Spanish-speaking programs long past the age when it is easiest to learn English—a policy finally outlawed when voters approved Proposition 227 in June 1998. The state education department pushed the education school nostrum "whole language," which left a generation unable to read or write standard English at levels acceptable in advanced workplaces—a mistake, the then-state superintendent later admitted, which shortchanged 5 million students. Civil liberties-minded legislators hobbled the criminal justice system, leaving teenage gangs to rule large swathes of central cities. Many of the newcomers prospered anyway. Nothing could keep the Asians down, not even the racial quotas which limited rather than increased their places at select high schools and universities. And many Latinos struggled successfully to move out on the freeways and up into the working middle class, ignoring the spoils-demanding politicians who claimed to speak in their name and the liberals' concentration on unionizing farm worker jobs that machines have rendered obsolete. Politicians have followed behind. The new Assembly speaker, Antonio Villaraigosa, is moving away from the leftish politics of most Latino legislators and toward the moderate programs of Governor Davis. And in Oakland, run for nearly two decades by leftish black politicians, rebellion has taken the form of the election in 1998 of former Governor Jerry Brown as mayor and the March 1999 victory of Green Party candidate Audie Bock in an Assembly race over Brown's predecessor.

Davis's election, and his moderate course in his first months as governor, may be the beginning of a moderate consensus replacing the clash and conflict between a liberal-left Democratic legislature on the one hand and a Republican governor or voters acting through referenda on the other—a conflict that characterized most of the years from 1978, when property-tax-cutting Proposition 13 was passed over Governor Jerry Brown's opposition, to the election in 1998 of Davis—who, interestingly, was Brown's chief of staff. That balance was never entirely stable: Governor George Deukmejian was first elected in 1982 by 1% and Governor Pete Wilson in 1990 by 3%; and Willie Brown, Assembly speaker from 1980–95 and now mayor of San Francisco, needed all of his political wiles and talents to maintain legislative control. The Republican executives set the tone, but Brown and Democratic legislators often surreptitiously set the policies, furthering the causes of their clients—teachers' unions, trial lawyers and the criminal defense bar. A consequence was government by referendum, usually a clumsy matter but sometimes effective, on criminal justice, aid to immigrants, racial quotas and preferences and the like. Another result was tax increases just as the recession hit, all proposed by politicians California voted for: George Bush's budget summit in 1990, Pete Wilson's state tax hikes in 1991, Bill Clinton's budget and tax package of 1993. California's nominal incomes (and living costs) are higher than the rest of the country's, and many more people are self-employed or own small businesses, so these soak-the-rich measures were really soak-California.

Yet as the prophets were crying doom, California's economy was recovering, as vibrantly as ever but in different form. No longer were big units, big corporations or big government leading the way; instead there was small unit growth. As Joel Kotkin of Pepperdine University pointed out, California's knowledge-intensive industries were growing vigorously—telecommunications, biomedical research, computer software, medical equipment, entertainment, international trade. Small factories humming quietly in squat stucco buildings in the Los Angeles Basin made California the world's leading manufacturing center, with huge production of apparel, furniture, computer equipment. In the Bay Area, vast numbers of small computer and high-tech companies spawn and grow lustily, financed by the world's largest concentration of sophisticated venture capital. Increasingly, Californians were "wired workers," busy at computers, either for small companies with flexible management, or often working for themselves at home. The Central Valley, long the home of the nation's largest and most productive farms, is now also growing industry, both high- and low-tech. Fueling this process are immigrants. Even as more Californians left for other states than people from other states left for California, starting in the recession year of 1990, the flow of immigrants continued steadily, from 217,000 to 269,000 every year from 1990 to 1998. Their contribution, seldom heralded by the press, is vast. One-third of Silicon Valley engineers are immigrants; most Orange County technicians are Vietnamese; immigrants from Korea, Iran, Armenia and Israel are upgrading inner Los Angeles neighborhoods. And for only four years, from 1992–96, was the total migration figure negative; California is once again growing, though not as rapidly as in the 1980s.

As in the days of heavy immigration early in the century, there have been clashes and discord. But the assumption, voiced years ago by Willie Brown, that "people of color" would form a Third World majority, a united proletariat ready to end white oppression, has not been proven out. Instead, Californians asserting the value of traditional American values and folkways have prevailed, sometimes through sharp political conflict, to the point that Gray Davis in 1998 and 1999 could plausibly claim to represent a widespread consensus and argue that further divisions are unnecessary. The battle over racial quotas and preferences, condemned in Proposition 209 in 1996, came in the wake of the O.J. Simpson murder trial, in which large majorities of blacks considering him innocent while even larger majorities of non-blacks—including Hispanics and Asians—thought him guilty. But this polarization cannot be explained as a response to poverty or political powerlessness. California blacks' incomes are well above the national black average; residential integration in much of California is the norm, and the big growth in black population is in prosperous neighborhoods in southwest Los Angeles. Politically blacks have had more power than their numbers, for they are only 7% of the state's population, 11% in Los Angeles County, and yet the mayor of Los Angeles for 20 years and the Assembly speaker for 15 years were black, as are a disproportionate number of state legislators; blacks were elected to statewide office by 1970. The separate mindset symbolized by reactions to Simpson was less the result of overt racism by whites than of the separateness in universities, government employment and the corporate sector which is the proximate result of racial quotas: the natural reaction of those who are stigmatized as inferior and in need of help to turn aside from the larger society. Nor did the abolition of quotas and preferences enforce racial segregation on California's state universities, as was widely predicted. In 1999 they admitted almost exactly the same number of blacks as they had before quotas, with the difference that none entered with the stigma of inferiority which any quota system imposes on its intended beneficiaries.

As for Latinos and Asians—two large categories which contain many very different subgroups—they have been poorly served by the civil rights paradigm which sees the central problem as discrimination and the central remedy as government-imposed quotas. Latinos have been badly served by an education system that lost its capacity to teach basic skills and insists on holding pupils back in Spanish—in vivid contrast to the public schools earlier in this century which helped immigrants' children enter the mainstream. Asians were badly served by quotas which fenced them off from opportunity. A greater problem results from the withdrawal of the affluent into gated subdivisions and distant suburbs, especially in greater Los Angeles, which has created a sense of isolation and separateness on all sides. Vast tracts of city and suburb, once peopled by migrants from the Midwest, are now filled with newcomers from Mexico and Korea, El Salvador and Taiwan, Iran and Armenia; young men stand on street corners in affluent areas from dawn, mutely looking for work, sometimes staying all day. It is against this background that Davis could campaign in 1998 for an end to controversy and confrontation, for the sogginess of his rhetoric was underpinned by the crunchiness of the rules which his political rivals and California voters wisely insisted on.

Davis's smashing 58%–38% victory produced the first Democratic governor in 16 years and may produce an end to the upheaval and political controversies of the 1990s. In effect Davis won heavy margins among two groups of voters which were miniscule 10 years before, but are growing toward making a majority now—"wired workers" and immigrants. The recession of the early 1990s and George Bush's seeming indifference to it, produced an across-the-board Democratic victory in 1992, when Bill Clinton carried California 46%–33%. Democrats down the line won as well, carrying the House vote 52%–41% and winning several districts they had not expected. Democrats Dianne Feinstein and Barbara Boxer won the state's two Senate seats in "the year of the woman" (Feinstein won the remaining two years of Pete Wilson's term). In 1994, Clinton's support slumped here, but not nearly as much as nationally, as he visited frequently and tended carefully to state crises and disasters. Wilson, who had been far down in the polls, responded by stressing his support of capital punishment, which was opposed by his Democratic opponent, state Treasurer Kathleen Brown. And he complained loudly about the billions the state was forced to spend on services to illegal aliens and endorsed Proposition 187. Wilson won 55%–41%, as 187 passed by an even wider margin; Republicans edged Democrats in House races 49%–48%. Feinstein prevailed over Republican Congressman Michael Huffington by only 47%–45% in what was then the most expensive Senate campaign in history. Republicans won most statewide offices for the first time since 1966.

The wheel turned again in 1996 and 1998. Clinton carried California over Bob Dole, 51%–38%—the same 13% margin by which he had beaten Bush four years before. But in much of the state the Clinton percentage margin fell, as some Perot voters moved back to the Republican column. Where the Clinton percentage margin increased was in areas with many Latino voters, who favored him 71%–20% over Dole and who turned out in significantly larger numbers than in 1992, partly because of Clinton Administration efforts to speed up naturalization of immigrants, partly because of delayed reaction to Proposition 187 and to the Republican-passed (though Clinton-signed) 1996 welfare reform which cut off aid to legal immigrants. Ironically, it was mostly Republicans (though also some Democrats, notably California's Howard Berman) who prevented Congress from reducing legal immigration; and it was the Democratic administration, building upon the El Paso programs of U.S. Border Patrol agent Silvestre Reyes (now a Democratic Congressman from Texas), which deployed many more INS agents on the border and cut down the illegal migration across the border in California which Wilson's 1994 ads decried. But this was not an unalloyed victory for the political left. Clinton's total was a bare majority, and he lost the Central Valley—indeed all of California outside the Bay Area and Los Angeles County—to Dole. Democratic legislative candidates led Republicans, but by narrower margins than in 1992, 50%–45% for the House, 50%–46% for the Assembly. In 1998 Democrats won stunning victories at the top of the ticket. Gray Davis's 20% margin was reminiscent of those of Ronald Reagan in 1966 and Pat Brown in 1958, and Republicans were able to hold on narrowly to only two statewide offices. Senator Barbara Boxer, elected with a 48%–43% plurality in 1992, this time beat lightly-funded Republican Matt Fong by 53%–43%. But Democrats only narrowly bettered their showing in legislative elections, to 51%–44% for the House and 52%–46% for the Assembly. The parties traded two House seats in northern California; in the Assembly Democrats improved their majority from 43–37 to 48–32 by winning several close contests and taking advantage of demographic changes. Davis's success in bringing immigrants and wired workers into his coalition was echoed but not equalled by other Democrats.

Partisan divisions in California, even more than elsewhere, run along cultural rather than economic lines. Consider the results in the Boxer-Fong Senate race, in which the numbers were similar to the Clinton-Dole race two years before. Non-Hispanic whites voted 50%–46% for Fong over Boxer, while blacks favored Boxer 85%–13%, Hispanics 72%–23% and Asians 54%–44%. Religion, in this relatively secular state, was another sharp divider: for Fong were Protestants (59%–39%) and other Christians (50%–47%); for Boxer were Jews (81%–19%), those with other religions (62%–32%) and those with no religion (70%–26%). By education, those with graduate school degrees, who are so often unionized teachers, social workers and other government employees, went for Boxer (56%–41%), while college graduates were for Fong (50%–48%).

It is as if these groups of voters were living in different Californias. And to some considerable extent they are. The traditional division is between a San Francisco-dominated North and a Los Angeles-dominated South, but that makes little sense today when Los Angeles is leftish and Orange County conservative, or when San Francisco and the Central Valley seem to vote the opposite way on everything. Since the 1970s a more illuminating division has been between coastal and inland California. Coastal California, the big population gainer in the 1970s, tends toward cultural liberalism. The Big Sur coast or the Redwood Empire, San Francisco and Marin County or Westside Los Angeles—this is the political base of most Democrats. But go inland, even just a few miles, and the cultural climate changes as rapidly as the weather. This California is sunnier in summer, colder in winter, more arid. And from the Central Valley and the Sierra foothills to the San Ramon Valley, or the "Inland Empire" at the east end of the Los Angeles Basin around San Bernardino, Riverside and the desert beyond, this big growth area of the 1980s has attracted cultural conservatives. While coastal California protected itself

from growth with environmental restrictions, new subdivisions and factories and cities proliferated inland. Today's cultural politics turns partisan history on its head. The affluent coastal
counties were solidly Republican as late as the 1960s, while the dusty roads of the Central
Valley and the inland industrial suburbs were the heartland of the Democratic Party that carried
California for Lyndon Johnson in 1964. Another way to understand California is to divide the
state into four major political regions, each with about one-quarter of the voters, each of which
by itself would be one of the 10 largest states.

Los Angeles County. If no state is culturally more diverse than California, no county is
more diverse than Los Angeles County, which is to the America of the 1990s what New York
City was to the America of the 1910s: the great entry point for immigrants and the venue of
their rapid upward mobility. It is also inevitably, like New York, messy and disorganized, crime-
ridden (though crime rates are down) and anxiety-prone. Although there are some suburban
tracts here, Los Angeles County increasingly has taken on the function of a central city, but
not a population-losing industrial enclave, like most American central cities of the 1960s and
1970s, but a population-surging, economically vital immigrant metropolis. Los Angeles now,
like New York then, is the starting point not only of the immigrant but of the small-time
entrepreneur—often the same person—who starts a small business in a garage, hires people
newly-arrived into town, sells products out of a van, and makes enough money to expand the
business and buy a home. Low-lying stucco buildings all over the Los Angeles basin house
these businesses, run and staffed by Mexicans, Koreans, Vietnamese, Russian Jews, Armenians
and Iranians. This Los Angeles, like the great surging cities of the past—Dickens's London,
Balzac's Paris, Edith Wharton's New York and Theodore Dreiser's Chicago—is not a comfortable place. Traffic is choking; the air has a sour, burnt look. Housing is cramped, with most
people living in tightly-packed subdivisions or garden apartments on tiny plots of land that a
Midwesterner would find claustrophobic. Los Angeles County was hit hard by 1990s defense
cutbacks, the 1992 riot and the 1994 earthquake; but like New York after the panic of 1907
and the Triangle fire of 1911, it surges ahead.

Politically, Los Angeles County, like that New York of long ago, leans Democratic but is
subject to vast shifts of votes as new ethnic groups take—or change—their places. Unlike the
riot-torn cities of the 1960s, Los Angeles County is not headed toward black majorities; it was
11% black in 1990, with a large affluent black population and net outmigration among blacks.
The areas where blacks and recent Central American migrants rioted are demographically a
small part of LA County, far smaller than heavily Mexican East Los Angeles or affluent black
Baldwin Hills or the heavily Asian San Gabriel Valley. Los Angeles's boom, as Joel Kotkin
points out, is based less on big defense contractors than on small factories, less on highly visible
tenants of downtown office towers than on the self-employed, who are more numerous than
union members. After blacks, the most reliably Democratic bloc are Westside Jews, exceedingly
affluent by national standards, with political clout amplified by many Hollywood figures. In
national politics they are heavily Democratic, enraged by Bill Clinton's accusers and fearful of
the religious right; locally, they backed Republican Mayor Richard Riordan over leftish challenger Tom Hayden in 1997. Potentially a much larger constituency are Latinos, who were
moving mildly toward Republicans in the late 1980s but powerfully toward Democrats in the
late 1990s. Their turnout is still low, because so many are children or non-citizens, but it is
increasing: in 1996 one central Los Angeles Assembly district cast only 29,000 votes, but in
the offyear of 1998 it cast 26,800, almost as many. Latino voters were a key factor in Riordan's
re-election, voting about 60% for him over Hayden. Latinos have high rates of family formation
and work and low rates of divorce and (outside a few central neighborhoods) crime; in some
ways they resemble the white Anglo young families who voted for Pat Brown in 1958 and
Reagan in 1966, though the schools the education professionals and teachers' unions have
provided them are far inferior. Asians have moved around on the political spectrum. In 1992
and 1994 they voted narrowly Republican, presumably in reaction to civic leaders' sympathy
for rioters and indifference toward Asian storeowners; in 1996 and 1998 they voted narrowly

Democratic, perhaps because the Republican welfare bill cut off aid to legal aliens, including the many aged parents Asians had brought over and put on Supplemental Security Income. Los Angeles County voted solidly for Clinton in 1996, 59%–31%, better than his 53%–29% margin in 1992; it was 61%–36% for Boxer over Fong in 1998. But Proposition 209 lost here by only 54%–46%, as most Asians and a large number of Latinos voted against it.

Southern California. The rest of southern California outside Los Angeles County looks more like the Los Angeles of the 1940s: predominantly white, middle class, of Midwestern origin (if you go back a couple of generations). But it also has more Asians and Hispanics than East Coast experts usually imagine. Essentially, the old Los Angeles has grown out past the freeways into Orange County and the Inland Empire at the east end of the Los Angeles basin, and west out into the desert, past the San Fernando Valley into Ventura County, down south of San Juan Capistrano and Camp Pendleton, where it merges with fast-growing San Diego. Of these four major regions, this is now the most populous, casting 28% of the state's votes. Until the early 1990s southern California radiated the optimism, the somewhat innocent confidence and the know-how of its pioneers, contemporaries of its natural hero, Reagan, who came out here in hard times and created a new Middle America more tidy and square and cheerful than the original Middle America ever was. Now the mood seems more guarded, and changeable: in the 1990s southern California soured first on the Republicans for their indifference and next on the Democrats for their indiscipline. In 1992, southern California outside LA voted only 38%–35%–24% for Bush over Clinton and Perot. In 1994 it voted 68% for Proposition 187 and 65%–31% for Wilson over Brown. In 1996 it voted narrowly, 47%–42% for Bob Dole, but 63%–37% for Proposition 209. But it also voted narrowly for legalizing marijuana for medical purposes: it is more libertarian than culturally conservative. In 1998 it voted 51%–44% for Matt Fong, not the margin he needed; amazingly, it preferred Gray Davis to Dan Lungren by a 49%–47% margin.

San Francisco Bay Area. The Bay Area is affluent, preoccupied with the environment and with identity politics, not propelled by economic necessity. For years San Francisco and much of the Bay Area has attracted those who felt their personal lifestyles were not accepted elsewhere or who relished the atmosphere of counter-culture and revolt that has roots here in the turn-of-the-century artists and writers and the Beat Generation of the 1950s—gays and perpetual graduate students, radicals and perennial rebels. In recent years the population surge has been to the south, in and around Silicon Valley; the new voters here are passionate techies, united by a hatred of Microsoft, inclined toward market economics but, repulsed by the Republicans' religious conservatism, eager to believe their views are shared by Democrats like Clinton and Davis. It has lots of voters with graduate degrees, who vote heavily Democratic: California's Democratic base is made up less of blacks and factory workers than it is of teachers, lawyers, nurses, environmental enthusiasts and public sector administrators. Once closely divided politically, the Bay Area is now so overwhelmingly Democratic that many campaigns don't bother to buy ads in the San Francisco media market. The Bay Area voted 55%–27% for Clinton in 1992, 63%–30% for Senator Dianne Feinstein when she nearly lost in 1994, 61%–28% for Clinton in 1996 and 64%–33% for Boxer in 1998; her margin would have been larger but for Fong's appeal to Asian-American voters (his mother was once a Democratic Assemblywoman from the East Bay).

The rest of California. Little attention is usually given to the rest of California, the relatively lightly populated coastal counties and the huge Central Valley. Yet 8 million people live here, more than in Georgia or Massachusetts, almost as many as Missouri and Minnesota put together; the media markets of Sacramento and Fresno in the Central Valley taken together would be the nation's eleventh largest. This is the most culturally conservative part of the state, though not nearly so much as the Midwest or South; many new residents are young families fleeing from the smog and crime of the Los Angeles basin to the cleaner and safer Central Valley or Mother Lode country or Sacramento area. Historically Democratic, this part of California trended against liberal Democrats in the 1980s. It voted narrowly for Clinton in 1992, 39%–36%, but was 61%–35% for Wilson in 1994. In 1996 it voted 46%–44% for Dole, and 50%–44% and 54%–41% for Republican House and Assembly candidates. It voted 63% for Proposition 209 and 52% against medical marijuana: middle America on the Pacific Rim. In 1998 it crossed lines, and voted for Davis 50%–45%, but it also delivered a 50%–45% margin for Fong; Boxer lost almost every county in the Central Valley.

Where is California headed? Economically, California seems headed for growth again; with its creativity, suppleness, Pacific Rim location and brains, it cannot be kept permanently down. Culturally, California seems to want both therapy and discipline, the right to dispense medical marijuana on a casual basis and the liberty to divorce and remarry frequently and to practice alternative lifestyles, but also stern punishment of criminals, strict enforcement of immigration laws and an end to racial quotas and preferences. In partisan terms, Democrats have a clear but not enormous advantage. They profited in 1998 from revulsion against the impeachment process, and from a desire, widespread in America, to get beyond the political clash and confrontations of the early 1990s and into some comfortable consensus. So long as Democrats remain reliably moderate—and in his first months as governor, Davis with steely discipline did so—they have a statewide advantage. They have a further advantage in that most California Republican politicos bring to mind Benjamin Disraeli's description of his fellow Conservatives as "the stupid party."

In all this it is important to keep in mind how invisible politics is in California. There is nothing here like the tabloid cultures of the East Coast, with their screaming headlines about the minutiae of local political feuds; California television stations present almost no news of politics or government at all, and the newspapers present leftish-biased coverage which most voters seem blithely to ignore. Much public policy has been made surreptitiously, especially by Democrats in the legislature; other important policies have been adopted by the clumsy yet sometimes effective device of initiative and referendum. Great success has come to politicians who, like Governors Pete Wilson and Gray Davis, have the art to present their message succinctly in the few moments when they have the voters' attention and the political insider skills to follow through on their promises or at least to not disappoint the voters' mild expectations too frontally. Davis and the Democrats, many of whom consider him a moderate squish, have the opportunity now to preside over a consensus which, much like that of British Prime Minister Tony Blair, has been forged by their conservative predecessors' willingness to risk confrontation and wage war on liberal shibboleths. It is the best opportunity American Democrats have, outside of Washington, to demonstrate that they can be a successful governing party—even if it is in a state whose achievements and challenges are increasingly idiosyncratic and atypical of the country of which they are the largest constituent part.

Governor. Gray Davis, elected governor in 1998, is only the fourth Democratic governor of California in this century (and only the second not named Brown). Davis grew up in Connecticut and, after age 11, in Los Angeles; he graduated from Stanford and Columbia Law School, then served in the Army in Vietnam, where he earned a Bronze Star. In 1969 he returned to California and almost immediately plunged into politics. In 1972 he worked on Tom Bradley's first successful campaign for mayor; in 1974, at 31, Davis ran for state treasurer, and lost the primary to former Speaker Jess Unruh. Later that year, he worked on Jerry Brown's successful campaign for governor, and in 1975 he became Brown's chief of staff. To the always improvisatory and provocative Brown, Davis was a balance wheel: well-organized, unflappable, propitiating conventional politicians and bureaucrats, learning the ways of the powers-that-be not only in Sacramento but across the state. When Brown launched into the 1982 Senate campaign which he lost to Pete Wilson, Davis moved to Westside Los Angeles and, pre-empting serious primary opposition, won a safe Democratic seat in the Assembly. There he served two terms as a conventional California liberal, during which he had surgery for removal of a benign brain tumor. No other state legislative seat in the country has as many big Democratic contributors, and Davis cultivated them tirelessly.

That enabled him to move from top-level staffer and Assembly insider to statewide office.

In 1986 he ran for controller, the one statewide position with significant patronage, and won; in 1990, when Attorney General John Van de Kamp and former San Francisco Mayor Dianne Feinstein slugged it out for the gubernatorial nomination (Feinstein eventually lost 49%–46% to Pete Wilson), Davis was cruising to re-election. In 1992 he made his one false step, running against Feinstein for the nomination for the last two years of Wilson's Senate term; he ran ads comparing Feinstein to convicted tax evader Leona Helmsley and enraged her and many feminists in the "year of the woman." He lost the primary 57%–33%. But in 1994 he recovered and ran for lieutenant governor. As in 1986, he chose his spot well. His fundraising capacity deterred other potentially strong candidates; his base in the liberal Westside was strong enough to allow him to take moderate positions on some issues, like supporting the death penalty; his braininess and knowledge of state government made him an eminently respectable choice for editorial writers and endorsement groups. He won the primary easily and, while Pete Wilson was beating Democrat Kathleen Brown by 55%–40%, Davis was elected by 52%–40% over little-known and poorly-financed Simi Valley state Senator Cathie Wright.

It was no secret that Davis was aiming to run to succeed the term-limited Wilson, with whom he had almost no relationship. Politics and government are everything to Davis: he and his wife live in a tiny West Hollywood apartment; he has never made large amounts of money and his taste for California social life is undetectable. It was widely thought also that he was unelectable—too boring and uncharismatic, many said, too gray. Two seemingly dazzling and self-financed candidates entered the Democratic primary. Former Northwest Airlines Co-Chairman Al Checchi, who boasts a net worth around $550 million, conducted a serious study of California government and called for striking education reforms; he was articulate, attractive (with a Spanish-speaking wife) and he spent more than $38 million on his campaign. And Congresswoman Jane Harman, after three terms representing the Los Angeles beachfront, decided to enter the race in March 1998 after Senator Dianne Feinstein, wary of another contest against Davis, declined to run in what would have been her fourth statewide campaign in eight years. Harman also spent freely of her own money and raised more to spend $20 million. She argued that as a woman she was better able to listen to Californians and understand their needs: a seemingly strong platform in a state where Democrats had not nominated a man for governor or senator in 10 years.

But Davis was able to take advantage of mistakes made by the big money candidates. In March Harman surged momentarily into a lead in the polls, and Checchi ran negative ads against her. The result was that both sank in the polls. But their candidacies had deeper flaws. Checchi had already run millions of dollars of ads proclaiming him the candidate of change, and presenting substantive programs for improving government. But California Democrats, in a pro-incumbent year and particularly after Bill Clinton was being threatened with impeachment for lying under oath about his affair with Monica Lewinsky, were interested not in making change but in preserving the status quo. And Harman, it quickly became apparent, despite her competence at dealing with issues in the House, was not well schooled in state government. Davis's slogan was "Experience money can't buy," which established his incumbent status and his knowledge of state government. And if he was heavily outspent by his rivals, he was able to use his Westside contacts to raise $10 million, an impressive amount in any context except this one. Davis had the forethought to save most of his money to run ads in the last weeks before the June primary, during which he was able to match his opponents' ad buys; indeed, amid the heavy spending by Checchi and Harman, and by Senator Barbara Boxer and Republican challengers Darrell Issa and Matt Fong and by candidates for statewide and legislative office, the TV stations almost ran out of time to sell. The result was a blowout victory for Davis: of the votes cast for Democrats, he won 58%, to 21% for Checchi and 20% for Harman.

Democrats, hungry for victory after 16 years of Republican governors, were happy to rejoice in Davis's victory; his mostly positive message had antagonized no one. But Davis had more going for him. Sensing the mood of the voters accurately, he had been calling for months to an end to the confrontations promoted by Republicans over issues like capital punishment, welfare for immigrants and racial quotas and preferences, and for an era of cooperation and amity: sogginess over crunchiness. He took some of these controversial issues off the table: although he had opposed Propositions 187, 209 and 227, he promised to respect the voters' choice and enforce them. Others he embraced: for years he had supported capital punishment, backed by some 80% of voters and the key issue in Pete Wilson's defeat of Kathleen Brown. Despite the fact that he had voted in the Assembly in lockstep with the teachers' unions, he proposed education reforms which, while crafted carefully to minimally annoy union leaders, still diverged from the liberal policies which had destroyed California's public schools. He joked about his lack of charisma, especially when welcoming Vice President Al Gore to the state, and emphasized at every turn his status as a Vietnam veteran.

Once again, Davis's shrewdness, his dogged preparation and his strategy over a very long haul enabled him to take advantage of the opposition's mistakes. The Republican nominee, not seriously opposed in the primary, was Dan Lungren, a congressman from 1978–88 and attorney general since 1990. Lungren has an outgoing personality, the aggressive friendliness of the California of the 1950s he grew up in, in the then-Middle American city of Long Beach, the son of Richard Nixon's doctor. In polls until midyear he ran roughly even with Davis and the other Democrats. But he did not adapt well to circumstances. Until well into October he emphasized the crime issue, and tried to argue that Davis was a closet liberal. But Davis's long record against capital punishment gave him little opening to do what Pete Wilson had done to Kathleen Brown. Lungren tried to portray Davis as a clone of Jerry Brown, who after three quixotic presidential campaigns was attracting attention as a candidate for mayor of Oakland. But Davis's differences on issues made this unpersuasive. Lungren ran few ads and talked little about education, which polls showed to be far and away the number one issue; so Davis, whose party had mostly run the public schools, was able to establish himself as the candidate who would reform them. Davis in the meantime dredged up old congressional votes and argued that Lungren was far to the right, and he emphasized his opposition to choice. About this Lungren could only say that as a believing Catholic he opposed abortion—not a good excuse for many voters in this increasingly secular state—and that the only relevant issues were parental consent and partial-birth abortions.

Davis won by the landslide margin of 58%–38%—a margin of the magnitude of George Deukmejian's 61%–37% in 1986, Jerry Brown's 56%–36% in 1978, Ronald Reagan's 58%–42% in 1966 and Pat Brown's 60%–40% in 1958. Davis carried the Bay Area 69%–28% and Los Angeles County by nearly as much, 66%–31%; he even carried the South 49%–47% and the rest of the state 50%–45%. Davis carried blacks with 83% of the vote, Hispanics with 78%, Asians with 67%, white women with 60% and even white men with 54%. Democrats increased their hold on the Assembly to 48–32 and on the state Senate to 25–15; California became only the second state (Hawaii is the other) with a Democratic governor, two Democratic senators, and a Democratic House delegation and a Democratic legislature. It was a victory as sweeping as that of Tony Blair's New Labour party in Britain in May 1997 and left Davis, like Blair, with a mandate to pursue conciliatory moderate policies not so far out of line as one might think with the confrontational policies of his increasingly inept conservative predecessors. He also came into office at a time when California's surging economy was producing budget surpluses—very different from the early 1990s, when Pete Wilson announced a $14 billion deficit.

Very much like Blair, Davis pledged to "govern neither from the left nor the right, but from the center." He continued to talk tough on crime and denied clemency and allowed the execution of double-murderer Jaturun Siripongs. Education he proclaimed as his "first, second and third" priorities. At his first meeting in 1995 of the California State University board of regents, on which he served ex officio as lieutenant governor, he was shocked to find that most students had to take remedial reading courses—to learn what California's public schools had failed to teach. Davis called a special session of the legislature and presented four bills—for peer review for teachers, enhanced reading instruction, a school-rating system and a standardized test for high schools. Democratic legislators watered them down and delayed some reforms until 2003 and 2004, but in March 1999 versions of all four were passed, and Davis claimed victory.

On the national level, he backed the House Republicans' EdFlex bill, arguing that California didn't need money to reduce class sizes for the first four grades—a Clinton targeted program—because it had just done so under a law Pete Wilson proposed and Davis backed; it needed the flexibility to spend money on classrooms for higher grades. At home he angered liberals by agreeing to phase out a gasoline additive backed by environmentalists and to support the flag burning amendment. He opposed a plan to renovate the Bay Bridge supported by Mayors Willie Brown and Jerry Brown as too expensive. He opposed trial lawyers' proposal to raise the cap on medical malpractice awards. He opposed gay marriage. He supported Wilson's reduction in car taxes and opposed taxes on Internet commerce. He agreed, against the angry protests of liberals, to allow a court of appeals to mediate over Proposition 187; he proposed a university admissions plan consistent with Proposition 209; he supported implementation of Proposition 227. Liberal legislators lay in wait, with bills to reward trial lawyers, teachers' unions and gays. But Davis seemed guided by conviction and, as always in his long political career, by a desire to be in line with the electorate in the next election. He said he would not accept the vice presidency if it were offered to him; his whole ambition was to be governor. His chances for re-election, more than three years out, looked good; mentioned as possible opponents were Insurance Commissioner Chuck Quackenbush and Secretary of State Bill Jones—the only two Republican statewide officials—and Congressman Tom Campbell and unsuccessful 1998 Senate candidate Darrell Issa.

Senior Senator. Dianne Feinstein was elected in 1992 with the most votes cast for a senator in U.S. history. She grew up in San Francisco, in lush Presidio Heights, went to Stanford and later studied criminology. She was appointed by Governor Pat Brown to the women's parole board in 1960, at 27. In 1969 she was elected to the San Francisco County Board of Supervisors—the city's council—and twice ran for mayor and lost. As president of the board, she became mayor when Mayor George Moscone and Supervisor Harvey Milk were murdered by former Supervisor Dan White; she discovered Moscone's body and showed steadiness and a sense of command that calmed the city. In 1984, Walter Mondale seriously considered her for vice president, but passed over her for Geraldine Ferraro because of qualms about the business dealings of her husband, Richard Blum. Feinstein presided gracefully that year over the Democratic National Convention in San Francisco—while Ferraro juggled questions about *her* family's business. In fact, Feinstein and Blum's investments have thrived; the Capitol Hill newspaper *Roll Call* estimated their net worth in 1999 at $50 million, the fifth highest in Congress.

Ineligible for a third full term in 1987, Feinstein ran for governor in 1990, won the Democratic primary impressively, then lost 49%–46% to Pete Wilson. When Wilson appointed Orange County state Senator John Seymour—an unknown and bland choice—to replace him in the Senate, Feinstein quickly announced for the seat, even though the 1992 race was for only the last two years of Wilson's term, and she could have run for the seat being vacated by Alan Cranston the same year. She had primary competition from Gray Davis, then state controller, who ran a spot against her campaign finance practices comparing her to Leona Helmsley; Feinstein won 58%–33%. In the general she faced appointed Senator John Seymour, who had just switched to pro-choice and anti-offshore oil drilling positions. Nothing worked for Seymour—not Feinstein's arguably tricky financing of her 1990 gubernatorial campaign (which resulted in a $190,000 fine), nor fears of immigration, nor Seymour's tending to agricultural interests. Feinstein won 54%–38%, coming close even in Seymour's southern California base.

California has a long tradition of having one senator who expresses ideological views and another who works hard to represent the state's economic interests. Feinstein chose the latter workhorse role, as did her predecessors Wilson, Cranston and Thomas Kuchel. She got a seat on Appropriations, where she could funnel money to California, and on Judiciary, where she was one of the women chosen by then-chairman Joseph Biden, who sought to spare himself the flak he got for allowing cross-examination of Anita Hill. Feinstein has a generally but not uniformly liberal voting record; she also has a tough, prosecutorial demeanor, and on the podium she can be one of the best speakers in American politics today. She has kept her distance from the Clinton Administration, negotiating for changes before voting for the 1993 budget, voting against NAFTA, withdrawing her support of the Clinton health care plan in May 1994, condemning Bill Clinton's "I did not have sexual relations with that woman, Miss Lewinsky" comment which she had witnessed in person.

In her first two years she had two major legislative achievements. One was the attachment of the assault weapons ban to the 1994 crime bill—good politics for her and many Democrats in metropolitan states, but a liability to Democrats in much of the West and South. When Idaho's Larry Craig argued that her definition of assault weapons was not rigorous enough and challenged her knowledge of firearms, she responded by saying: "I know something about what firearms can do; I came to be mayor of San Francisco as a product of assassination." Her other major achievement was a California Desert Protection Act. Similar measures had been stymied by the state's Republican senators as too restrictive, but now that there was no Republican senator, Feinstein managed it through enactment. In October 1994, the retiring Republican Malcolm Wallop of Wyoming tried to kill the bill by end-of-session filibuster, but other senators, apparently sympathetic to Feinstein's case or her political plight, helped it to pass.

Feinstein surely hoped that she would face weak competition in 1994 and that her early and hard work raising money would enable her to win essentially unopposed. But then came Michael Huffington, with the determination and the cash to be the biggest spending Senate candidate ever. Texas-born, Huffington moved to Santa Barbara in 1991 and in 1992 beat an 18-year Republican congressman in the primary by spending over $3 million. He won the general election easily. Huffington started off with an ad in which he promoted William Bennett's *The Book of Virtues*, addressing Californians' sense of moral deficiency. Feinstein ran an ad accusing Huffington of refusing to act as an advocate for Raytheon in Congress, a company located in his district. This was political jujitsu, using her strength of constituency service to prove his claim that she was a "career politician." Feinstein was clearly flustered and angry that a politician who had put in so little time and effort had pulled even with her in the polls by September, and that she could not count on heavily outspending him. Huffington's spending—nearly $30 million altogether—moved him even with Feinstein in September and October polls; when it was revealed that he and his wife employed an illegal alien as a nanny, his poll numbers went down. On the Thursday before the election, it was revealed that Feinstein, despite her earlier denials, had employed a woman whose work permit had expired. But the news media ran stories saying that federal officials cast doubt on whether the woman was an illegal. This alibi turned out to be false, but it probably made the difference; it is a sign of Democratic weakness in 1994 that Feinstein, for all her strength and achievements, was in such straits. Feinstein won 47%–45%, carrying the Bay Area 63%–30% and Los Angeles County 52%–40%, while losing the rest of southern California 56%–35% and the north outside the Bay Area 51%–40%.

In the minority for the first time in her career, Feinstein worked on anti-crime legislation, passing the Comprehensive Methamphetamine Control Act of 1996 and proposing a Federal Gang Violence Act (doubling penalties to gang members). She opposed the immigration bill until the Gallegly amendment, allowing states to exclude children of illegal immigrants from schools, was dropped. She opposed the Welfare Reform Act provisions cutting off aid to elderly legal immigrants, and sought in 1997 to repeal that provision. She sought to link trade ties to Mexico with changes in its drug enforcement. Toward China she was more friendly. When San Francisco and Shanghai became sister cities in 1979, Feinstein got to know Mayor Jiang Zemin, now president of China. Every year she strongly supports renewal of normal trade relations with China; she argues that trade is driving political change in China and that if trade ties are cut China will just withdraw and remain dictatorial. But her strong stand prompted her husband to give up any profits he makes on investments in China.

Feinstein co-sponsored the bill to ban denial of hospitalization for mastectomies. She opposed the McCain-Feingold campaign finance bill because it limits ideological PACs like EM-

ILY's List, which gave her much support. With Republican Orrin Hatch, she promoted legislation to address gang violence and another to curb the practices of photographers who stalk celebrities; with Republican Jon Kyl she sponsored a constitutional amendment to give victims of crime fundamental rights. She sponsored the law that created the breast cancer stamp and raised millions for research. In September 1998 she sponsored a bill to prohibit human cloning.

In October 1997 Feinstein gave a speech stingingly criticizing California's public school system, spotlighting relatively low spending and dismal results, and calling for "nothing short of a major restructuring," including an end to social promotion, longer school days and standards to measure each school's achievement. By some this was seen as a prelude to another run for governor in 1998, and December 1997 polls showed Feinstein to be the strongest Democratic competitor. For some weeks she considered it seriously, but in January 1998 she announced she would not run; the prospect of running a fourth statewide race in eight years and the presence of the free-spending Al Checchi and her 1992 nemesis Gray Davis were perhaps unappealing.

In December 1998, as the House was preparing to vote impeachment, Feinstein wrote a proposal to censure Clinton for "immoral and reckless behavior." But it was never able to get the support of some Democrats who wanted Clinton let off scot-free or of some Republicans who believed that censure was extraconstitutional or that it provided Clinton an easy way out. When impeachment was defeated, she dropped the proposal for censure. At the same time, she was still working on California issues, successfully brokering a deal for Pacific Lumber to sell redwood groves in the Headwaters Forest on the north coast. She and Barbara Boxer shifted committee seats, giving Feinstein a seat on Appropriations where she could fund California projects during the last two years of her term. Predicting California Senate races is a tricky business: Feinstein won the 1994 race by less than almost anybody expected 18 months before, Boxer won the 1998 race by more. California Democrats' solid wins in 1998 and Feinstein's good poll ratings made her the heavy favorite, and no Republican has the statewide name identification to be a strong candidate initially.

Cook's Call. *Probably Safe.* The enormous expense of running a credible, top-level statewide campaign in California has grown to the point that only the incredibly wealthy or the very best of fundraising candidates can seriously contemplate running, making it highly unlikely that Feinstein will have a difficult race. But she is not without her vulnerabilities. On the Republican side, San Diego County Supervisor and rancher Bill Horn has announced, although other candidates could get in. Horn is not known outside his base and will have difficulty raising enough money. There is also speculation on whether Feinstein will get the nod as the vice presidential running mate; California law allows her to run for both offices.

Junior Senator. Barbara Boxer, by most measures, is one of the most liberal members of Congress. She grew up in Brooklyn, where she was a victim of sexual harassment by a college professor and was refused work as a stockbroker; she moved to California in 1965 and worked on civic and political campaigns and ultimately for Democratic Congressman John Burton. In 1972 she ran for the Marin County Board of Supervisors, in the ultra-trendy suburbs nestled between Mount Tamalpais and the Bay, north of the Golden Gate Bridge. She lost, but in 1976, when women candidates were more accepted, she won a seat on the board. Boxer is energetic, usually good-humored, unafraid to challenge authority, voluble in support of her issue positions but not always candid about her goals. When Burton retired unexpectedly in 1982, she ran for the House and was easily elected. She made many splashes in the House, unearthing the Air Force's $7,622 coffee pot in 1984, denouncing the Persian Gulf war with more ardor than anyone, and leading a march of angry women on the Senate when Anita Hill was testifying against Clarence Thomas. She also compiled the highest-dollar voting record in the House on spending in 1992.

Boxer began the 1992 Senate campaign not as the best-known or best-financed candidate, but as the most distinctive in a year in which the enthusiasm of the feminist left energized the Democratic Party and sped it to victory. In the primary, she faced Lieutenant Governor Leo

McCarthy, who had high name identification after four statewide races, and Congressman Mel Levine, who had strong financial backing from Los Angeles's Westside. Levine ran tough ads in favor of the Gulf war resolution and took a tough stand against the Los Angeles riot, but only managed to alienate liberal voters—who went to Boxer—without winning over moderates who stuck with the better-known but more liberal McCarthy. Boxer, despite 143 overdrafts at the House bank, won with 44% of the vote, to 31% for McCarthy and 22% for Levine. Her general election opponent was Bruce Herschensohn, a Los Angeles TV and radio commentator, Nixon speechwriter and Reagan enthusiast, backer of a flat tax and offshore oil drilling and opponent of abortion. Herschensohn had edged Silicon Valley moderate Congressman Tom Campbell 38%–36% in the primary, with the help of then-Palm Springs Mayor Sonny Bono, who won 17% of the vote. The Boxer-Herschensohn race was a battle of opposites, the far left versus the far right of the American electoral spectrum. Boxer was helped by the collapse of the Bush candidacy in California, by hearty support from Feinstein and by the revelation by the state Democratic political director during the last week of the campaign that Herschensohn attended nude dancer night clubs. In a race where neither candidate won a majority, Boxer won 48%–43%, carrying the Bay Area 61%–30% and Los Angeles County 53%–40%, while losing southern California 52%–38% and the rest of the state 49%–42%.

Boxer's voting record has been strongly liberal; Bob Dole once called her "the most partisan senator I've ever known." She is one of the strongest proponents of abortion rights in the Senate; she vehemently opposed the partial-birth abortion ban. She crusaded in 1995 for open Ethics Committee hearings on Bob Packwood. Her relations with the Clinton White House are close—her daughter is married to Hillary Rodham Clinton's brother—and caused her to switch her positions on charges of sexual misconduct. In 1998, the senator who had marched across the Capitol to protest the cross-examination of Anita Hill, found little to believe in the charges against Clinton until he admitted their truth, and even then limited her condemnation to a perfunctory statement combined with a total commitment to defeat impeachment. And in 1999 the crusader against the Gulf war resolution solidly backed the bombing campaign against Serbia.

On other issues, Boxer voted against the 1996 welfare reform. She was one of the first to sponsor a bill to require child-proof safety locks on all handguns. She has sought out some popular California causes as well. She calls for full reimbursement of border states for the costs of illegal immigration. In the early 1990s she sponsored defense reconversion bills and funding. She has worked to pass a dolphin-safe tuna labeling law and the California Cruise Industry Revitalization Act. She scored a great success in pushing the public-private trust for the Presidio in the 1996 parks bill, and helped broker a last-minute compromise between the White House and Alaska Senator Frank Murkowski on the Tongass National Forest, which enabled the bill to pass. In December 1996 she got Feinstein to yield her a seat on the Appropriations Committee, where she worked on California projects for two years; after the 1998 election, she gave the seat back to Feinstein and took one on Foreign Relations. Some of her stands have divided her supporters. She opposed the Defense of Marriage Act, but refused to support government recognition of gay marriages. She sided with writers and directors and against the studios by backing a bill for disclaimers on altered films.

During Boxer's first three years in the Senate her job rating was among the chamber's lowest, and Republicans seemed lined up to run against her. But by early 1997, as Democratic fortunes advanced in California, her job rating cleared 50%, and fewer Republicans seemed interested. Congressman Tom Campbell, who nearly won the 1992 nomination, and Michael Huffington, the nearly successful 1994 candidate, both decided not to run. San Diego Mayor Susan Golding, who has had much success in the state's third largest city, pulled out of the race in January 1998 after campaigning for seven months. That left two Republican nominees, neither particularly strong. One was state Treasurer Matt Fong, whose mother was a Democratic Assemblywoman and secretary of State; he was an Air Force officer who entered politics as a Republican, but took some stands—neutrality on Proposition 187—which irritated conservatives. The other was car alarm magnate Darrell Issa, a solid conservative who spent more than $10 million—much of it his own—on his primary campaign. Congressman Frank Riggs, facing an uphill battle in his Democratic-leaning 1st District, also entered the race in January but left in April. This was not the most closely watched primary in California in 1998, and was run under the all-party primary rules adopted by voters in 1996; in the other states with that system, Washington and Alaska, an incumbent's performance in the primary is often a good forecast for November. In June the news was not good for Boxer. The more moderate Fong won the Republican nomination, winning 21% of all votes to Issa's 18%. And Boxer won only 41%—well below a majority.

But in the next five months Boxer rallied and won convincingly. She raised more than $15 million altogether, and launched an ad campaign attacking Fong for his ambiguous stances on issues like abortion. She guarded herself from contact with reporters so she would not have to answer questions about Clinton; at one point her staff told reporters she had a bad back though she danced at a Democratic gathering soon after. Fong attacked her for the hypocrisy of her stand on the Clinton scandals. He hoped also to run well among the growing number of Asian-American voters. But Fong, though he could talk convincingly on issues if given a few minutes to expound his remarks, spoke hesitantly and unconvincingly in the sound bites which are the staple of California politics. And he never succeeded in raising the money he needed. For much of September and October he was off the air, while Boxer was pounding the airwaves mercilessly. Californian's vehement opposition to prosecution of the Clinton scandal surely helped Boxer as well.

By October Boxer had a big lead in polls; in November she won 53%–43%. She won 61%–36% in Los Angeles County, a big improvement over 1992, in a county from which hundreds of thousands of Anglos had fled and in which many immigrants were just getting on the voting rolls; she won 64%–33% in the Bay Area, by the same margin as in 1992, in the part of the state with the largest Asian population. She lost by 51%–44% in the South, not a bad margin for a Democrat, and by 50%–45% in the rest of the state. In the one part of California that has been moving to Republicans in the 1990s, the Central Valley, she ran poorly, carrying Sacramento with only 50% of the vote and otherwise carrying only two small counties, Merced and Yolo, site of the leftish U.C.-Davis campus. But she made up for that with good showings in coastal counties, even carrying historically Republican Santa Barbara. This was a gender gap race, an even 48%–48% among men and 57%–39% for Boxer among women.

Presidential politics. With 54 electoral votes, California is the gorilla of American politics: it may be geographically far away from the rest of the action, but ignore it at your peril. In the 1970s and 1980s, it was the state that accounted for what people called the Republican lock on the presidency. Republicans won handily when they nominated Californians—Richard Nixon in 1972 and Ronald Reagan in 1980 and 1984—but they won only narrowly in 1976 and 1988 when they didn't. In the 1990s it was the Democrats who seemed to have a lock on California and the presidency. Bill Clinton, not a Californian but adapting eagerly to the California environment, lavishing attention and his presence on the state, led in California polls in 1992 and 1996 by such wide margins that he was free to prospect for votes in the Midwest and South, while Republicans felt obliged to spend money and time there (including the 1996 convention in San Diego) that turned out to be wasted. Clinton was clearly aware of California's importance, visiting the state with regularity during the 1992 campaign and afterwards as if the campaign never stopped, paying homage to different subgroups of this culturally diverse state's population. Indeed, sometimes too much homage: it is unlikely that Al Gore will appear at any fundraisers in Buddhist temples in 2000 as he did in 1996. Instead he hopes to be appear in triumph at the Democratic National Convention in Los Angeles.

But neither the convention nor the 1998 results guarantee that the Democrats' lock on California will continue in 2000 and after any more than the Republicans' lock continued after 1990. Clinton's margins here have been large, but his percentages in three-way races—46% in 1992 and 51% in 1996—have not been overwhelming. They are not as high as Reagan's 53%

(in a three-way race) in 1980 and 58% in 1988, and more like Bush's 51% in 1988. And if coastal California has clearly trended in Clinton's direction, much of inland California has gone the other way. Democrats' striking success with Latino voters—increasing their turnout and their Democratic percentages at the same time—may continue in 2000, and may not; most Republican state legislators here endorsed George W. Bush in early 1999, in the hopes that he could do what none of them has the foggiest idea of how to do: win the near-majority among Latinos as he did in Texas in 1998. It seems a tall order, yet it is also probably true that Latinos today, like some immigrant groups in the past, have not in their first years in the voting stream developed a firm attachment to either party. Early 1999 polls showing Bush leading Gore in California give Republicans hope, perhaps falsely; but it is almost sure that, whatever the polls, California will be seriously contested by both major parties in 2000. It is just too big to ignore.

California's presidential primary will surely get close attention, for the first time since 1972. Then it was held in June, a time when under old rules no one usually had the nomination sewn up; California, with its winner-take-all primary (abolished by the Democrats in 1976 but not by Republicans) could determine the nomination. California was the center of national attention when Nelson Rockefeller lost here to Barry Goldwater in 1964, when Robert Kennedy and Eugene McCarthy slugged it out in 1968, and when George McGovern edged Hubert Humphrey in 1972.

Then the new rules enabled candidates to sew up nominations long before June. In belated response, California rescheduled its 1996 primary for March 26. But even that was too late: the Republican nomination was already decided and the Democratic not even contested. So for 2000 California has scheduled its primary for March 7. There are still problems. The all-party primary allows anyone, not just registered Democrats, to vote for a Democrat: not kosher under Democratic Party rules. But Secretary of State Bill Jones, a Republican, came up with a computer-assisted double counting procedure, which would allow a total of just registered Democrats' votes to be counted for Democratic delegates. California, of course, wants to increase its influence and diminish that of Iowa and New Hampshire; but the primary date may give enormous leverage to Iowa and New Hampshire winners. The history of presidential delegate selection processes in the late 20th Century is a history of unintended consequences. The Founding Fathers who set up a framework of elections which, with only minor changes, has served the nation well for more than 200 years, unfortunately never gave any thought to how parties select presidential candidates, and so we lesser beings thrash around, trying to come up with a system that works tolerably well—and will probably find ourselves thrashing some more, well into the 21st century.

Congressional districting. California grows so fast and is so populous that redistricting matters here more than anywhere else. The tradition of partisan redistricting goes way back: Republicans drew the lines to their advantage in the 1940s and 1950s, Democrats in the 1960s, 1970s and 1980s, as the California House delegation grew from 23 in the 1940s to 30, 38, 43, 45 and 52, the largest for any state in history. The great genius of redistricting here was Democratic Congressman Phillip Burton, who dominated the line-drawing for House seats and for the state Senate and Assembly as well (and intervened behind the scenes in other states too); his 1982 plan, slightly revised for 1984–90, left Democrats in secure control of the delegation even though he died in 1983. Thus, in 1984 Democrats had a 27–18 edge in the House delegation, even though Republicans won the popular vote 49%–48%. But in the 1990s the man who made the difference was Governor Pete Wilson, who after hard-nosed bargaining with the Democratic legislature in 1991 persuaded the state Supreme Court (Republican ever since voters threw out three Jerry Brown appointees in 1986) to adopt a plan drawn up by his appointed commission in 1992. This was a relatively evenhanded plan, with generally regular boundaries. As a result, when Republicans won the popular vote in 1994 by 49%–48%, the district lines again produced 27 Democrats but now also 25 Republicans. When Democrats won the House vote 51%–44% in 1998, the result was a delegation of 29 Democrats and 23 Republicans—a reasonably fair result.

California is the great prize in the battle over redistricting—and over the Census—for 2000. In the wake of the 1998 elections, Democrats hold the governorship and have such large margins in the legislature that they are extremely unlikely to be overturned in 2000. But Democratic control is threatened by an initiative sponsored by Ron Unz, which would create a nonpartisan commission to draw the lines, and by the possibility that state judges, mostly appointed by Republican governors in their 16 years of office, would overturn a state law.

The census comes in here: national Democrats have insisted that the census be conducted by sampling, which would allow manipulation by Clinton appointees; national Republicans insist on a head count. The Supreme Court ruled in early 1998 that a head count was required for apportionment of districts among the states, but left open the possibility of using sampling results for the drawing of district lines within states. In most states this is academic: small states don't have that many districts to draw lines for, and large states mostly have Republican governors or Republicans in control of at least one house of the legislature, none of whom will use sampling results if they give the Democrats the partisan advantage. But California Democrats will jump at using them, for just that reason. A sampling formula that is jiggered to overcounting Hispanics will allow them to create two or three more heavily Democratic congressional districts, and more Assembly districts, than could be done using head count numbers.

But the Democrats will run into two limits on their ability to use sampling numbers for partisan advantage. One is that California, which did not grow by its usual lusty percentages in the first half of the 1990s, is likely to gain only one or two new districts, not eight as in 1962 or seven as in 1992. Second, the Voting Rights amendments of 1982 has been interpreted as requiring the maximization of the number of majority-minority districts; translated into English, this means that Democratic district-drawers will feel obliged by this law, and by the demands of their Latino-left legislators, to create more Hispanic-majority districts. That will limit their ability to put Democratic precincts into formerly Republican districts and will also cause them distress as they attempt to protect non-Latino Democratic incumbents who seek new safe districts. Bottom line: the Democrats likely to be in control of redistricting may be willing, or may feel obliged, to offer the Republicans a deal safeguarding all or all but one or two of the current Republicans and allotting the new one or two districts to Democrats. This will help Democrats nationally, but not enough to compensate for the losses they could easily sustain through redistricting in Texas, Michigan and Pennsylvania, where Republicans stand to make significant gains.

The People: Est. Pop. 1998: 32,666,550; Pop. 1990: 29,760,021, up 9.7% 1990–1998. 12.1% of U.S. total, 1st largest; 7.4% rural. Median age: 32.7 years. 11% 65 years and over. 69.1% White, 7.4% Black, 9.6% Asian, 0.8% Amer. Indian, 13.1% Other; 25.4% Hispanic Origin. Households: 52.7% married couple families; 26.9% married couple fams. w. children; 53.9% college educ.; median household income: $35,798; per capita income: $16,409; 55.6% owner occupied housing; median house value: $195,500; median monthly rent: $561. 5.9% Unemployment. 1998 Voting age pop.: 23,665,000. 1998 Turnout: 8,621,121; 41% of VAP. Registered voters (1998): 14,969,185; 6,989,006 D (47%), 5,314,912 R (36%), 2,665,267 unaffiliated and minor parties (18%).

Political Lineup: Governor, Gray Davis (D); Lt. Gov., Cruz Bustamante (D); Secy. of State, Bill Jones (R); Atty. Gen., Bill Lockyer (D); Treasurer, Phil Angelides (D); State Senate, 40 (25 D, 15 R); Majority Leader, Richard Polanco (D); State Assembly, 80 (47 D, 32 R, 1 Green); Assembly Speaker, Antonio Villaraigosa (D). Senators, Dianne Feinstein (D) and Barbara Boxer (D). Representatives, 52 (28 D, 24 R).

Elections Division: 916-657-2166; **Filing Deadline for U.S. Congress:** December 10, 1999.

1996 Presidential Vote

Clinton (D) 5,119,815 (51%)
Dole (R) 3,828,368 (38%)
Perot (I) 697,845 (7%)
Others 372,553 (4%)

1996 Republican Presidential Primary

Dole (R) 1,619,931 (66%)
Buchanan (R) 450,695 (18%)
Forbes (R) 183,367 (7%)
Keyes (R) 93,577 (4%)
Others 104,742 (5%)

1992 Presidential Vote

Clinton (D) 5,121,249 (46%)
Bush (R) 3,630,566 (33%)
Perot (I) 2,296,004 (21%)

GOVERNOR

Gov. Gray Davis (D)

Elected 1998, term expires Jan. 2003; b. Dec. 26, 1942, New York, NY; home, Los Angeles; Stanford U., B.A. 1964, Columbia U., J.D. 1967; Catholic; married (Sharon).

Military Career: Army, 1967–69 (Vietnam).

Elected Office: CA Assembly, 1982–86; U.S. Senate candidate, 1992; CA Lt. Gov., 1995–98.

Professional Career: Finance Dir., Tom Bradley mayoral campaign, 1972–74; Chief of Staff, Gov. Jerry Brown Jr., 1974–82; CA Controller, 1986–94.

Office: State Capitol Bldg., Sacramento, 95814, 916-445-2841; Fax: 916-445-4633; Web site: www.state.ca.gov.

Election Results

1998 gen.	Gray Davis (D)	4,858,817	(58%)
	Dan Lungren (R)	3,216,749	(38%)
	Others	306,305	(4%)
1998 prim.	Gray Davis (D)	2,083,396	(35%)
	Dan Lungren (R)	2,023,618	(34%)
	Al Checchi (D)	748,828	(12%)
	Jane Harman (D)	741,251	(12%)
	Others	399,697	(7%)
1994 gen.	Pete Wilson (R)	4,777,674	(55%)
	Kathleen Brown (D)	3,517,777	(41%)
	Others	363,430	(4%)

SENATORS

Sen. Dianne Feinstein (D)

Elected 1992, seat up 2000; b. June 22, 1933, San Francisco; home, San Francisco; Stanford U., B.A. 1955; Jewish; married (Richard C. Blum).

Elected Office: San Francisco Bd. of Supervisors, 1970–78, Pres., 1970–71, 1974–75, 1978; San Francisco Mayor, 1978–88.

Professional Career: CA Women's Parole Bd., 1960–66.

DC Office: 331 HSOB, 20510, 202-224-3841; Fax: 202-228-3954; Web site: www.senate.gov/~feinstein.

State Offices: Fresno, 559-485-7430; Los Angeles, 310-914-7300; San Diego, 619-231-9712; San Francisco, 415-536-6868.

Committees: *Appropriations* (12th of 13 D): Agriculture & Rural Development; Interior; Labor & HHS; Legislative Branch (RMM). *Judiciary* (5th of 8 D): Immigration; Technology, Terrorism & Government Information (RMM); Youth Violence. *Rules & Administration* (5th of 7 D). *Joint Committee on Printing* (4th of 5 Sens.).

Group Ratings

	ADA	ACLU	AFS	LCV	CON	NTU	NFIB	COC	ACU	NTLC	CHC
1998	90	86	89	100	30	14	33	61	4	14	10
1997	85	—	67	—	36	32	—	50	4	—	—

National Journal Ratings

	1997 LIB — 1997 CONS	1998 LIB — 1998 CONS
Economic	67% — 31%	65% — 33%
Social	71% — 0%	74% — 0%
Foreign	62% — 32%	73% — 21%

Key Votes of the 105th Congress

1. Bal. Budget Amend.	N	5. Satcher for Surgeon Gen.	Y
2. Clinton Budget Deal	Y	6. Highway Set-asides	Y
3. Cloture on Tobacco	Y	7. Table Child Gun locks	N
4. Education IRAs	Y	8. Ovrd. Part. Birth Veto	N

9. Chem. Weapons Treaty	Y
10. Cuban Humanitarian Aid	Y
11. Table Bosnia Troops	Y
12. $ for Test-ban Treaty	Y

Election Results

1994 general	Dianne Feinstein (D)	3,977,063	(47%)	($14,407,179)
	Michael Huffington (R)	3,811,501	(45%)	($29,969,695)
	Others	714,500	(8%)	
1994 primary	Dianne Feinstein (D)	1,635,837	(74%)	
	Ted Andromidas (D)	297,128	(13%)	
	Daniel O'Dowd (D)	271,615	(12%)	
1992 general	Dianne Feinstein (D)	5,853,621	(54%)	($8,054,222)
	John Seymour (R)	4,093,488	(38%)	($6,849,805)
	Others	832,581	(8%)	

Sen. Barbara Boxer (D)

Elected 1992, seat up 2004; b. Nov. 11, 1940, Brooklyn, NY; home, Greenbrae; Brooklyn Col., B.A. 1962; Jewish; married (Stewart).

Elected Office: Marin Cnty. Bd. of Supervisors, 1976–82; U.S. House of Reps., 1982–92.

Professional Career: Stockbroker & researcher, 1962–65; Journalist, *Pacific Sun*, 1972–74; Dist. aide, U.S. Rep. John Burton, 1974–76.

DC Office: 112 HSOB, 20510, 202-224-3553; Fax: 202-228-4056; Web site: www.senate.gov/~boxer.

State Offices: El Segundo, 310-414-5700; Fresno, 209-497-5109; Los Angeles, 213-894-5000; Sacramento, 916-448-2787; San Bernardino, 909-888-8525; San Diego, 619-239-3884; San Francisco, 415-403-0100.

Committees: *Budget* (5th of 10 D). *Environment & Public Works* (7th of 8 D): Clean Air, Wetlands, Private Property & Nuclear Safety; Fisheries, Wildlife & Drinking Water; Superfund, Waste Control & Risk Assessment. *Foreign Relations* (7th of 8 D): International Economic Policy, Export & Trade Promotion; International Operations (RMM); Western Hemisphere, Peace Corps, Narcotics & Terrorism.

Group Ratings

	ADA	ACLU	AFS	LCV	CON	NTU	NFIB	COC	ACU	NTLC	CHC
1998	95	86	100	88	7	14	33	59	4	0	0
1997	100	—	89	—	12	14	—	50	0	—	—

National Journal Ratings

	1997 LIB — 1997 CONS		1998 LIB — 1998 CONS	
Economic	96%	0%	83%	10%
Social	71%	0%	63%	26%
Foreign	92%	0%	86%	12%

Key Votes of the 105th Congress

1. Bal. Budget Amend.	N	5. Satcher for Surgeon Gen.	Y	9. Chem. Weapons Treaty	Y
2. Clinton Budget Deal	N	6. Highway Set-asides	Y	10. Cuban Humanitarian Aid	Y
3. Cloture on Tobacco	Y	7. Table Child Gun locks	N	11. Table Bosnia Troops	Y
4. Education IRAs	N	8. Ovrd. Part. Birth Veto	N	12. $ for Test-ban Treaty	Y

Election Results

1998 general	Barbara Boxer (D)	4,410,056	(53%)	($13,737,548)
	Matt Fong (R)	3,575,078	(43%)	($10,764,892)
	Others	326,771	(4%)	
1998 primary	Barbara Boxer (D)	2,574,264	(41%)	
	Matt Fong (R)	1,292,662	(21%)	
	Darrell Issa (R)	1,142,567	(18%)	
	John M. Brown (R)	489,741	(8%)	
	Frank D. Riggs (R)	295,886	(5%)	
	Others	507,257	(8%)	
1992 general	Barbara Boxer (D)	5,173,443	(48%)	($10,415,811)
	Bruce Herschensohn (R)	4,644,139	(43%)	($7,649,072)
	Others	981,781	(9%)	

FIRST DISTRICT

The North Coast of California is unlike any other place in America. It is the only part of the Lower 48 states first settled by Russians, who built Fort Ross in 1812; they sold it in 1841 to a Swiss named John Augustus Sutter, whose discovery of gold near Sacramento started the Gold Rush eight years later. It is the only part of the world with large numbers of redwood trees, shooting up in the moist and drizzly air hundreds of feet toward the sky. It is wet country, and for years it has been one of America's prime lumbering areas: Eureka and smaller lumber towns are filled with filigreed Victorian houses and old lumber mills, saloons and waterfront hotels. It has moved on to other crops: in sunny valleys sealed off the from Coast Range ridges grow some of the nation's premium wine grapes, and Mendocino County has been known since the late 1960s for its premier marijuana fields. Twenty years ago, there were only 20 wineries in Napa Valley; today there are more than 200, with another 100 just west of the ridges in Sonoma County. These valleys were some of California's earliest literary haunts: Robert Louis Stevenson took his honeymoon near Calistoga in Napa, and Jack London owned a giant house in Sonoma which mysteriously burned down in 1913.

The 1st Congressional District consists of most of the North Coast (though just missing Fort Ross), plus much of the wine-growing area inland and just a bit of the vast Central Valley interior. The North Coast lumbering area from Mendocino on north, once filled with rough-hewn working men, was historically Democratic country, but it backlashed toward the Republicans on cultural issues. As veterans of the counterculture settled in Mendocino County and along the coast, it has moved toward the cultural left. Inland, the wine-growing country around Healdsburg and in Napa County is politically more conservative, with neither the blue-collar tradition nor the counterculture past of the coast, though there is often partisan competition. The district's inland portion is around Fairfield, home of Travis Air Force Base. The mix of different economies and cultures, of generations with sharply different experiences and outlooks, makes this one of California's politically most unstable districts, and it has changed partisan hands in four of the last five elections.

The congressman from the 1st District is Mike Thompson, a Democrat elected in 1998. Thompson grew up in the Napa Valley town of St. Helena, served in the Army in Vietnam, earning a Purple Heart, and later owned a vineyard and worked as a maintenance supervisor for Beringer, a big winery in the valley. He taught at San Francisco State University and California State University-Chico. In 1982 he was chosen an Assembly Fellow, and from 1984–90 was chief of staff to two veteran Bay Area Assembly members. In 1990 he ran for the state Senate, survived redistricting, and was elected again in 1994. He chaired the Senate Budget Committee and helped broker the controversial Headwaters Forest deal, an on-again, off-again plan, finally approved in March 1999, to buy out and preserve the last privately held stand of redwoods owned by the corporate raider Charles Hurwitz.

In 1998, facing California's legislative term limits, he decided to run for the House seat held, precariously, by Republican Frank Riggs. Riggs, whose background is in law enforcement, was first elected in 1990, lost the seat in 1992, then was elected again in 1994 and 1996. In 1990 he won 43%–42% over Democrat Doug Bosco, who was opposed on the left by a Peace and Freedom candidate who won 15% of the vote. In 1992 Riggs lost the seat to a very different Democrat, Dan Hamburg, who moved to Mendocino County to found an "alternative school," and taught Chinese culture and language to foreigners in China. In 1994 Hamburg lost to Riggs 53%–47%—the only absolute majority for anyone in this culturally fractured district from 1988–98. In 1996 Riggs defended the seat against Michela Alioto, 28-year-old granddaughter of former San Francisco Mayor Jospeh Alioto. But she had serious problems—blatant unfamiliarity with the district, liens for unpaid taxes—and even as Bill Clinton was carrying the district 48%–35%, Riggs carried every county but Mendocino and won 50%–43%—the only time a member has been re-elected here since 1988.

By 1998 the political terrain had changed. Loggers who had lost their jobs had moved away; the Headwaters Forest deal seemed on the way to completion. Possibly fearing a primary from Thompson, who had had been eyeing the seat, Riggs in January 1998 announced he would run for Barbara Boxer's Senate seat; with no name identification beyond the district and little money, he left that race in April. Thompson announced in April, facing weak opposition and winning support from almost every interest group—unions, medical providers, vintners, oil and timber interests, law enforcement groups, fishermen. His issue stands—opposition to oil drilling off the California coast, support of abortion rights and the death penalty—were broadly popular. He won the June primary easily, 78%–22% over the only other Democrat, and Republicans essentially conceded the district to him. He won in November by 62%–33%.

Thompson won seats on the Agriculture and Armed Services committees. His strong performance in 1998 and his success at bridging over the differences that have shaped politics in this district for a decade, suggest that he will have a longer and more serene tenure than his immediate predecessors.

Cook's Call. *Probably Safe.* Thompson, a popular former state senator, cruised to an easy victory in 1998 and his political savvy and moderate political views should insulate him from a tough challenge. He is a strong favorite for re-election in 2000.

The People: Pop. 1990: 572,870; 33.4% rural; 13.3% age 65 + ; 85.1% White, 3.9% Black, 3.6% Asian, 2.8% Amer. Indian, 4.6% Other; 10.9% Hispanic Origin. Households: 56.5% married couple families; 26.9% married couple fams. w. children; 52.3% college educ.; median household income: $30,943; per capita income: $14,298; median house value: $136,400; median gross rent: $438.

1996 Presidential Vote		
Clinton (D)	113,861	(48%)
Dole (R)	83,669	(35%)
Perot (I)	23,024	(10%)
Others	15,695	(7%)

1992 Presidential Vote		
Clinton (D)	119,491	(46%)
Bush (R)	74,597	(29%)
Perot (I)	61,160	(24%)

Rep. Mike Thompson (D)

Elected 1998; b. Jan. 24, 1951, St. Helena; home, St. Helena; CA St. U., B. A. 1982, M. A. 1996.; Catholic; married (Janet).

Military Career: Army, 1969–73 (Vietnam).

Elected Office: CA Senate, 1990–98.

Professional Career: Owner, Beringer Winery; CA Assembly fellow, 1982–83; Chief of Staff, CA Assemblyman Lou Papan, 1984–87; Chief of Staff, CA Assemblywoman Jacqueline Speier, 1987–90.

DC Office: 415 CHOB 20515, 202-225-3311; Fax: 202-225-4335; Web site: www.house.gov/mthompson.

District Offices: Eureka, 707-269-9595; Fort Bragg, 707-962-0933; Napa, 707-226-9898.

Committees: *Agriculture* (23d of 24 D): Department Operations, Oversight, Nutrition & Forestry; Risk Management, Research & Specialty Crops. *Armed Services* (27th of 28 D): Military Installations & Facilities; Military Personnel.

Group Ratings and Key Votes: Newly Elected

Election Results

1998 general	Mike Thompson (D)	121,710	(62%)	($941,795)
	Mark Luce (R)	64,622	(33%)	($123,061)
	Others	10,437	(5%)	
1998 primary	Mike Thompson (D)	77,544	(51%)	
	Mark Luce (R)	30,532	(20%)	
	Jim Hennefer (D)	21,841	(14%)	
	R J (Jim) Chase (R)	13,729	(9%)	
	Others	7,754	(5%)	
1996 general	Frank D. Riggs (R)	110,242	(50%)	($1,390,399)
	Michela Alioto (D)	96,522	(43%)	($1,228,870)
	Emil Rossi (Lib)	15,354	(7%)	

SECOND DISTRICT

Rising 14,000 feet over low foothills and the Central Valley, visible for 100 miles, is the snow-capped volcanic cone of Mount Shasta, one of a string of (presumably) burnt-out volcanoes that march up and down the Pacific Coast states. This is the far northern end of California, where truck traffic on Interstate 5 is the only reminder of the choked metropolitan areas where most of the state's people live. This is lumber country mostly, where the mountains that rise on all sides—the Coast Range to the east, the Sierra Nevada to the west, the scattered mountains sealing off the Central Valley north of Redding—are carpeted with trees; rough flannel-shirt, two-lane-road country that was left behind economically when greater Los Angeles and San Francisco boomed after World War II. In the last dozen years, however, the northern end of California has been attracting people, mostly young families who come here to raise their children in a small town atmosphere, but also retirees looking for a calm atmosphere and low cost of living. There are few minorities here; the population is 92% white, the highest in any California district.

The 2d Congressional District of California covers most of this area. The district has two major population areas: one around Redding, just below Mount Shasta, and the other farther south, at the edge of the Sierra foothills, around the Butte County communities of Paradise and Chico. Chico is a liberal oasis amid sprawling orchards—home to a state university and Sierra Nevada Pale Ale—but the rest of the 2d District is culturally conservative and angry at the diktats of urban environmentalists. The region has a Democratic heritage: from 1943–80, it elected rough-and-ready Democrats who pulled strings in Sacramento and Washington to build roads and dams. Now it elects abstemious and circumspect Republicans who have solidly conservative voting records and tend to local needs.

The congressman from the 2d District is Wally Herger, a Republican, businessman and rancher first elected to the Assembly in 1980. In 1986 he was elected to Congress after winning solid margins over the mayor of Redding in the primary and a Shasta County supervisor in the general. He has served rather quietly on the Ways and Means Committee and Budget commit-tees, favoring balanced budgets and lower taxes. He pushed for the timber-salvage bill passed in the 104th Congress, to allow 18 months to remove dead and dying trees from federal forests. He tends to local water projects, lamenting in the January 1997 floods the failure to shore up levees and opposing the Central Valley Project water bill for legislating "a permanent drought." He has attacked racial quotas and preferences in civil service and arts funding for basket-weavers, some in his district. He sponsored an exemption of flood control activities from the Endangered Species Act. He passed as part of welfare reform a law to prevent prisoners in local and state jails from collecting Supplemental Security Income benefits. Sheriffs and prison departments were given a bonus for identifying prisoners who receive illegal beneits, and in 1998 the program was estimated to save the taxpayers $3.46 billion over seven years.

Perhaps Herger's most significant effort was providing clout for the Quincy Library Group, a collection of loggers and (some) local environmentalists in Plumas County in the Sierras who decided to meet at the library in Quincy—the only place where they couldn't shout at each other. They hammered out a plan that permitted the logging of smaller, more crowded trees in national forests as a way to reduce wildfires and provide a steady supply of timber for local mills. (After decades of resource extraction, there are few old-growth forests still left here.) Initially, even the Clinton Administration backed the proposal, believing it melded with a Clinton-Gore effort to promote collaboration, rather than litigation, to solve environmental problems. In 1997 the House passed the Quincy plan 429–1. But then national environmental groups came out full-bore against it, fearing it would set a precedent for greater local control of federal lands. Senator Barbara Boxer, who needed environmentalists' support in what seemed then like a tough re-election campaign, stalled Herger's bill for months, but legislators did an end-run around her by inserting language into the omnibus spending package that passed in October 1998. Forest-use policy may or may not change radically as a result, but the acrimony generated by the Washington-based enviros tended to undercut the notion of collaborative policymaking.

Herger was reelected in 1998, by 63%–34%, a bit better than his 61%–34% in 1996.

Cook's Call. *Safe.* This solidly conservative district has easily elected Herger for seven elections. Nothing appears on the horizon to change that. Consider Herger a safe bet for 2000.

The People: Pop. 1990: 573,226; 40.5% rural; 16.2% age 65 + ; 91.7% White, 1.5% Black, 2.4% Asian, 2.5% Amer. Indian, 1.9% Other; 5.9% Hispanic Origin. Households: 56.7% married couple families; 24.4% married couple fams. w. children; 50.7% college educ.; median household income: $24,807; per capita income: $12,458; median house value: $94,300; median gross rent: $351.

1996 Presidential Vote			1992 Presidential Vote		
Dole (R)	126,430	(51%)	Bush (R)	101,505	(38%)
Clinton (D)	89,736	(36%)	Clinton (D)	93,823	(35%)
Perot (I)	22,161	(9%)	Perot (I)	67,298	(25%)
Others	10,058	(4%)			

Rep. Wally Herger (R)

Elected 1986; b. May 20, 1945, Yuba City; home, Marysville; American River Comm. Col., A.A. 1967, CA St. U., 1968–69; Mormon; married (Pamela).

Elected Office: CA Assembly, 1980–86.

Professional Career: Rancher; Owner, Herger Gas Inc., 1969–80.

DC Office: 2433 RHOB 20515, 202-225-3076; Web site: www.house.gov/herger.

District Offices: Chico, 530-893-8363; Redding, 530-223-5898.

Committees: *Budget* (4th of 24 R). *Ways & Means* (7th of 23 R): Trade.

Group Ratings

	ADA	ACLU	AFS	LCV	CON	NTU	NFIB	COC	ACU	NTLC	CHC
1998	0	6	0	0	45	73	100	88	100	95	100
1997	5	—	25	—	49	64	—	90	96	—	—

National Journal Ratings

	1997 LIB	—	1997 CONS		1998 LIB	—	1998 CONS
Economic	15%	—	84%		19%	—	79%
Social	20%	—	71%		0%	—	97%
Foreign	0%	—	88%		7%	—	83%

Key Votes of the 105th Congress

1. Clinton Budget Deal	Y	5. Puerto Rico Sthood. Ref.	N	9. Cut $ for B-2 Bombers	N
2. Education IRAs	Y	6. End Highway Set-asides	Y	10. Human Rights in China	N
3. Req. 2/3 to Raise Taxes	Y	7. School Prayer Amend.	Y	11. Withdraw Bosnia Troops	Y
4. Fast-track Trade	Y	8. Ovrd. Part. Birth Veto	Y	12. End Cuban TV-Marti	N

Election Results

1998 general	Wally Herger (R)	128,372	(63%)	($608,996)
	Roberts Braden (D)	70,837	(34%)	($35,424)
	Others	6,158	(3%)	
1998 primary	Wally Herger (R)	102,806	(63%)	
	Roberts Braden (D)	45,049	(27%)	
	Bob Todd (R)	11,487	(7%)	
	Others	5,117	(3%)	
1996 general	Wally Herger (R)	144,913	(61%)	($536,724)
	Roberts Braden (D)	80,401	(34%)	($161,918)
	Others	13,019	(5%)	

THIRD DISTRICT

California's Sacramento Valley is one of nature's—and man's—miracles. Nature has sculpted a floor of almost perfectly flat land, surrounded on three sides by mountains, alternately purple and brown in the light. To this fertile lush black loam, man has added roads and fences—as straight as the lines in a geometry text—and, most importantly, water. Pacific clouds pour rain into the mountains, but the water used to run off quickly before it was penned in reservoirs and distributed through a system of canals and aqueducts, levees and pumping plants. The Sacramento and Central valleys now produce a marvelous variety of crops: rice, plums, almonds, olives, asparagus, pears, hops, beans, celery, onions, potatoes. The Sacramento Valley has always guarded its water jealously, and in the days before one-person-one-vote, it had enough seats in the California Senate to veto water decisions it didn't like; today it must fight to keep enough for its farms against the demands of the cities to the south and to maintain the levees which broke during the floods of January 1997.

The metropolis of this valley is Sacramento. Its historic foundation is apparent, coming into town on the West Sacramento Freeway, elevated above utterly flat rice lands painstakingly drained by a network of canals. As you hurtle over the Sacramento River on the M Street Bridge you see, framed perfectly in its arch, California's glorious golden-domed Capitol. On this landing Sacramento was born, and the state government, along with the agriculture symbolized by those rice fields, were for years its lifeblood. Now Sacramento spreads far to the south, east and north, with 1.5 million people—one of the fastest-growing major metropolitan areas during the last two decades.

The 3d Congressional District includes part of metropolitan Sacramento and much of the Sacramento Valley to the north. It takes in many of the suburbs just north of Sacramento and the American River—all or part of Carmichael, Citrus Heights, North Highlands and Foothills Farms. Sacramento, filled with government employees, is historically Democratic, but these suburbs are increasingly Republican. The 3d also includes heavily Democratic Yolo County, with industrial West Sacramento just across the Sacramento River from the Capitol and, on the flat farmlands, the tree-shaded, bicycle-pathed town of Davis, with its University of California campus. In the Sacramento Valley it extends north along I-5 to Red Bluff.

The congressman from the 3d District is Doug Ose, a Republican elected in 1998 to a seat which, in its various versions, had elected only Democrats since it was created in 1962. Ose grew up in Sacramento and went into the family real estate development business after graduating from Berkeley in 1977. In 1985, he struck out on his own, mainly to build mini-storage units. This is a booming business in a fast-growing metropolitan area filling up with subdivision houses on narrow lots and garden apartments with little room to store a lifetime's paraphernalia. Ose had accumulated enough of a fortune to be able to self-finance a House campaign. The occasion came in November 1997, when 3d District Congressman Vic Fazio announced he would not seek re-election after 20 years in the House.

Fazio was chairman of the Democratic Caucus, the third-ranking leadership position; he used to chair the Legislative Subcommittee, which determines Congress's own budget. In his efforts to save Sacramento's McClellan Air Force Base from the 1995 round of base closures, the Clinton Administration came up with a "privatization-in-place" program that saved McClellan's jobs and eliminated those in other military depots—a breaking of the rules that has killed the base-closing procedure ever since. Despite his prominence in Washington and connections in Sacramento, redistricting in 1992 gave Fazio this Republican-leaning district, which he had to fight hard to hold. He spent $1.9 million in 1992, $1.9 million again in 1994, $2.3 million in 1996, and won by just 51%–40%, 50%–46% and 54%–41%.

Fazio's retirement made Republicans the clear favorite for the district. Their two leading candidates were Ose, who had not run for office before, and Assemblywoman Barbara Alby, a strong conservative. Spending freely of his own money, Ose ran a stream of television and radio attacks against Alby; one ad asserted that Alby had missed two of every 10 legislative votes in 1997 (some of them due to a "junket to Hawaii," a charge that was accompanied in the ad by dancing hula dolls). The attacks worked. In the nine-candidate all-party June primary, Ose finished first, with 30% of the vote, to Alby's 19%. Sandie Dunn, a water and land-use attorney endorsed by Fazio, took 23% and won the Democratic nomination.

Both candidates showed strengths in the general election campaign. Dunn campaigned as a moderate, with special expertise in water law and experience in the Sacramento Valley on this issue; she came out and opposed the moribund Auburn Dam. Ose campaigned as a strong supporter of tax cuts and for giving local governments control over environmental protection. His manner on the stump was perhaps not as effective as hers, but he made up for it in money. The two candidates raised roughly comparable sums from individuals and PACs—$530,000 for Dunn, $735,000 for Ose. But Ose spent a total of $1.43 million of his own money, for almost $2.4 million; this was the sixth most expensive House contest of 1998. With turnout low, the district's Republican lean prevailed, and Ose won won 53%–45%. Yolo County, which cast one-quarter the district's votes, went 57%–41% for Dunn. But Sacramento County and the Sacramento Valley counties, each with three-eighths of the district's votes, went for Ose by 52%–45% and 60%–37% respectively.

In Washington, Ose was assigned to the Agriculture, Government Reform, and Banking committees. He looks to be politically safe, though he could face a conservative challenge in the primary or a serious Democrat in the general. But as Republican state Senator Maurice Johannessen said during the 1998 campaign, "If the Democrats cannot get this seat now, they might as well forget it for decades."

Cook's Call. *Competitive.* This is a district that would be problematic at best for any Democrat but fairly safe for any Republican who works hard and doesn't move too far from the middle. Ose, a moderate, wealthy businessman, looks well-positioned to hold onto the district. Democrats, who had trouble finding a top-tier candidate here in 1998, look like they may have that same problem in 2000. There is serious talk that the governor and Democratic-controlled legislature may play havoc with this district and, given the abundance of Democratic voters in the next door 5th District, it is a possibility.

The People: Pop. 1990: 571,545; 18.2% rural; 11.5% age 65 +; 82.2% White, 3.2% Black, 5.6% Asian, 1.4% Amer. Indian, 7.5% Other; 13.8% Hispanic Origin. Households: 55% married couple families; 27% married couple fams. w. children; 52.9% college educ.; median household income: $30,296; per capita income: $13,786; median house value: $118,400; median gross rent: $438.

1996 Presidential Vote			1992 Presidential Vote		
Clinton (D)	103,507	(45%)	Clinton (D)	99,781	(41%)
Dole (R)	101,651	(44%)	Bush (R)	90,799	(37%)
Perot (I)	15,921	(7%)	Perot (I)	53,323	(22%)
Others	7,858	(3%)			

Rep. Doug Ose (R)

Elected 1998; b. June 27, 1955, Sacramento; home, Sacramento; U. of CA at Berkeley, B.S. 1977; Lutheran; married (Lynnda).

Professional Career: Project mgr., Ose Properties, 1977–85; Real estate developer, 1985-present.

DC Office: 1508 LHOB 20515, 202-225-5716; Fax: 202-226-1298; Web site: www.house.gov/ose.

District Office: Woodland, 530-669-3540.

Committees: *Agriculture* (25th of 27 R): General Farm Commodities, Resource Conservation & Credit; Risk Management, Research & Specialty Crops. *Banking & Financial Services* (27th of 32 R): Domestic & International Monetary Policy; Housing & Community Opportunity. *Government Reform* (21st of 24 R): Criminal Justice, Drug Policy & Human Resources; Government Management, Information & Technology.

Group Ratings and Key Votes: Newly Elected

Election Results

1998 general	Doug Ose (R)	100,621	(52%)	($2,373,133)
	Sandie Dunn (D)	86,471	(45%)	($622,964)
	Others	4,914	(3%)	
1998 primary	Doug Ose (R)	44,866	(30%)	
	Sandie Dunn (D)	34,012	(23%)	
	Barbara Alby (R)	27,988	(19%)	
	Howard Beeman (D)	13,768	(9%)	
	Charles Schaupp (R)	12,277	(8%)	
	Bob Kent (D)	6,403	(4%)	
	Others	8,397	(6%)	
1996 general	Vic Fazio (D)	118,663	(54%)	($2,320,330)
	Tim Lefever (R)	91,134	(41%)	($645,209)
	Others	11,940	(5%)	

FOURTH DISTRICT

California sprang suddenly into existence: The Gold Rush of 1849 was followed by statehood and the creation of the first 27 counties in 1850. The new state's first boom area was the Mother Lode country in the foothills of the Sierras above Sacramento. Mining camps the size of eastern cities grew up in vacant valleys locked amid steep hills, with thousands of would-be millionaires gathered to find gold—though most of those who actually got rich did so by catering to miners' needs. In Placerville, John Studebaker had a buggy shop, Phillip Armour ran a butcher shop and Mark Hopkins had a dry goods store. The biggest mine in California was sunk in Grass Valley in 1857 and worked for half a century. But long before that, most of the Mother Lode country emptied out, leaving ghost towns and villages with hundreds of deserted houses—an antique vacation country left behind in time.

As they celebrated the sesquicentennial, local residents have sought to resurrect their area into a booming ex-urban and tourist mecca. "The American River near Coloma becomes a virtual freeway of whooping rafters on summer weekends," reported *USA Today*. "The Mother Lode also offers modern-day prospectors an intriguing pastiche of bed-and-breakfast inns, musty antique stores and such blink-and-you'll-miss-'em outposts as Volcano, Fiddletown, Rough and Ready"— named after President Zachary Taylor. Thousands of Californians—many of them families from smog-filled, middle-class suburbs of the Los Angeles Basin and the San Francisco Bay area—looking for a more pleasant, small-town, orderly environment, have found it here along fast-flowing creeks where the '49ers camped. For the first time since the 1860 Census, county populations rose sharply in the past two decades. Politically, this migration has changed the Mother Lode country from Democrat to Republican. The new migrants are tired of the cultures of therapy of the big metro areas and ready for more discipline. In 1976, nine Mother Lode counties from Sierra to Mariposa cast 118,000 votes, 50% for Jimmy Carter and 47% for Gerald Ford—close to the California average. In 1996 they cast 264,000 votes, 51% for Bob Dole and 38% for Bill Clinton, results closer to Idaho than coastal California. In 1998, Republican Dan Lungren's 54% in Placer County, the largest in the district, was among his strongest performances in the state—better than in Orange County.

The 4th Congressional District consists of most of the Mother Lode country plus the northeastern suburbs of Sacramento—Fair Oaks, Citrus Heights, Orangevale—and the old town of Folsom. The district runs northeast along I-80 into Auburn and Roseville in Placer County where the Mother Lode hills start, then up to the crest of the Sierra Nevada and over to the California shore of Lake Tahoe and the arid salt flats around Mono Lake. Politically, this is about as solidly Republican an area as there is in California these days.

The congressman from the 4th District is John Doolittle, a Republican with one of the most conservative voting records in the House. Doolittle grew up in the Los Angeles area and went to high school in Cupertino, in what now is Silicon Valley. His conservatism was annealed in the fires of adversity: He graduated from the University of California at Santa Cruz in 1972, when the campus was 97% for George McGovern. After law school he moved to the edge of the Sacramento metro area where the foothills begin, and in 1980 was elected at 30 to the state Senate from a district that stretched up to the Oregon border. As a senator he opposed gun control and abortion, and favored a crime victims' bill of rights and widespread AIDS testing. When the incumbent retired in 1990 in a district that then stretched from the Mother Lode country to Stockton, Doolittle ran for the seat. He had tougher competition than expected from Democrat Patricia Malberg, who was pro-choice on abortion, against nuclear power and for defense spending cuts; Doolittle won by just 50%–46%.

As a freshman, Doolittle was one of the Republicans' Gang of Seven, who were the advance guard for Newt Gingrich's 1994 revolution. He was California House Republicans' point man on redistricting, but he supported a plan that only protected Republican incumbents and gave them no shot at California's seven new seats; this was nixed by Governor Pete Wilson. Perhaps to curry favor with the 25% of the district who voted for Ross Perot in 1992, Doolittle joined "United We Stand America." In 1994, he seemed finally to get a firm hold on the district, raising his vote above 60%.

In the Republican House, Doolittle was given a subcommittee chair the old Democrats who represented this area would have relished: Water and Power. But his agenda resembled theirs only in his support for the Auburn Dam, which he and other Sacramento area congressmen wanted built on the American River, 35 miles east of Sacramento. Doolittle insisted on a design that could supply water to the Mother Lode. But in 1996 the dam was rejected in committee, 35–28, by a combination of environmentalists and spending opponents. When he continued the fight, the Senate Environment and Public Works Committee, led by the Bay Area's Barbara Boxer, blocked his efforts in 1998. Doolittle then blocked Robert Matsui's proposal for higher levees and to create more outlets in the Folsom Dam. The deadlock left unresolved attempts to address Sacramento's flood-control needs.

Doolittle's other subcommittee plans are longer range, and also unrealized. He seeks to sell the government's Power Marketing Administrations, which subsidize electric power in some areas because they needed power lines built in the 1930s. But Doolittle's efforts to sell the Southeastern Power Administration was nixed in October 1995 when Speaker Gingrich heeded the plea of the Republican gubernatorial nominee (who lost anyway). Doolittle also seeks to change the environmental provisions imposed on the Central Valley Project in 1992, but the Environmental Protection Agency in 1998 blocked his effort to build a water pipeline out of the Lake Tahoe basin.

Doolittle worked with Majority Whip Tom DeLay in 1998 to oppose the Shays-Meehan campaign-finance reform by proposing their own alternative to remove existing restrictions on fundraising but provide daily disclosure of contributions: free expression and transparency. (This is also the position of former Senator Eugene McCarthy.) This was derided as the enemy of "reform," but Doolittle reintroduced it in the 106th Congress; its prospects seem nil. Interestingly, Doolittle's 1998 opponent tried his own reform by not taking contributions at all; Doolittle won by his biggest margin ever. In early 1999, Doolittle hoped that DeLay would tap him to replace Denny Hastert as the Republican's chief deputy whip, but he was passed over. He boycotted the 1999 State of the Union address, calling Clinton "guilty as sin" and "not fit to hold office." In March 1999, he and Bill Thomas revived an old proposal—in lieu of a pay raise, per-diem allowances to cover expenses, of the kind they received as California Assemblymen; others said this would be attacked as an $18,000 tax-free pay increase, and the proposal seemed sure to go nowhere. In 1999, Doolittle began to become more active in the House Republican Caucus; he is one of six vice chairs of the National Republican Congressional Committee.

Cook's Call. *Safe.* Doolittle's past electoral experience suggests that when faced with a high quality challenger, he can be pushed into a competitive race but perhaps not beaten; against weak opposition he will win comfortably every time. It's unclear whether Democrats will expend the effort to target Doolittle, but it's unlikely that he would lose in any case.

The People: Pop. 1990: 571,027; 38.4% rural; 12.5% age 65 + ; 92.7% White, 1.7% Black, 2.1% Asian, 1.4% Amer. Indian, 2.1% Other; 7.2% Hispanic Origin. Households: 61.8% married couple families; 28.2% married couple fams. w. children; 57.5% college educ.; median household income: $35,772; per capita income: $16,263; median house value: $152,400; median gross rent: $488.

1996 Presidential Vote

Dole (R) 145,223 (51%)
Clinton (D) 107,076 (38%)
Perot (I) 21,233 (7%)
Others 9,775 (3%)

1992 Presidential Vote

Bush (R) 117,155 (40%)
Clinton (D) 97,501 (34%)
Perot (I) 73,060 (25%)

Rep. John Doolittle (R)

Elected 1990; b. Oct. 30, 1950, Glendale; home, Rocklin; U. of CA at Santa Cruz, B.A. 1972, U. of the Pacific, J.D. 1978; Mormon; married (Julia).

Elected Office: CA Senate, 1980–90, Repub. Caucus Chmn., 1987–90.

Professional Career: Practicing atty., 1978–80.

DC Office: 1526 LHOB 20515, 202-225-2511; Fax: 202-225-5444; Web site: www.house.gov/doolittle.

District Office: Roseville, 916-786-5560.

Committees: *Government Reform* (23d of 24 R): Census (Vice Chmn.); National Economic Growth, Natural Resources & Regulatory Affairs. *Resources* (8th of 28 R): Forests & Forest Health; Water & Power (Chmn.). *Transportation & Infrastructure* (32d of 41 R): Aviation; Oversight, Investigations & Emergency Management; Water Resources & Environment. *Joint Economic Committee* (3d of 10 Reps.).

Group Ratings

	ADA	ACLU	AFS	LCV	CON	NTU	NFIB	COC	ACU	NTLC	CHC
1998	5	6	11	0	13	55	100	89	100	95	100
1997	0	—	13	—	19	61	—	80	96	—	—

National Journal Ratings

	1997 LIB — 1997 CONS		1998 LIB — 1998 CONS	
Economic	10% —	86%	15% —	85%
Social	0% —	90%	11% —	88%
Foreign	0% —	88%	0% —	93%

Key Votes of the 105th Congress

1. Clinton Budget Deal	Y	5. Puerto Rico Sthood. Ref.	*	9. Cut $ for B-2 Bombers	N
2. Education IRAs	Y	6. End Highway Set-asides	Y	10. Human Rights in China	N
3. Req. 2/3 to Raise Taxes	Y	7. School Prayer Amend.	Y	11. Withdraw Bosnia Troops	Y
4. Fast-track Trade	N	8. Ovrd. Part. Birth Veto	Y	12. End Cuban TV-Marti	N

Election Results

1998 general	John Doolittle (R)	155,306	(63%)	($489,083)
	David Shapiro (D)	85,394	(34%)	
	Others	7,524	(3%)	
1998 primary	John Doolittle (R)	119,812	(65%)	
	David Shapiro (D)	56,829	(31%)	
	Dan Winterrowd (Lib)	8,108	(4%)	
1996 general	John Doolittle (R)	164,048	(60%)	($604,778)
	Katie Hirning (D)	97,948	(36%)	($199,179)
	Others	9,319	(3%)	

FIFTH DISTRICT

Sacramento, capital of the nation's largest state, focus of California's third-largest media market, home of a national sports franchise (the NBA's Sacramento Kings) and an 18-mile light rail system, is no longer just a small city with a lot of civil servants and a vegetable-packing economy. It is a vibrant major American metropolis, with some of the nation's highest job growth. Sacramento started as a river port on the sluggish waters of the Sacramento and American rivers. It was the destination of many overland migrants, the site of Sutter's Fort, where John Augustus Sutter found the gold that set off the Gold Rush of 1849, and the western terminus of the Pony Express in 1860. This was the natural choice to be California's capital, halfway between the San Francisco Bay and the Mother Lode country in the foothills of the Sierras, and in the middle of California's vast valley. Agriculture continues to be important today in Sacra-tomato (as some call it)—it has the world's largest almond processing plant.

In the old days, government was not a big business. Just a few lobbyists hung out in saloons on K or J streets, the governor's mansion was a musty antique, and the 100-plus degree summers emptied out what there was of the city. But air conditioning has replaced awnings, freeways and shopping malls have followed the city's growth east and north toward the Sierra foothills, and affluence has made this one of America's higher income metropolitan areas. In the 1980s metropolitan Sacramento grew 35%, more than any other large metro area except that other western capital, Phoenix, to more than 1.5 million; it has grown about 15% more in the 1990s. Even military base closedowns have not stopped the surge; the city extended benefits to get the computer maker Packard Bell to move to the Sacramento Army Depot after its headquarters was destroyed in the 1994 Northridge earthquake. Government expanded, too, even under Republicans George Deukmejian and Pete Wilson from 1983–99, and the platoons of lobbyists, lawyers and consultants is growing anew since Democrat Gray Davis reclaimed the governor's office.

As Sacramento has grown, this once Democratic, pro-government, working-class bastion has become closer to an upscale Sun Belt boom town. A long generation ago, in 1966, the Sacramento area was just about the only part of California beyond the Bay Area that stuck with Pat Brown over challenger Ronald Reagan. In 1998, the Sacramento area favored Democrat Gray Davis, but with 55%, 3% below his statewide average.

The 5th District consists of the center of metropolitan Sacramento; the area now includes parts of three other districts. The 5th contains affluent neighborhoods on older grid streets and scattered low-income black, Mexican-American and Hmong neighborhoods, plus new condominiums north of the American River and middle-class subdivisions south of downtown. Politically, this includes most of Sacramento's remaining Democratic neighborhoods, and it is the most Democratic district in the great valley from Bakersfield north to Oregon.

The congressman from the 5th is Robert Matsui, a Democrat first elected in 1978, third-ranking Democrat on the Ways and Means Committee. Born in 1941, the infant Matsui and his family were among the West Coast Japanese Americans forced into internment camps in 1942, and although he has no memory of the experience himself, he does remember the silence his family and others maintained about it. It was Asian shame, when none of the victims had anything to be ashamed about. He was one of the lead sponsors of the 1988 Japanese American redress law which apologized for the internment policy and provided monetary compensation for every survivor of the camps and for so-called "voluntary evacuees." He also sponsored the creation of the Manzanar National Historic Site, near Bishop, California, to preserve the memory of this episode.

For most of the 1990s Matsui has been a national leader on trade issues. In early 1993 he took the lead among House Democrats in seeking approval of the North American Free Trade Agreement, at a time when the Clinton Administration was lukewarm, then-Majority Leader Dick Gephardt was opposed and then-Minority Whip Newt Gingrich was not engaged in the issue. Working with Republican Jim Kolbe of Arizona, he rallied support and let the White House know that NAFTA was foundering and would not pass without a major push. Both the White House and Gingrich went all out, and NAFTA passed by a comfortable majority. Matsui, by now ranking Democrat on the Trade Subcommittee, hoped for a similar outcome on fast-track negotiating authority in 1997. But he found himself isolated as one of very few Democrats strongly supporting fast track, and when he and the White House were unable to produce the number of Democratic votes they had promised, Speaker Newt Gingrich pulled the measure at the last minute. The Republicans brought it back up for a vote in September 1998, even though it was apparent it had lost rather than gained votes. Matsui bitterly termed the vote "an attempt to embarrass members of my party," though the question might be asked whether the Democrats, only 29 of whom voted for fast track, embarrassed themselves.

When the ranking Democratic seat on the Social Security Subcommittee opened up in 1999, Matsui was eager to switch, and he found himself more comfortably arguing Democratic dogma on a conventional partisan issue. On another issue which has crossed party lines, Matsui has always favored normal trade relations for China, but his stand was reinforced when he was approached in Frank Fat's (the prime politicians' restaurant in Sacramento) by owner Frank Fat who asked him to support it. He continued to rally support for normal trade relations with China after revelations of illegal Chinese campaign contributions and illegal transfers of missile launch technology.

Starting in the early 1990s, before Clinton was elected, Matsui became a player in Democratic fundraising, as treasurer of the Democratic National Committee from 1991–95 and deputy chairman in 1995 and 1996; his wife Doris Matsui was deputy director of public liaison in the Clinton White House until early 1999. In April 1996 Matsui introduced Vice President Al Gore at the luncheon in the Buddhist temple in Hacienda Heights where nuns were reportedly making $5,000 contributions to the DNC. Matsui said in 1997 that he understood all along that the luncheon was both a "community outreach" event and a fundraiser. But as news of Clinton finance scandals came out, it became evident that neither Matsui was involved in any wrongdoing.

The retirement of Vic Fazio in the 3rd district has increased the burden on Matsui to work on local projects. The Sacramento delegation worked together for years to build the Auburn Dam to provide greater flood protection for Sacramento, but after that was beaten by a coalition of environmentalists and fiscal conservatives, the delegation split. The 4th district's John Doolittle wanted to push building the dam by transferring the land to the state government; Matsui conceded that the Auburn Dam would not be built and introduced a plan, endorsed by the Clinton Administration, to raise the height of downstream American River levees. As a result, neither plan was approved in 1998. But in April 1999, the House approved a water resources bill that contained some improvements for Sacramento's flood control system; Matsui is pushing for even more. On other issues, Matsui has a bill to preserve health care services for military retirees—important locally because Sacramento's McClellan Air Force Base is, technically, being closed, though the Clinton administration's "privatization in place" program is designed to maintain jobs there at the expense of other federal depots.

In the past, Matsui has flirted with running for statewide office—against then-Senator Pete Wilson in 1988, for attorney general in 1990, for the Senate seat Alan Cranston vacated in 1992—but decided each time not to. He has been re-elected easily every two years.

Cook's Call. *Safe.* This Sacramento-based district is strongly Democratic and has re-elected Matsui easily for over 20 years; he is a cinch for re-election in 2000. Democrats, who will control the redistricting process in 2001, may draw some of the surplus Democrats in the 5th into adjacent districts to boost their chances in those seats.

The People: Pop. 1990: 573,659; 0.5% rural; 11.9% age 65 + ; 65.7% White, 12.8% Black, 13.2% Asian, 1.3% Amer. Indian, 7% Other; 14.4% Hispanic Origin. Households: 44.4% married couple families; 21.5% married couple fams. w. children; 57.1% college educ.; median household income: $29,974; per capita income: $14,661; median house value: $122,500; median gross rent: $441.

1996 Presidential Vote			1992 Presidential Vote		
Clinton (D)	119,678	(57%)	Clinton (D)	120,577	(50%)
Dole (R)	70,925	(34%)	Bush (R)	73,562	(31%)
Perot (I)	10,863	(5%)	Perot (I)	42,566	(18%)
Others	8,159	(4%)			

Rep. Robert T. Matsui (D)

Elected 1978; b. Sept. 17, 1941, Sacramento; home, Sacramento; U. of CA at Berkeley, A.B. 1963, J.D. 1966; United Methodist; married (Doris).

Elected Office: Sacramento City Cncl., 1971–78.

Professional Career: Practicing atty., 1967–78.

DC Office: 2308 RHOB 20515, 202-225-7163; Fax: 202-225-0566; Web site: www.house.gov/matsui.

District Office: Sacramento, 916-498-5600.

Committees: *Ways & Means* (3d of 16 D): Human Resources; Social Security (RMM).

Group Ratings

	ADA	ACLU	AFS	LCV	CON	NTU	NFIB	COC	ACU	NTLC	CHC
1998	95	81	89	100	55	10	7	39	4	8	0
1997	90	—	88	—	62	20	—	40	20	—	—

National Journal Ratings

	1997 LIB — 1997 CONS	1998 LIB — 1998 CONS
Economic	71% — 28%	79% — 0%
Social	85% — 0%	72% — 27%
Foreign	79% — 19%	90% — 5%

Key Votes of the 105th Congress

1. Clinton Budget Deal	N	5. Puerto Rico Sthood. Ref.	Y	9. Cut $ for B-2 Bombers	N
2. Education IRAs	N	6. End Highway Set-asides	N	10. Human Rights in China	Y
3. Req. 2/3 to Raise Taxes	N	7. School Prayer Amend.	N	11. Withdraw Bosnia Troops	N
4. Fast-track Trade	N	8. Ovrd. Part. Birth Veto	N	12. End Cuban TV-Marti	Y

Election Results

1998 general	Robert T. Matsui (D)	130,715	(72%)	($586,491)
	Robert S. Dinsmore (R)	47,307	(26%)	($17,530)
	Others	3,816	(2%)	
1998 primary	Robert T. Matsui (D)	94,745	(71%)	
	Robert S. Dinsmore (R)	23,905	(18%)	
	Edward E. Gorre (R)	12,947	(10%)	
	Others	2,670	(2%)	
1996 general	Robert T. Matsui (D)	142,618	(70%)	($814,857)
	Robert S. Dinsmore (R)	52,940	(26%)	($18,792)
	Others	6,902	(3%)	

SIXTH DISTRICT

When the Golden Gate bridge was opened in 1937, San Francisco was one of the nation's best-known cities, but few knew much about the land beyond the bridge's north pierhead. There were fewer than 50,000 people in Marin County then and another 65,000 just to the north in Sonoma County. For San Franciscans, Marin was known for the ferry terminus in Sausalito, a fishing village and art colony, and as the beginning of the Redwood Empire, with its giant trees in Muir Woods; near the Bay was the state prison at San Quentin, with its infamous gas chamber.

Farther north, in a sunny valley protected from the fog by the Coast Range, was Santa Rosa, site of agronomist Luther Burbank's laboratory, a town that looked Middle American enough to be the set for dozens of movies. Politically, the area was then typical of the nation: traditionally Republican, but favoring Franklin Roosevelt in the 1930s.

Today this part of California is far more populous, with 230,000 people in Marin and 388,000 in Sonoma, solidly a part of the San Francisco Bay Area, affluent beyond the dreams of Americans of 50 years ago and extreme in its cultural attitudes. Trendy Marin, with its hot tubs and its fashionable people getting in touch with themselves, became a national caricature in the late 1970s: economically affluent, culturally liberationist. After a while such an image feeds on itself; a place like Marin attracts affluent people who share its values, while those who don't go elsewhere—in the Bay Area to the much more conservative San Ramon Valley, beyond the mountains east of Oakland. Indeed the Bay Area as a whole seems to attract liberals and repel conservatives, just as Phoenix does the opposite. And Marin and Sonoma are attracting the most liberal of the liberal—averse to traditional religion, derisive of traditional sexual and marriage mores, viscerally anti-military.

The 6th Congressional District includes all of Marin County and Sonoma except for its most rural corner. Republican as recently as 1980, the 6th voted 57%–29% for Bill Clinton over Bob Dole in 1996 and 66%–28% for Gray Davis over Dan Lungren in 1998. The public dialogue here is increasingly monopartisan, and, in this community priding itself on its tolerance, nary a dissenting word is heard.

The congresswoman from the 6th District is Lynn Woolsey, a Democrat elected in 1992 when 10-year incumbent Barbara Boxer was elected to the Senate. Woolsey grew up in the Pacific Northwest, moved to Marin 30 years ago and was a housewife with three children under 6 when her marriage ended in 1968. She went on welfare, got a low-paying job and left her children with 13 different babysitters in a year. Deliverance appeared in the form of a job with a high-tech startup firm where she rose to become a top executive. She remarried and moved to a house in Petaluma where her mother could live and look after the kids. As she wrote in her campaign literature, "Finally I could concentrate on work. The children had good care at last!" She put herself through business school at night, earned a degree in human resources and started her own personnel service.

In 1984 Woolsey won a seat on the Petaluma Council and was proud of its record in limiting growth, setting up affirmative action programs and a Women of Color Task Force, requiring that 15% of new housing be reserved for low-income buyers and establishing a voucher system for low-income families' child care. In 1992 she won the House seat in a nine-candidate primary against well-known members of the Marin and Sonoma boards of supervisors and the well-financed J. Bennett Johnston III, son of the former Louisiana senator. In that year of the woman, she led the primary with 26%, well ahead of the next candidate's 19%. In the general she faced liberal Republican Assemblyman Bill Filante. But he had surgery for a brain tumor and stopped campaigning, and she won 65%–34%.

Woolsey has one of the most liberal voting records in the House. As the only known former welfare recipient in Congress, she co-chaired the Democrats' task force on welfare reform. She opposed the 1996 Welfare Reform Act and calls for easing work requirements and providing more child care; she wants mothers to be able to stay at home until their children are 11, not 6. She pushed successfully for $100 million from the federal government to match low-income savers' money in Individual Development Accounts. She lobbied against banning gays in the military, accompanied by her son who is gay. She wants to let school districts use federal aid to provide health services. When the child-nutrition program was renewed in the 105th Congress, she took credit for a pilot program to expand school breakfast to all children regardless of income and for opening eligibility to teenagers in after-school snack programs. On occasion, Woolsey has teamed with Republicans: with Henry Hyde on a proposal to have the IRS enforce child-support collection and with Wally Herger on moving Social Security revenues out of federal budget calculations.

Her big local project has been to expand the protected area around the Point Reyes National Seashore by purchasing easements from nearby farmers and barring them from selling their land to nonagricultural users. But many farmers have complained about a federal "land grab" and the proposal has languished. In 1998, she brokered the sale of Hamilton Field, closed by the Navy 20 years ago, to the city of Novator. Another local favorite is Woolsey's call for export subsidies for winemakers. She worked for a larger antenna for the Rohnert Park public radio station and federal buyouts of landslided properties in Sonoma County.

Politically, she was "deeply disappointed" with President Clinton in the Lewinsky affair but she said in 1998 her greatest disappointment would be "if the country cannot move beyond this." Woolsey has been easily re-elected.

Cook's Call. *Safe.* This Marin and Sonoma based district has consistently supported liberal women representatives for the past 16 years and it looks like Woolsey will keep the tradition going strong in 2000. While not as overwhelmingly Democratic as other Bay Area districts, the 6th retains a strong Democratic core.

The People: Pop. 1990: 571,360; 18.7% rural; 13.6% age 65 + ; 90.1% White, 2.3% Black, 3.4% Asian, 0.8% Amer. Indian, 3.3% Other; 8.5% Hispanic Origin. Households: 51.3% married couple families; 22.9% married couple fams. w. children; 67.1% college educ.; median household income: $40,564; per capita income: $21,603; median house value: $257,400; median gross rent: $644.

1996 Presidential Vote

Clinton (D)	155,513	(57%)
Dole (R)	78,166	(29%)
Perot (I)	18,431	(7%)
Others	21,199	(8%)

1992 Presidential Vote

Clinton (D)	169,301	(56%)
Bush (R)	71,564	(24%)
Perot (I)	60,920	(20%)

Rep. Lynn Woolsey (D)

Elected 1992; b. Nov. 3, 1937, Seattle, WA; home, Petaluma; U. of San Francisco, B.A. 1980; Presbyterian; divorced.

Elected Office: Petaluma City Cncl., 1985–92, Vice Mayor, 1986, 1991.

Professional Career: Human Resources Mgr., Harris Digital Telephone, 1969–80; Owner, Woolsey Personnel Svc., 1980–92.

DC Office: 439 CHOB 20515, 202-225-5161; Fax: 202-225-5163; Web site: www.house.gov/woolsey.

District Offices: San Rafael, 415-507-9554; Santa Rosa, 707-542-7182.

Committees: *Education & the Workforce* (11th of 22 D): Early Childhood, Youth & Families; Workforce Protections. *Science* (9th of 22 D): Basic Research.

Group Ratings

	ADA	ACLU	AFS	LCV	CON	NTU	NFIB	COC	ACU	NTLC	CHC
1998	100	93	100	100	38	18	21	28	8	5	0
1997	100	—	88	—	74	30	—	30	0	—	—

National Journal Ratings

	1997 LIB — 1997 CONS			1998 LIB — 1998 CONS		
Economic	93%	—	0%	79%	—	0%
Social	85%	—	0%	85%	—	15%
Foreign	94%	—	3%	84%	—	11%

Key Votes of the 105th Congress

1. Clinton Budget Deal	N	5. Puerto Rico Sthood. Ref.	Y	9. Cut $ for B-2 Bombers	Y
2. Education IRAs	N	6. End Highway Set-asides	N	10. Human Rights in China	Y
3. Req. 2/3 to Raise Taxes	N	7. School Prayer Amend.	N	11. Withdraw Bosnia Troops	N
4. Fast-track Trade	N	8. Ovrd. Part. Birth Veto	N	12. End Cuban TV-Marti	Y

Election Results

1998 general	Lynn Woolsey (D)	158,446	(68%)	($634,563)
	Ken McAuliffe (R)	69,295	(30%)	($97,352)
	Others	5,240	(2%)	
1998 primary	Lynn Woolsey (D)	110,364	(65%)	
	Ken McAuliffe (R)	31,153	(18%)	
	Gisele Stavert (R)	24,187	(14%)	
	Others	3,882	(2%)	
1996 general	Lynn Woolsey (D)	156,958	(62%)	($542,131)
	Duane C. Hughes (R)	86,278	(34%)	($292,181)
	Others	10,600	(4%)	

SEVENTH DISTRICT

The journey inward from the Pacific Ocean to the vast flatness of California's Central Valley passes through wondrous terrain. The traveler starts at the Golden Gate, with the lush green Presidio on one side and the bluff of the Marin mountains on the other; through the waters of San Francisco Bay, looked down upon by ridges above the East Bay on one side and the cone of Mount Tamalpais on the other; through the narrow Carquinez Strait to Suisun Bay, with its sloughs and marshes, fed by the sluggish waters of the Sacramento and San Joaquin Delta; and finally past the mountains and waters, to the flat, fertile expanse of California's great interior. This is not a journey most tourists make, but it was a familiar route to the first Californians and it passes by much of the industrial base of the Bay Area. On the east side of the bay is Richmond, developed almost instantaneously during World War II when Henry J. Kaiser built a shipyard in its deep-water port and 91,000 people from all over the country were put to work building ships for the Pacific theater; it now has a large black population and is attracting high-tech spinoffs. Across Carquinez Strait is Vallejo, named for a Mexican general and member of the first California Senate, the site since 1853 of the giant Mare Island Naval Shipyard that was closed in 1996 and is now being redeveloped. Across the strait are tank farms and factories in Rodeo and Pittsburg and Martinez, the seat of Contra Costa County (literally, the coast opposite San Francisco).

The 7th Congressional District includes most of this passage, from Richmond and El Cerrito along both sides of Carquinez Strait and Suisun Bay to Vallejo, Rodeo, Martinez and Pittsburg. It also proceeds inland through the intermountain interstices of Contra Costa County to include most of middle-income Concord, but excludes the heavily Republican and higher-income interior Contra Costa communities around Walnut Hill and the San Ramon Valley. Politically, this industrial area was blue-collar, labor-union Democratic back in the days when San Francisco, with its larger white-collar population, often voted Republican. Today it is heavily Democratic, liberal on most issues, though not so far left as San Francisco or Berkeley.

The congressman from the 7th District is George Miller, one of four remaining Democrats of the Watergate class of 1974, the first baby-boom liberal to chair a House committee. He is also heir to a tradition of Bay Area working-class politics. His father was chairman of the state

Senate Finance Committee; when he died in 1969, Miller lost the race to succeed him, but became a staffer for Senate Leader (and later San Francisco Mayor) George Moscone. Miller was also a protege of San Francisco Congressman Phillip Burton, who did so much to establish liberal hegemony in the House in the 1970s. To his work Miller brings an aggressiveness and zest for political combat reminiscent of Burton. He is a strong backer of protecting the environment against what he sees as greedy private sector operators and of furthering the causes of labor unions.

Miller began the 1990s in a position of power, able to advance his causes forward; in the mid-1990s he found himself defending yesterday's gains and trying to prevent losses. In 1991 he became chairman of Interior (he renamed it Natural Resources in 1993 and Republicans renamed it Resources in 1995) and proceeded, in his words, "to kick ass and take names." He had long crusaded against water reclamation projects that provided cheap water to farmers. In 1992, amid a California drought, he passed a Central Valley Project law that raised farmers' prices closer to urban users and imposed environmental restrictions, over the fierce opposition of Central Valley politicians and Governor Pete Wilson. The victory was sealed when Bill Clinton appointed a top Miller aide as head of the Bureau of Reclamation. But the Clinton Administration was not always helpful on other matters. Miller strongly backed higher mining, grazing and timber fees for companies operating on federal lands, and he was dismayed when Clinton dropped Interior Secretary Bruce Babbitt's proposal for these in March 1993. He was successful in passing the California desert bill, with Senator Dianne Feinstein; it was the last major legislation of the Democratic Congress in October 1994.

Miller's successes since 1994 have been more in preventing change than making change. He helped to stymie John Doolittle's attempt to revise the Central Valley Project and was part of the coalition opposing the Auburn Dam sought by Doolittle and other Sacramento-area congressmen. He harshly criticized Republicans for trying to change the Endangered Species Act, EPA regulations, Arctic National Wildlife Refuge oil drilling, Tongass Forest logging and commercial sponsorship of national parks. He worked for the Presidio private-public trust fund and Bay-Delta funding in the successful 1996 parks bill, for the Manzanar National Historic Site commemorating one of the Japanese American detention camps in World War II; he successfully moved to award Congressional Medals of Honor to black World War II veterans who were unfairly overlooked, and has moved to reopen the mutiny verdicts of black sailors who refused to report for duty after munitions explosions at Port Chicago in 1944. He showed open-mindedness by working with Republican Senator Mike DeWine to change the focus of the Family Reunification Act, which Miller sponsored in 1980, to the best interests of children. He continued to be interested in California water, opposing a Utah radioactive waste dump in the Colorado River basin, favoring conservation over new CALFED projects, seeking a tougher law on agricultural runoff. And he ventured far afield, criticizing the Park Service's proposals for a visitors' center at Gettysburg and attacking Republican Whip Tom DeLay for supporting what Miller considers sweatshops in the Commonwealth of the Northern Mariana Islands.

From time to time Miller's short fuse is on display. In April 1997 he and DeLay had a red-faced confrontation over Miller's charge that DeLay let lobbyists write legislation in his office. In September 1997 he obstructed the House by objecting to routine procedures in order to force a vote on the campaign finance bill. Miller mocked what he considered Republicans' obsession with Monica Lewinsky, speculating they would take her blue dress "through their districts like the Olympic torch or something and see if that helps." But he was the one member who did not vote on impeachment in December 1998, for a good reason: he had just had hip-replacement surgery and his California doctor advised against air travel.

Miller has no cause for concern in his district. But he was part of an Election Day ruckus in 1998, when Republicans apparently sent a fraudulent mailer opposing Ellen Tauscher in the neighboring 10th district, with Miller's name on the letterhead of a fictitious group.

Cook's Call. *Safe.* A fixture of Bay Area and California politics for more than 25 years, Miller has not had to worry about a race in a long time. Don't look for any upsets here.

The People: Pop. 1990: 572,857; 0.3% rural; 10.7% age 65+; 62.7% White, 16.6% Black, 14.4% Asian, 0.8% Amer. Indian, 5.5% Other; 12.9% Hispanic Origin. Households: 52.2% married couple families; 26.7% married couple fams. w. children; 56.8% college educ.; median household income: $38,608; per capita income: $16,006; median house value: $168,100; median gross rent: $562.

1996 Presidential Vote

Clinton (D)	131,707	(65%)
Dole (R)	50,140	(25%)
Perot (I)	12,178	(6%)
Others	7,321	(4%)

1992 Presidential Vote

Clinton (D)	140,159	(60%)
Bush (R)	51,356	(22%)
Perot (I)	39,038	(17%)

Rep. George Miller (D)

Elected 1974; b. May 17, 1945, Richmond; home, Martinez; San Francisco St. U., B.A. 1968, U. of CA at Davis, J.D. 1972; Catholic; married (Cynthia).

Professional Career: Legis. aide, CA Senate Majority Ldr., 1969–74; Practicing atty., 1972–74.

DC Office: 2205 RHOB 20515, 202-225-2095; Fax: 202-225-5609; Web site: www.house.gov/georgemiller.

District Offices: Concord, 925-602-1880; Richmond, 510-262-6500; Vallejo, 707-645-1888.

Committees: *Education & the Workforce* (2d of 22 D): Early Childhood, Youth & Families; Workforce Protections. *Resources* (RMM of 24 D): Water & Power.

Group Ratings

	ADA	ACLU	AFS	LCV	CON	NTU	NFIB	COC	ACU	NTLC	CHC
1998	100	93	100	100	77	30	7	19	8	3	0
1997	95	—	100	—	32	25	—	11	4	—	—

National Journal Ratings

	1997 LIB — 1997 CONS		1998 LIB — 1998 CONS	
Economic	91% —	7%	79% —	0%
Social	85% —	0%	93% —	0%
Foreign	85% —	15%	61% —	37%

Key Votes of the 105th Congress

1. Clinton Budget Deal	N	5. Puerto Rico Sthood. Ref.	Y	9. Cut $ for B-2 Bombers	Y
2. Education IRAs	N	6. End Highway Set-asides	N	10. Human Rights in China	Y
3. Req. 2/3 to Raise Taxes	N	7. School Prayer Amend.	N	11. Withdraw Bosnia Troops	N
4. Fast-track Trade	N	8. Ovrd. Part. Birth Veto	N	12. End Cuban TV-Marti	Y

Election Results

1998 general	George Miller (D)	125,842	(77%)	($343,658)
	Norman H. Reece (R)	38,290	(23%)	($28,183)
1998 primary	George Miller (D)	87,533	(76%)	
	Norman H. Reece (R)	27,142	(24%)	
1996 general	George Miller (D)	137,089	(72%)	($434,745)
	Norman H. Reece (R)	42,542	(22%)	($41,147)
	Others	11,286	(6%)	

EIGHTH DISTRICT

On February 20, 1915, Governor Hiram Johnson and Mayor James Rolph led 150,000 people onto the grounds of the Panama-Pacific International Exposition to see the Spanish-Italian baroque style building built on reclaimed land in what became San Francisco's Marina district. The Exposition ostensibly celebrated the completion of the Panama Canal, but it was clearly intended to show off San Francisco's recovery from the 1906 earthquake. It also spotlighted San Francisco as the central focus of an America that was becoming, with its acquisition of Hawaii and the Philippines and its interest in an open-door policy with China and trade with Japan, a power in what we now call the Pacific Rim. The Exposition set the physical style of San Francisco: it encouraged the use of Mediterranean color, accent and detail that characterizes most post-Victorian houses and commercial structures in The City (as the *San Francisco Examiner* still calls it). It created the picturesque Marina district, whose old buildings were among the those damaged in the 1989 earthquake, and today's tourist waterfront around Fisherman's Wharf and Ghirardelli Square. This San Francisco has many facets: on a sunny day it looks almost tropical, with brown mountains baking in the sun and light shining off the pastel stucco buildings; when the clouds scud in from the Pacific, it can look sinister, full of dark corners where a private detective's partner might be ambushed by a pretty girl. The buildings can be majestic, like the monumental Beaux Arts City Hall, or tawdry, like the hotels of the Tenderloin; it is a city that looks exotic at first but, when you look closely, can only be American.

San Francisco has been a dynamic city, capable of great growth, carrying the American tradition of tolerance of diversity to new lengths; it grew from nothing to a major city in the single year of 1850; its American origins are obvious from the regular grids of streets named after politicians and local developers. The San Francisco of 1915 was proud of the writers who had flourished there—Jack London, Ambrose Bierce, Frank Norris—and of the home-town traditions of the arts and crafts movement, just as San Francisco later would have a Herb Caenish pride in the beats of the 1950s North Beach, the hippies who thronged Haight-Ashbury in 1967, and the gays of Castro in the 1970s and 1980s. Over the years, the city's booming economy, based initially on food processing, but now on finance, high-tech and clothing (Levi Strauss, The Gap) has attracted talented newcomers, weighted increasingly toward those who find its liberation-minded cultural attitudes congenial.

Politically, San Francisco was a progressive Republican town, like the two men who led the way into the Exposition. The sour-tempered Hiram Johnson made his name as a reformer throwing out crooked city politicians; his administration gave California primary elections, referenda and recall, and strong civil service laws. "Sunny Jim" Rolph, mayor from 1911–30 and then governor, built the civic center, parks, schools, streetcars and the Hetch Hetchy power lines—the antique infrastructure of San Francisco today. Sympathetic to the conservation movement, willing to deal with organized labor in a union town that had America's only general strike in 1934, tolerant of the diversity of California, these progressive Republicans were the recognizable ancestors of, though certainly not identical to, the San Franciscans who in the 1970s and 1980s became increasingly liberal and even radical.

But San Francisco's hipness can be overstated. For if its distinctive style attracted liberal singles and gays in increasing numbers, its economic dynamism on the Pacific Rim has attracted Asians—as indeed San Francisco did from 1850 until immigration was shut off by the Chinese Exclusion Act in 1882. The city has elected strong liberal politicians at least since the 1975 elections of Mayor George Moscone and openly gay Supervisor Harvey Milk, who were shot to death in 1978 by a political opponent who was acquitted of murder by a liberal jury on the bizarre theory that he had been crazed by junk food. Over the next decade, the city's cultural liberalism was tempered by Mayor Dianne Feinstein, who vetoed a gay marriage ordinance and opposed commercial rent control. In 1995, Willie Brown, ousted after 15 years as speaker of the Assembly, returned home. After the first two years, in which he reaped admiring publicity, Brown's record suddenly seemed dismal. The homeless, attracted by promises of toleration and aid, thronged on public streets and in the parks. While the affluent neighborhoods were enriched with new Silicon Valley millionaires, the Chinese, Filipino and other Asian immigrants in the southern and western parts of the city were beleaguered by high taxes that supported the pampered public employee unions.

The 8th Congressional District takes in four-fifths of San Francisco, all but the southwest corner. It has all of San Francisco's high-rise downtown, the increasingly crowded and bustling Chinatown, Telegraph, Nob and Russian Hills, North Beach (which was once really a beach), Pacific Heights (which is still on heights) and the Marina District (which does not have a very big marina). It extends to the ocean to include Sea Cliff overlooking the Golden Gate Bridge, and the Richmond area with its many Asian Americans. In the valleys are the mostly black Fillmore and Western Addition areas, but only 12% of the district's residents are black, as compared to 16% Hispanic and 27% Asian—the highest Asian percentage of any district outside Hawaii. The 8th also has the gay Castro district and Noe Valley, Haight-Ashbury, once the bedraggled center of hippiedom and now another yup-and-coming San Francisco neighborhood, and Portrero Hill with its restored houses overlooking downtown. Farther south are the old residential areas overlooking I-280, with pastel houses strewn along grid streets which hug the steep hills.

The 8th District is represented by Nancy Pelosi, a Democrat with deep political roots, who was elected in June 1987. She has the energy and shrewdness of one who has handled the most delicate political chores and the charm and unflappability of one who is the parent of five children. Pelosi grew up in Maryland; her father, Thomas D'Alessandro, served in the House from 1939–47 and was mayor of Baltimore for 12 years after that, and her brother, Thomas D'Alessandro Jr., was mayor from 1967–71. Married to a successful San Francisco business-man, Nancy Pelosi was California Democratic Party chair in the early 1980s, chaired the national party's Compliance Review Commission on delegate rules for 1984, and served as the Democratic Senatorial Campaign Committee's finance chair in 1985. She never considered running for the House when San Francisco's congressional politics was dominated by Phillip Burton, an old-fashioned labor-liberal Democrat. But Burton died in 1983 and his widow Sala, elected to succeed him, died in 1987. Pelosi ran and won 35%–31% in a June 1987 special against gay supervisor Harry Britt.

Pelosi has taken the lead on important issues of local sensitivity. One is human rights, especially in China. After the Tiananmen Square massacre, Pelosi sponsored an amendment to give Chinese students the right to remain in the United States; it passed but was vetoed by President Bush. In 1991 she became the lead sponsor of the bill to condition China's Most Favored Nation status on human rights reforms; Bush's veto was overridden in the House but upheld in the Senate. Since then Pelosi has led the fight against normal trade relations status and has sharply criticized China. "I don't believe in the concept of trickle-down liberty. Economic reform does not necessarily lead to political reform," she has said, arguing that the Chinese make concessions not when the U.S. bows to their wishes but when it threatens to walk away. As co-chair of the Congressional Working Group on China, she said that Clinton was either in denial or ill-informed about what's going on in China. When President Jiang Zemin visited Washington in 1997, she termed the White House state dinner shameful and attended a stateless dinner hosted by actor and pro-Tibet activist Richard Gere. All this is done at some political risk: Pelosi's position is by no means universally popular with Asian Americans in her district; many think the U.S. should trade and negotiate quietly with China. And one of her chief adversaries is her San Francisco neighbor, Senator Dianne Feinstein.

A second Pelosi cause is AIDS funding. She has used her Appropriations seat to get money for people with AIDS and wants access to new therapies and drugs without regard to ability to pay; she got AIDS spending increased even in the Republican Congress. In early 1999 she planned to sponsor a bill to expand Medicaid coverage of AIDs. Another Pelosi cause was the Presidio, for which Burton years ago got a law turning it over to the Interior Department if it was abandoned by the military; it was transferred to the National Park Service in 1995. There is no more stunning piece of urban property in America, but it is extremely expensive to maintain. Pelosi spent four years trying to devise a private-public trust fund for the Presidio. Her bill passed the House in 1994 but was killed by Senate Republicans. She succeeded in 1996 by getting Republican support for a trust that would lease the buildings to provide enough revenue to pay the Park Service to maintain the open spaces and renovate the old buildings, with the proviso, insisted on by Republicans, that it be self-supporting in 15 years.

On other issues Pelosi has a perfectly liberal voting record. She has worked to restore welfare for legal immigrants, has supported needle exchanges and opposed fast-track trade legislation. Although she works well with Republicans on China and the Presidio, she is a strong partisan, and, as a member of the ethics committee and the subcommittee that investigated Newt Gingrich, believed Republicans were obstructing the process and favored censure. As ranking member on the Foreign Operations Subcommittee, she wants aid programs to encourage family planning and environmental protection and has advocated the International Monetary Fund.

Pelosi has shown no interest in statewide office, but told House Democrats in 1998 that she would run for whip if they regained the majority. After the election, she turned down Dick Gephardt's entreaties to lead the Democratic Congressional Campaign Committee. As the Californian perhaps best-positioned for a House Democratic leadership position, her career continues to flourish. Pelosi has been re-elected by huge margins.

Cook's Call. *Safe.* It's almost impossible to imagine how Democrats could lose the 8th District, which is among the two dozen most Democratic and liberal in the nation. It's safe to say that the seat is Pelosi's until she decides to give it up.

The People: Pop. 1990: 573,192; 14.4% age 65+; 52.1% White, 12.8% Black, 27.8% Asian, 0.5% Amer. Indian, 6.8% Other; 15.1% Hispanic Origin. Households: 29.7% married couple families; 12.7% married couple fams. w. children; 58.4% college educ.; median household income: $31,659; per capita income: $19,377; median house value: $274,700; median gross rent: $594.

1996 Presidential Vote		
Clinton (D)	114,906	(66%)
Dole (R)	31,282	(18%)
Perot (I)	7,104	(4%)
Others	20,853	(12%)

1992 Presidential Vote		
Clinton (D)	187,201	(75%)
Bush (R)	39,396	(16%)
Perot (I)	21,180	(8%)

Rep. Nancy Pelosi (D)

Elected June 1987; b. Mar. 26, 1940, Baltimore, MD; home, San Francisco; Trinity Col., B.A. 1962; Catholic; married (Paul).

Professional Career: CA Dem. Party, Northern Chmn., 1977–81, St. Chmn., 1981–83; DSCC Finance Chmn., 1985–87; PR exec., Ogilvy & Mather, 1986–87.

DC Office: 2457 RHOB 20515, 202-225-4965; Fax: 202-225-8259; Web site: www.house.gov/pelosi.

District Office: San Francisco, 415-556-4862.

Committees: *Appropriations* (9th of 27 D): Foreign Operations & Export Financing (RMM); Labor, HHS & Education. *Permanent Select Committee on Intelligence* (2d of 7 D): Human Intelligence, Analysis & Counterintelligence.

Group Ratings

	ADA	ACLU	AFS	LCV	CON	NTU	NFIB	COC	ACU	NTLC	CHC
1998	95	94	100	100	38	15	7	33	12	3	8
1997	100	—	100	—	19	26	—	20	4	—	—

National Journal Ratings

	1997 LIB — 1997 CONS		1998 LIB — 1998 CONS	
Economic	93%	— 0%	72%	— 23%
Social	85%	— 0%	93%	— 0%
Foreign	85%	— 13%	71%	— 27%

Key Votes of the 105th Congress

1. Clinton Budget Deal	N	5. Puerto Rico Sthood. Ref.	Y	9. Cut $ for B-2 Bombers	Y
2. Education IRAs	N	6. End Highway Set-asides	N	10. Human Rights in China	Y
3. Req. 2/3 to Raise Taxes	N	7. School Prayer Amend.	N	11. Withdraw Bosnia Troops	N
4. Fast-track Trade	N	8. Ovrd. Part. Birth Veto	N	12. End Cuban TV-Marti	Y

Election Results

1998 general	Nancy Pelosi (D)	148,027	(86%)	($523,136)
	David J. Martz (R)	20,781	(12%)	
	Others	3,654	(2%)	
1998 primary	Nancy Pelosi (D)	106,001	(85%)	
	David J. Martz (R)	15,374	(12%)	
	Others	3,714	(3%)	
1996 general	Nancy Pelosi (D)	175,216	(84%)	($465,863)
	Justin Raimondo (R)	25,739	(12%)	
	Others	6,805	(3%)	

NINTH DISTRICT

Oakland and Berkeley, on the East Bay opposite San Francisco, stand today on one of the lushest sites in America, overlooking the Bay Bridge and the Golden Gate, basking in the sunshine that is more common here than across the Bay. Both cities are the homes of great institutions, but in different ways they are also museum pieces, antiques from a moment in the 1960s when both, especially Berkeley, gained identities that became hard to shake. Berkeley was founded as a university town, named after the 18th Century Irish philosopher Bishop George Berkeley, for his proclamation, "Westward the course of empire takes its way." Famous for years as the home of first-rate scholarship at the University of California, Berkeley became famous politically in 1964 as the home of student rebellion when the Free Speech Movement, protesting an administrator's refusal to let students set up a card table to sign up volunteers for Lyndon Johnson's 1964 campaign, led to months of riots, student strikes and classroom confrontation. In 1969, students led protests at "People's Park," a lot owned by the university, and Governor Ronald Reagan sent in the National Guard to protect state property from conversion to a playground: an episode in which both sides relished confrontation more than success. Berkeley in the 1960s gave birth to a street culture that still exists (in 1993, a student went about campus naked and was expelled only when administrators had the ingenuity to charge him with sexual harassment). Its denizens made common cause with the Black Panthers, a violent quasi-political gang from nearby Oakland, and smoked marijuana with the Hell's Angels motorcycle gang, also once based in Oakland. Berkeley's city council features bizarre political wars in which Democrats very liberal by national standards are the right wing. The Berkeley campus, with its view of the Bay, remains beautiful, and old buildings like the shingled Claremont Hotel are grand. But Berkeley has had little commercial development, and its public facilities have a low-maintenance, almost Third World look.

Oakland has a different history, centered around commerce and building its own civic institutions (Gertrude Stein was wrong: there is a there there). It became the western terminus of the transcontinental railroad in 1870 and was connected by ferry to San Francisco; it has always had heavy industry, and its port today is the busiest on the bay. The docks attracted young roustabouts like the writer Jack London, after whom a downtown square is named; civic affairs were run by the local elite, like the Knowland family who owned the *Oakland Tribune*. With the Bay Area's largest black community, Oakland spawned the Black Panthers in the 1960s; blacks took control of city government in the 1970s and, through the late editor-owner Bob Maynard, the *Tribune* in the 1980s. But for much of the 1990s, Oakland was anything but thriving, with high crime rates, poor public schools and little economic development.

Onto the scene came Jerry Brown, governor of California 20 years before, unsuccessful presidential candidate in 1976, 1980 and 1992; he ran an unorthodox campaign for mayor, and in June 1998 won without a runoff. Brown irritated local politicos by firing department heads and ignoring political alliances, but he seemed to be taking seriously his mission of propelling Oakland to the prominence its geographic position suggests it can occupy. And at least implicitly he criticized the city's liberal policies by campaigning to make the city safer, to improve its schools and to bring businesses back to downtown. If Brown's victory was a rejection of the Oakland political establishment, so even more was the victory in a March 1999 special election to the Assembly of Green Party nominee Audie Bock over Brown's predecessor as mayor, Elihu Harris.

The 9th Congressional District consists of Oakland and Berkeley, plus adjacent towns like Alameda, site of an old Navy base on the bay. It had in 1990 the largest black percentage of any northern California district, but not a majority (31%); it was 15% Asian and 11% Hispanic. Politically, it is leftish Democratic: 75%–13% for Bill Clinton in 1996.

The congresswoman from the 9th District is Barbara Lee, a Democrat chosen in an April 1998 special election. She grew up in Texas and the San Fernando Valley, graduated from Mills College in Oakland and got a social work degree at Berkeley. She started a community mental health center in Berkeley and then worked as a staffer from 1975–87 for Congressman Ronald Dellums, elected in 1970 as a left Democrat and, in time, chairman of the Armed Services Committee. In 1990 Lee was elected to the California Assembly; in 1996, she was elected to the California Senate from a constituency almost as large as the congressional district. She chaired the Housing and Land Use Committee, and worked to promote the Sonoma Baylands project, which broke the logjam on bay dredging. She passed laws on a variety of subjects and worked for closer ties between California and Africa. After Dellums announced he was re-signing in February 1998, he endorsed Lee as his successor, and she won the special election without a runoff, with 67% of the vote. She had the good fortune to be running before Oakland was swept by the vote-for-a-change attitude that elected Jerry Brown and Audie Bock.

During the campaign, Lee said that she would work to reduce the nation's weapons stockpile and Pentagon spending. She promised to continue Dellums's efforts to convert closed military bases in Oakland to civilian use. On foreign policy, she moved quickly to revive the tradition of the "People's Republic of Berkeley." After a visit to Cuba, she called for a review of U.S. policy, including steps to end the 40-year embargo of Castro's island. Lee criticized President Clinton's renewed bombing of Iraq in late 1998, saying, "The United States has not explored and exhausted all possible means for a peaceful resolution to this conflict." And as most Democrats voted to authorize bombing of Serbia in March 1999, Lee was the only member of the House to vote against a resolution supporting U.S. troops; she argued that it wrongfully "embraces the notion that the president can authorize the commitment of U.S. troops to war without congressional approval."

Cook's Call. *Safe.* This Oakland-based district is one of the safest Democratic seats in the nation. Lee will hold this seat for as long as she wants it.

The People: Pop. 1990: 573,669; 12.6% age 65 +; 45.4% White, 31.8% Black, 15.8% Asian, 0.6% Amer. Indian, 6.5% Other; 11.4% Hispanic Origin. Households: 35.5% married couple families; 16.7% married couple fams. w. children; 61.9% college educ.; median household income: $30,067; per capita income: $16,833; median house value: $223,900; median gross rent: $490.

1996 Presidential Vote

Clinton (D)	156,998	(75%)
Dole (R)	26,321	(13%)
Perot (I)	6,277	(3%)
Others	19,498	(9%)

1992 Presidential Vote

Clinton (D)	186,714	(78%)
Bush (R)	29,394	(12%)
Perot (I)	21,207	(9%)

Rep. Barbara Lee (D)

Elected April 1998; b. July 16, 1946, El Paso, TX; home, Oakland; Mills Col., B.A. 1973, U. of CA at Berkeley, M.A. 1975; no religious affiliation; divorced.

Elected Office: CA Assembly, 1990–96; CA Senate, 1996–98.

Professional Career: Chief of Staff, U.S. Rep. Ron Dellums, 1975–87.

DC Office: 414 CHOB 20515, 202-225-2661; Fax: 202-225-9817; Web site: www.house.gov/lee.

District Office: Oakland, 510-763-0370.

Committees: *Banking & Financial Services* (19th of 27 D): Domestic & International Monetary Policy; Housing & Community Opportunity. *International Relations* (21st of 23 D): Africa.

Group Ratings (Only Served Partial Term)

	ADA	ACLU	AFS	LCV	CON	NTU	NFIB	COC	ACU	NTLC	CHC
1998	75	92	100	100	98	31	0	14	5	7	0
1997	*	—	—	—	*	*	—	*	*	—	—

National Journal Ratings (Only Served Partial Term)

	1997 LIB — 1997 CONS			1998 LIB — 1998 CONS		
Economic	*	—	*	79%	—	0%
Social	*	—	*	93%	—	0%
Foreign	*	—	*	89%	—	11%

Key Votes of the 105th Congress (Only Served Partial Term)

1. Clinton Budget Deal	*	5. Puerto Rico Sthood. Ref.	*	9. Cut $ for B-2 Bombers	*
2. Education IRAs	*	6. End Highway Set-asides	*	10. Human Rights in China	*
3. Req. 2/3 to Raise Taxes	N	7. School Prayer Amend.	N	11. Withdraw Bosnia Troops	*
4. Fast-track Trade	N	8. Ovrd. Part. Birth Veto	N	12. End Cuban TV-Marti	Y

Election Results

1998 general	Barbara Lee (D)	140,722	(83%)	($504,240)
	Claiborne (Clay) Sanders (R)	22,431	(13%)	($9,555)
	Others	6,742	(4%)	
1998 primary	Barbara Lee (D)	87,389	(70%)	
	Claiborne (Clay) Sanders (R)	13,833	(11%)	
	Greg Harper (D)	13,103	(11%)	
	Randal Stewart (D)	5,812	(5%)	
	Others	4,352	(3%)	
1998 special	Barbara Lee (D)	31,025	(67%)	($268,351)
	Greg Harper (D)	7,504	(16%)	($35,743)
	Clairborne (Clay) Sanders (R)	5,617	(12%)	($7,565)
	Randal Stewart (D)	2,265	(5%)	($21,875)
1996 general	Ronald V. Dellums (D)	154,806	(77%)	($415,090)
	Deborah Wright (R)	37,126	(18%)	($34,491)
	Others	9,044	(5%)	

TENTH DISTRICT

In the 1950s, when the streets of San Francisco and Oakland were already crowded, the rolling grasslands on the east of the mountain ridges, over the hill and through the tunnel from Oakland, were still mostly empty. In the years since, they have filled up. Freeways took the first commuters through the Caldecott Tunnel to the woodsy trail-like roads of Orinda and Lafayette; I-580 brought people east from the southern East Bay towns to the Amador Valley and Livermore, site of one of the nation's nuclear laboratories; I-680 running north-south provided a spine for businesses and shopping centers up and down the San Ramon Valley, from burgeoning Concord through Walnut Creek, Danville and Dublin; BART stations in Walnut Creek and Orinda took commuters to downtown San Francisco. Not all this area is filled in yet, and there is resistance to overdevelopment. But what has evolved in this sunny land, shielded by the mountains from the ocean fogs and rains, is an advanced civilization of highly skilled and educated people. Affluent and generally tolerant of—if a little put off by—what happens in San Francisco, they are respectful of economic markets and wary of government, but concerned about preserving a physical environment that is one of America's most pleasant. Or as Bruce Cain of Berkeley's Institute of Governmental Studies put it, "These are basically secular professionals."

This is the land of the 10th Congressional District, a seat created by the redistricting of 1992. It consists almost entirely of the interior portion of the Bay Area, with just a few salients beyond—the suburb of Castro Valley on the East Bay, the working class town of Antioch on the San Joaquin River Delta. This area had been voting Republican for years but was split up between four Democratic districts. It is now easily the most Republican Bay Area district, but not very Republican by national standards.

The congresswoman from the 10th District is Ellen Tauscher, a Democrat elected in 1996. Tauscher grew up in New Jersey, where her father ran a grocery store; she won a seat on the New York Stock Exchange at 25, where she was a stock trader and investment banker. In 1989, she and her husband, owner of Vanstar (formerly ComputerLand), moved to California. In 1992, after a difficult childbirth, Tauscher started the ChildCare Registry, the first company to offer (for $140) background information on child-care providers. "Here we are, on the front porch of the 21st Century, and we don't have standards for caring for the most precious things in the world," she has said. Politically, she raised money for Senator Dianne Feinstein and Superintendent of Public Instruction Delaine Eastin.

In 1995 she decided to run against Republican Bill Baker, who had a reputation for knowledgeable fiscal conservatism, but was also a tart-tongued conservative on cultural issues. She ran as a moderate Democrat and spent liberally of her own money, some $1.73 million in all, second highest in the nation. Baker responded by calling her a "tax-and-spend" liberal and ran ads comparing her to a lottery winner buying a congressional seat. Tauscher spent heavily on San Francisco TV stations. Her ads called Baker an "extremist" on gun control, abortion and the environment; a brochure opened with, "Did you vote for Newt Gingrich?" On issues, Tauscher came out against the Defense of Marriage Act, for the 1996 welfare reform act and the death penalty. In mid-campaign she published *The ChildCare Source Book*. She claimed not to have special interests supporting her, but union workers were out working precincts. All of this proved a winning combination, though only barely. In by far the highest turnout of any Bay Area district, Tauscher won 49%–47%, slightly ahead of Bill Clinton's 48%–43% margin here. Money made much of the difference; Baker had won when Clinton's margin was wider in 1992.

In the House, Tauscher has a more moderate voting record than other Bay Area Democrats— "Tauscherism," as *Time* once called it. She joined the moderate Blue Dog Democrats and the New Democrat Coalition and chaired its entitlement reform task force. As the region's only Transportation and Infrastructure Committee member, she took the lead on behalf of both highway projects in her district and Bay Area transit plans in the 1998 highway bill. In late 1998, she won a seat on the Armed Services Committee; the 10th District is home to two national defense labs. She sponsored model child care and school infrastructure bills. She co-sponsored the bill to prohibit abortions after the fetus is viable, though with an exception for the mother's health which courts have interpreted as meaning just about anything. She voted for the Republicans' impeachment inquiry resolution and called on Bill Clinton to stop "legal hairsplitting and speak plain English to the American people." Though a junior member of the minority party, she said she had the ability to make bipartisan deals: "I feel like I'm back on Wall Street. If you have a sensory touch that can tell there's a deal in the room—and I have a great one—you can get things done." But she has also been an active partisan Democrat; after the 1998 election Dick Gephardt named her one of three co-chairs of the Democrats' campaign committee.

Tauscher did not win re-election without a contest. The Republican nominee, Charles Ball, a national-security analyst at the Lawrence Livermore National Laboratory, where he tracked proliferation of nuclear, chemical and biological weapons, put together a serious platform and raised serious money, spending $1 million to Tauscher's $1.3 million. The national Republican Party spent another $500,000 on ads attacking Tauscher on taxes. Ball argued that Tauscher's record in Washington was more liberal than she advertised, while he took more moderate positions on cultural issues than Baker. Tauscher led Ball 55%–24% in the June all-party primary, which turned out to be a good forecast of her strength in the general. She won 53%–43%, a solid margin, but not perhaps enough to bar another serious challenge in this basically Republican district.

Cook's Call. *Competitive.* The most marginal of the Bay Area districts, the 10th is the most Republican district in California held by a Democrat. Tauscher's personal wealth (she spent $1.6 million of her own money to win the seat in 1996) and her pro-business political agenda helped keep her safe from a top-tier challenge in 1998. Still, against a relatively unknown challenger, Tauscher took only 53% of the vote in what was a good year for Democrats. Tauscher is always going to be an attractive target for Republicans, but to beat her, they will need either a very strong candidate or a very good year—or both—to pull her under.

The People: Pop. 1990: 571,979; 3% rural; 10.8% age 65 +; 88% White, 2.3% Black, 6.3% Asian, 0.6% Amer. Indian, 2.9% Other; 8.7% Hispanic Origin. Households: 61.6% married couple families; 29.4% married couple fams. w. children; 68.5% college educ.; median household income: $52,378; per capita income: $23,972; median house value: $275,100; median gross rent: $684.

1996 Presidential Vote

Clinton (D)	138,386	(48%)
Dole (R)	122,296	(43%)
Perot (I)	17,930	(6%)
Others	8,375	(3%)

1992 Presidential Vote

Clinton (D)	127,450	(42%)
Bush (R)	107,191	(35%)
Perot (I)	66,180	(22%)

Rep. Ellen Tauscher (D)

Elected 1996; b. Nov. 15, 1951, E. Newark, NJ; home, Pleasanton; Seton Hall U., B.A. 1973; Catholic; married (William).

Professional Career: Wall Street Invest. Banker, 1974–88, NYSE member, 1977–79; Founder & CEO, Registry Cos., 1992–96.

DC Office: 1239 LHOB 20515, 202-225-1880; Fax: 202-225-5914; Web site: www.house.gov/tauscher.

District Offices: Antioch, 925-757-7187; Dublin, 925-829-0813; Walnut Creek, 925-932-8899.

Committees: *Armed Services* (23d of 28 D): Military Personnel; Military Procurement. *Transportation & Infrastructure* (24th of 34 D): Aviation; Water Resources & Environment.

Group Ratings

	ADA	ACLU	AFS	LCV	CON	NTU	NFIB	COC	ACU	NTLC	CHC
1998	75	81	67	85	26	22	29	72	12	13	8
1997	85	—	63	—	91	36	—	50	20	—	—

National Journal Ratings

	1997 LIB — 1997 CONS		1998 LIB — 1998 CONS	
Economic	61% —	39%	57% —	43%
Social	76% —	23%	73% —	25%
Foreign	79% —	19%	71% —	27%

Key Votes of the 105th Congress

1. Clinton Budget Deal	N	5. Puerto Rico Sthood. Ref.	Y	9. Cut $ for B-2 Bombers	Y
2. Education IRAs	Y	6. End Highway Set-asides	N	10. Human Rights in China	Y
3. Req. 2/3 to Raise Taxes	N	7. School Prayer Amend.	N	11. Withdraw Bosnia Troops	N
4. Fast-track Trade	Y	8. Ovrd. Part. Birth Veto	N	12. End Cuban TV-Marti	Y

Election Results

1998 general	Ellen Tauscher (D)	127,134	(53%)	($1,355,053)
	Charles Ball (R)	103,299	(43%)	($1,066,829)
	Others	7,376	(3%)	
1998 primary	Ellen Tauscher (D)	89,275	(55%)	
	Charles Ball (R)	38,739	(24%)	
	Gordon Thomas Blake (R)	17,020	(10%)	
	Dave Williams (R)	9,021	(6%)	
	Others	9,216	(6%)	
1996 general	Ellen Tauscher (D)	137,726	(49%)	($2,571,595)
	Bill Baker (R)	133,633	(47%)	($1,398,556)
	Others	11,824	(4%)	

ELEVENTH DISTRICT

People from back East looking for clues about California might consider avoiding Beverly Hills and Nob Hill and taking a look at Stockton. For Stockton, just 50 miles south of Sacramento, is in the middle of the Central Valley, which saw much of California's most rapid growth in the 1980s and is now subject to some growing problems of it own. This is not a new part of the state: Stockton was a Gold Rush trading town founded in 1847, named after Robert Stockton, the second U.S. military governor of California, who captured Santa Barbara and Los Angeles from Mexico and proclaimed California United States territory. The Central Valley, criss-crossed with railroads and canals, became one of the world's greatest agriculture areas; the San Joaquin River channel was deepened to 37 feet and Stockton today is the Central Valley's ocean port. The rich farming attracted immigrants from all over: Mexicans coming up Route 99 joined North Dakotans flocking to the town of Lodi; Italian and Yugoslav immigrants bringing their Old World crops; Yankees and Okies bringing their distinct churches and systems of belief; and now Southeast Asian refugees crowd into the older streets of Stockton. The 1980s growth brought traffic congestion and air-quality problems to the Central Valley.

In the 1990s, Stockton positioned itself to take advantage of the region's economic strength by turning into a warehouse and distribution center for northern California; in 1998, building permits in the county were the highest since 1990. This economic growth comes when farms are being squeezed by two inexorable economic factors: the move away from subsidized water and water prices that reflect market forces, and the alleged increasing difficulty of attracting migrant workers for harvests. Some preservationists and agricultural officials worry about the slow disappearance of farmland, but this seems to be the natural result of economic forces.

The 11th Congressional District includes Stockton and most of surrounding San Joaquin County, plus the southern part of Sacramento County, an area of farms and a few subdivisions, dredge tailings and marshy, rich-soiled islands in the delta of the Sacramento and San Joaquin Rivers. This was once a solidly Democratic area; towns near Stockton were the home base of two House Democratic whips, John McFall, who was defeated for re-election in 1980, and Tony Coelho, who resigned in 1989 and in May 1999 was appointed general chairman of Al Gore's presidential campaign. But today the Valley has increasingly moved to the right, angry at the intrusiveness of federal environmental regulators, puzzled by the cultural liberalism of Bay Area and Los Angeles Democrats.

The congressman from the 11th District is Richard Pombo, a Republican elected when the district was created in 1992 and one of the leaders of the property rights movement in Congress. Pombo grew up in Tracy, attended Cal Poly Pomona, worked on the family cattle ranch; he often wears a cowboy hat. The favorite in the Republican primary was former Sacramento County Supervisor Sandy Smoley, a moderate who lost to Robert Matsui in a Sacramento-based district in 1978. Pombo called Smoley "the surefire choice of the hard-line feminists" and attacked her support of Governor Pete Wilson's gay rights bill; when liberal Massachusetts Congressman Barney Frank called Pombo a "low-rent Pat Buchanan," Pombo embraced the label. Pombo won 36%–27%, with 24% for a former aide to a former Stockton congressman. In the general, Pombo faced Patti Garamendi, wife of 1994 gubernatorial candidate John Garamendi, who had twice run and lost for the legislature in the 1990s. Pombo stressed his opposition to abortion, his support of property rights and opposition to the Endangered Species Act and, though solidly outspent, won 48%–46%.

"I'm not going to fit in too well, because I'm anything but politically correct," Pombo said in his first term; his voting record has been almost perfectly conservative, and he tilted with environmentalists on the Resources Committee and with subsidy advocates on Agriculture. Suddenly after 1994 he was in the majority. Resources Chairman Don Young put him in charge of rewriting the Endangered Species Act; he held hearings with stories of absurd regulations (one Fish and Wildlife Service official wanted to reduce the speed limit on a section of I-10 to 15 miles an hour to avoid bothering a rare fly) and produced a bill which would provide compensation to landowners whose property values declined greatly. It passed the committee but, as Republican environmental measures came under attack, was never brought to the floor. Similarly, a Pombo amendment for a new 250,000-worker migrant labor program was defeated in March 1996. That same year he and liberal Republican Sherwood Boehlert co-chaired a Speaker's Task Force on the Environment, and in fact the Republican 104th produced more environmental legislation than the Democratic 103d—the Safe Drinking Water, Coastal Zone Management, Food Quality Protection and Water Resources Development Acts, plus Freedom to Farm conservation sections and Everglades protection amendments. In May 1997 an environmental coalition defeated by 227–196 Pombo's efforts to give flood control projects priority over threatened animals and plants. Pombo opposed Robert Matsui's proposal for higher levees on the American River, and he also sought to have the American Heritage Rivers program declared unconstitutional.

However harshly Pombo is criticized in Washington or San Francisco, he is well thought of in the Central Valley. He has been re-elected easily three times, even in 1998, when Democrat Gray Davis was carrying the district for governor.

Cook's Call. *Probably Safe.* Though this Stockton-based district has Democratic roots (this was part of Tony Coehlo's district until he resigned and was remapped in 1991), it has moved farther to the right in the 1990s, especially on social and cultural issues. Pombo has a good profile for this agriculture-based district. If, however, Democrats get a strong candidate to run this could be a race worth watching.

The People: Pop. 1990: 571,650; 15% rural; 11.2% age 65 +; 75% White, 5.8% Black, 11.5% Asian, 1.2% Amer. Indian, 6.5% Other; 20.4% Hispanic Origin. Households: 57% married couple families; 29.8% married couple fams. w. children; 45.9% college educ.; median household income: $31,605; per capita income: $13,299; median house value: $124,000; median gross rent: $427.

1996 Presidential Vote

Clinton (D)	85,117	(46%)
Dole (R)	84,303	(45%)
Perot (I)	12,373	(7%)
Others	4,187	(2%)

1992 Presidential Vote

Clinton (D)	79,432	(40%)
Bush (R)	75,319	(38%)
Perot (I)	41,006	(21%)

Rep. Richard Pombo (R)

Elected 1992; b. Jan. 8, 1961, Tracy; home, Tracy; CA Polytechnic Inst., 1979–82; Catholic; married (Annette).

Elected Office: Tracy City Cncl., 1990–92.

Professional Career: Cattle rancher; Co-founder, Citizens Land Alliance, 1986.

DC Office: 2411 RHOB 20515, 202-225-1947; Fax: 202-225-0861; Web site: www.house.gov/pombo.

District Office: Stockton, 209-951-3091.

Committees: *Agriculture* (6th of 27 R): Department Operations, Oversight, Nutrition & Forestry; Livestock & Horticulture (Chmn.). *Resources* (11th of 28 R): Fisheries Conservation, Wildlife & Oceans; National Parks & Public Lands; Water & Power.

Group Ratings

	ADA	ACLU	AFS	LCV	CON	NTU	NFIB	COC	ACU	NTLC	CHC
1998	10	6	11	0	13	56	86	89	96	95	100
1997	0	—	25	—	0	57	—	60	92	—	—

National Journal Ratings

	1997 LIB — 1997 CONS		1998 LIB — 1998 CONS	
Economic	16% —	82%	12% —	85%
Social	0% —	90%	21% —	76%
Foreign	0% —	88%	0% —	93%

Key Votes of the 105th Congress

1. Clinton Budget Deal	Y	5. Puerto Rico Sthood. Ref.	Y	9. Cut $ for B-2 Bombers	N
2. Education IRAs	Y	6. End Highway Set-asides	Y	10. Human Rights in China	N
3. Req. 2/3 to Raise Taxes	Y	7. School Prayer Amend.	Y	11. Withdraw Bosnia Troops	Y
4. Fast-track Trade	N	8. Ovrd. Part. Birth Veto	Y	12. End Cuban TV-Marti	N

Election Results

1998 general	Richard Pombo (R)	95,496	(61%)	($517,830)
	Robert L. Figueroa (D)	56,345	(36%)	($12,625)
	Others	3,608	(2%)	
1998 primary	Richard Pombo (R)	72,378	(64%)	
	Robert L. Figueroa (D)	37,285	(33%)	
	Others	3,713	(3%)	
1996 general	Richard Pombo (R)	107,477	(59%)	($470,749)
	Jason Silva (D)	65,536	(36%)	($17,862)
	Others	8,083	(4%)	

TWELFTH DISTRICT

Running south from San Francisco is the Peninsula, which connects the city with the mainland of the United States. This is geologically interesting, and active, country: the San Andreas Fault runs just east of the Coast Range, underneath the reservoirs that store San Francisco's water supply. To the west are green mountains splashing down into the foggy ocean. To the east is a zone of flat land between mountain and bay, an unbroken chain of suburbs and urban settlement, with light industry and salt flats along the bay front, and residential neighborhoods and some commercial strips from the Bayshore Freeway up through the Junipero Serra Freeway atop the mountain ridge. Historically, the Peninsula has seemed separate from San Francisco. Today, increasingly, the action is on the Peninsula, which separates the Silicon Valley workplaces of some of the Bay Area's most productive people from the San Francisco neighborhoods where they like to cocoon.

The 12th Congressional District consists of the northern Peninsula suburbs plus the southwest quadrant of San Francisco—the city's middle-income Sunset district, with older houses amid unburied telephone and electric wires, lying on curving hills that were once sand dunes, and affluent St. Francis's Wood. Just to the south, across the San Mateo County line at the southern extension of the BART lines, is Daly City, with substantial numbers of Mexican-Americans and Asians; nearby, South San Francisco proclaims itself "the industrial city" in big letters on San Bruno Mountain near the Bayshore Freeway; the streets lined with boxy houses in San Bruno and Pacifica wind over sweeping hillsides facing cemeteries where many San Franciscans and veterans of Pacific wars are buried. That is the view from one side of the Junipero Serra Freeway; from the other, the vista is of San Francisco Bay, broader than one might expect, and the airport next door, connecting this metropolis with others on the Pacific Rim; to the south is the neat suburban city of San Mateo and, on twisting streets in the hills above the Burlingame Country Club, the rich suburb of Hillsborough, home to much of the city's WASP elite.

This is an ethnically diverse and economically prosperous constituency. Fully 26% of its residents are Asian—the second highest of any mainland district, after San Francisco's 8th just to the north—and another 14% are Hispanic. Income levels are, if not among the highest in the country, very far above average, more than 25% higher than the average in California. The economic orientation here was historically toward San Francisco but now is increasingly south toward Silicon Valley; the political heritage is mostly Democratic, from ethnic heritage and historic labor union ties, and from liberal cultural attitudes. Bill Clinton carried the 12th 70%–21% in 1996.

The congressman from the 12th District, Tom Lantos, has several distinctions, but none more important than the fact that he is the only Holocaust survivor ever to serve in Congress. Lantos was born in Hungary and as a teenager fought in the underground against the Nazis; he was imprisoned and was one of the Jews saved by Swedish diplomat Raoul Wallenberg. So was his wife Annette, his childhood sweetheart and now his unpaid assistant; these two Holocaust survivors have two daughters and 17 grandchildren. Lantos has shown energy and competence throughout his career. He taught economics at San Francisco State, made money as an investor, appeared on television as a foreign policy expert. He had the political insight to challenge a Republican incumbent in the Peninsula in 1980, a Republican year nationally but not so much here, and he has shown great capacity for publicizing his crusades in congressional hearings and on television. In early 1999, he was featured in the release of a documentary by Steven Spielberg, *The Last Days*, which recounts the Nazis' 1944 destruction of Hungary's Jewish community. "It's been very difficult to watch it," Lantos said of the Oscar-winning film, which he promoted in four cities across the country.

Lantos has spent much of his time in the House on foreign policy. Unlike other Bay Area Democrats, he did not bring to his work an instinctive mistrust of American policy or doubts of American good intentions. He founded the Congressional Human Rights Caucus, focusing on Communist regimes as well as the right-wing dictatorships other liberal Democrats denounced. He is among the most enthusiastic supporters of Israel and called for economic sanctions against Iraq back in 1988 for its gassing of the Kurds. Lantos stayed in close touch with Eastern Europe, especially Hungary, as Communism collapsed and new democracies rose up; in 1990 he was the first American official to visit Albania since 1946. He sponsored the first U.S. aid to the newly free countries of Eastern Europe and strongly backed NATO expansion. He advocated a more active American role in Bosnia and other parts of the former Yugoslavia. He has attacked human rights violations in China and opposes normalizing of Chinese trade status. Lantos has been part of the U.S. delegations to the European Parliament and the United Nations; he became friends with Secretary General Kofi Annan, whose wife Nane Annan is Raoul Wallenberg's niece. He sponsored the bust of Wallenberg which was unveiled in the Capitol in 1995 and the conferring of honorary U.S. citizenship on him—the only person besides Winston Churchill ever so honored. He and Republican Chris Smith have sponsored a Torture Victims Relief Act and, with other colleagues, a Human Rights Information Act.

Lantos has displayed a flair for showmanship and confrontation in Government Operations Committee investigations. In 1989 and 1990 he conducted hearings on alleged misconduct under Reagan HUD Secretary Samuel Pierce, which resulted in an independent counsel and prosecutions. Unlike almost all other congressional Democrats, he initially pursued Clinton Administration scandals. He aggressively probed administration actions in the Waco massacre. And he grilled former White House aide Craig Livingstone in the hearing on FBI files in the White House. He sponsored resolutions condemning Louis Farrakhan's antisemitic statements and his meetings with the leaders of Libya, Iran and Iraq, and did not back down when criticized by members of the Congressional Black Caucus. But he became a harsh critic when chairman Dan Burton began investigating Bill Clinton's 1996 campaign-finance abuses, terming the inquiry authoritarian and dictatorial. Lantos's defense of the Clinton Administration grew more heated at a committee hearing when he compared Independent Counsel Donald Smaltz's investigation of former Agriculture Secretary Mike Espy to the conduct of ex-United Nations Secretary General and Nazi war criminal Kurt Waldheim. Republicans, aghast at the comparison, said that Lantos had lost his credibility.

Locally, Lantos has worked to build a tunnel to avoid the hazardous Devil's Slide area where a mudslide closed Route 1 just south of Pacifica in 1983, and for funding of the BART subway to San Francisco International Airport. He supports expansion of the Golden Gate National Recreation Area and retention of the San Bruno National Archives facility. He has a bill to regulate child labor among migrant farm workers.

Lantos spent $1.7 million on his 1980 and 1982 campaigns and has won easily ever since. More recently his fundraising has been targeted to his son-in-law Dick Swett, who was elected congressman from New Hampshire in 1990 and 1992, but was defeated in 1994 and lost for the Senate in 1996.

Cook's Call. *Safe.* Lantos has won effortlessly in this Bay Area district ever since he was first elected in 1980 with just 46% of the vote. There have been rumors that the 71-year old Lantos may retire, but even then the seat is solidly in Democratic hands.

The People: Pop. 1990: 571,667; 14.5% age 65 + ; 65.4% White, 4% Black, 25.7% Asian, 0.5% Amer. Indian, 4.5% Other; 14% Hispanic Origin. Households: 51.5% married couple families; 23.2% married couple fams. w. children; 62.3% college educ.; median household income: $44,720; per capita income: $20,984; median house value: $324,100; median gross rent: $723.

1996 Presidential Vote

Clinton (D)	191,973	(70%)
Dole (R)	58,260	(21%)
Perot (I)	11,994	(4%)
Others	10,291	(4%)

1992 Presidential Vote

Clinton (D)	139,281	(57%)
Bush (R)	64,984	(27%)
Perot (I)	38,129	(16%)

Rep. Tom Lantos (D)

Elected 1980; b. Feb. 1, 1928, Budapest, Hungary; home, San Mateo; U. of WA, B.A. 1949, M.A. 1950, U. of CA, Ph.D. 1953; Jewish; married (Annette).

Professional Career: Economist, Bank of America, 1952–53; TV Commentator, San Francisco, 1955–63; Dir. of Intl. Programs, CA St. U., 1962–71; Advisor, U.S. Sen. Joseph R. Biden Jr., 1978–79; Mbr., Pres. Task Force on Defense & Foreign Policy, 1976; Prof., San Francisco St. U., 1950–80.

DC Office: 2217 RHOB 20515, 202-225-3531; Web site: www.house.gov/lantos.

District Office: San Mateo, 650-342-0300.

Committees: *Government Reform* (2d of 19 D): National Economic Growth, Natural Resources & Regulatory Affairs; National Security, Veterans' Affairs & Intl. Relations. *International Relations* (2d of 23 D): Asia & the Pacific (RMM).

Group Ratings

	ADA	ACLU	AFS	LCV	CON	NTU	NFIB	COC	ACU	NTLC	CHC
1998	100	79	100	100	62	14	14	33	8	5	0
1997	80	—	88	—	46	25	—	33	8	—	—

National Journal Ratings

	1997 LIB — 1997 CONS			1998 LIB — 1998 CONS		
Economic	93%	—	0%	79%	—	0%
Social	80%	—	19%	80%	—	19%
Foreign	84%	—	15%	59%	—	40%

Key Votes of the 105th Congress

1. Clinton Budget Deal	N	5. Puerto Rico Sthood. Ref.	Y	9. Cut $ for B-2 Bombers	Y
2. Education IRAs	N	6. End Highway Set-asides	N	10. Human Rights in China	Y
3. Req. 2/3 to Raise Taxes	N	7. School Prayer Amend.	N	11. Withdraw Bosnia Troops	N
4. Fast-track Trade	N	8. Ovrd. Part. Birth Veto	N	12. End Cuban TV-Marti	N

Election Results

1998 general	Tom Lantos (D)	128,135	(74%)	($254,400)
	Robert H. Evans Jr. (R)	36,562	(21%)	
	Michael J. Moloney (Lib)	8,515	(5%)	
1998 primary	Tom Lantos (D)	88,917	(72%)	
	Robert H. Evans Jr. (R)	27,038	(22%)	
	Michael J. Moloney (Lib)	8,372	(7%)	
1996 general	Tom Lantos (D)	149,052	(72%)	($591,305)
	Storm Jenkins (R)	49,278	(24%)	($4,016)
	Others	9,583	(5%)	

THIRTEENTH DISTRICT

The East Bay is the workaday, unglamorous side of metropolitan San Francisco—the margin of land perhaps five miles wide between San Francisco Bay and the surprisingly high mountains that rise just to the east. The shoreline is not picturesque, with its closed-down Navy bases, docks, airports and salt evaporators; the Bay Bridge, bisected by Yerba Buena Island, cuts an inspiring figure, but the San Mateo Bridge to the south is at best utilitarian. Fifty years ago, when the shipyards of Richmond and the Navy yard in Oakland were buzzing, the East Bay south of Oakland was still largely uninhabited farm fields. In the postwar years, it has filled up, south along Route 17: San Leandro, originally settled by Portuguese, Castro Valley with its Japanese Gardens, Hayward with its Cal State University campus, Union City with its rail yards, and Fremont, home of the famous NUMMI auto plant where Chevrolets and Toyotas are produced together, and of the California School for the Deaf. Underneath is the Hayward Fault, not as famous as the San Andreas, but equally—if not more—hazardous.

The 13th Congressional District is made up of this string of East Bay towns, somewhat lower income than the Peninsula towns across the Bay. The district is racially and ethnically mixed in the California manner—19% Asian, 18% Hispanic, 7% black—and with a Democratic heritage not yet dampened by high crime (crime rates are much lower here than in Oakland) or revulsion toward cultural liberalism (these people are used to TV newscasts from San Francisco). This area looks like much of the Bay Area, with stucco houses and shopping centers, but house prices are below the ridiculously high Bay Area average and the stores are discount chains more than upscale. Still, income levels are well above the national average.

The congressman from the 13th District is Pete Stark, a liberal Democrat and product of the peace movement of the 1960s who in the first half of the 1990s was one of four senior Democratic House committee and subcommittee chairmen elected from four East Bay districts. Now, in the second half of the 1990s, two of the others have retired from Congress and Stark is a senior member of the minority. Stark grew up in Wisconsin, served in the Air Force, got an engineering degree at MIT and an M.B.A. at Berkeley and in 1961 started a bank in Walnut Creek. He attracted attention, and accounts, all over the Bay Area when he put a giant peace symbol atop the bank headquarters and peace symbols on all checks. In 1972 he ran for Congress, spending his own money freely; he beat an 81-year-old incumbent in the primary 56%–22% and held on in the McGovern undertow to win the general with 53%. By his third term he was on Ways and Means, on which he now is the second ranking Democrat; he chaired its Health Subcommittee from 1985–95.

Stark brought to that post a desire to use government powers to make health care more available—and a habit of infelicitous quips that got him into trouble. He was not always successful on policy. He did expand Medicare benefits and provided COBRA benefit continuation to younger workers. But his major achievement was the Catastrophic Health Care Act of 1988, which created a new benefit for Medicare recipients but was repealed by an overwhelming vote in 1989 after an outpouring of public protest: the problem was that its tax on the high-income elderly was very unpopular while benefits seemed puny. Since 1991 he has supported universal health insurance in various forms. This was overtaken by the Clinton health care plan, from whose formulation Stark and other members complained that they were shut out. In the spring of 1994, Stark worked his subcommittee hard, eventually producing a majority for a bill that modified the Clinton plan with some Stark features; that narrowly passed Ways and Means. But, with moderate swing Democrats fearful of its big-government features, it never had majority support in the House and was not brought to the floor.

Stark's sharp tongue has gotten him in trouble. In 1991, he attacked "Jewish colleagues" for voting for the Gulf war resolution to help Israel. In 1994, when Republican Nancy Johnson, who is married to a physician, attacked Stark's proposals, he said, "The gentlelady got her medical degree through pillow talk and the gentleman from Washington [Jim McDermott, a committee member trained as a psychiatrist] got his medical degree by going to school." Johnson said that was insulting, and 35 Republicans insisted Stark apologize; after an uncomfortable interval he did. Then in March 1995, Stark called Johnson a "whore" for the insurance industry. This time women members from both sides of the aisle demanded an apology, which he made in writing. His 1996 opponent said, "If Pete Stark were not a congressman, he would deserve to be sued for sexual harassment."

The Republican capture of Congress in 1994 left Stark often on the sidelines. He was one of two votes against the 1996 Kennedy-Kassebaum bill, on the grounds it did not include mental health coverage and extended patent protection for a drug. He denounced Blue Cross of California as "a greed-driven vampire," and Newt Gingrich as a "messianic megalomaniac." But he worked more amicably with fellow Californian Bill Thomas and called his 1997 Medicare bill "not bad," except for its provisions encouraging medical savings accounts. He defended the Clinton Administration's provision banning doctors for two years from Medicare if they accept payment for Medicare-provided services; he argues that would create "boutique health care" for the rich and leave Medicare with the poorest and sickest. He argues that Medicare would save money if it could buy drugs at the prices the Veterans Administration pays, saying, "Drug industry charges to Medicare are a scandal." He opposes allowing association health plans that don't meet state standards and has sponsored a law to require safer hypodermic needles in hospitals.

Stark has been re-elected by wide margins, and his insouciance continues. When he missed the January 1999 swearing-in because he stayed in Hawaii with his three-year-old who had an ear infection, he told a reporter, "I didn't think it made a difference if I was there."

Cook's Call. *Safe.* Stark has not had a truly competitive race since winning this seat in 1972 with 53% of the vote. Like so many other Bay area districts, the 13th is congenitally Democratic; when Stark decides to retire, this seat should remain safely in Democratic hands.

The People: Pop. 1990: 572,333; 0.1% rural; 9.7% age 65 +; 64.4% White, 7.3% Black, 19.4% Asian, 0.7% Amer. Indian, 8.1% Other; 17.8% Hispanic Origin. Households: 57.4% married couple families; 29.9% married couple fams. w. children; 54.5% college educ.; median household income: $43,877; per capita income: $17,335; median house value: $223,700; median gross rent: $669.

1996 Presidential Vote

Clinton (D)	115,633	(62%)
Dole (R)	51,084	(28%)
Perot (I)	13,085	(7%)
Others	5,843	(3%)

1992 Presidential Vote

Clinton (D)	116,829	(54%)
Bush (R)	55,100	(25%)
Perot (I)	43,026	(20%)

Rep. Fortney H. (Pete) Stark (D)

Elected 1972; b. Nov. 11, 1931, Milwaukee, WI; home, Fremont; MIT, B.S. 1953, U. of CA at Berkeley, M.B.A. 1960; Unitarian; married (Deborah).

Military Career: Air Force, 1955–57.

Professional Career: Founder, Beacon Savings & Loan Assn., 1961; Founder & Pres., Security Natl. Bank, Walnut Creek, 1963–72.

DC Office: 239 CHOB 20515, 202-225-5065; Fax: 202-226-3805; Web site: www.house.gov/stark.

District Office: Fremont, 510-494-1388.

Committees: *Ways & Means* (2d of 16 D): Health (RMM); Human Resources. *Joint Committee on Taxation* (5th of 5 Reps.). *Joint Economic Committee* (7th of 10 Reps.).

Group Ratings

	ADA	ACLU	AFS	LCV	CON	NTU	NFIB	COC	ACU	NTLC	CHC
1998	90	93	100	92	98	38	0	6	8	3	0
1997	100	—	100	—	11	23	—	10	4	—	—

National Journal Ratings

	1997 LIB — 1997 CONS		1998 LIB — 1998 CONS	
Economic	93%	— 0%	79%	— 0%
Social	85%	— 0%	93%	— 0%
Foreign	81%	— 19%	82%	— 18%

Key Votes of the 105th Congress

1. Clinton Budget Deal	N	5. Puerto Rico Sthood. Ref.	Y	9. Cut $ for B-2 Bombers	Y
2. Education IRAs	N	6. End Highway Set-asides	N	10. Human Rights in China	Y
3. Req. 2/3 to Raise Taxes	N	7. School Prayer Amend.	N	11. Withdraw Bosnia Troops	N
4. Fast-track Trade	N	8. Ovrd. Part. Birth Veto	N	12. End Cuban TV-Marti	Y

Election Results

1998 general	Fortney H. (Pete) Stark (D) 101,671	(71%)	($313,711)
	James R. Goetz (R) 38,050	(27%)	
	Others 3,066	(2%)	
1998 primary	Fortney H. (Pete) Stark (D) 69,405	(69%)	
	James R. Goetz (R) 28,613	(28%)	
	Others 2,908	(3%)	
1996 general	Fortney H. (Pete) Stark (D) 114,408	(65%)	($630,357)
	James S. Fay (R) 53,385	(30%)	($60,106)
	Terry C. Savage (Lib) 7,746	(4%)	($3,532)

FOURTEENTH DISTRICT

Silicon Valley is a place and a state of mind, an area that had no distinctive identity two decades ago but which people all over the world now recognize, admire and try to imitate. For Silicon Valley has been the center of America's computer industry, a place where creative minds have developed products that large corporations never thought would sell. Its beginnings can be traced back to 1939, when William Hewlett and David Packard started their electronics firm in a Palo Alto garage, or perhaps to 1891, when Stanford University was founded on the estate of a California governor and senator.

But Silicon Valley did not achieve critical mass until the late 1970s and early 1980s, when Steve Jobs started Apple in a garage in Cupertino with the idea of making a computer ordinary people could use, and Gordon Moore, Robert Noyce and Andrew Grove started Intel in nearby Santa Clara to make the microchips that let computers process data much faster than almost anyone thought possible. What follows was suggested by Moore's law: that computer capacity tends to double every 18 months. Physically, Silicon Valley's office parks are unremarkable—large anonymous buildings in Cupertino, Sunnyvale, Mountain View and Palo Alto, the line of towns between the Junipero Serra and Bayshore freeways running south from San Francisco to San Jose. Yet this is where computer hackers have turned tinkerers' dreams into multi-billion dollar companies and innovators have produced business after business that out-think public planners and out-compete subsidized foreign consortiums.

Silicon Valley is not without its challengers—a conversation in a Palo Alto espresso shop or bar quickly turns into a denunciation of Microsoft—but it primacy continues. Rapidly growing businesses are inherently unstable, but the Valley's enduring advantages have made it amazingly adaptable. One is Stanford, the students it attracts and produces (including the daughters of both Bill Clinton and Kenneth Starr), and the encouragement of profit-making activity by faculty. Another is venture capital, widely available from innovation-minded San Francisco. A third, perhaps the greatest, is that Silicon Valley is the kind of place where smart young innovators like to live. Counterculture veterans may cluster around the liberal university towns; elite law and medical school graduates head to the prestigious, high-salary jobs of central cities; but techies are free to live in this pleasant, healthy environment. Sheltered by hills from coastal fogs and rains, Silicon Valley boasts a sunny climate with perceptible but gentle seasons, perfect for year-round outdoor sports; there may well be more jogging trails and bicycle paths here than anywhere else in the country. There is a sort of pure Americana here: these communities were rustic but never poor, rural but never bigoted, country-like but still easily accessible to the luxuries of civilization. People here were ahead of the rest of the nation in fighting for the environment, in favoring natural over processed foods, and in indulging in regular exercise. Innovation extends even to government. The city of Sunnyvale, with its results-oriented management and flexible job definitions in the semi-conductor, aerospace and biotechnology firms, is the hero of David Osborne's *Reinventing Government*, and Bill Clinton and Al Gore have visited Sunnyvale as well as Silicon Valley for instruction.

The 14th Congressional District coincides almost exactly with Silicon Valley. Though it reaches to the Pacific and homey Half Moon Bay with its pumpkin farms, the 14th's population lies mostly on the San Francisco Bay side of the mountains, in the strip of flat land from Belmont, not far south of San Francisco Airport, through Redwood City, Menlo Park, Palo Alto (home of Stanford), Mountain View, Sunnyvale and Cupertino (home of Apple). There are a few ultra-wealthy enclaves, with real estate prices pushed skyward by entrepreneurs' paper profits: Atherton, with its stone-walled lots; Woodside, with its 1850s country store and mansions dotting the hills; Portola Valley and Los Altos Hills, with stark contemporary homes overlooking the Bay. The 14th's political heritage is progressive—a sort of environmentalist, dovish, healthy-lifestyle, but entrepreneurial Republicanism, typified by former Congressmen Pete McCloskey (1967–83), Ed Zschau (1983–87) and Tom Campbell (1989–93), each of whom ran unsuccessfully for the Senate; Campbell is now back in the House, from the 15th District directly to the south. But as this kind of Republican has become rarer, Silicon Valley has become very Democratic. It took immediately to Clinton in 1992 and was not much dismayed even when he vetoed the securities litigation bill high-tech entrepreneurs wanted at the behest of trial lawyer William Lerach; Congress overrode the veto. The 14th voted 58%–31% for Clinton in 1996.

The congresswoman from the 14th District is Anna Eshoo, a Democrat elected in 1992. Born back East, she is the only member of Congress of Assyrian descent. She was a full time homemaker, then chaired the San Mateo County Democratic Party and was elected to the San Mateo Board of Supervisors in 1982. In 1988, she ran for the House, facing Tom Campbell, a

Stanford Law professor and economics Ph.D. with high-tech backing. The two spent a total of $2.5 million, and Eshoo was the first congressional candidate to distribute videotapes to voters—a slick video with hip music, showing her in a postmodern office, telling voters that the Silicon Valley, unlike Orange County or Iowa, should be represented by someone special. Campbell won 52%–46%. But in 1992 he ran for the Senate (losing the Republican primary 38%–36% to conservative Bruce Herschensohn), and Eshoo ran for the House. In the primary she beat an assemblyman redistricted out of his seat at age 30, by 40%–36%; in the general, she distributed a Paul Tsongas-like 58-page booklet of her issue positions and boasted of her work on setting up a managed-competition health plan for county government; she outspent her Republican opponent and while George Bush was winning only 26% of the vote here, Eshoo won 57%–39%.

In the House Eshoo's voting record is solidly liberal. She seemed a bit nervous about supporting the Clinton budget and tax package, which hit this high-income area hard, and hesitated long before supporting NAFTA and fast track. In the Republican Congress she has crossed the aisle—sometimes to the dismay of liberal Democrats and consumerists—to work successfully for several bills: securities litigation reform (including the original 1996 bill passed over Bill Clinton's veto and the 1998 bill taking cases out of state courts), liability relief for Y2K computer problems, and FDA reform, in which she focused on gaining quicker regulatory approval for new medical devices from the biotechnology industry. In telecommunications reform she passed an amendment barring the FCC from setting a standard for cable compatibility and from establishing gatekeeper technology for home automation systems. She sought looser controls on high-tech exports, exports of encryption software as powerful as software already available in affected countries, and opposed the FASB accounting board proposal to charge stock options against earnings: Silicon Valley stands, all. She got into the October 1998 omnibus budget a bill requiring federal agencies to make forms available online and allowing people to sign them with digital signatures. She sponsored a bill to improve the safety of imported fruits and vegetables. She worked to complete the Phleger estate purchase for the Golden Gate National Recreation Area and got $10 million to purchase Bair Island for the Don Edwards San Francisco Bay National Wildlife Refuge.

Cook's Call. *Safe.* This affluent Silicon Valley district routinely elected culturally liberal, but pro-business Republicans for almost three decades; since 1992 voters here have taken to electing Eshoo easily. Without Eshoo on the ballot, it's easy to see how a moderate to liberal Republican could win this seat, but it's highly unlikely that she will be unseated.

The People: Pop. 1990: 571,058; 1.5% rural; 11.9% age 65 + ; 78.1% White, 4.9% Black, 12.2% Asian, 0.4% Amer. Indian, 4.3% Other; 13.3% Hispanic Origin. Households: 50.5% married couple families; 21.7% married couple fams. w. children; 72.6% college educ.; median household income: $50,078; per capita income: $26,047; median house value: $404,400; median gross rent: $727.

1996 Presidential Vote			1992 Presidential Vote		
Clinton (D)	137,561	(58%)	Clinton (D)	143,765	(53%)
Dole (R)	73,302	(31%)	Bush (R)	71,754	(26%)
Perot (I)	13,939	(6%)	Perot (I)	53,047	(20%)
Others	13,193	(6%)			

Rep. Anna G. Eshoo (D)

Elected 1992; b. Dec. 13, 1942, New Britain, CT; home, Atherton; Canada Col., A.A. 1975; Catholic; divorced.

Elected Office: San Mateo Cnty. Bd. of Supervisors, 1982–92, Pres., 1986.

Professional Career: Chmn., San Mateo Cnty Dem. Party, 1980; Chief of Staff, CA Assembly Speaker McCarthy, 1981.

DC Office: 205 CHOB 20515, 202-225-8104; Fax: 202-225-8890; Web site: www-eshoo.house.gov.

District Office: Palo Alto, 650-323-2984.

Committees: *Commerce* (12th of 24 D): Health and Environment; Telecommunications, Trade & Consumer Protection.

Group Ratings

	ADA	ACLU	AFS	LCV	CON	NTU	NFIB	COC	ACU	NTLC	CHC
1998	90	80	89	100	84	25	14	39	0	5	0
1997	100	—	88	—	66	36	—	40	8	—	—

National Journal Ratings

	1997 LIB — 1997 CONS	1998 LIB — 1998 CONS
Economic	85% — 15%	79% — 21%
Social	78% — 21%	90% — 7%
Foreign	82% — 16%	84% — 11%

Key Votes of the 105th Congress

1. Clinton Budget Deal	N	5. Puerto Rico Sthood. Ref.	Y	9. Cut $ for B-2 Bombers	Y
2. Education IRAs	N	6. End Highway Set-asides	N	10. Human Rights in China	Y
3. Req. 2/3 to Raise Taxes	N	7. School Prayer Amend.	N	11. Withdraw Bosnia Troops	N
4. Fast-track Trade	Y	8. Ovrd. Part. Birth Veto	N	12. End Cuban TV-Marti	Y

Election Results

1998 general	Anna G. Eshoo (D)	129,663	(69%)	($450,368)
	John C. (Chris) Haugen (R)	53,719	(28%)	($35,529)
	Others	5,528	(3%)	
1998 primary	Anna G. Eshoo (D)	85,511	(66%)	
	John C. (Chris) Haugen (R)	17,549	(14%)	
	Henry E. (Bud) Manzler (R)	15,706	(12%)	
	George Kiehle (D)	5,512	(4%)	
	Others	4,845	(4%)	
1996 general	Anna G. Eshoo (D)	149,313	(65%)	($544,566)
	Ben Brink (R)	71,573	(31%)	($432,849)
	Others	9,289	(4%)	

FIFTEENTH DISTRICT

The broad valley of Santa Clara County around San Jose a few decades ago was mostly orchards and vineyards. Sheltered by mountains from the chilly ocean fogs, with soil incredibly fertile once it was irrigated, this valley produced peaches, plums, prunes, apricots and grapes and made San Jose half a century ago the nation's biggest fruit-packing center. Today, almost all the orchards have been replaced by subdivisions and shopping centers and office buildings, for

Santa Clara County has become a metropolitan area of 1.6 million people. San Jose, with a growing downtown, an arena for its National Hockey League team (the San Jose Sharks), and a population of 782,000, has become a major American city. Santa Clara County is also the center of Silicon Valley, site of many creative firms that have made the United States the world's computer and microchip industry center, a phenomenon predicted by few if any national policymakers or corporate leaders a quarter-century ago.

The 15th Congressional District is made up of the central slice of Santa Clara County, plus, over the mountains to the south, a portion of Santa Cruz County. Downtown San Jose is in the 16th District to the east, and Silicon Valley towns like Cupertino and Mountain View are in the 14th District to the northwest; the 15th District lies in between. At its northern end, near the salt evaporators and wetlands around San Francisco Bay, is the Great America theme park, not far from where a huge Lockheed plant was once the nation's largest defense contractor. Just to the south is Santa Clara, with its old mission and Santa Clara University. The 15th includes much of the upscale and middle-income neighborhoods of western San Jose, with more than 300,000 people. It also has high-income suburbs nestled in what used to be vineyards beneath the encroaching mountains: Saratoga, Los Gatos, Monte Sereno. After all this settlement, the mountains remain surprisingly wild, a haunt of Ken Kesey's Merry Pranksters in the 1960s, now inhabited with rustic cabins and high-income houses in narrow valleys. Prosperous and pleased with its environment, confident in free-market economics and uneasy about the performance of the public sector, people here have been somewhat more conservative than in other quadrants of the Bay Area. There are fewer singles and gays here than farther north, fewer Mexican-Americans than farther east; the 11% who are Asian Americans are far likelier to be high-income producers than low-income supplicants. But the 1990s trend here, as elsewhere in the Bay Area and in contrast to much of the country, has been toward the Democrats. This is a place where any trace of cultural conservatism hurts the Republicans.

The congressman from the 15th District is Republican Tom Campbell, chosen in a special election in December 1995; he also was elected in what is now the 14th District in 1988 and 1990. Campbell grew up in Chicago, where his father was a federal judge and an ally of the Daley Democratic machine. He was an outstanding student at the University of Chicago and at Harvard Law School, served as a Supreme Court law clerk and earned an economics Ph.D. at Chicago. A believer in free markets, he worked at the Reagan FTC, then became a law professor at Stanford. In 1988 he ran for the House, defeating a one-term conservative Republican incumbent in the primary and Anna Eshoo, now the neighboring congresswoman, in the general, 52%–46%. Conservative on economics, liberal on cultural issues, in 1992 he ran for the Senate. In the Republican primary he lost narrowly, 38%–36%, to conservative Bruce Herschensohn, with then-Palm Springs Mayor Sonny Bono trailing. Herschensohn lost in the general to Barbara Boxer, 48%–43%; many thought Campbell would have won. Campbell went back to California and in 1993 won a special election to the state Senate.

Then in October 1995, 15th District Congressman Norman Mineta, former chairman of the Public Works and Transportation Committee, resigned to become a Lockheed Martin executive. In the special election, Campbell was the only Republican and Jerry Estruth, a San Jose councilman more than a decade before, the only Democrat. Campbell was the clear favorite, but Democrats decided to make this a test case of their strategy of campaigning against Newt Gingrich, who was very unpopular here, and ran ads showing Campbell cloning into Gingrich. Campbell, much better financed with his Silicon Valley connections, talked of balancing the budget and improving education; he also blamed Estruth for a $60 million investment loss for San Jose in 1984. Campbell won 59%–36%, a lesson that the get-Gingrich tactic would not sweep all before it, at least against a well-financed candidate who had other things going for him. Campbell's win also cost Democrats a majority in the California delegation for the first time in 37 years, but they won it back in 1996.

Campbell is pleasant, professorial, not at all an arm-twister; "I cannot," he says, "see myself trading a vote." He did have some legislative successes: an amendment allowing House committees to use dynamic scoring, taking effects of taxes on behavior for informational purposes; and another, to allow illegal immigrants to receive federal aid for immunization and treatment of communicable diseases. In California he got passed in March 1996 an open primary initiative, allowing voters to choose candidates in primaries regardless of party registration; he figured he might have won the Senate primary in 1992 under this system, and that it would help moderate candidates and hurt extremists. In January 1997 he voted for Jim Leach and against Newt Gingrich for speaker because Gingrich had admitted making a misleading statement to the ethics committee on a material issue: this angered many Republicans. In April 1998 he joined Bob Barr's petition for an impeachment inquiry, despite the Republican leadership's cautious stance: this angered many of his constituents. He was one of 12 Republicans who opposed the Republican managed care bill and the only Republican to vote against the $500 per child tax credit. He worked with other Republicans on legislation to end the use of gender and race as measures in awarding billions of dollars of federal contracts, and worked with Jesse Jackson Jr. to find ways to encourage privately built affordable housing. He worked to find a compromise to pass an increase in H-1B visas for high-tech workers.

Campbell led an unsuccessful effort to require a War Powers Resolution vote to approve the deployment of U.S. forces in Bosnia (it lost in March 1998, 225–193) and he voted against supplemental funds for Bosnia because Congress hadn't authorized the deployment. Campbell again invoked the War Powers Resolution in April 1999 with the bombing campaign underway against Yugoslavia; the House voted 290–139 against withdrawing U.S. troops and 427–2 against declaring war. He was the head of a bipartisan group of 25 House members who filed a lawsuit against Clinton accusing him of acting illegally in sending bombers to Yugoslavia without congressional approval. Campbell's most controversial, and politically perilous, decision was to vote for the impeachment of Clinton, an action that influenced other moderate Republicans who respect Campbell as a constitutional scholar but offended many of his constituents. Within days of the vote, groups of local Republicans—including a dozen Stanford professors—switched parties in protest and Democratic Party officials pledged to run a strong candidate in 2000. But Campbell's October vote for the impeachment inquiry did not much damage him in November; he won by 61%–38%, an improvement over his 1996 showing.

Campbell has been mentioned often as a candidate for another statewide race. But in 1998 he declined to challenge Senator Barbara Boxer because he had made a commitment not to. He has retained tenure by teaching an undergraduate law and public policy course at Stanford's Washington, D.C. campus.

Cook's Call. *Potentially Competitive.* The 15th District will be a good test of whether the impeachment backlash felt in early 1999 has legs in the 2000 general election. Campbell won this normally Democratic-leaning seat easily in a 1995 special election and has been re-elected easily since. But Democrats are working hard to convince a first-tier challenger to take him on. It's very unlikely that he will be unseated, no matter how hot the out-year rhetoric may sound.

The People: Pop. 1990: 572,360; 4% rural; 9.9% age 65 + ; 82.5% White, 2.1% Black, 11.4% Asian, 0.5% Amer. Indian, 3.5% Other; 10.3% Hispanic Origin. Households: 55.5% married couple families; 25.6% married couple fams. w. children; 68.4% college educ.; median household income: $50,823; per capita income: $22,833; median house value: $291,500; median gross rent: $729.

1996 Presidential Vote

Clinton (D)	125,438	(53%)
Dole (R)	83,846	(35%)
Perot (I)	17,506	(7%)
Others	11,155	(5%)

1992 Presidential Vote

Clinton (D)	127,060	(46%)
Bush (R)	83,301	(30%)
Perot (I)	64,192	(23%)

Rep. Tom Campbell (R)

Elected Dec. 1995; b. Aug. 14, 1952, Chicago, IL; home, Campbell; U. of Chicago, B.A., M.A., 1973, Ph.D. 1980, Harvard Law Schl., J.D. 1976; Catholic; married (Susanne).

Elected Office: U.S. House of Reps., 1988–92; CA Senate, 1993–95.

Professional Career: Law Clerk, U.S. Supreme Court, 1977–78; Practicing atty., 1978–80; White House Fellow, 1980–81; Exec. Asst. to Dpty. U.S. Atty. Gen., 1981; Dir., Federal Bureau of Competition, 1981–83; Prof., Stanford U., 1983–95.

DC Office: 2442 RHOB 20515, 202-225-2631; Fax: 202-225-6788; Web site: www.house.gov/campbell.

District Office: Campbell, 408-371-7337.

Committees: *Banking & Financial Services* (10th of 32 R): Financial Institutions & Consumer Credit; Housing & Community Opportunity. *International Relations* (19th of 26 R): Africa; International Economic Policy & Trade. *Joint Economic Committee* (4th of 10 Reps.).

Group Ratings

	ADA	ACLU	AFS	LCV	CON	NTU	NFIB	COC	ACU	NTLC	CHC
1998	35	56	44	46	96	68	71	72	52	55	42
1997	50	—	13	—	100	69	—	80	68	—	—

National Journal Ratings

	1997 LIB — 1997 CONS		1998 LIB — 1998 CONS	
Economic	46%	— 54%	51%	— 49%
Social	61%	— 39%	62%	— 37%
Foreign	41%	— 58%	53%	— 45%

Key Votes of the 105th Congress

1. Clinton Budget Deal	N	5. Puerto Rico Sthood. Ref.	N	9. Cut $ for B-2 Bombers	N
2. Education IRAs	Y	6. End Highway Set-asides	Y	10. Human Rights in China	N
3. Req. 2/3 to Raise Taxes	N	7. School Prayer Amend.	Y	11. Withdraw Bosnia Troops	Y
4. Fast-track Trade	Y	8. Ovrd. Part. Birth Veto	Y	12. End Cuban TV-Marti	N

Election Results

1998 general	Tom Campbell (R)	111,876	(61%)	($791,634)
	Dick Lane (D)	70,059	(38%)	($15,484)
	Others	2,851	(2%)	
1998 primary	Tom Campbell (R)	86,248	(66%)	
	Dick Lane (D)	33,767	(26%)	
	Connor Vlakancic (D)	8,335	(6%)	
	Others	2,409	(2%)	
1996 general	Tom Campbell (R)	132,737	(59%)	($527,125)
	Dick Lane (D)	79,048	(35%)	($64,732)
	Others	15,101	(7%)	

SIXTEENTH DISTRICT

With more people than San Francisco, higher per capita incomes than San Diego, a tradition of high-tech innovation that rivals any on earth, and a major league sports team housed in California's biggest indoor arena, San Jose has great claims on national attention and respect.

Yet San Jose—with the 11th largest population within city limits in the United States—does not yet bulk as large in the national consciousness as it should. At the southern end of the Bay, it remains in the shadow. San Francisco is every tourist's idea of a city: geographically compact, with picturesque public transportation, old-time and new immigrant groups, an economy historically based on heavy industry and sea trade, a large city bureaucracy symbolized by a monumental city hall. San Jose is quite different. It got its start as a farm-market town, with canneries and fruit-packing operations for the produce from the surrounding fertile plains. It sits not on the Bay, but on the Southern Pacific line above the marshes and salt evaporators; its major transportation arteries are the freeways—U.S. 101, Interstates 280 and 680, California 17—which encircle its revitalized downtown. The main minority group here is Mexican-Americans, who initially came as farm workers but now inhabit every occupational niche and, while concentrated on the east side, are also scattered throughout San Jose and adjacent towns; there are also increasing numbers of Asian Americans. Scattered is the right word to describe San Jose's growth. Starting in the 1950s, San Jose has grown out in every direction, developers hip-hopping across the farmland, putting up subdivisions faster sometimes than the few city employees could update the street map. Economically, San Jose has been sustained by everything from its traditional agriculture to manufacturing to the high-tech businesses that are centered in Silicon Valley towns just to the west but are omnipresent here: an American city, 21st Century style.

The 16th Congressional District consists of the larger part of San Jose, plus its urban fringe to the east and the still agricultural Santa Clara Valley to the south, including Gilroy, the garlic capital of the United States. It includes the old and new downtown and the heavily Mexican-American areas to the east. This is the most heavily Hispanic district in the Bay Area (36%) and is also heavily Asian (20%), with the largest concentration of Vietnamese in the U.S. Politically, it has become Democratic, and its future leanings depend on the trends among Latinos, who are family-oriented and not as favorable to big government as blacks, and Asians, who are more often the victims than the beneficiaries of liberals' quota schemes.

The congresswoman from the 16th District is Zoe Lofgren, a Democrat elected in 1994. Lofgren grew up in the Bay Area, where her father was a Teamster truck driver and her mother worked for the Machinists Union, went to Stanford and Santa Clara Law School, worked for eight years as a staffer to Congressman Don Edwards; while still a law student, she worked for him while he served on the Judiciary Committee that voted to impeach Richard Nixon. In 1980 she was elected to the Santa Clara County Board of Supervisors, where she spearheaded a 1984 ballot proposition to give local governments control of freeway building and moved the jails from the sheriff's office to the local corrections department. In 1994, when Edwards retired after 32 years in the House, Lofgren ran for the seat. Her main primary opponent, former (1983–90) San Jose Mayor Tom McEnery, started off better known. But Lofgren raised almost twice as much money with the support of the National Women's Political Caucus, the National Organization for Women, EMILY's List, Senator Barbara Boxer and Congresswomen Anna Eshoo and Lynn Woolsey. She won the primary 45%–42%. She easily won the general election and looked forward to putting into effect her ideas for early intervention to fight gun violence and drug abuse and to help underprivileged children.

To her surprise she found herself in the minority. "It has been frustrating because so much of what the Gingrich agenda has been is stuff I don't agree with," she said. Nonetheless she has had some legislative impact, and her voting record, while mostly liberal, includes some free-market positions responsive to local businesses. She has worked to expand the H-1B visa program for high-tech workers, which went through in October 1998. She passed an amendment to exempt AIDS drugs from some FDA procedures. A major cause has been to get schools wired to the Internet; she strongly supports the "e-rate," the tax on telephones devoted to wiring schools to the Internet. She also has pushed for looser controls on encryption exports. She supported securities litigation reform, a big Silicon Valley cause, and after much hesitation voted for fast track. She opposed the Communications Decency Act and sponsored a bill to require Internet service providers to offer filtering software. She has expressed concern about the high cost of housing in the San Jose area, and sponsored a bill to encourage local school districts to start the school day later, at 9 a.m. She and Colorado Republican Joel Hefley head up the subcommittee investigating ethics charges against Transportation Chairman Bud Shuster.

The impeachment inquiry suddenly put Lofgren in the national spotlight. She was the only Judiciary member to have served as a staffer during the Nixon impeachment proceedings, and she attempted to put her experience to use. She brought forward the 1974 committee staff report that had set forth grounds for impeachment, and insisted the committee members vote on what is an impeachable offense now—though of course Judiciary had not had such a vote 24 years before. This argument suited Democrats' partisan purpose, and they included it in their impeachment resolution, which is presumably why it was not acceptable to Chairman Henry Hyde and the Republicans. For the definition of an impeachable offense is a constitutional question, and no member of Congress can be bound, even by majority vote, to any view of what the Constitution requires. But the partisan atmosphere engendered by the vote on which party's impeachment inquiry to adopt pervaded the entire process. To this Lofgren contributed. Impeachment was a "national embarrassment," she said, and laughed loudly at arguments made by the other side. She argued that a Senate trial would paralyze the nation for six months and prevent the Supreme Court from doing business—which did not turn out to be true. And she said that Clinton's acts did not impair the operations of government, though they did impair the operations of the federal courts, which are part of government. Nevertheless her stand was popular with her constituents and was praised by the Bay Area press.

Cook's Call. *Safe.* Another California Democrat with not a re-election woe in the world is Lofgren. This San Jose-based seat is about as safe as they come.

The People: Pop. 1990: 571,460; 4% rural; 7.3% age 65+; 55.3% White, 5.2% Black, 21.1% Asian, 0.8% Amer. Indian, 17.7% Other; 36.2% Hispanic Origin. Households: 55.9% married couple families; 33.3% married couple fams. w. children; 48.8% college educ.; median household income: $42,223; per capita income: $14,614; median house value: $234,500; median gross rent: $652.

1996 Presidential Vote			1992 Presidential Vote		
Clinton (D)	91,786	(61%)	Clinton (D)	86,418	(52%)
Dole (R)	43,257	(29%)	Bush (R)	44,693	(27%)
Perot (I)	9,659	(6%)	Perot (I)	33,882	(20%)
Others	5,195	(3%)			

Rep. Zoe Lofgren (D)

Elected 1994; b. Dec. 21, 1947, San Mateo; home, San Jose; Stanford U., B.A. 1970, U. of Santa Clara Law Schl., J.D. 1975; Protestant; married (John Collins).

Elected Office: Santa Clara Bd. of Supervisors, 1980–94.

Professional Career: Staff Asst., U.S. Rep. Don Edwards, 1970–78; Practicing atty., 1978–80; Prof., U. of Santa Clara Law Schl., 1981–94.

DC Office: 318 CHOB 20515, 202-225-3072; Fax: 202-225-3336; Web site: www.house.gov/lofgren.

District Office: San Jose, 408-271-8700.

Committees: *Judiciary* (8th of 16 D): Courts & Intellectual Property; Immigration & Claims. *Science* (8th of 22 D): Energy & Environment; Space & Aeronautics. *Standards of Official Conduct* (5th of 5 D).

Group Ratings

	ADA	ACLU	AFS	LCV	CON	NTU	NFIB	COC	ACU	NTLC	CHC
1998	95	88	89	85	95	30	21	47	0	5	0
1997	95	—	88	—	42	31	—	40	8	—	—

National Journal Ratings

	1997 LIB — 1997 CONS		1998 LIB — 1998 CONS	
Economic	93%	— 0%	72%	— 23%
Social	85%	— 0%	78%	— 21%
Foreign	88%	— 10%	96%	— 2%

Key Votes of the 105th Congress

1. Clinton Budget Deal	N	5. Puerto Rico Sthood. Ref.	Y	9. Cut $ for B-2 Bombers	Y
2. Education IRAs	N	6. End Highway Set-asides	N	10. Human Rights in China	Y
3. Req. 2/3 to Raise Taxes	N	7. School Prayer Amend.	N	11. Withdraw Bosnia Troops	N
4. Fast-track Trade	Y	8. Ovrd. Part. Birth Veto	N	12. End Cuban TV-Marti	Y

Election Results

1998 general	Zoe Lofgren (D)	85,503	(73%)	($221,568)
	Horace Eugene Thayn (R)	27,494	(23%)	
	Others	4,417	(4%)	
1998 primary	Zoe Lofgren (D)	58,947	(72%)	
	Horace Eugene Thayn (R)	18,414	(23%)	
	John H. Black (NL)	4,308	(5%)	
1996 general	Zoe Lofgren (D)	94,020	(66%)	($191,393)
	Chuck Wojslaw (R)	43,197	(30%)	($77,796)
	Others	5,990	(4%)	

SEVENTEENTH DISTRICT

The California coast around Monterey Bay is for many a working definition of paradise. This kernel of California, where Spanish and then Mexicans governed a virtually empty land and Californians set up their first state capital, still makes a fine living, as it has for nearly 150 years, off the land and sea. The fields around Salinas supply much of the nation's lettuce and cauliflower, the fields around Castroville supply almost all of its artichokes, and the vast greenhouses around Watsonville supply a goodly portion of its roses. The fishing fleet and 18 canneries of Monterey are not the major industry they were half a century ago (the last cannery closed nearly 30 ago), but they have generated a new industry: Cannery Row is refurbished with upscale shops and hotels, and the magnificent Monterey Bay Aquarium has become one of California's top tourist destinations. Monterey Bay has become the language learning capital of the United States, with the Defense Language Institute, the AT&T Language Line and the Cal State University Monterey Bay Center for Intensive Language and Culture. There are other attractions on the Monterey peninsula as well, like the Pebble Beach golf courses and the Del Monte Lodge, and Carmel, whose restrictive laws—no house numbers, no door-to-door mail delivery, no live entertainment, no stop lights, no cutting trees without city council permission—reflect an effort to maintain the atmosphere of 80 years ago, when it really was an artists' colony.

The 17th Congressional District includes all the coast of Monterey Bay and then follows the Big Sur coastline south almost to William Randolph Hearst's castle, San Simeon, past perhaps the most beautiful scenery in America. The district extends inland, into sunny valleys sheltered from ocean mists, and covers some of the nation's richest farmland. This area is a prime example of how the California coast has trended Democratic. The older residents—landowners in Salinas and the townspeople who sympathize with them, retirees in Santa Cruz and the Monterey Peninsula—still vote Republican. But an influx of liberation-minded young people now in their prime years, attracted less by the economy than by the atmosphere, moved the coast to the left. Also, the branch of the University of California at Santa Cruz is so liberal (97% for McGovern in 1972) that it has changed the political balance of the whole county. As late as 1980, Monterey and Santa Cruz counties were voting less Democratic than the nation. But since 1984 they have been 6% to 10% more Democratic than the nation. In 1998, Democratic gubernatorial candidate Gray Davis won more than 60% of the vote in this district that was carried four times by Ronald Reagan.

The congressman from the 17th is Sam Farr, a Democrat elected in June 1993. Farr, a fifth-generation Californian, grew up in the area, where his father Fred Farr was a state senator for many years. Sam Farr after college signed up for the Peace Corps, learned Spanish at the Monterey Institute of International Studies and served two years in Colombia. He was a staffer in the California Assembly for a decade, became a Monterey County supervisor in 1975, and was elected to the Assembly in 1980. There he wrote one of the nation's strictest oil spill liability laws and expanded the state park system. In 1993 the 17th's congressman since 1976, Leon Panetta, resigned to become Office of Management and Budget director, and Farr ran for the House. He entered the race as the overwhelming favorite, and in the all-party primary won 26% to beat two other Democrats who had 19% and 14%. But in the June runoff, after the Clinton budget and tax increase had been introduced, he had trouble against Republican Bill McCampbell, who had been beaten 72%–24% by Panetta seven months before. Farr won, but by just 52%–43%.

The 1991 base-closing law had shut Fort Ord, site of the Language Institute—one of the biggest closures in the country. Farr in his first term worked to get $15 million to help start the California State University campus there (in his second term he got an additional $36 million) and to install a Defense Department finance center. In November 1994 Farr again faced McCampbell and lost Monterey County, winning by enough in Santa Cruz for a 52%–44% victory. After the election there was terrible flooding. A local official "asked me whether, being in the minority, I was able to handle disasters. I said becoming the minority was a disaster. I am disaster equipped." But Farr had some successes, as well as some failures, in the Republican Congress. He got more funding for Cal State and a new veterans' clinic. He saved 300 jobs at Social Security's Salinas Data Operations Center. He opposed Richard Pombo's bill to allow 250,000 foreign farm workers in, arguing that growers who pay good wages don't need to import workers; this was a contrast to Panetta's sponsorship in the 1980s of guest worker programs. In voting against Clinton's 1997 fast-track trade bill, Farr cited the administration's failure to restrict imports of duty-free cut flowers from Colombia, which have harmed a major local industry; the flowers are allowed across the border with no tariff as an incentive for Columbia to grow crops other than narcotics. But the trade dispute did not prevent Farr from bringing Clinton and Vice President Gore to Monterey in June 1998 for the first-ever National Ocean Conference, where environmentalists, scientists and politicians made a renewed commitment to protect the seas.

After the 1998 election Farr won a seat on the Appropriations Committee. His subcommittee assignments will allow him to focus on two major local issues—farming and military bases. Farr also was elected chairman of the California Democratic delegation in the House. Farr was re-elected by wide margins in 1996 and 1998.

Cook's Call. *Probably Safe.* After a couple close calls in the early 1990s, Farr looks like he finally has a handle on this district. He is a strong favorite for 2000, but this is a district where Republicans have at least a toe-hold and with the right candidate could give Farr a fight.

The People: Pop. 1990: 571,077; 15.4% rural; 11.1% age 65 + ; 69.6% White, 4.4% Black, 6.3% Asian, 0.9% Amer. Indian, 18.8% Other; 30.9% Hispanic Origin. Households: 55.4% married couple families; 29.3% married couple fams. w. children; 53.6% college educ.; median household income: $33,911; per capita income: $15,006; median house value: $220,800; median gross rent: $586.

1996 Presidential Vote

Clinton (D)	109,941	(55%)
Dole (R)	64,178	(32%)
Perot (I)	12,795	(6%)
Others	12,020	(6%)

1992 Presidential Vote

Clinton (D)	111,937	(52%)
Bush (R)	57,990	(27%)
Perot (I)	42,317	(20%)

Rep. Sam Farr (D)

Elected June 1993; b. July 4, 1941, San Francisco; home, Carmel; Willamette U., B.S. 1963; Episcopalian; married (Shary).

Elected Office: Monterey Cnty. Bd. of Supervisors, 1975–80, Chmn., 1979; CA Assembly, 1980–93.

Professional Career: Peace Corps, Columbia, 1963–65; Staff, CA Assembly, 1965–75.

DC Office: 1221 LHOB 20515, 202-225-2861; Fax: 202-225-6791; Web site: www.house.gov/farr.

District Offices: Salinas, 408-424-2229; Santa Cruz, 408-429-1976.

Committees: *Appropriations* (24th of 27 D): Agriculture, Rural Development, & FDA; Military Construction.

Group Ratings

	ADA	ACLU	AFS	LCV	CON	NTU	NFIB	COC	ACU	NTLC	CHC
1998	100	80	100	100	76	15	29	44	0	5	0
1997	95	—	88	—	46	25	—	40	4	—	—

National Journal Ratings

	1997 LIB — 1997 CONS			1998 LIB — 1998 CONS		
Economic	85%	—	10%	79%	—	0%
Social	77%	—	23%	81%	—	16%
Foreign	85%	—	15%	96%	—	2%

Key Votes of the 105th Congress

1. Clinton Budget Deal	N	5. Puerto Rico Sthood. Ref.	Y	9. Cut $ for B-2 Bombers	Y
2. Education IRAs	N	6. End Highway Set-asides	N	10. Human Rights in China	Y
3. Req. 2/3 to Raise Taxes	N	7. School Prayer Amend.	N	11. Withdraw Bosnia Troops	N
4. Fast-track Trade	N	8. Ovrd. Part. Birth Veto	N	12. End Cuban TV-Marti	Y

Election Results

1998 general	Sam Farr (D)	103,719	(65%)	($413,023)
	Bill McCampbell (R)	52,470	(33%)	($108,905)
	Others	4,501	(3%)	
1998 primary	Sam Farr (D)	73,337	(60%)	
	Bill McCampbell (R)	36,089	(30%)	
	Art Dunn (D)	5,966	(5%)	
	Others	6,589	(5%)	
1996 general	Sam Farr (D)	115,116	(59%)	($563,235)
	Jess Brown (R)	73,856	(38%)	($455,239)
	Others	6,573	(3%)	

EIGHTEENTH DISTRICT

The Central Valley of California is a miraculous man-made landscape, an outdoor factory stretching as far as the eye can see. Nature created the vast flatlands, rimmed by mountains rising surreally in the distant haze. But man in the last century has disciplined the land with a remorseless mile-square grid of roads, and the sluggish-flowing California Aqueduct and dozens of arrow-straight canals; pipes fitted with valves and gauges to pump water and fertilizer and pesticides to the fields in measured quantities give an air of industrial precision. The crops grow in carefully spaced rows, filling the fields, for the rich soil and the irrigated water are too precious to waste on decoration or flower gardens: the Valley is business. Farming here has never been a way of life, but a business; in the 19th Century the land was not given to 160-acre homesteaders but sold to thousands-of-acres capitalist enterprises.

The Central Valley has been one of California's surprise boom areas in the 1980s and 1990s, growing not just crops but people. Middle-wage employees in the San Francisco Bay area drive east at the end of the day on I-580, past surreal windmills whirling on the bare hills of the Altamont pass, across the Westlands fields to modestly priced homes in Modesto, the town immortalized (when it was much smaller) in *American Graffiti*. Warehouses and factories have sprung up on land that, for all its farming value, is cheaper than industrial land in the Bay Area, and some croplands have been given over to pasture, as subsidized water was cut off from cultivators of cotton and water prices are moving slowly toward market levels far above those of government subsidy. The result, however, is not stagnation but growth, and a more well-rounded economy. But there are costs. Traffic is a problem, air pollution on bad days approaches coastal metropolitan levels, and the pace of life is getting more hectic.

The 18th Congressional District includes a large chunk of the Central Valley from Modesto and Stanislaus County south through Merced almost to Fresno. The political tradition here is Democratic: Democrats in Washington and Democratic Governor Pat Brown built the irrigation canals and authorized the water subsidies; Democrats own the McClatchy newspapers, the predominant Valley chain; Democrats staffed the Bank of America, long the dominant financial force here; on the walls of insider law firms are signed pictures of Franklin Roosevelt and Pat Brown, not Ronald Reagan and Pete Wilson. Today the voters of the 18th District remain fairly heavily Democratic. There are many Latinos here, and an increasing number of Asians, though neither group produces the overwhelming Democratic majorities blacks do; there are some voters of white Southern ancestry, used to voting for local Democrats though happy to vote Republican for president. The Central Valley is the part of California with the highest proportion of families and children, and there is a natural cultural conservatism here, shared by successful local Democratic politicians.

The congressman from the 18th District is Gary Condit, a Democrat chosen in a September 1989 special election to replace the far more-partisan Democratic Whip Tony Coelho after he resigned, and now one of the key Democrats in a closely-divided House. Condit grew up in Oklahoma, the son of a Baptist minister; at 19 he married and, with his young family and father, moved to Ceres in the Central Valley; he worked his way through college and in 1972, the year he graduated, he was elected to the Ceres Council. In 1982, at 34, he was elected to the California Assembly; there he made a moderate to conservative record on crime and taxes and was one of the "Gang of Five" Democrats who nearly toppled Speaker Willie Brown in 1988— and were fiercely retaliated against. When Coelho surprised everyone by resigning, Condit seized the chance to run for Congress. Against former state Senator Clare Berryhill, Condit raised money efficiently and ran an absentee voter drive which essentially won the election before the polls opened. Some 35% of all votes were cast absentee, the large majority Democratic, and Condit won 57%–35%.

Condit has the most conservative voting record of any California Democrat: for the balanced budget amendment and line-item veto, against publicly funded abortions, for relaxed environmental restrictions. He had little influence when Democrats held the majority, but became a key member after the 1994 election. He was the prime Democratic co-sponsor of the 1995 unfunded mandates act, which disclosed the costs bills would impose on state and local governments. When Dick Gephardt refused to appoint him to the conference committee, Newt Gingrich did instead. Condit backed regulatory reform, including risk assessment and cost-benefit analysis. He supported tort reform, product liability reform, and sunsetting of the Internal Revenue Code. He opposed school vouchers, NAFTA and privatizing Social Security.

In 1995 Condit was a founding member of the Blue Dog Democrats; they are not yellow dog Democrats, they said, always faithful to the party, but dogs who were choked till they were blue by liberal Democrats. "We are not a hostile group and we are not mad at anyone. We just want to do what's right for the country and vote our conscience," he insists. But "the fact is, our leadership did not want to have a balanced budget and did not want welfare reform. With all due respect, that's unacceptable." The Blue Dogs produced their own budget in 1995, which went nowhere as Gingrich's Republicans and the Clinton White House slugged it out. But the May 1997 balanced budget deal partook of the Blue Dog approach, and as the federal deficit became (at least for a while) history, Condit could take satisfaction in achieving one of his goals. And now he was let in on the top negotiations, in which he became friends with Budget Chairman John Kasich. They even attended Pearl Jam and Rolling Stones concerts together, and Kasich pledged to contribute to Condit's campaign, which later led angry California Republicans to block his participation at a February 1999 Republican presidential candidates "cattle show."

Condit's friendliness and apparent lack of guile has enabled him to make friends across all lines. In 1997 he assembled a coalition of Blue Dog, New Democrat Coalition and Congressional Black Caucus members to support reform of Superfund, most of whose money goes to lawyers, not environmental cleanup. Condit voted for the Republicans' tax cut in September 1998 and against the omnibus budget in October. In February 1999 he sponsored an unfunded mandates bill which required the CBO to estimate the costs of bills on private businesses; it passed by 274–149. He was one of 31 House Democrats to vote for the Clinton impeachment inquiry, though he later voted against impeachment. Republicans often urged Condit to switch parties, but after 1995 he said switching was "over with." And in the closely divided House he has more leverage than ever. Gephardt, who once snubbed him, in February 1999 invited him to serve on the party's leadership council.

He does not neglect local issues. As air pollution in the Central Valley has increased, Condit and George Radanovich moved to ban Mexican-registered cars unless they can meet California clean air standards, and he pushed for tougher air standards on the San Francisco Bay Area, whose air blows through the passes into the Central Valley. In 1997 he organized Team California, a bipartisan group of California federal, state and local officials, to get the ideologically divided California delegation moving in the same direction on at least some state issues. He endorsed Gray Davis for governor in January 1998, when he seemed mired in third place in the primary, and accompanied him to Valley events. After the election, Davis named Condit one of three co-chairmen of a 33-member commission on farm and water policy—a clear sign Davis would not pursue the anti-Valley policies of the governor he had once served as chief of staff, Jerry Brown.

Condit, who rides a Harley when he is back home, is confident enough of re-election that he gives campaign funds to charities. He was opposed by only a Libertarian candidate in 1998.

Cook's Call. *Safe.* Though many Democrats begrudge Condit for his conservative record, it is this profile that has helped him to get re-elected in this conservative, agriculturally-dependent, Central Valley district. As one of the founders of the Blue Dog faction of House Democrats, Condit appears to have found the right recipe for this district but in an open seat situation, there could be a real fight here.

The People: Pop. 1990: 571,358; 19.2% rural; 10.7% age 65 +; 75.8% White, 2.8% Black, 5.9% Asian, 1.1% Amer. Indian, 14.4% Other; 25.6% Hispanic Origin. Households: 60.1% married couple families; 33.4% married couple fams. w. children; 41.2% college educ.; median household income: $28,324; per capita income: $12,013; median house value: $114,800; median gross rent: $393.

1996 Presidential Vote		
Clinton (D)	77,560	(46%)
Dole (R)	76,217	(45%)
Perot (I)	12,161	(7%)
Others	3,470	(2%)

1992 Presidential Vote		
Clinton (D)	74,357	(41%)
Bush (R)	67,898	(37%)
Perot (I)	39,645	(22%)

Rep. Gary Condit (D)

Elected Sept. 1989; b. Apr. 21, 1948, Salina, OK; home, Ceres; Modesto Jr. Col., A.A. 1970, CA St. U., B.A. 1972; Protestant; married (Carolyn).

Elected Office: Ceres City Cncl., 1972–76; Ceres Mayor, 1974–76; Stanislaus Cnty. Bd. of Supervisors, 1976–82; CA Assembly, 1982–89.

DC Office: 2234 RHOB 20515, 202-225-6131; Fax: 202-225-0819; Web site: www.house.gov/gcondit.

District Offices: Merced, 209-383-4455; Modesto, 209-527-1914.

Committees: *Agriculture* (3d of 24 D): Livestock & Horticulture; Risk Management, Research & Specialty Crops (RMM). *Permanent Select Committee on Intelligence* (5th of 7 D): Human Intelligence, Analysis & Counterintelligence; Technical & Tactical Intelligence.

Group Ratings

	ADA	ACLU	AFS	LCV	CON	NTU	NFIB	COC	ACU	NTLC	CHC
1998	60	47	78	15	63	49	71	67	56	58	50
1997	60	—	50	—	76	53	—	60	52	—	—

National Journal Ratings

	1997 LIB — 1997 CONS			1998 LIB — 1998 CONS	
Economic	52%	—	48%	52%	—	47%
Social	57%	—	42%	53%	—	46%
Foreign	38%	—	60%	43%	—	53%

Key Votes of the 105th Congress

1. Clinton Budget Deal	Y	5. Puerto Rico Sthood. Ref.	Y	9. Cut $ for B-2 Bombers	Y
2. Education IRAs	Y	6. End Highway Set-asides	N	10. Human Rights in China	Y
3. Req. 2/3 to Raise Taxes	Y	7. School Prayer Amend.	Y	11. Withdraw Bosnia Troops	Y
4. Fast-track Trade	N	8. Ovrd. Part. Birth Veto	Y	12. End Cuban TV-Marti	N

Election Results

1998 general	Gary Condit (D)	118,842	(87%)	($439,331)
	Linda M. Degroat (Lib)	18,089	(13%)	
1998 primary	Gary Condit (D)	83,512	(89%)	
	Ken Aaroe (Lib)	10,262	(11%)	
1996 general	Gary Condit (D)	108,827	(66%)	($678,001)
	Bill Conrad (R)	52,695	(32%)	($75,271)
	Others	4,064	(2%)	

NINETEENTH DISTRICT

Fresno, in California's Central Valley, between the flat Westlands and the Sierras, is a city both agricultural and industrial, middle American and ethnically diverse. It is a creation of the industrial age, founded by the Central Pacific Railroad; its city fathers bred the local wine grape, developed the raisin industry and introduced the Smyrna fig. But these are not all of Fresno County's crops, which include cotton, lima beans, tomatoes, cantaloupes, plums, peaches and alfalfa: Fresno produces more farm products in dollar value than any other county in the United States. Central Valley agriculture is industrial in its precision, its thoroughness and its ownership by large corporations: the vineyards outside Fresno radiate in mechanical precision, with vines just 10 feet apart and exposed to the relentless summer sun—nothing romantic or quaint here. The city of Fresno started off as a farm-marketing center—one high-income neighborhood is called Fig Garden because that's what it used to be—and as a tourists' stop-off point on the way to Yosemite National Park. But it has long since grown out north, east and west from its old downtown, and its economy has diversified.

Like all the Central Valley, Fresno has always been ethnically diverse, with a telephone book that reads like the United Nations. It has America's second largest Armenian community, after Los Angeles; Fresno's great chronicler was William Saroyan. Its already large Latino population has more than doubled in the last 20 years; Asians, including Chinese, Filipinos, Vietnamese and Hmong, may number as many as 50,000. Fresno had its troubles in the 1990s, as immigration continued despite high unemployment; there were violent teenage gangs and air pollution that made the Sierra Nevada invisible on many days. Historically, Fresno was a Democratic town, the prime Democratic bastion in the Valley south of Sacramento. But in the 1990s it has trended Republican. Fresno elected a Republican mayor, religious broadcaster Jim Patterson, in 1993, who cut crime and tried to reduce burdens on business. In 1996 Fresno County favored Bob Dole over Bill Clinton 47%–45%, and in the 1998 gubernatorial election it favored Republican Dan Lungren over Democrat Gray Davis 49%–48%, even as Davis was winning 58%–38% statewide; it was the largest county Lungren won.

The 19th Congressional District of California includes most of Fresno, all but the old down-town and a Latino area in the Hispanic-majority 20th District. The 19th spreads with an erose boundary over the farm country below the Sierra foothills from Visalia, south of Fresno, to mountainous Mariposa County. Most of its land mass is part of the Sierra Nevada, and it contains most of three major national parks: Yosemite, Kings Canyon and Sequoia.

The congressman from the 19th District is George Radanovich, a Republican elected in 1994. Radanovich is the son of Croatian immigrants, with relatives all over the Valley. He worked on the family farm, served on the Mariposa County Planning Commission in the 1980s and won a seat on the Board of Supervisors in 1989. In 1986, after studying local microclimates, he opened the first winery in Mariposa County and made it work; the Radanovich Winery now ships 4,500 cases of sauvignon blanc, zinfandel and cabernet sauvignon. In 1992 he ran for Congress, losing the primary 33%–30% to 28-year-old Tal Cloud, who lost to incumbent Democrat Richard Lehman 47%–46%. Lehman was an adept professional politician, but all his fundraising and skills could not avail him in 1994 as Radanovich, an easy winner in this primary, attacked him for supporting the Clinton Administration's and California Democrat George Miller's attempts to raise the price of Valley water. Radanovich won 57%–40% in the widest defeat of a non-freshman incumbent in 1994. Radanovich became the first full-time professional winemaker to serve in the House.

In the House, Radanovich was elected president of the 74-member freshmen Republican class. Sometimes moderate on economics, he has mostly had a conservative voting record. He defended the government shutdown, even when it closed Yosemite during the holiday season, and said he would prefer government default before voting to increase the debt limit. In June 1996 his and David Bonior's amendment to require Turkey to acknowledge the Armenian genocide of 1915 passed the House 268–153; Turkey spurned aid under such conditions. He also sponsored a bill to redirect the $22 million in aid for Turkey to Armenia; he got the House to extend the foreign aid embargo on Azerbaijan by 231–182 in September 1998. He strongly opposes George Miller's 1992 Central Valley water act; he prefers the "stakeholder process" of the Bay-Delta Accord of 1994. He held out on fast track, agreeing to support it only after the administration agreed to address Mexican wine tariffs. On Capitol Hill, he sold his wine at a local market but he drew consumerists' attacks when he filed legislation to benefit winemakers. In June 1995 he stopped answering constituent mail, sending a form letter explaining how expensive the average member's mail is; the Democratic *Fresno Bee* applauded. He worked on local issues, calling for light rail in Yosemite even if other parks had to be closed to fund it, and getting 67 families continued access to isolated cabins in Sequoia National Park. After the winter 1997 Yosemite flood, he worked to schedule federal repairs so as to minimize harm to the tourist business. With Gary Condit, he moved to ban from California cars from Mexico which do not meet the state's air-quality standards.

Radanovich has been highly popular at home. In 1998, no Democrat ran in this district which a Democrat had held only four years before. Two days after the 1998 election, Radanovich challenged House Republican Conference chairman John Boehner, but switched to support J.C. Watts when he entered the race.

Cook's Call. *Safe.* Though this district was held by Democrat Richard Lehman for 10 years, redistricting in 1991 slashed Democratic registration by 12 points and added more rural sections to the district, making it a safe Republican seat. There is little hope of Democrats mounting a competitive effort unless the lines are moved substantially.

The People: Pop. 1990: 573,077; 20.3% rural; 11.7% age 65 +; 73.7% White, 3.3% Black, 7.4% Asian, 1.3% Amer. Indian, 14.3% Other; 23.1% Hispanic Origin. Households: 56% married couple families; 28.4% married couple fams. w. children; 51.5% college educ.; median household income: $29,153; per capita income: $13,516; median house value: $90,800; median gross rent: $378.

1996 Presidential Vote			1992 Presidential Vote		
Dole (R)	111,666	(52%)	Bush (R)	97,124	(43%)
Clinton (D)	85,744	(40%)	Clinton (D)	85,049	(38%)
Perot (I)	12,495	(6%)	Perot (I)	41,052	(18%)
Others	4,816	(2%)			

Rep. George Radanovich (R)

Elected 1994; b. June 20, 1955, Mariposa; home, Mariposa; CA Polytechnic U., B.S. 1978; Catholic; married (Ethie).

Elected Office: Mariposa Cnty. Planning Comm., 1982–86, Chmn., 1985–86; Mariposa Cnty. Bd. of Supervisors, 1989–92.

Professional Career: Farmer; Founder & Owner, Radanovich Winery, 1986–present.

DC Office: 123 CHOB 20515, 202-225-4540; Fax: 202-225-3402; Web site: www.house.gov/radanovich.

District Office: Fresno, 209-248-0800.

Committees: *Budget* (9th of 24 R). *International Relations* (24th of 26 R): Africa; International Economic Policy & Trade. *Resources* (14th of 28 R): National Parks & Public Lands; Water & Power.

Group Ratings

	ADA	ACLU	AFS	LCV	CON	NTU	NFIB	COC	ACU	NTLC	CHC
1998	0	7	0	0	42	65	86	94	100	95	100
1997	0	—	13	—	62	59	—	80	96	—	—

National Journal Ratings

	1997 LIB — 1997 CONS			1998 LIB — 1998 CONS	
Economic	28%	—	67%	0% — 88%	
Social	0%	—	90%	13% — 86%	
Foreign	0%	—	88%	0% — 93%	

Key Votes of the 105th Congress

1. Clinton Budget Deal	Y	5. Puerto Rico Sthood. Ref.	N	9. Cut $ for B-2 Bombers	N
2. Education IRAs	Y	6. End Highway Set-asides	*	10. Human Rights in China	N
3. Req. 2/3 to Raise Taxes	Y	7. School Prayer Amend.	Y	11. Withdraw Bosnia Troops	Y
4. Fast-track Trade	Y	8. Ovrd. Part. Birth Veto	Y	12. End Cuban TV-Marti	N

Election Results

1998 general	George Radanovich (R)	131,105	(79%)	($452,642)
	Jonathan Richter (Lib)	34,044	(21%)	
1998 primary	George Radanovich (R)	101,169	(82%)	
	Jonathan Richter (Lib)	21,623	(18%)	
1996 general	George Radanovich (R)	137,402	(67%)	($618,220)
	Paul Barile (D)	58,452	(28%)	($6,509)
	Others	10,525	(5%)	

TWENTIETH DISTRICT

California's Central Valley by car seems a monotonous landscape: mile after mile of farmland with mile-square grid roads, cut across by diagonal railroads and canals, with an occasional cluster town. The land is hilly and gets more water near the Sierra Nevada, and this is where the larger cities cluster. On the other side is the Westlands, where the land is flatter and the water scarcer. Here the land was always developed and sold in large plots, and it has some of the world's largest farming operations today. And it produces plenty: alfalfa, cantaloupes, cotton, grapes, lima beans, olives, peaches, plums, raisins, sugar beets, tomatoes, walnuts, wheat. The owners are a hardy lot, but like most entrepreneurs they have been happy to have government help: crop price supports, agricultural research, exceptions to the immigration laws, irrigation systems and (most important) subsidized water. They have fought hard against liberals' efforts at change, from Governor Jerry Brown's attempts to encourage Cesar Chavez's United Farm Workers in the 1970s to former House Natural Resources Committee Chairman George Miller's 1992 law to draw off more water to the Sacramento delta and charge higher prices for it in the Valley. But the greatest threats may come from conservatives: In a free market for water, Los Angeles users may outbid the farmers, and tighter restrictions on illegal immigrants have cut into the supply of farm workers; Congress has so far declined to approve guest worker programs pushed by Valley members.

The 20th Congressional District includes most of the Westlands of the Central Valley, from south of Bakersfield to north of Fresno. Its irregular boundaries were drawn to maximize the Hispanic population and possibly elect a Hispanic congressman, so the 20th includes the old downtown neighborhoods of both Bakersfield and Fresno, but none of their newer suburbs; it includes heavily Latino towns like Delano, long Chavez's headquarters, but not more Anglo places like Tulare. The 20th's Hispanic percentage was 55% in 1990, compared to 20%–26% in other Central Valley districts, but the percentage of voters who are Latino is lower, 34% in 1990 and 39% in 1997. Still, this is the most Democratic Valley seat between Sacramento and Los Angeles.

The congressman from the 20th is Calvin Dooley, a Democrat elected in 1990. He is a farmer, growing cotton, alfalfa and walnuts as his great-grandfather did before him. In the late 1987 he became a staffer for Tulare state Senator Rose Ann Vuich. In 1990, he ran for Congress in a more Republican-leaning district. Luck was with him: The incumbent had accepted contributions from S&L operator Charles Keating and then interceded with regulators on his behalf. Dooley won with a solid 55%. When new district lines were announced in 1992, Dooley and 10-year incumbent Democrat Richard Lehman both eyed the 20th, but Dooley staked it out solidly and Lehman ran in the much more Republican 19th District, which he won narrowly that year and then lost in 1994, while Dooley has been re-elected without difficulty.

Dooley's endurance has been partly a testimonial to his moderate voting record, which vies with Gary Condit's for being the most conservative of California Democrats. He tottered before voting for the Clinton budget and tax package, and he supported the balanced budget amendment and the line-item veto. In the Republican 104th Congress, Dooley voted for much of the Contract with America and supported most of welfare reform. In his committee work he tended to district interests. On the Agriculture Committee, he worked on the complex dairy issues, co-sponsoring an amendment with New York Republican Gerald Solomon to phase out butter, cheese and powder price supports and consolidate the 33 milk marketing orders into no more than 14, with a guarantee that California could set its own standard for pricing and milk solids. He was one of three committee Democrats to vote for Richard Pombo's guest worker bill. In August 1995 he switched his vote on maintaining EPA's powers because he learned that EPA would force Fresno to spend $197 million and Hanford $30 million to remove radon and arsenic from water; the amendment failed 210–210 and EPA lost. He serves on the Resources Committee and is co-chairman of the Congressional Beef Caucus and the Western Water Caucus. He backed Superfund reform and supported $18 billion for the IMF in 1998 and normal trading relations with China.

Dooley is also active on local issues, helping to secure $1.2 million for a flood control project on Arroyo Pasajero and $1.1 million to increase the capacity of Kaweah Lake behind the Terminus Dam. He helped get $3.5 million to upgrade the Fresno Yosemite International Airport and hailed the arrival of 30 new F/A-18E/F Super Hornet jets at Lemoore Naval Air Station. He helped obtain a $3.8 million grant to assist Southeast Asian refugees in Fresno County learn English and get jobs; he supported the bill to waive the English language requirement for citizenship for Hmong and Lao veterans who were recruited by the U.S. military in the 1960s and 1970s.

Dooley is a founder and co-chairman of the New Democrat Coalition, formerly the Mainstream Forum, a group of about 50 moderate House Democrats who bill themselves as seeking bipartisan solutions to the nation's problems. After the 1998 election, he ran for the vacant vice-chairmanship of the House Democratic Caucus, seeking to assemble a coalition of conservatives and Californians. But he failed to lock up either camp, and lost 124–81 on the second ballot to Robert Menendez of New Jersey. Afterward, Minority Leader Dick Gephardt asked Dooley to be one of five members of a new Democratic Leadership Council designed to encourage dialogue among Democratic factions.

Dooley had a well-financed opponent in 1996, term-limited Assemblyman Trice Harvey, and still won 57%–39%. In the small turnout of 1998 he won 61%–39%.

Cook's Call. *Potentially Competitive.* Dooley has a strong, but not solid lock on this relatively conservative Central Valley district. A well-funded, well-organized challenger could give him a credible fight, but in the end it would be hard to unseat him.

The People: Pop. 1990: 573,555; 27.3% rural; 9.1% age 65 + ; 48.8% White, 6.4% Black, 5.5% Asian, 1.1% Amer. Indian, 38.2% Other; 54.7% Hispanic Origin. Households: 58.5% married couple families; 36% married couple fams. w. children; 26% college educ.; median household income: $21,140; per capita income: $8,097; median house value: $64,000; median gross rent: $304.

1996 Presidential Vote			1992 Presidential Vote		
Clinton (D)	62,164	(52%)	Clinton (D)	55,942	(47%)
Dole (R)	48,446	(41%)	Bush (R)	44,674	(37%)
Perot (I)	6,617	(6%)	Perot (I)	18,568	(16%)

Rep. Calvin Dooley (D)

Elected 1990; b. Jan. 11, 1954, Visalia; home, Visalia; U. of CA at Davis, B.S. 1977, Stanford U., M.A. 1987; Methodist; married (Linda).

Professional Career: Farmer, 1978–91; A.A., CA Sen. Rose Ann Vuich, 1987–89.

DC Office: 1201 LHOB 20515, 202-225-3341; Fax: 202-225-9308; Web site: www.house.gov/dooley.

District Office: Hanford, 559-585-8171.

Committees: *Agriculture* (5th of 24 D): Livestock & Horticulture; Risk Management, Research & Specialty Crops. *Resources* (11th of 24 D): Energy & Mineral Resources; Water & Power (RMM).

Group Ratings

	ADA	ACLU	AFS	LCV	CON	NTU	NFIB	COC	ACU	NTLC	CHC
1998	85	75	89	38	93	25	43	67	4	34	0
1997	65	—	38	—	96	39	—	90	12	—	—

National Journal Ratings

	1997 LIB — 1997 CONS		1998 LIB — 1998 CONS	
Economic	57%	— 42%	60%	— 39%
Social	76%	— 24%	76%	— 23%
Foreign	64%	— 33%	90%	— 5%

Key Votes of the 105th Congress

1. Clinton Budget Deal	Y	5. Puerto Rico Sthood. Ref.	Y	9. Cut $ for B-2 Bombers	N
2. Education IRAs	N	6. End Highway Set-asides	N	10. Human Rights in China	N
3. Req. 2/3 to Raise Taxes	N	7. School Prayer Amend.	N	11. Withdraw Bosnia Troops	N
4. Fast-track Trade	Y	8. Ovrd. Part. Birth Veto	N	12. End Cuban TV-Marti	Y

Election Results

1998 general	Calvin Dooley (D)	60,599	(61%)	($634,240)
	Cliff Unruh (R)	39,183	(39%)	($222,368)
1998 primary	Calvin Dooley (D)	30,781	(43%)	
	Cliff Unruh (R)	16,213	(23%)	
	Devin G. Nunes (R)	15,124	(21%)	
	John Estrada (D)	7,129	(10%)	
	Others	1,540	(2%)	
1996 general	Calvin Dooley (D)	65,381	(57%)	($662,818)
	Trice Harvey (R)	45,276	(39%)	($505,054)
	Jonathan J. Richter (Lib)	5,048	(4%)	

TWENTY-FIRST DISTRICT

Bakersfield, at the apex of the southern end of California's Central Valley, has been the focus of great migrations four times—in a gold rush in 1885, when oil was discovered here in 1899, during the 1930s when the Okies drove their jalopies from the Dust Bowl of Oklahoma and Kansas and Texas across the Southwest on U.S. 66, and again in the 1980s, when Bakersfield and Kern County grew more rapidly than California's biggest metro areas. Bakersfield's gold is gone, its oil rigs pump more oil than is produced annually in Oklahoma, but the migration that made the deepest imprint was in the 1930s. The Okies drove over one thousand miles of brown landscape, then through the Tehachapi Pass, and found this vast green valley, with its irrigated fields and its eucalyptus-shaded towns, the richest farming country in the world. The story is told vividly in John Steinbeck's *The Grapes of Wrath*, though his vision of the Okies as workers eager to join together with their fellow proletarians and rise up against their bosses did not get the picture quite right. More accurate is Dan Morgan's *Rising in the West*, which shows the strong Pentecostal beliefs which drove many migrants and, unlike Steinbeck, explains how they prospered in California.

The area around Bakersfield has become the one Southern-accented part of California, the home of country singers Buck Owens and Merle Haggard and a thriving contemporary country music scene, culturally conservative with a strong drive toward discipline and little empathy for the therapy that is so common in Los Angeles, 110 miles south. "I hope you all agree with me that Bakersfield is boring," LA Mayor Richard Riordan once said on radio—and then came up for a tour in 106-degree heat and heard the Kern County DA tell him that motorists are not fired at on Bakersfield's freeways, its citizens don't riot when they don't like a jury verdict and its celebrities are not on trial for murder.

The 21st Congressional District, the southernmost district in the Central Valley, is centered on Bakersfield and takes in most of Kern and Tulare counties; it also includes Edwards Air Force Base where Chuck Yeager flew the X-1 and where the space shuttle frequently lands. The district's boundaries are irregular to maximize the Hispanic percentage of the next-door 20th District. The 21st includes most of Bakersfield and its surroundings, oil fields and high-income subdivisions, and Kern County desert and mountain communities. The rich farm land produces a majority of the olives grown in the United States and is the nation's largest dairy-producing region. Politically, this was Democratic territory in the early 1960s—when, for that matter, so was Oklahoma; by the late 1960s, both had become solidly Republican in national politics, and today both seem Republican up and down the ticket. In 1996 the 21st District voted 56%–34% for Bob Dole, a showing he matched in only one other California district, the 48th in San Diego County; in 1998 the district solidly backed Republican Dan Lungren over Democrat Gray Davis.

The congressman from the 21st, Bill Thomas, is now one of the senior Republicans in the House after years of frustration in the minority. He chairs the House Administration Committee, is a senior member of Ways and Means and chairman of its Health Subcommittee. Thomas grew up in Orange County; his parents were not high school graduates and he lived for a time in public housing. He graduated from San Francisco State and taught political science from 1965–74 in the community college in Bakersfield. In 1974 he was elected to the Assembly, a conservative in a liberal-run legislature; when Congressman Bill Ketchum died after the 1978 primary, he ran as the relative moderate at the party convention and won the seat. He is bright and testy; he has, wrote Faye Fiore in the *Los Angeles Times*, "an intellect so sharp he is considered one of the brightest members of the House and a temper so mercurial some say he may be one of the meanest." Some of that may come from working on elections issues. He lost on the challenge to the Indiana 8th District result in 1985 and failed to stop motor-voter registration; he worked successfully on bills to encourage uniform poll closings and restrict franked mail. (When in the majority, Thomas superintended Robert Dornan's challenge to the election in 1996 of Loretta Sanchez; eventually, the committee ruled against Dornan.) In December 1992 some younger conservatives considered Thomas too accommodating, and—with the encouragement of then-Minority Whip Newt Gingrich, who had once roomed with Thomas—ran Paul Gillmor of Ohio against him for ranking-member on House Administration, losing by only 12 votes. Thomas fought George Miller's 1992 Central Valley Water Project Act and the 1994 Desert Protection Act, unsuccessfully. He has generally been a free trader, with an eye out for California pistachios; on Ways and Means, he voted for NAFTA and backed fast-track trade authority.

Once in the majority, things have been different, though not peaceful. Thomas was given two tough assignments by Gingrich. As chairman of House Administration (which regained its original name after being called House Oversight during the first four years of the Republican majority), Thomas managed the Republicans' bills reducing the House budget by $50 million, reducing committee staffs by one-third, providing an independent audit of the House and applying to Congress the laws it applies to others. He opposed Democratic campaign finance measures and proposed his own reforms: in 1996 to limit both PAC and individual contributions to about $2,500 and to require candidates to raise most of their money in their own districts; in 1998 to restrict spending by unions and require written permission from members before using their dues. Following the July 1998 murder of two Capitol policemen, Thomas took control of efforts to impose additional security restrictions, including the long-planned construction of a visitors center under the Capitol's east plaza.

Thomas has been the Republicans' point man on Medicare. He studied the issue intensively and reflected on the situation of his parents (his mother was killed and his father gravely injured in a Kern County car crash). He managed to passage in the House the 1995 Medicare reform reducing the rate of spending increases and giving seniors more choices. Democrats howled with disapproval. Though Democratic candidates hammered Republicans hard on Medicare, polling after the Republican counteroffensive in October 1996 showed that it was not a net minus for Republican House candidates, who ran even with Democrats among the elderly. After the 1996 election, Thomas played a key role in drafting the Medicare-reform package—including steps to give senior citizens additional private-insurance options—that finally was enacted as part of the 1997 balanced budget deal. He became co-chairman, with Senator John Breaux, of the National Bipartisan Commission on the Future of Medicare set up under the law. Breaux and Thomas produced a "premium support" package, modeled on the Federal Employees Health Benefits Plan, which would give seniors enough money to pay for a certain minimum amount of coverage, plus the option of entering into other plans; in March 1999 it got the votes of 10 members of the 17-member commission, but not the 11-vote supermajority required to be its official recommendation. It was spurned by President Clinton, though he had no reform of his own to offer; but Breaux and Thomas promised to try to move it ahead in the Senate and House.

On other health issues, Thomas took the lead in establishing deductibility of health care insurance for the self-employed. On Ways and Means he has supported additional tax incentives for oil drilling. He has called for replacing the income-tax code with some form of consumption tax. Thomas would like to succeed Bill Archer as Ways and Means chairman after the 2000 election, provided Republicans retain their majority. But the elevation of Speaker Denny Hastert of Illinois could be a setback if Hastert backs fellow Illinoisan Philip Crane, who is senior to Thomas. Thomas must depend on his cerebral skills; he is not a convivial backslapper and even his hobbies are unsociable: He likes to detail cars and take apart computers. "Other people have other skills, interpersonal maybe, or backslappers, or whatever it is they do. My stock in trade has always been knowledge," he said.

Thomas has been re-elected by wide margins in the 21st District.

Cook's Call. *Safe.* The 21st is about as solid Republican as they come. Thomas should have no re-election concerns.

The People: Pop. 1990: 571,143; 18.6% rural; 11.2% age 65+; 77.9% White, 4% Black, 3.2% Asian, 1.5% Amer. Indian, 13.4% Other; 20% Hispanic Origin. Households: 58% married couple families; 30.3% married couple fams. w. children; 46.7% college educ.; median household income: $29,943; per capita income: $12,983; median house value: $85,000; median gross rent: $375.

1996 Presidential Vote

Dole (R)	109,344	(56%)
Clinton (D)	66,492	(34%)
Perot (I)	15,000	(8%)
Others	3,513	(2%)

1992 Presidential Vote

Bush (R)	94,727	(46%)
Clinton (D)	66,284	(32%)
Perot (I)	43,016	(21%)

Rep. Bill Thomas (R)

Elected 1978; b. Dec. 6, 1941, Wallace, ID; home, Bakersfield; San Francisco St. U., B.A. 1963, M.A. 1965; Baptist; married (Sharon).

Elected Office: CA Assembly, 1974–78.

Professional Career: Prof., Bakersfield Comm. Col., 1965–74.

DC Office: 2208 RHOB 20515, 202-225-2915; Fax: 202-225-8798; Web site: www.house.gov/billthomas.

District Offices: Bakersfield, 805-327-3611; Visalia, 209-627-6549.

Committees: *House Administration* (Chmn. of 6 R). *Ways & Means* (3d of 23 R): Health (Chmn.); Trade. *Joint Committee on Printing* (1st of 5 Reps.). *Joint Committee on Taxation* (3d of 5 Reps.). *Joint Committee on the Library of Congress* (Vice Chmn. of 6 Reps.).

Group Ratings

	ADA	ACLU	AFS	LCV	CON	NTU	NFIB	COC	ACU	NTLC	CHC
1998	0	25	11	8	2	52	93	100	92	92	67
1997	10	—	25	—	42	47	—	100	80	—	—

National Journal Ratings

	1997 LIB — 1997 CONS		1998 LIB — 1998 CONS	
Economic	19%	— 76%	30%	— 67%
Social	52%	— 47%	52%	— 48%
Foreign	41%	— 59%	39%	— 58%

Key Votes of the 105th Congress

1. Clinton Budget Deal	Y	5. Puerto Rico Sthood. Ref.	N	9. Cut $ for B-2 Bombers	N
2. Education IRAs	Y	6. End Highway Set-asides	Y	10. Human Rights in China	N
3. Req. 2/3 to Raise Taxes	Y	7. School Prayer Amend.	Y	11. Withdraw Bosnia Troops	Y
4. Fast-track Trade	Y	8. Ovrd. Part. Birth Veto	Y	12. End Cuban TV-Marti	N

Election Results

1998 general	Bill Thomas (R)	115,989	(79%)	($1,172,167)
	John Evans (RP)	30,994	(21%)	($6,464)
1998 primary	Bill Thomas (R)	82,892	(79%)	
	John Evans (RP)	22,206	(21%)	
1996 general	Bill Thomas (R)	125,916	(66%)	($768,689)
	Deborah A. Vollmer (D)	50,694	(27%)	($33,295)
	John Evans (RP)	8,113	(4%)	($5,505)
	Others	6,601	(3%)	

TWENTY-SECOND DISTRICT

Santa Barbara is one of California's most paradisical cities, a collection of red tile roofs and leafy live oaks, sheltered by towering mountains just above the sea. The impression is a bit misleading, for Santa Barbara has its problems, and its Spanish style is a creation not of 18th-Century Mission culture, but of the 20th Century. Most of its white stucco buildings were put up after a 1925 earthquake leveled much of the town and the most distinguished of the Spanish Revival buildings were designed by an architect with the marvelously un-Latin name of George Washington Smith. Santa Barbara, like Disneyland, does not reproduce the past but presents a bigger, more attractive, cleaner version of it, maintained not by a company but by an architectural review board. But Santa Barbara's affluence isn't ersatz. This has long been one of the nation's richest retirement communities, and one increasingly devoted to preserving its environment and serenity. Both features came under threat spectacularly in 1969, when an underwater oil well ruptured, coating the beach with oil; pictures of the oil slick in the channel and of volunteers trying to wash oil off grounded birds, helped to launch the environmental movement of the 1970s. Almost all the wells are closed now (though some old 19th Century wells still send globs of oil to the beach at nearby Summerland), but the oil spill did leave a residue in Santa Barbara's politics—and helped attract high-tech businesses to replace the defense jobs lost in the early 1990s. This has been a Republican community, uninterested in redistribution of wealth, but very concerned about the environment (it has built the nation's largest desalination plant) and moderate to liberal on cultural issues.

The 22d Congressional District consists of all of Santa Barbara County except the town of Carpinteria at its southeast corner, plus San Luis Obispo County to the north. Not all of this area resembles Santa Barbara. The most notable feature in northern Santa Barbara County, across the Santa Ynez Mountains from Ronald Reagan's former ranch, is Vandenberg Air Force Base, and the nearby town of Santa Maria is pro-military and conservative. San Luis Obispo County is pleasant and as untrendy a place as you could find on this coast, culturally more Middle American than Santa Barbara.

The congresswoman from the 22d District is Lois Capps, a Democrat selected in a March 1998 special election, and the fourth person to represent this district in the 1990s. Capps grew up in Wyoming and Montana, the daughter of a Lutheran minister; she graduated from college with a nursing degree and was head nurse at Yale New Haven Hospital where she met her husband, Walter Capps, a student at Yale Divinity School. In 1964 he became a professor at the University of California at Santa Barbara. Lois Capps became the head elementary school nurse for the Santa Barbara school system, director of the county's teenage pregnancy and parenting project, and a part-time instructor at Santa Barbara City Community College. In 1994 Walter Capps ran for the House, and lost 49.3%–48.5% to Andrea Seastrand, a conservative Republican assemblywoman from San Luis Obispo County. In 1996 he ran again and won 48%–44%. Capps said he wanted to promote conciliation in the House and was put off by partisan confrontations on procedure. He died suddenly in October 1997.

National Republicans had great hopes of picking up the seat in the special election. Speaker Newt Gingrich encouraged the candidacy of Assemblyman Brooks Firestone, who abandoned his campaign for lieutenant governor. Firestone, an heir to the Firestone tire fortune and successful winemaker, was a centrist candidate in favor of abortion rights and gun control. But also running was Assemblyman Tom Bordonaro, the favorite of Christian conservatives. Bordonaro, a paraplegic since a car accident in college, emphasized his "blue-collar roots and common values" and attacked Firestone's wealthy status; after a Firestone fundraiser with former President Gerald Ford, Bordonaro said caustically, "I don't have the luxury of hobnobbing with celebrities from Palm Springs." House conservatives were angered by Gingrich's support of Firestone; Majority Whip Tom DeLay steered about $30,000 to Bordonaro during the primary.

Meanwhile, Lois Capps announced her candidacy, with support from many of Walter Capps's admirers as well as from labor and environmental groups; she got a campaign visit from Hillary Rodham Clinton. Both Capps and Firestone spent about $450,000 in the primary compared to Bordonaro, who spent only $130,000. In the January 1998 all-party primary, Capps finished first with 45%, Bordonaro was second with 29% and Firestone had 25%. The turning point for Bordonaro may have been a $100,000 independent ad campaign sponsored by the Campaign for Working Families, featuring Bordonaro's opposition to partial-birth abortions. In the fiercely-contested March 1998 runoff, Capps ran a better-organized campaign, including a superior absentee-ballot effort, and Bordonaro suffered from lingering animosity of Firestone supporters plus voter backlash against the outside groups' advertising. Also, term limits advocates ran ads against the younger Bordonaro, who refused to limit his terms, and in effect for Capps, who said that at her age she was happy to limit herself. She won by a surprisingly large 53%–45%. That did not end their competition; both were on the ballot again in November. But national Republicans had few hopes of winning this time, and it was not a priority race. Even the San Luis Obispo *Telegram-Tribune*, which had endorsed Bordonaro in the spring, came out for Capps who, it said, "has allayed fears that she would be overwhelmed as a political neophyte." She won 55%–43%, carrying San Luis Obispo narrowly and winning Santa Barbara 58%–40%.

With her background as a health-care professional, Capps won a seat on the Commerce Committee in December 1998, where she planned to focus on gaining patients' bill of rights legislation. After going through four seriously contested campaigns in four years, she was an advocate of campaign-finance reform. She also backed legislation to bar offshore oil drilling off the Santa Barbara and San Luis Obispo coasts. But she was not a down-the-line liberal. She broke ranks with Democrats in September 1998 to support House Republicans' tax cut.

Cook's Call. *Competitive.* For the past four elections, this swing district has been famous for hotly contested races, which makes Capps' solid 55% win in 1998 look like a landslide. Though a well-funded, moderate Republican could give her a real race, particularly in a down year for Democrats, Capps is projecting a more moderate image herself, which gives her more staying power than might have been expected.

The People: Pop. 1990: 572,956; 11.5% rural; 13.7% age 65+; 81.7% White, 2.8% Black, 3.9% Asian, 1.1% Amer. Indian, 10.6% Other; 20.8% Hispanic Origin. Households: 53.3% married couple families; 24.2% married couple fams. w. children; 59% college educ.; median household income: $33,680; per capita income: $16,458; median house value: $230,100; median gross rent: $569.

1996 Presidential Vote		
Dole (R)	108,722	(44%)
Clinton (D)	108,208	(44%)
Perot (I)	17,311	(7%)
Others	11,656	(5%)

1992 Presidential Vote		
Clinton (D)	106,815	(41%)
Bush (R)	92,045	(35%)
Perot (I)	61,030	(23%)

Rep. Lois Capps (D)

Elected March 1998; b. Jan. 10, 1938, Ladysmith, WI; home, Santa Barbara; Pacific Lutheran U., B.S. 1959, Yale U., M.A. 1964, U. of CA at Santa Barbara, M.A. 1990; Lutheran; widowed.

Professional Career: Staff nurse, Visiting Nurses Assn., 1963–64; Head nurse, Yale New Haven Hospital, 1960–63; Instructor, Santa Barbara City Col., 1983–95; Nurse, Santa Barbara Schl. Dist., 1979–96.

DC Office: 1118 LHOB 20515, 202-225-3601; Fax: 202-225-5632; Web site: www.house.gov/capps.

District Offices: San Luis Obispo, 805-546-8348; Santa Barbara, 805-730-1710; Santa Maria, 805-349-9313.

Committees: *Commerce* (24th of 24 D): Finance & Hazardous Materials; Health and Environment.

Group Ratings (Only Served Partial Term)

	ADA	ACLU	AFS	LCV	CON	NTU	NFIB	COC	ACU	NTLC	CHC
1998	85	83	89	83	7	17	22	71	18	17	0
1997	*	—	*	—	*	*	—	*	*	—	—

National Journal Ratings (Only Served Partial Term)

	1997 LIB — 1997 CONS		1998 LIB — 1998 CONS	
Economic	*	— *	61%	— 39%
Social	*	— *	79%	— 21%
Foreign	*	— *	64%	— 31%

Key Votes of the 105th Congress (Only Served Partial Term)

1. Clinton Budget Deal	*	5. Puerto Rico Sthood. Ref.	*	9. Cut $ for B-2 Bombers	*
2. Education IRAs	*	6. End Highway Set-asides	N	10. Human Rights in China	*
3. Req. 2/3 to Raise Taxes	N	7. School Prayer Amend.	N	11. Withdraw Bosnia Troops	N
4. Fast-track Trade	N	8. Ovrd. Part. Birth Veto	N	12. End Cuban TV-Marti	Y

Election Results

1998 general	Lois Capps (D)	109,517	(55%)	($990,611)
	Tom J. Bordonaro Jr. (R)	85,927	(43%)	($392,149)
	Others	3,820	(2%)	
1998 primary	Lois Capps (D)	79,787	(52%)	
	Tom J. Bordonaro Jr. (R)	63,550	(41%)	
	James Harrison (R)	7,901	(5%)	
	Others	2,917	(2%)	
1998 special	Lois Capps (D)	93,392	(53%)	($1,602,656)
	Tom J. Bordonaro Jr. (R)	78,224	(45%)	($861,438)
	Others	3,079	(2%)	
1996 general	Walter Capps (D)	118,299	(48%)	($904,831)
	Andrea Seastrand (R)	107,987	(44%)	($1,232,118)
	Steven Wheeler (I)	9,845	(4%)	
	Others	8,055	(3%)	

TWENTY-THIRD DISTRICT

On a golden mountainside, looking westward over a valley hemmed in by mountains north and south, five United States presidents gathered in November 1991 to dedicate the Ronald Reagan Library. This was the first time in 202 years that five presidents stood together in one place—one which the Founding Fathers surely did not imagine would ever be American and yet today seems quintessentially so. Simi Valley, famous a few months later as the site of the trial of police officers accused of assaulting Rodney King, is a product of the 1960s, the expansive and still optimistic postwar years when the vast stream of migrants who had come from all over the United States to Los Angeles spread beyond city and county limits to fill up barren valleys between golden mountains. They brought a willingness to work hard, high competence and high tech, an appreciation of the local environment and a distaste for crime and rioting that seemed all too common in the Los Angeles basin they left behind.

Simi Valley is just one of several communities in the valleys and narrow coastal margins of Ventura County, west of Los Angeles, that have been filling up with people leaving Los Angeles and the San Fernando Valley and building new communities in what had been an agricultural county with a gritty port and Navy base; Simi Valley claims more cars per capita than anywhere else in the United States. After the King trial, Simi Valley was criticized for being all-white and racist. In fact it is ethnically diverse: Ventura County was 26% Hispanic and 5% Asian in the 1990 Census, and its white Anglo residents include many with names and backgrounds that would have been called hyphenated-American at best not so long ago. It also has some of the nation's lowest crime rates, a stark contrast with gang warfare in Los Angeles, and some of the highest percentages of intact families in California, a vivid contrast with the showbiz life-styles of Westside LA. It also has a reminder, where the five presidents met in 1991, that traditional American values are not just material but are also moral: Pieces of the Berlin Wall, which President Reagan called on Mikhail Gorbachev to tear down, stand at the edge of the hill as you look toward the west.

The 23d Congressional District includes almost all of Ventura County except the Thousand Oaks area—Simi Valley, Moorpark, Camarillo, Ventura, Oxnard, and the Point Mugu Navy base—plus just a corner of Santa Barbara County and the town of Carpinteria. Politically, this was strong Reagan country when he was elected governor and president, though it lost some of its cheerful optimism in the more downbeat years of his successors, Jerry Brown in California and George Bush in Washington. It has trended conservative in recent local elections, but it is closely enough balanced to go Democratic occasionally; Bill Clinton carried it narrowly in 1992 and 1996, and Governor Gray Davis won by 53%–44% in 1998.

The congressman from the 23d District is Elton Gallegly. He grew up in the working class suburb of Huntington Park (now almost entirely Hispanic), dropped out of college and became a real estate broker. He was elected at 35 to the Simi Valley city council, became mayor in 1980, then was elected to Congress in 1986 after the incumbent ran for the Senate. In 1992, when redistricting moved much of fellow Republican Robert Lagomarsino's district into the new Ventura County-based seat, Gallegly moved fast to push Lagomarsino into running in the 22d District to the north, where he lost the primary to Michael Huffington's $3 million campaign. Gallegly had minimal primary opposition but a spirited challenge from Democrat Anita Perez Ferguson, who raised large sums from the feminist left in "the year of the woman" and held Gallegly to a 54%–41% margin. Since then he has been re-elected easily.

Gallegly has a very conservative voting record and has played a part on major issues. Foremost among them is illegal immigration. He has called for a tougher Border Patrol, a tamperproof identification card for legal aliens and an end to welfare for illegal immigrants. He criticizes the current INS IDs as easily forgeable, carrying one around himself as evidence. "One of the reasons that I am such a strong opponent of illegal immigration, other than the fact that it's illegal, is because it poses the greatest threat to legal immigration," he said; he has never supported a major cut in legal immigration. In 1995, Speaker Newt Gingrich named him head of a bipartisan Immigration Reform Task Force. In March 1996, Gallegly got the full House to pass his amendment allowing states to deny education to children who are illegal immigrants. This was heartily supported by Bob Dole, campaigning in California, and opposed by Clinton. After a filibuster threat in the Senate, Republicans agreed to drop it.

Gallegly has worked on other issues as well. He sought to minimize labeling requirements on vitamins and dietary supplements issued by the Food and Drug Administration in response to a 1990 law sponsored by Henry Waxman. Locally, he worked hard to save the Point Mugu Navy base, threatened with closure for six weeks in early 1996, and, with 18,000 related jobs, Ventura County's largest employer; in 1998 he worked, even buttonholing an admiral at a refueling stop, to get a wing of 16 E-2 radar planes assigned there. He passed a law to identify criminal aliens in U.S. prison, with a view toward deportation, and another to allow government agencies to give away their dogs—superannuated drug-sniffers and guard dogs—to their handlers. He sponsored a bill, supported by many real estate developers, to allow those who believe their property has been taken by government regulation, to challenge it directly in federal court without exhausting state and local remedies. In committee, he switched his vote in November 1997 to oppose Charles Canady's bill to outlaw racial quotas and preferences. Gallegly was the first non-lawyer to serve on the Judiciary Committee; he declined the opportunity to serve as a House manager during the Senate impeachment trial of Clinton.

Cook's Call. *Safe.* The 23rd District does not seem to be as conservative as it once was. But, with Gallegly rarely making it onto Democratic target lists, it's unlikely that he will face a tough race in 2000. A well-funded challenger, or a bit of tinkering with the lines before 2002 and this could become a competitive district.

The People: Pop. 1990: 571,562; 5.4% rural; 9.9% age 65 + ; 77% White, 2.5% Black, 5.2% Asian, 0.8% Amer. Indian, 14.4% Other; 29.8% Hispanic Origin. Households: 61% married couple families; 32.9% married couple fams. w. children; 54.4% college educ.; median household income: $42,989; per capita income: $16,617; median house value: $235,600; median gross rent: $676.

1996 Presidential Vote

Clinton (D)	93,046	(45%)
Dole (R)	85,508	(42%)
Perot (I)	19,237	(9%)
Others	6,745	(3%)

1992 Presidential Vote

Clinton (D)	82,613	(38%)
Bush (R)	74,106	(34%)
Perot (I)	58,177	(27%)

Rep. Elton Gallegly (R)

Elected 1986; b. Mar. 7, 1944, Huntington Park; home, Simi Valley; Los Angeles St. Col., 1962–63; Protestant; married (Janice).

Elected Office: Simi Valley City Cncl., 1979–80; Simi Valley Mayor, 1980–86.

Professional Career: Owner, real estate firm.

DC Office: 2427 RHOB 20515, 202-225-5811; Fax: 202-225-1100; Web site: www.house.gov/gallegly.

District Office: Oxnard, 805-485-2300.

Committees: *International Relations* (8th of 26 R): Western Hemisphere (Chmn.). *Judiciary* (7th of 21 R): Courts & Intellectual Property; Immigration & Claims. *Resources* (5th of 28 R): National Parks & Public Lands.

Group Ratings

	ADA	ACLU	AFS	LCV	CON	NTU	NFIB	COC	ACU	NTLC	CHC
1998	15	13	22	8	13	48	100	83	76	87	100
1997	5	—	13	—	34	46	—	100	80	—	—

National Journal Ratings

	1997 LIB — 1997 CONS			1998 LIB — 1998 CONS		
Economic	24%	—	73%	23%	—	74%
Social	30%	—	64%	38%	—	60%
Foreign	30%	—	68%	25%	—	74%

Key Votes of the 105th Congress

1. Clinton Budget Deal	Y	5. Puerto Rico Sthood. Ref.	Y	9. Cut $ for B-2 Bombers	N
2. Education IRAs	Y	6. End Highway Set-asides	Y	10. Human Rights in China	N
3. Req. 2/3 to Raise Taxes	Y	7. School Prayer Amend.	Y	11. Withdraw Bosnia Troops	Y
4. Fast-track Trade	N	8. Ovrd. Part. Birth Veto	Y	12. End Cuban TV-Marti	N

Election Results

1998 general	Elton Gallegly (R)	96,322	(60%)	($282,187)
	Daniel Gonzalez (D)	64,032	(40%)	($33,777)
1998 primary	Elton Gallegly (R)	71,151	(63%)	
	Daniel Gonzalez (D)	41,054	(37%)	
1996 general	Elton Gallegly (R)	118,880	(60%)	($294,940)
	Robert R. Unruhe (D)	70,035	(35%)	($24,642)
	Gail Lightfoot (Lib)	8,346	(4%)	

TWENTY-FOURTH DISTRICT

The San Fernando Valley, in the early 20th Century when the movie business was young, was a vast expanse of empty land, annexed to Los Angeles in 1915; moviemakers, looking for filming sites for a western, drove past the vacant lots of Westwood, up narrow roads through the Santa Monica Mountains and over into the vast Valley, sheltered from ocean breezes and rain-bearing clouds by the mountains. Over the past 80 years this vast bowl of land has been transformed, first into 1950s suburbia, then into a postmodern city of its own, economically vital and yeastily ethnic. Even in its suburban years, the San Fernando Valley was not entirely residential: Big factories—the General Motors Van Nuys assembly plant, the Anheuser Busch brewery, Rockwell and Litton defense plants—provided jobs. In the 1950s and 1960s this was fast-growing, family-friendly territory; politically, it was turf fought over hard by Republicans and Democrats. By the 1970s young white Anglo families were fleeing, as the Los Angeles Unified School District was hit by a busing order. There is plenty of upscale territory left in the uplands in the rims of the Valley, in heavily Jewish Sherman Oaks and Encino and to the west in Woodland Hills and Chatsworth; the office blocks and mini-malls along Ventura and Woodland Hills Boulevard show unmistakable signs of affluence. In the inner lowlands of the Valley, new immigrants have moved in. Some old neighborhoods have become rough Latino enclaves, with youth gangs and boarded-up houses and apartments weakened by the Northridge earthquake; Iranians and Chinese, Mexicans and Koreans, Israelis and Filipinos are keeping other neighborhoods solidly middle-class.

The 24th Congressional District includes most of the southern and western San Fernando Valley, from the hillside mansions of Encino to the gang territory around the Van Nuys plant. Two-thirds of the 24th's people live in the Valley; another one-fifth live directly west, in new communities nestled amid mountains along U.S. 101—ranch-like Agoura, jewel-like Westlake Village and sprawling Thousand Oaks, home of the biotechnology giant Amgen. The 24th also takes in Malibu, with $1 million beach houses five feet from each other and Pepperdine University's campus in the hills. Politically, this is a mixed area. The Jewish precincts are solidly Democratic, and have become more so in the 1990s; Thousand Oaks is heavily Republican; the immigrant areas fluctuate and could go any which way; Malibu is trendy showbiz liberal.

The congressman from the 24th is Brad Sherman, a Democrat elected in 1996. Sherman grew up in Monterey Park, in the San Gabriel Valley east of Los Angeles; he started working on Democratic campaigns at age 6, licking stamps and stuffing envelopes, and set up his own stamp wholesaling firm at 14. He graduated with high honors from UCLA, worked as an accountant, then went to Harvard Law and practiced tax law in Los Angeles. But he always had the political bug, and in 1990 sought offices to run for and settled on the state Board of Equalization. This is a five-member body which is a sort of tax court; Sherman's district was most of Los Angeles County. He was known as a stickler for detail, a "tax nerd," as one former staffer said, who used the office with a keen scent for political advantage. He led the fight against Pete Wilson's snack tax in 1991, and got Bill Clinton to side with his opinion on taxing foreign-owned businesses, which he says saved California $2 billion in revenue. But he irritated cartoonists with a ruling that exempted them from state tax on artwork but not on illustrations; they set up a Website, the Sherman gallery, in which they vied in caricaturing the balding and bespectacled Sherman.

Sherman decided to run for Congress, and moved his residence from Santa Monica to Sherman Oaks, when 24th District Congressman Anthony Beilenson announced his retirement in 1995 after 20 years in the House and after beating businessman Rich Sybert by only 49%–48% in 1994. Sybert worked as Pete Wilson's head of planning, then went into the toy business. He kept running after 1994, and in March 1996 both he and Sherman won multi-candidate primaries easily—Sherman with 54%, Sybert with 68%. Both stressed their moderation. Sherman ran against Newt Gingrich and the Republican Congress, which was especially unpopular among Jewish voters; but he also supported the death penalty, said he wanted racial quotas and preferences phased out and favored tough measures on illegal immigration. Sybert stressed his independence of Gingrich and the Republican leadership, favoring abortion rights and environmental protections. Sybert was intense, Sherman a bit humorous (he handed out combs to voters, saying "You'll be able to use it more than I can"). Sherman won 49%–44%.

Sherman's voting record in the House has been notably more moderate than those of other Los Angeles County Democrats. One of the few CPAs in Congress, he served on the Budget Committee and is now on Banking. He passed an amendment appropriating an extra $599 million for parkland acquisition and claimed credit for $5 million for the Santa Monica Mountains National Recreation Area; he also announced money for the Backbone Trail for hikers in the mountains. He sponsored a national hotline for parents to check if teachers and coaches were convicted sexual predators, which became law. He pushed for a $500,000 study of the San Diego-Ventura Freeway interchange in the Valley, the fourth busiest in California, and urged a mandatory curfew at Burbank Airport.

In 1998, national Republican leaders backed Randy Hoffman, a Harvard Business graduate who founded Magellan Systems, a manufacturer of global satellite positioning systems. Hoffman won publicity when his neighbor and Melrose Place actress Heather Locklear stood in for Speaker Gingrich at a campaign breakfast, and he produced a platform calling for better education and revamping the criminal justice system. Hoffman spent $1 million, $426,000 of his own money; Sherman, who spent $578,000 of his own money in 1996, spent only $65,000 of it this time, but spent $1.2 million altogether: the benefits of incumbency. Sherman won 57%–38%; he carried the Los Angeles County portion of the district 61%–35% while losing the smaller Ventura County part of the district by 51%–45%. This was evidence of the leftward trend in the Valley and the Los Angeles area generally.

In Washington, though he has sometimes cast independent votes, he was invited to be one of 45 Democratic deputy whips. "I will work with the whip organization only when I agree strongly with the outcome," he said. That view may not endear him to party leaders, but it plays well back home.

Cook's Call. *Probably Safe.* Brad Sherman's strong showing in 1998 offers the first clue that he may have begun to lock up the 24th District. And, given the obscenely-expensive Los Angeles media market, only a phenomenally well-financed challenger could have any expectation of giving Sherman a race under the current lines.

The People: Pop. 1990: 572,287; 2.8% rural; 11.6% age 65 + ; 84.7% White, 2% Black, 6.4% Asian, 0.4% Amer. Indian, 6.5% Other; 13.3% Hispanic Origin. Households: 53.8% married couple families; 24.3% married couple fams. w. children; 66.1% college educ.; median household income: $48,433; per capita income: $25,767; median house value: $305,700; median gross rent: $711.

1996 Presidential Vote			1992 Presidential Vote		
Clinton (D)	117,724	(52%)	Clinton (D)	128,572	(48%)
Dole (R)	83,412	(37%)	Bush (R)	79,728	(30%)
Perot (I)	16,165	(7%)	Perot (I)	57,625	(22%)
Others	8,054	(4%)			

Rep. Brad Sherman (D)

Elected 1996; b. Oct. 24, 1954, Los Angeles; home, Sherman Oaks; U.C.L.A., B.A. 1974, Harvard U., J.D. 1979; Jewish; single.

Elected Office: CA St. Board of Equalization, 1990–95, Chmn., 1991–95.

Professional Career: Accountant, 1980–90.

DC Office: 1524 LHOB 20515, 202-225-5911; Fax: 202-225-5876; Web site: www.house.gov/sherman.

District Offices: Thousand Oaks, 805-449-2372; Woodland Hills, 818-999-1990.

Committees: *Banking & Financial Services* (16th of 27 D): Domestic & International Monetary Policy; Financial Institutions & Consumer Credit. *International Relations* (14th of 23 D): International Economic Policy & Trade; International Operations and Human Rights.

Group Ratings

	ADA	ACLU	AFS	LCV	CON	NTU	NFIB	COC	ACU	NTLC	CHC
1998	95	75	89	92	30	25	43	61	20	18	8
1997	75	—	75	—	84	40	—	50	32	—	—

National Journal Ratings

	1997 LIB	—	1997 CONS	1998 LIB	—	1998 CONS
Economic	59%	—	40%	58%	—	42%
Social	71%	—	27%	76%	—	23%
Foreign	56%	—	42%	59%	—	40%

Key Votes of the 105th Congress

1. Clinton Budget Deal	Y	5. Puerto Rico Sthood. Ref.	N	9. Cut $ for B-2 Bombers	N
2. Education IRAs	N	6. End Highway Set-asides	N	10. Human Rights in China	Y
3. Req. 2/3 to Raise Taxes	Y	7. School Prayer Amend.	N	11. Withdraw Bosnia Troops	N
4. Fast-track Trade	N	8. Ovrd. Part. Birth Veto	N	12. End Cuban TV-Marti	N

Election Results

1998 general	Brad Sherman (D)	103,491	(57%)	($1,185,937)
	Randy Hoffman (R)	69,501	(38%)	($1,040,934)
	Others	7,588	(4%)	
1998 primary	Brad Sherman (D)	62,185	(54%)	
	Randy Hoffman (R)	24,011	(21%)	
	Joe Gelman (R)	13,566	(12%)	
	William Westmiller (R)	8,003	(7%)	
	Others	7,096	(6%)	
1996 general	Brad Sherman (D)	106,193	(49%)	($1,364,516)
	Rich Sybert (R)	93,629	(44%)	($898,786)
	Others	15,026	(7%)	

TWENTY-FIFTH DISTRICT

One of the tragedies of the 1994 Northridge earthquake was at the intersection of the I-5 and Route 14 freeways at the north edge of the San Fernando Valley, where an overpass collapsed and a motorcycle patrolman hurtled to his death. Destruction of the interchange had an economic and personal impact for months afterwards, for the settled area of Los Angeles County no longer ends at the mountains at the northern rim of the San Fernando Valley. It continues along Route 14 past the mountain-surrounded city of Santa Clarita, with 110,000 people in 1990, and 25 miles beyond, where the mountains stop at the San Andreas Fault and the desert stretches out low and flat, divided into mile-square grids—the Antelope Valley, with huge aerospace plants and military bases around the fast-growing towns of Palmdale and Lancaster, where nearly 200,000 people live. Because of mountain terrain, these areas are connected by just one freeway, over which thousands travel each day; when the chokepoint intersection was crushed, commuters lined up for hours to get to work.

The 25th Congressional District covers all three of these areas. It includes the northwest quadrant of the San Fernando Valley, Granada Hills and Chatsworth, with 180,000 mostly affluent Anglos inside the LA city limits; it takes in Santa Clarita, with its Old West air and its industrial park, spreading subdivisions and Six Flags Magic Mountain theme park, home of a boosterish Republicanism; it includes the aerospace country of the Antelope Valley, with somewhat lower-income. All three parts of the district are heavily Republican, especially the desert area; this is a safe Republican district, newly created after the 1990 Census.

The congressman from the 25th is Howard "Buck" McKeon, who grew up in Southern California, graduated from Brigham Young University and is a co-owner of Howard and Phil's Western Wear, a family business which expanded to 52 stores in California, Arizona, Nevada and Utah in the early 1990s, then cut back in 1999 to 16. McKeon was the first mayor of Santa Clarita, when it was incorporated by joining several towns, and served five years on the council. He won the 1992 primary 40%–38% over Assemblyman Phil Wyman, who once had a bill to ban the allegedly satanic practice of recording certain words into songs backwards.

McKeon, the 1992 Republican freshman class president, talked about reforming the House and in 1993 helped abolish four select committees. With a seat on the Armed Services Committee, he worked to save local defense jobs—this is the production base for the B-1 and B-2 bombers, and the F-117 and SR-71 fighter planes. "The B-2 bomber is our nation's only advanced bomber and remains the most cost-effective means of rapidly projecting force over great distances," he said. He helped get new contracts for the X-33, the next generation Space Shuttle and the Joint Strike Fighter. He is trying to authorize more B-2s and to get NASA to perform Space Shuttle modifications to Air Force Base Plant 42 in Palmdale, and has criticized the Clinton Administration for failing to meet military readiness needs. He opposed the 1994 Desert Protection Act, which, he said, "does little more than create pork projects." He fought an Equal Employment Opportunity Commission religious harassment guideline which, he felt, would bar people from keeping a Bible on their desk or wearing religious symbols like the Star of David at work.

After the 1994 election, McKeon got bigger assignments. He chairs the Post-Secondary Education, Training and Lifelong Learning Subcommittee on Education and the Workforce, and put together a bill restructuring job training, literacy and youth employment programs which passed the House 345–79 in September 1995, but it was never successfully reconciled with the Senate version. In 1998, his subcommittee reauthorized the Higher Education act, brokering a truce with the Clinton Administration over student loan programs; bank-based and government-run programs would continue to coexist. On the agenda for the 106th Congress is work on teacher issues in reauthorization of the Elementary and Secondary Education Act. After the 1998 election, he briefly considered a challenge to Majority Leader Dick Armey, but correctly concluded that Armey would prevail. Instead, he moved into the inner circle of Speaker-designate Bob Livingston, who named McKeon one of his top lieutenants. But that assignment disappeared with Livingston's surprise announcement December 19 that he was resigning.

On local issues, in 1996 he got the House to pass a bill blocking the Forest Service from transferring land for a proposed dump in Elsmere Canyon, just east of Santa Clarita. He also has pressed for transportation improvements for his rapidly-growing district, including and development of a Palmdale regional airport; he opposed Los Angeles's request for $100 million for the Red Line subway and got funding for interchange improvements in Santa Clarita and the Antelope Valley. He got into the October 1998 omnibus a ban on a 190 million ton trash dump in Elsmere Canyon.

McKeon has been re-elected without serious opposition. In the June 1998 primary a Democrat failed to win the number of write-in votes she needed to get on the November ballot.

Cook's Call. *Safe.* This district is unlikely to give a Republican incumbent any problem at all. McKeon is safe.

The People: Pop. 1990: 573,189; 10.2% rural; 7.9% age 65+; 80% White, 4.5% Black, 6.4% Asian, 0.8% Amer. Indian, 8.2% Other; 16.2% Hispanic Origin. Households: 62.3% married couple families; 34.2% married couple fams. w. children; 58.6% college educ.; median household income: $46,480; per capita income: $18,849; median house value: $214,100; median gross rent: $616.

1996 Presidential Vote			1992 Presidential Vote		
Dole (R)	97,002	(47%)	Bush (R)	89,987	(39%)
Clinton (D)	84,212	(41%)	Clinton (D)	83,305	(36%)
Perot (I)	18,320	(9%)	Perot (I)	57,398	(25%)
Others	5,775	(3%)			

Rep. Howard P. (Buck) McKeon (R)

Elected 1992; b. Sept. 9, 1939, Los Angeles; home, Santa Clarita; Brigham Young U., B.S. 1985; Mormon; married (Patricia).

Elected Office: William S. Hart School District Bd., 1979–87; Santa Clarita Mayor, 1987–88; Santa Clarita City Cncl., 1988–92.

Professional Career: Small businessman; Owner, Howard & Phil's Western Wear, 1973–present; Chmn., Valencia Natl. Bank, 1987–88.

DC Office: 2242 RHOB 20515, 202-225-1956; Fax: 202-226-0683; Web site: www.house.gov/mckeon.

District Offices: Palmdale, 805-274-9688; Santa Clarita, 805-254-2111.

Committees: *Armed Services* (16th of 32 R): Military Installations & Facilities; Military Research & Development. *Education & the Workforce* (8th of 27 R): Employer-Employee Relations; Postsecondary Education, Training & Life-Long Learning (Chmn.). *Veterans' Affairs* (14th of 17 R): Health.

Group Ratings

	ADA	ACLU	AFS	LCV	CON	NTU	NFIB	COC	ACU	NTLC	CHC
1998	5	6	0	8	19	51	100	100	96	95	100
1997	0	—	13	—	62	54	—	90	92	—	—

National Journal Ratings

	1997 LIB — 1997 CONS		1998 LIB — 1998 CONS	
Economic	16% —	82%	0% —	88%
Social	0% —	90%	32% —	67%
Foreign	0% —	88%	19% —	75%

Key Votes of the 105th Congress

1. Clinton Budget Deal	Y	5. Puerto Rico Sthood. Ref.	Y	9. Cut $ for B-2 Bombers	N
2. Education IRAs	Y	6. End Highway Set-asides	Y	10. Human Rights in China	N
3. Req. 2/3 to Raise Taxes	Y	7. School Prayer Amend.	Y	11. Withdraw Bosnia Troops	Y
4. Fast-track Trade	Y	8. Ovrd. Part. Birth Veto	Y	12. End Cuban TV-Marti	N

Election Results

1998 general	Howard P. (Buck) McKeon (R) 114,013	(75%)	($405,024)
	Bruce R. Acker (Lib) 38,669	(25%)	
1998 primary	Howard P. (Buck) McKeon (R) 76,006	(78%)	
	Bruce R. Acker (Lib) 20,465	(21%)	
	Others 539	(1%)	
1996 general	Howard P. (Buck) McKeon (R) 122,428	(62%)	($384,011)
	Diane Trautman (D) 65,089	(33%)	($16,434)
	Others 8,686	(4%)	

TWENTY-SIXTH DISTRICT

A hiker looking north from the crest of the Santa Monica Mountains in 1910 would have seen spread out, almost totally empty and barren, 20 miles wide and 12 miles deep, the San Fernando Valley. Separated by the Cahuenga Pass from rapidly growing Los Angeles and Hollywood, the Valley was bought up in massive tracts by civic leaders even as they were urging city engineer William Mulholland to build a huge 250-mile aqueduct from the Owens Valley to give Los Angeles water and persuading the city in 1915 to annex 200 square miles of the Valley. In the years after World War II, this was modern suburbia, filled with *Leave It to Beaver* families. Today the San Fernando Valley is postmodern urban, with a look you can see in exaggerated form in Disney headquarters buildings in Burbank or Universal City's CityWalk shopping mall: The driver topping the crest today sees office towers looming out over slightly hazy air, shopping centers, occasional palm trees, lines of grid streets stretching out into the distance beyond stucco subdivisions and the squat factory and warehouse buildings that make Los Angeles County the nation's number-one manufacturer.

The people in the Valley have also changed. The white Anglo families with stay-at-home moms in the 1950s have been replaced by hard-working Latino families, with children waiting at the bus stops for schools and parents juggling two jobs. But there is continuity: These remain places where people work hard and try to raise children who will have better chances and make better livings than they have. Pacoima, at the northern end of the Valley, where Rodney King was pulled over and beaten and arrested, is mostly black and Latino. Farther south, in Canoga Park, Van Nuys and Burbank, are the big aerospace plants and the GM assembly plants that have been shut down since 1989, with thousands of jobs lost; less visible are the hundreds of small factories and multimedia plants where thousands of jobs have been created. The lower income areas here are farther from the central city; the southern rim of the Valley, around Studio City and North Hollywood, is still heavily Jewish and is attracting new families who often send their kids to religious schools.

The 26th Congressional District consists of the Golden State and Hollywood Freeway corridors of the Valley—roughly its eastern half—proceeding as far west as Van Nuys and the San Diego Freeway. Overall, the district was 53% Hispanic in 1990, but even in the late 1990s Latinos are not the major voting bloc here; many are not citizens, many are children or young people not yet in the voting stream; and the tradition among Latinos in the 1990s, as among Italians in the 1910s, is to trust family and hard work, not politics and government, to get ahead. The rising Democratic percentages here are due as much to Jewish as to Latino voters, who have both trended Democratic in the late 1990s, one group in response to the emergence of the Christian right, the other in response to the campaign for cutting off aid to illegal aliens which suggested, wrongly, that Latinos are interested more in welfare than hard work.

The congressman from the 26th is Howard Berman, one of the most aggressive and creative members of the House—and one of the most clear-sighted operators in American politics. He grew up in Los Angeles in modest circumstances, got involved in politics, and was elected to the Assembly from a formerly Republican Hollywood Hills district in 1972, at 31. This was the beginning of the so-called Berman-Waxman political machine—not so much a precinct organization as a group of consultants who raised money, redrew district lines and endorsed candidates through direct mail. Their core constituency was liberal Westside Jews. Berman became Assembly majority leader in his first term. In 1980 he tried to unseat Speaker Leo McCarthy; ultimately both lost to Willie Brown, who served 15 years. Berman's consolation prize was a Valley-based congressional seat in 1982. The machine fell on hard times in the 1990s, as Republicans seized control of redistricting, the feminist left became the Democratic Party's driving force and Berman-Waxman ally Mel Levine lost the 1992 Senate primary to Barbara Boxer. Since then, Berman has been a political force on his own, with a record that is mostly but not always liberal.

Berman has been an active legislator even more than a political operator, and on all manner of issues. On foreign policy, he started off less as a Vietnam war dove than as a backer of Israel, and he is not one of those Democrats who think America has habitually been on the wrong side in the world. For a decade he floor-managed foreign aid bills, defending aid to many countries as well as Israel. With Henry Hyde he wrote the law authorizing embargoes on nations that condone terrorism; in April 1990 he called for sanctions on Iraq, four months before Saddam Hussein invaded Kuwait. Berman voted for the Gulf war resolution, but was understandably critical of the administration—if it had followed his advice there might well have been no need for war. More recently, Berman has worked to stop the export of missile and nuclear weapons technology—an uphill battle in the Clinton years. He also was among the few Democrats to buck organized labor and back President Clinton's request for fast-track trade authority. "We can't afford to sit on the sidelines while the rest of the world hammers out new trade agreements," he said.

Berman passed a law banning the double-issuing of U.S. passports to coddle Arab countries who refuse to honor passports with Israeli marks. He pushed through the International Broadcasting Act of 1994, consolidating and downsizing agencies but maintaining Radio Free Europe and establishing Radio Free Asia. He worked hard to save the National Endowment for Democracy. He led the successful fight to scuttle the Republicans' Contract With America call for reducing U.S. participation in UN-led peacekeeping operations. He has worked on reorganizing the State Department and other foreign policy agencies.

On the Judiciary Committee, Berman has been a major force on immigration. In 1988 he sponsored the provision allowing 20,000 immigrant visas for migrants without close relatives here, to be selected randomly by computer—"Berman visa applications," they are called. He secured in 1990 more family reunification slots, expediting the immigration of Soviet Jews (a vivid presence in L.A. these days), and gaining amnesty provisions for more family members to remain in this country. He worked to get the federal government to acknowledge responsibility for state spending on illegal immigrants. On the 1996 immigration bill he made two major contributions. With Republican Dick Chrysler, he sponsored the amendment separating legal and illegal immigration; its passage on the floor by 238–183 in March 1996 and the nearly simultaneous passage of a similar amendment by Republican Spencer Abraham in the Senate Judiciary Committee ended the drive by the two immigration subcommittee chairmen to cut legal immigration. Berman also weighed in heavily against Republican Richard Pombo's amendment to let in 250,000 guest farm workers.

Some of Berman's issues have local angles. He worked to get $8.6 billion in emergency aid after the January 1994 Northridge earthquake. In 1991 he helped establish CALSTART, to produce electric cars in the Valley; in a closed defense plant in Burbank, electric car parts and infrastructure for electric vehicles and electric buses are now produced. Berman is not without leverage in the Republican House, but he is clearly frustrated being in the minority. In the spring of 1996 he contemplated running in the April 1997 election for mayor of Los Angeles. But he banked on a Democratic majority returning and made no move to run, and when Republicans retained the House in 1996 he judged it was too late to challenge incumbent Republican Richard Riordan. That was not all the bad news: In 1997 Minority Leader Richard Gephardt prevailed on him to become ranking minority member of the ethics committee, badly scarred by partisanship during the investigation of Newt Gingrich. "In the end I decided that there is an obligation to the House . . . to devote some portion of your time to the institution rather than issues," he said.

In 1998 Berman faced his first vocal electoral opposition. The Latino population in the district had been growing, and more Latinos were registering to vote, with the Latino percentage of registered voters rising from 18% in 1990 to 30% in 1997. A vitriolic primary in the 20th state Senate district between Anglo Richard Katz, a former Assembly speaker, and Latino Richard Alcaron, a city councilman, was won by Alarcon in June 1998 by only 29 votes. In December 1997 Berman sent a letter to constituents warning about "vandals, burglars, rapists and murderers that roam our streets," and arguing that though improvements have been made, "the crime rate in our area remains appallingly high!" Raul Gordinez, mayor of the enclave-town of San Fernando, took umbrage, noting that crime in San Fernando was down 20% in three years. Berman responded, "The crime rate is still too high." In March Godinez started running for the 26th District seat, portraying himself as a David challenging a Goliath, criti-cizing Berman's efforts to create a recreation area at Hansen Lake in the northern Valley. Berman campaigned hard in district neighborhoods, and in the June primary got 61% to 30% for Godinez. No Republican ran, and Berman was easily re-elected in November.

After the election Berman, as a senior member of the Judiciary Committee, became a part of the impeachment debate. But unlike other Judiciary members of both parties, he avoided television interviews and public comment. He met with some Republican members early in the hearings and avoided incendiary comment; in debate he conceded that Bill Clinton had probably lied under oath but argued that his offense did not rise to the level requiring removal; he refrained from the partisan attacks on Chairman Henry Hyde or Independent Counsel Kenneth Starr that so many other Democrats reveled in. This showed some considerable restraint.

In the 106th Congress, Berman gave up his ranking position on the Asia and Pacific Sub-committee of International Affairs, and took the ranking position on the Courts and Intellectual Property Subcommittee of Judiciary, one of vital importance to Hollywood interests. He can certainly be re-elected as long as he likes; though redistricting looms, he has been the Demo-cratic delegation's chief redistricting impresario.

Cook's Call. *Safe.* This overwhelmingly Democratic district has been easily carried by Berman for the last 16 years. Don't expect a competitive race here.

The People: Pop. 1990: 571,538; 8.3% age 65 + ; 53.6% White, 6.1% Black, 7.3% Asian, 0.5% Amer. Indian, 32.4% Other; 52.2% Hispanic Origin. Households: 48.4% married couple families; 28.9% married couple fams. w. children; 40.1% college educ.; median household income: $32,134; per capita income: $12,198; median house value: $186,600; median gross rent: $561.

1996 Presidential Vote			1992 Presidential Vote		
Clinton (D)	71,416	(65%)	Clinton (D)	72,673	(56%)
Dole (R)	27,129	(25%)	Bush (R)	31,013	(24%)
Perot (I)	7,930	(7%)	Perot (I)	24,167	(19%)
Others	3,150	(3%)			

Rep. Howard L. Berman (D)

Elected 1982; b. Apr. 15, 1941, Los Angeles; home, N. Hollywood; U.C.L.A., B.A. 1962, LL.B. 1965; Jewish; married (Janis).

Elected Office: CA Assembly, 1973–82, Majority Ldr., 1974–79.

Professional Career: Practicing atty., 1967–72.

DC Office: 2330 RHOB 20515, 202-225-4695; Fax: 202-225-5279; Web site: www.house.gov/berman.

District Office: Mission Hills, 818-891-0543.

Committees: *International Relations* (3d of 23 D): Asia & the Pacific. *Judiciary* (3d of 16 D): Courts & Intellectual Property (RMM); Immigration & Claims. *Standards of Official Conduct* (RMM of 5 D).

Group Ratings

	ADA	ACLU	AFS	LCV	CON	NTU	NFIB	COC	ACU	NTLC	CHC
1998	90	88	100	92	71	17	15	36	5	8	0
1997	80	—	88	—	58	27	—	33	9	—	—

National Journal Ratings

	1997 LIB — 1997 CONS		1998 LIB — 1998 CONS	
Economic	93%	— 0%	79%	— 0%
Social	85%	— 0%	89%	— 11%
Foreign	85%	— 15%	84%	— 11%

Key Votes of the 105th Congress

1. Clinton Budget Deal	N	5. Puerto Rico Sthood. Ref.	*	9. Cut $ for B-2 Bombers	N
2. Education IRAs	N	6. End Highway Set-asides	N	10. Human Rights in China	Y
3. Req. 2/3 to Raise Taxes	N	7. School Prayer Amend.	N	11. Withdraw Bosnia Troops	N
4. Fast-track Trade	N	8. Ovrd. Part. Birth Veto	N	12. End Cuban TV-Marti	Y

Election Results

1998 general	Howard L. Berman (D)	69,000	(82%)	($690,408)
	Juan Carlos Ros (Lib)	6,556	(8%)	($672)
	Maria Armoudian	4,858	(6%)	
	Others	3,248	(4%)	
1998 primary	Howard L. Berman (D)	39,244	(61%)	
	Raul Godinez II (D)	19,676	(30%)	
	Others	5,728	(9%)	
1996 general	Howard L. Berman (D)	67,525	(66%)	($408,096)
	Bill Glass (R)	29,332	(29%)	($78,469)
	Others	5,658	(6%)	

TWENTY-SEVENTH DISTRICT

In the early years of the 20th Century, when Los Angeles was growing to become one of America's major cities, its richest citizens settled not on the beach (too clammy and cold) or on the west side (too dusty and remote), but in communities they built at the base of the San Gabriel Mountains that rise 10,000 feet above the city, their snow-capped peaks visible most of the year. The premier such community was Pasadena, with its institutions of national stature—the Rose Bowl, Cal Tech—and the premier structures were Pasadena's baroque-domed

City Hall and railroader Henry Huntington's house in next-door San Marino, now the Huntington Library, one of the world's great scholarly institutions. Pasadena and South Pasadena have proudly preserved their bungalow neighborhoods, and Pasadena preserved and rebuilt the 80-year old curving Colorado Boulevard Bridge over Arroyo Seco. More middle class is Glendale, north of downtown Los Angeles, site of Forest Lawn Cemetery; just west, beneath the Verdugo Mountains, is Burbank (named not for botanist Luther Burbank but for a local dentist-developer), famous now for the NBC Studios and Disney headquarters and home to many small entertainment multimedia companies as well. With its lower taxes and business-friendly attitude, and despite its earlier loss of aerospace jobs, Glendale and Burbank are booming while inside the city limits of high-tax and high-regulation Los Angeles, Hollywood has become seedy and commercial buildings have huge vacancy rates.

The 27th Congressional District takes in all these affluent foothill communities plus—sandwiched between the Verdugo and San Gabriel Mountains—La Canada, La Crescenta, Sunland and Tujunga. For years these places were traditionally, indeed stereotypically, Republican, but in recent years they have been moving toward the Democrats. The black communities in Pasadena and Altadena, the boyhood home of Jackie Robinson, are expanding. Affluent Asians are moving into San Marino and style-conscious young couples are moving into South Pasadena. Glendale is now the center of the nation's largest Armenian community and has many Iranians, Koreans, Filipinos—nearly half its residents are foreign-born. There are also immigrants as well as upscale singles in showbizzy Burbank. The district gave Bill Clinton 8% pluralities in both 1992 and 1996, and in 1996 the two Assembly districts that cover the area, safe Republican seats since the 1940s, both elected Democrats.

The congressman from the 27th is James Rogan, a Republican elected in 1996. He grew up in San Francisco, raised mostly by his grandfather, a longshoreman; his mother was a convicted felon and welfare recipient, his stepfather an alcoholic. He dropped out of high school, then worked his way through Berkeley and UCLA Law, with jobs such as bartender and adult-theater bouncer. He practiced law with a large Los Angeles firm, then became an deputy district attorney, a member of the Hardcore Gang Unit who got death penalties, and a resourceful prosecutor whose wordless summation of a drunk driving case was to pour ten cans of beer into ten cups and then snap his fingers. In 1990 he was appointed to the Glendale municipal court and at 33 was the youngest judge in California. In 1993 he won a special election to replace Pat Nolan, once Republican leader in the Assembly, who had pleaded guilty to a federal racketeering charge. In an Assembly bitterly divided on partisan lines, he became noted for combining conservative positions with a judicial manner. He was named the best Assembly member by the *California Journal*, and after Republicans, in a 41–39 majority, succeeded in getting rid of three successive Republicans who had been co-opted by Willie Brown to run as his puppet speaker, he was elected majority leader in his first full term. He rallied Republicans to repeal the motorcycle helmet law, but was less successful on a bill to allow police to spank graffiti vandals, and was unable to pass the Contract with California to roll back business taxes and regulations. But he also supported Democrats' bills on domestic violence, medical marijuana and penalties for carrying concealed weapons. He hosted a February 1996 dinner for Laurence Powell, one of the policemen in the Rodney King case, because Rogan felt he'd been subjected to double jeopardy.

Rogan was an obvious candidate for Congress once 24-year veteran Carlos Moorhead announced his retirement in August 1995; despite his seniority, Moorhead had been passed over by Speaker Newt Gingrich for the chairs of both Judiciary and Commerce, and as chairman of the Intellectual Property Subcommittee had been opposed by some Republicans on patent reform. The Democrats had a close primary between Doug Kahn (who held Moorhead to 50%–39% and 53%–42% victories in 1992 and 1994) and Barry Gordon, for seven years president of the Screen Actors Guild. Gordon had endorsements from unions and Congressman Howard Berman, but Kahn—a computer graphics artist who financed most of his campaign—attacked Gordon for carpetbagging and condoning sexual harassment (for which Kahn later apologized) and won 51%–49%. Kahn argued Rogan—against abortion and gun control, for Proposition 187 and school vouchers—was too extreme. Rogan won 50%–43% in November.

Once elected, Rogan moved as quickly to become a player in Washington as he had in Sacramento, gaining seats as a freshman on the Commerce and Judiciary committees. On Commerce, he helped to broker a deal for auctioning radio spectrum space. But Judiciary proved to be the place where he gained fame for his work on the Clinton impeachment. In early 1998, Speaker Newt Gingrich asked Rogan to review recent precedents for possible Judiciary Committee proceedings. Then, in September, after Independent Counel Kenneth Starr submitted his report with possible impeachable offenses, Rogan became one of the leading players within committee deliberations and a common-sense spokesman for House Republicans to the news media. During the Senate impeachment trial, Rogan was among the most articulate House managers making their case for Clinton's removal. The result gave him more name recognition than most House members receive in a lengthy career. But there was a big downside: He made himself vulnerable to Democratic attack, both nationally and in the district. Back home, Hollywood Democrats were almost hysterical in defense of Clinton.

In the 1998 campaign, Barry Gordon, running again for the Democratic nomination, used similar rhetoric. In the June 1998 all-party primary, before the Starr referral, Rogan won 59% of the vote to Gordon's 37%; in Washington and Alaska, which have similar open primaries, these results are a pretty good forecast of the general election. As the impeachment hearings proceeded, Gordon, once a TV regular on *The New Dick Van Dyke Show* and *Archie Bunker's Place*, raised $525,000 and attacked Rogan as out of touch with his district on issues such as education vouchers, campaign-finance, abortion, guns and tobacco, and attacked him for not being consistent on procedural votes on impeachment. Rogan won in November, but by only 51%–46%, a narrower margin than in 1996 even in this pro-incumbent year, and an indication that the impeachment issue had cost him votes between June and November. Rogan's lead role as a House manager in January and February 1999 and his earnest, relentless prosecution of the case may have cost him more votes at home. Hollywood record mogul David Geffen promised to raise millions to oppose him. "Jim Rogan is done," California Democratic Chairman Art Torres said in February 1999. "Now he has been exposed as the far-right zealot he is."

But the impeachment trial may not be the last time most Americans hear from Jim Rogan. In early 1999, he began to explore the possibility of running against Senator Dianne Feinstein in 2000. But by the end of April, he ruled out a Senate challenge, despite the support of many state Republicans. Meanwhile, the district has become even more Hispanic and Rogan's high-profile opposition to Clinton may have damaged him with the area's increasingly liberal Anglos. He now faces a strong re-election challenge from state Senator Adam Schiff. And if he survives in 2000, Rogan faces the prospect that the heavily Democratic legislature would hurt him in redistricting. The easy way to create a more Democratic 27th is to include heavily Latino areas to the east, west and south, but there will be pressure on Democrats to reserve these precincts to maximize the number of Latino-majority districts.

Cook's Call. *Highly Competitive.* The 27th is a competitive district but does have a bit of a Democratic tilt to it. In state Senator Adam Schiff, Democrats have recruited a first-tier challenger to run in 2000. Many insiders believe that after the 2001 remapping this district could become even more hostile territory for Republicans. This is likely to be the most competitive and closely watched race for 2000.

The People: Pop. 1990: 572,629; 0.1% rural; 13.6% age 65 + ; 71.1% White, 8.2% Black, 10.5% Asian, 0.5% Amer. Indian, 9.7% Other; 20.1% Hispanic Origin. Households: 48.7% married couple families; 23.1% married couple fams. w. children; 61.2% college educ.; median household income: $37,929; per capita income: $20,344; median house value: $296,000; median gross rent: $608.

1996 Presidential Vote

Clinton (D) 98,348 (49%)
Dole (R) 81,282 (41%)
Perot (I) 13,324   (7%)
Others 7,540   (4%)

1992 Presidential Vote

Clinton (D) 98,057 (44%)
Bush (R) 80,986 (36%)
Perot (I) 42,071 (19%)

Rep. James E. Rogan (R)

Elected 1996; b. Aug. 21, 1957, San Francisco; home, Glendale; U. of CA at Berkeley, B.A. 1979, U.C.L.A., J.D. 1983; Christian; married (Christine Apffel).

Elected Office: CA Assembly, 1993–96, Majority Ldr., 1996.

Professional Career: Practicing atty., 1983–85; Los Angeles Cnty. Dpty. District Atty., 1985–90; Glendale Municipal Court Judge, 1990–94.

DC Office: 126 CHOB 20515, 202-225-4176; Fax: 202-225-5828; Web site: www.house.gov/rogan.

District Office: Pasadena, 626-577-3936.

Committees: *Commerce* (21st of 29 R): Energy & Power; Telecommunications, Trade & Consumer Protection. *Judiciary* (17th of 21 R): Courts & Intellectual Property.

Group Ratings

	ADA	ACLU	AFS	LCV	CON	NTU	NFIB	COC	ACU	NTLC	CHC
1998	0	6	0	15	60	59	85	100	100	95	100
1997	5	—	13	—	46	54	—	80	92	—	—

National Journal Ratings

	1997 LIB — 1997 CONS	1998 LIB — 1998 CONS
Economic	24% — 73%	30% — 67%
Social	0% — 90%	11% — 88%
Foreign	0% — 88%	19% — 75%

Key Votes of the 105th Congress

1. Clinton Budget Deal	Y	5. Puerto Rico Sthood. Ref.	N	9. Cut $ for B-2 Bombers	N
2. Education IRAs	Y	6. End Highway Set-asides	Y	10. Human Rights in China	N
3. Req. 2/3 to Raise Taxes	Y	7. School Prayer Amend.	Y	11. Withdraw Bosnia Troops	Y
4. Fast-track Trade	Y	8. Ovrd. Part. Birth Veto	Y	12. End Cuban TV-Marti	N

Election Results

1998 general	James E. Rogan (R)	80,702	(51%)	($1,259,523)
	Barry A. Gordon (D)	73,875	(46%)	($516,259)
	Others	4,489	(3%)	
1998 primary	James E. Rogan (R)	62,305	(59%)	
	Barry A. Gordon (D)	38,699	(37%)	
	Bob New (Lib)	4,441	(4%)	
1996 general	James E. Rogan (R)	95,310	(50%)	($763,574)
	Doug Kahn (D)	82,014	(43%)	($1,052,335)
	Others	12,606	(7%)	

TWENTY-EIGHTH DISTRICT

It is the great route west to California: Passengers on the Santa Fe railroad's *Super Chief* or motorists on U.S. 66, after hours and days in barren desert, descended through the El Cajon

Pass into the Los Angeles Basin, moving in a stately procession beneath the 10,000-foot snow-capped San Gabriel Mountains, marveling at orange groves and exotic plants. The railroad and highway ran through a line of towns, built by Midwestern Protestants as independent communities and now mostly high-income suburbs with their own civic institutions: Claremont, home of the academically strong Claremont Colleges; La Verne and Glendora; Azusa, named by a Chicago manufacturer for his wife; Duarte, with the City of Hope Medical Center; Monrovia and Arcadia, site of the Santa Anita race track and the Los Angeles County Arboretum. Today, the traveler arriving in Los Angeles can see the same sights—if the air is clear—as the jet glides down the flightpath to LAX.

The 28th Congressional District covers much of this territory, with the exception of Azusa, which is part of the Hispanic-majority 31st District. Its eastern end reaches south from Claremont and Glendora to include Covina and West Covina, classic 1950s suburbs now with many Mexican-Americans, where city ordinances require that lawns be kept watered: 1950s homeowner values continue to govern here. The District's western end reaches south from Monrovia and Arcadia to include Temple City, where many towns are trying to revive their old downtowns. It is far from mono-cultural: 24% Hispanic and 13% Asian in 1990. The 28th has a strong Republican heritage, but it has been trending Democratic lately; Bill Clinton, after losing it by 3% in 1992 carried it by 1% in 1996.

David Dreier, the congressman from the 28th, grew up in Kansas City, Missouri, then spent a decade mostly on the Claremont McKenna campus, as a student and administrator, before he was elected to Congress in 1980. He personifies the intellectually rigorous conservatism and free market economics that thrived for years in this area and maintains a cheerfulness and good humor characteristic of California—even though he served for 14 years in the minority, chiefly on the Rules Committee, where Republicans were outnumbered 9–4 and lost almost every vote. Now the tables are turned: Dreier is on the long end of the 9–4 split, and, since Gerald Solomon retired in 1998, he has been chairman. He had already exerted influence in his first months in the majority when, as co-chairman of the Joint Committee on the Organization of Congress, he worked to realign the House's committee structure: Three committees were abolished, almost half the other panels were renamed and saw some shifting of jurisdictional lines, committee staff was cut by one-third, and six-year term limits were established on committee and subcommittee chairmen. Dreier encouraged committees to establish websites on the Internet, and held the first interactive subcommittee hearing in May 1996; his reforms adopted in January 1997 include Internet access, allowing members to ask questions for more than five minutes and allowing committees to sit while the House is considering amendments.

The Rules chairman, once upon a time an independent operator, has become an operating member of the House leadership since Democrats instituted election of committee chairmen in 1974. Rules sets the terms for debate and limits the amendments that can be offered—an essential procedural function in a legislature with 435 members, and one which can be and often is used to shape substantive outcome. The 9–4 ratio and the careful selection of members guarantee the chairman control over committee votes, but over time it must be tempered by a sense of fairness: An outraged minority party can store up grievances and wait for a chance to overturn a rule on the floor (as Republicans did in 1994 and Democrats did in 1997). The strategy of Speaker Newt Gingrich and Solomon was to hold together the narrow Republican majority and make minimal concessions to Democrats. The strategy of Speaker Denny Hastert and Dreier in early 1999 seemed to be to shape legislation and rules so as to win over a sizable number of Democrats—a necessary response, perhaps, to the fact that their Republican majority is even narrower than Gingrich's.

With his youthful, photogenic demeanor, Dreier's skill and stubbornness can be underestimated. "His ambition is masked by an easygoing style, an infectious grin, a charming spontaneity," wrote Nina Easton and Gebe Martinez in the Los Angeles Times. But he's often "closed-lipped" and plays his cards close to his chest, said Porter Goss, second-ranking Republican on Rules. In contrast to Rules Committee chairmen from both parties in recent years,

Dreier also has a clear-cut policy agenda of his own, which he likely will continue to pursue. A strong backer of free trade, he was one of the leading Republicans rounding up votes for NAFTA in 1993, was chief Republican negotiator with the Clinton Administration in getting 1994 approval for the new General Agreement on Tariffs and Trade, has been a leader in normalizing trade relations with China and in 1997 unsuccessfully urged fast-track trade authority for Clinton. Dreier is an aggressive advocate of reducing capital-gains taxes and other tax burdens on business, and has been a leading sponsor of legislation to remove Depression-era regulations on banking. In May 1999 he became chief sponsor of legislation to limit liability in law suits stemming from the Y2K computer problem. Although he usually votes with conservatives, he prefers to avoid conflict on hot-button social issues like abortion.

Dreier lost his first race for Congress in 1978, at 25, against Democrat Jim Lloyd; but he beat Lloyd in 1980 and then fellow Republican Wayne Grisham after they were redistricted together in 1982. At that point, Dreier evidently decided never to be pressed for funds again; he raised plenty and spent little, which takes more self-discipline than one might think. After the 1998 campaign, in which he spent $893,000, he had $2.6 million cash on hand, the highest in the House. Although he has contemplated Senate races, Dreier's key position in the House and the relish he has for its work—plus California's recent Democratic trend—will probably keep him in the House. He doesn't deny interest in seeking the speakership at some point.

Dreier has not neglected the interests of his home state. Before chairing the Rules Committee, he led a Republican task force to respond to California's legislative priorities. He was the only Republican congressman named by *California Journal* as one of 25 Californians "with the power, influence and ideas to shape the dream for generations to come." Janice Nelson, a Los Angeles County pathologist who was his Democratic opponent in 1998, criticized Dreier as a professional politician who is the poster child for what is wrong with the system. But he easily won re-election. Dreier joked that probably the most frightening race of my life happened earlier in 1998, when he crashed down an icy run on a sled at Lake Placid, New York and ended up with his arm in a sling. That incident may have been good preparation for his work in the closely-divided House.

Cook's Call. *Safe.* Though Dreier's election percentages dropped in each of three non-Reagan Presidential elections, it certainly shouldn't be enough to jeopardize him. The district may be trending more Democratic but given that Dreier traditionally amasses one of the largest war chests in in Congress, it's unlikely that he will have too much difficulty winning in 2000.

The People: Pop. 1990: 572,189; 0.1% rural; 11.4% age 65 + ; 71.1% White, 5.7% Black, 13.1% Asian, 0.5% Amer. Indian, 9.7% Other; 23.6% Hispanic Origin. Households: 59.3% married couple families; 30.8% married couple fams. w. children; 59% college educ.; median household income: $43,508; per capita income: $18,064; median house value: $233,700; median gross rent: $639.

1996 Presidential Vote

Clinton (D)	88,709	(45%)
Dole (R)	86,358	(44%)
Perot (I)	15,215	(8%)
Others	5,441	(3%)

1992 Presidential Vote

Bush (R)	90,644	(41%)
Clinton (D)	82,958	(38%)
Perot (I)	45,623	(21%)

Rep. David Dreier (R)

Elected 1980; b. July 5, 1952, Kansas City, MO; home, San Dimas; Claremont McKenna Col., B.A. 1975, Claremont Grad. Schl., M.A. 1976; Christian Scientist; single.

Professional Career: Corp. Relations Dir., Claremont McKenna Col., 1975–78; Mktg. Dir., Industrial Hydrocarbons, 1979–80; Vice Pres., Dreier Development Co., 1985–present.

DC Office: 237 CHOB 20515, 202-225-2305; Fax: 202-225-7018; Web site: www.house.gov/dreier.

District Office: Covina, 626-339-9078.

Committees: *Rules* (Chmn. of 9 R): Rules & Organization of the House; The Legislative & Budget Process.

Group Ratings

	ADA	ACLU	AFS	LCV	CON	NTU	NFIB	COC	ACU	NTLC	CHC
1998	0	13	11	8	33	54	85	100	92	97	100
1997	0	—	13	—	23	54	—	100	88	—	—

National Journal Ratings

	1997 LIB — 1997 CONS	1998 LIB — 1998 CONS
Economic	10% — 86%	0% — 88%
Social	30% — 70%	36% — 63%
Foreign	12% — 81%	39% — 58%

Key Votes of the 105th Congress

1. Clinton Budget Deal	Y	5. Puerto Rico Sthood. Ref.	N	9. Cut $ for B-2 Bombers	N
2. Education IRAs	Y	6. End Highway Set-asides	Y	10. Human Rights in China	N
3. Req. 2/3 to Raise Taxes	Y	7. School Prayer Amend.	Y	11. Withdraw Bosnia Troops	Y
4. Fast-track Trade	Y	8. Ovrd. Part. Birth Veto	Y	12. End Cuban TV-Marti	N

Election Results

1998 general	David Dreier (R)	90,607	(58%)	($893,029)
	Janice M. Nelson (D)	61,721	(39%)	($122,994)
	Others	4,872	(3%)	
1998 primary	David Dreier (R)	63,801	(60%)	
	Janice M. Nelson (D)	33,678	(32%)	
	Others	8,601	(8%)	
1996 general	David Dreier (R)	113,389	(61%)	($396,104)
	David Levering (D)	69,037	(37%)	($50,651)
	Others	4,459	(2%)	

TWENTY-NINTH DISTRICT

The Westside: The term was not much used 20 years ago, but is now shorthand for what might be the biggest and flashiest concentration of affluence in the world. It is the heartland of one of America's most productive and creative industries and one of the nation's major exports, show business. The first moviemakers came here earlier in the century, looking for a place to shoot silent films where the sunlight was more dependable than Astoria, Queens, or Englewood, New Jersey. They found it in Hollywood, a suburb just annexed by burgeoning Los Angeles when the first movie studio was built in 1911. In 1923 came the Hollywood sign, overlooking the soon-famous intersection of Hollywood and Vine. By the 1930s, big studio lots were scattered around town, over the mountains in Burbank or out toward the ocean in Westwood and Culver City. Miraculously, the studio bosses of that era—most of them Jewish immigrants with little ancestral experience of America—created a popular culture that was universally accessible and embodied the American spirit in a way that still captures the imagination. This was the universal American culture of the 1940s movies that Ronald Reagan understood and transferred into politics. Today's showbiz moguls, by contrast, have been absorbed in the enterprise of putting their own personal idiosyncrasies on the screen or the tube or tapes or CDs.

Showbiz still sets the tone for the Westside. It remains tremendously profitable, in large part because it's not run by big business units but by thousands of craftsmen and entrepreneurs who keep it anchored in Los Angeles because so many of them remain here. People on the Westside like to portray themselves as artists in a garret, willing to risk starving to make art and speak truth to bourgeois society. But their yen for fashionable new moral standards make them disdainful of the ordinary people who are the market of any mass entertainment. The Westside loves to congratulate itself on its moral daring when it makes a movie or TV show revealing businessmen or priests as criminals. And yet the marketplace may be teaching showbiz some lessons. As Michael Medved, movie critic and author of *Hollywood vs. America*, has pointed out, Hollywood's most obscene, anti-business and anti-religious products don't sell nearly as well as its family fare; and television shows and movies started reflecting a wider range of subjects and values. Showbiz rejoiced in the election of Bill Clinton and in his frequent forays into California and obvious fascination with entertainers, and it rejected with fury the notion that there was something wrong about his affair with a White House intern from the Westside or with lying under oath in a sexual harassment case in a United States District Court.

Not everyone on the Westside is in show business, of course. This is also the home of thousands of small entrepreneurs, manufacturers, and inventors and marketers of everything imaginable, who sparked the Los Angeles Basin growth of the 1980s, and there are even traces of pre-show business Los Angeles money, which is also plentiful. There are large numbers of singles and gays here: apartment-renters provided majorities for Santa Monica's city government, which thrived when it imposed rent control but foundered when it invited in more homeless. The core of Hollywood itself has gone seedy and is the home now of many Central American immigrants, a high-crime and riot zone, but the Fairfax neighborhood remains solidly middle-class Jewish—though many of its Jews today are recent Russian immigrants. Hancock Park looks as aristocratic as it did when it was built, when Beverly Hills was vacant land. The Westside has been the home of a former president who does not at all exemplify its politics, Ronald Reagan; it is also the home, notably on the former Fox lot that is now Century City where Reagan keeps his office, of the largest office square footage in the Los Angeles area. It is the center of the second largest Jewish community in the United States, as well as the focus of the 1980s immigration of Iranians to the United States. It is also the locus of some of America's most expensive residential real estate, where people buy houses for multiples of $1 million, knock down the structure and build something new for a few more millions, and of one of the world's premier high-priced shopping areas—Rodeo Drive, a quite ordinary shopping street 20 years ago.

The 29th Congressional District contains almost all the major elements of Westside Los Angeles, from old, high-income Los Feliz and the gay neighborhood around Silver Lake through Hollywood and Hancock Park, west through Beverly Hills and Westwood, Bel Air and Brentwood, Santa Monica and Pacific Palisades. It is solidly Democratic and not just in votes: It probably contributes more money to Democratic candidates and liberal causes than any other district with the possible exception of Manhattan's New York 14th. Its boundaries are carefully sculpted to put blacks in the 32nd District to the south and Hispanics and Asians in the 30th to the east; far from being racially diverse, it has the highest percentage of non-Hispanic whites of any Los Angeles Basin district except the 24th on the other side of Mulholland Drive.

The congressman from the 29th is Henry Waxman, a Democrat elected in 1974, one of the ablest members of the House, a shrewd political operator who is a skilled and idealistic policy entrepreneur. There is no Westside glitz about him: He grew up over his family's store in Watts, his personal demeanor is quiet, he has never attended the Oscars ceremony. At each stage of his career, he has seen political openings before others did and gone smartly through them. He ran against Assemblyman Lester McMillan in the mostly Jewish Fairfax area in 1968, at 28, and won 64% in the primary. From 1971–72 he chaired the redistricting committee, a good place to make friends, but he went to Congress in 1974 in a district designed, he points out, not by his committee but by a court. Waxman's biggest break came after the 1978 election, when he was elected chairman of the Commerce Committee's Health and Environment Sub-committee. This was one of the first times House Democrats decided to ignore seniority in handing out subcommittee chairs. Nevertheless, Waxman argued his case on the issues and—in a move quite unprecedented at the time, though common in Sacramento and now also in Washington—made campaign contributions to other Democrats on the full committee, and won the post, 15–12, over the competent and widely respected Richardson Preyer of North Carolina.

The campaign contributions were no accident. Waxman and his friends Howard Berman and former Congressman Mel Levine built their own political machine in Los Angeles. Its power came not from patronage but from fundraising and savvy. Their specialty was targeted direct mail, with hundreds of customized letters and endorsement slates sent out to different lists of people. In the apolitical commonwealth of California, where television advertising is exceedingly expensive and people seem to avoid politics, this made them critical though not always successful players. But in 1992 their machine seemed to founder: Westsider Mel Levine lost the Senate nomination to Barbara Boxer in "the year of the woman," and Tom Hayden beat a Waxman-Berman ally for state senator.

Waxman has been a major national policymaker for two decades. In 1981 and 1982 he prevented the Reagan Administration and Commerce Committee Chairman John Dingell from revising the Clean Air Act; biding his time, he worked to strengthen the law in its 1990 revision. He and Dingell—frequent shouting-match partners who nevertheless maintained a working relationship—hammered out a compromise, delaying stricter California-type auto standards until 1994 and moving more aggressively on non-auto issues. Another great Waxman project has been expanding Medicaid for the poor. His strategy was to threaten to hold up budget reconciliation bills unless they required states to expand Medicaid eligibility. Between 1984 and 1990, he got coverage for all poor children up to 18, all children under seven and pregnant women in families under 133% of poverty income. This helped raise Medicaid from 9% to 14% of state spending in the 1980s, and helps to explain why Waxman is so disliked by many governors.

Waxman had less success on reforming national health care. He wanted to move to some-thing like a single-payer program and supported the Clinton plan but to no avail. He has secured more funding for AIDS research, important in the 29th District with its large gay population. He passed a law providing damages to children injured by required immunizations, sponsored measures to require testing of mammography devices, expanded the availability of generic drugs, extended patent protection for drugs for time spent during the approval process, and tried unsuccessfully to legalize the use of heroin to reduce the pain of terminal cancer patients. In early 1994, in widely publicized hearings, he lined up the chief executive officers of leading tobacco companies and accused them of adding nicotine and other substances to cigarettes and of lying in their testimony. All this had no immediate legislative result, and when Thomas Bliley of Virginia, became Commerce Committee chair, the hearings stopped. But Waxman brought the tobacco issue into public view and FDA head David Kessler's proposal to regulate tobacco as a drug proved to be a good campaign issue for Clinton and most Democrats in 1996, and it helped to inspire the lawsuits against tobacco companies which have resulted in the biggest redistribution of corporate assets—from the tobacco companies to state governments and trial lawyers—in history.

Waxman reacted with dismay to the Republican takeover of Congress, but with no slackening of effort. On some issues, he worked to negotiate compromises with Republicans, notably the Safe Drinking Water Act and the pesticide standards in the Food Quality Provision Act of 1996; part of his strategy was "right-to-know" amendments listing contaminants. He led the fight against Republicans' regulatory reform and Medicare and Medicaid changes. He was the senior Democrat on the Corrections Day Advisory Group, working to prevent liberal laws from being quickly repealed. In 1997 he gave up the ranking position on Health to be the lead Democrat on the Government Reform Committee. There he sharply attacked Chairman Dan Burton's investigation of Clinton campaign misdeeds, arguing that Burton had given himself unprecedented subpoena power and was misusing it, and he emerged as perhaps the House's most articulate defender of Clinton against scandal charges. *The Weekly Standard*, no admirer of his type, headlined him "Washington's Most Formidable Liberal" for his skill in undercutting Burton. "He's smart, intense, partisan, highly ideological, and works harder than almost any other member of Congress," wrote Matthew Rees. "In the process, he's scored more legislative victories than almost any other member of Congress in recent memory."

Waxman has always won re-election easily, and has contributed generously to other Democrats' campaigns. He continues to hope the Democrats will win back control of the House, and looks forward to chairing Governmental Affairs. His 1996 Republican opponent, Paul Stepanek, denied party funding in this hopeless district, endorsed Bill Clinton and denounced Newt Gingrich and Dick Armey. It availed him nothing. Nor would any other Republican strategy.

Cook's Call. *Safe.* Waxman is another incumbent with no re-election concerns. Since winning the seat in 1974, his closest electoral call was a 61% win in 1992. This seat will stay firmly planted in the Democratic column.

The People: Pop. 1990: 571,386; 16.9% age 65 + ; 83.9% White, 3.5% Black, 7.6% Asian, 0.3% Amer. Indian, 4.7% Other; 12.8% Hispanic Origin. Households: 32.9% married couple families; 11.6% married couple fams. w. children; 70.5% college educ.; median household income: $37,540; per capita income: $34,253; median house value: $500,001; median gross rent: $636.

1996 Presidential Vote

Clinton (D)	150,771	(66%)
Dole (R)	53,354	(24%)
Perot (I)	10,639	(5%)
Others	12,002	(5%)

1992 Presidential Vote

Clinton (D)	183,233	(66%)
Bush (R)	55,924	(20%)
Perot (I)	37,217	(13%)

Rep. Henry A. Waxman (D)

Elected 1974; b. Sept. 12, 1939, Los Angeles; home, Los Angeles; U.C.L.A., B.A. 1961, J.D. 1964; Jewish; married (Janet).

Elected Office: CA Assembly, 1968–74.

Professional Career: Practicing atty., 1965–68.

DC Office: 2204 RHOB 20515, 202-225-3976; Fax: 202-225-4099; Web site: www.house.gov/waxman.

District Office: Los Angeles, 323-651-1040.

Committees: *Commerce* (2d of 24 D): Health and Environment; Oversight & Investigations. *Government Reform* (RMM of 19 D).

Group Ratings

	ADA	ACLU	AFS	LCV	CON	NTU	NFIB	COC	ACU	NTLC	CHC
1998	100	88	100	100	91	18	0	18	4	5	0
1997	95	—	100	—	22	28	—	20	0	—	—

National Journal Ratings

	1997 LIB — 1997 CONS		1998 LIB — 1998 CONS	
Economic	93% —	0%	79% —	0%
Social	85% —	0%	88% —	11%
Foreign	94% —	3%	84% —	11%

Key Votes of the 105th Congress

1. Clinton Budget Deal	N	5. Puerto Rico Sthood. Ref.	Y	9. Cut $ for B-2 Bombers	Y
2. Education IRAs	N	6. End Highway Set-asides	N	10. Human Rights in China	Y
3. Req. 2/3 to Raise Taxes	N	7. School Prayer Amend.	N	11. Withdraw Bosnia Troops	N
4. Fast-track Trade	N	8. Ovrd. Part. Birth Veto	N	12. End Cuban TV-Marti	Y

Election Results

1998 general	Henry A. Waxman (D)	131,561	(74%)	($276,306)
	Mike Gottlieb (R)	40,282	(23%)	($47,641)
	Others	6,251	(4%)	
1998 primary	Henry A. Waxman (D)	78,151	(70%)	
	Mike Gottlieb (R)	15,397	(14%)	
	David Churchman (R)	12,203	(11%)	
	Others	5,130	(5%)	
1996 general	Henry A. Waxman (D)	145,278	(68%)	($365,082)
	Paul Stepanek (R)	52,857	(25%)	($135,677)
	John Peter Daly (P&F)	8,819	(4%)	
	Others	7,863	(4%)	

THIRTIETH DISTRICT

Surrounding downtown Los Angeles are neighborhoods just now becoming antique, as the early 20th Century buildings stop looking familiar and start taking on the patina of the historic. Downtown LA, with its 1980s marble slabs and pink cylinders jutting up to 70 stories from what was once a low-rise business district, seems soulless and detached from its neighborhoods, which change character with every new immigration flow. Not far east, over the Los Angeles River, is Boyle Heights, once an entry neighborhood for Irish and Jewish immigrants and for the last 30 years predominantly Mexican-American, poor in income but with enough community cohesion not to riot in April 1992. In between downtown and Boyle Heights is Toytown, the center now of toy manufacturing and importing in the United States. South of downtown is the garment district, with factories in nondescript buildings, an economically vibrant area and one of the reasons Los Angeles is the number one manufacturing city in America today. To the north of downtown is Lincoln Heights, a heavily Hispanic area centering on the busy shopping street of North Broadway, plus the neighborhoods of Highland Park and Eagle Rock, white middle-class 30 years ago, now mostly Hispanic but with Asians as well. West of downtown are Pico Union, an entry point for new immigrants, lower Sunset Boulevard, the Koreatown strip along Western Avenue, site of the worst damage during the April 1992 riot, and much of Hollywood and some of South Central. Hollywood has a seedy look, for it has not sprouted the office buildings you can see in Burbank or Glendale because of Los Angeles's high taxes and daffy regulations; Central Americans rioted in Hollywood in 1992, and the subway line on Hollywood Boulevard caved in during the 1994 earthquake: not auspicious signs.

All of these neighborhoods are populated more thickly than they were a quarter-century ago, with small houses and garden apartments full of large families and many children; new migrants stay with those who have been here a few years, with beds assigned to family members working different shifts so they're slept in 24 hours a day. To most American eyes, these look like poverty neighborhoods, but this is the snapshot view; in the video version they are the first frames on the way to prosperity, the first way-station on freeways out to middle-income American comfort.

Almost all of these areas, centering geographically on Dodger Stadium, are part of California's 30th Congressional District. The population here in 1990 was recorded as 60.5% Hispanic and 21% Asian. But many of these are recent immigrants; only 34% of registered voters were Latino and 7% Asian. There are some 600,000 people living here, but in 1998 only 57,000 voted in the Democratic primary and only 78,000 in the general election, compared to 124,000 in the primary and 190,000 in the general in the adjacent Westside 29th District.

The congressman from the 30th District is Xavier Becerra, a Democrat elected in 1992. He grew up in California, went to college and law school at Stanford, worked for legal services, then worked for state Senator Art Torres and Attorney General John Van de Kamp, and married a Harvard Medical School graduate who teaches at George Washington University. In 1990 he was elected to the Assembly, and had a liberal record on the environment and making AIDS drugs available; he backed campaign finance reform and tougher penalties for gang activities near schools. In 1992, the newly-redrawn 30th District was expected to re-elect Edward Roybal, California's first Latino congressman, elected 30 years before; his daughter, Assemblywoman Lucille Roybal-Allard, was running in the neighboring 33d District. But Roybal announced late in the game that he was retiring, and Becerra jumped into the race, although his residence was in Monterey Park outside the district. Becerra's main Latino competitor, Leticia Quezada, was a member of the Los Angeles school board, a powerful engine for publicity, and had the endorsement of Councilman Richard Alatorre and Assemblyman Richard Polanco. But Becerra had the endorsements of Roybal, 34th District Congressman Esteban Torres and County Supervisor Gloria Molina. In a primary in which only 33,000 voters turned out, Becerra won with 32% to 22% for Quezada. Becerra's 10,417 votes effectively made him the representative of 573,000 people; he won the general in this heavily Democratic district 58%–24%.

The fast-moving Becerra initially was slowed down in the House. He did not get on the Commerce Committee, where he had hoped to work on health care reform. But even with Republicans in control, he was legislatively active, if not always successful. On the Judiciary Committee he moved for refunds of the $80 fee paid by the one million visa applicants who would be ineligible under the proposed immigration rules and called for an appeals process for workers denied jobs by errors in the proposed new identification program. He said declaring English as the official language "sends a message of intolerance for those trying to learn English." He opposed a law to allow local law enforcement agents to enter pacts with the Department of Justice to enforce immigration laws. He struggled to oppose restrictions on bilingual education and to oppose Republican restrictions on census sampling techniques.

After the 1996 election, Becerra visited Cuba and met with Fidel Castro; he did not denounce his regime or demand free elections as other members, including California Democrat Tom Lantos, have done on such visits. In January 1997 he was elected chairman of the Hispanic Caucus by 12–7, at which point Republican members Ileana Ros-Lehtinen and Lincoln Diaz-Balart resigned because of his trip to Cuba. As chairman of the caucus, he found himself often on the defensive. In 1997, he also became a member of the Ways and Means Committee.

Becerra's pleasant and businesslike manner combined with his obvious ambition could make him a force in the House, though his leftish views, for the moment anyway, make him not very effective. Nor has he ruled out other elective office, possibly a run for Los Angeles mayor.

Cook's Call. *Safe.* Becerra has won easily here since 1992 and should have no problems in 2000. This district is a lock for Democrats.

The People: Pop. 1990: 572,604; 8.5% age 65 +; 43.7% White, 3.4% Black, 21.4% Asian, 0.4% Amer. Indian, 31.1% Other; 60.5% Hispanic Origin. Households: 43.4% married couple families; 27.5% married couple fams. w. children; 35.2% college educ.; median household income: $23,435; per capita income: $9,637; median house value: $189,000; median gross rent: $483.

1996 Presidential Vote		
Clinton (D)	61,114	(71%)
Dole (R)	17,053	(20%)
Perot (I)	4,165	(5%)
Others	3,713	(4%)

1992 Presidential Vote		
Clinton (D)	56,378	(62%)
Bush (R)	21,750	(24%)
Perot (I)	11,842	(13%)

Rep. Xavier Becerra (D)

Elected 1992; b. Jan. 26, 1958, Sacramento; home, Los Angeles; Stanford U., B.A. 1980, J.D. 1984; Catholic; married (Carolina Reyes).

Elected Office: CA Assembly, 1990–92.

Professional Career: Staff Atty., Legal Assistance Corp. of Central MA; Dist. Dir., CA Sen. Art Torres, 1986; CA Dep. Atty. Gen., 1987–90.

DC Office: 1119 LHOB 20515, 202-225-6235; Fax: 202-225-2202; Web site: www.house.gov/becerra.

District Office: Los Angeles, 213-483-1425.

Committees: *Ways & Means* (14th of 16 D): Trade.

Group Ratings

	ADA	ACLU	AFS	LCV	CON	NTU	NFIB	COC	ACU	NTLC	CHC
1998	90	88	100	77	74	16	7	35	0	6	0
1997	90	—	100	—	15	28	—	30	0	—	—

National Journal Ratings

	1997 LIB	—	1997 CONS	1998 LIB	—	1998 CONS
Economic	93%	—	0%	79%	—	0%
Social	85%	—	0%	89%	—	10%
Foreign	94%	—	3%	98%	—	0%

Key Votes of the 105th Congress

1. Clinton Budget Deal	N	5. Puerto Rico Sthood. Ref.	Y	9. Cut $ for B-2 Bombers	Y
2. Education IRAs	N	6. End Highway Set-asides	N	10. Human Rights in China	Y
3. Req. 2/3 to Raise Taxes	N	7. School Prayer Amend.	N	11. Withdraw Bosnia Troops	N
4. Fast-track Trade	N	8. Ovrd. Part. Birth Veto	N	12. End Cuban TV-Marti	Y

Election Results

1998 general	Xavier Becerra (D)	58,230	(81%)	($361,813)
	Patricia Parker (R)	13,441	(19%)	
1998 primary	Xavier Becerra (D)	38,925	(80%)	
	Patricia Parker (R)	9,856	(20%)	
1996 general	Xavier Becerra (D)	58,283	(72%)	($223,890)
	Patricia Parker (R)	15,078	(19%)	
	Others	7,229	(9%)	

THIRTY-FIRST DISTRICT

Anyone interested in the future of America and today's immigrants should drive straight east from downtown Los Angeles on the San Bernardino Freeway, through the string of suburbs that grew up in the 1940s and 1950s. These were once white middle-class communities, with grids of stucco houses above the dry river beds; they were filled with Midwest and East Coast migrants who discovered California during World War II and decided to stay, or who learned of its golden reputation from the new medium of television in the days before smog became part of the language. The atmosphere then was Midwestern, cheerful, busy, with children always underfoot. Over the next generation or so, there has been almost a complete population turnover here, but some things remain the same. Mexican-Americans have spread out from their original East Los Angeles base to become majorities in blue-collar suburbs like El Monte, Baldwin Park and Azusa, all with many more residents than in their Anglo days. Monterey Park and San Gabriel have sprouted Chinese and Korean shopping centers and storefronts, and have become the American center for Taiwanese. In next-door Alhambra, the Asians have made the local high school "an academic giant," reports *The Washington Post*'s Jay Mathews. "Its name is . . . at the top of lists of the leading science and mathematics programs in American education." But these are not mono-ethnic communities, and East Los Angeles has not become a slum. There are no empty storefronts, but busy shops with new signs; no housing riddled with vandalism and neglect, but newly painted homes with carefully tended gardens; these are neighborhoods still filled with children whose parents believe in traditional values. When blacks and Latinos were rioting in South Central and Hollywood, East Los Angeles and the San Gabriel Valley were quiet and orderly. Sometime in the 21st Century, novels will be written describing the by-then vanished atmosphere of these immigrant suburbs, that will surely tell more about the human condition than TV series about the "horrors" of growing up rich in Beverly Hills.

In the 1950s, these were Democratic areas—New Dealers bringing their voting habits west—but the new Latinos and Asians seem up for grabs. They voted strongly for Ronald Reagan in 1984 and were only 5% to 8% more Democratic than average in the 1988 and 1990 elections; in 1992, Latinos moved toward the Democrats, but Asians, dismayed by responses to the riot, trended Republican. In 1996 Latinos, less because of Proposition 209's prohibition of racial quotas than because of Republican immigration and welfare laws removing aid to legal immigrants and because the Republican campaign ads suggested Latinos were more interested in welfare than work, moved heavily toward the Democrats; Asians moved a bit in the same direction. The movement continued, and voter registration increased among Latinos in 1998. Though the 31st is unlikely to go Republican, the battle for these voters and others like them in California could be crucial in the 2000 presidential race. The potential for movement is great. Democrats hope to replicate the showing among Latinos of California Governor Gray Davis, who carried them 78%–14%; Republicans hope to replicate the showing of Texas Governor George W. Bush, who lost Hispanics in his state by only 51%–49%.

The 31st Congressional District covers much of the territory from the LA city limit east through East Los Angeles, Alhambra, San Gabriel, Rosemead, El Monte, Baldwin Park and Azusa; it brushes, but excludes, higher-income suburbs up against the San Gabriel Mountains. It was 58.2% Hispanic in 1990, and 23% Asian, with one of the lowest percentages of non-Hispanic whites (18%) in California, and is solidly Democratic.

The congressman from the 31st is Matthew Martinez, a Democrat elected in 1982. The owner of an upholstery company, he was elected to the Monterey Park City Council in 1974 and became mayor in 1976. He was tapped in 1980 to run for the Assembly by Howard Berman, who was running for speaker, and the Berman-Waxman machine superintended Martinez's campaign to a win. Their ally, Phil Burton, in the 1982 redistricting plan forestalled a Republican-Hispanic alliance by creating two Hispanic districts in the eastern Los Angeles Basin. One was for Martinez, and after a desultory campaign he beat incumbent Republican and former John Birch Society organizer John Rousselot 54%–46%.

By 1993, Martinez was a subcommittee chairman and the lead sponsor of the Clinton Administration's National Community Service Bill and the reauthorizations of the Older Americans Act and the Juvenile Justice Act and Delinquency Prevention Act, all signed into law. He also passed a Native American Languages Act to record these languages before they die out. His pet cause is regulating private security guards, omnipresent in southern California and on occasion the perpetrators of horrible crimes; he had a bill to require states to set minimum training and screening standards and another to open up FBI crime records to state regulators. Martinez sought to exempt the Census from the English-official-language bill and opposed the Republican bill prohibiting the Labor Department from advising pension fund managers to make investments based on social criteria. With Democrats in the minority, he has sought to mediate between Republicans and the White House on education, Head Start and other human-service programs. In 1998 he showed political savvy by delivering belated support for fast track in exchange for a Clinton Administration agreement to approve the long-delayed $1.4 billion Long Beach freeway extension in the district. In 1999, he plans to push teacher training and class size reduction as the Education and the Workforce Committee reauthorizes the Elementary and Secondary Education Act.

Martinez's hold on the seat does not seem solid: he won only 43% and 55% in primaries in 1992 and 1994, though he has not had party opposition since then.

Cook's Call. *Safe.* With the exception of two recent contested primaries, Martinez has had smooth sailing here. Martinez should not have any redistricting concerns, at least so far as the general election is concerned, but given his past primary difficulties, how the lines are drawn and how much his district is reconstituted could be important in his Democratic primary.

The People: Pop. 1990: 572,758; 9.5% age 65 + ; 48.4% White, 1.6% Black, 22.9% Asian, 0.4% Amer. Indian, 26.7% Other; 58.2% Hispanic Origin. Households: 55.5% married couple families; 34.1% married couple fams. w. children; 35.5% college educ.; median household income: $30,667; per capita income: $10,264; median house value: $180,100; median gross rent: $563.

1996 Presidential Vote		
Clinton (D)	70,288	(65%)
Dole (R)	27,736	(26%)
Perot (I)	7,043	(7%)
Others	2,468	(2%)

1992 Presidential Vote		
Clinton (D)	59,616	(51%)
Bush (R)	37,250	(32%)
Perot (I)	18,449	(16%)

Rep. Matthew G. Martinez (D)

Elected 1982; b. Feb. 14, 1929, Walsenburg, CO; home, Monterey Park; Los Angeles Trade Tech. Col., 1950; Catholic; married (Elvira).

Military Career: Marine Corps, 1947–50.

Elected Office: Monterey Park City Cncl., 1974–80; Monterey Park Mayor, 1976, 1980; CA Assembly, 1980–82.

Professional Career: Businessman, 1950–70; Monterey Park Planning Cmte., 1971–74.

DC Office: 2269 RHOB 20515, 202-225-5464; Fax: 202-225-5467; Web site: www.house.gov/martinez.

District Office: Alhambra, 818-458-4524.

Committees: *Education & the Workforce* (4th of 22 D): Postsecondary Education, Training & Life-Long Learning (RMM); Workforce Protections. *International Relations* (6th of 23 D): Asia & the Pacific; Western Hemisphere.

Group Ratings

	ADA	ACLU	AFS	LCV	CON	NTU	NFIB	COC	ACU	NTLC	CHC
1998	75	87	100	62	48	10	14	41	29	19	8
1997	70	—	75	—	58	26	—	60	22	—	—

National Journal Ratings

	1997 LIB	—	1997 CONS	1998 LIB	—	1998 CONS
Economic	70%	—	30%	79%	—	0%
Social	73%	—	24%	77%	—	22%
Foreign	72%	—	26%	70%	—	29%

Key Votes of the 105th Congress

1. Clinton Budget Deal	N	5. Puerto Rico Sthood. Ref.	Y	9. Cut $ for B-2 Bombers	N
2. Education IRAs	N	6. End Highway Set-asides	N	10. Human Rights in China	Y
3. Req. 2/3 to Raise Taxes	N	7. School Prayer Amend.	N	11. Withdraw Bosnia Troops	*
4. Fast-track Trade	*	8. Ovrd. Part. Birth Veto	Y	12. End Cuban TV-Marti	Y

Election Results

1998 general	Matthew G. Martinez (D)	61,173	(70%)	($124,583)
	Frank Moreno (R)	19,786	(23%)	
	Krista Lieberg-Wong	4,377	(5%)	
	Others	2,024	(2%)	
1998 primary	Matthew G. Martinez (D)	42,162	(67%)	
	Frank Moreno (R)	14,584	(23%)	
	Krista Lieberg-Wong	4,308	(7%)	
	Others	2,058	(3%)	
1996 general	Matthew G. Martinez (D)	69,285	(67%)	($83,015)
	John V. Flores (R)	28,705	(28%)	($39,439)
	Michael B. Everling (Lib)	4,700	(5%)	

THIRTY-SECOND DISTRICT

One of the myths of the Los Angeles riots of 1992 and 1965 is that black Angelenos live in conditions of isolation and poverty. Some do, but in levels of income and in degree of residential integration with non-blacks, Los Angeles blacks rank among the top in the United States, and its black-owned businesses have the highest revenues of any city in the nation. Californians have historically shown less prejudice against blacks than most Americans, and job opportunities in Los Angeles—up to and including the office of mayor for 20 years—have been plenteous for blacks. This is apparent in the hills just west of Crenshaw, an Art Deco neighborhood built in the 1920s and 1930s in vacant flat land southwest of downtown LA. Here, in Baldwin Hills, where on clear days you can see the towers of downtown and the snow-capped San Gabriel Mountains beyond, is a high-income black neighborhood, one of the strongest in the country, and where Magic Johnson has built his successful multiplex theaters. To the north and west are other comfortable black-majority neighborhoods; on the flatlands south of Beverly Hills and the Fairfax district not far away, many affluent blacks are buying houses.

This part of Los Angeles is the heart of the 32d Congressional District, which runs approximately from the Harbor Freeway west past Baldwin Hills to Culver City almost to the ocean, and south from Olympic Boulevard past the Santa Monica Freeway down almost to Inglewood and the LAX airport. The 32d vies with the Maryland 4th and New York 6th for the largest numbers of affluent blacks in any district. Politically there has been no serious trend toward Republicans. Indeed, affluent, well-educated blacks seem if anything to be culturally more liberal than low-income black voters who may have closer ties to church and tradition. Many have profited on the way up from some form of government intervention—a student loan, a public sector job, an affirmative action program—and many hold public sector jobs.

262 CALIFORNIA

The congressman from the 32d District is Julian Dixon, a Democrat elected in 1978. Dixon went to college and law school in southern California after serving in the Army. He practiced law in Los Angeles and was elected in 1972 to the Assembly, where he was a Henry Waxman ally; in 1978, when incumbent Yvonne Burke ran for attorney general, Dixon was elected to the House. Intelligent, politically savvy, a team player with high ethics and a discreet style, he got good positions and tough assignments. In 1984 he chaired the rules committee at the Democratic National Convention and dealt effectively with Jesse Jackson's challenges to the rules. As House ethics committee chairman, he supervised the task of passing judgment on Speaker Jim Wright. This was as high-pressure an assignment as could be imagined: Republicans led by Newt Gingrich were furiously pursuing Wright, Democrats were nervously defending him. Dixon proceeded deliberately, maintaining bipartisanship on the committee and let the evidence come out that prompted Wright to resign in June 1989.

Early on Dixon got a seat on the Appropriations Committee and rose quickly to become chairman of the District of Columbia Subcommittee—a thankless post. At first he sought to help then-Mayor Marion Barry obtain plenty of funds for the large District government. But when Barry returned to office in 1995 after serving time in prison, Dixon, now in the minority, became a harsh critic and called for privatization of some services and federalization of others, like corrections; but he sometimes opposed Republican plans as over-stringent. In 1999, he became ranking Democrat on the Select Intelligence Committee, which shuns publicity but quietly battles the Appropriations and Armed Services committees for influence on national-security policy.

On Appropriations, Dixon has been attentive to local issues. On the Defense Subcommittee he worked for Los Angeles area defense contractors, and sponsored a loan guarantee act for small businesses hurt by military base closings and defense contract terminations. His voting record, very liberal for the most part, is more moderate on foreign issues. He stepped in with "dire emergency" supplementals for Los Angeles after the riot in 1992 and the Northridge earthquake in 1994. He has been the chief funder of Los Angeles's Metro subway, an often troubled venture; when Waxman objected to building on the Wilshire Boulevard corridor, one of the most densely populated parts of the Los Angeles Basin, because of methane gas deposits, Dixon steered the route farther into his own district, though unaccountably, no route is planned to nearby LAX; later, Latinos feuded with him on directing more transit funds to the Eastside. He has pushed for more funding of INS and Border Patrol guards and for reimbursing states for the costs of jailing illegal aliens. He got a $400 million federal loan for the Alameda Corridor, an underground connection between Los Angeles's huge port and the major east-west rail lines.

Dixon has been regularly re-elected without significant opposition. He has declined calls in 1992 to run for the Los Angeles Board of Supervisors (instead his predecessor Yvonne Burke was elected) and in 1997 to run for mayor of Los Angeles.

Cook's Call. *Safe.* There are few members in either party with safer constituencies than Dixon. Don't expect a competitive race here.

The People: Pop. 1990: 572,630; 12.1% age 65 +; 32.2% White, 40.4% Black, 7.9% Asian, 0.4% Amer. Indian, 19.2% Other; 29.6% Hispanic Origin. Households: 36.5% married couple families; 18.2% married couple fams. w. children; 50% college educ.; median household income: $28,332; per capita income: $14,520; median house value: $234,800; median gross rent: $529.

1996 Presidential Vote		
Clinton (D)	130,394	(81%)
Dole (R)	19,348	(12%)
Perot (I)	5,764	(4%)
Others	4,854	(3%)

1992 Presidential Vote		
Clinton (D)	147,623	(77%)
Bush (R)	23,956	(13%)
Perot (I)	17,561	(9%)

Rep. Julian C. Dixon (D)

Elected 1978; b. Aug. 8, 1934, Washington, D.C.; home, Culver City; CA St. U., Los Angeles, B.S. 1962, Southwestern U., LL.B. 1967; Episcopalian; married (Betty).

Military Career: Army, 1957–60.

Elected Office: CA Assembly, 1972–78.

Professional Career: Practicing atty., 1960–73.

DC Office: 2252 RHOB 20515, 202-225-7084; Fax: 202-225-4091.

District Office: Los Angeles, 323-678-5424.

Committees: *Appropriations* (5th of 27 D): Commerce, Justice, State & the Judiciary; Defense; District of Columbia. *Permanent Select Committee on Intelligence* (RMM of 7 D).

Group Ratings

	ADA	ACLU	AFS	LCV	CON	NTU	NFIB	COC	ACU	NTLC	CHC
1998	100	93	100	92	46	9	7	29	0	3	0
1997	90	—	100	—	11	14	—	30	12	—	—

National Journal Ratings

	1997 LIB — 1997 CONS		1998 LIB — 1998 CONS	
Economic	82%	— 15%	79%	— 0%
Social	85%	— 0%	93%	— 0%
Foreign	69%	— 28%	81%	— 18%

Key Votes of the 105th Congress

1. Clinton Budget Deal	N	5. Puerto Rico Sthood. Ref.	Y	9. Cut $ for B-2 Bombers	N
2. Education IRAs	N	6. End Highway Set-asides	N	10. Human Rights in China	Y
3. Req. 2/3 to Raise Taxes	*	7. School Prayer Amend.	N	11. Withdraw Bosnia Troops	Y
4. Fast-track Trade	N	8. Ovrd. Part. Birth Veto	N	12. End Cuban TV-Marti	Y

Election Results

1998 general	Julian C. Dixon (D)	112,253	(87%)	($79,412)
	Laurence Ardito (R)	14,622	(11%)	
	Others	2,617	(2%)	
1998 primary	Julian C. Dixon (D)	76,661	(86%)	
	Laurence Ardito (R)	10,347	(12%)	
	Others	2,451	(3%)	
1996 general	Julian C. Dixon (D)	124,712	(82%)	($97,495)
	Laurence Ardito (R)	18,768	(12%)	
	Neal Donnoer (Lib)	6,390	(4%)	

THIRTY-THIRD DISTRICT

A block from Los Angeles's "modern architecture" City Hall, whose 452-foot white tower—long the symbol of the city but now dwarfed by 60- and 70-story postmodern marble slabs and pink cylinders a few blocks away—is the huge retail shopping street of Broadway. The sidewalks are thronged, the signs are mostly in Spanish, the merchandise is often strewn on tables: this could be Mexico City or Lima, Latin America transplanted a block from a gleaming symbol of Yankee propriety and gaudy emblems of North American prosperity. Broadway, now somewhat in decline from its retail heyday, is neither the geographical nor spiritual center of Los

Angeles's Latino communities and it is by no means their only major shopping area. But it is an emblem of the entry-level Latino neighborhoods of the nation's second largest city, the places where many immigrants, not only from Mexico but from Central and South America, come to find a cheap place to live—doubling and tripling up with other families and single newcomers, close enough to drive an old car to work in factories and warehouses that fill so much of the acreage south and east of downtown.

Broadway and many of these entry-level neighborhoods make up much of the 33d Congressional District. It includes downtown and MacArthur Park, once beautiful and now a drug dealers' hangout, and Pico Union, where many Central and South American immigrants make their first homes. It also includes the giant factories south of downtown along the Southern Pacific Railroad and Santa Ana Freeway and it takes in part of East Los Angeles. To the south it includes the garment factories of Vernon and the 1940s working-class suburbs—Huntington Park, with its vibrant shopping strip on Atlantic Boulevard, South Gate, Bell and Bell Gardens, Commerce, Maywood and Cudahy—which are now heavily Latino. The 33d District in 1990 was 83% Hispanic, by far the highest figure of any California district, and the only one that can be called monocultural. Politically, these neighborhoods are more Democratic than when they were white but less Democratic than when they were black. The lag in voter participation is growing smaller: in 1990 the registered votes were 48% Latino, in 1997 62%—the highest percentage in California. This is mostly a non-voting constituency: Newcomers may not be citizens, many residents are children, workers at two jobs may be too busy to register, and Latinos tend to see private sector work, not public sector protections, as their way up in the world. As a result, in 1996 only 14,445 people voted in the 33d District's Democratic primary and only 58,000 in the general election, compared to 215,000 in the Westside 29th District and 103,000, and 75,000, 103,000 and 138,000 in the Hispanic-majority 26th, 30th, 31st and 34th Districts. The 33d District looks like a late 20th Century version of a rotten borough, Old-Sarum-on-the-Pacific-Rim, but it is a district where people work hard and play by the American rules, with high rates of family stability and low levels of people who count on Aid to Families with Dependent Children—the home of people rising into the middle class.

The 33d District's congresswoman is Lucille Roybal-Allard, first elected in 1992, the daughter of 30-year Congressman Edward Roybal, whose roots were in New Mexico, not Mexico, and was the first Latino elected to the Los Angeles city council. Roybal-Allard was elected to the Assembly in 1986 and there sponsored bills on sexual assault, domestic violence and such causes as requiring more environmental impact reports for toxic waste incinerators (a move prompted by protests against a proposed incinerator in Vernon.) She entered the 1992 House race even before her father announced his retirement, and she won 75% in the Democratic primary and 63% in the general election. She says she is "dedicated to community empowerment at all levels," and compiled an almost perfectly liberal voting record. She has urged that the Los Angeles Metro line be extended in her Eastside area. From 1997–99 she was co-chair of the California Democratic delegation. In 1999, she won two important assignments: membership on the Appropriations Committee, where her subcommittee work will deal heavily with immigration issues, and chairmanship of the Hispanic Caucus, where she plans to take a more visible role to challenge what she calls the "East coast mentality in Washington."

Back home, Roybal-Allard sponsors health fairs and workshops on home-buying and U.S. citizenship. She has been re-elected without difficulty.

Cook's Call. *Safe.* This seat was almost Roybal-Allard's birthright. Before she won it in 1992, her father represented most of this area for 30 years. Districts don't come any safer than this.

The People: Pop. 1990: 570,893; 6.9% age 65 + ; 35.8% White, 4.3% Black, 4.3% Asian, 0.6% Amer. Indian, 55% Other; 83.2% Hispanic Origin. Households: 48.2% married couple families; 35.5% married couple fams. w. children; 17.3% college educ.; median household income: $20,708; per capita income: $6,997; median house value: $156,200; median gross rent: $447.

1996 Presidential Vote

Clinton (D)	48,636	(80%)
Dole (R)	8,538	(14%)
Perot (I)	2,691	(4%)
Others	1,146	(2%)

1992 Presidential Vote

Clinton (D)	33,642	(63%)
Bush (R)	12,607	(23%)
Perot (I)	7,149	(13%)

Rep. Lucille Roybal-Allard (D)

Elected 1992; b. June 12, 1941, Los Angeles; home, Los Angeles; CA St. U. at Los Angeles, B.A. 1965; Catholic; married (Edward Allard).

Elected Office: CA Assembly, 1986–92.

DC Office: 2435 RHOB 20515, 202-225-1766; Fax: 202-226-0350; Web site: www.house.gov/roybal-allard.

District Office: Los Angeles, 213-628-9230.

Committees: *Appropriations* (23d of 27 D): Commerce, Justice, State & the Judiciary; Treasury, Postal Service & General Government.

Group Ratings

	ADA	ACLU	AFS	LCV	CON	NTU	NFIB	COC	ACU	NTLC	CHC
1998	100	86	100	92	72	15	7	29	0	3	0
1997	100	—	100	—	27	22	—	30	8	—	—

National Journal Ratings

	1997 LIB — 1997 CONS			1998 LIB — 1998 CONS		
Economic	85%	—	10%	79%	—	0%
Social	85%	—	0%	87%	—	13%
Foreign	88%	—	10%	96%	—	2%

Key Votes of the 105th Congress

1. Clinton Budget Deal	N	5. Puerto Rico Sthood. Ref.	Y	9. Cut $ for B-2 Bombers	Y
2. Education IRAs	N	6. End Highway Set-asides	N	10. Human Rights in China	Y
3. Req. 2/3 to Raise Taxes	N	7. School Prayer Amend.	N	11. Withdraw Bosnia Troops	N
4. Fast-track Trade	N	8. Ovrd. Part. Birth Veto	N	12. End Cuban TV-Marti	Y

Election Results

1998 general	Lucille Roybal-Allard (D)	43,310	(87%)	($143,600)
	Wayne Miller (R)	6,364	(13%)	
1998 primary	Lucille Roybal-Allard (D)	30,194	(86%)	
	Wayne Miller (R)	4,899	(14%)	
1996 general	Lucille Roybal-Allard (D)	47,478	(82%)	($144,278)
	John P. Leonard (R)	8,147	(14%)	($6,208)
	Howard Johnson (Lib)	2,203	(4%)	

THIRTY-FOURTH DISTRICT

One of the great population surges in the United States is the upward social and outward geographic movement of the hundreds of thousands of immigrants to the Los Angeles Basin, from crowded entry-level neighborhoods out on freeways to the suburbs. It is visible east and southeast of Los Angeles, in suburbs that over a generation have changed from solidly white Anglo to largely Latino. Many have made their way up working in small smokeless factories— these have made Los Angeles the nation's number-one manufacturing metro area—along rail- road tracks and near river beds, beneath roaring freeways and on grid streets near stucco garden apartment blocks and in small business offices and stores. These people came to the United States not to re-create their Third World environment but to rise above it, and they see this country not as a land of oppression but of opportunity. Their values resemble those of working- class Americans of the pre-Vietnam 1960s: pro-family and respectful of traditional personal morals (LA-area Latinos have lower than average divorce rates and are more likely to raise children in two-parent families), patriotic and pro-military (they are more likely than average to volunteer for military service), working for economic advancement (Latino males have the highest work force participation of any measured group and the incomes of U.S.-born Los Angeles County Latino incomes are at the county average.)

Vast numbers of these new residents—whose rise through hard work has gone shamefully unnoticed in a mainstream press—live in the 34th Congressional District. The percentage of Latino voters rose from 43% in 1990 to 51% in 1997—the second highest of any California district. This is a swath of suburban Los Angeles County anchored by three suburbs. On the northwest is Montebello, a working-class suburb just beyond East Los Angeles, now heavily Latino. To the east is La Puente, a center of the light-manufacturing economy that created hundreds of thousands of jobs in the Los Angeles Basin in the 1980s, and in which increasing numbers of small businesses are owned by Asians, Latinos and blacks. To the south is Whit- tier—a town founded by Midwestern Quakers, where Richard Nixon grew up and went to Whittier College—and Norwalk, farther south astride the Santa Ana Freeway. The 34th Dis- trict's population in 1990 was 62% Hispanic, the second highest figure in California.

The congresswoman from the 34th District is freshman Grace Flores Napolitano, a Democrat elected in 1998. Napolitano grew up in the Lower Rio Grande Valley of Texas, married at 18, and had five children and moved to California by the time she was 23. She worked as a secretary at Ford Motor Company for 22 years. After her first husband died, she married Frank Napolitano and in 1980 they started a pizzeria business. She served on the city council in Norwalk from 1986–92, and served one term as mayor, becoming the first Latina to hold either position. In 1992 she was elected to the California Assembly from a district that covered 60% of this congressional district. She chaired the International Trade and Development Committee and got a 100% rating from the AFL-CIO.

Term-limited from another race for the Assembly, she got the opportunity to run for Congress when 16-year incumbent Esteban Torres announced three days before the filing deadline that he was retiring. Torres's surprise move seemed designed to promote the election of Jamie Casso, his son-in-law and chief of staff, who immediately announced his candidacy. But Napolitano was not deterred. She convinced the state AFL-CIO to vote an "open endorsement" although the executive board had backed Casso, and Torres had been a senior United Auto Workers official under Walter Reuther in the 1960s.

Napolitano and Casso waged a fierce campaign. She criticized his failure to live in the district; he criticized her $180,000 loan to her campaign at an unusual 18% interest rate, which he said left her little reason to repay the principal. Torres was featured prominently in Casso's campaign literature and appearances. Napolitano had the financial backing of national women's organization, including EMILY's List, plus the benefit of higher name-identification. There were few differences between the two candidates on major issues, except that Napolitano signed a U.S. Term Limits pledge to serve only three terms. Napolitano won by 618 votes, 51%–49% among Democratic voters. Her victory in November was routine. But the bitter primary left the possibility of a serious Democratic challenger in 2000.

On arrival in Washington, Napolitano fared poorly with committee assignments, receiving Resources and Small Business.

Cook's Call. *Safe.* Napolitano seamlessly took over this suburban Los Angeles County seat from eight-term Congressman Esteban Torres in 1998 and should be able to hold this seat for as long as she wants.

The People: Pop. 1990: 573,456; 9.3% age 65 + ; 56.9% White, 2% Black, 9.3% Asian, 0.6% Amer. Indian, 31.2% Other; 61.7% Hispanic Origin. Households: 60.2% married couple families; 35.4% married couple fams. w. children; 36.7% college educ.; median household income: $36,224; per capita income: $12,012; median house value: $174,400; median gross rent: $582.

1996 Presidential Vote				1992 Presidential Vote			
Clinton (D)		91,603	(64%)	Clinton (D)		78,889	(51%)
Dole (R)		39,277	(27%)	Bush (R)		48,181	(31%)
Perot (I)		10,396	(7%)	Perot (I)		27,944	(18%)
Others		2,930	(2%)				

Rep. Grace Napolitano (D)

Elected 1998; b. Dec. 4, 1936, Brownsville, TX; home, Norwalk; Catholic; married (Frank).

Elected Office: Norwalk City Cncl., 1986–92; Norwalk Mayor, 1989–92; CA Assembly, 1992–98.

Professional Career: Employee, Ford Motor Co., 1970–1992.

DC Office: 1407 LHOB 20515, 202-225-5256; Fax: 202-225-5256; Web site: www.house.gov/napolitano.

District Office: Montebello, 323-728-0112.

Committees: *Resources* (20th of 24 D): Forests & Forest Health; Water & Power. *Small Business* (14th of 17 D): Tax, Finance & Exports.

Group Ratings and Key Votes: Newly Elected

Election Results

1998 general	Grace Napolitano (D)	76,471	(68%)	($618,421)
	Ed Perez (R)	32,321	(29%)	($15,819)
	Others	4,283	(4%)	
1998 primary	Grace Napolitano (D)	30,134	(37%)	
	James M. Casso (D)	29,516	(37%)	
	Ed Perez (R)	18,037	(22%)	
	Others	2,962	(4%)	
1996 general	Esteban E. Torres (D)	94,730	(68%)	($207,398)
	David G. Nunez (R)	36,852	(27%)	($11,171)
	Others	6,858	(5%)	

THIRTY-FIFTH DISTRICT

In April 1992, the corner of Florence and Normandie in South Central Los Angeles became for a moment the most famous intersection in America: the epicenter of the Los Angeles riot. This was not, as was commonly said, simply an outpouring of anger at the Rodney King verdict; if it were, there would have been rioting everywhere in the Los Angeles Basin, since few citizens agreed with the Simi Valley jury. It was rather, like the urban riots of the 1960s, a collection of criminal acts suddenly committed by people in the expectation that so many others would be doing the same thing that all would have impunity; and even so, the rioting this time clearly would have been stopped but for the dereliction of Los Angeles Police Department Chief Daryl Gates, who had prepared no contingency plan and spent hours on his way to and from a political fundraiser as the rioting broke out. The definitive story is told by the brilliant reporter Lou Cannon in his book *Official Negligence*. The rioting stopped after some 36 hours once Governor Pete Wilson and President George Bush announced that 25,000 troops were being ordered to Los Angeles, eliminating potential rioters' expectation that they would not be punished.

The commitment of troops was much greater than in the big 1960s riots, and this riot ended far sooner. But in the meantime great damage was done. Most visible was the harm to individuals: black and Latino onlookers were killed and injured by rioters and law enforcement personnel; a white truck driver was viciously beaten at Florence and Normandie; Asian and Latino storeowners were singled out by black and Central American rioters and treated as oppressors, when in fact they were providing goods and services which no one else—for reasons later painfully apparent—was willing to provide. Even more harmful may be the damage to Los Angeles's civic culture. For in the riot's aftermath it was widely repeated that blacks were helpless victims of racism and poverty, when in fact most LA area blacks have moved upward economically and out geographically from the old South Central and Watts ghettos in the 27 years since the 1965 riot, and African-Americans are well-represented in LA and California politics.

Among those commenting most vociferously on the riot was Congresswoman Maxine Waters, whose 35th Congressional District includes Florence and Normandie as well as much of the South Central and Watts corridors which formed California's first black-majority district 30 years ago. The 35th also includes the majority-black middle-income suburb of Inglewood, home of the Los Angeles Forum; Hawthorne, birthplace of the Beach Boys; and Gardena, with California's first licensed poker clubs at which some of the most cutthroat games in the country are played. Latinos have been moving for two decades into South Central and Watts, and in 1990 the 35th District was 43% Hispanic. Another 42% of its residents and a solid majority of its voters were black, and Waters seems to regard her constituency as essentially black, whatever the Census numbers. Waters came to California in 1961, worked in a garment factory and raised two children, got a sociology degree at California State University in Los Angeles and became an assistant Head Start teacher after the Watts riot of 1965. In 1976 she won a seat in the California Assembly. There she supported Willie Brown and passed minority, women's and tenants' rights laws, limits on police strip searches and a provision mandating divestiture of state pension funds from South Africa. She became a Democratic National Committeewoman in 1980 and Phil Burton consulted her on 1982 redistricting. When Augustus Hawkins retired in 1990 after 28 years in the House and 28 years in the California Assembly, Waters was the obvious choice for the seat and won it easily. She had already made a national name for herself as a vocal supporter of Jesse Jackson in 1984 and 1988 and was probably the most prominent freshman in the 102d Congress.

Waters brings to her work a fury that is almost palpable, and an insistence that she will assert herself regardless of protocol, partly perhaps a result of anger but also a weapon she uses shrewdly and cynically to get both publicity and results. "I don't have time to be polite," she says, beginning her career by getting herself included in a post-riot White House meeting with George Bush after learning of the meeting on a morning TV show. Sometimes she over-blusters: She missed the chance to demand a roll call for one of her amendments, which was beaten, because she was outside the House participating in a press conference.

The Los Angeles riot was occasion for both Waters' best and worst moments. She flew home immediately and roused the Department of Water and Power to restore water to the riot area, and was effective in gaining provisions to the post-riot emergency act that eventually made it through Congress and was signed into law. But she also over-emotionally claimed,

"Los Angeles is under siege . . . the violence could spill over to many other cities in this country." Which, of course, it didn't. And she made statements suggesting that the rioters were morally justified, that somehow street thugs were speaking for the black community instead of destroying it.

Waters comes from a poor background and believes with fervor in federal aid for the poor and for racial preferences to help blacks overcome years of slavery, segregation and discrimination; she favors drastic reductions in defense spending and was one of six members who voted against supporting the Gulf war once it started, asking how urban gang members could be expected to stop fighting when America's own leaders were waging battles.

But she has also produced specific legislation, including the Community Reinvestment Act racial quotas, a "Youth Fair Chance Act" with job training and counseling for unemployed young men 17 to 30, and a Center for Women Veterans within the Department of Veterans Affairs. She has worked for many set-asides for women and minorities. She was an early but unillusioned supporter of Bill Clinton for the Democratic nomination, and traveled often with Clinton. At the 1992 Democratic convention, insisting that "this is the last time I support an all-white anything," she said she would support the Democratic ticket in 2000 only if it has a black or a woman on it. Her husband, a former professional football player and Mercedes Benz salesman, became President Clinton's Ambassador to the Bahamas. Even so, she voted against the crime bill rule in August 1994 when the administration desperately needed votes, because she said she "could not vote for a crime bill that sweepingly expands the death penalty to include sixty new crimes." In 1994 she protested Clinton's cutoff of Haitian refugees and was arrested at the gates of the White House. In 1996, again opposing Clinton, she denounced his signing of the welfare bill and called for a vast expansion of government spending and powers.

Waters finds unconventional ways to make news. In 1997, she pushed the theory, supported in a story in the *San Jose Mercury News* (which later cast doubt on it) but by little else, that the CIA had worked with Nicaraguan Contras to import crack cocaine into South Central Los Angeles. "When you understand the totality of the CIA connection, you can't help but conclude they were either directly involved in the trafficking or they turned a blind eye," she said. As chairman of the Congressional Black Caucus, she promised a "real war on drugs," an 800 line for complaints of discrimination and a business development initiative for minorities. Waters gained her greatest national publicity during the Judiciary Committee's Clinton impeachment inquiry, where she assailed "trumped-up charges"; said that Clinton was "guilty of being a populist leader who opened up government and access to the poor, to minorities, to women, and to the working class"; and termed Kenneth Starr "guilty" of "raw, unmasked, unbridled hatred and meanness that drives this impeachment coup d'etat." Republicans not surprisingly tended to ignore her, some Democrats felt uncomfortable with her unvarnished defense, and Chairman Henry Hyde visibly sighed when she would, out of order, seek recognition to make another protest. But she helped to delegitimize the impeachment proceedings for many Americans, black and non-black, and she was undoubtedly acting with an eye to seeking advantage from the Clinton Administration later.

Waters has been re-elected without difficulty.

Cook's Call. *Safe.* When Waters mounted her outspoken defense of President Clinton during the 1998 impeachment battle, she could do so with a clean political conscience, knowing that it would cause her no problems at home. This is solid Democratic territory.

The People: Pop. 1990: 570,697; 7.8% age 65 +; 21.4% White, 42.7% Black, 6% Asian, 0.3% Amer. Indian, 29.6% Other; 42.2% Hispanic Origin. Households: 40.6% married couple families; 25.5% married couple fams. w. children; 35.3% college educ.; median household income: $25,481; per capita income: $9,761; median house value: $150,500; median gross rent: $518.

1996 Presidential Vote		
Clinton (D)	92,773	(84%)
Dole (R)	12,063	(11%)
Perot (I)	4,129	(4%)
Others	1,727	(2%)

1992 Presidential Vote		
Clinton (D)	100,432	(77%)
Bush (R)	16,685	(13%)
Perot (I)	11,950	(9%)

Rep. Maxine Waters (D)

Elected 1990; b. Aug. 15, 1938, St. Louis, MO; home, Los Angeles; CA St. U. at Los Angeles, B.A. 1970; Christian; married (Sidney Williams).

Elected Office: CA Assembly, 1976–90.

Professional Career: Head Start teacher, 1966; Dpty., City Councilman David Cunningham, 1973–76.

DC Office: 2344 RHOB 20515, 202-225-2201; Fax: 202-225-7854; Web site: www.house.gov/waters.

District Office: Los Angeles, 323-757-8900.

Committees: *Chief Deputy Minority Whip. Banking & Financial Services* (5th of 27 D): Capital Markets, Securities & Government Sponsored Enterprises; Domestic & International Monetary Policy (RMM). *Judiciary* (10th of 16 D): The Constitution.

Group Ratings

	ADA	ACLU	AFS	LCV	CON	NTU	NFIB	COC	ACU	NTLC	CHC
1998	80	93	100	69	79	19	0	21	0	6	0
1997	95	—	100	—	7	21	—	20	8	—	—

National Journal Ratings

	1997 LIB — 1997 CONS			1998 LIB — 1998 CONS		
Economic	75%	—	22%	79%	—	0%
Social	85%	—	0%	93%	—	0%
Foreign	90%	—	10%	90%	—	5%

Key Votes of the 105th Congress

1. Clinton Budget Deal	N	5. Puerto Rico Sthood. Ref.	Y	9. Cut $ for B-2 Bombers	N
2. Education IRAs	N	6. End Highway Set-asides	*	10. Human Rights in China	Y
3. Req. 2/3 to Raise Taxes	N	7. School Prayer Amend.	N	11. Withdraw Bosnia Troops	N
4. Fast-track Trade	N	8. Ovrd. Part. Birth Veto	N	12. End Cuban TV-Marti	Y

Election Results

1998 general	Maxine Waters (D)	78,732	(89%)	($177,584)
	Gordon Michael Mego (AI)	9,413	(11%)	
1998 primary	Maxine Waters (D)	48,892	(86%)	
	Gordon Michael Mego (AI)	7,677	(14%)	
1996 general	Maxine Waters (D)	92,762	(86%)	($235,851)
	Eric Carlson (R)	13,116	(12%)	($2,428)
	Others	2,610	(2%)	

THIRTY-SIXTH DISTRICT

For many southern Californians, there is no better place to be than the beach. It is not a perfect environment: In the morning there may be mists, the winter air is damp and clammy, even in summer the weather can be chilly, the water is never very warm and is sometimes polluted. But for many this is echt-California, and in this democratic polity, there is a beach to suit the taste of just about everyone. The funkiest of all is Venice, with its beach houses jammed together and the long-stagnant canals dug by a developer in 1904, with the boardwalk where skateboarding got its start. Right behind is Marina Del Rey, with sleek modern apartment complexes and expensive yacht moorings. Just south, across an inlet, is LAX, the only major American airport commonly known by its three-letter code; the swooping arches of its theme building, intended in 1961 to symbolize the jet era, are now an historic landmark, like Disneyland's Tomorrowland or the *Jetsons*, an antique version of a surpassed future. To the south is El Segundo, named for Socal's second oil refinery. Next are Manhattan Beach, one of the favorites three decades ago of the Beach Boys who grew up a couple of miles inland in Hawthorne, and tiny Hermosa Beach, with tightly packed frame houses originally the homes of elderly retirees; the current attitude here is suggested by Councilman Robert (Burgie) Benz, who sponsors a beer drinking and vomiting fest every Fourth of July. To the south are the flower-planted rises of Redondo Beach and Torrance, whose vast inland expanse is filled with the American headquarters of Japanese companies. The South Bay beaches end where the Palos Verdes Peninsula looms high over the ocean, seismically active and socioeconomically upscale. Just to the east is the harbor town of San Pedro, once working-class, but moving up as well, overlooking LA's eerily modern containerport.

All this beach territory, from Venice south to San Pedro (both of which technically are part of Los Angeles, though the area in between is not), makes up the 36th Congressional District. Historically Republican, this area is still leery of taxes, but culturally it is libertarian—against restrictions or even aspersions on its various lifestyles. When those issues are paramount, the Beach area trends Democratic, as in the mid-1970s and mid-1990s; when economics and defense are more important, it is solidly Republican, as in the 1960s and early-1980s. For this has been one of America's leading defense and aerospace areas, where Howard Hughes built planes half a century ago and where so much of the 1980s defense buildup took place.

The congressman from the 36th is Republican Steven Kuykendall, a Republican elected in 1998. Kuykendall grew up in Oklahoma and graduated from college there; he joined the Marine Corps and served two tours of duty in Vietnam; he moved to California, got a business degree and worked as a real estate broker and for firms specializing in commercial and residential real estate financing. He was elected to the Rancho Palos Verdes City Council, and served a term as mayor; in 1994 he was elected to the California Assembly, where he served as a Republican whip. In 1998, facing his third and final term because of California's term limits, he jumped at the chance to run for Congress when Democratic incumbent Jane Harman announced in January she was running for governor. Harman had a record that was economically conservative and culturally liberal, helping the area's defense industries and spending more than $1 million in each of her three campaigns.

In the 1998 campaign Kuykendall faced competition from two women, very different from each other but both political outsiders. His chief primary opponent was Susan Brooks, a prochoice, pro-gun, pro-Contract with America Republican who was the nominee against Harman in 1994 and 1996, losing 48%–47.6% the first time and then 52%–44% as Bill Clinton carried the district 47%–41%. This time Brooks ran an aggressive primary campaign and promised to serve only three terms. Kuykendall ran as the experienced legislator and argued he had a better chance of winning in November. In the all-party primary, he ran ahead of Brooks 37%–29% among Republican votes; Rudy Svorinich, a liberal Los Angeles councilman endorsed by Mayor Richard Riordan, got 26% of the party votes.

Altogether Republican candidates got 61% in the primary, Democrats only 34%—a misleading indicator for November, perhaps because there was no serious contest for the Democratic nomination. She was Janice Hahn, a public affairs manager for Southern California Edison who was known best as the daughter of longtime Los Angeles County Supervisor Kenneth Hahn, who died in 1997 after leaving office in 1992; supervisors represent one-fifth of the county, nearly 2 million people today, and Hahn represented much of this area, as well as the black neighborhoods of South Central, where he is fondly remembered even years after leaving office. Kuykendall talked about his record against crime and efforts to improve schools; Hahn insisted she was a moderate and attacked Kuykendall for taking money from tobacco companies. Both were well financed.. The strong reaction of southern Californians against the impeachment inquiry and the surge of support for Democratic governor candidate Gray Davis may have helped Hahn. Kuykendall won, but by only 49%–47%.

In the House, Republican leaders saw that Kuykendall got a seat on the Armed Services Committee, where he can help local defense industries. But given his narrow margin, he may have serious competition again in 2000.

Cook's Call. *Competitive.* This is a swing district and Republicans have every reason to be nervous about it, particularly since that, as of early 1999, they had less than encouraging poll numbers on the West Coast. Kuykendall, a moderate with good political sense, is as well positioned as a Republican could be in this district. Democrats surely will target this district and if Kuykendall isn't careful, or if Democrats run a particularly good candidate in a favorable year for their party, this is a possible turnover.

The People: Pop. 1990: 573,665; 0.1% rural; 10.9% age 65 + ; 77.9% White, 3.1% Black, 12.5% Asian, 0.5% Amer. Indian, 6% Other; 14.7% Hispanic Origin. Households: 48.5% married couple families; 20.6% married couple fams. w. children; 67.2% college educ.; median household income: $48,522; per capita income: $25,534; median house value: $371,100; median gross rent: $758.

1996 Presidential Vote		1992 Presidential Vote	
Clinton (D)	109,244 (47%)	Clinton (D)	111,014 (41%)
Dole (R)	96,872 (41%)	Bush (R)	95,646 (35%)
Perot (I)	18,510 (8%)	Perot (I)	62,458 (23%)
Others	9,375 (4%)		

Rep. Steven T. Kuykendall (R)

Elected 1998; b. Jan. 27, 1947, Oklahoma City, OK; home, Rancho Palos Verdes; OK City U., B.S. 1968, San Diego St. U., M.B.A. 1974; Presbyterian; married (Jan).

Military Career: Marine Corps, 1968–73 (Vietnam).

Elected Office: Rancho Palos Verdes City Council, 1992–94; Mayor, Rancho Palos Verdes, 1994; CA Assembly, 1994–98.

Professional Career: Banker, 1973–94; Real Estate Broker.

DC Office: 512 CHOB 20515, 202-225-8220; Fax: 202-225-7119; Web site: www.house.gov/kuykendall.

District Office: Torrance, 310-543-1098.

Committees: *Armed Services* (31st of 32 R): Military Personnel; Military Research & Development; Special Oversight Panel on the Merchant Marine (Vice Chmn.). *Science* (21st of 25 R): Space & Aeronautics; Technology. *Transportation & Infrastructure* (39th of 41 R): Aviation; Water Resources & Environment.

Group Ratings and Key Votes: Newly Elected

Election Results

1998 general	Steven T. Kuykendall (R)	88,843	(49%)	($785,085)
	Janice Hahn (D)	84,624	(47%)	($692,076)
	Others	8,239	(5%)	
1998 primary	Janice Hahn (D)	35,732	(30%)	
	Steven T. Kuykendall (R)	26,950	(23%)	
	Susan Brooks (R)	20,789	(17%)	
	Rudy Svorinich Jr. (R)	19,221	(16%)	
	Others	16,431	(14%)	
1996 general	Jane Harman (D)	117,752	(52%)	($1,579,938)
	Susan Brooks (R)	98,538	(44%)	($486,564)
	Others	8,169	(4%)	

THIRTY-SEVENTH DISTRICT

Los Angeles is the creation not of nature but of man: there is little natural water supply here and no natural port, little in the way of natural resources except for oil which turned out not to be enough for California; it is a place for people who plan big. Nearly a century ago, Los Angeles's city fathers decided to build a port where the usually-dry Los Angeles River debouches into the ocean; in 1906 they annexed an eight-mile-long, four-block-wide corridor of land (christened Harbor Gateway in 1984) and the harbor areas of Wilmington and San Pedro, and converted a shallow bay with a few marshy inlets into the biggest port on the West Coast, ahead of the splendid natural harbors of San Francisco and San Diego. Inland, along the rail lines that hug the river bed, heavy and light industry developed—oil tank farms and big factories, small job shops and warehouses. Interspersed were subdivisions; to the north was Watts, the epicenter of the 1965 riot and also the site of one of the strangest made-by-man structures in this made-by-man city, the 107-foot-high Watts Tower, built from 1921–54 by Simon Rodia out of all manner of salvaged material.

The 37th Congressional District takes in a swath of low-income industrial suburbs from Watts and the new Century Freeway, the most expensive road in history (with pavement buckling in Downey because it was built too close to the water table), south to Wilmington and the port. Here are Compton and Lynwood, which switched from all-white to all-black in the 1960s and in the 1980s became heavily Latino; here also is Carson, with recent subdivisions amid freeway interchanges and tank farms; and Wilmington, facing a spankingly modern port. Overall, the 37th District's population in 1990 was 34% black and 44.5% Hispanic, but 55% of registered voters were black and only 16% Latino in 1996.

The congresswoman from the 37th District is Juanita Millender-McDonald, chosen in a March 1996 special election. She was born in Alabama, raised a family in Carson, and earned a bachelor's degree in 1979, at 40; she worked as a teacher and editor/writer for the Los Angeles Unified School District and was manuscript editor for *IMAGES*, a state textbook designed for young women to enhance self-esteem and explore non-traditional careers. She later became director of gender equity programs for the district and was appointed to the National Commission on Teaching and America's Future, chaired by North Carolina Governor Jim Hunt. In April 1990 she was elected to the Carson City Council. In 1992 she ran for the Assembly and beat an incumbent in the primary. She chaired the Insurance and the Revenue and Taxation Committees for a year each and sponsored the bill qualifying for designation as a National Transportation Artery the Alameda Corridor—a proposed $1.8 billion combination of underground rail lines and freeway lanes connecting the port to major east-west rail lines and freeways. She favored homeless voting rights and domestic violence insurance, sponsored tax incentives for business and workmen's compensation reform and opposed the motorcycle helmet law. She supported the state takeover of Lincoln Park Cemetery in Carson amid talk of embezzlement.

Her opening to run for Congress came in December 1995, when two-term Congressman

Walter Tucker was convicted of extortion and tax fraud as mayor of Compton and sentenced to 27 months in federal prison. A special election was set for March 26, 1996, the same day as the regular primary, and since no Republicans ran, it determined the winner. Already running for months was Assemblyman Willard Murray, chief of staff to former (1981–93) Congressman Mervyn Dymally. But with help from EMILY's List Millender-McDonald raised much more money. Murray may have started off best known, but he had problems: He favored building a prison for Compton, which voters turned down 87%–13%, and he favored the state takeover of Compton's public schools. Millender-McDonald won the nine-candidate special with 27% to 20% for Murray. Among other candidates were Compton Mayor Omar Bradley, Lynwood Mayor Paul Richards and Tucker's wife Robin. The regular primary on the same ballot was a bit closer because of the presence of another candidate, Susan Carrillo, who got 15%. Millender-McDonald won this contest by just 24%–21%. The victory was a bit bittersweet, since Millender-McDonald's son Keith McDonald on the same day lost the primary for her Assembly seat to her predecessor Richard Floyd.

In the House, the Democratic leadership gave Millender-McDonald a seat on the Transportation and Infrastructure Committee, where she made the Alameda Corridor her first priority. She also made national news on another issue, when after the *San Jose Mercury News* charged that the CIA aided Nicaraguan Contras in smuggling crack cocaine to Los Angeles, she invited CIA Director John Deutsch to a public meeting in her district in November 1996. Astonishingly, he accepted, and was denounced by dozens of speakers and booed and interrupted with obscenities by many others despite Millender-McDonald's pleas for order. Other causes included a cervical cancer awareness resolution, the Faces of AIDS stamp, expanding the bone marrow registry for minorities and people of mixed ancestry and preventing minors from buying alcohol on the Internet. She is vice-chair of the Women's Caucus. She was a prime organizer during the September 1998 impeachment of a delegation of House Democratic women to visit First Lady Hillary Rodham Clinton to "refocus the political dialogue on issues that really matter." She backs the Chinese-government-owned China Ocean Shipping Company's bid to build a container terminal at the former Long Beach Naval Air Station. "I'm trying to help the people of Long Beach and restore the economic wherewithal that had been part of the military presence there," she explained.

In the June 1998 primary her Republican opponent urged voters to vote for her Democratic opponent Amen Rahh; Millender-McDonald won 61%–25% then and 85%–15% in November.

Cook's Call. *Safe.* This district is pretty barren territory for any Republican. Millender-McDonald has not had a close race since her special election win in 1996. She is very safe.

The People: Pop. 1990: 572,191; 7.3% age 65 + ; 26.2% White, 33.8% Black, 10.8% Asian, 0.5% Amer. Indian, 28.9% Other; 44.5% Hispanic Origin. Households: 49.7% married couple families; 32.7% married couple fams. w. children; 32.4% college educ.; median household income: $27,127; per capita income: $9,104; median house value: $142,800; median gross rent: $489.

1996 Presidential Vote			1992 Presidential Vote		
Clinton (D)	88,877	(81%)	Clinton (D)	90,523	(73%)
Dole (R)	13,874	(13%)	Bush (R)	19,299	(16%)
Perot (I)	4,798	(4%)	Perot (I)	12,905	(10%)

Rep. Juanita Millender-McDonald (D)

Elected March 1996; b. Sept. 7, 1938, Birmingham, AL; home, Carson; U. of Redlands, B.S. 1979, CA St. U., M.Ed. 1981; Baptist; married (James).

Elected Office: Carson City Cncl., 1990–92; Carson Mayor Pro-Tem, 1991–92; CA Assembly, 1993–96.

Professional Career: Teacher & Schl. Admin., 1981–90.

DC Office: 419 CHOB 20515, 202-225-7924; Fax: 202-225-7926; Web site: www.house.gov/millender-mcdonald.

District Office: Torrance, 310-538-1190.

Committees: *Small Business* (2d of 17 D): Empowerment (RMM). *Transportation & Infrastructure* (20th of 34 D): Aviation; Ground Transportation.

Group Ratings

	ADA	ACLU	AFS	LCV	CON	NTU	NFIB	COC	ACU	NTLC	CHC
1998	95	94	100	69	55	14	9	31	4	5	0
1997	90	—	100	—	11	18	—	30	12	—	—

National Journal Ratings

	1997 LIB — 1997 CONS		1998 LIB — 1998 CONS	
Economic	85%	— 10%	79%	— 0%
Social	85%	— 0%	93%	— 0%
Foreign	72%	— 26%	90%	— 5%

Key Votes of the 105th Congress

1. Clinton Budget Deal	N	5. Puerto Rico Sthood. Ref.	Y	9. Cut $ for B-2 Bombers	N
2. Education IRAs	N	6. End Highway Set-asides	N	10. Human Rights in China	Y
3. Req. 2/3 to Raise Taxes	N	7. School Prayer Amend.	N	11. Withdraw Bosnia Troops	N
4. Fast-track Trade	N	8. Ovrd. Part. Birth Veto	N	12. End Cuban TV-Marti	Y

Election Results

1998 general	Juanita Millender-McDonald (D)	70,026	(85%)	($205,223)
	Saul E. Lamkster (R)	12,301	(15%)	
1998 primary	Juanita Millender-McDonald (D)	31,995	(61%)	
	Amen Rahh (D)	13,357	(25%)	
	Saul E. Lamkster (R)	7,467	(14%)	
1996 general	Juanita Millender-McDonald (D)	87,247	(85%)	($113,081)
	Michael E. Voetee (R)	15,399	(15%)	($42,972)

THIRTY-EIGHTH DISTRICT

Long Beach, founded in 1888, with 434,000 people in 1990, would be a major metropolis anywhere but in Los Angeles County where it seems just the largest of many suburbs. But it has an identity of its own. Started as a beach resort, it soon became a port when Los Angeles civic leaders decided that if their town were to be a world-class city it must have a world-class harbor; nature not having provided one, they built it where the Los Angeles River merges into the ocean at Long Beach. By 1909, Los Angeles had annexed the harbor towns of San Pedro and Wilmington next to Long Beach; over the next decades the two cities persuaded the government to dredge channels and build a breakwater and turning basins. Long Beach was developing other businesses as well: it sprouted oil derricks in the 1920s and briefly became one of the nation's big oil producers; it was the site of major aircraft plants in the 1940s and after. By the 1980s, the Los Angeles-Long Beach port was the nation's largest, the fastest-growing major cargo center in the world, with huge steel-gray container ships pulling quietly up to enormous automated loading facilities—a 21st Century contrast to the rotting docks of New York and San Francisco. Long Beach even acquired the *Queen Mary*, which became its biggest tourist attraction, plus, until it was sawed apart and taken to a museum in Oregon, Howard Hughes's *Spruce Goose*, the huge cargo seaplane that was piloted just once across this harbor in 1946. Long Beach's downtown, once full of rundown 1920s buildings and pawn shops, now has an array of glittering 1980s high-rises and the area has become a favorite for Japanese and Asian companies' American headquarters. Long Beach was hurt by closure of its naval shipyard and cutbacks at the huge McDonnell Douglas plant before the company was purchased by Boeing, but small businesses have grown. Long Beach's school system was the first in the state to make school uniforms mandatory; three-quarters of students go on to college.

The 38th Congressional District includes most of Long Beach—the beachfront, harbor and airport. It extends north and inland to include the post-World War II suburbs of Lakewood, Paramount, Bellflower and Downey. This is middle-class country, but not monochromatic; the 38th excludes some black areas of Long Beach but in 1990 was 25% Hispanic and 9% Asian. It has a large Cambodian community, a core of union members, and a large gay population. Defense contracts and bases remain important in Long Beach, and Downey has the Boeing (formerly Rockwell) plant that built the space shuttle. Politically, the 38th is marginal, voting for the winners in all recent presidential and gubernatorial elections.

The congressman from the 38th is Steve Horn, a Republican first elected in 1992. Horn grew up on a farm near San Juan Bautista, California, and worked his way through Stanford and Harvard. He was an aide to President Eisenhower's labor secretary in the 1950s and to California Senator Thomas Kuchel in the 1960s. He was in Everett Dirksen's office helping draft the Voting Rights Act in those stirring days of 1965, and he served on the U.S. Commission on Civil Rights from 1969–82. Horn is also a political scientist and has written books on parliamentary procedures, the Senate Appropriations Committee and campaign finance. He worked at the Brookings Institution, was a dean at American University in Washington, and then from 1970–88 was president of Cal State at Long Beach, leaving the job when he first ran for Congress. That race was in a district that stretched from Long Beach far into Orange County, and he ran third in the primary, with 20%, behind the more conservative and flamboyant Dana Rohrabacher. In 1992 he ran in the newly drawn 38th. In the primary, the pro-choice Horn beat anti-abortion former Assemblyman Dennis Brown by 105 votes out of 45,000 cast, 29.8%–29.5%. In the general, he faced Long Beach Councilman Evan Anderson Braude, step-son of 22-year incumbent and Public Works Chairman Glenn Anderson. Horn accepted no PAC money and ran his campaign out of his son's apartment, sending out 50,000 15-minute videos to voters. He won 49%–43%.

In the House, Horn has a mostly moderate voting record, but has been downright liberal on cultural issues (for abortion rights, gun control, gays in the military). He opposes non-emergency health care for illegal aliens, sought more Border Patrol guards and favors a tamperproof Social Security card. He obtained flood control projects for the Los Angeles and Rio Hondo Rivers and he worked to save the C-17 transport plane assembled at Long Beach. He plays a key role in obtaining funds for the Alameda Corridor, the $1.8 billion underground rail and freeway connection from the port to the main east-west links.

In 1995 Horn became chairman of the Subcommittee on Government Management, Information and Technology. Working often in bipartisan fashion with Democrat Carolyn Maloney, he produced a Debt Collection Act, aimed at getting back some $2 billion the government is owed but is not able to collect. He took the lead in raising concerns about the capacity of government agencies to meet the Y2K problem. Like an old-time professor, he took to grading government agencies on how they're handling it: He gave the administration on overall grade of "F" in May 1998, and later said the White House needs more management expertise to tackle problems such as the Y2K. Horn noted the agencies' progress every three months, and by February 1999 the administration received a "C+," its first passing grade. In 1998 Horn offered legislation, which won a majority but needed 2/3 to pass, to permit election officials in five states with large immigrant populations to verify the citizenship of voter-registration applicants.

Horn's usually moderate record and taste for bipartisanship has sparked opposition from several quarters. Rick Dykema, an aide to Representative Dana Rohrabacher, started to challenge him from the right in 1996, but was talked out of running by Tom DeLay and Bill Paxon. The leftward trend in southern California has narrowed Horn's margin, from 58%–37% in 1994 to 53%–43% in 1996 and 53%–44% in 1998. Horn may be on the Democrats' target list again in 2000, before district lines change; his 1998 opponent, Peter Matthews, backed a $6.15 minimum wage, and announced after Horn voted for impeachment that he would run again. Even if Horn wins, he may be in more trouble in 2002, since Democrats will likely control the redistricting process.

Cook's Call. *Competitive.* As a Republican in a Democratic-tilting district, Horn has his work cut out for him. Horn, who has only been a second or third tier target in the last two elections, may well find himself near the top of the Democratic list in 2000. But his moderate, sometimes liberal voting record and aversion to some of the more conservative elements of his party has helped him survive here. Should he step down, this will be a very difficult district for Republicans to hold.

The People: Pop. 1990: 572,676; 12.5% age 65+; 69.3% White, 7.7% Black, 9.1% Asian, 0.7% Amer. Indian, 13.1% Other; 25.3% Hispanic Origin. Households: 45.1% married couple families; 21.7% married couple fams. w. children; 52.5% college educ.; median household income: $34,364; per capita income: $16,497; median house value: $224,700; median gross rent: $582.

1996 Presidential Vote		
Clinton (D)	91,673	(53%)
Dole (R)	62,053	(36%)
Perot (I)	14,310	(8%)
Others	5,472	(3%)

1992 Presidential Vote		
Clinton (D)	88,728	(44%)
Bush (R)	66,647	(33%)
Perot (I)	43,596	(22%)

Rep. Steve Horn (R)

Elected 1992; b. May 31, 1931, San Juan Bautista; home, Long Beach; Stanford U., A.B. 1953, Harvard U., M.P.A. 1955, Stanford U., Ph.D. 1958; Protestant; married (Nini).

Military Career: Army Reserves, Strategic Intelligence, 1954–62.

Professional Career: A.A., U.S. Labor Secy. James Mitchell, 1959–60; Legis. Asst., U.S. Sen. Thomas Kuchel, 1960–66; Sr. Fellow, Brookings Inst., 1966–69; Dean, Grad. Studies, American U., 1969–70; Vice Chmn./Mbr., U.S. Commission on Civil Rights, 1969–82; Pres., CA St. U. at Long Beach, 1970–88; Chmn., Amer. Assn. of State Cols. & Universities, 1985–86; Prof., CA St. U. at Long Beach 1988–92.

DC Office: 2331 RHOB 20515, 202-225-6676; Fax: 202-226-1012; Web site: www.house.gov/horn.

District Office: Lakewood, 562-425-1336.

Committees: *Government Reform* (7th of 24 R): District of Columbia; Government Management, Information & Technology (Chmn.). *Transportation & Infrastructure* (10th of 41 R): Ground Transportation; Water Resources & Environment.

Group Ratings

	ADA	ACLU	AFS	LCV	CON	NTU	NFIB	COC	ACU	NTLC	CHC
1998	20	50	33	54	26	42	79	83	56	53	33
1997	50	—	38	—	76	48	—	60	44	—	—

National Journal Ratings

	1997 LIB — 1997 CONS		1998 LIB — 1998 CONS	
Economic	51%	— 48%	43%	— 56%
Social	66%	— 33%	62%	— 38%
Foreign	51%	— 46%	27%	— 68%

Key Votes of the 105th Congress

1. Clinton Budget Deal	Y	5. Puerto Rico Sthood. Ref.	N	9. Cut $ for B-2 Bombers	N
2. Education IRAs	Y	6. End Highway Set-asides	Y	10. Human Rights in China	Y
3. Req. 2/3 to Raise Taxes	Y	7. School Prayer Amend.	N	11. Withdraw Bosnia Troops	Y
4. Fast-track Trade	Y	8. Ovrd. Part. Birth Veto	N	12. End Cuban TV-Marti	N

Election Results

1998 general	Steve Horn (R)	71,386	(53%)	($238,560)
	Peter Mathews (D)	59,767	(44%)	($165,594)
	Others	3,722	(3%)	
1998 primary	Steve Horn (R)	48,462	(53%)	
	Peter Mathews (D)	32,147	(35%)	
	Margherita Underhill (R)	7,884	(9%)	
	Others	2,206	(2%)	
1996 general	Steve Horn (R)	88,136	(53%)	($470,077)
	Rick Zbur (D)	71,627	(43%)	($1,011,672)
	Others	7,882	(5%)	

THIRTY-NINTH DISTRICT

When Walt Disney began planning Disneyland in the late 1940s, he did not have to drive far from downtown Los Angeles before arriving at agricultural land. Dairy farms and orange groves covered most of southeast Los Angeles County and Orange County, which had only 216,000 people in 1950. As Disneyland opened there in 1955 and became a vast success, the area around it—a mass of flat land surrounded by mountains and sea—found itself directly in the path of the most explosively growing metropolitan area in the United States. Orange County's population rose to 703,000 in 1960, 1.4 million in 1970, 1.9 million in 1980, 2.4 million in 1990, 2.7 million in 1998—the nation's fifth largest county.

Always Republican, Orange County became a symbol of conservatism first in California and then nationally: In 1988, its 317,000-vote plurality for George Bush was the largest of any county; even in 1996, it gave Bob Dole a 119,000-vote margin. Orange County's conservatism reflected a belief in technological progress and traditional values as unyielding as the mile-square grid the county's founders imposed on most of its land, a belief in the market economics that had produced such wonders as Disneyland and the area's advanced military technologies. These faiths have been tried on occasion, in the recession and amid the defense cutbacks of the early 1990s; in December 1994, the county government declared bankruptcy because of the county treasurer's sloppy investment and bookkeeping practices. Shortly afterwards, the Disney company shelved plans for a $2 billion resort development that would have doubled the size of Disneyland, a further blow to local officials and businesses.

The 39th Congressional District consists of an area that was mostly farmland when Disneyland was being laid out. In Los Angeles County, its largest community is Cerritos, once all dairy farms, now a suburb with a harmonious Angeleno mix: 45% Asian, 36% white Anglos, 12% Hispanic. La Mirada to the north is more upscale, as are the La Habra communities which span the LA-Orange County line. The biggest Orange County city here is Fullerton, with its own branch of Cal State University; to the southwest are Buena Park, home of the earliest theme park (c. 1940), Knott's Berry Farm, plus Cypress, Los Alamitos and Rossmoor. The 39th also pushes east of Fullerton to include, by just a few blocks, the Richard Nixon Library and birthplace in Yorba Linda.

The life of the 39th District's congressman, Ed Royce, almost precisely covers the area's growth. Like Orange County, he has long been conservative: He was in the Young Americans for Freedom at Cal State Fullerton; he worked several years as a tax and capital projects manager for a cement company. In 1982, a bunch of conservative legislators known as "the Cave Men" took him to a Black Angus restaurant—no avocado and sprout sandwiches for them—and after a few beers persuaded him to run for the state Senate. He did and won at age 31. There he sponsored the 1990 law making stalking a crime, now copied in most other states. When the legislature refused to pass his legislation allowing crime victims to object to trial delays, giving grand juries more power and ending shopping for juries, he put it on the ballot as an initiative and it passed by a wide margin in 1990. With many Vietnamese in Orange County, Royce passed a law making it easier for University of Saigon medical graduates to practice in California.

In 1992 Royce ran for the House when the 39th's incumbent made a quixotic run for the Senate. With the blessing of Orange County Republican leaders, Royce had no opposition in the decisive Republican primary and easily won the general. In the House, Royce has a conservative voting record, though a bit less so on foreign issues; he surprised some by voting against NAFTA. He worked to pass anti-stalking legislation, first in the 1994 crime bill, then as part of a defense appropriation in September 1996; in the signing ceremony Royce was shunted off to the side and was not mentioned by Bill Clinton. He continues to push a victim's rights constitutional amendment. Another amendment he has pressed without success is a ban on retroactive taxation. He is co-chairman, with Democrat David Minge, of the House "porkbusters," risking others' wrath by opposing appropriations bills with dubious projects. In 1995, for example, he targeted the Puget Sound Naval Shipyard gym ("there is a YMCA less than a mile away"); in 1996 he targeted a new Army museum and demolition of the West Side Highway in Manhattan, and in 1997 he targeted timber company subsidies. Not all his projects are successful: He worked with appropriator Frank Wolf to stop highway "demonstration projects," but the 1998 transportation bill had a record number of "earmarks." He called unsuccessfully for a breakup of the Energy Department and the abolition of the Overseas Private Investment Corporation, which guarantees foreign investments, as a form of corporate welfare. As an offshoot of porkbusters, he backed the deficit lockbox amendment, requiring spending cuts to be deposited in the Treasury; he got a rules change requiring unauthorized spending to be listed separately in appropriations bills.

Since becoming chairman of the International Relations Subcommittee on Africa in 1997, he has been backing an Africa free trade bill, co-sponsored by ranking Ways and Means Democrat Charles Rangel; it comes at a time when, after three decades of economic stagnation and dictatorship, several African countries are moving toward democracy and market economics. Despite Rangel's support, the issue has caused divisions within the Black Caucus; Jesse Jackson Jr. called for forgiving of African nations' foreign debts instead, and Maxine Waters seemed dubious. But in March 1998 Royce was able to steer the bill to passage in the House; the Senate didn't act, but he reintroduced it in February 1999. Royce was the only Republican on Clinton's 1998 visit to Africa, where he said the President should do more to promote the trade bill.

Back home Royce has been re-elected easily.

Cook's Call. *Safe.* Royce has had little problem holding onto this Orange- and Los Angeles County-based seat. He is a sure bet in 2000.

The People: Pop. 1990: 573,941; 9.8% age 65 +; 73% White, 2.5% Black, 13.8% Asian, 0.6% Amer. Indian, 10.1% Other; 22.4% Hispanic Origin. Households: 61% married couple families; 30.4% married couple fams. w. children; 58.3% college educ.; median household income: $46,196; per capita income: $18,190; median house value: $239,000; median gross rent: $682.

1996 Presidential Vote			1992 Presidential Vote		
Dole (R)	97,247	(48%)	Bush (R)	100,669	(44%)
Clinton (D)	83,246	(41%)	Clinton (D)	78,305	(34%)
Perot (I)	15,909	(8%)	Perot (I)	50,834	(22%)
Others	4,841	(2%)			

Rep. Ed Royce (R)

Elected 1992; b. Oct. 12, 1951, Los Angeles; home, Fullerton; CA St. U., Fullerton, B.A. 1977; Catholic; married (Marie).

Elected Office: CA Senate, 1982–92.

Professional Career: Tax Mgr., 1979–82.

DC Office: 1133 LHOB 20515, 202-225-4111; Fax: 202-226-0335; Web site: www.house.gov/royce.

District Office: Fullerton, 714-992-8081.

Committees: *Banking & Financial Services* (11th of 32 R): Capital Markets, Securities & Government Sponsored Enterprises; Financial Institutions & Consumer Credit. *International Relations* (13th of 26 R): Africa (Chmn.); Asia & the Pacific.

Group Ratings

	ADA	ACLU	AFS	LCV	CON	NTU	NFIB	COC	ACU	NTLC	CHC
1998	5	6	14	15	84	83	100	71	100	94	100
1997	10	—	0	—	73	85	—	80	100	—	—

National Journal Ratings

	1997 LIB — 1997 CONS			1998 LIB — 1998 CONS		
Economic	0%	—	90%	28%	—	72%
Social	0%	—	90%	25%	—	75%
Foreign	32%	—	65%	27%	—	68%

Key Votes of the 105th Congress

1. Clinton Budget Deal	Y	5. Puerto Rico Sthood. Ref.	N	9. Cut $ for B-2 Bombers	N
2. Education IRAs	Y	6. End Highway Set-asides	*	10. Human Rights in China	Y
3. Req. 2/3 to Raise Taxes	Y	7. School Prayer Amend.	Y	11. Withdraw Bosnia Troops	Y
4. Fast-track Trade	N	8. Ovrd. Part. Birth Veto	Y	12. End Cuban TV-Marti	N

Election Results

1998 general	Ed Royce (R)	97,366	(63%)	($487,001)
	Cecy R. Groom (D)	52,815	(34%)	($120,134)
	Others	5,284	(3%)	
1998 primary	Ed Royce (R)	70,528	(67%)	
	Cecy R. Groom (D)	15,151	(14%)	
	Charlie Ara (D)	14,768	(14%)	
	Others	4,156	(4%)	
1996 general	Ed Royce (R)	120,761	(63%)	($489,076)
	Bob Davis (D)	61,392	(32%)	
	Jack Dean (Lib)	10,137	(5%)	

FOURTIETH DISTRICT

Over the last two decades the great American movement west has turned back east, at least in California. As settlement reached the Pacific Coast, young families looking for affordable houses, neighborhoods and schools, where traditional values are respected, moved away from the liberation-minded and high-crime coast and toward the sunny, often hot, valleys inland. This impulse has resulted in rapid growth in the Central Valley, the repopulation of the Mother Lode country in the foothills of the Sierras and the startling growth in the eastern end of the Los Angeles Basin, around San Bernardino and Riverside, and east and north past the mountain rims into the desert. This "Inland Empire" of San Bernardino grew so robustly in the 1980s, from 1.6 to 2.6 million, that it increased from three congressional districts to five in 1992.

One of these is the 40th Congressional District, which covers most of the land area of continental America's physically largest county, San Bernardino, though its population is concentrated in just a few places. About one-third of its people live on the eastern edge of San Bernardino itself, or around Loma Linda, Redlands and Yucaipa—small towns formed by pious Midwesterners at the base of 10,000-foot mountains, now part of the expanding Los Angeles suburban strip. North of the mountains, out beyond the wind-torn El Cajon Pass in the scorching desert, with its Joshua trees and California poppies, are Victorville and Apple Valley, once tiny gas station stops on the road to Las Vegas; Roy Rogers and Dale Evans lived for years on a ranch here, with their stuffed Trigger, Buttermilk and Bullet in a nearby museum. Now vast subdivisions and the new city of Hesperia have grown up here, housing more than 150,000 people. The rest of the people of the 40th are scattered across the desert, in ghost towns and weapons testing sites, in Twentynine Palms and its Marine base. The 40th has some of the nation's hottest temperatures and some of its lowest rainfall, the lower 48 states' highest point at Mount Whitney and lowest point in Death Valley.

The congressman from the 40th is Jerry Lewis, a House member since 1978, an assemblyman for 10 years before that and a House Republican leader from 1984–92. Up to that point his career followed the usual path of House Republican leaders of earlier generations. He was an insurance agent in Redlands, a joiner in civic causes, when he was elected to the Assembly at 34. In the House, he got a seat on the Appropriations Committee, where bipartisan cooperation was the norm, enabling even minority members to confer favors on their districts. He eventually became ranking Republican on the Legislative Subcommittee, working amicably on Congress's budget with fellow Californian and friend from their Assembly days, chairman Vic Fazio. Lewis seemed to be following Robert Michel's route to the minority leadership: chairman of the Republican Research Committee in 1984, chairman of the Policy Committee in 1986, Conference chairman in 1988. But conservatives resented Lewis's cooperation with Democrats and his support of the 1990 tax increases. In 1990, California Republicans voted him out as their representative on the committee on committees. In late 1992, Dick Armey—with support from Newt Gingrich—challenged his re-election as Conference chairman and won 88–84. That narrow margin, plus Gingrich's 87–85 victory for whip in March 1989, put in place the two top leaders of the Republican majority that emerged after November 1994.

Lewis was unhappy with that setback, but has rebounded well. He has a moderately conservative voting record and supported the Contract with America except for term limits. He is a member of the "college of cardinals," as chairman of the VA-HUD Appropriations Subcommittee from 1995–99 and, after Bob Livingston left the committee and Bill Young became full committee chairman, the Defense Appropriations Subcommittee from January 1999. At VA-HUD, Lewis focused on eliminating waste and fraud in federal housing programs to assure, he said, that federal dollars actually get to people they are intended to help. Lewis also has worked for relief appropriations after the Northridge earthquake of 1994 and has promoted the Alameda Corridor rail connection between the Los Angeles-Long Beach port and main east-west rail lines. He worked for a medical facility at Loma Linda University and on behalf of a national bone marrow transplant registry; he wants to widen I-15 and I-40 in fast-growing desert areas. With his new assignment in charge of Pentagon spending, Lewis pledged to focus on readiness and quality of life issues for the troops, many of whom are based in his district.

Lewis is now chairman of the California Republican delegation and in 1997 initiated California Day, which brought the California delegation of both parties together with state and local officials. "People from Texas and New York have been laughing at us. . . . We've got the largest delegation and we're like six states," he said, but in the past the ideologically polarized California delegations had seldom worked together. He has many friends among Democrats: He saved Speaker Jim Wright from drowning in Hawaii and asked the Pope to pray for Vic Fazio's cancer-stricken daughter. Ironically, given their earlier conflicts, Lewis was a leading defender of Speaker Gingrich when some conservatives and other party leaders moved to depose him in 1997. Lewis retains a certain aggressiveness: One evening in May 1994 he saw a thief driving his 1984 Oldsmobile from a Capitol Hill parking place and chased the car down Pennsylvania Avenue until it crashed and police arrested the man two blocks away.

One issue which Lewis has fought fiercely is the Desert Protection Act sponsored by Dianne Feinstein and George Miller and passed over Lewis's opposition, but with some of his limiting amendments, in 1994. In 1995 Lewis sought to reduce the appropriation for National Park Service management to $1 and transfer authority to the Bureau of Land Management, which is less inclined to close roadways to hunters, grazers and four-wheel drive enthusiasts. But the Clinton Administration objected.

Lewis has been re-elected easily in this Republican district. But worried that redistricting could move him into heavily Hispanic and Democratic precincts of San Bernardino County, he has been tutoring himself by taking Spanish lessons, including time spent with a family in Mexico City.

Cook's Call. *Safe.* Lewis has had little difficulty holding onto this San Bernardino County district in his 11 general elections. He should have no problem in 2000.

The People: Pop. 1990: 573,939; 17.8% rural; 12.2% age 65 +; 82.1% White, 5.5% Black, 3.5% Asian, 1.6% Amer. Indian, 7.3% Other; 15.8% Hispanic Origin. Households: 59.5% married couple families; 30.3% married couple fams. w. children; 49.2% college educ.; median household income: $30,408; per capita income: $13,568; median house value: $110,300; median gross rent: $439.

1996 Presidential Vote		
Dole (R)	94,916	(49%)
Clinton (D)	73,316	(38%)
Perot (I)	20,719	(11%)
Others	5,467	(3%)

1992 Presidential Vote		
Bush (R)	86,453	(39%)
Clinton (D)	76,363	(35%)
Perot (I)	53,955	(25%)

Rep. Jerry Lewis (R)

Elected 1978; b. Oct. 21, 1934, Seattle, WA; home, Redlands; U.C.L.A., B.A. 1956; Presbyterian; married (Arlene).

Elected Office: CA Assembly, 1968–78.

Professional Career: Insurance exec., 1959–78; Field rep., U.S. Rep. Jerry Pettis, 1968.

DC Office: 2112 RHOB 20515, 202-225-5861; Fax: 202-225-6498; Web site: www.house.gov/jerrylewis.

District Office: Redlands, 909-862-6030.

Committees: *Appropriations* (3d of 34 R): Defense (Chmn.); Foreign Operations & Export Financing; The Legislative Branch. *Permanent Select Committee on Intelligence* (Vice Chmn. of 9 R): Human Intelligence, Analysis & Counterintelligence.

Group Ratings

	ADA	ACLU	AFS	LCV	CON	NTU	NFIB	COC	ACU	NTLC	CHC
1998	10	31	22	15	13	44	100	100	75	73	73
1997	20	—	25	—	38	43	—	80	63	—	—

National Journal Ratings

	1997 LIB — 1997 CONS	1998 LIB — 1998 CONS
Economic	42% — 57%	33% — 66%
Social	43% — 57%	46% — 53%
Foreign	48% — 52%	43% — 53%

Key Votes of the 105th Congress

1. Clinton Budget Deal	Y	5. Puerto Rico Sthood. Ref.	N
2. Education IRAs	Y	6. End Highway Set-asides	Y
3. Req. 2/3 to Raise Taxes	Y	7. School Prayer Amend.	N
4. Fast-track Trade	Y	8. Ovrd. Part. Birth Veto	Y

9. Cut $ for B-2 Bombers	N
10. Human Rights in China	*
11. Withdraw Bosnia Troops	N
12. End Cuban TV-Marti	N

Election Results

1998 general	Jerry Lewis (R)	97,406	(65%)	($465,377)
	Robert Conaway (D)	47,897	(32%)	($7,017)
	Others	4,822	(3%)	
1998 primary	Jerry Lewis (R)	60,371	(61%)	
	Robert Conaway (D)	25,179	(25%)	
	George Craig (R)	10,836	(11%)	
	Others	2,713	(3%)	
1996 general	Jerry Lewis (R)	98,821	(65%)	($239,448)
	Robert Conaway (D)	44,102	(29%)	($12,085)
	Others	9,338	(6%)	

FORTY-FIRST DISTRICT

One area of explosive growth in the 1980s boom years in California was in the eastern end of the Los Angeles Basin—the Inland Empire, as it is now called. Mostly orange groves a couple of decades ago, this territory now is the site of a booming economy, personal upward mobility and ethnic and cultural harmony. The economic-growth secret is small entrepreneurial businesses, usually started by people with no particular connections or advantages—often, of Asian or Latino immigrant background. California has never been a land of leisure, as stereotype would have it, but rather a place for hard work, where the amazing fertility of the soil and the amazing productivity of the people have happened with a lot of effort and a tolerant attitude toward newcomers. California hasn't always welcomed people from strange places—anti-Asian feeling expressed itself in the Chinese Exclusion Act of 1882 and the Japanese American internment camps of 1942–44—but certainly since World War II this has been one of the least prejudiced and most welcoming places on earth, which helps to explain why it has received more immigrants than any other state.

The 41st Congressional District is one place where such trends are visible. It is centered in the Inland Empire on the point where Los Angeles, San Bernardino and Orange Counties come together. In San Bernardino County it includes most of Ontario and its airport and industrial zone, plus the higher income towns of Montclair and Upland, plus Chino, site of a low-security prison, and subdivisions below the Chino Hills. In Los Angeles County it includes the old town of Pomona, now much expanded, site of the Los Angeles County Fair, and fast-growing Diamond Bar. Over the hills in Orange County it includes Yorba Linda, site (just beyond the district line) of the birthplace of Richard Nixon in 1913 (when Orange County had only 40,000 residents). This was all rapidly growing country in the 1980s, filling up with two-worker households, and it grew even in the economically troubled early 1990s. Ethnically diverse, in the 1990s its residents were 32% Hispanic and 10% Asian, believers still in traditional values, working their way up through the private sector—and leaning toward Republicans.

The congressman from the 41st, a new district created after the 1990 Census, is Gary Miller, a Republican elected in 1998. He was born in Arkansas but grew up in Whittier, and in his early 20s became a home builder, and developed planned communities. His public service began in 1988 when Los Angeles County Supervisor Pete Schabarum appointed him to the Diamond Bar Municipal Advisory Council. A year later, after Diamond Bar was incorporated, Miller was elected to the city council and served as mayor. In 1995, he was elected to the state Assembly in a special election to replace Republican Paul Horcher, who was recalled after he supported Democrat Willie Brown for Assembly speaker. In Sacramento, Miller became chairman of the Budget Committee in his freshman year. He helped pass many law-enforcement bills in addition to his work on budget and tax issues.

In November 1997 he decided to run for the House against scandal-tarred incumbent Jay Kim, who lived just two blocks away in Diamond Bar. Kim was first elected in 1992, the first Korean-American in Congress, after running an engineering firm that worked mostly on public projects. In August 1997 Kim and his wife pleaded guilty to accepting and concealing $230,000 in illegal campaign contributions between 1992 and 1996. After his conviction, Kim in an interview apologized for his mistake and said that he wished he had remained an engineer. Kim was sentenced in March 1998 to be placed under house arrest, confined to the House and his apartment in suburban Virginia, and was required to wear an electronic bracelet around his ankle for two months. As a result, he could not campaign back home in the June primary. He refused to speak to reporters and ran his bizarre campaign through surrogates. Not surprisingly, he had trouble raising campaign funds. "I'm sorry I can't be there in person," he said in a videotape message played to a neighborhood meeting of constituents. "But due to unforeseen circumstances, I must remain here in Washington." Local leaders appealed to Miller to run, and he was endorsed by Governor Pete Wilson, and the National Republican Congressional Committee, which normally endorses incumbents, remained neutral. Miller emphasized standard Republican themes—lower taxes, tougher penalties for crime, improved local education—and largely financed his own campaign.

The result was unambiguous. Two-thirds of the votes in the all-party primary were cast for Republican candidates, and Miller won 48% of Republican votes, to 26% for Kim and 22% for Orange County-based Pete Pierce. This was not a seriously contested race in November, and Miller won 53%–41%.

While he did not get any of his top three committee choices—he ended up on Budget,

Transportation, and Science—Miller should be able to produce some good work and allow local voters to forget their recent nightmare.

Cook's Call. *Probably Safe.* That Miller only won this seat by a small margin in 1998 is probably more of a sign of the tumultuous transition from Jay Kim than any real weakness on Miller's part. However, if Miller doesn't substantially improve upon his performance in this very Republican district in 2000, it would be a sure sign that he is an underperformer and Democrats might start sniffing around for an opponent.

The People: Pop. 1990: 572,529; 1.2% rural; 6.1% age 65 + ; 68.1% White, 6.8% Black, 10.1% Asian, 0.5% Amer. Indian, 14.5% Other; 31% Hispanic Origin. Households: 63.4% married couple families; 38.3% married couple fams. w. children; 54.9% college educ.; median household income: $44,607; per capita income: $16,002; median house value: $204,600; median gross rent: $591.

1996 Presidential Vote			1992 Presidential Vote		
Dole (R)	76,867	(47%)	Bush (R)	78,902	(42%)
Clinton (D)	71,393	(43%)	Clinton (D)	64,666	(35%)
Perot (I)	13,007	(8%)	Perot (I)	41,112	(22%)
Others	3,732	(2%)			

Rep. Gary Miller (R)

Elected 1998; b. Oct. 16, 1948, Huntsville, AR; home, Diamond Bar; Mt. San Antonio Col. 1971, 1988–89; Christian; married (Cathy).

Military Career: Army, 1967.

Elected Office: Diamond Bar City Cncl., 1989–95; Diamond Bar Mayor, 1992; CA Assembly, 1995–98.

Professional Career: Businessman, real estate developer, G. Miller Development Co., 1971–98.

DC Office: 1037 LHOB 20515, 202-225-3201; Fax: 202-226-1485; Web site: www.house.gov/garymiller.

District Office: Diamond Bar, 909-612-4677.

Committees: *Budget* (22d of 24 R). *Science* (22d of 25 R): Energy & Environment (Vice Chmn.); Technology. *Transportation & Infrastructure* (35th of 41 R): Aviation; Ground Transportation.

Group Ratings and Key Votes: Newly Elected

Election Results

1998 general	Gary Miller (R)	68,310	(53%)	($569,494)
	Eileen R. Ansari (D)	52,264	(41%)	($100,802)
	Others	7,840	(6%)	
1998 primary	Gary Miller (R)	26,809	(32%)	
	Eileen R. Ansari (D)	23,067	(28%)	
	Jay Kim (R)	14,174	(17%)	
	Pete Pierce (R)	12,211	(15%)	
	Others	7,029	(8%)	
1996 general	Jay Kim (R)	83,934	(58%)	($579,673)
	Richard L. Waldron (D)	47,346	(33%)	
	Richard G. Newhouse (Lib)	7,135	(5%)	
	Others	5,150	(4%)	

FORTY-SECOND DISTRICT

The gateway to the Los Angeles Basin for decades was San Bernardino, situated on flat land where the route through the twisting, windy El Cajon Pass took passengers on the Santa Fe Railroad and motorists on U.S. 66 from the hot and dusty desert to the greener, tree-lined Los Angeles basin. There were orange groves around the little railroad towns and vineyards to the west; this was an agricultural zone until World War II, when Henry J. Kaiser built the West Coast's first major steel mill between the Santa Fe and Southern Pacific lines in Fontana, just west of San Bernardino. Today, these lands have largely filled up. This Inland Empire, as it is called, may be where the smog piles up against the mountains, but it also has some of the lowest real estate prices in the Los Angeles Basin and an energetic small business economy.

The 42d Congressional District consists of most of San Bernardino and the towns running west—low-income Rialto, Fontana with many other businesses replacing the closed steel mill (the blast furnaces were dismantled in 1994 and reassembled in China), fast-growing Rancho Cucamonga. Politically this area trended Republican in the 1980s, as the cultural liberalism of California Democrats repelled family-oriented residents, but when the economy slowed and real estate prices plummeted in the early 1990s, it swung toward Bill Clinton and the Democrats.

The congressman from the 42d District is George Brown, a Democrat serving his 18th term, the oldest member of the House. He is one of only two congressmen (John Dingell is the other) who served in the House when John Kennedy was president. Brown grew up in the Imperial Valley, served in the Army in World War II, and got a degree in physics from UCLA. An engineer with a Quaker upbringing who has long cared about arms control issues, Brown worked for many years for the city of Los Angeles. In 1958 he was mayor of Monterey Park and served on the council, far to the west of his current district; in that banner Democratic year, he was elected to the California Assembly and served on the redistricting committee. Lo and behold, he got one of California's eight new House seats in 1962. He ran for the Senate in 1970 and almost beat John Tunney in the primary; if he had, he might well have won the general. Brown found a new district in 1972 in the Inland Empire, and Phil Burton redrew the lines in 1982 to help him through another decade. But Brown has not won by landslides: Against a religious fundamentalist, a small town businessman and a San Bernardino County supervisor, he won between 53% and 57% in the 1980s. His military dovishness over the years has moderated into support for local defense installations, and he has long been a supporter of space exploration. In 1990 he became chairman of the House Science Committee. There he supported both manned and unmanned space exploration, backing a new space launch vehicle and the space shuttle. He worked to restructure the national weapons laboratories and maintain the Landsat remote-sensing system. He supported federal aid for emerging technologies and development of electric vehicles and solar energy. He looked forward to working with Vice President Albert Gore, a former Science Committee member, as "heaven on earth," and he had the pleasure of seeing Science become a sought-after assignment in 1993. In July 1995, fearing the overall space budget was getting out of control, he voted against the space station. Since then, Brown has supported the station and continues to advocate a vigorous national science and technology focus in Congress.

Brown continued to have serious challenges at home in the 1990s, as the new district lines became less favorable. In 1992 he faced Dick Rutan, pilot of the *Voyager* plane which circled the earth without refueling in 1986; with gobs of PAC money, Brown outspent him 2–1 and won 51%–44%. In 1994 he was opposed by Rob Guzman, owner of a workplace training business called Templo Calvario Legalization & Education; Brown outspent him by a narrower margin and won 51%–49% in a Republican year. Then came the closest race yet, a 996-vote win in 1996 against Linda Wilde, a Superior Court Judge on leave of absence to run. But in pro-incumbent 1998 he rebounded to a 55%–40% victory over real estate developer Eliz Pirozzi, who criticized Brown's liberal voting record, office perks and congressional pay. It was Brown's biggest margin since 1978 when he won 63%–37%. There has been talk that Brown would retire, but with his larger margin of victory and the possibility of gaining a chairmanship if Democrats retake the House in 2000, he is looking favorably on seeking a 19th term. He has been under pressure from San Bernardino Democrat Joe Baca, who had served the three terms allowed in the Assembly and wanted to run for the House in 1998; instead he was elected to a four-year term in the state Senate, and so can run for the House in 2000 without losing his seat. But Brown's wife Marta, who also serves as his press secretary, has not ruled out an effort to succeed her husband. And there could easily be a serious Republican candidate in this district which has seen so many close contests.

Brown, meanwhile, plans to pursue his continuing interest in a vigorous national science and technology policy, including improved high-tech schools and internships with computer companies. He also has teamed up with neighboring Republican Jerry Lewis, a senior appropriator, to promote local projects and to reduce HUD foreclosures, which were common in the recession of the early 1990s.

Cook's Call. *Competitive.* Few members in modern history have held onto highly competitive districts with as many tough races as has Brown. But the Republican effort to drive Brown out in 1998 lacked the enthusiasm of past efforts and it would seem that they have decided to just wait the 79-year-old incumbent out. As presently configured, a sharp Republican in a good year could win the district, though it seems more likely that their best shot will be when Brown eventually steps aside.

The People: Pop. 1990: 571,595; 0.5% rural; 7.5% age 65 + ; 66.1% White, 11.1% Black, 3.9% Asian, 0.9% Amer. Indian, 18% Other; 34% Hispanic Origin. Households: 56.9% married couple families; 35.3% married couple fams. w. children; 45.7% college educ.; median household income: $33,737; per capita income: $12,308; median house value: $127,000; median gross rent: $496.

1996 Presidential Vote

Clinton (D)	76,745	(53%)
Dole (R)	51,106	(36%)
Perot (I)	12,342	(9%)
Others	3,329	(2%)

1992 Presidential Vote

Clinton (D)	76,964	(45%)
Bush (R)	54,978	(32%)
Perot (I)	35,828	(21%)

Rep. George Brown (D)

Elected 1972; b. Mar. 6, 1920, Holtville; home, San Bernardino; U.C.L.A., B.A. 1946; Protestant; married (Marta).

Military Career: Army, 1942–46 (WWII).

Elected Office: Monterey Park City Cncl., 1954–58, Monterey Park Mayor, 1955–56; CA Assembly, 1958–62; U.S. House of Reps., 1962–70.

Professional Career: City of Los Angeles, Personnel & Engineering, Mgmt. Consult. 1940–42, 1946–57.

DC Office: 2300 RHOB 20515, 202-225-6161; Fax: 202-225-8671; Web site: www.house.gov/georgebrown.

District Office: San Bernardino, 909-383-1233.

Committees: *Agriculture* (2d of 24 D): Department Operations, Oversight, Nutrition & Forestry; Risk Management, Research & Specialty Crops. *Science* (RMM of 22 D).

Group Ratings

	ADA	ACLU	AFS	LCV	CON	NTU	NFIB	COC	ACU	NTLC	CHC
1998	100	87	100	77	46	17	7	29	0	3	0
1997	100	—	100	—	20	37	—	30	4	—	—

National Journal Ratings

	1997 LIB — 1997 CONS	1998 LIB — 1998 CONS
Economic	93% — 0%	79% — 0%
Social	85% — 0%	90% — 7%
Foreign	92% — 8%	98% — 0%

Key Votes of the 105th Congress

1. Clinton Budget Deal	N	5. Puerto Rico Sthood. Ref.	Y	9. Cut $ for B-2 Bombers	Y
2. Education IRAs	N	6. End Highway Set-asides	N	10. Human Rights in China	*
3. Req. 2/3 to Raise Taxes	*	7. School Prayer Amend.	N	11. Withdraw Bosnia Troops	N
4. Fast-track Trade	N	8. Ovrd. Part. Birth Veto	N	12. End Cuban TV-Marti	Y

Election Results

1998 general	George Brown (D)	62,007	(55%)	($676,044)
	Elia Pirozzi (R)	45,328	(40%)	($585,522)
	Others	4,985	(4%)	
1998 primary	George Brown (D)	36,533	(54%)	
	Elia Pirozzi (R)	12,734	(19%)	
	Rob Guzman (R)	12,222	(18%)	
	Bernard McClay (R)	3,802	(6%)	
	Others	2,935	(4%)	
1996 general	George Brown (D)	52,166	(50%)	($722,544)
	Linda M. Wilde (R)	51,170	(50%)	($685,623)

FORTY-THIRD DISTRICT

Riverside was a sleepy town of 34,000, a couple hours' drive from Los Angeles, when Richard and Pat Nixon were married in 1940 in the gaudy Mission Inn, with its bell towers, altars, fountains, rotunda, stained-glass windows and wrought-iron grilles. Riverside was not much larger, with 46,000 people, when Ronald and Nancy Reagan spent their honeymoon at the Mission Inn a dozen years later, in 1952. Riverside then was a citrus center, a market town amid orange groves, where the local agricultural college developed among other things the navel orange. Today the Mission Inn is still doing business, but Riverside has changed completely. The city has expanded to some 240,000 people, and Riverside County, which had 105,000 people in 1940, has more than doubled since 1980, growing from 663,000 then to more than 1.4 million in 1998. Riverside County stretches east to Arizona, so some of this increase was in the desert, but much was in the Inland Empire around Riverside, where the flat Los Angeles Basin plains are interrupted by odd-shaped hills and ridges and the vegetation has an other-worldly air. There are odd by-products from such rapid development, like the dozens of 300-pound pigs that live in the river bed just outside Riverside. This was one of the boom parts of California in the 1980s, where modest-income families found new houses in inexpensive developments and small businesses expanded mightily; it was hit hard by the recession of the early 1990s but has rebounded and now is growing strongly again.

The 43d Congressional District is one of two that were formed from the old 37th District, which included most of Riverside County and was the fastest-growing congressional district in the nation in the 1980s. This was a seat without an incumbent and with great political volatility—not accidental in an area where few voters have deep roots, where neither ethnic ties nor economic security produces strong commitment to either party, and where the economy has changed so sharply. The 43d District includes all of Riverside and the towns immediately nearby; another population node just to the west, around Corona; and new subdivisions scattered around I-215 and I-15, which run south from Riverside and Corona until they join at Murietta Hot Springs, just north of the new town of Temecula.

The congressman from the 43d is Ken Calvert, a Republican elected in 1992. Calvert grew up in Corona; after college, he ran a restaurant there and in 1980 started in the commercial real estate business. In 1982, at 29, he ran for Congress in the old Riverside County district and lost a nine-candidate primary to Al McCandless by a 25%–24% margin: 868 votes kept him out of Congress for 10 years. He remained active in civic affairs and chaired the local Republican Party. In 1992 he ran for Congress in the new 43d—one of seven Republican candidates and seven Democrats—and won the primary with 28%, followed by business professor Joseph Khoury, with 21%, and Larry Arnn, president of the Claremont Institute, with 18%. His Democratic opponent was Mark Takano, an eighth grade teacher and Riverside Community College trustee with institutional support from teachers' unions and financial support from Japanese Americans. The 43d is a good example of the return of straight ticket voting in the 1990s: George Bush beat Bill Clinton by 797 votes, and Calvert beat Takano by 519 votes.

In the House, Calvert compiled a conservative voting record and served quietly in the minority on the Science and Resources Committees. But he ran into trouble back home. In November 1993 the Corona police stopped him with a convicted prostitute in his car; not much was reported about the incident but the Riverside *Press-Enterprise* brought suit to recover police records, and in April 1994 it revealed the reports. Calvert apologized and said that he was upset because his wife had divorced him the month before and his father had recently committed suicide. Also, it was reported that Calvert and his ex-wife owed $16,000 in back taxes on a nine-acre lot. He argued that the tax liability had been overlooked during his divorce, and his ex-wife defended him against charges of intentional tax avoidance. But it was, as he said, "an extremely embarrassing situation," of which his opponents rushed to take advantage. Khoury, running again, was already attacking Calvert as insufficiently conservative and chimed in on the scandal. Calvert won the primary 51%–49%, with only an 884-vote margin. Takano, running again in the general, ran an ad with the song "The Liar" and accused him of "flagrant womanizing." At a public meeting, Republican Assemblyman Ray Haynes called Takano a "nutzoid" liberal homosexual. Calvert was rated the most endangered incumbent by *Roll Call*. The Republican tide of the year showed up in the election results, with Calvert winning by a thumping 55%–38%.

In 1995, Calvert found himself, after his near-political-death experiences, chairman of the Energy and Mineral Resources Subcommittee. He produced a bill to reform the Mining Law of 1872, which allows mining companies to stake claims on federal lands for absurdly low fees; he would have required them to pay fair market value and a royalty of 3%. But Democrats and some Republicans called that "anemic," and no legislation passed. In 1996 he was easily re-elected. In 1997, Calvert took over as chairman of the Energy and Environment Subcommittee of Science. In that position, he challenged the Clinton Administration's support of the global-warming pact that was negotiated in Kyoto, Japan, where Calvert was an outspoken critic. Meanwhile, he gained stature in office, and neighboring George Brown, the senior Democrat on Science, said moving into the majority "has really made [Calvert] a new man." But in the June 1998 primary, Khoury ran a third time, citing the Clinton scandal and arguing that both Calvert and Clinton "have shown they lack the common decency, sense of right and wrong, concern for the truth and respect for women that the rest of us learned as children." Calvert responded that the Khoury mailing was "unfortunate" and that he wanted to discuss the issues. Calvert won by 56%–35% amongst Republican voters, and won by a 56%–38% margin in November.

Cook's Call. *Probably Safe.* Though this district only leans Republican, Calvert seems to have solidified himself here, even while weathering scandal along the way. Democrats will often take a look at—but generally not target—this district, since there are far more attractive and promising opportunities elsewhere in the state.

The People: Pop. 1990: 571,090; 14% rural; 8.8% age 65+; 75.8% White, 5.9% Black, 4.3% Asian, 0.9% Amer. Indian, 13.1% Other; 24.5% Hispanic Origin. Households: 62.1% married couple families; 35.1% married couple fams. w. children; 50% college educ.; median household income: $37,806; per capita income: $14,449; median house value: $153,700; median gross rent: $528.

1996 Presidential Vote

Dole (R)	82,940	(45%)
Clinton (D)	78,384	(43%)
Perot (I)	16,406	(9%)
Others	4,687	(3%)

1992 Presidential Vote

Bush (R)	76,837	(38%)
Clinton (D)	76,040	(38%)
Perot (I)	48,197	(24%)

Rep. Ken Calvert (R)

Elected 1992; b. June 8, 1953, Corona; home, Corona; San Diego St. U., B.A. 1975; Protestant; divorced.

Professional Career: Restaurant owner, 1975–80; Real estate broker, 1980–92; Chmn., Riverside Cnty. Repub. Party, 1984–88.

DC Office: 1034 LHOB 20515, 202-225-1986; Fax: 202-225-2004; Web site: www.house.gov/calvert.

District Office: Riverside, 909-784-4300.

Committees: *Agriculture* (20th of 27 R): Livestock & Horticulture. *Resources* (10th of 28 R): Water & Power. *Science* (8th of 25 R): Energy & Environment (Chmn.); Space & Aeronautics.

Group Ratings

	ADA	ACLU	AFS	LCV	CON	NTU	NFIB	COC	ACU	NTLC	CHC
1998	0	13	0	8	13	49	100	100	92	100	100
1997	0	—	13	—	42	50	—	100	92	—	—

National Journal Ratings

	1997 LIB — 1997 CONS		1998 LIB — 1998 CONS	
Economic	10% —	86%	15% —	81%
Social	18% —	81%	34% —	64%
Foreign	12% —	81%	34% —	62%

Key Votes of the 105th Congress

1. Clinton Budget Deal	Y	5. Puerto Rico Sthood. Ref.	Y	9. Cut $ for B-2 Bombers	N
2. Education IRAs	Y	6. End Highway Set-asides	Y	10. Human Rights in China	N
3. Req. 2/3 to Raise Taxes	Y	7. School Prayer Amend.	Y	11. Withdraw Bosnia Troops	Y
4. Fast-track Trade	Y	8. Ovrd. Part. Birth Veto	Y	12. End Cuban TV-Marti	N

Election Results

1998 general	Ken Calvert (R)	83,012	(56%)	($790,556)
	Mike Rayburn (D)	56,373	(38%)	
	Others	9,686	(6%)	
1998 primary	Ken Calvert (R)	36,952	(39%)	
	Mike Rayburn (D)	23,210	(25%)	
	Joe Khoury (R)	23,016	(24%)	
	R. M. (Cook) Barela (R)	6,480	(7%)	
	Others	4,935	(5%)	
1996 general	Ken Calvert (R)	97,247	(55%)	($594,665)
	Guy C. Kimbrough (D)	67,422	(38%)	($46,590)
	Others	13,055	(7%)	

FORTY-FOURTH DISTRICT

From the air two decades ago, a night flight east from Los Angeles showed the lights of 10 million persons' streets and houses and then almost perfect darkness: a vast metropolis surrounded by almost uninhabited territory. Today the sprinkled pattern of white lights has spread into the Inland Empire around Riverside and San Bernardino and is multiplying outward into the desert. The Inland Empire has filled up with instant towns like Moreno Valley, which did not exist in 1980 and had 118,000 people in 1990. The surreal landscape to the south and east, around the old towns of Perris and Hemet, is filling up with new places like Sun City and Valle Vista. Over the 10,000-foot San Jacinto Mountains, desert communities have boomed: Palm Springs, once the lone winter resort for the stars, is now one of a string of communities along Highway 111 and Frank Sinatra and Bob Hope Drives. Among rich retirees, the vogue for the coast lessened as beach cities filled up with enviro-activists and rent control crusaders; the clean, dry, roomy desert, where the days are almost always crystal clear and the sky usually blue and cloudless, became more attractive, and, with everything air-conditioned, a comfortable year-round home for more than 150,000 in 1990. That's 200,000 if you count Indio, the heavily Latino center of the Coachella Valley, which has 98% of the country's date palms and features camel races at its annual date festival. Two presidents retired to the desert, Dwight Eisenhower in Palm Desert for the winters and Gerald Ford in nearby Rancho Mirage.

The 44th Congressional District, one of two created from the fastest-growing district in the United States in the 1980s, covers all the desert in Riverside County and proceeds west to Moreno Valley, including most of the region around Perris and Hemet. It is heavily Republican in most elections, but trended Democratic and voted for Bill Clinton in 1992. Then, unlike coastal California but like inland California and most of the Rocky Mountain area, it returned toward Republicans and voted for Bob Dole in 1996.

The congresswoman from the 44th District is Mary Bono, who won the seat held until his death in January 1998 by her husband Sonny Bono, onetime showbiz celebrity, restauranteur and mayor of Palm Springs. As an entertainer, Sonny always portrayed himself as a worse singer than Cher and the object of her putdowns; he carried that image over into his political career. "I feel kind of like the black sheep in Congress, but here I am," he once said. But behind his seeming klutziness was a sense of humor that suggested a shrewdness as well. When asked to talk about illegal immigration, he replied, "What's to talk about? It's illegal"—a response that nicely anticipated the success of Proposition 187. He was on a family vacation in January 1998 when he died in a skiing accident in South Lake Tahoe, California. His widow later said that he had become addicted to prescription painkillers that impaired his judgment. His funeral—televised by CNN—was attended by Hollywood stars, his constituent former President Ford, Governor Pete Wilson and dozens of congressmen, including Speaker Newt Gingrich.

Under strong encouragement from House Republican leaders who feared that she was the only one who could avert a Republican primary bloodbath and the possible loss of the seat, Mary Bono decided to run to fill the remainder of the term. "Sonny would have encouraged me to continue his work," she said. She grew up as Mary Whitaker in South Pasadena, where she was an accomplished gymnast; she remains a fitness buff, a certified personal fitness instructor who has studied karate and Tae Kwan Do. They met when she was celebrating her college graduation at his Los Angeles restaurant in 1984 and were married two years later. Before her campaign, she had no political experience and was little known in Washington. She calls herself a "mainstream conservative," and has more-centrist views on the environment and on labor protections than did her husband. Her chief opponent in the April 1998 special election was actor Ralph Waite, best known as "Pa" Walton in *The Waltons*, who had run in the larger district in 1990. But Waite was handicapped during the brief special election campaign because he kept a commitment to play Willy Loman in *Death of a Salesman* six times a week in a New Jersey theater. The campaign's biggest controversy came when Sonny's 83-year-old mother said that her son would have opposed Mary's candidacy, preferring that she care for their children (did that win Mary Bono the anti-mother-in-law vote?). But it was no contest: Bono won 64%–29%, a bigger margin than Sonny's two victories.

But that was only the start of Mary Bono's unusual year. Bono won her husband's former seat on the Armed Services Committee to tend to the region's ample military facilities. Her chief legislative priority was passage of the bill sponsored by Sonny Bono to restore the Salton Sea, an artificial body of water in the desert created when a canal burst early in the century, which in recent decades has been shrinking, increasing the salinity of the water and the pollution from agricultural runoff. Although some Democrats objected to taking funds from other California projects, Mary Bono finally secured $13.4 million for this project. In November she beat Waite by 60%–36%.

In November 1998, as the only female Republican on the Judiciary Committee and the panel's most junior member, the non-lawyer played a highly visible role in the impeachment inquiry. "When Bono finally got the floor," reported *Newsweek*, "she was more Kathie Lee [Gifford] than Bob Barr. She joked about being a Washington outsider, sympathized with Starr's family, and asked, 'What motivates you to keep going forward?' Bono was citizen Jane—the everywoman in a room of blowhards." She voted for impeachment.

Cook's Call. *Probably Safe.* Bono picked up right where her late husband left off, winning by large margins in her special and general election contests. Though not an overwhelmingly Republican district, it does have a strong tilt to it. Bono is unlikely to face a tough race under these lines, though given the high growth rates here, the lines will change a lot in 2001.

The People: Pop. 1990: 571,843; 13.6% rural; 18.9% age 65 + ; 76.6% White, 5.1% Black, 2.8% Asian, 1.1% Amer. Indian, 14.3% Other; 27.7% Hispanic Origin. Households: 57.4% married couple families; 25.6% married couple fams. w. children; 44.8% college educ.; median household income: $29,049; per capita income: $14,417; median house value: $121,800; median gross rent: $471.

1996 Presidential Vote

Dole (R)	86,414	(45%)
Clinton (D)	85,397	(44%)
Perot (I)	17,830	(9%)
Others	3,914	(2%)

1992 Presidential Vote

Clinton (D)	87,180	(40%)
Bush (R)	76,772	(36%)
Perot (I)	50,867	(24%)

Rep. Mary Bono (R)

Elected April 1998; b. Oct. 24, 1961, Cleveland, OH; home, Palm Springs; U. of S. CA, B.F.A. 1984; Protestant; widowed.

Professional Career: Gen. Mgr., Bono restaurant, 1986–90.

DC Office: 516 CHOB 20515, 202-225-5330; Fax: 202-225-2961; Web site: www.house.gov/bono.

District Offices: Hemet, 909-658-2312; Moreno Valley, 909-485-4827; Palm Springs, 760-320-1076.

Committees: *Armed Services* (28th of 32 R): Military Personnel; Military Procurement. *Judiciary* (19th of 21 R): Commercial & Administrative Law; Courts & Intellectual Property. *Small Business* (19th of 19 R): Government Programs & Oversight (Vice Chmn.).

Group Ratings & Key Votes (Only Served Partial Term)

Election Results

1998 general	Mary Bono (R)	97,013	(60%)	($364,834)
	Ralph Waite (D)	57,697	(36%)	($34,184)
	Jim J. Meuer (NL)	6,818	(4%)	
1998 primary	Mary Bono (R)	66,504	(58%)	
	Ralph Waite (D)	34,300	(30%)	
	Anna Nevenich (D)	6,808	(6%)	
	Others	8,016	(7%)	
1998 special	Mary Bono (R)	50,841	(64%)	($423,184)
	Ralph Waite (D)	22,787	(29%)	($172,429)
	Others	5,656	(7%)	
1996 general	Sonny Bono (R)	110,643	(58%)	($458,527)
	Anita Rufus (D)	73,844	(39%)	($116,240)
	Others	7,141	(4%)	

FORTY-FIFTH DISTRICT

In the 1950s, when the Beach Boys were at Hawthorne High School, surfers would drive far down the coast to the vast expanse of Huntington Beach in Orange County to catch a wave. This was empty country then, vegetable fields and orange groves, with nary a freeway or shopping center in sight. Today the beach itself is eerily empty, with swampland across the highway where surfers' pickups are parked; but the rest of Orange County is pretty much filled in. Huntington Beach is a city of 181,000, a mixture of family subdivisions and garden apartments. To the north are Stanton and Westminster, the latter the center of the nation's biggest Vietnamese-American community. South along San Diego Freeway is Fountain Valley, the central focus of many Asian-owned high-tech businesses, an engine of Southern California growth. Near the coast is Costa Mesa, site of South Coast Plaza's luxury stores, and Newport Beach, with its large harbor and expensive mansions a block or two from the ocean.

The 45th Congressional District includes all this territory. Politically, it is heavily Republican, though Democrats have sometimes been competitive in Stanton and Westminster. The Vietnamese here are conservative, angry with America—not for going into Vietnam but for leaving it. There is confidence here in free enterprise despite the early 1990s recession and despite the Orange County bankruptcy of 1994 (the speculative excess of the county's one Democratic office-holder, Treasurer Robert Citron, but accepted by local government Republicans greedy for revenue). There is also a desire, despite the wildness of the beach and the seeming anarchy of the freeway, for discipline to supplant therapy and reassert the order that seemed so solid when Orange County was starting to grow in the 1950s.

The congressman from the 45th is Dana Rohrabacher, a Republican elected in 1988. Rohrabacher calls himself a surfer Republican, wears a Reagan baseball cap and sports an American flag surfboard. He grew up in southern California, went to college and experimented with drugs and once had a folk band called the Goldwaters. He worked on the 1976 and 1980 Reagan presidential campaigns, wrote editorials for *The Orange County Register* and served in the Reagan White House speechwriting shop. He returned to Southern California in 1988 when Long Beach-based Congressman Dan Lungren decided not to run again (Lungren went on to be elected attorney general in 1990 but lost for governor in 1998). Rohrabacher, with fund-raising help from Oliver North, won the primary with 35%, compared to 22% for an Orange County supervisor who had padded her resume, and 20% for Steve Horn, now congressman from the Long Beach-based 38th District. After redistricting, Rohrabacher tussled with Robert Dornan and won, running in this heavily Republican district while Dornan ran in the marginal 46th, where he lost in 1996. Rohrabacher persuaded the mayor of Huntington Beach not to run and won the 1992 primary with 48% of the vote against three Costa Mesa and Huntington Beach councilmen.

Rohrabacher has made waves on several issues in the House. As chairman of the Space and Aeronautics Subcommittee on Science, he worked for the single stage-to-orbit vehicle. In 1997, he cut a deal with House Democrats to give them their weather-observing satellite project—which he had publicly derided as trendy science aimed at ozone depletion and other "liberal clap-trap"— in exchange for his reusable rockets. He strongly opposes illegal immigration, which he says is "going to bankrupt America," but he draws a sharp distinction between legals and illegals: He is not against government benefits for aliens legally resident in the United States. In 1993, Rohrbacher was one of 15 congress members who asked the Clinton Administration to lift the ban on the launching from China of satellites manufactured by Los Angeles-based Hughes Electronics. But in the spring of 1998, Rohrabacher made an impassioned speech on the House floor criticizing Clinton for his 1996 decision to relax export controls on satellites to China. Rohrabacher said the administration and watchdog groups had convinced him that no technology could be transferred to the Chinese. "In retrospect, I shouldn't have believed the administration's assurances," he later said. He has been a long-time critic of China's rulers, one of those unusual issues that unites activists left and right. When Bill Clinton ordered renewed bombing of Iraq on the eve of the House's December 1998 impeachment debate, Rohrabacher called him a "shameless liar" and added, "Nobody should rule out the possibility that this military operation is politically motivated on his part." He also has strongly criticized the dispatch of U.S. troops to the former Yugoslavia.

In 1996, his opponent was 82-year-old Sally Alexander; he said he would not challenge her to his usual surfing contest, but she went out surfing anyway. Rohrabacher won 61%–33%. In 1997 Orange County District Attorney Michael Capizzi, a Republican, prosecuted Rhonda Carmony—Rohrabacher's surfing partner, 1996 campaign manager, then-fiance and current wife—for falsifying election documents on behalf of a Democratic decoy candidate in a 1995 Assembly special election won by Rohrabacher ally Scott Baugh. Carmony pleaded guilty to two felony charges related to election fraud, which were immediately reduced to misdemeanors. She was sentenced to three years probation, 300 hours of community service and a $2,800 fine. After the December 1997 guilty plea, Rohrabacher attacked Capizzi for prosecuting the case to advance his own career. "This is a man who has grandiose ideas about himself," Rohrabacher said; Capizzi ran for state attorney general in 1998 and won only 34% of Republican votes in the primary.

In 1998 Rohrabacher had the unusual experience of a serious re-election challenge from Patricia Neal, a local real-estate agent and former president of the California Association of Realtors. For the first time in Rohrabacher's career, organized labor actively opposed him, believing he might be defeated. "Dana does not have any other verbiage except 'pinko, communist, liberal, tax-and-spend left,' " Neal said. She also criticized him for avoiding the draft during the Vietnam war years. Rohrabacher conceded, "I respect those guys who went a lot more than I respect myself for showing that X-ray" of a high school hip injury to win his deferment. Neal spent more than $200,000 of her own money and outspent the incumbent. But in a pro-incumbent year in this Republican district, he won 59%–37%.

Former Congressman Bob Dornan has threatened to primary Rohrabacher in 2000. Their feud goes back to the 1991 redistricting, when the two narrowly avoided a primary after Dornan agreed to run in the 46th District, and flared up when Rohrabacher refused to endorse Dornan's 1998 challenge to Loretta Sanchez.

Cook's Call. *Probably Safe.* It's hard to see how Rohrabacher will have a tough general election in 2000. This district could be changed drastically in 2001 as it is one of the fastest growing areas of the state.

The People: Pop. 1990: 570,991; 10.7% age 65 + ; 82.1% White, 1.2% Black, 11% Asian, 0.6% Amer. Indian, 5% Other; 14.5% Hispanic Origin. Households: 51% married couple families; 23% married couple fams. w. children; 63.2% college educ.; median household income: $45,074; per capita income: $21,046; median house value: $266,300; median gross rent: $750.

1996 Presidential Vote		
Dole (R)	108,240	(50%)
Clinton (D)	81,299	(38%)
Perot (I)	17,831	(8%)
Others	6,972	(3%)

1992 Presidential Vote		
Bush (R)	105,893	(42%)
Clinton (D)	80,646	(32%)
Perot (I)	63,609	(25%)

Rep. Dana Rohrabacher (R)

Elected 1988; b. June 21, 1947, Coronado; home, Huntington Beach; Long Beach St. Col. B.A. 1969, U. of S. CA, M.A. 1975; Baptist; married (Rhonda).

Professional Career: Radio & print journalist, 1970–80; Sr. Speechwriter, Special Asst. to Pres. Reagan, 1981–88.

DC Office: 2338 RHOB 20515, 202-225-2415; Fax: 202-225-0145; Web site: www.house.gov/rohrabacher.

District Office: Huntington Beach, 714-960-6483.

Committees: *International Relations* (11th of 26 R): Asia & the Pacific; International Economic Policy & Trade. *Science* (6th of 25 R): Energy & Environment; Space & Aeronautics (Chmn.).

Group Ratings

	ADA	ACLU	AFS	LCV	CON	NTU	NFIB	COC	ACU	NTLC	CHC
1998	5	13	22	15	96	81	93	67	100	97	100
1997	10	—	13	—	29	78	—	80	92	—	—

National Journal Ratings

	1997 LIB — 1997 CONS			1998 LIB — 1998 CONS		
Economic	0%	—	90%	28%	—	70%
Social	0%	—	90%	34%	—	64%
Foreign	32%	—	65%	19%	—	75%

Key Votes of the 105th Congress

1. Clinton Budget Deal	Y	5. Puerto Rico Sthood. Ref.	N	9. Cut $ for B-2 Bombers	N
2. Education IRAs	Y	6. End Highway Set-asides	Y	10. Human Rights in China	Y
3. Req. 2/3 to Raise Taxes	Y	7. School Prayer Amend.	Y	11. Withdraw Bosnia Troops	Y
4. Fast-track Trade	N	8. Ovrd. Part. Birth Veto	Y	12. End Cuban TV-Marti	N

Election Results

1998 general	Dana Rohrabacher (R)	94,296	(59%)	($275,748)
	Patricia W. Neal (D)	60,022	(37%)	($587,903)
	Others	6,452	(4%)	
1998 primary	Dana Rohrabacher (R)	58,537	(54%)	
	Patricia W. Neal (D)	21,170	(20%)	
	Charmayne Bohman (R)	11,788	(11%)	
	Long K. Pham (R)	6,486	(6%)	
	Lud Gerber (D)	6,295	(6%)	
	Others	3,624	(3%)	
1996 general	Dana Rohrabacher (R)	125,326	(61%)	($272,859)
	Sally J. Alexander (D)	68,312	(33%)	($51,491)
	Mark F. Murphy (Lib)	8,813	(4%)	

FORTY-SIXTH DISTRICT

Orange County is the sixth most populous county in the United States, having grown steadily from 130,000 in 1940 to 216,000 in 1950, 703,000 in 1960, 1.4 million in 1970, 1.9 million in 1980, 2.4 million in 1990 and 2.7 million in 1998. It is now a community with the patina of maturity—in some places an aging community, fraying around the edges. The county is no longer capable of its early growth, when Disneyland sprung up on empty land and mile-square grids of orange groves and bean fields were transformed into one suburban subdivision, shopping center or office tower after another. A distinctive civilization was implanted here: mostly white and middle-class, confident of its traditional values and its market capitalism, proud of American principles and American military might. Orange County has been troubled in years since, transformed by its own openness to economic and ethnic change. Its economy was constantly reshaped by the inevitable upheavals of capitalism: There is no single industry here— not even defense—that is totally responsible for the prosperity of Orange County, and people here must be ready to adapt almost as deftly as the Taiwanese on the other side of the Pacific Rim. It was hit hard by the defense cutbacks and recession of the early 1990s but has been bouncing back, pitched forward by new startups and small entrepreneurial successes not anticipated by government or corporate planners. Local progress also was shaken by bankruptcy of the county government in December 1994, caused by the improvident investments of County Treasurer Robert Citron.

Just as Orange County was once transformed by newcomers from Los Angeles County and the Midwest, so Orange County is again being transformed by immigrants from the Pacific Rim, from Mexico and other parts of Latin America, and from Vietnam, Taiwan, Korea and other parts of East Asia. By 1990 the county's population was about one-quarter Hispanic and one-tenth Asian; now the figures are higher. Some of these new Orange County residents are direct migrants: Santa Ana, the county seat, is one of two major arrival points for immigrants from Mexico, and its population now more than 70% Latino. Others have moved out along the freeways, like so many southern Californians before them, working hard at jobs, commuting on freeways and living in stucco subdivisions like anyone else. There are concentrations in various places—Latinos in Santa Ana and much of Anaheim, Vietnamese in Westminster and Garden Grove—but many of these new Californians are just speckled through the county. These changes have made for some political wobble—but until the mid-1990s not very much: Asians tend to vote Republican and Latinos were registered in very small numbers. In the past couple of years, the number of Latino voters has increased sharply, even as they have switched toward the Democrats, giving central Orange County a Democratic constituency for the first time.

The 46th Congressional District is the geographic heart of Orange County. About half its people live in Santa Ana, most of them Latino, in neighborhoods full of large families and many workers. The district also includes most of Garden Grove, with many Latinos and some Vietnamese—though the main Vietnamese shopping area is across the line in Westminster—and most of Anaheim, including Disneyland and territory just across the street from Orange County landmarks—Anaheim Stadium, Knott's Berry Farm and John Wayne Airport. Overall, the population in 1990 was 49% Hispanic and 12% Asian; registered voters, only 18% Latino in 1990, were 25% Latino in 1997. Even before these population influxes, this was the least Republican part of Orange County, and from 1962–82 redistricters carefully sculpted Democratic districts here. In the mid-1980s the Vietnamese tilted the district toward the Republicans; now, increasing numbers of Latino voters are tilting it toward the Democrats.

The congresswoman from the 46th District is Loretta Sanchez, a Democrat who in 1996 upset one of the loudest voices of American conservatism, Robert Dornan. Sanchez grew up in Anaheim and graduated from Chapman University in Orange. She worked as a financial analyst, providing advice to public agencies and private businesses; she established her own firm in the early 1990s, though it had no listed phone number. For a time she and her husband lived in Palos Verdes Estates, but in 1994 she ran for the city council in Anaheim under her married name, Loretta Sanchez-Brixey, and lost. She ran for the House in the 1996 primary against three Anglo male Democrats (she had registered as a Democrat in February 1992), and won with 35% of the vote; she carried the Latino vote heavily, winning 72 of 85 precincts in Santa Ana. She ran her primary campaign out of the office of sometime business associate Howard Kieffer, who went to prison for tax fraud and was ordered to pay $213,000 in restitution in 1989—something for which Dornan attacked Sanchez later.

Sanchez's primary victory in March 1996 attracted little attention, not even from Dornan. But she shrewdly counted on increasing Latino turnout ("Latinos will vote for Latinos," she said) and also dropped Kieffer as an advisor. Sanchez must have calculated that, if she could make her candidacy plausible, she could attract contributions from many of Dornan's political enemies—Dornan had made many over a long political career that went back to 1976 and included three terms from a Westside Los Angeles district, a losing Senate race in 1982, then a move to central Orange County and victory over an incumbent Democrat in 1984, and a quixotic presidential campaign that took him far from Orange County through much of 1995 and 1996 (he won only 1,029 votes for president in the 46th District). He was a hero to many and a villain to many others for his attacks on Bill Clinton and liberals generally, a popular substitute guest host on Rush Limbaugh's talk show.

Meanwhile, Sanchez was running close to even in polls, was touted by national Democrats and was raising large sums from labor unions, Hollywood liberals, feminists and gays; she outspent Dornan by $811,000 to $742,000. The campaign was acrimonious: Dornan would not debate Sanchez because of her past association with Kieffer; Sanchez's husband tore down two Dornan signs and was prosecuted and fined $640. Dornan predicted he would win 50%–41%, as he had in 1992 against another Latino; but this time Latino turnout was up from 14% to 20% of the total, and it went heavily against him. Bill Clinton came to Santa Ana late in the campaign to stump for Sanchez, and this may have made the difference. She won by 984 votes, 47%–46%.

There was great cheering in the White House and in many liberal precincts at Dornan's defeat. From Dornan there were bellows of rage and charges of vote fraud; if he had put as much effort into his congressional campaign earlier as he did in fighting his loss later, he probably would have won. Dornan brought his case to the House Contested Elections Task Force, which in February 1997 issued many subpoenas and promised a hearing in Orange County. Dornan argued that there were 1,789 illegal voters and by spring 1997 Dornan came up with proof that 547 non-citizens voted in Orange County and that 303 ineligibles had been registered to vote in the 46th District by a group called Hermandad Mexicana Nacional; this fell short of proving the result was wrong, but raised questions about the netherworld of voter registration in Orange County. California's registration laws make it easy to get anyone on the voter rolls (the accused assassin of Mexican presidential candidate Luis Donaldo Colosio was a registered Democrat in San Pedro), and the Clinton Administration INS made great efforts to process new citizens and dispensed with the usual check for criminal records if the FBI did not respond within sixty days.

Throughout 1997, Dornan, using the privileges afforded to former members, appeared on the House floor trying to convince his ex-colleagues to call for a special election in the 46th District; Democrats charged that he was abusing his privileges by promoting a personal agenda and the House voted to bar him from the floor after a heated discussion between Dornan and New Jersey Democrat Bob Menendez. Finally, in February 1998 the House Oversight Committee (which later regained its name as House Administration) upheld Sanchez's victory. Later, the committee voted to reimburse the two candidates for nearly $600,000 in legal expenses. The vote was along party lines and Democrats argued that the action was a move to finance Dornan's next campaign.

Sanchez maintained a busy schedule in her district, including her call for reparations for South Vietnamese soldiers who served under United States command during the Vietnam War and were prisoners of war (30 of whom live in her district). She also supported an INS pilot project to determine whether inmates at the Anaheim jail were in the country legally and also helped obtain a $2.5 million federal grant to study and design a proposed 28-mile light rail system for Orange County. When Dornan sought vindication in the 1998 election, many dubious Republican leaders sought a less controversial candidate and backed lawyer Lisa Hughes. But in the June primary Dornan beat her among Republicans by 49%–27%—a victory, but less than a stunning result for a long-time incumbent.

By the fall it was obvious to everyone, except perhaps Dornan, that Sanchez would win. Latino registration was up, and Sanchez herself had become a celebrity: Dornan's challenge had been featured prominently on the Spanish-language TV networks Telemundo and Univision, and Sanchez became the third-biggest fundraiser in the House in 1998. She won by the convincing margin of 56%–39%. After the election, she was named general co-chairwoman of the Democratic National Committee to lead a Hispanic voter-registration drive, and Vice President Gore tapped her as honorary chair of his political action committee.

Cook's Call. *Competitive.* With two big wins under her belt, Sanchez may well have bought herself enough time to lock up the district and thus make it difficult for Republicans to dislodge her. However, Sanchez in early 1999 had a parting of the ways with her highly-regarded chief of staff who shepherded her through her 1997 election challenge and 1998 re-election campaign, prompting some to question how she will do in 2000 without him.

The People: Pop. 1990: 570,963; 7.3% age 65 + ; 66.6% White, 2.5% Black, 12.4% Asian, 0.5% Amer. Indian, 17.9% Other; 49.4% Hispanic Origin. Households: 55.8% married couple families; 34.1% married couple fams. w. children; 38.3% college educ.; median household income: $35,416; per capita income: $11,297; median house value: $188,500; median gross rent: $667.

1996 Presidential Vote

Clinton (D)	51,330	(49%)
Dole (R)	42,780	(41%)
Perot (I)	8,229	(8%)
Others	2,609	(2%)

1992 Presidential Vote

Bush (R)	47,689	(40%)
Clinton (D)	44,352	(37%)
Perot (I)	27,542	(23%)

Rep. Loretta Sanchez (D)

Elected 1996; b. Jan. 7, 1960, Lynwood; home, Anaheim; Chapman U., B.A. 1982, American U., M.B.A. 1984; Catholic; married (Stephen Brixey).

Professional Career: Mgr. & Financial Analyst, Orange Cnty. Transp. Auth., 1984–87; Asst. Vice Pres., Fieldman, Rolapp & Assoc., 1987–90; Assoc., Booz, Allen & Hamilton, 1990–93; Principal, Amiga Advisors.

DC Office: 1529 LHOB 20515, 202-225-2965; Fax: 202-225-5859; Web site: www.house.gov/sanchez.

District Office: Garden Grove, 714-621-0102.

Committees: *Armed Services* (18th of 28 D): Military Personnel; Military Research & Development. *Education & the Workforce* (18th of 22 D): Early Childhood, Youth & Families; Workforce Protections.

Group Ratings

	ADA	ACLU	AFS	LCV	CON	NTU	NFIB	COC	ACU	NTLC	CHC
1998	95	69	100	62	82	24	36	44	8	24	8
1997	65	—	50	—	53	42	—	60	28	—	—

National Journal Ratings

	1997 LIB — 1997 CONS		1998 LIB — 1998 CONS	
Economic	57%	— 43%	61%	— 37%
Social	71%	— 29%	73%	— 25%
Foreign	67%	— 32%	71%	— 27%

Key Votes of the 105th Congress

1. Clinton Budget Deal	Y	5. Puerto Rico Sthood. Ref.	Y	9. Cut $ for B-2 Bombers	N
2. Education IRAs	N	6. End Highway Set-asides	N	10. Human Rights in China	Y
3. Req. 2/3 to Raise Taxes	Y	7. School Prayer Amend.	N	11. Withdraw Bosnia Troops	N
4. Fast-track Trade	N	8. Ovrd. Part. Birth Veto	N	12. End Cuban TV-Marti	Y

Election Results

1998 general	Loretta Sanchez (D)	47,964	(56%)	($2,535,243)
	Bob Dornan (R)	33,388	(39%)	($3,864,920)
	Others	3,650	(4%)	
1998 primary	Loretta Sanchez (D)	25,543	(45%)	
	Robert Dornan (R)	14,893	(26%)	
	Lisa Hughes (R)	8,323	(15%)	
	James P. Gray (R)	6,327	(11%)	
	Others	2,176	(4%)	
1996 general	Loretta Sanchez (D)	47,964	(47%)	($811,219)
	Robert Dornan (R)	46,980	(46%)	($741,984)
	Others	7,540	(7%)	

FORTY-SEVENTH DISTRICT

As one drives southeast in Orange County, there are still some patches of vacant land, places where one can see what this metropolis must have looked like before the vast growth starting in the 1950s. The Irvine Ranch, originally stretching 10 miles along the Pacific Coast and 22 miles inland to the mountains, was sold to developers by the Irvine family in the late 1970s but is still not entirely inhabited. Arrayed at the edges of the Irvine Ranch are Orange County landmarks. One is John Wayne Airport, named after the movie star who lived in Newport Beach and who symbolized patriotism though he never served in the military himself. Another is South Coast Plaza, the highest-volume upscale shopping center in southern California, standing in what not so long ago was a lima bean field. Another is University of California-Irvine, with 1,000 acres donated by the Irvine Ranch developers. On all sides are comfortable settlements—Orange, an orderly community, within sight of the hills, where even the street signs are orange; Newport Beach around its harbor; Irvine, with its planned communities, handsome clusters of office towers, landscaped shopping plazas and groups of houses and condominiums (but no cemeteries); artsy-craftsy Laguna Beach between mountains and the sea. Orange County is assailed by some as monotonous and sterile and boring, but for most of its residents it is a promised land, economically creative and ethnically diverse, orderly without being authoritarian, crowded perhaps but with privacy, sunny without being too hot.

The 47th Congressional District is centered geographically on the Irvine Ranch lands. On the coast it includes about half of Newport Beach as well as most of Irvine and runs south to Laguna Beach. It includes the growing subdivisions near the now closed El Toro Marine Corps Air Station in Lake Forest (the name was changed from El Toro) and Laguna Hills. About half its residents live to the north, in and around Orange; the other half are split between the ocean communities and those inland. Politically, this is a conservative area, one of the most Republican districts in the United States. Its people like the sense of order conveyed by its grid street patterns and the feeling of protection imparted by subdivision walls. They have felt comfortable as well with the military nearby. Although there are some distinctively rich communities here, the people do not feel that they are some kind of elite; they tend to see themselves as ordinary Americans with classic values who have worked hard and are entitled to enjoy their comfort.

The congressman from the 47th is Christopher Cox, a Republican elected in 1988, one of the intellectual leaders of his party in the House. Cox grew up in St. Paul, Minnesota, graduated from Southern California in three years, went to Harvard Law and Business Schools jointly, practiced law at Latham & Watkins in Orange County, then was part of the Reagan White House counsel's staff. In 1988, when the local incumbent retired, Cox ran for the House—one of 14 Republican candidates. With the support of Oliver North, Robert Bork and members of the Irvine family, he won the primary with 31%. He has since won primary and general elections without difficulty. Cox's intellect and range of interests are impressive: from the former Soviet Union (he and his father published an English translation of *Pravda* from 1984–88) to lobbying for more local control of highway funds and a proposed monorail system in Orange County. In 1995 and 1996 he called for abolition of the Interstate Commerce Commission and teamed up with law school classmate Barney Frank to eliminate the military's helium program. Cox did more than lament Orange County Treasurer Robert Citron's reckless investments, which bankrupted the county government; he backed local Republican John Moorlach's criticism of Citron's practices and afterwards proposed that public sector investors be required to make the same disclosures as private.

With the Republican victory in 1994, Cox came into his own, becoming chairman of the Republican Policy Committee and a leading legislator on many fronts. On the first day of the new Congress, he led the move to end baseline budgeting, which typically had given each agency and department either an inflation increase or the previous year's increase, whichever was higher, and an opportunity to argue for even more: This practically insured that government grew faster than the private economy. His radical idea was to state budget totals in dollar terms, so that an increase is an increase and a cut is a cut. Later, he proposed to overhaul the congressional budget process so that the annual resolution is legally binding and there are additional enforcement tools to limit spending. Another specialty is tort reform. Cox passed through the House bills limiting "injured feelings" recovery to $250,000 and repealing joint and several liability. He wrote the securities litigation reform to prevent predatory suits against high-tech and other companies, which got two-thirds support in both houses and was the only bill passed over Bill Clinton's veto in his first term. His bill to limit appeals of death penalties became law in April 1995.

Cox's interests extend abroad as well. His response to the Mexico bailout was a bill that passed the House in July 1995 barring the president from spending Exchange Stabilization Funds to bolster a currency. Opposed to normal trade relations with China, he oversaw House passage in 1997 of the "Policy for Freedom" package of 11 bills dealing with a range of human rights and free market issues in China. In 1998, Speaker Newt Gingrich tapped Cox to investigate reports of technology transfers from U.S. companies to China; the closed-door review release found that over the last 20 years, China had obtained some of the most sensitive of U.S. military technology, including nuclear weapons design. It faulted the policies of the Reagan, Bush and Clinton Administrations. This was one investigating committee that Cox and ranking Democrat Norman Dicks of Washington made sure was run on a bipartisan basis, and with no leaks to the press; the only leaks came out after the report was presented in early 1999 to the White House. It was finally made public in May 1999, after more than four months of negotiations with the White House over what material could be declassified. Cox won much bipartisan praise over his handling of the report. "Chris Cox has been a man of his word," said Dicks. An Internet surfer, Cox won enactment in 1998 of an important proposal for the emerging marketplace. With Democratic Senator Ron Wyden of Oregon, he passed the Internet Tax Freedom Act, which places a three-year moratorium on state and local governments from imposing special taxes on electronic commerce. It also directs the Clinton Administration to take action to keep foreign taxes and tariffs off the Internet.

Amid all these big issues, Cox also works on small ones. He passed a Corrections Day bill easing requirements for metric conversion in federal projects to what is practical. He passed a law allowing FedEx, UPS and other private delivery services to meet the IRS "timely-mailing-as-timely-filing" requirement. He sponsored a law to allow deputization of state and local law enforcement officers to enforce immigration law. And he pushed through a land exchange between the Orange County Boy Scouts Council and the U.S. Forest Service.

Cox has been re-elected easily in the 47th District. He considered running for the Senate in 1994 against Dianne Feinstein, but decided not to enter the primary against Michael Huffington, who spent freely of his own money. Cox also was mentioned as a candidate against Senator Barbara Boxer in 1998 and against Feinstein again in 2000, but declined to run. He may decide that he can influence national policy more from the House—and in national politics too: George Will has suggested he would be a good choice for vice president. During the House Republican turmoil in late 1998, Cox twice showed interest in running for speaker but he backed off each time—first in November, when Bob Livingston wrapped up support a few days after Newt Gingrich decided to quit; then, for a few hours December 19, until Republicans decided to quickly rally behind Denny Hastert after Bob Livingston's sudden resignation. The sobering lesson for Cox was that to win he needed to work harder at the House's inside game. (Winning the endorsement of the *Wall Street Journal* editorial page, as Cox did, doesn't count for much in a contest for speaker, even among House Republicans.) On the other hand, he has already shown the capacity for handling national and international issues of the highest importance.

Cook's Call. *Safe.* In six general elections, Cox's worst showing was 65% in 1992. This Orange County district is clearly Republican country, and Cox should have no problem in 2000.

The People: Pop. 1990: 571,605; 0.5% rural; 11.3% age 65 + ; 83.6% White, 1.8% Black, 9.6% Asian, 0.4% Amer. Indian, 4.6% Other; 12.9% Hispanic Origin. Households: 56.9% married couple families; 26.9% married couple fams. w. children; 72% college educ.; median household income: $51,554; per capita income: $25,268; median house value: $280,800; median gross rent: $797.

1996 Presidential Vote

Dole (R)	137,024	(54%)
Clinton (D)	91,916	(36%)
Perot (I)	17,680	(7%)
Others	7,206	(3%)

1992 Presidential Vote

Bush (R)	127,700	(46%)
Clinton (D)	86,279	(31%)
Perot (I)	64,227	(23%)

Rep. Christopher Cox (R)

Elected 1988; b. Oct. 16, 1952, St. Paul, MN; home, Newport Beach; U. of S. CA, B.A. 1973, Harvard U., M.B.A., J.D., 1977; Catholic; married (Rebecca).

Professional Career: Clerk, U.S. Court of Appeals, Judge Hebert Choy, 1977; Practicing atty., 1978–86; Lecturer, Harvard Bus. Schl., 1982–83; Sr. Assoc. Cnsl., White House, 1986–88.

DC Office: 2402 RHOB 20515, 202-225-5611; Fax: 202-225-9177; Web site: www.house.gov/chriscox.

District Office: Newport Beach, 949-756-2244.

Committees: *Republican Policy Committee Chairman. Commerce* (10th of 29 R): Finance & Hazardous Materials; Oversight & Investigations; Telecommunications, Trade & Consumer Protection.

Group Ratings

	ADA	ACLU	AFS	LCV	CON	NTU	NFIB	COC	ACU	NTLC	CHC
1998	0	13	11	15	79	75	93	83	100	97	100
1997	10	—	33	—	33	64	—	75	96	—	—

National Journal Ratings

	1997 LIB — 1997 CONS			1998 LIB — 1998 CONS		
Economic	15%	—	84%	0%	—	88%
Social	20%	—	71%	33%	—	66%
Foreign	23%	—	77%	32%	—	67%

Key Votes of the 105th Congress

1. Clinton Budget Deal	Y	5. Puerto Rico Sthood. Ref.	N	9. Cut $ for B-2 Bombers	*
2. Education IRAs	Y	6. End Highway Set-asides	Y	10. Human Rights in China	Y
3. Req. 2/3 to Raise Taxes	Y	7. School Prayer Amend.	Y	11. Withdraw Bosnia Troops	N
4. Fast-track Trade	Y	8. Ovrd. Part. Birth Veto	Y	12. End Cuban TV-Marti	N

Election Results

1998 general	Christopher Cox (R)	132,711	(68%)	($1,417,508)
	Christina Avalos (D)	57,938	(30%)	($9,781)
	Others	5,667	(3%)	
1998 primary	Christopher Cox (R)	91,638	(71%)	
	Christina Avalos (D)	32,516	(25%)	
	Others	5,397	(4%)	
1996 general	Christopher Cox (R)	160,078	(66%)	($527,738)
	Tina Louise Laine (D)	70,362	(29%)	($73,980)
	Others	13,337	(5%)	

FORTY-EIGHTH DISTRICT

The California coast between Los Angeles and San Diego has never entirely filled up with development and never will as long as the Marine Corps retains custody of Camp Pendleton, the giant training base just south of the Orange-San Diego County line. But on both sides of Pendleton up and down the coast and for miles inland on the pleasant hills and in sunny valleys, there has been tremendous growth over the past two decades. Little wonder: This area has perhaps the most agreeable climate in the continental United States, beautiful scenery, the physical infrastructure typical of California and much lower crime rates than Los Angeles or even San Diego. A quarter century ago, this was largely empty territory—never fertile enough to produce a large farm community, never endowed with much manufacturing, never actively promoted as a retirement community. In 1990 there were half a million people just north and south of Pendleton, and the Interior Department was struggling to come up with a district plan that would protect the ecosystem of the 4-inch gnat-catcher bird and other endangered species in the area.

The 48th Congressional District occupies the southernmost portion of Orange County, the North County part of San Diego County and a small slice of Riverside County, the instant town of Temecula. It includes the seaside communities of San Clemente, where Richard Nixon lived just after leaving the White House, and San Juan Capistrano, to which the swallows famously return every year. Inland, there are the newer condominium communities of Mission Viejo and Laguna Niguel; just south of Pendleton in San Diego County are Oceanside and Vista. Farther inland amid the hills are Fallbrook and, in Riverside County, Temecula, in the mid-1980s a corner-grocery town serving a vineyard district, now the center of an area with 100,000 people, mostly commuters to Orange County and Riverside attracted by low-priced homes and traditional values. People in all these areas tend to be Republicans; they are affluent enough to identify with the party of property, conventional enough in their personal lives to identify with what describes itself as the party of traditional values, undivided enough by ethnic differences to identify with the party that fancies it is made up of an unethnic majority.

The congressman from the 48th, Ron Packard, is a Republican who first won when a new district was created for this area in 1982. Packard is a Mormon from Idaho, a dentist who served in the Navy Dental Corps in Camp Pendleton in the 1950s, then moved his growing family (now 7 children and 34 grandchildren and two great-grandchilden) to Carlsbad. There he served on the school board, the Chamber of Commerce and city council, was a director of the North County Transit District and mayor: one of the people who keeps things working in these growing communities. He was mayor of Carlsbad in 1982 when he ran for Congress in the new district, losing an 18-candidate Republican primary by 92 votes to Johnnie Crean, who spent his own money on ads fraudulently claiming President Reagan's endorsement. Packard promptly ran as a write-in and won with 37%, to 32% for the Democrat and 31% for Crean. He has been easily re-elected since; Democrats failed to nominate an opponent in 1998.

In the minority, Packard was a conservative backbencher; but since 1994 he has been chairmen of three Appropriations subcommittees. The first was Legislative Branch, which cut spending on Congress by 9% and would have cut more but for resistance by the Senate. He spurred privatization of services by the Architect of the Capitol and worked to create a "cyber-Congress" with up-to-date computer systems in all offices; the latter created pressure for more spending. In 1997 Packard switched to chair the Military Construction Subcommittee, on which he set his first priority on improving base housing, including at Camp Pendleton. But chairing that subcommittee also gave Packard the opportunity to receive specific requests from more than half of the 435 House members seeking construction projects for their district. "It doesn't satisfy my ego to have a lot of people come and seek the things I have to give," he said. "But I do enjoy being able to determine what programs are worthy of funding. I've waited a long time for that." Then, in 1999, he moved a step further up the Appropriations ladder to become chairman of the Energy and Water Development Subcommittee, an especially auspicious panel for a southern Californian; as Packard said, water is "the lifeblood of the state." The subcommittee's $21 billion annual budget also includes the Energy Department's nuclear programs.

In each case, Packard benefited from his close friendship with Bob Livingston, who chaired Appropriations for four years. So it was no surprise that Packard reciprocated their friendship by spending much of 1998 as campaign manager for Livingston's unconventional bid for a speaker's post that was not yet vacant. But Packard's nine months of work unexpectedly bore fruit when Speaker Newt Gingrich announced his resignation three days after the November 1998 election, and Livingston quickly showed that he had locked up the succession. Suddenly Packard was one of the most important members of the House, which Livingston reinforced by naming his "trusted friend" as co-chair of his transition team. Packard had become in political parlance the speaker-designate's "go-to guy," a nice slice of political power; he quickly sent out the message that the new speaker would be far more inclusive, far less partisan than the exiting Gingrich. But, alas, what blossomed so quickly faded to a nightmare for his allies, with Livingston's stunning December 19 resignation announcement. Still, Packard kept his new Energy and Water chairmanship; his collegial style should play well in Denny Hastert's narrowly-divided House.

On local issues, he has crusaded against illegal immigration. He responded to what he considered an egregious case of an illegal alien receiving $12,000 in federal funds to leave her previous home, which was becoming a federal housing project. Packard won enactment of a bill to ban that.

Cook's Call. *Safe.* Packard is a sure bet in this overwhelmingly Republican district. He can have this seat as long as he wants it.

The People: Pop. 1990: 573,211; 10.9% rural; 11% age 65 +; 83.3% White, 4% Black, 4.6% Asian, 1.1% Amer. Indian, 6.9% Other; 16.9% Hispanic Origin. Households: 62.1% married couple families; 30.4% married couple fams. w. children; 65% college educ.; median household income: $42,389; per capita income: $19,435; median house value: $237,300; median gross rent: $646.

1996 Presidential Vote		
Dole (R)	132,545	(56%)
Clinton (D)	80,646	(34%)
Perot (I)	18,731	(8%)
Others	6,462	(3%)

1992 Presidential Vote		
Bush (R)	108,581	(44%)
Clinton (D)	71,621	(29%)
Perot (I)	65,980	(27%)

Rep. Ronald C. Packard (R)

Elected 1982; b. Jan. 19, 1931, Meridian, ID; home, Oceanside; Brigham Young U., 1948–50, Portland St. U., 1952–53, U. of OR, D.M.D. 1957; Mormon; married (Jean).

Military Career: Navy Dental Corps, 1957–59.

Elected Office: Carlsbad Schl. Dist. Bd., 1962–74; Carlsbad City Cncl., 1976–78; Carlsbad Mayor, 1978–82.

Professional Career: Practicing dentist.

DC Office: 2372 RHOB 20515, 202-225-3906; Fax: 202-225-0134; Web site: www.house.gov/packard.

District Offices: San Clemente, 949-496-2343; Vista, 760-631-1364.

Committees: *Appropriations* (10th of 34 R): Energy & Water Development (Chmn.); Foreign Operations & Export Financing; Transportation.

Group Ratings

	ADA	ACLU	AFS	LCV	CON	NTU	NFIB	COC	ACU	NTLC	CHC
1998	5	7	0	8	13	50	100	100	96	95	100
1997	5	—	13	—	42	45	—	100	84	—	—

National Journal Ratings

	1997 LIB	—	1997 CONS	1998 LIB	—	1998 CONS
Economic	34%	—	66%	19%	—	79%
Social	10%	—	82%	12%	—	87%
Foreign	38%	—	60%	7%	—	83%

Key Votes of the 105th Congress

1. Clinton Budget Deal	Y	5. Puerto Rico Sthood. Ref.	N	9. Cut $ for B-2 Bombers	N
2. Education IRAs	Y	6. End Highway Set-asides	Y	10. Human Rights in China	N
3. Req. 2/3 to Raise Taxes	Y	7. School Prayer Amend.	Y	11. Withdraw Bosnia Troops	Y
4. Fast-track Trade	Y	8. Ovrd. Part. Birth Veto	Y	12. End Cuban TV-Marti	N

Election Results

1998 general	Ronald C. Packard (R)	138,948	(77%)	($288,822)
	Sharon K. Miles (NL)	23,262	(13%)	
	Daniel L. Muhe (Lib)	18,509	(10%)	
1998 primary	Ronald C. Packard (R)	85,485	(71%)	
	James Luke (R)	10,401	(9%)	
	Sharon K. Miles (NL)	10,079	(8%)	
	Daniel L. Muhe (Lib)	7,979	(7%)	
	Edward Mayerhofer (R)	6,492	(5%)	
1996 general	Ronald C. Packard (R)	145,814	(66%)	($264,625)
	Dan Farrell (D)	59,558	(27%)	($10,645)
	Others	16,019	(7%)	

FORTY-NINTH DISTRICT

When the United States was dictating the terms of the Treaty of Guadalupe Hidalgo in 1848, after its successful war with Mexico, it made sure the southern boundary of its new California territory was just south of the port of San Diego. This is one of three splendid natural harbors on the Pacific Coast and the major West Coast U.S. Navy base for more than 50 years. The port and Navy base in the sheltered harbor remain the central focus of a metropolis which has grown tenfold over that time span and now stretches far inland and to the north. On one side is its downtown, blooming with post-modern buildings like the Horton Plaza amid a few well-preserved early 20th Century relics like the Spreckels Theatre. Across the harbor, on the sand spit that guards it against the ocean, is the white frame castle of the Hotel Del Coronado, with its surprisingly dark wooden interior, the world's largest wooden structure and a favored resort of past American presidents; the town of Coronado has long been a favorite retirement place for Navy admirals and captains.

But San Diego is not all harbor and Navy. To the north, the Pacific waves pound against the beach beneath erose cliffs of unique rock formations that stride up and down the coast on which stand some of San Diego's great cultural institutions: the Scripps Institute of Oceanography, the University of California San Diego campus, the Salk Institute and the Torrey Pines reserve, home of this unique, wide-spreading pine tree. They look out over the ocean through clear and gentle air south to La Jolla, the city's highest-income neighborhood, and north toward Del Mar and the race track that made San Diego a tourist mecca 50 years ago when the track was owned by Bing Crosby and friends. The weather—a sunny 70% of the time—has lured people to San Diego; the informal resort atmosphere of La Jolla and Mission Beach appeal to tourists. But this is a working town as well, a sophisticated high-tech center with nearly 200,000 full- and part-time students at its colleges and universities and growing biotech, electronics, software and telecommunications industries; someone who looks like a professional surfer may turn out to be a high-tech engineer. And it is a manufacturing center as well, with maquiladora factories clustering near the Mexican border.

The 49th Congressional District, which includes about half the population of San Diego plus Coronado and Imperial Beach, takes in most of the harbor and Navy bases and much of its high-tech businesses and workers. It reaches as far south as the Mexican border and includes most of downtown San Diego and Balboa Park, with its justly famous zoo. It reaches inland where the city's freeway network, denser and more practical than San Francisco's or even Los Angeles's, efficiently shuttles commuters from scattered employment centers to their homes on hilltop subdivisions. San Diego under then-Mayor (1971–82) Pete Wilson wouldn't let developers build on the sides of the hills, so San Diego doesn't have the picturesque but precarious hillside streets of the Hollywood Hills or Pacific Heights—but rather the natural landscape that the Portuguese explorer Cabrillo saw in the 1500s and the American adventurer Richard Henry Dana saw three centuries later, though the hills are now topped unobtrusively by subdivisions. The district includes Ocean Beach and Mission Bay and La Jolla and reaches as far north as Torrey Pines and as far inland as the outer boundary of Miramar Naval Air Station.

With its climate, scenery and friendliness, this should be paradise, but politically San Diego was in a foul temper in the early 1990s, kicking out incumbents of both parties all over town. Voters here tend to be Republican and free market on economics but liberal on cultural issues like abortion and the environment—much like Pete Wilson and, later, Susan Golding, elected mayor in 1992 and re-elected with 78% in 1996, with her brand of governance—lower taxes, slimmer but more proactive government—which did much to attract the Republican National Convention here in 1996. "If the GOP wants to present itself as the party for the 21st Century," she said to National Journal's *Convention Daily* "there's no better city than San Diego. We are at the center of the Pacific Rim, and we target the fastest-growing markets in the world."

The congressman from the 49th is Brian Bilbray, a Republican who was born in Coronado and grew up on naval bases and in Imperial Beach. He owns a tax preparation business and was elected to the Imperial Beach Council in 1976, at 25, then mayor two years later, and to the San Diego County Board of Supervisors in 1984, where he worked for environmental protections and economic development. He made his first big splash in 1980, when he mounted a skiploader and built a berm to keep the sewage-polluted Tijuana River from seeping into San Diego County beaches. An experienced surfer, he made news again in 1984 when he paddled out on his surfboard to battle a fire raging on the city pier. In 1994 he ran for the House seat won two years earlier by Democrat Lynn Schenk. Schenk had a moderate voting record and had worked hard on the base closure issue and aiding high-tech businesses, but she voted for the 1993 Clinton budget and tax increase. Bilbray attacked her for that and supported the Contract with America, and won 49%–46%.

In the House Bilbray, got a seat on the Commerce Committee and, as the only member living within sight of the Mexican border, worked constructively on many immigration-related issues. He got the Republican budget to include funds for hospitals treating illegal immigrants. He also worked to get 1,400 new Border Patrol agents and $425 million to reimburse states for costs of incarcerating illegal immigrants. He backed reduced levels of legal immigration and a pilot program for an electronic verification system. He sponsored a bill to allow customs inspectors at the border to impose fines and seize vehicles for violations of emission standards or failure to meet California insurance requirements. He helped pass the California Cruise Ship Industry Revitalization bill, which allowed ships with gambling to stop in more than one California port; they had been skipping San Diego. In April 1999, his proposal to encourage coastal states to test their swimming waters unanimously passed the House.

This was naturally a Democratic target seat. In 1996, after Schenk waited until the last minute before deciding not to run, the Democratic nominee was Peter Navarro, who lost to Golding in 1992. Bilbray said he stood up to Speaker Newt Gingrich on hospital funding and the assault weapons ban. He campaigned as "San Diego's independent voice for change" and his radio ads proclaimed "Brian has been there when we needed him." Unlike 1994, when he was outspent almost 2–1, Bilbray had a better than 2–1 money advantage. Despite Clinton's local strength, Bilbray won 53%–42%.

In 1998, Bilbray had a tougher re-election challenge, this time from Christine Kehoe, a San Diego councilwoman who acknowledged but did not highlight her lesbianism, except to bolster her fundraising. "History is about to be made and you can be part of it," read a Kehoe campaign flier seeking dollars. When Bilbray sought to deny Kehoe's attacks for his Social Security, Medicare and environment votes, she responded that he was engaging in "Washington double-speak." In June, Bilbray led 53%–41% in California's new all-party primary, which in the other states which use it, Washington and Alaska, has usually been a good forecast of the general election. But southern Californians' disdain for House Republicans' prosecution of the Clinton scandal evidently shifted opinion toward the Democrats. Bilbray won by only 49%–47% and blamed impeachment: "It may be the issue that finally drives a nail through my political coffin," he said.

Still, Bilbray said that he was comfortable with his pro-impeachment votes for a President he called "a perpetual liar." And he quickly became a booster of new speaker Denny Hastert, challenging critics to "point to any speaker who's more fair-minded and open to advice." But Bilbray may still face serious challenges. In March 1999 Assemblywoman Susan Davis announced she would run against him; she should be able to tap Sacramento and feminist moneygivers. Democrats will likely control the redistricting process for 2002. Their only problem is that the best way to weaken Bilbray, should he win again, is to add Democratic territory in the current 50st District, which Democratic incumbent Bob Filner will be loath to relinquish.

Cook's Call. *Highly Competitive.* After three close races, Bilbray is once again a top target for Democrats in 2000. This should be a great race, one of the best in the country to watch.

The People: Pop. 1990: 573,437; 13.5% age 65 + ; 82.1% White, 5.2% Black, 6.6% Asian, 0.8% Amer. Indian, 5.2% Other; 12.3% Hispanic Origin. Households: 39.6% married couple families; 15.2% married couple fams. w. children; 67.3% college educ.; median household income: $32,562; per capita income: $19,184; median house value: $226,000; median gross rent: $570.

1996 Presidential Vote			1992 Presidential Vote		
Clinton (D)	110,920	(49%)	Clinton (D)	114,081	(43%)
Dole (R)	91,478	(40%)	Bush (R)	82,834	(31%)
Perot (I)	15,084	(7%)	Perot (I)	65,856	(25%)
Others	9,514	(4%)			

Rep. Brian P. Bilbray (R)

Elected 1994; b. Jan. 28, 1951, Coronado; home, Imperial Beach; SW Commun. Col., 1972; Catholic; married (Karen).

Elected Office: Imperial Beach Cncl., 1976–78; Imperial Beach Mayor, 1978–85; San Diego Cnty. Supervisor, 1985–94.

Professional Career: Tax consultant, 1972–present.

DC Office: 1530 LHOB 20515, 202-225-2040; Fax: 202-225-2948; Web site: www.house.gov/bilbray.

District Office: San Diego, 619-291-1430.

Committees: *Commerce* (14th of 29 R): Finance & Hazardous Materials; Health and Environment; Oversight & Investigations.

Group Ratings

	ADA	ACLU	AFS	LCV	CON	NTU	NFIB	COC	ACU	NTLC	CHC
1998	20	20	33	85	74	52	79	61	64	63	75
1997	15	—	25	—	76	53	—	80	76	—	—

National Journal Ratings

	1997 LIB — 1997 CONS	1998 LIB — 1998 CONS
Economic	42% — 58%	46% — 54%
Social	37% — 61%	46% — 54%
Foreign	24% — 72%	34% — 62%

Key Votes of the 105th Congress

1. Clinton Budget Deal	Y	5. Puerto Rico Sthood. Ref.	N	9. Cut $ for B-2 Bombers	N
2. Education IRAs	Y	6. End Highway Set-asides	Y	10. Human Rights in China	N
3. Req. 2/3 to Raise Taxes	Y	7. School Prayer Amend.	Y	11. Withdraw Bosnia Troops	Y
4. Fast-track Trade	Y	8. Ovrd. Part. Birth Veto	Y	12. End Cuban TV-Marti	N

Election Results

1998 general	Brian P. Bilbray (R)	90,516	(49%)	($1,278,210)
	Christine Kehoe (D)	86,400	(47%)	($1,263,299)
	Others	8,603	(5%)	
1998 primary	Brian P. Bilbray (R)	62,571	(53%)	
	Christine Kehoe (D)	48,288	(41%)	
	Others	7,380	(6%)	
1996 general	Brian P. Bilbray (R)	108,806	(53%)	($1,122,073)
	Peter Navarro (D)	86,657	(42%)	($450,424)
	Others	11,305	(5%)	

FIFTIETH DISTRICT

San Diego, at one corner of the continental United States, not so long ago a small Navy town known for its good harbor and splendid weather, is now a major metropolis, a city of 1.1 million people and the center of a metro area of 2.7 million. It is also, to its increasing discomfort, one of the largest cities anywhere directly on an international border and between countries with strikingly different economic conditions, political systems and cultural traditions. Not many other Americans think about it, but Mexican presidential candidate Luis Donaldo Colosio was murdered in March 1994 just a few blocks from the border in Tijuana.

This is, in fact, the busiest border crossing in the world, but most of San Diego seems to look away, toward the ocean. Tijuana looks to the United States, to the lower-income part of San Diego—the industrial zone on brown hills in Otay Mesa and San Ysidro, the industrial suburbs of Chula Vista and National City toward the bay and the grid streets south of downtown and behind the harbor in San Diego itself. Latinos are scattered in various parts of the city, in the southern corridor and in Encanto and Chollas Park in the east. Oddly, there is not much evidence of Mexican style in San Diego—less even than in Los Angeles, as if the border city was insisting on its Yanqui origins, just as San Diego's civic leaders bridle at the idea of a bi-national airport on the border. Even San Diego's favorite symbol, the red Tijuana Trolley that takes tourists from downtown to the San Ysidro-Tijuana border station, is as resolutely Yanqui as Main Street in Disneyland.

The 50th Congressional District—the first 50th district in the history of the House—covers the southern and eastern ends of San Diego and includes National City and Chula Vista toward the border. The district's population was 40% Hispanic in 1990, and is by far the most Democratic district in the San Diego area; the Latino percentage of registered voters rose from 22% in 1990 to 30% in 1997. Even so, districts in this general territory ousted incumbent Democratic congressmen in 1980 and again in 1990, both times electing Republicans who after the ensuing redistricting chose to run in more heavily Republican seats farther from the central city: Duncan Hunter, who now represents the 52d District, and Duke Cunningham, who represents the 51st.

The congressman from the 50th District is Bob Filner, a Democrat elected in 1992, the close winner of primaries that year and in 1996. Filner grew up in New York and was a Freedom Rider in 1961, imprisoned for two months in Mississippi. He earned a Ph.D. at Cornell and taught history at San Diego State and directed the Lipinsky Institute for Judaic Studies; he took time off to work on Senator Hubert Humphrey's staff in the 1970s and was elected to the San Diego school board in 1979 and to the city council in 1987. In the 1992 primary he had strong backing from blacks and Latinos although he had two better-known rivals. Filner won with 26%; to 23% for Waddie Deddeh, state senator and assemblyman since 1966, but 71 and recovering from heart surgery; 20% for Jim Bates, four-term congressman beaten in 1990 after being disciplined for sexual harassment; and 19% for Juan Carlos Vargas, returned to San Diego after training to be a Jesuit priest and then switching to Harvard Law School.

Filner is politically savvy, with some original ideas about policy, aggressive to the point of abrasiveness. He told the 1993 Democratic freshmen they should vote as a bloc for reform; they did not, and many lost, as Filner foresaw. He killed the proposed bi-national airport by cutting funds for planning. Filner won handily in 1994 and said "The shaking up of the system probably helped me more than hurt me." In 1995, he worked with freshman Republican Brian Bilbray to get funding for the international sewage treatment center (taking too much of the credit, Bilbray thought) and supported the permanent waiver Bilbray obtained from the sewage treatment standards. He crashed a Newt Gingrich press conference in Mission Valley to attack him on Medicare even as he conceded that the Republicans' $2.2 billion reimbursement of hospitals for treatment of illegal immigrants was "needed and appreciated." He was frustrated on his own proposal for a "Jobs Train" to reopen the now-defunct San Diego and Arizona Eastern Railroad, providing a connection between the port of San Diego and the east. He wanted only $490,000 so as to trigger a $7.9 million loan guarantee, but his proposal, supported also by Bilbray, lost 238–162 when the other three San Diego Republicans voted against it; it would dip into Mexico and, Duncan Hunter said, be a conduit for Mexican drug smugglers. Filner was one of only five House members to vote against both parties' impeachment inquiries.

As the number-two Democrat on the Veterans' Affairs Committee, Filner has become an eager advocate of veterans' rights, a popular cause in his district of many military retirees. He has paid particular attention to restoring benefits up to now denied to Filipino veterans who fought for the U.S. in World War II; in 1997 he and 15 of the veterans were arrested after they chained themselves to a White House fence. In March 1999, he was one of only two members to vote against further restrictions on burials at Arlington Cemetery.

In the March 1996 primary, Filner was challenged by Vargas, who had been elected to succeed him on the council in 1993, where he made a name favoring graffiti removal and expansion of Jack Murphy Stadium. Vargas ran as a moderate and could expect support from many Latinos. Filner, who ran ads saying Vargas was "anti-choice," bragged of fighting Gingrich on Medicare and saving taxpayers $3 billion on sewage treatment. Vargas responded with an ad showing his wife praising his positive, door-to-door campaign ("a candidate who doesn't throw mud to win elections") and with him saying, "It's wrong to cut Medicare and veterans' benefits, and it's wrong to burn the American flag"—a reference to Filner's vote against the flag amendment. Filner won, but by just 55%–45%. In 1998, by contrast, Filner had no opposition in the primary or general election.

Asked if he was interested in running to succeed term-limited Mayor Susan Golding, he responded with his own detailed economic plan for the city. But he announced in February 1999 that, even though he thought he could have won, he decided not to run for mayor because he could accomplish more for the city by working to create a Democratic-controlled House in which he might chair a committee.

Cook's Call. *Safe.* This San Diego-based seat is very Democratic and rather barren territory for Republicans. Filner is heavily favored in 2000.

The People: Pop. 1990: 573,244; 0.9% rural; 8.9% age 65 + ; 46.6% White, 14.4% Black, 14.9% Asian, 0.6% Amer. Indian, 23.5% Other; 39.7% Hispanic Origin. Households: 53.1% married couple families; 31.5% married couple fams. w. children; 43.5% college educ.; median household income: $27,655; per capita income: $10,577; median house value: $137,300; median gross rent: $495.

<table>
<tr><td colspan="3">1996 Presidential Vote</td><td colspan="3">1992 Presidential Vote</td></tr>
<tr><td>Clinton (D)</td><td>78,881</td><td>(60%)</td><td>Clinton (D)</td><td>69,546</td><td>(48%)</td></tr>
<tr><td>Dole (R)</td><td>42,730</td><td>(32%)</td><td>Bush (R)</td><td>42,830</td><td>(30%)</td></tr>
<tr><td>Perot (I)</td><td>7,764</td><td>(6%)</td><td>Perot (I)</td><td>30,267</td><td>(21%)</td></tr>
<tr><td>Others</td><td>2,765</td><td>(2%)</td><td></td><td></td><td></td></tr>
</table>

Rep. Bob Filner (D)

Elected 1992; b. Sept. 4, 1942, Pittsburgh, PA; home, San Diego; Cornell U., B.A. 1963, Ph.D. 1973, U. of DE, M.A. 1969; Jewish; married (Jane).

Elected Office: San Diego Schl. Bd., 1979–83, Pres., 1982–83; San Diego City Cncl., 1987–92, Dpty. Mayor, 1991.

Professional Career: Prof., San Diego St. U., 1970–92; Legis. Asst., U.S. Sen. Hubert Humphrey, 1974; Legis. Asst., U.S. Rep. Don Fraser, 1975.

DC Office: 330 CHOB 20515, 202-225-8045; Fax: 202-225-9073; Web site: www.house.gov/filner.

District Office: Chula Vista, 619-422-5963.

Committees: *Transportation & Infrastructure* (16th of 34 D): Aviation; Ground Transportation. *Veterans' Affairs* (2d of 14 D): Benefits (RMM).

Group Ratings

	ADA	ACLU	AFS	LCV	CON	NTU	NFIB	COC	ACU	NTLC	CHC
1998	100	86	100	100	85	24	0	22	4	0	0
1997	95	—	100	—	8	23	—	30	8	—	—

National Journal Ratings

	1997 LIB — 1997 CONS		1998 LIB — 1998 CONS	
Economic	93% —	0%	79% —	0%
Social	78% —	22%	88% —	11%
Foreign	76% —	22%	71% —	27%

Key Votes of the 105th Congress

1. Clinton Budget Deal	N	5. Puerto Rico Sthood. Ref.	Y	9. Cut $ for B-2 Bombers	N
2. Education IRAs	N	6. End Highway Set-asides	N	10. Human Rights in China	Y
3. Req. 2/3 to Raise Taxes	N	7. School Prayer Amend.	N	11. Withdraw Bosnia Troops	Y
4. Fast-track Trade	N	8. Ovrd. Part. Birth Veto	N	12. End Cuban TV-Marti	Y

Election Results

1998 general	Bob Filner (D)	77,354	(99%)	($433,671)
	Others	596	(1%)	
1998 primary	Bob Filner (D)	46,636	(99%)	
	Others	334	(1%)	
1996 general	Bob Filner (D)	73,200	(62%)	($1,142,370)
	Jim Baize (R)	38,351	(32%)	($120,562)
	Others	6,789	(6%)	

FIFTY-FIRST DISTRICT

When FBI director J. Edgar Hoover came to the races at Del Mar for two weeks every summer in the 1940s and 1950s, the rest of north San Diego County, from the track north to the Marine Corps's Camp Pendleton, was mostly uninhabited: There were a few thousand people in the beach towns of Oceanside and Carlsbad and a few thousand more scattered over the dry, brownish hills that rolled inland. Today about 650,000 people live in North County, and who can blame them? For this is one of America's most beautiful and comfortable environments, with ocean and mountain scenery, sunny and warm weather, no rural poverty and low crime. Here, amid dry but not desert landscape, you can see miles of rolling hills, with occasional surrealistic trees and sagebrush-like bushes; mountains clump up not in ridges, but here and there, seemingly at random. This land has attracted thousands of new migrants, many, but by no means all, retirees. Outside the Los Angeles media market, not frequented by many entertainment celebrities, North County does not have a high media profile, which probably suits the quietly successful people who have moved here just fine.

The 51st Congressional District covers much of North County. It includes some 200,000 people in San Diego itself—not in its urbanized core, but in land it annexed during Governor Pete Wilson's long tenure as mayor, including the Rancho Bernardo planned community and Miramar Naval Air Station, whose Navy fliers were made famous in *Top Gun*. It also includes the gorgeous suburb of Rancho Sante Fe, where 39 members of the Heaven's Gate cult—under the direction of New Age philosophist Marshall Applewhite—committed mass suicide in March 1997, apparently in an attempt to hitch a ride on the "spaceship" trailing Comet Hale-Bopp. The 51st takes in the beach communities from Del Mar north to Carlsbad and the nearby La Costa resort. Inland, with its red-tile roofs filling a sunny valley and its splendid arts center, is fast-growing Escondido, with 108,000 people in 1990. Politically, this is overwhelmingly Republican territory, though with a taste for Ross Perot in 1992; rather conservative on cultural issues, against bigger government, patriotic and nationalistic on foreign policy.

The congressman from the 51st is Randy (Duke) Cunningham, a Republican elected in 1990. Born the day after Pearl Harbor, he taught and coached swimming in Hinsdale, Illinois, and San Diego; in 1966, at 25, he joined the Navy and became one of the most decorated pilots in the Vietnam war. He then trained pilots at Miramar in the Top Gun program; he retired from the Navy in 1987 and started a business in San Diego. In 1990 he ran in a Democratic district against Democratic Congressman Jim Bates, who was charged with sexual harassment; Cunningham beat a former ambassador to Qatar in the Republican primary 46%–30%, and in the general beat Bates 46%–45%. In 1992, faced with a choice of districts to run in, he passed up the marginal and culturally more liberal 49th on the coast and ran in the 51st. Incumbent Bill Lowery, a Republican who had 300 overdrafts at the House bank, withdrew from the race in April 1992, and Cunningham comfortably won the primary and general.

Cunningham arrived just in time for the Gulf war debate and in his first years worked to make Filipino Gulf war veterans eligible to apply for U.S. citizenship and to prevent base closings in the San Diego area. He was one of four congressmen who in October 1992 met with George Bush and prompted him to ask questions about Bill Clinton's student trip to Moscow and Eastern Europe, an issue that hurt the Republican ticket. With Republican control, he has switched to the Appropriations panel and has won assignments to its two subcommittees with the largest budgets: Defense; and Labor, Health and Human Services, and Education. He has emerged as one of the most forceful advocates of more Pentagon spending: "Simply put, the administration is stretching our military to the breaking point," he said, complaining about aging equipment and the forces' high operational tempo. Cunningham was the lead sponsor of the English-as-official-language bill passed by the House in August 1996. "We must take this defining step to avoid our nation becoming divided into many ethnic enclaves." He has pressed for stricter enforcement of immigration laws and criticized the Operation Gatekeeper program of the INS. He sponsored a "no frills prison act."

Cunningham has a gift for pungent comments. At one hearing, he said, "I do not believe they [troops] can be well led when they have a commander-in-chief who has turned his back on them." He said that Clinton's anti-war past would result in being "tried as a traitor and even shot" if he had lived in another country. After he said Jim Moran "switched his vote and turned his back on Desert Storm," Moran pushed him in the hall, then apologized. In 1995, he triggered a firestorm by calling gays "homos" on the House floor. And in 1998 he dressed down an Army official at a Defense subcommittee hearing about "B.S." efforts to combat sexual harassment and discrimination in the military. "Our kids don't like that. They don't like the political correctness," Cunnningham lectured.

In recent years, he has had several personal setbacks. Cunningham unsuccessfully ran for the Republican Conference secretary position in the July 1997 leadership shuffle caused by the retirement of Susan Molinari; he was winnowed out on the second ballot, with just 42 votes to Sue Myrick's 65 and Deborah Pryce's 110. In January 1997 his 27-year-old son was arrested and charged with flying a plane to Boston with 400 pounds of marijuana. He said, "As a parent this is the most anguishing thing that can happen to you. We love him. If the charges are true, we are disappointed, and he must face his responsibilities." When his son later was sentenced to two years in federal prison, Cunningham appeared in court for the sentencing and admitted in a tear-choked voice that he had not spent much time with the boy when he was growing up. Also in 1998, he underwent surgery for prostate cancer, crediting early detection with saving his life. His 1998 margin, while comfortable, was his smallest since 1992.

Cook's Call. *Safe.* Former Top Gun instructor Cunningham is also a high flier in this district. He should have no trouble in 2000.

The People: Pop. 1990: 572,850; 3.3% rural; 11.9% age 65 + ; 84.8% White, 1.6% Black, 8.1% Asian, 0.6% Amer. Indian, 4.8% Other; 13.3% Hispanic Origin. Households: 59.7% married couple families; 28.6% married couple fams. w. children; 68.2% college educ.; median household income: $45,186; per capita income: $20,586; median house value: $231,000; median gross rent: $671.

1996 Presidential Vote		
Dole (R)	130,459	(52%)
Clinton (D)	97,128	(38%)
Perot (I)	16,963	(7%)
Others	7,918	(3%)

1992 Presidential Vote		
Bush (R)	108,470	(40%)
Clinton (D)	86,870	(32%)
Perot (I)	73,580	(27%)

Rep. Randy (Duke) Cunningham (R)

Elected 1990; b. Dec. 8, 1941, Los Angeles; home, San Diego; U. of MO, B.A. 1964, M.S. 1965, National U., M.B.A. 1985; Christian; married (Nancy).

Military Career: Navy, 1966–87 (Vietnam).

Professional Career: Businessman, 1987–90.

DC Office: 2238 RHOB 20515, 202-225-5452; Fax: 202-225-2558; Web site: www.house.gov/cunningham.

District Office: Escondido, 760-737-8438.

Committees: *Appropriations* (25th of 34 R): Defense; District of Columbia; Labor, HHS & Education.

Group Ratings

	ADA	ACLU	AFS	LCV	CON	NTU	NFIB	COC	ACU	NTLC	CHC
1998	0	8	0	8	21	54	100	100	100	91	100
1997	0	—	25	—	62	58	—	100	92	—	—

National Journal Ratings

	1997 LIB — 1997 CONS		1998 LIB — 1998 CONS	
Economic	10%	— 86%	22%	— 78%
Social	0%	— 90%	21%	— 79%
Foreign	0%	— 88%	18%	— 82%

Key Votes of the 105th Congress

1. Clinton Budget Deal	Y	5. Puerto Rico Sthood. Ref.	N	9. Cut $ for B-2 Bombers	N
2. Education IRAs	Y	6. End Highway Set-asides	Y	10. Human Rights in China	N
3. Req. 2/3 to Raise Taxes	Y	7. School Prayer Amend.	Y	11. Withdraw Bosnia Troops	Y
4. Fast-track Trade	Y	8. Ovrd. Part. Birth Veto	Y	12. End Cuban TV-Marti	*

Election Results

1998 general	Randy (Duke) Cunningham (R)	126,229	(61%)	($436,528)
	Dan Kripke (D)	71,706	(35%)	($92,708)
	Others	8,943	(4%)	
1998 primary	Randy (Duke) Cunningham (R)	88,542	(67%)	
	Dan Kripke (D)	36,876	(28%)	
	Others	7,514	(6%)	
1996 general	Randy (Duke) Cunningham (R)	149,032	(65%)	($425,525)
	Rita Tamerius (D)	66,250	(29%)	($19,935)
	Others	13,742	(6%)	

FIFTY-SECOND DISTRICT

San Diego began as a port, but today most metropolitan area residents live out of sight of the sea, in hilltop neighborhoods inland that look out over distant ridges and freeways or in warm, sunny valleys amid the mountains which become denser and higher as one travels east from the Pacific. There is a discernible difference in attitudes and values between those who have settled inland and those nearer the ocean, part of the split which became critical in California's political struggles and culture wars since the 1980s. In San Diego, both groups tend to identify as Republicans, and coastal people may be more affluent. But those who settle inland are more likely to be conventionally religious and to have traditional moral values; they tend to be more supportive of the military and assertive foreign policy; they are more dubious about the ability of government to shape poor citizens' lives. They are more conservative on most of the cultural and foreign issues of recent times, and therefore more reliably Republican: When oceanfront voters in San Diego shifted sharply toward Democrats in 1992, those in inland suburbs shifted more to Ross Perot but stayed Republican in other races.

The 52d Congressional District—the highest-numbered House district in American history—takes in many of the inland San Diego suburbs and proceeds eastward across mountains and desert and the man-made Salton Sea to the drained-dry Colorado River on the Arizona border. More than half its people are clustered in suburbs directly east of San Diego, off I-8 and Routes 94 and 67: Lemon Grove, La Mesa, Spring Valley, El Cajon, Santee. The rest are scattered in pockets around rural San Diego County and in the Imperial Valley, irrigated desert land where low-paid farm workers harvest some of America's most bounteous crops.

The congressman from the 52d is Duncan Hunter, who came to the House in 1980 as an upset winner in the Reagan landslide and now leads a strain of America-first Republicanism, which is not represented in large numbers in the House, but which Hunter thinks has greater support among ordinary voters. Hunter served in the Army in Vietnam in helicopter combat assaults, and was an antipoverty lawyer afterwards. In 1980, at 32, he beat an incumbent Democrat and came to the House brash and confident he had the right answers. In the 1980s he was part of the group of young conservative Republicans around Newt Gingrich. On the Armed Services Committee, he was an ardent backer of the Strategic Defense Initiative and of the buildup of the Navy. He worked to block relaxation of export controls on high-tech products. In the early 1990s he developed on his own a politics very much like Patrick Buchanan's. He has continued to work for higher defense expenditures on particular programs. But he has strongly opposed free trade measures, once taking a sledgehammer to a Japanese car. And, representing a district with hundreds of miles along the Mexican border, he has prosecuted a crusade for more fences and barriers along the border.

On Armed Services he remains in line with the Republican leadership. He is a strong backer of Republican proposals to keep U.S. troops from serving under U.N. command. As chairman of the Military Procurement Subcommittee, he called for accelerated F-22 development because of its stealth capabilities even though the F-15 has a long shelf life; he notes that the F-117s that Congress provided over the Pentagon's objections worked well in the Gulf war. He supported building more B-2s, and has tried to push the Pentagon to build more nuclear submarines and match apparent Russian gains in quiet technology. He said that President Clinton's February 1999 defense budget was $11 billion too low and that Clinton "has brought our defenses to dangerously low levels." He opposed the 1998 pork-laden highway bill because it would take money from national defense.

Hunter's most open break with the Republican leadership came in the debate over NAFTA, of which he was one of the most ardent opponents. He decried Mexican abuses of human rights and in 1996 said that NAFTA cost the United States 250,000 jobs. He also vociferously opposed GATT in 1994, the Mexico bailout in 1995, and fast track in 1997. "We're engaged in what I call dumb trade." In October 1995 he warned that he would vote against the Republican budget unless fast-track authority for extending NAFTA to Chile was removed; it was. He also became a vociferous opponent of expanding trade with China. In 1998, he led the successful effort to deny Clinton the authority to issue a waiver allowing the China Ocean Shipping Company to lease a terminal at the former Long Beach naval station: "For all practical purposes, COSCO is the merchant marine of the Chinese military." And he sponsored passage of an amendment banning satellite technology transfers to China, stifling what he said might be "the greatest triumph of greed over national security in history."

In the early 1990s, Hunter called for a 10-foot steel wall to replace the chain link fence between San Diego and Tijuana and worked to use military personnel to repair border fences and improve border roads. And he enacted a "return-to-sender" system to intercept sewage flows from across the border in Tijuana and return them to Mexico before sewage can enter the Tijuana River and pollute San Diego beaches. More recently, he has pushed for a three-layer fence, with barriers 30 feet apart, along the border. Border concerns also prompted Hunter's opposition to funds to secure a federal loan guarantee to rebuild the San Diego & Arizona Eastern Railroad. San Diego Democrat Bob Filner argued that it would provide the port of San Diego with a direct connection to an east-west railroad. But Hunter noted that the railroad dips into Mexico and said it would attract Mexican bandits, border crossers and cocaine smugglers, and the proposal lost 238–162 in June 1996. He objected to a 1999 INS plan to release criminal aliens from crowded U.S. jails, saying "tents which are good enough for housing our soldiers . . . should be good enough for housing criminals."

Hunter has usually been re-elected without difficulty. In 1992 he was troubled by 399 House bank overdrafts totalling $129,000, and for three days set up a card table in front of the El Cajon courthouse with copies of his checks, ready to explain each one to any voter. He was re-elected with a closer than usual 53%–41%. In 1998, he had no major party opposition.

Cook's Call. *Safe.* Hunter's only close race this decade was due to a combination of remapping and his 399 bounced checks at the House bank in 1992. Without those factors at work in 2000, Hunter is a sure bet for re-election.

The People: Pop. 1990: 573,355; 11% rural; 11.4% age 65 + ; 83.7% White, 3% Black, 3% Asian, 1.2% Amer. Indian, 9% Other; 22.3% Hispanic Origin. Households: 57.1% married couple families; 29.4% married couple fams. w. children; 52.1% college educ.; median household income: $33,046; per capita income: $14,075; median house value: $155,400; median gross rent: $516.

1996 Presidential Vote

Dole (R)	94,035	(48%)
Clinton (D)	81,401	(41%)
Perot (I)	16,657	(8%)
Others	5,531	(3%)

1992 Presidential Vote

Bush (R)	81,421	(37%)
Clinton (D)	74,913	(34%)
Perot (I)	63,176	(29%)

Rep. Duncan Hunter (R)

Elected 1980; b. May 31, 1948, Riverside; home, Alpine; U. of MT, U. of CA, Western St. U., B.S.L & J.D. 1976; Baptist; married (Lynne).

Military Career: Army, 1969–71 (Vietnam).

Professional Career: Practicing atty., 1976–80.

DC Office: 2265 RHOB 20515, 202-225-5672; Fax: 202-225-0235; Web site: www.house.gov/hunter.

District Offices: El Cajon, 619-579-3001; Imperial, 760-353-5420.

Committees: *Armed Services* (3d of 32 R): Military Procurement (Chmn.); Military Readiness; Special Oversight Panel on the Merchant Marine.

Group Ratings

	ADA	ACLU	AFS	LCV	CON	NTU	NFIB	COC	ACU	NTLC	CHC
1998	5	6	13	8	42	66	86	71	100	97	100
1997	0	—	25	—	9	53	—	80	88	—	—

National Journal Ratings

	1997 LIB — 1997 CONS			1998 LIB — 1998 CONS		
Economic	14%	—	85%	23%	—	74%
Social	0%	—	90%	3%	—	90%
Foreign	24%	—	72%	27%	—	68%

Key Votes of the 105th Congress

1. Clinton Budget Deal	Y	5. Puerto Rico Sthood. Ref.	N	9. Cut $ for B-2 Bombers	N
2. Education IRAs	Y	6. End Highway Set-asides	Y	10. Human Rights in China	Y
3. Req. 2/3 to Raise Taxes	Y	7. School Prayer Amend.	Y	11. Withdraw Bosnia Troops	N
4. Fast-track Trade	N	8. Ovrd. Part. Birth Veto	Y	12. End Cuban TV-Marti	N

Election Results

1998 general	Duncan Hunter (R)	116,251	(76%)	($605,857)
	Lynn Badler (Lib)	21,933	(14%)	
	Adrienne Pelton (NL)	15,380	(10%)	
1998 primary	Duncan Hunter (R)	84,703	(78%)	
	Lynn Badler (Lib)	13,090	(12%)	
	Adrienne Pelton (NL)	10,320	(10%)	
1996 general	Duncan Hunter (R)	116,746	(65%)	($632,305)
	Darity Wesley (D)	53,104	(30%)	($40,178)
	Others	8,471	(5%)	

COLORADO

Colorado in the 1990s, at the Front Range of the Rocky Mountains, has also been at the front edge of economic, cultural and political change. Colorado is an island of nearly 4 million people surrounded by the sea of the Great Plains and the ramparts of the Rockies. With vistas of vast emptiness, it is mostly an urban state: more than half its people live in metropolitan Denver and four-fifths in the urban strip paralleling the Front Range, where the Rockies rise suddenly from the mile-high plateau. And its very ruggedness is inviting more settlement: as the eastern plains continue to lose population, the valley-crevices between the mountains are being filled with second-home condominiums and ranchettes. While much of Colorado's positive change has gone unnoticed in the rest of the country, the state came glaringly into the national spotlight when Columbine High School, in the Denver suburb of Littleton, became the site of the deadliest school massacre in the nation's history.

Colorado started off with a boom, with the discovery of gold and silver in the crevasses of the Rockies. Evidence of this mining boom can be seen still in the opera houses and storefronts of Cripple Creek and Central City, Aspen and Telluride, built when Denver was just a village on the creek that is the South Platte River. Then Denver grew, as a meatpacking, banking and manufacturing center, and also as the state capital and regional headquarters of the federal government: growth that is evident in the orderly neighborhoods and pleasant parks of older Denver neighborhoods. Then came the booms of the 1960s and the high-energy-priced 1970s, when the Denver skyline sprouted new buildings overlooking the Capitol's golden dome and entrepreneurs built ever more ski resorts and year-round mountain condominiums.

The pre-1970s Colorado was politically just a bit more Republican than the nation as a whole, with cautious Democrats alternating in office with conventionally conservative Republicans. But in the decades since, two waves of young newcomers produced two distinctly Coloradan generations of politicians: liberal Democrats starting in the 1970s, conservative Republicans coming to power in the 1990s. The newcomers of the 1970s, entranced by the splendor of the Rockies and enjoying the long 1960s prosperity, wanted to slow down development and protect the environment. They disliked the boosterism of traditional politicians of both parties, and sponsored a referendum in 1972 preventing the Winter Olympics from coming to Colorado. That same year they elected Patricia Schroeder to the House. In 1974 they elected Dick Lamm governor, Gary Hart U.S. senator, and Tim Wirth congressman. All had grown up elsewhere and chosen to live in Colorado; all went on to long careers, intent on limiting growth and limiting the reach of U.S. military power; they set the tone of Colorado politics for years. There were countervailing trends. The oil-driven prosperity of the late 1970s produced a new entrepreneurial class, and Republicans controlled the legislature from 1976. Denver Mayor Federico Pena built grand new projects: a convention center, Coors Field baseball stadium, the cost-overrun-plagued Denver International Airport far out in the plains. But these slightly-older-than-baby-boomer Democrats set the tone of Colorado's public life. Lamm, who called for less immigration and for older people to move on, remained governor until 1986. His successor, Roy Romer, though from rural eastern Colorado, had somewhat different priorities—higher taxes for education—but also pushed for regional planning and a light rail system. Metropolitan Denver casts most of Colorado's votes, and for years Denver seemed guided by the values of Boulder, home of the University of Colorado and beacon of upscale environmentalism.

The conservative wave of the 1990s came in less visibly and without the dazzling cadre of election winners that propelled the liberal wave of the 1970s. It has been sparked by newcomers. Colorado's economy boomed in the 1990s, fueled not by energy as in the 1970s but by high-tech: this is the headquarters of cable giant TCI and QWest and dozens of smaller high-tech companies. Since 1990 some 300,000 people have moved here, many of them refugees from southern California's recession—and moral climate. One such was Dr. James Dobson, who in 1994 moved to Colorado Springs, where the headquarters of his Focus on the Family has a stunning view centered on Pike's Peak. Colorado Springs, the home of the Air Force Academy and Fort Carson, has always been conservative, but in the 1990s it became almost monopartisanly Republican and a stronghold of religious and family-oriented conservatives—a contrast to environment-conscious and secular Boulder. Just as Boulder's spirit seemed to migrate down the old U.S. 36 to Denver in the 1970s, so Colorado Springs's spirit seemed to surge up the wide Interstate 25, through the spanking-new subdivisions of Douglas County, one of the fastest-growing counties in the United States.

Politically, the conservative movement won its first big victories in two of Colorado's frequent referendums. In 1990 Colorado became one of the first states to pass term limits; in 1992 it passed a measure requiring a popular vote to raise taxes—much to the frustration of Governor Roy Romer, since his proposed tax increases were routinely voted down in the years ahead. In 1992 Democrats still seemed strong in Colorado: Congressman Ben Nighthorse Campbell from the Western Slope was elected to the U.S. Senate and Bill Clinton carried the state, even as Ross Perot won 23%, one of his highest percentages. But the movement was actually in the other direction. In 1995 Campbell switched parties, and Colorado had two Republican senators for the first time since 1972; since a Republican won his House seat in 1992, the House delegation was 4–2 Republican. Colorado was one of three states which went for Clinton in 1992 and then switched to Bob Dole in 1996 (the others were rural Montana and fast-growing Georgia). The region which set the tone was not the central city of Denver (62%–30% for Clinton) or Boulder (52%–35% for Clinton) but Colorado Springs and El Paso County (59%–32% for Dole), which cast nearly as many votes. Perot's vote was down to 7%, with most of his old supporters going to Dole. Turnout, down in most of the state, was up in El Paso County and up heavily in Douglas. Also in 1996 Republican Wayne Allard won the open Senate seat, 51%–46%, though he was outspent $2.8 million to $2.2 million by a Democrat with close ties to Denver developers and political insiders.

Colorado has continued to grow, and to grow more Republican. Its importance was recognized when both major parties chose Coloradans as national party chairmen. (The last state with that distinction was Texas in 1973.) Clinton, dogged by charges of campaign finance violations, picked Romer, widely respected for his integrity and candor. The Republicans elected longtime party official Jim Nicholson, real estate developer and Vietnam veteran. Party registration switched from a 30,000 Democratic plurality in 1992 to a 120,000 Republican plurality in 1998, a 52%–48% Republican edge. These newcomers tend to be high-tech, family-oriented cultural conservatives: in the 1990s public school enrollment rose 14%, while private school enrollment was up 33% and the number of home-schooled children tripled. To explain these trends, Nicholson invoked tradition: "The spirit of the Rocky Mountain West, the emphasis on freedom and rugged individualism, coincides well with Republican values." The

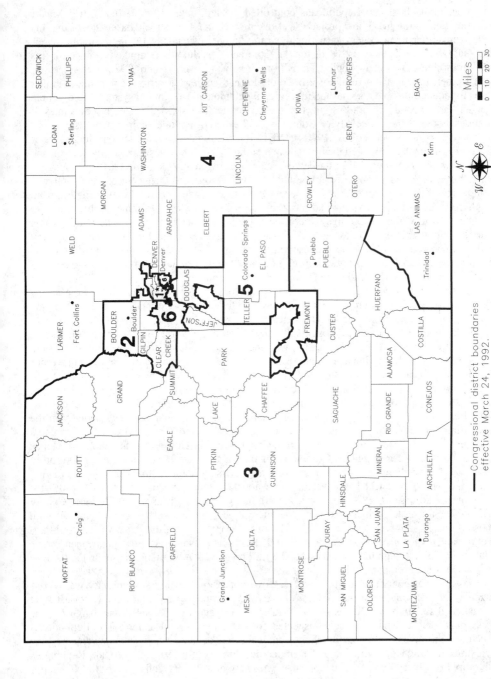

Congressional district boundaries effective March 24, 1992.

Republican ascendancy was sealed by the election of 1998. Term limits prevented Romer from running again, and kicked in on legislators as well. Both parties put forward attractive and well-financed candidates: Romer's Lieutenant Governor Gail Schoettler, and state Treasurer Bill Owens. Owens's win gave conservative Republicans control of state government for the first time since the liberal Democrats of the 1970s won their first victories. But they did not carry quite all before them in this changing state. In referenda, voters approved a requirement of parental consent for abortions but rejected a partial-birth abortion ban; they voted against tax credits for private schools and against a measure to let the state keep a larger share of the income tax. Coloradans voted for regulating hog lots (with a 20 cent per piglet fee) and Denver voted for a tax for a new Broncos stadium (the Broncos' Super Bowl victory helped this pass).

Governor. Bill Owens grew up in Texas and was appointed a page by Congressman Jim Wright, whom Owens's father had supported in his first victory in 1954. He went to Austin State University, where he demonstrated with a red-white-and-blue armband against anti-Vietnam war demonstrators, and to the University of Texas's Lyndon B. Johnson School, where he was one of the few Republicans during the Watergate scandal. He moved to Colorado and went to work for an oil producers' association. In 1982 he was elected to the state House and in 1988 to the state Senate. There he sponsored a successful charter schools law in 1993 and public school choice in 1994. He opposed Roy Romer's 1% tax for education. He worked for deregulation of taxis, limousines, messengers and off-road charters, and for the three-strikes law. In 1994 he was elected state treasurer.

Colorado's choice for governor was, as the country's choice for president in 2000 may be, one between a New Republican and New Democrat. With support from conservative activists, Owens won the party nomination in convention, but was challenged in the primary by state Senate President Tom Norton, who favored Referendum B, which would have given the state a larger share of the income tax. Owens from July 1998 on had to admit that he had stated wrongly that he had not sought military deferments while in college, and he had to deal with a Republican state chairman who refused to endorse him and changed the locks on party headquarters to keep the vice-chairman out. Owens won the primary, despite the draft issue, by 59%–41%. Meanwhile, Schoettler was opposed by state Senate Minority Leader Mike Feeley, who was endorsed by the AFL-CIO and the Colorado Education Association; she won 53%–45%.

In the general the issues were squarely raised. Owens favored cutting the state income tax and eliminating the property tax on business property like computers and machines; he called for tort reform; he called for holding teachers and students accountable for results, while reducing education regulation; he wanted more emphasis on buses rather than light rail. Schoettler, riding across the state on a Tennessee walking horse named Sam to promote her views, represented continuity with past policies; she had worked for Governor Dick Lamm and then was elected treasurer and lieutenant governor. Schoettler cut into the usual Republican vote among high-earning and high-education voters; Owens depended heavily on the support of the elderly. Schoettler claimed, "Colorado is on the right track," with the economy booming, crime down and the state budget in surplus. Owens said, "This is a system controlled by one party way too long. We need change and we need change at the top." Romer argued that it would be dangerous to turn over control to "an increasingly conservative legislature and a very conservative governor." It was a close election, but Owens won 49%–48%. Schoettler had a 65%–45% margin in metro Denver, but Owens carried the rest of the state by 51%–46%, including 61%–36% in El Paso County.

The very close result suggested that many voters shared Romer's qualms. But Owens did win, and Republicans have solid majorities in the legislature. Now 1990s Republicans have the opportunity 1970s Democrats once had to govern. Owens is likely to move to cut taxes, restrict abortions, and overturn Romer vetoes on issues like workmen's comp reform and streamlining of air quality provisions. He was widely credited for his prominent role in dealing with the Columbine High School shootings.

Senior Senator. Ben Nighthorse Campbell is the only Native American Indian in the Senate—only the eighth to serve in Congress, and a former Democrat who switched to the Republican Party in March 1995. He is a distinctive figure, with his bolo ties and his pony tail, riding a motorcycle as he did in a parade at the 1996 Republican National Convention, or riding a horse wearing full Indian headdress as he did at the 1993 Presidential Inaugural Parade. Campbell had a rough early life; he was placed in an orphanage, dropped out of high school, joined the Air Force and served in Korea. He studied judo for four years in Japan and was captain of the 1964 U.S. Olympic judo team and carried the American flag in the opening ceremonies. He settled not in one of the trendy "granola belt" ski resorts but in the small town of Ignacio, on the plain below Durango, near the New Mexico border, where he bred horses and built a successful jewelry-making business. He is a member of the Northern Cheyenne tribe and attends tribal ceremonies every year in Montana.

Campbell got into politics serendipitously. One day in 1982 his plane was grounded and he attended a Democratic Party meeting for a friend being nominated for sheriff; Campbell spoke briefly and was soon drafted to run for the legislature. He spent $13,000 of his own money and won. In 1986 he ran for Congress and beat a Republican incumbent who had personal financial problems. In the House he had a moderate record, showing more interest in economic growth than in preserving the environment. In 1992, when Tim Wirth made his surprise announcement to retire from the Senate, Campbell plunged into the race. He faced two tough Denver-based candidates. First was three-term Governor Dick Lamm, out of office for six years, often known as "Governor Gloom" for his forebodings about population growth and immigration; the terminally ill have a "duty to die," he once said. In the primary, Campbell, with backing from the Western Slope and other non-upscale areas, won 46%, while Lamm, carrying Denver, its affluent suburbs, and the "granola belt" of mountain resorts, won 36%. In the general election Campbell faced entrepreneur Terry Considine, a former state senator who started the national term limits movement in Colorado. In the weeks before his election, Campbell kept with him a ceremonial eagle feather tuft and Northern Cheyennes held a series of ritual ceremonies and prayer meetings on his behalf. Campbell benefited from Bill Clinton's victory in Colorado, from the endorsement of the active Colorado Perot organization, and from the fact that he backed some of Considine's conservative reforms. Campbell won 52%–43%.

In the Senate, Campbell criticized Clinton's stands on grazing fees and Mining Act revision. Then, in March 1995, the day after the balanced budget amendment failed in the Senate by one vote, he switched parties. He acted partly out of irritation with Denver area liberals, for their environmental stands and also maybe their penchant for reform: he was upset when he was denied an exemption from congressional income limits on his jewelry making, even though book royalties and investment income is exempted. At the Republican convention in San Diego, he said, "The Democratic Party has become a party of special interests, not the people's interests," while Republicans are "the party that will protect private property rights and your right to use the public lands."

As a Republican, he switched on some issues—the partial-birth abortion ban, oil-drilling in the Arctic National Wildlife Reserve, the assault weapons ban. But he continued to support labor unions' positions on many issues, and his voting record on economic and cultural issues has been right in the middle of the Senate. He sponsored laws to aid police departments in buying bulletproof vests and to pay for stationing cops in schools. He called for "probationary certification" of Mexico's drug-fighting program in 1997 and sponsored a ban on human cloning in 1998. He commissioned a GAO report showing that the Army overpaid for the Rocky Mountain Arsenal cleanup. With Olympia Snowe he sponsored a repeal of the federal law penalizing states without mandatory motorcycle helmet laws. As chairman of Appropriations Treasury and General Government Subcommittee, he has worked on Colorado causes, on getting money for a juvenile drug court in Fort Collins, a multipurpose juvenile facility in Montrose and the Denver women's business center, Mi Casa.

He has worked on, and gotten some criticism for, other bills close to home. He was criticized in 1998 for a bill to sell the Vallecito Reservoir to the Pine River Irrigation District, in which as a rancher he owns shares; critics said the price was too low. In March 1999 the Citizens Progressive Alliance filed a complaint with the Senate Ethics Committee on Campbell's failure to disclose his interest in the deal. He has been a strong backer of the Animas-LaPlata water project—originally a $700 million project for irrigation and industrial development, now thanks to environmental opposition and budget constraints a $200 million project billed as settling the water claims of the Mountain and Southern Utes. Campbell shepherded to passage a law to find and purchase the site of the 1864 Sand Creek massacre. He is chairman of the Indian Affairs Committee, and has opposed, so far successfully, Slade Gorton's attempts to waive tribes' sovereign immunity from civil litigation, and to means-test assistance to tribes. In 1998 he attacked Democratic lobbyist Nathan Landow for seeking the business of the Cheyenne-Arapahoe tribe, which though poor contributed $107,000 to the Democrats. He wants to have Indian nickels minted again, in Denver.

Campbell was re-elected in 1998, the first Colorado senator to seek re-election since 1984 and the first to have been elected while in two different parties since Henry Teller in 1903. But this result was not always certain. His 1996 annoucement for re-election infuriated Western Slope Congressman Scott McInnis; based on Campbell's assurance that he would run for governor, McInnis had started running for Senate and raised $850,000. For months he vowed to run anyway; this irritated national Republican leaders, who didn't want to see a prominent party-switcher beaten in a primary; in October McInnis abruptly withdrew. On the Democratic side, Governor Roy Romer withdrew early, and 2d District Congressman David Skaggs in October not only took himself out of the Senate race but decided to retire from the House too. That left Dottie Lamm, Dick Lamm's wife and for 17 years a *Denver Post* columnist, to hold the Democratic torch.

Both Campbell and Lamm had primary opposition and it turned out that the Democrats were more damagingly divided than the Republicans. Conservative Bill Eggert charged that Campbell was too liberal on abortion and union issues; he got 43% against him at the state convention. But the Senate Republicans campaign committee took the unusual step of mailing postcards endorsing Campbell, and he won the Republican primary 71%–29%. Lamm did not fare so well. Denver's graying boomer liberals remain concerned about the environment and fiscally cautious, but Lamm found that unions were hostile to her and Hispanics put off by her husband's opposition to immigration. Lightly-financed state Senator Gil Romero (who got out of the 3d District House race when Scott McInnis got back in) actually beat Lamm in the convention and held her to a 58%–42% in the Democratic primary, whose turnout was far below that of the Republican contest.

In the general Lamm ran an ingenious ad campaign hitting Campbell for his flip-flops on issues from gay rights to campaign finance reform. She noted his switch on ANWR and his opposition to the tobacco settlement—and the contributions he received from oil and tobacco PACs. Campbell countered with radio ads of a clock repairman discussing Lamm's columns—17 years of potentially controversial material!—with his wife. As he read words questioning organ transplants to seniors and life support for the smallest premature babies, the listener suddenly heard, "Cuckoo, cuckoo." The teachers' union endorsed Lamm and the Sierra Club ran ads against Campbell. But Lamm was reduced to bedrock granola: she carried the counties containing Denver, Boulder, Aspen and Telluride, and lost everything else. These counties cast only 21% of the state's votes, and Lamm's 53%–45% win there produced only a 22,000-vote margin. Colorado Springs's El Paso County and the four suburban counties around Denver cast 46% of the state's votes and Campbell won them 66%–32%, for a 210,000-vote margin. The rest of the state cast 33% of the vote, and was carried 69%–29% by Campbell, for a 177,000-vote majority. Overall, Campbell won 62%–35%, a big enough margin to make him a favorite to win in 2004 the second full term to which he limited himself.

Junior Senator. Wayne Allard is a Republican elected in 1996. He grew up in the northern end of the Front Range, attended veterinary school, and built a veterinary practice in Loveland—a lively business in an area with vast feedlots. In 1982 he was elected to the state Senate, where he succeeded in limiting the length of legislative sessions—so legislators would be more in touch with their constituents, he said. In 1990, when Congressman Hank Brown, a moderate on cultural issues but a workfare advocate and porkbuster in the House, ran for the Senate, the solidly conservative Allard ran for the House in the 4th District, which covered much of the High Plains and the northern end of the Front Range. Against a former local university president and legislator, Allard barely carried the Front Range, but he won 61% on the conservative High Plains, for a solid 54% victory. He was easily re-elected in 1992 and 1994 and, when Brown retired from the Senate after just one term, Allard ran for the seat.

Allard's voting record was one of the most conservative in the House. He returned more than $1 million in unspent office funds, and sponsored a Citizens Congress Act, to abolish the congressional pension system, require votes on pay raises, ban personal use of frequent flier miles, and ban unsolicited mailings. "I have always felt it was important that whoever serves in the House and Senate be able to walk in the shoes of the people they represent," he said. He moved to defund the National Biological Survey in 1994, charging that it leads to misuse of the Endangered Species Act. He sponsored a bill for regulatory relief for the farm credit system and a bill to improve the process of approving drugs for animals, both of which passed.

Allard was scarcely the best known possible candidate going into 1996, but others better known declined to run—former Senator Gary Hart, Governor Roy Romer, former Governor Dick Lamm. His primary opponent, Attorney General Gale Norton, lost in the Supreme Court defending Colorado's anti-gay rights Amendment 2 a month before the June 1996 nominating convention, and her support of abortion rights rankled many Republican activists and voters. With strong support from religious conservatives, Allard led 40%–31% at the convention. With more money, he ran a blitz of ads before the primary, stressing his background as a veterinarian: "Four candidates for the U.S. Senate. Three more lawyers and Wayne Allard." In the August 13 primary, Norton ran close to even in metro Denver, but Allard took 62% in the rest of the state, and won 57%–43%. The Democratic nominee was Tom Strickland, law partner of Phil Brownstein, one of the key fundraisers and political insiders in Colorado; Strickland lost the convention to a campaign finance reformer, but with far more money won the primary 66%–34%.

In the general Strickland had more money and sophistication, but Allard ended up with more votes. Strickland held fundraisers with Robert Redford and Gloria Steinem. Strickland attacked Allard's "Neanderthal" positions on the environment; Allard said he was interested in "sound science" rather than emotional appeals, more local decision-making and less bureaucracy. Allard went on to run ads attacking Strickland for defending clients with environmental problems, including one company trying to build a medical waste incinerator in a poor Denver neighborhood. Strickland delayed releasing his tax records, then revealed he made $886,000 in 1995. His image as a lobbyist hurt; as one former Romer aide said, "Tom's OK with me, but I don't like the people around Tom. I don't believe you can swim with the sharks and say you're a trout." Allard won 51%–46%, trailing only narrowly in metro Denver (47%–51%) and winning solidly in the rest of the state (56%–41%).

Allard has a very conservative voting record in the Senate. He has often been part of small minorities taking conservative stands—on the Chemical Weapons convention and the May 1997 budget deal, for instance. He has his own special causes. He wants to eliminate the Overseas Private Investment Corporation, which insures foreign investments by U.S. companies; he calls it corporate welfare, with a Democratic twist (because it helped many companies who gave to Democrats). He has a bill to pay back $11.65 billion of the national debt every year from 1999 to 2028. He wants to eliminate the estate tax and pass a constitutional amendment authorizing the line-item veto. He has tended to small Colorado issues. He pushed through a privately funded visitor center at Rocky Mountain National Park and a ban on commercial flights over the park. He put a hold on the Spanish Peaks Wilderness bill because of local concerns and pushed a Greeley reservoir land swap. He held up an EPA appointee in February 1998 until the EPA approved Colorado's environmental audit law and he put a hold on a DOT appointee to try to get approval of a British Airways Denver-London flight. He called for more flexibility on the leaking underground storage tank fund. He served on the Environment and Public Works Committee which passed the transportation bill in 1998 and, despite his leeriness about spending, he hailed Colorado's 52% increase in spending, to $1.8 billion, and sponsored an amendment to change the mass transit funding formula to give more money to smaller metro areas like Denver. For 1999 he received the chair of the Housing and Transportation Subcommittee on Banking; in 1998 he introduced a bill to make it easier for community banks to convert to taxsaving Subchapter S corporations.

Allard promised to hold town meetings in all 63 counties in his first year; he had kept his word by September 1997. This close attention to oft-ignored areas he surely hopes will pay off in even greater rural margins in 2002, when his seat comes up. He had perfect attendance on all 298 recorded votes in his first year in the Senate.

Presidential politics. Colorado has been one of the most closely contested states in presidential elections in the 1990s; a reporter could do worse than cover the race from the Denver media market. In 1988 and 1992 it voted close to the national average; in 1996, with the rising voice of Colorado Springs and family-oriented conservatism here, it switched and voted for Bob Dole.

Colorado in the 1990s has had an early March presidential primary. It has produced one interesting result, the victory of Jerry Brown in March 1992, but has otherwise been mostly predictable. It will be part of the Big Sky primary on March 10 in 2000.

Congressional districting. Colorado did not gain a new House seat out of the 1990 Census, for the first time in three decades, because of sagging population growth in the mid-1980s. Redistricting by the Republican legislature and Democratic Governor Roy Romer didn't change the districts much. Now that Republicans control the legislature and governorship, the likelihood is that they will try to create another Republican district for 2002.

The People: Est. Pop. 1998: 3,970,971; Pop. 1990: 3,294,394, up 20.5% 1990–1998. 1.5% of U.S. total, 24th largest; 17.6% rural. Median age: 35 years. 10.4% 65 years and over. 88.3% White, 4% Black, 1.8% Asian, 0.9% Amer. Indian, 5% Other; 12.7% Hispanic Origin. Households: 53.8% married couple families; 26.7% married couple fams. w. children; 57.9% college educ.; median household income: $30,140; per capita income: $14,821; 62.3% owner occupied housing; median house value: $82,700; median monthly rent: $362. 3.8% Unemployment. 1998 Voting age pop.: 2,961,000. 1998 Turnout: 1,321,305; 45% of VAP. Registered voters (1998): 2,563,441; 783,044 D (31%), 914,486 R (37%), 865,911 unaffiliated and minor parties (34%).

Political Lineup: Governor, Bill Owens (D); Lt. Gov., Joe Rogers (R); Secy. of State, Victoria Buckley (R); Atty. Gen., Ken Salazar (D); Treasurer, Mike Coffman (R); State Senate, 35 (15 D, 20 R); Majority Leader, Tom Blickensderfer (R); State House, 65 (25 D, 40 R); House Speaker, Russell George (R). Senators, Ben Nighthorse Campbell (R) and Wayne Allard (R). Representatives, 6 (2 D, 4 R).

Elections Division: 303-894-2680; **Filing Deadline for U.S. Congress:** June 13, 2000.

1996 Presidential Vote

Dole (R)	691,846	(46%)
Clinton (D)	671,150	(44%)
Perot (I)	99,628	(7%)
Others	45,646	(3%)

1996 Republican Presidential Primary

Dole (R)	108,065	(44%)
Buchanan (R)	53,314	(22%)
Forbes (R)	51,557	(21%)
Alexander (R)	24,164	(10%)
Keyes (R)	9,049	(4%)

1992 Presidential Vote

Clinton (D)	629,681	(40%)
Bush (R)	562,850	(36%)
Perot (I)	366,010	(23%)

GOVERNOR

Gov. Bill Owens (D)

Elected 1998, term expires Jan. 2003; b. Oct. 22, 1950, Ft. Worth, TX; home, Aurora; Austin St. U., B.S. 1973; U. of TX, M.P.A. 1975; Catholic; married (Frances).

Elected Office: CO House of Reps., 1982–88; CO Senate, 1988–94; CO Treasurer, 1994–98.

Professional Career: Consultant, Touche Ross & Co., 1975–77; Project Mgr., Gates Corp., 1977–80, Assoc. Dir., 1980–82; Exec. Dir., CO trade assn., 1982–95.

Office: 136 State Capitol, Denver, 80203, 303-866-2471; Fax: 303-866-2003; Web site: www.state.co.us.

Election Results

1998 gen.	Bill Owens (R)	648,202	(49%)
	Gail Schoettler (D)	639,905	(48%)
	Others	33,200	(3%)
1998 prim.	Bill Owens (R)	126,613	(59%)
	Tom Norton (R)	87,269	(41%)
1994 gen.	Roy Romer (D)	619,205	(55%)
	Bruce Benson (R)	432,042	(39%)
	Others	65,060	(6%)

SENATORS

Sen. Ben Nighthorse Campbell (R)

Elected 1992, seat up 2004; b. Apr. 13, 1933, Auburn, CA; home, Ignacio; San Jose St. U., B.A. 1957, Meiji U., Japan, 1960–64; no religious affiliation; married (Linda).

Military Career: Air Force, 1951–53 (Korea).

Elected Office: CO House of Reps., 1982–86; U.S. House of Reps, 1986–92.

Professional Career: Rancher; Horse trainer; Jewelry designer.

DC Office: 380 RSOB, 20510, 202-224-5852; Fax: 202-224-1933; Web site: www.senate.gov/~campbell.

State Offices: Colorado Springs, 719-636-9092; Denver, 303-866-1900; Ft. Collins, 970-224-1909; Grand Junction, 970-241-6631; Pueblo, 719-542-6987.

Committees: *Appropriations* (12th of 15 R): Commerce, Justice, State & the Judiciary; Foreign Operations & Export Financing; Interior; Transportation; Treasury & General Government (Chmn.). *Energy & Natural Resources* (5th of 11 R): Forests & Public Land Management; National Parks, Historic Preservation & Recreation (Vice Chmn.); Water & Power. *Indian Affairs* (Chmn. of 8 R). *Veterans' Affairs* (5th of 7 R).

Group Ratings

	ADA	ACLU	AFS	LCV	CON	NTU	NFIB	COC	ACU	NTLC	CHC
1998	25	29	33	0	0	54	89	83	76	71	82
1997	25	—	11	—	54	72	—	60	72	—	—

National Journal Ratings

	1997 LIB — 1997 CONS		1998 LIB — 1998 CONS	
Economic	48% —	51%	38% —	57%
Social	51% —	45%	31% —	64%
Foreign	0% —	77%	51% —	36%

Key Votes of the 105th Congress

1. Bal. Budget Amend.	Y	5. Satcher for Surgeon Gen.	N	9. Chem. Weapons Treaty	N
2. Clinton Budget Deal	Y	6. Highway Set-asides	Y	10. Cuban Humanitarian Aid	N
3. Cloture on Tobacco	N	7. Table Child Gun locks	Y	11. Table Bosnia Troops	Y
4. Education IRAs	Y	8. Ovrd. Part. Birth Veto	Y	12. $ for Test-ban Treaty	Y

Election Results

1998 general	Ben Nighthorse Campbell (R)	829,370	(62%)	($3,045,982)
	Dottie Lamm (D)	464,754	(35%)	($1,818,801)
	Others	33,111	(3%)	
1998 primary	Ben Nighthorse Campbell (R)	154,702	(71%)	
	Bill Eggert (R)	64,347	(29%)	
1992 general	Ben Nighthorse Campbell (D)	803,725	(52%)	($1,561,347)
	Terry Considine (R)	662,893	(43%)	($2,215,791)
	Others	85,671	(6%)	

Sen. Wayne Allard (R)

Elected 1996, seat up 2002; b. Dec. 2, 1943, Fort Collins; home, Loveland; CO St. U., D.V.M. 1968; Protestant; married (Joan).

Elected Office: CO Senate, 1982–90; US House of Reps., 1990–96.

Professional Career: Veterinarian, 1968–present; Loveland City Health Officer, 1970–78; Owner, Allard Animal Hosp., 1970–90.

DC Office: 513 HSOB, 20510, 202-224-5941; Fax: 202-224-6471; Web site: www.senate.gov/~allard.

State Offices: Colorado Springs, 719-634-6071; Englewood, 303-220-7414; Grand Junction, 970-245-9553; Greeley, 970-351-7582; Pueblo, 719-545-9751.

Committees: *Armed Services* (9th of 11 R): Airland Forces; Personnel (Chmn.); Strategic Forces. *Banking, Housing & Urban Affairs* (6th of 11 R): Financial Institutions; Housing & Transportation (Chmn.); Securities. *Intelligence* (9th of 9 R).

Group Ratings

	ADA	ACLU	AFS	LCV	CON	NTU	NFIB	COC	ACU	NTLC	CHC
1998	5	14	0	0	81	74	89	83	100	96	100
1997	0	—	0	—	25	81	—	80	100	—	—

National Journal Ratings

	1997 LIB — 1997 CONS		1998 LIB — 1998 CONS	
Economic	11% —	76%	18% —	72%
Social	0% —	83%	0% —	88%
Foreign	0% —	77%	12% —	75%

Key Votes of the 105th Congress

1. Bal. Budget Amend.	Y	5. Satcher for Surgeon Gen.	N	9. Chem. Weapons Treaty	N
2. Clinton Budget Deal	Y	6. Highway Set-asides	N	10. Cuban Humanitarian Aid	N
3. Cloture on Tobacco	N	7. Table Child Gun locks	Y	11. Table Bosnia Troops	N
4. Education IRAs	Y	8. Ovrd. Part. Birth Veto	Y	12. $ for Test-ban Treaty	N

Election Results

1996 general	Wayne Allard (R) 750,325	(51%)	($2,233,429)
	Tom Strickland (D) 677,600	(46%)	($2,894,916)
	Others 41,686	(3%)	
1996 primary	Wayne Allard (R) 115,064	(57%)	
	Gale Norton (R) 87,394	(43%)	
1990 general	Hank Brown (R) 569,048	(56%)	($3,684,020)
	Josie Heath (D) 425,746	(42%)	($1,943,422)

FIRST DISTRICT

One mile above sea level (as the plaque on the 14th step of the gold-domed Capitol reads), a few miles from where the High Plains yield to the sharp peaks of the Front Range of the Rockies, on no historic trade route and with a fresh water supply adequate for a town one-tenth of its size, stands the great metropolitan center of Denver. With 2 million people, it has been the economic and cultural capital for 100 years of the whole Rocky Mountain region. On top of its Old West heritage and early 20th Century elegance, Denver has developed an exuberant postmodern style. The National Western Stock Show held here every year and the LoDo entertainment district redeveloped near the railyards along the South Platte evoke the Old West; the Capitol, the spacious parks, the aspens which line so many streets, give the city a lush, burnished air, in contrast to the dry high plains and the stark Rocky peaks. Amid its downtown grid, slanted on a 45-degree angle to align with the South Platte and the railroads, are the skyscrapers of the 1970s energy and 1990s high-tech booms, plus the new-old Coors Stadium and Elitch Gardens amusement park. Denver has not lost population as many central cities have, and most of its neighborhoods have vitality, including the black neighborhoods of northeastern Denver, filled with well maintained 1950s bungalows, and the Hispanic quarter northwest of downtown. But three-quarters of the metro area's people now live in the suburbs, and Denver has disproportionate numbers of singles and cultural liberals who value an urban lifestyle, in the gentrified areas south of the Capitol and the rich neighborhood where the Tattered Cover, among the nation's premier independent book stores, sits opposite posh Cherry Creek Shopping Center.

Denver increasingly is the liberal heart of Colorado, heavily Democratic as the state mostly votes Republican, strongly liberation-minded on cultural issues, cautiously liberal on economic issues. Though it remains majority white Anglo, it has elected Hispanic and black mayors since 1983—Federico Pena, who became Bill Clinton's Transportation and then Energy secretary, and the current incumbent Wellington Webb. In the early 1970s Denver liberals were hostile to growth and boosterism; today's Denver has shown that growth can improve a city and that a little local pride is not so bad. Twenty years ago Denver's winters were palled by "brown cloud" air pollution. But the city has cut down on wood fires and used non-polluting de-icing agents and oxygenated gasoline, and in 1998 it had its second consecutive brown-cloudless winter. From Cherry Creek to LoDo, Denver has shown that growth can produce more of the distinctiveness that people here like.

The 1st Congressional District of Colorado includes all of Denver and extends northeast toward DIA, taking in Commerce City and the northern part of Aurora, places with warehouses and trucking terminals on main streets and curved-street subdivisions behind. This is a heavily Democratic district, including most of metro Denver's blacks and Hispanics, singles and gays:

the percentage of households with married couples and children is among the lowest in America. In an era when cultural attitudes are a better clue to voting behavior than economic status, this once politically marginal area has become a solidly Democratic constituency.

The congresswoman from the 1st District is Diana DeGette, a Democrat elected in 1996. DeGette is a fourth-generation Denverite who went away to law school and returned to practice employment law and became involved in politics. In 1992, at 35, she was elected to the Colorado House, where she was surprisingly productive for a member of the minority. She sponsored a "bubble" bill placing a zone of protection around abortion clinics and their clients; she worked on rewriting domestic violence laws; she developed a Voluntary Cleanup and Redevelopment Act to encourage businesses and citizens to clean up the environment; she passed a bill protecting families of accident victims from being contacted by lawyers within 30 days.

In 1995, Denver Congresswoman Patricia Schroeder announced she was retiring after 24 years in the House; she was a pioneer of the feminist left, whose persistence on the Armed Services Committee helped change the military culture and who in 1987 gave serious consideration to running for president. Today, in a place like Denver, the feminist left is the heart of the Democratic Party (as the religious right is the heart of the Republican Party in Colorado Springs) and DeGette—feminist, organizationally adept and legislatively creative—seemed a natural candidate. After leading in the June nominating convention, she won the August primary by 56%–44% over former Denver Councilman Tim Sandos. In the general DeGette faced Joe Rogers (who in 1998 was elected lieutenant governor). He waged a vigorous campaign, but DeGette, with help from EMILY's List and feminists nationwide, raised far more money and won 57%–40%.

In the House DeGette has a very liberal voting record. She won a seat on the Commerce Committee and, as she had in Denver, had some legislative successes even though in the minority. One was an amendment creating "presumptive eligibility" for Medicaid for poor families with children. The idea is to let hospitals and care-givers initiate the application for government aid, so that they get paid rather than provide their services for free. Cooperating with then-6th District Republican Dan Schaefer, fifth-ranking Republican on Commerce, she got this in the May 1997 budget agreement. In October 1997 she passed an amendment barring insurance companies from considering survivors of domestic abuse as higher risks; that made it into the banking bill the House passed in May 1998. With help from Schaefer, she pushed an amendment to restore EPA funding for pilot brownfields projects, three of them in the Denver area. DeGette fell short on other goals, including an amendment to end crop insurance for tobacco farmers. She has shown skill in getting measures through the Republican House, but will need another Republican partner since Schaefer retired in 1998.

The 1998 election was anticlimactic. DeGette's opponent Nancy McClanahan proved correct when she said she had a snowball's chance in hell; DeGette won 67%–30%.

Cook's Call. *Safe.* As the most Democratic district in the state, this Denver-based district is unlikely to show up on any Republican target list. DeGette is a solid favorite for 2000.

The People: Pop. 1990: 549,053; 13.8% age 65 + ; 73% White, 12.9% Black, 2.4% Asian, 1.2% Amer. Indian, 10.5% Other; 21.7% Hispanic Origin. Households: 38% married couple families; 16.6% married couple fams. w. children; 53.9% college educ.; median household income: $24,870; per capita income: $14,942; median house value: $75,500; median gross rent: $335.

1996 Presidential Vote		
Clinton (D)	133,032	(61%)
Dole (R)	66,427	(31%)
Perot (I)	10,367	(5%)
Others	7,676	(4%)

1992 Presidential Vote		
Clinton (D)	135,016	(55%)
Bush (R)	63,283	(26%)
Perot (I)	43,245	(18%)

Rep. Diana DeGette (D)

Elected 1996; b. July 29, 1957, Tachikawa, Japan; home, Denver; CO Col., B.A. 1979, N.Y.U., J.D. 1982; Presbyterian; married (Lino Lipinsky).

Elected Office: CO House of Reps., 1992–96, Asst. Minority Ldr., 1994–95.

Professional Career: Practicing atty., 1982–96.

DC Office: 1339 LHOB 20515, 202-225-4431; Fax: 202-225-5657; Web site: www.house.gov/degette.

District Office: Denver, 303-844-4988.

Committees: *Commerce* (21st of 24 D): Finance & Hazardous Materials; Health and Environment; Oversight & Investigations.

Group Ratings

	ADA	ACLU	AFS	LCV	CON	NTU	NFIB	COC	ACU	NTLC	CHC
1998	95	94	100	100	89	21	7	22	4	5	0
1997	100	—	100	—	29	30	—	22	13	—	—

National Journal Ratings

	1997 LIB	—	1997 CONS	1998 LIB	—	1998 CONS
Economic	93%	—	0%	79%	—	0%
Social	85%	—	0%	93%	—	0%
Foreign	93%	—	6%	90%	—	5%

Key Votes of the 105th Congress

1. Clinton Budget Deal	N	5. Puerto Rico Sthood. Ref.	Y	9. Cut $ for B-2 Bombers	Y
2. Education IRAs	N	6. End Highway Set-asides	N	10. Human Rights in China	Y
3. Req. 2/3 to Raise Taxes	N	7. School Prayer Amend.	N	11. Withdraw Bosnia Troops	N
4. Fast-track Trade	N	8. Ovrd. Part. Birth Veto	N	12. End Cuban TV-Marti	Y

Election Results

1998 general	Diana DeGette (D)	116,628	(67%)	($775,271)
	Nancy McClanahan (R)	52,452	(30%)	($42,440)
	Others	5,225	(3%)	
1998 primary	Diana DeGette (D)	unopposed		
1996 general	Diana DeGette (D)	112,631	(57%)	($889,219)
	Joe Rogers (R)	79,540	(40%)	($423,755)
	Others	5,668	(3%)	

SECOND DISTRICT

Boulder, Colorado, nestled right up against the Front Range of the Rockies, the home of the University of Colorado, is billed by its convention bureau as "a combination of lycra-clad athletes, New Age artists, and thoughtful intellectuals sipping cappuccinos." It was called the nation's number one town for outdoor sports by *Outdoor* magazine, and an "international mecca for people who thrive on physical challenge and risk" by Colorado journalist Clifford May. Boulder is the nation's leading center for bungee jumping, mountain biking, snowshoe running, rock and ice climbing, downhill skiing, land surfing and hot-air ballooning, plus the home of the Buddhist Naropa Institute and the Boulder School of Massage Therapy. All of which is suggested by the terrain: Boulder literally looks up at erose rows of peaks rising to 14,000 feet from a mile-high plain laid out in mile-square grids much farther than the eye can see. Its pedestrian mall lined by kicky restaurants and shops is full of friendly fit people. But not all is happy in this paradise: Boulder is where JonBenet Ramsey was murdered in 1996, and where a police detective charged in 1998 that District Attorney Alex Hunter "effectively crippled" the investigation of the killing.

The 2d Congressional District of Colorado is centered on Boulder. It extends west to some lightly-populated but picturesque Rocky Mountains acreage, including Central City with its new gambling casino, and south to north and northwest of Denver—Arvada, Wheat Ridge, Westminster, Thornton, Northglenn, Broomfield. Here families of comfortable affluence and struggling finances, of fundamentalist religion and environment-loving liberalism, live in subdivisions with views of the mountains, close to metro Denver's biggest shopping malls. In the 1990s, greater Boulder grapples with the effects of commercial and residential "growth management," as development is restricted to just one percent annually and open space is protected by a "blue line" barrier, causing housing prices to soar. The Metro North area is politically marginal while Boulder is heavily Democratic. Overall, this is one of just a few Democratic-leaning districts in the Rocky Mountain states. But it has been trending Republican, as Boulder limits its growth while Metro North continues to grow.

The congressman from the 2d District is Mark Udall, a Democrat elected in a close race in 1998. Udall is the son of longtime (1961–91) Arizona Congressman Morris Udall, who ran for president in 1976 and died in December 1998 after a long battle with Parkinson's disease, and the nephew of Stewart Udall, who served in the House before his brother and was Interior secretary from 1961–68. "I can remember the excitement I felt sitting in a corner of Stewart's kitchen listening to my father, Stewart, Bob McNamara, Bobby Kennedy and Justice Douglas talk about the issues of the day and there was a sense of optimism and sense of involvement and sense of meaning," Mark said. He is also a cousin of Oregon Senator Gordon Smith, a Republican, and of Tom Udall, who was elected in the New Mexico 3d District in 1998. "Vote for the Udall nearest you," as Mark put it.

Soon after college, Udall moved to Boulder to work for the Colorado Outward Bound School and headed it for 10 years; he is an accomplished mountaineer (though he didn't quite make it to the top of Mount Everest), rock climber and kayaker. In 1996 he ran for the state House, and with his family and ideological connections—his wife is regional director of the Sierra Club—raised 40% of his money out of state and won. In October 1997, Udall was one of several candidates spurred to run when incumbent Democrat David Skaggs, who had been mulling a Senate race, announced he was not running for either Senate or House in 1998. First elected in 1986, Skaggs could take satisfaction in the success of the March 1997 "civility summit" he co-hosted with Ray LaHood and his lawsuit challenging the constitutionality of the line-item veto. In the primary Udall faced Gene Nichol, a University of Colorado law professor who had run for the Senate in 1996 as a backer of campaign finance reform; outspent, Nichol lost the primary 66%–34%. This time the race was closer: Udall didn't compete at the district convention, and he attributed his success to the 7,000 doors he knocked on to get enough signatures to get on the primary ballot. There he won 44%–37%.

The Republican nominee was Bob Greenlee, mayor of Boulder, member of the Boulder Council for 15 years and successful entrepreneur—the Rock Bottom Brewery, the Black Hawk casino, KXPK "The Peak" radio. Greenlee put more than $1 million into his own campaign and won the primary 66%–34%. He focused on cutting taxes and regulation; Udall stressed environmental protection, growth management and education. Udall pounced when Greenlee argued that global warming theory was based on "phony science," and he ran ads, much resented by Greenlee, attacking him for missing Council votes and firing a casino employee. He also ridiculed him for copying policy statements from a Heritage Foundation paper. Greenlee spent more and ran well in the suburbs, carrying the relatively affluent Jefferson County suburbs 55%–42% and working-class Adams County suburbs 50%–47%. But even with all his involvement in local government and charities in Boulder, he still lost Boulder County, where nearly half the votes were cast, 56%–41%. That gave Udall a 50%–47% victory; local difficulties in vote-counting made it one of the last results announced.

Udall got seats on the Resources and Science Committees and was elected western regional whip by his colleagues. As an incumbent, Udall should be favored to win re-election. But demographic trends, so long as Boulder sticks to its zero-growth policy, favor Republicans, and redistricting, likely to be controlled by Republicans, could change the political balance. Greenlee has said he will not run for office again.

Cook's Call. *Competitive.* The district leans Democratic, but not overly so. The right Republican in the right year could upset Udall but the stars would have to line up perfectly. Redistricting is probably Udall's biggest concern as there is talk about a remapping that would move some of the more Democratic parts of the district into the 1st.

The People: Pop. 1990: 548,953; 8% rural; 8.2% age 65 +; 92.9% White, 0.7% Black, 2.4% Asian, 0.6% Amer. Indian, 3.4% Other; 9.3% Hispanic Origin. Households: 55.2% married couple families; 28.1% married couple fams. w. children; 61.3% college educ.; median household income: $35,117; per capita income: $15,823; median house value: $89,900; median gross rent: $418.

1996 Presidential Vote		
Clinton (D)	127,702	(49%)
Dole (R)	102,107	(40%)
Perot (I)	16,605	(6%)
Others	12,074	(5%)

1992 Presidential Vote		
Clinton (D)	123,144	(45%)
Bush (R)	83,209	(30%)
Perot (I)	66,678	(24%)

Rep. Mark Udall (D)

Elected 1998; b. July 18, 1950, Tucson, AZ; home, Boulder; Williams Col., B.A. 1972; no religious affiliation; married (Maggie L. Fox).

Elected Office: CO House of Reps., 1996–98.

Professional Career: CO Outward Bound Course Dir., 1975–85, Exec. Dir., 1985–95.

DC Office: 128 CHOB 20515, 202-225-2161; Fax: 202-226-7840; Web site: www.house.gov/markudall.

District Office: Westminster, 305-457-4500.

Committees: *Resources* (22d of 24 D): Forests & Forest Health; National Parks & Public Lands. *Science* (16th of 22 D): Space & Aeronautics; Technology. *Small Business* (16th of 17 D).

Group Ratings and Key Votes: Newly Elected

Election Results

1998 general	Mark Udall (D)	113,946	(50%)	($1,226,580)
	Bob Greenlee (R)	108,385	(47%)	($1,879,887)
	Others	6,111	(3%)	
1998 primary	Mark Udall (D)	12,147	(44%)	
	Gene Nichol (D)	10,233	(37%)	
	Paul Weissman (D)	2,545	(9%)	
	Dave Thomas (D)	2,376	(9%)	
1996 general	David E. Skaggs (D)	145,894	(57%)	($778,880)
	Patricia Miller (R)	97,865	(38%)	($458,442)
	Others	12,025	(5%)	

THIRD DISTRICT

On a clear night from the air they look like tiny mottled veins with small clots here and there, thicker near Denver but never very bright: the lights of the civilization Americans have built on the Western Slope of the Rockies in Colorado. The lights follow the trails of valley roads and mountainside switchbacks; the nodes mark the dozens of little towns built during mining boom years: the gold rush of the 1870s, the uranium boom of the 1950s, the oil shale boomlet of the 1970s. The Western Slope—everything west of the Front Range, with dozens of peaks over 14,000 feet—has always blocked east-west movement; except for mining and now skiing, no one would have followed the Ute Indians and settled here. The miners who tracked gold and silver and lead ores also built Victorian towns with opera houses and gingerbread storefronts in Leadville and Salida in valleys and defiles scarcely accessible to the outside world. Now many of these towns have been restored by ski resort operators and joined by dozens of new condominiums and shopping malls. Cries of overdevelopment have followed, and stimulated different responses. One is extreme: the "Earth Liberation Front" has announced it burned $12 million of Vail's resort expansion facilities "on behalf of the lynx," whose reintroduction to the area began in February 1999. But there is also consensus between former adversaries: cattlemen and environmentalists are using land trusts to preserve open land in pastures around Steamboat Springs.

The political map of the Western Slope is as diverse as its history. Aspen and Telluride, with Victorian houses and counter-cultural substrata, are liberal and Democratic: the "granola belt." Vail and Crested Butte, with contemporary condominiums, formerly Republican, are trending left. The rough-handed mining area around Grand Junction, where piles of tailings still crackle with radioactivity, and the northwest corner of the state, where people remember the oil shale boom with nostalgia, is hostile to environmentalists and heavily Republican.

The 3d Congressional District of Colorado includes all the Western Slope plus the small industrial city of Pueblo. There, on the banks of the Arkansas River, the Rockefellers built large steel factories before World War I to make barbed wire and rails; now this blue-collar town has attracted new plants from Unisys and B.F. Goodrich. Pueblo is heavily Democratic and so are Hispanic Conejos and Costilla counties just to the south. Hispanic, not Mexican-American: Spanish-speaking people have been living here, as in northern New Mexico, for 350 years. Politically, the 3d District has been moving to the right, voting for Bill Clinton in 1992 and for Bob Dole in 1996.

The congressman from the 3d District is Scott McInnis, a Republican elected in 1992, when then-Democratic Congressman Ben Nighthorse Campbell was elected to the Senate. McInnis grew up in Glenwood Springs, in a crevassed valley west of Aspen and Vail. He worked as a local policeman and went to law school, practiced law and was elected to the legislature in 1982, at 29. Colorado was one of the few states in the 1980s with a Republican legislature, and McInnis became House majority leader in 1990. In 1992 he won the 3d District Republican nomination unopposed and outworked and outcampaigned Lieutenant Governor Mike Callihan to win 55%–44%.

McInnis has a moderate-to-conservative voting record, with some unusual features; he supports funding for the National Endowment for the Arts and for Denver's light rail, for example. But he is enough of a party regular to have been placed on the Rules Committee by Newt Gingrich in 1995. Gingrich has also named him a party representative on problems in Korea, in Bosnia after the Dayton accords, and in the tobacco settlement talks. McInnis travels back to his district every weekend, and he is much involved in local issues. He worked with David Skaggs on a federal-Gilpin County land transfer and, with Wayne Allard and Campbell, fought proposals to sell off federal ski resort land for deficit reduction. He worked for the Animas-La Plata project, a favorite of Campbell's, which lost in the House but was saved in the Senate. He worked with Skaggs to protect the Spanish Peaks against logging and mining, though neither Campbell nor Allard would sponsor it in the Senate.

For years McInnis worked closely with Campbell. Campbell did not endorse his Democratic opponents in 1992 and 1994, and he helped persuade Campbell to switch to the Republican Party in 1995. McInnis passed up the 1996 Senate seat and, expecting Campbell to run for governor, planned to run in 1998. But in December 1996 Campbell announced for re-election, and McInnis angrily stayed in the race—even though Wayne Allard endorsed Campbell in June 1997 and Newt Gingrich urged McInnis to stay in the House in early October, and even sent flowers. McInnis raised $850,000 for the race, then in late October grudgingly dropped out. He ran for re-election to the House, and let voters know he no longer felt bound by his 1992 pledge to limit himself to four terms. That was based on the assumption that everyone would be bound by term limits, he said; instead he would abide by the 12-year limit set in Colorado's 1990 referendum. That would leave him free to serve in the House until Campbell's seat comes up again in 2004.

McInnis's switch on term limits didn't seem to bother his constituents much; neither did his September 1998 call for Clinton's resignation. He has a zest for getting around the district and for political combat: "I love campaigning. I don't feel good unless I wake up in the morning and know I'm going to have a good fight." In 1998, against the husband of the candidate he beat in his first legislative election in 1982, he won by 66%–31%. Later in November he was awarded a seat on Ways and Means, for which he gave up Rules; a parting gift from Gingrich?

Cook's Call. *Safe.* McInnis's big wins over the past three cycles are due to a combination of his own strengths and the fact that he has had relatively weak opponents. Though this district is not as solidly Republican as others in the state, McInnis should have no trouble in 2000.

The People: Pop. 1990: 549,120; 46% rural; 13% age 65 +; 91.8% White, 0.6% Black, 0.5% Asian, 1.4% Amer. Indian, 5.7% Other; 17.3% Hispanic Origin. Households: 56.6% married couple families; 26.8% married couple fams. w. children; 49.2% college educ.; median household income: $24,521; per capita income: $12,115; median house value: $62,300; median gross rent: $293.

1996 Presidential Vote			1992 Presidential Vote		
Dole (R)	122,826	(45%)	Clinton (D)	107,227	(40%)
Clinton (D)	116,628	(43%)	Bush (R)	92,292	(34%)
Perot (I)	23,571	(9%)	Perot (I)	67,210	(25%)
Others	8,711	(3%)			

Rep. Scott McInnis (R)

Elected 1992; b. May 9, 1953, Glenwood Springs; home, Grand Junction; Ft. Lewis Col., B.A. 1975, St. Mary's U., J.D. 1980; Catholic; married (Lori).

Elected Office: CO House of Reps., 1982–92, Majority Ldr., 1990–92.

Professional Career: Glenwood Springs Police Officer, 1976; Practicing atty., 1980–92.

DC Office: 320 CHOB 20515, 202-225-4761; Fax: 202-226-0622; Web site: www.house.gov/mcinnis.

District Offices: Durango, 970-259-2754; Glenwood Springs, 970-928-0637; Grand Junction, 970-245-7107; Pueblo, 719-543-8200.

Committees: *Ways & Means* (21st of 23 R): Human Resources; Oversight.

Group Ratings

	ADA	ACLU	AFS	LCV	CON	NTU	NFIB	COC	ACU	NTLC	CHC
1998	5	6	0	15	26	53	100	100	96	94	92
1997	0	—	0	—	94	61	—	90	91	—	—

National Journal Ratings

	1997 LIB — 1997 CONS			1998 LIB — 1998 CONS		
Economic	24%	—	73%	0%	—	88%
Social	39%	—	61%	40%	—	60%
Foreign	29%	—	71%	26%	—	73%

Key Votes of the 105th Congress

1. Clinton Budget Deal	Y	5. Puerto Rico Sthood. Ref.	N	9. Cut $ for B-2 Bombers	N
2. Education IRAs	Y	6. End Highway Set-asides	Y	10. Human Rights in China	Y
3. Req. 2/3 to Raise Taxes	Y	7. School Prayer Amend.	Y	11. Withdraw Bosnia Troops	Y
4. Fast-track Trade	Y	8. Ovrd. Part. Birth Veto	Y	12. End Cuban TV-Marti	*

Election Results

1998 general	Scott McInnis (R) 156,501	(66%)	($410,491)
	Robert Reed Kelley (D) 74,479	(31%)	($47,101)
	Others 5,673	(2%)	
1998 primary	Scott McInnis (R) .... unopposed		
1996 general	Scott McInnis (R) 183,523	(69%)	($270,892)
	Albert L. Gurule (D) 82,953	(31%)	($79,406)

FOURTH DISTRICT

The High Plains of eastern Colorado are dusty brown, gently rolling grasslands that seem flat but actually slope imperceptibly downward toward the Mississippi River. The land is fertile but dry: rainfall is rare, the rivers are just a trickle most of the year, and in many places groundwater is equally scarce. It is fine wheat country when irrigated and one of the foremost beef cattle regions. But it has been squeezed in recent decades between declining prices for wheat and declining demand for beef on the one hand, and increased prices for water because of high demand in Denver and along the Front Range on the other. The prairie lands and small towns of the High Plains have small reminders of their past: the Pawnee National Grasslands, where antelope, coyotes and prairie dogs still roam, and Burlington's 1905 carousel, one of the few with the original paint. But the free market that once peopled the High Plains with farmers and ranchers and made it the scene of farm protests and revolts is now causing it to empty out and revert to untamed land, ready again for now increasingly numerous buffalo.

The 4th Congressional District of Colorado contains almost all of the High Plains plus the medium-sized towns of Greeley, Fort Collins and Loveland—the northern end of the densely populated Front Range. By heritage and usually by inclination, this is Republican territory: it was evenly split in 1992 but gave solid margins to Bob Dole and Wayne Allard in 1996. The only Democratic parts are the working-class Adams County suburbs north of Denver and Las Animas County on the New Mexico border.

The congressman from the 4th District is Bob Schaffer, a Republican elected in 1996. Schaffer grew up in Cincinnati and went to the same high school as House Republican Conference Chairman John Boehner; after college in Ohio, he moved to Fort Collins and bought and managed rental property. In 1986, at 24, he was elected to the state Senate, where he favored tax cuts, education reform, tougher sentences and welfare reform. A solid conservative, he seized AIDS pamphlets on display at the Capitol in 1993 as unsuitable for children and supported a bill to enable parents to take children out of sex education classes more easily. He sponsored a law to end judicial review of initiatives passed by the voters. In 1994 he was a Republican candidate for lieutenant governor.

In 1996, when Allard ran for the Senate, Schaffer was one of three Republican legislators running for the House. Schaffer portrayed himself as a "true conservative" and gun control opponent whose first priority was balancing the budget. Pat Sullivan, a urologist from Fort Collins, focused on the budget and agriculture, calling himself a "mainstream conservative."

He and Don Ament, a farmer and rancher, both supported limited abortion rights. Ament won 30%, carrying his base in northeast Colorado, and Sullivan won 29%, barely carrying the Fort Collins area. Schaffer, with support from all over the district, won with 40%.

In the general Schaffer faced University of Colorado Regent Guy Kelley. Schaffer ran on the balanced budget amendment and a plan to eliminate the Commerce, Education, and other departments; in the aftermath of the Republicans' phasing-out of farm subsidies, he called for lower taxes on farmers, opening up foreign markets to agricultural exports, and revision of the Endangered Species Act. Kelley accused Schaffer of running on a right-wing agenda undermining public education, abortion rights and gun control. Schaffer won 56%–38%, carrying the Adams County suburbs and losing only two southern counties to Kelley; he nearly lost another to Wes McKinley, a rancher and foreman of the grand jury investigating the Rocky Flats plutonium plant, who rode a mule 1,200 miles up and down the district and won 3% of the votes.

In the House, Schaffer has made a mostly conservative voting record and was elected president of his freshman class. "It's far, far more partisan here than in the state legislature," he said. But, he noted, "I didn't come to Washington to make friends with the alligators. I want to help drain the swamp." Schaffer worked on some local issues, including a land swap between the National Forest Service and the city of Greeley, and a survey to establish the Sand Creek Massacre site. He opposed the Forest Service's proposed moratorium on road-building. On taxes, he proposed to eliminate the marriage penalty, exempt small amounts of interest income, institute 100% deductibility for health insurance for the self-employed, expand prepaid tuition programs and exempt family farms and ranches from the estate tax. He sponsored the measure to prevent union dues from being used for politics without permission in the House, but dropped a similar state ballot measure when nonprofits objected. He has a bill to hold states liable if a released murderer, rapist or child molester commits a crime in another state. He sued Bill Clinton in 1997 to stop the American Heritage Rivers Initiative, and lost. He and the 6th District's Tom Tancredo chose not to attend the State of the Union in 1999.

Schaffer had a vigorous opponent in 1998, a college professor who served as mayor of Fort Collins. Schaffer focused on tax cuts, and won easily 59%–41%, carrying their common home county by 54%–46%.

Cook's Call. *Safe*. With the 4th District decidedly Republican in its voting, Schaffer should have few re-election problems in 2000.

The People: Pop. 1990: 549,216; 35.4% rural; 11.4% age 65 + ; 91.5% White, 0.7% Black, 1.1% Asian, 0.7% Amer. Indian, 6.1% Other; 14.7% Hispanic Origin. Households: 59.2% married couple families; 30.1% married couple fams. w. children; 49.9% college educ.; median household income: $26,577; per capita income: $12,387; median house value: $70,200; median gross rent: $323.

1996 Presidential Vote			1992 Presidential Vote		
Dole (R)	122,840	(49%)	Bush (R)	96,638	(38%)
Clinton (D)	102,355	(41%)	Clinton (D)	94,234	(37%)
Perot (I)	18,644	(7%)	Perot (I)	63,203	(25%)
Others	6,683	(3%)			

Rep. Bob Schaffer (R)

Elected 1996; b. July 24, 1962, Cincinnati, OH; home, Fort Collins; U. of Dayton, B.A. 1984; Catholic; married (Maureen).

Elected Office: CO Senate, 1986–96.

Professional Career: Legis. Research, OH Senate, 1984–85; Press Secy., CO Senate, 1985–87; Owner, Northern Front Range Mktg. Co., 1989–94.

DC Office: 212 CHOB 20515, 202-225-4676; Fax: 202-225-5870; Web site: www.house.gov/schaffer.

District Offices: Fort Collins, 970-493-9132; Greeley, 970-353-3507; LaJunta, 719-384-7370; Sterling, 970-522-1788.

Committees: *Agriculture* (16th of 27 R): Livestock & Horticulture. *Education & the Workforce* (18th of 27 R): Early Childhood, Youth & Families (Vice Chmn.); Oversight & Investigations. *Resources* (21st of 28 R): Energy & Mineral Resources; Forests & Forest Health.

Group Ratings

	ADA	ACLU	AFS	LCV	CON	NTU	NFIB	COC	ACU	NTLC	CHC
1998	5	19	0	8	60	82	100	78	100	97	100
1997	5	—	0	—	80	69	—	90	96	—	—

National Journal Ratings

	1997 LIB	—	1997 CONS	1998 LIB	—	1998 CONS
Economic	0%	—	90%	0%	—	88%
Social	37%	—	61%	21%	—	76%
Foreign	0%	—	88%	0%	—	93%

Key Votes of the 105th Congress

1. Clinton Budget Deal	Y	5. Puerto Rico Sthood. Ref.	N	9. Cut $ for B-2 Bombers	N
2. Education IRAs	Y	6. End Highway Set-asides	Y	10. Human Rights in China	N
3. Req. 2/3 to Raise Taxes	Y	7. School Prayer Amend.	Y	11. Withdraw Bosnia Troops	Y
4. Fast-track Trade	Y	8. Ovrd. Part. Birth Veto	Y	12. End Cuban TV-Marti	N

Election Results

1998 general	Bob Schaffer (R)	131,318	(59%)	($514,662)
	Susan Kirkpatrick (D)	89,973	(41%)	($291,909)
1998 primary	Bob Schaffer (R)	unopposed		
1996 general	Bob Schaffer (R)	137,012	(56%)	($464,165)
	Guy Kelley (D)	92,837	(38%)	($261,425)
	Others	14,218	(6%)	

FIFTH DISTRICT

In 1893 Katherine Lee Bates took the cog railway up from Colorado Springs to the top of 14,110-foot Pikes Peak and, looking out at the purple mountain's majesty above amber waves of grain, wrote the lines of "America the Beautiful." Pike's Peak, first espied by Zebulon Pike in 1806, and Colorado Springs, with the Garden of the Gods and the Broadmoor Hotel, have been tourist attractions for more than 100 years. In the second half of the 20th Century, Colorado Springs, safe in the fastness of North America, has also become a great American military fortress, the home of Fort Carson, the site of the Air Force Academy, and, most recently, at Falcon Air Force Base, site of space-based defense research.

Around them Colorado Springs has built a high-tech, innovative economy—"silicon mountain." And with the arrival of Dr. James Dobson's Focus on the Family and dozens of other Christian organizations, it has been a center of conservative Christianity, the home of Colorado's young conservatism, the counterpoint to Denver's aging liberalism. This was the birthplace of Amendment 2, which in 1992 repealed city gay rights ordinances but was overturned by the U.S. Supreme Court, and of Colorado's anti-tax initiatives. More recently, Colorado Springs's conservative activists have had some local opposition; the city even passed a tax increase to fund purchases of open land. But overall, this is one of America's most Republican metropolitan areas, voting 59%–33% for Bob Dole over Bill Clinton in 1996.

Between Colorado Springs and Denver is Douglas County, which until the 1970s was a sparsely-populated patch of the High Plains just east of the Front Range. In the 1990s it has become one of the fastest-growing counties in the United States, as young families move into huge subdivisions around Castle Rock and Parker. This is a high-tech, highly educated, culturally traditional population, even more conservative by most measures than Colorado Springs's El Paso County. One big issue here is the status of the Preble's meadow-jumping mouse; Interior Secretary Bruce Babbit in May 1998 named it a threatened rather than endangered species, which means local governments must develop a habitat plan to protect it but need not stop development altogether. Douglas County voted 62%–31% for Dole in 1996; in 1998 it cast more votes than in the presidential year—evidence of surging growth.

El Paso County and most of Douglas County make up almost all of Colorado's 5th Congressional District, which spreads into a couple of mountain counties as well. This is by any measure Colorado's most Republican district, and one of the nation's.

The congressman from the 5th District is Joel Hefley, a Republican first elected in 1986. Hefley grew up in Oklahoma, and originally came to Colorado seeking work as a cowboy. He moved to Colorado Springs in 1965, became a professional civic leader, and was elected to the legislature in 1976. In the House he has a very conservative voting record. Long before the Contract with America, he called for zeroing out the National Endowment for Democracy, the EDA and the then-Interstate Commerce Commission, issued a Porker of the Week award for greedy colleagues, sought to end unfunded mandates and called for a three-fifths supermajority for tax increases.

Hefley came to Congress just as defense cutbacks were beginning; he now supports increased military spending, and has long been a staunch supporter of missile defense. In November 1995 he sought to bar U.S. troops from Bosnia until Congress voted funds; that passed the House but was ignored in the Senate. Hefley is now chairman of the Armed Services Subcommittee on Military Installations and Facilities, which has jurisdiction over base closings. The Clinton Administration has sought authority for new rounds of closings, so far in vain; many in Congress were dismayed by the administration's jiggering the rules in order to keep open depot bases in electoral-vote-rich California and Texas. Hefley is concerned that the high cost of environmental cleanup of closed bases will impinge on military needs. "To go through another round of base closures, when we are still spending billions of dollars trying to close bases because of the cleanup makes no sense at all," he said. Perhaps in response, the 5th District has not been a favorite of the Clinton Administration: a Colorado Springs railyard was one of the items in Bill Clinton's line-item veto, and most of the civilian jobs cut nationwide by the Air Force Space Command in September 1997 were in Colorado Springs.

On other issues, Hefley favors abolishing the IRS and moving to a flat or sales tax. For years he crusaded for a base-closing-like commission on national parks, so that worthy parks could be funded more generously; in 1998 he called less controversially for the Park Service to encourage filmmakers to use the parks, for a $3,000 a day fee. He has backed a number of so-far lost causes—blocking the Clinton Administration ban on discrimination against gay federal workers, passing a federal law like Colorado's grant of immunity to polluters who voluntarily disclose their violations, setting a 10-year term for federal judges. In January 1998, he became head of a four-member panel investigating Transportation and Infrastructure Chairman Bud Shuster and his former staffer Ann Eppard; in response to criticism, Hefley announced he would seek no transportation projects from Shuster.

Hefley essentially won this seat in the 1986 primary and has held it easily ever since. In 1996 he told Senator Ben Nighthorse Campbell that he would like to run for his Senate seat if Campbell didn't run; but Campbell did and Hefley supported him as promised. In 1998 Hefley's wife was elected to the Colorado House by 76%–24% while he was winning re-election in the 5th Congressional District by a 73%–26% margin.

Cook's Call. *Safe.* Joel Hefley has not dropped below 66% in any of his seven general elections, and should win easily in 2000.

The People: Pop. 1990: 549,264; 11.3% rural; 7.6% age 65 + ; 88.9% White, 5.5% Black, 2.2% Asian, 0.8% Amer. Indian, 2.6% Other; 7.2% Hispanic Origin. Households: 61.8% married couple families; 33.1% married couple fams. w. children; 65.5% college educ.; median household income: $33,348; per capita income: $15,370; median house value: $90,600; median gross rent: $372.

1996 Presidential Vote			1992 Presidential Vote		
Dole (R)	158,790	(59%)	Bush (R)	125,749	(49%)
Clinton (D)	88,057	(33%)	Clinton (D)	71,185	(28%)
Perot (I)	16,583	(6%)	Perot (I)	57,488	(22%)
Others	5,928	(2%)			

Rep. Joel Hefley (R)

Elected 1986; b. Apr. 18, 1935, Ardmore, OK; home, Colorado Springs; OK Baptist U., B.A. 1957; OK St. U., M.S. 1962; Baptist; married (Lynn).

Elected Office: CO House of Reps., 1976–78; CO Senate, 1978–86.

Professional Career: Exec. Dir., Community Planning & Research Cncl., 1966–86.

DC Office: 2230 RHOB 20515, 202-225-4422; Fax: 202-225-1942.

District Offices: Colorado Springs, 719-520-0055; Englewood, 303-792-3923.

Committees: *Armed Services* (8th of 32 R): Military Installations & Facilities (Chmn.); Military Research & Development. *Resources* (7th of 28 R): National Parks & Public Lands. *Small Business* (3d of 19 R). *Standards of Official Conduct* (2d of 5 R).

Group Ratings

	ADA	ACLU	AFS	LCV	CON	NTU	NFIB	COC	ACU	NTLC	CHC
1998	0	6	11	15	66	72	100	75	100	100	100
1997	5	—	13	—	70	67	—	80	96	—	—

National Journal Ratings

	1997 LIB — 1997 CONS			1998 LIB — 1998 CONS		
Economic	0%	—	90%	0%	—	88%
Social	30%	—	64%	14%	—	81%
Foreign	12%	—	81%	7%	—	83%

Key Votes of the 105th Congress

1. Clinton Budget Deal	Y	5. Puerto Rico Sthood. Ref.	N	9. Cut $ for B-2 Bombers	N
2. Education IRAs	Y	6. End Highway Set-asides	Y	10. Human Rights in China	Y
3. Req. 2/3 to Raise Taxes	Y	7. School Prayer Amend.	Y	11. Withdraw Bosnia Troops	Y
4. Fast-track Trade	Y	8. Ovrd. Part. Birth Veto	Y	12. End Cuban TV-Marti	N

Election Results

1998 general	Joel Hefley (R)	155,790	(73%)	($151,194)
	Ken Alford (D)	55,609	(26%)	($5,422)
	Others	2,871	(1%)	
1998 primary	Joel Hefley (R)	unopposed		
1996 general	Joel Hefley (R)	188,805	(72%)	($329,794)
	Mike Robinson (D)	73,660	(28%)	($16,017)

SIXTH DISTRICT

A generation ago, most people in metro Denver lived in the city itself; at the city limits the tree-shaded sidewalks gave way to the empty High Plains. Today, three-quarters of metro Denver residents live outside the city. Just south of Denver, in Arapahoe County, are the comfortable and affluent suburbs, pioneered in the 1940s and 1950s, of Englewood, Cherry Hills and Littleton, the site in April 1999 of the nation's deadliest school massacre. Aurora, to the east, benefited at first from the growth around now-closed Stapleton Airport, but has grown big enough—from 50,000 in 1965 to 220,000 in 1990—to support its own regional mall. West in Jefferson County, which since 1992 has cast more votes than Denver, are Lakewood and Wheat Ridge, creations of the 1960s and 1970s, affluent but not elite suburbs with winding streets and office complexes, including Lakewood's gigantic Denver Federal Center. Up against the Front Range is Golden, the headquarters of Coors beer and the Coors family which funds so many conservative causes, and of the National Renewable Energy Laboratory, which develops solar energy exports.

The 6th Congressional District of Colorado covers most of this suburban territory. This is mostly Republican terrain. The dominant tone is technical and managerial, and many people here yearn for the certainty of traditional limits. They value their environment, but they also see the need for economic growth and scientific innovation—both of which they think liberals tend to underrate.

The congressman from the 6th District is Tom Tancredo, a self-described religious right Republican, who was elected after a turbulent campaign in 1998. Tancredo grew up on the northside of Denver, taught junior high school civics, and in 1976, at 30, was elected to the state House. He was part of a group called "the Crazies," who zeroed out the sales tax on food and utilities, the inheritance tax and the auto safety inspection tax. In 1981 he became head of the regional office of the Education Department; he cut its staff by two-thirds. In 1993 he became head of the Independence Institute, a libertarian think tank in Golden.

In January 1998, Dan Schaefer, the only congressman the 6th has ever had, announced he was retiring; he was elected in March 1983 after astronaut Jack Swygert, elected in November 1982, died in December before taking office. For four years Schaefer chaired the Energy and Power Subcommittee of Commerce; he exited saying his two main goals, ending the Cold War and eliminating the deficit, had been achieved. Tancredo, an energetic and active speaker, jumped into the race, but he was not the only candidate in the primary; there were rumors for a moment that Denver Broncos quarterback John Elway, a well-known Republican, would run. Instead, it was a contest of local pols: Tancredo and legislator Barry Arrington on the right; legislator Martha Kreutz, running to counter the influence of the religious right; former Ambassador Sam Zakhem, the only candidate with enough money to advertise on TV; legislator Bill Schroeder, a moderate endorsed by road contractors and home builders. Not until May did the Democrats have a candidate, 70-year-old businessman Henry Strauss. Tancredo campaigned by walking the district and running radio ads the last 10 days; his big break was an endorsement by former Senator (1979–91) Bill Armstrong, a religious conservative who has stayed active in the Denver area. Armstrong's endorsement was worth 5% of the vote Tancredo said, and he needed it: he led with 25% to 22% for Schroeder, 19% for Kreutz, 17% for Zakhem, and 16% for Arrington.

Tancredo's victory gave Democrats the idea they might win, and Strauss had enough money—he gave his campaign $230,000—to put on a real campaign. Tancredo campaigned on his issues: sunset the Internal Revenue code in 2003 and move to a flat tax, cut the federal and state governments out of education and let markets work, ban partial-birth abortions. Strauss, a refugee from Nazi Germany as a child, evidently regarded Tancredo, a lapsed Catholic who began attending an evangelical Presbyterian church in 1990, as a threat to democracy for opposing minimum wage increases, light rail funding and federal aid to education. Then Strauss ran a TV ad based on a speech Tancredo had given: "Gathering at night to lash out at our government—a militia group with featured speaker, Tom Tancredo. A militia linked to white supremacists and the racist Aryan Nation . . . and called 'dangerous' by the FBI." Then, "Tom Tancredo admits he's met with groups even more extreme than this militia." But Tancredo had spoken to many groups and the "more extreme" groups he mentioned were forums with Patricia Schroeder. The *Rocky Mountain News* called this ad a smear and wrote, "If Strauss really believes this, then he is one of the silliest men in America."

Tancredo won, not with anything like Schaefer's percentages, but by the comfortable margin of 56%–42%. Invited to the White House for a reception for new members, he declined: "I'm not going. I've been to the White House when we had a real president." He also declined to attend the 1999 State of the Union address. Tancredo's home is in Littleton, six bocks from Columbine High School. Gun ownership was prevalent in the working class neighborhood where Tancredo was raised, and he supports the Second Amendment, pointing out that Colorado has stronger gun-control laws than the federal government. "If I had my way, I would take away the evil in man's heart that makes it destructive," he said. Tancredo got seats on the Education and International Relations committees. He has promised to serve no more than the three terms imposed by Colorado's now invalidated term limits on congressmen.

Cook's Call. *Probably Safe.* Though Tancredo is certainly more controversial than his rather low-key predecessor, it's unlikely he will lose given the substantial Republican advantage in this suburban Denver district.

The People: Pop. 1990: 548,788; 4.8% rural; 8.3% age 65 +; 91.8% White, 3.5% Black, 2.3% Asian, 0.5% Amer. Indian, 1.9% Other; 6.2% Hispanic Origin. Households: 55.2% married couple families; 27.5% married couple fams. w. children; 68% college educ.; median household income: $37,333; per capita income: $18,289; median house value: $92,400; median gross rent: $414.

1996 Presidential Vote

Dole (R)	118,856	(49%)
Clinton (D)	103,376	(43%)
Perot (I)	13,858	(6%)
Others	4,574	(2%)

1992 Presidential Vote

Bush (R)	101,679	(38%)
Clinton (D)	98,875	(37%)
Perot (I)	68,186	(25%)

Rep. Tom Tancredo (R)

Elected 1998; b. Dec. 20, 1945, Denver; home, Littleton; U. of N. CO, B.A. 1968; Presbyterian; married (Jackie).

Elected Office: CO House of Reps., 1976–81.

Professional Career: Jr. high teacher, 1968–81; Regional rep., U.S. Dept. of Education, 1981–93; Pres., Independence Inst., 1993–98.

DC Office: 1123 LHOB 20515, 202-225-7882; Fax: 202-226-4623; Web site: www.house.gov/tancredo.

District Office: Littleton, 720-283-9773.

Committees: *Education & the Workforce* (24th of 27 R): Early Childhood, Youth & Families; Oversight & Investigations. *International Relations* (26th of 26 R): Africa; International Operations and Human Rights. *Resources* (28th of 28 R): Energy & Mineral Resources.

Group Ratings and Key Votes: Newly Elected

Election Results

1998 general	Tom Tancredo (R)	111,374	(56%)	($527,796)
	Henry L. Strauss (D)	82,662	(42%)	($393,280)
	Others	5,152	(3%)	
1998 primary	Tom Tancredo (R)	10,166	(25%)	
	Bill Schroeder (R)	8,903	(22%)	
	Martha Hill Kreutz (R)	7,476	(19%)	
	Sam H. Zakhem (R)	6,912	(17%)	
	Barry Arrington (R)	6,499	(16%)	
1996 general	Dan Schaefer (R)	146,018	(62%)	($760,648)
	Joan Fitzgerald (D)	88,600	(38%)	($119,224)

CONNECTICUT

Despite a rough economic patch in the 1990s, Connecticut remains the nation's highest-income state and quite likely the wealthiest, not through any natural advantage but by virtue of its own pluck. Through most of its history this small chunk of rocky terrain has been isolated and insular, while politically Connecticut has been an odd duck of a state: one of the last to renounce an established church (in 1818) and one of the last to impose an income tax (in 1991), one of the last to back the Federalist Party (1816) and one of the few to vote to reelect Herbert Hoover (1932). Most Connecticut residents today are descendants of Catholic immigrants who arrived here between 1840 and 1924, but life still bears the imprint of the original 17th Century settlers. Connecticut was established by Puritans who found Massachusetts too lenient and backsliding, and Connecticut Yankees for years have been flintier and more unyielding, more tight-fisted and set in their ways, than their Boston brethren.

These characteristics have yielded economic advantage. For Connecticut's affluence has come not from any windfall but from a knack for tinkering. In 1831, Alexis de Tocqueville was struck by how this spot on the map gave America "the clock-peddler, the schoolmaster, and the senator. The first gives you time, the second tells you what to do with it, and the third makes your law and civilization." Connecticut made clocks of wood and metal and hats of felt and invented vulcanized rubber; it produced combs, cigars, clocks, silk thread, pins, matches, furniture; it invented and still manufactures Pez candy in Orange, Pepperidge Farm bread and Nivea cream in Norwalk, the Stanley Powerlock tape measure in New Britain and the Wiffle ball in Shelton. Connecticut—one of the least violent parts of America—has always specialized in arms. The quintessential Connecticut Yankee, Eli Whitney, was the inventor not only of the cotton gin—which may have been the proximate cause of the Civil War—but also of the rifles with interchangeable parts with which so many were killed. Connecticut has been an arms maker ever since Samuel Colt won a War Department contract to manufacture guns for the Mexican-American War; during the Reagan defense buildup of the 1980s, it produced Air Force jets and Army helicopters and, in the Electric Boat Shipyard in New London, most of the Navy's nuclear submarines.

These arms industries, like Connecticut's civilian manufacturers, depend heavily on meticulous work. For years, the state was the center of the brass industry, the nation's main producer of precision instruments. Through decades of immigration Connecticut workers never lost the Yankee knack: Connecticut ranks among the highest in new patents per capita. Over the years Connecticut has accumulated capital and invested shrewdly, with great skill at assessing risk; it is the home of several of the nation's great insurance companies, and its laws are uniquely friendly to creditors and harsh on bankrupts.

For all its skills Connecticut fell on hard times in the early 1990s. The insurance companies were hit by huge casualty losses and have been downsizing and merging ever since. The end of the Cold War and cuts in defense spending cost Connecticut nearly 150,000 manufacturing jobs, down from a peak of 420,000 in 1982. Connecticut's small central cities—New Haven, Hartford, Bridgeport, Waterbury—have been plagued by crime and have lost manufacturing jobs and people (to the point that Hartford now casts far fewer votes than high-income Stamford). The 1990–91 recession struck hard at wealth by slashing housing values, and growth was retarded by passage in 1991 of a state income tax. For the first half of the decade Connecticut lost population. Now Connecticut is on the rebound. But its trajectory is a bit different. The state's biggest employer and taxpayer now is the Foxwoods Casino, opened in 1992, run by a battery of lawyers and lobbyists and developers working for the 550-member Mashantucket Pequot tribe. Housing values are booming, most spectacularly in wealthy Greenwich, in

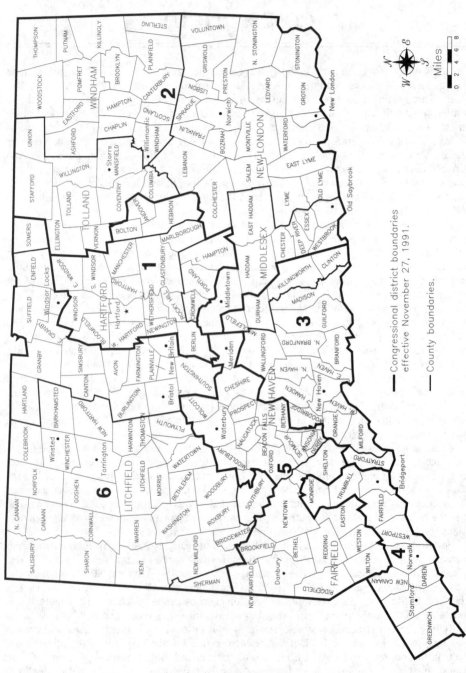

Congressional district boundaries effective November 27, 1991.

County boundaries.

the state's southwest corner and the state income tax has been reduced. The rebound has put Connecticut in a sunny political mood, like the country generally.

For most of the 20th Century, Connecticut politics has been an ethnic struggle between Yankee Republicans and Catholic Democrats. Slowly, as Catholic birthrates exceeded Protestant, Democrats gained ground; their great leader was John Bailey, state Democratic chairman from 1946–75, a master legislative strategist and ticket-balancer, who was one of the first to endorse John Kennedy for president. Traces of the old Protestant-Catholic divide are apparent today in geographic voting patterns, but not much in political rhetoric; splitting tickets is now common (at least one-third of voters did it in 1998) in a state where the straight-party lever dominated politics a generation ago. The guiding political temperament of Connecticut seems to be one of *laissez faire*, a hostility to taxes on the one hand and an aversion to imposition of old moral codes. All of which makes a certain sense in a state which is affluent economically and in which the orthodoxies of Puritan Protestantism and Roman Catholicism no longer claim many adherents. In the troubled early 1990s, Connecticut voters showed orneriness, electing Lowell Weicker as a third-party governor in 1990, then repudiating him with Republican John Rowland in 1994. Incumbents of both parties were threatened or beaten in House races; independents racked up significant totals. The later 1990s have been more placid. Bill Clinton, winner by 6% here in 1992, won by 18% in 1996; Democratic Senators Joseph Lieberman and Christopher Dodd were reelected with well over 60% in 1994 and 1998, as was Republican Governor John Rowland in 1998.

Governor. John Rowland, still in his 40s, is a grizzled veteran of Connecticut's political wars, with some scar tissue and muscular strength he didn't have when he started. Rowland grew up in Waterbury, the high-skill factory town that had America's highest percentage of Italian-Americans in the 1990 Census. His family has owned an insurance agency for four generations and his father and grandfather were city comptrollers. He was elected to the state House from a Democratic district, in 1980, at 23, and ran for Congress in 1984, upsetting a Democratic incumbent and becoming the youngest member of the House. He has run for governor in the last three elections, losing with 37% in 1990 (to former Republican Senator Lowell Weicker's 40%) and winning with 36% in 1994 (to Democrat Bill Curry's 33%). Dominating state politics then were issues of spending and taxes. State government spending went up by double-digit percentages yearly in the 1980s, as defense-driven revenues surged in; then the recession hit hard and resulted in huge deficits. Weicker's solution was a 4.5% income tax, enacted in 1991; it was unpopular, and he retired in 1994. Rowland campaigned against the income tax in 1990 and promised to repeal it in 1994. This probably made the difference in his victory over Curry, who said he would keep the tax and guarantee college educations, and two other candidates.

In his first year as governor, even with a divided legislature, Rowland had surprising success. Connecticut passed a "tough love" welfare bill limiting payments to 21 months and encouraging recipients to get a job and work their way up. By April 1998 welfare rolls had declined 25%. The income tax was cut marginally. Business taxes were lowered and unemployment and workmen's comp were made more business-friendly. Parents delinquent with child support were denied all state licenses. A new death penalty law and Megan's law to inform communities of released sex offenders were passed. The state workforce was cut by 2,500 and the lottery was privatized. State spending increases were minimal.

This was major conservative reform in a state that, in national politics, was moving toward Bill Clinton's Democrats. Although Democrats captured the state Senate in 1996 and held the House throughout, Rowland was able to push through tax cuts every year, as the state's economy revived and revenues rose. Democrats Bill Curry and Bridgeport Mayor Joseph Ganim thought about opposing him, until the field was preempted in September 1997 by 1st District Congresswoman Barbara Kennelly. Daughter of longtime Democratic Chairman John Bailey, widow of a speaker of the Connecticut House, Kennelly served on Ways and Means and adroitly navigated the corridors of power in Washington.

Polls in spring and fall 1997 showed the race about even. But Kennelly's insider skills and political lineage made less difference than her discomfort with campaigning. Voters believed Rowland when he talked of the Connecticut comeback, and many credited his tax cuts—which eventually totaled $1.5 billion—and welfare reform. In fall 1997 and spring 1998 Rowland unveiled proposals for redevelopment of ailing central cities, school construction, state purchase of open space, and a cut of 5,000 state employees. He got reluctant Democrats to approve an income tax rebate, over Kennelly's opposition. He even got a limited school choice program. Borrowing from Bill Clinton's 1995–96 playbook, Rowland in January 1998 started running ads touting his accomplishments. "Connecticut 1994—an economy in shambles," one said.

He certainly turned the campaign around. By early April Rowland had a 55%–31% lead in a Quinnipiac poll; in September it was 60%–23%. While Kennelly complained that he was stealing her issues, Rowland campaigned with gusto. The income tax rebates were sent out in July 1998 with the message, "It's your money. We're giving it back." Claims were made in the press that Rowland was cruising ahead because he had adopted Democratic stands; he supported health insurance for uninsured children in 1997, but insisted on using private insurers; he was happy to join a group headed by Robert Kennedy, Jr., suing New York City for polluting Long Island Sound. But the consensus Rowland formed was well to the right of state policy in 1994. Rowland was hit for changing positions on issues (abortion in 1990, school vouchers in 1997, the minimum wage and patients suing health insurers in 1998), but that had little impact; neither did ethics charges that he accepted discounted tickets to a Jimmy Buffett concert or that state troopers gave his children state surplus sleeping bags and canteens.

Rowland won by 63%–35%, carrying all but eight of Connecticut's cities and towns. He faces some challenges. Early on he was met with a huge political setback when in April 1999 the New England Patriots backed out of their plans to move to Hartford; city business leaders acknowledged that this essentially squashed any hopes for downtown redevelopment. Also, State Supreme Court rulings threaten the school aid formula and might force a merger of Hartford and suburban school systems. And, will Connecticut be able to reduce or hold down taxes when the inevitable economic slowdown finally occurs?

Senior Senator. Christopher Dodd was almost born into politics, one of three senators who are sons of senators (Evan Bayh and Bob Bennett are the others). His father Thomas Dodd, a prosecutor at the Nuremberg trials, was elected to the House in 1952, when Chris was eight; he lost a Senate race to Prescott Bush, George Bush's father, in 1956, then won in 1958. Chris Dodd served in the Peace Corps in the Dominican Republic from 1966–68. In 1967, the older Dodd was censured by the Senate for misuse of funds; he ran as an independent in 1970 and Chris Dodd managed his campaign, in which he finished behind Republican Lowell Weicker and Democrat Joseph Duffey, for whom Yale Law School student Bill Clinton was working as a volunteer. Almost immediately after law school, Christopher Dodd ran for the House in the open-seat eastern Connecticut 2d District and, in the Watergate year of 1974, won comfortably. He was reelected easily and in 1980 outmaneuvered fellow Watergate Democrat Toby Moffett to get the Democratic nomination to succeed Senator Abraham Ribicoff, and won that race by a wide margin.

In the 1980s Dodd, who speaks fluent Spanish, worked most visibly on Latin American issues. On the Western Hemisphere Subcommittee he took the lead in opposing U.S. military aid to El Salvador's government and aid to the Nicaraguan contras. Dodd also worked on the never-passed ABC child care bill, supported by the AFL-CIO and the Children's Defense Fund, which sought to put preschooling into much the same institutional mold as elementary and secondary schools. It passed the Senate but was rejected in the House in the late 1980s.

In the 1990s Dodd has emphasized other issues, with more success. He was the lead sponsor of the Family and Medical Leave Act vetoed by George Bush and signed by Bill Clinton in early 1993—and still cited by Clinton as one of his greatest achievements. Dodd's measures and his voting record have not been as uniformly liberal as they were in the 1980s. He has had a somewhat conservative voting record on foreign issues—and not just because he has worked for nuclear submarine contracts for Electric Boat in Groton. He sought to end the process of certifying anti-drug efforts of foreign countries each year, arguing that this causes needless friction with Latin countries, especially Mexico, without helping the anti-drug effort; Clinton signed the legislation in late 1997.

Dodd has emerged as one Democrat who has battled trial lawyers, and won. He was the chief Democratic sponsor of the securities litigation bill sought by high-tech companies and fought by trial lawyers; "People shouldn't make a business out of ambulance chasing when a stock simply fluctuates on the market," he said. When Clinton vetoed it, he immediately started lobbying Senate and House Democrats, and both houses in December 1995 voted to override. In 1996 and 1998 he worked with Phil Gramm and Alfonse D'Amato to successfully pass a law barring class-action securities litigation suits from state courts, requiring them to be heard in federal court where the rules are stricter. He was a lead sponsor of the product liability bill vetoed by Clinton in May 1996. He has supported bills easing regulation of the FDA. Still, with senior positions on Foreign Relations and Labor, where he ranks second behind Ted Kennedy, he takes more liberal than conservative stands; he is ranking Democrat on the sub-committee on Children and Families.

Dodd's greatest strength is his easy, confident articulateness; in his third decade in Congress and fifth decade of proximity to high office, he seems unfazed by opposition and approaches debates with an affable air, deflating opponents' indignation and suggesting that they are all in this game together. That has served him well when he took the national stage in 1996, though not in the role he first sought or with the encore he might have wished. In November 1994 he launched a quick and nearly successful campaign for Senate Democratic leader: Jim Sasser, his original choice, had lost in Tennessee, and after a month-long campaign Dodd lost to Tom Daschle by 24–23. Dodd was promptly asked by Bill Clinton to be Democratic National Committee chairman. Dodd performed ably in public debates and set-tos with Republican Chairman Haley Barbour, but was embarrassed in October 1996 when he followed White House orders to stonewall on charges that DNC top-level fundraiser John Huang raised millions in illegal foreign contributions. Dodd plausibly denied that he knew much about Huang, who was placed at the committee personally by Clinton; he was less plausible when he said he never thought the White House coffees, some of which he attended, were fundraisers.

With relief, Dodd dropped the chairmanship in January 1997, and mostly avoided investigations of the DNC thereafter. The next year he seemed genuinely angry at Bill Clinton for carrying on the Lewinsky affair and then lying about it for seven months. He said he had no intention of assuming the role of defense counsel and that he was undecided on impeachment. While meeting with editors of the *Connecticut Post* he said, "On issues, I've stood up and fought for things and all of a sudden, the idiot throws [the Lewinsky scandal] in the midst of all this."

None of this seemed to hurt on the campaign trail in 1998. His Republican opponent was Gary Franks, elected congressman in 1990 and defeated in 1996 in the often marginal 5th District, and one of the few black Republicans to serve in Congress. Franks's attacks on Dodd's closeness to Clinton and his attendance record struck no sparks, especially since Franks at the end of September had only $21,000 cash on hand compared to Dodd's $2.3 million. In October the *New Haven Register* reported that a lien had been placed on Franks's home in Waterbury; he had several unconvincing explanations, and Dodd actually scolded a reporter for raising the issue. "Why should I vote for you?" a student at Guilford High School asked. "Because I'm a hell of a guy," Dodd replied, with a big smile. Dodd had won reelection by wide margins against heavily outspent opponents in 1986 and 1992; so it was again. He won 65%–32%, carrying all but six of the state's cities and towns.

Junior Senator. In his second term Joseph Lieberman has come to occupy a unique place in the Senate, exerting influence out of proportion to his seniority, committee position or political clout, an influence that comes from respect for his independence of mind, civility of spirit and fidelity to causes in which he believes. In a bitterly partisan time he is one of the least partisan Democrats on Capitol Hill, one of the very few Democrats not to engage in lockstep White House defense in the Clinton scandals. Yet Lieberman is anything but a political innocent, and has had close associations with Bill Clinton at different points in his career. He grew up in Stamford, the son of a liquor store owner, went to Yale, became chairman of the *Yale Daily News*, worked summers for Senator Abraham Ribicoff and the Democratic National Committee. In college he wrote a revealing yet admiring biography of that quintessential political boss John Bailey. He helped found a reform and antiwar Caucus of Connecticut Democrats; in 1970 he ran for state Senate in New Haven against the Senate majority leader, and won with volunteer help from Yale Law student Bill Clinton. In 1980 he ran for an open House seat and lost 52%–46%; in 1982 he was elected attorney general, where he took action against fake charities, crooked car dealers and gouging merchants.

In 1988 Lieberman challenged Senator Lowell Weicker, another maverick, of a different sort. Weicker was well to the left of most Republicans on economic and cultural issues, Lieberman more conservative than most Democrats on cultural issues and foreign policy. Lieberman is an orthodox Jew—he didn't attend the convention that nominated him because it was held on Saturday—and a believer that "we in government should look to religion as a partner, as I think the Founders of our country did." He favored the death penalty and a moment of silence in schools, and opposed Weicker's proposed 30-cent gas tax increase. He ran witty ads, one showing a bear sleeping through work—a nice take-off on the growling but erratic Weicker. Lieberman won 50%–49%; the contest cut across party lines, with Lieberman running well in industrial towns and Weicker in Hartford, college towns and tony towns in Litchfield County.

Lieberman has made a distinctive mark in foreign policy. He was one of the leaders in the fight for the Gulf war resolution in January 1991, and without his earnest but vehement support it might not have passed. Presciently, he called for "final victory" over Saddam Hussein. He is a strong supporter of Israel but favored F-15 sales to Saudi Arabia in 1992; in spring 1998 he spoke against an American ultimatum to Israel. He favored U.S. ground troops in Bosnia and action against Bosnian Serb war criminals. He backed NATO expansion in Eastern Europe. In 1998 he successfully led a fight for sanctions to stop Russia from exporting missile technology to Iran.

On economic issues, he has backed capital gains tax cuts for small business ("you can't be pro-jobs and anti-business") and urged President Clinton to sign the 1996 welfare reform bill—both stands opposed by many Democrats. On HMO regulation, he co-sponsored a compromise that omits Medical Savings Accounts and would allow lawsuits against HMOs, but limit them to economic recovery and attorneys' fees only. He is a sponsor of Auto Choice reform, which would allow car owners to opt out of pain and suffering damages and get much cheaper insurance premiums. On environmental issues, Lieberman supported the Clinton position at the Kyoto air pollution conference but said China has to be part of the solution. He co-sponored the Clean Air Act of 1990 and supports an EPA project to allow companies greater flexibility to achieve specific pollution control goals.

In highly publicized campaigns Lieberman has joined with *Book of Virtues* author William Bennett and others to denounce obscene entertainment. His goal has been "to convince people who run the entertainment industry that they have enormous power to shape our culture, to affect our lives, particularly our children's lives." In 1995 they criticized gangsta rap records, and shamed Time Warner into selling their Interscope label; in 1998 they said the purchaser, Seagram, failed to keep its promises to clean up the words, and gave it a Silver Sewer award. In 1995 he attacked 10 daytime TV shows as "trash" and called on advertisers to avoid them, with some success. In 1998 he objected to government closed-captioning of the Jerry Springer show. He helped get a voluntary video games rating system in 1994 and helped prod the TV networks toward ratings.

Lieberman played a serious role on the Clinton scandals in 1997–98, though he had worked with Clinton in the Democratic Leadership Council and headed the organization those years. First, at the hearings on illegal campaign financing, after John Glenn denounced Chairman Fred

Thompson's claims of a Chinese conspiracy to affect the elections, Lieberman read the documents and got Glenn to join him in saying, "I conclude there was in fact a Chinese government plan to move money into congressional elections last year," though he added that there wasn't clear evidence that the presidential election was affected. He was dismayed by Clinton's August 17 speech in which he grudgingly admitted lying about the Lewinsky affair for seven months. When the Senate resumed in September, he took the floor and said, "Such behavior is not only inappropriate, it is immoral and it is harmful." And, "It is wrong and unacceptable and should be followed by some measure of public rebuke and accountablity." But he was persuaded by Minority Leader Tom Daschle not to call for censure, and he stopped well short of backing impeachment or resignation. After the speech he was seconded by Daniel Patrick Moynihan and Bob Kerrey, and he clearly changed the tenor of the public dialogue. Clinton accepted this rebuke, and it may have helped him, by showing other Democrats how to criticize his conduct while still not calling for removal.

As DLC chairman, Lieberman has argued that Clinton has helped lead the Democratic Party and the country his way, at least on many important issues. He has supported Clinton on many important issues—the 1993 tax increase, the 1994 crime bill, the 1996 welfare reform bill, the V-chip, the partial-birth abortion ban veto. He was reelected in Connecticut by a striking 67%–31% margin in the Republican year of 1994, and he should be in good shape for 2000.

Cook's Call. *Safe.* It does not appear Republicans will mount a credible challenge to Lieberman, who has figured out the recipe for popularity that transcends both parties and ideological lines.

Presidential politics. Connecticut voted Democratic for president in the 1960s and 1990s, Republican in the 1970s and 1980s. The shifts from party to party have resulted from fractures of old coalitions: the Democrats split in the culture wars of the Nixon years, the Republicans split amid the economic turmoil of the early 1990s. Both splits were symbolized and helped along by independent candidacies—Thomas Dodd's independent candidacy for the Senate in 1970, Lowell Weicker's successful third-party candidacy for governor in 1990, and Ross Perot's strong 22% here in 1992.

Connecticut's presidential primary, though held fairly early in the process, has not been quite early enough and has made little difference. Gary Hart won here in 1984, Jerry Brown in 1992; but they fared no better than the Federalists Connecticut favored in 1816. In 1996 Bob Dole won by a wide margin three days after he clinched the nomination in South Carolina.

Congressional districting. Connecticut's six districts were drawn by a nine-member commission appointed by legislative leaders that made only minimal changes for the 1990s. The state may lose a district after the 2000 Census; the 5th District is the likeliest candidate to be sliced up amongst its neighbors.

The People: Est. Pop. 1998: 3,274,069; Pop. 1990: 3,287,116, down 0.4% 1990–1998. 1.2% of U.S. total, 29th largest; 20.9% rural. Median age: 36.2 years. 14.2% 65 years and over. 87.1% White, 8.3% Black, 1.5% Asian, 0.2% Amer. Indian, 2.9% Other; 6.2% Hispanic Origin. Households: 55.6% married couple families; 25.1% married couple fams. w. children; 49.7% college educ.; median household income: $41,721; per capita income: $20,189; 65.6% owner occupied housing; median house value: $177,800; median monthly rent: $510. 3.4% Unemployment. 1998 Voting age pop.: 2,464,000. 1998 Turnout: 1,022,453; 41% of VAP. Registered voters (1998): 1,969,324; 699,766 D (36%), 477,684 R (24%), 791,874 unaffiliated and minor parties (40%).

Political Lineup: Governor, John G. Rowland (R); Lt. Gov., M. Jodi Rell (R); Secy. of State, Susan Bysiewicz (D); Atty. Gen., Richard Blumenthal (D); Treasurer, Denise Nappier (D); State Senate, 36 (19 D and 17 R); Majority Leader, George Jepson (D); State House, 151 (96 D, 55 R); House Speaker, Moira Lyons (D). Senators, Christopher J. Dodd (D) and Joseph I. Lieberman (D). Representatives, 6 (4 D, 2 R).

Elections Division: 860-509-6100; **Filing Deadline for U.S. Congress:** January 21, 2000.

1996 Presidential Vote

Clinton (D)	735,740	(53%)
Dole (R)	483,109	(35%)
Perot (I)	139,523	(10%)
Others	34,237	(2%)

1996 Republican Presidential Primary

Dole (R)	70,998	(54%)
Forbes (R)	26,253	(20%)
Buchanan (R)	19,664	(15%)
Alexander (R)	6,985	(5%)
Others	6,518	(5%)

1992 Presidential Vote

Clinton (D)	682,318	(42%)
Bush (R)	578,313	(36%)
Perot (I)	348,771	(22%)

GOVERNOR

Gov. John G. Rowland (R)

Elected 1994, term expires Jan. 2003; b. May 24, 1957, Waterbury; home, Hartford; Villanova U., B.S. 1979; Catholic; married (Patricia).

Elected Office: CT House of Reps., 1980–84; U.S. House of Reps., 1984–90.

Professional Career: Insurance Agent, 1979–84.

Office: Executive Chamber, State Capitol, Hartford, 06106, 860-566-4840; Fax: 860-566-4677; Web site: www.state.ct.us.

Election Results

1998 gen.	John G. Rowland (R)	628,707	(63%)
	Courtney Kennelly (D)	354,187	(35%)
	Others	16,641	(2%)
1998 prim.	John G. Rowland (R)	nominated	
1994 gen.	John G. Rowland (R)	415,201	(36%)
	Bill Curry (D)	375,133	(33%)
	Eunice Strong Groark (ACP)	216,585	(19%)
	Tom Scott (I)	130,128	(11%)

SENATORS

Sen. Christopher J. Dodd (D)

Elected 1980, seat up 2004; b. May 27, 1944, Willimantic; home, East Haddam; Providence Col., B.A. 1966, U. of Louisville, J.D. 1972; Catholic; divorced.

Military Career: Army Reserves, 1969–75.

Elected Office: U.S. House of Reps., 1974–80.

Professional Career: Peace Corps, Dominican Republic, 1966–68; Practicing atty., 1972–74.

DC Office: 444 RSOB, 20510, 202-224-2823; Fax: 202-224-1083; Web site: www.senate.gov/~dodd.

State Office: Wethersfield, 860-258-6940.

Committees: *Banking, Housing & Urban Affairs* (2d of 9 D): Economic Policy; Housing & Transportation; Securities (RMM). *Foreign Relations* (3d of 8 D): European Affairs; Near Eastern & South Asian Affairs; Western Hemisphere, Peace Corps, Narcotics & Terrorism (RMM). *Health, Education, Labor & Pensions* (2d of 8 D): Aging; Children & Families (RMM); Employment, Safety & Training. *Rules & Administration* (RMM of 7 D). *Joint Committee on the Library of Congress* (5th of 5 Sens.).

Group Ratings

	ADA	ACLU	AFS	LCV	CON	NTU	NFIB	COC	ACU	NTLC	CHC
1998	95	86	100	100	49	15	33	61	4	11	0
1997	90	—	89	—	32	22	—	50	4	—	—

National Journal Ratings

	1997 LIB — 1997 CONS		1998 LIB — 1998 CONS	
Economic	79%	— 18%	83%	— 10%
Social	71%	— 0%	74%	— 0%
Foreign	59%	— 38%	65%	— 27%

Key Votes of the 105th Congress

1. Bal. Budget Amend.	N	5. Satcher for Surgeon Gen.	Y
2. Clinton Budget Deal	N	6. Highway Set-asides	Y
3. Cloture on Tobacco	Y	7. Table Child Gun locks	N
4. Education IRAs	N	8. Ovrd. Part. Birth Veto	N

9. Chem. Weapons Treaty	Y
10. Cuban Humanitarian Aid	Y
11. Table Bosnia Troops	Y
12. $ for Test-ban Treaty	Y

Election Results

1998 general	Christopher J. Dodd (D)	628,306	(65%)	($4,442,567)
	Gary A. Franks (R)	312,177	(32%)	($1,478,307)
	Others	23,974	(2%)	
1998 primary	Christopher J. Dodd (D) ... nominated by convention			
1992 general	Christopher J. Dodd (D-ACP)	882,569	(59%)	($4,553,792)
	Brook Johnson (R)	572,036	(38%)	($2,395,262)
	Others	46,104	(3%)	

Sen. Joseph I. Lieberman (D)

Elected 1988, seat up 2000; b. Feb. 24, 1942, Stamford; home, New Haven; Yale U., B.A. 1964, LL.B. 1967; Jewish; married (Hadassah).

Elected Office: CT Senate, 1970–80, Majority Ldr., 1974–80; CT Atty. Gen., 1983–88.

Professional Career: Practicing atty., 1964–80.

DC Office: 706 HSOB, 20510, 202-224-4041; Fax: 202-224-9750; Web site: www.senate.gov/~lieberman.

State Office: Hartford, 860-549-8463.

Committees: *Armed Services* (6th of 9 D): Airland Forces (RMM); Emerging Threats & Capabilities; Strategic Forces. *Environment & Public Works* (6th of 8 D): Clean Air, Wetlands, Private Property & Nuclear Safety; Transportation & Infrastructure. *Governmental Affairs* (RMM of 7 D). *Small Business* (4th of 8 D).

Group Ratings

	ADA	ACLU	AFS	LCV	CON	NTU	NFIB	COC	ACU	NTLC	CHC
1998	80	71	89	100	47	17	33	56	16	25	9
1997	75	—	56	—	51	34	—	60	20	—	—

National Journal Ratings

	1997 LIB — 1997 CONS		1998 LIB — 1998 CONS	
Economic	56%	— 43%	55%	— 43%
Social	64%	— 29%	74%	— 0%
Foreign	51%	— 46%	51%	— 36%

Key Votes of the 105th Congress

1. Bal. Budget Amend.	N	5. Satcher for Surgeon Gen.	Y	9. Chem. Weapons Treaty	Y
2. Clinton Budget Deal	Y	6. Highway Set-asides	Y	10. Cuban Humanitarian Aid	N
3. Cloture on Tobacco	Y	7. Table Child Gun locks	N	11. Table Bosnia Troops	Y
4. Education IRAs	Y	8. Ovrd. Part. Birth Veto	N	12. $ for Test-ban Treaty	Y

Election Results

1994 general	Joseph I. Lieberman (D)	723,842	(67%)	($4,017,520)
	Jerry Labriola (R)	334,833	(31%)	($166,064)
	Others	20,989	(2%)	
1994 primary	Joseph I. Lieberman (D) ... nominated by convention			
1988 general	Joseph I. Lieberman (D)	688,499	(50%)	($2,570,779)
	Lowell P. Weicker, Jr. (R)	678,454	(49%)	($2,609,902)

FIRST DISTRICT

In 1871, Mark Twain moved to Hartford to become director of an insurance company, and in time became the Connecticut capital's most famous citizen. Hartford, already more than two centuries old, home of the nation's longest circulating newspaper (since 1764), *The Hartford Courant*, was becoming the nation's best-known insurance center. This was not what the harsh Puritans who founded Hartford had in mind, but Connecticut's Yankees turned out to be shrewd businessmen. Thanks to the broad Connecticut River, Hartford also became a seaport; its merchants, prevented from trading and writing marine insurance by Thomas Jefferson's Embargo Act of 1807, turned to writing fire insurance and using the capital they'd accumulated in the Napoleonic Wars to finance their ventures. One was Samuel Colt's gun factory just south of downtown Hartford, which became one of the nation's great arms plants—and whose company became a symbol of Connecticut's recession when it went into Chapter XI in 1992.

Insurance and arms are still economic mainstays of Hartford, Connecticut's capital and the center of its largest metropolitan concentration. Though affected by downsizing and mergers, Aetna, CIGNA and ITT Hartford are still big employers, and across the river is the Pratt and Whitney jet engine plant in East Hartford, cornerstone of Connecticut-based United Technologies. The small central city of Hartford is otherwise in bad shape, its high-crime neighborhoods abandoned and bedraggled, its school system contracted out to a private firm and declared unconstitutionally segregated by the state Supreme Court. But metropolitan Hartford has long since spread miles into pleasant hills, and most Hartford suburbs are in good shape, especially with the economic recovery of the late 1990s.

The 1st Congressional District of Connecticut is centered on Hartford, but the city now casts only 12% of its votes. Politically, the Hartford area has long been more Democratic than the rest of Connecticut: Hartford in Connecticut is something like Boston in Massachusetts, a great commercial metropolis more statist than is its surroundings. And it may owe some of its Democratic character to longtime Democratic state (1946–75) and national (1961–68) Democratic chairman, John Bailey an old-fashioned political boss with a scandal-free career who promoted a raft of first-class candidates.

The congressman from the 1st District is John Larson, a Democrat elected in 1998 to fill the place of Barbara Kennelly, Bailey's daughter, who ran for governor after 16 years in the House and lost by a wide margin. Larson grew up in the Mayberry Village public housing project in East Hartford, one of eight children; his father was a fireman at Pratt & Whitney, and his mother worked at the state Capitol. He graduated from Central Connecticut State and taught high school and coached athletics; in 1977 he became an insurance agent. He seems to come from a political family—his brother Timothy is now mayor of East Hartford—and in 1982, at 34, John was elected to the state Senate. Four years later he was Senate president.

There Larson sponsored one of the nation's first family medical leave laws, a prototype for the law sponsored by Senator Christopher Dodd and signed by Bill Clinton in 1993. He also created neighborhood resource centers for preschoolers, where parents could receive a variety of services. Larson seemed headed for the governorship, and in 1994 he ran and won the party designation at the state convention. But Comptroller Bill Curry built an organization of unionists and liberal activists, and beat him 55%–45% in the primary. Larson went back to private life and promoted a volunteer Connect '96 project to hook up libraries and schoolrooms to the information superhighway.

When Kennelly announced her retirement in September 1997, Larson was an obvious candidate; another was Secretary of State Miles Rapoport, from more affluent West Hartford, who had the support of unions, the Sierra Club, and the Connecticut Citizens Action group. They had clashed in the legislature, where Rapoport helped lead the push for a state income tax in 1991 and Larson was one of the few Democrats who opposed it. Rapoport led in polls and fundraising. But Larson raised impressive sums as well, built a local organization, did lots of door-to-door campaigning, and benefited from the support of former Hartford Mayor Mike Peters. Rapoport ran an ad attacking Larson for not backing ConnPace, a subsidized prescription program for the elderly; Larson denied that, and there may have been a backlash. Anyway, Larson had a surprise 46%–43% win. Rapoport won in the northwest part of the district, including Hartford, West Hartford, and heavily Jewish Bloomfield; Larson carried most of the rest, with a big vote in East Hartford.

The last time the Republicans won the 1st District was in 1956, when Edwin May rode the straight-party-lever coattails of Dwight Eisenhower; in July 1996 the Republican nominee withdrew after local party leaders failed to invite him to an appearance by Bob Dole. Nonetheless, Republicans found a vigorous candidate here in 1998. Kevin O'Connor, a 31-year-old former law clerk and SEC lawyer, returned to the Hartford area and enlisted his large extended family; he held fundraisers in sports bars, bought signs on buses, had his young nephews blow kisses to motorists as volunteers held signs. He called for revitalizing downtown Hartford and said he would bring "urgency and accountability" to the job, because "I know that every two years Democrats are going to be gunning for me." He generated enough enthusiasm to get the endorsement of *The Hartford Courant* and the dispatch of $70,000 for ads from the House Republican campaign committee.

But Larson had his own resources. One was an earnestness unusual in such an experienced politician: "I want to go to Washington not to make a difference in the House of Representatives, but to be the Representative who makes a difference in your house, the schoolhouse, and the workplace." He suppported gun control and gay rights, opposed late-term abortions, and boasted of his experience on family medical leave and neighborhood resources center. Of O'Connor he said, "He says all the time, 'a fresh face.' I think that's just another way of saying, 'I have no record.'" Republican Governor John Rowland carried the 1st District by a wide margin, but so did Democratic Senator Christopher Dodd, and for all the vigor of O'Connor's campaign, Larson won with 58%, just one point shy of Clinton's win here in 1996. Larson is likely to be a faithful member of the Democratic Caucus and seems unlikely to face a serious challenge here.

Cook's Call. *Safe*. Like his predecessor Barbara Kennelly, Larson should have little trouble holding on to this very Democratic Hartford-based district. The only question now is whether he will be able match the huge wins that Kennelly rolled up year after year.

The People: Pop. 1990: 547,979; 10.8% rural; 15% age 65 + ; 78.4% White, 14.2% Black, 1.7% Asian, 0.3% Amer. Indian, 5.5% Other; 9.8% Hispanic Origin. Households: 50.7% married couple families; 22.1% married couple fams. w. children; 48.7% college educ.; median household income: $39,961; per capita income: $18,644; median house value: $172,000; median gross rent: $497.

1996 Presidential Vote			1992 Presidential Vote		
Clinton (D)	136,775	(59%)	Clinton (D)	133,686	(50%)
Dole (R)	68,483	(30%)	Bush (R)	82,086	(31%)
Perot (I)	20,862	(9%)	Perot (I)	52,154	(19%)
Others	5,204	(2%)			

Rep. John Larson (D)

Elected 1998; b. July 22, 1948, Hartford; home, E. Hartford; Central CT St. U., B.S. 1971; Catholic; married (Leslie).

Elected Office: E. Hartford Bd. of Ed., 1977–79; E. Hartford Town Cncl., 1979–83; CT Senate, 1983–95, Pres. Pro-Tem 1986–95.

Professional Career: High schl. teacher, 1972–77; Insurance broker, 1977–98; Sr. Fellow, Yale Bush Ctr., 1995-present.

DC Office: 1419 LHOB 20515, 202-225-2265; Fax: 202-225-1031; Web site: www.house.gov/larson.

District Office: Hartford, 860-278-8888.

Committees: *Armed Services* (28th of 28 D): Military Personnel; Military Research & Development. *Science* (15th of 22 D): Basic Research; Space & Aeronautics.

Group Ratings and Key Votes: Newly Elected

Election Results

1998 general	John Larson (D)	97,681	(58%)	($1,181,517)
	Kevin O'Connor (R)	69,668	(41%)	($389,948)
	Others	915	(1%)	
1998 primary	John Larson (D)	19,877	(46%)	
	Miles S. Rapoport (D)	18,189	(42%)	
	Jim McCavanagh (D)	2,565	(6%)	
	Joseph M. Suggs Jr. (D)	2,185	(5%)	
1996 general	Barbara B. Kennelly (D)	158,222	(74%)	($543,033)
	Kent Sleath (R)	53,666	(25%)	($8,459)
	Others	3,248	(2%)	

SECOND DISTRICT

Eastern Connecticut, one of the longest-settled parts of the United States, has undergone great, and sometimes painful, change in the 1990s—a change comparable to those of the 1640s or 1810s or 1950s. When the Puritan settlers from Massachusetts and England arrived, these flinty hills were the home of small Indian tribes, whose numbers were slashed by warfare and even more by disease. This was never fertile farming country, but New London and Norwich were among the 13 colonies' leading workshops and ports. Not long after, factories sprang up around mills in little villages on the fast-flowing Quinebaug and Shetucket Rivers. Sandbars kept oceangoing ships out of the rivers, but they docked at New London. In the mid-20th Century new technology shaped the area. Four nuclear power plants were built here, more than in any similarly-populated part of the United States. And in Groton, across the Thames River from New London and downriver from the Coast Guard Academy, is General Dynamics' Electric Boat Company, where for four decades were built the nuclear submarines which may very well have deterred nuclear war.

By the 1990s this latest high-tech economy was in trouble. Nuclear plants were wearing out and being shut down across the country and no new ones built. And with the end of the Cold War, most of the Electric Boat work force was laid off, though some remained lest we lose the knack of producing nuclear subs. Now the area's economic base has shifted from 1950s high-tech to 1990s entertainment. Eastern Connecticut has six of the state's leading tourist destinations, including Mystic Seaport and the Coast Guard Academy. The state's biggest employer is no longer Electric Boat but the Foxwoods Casino, the largest in the East, with hotels and golf courses and a convention center, which has 12,000 employees and attracts 50,000 visitors a day. Foxwoods was built by the 550-member Mashantucket Pequot tribe and the legions of managers and lawyers and lobbyists it has hired. The tribe has reaped enormous profits, donating $10 million to the National Museum of the American Indian and becoming one of the nation's biggest political contributors, doling out some $310,000 during the 1997–98 cycle. It is almost as if the Indians are reclaiming the land they seemed to have lost irrevocably in the last days of the Mohicans.

The 2d Congressional District includes most of eastern Connecticut, centering on New London and Norwich, including mill towns and the University of Connecticut town of Storrs nestled in the rocky hills to the north and home to the 1999 NCAA men's basketball champs. The 2d also stretches west to Middletown, once ethnic and now a college town, and affluent antique-filled small towns like Essex and Old Lyme on Long Island Sound. For many years this was a politically marginal district, with close battles between Yankee Republicans and Catholic Democrats. In the early 1990s it was the scene of political rebellions. It voted 27% for Ross Perot in 1992—his best showing in New England after the two Maine districts—and in 1994 it came within 21 votes of defeating its Democratic Congressman Sam Gejdenson. Then, with the economy revived, it gave Bill Clinton a wide margin in 1996 and in 1998 voted solidly to reelect a Democratic senator, Republican governor, and Democratic congressman.

Gejdenson was born in a German displaced persons camp, the son of concentration camp inmates, and grew up on a dairy farm in Bozrah, Connecticut; he likes to refer to himself wryly as "just a farm boy who spends his week in Washington." He was elected to the legislature in 1974, at 26, served as a staffer to Governor Ella Grasso, then in 1980, at 32, ran for the House when then-Congressman Christopher Dodd ran for the Senate. Gejdenson brings to his work good-humored energy and a set of beliefs characteristic of many of the liberals first elected in the Watergate year of 1974. He believes that an energetic and expanding government can help ordinary people, he has often been suspicious of the assertion of American power abroad, and he tends to champion liberal cultural values. Of course he worked hard and with considerable success to keep Electric Boat operating and is an active supporter of the Coast Guard.

He has had an almost entirely liberal voting record over the years and has been a mainstay supporter of the Democratic leadership. He was ranking Democrat on House Administration, which handles campaign finance issues, and is now the ranking Democrat on International Relations. He worked to relax export controls on China and Russia, and has strongly supported Israel; in 1991 he voted against the Gulf war resolution. He has a knack for introducing bills to attack problems that have hit the local headlines, or make them, as in his crusade against breakfast cereal prices. When the investment adviser of a Westbrook company's 401(k) defrauded it of $2 million, he introduced a bill in July 1998 to require that 401(k) managers must hold funds in a bank or (a Connecticut touch) insurance company. When some Medicare HMOs announced their withdrawal from eastern Connecticut in September 1998, he proposed a law to require them to stay put for three years rather than one. He sponsored a law to require negotiations for an international code of conduct for arms sales, opposing one that would impose unilateral restrictions on the U.S., which was opposed by Connecticut's United Technologies. He has worked for a four-lane U.S. highway on the 11 miles between Bolton and Columbia and for a National Heritage Corridor.

After easily winning reelection in the 1980s, Gejdenson had three tough challenges in the 1990s from Republican Ed Munster, a biostatistician at Pfizer in Groton. In 1992 he attacked Gejdenson for opposing "every weapons system except the bow and arrow" and charged that "Sam greased the wheels for Saddam." Gejdenson won by only 51%–49% after outspending Munster $1,014,000 to $140,000. In 1994, he faced Munster again, and this time—after the state Supreme Court's six-day hearing and final count—won by the less-than-landslide margin of 21 votes. In this contest Gejdenson spent $1,422,000 and Munster $426,000. In 1996, Gejdenson went on the attack against Newt Gingrich's "extreme agenda" and charged that Republicans were trying to cut Medicare. Munster criticized Gejdenson with some effect for voting against welfare reform and term limits. Even with Republicans in control of the House, Gejdenson got the lion's share of PAC money, outraising Munster $398,000 to $75,000 among them in 1996. Also Gejdenson raised $650,000 in individual contributions, many of them undoubtedly from Jewish contributors across the country; he was the nation's number one recipient of pro-Israel PAC money from 1987–95, with $126,000, according to *Congressional Quarterly*. The result was a 52%–45% Gejdenson victory.

The 1998 contest was much easier. The Republicans did not find a nominee until May, Mansfield businessman Gary Koval. He never raised much money, while Gejdenson spent over $1,000,000. Gejdenson's knack for jumping on headline issues, plus denunciations of Newt Gingrich and calls for HMO lawsuits, helped him win 61%–35%—better than Clinton's 1996 margin in the district; he carried every city and town but two.

Cook's Call. *Probably Safe.* While this district is Democratic, it's not nearly as liberal as Gejdenson, which may explain his numerous close calls in recent elections. Should Republicans pull out all the stops again, Gejdenson may well have another competitive race but the chances of him losing, in the absence of a very bad year for Democrats, is fairly small.

The People: Pop. 1990: 548,018; 45.2% rural; 12.5% age 65 + ; 93.2% White, 3.7% Black, 1.4% Asian, 0.4% Amer. Indian, 1.3% Other; 2.9% Hispanic Origin. Households: 57.9% married couple families; 27.2% married couple fams. w. children; 47.8% college educ.; median household income: $38,524; per capita income: $16,946; median house value: $151,300; median gross rent: $487.

1996 Presidential Vote		
Clinton (D)	123,595	(53%)
Dole (R)	73,863	(32%)
Perot (I)	29,790	(13%)
Others	6,991	(3%)

1992 Presidential Vote		
Clinton (D)	113,553	(43%)
Bush (R)	79,110	(30%)
Perot (I)	72,782	(27%)

Rep. Samuel Gejdenson (D)

Elected 1980; b. May 20, 1948, Eschwege, Germany; home, Bozrah; Mitchell Col., A.S. 1966, U. of CT, B.A. 1970; Jewish; married (Betsy Henley-Cohn).

Elected Office: CT House of Reps., 1974–78.

Professional Career: Legis. Liaison, CT Gov. Ella Grasso, 1979–80.

DC Office: 1401 LHOB 20515, 202-225-2076; Fax: 202-225-4977; Web site: www.house.gov/gejdenson.

District Offices: Middletown, 203-346-1123; Norwich, 203-886-0139.

Committees: *International Relations* (RMM of 23 D).

Group Ratings

	ADA	ACLU	AFS	LCV	CON	NTU	NFIB	COC	ACU	NTLC	CHC
1998	100	81	100	92	48	14	14	28	9	14	0
1997	95	—	88	—	80	27	—	40	12	—	—

National Journal Ratings

	1997 LIB — 1997 CONS			1998 LIB — 1998 CONS		
Economic	85%	—	10%	79%	—	0%
Social	85%	—	0%	88%	—	11%
Foreign	69%	—	28%	64%	—	31%

Key Votes of the 105th Congress

1. Clinton Budget Deal	N	5. Puerto Rico Sthood. Ref.	Y	9. Cut $ for B-2 Bombers	Y
2. Education IRAs	N	6. End Highway Set-asides	N	10. Human Rights in China	Y
3. Req. 2/3 to Raise Taxes	N	7. School Prayer Amend.	N	11. Withdraw Bosnia Troops	N
4. Fast-track Trade	N	8. Ovrd. Part. Birth Veto	N	12. End Cuban TV-Marti	Y

Election Results

1998 general	Samuel Gejdenson (D)	99,567	(61%)	($1,041,564)
	Gary M. Koval (R)	57,860	(35%)	($126,650)
	Others	5,774	(4%)	
1998 primary	Samuel Gejdenson (D)	nominated by convention		
1996 general	Samuel Gejdenson (D)	115,175	(52%)	($1,177,355)
	Edward W. Munster (R)	100,332	(45%)	($423,658)
	Others	7,740	(3%)	

THIRD DISTRICT

The beginnings of Connecticut's defense industry came two centuries ago, in 1798, when Eli Whitney, a young Yale graduate, won an order from the federal government to produce 10,000 muskets at $13.40 each. Six years before, Whitney had invented the cotton gin, which revolutionized the South but for years only embroiled him in a patent suit. On the musket contract, he was determined to make a profit right off, so he set up a system of interchangeable parts and invented a milling machine and gauges: the beginning of standardized American manufacturing. It was also the beginning of New Haven as a manufacturing center, for Whitney set up his factory along a small, rapidly flowing river just north of this town established more than 150 years before as a religious haven for strict Puritans. For the next 150 years or so, the town mass-produced rifles, clocks, locks, hardware and toys—anything its tinkerers and entrepreneurs could fashion. Today there are few factories left in New Haven, and Connecticut's defense contracts have been cut way back. Southern Connecticut around New Haven is mostly prosperous, but the city itself, with significant crime rates, has only two-thirds of its peak population. Yale, with its Gothic spires, redbrick halls and modernist skating rink, has always been the visual focus of the city; now Yale is left as New Haven's largest employer.

The 3d Congressional District of Connecticut covers the New Haven metropolitan area, which has long since spread beyond the narrow city limits over the hills of what were once Yankee villages and countryside; New Haven cast only 13% of its votes in 1998. Politics in the New Haven area for years was a three-cornered battle, between Yankee Republicans, Irish Democrats, and Italians who became its largest ethnic group and usually voted Republican. Though often regarded as a Democratic seat, the 3d has sometimes been marginal, changing partisan hands in the 1980s as well as the 1940s and 1950s.

Rosa DeLauro, congresswoman from the 3d District, is well connected in New Haven and Washington. She grew up in New Haven's Wooster Square, where her father Ted was alderman; today her mother, Luisa DeLauro, is New Haven's longest-serving alderman. Rosa's husband Stanley Greenberg was Bill Clinton's chief pollster from 1991–94 and worked for Tony Blair's New Labour Party in Britain. Rosa DeLauro has been in politics for years: she was a development administrator in New Haven in the 1970s, chief of staff to Senator Christopher Dodd from 1980–87, then spent a year working to stop U.S. military aid to Nicaraguan contras before going on to become director of EMILY's List, the spectacularly successful liberal women's fundraising group; in 1998 it raised more money than any other PAC. In 1990, when 3d District incumbent Bruce Morrison ran for governor, DeLauro ran for Congress, and won 52%–48% over anti-tax and anti-abortion legislator Tom Scott after spending an impressive $957,000.

DeLauro is now part of the Democrats' leadership and one of its loudest champions on the floor. In November 1998 she ran for Caucus chairman, and lost narrowly, 108–97, to Martin Frost of Texas. She has supported the Clinton Administration faithfully; she supported the 100,000 more teachers idea in 1998 and called for no tax cut in order to save Social Security. Like most House Democratic leaders, she voted against NAFTA. She has been an active and enthusiastic supporter of women's issues. A cancer survivor herself, she sponsored the law to require 48-hour hospital stays for mastectomies.

In 1991 she was formally called down for demanding the Senate hold "a full and public hearing" on Anita Hill's charges (House rules forbid urging the Senate to do anything). She argues that pharmaceutical company discounts to HMOs mean higher drug prices for seniors. She has sought defense contracts for locally built Black Hawk helicopters and retirement benefits for former workers at the Raymark brake factory in Stamford, for helping Longshoremen's Local 1398 buy the bankrupt New Haven Terminal port facilities and for land purchases to complete the Stewart McKinney Wildlife Reserve. She holds a seat on Appropriations and its Agriculture and Labor Subcommittees.

DeLauro's last serious competition in the 3d District came in 1992, when she outspent Scott

$1,022,000 to $219,000 and beat him 66%–34%. She was reelected easily in 1994 and by a 71%–28% margin in 1996 and again in 1998 over Martin Reust, a computer consultant. **Cook's Call.** *Safe.* After her initial narrow win in 1990, DeLauro has won easily in this solidly Democratic district and persuaded all but the most fool-hardy Republicans that this is no district to contest.

The People: Pop. 1990: 547,904; 12.2% rural; 15.2% age 65 + ; 84.2% White, 12% Black, 1.5% Asian, 0.2% Amer. Indian, 2.2% Other; 4.5% Hispanic Origin. Households: 53% married couple families; 23.2% married couple fams. w. children; 48.5% college educ.; median household income: $39,815; per capita income: $18,243; median house value: $173,800; median gross rent: $530.

1996 Presidential Vote			1992 Presidential Vote		
Clinton (D)	129,756	(57%)	Clinton (D)	121,163	(44%)
Dole (R)	71,009	(31%)	Bush (R)	96,085	(35%)
Perot (I)	22,916	(10%)	Perot (I)	54,147	(20%)
Others	5,531	(2%)			

Rep. Rosa DeLauro (D)

Elected 1990; b. Mar. 2, 1943, New Haven; home, New Haven; Marymount Col., B.A. 1964, London Sch. of Econ., 1962–63, Columbia U., M.A. 1966; Catholic; married (Stanley Greenberg).

Professional Career: Exec. Asst., New Haven Mayor Frank Logue, 1976–77; Exec. Asst. & Develop. Admin., City of New Haven, 1977–79; Chief of Staff, U.S. Sen. Christopher Dodd, 1980–87; Exec. Dir., Countdown '87, 1987–88; Exec. Dir., EMILY's List, 1989.

DC Office: 436 CHOB 20515, 202-225-3661; Fax: 202-225-4890; Web site: www.house.gov/delauro.

District Office: New Haven, 203-562-3718.

Committees: *Appropriations* (13th of 27 D): Agriculture, Rural Development, & FDA; Labor, HHS & Education.

Group Ratings

	ADA	ACLU	AFS	LCV	CON	NTU	NFIB	COC	ACU	NTLC	CHC
1998	100	81	100	100	55	13	14	28	8	11	0
1997	95	—	88	—	80	28	—	30	13	—	—

National Journal Ratings

	1997 LIB — 1997 CONS			1998 LIB — 1998 CONS		
Economic	91%	—	7%	79%	—	0%
Social	82%	—	15%	89%	—	11%
Foreign	79%	—	19%	78%	—	19%

Key Votes of the 105th Congress

1. Clinton Budget Deal	N	5. Puerto Rico Sthood. Ref.	Y	9. Cut $ for B-2 Bombers	Y
2. Education IRAs	N	6. End Highway Set-asides	N	10. Human Rights in China	Y
3. Req. 2/3 to Raise Taxes	N	7. School Prayer Amend.	N	11. Withdraw Bosnia Troops	N
4. Fast-track Trade	N	8. Ovrd. Part. Birth Veto	N	12. End Cuban TV-Marti	Y

358   CONNECTICUT

Election Results

1998 general	Rosa DeLauro (D)	109,726	(71%)	($463,460)
	Martin T. Reust (R)	42,090	(27%)	($22,274)
	Others	2,035	(1%)	
1998 primary	Rosa DeLauro (D)	nominated by convention		
1996 general	Rosa DeLauro (D)	150,798	(71%)	($424,582)
	John Coppola (R)	59,335	(28%)	

FOURTH DISTRICT

It was a fitting place, perhaps, for one of the most spectacular financial failures in history, the collapse in September 1998 of Long Term Capital Management, in Greenwich, Connecticut. In the far southwestern corner of New England, Greenwich never seemed destined for wealth, and yet it is arguably the wealthiest community of its size in the world. The Connecticut towns along Long Island Sound were lightly populated Yankee farm country in the 17th and 18th Centuries. In the 19th Century Bridgeport, several towns east of Greenwich, became a factory town, famous as the home of P. T. Barnum. By the early 20th Century, Greenwich and other Yankee villages clustered around commuter railroad stations became the home of some of New York's elite. Greenwich has beautifully manicured hills, elaborately simple boat docks, carefully casual roads, good manners and dull haircuts, 16 private clubs and 9 private schools—and houses which are routinely sold for more than $1 million and then torn down to make way for grander mansions. Starting in the 1950s, New York-based CEOs, eager to minimize their own commutes and avoid New York income taxes, moved their headquarters out to Greenwich and Stamford and Fairfield and points inland: General Electric, American Brands, Union Carbide, Champion International, Pitney Bowes, and Olin. Many other firms, including LTCM, followed, so that Stamford, just east of Greenwich, is now the focus of an edge city that is the biggest office center between Manhattan and Boston.

The 4th Congressional District of Connecticut covers all of Connecticut along Long Island Sound from industrial Bridgeport to Greenwich, plus several inland towns. It includes Stamford, chock full of office complexes; woodsy Darien and New Canaan; Norwalk, with its industrial zone and modest neighborhoods down by the tracks; artsy-craftsy Westport; Fairfield, home of GE; Bethel, where Duracell opened its $70 million headquarters in 1995; and Bridgeport, an odd duck, industrial and low-income, though spruced up when the state-financed Ballpark at Harbor Yard opened up for minor league baseball in 1998. The basic political balance has been the same since the 1940s, when the heavily affluent suburbs attracted enough people to outvote Bridgeport and elect Republican Clare Boothe Luce to the House in 1942 and 1944. More than the rest of Connecticut, the 4th is oriented to New York rather than Hartford or Boston. People here watch New York TV stations: they are Yankee, not Red Sox, fans; their political attitudes are shaped by what is happening in the City as much as in Hartford. Hatred of the state income tax has enabled Republican Governor John Rowland to win by big margins here three times in the 1990s. But the specter of the religious right eroded the Episcopalian Republican vote and helped Bill Clinton make a dead heat of the race here against Greenwich native George Bush in 1992 and to beat Bob Dole 51%–40% in 1996.

The 4th District's congressman, Christopher Shays, is a product of the upscale towns and one of the most pivotal Republicans in the House. Shays grew up in Stamford. After college he and his wife volunteered for the Peace Corps and served in Fiji; after graduate school he was elected to the Connecticut House at 29 and served for 12 years, working with Common Cause on rules reform. He won the U.S. House seat in a 1987 special election by beating a culturally conservative Democrat from Bridgeport. Shays is a pleasant man with a stubborn streak and considerable legislative savvy; his voting record is near the middle of the House on most issues, a bit left on cultural issues. When he feels strongly, he will risk everything: he registered for conscientious objector status during the Vietnam war, and says he would not have served if drafted; as a legislator, he went to jail for seven days in 1986 to protest judicial system corruption.

Despite his dissent from many Republicans' views—on campaign finance reform, abortion, gun control, subsidies to the arts, gay rights, the minimum wage, defense spending, Census sampling—he was long a partisan Republican from the time he was ignored by the House's Democratic leaders and impressed by a speech in Connecticut by a backbencher named Newt Gingrich. In August 1994 he withdrew his vote for the Clinton crime bill in protest over Democratic tactics, and with Gingrich's support negotiated a new version—an episode that helped break up the Democratic majority. And the first major bill passed the first day of the Republican Congress was managed by Shays, the Congressional Accountability Act, imposing on Congress the laws it imposes on others; it passed unanimously. Shays was also chief sponsor of the gift ban law and the Lobby Disclosure Act. Yet he soured on other House Republicans as Gingrich went to great lengths to sink his campaign finance reform bill in 1998. "I am very much a part of the Republican revolution—and I do think it is a revolution—but I am still an independent person," Shays said in January 1996, amid the budget fight; he supported Gingrich on ethics charges and warned him of the other leaders' coup in 1997. But during the campaign finance fight in June 1998, his tune was different: "I am a Republican who can't be proud of how my Republicans are conducting themselves."

Shays's two great causes in the 105th Congress were campaign finance reform and Gulf war illnesses. He was the lead sponsor of the Shays-Meehan bill, which in its latest version—it has been rewritten several times—would ban "soft money" in federal elections and bar non-candidate groups from running ads to help candidates within 60 days of an election. Most Republicans opposed it as harmful to their party, and added that some of its provisions would be unconstitutional under current Supreme Court precedents. Newt Gingrich, seeing that it could gain a majority and that neither argument was likely to outweigh its attractive label, tried to prevent a vote in March 1998, and failed. Then he moved to allow debate on some 200 amendments and allowed 10 other campaign finance measures to come to the floor, with the proviso that the one with the most votes would win. But Shays and his co-sponsor, Democrat Martin Meehan, beat the other amendments and held down the totals for the other reforms. Finally, the House passed Shays-Meehan on August 6, 252–179, with a surprising 61 Republicans voting for. "They gave it more life by the arrogance with which they tried to kill it," Shays said. Majority Leader Trent Lott was able to keep the issue off the floor in the Senate, but Shays reintroduced the bill in January 1999.

As chairman of a Government Reform subcommittee, Shays has zeroed in on the issue of Gulf war illnesses. A large number of veterans have reported various symptoms, some of which may be related to exposure to chemical weapons, and the Pentagon failed to reveal for years the use of some gas by Iraq or contact with it by American troops. Questions were raised whether an anti-gas drug given to American troops may have done damage. Shays became convinced that the Pentagon and the Veterans' Administration were "plagued by arrogant incuriosity and a pervasive myopia that sees lack of evidence as proof." After a 20-month investigation, the subcommittee voted to take jurisdiction away from the Pentagon and VA altogether—although it didn't say who would handle the issue.

Shays's cooperation with Gingrich and the Republican revolution may have cost him some votes. His 1996 opponent attacked him for supporting Gingrich, and his percentage dropped from 74% in 1994 to 60% in 1996. In the latter year he lost Bridgeport 64%–33%. But his much-publicized opposition to Gingrich on campaign finance reform and other issues seemed to help in 1998. Shays won overall 69%–30% and lost Bridgeport by only 51%–48%.

Cook's Call. *Safe.* This is not a rock-solid Republican district but a swing district that is well-suited for a moderate, reform-oriented Republican like Shays. As long as Shays runs, Republicans should have little difficulty holding onto this seat. Once it does open up, expect a very competitive race to replace him.

The People: Pop. 1990: 547,561; 4.5% rural; 14.5% age 65+; 80.2% White, 13.2% Black, 2% Asian, 0.1% Amer. Indian, 4.5% Other; 10.6% Hispanic Origin. Households: 53.8% married couple families; 23.4% married couple fams. w. children; 54.2% college educ.; median household income: $47,636; per capita income: $27,130; median house value: $277,400; median gross rent: $594.

1996 Presidential Vote

Clinton (D)	113,411	(51%)
Dole (R)	88,181	(40%)
Perot (I)	14,825	(7%)
Others	5,355	(2%)

1992 Presidential Vote

Bush (R)	110,072	(42%)
Clinton (D)	109,122	(42%)
Perot (I)	40,802	(16%)

Rep. Christopher Shays (R)

Elected Aug. 1987; b. Oct. 18, 1945, Stamford; home, Bridgeport; Principia Col., B.A. 1968, NYU, M.B.A. 1974, M.P.A. 1978; Christian Scientist; married (Betsi).

Elected Office: CT House of Reps., 1974–87.

Professional Career: Peace Corps, Fiji, 1968–70; Aide, Trumbull Mayor, 1971–72.

DC Office: 1126 LHOB 20515, 202-225-5541; Fax: 202-225-9629; Web site: www.house.gov/shays.

District Offices: Bridgeport, 203-579-5870; Norwalk, 203-866-6469; Stamford, 203-357-8277.

Committees: *Budget* (3d of 24 R). *Government Reform* (4th of 24 R): Criminal Justice, Drug Policy & Human Resources; National Security, Veterans' Affairs & Intl. Relations (Chmn.).

Group Ratings

	ADA	ACLU	AFS	LCV	CON	NTU	NFIB	COC	ACU	NTLC	CHC
1998	45	63	33	100	92	67	57	56	40	42	58
1997	55	—	38	—	97	72	—	70	56	—	—

National Journal Ratings

	1997 LIB — 1997 CONS			1998 LIB — 1998 CONS		
Economic	48%	—	52%	53%	—	47%
Social	64%	—	35%	65%	—	34%
Foreign	56%	—	42%	53%	—	45%

Key Votes of the 105th Congress

1. Clinton Budget Deal	Y	5. Puerto Rico Sthood. Ref.	N	9. Cut $ for B-2 Bombers	Y
2. Education IRAs	Y	6. End Highway Set-asides	N	10. Human Rights in China	N
3. Req. 2/3 to Raise Taxes	Y	7. School Prayer Amend.	N	11. Withdraw Bosnia Troops	Y
4. Fast-track Trade	Y	8. Ovrd. Part. Birth Veto	Y	12. End Cuban TV-Marti	N

Election Results

1998 general	Christopher Shays (R)	94,767	(69%)	($604,689)
	Jonathan Kantrowitz (D)	40,988	(30%)	
	Others	1,449	(1%)	
1998 primary	Christopher Shays (R)	..... nominated by convention		
1996 general	Christopher Shays (R)	121,949	(60%)	($552,597)
	Bill Finch (D)	75,902	(38%)	($183,061)
	Others	3,861	(2%)	

FIFTH DISTRICT

Central Connecticut's stony hills are physically isolated, the climate is forbidding, local manners are frosty, there is nothing to suggest lavishness: this might be the Switzerland of America. Yet in the last 200 years, the mountains of Switzerland and the hills of Connecticut have been transformed from subsistence farmland to some of the most productive and affluent places on earth. Their secrets have been thrift, hard work, inventiveness and an intolerance for imprecision. Keeping time is a common motif: Switzerland was long the world's leading watchmaker, and Connecticut has long been America's leading clockmaker. The comparison at some point breaks down: Switzerland has prospered by closing others out, its political neutrality and financial probity reassuring investors and undergirding its banking industry. Connecticut, like the rest of America, is an open society, welcoming newcomers and imbuing immigrants with the Yankee knack for tinkering and precision work. It has also been quick to adapt to market changes. Danbury was once the nation's leading producer of hats; now it cuts almost no felt but is a major corporate headquarters. Meriden once made ivory combs, clocks, cutlery, and silver; now it produces electrical signalling equipment, jewelry, biotech filters, and nuclear instruments. Waterbury, once the nation's largest producer of brass, saw the last of its big three brass fabricators shut down in 1985, but has replaced that with health care and now two local hospitals are the city's biggest employers; the old Scovill brass factory is now a shopping mall.

The 5th Congressional District is an irregularly shaped slice of central Connecticut, entirely inland, from Meriden west through Waterbury to Danbury and the high-income havens of Ridgefield and Wilton. This was the Federalist heartland in the early 19th Century. It voted Republican for nearly a century, then became Democratic as Catholics started outnumbering Protestants. Now, cultural conservatism and economic growth have tilted it toward Republicans again; it produced the lowest Clinton margin of any Connecticut district in 1996. But it is closely balanced enough to be marginal often, and has voted out incumbent congressmen of both parties in 1972, 1978, 1984, 1996, and came close to doing so in 1998. In recent years the 5th was represented by Republican Governor John Rowland, reelected by a wide margin in 1998, and by Republican Gary Franks, who lost to Senator Christopher Dodd by a wide margin the same year. Now it is represented by James Maloney, a Democrat from Danbury, who won the seat from Franks in 1996 and defended it against a tough challenge in 1998.

Maloney grew up in Danbury, and after college and law school spent a year as a Vista volunteer. From 1974–78 he headed Danbury's antipoverty agency. In 1986 he was elected to the state Senate, where he worked on a family leave act, voted against the state income tax, and supported business tax cuts. In 1994 he decided to run against Franks, then the only black Republican in the House. Maloney held him to a 52%–46% margin in 1994, the second lowest margin for a Republican incumbent that year, and in early 1996 decided to run again. He was helped when a primary candidate dropped out in July; this was the first uncontested Democratic primary here since 1990.

Maloney ran on a somewhat conservative platform—for the balanced budget amendment, favoring job opportunities and no cash payments for welfare recipients. Maloney also criticized Franks for receiving a $100,000 advance from HarperCollins for a book; unperturbed, Franks spent much of summer 1996 on a 17-city book tour. And he made it no secret that he was thinking of running against Senator Christopher Dodd in 1998. Maloney said, "I don't think Gary Franks is running for the Senate in 1998 because he's not going to be in Congress after this year. How about paying attention to the needs of the 5th district?" Right and wrong: Franks lost in 1996, but ran against Dodd anyway (and lost) in 1998.

Maloney won 52%–46%, and proceeded to compile a moderate voting record. He supported a tax cut and the partial-birth abortion ban. He sponsored a bill, which passed the House in October 1998, to spend $20 million on hiring police officers who would be stationed in schools. With Christopher Shays, he sponsored a brownfields bill, to help finance new construction on old factory sites, which was used to aid Danbury, Meriden, Derby, Seymour, and Waterbury. He also sponsored a bill to expand the Weir Hall National Historic Site.

Not surprisingly Maloney had serious opposition in 1998, from 34-year-old Danbury state Senator Mark Nielsen. Republican leaders called the 5th "one of our top targets in the nation," and Nielsen, whose opponent for the nomination dropped out before the primary, had nearly as much money as the incumbent. Scandal issues played some role. On August 18, the day after Bill Clinton's grand jury appearance, Nielsen called on him to resign. Maloney on October 8 voted for the Republican motion to hold impeachment hearings. "The only way to address it is to go through the inquiry process and get it resolved, one way or another," he said. Maloney was also dogged by campaign finance charges. In January 1998 his brother was convicted of reimbursing contributors to his 1996 campaign, and fined $256,000. Then in October the Maloney campaign returned $5,000 and redesignated $29,000 of contributions classified as pre-primary, but which were contributed between the July convention and the September primary where Maloney had no opposition. Nielsen ran ads attacking these irregularities. More positively, he called for welfare reform and tax cuts and called himself a "John Rowland Republican."

This was not quite enough, and Maloney won in one of the closest races in the East, by 50%–48%. He carried Meriden in the east and Danbury in the west, plus the Naugatuck valley factory towns narrowly, but he scarcely carried Waterbury and lost most of the smaller towns.

Cook's Call. *Highly Competitive.* Another competitively drawn district, this seat has seen its fair share of close races over the past few years. Maloney has never won big here and will likely face his 1998 opponent Mark Nielsen in 2000. Expect another battle here.

The People: Pop. 1990: 547,907; 20.8% rural; 13.4% age 65 +; 91.3% White, 4.8% Black, 1.3% Asian, 0.2% Amer. Indian, 2.4% Other; 5.9% Hispanic Origin. Households: 59.3% married couple families; 28.4% married couple fams. w. children; 49.9% college educ.; median household income: $44,056; per capita income: $20,316; median house value: $183,900; median gross rent: $474.

1996 Presidential Vote

Clinton (D)	110,596	(48%)
Dole (R)	92,570	(40%)
Perot (I)	24,265	(10%)
Others	4,694	(2%)

1992 Presidential Vote

Bush (R)	111,327	(42%)
Clinton (D)	93,966	(35%)
Perot (I)	60,891	(23%)

Rep. James H. Maloney (D)

Elected 1996; b. Sept. 17, 1948, Quincy, MA; home, Danbury; Harvard U., B.A. 1972, Boston U., J.D. 1980; Catholic; married (Mary Draper).

Elected Office: CT Senate, 1986–95.

Professional Career: Exec. Dir., Danbury Anti-Poverty Agency, 1974–78; Practicing atty., 1980–96.

DC Office: 1213 LHOB 20515, 202-225-3822; Fax: 202-225-5746; Web site: www.house.gov/jimmaloney.

District Office: Waterbury, 203-573-1418.

Committees: *Armed Services* (19th of 28 D): Military Procurement; Military Readiness; Special Oversight Panel on the Merchant Marine. *Banking & Financial Services* (12th of 27 D): Capital Markets, Securities & Government Sponsored Enterprises; Housing & Community Opportunity.

Group Ratings

	ADA	ACLU	AFS	LCV	CON	NTU	NFIB	COC	ACU	NTLC	CHC
1998	85	63	89	77	6	31	64	56	32	32	17
1997	75	—	63	—	34	41	—	60	32	—	—

National Journal Ratings

	1997 LIB	—	1997 CONS	1998 LIB	—	1998 CONS
Economic	61%	—	39%	58%	—	42%
Social	66%	—	33%	69%	—	31%
Foreign	64%	—	36%	49%	—	48%

Key Votes of the 105th Congress

1. Clinton Budget Deal	Y	5. Puerto Rico Sthood. Ref.	Y	9. Cut $ for B-2 Bombers	N
2. Education IRAs	N	6. End Highway Set-asides	N	10. Human Rights in China	Y
3. Req. 2/3 to Raise Taxes	Y	7. School Prayer Amend.	N	11. Withdraw Bosnia Troops	Y
4. Fast-track Trade	N	8. Ovrd. Part. Birth Veto	Y	12. End Cuban TV-Marti	N

Election Results

1998 general	James H. Maloney (D)	78,394	(50%)	($1,377,977)
	Mark Nielsen (R)	76,051	(48%)	($939,775)
	Others	2,712	(2%)	
1998 primary	James H. Maloney (D) ..... nominated by convention			
1996 general	James H. Maloney (D-ACP)	111,974	(52%)	($614,440)
	Gary A. Franks (R)	98,782	(46%)	($644,293)
	Others	4,374	(2%)	

SIXTH DISTRICT

From its Yankee past to its Ellis Islander present and ahead to its third wave of immigrants future, Connecticut has been a land of tinkerers specializing in precision work, of inventors able to transform vagrant ideas into profitable products. Over the years this stony soil has become the home of some of the most affluent people in the nation and the world. This is true even in the hills of northwest Connecticut, off the interstates and far from Connecticut's small urban capital of Hartford and its sometime booming edge city of Stamford. Here are exquisite Yankee towns like Washington and Kent, prosperous once in the post-Revolutionary era when Connecticut's ship owners accumulated capital and invested it in factories and mills, and now a country-home mecca for ultra-rich New Yorkers seeking to avoid the glitz of Southampton. Not far away are small industrial cities like New Britain, America's ball bearing capital for years, and Bristol, where sports announcer Bill Rasmussen dreamed up the idea of transmitting satellite feeds of UConn games to his neighbors by cable TV—an idea which became ESPN.

The 6th Congressional District of Connecticut covers approximately the northwest corner of the state, stretching from Enfield and Windsor Locks, north of Hartford on the Connecticut River, across the affluent Farmington valley suburbs of Hartford to industrial New Britain and Bristol, and includes all of Litchfield County. Historically, this was rock-ribbed Federalist and Republican territory; in the 20th Century, with Italian immigrants heading to Enfield and Windsor Locks and Poles to New Britain, it moved toward being politically marginal.

The congresswoman from the 6th District is Nancy Johnson, a Republican first elected in 1982. She grew up in Chicago, daughter of a Republican state legislator, came east to school, then lived in New Britain as a doctor's wife and a teacher, raising three children while active in charitable and community affairs. She was elected to the Connecticut Senate in 1976 from a heavily Democratic district. When 6th District Congressman Toby Moffett ran against Senator Lowell Weicker in 1982, Johnson won the House seat, beating Bill Curry, then a 30-year-old nuclear freeze organizer and later the 1994 Democratic candidate for governor and a Clinton White House aide.

Johnson has become one of the most active and productive legislators in the House, and was on her way to being so even before Republicans won control. Her record has been mostly market-oriented on economics, fairly liberal on cultural issues. She is pro-choice but has opposed what she considers statist legislation, from the Children's Defense Fund childcare bill in the 1980s to the Clinton healthcare package in 1994. She voted for the 1994 crime bill and was one of the few Republican dissenters from the Contract with America crime package. On Ways and Means she took the lead on eliminating the old childcare tax credit, which tended to help high-income parents, and replaced it with $300 million in vouchers to low-income working mothers. She works on local projects—redevelopment in New Britain, getting the Connecticut River designated an American Heritage River, building the Black Revolutionary War Patriots Memorial.

Johnson is now second-ranking Republican on the Ways and Means Health Subcommittee, and has worked on many health issues over the years. She participated in hearings on the Clinton healthcare plan, despite gratuitous and sexist insults from then-Chairman Pete Stark, and her efforts contributed to its demise. Johnson's bill to continue low-cost health care for seniors was the only healthcare law passed by Congress in 1994. On welfare reform in 1995, she worked with Clay Shaw and pushed successfully for a child support enforcement amendment and for guaranteed Medicaid benefits for welfare recipients with no private health insurance. She also helped put together the healthcare portability law in 1996 and was involved in constructing the Republican Medicare plan.

But the biggest headlines—and headaches—for her came from her work as chairman of the House ethics committee, when she was considering the case against Newt Gingrich. Johnson and Gingrich, despite her moderate record, had long been allies: he consulted her often on issues; she gave him key support in his 1989 race for Republican whip. In September 1996, after working for a year, outside counsel James Cole submitted a report on Gingrich which Johnson, following precedent, did not make public. That sparked Democratic cries of coverup and back home in Connecticut her Democratic opponent Charlotte Koskoff called her "Stonewall Johnson."

Johnson had beaten Koskoff 64%–32% in 1994 and in 1996 outspent her by about 4–1. But Bill Clinton ended up carrying the 6th District 50%–36%, and Newt Gingrich was highly unpopular there. The National Organization of Women, which had endorsed Johnson in six races and was neutral in 1994, endorsed the Democrat. The networks reported on election night that Johnson was beaten; in fact she ended up winning 50%–49%. Johnson readily admitted that her role on the ethics committee "absolutely hurt me." Although the ethics committee agreed just before Christmas on the Gingrich reprimand, Johnson did not make public the counsel's report until after Gingrich's reelection as speaker in January. Democrats harshly criticized her for truncating to one day the public hearings on Gingrich. On January 21 the House voted 395–28 to reprimand and fine Gingrich an unprecedented $300,000; and Johnson, her term up, immediately left the committee.

Johnson then went into legislative high gear. She was the lead sponsor of a bill to provide health insurance for uninsured children, which passed in July 1997. After many health insurers started paying for Viagra, she and Nita Lowey sponsored a bill to provide contraceptives to federal employees with health insurance covering prescriptions. As chairman of the Oversight Subcommittee, she was a chief sponsor of the IRS reform bill, which moved the presumption of correctness away from the agency and otherwise changed rules of many years standing. She sought full funding for the National Endowment for the Arts. When a parliamentary manuever she and Christopher Shays made in 1997 was interpreted as an anti-NEA measure, House leaders arranged for her to move the adoption of the full $98 million funding; it passed 253–173. She stepped up work on the American Heritage Rivers bill and in 1997 her rating from the League of Conservation Voters rose from 46% to 94%. Roused by incidents in a New Britain housing project, she sponsored a law barring convicted sex offenders from federally financed public housing; it became law in October 1998. In the fall of 1998, she and Sam Johnson proposed a "Johnson & Johnson" package of tax cuts, including higher standard deductions for married couples and earnings thresholds for seniors, making health insurance premiums 100% deductible, and making the research and development tax credit permanent.

Much of this was with a view to the 1998 election. Charlotte Koskoff was running again, and managed to elbow aside other Democrats without a primary. She called for a patient's right to sue HMOs and an infusion of the federal budget surplus into Social Security. "The bottom line is that she is an enabler and participant in the right-wing Republican agenda," she said of Johnson. This time Koskoff had solid support from national Democrats, the AFL-CIO, and EMILY's List. Johnson countered with endorsements from education, environment, and labor groups. She argued that, with Hartford's Barbara Kennelly leaving Congress and Ways and Means (to run for governor), Connecticut needed her more than ever.

The hottest argument came over a bill Johnson sponsored to prevent the Customs Bureau from changing the rule allowing companies to market tools including overseas-made components as "Made in the U.S.A." Among the companies interested was Stanley Works of New Britain, and in October 1997 it was revealed that Johnson owns over $100,000 of Stanley stock (her husband inherited it from his father, who was a Stanley foreman). Koskoff ran ads accusing Johnson of helping Stanley Works export jobs, and accusing her of trying to benefit herself and responding to $6,000 in contributions from Stanley Works executives. Johnson replied tartly that the bill would increase jobs in Connecticut and added, "I've busted my butt for local industry." Outspending Koskoff more than 3–1, Johnson rebounded, though not quite to her 1994 level. That year she won 64%–32%; in 1996, she squeaked through, 50%–49%; in 1998 she won 58%–40%, carrying practically all small towns but one and losing only in New Britain, Bristol, and (Koskoff's home town) Plainville.

Cook's Call. *Probably Safe.* Though the 6th District was also drawn to be very competitive, Johnson has carried it easily in seven of her nine general election campaigns. As a moderate Republican who isn't afraid to buck her party's leadership, Johnson has built a profile that is well-suited for this district. However, when she steps aside, expect a very competitive fight to replace her.

The People: Pop. 1990: 547,747; 31.7% rural; 14.5% age 65 + ; 95.1% White, 2.2% Black, 1.1% Asian, 0.1% Amer. Indian, 1.6% Other; 3.5% Hispanic Origin. Households: 59.2% married couple families; 26.5% married couple fams. w. children; 49.2% college educ.; median household income: $42,817; per capita income: $19,863; median house value: $166,400; median gross rent: $482.

1996 Presidential Vote

Clinton (D)	121,607	(50%)
Dole (R)	89,003	(36%)
Perot (I)	26,865	(11%)
Others	6,462	(3%)

1992 Presidential Vote

Clinton (D)	110,828	(40%)
Bush (R)	99,633	(36%)
Perot (I)	67,995	(24%)

Rep. Nancy L. Johnson (R)

Elected 1982; b. Jan. 5, 1935, Chicago, IL; home, New Britain; U. of Chicago, 1951–53, Radcliffe Col., B.A. 1957, U. of London, 1957–58; Unitarian; married (Theodore).

Elected Office: CT Senate, 1976–82.

Professional Career: Pres., Sheldon Community Guidance Clinic; Adjunct Prof., Central CT St. Col., 1968–71.

DC Office: 2113 RHOB 20515, 202-225-4476; Fax: 202-225-4488; Web site: www.house.gov/nancyjohnson.

District Office: New Britain, 860-223-8412.

Committees: *Ways & Means* (5th of 23 R): Health; Human Resources (Chmn.).

Group Ratings

	ADA	ACLU	AFS	LCV	CON	NTU	NFIB	COC	ACU	NTLC	CHC
1998	55	63	67	77	62	28	71	83	16	34	17
1997	55	—	50	—	62	40	—	80	36	—	—

National Journal Ratings

	1997 LIB — 1997 CONS	1998 LIB — 1998 CONS
Economic	52% — 48%	53% — 46%
Social	67% — 33%	70% — 28%
Foreign	51% — 46%	56% — 42%

Key Votes of the 105th Congress

1. Clinton Budget Deal	Y	5. Puerto Rico Sthood. Ref.	N	9. Cut $ for B-2 Bombers	N
2. Education IRAs	N	6. End Highway Set-asides	N	10. Human Rights in China	N
3. Req. 2/3 to Raise Taxes	N	7. School Prayer Amend.	N	11. Withdraw Bosnia Troops	Y
4. Fast-track Trade	Y	8. Ovrd. Part. Birth Veto	N	12. End Cuban TV-Marti	N

Election Results

1998 general	Nancy L. Johnson (R)	101,630	(58%)	($1,768,957)
	Charlotte Koskoff (D)	69,201	(40%)	($551,881)
	Others	3,950	(2%)	
1998 primary	Nancy L. Johnson (R)	..... nominated by convention		
1996 general	Nancy L. Johnson (R)	113,020	(50%)	($931,406)
	Charlotte Koskoff (D)	111,433	(49%)	($273,133)

DELAWARE

Delaware, the first state to ratify the Constitution, the second smallest state in area, fifth smallest in population, is a small corner of America, with some considerable claims on the national attention. The mouth of the Delaware River was explored by Henry Hudson, and the Dutch and Swedes built settlements on the west bank in the 1630s. But the three counties of Delaware owe their separate existence to the politics of the proprietors of William Penn's colony of Pennsylvania, and to Delawareans' own speed in ratifying the Constitution which made it literally the "First State."

Through most of its history Delaware has been unusually affluent. It had the nation's highest income levels during the early 20th Century and high incomes in the prosperous 1990s. It houses, in beautiful cobblestone mansions in its chateau country, many members of the most numerous wealthy family in America, the du Ponts. Delaware's ethnic and racial mixture is much like that along the rest of the East Coast and not that much different than the nation's, though with fewer than average Hispanics and Asians; there is a mixture here of suburbs, old immigrant neighborhoods, urban black neighborhoods and farmlands. If not all parts of the nation can follow Delaware's exact path to continued prosperity, perhaps they can get an idea of the direction to travel.

The central focus of Delaware's economy for two centuries was the business started when Eleuthere Irenee du Pont, the practical business-minded son of a dreamy, idealistic French immigrant, built a gunpowder mill on the banks of Brandywine Creek in 1802. This was the first enterprise of the family du Pont, and it expanded to become one of America's great munitions and chemical companies. It grew especially rapidly during World War I, generating so much capital that the Du Pont Company bought a huge block of stock in General Motors in the 1920s and controlled GM for thirty years while it was America's largest corporation. That capital also financed what was arguably the world's finest research and development program. In the years during and after World War II, Du Pont prospered by bringing to the consumer and industrial market new synthetics and plastics like rayon, nylon, cellophane, polyethylene, lucite and teflon: "Better Living Through Chemistry." Delaware continues to be a high-tech state today; it boasts that it ranks number one in scientists and engineers with Ph.Ds. per capita and highest in patents per capita.

Delaware has also thrived in finance. In the late 19th Century, it pioneered liberal laws of incorporation, giving more flexibility and power to managers and owners. A large share of the nation's big companies are incorporated in Delaware—their legal births take place in a federal-style building near the Capitol in Dover—which means that much of the nation's corporate law, especially on mergers and acquisitions and unfriendly takeovers, is made in Delaware courts. Banking prospered here starting in the 1980s when Governor Pete du Pont's succeeded in liberalizing Delaware's banking laws to encourage out-of-state banks to locate operations here. Today banking accounts for more than 30,000 jobs in Delaware, more than any other business. Du Pont's systematic lowering of the income tax rate, continued by his successors, Republican Mike Castle and Democrat Thomas Carper, has also contributed mightily to Delaware's prosperity. Its economy grew robustly in the 1980s, paused only a little in the recession of the early 1990s, and surged again as its population grew more than than any other Northeastern or Midwestern state.

On both sides of the Mason and Dixon line, with immigrants in Wilmington and southern-accented farmers in Kent and Sussex Counties, with suburbs ranging from very affluent to not-so-affluent in New Castle County, Delaware has long had a robust two-party politics. Democrats hold four of six statewide offices, Republicans occupy one of the two Senate seats and the

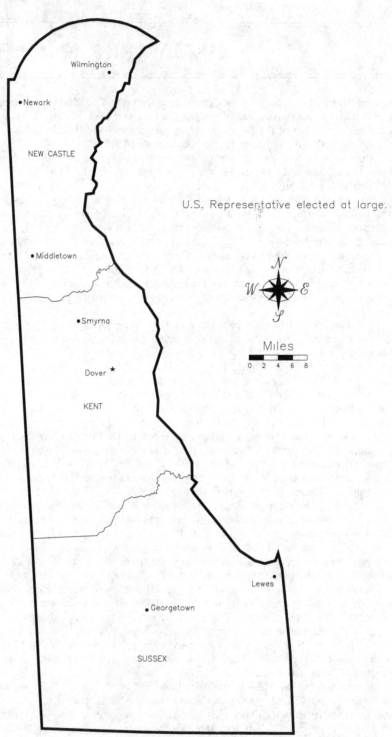

Wilmington

• Newark

NEW CASTLE

U.S. Representative elected at large.

• Middletown

N
W ✦ E
S

Miles
0 2 4 6 8

• Smyrna

Dover ★

KENT

Lewes

• Georgetown

SUSSEX

state's single seat in the House, close races nationally for president are close in Delaware as well; indeed Delaware has voted for the winning presidential candidate in every contest in the last half-century. But thanks to Delaware's small size there is still an intimacy to politics here. Most of Delaware is reached (though politically ignored) by Philadelphia TV, so personal campaigning is still important. The Thursday after the election is "Return Day," when winning and losing candidates—opponents ride in the same car—come back to the lower Delaware town of Georgetown to receive the bipartisan cheers of the voters. And everyone seems to know everyone else, which makes Delaware politics less angry and mean-spirited than in bigger East Coast states. But that intimacy can also be tragic, as it was when Thomas Capano, prominent lawyer and former counsel to former Governor Castle, was tried and in January 1999 convicted for murdering Anne Marie Fahey, scheduling secretary to Governor Carper, a ghastly crime which seemed to touch almost everyone in this small state.

Governor. Thomas R. Carper grew up in southside Virginia and went to college in Ohio. But out-of-state origins are not uncommon here: Delaware's two senators were born in Montana and Pennsylvania. Carper first came to Delaware as an ensign in the Navy, then returned after service in Southeast Asia to get his M.B.A. In 1976, he was elected state treasurer at 29; he ran for Congress in 1982 and beat a scandal-tarred incumbent. In the House, Carper had a moderate voting record and worked to let banks into the securities business and to prevent ocean sludge dumping, both causes supported by Delaware constituencies. In 1992, when Republican Mike Castle had served his two allotted terms and ran for Congress, Carper ran for governor and won the general with 65%.

As governor, Carper pursued an agenda in many ways more conservative than liberal. He continued du Pont's policy of cutting taxes, reducing income tax rates about 10% and also cutting small business and utility taxes; he claims the tax burden is the lowest between Vermont and West Virginia. Revenues kept gushing in from Delaware's strong economy, and he increased the "rainy day" fund and boosted the state's credit rating to an historic high. He inherited Mike Castle's standard-based education reform, raised standards, started testing students in 1998 and provided public school choice, utilized by 8% of students, tried to raise teacher salaries, and instituted charter schools. He worked to keep current industries and attract others; jobs rose 50,000 in his first five years. His June 1995 "A Better Chance" welfare reform imposed four-year limits on welfare payments, required recipients to work, and discouraged teen pregnancy by denying additional welfare aid to families that increase in size; it cut welfare rolls 23% in two years. He built more prisons, saw that violent criminals served 89% of their sentences, and required a year of drug counseling for inmates with addictions. He has tried to take action against chicken waste, a major problem in southern Delaware and called for a business-friendly "new environmentalism." His major defeats came when the legislature voted to allow slot machines at harness racing tracks over his opposition and refused to approve a higher tobacco tax. In 1998 he stopped Republicans from passing electricity deregulation and statewide property reassessment for school funding.

Carper has had high job approval ratings and in 1996 was re-elected by 70%–31% over then-Treasurer Janet Rzewnicki. He is barred from seeking a third term in 2000 and is widely considered a strong candidate for Senator William Roth's seat that year.

Cook's Call. *Highly Competitive.* Carper's departure after eight years as governor sets up a very competitive race. Democrats have touted Lieutenant Governor Ruth Ann Minner, owner of a towing service, as their frontrunner. Potential Republican candidates include Attorney General M. Jane Brady, a conservative; Philadelphia Maritime Exchange President Dennis Rochford; state House Speaker Terry Spence and Judge William Swain Lee, of the Capano murder case.

Senior Senator. Senator William V. Roth Jr., the third most senior Republican in the Senate, has now held high statewide office for longer than anyone else in Delaware's history. He served in the Army in World War II, settled in Delaware and practiced law, became Republican state chairman in 1961, and won the state's at-large House seat in 1966. In 1970, when Senator John

Williams retired after four terms, Roth was the obvious Republican choice. With his moderate voting record, friendly demeanor and frequent presence in Delaware with his St. Bernards at his side, he has been politically strong ever since. He remains an elusive figure to many in Washington: he is not stylish or dazzlingly articulate, and his wife is a federal judge back in Delaware. Yet he has sponsored important legislation and advanced powerful political ideas with increasing success, and he holds one of the key power positions on Capitol Hill, the chairmanship of the Senate Finance Committee.

Roth's overall voting record is middle-of-the-road in the Republican Senate, but his key initiatives have been in the direction of reducing taxes and giving citizens more leeway in spending what they earn. One early initiative was the Kemp-Roth tax cut, of which he was the chief Senate sponsor, the 30% across-the-board cut in income tax rates first proposed and backed by almost every Republican in 1978 and then largely enacted in 1981 after Ronald Reagan won in 1980. Another major Roth cause is promoting IRAs—adapting the Individual Retirement Accounts to allow tax-free savings for college educations and making IRAs available to homemakers. He sponsored the Roth IRAs enacted in 1997, which became the hottest investment vehicle of 1998: they allow the investment of $2,000 a year of after-tax money that grows tax-free, even when it is withdrawn. In January 1999 he proposed a Roth 401(k), which would have even less income restrictions than Roth IRAs. He has sponsored a $5,000 adoption tax credit, which was passed by the Republican Congress and signed by President Clinton in August 1996. In 1996 and again in 1997, he backed the House Republicans' $500 per child tax credit; it was passed the second time through. But he has gone against House Republicans on important issues, on which they sought political breakthroughs. He opposed separating Medicaid reform from welfare reform, which was done anyway and resulted in the signing of welfare reform in August 1996. And, with Budget Chairman Pete Domenici, he opposed major tax cuts in 1997 and 1998.

Roth has sought other bold reforms. With Finance ranking Democrat Daniel Patrick Moynihan, he assembled an expert panel on the Consumer Price Index that concluded it significantly overstated inflation. But they were unable to overcome opposition from the Bureau of Labor Statistics and some liberals to adjusting the CPI, which would have reduced Social Security costs, especially in out years. But Roth did win another victory in the 105th Congress. In September 1997 he conducted three days of hearings on IRS abuses, helping to create a political climate for IRS reform. That reform, passed in May 1998, for the first time shifted the burden of proof in some cases from the taxpayer to the IRS, and protected innocent spouses, provided for Saturday IRS hours and allowed telephone and computerized filing of returns.

Roth has been active on other issues. On the Governmental Affairs Committee, which he chaired in 1995, Roth helped pass the legislation authorizing Vice President Al Gore's reinventing government initiative. He was a leading proponent of NATO expansion, and chairman of the North Atlantic Assembly; he led the move to include Slovenia in the first round of NATO expansion, and presented his own plan for deployment of NATO forces in the post-Cold War era, which would dispense with the requirement of United Nations authorization. With Moynihan, he got the term "Most Favored Nation" status, controversial in votes on China every year, changed to the more accurate "Normal Trade Relations." He opposes ocean dumping and incineration of toxic waste, backs the Coastal Zone Management Act, and wants to protect the striped bass; he is a leading Republican opponent of oil drilling in Alaska's Arctic National Wildlife Refuge. In 1998 he came up with a clever plan to get $2.3 billion in capital improvements for Amtrak, more valued perhaps in Delaware than anywhere else; the idea was to name Amtrak as the successor of the freight railroads that paid $197 million back in 1970 to shed their passenger-carrying obligations, and to let Amtrak assume their net operating loss carrybacks. He has called for more effort to put through fast track and to strengthen the Caribbean Basin Initiative to helps nations devastated by Hurricane Mitch.

Roth was re-elected by comfortable margins in 1976, 1982 and 1988. He once promised not to run after he turned 70, but ran anyway in 1994. Attorney General Charles Oberly, the

Democratic nominee, spent over $1.5 million, but never got much traction; Roth, staying above the fray, won 56%–42%. He turns 79 when his seat comes up in 2000. His position as Finance chairman is obviously important to a state in which banking is the leading industry, and his recent successes—especially with Roth IRAs—make him better known than ever. In early 1999 he said simply, "I talked to my St. Bernards. They're ready." He could have serious competition from Governor Thomas Carper, a Democrat who has pushed many conservative policies and is barred from a third term in 2000. Carper is certainly likely to run if Roth doesn't. In that case, the strongest Republican would be Congressman-at-Large Mike Castle. But Castle seems pleased with his position as a crucial moderate Republican in the House and has a strong friendship with Carper. It is, after all, a small state.

Cook's Call. *Potentially Competitive.* Roth is high on the list of potential retirements, but most expect him to seek a sixth term. Democrats hope that Governor Carper will challenge Roth. Although Carper would be a formidable candidate, Roth would have the edge in that race. If Carper decides not to run, Roth would be a heavy favorite for re-election. If Roth opts to step down, the seat is up for grabs, with Republican Representative Mike Castle very likely to enter the fray.

Junior Senator. Joseph R. Biden Jr. is in his third decade as a senator and even in the minority has had influence on important policies. Biden grew up in 1950s white collar suburbia (his father was a car salesman and one grandfather was a state senator in Pennsylvania), a Catholic when it was still assumed that only a Protestant could be president, and a teenager with a stutter who taught himself to deliver a speech to his whole school. Born just a few years before the baby boom, Biden married and had a family while still in law school. He moved to the Wilmington suburbs, practiced law, and in 1970, at 27, was elected to the New Castle County Council. In 1972 he ran for the Senate, against a popular incumbent who seemed ready to retire, while this young challenger had energy, an attractive extended family and an ability to connect with voters' emotions. He won 51%–49%, though his victory was tempered a month later by the auto accident that killed his wife and daughter. He began his practice, kept to this day, of commuting from his home near Wilmington on Amtrak, 80 minutes to and from Washington every day. He remains a familiar figure in, and one familiar with, his constituency.

In the Senate, Biden has a moderate-to-liberal voting record, not so far to the left of his Republican colleague William Roth. He did much of his most visible work on the Judiciary Committee, which he chaired from 1987–95 and served as ranking Democrat on from 1981–87 and 1995–97. The issues that arise here—abortion, flag-burning, capital punishment, crime control—cut deeply, and for years the cultural liberals in the Democratic Party differed sharply on most of them from the constituents Biden saw in Delaware every day. As chairman, Biden presided over the most contentious Supreme Court confirmation hearings in history. In his 1987 hearings, nominee Robert Bork set a high standard for intellectual seriousness, but some of his opponents used his candor to vote against him for disgracefully dishonest reasons, from which Biden's attempts to construct an honestly based, anti-Bork rationale proved politically indistinguishable; no other nominee since has testified so frankly. The 1991 hearings on Clarence Thomas exploded when someone leaked charges of sexual harassment by Anita Hill against the nominee. Biden was bitterly criticized for covering up this information, but he had shared it with committee members, who agreed that Hill's initial unwillingness to testify publicly meant that any reference to it would be unfair to Thomas. Once the story was out though, Hill and then Thomas testified to fascinated television audiences. Despite the strong pro-Hill bias of the press, Thomas was confirmed, over Biden's opposition.

In the middle of the Bork hearings came a climactic moment for Biden's presidential candidacy. He announced in 1987, hoping to inspire a new generation as John Kennedy had inspired his. But Biden decided to leave the race when a Michael Dukakis staffer leaked an "attack video" showing similarities between Biden's stump speech about his background and a speech by British Labour Party leader Neil Kinnock. Paraphrasing someone else's words is not a political crime—most political discourse is conducted in familiar shorthand terms—but Biden in dramatizing his background actually distorted it, for unlike Kinnock he did not rise from working class roots, and unlike in Britain, upward social mobility is a common experience in the United States. In 1988, Biden nearly died of an aneurysm, but recovered fully.

After the Thomas hearings, Biden seemed defensive about attacks from the feminist left, the greatest source of activism in the Democratic Party, as the religious right is in the Republican Party; he sought out women to serve on Judiciary and worked hard on the 1994 Violence Against Women Act. Most of his energies in the early Clinton years were devoted to what became the 1994 crime bill, which came very close to being whipsawed between liberals who prefer therapy to harsh punishment and conservatives who oppose gun control and favor tough sentences. It was only after a characteristically eloquent and angry performance by Biden, and after tough negotiations between the Clinton Administration and House Republican moderates led by Delaware's Mike Castle, that the bill passed. After Republicans took control, Biden helped pass a methamphetamine control law, a nationwide tracking system for sex offenders and a bill to crack down on Rohypnol, the "date rape" drug. Biden has also worked on juvenile crime bills and has supported, with Jon Kyl and Dianne Feinstein, a victims' rights constitutional amendment. A long-time supporter of independent counsels, he criticized the work of Kenneth Starr and in March 1998 said, "It's going to be a cold day in hell" before another independent counsel is given the power Starr was.

In 1997 Biden shifted from ranking member on Judiciary to ranking member on Foreign Relations, where he has worked to a greater extent than most thought possible with Chairman Jesse Helms. Once part of a Democratic majority wary of another Vietnam and of the extension of American power, Biden now, after the U.S. victory in the Cold War, has sought to maintain American involvement in the world. When democracy in the former Yugoslavia was thwarted by state-led terrorism and when multilateral instrumentalities proved ineffective, Biden was among the strongest voices—and the best positioned, with his high-ranking seat on Foreign Relations—to call for lifting the arms embargo on Bosnia and training Bosnian Muslims, demanding that the United States and NATO investigate war crimes there, and arguing for NATO air strikes. He worked hard to preserve Radio Free Europe and Radio Liberty and to establish Radio Free Asia, and he is the author of the law setting up a separate international broadcasting agency, apart from the State Department or USIA. He favored NATO expansion, while remaining concerned about whether Europeans would share burdens equally, and with Helms led the move to approve expansion. He worked hard with Helms to achieve a long-delayed reorganization of foreign policy agencies, plus an increase in the State Department budget; they also agreed on a schedule for repaying unpaid U.S. dues to the United Nations. He opposed Helms on the Chemical Weapons Treaty, and managed its ratification; he says he wants to get ratification of the Comprehensive Test Ban Treaty as well.

On other issues, Biden was one of the Democrats who supported the balanced budget amendment in March 1997, when it failed by one vote. He co-sponsored a ban on federal funding for assisted suicides. Unlike most Democrats, he supported the Coverdell education savings account bill that passed the Senate. And of course he supported Amtrak funding. Biden's most visible gift is an articulateness that can verge on the mellifluous; he can inspire, but can also drone on at great length (being elected a senator at 29 does not curb a tendency to verbosity). But this has not reduced the appreciation most Delawareans have for his admirable personal qualities. He was re-elected by wide margins in 1984 (60%–40%), 1990 (63%–36%) and 1996 (60%–38%). He said he came close to retiring then, as 14 other senators did that year: "All the things I fought for were under siege." But his wife persuaded him otherwise: "You're not so special. But you're at the top of your game. You're not going to get any better. If you're going to quit now, why did you run in the first place?" His opponent was a Naval Academy graduate and businessman who walked, rode a bicycle and rollerbladed through the state, raised $1 million and questioned the sale of Biden's house to an executive of MBNA, the big credit card company whose top executives gave generously to Biden's campaign. But Biden won by his accustomed majority. He turns 60 just after his seat comes up in 2002, and is expected to run again. Will he run for president again? In September 1997 he said, "The honest-to-God truth is that I have no desire to run for president, no plans to run for president and I've taken no action to run for president. But who knows what will happen in four years or eight years if I'm still around?"

Representative-At-Large. Michael Castle, a Republican first elected in 1992, has been in public life his entire career. He grew up in Delaware and, after college and law school, returned to be a deputy attorney general, and in 1966, at 26, was elected to the Delaware House. Two years later he was elected to the Senate, and in time became minority leader; in 1980 he was elected lieutenant governor; he was elected governor in 1984 and 1988. In that office he cut tax rates, started a program to make health care services available to all children, developed an "Environmental Legacy" program to address issues in the coming decade, and increased teacher salaries. In 1992, barred by term limits after his second term, he traded jobs with Democratic Congressman-at-Large Thomas Carper. Castle won the primary by 56%–30% over state Treasurer Janet Rzewnicki, and won the general 55%–43% over former Senate candidate and Lieutenant Governor S. B. Woo, who raised more in individual contributions (mostly from Chinese-Americans) than any other non-incumbent in 1992.

At that point it seemed unlikely that Castle, as a moderate member of a conservative minority party, could be influential; yet he was. He was a leader of the bipartisan freshmen who offered their own budget cuts. In August 1994 he withdrew his support from the crime bill when he thought Democrats overreached, then at Newt Gingrich's suggestion led a group of moderate Republicans to negotiate with the administration. This delivered a stinging rebuke to Democrats it—broke their majority apart, in fact—and yet ultimately produced a crime bill with less spending on prevention but with the gun control provisions which Castle, unlike most Republicans, supported.

Castle has a voting record at the middle of the House; he was one of the 10 Republicans to support Clinton Administration positions on most issues and was a leader of the informal Tuesday Group of moderate Republicans. Castle was the "middle man," in *CongressDaily*'s phrase, in the Republican 104th Congress: "Take almost any contentious issue this Congress and at the center you will find Representative Michael Castle, like a magnet, attracting a bipartisan coalition of moderates just strong enough to give GOP leaders a headache. But he always seems to carry a remedy all sides are able to swallow." In August 1996, when Republicans revived their twice-vetoed welfare reform, Castle and Tennessee Democrat John Tanner proposed an alternative. It was rejected, but several of its provisions were included in the final bill, for which Castle voted. In March 1997 he came forward with his own budget plan, with no tax cuts until the budget was balanced; Castle and future Speaker Dennis Hastert called for considering tax cuts separately from the budget; in 1998 he attacked John Kasich's budget for cutting spending too much. He voted for the Republicans' Teamwork in Employees and Managers Act on labor law and the Republicans' HMO reform. Castle rejected the $15 million in local highway projects offered by Transportation Chairman Bud Shuster. In October 1997, there was talk of a coalition of Democrats and moderate Republicans electing Castle to replace Newt Gingrich as speaker; his response, "I don't have any interest in becoming speaker."

Castle is on the Banking Committee, which is of great importance to Delaware. He held hearings on the new $100 and $20 bills, and pushed for a new dollar coin, more distinctive than the failed Susan B. Anthony dollar; he pushed for the Statue of Liberty on one side, but Treasury Secretary Robert Rubin's panel chose the Indian guide Sacajawea instead. Castle sponsored the bill for the commemorative quarter, with different designs for each state. Castle was present when the first such coin was issued, which shows Delaware Revolutionary leader Caesar Rodney, atop a galloping horse, rushing to Philadelphia in 1776 to sign the Declaration of Independence. On Delaware issues, he has pushed successfully for beach replenishment and a study of *Pfiesteria piscicida*, which is ravaging rivers in the Delmarva peninsula.

Castle, who worked with Bill Clinton in governors' conferences, was counted by many as a Republican vote against impeachment. He seemed inclined toward censure, but in early

December said, "I have been frustrated by the line of defense so far. They have to get away from attacks on a whole procedure and a highly legalistic defense. They have to get into a factual defense." In the end he voted for impeachment.

Castle has proved highly popular in Delaware. He was re-elected 66%–32% in 1998, and ended up with $823,642 cash on hand. In mid-November, as Republican leadership contests swirled, Castle and Thomas Ewing of Illinois moved to draft Dennis Hastert to run for majority leader; Hastert demurred, because he had committed to Dick Armey, and his candidacy fizzled. But when Bob Livingston renounced the speakership December 19, Hastert was quickly selected to fill that higher post, and Castle can expect to be close to him. Castle has long been thought of as a likely candidate for the Senate, and has said that he surely would have run if William Roth had retired in 1994. But "as time has evolved, I have grown to like my role in the House," he said in 1998, and it is not clear whether he will run in 2000 even if Roth retires.

Cook's Call. *Safe*. As politically competitive as Delaware is, it has a soft spot for incumbents; the last incumbent House or Senate member to lose re-election was Senator Caleb Boggs in 1972. Though Castle can probably have this seat as long as he wants it, the fight to replace him would be extremely competitive.

Presidential politics. Delaware has been competitive in presidential elections since the Federalists were battling the Jeffersonians. Today it can claim to be the nation's presidential bellwether: it has voted for every winner since 1952, the longest winning streak of any state. Wilmington is heavily Democratic but casts relatively few votes, the two lower counties lean Republican and the balance is struck by the New Castle County suburbs. But Delaware, with its three electoral votes gets little national attention, and its two presidential candidates, Pete du Pont and Joseph Biden, got nowhere.

In 1996 Delaware vied for attention by holding its presidential primary February 24, just four days after New Hampshire. But New Hampshire Republicans put pressure on candidates to ignore Delaware, and only Steve Forbes and Alan Keyes showed up here. Forbes advertised heavily on Philadelphia TV and won the contest with 33% of the vote, to 27% for Bob Dole, 19% for Pat Buchanan, and 13% for Lamar Alexander. For 2000, Delaware has again scheduled its primary for the Saturday after New Hampshire's Tuesday, and New Hampshire has again objected. But Steve Forbes and Lamar Alexander made campaign appearances in Delaware in 1998 and 1999, and so Delaware may be seriously contested in 2000.

The People: Est. Pop. 1998: 743,603; Pop. 1990: 666,168, up 11.6% 1990–1998. 0.3% of U.S. total, 45th largest; 26.8% rural. Median age: 35 years. 12.7% 65 years and over. 80.4% White, 16.8% Black, 1.3% Asian, 0.3% Amer. Indian, 1.2% Other; 2.3% Hispanic Origin. Households: 55.8% married couple families; 26.3% married couple fams. w. children; 44.8% college educ.; median household income: $34,875; per capita income: $15,854; 70.3% owner occupied housing; median house value: $100,100; median monthly rent: $425. 3.8% Unemployment. 1998 Voting age pop.: 568,000. 1998 Turnout: 182,281; 32% of VAP. Registered voters (1998): 467,388; 196,145 D (42%), 161,443 R (36%), 109,800 unaffiliated and minor parties (23%).

Political Lineup: Governor, Thomas R. Carper (D); Lt. Gov., Ruth Ann Minner (D); Secy. of State, Edward J. Freel (D); Atty. Gen., M. Jane Brady (R); Treasurer, Jack Markell (D); State Senate, 21 (13 D, 8 R); Majority Leader, Thurman Adams Jr. (D); State House, 41 (15 D, 26 R); House Speaker, Terry Spence (R). Senators, William V. Roth Jr. (R) and Joseph R. Biden Jr. (D). Representative, 1 R at large.

Elections Division: 302-577-3464; **Filing Deadline for U.S. Congress:** July 28, 2000.

1996 Presidential Vote

Clinton (D) 140,355 (52%)
Dole (R) 99,062 (37%)
Perot (I) 28,719 (11%)

1996 Republican Presidential Primary

Forbes (R) 10,709 (33%)
Dole (R) 8,909 (27%)
Buchanan (R) 6,118 (19%)
Alexander (R) 4,375 (13%)
Keyes (R) 1,729 (5%)
Others 933 (3%)

1992 Presidential Vote

Clinton (D) 126,054 (44%)
Bush (R) 102,313 (35%)
Perot (I) 59,213 (20%)

GOVERNOR

Gov. Thomas R. Carper (D)

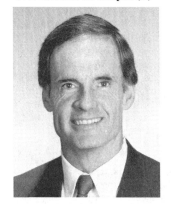

Elected 1992, term expires Jan. 2001; b. Jan. 23, 1947, Beckley, WV; home, Wilmington; OH St. U., B.A. 1968, U. of DE, M.B.A. 1975; Presbyterian; married (Martha).

Military Career: Navy, 1968–73 (Vietnam), Naval Reserves, 1973–91.

Elected Office: DE Treas., 1976–82; U.S. House of Reps., 1982–92.

Professional Career: Industrial Devel. Specialist, DE Div. of Econ. Devel., 1975–76.

Office: Legislative Hall, Dover, 19901, 302-739-4101; Fax: 302-739-2775; Web site: www.state.de.us.

Election Results

1996 gen.	Thomas R. Carper (D)	188,300	(70%)
	Janet C. Rzewnicki (R)	82,654	(30%)
1996 prim.	Thomas R. Carper (D)	unopposed	
1992 gen.	Thomas R. Carper (D)	179,365	(65%)
	B. Gary Scott (R)	90,725	(33%)
	Others	6,944	(3%)

SENATORS

Sen. William V. Roth, Jr. (R)

Elected 1970, seat up 2000; b. July 22, 1921, Great Falls, MT; home, Wilmington; U. of OR, B.A. 1944, Harvard U., M.B.A., LL.B. 1947; Episcopalian; married (Jane).

Military Career: Army, 1943–46 (WWII).

Elected Office: U.S. House of Reps., 1966–70.

Professional Career: Practicing atty., 1950–66; Chmn., DE Repub. St. Cmte., 1961–64.

DC Office: 104 HSOB, 20510, 202-224-2441; Web site: www.senate.gov/~roth.

State Offices: Dover, 302-674-3308; Georgetown, 302-856-7690; Wilmington, 302-573-6291.

Committees: *Finance* (Chmn. of 11 R): Health Care; International Trade. *Governmental Affairs* (2d of 9 R): Government Management, Restructuring and the District of Columbia; Investigations (Permanent). *Joint Committee on Taxation* (Vice Chmn. of 5 Sens.). *Joint Economic Committee* (2d of 10 Sens.).

Group Ratings

	ADA	ACLU	AFS	LCV	CON	NTU	NFIB	COC	ACU	NTLC	CHC
1998	15	33	11	38	39	59	78	78	65	67	55
1997	10	—	0	—	93	77	—	100	64	—	—

National Journal Ratings

	1997 LIB — 1997 CONS	1998 LIB — 1998 CONS
Economic	44% — 52%	45% — 54%
Social	45% — 50%	49% — 50%
Foreign	43% — 50%	44% — 55%

Key Votes of the 105th Congress

1. Bal. Budget Amend.	Y	5. Satcher for Surgeon Gen.	Y
2. Clinton Budget Deal	Y	6. Highway Set-asides	Y
3. Cloture on Tobacco	Y	7. Table Child Gun locks	Y
4. Education IRAs	Y	8. Ovrd. Part. Birth Veto	Y

9. Chem. Weapons Treaty	Y
10. Cuban Humanitarian Aid	N
11. Table Bosnia Troops	Y
12. $ for Test-ban Treaty	N

Election Results

1994 general	William V. Roth Jr. (R)	111,088	(56%)	($2,310,474)
	Charles M. Oberly III (D)	84,554	(42%)	($1,561,440)
	Others	3,387	(2%)	
1994 primary	William V. Roth Jr. (R)	unopposed		
1988 general	William V. Roth Jr. (R)	151,115	(62%)	($1,942,119)
	S.B. Woo (D)	92,378	(38%)	($2,235,318)

Sen. Joseph R. Biden, Jr. (D)

Elected 1972, seat up 2002; b. Nov. 20, 1942, Scranton, PA; home, Wilmington; U. of DE, B.A. 1965, Syracuse U., J.D. 1968; Catholic; married (Jill).

Elected Office: New Castle Cnty. Cncl., 1970–72.

Professional Career: Practicing atty., 1968–72.

DC Office: 221 RSOB, 20510, 202-224-5042; Fax: 202-224-0139; e-mail: www.senate.gov/~biden.

State Offices: Dover, 302-678-9483; Georgetown, 302-856-9275; Wilmington, 302-573-6345.

Committees: *Foreign Relations* (RMM of 8 D): European Affairs (RMM). *Judiciary* (3d of 8 D): Criminal Justice Oversight; Technology, Terrorism & Government Information; Youth Violence (RMM).

Group Ratings

	ADA	ACLU	AFS	LCV	CON	NTU	NFIB	COC	ACU	NTLC	CHC
1998	85	71	89	75	30	15	44	56	4	14	27
1997	70	—	56	—	45	34	—	70	16	—	—

National Journal Ratings

	1997 LIB — 1997 CONS	1998 LIB — 1998 CONS
Economic	64% — 35%	64% — 35%
Social	51% — 45%	63% — 26%
Foreign	62% — 32%	73% — 21%

Key Votes of the 105th Congress

1. Bal. Budget Amend.	Y	5. Satcher for Surgeon Gen.	Y	9. Chem. Weapons Treaty	Y
2. Clinton Budget Deal	Y	6. Highway Set-asides	Y	10. Cuban Humanitarian Aid	Y
3. Cloture on Tobacco	Y	7. Table Child Gun locks	N	11. Table Bosnia Troops	Y
4. Education IRAs	Y	8. Ovrd. Part. Birth Veto	Y	12. $ for Test-ban Treaty	Y

Election Results

1996 general	Joseph R. Biden Jr. (D)	165,465	(60%)	($2,466,499)
	Raymond J. Clatworthy (R)	105,088	(38%)	($1,126,427)
	Others	5,038	(2%)	
1996 primary	Joseph R. Biden Jr. (D)	unopposed		
1990 general	Joseph R. Biden Jr. (D)	112,918	(63%)	($2,550,061)
	M. Jane Brady (R)	64,554	(36%)	($240,669)

REPRESENTATIVE

Rep. Michael N. Castle (R)

Elected 1992; b. July 2, 1939, Wilmington; home, Wilmington; Hamilton Col., B.A. 1961, Georgetown U., LL.B. 1964; Catholic; married (Jane).

Elected Office: DE House of Reps., 1966–68; DE Senate, 1968–76, Minority Ldr., 1975–76; DE Lt. Gov., 1980–84; DE Gov., 1984–92.

Professional Career: DE Dep. Atty. Gen., 1965–66.

DC Office: 1227 LHOB, 20515, 202-225-4165; Fax: 202-225-2291; Web site: www.house.gov/castle.

District Offices: Dover, 302-736-1666; Wilmington, 302-428-1902.

Committees: *Banking & Financial Services* (8th of 32 R): Domestic & International Monetary Policy; Financial Institutions & Consumer Credit. *Education & the Workforce* (9th of 27 R): Early Childhood, Youth & Families (Chmn.); Postsecondary Education, Training & Life-Long Learning. *Permanent Select Committee on Intelligence* (4th of 9 R): Technical & Tactical Intelligence (Chmn.).

Group Ratings

	ADA	ACLU	AFS	LCV	CON	NTU	NFIB	COC	ACU	NTLC	CHC
1998	30	44	26	69	99	54	79	67	42	55	42
1997	50	—	25	—	97	54	—	90	56	—	—

National Journal Ratings

	1997 LIB — 1997 CONS		1998 LIB — 1998 CONS	
Economic	44%	— 55%	48%	— 51%
Social	50%	— 48%	59%	— 41%
Foreign	45%	— 55%	53%	— 45%

Key Votes of the 105th Congress

1. Clinton Budget Deal	Y	5. Puerto Rico Sthood. Ref.	N	9. Cut $ for B-2 Bombers	Y
2. Education IRAs	Y	6. End Highway Set-asides	N	10. Human Rights in China	N
3. Req. 2/3 to Raise Taxes	Y	7. School Prayer Amend.	N	11. Withdraw Bosnia Troops	N
4. Fast-track Trade	Y	8. Ovrd. Part. Birth Veto	Y	12. End Cuban TV-Marti	N

Election Results

1998 general	Michael N. Castle (R)	119,811	(66%)	($331,621)
	Dennis E. Williams (D)	57,446	(32%)	($1,297)
	Others	3,270	(2%)	
1998 primary	Michael N. Castle (R)	unopposed		
1996 general	Michael N. Castle (R)	185,576	(70%)	($376,350)
	Dennis E. Williams (D)	73,253	(27%)	($6,437)
	Others	7,996	(3%)	

DISTRICT OF COLUMBIA

There is hope for the District of Columbia. For most of the last 20 years, Washington, D.C., the capital of the most successful democracy in the history of the world, has been a dysfunctional polity, a city with above-average incomes and a vibrant commercial property base, but with a local government so bloated with employees yet so indifferent to its duties that it has destroyed one marginal neighborhood after another. Now, with the retirement of Marion Barry, mayor for 16 of the 20 years from 1978–98, and the election of Anthony Williams, there is reason to hope that the culture of the District government will be transformed and the city's neighborhoods made peaceful and prosperous.

The problem of how to govern the nation's capital is not new. In the 1790s the framers of the Constitution, familiar with contemporary London and Paris mobs and remembering how crowds had threatened Congress in Philadelphia, purposely gave the new federal government control of the 10-mile-square enclave that came to be called the District of Columbia. Over the years Congress kept control, for its own advantage and, later, out of distrust of the city's large black population. Blacks had consistently made up one-quarter of the population of Washington and surrounding counties since the 1790s, and the city was a center for free blacks even before the Civil War and Emancipation. Radical Republicans gave the District self-government in the era of Reconstruction in 1871, but Governor Alexander "Boss" Shepherd built great public works and spent the District into bankruptcy, and the experiment ended in 1874. Later Washington's vast growth, starting with the New Deal and World War II, resulted in the expansion of large, mostly white suburbs, and blacks became a larger percentage of the city's population—a majority in the 1960 Census. During the 1960s civil rights revolution, it began to seem absurd to deny the vote to Washington. So in 1964, Washingtonians began to cast three electoral votes for president, but the District is overwhelmingly Democratic and the presidential primary here receives little notice. In 1968 District residents were allowed to vote for school board; in 1971 they finally got to elect a non-voting delegate to Congress; and in 1974 they got home rule and could vote for a mayor and city council.

But the results were tragic, and the lead actor in the tragedy was Marion Barry, elected mayor in 1978, 1982 and 1986, then disgraced in January 1990 when he was videotaped and arrested in a D.C. hotel using crack cocaine, a crime for which he was eventually convicted and imprisoned—and then, astonishingly, elected mayor again in 1994. Barry is a man of great competence and charm, a Ph.D. candidate in chemistry from Tennessee who became a dashiki-clad protest leader in Washington in the 1960s. He inherited a government that was already overlarge and undermanaged, and over the years made it more so. He raised money from public employee unions and real estate developers and increasingly won votes from poor blacks by attacking any critic as racist.

Barry fostered a culture that combined a sense of entitlement to jobs and utter lack of accountability; the result was a public sector of Soviet magnitude and social problems of Third World dimensions. Crime rates have been among the nation's highest, while the police department, a 1997 audit showed, was in shambles: felony cases dismissed because of computer crashes or lost evidence, cases left unsolved through sheer negligence, an unguarded property warehouse and drug lab piled with guns, a morgue without air conditioning. Nor was the delivery of social services much better. Poor neighborhoods in the District have levels of infant mortality worse than in Sri Lanka or Jamaica. Meanwhile, the regulatory apparatus is so unwieldy and unresponsive that it is routinely ignored; the pothole-studded streets and frequently malfunctioning traffic signals remind even those in stable neighborhoods of the District's incompetence every day. The public schools are mostly dismal, despite brave efforts by some parents, and in 1997 could not be open for two months because roofs were unsafe. This is in vivid contrast to the high civic competence of suburban Maryland and Virginia jurisdictions (including majority-black Prince George's County, Maryland). Nor is all this for lack of personnel or money. District payrolls reached 51,300 at their peak in 1992, more per capita than anywhere else in America. Spending levels are above those of almost any other city in the country; and the District, with its prosperous downtown and its affluent liberals in Georgetown and Ward 3 west of Rock Creek Park, has tax resources other central cities would envy.

The result in the Barry years was not white flight (that happened long ago) but black flight. Washington's population in 1950 was 802,000; in 1998 it was 523,000; it lost an astonishing 14% of its population in the 1990s. One consequence is that the black percentage of the population is declining, from a peak of 70% in 1970s to about 60% today. Most Washington-area blacks live in the suburbs. Ward 3's population, in contrast, is on the rise, and people there are more likely to vote; the result is a 1998 electorate about 40% white.

Until Barry's arrest in 1990, he was widely considered "mayor-for-life." Instead he was succeeded in 1990 by Sharon Pratt Kelly, who ran on a platform of reform. But when it came time to cut the payroll, she flinched, asking for a larger federal payment (it reached $660 million at its peak), seeking to tax suburbanites working in the city (which will never happen as long as Virginia and Maryland are represented in Congress), and begging for statehood (a non-starter: The Democratic House voted it down 277–153 in 1993). When Barry emerged from prison, he ran for the Council and was elected in 1992; in 1994 he ran again for mayor. Building a coalition of welfare mothers, District employees and families of prisoners, he won the primary with 47%, to 37% for Councilman John Ray and only 13% for Kelly. The vote was highly uneven. Barry won 83% in Ward 8 and 66% in Ward 7, both in Anacostia; Ray beat him in Ward 3, 83% to 3%. In the general, Republican Carol Schwartz, a longtime Council member, ran a gallant campaign, but Barry won 56%–42%.

Barry's election coincided with the Republican takeover of Congress—and with a fiscal crisis. The District's credit rating was so low it could not borrow in the marketplace and its cash plunged toward zero. To the rescue came not the Clinton Administration, which showed scant interest in the District, but a pair of Republicans and D.C.'s delegate, Eleanor Holmes Norton. The Republicans were Speaker Newt Gingrich and Tom Davis, the suburban Virginia congressman who was formerly chairman of the Fairfax County Board of Supervisors and whom Gingrich named chairman of the subcommittee with jurisdiction over the District. They agreed on a five-member financial control board, which Congress passed without roll call votes in April 1995. Under Chairman Andrew Brimmer the control board demanded cuts in spending and payroll; Barry oscillated from cooperation to demagogic attacks. While he was on a trip to China and Korea, the control board took over the schools in November 1996. Then in August 1997 Congress stripped Barry of power over nine city departments, including Police, Public Works, Human Services, and Consumer and Regulatory Affairs; Barry kept the libraries and parks. The federal government assumed the District's $4.8 billion in unfunded pension liabilities in return for a two-thirds cut in the federal payment, and ordered closure of the scandal-tarred Lorton prison in northern Virginia. The control board's chief financial officer, Anthony Williams, a former city official in St. Louis and Boston, hacked away at the payroll, reformed management practices and literally cleaned up messes in District offices. In fall 1997 the police department audit came in: Barry's hand-picked police chief resigned after it was shown he shared a cut-rate luxury apartment with an officer who was blackmailing gay husbands.

Barry finally announced he would not run again in May 1998. That left four Council members in the race, Schwartz and three Democrats. But from the unlikely quarter of Ward 7 a move started to draft Anthony Williams, and he entered the race in late June. In many ways he was an unlikely candidate. He was not from Washington at all: Williams grew up in Los Angeles, the adopted son of postal workers; he was once an alderman in New Haven, Connecticut; when he took the CFO job in 1995 he moved first to Virginia and only later to Washington's Foggy Bottom. Williams had a history of changing course: he participated in anti-Vietnam war demonstrations, enlisted in the Air Force and served, then applied for conscientious objector status and got an honorable discharge. He graduated with honors from Yale, started an antique map business, then got degrees from Harvard Law and the Kennedy School and worked in Connecticut, Boston and St. Louis. Always dressed in a bow tie, diffident at first with crowds, he did not seem to have a political touch.

But this was quite a different electorate from 1994, with more affluent voters looking for good services and competent government; a harbinger was the victory in a special Council election in December 1997 of David Catania, a gay Republican. "It is about details," Williams said. "I think when all the smoke has cleared and all the lights have dimmed and you look behind the curtain, you'll find that no other candidate has as good a record in caring for people—and I've quit my job to show it." As CFO Williams had moved the District from huge deficits to a $185 million surplus in February 1998; he had cut payrolls deeply, provoking many squawks; he had changed the way many departments were managed. His leading primary opponent, Kevin Chavous, emphasized the need for a compassionate government and called Williams a bean counter. But Williams quickly surged and some key Barry supporters jumped on his bandwagon. He won the September Democratic primary by 50% to 35% for Chavous. He carried five of the eight wards, including Ward 3, where turnout was large and where he beat Chavous 77%-9%. In the general Schwartz attacked Williams as an interloper and a heartless bureaucrat who fired too many people. But Williams, endorsed by the conservative *Washington Times* as well as *The Washington Post*, won 66%-30%.

Right after the election, the control board delegated the power to run the city government to the new mayor; new board Chairman Alice Rivlin predicted Congress would restore full home rule in two years. Barry in November attempted to stay a political force by appointing 62 loyalists to city boards, including a new term for himself on the D.C. Sports Commission. But the District's fate depends not on whether Barry can insinuate himself into stadium negotiations and the like but on whether Williams can change the culture of the District government, and enable it to do what other city governments are increasingly doing around the country: Providing a safe place for people to live and work, holding down and reducing taxes and bureaucracy so that businesses can grow, providing schools that teach the basics of reading and math. If he can, the world's greatest democracy might have, for the first time in its history, a capital city with competent self-government.

D.C. Delegate. Eleanor Holmes Norton, first elected delegate from the District of Columbia in 1990, is a Washington native. She graduated from Antioch and Yale Law School, worked for the ACLU and the New York City Commission on Human Rights, and was head of the Equal Employment Opportunity Commission in the Carter administration. Afterward, she taught law at Georgetown. When the delegate seat came open in 1990, she ran and was criticized because her husband hadn't filed their income taxes for several years. But in the primary she edged past Councilwoman Betty Anne Kane, 39%-33%. Norton has been re-elected easily since.

In the House she has had the difficult and sometimes vexing task of responding to the fiscal collapse of the District government just as Republicans took over Congress. She has been hardworking, competent, intellectually honest, able to get along with opponents as well as fellow partisans and willing to take personal and political risks. She established good relations with Republicans active on District matters before 1994, even though she led the drive, much resented by Republicans in 1993 and repealed by them in 1995, to give her and the four territorial delegates to the House—all of whom were then Democrats—votes on most legislation in the House. In 1995 she worked with Tom Davis and Newt Gingrich to create the fiscal control board to superintend District finances; in 1997 she and Davis came up with the package that rescued District finances and removed control over most of the District government from Marion Barry. She initially hailed it as "a great day for the District," and with some cause: The federal government assumed the District's $4.8 billion unfunded pension debt and substantial Medicaid costs, it provided a $5,000 tax credit to first-time home-buyers and a $3,000 wage credit for hiring D.C. residents. In return, the District gave up the $660 million federal payment for a $198 million "contribution," but, as Norton argues, this should in the long run remove the District from the close superintendency of Congress. To that end she has made the sensible proposal to abolish the D.C. Appropriations subcommittee which has an institutional interest in meddling.

However, Norton changed her tone after Barry criticized the measure for stripping the mayor of effective power over most of the District government. "The country needs to hang its head low on this day of celebration," she said on Martin Luther King Jr. Day in January 1998. "There has been an usurpation of democracy." As it has turned out, the control board's success at restoring the city finances led it to cede power back to the mayor earlier than expected, and Norton's initial judgment that the District needed to take some medicine in order to get well seems likely to be vindicated.

In the process Norton has come up with lots of money for the District, including some $1 billion for much needed street repairs and $75 million for the water system (there was a drinking water scare in summer 1995). She also got District borrowing authority for a new convention center. She wants to stop new monuments from being built on the Mall and to reopen Pennsylvania Avenue in front of the White House; her camel's nose under the tent on that was a law to allow buses for the elderly and handicapped to drive there.

The People: Est. Pop. 1998: 523,124; Pop. 1990: 606,900, down 1.3% 1990–1998. 0.2% of U.S. total, 50th largest. Median age: 35.6 13.6% 65 years and over. ; 29.6% White, 65.9% Black, 1.9% Asian, 0.3% Amer. Indian, 2.4% Other; 5.2% Hispanic Origin. Households: 25.3% married couple families; 10.5% married couple fams. w. children; 51.9% college educ.; median household income: $30,727; per capita income: $18,881; 38.9% owner occupied housing; median house value: $123,900; median monthly rent: 441. 8.8% Unemployment. 1998 Voting age pop.: 414,000. 1998 Turnout: 141,977; 34% of VAP. Registered voters (1998): 353,503; 274,989 D (78%), 25,399 R (7%), 53,115 unaffiliated and minor parties (15%).

Political Lineup: Delegate, 1 D at large.

1996 Presidential Vote

Clinton (D)	158,220	(85%)
Dole (R)	17,339	(9%)
Perot (I)	3,611	(2%)
Others	6,566	(4%)

1996 Republican Presidential Primary

Dole (R)	2,256	(76%)
Buchanan (R)	283	(9%)
Others	448	(15%)

1992 Presidential Vote

Clinton (D)	192,619	(85%)
Bush (R)	20,698	(9%)
Perot (I)	9,681	(4%)

DELEGATE

Del. Eleanor Holmes Norton (D)

Elected 1990; ; b. June 13, 1937, Washington, D.C.; home, Washington, D.C.; Antioch Col., B.A. 1960, Yale, M.A. 1963, LL.B. 1964; Episcopalian; divorced.

Professional Career: Asst. Legal Dir., ACLU, 1965–70; New York City Human Rights Comm., 1970–77; Equal Empl. Oppor. Comm., 1977–81; Sr. Fellow, The Urban Inst., 1981–82; Prof., Georgetown U. Law Ctr., 1982–90.

DC Office: 1424 LHOB, 20515, 202-224-3424; Fax: 202-225-3002; Web site: www.house.gov/norton.

District Office: Washington, D.C., 202-678-8900.

Committees: *Government Reform* (9th of 19 D): Civil Service; District of Columbia (RMM). *Transportation & Infrastructure* (10th of 34 D): Aviation; Economic Development, Public Buildings, Hazardous Materials & Pipeline Transportation.

Election Results

1998 general	Eleanor Holmes Norton (D) 118,520	(90%)		($143,495)
	Edward Henry Wolterbeek (R) 8,288	(6%)		
	Others 4,910	(4%)		
1998 primary	Eleanor Holmes Norton (D) .... unopposed			
1996 general	Eleanor Holmes Norton (D) 134,996	(90%)		($119,818)
	Sprague Simonds (R) 11,306	(8%)		
	Others 3,696	(2%)		

FLORIDA

Florida is maturing. From its exotic past as the only Atlantic Coast state not among the original 13 states, as a forgotten swamp and semitropical resort, Florida has emerged as almost an empire of its own, a prototype in many ways of America's future, with an international flavor and sometimes almost with its own foreign policy. For many years, Florida was the place which millions of retirees looked forward to: the sunny, year-round warmth after eternal gray skies over winter factories and dark offices. But today, Florida's population of children is growing more rapidly (25%) than its population of seniors (22%), as young couples, from the South, various points north and Latin America, raise their families and make their livings in a booming economy, with jobs and opportunities in communities that did not exist a generation ago. For refugees from Cuba and Haiti and immigrants from all over the Caribbean and Latin America, Florida has been a land of freedom and security from the totalitarians that control everyday life in police states. For Americans and foreigners of all kinds—some 48.7 million of them in 1998, up from 23 million a dozen years before—Florida is the place to visit, with attractions, year-round swimming, restaurants and rooms to suit every taste and pocketbook. Yet all is not sunny: crime is down, but still a threat; the economic future is, as always, uncertain; the melting pot works slowly, and Florida's Hispanic population seems often to live in a world apart.

Florida is a creation not of America's elite—though a few millionaires like Henry Flagler and Marcus Plant pioneered tourism here—but a place for which ordinary people have voted with their feet. Half a century ago, it was the least populous state in the South, with 1.4 million people, isolated, disease-ridden, bigoted, with no mineral resources but phosphate mines, not much agriculture outside its citrus groves and hardly any manufacturing at all. Today it is America's fourth most populous state, with 14 million people (it passed Ohio, Illinois, and Pennsylvania in the 1980s and is now closing in on New York). Florida is on the leading edge of where the nation is going: this is a state one-fifth of whose economy is based on tourism in a country where tourism is one of the great growth industries; a state with an economy based on services in a country increasingly service-oriented; the state with the largest proportion of elderly and retired citizens in a country where an increasing percentage will live many years in retirement; a state also with a growing number of school children in a country which, replenished by immigration, is growing faster and more robustly than any other advanced nation. Florida's architectural style once seemed exotic—Flagler's vast luxury hotels, the pink stucco motels of the 1940s and 1950s, the art deco hotels of Miami Beach—but now they have become leading edge: the Disney World Dolphin Hotel, Arquitectonica's Miami towers. And Florida is becoming a show business center, with actual movie production on the lots at the Universal and Disney World theme parks near Orlando: tourist attractions becoming work-places, life imitating art imitating life.

Florida today has one of America's most buoyant economies, though its economic base may seem a mystery to outsiders: It is not all tourism and retirees, but also services and trade. Miami for two decades has been the economic and commercial capital of Latin America, as well as its mecca for political exiles. A sign in Miami, "Gateway to Latin America," was updated to "Bridge to Latin America" and then "Capital of the Americas." You can fly nonstop from Miami to just about any place in Latin America, both English and Spanish are commonly understood, it has been the one place where Latins could be sure their money and their persons were safe from government takeover. But Miami's position is not secure: as democracy, property rights and the rule of law become more secure in Latin America, Miami loses much of its uniqueness, and perhaps much of its business. Florida's economic future is tied up with trade, but the failure of fast track could lead to higher trade barriers and more protectionism; Florida's congressmen (though not its senators) have turned away from NAFTA and fast track in order to protect its politically adept, but economically not that important, agricultural interests, at the risk of discouraging the international trade whose potential for growth, in the right framework, is enormous.

What may be fragile in Florida is civil society; Florida can be disorderly and chaotic. Most people here do not have deep roots in the state, most communities sprang into existence within living memory and, if Florida gives people more freedom and options than they may ever have imagined, it has also given them more disruption and crime than they surely anticipated. Many of Florida's great fortunes were made elsewhere, and brought here partly because the state has no income or inheritance taxes. Government is weak here, and even in fighting crime Florida has let citizens take the lead. This was the first major state with a carrying-concealed-weapons law, which allows law-abiding citizens to routinely be licensed to carry guns. The result has been lower crime rates because, backers say, criminals hesitate to attack people who may be armed. Instead, muggers target foreign tourists who don't have guns—to the point that at Frankfurt Airport in Germany you can buy a kit with American bumper stickers and a Florida State decal for your rental car.

This new Florida, like today's America, has no real center. Its largest urban focus, Miami, is geographically off to one corner and culturally uniquely Cuban, with its eyes increasingly on Latin America. Its politics sometimes holds it up to ridicule, as in March 1998 when the Miami city elections were voided because of absentee ballot fraud. But Miami holds only 360,000 of the 2 million people in the recently renamed Miami-Dade County, which has among other things developed one of the largest and best community college systems in the country. The rest of the Gold Coast, north past West Palm Beach, while containing almost one-third of Floridians, is also atypical, with a population drawn heavily from New York (the largest migration between any two states is from New York to Florida) and other Northeastern metro

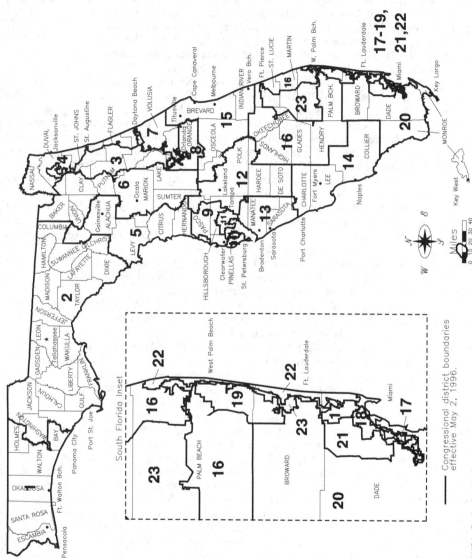

South Florida Inset

Congressional district boundaries
effective May 2, 1996.

areas, plus non-Latino migrants from Miami-Dade, with large numbers of Jews, and huge retiree condos lining the ocean front. Then there is Central Florida, the I-4 corridor from Tampa-St. Petersburg through citrus and tourist country and Orlando, then finally to the Space Coast. This is mostly family, not retiree, country, living off high-tech industries as much as tourism, a year-round rather than seasonal civilization. There is also the Gulf Coast, the affluent and burgeoning communities south of Tampa Bay and the more modest retirement counties to the north. Growing even more rapidly is the area along the hard-sand-beach Atlantic Coast around Jacksonville and Daytona Beach. Very Southern culturally is the western Panhandle, the "Redneck Riviera" around Pensacola and Panama City, which has Florida's most luxuriant white sand beaches.

Politically, this all adds up to a Florida that has become the most Republican of the nation's 10 largest states, but which like the nation has voted Democratic at the top of the ticket in important elections in the 1990s. Republican Jeb Bush was elected governor in 1998 after losing 51%–49% in 1994, and most statewide officals are Republicans. Republicans won control of the Florida Senate in 1994 and the House in 1996 (the first Republican-controlled legislature in 122 years), and now have large majorities in both. Republicans had been frustrated when Democrat Lawton Chiles was re-elected over Bush, and when Bill Clinton carried the state in 1996, after losing it in 1992, by a solid 48%–42% margin. But both of those Democrats were affected by Republican ideas and won only after making some concessions to them. Now Republicans must prove their experiments can work in this laboratory of democracy.

The experience of Florida's congressional delegation provides some clues. Florida has the second largest Republican delegation in the U.S. House, holding 15 of its 23 congressional districts by solid margins. But these Republicans have not proved to be rock-solid party loyalists or conservative ideologues. They have dissented increasingly on trade and, in the case of the two Cuban-Americans, on welfare reform. Like Florida's Democrats, they are adapting to the political environment. Interestingly, issues on which they haven't flinched from reform are Social Security and Medicare. The Democrats' oft-trumpeted charge that Republicans favored "cuts" in Medicare seemed to have only a marginal effect in 1996. Bob Dole actually ran better than George Bush in Gulf Coast counties heavily peopled by retirees, while he ran worse in the Gold Coast, especially in Miami-Dade County, and in the Orlando area, which has relatively few retirees. And congressmen supporting the Republican leadership on Social Security and Medicare were re-elected in districts with the largest elderly percentages in the nation.

More important are environmental issues. Migrants from New York or Illinois may not have cared much about environmental issues when they lived there, but they came to Florida in large part because of the climate and setting, and don't want to see oil drilled on the Gulf coast or the Everglades paved over. Awareness began in 1947, with the publication of *The Everglades: River of Grass* by Marjory Stoneman Douglas, who died in 1998 at 108. The water flows mostly south, from the Kissimmee River near Disney World, through Lake Okeechobee down to Florida Bay and the Gulf of Mexico. To stop floods and supply water to the Gold Coast, the Army Corps of Engineers built a network of canals and straightened the Kissimmee into concrete banks. In the 1990s, as demand for water and for protection of the unique environment grew, the Corps started a massive project to de-straighten the Kissimmee and in 1996 voters approved an amendment for cleaning up the Everglades (though disapproving a one-cent sugar tax to pay for it). In October 1998 Vice President Al Gore unveiled the administration's $7.8 billion Central and Southern Florida Project to build huge reservoirs above and under ground, a vast plant to recycle Miami waste water and a system of 70 massive pumps in the Everglades and to make the Tamiami Trail a causeway, like Alligator Alley 25 miles to the north. The two purposes seem contradictory—to reduce the outflow of water into the Gulf while maintaining the flow through the Everglades—and even the Corps admits it does not know exactly how or whether it will work. Meanwhile, a small but vocal number of farmers have protested against plans that will take their land. This will surely be a focus of Florida government and politics for some time to come.

Meanwhile, the partisan balance of Florida seems fairly well set. The Gold Coast, with about one-quarter of the votes, is heavily Democratic; heavily pro-Democratic Jewish voters are one major reason. Clinton increased his Gold Coast lead from 48%–36% in 1992 to 60%–33% in 1996, the main reason he carried the state; the rest of Florida went Republican by 44%–35% in 1992 and 48%–41% in 1996. The pattern in 1998 was much the same as in 1996: Jeb Bush, despite intensive campaigning aimed at softening his image among blacks and Jews in south Florida, lost the Gold Coast 56%–44% and carried the rest of the state 59%–41%. The I-4 corridor, with three-eighths of the votes, is marginal: The Tampa-St. Petersburg area was narrowly for Clinton and the Orlando area narrowly for Dole in 1996; Jeb Bush carried both, the latter more heavily. The rest of the state is mostly Republican, though for different reasons. The Panhandle and north Florida were historically Democratic and now are heavily Republican, except for black-majority enclaves and the capital of Tallahassee and the university town of Gainesville. The Gulf Coast is mixed, heavily Republican in affluent areas south of Tampa Bay, more marginal in the more modest retirement havens to the north. The historic trend favors the Republicans. From 1978–98 total registration in Florida rose from 4.2 million to 8.2 million, with Republican registration up 2.1 million and Democratic registration up only 800,000. The Democrats' registration edge dropped from 64%–30% in 1980 to 51%–41% in 1992 and 45%–40% in 1998. Counterbalancing this trend is the Florida media— generally liberal and pro-Democratic—which may be especially important in a state with eight media markets and dozens of newspapers, and hundreds of thousands of new voters unacquainted with Florida government or politics and no established civic ladders for developing political talent. And Florida's political season is brief, tucked into hurricane season, with a primary in September, a runoff in October, and then the November election. It's over in a flash: the wonder is that the results are as rational as they have been.

Governor. Jeb Bush is the second son of President George Bush to have been elected a big state governor in the 1990s. Jeb grew up in Midland and Houston, Texas. He majored in Latin American studies at the University of Texas and there met his wife, Columba, who is originally from Mexico. He speaks Spanish fluently—but with more a Mexican than Cuban accent, he notes. In 1981 he moved to Miami and started a real estate development company. For a year or so he was Commerce secretary under Republican Governor Bob Martinez. With a well-known name and strong convictions on issues, he decided to run for governor in 1994, vanquishing competition in the Republican primary and leading in polls during most of the fall. He called for fewer appeals for death row inmates and speedier executions, said Florida should withdraw from Aid to Families with Dependent Children and replace it with limited temporary assistance, and called for school choice and demanded voter approval of all state and local tax increases. There was a rigid tone to Bush's campaign; when one black man asked him what he would do to help him, Bush replied, "Probably nothing." Lawton Chiles responded with negative ads on Bush's business dealings; a Bush ad on crime backfired; Chiles started emphasizing his "cracker" roots and called himself "the he-coon [who] always walks before the light of day." The result was a 51%–49% Chiles victory. It was a polarized election: Blacks were 94% and Jews 75% for Chiles, Cubans 74% and Christian conservatives 91% for Bush.

Bush immediately started running again. He set up a foundation which produced intellectually serious government reform proposals and visited shelters for abused women and children in foster care. Challenged by the teachers' union head to spend more time in classrooms, he visited more than 200 schools and, with the Urban League of Miami, founded and taught at a charter school in Miami's Liberty City. In other ways this man who had lived among the elite got in closer touch with everyday life: His son George P. Bush started teaching school in south Miami-Dade County; his daughter attended Miami-Dade Community College; he converted to Catholicism. Bush lobbied the legislature to cut unemployment taxes in 1997 and to better handle abused children in foster care in 1998. "I started listening more," he said later and, while his positions on issues did not change much, his approach and his tone did. "I am more interested in how you lessen demands on government rather than how you beat government into submission," he said. Republican rule "does not mean that we don't need to create consensus and build some common ground." The consensus in Florida had been moving for some time toward Bush—Chiles had produced welfare and reinventing government reforms—and now Bush came some distance toward the consensus.

Bush entered 1998 as the heavy favorite for governor while Democrats inflicted damage on themselves. In January state House Democrats ousted party leader-designate Willie Logan, a black from Opa-Locka; asked why, they gave the answer that he wasn't a good enough fundraiser. Black legislators understandably protested, and Bush called Logan and held informal sessions with him and other black legislators; Logan said he had "free agency" in the governor race, and Bush got endorsements from a black legislator in Broward County and the mayor of Fort Lauderdale. Black legislators joined Republicans in overturning Chiles's vetoes of the partial-birth abortion ban, school vouchers and parental notification of abortions. After Senator Bob Graham announced in December 1997 he would run for re-election and not governor and Insurance Commissioner Bill Nelson announced in February 1998 he would not run, Democrats noisily looked for alternatives to the likely nominee, Lieutenant Governor Buddy MacKay, though MacKay had received good press for his work in office and nearly beat Connie Mack for senator in 1988. *Miami Herald* publisher David Lawrence was on the brink of running; state Senator Rick Dantzler got into the race, then left it in the summer to become MacKay's running mate. In time MacKay found his voice, bragging about the Healthy Kids insurance program and calling for higher education standards and a patients' bill of rights; he attacked Bush on vouchers, abortion and gun control, and criticized "questionable deals" and "mismanagement" in business. His efforts to put Bush on the spot on school prayer in an October 1998 debate did not work, as Bush ignored the issue.

Bush raised enough money to meet the state's spending cap by April 1998. In November he won 55%–45%. The electorate was a bit less polarized this time: Bush's percentage rose among blacks (to 14%) but was down among Christian conservatives (to 83%) and Hispanics (to 61%). Bush still lost Broward County and the Gold Coast by wide margins despite all his attentions, and his percentage rose most in the culturally conservative Panhandle and on the southern Gulf Coast. In mid-December Lawton Chiles unexpectedly died; his greatest legacy was the tobacco lawsuit which he initiated by pushing through a law changing the standard of proof; Buddy MacKay was governor for the last weeks of the term. In his first 100 days, Bush's legislative agenda met with stunning success. He canceled a plan for a high speed Miami-Orlando train, but passed a school voucher plan, got longer prison terms for gun-toting criminals, and instituted a $1 billion tax break.

Senior Senator. Bob Graham, Florida's senior senator, was first elected in 1986. He is careful, methodical, thorough, hard-working, reliable—always wearing his Florida ties, recording every meeting and meal in notebooks, scheduling meetings with every member of the Florida House delegation and with lobbyists on both sides of important issues. He comes from a prominent Florida family. His father started out with a Miami area dairy farm and developed the planned mini-city of Miami Lakes; his half-brother Philip Graham was publisher of *The Washington Post*. He has been in politics almost all his adult life; he was elected to the state House in 1966, at 30, and to the state Senate in 1970. In 1978 he ran for governor. After a come-from-behind win in the Democratic runoff, he won the general with a solid 56%. He was highly popular and easily won re-election in 1982. In 1986 he ran against Republican Senator Paula Hawkins, and after a spirited campaign won 55%–45%. His trademark campaign device since 1978 has been work days (invented by Senator Tom Harkin for his 1974 House race): Graham worked one day a week at some local job, from bagging groceries to construction. He keeps it up still, once a month, and in November 1998 logged his 340th work day, at a business on the Space Coast.

Graham's voting record in the Senate is just a little to the left of center. He has been a hardliner on crime legislation, supporting capital punishment, seeking federal reimbursement to states which jail criminal aliens, opposing a higher minimum wage for prisoners. A staunch opponent of Fidel Castro, Graham has argued for the embargo on Cuba. He wanted to stem the flow of Haitian refugees to Florida, and backed the dispatch of U.S. troops to Haiti. He worked for a new highway funding formula to guarantee states 95% of gas tax revenues; the 1998 transportation bill moved in that direction and gives $2 billion more to Florida. In 1997 he and Arizona's John McCain succeeded in getting changes in the veterans' health funding formula, to recognize the needs in rapidly growing states like Florida and Arizona. He urged action on Clinton Administration officials when a "surge" of tomato exports from Mexico threatened Florida growers' markets. He opposed taxation of prepaid college tuitions. He has worked hard to restore the Kissimmee River and the Everglades to their natural state, to ban oil drilling off the southwest Florida coast and to get the federal government to buy up existing leases, to make the Suwanee in north Florida a National Wild and Scenic River.

On national issues, he often supports Democratic policy but is sometimes willing to buck both party and constituency. He voted unhesitatingly for the Gulf war resolution. He supports the balanced budget amendment. He supports the McCain-Feingold campaign finance reform. In 1996 he called for means-testing Medicare and slightly reducing automatic increases in Social Security, in order to balance the budget—even as the Clinton campaign and AFL-CIO were excoriating Republicans for suggesting such things. But Graham coolly said that "it is appropriate to ask those able to contribute more to their health care premiums to do so" and, before the Boskin Commission report, that "there is ample evidence that the Consumer Price Index has overstated inflation."

On some major issues Graham has sought bipartisan solutions, sometimes successfully (as with the veterans' health formula), sometimes meeting with frustration, working often from the Finance Committee seat he has held since 1995. In 1998 he put together a compromise tobacco bill with John Chafee, with a $1.50 increase in the tobacco tax, a preservation of FDA authority to regulate, no immunity against future lawsuits and an $8 billion a year limit on tobacco company liability. But most Republicans preferred no bill at all, and none passed. Graham has repeatedly called on the federal government to file a tobacco lawsuit itself, claiming expenses from tobacco-caused health problems and eliminating by statute, as Florida under Governor Lawton Chiles did, the defense of contributory negligence. On HMO reform, Graham also worked with Chafee on a bill to guarantee direct access to specialists, assure continuity of coverage for the chronically ill, provide an internal appeals apparatus and provide for HHS to levy fines for refusal to provide care; but it did not have the right-to-sue feature favored by Democrats or the medical savings accounts favored by Republicans. This too did not pass, although something like it may. In March 1999, the House passed Graham's bill to prohibit nursing homes from evicting Medicaid patients; President Clinton signed it into law.

Graham perseveres in his middle-of-the-road approach: "I don't think being a centrist is necessarily a cautious position. It's a position that tries to get something accomplished." He sees Finance as a "laboratory for bipartisanship" and has worked there on Medicare, on protecting innocent spouses from IRS harassment, on curtailing IRS penalty and interest charges and on eliminating the capital gains on sales of most houses. He has worked closely with his Republican colleague Connie Mack on many Florida-related issues: to stop offshore oil drilling, to stiffen the trade embargo on Cuba, to clean up the Everglades, to prevent the deportation of 40,000 Haitians.

Graham was re-elected easily in 1992 and 1998. His 1998 opponent, state Senator Charlie Crist, had made headlines exposing the way top Democrats financed a Social Security telephone campaign with false charges against Jeb Bush in the last days of the 1994 campaign. Crist raised and spent more than $1 million, but that was not nearly enough to rival Graham, who won 62%–38%, winning over one-third of Republicans and Bush voters. In the impeachment trial, Graham seemed to be wavering for a time, but eventually voted with other Democrats.

Junior Senator. Connie Mack was first elected in 1988. He is the possessor of a famous name: his paternal grandfather was the longtime owner and manager of the Philadelphia Athletics from 1901–50; his maternal grandfather was Morris Sheppard, Texas senator from 1913–41. Mack grew up in Fort Myers, graduated from the University of Florida and became a banker in the Gulf Coast town of Cape Coral. In 1982, at 40, when he was president of the Florida National Bank of Lee County, he won a multi-candidate Republican primary for the House in a newly created Gulf Coast district. In the House, Mack became a supply-sider and one of the leaders of Newt Gingrich's Conservative Opportunity Society. He was the lead House sponsor of the Gramm-Rudman deficit-cutting measure that originated in the Senate; pro-choice on abortion, he switched when contemplating the 1988 Senate race. He entered that contest in October 1987, before incumbent Lawton Chiles and former Governor Reubin Askew decided not to run. "Hey, Buddy, you're liberal," Mack's ads said; his opponent was Congressman Buddy MacKay, later lieutenant governor and 1998 gubernatorial candidate. It was one of the closest Senate races of the year, and in Florida's history. Mack lost among those who went to the polls on election day, but with a big absentee margin won 50.4%–49.6%.

Mack has been chairman of the Republican Conference, the number three position in the leadership, since January 1997, and has a solidly conservative voting record. On economics, he opposed George Bush's tax increase in 1990 and Bill Clinton's in 1993. As chairman of the Joint Economic Committee from 1995–96 he made a major change by dropping the "current services budget" concept—the procedure which lets every government department get all the money it spent last year, plus more if it can claim more beneficiaries, plus the rate of inflation, all of which is based on an assumption that there can be no more efficient way of delivering government services than we have at present. He is a strong supporter of the balanced budget amendment. He favors merit pay for teachers and has sponsored legislation to allow states to opt out of federal surface transportation programs and keep the gas tax revenues generated there instead.

From early on he gave attention to issues of importance in Florida. He is a staunch opponent of Fidel Castro and pushed for tightening the Cuba embargo, helped set up TV Marti, and called for murder indictments against the Cuban pilots who shot down the Brothers to the Rescue in February 1996. He is a strong supporter of Israel. With his Democratic colleague Bob Graham he has worked to stop offshore oil drilling in the Gulf, to clean up the Everglades and prevent a water shortage there, to stop deportation of 40,000 Haitians. He was successful in helping Florida get two baseball teams—the Florida Marlins in Miami and the Devil Rays in Tampa Bay.

Mack has given special attention to health care issues. He is skeptical of government health care finance schemes and was one of the Republican responders to Bill Clinton's TV health care speech in September 1993. He looks very much more favorably on government health research. He and his wife are both cancer survivors, and were among the sponsors of "The March: Coming Together to Cure Cancer" on the Mall in September 1998. With ranking Democrat Tom Harkin he has called for doubling spending on NIH in five years. He also has a bill to prevent the tobacco companies from deducting their settlement costs from their corporate income taxes, and using the money for medical research.

Mack was re-elected easily in 1994 and looked good going in to 2000, so it was a surprise to most when he announced in March 1999 he would not run for a third term. For 1994 Democrats failed to recruit a well-known candidate (their nominee was Hugh Rodham, a Miami public defender who had never voted until 1992 and the brother of Hillary Rodham Clinton). Insurance Commissioner Bill Nelson is the strongest contender for the 2000 Democratic nomination; state Representative Willie Logan, who was ousted as speaker-designate by Democrats in January 1998, is considering running as an independent. On the Republican side, Bill McCollum of the 8th District is in the race and Education Commissioner Tom Gallagher is likely to run.

Cook's Call. *Highly Competitive.* A long line of potential successors quickly formed after Mack's retirement announcement but the field thinned out substantially once the financial realities of running here became apparent. Florida's political diversity and the expense of a campaign here will make this a competitive race.

Presidential politics. Florida, solidly Republican in presidential contests in the 1980s, became a fierce battleground in the 1990s: In 1992 and 1996 this was the only one of the four largest states to be seriously contested. George Bush carried it in 1992, but only by 41%–39%, and, after Lawton Chiles edged Jeb Bush in 1994, 51%–49%, Bill Clinton's strategists targeted Florida for 1996. It was a shrewd decision. Why did Florida change from the most Republican megastate in 1988 to a 48%–42% Clinton state in 1996? The Medicare and Social Security issues helped, though not nearly to the extent generally thought. Environmental issues probably switched more votes: People come to Florida looking for a kind of paradise, and are more concerned about the environment than they were when they lived in New York or Ohio or Illinois. Then there are Cuban-Americans, carefully cultivated by Clinton for years, helping him to be the first Democratic presidential nominee to carry Miami-Dade County since 1976.

Will these factors work for Al Gore or another Democrat in 2000? Envrionmental issues might well help; Social Security and Medicare depend on what if anything happens legislatively in 1999 and 2000; Cuban issues, after the Clinton Administration moved toward accommo-dating Fidel Casto in late 1999, are likely to work for Republicans.

Florida's mid-March presidential primary was once an early pivotal contest: Jimmy Carter's victory here in 1976 tossed George Wallace out of national politics and helped put Carter in the White House. It was around Florida that Southern Super Tuesday was built for the 1988 cycle; local Democrats hoped it would help a southern-based moderate clinch a nomination, and it did, but the southern-based moderate was George Bush and the party Republican. Seeking to boost their national clout for 2000, however, Florida attempted to move its primary up to March 7, a date which offered more clout for George W. Bush's presidential run. But in the last days of the legislative session, Senate President Toni Jennings attached campaign finance reform provisions to the bill, effectively killing it.

Congressional districting. Florida has gained congressional districts from every Census since 1940, when it was still the smallest state in the South. Now it is the fourth largest state in the nation, and with a growth rate converging on the national rate is expected to gain only one seat for 2002. This is not the only contrast with the 1990s redistricting. Then Florida picked up four seats, going from 19 to 23, and Democrats held the governorship and legislature and controlled the process. But they were so conflicted they could not produce a plan, and the current lines were drawn by a federal court in May 1992. The plan included three black-majority districts (two of them new) and two Hispanic-majority districts (one new), some with very peculiar shapes; boundaries of the other 18 districts were not so driven by politics, but some-times ended up grotesque because of next-door minority districts. The result was the election of three black congressmen, and a Republican edge that increased from 10–9 in 1990 to 15–8 after November 1994. In April 1996, the 3d District, which meandered through half the swamps of north Florida, was ruled unconstitutional, and redrawn amicably by a split-party legislature; its black percentage fell from 51% to 40%, but incumbent Democrat Corinne Brown has been re-elected since.

Republicans are all but certain to be in control in 2001, and will probably modify not too radically the lines that have served them well. The new district may end up in the fast-growing north central part of the peninsula. For most Florida members the lines don't matter much. Fifteen of its 23 members were re-elected without opposition in November 1998, and there is an unwritten rule against campaigning against a Florida colleague of the other party. Inciden-tally, 15 of the 23 Florida congressmen were born outside Florida—a reflection of this state's decades of growth and in-migration.

The People: Est. Pop. 1998: 14,915,980; Pop. 1990: 12,937,926, up 15.3% 1990–1998. 5.5% of U.S. total, 4th largest; 15.2% rural. Median age: 37.6 years. 19.1% 65 years and over. 83.1% White, 13.6% Black, 1.2% Asian, 0.3% Amer. Indian, 1.8% Other; 12% Hispanic Origin. Households: 54.4% married couple families; 21.5% married couple fams. w. children; 44.3% college educ.; median household income: $27,483; per capita income: $14,698; 67.2% owner occupied housing; median house value: $77,100; median monthly rent: $402. 4.3% Unemployment. 1998 Voting age pop.: 11,383,000. 1998 Turnout:

4,070,262; 38% of VAP. Registered voters (1998): 8,220,266; 3,691,742 D (45%), 3,292,589 R (40%), 1,235,935 unaffiliated and minor parties (15%).

Political Lineup: Governor, Jeb Bush (R); Lt. Gov., Frank Brogan (R); Secy. of State, Katherine Harris (R); Atty. Gen., Robert A. Butterworth (D); Treasurer and Insurance Commissioner, Bill Nelson (D); State Senate, 40 (15 D, 25 R); Majority Leader, Jack Latvala (R); State House, 120 (48 D, 72 R); House Speaker, John Thrasher (R). Senators, Bob Graham (D) and Connie Mack (R). Representatives, 23 (8 D,15 R).

Elections Division: 850-488-7697; **Filing Deadline for U.S. Congress:** May 12, 2000.

1996 Presidential Vote

Clinton (D)	2,545,690	(48%)
Dole (R)	2,242,951	(43%)
Perot (I)	483,761	(9%)

1992 Presidential Vote

Bush (R)	2,171,781	(41%)
Clinton (D)	2,071,651	(39%)
Perot (I)	1,052,481	(20%)

1996 Republican Presidential Primary

Dole (R)	511,108	(57%)
Forbes (R)	181,708	(20%)
Buchanan (R)	162,713	(18%)
Others	42,541	(6%)

GOVERNOR

Gov. Jeb Bush (R)

Elected 1998, term expires Jan. 2003; b. Feb. 11, 1953, Midland, TX; home, Miami; U. of TX, B.A. 1974; Catholic; married (Columba).

Elected Office: FL Commerce Secy., 1987–88; Candidate for FL Gov., 1994.

Professional Career: Pres. & COO, Codina Group, 1981–94; Founder & Chmn., Foundation for Florida's Future, 1995–98.

Office: The Capitol, Tallahassee, 32399, 904-488-7146; Fax: 904-487-0801; Web site: www.state.fl.us.

Election Results

1998 gen.	Jeb Bush (R)	2,192,105	(55%)
	Buddy MacKay (D)	1,773,054	(45%)
1998 prim.	Jeb Bush (R)	unopposed	
1994 gen.	Lawton Chiles (D)	2,135,008	(51%)
	Jeb Bush (R)	2,071,068	(49%)

SENATORS

Sen. Bob Graham (D)

Elected 1986, seat up 2004; b. Nov. 9, 1936, Coral Gables; home, Miami Lakes; U. of FL, B.A. 1959, Harvard, J.D. 1962; United Church of Christ; married (Adele).

Elected Office: FL House of Reps., 1966–70; FL Senate, 1970–78; FL Gov., 1978–1986.

Professional Career: The Graham Cos., Sengra Development Corp., 1962–66.

DC Office: 524 HSOB, 20510, 202-224-3041; Fax: 202-224-2237; Web site: www.senate.gov/~graham.

State Offices: Miami, 305-536-7293; Tallahassee, 904-422-6100; Tampa, 813-228-2476.

Committees: *Energy & Natural Resources* (4th of 9 D): Energy, Research, Development, Production & Regulation (RMM); National Parks, Historic Preservation & Recreation; Water & Power. *Environment & Public Works* (5th of 8 D): Clean Air, Wetlands, Private Property & Nuclear Safety (RMM); Fisheries, Wildlife & Drinking Water; Transportation & Infrastructure. *Finance* (6th of 9 D): Health Care; International Trade; Long-Term Growth & Debt Reduction (RMM). *Intelligence* (3d of 8 D). *Veterans' Affairs* (2d of 5 D).

Group Ratings

	ADA	ACLU	AFS	LCV	CON	NTU	NFIB	COC	ACU	NTLC	CHC
1998	85	86	89	100	30	12	56	61	4	14	9
1997	60	—	44	—	66	43	—	80	8	—	—

National Journal Ratings

	1997 LIB — 1997 CONS		1998 LIB — 1998 CONS	
Economic	65%	— 33%	61%	— 36%
Social	64%	— 29%	74%	— 0%
Foreign	55%	— 41%	51%	— 36%

Key Votes of the 105th Congress

1. Bal. Budget Amend.	Y	5. Satcher for Surgeon Gen.	Y	9. Chem. Weapons Treaty	Y
2. Clinton Budget Deal	Y	6. Highway Set-asides	Y	10. Cuban Humanitarian Aid	N
3. Cloture on Tobacco	Y	7. Table Child Gun locks	N	11. Table Bosnia Troops	Y
4. Education IRAs	N	8. Ovrd. Part. Birth Veto	N	12. $ for Test-ban Treaty	Y

Election Results

1998 general	Bob Graham (D)	2,436,402	(62%)	($5,094,581)
	Charlie Crist (R)	1,463,749	(38%)	($1,487,498)
1998 primary	Bob Graham (D)	unopposed		
1992 general	Bob Graham (D)	3,245,565	(65%)	($3,318,473)
	Bill Grant (R)	1,716,505	(35%)	($242,251)

Sen. Connie Mack (R)

Elected 1988, seat up 2000; b. Oct. 29, 1940, Philadelphia, PA; home, Cape Coral; U. of FL, B.A. 1966; Catholic; married (Priscilla).

Elected Office: U.S. House of Reps., 1982–88.

Professional Career: Banker, 1966–82.

DC Office: 517 HSOB, 20510, 202-224-5274; Fax: 202-224-8022; Web site: www.senate.gov/~mack.

State Offices: Ft. Myers, 941-275-6252; Jacksonville, 904-268-7915; Miami, 305-530-7100; Pensacola, 904-479-9803; Tallahassee, 904-425-1995; Tampa, 813-225-7683.

Committees: *Republican Conference Chairman. Banking, Housing & Urban Affairs* (3d of 11 R): Economic Policy (Chmn.); Financial Institutions; International Trade & Finance. *Finance* (10th of 11 R): Long-Term Growth & Debt Reduction; Taxation & IRS Oversight. *Joint Economic Committee* (Chmn. of 10 Sens.).

Group Ratings

	ADA	ACLU	AFS	LCV	CON	NTU	NFIB	COC	ACU	NTLC	CHC
1998	0	29	0	0	67	64	100	89	80	89	82
1997	0	—	0	—	85	76	—	80	88	—	—

National Journal Ratings

	1997 LIB — 1997 CONS		1998 LIB — 1998 CONS	
Economic	25% —	67%	31% —	63%
Social	17% —	72%	43% —	55%
Foreign	0% —	77%	29% —	58%

Key Votes of the 105th Congress

1. Bal. Budget Amend.	Y	5. Satcher for Surgeon Gen.	Y	9. Chem. Weapons Treaty	N
2. Clinton Budget Deal	Y	6. Highway Set-asides	N	10. Cuban Humanitarian Aid	N
3. Cloture on Tobacco	N	7. Table Child Gun locks	Y	11. Table Bosnia Troops	Y
4. Education IRAs	Y	8. Ovrd. Part. Birth Veto	Y	12. $ for Test-ban Treaty	N

Election Results

1994 general	Connie Mack (R)	2,894,726	(71%)	($5,729,359)
	Hugh E. Rodham (D)	1,210,412	(29%)	($617,190)
1994 primary	Connie Mack (R)	unopposed		
1988 general	Connie Mack (R)	2,049,329	(50%)	($5,181,639)
	Buddy MacKay (D)	2,015,717	(50%)	($3,714,852)

FIRST DISTRICT

The "Redneck Riviera" is the affectionate local name for the Gulf Coast beaches of Florida's Panhandle, from Pensacola east to Destin. This has been military country ever since John Quincy Adams persuaded Spain to sell Florida to the U.S. in 1819 to get the port of Pensacola. This was the site of the nation's first naval aviation training base and the birthplace of carrier aviation. The Air Force also has a massive presence in Eglin Air Force Base, which spreads over the lion's share of three counties. Culturally part of Dixie, this was economically backward land for years, dependent in the 1940s and 1950s on the military bases for growth. More recently, as the South has become more prosperous, this American Riviera has become a major vacation and retirement spot for southerners who enjoy its vast, fine-grained white sand beaches, perhaps the finest in the country, and its pleasant inlet-filled bays. Its cultural conservatism has remained ingrained from that earlier era, and it has become economically more conservative as well, while militarily it is supportive of assertive American policies around the world.

The 1st Congressional District includes the end of the Panhandle, so far west it's in the Central time zone. It stretches from Pensacola and the Alabama border east to include part of Panama City. Politically, this is Republican territory. George Bush and Bob Dole may not have run well elsewhere in the state, but they carried the 1st District smartly against Bill Clinton in 1992 and 1996. The Panhandle has become reliably Republican in statewide races and now elects mostly Republicans to the legislature; Jeb Bush won over 70% here in 1998.

The congressman from the 1st is Joe Scarborough, a Republican first elected in 1994. Scarborough grew up in Pensacola and taught high school and coached the football team, then practiced law and was active in community affairs. In October 1993 he helped collect 3,000 signatures to protest the city government's 65% property tax increase. He had never run for office, but had long been interested in politics: his family remembers him at 5, in 1968, coloring in states red and blue depending on whether they went Democrat or Republican. When Democratic Congressman Earl Hutto, with only 52% in 1990 and 1992, decided to retire, Scarborough ran for Congress. He was one of five Republicans in the race, and far from the best known. In the September primary Scarborough, conservative and anti-abortion, built on petition contacts and finished second with 30.6%, just behind Lois Benson, a pro-choice legislator and Pensacola council member, with 31.4%. Scarborough won the October runoff 54%–46%. His Democratic opponent, Vince Whibbs Jr., was just the kind of politician who had held such conservative seats for years—a Marine veteran and local businessman and lawyer, an opponent of gun control, supporter of school prayer and the balanced budget amendment. He argued he could do more for the district as part of the then-Democratic majority. Scarborough advocated a five-year federal spending freeze, school vouchers and tax credits for home schoolers and a ban on offshore oil drilling. Scarborough won by the whopping margin of 62%–38%.

Temperamentally Scarborough is a cheerful rebel. His fellow freshmen elected him their political director and then-Speaker Newt Gingrich named him to head a Republican task force on education. "Our goal is to get as much money, power and authority out of Washington and get as much money, power and authority into the classroom as possible," he said. Scarborough cast one of 10 Republican protest votes against the budget in 1995 and urged intransigence in the government shutdown; his plans to dismantle the Department of Education were never approved. One of the youngest freshmen, Scarborough kept a coonskin cap in his office and liked to wear jeans on Fridays. He called for ending corporate welfare, including royalty relief for offshore oil drillers and aid to large tobacco and sugar companies. He opposed offshore oil drilling in the Gulf of Mexico.

He has continued his rebel ways. He voted against increased committee funding in 1996, supported the coup against Gingrich in 1997 and voted against the transportation bill and omnibus budget in 1998. He worked to shut down the School of the Americas at Fort Benning and to fund D.C. advisory neighborhood commissions. He was one of the few congressmen to speak at the Tibet Freedom Rally on the steps of the Capitol. While appearing often on TV political programs, and singing a tasteless song at the DC's Funniest Celebrity Contest at the Improv in 1998, he also worked on TRICARE, the military's health insurance system, and on improving the quality of military life. He favored renaming a Pensacola street after Martin Luther King Jr. He brought to Washington Hunter Scott, a 13-year-old eighth grader, who wrote a school project claiming that Captain Charles B. McVay III of the *U.S.S. Indianapolis*, sunk in 1945, was "wrongly court-martialed."

Scarborough was re-elected against weak opposition in 1996 with 73%, the second highest for a contested Republican. In 1998 he was unopposed. Days later, he received a seat on the Appropriations Committee and its Military Construction Subcommittee, a position long held by Panhandle Congressman (1940–78) Bob Sikes.

Cook's Call. *Safe.* This Florida Panhandle district is very conservative and increasingly

Republican. Scarborough has made noises about running for Connie Mack's open Senate seat in 2000, but it's hard to see how Democrats can recapture this district, short of fielding an extraordinary candidate against a terribly-flawed Republican nominee.

The People: Pop. 1990: 562,575; 25.9% rural; 11.9% age 65 + ; 84% White, 12.8% Black, 1.7% Asian, 0.9% Amer. Indian, 0.5% Other; 2% Hispanic Origin. Households: 58.3% married couple families; 27% married couple fams. w. children; 48.6% college educ.; median household income: $25,866; per capita income: $12,505; median house value: $62,400; median gross rent: $310.

1996 Presidential Vote

Dole (R)	146,794	(59%)
Clinton (D)	77,070	(31%)
Perot (I)	24,322	(10%)

1992 Presidential Vote

Bush (R)	117,809	(51%)
Clinton (D)	59,316	(26%)
Perot (I)	53,250	(23%)

Rep. Joe Scarborough (R)

Elected 1994; b. Apr. 9, 1963, Atlanta, GA; home, Pensacola; U. of AL, B.A. 1985, U. of FL, J.D. 1990; Baptist; married (Melanie).

Professional Career: Teacher, 1985–87; Practicing atty., 1990–94.

DC Office: 127 CHOB 20515, 202-225-4136; Fax: 202-225-3414; Web site: www.house.gov/scarborough.

District Offices: Ft. Walton Beach, 850-664-1266; Pensacola, 850-479-1183.

Committees: *Armed Services* (22d of 32 R): Military Installations & Facilities; Military Research & Development; Special Oversight Panel on Morale, Welfare and Recreation; Special Oversight Panel on the Merchant Marine. *Government Reform* (12th of 24 R): Civil Service (Chmn.); District of Columbia. *Judiciary* (21st of 21 R): Commercial & Administrative Law; Immigration & Claims.

Group Ratings

	ADA	ACLU	AFS	LCV	CON	NTU	NFIB	COC	ACU	NTLC	CHC
1998	10	6	11	31	87	77	79	78	96	92	100
1997	10	—	25	—	8	70	—	70	100	—	—

National Journal Ratings

	1997 LIB — 1997 CONS		1998 LIB — 1998 CONS	
Economic	0% —	90%	12% —	85%
Social	20% —	71%	3% —	90%
Foreign	20% —	79%	7% —	83%

Key Votes of the 105th Congress

1. Clinton Budget Deal	Y	5. Puerto Rico Sthood. Ref.	N	9. Cut $ for B-2 Bombers	N
2. Education IRAs	Y	6. End Highway Set-asides	Y	10. Human Rights in China	Y
3. Req. 2/3 to Raise Taxes	Y	7. School Prayer Amend.	Y	11. Withdraw Bosnia Troops	Y
4. Fast-track Trade	N	8. Ovrd. Part. Birth Veto	Y	12. End Cuban TV-Marti	N

Election Results

1998 general	Joe Scarborough (R)	unopposed		($395,976)
1998 primary	Joe Scarborough (R)	unopposed		
1996 general	Joe Scarborough (R)	175,946	(73%)	($428,856)
	Kevin Beck (D)	66,495	(27%)	($30,613)

SECOND DISTRICT

Tallahassee seems an odd choice to be the capital of the nation's fourth largest state. Until recently it was not much more than a Spanish-mossed county seat with a handsome Creole capitol, built in 1845 and preserved opposite its 1977 skyscraper replacement, and two state universities. The site was chosen in the days when almost all Floridians lived along the state's northern edge and Tallahassee was near the population center. Ralph Waldo Emerson, visiting Tallahassee in the 19th Century, said it was a "grotesque place, rapidly settled by public officers, land speculators and desperadoes." The countryside around it is distinctly Dixie: cotton fields, soft pine stands, catfish farms, large families, small towns with big churches, both black and white. But Tallahassee itself and the subdivisions spreading beyond it are bringing to the state's north end some of the new urbanized Florida, with an additional pro-government tilt: 42% of Tallahassee area jobs are now in city and state government, compared to 15% statewide. Tallahassee has not attained the critical mass of the capitals of the three more populous states (Sacramento, Austin, and Albany), but it is on its way.

The 2d Congressional District is centered on Tallahassee, but extends westward to Panama City and eastward almost to Jacksonville. Historically, this was Democratic country, Jeffersonian and segregationist. Today, it is still mostly Democratic, though for different reasons; there is a large black percentage (23%, the fourth largest in Florida) and a strong Democratic preference among state employees and those dependent on them. Tallahassee's Leon County gave solid margins twice to Bill Clinton and, with two adjacent counties with high black percentages, favored Democrat Buddy MacKay for governor in 1998. But the rest of the district's counties gave majorities to Republican Jeb Bush.

The congressman from the 2d District is Allen Boyd, a Democrat first elected in 1996. A life-long farmer, Boyd grew up in Monticello in Jefferson County just east of Tallahassee. He served in Vietnam and received his degree from Florida State University. His political career began in 1989 when he was elected to the state House. There he was majority whip and chairman of two committees and helped form the Conservative Democratic Caucus.

Boyd decided to run for the House in 1995, when incumbent Pete Peterson, a moderate Democrat and Vietnam prisoner-of-war, decided to retire after three terms, saying he believed in term limits; in March 1996 he was named our first ambassador to Vietnam. A huge number, 141,000 people, voted in the Democratic primary and 117,000 in the runoff. Boyd ran well ahead, with 48% to 26% for Leon County Commissioner Anita Davis and 25% for retired Gulf County Judge David Taunton. Boyd then easily prevailed in the runoff 64%–36%. Republicans, with less than 23,000 voters in the primary and 15,000 in the runoff, had a contest in which a former state Commerce secretary edged a Christian Coalition-backed woman. In the general, Boyd campaigned with Blue Dog conservative House Democrats Pete Geren (who was retiring from Congress) and Bud Cramer. More important, he outspent the Republican by 2–1. The result was a solid 59%–40% victory for Boyd.

In the House Boyd increased the ranks of the conservative Blue Dogs to 21, and became Blue Dog whip himself. He sought to be a behind-the-scenes consensus builder and worked for the balanced budget agreement reached in 1997 and for a campaign finance bill; he called himself a "moderate Democrat with a social conscience." In 1998 he was head of the Blue Dogs' PAC and worked with Democratic campaign committee officials and elected several more Blue Dogs, whose ranks have now swelled to 29. He worked to get more money for Florida in the transportation bill and to keep open Tyndall Air Force Base near Panama City. At home he spearheaded a Coalition for a Drug-Free North Florida. He backed a bill to allow private timber harvesters to enter national forests and remove trees damaged in fires or floods. He was unperturbed when animal rights advocates picketed the Annual Boyd Family Dove Hunt in November 1998.

Boyd was re-elected over a write-in candidate in 1998. After the election he got a seat on Appropriations, as did 1st District Republican Joe Scarborough.

Cook's Call. *Safe.* Based on presidential voting patterns, Florida's 2d District looks like it should be a classic swing district. But Boyd, a conservative Democrat, has a good profile for this district and has had little difficulty winning here. He can probably hold this seat as long as he wants it, but don't be surprised to see a strong Republican make a very credible bid in an open seat situation.

The People: Pop. 1990: 562,359; 46.7% rural; 12.3% age 65+; 74% White, 24% Black, 0.9% Asian, 0.5% Amer. Indian, 0.5% Other; 1.9% Hispanic Origin. Households: 52.8% married couple families; 25.4% married couple fams. w. children; 41.6% college educ.; median household income: $22,839; per capita income: $11,341; median house value: $57,400; median gross rent: $282.

1996 Presidential Vote			1992 Presidential Vote		
Clinton (D)	114,601	(48%)	Clinton (D)	100,723	(42%)
Dole (R)	99,487	(42%)	Bush (R)	92,805	(39%)
Perot (I)	25,455	(11%)	Perot (I)	46,958	(20%)

Rep. Allen Boyd, Jr. (D)

Elected 1996; b. June 6, 1945, Valdosta, GA; home, Monticello; N. FL Jr. Col., A.A. 1966, FL St. U., B.S. 1969; Methodist; married (Cissy).

Military Career: Army 1969–71 (Vietnam).

Elected Office: FL House of Reps., 1989–96.

Professional Career: Farmer.

DC Office: 107 CHOB 20515, 202-225-5235; Fax: 202-225-5615; Web site: www.house.gov/boyd.

District Offices: Panama City, 850-785-0812; Tallahassee, 850-561-3979.

Committees: *Appropriations* (27th of 27 D): Agriculture, Rural Development, & FDA; Military Construction.

Group Ratings

	ADA	ACLU	AFS	LCV	CON	NTU	NFIB	COC	ACU	NTLC	CHC
1998	65	44	89	23	96	28	57	65	32	41	33
1997	55	—	50	—	76	32	—	80	44	—	—

National Journal Ratings

	1997 LIB — 1997 CONS			1998 LIB — 1998 CONS	
Economic	53%	—	46%	54%	—	46%
Social	62%	—	37%	63%	—	36%
Foreign	48%	—	52%	59%	—	40%

Key Votes of the 105th Congress

1. Clinton Budget Deal	N	5. Puerto Rico Sthood. Ref.	Y	9. Cut $ for B-2 Bombers	Y
2. Education IRAs	Y	6. End Highway Set-asides	N	10. Human Rights in China	N
3. Req. 2/3 to Raise Taxes	N	7. School Prayer Amend.	N	11. Withdraw Bosnia Troops	N
4. Fast-track Trade	N	8. Ovrd. Part. Birth Veto	Y	12. End Cuban TV-Marti	N

Election Results

1998 general	Allen Boyd Jr. (D)	unopposed		($281,015)
1998 primary	Allen Boyd Jr. (D)	unopposed		
1996 general	Allen Boyd Jr. (D)	138,151	(59%)	($807,103)
	Bill Sutton (R)	94,122	(40%)	($287,292)

THIRD DISTRICT

Before the Civil War, most of Florida was still an unchartered watery wilderness, festooned with exotic greenery, inhabited by unusual animals: a part of the United States so far out of the experience of most Americans as to seem foreign. As late as 1940, Florida had the smallest population of all the southern states, and most of the people here lived in classic Dixie rural counties with small courthouse towns, where civic affairs were run by the richest white men; blacks lived in poorly-constructed, unpainted shotgun houses propped up on blocks, with little money and no vote. This was a land of swamps and lakes and orange groves, of Marjorie Kinnan Rawlings's Cross Creek, where she wrote the great children's classic *The Yearling*, and the Florida of the broad St. Johns River, one of the few rivers in North America that flows (if only sluggishly) north, through the orange grove country to the port of Jacksonville, for many years Florida's largest city.

The 3d Congressional District occupies much of this old Florida terrain. The district was created in 1992 to be north Florida's black majority seat, and was modified for 1996, by an almost unanimous vote of the legislature, when it was overturned by a court order; it is now about 47% black. The district as drawn in 1992 collected the descendants of the slaves who worked on the plantations and farms of northern Florida over a century ago, plus blacks who have settled in the state since then. As redrawn in 1996, it no longer has a tentacle reaching out to Gainesville and Ocala, but extends more or less straight north and south, from Jacksonville to Orlando. Almost half of the district's population lives in Jacksonville, almost one quarter in and near Orlando (including all-black Eatontown, home of author Zora Neale Hurston). Much of it follows Florida watercourses: it touches on Cross Creek as well as the St. Johns River and numerous swamps.

The congresswoman from the 3d District is Corrine Brown, a Democrat elected in 1992. She grew up in Jacksonville, taught at the community college, was a guidance counselor and in 1982 was elected to the Florida House. With her Jacksonville base, she was the obvious favorite in 1992. In the Democratic primary she faced white talk radio host Andy Johnson who called himself "the blackest candidate in the race." Brown led 43%–31% in the primary and 64%–36% in the runoff; she won the general 59%–41%. Johnson brought the case challenging the district boundaries, but was not pleased with the results.

Brown has compiled a liberal record on most issues, though she supports more defense spending than many on the left; she stresses that the military can be a source of opportunity, a lesson many black Americans have learned from personal experience. She worked very hard and used her seats on Transportation and Veterans' Affairs to bring economic development to her district, working to secure an $86 million federal courthouse for Jacksonville and to promote LYNX in Orlando and cross-Florida high-speed rail. On the Transportation Committee she was a rock solid vote in 1998 for the new Step-21 formula which gives all states at least 95% of their gas tax revenues (Florida used to get 74%). As the only woman on the Veterans' Committee until 1997, she spearheaded a law to provide better health care for women in veterans' hospitals and clinics; in 1998 she helped pass the VERA (Veterans Equitable Resource Allocation) formula that gives Florida reimbursement for veterans who move there or use health facilities while visiting. She fought to preserve the Medicaid payments for disproportionate share hospitals (those with lots of low-income patients). On a trip to Ecuador she was appalled by its justice system and worked to help two Floridians imprisoned there; one was released in October 1997.

Brown has had spirited opposition, which is unusual for Florida incumbents; though she opposed the redistricting lawsuit, she embraced the legislature's new lines with enthusiasm and won 61%–39% in 1996. She faced her most difficult contest in 1998. That April the *St. Petersburg Times* reported that she received $10,000 from Baptist minister Henry Lyons, who since had been indicted on theft charges; she said the money was for his help in a rally protesting the redistricting case. In June the same paper reported that her daughter, attorney and EPA employee Shantrel Brown, was given a $50,000 Lexus by agents of African millionaire Foutanga Sissoko; he had been imprisoned in Miami on federal charges, and Corinne Brown had been working furiously to get him released, lobbying Attorney General Janet Reno to have him deported to Africa to continue his humanitarian work. A third charge came out: that she kept a jazz singer on her payroll as a "congressional outreach specialist"—though why that should be wrongful is unclear. Brown reacted with fury: she filed a criminal contempt charge against the *Times* reporters with the Capitol Police, claiming they "accosted" her and their questions made her cry. A federal prosecutor said there was not enough to indict them for impeding a member of Congress.

These charges attracted national Republican attention. They had a presentable candidate: Bill Randall, also black, a former General Motors management employee who had become a minister and worked as a sales manager for a cable company; he opposed abortion, favored local control of schools and school vouchers. As Randall admitted, "I think this race has gotten on the radar screen based on what this candidate has done to herself. It's not so much that I'm all that great a candidate or anything." But starting in June Randall outraised Brown, and was able to bring in Newt Gingrich, Christie Whitman and Alan Keyes. Democrats responded: in came Hillary Rodham Clinton, Jesse Jackson, Maxine Waters.

There were further wrinkles. Gingrich visited Monday, October 19. But on Sunday, October 18, the *Daytona News-Journal* reported two allegations against Randall. One was that he bounced a check for $1,300 in 1988 when the IRS froze his bank account because of failure to pay $30,000 in taxes. Randall said he was paying off the arrears and that one reason he was running was his mistreatment by the IRS. The paper also charged that Randall fathered a child with an unmarried woman in 1980. "An absolute lie," he said on October 19. But two days later, surrounded by his wife, daughter and grandchildren, he acknowledged the charge, and said it was the catalyst that got him to attend the seminary. This must have undercut the ad the Republicans were running: "We need public officials to be honest and preserve the rule of law. But look at Corinne Brown's record."

What did voters make of these charges, all of which analyzed with a bit of sympathy look like mistakes made at least partly out of good motives? They mostly reverted, as members of Congress mostly did to the charges against Bill Clinton, to partisan hype. They did cost Brown something: she won by 55%–45%, 6% down from 1996 though most incumbents of both parties saw their percentages rise. Brown won 60% in Jacksonville and 66% in the Orlando and Orange County parts of the district, both with black majorities; Randall made inroads among white Democrats in Putnam, Flagler and St. Johns counties and got 77% in very heavily Republican Clay County.

Brown promises to continue working for her constituency. The Congressional Accountability Project requested that the House ethics committee investigate the $10,000 contribution and the Lexus gift. But as of May 1999 no action had been taken.

Cook's Call. *Safe.* In 1998, Republicans had their best chance to knock the scandal-tainted Brown from this overwhelmingly-Democratic, majority-black district. Now that Brown has weathered her ethical storm, it's unlikely that Republicans will be able to replicate the situation with a better candidate; Brown is likely to remain comfortably in office, if a bit chastened.

The People: Pop. 1990: 562,080; 15.7% rural; 13.3% age 65 +; 50.4% White, 47% Black, 1% Asian, 0.3% Amer. Indian, 1.4% Other; 3.4% Hispanic Origin. Households: 44.8% married couple families; 21.3% married couple fams. w. children; 33.1% college educ.; median household income: $21,306; per capita income: $10,047; median house value: $50,500; median gross rent: $309.

1996 Presidential Vote			1992 Presidential Vote		
Clinton (D)	110,701	(58%)	Clinton (D)	93,446	(57%)
Dole (R)	66,057	(35%)	Bush (R)	49,198	(30%)
Perot (I)	12,633	(7%)	Perot (I)	21,225	(13%)

Rep. Corrine Brown (D)

Elected 1992; b. Nov. 11, 1946, Jacksonville; home, Jacksonville; FL A&M, B.S. 1969, M.S., 1971; Baptist; single.

Elected Office: FL House of Reps., 1982–92.

Professional Career: Prof., FL Commun. Col., 1977–82, Guidance Counselor, 1982–92.

DC Office: 2444 RHOB 20515, 202-225-0123; Fax: 202-225-2256; Web site: www.house.gov/corrinebrown.

District Offices: Jacksonville, 904-354-1652: Orlando, 407-872-0656.

Committees: *Transportation & Infrastructure* (14th of 34 D): Aviation; Ground Transportation. *Veterans' Affairs* (4th of 14 D): Oversight & Investigations (RMM).

Group Ratings

	ADA	ACLU	AFS	LCV	CON	NTU	NFIB	COC	ACU	NTLC	CHC
1998	95	87	100	77	55	12	9	31	4	14	0
1997	90	—	100	—	16	16	—	44	17	—	—

National Journal Ratings

	1997 LIB — 1997 CONS		1998 LIB — 1998 CONS	
Economic	79%	— 21%	79%	— 0%
Social	85%	— . 0%	87%	— 13%
Foreign	64%	— 36%	78%	— 19%

Key Votes of the 105th Congress

1. Clinton Budget Deal	N	5. Puerto Rico Sthood. Ref.	Y
2. Education IRAs	N	6. End Highway Set-asides	N
3. Req. 2/3 to Raise Taxes	N	7. School Prayer Amend.	N
4. Fast-track Trade	N	8. Ovrd. Part. Birth Veto	N

9. Cut $ for B-2 Bombers	N
10. Human Rights in China	Y
11. Withdraw Bosnia Troops	N
12. End Cuban TV-Marti	N

Election Results

1998 general	Corrine Brown (D)	66,621	(55%)	($488,690)
	Bill Randall (R)	53,530	(45%)	($465,865)
1998 primary	Corrine Brown (D)	unopposed		
1996 general	Corrine Brown (D)	98,085	(61%)	($330,201)
	Preston James Fields (R)	62,196	(39%)	($38,413)

FOURTH DISTRICT

With nearly 1 million people in the surrounding area, Jacksonville is one of Florida's major cities, with a National Football League franchise (the Jaguars) and bold new skyscrapers looming above a wide river and a shopping mall overshadowing grid streets of tiny shotgun houses. The wide freeways leading to huge beachfront subdivisions are not far from primeval wetlands and citrus groves. Mayport, one of the Navy's biggest bases, and other military installations are nearby. But Floridians tend to overlook Jacksonville. While its gleaming downtown is just one of a dozen in a state that had no commercial office development a generation ago, Jacksonville was known not long ago as a smelly, slow-growing insurance and paper mill town. Attracting big installations from AT&T, Brockway International, Prudential, Sears, UPS, American Express and the Mayo Clinic, Jacksonville has grown in the 1980s, while still maintaining its big military bases and insurance headquarters. In the 1990s, the counties just to the south of Jacksonville have been among the fastest-growing in Florida. Vast condominiums have been built along the Atlantic coastline from Amelia Island south through Ponte Vedra; farther south the new city of Palm Coast has grown up not far south of St. Augustine, the oldest European settlement in the United States. The growth has continued around Ormond Beach, where John D. Rockefeller used to spend his winters, and nearby Daytona Beach with its hard sand and stock car races. But like all of Florida it is not immune from disaster. In June and July 1998, wildfires swept 485,000 acres in northeast Florida; I-95 was closed for 125 miles south from Jacksonville; everyone in Flagler County and thousands to the north and south were evacuated; the Pepsi 400 stock car race was postponed. A massive fire-fighter effort stopped much damage, and finally the rains came.

The 4th Congressional District includes most of Jacksonville (minus the mostly black areas in the 3d District) and the beach areas to the north and south as far as Daytona Beach. The area is heavily Republican and voted solidly for Governor Jeb Bush in 1998.

The congresswoman from the 4th District is Tillie Fowler, a Republican elected in 1992. Fowler grew up in Milledgeville, Georgia—where writer Carson McCullers lived; her father was a druggist who served in the legislature. After law school she worked in Washington for Georgia Congressman Robert Stephens and the Nixon Administration—in the Office of Consumer Affairs with Elizabeth Dole. After marrying a Jacksonville businessman, she raised a family, did volunteer work and was elected to the City Council in 1985. In 1992 she was about to retire from the Council because of her support of "eight is enough" term limits, when 44-year incumbent House Democrat Charles Bennett retired. Fowler ran, with two retired admirals at her announcement and a promise from House Republican leaders that if elected she would get a seat on the Armed Services Committee. She pledged to make Mayport her top priority, while supporting abortion rights and the balanced budget amendment. Her Democratic opponent, a judge and former legislator, campaigned as a conservative, but Fowler, with a strong showing in Jacksonville, won with 57%. She has been unopposed since.

Fowler got her seat on Armed Services, long chaired by Carl Vinson, who was also from Milledgeville. She was elected co-chair of the Freshman Republican Task Force on Reform, and in her second term she became a deputy whip. She worked on an eight-year term limits amendment based on Florida's initiative, but was unable to get a vote on it. She has a moderate record on cultural issues, supporting the National Endowment for the Arts, and a strong conservative record on foreign and military policy. She fought hard and knowledgeably about the the relaxation of export controls, which allowed proliferation of dangerous high-tech weapons systems. In late 1996 Newt Gingrich gave Fowler and former Democratic Congresswoman Jane Harman the tough assignment of investigating sexual harassment in the Army. She has sought to upgrade Mayport so that it can accommodate nuclear carriers. And she has called for more defense spending, pointing out that deployments have increased dramatically in the Clinton years while forces have been cut back and defense spending in constant dollars has declined.

On Transportation and Infrastructure, Fowler worked on local projects and won authorization to replace Jacksonville's Fuller Warren Bridge on I-95. She supported the change in funding formula in 1998 which guaranteed Florida 95% of its gas tax revenues. Responding to the 1998 wildfires, she got eye drop manufacturers to drop cases of their product for fire fighters and co-sponsored a Disaster Mitigation Act to inventory government assistance before disasters occurred. She stopped designation of the St. Johns River as an American Heritage River, though Jacksonville Mayor John Delaney disagreed.

After the 1998 election, Fowler ran for vice chairman of the House Republican Conference, the number five position in the leadership. She started off with wide support, helped by her membership in Tom DeLay's whip organization; she promised to run again in 2000, despite her term-limits promise, to assure members she would serve the Conference post longer than two years. She led on the first ballot with 90 votes, to 43 for her closest competitor, Anne Northup. On the second ballot she won with 108 votes, to 58 for Northup and 42 for Peter

Hoekstra. Some said she was helped when Jennifer Dunn lost for majority leader, since many Republicans wanted a woman in the leadership; but three of the four members running were women. She voted for impeachment: "If our children are going to learn anything positive from this, then let them learn that the Constitution works, that the process will go forward, that lying under oath or otherwise will not be tolerated."

Term limits supporters promised to oppose Fowler for breaking her promise. But she is vulnerable only in a primary, if there. Her response: "I'm going to leave it up to my consituents. They know I have worked very hard for them."

Cook's Call. *Safe.* In early 1999, it's unclear whether Fowler will abide by her 1992 campaign pledge to serve only four terms and retire in 2000. Whatever her decision, this seat is likely to remain in Republican hands.

The People: Pop. 1990: 562,459; 11.1% rural; 14.3% age 65 + ; 91.1% White, 6.3% Black, 1.6% Asian, 0.3% Amer. Indian, 0.6% Other; 2.6% Hispanic Origin. Households: 56.7% married couple families; 25.3% married couple fams. w. children; 52.4% college educ.; median household income: $31,676; per capita income: $16,718; median house value: $80,900; median gross rent: $401.

1996 Presidential Vote			1992 Presidential Vote		
Dole (R)	145,760	(56%)	Bush (R)	132,023	(53%)
Clinton (D)	94,843	(37%)	Clinton (D)	75,035	(30%)
Perot (I)	19,071	(7%)	Perot (I)	41,075	(17%)

Rep. Tillie K. Fowler (R)

Elected 1992; b. Dec. 23, 1942, Milledgeville, GA; home, Jacksonville; Emory U., A.B. 1964, J.D. 1967; Episcopalian; married (Buck).

Elected Office: Jacksonville City Cncl., 1985–92, Pres., 1989–90.

Professional Career: Legis. Asst., U.S. Rep. Robert Stephens, 1967–70; White House Office of Consumer Affairs, 1970–71.

DC Office: 106 CHOB 20515, 202-225-2501; Fax: 202-225-9318; Web site: www.house.gov/fowler.

District Offices: Jacksonville, 904-739-6600; Ormond Beach, 904-672-0754.

Committees: *Republican Conference Vice Chairman. Armed Services* (11th of 32 R): Military Installations & Facilities; Military Readiness. *Transportation & Infrastructure* (14th of 41 R): Ground Transportation; Oversight, Investigations & Emergency Management (Chmn.).

Group Ratings

	ADA	ACLU	AFS	LCV	CON	NTU	NFIB	COC	ACU	NTLC	CHC
1998	5	25	14	15	28	46	100	94	88	86	67
1997	5	—	13	—	59	56	—	90	84	—	—

National Journal Ratings

	1997 LIB — 1997 CONS			1998 LIB — 1998 CONS		
Economic	28%	—	67%	33%	—	67%
Social	45%	—	54%	44%	—	55%
Foreign	0%	—	88%	34%	—	62%

Key Votes of the 105th Congress

1. Clinton Budget Deal	Y	5. Puerto Rico Sthood. Ref.	N	9. Cut $ for B-2 Bombers	N
2. Education IRAs	Y	6. End Highway Set-asides	Y	10. Human Rights in China	N
3. Req. 2/3 to Raise Taxes	Y	7. School Prayer Amend.	Y	11. Withdraw Bosnia Troops	Y
4. Fast-track Trade	*	8. Ovrd. Part. Birth Veto	Y	12. End Cuban TV-Marti	N

Election Results

1998 general	Tillie K. Fowler (R) .... unopposed		($162,361)
1998 primary	Tillie K. Fowler (R) .... unopposed		
1996 general	Tillie K. Fowler (R) .... unopposed		($280,593)

FIFTH DISTRICT

Over the past quarter century, Florida's urban areas have grown in every unlikely direction, occupying the high ground between the swamps and wetlands that still take up much of the state's peninsula. The pattern of development is clear in the North Sun Coast, the Gulf Coast counties north of St. Petersburg and Tampa, where subdivisions and trailer parks and shopping centers with Eckerd drug stores and Publix and Winn Dixie supermarkets sprang up in what were sleepy little towns with low brick buildings baking in the Florida sun. More than a half million people live in the towns starting with Clearwater and Tampa's northern suburbs that run up the spines of U.S. 19, just off the Gulf Coast, or U.S. 41 and I-75 inland near the orange groves. Though there are plenty of working people here, this is retirement country. People are comfortable though not usually affluent here, and if the existence of such communities is taken for granted by most Americans, their construction—the creation of an infrastructure of water and sewer lines, underground electricity, and phone and TV cables—is an example of the miracles of modern technology.

The 5th Congressional District, created after the 1990 census, occupies much of the fast-growing area, including the New Port Richey area on the Pasco County coast and fast-growing Citrus and Hernando counties to the north. The 5th travels northward to include Gainesville, home of the University of Florida, where students from the more wealthy urban corridors of central and south Florida study in a town with many flimsy houses from the impoverished South of 50 years ago; here they can become part of a Florida elite bonded by shared memories of the Gator Growl festivities. The population of this area quadrupled from 1960–90, and is growing still. Politically, the Gulf Coast counties are marginal territory, Democratic at the top of the ticket in 1996, Republican in 1998, and Gainesville is liberal and Democratic.

The congresswoman from the 5th District is Karen Thurman, a Democrat who has shown something like perfect political pitch while spending most of her adult lifetime in political office. An Air Force brat, she grew up in Florida and elsewhere, worked as a middle school math teacher for eight years before being elected to the Dunnellon Council, then became mayor. Elected to the Florida Senate in 1982, at 31, she was re-elected in 1986 with more votes than any other state senator. She sponsored an average of 60 bills a year on issues like education, the environment and agriculture, and, most important, as chairman of the reapportionment committee was careful to include her home town in the new 5th District for 1992. She easily won the primary and in the general faced a former prosecutor who called her a "professional, big money politician." She outraised him 2–1 and won 49%–43%.

In the House Thurman has compiled a moderate to liberal voting record. She casts conservative votes on many issues but has supported at some risk the Democratic position on some key votes, like the 1993 tax increase and term limits. One of her chief causes is regulatory relief: She was a lead Democrat for requiring EPA to conduct risk-assessment studies before issuing regulations. In the Republican 104th she was one of four Democrats to vote in committee to freeze new federal regulations until Congress can review the underlying statutes. She has also worked for local water and sewer projects, like a $29 million Tampa Bay water reuse project, and got a $13 million grant for equipment for the University of Florida's Brain Institute. She opposes offshore oil drilling and has pushed for changes in the formulas for federal highway funds. In 1995 she came up with an ingenious amendment to the line-item veto which passed with bipartisan support: To avoid giving the president too much leverage, it calls for separate override votes on projects if 50 members agree.

Thurman has been responsive to constituent problems; when a local woman got stuck paying for a $20,000 operation, she called for a six-month period for converting to individual insurance when a bankrupt employer's group policy is canceled. She backs tax-free pensions for survivors of police officers killed in the line of duty. She favors preserving 100% of the budget surplus for Social Security. She has a bill that would allow immediate small business deductions for purchases of $20,000 in computer equipment to cope with the Year 2000 problem. She has shown her political adroitness in other ways. In December 1996 when her constituents John and Alice Martin brought her a taped cell phone conversation involving Newt Gingrich, she refused to take it and sent them to the ethics committee; there they turned it over to ranking Democrat Jim McDermott, who evidently leaked it to *The New York Times*. The Martins were fined $500 each for illegal taping, but the Justice Department in October 1998 announced that Thurman was not and had not been the target of the investigation.

Thurman, who signs her letters "Karen" and still talks of herself as a math teacher, has performed well in elections. She was targeted by Republicans in 1994 and her opponent, former drag racing champion Don "Big Daddy" Garlits, attracted attention, calling for "medieval-style prisons" and public paddling of juveniles in town squares. Thurman raised more money and won more votes, carrying all but one county and winning 57%–43%. She was helped by a May 1996 redistricting case which added black and white liberal precincts in Gainesville and Alachua County from the formerly near black-majority 3d District. A Republican state senator dropped out of the race, and Thurman's anti-crime opponent was undercut when it turned out he was arrested in 1995 in Gainesville for carrying a concealed weapon without a permit. Thurman won 62%–38%. In 1998 her opponent was Jack Gargan, running on the Reform Party ticket. He promised to poll constituents and vote accordingly. To get enough ballot signatures, he promised to raffle off $50,000 of his salary to petition signers and campaign volunteers. He got the signatures, but his promise was mooted when Thurman won 66%–34%.

Cook's Call. *Safe.* Having carefully drawn this newly-created congressional district for herself while serving in the state Senate, Thurman has had a fairly easy time holding onto this Gainesville-based district. She should be pretty safe in the 5th for as long as she wants it.

The People: Pop. 1990: 562,926; 37.9% rural; 25.9% age 65 + ; 89.6% White, 8.4% Black, 1.1% Asian, 0.4% Amer. Indian, 0.5% Other; 2.6% Hispanic Origin. Households: 56.1% married couple families; 17.7% married couple fams. w. children; 39% college educ.; median household income: $21,434; per capita income: $11,876; median house value: $61,700; median gross rent: $320.

1996 Presidential Vote			1992 Presidential Vote		
Clinton (D)	135,496	(50%)	Clinton (D)	110,244	(42%)
Dole (R)	100,603	(37%)	Bush (R)	90,656	(34%)
Perot (I)	34,973	(13%)	Perot (I)	64,106	(24%)

Rep. Karen L. Thurman (D)

Elected 1992; b. Jan. 12, 1951, Rapid City, SD; home, Dunnellon; U. of FL, B.A. 1973; Episcopalian; married (John).

Elected Office: Dunnellon City Cncl., 1974–82; Dunnellon Mayor, 1979–81; FL Senate, 1982–92.

Professional Career: Middle schl. teacher, 1974–82.

DC Office: 440 CHOB 20515, 202-225-1002; Fax: 202-226-0329; Web site: www.house.gov/thurman.

District Offices: Gainesville, 352-336-6614; Inverness, 352-344-3044; New Port Richey, 813-849-4496.

Committees: *Ways & Means* (15th of 16 D): Health.

Group Ratings

	ADA	ACLU	AFS	LCV	CON	NTU	NFIB	COC	ACU	NTLC	CHC
1998	100	81	100	38	96	27	29	39	8	29	0
1997	75	—	75	—	70	27	—	60	24	—	—

National Journal Ratings

	1997 LIB	—	1997 CONS	1998 LIB	—	1998 CONS
Economic	73%	—	26%	64%	—	34%
Social	73%	—	24%	73%	—	25%
Foreign	56%	—	42%	75%	—	23%

Key Votes of the 105th Congress

1. Clinton Budget Deal	N	5. Puerto Rico Sthood. Ref.	Y	9. Cut $ for B-2 Bombers	N
2. Education IRAs	N	6. End Highway Set-asides	N	10. Human Rights in China	Y
3. Req. 2/3 to Raise Taxes	N	7. School Prayer Amend.	N	11. Withdraw Bosnia Troops	N
4. Fast-track Trade	N	8. Ovrd. Part. Birth Veto	N	12. End Cuban TV-Marti	Y

Election Results

1998 general	Karen L. Thurman (D)	132,005	(66%)	($472,959)
	Jack Gargan (Ref)	67,147	(34%)	($28,485)
1998 primary	Karen L. Thurman (D)	unopposed		
1996 general	Karen L. Thurman (D)	161,050	(62%)	($521,859)
	Dave Gentry (R)	100,051	(38%)	($62,164)

SIXTH DISTRICT

The flat rolling grasslands of central Florida, once bypassed by southbound tourists heading for the coast, by the 1980s had become a prime growth area in this high-growth state. In earlier decades, these areas depended economically on farming, on state institutions (the University of Florida in Gainesville, the big state prison in Raiford) and on passing tourists getting off the interstate to see attractions like Silver Springs, the world's largest formation of clear artesian springs. Then retirees began settling in places like the bluegrass country around Ocala (one of America's prime horse breeding grounds) and the plenteous lakes in Lake County to the south; the area was studded with trailer parks and mobile home developments. In the 1990s growth has accelerated, and pitched a bit more upscale; voter turnout around Ocala and Leesburg rose between 1990–98 more than in just about any other county in Florida.

The 6th Congressional District takes up much of this territory. Following the May 1996 redistricting, it takes in the small counties west of Jacksonville and much of Clay County. It includes all of Ocala and Marion County and most of Lake and Sumter counties just to the south. These counties, once marginal, are now solidly Republican. About half of its people live around Ocala or in Lake County; about one-third live on the west side of Jacksonville or in Clay County.

The congressman from the 6th District is Cliff Stearns, a Republican first elected in 1988. Stearns grew up and attended public schools in Washington, D.C., and served in the Air Force; he worked as an aerospace engineer, but then went into real estate and ended up owning five motels, three restaurants and other property—"someone who works in the community, goes to church with his neighbors, and doesn't live in Tallahassee," as he put it in his 1988 campaign, when he beat the favorite, state House Speaker Jon Mills, 54%–46%.

"I was elected to put the federal government on a diet," Stearns has said, and he has compiled a solidly conservative voting record. He was first noticed on Capitol Hill for cutting congressional staff pay raises. He sponsored a free market health care reform bill, pushed for funding cuts in the National Endowment for the Arts, chaired a Republican task force on gays in the military which surveyed generals and admirals and found 97% of them opposed lifting the ban. In June 1994, he penned the letter signed by 87 Republicans calling for the resignation of then-Surgeon General Joycelyn Elders. He worked out a consensus for returning to Florida government 77,000 acres set aside for the now-canceled Cross-Florida Barge Canal. He was able to convince HUD to issue rules protecting seniors-only housing developments from dis- crimination suits. As part of the majority on the Commerce Committee he has worked for privacy for health care and genetic records, and introduced bills on the subject. He is a leader for letting the states take the lead in utility deregulation, and sought Democratic support when other Republicans were working only inside the party. He wants to drop the requirement that utilities purchase power from renewable and non-traditional energy sources.

But Stearns is also interested in funds that mean jobs for north Florida. He took credit for situating a new 3,000-bed federal prison in Sumter County and then expanding it, for a new veterans' psychiatric facility and a VA ambulatory care center in Gainesville (near but not in the district) and for a Marion County veterans' outpatient clinic. As chairman of the Veterans' Health Subcommittee, he has been one of the leaders in urging recognition of Gulf war syn- drome and sponsored a research center on the subject. He got $6 million for an interchange on Florida's Turnpike on County Road 470 in Lake County. He opposed designation of the St. Johns River as an American Heritage River and attacked this administration initiative as unau- thorized spending.

After Republicans won a majority in 1994, he sought a leadership post, running for vice chairman of the House Republican Conference; he lost to Susan Molinari by 124–100 (now the vice chair is Tillie Fowler of the next-door 4th District). After that he has taken some anti- leadership positions. He opposed IMF funding and fast-track trade authority. He voted against the May 1997 budget agreement and the October 1998 omnibus budget.

Stearns has won re-election easily; in 1994 and 1998 he was unopposed. After the November 1998 election he said it was too early to say whether he would stick to the six-term limit promise he made in 1988. But his campaign treasury had $820,000 in cash on hand after the election—a strong disincentive for anyone to run against him.

Cook's Call. *Safe.* This is a safe Republican district, and Stearns should have this seat as long as he wants it.

The People: Pop. 1990: 562,219; 53.6% rural; 19.1% age 65 + ; 87.1% White, 11% Black, 0.8% Asian, 0.4% Amer. Indian, 0.7% Other; 2.8% Hispanic Origin. Households: 62.5% married couple families; 25.2% married couple fams. w. children; 36.8% college educ.; median household income: $25,036; per capita income: $12,026; median house value: $66,500; median gross rent: $314.

1996 Presidential Vote			1992 Presidential Vote		
Dole (R)	124,489	(50%)	Bush (R)	112,554	(47%)
Clinton (D)	96,135	(39%)	Clinton (D)	74,328	(31%)
Perot (I)	27,762	(11%)	Perot (I)	50,914	(21%)

Rep. Cliff Stearns (R)

Elected 1988; b. Apr. 16, 1941, Washington, DC; home, Ocala; George Washington U., B.S. 1963; Presbyterian; married (Joan).

Military Career: Air Force, 1963–67.

Professional Career: Data Control Systems Inc., 1967–68; Negotiator, CBS, 1969–70; Pres., Stearns House Inc., 1972–present.

DC Office: 2227 RHOB 20515, 202-225-5744; Fax: 202-225-3973; Web site: www.house.gov/stearns.

District Offices: Leesburg, 352-326-8285; Ocala, 352-351-8777; Orange Park, 904-269-3203.

Committees: *Commerce* (7th of 29 R): Energy & Power (Vice Chmn.); Health and Environment; Telecommunications, Trade & Consumer Protection. *Veterans' Affairs* (8th of 17 R): Health (Chmn.).

Group Ratings

	ADA	ACLU	AFS	LCV	CON	NTU	NFIB	COC	ACU	NTLC	CHC
1998	5	6	11	8	77	66	100	83	96	92	100
1997	10	—	25	—	62	59	—	70	100	—	—

National Journal Ratings

	1997 LIB — 1997 CONS			1998 LIB — 1998 CONS	
Economic	28%	—	67%	12%	—	85%
Social	20%	—	71%	3%	—	90%
Foreign	12%	—	81%	7%	—	83%

Key Votes of the 105th Congress

1. Clinton Budget Deal	Y	5. Puerto Rico Sthood. Ref.	N	9. Cut $ for B-2 Bombers	N
2. Education IRAs	Y	6. End Highway Set-asides	Y	10. Human Rights in China	Y
3. Req. 2/3 to Raise Taxes	Y	7. School Prayer Amend.	Y	11. Withdraw Bosnia Troops	Y
4. Fast-track Trade	N	8. Ovrd. Part. Birth Veto	Y	12. End Cuban TV-Marti	N

Election Results

1998 general	Cliff Stearns (R)	unopposed		($189,345)
1998 primary	Cliff Stearns (R)	unopposed		
1996 general	Cliff Stearns (R)	161,527	(67%)	($301,045)
	Newell O'Brien (D)	78,908	(33%)	($38,183)

SEVENTH DISTRICT

In ever-changing Florida, new communities and towns continue to spring up on the landscape, replacing older town centers with which tourists have been familiar. Just down the road from

Daytona Beach, where 340,000 motorcyclists gather each March for Bike Week, is New Smyrna Beach, a new town established on the site of an old settlement. Fifteen miles inland, close to Sanford, where Amtrak's Auto-Train unloads its Florida-bound travelers, is Deltona, a vast five-mile square development that drained part of a Florida swamp and designed curving streets meandering around small lakes and golf courses, set aside land for shopping centers and office space and then marketed the place nationwide. It became an instant city: in 1990, 51,000 people lived in Deltona—where there were 15,000 in 1980 and 4,800 in 1970.

The 7th Congressional District includes Deltona, New Smyrna Beach and part of Daytona Beach, as well as most of Sanford. Stretching from Daytona across the marshy St. Johns River basin to Seminole County, it includes large Orlando suburbs like Altamonte Springs and small old towns like Oviedo, and goes south to include part of Orlando itself. In most elections, this is a solidly Republican district, although the area around Daytona has a conservative Democratic heritage and was the site of two close legislative races in 1996, where Democrats failed to take Republican seats and lost control of the state House.

The congressman from the 7th is John Mica, a spirited Republican and a political veteran who came to office as an opponent of the status quo. He grew up in south Florida, in a bipartisan political family: His younger brother Dan Mica was a Democratic congressman from Palm Beach County from 1978–88, when he lost a primary for U.S. Senate, and another brother worked for Democratic Governor Lawton Chiles. But John Mica has always been a conservative Republican. He made a small fortune by turning 360 feet of New Smyrna beachfront into a real estate business, then served as a staffer to Florida Senator Paula Hawkins from 1981–85, then became a lobbyist. When attacked in the 1992 Republican primary as an insider representing special interests, Mica lobbied pro bono for the Daytona airport and got a runway extension, and won 53%–34%. In the general he outraised his opponent, attacked him as a liberal backed by trial lawyers and labor unions and won 56%–44%.

Mica started off as a brash reformer, leading the charge to abolish House select committees and to make public the names of those signing petitions to discharge legislation. In 1993, Mica also pushed a plan to require the EPA to subject new regulations to a cost-benefit analysis, versions of which ultimately passed. When Republicans took control after 1994, Mica became chairman of the Government Reform's Civil Service Subcommittee. There he helped pass the White House Accountability Act of 1996, imposing on the White House, as a Republican-pushed 1995 law imposed on Congress, the laws the legislative and executive branches impose on others. More recently, he has proposed to expand federal employees' health insurance to include long-term coverage at group rates. In 1998 he managed to put $100 million into the omnibus budget for a Capitol Visitors Center below the East Front of the Capitol; support increased after two Capitol Police officers were killed by a gunman that summer.

Mica has said that his biggest issue is fighting drugs. In May 1997 he complained that federal drug interdiction forces, like high-altitude radar balloons and sophisticated planes, had been shifted from Florida to the Mexican borders and Puerto Rico; federal drug authorities said they still patrolled Florida. With Senator Bob Graham, he announced in March 1998 a new Central Florida High Intensity Drug Trafficking Area, headquartered in the Orlando area; he told local police, "We want you to kick butt." In March 1998 he and Clay Shaw introduced a bill to revoke the administration's certification of Mexico's drug-fighting efforts. Also he sponsored a bill to bar federal employees convicted on drug charges from federal employment from five to 10 years.

On local issues he has supported the light-rail system in Orlando and proposed to build a bus, train and light-rail station in Sanford to connect with the Auto Train, Amtrak and LYNX. He worked to keep the Army simulation training command in Orlando, where it has spawned many local businesses. He has been re-elected by wide margins, with no opposition in 1998.

Cook's Call. *Safe.* Since first capturing this seat in 1992, Mica has had little trouble winning re-election in this very Republican district. He should have no concerns about winning in 2000.

The People: Pop. 1990: 563,552; 11.5% rural; 16.4% age 65 +; 93.1% White, 4.1% Black, 1.2% Asian, 0.4% Amer. Indian, 1.2% Other; 5.5% Hispanic Origin. Households: 59.1% married couple families; 24.9% married couple fams. w. children; 51.2% college educ.; median household income: $30,921; per capita income: $15,132; median house value: $80,600; median gross rent: $450.

1996 Presidential Vote			1992 Presidential Vote		
Dole (R)	108,636	(47%)	Bush (R)	105,519	(45%)
Clinton (D)	100,603	(43%)	Clinton (D)	81,180	(34%)
Perot (I)	22,863	(10%)	Perot (I)	49,588	(21%)

Rep. John L. Mica (R)

Elected 1992; b. Jan. 27, 1943, Binghamton, NY; home, Winter Park; Miami-Dade Commun. Col., A.A. 1965, U. of FL, B.A. 1967; Episcopalian; married (Patricia).

Elected Office: FL House of Reps., 1976–80.

Professional Career: Exec. Dir., Palm Beach & Orange Cnty. Govt. Charter Study Commissions, 1970–74; Pres., MK Development, 1975–92; A.A., U.S. Sen. Paula Hawkins, 1981–85; Partner, Mica, Dudinsky & Assoc., 1985–92.

DC Office: 2445 RHOB 20515, 202-225-4035; Fax: 202-226-0821; Web site: www.house.gov/mica.

District Offices: Casselberry, 407-657-8080; Deltona, 407-860-1499; Port Orange, 904-756-9798.

Committees: *Government Reform* (8th of 24 R): Civil Service; Criminal Justice, Drug Policy & Human Resources (Chmn.); National Security, Veterans' Affairs & Intl. Relations. *House Administration* (5th of 6 R). *Transportation & Infrastructure* (12th of 41 R): Aviation; Ground Transportation.

Group Ratings

	ADA	ACLU	AFS	LCV	CON	NTU	NFIB	COC	ACU	NTLC	CHC
1998	10	6	11	15	65	54	100	89	92	95	100
1997	0	—	13	—	6	56	—	100	100	—	—

National Journal Ratings

	1997 LIB — 1997 CONS		1998 LIB — 1998 CONS	
Economic	10%	— 86%	26%	— 72%
Social	10%	— 82%	37%	— 62%
Foreign	0%	— 88%	19%	— 75%

Key Votes of the 105th Congress

1. Clinton Budget Deal	Y	5. Puerto Rico Sthood. Ref.	Y	9. Cut $ for B-2 Bombers	N
2. Education IRAs	Y	6. End Highway Set-asides	Y	10. Human Rights in China	N
3. Req. 2/3 to Raise Taxes	Y	7. School Prayer Amend.	Y	11. Withdraw Bosnia Troops	Y
4. Fast-track Trade	N	8. Ovrd. Part. Birth Veto	Y	12. End Cuban TV-Marti	N

Election Results

1998 general	John L. Mica (R)	unopposed		($117,344)
1998 primary	John L. Mica (R)	unopposed		
1996 general	John L. Mica (R)	143,667	(62%)	($539,973)
	George Stuart Jr. (D)	87,832	(38%)	($165,921)

EIGHTH DISTRICT

Who would have supposed that the most popular tourist destination in the world would rise amid the swamps and orange groves of central Florida? The answer: Walt Disney, and just about no one else. In the middle 1960s Disney looked at the map and decided that the intersection of I-4 and Florida's Turnpike, the "crossroads of Florida," just a few miles southwest of Orlando, was the perfect place for the vast theme park he was planning. Metro Orlando in 1960 had less people—88,000—than the Orlando area has hotel rooms today—91,000; Walt Disney World's Magic Kingdom opened in 1971, and EPCOT Center, Disney/MGM Studios, Sea World, Universal Studios, Splendid China and dozens of other attractions bring in millions of visitors from all over the world each year. Orlando is the center of a 1 million-plus metropolitan area, with the biggest job gain, 74%, in the 1980s of any major metro area. And the economy has diversified beyond tourism: Martin Marietta built a big defense plant here way back in 1956, and greater Orlando has a high-tech economy and a population weighted toward young families with children rather than retirees.

The spirit of this place has been set by a man who never lived here but created something now taken for granted. Walt Disney conceived the first theme park in the flatlands of Orange County, California, but he perfected it in the 17,000 acres of swamp and lakes in Florida's Orange County. And with the invention of the theme park, Disney also pioneered sophisticated communications, utility, and waste disposal methods—all out of sight and underground. Yet Disney World is not just an engineering marvel; it requires some 36,000 people with know-how and unfailing cheerfulness. Disney's vision of a future that was labor-intensive as well as high-tech—in which the critical ingredient is the provision of services—accurately forecast the service-driven economy that has grown so lustily for decades now.

The 8th Congressional District includes most of Orlando and surrounding Orange County. It excludes most heavily black neighborhoods and towns placed in the 3d District—boundaries that, for the most part, survived redistricting in 1996. It includes central and eastern Orlando and all its suburbs directly to the east, plus most to the south and west. It also takes in most of the Kissimmee area in Osceola County just to the south and Disney World's Magic Kingdom. Politically, this Orange County is less Republican than the Orange County where the original Disneyland was built; it was historically Democratic, like all of central Florida, and can sometimes be persuaded to vote for Democrats, but it voted for George Bush and Bob Dole in 1992 and 1996, and for Jeb Bush in both 1994 and 1998.

The congressman from the 8th District is Bill McCollum, a Republican first elected in 1980 and now chairman of Judiciary's Crime Subcommittee. McCollum grew up in Brooksville, near the Gulf of Mexico, where, after his mother's death from cancer, he was raised in the house of his grandfather, one of the first active Republicans in the area. He went to college and law school at the University of Florida where he organized conservative groups designed to develop future leaders. He was a Navy lawyer for three years, then practiced law in the Orlando area defending insurance companies. In 1980, he ran for the House, against an incumbent implicated in the Abscam scandal, in a district that went west to the Gulf of Mexico and included his home town; with his Orlando area base he won the runoff and general.

McCollum is serious, dogged, a believer in firmly anchored principles. In the Democratic House he led the fight against the Brady bill, winning in 1988 but losing in 1993. On immigration he was not happy with the higher quotas in the 1990 bill. On the Iran-Contra Committee, he was a vocal critic of majority Democrats. He led the unsuccessful fight in 1992 to allow S&Ls to count goodwill as an asset. He led the fight in the House against the so-called "racial justice" provision, which would impose something like racial quotas on executions by allowing capital defendants to use statistics to challenge a death sentence as biased based on race; he lost 217–212 on the first vote, but many House Democrats, under the spotlight, switched, and by a 264–149 vote took it out of the 1994 crime bill. He favored 12-year term limits and, after

Republicans won control, his proposal for an amendment became the basis of the Contract with America version and won 227 votes—a majority but far short of the two-thirds required.

McCollum's effort to move into the House leadership failed: in 1994 he ran for vice chairman of the Republican Conference, but finished third with only 28 votes, far behind Tom DeLay (119) and Robert Walker (80). But he is now the third Republican on Judiciary and number two on Banking. He spotlighted law enforcement wrongdoing in the Waco massacre of 1993 and supported multipoint wiretapping in the anti-terrorism bill. He opposed gun control measures and pushed successfully for limits on death row appeals. On local issues he worked with John Mica to keep the military simulation center in the Orlando area.

McCollum had two major projects in the 105th Congress, neither of which became law. One was a juvenile justice bill. Prompted by the fact that so few juvenile offenders are put in secure confinement, he called for changing the federal rules for juveniles, with a presumption of adult prosecution for those 14 and over, establishing a program to apprehend armed youths and providing $500 million over three years for states' juvenile justice systems which passed the House but died in the Senate. The second major bill was bankruptcy reform. In the prosperous 1990s bankruptcies have been skyrocketing, enabling some to avoid paying their debts by increasing the cost of credit to everyone else. This passed the House 306–118 in June 1998, but was not voted on by the Senate. McCollum was more successful on other measures. A bill to help parents block Internet pornography and punish pedophile stalkers; it passed the House 416–0 in June 1998. He also helped pass federal penalties for failure to pay child support and a Western Hemisphere Drug Elimination Act, authorizing $3.3 billion over four years.

Much of McCollum's time in late 1998 and early 1999 was taken up by impeachment. Early on he said that if Bill Clinton committed perjury, he should be impeached; he voted for impeachment and was one of the House managers in the Senate. After the election, he denied that Republicans were on the wrong track politically and needed to become more moderate. "We represent the mainstream of America right now," he said. "I'm firmly convinced of that."

In the Florida 8th that is certainly true: McCollum has been re-elected easily. In 1996 and 1998 he was opposed by Al Krulick, an actor who plays Claude Frollo in *The Hunchback of Notre Dame* at Disney/MGM Studios; McCollum won by a 2–1 margin. In 1996, when he thought Bob Graham might vacate his Senate seat to run for governor, McCollum considered, then demured, running for the seat. When Senator Connie Mack announced he would not run again, McCollum immediately jumped into the race, hoping to disuade any other Republican hopefuls.

Cook's Call. *Probably Safe.* Though McCollum is stepping aside to run for the Senate in 2000, Republicans still have the upper hand in holding onto the Republican-leaning 8th District. While Democrats are looking closely at this seat, the district has not been all too friendly to them as McCollum and Republican statewide and presidential candidates have racked up big margins here in recent years.

The People: Pop. 1990: 562,244; 8.6% rural; 11.9% age 65 +; 88.9% White, 5.1% Black, 2.3% Asian, 0.4% Amer. Indian, 3.3% Other; 11% Hispanic Origin. Households: 53.9% married couple families; 24.7% married couple fams. w. children; 51.9% college educ.; median household income: $31,251; per capita income: $15,464; median house value: $85,100; median gross rent: $454.

1996 Presidential Vote			1992 Presidential Vote		
Dole (R)	95,300	(47%)	Bush (R)	101,707	(48%)
Clinton (D)	88,306	(44%)	Clinton (D)	68,840	(32%)
Perot (I)	17,231	(9%)	Perot (I)	42,901	(20%)

Rep. Bill McCollum (R)

Elected 1980; b. July 12, 1944, Brooksville; home, Altamonte Springs; U. of FL, B.A. 1965, J.D. 1968; Episcopalian; married (Ingrid).

Military Career: Navy, 1969–72, Naval Reserves, 1972–92.

Professional Career: Practicing atty., 1973–81; Chmn., Seminole Cnty. Repub. Cmte., 1976.

DC Office: 2109 RHOB 20515, 202-225-2176; Fax: 202-225-0999; Web site: www.house.gov/mccollum.

District Office: Orlando, 407-872-1962.

Committees: *Banking & Financial Services* (Vice Chmn. of 32 R): Domestic & International Monetary Policy; Financial Institutions & Consumer Credit (Vice Chmn.). *Judiciary* (3d of 21 R): Crime (Chmn.); Immigration & Claims. *Permanent Select Committee on Intelligence* (3d of 9 R): Human Intelligence, Analysis & Counterintelligence (Chmn.).

Group Ratings

	ADA	ACLU	AFS	LCV	CON	NTU	NFIB	COC	ACU	NTLC	CHC
1998	5	13	11	15	30	61	79	94	84	84	92
1997	5	—	25	—	20	49	—	90	88	—	—

National Journal Ratings

	1997 LIB	—	1997 CONS	1998 LIB	—	1998 CONS
Economic	28%	—	67%	23%	—	74%
Social	10%	—	82%	38%	—	60%
Foreign	12%	—	81%	7%	—	83%

Key Votes of the 105th Congress

1. Clinton Budget Deal	Y	5. Puerto Rico Sthood. Ref.	Y	9. Cut $ for B-2 Bombers	N
2. Education IRAs	Y	6. End Highway Set-asides	Y	10. Human Rights in China	N
3. Req. 2/3 to Raise Taxes	Y	7. School Prayer Amend.	Y	11. Withdraw Bosnia Troops	Y
4. Fast-track Trade	Y	8. Ovrd. Part. Birth Veto	Y	12. End Cuban TV-Marti	N

Election Results

1998 general	Bill McCollum (R)	104,298	(66%)	($648,553)
	Al Krulick (D)	54,245	(34%)	($38,882)
1998 primary	Bill McCollum (R)	unopposed		
1996 general	Bill McCollum (R)	136,515	(67%)	($421,409)
	Al Krulick (D)	65,794	(33%)	($34,066)

NINTH DISTRICT

Half a century ago, the land north of St. Petersburg and Tampa was scarcely inhabited. The Gulf is lined with swamps and inland the terrain is spotted with lakes and was covered with dense semitropical forests. Over the years, development has moved up the coast and up the major highways inland. Much of this area originally was designed for retirees—condominiums, garden apartments, trailer parks. But this is working country as well. Businesses grew up around

Clearwater in northern Pinellas County and inland in Pasco County off I-75. And people brought their ancestral political beliefs with them. In the 1950s and 1960s, only white-collar retirees could afford to buy new places in Florida, and they were heavily Republican. As blue-collar workers and union members became more affluent in the 1970s and 1980s, they came with their traditional Democratic Party identification and cultural conservatism. Those cross-currents have made this area prime marginal territory in Florida politics.

The 9th Congressional District covers much of this area north of St. Petersburg and Tampa. About half its population is in northern Pinellas County around Clearwater and Tarpon Springs, an old resort first settled by Greek sponge divers early in the 20th Century. Another quarter is in northern Hillsborough County, on the suburban fringe of Tampa. The final quarter is the inland portion of Pasco County, north of Tampa, where former crossroads like Zephyrhills have become significant population centers.

The congressman from the 9th District is Michael Bilirakis, a Republican who grew up near Pittsburgh; he served in the Air Force, and then worked his way through college toiling in a steel mill. He also worked for the government in Washington and an aerospace contractor in Florida, then practiced law. He believes strongly that Americans can work their way up, with occasional government assistance (like the G.I. Bill that helped him through school). Originally a Democrat, he switched to the Republican Party in 1980, and in 1982, when this district was created, he won though it had been designed for a Democrat. He has a moderate record on economics and is more conservative on other issues. He has made something of an environ-mental record, opposing Western water subsidies and offshore oil drilling on the Gulf Coast.

Early in his career Bilirakis won a seat on the Commerce Committee, and today he holds one of the most powerful chairmanships in Congress, that of the Health and Environment Subcommittee. In 1993, with Democrat Roy Rowland, he sponsored the Health Care Reform Consensus Act, which tried to make health insurance portable and to stop insurers from denying coverage for pre-existing conditions. That bill became a vehicle and could have passed if it came to a vote; but Democrats held out for the Clinton plan until it died in fall 1994. In 1995 Bilirakis sponsored a similar bill, very similar to the bill usually named after its Senate sponsors Nancy Kassebaum and Edward Kennedy which became law in 1996. Bilirakis also sponsored the 1996 Safe Drinking Water Act, which had bipartisan support, and the Food Quality Pro-tection Act, which eliminated the Delaney clause and substituted a provision allowing pesticides only when there is a reasonable certainty of no harm to the consumer. Also he sponsored reauthorization of the Ryan White Care Act and, as vice chairman of the Veterans' subcom-mittee on hospitals, passed a law prorating VA disability checks for spouses (the government had demanded their return the month the beneficiary died).

In the 105th Congress, Bilirakis helped to pass the 1997 FDA law intended to speed up approval of lifesaving drugs and a law to provide "forgotten widows" of veterans with a minimum annuity of $165 a month. He sought increased NIH funding, preventive coverage in Medicare and a law to cope with discrimination at the Veterans' Affairs Department. After a Tampa nursing home evicted beneficiaries in April 1998, Bilirakis, Jim Davis of Tampa and Senator Bob Graham sponsored a bill to prevent that practice; a version was signed by President Clinton in March 1999. Bilirakis was appointed to the national Medicare commission. He was proud of getting $20 million for a spinal injury VA center in Tampa.

Bilirakis has been re-elected by wide margins in the 1990s; in 1998 he was unopposed. His son Gus Bilirakis ran for the 48th state House District; this contest attracted attention when Democratic nominee Diane Ellis claimed that the younger Bilirakis had been dead since 1995 and the man running was a stand-in named Danny Divito. Gus Bilirakis proved that he was alive and won the race by a wide margin.

Cook's Call. *Safe.* Since capturing this newly-redrawn open seat in 1982, Bilirakis has consistently won victories far larger than might be expected even in this Republican-leaning district. It's unclear how long Bilirakis will want to stay in Congress; still, the 9th—at least as presently configured—will likely remain in Republican hands.

The People: Pop. 1990: 562,814; 19% rural; 22.4% age 65 + ; 94.7% White, 3.4% Black, 0.9% Asian, 0.3% Amer. Indian, 0.7% Other; 4% Hispanic Origin. Households: 59.4% married couple families; 21.8% married couple fams. w. children; 48.2% college educ.; median household income: $29,293; per capita income: $15,797; median house value: $85,300; median gross rent: $413.

1996 Presidential Vote

Dole (R) 119,658 (45%)
Clinton (D) 118,996 (45%)
Perot (I) 27,335 (10%)

1992 Presidential Vote

Bush (R) 113,853 (41%)
Clinton (D) 94,662 (34%)
Perot (I) 68,167 (25%)

Rep. Michael Bilirakis (R)

Elected 1982; b. July 16, 1930, Tarpon Springs; home, Palm Harbor; U. of Pittsburgh, B.S. 1959, U. of FL, J.D. 1963; Greek Orthodox; married (Evelyn).

Military Career: Air Force, 1951–55.

Professional Career: Steelworker, 1955–59; Govt. contract negotiator, 1959–60; Petroleum engineer, 1960–63; Practicing atty., 1969–83.

DC Office: 2369 RHOB 20515, 202-225-5755; Fax: 202-225-4085; Web site: www.house.gov/bilirakis.

District Offices: Clearwater, 727-441-3721; Land O'Lakes, 813-996-7441.

Committees: *Commerce* (4th of 29 R): Energy & Power; Health and Environment (Chmn.). *Veterans' Affairs* (3d of 17 R): Health.

Group Ratings

	ADA	ACLU	AFS	LCV	CON	NTU	NFIB	COC	ACU	NTLC	CHC
1998	5	6	11	46	2	53	100	89	92	89	100
1997	10	—	13	—	49	48	—	100	84	—	—

National Journal Ratings

	1997 LIB — 1997 CONS	1998 LIB — 1998 CONS
Economic	40% — 60%	26% — 74%
Social	10% — 82%	14% — 81%
Foreign	12% — 81%	7% — 83%

Key Votes of the 105th Congress

1. Clinton Budget Deal	Y	5. Puerto Rico Sthood. Ref.	N	9. Cut $ for B-2 Bombers	N
2. Education IRAs	Y	6. End Highway Set-asides	Y	10. Human Rights in China	N
3. Req. 2/3 to Raise Taxes	Y	7. School Prayer Amend.	Y	11. Withdraw Bosnia Troops	Y
4. Fast-track Trade	N	8. Ovrd. Part. Birth Veto	Y	12. End Cuban TV-Marti	N

Election Results

1998 general	Michael Bilirakis (R)	.... unopposed		($323,890)
1998 primary	Michael Bilirakis (R)	.... unopposed		
1996 general	Michael Bilirakis (R)	 161,708	(69%)	($846,392)
	Jerry Provenzano (D)	 73,809	(31%)	($84,370)

TENTH DISTRICT

St. Petersburg, established in 1888 and named for the then-Russian capital, known for decades as the American city with the largest percentage of elderly residents, in the 1990s finally reached

a certain balance. It started off promoting itself as a retirement center, and in the early 1900s
St. Petersburg Times editor W. L. Straub tried to stop the industrialization of the waterfront,
setting the city's character by establishing parks and park benches. By the 1950s, St. Petersburg
had become a national cliche, bringing to mind old folks trying to drum up a game of shuffle-
board. Starting off on the grid streets facing Tampa Bay, spreading later toward the beaches on
the Gulf Coast, St. Petersburg filled up to a greater extent than any other American city with
retirees, mostly from the North and modestly affluent. They adapted easily to a city whose civic
tone was set by the *St. Petersburg Times* and its longtime owners Nelson and Henrietta Poynter:
sober, good-humored, supportive of clean government and civil rights.

Like any retirement center, St. Petersburg has had rapid population turnover, reflected in its
political trends. White-collar Yankee retirees in the 1940s and 1950s made St. Petersburg the
first Republican center in ancestrally Democratic Florida; it voted for Thomas Dewey in 1948
and elected a Republican congressman in 1954. Then, as more blue-collar workers could afford
Florida retirement and the affluent moved farther down the Gulf Coast, St. Petersburg trended
Democratic in the 1970s and 1980s. Also, St. Petersburg developed more businesses, attracted
more young families with children, and its black and Hispanic communities grew larger. It
became a kind of central city, even hosting the 1996 vice presidential debate. In the process
St. Petersburg and Pinellas County became contested political territory.

St. Petersburg and southern Pinellas County, including Largo and the string of barrier island
beach towns from Mullet Key to Belleair Beach, make up the 10th Congressional District.

The congressman from the 10th District is Bill Young, a Republican first elected in 1970,
tied for second in seniority among House Republicans and chairman of the Appropriations
Committee. Young, originally from Pennsylvania, grew up in Florida, quit school to support
his ill mother, then ran an insurance agency. In the 1950s he worked for St. Petersburg's first
Republican congressman, William Cramer. Young was elected to the state Senate in 1960, at
29; then, when Cramer ran for the Senate in 1970, Young ran for the St. Petersburg House seat
and won. In the early 1970s, Social Security was vastly increased and indexed to inflation and
St. Petersburg basked in prosperity; Young delivered constituency services and had a moderate
to conservative voting record, and was easily re-elected.

Early on, Young got a seat on Appropriations, where he, like many Republicans, worked
closely with the Democratic chairmen. Young's special project has been the bone marrow donor
program, originated by Dr. Robert Good of All Children's Hospital in St. Petersburg. Working
from his seat on the Defense Subcommittee, he originally placed the program in the Pentagon;
in 1987 it started off with $2.1 million; by 1998 had $34 million, with 3.5 million volunteers,
and Young won its continuation for another five years. He has backed child health research
centers, juvenile diabetes centers, more money for pediatric AIDS, and the University of Florida's Brain Institute.

Despite his seniority, Young did not become full committee chairman after Republicans won
their majority in 1994. It was generally thought that Speaker-designate Newt Gingrich passed
over him and two more senior Republicans for being too accommodating to Democrats. Young
says that Gingrich offered him the job, but that he preferred to chair the Defense Subcommittee;
in 1998 he said, "To this day I think it was the right decision to make at the time." In that post
he worked to produce bipartisan appropriations out of the spotlight; he has one of the four
secret telephones in House offices and subcommittee markups are typically done behind closed
doors; he has said he knows every dime that goes into secret "black" military and intelligence
operations. "I do my job with as little fanfare as possible," he said. "I don't hold press conferences. I don't put out press releases except if it affects my district." Young has sharply
criticized the Clinton Administration for stretching the military too thin. His philosophy, he
says, goes back to his memories of hearing about Pearl Harbor as a child. In his office he keeps
a "horseshoe nail" list ("for want of the nail, the shoe was lost") of small items the military
needs; it is on a scroll, which strecthes across the room, and includes items like more training

hours for pilots, barracks repair and more bullets, compasses, tents and flashlights. This became the basis for the supplemental defense appropriation Young passed in October 1998.

On other issues Young has a moderate voting record; he backed Clinton projects like family and medical leave and the 1994 gun control laws. He also stays attentive to local issues. He intervened with Attorney General Janet Reno to object when the town of Pinellas Park was told to refund a $250,000 federal grant that was under dispute. In 1998 he got $5.6 million for replenishment of Upham and Sunset beaches.

Young has not had much electoral competition. In 1992 he was criticized in a series of articles in the *Tampa Tribune* for speech honoraria he received and trips he took, but beat Democrat Karen Moffitt by a 57%–43% margin. He was unopposed in 1994 and 1998 and won easily in 1996. Three days after the November 1998 election, Newt Gingrich decided to resign; Appropriations Chairman Bob Livingston quickly became the speaker-designate; so Young was suddenly elevated to the full committee chairmanship. He immediately promised to try to "avoid a train wreck" like that in 1998, and urged the 13 subcommittee chairmen to report their bills on schedule. Back in 1995, he said that he would abide by Florida's "eight is enough" term limits, and would not run again in 2000; after becoming chairman he said it was up to his constituents. Presumably that means he will run, and it would be surprising if the chairman of the Appropriations Committee in a pro-incumbent time were defeated.

Cook's Call. *Safe.* Based on presidential voting patterns, the 10th District should be at least competitive—if not Democratic. But Democrats have had little luck in even coming close to knocking off Young and, with Young now at the top of the Appropriations Committee, he's unlikely to lose. But when he does step down, Democrats have at least a 50–50 shot of picking up this seat.

The People: Pop. 1990: 562,301; 27.1% age 65 +; 88.7% White, 9.3% Black, 1.4% Asian, 0.3% Amer. Indian, 0.4% Other; 2.2% Hispanic Origin. Households: 48.1% married couple families; 15.1% married couple fams. w. children; 44.1% college educ.; median household income: $25,145; per capita income: $15,124; median house value: $69,000; median gross rent: $380.

1996 Presidential Vote			1992 Presidential Vote		
Clinton (D)	120,716	(52%)	Clinton (D)	107,121	(40%)
Dole (R)	89,928	(38%)	Bush (R)	96,956	(36%)
Perot (I)	23,579	(10%)	Perot (I)	63,765	(24%)

Rep. C. W. (Bill) Young (R)

Elected 1970; b. Dec. 16, 1930, Harmarville, PA; home, Indian Rocks Beach; United Methodist; married (Beverly).

Military Career: Army Natl. Guard, 1948–57.

Elected Office: FL Senate, 1960–70, Minority Ldr., 1966–70.

Professional Career: Aide, U.S. Rep. William Cramer, 1957–60.

DC Office: 2407 RHOB 20515, 202-225-5961; Fax: 202-225-9764.

District Offices: Largo, 813-581-0980; St. Petersburg, 813-893-3191.

Committees: *Appropriations* (Chmn. of 34 R): Defense; Labor, HHS & Education.

Group Ratings

	ADA	ACLU	AFS	LCV	CON	NTU	NFIB	COC	ACU	NTLC	CHC
1998	0	8	0	15	2	63	92	93	90	86	83
1997	10	—	29	—	34	44	—	100	79	—	—

National Journal Ratings

	1997 LIB — 1997 CONS		1998 LIB — 1998 CONS	
Economic	46%	— 53%	22%	— 78%
Social	39%	— 61%	21%	— 79%
Foreign	19%	— 80%	42%	— 57%

Key Votes of the 105th Congress

1. Clinton Budget Deal	Y	5. Puerto Rico Sthood. Ref.	N	9. Cut $ for B-2 Bombers	N
2. Education IRAs	Y	6. End Highway Set-asides	Y	10. Human Rights in China	*
3. Req. 2/3 to Raise Taxes	Y	7. School Prayer Amend.	Y	11. Withdraw Bosnia Troops	N
4. Fast-track Trade	Y	8. Ovrd. Part. Birth Veto	*	12. End Cuban TV-Marti	N

Election Results

1998 general	C.W. (Bill) Young (R) .... unopposed			($178,796)
1998 primary	C.W. (Bill) Young (R) .... unopposed			
1996 general	C.W. (Bill) Young (R)	114,443	(67%)	($265,355)
	Henry Green (D)	57,375	(33%)	($36,554)

ELEVENTH DISTRICT

Tampa is one of America's boom towns whose history goes back just a little more than a century. Its industrial past can be traced to 1886, when Cuban cigar-makers left Key West for what became the Ybor City neighborhood of Tampa. Soon after, it was the major takeoff spot for U.S. troops in the Spanish-American War of 1898. It also became a major citrus distribution center. The old industrial city developed along the waterfront, where today you can find the world's longest sidewalk (6.5 miles along Bayshore Boulevard) and still see the 13 minarets of Tampa pioneer Henry B. Plant's 1890s Arabian-style Tampa Bay Hotel (long since taken over by the University of Tampa). For a time, Tampa was Florida's one industrial city. Now, with a diversified economy, a fast-growing service sector, tourist attractions led by Busch Gardens, and a famously pleasant and convenient airport, it has moved ahead, with subdivisions and condominiums, office towers and low-rise commercial buildings spreading inland across swamps and lowlands.

Through all this, and in contrast to St. Petersburg with its many retirees, Tampa has remained a city of families and young people, a place with a blue-collar past which is quickly moving upscale as it expands—with a major league baseball franchise since 1995. The smell of cigars still wafts over Ybor City (though pollution controllers want to get rid of it) and Tampa is still an important military command center: Central Command, which ran the Gulf war, is head-quartered at the still-thriving MacDill Air Force Base, and General Norman Schwarzkopf remains a Tampa area resident.

The 11th Congressional District consists of Tampa and two-thirds of surrounding Hillsborough County. Tampa was historically Democratic as St. Petersburg was Republican, but in fact the two sides of Tampa Bay have more or less converged politically; in the 1992 and 1996 Florida governor races Tampa and Hillsborough cast higher percentages for Republican Jeb Bush. But the 11th District voted twice for Bill Clinton.

The congressman from the 11th District is Jim Davis, a Democrat first elected in 1996. Davis grew up in Tampa, returned after law school, was elected in 1988, at 31, to the state House. There he showed insider skills and interests, favoring a requirement that criminals serve

85% of their sentences and rewriting the education formula to help Hillsborough County. After the 1992 election he was elected House majority leader—the last Democrat to hold that job, since Republicans won a majority in 1996. In 1996, 11th District Sam Gibbons decided to retire after 34 years, including seven months as Ways and Means chairman and a frustrating last two years in the majority. Davis was far from the best known candidate, but he showed great skill at raising money and was the only candidate running TV ads for the September 3 primary. Sandy Freedman, Tampa's mayor from 1986–95, led that contest, with 35%, and Davis came in second with 25%, just 274 votes ahead of County Commissioner Busansky. Attacks were thrown back and forth, but they did agree on some issues: both supported the balanced budget amendment, the 1996 welfare reform and called for more managed care. Davis won the runoff 56%–44% and then faced Republican Mark Sharpe in the general.

Sharpe was born at MacDill, where his father was stationed, and spent eight years in the Navy as an intelligence officer. In 1992, he ran against Gibbons and held him to a 53%–41% margin—startling, considering that Gibbons outspent him $960,000 to $51,000. In 1994 he ran again, this time spending $472,000; Gibbons spent $1.1 million, and won by only 52%–48%. In 1996 Sharpe had a tougher target. He attacked Davis as a fan of higher taxes and a career politician. But the *St. Petersburg Times* wrote that Sharpe admitted to making up poll numbers in his 1992 primary. The *Tampa Tribune* printed the shocking news that he had been teaching history at a Presbyterian school without certification. Davis insisted he was a New Democrat, supporting the Defense of Marriage Act and opposing the penny-per-pound sugar tax on the Florida ballot; he also called for more education spending. Davis won by a very solid 58%–42%.

In his first term Davis was elected the Democratic freshman class president and got a seat on the Budget Committee, where he worked to balance the budget. His voting record was one of the least liberal among Democrats. He favored a number of New Democrat causes: fast track on trade, federal funding of charter schools, the partial-birth abortion ban. He supported a freshman campaign finance bill, with a ban on soft money and disclosure for those spending more than $25,000 on issue advocacy ads. He pushed a Medicare anti-fraud bill passed in 1997. He called for more spending on education to reduce class size. Prompted by eviction of Medicaid beneficiaries from a Tampa nursing home, he joined Republican Michael Bilirakis and Senator Bob Graham in sponsoring a bill to stop such evictions, which Clinton signed in 1999. On impeachment, he started off saying, "I'm not in the camp of 'I believe the president.' I'm in the camp of 'Let's have a thorough investigation and learn the facts.' " But he voted against the Republicans' impeachment inquiry resolution and against impeachment.

All of this left Republicans with few targets in 1998. Their nominee, an architect and county commissioner, raised little money and promised "creative campaigning." Not creative enough: Davis won by 65%–35%, the biggest margin here since 1990.

Cook's Call. *Probably Safe.* Though this is hardly a safe Democratic district, Davis appears to have secured it for now, contingent upon any major changes in redistricting.

The People: Pop. 1990: 562,293; 1.2% rural; 12.6% age 65 + ; 78.8% White, 17.1% Black, 1.5% Asian, 0.4% Amer. Indian, 2.2% Other; 13.8% Hispanic Origin. Households: 46.1% married couple families; 20.7% married couple fams. w. children; 45.8% college educ.; median household income: $26,166; per capita income: $13,578; median house value: $66,600; median gross rent: $368.

1996 Presidential Vote

Clinton (D)	98,028	(52%)
Dole (R)	75,004	(40%)
Perot (I)	14,849	(8%)

1992 Presidential Vote

Clinton (D)	81,849	(41%)
Bush (R)	77,942	(39%)
Perot (I)	39,148	(20%)

Rep. Jim Davis (D)

Elected 1996; b. Oct. 11, 1957, Tampa; home, Tampa; Wash. & Lee U., B.A. 1979, U. of FL, J.D. 1982; Episcopalian; married (Peggy).

Elected Office: FL House of Reps., 1988–96, Majority Ldr. 1994–96.

Professional Career: Practicing atty., 1982–96.

DC Office: 418 CHOB 20515, 202-225-3376; Fax: 202-225-5652; Web site: www.house.gov/jimdavis.

District Office: Tampa, 813-354-9217.

Committees: *Budget* (7th of 19 D). *House Administration* (3d of 3 D). *International Relations* (17th of 23 D): Asia & the Pacific; Western Hemisphere. *Joint Committee on the Library of Congress* (5th of 6 Reps.).

Group Ratings

	ADA	ACLU	AFS	LCV	CON	NTU	NFIB	COC	ACU	NTLC	CHC
1998	85	56	89	69	93	22	43	67	16	24	17
1997	75	—	63	—	99	37	—	60	16	—	—

National Journal Ratings

	1997 LIB — 1997 CONS		1998 LIB — 1998 CONS	
Economic	66%	— 34%	59%	— 41%
Social	64%	— 35%	60%	— 38%
Foreign	60%	— 40%	75%	— 23%

Key Votes of the 105th Congress

1. Clinton Budget Deal	N	5. Puerto Rico Sthood. Ref.	Y
2. Education IRAs	N	6. End Highway Set-asides	N
3. Req. 2/3 to Raise Taxes	N	7. School Prayer Amend.	N
4. Fast-track Trade	Y	8. Ovrd. Part. Birth Veto	Y

9. Cut $ for B-2 Bombers	Y
10. Human Rights in China	N
11. Withdraw Bosnia Troops	N
12. End Cuban TV-Marti	N

Election Results

1998 general	Jim Davis (D)	85,262	(65%)	($756,141)
	Joe Chillura (R)	46,176	(35%)	($48,041)
1998 primary	Jim Davis (D)	unopposed		
1996 general	Jim Davis (D)	108,500	(58%)	($935,314)
	Mark Sharpe (R)	78,856	(42%)	($755,184)

TWELFTH DISTRICT

With their skyscrapers rising over bays and rivers, the great gleaming cities of Florida are found near the Atlantic or Gulf coasts. Inland are parts of the state that were most heavily settled half a century ago. One is Polk County, the biggest inland county in Florida, with its small lakes and small cities of Lakeland, Bartow, Lake Wales and Winter Haven scattered about. The citrus business is still a mainstay of the local economy and orange groves abound, although periodic freezes have convinced some growers to move south or to produce tomatoes instead. Turpentine distilleries, dependent on the big stands of pine, and phosphate mining businesses can be found also; there are more manufacturing jobs here proportionally (though not that many) than almost anywhere else in Florida. Retired *Ladies Home Journal* editor Edward Bok built the most prominent landmarks here, the gothic Bok Tower and the surrounding Mountain Lake Sanctuary and gardens. But little of Bok's prestige remains here and the area has not become a major retiree haven.

Polk County historically was Democratic, the home of Spessard Holland and Lawton Chiles; Holland was senator 1946–71, after serving as governor, and Chiles was senator 1970–88 and then was elected governor in 1990 and 1994. But as in most of the Deep South, Republicans have picked up strength in Polk County. Chiles kept it in the Democratic column and stopped Republicans from picking up the two seats they needed for a state Senate majority in 1990. But it voted Republican in the 1990s, for George Bush and Bob Dole, for Jeb Bush against Chiles in 1994 and with a 59% majority in 1998.

The 12th District includes all but the northeast edge of Polk County, plus the western, rapidly suburbanizing edge of Tampa's Hillsborough County. It extends into old-fashioned Florida agricultural country north of Polk County, around Dade City in Pasco County, and to the south, in Hardee, DeSoto and a slice of Highlands counties. Historically Democratic, this has been a Republican seat since Congressman Andy Ireland switched parties in 1984.

The congressman from the 12th is Charles Canady, first elected in 1992. He grew up in Lakeland, went to Haverford College and Yale Law School, then practiced law in Lakeland; his father, Charles E. Canady, served for 18 years as Lawton Chiles's top staffer in Florida and Washington. The younger Canady was elected to the Florida House in 1984, at 30, served as majority whip, and switched parties in 1989, saying he had little in common with liberal Democrats. In 1990 he ran for the state Senate and, as Chiles swept Polk County, lost. In 1992, Canady ran for Congress. He was unopposed in the Republican primary but trailed Democratic legislator Tom Mims in the early polls. But Canady pledged to serve only four terms and attacked Mims sharply in mailings and in the end with TV spots calling him pro-tax and antibusiness, and won 52%–48%.

In a short time Canady became one of the most productive and effective members of the House. In his first two years he compiled a conservative voting record, opposing NAFTA because of citrus and tomato growers' concerns and voting for the 1994 crime bill. After the 1994 elections, Judiciary Chairman Henry Hyde named him chairman of the Constitution Subcommittee, one of the busiest and most controversial in the House. Canady is hard-working and soft-spoken ("when he was a kid, what he did for fun was read the encyclopedia," his father once said), strong in his convictions but businesslike in demeanor, bright enough to keep up with the subcommittee's ranking Democrat, Barney Frank, and a strong partisan Republican but willing to work with Frank and other Democrats on occasion. His first major bill was the private property protection bill, passed by the House as part of the Contract with America in March 1995, but never acted on by the Senate. He floor managed a bill to allow seniors-only housing; it passed the House in April 1995 and became law in December. Perhaps his biggest achievement was lobbying reform, where he worked with Frank and other Democrats, struggling to keep out maximalist amendments which would have doomed the bill while retaining its substance. As *National Journal*'s Eliza Newlin Carney wrote, "Canady's success on the lobby legislation, which was threatened with myriad roadblocks, reflected a combination of skilled coalition-building and legislative elbow grease." It was passed in November 1995 and was signed in December. In April 1996 Canady also led the fight for two key prison reforms, discouraging court-imposed limits on prison populations and curbing frivolous prisoner lawsuits; it was signed that month. Canady also managed the Defense of Marriage Act, grudgingly signed by Bill Clinton in September 1996.

Canady has had less success with other causes. He is chief sponsor of measures to ban racial quotas and preferences in federal hiring, contracting and program administration. "I want to look at the right kind of affirmative action—affirmative action that doesn't discriminate." But in 1995, even though (or perhaps because) his Senate sponsor was Bob Dole, it never came up. He persisted in 1997, but was beaten in committee when George Gekas opposed his bill; he tried to compromise by adding a requirement that federal agencies engage in outreach. He was stymied again when a similar measure died in committee. Canady was also chief House

422   FLORIDA

sponsor of the partial-birth abortion ban, which passed the House twice, in March 1997, and the Senate in 1998. The House had enough votes to override Bill Clinton's veto, but the Senate by a narrow margin did not. His English-as-the-official-language bill passed the House in August 1996, but not the Senate. On local matters, he has supported additional judgeships for the Middle District of Florida, though they would be appointed by Clinton, and he wants to do something about the Medicare HMOs that pulled out of Polk County in 1998.

Canady was an appellate lawyer in Polk County, and in the impeachment case he showed impressive skills as an advocate—original legal scholarship, a tightly disciplined use of language, strong powers of argument. For him early on Clinton's offenses were impeachable: "Unless evidence is forthcoming to rebut what I have heard so far, I will vote in favor of articles of impeachment." His argument to the Senate on the definition of impeachment under the Constitution brought praise even from pro-Clinton law professors.

Canady was re-elected without opposition in 1998. He insists he will keep to his term-limits pledge and not run in 2000; the fact that he raised little money in 1998 suggests he meant it when he said, "Come noon, January 1, 2001, I will be somewhere other than here."

Cook's Call. *Potentially Competitive.* With Canady abiding by his pledge to serve only three terms, Republicans are forced to defend this open seat in 2000. The seat has Republican leanings, however, and it is not yet clear whether Democrats can recruit the type of conservative candidate needed to be competitive here. In early 1999, Republicans seem to have settled on young, conservative state Representative Adam Putnam. On the Democratic side is state Senator Lori Edwards.

The People: Pop. 1990: 562,381; 33.7% rural; 17.8% age 65+; 84.2% White, 12.7% Black, 0.6% Asian, 0.4% Amer. Indian, 2.2% Other; 5.8% Hispanic Origin. Households: 60.4% married couple families; 25.7% married couple fams. w. children; 34.8% college educ.; median household income: $25,315; per capita income: $12,277; median house value: $62,200; median gross rent: $297.

1996 Presidential Vote

Dole (R) 96,140 (47%)
Clinton (D) 89,296 (43%)
Perot (I) 20,770 (10%)

1992 Presidential Vote

Bush (R) 90,694 (46%)
Clinton (D) 68,487 (34%)
Perot (I) 39,770 (20%)

Rep. Charles Canady (R)

Elected 1992; b. June 22, 1954, Lakeland; home, Lakeland; Haverford Col., B.A. 1976, Yale Law Schl., J.D. 1979; Presbyterian; married (Jennifer).

Elected Office: FL House of Reps., 1984–90.

Professional Career: Practicing atty., 1979–92.

DC Office: 2432 RHOB 20515, 202-225-1252; Fax: 202-225-2279; Web site: www.house.gov/canady.

District Office: Lakeland, 941-688-2651.

Committees: *Agriculture* (7th of 27 R): Department Operations, Oversight, Nutrition & Forestry. *Judiciary* (8th of 21 R): Crime; Immigration & Claims; The Constitution (Chmn.).

Group Ratings

	ADA	ACLU	AFS	LCV	CON	NTU	NFIB	COC	ACU	NTLC	CHC
1998	5	6	11	15	21	53	93	89	88	89	92
1997	10	—	13	—	49	54	—	100	92	—	—

National Journal Ratings

	1997 LIB — 1997 CONS			1998 LIB — 1998 CONS		
Economic	28%	—	67%	34%	—	64%
Social	0%	—	90%	3%	—	90%
Foreign	12%	—	81%	7%	—	83%

Key Votes of the 105th Congress

1. Clinton Budget Deal	Y	5. Puerto Rico Sthood. Ref.	N	9. Cut $ for B-2 Bombers	N
2. Education IRAs	Y	6. End Highway Set-asides	Y	10. Human Rights in China	N
3. Req. 2/3 to Raise Taxes	Y	7. School Prayer Amend.	Y	11. Withdraw Bosnia Troops	Y
4. Fast-track Trade	N	8. Ovrd. Part. Birth Veto	Y	12. End Cuban TV-Marti	N

Election Results

1998 general	Charles Canady (R)	unopposed		($116,254)
1998 primary	Charles Canady (R)	unopposed		
1996 general	Charles Canady (R)	122,584	(62%)	($213,131)
	Michael Canady (D)	76,513	(38%)	($12,818)

THIRTEENTH DISTRICT

Everyone else followed the circus to Sarasota. When the Ringling Brothers made a success of the circus they founded in the 1880s, they needed a place for performers and animals to rest during the winter months. They settled on the bayfront village behind a barrier island along the Gulf of Mexico. It was just far enough north to be reachable by railroad, just far enough south to be semitropical so the elephants would not get sick and die. Here, John Ringling established the Ringling Museum of Art, with its huge sculpture garden and built his own Venetian palace, the Ca'd'Zan. After World War II, when people began spending their retirement years in warmer climates, the Gulf Coast started attracting new settlers—affluent, WASPy Republicans from upper crust suburbs of northern cities. The population exploded, with Manatee and Sarasota counties growing from 63,000 in 1950 to 489,000 in 1990.

The 13th Congressional District includes Sarasota and Manatee counties and slivers of Tampa's Hillsborough County on the north and Charlotte County on the south. It is mostly a collection of Gulf Coast towns, from Tampa Bay south past Venice (where the circus now has its winter quarters). It is retiree country: almost 32% of the people here in 1990 were 65 or older (the highest percentage is the 22d District, the Gold Coast beachfront). The 13th is also very heavily Republican, with the second highest Republican registration of any Florida district (the highest is the 14th, just to the south).

The congressman from the 13th District is Dan Miller, a Republican first elected in 1992. Miller is a native of Michigan, with an M.B.A. and a Ph.D., who taught economics at Georgia State and then moved to Bradenton in the 1970s and practiced economics, starting small businesses—the Memorial Pier Restaurant, the Suncoast Manor Nursing Center, the Barnett Bank Building and Riverview Center. He served on local commissions, the hospital board of directors and the judicial nominating commission. After the 1992 redistricting, Congressman Andy Ireland, who had represented most of the new 12th and 13th Districts, retired. Miller was one of five Republicans and two Democrats running for the seat. Calling for less government, fewer regulations, and lower taxes, he ran second in the primary, 143 votes behind former Bush Administration appointee Brad Baker; in the runoff, with Ireland's endorsement, Miller won 53%–47%. Against Democrat Brad Snell, former aide to Lawton Chiles, he won 58%–42%.

Miller's voting record has been conservative on economics and moderate on cultural issues: He voted for the assault weapons ban and has supported abortion rights. He has taken some political risks. He spearheaded opposition to the Clinton health care plan in 1993 and 1994 and helped put together the Republican Medicare proposal in 1995. One area of spending he looks favorably on is medical research: He worked to appropriate more than Clinton requested for the National Institutes of Health and the Centers for Disease Control and Prevention. Every year he conducts a Congressional Classroom program, started by his predecessor Andy Ireland, bringing one junior from every high school in the district to meet Washington leaders and stage a mock Congress.

Miller has embarked on several crusades in his years in Congress. The first was against the sugar program, which places quotas on imports from other nations and subsidizes U.S. producers because the domestic price is double the world price—"corporate welfare," in Miller's view. It increases prices to U.S. consumers by more than $1 billion a year. It has stimulated overproduction in Florida and the phosphorus runoff has killed nourishing plants and wildlife in the Everglades. In 1995 Miller and Democrat Charles Schumer led an effort to kill the program; it was maintained in committee, to provide enough votes to pass the Freedom to Farm Act; in February 1996 their amendment lost on the floor by only 217–208. Miller has persisted, but has not come as close since. Another Miller cause is renegotiating the extradition treaty with Mexico. He was outraged when Mexico refused to extradite a man who murdered a Sarasota mother of six, even after the district attorney waived (as the treaty allows Mexico to demand) capital punishment. In September 1998 he got the House to urge renegotiation by voice vote. In February 1998 Miller formed a "Keep the Caps" coalition, to uphold the May 1997 budget agreement; he endorsed John Kasich's budget resolution in May 1998. He voted against the transportation bill in April 1998 (though it contained a Sarasota project) as having "more pork than a Memphis barbecue."

Then there is the Census. In a September 1997 floor debate he attacked the Clinton Administration proposal for Census sampling, pointing out that his Ph.D. is in marketing and statistics. "I used to make the statement, 'Tell me the point you want to make, and I will prove it with statistics,' because it can be done," he said. In November, just two weeks after he got a temporary slot on the Government Operations Committee, he was made chairman of a new Census Subcommittee; the issue had been handled by a panel headed by Dennis Hastert, now speaker. The Census has become a major struggle between Clinton and Congress. Miller argues that the Clinton plan to headcount just 90% of the population (instead of the 98.2% counted in 1990) and to use a 750,000-person sample to adjust the count leaves open the possibility of fraud (the sample would be conducted by local people, perhaps chosen by political operatives) and requires a far larger and faster survey than the Census Bureau has ever conducted. His position was strengthened in January 1999 when the Supreme Court upheld two appeals court decisions and said the sampling plan could not be used for apportionment of House seats among the states. The administration then said it would conduct two counts, and that sample-produced numbers could be used for redistricting within states; Miller, who has authorized larger sums than the administration requested in order to improve the head count, has said he will not support funding for two counts. In May 1999, as part of the $15 military spending bill, the House agreed to finance the Census Bureau for the summer—a sign that Republicans may be backing off their opposition to sampling, much to Miller's chagrin.

Miller has won re-election easily.

Cook's Call. *Safe.* Miller should have little difficult holding onto the Republican-leaning 13th District in 2000.

The People: Pop. 1990: 562,501; 10.8% rural; 31.8% age 65 + ; 92.7% White, 5.4% Black, 0.6% Asian, 0.3% Amer. Indian, 1% Other; 4.2% Hispanic Origin. Households: 57.9% married couple families; 15.6% married couple fams. w. children; 44.7% college educ.; median household income: $27,616; per capita income: $16,254; median house value: $81,800; median gross rent: $425.

1996 Presidential Vote			1992 Presidential Vote		
Dole (R)	133,005	(47%)	Bush (R)	124,394	(43%)
Clinton (D)	122,884	(43%)	Clinton (D)	100,831	(35%)
Perot (I)	29,634	(10%)	Perot (I)	65,283	(22%)

Rep. Dan Miller (R)

Elected 1992; b. May 30, 1942, Highland Park, MI; home, Bradenton; U. of FL, B.S./B.A. 1964, Emory U., M.B.A. 1965, Louisiana St. U., Ph.D. 1970; Episcopalian; married (Glenda).

Professional Career: Businessman, Miller Enterprises, 1973–present; Asst. Prof., Georgia St. U., 1969–73; Adjunct Prof., U. of S. FL, 1975–83.

DC Office: 102 CHOB 20515, 202-225-5015; Fax: 202-226-0828; Web site: www.house.gov/danmiller.

District Offices: Bradenton, 941-747-9081; Sarasota, 941-951-6643.

Committees: *Appropriations* (18th of 34 R): Commerce, Justice, State & the Judiciary; Labor, HHS & Education; Military Construction. *Government Reform* (16th of 24 R): Census (Chmn.); Civil Service; Postal Service.

Group Ratings

	ADA	ACLU	AFS	LCV	CON	NTU	NFIB	COC	ACU	NTLC	CHC
1998	10	40	11	31	92	78	100	76	88	95	83
1997	20	—	25	—	96	64	—	100	84	—	—

National Journal Ratings

	1997 LIB — 1997 CONS	1998 LIB — 1998 CONS
Economic	19% — 76%	0% — 88%
Social	45% — 54%	44% — 55%
Foreign	24% — 72%	33% — 66%

Key Votes of the 105th Congress

1. Clinton Budget Deal	Y	5. Puerto Rico Sthood. Ref.	N	9. Cut $ for B-2 Bombers	Y
2. Education IRAs	Y	6. End Highway Set-asides	Y	10. Human Rights in China	N
3. Req. 2/3 to Raise Taxes	Y	7. School Prayer Amend.	N	11. Withdraw Bosnia Troops	Y
4. Fast-track Trade	Y	8. Ovrd. Part. Birth Veto	Y	12. End Cuban TV-Marti	N

Election Results

1998 general	Dan Miller (R)	unopposed		($191,313)
1998 primary	Dan Miller (R)	unopposed		
1996 general	Dan Miller (R)	173,671	(64%)	($387,149)
	Sanford Gordon (D)	96,098	(36%)	($73,500)

FOURTEENTH DISTRICT

On the edge of the Tropics, in a physical environment once teeming with diseases and inhospitable to advanced civilization only two generations ago, Florida's Gulf Coast has sprung up as a model of what America will be for many when they retire. The wide white sand beaches with gentle breakers, the inlets and broad estuaries that abound for boating, the wetlands filled with exotic birds, made this prime resort country: Thomas Edison had his winter home in Fort Myers, Henry Ford used to visit here, Walter Reuther, after his gunshot wound, recuperated by building a modest house near the Caloosahatchee River. But the local economy could not support many permanent residents, and at the beginning of World War II, there were only 68,000 people living on the Gulf Coast from Sarasota south to Naples.

By 1990 there were 1.1 million: the climate and environment attracted affluent suburbanites from the Midwest and Northeast, with the added lure of no state income or inheritance taxes.

Developers like Barron Collier, who built the Tamiami Trail across the Everglades and designed Naples with the wealthy in mind (and gave his name to Collier County, the richest in Florida), were determined to avoid the high-rise canyons that line the Atlantic from Miami to Palm Beach. The alternative has been low-rise, city-sized developments like Cape Coral and Port Charlotte, with canals in most backyards, and thinly paved roads along the sand spits next to the sultry, lapping waves of the Gulf, or the luxurious town of Naples set amid preserved coastal islands and interior swamps. This is very much retirement country, with more than one in four residents over 65. The 14th Congressional District occupies the southern half of this Gulf Coast, from Charlotte County past Cape Coral and Fort Myers south to Naples. This district has the highest Republican registration of any in Florida, and continually casts among the highest Republican percentages.

The congressman from the 14th is Porter Goss, a Republican first elected in 1988, who worked 10 years in the CIA's Clandestine Services and then moved to Sanibel Island (whose famous shells are now scarce). There he founded a prize-winning newspaper, served on the city council and passed growth management laws and was appointed to the Lee County Commission by then-Governor Bob Graham. When incumbent Connie Mack ran for the Senate in 1988, Goss ran for this seat and effectively won it in the Republican primary, leading 38%–29%–19% over former Congressman Skip Bafalis and retired General Jim Dozier.

Goss's voting record has been mostly conservative and he has advanced proposals suggesting an active and original mind. In line with Gulf Coast opinion, he is something of an environmentalist; he has worked to extend, and wants to make permanent, the 1982 moratorium on oil drilling in the Outer Continental Shelf of the Gulf. He has also worked to increase Everglades funding above the $200 million voted in the 1995 farm bill. Goss is also something of a reformer. He pushed for the gift ban and has his own campaign finance reform proposal. He proposed charging members $600 from their office accounts for each insertion of extraneous matter into the *Congressional Record*. He introduced legislation to repeal the Ramspeck Act, a measure passed in 1940 to make it easier for displaced Hill staffers to enter the civil service system. He is the chief sponsor of the Ricky Ray Hemophilia Relief Fund Act, which compensates hemophiliacs who contracted AIDS through tainted transfusions. Ricky Ray was one of three south Florida brothers so infected; Goss introduced the bill in 1995 and it became law in October 1998. It sets up a $750 million fund to provide $100,000 to each recipient. "If there is ever any reason to serve in public this is it," Goss said when it passed the Senate.

Goss is chairman of the Intelligence Committee and second ranking Republican on Rules. On Intelligence he led efforts in 1998 to increase intelligence spending in the October 1998 omnibus budget bill. "There is no question in my view that we have hollowed out our defense unnecessarily, including our intelligence, and we have to rebuild," he said. He intended the increased spending to enable intelligence agencies to recapitalize technological intelligence collection, rebuild espionage capabilities, develop the ability to respond with covert action to transnational threats and hostile states and to increase analytic depth and breadth. He also calls on intelligence agencies to do more to learn about the drug trade in Latin America. He supported the bill to spend $2 billion on drug interdiction and $880 million for a national media campaign against drugs.

On Rules he has operated in tandem with the Republican leadership. He has called for changing the budget process so that Congress and the president would early on agree on a budget resolution. He served on the ethics committee from 1991–96, where he had to deal with the partisan contentiousness over the charges Democrats brought against Newt Gingrich. "I think we are going to have to make some procedural changes in order to get the politics out of the ethics process, or we are going to have to give up trying to pretend that we are conducting an efficient and responsible ethics oversight role amongst ourselves," he said. He has proposed a jury system so that randomly chosen panel members would investigate ethics complaints. On local matters, he has pushed for a new VA outpatient clinic and a new federal courthouse in Fort Myers and expansion of the Southwest Florida International Airport. Every year he conducts a Congressional Classroom program bringing one junior from every high school in the district to meet Washington leaders and stage a mock Congress.

Goss has been re-elected without difficulty.

Cook's Call. *Safe.* Goss hasn't had a real race since he first won the seat in 1982. He is heavily favored to win in this Republican district in 2000.

The People: Pop. 1990: 562,489; 17.8% rural; 26.4% age 65 + ; 91.9% White, 5.6% Black, 0.5% Asian, 0.3% Amer. Indian, 1.7% Other; 6.4% Hispanic Origin. Households: 61.3% married couple families; 17.9% married couple fams. w. children; 44% college educ.; median household income: $29,620; per capita income: $17,165; median house value: $90,900; median gross rent: $434.

1996 Presidential Vote

Dole (R) 140,921 (51%)
Clinton (D) 105,027 (38%)
Perot (I) 29,735 (11%)

1992 Presidential Vote

Bush (R) 129,493 (46%)
Clinton (D) 87,978 (31%)
Perot (I) 63,175 (23%)

Rep. Porter J. Goss (R)

Elected 1988; b. Nov. 26, 1938, Waterbury, CT; home, Sanibel; Yale U., B.A. 1960; Presbyterian; married (Mariel).

Military Career: Army Intelligence, 1960–62.

Elected Office: Sanibel City Cncl., 1974–82; Sanibel Mayor, 1974–77, 1980; Lee Cnty. Commissioner 1983–88.

Professional Career: CIA Clandestine Svcs. 1960–71; Business-man & newspaper publ., 1973–78.

DC Office: 108 CHOB 20515, 202-225-2536; Fax: 202-225-6820; Web site: www.house.gov/goss.

District Offices: Ft. Myers, 941-332-4677; Naples, 941-774-8060; Punta Gorda, 941-639-0051.

Committees: *Permanent Select Committee on Intelligence* (Chmn. of 9 R). *Rules* (2d of 9 R): The Legislative & Budget Process (Chmn.).

Group Ratings

	ADA	ACLU	AFS	LCV	CON	NTU	NFIB	COC	ACU	NTLC	CHC
1998	5	19	14	31	46	72	100	86	91	89	100
1997	10	—	13	—	76	59	—	80	88	—	—

National Journal Ratings

	1997 LIB — 1997 CONS	1998 LIB — 1998 CONS
Economic	19% — 76%	0% — 88%
Social	10% — 82%	36% — 64%
Foreign	29% — 70%	43% — 53%

Key Votes of the 105th Congress

1. Clinton Budget Deal	Y	5. Puerto Rico Sthood. Ref.	N	9. Cut $ for B-2 Bombers	N
2. Education IRAs	Y	6. End Highway Set-asides	Y	10. Human Rights in China	N
3. Req. 2/3 to Raise Taxes	Y	7. School Prayer Amend.	Y	11. Withdraw Bosnia Troops	N
4. Fast-track Trade	*	8. Ovrd. Part. Birth Veto	Y	12. End Cuban TV-Marti	N

Election Results

1998 general	Porter J. Goss (R) .... unopposed			($158,856)
1998 primary	Porter J. Goss (R) .... unopposed			
1996 general	Porter J. Goss (R) 176,992	(73%)		($372,563)
	Jim Nolan (D) 63,842	(27%)		($19,596)

FIFTEENTH DISTRICT

When Cape Canaveral was chosen as the nation's rocket testing site in the 1940s, there were only 20,000 people in all of Brevard County, which stretches along 63 miles of the coast north and south of the Cape. It was a backward place with no industry, picked because it was the sunny Atlantic coast: rockets here have to be launched eastward so spent parts fall into the ocean. Today, Brevard County north and south of the Cape has nearly 500,000 people. It is a prototype of America's future, with no city center but plenty of shopping centers along strip highways, with a white-collar, service economy, knit together by interest in the space program.

The 15th Congressional District includes all of the Space Coast and Brevard County and extends south into Indian River County and the fast-growing retirement areas around Vero Beach. It continues west past the vast new town of Palm Bay, now the district's largest city, to what is left of primeval Florida. More may come: the Army Corps of Engineers, which straightened out the Kissimmee River in the early 1970s, is now seeking to restore it to its natural snake-like course, while nearby in the Three Lakes Wildlife Management Area, whooping cranes were released to propagate in the wild. The Space Coast is heavily Republican, distrustful of many national Democrats' disdain for the space program.

The congressman from the 15th is Dave Weldon, a Republican first elected in 1994. Weldon grew up on Long Island, went to medical school in Buffalo, served in the Army in Fort Stewart, Georgia, then in 1987 joined Melbourne Internal Medicine Associates in Florida. In 1989 he founded the Space Coast Family Forum "to promote family-friendly issues and positions." Weldon ran for the House in 1994, when moderate Democrat Jim Bacchus retired, and was considered a weak candidate because of his strong conservative views on cultural issues. He led the seven-candidate Republican primary, but with only 24% of the vote, and in the runoff won 54%–46% over Carole Jordan, who campaigned as a pro-choice moderate. Democrats ran a pro-choice former Republican and Space Coast Chamber of Commerce head, Sue Munsey. Weldon called for phasing out welfare and banning abortion; Munsey said Speaker Thomas Foley promised her a seat on the Science Committee.

Weldon won 54%–46%, and Speaker Newt Gingrich, whom Weldon called an "idol," gave him a seat on Science and made him vice chairman of the Space and Aeronautics Subcommittee. Weldon started off defending the Kennedy Space Center and promoting the Space Shuttle, protecting their funding even when NASA funding was going down. But in time he moved from defending an existing program to transforming it. With Senator Bob Graham, he sponsored a bill passed in October 1998 to move toward commercialization of space. The idea was to increase U.S. commercial launching capacity, by using antiquated (and disposable) ballistic missiles; the U.S. currently produces 77% of commercial satellites, but has launching capacity for only about one-third of them; increased capacity would mean less reliance on countries like China, and less incentive for U.S. satellite companies to betray American technology to China, as some evidently did. The bill would also ease licensing requirements for commercial re-entry vehicles, to provide competition for NASA's Space Shuttle. And it orders NASA to improve its tracking machinery at launching sites. Weldon has continued to support the space station the U.S. is operating jointly with Russia, but has questioned whether Russia is providing the necessary financing.

Weldon continues to have a very conservative voting record; he favors revoking the marriage penalty, increased defense spending, a 17% flat tax, school vouchers and education IRAs. He has called for restoration of Brevard County beaches. He pestered Transportation Committee members so much for a $25 million earmark for widening two-lane U.S. 192 that they started referring to him as "192." But Weldon surprised many when he rejected a proposed VA hospital his predecessor had secured for the Space Coast; only an outpatient clinic was necessary, he said, and veterans' other needs could be taken care of in local hospitals. This struck hard at the rationale for the separate existence of a VA hospital system, not to mention the conventional wisdom that politicians should seek every available federal dime for their local districts; and Weldon was attacked for it by the 1996 Democratic nominee. On other fronts, Weldon attacked a "Murphy Brown" episode on medical marijuana in 1997 as medically inaccurate. And in July 1997 he passed 396–25 an amendment barring the National Park Service from posting "clothing-optional" signs at Playalinda Beach in the Canaveral National Seashore; Brevard County bars nude bathing as well as thongs, but defendants said that the federal permission overruled it. The president of the Florida Naturists attacked Weldon for charging the signs encouraged lewd behavior. Weldon said, "There are 20 other beaches these people can go to in Florida. My constituents don't want it in Brevard."

Weldon's reputation for outspoken conservatism—he is one of four members of Congress who home-schools his children—inspired strong opposition in 1996. But Weldon outraised his opponent and won 51%–43%–6%. In 1998 he had opposition in the primary and in the general was opposed by a ship's captain who had run as an independent in 1996. Weldon won the primary 79%–21% and the general 63%–37%—impressive margins.

Cook's Call. *Probably Safe.* While there is no doubt that this is a Republican-leaning district, it is also socially moderate, which may explain why Weldon has had a couple of close races here. Though quite conservative, Weldon is still not an easy target, and Democrats, with the right candidate in the right environment, could launch a credible race against him.

The People: Pop. 1990: 562,542; 17.8% rural; 19.2% age 65 + ; 90.2% White, 7.6% Black, 1.1% Asian, 0.4% Amer. Indian, 0.8% Other; 3.5% Hispanic Origin. Households: 59.3% married couple families; 22.1% married couple fams. w. children; 48.7% college educ.; median household income: $29,755; per capita income: $15,225; median house value: $75,500; median gross rent: $405.

1996 Presidential Vote			1992 Presidential Vote		
Dole (R)	125,430	(46%)	Bush (R)	117,206	(43%)
Clinton (D)	111,263	(41%)	Clinton (D)	83,507	(31%)
Perot (I)	34,594	(13%)	Perot (I)	69,605	(26%)

Rep. Dave Weldon (R)

Elected 1994; b. Aug. 31, 1953, Amityville, NY; home, Palm Bay; S.U.N.Y. Stony Brook, B.A. 1978, S.U.N.Y. Buffalo, M.D. 1981; Christian; married (Nancy).

Military Career: Army Medical Corps, 1981–87, Army Reserves, 1987–92.

Professional Career: Practicing physician, 1987–94.

DC Office: 332 CHOB 20515, 202-225-3671; Fax: 202-225-3516; Web site: www.house.gov/weldon.

District Office: Melbourne, 407-632-1776.

Committees: *Banking & Financial Services* (18th of 32 R): Domestic & International Monetary Policy; Financial Institutions & Consumer Credit. *Science* (12th of 25 R): Energy & Environment; Space & Aeronautics (Vice Chmn.).

Group Ratings

	ADA	ACLU	AFS	LCV	CON	NTU	NFIB	COC	ACU	NTLC	CHC
1998	0	13	0	15	42	54	93	89	92	92	100
1997	0	—	25	—	10	52	—	67	92	—	—

National Journal Ratings

	1997 LIB — 1997 CONS		1998 LIB — 1998 CONS	
Economic	24%	— 76%	19%	— 79%
Social	0%	— 90%	14%	— 81%
Foreign	0%	— 88%	7%	— 83%

Key Votes of the 105th Congress

1. Clinton Budget Deal	Y	5. Puerto Rico Sthood. Ref.	N	9. Cut $ for B-2 Bombers	N
2. Education IRAs	Y	6. End Highway Set-asides	Y	10. Human Rights in China	N
3. Req. 2/3 to Raise Taxes	Y	7. School Prayer Amend.	Y	11. Withdraw Bosnia Troops	Y
4. Fast-track Trade	Y	8. Ovrd. Part. Birth Veto	Y	12. End Cuban TV-Marti	N

Election Results

1998 general	Dave Weldon (R)	129,278	(63%)	($508,032)
	David Golding (D)	75,654	(37%)	($26,640)
1998 primary	Dave Weldon (R)	37,370	(79%)	
	Charles Talbot (R)	9,791	(21%)	
1996 general	Dave Weldon (R)	139,014	(51%)	($774,408)
	John L. Byron (D)	115,981	(43%)	($332,687)
	David Golding (I)	15,349	(6%)	

SIXTEENTH DISTRICT

Urban Florida has fanned far across the swamplands from its original nuclei in beachfront resort communities. Thus Palm Beach has spread out from its original locus at the Breakers Hotel, across Lake Worth and well beyond the less fashionable city of West Palm Beach: these are now just neighborhoods in a vast metropolitan area. Old beach towns, such as Hobe Sound, located northward along the ocean, have become the hub of extremely affluent developments that stretch all the way to Stuart in Martin County. Farther north, near the old town of Fort Pierce are larger, but more modest developments like Port St. Lucie. Entire square miles west and northwest of West Palm Beach have been reclaimed from swampland and made into condo communities surrounded by golf courses or tracts of factories and warehouses. Once, metro Palm Beach was a narrow stretch along Lake Worth; now it runs inland almost halfway to Lake Okeechobee.

The 16th Congressional District includes much of greater West Palm. Its boundaries include the beach towns from Jupiter north to Port St. Lucie, but they are convoluted to avoid the black-majority 23d District. The district also takes in many recently and soon-to-be developed parcels in inland Palm Beach County. One-sixth of the district's residents live in citrus and vegetable growing areas around Lake Okeechobee, and as far away as Sebring, site of an auto racing track: here is the source of the Everglades, the 50-mile-wide and six-inch-deep "river of grass" that flows slowly to the Gulf of Mexico. This is a Republican-leaning district, though much of Palm Beach County has been trending Democratic, and it can be competitive.

The congressman from the 16th District is Mark Foley, a Republican first elected in 1994. Foley was born in Massachusetts, moved to Florida at age 3, dropped out of Palm Beach Community College and opened The Lettuce Patch restaurant in Lake Worth at 20. He was active in politics, working for Democratic Congressman Paul Rogers; he was a real estate broker and served on civic boards. Foley was elected to the Lake Worth City Commission at 23, to the state House as a Republican in 1990 and the state Senate from a Democratic district in

1992. In 1994, when Republican Congressman Tom Lewis decided to retire after 12 years, he and the local Republican organization supported Foley, who won a three-way primary with 61% of the vote. In the general election he outraised the Democrat and outpolled him 58%–42%, though by only 52%–48% in Palm Beach County.

In the House, Foley's political skills caught the leadership's eye, and he was named one of 14 deputy whips and a member of task forces to abolish government departments. But Foley also displayed an independent streak and concentrated on issues with local ramifications—immigration and agriculture. He proved capable of shifting on issues, voting in 1995 to cut EPA monies and in 1996 against the cuts; his 1996 vote for repeal of the assault weapons ban contrasted with his support of some gun control measures in Florida. He supported funding of AIDS research, family planning, and public broadcasting. He pushed for the deportation of imprisoned illegal immigrants, and to amend the Constitution so that children born here are not automatically citizens. But he also worked to increase the number of immigrants admitted as farmworkers, although many overstay their visas and never return home.

Much of his work focused on the Everglades. In 1996 he got Newt Gingrich and Bob Dole to earmark $200 million for Everglades restoration—land acquisition and water filtration—into the farm bill. But he also took the side of the sugar industry, opposing the Florida referendum for a one-cent tax on sugar and opposing the Dan Miller-Charles Schumer effort to repeal the sugar program which imposes quotas on imports and doubles the U.S. price of sugar; Miller and Schumer argued that phosphorus runoff from sugar cultivation has killed off flora and fauna in the Everglades. The sugar program has not come up again, and Foley has continued to work for Everglades restoration, criticizing the Martin County Board of Commissioners for not acquiring the Allapattah Ranch; he unveiled in 1998 a 30-year, $8 billion plan to save the Everglades.

In his 1996 campaign, Foley described his record as "moderate, moderate, moderate." He was part of the Green Scissors Coalition seeking to eliminate expensive programs like the Gas Turbine Modular Helium Reactor. He sponsored an amendment to force insurance companies to open up records of policies of Holocaust victims. In 1998 his Volunteers for Children Act was passed; it would allow volunteer groups like the Boy Scouts to check records in the FBI database. He seeks to build an agricultural and science center in the northern part of the district.

Foley won re-election by 64%–36% in 1996 and was unopposed in 1998; he held "thank you" barbecues around the district and $609,000 cash on hand in mid-October. After the election he got a seat on Ways and Means; he has dissented from other Republicans on substantive issues but has been careful to stay loyal on procedural votes. Redistricting after the 2000 Census might be a problem for Foley, since Palm Beach County has been growing rapidly and growing more Democratic; the 16th had more registered voters in 1998 than any other Florida district. But the governor and legislature are both Republican, and Foley is likely to get a favorable district.

Cook's Call. *Safe.* Though there are certainly more Republican districts in Florida, Foley seems as safe as any incumbent can be. Foley took a look at running for Connie Mack's open Senate seat and then backed off, but don't be surprised to see him seek higher office down the road. For now, consider him safe.

The People: Pop. 1990: 561,856; 21.8% rural; 24.7% age 65 + ; 93.2% White, 3.9% Black, 0.8% Asian, 0.4% Amer. Indian, 1.8% Other; 6.2% Hispanic Origin. Households: 60.8% married couple families; 20.8% married couple fams. w. children; 44.9% college educ.; median household income: $30,582; per capita income: $16,952; median house value: $88,500; median gross rent: $483.

1996 Presidential Vote

Clinton (D) 131,252 (47%)
Dole (R) 116,630 (42%)
Perot (I) 29,321 (11%)

1992 Presidential Vote

Bush (R) 108,503 (39%)
Clinton (D) 98,154 (36%)
Perot (I) 68,543 (25%)

Rep. Mark Foley (R)

Elected 1994; b. Sept. 8, 1954, Newton, MA; home, West Palm Beach; Palm Beach Commun. Col., 1974; Catholic; single.

Elected Office: Lake Worth City Comm., 1977–83; Vice Mayor, 1983–84; FL House of Reps., 1990–92; FL Senate, 1992–94.

Professional Career: Restaurateur, 1974–84; Real estate broker, 1984–90.

DC Office: 113 CHOB 20515, 202-225-5792; Fax: 202-225-3132; Web site: www.house.gov/foley.

District Offices: Palm Beach Gardens, 561-627-6192; Port St. Lucie, 561-878-3181.

Committees: *Ways & Means* (23d of 23 R): Human Resources.

Group Ratings

	ADA	ACLU	AFS	LCV	CON	NTU	NFIB	COC	ACU	NTLC	CHC
1998	20	31	22	38	4	60	93	100	80	92	67
1997	30	—	13	—	84	59	—	100	84	—	—

National Journal Ratings

	1997 LIB — 1997 CONS		1998 LIB — 1998 CONS	
Economic	28%	— 67%	15%	— 81%
Social	50%	— 48%	53%	— 46%
Foreign	32%	— 65%	26%	— 73%

Key Votes of the 105th Congress

1. Clinton Budget Deal	Y	5. Puerto Rico Sthood. Ref.	Y	9. Cut $ for B-2 Bombers	Y
2. Education IRAs	Y	6. End Highway Set-asides	Y	10. Human Rights in China	N
3. Req. 2/3 to Raise Taxes	Y	7. School Prayer Amend.	Y	11. Withdraw Bosnia Troops	Y
4. Fast-track Trade	Y	8. Ovrd. Part. Birth Veto	Y	12. End Cuban TV-Marti	N

Election Results

1998 general	Mark Foley (R) .... unopposed			($399,472)
1998 primary	Mark Foley (R) .... unopposed			
1996 general	Mark Foley (R) 175,714	(64%)		($613,392)
	Jim Stuber (D) 98,827	(36%)		($84,523)

SEVENTEENTH DISTRICT

North from downtown Miami, alongside the railroad tracks that Henry Flagler built shortly after Miami was founded in 1896 and alongside I-95, Miami's main north-south artery, is the city's largest black community, stretching from the Orange Bowl near downtown Miami north through Allapattah and Liberty City toward the suburb of Opalocka. This has been a kind of frontierland in Miami, the scene where hostilities between Miami's blacks and its Cuban-American majority have been played out. In 1980, 18 people died in a riot after the acquittal of a police officer charged with killing a black insurance salesman; this was the first public crisis for Janet Reno, then in her first term as district attorney and now U.S. attorney general. Many Miami blacks have resented the economic upward mobility and political strength of the Cubans, the first generation of which rose while still speaking mostly Spanish, and of other Latins—including the Haitians in Little Haiti—who have been moving upward as well. There is a political dimension as well: blacks are Miami's most Democratic voting group, while Cuban-Americans usually vote heavily Republican.

The 17th Congressional District covers all of this territory, running along the I-95 and 27th Avenue corridors from the Miami River north to the Miami-Dade County line. The mostly white high-rise gated condominiums on the shore of Biscayne Bay and heavily Cuban Hialeah were carefully excluded from the district. It extends south along a narrow corridor on either side of Dixie Highway, expanding here and there to bring in heavily black areas all the way south to Homestead, site of Hurricane Andrew's worst damage in 1992.

The congresswoman from the 17th is Carrie Meek, a Democrat first elected in 1992. The granddaughter of a slave, Meek was born in Tallahassee and grew up near the old Capitol in a neighborhood called the Bottom. She was a gifted athlete when she attended Florida A&M's lab school; she went to Florida A&M and the University of Michigan (Florida government paid the tuition because its graduate schools were segregated). When she came back to Miami, she taught physical education at Miami-Dade Community College. Here she became active in politics and, when pioneer black legislator Gwen Cherry died in an auto accident, Meek was elected to the Florida House in 1978. Particularly effective in the legislature, Meek passed legislation to criminalize stalking, a Minority Business Enterprise law, and promoted literacy and dropout prevention programs. In the state Senate for a decade, she helped to draw the new 17th District after the 1990 Census. In this district she was clearly the best-known and best-liked politician and was nominated with 83% of the vote in the primary and elected with no Republican opposition.

Meek has had a very liberal record, except on some foreign policy issues; she is a strong critic of Fidel Castro. In her first term, she demonstrated her own determination and savvy by being the only freshman Democrat to win a seat on the Appropriations Committee. She said her first priority was creating jobs through federal programs and private initiatives to help blacks develop their own businesses and banks as, she notes, Cuban-Americans have. She worked successfully to change the rules for Social Security for household employees and sought to extend Supplemental Security Income to the aged, blind and handicapped legal aliens. The Republican capture of the House temporarily cost her her seat on Appropriations.

Meek has worked to pass a variety of bills: money for the Section 202 elderly housing program, funding for research on learning-disabled college students, funding for repairs after Hurricane Andrew. She is a strong advocate of Census sampling, and says there was a large undercount in her district in 1992: "My people died for the right to vote. And if you are going to skew the figures because you don't want to count them correctly, that removes the humor from this situation for me." After the Supreme Court ruled against sampling in January 1999, she persuaded Government Reform Census Subcommittee Chairman Dan Miller to support her bill to allow recipients of welfare to hold temporary census jobs without fear of losing benefits; the aim is to get a more accurate count of poor neighborhoods by using members of those communities to assist in the counting. She worked hard also to protect Haitian immigrants and refugees allowed to remain temporarily in the country but not included in the November 1997 Nicaraguan Adjustment and Central America Relief Act. In September 1998 she became vice chairwoman of the state Democratic Party after many blacks were furious when state Representative Willie Logan was dumped as speaker-designate in January.

Cook's Call. *Safe.* There are few members of Congress with safer seats than Meek in Miami's 17th District. She'll hold this seat as long as she wants it.

The People: Pop. 1990: 563,284; 10.4% age 65 + ; 36.6% White, 58.5% Black, 1.1% Asian, 0.2% Amer. Indian, 3.5% Other; 22.7% Hispanic Origin. Households: 40.5% married couple families; 22.4% married couple fams. w. children; 31.9% college educ.; median household income: $21,899; per capita income: $9,157; median house value: $64,100; median gross rent: $358.

1996 Presidential Vote

Clinton (D)	115,732	(85%)
Dole (R)	16,802	(12%)
Perot (I)	3,944	(3%)

1992 Presidential Vote

Clinton (D)	99,422	(74%)
Bush (R)	25,873	(19%)
Perot (I)	9,913	(7%)

Rep. Carrie P. Meek (D)

Elected 1992; b. Apr. 29, 1926, Tallahassee; home, Miami; FL A&M U., B.A. 1946, U. of MI, M.S. 1948; Primitive Baptist; divorced.

Elected Office: FL House of Reps, 1978–82; FL Senate 1982–92.

Professional Career: Admin., Miami-Dade Commun. Col., 1949–92.

DC Office: 401 CHOB 20515, 202-225-4506; Fax: 202-226-0777; Web site: www.house.gov/meek.

District Office: Miami, 305-381-9541.

Committees: *Appropriations* (17th of 27 D): Treasury, Postal Service & General Government; VA, HUD & Independent Agencies.

Group Ratings

	ADA	ACLU	AFS	LCV	CON	NTU	NFIB	COC	ACU	NTLC	CHC
1998	95	93	100	85	55	11	7	28	4	11	0
1997	80	—	100	—	11	19	—	40	17	—	—

National Journal Ratings

	1997 LIB — 1997 CONS		1998 LIB — 1998 CONS	
Economic	73% —	26%	79% —	0%
Social	85% —	0%	81% —	19%
Foreign	58% —	41%	73% —	26%

Key Votes of the 105th Congress

1. Clinton Budget Deal	N	5. Puerto Rico Sthood. Ref.	Y	9. Cut $ for B-2 Bombers	N
2. Education IRAs	N	6. End Highway Set-asides	N	10. Human Rights in China	Y
3. Req. 2/3 to Raise Taxes	N	7. School Prayer Amend.	N	11. Withdraw Bosnia Troops	N
4. Fast-track Trade	N	8. Ovrd. Part. Birth Veto	N	12. End Cuban TV-Marti	N

Election Results

1998 general	Carrie P. Meek (D)	unopposed		($267,089)
1998 primary	Carrie P. Meek (D)	unopposed		
1996 general	Carrie P. Meek (D)	114,638	(89%)	($257,039)
	Wellington Rolle (R)	14,525	(11%)	

EIGHTEENTH DISTRICT

A century ago it was a tiny tropical village where the Miami River empties into Biscayne Bay. Today it is a world-city, not just America's "Gateway to Latin America" but the "Capital of the Americas," as welcoming signs have proclaimed. The surrealistic high-rises of Brickell Boulevard, the reminders of the 1920s in the pseudo-Spanish Villa Vizcaya and the winding lanes of Coral Gables, the shimmer of orange and pink neon signs in the hot night air: the lights of the grid streets stretching for miles and then abruptly turning to darkness at the bayfront or the Everglades: this is Miami today. It lives on the cusp of two civilizations, North American and Latin American with different traditions, styles and sensibilities, converging in this one place, despite some friction, toward an amalgam with many strengths of both. Miami has become commercially and economically the capital of Latin America, the one place from which it is easiest to fly directly to any other part of Latin America, where top business and banking services are available to a sophisticated Spanish-speaking (and usually also English-speaking) clientele. And, with increasing tourism from Europe and in the trendy haunts of South Beach and Coconut Grove, Miami partakes of Europe as well.

The 1980s TV program "Miami Vice" showed the underside of Miami, the air of menace in streets where many are armed and vast quantities of drugs and cash regularly change hands and killings are not at all unusual. The news columns have focused on violence, the riots by blacks in 1980 and 1989, and on corruption, the shenanigans of the city's politicians in 1997 and 1998 when corruption charges were lodged at several officeholders and the mayor thrown out when the courts ruled that vote fraud produced his winning margin. But such episodes are common enough in the history of high-immigration American cities, and the negatives are often exaggerated: crime is down from the 1980s, the drug trade not as menacing, the city of Miami is just one small governmental unit in a giant county, recently renamed Miami-Dade, which provides most governmental services about as competently and honestly as most large American local governments. What is really striking about Miami is not its vices but its virtues—the vitality and creativity of entrepreneurs and artists, the cosmopolitan sophistication of people living and making their way ahead in two (or more) cultures, the successful Americanization of Cubans and other Latinos who make up more than half of Miami-Dade's population, together with the retention of a cultural flavor that is linked to the past but headed fast into the future.

John Quincy Adams believed that Cuba must inevitably become a part of the United States. That never happened, but a large part of the Cuban people have become Americans. And the epicenter of Cuban America has been, since the days the first refugees fled Fidel Castro's regime in 1959, Miami. That has caused a certain amount of resentment among those who were previously the majority. In the 1960s, as the Cuban population grew, the tone of Miami civic life was set by the large Jewish community and the liberal voice of the *Miami Herald*: Dade County was the one liberal Democratic bastion in a state dominated by George Wallace Democrats and rising conservative Republicans. But the Cubans, implacably opposed to the totalitarian Castro and estranged by John Kennedy's betrayal of their cause at the Bay of Pigs, entered the voting stream heavily Republican. The liberals bristled at comments like the late Cuban activist Jorge Mas Canosa's charges that the *Miami Herald* "manipulates information just like *Granma*," the Castro paper in Havana. On its face, the charge was absurd, yet it should be added that many goodhearted liberals have failed to appreciate the totalitarianism of Castro's regime and glossed over the brutality that has been its steady conduct. Typical was the liberal Miami politician who called the city's Cuban-Americans "emigres," the term leftists have used to disparage supposedly rich and selfish opponents of progressive revolutions since the French Revolution 200 years ago. Anglo-Americans, after years of politics in which the shades of difference between candidates are often subtle and in which basic liberties and property are not threatened, have a hard time understanding the enthusiasm of Americans with backgrounds in Latin America, where the differences between political creeds can be enormous and where liberties have frequently been in danger.

In the early 1960s Cubans were a noisy minority in the Miami area; now they are the dominant part of a Latino majority in Miami-Dade County. The Hispanic population is now more than 50%, blacks are about 20%, whites less than 30% and falling. South Florida's Jewish community has mostly moved north, to Broward and Palm Beach counties; elderly retirees from the Northeast have gone there, not to Miami-Dade, or to other parts of Florida. Other Latins have also come to Miami-Dade in large numbers, and form perhaps 40% of the Hispanic population: Little Havana around Calle Ocho (Southwest 8th Street in English) now has many

Nicaraguans, Hondurans and Peruvians; Spanish accents other than Cuban, and Haitian *patois*, are heard all over the county. Miami-Dade's Latinos tend to stay in the area, go to school at Miami-Dade Community College (one of the nation's largest) and Florida International University; they start businesses and practice professions in Miami's booming economy. Politically, Miami-Dade, once heavily Democratic, is now mostly Republican; it went for Bill Clinton in 1996, after he signed the Helms-Burton Act and responded angrily to the shooting down of two Brothers to the Rescue planes, but has soured on him since, as he has suspended Helms-Burton's operation and looked for ways to accommodate Castro.

The 18th Congressional District is one of two Hispanic-majority districts in Miami-Dade County, about two-thirds Cuban-American, and usually heavily Republican. It includes the corridor along Calle Ocho and spreads south and west toward Miami Airport and the suburb of Kendall. It stretches all the way down to Homestead, site of Hurricane Andrew's worst damage, and then extends back north, around the black-majority 17th, to include the neighborhoods of Coconut Grove and Miami Beach's trendy South Beach, with old art deco hotels that used to house elderly retirees now a temporary home to the glitziest celebrities of North America, Latin America and Europe.

The representative from the 18th District is Ileana Ros-Lehtinen, the first Cuban-American elected to Congress. She was born in Cuba, came to Miami at 7, graduated from Miami-Dade Community College and Florida International University. She became a teacher, then was the owner of a private school. She was elected to the Florida House in 1982, at 30, and to the state Senate in 1986; her husband Dexter Lehtinen also served in both houses of the legislature and served as U.S. Attorney in Miami as well. Ros-Lehtinen ran for the House in the special election called after the death in May 1989 of Claude Pepper, one of the most enduring liberals in American politics and a staunch opponent of Castro, who was chairman of the House Rules Committee and a great champion of Social Security. This was an acrimonious contest, and voting ran almost entirely on ethnic lines: exit polls showed that 96% of blacks and 88% of non-Hispanic whites voted for Democratic nominee Gerald Richman, while 90% of Hispanics voted for Ros-Lehtinen. Hispanic turnout was 58%, compared to 42% for non-Hispanic whites, and Ros-Lehtinen won with 53%. With a much more heavily Latino district since, she has won without serious opposition.

Ros-Lehtinen has a mixed voting record, moderate on economics and foreign policy, conservative on cultural issues. Despite the long-term local economic benefit, she opposed NAFTA (which extends only to Mexico), and spoke out against it. She refused to sign the Contract with America in 1994, and in 1995 and 1996 was a harsh critic of Republican attempts to pass English-only legislation, to cut off welfare for legal immigrants, and to reduce the immigration quota for relatives of U.S. citizens. "I wish our party would be more aggressive in courting this Hispanic vote but because of welfare and immigration reform and English-only issues we are afraid to try and solicit their support," she said. Noting that Miami-Dade has the highest percentage of immigrants in the United States—about half its residents were born in other countries—she says, "I think Miami is just a microcosm of all that's good in immigration. You take people in and give them an opportunity and look at what they've done with that opportunity." In 1998 she was chief sponsor of the Child Custody Protection Act, to bar the transport of minors across state lines for abortions; the House voted for it 276–150, just eight votes shy of a veto-proof majority, in July, but it was held up on a party-line vote in the Senate in September. She has sponsored a constitutional amendment on victims' rights.

Ros-Lehtinen serves on the International Relations Committee, and much of her energy has been devoted to Cuban and Latin issues. She strongly backed the Cuban Democracy Act and Helms-Burton. She opposed routing Cuban refugees to Guantanamo and then forcing them back to Cuba. In July 1998 after actor Jack Nicholson praised Castro as "a genius," Ros-Lehtinen said, "It seems Mr. Nicholson has really flown over the cuckoo's nest this time with his latest ludicrous statement about the Cuban tyrant." In October 1998, after a Spanish judge indicted former Chilean President Augusto Pinochet, she pressed Clinton to indict Castro for the shooting down of the Brothers to the Rescue planes in February 1996. With the two other Cuban-American members, Lincoln Diaz-Balart of Miami-Dade and Democrat Robert Menendez of New Jersey, she opposed Senator John Warner's proposal for a commission to review Cuban policy, saying it "would be a nice Christmas present for Castro." She worked to suspend the deportation of illegal immigrants from El Salvador, Guatemala, Honduras and Nicaragua after their countries were ravaged by Hurricane Mitch.

Ros-Lehtinen was re-elected without opposition in 1998. While theoretically vulnerable in a Republican primary, she seems unbeatable; she had over $1 million cash on hand at the end of 1998.

Cook's Call. *Safe.* Another safely ensconced Republican, Ros-Lehtinen hasn't had an opponent since 1992. Don't expect a race here.

The People: Pop. 1990: 562,394; 0.2% rural; 18.2% age 65 + ; 89.1% White, 3.9% Black, 1.1% Asian, 0.2% Amer. Indian, 5.7% Other; 66.7% Hispanic Origin. Households: 49.5% married couple families; 21.4% married couple fams. w. children; 42.2% college educ.; median household income: $25,537; per capita income: $14,779; median house value: $95,600; median gross rent: $397.

1996 Presidential Vote

Dole (R)	86,005	(52%)
Clinton (D)	71,673	(43%)
Perot (I)	7,788	(5%)

1992 Presidential Vote

Bush (R)	93,870	(57%)
Clinton (D)	54,113	(33%)
Perot (I)	16,988	(10%)

Rep. Ileana Ros-Lehtinen (R)

Elected Aug. 1989; b. July 12, 1952, Havana, Cuba; home, Miami; Miami-Dade Commun. Col., A.A. 1972, FL Intl. U., B.S. 1975, M.S. 1986; Catholic; married (Dexter).

Elected Office: FL House of Reps., 1982–86; FL Senate, 1986–89.

Professional Career: Teacher, Principal & Owner, Eastern Academy Elem. Schl., 1978–85.

DC Office: 2160 RHOB 20515, 202-225-3931; Fax: 202-225-5620; Web site: www.house.gov/ros-lehtinen.

District Office: Miami, 305-275-1800.

Committees: *Government Reform* (5th of 24 R): Criminal Justice, Drug Policy & Human Resources; National Security, Veterans' Affairs & Intl. Relations. *International Relations* (9th of 26 R): International Economic Policy & Trade (Chmn.); Western Hemisphere.

Group Ratings

	ADA	ACLU	AFS	LCV	CON	NTU	NFIB	COC	ACU	NTLC	CHC
1998	15	27	57	46	28	50	92	67	80	69	92
1997	20	—	25	—	59	48	—	90	76	—	—

National Journal Ratings

	1997 LIB — 1997 CONS			1998 LIB — 1998 CONS		
Economic	48%	—	51%	51%	—	48%
Social	10%	—	82%	44%	—	56%
Foreign	32%	—	65%	17%	—	83%

Key Votes of the 105th Congress

1. Clinton Budget Deal	Y	5. Puerto Rico Sthood. Ref.	Y	9. Cut $ for B-2 Bombers	Y
2. Education IRAs	Y	6. End Highway Set-asides	*	10. Human Rights in China	Y
3. Req. 2/3 to Raise Taxes	Y	7. School Prayer Amend.	*	11. Withdraw Bosnia Troops	Y
4. Fast-track Trade	N	8. Ovrd. Part. Birth Veto	Y	12. End Cuban TV-Marti	N

Election Results

1998 general	Ileana Ros-Lehtinen (R) .... unopposed	($152,709)
1998 primary	Ileana Ros-Lehtinen (R) .... unopposed	
1996 general	Ileana Ros-Lehtinen (R) .... unopposed	($163,902)

NINETEENTH DISTRICT

When the first millionaires came to Palm Beach in the 1920s to winter in their new Addison Mizner pseudo-Mediterranean mansions and as the first real estate speculators arrived in Miami, there was virtually nothing man-made between these two cites. In 1920, Dade, Broward and Palm Beach counties had some 66,000 residents. Now, more than 4 million are wedged almost entirely in the 5- to 15-mile strip between the Atlantic Ocean and the protected Everglades. The contrast between the 1920s and today's vast state is especially glaring in Boca Raton, where Mizner built what is now the Boca Raton Hotel and Club in 1926. Its azure-tiled fountains and red-tiled roofs, its pseudo-Moorish columns and pink stucco walls bespeak a vision of a holiday Florida, a bit mannered and antique to today's eye, but still exuberant. Now, Boca Raton has grown inland and is still solidly affluent, but also is more functional and workaday. Affluent retirees from the Northeast and Canada ("snowbirds") live in unadorned high-rise towers, enjoying the weather and the lack of a state income tax. But there are also major corporate headquarters here—W.R. Grace and an IBM-Intel joint venture: high-tech and big money at work in what used to be just paradise.

The 19th Congressional District includes former swampland and citrus groves in Palm Beach and Broward counties. It does not touch the ocean at all, kept from it by the majority-black 23d District which collects the black neighborhoods just inland from the Intracoastal Waterway. It stretches from the edge of West Palm Beach, travels through the Lantana headquarters of the *National Enquirer* to Boynton Beach, Boca Raton, Deerfield Beach and Sunrise. With the growth in northern Broward and southern Palm Beach counties during the 1970s and 1980s, the district's largest communities are no longer the beach towns, but new inland communities: Coral Springs, Margate, Tamarac. Liberal condominium associations, mobilized by "condo commandos," are political powers. The 19th has a large Jewish population, in both counties, and is heavily Democratic.

The congressman from the 19th is Robert Wexler, a Democrat first elected in 1996. Wexler grew up in Florida from age 10, and after law school went into practice in Boca Raton. In 1990, at 29, he was elected to the state Senate, where he sponsored tough prison sentencing guidelines, called for chemical castration of sex offenders, a cap on money taxpayers contributed to Everglades cleanup and more funds for education. When four-term Democrat Harry Johnston retired, Wexler was one of three Democratic legislators who jumped into the race. It was a close race in Broward County, but Wexler led in Palm Beach County, which cast over half the votes. Wexler won overall with 47% to 29% for state Senator Peter Weinstein and 21% for state Representative Benjamin Graber. The October 1 runoff was bitter. Wexler won 65%–35%, carrying Palm Beach County 83%–17% and losing Broward County 59%–41%; but afterwards Weinstein filed a $10 million defamation suit against him, citing an unflattering picture of Weinstein in a Wexler TV ad (the suit was dropped in early 1997). In this heavily Democratic district, Wexler won the general 66%–34%.

Wexler has had a fairly liberal voting record in the House and a flare for gaining attention. In March 1997 he and Republican Mark Foley proposed a constitutional amendment to allow states to change "gain time" rules for prisoners retroactively. In April 1997 he asked for an investigation of the price of matzoh in south Florida. "It's the biggest thing since the Pharoah let us out of Egypt," he said, surely not entirely seriously, and not very biblically correct either since the Pharoah tried to keep the Jews from leaving. His advice to constituents: "Get your family or friends to buy three five-pound boxes in the Bronx and FedEx it down here." He investigated the troubled FBI crime lab, and in June 1997 called for a neutral re-examination of the evidence against Dr. Jeffrey MacDonald, convicted of killing his wife and children. On the International Relations Committee, he traveled to the Middle East with Madeleine Albright and met with Benjamin Netanyahu; he was the only member of the House in attendance at the Wye Accords. He got a seat on the Western Hemisphere Subcommittee, in April 1998. Amid controversy over the gap between civilian and military standards of conduct, he told an Army lieutenant colonel, "Quite frankly, I think the military's standards are too high."

But Wexler made his greatest mark as an ardent defender of Bill Clinton. Producers of cable shows are always looking for someone who can be relied on to take one side of an issue and to bring energy to the broadcast: one look at Wexler convinced bookers that he would fill the bill, and he seemed to turn few invitations down. On MSNBC and CNBC, CNN and the Fox News Channel, on "Hardball" with Chris Matthews and "Upfront Tonight" with Geraldo Rivera and "The Big Show" with Keith Olbermann, there was Wexler almost every night, denouncing Clinton's personal conduct to be sure, but then bellowing with rage over the acts of Independent Counsel Kenneth Starr or House Judiciary Committee Republicans and everyone who was preventing him from working on issues like health care, education and Social Security. One typical plaint: "The president betrayed his wife; he did not betray his country. God help this nation if we fail to recognize the difference."

Some have speculated that Wexler was trying to strengthen himself in his district or to set himself up as a statewide candidate. But his standing in the 19th is solid—he was re-elected without opposition—and he has not accumulated anything like the money that would be needed to launch a statewide effort. After the 1998 race he had just $126,930 cash on hand, compared to $1.5 million for the 20th District's Peter Deutsch, who shares his base in heavily Jewish south Florida. Most likely, Wexler is a man of excitable temperament saying what he genuinely believes.

Cook's Call. *Safe.* Regardless of whether Wexler runs for Connie Mack's open Senate seat, it is hard to see how this strongly Democratic south Florida district slips from Democratic control.

The People: Pop. 1990: 562,978; 2.2% rural; 29% age 65 + ; 94.9% White, 2.7% Black, 1.4% Asian, 0.2% Amer. Indian, 0.9% Other; 6.1% Hispanic Origin. Households: 59.3% married couple families; 19% married couple fams. w. children; 50.4% college educ.; median household income: $34,396; per capita income: $20,029; median house value: $107,600; median gross rent: $588.

1996 Presidential Vote

Clinton (D) 189,336 (65%)
Dole (R) 81,020 (28%)
Perot (I) 20,094   (7%)

1992 Presidential Vote

Clinton (D) 159,284 (54%)
Bush (R) 89,698 (30%)
Perot (I) 46,946 (16%)

Rep. Robert Wexler (D)

Elected 1996; b. Jan. 2, 1961, Queens, NY; home, Boca Raton; U. of FL, B.A. 1982, George Washington U., J.D. 1985; Jewish; married (Laurie).

Elected Office: FL Senate, 1990–96.

Professional Career: Practicing atty., 1985–96.

DC Office: 213 CHOB 20515, 202-225-3001; Fax: 202-225-5974; Web site: www.house.gov/wexler.

District Offices: Boca Raton, 561-988-6302; Margate, 954-972-6454.

Committees: *International Relations* (15th of 23 D): Asia & the Pacific; Western Hemisphere. *Judiciary* (13th of 16 D): Courts & Intellectual Property.

Group Ratings

	ADA	ACLU	AFS	LCV	CON	NTU	NFIB	COC	ACU	NTLC	CHC
1998	100	75	100	100	96	31	14	18	0	5	0
1997	90	—	88	—	86	28	—	40	17	—	—

National Journal Ratings

	1997 LIB — 1997 CONS	1998 LIB — 1998 CONS
Economic	69% — 30%	79% — 0%
Social	76% — 23%	81% — 19%
Foreign	81% — 18%	71% — 27%

Key Votes of the 105th Congress

1. Clinton Budget Deal	N	5. Puerto Rico Sthood. Ref.	Y	9. Cut $ for B-2 Bombers	Y
2. Education IRAs	N	6. End Highway Set-asides	N	10. Human Rights in China	Y
3. Req. 2/3 to Raise Taxes	N	7. School Prayer Amend.	N	11. Withdraw Bosnia Troops	N
4. Fast-track Trade	N	8. Ovrd. Part. Birth Veto	N	12. End Cuban TV-Marti	N

Election Results

1998 general	Robert Wexler (D)	unopposed		($280,724)
1998 primary	Robert Wexler (D)	unopposed		
1996 general	Robert Wexler (D)	188,766	(66%)	($872,367)
	Beverly Kennedy (R)	99,101	(34%)	($121,117)

TWENTIETH DISTRICT

Fort Lauderdale, back when Connie Francis first made it famous in the 1960 spring break movie *Where the Boys Are*, was just a small town with a strip of motels along the beach and some nice houses fronting canals. Now it is the center of a vast metropolitan area with its own major airport. Fort Lauderdale and Broward County had fewer than 100,000 people in 1950; now it is about 1.5 million. The land from the strip of beach along the Atlantic Ocean west to the Sawgrass Expressway and the Everglades Wildlife Management Area has filled up with subdivisions, shopping centers, office complexes, warehouses and trucking terminals. Broward County is no longer just vacation country; it is also a major port and business center with high-tech companies and startups that have become national giants, including Blockbuster Video.

As it has grown, the ethnic composition of Broward County has changed. In the 1950s, it was understood that Jews couldn't buy houses or rent hotel rooms this far north of Miami.

Today, after three decades of Cubans moving into the Miami area and many Jews moving out, Broward County is the most heavily Jewish part of Florida, indeed one of the most heavily Jewish parts of the United States. Nearer the coast, especially in the huge high-rises of Hollywood and Hallandale, most of Broward's Jews are retirees from New York and other northeastern metro areas. But inland, in towns like Pembroke Pines and Davie, and Plantation and Sunrise that didn't exist a few decades ago, there are many young Jewish parents raising families in communities that pride themselves on fine schools and high property values. This is one reason that in the 1990s the number of children in Florida has been rising more rapidly than the number of seniors, with school enrollment rising more than 35% in Broward alone.

The 20th Congressional District includes most of southern Broward County, though not the precincts nearest the beach, which are in the 22d and 23d Districts. The district also takes in the mostly unpopulated Everglades west of the Sawgrass in Broward and Miami-Dade counties, plus the Florida Keys. At the end of the Overseas Highway is Key West, now a bustling tropical outpost that echoes its historic seafaring roots. This southern-most city in the continental United States was long accessible only by sea, and treasures from shipwrecks along the miles of coral reefs once gave its residents the highest per capita income in the nation. Key West has attracted famous residents—Ernest Hemingway, Tennessee Williams, Jimmy Buffett—and a large gay population, many living in restored "conch houses," quaint clapboard bungalows. Politically, this is a heavily Democratic district.

The congressman from the 20th District is Peter Deutsch, a Democrat first elected in 1992. Deutsch grew up in New York, graduated from Yale Law School in June 1982, moved to Florida and by November was elected to the state legislature. Two years later, he was re-elected with the largest vote in Florida and was unopposed in the next three elections. A *Miami Herald* reporter said Deutsch was "viewed by colleagues as bright but abrasive, and an expert at using procedural rules to advance or torpedo legislation." The newly drawn 20th District looked as if it were drawn for Deutsch. He became the first congressional candidate in Florida history to get on the ballot by petition. He started off his campaign by loaning it $350,000. Dante Fascell, chairman of the Foreign Affairs Committee, confronted with the prospect of a district dominated by unfamiliar Broward County, decided to retire after 38 years in the House. Deutsch won the primary nearly 2–1 and the general election 55%–39%.

Deutsch has a mostly liberal voting record and is a member of the New Democrat Coalition. He does not waste time: on his first day in Congress, while most freshmen were attending swearing-in ceremonies, he held a press conference to announce he had introduced a bill to increase flood insurance benefits. His early achievements were passage of a law to protect the health care benefits of police officers and fire fighters injured in the line of duty, named after two Plantation fire fighters injured in a 1995 explosion, and a $1.5 million law enforcement training program on missing children, named after 9-year-old Jimmy Ryce of Miami Beach who was abducted and murdered. He has opposed raising the Medicare age in tandem with Social Security, a $5 fee for home health visits and means-testing to determine Medicare premiums. He has worked to have Medicare reimbursements reflect cost in densely populated areas and opposed adjustment of the CPI.

Deutsch has spent much time on Everglades restoration. When appropriators called for cuts in planned spending, he helped negotiate a five-year agreement to keep money coming in for land acquisition and increasing water flow. In 1998 he helped settle a dispute with the Miccosukee Tribe, who wanted to develop new land near the Tamiami Trail. He opposed Florida legislation sought by the sugar industry, which would have increased federal land acquisition costs, and helped persuade Governor Lawton Chiles to veto it. On the International Relations Committee, he pursued matters of local interest. He went on trips with Bill Clinton and Chairman Benjamin Gilman to the Middle East. In 1998 he charged that a United Nations agency was funding antisemitic textbooks in Palestinian schools, and got language in the State Department appropriation to end it. He supports the Helms-Burton Act and Radio and TV Marti, and criticized Fidel Castro for building a Chernobyl-style nuclear reactor. The Florida Keys have different interests: he is faced with protests from a Conch Coalition of fishermen, real estate agents and treasure hunters opposed to government bureaucrats declaring, despite previous assurances, no-fishing zones in the Florida Keys National Marine Sanctuary established in 1990.

Deutsch has won re-election easily, but not without raising plenty of money: $2.3 million in the 1996 and 1998 cycles. He has handled it well too: he invested $700,000 of campaign funds in January 1997 and it grew to $1.1 million 15 months later. He was unopposed in 1998 and had $1.5 million cash on hand at the end of the year. All of which raises the question of whether he wants to run for statewide office. In late 1996 some thought he wanted to run for Bob Graham's Senate seat. But, after mulling the Senate race to replace Connie Mack in 2000, Deutsch opted out. With a safe Broward seat, he can wait and see if the state turns more Democratic.

Cook's Call. *Safe.* Deutsch will have no trouble holding on to this heavily Democratic seat.

The People: Pop. 1990: 562,673; 8.9% rural; 16.8% age 65 +; 92% White, 4.5% Black, 1.6% Asian, 0.4% Amer. Indian, 1.5% Other; 12% Hispanic Origin. Households: 58.2% married couple families; 24.7% married couple fams. w. children; 50.6% college educ.; median household income: $35,378; per capita income: $18,285; median house value: $103,200; median gross rent: $540.

1996 Presidential Vote			1992 Presidential Vote		
Clinton (D)	148,289	(59%)	Clinton (D)	116,568	(47%)
Dole (R)	78,699	(31%)	Bush (R)	83,485	(34%)
Perot (I)	23,296	(9%)	Perot (I)	48,687	(20%)

Rep. Peter R. Deutsch (D)

Elected 1992; b. Apr. 1, 1957, New York, NY; home, Lauderhill; Swarthmore Col., B.A. 1979, Yale Law Schl., J.D. 1982; Jewish; married (Lori).

Elected Office: FL House of Reps., 1982–92.

Professional Career: Practicing atty., 1983–92.

DC Office: 204 CHOB 20515, 202-225-7931; Fax: 202-225-8456; e-mail: pdeutsch@hr.house.gov.

District Office: Pembroke Pines, 954-437-3936.

Committees: *Commerce* (10th of 24 D): Energy & Power; Finance & Hazardous Materials; Health and Environment.

Group Ratings

	ADA	ACLU	AFS	LCV	CON	NTU	NFIB	COC	ACU	NTLC	CHC
1998	95	69	100	92	94	31	14	35	4	11	0
1997	80	—	75	—	96	35	—	60	21	—	—

National Journal Ratings

	1997 LIB — 1997 CONS		1998 LIB — 1998 CONS	
Economic	71% —	28%	67% —	32%
Social	71% —	27%	76% —	23%
Foreign	81% —	19%	71% —	27%

Key Votes of the 105th Congress

1. Clinton Budget Deal	N	5. Puerto Rico Sthood. Ref.	Y	9. Cut $ for B-2 Bombers	Y
2. Education IRAs	N	6. End Highway Set-asides	N	10. Human Rights in China	Y
3. Req. 2/3 to Raise Taxes	N	7. School Prayer Amend.	N	11. Withdraw Bosnia Troops	N
4. Fast-track Trade	N	8. Ovrd. Part. Birth Veto	N	12. End Cuban TV-Marti	N

Election Results

1998 general	Peter R. Deutsch (D) .... unopposed			($259,016)
1998 primary	Peter R. Deutsch (D) .... unopposed			
1996 general	Peter R. Deutsch (D) 159,256	(65%)		($435,604)
	Jim Jacobs (R) 85,777	(35%)		($29,928)

TWENTY-FIRST DISTRICT

Miami's Cuban-American community has been one of America's most dynamic over the last 40 years (see 18th District), growing from 50,000 in 1960, the year after Fidel Castro took over Cuba, to well over 1 million today. Over those years, the Cuban-American neighborhoods centered along 8th Street—Calle Ocho—expanded to the southwest, west and northwest. Development moved out in the 1960s and 1970s, filling up the land all the way to the Palmetto Expressway; in the 1980s, development reached outward to the Homestead Extension of Florida's Turnpike. The Cuban-Americans moved out and beyond Hialeah, whose now-closed race track was constructed in the 1920s beyond the edge of urban development, and which now has the highest percentage of Cuban-Americans in the Miami area. To the south, Westwood and Kendall Lakes—southwest suburbs of Miami with large Cuban-American populations—have been growing outward into what once was swampland. Here, planned communities and subdivisions often have just one guarded entrance, with streets fanning out around lakes and golf courses.

The 21st Congressional District includes most of these new Cuban-American communities, taking in Hialeah and, just to the north, the planned community of Miami Lakes developed in 1962 by Senator Bob Graham and his father. To the south, it is centered on Kendall Lakes, and its boundaries go out to the Everglades Wildlife Management Area. The district is 70% Hispanic—mostly but not all Cuban-American—and usually heavily Republican. Knowing first hand the evils of Communism, Cuban-Americans appreciate the blessings of free enterprise, cherish traditional moral values, and for years preferred Republicans to Democrats on all these counts. In 1996 Bill Clinton cut into the Cuban vote by condemning the Cubans who shot down the Brothers to the Rescue pilots, supporting the Helms-Burton Act, and opposing cutoffs of welfare to legal aliens; by 1998, after seeking accommodation with Castro, Clinton has lost some popularity here.

The congressman from the 21st District is Lincoln Diaz-Balart, a Republican first elected when the district was created in 1992. Diaz-Balart was born in Cuba where his grandfather and father served in the Cuban Congress; the family left Cuba in 1959, shortly after Castro took over and their house was looted and burned. His aunt was the former wife of Fidel Castro and the mother of Castro's only recognized child. Diaz-Balart started off as a poverty lawyer and a Democrat, but switched parties. He was elected to the state House as a Republican in 1986 with 78% of the vote and to the state Senate in 1989 with 82%, a year after his younger brother Mario was elected to the state House. In the legislature Diaz-Balart sponsored laws toughening sentences for crimes against law enforcement officers, increasing penalties for drug money-laundering, providing low-interest home construction loans, creating a statewide substance abuse program, and requiring prospectuses of Florida firms issuing securities to disclose whether they do business with Cuba.

In 1989, Jorge Mas Canosa's Cuban American National Foundation convinced Diaz-Balart not to run against Ileana Ros-Lehtinen in the then-18th District special election to replace

Claude Pepper. In 1992, the organization endorsed Diaz-Balart to run in the new 21st. But fellow state Senator Javier Souto, also Cuban-born, opposed him in the primary, charging that Diaz-Balart was backed by wealthy contributors and was not a lifelong Republican. Diaz-Balart won 69%–31%.

Diaz-Balart has a voting record that is rather liberal on economics, veering far from market principles on issues from the minimum wage to NAFTA, though he has said he believes a hemispheric common market is inevitable. Naturally he has favored sanctions against Cuba, and when the Clinton Administration announced in May 1995 that it would no longer give automatic safe haven in the U.S. to Cuban refugees and instead would return them to Cuba—a reversal of previous U.S. policy—Diaz-Balart was one of two people arrested while protesting this policy switch. When Colorado Democrat David Skaggs tried to cut funding for Radio Marti and TV Marti broadcasts to Cuba, Diaz-Balart moved successfully to cut $23 million in funding for the National Institute of Standards and Technology in Skaggs's district.

When Republicans took over the House, Speaker Newt Gingrich named Diaz-Balart to the Rules Committee. But he has not always followed the party line. He was one of three Republican incumbents who refused to sign the Contract with America in 1994, and he voted against the Republican welfare bills because of their provisions denying welfare to legal immigrants. Many older Cubans have not taken U.S. citizenship because they hoped some day to return to Cuba; many are dependent on Supplemental Security Income and other aid. "This is a disaster for my district," Diaz-Balart said. "I've been getting calls by the hour, I've been hearing stories from people in restaurants about the elderly, the disabled, who are going to be affected by this." He persevered, and his bill to restore SSI benefits to legal immigrants passed 345–74 in May 1997. Another Diaz-Balart measure established Florida's Jennifer Act as a national standard for dealing with criminals who target children.

Diaz-Balart has worked on other legislation regarding Cuba and Latin America. He wrote the section of Helms-Burton codifying the embargo against Cuba. He sponsored the Central American relief act of 1997 which prevented deportation of Nicaraguans, Salvadorans and Guatemalans—several hundred thousand—who qualified for legal resident or immigrant status temporarily, and had become law-abiding residents for many years. With the other Cuban-Americans in the House—Miami's Ileana Ros-Lehtinen and Robert Menendez of New Jersey—he sponsored in 1998 a bill to force the Clinton Administration to "directly assist" Cuban dissidents, opposed "in the strongest possible terms" the sending of food and medicine to Cuba and, in a meeting with Secretary of State Madeleine Albright, attacked big corporations ("gluttons of privilege") for seeking a commission to review U.S. policy toward Cuba. He objected to Cuba's building a Chernobyl-style nuclear reactor, called Canadian policy "racist" for boycotting Nigeria but not Cuba, and objected when the Clinton Administration declared almost all of Florida's coast a "security zone" requiring small vessels to get permits to enter Cuban waters. In October 1998, inspired by the Spanish prosecution of Chile's former President Augusto Pinochet, he and Ros-Lehtinen pressed Clinton to indict Castro for shooting down two Brothers to the Rescue planes in February 1996.

Diaz-Balart was one of the few Florida congressmen with opposition in 1998; he won 75%–25% and had $535,209 cash on hand at year's end.

Cook's Call. *Safe.* Diaz-Balart is safely ensconced in this solidly Republican, overwhelmingly Cuban district. With the Voting Rights Act insuring that minority representation will not be diluted, Diaz-Balart should have no problem winning in 2000 or for as long as he wants.

The People: Pop. 1990: 562,402; 0.8% rural; 10.4% age 65 +; 87.7% White, 4.2% Black, 1.5% Asian, 0.1% Amer. Indian, 6.6% Other; 69.5% Hispanic Origin. Households: 59.6% married couple families; 31.7% married couple fams. w. children; 45.3% college educ.; median household income: $32,043; per capita income: $13,173; median house value: $91,300; median gross rent: $507.

1996 Presidential Vote

Dole (R) 82,384 (51%)
Clinton (D) 72,844 (45%)
Perot (I) 7,901 (5%)

1992 Presidential Vote

Bush (R) 85,292 (58%)
Clinton (D) 45,778 (31%)
Perot (I) 15,545 (11%)

Rep. Lincoln Diaz-Balart (R)

Elected 1992; b. Aug. 13, 1954, Havana, Cuba; home, Miami; U. of S. FL, B.S. 1977, Case Western Reserve U., J.D. 1979; Catholic; married (Cristina).

Elected Office: FL House of Reps., 1986–89; FL Senate 1989–92.

Professional Career: Practicing atty., 1979–92; Asst. FL Atty., 1983–84.

DC Office: 404 CHOB 20515, 202-225-4211; Fax: 202-225-8576; Web site: www.house.gov/diaz-balart.

District Office: Miami, 305-470-8555.

Committees: *Rules* (5th of 9 R): Rules & Organization of the House (Vice Chmn.).

Group Ratings

	ADA	ACLU	AFS	LCV	CON	NTU	NFIB	COC	ACU	NTLC	CHC
1998	25	27	56	38	13	44	79	72	68	66	92
1997	20	—	38	—	42	44	—	70	72	—	—

National Journal Ratings

	1997 LIB — 1997 CONS		1998 LIB — 1998 CONS	
Economic	52%	47%	51%	49%
Social	18%	81%	45%	55%
Foreign	36%	63%	27%	68%

Key Votes of the 105th Congress

1. Clinton Budget Deal	Y	5. Puerto Rico Sthood. Ref.	Y	9. Cut $ for B-2 Bombers	N
2. Education IRAs	Y	6. End Highway Set-asides	N	10. Human Rights in China	Y
3. Req. 2/3 to Raise Taxes	Y	7. School Prayer Amend.	Y	11. Withdraw Bosnia Troops	N
4. Fast-track Trade	N	8. Ovrd. Part. Birth Veto	Y	12. End Cuban TV-Marti	N

Election Results

1998 general	Lincoln Diaz-Balart (R) 84,018	(75%)	($482,166)
	Patrick Cusack (D) 28,378	(25%)	($28,635)
1998 primary	Lincoln Diaz-Balart (R) .... unopposed		
1996 general	Lincoln Diaz-Balart (R) .... unopposed		($130,085)

TWENTY-SECOND DISTRICT

The barrier islands of Florida's Gold Coast have been developed in spasms of speculative frenzy, not just as vacation places and retirement homes but as embodiments of dreams and fantasies. Consider Palm Beach, the great beach resort of the 1920s, where rich WASPs would leave their snow-covered Tudor or Georgian mansions and live in Addison Mizner's pseudo-Mediterranean confections. Consider also Miami Beach: the great resort of the 1950s, where

Jews who had grown up amid prejudice and made their fortunes in ebullient postwar America vacationed in surrealistically curved and embellished skyscraper hotels—like Morris Lapidus's Fontainebleau and Eden Roc—giant variations on the themes set out in the much smaller Art Deco hotels at the beach's south end. Or think of the 1970s and 1980s, as the coastline of Miami-Dade, Broward and Palm Beach counties were lined with one high-rise condo after another, a promised land for retirees, free from winter frost and state and city income taxes.

Almost all of this beach area is now gathered together into Florida's 22d Congressional District, a thin strip of land 91 miles long and never more than three miles wide, along the barrier islands from Juno Beach in the north through Palm Beach south to the Lincoln Road mall in Miami Beach. Palm Beach has been maintained as if under glass by great wealth; the Fort Lauderdale beach went downhill and has now been refurbished; Miami's South Beach, its Art Deco buildings restored, has become a kind of amalgam of North American, Latin American and European cultures. Today's 22d District has the highest percentage of over-65 residents and quite possibly the highest percentage of high-rise dwellers, of any district in America. Politically, it is marginal territory, usually Republican on balance, but for Bill Clinton in the 1990s, and more Republican as you go farther north.

The congressman from the 22d District is Clay Shaw, first elected in 1980, and now a senior Republican. Shaw grew up in Fort Lauderdale, practiced law and served as a judge and councilman; in 1975, at 36, he became the city's mayor. In 1980 he ran for the House, and had the good fortune of seeing the Democratic incumbent lose his primary to a Miami lawyer. He won the seat handily and held it despite the Fort Lauderdale area's Democratic tilt. For eight years he served on Judiciary, working on drug and crime bills; he backed the death penalty for major drug dealers, a federal drug czar, and the use of the military to interdict drug smuggling. In July 1988 he switched to Ways and Means. There he drafted an alternative to the statist ABC child care bill, first supported and then in 1989 opposed the Catastrophic Health Care Act, worked on the nanny tax bill in 1993–94 and opposed taxes on Social Security earnings.

In the Republican Congress Shaw has taken on the really big issues, first welfare reform, then Social Security. After Republicans won control in 1994, Shaw became chairman of the Way and Means subcommittee handling welfare. His little-noticed 1993 bill, to end the federal entitlement to welfare and take most recipients off the rolls and require them to work after two years, now was part of the Contract with America and became one of House Republicans' major priorities. Shaw's bills were passed twice in 1995, in somewhat different form, and vetoed twice by Bill Clinton. They generally turned over control of welfare to the states, but not without some strings: cash benefits were barred for mothers under 18 and the two-years-and-work rule could not be dropped. In early 1996 House Republicans hoped that Bob Dole could use the welfare issue against Bill Clinton. By July 1996 they decided that Dole was likely to lose anyway, and so decided to pass welfare reform a third time, giving Dole an issue if Clinton vetoed it again and giving House Republicans an accomplishment if Clinton signed it. They had no idea what he would do, but in the end he signed, and a major change in American public policy was made.

Shaw continued to be involved in welfare issues in 1997 and 1998. He tried but failed to keep workfare participants exempt from the various requirements and conditions that unions have exacted for others on local public payrolls; he retreated in October 1997 when it was plain that the Senate wouldn't act. But around the country workfare continued. He introduced a fatherhood bill in February 1998, to encourage welfare fathers to get jobs and take more responsibility for their children's lives; but he had to admit that studies of pilot projects did not produce positive results. He stayed steady on main principles: "I'm not going to tear out the heart and soul of the program which is the requirement of work after two years."

After the 1998 election, Shaw, representing the House district with the nation's highest percentage of those 65 and over, became chairman of the Ways and Means Social Security Subcommittee. He said he wanted to reform the system and preserve it for baby boomers' retirements. But his efforts to persuade Clinton to submit a bill had not worked by February

1999 and Ways and Means Chairman Bill Archer seemed determined not to go forward with legislation unless Clinton did first. In 1999, Shaw and Archer introduced a bill which would give workers income tax credits to fund personal retirement accounts. But in April, some Republican leaders signaled they would abandon Social Security reform until after the 2000 elections.

Shaw has worked also on local issues. He asked for spot checks of pleasure boats, to stop drug smuggling, and for repeal of the 24 cent tax on recreational boat diesel fuel in 1997. In April 1997 he released the first snout beetles which biologists hope will nibble down the melaleuca trees that have been infesting the Everglades and driving out other species. He sought a delay in a government designation of Johnson's sea grass as a threatened species in 1998, fearing it would stop port operations. His bill for security checks for dock workers was killed by labor unions in October 1998. With Peter Deutsch he attacked a bill passed by the Florida legislature which would raise federal land acquisition costs in the Everglades; Governor Lawton Chiles vetoed it. He beat back a cutback in funds for the National Hurricane Center and got 60 emergency customs inspectors hired in 1997. The new 17th Street causeway bridge is named after him.

Shaw with his moderate voting record has run ahead of his party and has not had much serious competition. In 1992, when the district was newly created, he was opposed by state Senate President Gwen Margolis; he won 52%–37%. He was unopposed in 1998. Democratic state Representatives John Rayson and Elaine Bloom will mount challenges for 2000.

Cook's Call. *Probably Safe.* This district is more competitive than Shaw's past impressive margins of victory suggest; in fact, presidential election numbers suggests the district leans a little Democratic. While Shaw may well have safely ensconced himself in this district, should he step aside or the boundaries change significantly in 2002, this could become a prime Democratic target.

The People: Pop. 1990: 560,959; 32.1% age 65 + ; 94.4% White, 2.9% Black, 1% Asian, 0.2% Amer. Indian, 1.6% Other; 12.6% Hispanic Origin. Households: 43% married couple families; 10.7% married couple fams. w. children; 50.8% college educ.; median household income: $29,595; per capita income: $24,663; median house value: $118,200; median gross rent: $477.

1996 Presidential Vote			1992 Presidential Vote		
Clinton (D)	124,715	(55%)	Clinton (D)	115,912	(45%)
Dole (R)	86,668	(38%)	Bush (R)	96,986	(38%)
Perot (I)	17,418	(8%)	Perot (I)	44,845	(17%)

Rep. E. Clay Shaw, Jr. (R)

Elected 1980; b. Apr. 19, 1939, Miami; home, Ft. Lauderdale; Stetson U., B.A. 1961, U. of AL, M.B.A. 1963, Stetson U., J.D. 1966; Catholic; married (Emilie).

Elected Office: Ft. Lauderdale City Comm., 1971–73; Ft. Lauderdale Vice Mayor, 1973–75, Mayor, 1975–80.

Professional Career: Practicing atty., 1966–68; Ft. Lauderdale Chief Prosecutor, 1968–69; Assoc. Municipal Judge, 1969–71.

DC Office: 2408 RHOB 20515, 202-225-3026; Fax: 202-225-8398; Web site: www.house.gov/shaw.

District Offices: Ft. Lauderdale, 954-522-1800; West Palm Beach, 561-832-3007.

Committees: *Ways & Means* (4th of 23 R): Social Security (Chmn.); Trade.

Group Ratings

	ADA	ACLU	AFS	LCV	CON	NTU	NFIB	COC	ACU	NTLC	CHC
1998	10	38	11	31	33	36	86	100	72	76	75
1997	10	—	25	—	91	46	—	100	80	—	

National Journal Ratings

	1997 LIB — 1997 CONS		1998 LIB — 1998 CONS	
Economic	35%	— 63%	43%	— 56%
Social	46%	— 53%	50%	— 50%
Foreign	30%	— 68%	34%	— 62%

Key Votes of the 105th Congress

1. Clinton Budget Deal	Y	5. Puerto Rico Sthood. Ref.	N	9. Cut $ for B-2 Bombers	N
2. Education IRAs	Y	6. End Highway Set-asides	Y	10. Human Rights in China	N
3. Req. 2/3 to Raise Taxes	N	7. School Prayer Amend.	N	11. Withdraw Bosnia Troops	Y
4. Fast-track Trade	Y	8. Ovrd. Part. Birth Veto	Y	12. End Cuban TV-Marti	N

Election Results

1998 general	E. Clay Shaw Jr. (R) .... unopposed			($353,968)
1998 primary	E. Clay Shaw Jr. (R) .... unopposed			
1996 general	E. Clay Shaw Jr. (R) 137,098	(62%)		($548,109)
	Kenneth D. Cooper (D) 84,517	(38%)		($85,040)

TWENTY-THIRD DISTRICT

In the morning shadow of the high-rise condominiums that line the Atlantic Ocean from Palm Beach to Miami Beach, behind the waterways that separate the barrier islands from the mainland, usually a few blocks off of old U.S. 1 and behind the railroad lines, are the black neighborhoods of South Florida's Gold Coast. They are gatherings of older stucco homes and commercial storefronts, ranging from enclaves of upper-middle-class residents to rundown slums. These are neighborhoods overlooked by most tourists and feared by many local residents.

The 23d Congressional District, created by the May 1992 court redistricting, gathers together many of these black neighborhoods in a constituency that is ethnically defined and geographically grotesque. A little more than half its residents live in Broward County, with a little more than one-third living in Palm Beach County and the rest scattered—a few in north Miami-Dade County, more in a geographically expansive but lightly populated segment that includes migrant worker camps around Lake Okeechobee and the old black neighborhood of Fort Pierce, a small city 120 miles north of Miami.

The congressman from the 23d District is Alcee Hastings, a Democrat elected in 1992, the only member of Congress ever to have been impeached and removed from office as a federal judge. Hastings is articulate and charming, the son of a hotel maid from Orlando, who practiced law, ran for the U.S. Senate in 1970 and was appointed a federal judge in 1979. He was impeached by the House of Representatives by a vote of 413–3 in 1988 and convicted and removed from office by the Senate by a vote of 69–26. Hastings was charged with conspiring with a friend to take a $150,000 bribe and give two convicted swindlers light sentences. Hastings was acquitted by a Miami jury in 1983, but the friend was convicted. The 11th Circuit Court of Appeals called for impeachment in 1987 and referred the case to Congress. In the House the case for impeachment was made by John Conyers, senior member of the Congressional Black Caucus; the case was heard by a panel of 12 senators, and Hastings was removed in October 1989. Footnote: in 1997 the Department of Justice in investigating the FBI crime lab found that an agent falsely testified against Hastings, and Hastings and Conyers moved to reopen the case. Nothing came of that: can a removed federal judge be restored to office?

After his removal Hastings was unapologetic. In 1990, he ran an abortive campaign for governor, then lost in the primary for Florida secretary of State. When the 23d District was created, he sprang into that race. In the September primary Hastings edged out another black candidate for second place, 28%–27%. In the October runoff he faced Palm Beach County legislator Lois Frankel. He was helped by a ruling by federal Judge Stanley Sporkin that his removal from office was invalid since the charges were not heard by the full Senate; the Supreme Court ruled to the contrary in a case involving another federal judge in January 1993, but by that time, Hastings was in Congress. Frankel blasted Hastings for his record, and he responded, "The bitch is a racist," and won the runoff 58%–42%, with voting closely following racial lines. He won the general election 59%–31%.

"I sort of came back like gangbusters, didn't I?" he asked later, but in the House he treated colleagues pleasantly and respectfully. "I'm not a vengeful person," he said in 1993. His voting record is the most liberal in the Florida delegation. He became vice chairman of the Congressional Black Caucus in 1993, but in 1994 lost a run for the chair to Donald Payne 23–15. As a member of the International Relations Committee he traveled to Haiti, Bosnia, and Israel; he serves on the Organization for Security and Cooperation in Europe and in July 1998 was re-elected Rapporteur of the OSCE Committee on Political Affairs and Security. He has worked with Fort Lauderdale neighbor Clay Shaw for funds for Port Everglades and customs officers. In 1998 he passed a law allowing the Miccosukee Tribe to build on an additional 680 acres in the Everglades, but requiring them to obey federal restrictions.

Naturally, Hastings's opinion was sought when the subject of impeachment arose, and it was exuberantly given. Hastings saw Clinton's impeachment as being driven by prosecutors as his own was, in his view, by judges—in both cases abusing their powers. "In my case, they nullified a jury. In this case, they are nullifying an election." In September 1998 he moved to impeach Independent Counsel Kenneth Starr; his motion was voted down 340–71. When one senator estimated that a trial would take just three weeks, Hastings replied, "Hello? I don't think so. Over on Ego Mountain they don't have a clue."

But even as he was opposing Republicans in Congress, he was opposing Democrats back home. In January 1998 Florida House Democrats ousted Willie Logan, a black from Opa-Locke, as Speaker-designate, claiming that he wasn't a good fundraiser. Hastings respond with more outrage than Logan, who declared himself a "free agent." In a March special election for a Broward state Senate vacancy, he backed the Republican over a Democrat who had voted against Logan. The Democrat still won, but in black precincts where Jeb Bush had won 4% for governor in 1994 the Republican won 54% in 1998. Hastings had friendly meetings with Bush, and proclaimed that competition between the two parties for black votes was a good thing; he said he would back Democratic nominee Buddy MacKay, but not even lukewarmly. In the September primaries he backed a slate of candidates and scored a big victory when his choice ousted an incumbent state Senator from a Broward-Palm Beach black-majority district. Hastings has said before that he will retire in 2002, when the district lines must be redrawn. But in the meantime he has more clout than ever in his home base.

Cook's Call. Safe. Hasting's past judicial affliction certainly hasn't hurt him politically in this overwhelmingly minority and Democrat-dominated district. It is as solidly Democratic as they come, so don't look for any upsets here.

The People: Pop. 1990: 563,645; 4.7% rural; 13.6% age 65 + ; 45% White, 51.7% Black, 0.9% Asian, 0.2% Amer. Indian, 2.3% Other; 8.9% Hispanic Origin. Households: 41.8% married couple families; 20.1% married couple fams. w. children; 31.9% college educ.; median household income: $23,039; per capita income: $10,511; median house value: $67,600; median gross rent: $407.

1996 Presidential Vote		
Clinton (D)	107,884	(75%)
Dole (R)	27,531	(19%)
Perot (I)	9,193	(6%)

1992 Presidential Vote		
Clinton (D)	94,873	(62%)
Bush (R)	35,265	(23%)
Perot (I)	22,084	(15%)

Rep. Alcee L. Hastings (D)

Elected 1992; b. Sept. 5, 1936, Altamonte Springs; home, Miramar; Fisk U., B.A. 1958, Howard U., 1958–60, FL A&M, J.D. 1963; Methodist; single.

Elected Office: Broward Cnty. Circuit Court Judge, 1977–79.

Professional Career: Practicing atty., 1964–77; Federal Judge, U.S. District Court, 1979–89.

DC Office: 2235 RHOB 20515, 202-225-1313; Fax: 202-226-0690; Web site: www.house.gov/alceehastings.

District Offices: Ft. Lauderdale, 954-733-2800; West Palm Beach, 561-684-0565.

Committees: *International Relations* (11th of 23 D): Africa; Asia & the Pacific. *Permanent Select Committee on Intelligence* (7th of 7 D): Human Intelligence, Analysis & Counterintelligence (RMM).

Group Ratings

	ADA	ACLU	AFS	LCV	CON	NTU	NFIB	COC	ACU	NTLC	CHC
1998	80	93	100	92	74	28	0	22	5	3	0
1997	80	—	100	—	4	17	—	20	19	—	—

National Journal Ratings

	1997 LIB — 1997 CONS		1998 LIB — 1998 CONS	
Economic	82%	— 15%	79%	— 0%
Social	85%	— 0%	93%	— 0%
Foreign	74%	— 25%	81%	— 18%

Key Votes of the 105th Congress

1. Clinton Budget Deal	N	5. Puerto Rico Sthood. Ref.	Y	9. Cut $ for B-2 Bombers	Y
2. Education IRAs	N	6. End Highway Set-asides	N	10. Human Rights in China	Y
3. Req. 2/3 to Raise Taxes	*	7. School Prayer Amend.	N	11. Withdraw Bosnia Troops	N
4. Fast-track Trade	N	8. Ovrd. Part. Birth Veto	N	12. End Cuban TV-Marti	N

Election Results

1998 general	Alcee L. Hastings (D)	.... unopposed		($263,794)
1998 primary	Alcee L. Hastings (D)	.... unopposed		
1996 general	Alcee L. Hastings (D)	 102,161	(73%)	($276,708)
	Robert Paul Brown (R)	 36,907	(27%)	($13,417)

GEORGIA

At the close of the 1990s, Atlanta and Georgia have reason for satisfaction. New York was where the 1980s had happened; the 1990s are happening in Atlanta and Georgia—as evidenced by the three-day visit of author Tom Wolfe in November 1998 to publicize his first novel of the decade, *A Man in Full*. Wolfe's great novel of the 1980s, *Bonfire of the Vanities*, was about New York, about the bond traders of Wall Street and Park Avenue and the criminals and prosecutors of the South Bronx. His great novel of the 1990s was about Atlanta and Georgia, centered on a football player turned real estate developer with a mansion in Buckhead and a 29,000-acre hunting estate in south Georgia. The Atlanta *Journal-Constitution*'s "Wolfe Watch" chronicled the author as he dined at the exclusive Piedmont Driving Club and spoke to 1,100 at the Borders bookstore in upscale Buckhead. Sam Massell, the unofficial mayor of Buckhead, offended by a book that shows an Atlanta developer manufacturing a Ku Klux Klan rally to deflate the price of property he wants to buy, stayed away from a Wolfe lunch; Atlanta Mayor Bill Campbell, who denied the existence of the tension between light-skinned and dark-skinned blacks described by Wolfe, issued a calming statement. But other Atlantans were charmed as they heard Wolfe praise the city's ambition and optimism, good manners and unfailing generosity.

Atlanta and Georgia have been in many ways for many years the center of the South, at least since William Tecumseh Sherman marched here in 1864. This is where John Stith Pemberton invented Coca-Cola, where Margaret Mitchell wrote *Gone With the Wind*, where Martin Luther King Jr. grew up, and where most of the civil rights organizations that changed America were headquartered. But in growth and flamboyance, Georgia for decades was outdazzled by other parts of the South—by Texas with its oil wells and high-tech industries, by Florida with Miami Beach and Disney World, even by North Carolina with its Research Triangle and college basketball champions. But in the 1990s, Georgia has grown faster than any of them. In 1990 Georgia was the 11th largest state, with 6.4 million people; by 1998 Georgia had 7.6 million, with the fastest growth rate east of the Rockies, and had passed fast-growing North Carolina to become the tenth-largest state—the first time Georgia has been among the top ten since the 1850 Census. Almost all this growth has come in the booming Atlanta metropolitan area, not in the core city, but amid the hills of suburban counties for almost 100 miles around. Atlanta, long a regional capital, has become a world city, a status suitably memorialized when it hosted the 1996 Summer Olympics, and re-emphasized every day as travelers all over the world watch the news from the CNN Broadcast Center next door to the World Congress Center.

Atlanta's growth is not immediately apparent to the traveler. Heading into Hartsfield International Airport, the busiest in the world in 1998, you see mostly trees; even on the traffic-filled Route 400 toll road in the booming northern suburbs you see what looks like forest all around. Atlanta is expanding rapidly into what were once rural counties, and Atlantans drive more miles per day (34) than residents of any other major metro area. The urban landscapes here still have what author John Brinckerhoff Jackson called the disorderliness characteristic of the South; even the gleaming malls and office towers are never out of sight of kudzu vines and muddy creeks. The congestion may be too much: Local elections are being won by "smart growth" advocates and traffic jams and spiking real estate prices may be discouraging new businesses; Forsyth County was the fastest-growing in the U.S. from 1997 to 1998, increasing in population by 13%. The legislature in March 1999 passed a proposal by Governor Roy Barnes to create a transportation superagency with broad powers to impose transit systems and highways on local governments.

Neither Atlanta's rise to world eminence nor its rise as the capital of the South was inevitable.

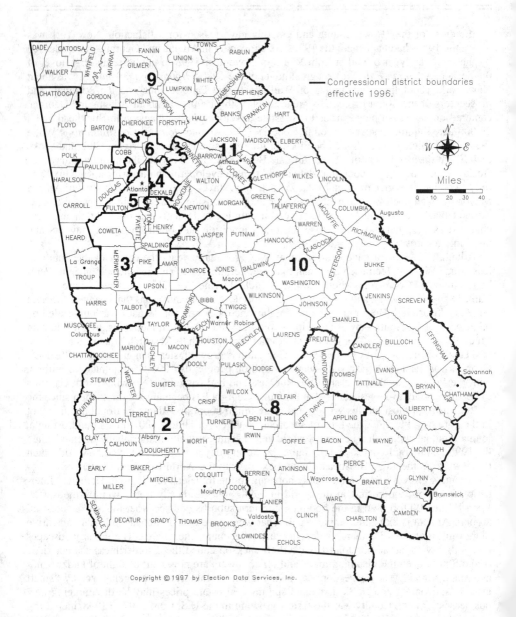

Congressional district boundaries effective 1996.

This was only a small, though well located, railroad crossroads when it was burned by General William Tecumseh Sherman's troops as they began their "march to the sea." Richmond, Charleston and New Orleans all had stronger claims to being the central focus of the South a century ago. But in the 20th Century, two figures imprinted Atlanta on the national imagination. One was Margaret Mitchell, whose 1936 novel *Gone with the Wind* inspired the 1939 movie in which Tara was improbably sited near a burning Atlanta. The other was Martin Luther King Jr., reared in Atlanta and based there during most of his career, as a leader and ultimately the national symbol of the civil rights revolution that changed the South and the nation. Linking the two was Atlanta's business community, notably Robert Woodruff, who headed Coca-Cola from 1932–60 and made Coke a worldwide enterprise. Perhaps aware that a world company could not indefinitely be associated with racial segregation, Woodruff and William Hartsfield, mayor from 1937–61, cooperated with blacks and promoted Atlanta as "the city too busy to hate." Hartsfield's successor, Ivan Allen, elected in 1961 and 1965, supported the Civil Rights Act of 1964, as Peachtree Center and the first atriumed Hyatt Regency were going up in downtown Atlanta.

This new Atlanta was growing up amid a mostly rural, deeply segregationist Georgia that as late as 1960 cast the second-highest Democratic percentage of any state for president: Memories of General Sherman were still strong. Political contests typically matched Atlanta-supported moderates against rural-supported segregationists, and the latter invariably won: Georgia's electoral votes were cast for Barry Goldwater in 1964 and George Wallace in 1968. Then came change in the person of Jimmy Carter, former nuclear submarine officer and one-term state senator, who was elected governor in 1970 with a rural base as well as conspicuous black support. On taking office he proclaimed a reconciliation of the races and installed a portrait of Martin Luther King Jr. in the Capitol. Carter thus became one of the first politicians from the rural South to celebrate and honor the civil rights revolution and set himself on the road to being elected President in 1976. Today he remains a prominent figure in Atlanta, promoting Habitat for Humanity, and around the world eager to employ his skills at conflict resolution. Without exactly saying so, Georgia has developed what Charles Moskos and John Sibley Butler in their book on races in the Army, *All We Can Be*, call an Anglo-African culture, a merger of traditions that were long associated intimately in private life but rigidly and even violently separated in public. This is the dominant culture of the Army, Moskos and Butler argue, and could turn out to be—though Tom Wolfe doesn't seem to think so—the dominant culture of Georgia. In politics, criticisms of Atlanta mayors are sometimes taken as racist, but two black congressmen are now from white-majority districts, and Andrew Young won in a white-majority district as long ago as 1972. Republicans have made a major effort to recruit black candidates, and more black Republicans ran for state and federal office in 1998 in Georgia than in any other state.

If for years Georgia was a heavily Democratic state, and if there were signs in the early 1990s it was headed toward being heavily Republican, it now seems excruciatingly closely divided between the parties. Bill Clinton carried Georgia by 43.5%–42.9% in 1992 and lost it by 47%–46% in 1996. In 1998 Democratic Governor Roy Barnes won by 52%–44% and Republican Senator Paul Coverdell won by 52%–45%, and these were veritable landslides compared to the 51%–49% results the last time those seats came up. Similarly, Democrat Max Cleland was elected to the Senate in 1996 by 49%–48%—a result that would have required a runoff under an old Georgia law that was repealed by the Democratic legislature because it had enabled Coverdell to win the 1992 Senate race after finishing behind on Election Day. One leading indicator: primary turnout. In 1998, 54% of the primary vote was cast in the Democratic contest; that November, 53% of the two-party vote for governor was cast for the Democrat.

In other races the results have see-sawed a bit. In House races, a racially driven redistricting plan backfired on its Democratic architects, as the delegation changed from eight white Democrats, one black Democrat and one Republican (Newt Gingrich) going into the 1992 election, to zero white Democrats (after the last one switched parties), three black Democrats and eight

Republicans (including the speaker of the House) in mid-1995. The balance has stayed the same since, despite some serious challenges by both parties. In the legislature, Republicans made serious gains in the mid-1990s, but fell back in House seats in 1998.

What are the lines of division? The inner core of metro Atlanta—Fulton, DeKalb and Clayton Counties—casts 22% of the state's votes: It is about half black, with many of the rest affluent whites with strong party allegiances on either side; in the top 1998 races it voted more than 60% Democratic. Then there is the ring of suburban counties—17 of them, by Census definition—reaching far into what was once countryside, which cast 30% of the state's votes. The population is heavily but not entirely white, and the voting preference heavily Republican; Senator Paul Coverdell carried the Atlanta ring 62%–34%. Then there is the rest of Georgia, slower growing, with 48% of the vote, and the bulk of the swing votes in close elections: Governor Roy Barnes carried it 55%–42% and Coverdell 54%–45%. Georgia's smaller cities look like miniature Atlantas, with Democratic cores and Republican rings; small-town counties in the north and on the coast lean Republican, those in the center and west lean Democratic.

Who owns the political future of Georgia? No one—or whoever is able to see past current conventional wisdom and articulate a vision for change. When Newt Gingrich in the early 1990s proclaimed that Georgia, the South and the House could go Republican, few believed him; but his energy and initiative helped make it happen. When the Republican Party seemed ascendant in state politics, longtime Democratic politician Zell Miller advanced a program—a state lottery, with proceeds to go for college scholarships for students who make good grades—that helped make him one of the nation's most popular governors, and helped to elect Democratic governors in 1998 not only in Georgia, but in neighboring South Carolina and Alabama. Georgia may have its travails—the farm drought of 1998, with low pecan, peanut and tobacco crops—but it is not yet through leading and redefining the South, and the nation as well.

Governor. Roy Barnes, elected governor in 1998, is a lawyer and professional politician who has spent almost all his adult life in public office—a political liability in the angry early 1990s, when he ran third in the 1990 Democratic gubernatorial primary, but an asset in the prosperous, contented late 1990s, when he won convincingly. Barnes grew up in Cobb County, when it was mostly rural and Marietta was a courthouse town dependent on the Lockheed aircraft factory, not a booming edge city with burgeoning small businesses. He returned from college and law school, became a prosecutor in the Cobb district attorney's office, and was elected to the state Senate in 1974, at 26, and served 16 years in the then-large Democratic majority, ran for governor and lost in 1990, then was elected to the state House from an increasingly Republican county in 1992.

In early 1997, Barnes was not even running for governor; he entered the race only in August, after Lieutenant Governor Pierre Howard declared he would not run. Leading the polls was Attorney General Mike Bowers, a stern conservative who had switched to become a Republican. But in June 1997 Bowers admitted he had had a 10-year affair with a former state employee, and he sunk like a stone. The Republican favorite then was Guy Millner, who started the Norrell temporary employee firm and spent freely of his $160-million-plus fortune to lose narrowly to Governor Zell Miller in 1994 and Senator Max Cleland in 1996. But Georgia voters were no longer as angry or as Republican in 1998. Governor Zell Miller had one of the highest job ratings in the nation. He had run in 1990 promising a state lottery; he used the proceeds to pass HOPE scholarships, guaranteeing tuition in any Georgia college to any Georgia student maintaining a B average. Miller was also popular for his two-strikes law (life for a second felony), welfare reform and statewide pre-kindergarten. Barnes also profited from the nature of the opposition. His chief primary opponent, Secretary of State Lewis Massey, was 36 and looked younger; two other intellectually serious candidates were poorly funded. Barnes raised $4 million by the primary and stressed the issue of the hour, providing more choice of doctors in managed care health insurance plans. He was anti-abortion and endorsed by the National Rifle Association; he had to apologize for a 1980s vote against the Martin Luther King Jr. holiday.

Barnes led Massey in the July 1998 primary by 49%–28%; two days later Massey withdrew from the runoff. Meanwhile, Guy Millner had beaten Bowers by only 50.4%–39.9%, avoiding a runoff by only 1,574 votes. Millner started by running ads accusing Barnes of being soft on crime; Barnes promised to cut residential property taxes. Millner constantly criticized Atlanta Mayor Bill Campbell and was accused of "playing the race card." Millner, who refused to appear in primary debates, made a show of bringing a flatbed truck to a joint appearance at the Gwinnett County convention center and calling on Barnes to debate right there. But Millner's previous races apparently did not leave all voters with a favorable impression. And the overall mood worked for Barnes. "I don't see all those negative things that Guy Millner sees. I see a Georgia that prospers," he said. Polls showed the race close throughout, but Barnes steadily made gains and Millner didn't. The final result was a solid 52%–44% victory for Barnes. He was helped by black turnout, which according to the VNS exit poll was 29% of the total, slightly higher than the black share of population; he also did especially well among the youngest voters—a good omen for Democrats. The question now is whether this politically experienced and talented governor can deliver on his promises as spectacularly as Zell Miller did.

Senior Senator. Paul Coverdell, Georgia's senior senator, first elected in 1992, has become a key part of the Republican leadership and in 1998 became the first senator re-elected to this seat since 1974. Coverdell grew up in Kansas City and went to the University of Missouri journalism school, then served in the Army in Okinawa, Taiwan and Korea. In 1964, at 25, he started working in his parents' insurance marketing business in Atlanta. In 1970, as the Republican Party was starting to rise in the South, he was elected to the state Senate; in 1974, when the Republican rise seemed stalled, he became minority leader (of 5 Republicans versus 51 Democrats). He was Republican state chairman in the mid-1980s, supporting George Bush in 1988, and served as Peace Corps director from 1989–91, leading the Peace Corps into Eastern Europe and Russia.

In 1992 Coverdell ran for the Senate and battled through four elections before winning by barely more than 1%. In the July primary he ran first, 37%–24% ahead of former U.S. Attorney and now 7th District Congressman Bob Barr. In the August runoff he beat Barr by 1,548 votes. In the general he faced incumbent Wyche Fowler, a politically savvy liberal who had represented the black-majority 5th District. Fowler had beaten Coverdell once before in a 1977 House special election. Coverdell attacked Fowler in the Senate race for opposing the Gulf war, supporting defense cuts, backing the congressional pay raise and defending the House bank. Fowler led in November, but only by 49%–48%, less than the absolute majority then required by Georgia law; so there was a runoff on November 24. Bill Clinton and Al Gore campaigned for Fowler; Coverdell got enthusiastic support from national and local Republicans, the Libertarian candidate who had deadlocked the first race, and the Georgia Ross Perot organization. Both national parties poured $1 million of soft money into the race, but Coverdell had the momentum and won 51%–49%.

In Georgia Coverdell had the reputation of an urban Republican; in the Senate he has become a leader, the Conference secretary since December 1996 and a close ally of Majority Leader Trent Lott. He supported the balanced budget amendment and line-item veto; inspired by the Clinton budget and tax package, he sponsored a constitutional amendment to ban retroactive tax increases. He opposed the Clinton health care plan and worked to include medical savings accounts in the 1996 health care portability law. Though pro-choice, he has opposed partial-birth abortions, abortions in military base hospitals and federal funding of abortions. He supported IRS reform and, struck that Georgia ranked fifth in random audits per taxpayer, called for abolishing random audits altogether.

Coverdell's most distinctive legislation has been his bill to establish education IRAs, cosponsored with New Jersey Democrat Bob Torricelli. It was attacked by most Democrats and stalled in November 1997; it passed the Senate in April 1998 but was vetoed by President Clinton. Coverdell also introduced a school choice bill in 1997 to allow parents of kids in high-violence schools to send them elsewhere. Much of Coverdell's work has revolved around drugs and peanuts. He was part of the successful move to preserve peanut programs in the 1996

Freedom to Farm Act, and in 1997 became chairman of the Agriculture Committee's Marketing, Inspection and Product Promotion Subcommittee, which will allow him to protect peanut programs. He sought to reform guest worker programs after an INS roundup of Vidalia onion harvesters in May 1998. Since 1995 he has chaired the Western Hemisphere Subcommittee on Foreign Relations, where he supported more money for drug interdiction in the Caribbean, opposed the nomination of William Weld to be ambassador to Mexico in 1997, and backed debt relief for countries stricken by Hurricane Mitch in 1998. He worked successfully with Joseph Biden to get tough penalties for felons who use drugs, such as the so-called date rape drug Rohypnol. He worked to amend the 1996 Immigration Act to get tougher sentences for drug smugglers and deportation of immigrants who commit crimes of domestic violence, stalking or rape. He opposed the Chemical Weapons Treaty and opposed any new round of base closings, which threatens the Warner Robins depot in south Georgia. He supported the 1998 Clinton proposal to double the number of Peace Corps volunteers.

Going into the 1998 election, Coverdell had little substantive recognition in Georgia, partly because the Atlanta *Journal-Constitution* devoted most of its Capitol Hill coverage to House Speaker Newt Gingrich. He avoided the toughest possible opponent when outgoing Governor Zell Miller adamantly refused to run. But he faced serious opposition from Michael Coles, a Cobb County millionaire (the Great American Cookie Company) who spent $2.4 million of his own money on an unsuccessful race against Gingrich in 1996. "Coverdell works," was the incumbent's slogan, and his ads showed him in rapid-fire motion; he emphasized his support of education IRAs and his efforts to stop the drug trade. Coles attacked Coverdell for undermining public schools and called for patients to have the right to sue HMOs—an issue also raised by Roy Barnes in his campaign for governor. But Coverdell's dogged fundraising enabled him to outspend Coles $6.9 million to $5 million, and Coverdell won 52%–45%—not overwhelming, but the biggest margin in this seat since 1974. He ran especially well with high-income and college (but not graduate school) educated voters, according to the VNS exit poll. That also suggested that his strongest issue was taxes, but that he ran about even with voters concerned about education, the economy and Social Security.

When Connie Mack announced in March 1999 he would not seek re-election, Coverdell became the leading candidate to succeed him as Senate Republican Conference chairman.

Junior Senator. Max Cleland was elected senator in 1996, after a long career in public life and having overcome grievous injuries sustained during the Vietnam war. Cleland grew up in Lithonia, now an Atlanta suburb in DeKalb County, but then a country town that could have been hundreds of miles from the city. After college and a master's degree in American history at Emory, he volunteered for the Army and went to Vietnam in 1967, at 25; he lost both legs and one arm when a loose grenade he thought to be his own accidentally exploded, but in March 1999 the marine who saved Cleland's life told him the grenade had belonged to another soldier, lifting Cleland's emotional burden from the accident. In 1970 Cleland was elected to the Georgia Senate, where he wrote a law to make public facilities accessible to the handicapped. In 1977 Jimmy Carter appointed him head of the Veterans Administration, the youngest ever. In 1982 he was elected Georgia secretary of State, and was re-elected by wide margins three times. In October 1995, Senator Sam Nunn surprised Georgians when he announced he would retire in 1996, at 58, after 24 years there and despite his position as ranking member of Armed Services. Cleland promptly announced he would run and had no primary opposition.

The leader in the Republican primary was Guy Millner, the 1994 (and later 1998) gubernatorial nominee who founded the Norrell temporary employee firm and made a fortune, and who ran on a staunch conservative platform. Also running were Johnny Isakson, the 1990 gubernatorial nominee (who succeeded Newt Gingrich in 1999), who was pro-choice on abortion, and Clint Day, scion of the Days Inn family, who ran as a Christian conservative. In the July 9 primary, Millner led Isakson, 42%–35%. The Summer Olympics began 10 days later, overshadowing the campaign. Millner won the August 6 runoff 53%–47%.

Cleland's campaign was mostly positive, making folksy, self-deprecating speeches, running soft-focus positive ads showing him shaving, putting on a tie, and driving, saying, "I was raised to believe you can't expect help if you don't help yourself." His issue stands were mostly conservative: for a balanced budget amendment, term limits, the 1996 welfare reform bill, the death penalty for drug dealers, victims' rights, and a constitutional amendment allowing limits on campaign spending. Millner spent more than $9 million altogether. He ran tough ads charging that Cleland sought parole for a killer with a politically connected father who, when released, committed another murder, and criticizing Cleland for a $300,000 settlement paid to a worker in his office when she blew the whistle on his use of state computers for political purposes. The result was exceedingly close. Cleland won 49%–48%; Millner had a microscopic edge in metro Atlanta and ran well in north Georgia, but he carried few counties south of Atlanta. These percentages were identical to those four years earlier, when Democrat Wyche Fowler led Republican Paul Coverdell, triggering a runoff three weeks later which Coverdell won. But in the meantime, the Democratic legislature, led by Speaker Tom Murphy, repealed the runoff law, and Millner did not have a second chance.

Cleland has a moderate voting record, just to the left of the Senate center. He got Sam Nunn's place on Armed Services, and also on the Personnel Subcommittee, where he became ranking Democrat. He authored a 1998 law to require the Defense and Veterans Affairs departments to cooperate on veterans health care and to mandate pilot tests of three health care options for military retirees. He made his first inspection trip to Europe in April 1998 and came home more supportive of continued American deployment in Bosnia. Also in 1998 he and Republican Chuck Hagel sponsored a new treatment of veterans' preference.

One great cause for Cleland is campaign finance reform; he is a strong supporter of the McCain-Feingold bill. He has sought more funding for women's business centers. He sponsored a bill to allow the confiscation of cash of anyone carrying more than $10,000 if found in an airport or on a highway hidden in a "highly unusual" manner; this is targeted at drug dealers. He worked with Congressman Jack Kingston for acquisition of the Greyfield tract on Cumberland Island. In 1997 he had health problems, including a sleeping disorder which triggered memories of the explosion that cost him his arm and legs. "I find life a constant series of being broken and then recovering and then moving on and overcoming." But he never missed a vote, and his health improved in 1998. In December 1998 he got a seat on the Commerce Committee. His seat comes up in 2002; 3d District Congressman Mac Collins has expressed interest in the race, and 1st District Congressman Jack Kingston is another possibility.

Presidential politics. Georgia used to be an outlier in presidential politics—the second-most Democratic state in 1960, for Barry Goldwater in 1964 and George Wallace in 1968, heavily Republican in 1972, strongly for native son Jimmy Carter in 1976 and 1980. In the 1990s it has emerged as one of the prime marginal states—for Bill Clinton by 13,000 votes in 1992, for Bob Dole by 27,000 votes in 1996. With many new voters every cycle, Georgia is likely to remain seriously contested and unpredictable—and more important as it rises after 2000 from 13 electoral votes to 14 or 15.

Georgia's 1992 presidential primary was scheduled one week before Super Tuesday at the insistence of Governor Zell Miller, who wanted to help Bill Clinton, and did: Clinton won smartly to balance losses in Maryland and Colorado the same day. George Bush's 64%–36% victory here over Pat Buchanan showed the Buchanan brigades were not about to overrun the South. Bob Dole similarly defeated Buchanan 41%–29%. Turnout here has been a gauge of changing partisan balance: Republican turnout increased from 200,000 in 1980 to 400,000 in 1988, 454,000 in 1992 and 561,000 in 1996. Democratic primary turnout fell from 684,000 in 1984 to 612,000 in 1988 and 454,600 in 1992.

Congressional districting. With a burgeoning population spreading rapidly across the hills of north Georgia within a nearly 100-mile radius of downtown Atlanta, Georgia is a redistricter's dream—or nightmare. For the 1990s, Democratic Speaker Tom Murphy drew up a plan that was intended to end the career of Newt Gingrich, safeguard Democratic incumbents and create three black-majority seats. But each of those goals was frustrated. Gingrich moved to a heavily Republican suburban Atlanta seat, was re-elected and became speaker. Democratic incumbents retired, were beaten or switched parties, to the point that a delegation 9–1 Democratic in October 1992 was 8–3 Republican by April 1995. And in June 1995 the Supreme Court ruled that the convoluted black-majority 11th District, extending from Atlanta to Savannah, was a "racial gerrymander," and a new plan, with just one black-majority district, was drawn up by a federal court in December 1995; it was approved by the Supreme Court in June 1997. In fact, all the black incumbents were re-elected; the idea that white Georgians are unwilling to vote for black candidates was refuted as long ago as 1972, when Andrew Young was elected in a majority-white district.

The 2000 Census is likely to give fast-growing Georgia one or two new districts. Democrats are likely once again to control the process, unless Republicans gain enough state legislative seats to control one house of the legislature in 2000—not an impossibility, but not something anyone expects to see happen. But the creation of more black-majority districts would, as the 1994 elections showed, take critical numbers of Democratic votes out of potentially marginal seats. The rearrangement of lines in south Georgia would probably not critically weaken the now well-entrenched Republican incumbents there, though it might give Democrats a pickup if one doesn't run for re-election. It might be possible to create a new Democratic district based in the Atlanta core of Fulton, DeKalb and Clayton Counties. But the fastest growth has been in the northern suburban ring, which is very heavily Republican. So the prospects for a majority-Democratic delegation seem distant.

The People: Est. Pop. 1998: 7,642,207; Pop. 1990: 6,478,216, up 18% 1990–1998. 2.8% of U.S. total, 10th largest; 36.8% rural. Median age: 33.3 years. 10.6% 65 years and over. 71.1% White, 26.9% Black, 1.1% Asian, 0.2% Amer. Indian, 0.6% Other; 1.6% Hispanic Origin. Households: 55.2% married couple families; 28.2% married couple fams. w. children; 41.3% college educ.; median household income: $29,021; per capita income: $13,631; 64.9% owner occupied housing; median house value: $71,300; median monthly rent: $344. 4.2% Unemployment. 1998 Voting age pop.: 5,678,000. 1998 Turnout: 1,792,808; 32% of VAP. Registered voters (1998): 4,016,542; no party registration.

Political Lineup: Governor, Roy Barnes (D); Lt. Gov., Mark Taylor (D); Secy. of State, Cathy Cox (D); Atty. Gen., Thurbert Baker (D); Auditor, Claude L. Vickers (D); State Senate, 56 (34 D, 22 R); Majority Leader, Charles Walker (D); State Assembly, 180 (102 D, 78 R); House Speaker, Thomas B. Murphy (D). Senators, Paul Coverdell (R) and Max Cleland (D). Representatives, 11 (3 D, 8 R).

Elections Division: 404-656-2871; **Filing Deadline for U.S. Congress:** April 28, 2000.

1996 Presidential Vote

Dole (R) 1,080,840 (47%)
Clinton (D) 1,053,848 (46%)
Perot (I) 146,337   (6%)

1996 Republican Presidential Primary

Dole (R) 226,732 (41%)
Buchanan (R) 162,627 (29%)
Alexander (R) 75,855 (14%)
Forbes (R) 71,278 (13%)
Others 22,577   (4%)

1992 Presidential Vote

Clinton (D) 1,008,966 (44%)
Bush (R) 995,252 (43%)
Perot (I) 309,657 (13%)

GOVERNOR

Gov. Roy Barnes (D)

Elected 1998, term expires Jan. 2003; b. Mar. 11, 1948, Atlanta; home, Marietta; U. of GA, A.B. 1969, J.D. 1972; Methodist; married (Marie).

Elected Office: Cobb County Asst. D.A., 1972–74; GA Senate, 1974–90; GA House of Reps., 1993–98.

Professional Career: Practicing atty., 1975–98.

Office: 203 State Capitol, Atlanta, 30334, 404-656-1776; Fax: 404-657-7332; Web site: www.state.ga.us.

Election Results

1998 gen.	Roy Barnes (D)	941,076	(52%)
	Guy Millner (R)	790,201	(44%)
	Others	61,531	(3%)
1998 runoff	Roy Barnes (D)	221,651	(83%)
	Lewis A. Massey (D)	45,735	(17%)
1998 prim.	Roy Barnes (D)	239,517	(49%)
	Lewis A. Massey (D)	135,920	(28%)
	David Poythress (D)	65,860	(14%)
	Steve Langford (D)	31,543	(6%)
	Others	14,001	(3%)
1994 gen.	Zell Miller (D)	788,926	(51%)
	Guy Millner (R)	756,371	(49%)

SENATORS

Sen. Paul Coverdell (R)

Elected 1992, seat up 2004; b. Jan. 20, 1939, Des Moines, IA; home, Atlanta; U. of MO, B.A., 1960; Methodist; married (Nancy).

Military Career: Army, 1962–64.

Elected Office: GA Senate, 1970–89, Minority Ldr., 1974–89.

Professional Career: Businessman, Coverdell & Co. Inc., 1964–89; Chmn., GA Repub. Party, 1985–87; Dir., Peace Corps, 1989–91.

DC Office: 200 RSOB, 20510, 202-224-3643; Fax: 202-228-3783; Web site: www.senate.gov/~coverdell.

State Offices: Atlanta, 404-347-2202; Augusta, 706-722-0032; Columbus, 706-322-7920; Dalton, 706-226-1925; Macon, 912-742-0205; Moultrie, 912-985-8113; Savannah, 912-238-3244.

Committees: *Republican Conference Secretary. Agriculture, Nutrition & Forestry* (5th of 10 R): Forestry, Conservation & Rural Revitalization; Marketing, Inspection & Product Promotion (Chmn.). *Foreign Relations* (3d of 10 R): East Asian & Pacific Affairs; European Affairs; Western Hemisphere, Peace Corps, Narcotics & Terrorism (Chmn.). *Small Business* (3d of 10 R).

Group Ratings

	ADA	ACLU	AFS	LCV	CON	NTU	NFIB	COC	ACU	NTLC	CHC
1998	0	14	11	0	2	66	100	89	92	93	82
1997	10	—	11	—	42	77	—	90	92	—	—

National Journal Ratings

	1997 LIB — 1997 CONS		1998 LIB — 1998 CONS	
Economic	37% —	57%	18% —	72%
Social	17% —	72%	23% —	76%
Foreign	0% —	77%	29% —	58%

Key Votes of the 105th Congress

1. Bal. Budget Amend.	Y	5. Satcher for Surgeon Gen.	Y	9. Chem. Weapons Treaty	N
2. Clinton Budget Deal	Y	6. Highway Set-asides	N	10. Cuban Humanitarian Aid	N
3. Cloture on Tobacco	N	7. Table Child Gun locks	Y	11. Table Bosnia Troops	Y
4. Education IRAs	Y	8. Ovrd. Part. Birth Veto	Y	12. $ for Test-ban Treaty	N

Election Results

1998 general	Paul Coverdell (R) 918,540	(52%)	($6,936,745)	
	Michael Coles (D) 791,904	(45%)	($5,275,419)	
	Others 43,467	(2%)		
1998 primary	Paul Coverdell (R) .... unopposed			
1992 runoff	Paul Coverdell (R) 635,114	(51%)	($3,193,774)	
	Wyche Fowler (D) 618,877	(49%)	($4,894,620)	
1992 general	Wyche Fowler (D) 1,108,416	(49%)		
	Paul Coverdell (R) 1,073,282	(48%)		
	Others 69,889	(3%)		

Sen. Max Cleland (D)

Elected 1996, seat up 2002; b. Aug. 24, 1942, Atlanta; home, Lithonia; Stetson U., B.A. 1964, Emory U., M.A. 1968; Methodist; single.

Military Career: Army, 1965–68 (Vietnam).

Elected Office: GA Senate, 1970–75; GA Secy. of State, 1982–96.

Professional Career: Staff Mbr., Senate Veterans' Affairs Cmte., 1975–77; Administrator, U.S. Veterans' Admin., 1977–81.

DC Office: 461 DSOB, 20510, 202-224-3521; Fax: 202-224-0072; Web site: www.senate.gov/~cleland.

State Offices: Albany, 912-430-7796; Atlanta, 404-331-4811; Augusta, 706-722-4040; Columbus, 706-649-7705; Dalton, 706-275-8905; Macon, 912-755-1779; Savannah, 912-352-8283.

Committees: *Armed Services* (7th of 9 D): Airland Forces; Personnel (RMM); Readiness & Management Support. *Commerce, Science & Transportation* (9th of 9 D): Aviation; Communications; Surface Transportation & Merchant Marine. *Governmental Affairs* (6th of 7 D): International Security, Proliferation & Federal Services; Investigations (Permanent). *Small Business* (6th of 8 D).

Group Ratings

	ADA	ACLU	AFS	LCV	CON	NTU	NFIB	COC	ACU	NTLC	CHC
1998	85	86	78	63	56	14	44	56	0	11	18
1997	75	—	67	—	36	28	—	80	8	—	—

National Journal Ratings

	1997 LIB — 1997 CONS		1998 LIB — 1998 CONS	
Economic	60% —	36%	59% —	39%
Social	64% —	29%	74% —	0%
Foreign	62% —	32%	65% —	27%

Key Votes of the 105th Congress

1. Bal. Budget Amend.	Y	5. Satcher for Surgeon Gen.	Y	9. Chem. Weapons Treaty	Y
2. Clinton Budget Deal	Y	6. Highway Set-asides	Y	10. Cuban Humanitarian Aid	Y
3. Cloture on Tobacco	Y	7. Table Child Gun locks	N	11. Table Bosnia Troops	Y
4. Education IRAs	Y	8. Ovrd. Part. Birth Veto	N	12. $ for Test-ban Treaty	Y

Election Results

1996 general	Max Cleland (D)	1,103,993	(49%)	($2,926,391)
	Guy Millner (R)	1,073,969	(48%)	($9,858,955)
	Others	81,270	(4%)	
1996 primary	Max Cleland (D)	unopposed		
1990 general	Sam Nunn (D)	unopposed		($1,214,695)

FIRST DISTRICT

Georgia's South Atlantic coast, long one of the poorest parts of the country, has been booming in recent years. The area was settled in the 1730s by James Oglethorpe as Britain's 13th coastal colony as a refuge and reformatory for convicts. It did not take long for the sea islands and lowlands along the wide rivers and inlets to become plantation country. Savannah, the state's first capital, was by the 1830s one of America's booming cotton ports; it languished after the Civil War, living off paper mills and chemical plants in the 20th Century, with impoverished blacks on the islands still speaking Gullah dialects. Then, a few decades ago, preservationists started restoring houses and churches on the grid punctuated by 24 squares that Oglethorpe had laid out more than 200 years before. Today Savannah is one of the most graciously preserved cities in the country, and a major tourism mecca thanks to the popularity of John Berendt's *Midnight in the Garden of Good and Evil*, a somewhat-based-on-facts story of eccentricity and murder that was on the bestseller lists from 1994 to 1998. Some of the islands have been preserved as well, for years by rich private owners, more recently by government; one such is Cumberland Island, now mostly government-owned, where John F. Kennedy Jr. married Carolyn Bessette in a private ceremony in September 1996.

The 1st Congressional District of Georgia includes all the state's Atlantic coast and goes 50 or so miles inland, through cotton and tobacco fields and softwood forests. There are more exotic products here as well: Toombs County is the home of the fragrant Vidalia onions that folks say are so sweet you can eat 'em like an apple, while Claxton in tiny Evans County has for nearly a century been home to two of the nation's prime fruitcake makers. The boundaries were changed a bit in the 1995 court-mandated redistricting, in which the 1st lost some rural counties and gained black neighborhoods in Savannah; the black percentage rose from 23% to 31%. Though the counties in the 1st District are ancestrally Democratic, most voters here are conservative on cultural and military issues. That, plus coastal prosperity, has made this area Republican at the top of the ticket and even in some statewide contests; in 1998 the 1st voted for Democrat Roy Barnes for governor and Republican Paul Coverdell for senator.

The congressman from the 1st District is Jack Kingston, a Republican first elected in 1992. Kingston grew up in Texas, Ethiopia, and Athens, Georgia, the son of a professor; after college he moved to Savannah in 1977 and became a commercial insurance agent. In 1984 he was elected to the Georgia House, at 29, and served eight years. In 1992, when incumbent Democrat Lindsay Thomas retired to work on the Summer Olympics, Kingston ran for Congress. Against Democrat Barbara Christmas, a school principal in four counties over the years, Kingston won decisively—58%–42%, with a 2–1 margin in his home base of Savannah and Chatham County.

In the House, Kingston has a mostly conservative voting record and has tended to district interests as have Democratic congressmen of yore. Opposing the House's 1998 five-day work week, he said, "I'm just enough of a populist to believe that the real action is on the streets of America and not in Washington." He has parted company with the Republican leadership on some issues, notably NAFTA and GATT, decrying the World Trade Organization. He serves on the Agriculture Subcommittee of Appropriations, where he has used his vote and lobbied his colleagues for district interests. One is sugar. The nation's largest sugar refinery, Savannah Foods, is in the 1st District, and in May 1996 he tried to get a cap of 21 cents a pound on the price of raw sugar, but faced spirited opposition from lawmakers from cane- and sugar beat-producing states, including then-Appropriations Chairman Bob Livingston of Louisiana. He also failed in his push for an amendment to the 1996 immigration reform bill to allow farmers to hire foreign workers to harvest crops like Vidalia onions, and withholding 25% of their wages until they are ready to return home.

More successful was a Kingston amendment to a spending bill barring requests for FBI files except for those of presidential appointees or regarding clear threats to national security, as attested by the attorney general or White House counsel; this was prompted by the fact that one of Kingston's top aide's files was among those found in the Clinton White House. On local issues, Kingston has fought for historic preservation and looked after Fort Stewart, with its 25,900 military and civilian employees. He has worked to bring in $7 million for replacing the Sidney Lanier drawbridge in Brunswick and $12 million for acquisition of the Greyfield tract on Cumberland Island, although a local Park Service official criticized him for holding onto the first $6.4 million until the Service developed a plan for a road to Plum Orchard mansion.

Kingston was re-elected by better than 2–1 margins in 1994 and 1996. In 1998 he was pleased to be unopposed and argued that was better for his constituents. "What happens is a lot of campaigning is rhetoric as opposed to really listening and learning. You have to repeat the message . . . over and over again. It's more of a debate than a dialogue, whereas governing is more of a dialogue."

Cook's Call. *Safe.* Although Kingston has continued to win by impressive margins, this district is theoretically competitive. Redistricting in 1996 boosted the black population from 23% to 31%, meaning that a Democrat capturing all the black vote would need only to pick up 19 points from other voters for the win. Kingston looks pretty secure, but, should he move on or if the district's white population is further diluted in 2002, this seat could be quite competitive.

The People: Pop. 1990: 588,541; 37.1% rural; 11.7% age 65+; 67.7% White, 30.5% Black, 0.8% Asian, 0.3% Amer. Indian, 0.7% Other; 1.6% Hispanic Origin. Households: 55.7% married couple families; 28.9% married couple fams. w. children; 36.7% college educ.; median household income: $24,779; per capita income: $11,429; median house value: $59,400; median gross rent: $275.

1996 Presidential Vote

Dole (R) 87,895 (49%)
Clinton (D) 81,804 (45%)
Perot (I) 11,491 (6%)

1992 Presidential Vote

Bush (R) 88,703 (47%)
Clinton (D) 71,770 (38%)
Perot (I) 28,292 (15%)

Rep. Jack Kingston (R)

Elected 1992; b. Apr. 24, 1955, Bryan, TX; home, Savannah; U. of GA, B.S. 1978; Episcopalian; married (Libby).

Elected Office: GA House of Reps., 1984–92.

Professional Career: Insurance agent, 1979–92.

DC Office: 1034 LHOB 20515, 202-225-5831; Fax: 202-226-2269; Web site: www.house.gov/kingston.

District Offices: Brunswick, 912-265-9010; Savannah, 912-352-0101; Statesboro, 912-489-8797.

Committees: *Appropriations* (20th of 34 R): Agriculture, Rural Development, & FDA; Foreign Operations & Export Financing; Interior.

Group Ratings

	ADA	ACLU	AFS	LCV	CON	NTU	NFIB	COC	ACU	NTLC	CHC
1998	0	6	0	8	66	69	100	82	100	100	100
1997	5	—	0	—	39	66	—	80	96	—	—

National Journal Ratings

	1997 LIB — 1997 CONS		1998 LIB — 1998 CONS	
Economic	0%	90%	15%	81%
Social	37%	61%	3%	90%
Foreign	24%	72%	19%	75%

Key Votes of the 105th Congress

1. Clinton Budget Deal	Y	5. Puerto Rico Sthood. Ref.	N	9. Cut $ for B-2 Bombers	N
2. Education IRAs	Y	6. End Highway Set-asides	Y	10. Human Rights in China	Y
3. Req. 2/3 to Raise Taxes	Y	7. School Prayer Amend.	Y	11. Withdraw Bosnia Troops	Y
4. Fast-track Trade	Y	8. Ovrd. Part. Birth Veto	Y	12. End Cuban TV-Marti	N

Election Results

1998 general	Jack Kingston (R)	unopposed		($232,812)
1998 primary	Jack Kingston (R)	unopposed		
1996 general	Jack Kingston (R)	108,616	(68%)	($452,178)
	Rosemary D. Kaszans (D)	50,622	(32%)	($46,023)

SECOND DISTRICT

The southwest corner of Georgia, plantation country before the Civil War, still is mostly farmland today: cotton fields, peanut acreage, pecan groves, pine lands. In the south, near the Florida border, is the Plantation Trace area around Thomasville, where rich Northerners have come to shoot quail and ducks in winters since the 1880s. A bit to the north is Albany, the largest city in these parts, with several factories, the site of Martin Luther King Jr.'s least successful civil rights protests in the 1960s. Two counties north is the village of Plains, the home since childhood of Jimmy Carter, and the center of the Free World during his presidency 20 years ago; his childhood home was bought by the government for $1.4 million in 1998. This is hardscrabble country: As recently as World War II, most rural residents lived in clapboard cabins without power or running water, eking a living out of over-tilled soil. Today this remains one of the low-income quarters of America. But rural electrification and then air-conditioning made homes and workplaces comfortable; automobiles and good roads have given people options they never had before (such as outlet malls); racial desegregation has given dignity to all in a way few dreamed possible thirty-some years ago (Albany has a civil rights museum).

This is the land of Georgia's 2d Congressional District. For the 1992 and 1994 elections this was a seat with ragged boundaries designed to make it black-majority; it included black neighborhoods in Columbus, Macon, and Valdosta, as well as Albany and the heavily black counties along the Alabama border. But the Supreme Court overturned the Georgia districting, and the 1995 court-drawn plan had new boundaries along county lines that excluded Columbus, Macon, and Valdosta, and reduced the black percentage from 57% to 39%.

The congressman from the 2d District is Sanford Bishop, a Democrat first elected in 1992. Bishop grew up in Mobile, Alabama, where his father was a state college president. He went to Morehouse College in Atlanta, where he was student body president in 1968 and sang at Martin Luther King Jr.'s funeral. He was an award-winning student at Emory Law School, then served in the Army. After a year in New York, he settled in Columbus, practiced law, joined the church choir and many civic organizations, and was elected to the state legislature in 1976, at 29. He served there until 1990, when he was elected to the Georgia Senate. There Bishop helped push through an ethics law, a training program for welfare recipients, and established the Commission on Equal Opportunity and the Office of Child Support Receiver. In 1992 he ran for the House against incumbent Charles Hatcher, who gained his greatest public notice when it was revealed he had 819 overdrafts on the House bank. Bishop was urged into the race by Columbus business leaders, and in the primary he edged another Hatcher challenger by 21%–19% for a runoff slot. Hatcher had 40%, but could not get many more votes, and Bishop won the runoff 53%–47%. He won the general election 64%–36%.

Bishop describes himself as "a moderate conservative on fiscal issues and a 'traditionalist' on so-called family issues." His style is not confrontational, and his voting record is far more moderate than that of Georgia's two other black Democrats, John Lewis and Cynthia McKinney. He supported the balanced budget, school prayer and anti-flag burning amendments. He voted for welfare reform in 1996 and the Republican tax cut in 1998. In his first term he voted for the assault weapons ban, but switched, joined the NRA and started hunting doves. He joined the conservative Blue Dog Democrats. He works to protect local military bases, like the School of the Americas at Fort Benning, and has gotten financing for road widenings and historic sites.

Most importantly, Bishop serves on the Agriculture Committee and on its Risk Management and Specialty Crops Subcommittee, which has jurisdiction over peanuts and tobacco. In the 1996 farm bill debate, Bishop realized he could not save the old peanut program and fashioned what he calls a "market-oriented, no-net cost" program. Working with 8th District Republican Saxby Chambliss, Bishop lobbied hard to pass it, and it prevailed in the House by three votes; he points out that 23 members of the Congressional Black Caucus voted for it, and suggests his work was crucial in getting these votes.

The 1995 redistricting made the seat much more difficult to hold: Clinton's 1992 percentage fell from 60% to 46% after the changes. Bishop moved to Albany in 1996, and regularly attends the Big Pig Jig in Vienna and Rattlesnake Roundup in Whigham. In 1996 Bishop was opposed by a former staffer who attacked him for supporting GATT and opposing gun control. Bishop carried every county and won 59%–33%. Then Republican Darrel Ealum ran ads calling Bishop "shockingly liberal," hitting his vote for the 1996 tax increase and charging that he got 92% of his funding from outside the district. But Bishop stayed cool and ran ads mentioning job security, the balanced budget amendment, and his work promoting local military bases. Bishop won by 54%–46%, losing seven counties, most with relatively well-off towns, running up big margins in the black-majority counties, and winning solidly in counties filled up with white farmers—the kind of people it was thought 30 years ago would never vote for a black congressman. House Republicans asked Bishop to switch parties; he "respectfully declined."

In 1998 Bishop attracted two serious Republican challengers. One was Dylan Glenn, a 29-year-old former Bush White House and Republican National Committee staffer, urged into the race by Speaker Newt Gingrich, who evidently thought a black Republican could dip into Bishop's black support. Glenn grew up in Columbus, but left for the D.C.-area while in high school. He got primary support from the national party. The other Republican was Joe McCormick, a 35-year-old Albany, Georgia, businessman, who grew up near Albany, New York, worked for the 1992 Bush-Quayle campaign and moved to Georgia in 1994 when he married a former national Peanut Queen. Both disputed the others' connections to their current home. The turnout in the Republican primary was low, though not so low as what it was in many of these counties 20 years ago (zero). McCormick won 53%–47%, in what seems to have been a friends-and-neighbors rather than racial pattern: He carried the counties clustered around Albany, plus Thomasville, while Glenn carried most counties to the northwest and southeast.

In the general election McCormick ran ads showing himself as a military school cadet and Army Ranger and said that economic times were bad; there was a fierce drought that summer. But Bishop was able to bank on positive economic feelings in even this low-income district, claiming that 41,000 new jobs had been created in the district since 1992. This was one of the districts where the Republican Party in the last weeks ran ads saying the choice was "reward Bill Clinton or vote Republican"; McCormick sought to distance himself from them. In the pro-incumbent climate Bishop increased his margin and won 57%–43%. He carried 27 of 31 counties and almost 40% of the white vote. The results here in 1996 and 1998 showed that white voters in the Deep South, and therefore presumably anywhere else in America, are ready and willing to vote for black candidates who work hard and favorably represent their views and interests. As Bishop put it in 1998, "There were people who never would have imagined voting for me, who didn't vote for me the first time. But the majority vote their pocketbooks. They understand the precarious situation that the farming community is in and they'll support people that help them."

Cook's Call. *Potentially Competitive.* Though Bishop's voting record could be described as moderately liberal, he has made enough of a distinction between himself and the more predictably liberal members of the Black Caucus as to make himself palatable with the more conservative and white voters. Bishop seems in reasonably good shape for re-election in 2000, but this is a district to keep an eye on, particularly after 2001 redistricting.

The People: Pop. 1990: 587,583; 50.3% rural; 12.7% age 65 + ; 59.5% White, 39.2% Black, 0.4% Asian, 0.3% Amer. Indian, 0.6% Other; 1.6% Hispanic Origin. Households: 53.2% married couple families; 27.4% married couple fams. w. children; 30.2% college educ.; median household income: $20,938; per capita income: $9,804; median house value: $47,700; median gross rent: $190.

1996 Presidential Vote		
Clinton (D)	82,429	(49%)
Dole (R)	72,934	(44%)
Perot (I)	11,494	(7%)

1992 Presidential Vote		
Clinton (D)	96,684	(60%)
Bush (R)	47,692	(29%)
Perot (I)	17,428	(11%)

Rep. Sanford D. Bishop, Jr. (D)

Elected 1992; b. Feb. 4, 1947, Mobile, AL; home, Albany; Morehouse Col., B.A. 1968, Emory U., J.D. 1971; Baptist; divorced.

Military Career: Army, 1970–71.

Elected Office: GA House of Reps., 1976–90; GA Senate, 1990–92.

Professional Career: Practicing atty., 1971–92.

DC Office: 1433 LHOB 20515, 202-225-3631; Fax: 202-225-2203; Web site: www.house.gov/bishop.

District Offices: Albany, 912-439-8067; Dawson, 912-995-3991; Valdosta, 912-247-9705.

Committees: *Agriculture* (11th of 24 D): General Farm Commodities, Resource Conservation & Credit; Risk Management, Research & Specialty Crops. *Permanent Select Committee on Intelligence* (3d of 7 D): Technical & Tactical Intelligence (RMM).

Group Ratings

	ADA	ACLU	AFS	LCV	CON	NTU	NFIB	COC	ACU	NTLC	CHC
1998	70	44	78	15	6	22	57	61	44	39	17
1997	75	—	75	—	53	26	—	60	29	—	—

National Journal Ratings

	1997 LIB — 1997 CONS		1998 LIB — 1998 CONS	
Economic	58%	— 42%	56%	— 44%
Social	71%	— 29%	55%	— 44%
Foreign	55%	— 44%	49%	— 48%

Key Votes of the 105th Congress

1. Clinton Budget Deal	N	5. Puerto Rico Sthood. Ref.	Y	9. Cut $ for B-2 Bombers	N
2. Education IRAs	Y	6. End Highway Set-asides	N	10. Human Rights in China	Y
3. Req. 2/3 to Raise Taxes	N	7. School Prayer Amend.	Y	11. Withdraw Bosnia Troops	N
4. Fast-track Trade	N	8. Ovrd. Part. Birth Veto	Y	12. End Cuban TV-Marti	N

Election Results

1998 general	Sanford D. Bishop Jr. (D)	77,953	(57%)	($626,373)
	Joe McCormick (R)	59,305	(43%)	($419,229)
1998 primary	Sanford D. Bishop Jr. (D)	unopposed		
1996 general	Sanford D. Bishop Jr. (D)	88,256	(54%)	($774,474)
	Darrel Ealum (R)	75,282	(46%)	($329,309)

THIRD DISTRICT

Running south from Atlanta, within an hour or so by car, you can see the most modern parts of Georgia and some of the most traditional. The modern is Atlanta's Hartsfield International Airport, built by Mayor William Hartsfield on the site of Candler Racetrack eight miles south of Atlanta's Five Points. Hartsfield was the mayor whose moderation on racial issues made Atlanta known as "the city too busy to hate," and whose airport, completely rebuilt in the 1980s, is the link between Atlanta's world corporations—Coca-Cola, CNN—and the world. Not far south are the old courthouse towns of Jonesboro and Fayetteville, now surrounded by new suburbs, but both with claims to be the spiritual homes of *Gone With the Wind*; near

Jonesboro is the mansion long owned by Senator (1957–81) Herman Talmadge, which looks a lot like Tara.

Eventually—farther south each year, it seems—the suburbs thin out, and you are in rural Georgia; a county past Sprayberry's Barbecue in booming Newnan is the village of Warm Springs and the faded hotel and pool where Franklin Roosevelt recuperated from polio in the 1920s, and where he died in 1945. Roosevelt liked to look over the wooded hills of Meriwether County, where few dwellings had central heat or indoor plumbing and almost everyone voted Democratic, just as they had since General Sherman marched his troops not too many miles away from Atlanta to the sea. Farther south is another Georgia, the small industrial city of Columbus and next-door Fort Benning, long the home of the Army's Infantry School, the place where George Marshall's brilliant talents were first noticed and where he kept his little book on the gifted officers whom he would make generals in World War II.

The 3d Congressional District of Georgia takes in all this territory, starting just south of the airport, passing through suburbs and fields to Columbus. About seven in ten votes here are cast in the Atlanta communities. These new communities are affluent but not dominated by any establishment, liberation-minded in much of their lifestyles but often tradition-minded in their yearnings. Politically, this is conservative country, full of young families moving up who prefer the relatively bucolic culture of the smaller counties. Mostly white, their ancestral politics may be Democratic but their current preferences lean Republican; these areas voted heavily for Bob Dole in 1996. The 1995 federal court redistricting removed some rural counties and added Warm Springs and black neighborhoods in Columbus; this increased the black percentage from 18% to 25%, and made the 3d somewhat more Democratic.

The congressman from the 3d is Mac Collins, a switcher to the Republican Party in the 1980s. Collins grew up in Jackson and started his trucking company at age 18, hauling logs for Georgia-Pacific; he is known, a local paper said, for "his lumbering stature and signature boots." He served as a Democrat on the Butts County Commission in the late 1970s, lost in 1980, then convinced the Butts County Republicans to elect him chairman. In 1988, he was elected to the state Senate, where he worked on welfare and ethics reforms and bills to fight drug dealing. In 1992, he ran for Congress in a newly fashioned district. Collins capitalized on a fierce Democratic primary battle between incumbent Congressman Richard Ray and David Worley, who came close to beating Gingrich in the old 6th District in 1990. Ray won 51%–32%. Collins, like Worley, attacked Ray as an insider; Ray spent 10 years as an aide to Senator Sam Nunn before running for Congress himself. Ray spent $1.1 million, but Collins won 55%–45%.

Collins has a mostly conservative voting record. Hartsfield International Airport was his chief early focus; he pushed for a repeal of the airline fuel tax slated for fall 1995, arguing the levy would cripple the industry, including Georgia-based Delta. He voted to pare spending at almost every opportunity, except for defense and 3d District projects—and made a point of opting out of the congressional pension plan. On Ways and Means since his second term, Collins backed welfare reform, the 1996 health care bill and a lower tax on earnings by Social Security recipients. He voted for the Freedom to Farm Act. On trade issues he voted against NAFTA and GATT. He has visited Bosnia, twice during December 1997, and supported deployment there. He came out for impeachment and removal of Bill Clinton in September 1998 and suggested the new president should nominate Sam Nunn for vice president.

Collins has been re-elected by robust margins. He won by 2–1 in 1994 though heavily outspent. After the 1995 redistricting, he dropped his opposition to PAC contributions and, in the new area around Columbus, won only 53% of the vote. But overall he won 61%–39%. In 1998 he was unopposed. In early 1998 he considered running for governor, but in February announced he would not. "If the voters are willing to give me two more terms in the House, then I'll be looking at running at the end of Cleland's term," in 2002, he said.

Cook's Call. *Safe.* Since beating incumbent Democrat Richard Ray in 1992, Collins has had few re-election concerns—even after federal courts boosted the district's black percentage. The district remains solidly Republican, and Collins should have no trouble in 2000.

The People: Pop. 1990: 589,718; 36.3% rural; 9.9% age 65 +; 73.2% White, 24.6% Black, 1.2% Asian, 0.2% Amer. Indian, 0.7% Other; 1.6% Hispanic Origin. Households: 60.1% married couple families; 31.5% married couple fams. w. children; 38.3% college educ.; median household income: $30,672; per capita income: $13,217; median house value: $70,100; median gross rent: $318.

1996 Presidential Vote

Dole (R)	104,286	(51%)
Clinton (D)	87,911	(43%)
Perot (I)	13,550	(7%)

1992 Presidential Vote

Bush (R)	105,731	(48%)
Clinton (D)	80,628	(37%)
Perot (I)	32,285	(15%)

Rep. Mac Collins (R)

Elected 1992; b. Oct. 15, 1944, Jackson; home, Hampton; Methodist; married (Julie).

Military Career: Army Natl. Guard, 1964–70.

Elected Office: Chmn., Butts Cnty. Commission, 1977–80; GA Senate, 1988–92.

Professional Career: Founder & Pres., Collins Trucking Co., 1962–92; Chmn., Butts Cnty. Repub. Party, 1981–82.

DC Office: 1131 LHOB 20515, 202-225-5901; Fax: 202-225-2512; Web site: www.house.gov/maccollins.

District Offices: Columbus, 706-327-7228; Jonesboro, 770-603-3395; Newnan, 770-304-8812.

Committees: *Budget* (18th of 24 R). *Ways & Means* (14th of 23 R): Social Security.

Group Ratings

	ADA	ACLU	AFS	LCV	CON	NTU	NFIB	COC	ACU	NTLC	CHC
1998	0	6	0	0	50	61	100	83	100	95	91
1997	5	—	25	—	76	61	—	80	83	—	—

National Journal Ratings

	1997 LIB — 1997 CONS		1998 LIB — 1998 CONS	
Economic	18% —	81%	0% —	88%
Social	0% —	90%	3% —	90%
Foreign	20% —	79%	19% —	75%

Key Votes of the 105th Congress

1. Clinton Budget Deal	Y	5. Puerto Rico Sthood. Ref.	N	9. Cut $ for B-2 Bombers	N
2. Education IRAs	Y	6. End Highway Set-asides	Y	10. Human Rights in China	N
3. Req. 2/3 to Raise Taxes	Y	7. School Prayer Amend.	Y	11. Withdraw Bosnia Troops	Y
4. Fast-track Trade	Y	8. Ovrd. Part. Birth Veto	Y	12. End Cuban TV-Marti	Y

Election Results

1998 general	Mac Collins (R)	unopposed		($335,801)
1998 primary	Mac Collins (R)	unopposed		
1996 general	Mac Collins (R)	120,251	(61%)	($485,354)
	Jim Chafin (D)	76,538	(39%)	($122,393)

FOURTH DISTRICT

In 1920, when Gutzom Borglum began sculpting Jefferson Davis, Robert E. Lee and Stonewall Jackson into the side of Stone Mountain, the huge outcropping of granite was a day's drive into the country from central Atlanta. Even when the memorial (the largest single piece of sculpture in the world) was completed in 1972, suburban development barely reached this far. But today, after two decades of some of the most explosive metropolitan growth in the country, DeKalb County, which Stone Mountain overlooks, is part of the core of the Atlanta metropolitan area, and this monument to the Confederacy sits in one of the most cosmopolitan and liberal constituencies in the South. Not far from Stone Mountain is Emory University, just beyond the old mansions of Druid Hills. A few miles away are the Centers for Disease Control and Prevention, one of the federal government's superb research institutions. All around in north DeKalb County are affluent suburbs, including much of Atlanta's Jewish community, with voting habits somewhat more liberal than other suburbs. Also, southern DeKalb is being transformed from mostly rural territory 25 years ago to one of the nation's largest collections of affluent black neighborhoods, rivalled only by Prince George's County, Maryland. This has pushed DeKalb County's politics well to the left: It was a Republican county when rural Georgia was almost all Democratic in the 1960s; now it is the most heavily Democratic major county in Georgia, even more so than next-door Fulton County which includes central Atlanta.

The 4th Congressional District consists of almost all of DeKalb County plus a small slice of the more Republican Gwinnett County to the northeast. It is the product of the 1995 redistricting, in which a federal court, enforcing a Supreme Court decision, reduced the number of black-majority districts in Georgia from three to one. It also produced some nimble district-hopping. Cynthia McKinney, elected in 1992 and 1994 from the old black-majority 11th District, which stretched from DeKalb County all the way to Savannah, decided to run here: South DeKalb is her political base. And Republican John Linder, who represented most of DeKalb in the old 4th District, moved to Gwinnett County to run in the new 11th District that stretches to the South Carolina border.

Cynthia McKinney grew up in Atlanta, just long ago enough to remember many of the great events of the civil rights revolution; she recalls riding on her father's shoulders as a child in civil rights marches. Her father, Billy McKinney, was elected to the legislature in 1973, just one year after Andrew Young was elected to Congress from a white-majority Atlanta district. Cynthia McKinney went to college in California, studied international relations in graduate school, taught at Spelman College, Clark Atlanta University, and Agnes Scott College, and is a doctoral candidate in international relations at the Fletcher School at Tufts. In 1988 she was elected to the Georgia House from south DeKalb County and became part of the only father-daughter legislative team in the country. She got a seat on the legislature's 1991 redistricting committee and worked long and hard to craft the two new black-majority districts. In 1992 she ran in the 11th, one of the districts she had helped create. With her DeKalb base, she led the Democratic primary with 31%, then won the runoff with 56%.

McKinney has a very liberal voting record and a confrontation-prone temperament. "I'm attracted to fights," she said when she insisted on wearing pants on the floor of the House. She complained loudly when White House guards in 1996 and again in 1998 did not recognize her and treat her like other members of Congress. "I am absolutely sick and tired of having to have my appearance at the White House validated by white people." She was one of the fiercest critics of her Atlanta neighbor Newt Gingrich, calling him "a little piglet who spent most of his days rolling around in a filthy ditch"; she was one of three members who brought the ethics complaint which resulted in his January 1997 reprimand. In 1998, she defended Jane Fonda after Fonda apologized to Governor Zell Miller for comparing parts of Georgia to starving nations of the Third World.

McKinney has spent much time and effort on Africa, traveling there four times in 1997 alone. She has called for respect for human rights and has hailed new African leaders who are willing to allow the private sector to get involved in economic development. She was appalled by the genocide in Rwanda in 1994 and later charged that the United Nations knew it was about to take place and failed to act. She supported Laurent Kabila's attempts to overthrow the Mobutu dictatorship in what is now Congo, but later called for investigation of the Kabila government's human rights abuses. She went to Liberia for the inauguration of President Charles Taylor in August 1997, but noted that he had a record of atrocities to overcome. In August 1998 she described IMF agreements as a "cruel hoax," because they require countries to spend money on repayment of loans they can never pay off rather than on health care and education.

As late as 1998 McKinney was still expressing resentment for the June 1995 Supreme Court decision calling her old 11th District a "racial gerrymander," and the December 1995 court-drawn plan which constructed her current district. At one point she blamed some Georgia producers of kaolin—the white clay used in china—for bringing the case, against whom she sought a price-fixing investigation. The new 4th District was only 33% black (compared to 60% in the old 11th) in 1990, but since then many middle-income blacks had moved into DeKalb from Atlanta, and many whites in the area proved entirely open to voting for a black candidate. In the 1996 Democratic primary McKinney was challenged by Comer Yates, who had run against John Linder in the old 4th two years earlier; McKinney won 67%–24%. In the general election, Republican John Mitnick attacked her for opposing school vouchers while sending her son to the elite Paideia school, for attending a 1995 panel discussion at Howard University with Louis Farrakhan and then for voting against a resolution to condemn him. She called Mitnick a Gingrich clone, while her ads talked of her support of the crime bill and increasing the minimum wage and opposition to "the extremists who tried to cut Medicare to fund tax breaks for the wealthy." In October 1996 Billy McKinney called Mitnick "a racist Jew." She asked him to apologize publicly—"he's my dad and I love him, but I am with him when he's right and I tell him when he's wrong"—and he withdrew from her campaign. McKinney won 58%–42%, carrying south DeKalb overwhelmingly and running well in north DeKalb. Overall she ran about 6% behind Bill Clinton and Democratic Senate candidate Max Cleland—a dropoff, but of similar magnitude to many across the country. McKinney argued that her victory was the result of incumbency, that she could not have won an initial election in such a district. Not, perhaps, if she had run the identical campaign she had in 1992, when she pitched her appeal entirely to black voters; but if she had taken the more moderate tone of her 1996 ads she might well have won then within the lines of the current district.

In 1998 McKinney was opposed by black Republican businesswoman Sunny Warren; three years earlier McKinney had told USA Today, "My impression of modern-day black Republicans is they have to pass a litmus test in which all black blood is extracted." Warren campaigned with verve and showed an attitude different from McKinney's: "I've broken all the barriers, and I'm still a black female doing it. The barriers have come down because I haven't made that an issue." But she had little money and McKinney won 61%–39%. In September McKinney issued a harsh criticism of Bill Clinton: "His reckless behavior with Monica Lewinsky has brought us to the brink of a constitutional crisis. His lost credibility means he is no help to me raising my son, his leadership is missing in action on Capitol Hill, he has shattered the confidence of too many people in my district."

Cook's Call. *Safe.* Though McKinney has won here by impressive margins even after redistricting slashed the black population almost in half, the district is not a safe one for her. McKinney is nowhere near the ideological 50-yard line for the district, she appears to have solidified herself well-enough to avoid serious challenge.

The People: Pop. 1990: 589,431; 2.3% rural; 8.1% age 65 + ; 58.4% White, 36.6% Black, 3.6% Asian, 0.2% Amer. Indian, 1.2% Other; 2.9% Hispanic Origin. Households: 48.4% married couple families; 23.5% married couple fams. w. children; 62.3% college educ.; median household income: $36,523; per capita income: $17,461; median house value: $91,800; median gross rent: $476.

1996 Presidential Vote			1992 Presidential Vote		
Clinton (D)	141,078	(64%)	Bush (R)	116,418	(46%)
Dole (R)	69,912	(32%)	Clinton (D)	101,990	(41%)
Perot (I)	8,014	(4%)	Perot (I)	33,226	(13%)

Rep. Cynthia McKinney (D)

Elected 1992; b. Mar. 17, 1955, Atlanta; home, Lithonia; U. of S. CA, B.A. 1978; Catholic; divorced.

Elected Office: GA House of Reps., 1988–92.

Professional Career: Diplomatic Fellow, Spelman Col., 1984; Atlanta Bd. of Health Svcs. Plng. Cncl., 1990–92; Adjunct Prof., Agnes Scott Women's Col., 1991–92.

DC Office: 124 CHOB 20515, 202-225-1605; Fax: 202-226-0691; Web site: www.house.gov/mckinney.

District Office: Decatur, 404-377-6900.

Committees: *Armed Services* (22d of 28 D): Military Personnel; Military Procurement. *International Relations* (10th of 23 D): International Operations and Human Rights (RMM).

Group Ratings

	ADA	ACLU	AFS	LCV	CON	NTU	NFIB	COC	ACU	NTLC	CHC
1998	100	93	100	100	85	23	14	22	8	3	0
1997	100	—	75	—	96	35	—	30	13	—	—

National Journal Ratings

	1997 LIB — 1997 CONS		1998 LIB — 1998 CONS	
Economic	79%	— 18%	72%	— 23%
Social	85%	— 0%	90%	— 7%
Foreign	79%	— 19%	71%	— 27%

Key Votes of the 105th Congress

1. Clinton Budget Deal	N	5. Puerto Rico Sthood. Ref.	Y	9. Cut $ for B-2 Bombers	Y
2. Education IRAs	N	6. End Highway Set-asides	N	10. Human Rights in China	Y
3. Req. 2/3 to Raise Taxes	N	7. School Prayer Amend.	N	11. Withdraw Bosnia Troops	N
4. Fast-track Trade	N	8. Ovrd. Part. Birth Veto	N	12. End Cuban TV-Marti	Y

Election Results

1998 general	Cynthia McKinney (D)	100,622	(61%)	($414,368)
	Sunny Warren (R)	64,146	(39%)	($160,593)
1998 primary	Cynthia McKinney (D)	unopposed		
1996 general	Cynthia McKinney (D)	127,157	(58%)	($1,015,197)
	John Mitnick (R)	92,985	(42%)	($654,287)

FIFTH DISTRICT

Venture out of the quiet of the Ebenezer Baptist Church or the shade of Martin Luther King Jr.'s boyhood home two blocks away and into the steamy heat of the sun on Auburn Avenue—Sweet Auburn—and you can see, a mile away, downtown Atlanta's atrium-skyscrapers towering in their glory. They are evidence of the wealth and vibrant growth of the commercial capital of the South, the metropolis that has grown up where there was little more than a railroad junction at the time of the War Between the States. But the awesome achievement that is downtown Atlanta is overshadowed by the revolution made in very large part by a man who grew up on Auburn Avenue, where people who never felt air-conditioning moved slowly in the sweltering heat, and around Morehouse and Spelman colleges, where proud professionals struggled and worked hard and raised their families. Atlanta's white establishment, led by

Mayors William Hartsfield and Ivan Allen and Coca-Cola's Robert Woodruff, deserve credit for abandoning segregation, but it was King and other civil rights leaders who took the risks that led them to do so. Atlanta's city fathers acted out of good will, but also with an eye for the economic growth of their city, which they knew would be hurt by violent resistance. White Atlanta's decision to desegregate has helped Atlanta prosper, but King's vision and movement to change the way Americans behave have made it possible for a nation to live up to its ideals.

Yet, sadly, not all is entirely well in Atlanta—on Peachtree Street or on Sweet Auburn. Downtown Atlanta's primacy in office buildings is being eclipsed by north-side edge cities in Buckhead and along I-285. Many of Atlanta's black neighborhoods today have been abandoned by families who have headed to subdivisions in DeKalb County, leaving the central city with vacant housing and street crime. Atlanta has its glories: The headquarters of world-girdling Coca-Cola and CNN, the gigantic Hartsfield International Airport, the modern Martin Luther King Jr. Center that depicts the triumphs of the civil rights movement, the antique Cyclorama that shows Atlanta burning during the Civil War, and the stadiums and sports facilities built for the 1996 Summer Olympics. As the world turned its attention to Atlanta for the Games, officials scurried to repave streets, build new parks, and revitalize inner-city neighborhoods such as Summerhill and Mechanicsville, spending more than $2 billion. But the bombing which killed one person at Centennial Olympic Park and complaints about run-down housing for athletes and inefficient transportation marred the festivities, and Atlanta was left with $500 million in new sports facilities but scant profits.

The 5th Congressional District includes most of Atlanta and a few suburbs, from posh Buckhead and Sandy Springs in the north to middle-class and increasingly black East Point in the south, plus rural southwest Fulton County and a black neighborhood around the airport in Clayton County. The district was 62% black in 1990; that number has probably declined, as middle-class blacks move outward to DeKalb County and heavily white Buckhead prospers and grows.

The congressman from the 5th District is John Lewis, who made history a generation ago as a hero of the civil rights movement, as he recounts in his 1998 autobiography, *Walking With the Wind*. A sharecropper's son from Troy, Alabama, he was seized by religious fervor as a child, preaching in the barnyard, determined to be a minister. Lewis was the first in his family to finish high school; he wrote to Ralph Abernathy for help in suing for the right to enter Troy State College; he met Martin Luther King Jr. when he was 18. In 1959, at 19, he helped organize the first lunch-counter sit-in, which was received with open hostility hard to imagine today. In 1960, the day after John Kennedy was elected, Lewis sat in the Krystal Diner in Nashville while a waitress poured cleansing powder down his back and water over his food; he went to talk to the manager, who turned a fumigating machine on him. In May 1961, he was on the first of the Freedom Rides, riding buses as they were attacked and burned; he was viciously beaten in Rock Hill, South Carolina, and Montgomery, Alabama. He spoke at the 1963 March on Washington, criticizing Kennedy liberals for inaction on civil rights and calling for massive help for the poor. In 1964, he helped coordinate the Mississippi Freedom Project. In 1965, he led the Selma-to-Montgomery march to petition for voting rights and was beaten by policemen who fractured his skull. Modestly, quietly, maintaining his poise and good judgment under harsh circumstances, Lewis was one of the people who risked their lives many times to make the civil rights revolution happen. He worked for Robert Kennedy for president in 1968, and was with him in Indianapolis when they heard King was killed, and in Los Angeles just before Kennedy himself was shot.

Lewis's tenure as head of the Voter Education Project in Atlanta and his work at ACTION during the Carter Administration did not give him the publicity and fame, however, that made a national celebrity of Jesse Jackson, whose civil rights movement credentials are much thinner. Lewis's first foray into electoral politics was unsuccessful: He ran in 1977 to replace Andrew Young in the House and was soundly beaten by Wyche Fowler (but ran ahead of Republican Paul Coverdell, who beat Fowler in the 1992 Senate election). After winning a seat on the

Atlanta Council in 1981, Lewis ran for Congress in 1986, and trailed Julian Bond 47%–35% in the primary. But even though Bond won more than 60% of the black vote, Lewis won the runoff by assembling a coalition of poor blacks and affluent whites: "Vote for the tugboat, not the showboat" was his slogan, stressing his hard work on local issues. He has been re-elected easily since, winning 79%–21% against an unrelated John H. Lewis Sr. in 1998.

Lewis has been a strong partisan, with one of the most liberal voting records in the House, and an impassioned supporter of Bill Clinton in the scandals of 1998. Usually quiet, he can speak in the cadences of black preachers, as he did on the Gulf war resolution in January 1991 and impeachment in November 1998. He is one of the Democrats' four chief deputy whips, an integral part of the leadership, and has a seat on Ways and Means. Only occasionally does he defect from his party, as when he opposed the 1994 crime bill because of his disapproval of capital punishment. He furiously voiced his disappointment when Republicans' captured the House in 1994, and his formerly pleasant relationship with Newt Gingrich ended in early 1995 when he attacked Gingrich for his book contract and called for an independent counsel investigation. Later, Lewis filed ethics complaints against Gingrich for the financing of his college course and use of GOPAC funds. Lewis argued passionately against the Republican welfare bills: "They're coming for the children. They're coming for the poor. They're coming for the sick, the elderly and the disabled." And he implicitly compared the Republicans to Nazis by quoting an anti-Nazi German theologian against them.

Lewis has worked to commemorate the civil rights revolution in which he played such a large part. He got a federal building in Atlanta named for Martin Luther King Jr. and got the route from Selma to Montgomery designated a National Historic Trail. His vision remains clear: "You can have an integrated society without losing diversity. But you can also have a society that transcends race, where you can lay down the burden of race . . . and treat people as human beings, regardless of the color of their skin." He called the court decision that overturned Georgia's congressional district lines a setback to black participation in politics, but prefers not to maximize black percentages to encourage bi-racial coalitions. He has said affirmative action should move from race to class as a criterion, but he has stoutly defended racial quotas and preferences and opposed school vouchers for low-income children in Washington, D.C. He gave Bill Clinton a long hug after the 1998 State of the Union speech and later said, "We should leave him alone. If he has sinned, we should be prepared to forgive."

In 1997 Lewis considered running against Senator Paul Coverdell, but in August announced he would not do so.

Cook's Call. *Safe.* To say that Lewis is safe is something of an understatement. Since first winning this seat in 1986 with 75% of the vote, he has consistently won re-election with 70% or more, only once dipping to 69%. There seems to be no reason why that should change now.

The People: Pop. 1990: 589,380; 2.6% rural; 11% age 65 +; 35.7% White, 61.9% Black, 1.3% Asian, 0.2% Amer. Indian, 0.8% Other; 1.9% Hispanic Origin. Households: 33.8% married couple families; 16% married couple fams. w. children; 47.3% college educ.; median household income: $25,547; per capita income: $15,003; median house value: $73,600; median gross rent: $375.

1996 Presidential Vote

Clinton (D)	134,597	(74%)
Dole (R)	41,346	(23%)
Perot (I)	4,980	(3%)

1992 Presidential Vote

Clinton (D)	140,175	(68%)
Bush (R)	52,191	(25%)
Perot (I)	15,241	(7%)

Rep. John Lewis (D)

Elected 1986; b. Feb. 21, 1940, Troy, AL; home, Atlanta; Amer. Baptist Theol. Seminary, B.A. 1961, Fisk U., B.A. 1963; Baptist; married (Lillian).

Elected Office: Atlanta City Cncl., 1981–86.

Professional Career: Chmn., Student Nonviolent Coord. Cmte., 1963–66; Field Foundation, 1966–67; Community Organization Dir., Southern Regional Cncl., 1967–70; Exec. Dir., Voter Educ. Project, 1970–76; Assoc. Dir., ACTION, 1977–80; Community Affairs Dir., Natl. Coop. Bank, 1980–82.

DC Office: 343 CHOB 20515, 202-225-3801; Fax: 202-225-0351; Web site: www.house.gov/johnlewis.

District Office: Atlanta, 404-659-0116.

Committees: *Chief Deputy Minority Whip. Ways & Means* (9th of 16 D): Health; Oversight.

Group Ratings

	ADA	ACLU	AFS	LCV	CON	NTU	NFIB	COC	ACU	NTLC	CHC
1998	90	93	100	62	84	29	7	13	0	3	0
1997	95	—	100	—	20	24	—	20	4	—	—

National Journal Ratings

	1997 LIB — 1997 CONS		1998 LIB — 1998 CONS	
Economic	85%	— 10%	79%	— 0%
Social	85%	— 0%	93%	— 0%
Foreign	94%	— 3%	95%	— 5%

Key Votes of the 105th Congress

1. Clinton Budget Deal	N	5. Puerto Rico Sthood. Ref.	Y	9. Cut $ for B-2 Bombers	Y
2. Education IRAs	N	6. End Highway Set-asides	N	10. Human Rights in China	Y
3. Req. 2/3 to Raise Taxes	N	7. School Prayer Amend.	*	11. Withdraw Bosnia Troops	N
4. Fast-track Trade	N	8. Ovrd. Part. Birth Veto	*	12. End Cuban TV-Marti	Y

Election Results

1998 general	John Lewis (D)	109,177	(79%)	($307,440)
	John H. Lewis Sr. (R)	29,877	(21%)	($11,938)
1998 primary	John Lewis (D)	unopposed		
1996 general	John Lewis (D)	unopposed		($207,661)

SIXTH DISTRICT

In the red clay hills north of Atlanta, over the last three decades, an almost wholly new metropolitan quarter has grown up as affluent Atlanta has spread out from Ansley Park, just north of downtown, and the rolling hills of Buckhead, within the city limit, past the I-285 Perimeter into territory that was once just farms, small towns and little factory cities. Where there were perhaps 100,000 people in the 1950s, there are one million today. No longer is downtown Atlanta the only focus: The edge cities of Buckhead, Perimeter Center and the area near Cumberland Mall are now not just shopping but major office centers, rivaling downtown Atlanta in square footage. Cobb County around Marietta is the headquarters of Home Depot and the Weather Channel; Dunwoody in northern DeKalb County is the home of Holiday Inn. Yet physically this Golden Crescent north of the Perimeter and between I-75 in Cobb County and

I-85 in Gwinnett County seems not to have changed greatly: The buildings are tree-shaded and lush foliage and large-lot requirements have given most of the communities a woodsy look.

The 6th Congressional District occupies a large portion of this Golden Crescent north of Atlanta, including most of Cobb County, Fulton County north of the Perimeter, and to the east a chunk of Gwinnett County. This was a newly created seat in 1992, the seat Georgia gained in the 1990 Census, in recognition of how much the affluent suburban ring around Atlanta has contributed to the state's growth. It would surely surprise Georgians a generation or two ago to learn that one of their congressional districts would rank among the nation's richest and most educated. The 6th ranks 11th of 435 districts in percentage of adults with college degrees, at 40%; it ranked 23d in median family income in 1990, behind districts all in larger metro areas. It is easily the most Republican district in Georgia, and by some measures one of the most heavily Republican districts in the country.

For three terms and just the beginning of a fourth, the congressman from the 6th District was Newt Gingrich, the 50th speaker of the House, and one of the most important. Gingrich's story, now well known, shows how in our politics one can come from obscurity and, with insight and effort and not a little luck, make an enormous difference. About 20 years ago, Gingrich was an untenured history professor in rural Georgia who had lost two races for the House. When he finally won in 1978, the House was 2–1 Democratic. There he argued that Republicans should work to advance Ronald Reagan's ideas and aggressively oppose rather than accommodate Democratic leaders. He pioneered the use of C-SPAN to propel issues and in December 1987 brought ethics charges against Speaker Jim Wright. In 1989, with crucial support from moderates, he was elected minority whip by 87–85—the first of many narrow margins that preserved and advanced his career. He proceeded to advance other allies and to plan the 1994 Contract With America campaign that he was the first to see could produce a Republican majority. As speaker he pushed the Contract through and led a budget fight that resulted in setbacks in the polls but success on the bottom line: Without the 1995 zero increase in spending, the budget would not be balanced today. It was Gingrich who decided in July 1996 to pass welfare reform a third time, when in an election season Bill Clinton would sign it. It was Gingrich who rounded up votes to pass NAFTA in November 1993 and who provided support and impetus for the expansive foreign policy that he commended in his last House speech in December 1998.

But Gingrich also aroused furious opposition. In 1996 ethics charges were filed against him, and he ended up settling them in January 1997 by paying a $300,000 fine. Several Republicans refused to vote for him for speaker and his election was in doubt until the last moments. In July 1997 other House Republican leaders tried to depose him, and nearly succeeded. In November 1998, after Republicans lost five House seats rather than, as everyone expected, gained a few, backbencher Matt Salmon announced that he and five other Republicans would not vote for Gingrich for speaker. On Friday, November 6, Gingrich announced he would stand down and resign from the House.

The only suspense in the six-candidate, nonpartisan special election was whether Gingrich's hand-picked successor, moderate, pro-choice Republican Johnny Isakson, would win with a majority and thus avoid a runoff. A real estate agent, Isakson became president of Sandy Springs-based Northside Realty in 1979. He was elected to the Georgia House in 1976, serving as Republican leader from 1983 until 1990, when he lost the gubernatorial election to Zell Miller, 53%–45%. He was elected to the state Senate in 1993, serving until 1996, when he sought to challenge Democratic Senator Max Cleland. But Isakson had tough competition from Guy Millner, the millionaire founder of the Norrell temporary employee firm (who lost to Miller in 1994) and Clint Day of the Days Inn family, and the race was overshadowed by the Summer Olympics. Millner won the primary with 42%, compared to 35% for Isakson and 19% for Day, and carried the runoff against Isakson 53%–47%. That December, Governor Miller appointed Isakson chairman of the state Board of Education.

Isakson was by far the best-known, most experienced and best-financed candidate in the

February 23 special, which included five Republicans and one Democrat, attorney Gary "Bats" Pelphrey, who had lost to Gingrich in November 1998, 71%–29%. The only other candidate with significant name recognition was Kennesaw State University professor Christina Jeffrey, who Gingrich hired and then dismissed as House historian in 1995 after Democrats attacked her criticism of a high school Holocaust course for not reflecting the views of the Nazis. Jeffrey ran as a conservative, pro-life alternative to Isakson, who embraced much of the Republican leadership's economic agenda while playing down his moderate stands on social issues. But no one could compete with the $1 million Isakson had raised and the additional $500,000 he contributed of his own money, which allowed him to maintain a steady advertising presence for weeks. Isakson avoided a runoff, winning 65% of the vote and carrying all four counties; Jeffrey finished second with 25%, Pelphrey third with 5%.

In the state House, Isakson authored and passed legislation on growth policy and regional planning, major issues in the sprawling Atlanta metro region. He won a seat on the Transportation Committee, which was his first choice, where he is expected to help push for securing $42 million for a study of transportation alternatives for the overburdened Georgia 400 corridor. Isakson, on his approach to politics: "I've always been one to build consensus. . . . I believe you make progress wherever you can find common ground, and that's what I'm going to do." In this Republican district, he stands a chance to have the time to prove his mettle.

Cook's Call. *Safe.* A moderate Republican, certainly by Republican and even national standards, Isakson may find himself harassed from time to time in primaries but should have no general election concerns in this quintessentially Republican district.

The People: Pop. 1990: 589,018; 10.8% rural; 5.6% age 65 + ; 91.1% White, 6.3% Black, 1.8% Asian, 0.2% Amer. Indian, 0.6% Other; 2.1% Hispanic Origin. Households: 60.5% married couple families; 31.8% married couple fams. w. children; 69.5% college educ.; median household income: $46,148; per capita income: $22,297; median house value: $118,100; median gross rent: $512.

1996 Presidential Vote			1992 Presidential Vote		
Dole (R)	186,084	(62%)	Bush (R)	155,739	(56%)
Clinton (D)	100,714	(33%)	Clinton (D)	82,381	(29%)
Perot (I)	15,416	(5%)	Perot (I)	41,874	(15%)

Rep. Johnny Isakson (R)

Elected Feb. 1999; b. Dec. 28, 1944, Atlanta; home, Marietta; U. of GA, B.B.A. 1966; Methodist; married (Dianne).

Military Career: GA Air Natl. Guard, 1967–71.

Elected Office: GA House of Reps., 1976–90, Repub. Ldr., 1983–90; GA gubernatorial candidate, 1990; GA Senate, 1993–96; U.S. Senate candidate, 1996.

Professional Career: Northside Realty, 1967–99, Pres., 1979–99; Co-chair, Dole GA presidential campaign, 1988, 1996; Chmn., GA Board of Ed., 1997.

DC Office: 2428 Rayburn 20515, 202-225-4501; Fax: 202-225-4656; e-mail: gao6@mail.house.gov.

District Office: Marietta, 770-565-6398.

Committees: *Education & the Workforce* (27th of 27 R): Postsecondary Education, Training & Life-Long Learning; Workforce Protections. *Transportation & Infrastructure* (41st of 41 R): Aviation; Oversight, Investigations & Emergency Management.

Group Ratings and Key Votes: Newly Elected

Election Results

1999 special	Johnny Isakson (R)	51,548	(65%)	($912,413)
	Christina Jeffrey (R)	20,115	(25%)	($215,736)
	Gary (Bats) Pelphrey (D)	4,014	(5%)	
	Others	3,536	(4%)	
1998 general	Newt Gingrich (R)	164,966	(71%)	($7,578,716)
	Gary (Bats) Pelphrey (D)	68,366	(29%)	($11,232)
1998 primary	Newt Gingrich (R)	unopposed		
1996 general	Newt Gingrich (R)	174,155	(58%)	($5,577,715)
	Michael Coles (D)	127,135	(42%)	($3,325,030)

SEVENTH DISTRICT

North Georgia, home of the Cherokee Nation before they were sent west in the 1830s on the Trail of Tears, has been manufacturing country for the last century. There are hundreds of textile mills and dozens of carpet mills located near the supply of natural cotton and along the railroad lines heading southwest at the base of the southern Appalachian chain. Factories were hailed as the vanguard of technological progress by the late 19th Century propagandists of the New South, and in fact the factories produced a higher standard of living than farms on this stubborn land. But mill work put scant premium on education or the cultivation of civic virtues and did little to bring in higher-skill white-collar work. All-white hiring practices maintained racial segregation in mostly white north Georgia. Today, north Georgia is developing a different kind of economy, as the example of Atlanta shines to the south and spreads out over highways north into what used to be mill towns. Cobb County, once centered on the Lockheed aircraft factory in Marietta, has been transformed into an upscale suburb and office center; places like the textile mill town of LaGrange or the carpet mill town of Rome are seeing change as well.

The 7th Congressional District includes much of this part of north Georgia. It extends along the state's western boundary from LaGrange to Rome, east to Cartersville, where U.S. 41 starts its four-lane roll toward Atlanta, and takes in a somewhat downscale part of western Cobb County, including the old center of Marietta. This was Democratic territory from the time of General Jackson and General Sherman until the civil rights revolution of the 1960s. In the 1970s, Carrollton, in the western part of the 7th, was the home of a West Georgia College professor who, in his third try, became a Republican congressman: Newt Gingrich.

The congressman from the 7th is Bob Barr, a Republican elected in 1994 who almost immediately became prominent on national issues. Like most members of the Georgia delegation, Barr grew up elsewhere; his father was in the Army and he went to high school in Tehran and college at the University of Southern California. In the 1970s he worked as a CIA analyst while he went to law school at Georgetown University. In 1978 he left the agency and moved to Georgia to practice law; in 1986 he became U.S. attorney in Atlanta—a high-profile job. Yet for all his successes he remains humorless, pessimistic, sarcastic, to the point that his wife beeps him when he is on TV, "Smile, honey." He told the *New York Times*, "When I was young, I was teased very maliciously at some times and I'm sensitive to that. I was short. I have scars on the side of my head from an operation I had after I was born." He says he has no close friends on Capitol Hill and usually sleeps in his office.

In 1992 Barr ran for the Senate, and with 24% in the primary just made it into a runoff with Paul Coverdell. Barr lost the runoff by 1,548 votes, 50.5%–49.5%. Undaunted, he ran for the House in 1994. Against a less conservative primary opponent, he won 57%–43%. In the general election, he faced incumbent Buddy Darden, a Democrat with a mixed voting record who stayed in office in a Republican-leaning district. Barr's campaign gave out t-shirts showing Darden jogging with Bill Clinton, and he attacked Darden for voting for the Clinton tax increase and the crime bill. Darden replied that he voted against the Clinton health care plan and for the balanced budget amendment, but he could not deny he was a Clinton supporter. Barr won 52%–48%.

Barr has a strongly conservative voting record, is a stern opponent of gun control and proponent of family values, though he is not a gun enthusiast and has been divorced twice. In his first term, while ranking 20th of 20 Republicans on Judiciary, he played a lead role in three national issues. The first was the anti-terrorism bill sought after the April 1995 Oklahoma City bombing. Barr led a fight to amend the committee bill and stitched together a coalition of conservative Republicans angry at government misconduct at Waco and Ruby Ridge and liberal Democrats long opposed to government infringements of civil liberties. His amendment deleted government authority to designate chosen foreign groups as terrorist and withhold entry visas to their members, and a provision to allow illegally obtained wiretap evidence in terrorism cases. It also struck the provisions lowering the standard of proof for prosecution when the guns used in crimes are provided in court, and restricted proposed smokeless powder and armor-piercing bullet studies. In March 1996 the amendment passed 246–171, with support from most Republicans and about one-third of Democrats.

Two months later Barr introduced the Defense of Marriage Act, allowing states to refuse to recognize same-sex marriages and to define marriage for federal benefit purposes as the legal union of one man and one woman. This was a response to the Hawaii court case that seemed likely to legalize same-sex marriages there, which ordinarily would cause them to be honored in every state by the Constitution's full faith and credit clause. Barr acted even though the fact that he had been married three times himself invited ridicule. The bill passed overwhelmingly and a reluctant but re-election-minded Bill Clinton signed it in the dark of night in September 1996. Barr's third accomplishment was sponsoring repeal of the assault weapons ban, which passed the House 239–173, but never came to a vote in the Senate.

Barr has been allied with the ACLU on some issues. "It's really come to the point of no return with government taking so much power. I really have a tremendous fear of government taking away our freedoms." He was the first House member to speak out against an FBI push for "roving wiretaps," which would allow tapping of all phones in any home or business used by or near a target. He opposes a national identification card and unique health identifers and won a one-year delay of a federal rule encouraging states to use Social Security numbers on drivers' licenses. He sees great dangers in giving the government access to burgeoning data-bases. He opposed a bill to provide every welfare recipient with a debit card so the government can track expenditures. In 1998 he joined Maxine Waters in opposing the Intelligence Author-ization Act.

Barr has other interests. He seeks to ban weightlifting equipment and intramural basketball in federal prisons. He criticized Atlanta Mayor Bill Campbell for not obeying a decree to stop illegal discharges in the Chattahoochee River, which runs through the 7th District. He is trying to bar a railroad switching yard from Austell in Cobb County. He and Georgia's two senators are seeking a new veterans' cemetery in Atlanta; the Marietta cemetery has been full since 1978. But what Barr is best known for is, of course, impeachment. Back in May 1997 he asked Independent Counsel Kenneth Starr to give the House Judiciary Committee any evidence that might be grounds to impeach Clinton. In November 1997, before Monica Lewinsky had been summoned as a witness in the Paula Jones case, he and 17 other members filed an inquiry of impeachment. "I care about the rule of law," he said, a theme he would repeat many times. In December 1998 Barr made his presentation to the House. "Anyone not possessing an infinite capacity for self-delusion knows," he said, "that the president perjured himself on multiple occasions and committed other acts of obstruction of justice." In January 1999 he made his presentation to the Senate—and seemed dour and pessimistic about the result. In December it was revealed he had spoken six months before to the Council of Conservative Citizens, a group with racist material on its Web site. Barr replied, "If I were aware white supremacists' views occupied any place in the Council's philosophy, I would never have agreed to speak."

No one doubts Democrats would like to defeat Barr. As he said, "I suspect that there are a lot of Democrats who hate me, and I don't think it's just a mild dislike." In 1996, state House Speaker Tom Murphy got House Banking Chairman Charlie Watts to run. Barr outspent him vastly and won 58%–42%. In 1998, Democrats had a much weaker nominee. He won by 55%–45%, a downtick in contrast to the upswings in votes for most incumbents of both parties. He barely carried Cobb County, though the 7th's share of the county is much less affluent and Republican than the 6th's. Was this a negative response to impeachment? It's not clear, but he did run about even with the winning showing of Senator Paul Coverdell in the district.

Cook's Call. *Probably Safe.* Though it's unlikely that Bob Barr will actually lose re-election in 2000, he had the lowest election percentage of the Georgia congressional delegation in 1998 and was in a three-way tie for 3d lowest in 1996. Barr is in a very comfortable, conservative, Republican district, but, simply put, he is a polarizing figure, likely to elicit strong opinions from just about anyone—positive and negative. Though never likely to run up big margins like some of his more get-along, go-along colleagues, Barr is likely to hold onto the seat.

The People: Pop. 1990: 589,915; 46.1% rural; 11.4% age 65+; 85.7% White, 13.2% Black, 0.5% Asian, 0.3% Amer. Indian, 0.4% Other; 1% Hispanic Origin. Households: 60.9% married couple families; 31.1% married couple fams. w. children; 31.2% college educ.; median household income: $28,898; per capita income: $12,446; median house value: $64,800; median gross rent: $306.

1996 Presidential Vote			1992 Presidential Vote		
Dole (R)	99,320	(51%)	Bush (R)	93,175	(47%)
Clinton (D)	77,741	(40%)	Clinton (D)	77,103	(38%)
Perot (I)	16,603	(9%)	Perot (I)	30,097	(15%)

Rep. Bob Barr (R)

Elected 1994; b. Nov. 5, 1948, Iowa City, IA; home, Smyrna; U. of S. CA, B.A. 1970, George Washington U., M.A. 1972, Georgetown U., J.D. 1977; Methodist; married (Jeri).

Professional Career: CIA Analyst, 1971–78; Practicing atty., 1978–86, 1990–94; U.S. Atty., N. GA District, 1986–90; Dir., SE Legal Foundation, 1990–92.

DC Office: 1207 LHOB 20515, 202-225-2931; Fax: 202-225-2944; Web site: www.house.gov/barr.

District Offices: Carrollton, 770-836-1776; LaGrange, 706-812-1776; Marietta, 770-429-1776; Rome, 706-290-1776.

Committees: *Banking & Financial Services* (15th of 32 R): Financial Institutions & Consumer Credit; General Oversight & Investigations; Housing & Community Opportunity. *Government Reform* (15th of 24 R): Criminal Justice, Drug Policy & Human Resources (Vice Chmn.); National Economic Growth, Natural Resources & Regulatory Affairs. *Judiciary* (12th of 21 R): Crime; The Constitution.

Group Ratings

	ADA	ACLU	AFS	LCV	CON	NTU	NFIB	COC	ACU	NTLC	CHC
1998	5	7	13	0	87	76	100	72	100	100	100
1997	5	—	13	—	56	72	—	80	96	—	—

National Journal Ratings

	1997 LIB — 1997 CONS			1998 LIB — 1998 CONS		
Economic	0%	—	90%	34%	—	64%
Social	20%	—	71%	13%	—	86%
Foreign	0%	—	88%	0%	—	93%

Key Votes of the 105th Congress

1. Clinton Budget Deal	Y	5. Puerto Rico Sthood. Ref.	N	9. Cut $ for B-2 Bombers	N
2. Education IRAs	Y	6. End Highway Set-asides	Y	10. Human Rights in China	N
3. Req. 2/3 to Raise Taxes	Y	7. School Prayer Amend.	Y	11. Withdraw Bosnia Troops	Y
4. Fast-track Trade	N	8. Ovrd. Part. Birth Veto	Y	12. End Cuban TV-Marti	N

Election Results

1998 general	Bob Barr (R) 85,982	(55%)	($1,424,519)
	James F. Williams (D) 69,293	(45%)	($13,633)
1998 primary	Bob Barr (R) .... unopposed		
1996 general	Bob Barr (R) 112,009	(58%)	($1,272,303)
	Charlie Watts (D) 81,765	(42%)	($308,368)

EIGHTH DISTRICT

South Georgia has been under attack and enemy occupation more than almost any other part of America. Most famously, of course, when General William Tecumseh Sherman's troops set out from Atlanta, without supplies or lines of communication, to march through Georgia to the sea, burning its antebellum mansions, destroying its crops, capturing its leader (the Jefferson Davis Memorial in Ocilla marks the spot where Union troops took him in May 1865), leaving memories of slaves freed, handed down as family lore for more than a century. But the land bears, if only on its road signs, the memory of another invasion, when poor white farmers aided by Andrew Jackson's troops drove the Cherokees and other Indians off this land, where Indians had lived for perhaps thousands of years, west over the Trail of Tears to what is now Oklahoma. And there was the oppression of blacks by whites under the old systems of slavery and legal segregation, the latter not long dead—a past recalled by Macon's Harriet Tubman Historical and Cultural Museum.

The 8th Congressional District runs down the center of Georgia, roughly along these lines of occupation, past immense stands of soft lumber pines, through counties where 60% of the world's kaolin (clay used for china and ceramics) is mined, all the way from Macon to the Okefenokee Swamp, where local officials are trying to raise $90 million to buy up a proposed DuPont titanium mine, and a private company is building a prison. The district lines were more regular for 1996 than for 1992 and 1994, thanks to a federally court-ordered plan handed down in 1995 after the Supreme Court overturned the former lines as a "racial gerrymander." The 8th now includes all of Macon, home of music legends Otis Redding, Little Richard and the Allman Brothers, a city proud of its restored houses and Japanese cherry trees (it has 20 times as many as Washington). This has been Democratic country since Sherman's troops came through, and the 1995 redistricting made the 8th even more Democratic, primarily by increasing the black percentage from 21% to 31%. The new 8th cast 47% of its votes for Bill Clinton in 1996, compared to 40% in the old 8th; all but two counties here were carried by Senator Max Cleland in 1996 while every county was carried by Governor Roy Barnes in 1998.

The congressman from the 8th District is Saxby Chambliss, a Republican elected in 1994 to replace a retiring conservative Democrat. Chambliss grew up in Shreveport, Louisiana, the son of an Episcopalian minister, went to college in Georgia, and practiced business and agriculture law in Moultrie starting in 1968. In 1992 he ran for the House and lost the Republican primary; in 1994 he was the sole Republican candidate, while Democrats, as in days of yore, had a multi-candidate contest. The winner was Craig Mathis, the 32-year-old son of one-time (1971–81) Congressman Dawson Mathis and a former staffer for Congressmen Ed Jenkins and Sonny Callahan. Chambliss called for targeting repeat offenders and reducing the deficit; he opposed Dick Armey's proposal to zero out peanut subsidies. Chambliss won 63%–37%.

In the House, Newt Gingrich saw that Chambliss had the committee assignments he needed most—National Security to look after Robins Air Force Base near Macon, and Agriculture to protect subsidies for peanut farmers in the counties to the south. In his first term Chambliss toured every military base in Georgia (80-plus years of Carl Vinson, Richard Russell and Sam Nunn is a tough legacy to follow) and worked with locals to remove Robins, an air logistics center, from the final Base Closing Commission list in 1995. He formed and co-chaired an Air Power Caucus and sought support for the F-22 Raptor.

To protect peanut farmers, he voted in committee against the Freedom to Farm Act in 1995 with four other Republicans, which defeated it temporarily; he opposed a provision to end the cotton marketing program as well. When the leadership folded the farm bill into the budget, Chambliss threatened not to support it but backed down under pressure. With Sanford Bishop of the 2d District, he devised a new "no-net-cost, market-oriented" peanut program, with a quota set at the projected domestic demand for edible peanuts; this was put into the final Freedom to Farm Act. He has sponsored measures to allow more foreign guest workers to be hired by farmers and to waive collateral for disaster loans for crop losses in 1997. When the Department of Transportation tried to force airlines to offer peanut-free zones around passengers who claimed allergies, Chambliss retaliated with a ban on such action that made its way into the October 1998 omnibus budget bill.

On other issues, Chambliss almost always votes with the Republican leadership, but he was one of the 1994 freshman class members who wanted a lower income cap on the $500 per-child tax credit. He staunchly opposed Clinton proposals for regulating tobacco like a drug. He opposes gun control and has become vice chairman of the Sportsmen's Caucus, which sponsored the first Congressional Shoot-out; he has proposed a Sportsmen's Bill of Rights, to allow hunting and fishing on federal land unless specifically forbidden by Congress. An avid outdoorsman, Chambliss said, "On one of those rare outdoor occasions when my mind turns to a pending issue in Congress, I have found no better place to be alone with my thoughts than my favorite fishing hole." He got $1 million for renovation of the Okefenokee Swamp visitors' center.

Democrats have tried to target Chambliss since the 1995 redistricting, which removed his own home from the district; he moved to an apartment in Macon. But Chambliss vastly outspent the 1996 nominee, Jim Wiggins, a Vietnam veteran and prosecutor, and ran as the savior of the peanut program. He won 53%–47%. In 1998 Democrats were frustrated when their choice, Judge John Ellington, announced in January he was not going to run. Chambliss spent time raising money for his PAC, the Common Sense Leadership Fund, which donated to other Republicans. He won 62%–38%, carrying all but two small counties. Three weeks after the election, Bob Livingston, then speaker-designate, named Chambliss vice chairman of the Budget Committee.

Cook's Call. *Potentially Competitive.* After the 1996 remapping, Chambliss is now in a competitive district but will only lose if Democrats field a strong candidate with a well-financed and organized campaign. Watch this seat closely in 2000; it will be an important test of candidate recruitment for Democrats.

The People: Pop. 1990: 587,912; 48.6% rural; 12.8% age 65 + ; 68% White, 31.1% Black, 0.4% Asian, 0.2% Amer. Indian, 0.3% Other; 0.8% Hispanic Origin. Households: 54.8% married couple families; 27.7% married couple fams. w. children; 30.3% college educ.; median household income: $23,577; per capita income: $11,038; median house value: $50,000; median gross rent: $213.

1996 Presidential Vote

Clinton (D) 90,662 (47%)
Dole (R) 85,224 (45%)
Perot (I) 14,643   (8%)

1992 Presidential Vote

Clinton (D) 93,643 (45%)
Bush (R) 83,976 (40%)
Perot (I) 32,068 (15%)

Rep. Saxby Chambliss (R)

Elected 1994; b. Nov. 10, 1943, Warrenton, NC; home, Macon; U. of GA, B.A. 1966, U. of TN, J.D. 1968; Episcopalian; married (Julianne).

Professional Career: Practicing atty., 1968–94.

DC Office: 1019 LHOB 20515, 202-225-6531; Fax: 202-225-3013; Web site: www.house.gov/chambliss.

District Offices: Macon, 912-752-0800; Waycross, 912-287-1180.

Committees: *Agriculture* (13th of 27 R): Department Operations, Oversight, Nutrition & Forestry; General Farm Commodities, Resource Conservation & Credit; Risk Management, Research & Specialty Crops. *Armed Services* (20th of 32 R): Military Readiness; Military Research & Development; Special Oversight Panel on Morale, Welfare and Recreation. *Budget* (2d of 24 R).

Group Ratings

	ADA	ACLU	AFS	LCV	CON	NTU	NFIB	COC	ACU	NTLC	CHC
1998	0	6	0	8	2	49	100	94	96	92	91
1997	5	—	0	—	70	55	—	88	88	—	—

National Journal Ratings

	1997 LIB — 1997 CONS		1998 LIB — 1998 CONS	
Economic	35%	— 65%	23%	— 74%
Social	29%	— 71%	3%	— 90%
Foreign	0%	— 88%	34%	— 62%

Key Votes of the 105th Congress

1. Clinton Budget Deal	Y	5. Puerto Rico Sthood. Ref.	N	9. Cut $ for B-2 Bombers	N
2. Education IRAs	Y	6. End Highway Set-asides	Y	10. Human Rights in China	N
3. Req. 2/3 to Raise Taxes	Y	7. School Prayer Amend.	Y	11. Withdraw Bosnia Troops	N
4. Fast-track Trade	Y	8. Ovrd. Part. Birth Veto	Y	12. End Cuban TV-Marti	N

Election Results

1998 general	Saxby Chambliss (R)	87,993	(62%)	($708,556)
	Ronald L. Cain (D)	53,079	(38%)	($10,459)
1998 primary	Saxby Chambliss (R)	unopposed		
1996 general	Saxby Chambliss (R)	93,619	(53%)	($1,081,914)
	Jim Wiggins (D)	84,506	(47%)	($277,400)

NINTH DISTRICT

In the last years of the 20th Century, the hills and mountains of north Georgia have suddenly become one of the boom areas of the South. This is a sharp turn in their history. Since the Cherokee were driven out early in the 19th Century, this has been poor country, where small farmers scratched a living off rocky land. It was devastated by the Civil War, by General Sherman's troops and because so many young men who left to fight for the Confederacy (and a few who left from mountain counties to fight for the Union) never returned. After the war not much changed for a while. Most communities lived in isolation; roads with hairpin curves led to remote hills where until very recently moonshine stills were more common than summer cabins. In time, textile mills began springing up along the railroads, around Gainesville poultry production became a big business, and in Dalton the craft tradition of tufted bedspread handiwork was transformed into the world's largest carpet industry, producing 60% of the world's tufted carpet. But these were low-wage industries and all-white; there had never been many slaves here, and in 1912 Forsyth County made headlines when it drove out its few black residents.

In the 1980s and especially the 1990s there has been a rush of change. Interstate highways have brought north Georgia in easy range of the world-city of Atlanta; the carpet industry has become more high-tech; small manufacturing is booming, with higher-skill work replacing low-tech mills; vacation and retirement communities have been built in mountains and around lakes. Forsyth and Cherokee counties are now part of the booming ring around Atlanta, even 50-plus miles from Peachtree Street. So tight are the labor markets that tens of thousands of Latinos from Texas and Latin countries have come to Dalton, Gainesville and the area around to snap up the jobs the boom is creating.

The 9th Congressional District covers the whole northern end of the state, from the Georgia suburbs of Chattanooga and Dalton in the west to the old Republican and new resort counties in the east. It extends south to include Forsyth County and part of Cherokee. A few counties here have always been Republican, many started switching in the 1970s and 1980s, and Cherokee and Forsyth now are among the most heavily Republican counties in the South—or anywhere. Economic prosperity and cultural traditionalism have sent politics here in one direction, even against national tides: Despite north Georgia native Governor Zell Miller's strong support for Bill Clinton, every county in the 9th District voted for Bob Dole in 1996.

The congressman from the 9th District is Nathan Deal, first elected in 1992, who switched parties and became a Republican in April 1995. Deal grew up in Gainesville, went to Mercer University, then served in the Army from 1966–68; he returned home to practice "street level law," with offices always on the ground floor, and public offices a young lawyer takes as civic duty: assistant district attorney, juvenile court judge, county attorney. In 1980, at 38, he was elected to the state Senate as a Democrat; Jimmy Carter was still president, the legislature was overwhelmingly Democratic, and it would have been quixotic to run as a Republican. He proved a capable legislator and was elected Senate president pro tem in 1989 and 1991. In 1992, with the retirement of 16-year incumbent Ed Jenkins, a power on the Ways and Means Committee, Deal ran, defeating a Republican abortion opponent with 59% of the vote.

In the House, Deal opposed the new Clinton Administration's economic policies, voting against the 1993 budget, for the line-item veto and balanced budget amendment; he helped found a 26-Democrat Fiscal Caucus and in 1994 co-sponsored a version of the "A to Z" spending cuts plan, which called for a special session of the House to consider budget cuts. Many saw Deal as a potential party-switcher, but while campaigning in 1994 he said, "If I choose to switch during the term, I think the honest thing to do is resign and have a special election." He beat an underfunded Republican, but with only 58%—a sign of increasing Republican sentiment.

In early 1995 he soldiered on as a Democrat and worked with other Democrats to offer an alternative to the Republicans' welfare reform package, which got the votes of every Democrat and a few Republicans as well. On Monday, April 3, Deal was saying how pleased he was by Democrats' support for his welfare reform package. On Wednesday, April 5, he found himself at odds with Democrats' opposition to tax cuts and with senior Democrats' criticisms of Clean Water Act revision proposals he and Louisiana's Jimmy Hayes (later a party-switcher himself) had gotten approved on a bipartisan committee vote. On Monday, April 10, back home in Gainesville for the congressional recess, Deal announced he was switching—the first party-switcher in the 104th Congress. He said the national Democratic Party was unwilling to admit it was "out of touch with mainstream America," and "I think that it is important that at some point you get away from the schizophrenia I have had to deal with." Democrats were stunned, and Newt Gingrich was clearly delighted; Deal was rewarded with a seat on the Commerce Committee. He also sits on Education—both his parents and his wife were teachers.

Deal has not proved to be a totally party-line Republican. In July 1996 he backed the minimum wage increase and in August 1998 he supported the Shays-Meehan campaign finance bill. But his voting record was mostly conservative, and constituents did not protest vehemently at the Tailgate Talk public meetings he holds in town squares every summer. Deal worked to get a community veterans' clinic opened in Gainesville in October 1998, sponsored a Web site for disabled people to become aware of assistive technology, and was a co-sponsor of Megan's Law. He worked on the 1996 immigration law and in 1997 opposed extension of a provision allowing green card applicants to pay a $1,000 fine and file for legal residency while staying in the United States. He sponsored higher penalties for illegal aliens and smugglers of aliens. Deal said he was aware that this may hurt politically in a district with a rapidly-growing Hispanic population, but "We're a nation of laws. It's our responsibility to forge support for the concept of law."

Deal had no opposition in the 1996 Republican primary, and in the general election, against a well-funded state legislator, he won 66%–34%, running especially strong among suburbanites in Cherokee (73%) and Forsyth (79%) Counties. In 1998 he was unopposed.

Cook's Call. *Safe.* Sometimes party-switches take, sometimes they don't; clearly, Deal's 1995 switch worked, as he has won by large margins since 1995. This is a solidly conservative, Republican district, and Deal has a good hold on it.

The People: Pop. 1990: 589,355; 78% rural; 12.2% age 65 + ; 94.8% White, 3.6% Black, 0.4% Asian, 0.3% Amer. Indian, 0.9% Other; 1.5% Hispanic Origin. Households: 64.9% married couple families; 31.8% married couple fams. w. children; 29.6% college educ.; median household income: $26,631; per capita income: $12,062; median house value: $62,700; median gross rent: $276.

1996 Presidential Vote		
Dole (R)	115,306	(55%)
Clinton (D)	73,861	(35%)
Perot (I)	20,809	(10%)

1992 Presidential Vote		
Bush (R)	98,205	(49%)
Clinton (D)	70,943	(35%)
Perot (I)	32,808	(16%)

Rep. Nathan Deal (R)

Elected 1992; b. Aug. 25, 1942, Millen; home, Lula; Mercer U., B.A. 1964, J.D. 1966; Baptist; married (Sandra).

Military Career: Army, 1966–68.

Elected Office: Hall Cnty. Juvenile Court Judge, 1971–72; GA Senate, 1980–92, Pres. Pro-Tem, 1989–90, 1991–92.

Professional Career: Hall Cnty. Atty., 1966–70; Asst. Dist. Atty., NE Judicial Circuit, 1970–71; Practicing atty., 1971–92.

DC Office: 2437 RHOB 20515, 202-225-5211; Fax: 202-225-8272; Web site: www.house.gov/deal.

District Offices: Dalton, 706-226-5320; Gainesville, 770-535-2592; Lafayette, 706-638-7042.

Committees: *Commerce* (11th of 29 R): Health and Environment; Telecommunications, Trade & Consumer Protection. *Education & the Workforce* (20th of 27 R): Postsecondary Education, Training & Life-Long Learning.

Group Ratings

	ADA	ACLU	AFS	LCV	CON	NTU	NFIB	COC	ACU	NTLC	CHC
1998	10	0	11	8	81	73	100	67	88	97	100
1997	0	—	13	—	49	62	—	90	96	—	—

National Journal Ratings

	1997 LIB — 1997 CONS			1998 LIB — 1998 CONS		
Economic	0%	—	90%	12%	—	85%
Social	20%	—	71%	3%	—	90%
Foreign	12%	—	81%	27%	—	68%

Key Votes of the 105th Congress

1. Clinton Budget Deal	Y	5. Puerto Rico Sthood. Ref.	N	9. Cut $ for B-2 Bombers	N
2. Education IRAs	Y	6. End Highway Set-asides	Y	10. Human Rights in China	N
3. Req. 2/3 to Raise Taxes	Y	7. School Prayer Amend.	Y	11. Withdraw Bosnia Troops	Y
4. Fast-track Trade	N	8. Ovrd. Part. Birth Veto	Y	12. End Cuban TV-Marti	Y

Election Results

1998 general	Nathan Deal (R)	unopposed		($224,137)
1998 primary	Nathan Deal (R)	unopposed		
1996 general	Nathan Deal (R)	132,532	(66%)	($865,898)
	Ken Poston (D)	69,662	(34%)	($429,454)

TENTH DISTRICT

Augusta, Georgia, is one of those small American cities that pops up now and again in our history. Founded in 1735 on the site of a fur-trading post, it is far older than Atlanta and just about as old as coastal Savannah. It was missed, fortunately, on General Sherman's march through Georgia; in those same years it was the boyhood home of Woodrow Wilson. Its antique Medical College of Georgia dates back to 1835. It is best known for its Augusta National Golf Course, where President Eisenhower used to tee off, and where the Masters Tournament is held every year. Augusta was once a cotton port on the Savannah River, with its own Cotton Exchange; now it has a Riverwalk on the site of the old levee. The paper industry, stoked by the pines that grow in profusion on the flat Piedmont land, is important here; so are nuclear weapons, produced until 1989 and now under disarmament downriver in South Carolina at the Savannah River site.

The 10th Congressional District includes Augusta and its fast-growing suburbs—they account for more than half the population and votes—plus 22 mostly rural counties in every direction. This district was very much changed by the redistricting of December 1995, which followed a Supreme Court decision overturning the boundaries used in 1992 and 1994 as a "racial gerrymander." The old 10th District did not include the black neighborhoods of Augusta, and most of its other counties were to the north and west, toward the Gwinnett County suburbs of Atlanta. Only 18% of its residents were black, and most of its smaller counties had been trending Republican for years. The new 10th includes all of Augusta, plus several black-majority counties to the south—once big plantation country. In all, the district lost 12 of its 19 counties and gained 17 new ones. Its population now is 38% black; the redistricting changed the 10th from a 47%–39% Bush district in 1992 to a 48%–46% Clinton district in 1996.

The congressman from the 10th District is Charlie Norwood, a Republican elected by a smashing margin in 1994. Norwood grew up in Valdosta, went to college and dental school, served in the Army in Vietnam and at Fort Gordon, then practiced dentistry in Augusta. He was president of the Georgia Dental Association and also started small businesses—Northwood Tree Nursery and Park Avenue Fabrics. In 1993 he decided to sell his dental practice and run against Congressman Don Johnson, a freshman elected in 1992. "I calculated one time that if my grandson was a dentist and we kept going the way we were going, he'd have to do 900 crowns just to pay his part of the interest on the national debt." Johnson was the kind of Democrat who had held such Southern seats for years: A former congressional staffer and state senator, with strong local connections and good political instincts. But he came under scathing criticism when he broke a campaign promise to vote against any tax increase and supported the Clinton budget and tax package in 1993. Norwood's toughest race in 1994 turned out to be the primary; he came from behind to beat Ralph Hudgens in the runoff 51%–49%. When Johnson said he wanted Bill Clinton or Al Gore to visit the 10th District only if "they are coming down to endorse my opponent," Norwood invited Clinton and offered to pay his plane fare. Norwood won 65%–35%, as Johnson took one of the worst lickings of a non-scandal-tarred incumbent in recent history.

In his first term, Norwood had a conservative voting record, with seats on the Commerce and the Education and the Workforce committees. His one major dissent from the leadership was his successful opposition in 1995 to the sale of the Southeastern Power Administration for the purpose of deficit reduction; he was afraid private utilities would charge higher rates. Redistricting put him in obvious political danger. The Democratic nominee, state legislator David Bell, campaigned as a conservative and said he would support the Blue Dog Democrats in the House, but criticized Norwood on education, the environment, Medicare and the minimum wage. The AFL-CIO also targeted Norwood, running ads accusing him of cutting Medicare and college loans. But Norwood excelled in fundraising: In 1995 he ranked fifth among the 73 Republican freshmen in raising PAC money, and collected $664,000 in PAC contributions for the 1996 election. Norwood challenged the accuracy of the AFL-CIO ads and persuaded all but one Augusta station not to run them; he purchased his own ads, to be run right after the AFL-CIO spots, calling them lies and urging viewers to switch channels. And when Bell ran an ad in which a cartoon fish said, "Sorry, Charlie," Norwood's campaign alerted StarKist Tuna, which called it a trademark infringement on their Charlie the Tuna ads and demanded it be yanked. This was the closest House election in Georgia in 1996. Norwood carried the Augusta area 55%–45%; in the rest of the district Bell won narrowly; overall Norwood won 52%–48%.

In his second term, Norwood suddenly became one of the most influential members in the House. The reason was PARCA, the Patient Access to Responsible Care Act, regulating health maintenance organizations, which Norwood sponsored and pushed with great vehemence. "This is something that has been festering in my soul for a long time. People are trying to deny our patients treatment." In his dental practice, Norwood was in an HMO for three years and decided, "This was no way to go." To some critics, PARCA looked like "provider protection." But Norwood insisted, "This is not about money for physicians. It is about them losing control of their ability to practice medicine." To push his bill, Norwood pestered Newt Gingrich on flights to Atlanta and, more importantly, assembled at one point 230 co-sponsors, including 90 Republicans—a majority of the House. PARCA provided that patients could sue HMOs when they overrule doctors and refuse to pay for treatments that turn out to have been needed; that patients can visit emergency rooms without the permission of the insurer; that doctors couldn't be prohibited from discussing alternative treatments (the gag rule); and that patients have free selection of doctors, hospitals and treatments; that patients can see specialists on a doctor's recommendation. Ironically, it would be enforced mainly by the Labor Department; it was heavy-handed OSHA regulation that inspired Norwood to get into politics.

PARCA produced new political alliances and results. Large businesses and the Chamber of Commerce were appalled, and predicted it would raise insurance costs by something like 35%. HMOs and the Blues were against it as well. The American Medical Association, American Dental Association and the American College of Emergency Physicians came out in favor. Most Democrats favored the idea, as did Republican Greg Ganske, an Iowa plastic surgeon; but many Republicans who had stoutly opposed the Clinton health care plan favored PARCA just as strongly. In January 1998, as momentum for PARCA was growing, Speaker Newt Gingrich appointed a Republican working group headed by Chief Deputy Whip Dennis Hastert. Through breakfast meetings and negotiating sessions, there seemed to be genuine interaction. Norwood judged that he couldn't get his full bill through a conference committee, and so was ready to compromise; Greg Ganske, in contrast, joined with Democrats to back their bill. On

June 24, the working group came up with a bill. It did not include the right to sue, but did include a ban on the gag rule, emergency room visits without previous approval, and allowing patients to appeal decisions to an outside arbitrator. Some of Hastert's initiatives were added: "HealthMarts," cooperative purchasing agreements to give small businesses access to lower-cost insurance, and malpractice reforms. In August the House voted on the two bills. The working group's proposal, the Patient Protection Act, passed 216–210; a Democratic "Patient Bill of Rights" failed 212–217. The Senate did not act, but the issue seems sure to return in the 106th Congress.

Back in the 10th District Norwood seemed stronger than in 1996. David Bell declined to run again, and local Democratic Chairman Chuck Pardue, who thought about running, declined because of Norwood's funding advantage. Norwood bragged about PARCA and about his attaching a rider to the 1997 disaster relief bill to allow a local ophthamologist to bring back a polar bear he shot in Canada. Against weak opposition Norwood raised $1.1 million, but didn't spend it all. He won 60%–40%, running well ahead of party lines. Bell is seriously considering another run in 2000.

Cook's Call. *Potentially Competitive.* After the 1996 redistricting, Norwood, like Saxby Chambliss in the 8th District, is now in a competitive district. The question here is whether Democrats will field a strong enough candidate and fund him sufficiently to take advantage of it. Watch the 10th in 2000; Norwood could face a real race but would still be favored.

The People: Pop. 1990: 588,046; 47.3% rural; 11.7% age 65 + ; 60.9% White, 37.5% Black, 1% Asian, 0.2% Amer. Indian, 0.4% Other; 1% Hispanic Origin. Households: 54% married couple families; 27.9% married couple fams. w. children; 32.5% college educ.; median household income: $24,666; per capita income: $11,159; median house value: $55,600; median gross rent: $241.

1996 Presidential Vote			1992 Presidential Vote		
Clinton (D)	94,968	(48%)	Bush (R)	99,336	(47%)
Dole (R)	90,213	(46%)	Clinton (D)	81,960	(39%)
Perot (I)	11,669	(6%)	Perot (I)	30,662	(14%)

Rep. Charlie Norwood (R)

Elected 1994; b. July 27, 1941, Valdosta; home, Evans; GA S. U., B.S. 1964, Georgetown U., D.D.S. 1967; Methodist; married (Gloria).

Military Career: Army, 1967–69 (Vietnam).

Professional Career: Small businessman, 1969–present; Practicing dentist, 1969–93; Pres., GA Dental Assn., 1983.

DC Office: 1707 LHOB 20515, 202-225-4101; Fax: 202-225-0279; Web site: www.house.gov/norwood.

District Offices: Augusta, 706-733-7066; Dublin, 912-275-2814; Milledgeville, 912-453-0373.

Committees: *Commerce* (17th of 29 R): Energy & Power; Health and Environment. *Education & the Workforce* (16th of 27 R): Oversight & Investigations (Vice Chmn.).

Group Ratings

	ADA	ACLU	AFS	LCV	CON	NTU	NFIB	COC	ACU	NTLC	CHC
1998	5	6	11	8	21	50	100	83	100	97	100
1997	0	—	0	—	70	69	—	90	96	—	—

National Journal Ratings

	1997 LIB — 1997 CONS		1998 LIB — 1998 CONS	
Economic	0% —	90%	15% —	85%
Social	0% —	90%	19% —	80%
Foreign	22% —	77%	7% —	83%

Key Votes of the 105th Congress

1. Clinton Budget Deal	Y	5. Puerto Rico Sthood. Ref.	N	9. Cut $ for B-2 Bombers	N
2. Education IRAs	Y	6. End Highway Set-asides	Y	10. Human Rights in China	N
3. Req. 2/3 to Raise Taxes	Y	7. School Prayer Amend.	Y	11. Withdraw Bosnia Troops	Y
4. Fast-track Trade	N	8. Ovrd. Part. Birth Veto	Y	12. End Cuban TV-Marti	N

Election Results

1998 general	Charlie Norwood (R)	88,527	(60%)	($1,104,431)
	Marion Spencer Freeman (D)	60,004	(40%)	($48,136)
1998 primary	Charlie Norwood (R)	unopposed		
1996 general	Charlie Norwood (R)	96,723	(52%)	($1,622,486)
	David Bell (D)	88,054	(48%)	($604,043)

ELEVENTH DISTRICT

Greater Atlanta has grown out in every direction, south past the airport, west over the Chattahoochee, north past Buckhead and the Perimeter Mall, and east and northeast past Stone Mountain. Gwinnett County, on I-85, has become an urban community of its own: It cast 21,000 votes in 1972 and 162,000 in 1996, a level approaching Fulton County, which includes central Atlanta or DeKalb just to the east. Now similar growth is heading east to Walton and Barrow Counties, the then-rural home of Senator (1933–71) Richard Russell, and south to Rockdale County, where spiritualist Nancy Fowler channelled messages said to be from the Virgin Mary. Politically, these new growth areas favor market forces over government regulation on economic issues and traditional values over liberal ones on cultural issues; they vote overwhelmingly Republican.

But there is another Georgia in the counties beyond, a state of still rural communities, and Athens, home of the University of Georgia, the country's oldest chartered state university. Athens is the site of one of America's finest collections of Greek Revival buildings—gleaming white columns, perfectly proportioned little Parthenons and flat-roofed square houses surrounded by fluted columns with Corinthian capitals, all dating from the 1830s-50s. Politically, Athens remains liberal and Democratic, though neighboring Oconee County has been—Gwinnett-like—growing and trending Republican.

The 11th Congressional District consists of much of this territory, from Gwinnett County east to Athens, then northeast to the Savannah River. Gwinnett and the other counties in metro Atlanta cast 70% of the votes here in 1996 and 1998, with the rest split about equally between Athens and Oconee County and the rural counties. The current 11th District was created when the Supreme Court in 1995 declared Georgia's district lines a "racial gerrymander." The former 11th was a black-majority district that snaked from heavily black south DeKalb County across the state to black precincts in Savannah and Augusta; none of the new 11th is contained within these lines. Athens and most of the rural counties were formerly part of the 10th District.

The congressman from the 11th District is John Linder, a Republican elected in 1992 and 1994 in the old 4th District, which combined north DeKalb County and half of Gwinnett. Like most of the Georgia delegation, Linder grew up elsewhere, in his case Minnesota, where he went to college and dental school. Then after two years in the Air Force he moved to greater Atlanta and practiced dentistry for 13 years. In 1977 he started Linder Financial Corporation, a lending institution for entrepreneurial ventures in the South. In 1974, at 32, he was elected to the Georgia House, where he served all but two of the next 14 years. In 1990 he challenged Democratic Congressman Ben Jones, known to TV watchers as Cooter in the *Dukes of Hazzard*, and lost 52%–48%. When 1992 redistricting removed black middle- and upper-income south DeKalb from the 4th, Jones decided to run in the new 10th, where he lost the Democratic primary. Linder ran again in the 4th, where he finished first in a six-candidate primary with 38%, then won the runoff with 62%. In the general, he faced Democratic state Senator Cathey Steinberg and, in a race that ran along national party lines, won by just 51%–49%.

From this tenuous beginning Linder quickly became an important congressman. One reason was electoral security: In heavily Republican 1994 he won 58%–42%, and since 1996 he has had a safe seat in the 11th. Another is that he was a very close ally to Newt Gingrich. That goes back a ways: In 1975 Linder, Gingrich and Paul Coverdell began meeting to try to build a strong Georgia Republican Party, surely not imagining that within 20 years they would be congressman, speaker and senator; in 1984 they developed Operation Breakthrough for electing Republicans in conservative-leaning legislative districts which had never been seriously contested before.

Linder has a calm, usually humorous demeanor; his views are solidly conservative. He says his "over-arching ideology [is] that individuals will make better decisions for their families than the government." In his first term he sponsored the Republicans' three-term limit on service as a committee's ranking member—an important procedural change now that Republicans are chairmen and one that is becoming increasingly unpopular as they serve their third term in the majority. After Republicans won control, Gingrich gave Linder a seat on the Rules Committee and called on him often to preside over contentious debates; he floor-managed rules on complex bills like the 1996 Telecommunications Act. He differed from the leadership only occasionally, favoring a balanced budget amendment with a three-fifths vote to raise taxes and calling term limits "a bad idea whose time has come." Linder also became the informal head of a group of Republicans determined to defend Gingrich on ethics charges. In September 1996 he introduced a resolution demanding a special counsel in the ethics probe against Democratic Leader Dick Gephardt, whom the ethics committee found had filed an inaccurate statement on the ownership of a beach house. That same month he attacked ethics committee ranking Democrat Jim McDermott as "the least ethical person in the House."

After the 1996 election, Gingrich chose Linder to replace Bill Paxon as chairman of the National Republican Congressional Committee. He still continued to be active legislatively. He floor-managed rules on issues like bankruptcy reform, the transportation appropriation and national education testing. He served on the Republican health care and tobacco settlement working groups. He sought a delay in regulations imposed on Atlanta by EPA for purported air-quality violations whose accuracy he doubted. Into the October 1998 omnibus budget, he put a measure to help dialysis patients get insurance; he got funding for an Athens-Atlanta rail line and made sure both Elbert and Hart counties were included in the Appalachian Regional Commission.

But Linder's main focus in 1998 was on the campaign committee job. He excelled at fundraising, amassing some $40 million for the committee and relentlessly prevailing on incumbents to contribute to Republican challengers. He did a good job at recruiting candidates. He shared the assumption of most observers that Republicans would gain seats as the out party in a presidential off-year election and predicted gains. His assessment of the overall attitude, made with respect to his own race, was not far off the mark: "The public is quite content. Approval ratings for Congress are the highest ever. This will be a status quo election. It will be a light turnout." He tried to change that with Operation Breakthrough, heavy funding and national ads in long-shot Democratic districts. His targeting was good but one of his ads misfired: It raised the trust and impeachment issues against Bill Clinton, and while run in only a few districts, it was publicized nationally, yielding a minimum of gain and a maximum of pain.

After the election, when the Republicans actually lost five seats, Linder was obviously in deep trouble. He could argue that the party came closer to predictions than it often has, and that Republicans won more seats and more votes than Democrats. He could argue that Democrats did better at turnout, which made a bit of difference, and that the Republican base was disheartened by the October 1998 omnibus budget. Linder said the problem was the lack of a "strong message," which "was not my responsibility." In fact, Republicans had a net open-seat loss of only one, an excellent result since the retirement of several popular Republicans in Democratic-leaning states left them vulnerable. But five Republican incumbents and only one Democrat lost: in a pro-incumbent year, only the weakest animals were culled from the herd, and the Republicans had more of them.

Gingrich, under attack himself, said that the next NRCC head would be elected by the conference rather than appointed by him, and Tom Davis, a highly competent election buff, started running for the job, with the support of Whip Tom DeLay. Linder reacted bitterly, his two decades-long alliance with Gingrich at an end. "I remember when Newt Gingrich's wife left a press conference in tears when he blamed her. So I don't think he has any compunction about blaming me." That was Thursday; Gingrich announced his retirement late on Friday; 12 days later Linder lost to Davis 130–77. Linder said, "There clearly was a desire for change, and I was a perfect target for that." The question now is whether Linder will resume his legislative work and get on well with the new Republican leadership; Rules is not a good committee for a party rebel. He was re-elected with 69% in the 11th District, and can stay in the House as long as he wants.

Cook's Call. *Safe.* Though Linder lost his chairmanship of the National Republican Congressional Committee, he should have no trouble holding onto his congressional seat, should he decide to run again. Even if he was to step aside, the district should remain safely in Republican hands.

The People: Pop. 1990: 589,317; 45.1% rural; 9.2% age 65 + ; 86.6% White, 11.8% Black, 1.1% Asian, 0.2% Amer. Indian, 0.4% Other; 1.2% Hispanic Origin. Households: 63% married couple families; 34% married couple fams. w. children; 43.3% college educ.; median household income: $32,761; per capita income: $14,001; median house value: $83,500; median gross rent: $348.

1996 Presidential Vote		
Dole (R)	128,320	(55%)
Clinton (D)	88,083	(38%)
Perot (I)	17,668	(8%)

1992 Presidential Vote		
Clinton (D)	121,356	(67%)
Bush (R)	44,419	(24%)
Perot (I)	15,676	(9%)

Rep. John Linder (R)

Elected 1992; b. Sept. 9, 1942, Deer River, MN; home, Tucker; U. of MN, B.S. 1964, D.D.S., 1967; Presbyterian; married (Lynne).

Military Career: Air Force, 1967–69.

Elected Office: GA House of Reps., 1974–80, 1982–90.

Professional Career: Practicing dentist, 1969–82; Founder & Pres., Linder Financial Corp., 1977–92.

DC Office: 2447 RHOB 20515, 202-225-4272; Fax: 202-225-4696; Web site: www.house.gov/linder.

District Offices: Athens, 706-355-9909; Duluth, 770-931-9550.

Committees: *Rules* (3d of 9 R): Rules & Organization of the House (Chmn.).

Group Ratings

	ADA	ACLU	AFS	LCV	CON	NTU	NFIB	COC	ACU	NTLC	CHC
1998	0	6	0	8	26	53	100	100	100	97	100
1997	0	—	13	—	70	55	—	100	87	—	—

National Journal Ratings

	1997 LIB — 1997 CONS		1998 LIB — 1998 CONS	
Economic	19% —	76%	0% —	88%
Social	20% —	71%	3% —	90%
Foreign	37% —	62%	32% —	67%

Key Votes of the 105th Congress

1. Clinton Budget Deal	Y	5. Puerto Rico Sthood. Ref.	N	9. Cut $ for B-2 Bombers	N
2. Education IRAs	Y	6. End Highway Set-asides	Y	10. Human Rights in China	N
3. Req. 2/3 to Raise Taxes	Y	7. School Prayer Amend.	Y	11. Withdraw Bosnia Troops	Y
4. Fast-track Trade	Y	8. Ovrd. Part. Birth Veto	Y	12. End Cuban TV-Marti	N

Election Results

1998 general	John Linder (R)	120,909	(69%)	($717,543)
	Vincent Littman (D)	53,510	(31%)	($11,541)
1998 primary	John Linder (R)	unopposed		
1996 general	John Linder (R)	145,821	(64%)	($780,653)
	Tommy Stephenson (D)	80,940	(36%)	($58,200)

HAWAII

Trouble in paradise. That has been the story of Hawaii in the 1990s. While the rest of the nation has surged to prosperity, Hawaii has fallen behind. The number of jobs peaked in 1991, then fell 4% by 1997. Unemployment, at 3% in 1990, nearly doubled by mid-1998. Foreign investment plummeted from $3.6 billion in 1990 to half a billion four years later. Bankruptcies increased fivefold between 1990 and 1997. While the 49 other states have cut welfare rolls since 1993, Hawaii had a 36% increase in caseloads during the same period. Home sales dropped 55% from 1990 to 1997, and Hawaii was the only state with falling house prices in 1997. The key number is that tourism, the mainstay of Hawaii's economy, declined from a peak of 7 million in 1990 to 6.1 million in 1993, then rebounded to only 6.8 million in 1996 and 1997. But Hawaii's troubles are not just economic. There are threats as well that some of the defining characteristics that have made Hawaii strong and tolerant in the nearly six decades after Pearl Harbor might turn sour.

Hawaii was settled only about a thousand years ago by Polynesians who paddled across vast Pacific expanses in small outrigger canoes; when Captain Cook came here in 1776, he found his Maori interpreter from New Zealand could understand Hawaiian. On these geologically young islands, teeming with food and seldom inconvenienced by bad weather, Hawaiians built a fierce civilization, with harsh taboos and cannibalism as well as alluring music and dance. The islands were united politically in 1779 by King Kamehameha I, who ate one of his rivals and maintained the old culture. In 1819, within a year of his death, his consort Kaahumanu outlawed the Hawaiian religious taboos and welcomed the American missionary Hiram Bingham. New England missionaries and their trader cousins came—while British and Russian ships occasionally put into port—and established the predominant culture. By the 1850s, they were importing laborers from China, Japan, Portugal and the Philippines to work their sugar and pineapple plantations. American planters and businessmen bridled at the caprices of the royal line and, in January 1893, with the help of U.S. Marines, ousted Queen Liliuokalani from the Iolani Palace and called on the United States to annex Hawaii. President Grover Cleveland demurred, and Hawaii for five years was a republic; it was annexed by President William McKinley in July 1898.

This history is a source of regret for some; an *Onipa'a* ceremony remembering Liliuokalani's overthrow was staged by John Waihee, the first governor of native Hawaiian descent, in January 1993, with the American flag conspicuously absent; in 1998, native Hawaiians staged a protest demonstration on the Mall in Washington. Yet Hawaii is a civilization both American and Pacific, which has created a better life for its citizens than almost any island or native commonwealth of 100 years ago. Its ethnic mixing began a century ago when disease reduced the native Hawaiians to 45,000; they shared Liliuokalani's Hawaii with 3,000 Americans, 20,000 Chinese and 25,000 Japanese. Hawaii was well on it way to being "the gathering place of peoples," as Walter McDougall called it in his history of the North Pacific, *Let the Sea Make a Noise*.

To that Americana, each group has made a positive contribution. The Asian migrant laborers brought traditions of hard work, family loyalty and group solidarity that found expression most vividly in the performance of the 442d "Go for Broke" Regimental Combat Team, made up mostly of sons of Japanese immigrants, which became the most decorated unit in U.S. military history. The Yankee spirit has been evident in Hawaii's commercial success and in its attachment to the rule of Anglo-American law. The Hawaiian spirit is alive in the vitality of the *aloha* ambience, the welcoming of others despite their differences, and a willingness to absorb the teachings of others while maintaining a certain Polynesian attitude toward life. When Pearl Harbor was attacked by the Japanese in December 1941, no one in Hawaii or on the Mainland doubted that this was part of America. Ironically, it was Hawaii's super-American tolerance that inspired segregationist Southern Democrats to block its admission to the Union for years. Today, Hawaiians retain pride in their ethnic heritage—or heritages: about half of non-military weddings are "out" marriages and most babies are of mixed ethnicity.

Hawaii's economy was built first on agriculture, by the Big Five trading companies that shipped out sugar and pineapple and shipped in almost anything else; then on the military, important for nearly 100 years in this strategic site in the middle of the world's largest ocean. But the sugar and pineapple plantations have become uneconomic; there were just 7,200 farming jobs by 1997 compared to 11,300 in 1982. The total number of military and civilian federal employees has also fallen from 97,800 in 1988 to 74,100 in 1997. The real engine of Hawaii's economy—a sputtering engine today—is tourism, which accounts for one-quarter of Hawaii's economy and one-third of its jobs. Tourism peaked in 1990, as recessions began in its two chief sources of vacationers, California and Japan. The drop was sharpest in westbound (California-based) tourists, but as soon as California snapped out of recession, in 1995, the Japanese yen depreciated and eastbound tourism plummeted. (Japanese tourists spend an average $286 a day, compared to $137 for Americans.) In addition, Hurricane Iniki caused $1.6 billion damage on the island of Kauai in 1992. Hawaii, which had never done much to promote tourism, now found it could not match the attractions of California or Florida, while its costs were far higher; attempts to attract Koreans, Thais and other Asians fizzled with the devaluations of 1997.

Hawaii seems unable to support the expensive and intrusive governmental apparatus constructed by the Democrats who have controlled state government since 1962 and, despite a near-loss of the governorship in 1998, still control it today. This machine had its beginning in the 1950s, when returning World War II veterans like Daniel Inouye, Spark Matsunaga and George Ariyoshi joined forces with former Mainlander John Burns, who as a policeman during the war helped prevent persecution of Japanese Americans. They allied themselves with the then-powerful International Longshoremen's and Warehousemen's Union, and cemented the allegiance of Japanese American voters. In the 1950s, Hawaii, resenting Mainland Southern

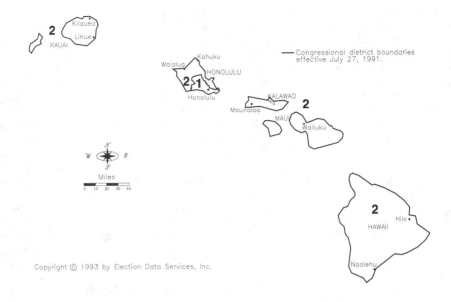

Democratic senators who delayed statehood, tended to vote Republican. But the Burns-Inouye machine built on the grievances against the *haole* (white) owners of the big companies and triumphed. Inouye was elected as a Democrat to the House in 1959 and to the Senate in 1962; Burns was elected governor in 1962, and the office has been passed down in lineal succession to George Ariyoshi, John Waihee and now Benjamin Cayetano—a balanced ticket, of Japanese, native Hawaiian and Filipino descent. As agriculture and the docks became less important, the ILWU's power waned; it has been replaced by the public employee unions which are strongly Democratic. Voting has long tended to run along ethnic lines. Japanese Americans, used to working in organizations in unions and government, have tended to be the heart of the Democratic Party; whites, with relatively high incomes, tend toward Republicans; Filipinos, often in menial jobs, are heavily Democratic; Chinese, somewhat less so; native Hawaiians, heavily Democratic but not as likely to be active in politics.

Over the years this machine has built a large government. Hawaii has the fifth highest per capita tax burden in the nation and the third toughest income tax scale in the nation. Of state and local governments with more than $1 billion in revenue, it has more public employees per capita than any but the District of Columbia and New York City. This is centralized government: Hawaii has four counties (with one, Honolulu, covering 71% of the population), one school district, one statewide health care plan. And it is thick with regulations. Cayetano's business department director Seija Naya, looking back at the 1980s, said, "This was a boom period, and government wanted to stay in control. They added more regulations, charged more fees and made it harder for businesses to receive approvals." The culture created by one-party control and a large state apparatus seems to be characterized in a phrase of Cayetano's, "You've got to support your friends and you have to punish your enemies." Law professor Randall Roth, a backer of Republican governor candidate Linda Lingle in 1998, explains her failure to win support among business groups by saying, "There is a fear of retribution. With regulation and centralized government, you just can't afford to be seen as an enemy of the administration."

Eight public and private entities own 70% of Hawaii's land: the federal government 16%, the state 29%, and six private landowners 25%. The Bishop Estate (Mrs. Bishop was the last surviving descendant of Kamehameha I) owns 8%; its five trustees, appointed by the state

Supreme Court, which is to say the Democratic machine, and paid more than $800,000 a year, are supposed to spend the Estate's huge income on the Kamehameha School for native Hawaiians. A 1984 U.S. Supreme Court decision upheld a Hawaii law forcing the Bishop Estate to sell land held in 99-year leaseholds when they expire, and with the resulting cash the Estate has made vast investments, including the Royal Hawaiian Shopping Center, a bank and aluminum factory in China, and 10% of the investment firm of Goldman Sachs; it also guarantees against loss the blind trust of Treasury Secretary and former Goldman partner Robert Rubin in return for $291,000 a year. The Bishop Estate's total net worth is some $10 billion. In 1998 its five trustees were embroiled in lawsuits: a criminal charge of breach of fiduciary duty was brought against one; an ouster suit was brought against four; one trustee sought the ouster of two others. Meanwhile, students at the Kamehameha School charged one trustee with intruding on the headmaster and ending an outreach program to save $11 million and dismissing 170 teachers. In 1999 a state judge ordered the removal of four trustees and accepted the resignation of the fifth after the IRS threatened to take away the Estate's tax-exempt status.

The burden of Hawaii's expensive and officious welfare state seems to be too much for its tourism-dominated economy to bear. Hawaii has great advantages as a central Pacific emporium—the stability of the American flag and dollar, the openness to diversity, the wondrous climate and physical beauty of these islands. (The last is almost too good: Hawaii's island ecology means there are few species here and that the islands can be easily overrun by intruders; Hawaiians are desperate to keep out the tree snake that has infested Guam and the Miconia calvescens plant that has overrun Tahiti.) But despite these advantages, jobs and people have been fleeing. In contrast, Alaska, facing falling oil revenues, military cutbacks and Asian recession, has much lower taxes and has been adding jobs. The response of the political system has been tepid. In fall 1997, a commission of business, labor and government leaders proposed a stimulus package of lower personal and corporate taxes, a higher sales tax and many recommendations for streamlining government and privatizing services. But the legislature voted only a four-year phased in lowering of income tax and a few structural recommendations. Hawaii's generous welfare system with its increasing rolls was left mostly untouched. And this was while Cayetano was trailing in the polls as Republican Linda Lingle called for more drastic reform. In November, Cayetano, primarily through ethnic appeals, eked out a 50%–49% victory, and many Democrats concluded the need for major change had passed. Tourism may expand again. And in May 1999, the state convinced the popular TV series "Baywatch" to begin filming here, under the new name "Baywatch Hawaii"; the legislature allocated $1.7 million to help build the set and Cayetano personally helped negotiate concessions with the Teamsters union to cut costs.

Change may be coming from another quarter, however: the native Hawaiian sovereignty movement. Consciousness of native ancestry has been growing in the 1990s: 12.5% of Hawaiians classified themselves as partly native in the 1990 Census, but that number has risen to about 19% in recent surveys (less than 1% of Hawaii residents are of entirely native ancestry). More people are learning the Hawaiian language. The centennials of the overthrow of Queen Liliuokolani (1993) and of U.S. annexation of Hawaii (1998) inspired demonstrations and expressions of bitterness over the end of the Hawaiian kingdom. A state sovereignty commission met for two years and in 1996 sponsored a referendum of native Hawaiians; 73% of those eligible (with some native blood) voted yes on the question, "Shall the Hawaiian people elect delegates to propose a native Hawaiian government?" The problem is that no one is quite sure what sovereignty means. A few activists have called for independence; others seek a commonwealth status something like Puerto Rico's (though in Puerto Rico support for statehood is rising); some want native Hawaiians to be a "nation within a nation," like various North American Indian tribes. But few if any native Hawaiians live in aboriginal communities, and the condition of life on Indian reservations is not an appealing one. Nor is Indian gambling likely to be approved in Hawaii, which is one of the three states (Utah and Tennessee are the others) with no legalized gambling.

Hawaii's officeholders take a typically tolerant view. Cayetano says sovereignty will be fine if it is "acceptable to the non-Hawaiians, as well as the United States government"; the four-member Hawaiian congressional delegation promised to abide by the results of the referendum. But this verges on sanctioning separatism. Surely the sensible future for Hawaii is not to create ethnic enclaves or racial preference, but to nurture the special strengths of all the peoples who have made Hawaii tolerant and affluent—just as Hawaii, to protect its 10,000 unique biological and botanical species, needs not to put them under glass but to maintain the environment in which they have flourished. But Western ideology has made Hawaii a free, tolerant, and prosperous state, and the stability of being an unquestioned part of the United States is one of the assets Hawaii can deploy to diversify its economy beyond tourism.

There is one other aspect of diversity that needs to be mentioned. Since 1993 Hawaii's Supreme Court has been on the verge of legalizing gay marriages. This prompted Congress to pass and Bill Clinton to sign the 1996 Defense of Marriage Act, which purported to let states refuse to recognize such marriages, though that seems contrary to the Constitution's full-faith-and-credit clause. But Hawaiian legislators and voters have made the issue moot. In 1997, the legislature authorized a domestic partners referendum, which would to provide for shared health insurance, state pensions, inheritance rights, property ownership and wrongful death suits. But in November 1998, Hawaiians voted 69%–30% to reserve marriage for male-female couples.

Governor. Benjamin J. Cayetano has twice been elected governor by narrow margins. He grew up in Honolulu, went to college and law school in Los Angeles, then went into private practice in Hawaii; he was elected to the legislature in 1974, at 34, and served 12 years, working on low-income housing loans, auto insurance premium rollbacks and Agent Orange compensation. He was elected lieutenant governor in 1986 and was former Governor John Waihee's choice for succession. But Cayetano had serious competition in 1994. In the September primary he beat state health care program director Jack Lewin by 55%–38%. In the general he faced former Congresswoman Pat Saiki, a strong though losing candidate against Senator Daniel Akaka in 1990, and of Japanese descent; and Frank Fasi, who formed his own The Best Party using as his symbol the Hawaiian good luck gesture of a raised thumb and little finger. Fasi is the termagent of Hawaii politics, mayor of Honolulu for all but four years from 1968–94, a candidate for governor five times on the Democratic, Republican and Best Party tickets, accusing Democratic machine politicians of corruption and accused by them of it in turn. Cayetano said he was concerned about education and ran a half-hour ad telling his personal story; Saiki ran an unfocused campaign; Fasi rallied his supporters in Honolulu and came near to winning. Cayetano won with 37%, to 31% for Saiki and 29% for Fasi.

In office, Cayetano, facing big deficits, moved to hold down spending and cut the state work force by more than 3,000. He reformed workmen's compensation and gave more authority to local schools. Telecom was deregulated. He doubled to $60 million the state's marketing budget for tourism and built a $350 million convention center on the Honolulu waterfront. But he insisted that he wanted to maintain state government's safety net, and the economy still sputtered. Only parts of the fall 1997 commission stimulus package were passed by the heavily Democratic legislature, and the expensive welfare system was little touched by reform.

Linda Lingle, Republican mayor of Maui since 1990, mounted a challenge. Maui had been gaining jobs during the recession: "the Maui miracle," she called it: "It's time for a change, and change is about joining the other 49 states with economic revitalization that is taking place across the country." In February 1998 voters said Hawaii was off on the wrong track by a 67%–18% margin, and Lingle led in polls right up through the campaign.

Yet Cayetano won, 50%–49%. If Lingle was calling for change, Cayetano was appealing to values. "We Democrats have built this state," he insisted. In a June 1998 poll, voters by a 49%–23% margin said Republicans were better for the economy, but by a 68%–19% said Democrats were closer to Hawaii's mainstream. Cayetano ads recounted his humble background and appealed to the traditional Democratic loyalties of Filipinos and Japanese Americans, back to the days when they felt oppressed by the sugar and pineapple growers and the

"Big Five" companies that ran the docks. In August, Lingle accused the Cayetano campaign of spreading the false rumor that she is gay. But Senator Daniel Inouye did say later, "I would prefer to have a governor who's had a family. Ben's my man." The outcome may have been determined by Lingle's decision to take state matching funds and abide by a $2.7 million spending limit. While she had great success raising money on the Mainland, she was heavily outspent by Cayetano in the last two weeks. Voting tended to fall on ethnic lines, with Cayetano carrying heavily Filipino and Japanese American areas, and Lingle carrying 21 of the 29 state House districts where Caucasians are the largest ethnic group.

Was 1998 a year the Democratic machine survived a challenge at a moment when it was peculiarly vulnerable? Or was it a year that saw movement away from the Democratic machine that has run state government for nearly 40 years? The 2002 election will tell. Lingle said she is running again; Lieutenant Governor Mazie Hirono, of Japanese descent, would be an attractive candidate for Democrats—and if she wins would become the fourth consecutive lieutenant governor to be elected governor.

Senior Senator. The largest figure in Hawaii's public life remains Senator Daniel K. Inouye, who has held elective office here since Hawaii attained statehood in 1959. Inouye was a severely wounded veteran of the 442d Regimental Combat Team in World War II, then became a lawyer, and was elected to the state legislature in 1954, the House in 1959, and the Senate in 1962. He was keynoter at the turbulent 1968 Democratic National Convention, a tenacious member of the Senate Watergate Committee in 1973–74 and the first chairman of the Senate Intelligence Committee, in 1976. Inouye believes in the Senate, the Democratic Party, Hawaii, the armed services, and Native Americans—among other things. He is the fourth most senior member of the Senate, and a stickler for its prerogatives. He went out of his way to defend senators in his view unjustly attacked—Harrison Williams during the Abscam scandal, Dennis DeConcini of the Keating Five—but was also quick to call for the resignation of Bob Packwood after the Senate voted in 1993 to subpoena his diaries.

Inouye is ranking Democrat on the Appropriations Defense Subcommittee; the committee's chairman is Ted Stevens of Alaska, which gives enormous clout to two senators in office since the 1960s from the two states most recently admitted to the Union, both with their own special claims on the federal government. Inouye's voting record is very liberal on economic and cultural issues, but on foreign and defense issues he is close to the center of the Senate; he never shared many liberals' skepticism or hostility to American foreign and defense policies in the 1970s and 1980s. He and Hawaii colleague Daniel Akaka were two of the four Democrats who joined all Republicans in seeking to deploy a ballistic missile defense system; they were one vote short of stopping a filibuster in May and September of 1998. The Clinton Administration's opposition to deployment is based in part on an intelligence estimate that there will be no missile threat within the next 10 years to the continental 48 states—which seems to exclude Hawaii and Alaska from the "common defense" the Constitution promises.

Inouye has long used his seat on Appropriations to fund projects he finds worthy, from his alma mater of George Washington University to the Pacific Island Technical Assistance Program to native Hawaiian education. He has proudly earmarked projects for Hawaii in the defense appropriations bill—$255 million in 1997, $240 million in 1998. The 1998 bill included such items as funds to keep the brown tree snake that has ravaged Guam out of Hawaii and a 30-year monopoly on the Hawaiian cruise business for Sam Zell's American Classic Voyages (to encourage Zell to build two ships; the Jones Act requires U.S. ships to be built in expensive U.S. shipyards and requires all shipping from the mainland to be in U.S.-flag ships). He is pleased that the Navy decided that the *U.S.S. Missouri*'s final berth would be in Pearl Harbor. He is persistent but can also move fast. After many years, he got the target range island of Kahoolawe turned back to the state with $445 million for cleanup, and he got a cool $1.2 billion to repair the damage of 1992's Hurricane Iniki. He persisted 25 years to build the "interstate" highway H-3 from the Windward Coast to Pearl Harbor, finally opened in 1997. His priority for 1999 is to develop Ford Island in Pearl Harbor, with job-creating businesses, tourist destinations and a military community. He opposes closing any Hawaii bases and wants changes in the Jones Act. He has supported many appropriations for Native Hawaiian organizations, like the Papa Ola Lokahi health care program, which supports traditional healing methods for natives, and he weighed in to allow shipment of Hawaiian avocados to the Mainland in early 1996. He has supported transfer of federal lands to the Hawaiian Homes program, and argues that the 1995 Hawaiian Homes Recovery Act creates a special trust relation between the federal government and native Hawaiians, whom he says should be regarded as Native Americans.

On the Commerce Committee, Inouye was long involved in communications issues and tended to favor government regulation over markets. He backed cable reregulation and was pleased that the Telecommunications Act of 1996 imposed a competition checklist for local services on the Regional Bells before they could enter the long-distance market. Inouye wanted to set aside up to 20% of the information superhighway for libraries, schools, state and local governments and nonprofits, but the provision was not included in the final bill. He chaired the Indian Affairs Committee from 1989–94, where he worked to authorize a new building on Washington's Mall to house part of the American Indian Museum collection and in 1990 got those living on Indian reservations exempted from the federal death penalty. He was an early backer of Indian gaming. He sponsored a 1993 bill in which the United States apologized for overthrowing the Hawaiian monarchy, and is sympathetic to the claim of native Hawaiians for some form of sovereignty. On cultural issues, he voted against the partial-birth abortion ban, against the Defense of Marriage Act (though he opposes same-sex marriage), and against the 4-cent gas tax repeal.

Honolulu is a long two flights from Washington, and Inouye's local influence has varied. But he is very much the senior member of the state's governing Democratic organization, and his support surely helped Senator Daniel Akaka and Governors John Waihee and Ben Cayetano win close races. In 1992, Republican Rick Reed ran an ad with tapes of a woman who was long Inouye's barber making charges about events many years before. On election day, Inouye won with a much reduced percentage, 57%, to 27% for Reed and 14% for the Green Party's Linda Martin. In 1998 he faced less controversy. In October, Republican Crystal Young alleged that actress Shirley MacLaine implanted electromagnetic needles in her. MacLaine said she had not been in Hawaii in "years and years and years," and added, "I don't know anything about this and she certainly won't get my vote." She didn't get many others, either. Inouye won 81%–18%.

Junior Senator. Daniel K. Akaka is the first native Hawaiian senator. Born four days after Daniel Inouye, he served in the Army Corps of Engineers in the 1940s, went to college, taught school and became a principal. In 1971, at 47, he became director of the Hawaii antipoverty program; in 1975, he became an assistant to Governor George Ariyoshi. The next year, when both of Hawaii's congressmen ran for the Senate, he was elected to the House, where he served quietly on the Appropriations Committee. In May 1990, after the death of Senator Spark Matsunaga, Governor John Waihee appointed Akaka to the Senate. He has thus been an integral part of the dominant Democratic organization and a quiet but diligent worker on Hawaii issues for nearly 30 years.

Akaka has a mostly liberal voting record, somewhat less so on foreign and defense issues; he and Inouye were two of the four Democrats supporting deployment of a ballistic missile defense in 1998. Hawaii, out in the Pacific, is much more vulnerable to North Korean missiles than the U.S. Mainland. Akaka also worked for a 1991 ban on German chemical weapons dumping on Johnston Island, 700 miles southwest of Hawaii, and in 1996 he opposed a proposed nuclear waste dump on Palmyra Island, 1,000 miles southwest. He vehemently opposed French nuclear testing in the South Pacific. He sponsored the Hawaiian Home Lands Recovery Act of 1995, to reclaim Native lands in Lualualei unlawfully withdrawn from the home lands when Hawaii was a territory; it was partly implemented in 1998. He sponsored a 1998 law to allow Hawaii energy companies during an emergency to buy oil at the average price of successful bids for Strategic Petroleum Reserve oil.

Akaka is not well known in Washington. "I do much of my work with members in committees," he said. "I do it that way because it works, it's where you find out whether you have heavy opposition, which could cause you to change tactics or not even bring [the issue] up." In 1997, as a member of the Governmental Affairs Committee investigating Clinton-Gore campaign finances, Akaka charged that Clinton had dropped Asian-Americans from consideration for Cabinet posts because of the controversy and criticized the Democratic National Committee for having auditors ask Asian-Americans about "whether they were citizens, how they earn their money, if they would provide their tax returns, and other intrusive questions." In July 1997 he said, "I am seriously concerned with the negative impact that the allegations of fundraising abuse have had on the Asian-Pacific-American community."

Akaka had one tough election in 1990—indeed the only Senate election in Hawaii that has generated any suspense since 1976. His opponent, Republican Congresswoman Pat Saiki, conceded that Akaka was congenial, but suggested he was ineffective and not too bright. Akaka struck back with ads attacking drugs and his work to end the use of the island of Kahoolawe as a target range. The Democratic organization worked hard and Akaka won 54%–45%, carrying not just the Democratic Neighbor Islands and poorer areas of Honolulu, but most of Oahu as well. In 1994 Akaka was easily re-elected, 72%–24%. In 2000, when his seat comes up, he will be 76. He intends to run again.

Cook's Call. *Safe.* Hawaii remains one of the most Democratic states in the country. Republicans came as close as they have ever come to winning the governor's office in 1998, and were disheartened by their narrow loss. As a result, there does not appear to effort to mount a serious challenge to Akaka.

Presidential politics. Hawaii's presidential voting over the years has been the product of two sometimes countervailing forces. One is the Islands' strong Democratic partisan preference, since voters tend to favor big government and value racial tolerance and diversity. This helps explain why Hawaii voted Democratic when most states didn't in 1980 and 1988. The other is an inclination to support incumbents in a state that takes patriotism very seriously, in part because the patriotism of so many of its citizens was once unjustly questioned and in part because, in these heavily fortified Pacific islands, foreign threats seem more menacing. This helps explain why Hawaii supported President Reagan solidly in 1984 and came close to voting for President Ford in 1976, though it wasn't nearly enough to help George Bush in 1992: Ross Perot's military background, and the presence of Hawaiian Orson Swindle among his top leaders, gave him 14% and helped Bill Clinton carry Hawaii 48%–37%. In 1996, as in 1968 and 1980, both forces were moving in the same direction, and Bill Clinton, incumbent and Democrat, carried Hawaii 57%–32%—his fifth highest percentage.

Hawaii chooses presidential delegates by caucus. Sometimes insurgents have been able to swamp thinly-attended meetings and win, as Jesse Jackson and Pat Robertson did in 1988. But in the 1990s, Hawaii's caucus-goers went for the frontrunners.

Congressional districting. Hawaii has two congressional districts: the 1st includes urban Honolulu (city elections now cover all of Oahu) and extends westward to Pearl Harbor and the rural area beyond; the 2d includes the rest of Oahu and the Neighbor Islands. Both districts are represented by liberal Democrats who had served in the past, then lost elections, ran again and won in 1990 and have been re-elected since.

The People: Est. Pop. 1998: 1,193,001; Pop. 1990: 1,108,229, up 7.6% 1990–1998. 0.4% of U.S. total, 41st largest; 11% rural. Median age: 35.1 years. 11.8% 65 years and over. 33.4% White, 2.4% Black, 61.9% Asian, 0.5% Amer. Indian, 1.7% Other; 7.1% Hispanic Origin. Households: 59.1% married couple families; 31.1% married couple fams. w. children; 51.3% college educ.; median household income: $38,829; per capita income: $15,770; 53.9% owner occupied housing; median house value: $245,300; median monthly rent: $599. 6.2% Unemployment. 1998 Voting age pop.: 878,000. 1998 Turnout: 412,520; 47% of VAP. Registered voters (1998): 601,404; no party registration.

Political Lineup: Governor, Benjamin J. Cayetano (D); Lt. Gov. & Secy. of State, Mazie Hirono (D); Atty. Gen., Margery Bronster (D); Comptroller, Raymond Sato (D); State Senate, 25 (23 D, 2 R); Majority Leader, Les Ihara Jr. (D); State House, 51 (39 D, 12 R); House Speaker, Calvin Say (D). Senators, Daniel K. Inouye (D) and Daniel K. Akaka (D). Representatives, 2 (2 D).

Elections Division: 808-453-8683; **Filing Deadline for U.S. Congress:** July 25, 2000.

1996 Presidential Vote

Clinton (D)	205,012	(57%)
Dole (R)	113,943	(32%)
Perot (I)	27,362	(8%)
Others	13,807	(4%)

1992 Presidential Vote

Clinton (D)	179,310	(48%)
Bush (R)	136,822	(37%)
Perot (I)	53,003	(14%)

GOVERNOR

Gov. Benjamin J. Cayetano (D)

Elected 1994, term expires Jan. 2003; b. Nov. 14, 1939, Honolulu; home, Honolulu; U. of CA, B.A. 1968, Loyola Law Schl., J.D. 1971; Christian; married (Vicki).

Elected Office: HI House of Reps., 1974–78; HI Senate 1978–86; HI Lt. Gov., 1986–90.

Professional Career: Practicing atty., 1971–86.

Office: State Capitol, Executive Chambers, Honolulu, 96813, 808-586-0034; Fax: 808-586-0006; Web site: www.state.hi.us.

Election Results

1998 gen.	Benjamin J. Cayetano (D)	204,206	(50%)
	Linda Lingle (R)	198,952	(49%)
	Others	4,398	(1%)
1998 prim.	Benjamin J. Cayetano (D)	95,797	(86%)
	Jim Brewer (D)	6,169	(6%)
	Others	8,914	(8%)
1994 gen.	Benjamin J. Cayetano (D)	134,978	(37%)
	Frank F. Fasi (Best)	113,158	(31%)
	Patricia F. Saiki (R)	107,908	(29%)
	Others	12,969	(4%)

SENATORS

Sen. Daniel K. Inouye (D)

Elected 1962, seat up 2004; b. Sept. 7, 1924, Honolulu; home, Honolulu; U. of HI, B.A. 1950, George Washington U., J.D. 1952; United Methodist; married (Margaret).

Military Career: Army, 1943–47 (WWII).

Elected Office: HI House of Reps., 1954–58; HI Senate, 1958–59; U.S. House of Reps., 1959–62.

Professional Career: Honolulu Dpty. Public Prosecutor, 1953–54.

DC Office: 722 HSOB, 20510, 202-224-3934; Fax: 202-224-6747; Web site: www.senate.gov/~inouye.

State Offices: Hilo, 808-935-0844; Honolulu, 808-541-2542; Kauai, 808-245-4610; Kona, 808-935-0844; Maui, 808-242-9702; Molokai, 808-642-0203.

Committees: *Appropriations* (2d of 13 D): Commerce, Justice, State & the Judiciary; Defense (RMM); Foreign Operations & Export Financing; Labor & HHS; Military Construction. *Commerce, Science & Transportation* (2d of 9 D): Aviation; Communications; Oceans & Fisheries; Surface Transportation & Merchant Marine (RMM). *Indian Affairs* (RMM of 6 D). *Rules & Administration* (3d of 7 D). *Joint Committee on Printing* (5th of 5 Sens.).

Group Ratings

	ADA	ACLU	AFS	LCV	CON	NTU	NFIB	COC	ACU	NTLC	CHC
1998	80	86	100	75	88	15	33	44	9	12	0
1997	75	—	100	—	10	13	—	50	4	—	—

National Journal Ratings

	1997 LIB — 1997 CONS	1998 LIB — 1998 CONS
Economic	94% — 5%	80% — 19%
Social	71% — 0%	63% — 26%
Foreign	51% — 46%	48% — 51%

Key Votes of the 105th Congress

1. Bal. Budget Amend.	N	5. Satcher for Surgeon Gen.	Y
2. Clinton Budget Deal	N	6. Highway Set-asides	Y
3. Cloture on Tobacco	Y	7. Table Child Gun locks	N
4. Education IRAs	N	8. Ovrd. Part. Birth Veto	N

9. Chem. Weapons Treaty	Y
10. Cuban Humanitarian Aid	Y
11. Table Bosnia Troops	Y
12. $ for Test-ban Treaty	*

Election Results

1998 general	Daniel K. Inouye (D)	315,252	(79%)	($1,375,601)
	Crystal Young (R)	70,964	(18%)	
	Others	11,908	(3%)	
1998 primary	Daniel K. Inouye (D)	108,891	(93%)	
	Richard Thompson (D)	8,468	(7%)	
1992 general	Daniel K. Inouye (D)	208,266	(57%)	($3,515,722)
	Rick Reed (R)	97,928	(27%)	($438,851)
	Linda B. Martin (Green)	49,921	(14%)	($6,687)
	Others	7,547	(2%)	

Sen. Daniel K. Akaka (D)

Appointed May 1990, seat up 2000; b. Sept. 11, 1924, Honolulu; home, Honolulu; U. of HI, B.A. 1953, M.A. 1966; Congregationalist; married (Mary Mildred).

Military Career: Army Corps of Engineers, 1945–47 (WWII).

Elected Office: U.S. House of Reps., 1976–90.

Professional Career: Public schl. teacher, principal & admin., 1953–71; Dir., HI Office of Econ. Oppor., 1971–74; Asst., HI Gov. Ariyoshi, 1975–76; Dir., Progressive Neighborhoods Program, 1975–76.

DC Office: 720 HSOB, 20510, 202-224-6361; Fax: 202-224-2126; Web site: www.senate.gov/~akaka.

State Offices: Hilo, 808-935-1114; Honolulu, 808-522-8970.

Committees: *Energy & Natural Resources* (2d of 9 D): Energy, Research, Development, Production & Regulation; Forests & Public Land Management; National Parks, Historic Preservation & Recreation (RMM). *Governmental Affairs* (3d of 7 D): International Security, Proliferation & Federal Services (RMM); Investigations (Permanent). *Indian Affairs* (4th of 6 D). *Veterans' Affairs* (3d of 5 D).

Group Ratings

	ADA	ACLU	AFS	LCV	CON	NTU	NFIB	COC	ACU	NTLC	CHC
1998	85	83	100	88	19	9	33	41	10	3	0
1997	95	—	89	—	12	12	—	60	4	—	—

National Journal Ratings

	1997 LIB	—	1997 CONS	1998 LIB	—	1998 CONS
Economic	96%	—	0%	90%	—	0%
Social	71%	—	0%	74%	—	0%
Foreign	73%	—	19%	65%	—	27%

Key Votes of the 105th Congress

1. Bal. Budget Amend.	N	5. Satcher for Surgeon Gen.	Y	9. Chem. Weapons Treaty	Y
2. Clinton Budget Deal	N	6. Highway Set-asides	Y	10. Cuban Humanitarian Aid	Y
3. Cloture on Tobacco	Y	7. Table Child Gun locks	N	11. Table Bosnia Troops	*
4. Education IRAs	*	8. Ovrd. Part. Birth Veto	N	12. $ for Test-ban Treaty	Y

Election Results

1994 general	Daniel K. Akaka (D) 256,189	(72%)	($1,017,872)
	Maria M. Hustace (R) 86,320	(24%)	($29,293)
	Richard O. Rowland (Lib) 14,393	(4%)	
1994 primary	Daniel K. Akaka (D) .... unopposed		
1990 general	Daniel K. Akaka (D) 188,901	(54%)	($1,691,384)
	Patricia Saiki (R) 155,978	(45%)	($2,398,961)

FIRST DISTRICT

Tourists in Honolulu see the airport and adjacent Hickam Air Force Base, the *Arizona* monument in Pearl Harbor, perhaps the downtown with its wondrously Victorian Iolani Palace, and of course Waikiki, with its 40-story hotels rising within a few feet of one another. This is tight-packed Hawaii, between the 3,000-foot Koolau Range and the beaches and harbor, where tropical bungalows and garden apartments house Hawaiians of all incomes. Here are Hawaii's largest shopping centers and its state university; here are neighborhoods where the rich overlook the ocean and neighborhoods where the relatively poor are packed into people-clogged streets. Hawaii's topography also jams cars into just a few freeways and avenues, where traffic slows during rush hour and the *aloha* spirit is sorely tested.

Politically, the neighborhoods around Honolulu's downtown and the university campus are lower income and usually Democratic. To the west, around the harbor, are many military families in modest neighborhoods who may vote for Democrats but can be attracted to Republicans. To the east, past Waikiki, around Diamond Head and out to the Kahala and Koko Head beach areas, is higher-income territory, voting for Republicans when they seriously contest a race.

The congressman from the 1st District is Neil Abercrombie, a Democrat with a graying beard who used to sport a pony tail; he has been called an aging hippie but celebrated his 60th birthday by bench-pressing 260 pounds in the House gym; he debates with an aggressiveness and bombast tempered by enthusiasm and good humor. After college in Upstate New York, he taught school, moved to Hawaii, earned a Ph.D. in sociology; he was elected to the Hawaii legislature in 1974 and served 12 years. Abercrombie first came to the House in 1986, when he won a special election, and served only three months; he lost a primary for the full term to a Democrat who then lost to Republican Pat Saiki. When she ran for the Senate, Abercrombie won a three-way primary in 1990 for the House seat and won the general election easily.

Abercrombie is one of the distinctive and often delightful figures in the House. His voting record is mostly, but not entirely, liberal. He has the '60s liberal's visceral skepticism about military spending, but he has used his Armed Services Committee seat to work for $50 million in military housing at Schofield Barracks and Kaneohe. He wants to stop a nuclear waste dump on Palmyra Island, 1,000 miles from Hawaii, and make it easier for Koreans to get U.S. tourist visas. Recalling his backpacking trip across India, he co-sponsored an Asian Elephant Conservation Fund and has kept tabs on human rights practices (improved, he says) in Punjab. He co-sponsored a $13 million National Oceanographic Partnership Act included in the 1997 defense spending bill. After the Republican takeover of the House, he co-authored *Blood of Patriots*, a thriller in which two terrorists disguised as staffers walk into the House during a vote and murder 125 members of Congress. He opposes repeal of the Jones Act and called for retaliation against the European Union for barriers to banana imports.

Abercrombie has survived spirited competition in the 1st District. In 1994 and 1996 he faced Orson Swindle, Marine Corps pilot and Vietnam POW, a national leader of Ross Perot's United We Stand America in 1992. In 1994 Swindle charged that Abercrombie was too dovish, but Abercrombie outraised him and won 54%–43%. In 1996 Swindle labeled Abercrombie a far left hippie and called for big spending cuts. Abercrombie only narrowly outspent him, and won by only 50%–46%, even as Bill Clinton was smashing Bob Dole locally.

In early 1998, with Hawaii's economy still declining and Governor Ben Cayetano trailing in polls, Abercrombie seemed to be in trouble again. His likely opponent seemed to be Quentin Kawananakoa, a descendant of King Kalakaua and Queen Kapiolanoi and minority leader—of 12 Republicans—in the state House. In a November 1997 poll Abercrombie led by an insignificant 38%–35%; in August his lead was an uninspiring 47%–37%. But on August 26, Kawananakoa, hospitalized for hypertension, though only 36, abruptly withdrew from the race for health reasons. This left the nomination to Gene Ward, another legislator with Christian right ties, who in the same August poll trailed Abercrombie 52%–26%. Ward emphasized his record as a Peace Corps volunteer and Vietnam veteran, said he would be a business advocate and argued that he could do more for Hawaii as part of the majority party. Oddly, he said he wanted to use the House to head a United Nations agency or be appointed ambassador. Abercrombie argued that the all-Democratic Hawaii delegation had reduced the economic damage of Hawaii's recession and accused Ward of voting against smaller class sizes and against notifying communities about polluters. And he outspent Ward 2–1.

The polls appear to have been right: Abercrombie won 62%–26%, his best since showing since 1992. Whether he will have a tough contest in 2000 depends on the strength of the Republican nominee.

Cook's Call. *Potentially Competitive.* This is not a particularly competitive district—and indeed should be relatively safe. But Abercrombie has yet to nail it down. Though he is certainly favored in 2000, his close calls in 1994 and 1996 warrant watching this district very closely for a possible upset.

The People: Pop. 1990: 554,174; 0.2% rural; 13.1% age 65+; 29.1% White, 2.4% Black, 66.7% Asian, 0.4% Amer. Indian, 1.4% Other; 5.3% Hispanic Origin. Households: 56.2% married couple families; 27.6% married couple fams. w. children; 54.4% college educ.; median household income: $40,257; per capita income: $17,508; median house value: $311,200; median gross rent: $615.

1996 Presidential Vote

Clinton (D)	99,351	(57%)
Dole (R)	58,906	(34%)
Perot (I)	10,741	(6%)
Others	5,521	(3%)

1992 Presidential Vote

Clinton (D)	87,664	(47%)
Bush (R)	72,182	(39%)
Perot (I)	23,442	(13%)

Rep. Neil Abercrombie (D)

Elected 1990; b. June 26, 1938, Buffalo, NY; home, Honolulu; Union Col., B.A. 1959, U. of HI, M.A.1964, Ph.D. 1974; no religious affiliation; married (Nancie Caraway).

Elected Office: HI House of Reps., 1974–78; HI Senate, 1978–86; U.S. House of Reps., 1986–87; Honolulu City Cncl., 1988–90.

Professional Career: College teacher, 1959–63; Probation Officer, Marin Cnty., CA, 1964–67; Sociologist, 1967–74; Asst. prof., HI Loa Col., 1979–80; Consultant, 1983–87, 1989–90; Asst., HI Superintendent of Educ., 1987–88.

DC Office: 1233 LHOB 20515, 202-225-2726; Fax: 202-225-4580; Web site: www.house.gov/abercrombie.

District Office: Honolulu, 808-541-2570.

Committees: *Armed Services* (8th of 28 D): Military Installations & Facilities; Military Personnel (RMM); Special Oversight Panel on the Merchant Marine. *Resources* (7th of 24 D): Fisheries Conservation, Wildlife & Oceans.

Group Ratings

	ADA	ACLU	AFS	LCV	CON	NTU	NFIB	COC	ACU	NTLC	CHC
1998	95	81	100	85	55	12	14	22	12	5	0
1997	95	—	88	—	37	23	—	30	20	—	—

National Journal Ratings

	1997 LIB — 1997 CONS		1998 LIB — 1998 CONS	
Economic	75% —	22%	79% —	0%
Social	82% —	15%	81% —	16%
Foreign	74% —	26%	78% —	19%

Key Votes of the 105th Congress

1. Clinton Budget Deal	N	5. Puerto Rico Sthood. Ref.	Y	9. Cut $ for B-2 Bombers	Y
2. Education IRAs	N	6. End Highway Set-asides	N	10. Human Rights in China	Y
3. Req. 2/3 to Raise Taxes	N	7. School Prayer Amend.	N	11. Withdraw Bosnia Troops	N
4. Fast-track Trade	N	8. Ovrd. Part. Birth Veto	N	12. End Cuban TV-Marti	Y

Election Results

1998 general	Neil Abercrombie (D)	116,693	(62%)	($1,082,330)
	Gene Ward (R)	68,905	(36%)	($701,480)
	Others	3,973	(2%)	
1998 primary	Neil Abercrombie (D)	40,492	(91%)	
	Alexandra Kaan (D)	2,089	(5%)	
	Al Canopin Jr. (D)	1,783	(4%)	
1996 general	Neil Abercrombie (D)	86,732	(50%)	($674,404)
	Orson Swindle (R)	80,053	(46%)	($627,839)
	Others	5,421	(3%)	

SECOND DISTRICT

The 2d District of Hawaii includes not only the Neighbor Islands but most of Oahu's acreage beyond the city of Honolulu. It has Wheeler Air Force Base, still looking much as it did in December 1941, and the farmlands north of Pearl Harbor, between two jagged chains of mountains that lift the island out of the sea. Over the mountains to the west is the Leeward Coast— calm, sultry and lightly populated; over the mountains to the northeast is the Windward Coast with many prosperous and Republican subdivisions in and around Kaneohe and Kailua. The Neighbor Islands have distinct personalities. Hawaii, the Big Island, is large enough to boast huge cattle ranches, the active volcano of Kilauea, and Mauna Kea, the highest mountain in the world if you count from its base far under the ocean to the peak. On the north shore, with heavy rainfall and tropical foliage, is the old port of Hilo and Hawaii's macadamia nut industry; this is a blue-collar Democratic area. On the Kona Coast, where there is little rainfall and the landscape is dominated by lava flows, there are retirement condominiums and a higher-income, more Republican population. Maui, favored more by North American than Asian tourists, has dozens of luxury condominiums and vast upscale resorts. Kauai, much of which was devastated by Hurricane Iniki in 1992, is the least-developed and most agricultural of the main islands; parts of it have the nation's highest rainfall, while others seldom get wet. Its large farm work force makes it the most Democratic of the islands.

The 2d District is represented by Patsy Mink, still exuberant and enthusiastically liberal after a long political career. She grew up in Hawaii, went to law school in Chicago, then practiced law in Honolulu starting in 1953 and became involved in politics while Hawaii was still a territory. She was first elected to the House in 1964, gave up the seat to run unsuccessfully for the Senate in 1976, then, after losing races for governor in 1986 and mayor of Honolulu in 1988, won the House seat again in 1990 after incumbent Daniel Akaka was appointed to the Senate. She helped feminism grow from a fringe cause to one of the main rallying cries for Democrats, and sponsored a gender equity act, which passed the House and then the Senate— though in a more diluted form—and women's health care measures. She spoke with special vehemence in March 1995 against product liability reform. (She sued a drug company and hospital 44 years ago after she was prescribed the anti-miscarriage drug DES; it was later thought to expose children to a greater risk of cancer, and Mink collected a $250,000 settlement.) After the French resumed nuclear testing in the South Pacific, she boycotted a February 1996 speech by President Jacques Chirac before a joint session of Congress. In 1997 she introduced a bill for reparations for Latin Americans of Japanese descent who were put in U.S. internment camps during World War II.

After spending most of her legislative career in the majority—often a large one, the minority seems not to suit Mink. She served for many years on the committee now called Education and the Work Force, on which union leaders made sure they had a solid majority after losing a committee vote on the Landrum-Griffin Act in 1959. But the Republican victory of 1994 changed all that. With great vehemence Mink has criticized the Republicans. She opposed a $1.4 million review of labor laws. As ranking member on Peter Hoekstra's Oversight Subcommittee, she called his hearings on the Teamsters a "sham," sought delays at many turns and opposed issuance of subpoenas.

Mink won the seat in 1990 by narrowly edging former 1st District nominee Mufi Hannemann in the primary; she won easily in 1992 and 1994. In 1996 she had primary opposition from four Democrats, including state Senator Robert Bunda who ran as a "moderate alternative." Controversy ensued when Bunda cited Mink's vote against the Defense of Marriage Act; Mink ran newspaper ads saying she voted that way because she thought the measure was unconstitutional, but that she was against the principle of same-sex marriage. Mink won the primary by 60%–32%, a wide margin. In 1998 she was easily re-elected.

Cook's Call. *Safe.* While Neil Abercrombie's situation in the 1st District is somewhat problematic, Patsy Mink has had no such difficulties in the 2d. This is the more liberal and more solidly-Democratic of Hawaii's two districts, and Mink should be able to hold onto this district for as long as she wants it.

The People: Pop. 1990: 554,055; 21.9% rural; 10.5% age 65+; 37.8% White, 2.4% Black, 57.1% Asian, 0.6% Amer. Indian, 2.1% Other; 8.9% Hispanic Origin. Households: 62.3% married couple families; 35.1% married couple fams. w. children; 48% college educ.; median household income: $37,247; per capita income: $14,032; median house value: $190,900; median gross rent: $564.

1996 Presidential Vote			1992 Presidential Vote		
Clinton (D)	105,661	(57%)	Clinton (D)	91,646	(49%)
Dole (R)	55,037	(30%)	Bush (R)	64,640	(34%)
Perot (I)	16,621	(9%)	Perot (I)	29,561	(16%)
Others	8,286	(4%)			

Rep. Patsy Mink (D)

Elected Sept. 1990; b. Dec. 6, 1927, Paia, Maui; home, Hilo; U. of HI, B.A. 1948, U. of Chicago, J.D. 1951; Protestant; married (John Francis).

Elected Office: HI House of Reps., 1956–58; HI Senate, 1959, 1963–64; U.S. House of Reps., 1964–76; Honolulu City Cncl., 1983–87.

Professional Career: Practicing atty., 1953–64, 1987–90; U.S. Asst. Secy. of State for Oceans, Intl. Environment & Scientific Affairs, 1977–78; Pres., Americans for Democratic Action, 1978–81.

DC Office: 2135 RHOB 20515, 202-225-4906; Fax: 202-225-4987; Web site: www.house.gov/mink.

District Offices: Hilo, 808-935-3756; Honolulu, 808-541-1986; Kauai, 808-245-1951; Maui, 808-242-1818.

Committees: *Education & the Workforce* (7th of 22 D): Early Childhood, Youth & Families; Postsecondary Education, Training & Life-Long Learning. *Government Reform* (7th of 19 D): Criminal Justice, Drug Policy & Human Resources (RMM); Government Management, Information & Technology.

Group Ratings

	ADA	ACLU	AFS	LCV	CON	NTU	NFIB	COC	ACU	NTLC	CHC
1998	95	87	100	100	55	16	7	22	8	5	0
1997	100	—	100	—	4	18	—	20	12	—	—

National Journal Ratings

	1997 LIB — 1997 CONS			1998 LIB — 1998 CONS		
Economic	85%	—	10%	79%	—	0%
Social	85%	—	0%	90%	—	7%
Foreign	76%	—	22%	90%	—	5%

Key Votes of the 105th Congress

1. Clinton Budget Deal	N	5. Puerto Rico Sthood. Ref.	Y	9. Cut $ for B-2 Bombers	Y
2. Education IRAs	N	6. End Highway Set-asides	N	10. Human Rights in China	Y
3. Req. 2/3 to Raise Taxes	N	7. School Prayer Amend.	N	11. Withdraw Bosnia Troops	N
4. Fast-track Trade	N	8. Ovrd. Part. Birth Veto	N	12. End Cuban TV-Marti	Y

Election Results

1998 general	Patsy Mink (D)	144,254	(69%)	($221,165)
	Carol J. Douglas (R)	50,423	(24%)	($9,495)
	Noreen Leilehua Chun (Lib)	13,194	(6%)	
1998 primary	Patsy Mink (D)	61,382	(90%)	
	David L. Bourgoin (D)	7,106	(10%)	
1996 general	Patsy Mink (D)	109,178	(60%)	($315,187)
	Tom Pico Jr. (R)	55,729	(31%)	($88,935)
	Nolan Crabbe (I)	7,723	(4%)	
	Others	8,333	(5%)	

IDAHO

Idaho has been at the leading edge of America's growth for most of the 1990s. It surged out of the early 1990s recession and led the nation in population growth, technological progress and economic creativity; it also led at least part of the nation in cultural attitudes and politics, in a direction that many, especially the national media, resented and resisted. Idaho's growth tapered off a bit in the late 1990s, but it still has a robust and growing economy. Its biggest businesses are big: J.R. Simplot is the nation's largest potato processer; Micron Technology, the state's number one employer, is a leader in semiconductors; Albertson's, after buying Lucky and Jewel Tea, is the nation's largest supermarket chain. And dozens of smaller high-tech and service businesses have sprung up. From California a few highly publicized liberal entertainment personalities and a much larger number of conservative engineers and entrepreneurs have come to Idaho for a fresh environment and fresh start, clean air and few crowds, and no cumbersome and expensive regulations, where family lifestyles are still prevalent, traditional values respected, and traditional rules enforced.

The wilderness is never far away in Idaho, nor is the experience of the first settlers. Towering over the state Capitol in Boise is the vast peak of Shafer Butte, and not far away are impassable mountains of the Frank Church River of No Return Wilderness: Idaho ranks third in National Wilderness lands, behind California and Alaska. This was the last North American area European pioneers—fur traders—set eyes on. In the 1840s, New England Yankees led by ministers made their way west on the Oregon Trail through southern Idaho. Idaho's northern panhandle, an extension of Washington's Columbia Valley, was first settled by miners seeking gold and silver, then by loggers seeking timber. Mormons moved north from Utah and settled eastern Idaho. But federal water reclamation projects first authorized in 1894 brought the most settlers, and they transformed the barren Snake River Valley into some of the nation's best volcanic soil-enriched farmland. Fresh in family lore are the people who pioneered this state, built the first towns and farms, established the first churches and schools and became its community leaders. Yet Idaho is also cosmopolitan. It exports potatoes—mostly frozen french fries—across the Pacific Rim, and its high-tech companies have competitors all over the world. If Idaho politicians used to concentrate on water and maintaining irrigation, now they work to curb Canadian potato imports and South Korean semiconductor subsidies.

Idaho politics for years was run by two bosses—Democrat Tom Boise from the panhandle and Republican Lloyd Adams from the Mormon east—who could patch together statewide alliances from the regional divisions still apparent today. Although its first settlers had a Republican heritage, silver-mining Idaho went for William Jennings Bryan and free silver in 1896, and then supported Woodrow Wilson and Franklin D. Roosevelt; as late as 1960, John F. Kennedy won 46% of the vote here. Idaho produced prominent national politicians of both parties—notably, Senate Foreign Relations Committee Chairmen William Borah, a Republican, and Frank Church, a Democrat. Democrats—Cecil Andrus, John Evans, then Andrus again—held the governorship from 1970–94.

But that is in the past. Logging and unions have declined in the panhandle, while the Mormon east is growing and Boise has become heavily Republican. The result is that Idaho is arguably the nation's most one-sidedly Republican state. Bob Dole carried it easily in 1996, winning all but four counties—Sun Valley with its trendy newcomers and three northern panhandle counties, with university professors and mill hands. Today most Idahoans think of themselves not as downtrodden employees of absentee corporations needing a protective federal government, but as pioneering entrepreneurs who need to get a bloated, bossy federal government off their backs. The federal government owns 65% of Idaho's land, and when it tries to block logging roads or raise grazing fees—or, even worse, reintroduce grizzly bears into the wilderness—Idahoans howl in protest; against the bears, Custer County passed an "unacceptable species ordinance." Some go to extremes: a group called Aryan Nation insists on parading in Coeur d'Alene, militias spring up in some counties, and there are bitter memories of how the wife and son of recluse and protester Randy Weaver were killed at Ruby Ridge in 1992 by an FBI sharpshooter who was indicted for manslaughter in 1997. Nearby the Coeur d'Alene tribe started gambling by Internet in 1998, with instant-win bingo and a scratch lottery. In eastern Idaho the federal government has done a dismal job of cleaning up toxic waste at the Idaho National Engineering and Environmental Laboratory (INEEL) plant near Idaho Falls, in central Idaho the Forest Service infuriated locals by curtailing whitewater rafting, and in southwest Idaho B-1s flying at 500 feet threaten bighorn sheep. The *Idaho Statesman* has even called for the destruction of the biggest federal monuments here: the dams on the Snake River which stop salmon from migrating upstream. All this friction, added to almost universal opposition to Interior Secretary Bruce Babbitt's grazing fee increase and proposals for reforming the Mining Act of 1872, undercut local Democrats and provided a setting where Idaho's normally Republican strength was amplified.

Today Republicans hold almost all of Idaho's elective offices, and have won most by wide margins. In 1998, Senator Dirk Kempthorne won 68% of the votes for governor and Congressman Mike Crapo won 70% for the Senate. In House races, incumbent Republican Helen Chenoweth and non-incumbent Republican Mike Simpson both won despite serious weaknesses. Senator Larry Craig won in 1990 and 1996 by comfortable margins. In the legislature, Republicans' overall lead is 89–16. Republicans hold all but two of the seven statewide offices. Republican successes cannot be ascribed to low turnout: Idaho has one of the highest voter turnouts in the nation. Nor is it just a matter of tradition: the VNS exit poll showed the highest percentages for Kempthorne and Crapo came from voters under 30. State Republican Chairman Ron McMurray had an unsentimental explanation: "I don't mean this to sound harsh, but you have to be more like Idaho. When you have a trial lawyer that's the head of the party from Boise, a trial lawyer from Boise running for governor, a trial lawyer from Boise running for Congress, and a trial lawyer from Boise running for the Senate, that's not Idaho." But Republican majorities are not monolithic, or everlasting: term limits will help give Democrats a chance to fasten on local grievances and raise new issues which will surely some day yield them more than they have now.

Governor. Governors are often elected to the Senate, but between the mid-1950s and 1990 no senator was elected governor. Now, in the 1990s, senators have been elected governor: Pete Wilson of California in 1990 and, after two years out of office, Lawton Chiles of Florida and

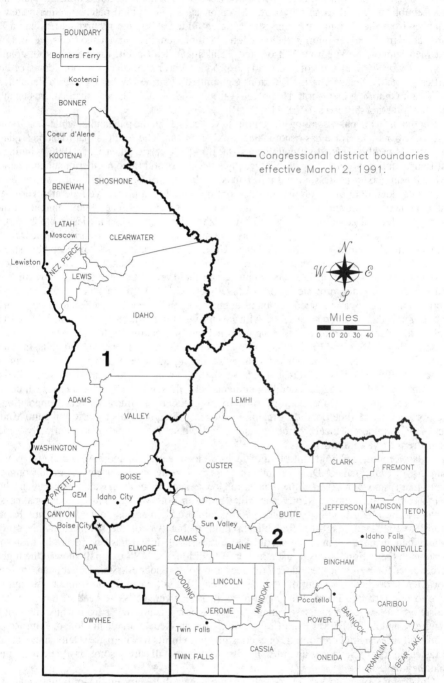

Congressional district boundaries effective March 2, 1991.

Lowell Weicker of Connecticut in 1990; the latest is Dirk Kempthorne of Idaho in 1998. Kempthorne was born in San Diego, grew up in Spokane, Washington, and graduated the University of Idaho. He has spent most of his adult life in the political arena, starting in state government, then working for the Idaho Home Builders Association and FMC Corporation. He managed Phil Batt's unsuccessful gubernatorial campaign in 1982 (Batt finally won in 1994) and was mayor of Boise for seven boom years from 1986–93. Kempthorne was elected to the Senate seat vacated in 1992 by two-term incumbent Republican Steve Symms and over tough competition from Democratic Congressman Richard Stallings, a Mormon and a conservative on abortion and gun control, three-time congressman from the eastern Idaho 2d District. Kempthorne won with 57%, barely carrying the panhandle, but running far ahead in the Boise market and carrying the Mormon areas in the east.

Kempthorne started off 100th in seniority in a Democratic Senate, concentrating on the nonstarter issue of unfunded mandates. But after the Republicans's 1994 victory, Bob Dole made Kempthorne's unfunded mandates bill S.1, the first order of legislative business. Kempthorne impressed colleagues with his knowledge of detail and his willingness to face off with Robert Byrd, who fought mightily against the bill as an infringement of congressional prerogatives; it passed the Senate easily with bipartisan support. Kempthorne also worked hard on the Safe Drinking Water Act, which passed with bipartisan support in 1996. He worked on a bipartisan Endangered Species Act revision which never passed the House and chaired the Armed Services Personnel Subcommittee.

But Idaho beckoned. Phil Batt, elected at 67, decided to retire after a long career in state politics and one successful four-year term as governor. Welfare rolls were cut more than 75%, crime was sharply down, taxes and state payrolls were cut, and in 1996, voters had endorsed by 63%–37% the 40-year compact with the federal government Batt negotiated on nuclear waste disposal. In September 1997 Batt announced his decision to retire; in October 1997 Kempthorne announced he was running. He was willing to give up what easily could have been a lifetime Senate seat for, at most, two term-limited terms as governor. "I truly do believe power now is irreversibly returning to the states, and that is where the important action will be," he said. Once Kempthorne was in, the race was essentially over. Former state Supreme Court Justice Robert Huntley ran, he said, to maintain two-party competition. There was not very much: 128,000 voted in the Republican primary, 27,000 in the Democratic. Huntley proposed tax increases and breaching the Snake River dams to save migrating salmon, saying, "I'm a little bit arrogant. If the people don't like my programs, I'll be damned if I want to be their governor." Kempthorne won 68%–29%, carrying every county but the one including Sun Valley.

Kempthorne called for an end to the marriage penalty and a tax credit for tuition to private schools. He favors parental consent for abortion and birth-control pills and cracking down on methamphetamine use. For the salmon, he favored "fish-friendly" turbines on the river and for moving salmon-eating terns and cormorants off a man-made island in the Columbia.

Senior Senator. Larry Craig brings to politics stentorian argumentation and a controlled fervor in support of his conservative positions. Born on a ranch homesteaded by his grandfather in 1899, he was elected to the state Senate in 1974, at 29, and to the U.S. House in 1980, at 35. In 1990, when Senator James McClure retired, he was elected to the Senate. Throughout his career he has had a very conservative voting record and has been a well-informed and persistent critic of Western lands policies favored by environmentalists or, as he says, "environmental extremism." In the Senate he became chairman of the informal conservative Steering Committee, whose members seemed to win most of the leadership positions. After Bob Dole's resignation in June 1996, Craig became chairman of the Republican Policy Committee, the number four leadership position. He was, Idaho reporter Dan Popkey wrote, "poised to become the fourth face on Idaho's Mount Rushmore, joining Senators William Borah, Frank Church, and Jim McClure.

One major Craig cause has been the balanced budget constitutional amendment. Back in

1982, when he and Democrat Charles Stenholm co-sponsored it in the House, it got just 153 votes; in February 1995 it exceeded the required two-thirds and got 300. By that time Craig was in the Senate, working with Democrat Paul Simon, and in March 1995 their amendment on a cliff-hanger 65–35 vote fell barely short of gaining two-thirds, with all the 53 Republicans except for Mark Hatfield voting in favor and with six Democrats who had previously supported other versions switching to oppose it. (The bill actually had 66 votes, one short of the two-thirds required, but Bob Dole switched to vote against it so that he could call it up for reconsideration.) Another Craig cause is nuclear waste. He has been pushing relentlessly for the government to meet its commitment to establish a permanent nuclear waste repository at Yucca Mountain in Nevada. The opposition comes from Nevada's two senators and from Bill Clinton, who carried Nevada twice by narrow margins after promising to veto bills to establish a temporary waste facility there. In August 1997 Craig got the Senate to pass his nuclear waste policy act by 65–34—just two votes short of what is needed to override a veto. In July 1998 he held up the confirmation of Bill Richardson as Energy Secretary until Clinton had given him in writing full authority to handle nuclear waste issues. Back in Idaho, he backed former Governor Phil Batt's compact with the federal government, approved by voters in 1996, to open an interim waste site in Idaho, but that has increased his concern that waste from Idaho's INEEL be eventually transported to Yucca Mountain.

Craig has used his seats on the Appropriations, Agriculture and Energy committees to fight for what he considers sensible environmental policies. He opposed Clinton efforts to revise the Mining Act of 1872 and increase grazing fees. He opposes the introduction of grizzly bears into Idaho's Selway wilderness and the moratorium on logging roads in the national forests. He is against breaching the Snake River dams to allow salmon to swim more easily upstream. As chairman of the Forests and Public Land Management Subcommittee, he seems engaged in a continual battle to change the policies and institutional culture of the Forest Service. He has a reorganization bill to streamline planning procedures, limit court challenges to people who commented during the planning process, and forbid deviations from the plan once adopted. It would allow states and private organizations, with congressional approval, to take over management of National Forest and Bureau of Land Management lands. Frustrated with the agency's attempts to close roads and deny timber sales, he called in February 1998 for cuts in the Forest Service payrolls because "we are just flat tired of them giving us lip service and doing nothing."

Some of Craig's initiatives are prompted by Idaho causes. He and Dirk Kempthorne got a ban on IMF funds to subsidize semiconductor firms in other countries in the IMF bailout; a matter of much interest to Idaho's Micron Technology. He tried but failed to get Indian gambling exempted from the ban on Internet gambling that passed the Senate easily; the Coeur d'Alene tribe has started a gambling Web site. He got a pilot Superfund program for the Coeur d'Alene basin through the Environment Committee. He sponsored the lifting of sanctions on farm product sales to India and Pakistan in July 1998. But Craig's interests go farther afield. He sponsored a Puerto Rico status bill similar to the one which passed the House 209–208 in March 1998. He worked on Republican child care proposals in January 1998. He has served on the ethics committees in both House and Senate, passing judgment on Jim Wright and Bob Packwood. He is one of the "Singing Senators," with Trent Lott, Jim Jeffords and John Ashcroft. And he has was one of the leaders in the gun control debate in the Senate in 1999, sponsoring a measure to allow (but not force) unlicensed sellers at gun shows to conduct background checks.

Craig won the seat relatively easily in 1990, with 59% in the primary against Attorney General Jim Jones and with 61% in the general. For a while the 1996 race looked tougher. Democratic Senatorial Campaign Committee Chairman Bob Kerrey recruited building materials millionaire Walt Minnick, who had testified against Craig's plans for deficit timber sales and road building in the national forests. He spent $945,000 of his own money, attacked Craig sharply for backing Batt's nuclear waste compact and ran "Lying Larry" ads associating him with nuclear pollution, clear-cutting, gill-netting and national parks destruction. Craig responded by rafting down the river with his family and running ads predicting toxic desolation if the nuclear waste compact was not carried out. In what is likely to be the toughest test he will get, Craig won 57%–40%, losing only three counties.

Junior Senator. Mike Crapo is a Republican elected to the House in 1992 and the Senate in 1996. He grew up in Idaho Falls, went to Brigham Young University and Harvard Law School, is a faithful Mormon who became a bishop in the church at 31. He was elected to the state Senate in 1984, at 33, and became state Senate leader in 1988; he was described by an Idaho Falls *Post Register* reporter as "intelligent, approachable and even-tempered." Crapo won the 1992 primary 68%–32% and campaigned against all tax increases, for spending cuts, a balanced budget amendment and the line-item veto—the Contract with America two years early. "Cowboy Democrat" J. D. Williams, the state controller, ran on a "put America first" stand on industrial policy and trade. Crapo won 61%–35%.

With a self-professed "passion for reform," Crapo became Republican freshman class leader and championed institutional reforms—on discharge petitions, select committees, closed rules, closed committee meetings, open voting—many of which were adopted after Republicans won control in 1994. Like many Republicans, he favored simple, hard-and-fast rules—a balanced budget, term limits, across-the-board discretionary spending cuts (excluding Social Security)—to force tough decisions. He sponsored the deficit reduction lock box bill which passed the House in 1995, setting aside program savings for reducing the deficit; he served on Agriculture as it passed the Freedom To Farm Act. He was a founding member of the Congressional Water Caucus and a member of the fabled Congressional Boot Caucus, an informal group of Western lawmakers who wear boots.

His overall voting record has been very conservative, with some exceptions on economics; he opposed NAFTA in 1993 and the Republican HMO regulation in 1998. Crapo seems less confrontation-minded than his Idaho colleagues Larry Craig and Helen Chenoweth, though not much less conservative. He opposed a Craig bill to transfer 270 million acres of Bureau of Land Management land to private ownership. He got funding for the Sawtooth Recreation Area, opposed by colleague Helen Chenoweth, though he also opposed the Forest Service's increases in rental fees in 1997. He wants decisions on issues like grazing, water quality and grizzly bear management to be made at local forums.

Crapo supported former Governor Phil Batt's nuclear waste compact with the federal government, allowing waste to be transported now to INEEL in the 2d District in return for a promise of later shipment to waste sites in New Mexico and Nevada. He has pressed for funds for the cleanup of INEEL facilities, whose troubles have threatened the compact. Crapo has said he would like a scientific solution for maintaining the salmon in the Snake River, but he strongly opposes breaching the Snake dams and he opposes spring drawdowns on lower Snake River dams; he wants to maintain the flow of Snake River water to Idaho farms. On the House Commerce Committee, he declined to support federal electricity deregulation, for fear it would raise the Pacific Northwest's traditionally low utility costs. At one point he insisted that Idaho and the other Northwest states must get full control of the Snake and Columbia River water before he would support deregulation. With Craig and Dirk Kempthorne, he backed the amendment banning the IMF from subsidizing Korean semiconductor companies, which compete with Idaho's Micron.

In fall 1997, Crapo, who prides himself on returning to Idaho Falls every weekend, faced a career choice that many House members would like to face. In September Governor Phil Batt announced his retirement and in October Senator Dirk Kempthorne said he would run for governor. Within days Crapo announced he would run for the Senate. His opponent was former Democratic chairman and Boise trial lawyer Bill Mauk. He attacked Crapo for accepting tobacco PAC money; Crapo replied he had stopped taking it some time ago. Mauk also attacked Crapo for switching positions on school vouchers, as indeed he had. But voters apparently didn't much mind. Idaho, one-quarter Mormon, had never elected a Mormon senator. This time it did. Crapo led in polls by a wide margin and Mauk, vastly outspent, made little headway. Crapo won 70%–28%, carrying every county. In the Senate he got seats on the Environment and Banking Committee and, taking his seat at 47, has the prospect of a long career.

Presidential politics. Idaho is one of the most Republican states in national politics. Bob Dole and George Bush carried it easily; in 1992 Bill Clinton only narrowly beat out Ross Perot for second place, 28%–27%. From 1988–96, Idaho's presidential primary was held in late May, but was not binding for Democrats, who select their presidential nominee in the early March caucus. Idaho considered joining other Rocky Mountain states voting in an early March 2000 primary, but the state House voted it down in March 1999.

Congressional districting. Idaho has two congressional districts, which split Boise between them. After the 2000 Census, a bipartisan commission is scheduled to draw new boundaries; given Idaho's geography, it will most likely push the boundary west a couple of miles to Maple Grove Road.

The People: Est. Pop. 1998: 1,228,684; Pop. 1990: 1,006,749, up 22% 1990–1998. 0.5% of U.S. total, 40th largest; 42.6% rural. Median age: 33 years. 12.5% 65 years and over. 94.4% White, 0.4% Black, 0.9% Asian, 1.5% Amer. Indian, 2.8% Other; 5.1% Hispanic Origin. Households: 62.2% married couple families; 31.7% married couple fams. w. children; 49.3% college educ.; median household income: $25,257; per capita income: $11,457; 70.1% owner occupied housing; median house value: $58,200; median monthly rent: $261. 5% Unemployment. 1998 Voting age pop.: 888,000. 1998 Turnout: 386,720; 44% of VAP. Registered voters (1998): 661,433; no party registration.

Political Lineup: Governor, Dirk Kempthorne (R); Lt. Gov., C. L. (Butch) Otter (R); Secy. of State, Pete T. Cenarrusa (R); Atty. Gen., Alan Lance (R); Treasurer, Ron Crane (R); State Senate, 35 (4 D, 31 R); Majority Leader, Jim Risch (R); State House, 70 (12 D, 58 R); House Speaker, Bruce Newcomb (R). Senators, Larry Craig (R) and Mike Crapo (R). Representatives, 2 (2 R).

Elections Division: 208-334-2852; **Filing Deadline for U.S. Congress:** March 31, 2000.

1996 Presidential Vote

Dole (R) 256,595 (52%)
Clinton (D) 165,443 (34%)
Perot (I) 62,518 (13%)

1996 Republican Presidential Primary

Dole (R) 74,011 (62%)
Buchanan (R) 26,461 (22%)
Keyes (R) 5,904 (5%)
Others 12,339 (10%)

1992 Presidential Vote

Bush (R) 202,645 (42%)
Clinton (D) 137,013 (28%)
Perot (I) 130,395 (27%)

GOVERNOR

Gov. Dirk Kempthorne (R)

Elected 1998, term expires Jan. 2003; b. Oct. 29, 1951, San Diego, CA; home, Boise; U. of ID, B.A. 1975; Methodist; married (Patricia).

Elected Office: Boise Mayor, 1986–92; U.S. Senate, 1992–98.

Professional Career: Exec. Asst. to Dir., ID Dept. of Public Lands, 1976–78; Exec. V.P., ID Home Builders Assn., 1978–81; Campaign Mgr., Phil Batt for Gov., 1982; ID Public Affairs Mgr., FMC Corp, 1983–86.

Office: State House, Boise, 83720, 208-334-2100; Fax: 208-334-2175; Web site: www.state.id.us.

Election Results

1998 gen.	Dirk Kempthorne (R)	258,095	(68%)
	Robert C. Huntley (D)	110,815	(29%)
	Others	12,338	(3%)
1998 prim.	Dirk Kempthorne (R)	111,658	(87%)
	David Shepherd (R)	16,332	(13%)
1994 gen.	Phil Batt (R)	216,123	(52%)
	Larry EchoHawk (D)	181,363	(44%)
	Ronald D. Rankin (I)	15,793	(4%)

SENATORS

Sen. Larry Craig (R)

Elected 1990, seat up 2002; b. July 20, 1945, Midvale; home, Payette; U. of ID, B.A. 1969; United Methodist; married (Suzanne).

Military Career: Army Natl. Guard, 1970–74.

Elected Office: ID Senate, 1974–80; U.S. House of Reps., 1980–90.

Professional Career: Rancher, farmer.

DC Office: 520 HSOB, 20510, 202-224-2752; Fax: 202-228-1067; Web site: www.senate.gov/~craig.

State Offices: Boise, 208-342-7985; Coeur d'Alene, 208-667-6130; Idaho Falls, 208-523-5541; Lewiston, 208-743-0792; Pocatello, 208-236-6817; Twin Falls, 208-734-6780.

Committees: *Republican Policy Committee Chairman. Aging (Special)* (3d of 11 R). *Agriculture, Nutrition & Forestry* (9th of 10 R): Forestry, Conservation & Rural Revitalization (Chmn.); Production & Price Competitiveness. *Appropriations* (13th of 15 R): Energy & Water Development; Labor & HHS; Legislative Branch; Military Construction; VA, HUD & Independent Agencies. *Energy & Natural Resources* (4th of 11 R): Energy, Research, Development, Production & Regulation; Forests & Public Land Management (Chmn.); Water & Power. *Veterans' Affairs* (6th of 7 R).

Group Ratings

	ADA	ACLU	AFS	LCV	CON	NTU	NFIB	COC	ACU	NTLC	CHC
1998	5	14	0	0	14	65	100	100	84	86	91
1997	5	—	0	—	89	82	—	100	84	—	—

National Journal Ratings

	1997 LIB — 1997 CONS	1998 LIB — 1998 CONS
Economic	11% — 76%	18% — 72%
Social	17% — 72%	12% — 79%
Foreign	0% — 77%	0% — 88%

Key Votes of the 105th Congress

1. Bal. Budget Amend.	Y	5. Satcher for Surgeon Gen.	N	9. Chem. Weapons Treaty	N
2. Clinton Budget Deal	Y	6. Highway Set-asides	N	10. Cuban Humanitarian Aid	N
3. Cloture on Tobacco	N	7. Table Child Gun locks	Y	11. Table Bosnia Troops	N
4. Education IRAs	Y	8. Ovrd. Part. Birth Veto	Y	12. $ for Test-ban Treaty	N

Election Results

1996 general	Larry Craig (R) 283,532	(57%)	($2,992,451)
	Walt Minnick (D) 198,422	(40%)	($2,140,878)
	Others 15,279	(3%)	
1996 primary	Larry Craig (R) .... unopposed		
1990 general	Larry Craig (R) 193,641	(61%)	($1,620,304)
	Ron J. Twilegar (D) 122,295	(39%)	($544,419)

Sen. Mike Crapo (R)

Elected 1998, seat up 2004; b. May 20, 1951, Idaho Falls; home, Idaho Falls; Brigham Young U., B.A. 1973, Harvard U., J.D. 1977; Mormon; married (Susan).

Elected Office: ID Senate, 1984–92, Senate Ldr., 1988–92; U.S. House of Reps., 1992–98.

Professional Career: Practicing atty., 1977–92.

DC Office: 111 RSOB, 20510, 202-224-6142; Fax: 202-228-1375; Web site: www.senate.gov/~crapo.

State Offices: Boise, 208-334-1776; Caldwell, 208-455-0360; Coeur D'Alene, 208-664-5490; Idaho Falls, 208-522-9779; Moscow, 208-883-9783; Pocatello, 208-236-6775; Twin Falls, 208-734-2515.

Committees: *Banking, Housing & Urban Affairs* (11th of 11 R): Financial Institutions; International Trade & Finance (Vice Chmn.); Securities. *Environment & Public Works* (8th of 10 R): Fisheries, Wildlife & Drinking Water (Chmn.); Superfund, Waste Control & Risk Assessment. *Small Business* (8th of 10 R).

Group Ratings (as Member of U.S. House of Representatives)

	ADA	ACLU	AFS	LCV	CON	NTU	NFIB	COC	ACU	NTLC	CHC
1998	10	13	25	15	21	51	92	94	83	73	100
1997	0	—	25	—	15	58	—	70	92	—	—

National Journal Ratings as Member of U.S. House of Representatives

	1997 LIB — 1997 CONS	1998 LIB — 1998 CONS
Economic	27% — 73%	50% — 49%
Social	0% — 90%	21% — 76%
Foreign	0% — 88%	7% — 83%

Key Votes of the 105th Congress as Member of U.S. House of Representatives

1. Clinton Budget Deal	Y	5. Puerto Rico Sthood. Ref.	N	9. Cut $ for B-2 Bombers	N
2. Education IRAs	Y	6. End Highway Set-asides	Y	10. Human Rights in China	N
3. Req. 2/3 to Raise Taxes	Y	7. School Prayer Amend.	Y	11. Withdraw Bosnia Troops	Y
4. Fast-track Trade	N	8. Ovrd. Part. Birth Veto	Y	12. End Cuban TV-Marti	N

Election Results

1998 general	Mike Crapo (R)	262,966	(70%)	($1,563,811)
	Bill Mauk (D)	107,375	(28%)	($241,443)
	Others	7,833	(2%)	
1998 primary	Mike Crapo (R)	unopposed		
1992 general	Dirk Kempthorne (R)	270,468	(57%)	($1,305,338)
	Richard Stallings (D)	208,036	(43%)	($1,222,222)

FIRST DISTRICT

The 1st District of Idaho stretches from the Nevada border to Canada, including most of usually Republican Boise and all of the panhandle, historically Democratic but more recently known as the home of militias. It includes two of Idaho's big growth areas, the west side of Boise and the Coeur d'Alene area; high-tech and tourism dominate the economy. Politically, it is marginally less Republican than the 2d, but not very Democratic: Bill Clinton has not won more than 35% here. Northern mining counties were once the district's Democratic base; it is now the university town of Moscow.

The congressman from the 1st District is Helen Chenoweth (don't call her congresswoman, please), one of the most distinctive members of the Republican class of 1994. Chenoweth grew up in Oregon, lived with her husband in the timber town of Orofino, then divorced and moved to Boise in the 1970s, where she was a medical office manager and a lobbyist for timber and mining industries. She worked in political campaigns for former Senator Steven Symms and former Lieutenant Governor David Leroy, but left after disagreements. In 1994 she ran for Congress, against incumbent Democrat Larry LaRocco, who won the seat as a moderate in 1990 and 1992. Chenoweth's core support came from religious conservatives, sympathizers with militia and patriot movements, and from believers in Wise Use, an organization she helped found to combat what she considers environmental extremism. In the primary she beat Leroy 42%–28%, carrying all but one remote county. In the general she attracted attention when she held "endangered salmon bakes" throughout the district, ridiculing the listing of Idaho salmon as an endangered species. Chenoweth attacked the "Clinton war on the West" and led in a poll after the May primary—a harbinger of the Republican tsunami. Chenoweth won 55%–45%, carrying 58% in Boise's Ada County and losing the panhandle by only 51%–49%.

In the House, Chenoweth has a strongly conservative record, voting against some measures even other Idaho Republicans supported—Sawtooth Recreation Area funding, Governor Phil Batt's "share the risk" salmon initiative, MFN status for China despite pressure from big Boise employer Hewlett-Packard. She was one of 15 Republicans who voted against the bill to get the government running again in January 1996. To the Oklahoma City bombing in April 1995 she reacted, "While we can never condone this, we still must begin to look at the public policies that may be pushing people too far." With the FBI misuse of power at Ruby Ridge in mind, she sponsored a bill to require federal agents to get written authorization from local sheriffs before enforcing federal law. "Chenoweth camps on the political parapet," wrote Ken Miller of the *Idaho Statesman*, "tightening races with 12-gauge rhetoric and sometimes impolitic remarks. Those offhand comments range from whether minorities can handle Idaho's cool weather to white males being an 'endangered species' to the abundance of salmon on supermarket shelves." Her Boise office displays Hamburger Helper repackaged as Spotted Owl Helper. She co-sponsored Bob Barr's impeachment resolution in November 1997. In 1997 Resources Chairman Don Young created a Forests and Forest Health Subcommittee for her to chair. There she challenged the 1998 moratorium on logging roads and sought to bar the president from establishing National Monuments without congressional approval. In 1998 she cut money from Forest Service administration and gave it to wildfire suppression. She also backed less controversial legislation, like country-of-origin labeling of meat.

Chenoweth's penchant for controversy has cheered some constituents and enraged others. She seemed in trouble in 1995 when she admitted (just one day after the deadline for bringing House ethics charges before the election) after an FEC investigation that she had failed to report an unsecured $50,000 loan after the 1994 campaign and when it was suggested that land she sold near the end of her 1994 campaign was worth only one-sixth of its $60,000 price; but the FEC ultimately rejected the charges. Some Republicans were turned off: her 1996 primary opponent won 32% even after removing most of his clothes in a TV interview and being sent to a mental hospital. Her Democratic opponent, attorney Dan Williams, took moderate stands—against gun control, for a capital gains tax cut—and called her an extremist. Chenoweth raised more money, but Williams had help from ads paid for by the AFL-CIO. She lost ground in Boise and Ada County, leading Williams there by only 50%–48%, but she won overall by the same margin.

In 1998 Chenoweth had serious opposition again. Computer entrepreneur Tony Pacquin challenged her in the primary, then withdrew in March. But in the May primary a disgruntled constituent got 29% of the vote; in fact, if the two party primary results are taken together, Chenoweth got 56% of the vote—almost exactly what she did get in November. Williams, running again, attacked Chenoweth's plan for "selling off public lands" to private interests; the reference is to a proposal she backed for the federal government to turn over public lands to the state government, which would make land use decisions. Williams also called for federal spending to rebuild schools and hire more teachers. Williams was supported again by the AFL-CIO, and the League of Conservation Voters again put Chenoweth on its "Dirty Dozen" list. These helped compensate for Chenoweth's edge in fundraising. In September 1998 Chenoweth began running an ad criticizing Bill Clinton for his "sordid spectacle" and arguing that "personal conduct does count." A day later it was reported that Chenoweth had had an affair with former state legislator Vern Ravenscroft from 1978–84, when she was not married but he was and neither was in public office. The race was even in September and October polls. But Chenoweth won by a larger-than-expected 55%–45%, carrying Boise and Ada County 54%–46% and the panhandle 52%–48% and losing only three counties. Compared with 1994, her overall percentage was the same, but she improved her standing in rural counties and lost ground in Boise.

Chenoweth is one of those Republicans who promised to serve only three terms in 1994. By 1998 she said she had come to believe that term limits were a mistake, but said, "I gave my word. It was part of the bargain between the voters and me." She filed papers for a 2000 committee, but said it was just to keep her fundraising committees going. In all likelihood, another Republican nominee will do better than the controversial Chenoweth, and the list of possibilities is long. Most likely to run are Lieutenant Governor Butch Otter (the former son-in-law of J.R. Simplot), state party chairman Ron McMurray (who finished third in the 1994 primary) and Boise Family Forum head Dennis Mansfield.

Cook's Call. *Probably Safe.* Despite Chenoweth's narrow victories in 1996 and 1998, it doesn't necessarily follow that Democrats have a great chance to pick up the seat in 2000, now that she has announced her retirement. Idaho is so thoroughly conservative and Republican that Democrats probably had a better chance beating the controversial Chenoweth than winning an open seat.

The People: Pop. 1990: 503,141; 45.8% rural; 13.4% age 65 + ; 94.9% White, 0.3% Black, 0.9% Asian, 1.5% Amer. Indian, 2.5% Other; 4.7% Hispanic Origin. Households: 62.2% married couple families; 30.2% married couple fams. w. children; 47.4% college educ.; median household income: $25,086; per capita income: $11,530; median house value: $60,300; median gross rent: $264.

1996 Presidential Vote			1992 Presidential Vote		
Dole (R)	134,783	(51%)	Bush (R)	101,787	(41%)
Clinton (D)	91,297	(35%)	Clinton (D)	75,499	(30%)
Perot (I)	33,130	(13%)	Perot (I)	67,677	(27%)
Others	4,142	(2%)			

Rep. Helen Chenoweth (R)

Elected 1994; b. Jan. 27, 1938, Topeka, KS; home, Boise; Whitworth Col., B.A. 1962; Christian; divorced.

Professional Career: Legal/Medical Mgmt. Consultant, 1964–75; Exec. Dir., ID Repub. Party, 1975–77; Chief of Staff, U.S. Rep. Steve Symms, 1977–78; Founder & Pres., Consulting Associates Inc., 1978–94.

DC Office: 1727 LHOB 20515, 202-225-6611; Fax: 202-225-3029; Web site: www.house.gov/chenoweth.

District Offices: Boise, 208-336-9831; Coeur d'Alene, 208-667-0127; Lewiston, 208-746-4613.

Committees: *Agriculture* (11th of 27 R): Livestock & Horticulture. *Government Reform* (24th of 24 R): National Economic Growth, Natural Resources & Regulatory Affairs; National Security, Veterans' Affairs & Intl. Relations. *Resources* (13th of 28 R): Forests & Forest Health (Chmn.); Water & Power. *Veterans' Affairs* (11th of 17 R): Health.

Group Ratings

	ADA	ACLU	AFS	LCV	CON	NTU	NFIB	COC	ACU	NTLC	CHC
1998	20	6	33	8	33	60	86	67	92	84	100
1997	0	—	25	—	13	62	—	70	96	—	—

National Journal Ratings

	1997 LIB — 1997 CONS			1998 LIB — 1998 CONS		
Economic	15%	—	84%	48%	—	51%
Social	0%	—	90%	0%	—	97%
Foreign	12%	—	88%	0%	—	93%

Key Votes of the 105th Congress

1. Clinton Budget Deal	Y	5. Puerto Rico Sthood. Ref.	N	9. Cut $ for B-2 Bombers	N
2. Education IRAs	Y	6. End Highway Set-asides	Y	10. Human Rights in China	N
3. Req. 2/3 to Raise Taxes	Y	7. School Prayer Amend.	Y	11. Withdraw Bosnia Troops	Y
4. Fast-track Trade	N	8. Ovrd. Part. Birth Veto	Y	12. End Cuban TV-Marti	N

Election Results

1998 general	Helen Chenoweth (R)	113,231	(55%)	($1,331,487)
	Dan Williams (D)	91,653	(45%)	($876,308)
1998 primary	Helen Chenoweth (R)	43,941	(71%)	
	Jim Pratt (R)	17,926	(29%)	
1996 general	Helen Chenoweth (R)	132,344	(50%)	($1,129,263)
	Dan Williams (D)	125,899	(48%)	($659,753)
	Others	6,535	(2%)	

518   IDAHO

SECOND DISTRICT

The 2d District of Idaho, from central Boise east to the Utah border, is one of America's most Republican districts in presidential elections. Southeast Idaho is part of the Mormon heartland, and the district is almost half Mormon. Most of the farm counties and towns here are heavily Republican, but the old frontier and railroad town of Pocatello is Democratic. The 2d's portion of Boise includes the city's few Denverish-liberal neighborhoods.

The congressman from the 2d District is Mike Simpson, a Republican elected in 1998 when incumbent Republican Mike Crapo was elected to the Senate. But Simpson's elevation was not automatic. He grew up in Blackfoot, became a dentist and joined his father's practice there and was elected to the city council in 1982 and the state House in 1984; he didn't declare himself as a Republican until then and was opposed by the local party organization. In 1993 he became speaker, but kept up his dental practice as well. In the legislature he was known as a moderate in a conservative House, affable and able to get differing sides together. He pushed the Martin Luther King Jr. holiday, workmen's compensation for farm workers and property tax relief. When Governor Phil Batt announced he would retire in 1998, Simpson wanted to run for his office. But Senator Dirk Kempthorne's decision to go for governor closed that option. Then 2d District Congressman Mike Crapo ran for Kempthorne's Senate seat, and Simpson entered the 2d District race.

In the Republican primary Simpson was opposed by state Representative Mark Stubbs and two former state senators. Simpson called for tax reform, Stubbs for lower payroll taxes; Stubbs had opposed nuclear programs at the Idaho Nation Engineering and Environmental Laboratory in the 1980s, while Simpson wanted more work at the facility. But the big issue was term limits. Simpson refused to take US Term Limits's pledge to serve only three terms; the other three did. Americans for Term Limits spent thousands to run TV ads against Simpson. Enraged by these ads, Governor Phil Batt endorsed Simpson five days before the election; Simpson ran ads against "outsiders" and "out-of-state folk"; Batt recorded a message for him which was delivered to 47,000 households by telemarketing. Simpson beat Stubbs, 47%–41%.

The Democratic nominee was Richard Stallings, a former history professor elected to the House in 1984 and re-elected three times; in 1992 he ran against Kempthorne for the Senate and lost 57%–43%. Stallings talked about his conservative voting record in the House, called for more education spending and pointed with anxiety at falling farm commodity prices. Simpson wanted a smaller federal role in education. He favored tax cuts and Republican Social Security reform. As farm prices plummeted, Simpson called for trade talks to open markets, with possible tariffs if others didn't go along, and renegotiating NAFTA. "We need to take a look at why commodity prices have been so low and try to make sure it doesn't happen again," he said. Stallings called for export incentives and exemption of food from diplomatic sanctions. On two issues they clashed sharply. Stallings attacked Simpson for not spending enough in Boise on education: "You've balanced the budget, Mr. Simpson, you have balanced it on the backs of children by funding prisons." Simpson said that state spending on education increased as a share of the budget. Simpson accused Stallings of voting for a tax increase when he voted for a budget resolution in 1987. Not so, said Stallings, a budget resolution doesn't tax anyone. "Mr. Stallings believes there's a federal solution for every problem," summed up Simpson. That basic sentiment, plus Simpson's larger campaign budget, evidently overcame Stallings's past service. Simpson won 53%–45%, losing the most visible parts of the district—Pocatello, Sun Valley, Boise—but carrying just about everything else, and in the Mormon southeast and ultraconservative northeast by considerable margins.

In the House, Simpson got seats on Agriculture and on Resources, always important in Idaho.

Cook's Call. *Safe.* The 1998 election proved just how Republican Idaho really is: Democrats ran their best possible candidate, former Representative Richard Stallings, yet still came up short in what elsewhere was a good year for them. This is one of the most Republican districts in the nation, and Simpson should be able to hold onto this seat for as long as he wants.

The People: Pop. 1990: 503,608; 39.3% rural; 11.6% age 65 + ; 94% White, 0.5% Black, 0.9% Asian, 1.4% Amer. Indian, 3.2% Other; 5.6% Hispanic Origin. Households: 62.2% married couple families; 33.3% married couple fams. w. children; 51.5% college educ.; median household income: $25,446; per capita income: $11,384; median house value: $55,900; median gross rent: $259.

1996 Presidential Vote			1992 Presidential Vote		
Dole (R)	121,812	(53%)	Bush (R)	100,858	(43%)
Clinton (D)	74,146	(32%)	Perot (I)	62,718	(27%)
Perot (I)	29,388	(13%)	Clinton (D)	61,514	(26%)
			Others	8,925	(4%)

Rep. Mike Simpson (R)

Elected 1998; b. Sept. 8, 1950, Burley; home, Blackfoot; UT St. U., 1968–72; WA U. Dental Schl., D.D.S. 1977; Mormon; married (Kathy).

Elected Office: Blackfoot City Cncl., 1982–86; ID House of Reps., 1984–98, Speaker, 1993–98.

Professional Career: Practicing dentist, 1977-present.

DC Office: 1440 LHOB 20515, 202-225-5531; Fax: 202-225-8216; Web site: www.house.gov/simpson.

District Offices: Boise, 208-334-1953; Idaho Falls, 208-523-6701; Pocatello, 208-478-4160; Twin Falls, 208-734-7219.

Committees: *Agriculture* (24th of 27 R): Risk Management, Research & Specialty Crops. *Resources* (27th of 28 R): Fisheries Conservation, Wildlife & Oceans; Water & Power. *Transportation & Infrastructure* (40th of 41 R): Aviation; Water Resources & Environment. *Veterans' Affairs* (16th of 17 R): Health.

Group Ratings and Key Votes: Newly Elected

Election Results

1998 general	Mike Simpson (R)	91,337	(53%)	($888,208)
	Richard H. Stallings (D)	77,736	(45%)	($648,952)
	Others	4,872	(3%)	
1998 primary	Mike Simpson (R)	26,620	(47%)	
	Mark D. Stubbs (R)	23,336	(41%)	
	Ann Rydalch (R)	6,844	(12%)	
1996 general	Mike Crapo (R)	157,646	(69%)	($755,679)
	John D. Seidl (D)	67,625	(30%)	($163,532)
	Others	3,977	(2%)	

ILLINOIS

A century ago America seemed destined to center on Chicago. This brash new city on the lake had grown from 112,000 residents in 1860, when it was host to the Republican Convention that nominated Illinois's Abraham Lincoln, to 1,400,000 when it hosted the Columbian Exposition in 1893. "Make no little plans," Chicago architect Daniel Burnham exhorted, and Chicago was making vast plans, building grand parks on the lakefront, erecting America's first downtown of skyscrapers, building expansive retail palaces, becoming the headquarters of the new American Medical and American Bar Associations, creating a great university from scratch on the Exposition's Midway Plaisance, housing the union agitators and their liberal advocate Clarence Darrow as well as the corporate leaders and attorneys who bested them, hosting the Democratic Convention of 1896 that nominated 36-year-old William Jennings Bryan after his "cross of gold" speech, and becoming the headquarters of the brilliant campaign Marcus Hanna waged for William McKinley which beat Bryan in the fall. Chicago started with the advantage of a great location, where the Great Lakes met the prairies of the vast Mississippi Valley, and Chicago's entrepreneurs made it the hub of the nation's railroad network and the center of the nation's trade in lumber, grain and meat, as William Cronon describes in *Nature's Metropolis*.

A century later, Chicago is the nation's third largest metropolis, sometimes overshadowed by and often ignored by the media of coastal New York and Los Angeles; but it is still a productive and creative world-city. In commerce, Chicago remains a prime producer and processor of food products, a great manufacturing center with the strongest white-collar and service economy between the coasts, the home of the world's greatest commodities exchanges and futures markets. O'Hare Airport, built with care by longtime (1955–76) Mayor Richard J. Daley and long the world's busiest airport, was edged into second place by Atlanta's Hartsfield in 1998. Chicago and Illinois remain a focus of national attention. In the great home run duel of 1998, Illinois was split, between Cubs fans on the North Side of Chicago and suburbs rooting for Sammy Sosa and St. Louis Cardinals fans in much of Downstate rooting for Mark McGwire. All the nation joined Chicago in celebrating the career and lamenting the retirement of Michael Jordan in January 1999. Chicago's natural and man-made disasters are outsized as well: the police charges of two 7- and 8-year-old boys as accused killers, later dropped, horrified millions in July 1998; the massive 22-inch snowstorm of January 1999 tied up O'Hare and therefore much of the nation's end-of-holiday air travel.

Politically, Chicago and Illinois have not produced any presidents in the 20th Century, but they have produced crucial votes and pivotal politicians. Start with Charles Dawes, a 30-year-old lawyer sent to Chicago by Hanna to manage McKinley's campaign; later he was a World War I general, the first Budget Bureau (now Office of Management and Budget) director, and vice president under Calvin Coolidge. Or Chicago lawyer Harold Ickes, who was Franklin Roosevelt's great Interior secretary. Prominent Illinois Republicans have included Speaker Joseph Cannon, Senate Republican Leader Everett Dirksen, Senator Charles Percy and House Republican Leader Robert Michel; prominent Democrats have included Governor Adlai Stevenson, Mayor Richard J. Daley and Ways and Means Chairman Dan Rostenkowski. Currently, Illinois has 22 electoral votes and with percentages near the national average of blacks and Hispanics, immigrants and pioneers, city-dwellers and suburbanites and farmers, the affluent and the impoverished, heavy industry and high-tech, they tend to reflect national divisions. Illinois is furiously contested in close presidential elections and, since Bryan orated and Dawes set up shop, it has voted for the losing presidential candidate only twice, in 1916 and 1976. Increasingly, its aberrations from the national average reflect the views of the Chicago suburbs which cast 40% of the state's vote, pro-market on economics and *laissez faire* on cultural issues:

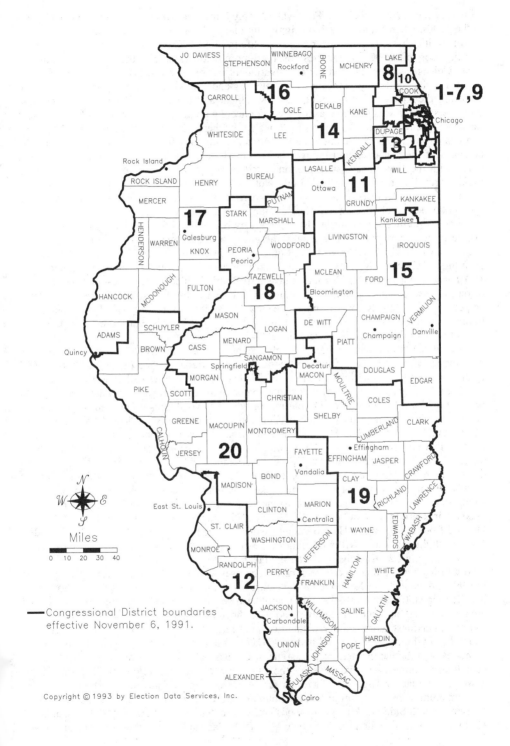

Congressional District boundaries
effective November 6, 1991.

these sent Illinois toward Gerald Ford when Jimmy Carter was winning and toward Bill Clinton in the 1990s, when Illinois was by a significant margin his best Midwestern state.

But politics has not always been central to life in Illinois. This was a state of farmers, whose families, communities and churches absorbed more of their energies than politics or government. Chicago was established not by government but by markets; it has always been a free enterprise city, settled by pioneers from New England and Kentucky, by immigrant Irishmen who dug the first canal connecting Lake Michigan and the Illinois River, and by railroad promoters who saw its potential as the great connecting point between East and West, the Great Lakes and the Mississippi Valley. Its factories, built where iron ore from Great Lakes freighters and coal from inland hills came together, attracted migrants from near and far. To meet the demands of these masses and referee their cultural struggles, political machines sprang up, allied with the Republicans who predominated in northern Illinois and the Democrats who usually prevailed from Springfield south. Not until the Depression of the 1930s did Chicago become reliably Democratic, and that was in part because so many Republicans had moved to the Cook County suburbs and the Collar Counties surrounding Chicago.

Illinois's political trends have also been set by reactions to the political officeholder most visible to the voters, who is not usually the governor off in remote Springfield and certainly not the senators who have to work "out of town" in Washington, but the mayor of Chicago—even though Chicago itself now casts only 20% of the state's votes. During the years Richard J. Daley served as "Da Mare"—and as boss of the fabled Chicago machine—politics here was a contest between Chicago and Downstate, typified by the 1960 presidential race when Daley helped John F. Kennedy carry Illinois by exactly (or so it was reported) 8,858 votes out of 4.7 million cast. Only twice since then, in 1984 and 1992, has Illinois cast more votes; the 1996 turnout of 4.3 million was the lowest since 1948.

Elected in 1989, his son, Richard M. Daley, came to office with a reputation as an inarticulate heir but has proved to be innovative, thoughtful and effective—one of the most successful Democratic public officials in the country. Richie Daley, as he is often called, was a state senator and Cook County state's attorney whose one major setback was his defeat in the 1983 mayoral primary to Harold Washington, an able mayor who was vociferously opposed by white politicians in "the council wars." After Washington's death Daley was elected by winning the white bungalow wards plus Hispanic and lakefront wards his opponents took for granted. Daley's first achievement was racial reconciliation; his approval ratings among blacks have topped 50% and among others, including suburbanites, are up around 80%. He worked to downsize and privatize city government. Daley has had limited success in Illinois's airport wars: His plans for a new airport around Lake Calumet were abandoned when the legislature would not meet his terms; he blocked former Governor Jim Edgar's and Congressman Jesse Jackson Jr.'s proposed new airport at Peotone, 45 miles south of Chicago; Daley has been blocked from expanding O'Hare by congressmen Henry Hyde, whose constituency is underneath its flight paths, and William Lipinski, the great protector of Midway; Edgar blocked him from closing until 2002 Meigs Field on the lakefront, to make it a park.

But Daley has had other, perhaps smaller successes which, added together, are much greater. In 1995 Edgar and the Republican legislature gave him control of the public schools. He installed top staffer Paul Vallas as CEO, abolished social promotion, ran huge summer school programs to get kids up to grade level and used the authority to reassign and remove teachers and principals; test scores have risen and dropout rates declined. Like his father, he seems to know the city block by block, and he has worked to improve both struggling and rising neighborhoods; and the fact is that, even as some of Chicago's big units— companies like Sears or huge housing projects—leave or decay, the city as a whole has marvelous vitality. Small businesses are replacing large; old factories far from the lakefront are being rebuilt as luxury condominium complexes; immigrant communities are vibrant in precincts that once seemed to be dying. South Side black neighborhoods are well maintained and growing rather than being abandoned; the new United Center, where Michael Jordan played basketball and Al Gore moved to the macarena, is bringing signs of life to the bedraggled West Side. Symbolic of Daley's approach is his zest for wrought iron fences, in parks, around new developments, in neighborhoods: strong fences making good neighbors.

Daley and his brother William, a smart political strategist, smiled on Bill Clinton as he won his clinching primary victory in Illinois in 1992. Bill Daley was passed over for Transportation secretary, but was Clinton's chief lobbyist for NAFTA in November 1993. Chicago was awarded the Democratic National Convention in 1996, a grand occasion for Daley to show off the city and erase memories of 1968; after the election, Bill Daley was named Commerce secretary. There is nothing resembling the Daley machine of old, and Daley does not determine statewide nominations; he has taken advantage of his ability to fill vacancies in the City Council and to parcel out projects that there is no effective opposition. In February 1999 Daley was re-elected 72%–28% and won 45% of the black vote, against a serious black candidate, Congressman Bobby Rush.

Republicans control the Illinois Senate, Democrats the Illinois House. Both parties elect downballot statewide officials. The U.S. House delegation has been evenly split in 1994, 1996 and 1998, with only a handful of close races. In the early 1990s, the most notable members of the delegation were Democrat Dan Rostenkowski and Republican Robert Michel. Both were eclipsed by the Republican tide of 1994: Rostenkowski lost his seat amid scandal charges, while Michel was pushed into retirement by Newt Gingrich. But Illinois became prominent again as Gingrich was eclipsed in 1998: leading the effort to impeach Bill Clinton was Henry Hyde, and presiding over the debate was Michel's successor Ray LaHood; and the new speaker, elected after Gingrich and then Bob Livingston stepped down, was Dennis Hastert, from the 14th District, which spans the suburbs and Downstate. A common theme to all these Illinois careers, and to that of Governor George Ryan as well, is an ability to get along—and make deals—across party lines.

Bill Clinton twice carried Illinois by effective margins—49%–34% over George Bush in 1992 and 54%–37% over Bob Dole in 1996, when Clinton carried the suburbs 48%–43% as well as the city 79%–16%. The suburbs—anti-tax, secular if not liberal on cultural issues—seemed largely satisfied with Clinton by 1996; but they were also satisfied with the moderate Republican governors who succeeded fellow Republican James Thompson, Jim Edgar in 1990 and George Ryan in 1998. In the latter year, the suburbs, with much bigger turnout than eight years before, reacted negatively to Democratic nominee Glenn Poshard, a Downstater who opposed abortion and gun control. Yet they also gave a solid margin in the Senate race to conservative Republican Peter Fitzgerald over scandal-scarred Democratic incumbent Carol Moseley-Braun. The Republican margin in the suburbs was narrower in 1996, when conservative Al Salvi lost statewide to Downstate Democratic Congressman Richard Durbin, who took advantage of hometown strength to carry Downstate.

The Illinois primary has sometimes been a bellwether: The defeat of Senator Alan Dixon and four congressmen in the 1992 primary was a harbinger of the anti-incumbent trend that year. Michel's decision to retire, which had to be made by the December 1993 filing deadline, gave Gingrich plenty of time to consolidate his leadership of House Republicans before the 1994 campaign, and signalled a new kind of Republican Party in the House. And the fizzling of challenges to incumbents in March 1996 and 1998 foreshadowed the pro-incumbent sentiments in those years.

Governor. George Ryan was elected governor in 1998 after a long career in politics. He grew up in Kankakee, served in Korea, got a degree in pharmacy and ran a family pharmacy in Kankakee—a town on the border of Chicagoland and Downstate Illinois. In 1966, prodded by a friend after complaining about local government, he ran for the County Board, and served six years. In 1972 he was elected to the state House, becoming minority leader in 1976 and speaker in 1980; that was the last term before Illinois's 177-member "Big House," with each district electing two from one party and one from the other, was slimmed down to 118.

The Big House was an environment that encouraged accommodation and deal-making (good and bad words for the same thing), in which Ryan continued to excel. In 1982 he was elected lieutenant governor and served eight years; in 1990 he was edged out of the race for governor by Jim Edgar, and was elected secretary of state instead. Ryan used the office, which issues driver's licenses and other documents, to maximum advantage. He continued Edgar's crusade against drunk drivers and in 1997 got the legislature to reduce the alcohol level for DUIs to .08%. He opened offices on Saturdays and placed his name everywhere, on drunken driving pamphlets, ads for organ donations, refrigerator magnets for a seniors' hot line, promotions for family reading night. When Edgar stunned everyone by announcing in August 1997 his retirement from elective politics, Ryan jumped into the race.

So did several Democrats, hungry for an office their party has not occupied since 1976. They included John Schmidt, a wealthy lawyer and former Daley aide, who left a high post in the U.S. Justice Department and seemed to have Daley's backing; Chicago-based U.S. Attorney Jim Burns; former state Attorney General Roland Burris, confident of a large base among black voters; and Glenn Poshard, a congressman from far Downstate Illinois—closer to Jackson, Mississippi, than Jackson Boulevard in Chicago, noted George Will—who had reached his self-imposed limit of five terms. The primary was typically raucous. Burris started out with a large lead, but never raised enough money for a big ad campaign; he hurt himself by calling his opponents "non-qualified white boys." Schmidt and Poshard, with more ad money, launched attacks on each other. Schmidt blasted Poshard for opposing abortion, gun control and environmental bills; Poshard complained that an ad made him look like a "Hitler-style" dictator. Poshard pledged not to accept PAC money and to limit contributions to $4,000 from individuals and $50,000 from candidates; he was endorsed in January by the Illinois AFL-CIO. The primary results showed the competing strength of Democratic constituencies. The labor-backed Poshard won with 38%; he carried all but two Downstate counties, with a total of 70%. Burris, with backing from blacks, who formed almost one-quarter of the primary electorate, won 31%. Chicago-backed Schmidt had 25%; Burns trailed with 6%.

The results left Ryan with a big fundraising advantage (he eventually raised $15 million to Poshard's $5.9 million) and Poshard with problems on his Democratic flanks. Over the spring and summer Poshard was battered by Chicago area liberals who disliked his opposition to abortion (even greater than that of Ryan, who would make an exception for rape and incest), his votes against some gay rights positions, his opposition to some gun control measures. He got criticism for favoring corporal punishment in schools. The Independent Voters of Illinois refused to endorse him, and gay rights leaders, after meeting with Poshard, announced they were sticking with Ryan. Poshard was hit for opposing the Clean Air Act (he opposed limits on southern Illinois's high-sulfur coal). His opposition to expanding gambling angered others. Mayor Daley did support Poshard, but admitted he had always gotten on well with Ryan.

On most of these issues Ryan took more politic stands. He had backed gun control since 1989, supported gay rights, opposed corporal punishment, favored the beginning of a Peotone airport (with only two runways), opposed more riverboat gambling but favored changes to make Illinois's boats more competitive with those in Indiana, Iowa and Missouri. He set out his own priorities: putting 51% of new state revenues into schools, life sentences for criminals who use guns and injure or kill people, disentangling the "Hillside Strangler" intersection of the Eisenhower Expressway and two tollways. Ryan has an instinct for centrism and a disinclination to be pinned down. When a reporter asked him if he would ever back a tobacco or liquor tax increase, he said, "Ever is for a long time." When he went on TV in July, an ad showed him striding down the center aisle of the legislature and quoted him as saying he could always work with people on both sides of the aisle.

In the pro-incumbent mood of 1998, with far more money than Poshard, Ryan seemed to be coasting platitudinously to victory. His October ads hit Poshard as too conservative and "extreme, extreme, extreme." Poshard was on the defensive as he refrained from appearing at a September fundraiser with Bill Clinton, pleading that he had to vote on important issues in the House. But Poshard came charging back with negatives. Employees at a Melrose Park

Secretary of State's office were accused of bribery for issuing more than 250 truck driver's licenses to unqualified applicants; a federal probe that began in September led to charges against 12 individuals and allegations of corruption in the state Department of Transportation. Ryan was also criticized for getting campaign contributions from employees in his office (he pointed out that 75% of them did not contribute). In the end, Ryan won by just 51%–47%, after leading by much wider margins in the polls. He made some inroads into the Democratic base—18% among blacks, 62% among Jews, 26% of self-identified Democrats—but Poshard also was strong in his home base, winning his old district convincingly, and holding Ryan to a 50%–49% margin Downstate. The difference was the suburbs, which went about 2–1 for Ryan.

As governor, Ryan moved successfully to avoid being put on the spot by gambling bills, and worked to increase education spending, but without the $1,000 vocational school scholarships he had promised for high school graduates. He said he hoped to convince Mayor Daley to approve a startup airport at Peotone and to keep open Meigs Field on Chicago's lakefront, which Daley wants to make a park. In March 1999, Ryan proposed a scaled-down third airport with just one runway as a compromise. He seems likely to govern through negotiation, with Daley, with Senate President James "Pate" Philip, a crusty Republican from suburban DuPage County, with House Speaker Michael Madigan, a southwest Chicago Democrat who is not necessarily friendly with Daley (Madigan favors Midway Airport, Daley favors O'Hare), and with House Minority Leader Lee Daniels, a DuPage County Republican who is only a few votes from the speakership he formerly held. In his first 100 days, he supported a stiffer seatbelt law and helped broker a compromise on regulating hog farms.

Senior Senator. Richard Durbin, the senior senator, is a Democrat elected in 1996. Durbin grew up in East St. Louis, and for almost all his adult life has been in politics: right out of law school he joined Paul Simon's staff when he was lieutenant governor (1969–73), then was a state Senate staffer in the 1970s. He taught in medical school and lost two races for office in the 1970s, but in 1982 won the nomination to oppose Republican Congressman Paul Findley, who had characterized himself as Yasir Arafat's best friend in Congress; that helped Durbin raise large sums from Israel supporters. Durbin won that race, got a seat on the Agriculture Committee and then moved to Appropriations, where in January 1993 he became chairman of the Agriculture Subcommittee. There Durbin worked on Illinois projects—not just Downstate projects like the research center at the Lincoln home, but the $750 million Chicago Circulator trolley project as well. He worked to promote ethanol and soybean-based ink in government documents—big causes in the homeland of Dwayne Andreas's Archer-Daniels-Midland. Durbin's father died of lung cancer when he was 14, and Durbin's most prominent achievement was the 1988 ban on smoking on domestic airline flights; he followed that up by trying to limit tobacco subsidies and in 1994 moved unsuccessfully to direct the FDA to regulate tobacco as a health hazard.

Senator Paul Simon announced his retirement in November 1994, and in June 1995, Durbin decided to run for the seat. He had lost his subcommittee chair after Republicans won the House in 1994. His recent House races had been uncomfortably close; he won against a serious opponent with 57% in 1992, then won with just 55% in 1994 against a construction worker and John Birch Society member who spent only $55,000. So he jumped at the chance to run for the Senate. Simon immediately endorsed him, which surely helped him Downstate. His chief problem—an almost total lack of name identification in Chicago, which cast nearly half the primary votes—was solved with money: Durbin raised more than $1 million for the March 19 primary, vastly outspending his only serious opponent, former state Treasurer Pat Quinn. Durbin went on TV in early February, talking of his working class roots and fights against tobacco and gun lobbies; he won the primary 65%–30%. Meanwhile, the Republican primary was won in an upset. Governor Jim Edgar and other insiders had worked to persuade a reluctant Lieutenant Governor Bob Kustra to run. But Kustra, who at one point in 1994 announced he was retiring from politics to be a talk radio host, seemed to have little fire in his belly. His opponent, trial lawyer and abortion opponent Al Salvi, did, and spent more than $1 million of his own money in the primary. Despite a meek demeanor and total lack of name identification, Salvi came from behind to edge Kustra 48%–43%.

The general election was a battle of broad-brush charges in a state where few voters knew much about either candidate. Salvi called Durbin a tax-raiser, hit him for opposing the balanced budget amendment; a bartender in one of his ads called Durbin "a big-taxin', big-spendin', pay-grabbin' liberal congressman." Durbin constantly called Salvi an "extremist," and hit him for opposing the assault weapons ban and taking tobacco money. Perhaps the leading issue was gun control. Salvi's opposition to the assault weapons ban was undoubtedly unpopular, especially in the suburbs, and an October endorsement from gun control activists Jim and Sarah Brady surely helped Durbin. But more important was an astonishing mistake by Salvi: In late October, someone he met at a rally told him that Jim Brady used to sell machine guns and, without checking out the story, Salvi repeated it in a radio interview. It was totally untrue and Salvi had to apologize, but any chance of his overtaking Durbin was gone. Durbin won 56%–41%, with a huge margin in Chicago and narrow edges in the suburbs and Downstate. Durbin's 56% was almost exactly identical to Bill Clinton's 54% and Democratic House candidates' 55%.

In the Senate Durbin has a liberal voting record and has been a leading partisan defender of Bill Clinton. He started off by failing to get the Appropriations seat he wanted (he got it two years later). His move to waive the balanced budget requirement by a simple majority in times of serious economic problems was rejected 64–35. He defended the Clinton-Gore campaign resolutely in Fred Thompson's 1997 investigation of campaign finance irregularities, including Chinese contributions. Durbin supported the McCain-Feingold campaign finance bill and tried to move his goal of gun control incrementally forward. He called for a ban on gun possession by foreigners on non-immigrant visas, a ban on certain cheap handguns, criminal penalties for parents whose children get hold of guns and a permanent extension of the Brady bill's five-day waiting requirement (the original bill had it lapse to be replaced by an instant criminal background check). He worked for food protection laws and a bill to prevent "slamming" of long-distance telephone customers. He opposed patent extensions for drug manufacturers. In March 1999 he was one of three senators to oppose a national missile defense system.

On tobacco, Durbin took a lead role at several stages. He moved to repeal the tax credit for tobacco companies; he lost 78–22 in July 1997, then won 95–3 in September 1997. He opposed provisions to limit FDA regulation of tobacco or "any additive ingredient of a tobacco product." In July 1998 he moved to ban smoking on international flights. With colleague Carol Moseley-Braun he was attentive to Illinois business interests. He helped block the reappointment of Commodity Futures Trading Commission member Joseph Dial, who opposed a Chicago Board of Trade proposal to change points at which corn and soybeans could be delivered to fulfill contracts. He opposed Chinese imports shipped in raw wood packing that can harbor the tree-killing Asian long-horned beetle, which was infesting trees in the Chicago area. He protested the fact that more women than men were subjected to drug searches at O'Hare Airport. He supported the bankruptcy bill that passed the Senate near unanimously, but opposed the House version, which bans class action lawsuits against creditors that demand payment on unpaid debt contrary to bankruptcy law.

Junior Senator. Peter Fitzgerald, a Republican elected at 38 in 1998, is the youngest member of the Senate. He grew up in the affluent northwest suburb of Inverness— as Republican as Chicago is Democratic. His father started a suburban bank chain the year he was one and sold it to the Bank of Montreal in 1991, netting Peter Fitzgerald some $40 million in stock; he was always interested in politics, and now had the means to run for office. He went to Catholic schools and majored in Latin and Greek at Dartmouth; after a year in Greece he went to Michigan Law School. In his college years he was an intern for Congressman Philip Crane, now the senior Republican in the House, and organized a New Hampshire rally for Crane's presidential campaign. In 1988 Fitzgerald lost a close primary for the state House; in 1992 he was elected to the state Senate. There he opposed tax increases and was known as one of the

"Fab Five" conservatives. He voted to allow law-abiding citizens to carry concealed weapons and favored competitive bidding for casino licenses. In 1994 he spent more than $700,000 of his own money challenging Crane in the primary, and lost by only 40%–33%.

Fitzgerald was not the only Illinois politician with an eye on the 1998 Senate race. Incumbent Carol Moseley-Braun was elected by a solid 53%–43% in 1992, after winning a three-way primary in which the other two candidates bloodied each other up: thus she became the first black woman senator. She had a mostly liberal record but tended closely to Chicago and Downstate business interests; she was articulate, with a winning manner. But she also had terrible problems. In September 1992 it was revealed that in 1989 she split among herself and siblings a $28,750 timber royalty inheritance owed to her mother, a nursing home resident who was supposed to have reimbursed Medicaid with the money. After her election, Mosely-Braun and her South African campaign manager and ex-fiance Kgosie Matthews embarked on a month-long trip to Africa, allegedly spending some $281,000, apparently in campaign funds, on travel, clothes, stereo equipment, jewelry and two Jeeps. Then in August 1996, she and Matthews, a former registered agent of the Nigerian government, paid a "private" visit to Nigeria where they met with now-deceased dictator General Sani Abacha, without the normal checking in with the State Department. Her poll numbers dropped to near-record lows. But Democratic challengers shied away from running against the only black senator and Daley, perhaps with an eye to black voters in the February 1999 mayor race, endorsed her and started raising money for her in early 1997. Michael Bakalis, Democratic candidate for governor in 1978, weighed running but got out of the race in September 1997. What was surprising was that the Republican nomination seemed to go begging. Governor Jim Edgar, widely popular, announced in August 1997 that he wouldn't run for office again. Secretary of State George Ryan, often mentioned for the Senate race, immediately ran for governor. Attorney General Jim Ryan, recovering from cancer, took himself out of the race in September 1997.

Fitzgerald, who announced in April 1997, seemed to have this desirable nomination to himself. But Edgar and other Republican leaders, fresh from watching abortion opponent Al Salvi lose the 1996 Senate race, did not want abortion opponent Peter Fitzgerald as the nominee. They encouraged Comptroller Loleta Didrickson to run, though she was reluctant to do so. Fitzgerald spent some $7 million in the primary, starting off with warm ads showing him as a basic suburban father, then calling for lower taxes. When Moseley-Braun said, "Loleta Didrickson and I voted very much alike when we were in the state legislature together," Fitzgerald seized on the theme and attacked Didrickson as a tax-raiser. A suburban official sued Didrickson for using state workers, phones, cars and airplanes in her campaign; only after the primary was it revealed that Fitzgerald's campaign paid the lawyers. Didrickson called him "the trust fund kid" and argued that he would lose the general election. After being outspent, she complained, "I can't compete effectively." Actually it was close. Fitzgerald won 52%–48%, losing the suburbs narrowly but carrying Downstate 59%–41%.

In the general, Fitzgerald attacked "six years of scandal and controversy" and said that Moseley-Braun had "been to Nigeria more than she's been to Rockford." When it was revealed in July that the Justice Department had twice turned down IRS requests to begin a criminal investigation into her post-1992 campaign spending spree, he called for her to release the underlying documents. Moseley-Braun fought back. In ads she conceded, "I know I've made some mistakes and disappointed some people. But I want you to know that I've always tried to do what's best for Illinois." Bill Clinton, Al Gore and Illinois native Hillary Rodham Clinton came in to raise money and campaign for her, as did Ann Richards and Maya Angelou. Mosely-Braun accused Fitzgerald of running a stealth campaign and relying on ads, and she performed creditably in debate. She attacked him for backing carry-concealed weapon laws; he responded that he supported the Brady bill's waiting period and the 1994 assault weapons ban. But Fitzgerald, with more than $14 million of his own money, outspent her 2–1. And Moseley-Braun stumbled when she accused columnist (and Illinois native) George Will of accusing her of being corrupt "because he could not say [racial epithet]." Actually, he didn't use the word "corrupt" either, and Moseley-Braun faxed an apology.

Fitzgerald won by just 50%–47%, losing Cook and four small Downstate counties and carrying the other 97. Moseley-Braun carried Cook County heavily, but Fitzgerald was ahead in the suburbs and he carried the rest of the state 60%–36%, even though it went for George Ryan over Downstater Glenn Poshard by only 50%–49%. She carried blacks 93%–7%; he carried white Protestants 65%–32% and white Catholics 69%–30%.

Presidential politics. Illinois's presidential primary, for years held fittingly on or around St. Patrick's Day, has played a decisive role in most recent presidential years. It certified Republican victors Gerald Ford in 1976, Ronald Reagan in 1980 and George Bush in 1988 and Democratic victors Jimmy Carter in 1980, Walter Mondale in 1984 and Bill Clinton in 1992. In 1988, the Democratic nomination would probably have been clinched here for Michael Dukakis, except for the dominance of two Illinois candidates, Paul Simon and Jesse Jackson. In 1996 it was less decisive. Bill Clinton was unopposed, and the Republican nomination had already been decided March 2 in South Carolina, with Bob Dole's 65%–23% victory over Pat Buchanan here just icing on his cake. Illinois's Republican primary voters, by the way, are about evenly split between the suburbs, with their affluent free-marketeer dislike for taxes, and Downstate, with their old-fashioned, practical-minded Midwestern politics. Illinois's Democratic primary voters are more evenly split between Chicago, the suburbs, and Downstate.

Illinois's importance in the presidential nominating process was greatly diminished when California and other states moved up their primary dates. For 2000, the Illinois primary is set for March 21, after both California and New York.

Congressional districting. Illinois's congressional district lines for the last 20 years have been drawn by courts. The 1980s plan favored Democrats, the 1990s plan the Republicans. The advent of new lines can cause political upsets: four incumbents lost in the 1992 primary. But by 1998 most incumbents were pretty well entrenched. Illinois could lose one seat in redistricting for 2000. The suburbs have been gaining population smartly, and incumbents there will probably scamper to victory. Downstate counties have not gained much, and there could be some defeats there, or party shifts. Chicago's seats are all held by Democrats, and some of them may be squeezed. Of particular interest is what happens to the U-shaped, Hispanic-majority 4th District; it may get mixed together with the grotesquely shaped 5th. The 4th's boundaries would probably not stand muster with the courts today, but Hispanics have been streaming into Chicago's outer neighborhoods, which are also home to many recent immigrants from Poland, India, and former Soviet republics.

The People: Est. Pop. 1998: 12,045,326; Pop. 1990: 11,430,602, up 5.4% 1990–1998. 4.5% of U.S. total, 5th largest; 15.4% rural. Median age: 34.3 years. 13.1% 65 years and over. 78.4% White, 14.8% Black, 2.5% Asian, 0.2% Amer. Indian, 4.1% Other; 7.7% Hispanic Origin. Households: 54.1% married couple families; 26.4% married couple fams. w. children; 46.2% college educ.; median household income: $32,252; per capita income: $15,201; 64.2% owner occupied housing; median house value: $80,900; median monthly rent: $369. 4.5% Unemployment. 1998 Voting age pop.: 8,755,000. 1998 Turnout: 3,541,379; 40% of VAP. Registered voters (1998): 6,754,998; no party registration.

Political Lineup: Governor, George H. Ryan (R); Lt. Gov., Corinne Wood (R); Secy. of State, Jesse White (D); Atty. Gen., James E. Ryan (R); Treasurer, Judy Baar Topinka (R); State Senate, 59 (27 D, 32 R); Senate President, James (Pate) Philip (R); State Assembly, 118 (62 D, 56 R); Assembly Speaker, Mike Madigan (D). Senators, Richard J. Durbin (D) and Peter G. Fitzgerald (R). Representatives, 20 (10 D, 10 R).

Elections Division: 217-782-4141; **Filing Deadline for U.S. Congress:** December 20, 1999.

1996 Presidential Vote

Clinton (D) 2,341,744 (54%)
Dole (R) 1,587,021 (37%)
Perot (I) 346,408 (8%)

1996 Republican Presidential Primary

Dole (R) 532,467 (65%)
Buchanan (R) 186,177 (23%)
Forbes (R) 39,906 (5%)
Keyes (R) 30,052 (4%)
Others 29,762 (4%)

1992 Presidential Vote

Clinton (D) 2,453,350 (49%)
Bush (R) 1,734,096 (34%)
Perot (I) 840,515 (17%)

GOVERNOR

Gov. George H. Ryan (R)

Elected 1998, term expires Jan. 2003; b. Feb. 24, 1934, Maquoketa, IA; home, Springfield; Butler U. 1952, Ferris State Col., B.S., 1961; Methodist; married (Lura Lynn).

Military Career: Army, 1954–56 (Korea).

Elected Office: Kankakee Cnty. Bd., 1966–72; IL House of Reps., 1972–82, Minority Ldr., 1977–81, Speaker, 1981–82; IL Lt. Gov., 1982–90; IL Secy. of State, 1990–98.

Professional Career: Pharmacist & co-owner, family pharmacy, 1962–90.

Office: 207 State House, Springfield, 62706, 217-782-6830; Fax: 217-524-1676; Web site: www.state.il.us.

Election Results

1998 gen.	George H. Ryan (R)	1,714,094	(51%)
	Glenn Poshard (D)	1,594,191	(47%)
	Others	50,420	(2%)
1998 prim.	George H. Ryan (R)	608,940	(86%)
	Chad Koppie (R)	98,466	(14%)
1994 gen.	Jim Edgar (R)	1,984,318	(64%)
	Dawn Clark Netsch (D)	1,069,850	(34%)
	Others	52,398	(2%)

SENATORS

Sen. Richard J. Durbin (D)

Elected 1996, seat up 2002; b. Nov. 21, 1944, E. St. Louis; home, Springfield; Georgetown U., B.S. 1966, J.D. 1969; Catholic; married (Loretta).

Elected Office: U.S. House of Reps., 1982–96.

Professional Career: Staff, Lt. Gov. Paul Simon, 1969–72; Legal Cnsl., IL Sen. Judiciary Cmte., 1972–82; Prof., S. IL Schl. of Medicine, 1978–82.

DC Office: RSOB, 20510, 202-224-2152; Fax: 202-228-1374; Web site: www.senate.gov/~durbin.

State Offices: Chicago, 312-353-4952; Marion, 618-998-8812; Springfield, 217-492-4062.

Committees: *Appropriations* (13th of 13 D): Agriculture & Rural Development; Defense; District of Columbia (RMM); Legislative Branch. *Budget* (10th of 10 D). *Ethics (Select)* (3d of 3 D). *Governmental Affairs* (4th of 7 D): Government Management, Restructuring and the District of Columbia (RMM); Investigations (Permanent).

Group Ratings

	ADA	ACLU	AFS	LCV	CON	NTU	NFIB	COC	ACU	NTLC	CHC
1998	95	86	100	100	7	11	33	50	8	3	0
1997	100	—	100	—	40	17	—	40	4	—	—

National Journal Ratings

	1997 LIB — 1997 CONS			1998 LIB — 1998 CONS		
Economic	90%	—	6%	90%	—	0%
Social	71%	—	0%	74%	—	0%
Foreign	83%	—	14%	79%	—	15%

Key Votes of the 105th Congress

1. Bal. Budget Amend.	N	5. Satcher for Surgeon Gen.	Y	9. Chem. Weapons Treaty	Y
2. Clinton Budget Deal	N	6. Highway Set-asides	Y	10. Cuban Humanitarian Aid	Y
3. Cloture on Tobacco	Y	7. Table Child Gun locks	N	11. Table Bosnia Troops	N
4. Education IRAs	N	8. Ovrd. Part. Birth Veto	N	12. $ for Test-ban Treaty	Y

Election Results

1996 general	Richard J. Durbin (D)	2,384,028	(56%)	($4,966,804)
	Al Salvi (R)	1,728,824	(41%)	($4,696,065)
	Others	137,870	(3%)	
1996 primary	Richard J. Durbin (D)	512,520	(65%)	
	Pat Quinn (D)	233,138	(30%)	
	Others	44,397	(6%)	
1990 general	Paul Simon (D)	2,115,377	(65%)	($8,665,789)
	Lynn Martin (R)	1,135,628	(35%)	($4,921,613)

Sen. Peter G. Fitzgerald (R)

Elected 1998, seat up 2004; b. Oct. 20, 1960, Elgin; home, Inverness; Dartmouth Col., A.B. 1982, U. of MI Law Schl., J.D. 1986; Catholic; married (Nina).

Elected Office: IL Senate, 1992–98.

Professional Career: Practicing atty., 1986–96.

DC Office: 555 DSOB, 20510, 202-224-2854; Fax: 202-228-1372; Web site: www.senate.gov/~fitzgerald.

State Offices: Chicago, 312-886-3506; Springfield, 217-492-5089.

Committees: *Agriculture, Nutrition & Forestry* (7th of 10 R): Forestry, Conservation & Rural Revitalization; Research, Nutrition & General Legislation (Chmn.). *Energy & Natural Resources* (9th of 11 R): Energy, Research, Development, Production & Regulation; Forests & Public Land Management. *Small Business* (7th of 10 R).

Group Ratings and Key Votes: Newly Elected

Election Results

1998 general	Peter G. Fitzgerald (R)	1,709,041	(50%)	($17,678,198)
	Carol Moseley-Braun (D)	1,610,496	(47%)	($7,200,895)
	Others	74,984	(2%)	
1998 primary	Peter G. Fitzgerald (R)	372,916	(52%)	
	Loleta Didrickson (R)	346,606	(48%)	
1992 general	Carol Moseley-Braun (D)	2,631,229	(53%)	($6,699,942)
	Richard S. Williamson (R)	2,126,833	(43%)	($2,300,924)
	Others	181,496	(4%)	

FIRST DISTRICT

The South Side of Chicago has been the nation's largest urban black community for nearly a century now. At first there were just a few blocks where black families from the South would settle; this ghetto grew rapidly with the first influx of blacks from the Mississippi Delta in the 1910s. By the 1920s, the South Side was well established, a center of blues music in America and of black-owned businesses. Politically, the South Side was a heavily Republican constituency throughout those years; the comfortable white Protestants who settled in solid brick houses here believed in the party of Yankee propriety, and the blacks had faith in the party of Lincoln. This was one of the heartlands of the Republican Party, represented in Congress by Republican Minority Leader James R. Mann, and then Appropriations Chairman Martin Madden. After Madden died in the Appropriations Committee room in 1928, the 1st District elected Oscar DePriest, the first black elected to the House in the 20th Century. Blacks remained faithful to the party of Lincoln even during the Depression, voting for Herbert Hoover and DePriest in 1932.

The New Deal and the racial liberalism of New Dealers like Eleanor Roosevelt and Interior Secretary Harold Ickes (a former Chicago Republican himself) attracted blacks to the Democratic Party, and DePriest was beaten by a black Democrat in 1934. The South Side has been Democratic ever since. For 40 years, it was a cooperative part of Chicago's Democratic machine; then, after the death of longtime Congressman William Dawson, it rebelled against Mayor Richard J. Daley. The South Side seemed to take over the city when Congressman Harold Washington was elected mayor in 1983 and 1987. But control of political office does not mean what it once did. Patronage jobs became fewer as a result of court decisions. After

Washington died in November 1987, other South Side black politicians flailed at each other, even though Chicago's electorate is only 40% black and a black candidate needs non-black voters to win.

The 1st Congressional District of Illinois includes about half of Chicago's South Side black community within its oddly shaped boundaries. It also extends out into the suburbs, and is no longer the nation's highest-percentage black district, but is by most measures Illinois's most Democratic. It includes the Gothic spires of the University of Chicago and the mansions of Kenwood, once the home of Chicago's Jewish aristocracy and more recently the headquarters of the Nation of Islam and home to its leader, Louis Farrakhan. Miles and miles of the district are made up of bungalow neighborhoods, with single-family houses lining arrow-straight streets. Many of these neighborhoods have shown signs of vitality and growth in recent years. Citizens have banded together to fight crime using high-sodium streetlights and roadblocks. The South Shore Development Bank, much touted by Bill Clinton, has provided loans to minority business owners.

The 1st District's odd shape follows historic patterns: the eastern half of the district roughly approximates the boundaries of 1st Districts going back to the 1960s; the western half, to which it is connected by a strip a mile wide, has some all-black neighborhoods, but also includes the higher-income Irish-American neighborhoods of Morgan Park and Beverly, where the annual South Side Irish St. Patrick's Day Parade is held. It goes as far south as the industrial suburbs of Alsip and Blue Island.

The congressman from the 1st District is a man who has gone through several transformations. Bobby Rush grew up on the North Side, a Boy Scout whose mother was a Republican precinct captain. In the Army, he became involved in the Student Non-Violent Coordinating Committee in the South, then founded the Illinois Black Panthers, where he recruited Fred Hampton, later killed in a raid by police in 1969. Rush served six months in prison for illegal possession of firearms, but also during his time with the Black Panthers he had run a medical clinic which developed the nation's first mass sickle cell anemia testing program. "I don't repudiate any of my involvement in the Panther party—it was part of my maturing," he has since said. In 1983, he was elected 2d Ward alderman and became a strong Harold Washington supporter; after 1989, he worked amicably with Mayor Richard M. Daley as well. In 1992, with the district expanded, he challenged incumbent Congressman Charles Hayes, an older generation politician with a union background. Just before the March 1992 primary it was revealed that Hayes had 716 overdrafts on the House bank. In a big primary turnout of 128,000, Rush beat Hayes 42%–39%, carrying eight of 12 black wards plus Morgan Park and Beverly, where many white police veterans live and where Rush was helped by House Speaker and 13th Ward Committeeman Michael Madigan.

Rush's rhetoric has toned down over the years. "Most African-Americans just want a comfortable, middle-class lifestyle," he said in 1992. "Twenty-five years ago, I didn't know that." On crime, he said, "Blacks are killing blacks. Young blacks are killing other young blacks. We don't need to make excuses for our young people. We need to challenge them." He called for laws to reduce crime in high schools, increase youth employment and establish community-based organizations, articulating surely the yearnings of constituents struggling to keep safe neighborhoods where they can raise their families and work their way up.

In the House, Rush has a liberal voting record and a seat on the Commerce Committee; he served on the conference committee on telecom. He voted for the securities litigation reform bill that was passed over President Clinton's veto. On locally oriented issues, he sought to ban handguns in housing projects and to get federal penalties for drug dealing near schools. He sponsored a bill to ban handguns except for law enforcement and increase the licensing fee for gun dealers from $10 to $3,000. But he has also been willing to protest what he considers injustice. He was so angry that Bill Clinton signed the 1996 welfare bill that he would have thrown away his delegate credential for the 1996 Democratic National Convention but for his wife's urging. In May 1997 he called the requirement of community service for public housing tenants "involuntary servitude." In 1998 he attacked Chicago's anti-gang loitering law as "police state tactics [that] make scapegoats and criminals of innocent people."

This protest politics presumably is due to his ambition to be mayor. He was thinking about running in 1995, but in October 1994 his Republican opponent crashed a press conference and accused him of owing $55,000 in back taxes; this was a civil case, and he was in the process of paying off arrears. In 1998 he was re-elected routinely. Three weeks later he announced he was running against Mayor Richard M. Daley, and criticized him for police brutality and CTA service cuts. Two House colleagues—Jesse Jackson Jr. and Danny Davis—were at his announcement, but none of the 50 aldermen; many had been appointed by Daley to fill vacancies and he worked with almost all of them on local projects. Rush insisted that he wanted to build a multiracial coalition, but for practical purposes his only chance was with black voters, and not all of them supported him. Daley's record was simply too popular and his financial advantage overwhelming. Daley won the February election by 72%–28%, winning 45% of the black vote, an achievement that reflects more on his record than on Rush. It is not clear whether Rush will run for mayor again, but he seems safe in the 1st District seat.

Cook's Call. *Safe.* Rush is sitting in what must be among the half dozen or so most Democratic districts in the nation. Suffice it to say, Rush will be safe in 2000.

The People: Pop. 1990: 571,908; 14.7% age 65 +; 27.3% White, 69.6% Black, 1.1% Asian, 0.1% Amer. Indian, 1.9% Other; 3.5% Hispanic Origin. Households: 34% married couple families; 15.8% married couple fams. w. children; 45% college educ.; median household income: $24,140; per capita income: $11,709; median house value: $73,100; median gross rent: $361.

1996 Presidential Vote		
Clinton (D)	179,767	(85%)
Dole (R)	22,914	(11%)
Perot (I)	6,378	(3%)

1992 Presidential Vote		
Clinton (D)	214,104	(81%)
Bush (R)	32,803	(12%)
Perot (I)	17,355	(7%)

Rep. Bobby Rush (D)

Elected 1992; b. Nov. 23, 1946, Albany, GA; home, Chicago; Roosevelt U., B.A. 1973, U. of IL, M.A. 1994, McCormick Seminary, M.A. 1998; Baptist; married (Carolyn).

Military Career: Army, 1963–68.

Elected Office: Chicago City Alderman, 1983–92; 2nd Ward Committeeman, 1984–present.

Professional Career: Member, Student Non-Violent Coord. Cmte., 1966–68; Co-founder, IL Black Panther Party, 1968; Med. Clinic Dir., 1970–1973.

DC Office: 2416 RHOB 20515, 202-225-4372; Fax: 202-226-0333; Web site: www.house.gov/rush.

District Offices: Chicago, 773-224-6500; Evergreen Park, 708-422-4055.

Committees: *Commerce* (11th of 24 D): Energy & Power; Finance & Hazardous Materials; Telecommunications, Trade & Consumer Protection.

Group Ratings

	ADA	ACLU	AFS	LCV	CON	NTU	NFIB	COC	ACU	NTLC	CHC
1998	95	87	100	92	55	20	7	33	8	5	0
1997	100	—	100	—	8	23	—	40	4	—	—

National Journal Ratings

	1997 LIB — 1997 CONS			1998 LIB — 1998 CONS		
Economic	79%	—	18%	72%	—	23%
Social	78%	—	22%	85%	—	14%
Foreign	97%	—	0%	96%	—	2%

Key Votes of the 105th Congress

1. Clinton Budget Deal	N	5. Puerto Rico Sthood. Ref.	N	9. Cut $ for B-2 Bombers	Y
2. Education IRAs	N	6. End Highway Set-asides	N	10. Human Rights in China	Y
3. Req. 2/3 to Raise Taxes	N	7. School Prayer Amend.	N	11. Withdraw Bosnia Troops	N
4. Fast-track Trade	N	8. Ovrd. Part. Birth Veto	N	12. End Cuban TV-Marti	Y

Election Results

1998 general	Bobby Rush (D)	151,890	(87%)	($243,587)
	Marlene White Ahimaz (R)	18,429	(11%)	
	Others	4,046	(2%)	
1998 primary	Bobby Rush (D)	85,696	(89%)	
	Caleb A. Davis Jr. (D)	10,785	(11%)	
1996 general	Bobby Rush (D)	174,005	(86%)	($156,219)
	Noel Naughton (R)	25,659	(13%)	($20,220)
	Others	3,449	(2%)	

SECOND DISTRICT

Chicago is a great center of both commerce and industry, and if its white collar offices are heavily concentrated in the Loop, its blue collar heavy industries are most visible on the far South Side. This heavy industry Chicago, diminished in importance economically today, is historically significant and, with the remnants of its great hulking factories around Lake Calumet and the nearby rail yards, has a certain undeniable majesty. Thomas Geoghegan, who writes more poetically than a lawyer ought to be able to, has told in his book, *Which Side Are You On?*, of the fights to wrest severance benefits and pension rights for the workers whose steel mills shut down, of the decline in the labor movement in a place where it got much of its inspiration. This is where the Pullman strike of 1894 was broken by federal troops and where policemen killed 10 union supporters in the Little Steel strike of 1937. Over the years, Chicago grew around the tight ethnic neighborhoods where workers went home at shift break each afternoon or midnight; today, they are mostly empty buildings that suburbanites speed by on the Calumet and Dan Ryan Expressways.

The 2d Congressional District includes much of Chicago's old South Side industrial area plus many suburbs to the south. About two-thirds of its people live in Chicago, in widely separated neighborhoods. Some are in the old factory towns around Lake Calumet, some in the once heavily Jewish South Shore neighborhood, some in black wards west of Halsted Street. The Chicago portion of the 2d is overwhelmingly black; many blacks, especially young parents fleeing Chicago public schools, are moving into suburbs directly to the south—Harvey, Dolton, Posen (a reminder of its Polish origin), Markham. Farther south are Homewood and Flossmoor, with significant Jewish populations, high-income Olympia Fields, the planned town of Park Forest, and Chicago Heights, home town of America's premier political reporter for three decades now, David Broder. Two-thirds of the district's voters are black, and most are middle class.

The congressman from the 2d District is Jesse Jackson Jr., a Democrat first elected in December 1995, and son of civil rights activist and 1984 and 1988 presidential candidate Jesse Jackson. Jesse Jackson Jr. was born in Greenville, South Carolina, while his father was marching to Selma; he went to St. Albans School in Washington (as did Vice President Al Gore), then to North Carolina A&T (as did his father), and got a masters degree at Chicago Theological Seminary and a law degree at the University of Illinois. He worked for his father's Rainbow Coalition and did not run for office until the spectacular rise and fall of 2d District Congressman Mel Reynolds, who was hailed nationally when he defeated the anti-Semitic Gus Savage in the 1992 primary and then disgraced when he was convicted and sentenced to five years in prison for having sexual relations with a teenage campaign worker. When Reynolds announced he would resign, Jackson promptly decided to run. He faced serious opposition in Emil Jones, a 23-year legislator and state Senate minority leader who had the support of Mayor Richard M. Daley and two other legislators. Jones boasted of his clout and political experience; Jackson said being his father's son was a lifetime of political experience. He talked of bringing dollars to the South Side and, echoing the argument Dan Rostenkowski made to Mayor Richard J. Daley in 1957, said, "The only way one grows into leadership in Congress is to get elected young enough that you become speaker of the House or chairman of the Ways and Means Committee." The November 1995 primary was a close contest, but Jackson won with 46% to Jones's 37%; a state legislator endorsed by Louis Farrakhan and Gus Savage won only 2%. Jackson easily won the special general election with 76%.

In office, Jackson has combined advocacy of liberal positions with careful attention to the interests of his district. He called for a law to create full employment through job training and a single-payer universal health care system—both nonstarters even in a Democratic Congress. He bitterly opposed the 1997 budget agreement. He opposed requiring eight hours per month community service by public housing tenants—"Will picking cotton qualify?" he caustically asked. In 1997 he criticized Bill Clinton's race initiative as "race entertainment." He said Clinton's proposal to apologize for slavery was a "valid . . . symbolic act" but was not enough. In a 10-page dear-colleague letter he called Promise Keepers a "political Trojan horse" designed to split minority voters from the Democratic Party. He showed much the same suspicion of assertions of military power as his father did in the 1980s: "The drumbeat and path to war here in Washington is reaching insane proportions," he said as Clinton confronted Iraq in February 1998. He opposed the Crane-Rangel Africa trade bill in March 1998, saying that he feared exploitation of African workers, and proposed an alternative HOPE for Africa Act in February 1999. Some of his stands defy categorization. He joined Budget Chairman John Kasich to oppose reauthorization of the Overseas Private Investment Corporation as "corporate welfare" and co-sponsored the $18 billion IMF replenishment.

Jackson worked on local projects, notably on flooding and the unpotable water supply in Ford Heights; he took advantage of funding formulas and found Agriculture Department money for a water tower, pump house and water mains. His great cause has been the building of a third Chicago area airport in Peotone, 45 miles south of the Loop and just south of the 2d District along Interstate 57. He sees it as an economic development project: "The point is, the third airport will provide 236,000 jobs . . . on the South Side and in the south suburbs. . . . It means a livable wage and union jobs. It means school funding." This fight has pitted him against fellow Democrats, including Congressman William Lipinski, the great protector of Midway Airport in his 3d District, and Mayor Richard M. Daley, the great protector of O'Hare; his allies have included Republicans like former Governor Jim Edgar, who first suggested Peotone, Congressman Henry Hyde, who is worried about O'Hare noise over his suburban 6th District, and Governor George Ryan. In the 1998 gubernatorial race, Jackson refused to endorse Democrat Glenn Poshard, who opposed Peotone, and made friendly noises about Ryan.

Jackson has been mentioned as a candidate for higher office but seems bent on remaining in the House. "I told the people of my district I'd be their member of Congress for as long as they'll have me," he said in 1998. He has taken pains to be on good personal terms with Republicans, and, in the December 1996 Democratic Caucus, delivered a stirring speech for "one more term" for 80-year-old Banking ranking Democrat Henry Gonzalez, which helped persuade John LaFalce to withdraw his candidacy after the first ballot. In the 1998 cycle he campaigned intensively for 30 House Democratic colleagues. He became ranking Democrat on a Small Business subcommittee in March 1997 and in December 1998 won a seat on Appropriations.

In the 1999 mayor's race, Jackson endorsed his House colleague Bobby Rush with considerable enthusiasm, but also made a point of saying nice things about Mayor Richard M. Daley, who was re-elected easily in February: "As you know, this Mayor Daley has issued no 'shoot to kill' orders. This Mayor Daley has positioned African-Americans on the School Board, in the Police Department . . . and has done a fairly decent job of fighting to include more African-Americans at every level of his administration." Middle-class blacks, the heart of Jackson's constituency, are moving in large numbers from Chicago to the suburbs, which reduces his core constituency for some future race for mayor, and redistricting after the 2000 Census may make this a mostly suburban district. His advocacy of the Peotone airport suggests Jackson has anticipated this and is set on representing a mostly-suburban, mostly-black district for some time.

Cook's Call. *Safe.* Like Bobby Rush's 1st District, Jackson enjoys a commandingly Democratic district. He is a sure bet in 2000.

The People: Pop. 1990: 572,188; 0.2% rural; 10% age 65 + ; 27.3% White, 68.4% Black, 0.5% Asian, 0.2% Amer. Indian, 3.7% Other; 6.4% Hispanic Origin. Households: 45% married couple families; 23.9% married couple fams. w. children; 41.7% college educ.; median household income: $30,217; per capita income: $11,468; median house value: $65,000; median gross rent: $368.

1996 Presidential Vote

Clinton (D) 170,819 (85%)
Dole (R) 22,204 (11%)
Perot (I) 6,395 (3%)

1992 Presidential Vote

Clinton (D) 194,639 (80%)
Bush (R) 31,634 (13%)
Perot (I) 16,950 (7%)

Rep. Jesse Jackson, Jr. (D)

Elected Dec. 1995; b. Mar. 11, 1965, Greenville, SC; home, Chicago; NC A&T, B.S. 1987, Chicago Theological Seminary, M.A. 1990, U. of IL, J.D. 1993; Baptist; married (Sandra).

Professional Career: Civil rights activist; Pres., Keep Hope Alive PAC, 1989–90; V.P., Operation PUSH 1991–95; Field Dir., Natl. Rainbow Coalition 1993–95.

DC Office: 313 CHOB 20515, 202-225-0773; Fax: 202-225-0899; Web site: www.jessejacksonjr.org.

District Office: Homewood, 708-798-6000.

Committees: *Appropriations* (25th of 27 D): Foreign Operations & Export Financing; Labor, HHS & Education.

Group Ratings

	ADA	ACLU	AFS	LCV	CON	NTU	NFIB	COC	ACU	NTLC	CHC
1998	100	94	100	100	55	20	0	22	8	0	0
1997	100	—	100	—	3	24	—	20	4	—	—

National Journal Ratings

	1997 LIB	—	1997 CONS	1998 LIB	—	1998 CONS
Economic	85%	—	10%	72%	—	23%
Social	85%	—	0%	93%	—	0%
Foreign	97%	—	0%	78%	—	19%

Key Votes of the 105th Congress

1. Clinton Budget Deal	N	5. Puerto Rico Sthood. Ref.	Y	9. Cut $ for B-2 Bombers	Y
2. Education IRAs	N	6. End Highway Set-asides	N	10. Human Rights in China	Y
3. Req. 2/3 to Raise Taxes	N	7. School Prayer Amend.	N	11. Withdraw Bosnia Troops	N
4. Fast-track Trade	N	8. Ovrd. Part. Birth Veto	N	12. End Cuban TV-Marti	Y

Election Results

1998 general	Jesse L. Jackson Jr. (D)	148,985	(89%)	($245,478)
	Robert Gordon III (R)	16,075	(10%)	
	Others	1,608	(1%)	
1998 primary	Jesse L. Jackson Jr. (D)	unopposed		
1996 general	Jesse L. Jackson Jr. (D)	172,648	(94%)	($260,163)
	Frank H. Stratman (Lib)	10,880	(6%)	

THIRD DISTRICT

A century ago, Finley Peter Dunne's fictional Mr. Dooley pontificated on matters political in a saloon on Archer Avenue. This was, and is, Archer Avenue on the South Side of Chicago, one of the radial streets that cuts across what was once open prairie near the Loop and out the Chicago River and the Chicago and Sanitary Ship Canal. Archer Avenue was one of the paths of outward migration and upward mobility for the children and grandchildren of Chicago's various ethnic and cultural groups, and still is. Italians from the river wards along the Canal moved west; the South Side Irish moved west and south along Cicero Avenue toward Oak Lawn; the Bohemians (as they were called then, now Czechs) were heavily concentrated in the neat bungalows of the industrial suburbs of Berwyn and Cicero, famous as a haven for Al Capone's mobsters in the 1920s. Cicero has continued to be plagued by gang activity, and in April 1999, Cicero's town board passed an ordinance giving gang members 60 days to leave its working class streets—the nation's first gang-eviction law. The town board followed up the ordinance with lawsuits filed in May 1999, declaring two major gangs public nuisances and claiming $11 million in property damage and emotional distress. Today, Latinos are driving these same avenues, up before dawn to arrive at large factories and small, or heading to the Loop on the CTA or to edge city jobs out the expressways or the Tollway, then home to old bungalows carefully refurbished and tended by kids home from school.

The 3d Congressional District of Illinois consists of much of this territory, criss-crossed by the Canal, the radial streets and the railroad lines and switching yards so common in this, the center of the nation's rail network. It includes the far west edge of Chicago and most of Cicero and Berwyn; Riverside, with its early 20th Century prairie-style houses; a few older affluent suburbs like Western Springs and the more recent and middle-income expanses of Oak Lawn and Palos Heights. Politically, this is marginal territory. Ancestral political preferences are mostly Democratic, but this is a culturally conservative area, with a sense of patriotism; Cicero, hostile to blacks in the 1960s, is now growing with an influx of Hispanic families. This is an area with a strong Democratic machine tradition and a deep faith in traditional values.

The congressman from the 3d District, Democrat William Lipinski, grew up in southwest Chicago, started off as a patronage employee with the Parks District, was elected 23d Ward alderman and ward committeeman in 1975; he still holds the latter position in the ward that includes Midway Airport and Chicago's westernmost stretch of Archer Avenue. He ran for Congress and beat an aging incumbent in the 1982 primary 61%–36%. His credo: "I know the people of the 3d District—what they believe in, what they want for their future and their children's future. . . . I have never been so involved in what was happening in Washington that I lost sight of my constituents and their needs."

Lipinski's views on issues seem to mirror those of his constituents. He is anti-abortion, supported the partial-birth abortion ban and lobbied to have the 1996 Democratic platform include "toleration" of anti-abortion views. He was strongly against gays in the military and for the Defense of Marriage Act. He favors the death penalty and opposed NAFTA, GATT and fast track. He was one of the few Democrats for vouchers for poor children in Washington, D.C., and for tax-free education savings accounts. He called for lifting the 750,000 ceiling on medical savings accounts. He was one of 30 Democrats to vote for the Republican welfare reform. He was proud of the passage of his amendment, co-sponsored by two Republicans, denying welfare benefits to fugitive criminals (previously, it barred benefits only to those in jail; those who escaped were entitled). He supported restrictions on welfare for legal immigrants, but also got an amendment to help 832 refugees, who had left Poland and Hungary before fall 1989, gain permanent resident status. He helped write the flag burning amendment, which passed 310–114 in June 1997: "The flag, being the symbol of American freedom and ideas, ought to be protected with the same vigor with which we protect the very freedoms and rights it represents."

Lipinski is on the Transportation Committee and is ranking Democrat on the Aviation Subcommittee. He is a staunch advocate of Midway Airport, which generates more jobs than any other site in the 3d District. He supported Mayor Richard M. Daley's $3 per passenger charge but insisted that the money be used to upgrade Midway and O'Hare, not used to start a third airport in Peotone, 45 miles south of Chicago; part of that money has been used for rehabilitating Midway and rebuilding its terminal. In 1996 he kept Jesse Jackson Jr., a strong backer of Peotone, off the Transportation Committee for that reason. On other aviation issues, he opposed the naming of Washington National Airport for Ronald Reagan (but said he'd vote to put him on Mount Rushmore), called for requiring FAA and Department of Justice approval of airline alliances and congressional approval of international aviation agreements, sought tougher scrutiny of foreign repair certification and called for studying the need for defibrillators on airliners. He favors the policy of limiting carry-ons to one item.

Lipinski secured about $50 million for projects for the Chicago area and the district in the 1998 transportation bill. He is proud of his work to complete the CTA Orange Line and reconstruction of the CTA Blue Line Douglas branch, to rebuild the Stevenson Expressway and Lower Wacker Drive. In 1998 he forced disclosure of the Navy's route to ship by rail napalm supplies from San Diego to East Chicago, Indiana; lo and behold, a new route was adopted that avoided the 3d District, and in the end the napalm was turned around in Kansas and sent back to California. In the 1996 FAA reauthorization he included a provision allowing local communities to regulate train whistles; it may not sound like much, but when your district has (probably) the largest number of freight yards and surface crossings in the nation and whistle-blowing is mandatory, you will hear about it.

Lipinski is often out of line with the national Democratic Party and sometimes with Mayor Richard M. Daley, and is a close ally with Michael Madigan, who is speaker of the Illinois House, but, perhaps more important, 13th Ward committeeman, just south of the 23d. "Unless the ethnic position is listened to and we're not looked upon as outsiders," Lipinski once warned, "I think that there will be an even greater exodus from the Democratic Party among ethnic voters." From March 1997 he supported the gubernatorial candidacy of Glenn Poshard, his Downstate conservative colleague, and helped him win the Democratic nomination; despite his efforts Poshard lost to George Ryan 51%–47%, but Poshard did carry the 23d Ward in both the primary and general. Lipinski took a stern attitude toward Bill Clinton in 1998. He was one of 31 Democrats to vote for the Republican impeachment inquiry in October 1998 and only the day before the final vote said he "unfortunately" would not vote for impeachment.

Surprisingly, Lipinski had to fight hard to win re-election earlier in the decade. In 1992, redistricting put him in the same district with Democratic incumbent Marty Russo, a member of Ways and Means. Russo vastly outspent him (over $1 million to $375,000), but, with quiet support from Mayor Daley and an endorsement from the *Chicago Tribune* calling him "more important to the future of Illinois," Lipinski won 58%–37%. In 1994, Lipinski had serious competition from Republican Jim Nalepa, and in the anti-incumbent, anti-Democratic mood of that year, Lipinski won by just 54%–46%. In more pro-incumbent 1996, as Clinton was carrying the district easily, Lipinski beat Nalepa 65%–32%; in 1998 he defeated a radiologist 72%–28%.

Cook's Call. *Probably Safe.* Lipinski's past wins belie the fact that the 3d District is not reliably Democratic. As currently configured, the 61-year-old Lipinski can probably hold onto this seat as long as he wants, but, with too much change in the lines or when he steps aside, Republicans could have a shot here.

The People: Pop. 1990: 570,902; 16.9% age 65 + ; 93.3% White, 1.9% Black, 1.5% Asian, 0.2% Amer. Indian, 3.2% Other; 7.1% Hispanic Origin. Households: 57% married couple families; 25.7% married couple fams. w. children; 40.3% college educ.; median household income: $36,250; per capita income: $15,854; median house value: $92,800; median gross rent: $436.

1996 Presidential Vote

Clinton (D)	114,089	(53%)
Dole (R)	78,853	(37%)
Perot (I)	19,441	(9%)

1992 Presidential Vote

Clinton (D)	108,342	(41%)
Bush (R)	102,632	(39%)
Perot (I)	52,905	(20%)

Rep. William Lipinski (D)

Elected 1982; b. Dec. 22, 1937, Chicago; home, Chicago; Loras Col., 1956–57; Catholic; married (Rose Marie).

Military Career: Army Reserves, 1961–67.

Elected Office: Chicago City Alderman, 1975–83; Committeeman, 23d Ward, 1975–present.

Professional Career: Chicago Parks & Recreation Dept., 1958–75.

DC Office: 1501 LHOB 20515, 202-225-5701; Fax: 202-225-1012.

District Offices: Chicago, 312-886-0481; LaGrange, 708-352-0524; Oak Lawn, 708-952-0860.

Committees: *Transportation & Infrastructure* (4th of 34 D): Aviation (RMM); Ground Transportation.

Group Ratings

	ADA	ACLU	AFS	LCV	CON	NTU	NFIB	COC	ACU	NTLC	CHC
1998	45	0	67	62	68	18	29	50	48	32	64
1997	40	—	75	—	38	33	—	40	46	—	—

National Journal Ratings

	1997 LIB — 1997 CONS			1998 LIB — 1998 CONS		
Economic	60%	—	39%	54%	—	45%
Social	44%	—	56%	36%	—	63%
Foreign	48%	—	51%	39%	—	61%

Key Votes of the 105th Congress

1. Clinton Budget Deal	Y	5. Puerto Rico Sthood. Ref.	N	9. Cut $ for B-2 Bombers	*
2. Education IRAs	Y	6. End Highway Set-asides	N	10. Human Rights in China	Y
3. Req. 2/3 to Raise Taxes	N	7. School Prayer Amend.	Y	11. Withdraw Bosnia Troops	*
4. Fast-track Trade	N	8. Ovrd. Part. Birth Veto	Y	12. End Cuban TV-Marti	N

Election Results

1998 general	William Lipinski (D)	115,887	(72%)	($326,204)
	Robert Marshall (R)	44,012	(28%)	($100,518)
1998 primary	William Lipinski (D)	unopposed		
1996 general	William Lipinski (D)	137,153	(65%)	($455,967)
	Jim Nalepa (R)	67,214	(32%)	($202,334)
	Others	5,549	(3%)	

FOURTH DISTRICT

Just west of the Loop, the Chicago River splits into North and South branches, both penetrating the heart of old neighborhoods where immigrants fresh off the boat first got their start in Chicago. The South Branch is the guts of Chicago, the site of one of Western civilization's astonishing engineering feats: here in 1900, the course of the river was reversed so that sewage flowed Downstate through a canal rather than out into Lake Michigan. Just blocks away was Maxwell Street, thronged with market stalls (now closed), long the arrival neighborhood for Chicago's Jews; not far away, in an Italian-American neighborhood on Halsted Street, was Jane Addams's Hull House, the original settlement house, where social workers told new immigrants not how to rebel against middle-class American mores but how to live them. To the south were Bridgeport, home of the Irish and of the mayors of Chicago from 1933–79 and again from 1989 until recently, when the Daleys moved to the South Loop, and Pilsen, arrival neighborhood for the Bohemians (Czechs). Off the North Branch of the River was Milwaukee Avenue, the main street of Polish-Americans and Ukrainian-Americans for a century now.

Today, many of these places are arrival neighborhoods again, mostly for Chicago's wide variety of Hispanic immigrants. On the South Side, in the old river wards, is Chicago's Mexican-American community, extending west into the once Bohemian suburb of Cicero; on the North Side are many Puerto Ricans and other Hispanics. Altogether, the 1990 Census counted 545,000 Hispanics in Chicago, by far the largest Latino concentration north of Texas and Florida and between the two coasts. They have been attracted, as immigrants were 100 years ago, by a vibrant economy that provides opportunity to those who work hard, and by a culture which can be portrayed as unwelcoming only because of its own high standards.

The 4th Congressional District of Illinois is the Hispanic-majority district which was deemed mandatory under the Voting Rights Act amendments of 1982. The problem was that the South Side Mexican-American and the North Side Puerto Rican communities were separated by the West Side black ghetto. The solution was today's 4th Congressional District, with arguably the most convoluted shape of any district in the country. Essentially these two Latino communities, defined by erose boundaries to maximize the Hispanic percentage, are connected by a thin line of territory which stretches around the West Side black-majority 7th District to meet at the Cook-DuPage County line. Most of this salient consists of parkland, railroad yards and cemeteries; more than 95% of the votes are in Chicago or Cicero. Even so, Hispanics may not be a voting majority here, though they included about 58% of voting-age residents in 1990 and some larger percentage today.

Not surprisingly, the lines came under challenge in court. In November 1996 the Supreme Court sent the case back to a three-judge federal district court, which in August 1997 ruled the lines in order; in January 1998 three Supreme Court justices, but not the required four, voted to hear the appeal. The filing deadline had already passed for the 1998 election, and one wonders whether the judges, a bit weary of these cases, just decided to let the lines stay in place for two more elections and wait for the issue to arise again—if it does—after the redistricting following the 2000 Census.

The congressman from the 4th District since it was created has been Democrat Luis Gutierrez. He is of Puerto Rican descent, grew up in Chicago and lived two years in Puerto Rico as a teacher after college. Back in Chicago he worked as a cab driver and social worker. In

1983 he ran for 32d Ward committeeman against Dan Rostenkowski (who with his father had held the post for more than 50 years), and lost. Then he became a staffer for Mayor Harold Washington, ran for alderman in 1984 and lost, then ran again in 1986 in one of two new Hispanic-majority seats. He and Juan Soliz won—crucial victories that gave Washington a majority on the City Council for the first time. Then Washington died in November 1987 and, in the 1989 election to succeed him, Gutierrez backed (and Soliz opposed) Richard M. Daley. For that, Gutierrez was richly rewarded: he became chairman of the Housing Committee and pushed through his "New Homes for Chicago" affordable housing plan. He also authored a bill prohibiting discrimination against gays and the disabled. In both cases, he helped Daley cement his support with crucial groups in the middle 20% of the electorate: Latinos and gays.

Another "payback," as Gutierrez called it, came in the 1992 race for the new 4th District. Gutierrez and Soliz were again rivals. Gutierrez called crime the number one problem and bragged of his council record; Soliz talked about trade and health care and called Gutierrez a machine candidate. Certainly Gutierrez seemed a multi-ethnic candidate: "There is a Hispanic agenda . . . it's the same as the Polish, Irish and Lithuanian agenda. If you work hard, sweat and toil and play by the rules, you will be rewarded . . . with clean streets, safer and better schools, the opportunity to send your kids to college. Tell me who in America and in the 4th Congressional District doesn't want these things?" Gutierrez won 60%–40%. The 1994 primary was a rematch and Gutierrez won again, 64%–36%; he has not had serious competition since. Gutierrez has a high profile in the district, running recycling drives, a Gutierrez Community Corps to paint out graffiti and citizenship enrollment meetings.

In the House, Gutierrez's in-your-face style has produced mixed results. His outspoken opposition to congressional pay raises and his appearance on a February 1994 *60 Minutes* broadcast, in which he called the House "the belly of the beast" and charged that the Democratic leadership stifled reform and that some freshmen Democrats "sold out," was not well received. "I've gotten my rear end kicked around here," Gutierrez told *The Washington Post*; a leadership staffer said Gutierrez "will never get a choice committee assignment" and "will always end up on the Banking Committee." He's still there. Gutierrez has staked out liberal positions on issues and has been more a commentator than a legislative craftsman. He called for setting aside $1.5 billion for AIDS research; the North Shore's John Porter, the generous appropriator for NIH, said no. He called for raising mass transit aid from $4.8 billion to $7 billion while Bud Shuster and others crafted the 1998 transportation bill. In a deft manuever, he criticized the Clinton Administration's national education testing standards, while praising those set by Daley and Chicago public schools CEO Paul Vallas. His move to limit public housing tenants' rental to 30% was brusquely rejected.

Gutierrez is chairman of the Hispanic Caucus task force on immigration and naturalization, and has cheered on efforts to restore food stamp eligibility and other benefits to legal immigrants; his own bill to restore all aid didn't pass. He opposed the INS's increase from $95 to $200 or more of the fee for processing applications as "a glaring example of the government imposing a higher price on its customers while continuing to offer inadequate and inefficient service." He supported measures to hold off deportation of illegal aliens from Haiti, Honduras, El Salvador and Guatemala by applying the rules for those from Nicaragua and Cuba; some temporary stays were adopted after Hurricane Mitch in fall 1998. In the debate on Don Young's bill authorizing a status referendum in Puerto Rico, Gutierrez took the lead for the opposition. He has long backed independence ("Puerto Rico is not just a territory, it is a nation"), a position favored by fewer than 3% of Puerto Ricans, and argued that Young's bill was tilted toward statehood. It passed 209–208 in March 1998, despite Gutierrez's attempt to switch votes at the last minute; but there was never any chance the Senate would take it up.

One preoccupation now must be redistricting. It is by no means clear that the courts will approve a similar-shaped district after the 2000 Census, and Gutierrez has already been thinking of alternatives; during the pendency of the suit against this district he was reported to have talked to Danny Davis of the 7th District about preparing a backup map. One possibility would be to join the North Side and South Side nodes of Hispanic neighborhoods and push Davis's black-majority district farther west; that would produce more compact districts, though presumably with lower Hispanic and black percentages. A crucial role could be played by Daley, who has been highly popular with Hispanic voters and would presumably like to maintain a Hispanic district.

Cook's Call. *Safe.* Since reconfigured to be a Hispanic district in 1992, Gutierrez has easily won and held this seat. Though the 4th will probably have to expand to make up for population loss, Gutierrez should be able to hold on to this seat for as long as he wants.

The People: Pop. 1990: 571,162; 8.1% age 65 +; 48.9% White, 6.2% Black, 2.6% Asian, 0.3% Amer. Indian, 42% Other; 64% Hispanic Origin. Households: 45.8% married couple families; 30.6% married couple fams. w. children; 23.5% college educ.; median household income: $23,083; per capita income: $8,352; median house value: $64,900; median gross rent: $308.

1996 Presidential Vote			1992 Presidential Vote		
Clinton (D)	82,225	(80%)	Clinton (D)	82,271	(65%)
Dole (R)	14,661	(14%)	Bush (R)	29,093	(23%)
Perot (I)	5,160	(5%)	Perot (I)	15,272	(12%)

Rep. Luis Gutierrez (D)

Elected 1992; b. Dec. 10, 1953, Chicago; home, Chicago; NE IL U., B.A. 1975; Catholic; married (Soraida).

Elected Office: Chicago City Alderman, 1986–92, Pres. Pro Tem, 1989–92.

Professional Career: Teacher, Puerto Rico, 1977–78; Social Wkr., Chicago Dept. of Children & Family Svcs., 1979–83; Advisor, Chicago Mayor Harold Washington, 1984–86.

DC Office: 2438 RHOB 20515, 202-225-8203; Fax: 202-225-7810; Web site: www.house.gov/gutierrez.

District Offices: Chicago, 773-579-0902; Chicago, 773-509-0999.

Committees: *Banking & Financial Services* (7th of 27 D): Financial Institutions & Consumer Credit; General Oversight & Investigations. *Veterans' Affairs* (3d of 14 D): Health (RMM).

Group Ratings

	ADA	ACLU	AFS	LCV	CON	NTU	NFIB	COC	ACU	NTLC	CHC
1998	90	87	100	92	48	18	0	28	16	8	0
1997	95	—	100	—	12	29	—	13	13	—	—

National Journal Ratings

	1997 LIB	—	1997 CONS	1998 LIB	—	1998 CONS
Economic	82%	—	15%	79%	—	0%
Social	81%	—	18%	85%	—	14%
Foreign	81%	—	18%	60%	—	40%

Key Votes of the 105th Congress

1. Clinton Budget Deal	N	5. Puerto Rico Sthood. Ref.	N	9. Cut $ for B-2 Bombers	Y
2. Education IRAs	N	6. End Highway Set-asides	N	10. Human Rights in China	Y
3. Req. 2/3 to Raise Taxes	N	7. School Prayer Amend.	N	11. Withdraw Bosnia Troops	*
4. Fast-track Trade	N	8. Ovrd. Part. Birth Veto	N	12. End Cuban TV-Marti	N

Election Results

1998 general	Luis Gutierrez (D) 54,244	(82%)	($349,887)
	John Birch (R) 10,529	(16%)	
	Others 1,583	(2%)	
1998 primary	Luis Gutierrez (D) .... unopposed		
1996 general	Luis Gutierrez (D) 85,278	(94%)	($261,252)
	William Passmore (Lib) 5,857	(6%)	

FIFTH DISTRICT

No place in America today has more variety—ethnic and cultural—than the North Side of Chicago. From the air, the geometric grid streets lit by high-sodium lamps seem monotonous; on the ground, on a winter's day with snow swirling, its brick buildings look stolid and forbidding. This has been the homeland of one immigrant group after another and the chosen neighborhoods of all manner of successful middle-class people. Wooden workingman's cottages from the late 19th Century give way to sturdy huge brick houses of the early 1900s and then to the prairie bungalows of the 1920s and white-shuttered, orange-brick colonials of the 1950s. Chicago was America's number one immigrant destination for Poles, Lithuanians, Czechs, Slovaks, Ukrainians and Romanians; something about the heavy dull clouds of the long winters, the short hot summers, a climate suited to potatoes and cabbage and other hardy vegetables, may have reminded them of central and eastern Europe. By the late 1980s, new upwardly mobile immigrants from Mexico and Guatemala, Korea and the Philippines, have moved in; the 1990s have seen immigrants from Poland and Ukraine, Pakistan and India. Family ties, webs of acquaintance that reach back to ancestral villages, have made the North Side of Chicago a natural port of entry for Eastern bloc migrants coming to America.

The 5th Congressional District of Illinois covers an oddly-shaped slice of Chicago's North Side, running from the Lakefront all the way to the suburbs directly south of O'Hare Airport. Its boundaries were carefully drawn to put most Hispanics in the 4th District just to the south, but otherwise it reflects the full variety of the North Side. It includes Chicago's most glamorous lakefront apartments facing the Oak Street beach and the gentrified neighborhoods of Old Town, where old houses and factories are being converted into upscale condominiums. It takes in the Polish-American and Ukrainian-American neighborhoods around Milwaukee Avenue, and the old Italian neighborhoods running west on Grand Avenue. It includes, a couple of blocks from the Chicago River, the old church of St. Stanislaus Kostka, a traditional center of the Polish community since the 19th Century, and the residence across Pulaski Park of Dan Rostenkowski, chairman of the House Ways and Means Committee from 1981 to 1995, for whom the district was originally designed.

The congressman from the 5th District now is Rod Blagojevich, a Democrat elected in 1996 over the Republican who upset Rostenkowski in 1994, Michael Flanagan. Blagojevich is of Serbian descent; he was a Golden Gloves boxer who graduated from Northwestern and Pepperdine Law School. He practiced law and worked two years in State's Attorney Richard M. Daley's office in the 1980s. In 1992 he was elected state Representative. Politics in Chicago is often a matter of genealogy, and it did not hurt that Blagojevich is the son-in-law of 33d Ward Alderman Dick Mell, one of the major powers in Chicago politics.

Blagojevich was surely as surprised as anyone when Flanagan beat Rostenkowski 54%–46%, and he immediately began eyeing this Democratic seat. Flanagan's record was mostly conservative, and he seemed to have few political skills and little institutional backing. Not surprisingly, Blagojevich had primary opposition, the strongest from state Representative Nancy Kaszak. They had similar records, except on the death penalty—Blagojevich blasted her for switching from opposition to endorsement. Blagojevich had Mell's organization, one of the more active ward operations in the city, and the backing of Mayor Daley; Kaszak had fundraising help from EMILY's List and roughly matched him in money. But Blagojevich had more votes, winning 50%–38%. In the general, Blagojevich focused on guns and tobacco, saying that Flanagan might as well be a lobbyist for the National Rifle Association and the American Tobacco Institute. To lakefront voters Blagojevich introduced himself as the pro-choice candidate; to others he promised to seek laws to help cities fight crime and gang violence. It was no contest: Clinton ran far ahead in this district, Blagojevich outspent and out-organized Flanagan, and the Democrat won by a 64%–36% margin.

In the House, Blagojevich has pushed for gun control legislation and made news by opposing napalm shipments through the Chicago area. He sponsored bills to require child-proof locks on handguns, to abolish the Civilian Marksmanship program and to require federal licenses for gun buyers at gun shows. He sponsored $10 million to get prosecutors to work in local neigh-borhoods on quality of life offenses, like graffiti. None of this passed the Republican Congress, but he was more successful on napalm. In December 1997 he heard of the Navy's plans to ship old napalm from San Diego to East Chicago, Indiana. He held a press conference at Canal Street and Roosevelt Road in January 1998, comparing napalm (which is less hazardous than many materials routinely shipped by rail) to Hiroshima-type nuclear bombs. The 3d District's William Lipinski got the shipping route changed so the train wouldn't go through his district; at the last minute, the train was turned back in Kansas and the napalm sent back to San Diego.

Blagojevich also serves on the Census Subcommittee, and has decried census undercounts and backed Census sampling. He opposed fast track and the B-2 stealth bomber. He remains a fine athlete, recruited for the Democratic team in the congressional baseball game. He continued to run marathons, even training during a congressional visit to 8,500-foot-high, heavily-air-polluted, narcoterrorist-threatened Bogota; a Coast Guard lieutenant detailed to accompany him on his run couldn't keep up. He said he was frustrated by having low seniority, but understands where he is in the Chicago political firmament: "I'm just a Congressman. In Chicago, I'm not even [as high up] as an Alderman yet." His political rank was certainly heightened in May 1999, however, when he traveled to Serbia with Jesse Jackson to successfully secure the release of three American POWs. Blagojevich, who used his Serbian-American contacts to set up the historic meeting with Milosevic, is fluent in Serbian and served as chief negotiator.

Blagojevich will surely be re-elected in 2000, but he must worry about redistricting in 2000. Illinois will probably lose one seat, and the 5th District, with its attenuated shape, could be carved up among its neighbors. One possibility would be to put the lakefront wards into the 9th District and to push the 5th north and west inland, which would reduce its Democratic percentage, but probably not fatally.

Cook's Call. *Safe.* The 1995–97 Republican hold on this reliably Democratic district was purely a fluke, and is unlikely to be replicated under these lines. Blagojevich should have no trouble holding onto this seat in 2000, but the district has been losing a lot of population and may be impacted by redistricting in 2001.

The People: Pop. 1990: 571,053; 15.9% age 65 + ; 86.9% White, 1.4% Black, 5.8% Asian, 0.2% Amer. Indian, 5.6% Other; 13.1% Hispanic Origin. Households: 42.5% married couple families; 18% married couple fams. w. children; 47.4% college educ.; median household income: $33,262; per capita income: $19,242; median house value: $109,900; median gross rent: $457.

1996 Presidential Vote		
Clinton (D)	120,132	(63%)
Dole (R)	56,532	(30%)
Perot (I)	12,915	(7%)

1992 Presidential Vote		
Clinton (D)	124,273	(51%)
Bush (R)	80,036	(33%)
Perot (I)	39,113	(16%)

The *Almanac* is now on the Web —

...........➤ with updates!

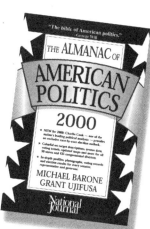
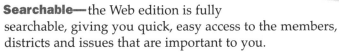

Need quick, easy access to the Washington power structure?

Look to *The Capital Source.*

The one resource that puts you in instant contact with the 7,000 most important people and organizations in Washington, DC.

The Capital Source provides you with contact and organization names, mailing addresses, phone and fax numbers, and Web addresses. And because it's published twice a year, you can be confident that the information is completely up to date and accurate.

If you need to contact:

The White House, The Cabinet, Congressional Committees, U.S. Senate, Senate Staff, U.S. House of Representatives, House Staff, Federal & Related Agencies, Foreign Embassies, The Courts, State & Local Government, Corporations, Financial Institutions, Labor Unions, Think Tanks, Interest Groups, Real Estate, Trade & Professional Associations, Political Consultants & Lobbyists, Advertising & Public Relations, Law Firms, Private Clubs, Restaurants, TV, Radio, Talk Shows, Syndicated Columnists, News Services, Publishing Companies, Magazines & Trade Publications, Newspapers, Media Organizations & Electronic Publishers, Foreign Press, Newsletters, and more.

...then you need The Capital Source.

The Spring edition is available in early May and the Fall edition is available in late October.

Pricing

You can purchase either the Spring or Fall edition for $26.95. Or you can purchase both editions at once and pay just $46.95—over a 10% savings off the single-edition price. In addition, you can choose to be put on standing order and receive future editions automatically.

Order your copy today.
Call us toll free at 1-800-356-4838.

> *The Capital Source:*
> **The Who's Who, What, Where in Washington**

Rep. Rod R. Blagojevich (D)

Elected 1996; b. Dec. 10, 1956, Chicago; home, Chicago; North-western U., B.A. 1979, Pepperdine U., J.D. 1983; Eastern Orthodox; married (Patti).

Elected Office: IL House of Reps., 1992–96.

Professional Career: Practicing atty., 1984–96; Asst. Cook County Atty., 1986–88.

DC Office: 501 CHOB 20515, 202-225-4061; Fax: 202-225-5603; Web site: www.house.gov/blagojevich.

District Offices: Chicago, 773-868-3240; Elmwood Park, 708-583-1948.

Committees: *Armed Services* (12th of 28 D): Military Procurement; Military Readiness. *Government Reform* (13th of 19 D): Criminal Justice, Drug Policy & Human Resources; National Security, Veterans' Affairs & Intl. Relations (RMM).

Group Ratings

	ADA	ACLU	AFS	LCV	CON	NTU	NFIB	COC	ACU	NTLC	CHC
1998	100	69	100	85	68	14	29	39	8	11	0
1997	90	—	88	—	88	29	—	40	16	—	—

National Journal Ratings

	1997 LIB — 1997 CONS			1998 LIB — 1998 CONS		
Economic	79%	—	18%	72%	—	28%
Social	73%	—	24%	70%	—	30%
Foreign	69%	—	28%	75%	—	23%

Key Votes of the 105th Congress

1. Clinton Budget Deal	N	5. Puerto Rico Sthood. Ref.	Y	9. Cut $ for B-2 Bombers	Y
2. Education IRAs	N	6. End Highway Set-asides	N	10. Human Rights in China	Y
3. Req. 2/3 to Raise Taxes	N	7. School Prayer Amend.	N	11. Withdraw Bosnia Troops	N
4. Fast-track Trade	N	8. Ovrd. Part. Birth Veto	N	12. End Cuban TV-Marti	N

Election Results

1998 general	Rod R. Blagojevich (D) 95,738	(74%)	($384,964)
	Alan Spitz (R) 33,687	(26%)	($20,509)
1998 primary	Rod R. Blagojevich (D) .... unopposed		
1996 general	Rod R. Blagojevich (D) 117,544	(64%)	($1,552,073)
	Michael Patrick Flanagan (R) 65,768	(36%)	($724,124)

SIXTH DISTRICT

The nation's second-busiest airport today was half a century ago an airstrip in an apple orchard (hence its current three-letter code: ORD); to the east was the Forest Preserve along the Des Plaines River, to the west little suburban villages strung along rail lines, separated by cornfields. But in the 1950s, Mayor Richard J. Daley decided that Chicago needed a new airport, annexed the orchard, and named it after a World War II Medal of Honor winner from a good Chicago Irish Catholic family. Today, O'Hare is surrounded on all sides by suburbs as densely settled as the bungalow wards of the city, with hotels and office buildings clustered near the interchanges in Rosemont, and characteristic Chicago yellow-orange brick houses in orderly rows in suburbs like Park Ridge, where Hillary Rodham Clinton grew up at 235 Wisner, just three blocks west of Chicago. Politically, these suburbs have long been solidly Republican, as were the Rodhams, convinced that civic virtues could best be realized by opposing the party of City Hall in Chicago and economic growth could best be assured by opposing the party that backed stifling government regulation. Indeed, Maine Township, which includes Park Ridge, has remained true to the principles which its most famous daughter has renounced, voting for Paul Tsongas over Bill Clinton in the 1992 Illinois primary and for Bush/Quayle and Dole/Kemp over Clinton/Gore.

The 6th Congressional District of Illinois includes much of this suburban area. It includes Park Ridge and Des Plaines just north of O'Hare and to the west the newer suburb of Elk Grove Village, the headquarters of United Airlines. The larger part of the district is over the line in DuPage County, including the string of long-settled suburbs directly west of the Loop: Elmhurst, Villa Park, Lombard, Glen Ellyn, Wheaton. It also takes in the newer suburbs along I-290 and Lake Street: Bensenville, Addison, Wood Dale, Bloomingdale. Economically, this is high income territory; culturally, it is cautiously moderate; politically, it is one of the most Republican districts in Illinois.

The congressman from the 6th is Henry Hyde, chairman of the House Judiciary Committee, chief manager of the impeachment of Bill Clinton and one of the most respected and intellectually honest members of the House. Hyde springs from Chicago earth, was raised a Catholic and a Democrat; he was an all-city basketball center and played against basketball great George Mikan; he went off to college at Georgetown and enlisted in the Navy and served at Lingayen Gulf. After the war, he finished college and law school, practiced law in Chicago, and in 1958 switched parties, convinced that Republicans were more in line with his anti-Communist beliefs. He ran for the House in 1962 in northwest Chicago and lost 53%–47% to incumbent Roman Pucinski. He was elected to the Illinois House in 1966 and in the Democratic year of 1974 was elected, as one of only 144 Republicans, to the U.S. House.

There he first made his name as an opponent of abortion, attaching to Appropriations subcommittee bills his Hyde amendments prohibiting the use of federal funds to pay for abortions in various circumstances. He had been appalled by abortion since a colleague in Springfield asked him to support a liberalized abortion law in 1968. "I look for the common thread in slavery, the Holocaust and abortion," he said in 1998. "To me, the common thread is dehumanizing people." In 1976 he was asked by conservative Robert Bauman to sponsor an amendment to an appropriation bill cutting spending on abortion; that year the first Hyde amendment was passed, banning Medicaid abortions. It has remained in force ever since, though states can spend their own money on abortions, and about 14 do, and exceptions of saving the life of the mother, and victims of rape and incest were added in 1993. Hyde is concerned about born as well as unborn children. He was one of the few Republicans who supported the family leave bill, and, with abortion rights advocate Nita Lowey, he sponsored a law to provide pregnancy benefits under the children's health insurance program for pregnant women ineligible for Medicaid but with incomes below 225% of poverty. He has worked to outlaw commercial surrogate motherhood contracts and to facilitate adoption of Romanian children. Hyde also joined the bipartisan effort on the 1995 welfare bill to add tough measures against "deadbeat dads" who fail to support their family, proposing that the IRS collect child support through wage withholding, a step resisted by Ways and Means Chairman Bill Archer. He opposes assisted suicide as part of a "culture of death" and pressed federal officials to say that dispensing a drug to cause death, as appeared to be legal under Oregon's assisted suicide law, was contrary to federal drug laws.

On many occasions, including several times during the impeachment process, Hyde has proven himself one of the most eloquent members of the House. His speeches against term limits and in favor of the flag-burning amendment are classics; his evisceration of the nuclear freeze resolution helped turn the tide on foreign policy in the House in the 1980s. He defended the Reagan Administration on Iran-contra and in the process said, somewhat to his embarrassment in the impeachment debate, that to condemn all lying "seems to me too simplistic. In the murkier grayness of the real world, choices must often be made." He irked many junior Republicans by opposing term limits, though he reported the amendment to the floor in 1995, and he supported reauthorization of the independent counsel bill in 1994 when it was passed by the Democratic Congress and signed, presumably to his later regret, by Bill Clinton. He voted for the Brady bill waiting period for gun purchases. He steered to passage the antiterrorism bill of 1995 (divested of its wiretapping provisions by a combination of liberal Democrats and conservative Republicans), a bill enforcing in the U.S. the international treaty against war crimes, and the church arson law of 1996. He fought through to passage a victim restitution law, an act limiting death penalty appeals, Megan's Law (requiring released sex offenders to report their addresses), a law allowing senior citizen housing to discriminate by age, a law banning state taxes on pensions of nonresidents, and the Lobbying Disclosure Act of 1995. Three major Hyde measures passed both houses but were vetoed by Clinton: the partial-birth abortion ban, product liability and tort reform. He passed another Hyde amendment, to allow targets of government prosecution to collect legal fees if a case was "vexatious, frivolous or in bad faith."

On other issues, Hyde headed a select subcommittee on the U.S. policy of secretly allowing shipment of Iranian arms to Bosnia: not a scandal, he said, but "ineptitude in foreign policy." He chaired the Republican platform committee in San Diego and preserved the party's anti-abortion plank. In 1998 he tried to delink federal judges' and congressmen's salaries, arousing the fury of the Republican leadership. Much of his district lies under O'Hare flight paths, and he has been a champion of building a third Chicago area airport in Peotone in Will County; in this his chief ally has been the 2d District's Jesse Jackson Jr.

None of these challenges he had faced before was as great or as public as the challenge of impeachment. From the first Hyde had little taste for the subject, yet realized he had the responsibility to handle it. Early on he said that any impeachment resolution must be bipartisan if it were to be credible, but it became clear by September that almost every Democrat was determined to defend Bill Clinton at every turn. He noted that "bipartisanship is defined by Democrats as Republican surrender." Hyde assembled a staff headed by David Schippers, a longtime Chicago lawyer and a Democrat, and modeled his procedures on those used by Chairman Peter Rodino in the impeachment of Richard Nixon 24 years before. Democrats resisted his resolution for an impeachment inquiry but felt obliged to advance one of their own, with time limits and with Zoe Lofgren's requirement that members vote first on the definition of an impeachable offense. All Republicans and 31 Democrats voted for the Republican resolution; October was taken up with investigation and the hearings started after the November 3 elections.

These were again fractious, and Clinton backers tried to put Hyde on the defensive. In September, *Salon* magazine, often a White House mouthpiece, reported that Hyde had had an affair 30 years before; "youthful indiscretions," Hyde said in response. Others recalled that Hyde was a defendant with other directors in a suit brought by the FDIC against a savings and loan; a settlement had been reached in November 1996 in which Hyde had to pay nothing. As the facts of Clinton's conduct became known, Hyde obviously decided that the president had lied under oath in a United States District Court proceeding, and that that could not be forgiven, "because he has attacked the rule of law, eroded equal justice under the law. I don't see how I can look the other way." He ran the hearings with scrupulous fairness, despite the diatribes of some Democrats, and even with occasional humor. In his summation to the House he was genuinely eloquent, and impeachment was voted on two of four counts.

Then came the historic march of Hyde and the 12 other House managers to the Senate presided over by Chief Justice William Rehnquist. The managers were pitted against Clinton's professional litigators, and the discomfort of almost all senators was obvious. (In 1996, Hyde turned down requests that he run for the Senate, adding "I'd be a great senator—God, I'd be so arrogant.") Remembering his own experience in combat, he summoned up memories of Americans who had fallen in battle and urged the senators to uphold the rule of law. But Democrats did not waver, and the articles of impeachment were rejected, the first by 55–45, the second by 50–50.

Hyde has said, "You want to be thought well of by the people you work with. You like to earn their respect. I would like that to be my legacy." He has reached that standard and more. In January 1999 a poll showed his standing in his district slightly reduced, but there is no reason to think he will have trouble winning re-election. A greater problem is that under the Republican six-year rule, he can no longer serve as Judiciary chairman (or ranking member) after 2000. He might claim the same post of Foreign Affairs, on which he is second in seniority. Some have speculated that this opponent of term limits might retire; that will be clear by Illinois's early filing deadline of December 1999.

Cook's Call. *Safe.* By mid-1999, it was unclear whether Hyde would run for re-election. However, there is very little chance that this seat will fall into Democratic hands as it is safe Republican territory.

The People: Pop. 1990: 572,268; 12.5% age 65 +; 91.9% White, 1.4% Black, 5% Asian, 0.1% Amer. Indian, 1.5% Other; 4.9% Hispanic Origin. Households: 61.6% married couple families; 29.1% married couple fams. w. children; 57.3% college educ.; median household income: $44,216; per capita income: $19,405; median house value: $130,400; median gross rent: $548.

1996 Presidential Vote			1992 Presidential Vote		
Dole (R)	105,797	(48%)	Bush (R)	121,868	(47%)
Clinton (D)	93,358	(42%)	Clinton (D)	86,448	(33%)
Perot (I)	18,796	(9%)	Perot (I)	52,734	(20%)

Rep. Henry J. Hyde (R)

Elected 1974; b. Apr. 18, 1924, Chicago; home, Wood Dale; Georgetown U., B.S. 1947, Loyola U., J.D. 1949; Catholic; widowed.

Military Career: Navy, 1944–46 (WWII); Naval Reserves, 1946–68.

Elected Office: IL House of Reps., 1966–74, Majority Ldr., 1971–72.

Professional Career: Practicing atty., 1950–75.

DC Office: 2110 RHOB 20515, 202-225-4561; Fax: 202-225-1166; Web site: www.house.gov/hyde.

District Office: Addison, 630-832-5950.

Committees: *International Relations* (4th of 26 R): International Operations and Human Rights. *Judiciary* (Chmn. of 21 R): The Constitution.

Group Ratings

	ADA	ACLU	AFS	LCV	CON	NTU	NFIB	COC	ACU	NTLC	CHC
1998	0	6	0	8	40	61	79	88	92	89	92
1997	20	—	38	—	17	44	—	70	68	—	—

National Journal Ratings

	1997 LIB — 1997 CONS			1998 LIB — 1998 CONS	
Economic	37%	—	62%	28%	—	70%
Social	0%	—	90%	11%	—	88%
Foreign	48%	—	52%	43%	—	53%

Key Votes of the 105th Congress

1. Clinton Budget Deal	Y	5. Puerto Rico Sthood. Ref.	N	9. Cut $ for B-2 Bombers	N
2. Education IRAs	Y	6. End Highway Set-asides	Y	10. Human Rights in China	N
3. Req. 2/3 to Raise Taxes	Y	7. School Prayer Amend.	Y	11. Withdraw Bosnia Troops	Y
4. Fast-track Trade	Y	8. Ovrd. Part. Birth Veto	Y	12. End Cuban TV-Marti	N

Election Results

1998 general	Henry J. Hyde (R)	111,603	(67%)	($514,349)
	Thomas A. Cramer (D)	49,906	(30%)	
	Others	4,199	(3%)	
1998 primary	Henry J. Hyde (R)	unopposed		
1996 general	Henry J. Hyde (R)	132,401	(64%)	($434,160)
	Stephen De La Rosa (D)	68,807	(33%)	($11,139)
	Others	4,746	(2%)	

SEVENTH DISTRICT

The cross-country flyer on a lucky day can get a clear view of the biggest man-made cityscape between the Atlantic and Pacific Oceans: Chicago's Loop. High-rise buildings were pioneered a century ago in the Loop—named in 1897 for the circle the "El" train forms around the city's center—by architects like Louis Sullivan and Daniel Burnham. International School modernists built their most impressive collection of buildings here and along Lake Shore Drive in the years after World War II; in the last dozen years, postmodernists have decorated the Chicago River and reinvented the skyscraper. The Loop now spreads beyond the El, up the wondrous shopping street of North Michigan Avenue with a peak at the John Hancock Tower, and west beyond the commodities exchanges to the Sears Tower on the Chicago River. This is the face Chicago likes to present to the world: giant structures rising where the prairies meet the inland sea, a vast concentration of brains and muscle, the nerve center of the markets of the nation and the world.

Behind the lakefront, where the air traveler sees the grid spread out below with occasional radials, is the muscle and sinew, gristle and fat of the city. And also the parts that do not work so well: houses and apartment buildings are abandoned; commercial space stands empty and vandalized; giant housing projects, like the Robert Taylor Homes off the Dan Ryan Expressway, rise starkly, their playgrounds empty because of the ever-present threat of gunfire. The West Side of Chicago, the vast acres directly west of the Loop, for years was a dreadful slum, with some areas almost emptied out; the decay has spread west to the Austin neighborhood, just before the border of upper income—and for two decades racially integrated—Oak Park. In the 1990s there has been some revival. The United Center, home court of Michael Jordan and site of the 1996 Democratic National Convention, has sparked commercial development of the West Side; wrought iron fences, a favorite of Mayor Richard M. Daley, signal that commercial property owners and homeowners are there to stay; lower crime rates have raised the value of land once again.

The 7th Congressional District contains the Loop and most of the North Michigan corridor and the Near North Side, with the infamous Cabrini-Green housing project. It also goes south, past 19th Century Prairie Avenue mansions to the Taylor homes and takes in a few heavily black South Side neighborhoods. Its heart, demographically and spiritually, is the black ghetto of the West Side, more depopulated and socially disorganized than the South Side. To the west are Oak Park—the boyhood home of Ernest Hemingway and location of the Frank Lloyd Wright home and museum and many of his prairie-style houses, River Forest, and the much more modest Maywood, which is black-majority, and Broadview and Hillside. About two-thirds of the people here are black; there are few Hispanics since they were confined by painstaking boundary-drawing to the 4th District, which practically encircles the 7th on three sides.

The congressman from the 7th District is Danny Davis, a Democrat first elected in 1996 after two unsuccessful tries in 1984 and 1986. Davis grew up on a cotton farm in Arkansas, graduated from college there, then moved to Chicago and worked as a teacher, assistant principal and guidance counselor in Chicago public schools. For 10 years he ran a community health project on the West Side. He was elected alderman in the 29th Ward on the boundary of Oak Park in 1979 and supported Mayor Harold Washington in the council wars of the 1980s;

he is also 29th Ward committeeman. In 1990 he was elected a Cook County commissioner; in 1991 he made a quixotic run against Mayor Richard M. Daley.

In 1996, when Cardiss Collins retired after nearly 24 years in the House, Davis decided to run. His toughest opponent in the primary, Alderman Percy Giles, was hurt when he was linked to the "Operation Silver Shovel" waste-dumping kickback scandal; the other major contenders were 3d Ward Aldermen Dorothy Tillman, an ally now of Mayor Daley, and 37th Ward Alderman Ed Smith. The fiery Tillman told one crowd she had a "contract" on Newt Gingrich; Smith was for reform of welfare, and had once called for martial law on the West Side. Davis campaigned as a big-government liberal, calling for a $7.60 minimum wage, affirmative action, and a national health care plan; he said his goal was "the development of an urban strategy, and urban agenda, that reclaims the inner cities of America." Like teacher unions, he opposed school vouchers and favored more money to local districts, even ones like Chicago which have performed poorly. Davis won with 33%, followed by Tillman with 20%, Smith with 12%, Bobbie Steele with 12%, and Giles with 11%. He won the general with ease.

In the House, Davis has a very liberal voting record; he is listed on the Web page of the leftish New Party and says he likes its "freshness, its openness, its willingness to keep dreaming." He was one of three Illinois Democrats to vote against the 1997 tax cuts: "We cannot have a great, civilized and humane nation without paying the cost; if all we can do is cut, cut, cut, all that we will get is blood, blood, blood." With Republicans Jim Talent and J. C. Watts he has sponsored the American Community Renewal Act, which would provide tax cuts for businesses locating in troubled central city neighborhoods. He opposed the sugar program as corporate welfare and called charter schools a "sinister move to dismantle public education." He opposed air strikes in Iraq in February 1998. In late 1998 he protested the low percentage of minority law clerks on the Supreme Court, a protest brusquely rejected by Chief Justice William Rehnquist.

Davis speaks in impressive sepulchral tone, and his self-evident sincerity and concern for the poor has helped him achieve some legislative success in a mostly conservative House. In 1998 he was the only member to get Transportation Chairman Bud Shuster not to oppose an amendment to the big transportation bill; Davis moved to increase from $42 million to $150 million a pilot program to provide transportation for low-income central city residents to get to work sites in the suburbs. This was supported by UPS and United Airlines, and was passed with 48 Republican votes. The bill also contained $250 million for the reconstruction of Wacker Drive, which is in the district. Davis sponsored a $100 million increase in federal community health care centers, and called for relief from the interim payment system for home health care providers and a one-year delay of a 15% payment cut. In January 1999 he and Bobby Rush sought additional funds for the Chicago Housing Authority, which had to close two high-rise project buildings without heat or hot water because of cold weather.

In the March 1998 primary Davis's opponent was backed by his old enemy Percy Giles, furious because Davis had not supported another alderman's wife for his old slot on the Cook County Commission. Davis won handsomely, 85%–15%, and won the general with no major party opposition. He backed Roland Burris for governor in the primary, but agreed to cut radio spots for nominee Glenn Poshard, despite his conservative voting record. Davis's hold on the district seems secure, but redistricting could be a problem. If the Hispanic-majority 4th District's boundaries are changed, he could get a district with a lower black percentage in 2002.

Cook's Call. *Safe.* This Chicago district is ranked as one of the 15 most Democratic in the country. Davis should have no problem holding onto this majority black seat.

The People: Pop. 1990: 572,039; 10.6% age 65 + ; 29.1% White, 65.6% Black, 3.2% Asian, 0.1% Amer. Indian, 1.9% Other; 4% Hispanic Origin. Households: 31.9% married couple families; 15.5% married couple fams. w. children; 43.1% college educ.; median household income: $25,220; per capita income: $13,056; median house value: $89,500; median gross rent: $362.

1996 Presidential Vote

Clinton (D) 152,606 (82%)
Dole (R) 25,757 (14%)
Perot (I) 5,037 (3%)

1992 Presidential Vote

Clinton (D) 184,966 (78%)
Bush (R) 35,530 (15%)
Perot (I) 15,992 (7%)

Rep. Danny K. Davis (D)

Elected 1996; b. Sept. 6, 1941, Parkdale; home, Chicago; AR AM&N Col., B.A. 1961, Chicago St. U., M.S. 1968, Union Inst., Ph.D. 1977; Baptist; married (Vera).

Elected Office: Chicago City Alderman, 1979–90; Cook Cnty. Commissioner, 1990–96.

Professional Career: Teacher, Chicago Public Schls., 1962–69; Health Care Planner, 1969–79.

DC Office: 1222 LHOB 20515, 202-225-5006; Fax: 202-225-5641; Web site: www.house.gov/davis.

District Office: Chicago, 773-533-7520.

Committees: *Government Reform* (14th of 19 D): Census; Postal Service. *Small Business* (3d of 17 D): Government Programs & Oversight (RMM).

Group Ratings

	ADA	ACLU	AFS	LCV	CON	NTU	NFIB	COC	ACU	NTLC	CHC
1998	95	81	100	85	55	20	0	28	8	5	0
1997	100	—	100	—	2	23	—	10	8	—	—

National Journal Ratings

	1997 LIB	—	1997 CONS	1998 LIB	—	1998 CONS
Economic	82%	—	15%	79%	—	0%
Social	85%	—	0%	85%	—	15%
Foreign	90%	—	10%	82%	—	16%

Key Votes of the 105th Congress

1. Clinton Budget Deal	N	5. Puerto Rico Sthood. Ref.	N	9. Cut $ for B-2 Bombers	Y
2. Education IRAs	N	6. End Highway Set-asides	N	10. Human Rights in China	Y
3. Req. 2/3 to Raise Taxes	N	7. School Prayer Amend.	N	11. Withdraw Bosnia Troops	*
4. Fast-track Trade	N	8. Ovrd. Part. Birth Veto	N	12. End Cuban TV-Marti	N

Election Results

1998 general	Danny K. Davis (D)	130,984	(93%)	($160,147)
	Dorn E. Van Cleave III (Lib)	9,984	(7%)	
1998 primary	Danny K. Davis (D)	57,200	(85%)	
	Wilner J. Jackson (D)	10,046	(15%)	
1996 general	Danny K. Davis (D)	149,568	(83%)	($410,662)
	Randy Borow (R)	27,241	(15%)	($33,155)
	Others	4,286	(2%)	

EIGHTH DISTRICT

Schaumburg may not be nationally known, but it is one of America's major corporate headquarters cities and one of several edge cities northwest of Chicago. Fifty years ago, this was farmland, half a dozen miles beyond the orchard which is now O'Hare Airport. Today, Schaumburg, near the intersection of the Northwest Tollway and I-290, with lots of office space and Woodfield Mall and miles of subdivisions, with moderately-priced apartments and with some black residents, is the site of the headquarters of Motorola and Zurich American Life Insurance; nearby are the headquarters of Sears and Kemper Insurance. Yet Schaumburg yearns for traditions: It built a performing arts center, formed an orchestra for young people and has built from scratch a traditional downtown.

The 8th Congressional District is made up of Schaumburg and dozens of similar communities, on the prairies and hilly lakelands northwest of Chicago. Near Schaumburg are Streamwood, Hoffman Estates, Arlington Heights, Rolling Meadows, Palatine: Over half the district's population is in the far northwest extremity of Cook County. The 8th also includes the filling-up western half of Lake County, with little lake communities being surrounded by new suburbs. The tone of life here is not elite, but it is highly affluent; culturally, this is part of the great rural Midwest as much as—perhaps more than—it is of yeasty, lusty Chicago. Economically, it is suspicious of government spending, which it associates with the corrupt big city of yore. By most measures, this is the most Republican district in Illinois, and one of the most Republican in the nation.

The congressman from the 8th District is Philip Crane, a conservative Republican first elected in a 1969 special election, now the most senior Republican in the House. Crane grew up in Indiana, one of several sons of a doctor who had his own radio program; he went to college at Hillsdale, got a Ph.D. at Indiana University, was a conservative intellectual when that seemed an oxymoron. He moved to the Chicago area in 1967, and, at 39, won a November 1969 special election to the House, replacing Donald Rumsfeld, who was then Richard Nixon's poverty program director, before becoming chief of staff and Defense secretary under Gerald Ford. Crane supported a set of ideas which then seemed backward-looking but which have been on the ascendant in the nation and the world since—free market economics, a strong national defense, traditional values.

In his first years in the House he sat largely unnoticed on the back benches and had meager influence. In 1980 he ran for president, hoping, as the truer libertarian, to cut in on the elderly Ronald Reagan's support and then take it over when the Reagan candidacy faded. But his strategy totally failed, and through the 1980s he seemed embittered and unfocused; he was never a part of the young conservative movement led by Jack Kemp, Newt Gingrich and Trent Lott. By the early 1990s he was in trouble back home. In 1992 he had primary opposition from Gary Skoien, a former aide to then-Governor James Thompson; Crane, who declined the PAC money he could easily collect as a senior member of Ways and Means, won by only 55%–45%. That fall he won unimpressively, 56%–40%. In 1994 Crane once again had serious primary opposition, from Skoien and from state Senator Peter Fitzgerald, a former Crane volunteer and now U.S. senator. Fitzgerald spent $700,000 of his own money and did little to conceal statewide ambitions, but Crane won 40% of the vote to Fitzgerald's 33% and Skoien's 21%.

After those close scrapes Crane suddenly found himself part of a Republican majority. He was not a committee chairman—Bill Archer had seniority over him on Ways and Means—but Crane did become chair of that committee's Trade Subcommittee, and seemed to become engaged in legislation. Crane inserted in the unvetoable minimum wage bill several provisions—the adoption tax credit, expanding Employee Stock Ownership Plans, Subchapter S changes to help small businesses and various insurance provisions. He pushed for extending the General System of Preferences and shepherded through Most Favored Nation status for Bulgaria, Romania and Cambodia. He also supported renewal of MFN status for China; "Illinois exports to China grew 25% last year," he pointed out in 1996. He supported NAFTA, GATT and fast track. Crane is the lead sponsor of the Africa trade bill originated by the Congressional Black Caucus; he angered some members by threatening to tie it with fast track in February 1998— it passed the House in March 1998 but stalled in the Senate, where it faces competition from a different version by Jesse Jackson Jr. In May 1998 the House passed Crane's bill to change overtime policies and allow waivers of collective bargaining agreements in our northern and southern border patrols; this was held up in the Senate at the behest of labor unions. Crane proposed in 1997 to allow non-itemizing taxpayers to deduct half of all charitable contributions exceeding a total of $500. He has worked on Medicare reimbursement rules, with some attention to the needs of Chicago area hospitals.

Crane also tended, as he had not much in the past, to local projects. He boasted that he called Appropriators Bob Livingston and Bill Young and got money for ALQ-135 radar jammers for F-15s restored; they account for 1,300 jobs at the Rolling Meadows Northrop plant. He worked with John Porter to get reauthorization for the Des Plaines River Wetlands Demonstration Project and with Don Manzullo to get more floodgates in the Fox River region.

Crane has had primary opposition in each of the past four elections, but won with 75% in 1996 and 65% in 1998; he has won by wide margins in November. Stung by party leaders' requests for more funds for Operation Breakout in October 1998 he sent in $25,000 with a tart note: "I understand, however, that a career of service to our party and our candidates means little today, and the only question that now apparently matters, at least when it comes to 'properly securing' a chairmanship, is 'what have you done for me lately?' " Archer has announced he will retire in 2000, when he will have served the six years as Ways and Means chairman the Republican rule allows. Crane is next in line, and certainly looks forward to becoming chairman (or, but surely less so, to be ranking minority member if Republicans lose their majority). But there were rumors that Bill Thomas, who is next in line after Crane, might contest the chairmanship in the Republican Conference.

Cook's Call. *Safe.* For years now, Crane has found himself in competitive primary contests. But Crane has had little trouble winning general elections in this conservative, rock-ribbed Republican suburban district.

The People: Pop. 1990: 571,464; 5.5% rural; 7.7% age 65 + ; 92.3% White, 1.6% Black, 4% Asian, 0.2% Amer. Indian, 1.9% Other; 5.3% Hispanic Origin. Households: 63.9% married couple families; 33.5% married couple fams. w. children; 60.8% college educ.; median household income: $47,374; per capita income: $20,488; median house value: $132,300; median gross rent: $599.

1996 Presidential Vote			1992 Presidential Vote		
Dole (R)	105,742	(49%)	Bush (R)	118,714	(47%)
Clinton (D)	86,907	(41%)	Clinton (D)	76,327	(31%)
Perot (I)	19,482	(9%)	Perot (I)	54,269	(22%)

Rep. Philip M. Crane (R)

Elected Nov. 1969; b. Nov. 3, 1930, Chicago; home, Wauconda; Hillsdale Col., B.A. 1952, IN U., M.A. 1961, Ph.D. 1963; Protestant; married (Arlene).

Military Career: Army, 1954–56.

Professional Career: Instructor, IN U., 1960–63; Asst. Prof., Bradley U., 1963–67; Dir., Westminster Academy, 1967–68.

DC Office: 233 CHOB 20515, 202-225-3711; Fax: 202-225-7830; Web site: www.house.gov/crane.

District Offices: Lake Villa, 847-265-9000; Palatine, 847-358-9160.

Committees: *Ways & Means* (2d of 23 R): Health; Trade (Chmn.). *Joint Committee on Taxation* (2d of 5 Reps.).

Group Ratings

	ADA	ACLU	AFS	LCV	CON	NTU	NFIB	COC	ACU	NTLC	CHC
1998	0	7	0	0	87	83	92	81	96	100	100
1997	5	—	25	—	31	66	—	80	96	—	—

National Journal Ratings

	1997 LIB — 1997 CONS		1998 LIB — 1998 CONS	
Economic	10% —	86%	19% —	81%
Social	20% —	71%	10% —	89%
Foreign	0% —	88%	25% —	74%

Key Votes of the 105th Congress

1. Clinton Budget Deal	Y	5. Puerto Rico Sthood. Ref.	N	9. Cut $ for B-2 Bombers	N
2. Education IRAs	Y	6. End Highway Set-asides	Y	10. Human Rights in China	N
3. Req. 2/3 to Raise Taxes	Y	7. School Prayer Amend.	Y	11. Withdraw Bosnia Troops	Y
4. Fast-track Trade	Y	8. Ovrd. Part. Birth Veto	Y	12. End Cuban TV-Marti	N

Election Results

1998 general	Philip M. Crane (R)	104,242	(69%)	($833,853)
	Mike Rothman (D)	47,614	(31%)	
1998 primary	Philip M. Crane (R)	34,543	(65%)	
	S. David McSweeney (R)	18,221	(35%)	
1996 general	Philip M. Crane (R)	127,763	(62%)	($534,151)
	Elizabeth Anne Hull (D)	74,068	(36%)	($30,804)
	Others	3,474	(2%)	

NINTH DISTRICT

"Make no little plans," commanded architect Daniel Burnham, who made no little plans for the Chicago lakefront: the glorious parks he designed are still among America's urban jewels, and the row of high-rise apartment buildings—some austere works of masters of the International style, some in traditional styles evocative of some other place and time, some sleek Art Deco works of the 1920s and 1930s—are a splendid accompaniment. Behind the lakefront is all the diversity of Chicago. In sturdy brick houses, with scarcely a shoe horn's space between them, or in stubby apartment buildings, are ethnic and racial groups of all sorts, from Argentinians to Slavs, Plains Indians to Indian plainsmen. In the 1970s, the neighborhoods behind the lakefront seemed to be getting grimier and heading downhill. Since the late 1980s, they have been busy gentrifying, as young marrieds and gays, professionals and entrepreneurs renovate old houses and open new businesses.

The lakefront has long been the most heavily Jewish part of Chicago. Chicago's Jewish community, prominent for more than a century, has never been as much a force for big government as in New York, nor is it connected as much to a glamorous industry as in Los Angeles. Yet among Jewish voters liberal impulses have been strong: the 19th Century impulse to resist state authority and imposition of cultural uniformity and the 20th Century impulse to increase state responsibility for individuals' lives. Chicago's North Side Jews, on the lakefront or in neighborhoods like Rogers Park and nearby suburbs like Skokie and Niles, have been a solidly Democratic voting bloc, involved with—but skeptical of—the old Democratic machine. In the racial city politics of the 1980s, as in state politics, Jewish voters and lakefront liberals of all backgrounds have been a key swing group.

The 9th Congressional District covers most of Chicago's lakefront, from Diversey Harbor north to Evanston, the home of Northwestern University and a city that has moved gracefully from historic Yankee Republican-ness to trendy post-graduate Democratic-ness. The 9th presses inland from the Rogers Park neighborhood at the north end of Chicago west into Polish-American areas at the northwest edge of the city; from Evanston it reaches west through heavily Jewish Skokie to Morton Grove and Niles.

The representative from the 9th District is Jan Schakowsky, a Democrat elected in 1998. She was selected in the March Democratic primary to replace Sidney Yates, who had represented the Lakefront in Congress for all but two of the last 50 years; he was first elected in 1948, ran for the Senate and nearly beat Everett Dirksen in 1962, returned to the House two years later, and as ranking Democrat on the Interior Appropriations Subcommittee shepherded programs from the national parks to the National Endowment for the Arts; he was still vigorous when he decided to retire at 89. Schakowsky grew up in Rogers Park, worked two years as a teacher; in 1969 she formed National Consumers Unite and worked for date-of-freshness labels on food. Later she joined Illinois Public Action, a consumer group that worked to stop utilities from shutting off heat for delinquent bills in winter; in 1985 she became executive director of the Illinois State Council of Senior Citizens. In 1990 she was elected to the state House from Evanston and Skokie. There she worked for day care centers and hate crime laws and chaired the Labor and Commerce Committee.

Yates announced his retirement way back in October 1996, giving Schakowsky and two other Democrats, state Senator Howard Carroll and venture capitalist J.B. Pritzker plenty of time to run. Schakowsky's strategy was to run from the left—"I don't think I can be defined as too far left in a district like this"—and to build a volunteer organization. With ads in college papers, she got 400 young people to apply for 20 field organizer jobs; they set about identifying 30,000 Schakowsky voters. She also raised plenty of money, $1.4 million, with help from EMILY's List; she survived attacks based on the fact that her husband Robert Creamer had resigned as head of Citizens Action of Illinois because of a federal investigation. On primary day, Schakowsky's campaign fielded 1,500 workers, 250 from unions; she won 31,443 votes, enough for a 45% win.

Schakowsky's two opponents had a different strategy. Longtime state Senator Howard Carroll, with roots in the heavily Jewish 50th Ward, had the support of most Democratic ward committeemen. He attacked Schakowsky for her opposition to the death penalty, "even for murderous acts like the bombing in Oklahoma and New York." In response, Schakowsky brought in the father of a victim of the Oklahoma City bombing to show his disgust with the ad. J. B. Pritzker, a member of the billionaire family that started Hyatt hotels, put $1.5 million into his own campaign. Perhaps the most fiscally conservative candidate, Pritzker highlighted his experience working for Congressman Tom Lantos and former Senators Alan Dixon and Terry Sanford. He attacked Carroll for taking money from the American Muslim Council, whose leader he said supported terrorism.

On winning the primary, Schakowsky said, "Now the men's club delegation to the U.S. House of Representatives will have a woman's voice." Of course she easily won the general election; the Republican nominee was once her physician. She is likely to be on the left in the House, and has policy positions that sound closer to those of the 1940s British Labour government than to those of most American politicians. She says she wants to expand Medicare to cover everybody—single payer government health insurance, in effect—and has advanced a proposal, worked out with Northwestern economist Robert Eisner, to have a government-run investment fund that taxpayers could use to supplement Social Security—similar to the USA Accounts Bill Clinton proposed in January 1999.

Cook's Call. *Safe.* Schakowsky will have little trouble retaining this liberal Democratic district. Like many Chicago-based members, her biggest worry should be redistricting; there are rumors that Illinois will lose one seat and that her district may be affected. Until then Schakowsky remains very safe.

The People: Pop. 1990: 571,611; 17.3% age 65 +; 73.1% White, 12% Black, 10% Asian, 0.3% Amer. Indian, 4.5% Other; 9.5% Hispanic Origin. Households: 40.9% married couple families; 16.8% married couple fams. w. children; 60.2% college educ.; median household income: $32,183; per capita income: $18,691; median house value: $145,800; median gross rent: $465.

1996 Presidential Vote			1992 Presidential Vote		
Clinton (D)	139,166	(69%)	Clinton (D)	155,446	(61%)
Dole (R)	52,263	(26%)	Bush (R)	68,418	(27%)
Perot (I)	9,732	(5%)	Perot (I)	29,294	(12%)

Rep. Jan Schakowsky (D)

Elected 1998; b. May 26, 1944, Chicago; home, Evanston; U. of IL, B.S. 1965; Jewish; married (Robert Creamer).

Elected Office: IL House of Reps., 1990–98.

Professional Career: Prog. Dir., IL Public Action, 1976–85; Exec. Dir., IL State Cncl. of Sr. Citizens, 1985–90.

DC Office: 515 CHOB 20515, 202-225-2111; Fax: 202-226-6890; Web site: www.house.gov/schakowsky.

District Office: Evanston, 847-328-3399.

Committees: *Banking & Financial Services* (23d of 27 D): Domestic & International Monetary Policy; Housing & Community Opportunity. *Government Reform* (19th of 19 D): National Security, Veterans' Affairs & Intl. Relations.

Group Ratings and Key Votes: Newly Elected

Election Results

1998 general	Jan Schakowsky (D)	107,878	(75%)	($1,440,606)
	Herbert Sohn (R)	33,448	(23%)	($24,631)
	Others	3,284	(2%)	
1998 primary	Jan Schakowsky (D)	31,443	(45%)	
	Howard W. Carroll (D)	23,963	(34%)	
	Jay "J.B" Pritzker (D)	14,256	(20%)	
1996 general	Sidney R. Yates (D)	124,319	(63%)	($184,005)
	Joseph Walsh (R)	71,763	(37%)	($115,401)

TENTH DISTRICT

Since 1855, when the first Chicago & Northwestern opened the railroad line from downtown Chicago north along the lakeshore, the North Shore suburbs along Lake Michigan have been the favorite residence for Chicago's elite. The North Shore starts in Evanston, founded by Methodists to promote temperance (a cause that has never prospered in Chicago), and goes on to Wilmette, Winnetka, Glencoe, Highland Park, Lake Forest—each with a slightly different personality and character, each long established, mightily prosperous and with a patina of age. Not far from the gritty, monosyllabic city, these are communities of pleasant, affluent, well-educated people living in an environment whose natural beauty—the long water vista and blue light off the lake, the gentle hills and fine trees—is kept carefully disciplined.

The 10th Congressional District is the North Shore district, starting at the Baha'i Temple on the Wilmette lakefront, just north of Evanston, reaching up past Fort Sheridan (which was closed in 1993) to the city of Waukegan (once famous as the home of comedian Jack Benny) and the Wisconsin border beyond. The district also goes inland to what for many years was just cornfields to Northbrook and Deerfield, just west of Glencoe and Highland Park. Farther inland are suburbs like Arlington Heights, developed in the 1950s and 1960s on the Northwestern railroad line, and Wheeling, developed in the 1960s and 1970s near I-294. To the north are Long Grove and Libertyville, near where the Adlai Stevensons, the late presidential candidate and his son the former senator, have what is now one of the last farms only a few miles from Lake Michigan and the Onwentsia Club.

The congressman from the 10th District is John Porter, a Republican who has long seemed to fit the district well. He is a North Shore native, the son of an Evanston judge, a graduate of Northwestern, a Republican who is against tax increases and looks with favor on free markets, but who takes liberal stands on some foreign and cultural issues. He practiced law and was elected to the Illinois House in 1972. In 1980 he won election to the House from a district that then included Democratic Evanston. Since 1995 he has been chairman of the Appropriations' Labor-HHS-Education Subcommittee, with much say about vast flows of money and important public programs.

When Republicans gained control in 1994, Porter suddenly had the responsibility of managing an appropriations bill slated for most of the Republicans' reductions in domestic discretionary spending, and to navigate between the subcommittee's able and aggressive ranking Democrat, David Obey, and its strong conservative Republicans, like Ernest Istook. Of all this, Porter has proved himself capable. He has held out against plans for increased education funding, including former Senator Carol Moseley-Braun's school construction bill in November 1997, on the grounds that this is primarily a state and local responsibility. Instead he has worked to increase spending for the National Institutes of Health and biomedical research, with a view toward doubling NIH spending from 1997 to 2002, where the federal government plays a unique role which he has compared to Prince Henry the Navigator's encouragement of ocean exploration in 15th Century Portugal. He has cast crucial votes to save international family planning programs and Medicaid funding of abortions in cases of rape and incest.

Porter voted against the Republican tax cut, saying that spending should be cut first, and against the balanced budget amendment with a supermajority required to raise taxes. On other issues, he led opposition to repeal of the assault weapons ban and the 1993 gas tax, opposed term limits and defended the funding of public broadcasting. He has worked to cut away at the subsidy for logging roads in national forests. He is a House reformer, sponsor of the limit on ranking Republican committee positions to six years that now restricts their service as chairmen. He has opposed the B-2 bomber, the Seawolf submarine, and the space station; he is a strong supporter of Radio Free Asia and has denounced Turkey and Iran for their persecutions of Armenians, Kurds, and Baha'i (he is co-chair of the Caucus on Armenian Issues). He retreated from his opposition to MFN status for China in 1997, but advanced a series of proposals to advance human rights there—24-hour Radio Free Asia broadcasts, denial of visas to human rights abusers, disclosure of Chinese companies ties to the military. On the night Bill Clinton entertained Jiang Zemin, Porter attended a "stateless dinner" and toasted Jigme Zangpo, a Tibetan teacher jailed nearly 40 years for political activity. His wife took part in a hunger strike and vigil on the Capitol steps to protest Turkish oppression of Kurds.

Porter was one of the first Republicans to propose, in 1997, a Social Security reform, with the option of putting up to 5% of the payroll tax into individual investment accounts. He passed through the House a bill to protect volunteers—from Little League coaches to disaster relief workers—from liability lawsuits. He has sought to repeal the federal requirement of bilingual ballots, to make sure English remains the common language of political discourse. Porter declared early on that he would vote against impeachment, but changed his mind as the case was argued. "I get the impression that the president considers himself above the law. I have concluded that I will support at least the first two articles of impeachment."

Porter tends to local issues as well. In April 1998 he saved impact aid for schools in the

North Chicago School District 187, where 40% of pupils are from Great Lakes Naval Training Center. He stopped Senator Richard Durbin from preventing the sale of a 14-acre Army site to Lake Forest for a public works center. Porter's moderate record has inspired primary opposition in the 1990s, but as pro-incumbent feelings have grown, he has done better: He won primaries with 60% in 1992, 66% in 1994, and 68% in 1996. In 1998 he had no opposition at all. He gave some consideration to running for the Senate in 1996 and 1998, but in both cases decided not to. Angered by Porter's impeachment vote and encouraged by the moderate nature of the district, Democratic state Reps. Lauren Beth Gash and Jeffrey Schoenburg are seriously considering challenging him in 2000.

Cook's Call. *Probably Safe.* This is another Republican-leaning, but socially moderate, suburban district where Democrats are hoping that the impeachment backlash will hurt sitting Republicans. But Porter is a good fit for the district and it is hard to see how he could lose in 2000.

The People: Pop. 1990: 571,501; 0.6% rural; 10.8% age 65 +; 86.6% White, 6.1% Black, 4% Asian, 0.2% Amer. Indian, 3% Other; 6.8% Hispanic Origin. Households: 64.8% married couple families; 32.3% married couple fams. w. children; 66.4% college educ.; median household income: $50,355; per capita income: $26,405; median house value: $181,400; median gross rent: $539.

1996 Presidential Vote

Clinton (D)	112,105	(50%)
Dole (R)	97,434	(43%)
Perot (I)	13,418	(6%)

1992 Presidential Vote

Bush (R)	112,401	(43%)
Clinton (D)	108,149	(41%)
Perot (I)	40,719	(16%)

Rep. John Edward Porter (R)

Elected 1980; b. June 1, 1935, Evanston; home, Wilmette; M.I.T., 1953–54, Northwestern U., B.S.B.A. 1957, U. of MI, J.D. 1961; Presbyterian; married (Kathryn).

Military Career: Army Reserves, 1958–64.

Elected Office: IL House of Reps., 1972–78.

Professional Career: Atty., U.S. Dept. of Justice, 1961–63; Practicing atty., 1963–80.

DC Office: 2373 RHOB 20515, 202-225-4835; Web site: www.house.gov/porter.

District Offices: Arlington Heights, 847-392-0303; Deerfield, 847-940-0202; Waukegan, 847-662-0101.

Committees: *Appropriations* (4th of 34 R): Foreign Operations & Export Financing; Labor, HHS & Education (Chmn.); Military Construction.

Group Ratings

	ADA	ACLU	AFS	LCV	CON	NTU	NFIB	COC	ACU	NTLC	CHC
1998	15	38	11	69	78	51	86	83	46	45	50
1997	40	—	14	—	98	53	—	90	46	—	—

National Journal Ratings

	1997 LIB — 1997 CONS		1998 LIB — 1998 CONS	
Economic	48% —	52%	48% —	52%
Social	47% —	52%	58% —	42%
Foreign	60% —	38%	55% —	44%

Key Votes of the 105th Congress

1. Clinton Budget Deal	Y	5. Puerto Rico Sthood. Ref.	N
2. Education IRAs	Y	6. End Highway Set-asides	Y
3. Req. 2/3 to Raise Taxes	N	7. School Prayer Amend.	N
4. Fast-track Trade	Y	8. Ovrd. Part. Birth Veto	Y

9. Cut $ for B-2 Bombers	Y
10. Human Rights in China	N
11. Withdraw Bosnia Troops	Y
12. End Cuban TV-Marti	N

Election Results

1998 general	John Edward Porter (R) .... unopposed			($489,275)
1998 primary	John Edward Porter (R) .... unopposed			
1996 general	John Edward Porter (R)	145,626	(69%)	($726,615)
	Philip R. Torf (D)	65,144	(31%)	($54,367)

ELEVENTH DISTRICT

South of Chicago, sluggishly flowing rivers run circles around industrial sites. This low-lying land is a great divide, over which French explorers portaged, the easiest path from the inland oceans of the Great Lakes to the widened-out channels of communication through North America, the Mississippi River and all its tributaries. Today, there is still a kind of borderland here, as the factories and shopping centers and subdivisions stop somewhere past the Cook County line and Downstate Illinois prairies begin, cornfields bisected by highways and railroads radiating out from the Loop and the railyards of the nation's transportation hub. Politically, this is a borderland as well, between the traditionally Democratic Chicago metropolitan area, with its hard-bitten machine politics, and heavily Republican Downstate Illinois, with its tradition of governance by local civic leaders that stretches back to the days of Abraham Lincoln.

The 11th Congressional District covers much of this borderland. It includes the old 10th Ward of Chicago plus the suburbs of South Holland, Calumet City and Lansing near the Indiana line. This is heavy industry country; many of the factories around Lake Calumet are empty now—if not torn down—but the rows of workers' houses on the grid streets remain. This is the home of the struggling white working class, ancestrally Democratic. To the west is Joliet. Once a canal boat town, and later the producer of one-third of America's wallpaper, Joliet now has two big prisons; the federal Joliet Arsenal has been closed, and Joliet owes its current prosperity to four riverboat casinos built since 1992. To the south is Kankakee, a Downstate county seat amid rich prairie earth on the Illinois Central main line and the home town of Governor George Ryan; this is heavily Republican territory. Farther west, on bluffs above the Illinois River heading down to the Mississippi, are the factory towns of Ottawa and LaSalle and, to the south, Streator; this is LaSalle County, the politically marginal area in this part of Downstate Illinois.

The congressman from the 11th District is Jerry Weller, a hard-working, politically savvy Republican who won the seat in 1994 and has held it since. Weller grew up on a Grundy County farm, where his family still raises hogs; out of college, he was a staffer to Congressman Tom Corcoran and Agriculture Secretary John Block; in the mid-1980s he returned to Illinois and was elected to the state House in 1988. In 1994, when Democratic Congressman George Sangmeister retired "to smell the proverbial roses," Weller was one of six Republicans and seven Democrats to run for the seat. He boasted of reforming health care via market-based principles, holding criminals accountable and promoting markets for ethanol fuels and soybean inks; he was proud of replacing the "granny tax" on nursing home residents with a cigarette tax as a way to pay for health care. In the Republican primary he edged 1992 nominee Robert Herbolsheimer, 32%–29%; in the general, against Democrat Frank Giglio, a legislator for 20 of the previous 22 years, who said of Congress, "Wouldn't this be a nice way to finish my career?," Weller won 61%–39%.

In the House, Weller showed impressive insider skills. With the help of then Chief Deputy Whip Dennis Hastert, he was named one of three freshmen on the Republican Steering Committee. On the Veterans Affairs' Committee he steered to passage a law allowing the Veterans' Administration to contract outpatient care with private clinics and hospitals. On Transportation, he promoted the third Chicago area airport proposed for Peotone, 45 miles south of Chicago and a few miles north of Kankakee. He got money for the conversion of the 23,500-acre Joliet Arsenal into a 19,000-acre Midewin National Tallgrass Prairie, the biggest east of the Mississippi.

Weller was nonetheless hard pressed in the 1996 election. Bill Clinton ran well in the southern suburbs of Chicago, and Democrats picked up several crucial state House seats there. Democrat Clem Balanoff made a late TV buy and carried the Cook County portion of the district and ran even in LaSalle; though he spent $1.1 million and had campaigned nonstop around the district, Weller won by only 52%–48%. He immediately started running hard for a seat on the Ways and Means Committee, arguing that with the defeat of Michael Flanagan, no one on the committee represented Chicago. With help from Hastert, he won one of four open seats. Weller became one of the prime sponsors of ending the marriage penalty; he would give couples the option of the current system or his new provision. He also worked up a proposal, with the help of Chicago Mayor Richard M. Daley, for tax incentives to clean up brownfields, old factory sites which are environmentally contaminated; he wants to allow deductions of up to $500,000 a year, with the rest of the cost amortized over five years. He has also proposed reducing the World War I-era 3% telephone tax to 1% and dedicating revenues to school and library Internet access. He wants to give spouses shortchanged on child support tax breaks, with deadbeat parents penalized by the IRS. After a Joliet nine-year-old was targeted by sexual predators on the Internet, he proposed higher penalties for Internet sex crimes; this passed the House in June 1998 after Weller brought in the girl's parents to testify and the language was modified to satisfy Judiciary Committee Republicans.

Weller did not neglect local concerns. He has pushed for a feasibility study of a Calumet Ecological Park in the old industrial zone of the south suburbs; he placed veterans' medical clinics in the south suburbs and LaSalle County; he fought to save impact aid for schools near the closed Joliet Arsenal; he got $940,000 for a Kankakee River cleanup; he got $17 million for the Deep Tunnel and Reservoir Project in the often flood-sodden south suburbs. But his attempt to name a new Joliet veterans' cemetery after Abraham Lincoln was foiled by Raymond LaHood, who feared confusion with the cemetery in Springfield where Lincoln is buried.

He was unsuccessful in his pursuit of a leadership position. Weller lost a race for Republican Conference secretary in July 1997, after some bad publicity when he held a breakfast and promised $1,500 contributions to each member who attended; he withdrew from a race for chairman of the Policy Committee in November 1998. But in December 1998, when Bob Livingston stunned everyone by announcing his retirement, he worked the phones for Dennis Hastert for speaker, along with Tom DeLay and Tom Davis, and helped Hastert win within hours.

Weller had an easier time of it in the 1998 election than in 1996. Clem Balanoff dropped out a few days after the filing deadline, and the Democratic nominee, Gary Mueller, a lawyer in George Sangmeister's law firm, never raised enough money to get himself put on the House Democrats' campaign committee's support list. Mueller did attract notice in August when he signed an "affidavit of integrity" about his personal life; Weller briskly replied, "An honest man does not have to sign a piece of paper to prove his integrity." More to the point, Weller raised $1.5 million and won 59%–41%, a margin that seems to put this potentially marginal seat in the safe Republican category so long as he runs.

Cook's Call. *Probably Safe.* Weller has taken what should be a very competitive seat and, with a combination of political skill and solid fundraising, made it relatively safe. Still, this unwieldy district is not safe Republican territory and can feel the impact of a national tide.

The People: Pop. 1990: 571,050; 20.3% rural; 13.7% age 65 +; 87.4% White, 8.5% Black, 0.6% Asian, 0.2% Amer. Indian, 3.2% Other; 6.2% Hispanic Origin. Households: 60.6% married couple families; 30.2% married couple fams. w. children; 39.3% college educ.; median household income: $33,632; per capita income: $13,838; median house value: $67,400; median gross rent: $329.

1996 Presidential Vote

Clinton (D) 112,110 (51%)
Dole (R) 83,648 (38%)
Perot (I) 23,162 (11%)

1992 Presidential Vote

Clinton (D) 108,456 (43%)
Bush (R) 90,058 (36%)
Perot (I) 50,186 (20%)

Rep. Gerald C. (Jerry) Weller (R)

Elected 1994; b. July 7, 1957, Streator; home, Morris; U. of IL, B.S. 1979; Christian; divorced.

Elected Office: IL House of Reps., 1988–94.

Professional Career: Farmer; Aide, U.S. Rep. Tom Corcoran, 1980–81; Aide, U.S. Agriculture Secy. John Block, 1981–85.

DC Office: 424 CHOB 20515, 202-225-3635; Fax: 202-225-3521; Web site: www.house.gov/weller.

District Office: Joliet, 815-740-2028.

Committees: *Ways & Means* (19th of 23 R): Oversight; Social Security.

Group Ratings

	ADA	ACLU	AFS	LCV	CON	NTU	NFIB	COC	ACU	NTLC	CHC
1998	15	13	44	31	13	47	86	88	92	76	100
1997	5	—	25	—	42	46	—	80	84	—	—

National Journal Ratings

	1997 LIB — 1997 CONS			1998 LIB — 1998 CONS		
Economic	46%	—	53%	39%	—	59%
Social	30%	—	64%	29%	—	71%
Foreign	24%	—	72%	19%	—	75%

Key Votes of the 105th Congress

1. Clinton Budget Deal	Y	5. Puerto Rico Sthood. Ref.	N	9. Cut $ for B-2 Bombers	N
2. Education IRAs	Y	6. End Highway Set-asides	Y	10. Human Rights in China	Y
3. Req. 2/3 to Raise Taxes	Y	7. School Prayer Amend.	Y	11. Withdraw Bosnia Troops	Y
4. Fast-track Trade	N	8. Ovrd. Part. Birth Veto	Y	12. End Cuban TV-Marti	N

Election Results

1998 general	Gerald C. (Jerry) Weller (R) 100,597	(59%)	($1,514,474)
	Gary S. Mueller (D) 70,458	(41%)	($195,774)
1998 primary	Gerald C. (Jerry) Weller (R) .... unopposed		
1996 general	Gerald C. (Jerry) Weller (R) 109,896	(52%)	($1,116,062)
	Clem Balanoff (D) 102,388	(48%)	($481,979)

TWELFTH DISTRICT

The nation's two mightiest rivers, the Mississippi and Missouri, their waters roiling together, join just a few miles above St. Louis and just a few miles below Alton, Illinois. Most views of this center of the Mississippi Valley focus on the Gateway Arch and the buildings of downtown St. Louis. But the Mississippi shoreline of Illinois is worthy of attention as well. Alton's 19th Century buildings recall its turbulent history, when it was the home of the anti-slavery agitator Elijah Lovejoy, murdered by a mob; more recently it was the longtime home of conservative crusader and columnist Phyllis Schlafly. Just across from the Gateway Arch is East St. Louis, where dozens of rail lines and highways funnel into bridges over the river. Once a rail and stockyards center second only to Chicago, East St. Louis is now one of America's poorest and most troubled cities, a half-abandoned slum with one of the nation's highest crime rates and a rapidly declining tax base, almost entirely dependent on a riverboat casino for its tax revenue.

South of East St. Louis and the industrial area around Belleville, the river counties are lightly inhabited, but they were not always unimportant: This was the site of the French Kaskaskia settlement that became Illinois's first capital in 1818. Farther south, the river abuts the coal country and the town of Carbondale, once a coal center but now as the home of Southern Illinois University bustling with students from Downstate Illinois and Chicago and the retirement base of former Senator Paul Simon. The land here is sometimes known as Egypt, the southern end of Illinois where the Ohio River meets the Mississippi: flat, fertile farmland, protected by giant man-made levees because it is susceptible to yearly floods. There is more than a touch of Dixie here: the unofficial capital of Egypt, Cairo (pronounced *KAYroh*), is a declining town closer to Mississippi than to Chicago with its own occasional racial violence.

The 12th District covers all of this riverfront from Alton south to Cairo, with some inland territory as well. Most of its population is in St. Clair (East St. Louis and Belleville) and Madison (Alton) counties, but one-third of the votes are cast in counties running south to Cairo.

The congressman from the 12th District is Jerry Costello, a Democrat first elected in 1988. He grew up in a St. Clair County political family, he worked for the courts after college, then became chairman of the St. Clair County Board of Supervisors in 1980. In the late 1980s he waited with some impatience for the retirement of Congressman Mel Price, first elected in 1944, who was re-elected by only 943 votes in 1986, and announced his retirement not long after; he died while in office in April 1988. Experienced, well-connected, supported by organized labor, Costello was the obvious successor when Price finally retired. Yet he received only 51% of the votes in the August 1988 special and 53% in November.

Costello is a practical-minded politician with a seat on Transportation and Infrastructure and a voting record more liberal on economics than on cultural and foreign issues. He opposed George Bush's Clean Air Act and Bill Clinton's NAFTA, bucked Clinton on the balanced budget amendment and House Republicans on public works votes. He trumpets his accomplishments without subtlety. Bridges are important in a river district: Costello has worked to replace the Clark Bridge in Alton and, with the late Congressman Bill Emerson of Missouri, to build a new bridge to Cape Girardeau to be named after Emerson. His biggest ongoing project was building the Mid-America Airport at Scott Air Force Base near Belleville; it opened in 1997 but, alas, has no scheduled airline service. He kept the Mel Price Army Support Center in Granite City off the 1995 base-closing list and worked to extend the MetroLink light rail line from St. Louis's Laclede Landing to Belleville. In the 1998 transportation bill he got funding for a $4.8 million I-64 interchange in O'Fallon, $5.6 million for an industrial park in Alton and $4.5 million for a two-mile road through the new Sauget Business Park. In May 1998 he got Army officials to scrap a plan to ship hazardous waste to Sauget from Johnston Island in the Pacific.

But a cloud has hung over Costello. In September 1996 federal prosecutors indicted Amiel Cueto, a longtime friend and business partner of Costello's, for trying to stop an investigation of a gambling operation run by a client and for conspiring to get himself installed as St. Clair County State's Attorney. In May 1997 a federal judge ruled that Costello was an "unindicted co-conspirator," and prosecutors said he was a silent partner in a plan to build an Indian casino and he worked in Congress to get recognition of an Indian tribe to sponsor it. Costello denied all in June 1997, arguing that he had no interest in the casino, his role in the Indian designation was minimal, and he had tried to get a rival to vacate the State's Attorney job only to avoid the political fuss of a primary.

Cueto was convicted, and Costello was never indicted. But he put aside his plans to run for secretary of State and found himself opposed by Bill Price, an orthopedic surgeon and son of Mel Price, who switched parties and was running as a Republican. "Mr. Costello is in office to serve his own interests and those of his benefactors," Price said. "He is an unindicted co-conspirator in a federal criminal case. This is not a tactic we're using. It's a cause of why I am running." The men agreed on many substantive issues; they were against abortion, against tax increases, for medical savings accounts; they disagreed on school vouchers and Medicare. Price said Costello was taking credit for projects that were his father's (the Clark Bridge, MidAmerica Airport), that he was undercutting MidAmerica Airport by backing the new W-1W runway for Lambert Airport in St. Louis County, Missouri, and that he allowed southern Illinois highway money to be shifted to Chicago projects. Costello said that his seniority gave him the better chance to get a four-lane road from Carbondale to Metro East and to protect Scott Air Force Base.

Price raised large sums and came close to equalling Costello's $1 million in spending. But Costello won by a solid 60%–40%. Interestingly, he ran weakest in his home territory, where knowledge of the Cueto case was presumably greatest; he won just 55% in St. Clair County, and lost fast-growing Monroe County just to the south. Evidently voters in new communities away from the river did not find this well-entrenched politician attractive. The overall result, though, suggests that Costello is safe in this basically Democratic district. He could have more trouble, however, after redistricting in 2002, or if there are further legal developments.

Cook's Call. *Probably Safe.* Even as an unindicted co-conspirator with a credible challenger, Costello managed to rack up an impressive victory in 1998. Don't look for Costello to be in much danger in 2000.

The People: Pop. 1990: 571,441; 22.5% rural; 14.2% age 65 + ; 81.5% White, 17% Black, 0.8% Asian, 0.3% Amer. Indian, 0.4% Other; 1.2% Hispanic Origin. Households: 53% married couple families; 25.4% married couple fams. w. children; 39.5% college educ.; median household income: $25,032; per capita income: $11,547; median house value: $48,000; median gross rent: $258.

1996 Presidential Vote		
Clinton (D)	120,389	(56%)
Dole (R)	72,652	(34%)
Perot (I)	19,777	(9%)

1992 Presidential Vote		
Clinton (D)	132,570	(54%)
Bush (R)	69,829	(28%)
Perot (I)	42,169	(17%)

Rep. Jerry F. Costello (D)

Elected Aug. 1988; b. Sept. 25, 1949, E. St. Louis; home, Belleville; Belleville Area Col. A.A. 1970, Maryville Col. B.A. 1972; Catholic; married (Georgia).

Elected Office: Chmn., St. Clair Cnty. Bd. of Supervisors, 1980–88.

Professional Career: Dir., IL Court Svcs. & Probation, 1973–80; Chmn., Region's Cncl. of Govts., 1980–84.

DC Office: 2454 RHOB 20515, 202-225-5661; Fax: 202-225-0285; Web site: www.house.gov/costello.

District Offices: Belleville, 618-233-8026; Carbondale, 618-529-3791; Chester, 618-826-3043; E. St. Louis, 618-397-8833; Granite City, 618-451-7065.

Committees: *Science* (4th of 22 D): Energy & Environment (RMM). *Transportation & Infrastructure* (9th of 34 D): Aviation; Water Resources & Environment.

Group Ratings

	ADA	ACLU	AFS	LCV	CON	NTU	NFIB	COC	ACU	NTLC	CHC
1998	90	33	100	77	82	22	31	28	25	16	45
1997	85	—	88	—	66	31	—	40	25	—	—

National Journal Ratings

	1997 LIB — 1997 CONS		1998 LIB — 1998 CONS	
Economic	82%	15%	77%	22%
Social	49%	51%	47%	52%
Foreign	59%	40%	55%	44%

Key Votes of the 105th Congress

1. Clinton Budget Deal	N	5. Puerto Rico Sthood. Ref.	N	9. Cut $ for B-2 Bombers	Y
2. Education IRAs	N	6. End Highway Set-asides	N	10. Human Rights in China	Y
3. Req. 2/3 to Raise Taxes	N	7. School Prayer Amend.	N	11. Withdraw Bosnia Troops	N
4. Fast-track Trade	N	8. Ovrd. Part. Birth Veto	Y	12. End Cuban TV-Marti	N

Election Results

1998 general	Jerry F. Costello (D)	99,605	(60%)	($1,097,159)
	Bill Price (R)	65,409	(40%)	($846,057)
1998 primary	Jerry F. Costello (D)	47,334	(87%)	
	Kenneth Charles Wiezer (D)	6,807	(13%)	
1996 general	Jerry F. Costello (D)	150,005	(72%)	($506,257)
	Shapley R. Hunter (R)	55,690	(27%)	($4,261)
	Others	3,824	(2%)	

THIRTEENTH DISTRICT

Most residents of Chicagoland now live not in the city but in the suburbs, and increasingly not even in Cook County but in the Collar Counties all around. DuPage County, straight west of Chicago, had 103,000 residents in 1940; in 1990, there were 781,000, with new subdivisions still springing up. Nor are these just bedroom communities. Here in Oak Brook are the head-quarters of Ace Hardware, Federal Signal, the Spiegel catalogue, and most prominently, McDonald's and its Hamburger University. One out of eight young Americans has worked at McDonald's, and millions have learned from this corporation the basics of arithmetic and literacy, good work habits and cheerful service, lessons not always taught in today's public schools. Nearby are gracefully older railroad commuter towns like Hinsdale and Downers Grove, but also Naperville, once a country village, now an edge city. And vast government laboratories have sprung up, sparking private research firms, the Argonne National Laboratory along the Sanitary and Ship Canal and the Des Plaines River.

The 13th Congressional District includes the southern slice of DuPage County, including Oak Brook, Downers Grove and Naperville, the southwest corner of Cook County around Palos Hills, and the northern slice of Will County north of Joliet. Politically, this is a heavily Repub-lican area, suspicious of the motives and operations of Chicago's Democrats, devoted to free enterprise and hostile to higher taxes. DuPage County has indeed become Illinois's Republican powerhouse, the home base of state Senate President Pate Philip and House Minority Leader (and former Speaker) Lee Daniels.

The congresswoman from the 13th is Judy Biggert, a Republican elected in 1998. She grew up in Kenilworth, on the affluent North Shore, graduated from New Trier Township High School, Stanford and Northwestern Law School and clerked for a federal appeals judge. She raised four children in Hinsdale, practicing estate and real estate law out of her home, served on the Hinsdale Township Board of Education, was chairman of the Visiting Nurses Association of Chicago—a "former car pool mom and assistant soccer coach," as her campaign put it. In

1992 she was elected to the state House, and was soon part of the leadership. There she supported tort reform, property tax caps, repeal of the Structural Work Act, tougher sentencing for child pornographers and a "quality first" education reform. In August 1997 Congressman Harris Fawell, a Republican leader on labor issues, announced he would not run again; he endorsed Biggert in November. She ran as a supporter of abortion rights. "I strongly believe that the government should not interfere with a woman's most personal and private decision." She said she opposed most gun control measures for constitutional reasons, though she had campaigned for gun control in 1992, and she said she was against "drive-by" health care.

Biggert had primary opposition from state Representative Peter Roskam, who moved into the district to run. He attacked her on abortion, and criticized her for voting for a $485 million school funding bill that included tax increases on cigarettes, casino gambling and telephones. Gary Bauer's Campaign for Working Families ran ads against Biggert, and she was opposed by some corporations because of her stand on health care. But Biggert raised far more money, including $402,000 of her own funds and contributions from Planned Parenthood and the Human Rights Campaign (she has voted for gay rights bills). And she won the endorsement of Governor Jim Edgar as well as Fawell. Biggert won the March 1998 primary by 45%–40%, carrying DuPage 50%–38% and trailing in Will and Cook counties.

In the general election Biggert was opposed by Susan Hynes, a Democrat who held Fawell to a career-low 60% in 1996. She argued that the district's demographics had changed and charged that Biggert voted against a patient's rights bill and against a partial birth abortion ban in the legislature; Biggert argued that she voted for different versions of each. But Hynes was vastly outspent, and the demographic changes proved not to be enough for her to prevail. Biggert won 61%–39%, carrying 65% in DuPage County, 57% in Will and 55% in Cook. She has pledged to limit herself to three terms.

Cook's Call. *Safe.* This western Chicagoland district is one of the most reliably Republican in the state and Biggert should win here easily in 2000.

The People: Pop. 1990: 571,344; 4.2% rural; 8% age 65 +; 91.6% White, 3.1% Black, 4.2% Asian, 0.1% Amer. Indian, 0.9% Other; 2.9% Hispanic Origin. Households: 67.5% married couple families; 37% married couple fams. w. children; 64.6% college educ.; median household income: $50,087; per capita income: $20,912; median house value: $140,300; median gross rent: $562.

1996 Presidential Vote		
Dole (R)	126,594	(50%)
Clinton (D)	104,713	(41%)
Perot (I)	21,701	(9%)

1992 Presidential Vote		
Bush (R)	128,612	(47%)
Clinton (D)	88,314	(32%)
Perot (I)	58,123	(21%)

Rep. Judy Biggert (R)

Elected 1998; b. Aug. 15, 1937, Chicago; home, Hinsdale; Stanford U., B.A. 1959, Northwestern U., J.D. 1963; Episcopalian; married (Rody).

Elected Office: IL House of Reps., 1992–98.

Professional Career: Clerk, U.S. Ct. of Appeals, 1963–64; Practicing atty., 1975–98.

DC Office: 508 CHOB 20515, 202-225-3515; Fax: 202-225-9420.

District Office: Clarendon Hills, 630-655-1061.

Committees: *Banking & Financial Services* (29th of 32 R): Capital Markets, Securities & Government Sponsored Enterprises; Domestic & International Monetary Policy. *Government Reform* (19th of 24 R): Government Management, Information & Technology (Vice Chmn.); National Security, Veterans' Affairs & Intl. Relations. *Science* (23d of 25 R): Basic Research (Vice Chmn.); Energy & Environment.

Group Ratings and Key Votes: Newly Elected

Election Results

1998 general	Judy Biggert (R)	121,889	(61%)	($1,294,853)
	Susan W. Hynes (D)	77,878	(39%)	($222,656)
1998 primary	Judy Biggert (R)	24,482	(45%)	
	Peter Roskam (R)	21,784	(40%)	
	David J. Shestokas (R)	2,574	(5%)	
	Michael J. Krzyston (R)	2,566	(5%)	
	Others	2,961	(5%)	
1996 general	Harris Fawell (R)	141,651	(60%)	($537,449)
	Susan W. Hynes (D)	94,693	(40%)	($130,612)

FOURTEENTH DISTRICT

A few dozen miles beyond the Loop there is an invisible line marking two different Chicagos. One is the Chicago dominated by blacks and descendants of the vast immigrations of 1840–1924 and 1970–90, a Chicago where certain loyalties are taken for granted: loyalty to ethnic group, to church (usually the Catholic Church, often with an ethnic prefix), and to party (almost always the Democrats). This Chicago is a gritty city, where personal cheerfulness and courtesy lighten up days otherwise as cold and impersonal as the gray winter sky. The other Chicago is the beginning of the Great Plains, originally a white Anglo-Saxon Protestant Chicago, a place whose residents are products of the first great wave of immigration to America. The tone of this Chicago is lighter, its streets and highways cleaner and neater, its daily life generally free from evidence of unpleasantness and deprivation. People in this Chicago think of themselves as typical Americans, and their geographical vision takes in the vast plains. Ronald Reagan grew up in Downstate Illinois within the orbit of this Chicago (though he did live in the city briefly), and its spirit helped to characterize his presidency. His migration to southern California, incidentally, is not atypical: you can see in the geometric grids and Republican voting patterns of Orange County or Phoenix almost exact replicas of the grids and patterns in Chicago's suburban "Collar Counties," transported to the once-empty Southwest on the Atchison, Topeka & Santa Fe or out the old U.S. 66 from their beginnings in Chicago's Loop.

The 14th Congressional District straddles this line between metropolitan Chicago and Downstate Illinois. It gets as close as 30 miles to Chicago's Loop, in western DuPage County, with two great Chicagoland landmarks—Cantigny, the estate of Colonel Robert McCormick, long-time publisher of the *Chicago Tribune*, and FermiLab, the world's fastest energy particle accelerator and employer of some 2,000 people— icons of political conservatism and high technology within two miles of each other. The 14th also contains the Fox River Valley, and its industrial cities of Elgin and Aurora (the home of Garth and Wayne in *Wayne's World*), and antique St. Charles in the heart of the Collar Counties. Farther west, amid what may be the world's richest cornfields, the 14th passes through DeKalb, long the world's leading manufacturer of barbed wire, and goes on to Kendall and Lee counties, including Reagan's boyhood home in Dixon. This is some of the most heavily Republican territory in the country. Northern Illinois was settled, when Chicago was just a frontier village, by Yankees from Ohio, Indiana, Upstate New York and New England, and by Germans emigrating after the failed revolutions of 1848: people who formed the heart of the Republican Party from its founding in 1854, and who would form the core of the Grand Army of the Republic a few years later. Their descendants, in this extension of Chicagoland, remain solidly Republican today.

The congressman from the 14th is Dennis Hastert, a Republican first elected in 1986, and today the 51st man to become speaker of the House. Like many congressmen from high-income districts he comes from a modest background. He grew up on a farm; his father had a feed supply business, and Denny and his brothers hoisted 100-pound bags and delivered milk in the early morning. At high school in Oswego—then a rural town, now exploding with subdivisions—he wrestled and played football; after graduating from Wheaton College, he became a high school teacher at Yorkville High School, a rural town a few miles farther from Chicago. There he taught history and coached wrestling for 16 years. But his experience was not as limited as that description may suggest. In summers he traveled as a teacher for the YMCA or other groups to Japan, Columbia, Venezuela, Europe and the Soviet Union. "Almost every summer before I got married, I was in Japan or Europe or South America. I'd take slides and bring that experience back to the classroom." And as a wrestling coach he excelled: He took his teams to training camps and tournaments in other states to learn new holds; his team won the state championship and he was named the national coach of the year in 1976.

After a trip to Washington in 1978, when Democrats had a 2–1 majority in the House, he got involved in politics, interning with state Senator John Grotberg. In 1980 he finished third in an Illinois House primary, then the incumbent became fatally ill and Hastert was chosen to take his place on the November ballot. In the Illinois House he sat next to Tom Ewing, now congressman from the 15th District; the speaker was George Ryan, now governor of Illinois. After the March 1986 primary, Grotberg, now a member of Congress, was fatally stricken with cancer and Hastert again was chosen by the party as a replacement. The election was unusually close, but Hastert won 52%–48%.

In the House, Hastert had a conservative voting record and made few waves. But he gained valuable experience. He got a seat on the Commerce Committee and on the subcommittees handling health, energy and telecommunications issues. He built a relationship with Minority Leader Robert Michel, from Illinois's 18th District. He worked together with Tom DeLay of Texas for Ed Madigan in the race for minority whip in March 1989; Madigan lost by just two votes to an upstart from Georgia named Newt Gingrich. In the 1992 campaign he and Bill Emerson of Missouri worked hard for the House Republicans' campaign committee. In 1994 he was chief organizer for Tom DeLay's campaign for whip, the one leadership post won by a non-Gingrichite after the big Republican gains that fall. Afterwards, Hastert was named chief deputy whip and shared an office and staff with DeLay.

To his work Hastert brought the habits of a coach, listening long to colleagues' goals and complaints, sizing up their character and capacity, then insisting firmly on a course of action when he reached a judgment. He operated with minimal ego and a bear-like friendliness, putting his arm around a colleague when asking advice or seeking intelligence; increasingly he was looked to by other leaders to help Republicans reach consensus and to negotiate difficult issues with Democrats, particularly health care. In 1993 he was on a Republican task force responding to Hillary Rodham Clinton's health care plan. In 1996 he worked on the portability bill passed by both houses of Congress; it included removal of preexisting conditions, allowed small businesses to use pools to buy insurance, created medical savings accounts, increased on a sliding scale tax deductibility of health insurance for the self-employed and reformed malpractice laws. In 1997 he helped put together the Republicans' Medicare bill. Gingrich made him head of a task force that hammered out a patients' rights bill. This was delicate stuff: He worked with Charlie Norwood, who wanted patients to have the right to sue HMOs, and Bill Thomas, who was strongly against it. The Republican bill, passed by the House in August 1998, did not include the right to sue, but did include a ban on the gag rule, permitted emergency room visits without previous approval, and allowed patients to appeal decisions to an arbitrator.

Hastert was active in negotiations on the 1996 telecommunications bill and on repealing the Social Security "earnings tax"—the deduction of benefits among senior citizens who earn over a certain figure—in the 1995 Contract With America. Gingrich made him the Republicans' lead negotiator on the 2000 Census in 1997. He strongly opposed the Clinton Administration plan for census sampling, which he said would be open to fraud and abuse, and argued that the Constitution required an "enumeration" which could only be done by head-count. He eventually moved the issue to a new subcommittee headed by Dan Miller of Florida and held to a hard line against Democrats and the Clinton Administration. Over the years, Hastert has continued his trips abroad, including to Japan, and has been supportive of free trade; central Illinois, where the largest company is Caterpillar, produces more exports than just about anywhere else in the country. He tended to support the regional Bells on telecom issues and favored encryption controls on the Internet. He has helped get funding for FermiLab and Argonne National Laboratory, and in 1998 got $250,000 in the defense budget for "pharmacokinetics research," which turned out to be a study of caffeinated chewing gum by Amurol Confections Company of Yorkville.

Until December 1998, Hastert, well known in the House, was almost unknown to the general public. Then, three days after Republicans lost five seats in the November elections, Speaker Newt Gingrich announced his retirement. Challenges loomed against everyone in the leadership, with the conspicuous exception of DeLay. Many members urged Hastert to run against Majority Leader Dick Armey. But Hastert had pledged to support him; when he asked to be released from the pledge, Armey said no; and so he stuck to it and didn't run for a position he could probably have won. This behavior, unusual among Republican leaders who had been targeting each other for more than a year, was recalled on December 19, when just before the impeachment vote Speaker-designate Bob Livingston announced his retirement too. Gingrich told Hastert, "You are the only one in this conference who could pull this body together. You are going to have to be the next speaker of the House." At one 1 p.m. he announced; by the end of the day he had more than 100 votes, and the speakership.

In his opening speech January 6, Hastert made a point of walking down from the podium and speaking from the well of the House. "My legislative home is here on the floor with you, and so is my heart." He invoked the spirit of bipartisanship so widely longed for, but with an edge: "To my Democratic colleagues, I say I will meet you halfway, maybe more so on occasion. But cooperation is a two-way street, and I expect you to meet me halfway, too." He invoked his authority as a coach: "Everyone on the squad has something to offer. You never get to the finals without a well-rounded team. Above all, a coach worth his salt will instill in his team a sense of fair play, camaraderie, respect for the game and for the opposition. . . . It it is work, not talk, that wins championships." As speaker, he seems more likely to defer to committee chairmen and more eager to meet appropriations deadlines than Gingrich, who passed over seniority to create his own chairmen in 1994 and often created task forces to make end runs around them. At the same time, Hastert did not offer the kind of deference to appropriators that Livingston had demanded in November as Gingrich and, as a regular commuter home to Yorkville (where his wife still teaches school) every weekend, he rejected Livingston's proposal of a five-day work week. He told the *Chicago Sun-Times*, "I was never a Newt Gingrich. I wasn't very articulate and philosophical and a visionary that certainly Gingrich was. . . . My strong point is I can really identify problems and work through the process to solve the problems." In place of the dinosaur skeleton Gingrich put in the Speaker's office, he installed a ship captain's bell.

Many Democrats saw Hastert as an interim speaker, serving only until what they considered their inevitable victory in the House elections of 2000. Republicans hoped that he could produce solid enough achievements to commend their majority to pro-incumbent voters. Despite his unwillingness to give the wide-ranging overviews Gingrich loved, Hastert seemed in early months to have something of a strategy. Noting the importance of education, the House and Senate passed "EdFlex" bills, block-granting dollars to the states, a proposal supported by all 50 governors. As Hastert said in his opening speech, "In my 16 years as a teacher, I learned that most of the decisions having to do with education are best left to the people closest to the situation: parents, teachers and school board members. What should the federal government's role be? It should be to see that as many education dollars as possible go directly to the classrooms, where they will do the most good." Republicans invited Bill Clinton to propose specific Social Security and Medicare reforms—invitations he seemed determined to spurn. And they targeted defense and foreign policy. They moved quickly to pass a bipartisan missile defense bill. And on Kosovo, Hastert insisted on a debate over a resolution supporting the deployment of U.S. troops, with an open rule for amendments barring or limiting it. He said that he started off neutral, but weighed in quietly in support of the authorization, but with requirements that the administration specify objectives and means: an assertion of congressional authority that had been allowed to lapse and the basis for a critique of administration policy if things turn sour. It was not a bad start for a leader with a 223–212 majority, and it may be a sign that this former wrestling coach, who drives a pickup truck and carves duck decoys on the weekend, was being underestimated in early 1999 as he had been in the past.

Cook's Call. *Safe.* Speaker of the House Hastert will have no trouble winning his eighth election in this Republican district.

The People: Pop. 1990: 571,540; 21% rural; 9.6% age 65 +; 88.9% White, 4.2% Black, 1.7% Asian, 0.2% Amer. Indian, 5% Other; 9.5% Hispanic Origin. Households: 63.6% married couple families; 34.8% married couple fams. w. children; 50.3% college educ.; median household income: $39,815; per capita income: $15,769; median house value: $100,600; median gross rent: $412.

1996 Presidential Vote

Dole (R)	103,773	(48%)
Clinton (D)	89,939	(41%)
Perot (I)	22,148	(10%)

1992 Presidential Vote

Bush (R)	105,700	(44%)
Clinton (D)	83,109	(34%)
Perot (I)	52,914	(22%)

Rep. J. Dennis Hastert (R)

Elected 1986; b. Jan. 2, 1942, Aurora; home, Yorkville; Wheaton Col., B.A. 1964, N. IL U., M.A. 1967; Protestant; married (Jean).

Elected Office: IL House of Reps., 1980–86.

Professional Career: High schl. teacher & coach, 1965–80.

DC Office: 2263 RHOB 20515, 202-225-2976; Fax: 202-225-0697; Web site: www.house.gov/hastert.

District Office: Batavia, 630-406-1114.

Committees: *Speaker of the House.*

Group Ratings

	ADA	ACLU	AFS	LCV	CON	NTU	NFIB	COC	ACU	NTLC	CHC
1998	0	6	0	23	26	51	100	100	100	97	100
1997	0	—	13	—	49	51	—	100	88	—	—

National Journal Ratings

	1997 LIB — 1997 CONS		1998 LIB — 1998 CONS	
Economic	19%	— 76%	19%	— 79%
Social	0%	— 90%	14%	— 81%
Foreign	22%	— 77%	17%	— 82%

Key Votes of the 105th Congress

1. Clinton Budget Deal	Y	5. Puerto Rico Sthood. Ref.	N	9. Cut $ for B-2 Bombers	N
2. Education IRAs	Y	6. End Highway Set-asides	Y	10. Human Rights in China	N
3. Req. 2/3 to Raise Taxes	Y	7. School Prayer Amend.	Y	11. Withdraw Bosnia Troops	Y
4. Fast-track Trade	Y	8. Ovrd. Part. Birth Veto	Y	12. End Cuban TV-Marti	N

Election Results

1998 general	J. Dennis Hastert (R) 117,304	(70%)	($971,137)
	Robert A. Cozzi Jr. (D) 50,844	(30%)	($24,152)
1998 primary	J. Dennis Hastert (R) .... unopposed		
1996 general	J. Dennis Hastert (R) 134,432	(64%)	($968,055)
	Doug Mains (D) 74,332	(36%)	($125,997)

FIFTEENTH DISTRICT

South from Chicago, the Illinois Central Railroad heads to the city of New Orleans on a railbed elevated a few feet above the rich black soil of the Illinois prairie, topsoil reaching down not just inches but feet. This land dazzled its first settlers, who were used to land that had to be cleared of trees and stumps before it could be plowed; this treeless prairie could be cultivated almost immediately, and with bounteous results. Today, this remains farming country, made up not of small family farms but of large commercial operations, typically of 1,000 acres or more. Cultivating this soil is a business, requiring informed decisions about crop selection (soybeans and corn are the current favorites), maximizing yields, proper pesticides, marketing decisions, watching farm export prospects and, until the 1996 Freedom to Farm Act, taking advantage of government programs. The landscape on the prairies of eastern Illinois is marked by only a few towns, the largest of which, Champaign-Urbana and Bloomington-Normal, are the sites of universities (the University of Illinois and Illinois Normal). Politically, these prairie lands have been Republican, often very Republican; they incline much more to the party of former House Speaker Joseph Cannon, a Republican from the manufacturing city of Danville east of Urbana, than to that of Vice President Adlai Stevenson, a Democrat from Bloomington, who served under *laissez-faire* Democrat Grover Cleveland and was the grandfather of the Adlai Stevenson nominated by Democrats for president in 1952 and 1956.

The 15th Congressional District occupies much of this prairie, beginning 60 miles from Chicago, where the Illinois Central heads toward Kankakee, and moving over 150 miles of prairie to the courthouse town of Monticello. It includes Bloomington, Champaign-Urbana and Danville, and runs south almost to the National Road and U.S. 40, traditionally the line between northern Republican and southern Democratic Illinois. Today, the area is strongly Republican and has been represented for years by Republicans who have been active in local businesses, civic affairs and state legislative politics.

The congressman from the 15th, Tom Ewing, fits that description. He is a descendant of General Thomas Ewing Jr., who settled in these parts in the 1850s, and grew up in Georgia; he served in the Army in the 1950s, then headed the Pontiac and Harvey chambers of commerce, got a law degree and became an assistant state's attorney, then was elected to the Illinois House in 1974, at 39. His political history is intertwined with that of speakers of the U.S. House. In 1981 and 1982 his seatmate in Springfield was a freshman named Dennis Hastert; Ewing owes his own election to the victory of Newt Gingrich, speaker from 1995–99, by an 87–85 margin in the race for minority whip in March 1989 over Edward Madigan, then congressman from the 15th. After losing, Madigan retired and was appointed secretary of Agriculture; Ewing entered the race for the vacancy. As assistant and deputy minority leader in Springfield from 1982, he was the overwhelming favorite, and beat the Democrat 66%–31% in the July 1991 special election.

Ewing has compiled a solidly conservative voting record, and has concentrated on issues of local import. Thanks to then-Minority Leader Robert Michel, he got a seat on the Agriculture Committee; thanks to Gingrich, and the work he did to enable Republicans to win a majority, just three years later Ewing became chairman of the Agriculture Subcommittee on Risk Management, Research and Specialty Crops. This has jurisdiction over commodity futures, crop insurance, and the crops other than cotton, wheat, corn, soybeans, rice, which traditionally have had their own subcommittees. Ewing is a promoter of ethanol, produced from Illinois prairie grain and by Decatur-based Archer Daniels Midland; he took the lead in the successful fight in 1998 to continue the ethanol subsidy until 2007. He fought hard against eliminating sugar import quotas; high sugar prices guarantee a market for manufacturers of high-fructose syrup (ADM again). Ewing and Mark Foley of Florida led the sugar coalition to a 217–208 victory, and sugar joined cotton as the crop subsidies which the Republicans were not able to wipe out in the Freedom to Farm Act. Like most farm state congressmen, Ewing favored MFN status for China every year, and was co-sponsor of a 1997 bill to make it permanent if China made necessary reforms. His 1998 proposal to deregulate professional traders in futures markets was foiled after a dispute between the Chicago Board of Trade and the Chicago Mercantile Exchange. Prompted by local concerns over large hog and poultry lots, he included research on odor control and environmental management of these facilities in the 1998 bill which also extended crop insurance subsidies and restored food stamps for legal immigrants who are children, elderly or disabled. He has proposed that Medicare pay for insulin infusion pumps. Ewing has supported overturning the conviction of Dr. Samuel Mudd, who treated an injured John Wilkes Booth and was defended by General Thomas Ewing, for complicity in the assassination of Abraham Lincoln on the grounds that he was illegally tried by a military commission.

In the leadership shakeup after the November 1998 election, Ewing and Mike Castle nominated Dennis Hastert for majority leader at the Republican caucus, although Hastert declined to run and kept his promise to support Dick Armey. But this may have had some subliminal effect a month later, when Speaker-designate Bob Livingston stunned the House by announcing his retirement, and Hastert emerged within hours as the choice for speaker. Ewing got no position on the leadership himself, but is widely considered influential with Speaker Hastert.

At home, Ewing received vigorous opposition from a former Champaign County auditor in 1996 and 1998. In that first year, she held him to 57%, his lowest percentage; two years later he won 62%–38%.

Cook's Call. *Safe.* Although this district picked up some Democratic areas in the 1992 redistricting plan, it still retains a Republican leaning. Ewing should have no fear of losing here in 2000.

The People: Pop. 1990: 571,292; 33.7% rural; 13.5% age 65 + ; 89.8% White, 7.5% Black, 1.9% Asian, 0.2% Amer. Indian, 0.6% Other; 1.4% Hispanic Origin. Households: 54.6% married couple families; 25.9% married couple fams. w. children; 44.8% college educ.; median household income: $26,760; per capita income: $12,709; median house value: $52,500; median gross rent: $289.

1996 Presidential Vote			1992 Presidential Vote		
Clinton (D)	100,016	(45%)	Clinton (D)	107,914	(42%)
Dole (R)	98,926	(45%)	Bush (R)	98,378	(39%)
Perot (I)	19,478	(9%)	Perot (I)	47,280	(19%)

Rep. Tom Ewing (R)

Elected July 1991; b. Sept. 19, 1935, Atlanta; home, Pontiac; Milliken U., B.S. 1957, John Marshall, J.D. 1968; Methodist; married (Connie).

Military Career: Army, 1957–59; Army Reserves, 1959–63.

Elected Office: IL House of Reps., 1974–91.

Professional Career: Farmer; Exec. Dir., Pontiac & Harvey Chambers of Commerce, 1963–68; Asst. St. Atty., Livingston Cnty., 1968–73; Practicing atty., 1968–91.

DC Office: 2417 RHOB 20515, 202-225-2371; Fax: 202-225-8071; Web site: www.house.gov/ewing.

District Offices: Bloomington, 309-662-9371; Danville, 217-431-8230; Pontiac, 815-844-7660; Urbana, 217-328-0165.

Committees: *Agriculture* (4th of 27 R): Department Operations, Oversight, Nutrition & Forestry; Risk Management, Research & Specialty Crops (Chmn.). *House Administration* (6th of 6 R). *Science* (14th of 25 R): Basic Research; Technology. *Transportation & Infrastructure* (8th of 41 R): Aviation; Economic Development, Public Buildings, Hazardous Materials & Pipeline Transportation.

Group Ratings

	ADA	ACLU	AFS	LCV	CON	NTU	NFIB	COC	ACU	NTLC	CHC
1998	0	7	0	23	26	50	100	100	91	84	92
1997	20	—	13	—	62	52	—	80	84	—	—

National Journal Ratings

	1997 LIB — 1997 CONS			1998 LIB — 1998 CONS		
Economic	41%	—	58%	0%	—	88%
Social	10%	—	82%	25%	—	75%
Foreign	24%	—	72%	39%	—	61%

Key Votes of the 105th Congress

1. Clinton Budget Deal	Y	5. Puerto Rico Sthood. Ref.	N	9. Cut $ for B-2 Bombers	N
2. Education IRAs	Y	6. End Highway Set-asides	Y	10. Human Rights in China	N
3. Req. 2/3 to Raise Taxes	Y	7. School Prayer Amend.	Y	11. Withdraw Bosnia Troops	Y
4. Fast-track Trade	Y	8. Ovrd. Part. Birth Veto	Y	12. End Cuban TV-Marti	N

Election Results

1998 general	Tom Ewing (R) 104,255	(62%)	($546,599)
	Laurel Lunt Prussing (D) 65,054	(38%)	($140,733)
1998 primary	Tom Ewing (R) .... unopposed		
1996 general	Tom Ewing (R) 121,019	(57%)	($664,934)
	Laurel Lunt Prussing (D) 90,065	(43%)	($369,185)

SIXTEENTH DISTRICT

The far northwest corner of Illinois is one of the heartlands of the Republican Party. Here, in the town square of Freeport, some 15,000 people came to hear Abraham Lincoln and Stephen Douglas in one of their seven debates, and on terrain most partial to Lincoln. Settled by New England Yankees, northern Illinois was one of the strongest Republican constituencies in 1860 and for years after. Not far away, on a little river once navigable by Mississippi River steamboats, is Galena, one of the earliest settlements in northern Illinois, the home of Ulysses S. Grant before he became general and then president; not far away are Tampico and Dixon, birthplace and boyhood home of Ronald Reagan. Farther up on the Rock River is Rockford, settled by Swedes as well as Yankees, one of America's leading furniture manufacturers at one time, then a major center for machine tools. Politically, northern Illinois, perhaps inspired by Democratic Chicago, remained steadfastly Republican; it backed Herbert Hoover in 1932, Barry Goldwater in 1964 and George Bush in 1992 when most of America and Illinois were going the other way.

The 16th Congressional District consists of much of northwest Illinois, which extends west to the hilly, almost mountainous country around Galena and the Mississippi River, and east to McHenry County, full of new subdivisions surrounding old towns, where Motorola has been opening new cellular phone plants to supply Japan, and affluent young families make their way up through free enterprise and have conservative cultural values. Rockford is a big exporter of machine tools, and Caterpillar, one of the nation's leading exporters, is headquartered nearby and has many subcontractors here.

The congressman from the 16th District is Donald Manzullo, a Republican first elected in 1992. He grew up in Rockford, where his father ran a grocery store, and his brother owns Manzullo's Drive-In Restaurant and Italian Villa. While in college in Washington in the mid-1960s, he worked for Republican candidates, and he has practiced law in Illinois since 1970. He lives on a cattle-breeding farm, writes poetry and books on constitutional law, and ran a radio talk show; he and his wife home-school two of their three children. He ran in 1990 and lost the primary 54%–46% to a moderate, who after revelations of personal problems then lost the general to Democrat John Cox. Cox favored increased taxes, opposed capital punishment and was hurt when ultra-Republican McHenry County was added in redistricting. Manzullo ran again and, with support from conservative Christians, beat a moderate 56%–44% in the primary, attacking him for supporting gasoline, cigarette and computer software tax increases in the legislature. Cox campaigned for higher taxes; Manzullo for a 10% across-the-board income tax cut. Manzullo lost narrowly in Rockford and in Winnebago County but he won nearly 2–1 in McHenry County and won overall with 56%.

Manzullo's focus in the House has been on increasing manufactured exports. He supported NAFTA, GATT and the WTO: "opening new markets benefits the United States." He favored reauthorization of the Export-Import Bank, saying that otherwise Caterpillar would lose Three

Gorges Dam contracts to Japanese firms, and of the Overseas Private Investment Corporation, though some conservatives and liberals labeled it "corporate welfare," but only for two years and with a proviso requiring congressional approval of any commitment over $200 million. In 1997 he pressed unsuccessfully for approval of fast track. But he joined many protectionists in arguing against an FTC proposal to reduce the percentage of U.S. content to 75% in goods labeled "Made in U.S.A."

On a variety of legislation Manzullo has taken what might be considered common sense initiatives. He amended the Clean Air Act to make the car pooling provisions voluntary. He got the Navy to stop giving away deactivated ships to allies; it now leases or sells them, generating $600 million in revenue. Prompted by a school desegregation decree which forced Rockford to raise school taxes by $180 million, he wants to limit the power of federal judges to raise state and local taxes by requiring judges to take their decisions' impact on the community into account before they are issued. The House rejected his position 230–181 in April 1998. Prompted by a case in which a 38-year-old McHenry County teacher took a 14-year-old girl to a health clinic for an anti-pregnancy drug, he pressed to require federally funded health clinics to notify parents before dispensing birth control devices or contraceptives; this was beaten in the House in September 1997 by 220–201, but passed in October 1998 (too late for Senate action) by 224–220. In 1998 he also pushed a bill to relieve firms of Y2K liability. Manzullo favors a 10% tax cut, likes a flat tax provided home mortgage interest and charitable deductions are retained, and looks well on Social Security individual investment accounts. He sees no contradiction in backing these and supporting the 1998 transportation bill, which included $12 million for congestion relief in Algonquin, $7.5 million for an I-90 interchange near Rockford and $5.1 million to upgrade U.S. 20 Business Route in Freeport. He has entered Illinois's airport wars by arguing that any third Chicago area airport should be based in Rockford which, as he points out, is close to the fastest-growing part of the metropolitan area.

Cook's Call. *Safe.* Though this northern Illinois district has a Democratic core in Rockford, it is still pretty safe Republican territory. Manzullo is well entrenched here.

The People: Pop. 1990: 571,488; 26% rural; 12.5% age 65 + ; 92.8% White, 4.7% Black, 0.9% Asian, 0.2% Amer. Indian, 1.4% Other; 2.9% Hispanic Origin. Households: 62% married couple families; 31% married couple fams. w. children; 43.5% college educ.; median household income: $34,668; per capita income: $15,107; median house value: $73,700; median gross rent: $311.

1996 Presidential Vote			1992 Presidential Vote		
Dole (R)	111,641	(47%)	Bush (R)	108,949	(42%)
Clinton (D)	99,397	(42%)	Clinton (D)	95,103	(36%)
Perot (I)	24,153	(10%)	Perot (I)	56,169	(21%)

Rep. Donald Manzullo (R)

Elected 1992; b. Mar. 24, 1944, Rockford; home, Egan; American U., B.A. 1967, Marquette U., J.D. 1970; Baptist; married (Freda).

Professional Career: Practicing atty., 1970–92; author.

DC Office: 409 CHOB 20515, 202-225-5676; Fax: 202-225-5284; Web site: www.house.gov/manzullo.

District Offices: Crystal Lake, 815-356-9800; Rockford, 815-394-1231.

Committees: *Banking & Financial Services* (24th of 32 R): Capital Markets, Securities & Government Sponsored Enterprises. *International Relations* (12th of 26 R): Asia & the Pacific; International Economic Policy & Trade. *Small Business* (4th of 19 R): Tax, Finance & Exports (Chmn.).

Group Ratings

	ADA	ACLU	AFS	LCV	CON	NTU	NFIB	COC	ACU	NTLC	CHC
1998	0	6	0	23	63	63	100	94	92	89	100
1997	5	—	13	—	67	64	—	90	100	—	—

National Journal Ratings

	1997 LIB — 1997 CONS		1998 LIB — 1998 CONS	
Economic	14%	— 85%	15%	— 81%
Social	20%	— 71%	3%	— 90%
Foreign	12%	— 88%	27%	— 68%

Key Votes of the 105th Congress

1. Clinton Budget Deal	Y	5. Puerto Rico Sthood. Ref.	N	9. Cut $ for B-2 Bombers	N
2. Education IRAs	Y	6. End Highway Set-asides	Y	10. Human Rights in China	N
3. Req. 2/3 to Raise Taxes	Y	7. School Prayer Amend.	Y	11. Withdraw Bosnia Troops	Y
4. Fast-track Trade	Y	8. Ovrd. Part. Birth Veto	Y	12. End Cuban TV-Marti	N

Election Results

1998 general	Donald Manzullo (R) .... unopposed			($439,914)
1998 primary	Donald Manzullo (R) .... unopposed			
1996 general	Donald Manzullo (R)	137,523	(60%)	($786,063)
	Catherine M. Lee (D)	90,575	(40%)	($391,414)

SEVENTEENTH DISTRICT

Illinois's western prairies are some of America's richest agricultural land. They were first settled by Yankees coming overland from northern Indiana and Ohio and Upstate New York. After 1848, Germans left their homeland in search of better opportunities and settled this land that in so many ways resembles the flat, orderly plains of northern Germany. All these migrants farmed quarter-sections and built small towns, with banks and stores, community churches and libraries. In time, investors built farm machinery factories, and the Quad Cities of the Mississippi—Davenport and Bettendorf, Iowa, and Rock Island and Moline, Illinois—became one of the nation's biggest agricultural equipment manufacturing centers. These plants were unionized in the 1930s and 1940s, and in post-World War II America their wages went up as the demand for ever more sophisticated machines rose among the Midwest's government-subsidized farmers. But eventually the cost of subsidies rose too high and the market had its revenge. In the early 1980s, farm profits vanished, land values declined and orders for new machinery and equipment dried up. The result was a depression in western Illinois and neighboring Iowa, and a political swing toward the Democrats and away from the Republicans who had been the ancestral party in most of this area. Now Republicanism seems to be returning, but not with the speed of the Democratic trend a dozen years ago.

The 17th Congressional District includes most of Illinois's Mississippi River border with Iowa plus half a dozen more prairie counties to the east. For years, its Democratic base in the Quad Cities was outvoted by Republican counties elsewhere. But in 1982, longtime Republican congressman Tom Railsback lost to a conservative in the primary; ready to take advantage of this opening was Democrat Lane Evans, a local legal services attorney angry at the Reagan recession who took a gamble in running and ended up winning with 53%.

Evans remains, after two aggressive challenges, congressman from the 17th District. He grew up in Rock Island, the son of a union firefighter. He joined the Marine Corps in 1969, after high school, and served two years; then went to college and law school and worked as a legal services lawyer. He brings to his work an earnestness that is almost square, a pleasant, boyish demeanor that will never be mistaken for East Coast slick. He calls himself a "populist" rather than a liberal; by most standards, his voting record is solidly liberal and one of the most pro-union in the House. He was a strong opponent of NAFTA and GATT. He fervently favored higher agricultural subsidies during his five-year tenure on the Agriculture Committee, but left that post to take a seat on Armed Services in 1988, even as farm subsidies were cut back in 1985 and 1990 and phased out in 1996.

Evans is ranking Democrat on the Veterans Affairs Committee and has devoted much time to veterans' issues. He worked hard for years to get compensation for veterans who claimed they were harmed by exposure to Agent Orange, and ultimately succeeded. In 1996 he passed a bill providing benefits to children of Vietnam veterans exposed to Agent Orange who were born with spina bifida—the first entitlement for children of veterans. In 1992, he passed measures to provide mental health services for women veterans who are sexually traumatized on active duty. In 1994 he began to investigate what he and others have characterized as Gulf war syndrome, despite lack of evidence of causal connection between the variety of ailments complained of and Gulf war conditions. Evans's approach to traditional veterans' organizations and to Agent Orange was very different from that of longtime Chairman Sonny Montgomery, whom Evans challenged in the Democratic Caucus after the 1992 election; Montgomery won by only 127–123, but Evans did not challenge him for the ranking minority position in 1994 and Montgomery retired in 1996.

On Armed Services, Evans worked on finding alternatives to tritium production; he also questioned how much export controls should be relaxed on critical weapons materials. His major cause on the committee has been a ban on land mines, which continue to injure thousands years after wars are over. In 1997 he co-sponsored, with Republican Jack Quinn, a total ban along the lines championed by Canada and agreed to by many other nations; his ban would include "smart" mines, those which remain explosive for only a limited time and, after a 12-year exemption, all mines in South Korea. This approach was rejected by the Clinton Administration, which wanted to keep mines in South Korea to repel any attack by North Korea.

Evans is also co-chairman of the Alcohol Fuels Caucus; he helped the ethanol tax credit get extended from 2000 to 2007 in the 1998 transportation bill. He supports federal regulation of hog lots and attacked the VA for not seeking a share of the $385 billion settlement agreed to by the tobacco industry in 1997. In December 1997 he asked the GAO to study whether political contributions influenced decisions to bury people into Arlington National Cemetery lots. And he was one of 31 Democrats who voted for the Republicans' impeachment inquiry in October 1998, though he later voted solidly against impeachment.

In the years of agricultural unrest and high unemployment in western Illinois, Evans was re-elected by wide margins. But in the more prosperous mid-1990s, his margins have been narrower. In 1994 against an underfunded candidate he won with 55%. In 1996 and 1998 he faced Mark Baker, a TV anchor until 1996 in Quincy, in the southern end of the district, and after that a regional representative for the Illinois Chamber of Commerce. In 1996 Baker argued that Evans was ignoring the area's agricultural and transportation needs, and accused him of "a far-left social agenda and tax-and-spend record." Evans campaigned against Newt Gingrich and Medicare "cuts" and attacked Baker's opposition to gun control and abortion. The final result was a 52%–47% Evans victory. He carried Rock Island and the central part of the district, but lost the northern end and the area around Quincy by wide margins.

In 1998 Baker ran again. This time the race was targeted early by Republicans and Baker raised more PAC money than any other challenger. An additional factor came in May 1998 when Evans announced he had Parkinson's disease; he said he cannot stand long without pain or smile easily, but he still can jog and he lost weight under doctor's orders. The second Evans-Baker race presented strong contrasts in issue positions and tactics. Baker argued that Evans's positions hurt the farm economy, especially his opposition to NAFTA and fast track. He ultimately raised and spent almost $1.3 million and appealed strongly to the 38,000 Farm Bureau members in the district. Evans depended heavily on organized labor and liberal volunteers. He raised and spent almost $1.2 million, most of it from PACs, and was the beneficiary of $100,000 of TV ads by the Sierra Club (attacking hog lots) and $20,000 from the AFL-CIO. He also ran a campaign school, putting into the field as many as 6,000 volunteers and seven phone banks, and appealed heavily to the district's 58,000 union members.

The result of all this was almost exactly the same as in 1996: Evans won 52%–48%. He increased his percentages in Rock Island County and the counties immediately east and south; Baker increased his percentages in the north and south parts of the district. Evans said right after the election that he would run again in 2000; it is possible he will have another serious challenge.

Cook's Call. *Highly Competitive.* With two tight races under his belt and a district continuing to trend away from the Democrats, Evans remains one of the more vulnerable incumbents in the country. However, after putting up their best candidate (and lots of money) in 1998, it is hard to see what more Republicans can do to try to knock out Evans. If Evans decides to leave (his health may be a factor), Republicans have a good shot of picking it up. There are also rumors that Republican mapmakers in Illinois may try to draw this seat a little more favorably to Republicans for the 2002 election.

The People: Pop. 1990: 571,585; 38.3% rural; 17.1% age 65 + ; 94.7% White, 3.2% Black, 0.6% Asian, 0.2% Amer. Indian, 1.3% Other; 2.9% Hispanic Origin. Households: 57.7% married couple families; 25.9% married couple fams. w. children; 37.8% college educ.; median household income: $25,195; per capita income: $12,052; median house value: $41,600; median gross rent: $223.

1996 Presidential Vote

Clinton (D) 119,918 (51%)
Dole (R) 89,447 (38%)
Perot (I) 23,176 (10%)

1992 Presidential Vote

Clinton (D) 124,175 (47%)
Bush (R) 95,554 (36%)
Perot (I) 45,566 (17%)

Rep. Lane Evans (D)

Elected 1982; b. Aug. 4, 1951, Rock Island; home, Rock Island; Augustana Col., B.A. 1974, Georgetown U., J.D. 1978; Catholic; single.

Military Career: Marine Corps, 1969–71.

Professional Career: Practicing atty., 1978–82.

DC Office: 2335 RHOB 20515, 202-225-5905; Fax: 202-225-5396; Web site: www.house.gov/evans.

District Offices: Galesburg, 309-342-4411; Moline, 309-793-5760.

Committees: *Armed Services* (6th of 28 D): Military Procurement. *Veterans' Affairs* (RMM of 14 D).

Group Ratings

	ADA	ACLU	AFS	LCV	CON	NTU	NFIB	COC	ACU	NTLC	CHC
1998	90	94	100	100	62	15	14	22	16	8	8
1997	100	—	100	—	17	29	—	20	16	—	—

National Journal Ratings

	1997 LIB — 1997 CONS		1998 LIB — 1998 CONS	
Economic	85%	— 10%	72%	— 23%
Social	85%	— 0%	85%	— 14%
Foreign	76%	— 22%	64%	— 31%

Key Votes of the 105th Congress

1. Clinton Budget Deal	N	5. Puerto Rico Sthood. Ref.	Y	9. Cut $ for B-2 Bombers	Y
2. Education IRAs	N	6. End Highway Set-asides	N	10. Human Rights in China	Y
3. Req. 2/3 to Raise Taxes	N	7. School Prayer Amend.	N	11. Withdraw Bosnia Troops	N
4. Fast-track Trade	N	8. Ovrd. Part. Birth Veto	N	12. End Cuban TV-Marti	Y

Election Results

1998 general	Lane Evans (D)	100,128	(52%)	($1,203,109)
	Mark Baker (R)	94,072	(48%)	($1,306,748)
1998 primary	Lane Evans (D)	unopposed		
1996 general	Lane Evans (D)	120,008	(52%)	($629,624)
	Mark Baker (R)	109,240	(47%)	($506,793)

EIGHTEENTH DISTRICT

Old vaudeville bookers, presented with a new act, used to ask, "Will it play in Peoria?" The implication was that if an act went over in this small city on the bluffs above the Illinois River, 154 miles from Chicago and 171 miles from St. Louis, it would go over just about anywhere. In the first half of this century, Peoria did seem pretty typical of America. If its citizens were mostly of British or German descent, with a small percentage of blacks, that was the image of ordinary America that prevailed up through the 1960s, despite the great immigrations of 1880–1924 and the northward urban migrations of southern rural blacks of 1940–1965. For years, Peoria was a good test market for commercial products. But Peoria's economy, arguably typical at mid-century, is less so today. This is still a heavy manufacturing town, dominated by big plants that produce farm machinery and earth-moving equipment. Its biggest employer is

Caterpillar, the world's standard producer of earth-moving and construction equipment, and one of America's major exporters. There are more than just memories here of the sharp divide between blue collar and white collar, union and management, Democrat and Republican—the basis of the class warfare politics that was the norm in the heavy industrial metropolises of the Great Lakes region for three or four decades starting with the sitdown strikes of the late 1930s. But the blue collar workers now are not as numerous and the unions not as strong. The Peoria area went through terrible times in the 1980s, as big farm machinery plants laid off workers and even closed down; now employment seems permanently down. And Caterpillar, struck by the United Auto Workers in 1992, hired replacement workers and continued to operate—not without some friction and inefficiency, but profitably—something unheard of a dozen or more years before. Not until March 1998 did union members approve a settlement, pretty much on the company's terms.

The 18th Congressional District, variously configured, has been the Peoria district since the 1940s. It has been represented by two national Republican leaders: from 1934–48 by Everett McKinley Dirksen, who was elected senator in 1950 and was Senate Republican leader from 1959–69, and Robert Michel, congressman from 1956–94 and Republican House leader from 1980–94. The 18th's boundaries have changed considerably over that time; currently they extend south along the Illinois River and to the northern edge of Springfield, away from historically Republican Peoria toward the historically marginal counties of central Illinois.

The congressman from the 18th District is Ray LaHood, a Republican elected in 1994. LaHood grew up in Peoria, the grandson of an immigrant from Lebanon and son of a restaurant manager. He worked his way through school, spent six years teaching in Catholic schools, then moved to Rock Island, where he worked with delinquent teens and became a staffer for Congressman Tom Railsback. He served in the Illinois House in 1982 (when the speaker was George Ryan, now governor), then worked for Congressman Robert Michel in Peoria and, from 1990–94, as his chief of staff in Washington. Michel had represented the 18th district since 1956, a pleasant and decent man who could be a tough partisan on occasion but always maintained amicable relations with Democratic leaders. It was an approach very different from that of Newt Gingrich, whose election as minority whip in March 1989 Michel opposed; and although they worked together there was also tension. Gingrich pointedly declined to rule out running against Michel for Republican leader after the 1994 election; Michel, faced with a December 1993 filing deadline, decided to retire.

LaHood ran to replace his boss, and in the Republican primary beat state Representative Judy Koehler 50%–40%, carrying the Peoria area but running behind in the rest of the district. In the general, LaHood's Democratic opponent was Douglas Stephens, a labor lawyer and small businessmen, who held Michel to 52% in 1982 and 55% and 1988. Stephens favored school prayer, term limits and abortion restrictions, and called for House members to debate and vote from their districts via interactive television. He put on an energetic campaign, but in this Republican year LaHood carried all but one county and won 60%–39%.

LaHood, odd man out in the Gingrich House, became one of its most visible members in Gingrich's last days as speaker. LaHood was one of only three Republicans who did not sign the Contract with America; he had reservations about voting for tax cuts until the budget was balanced. He lost his bid for a seat on the Appropriations Committee. His voting record has been toward the middle of the House. He worked on the 1996 Freedom to Farm Act, which phased out most farm subsidies, and went after food stamp fraud as well; he balked at making any changes in the law as farm prices sagged in 1998. He voted for Republican Medicare reforms, but has also said, "There ought to be a way for people who don't have health insurance to have health insurance." But he disliked the Republicans' confrontational strategy in the 1995–96 budget crisis.

LaHood has worked for district interests. He says that he has supported Caterpillar 90% of the time and in 1998 worked to lift duties off four chemicals used to produce herbicides at DuPont's request. With neighbor Tom Ewing, he sponsored an extension of the ethanol tax credit from 2000 to 2007; this was voted in the final 1998 transportation bill. That bill also included $13 million to improve I-74 in Peoria, $3.5 million to restore a city street and $4 million to build a new parking garage. He called on TWA to provide at least one jet flight to Peoria each day. He has been willing to tangle with colleagues in behalf of local interests. He wants to promote the Illinois River, for both transportation and recreation; he bristled when the 20th District's John Shimkus came out against its designation as an American Heritage River. And when the 11th District's Jerry Weller got Joliet's new veterans' cemetery named after Abraham Lincoln, LaHood got a sentence in an appropriations bill revoking that, for fear of confusion with Springfield's Oak Ridge Cemetery, where Lincoln is buried.

Decrying the angry tone of House debate, LaHood and Democrat David Skaggs started the Bipartisan Retreat at Hershey, Pennsylvania, in March 1997, "to foster a Congress that is more civil and to create better communication among members." A second retreat in March 1999 drew only 187 members, including 80 Democrats. When Republican leaders attempted a coup against Newt Gingrich in July 1997, LaHood was on the new speaker's side. He remembered that when Michel was speaker, "they were always conniving about something. The Michel team was a family and we were very saddened by the way that these guys were cavorting in the background against Michel, trying to gut him." Gingrich held on, and LaHood led a drive to get the 50 signatures necessary to hold a Republican Conference meeting, over the leaders' objections. "The point is these people are the highest elected leaders of our conference and they needed to be held accountable." The meeting was held on July 23, the leaders asked forgiveness and the Republicans began working together, after a fashion, again.

LaHood has probably presided over the House more often than any other member in the past half-decade. The new Republican majority had no members with experience presiding (except for a few party-switchers), and Gingrich called on LaHood, who often monitored the floor for Michel, to do so. His evenhanded rulings, his surefooted mastery of parliamentary procedure and his determination to maintain decorum were widely appreciated. He was called on often to preside when controversial issues were debated—the partial-birth abortion ban, the Medicare overhaul, and finally, the impeachment of Bill Clinton. Even when LaHood had self-evident feelings about the issue himself—and he had called on Clinton to pay the $4.4 million cost of the Monica Lewinsky investigation—there were few if any complaints about his fairness; as he said, "People recognize that I have the ability to handle controversial matters but do it in a very fair way." After the impeachment debate, he received bipartisan applause.

At home he has been re-elected by wide margins.

Cook's Call. *Safe.* Although some local Democrats have vowed to take LaHood to task for his role in the impeachment trial (he served as the chair during the House debate), it is hard to see how they will be able to oust him. Though this district is not as Republican as it once was, LaHood has carved out a moderate, pragmatic image that the voters in this Peoria-based district have appreciated in their congressmen for years.

The People: Pop. 1990: 572,238; 36.9% rural; 14.7% age 65 + ; 93.7% White, 5.2% Black, 0.6% Asian, 0.2% Amer. Indian, 0.3% Other; 0.9% Hispanic Origin. Households: 59.6% married couple families; 28% married couple fams. w. children; 43.2% college educ.; median household income: $30,189; per capita income: $13,792; median house value: $52,000; median gross rent: $258.

1996 Presidential Vote			1992 Presidential Vote		
Dole (R)	118,572	(47%)	Clinton (D)	117,483	(42%)
Clinton (D)	112,678	(44%)	Bush (R)	114,090	(41%)
Perot (I)	20,975	(8%)	Perot (I)	47,087	(17%)

Rep. Ray LaHood (R)

Elected 1994; b. Dec. 6, 1945, Peoria; home, Peoria; Canton Jr. Col., 1963–65, Bradley U., B.S. 1971; Catholic; married (Kathy).

Elected Office: IL House of Reps., 1982.

Professional Career: Jr. High Schl. Teacher, 1971–77; Dir., Rock Island Youth Svcs., 1972–74; Chief Planner, Bi-state Planning Comm., 1974–76; Dist. A.A., U.S. Rep. Tom Railsback, 1977–82; Dist. A.A., U.S. Rep. Bob Michel, 1983–90, Chief of Staff, 1990–94.

DC Office: 329 CHOB 20515, 202-225-6201; Fax: 202-225-9249; Web site: www.house.gov/lahood.

District Offices: Jacksonville, 217-245-1431; Peoria, 309-671-7027; Springfield, 217-793-0808.

Committees: *Agriculture* (14th of 27 R): Department Operations, Oversight, Nutrition & Forestry; Risk Management, Research & Specialty Crops. *Permanent Select Committee on Intelligence* (8th of 9 R): Human Intelligence, Analysis & Counterintelligence; Technical & Tactical Intelligence. *Transportation & Infrastructure* (19th of 41 R): Aviation; Ground Transportation. *Veterans' Affairs* (12th of 17 R): Benefits.

Group Ratings

	ADA	ACLU	AFS	LCV	CON	NTU	NFIB	COC	ACU	NTLC	CHC
1998	20	13	44	31	76	45	64	83	60	68	83
1997	20	—	38	—	42	45	—	80	64	—	—

National Journal Ratings

	1997 LIB — 1997 CONS	1998 LIB — 1998 CONS
Economic	46% — 53%	48% — 51%
Social	10% — 82%	40% — 59%
Foreign	43% — 55%	43% — 53%

Key Votes of the 105th Congress

1. Clinton Budget Deal	Y	5. Puerto Rico Sthood. Ref.	N	9. Cut $ for B-2 Bombers	N
2. Education IRAs	Y	6. End Highway Set-asides	N	10. Human Rights in China	N
3. Req. 2/3 to Raise Taxes	Y	7. School Prayer Amend.	Y	11. Withdraw Bosnia Troops	Y
4. Fast-track Trade	Y	8. Ovrd. Part. Birth Veto	Y	12. End Cuban TV-Marti	N

Election Results

1998 general	Ray LaHood (R)	unopposed		($489,326)
1998 primary	Ray LaHood (R)	unopposed		
1996 general	Ray LaHood (R)	143,110	(59%)	($699,963)
	Mike Curran (D)	98,413	(41%)	($113,363)

NINETEENTH DISTRICT

Southern Illinois is a land of prairies, of flat, treeless land sloping imperceptibly down to the Ohio and Mississippi rivers. It was settled almost entirely from the south by farmers coming overland from Kentucky, such as Abraham Lincoln's family. Just beyond the Ohio River, they found hilly terrain, some of which turned out to have coal deposits. To the north they must have been astonished, after miles of thick forest, to see the great American prairie stretch before them, a vast sea of empty land extending past the horizon. The prairie lands proved wondrously rich, and were soon criss-crossed by rail lines taking their produce away and bringing in products of industrial civilization from Chicago and St. Louis and points east. About the same time, vast coal deposits were found in southern Illinois, producing one mining town after another: This was the home turf of John L. Lewis, the imperious leader of the United Mine Workers for half a century and, in the late 1930s and early 1940s, one of the most powerful and eloquent figures in American politics.

The 19th Congressional District covers most of the eastern half of southern Illinois. Mostly it is south of the old National Road, which became U.S. 40 and is paralleled by Interstate 70, the traditional boundary between the part of Downstate Illinois settled by southerners and the Downstate settled by Yankees—a boundary also between traditional Democrats and traditional Republicans. North of that line, the 19th includes Decatur, a small city that is home of the giant Archer Daniels Midland Company, a major processor of corn and soybeans and the major producer and promoter of government-subsidized ethanol. About a third of the 19th is prairie, straddling or south of the National Road; the other third is far Downstate, the Egypt region as it is called, where people speak with what Yankees regard as Southern accents and Southern mores prevail, including an attachment to a conservatively inclined Democratic Party.

The congressman from the 19th District is David Phelps, a Democrat elected in 1998 to replace Democrat Glenn Poshard, who after 10 years in the House ran for governor, won the Democratic nomination, but lost the general election. Phelps grew up in Eldorado, about 20 miles from Kentucky and graduated from Southern Illinois University. His family always led the singing at the General Baptist Church and David, the youngest son, developed a good tenor and a gift for songwriting. With his brothers he formed the Phelps Brothers Gospel Singing Group; they had offers to tour nationally, but instead sang in southern Illinois a couple of hours driving distance away. But they did travel to Nashville—much closer in every way to this part of Illinois than Chicago—to cut records, and their songs were performed by the Oak Ridge Boys. Phelps was twice elected Saline County clerk and recorder; in 1984, he was elected to the Illinois House, beating a five-term Republican incumbent. In the House, his voting record was anti-abortion, anti-gun control and for the death penalty; he worked to improve health care and education in rural areas.

Phelps stressed his similarities to Poshard: "I grew up 15 miles from Glenn Poshard. We go way back. We taught together. We came to Springfield together, with the same agenda." This certainly helped: In the district, Poshard won 92% of the votes in the four-candidate March 1998 primary, enough to propel him to an upset win for the Democratic nomination, even as Phelps was winning without serious competition. Poshard's victory meant that there would be a strong Democratic turnout in November, when Poshard—weak in the suburbs and northern Downstate—carried the district over George Ryan 70%–30%, while losing 51%–47% state-wide.

Meanwhile, the Republicans had a seriously contested primary. Evangelical minister and attorney Brent Winters, his party's nominee in the last two elections, was running again. But Winters had not run well against Poshard in the past—just 41% in 1994 and 32% in 1996. This pushed Republican leaders to persuade Chicago area banker Jerry Berg to return to his home town near Decatur to run, and a former state legislator from the southern part of the district ran also. Winters campaigned as a lifelong resident of southern Illinois and, to raise money, sold for $50 one-square-inch plots of land near Charleston that was once owned by Abraham Lincoln. Winters won the primary by 56%–29% over Berg. But he had little money left; by June 30 Phelps had $183,000 cash on hand and Winters had less than $11,000.

Phelps had other advantages. He could argue that his record in Springfield proved he was conservative on many issues; the best Winters could do was to argue that Phelps had sometimes voted for tax increases. Phelps had support from the Blue Dogs and New Democrats, and plenty of money from party sources; national Republicans discounted Winters's chances. Winters tried to raise the impeachment issue in August, when Phelps said he was "disappointed," but still supported Clinton. Winters's themes sometimes sounded simplistic. "Government is not the answer. If you just cut taxes, everything takes care of itself." Phelps had more of a rounded theme: "What's at stake in this election," he said, "is the stability of rural life." He called for a new look at the Freedom to Farm Act and for tougher school standards and more infrastructure spending. A June Democratic poll showed Phelps ahead 43%–29%; a September Republican poll showed him ahead by only 39%–35%, but by November the margin was wider. Winters carried six counties around his home base of Charleston and in the middle of the district. But Phelps won by a solid margin in the northern area around Decatur and carried the southern counties in and near his state legislative district by more than 2–1 margins, for a 58%–42% win overall.

Cook's Call. *Probably Safe.* This rural, downstate district is socially conservative but still retains a rock solid Democratic base. Phelps won here probably too easily in 1998 as Republicans failed to find a top notch challenger. Baring any self-inflicted political wounds, Phelps should have smooth sailing in 2000.

The People: Pop. 1990: 571,390; 50.8% rural; 18% age 65 + ; 95.5% White, 3.9% Black, 0.3% Asian, 0.2% Amer. Indian, 0.1% Other; 0.5% Hispanic Origin. Households: 58.9% married couple families; 26.6% married couple fams. w. children; 34.4% college educ.; median household income: $22,979; per capita income: $11,333; median house value: $38,800; median gross rent: $199.

1996 Presidential Vote			1992 Presidential Vote		
Clinton (D)	113,635	(47%)	Clinton (D)	131,396	(47%)
Dole (R)	97,977	(41%)	Bush (R)	95,759	(34%)
Perot (I)	28,653	(12%)	Perot (I)	50,706	(18%)

Rep. David Phelps (D)

Elected 1998; b. Oct. 26, 1947, Eldorado; home, Eldorado; S. IL U., B.S. 1969; Baptist; married (Leslie).

Elected Office: Saline Cnty. Clerk & Recorder, 1980–84; IL House of Reps., 1984–98.

Professional Career: Gospel singer/songwriter; Public schl. teacher & Asst. Principal, 1969–73; Small Businessman, 1973–80.

DC Office: 1523 LHOB 20515, 202-225-5201; Fax: 202-225-1541; Web site: www.house.gov/phelps.

District Offices: Charleston, 217-345-9166; Decatur, 217-425-8819; Effingham, 217-342-7220; Eldorado, 618-273-8203; Lawrenceville, 618-943-6036; Marion, 618-997-6004; West Frankfort, 618-937-6402.

Committees: *Agriculture* (21st of 24 D): Department Operations, Oversight, Nutrition & Forestry; General Farm Commodities, Resource Conservation & Credit. *Small Business* (13th of 17 D): Rural Enterprise, Business Opportunities & Special Small Business Problems.

Group Ratings and Key Votes: Newly Elected

Election Results

1998 general	David Phelps (D)	122,430	(58%)	($642,177)
	Brent Winters (R)	87,614	(42%)	($424,347)
1998 primary	David Phelps (D)	61,037	(83%)	
	Jerry Eckl (D)	12,254	(17%)	
1996 general	Glenn Poshard (D)	158,668	(67%)	($237,030)
	Brent Winters (R)	75,751	(32%)	($100,055)

TWENTIETH DISTRICT

Springfield, the capital of Illinois, has changed rather little since its great moment in history—when it was the home of Abraham Lincoln, lawyer, unsuccessful candidate for re-election to Congress and 16th president of the United States. Today, beyond the suburban fringe, the prairie countryside outside Springfield is still mostly farmland with few towns. Farming technology has changed vastly, but the patterns of cultivation, the contours of the land, even the shape of the ribbons of back country roads, cannot be entirely different from what Lincoln saw as a lawyer making his way from one county seat to another on the circuit. Nor has downtown Springfield changed as much since Lincoln's time as have downtown Columbus or Indianapolis or even Des Moines. If most of the officefronts and houses captured in the old photographs are gone, some remain; and the scale has not changed utterly. Lincoln's clapboard house is still in Springfield, and so is the courtroom where he argued cases before federal judges; the Greek revival downtown block where Lincoln & Herndon kept their law offices is open for inspection, as is the state Capitol building built here in 1839. Much of today's Springfield is tawdry, but unlike other state capitals it has not lost its 19th Century scale.

The 20th Congressional District is one of only 19 which can claim to be the lineal descendant of a district whose representative also became a president of the United States. It includes the southern half of Springfield and much of the Downstate Illinois prairie, which in 1846 elected a 37-year-old railroad lawyer and Whig opponent of the Mexican War named Abraham Lincoln to his single term in the House. Lincoln's denunciation of the Mexican War was so strong that he gave up any chance of a second term, for the countryside south and west of Springfield, straddling the National Road and along the Illinois River, both avenues of migration from the South, were strongly supportive of that war. Similar sentiments—a cultural conservatism, strong national pride—are still apparent here today.

The congressman from the 20th District is John Shimkus, a Republican elected in 1996. Shimkus grew up in Collinsville, a county seat in Madison County, on the other side of the Mississippi River from St. Louis; he is of Lithuanian descent, as is his predecessor in the seat, Senator Richard Durbin. Shimkus graduated from West Point, trained in the Army as a Ranger and paratrooper, studied in California, then came back to Collinsville to teach high school. Almost immediately he began running for local office. In 1988 he ran for the Madison County Board, and lost; in 1989, he was elected Collinsville Township Trustee; in 1990, at 32, he beat a 12-year incumbent and was elected Madison County treasurer, the only Republican county-wide officer, and was re-elected in 1994. In 1992 he ran against Congressman Richard Durbin, and, though heavily outspent ($921,000 to $278,000), held him to a 57%–43% victory. In 1995, when Durbin decided to run for the Senate seat being vacated by Paul Simon, Shimkus decided to run for Congress again.

He had plenty of competition. Shimkus was one of eight Republicans in the March primary, which he won with 51%, far ahead of the 19% of his nearest rival. In the general election he faced state Representative Jay Hoffman. Both were anti-abortion, anti-gun control, and pro-balanced budget amendment. But Shimkus took and Hoffman refused to take Americans for Tax Reform's pledge not to raise taxes. Shimkus supported the Republican budget; Hoffman attacked Newt Gingrich and decried Medicare "cuts." Hoffman bragged of his legislative record as Democratic floor leader and on child welfare, victims' rights, and truth-in-sentencing laws. Shimkus called for tougher border control to keep out drugs, more access to health insurance for the self-employed and employees of small business. Hoffman raised more money and had the benefit of AFL-CIO ads, but Shimkus won by 50.3%–49.7%, a margin of 1,238 votes. Hoffman carried the Democratic counties between Springfield and Madison County and the coal country in the southeast; Shimkus, campaigning in a Winnebago with his wife and two infant sons, did well in the farthest rural corners of the district and, critically, carried both Madison County and Springfield.

In the House, Shimkus got a seat on the Commerce Committee—a feat for a freshman—

and used it to sponsor one small but locally important piece of legislation. This was his amendment that qualified the soybean-diesel fuel blend B-20 for the alternative fuels program. This would make vehicles able to use B-20 qualify for the federal environmental quotas, and the Clinton Administration opposed it, arguing that any standard diesel fuel engine would qualify. But Shimkus, working with Democrat Karen McCarthy, got it passed by committee in August 1998 and by the full House in September; it became law in October. Local experts predicted that soybean prices, plummeting lately, would increase by 7 to 11 cents per bushel. On other commerce issues, he supported financial services deregulation, reducing Superfund litigation and reducing the FCC's regulatory power. He opposed further restriction on tobacco advertising, for fear it would raise a constitutional issue. After some indecision, he voted for fast track in 1997—farm exports are big here. He is a strong advocate of normal trade status for China. "I truly believe this is the best way to free the Chinese people. Trade is the best way to create religious freedom and the best way to aid the persecuted." Once pledging to abolish the Commerce Department, he said in June 1997, "I think you could safely say that I'm re-evaluating that position." He voted for the Shays-Meehan campaign finance bill. He vetoed inclusion of his part of the Illinois River in the American Heritage Rivers program. He is co-chairman of the Baltic Caucus and wants Commerce to have a presence in the Baltic states.

Shimkus's moderate voting record and his continual presence in the district made him a strong competitor in 1998. Indeed at one point it seemed he would have no competition at all. His 1996 opponent, Jay Hoffman, spent months deciding whether to run, then not long before the December 1997 filing deadline decided to run for the state House again. Democrats recruited community development official Dave Loebach, but he withdrew in January 1998 when it was ruled that he was covered by the Hatch Act and would have to quit his job to run. Meanwhile, as local station WILL-TV Channel 12 ran a documentary on Shimkus, starting with election night '96 and showing him commute from Washington to his young family in Collinsville, Macoupin County lawyer, Rick Verticchio launched a write-in campaign. Considering the many possible misspellings of his name, he did well, tallying some 3,100 votes, far above the 641 required. But Verticchio was not fully prepared; in March he was unable to say which side of abortion or gun control he was on, and his car slid off snowy I-55 into a ditch on his way to his announcement. As the campaign went on, he read from the Clinton script, blasting Shimkus for not backing school construction dollars (instead of block grants), for opposing a bill to penalize parents whose children commit crimes with guns (Shimkus said he didn't want to criminalize parents for their children's acts), for taking money from tobacco PACs (Shimkus said he got more from labor PACs, so that if anybody had bought him it was the unions), for not seeking money for a bridge to St. Louis (Shimkus said it was in Jerry Costello's district, and he hadn't asked for help). More decisive was the fact that Shimkus, from his seat on the Commerce Committee, had raised $869,000 and had $204,000 left after the election. Shimkus won 61%–39%, carrying every county but Macoupin, which he lost 51%–49%.

Cook's Call. *Probably Safe.* This is the most marginal of the downstate districts, but, after coming close in 1996, Democrats were unable to field a top-tier candidate in 1998, helping Shimkus to establish a pretty good hold on this seat. A bad year for Republicans or a top tier opponent could still give Shimkus a race, but Democrats' best chance may have already passed them by.

The People: Pop. 1990: 571,138; 48.4% rural; 16.5% age 65 + ; 94.9% White, 4.2% Black, 0.5% Asian, 0.2% Amer. Indian, 0.2% Other; 0.6% Hispanic Origin. Households: 58.7% married couple families; 27.5% married couple fams. w. children; 36.2% college educ.; median household income: $26,173; per capita income: $12,289; median house value: $47,200; median gross rent: $242.

1996 Presidential Vote			1992 Presidential Vote		
Clinton (D)	117,775	(47%)	Clinton (D)	129,865	(46%)
Dole (R)	101,634	(41%)	Bush (R)	94,038	(34%)
Perot (I)	26,431	(11%)	Perot (I)	55,712	(20%)

Rep. John M. Shimkus (R)

Elected 1996; b. Feb. 21, 1958, Collinsville; home, Collinsville; West Point Military Acad., B.S. 1980, Christ Col., Teaching Cert., 1990, S. IL U., M.B.A. 1997; Lutheran; married (Karen).

Military Career: Army 1980–85; Army Reserves, 1985-present.

Elected Office: Collinsville Township Trustee, 1989–93; Madison Cnty. Tres., 1990–96.

Professional Career: High schl. teacher, 1986–90.

DC Office: 513 CHOB 20515, 202-225-5271; Fax: 202-225-5880; Web site: www.house.gov/shimkus.

District Offices: Collinsville, 618-344-3065; Springfield, 217-492-5090.

Committees: *Commerce* (22d of 29 R): Energy & Power; Finance & Hazardous Materials; Telecommunications, Trade & Consumer Protection.

Group Ratings

	ADA	ACLU	AFS	LCV	CON	NTU	NFIB	COC	ACU	NTLC	CHC
1998	10	6	33	8	13	50	86	94	88	89	100
1997	10	—	25	—	34	49	—	80	88	—	—

National Journal Ratings

	1997 LIB — 1997 CONS		1998 LIB — 1998 CONS	
Economic	40%	— 59%	37%	— 61%
Social	10%	— 82%	24%	— 75%
Foreign	32%	— 65%	19%	— 75%

Key Votes of the 105th Congress

1. Clinton Budget Deal	Y	5. Puerto Rico Sthood. Ref.	*	9. Cut $ for B-2 Bombers	N
2. Education IRAs	Y	6. End Highway Set-asides	Y	10. Human Rights in China	Y
3. Req. 2/3 to Raise Taxes	Y	7. School Prayer Amend.	Y	11. Withdraw Bosnia Troops	Y
4. Fast-track Trade	Y	8. Ovrd. Part. Birth Veto	Y	12. End Cuban TV-Marti	N

Election Results

1998 general	John M. Shimkus (R)	121,103	(61%)	($677,009)
	Rick Verticchio (D)	76,475	(39%)	($245,796)
1998 primary	John M. Shimkus (R)	unopposed		
1996 general	John M. Shimkus (R)	120,926	(50%)	($647,796)
	Jay C. Hoffman (D)	119,688	(50%)	($812,397)

INDIANA

Every Memorial Day the nation's eyes turn to Indianapolis, the center of a state with the nation's most distinctive nickname and some of its least distinctive borders, for a sports spectacle celebrating the knack for tinkering and the taste for powerful machines that make the Midwest the nation's manufacturing center: the Indianapolis 500. This combination of sports and manufacturing is symbolic of Indiana's strengths and successes. The image of its manufacturing base and sports heritage seems as antique as the bricks with which the Indianapolis Speedway was originally paved, though all but one yard at the start/finish line has long since been asphalted. Indiana's manufacturing economy, after rough years in the early 1980s, is now humming: high-skill, high-employment and high-tech. The Speedway is literally at the center of American manufacturing: Almost precisely half the country's manufacturing jobs are east of Indiana and the other half west, almost half are north and half south. Indiana itself has the nation's highest percentage of workers in manufacturing and is the number one steel producer with its giant, heavily automated steel mills on the south shore of Lake Michigan. Indiana leads the nation in making elevators, refrigerators, engines, engine electrical equipment, recreational vehicles, mobile homes and truck and bus bodies. It gave the world canned pork and beans, tomato juice, the Coca-Cola bottle and Alka-Seltzer.

Nor are Indiana's days of innovation over. Just as it has attracted new teams and events to Indianapolis's sports facilities, the small factories set amidst farm landscape or at the edge of small cities have become centers of advanced manufacturing innovation. Indiana's job growth was slow in the 1980s as it shed low-wage, low-skill jobs. Today, its income levels are slightly less than the national average and well below those not only of the coasts but also of the Chicago area just over the state line. But housing and health care costs are also lower than average, and the tax burden lower and tort laws are generally less onerous.

Culturally, Indiana is like an older America; it retains some of the old norms that in the 1920s and 1930s brought sociologists Robert and Helen Lynd in their search for the typical American place to "Middletown" (actually Muncie). Ethnically, Indiana seems older too: Except for the steel area around Gary—really an extension of the Chicago metropolitan area—Indiana has relatively few descendants from the 1840–1924 wave of immigration and few recent Hispanic or Asian migrants. The major metropolitan area, Indianapolis, now has 1.5 million people but still doesn't have the big singles and gay neighborhoods of larger cities. What it does have is the nation's largest foundation, the Lilly Endowment (which gives much of its money locally) and a willingness to create and innovate. In the 1980s the Lilly Endowment urged Indianapolis to make itself a sports center. The city attracted the Colts professional football team to the Hoosier Dome (now the RCA Dome), hosted the Pan-American games in 1987, several trials for the 1996 Olympics, the NCAA Final Four in 1991, and the Big Ten Women's Basketball Championship in 1995. In the late 1990s Indianapolis's downtown filled with new construction projects: the pro basketball Pacers' Indiana Fieldhouse, the new NCAA headquarters, a conservatory and the Indiana State Museum; the Convention Center and Eiteljorg Museum of Native American Art were expanded and the Circle Center Mall filled with shoppers. Longtime Indianapolis Mayor Stephen Goldsmith, a Republican, pioneered the privatization of city services for everything but police, fire and zoning. The results are that costs are down by nearly one-quarter and the public work force by one-third, while taxes were cut some $240 million. In the state Capitol four blocks away, Governors Evan Bayh and Frank O'Bannon, both Democrats, have cut taxes. Government has been not a drain on the private economy, but a booster.

The last decade has seen innovation in Indiana's government. But its partisan politics some-

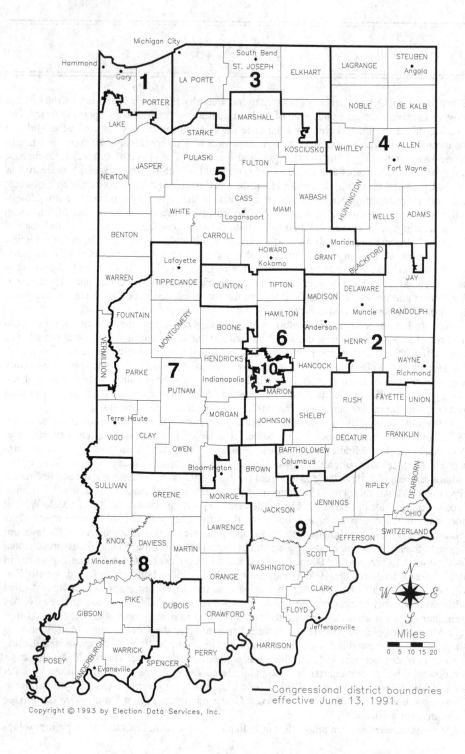

Michigan City

Hammond
Gary
1
PORTER
LAKE
NEWTON

LA PORTE
STARKE
JASPER

South Bend
ST. JOSEPH
3
MARSHALL
PULASKI
5
FULTON
WHITE
CASS
Logansport
BENTON
CARROLL

ELKHART
KOSCIUSKO
WABASH
MIAMI
HOWARD

LAGRANGE
NOBLE
WHITLEY
HUNTINGTON
WELLS
GRANT

STEUBEN
Angola
DE KALB
4   ALLEN
Fort Wayne
ADAMS

WARREN
FOUNTAIN
VERMILLION
PARKE

Lafayette
TIPPECANOE
MONTGOMERY
CLINTON
BOONE
7
PUTNAM

Kokomo
TIPTON
HAMILTON
HENDRICKS
10
Indianapolis
MARION

Marion
GRANT
MADISON
Anderson
6
HANCOCK

DELAWARE
Muncie
HENRY
2

BLACKFORD
JAY
RANDOLPH
WAYNE
Richmond

Terre Haute
VIGO
CLAY
MORGAN
OWEN
Bloomington
GREENE
MONROE

JOHNSON
SHELBY
BROWN
Columbus
BARTHOLOMEW
JACKSON
9

RUSH
DECATUR
FAYETTE   UNION
FRANKLIN
RIPLEY
JENNINGS
SCOTT
JEFFERSON
DEARBORN
OHIO
SWITZERLAND

SULLIVAN
KNOX
Vincennes
DAVIESS
MARTIN
LAWRENCE
ORANGE
WASHINGTON
CLARK

8
PIKE
GIBSON
DUBOIS
CRAWFORD
WARRICK
POSEY
VANDERBURGH
Evansville
SPENCER
PERRY
HARRISON
FLOYD
Jeffersonville

N
W   E
S
Miles
0 5 10 15 20

— Congressional district boundaries
effective June 13, 1991.

times seems typical of an older America, with preferences anchored in the Civil War era and a small overlay of change from the union-organizing days of the 1930s. Indiana's cultural conservatism has kept it Republican in presidential elections for the last generation, but for many years it was a crucial state from the Civil War to the New Deal in the struggles between Republicans and Democrats. Party identification was handed down like religious affiliation—the Lynds noted that Presbyterians had little to do with Methodists, but that was nothing next to divisions between Republicans and Democrats—in a state still peopled largely by descendants of its original settlers, Yankees from Ohio and New England and "Butternuts" (as they were called in the Civil War years) from Kentucky and the South.

Most Yankees became Republicans and most Butternuts Democrats, and that split has persisted over generations and can still be seen in election returns today. Of the 26 Indiana counties carried by Bill Clinton in 1996, 18 are south of Indianapolis, most near the Ohio River. The others are clustered around industrial towns which were organized by the CIO unions, the United Steelworkers and the United Auto Workers, in the 1930s. In the 1920s the Lynds, liberal academics influenced by Marx's idea that political beliefs were determined by economic interests, were puzzled why the factory workers in "Middletown" didn't vote against the bosses; in the 1930s and since, in some parts of industrial Indiana, they have. But not in other cities, including Indianapolis, which is by far the largest. Why not? One answer is that cultural identity and personal values tend to be permanent and so have usually been the critical determinants of political allegiance in an America where economic status can often be changeable. Another is that the economic interests of Indiana's high-skill workers and its small and large factory owners are not nearly as adversarial as academics and Washington liberals suppose.

Indiana's partisan allegiances have remained remarkably steady. There is an historic base here large enough to allow Democrats to win: Evan Bayh broke a 20-year Republican hold on the governorship in 1988, with his strongest support from southern Indiana and the far northwest industrial zone. In 1996 his lieutenant governor, Frank O'Bannon, won the race to succeed him, 52%–47%, over Indianapolis's Stephen Goldsmith, and the patterns were much the same as in 1988. But Hoosier politicians of both parties have been able to transcend the ancient allegiances: Richard Lugar, the only four-term senator in Indiana's history, was re-elected by 2–1 margins in 1988 and 1994; Bayh won re-election in 1992 and his Senate seat in 1998 by nearly as much; and Frank O'Bannon has had very high job ratings and could do the same in 2000. But the historic patterns were apparent in the 1996 presidential race: Bob Dole carried Indiana 47%–42%, in large part because of his strength in metro Indianapolis, which he carried 54%–36%. In the rest of the state his lead was thin, 45%–43%, with Bill Clinton carrying the unionized north and the Butternut south.

Governor. Frank O'Bannon, elected governor in 1996, grew up in the old town of Corydon, near the Ohio River, went to Indiana University, served in the Air Force, then went to law school. He returned to Corydon, practiced law and published weekly newspapers. In 1970, at 40, he was elected to the state senate from a district adjacent to the Ohio River; from 1979 he was Democratic floor leader. In 1988 he was elected as Evan Bayh's lieutenant governor and was given serious responsibilities as head of the state departments of Agriculture and Commerce. He worked on training programs and attracting business and hailed the creation of 370,000 new jobs in Indiana and the sharp drop in welfare rolls while he and Bayh were in office.

In 1996 Bayh retired after his two terms and O'Bannon ran. The favorite was Republican Mayor Stephen Goldsmith of Indianapolis, one of the nation's leading innovators in privatizing government and cutting spending and taxes. But Goldsmith had a primary opponent who campaigned against the big city of Indianapolis, and Goldsmith won by only 54%–37%. Goldsmith's call for startling change did not go over as well as O'Bannon's pledge, as a "compassionate conservative," to continue Bayh's highly popular policies at a time when most voters believed Indiana was moving in the right direction. Goldsmith was hurt politically in the last days of the campaign when four off-duty Indianapolis policemen used racial epithets in a downtown brawl and were indicted, though a Marion jury subsequently failed to reach a verdict against the officers. O'Bannon won 52%–47%, carrying Indianapolis. Possibly voters there (like New York Democrats in the 1982 primary between Mario Cuomo and Edward Koch) wanted to support a popular candidate for governor and keep a popular mayor.

Sparked by a $1.8 billion surplus, O'Bannon has cut taxes and promised more cuts for 1999. He has called for forgiving college loans for students with at least a B-average, a property tax credit for families, a welfare-to-work income tax credit, and 500 new police officers over four years. He has not always been successful: His campaign finance reform plan was beaten by labor Democrats in 1997, but he hopes to raise it again. And the Democratic teachers' unions in 1998 opposed his four major education proposals: an academic standards commission, paying high school students to take college entrance exams, tutoring of 10th graders who fail graduation tests, and increasing the number of credits needed for high school graduation. In 1998 he helped Democrats pick up three seats and a 53–47 majority in the state House; a mixed blessing, since Democrats opposed him on education and campaign finance. O'Bannon appears to be a strong candidate for re-election in 2000. Possible Republican candidates include Congressman David McIntosh, 1998 Senate candidate John Price and 1996 lieutenant governor candidate George Witwer.

Cook's Call. *Potentially Competitive.* O'Bannon will be safe unless Representative David McIntosh gets into the race. McIntosh is a very popular figure in state Republican circles. If he does not run in 2000, he will look at 2004 when the seat will be open. An O'Bannon-McIntosh race would be very competitive, but O'Bannon is the strong favorite if McIntosh decides to sit out.

Senior Senator. Richard Lugar, still running 5K races at the annual Dick Lugar Run and Walk in Indianapolis, has a career in public life going back to the late 1950s, when as a young Navy officer he prepared intelligence briefings for Chief of Naval Operations Arleigh Burke and briefed President Eisenhower over closed-circuit television. Now he is the first Indiana senator ever elected to a fourth term, chairman of the Senate Agriculture Committee and a powerful voice on foreign policy. Lugar grew up in Indianapolis, near his family's farm and food machinery firm, which was founded in 1893. He was an Eagle Scout, straight-A student and Rhodes scholar. After the service he returned to the family business, was elected to the school board in 1964, then was elected mayor of Indianapolis in 1967, at 35. As mayor he consolidated the city and county into Unigov, which brought in tax resources and suburban voters, keeping the city both solvent and Republican. In the late 1960s Lugar bucked fashion and called for fewer rather than more federal programs and became known as Richard Nixon's favorite mayor; not a political asset in 1974, when Lugar ran against Senator Birch Bayh, father of his new junior colleague, and lost 51%–46%. But in the more favorable climate of 1976 and against a weaker Democratic incumbent, Vance Hartke, Lugar won 59%–40%.

Throughout his public life Lugar's strength has been that he has followed where his stubborn convictions and his considerable intellect led, regardless of political risk or reward: He has plenty of accomplishments but also some disappointments to show for it. His lone course has served him well in Indiana, but has had mixed results in the Senate and in the national arena. He is a conservative on some, but not all, of the hot-button issues of today's conservative activists. He is an internationalist at a time when the president's attention to foreign issues is episodic and some in Lugar's own party are tempted to revert to isolationism. Lugar started off in the Senate leading the 1978 filibuster to defeat the AFL-CIO's labor law reform bill, although unions were then big in Indiana. He strongly supported NAFTA in 1993, in a Midwestern state where many thought foreigners were taking their jobs. In 1994, he doggedly raised questions about the ethical conflict posed by the investment in Lloyds of London by Supreme Court nominee Stephen Breyer. He voted against the Civil Rights Act of 1990, saying it imposed racial quotas. He ran for president in 1996 on his own platform and without any concessions to the political shorthand or the TV sensibility of the day, but his candidacy made little impact. Lugar based his campaign on what he thought were central goals: "nuclear security and fiscal sanity." He emphasized his work on deterring nuclear terrorism, running a series of four ads showing a president having to respond to such a threat, and he showcased his April 1995 proposal for a 17% national sales tax to replace the income tax and abolish the IRS. But Lugar's serious speeches got little coverage, and he finished 7th in Iowa and 5th in New Hampshire. His high point came when he campaigned intensively in Vermont and got 14% of the vote. On March 6 he withdrew from the race and endorsed Bob Dole.

Even amid Lugar's ill-fated presidential campaign, he achieved a staggering legislative success in the passage of the Federal Agriculture Improvement and Reform Act of 1996: the Freedom to Farm Act. Lugar is a farmer himself, raising corn, soybeans and wheat on a 600-acre spread outside Indianapolis. But for years he opposed the complex system of farm subsidies which had many farmers responding to government regulations and subsidies rather than to the market. As the ranking Republican on Agriculture since 1987, he has worked doggedly toward dismantling the system. In 1990 his farm bill froze target prices and dairy supports, in 1992 he led a crusade to close many of the 11,000 USDA field offices, and in 1995 he called for reducing target prices to zero over five years. Then, in the 1996 bill, Lugar's stance convinced House Agriculture Chairman Pat Roberts (now a Kansas senator) that subsidies had to go. After outmaneuvering Dakota Democrats on key votes in January 1996, he paved the way for the law zeroing out most subsidies over seven years and encouraging farmers to produce for foreign markets. He was especially proud of its environmental provisions: $200 million for the Everglades, an expansion of the Conservation Reserve program for wetlands, and an incentive program for waste containment facilities.

In 1998 low crop prices sparked demands for a return to subsidies. But Lugar managed to limit that drive to some temporary aid; he resisted disaster aid for fear it would discourage farmers from buying crop insurance. He tried to move the focus of farm policy elsewhere. Lugar proposed buying out farmers' tobacco quotas at $8 a pound, at a one-time cost of $15 billion. He passed a large agricultural research program aimed at improving productivity without environmental degradation, adding food stamps and crop insurance reform to assemble a bipartisan coalition. He also sponsored a Tropical Forest Conservation Act, which would allow developing countries to swap external debt for setting up trust funds to protect rain forests. In a rare move against expanding committee jurisdiction, he suggested that any regulations of hedge funds, swaps and derivatives should be handled by banking regulators, not the CFTC.

Lugar's other great interest is foreign policy. For 1985–86 he was chairman of the Foreign Relations Committee, where he quickly took command over a committee sharply divided between Jesse Helms, inclined to conduct his own foreign policy, and liberal Democrats. Lugar was in the middle, backing Contra aid and favoring sanctions on South Africa. On the Philippines, he took the lead, quickly concluding that Ferdinand Marcos's 1986 "victory" over Corazon Aquino was fraudulent and, at a decisive point, called on Marcos to leave office. After Republicans lost control of the Senate in 1986, Helms invoked seniority to take the ranking minority position on Foreign Relations, and after 1994 became chairman. Helms left Lugar off conference committees, supposedly to give junior members experience; the two engage in arch correspondence more than collegial conversation. In April 1997 Lugar led the fight to ratify the Chemical Weapons Agreement over Helms's opposition, and won. He also criticized Helms for blocking a vote on William Weld's appointment as ambassador to Mexico, and suggested he would retaliate on the Agriculture Committee.

On other foreign policy issues, Lugar favored the INF treaty in 1988, START I in 1992 and START II in 1996. He supported NATO expansion and U.S. payment of U.N. dues. Beginning in 1991 he developed the Nunn-Lugar Cooperative Threats Reduction program to pay Russia, Ukraine and Belarus to dismantle and destroy their nuclear weapons and some chemical and biological weapons as well, to prevent them from falling into the hands of hostile powers or terrorists. By 1998 nearly 5,000 nuclear warheads had been dismantled and more than $1 billion spent, with $2 billion in the pipeline; Lugar called for increasing the $425 million appropriated for 1999. But he is also capable of taking a hard line. Consistently since August 1990 he has called for an end to Saddam Hussein's regime and said that Saddam might have to be killed and U.S. ground troops needed to accomplish that. "A Saddam with the potential and ability to build weapons of mass destruction . . . poses a menace, because he has the will to use them."

Lugar has a generally moderate but not wishy-washy voting record. He is a strong free trader, backing fast track, IMF funding, and knocking down barriers to U.S. manufacturing and farm exports. Lamenting the application of automatic trade sanctions to half the nations in the world, he sponsored a sanctions-reform bill with Phillip Crane and now-retired Indiana Congressman Lee Hamilton. Two other Lugar causes: He fought to keep the federal school lunch program in the 1996 welfare reform bill, and he is leery of the effects of legalized gambling and co-sponsored the Gambling Study Commission.

In Indiana Lugar has remained vastly popular, more so probably than any politician in state history. He was re-elected in 1988 with 68% of the vote, a state record, and in 1994 with 67%. He is in fine shape for re-election in 2000, with no serious opposition in sight.

Cook's Call. *Safe.* Dispelling rumors that he might retire, Lugar made his intentions to run for another term known early. There have been a few Democratic names mentioned, but Lugar's victories of 68% in 1988 and 67% in 1994 are likely to scare off the most credible potential rivals, and his new Democratic colleague, Evan Bayh, is showing little interest in encouraging a challenge to Lugar.

Junior Senator. Evan Bayh was elected in 1998 to the Senate seat his father Birch Bayh first won in 1962 when Evan was just 6. He grew up mostly in Washington, graduated from Indiana University and the University of Virginia Law School, then returned to Indiana to practice law—and politics. His father, a charismatic candidate, beat three serious opponents: incumbent Senator Homer Capehart in 1962, later-Deputy Attorney General William Ruckelshaus in 1968, and future Senator Richard Lugar in 1974. But in 1980, with Evan helping run the campaign, he finally lost to Dan Quayle. In 1986, at 30, Evan was elected secretary of State, an office that is often a steppingstone. In 1988, at 32, he ran for governor. Republicans had controlled the office, and most of Indiana state government, for 20 years. However, their smoothly run machine had grown sluggish: The Republican nominee promised innovation, but Bayh was a young and fresh face.

Unlike his father's mostly liberal Senate voting record, Bayh was, for a Democrat, relatively conservative. He calls himself "pragmatic" and says he wants to find "the sensible center"; liberal Democrats call him a "Republicrat." As governor, he balanced the budget, cut taxes and piled up a $1.6 billion budget surplus. He trimmed a deficit in state pension plans and sliced Medicaid spending. He claimed credit for 350,000 jobs, as Indiana's manufacturing economy revived. He did less to reform education and other government services, but he was immensely popular and left office with high job ratings, over $1.3 million in a campaign treasury and a lead in the polls over incumbent Senator Dan Coats.

Coats had been elected in 1989 to replace Dan Quayle, who he had also succeeded in the House. Coats had a strong conservative voting record in the House, made a cause of stopping shipments of out-of-state garbage to Indiana and sought with some success to reframe government programs to encourage voluntary associations, charities and faith-based organizations to provide services in place of government. In December 1996 Coats announced he would not run again; everyone knew Bayh would, the only question was whether the Republicans could find a strong candidate.

Three Republicans ran: two conservatives, John Price and former Reagan aide Peter Rusthoven, and one moderate, Fort Wayne Mayor Paul Helmke. None was well financed or well known. Price called for Bill Clinton's immediate removal from office, Rusthoven talked about restoring integrity to Washington, and Helmke talked about his record in Fort Wayne. Helmke also had kind words for Bill and Hillary Rodham Clinton, whom he had known since law school and who invited him to White House events. Price held a press conference with anti-Clinton author Gary Aldrich, and Rusthoven was endorsed by writer Peggy Noonan. Helmke was calm enough to attend the Kentucky Derby just before the May primary. It was a squeaker: Helmke won with 35% to 33% for Price and 31% for Rusthoven.

Helmke was not uncritical of Bayh. "Evan still comes across a little the empty suit. He looks good. He sounds good. But there's a sense that he's trying to be all things to all people." It was the Republican, however, whose record included tax increases, and at mid-year Bayh had a $3.7 million warchest compared to Helmke's $64,000. Bayh said he wanted to maintain a balanced budget, save Social Security, raise education standards and move to a "fairer, flatter" tax. He ran ads showing his wife extolling his accomplishments, saying he "cracked down on deadbeat dads, sponsored Indiana's fatherhood initiative . . . worked to make our schools safer and drug-free and to move people from welfare to work." Though Helmke has been a talented and successful officeholder, this was not a seriously contested race. Bayh's record as governor cinched his victory; though one might say that if Birch Bayh had not beaten Homer Capehart by 10,000 votes in 1962, Evan Bayh would have never been elected governor at 32 and have a chance to achieve such popularity. Bayh won 64%–35%, carrying 88 of Indiana's 92 counties.

Presidential politics. Indiana, for all of Evan Bayh's popularity, remains one of the most Republican of the larger states; the only larger states with higher percentages for Bob Dole in 1996 were Texas and North Carolina. So Indiana sees little of presidential candidates in election year autumns. Nor does it see much of them in spring or summer: Indiana's May presidential primary has not been influential since 1968.

Congressional districting. Indiana's 1991 districting plan is a mild revision of a 1981 plan enacted by Republicans and upheld in a Supreme Court decision important to redistricting law. Legislative control was split between the parties in 1991, and it will likely be again in 2001, since Democratic Governor Frank O'Bannon is highly popular and Republicans have a big margin in the state Senate.

The People: Est. Pop. 1998: 5,899,195; Pop. 1990: 5,544,159, up 6.4% 1990–1998. 2.2% of U.S. total, 14th largest; 35.1% rural. Median age: 34.8 years. 13.1% 65 years and over. 90.6% White, 7.8% Black, 0.7% Asian, 0.3% Amer. Indian, 0.7% Other; 1.7% Hispanic Origin. Households: 58.2% married couple families; 28.4% married couple fams. w. children; 37.4% college educ.; median household income: $28,797; per capita income: $13,149; 70.2% owner occupied housing; median house value: $53,900; median monthly rent: $291. 3.1% Unemployment. 1998 Voting age pop.: 4,410,000. 1998 Turnout: 1,588,617; 36% of VAP. Registered voters (1998): 3,693,982; no party registration.

Political Lineup: Governor, Frank O'Bannon (D); Lt. Gov., Joe Kernan (D); Secy. of State, Sue Anne Gilroy (R); Atty. Gen., Jeff Modisett (D); Treasurer, Tim Berry (R); State Senate, 50 (19 D, 31 R); Majority Leader, Joseph Harrison (R); State House, 100 (53 D, 47 D); House Speaker, John Gregg (D). Senators, Richard G. Lugar (R) and Evan Bayh (D). Representatives, 10 (4 D, 6 R).

Elections Division: 317-232-3939; **Filing Deadline for U.S. Congress:** February 18, 2000.

1996 Presidential Vote

Dole (R)	1,006,632	(47%)
Clinton (D)	887,454	(42%)
Perot (I)	224,280	(11%)

1996 Republican Presidential Primary

Dole (R)	365,860	(71%)
Buchanan (R)	100,245	(19%)
Forbes (R)	50,802	(10%)

1992 Presidential Vote

Bush (R)	989,375	(43%)
Clinton (D)	848,420	(37%)
Perot (I)	455,934	(20%)

GOVERNOR

Gov. Frank O'Bannon (D)

Elected 1996, term expires Jan. 2001; b. Jan. 30, 1930, Louisville, KY; home, Indianapolis; IN U., B.A. 1952, J.D. 1957; Methodist; married (Judy).

Military Career: Air Force, 1952–54.

Elected Office: IN Senate, 1971–88; IN Lt. Gov., 1989–96.

Professional Career: Practicing atty., 1957–88; Dir. & Chmn., O'Bannon Publishing Co., 1970–88.

Office: 206 State House, Indianapolis, 46204, 317-232-4567; Fax: 317-232-3443; Web site: www.state.in.us.

Election Results

1996 gen.	Frank O'Bannon (D)	....	1,087,128	(52%)
	Stephen Goldsmith (R)	....	986,982	(47%)
	Others	....	35,937	(2%)
1996 prim.	Frank O'Bannon (D)	....	unopposed	
1992 gen.	Evan Bayh (D)	....	1,382,151	(62%)
	Linley E. Pearson (R)	....	822,853	(37%)

SENATORS

Sen. Richard G. Lugar (R)

Elected 1976, seat up 2000; b. Apr. 4, 1932, Indianapolis; home, Indianapolis; Denison U., B.A. 1954, Rhodes Scholar, Oxford U., M.A. 1956; Methodist; married (Charlene).

Military Career: Navy, 1957–60.

Elected Office: Indianapolis Bd. of Schl. Commissioners, 1964–67; Indianapolis Mayor, 1968–75.

Professional Career: Mgr., family farm; V.P. & Treas., Thomas L. Green & Co., 1960–67; Prof., U. of Indianapolis, 1976.

DC Office: 306 HSOB, 20510, 202-224-4814; Fax: 202-228-0360; Web site: www.senate.gov/~lugar.

State Offices: Evansville, 812-465-6313; Ft. Wayne, 219-422-1505; Indianapolis, 317-226-5555; Jeffersonville, 812-288-3377; Merrillville, 219-736-9084.

Committees: *Agriculture, Nutrition & Forestry* (Chmn. of 10 R). *Foreign Relations* (2d of 10 R): European Affairs; International Economic Policy, Export & Trade Promotion; Western Hemisphere, Peace Corps, Narcotics & Terrorism. *Intelligence* (3d of 9 R).

Group Ratings

	ADA	ACLU	AFS	LCV	CON	NTU	NFIB	COC	ACU	NTLC	CHC
1998	0	29	0	13	91	63	100	94	68	68	82
1997	30	—	0	—	77	67	—	90	64	—	—

National Journal Ratings

	1997 LIB — 1997 CONS		1998 LIB — 1998 CONS	
Economic	37% —	57%	38% —	57%
Social	28% —	62%	39% —	58%
Foreign	59% —	38%	45% —	52%

Key Votes of the 105th Congress

1. Bal. Budget Amend.	Y	5. Satcher for Surgeon Gen.	N	9. Chem. Weapons Treaty	Y
2. Clinton Budget Deal	Y	6. Highway Set-asides	N	10. Cuban Humanitarian Aid	Y
3. Cloture on Tobacco	N	7. Table Child Gun locks	Y	11. Table Bosnia Troops	Y
4. Education IRAs	Y	8. Ovrd. Part. Birth Veto	Y	12. $ for Test-ban Treaty	N

Election Results

1994 general	Richard G. Lugar (R) 1,039,625	(67%)	($4,688,326)
	James Jontz (D) 470,799	(31%)	($472,788)
	Others 33,144	(2%)	
1994 primary	Richard G. Lugar (R) .... unopposed		
1988 general	Richard G. Lugar (R) 1,430,525	(68%)	($3,244,601)
	Jack Wickes (D) 668,778	(32%)	($314,233)

Sen. Evan Bayh (D)

Elected 1998, seat up 2004; b. Dec. 26, 1955, Shirkieville; home, Indianapolis; Indiana U., B.A. 1978, U. of VA, J.D. 1982; Episcopalian; married (Susan).

Elected Office: IN Secy. of State, 1986–89; IN Gov., 1989–97.

Professional Career: Practicing atty., 1981–86, 1997–98; Visiting Prof., Indiana U., 1997–98.

DC Office: 717 HSOB, 20510, 202-224-5623; Fax: 202-228-1377; Web site: www.senate.gov/~bayh.

State Office: Indianapolis, 317-554-0757.

Committees: *Aging (Special)* (8th of 9 D). *Banking, Housing & Urban Affairs* (8th of 9 D): Financial Institutions; International Trade & Finance; Securities. *Energy & Natural Resources* (8th of 9 D): Energy, Research, Development, Production & Regulation; Forests & Public Land Management; National Parks, Historic Preservation & Recreation.

Group Ratings and Key Votes: Newly Elected

Election Results

1998 general	Evan Bayh (D) 1,012,244	(64%)	($3,914,375)
	Paul Helmke (R) 552,732	(35%)	($642,784)
	Others 23,641	(1%)	
1998 primary	Evan Bayh (D) .... unopposed		
1992 general	Daniel R. Coats (R) 1,267,972	(57%)	($3,802,077)
	Joseph H. Hogsett (D) 900,148	(41%)	($1,584,173)
	Others 43,306	(2%)	

FIRST DISTRICT

At the southernmost shore of Lake Michigan is a part of America made by steel. Here, in the northwest corner of Indiana, where the water highway of the Great Lakes comes closest to the rail highway of the transcontinental railroads, America's leading capitalists nearly a century ago recognized the best possible site for manufacturing steel. On empty sand dunes United States Steel, then the nation's largest corporation, founded Gary in 1906 and named it for the company's chairman, Chicago Judge Elbert Gary. For nearly 70 years the steel mills attracted a diverse work force, like Chicago and quite unlike the rest of Indiana: Irish, Poles, Czechs, Ukrainians and blacks from the American South. Politics here has always been turbulent, from the Communist-led long and unsuccessful steel strike of 1919 to the racially polarized politics of the 1960s and 1970s. The tone of public life—the clash between union stewards and management foremen, between blacks and eastern European ethnics, between the stalwarts of different factions vying for control of Gary's massive City Hall—was always abrasive, like the clash of steel on steel.

Steel brought sudden growth and sudden depression to northwest Indiana. The massive storefronts built on Gary's aptly named Broadway bear witness to the confidence and exuberance of the 1920s. But today they stand vacant—vandalized, sometimes burnt down—witness to the steel layoffs and crime waves of the 1970s. The steel mills went cold during the Depression of the 1930s, but were thronged with workers during World War II, and in the years afterward their massiveness helped create the illusion that life in the steel towns of Gary, Hammond and East Chicago would go on forever just like it was in the 1950s. The companies granted generous union contracts, confident they could sell as much steel as they could make for any price they chose to charge. But technological advances inevitably replaced increasingly expensive workers with increasingly efficient machines. And the efforts to seal off the U.S. steel market from the world inevitably failed. The oil crunch of 1979 was the catalyst for change, reducing the demand for large-sized autos, the biggest customer for steel. Steel employed 70,000 workers in northwest Indiana in 1979, and just 35,000 a few years later. Obsolete mills were closed, old mills modernized and new ones built which cut the number of manhours needed by two-thirds. Just-in-time methods were introduced, management and high-skill workers cooperated to engineer higher-quality, less expensive steel to meet customers' needs. For the last decade Indiana has been the number one steel-producing state. But trouble arose in 1998, when recession-stricken steel-producing countries—Russia, Japan and others—were selling steel at distress prices, and American steel producers called for import quotas.

As the steel industry was changing, Gary was falling almost into ruins. As long ago as 1967, Gary elected a black mayor, Richard Hatcher, who was determined to use city government to cure poverty. But high crime rates produced a flight to the suburbs and left Broadway's storefronts empty, and Gary's publicly financed convention center and airport have done little business. In 1993 and 1995 Gary was the nation's murder capital, with Governor Evan Bayh dispatching 50 state troopers to help Gary police for three months in 1995. In 1995 Gary responded by electing a white Democrat mayor, Scott King, with 78% of the vote. The city's latest hope is for salvation by riverboat (actually, lakeboat) gambling. But most of northwest Indiana's people have long since scattered out to suburbs and countryside, making it part of the greater Chicago area, distinctive mainly for its lower sales tax.

Indiana's 1st Congressional District stretches from Gary and Hammond along the Lake Michigan shore, east almost to Michigan City. Politically, this has been a heavily Democratic area since the Depression of the early 1930s and the United Steelworkers' organizing drives of the late 1930s. It is the most Democratic part of mostly Republican Indiana.

The congressman from the 1st District is Pete Visclosky, a Democrat first elected in 1984. Visclosky grew up in northwest Indiana (his father was once mayor of Gary), went to college there and law school at Notre Dame, not far away. He practiced law, then worked for six years for 1st District Congressman Adam Benjamin. Benjamin died suddenly in 1982 and Visclosky returned to Indiana. In 1984 he ran against Katie Hall, a black state senator who had been given the 1982 nomination—and thus the election, in this area—by Richard Hatcher, then district party chairman. But Hall was able to win only 33% of the 1984 primary vote; Visclosky had 34% and another white candidate 31%. Visclosky beat Hall again 57%–35% in 1986 and 51%–30% in 1990. He has not had serious opposition since.

Visclosky has a somewhat moderate voting record and concentrates much of his effort on projects to help the local economy. He supports the balanced budget amendment and has sometimes voted with Republicans on budget issues. He has voted against programs like the Market Promotion Program, calling them corporate welfare. He has a solid pro-union voting record, opposing Bacon-Davis repeal, the TEAM Act and the Republican measure to allow workers to choose compensatory time instead of premium overtime pay. He is vice chair of the executive committee of the 82-member Congressional Steel Caucus and supported the October 1998 resolution asking the president to conduct quick 10-day scrutiny of 10 steel-producing countries and punish offenders with a one-year ban on imports. Pointing to other countries' quotas, Visclosky asked, "If they're smart enough not to allow it to be dumped in Europe and Japan, why can't we protect ourselves too?"

In 1999 Visclosky became ranking Democrat on the Appropriations Subcommittee on Energy and Water Development. There he has pushed for $32 million in flood control and harbor reconstruction for the Little Calumet River, Burns Harbor, Cady Marsh Ditch and Mondaldi Barons; $2.2 million for beach renourishment at the Indiana Dunes National Lakeshore; $15 million for beach erosion at Ogden Dunes; and brownfield grants for Gary, East Chicago and Hammond. He pushed through an exception to the Johnson Act, making Lake Michigan waters eligible for gambling and thus allowing riverboat casinos for Gary. He worked to fund a 760-job postal encoding facility in Gary and to stop the FAA from closing its air tower at Gary Regional Airport, which he had once tried to make Chicago's third major airport. Years ago his mother's car was hit by a train at a crossing in Gary; he has pushed for funds for rail safety.

Alarmed by crime in Gary, he got northwest Indiana declared a High Intensity Drug Trafficking Area, bringing in the National Guard to tear down crack houses. He secured funding for 82 additional policemen, two military helicopters and night-vision goggles. Stunned that crack dealers had bulletproof vests and policemen did not, Visclosky introduced the Bulletproof Vest Partnership Grant Act, which passed in June 1998.

Visclosky encountered some competition in 1994; against a Republican who spent more than $100,000, he lost some conservative suburbs and won by just 56%–44%. In 1996 and 1998 he won without difficulty.

Cook's Call. *Safe.* Visclosky is deeply entrenched in this heavily Democratic district. Don't expect any upsets here.

The People: Pop. 1990: 554,514; 9% rural; 12.4% age 65 + ; 74.2% White, 21.1% Black, 0.6% Asian, 0.2% Amer. Indian, 3.9% Other; 8.3% Hispanic Origin. Households: 55.2% married couple families; 27.5% married couple fams. w. children; 36.8% college educ.; median household income: $31,300; per capita income: $13,161; median house value: $57,000; median gross rent: $297.

1996 Presidential Vote

Clinton (D) 116,355 (58%)
Dole (R) 62,595 (31%)
Perot (I) 19,530 (10%)

1992 Presidential Vote

Clinton (D) 117,115 (52%)
Bush (R) 68,392 (31%)
Perot (I) 37,129 (17%)

Rep. Peter J. Visclosky (D)

Elected 1984; b. Aug. 13, 1949, Gary; home, Merrillville; IN U. Northwest, B.S. 1970, U. of Notre Dame, J.D. 1973, Georgetown U., LL.M. 1982; Catholic; divorced.

Professional Career: Practicing atty., 1973–76, 1983–84; Aide, U.S. Rep. Adam Benjamin, 1976–82.

DC Office: 2313 RHOB 20515, 202-225-2461; Fax: 202-225-2493; Web site: www.house.gov/visclosky.

District Offices: Gary, 219-884-1177; Portage, 219-763-2904; Valparaiso, 219-464-0315.

Committees: *Appropriations* (10th of 27 D): Defense; Energy & Water Development (RMM).

Group Ratings

	ADA	ACLU	AFS	LCV	CON	NTU	NFIB	COC	ACU	NTLC	CHC
1998	80	69	100	77	68	17	21	28	12	13	27
1997	65	—	63	—	80	36	—	50	29	—	—

National Journal Ratings

	1997 LIB — 1997 CONS		1998 LIB — 1998 CONS	
Economic	63%	37%	71%	28%
Social	67%	33%	63%	37%
Foreign	60%	38%	64%	31%

Key Votes of the 105th Congress

1. Clinton Budget Deal	N	5. Puerto Rico Sthood. Ref.	Y	9. Cut $ for B-2 Bombers	N
2. Education IRAs	*	6. End Highway Set-asides	N	10. Human Rights in China	Y
3. Req. 2/3 to Raise Taxes	N	7. School Prayer Amend.	N	11. Withdraw Bosnia Troops	N
4. Fast-track Trade	N	8. Ovrd. Part. Birth Veto	Y	12. End Cuban TV-Marti	Y

Election Results

1998 general	Peter J. Visclosky (D)	92,634	(73%)	($277,447)
	Michael Petyo (R)	33,503	(26%)	($31,151)
	Others	1,617	(1%)	
1998 primary	Peter J. Visclosky (D)	45,845	(87%)	
	Cyril B. (Cy) Huerter (D)	7,027	(13%)	
1996 general	Peter J. Visclosky (D)	133,553	(69%)	($318,769)
	Michael Petyo (R)	56,418	(29%)	($47,379)
	Others	3,142	(2%)	

SECOND DISTRICT

Muncie, Indiana, became famous as the "Middletown" that sociologists Robert and Helen Lynd lived in and reported on in 1924–25 and again in 1935, and where a team of sociologists investigated again in 1976–78. The Lynds were attracted to Muncie by its typicalness—"every small city from Maine to California," *Life* said. But it wasn't exactly: It was a factory town in a country still almost half rural, it was almost entirely Protestant and Northern in a country one-quarter Catholic and one-third Southern. Muncie was more typical in being culturally homogeneous but economically riven. In the 1920s, Muncie celebrated its common values and was loath to admit its economic disparities; in the 1930s, the latter came out into the open when

Muncie, like most of the industrial Midwest, was unionized in what were sometimes violent uprisings. The business elite—local bankers, merchants, executives at General Motors and the Ball family's glass company—was fiercely opposed by workers who were joining CIO unions and voting for Democrats. Partisan politics took on the sharp, bitter tone of a struggle for wealth between two rival classes whose claims seemed irreconcilable.

Echoes of this class-warfare politics reverberate only faintly today. They grow louder with local economic distress, as Muncie suffered years ago in layoffs at GM and more recently when the Ball headquarters moved to Colorado. And there are higher Democratic percentages in towns with union traditions, like Muncie and Anderson, than in others such as Richmond and Kokomo. But Indiana's late 1990s prosperity, based on high-skill manufacturing, has brought something like a political consensus here for tax cuts, holding down budgets and quiet support of traditional values, with strong support for candidates of either party who agree.

The 2d Congressional District covers most of east-central Indiana. It includes Muncie and Anderson, with their big GM factories, in the north; Richmond, founded by a major branch of American Quakers and the home of their Earlham College; and Columbus, the home of Cummins Engine, whose longtime head J. Irwin Miller paid major international architects to design most of the town's important buildings, public and private. The 2d leans Republican in presidential politics and is a swing district in Indiana races.

The congressman from the 2d District is David McIntosh, a Republican first elected in 1994. McIntosh was born in California, and moved to Kendallville, north of Fort Wayne, when his mother returned home after his father's death; his mother became a Democratic city judge. His interest in politics began in 1976, at 18, when he saw 29-year-old Dan Quayle in his first campaign for Congress. McIntosh went to Yale and the University of Chicago Law School, where he studied under Antonin Scalia and was one of the founders of the conservative Federalist Society. McIntosh worked in the Reagan Justice Department and White House, then became director of the White House Council on Competitiveness headed by then-Vice President Quayle. After 1992, McIntosh worked for the Hudson Institute in Indianapolis and lived in Muncie, with a view of running against Philip Sharp, a Democrat who held the seat for 20 years by narrow margins and who decided in February 1994 to retire. Other Republicans with more time in local politics also were running. But state Auditor Ann DeVore astonishingly missed a noon deadline for filing nomination papers in an office down the hall from her own. Bill Frazier, who ran three times against Sharp, spent $616,000 of his own money. But McIntosh won the primary 43%–42%. In the general, McIntosh faced Secretary of State Joe Hogsett, a protege of Governor Evan Bayh, who ran for the Senate in 1992. McIntosh attacked him as a Clinton supporter and called the 1994 crime bill "the Clinton/Hogsett hug-a-thug bill." McIntosh won 54%–46%.

In the House, McIntosh has been a leader in the move for regulatory reform and one of the leading conservative critics of its Republican leadership. Immediately after the 1994 election he became the freshman liaison to the leadership and was picked by incoming Speaker Newt Gingrich to chair the subcommittee handling regulatory reform. McIntosh promptly called for a moratorium on new regulations and wrote a bill requiring agencies like EPA and OSHA to make cost-benefit analyses and risk assessments and hear challenges in court before issuing regulations—placing on government the same kind of burdens it delighted in placing on business. Though it passed the House in February 1995, it died in conference committee and was attacked by Democrats as an assault on the environment and workplace safety. In late 1995 he supported the effort to close down the government, and in January 1996 he was one of 15 Republican freshmen to vote against the bill to reopen it. He called for reform of Superfund and total repeal of retroactive liability. He also called for periodic review of regulations costing more than $100 million. McIntosh took the lead on Ernest Istook's bill to limit non-profit organizations that receive federal funds from spending more than 5% of their budgets on lobbying; this was attacked as an abridgement of free speech. McIntosh replied, "All we are asking is that these groups make a choice. Be a lobbying organization or be a grant recipient." He amended the March 1996 debt-limit bill to give Congress power to veto or change proposed regulations within 60 legislative days. "The act is the most significant change in regulatory law in 50 years," he said, "yet no one noticed. Most observers failed to read it carefully." McIntosh was even more adroit in finding Hoosier examples of people hurt by regulation and helped by his deregulatory work: He cited the case of an Anderson girl in need of a drug awaiting FDA approval; McIntosh called the FDA head and the drug was approved.

In 1996 McIntosh raised and spent more than $1 million and was re-elected by 58%–40%, losing narrowly in Muncie's Delaware County and winning elsewhere. As a member of the sophomore class, he grumbled about Newt Gingrich's ethics problems, and he zeroed in on those of the Clinton White House, focusing on its 200,000-name database. He was mentioned as a candidate when Senator Dan Coats announced his retirement, but did not run. In February 1998 he was elected chairman of the Conservative Action Team, which tried without much success to get the leadership to take more assertive stands. He called the House Republicans' 1998 budget's tax cuts "anemic and embarrassing" and said the Senate's regulatory reform bill made too many concessions. He did not back the Shays-Meehan campaign finance reform bill, instead favoring a requirement of immediate reporting, a ban on foreign contributions, and a bar on unions spending dues money on politics without members' approval.

In 1998 McIntosh was re-elected 61%–38% after raising another $1.3 million; this time he carried every county. On election night he was on the phone talking to members about running for speaker, but he ended up not seeking a leadership post. Frustrated with his inability, despite his subcommittee chair, to get his reforms passed by the Senate or signed by the president, he has thought out loud about running for governor in 2000. "There is something exciting about being involved in state government . . . Indiana has the potential to show how a pragmatic conservative government could work." But given Frank O'Bannon's strength, McIntosh seems likely to wait until 2004, two years before his self-imposed 12-year term-limit ends.

Cook's Call. *Probably Safe.* With McIntosh pretty firmly planted in this district, the biggest issue in 2000 will be whether or not he runs for governor. Although this industrial-dependant district has been trending more Republican in recent years, in an open seat situation the right Democrat could make this seat competitive, although Republicans would retain an edge.

The People: Pop. 1990: 554,321; 42.9% rural; 14.3% age 65 + ; 95.1% White, 4.1% Black, 0.4% Asian, 0.2% Amer. Indian, 0.2% Other; 0.6% Hispanic Origin. Households: 59% married couple families; 27.2% married couple fams. w. children; 32% college educ.; median household income: $26,185; per capita income: $12,311; median house value: $43,400; median gross rent: $243.

1996 Presidential Vote			1992 Presidential Vote		
Dole (R)	97,406	(45%)	Bush (R)	101,370	(43%)
Clinton (D)	89,038	(42%)	Clinton (D)	82,008	(35%)
Perot (I)	26,483	(12%)	Perot (I)	50,458	(22%)

Rep. David McIntosh (R)

Elected 1994; b. June 8, 1958, Oakton, CA; home, Muncie; Yale U., B.A. 1980, U. of Chicago Law Schl., J.D. 1983; Episcopalian; married (Ruthie).

Professional Career: Spec. Asst., U.S. Atty Gen., 1986–87; White House Spec. Asst., Domestic Affairs, 1987–88; Spec. Asst., Vice Pres. Dan Quayle, 1989–91; Exec. Dir., Cncl. of Competitiveness, 1989–92; Sr. Fellow, Hudson Inst., 1993–94.

DC Office: 1610 LHOB 20515, 202-225-3021; Fax: 202-225-3382; Web site: www.house.gov/mcintosh.

District Offices: Anderson, 765-640-2919; Columbus, 812-372-3637; Muncie, 765-747-5566; Richmond, 765-962-2883.

Committees: *Education & the Workforce* (15th of 27 R): Early Childhood, Youth & Families; Postsecondary Education, Training & Life-Long Learning. *Government Reform* (10th of 24 R): National Economic Growth, Natural Resources & Regulatory Affairs (Chmn.); National Security, Veterans' Affairs & Intl. Relations. *Small Business* (10th of 19 R): Regulatory Reform & Paperwork Reduction.

Group Ratings

	ADA	ACLU	AFS	LCV	CON	NTU	NFIB	COC	ACU	NTLC	CHC
1998	0	7	0	8	45	66	92	94	100	91	100
1997	15	—	38	—	9	62	—	67	100	—	—

National Journal Ratings

	1997 LIB — 1997 CONS	1998 LIB — 1998 CONS
Economic	37% — 63%	0% — 88%
Social	20% — 71%	0% — 97%
Foreign	23% — 77%	19% — 75%

Key Votes of the 105th Congress

1. Clinton Budget Deal	Y	5. Puerto Rico Sthood. Ref.	N
2. Education IRAs	*	6. End Highway Set-asides	Y
3. Req. 2/3 to Raise Taxes	Y	7. School Prayer Amend.	Y
4. Fast-track Trade	Y	8. Ovrd. Part. Birth Veto	Y

9. Cut $ for B-2 Bombers	*
10. Human Rights in China	Y
11. Withdraw Bosnia Troops	Y
12. End Cuban TV-Marti	N

Election Results

1998 general	David McIntosh (R)	99,608	(61%)	($714,843)
	Sherman Boles (D)	62,452	(38%)	($124,185)
	Others	2,236	(1%)	
1998 primary	David McIntosh (R)	unopposed		
1996 general	David McIntosh (R)	123,113	(58%)	($1,050,616)
	R. Marc Carmichael (D)	85,105	(40%)	($182,508)
	Others	4,665	(2%)	

THIRD DISTRICT

When Notre Dame University was founded in 1842, Catholics were still a rarity in most of America and certainly rare on the limestone-bottomed plains of northern Indiana. This was still farm country and South Bend no more than a crossroads on the St. Joseph River. But by the 1920s, both had grown. Notre Dame, thanks to its football team, "the Fighting Irish," was the most famous Catholic university in the land, and South Bend was a significant industrial city, home of Studebaker and Bendix and dozens of other factories. In the last 50 years Notre Dame has grown in size and reputation, but South Bend has had the experience of many Midwestern industrial cities: In the 1960s Studebaker went out of business, in the early 1980s there were big layoffs at big factories, and in the early 1990s there were well-publicized layoffs in nearby Elkhart. But more important than these high-visibility job losses was the largely invisible creation of jobs in small factories throughout the region. The work here requires more skill than did the old assembly lines, and the products must be more responsive to just-in-time prime contractors or computer-inventory retailers. By the late 1990s unemployment in northern Indiana was down to 3% and below, and the economic base was more secure than when it depended on the fate of two or three big companies.

The 3d Congressional District of Indiana has centered on South Bend for decades. This is an industrial and ethnic city—with the nation's largest percentage of Hungarian-Americans—which has long been Democratic; so is LaPorte County around Michigan City. Elkhart County, in contrast, is decidedly Republican.

The congressman from the 3d District is Tim Roemer, a Democrat first elected in 1990. Roemer grew up in South Bend and went to college in San Diego, then received a masters and Ph.D. from Notre Dame; he worked for 3d District Congressman John Brademas and Arizona Senator Dennis DeConcini and is married to the daughter of former Louisiana Senator Bennett Johnston. Roemer returned to South Bend and ran for Congress in 1990, raised more PAC money than Republican incumbent John Hiler and sounded outsider themes with insider skill.

Roemer is one of the House's most visible moderate Democrats, a co-chair of the New Democrats group formed in 1997, which claims 50 members in the 106th Congress. His voting record is squarely in the middle of the House. He supports the balanced budget amendment, votes against pork barrel projects and supported much of the Contract With America. Even before Republicans won control, his position on OSHA angered organized labor, long a force in South Bend. In 1995 he voted for the conservative Democrat Blue Dog balanced budget and moved to cut one-third of the employees in Energy Department labs. In November 1995 he and Fred Upton, a Republican from next-door St. Joseph, Michigan, wrote Speaker Gingrich and called for temporary appropriations, with the lower of Senate or House figures; Roemer was booed and hissed by fellow Democrats when he spoke for it on the floor and was paid little heed by Gingrich. In 1996 Roemer supported welfare reform and was one of 37 House Democrats who wrote Clinton urging him to sign the August 1996 Welfare Reform Act.

Since he came to Congress, Roemer has challenged the space station: In July 1998 his motion to zero it out was defeated 323–109. On education, he has bucked teachers' unions by devising bills to use federal funds to encourage charter schools and to change credentialing to allow lateral entry into teaching jobs. He supported military action against Iraq in 1998, though he voted against the Gulf war resolution in 1991; he opposed both NAFTA and fast track. Roemer has long decried the harsh partisan atmosphere of the House and called for "bipartisanship and civility"; he bristled when Minority Leader Richard Gephardt seemed to attack centrist Democrats in December 1997. In September 1998 he called for censure of Bill Clinton, but declined to call for his resignation; he voted against all counts of impeachment.

Roemer has run well ahead of his party in a district that was always marginal between 1980 and 1990. He won with 57% in 1992 when George Bush carried the district, with 55% in 1994 when Republicans carried it for all statewide offices, and with 58% when Bob Dole carried it in 1996. In 1998 he again won with 58%.

Cook's Call. *Probably Safe.* Though he had a couple of close calls in the early 1990s, Roemer looks to have secured himself pretty well in this very marginal district. However, this conservative district can swing with the national tide, and Roemer could find himself in trouble in a down year for Democrats.

The People: Pop. 1990: 554,482; 28.6% rural; 13.5% age 65 + ; 90.7% White, 7.4% Black, 0.7% Asian, 0.3% Amer. Indian, 0.9% Other; 1.9% Hispanic Origin. Households: 57.9% married couple families; 28.1% married couple fams. w. children; 37.4% college educ.; median household income: $29,470; per capita income: $13,385; median house value: $55,500; median gross rent: $314.

1996 Presidential Vote		
Dole (R)	91,427	(46%)
Clinton (D)	86,715	(43%)
Perot (I)	20,374	(10%)

1992 Presidential Vote		
Bush (R)	91,708	(42%)
Clinton (D)	82,483	(38%)
Perot (I)	41,358	(19%)

Rep. Tim Roemer (D)

Elected 1990; b. Oct. 30, 1956, South Bend; home, South Bend; U. of CA at San Diego, B.A. 1979, U. of Notre Dame, M.A., 1981, Ph.D. 1985; Catholic; married (Sally).

Professional Career: Staff Asst., U.S. Rep. John Brademas, 1980; Legis. Advisor, U.S. Sen. Dennis DeConcini, 1985–89; Instructor, American U., 1988.

DC Office: 2352 RHOB 20515, 202-225-3915; Fax: 202-225-6798; Web site: www.house.gov/roemer.

District Office: South Bend, 219-288-3301.

Committees: *Education & the Workforce* (9th of 22 D): Oversight & Investigations (RMM); Postsecondary Education, Training & Life-Long Learning. *Permanent Select Committee on Intelligence* (6th of 7 D): Technical & Tactical Intelligence.

Group Ratings

	ADA	ACLU	AFS	LCV	CON	NTU	NFIB	COC	ACU	NTLC	CHC
1998	65	31	89	62	65	33	64	78	44	32	50
1997	55	—	50	—	56	49	—	70	32	—	—

National Journal Ratings

	1997 LIB — 1997 CONS			1998 LIB — 1998 CONS		
Economic	58%	—	41%	55%	—	45%
Social	50%	—	48%	50%	—	50%
Foreign	67%	—	32%	59%	—	40%

Key Votes of the 105th Congress

1. Clinton Budget Deal	Y	5. Puerto Rico Sthood. Ref.	Y	9. Cut $ for B-2 Bombers	Y
2. Education IRAs	N	6. End Highway Set-asides	N	10. Human Rights in China	N
3. Req. 2/3 to Raise Taxes	Y	7. School Prayer Amend.	Y	11. Withdraw Bosnia Troops	N
4. Fast-track Trade	N	8. Ovrd. Part. Birth Veto	Y	12. End Cuban TV-Marti	Y

Election Results

1998 general	Tim Roemer (D)	84,625	(58%)	($489,658)
	Daniel A. Holtz (R)	61,041	(42%)	($270,523)
1998 primary	Tim Roemer (D)	unopposed		
1996 general	Tim Roemer (D)	114,288	(58%)	($525,727)
	Joe Zakas (R)	80,699	(41%)	($310,084)

FOURTH DISTRICT

The northeast corner of Indiana, in the center of a flat agricultural area, can claim to be the center of Middle America. Its first settlers were of New England Yankee stock, establishing orderly communities with public schools and even colleges; they were joined by German immigrants, who built tidy farms and their own civic institutions. In the northern part of the state there are hills and lakes, and the strange swamp that is the central focus of Gene Stratton Porter's children's classic, *Girl of the Limberlost*. The one large city here, Fort Wayne, was built on the flat terrain along the Maumee River that flows to Toledo, Ohio; it grew as a factory town, surging ahead and then falling back as large factories, often tied to the auto industry, opened and closed over the years. Today Fort Wayne has more white-collar jobs.

The 4th Congressional District consists of nine counties in northeast Indiana, plus a bit of Jay County. It includes Fort Wayne, Huntington and Columbia City but not North Manchester. Politically this area is ancestrally Republican since the Civil War years. Since the New Deal, it has sometimes veered Democratic in times of economic distress. This part of Indiana is also a cradle of vice presidents: Thomas Marshall, Woodrow Wilson's vice president, was born in North Manchester and practiced law in Columbia City; Dan Quayle spent his high school years and later practiced law in Huntington. Quayle won this seat in 1976 and represented the district for two terms.

The congressman from the 4th District is Mark Souder, a Republican first elected in 1994. Souder grew up in Grabill, 10 miles from Fort Wayne, where his Amish great-great-grandfather's family settled. There the family started Souder's of Grabill in 1907, originally a harness shop and now a furniture store and manufacturer of store fixtures. Souder worked in the furniture business, returned to Grabill, then went to work in 1984 for Dan Coats as minority staff director of the Select Committee on Children, Youth and Families. He moved with Coats to the Senate in 1989, where he served as his legislative director and deputy chief of staff. In 1993 he returned to Fort Wayne and started running against Jill Long, a Democrat elected to replace Coats. With a moderate record and a farm background, she was not an easy target. But Souder raised more money and won a six-candidate primary with 40%; the state Republican ticket was also running far ahead of the Democrats in the 4th District. The result was a 55%–45% Souder victory.

Despite his Washington experience, Souder has continued to be something of a rebel in the House, even against his own party's leaders. Souder says that he is "most defined by the fact that I'm an evangelical Christian." Elected vice president of the freshman class, he voted against the balanced budget amendment because it did not require a supermajority to raise taxes. Majority Leader Dick Armey once said, "Tell Souder I always assume that if there's trouble, it's him." When Souder and John Hostettler cast two of the 17 votes against a continuing resolution in January 1996, Gingrich announced that he would not appear at fundraisers for them. Said Souder, "This is a test of whether you can vote your conscience." He refused to sponsor a National Right-to-Work Committee though he favored it after the group sent a mailing to his district urging voters to demand he sponsor it.

Souder has been active on drug issues and served on Gingrich's drugs task force. In 1996 he proposed cutting off assistance to Mexico if it did not stop the drug flow. A modified version passed the conference committee, but the administration has continued to endorse Mexico's anti-drug efforts. He blamed Bill Clinton's "half-hearted" anti-drug message for increased drug use by teens. Frustrated that the House would not do so, Souder imposed drug testing on his own staff. He helped manage the drug-free workplace law that passed the House by a wide margin in June 1998 and sponsored an amendment to require those who lose student loans because of drug convictions to test negative before loans are resumed; with that adopted, he voted for the Higher Education Act. On other education issues, Souder sponsored a High Hopes program with Democrat Chaka Fattah sending letters to low-income sixth and seventh graders informing them of the availability of aid for college. He also sponsored a five-year test of IRA-type savings accounts for low income families, to be used for first homes, higher education, emergency medical service and business capitalization.

In September 1996 Souder called for an investigation of the INS program Citizenship USA; charging, presciently, that the Clinton Administration was seeking to naturalize new citizens unduly quickly so they could vote in November. But after being re-elected easily, he agonized before announcing finally on January 2, 1997, that he would vote to re-elect Newt Gingrich as speaker. In July 1997, when the coup against Gingrich failed, Souder said that turmoil was likely to continue as long as he was speaker. "He changes positions on fundamental legislation without telling anyone," Souder complained. Yet he also complained that the Gingrich leadership didn't have "A-B-C fallback plans" (which presumably require such maneuvers), just "A-whoops." In November 1997, even before the Monica Lewinsky scandal became public, he called for the impeachment of Bill Clinton for his "systematic abuses of office." But in November 1998, when impeachment was looming, he announced he would vote against; in December he voted for the third article and against the others.

Souder was comfortably re-elected in 1998.

Cook's Call. *Probably Safe.* Souder's vote against three of the impeachment articles has already drawn him a Republican opponent: Allen County Chief Deputy Prosecutor Mike Loomis. It remains to be seen, however, whether Souder, who has racked up big winning margins of late, is all that vulnerable, even in a primary. Regardless, the district (despite a lapse in the early 1990s when it elected a Democrat for two terms) remains fundamentally Republican and conservative.

The People: Pop. 1990: 554,577; 40.4% rural; 12.5% age 65 + ; 92.9% White, 5.5% Black, 0.6% Asian, 0.3% Amer. Indian, 0.7% Other; 1.5% Hispanic Origin. Households: 60.7% married couple families; 30.8% married couple fams. w. children; 40% college educ.; median household income: $30,859; per capita income: $13,436; median house value: $56,500; median gross rent: $295.

1996 Presidential Vote

Dole (R)	110,538	(53%)
Clinton (D)	75,185	(36%)
Perot (I)	19,641	(9%)

1992 Presidential Vote

Bush (R)	102,779	(46%)
Clinton (D)	69,292	(31%)
Perot (I)	49,565	(22%)

Rep. Mark Souder (R)

Elected 1994; b. July 18, 1950, Ft. Wayne; home, Grabill; IN U., B.S. 1972, Notre Dame U., M.B.A. 1974; Protestant; married (Diane).

Professional Career: Furniture salesman, 1976–83; Staff Dir., U.S. House Select Cmte. on Children, Youth & Families, 1984–89; Legis. Dir., U.S. Sen. Dan Coats, 1989–91, Dep. Chief of Staff, 1991–93.

DC Office: 109 CHOB 20515, 202-225-4436; Fax: 202-225-3479; Web site: www.house.gov/souder.

District Office: Ft. Wayne, 219-424-3041.

Committees: *Education & the Workforce* (14th of 27 R): Early Childhood, Youth & Families; Postsecondary Education, Training & Life-Long Learning. *Government Reform* (11th of 24 R): Census; Criminal Justice, Drug Policy & Human Resources; National Security, Veterans' Affairs & Intl. Relations (Vice Chmn.). *Resources* (23d of 28 R): Fisheries Conservation, Wildlife & Oceans; National Parks & Public Lands.

Group Ratings

	ADA	ACLU	AFS	LCV	CON	NTU	NFIB	COC	ACU	NTLC	CHC
1998	15	13	25	8	66	63	100	76	83	89	100
1997	5	—	13	—	62	64	—	80	100	—	—

National Journal Ratings

	1997 LIB — 1997 CONS			1998 LIB — 1998 CONS		
Economic	18%	—	81%	34%	—	64%
Social	20%	—	71%	29%	—	69%
Foreign	12%	—	81%	17%	—	83%

Key Votes of the 105th Congress

1. Clinton Budget Deal	Y	5. Puerto Rico Sthood. Ref.	N	9. Cut $ for B-2 Bombers	N
2. Education IRAs	Y	6. End Highway Set-asides	N	10. Human Rights in China	Y
3. Req. 2/3 to Raise Taxes	Y	7. School Prayer Amend.	Y	11. Withdraw Bosnia Troops	Y
4. Fast-track Trade	N	8. Ovrd. Part. Birth Veto	Y	12. End Cuban TV-Marti	N

Election Results

1998 general	Mark Souder (R)	93,671	(63%)	($221,310)
	Mark J. Wehrle (D)	54,286	(37%)	($6,932)
1998 primary	Mark Souder (R)	unopposed		
1996 general	Mark Souder (R)	121,344	(58%)	($438,384)
	Gerald L. Houseman (D)	81,740	(39%)	($65,093)
	Others	4,796	(2%)	

FIFTH DISTRICT

Across the plains of northern Indiana runs the Hoosier Heartland Corridor: The HHC, a publicist's name for U.S. 24 as it runs west from Fort Wayne along the Wabash River through Wabash, Peru and Logansport, and then overland toward the Illinois prairie. Scattered on the major east-west railroad and highway lines that connect the East Coast and Chicago, the Hoosier Heartland's small cities and large towns display a geometric order and heartland American values. It is also an economically creative place: In Kokomo, Elwood Haynes built one of the first gas-powered automobiles and invented stainless steel. This area was hit hard by recession in the early 1980s, but it has rebounded smartly: Its large factories, like Delco and Chrysler, are expanding, and its small manufacturers have proved high-skill and adaptive. This is a part of America with little immigrant heritage from the early waves of immigration, relatively few blacks, and only a handful of the more recent Latin and Asian immigrants. Basic values have not been shaken so much here as in other parts of the nation: This area has one of the nation's highest percentages of households with families, married couples and children. It is also a place that has given America such icons as James Dean, who grew up in Fairmount and Cole Porter, who grew up in Peru.

The 5th Congressional District occupies most of the land on either side of the HHC. There are no big cities within the district; it just skirts Indianapolis, Fort Wayne, South Bend and Gary. Though farming is important here, factories large and small employ many more people; this is one of the centers of American manufacturing. Since the Civil War, this has mostly been Republican country, and the western part of the district was the home base of House Minority Leader (1959–65) Charles Halleck. But in much of the 1970s and 1980s, Democrats were competitive.

The 5th District's congressman is Steve Buyer (pronounced *BOOyer*), a Republican elected in 1992. Buyer grew up in White County, graduated from The Citadel, served in the Army, worked in Indianapolis and started a family law practice in Monticello, where he joined all the civic organizations. A major in the military reserves, he was called to active duty in fall 1990, serving as legal adviser at a prisoner-of-war camp in the Persian Gulf. Buyer was enraged that two-thirds of House Democrats, including the 5th District's Democratic Congressman Jim Jontz, voted against the war. After he returned to Indiana, where he was White County Republican vice chairman, he began making speeches around the Hoosier Heartland attacking Jontz on his Gulf war stand. In October 1991 Buyer met with all of Jontz's former opponents, then launched his own campaign. In 1992 he focused on the House bank and post office scandals and called for term limits and application of laws passed by Congress to Congress itself, an anticipation of the Contract with America. He attacked Jontz for switching committees in order to protect the spotted owl in Oregon. Jontz was a skilled politician, but Buyer won 51%–49%, carrying the Hoosier Heartland but losing counties at the edge of the district.

Buyer has made far more of a legislative mark than one would have expected back in 1993 for a conservative-to-moderate Republican in a then-Democratic House. On the Veterans' Affairs Committee, he has spent much time on "Gulf war syndrome." Since his return from the Gulf, Buyer has suffered from flu, pneumonia, spastic colon, kidney infection, bronchitis and a constant cough. He investigated and discovered there may have been chemical weapons in a bunker destroyed by U.S. Army troops at Khamisiyay, Iraq. In 1994 he successfully co-sponsored legislation that allows the VA to compensate Gulf war veterans suffering from chronic disabilities resulting from undiagnosed illnesses that became manifest to a degree of 10% or more within a year of the Gulf war—a real departure in veterans' law. Buyer supports continued investigation for Gulf war illness. On Veterans, Buyer also worked on the Benefits Improvement Act of 1996 and on the measure to extend veterans' preferences (to the federal judiciary, for the first time).

In 1997 Buyer became chairman of the Military Personnel Subcommittee of Armed Services, which originates legislation extending the U.S. military presence in Bosnia. In October 1995 he sponsored a resolution with fellow Gulf war veteran Paul McHale saying that U.S. deployment should not be a requisite for a peace agreement; it passed 315–104. In December 1995 he and Ike Skelton wrote a resolution reiterating opposition to deployment; it passed 287–141. But after visiting Bosnia with Bill Clinton and Bob Dole in December 1997, he agreed—at Newt Gingrich's urging—to sponsor a deployment bill, but with strings: Buyer wants to set measurable objectives for implementing the Dayton accords and authorize U.S. partial or total withdrawal if they are not met. "I'm going to try to change the dynamic so we can push these people in Bosnia to either start moving on the civil implementations of the peace accord, or figure out what they want to do with their own destiny." He also held hearings on sexual misconduct in the military, bringing to light problems with recruit housing and training.

On local issues, Buyer co-sponsored the Step 21 funding formula in the 1998 transportation bill, which gave Indiana an extra $1.2 billion; Governor Frank O'Bannon promised it would be used to complete four-laning the HHC. Buyer has blocked the Fish and Wildlife Service from creating a Grand Kankakee Marsh Wildlife Refuge until it works with the Army Corps of Engineers on flood control.

Buyer is best known nationally for his work on the Judiciary Committee on the impeachment of Bill Clinton. He used his time for questions to compare Clinton's conduct with military standards. "Should we ask the members of the armed forces to accept a code of conduct that is higher for troops than for the commander-in-chief?" And he criticized advocates of civil rights who seemed prepared to condone perjury in civil rights cases. He got into one military appropriations bill an amendment that would subject the president and civilian Pentagon officials to military standards on lying and adultery, but it was not binding.

Buyer has proved very strong politically for this not-too-long-ago Democratic seat; he was re-elected 63%–36% in 1998.

Cook's Call. *Safe.* Not even his high-profile role as a House manager during the impeachment trial should threaten Buyer's re-election prospects in this Republican-leaning district.

The People: Pop. 1990: 554,240; 57.7% rural; 13.8% age 65 + ; 96.8% White, 2.1% Black, 0.3% Asian, 0.4% Amer. Indian, 0.4% Other; 1.2% Hispanic Origin. Households: 63.3% married couple families; 30.6% married couple fams. w. children; 31.1% college educ.; median household income: $27,893; per capita income: $12,252; median house value: $46,700; median gross rent: $241.

1996 Presidential Vote

Dole (R)	105,906	(50%)
Clinton (D)	78,270	(37%)
Perot (I)	27,469	(13%)

1992 Presidential Vote

Bush (R)	103,124	(45%)
Clinton (D)	70,891	(31%)
Perot (I)	52,354	(23%)

Rep. Stephen Buyer (R)

Elected 1992; b. Nov. 26, 1958, Rensselaer; home, Monticello; The Citadel, B.S. 1980, Valparaiso U., J.D. 1984; Methodist; married (Joni).

Military Career: Army, 1984–87, 1990–91 (Persian Gulf); Army Reserves, 1980–84, 1987–present.

Professional Career: IN Dep. Atty. Gen., 1987–88; Vice Chmn., White Cnty. Repub. Party, 1988–90; Practicing atty., 1988–92.

DC Office: 227 CHOB 20515, 202-225-5037; Fax: 202-225-2267; Web site: www.house.gov/buyer.

District Offices: Kokomo, 317-454-7551; Monticello, 219-583-9819.

Committees: *Armed Services* (10th of 32 R): Military Installations & Facilities; Military Personnel (Chmn.). *Veterans' Affairs* (6th of 17 R): Oversight & Investigations.

Group Ratings

	ADA	ACLU	AFS	LCV	CON	NTU	NFIB	COC	ACU	NTLC	CHC
1998	15	14	22	8	13	45	100	94	88	95	91
1997	0	—	13	—	22	53	—	100	83	—	—

National Journal Ratings

	1997 LIB — 1997 CONS			1998 LIB — 1998 CONS		
Economic	27%	—	73%	36%	—	64%
Social	29%	—	70%	34%	—	66%
Foreign	32%	—	68%	39%	—	58%

Key Votes of the 105th Congress

1. Clinton Budget Deal	Y	5. Puerto Rico Sthood. Ref.	Y	9. Cut $ for B-2 Bombers	N
2. Education IRAs	Y	6. End Highway Set-asides	Y	10. Human Rights in China	N
3. Req. 2/3 to Raise Taxes	Y	7. School Prayer Amend.	Y	11. Withdraw Bosnia Troops	N
4. Fast-track Trade	N	8. Ovrd. Part. Birth Veto	Y	12. End Cuban TV-Marti	N

Election Results

1998 general	Stephen Buyer (R)	101,567	(63%)	($457,278)
	David F. Steele III (D)	58,504	(36%)	($69,541)
	Others	2,317	(1%)	
1998 primary	Stephen Buyer (R)	unopposed		
1996 general	Stephen Buyer (R)	133,627	(65%)	($227,204)
	Douglas L. Clark (D)	66,628	(32%)	($6,764)
	Others	5,253	(3%)	

SIXTH DISTRICT

Indianapolis is one of America's most symmetrical cities, sited in almost the exact center of Indiana, centered on Monument Circle with eight avenues radiating like wheel spokes, with the city occupying the nearly square Marion County. In the seven surrounding suburban counties, the irregularities of the physical landscape and the asymmetries of the original settlers' boundaries intrude, but a respected order has been established here. The more affluent areas are typically farther out, starting on the north side somewhere north of the home of Benjamin Harrison, Indiana's one president, and the 1920s-era Governor's Mansion built on North Meridian Street by the man who more or less invented the gas station. Here are comfortable in-town neighborhoods built in the 1940s and 1950s, the cul-de-sac subdivisions and condominiums of the 1970s and 1980s, and new developments set out on hills in the once rural counties.

The 6th Congressional District includes most of the suburban territory around the core of Indianapolis, which forms the 10th District. The exception is to the west of the city, where most of Hancock and Boone Counties are in the 7th District. But the 6th includes the north side of Indianapolis and the affluent Hamilton County suburbs of Carmel and Fishers; it includes Hancock County to the east and takes in the less affluent but still conservative suburban territory to the south. This is by far the most Republican district in Indiana and indeed one of the most Republican districts in the country.

The congressman from the 6th District is Dan Burton, an active and enthusiastic Republican who was confrontation-minded long before most of today's feisty young House Republicans appeared on the scene (or started shaving). He has been running for office since he was in his 20s. He had a horrific childhood: His father was abusive and left the family, his mother worked as a waitress and bought the kids' clothes at Goodwill, his father ultimately kidnapped his mother and went to jail, and the kids were sent to the county home. "Looking back on my life, I think one of the reasons I'm so aggressive is because all through my childhood we were looked upon as second-class citizens," he has said. Burton earned money as a teenager shining shoes and at 18 enlisted in the Army. He never finished college but made his way up as a real estate broker and insurance salesman. He also ran for public office, often unsuccessfully. He was elected to the Indiana House in 1966, 1976 and 1978 and to the Indiana Senate in 1968 and 1980; he lost races for Congress in 1970 and 1972 and was first elected to the House in 1982, when the legislature created this heavily Republican suburban seat.

As chairman of the Government Reform Committee (which dropped "Oversight" from its title in 1999), he conducted the tumultuous Clinton-Gore campaign finance hearings in 1997 and 1998. He is one of the heads of the 40-member Conservative Action Team, a force independent of—and sometimes at odds with—the Republican leadership. He was regarded for years by many Democrats as a nut, excitably pursuing lost causes. He opposed sanctions on South Africa, backed UNITA in Angola and Renamo in Mozambique, offered dozens of spending cuts that were overwhelmingly defeated, and pushed for universal mandatory AIDS testing. But he has also been vindicated by events for some stands which were widely scorned, from his hard-line opposition to the Soviet Union to his lonely vote against the later-repealed Catastrophic Health Care Act of 1988. And, admirers say, through his tirades shines an uncynical sincerity and certain friendliness.

Going into the controversial campaign finance hearings, Burton had some significant legislative achievements. He co-sponsored the V-chip legislation with Massachusetts Democrat Edward Markey; it passed as part of the 1996 Telecommunications Act, over the strong objection of the broadcast lobby. His biggest achievement was the Helms-Burton Act. It was a response to the shooting down of the Brothers to the Rescue planes by the Cuban Air Force, and stated that foreign companies could be sued in American courts if, as part of business deals with Fidel Castro's regime, they took over property expropriated from American owners. Helms-Burton passed both houses in fall 1995 and was signed by Bill Clinton, but Clinton has delayed its full implementation. In the 105th Congress Burton steered to passage the Results Act, which requires federal agencies to set specific performance goals and to report on their progress—or lack of it—in meeting them.

On International Affairs, Burton has bucked the tide on several issues. He opposed normalization of relations with Vietnam. He opposed cutting off aid to Turkey: "I'm awfully tired of watching Turkey get kicked in the teeth on the floor and in this committee." He moved to reduce aid to India, because of its treatment of the Sikhs and Kashmiris, whose American counterparts contributed heavily to his 1996 campaign. Some of these stands have led Burton to campaign finance troubles. He had to return contributions to Sikh temples in April 1997 and to a lobbyist for Zaire President Mobutu Sese Seko a month later. And, as his hearings on Clinton-Gore were about to start, he was accused by a former lobbyist for Pakistan of threatening to cut off his access to other Republicans unless he raised $5,000 for Burton's campaign; Burton denied making any threats and the investigation is ongoing.

In late 1996, many Republicans were queasy about having Burton conduct the hearing; they felt he was too excitable and vulnerable to attack by Democrats and remembered with dismay his 1994 speech questioning whether White House counsel Vincent Foster had been murdered and his body moved. Burton promised a bipartisan approach but encountered early and fierce opposition. Ranking Democrat Henry Waxman, one of the brainiest Democrats in the House, set the tone, calling it "a partisan witch hunt." Burton helped that impression along when, in reference to Clinton, he told *The Indianapolis Star* editorial board in April 1998, "This guy's a scumbag. That's why I'm after him."

Democrats yelped, and the *New York Times* demurely refused to print the epithet. More damaging was the partial release of taped conversations between Webster Hubbell and his wife in a prison visiting room. Democrats said they were unfairly edited and a violation of privacy. But Burton said they were evidence that Hubbell was anticipating being paid off, through legal retainers for no work, and that prisoners have no rights of privacy. Regardless, Burton was forced to fire his investigator, David Bossie. In fact, Burton was facing what shows every sign of being a coverup: Some 90 witnesses took the Fifth Amendment or left the country, and there was no cooperation from the likes of John Huang, Charlie Trie or James Riady. In July 1997 the FBI subpoenaed Burton's finance records of his House campaigns. In August 1998 Burton recommended holding Attorney General Janet Reno in contempt for refusing to produce memos from FBI Director Louis Freeh and her own adviser Charles LaBella on campaign finance, which contradicted her own stand. She eventually relented, but rejected the demand for an independent counsel or outside investigation of the Clinton-Gore finances. The Burton investigation wound down in fall 1998 with little immediate impact and few new findings.

For all the pasting Burton took from the national press, he was never in trouble for re-election in 1998. Not even when it was revealed that he had fathered an illegitimate son some 15 years before: Burton had not been notified by the woman until her companion, long presumed to be the father, left her five years later. Burton took a blood test and afterward paid child support. But the Democratic nominee was not well positioned to take advantage of this. He was Bob Hidalgo Kern, convicted of fraud a decade earlier, who made calls around town impersonating a female Indianapolis judge and a Hollywood actress. The Democrats tried to get the state Recount Commission to take him off the ballot, but he won 50% of the primary vote to 27% and 23% for two others and the commission upheld the result. Kern no doubt benefited from placement at the top of the ballot and the fact that party favorite Nag Nagarajan's did not have high name recognition. The 6th District Democratic chairman said, "If people think I'm sending a signal to pass on that race, that's fine with me . . . I think both parties can do a lot better." Voters were less equivocal: 72% voted for Burton, 17% for Kern and 11% for Libertarian Joe Hauptmann.

Cook's Call. *Safe.* Although Burton has gotten himself into some political hot water over the years, his overwhelmingly Republican district helps insulate him from political fall-out. Democrats are not going to get much traction here, even under the best of political times.

The People: Pop. 1990: 553,865; 23.8% rural; 11.6% age 65 + ; 97.7% White, 1% Black, 0.9% Asian, 0.1% Amer. Indian, 0.2% Other; 0.8% Hispanic Origin. Households: 64.2% married couple families; 31.8% married couple fams. w. children; 52% college educ.; median household income: $38,644; per capita income: $17,971; median house value: $81,400; median gross rent: $386.

1996 Presidential Vote

Dole (R) 168,497 (63%)
Clinton (D) 75,285 (28%)
Perot (I) 22,404 (8%)

1992 Presidential Vote

Bush (R) 153,269 (57%)
Clinton (D) 61,030 (23%)
Perot (I) 54,909 (20%)

Rep. Dan Burton (R)

Elected 1982; b. June 21, 1938, Indianapolis; home, Indianapolis; IN U., 1958–59, Cincinnati Bible Seminary, 1959–60; Protestant; married (Barbara).

Military Career: Army, 1956–57, Army Reserves, 1958–63.

Elected Office: IN House of Reps., 1966–68, 1976–80; IN Senate, 1968–70, 1980–82.

Professional Career: Real estate broker; Founder, Dan Burton Insurance Agency, 1968.

DC Office: 2185 RHOB 20515, 202-225-2276; Fax: 202-225-0016; Web site: www.house.gov/burton.

District Offices: Greenwood, 317-882-3640; Indianapolis, 317-848-0201.

Committees: *Government Reform* (Chmn. of 24 R). *International Relations* (7th of 26 R): International Operations and Human Rights; Western Hemisphere.

Group Ratings

	ADA	ACLU	AFS	LCV	CON	NTU	NFIB	COC	ACU	NTLC	CHC
1998	5	7	0	0	5	51	100	93	96	95	100
1997	5	—	13	—	42	64	—	80	96	—	—

National Journal Ratings

	1997 LIB	—	1997 CONS	1998 LIB	—	1998 CONS
Economic	24%	—	73%	22%	—	77%
Social	20%	—	71%	21%	—	76%
Foreign	12%	—	81%	0%	—	93%

Key Votes of the 105th Congress

1. Clinton Budget Deal	Y	5. Puerto Rico Sthood. Ref.	Y	9. Cut $ for B-2 Bombers	N
2. Education IRAs	Y	6. End Highway Set-asides	Y	10. Human Rights in China	Y
3. Req. 2/3 to Raise Taxes	Y	7. School Prayer Amend.	Y	11. Withdraw Bosnia Troops	Y
4. Fast-track Trade	*	8. Ovrd. Part. Birth Veto	Y	12. End Cuban TV-Marti	N

Election Results

1998 general	Dan Burton (R) 135,250	(72%)	($902,183)
	Bob Kern (D) 31,472	(17%)	
	Joe Hauptmann (Lib) 21,032	(11%)	($11,741)
1998 primary	Dan Burton (R) 56,793	(84%)	
	George Thomas Holland (R) 10,922	(16%)	
1996 general	Dan Burton (R) 193,193	(75%)	($491,082)
	Carrie Jean Dillard-Trammell (D) 59,661	(23%)	($11,273)
	Others 5,003	(2%)	

SEVENTH DISTRICT

Of the railroad passenger trains that used to run on the lines criss-crossing the township grids of the Midwest, none had a more romantic name than the *Wabash Cannonball* that rumbled along the Wabash River, across the rolling farmland of northern Indiana on its way from Detroit to St. Louis, crossing the old National Road, now U.S. 40, which runs in a nearly straight line from Indianapolis to St. Louis. The landscape here is some of the most prosaic in the United States, mostly flat, with neat farms and frame-bungalowed towns, looking unchanged from years ago. Today the *Cannonball* no longer runs: People bounce around the Midwest on commuter airlines from small city to hub, and the National Road and U.S. 40 have been replaced for through traffic by Interstate 70.

The 7th Congressional District covers much of the routes of the *Wabash Cannonball* and the National Road in western Indiana, starting from the Indianapolis city limits. Its two largest towns are quite different in character. Terre Haute is an old manufacturing town, the boyhood home of Socialist Eugene Debs, and now has a Sony compact disc plant. The town has not gained population in years and tends to vote Democratic—a lonely stand in central Indiana. The other major town is Lafayette, where the main business is Purdue University, Indiana's land-grant college and the alma mater of C-SPAN founder Brian Lamb. Growing and prosperous, Lafayette tends to vote Republican. Even more Republican are the small counties and the suburban territory in Hendricks and Boone Counties outside Indianapolis.

The congressman from the 7th District is Edward Pease, a Republican elected in 1996 to replace 30-year incumbent John Myers. Pease grew up in Terre Haute, where he was an Eagle Scout and high school valedictorian. After college and law school at Indiana University, he practiced law in Brazil, the Clay County seat; he was active in many charities, including the Boy Scouts. In 1980 he was elected to the state Senate, where he served 12 years. In 1984 he went to work as Indiana State University's general counsel in Terre Haute, then became its vice president in 1993.

In 1996 Pease was one of 15 Republicans and four Democrats who ran for the seat being vacated by Myers. Initially Myers said he would endorse no one. But his daughter was supporting Pease and his son-in-law was Pease's communications and finance director. In late April Myers endorsed Pease for the May primary; Pease immediately began running radio and TV ads featuring the endorsement. It may have made the difference: Pease won 30% of the vote, to 17% for former prosecutor John Meyers. Three other candidates carried their home counties, while Pease carried pretty much everything else. In the general election Pease faced Democrat Robert Hellmann, a Terre Haute neighbor, longtime state legislator, and a self-described conservative. Hellmann attacked Pease for selling his house to a cousin for $350,000, renting it back, and donating $155,000 to his own campaign. But Pease won 62%–35%, carrying every county but Vigo, which includes Terre Haute, where he lost by only 159 votes, and next-door Vermillion. He had 57% in the county that includes Lafayette and 73% and 70% in Hendricks and Boone Counties, outside Indianapolis.

Pease wanted a seat on Appropriations, but settled for Transportation and Infrastructure, where he was the only Indiana member while the committee reauthorized the highway bill, in which Indiana got $1.3 billion more than before. He compiled a very conservative voting record and yet indicated a desire for comity rather than confrontation.

In Washington he seemed to make news mostly as a victim of crime: In March 1997 burglars stole his valuables, casual clothes and two sandwiches ("I guess they must have been hungry and cold"), and in November 1998 he was robbed at gunpoint in Arlington. He made more news as a member of the Judiciary Committee during impeachment hearings. Pease's comments were calm, concise, respectful—and solidly for impeachment.

Back home Pease's opponents made no attempt to raise money. "Basically, you're looking at a nonelection," said Indiana State University professor James McDowell. Pease won 69%–28%.

Cook's Call. *Safe.* This district has consistently elected Republicans for years and shows no signs of doing any differently in 2000. Pease is a safe bet in 2000.

The People: Pop. 1990: 554,500; 48% rural; 13% age 65 +; 96.4% White, 1.9% Black, 1.2% Asian, 0.2% Amer. Indian, 0.2% Other; 0.8% Hispanic Origin. Households: 60.5% married couple families; 29.4% married couple fams. w. children; 38.9% college educ.; median household income: $28,080; per capita income: $12,536; median house value: $54,700; median gross rent: $279.

1996 Presidential Vote			1992 Presidential Vote		
Dole (R)	111,500	(52%)	Bush (R)	103,801	(46%)
Clinton (D)	75,150	(35%)	Clinton (D)	71,273	(32%)
Perot (I)	25,773	(12%)	Perot (I)	48,916	(22%)

Rep. Ed Pease (R)

Elected 1996; b. May 22, 1951, Terre Haute; home, Seelyville; IN U., A.B. 1973, J.D. 1977; Methodist; single.

Elected Office: IN Senate, 1980–92.

Professional Career: Practicing atty., 1977–84; Gen. Cnsl., IN State U., 1984–93, Vice Pres., 1993–96.

DC Office: 119 CHOB 20515, 202-225-5805; Web site: www.house.gov/pease.

District Offices: Danville, 317-718-0307; Lafayette, 765-423-1661; Terre Haute, 812-238-1619.

Committees: *Judiciary* (15th of 21 R): Courts & Intellectual Property; Immigration & Claims. *Small Business* (17th of 19 R): Empowerment. *Transportation & Infrastructure* (24th of 41 R): Aviation; Ground Transportation.

Group Ratings

	ADA	ACLU	AFS	LCV	CON	NTU	NFIB	COC	ACU	NTLC	CHC
1998	0	6	11	31	13	51	86	100	100	89	100
1997	15	—	13	—	34	56	—	90	96	—	—

National Journal Ratings

	1997 LIB — 1997 CONS		1998 LIB — 1998 CONS	
Economic	16%	— 82%	30%	— 67%
Social	0%	— 90%	3%	— 90%
Foreign	0%	— 88%	19%	— 75%

Key Votes of the 105th Congress

1. Clinton Budget Deal	Y	5. Puerto Rico Sthood. Ref.	N	9. Cut $ for B-2 Bombers	N
2. Education IRAs	Y	6. End Highway Set-asides	Y	10. Human Rights in China	N
3. Req. 2/3 to Raise Taxes	Y	7. School Prayer Amend.	Y	11. Withdraw Bosnia Troops	Y
4. Fast-track Trade	Y	8. Ovrd. Part. Birth Veto	Y	12. End Cuban TV-Marti	N

Election Results

1998 general	Ed Pease (R)	109,712	(69%)	($489,357)
	Samuel (Dutch) Hillenberg (D)	44,823	(28%)	
	Others	4,779	(3%)	
1998 primary	Ed Pease (R)	52,108	(83%)	
	Douglas E.(Doug) Hess (R)	10,808	(17%)	
1996 general	Ed Pease (R)	130,010	(62%)	($586,448)
	Robert F. Hellmann (D)	72,705	(35%)	($340,816)
	Others	7,125	(3%)	

EIGHTH DISTRICT

"Evansville," wrote John Bartlow Martin in 1947, "is the capital of a tri-state area comprising the neglected tag ends of Indiana, Kentucky and Illinois." It was a factory town then, building car parts and refrigerators, drawing workers from Kentucky, Tennessee and the picturesque but not very fertile hills of southern Indiana. It has seen hard times, such as the terrible flood of March 1997, but it has also been buzzing with small-employer job growth and a certain amount of civic spirit: It claims to have the nation's second largest street festival, second only to New Orleans's Mardi Gras celebration.

Evansville is one of two major focuses of the 8th Congressional District of Indiana which, within irregular borders, covers most of the southwest portion of the state. The other is Bloomington, quite a different place, the home of Indiana University and a limestone quarrying center. This southwest corner of Indiana was the first part of the state settled by whites. Vincennes, now a small town on the banks of the Wabash River, was once the metropolis of Indiana, and Scottish philanthropist and visionary Robert Owen established the town of New Harmony downstream. Owen's son was the first congressman from the area, elected in 1842 and 1844.

More recently the district has become known as the "Bloody Eighth," for its close congressional races. At one point in the 1970s it elected four different congressmen in four successive elections, the only district in the country to do so in that decade. In 1984 the state counted the Republican the winner by exactly 34 votes, but the result was overturned by the Democratic House, in a fight that left many House Republicans bitterly aggrieved. In the 1990s it has been as fiercely contested as ever.

The congressman from the 8th District is John Hostettler, a Republican elected in 1994, an ingenuous and idealistic man who seems miscast in politics. Hostettler is from Posey County, just west of Evansville; he went to Rose-Hulman Institute of Technology in Terre Haute and in 1983 became a Southern Indiana Gas & Electric Company engineer. He had never run for office, but in 1994, at 33, he was one of six Republican candidates vying to run against 12-year incumbent Democrat Frank McCloskey. Hostettler's great strength was his support from anti-abortion and Christian fundamentalist groups; he also had obvious regional strength in the western edge of the district, along the Wabash. He won the primary with 35%, to 23% for his next competitor. In the general, Hostettler refused to take PAC money; his biggest fund raiser was a $100-per-family fried chicken dinner with Marilyn Quayle. Hostettler attacked McCloskey on taxes, gay rights, gun control, the environment, school prayer, his 65 overdrafts at the House bank and constantly referred to him as "Frank McClinton." McCloskey accused Hostettler of wanting to outlaw all abortions and called him "John McGingrich." McCloskey carried Evansville and Bloomington by microscopic margins, but Hostettler carried most of the rural counties and won 52%–48%.

In the House Hostettler has been a conservative willing to buck conventional political wisdom and his party leadership. He and fellow Indiana freshman Mark Souder were the only two Republicans to vote against the balanced budget amendment in 1995 because it did not require a supermajority to raise taxes. He opposed term limits out of opposition to amending the Constitution except where there is no alternative. In January 1996 he was one of 15 Republican members to vote against the continuing resolution to reopen the federal government. In response Newt Gingrich canceled his appearance at a Hostettler fundraiser. Hostettler then wrote Gingrich, "I cannot allow my fund-raising to be tied in any way to specific votes," and invited Dick Armey instead. In January 1997 Hostettler voted "present" for speaker.

In June 1996 Hostettler opposed Western conservatives and teamed with Democrat Joe Kennedy to eliminate timber road purchaser credits for logging in national forests. "If private companies don't think it is economically feasible to pay for the roads, why should taxpayers have to?" The amendment passed late one night, 211–210, then was brought up the next afternoon and was rejected on a tie vote, 211–211. In February 1997 he turned down a $4.5 million wetland status for Goose Pond and Beehunter Marsh in Greene County, though it was supported by Senator Richard Lugar; Hostettler said the money should go to pay off the national debt instead. In May 1998 he opposed proposing the Ohio River for inclusion in Bill Clinton's American Heritage Rivers program, for fear of threatening private property rights. The mayors of Evansville and Mount Vernon, who favored it, complained they had not been consulted, but the Ohio didn't make the list.

One federal project Hostettler does favor is the construction of a Canada-to-Mexico highway by extending I-69 from Indianapolis southwest, through Bloomington and Evansville, to Laredo, Texas. He formed the Interstate 69 Mid-Continent Highway Caucus, with 25 congressmen and 12 senators, and is co-chairman with Tom DeLay. To those who say his efforts to earmark $27 million for I-69 in southern Indiana are inconsistent with his philosophy, he responds, "Read the Constitution: It talks about roads."

With his unpolitical ways and the closeness of the district—it went for Bill Clinton by 2% twice—Hostettler has been a natural Democratic target. In 1996 he faced Jonathan Weinzapfel, a former McCloskey aide. A narrow primary winner, Weinzapfel was a good fundraiser and raised almost as much as Hostettler, who continued to refuse PAC money. In addition, this was one of the districts where the AFL-CIO spent at least $100,000, which buys a lot of television time in Evansville. But Hostettler turned these liabilities into assets by attacking Weinzapfel for taking PAC money, especially from the Laborers' Union, which the Clinton Justice Department said had "ties to organized crime." Hostettler eked out a 50%–48% victory, carrying most of the rural counties, some by handsome margins, while losing narrowly in the Evansville and Bloomington areas.

In 1998 Hostettler was a target again. This time his opponent, Evansville Councilwoman Gail Riecken, had no primary opposition, and with support from EMILY's List and other national feminist contributions, actually outraised the incumbent throughout the cycle. Riecken, a real estate broker and former river boat pilot, pointed to her work setting up Ark Crisis Nursery, a child abuse center, and on domestic violence, downtown development and the Pigeon Creek Greenway Passage Bike Path. But she was hurt in July when the *Evansville Courier* reported that her husband owed $6,000 in back taxes on his marina.

In September Riecken went on the air with ads attacking Hostettler for Congress' failure to pass HMO reform. One showed two parents and their brain-damaged infant: The wife said her child was harmed because her HMO wouldn't approve a Caesarean section, and the husband attacked Hostettler for saying managed care isn't causing problems in southern Indiana. "Exploitative," Hostettler responded. Riecken also talked about Social Security, Medicare for home health care, and criticized Hostettler for not backing the American Heritage River designation. She said she favored censure and opposed impeachment.

Democrats had great hopes for this district, but in a turnout lower than 1994, Hostettler won 52%–46%; a result midway between his 1994 and 1996 margins. He won big margins in rural counties and carried Evansville's Vanderburgh County, which begs the question of whether voters care more for I-69 than the American Heritage River. The 8th seems likely to be bloody again in 2000.

Cook's Call. *Competitive.* Hostettler is probably too conservative for this marginal district, and Democrats have come close to beating him. But it remains to be seen whether they can finally put together that magic combination of factors needed to knock him out.

The People: Pop. 1990: 554,347; 41.8% rural; 14.6% age 65 + ; 95.8% White, 3.1% Black, 0.8% Asian, 0.2% Amer. Indian, 0.1% Other; 0.5% Hispanic Origin. Households: 57.1% married couple families; 26.9% married couple fams. w. children; 36.8% college educ.; median household income: $25,242; per capita income: $12,153; median house value: $49,200; median gross rent: $261.

1996 Presidential Vote			1992 Presidential Vote		
Clinton (D)	100,171	(45%)	Clinton (D)	103,844	(42%)
Dole (R)	96,956	(43%)	Bush (R)	97,062	(40%)
Perot (I)	23,905	(11%)	Perot (I)	43,177	(18%)

Rep. John Hostettler (R)

Elected 1994; b. July 19, 1961, Evansville; home, Wadesville; Rose-Hulman Inst. of Tech., B.S. 1983; Baptist; married (Elizabeth).

Professional Career: Mechanical Engineer, S. IN Gas & Electric Co., 1983–94.

DC Office: 1507 LHOB 20515, 202-225-4636; Fax: 202-225-3284; Web site: www.house.gov/hostettler.

District Offices: Bloomington, 812-334-1111; Evansville, 812-465-6484.

Committees: *Agriculture* (12th of 27 R): Department Operations, Oversight, Nutrition & Forestry; Livestock & Horticulture. *Armed Services* (19th of 32 R): Military Installations & Facilities; Military Research & Development (Vice Chmn.).

Group Ratings

	ADA	ACLU	AFS	LCV	CON	NTU	NFIB	COC	ACU	NTLC	CHC
1998	10	19	11	0	65	58	93	78	92	89	92
1997	5	—	13	—	67	65	—	80	88	—	—

National Journal Ratings

	1997 LIB	—	1997 CONS	1998 LIB	—	1998 CONS
Economic	19%	—	76%	28%	—	70%
Social	37%	—	61%	26%	—	72%
Foreign	20%	—	79%	19%	—	75%

Key Votes of the 105th Congress

1. Clinton Budget Deal	Y	5. Puerto Rico Sthood. Ref.	N	9. Cut $ for B-2 Bombers	N
2. Education IRAs	Y	6. End Highway Set-asides	Y	10. Human Rights in China	N
3. Req. 2/3 to Raise Taxes	N	7. School Prayer Amend.	N	11. Withdraw Bosnia Troops	N
4. Fast-track Trade	N	8. Ovrd. Part. Birth Veto	Y	12. End Cuban TV-Marti	N

Election Results

1998 general	John Hostettler (R)	92,785	(52%)	($658,886)
	Gail Riecken (D)	81,871	(46%)	($799,118)
	Others	3,401	(2%)	
1998 primary	John Hostettler (R)	unopposed		
1996 general	John Hostettler (R)	109,860	(50%)	($528,325)
	Jonathan Weinzapfel (D)	106,201	(48%)	($470,027)
	Others	3,803	(2%)	

NINTH DISTRICT

The southeastern corner of Indiana, in the national eye only during the awful flood of March 1997, was a busy place when settlers rafted down the Ohio River in the early 19th Century. They were mostly southerners, "Butternuts," from across the river in Kentucky or over the mountains in Virginia, and they built the first large Indiana settlements. Today, you can see their work in the marvelous old buildings of Madison, now quiet but once one of the busiest ports on the Ohio River. Farther down the river is Corydon, from 1816–25 the state capital, now home town of Indiana's Governor Frank O'Bannon. The early 19th Century buildings here have been well preserved because these towns were bypassed first by the railroads, then by U.S. routes and interstate highways, and they certainly are remote from major airports. The river is still an artery of commerce, but utilitarian barges have replaced steamers, except for "riverboat" casinos.

Butternut Indiana retained its affection for things Southern into the Civil War and beyond. Local politician Jesse Bright was expelled from the U.S. Senate in 1862 for "supporting the rebellion." To this day, the hills along the Ohio River typically vote Democratic, as do the Indiana suburbs of Louisville. But to the east Indiana is now filling up with migrants from Cincinnati—a Yankee and German abolitionist bastion in Jesse Bright's time, an overwhelmingly Republican stronghold in ours—who are moving the southeast corner of Indiana away from its ancestral party.

The 9th Congressional District is made up of most of the state's Ohio River counties and an oddly shaped collection of lightly populated counties to the north. It is ancestrally Democratic, culturally conservative and recently trending Republican. For 34 years this was the district represented by Lee Hamilton, a Democrat who became chairman of the Intelligence and Foreign Affairs Committees and co-chairman of the Iran-Contra committee of 1987–88. Hamilton was temperamentally inclined to a bipartisan foreign policy but frequently opposed Reagan and Bush administration policies; he was seriously considered for the vice presidential nomination in 1988 and 1992.

The new congressman from the 9th is Baron Hill, a Democrat elected in a close contest in 1998. Hill grew up in Seymour, the small town of John Mellencamp's song "Small Town." He played basketball for Furman and returned home to a family insurance business. In 1982, at 29, he was elected to the state House and served eight years. In 1990 he ran against Senator Dan Coats and, despite a huge money disadvantage, held him to a 54%–46% win. Governor Evan Bayh appointed Hill to head the state student assistance agency, then he worked for Merrill Lynch. When Hamilton announced his retirement in February 1997—he was the tenth Democratic former committee chairman to decide to retire after the Republicans won control of the House—Hill plunged into the race.

Hill's opponent was Jean Leising, a former (1988–96) state senator who held Hamilton to a surprisingly low 52%–48% margin in 1994 and then lost to him 56%–42% in 1996. Leising campaigned as an opponent of all abortions and all gun control and a proponent of welfare reform. In 1998 she had primary opposition from Michael Bailey, who attracted media attention in the 1992 general and 1994 primary by trying to run ads showing aborted fetuses. But in 1998 the media gave him more heed than the voters: Leising won the primary 67%–25%.

Leising began the campaign ahead, presumably because she was better known. She called for lower spending and taxes and support of "the right to life" and "the right to bear arms." She featured Charlton Heston in TV ads and called in national Republicans to campaign. She called for saving Social Security and local control of schools, and criticized Hill for shifting to liberal positions on abortion and capital punishment. Hill raised nearly twice as much money, including more from PACs and party committees. He also had a clever way of attracting attention: In his 1990 Senate race he walked the state, from the Ohio River to Lake Michigan; this time he walked 400 miles through all 21 counties of the district starting in July. Hill promised to "save Social Security once and for all" and to support the Democrats' HMO reform. He called for smaller class sizes and alternative schools for troubled kids. Leising ran on crisp enunciation of hard-edge positions. Hill said, "I'm a person who's running for Congress, not to save the world from all its problems. What really gets me juiced is being able to help build our local communities here in southern Indiana."

Hill was behind in polls in late October. But he unleashed two ads which may have made the difference. In one he said Leising wanted to abolish federal education funding (she said she wanted the money to go to local schools without strings), in the other he said she wanted to privatize Social Security (Leising said she was looking for ways for young people to invest a portion of Social Security taxes). He also ran an ad showing Hamilton, and in the last days

Hamilton and O'Bannon campaigned for him. With the aid of a good get-out-the-vote campaign, Hill won 51%–48%.

In the House Hill was chosen by his fellow freshmen to serve on the Social Security task force. Hill has demonstrated good political talents, but this could be a seriously contested seat again in 2000.

Cook's Call. *Highly Competitive.* As a freshman Democrat sitting in one of the most marginal districts in the state, Baron Hill has his work cut out for him in holding on to this rambling, rural district in 2000. Republicans are committed to finding a stronger candidate than three-time nominee Jean Leising, and this bellwether district is certainly vulnerable to changes in the national political environment; a strong Republican tide could be felt here. With a good Republican candidate, this race has the potential to be close.

The People: Pop. 1990: 554,516; 59.3% rural; 13.3% age 65 + ; 97.7% White, 1.7% Black, 0.3% Asian, 0.2% Amer. Indian, 0.1% Other; 0.4% Hispanic Origin. Households: 63.2% married couple families; 31.8% married couple fams. w. children; 29.1% college educ.; median household income: $26,900; per capita income: $11,727; median house value: $49,300; median gross rent: $239.

1996 Presidential Vote			1992 Presidential Vote		
Clinton (D)	101,434	(44%)	Clinton (D)	97,970	(41%)
Dole (R)	99,915	(44%)	Bush (R)	97,412	(40%)
Perot (I)	26,154	(11%)	Perot (I)	44,839	(19%)

Rep. Baron Hill (D)

Elected 1998; b. June 23, 1953, Seymour; home, Seymour; Furman U., B.A. 1975; Christian; married (Betty).

Elected Office: IN House of Reps., 1982–90.

Professional Career: The Hill Agency (insurance), 1975–90; Exec. Dir., IN Student Assistance Comm., 1990–94; Financial analyst, Merrill Lynch, 1994–98.

DC Office: 1208 LHOB 20515, 202-225-5315; Fax: 202-226-6866; Web site: www.house.gov/baronhill.

District Office: Jeffersonville, 812-288-3999.

Committees: *Agriculture* (24th of 24 D): Department Operations, Oversight, Nutrition & Forestry; General Farm Commodities, Resource Conservation & Credit. *Armed Services* (26th of 28 D): Military Research & Development.

Group Ratings and Key Votes: Newly Elected

Election Results

1998 general	Baron Hill (D)	92,973	(51%)	($1,009,101)
	Jean Leising (R)	87,797	(48%)	($647,330)
	Others	2,406	(1%)	
1998 primary	Baron Hill (D)	43,970	(70%)	
	James R. McClure Jr. (D)	10,776	(17%)	
	Fred Holt (D)	7,707	(12%)	
1996 general	Lee H. Hamilton (D)	128,123	(56%)	($967,859)
	Jean Leising (R)	96,442	(42%)	($451,475)

TENTH DISTRICT

Indianapolis, radiating outward from the Soldiers and Sailors statue in Monument Circle, is precisely at the center of Indiana, dominating it as few other cities do a state. It is the political and governmental capital, industrial and financial center, and the intellectual center of Indiana as well. It is symmetrically laid out: Just to the west of the circle is the state Capitol, to the north is the American Legion headquarters, to the east is the City-County building, and to the south is the Circle Center mall, and the RCA Dome (formerly Hoosier Dome). Farther out are some classic and some new Indianapolis institutions: the Indiana University Medical Center, the Convention Center, the Eiteljorg Museum of Native American and Western Art and, under construction, the new Indiana State Museum, the Indiana Fieldhouse and the NCAA headquarters. In the 1980s Indianapolis became the nation's amateur sports capital; it has also become one of the most popular places for religious conventions. It has the world's biggest children's museum and is home to the Hudson Institute, a conservative think tank.

Politically, Indianapolis has long had robust competition in national as well as local races. Republicans have held the mayor's office since Richard Lugar won it in 1967, and Mayor Stephen Goldsmith, whose term ends at the end of 1999, has made Indianapolis a national innovator in privatization of services. By putting services up for bid, he has saved taxpayers money and spurred many incumbent city employees to come up with innovations. Lugar expanded Indianapolis's city limits to include all of Marion County, which made it a solidly Republican constituency then. But more recently, affluent young people have been moving to counties farther out, and Marion County is trending Democratic. Indiana's 10th Congressional District includes most but not all of Indianapolis and Marion County. It includes all of Center Township, with its large black population, and does not include much of the affluent, Republican northern edge of the county. It extends west toward Speedway, where the Indianapolis 500 is held, and southward and east to modest neighborhoods. Within these boundaries, the 10th District leans Democratic, and it has twice given Bill Clinton good-sized margins.

The congresswoman from the 10th District is Julia Carson, a Democrat elected in 1996. Carson was born to an unmarried teenage mother and grew up in poverty, working as a waitress, newspaper deliverer and summer farm laborer; she can remember going to the welfare office for a ration of cornmeal and lard. As a divorced mother she raised two children and then two grandchildren. In 1965 she was hired away from her job as a secretary at UAW Local 550 by newly elected Congressman Andy Jacobs to do casework in his Indianapolis office. When his election prospects looked dim in 1972 (he did lose, but won the seat back two years later), he encouraged Carson to run for the state House; she won, then was elected to the state Senate in 1976. In 1990 she ran for Center Township trustee, the position responsible for running welfare in central Indianapolis; the agency was $17 million in debt and accused of mismanagement of taxpayer funds and mistreatment of welfare applicants. As trustee, she instituted a workfare program, requiring recipients to work cleaning the streets, highways and riverbanks. The debt was paid off and property taxes lowered; the Republican Marion County auditor said, "Julia Carson wrestled that monster to the ground."

In 1996 Jacobs decided to retire after spending 30 of 32 unorthodox and humor-filled years in the House, and Carson decided to run. She won Jacobs's endorsement and that of the local Democratic organization. She was outspent by former prosecutor and party chairman Ann DeLaney, but won the primary 49%–31%. The Republican nominee was Virginia Blankenbaker, a stockbroker and state senator from 1980–92. In this youth-prone age, this turned out to be a race between two grandmothers. Both were also more liberal than many in their parties, pro-choice on abortion and against the death penalty. Carson cited her work as Center Township trustee and said she supported welfare reform, though not the 1996 act; she was for "universal" health care but not "nationalized" medicine. "Every poor kid in the country ought to have a laptop computer. I don't think you respond effectively to juvenile delinquency when you keep your foot on the neck of children who are not responsible and shouldn't be held accountable," she said. Many commentators wondered whether a black Democrat could beat a white Republican in this 30% black district, but Carson raised and spent almost as much as Blankenbaker and won 53%–45%. As she said later, "This is a wonderful city. A lot of people see you beyond the color of your skin. That becomes passe."

Carson, who had heart surgery in January 1997 and arterial surgery in February, finally arrived in Washington on March 5. She had seats on the Banking and Veterans' Affairs Committees and compiled a mostly liberal voting record. She sponsored a law to require trigger locks on guns and to penalize adults who let children have access to loaded guns without supervision; she obtained a $518,000 grant for the city to work on domestic violence. She strongly favored the Democrats' and denounced the Republicans' HMO reforms.

Republicans did not concede this seat. Blankenbaker ran again, but was beaten 44%–37% in the 1998 primary by Gary Hofmeister, owner of Hofmeister Personal Jewelers since 1973; he had not run for office before, but traveled to Latin America and Eastern Europe with human rights groups and taught entrepreneurship on 14 trips to the former Soviet Union. Hofmeister said he was running on faith, families, freedom, and called for "tough love" solutions to criminal rehabilitation and education. He emphasized his opposition to abortion and support of school vouchers and attacked Carson's liberal record. But Hofmeister was dogged by lurid rumors: In an interview with *NUVO Newsweekly*, he denied most of the charges but admitted he had had a drinking problem 15 years before.

Polls showed only narrow Carson leads during most of the campaign. But in November, after a campaign in which both spent liberally, she won 58%–39%; a margin similar to Clinton's here in 1996. Carson's explanation: "Once my opponent went on the attack and stayed on the attack, I was optimistic. The more he did it, the more determined people were to get out and vote for Julia."

Cook's Call. *Probably Safe.* This Indianapolis-based district is reliably but not overwhelmingly Democratic. Carson's solid victory in 1998, albeit against a flawed challenger, was probably good enough for Republicans to seriously consider removing her from the top-tier target list in 2000.

The People: Pop. 1990: 554,797; 12.1% age 65 + ; 68.7% White, 29.7% Black, 0.9% Asian, 0.3% Amer. Indian, 0.5% Other; 1.2% Hispanic Origin. Households: 42.2% married couple families; 20.3% married couple fams. w. children; 40.1% college educ.; median household income: $25,304; per capita income: $12,562; median house value: $46,200; median gross rent: $324.

1996 Presidential Vote		
Clinton (D)	89,851	(54%)
Dole (R)	61,892	(37%)
Perot (I)	12,547	(8%)

1992 Presidential Vote		
Clinton (D)	92,514	(47%)
Bush (R)	70,458	(36%)
Perot (I)	33,229	(17%)

Rep. Julia Carson (D)

Elected 1996; b. July 8, 1938, Louisville, KY; home, Indianapolis; Baptist; divorced.

Elected Office: IN House of Reps., 1972–76; IN Senate, 1976–90; Marion Cty. Center Township Trustee, 1991–96.

Professional Career: Secy., UAW, 1962–63; Legis. Aide, U.S. Rep. Andy Jacobs, 1965–72.

DC Office: 1541 LHOB 20515, 202-225-4011; Fax: 202-225-5633; Web site: www.house.gov/carson.

District Office: Indianapolis, 317-283-6516.

Committees: *Banking & Financial Services* (14th of 27 D): Domestic & International Monetary Policy; Housing & Community Opportunity. *Veterans' Affairs* (7th of 14 D): Health.

Group Ratings

	ADA	ACLU	AFS	LCV	CON	NTU	NFIB	COC	ACU	NTLC	CHC
1998	95	86	100	100	72	17	21	22	0	8	0
1997	90	—	86	—	74	31	—	30	9	—	—

National Journal Ratings

	1997 LIB	—	1997 CONS		1998 LIB	—	1998 CONS
Economic	82%	—	15%		79%	—	0%
Social	79%	—	20%		93%	—	0%
Foreign	82%	—	16%		64%	—	36%

Key Votes of the 105th Congress

1. Clinton Budget Deal	N	5. Puerto Rico Sthood. Ref.	Y	9. Cut $ for B-2 Bombers	Y
2. Education IRAs	N	6. End Highway Set-asides	N	10. Human Rights in China	Y
3. Req. 2/3 to Raise Taxes	N	7. School Prayer Amend.	N	11. Withdraw Bosnia Troops	N
4. Fast-track Trade	N	8. Ovrd. Part. Birth Veto	N	12. End Cuban TV-Marti	Y

Election Results

1998 general	Julia Carson (D)	69,682	(58%)	($773,835)
	Gary A. Hofmeister (R)	47,017	(39%)	($773,589)
	Others	2,737	(2%)	
1998 primary	Julia Carson (D)	20,284	(87%)	
	Suzann Fischman (D)	2,984	(13%)	
1996 general	Julia Carson (D)	85,965	(53%)	($572,617)
	Virginia Blankenbaker (R)	72,796	(45%)	($638,275)
	Others	3,612	(2%)	

IOWA

As Americans were surging westward in the 1840s, Iowa was filling up with Yankee farmers and German immigrants, watching as wagon trains headed to the Oregon Trail and the Mormon thousands mustered by Brigham Young headed from the Mississippi across the rolling hills to Council Bluffs on the Missouri and then west. Iowa was a young state then, proud of its hundreds of schools and dozens of colleges, sending more than its share of young men to fight for the cause of the Union back east. After that war, Iowans built a solid civilization based on farming, farm-machine making and meat processing that resisted the blandishments of William Jennings Bryan's populism and cheap money, and Iowa became one of the most solidly Republican states in the nation.

But starting around 1900, Iowa grew old. "Build it and they will come" was the theme from the movie *Field of Dreams*, set in Iowa. In the 19th Century Iowans built a model society. But in the 20th Century very few people have come. Iowa's commercial and financial center remained stuck in the railroad hub of Chicago, its economy failed to diversify and develop the dense manufacturing base of the Great Lakes states, and its young people started to move away to make their fortunes. Iowa's population, up from 674,000 in 1860 to 2.2 million in 1900, increased only slowly, and has not reached 3 million to this day: in 1900 Iowa had 11 congressional districts and California seven; in 2000 Iowa has five and California 52. Its solid Capitol and courthouses, its sturdy but mostly old housing stock, give testimony to Iowa's strengths but also bespeak its lack of dynamism. Even its great economic achievement—the development of high-tech, ever-more-productive, but also less labor-intensive agriculture—has made this a state that did not grow much.

Indeed, for much of the 20th Century Iowa has been a culturally and politically counter-cyclical state, headed in just the opposite direction of the rest of the nation—determinedly, with confidence in its own chipper rectitude, unembarrassedly out of step. In the industrial New Deal era, it stayed mostly agricultural and Republican, even as one-time Des Moines radio announcer Ronald Reagan became an enthusiastic Roosevelt Democrat and headed to Holly-wood. It partook little of postwar economic growth. It was dovish during the Vietnam war and after. In the 1980s, as Reagan, now a conservative Republican, became president, Iowans watched helplessly as farm prices and land values plummeted downward, farm implement factories closed, and 7% of its citizens left; its population fell more than any other state except West Virginia. Self-pity became the dominant note of Iowa's politics, as voters sought protection from the vagaries of the market even as commercial real estate and stock prices boomed else-where. By 1988 once-Republican Iowa had become one of the most Democratic states, sending 1988 caucus winner Dick Gephardt's politics solidly to the left and producing the second-highest percentage for Michael Dukakis in November.

In the 1990s Iowa and the nation have seemed to converge. If its economic rebellion against America's move toward free markets failed in the 1980s, its cultural qualms about America's move away from traditional values may be setting an example for the rest of the country in the 1990s. For Iowa has managed to combine over the years steady habits and tolerance of diversity. Iowans' incomes dropped in the 1980s, but in the 1990s its high level of literacy and good work habits have produced white-collar and high-tech growth in and around its pleasant small cities, even as many old factories have closed. Iowa's unemployment rate is now among the nation's lowest, it was voted by the Children's Rights Council in 1998 as the best state to raise a child, and its farm land values have revived even as Congress voted in 1996 to phase out most crop subsidies. Iowa's problems have not ceased entirely. In 1997 Iowans were complain-ing of the stench from giant hog lots, built to service new giant meatpacking plants. But by 1998 the hog lots had overproduced, the meatpacking plants had run out of capacity and pork prices fell from $58 per hundred pounds in July 1997 to $17 in November 1998. Agricultural markets, like real estate markets, take some time to clear, but there's likely to be less stench from hog lots in years ahead.

Politically, Iowa has moved in tandem with the nation in the 1990s, voting twice for Bill Clinton, electing mostly Republicans to Congress and lower offices, and surprising everyone with an upset Democratic victory in 1998 for Governor Tom Vilsack. Collectively these results indicate a sort of steady moderation, a desire to accept the verdict of the markets and to honor traditional values with some hedging on both counts. Iowa remains quirky in some respects. It is still probably one of the most dovish, isolationist-prone states, though very much aware of its role as an international exporter. It is thrift-minded, seeing a balanced budget more as a badge of moral rectitude than as a prudent economic policy. It pioneered legal riverboat gam-bling in 1989, but also has a large anti-abortion movement. Iowa remains ready to complain when pork prices dip or Chicago-Des Moines airfares spike, and they are quick to take offense at presidential candidates who do not pay homage to its caucuses, but Iowa seems increasingly confident, as growth continues into a second decade, that, to what they have built, people this time really will come.

Governor. Tom Vilsack, the Democrat elected governor of Iowa in 1998, was probably the biggest upset winner of that year. He grew up in Pennsylvania (he was adopted, as was his Republican opponent Jim Lightfoot), went to college and law school in Upstate New York, visited Iowa courting his wife and decided to live there. They moved to Mount Pleasant in southeast Iowa where he joined his father-in-law's law firm and won notable verdicts for farm-ers defrauded in the Prairie Grain Elevator case and in a class action that returned $13 million to 86,000 insurance policyholders (average: $151 each). In 1987 he became mayor of Mount Pleasant (after a gunman killed Mayor Edd King) and was elected to the state Senate in 1992

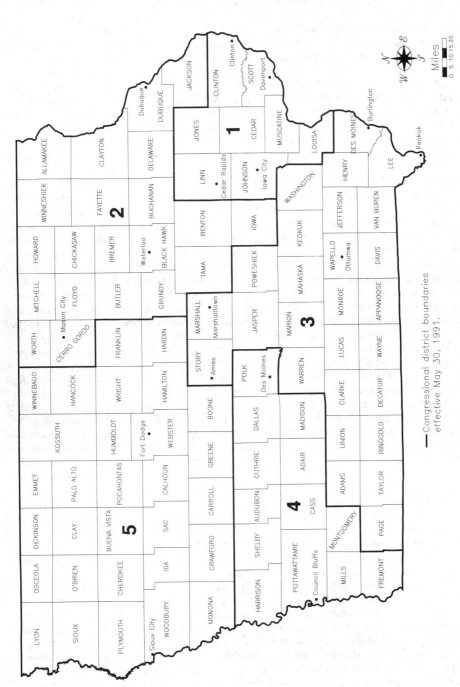

— Congressional district boundaries
effective May 30, 1991.

with 50% of the vote. He nearly retired from the state Senate in 1996, but decided to stay; now he is governor.

Vilsack did not even start off as the favorite in the Democratic primary. Republicans had held the governorship for 30 years; they had just gained control of the state House in 1994 and the state Senate in 1996. The state had a record surplus, unemployment was down to 3% and it was widely assumed Republicans would win again. Governor Terry Branstad had held office for a record 16 years; in March 1997, when Branstad announced he would retire, the focus was first on Senator Charles Grassley, but he decided not to run. Then attention turned to Senator Tom Harkin, in the opinion of many the only Democrat with a good chance to win; it was noted that he had bought a farm south of Des Moines in 1997 to replace an apartment as his Iowa residence. And he had a grievance against the likely Republican nominee, former Congressman Jim Ross Lightfoot: After the 1996 Senate race, in which he beat Lightfoot by just 52%–47%, he had vowed Lightfoot would never be elected governor and set up a PAC, the Iowa Future Fund, for that purpose.

But Harkin didn't run and Democrats had no distinct nominee. The better known candidate was former state Supreme Court Justice Mark McCormick, who campaigned as a moderate and said the party had to broaden its appeal—it had lost nine gubernatorial elections in a row, sometimes with able nominees. But Vilsack took a different tack. With a liberal record in the legislature (he pushed for a state takeover of county mental health and for a higher percentage of special education costs to be paid for by state government), he was endorsed by the United Auto Workers days after he announced and later by other unions. Thirty years of Republican rule, he said, is like "a stew cooking on the stove. You need to stir it once in a while; otherwise it will burn at the bottom." In a light turnout he beat McCormick 51%–48%, while Lightfoot received almost as many votes in the three-candidate Republican primary as both Democrats put together. This was very much a friends-and-neighbors victory. Vilsack carried Cedar Rapids and Davenport, but lost Des Moines and the university towns of Iowa City and Ames, as well as most small counties. But the counties wholly or partly within his state Senate district, one of 50, cast 6% of the state's votes, which Vilsack carried 87%–13%, or by 5,400 votes, enough to offset McCormick's 2,220-vote margin in the rest of the state.

For the general election campaign, Lightfoot raised more money and promised a major tax cut. Vilsack called for upgrading education and attracting agribusinesses to make Iowa "the Silicon Valley of food." Lightfoot, who even aides admitted disliked campaigning, ran mainly on the tax cut and ended with hamhanded negative ads. But the key role in the election was probably played by Harkin. He insisted that he was against Lightfoot on issues rather than personal grounds: "His beliefs are narrow, they're constricted and they're not in keeping with the beliefs of the people of Iowa." Harkin helped raise $300,000 of Vilsack's $2.3 million treasury and Harkin himself campaigned for the last two weeks all over the state. Vilsack ran a 23-city bus caravan and advanced steadily in polls, from a 53%–35% deficit in an early October Mason-Dixon poll to a 47%–42% deficit in the last week of the month. On election night Vice President Al Gore called Vilsack to tell him he'd won; Vilsack was watching *All the President's Men* instead of the televised results. His margin was 52%–47%, the same margin by which Harkin beat Lightfoot two years earlier.

Vilsack's goals include reducing class sizes, implementing student competency tests, lowering tax rates by eliminating federal deductibility, and having more comprehensive ground- and surface-water monitoring near hog lots and some local control over hog lot sites. In his first 100 days, he was able to sign into law two pieces of legislation that addressed campaign promises: one to deal with the methamphetamine addiction problem among Iowa's youth, and the other to reduce class sizes in early grades. He has a Republican legislature to work with; possible 2002 candidates include state House Speaker Ron Corbett and Majority Leader Brent Siegrist. Of course, he will seek to protect Iowa's first-in-the-nation presidential caucuses.

Senior Senator. Charles Grassley, the Republican senator from Iowa, is a farmer who worked as a machinist, unquestionably honest, preternaturally thrifty. He grew up on a farm in

Butler County near Waterloo; his parents switched parties when Franklin Roosevelt ran for a third term in 1940, and he ran for the state legislature in 1956 and lost by 70-some votes. While in graduate school he ran for the state House in the Democratic year of 1958 and was elected, at 25; he won an U.S. House seat in the Democratic year of 1974 and a Senate seat by beating a strong incumbent, John Culver, in 1980. Grassley combines political shrewdness with a seeming naivete that at some level is surely genuine. "People that feel that Chuck Grassley isn't smart enough to serve in the United States Senate soon find out that I've got some brains and I work hard," he said in 1998. He describes himself as "just a hog farmer from New Hartford," and says, "I don't know how you're going to have a strong farm economy if we don't have some farmers in Congress. I can't tell you how many people I have to tell that food doesn't grow on grocery shelves." Starting in 1997 he led the Senate in consecutive roll call votes; the last one he missed came when he was inspecting flood damage in Iowa in 1993. He goes back home to Iowa every weekend, helps his son run the family farm and holds open meetings in every one of Iowa's 99 counties each year.

Grassley's record in Congress has been guided by three issues: thrift, agriculture and dovishness on defense; he is ever alert for abuse of power. His first major legislation was the 1986 Federal False Claims Act, which authorizes suits for fraud on behalf of the government; he says it has brought in $1.8 billion. He long sponsored the bill to apply to Congress the laws it applies to others, and was the chief sponsor of the Congressional Accountability Act of 1995. He worked for years on IRS reform and helped pass it in 1998. He led the investigation in the FBI crime lab, and got release of one million pages of documents on POWs and MIAs. In 1998 he got the ethanol tax credit extended to 2007. He is a strong supporter of free trade as chairman of the International Trade Subcommittee and has worked to open up agricultural trade with Europe. In 1997 he became chairman of the Senate Aging Committee and in 1998 said he had an "open mind" on reforming Social Security, calling it "the most successful social program in the history of the country." He has worked on numerous rural health care programs.

Grassley is usually a partisan Republican but does not hesitate to vote against other Republicans on issues he thinks important: he was one of two Republicans who voted against the Gulf war resolution in 1991. He has worked for compromises on some programs, like AmeriCorps, and was a chief sponsor of the wind-energy tax credit and the conservation measures in the Freedom to Farm Act. He got a seat on Agriculture in 1995 and supported the Freedom to Farm Act, a "farm program in which no Washington bureaucrat dictates what [farmers] must plant." In 1998 he got a six-month extension of Chapter 12 of the Bankruptcy Act, which applies to farmers, as overall bankruptcy reform failed in the House. In late 1998 he said high airfares in Iowa were his toughest problem, and added that a solution is "probably going to come more when we get more competition than when we get more regulation."

Grassley has been a stern critic of the defense budget. In 1995 he said, "The defense budget should be leveling off, not going up." And in 1998 he did not join other Republicans' calls for more defense spending. He is quick to seize on outrages: he shellacked the Pentagon when he found out that an Air Force general, his wife, and cat were flown from Italy to Colorado in an otherwise empty 200-seat plane. On the Judiciary Committee, he has taken the same attitude toward lawyers and judges. He worked to block a 12th judgeship for what he considered the underworked D.C. Circuit, and sent a questionnaire to federal judges to see how they spend their money. "Some of these people should get out of their offices and they would see the poor John Deere worker in Waterloo, Iowa, is as concerned about judges wasting his money as the generals wasting his money."

If he is politically shrewder than he appears, Grassley seems to lack any element of cynicism. Since 1980 he has been the most popular politician in Iowa. In 1986 he became the first Iowa senator to win re-election in 20 years, with a record 66% of the vote. In 1992 he broke the record when he won 70%–27%, carrying all 99 counties. In 1998, against a Democrat who campaigned by taking trips down Iowa rivers, he fell back to 68%–30%, carrying all 99 counties again, from college town Iowa City's Johnson County (53%–45%) to heavily Dutch-American

Sioux County (91%–9%). If he serves out his term, Grassley will tie Bourke Hickenlooper for the second-longest tenure of an Iowa senator; he will beat the record set by William B. Allison if he serves until June 2016, three months before he turns 83.

Junior Senator. Tom Harkin, first elected to the Senate in 1984, is an accomplished veteran of Capitol Hill who still brings the attitude of the resentful outsider to his work. Harkin grew up poor in a rural town, where his father was a coal miner and his mother, a Slovenian immigrant, died when he was 10. His desire to use government to help those who are struggling comes not from academic theory but from tough personal experience. He worked his way through college and law school, spent five years in the Navy during the 1960s, ferrying planes from Vietnam for repair. Returning there in 1970 as an aide to Congressman Neal Smith, he discovered the infamous "tiger cages" prison cells. After a narrow loss in 1972, Harkin ran for Congress again in 1974 and invented "work days," a campaign technique widely imitated since: he spent a day working at each of a dozen or so local jobs. He won solidly and held the seat with good percentages. Well before the 1984 election, he cornered the Democratic nomination to run against Senator Roger Jepsen. This was in the midst of Iowa's farm depression of the 1980s and Harkin was elected with 55% of the vote.

Harkin's record in the Senate may fairly be characterized as liberal, though not always on economic issues; he voted for the balanced budget amendment in 1995 and 1997. His biggest disappointment surely has been on farm policy. He came to the Senate as a self-styled populist, eager to expand government farm programs. His big initiative was the 1987 Harkin-Gephardt supply management farm bill, which would have raised overall food costs in order to benefit small farmers. But it was a nonstarter even in the 1980s, when Iowa farmers were hurting, and farm policy since has moved in the other direction: in 1996 Harkin voted—to no avail—against the Freedom to Farm Act which phased out most subsidies over seven years. With some reluctance, he voted for NAFTA: Iowa is the nation's leading producer of corn and pork, staples of Mexican cuisine.

Harkin's greatest impact has been on health policy. Two of his sisters died from breast cancer and one brother of thyroid cancer; another brother became deaf at age nine. At Gallaudet University in Washington, D.C., a noted school for the hearing impaired, Harkin gave part of his speech in sign language when he withdrew from the 1992 presidential race; he used his chairmanship of the Labor-HHS Appropriations Subcommittee to establish grants for "assistive technology" for the handicapped and set up a new NIH Institute on Deafness and Other Communication Disorders. His interest in deafness prompted him and Senator Jennings Randolph to bring the first closed-caption TV to the Carter White House; in 1991 he passed a law requiring close-captioning on all 13-inch-plus TVs starting in 1995. As he notes, this is useful not only for the deaf but for a senator watching debate on C-SPAN while making phone calls.

Harkin also used that chair to promote the Americans with Disabilities Act of 1990. This was a great achievement, one that required overcoming resistance based on cost and qualms about the real-world effect of regulations, to build up a bipartisan coalition with the Bush Administration. Harkin, after he got relief from allergies by eating morsels of bee pollen, used his chairmanship in 1992 to create the National Center for Alternative and Complementary Medicine at NIH, then even in the minority got it elevated to an independent status within NIH, over the opposition of many medical scientists. Not all his health initiatives have been successful. The Harkin-Chafee-Graham tobacco bill was endorsed by Bill Clinton in March 1998 but no legislation was enacted that year. He favored funding of human cloning, to help understand diseases; but that was opposed by most senators and the Clinton Administration. Inspired perhaps by Iowa's giant hog lots, he has called for more research on animal waste and, by publicized incidents, for giving the USDA more powers to deal with meat contamination. He has taken on a crusade against child labor, in this country and abroad, trying to get rid of exceptions to current laws and double penalties; in Nepal in January 1998 he whipped out his camera to show the conditions under which 8-year-olds worked, much as he photographed the tiger cages 28 years before.

On foreign policy, Harkin is very much a product of the Vietnam experience. He opposed Contra aid and verged on being an apologist for the Nicaraguan Sandinista government in the 1980s and fervently opposed the Gulf war in 1991, bringing a lawsuit against President Bush to try to prevent him from using force without congressional approval. But Harkin was just as fervent a sponsor of an embargo on Haiti in 1994 when the military was in power and of threatening to use force to install then-exiled President Aristide.

Harkin has never had the widespread support enjoyed by Charles Grassley, but has become the first Iowa Democrat to win three full terms in the Senate. In 1990 he won re-election with 54% against a tough Republican opponent, Congressman Tom Tauke. In 1991 he surprised many by running for president. In angry phrases, with a Trumanesque zest, Harkin preached that George Bush and the Republicans helped only the rich and that government must get involved to help the poor and middle class. But organized labor withheld an early endorsement despite his 90%-plus AFL-CIO voting record—a great tactical victory for Bill Clinton. Harkin's sweep of the Iowa caucuses February 10, actually an impressive testimonial to his home state popularity, was mostly discounted by the media. He finished with only 10% in New Hampshire; though he won the Minnesota and Idaho caucuses March 3, he got only 7% in South Carolina March 7 after campaigning there with Jesse Jackson. In debt and ineligible for matching funds, Harkin quit the race.

Harkin went on to campaign gamely for Clinton; after the election, Clinton appointed his wife Ruth Harkin—a Washington lawyer who combines good humor, competence and strong beliefs—to head the Overseas Private Investment Corporation. But he opposed Clinton in 1996, when he put a hold on Alan Greenspan's nomination for another term as Federal Reserve chairman and delayed his confirmation from February to June 1996. The chairman's four-year term starts on confirmation, which means Clinton may be forced to renominate Greenspan in 2000, or hold him over for appointment by the next president—not the result Harkin wanted.

In 1996 Harkin had tough opposition from 3d District Congressman Jim Ross Lightfoot, who noted that Harkin had voted for pay raises and higher taxes and that he lived in a big house in northern Virginia, saying Harking was out of touch with Iowa. The race was tight, but Harkin had far more money and got a crucial late appearance from Clinton. Harkin won 52%–47%, his closest margin, and embarked on a project of preventing Lightfoot from being elected governor in 1998. Despite some speculation, he declined to run himself in May 1997. After the little-known Tom Vilsack won the June primary, Harkin was responsible for an estimated $300,000 raised for Vilsack. Harkin enlisted his topnotch political consultants in the campaign and campaigned himself solidly for the last two weeks.

Harkin enlisted just as heartily in the fight against the impeachment of Bill Clinton. The House managers' case against Clinton, he declared "a pile of dung." He made the only objection during the presentation of the House managers' case, arguing that senators should not be called "jurors" because their duties went beyond those of jurors and they were not limited by the Constitution or the Federalist Papers to just a narrow finding of fact. Chief Justice William Rehnquist, presiding over the trial, agreed.

Presidential politics. On a frosty evening in early February, upwards of 150,000 Iowans troop to caucuses in some 2,142 precincts and begin the process of choosing a president of the United States. (In 1996, there were caucuses earlier in Louisiana and Alaska, but few paid them much heed.) The precinct caucuses were scheduled early in the cycle for 1972 by Democratic doves who wanted more leverage for their views, and that year they started George McGovern on his way to the Democratic nomination. But the caucuses have had other, unanticipated consequences. In 1976, Jimmy Carter's strategist Hamilton Jordan determined that intensive campaigning could produce a surprise victory that could make a little-known candidate a national contender: without Iowa and the next-week New Hampshire primary, Carter would never have become president. By 1980, Iowans were so used to candidates courting them that when Ronald Reagan ducked an Iowa debate he was beaten by George Bush, even as Carter, still profiting from his 1976 contacts, was trouncing Edward Kennedy. But Reagan recovered in

New Hampshire, where he did show up for a debate ("I paid for this microphone") and Carter lost in November: a forecast of Iowa's irrelevance in cycles to come.

Iowa's 1980s economic angst made George Bush, the 1980 winner, a poor third in 1988, behind Bob Dole and Pat Robertson—a sign of the increasing presence of Christian conservatives in the Republican Party. Iowa's leftish economic policies had a substantial effect on Dick Gephardt, who won the state's Democratic contest in 1988. But Democrats have not had a contest since: Iowa's Tom Harkin pre-empted the field in 1992 and Bill Clinton was unopposed in 1996. Indeed there were no contests here at all in 1992, for Pat Buchanan started his insurgent campaign in New Hampshire, where he had the strong backing from the Manchester *Union Leader*; but he would have been staunchly opposed by the *Des Moines Register*. In 1996 Bob Dole had the support of leading Republicans, led by Governor Terry Branstad and Senator Charles Grassley, and farm state roots as well: Dole's very narrow victory was an omen of the weakness of his candidacy later, and the negative ads run against him by Steve Forbes and others may have contributed to his weak showing in Iowa in the fall. But no one pays close attention to Iowa in the fall, with its seven electoral votes, even though the state has voted close to the national average in the 1990s; in 1996 Bill Clinton won solidly, 50%–40%, carrying 80 of 99 counties.

A case can be made that the Iowa caucuses haven't determined a nomination since 1984. But Iowans are determined to preserve their first-in-the-nation status, enshrined in national Democratic (but not Republican) rules. Iowa Republicans pushed their caucus ahead to February 7, 2000, and Iowa Democrats are expected to hold their caucus on the same day if they can convince the DNC to change its rule of not holding caucuses before February 21. Branstad established a commission with New Hampshire Governor Jeanne Shaheen to preserve the status quo; "We want to protect a system that has worked well for the American people." Incoming Governor Tom Vilsack quickly made the usual case for retail politics: "Iowa is a good barometer of political candidates. . . . They have to come into our living rooms. They have to go into cafes. They have to go into coffee shops. They have to stand the test of time."

Iowa has the potential to shape, if not determine, the 2000 campaign. Al Gore would like it forgotten that he skipped the caucuses, which he called "madness" in "the small state of Iowa," when he ran for president in 1988. But by June 1997 he proclaimed, "I love Iowa," and in November 1998 he was on the phone congratulating Vilsack before Vilsack himself realized he had been elected governor. Second place can also be worth winning here. In 1984, against seven other candidates, Walter Mondale took about 50% of the vote (it is hard to measure Democratic votes, reported by national-convention-delegate-equivalent), an impressive score by any measure, while Gary Hart was second with about 16%. But the headlines were "Gary Hart surge!" and Hart came close to upsetting Mondale for the nomination. In any contest someone has to finish second and that someone, no matter how far behind, may have what George Bush in 1980 called "big mo" going into New Hampshire and other contests.

As for Republicans, Iowa could pose a problem for the man leading the polls in early 1999, George W. Bush. Can Bush, as incumbent Governor of Texas, spend the time and assemble the local organization which Iowans have come to expect? Especially since as of early 1999 he had not gone near the state, while potential opponents—Lamar Alexander, Gary Bauer, Steve Forbes, John Kasich, John McCain, Dan Quayle, Bob Smith—were visiting in 1998 and in many cases earlier.

Congressional districting. In May 1991, Iowa's Democratic legislature and Governor Branstad approved congressional district lines drawn by the non-partisan Legislative Services Bureau. These lines were not drawn consistently to the convenience of anyone—Democrats, Republicans, incumbents—and have resulted in a 4–1 Republican delegation, few of whose members are totally safe. If Iowa's Democratic governor and Republican legislature adopt a nonpartisan commission report again, the political consequences are unpredictable. The more so since Iowa, though growing again, seems set to lose another seat after the 2000 Census.

The People: Est. Pop. 1998: 2,862,447; Pop. 1990: 2,776,755, up 3.1% 1990–1998. 1.1% of U.S. total, 30th largest; 39.4% rural. Median age: 36.1 years. 16% 65 years and over. 96.7% White, 1.7% Black, 0.9% Asian, 0.3% Amer. Indian, 0.4% Other; 1.1% Hispanic Origin. Households: 59.2% married couple families; 27.5% married couple fams. w. children; 41.6% college educ.; median household income: $26,229; per capita income: $12,422; 70% owner occupied housing; median house value: $45,900; median monthly rent: $261. 2.8% Unemployment. 1998 Voting age pop.: 2,157,000. 1998 Turnout: 973,032; 45% of VAP. Registered voters (1998): 1,769,827; 567,441 D (32%), 588,061 R (33%), 614,325 unaffiliated and minor parties (35%).

Political Lineup: Governor, Thomas J. Vilsack (D); Lt. Gov., Sally Pederson (D); Secy. of State, Chester Culver (D); Atty. Gen., Tom Miller (D); Treasurer, Michael L. Fitzgerald (D); State Senate, 50 (20 D, 30 R); Senate President, Mary Kramer (R); State House, 100 (44 D, 56 R); House Speaker, Ron Corbett (R). Senators, Charles Grassley (R) and Tom Harkin (D). Representatives, 5 (1 D, 4 R).

Elections Division: 515-281-5865; **Filing Deadline for U.S. Congress:** March 17, 2000.

1996 Presidential Vote			1992 Presidential Vote		
Clinton (D)	620,258	(50%)	Clinton (D)	586,353	(43%)
Dole (R)	492,644	(40%)	Bush (R)	504,891	(37%)
Perot (I)	105,159	(9%)	Perot (I)	253,468	(19%)

GOVERNOR

Gov. Thomas J. Vilsack (D)

Elected 1998, term expires Jan. 2003; b. Dec. 13, 1950, Pittsburgh, PA; home, Mt. Pleasant; Hamilton Col., B.A. 1972, Albany Law Schl., J.D. 1975; Catholic; married (Christie).

Elected Office: Mt. Pleasant Mayor, 1987–92; IA Senate, 1992–98.

Professional Career: Practicing atty., 1975–98.

Office: State Capitol, Des Moines, 50319, 515-281-5211; Fax: 515-281-6611; Web site: www.state.ia.us.

Election Results

1998 gen.	Thomas J. Vilsack (D)	500,231	(52%)
	Jim Ross Lightfoot (R)	444,787	(47%)
	Others	11,397	(1%)
1998 prim.	Thomas J. Vilsack (D)	59,130	(51%)
	Mark McCormick (D)	55,950	(48%)
1994 gen.	Terry E. Branstad (R)	566,395	(57%)
	Bonnie J. Campbell (D)	414,453	(42%)
	Others	16,400	(2%)

SENATORS

Sen. Charles Grassley (R)

Elected 1980, seat up 2004; b. Sep. 17, 1933, New Hartford; home, New Hartford; U. of N. IA, B.A. 1955, M.A. 1956, U. of IA, 1957–58; Baptist; married (Barbara).

Elected Office: IA House of Reps., 1958–74; U.S. House of Reps., 1974–80.

Professional Career: Farmer.

DC Office: 135 HSOB, 20510, 202-224-3744; Fax: 202-224-6020; Web site: www.senate.gov/~grassley.

State Offices: Cedar Rapids, 319-363-6832; Council Bluffs, 712-322-7103; Davenport, 319-322-4331; Des Moines, 515-284-4890; Sioux City, 712-233-1860; Waterloo, 319-232-6657.

Committees: *Aging (Special)* (Chmn. of 11 R). *Agriculture, Nutrition & Forestry* (8th of 10 R): Forestry, Conservation & Rural Revitalization; Production & Price Competitiveness. *Budget* (2d of 12 R). *Finance* (3d of 11 R): Health Care; International Trade (Chmn.); Taxation & IRS Oversight. *Judiciary* (3d of 10 R): Administrative Oversight & the Courts (Chmn.); Immigration; Technology, Terrorism & Government Information. *Joint Committee on Taxation* (3d of 5 Sens.).

Group Ratings

	ADA	ACLU	AFS	LCV	CON	NTU	NFIB	COC	ACU	NTLC	CHC
1998	5	14	22	0	92	56	89	83	80	75	91
1997	5	—	0	—	98	75	—	100	80	—	—

National Journal Ratings

	1997 LIB — 1997 CONS		1998 LIB — 1998 CONS	
Economic	11%	— 76%	48%	— 51%
Social	17%	— 72%	12%	— 79%
Foreign	23%	— 76%	26%	— 71%

Key Votes of the 105th Congress

1. Bal. Budget Amend.	Y	5. Satcher for Surgeon Gen.	N	9. Chem. Weapons Treaty	N
2. Clinton Budget Deal	Y	6. Highway Set-asides	N	10. Cuban Humanitarian Aid	N
3. Cloture on Tobacco	Y	7. Table Child Gun locks	Y	11. Table Bosnia Troops	N
4. Education IRAs	Y	8. Ovrd. Part. Birth Veto	Y	12. $ for Test-ban Treaty	N

Election Results

1998 general	Charles Grassley (R)	648,480	(68%)	($2,781,940)
	David Osterberg (D)	289,049	(30%)	($165,429)
	Others	10,378	(1%)	
1998 primary	Charles Grassley (R)	unopposed		
1992 general	Charles Grassley (R)	899,761	(70%)	($2,486,030)
	Jean Lloyd-Jones (D)	351,561	(27%)	($410,894)
	Others	40,879	(3%)	

Sen. Tom Harkin (D)

Elected 1984, seat up 2002; b. Nov. 19, 1939, Cumming; home, Cumming; IA St. U., B.S. 1962, Catholic U., J.D. 1972; Catholic; married (Ruth).

Military Career: Navy, 1962–67; Naval Reserves, 1969–72.

Elected Office: U.S. House of Reps., 1974–84.

Professional Career: Practicing atty., 1972–74; Staff Aide, House Select Cmte. on U.S. Involvement in SE Asia, 1973–74.

DC Office: 731 HSOB, 20510, 202-224-3254; Fax: 202-224-9369; Web site: www.senate.gov/~harkin.

State Offices: Cedar Rapids, 319-365-4504; Davenport, 319-322-1338; Des Moines, 515-284-4574; Dubuque, 319-582-2130; Sioux City, 712-252-1550.

Committees: *Agriculture, Nutrition & Forestry* (RMM of 8 D). *Appropriations* (6th of 13 D): Agriculture & Rural Development; Defense; Foreign Operations & Export Financing; Labor & HHS (RMM); VA, HUD & Independent Agencies. *Health, Education, Labor & Pensions* (3d of 8 D): Employment, Safety & Training; Public Health. *Small Business* (3d of 8 D).

Group Ratings

	ADA	ACLU	AFS	LCV	CON	NTU	NFIB	COC	ACU	NTLC	CHC
1998	95	100	100	100	35	10	50	50	5	4	10
1997	85	—	89	—	61	29	—	70	12	—	—

National Journal Ratings

	1997 LIB — 1997 CONS		1998 LIB — 1998 CONS	
Economic	75%	— 24%	81%	— 17%
Social	71%	— 0%	74%	— 0%
Foreign	92%	— 0%	95%	— 0%

Key Votes of the 105th Congress

1. Bal. Budget Amend.	Y	5. Satcher for Surgeon Gen.	Y	9. Chem. Weapons Treaty	Y
2. Clinton Budget Deal	N	6. Highway Set-asides	Y	10. Cuban Humanitarian Aid	Y
3. Cloture on Tobacco	Y	7. Table Child Gun locks	N	11. Table Bosnia Troops	Y
4. Education IRAs	N	8. Ovrd. Part. Birth Veto	N	12. $ for Test-ban Treaty	Y

Election Results

1996 general	Tom Harkin (D)	634,166	(52%)	($6,070,137)
	Jim Ross Lightfoot (R)	571,807	(47%)	($2,439,679)
1996 primary	Tom Harkin (D)	unopposed		
1990 general	Tom Harkin (D)	529,571	(54%)	($5,628,242)
	Thomas J. Tauke (R)	453,273	(46%)	($5,060,104)

FIRST DISTRICT

A century and a half ago settlers surged west across the Mississippi River into the fertile, hilly lands that became Iowa. There New England and Midwestern Yankees built on the strange, open terrain their characteristic farmhouses, barns, town halls, church spires and small colleges; Germans, after crossing the ocean, stopped at the river bluffs reminiscent of their native land and built neat farmhouses and substantial towns; railroad builders, headquartered in Chicago, extended their networks of steel rails over the plains and rivers. Today some of the distinctiveness of these settlers remains in eastern Iowa, though the old ethnic folkways have faded, the old river craft have been replaced by giant barges and riverboat casinos, and the old rail lines have been modernized and employ fewer men. Davenport, on the hills over the Mississippi River (which, with Bettendorf, and Rock Island and Moline, Illinois, are called the Quad Cities) still has the look of the city where Ronald Reagan got his first radio job more than 60 years ago—plus a riverboat casino. Cedar Rapids, a couple of counties west of the river, looks more contemporary, with big high-tech employers (Rockwell has large avionics and electronics operations here). Iowa City, to the south, is a university town complete with trendy bookstores and vegetarian eateries.

Eight counties in eastern Iowa, with Davenport in one corner and Cedar Rapids in another, make up Iowa's 1st Congressional District. Historically Republican, in the 1970s and 1980s it became Democratic, though not as much as across the River in Illinois; now it can be labeled marginal.

The congressman from the 1st District is Jim Leach, chairman of the House Banking Committee, and one of the most senior and independent Republicans in the House. Leach grew up in Davenport, where his family owns propane gas and wholesale businesses, attended Princeton, studied Soviet politics at Johns Hopkins and the London School of Economics. He became a Foreign Service Officer in 1968, worked for Donald Rumsfeld at the Office of Economic Opportunity, then was assigned to the Arms Control and Disarmament Agency and served in the United Nations when George Bush was U.S. ambassador there. In 1973 he resigned after Richard Nixon fired special prosecutor Archibald Cox and returned to the family businesses in Davenport; in 1976 ran for the House and beat incumbent Democrat Edward Mezvinsky.

A believer in free enterprise with hands-on experience in a regulated business, Leach remains market-oriented on most economic issues. On cultural issues, he looks with some favor on international family planning and affirmative action. On foreign policy, like many Iowa Republicans, he has shown caution about asserting U.S. military power, but supported the Gulf war resolution in 1991, continued deployment of troops in Bosnia in 1997, and additional loan dollars for the International Monetary Fund in 1998.

On the Banking Committee Leach has often been ahead of his time in pointing to problems. In the 1980s he warned early on that allowing the states to liberate their savings and loans from investment limits while maintaining federal deposit insurance and not increasing capital requirements would lead to trouble. And so it did: the S&L crisis of the late 1980s cost taxpayers something on the order of $500 billion. On the Whitewater scandal, as part of the minority in 1994 he called for subpoenas and an investigation; Democrats stonewalled. In summer 1995, as chairman, he conducted four days of hearings, in which Democrats honed the tactics they have used on Clinton scandals ever since: making loud partisan objections and then trying to discredit the investigation as partisan.

On financial regulation issues, Leach has tended toward market solutions but has had to deal with issues that are among Capitol Hill's most complex and heavily lobbied. He resisted calls for regulations on derivatives and other high-risk investments. He has rejected the Clinton Administration's efforts to consolidate banking regulation in the Treasury, favoring the Federal Reserve instead, partly because it is less subject to political manipulation. He criticized government-sponsored Freddie Mac for buying Philip Morris bonds, and Fannie Mae for providing free life insurance to certain low-income homebuyers. Despite widespread agreement that the 1933 Glass-Steagall's firewalls between banks, investment banks and insurance companies should be dismantled, Leach has had a difficult time passing financial services deregulation. In 1996 his efforts were stymied by insurance interests and an inability to settle jurisdictional issues with Commerce Chairman Thomas Bliley. In a June 1997 markup, he lost on so many amendments he considered opposing the committee bill. In March 1998 his bill was yanked from the floor by the leadership, which judged it couldn't pass. A compromise bill passed by one vote (214–213) in May 1998 before dying in the Senate that October. Leach's unwillingness to take the head-cracking approach of some committee chairmen has made it difficult to get this bill through. But he reintroduced the measure in January 1999 with the "strong support" of the Clinton Administration.

At home Leach was re-elected without difficulty from 1978 to 1994. In 1996, after the Whitewater hearings, he had spirited opposition from former state Senator Bob Rush, who got a late-campaign appearance by Bill Clinton. Rush charged that Leach used to be a "nonpartisan, independent thinker" but had become more conservative and partisan. Leach's race was made more difficult by his refusal to accept contributions over $500, from outside Iowa or from PACs. Thus, the chairman of the Banking Committee was outraised by his challenger, $370,000 to $420,000. The 1st District went solidly for Clinton in 1996 as it had in 1992, and Leach said resignedly that he was "at peace" with himself whatever the result. He won narrowly, 53%–46%.

Leach continued to go his own way. In January 1997 he was the second Republican (after Michael Forbes) to announce he would not vote for Newt Gingrich for speaker and said that Gingrich's defense against ethics charges was "simply inadequate for a maker of laws." There was talk that Leach might lose his chairmanship. In April 1998 he was dressed down by Gingrich in a closed meeting for signing a discharge petition for campaign finance reform, and in June 1998 Bob Ehrlich drafted a proposal to strip Leach of his chairmanship. But nothing came of that and in August the campaign finance bill passed the House. Meanwhile, he firmly supported an additional $18 billion in loan guarantees for the IMF, strongly opposed by Majority Leader Dick Armey. "It is a dangerous time, requiring firm, bipartisan American leadership. . . . The honor, prosperity and security of the United States are at stake," Leach said. He proposed to improve its mixed record by requiring less secrecy, disclosure of bailout agreements and ways to make investors in foreign projects bear some risk; and the $18 billion eventually passed.

Leach was one of the Republicans most reluctant to vote for impeachment. The day after Clinton's August 18 speech he said, "There is a distinction between character flaws, political embarrassments and constitutional challenges. We have the first two, but as yet we certainly don't have the third." He finally decided to vote for impeachment in December. In Iowa Bob Rush ran against him again, and by mid-year had three times as much cash as in 1996. But Leach, even with his self-imposed limitations, eventually raised and spent more than the Democrat. Rush attacked Leach as "asleep at the wheel" for not getting enough pork barrel projects out of the transportation bill, and said Leach was not attentive enough to the district; he also hit him for favoring fast track. But Leach profited from the perception, in the *Des Moines Register*'s James Flansburg's words, that he "has a moral compass and follows its directions when it would be far easier to be blown along by the political winds." He won by a wider margin than in 1996, 57%–42%, benefiting from the pro-incumbent tide of 1998; he carried Scott County and Davenport by better than 2–1 and Linn County and Cedar Rapids as well. Under House rules, this is his last term as Banking chairman.

Cook's Call. *Probably Safe.* The notoriously low-key Leach does not raise the kind of money or run the kind of campaign that most committee chairmen and/or members in marginal districts would. There is no doubt that once he decides to retire this marginal—if somewhat Democratic leaning—district, will be hotly contested. Until then, Leach remains a solid favorite.

The People: Pop. 1990: 555,229; 23.6% rural; 12.6% age 65 + ; 95.1% White, 2.6% Black, 1.3% Asian, 0.3% Amer. Indian, 0.8% Other; 1.9% Hispanic Origin. Households: 56.5% married couple families; 27.3% married couple fams. w. children; 49.1% college educ.; median household income: $29,544; per capita income: $13,660; median house value: $55,800; median gross rent: $298.

1996 Presidential Vote			1992 Presidential Vote		
Clinton (D)	135,839	(54%)	Clinton (D)	128,655	(46%)
Dole (R)	92,207	(37%)	Bush (R)	95,660	(34%)
Perot (I)	19,027	(8%)	Perot (I)	52,983	(19%)
Others	4,409	(2%)			

Rep. Jim Leach (R)

Elected 1976; b. Oct. 15, 1942, Davenport; home, Davenport; Princeton U., B.A. 1964, Johns Hopkins U., M.A. 1966, London Schl. of Econ., 1966–68; Episcopalian; married (Elisabeth).

Professional Career: Staff Asst., U.S. Rep. Donald Rumsfeld, 1965–66; U.S. Foreign Svc., 1968–69, 1971–72 (Arms Control & Disarmament Agency); A.A. to Dir., U.S. Office of Econ. Opp., 1969–70; Pres., Flamegas Co., 1973–75; Dir., Fed. Home Loan Bank Bd., Midwest Reg., 1975–76.

DC Office: 2186 RHOB 20515, 202-225-6576; Fax: 202-226-1278; Web site: www.house.gov/leach.

District Offices: Cedar Rapids, 319-363-4773; Davenport, 319-326-1841; Iowa City, 319-351-0789.

Committees: *Banking & Financial Services* (Chmn. of 32 R). *International Relations* (3d of 26 R): Asia & the Pacific.

Group Ratings

	ADA	ACLU	AFS	LCV	CON	NTU	NFIB	COC	ACU	NTLC	CHC
1998	45	56	50	85	30	42	71	89	32	50	33
1997	45	—	38	—	95	52	—	100	60	—	—

National Journal Ratings

	1997 LIB — 1997 CONS		1998 LIB — 1998 CONS	
Economic	43%	— 56%	52%	— 48%
Social	58%	— 40%	60%	— 38%
Foreign	51%	— 46%	64%	— 31%

Key Votes of the 105th Congress

1. Clinton Budget Deal	Y	5. Puerto Rico Sthood. Ref.	Y	9. Cut $ for B-2 Bombers	Y
2. Education IRAs	Y	6. End Highway Set-asides	N	10. Human Rights in China	N
3. Req. 2/3 to Raise Taxes	Y	7. School Prayer Amend.	N	11. Withdraw Bosnia Troops	N
4. Fast-track Trade	Y	8. Ovrd. Part. Birth Veto	Y	12. End Cuban TV-Marti	N

Election Results

1998 general	Jim Leach (R)	106,419	(57%)	($673,673)
	Bob Rush (D)	79,529	(42%)	($468,465)
	Others	2,260	(1%)	
1998 primary	Jim Leach (R)	23,667	(99%)	
	Others	140	(1%)	
1996 general	Jim Leach (R)	129,242	(53%)	($369,864)
	Bob Rush (D)	111,595	(46%)	($419,647)
	Others	3,759	(2%)	

SECOND DISTRICT

Northeast Iowa, along the Mississippi River and westward, has some of the loveliest landscape in America. Here the Mississippi flows past green bluffs, then broadens out in great quiet pools and flows past picturesque German-style towns. Inland from the river are the rolling hills portrayed with surprisingly little exaggeration in the paintings of Iowa's Grant Wood. These lands were settled by immigrants in the late 19th Century. German Catholics settled Dubuque, whose giant Victorian courthouse looks down on the Mississippi and up at the Fenelon Place Elevator that rides up the bluff. Just west of Dubuque is Dyersville, where *Field of Dreams* was filmed and to which baseball buffs now repair: "If you build it, they will come." Farther west is Waterloo, which grew rapidly after 1900 as the John Deere tractor factory expanded and the eight-floor Rath factory became the largest meat-packing plant in the world; Rath closed in 1984 and Deere had thousands of layoffs, but Waterloo has rebounded somewhat with new businesses from a dog track to telemarketing to a high-tech Iowa Beef Processing (IBP) factory. To the south are the Amana colonies, settled in the 1850s by the Community of True Inspiration, German pietists who have retained many of their old customs even as they have built the Amana appliance business.

The 2d Congressional District of Iowa covers most of northeast Iowa, including Dubuque and Waterloo, Dyersville and the Amana colonies. There is considerable political variation here. Dubuque, heavily German Catholic, was for years Iowa's most Democratic city, and still often is unless abortion is the issue. But the rural counties along the river and farther west—more German Protestant, Scandinavian and Yankee—were traditionally Republican. Waterloo, originally Republican, trended sharply Democratic as the Rath plant shut down and Deere had big layoffs.

The congressman from the 2d District is Jim Nussle, first elected in 1990, at 30 the youngest member of the 102nd Congress. Nussle grew up in Chicago, attended a Lutheran college (he is Danish-American and speaks Danish) and law school and then moved back to his native Iowa. In the small town way, he soon became Delaware County attorney, known for prosecuting a local day care employee for child abuse. He coupled his anti-abortion stance with support for helping expectant mothers with the expenses of parenthood. When Republican Congressman Tom Tauke ran for the Senate in 1990, Nussle ran for his seat, narrowly winning the Republican primary and then facing a better-financed Democrat. Nussle emphasized his experience in law enforcement, called for more informed parental involvement in the drug war as well as in choosing day care. This was enough for him to win 50%–49%, one of the closest margins in the country that year.

Nussle quickly became one of the leaders of the nascent Republican revolution. He was one of the Gang of Seven, a group of freshman Republican reformers who attacked the Democratic leadership. In October 1991 he made national news by coming into the House with a paper bag over his head to protest Democratic leaders' refusal to make full disclosure of House bank overdrafts. He voted against agricultural appropriations, to the dismay of senior Iowa Democrats, and moved to cut congressional salaries 5% every year the federal budget is not balanced. For 1992, redistricting put Nussle into a district with incumbent Dave Nagle, a Democratic who had helped organize the defense of Speaker Jim Wright against Newt Gingrich's charges in 1989. Nagle had represented more of the new district's territory, but Nussle won again by 50%–49%. Two years later Nagle tried again, and Nussle won more easily, 56%–43%.

After the election, Gingrich appointed Nussle director of the transition to Republican rule: from paper bag to power in just three years. Nussle froze hiring, demanded detailed accountings, and supervised an overhaul of House administration. He also got a seat on Ways and Means, where he again took risks, voting in September 1995 for a bill that reduced the tax credit for (but also reduced tax rates for) ethanol. He defended the Republican Medicare program while trying to raise reimbursement rates for rural health care providers. Nussle had an unexpectedly tough time of it in the 1996 election. He vastly outspent Democrat Donna Smith, a 17-year Dubuque County supervisor, but she hammered home his closeness to Gingrich, attacked "Georgia Jim" for supporting big hog feedlots, and, when Nussle announced he was getting divorced, Smith said that he "divorced" Iowans by voting for the tax bill cutting the ethanol subsidy. Nussle continued to sound his conservative themes; of the Freedom to Farm Act he said, "By and large farmers make much better decisions than Washington can." But he added defensively that his ties to Gingrich "allowed us to save several programs." Nussle won by just 53%–46%, losing Dubuque County and Waterloo's Black Hawk County.

After that election Nussle sounded a much less revolutionary note. He was passed over by Gingrich for the chair of the Republicans' campaign committee and in July 1997 ran for Conference vice chairman against Jennifer Dunn, Gingrich's choice, but lost 129–85. Nussle turned to issues with local appeal. He became the loudest House supporter of extending the ethanol tax credit beyond 2000 and, though he was barred from taking that to the House floor, he served on the conference committee which adopted Senator Charles Grassley's move to extend it to 2007. In the 1998 tax bill he made income averaging for farmers permanent and accelerated the full deductibility of health insurance for the self-employed. And when the tax bill died in the Senate, Nussle got these provisions included in the omnibus spending bill that passed in October 1998. That year he also succeeded in changing the formula for Medicare reimbursement in rural areas. Nussle and Democrat Ben Cardin in October 1998 produced a proposal to change the budget process: it would make the budget resolution law, to be signed by the president; require agreement of maximum spending for seven categories of programs; and take inflation factors (which studies have shown are overestimates) from baseline budgeting. In the highway bill, this one-time scorner of pork got $28 million for the Julian Dubuque Bridge expansion. Nussle for some years has refused to talk to the *Des Moines Register*, whose editor Dennis Ryerson notes, "He feels we go out of our way to make him look bad. . . . He has been very frustrated by the tone of our stories."

Given Nussle's weak showing in 1996, Democrats targeted him in 1998. Rob Tully, former head of the Iowa Trial Lawyers Association, moved from Des Moines to his native Dubuque to run in fall 1997. His anti-abortion position took the issue off the table; he charged Nussle was out of touch with the district (he had sold his family home in Manchester after his divorce). Nussle outspent Tully significantly but not overwhelmingly, thanks to large amounts of PAC money. He won 55%–44%, losing Dubuque and Black Hawk Counties by very narrow margins and winning elsewhere.

Cook's Call. *Probably Safe.* While Nussle has not yet proven he has a solid lock on this rather marginal district, his strong 1998 victory is certainly a sign that he has established a solid foothold here. Nussle needs to be wary of changes in the political climate; he was caught off guard in the Democratic year of 1996, but he seems well-prepared for the 2000 challenge.

The People: Pop. 1990: 555,494; 48.9% rural; 17% age 65 + ; 97.4% White, 1.7% Black, 0.5% Asian, 0.3% Amer. Indian, 0.2% Other; 0.6% Hispanic Origin. Households: 61% married couple families; 28.4% married couple fams. w. children; 35.8% college educ.; median household income: $25,010; per capita income: $11,611; median house value: $42,600; median gross rent: $223.

1996 Presidential Vote			1992 Presidential Vote		
Clinton (D)	129,148	(53%)	Clinton (D)	120,228	(44%)
Dole (R)	91,155	(37%)	Bush (R)	95,005	(35%)
Perot (I)	21,377	(9%)	Perot (I)	55,279	(20%)

Rep. Jim Nussle (R)

Elected 1990; b. June 27, 1960, Des Moines; home, Manchester; Luther Col., B.A. 1983, Drake U., J.D. 1985; Lutheran; divorced.

Elected Office: Delaware Cnty. Atty., 1986–90.

Professional Career: Practicing atty., 1985–86.

DC Office: 303 CHOB 20515, 202-225-2911; Fax: 202-225-9129; Web site: www.house.gov/nussle.

District Offices: Dubuque, 319-557-7740; Manchester, 319-927-5141; Mason City, 515-423-0303; Waterloo, 310-235-1109.

Committees: *Budget* (7th of 24 R). *Ways & Means* (11th of 23 R): Trade.

Group Ratings

	ADA	ACLU	AFS	LCV	CON	NTU	NFIB	COC	ACU	NTLC	CHC
1998	10	13	11	31	42	49	100	100	84	92	100
1997	10	—	13	—	91	60	—	100	92	—	—

National Journal Ratings

	1997 LIB — 1997 CONS		1998 LIB — 1998 CONS	
Economic	34% —	65%	39% —	59%
Social	0% —	90%	14% —	81%
Foreign	32% —	65%	39% —	58%

Key Votes of the 105th Congress

1. Clinton Budget Deal	Y	5. Puerto Rico Sthood. Ref.	N	9. Cut $ for B-2 Bombers	Y
2. Education IRAs	Y	6. End Highway Set-asides	Y	10. Human Rights in China	N
3. Req. 2/3 to Raise Taxes	Y	7. School Prayer Amend.	Y	11. Withdraw Bosnia Troops	Y
4. Fast-track Trade	Y	8. Ovrd. Part. Birth Veto	Y	12. End Cuban TV-Marti	N

Election Results

1998 general	Jim Nussle (R)	104,613	(55%)	($902,684)
	Rob Tully (D)	83,405	(44%)	($687,083)
	Others	1,556	(1%)	
1998 primary	Jim Nussle (R)	unopposed		
1996 general	Jim Nussle (R)	127,827	(53%)	($679,904)
	Donna L. Smith (D)	109,731	(46%)	($69,796)

THIRD DISTRICT

As the pioneers did a century and a half ago, the rolling farmland of southern Iowa heads west, from the railroad towns perched below the bluffs on the Mississippi River to the dusty plains above the Missouri River looking over to Nebraska and the West. The southern two tiers of Iowa's counties have none of the state's large cities; the accent here sounds a bit like rural Missouri. Population here has been declining for many years, as the numerous children of large farm families seek opportunity elsewhere, since mechanization and technology require fewer people to work the land.

The 3d Congressional District covers 27 counties in southern Iowa, including almost all of the southern tier, from the Mississippi River border with Illinois almost to the Missouri River border with Nebraska. The 3d also juts north as far as Ames, the home of Iowa State University. There are dozens of notable towns here: Pella, home of the Pella window firm; Newton, home of Maytag appliances; Grinnell, with Grinnell College; Marshalltown, memorialized in *The Music Man*; and Fairfield, the home of Maharishi University and national headquarters of the Natural Law Party, whose presidential nominee John Hagelin got 21% of the vote in surrounding Jefferson County. The historical preference here is mostly Republican, but there are Democratic counties as well, next to heavily Democratic counties in northern Missouri.

The congressman from the 3d District is Leonard Boswell, a Democrat elected in 1996, the first new Iowa Democrat elected to the House in 10 years. He was not the stereotypical freshman, however; he was elected at 62. Boswell grew up on farms in Ringgold and Decatur Counties, near the Missouri border. He was drafted in 1956, at 22, and was a private in the Army. He re-enlisted, graduated first in his class in both fixed wing and helicopter flying school, served two years in Vietnam, and retired as a lieutenant colonel in 1976. Boswell settled down on his farm in Decatur County and became head of the local Farmers' Co-op. He managed to keep it out of bankruptcy during the farm depression of the 1980s and decided to go into politics. He was elected state senator from a six-county Republican district in 1984, served as chairman of Appropriations and, after 1992, Senate president; he was the Democratic nominee for lieutenant governor in 1994.

In 1996, when 3d District conservative Republican Congressman Jim Ross Lightfoot ran for the Senate, Boswell ran for the House. In the primary against state Deputy Attorney General Charles Krogmeier, he won with 58% of the vote, helped by 93% in his state district. The general election contest with Poweshiek County attorney Mike Mahaffey was very much a contest of nice guys. Boswell flew his four-seater Piper Comanche 250 around the district and called for balancing the budget, higher education aid and protections against Medicare reductions, all to be financed with Pentagon cuts and elimination of Medicare waste. Mahaffey ran as a moderate Republican, budget-balancer and term-limits advocate. Boswell drew on his experience: "I'm a farmer, he's a lawyer. I have experience in budgeting. I've been there, done it."

But Boswell was not a political naif. He was endorsed by the Farm Bureau, which usually backs Republicans. He raised more money than Mahaffey and, like other Democrats, ran ads attacking Newt Gingrich and the Republican Medicare plan. This looked all along like one of the closest races in the country, and it was. Mahaffey ran well ahead of Lightfoot's showing in the Senate race in the eastern and northern part of the district. But Boswell ran nearly 20 points ahead of Senator Tom Harkin's showing in his old state Senate district. The result was a 49%–48% Boswell victory, with a margin of 4,019 votes.

Boswell got a seat on Agriculture and, amid dropping farm prices, continued to support the Freedom to Farm Act. He voted for the partial-birth abortion ban and for $18 billion in IMF loans. He voted against fast track in November 1997 because it didn't contain language he wanted on child labor. Republicans charged that he was acting at the behest of unions, which had contributed heavily to his campaign. In September 1998, he switched and voted for fast track, after language was inserted requiring the president to consider child labor laws when negotiating trade agreements. He voted for the 1998 Republican tax bill because of its provisions for farmers. "They can't label me as liberal," he said. "They can't say I'm a tax-and-spend guy."

Boswell did not neglect Iowa issues. On the Transportation Committee he worked for continuation of the ethanol subsidy and got $33 million in road projects, including Highway 330 near Marshalltown, known as "the Ho Chi Minh Trail" because of its high death toll. In 1997 he considered running for governor, but decided against it in June. He conducted more than 50 "listening posts" meetings and 650 staff open office hours in nearly 100 communities.

Because of his narrow 1996 margin, Boswell was one of the Republicans' top 10 incumbent targets. State Senator Larry McKibben won the Republican primary and raised nearly as much money as Boswell. He attacked Boswell for not voting for fast track earlier and for not backing drug sanctions against Mexico; Boswell attacked McKibben for voting against a bill to spend more on anti-drug programs. But Boswell did not present a partisan image. In September 1998 he declined campaign help from Bill Clinton, who had been so helpful in 1996. In October 1998 he was one of 31 Democrats to vote for the Republicans' impeachment inquiry. In a year when most voters' mood was positive, Boswell seemed a comforting figure. As Democratic state chairman John Norris said, "People like Leonard. . . . He's got that kind of easygoing personality and soft-spoken style." Boswell won 57%–41%, carrying 22 of 27 counties.

Cook's Call. *Potentially Competitive.* Boswell's solid 1998 victory belies the underlying competitiveness of this district. Should a down year for Democrats or an anti-incumbent wave hit the state, Boswell could find himself in trouble. Until then, the affable Boswell has a background and a voting record that pretty well mirrors the district and he may avoid a top-tier challenger in 2000.

The People: Pop. 1990: 555,299; 46.3% rural; 17.2% age 65 + ; 97.6% White, 0.9% Black, 1% Asian, 0.2% Amer. Indian, 0.3% Other; 0.7% Hispanic Origin. Households: 60.1% married couple families; 27.1% married couple fams. w. children; 39.1% college educ.; median household income: $24,767; per capita income: $11,567; median house value: $41,400; median gross rent: $236.

1996 Presidential Vote

Clinton (D)	123,246	(50%)
Dole (R)	95,308	(39%)
Perot (I)	21,408	(9%)
Others	4,576	(2%)

1992 Presidential Vote

Clinton (D)	120,495	(45%)
Bush (R)	96,515	(36%)
Perot (I)	47,028	(18%)

Rep. Leonard L. Boswell (D)

Elected 1996; b. Jan. 10, 1934, Harrison Cnty., MO; home, Davis City; Graceland Col., B.A. 1969; Reorganized Latter Day Saints; married (Dody).

Military Career: Army, 1956–76 (Vietnam).

Elected Office: IA Senate, 1984–96, Pres., 1992–96.

Professional Career: Farmer.

DC Office: 1029 LHOB 20515, 202-225-3806; Fax: 202-225-5608; Web site: www.house.gov/boswell.

District Office: Osceola, 515-342-4801.

Committees: *Agriculture* (20th of 24 D): Livestock & Horticulture; Risk Management, Research & Specialty Crops. *Transportation & Infrastructure* (26th of 34 D): Aviation; Water Resources & Environment.

Group Ratings

	ADA	ACLU	AFS	LCV	CON	NTU	NFIB	COC	ACU	NTLC	CHC
1998	65	56	78	38	6	23	50	83	36	29	17
1997	65	—	63	—	80	34	—	70	28	—	—

National Journal Ratings

	1997 LIB — 1997 CONS			1998 LIB — 1998 CONS		
Economic	61%	—	39%	57%	—	43%
Social	66%	—	33%	63%	—	37%
Foreign	60%	—	38%	53%	—	45%

Key Votes of the 105th Congress

1. Clinton Budget Deal	Y	5. Puerto Rico Sthood. Ref.	Y	9. Cut $ for B-2 Bombers	Y
2. Education IRAs	N	6. End Highway Set-asides	N	10. Human Rights in China	Y
3. Req. 2/3 to Raise Taxes	Y	7. School Prayer Amend.	N	11. Withdraw Bosnia Troops	N
4. Fast-track Trade	Y	8. Ovrd. Part. Birth Veto	Y	12. End Cuban TV-Marti	N

Election Results

1998 general	Leonard L. Boswell (D)	107,947	(57%)	($1,041,955)
	Larry McKibben (R)	78,063	(41%)	($847,794)
	Others	3,742	(2%)	
1998 primary	Leonard L. Boswell (D)	unopposed		
1996 general	Leonard L. Boswell (D)	115,914	(49%)	($634,351)
	Mike Mahaffey (R)	111,895	(48%)	($439,269)
	Others	7,066	(3%)	

FOURTH DISTRICT

Iowa, which today seems very much in the middle of the country, was once part of the West. It was not only the home of sober farmers and pious burghers, but also the eastern terminus of the first Transcontinental Railroad, a waystop for people in a hurry to get across the Great Plains to the Rockies and the Pacific Northwest. Those who stayed behind were determined to use the wealth accumulated by methodical husbandry of their fertile farmlands to implant firmly the glories of Western civilization. You can feel that impulse today in Des Moines when you look across the river from downtown at the Victorian Capitol, its gold dome above a Corinthian pediment, or Terrace Hill, the beautifully restored governor's mansion, atop a hill overlooking the Raccoon River. The nearby Living History Farms, which recreate Indian villages, frontier towns and turn-of-the-century farms, show the effort the new settlers made to put their imprint on the environment. The same civilizing impulse can be seen farther west, in the city of Council Bluffs, in the mansion of General Grenville Dodge, who in 1859 lobbied Illinois lawyer Abraham Lincoln on the need for a transcontinental railroad; Lincoln got it through Congress in 1863, Dodge became its chief engineer, and Council Bluffs became its eastern terminus when it was completed in 1869.

Today Iowa is, as one voter said with satisfaction, "in the heart of middle America." Around 1987, after nearly a decade of farm depression, Iowa's economy started to grow again—mostly in and around its cities, especially Des Moines, now spreading into the countryside even as farm counties' population continues to decline. Insurance and printing and service businesses are expanding in office centers downtown and at freeway interchanges; Iowans are driving 100 miles or more to fill the shopping malls at cities' edges. Missing perhaps is the heady confidence of Iowans when they were pushing the frontier west; but missing also is the bedraggled feeling of the 1980s: Des Moines is leading Iowa deliberately into the future.

The 4th Congressional District of Iowa includes Des Moines and most of its expanding suburban fringe, into fast-growing Dallas County and even into Madison County, site of the famous novel and movie. It also proceeds west to Council Bluffs and the Missouri River, along the interstate where communities are growing again. Historically, Des Moines, with its unionized workers and in the midst of corn and hog country and the liberal *Des Moines Register* setting the tone, yearned after farm subsidies and voted heavily Democratic; in the early 1990s it trended mildly toward the Republicans, though it voted for Senator Tom Harkin in 1996 and Governor Tom Vilsack in 1998. Council Bluffs, surrounded by beef grazing territory, where federal intrusion has long been resented, looks west to Omaha, taking on the culturally more conservative tone of Nebraska and the conservative politics of the *Omaha World-Herald*.

The congressman from the 4th District is Greg Ganske, a Republican first elected in a stunning upset in 1994. Ganske grew up in Manchester, where he worked in his father's grocery store, earning his way through the University of Iowa. After medical school he served in the Army Reserves and started a plastic surgery practice in Des Moines, specializing in reconstructive surgery for birth defects and victims of accidents, burns and crimes. He and his wife, a physician, made plenty of money, raised a family and bought a farm.

Ganske decided to run for Congress in 1994. The incumbent was Neal Smith, a Democrat first elected in 1958, chairman of an Appropriations subcommittee, who had not had strong opposition for years. Redistricting had added Council Bluffs in 1992 but Smith won easily that year. Ganske put his own money, ultimately $618,000, into the campaign and, at Newt Gingrich's suggestion, bought a rusty beige 1958 DeSoto, made in the year Smith first won, and drove it around the district with a sign reading, "'58 Nealmobile—WHY is it still running?" Ganske opposed the Clinton health care plan and attacked Smith for "logrolling," saying, "What do 36-year career politicians like Neal Smith always do? They blame each other, spend more money and then raise your taxes." Smith raised and spent more than $1 million, but his claims of clout were undermined when Appropriations Chairman William Natcher died in February 1994 and Smith lost 152–106 in the race to succeed him to the younger and less senior David Obey. Ganske was leading in polls as early as June 1994, and in November he won 53%–46%, winning 65% in Council Bluffs and 62% in rural counties, and losing to Smith in the Des Moines area by only 48%–51%.

In the House Ganske got a seat on the Commerce Committee and compiled a moderate voting record. In Iowa fashion, he condemned plans to build a new Seawolf submarine and NASA plans to send a monkey into space. In spring 1995 he and Pat Roberts assembled 105 Republicans to sign a letter calling for reducing the upper limit on the $500-per-child tax credit from $200,000 to $95,000. He proposed an amendment to this end but it was rejected by the Rules Committee. After expressing some concern about the Republican Medicare plan, he successfully fought to include higher rural reimbursement rates for health plans, and voted for the bill. In 1996 he had serious competition from former nurse and Des Moines weathercaster Connie McBurney, and was a target of the AFL-CIO's barrage of TV ads; in the summer Ganske was trailing in polls. But he fought back. Ganske persuaded TV stations not to run ads charging that he voted to "cut" Medicare, and when the Teamsters ran an ad charging that he took tobacco money, he roared in protest and demonstrated that he did not. Altogether Ganske spent $2.3 million, including $553,000 of his own money; he also raised $668,000 from PACs and over $1 million from individuals. During the August 1996 recess Ganske traveled to Peru, not to junket, but to do charity medical work, operating on children with cleft palates and other disfigurements. In the process he contracted post-viral encephalitis, and was hospitalized in Des Moines and off the campaign trail for weeks. It became difficult to portray him as a picture of greed or indifference. He regained the lead in polls, and won 52%–47% on election day. He lost ground in Council Bluffs and the rural counties, which he carried with 57% and 58% of the votes. But he ran almost exactly even in metro Des Moines.

In his second term Ganske became a major legislator on health issues. From the start he supported HMO reform to allow patients to sue insurers. "I don't see this as a provider issue; I see this as a patient issue," he insisted. But he was clearly influenced by experience. He showed pictures of disfigured children and said that hundreds of patients had HMO coverage denied for surgery as "cosmetic." "People who pay good money for their HMO should not have to rely on charity so their child can have a normal face." Speaker Gingrich appointed him to the bipartisan Medicare Commission, but when it became known in July 1998 that he was going to appear with Bill Clinton in support of the Democrats' HMO reform, other Republicans protested, and Ganske resigned, apparently without rancor or retaliation. "The fact that I would appear at a press conference with the president creates among some Republicans some real heartburn. I want the commission to succeed and I don't want to be the cause of disharmony." Ganske had already joined Democrat John Dingell in seeking a discharge petition for their HMO bill; it was brought to the floor in July 1998 and defeated 217–212, and a Republican alternative passed 216–210. Ganske said there was no retaliation or even unpleasantness from other Republicans. But after the election, he insisted, "The issue is there, and it will be a big one in 1999. . . . I think there will be a number of Republicans who want to do something on this."

On other health issues, Ganske voted against the budget in 1997 because of concerns about Medicare and praised the FDA for allowing irradiation of red meat (contaminated food caused his encephalitis); he continued his volunteer medical work. He backed the Democrats on campaign finance reform. He supported ethanol tax credits and fast track. He worked for road improvements in Des Moines and Council Bluffs. On impeachment, Ganske was considered an uncertain vote but ended up voting in favor.

The 1998 election was effectively settled in March 1998, when Council Bluffs Mayor Tom Hanafan announced he wouldn't run. Democratic nominee Jon Dvorak said in October, "I kind of regret getting into it now"; he had once worked for George McGovern and wondered out loud whether the Watergate burglars may have been trying to see if the Democratic headquarters had information about him. He lost 65%–34%.

Cook's Call. *Potentially Competitive.* Although Ganske avoided a serious challenge in 1998, this does not mean that he is entirely safe from political danger in this swing district. A good candidate could make this a competitive race, but the longer Ganske sits in this seat, the more difficult it will be to dislodge him.

642   IOWA

The People: Pop. 1990: 555,276; 25.6% rural; 14.3% age 65 +; 95.4% White, 2.7% Black, 1.1% Asian, 0.3% Amer. Indian, 0.6% Other; 1.5% Hispanic Origin. Households: 56.8% married couple families; 26.7% married couple fams. w. children; 45.7% college educ.; median household income: $28,591; per capita income: $13,813; median house value: $52,900; median gross rent: $335.

1996 Presidential Vote

Clinton (D) 127,250 (49%)
Dole (R) 107,359 (42%)
Perot (I) 20,296   (8%)

1992 Presidential Vote

Clinton (D) 117,863 (43%)
Bush (R) 107,745 (39%)
Perot (I) 47,835 (17%)

Rep. Greg Ganske (R)

Elected 1994; b. Mar. 31, 1949, New Hampton; home, Des Moines; U. of IA, B.S. 1972, M.D. 1976; Catholic; married (Corrine).

Military Career: Army Reserves, 1986–present.

Professional Career: Farmer; Surgeon, 1976–present.

DC Office: 1108 LHOB 20515, 202-225-4426; Fax: 202-225-3193; Web site: www.house.gov/ganske.

District Offices: Council Bluffs, 712-323-5976; Des Moines, 515-284-4634.

Committees: *Commerce* (16th of 29 R): Finance & Hazardous Materials; Health and Environment; Oversight & Investigations.

Group Ratings

	ADA	ACLU	AFS	LCV	CON	NTU	NFIB	COC	ACU	NTLC	CHC
1998	5	20	33	46	38	36	67	81	64	63	83
1997	30	—	25	—	73	58	—	70	76	—	—

National Journal Ratings

	1997 LIB — 1997 CONS		1998 LIB — 1998 CONS	
Economic	28%	67%	48%	52%
Social	45%	54%	51%	49%
Foreign	54%	45%	43%	53%

Key Votes of the 105th Congress

1. Clinton Budget Deal	Y	5. Puerto Rico Sthood. Ref.	N	9. Cut $ for B-2 Bombers	Y
2. Education IRAs	Y	6. End Highway Set-asides	Y	10. Human Rights in China	Y
3. Req. 2/3 to Raise Taxes	Y	7. School Prayer Amend.	Y	11. Withdraw Bosnia Troops	Y
4. Fast-track Trade	Y	8. Ovrd. Part. Birth Veto	Y	12. End Cuban TV-Marti	Y

Election Results

1998 general	Greg Ganske (R)	129,942	(65%)	($1,364,326)
	Jon Dvorak (D)	67,550	(34%)	($45,003)
	Others	1,904	(1%)	
1998 primary	Greg Ganske (R)	unopposed		
1996 general	Greg Ganske (R)	133,419	(52%)	($2,334,251)
	Connie McBurney (D)	119,790	(47%)	($853,104)

FIFTH DISTRICT

Sioux City, one of the oldest market towns on the Great Plains, is situated picturesquely, nestled below and running up the loess bluffs above the Missouri River. Although still the largest city on the Plains west of Des Moines and north of Omaha, Sioux City has not grown much in the last five decades. Its original economic base has become obsolete, and so has some of the city itself: the waterfront, once raucous with boatmen and stockyard workers, is now quiet; stock-yards have been replaced by IBP's modern (and low-wage) beef factory across the river in Dakota City, Nebraska; downtown stores have been replaced by shopping malls at the edge of town where people will still drive for 100 miles to spend a day doing a season's shopping. Yet many neighborhoods still look as they did during the childhood days of the Friedman twins, Eppie and Popo, better known these last 40-some years as Ann Landers and Abigail Van Buren.

Sioux City is the largest city in the 5th Congressional District of Iowa, which covers most of northern and northwest Iowa, politically an area that, on balance, is a few points more Republican than the rest of the state. Its biggest population centers are Sioux City and Fort Dodge, northwest of Des Moines, to the east. The counties on the gently rolling landscape in between are an ethnic melange: Irish Catholics in Palo Alto, Dutch in Sioux (the most heavily Republican county in Iowa), and the descendants of the English lords who built huge cattle ranches around Le Mars in Plymouth County.

The congressman from the 5th District is Tom Latham, a Republican first elected in 1994. Latham grew up on a farm in Franklin County, near Alexander (population 168) where his family has owned a seed company—a very Iowa business!—since 1947. For years Tom Latham was active in Republican politics, attending the national convention and serving as a farm adviser to Congressman Fred Grandy. In 1994 Grandy ran against Governor Terry Branstad and lost a close primary; Latham fared more happily. Running as an opponent of the Clinton health care plan and supporting Contract with America principles before the Contract existed, he easily beat Sioux City state Senator Brad Banks 62%–38% in the primary and in the general soundly outpolled Democrat Sheila McGuire, one of 47 medical care professionals selected to sit on a White House advisory panel to review the Clinton health care program. "Professor McGuire helped write the Clinton health care plan that would put a bureaucrat between you and your doctor, raise your taxes and close many rural hospitals," a Latham ad said. He won 61%–39%.

In the House Latham has a solidly conservative record. He served one term on the Agriculture Committee and supported the Freedom to Farm Act, which phased out subsidies for most crops—that evidently have little support left in northwest Iowa. Inspired by the gruesome murder of a 19-year-old in Hawarden, he sponsored a successful amendment to allow local law enforcement officers to enter into agreements with the INS to detain illegal immigrants. He helped set up a center on methamphetamines—a big problem in rural Iowa—a media-intensive anti-drug initiative called the Latham project, and wants to allow drug users to sue dealers on product liability grounds. In 1997 he got a seat on the Appropriations Committee and its Agriculture Subcommittee. He rarely speaks on the House floor and doesn't seem to seek media attention beyond his district. "I don't think you judge your effectiveness by how many bills you put forth around here. . . . I'd just as soon we go through at least one session, if not a whole term of Congress, and not pass any new legislation and just do our oversight role of the agencies and bureaucracies here." He protested against an amendment to place a 14 million acre limit on enrollments in the Conservation Reserve Program. He helped rally 800 letters of protest when the FTC threatened to order Nestle to sell the Friskies pet food plant in Fort Dodge; the agency demurred. When the new transportation bill allotted $10 million for a light-rail system for Sioux City, he protested. "Just to pull this pie out of the sky and drop a $10 million bomb on Sioux City does not make sense."

Latham was re-elected easily in 1996 and without opposition in 1998.

Cook's Call. *Safe.* Tom Latham represents the most Republican district in the state and can keep a hold of it until the cows come home.

644   IOWA

The People: Pop. 1990: 555,457; 52.5% rural; 18.8% age 65 + ; 98.1% White, 0.6% Black, 0.6% Asian, 0.4% Amer. Indian, 0.3% Other; 0.8% Hispanic Origin. Households: 61.5% married couple families; 28.3% married couple fams. w. children; 38.3% college educ.; median household income: $24,150; per capita income: $11,461; median house value: $37,200; median gross rent: $205.

1996 Presidential Vote			1992 Presidential Vote		
Dole (R)	106,615	(45%)	Bush (R)	109,966	(42%)
Clinton (D)	104,775	(44%)	Clinton (D)	99,112	(38%)
Perot (I)	23,051	(10%)	Perot (I)	50,343	(19%)

Rep. Tom Latham (R)

Elected 1994; b. July 14, 1948, Hampton; home, Alexander; Wartburg Col., 1966–67, IA St. U., 1967–70; Lutheran; married (Kathy).

Professional Career: Farmer; Bank Teller/Bookkeeper, 1970–72; Independent Insurance Agent, 1972–74; Hartford Insurance Mktg. Rep., 1974–76; Co-Owner, Latham Seed Co., 1976–present.

DC Office: 324 CHOB 20515, 202-225-5476; Fax: 202-225-3301; Web site: www.house.gov/latham.

District Offices: Ft. Dodge, 515-573-2738; Orange City, 712-737-8708; Sioux City, 712-277-2114; Spencer, 712-262-6480.

Committees: *Appropriations* (28th of 34 R): Agriculture, Rural Development, & FDA; Commerce, Justice, State & the Judiciary; Energy & Water Development.

Group Ratings

	ADA	ACLU	AFS	LCV	CON	NTU	NFIB	COC	ACU	NTLC	CHC
1998	0	6	0	15	13	48	100	100	92	95	100
1997	10	—	13	—	62	53	—	100	76	—	—

National Journal Ratings

	1997 LIB — 1997 CONS		1998 LIB — 1998 CONS	
Economic	16%	82%	15%	81%
Social	0%	90%	0%	97%
Foreign	46%	53%	47%	51%

Key Votes of the 105th Congress

1. Clinton Budget Deal	Y	5. Puerto Rico Sthood. Ref.	N	9. Cut $ for B-2 Bombers	Y
2. Education IRAs	Y	6. End Highway Set-asides	Y	10. Human Rights in China	N
3. Req. 2/3 to Raise Taxes	Y	7. School Prayer Amend.	Y	11. Withdraw Bosnia Troops	Y
4. Fast-track Trade	Y	8. Ovrd. Part. Birth Veto	Y	12. End Cuban TV-Marti	N

Election Results

1998 general	Tom Latham (R)	unopposed		($450,391)
1998 primary	Tom Latham (R)	unopposed		
1996 general	Tom Latham (R)	147,576	(65%)	($477,173)
	MacDonald Smith (D)	75,785	(34%)	($126,516)

KANSAS

"Like everyone else," James Dickenson writes of his grandmother Mary Phipps, who lived her 91 years in Kansas, "she was taught that the earth and the other planets circled the sun, but deep down she had the feeling that the sun and the rest of the cosmos really revolved around western Kansas. . . . She took as the First Principle that bread, the staff of life, was one of the bases of existence itself, along with air and water. From this flowed the inescapable conclusion that wheat farmers were truly engaged in the Lord's work." These words open the book *Home on the Range*, in which Dickenson, for three decades a top national political reporter, starts with his own family and boyhood in Rawlins County to explain how Kansas came to be what it was, and how it is ceasing to be that and becoming something else.

But Kansas has always been quintessentially American, which is not to say entirely placid or entirely unflavorful. In 1989 when Russia's onetime prime minister Yevgeny Primakov wanted to see "real Americans," he flew out with Bob Dole to Dodge City, to visit Boot Hill Museum and the Long Branch Saloon. Kansas, like so much of Russia, may look quiet, full of solid farmers who work hard and have deep roots in the soil, the place around which the cosmos revolves. But Kansas's history, like Russia's, has also been punctuated by uprisings, intellectual and violent, by moments of anger and rage sweeping through the tall sheaves like a tornado wind. The difference, of course, is that Russian traditions of law and liberty, culture and civility are weak, while in Kansas, as in all America, they are remarkably strong.

Kansas literally began in a moment of violence, the Bleeding Kansas of the 1850s, that led proximately to the terrible war that split the whole nation. The trigger was the Kansas-Nebraska Act of 1854, which left to local settlers the question of whether this new Kansas Territory would be a free or slave state. Pro-slavery "bushwhackers" rode over the line from Missouri, stealing elections and writing a pro-slavery constitution. But much larger numbers of free-soil "jayhawkers" from New England and the New England-Yankee-settled Great Lakes states put down roots and, despite the massacres of the mad John Brown, prevailed and established their own law and order. The effect on national politics was tumultuous: the Democratic Party was split, the Republican Party was created, the nation was plunged into Civil War. The effect on Kansas was calming: the anti-slavery majority bent the soil to the plow and built small towns thick with schools, churches and colleges, to the point that in the 1939 color movie, *Wizard of Oz*, the Kansas scenes were shot in dreary black and white as the image of dull, prim, old-fashioned Middle America. But the rebellious impulse did not totally die out. Kansans' livelihoods were always at risk: hailstorms, grasshopper invasions, dry seasons or a drop in world farm prices could mean disaster for thousands. The high-rainfall 1880s attracted hundreds of thousands of new settlers to Kansas; the low-rainfall 1890s produced a bust and a populist rebellion. "What you farmers should do," said orator Mary Ellen Lease, "is to raise less corn and more hell." For a few years in the 1890s, and then in farm rebellions of the 1930s, 1950s and 1970s, Kansans did, but afterwards always returned to jayhawker Republicanism.

Kansas remains Republican in the late 1990s, but not in quite the same old way. Its most famous politician, Bob Dole, still returns occasionally to his small home town of Russell, out on the plains. But Kansas's population is increasingly metropolitan. Some 35% of Kansas's votes in 1998 were cast in the mostly suburban counties from Kansas City west to Topeka, and another 14% in Wichita's Sedgwick County. These suburban Kansans have produced their own kind of rebellion. In 1992 27% of Kansans voted for Ross Perot—his fifth best showing in the nation—and his vote was heaviest not in the wheat country but from just at the edge of metropolitan expansion and in the sparsely populated Flint Hills, places where young families live, commuting to jobs and shopping malls 50 or even 100 miles away. In 1994 the Kansas Re-

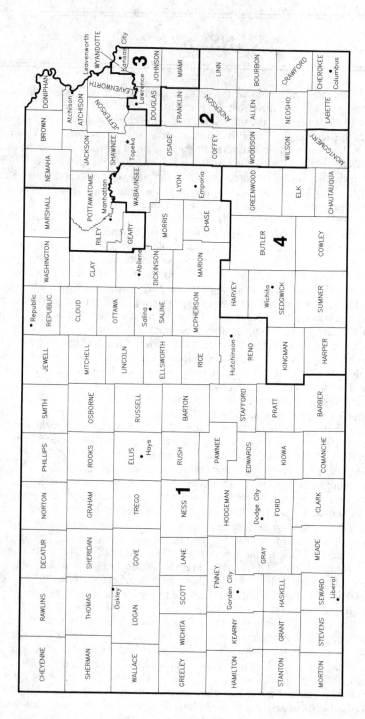

—— Congressional district boundaries
effective June 3, 1992.

Miles

0 10 20 30 40

publican Party apparatus was taken over by Christian conservatives, as two conservative Republicans won Topeka- and Wichita-centered House seats formerly held by Democrats. In 1996 Kansas's two Republican Senators left the scene—Bob Dole when he resigned from the Senate in June 1996, to spark up his presidential campaign, and Nancy Kassebaum when she decided not to run for reelection that fall after three terms. Replacing them was Pat Roberts, the chairman of the House Agriculture Committee and author of the 1996 Freedom to Farm Act, and 2d District freshman Sam Brownback, who beat interim appointee and party moderate Sheila Frahm in the primary.

That seemed to signal a rebellion against moderate Republican Governor Bill Graves, and conservatives did take over leadership positions in the legislature. They especially resented his support of abortion rights. But when state party Chairman David Miller ran against Graves in the 1998 primary, he was crushed, 73%–27%. Graves went on to win re-election by a similar margin, 73%–23%, and Sam Brownback was re-elected to a six-year term, 65%–32%. These incumbent victories were all evidence of a strong contentment. Yet after a record harvest in 1997, wheat prices plummeted in 1998. In the old days, that would have triggered a farm rebellion and a demand for goverment aid, and there was a little of that, but not very much. More visible (or smellable) was the protest against corporate hog lots in southwest Kansas, where Graves nearly lost a few counties in the primary. With rising wages and low unemployment (Hispanics are flocking to work in meatpacking factories in towns like Dodge City, because no locals are interested in the $22,000 wages), with many fewer family farmers dependent on wheat prices, Kansas seems to be well on its way to becoming a suburban, fairly conservative, quite Republican state. What would Mary Ellen Lease or John Brown have said?

Governor. Kansas's governor is Bill Graves, a Republican elected in 1994. Graves grew up in Salina, where his family had a trucking firm; he worked in the business from loading dock to management, even though he moved to a suburb of Kansas City (his wife practiced law in Missouri). In 1986 he was elected secretary of State. In 1994 he ran for governor. Republican Kansas has elected Democratic governors more often than not over the last 30 years, and the initial favorite was Democratic Congressman Jim Slattery, a 12-year moderate who in spring 1994 cast a decisive vote against Democratic health care plans in the Commerce Committee. Slattery won a five-candidate primary with an impressive 53%. Graves meanwhile won a six-candidate Republican primary with 41%. "Load 'em high and tight," he repeated over and over again, as his family had loaded the trailers of 18-wheelers with cartons of goods. Graves called Slattery a "double-dealing Washington congressman" and pledged to keep spending down, to rein in government. The race blew open in the last weeks, and Graves won 64%–36%—the widest margin in more than 20 years—carrying 102 of 105 counties.

In his first term, Graves had a mostly conservative record, producing tax cuts every year, cutting spending one year and reducing regulation. He was comfortable with business-oriented Republicans but clashed with the new conservatives who controlled the state House and state party. The House pushed for even bigger tax cuts, and conservatives attacked Graves's opposition to abortion restrictions and school vouchers and opposed his appointment of moderate Lieutenant Governor Sheila Frahm to Bob Dole's Senate seat in June 1996; Sam Brownback, already in the race, beat her in the August primary. In the 1998 legislative session Graves sought to mollify critics, even as his job rating soared to 75%. He signed a partial-birth abortion ban and a law to regulate hog lots. He signed a campaign finance law that requires identification of organizations that "expressly advocate" the election or defeat of "clearly identified candidates"; this was aimed at the Triad group that supported Brownback in 1996. When the two houses disagreed on which tax cut to back, Graves compromised by backing both, for a $247 million cut.

Even so, Republican Party Chairman David Miller jumped into the race in May, to end "moral free fall." Evidently he assumed he could turn activist support into votes. But Graves kept trotting out attractive positions: taking away driver's licenses of violent high schoolers, strong penalties for methamphetamines, generous adoption tax credits, a four-year elimination of the property tax on vehicles, relaxed restrictions on grain elevators to accommodate farmers. The teachers' union and the AFL-CIO supported Graves. In a climate of contentment, Graves won 73%–27%. Graves carried all 105 counties; Miller came closest where the issue was not abortion but hog lots. The Democratic candidate in the general was 12-year state legislator Tom Sawyer. He was heavily outspent and never got his message out. And voters seemed uninterested. Graves won 73%–23%, carrying every county and winning the highest percentage for governor in Kansas's history.

After the election, Graves may have set the conservatives' teeth on edge. He noted the defeat of conservative 3d District Congressman Vince Snowbarger: "I think to an extent some of the more strident views and positions of conservatives just don't sit well with a majority of voters" He announced that his elimination of the vehicle tax might take five rather than four years. But he also called for more tax cuts and promised a transportation package and increased per pupil education funding.

Senior Senator. Sam Brownback grew up on a farm in Anderson County, some 50 miles from Kansas City, was student body president at Kansas State University and briefly was a farm broadcaster. After law school, Brownback practiced law for four years in Manhattan, Kansas, in the 1980s; he was appointed secretary of the state Board of Agriculture in 1986 and served until it was abolished in 1993. He claims credit for encouraging the use of wheat to make plastics and cattle hides to make wound dressings. He was a White House Fellow, working from 1990–91 for U.S. Trade Representative Carla Hills. In March 1994 he announced for Congress, condemning "a welfare system that discourages the work ethic and encourages the disintegration of families and a government that can't say no to spending or yes to reform." Brownback won the three-way House primary 48%–35%–16%. In the general he faced John Carlin, governor from 1978–86. Brownback won 66%–34%, carrying every county.

Brownback was one of the enthusisatic 1994 freshmen who tried to shake up the House. He was put in charge of selling off a House annex building, which proved harder than expected. He pushed successfully to reduce Congress's own budget. He headed a group of "New Federalists," who sought to abolish three cabinet departments. He pushed hard for the gift ban rule which Republicans, after hesitating, passed. He backed the McCain-Feingold campaign finance bill and in 1995 spoke at Ross Perot's United We Stand convention denouncing "influence peddling" in Washington. On immigration he played a key role in separating the legal and illegal immigration issues, which led to passage of a tough measure against illegal immigrants but no major reductions in the number of legal immigrants.

On May 15, 1996, Bob Dole surprised just about everyone when he announced he was resigning from the Senate on June 11. On May 17, Brownback announced he would seek the seat, noting, "They are size 25 shoes that even Michael Jordan couldn't fill." Governor Bill Graves's choice to fill the vacancy, Lieutenant Governor Sheila Frahm, delayed ten days before accepting. Though both were labeled conservative, Frahm and Brownback presented a strong contrast. She was pro-choice on abortion, he anti-abortion. Brownback accused her of voting as a state legislator to raise taxes $500 million; she criticized his "slash and burn" approach to federal spending. Graves and Senator Nancy Kassebaum endorsed Frahm; William Bennett of Empower America and James Dobson of Focus on the Family endorsed Brownback. In the August primary, Brownback won 55%–42%.

In the general election for the remaining two years of Dole's term, Brownback faced a Democrat with a great political name, Wichita stockbroker Jill Docking, wife of a former lieutenant governor whose father and grandfather both served as governor. Docking promised "Kansas common sense," likened herself to Kassebaum, and when charged with being a Ted Kennedy liberal asked: "Did you ever meet a liberal stockbroker?" Brownback campaigned on the 3 Rs: "Reduce, reform and return. Reduce the size and scope of the federal government. Reform the Congress. Return to the basic values that built the country: work and family and the recognition of a higher moral authority." He promised to serve only two terms—presumably two full terms. Both candidates spent liberally, and some fall polls showed the race close. But Brownback won by the convincing though not overwhelming margin of 54%–43%.

Brownback brought his strongminded politics to the Senate—he has had a near-perfect conservative voting record—but has modulated some stands. With a dollop more seniority than other senators elected in 1994, he ended up with two subcommittee chairmanships. One was the Governmental Affairs Subcommittee on the District of Columbia, where he backed a 15% flat tax for D.C. residents and held hearings on shock rock and gangsta rap. The other was Foreign Affairs' Near Eastern and South Asian Affairs; he soon traveled to see Binyamin Netanyahu, Yasir Arafat and Hosni Mubarak; later he co-sponsored the law to aid opponents of Saddam Hussein. He criticized the Clinton Administration strongly for discouraging UNSCOM inspections in Iraq. He moved to repeal the Pressler amendment that had barred U.S. military aid to Pakistan since 1990. He backs a "Silk Road strategy" to encourage east-west ties between the U.S. and oil-rich Central Asia. He led the effort to present the Congressional Gold Medal to Mother Teresa, which was done in June 1997.

Brownback seeks a limited antitrust exemption for television networks so they can work together to limit TV violence. He was a chief sponsor of the repeal of the marriage penalty (which didn't pass) and for eliminating the Internal Revenue Code at the end of 2000 to force tax simplification and reform. He wants to require local government approval before rail-to-trail conversions. Once in the Senate, he dropped his support of McCain-Feingold, and, agreeing with Campaign Chairman Mitch McConnell, in May 1997 said, "McCain-Feingold is based on an unconstitutional premise of trying to restrict political speech." He would require 50% of individual contributions to be in-state. Common Cause, which opposes advocacy ads, ran them against Brownback in October 1997.

Campaign finance might have caused Brownback some embarrassment in 1998, as he sought reelection to a full six-year term. In March 1997 the *Kansas City Star* ran stories revealing that Brownback's in-laws gave $32,500 to seven PACs which promptly gave his campaign $31,500. All involved denied any earmarking. Then it was revealed that an organization called Triad directed money into Kansas conservatives' 1996 campaigns and also ran issue ads boosting Brownback in October 1996. There was no proof of wrongdoing, but an articulate opponent might have made something of it. But in January 1998 Docking declined to run again. Neither Wichita oil billionaire Bill Koch nor Agriculture Secretary and former 4th District Congressman Dan Glickman was interested. His Democratic opponent, Paul Feleciano, charged that Brownback was "bigoted," but he raised virtually no money. Brownback won 65%–32%, well above his 1996 showing.

Junior Senator. Pat Roberts is from a fine Kansas Republican background: his abolitionist great-grandfather founded Kansas's second oldest newspaper, and his father, Wes Roberts, was briefly Republican National Committee chairman during the Eisenhower years. Pat Roberts has spent most of his adult life preparing for the place he is in now. After four years in the Marine Corps and five years running an Arizona newspaper, he worked for two years as an aide to Senator Frank Carlson and 12 years as chief aide to 1st District Congressman Keith Sebelius. When Sebelius retired in 1980, Roberts won the seat with 56% in a three-candidate Republican primary. For 14 years, in the minority in the House, he concentrated on farm issues, learning their intricacies and minutiae, traveling in a van to keep in touch with constituents in a district so large that it took two weeks to visit every county seat. His voting record was moderate, and he looked after Kansas interests—raising Medicare payments for rural areas and changing wetlands law that protect "some low spot in your field where no self-respecting duck would ever land."

Then, in January 1995, Roberts became chairman of the House Agriculture Committee. He had long understood that the huge subsidies of the early 1980s would never return: "Farm programs have declined an average of 9% since 1986 and are going to go on declining." Faced with Republican budget parameters, Roberts fashioned a Freedom to Farm bill which would phase out subsidies over seven years. In September 1995 his bill failed in committee when

Southern Republicans eager to protect cotton, rice and peanut subsidies voted against it. But in November 1995, Roberts persuaded Agriculture conferees to include most of his bill in the 1996 budget reconciliation bill, which Clinton vetoed. He agreed to maintain cotton and rice marketing loans and managed to preserve the conservation reserve program popular in Kansas. But the overall thrust of his bill was revolutionary, the biggest change in agriculture policy since the New Deal act of 1933. Roberts's new bill passed the Agriculture Committee 29–17 in January 1996, the full House in February, and became law in April. There was tension with appropriators Bob Livingston and Joe Skeen, who resented Roberts's mandatory payments, and he resented their budget limits; but the reform passed. In 1998 it was threatened after crop prices plunged; in May Roberts, who chairs the Agriculture subcommittee on Production and Price Competitiveness, pleaded that reopening the farm bill was like "asking the Boston strangler for a neck massage." Instead, the House and Senate passed a farm aid bill in mid-summer to accelerate $5.5 billion in payments.

Roberts has tried to encourage farm exports in several ways, opposing cargo preferences, urging passage of fast track for trade agreements and replenishment of IMF funds. He worked in 1998 to get farm commodities removed from sanctions against India and Pakistan after their nuclear tests, and with Sam Brownback sponsored a unanimously passed resolution to revise the Glenn anti-proliferation law by giving the president authority to temporarily waive unilateral economic sanctions; he supports a permanent change in the law. Roberts serves on Armed Services and has criticized the military's state of readiness and personnel retention, and has a bill to reverse the 1986 law reducing 20-year retirement benefits from 50% to 40% of base pay. He criticized the administration in 1997 for lack of candor on Bosnia, and in September 1998 sponsored an amendment to require an explanation of mission, disclosure of costs and timetable for American involvement in Kosovo. "The Clinton Administration's foreign policy lacks focus and direction," he said.

Roberts was the first House member to give up a committee chairmanship to run for the Senate since Lister Hill in 1938 (and Hill got appointed to his Senate seat). When Nancy Kassebaum announced her retirement from the Senate in November 1995, Roberts was busy working on the Freedom to Farm Act and declined to run. When the bill's fortunes improved, he announced his candidacy in January 1996; the law would remove much of the power of the committee, and under new Republican rules he was limited to three terms as chairman. He won the August primary with an overwhelming 78% in a four-way race and in the general election faced state Treasurer Sally Thompson. She called Roberts a Washington insider who had lost touch with Kansas and who profited personally in Washington. Roberts responded, "My experience is the right kind to continue getting government out of our lives and pocketbooks," and he charged that she mismanaged funds in the Municipal Investment Pool, losing $20 million. Roberts won easily, 62%–34%, losing only the county that contains Kansas City and carrying the 104 others.

Presidential politics. Except for 1964, when it narrowly favored Lyndon Johnson over Barry Goldwater, Kansas has voted Republican for president throughout the last 60 years. It was also one of Ross Perot's best states in 1992. In 1996 Kansans were so elated with Dole's early success in wrapping up the Republican nomination that the state legislature voted to cancel the April primary, ensuring unanimous support for their native son at the San Diego Republican Convention.

Congressional districting. Kansas lost one of its five seats in the 1990 Census. There has been much reshuffling since. The House delegation has shifted from 2–2 to 4–0 and now 3–1 Republican.

The People: Est. Pop. 1998: 2,629,067; Pop. 1990: 2,477,574, up 6.1% 1990–1998. 1% of U.S. total, 32d largest; 30.9% rural. Median age: 34.7 years. 14.4% 65 years and over. 90.2% White, 5.7% Black, 1.3% Asian, 0.9% Amer. Indian, 1.9% Other; 3.6% Hispanic Origin. Households: 58.5% married couple families; 28.3% married couple fams. w. children; 48.4% college educ.; median household income: $-

27,291; per capita income: $13,300; 67.9% owner occupied housing; median house value: $52,200; median monthly rent: $285. 3.8% Unemployment. 1998 Voting age pop.: 1,925,000. 1998 Turnout: 743,288; 39% of VAP. Registered voters (1998): 1,513,685; 433,759 D (29%), 685,107 R (45%), 394,819 unaffiliated and minor parties (26%).

Political Lineup: Governor, Bill Graves (R); Lt. Gov., Gary Sherrer (R); Secy. of State, Ron Thornburgh (R); Atty. Gen., Carla Stovall (R); Treasurer, Tim Shallenburger (R); State Senate, 40 (13 D, 27 R); Majority Leader, Tim Emert (R); State House, 125 (48 D, 77 R); House Speaker, Robin Jennison (R). Senators, Sam Brownback (R) and Pat Roberts (R). Representatives, 4 (1 D, 3 R).

Elections Division: 785-296-4561; **Filing Deadline for U.S. Congress:** June 10, 2000.

1996 Presidential Vote

Dole (R)	583,245	(54%)
Clinton (D)	387,659	(36%)
Perot (I)	92,639	(9%)

1992 Presidential Vote

Bush (R)	449,469	(39%)
Clinton (D)	389,704	(34%)
Perot (I)	311,316	(27%)

GOVERNOR

Gov. Bill Graves (R)

Elected 1994, term expires Jan. 2003; b. Jan. 9, 1953, Salina; home, Lenexa; KS Wesleyan U., B.A. 1975, U. of KS, 1976–79; Methodist; married (Linda).

Elected Office: KS Secy. of State, 1986–94.

Professional Career: Graves Truck Line; KS Deputy Secy. of State, 1980–84; KS Asst. Secy of State, 1984–85.

Office: State Capitol, 2d Fl., Topeka, 66612, 913-296-3232; Fax: 913-296-7973; Web site: www.state.ks.us.

Election Results

1998 gen.	Bill Graves (R)	544,882	(73%)
	Tom Sawyer (D)	168,243	(23%)
	Others	29,540	(4%)
1998 prim.	Bill Graves (R)	225,782	(73%)
	David Miller (R)	84,368	(27%)
1994 gen.	Bill Graves (R)	526,113	(64%)
	Jim Slattery (D)	294,733	(36%)

652   KANSAS

SENATORS

Sen. Sam Brownback (R)

Elected 1996, seat up 2004; b. Sept. 12, 1956, Garnett; home, Topeka; KS St. U., B.S. 1978, U. of KS, J.D. 1982; Methodist; married (Mary).

Elected Office: U.S. House of Reps., 1994–96.

Professional Career: Radio broadcaster, KKSU, 1978–79; Practicing atty., 1982–86, 1993; Prof., KS St. U. Law Schl., 1982–86; Ogden & Leonardville City Atty., 1983–86; KS Secy. of Agriculture, 1986–93; White House Fellow, Office of USTR, 1990–91.

DC Office: 303 HSOB, 20510, 202-224-6521; Fax: 202-228-1265; Web site: www.senate.gov/~brownback.

State Offices: Garden City, 316-275-1124; Overland Park, 913-492-6378; Pittsburg, 316-231-6040; Topeka, 785-233-2503; Wichita, 316-264-8066.

Committees: *Commerce, Science & Transportation* (11th of 11 R): Aviation; Communications; Consumer Affairs, Foreign Commerce & Tourism; Manufacturing & Competitiveness; Surface Transportation & Merchant Marine. *Foreign Relations* (7th of 10 R): African Affairs; International Operations; Near Eastern & South Asian Affairs (Chmn.). *Health, Education, Labor & Pensions* (8th of 10 R): Children & Families; Public Health. *Joint Economic Committee* (5th of 10 Sens.).

Group Ratings

	ADA	ACLU	AFS	LCV	CON	NTU	NFIB	COC	ACU	NTLC	CHC
1998	0	14	0	0	52	68	100	94	92	100	100
1997	0	—	0	—	89	84	—	100	100	—	—

National Journal Ratings

	1997 LIB — 1997 CONS	1998 LIB — 1998 CONS
Economic	0% — 89%	12% — 85%
Social	0% — 83%	12% — 79%
Foreign	0% — 77%	12% — 75%

Key Votes of the 105th Congress

1. Bal. Budget Amend.	Y	5. Satcher for Surgeon Gen.	N	9. Chem. Weapons Treaty	N
2. Clinton Budget Deal	Y	6. Highway Set-asides	N	10. Cuban Humanitarian Aid	N
3. Cloture on Tobacco	N	7. Table Child Gun locks	Y	11. Table Bosnia Troops	N
4. Education IRAs	Y	8. Ovrd. Part. Birth Veto	Y	12. $ for Test-ban Treaty	N

Election Results

1998 general	Sam Brownback (R)	474,639	(65%)	($1,719,612)
	Paul Feleciano Jr. (D)	229,718	(32%)	($39,500)
	Others	22,879	(3%)	
1998 primary	Sam Brownback (R)	unopposed		
1996 general	Sam Brownback (R)	574,021	(54%)	($2,269,550)
	Jill Docking (D)	461,344	(43%)	($1,125,844)
	Others	29,351	(3%)	

Sen. Pat Roberts (R)

Elected 1996, seat up 2002; b. Apr. 20, 1936, Topeka; home, Dodge City; KS St. U., B.A. 1958; United Methodist; married (Franki).

Military Career: Marine Corps, 1958–62.

Elected Office: U.S. House of Reps., 1980–96.

Professional Career: Co-owner, editor, *The Westsider* (AZ newspaper) 1962–67; A.A., U.S. Sen. Frank Carlson, 1967–68; A.A., U.S. Rep. Keith Sebelius, 1968–80.

DC Office: 302 HSOB, 20510, 202-224-4774; Fax: 202-224-3514; Web site: www.senate.gov/~roberts.

State Offices: Dodge City, 316-227-2244; Prairie Village, 913-648-3103; Topeka, 785-295-2745; Wichita, 316-263-0416.

Committees: *Agriculture, Nutrition & Forestry* (6th of 10 R): Production & Price Competitiveness (Chmn.); Research, Nutrition & General Legislation. *Armed Services* (8th of 11 R): Airland Forces; Emerging Threats & Capabilities (Chmn.); Readiness & Management Support. *Ethics (Select)* (2d of 3 R). *Intelligence* (8th of 9 R).

Group Ratings

	ADA	ACLU	AFS	LCV	CON	NTU	NFIB	COC	ACU	NTLC	CHC
1998	0	14	0	0	4	56	88	100	84	79	91
1997	15	—	0	—	59	71	—	90	68	—	—

National Journal Ratings

	1997 LIB — 1997 CONS		1998 LIB — 1998 CONS	
Economic	35%	— 64%	18%	— 72%
Social	28%	— 62%	12%	— 79%
Foreign	50%	— 49%	12%	— 75%

Key Votes of the 105th Congress

1. Bal. Budget Amend.	Y	5. Satcher for Surgeon Gen.	N	9. Chem. Weapons Treaty	Y
2. Clinton Budget Deal	Y	6. Highway Set-asides	N	10. Cuban Humanitarian Aid	Y
3. Cloture on Tobacco	N	7. Table Child Gun locks	Y	11. Table Bosnia Troops	N
4. Education IRAs	Y	8. Ovrd. Part. Birth Veto	Y	12. $ for Test-ban Treaty	N

Election Results

1996 general	Pat Roberts (R)	652,677	(62%)	($2,305,898)
	Sally Thompson (D)	362,380	(34%)	($659,066)
	Others	37,243	(4%)	
1996 primary	Pat Roberts (R)	245,411	(78%)	
	Tom Little (R)	25,052	(8%)	
	Thomas L. Oyler (R)	23,266	(7%)	
	Richard L. Cooley (R)	20,060	(6%)	
1990 general	Nancy Landon Kassebaum (R)	578,605	(74%)	($521,140)
	Dick Williams (D)	207,491	(26%)	($16,627)

FIRST DISTRICT

"A prairie is not any old piece of flatland in the Midwest," writes Kansas-born reporter Dennis Farney. "No, a prairie is wine-colored grass, dancing in the wind. A prairie is a sun-splashed hillside, bright with wild flowers. A prairie is a fleeting cloud shadow, the song of the meadowlark. It is the wild land that has never felt the slash of the plow." This prairie once covered almost all of Kansas. Now only a little virgin prairie can still be found, in the Flint Hills region west and south of Topeka, where the waist-deep sea of grass still waves in the wind as it did when the pioneers on the Santa Fe Trail went west through here some 150 years ago; the Tallgrass Prairie National Preserve was created in 1996 to protect this unique landscape. Much of it was grazing land, first for buffalo, then for the cattle driven to Kansas railheads like Abilene and Dodge City in the 1870s and 1880s, a brief moment in history recaptured with varying accuracy in movies over a much longer span, and commemorated in Dodge City's Boot Hill Museum.

Then, after the harsh winter of 1886–87 wiped out the cattle herds, came the plow and barbed wire (commemorated in LaCrosse's Barbed Wire Museum), which enabled farmers to keep livestock out of their wheatfields. The farmers also brought to this vacant landscape Yankee civilization, with its schools and churches, and some foreign traditions as well, like the Cathedral of the Plains built by German Catholics. Now this civilization is threatened. "My great-grandparents and grandparents were part of the stream of settlers who migrated to western Kansas after the Civil War to become wheat farmers," writes James Dickenson in his elegiac *Home on the Range*. "They broke the virgin sod, erected houses, barns, schools, churches and towns, and made the area one of the most agriculturally productive in the world. A little more than a century later, the population has ebbed away from this area and many of the farms, schools, churches and towns lie vacant, dilapidated and boarded up like old boomtowns."

The 1st Congressional District consists of most of this expanse of Kansas, almost everything from the Flint Hills and Abilene west. Its 66 counties (only the Nebraska 3d and South Dakota at-large have more) increased from 76,000 people in 1870 to 570,000 in 1890; then growth slowed to 666,000 in 1940 and dropped to 619,000 in 1990. Population here has dropped since 1980 almost everywhere except the natural gas exploration areas around Dodge City, its largest town, Salina, and German-Catholic Ellis County, with the high birth rates most Catholic communities had 30 years ago. For years young people left here and community institutions were threatened by slow growth; in the late 1990s unemployment has been low and new meatpacking plants have attracted Latinos from Texas and California to fill jobs. Politically, the 1st remains heavily Republican—indeed in the prosperous middle 1990s more so than in the economically troubled 1890s.

The congressman from the 1st District is Jerry Moran, elected in 1996. Moran grew up in Plainville in Rooks County and got his start in politics as an intern for Representative Keith Sebelius, where Moran's predecessor, now Senator Pat Roberts, was a long-time aide. He worked as a banker for four years before attending law school at the University of Kansas. He was elected to the state Senate in 1988 where he fought to cut taxes and, as chairman of Judiciary, pushed to give judges greater flexibility on juvenile crime. In 1995 he became state Senate majority leader, succeeding Sheila Frahm who became lieutenant governor and then U.S. senator from June to November 1996. When Pat Roberts announced in January 1996 that he would run for the Senate, Moran stepped into the 1st District race and, with the help of other Republicans, avoided serious primary competition. He won 76% of the vote in the August primary, which was tantamount to election; in November he was elected 73%–24%.

His voting record has been moderate on economic and cultural issues, and he has pursued district causes. He argued that Medicare's Interim Payment System imposed too great a burden on rural home health care agencies, and wants greater reimbursement. He called for government help in transporting grain and guaranteed loans for short line railroads as the newly merged Union Pacific seemed unable to carry Kansas's record harvests in 1997 and 1998. He sponsored laws to allow farmers ousted from the Conservation Reserve Program to let land lie fallow one more season if they hadn't planted winter wheat. He protested when CRP credits to farmers providing habitat for the endangered burying beetle were endangered when USDA bureaucrats decided the beetle doesn't live in the region.

During recesses, Moran has logged 5,000 miles around the district; in August 1998 he conducted 61 town hall meetings (people here expect to see their congressman without driving to the next county over). He was rewarded at election time 1998 with a record 81% of the vote.

Cook's Call. *Safe.* Barring a self-inflicted political wound, Moran should not have trouble holding onto this very Republican district.

The People: Pop. 1990: 619,371; 51.3% rural; 17.8% age 65 + ; 94.3% White, 1.3% Black, 0.8% Asian, 0.5% Amer. Indian, 3.2% Other; 5.1% Hispanic Origin. Households: 60.9% married couple families; 28.3% married couple fams. w. children; 42.8% college educ.; median household income: $23,433; per capita income: $11,328; median house value: $38,200; median gross rent: $218.

1996 Presidential Vote		
Dole (R)	167,237	(62%)
Clinton (D)	75,840	(28%)
Perot (I)	25,055	(9%)

1992 Presidential Vote		
Bush (R)	122,621	(42%)
Perot (I)	85,004	(29%)
Clinton (D)	81,423	(28%)

Rep. Jerry Moran (R)

Elected 1996; b. May 29, 1954, Great Bend; home, Hays; U. of KS, B.S. 1976, J.D. 1981; Methodist; married (Robba).

Elected Office: KS Senate, 1988–96, Majority Ldr., 1995–97.

Professional Career: Operations Officer, Consolidated State Bank, 1975–77; Mgr., Farmers State Bank & Trust Co., 1977–78; Practicing atty., 1981–96; Instructor, Ft. Hays St. U., 1986.

DC Office: 1519 LHOB 20515, 202-225-2715; Fax: 202-225-5124; Web site: www.house.gov/moranks01.

District Offices: Hays, 785-628-6401; Hutchinson, 316-665-6138.

Committees: *Agriculture* (15th of 27 R): Department Operations, Oversight, Nutrition & Forestry; General Farm Commodities, Resource Conservation & Credit; Risk Management, Research & Specialty Crops. *Transportation & Infrastructure* (31st of 41 R): Aviation; Ground Transportation. *Veterans' Affairs* (9th of 17 R): Health.

Group Ratings

	ADA	ACLU	AFS	LCV	CON	NTU	NFIB	COC	ACU	NTLC	CHC
1998	10	19	11	15	13	55	100	100	92	87	92
1997	10	—	38	—	17	52	—	90	96	—	—

National Journal Ratings

	1997 LIB — 1997 CONS			1998 LIB — 1998 CONS		
Economic	28%	—	67%	30%	—	67%
Social	30%	—	64%	32%	—	67%
Foreign	0%	—	88%	19%	—	75%

Key Votes of the 105th Congress

1. Clinton Budget Deal	Y	5. Puerto Rico Sthood. Ref.	N	9. Cut $ for B-2 Bombers	N
2. Education IRAs	Y	6. End Highway Set-asides	Y	10. Human Rights in China	N
3. Req. 2/3 to Raise Taxes	Y	7. School Prayer Amend.	Y	11. Withdraw Bosnia Troops	Y
4. Fast-track Trade	Y	8. Ovrd. Part. Birth Veto	Y	12. End Cuban TV-Marti	N

Election Results

1998 general	Jerry Moran (R)	152,775	(81%)	($295,696)
	Jim Phillips (D)	36,618	(19%)	($10,165)
1998 primary	Jerry Moran (R)	unopposed		
1996 general	Jerry Moran (R)	191,899	(73%)	($430,261)
	John Divine (R)	63,948	(24%)	($82,631)
	Others	5,298	(2%)	

SECOND DISTRICT

The green plains of eastern Kansas have seen more than their share of American history. Here, on bluffs above the Missouri River, Fort Leavenworth was built in 1827, famous for years for its war college and military prison and now the oldest U.S. fort west of the Mississippi. In the 1850s, newly founded towns along the Kansas River and along the Missouri line were the centers of Bleeding Kansas, where the pro-slavery bushwhackers set up a state capital in tiny Lecompton and anti-slavery New Englanders set up their stronghold down the river at Lawrence. Farther up the river is Fort Riley, once an outpost against the Indians, now a major Army base threatened with closure, and Manhattan, home of Kansas State University. Topeka, the state capital, sits here on a low bluff above the river; it was this city whose system of legal segregation was overturned in the 1954 landmark case, *Brown v. Board of Education*. Farther south, on the Missouri border, are the hills called "the Balkans." Here coal miners, often of Eastern European origin, lived in and near towns like Pittsburg and Girard, once a center of American socialism, where Clarence Darrow and Upton Sinclair made pilgrimages, and its paper, *Appeal to Reason*, had a nationwide 750,000 circulation.

These disparate areas, Topeka and Manhattan, Fort Riley and Fort Leavenworth, wheat-growing counties and the Balkans—most of eastern Kansas except the Kansas City metropolitan area—make up the 2d Congressional District. The heritage here has been Republican ever since the jayhawks defeated the bushwhacks once the votes were counted honestly in the 1850s. Yet Democrats in recent decades have been competitive here in state and local races, especially in Topeka. For 20 of the 24 years from 1970–94, Democrats were elected to fill the 2d District seat. But in the last three elections it has voted for strongly conservative Republicans.

The congressman from the 2d is Jim Ryun, famous more than 20 years before he ran. He grew up in Wichita, where in 1965 he was the first high-schooler to break the four-minute mile; his 3:55.3 time is still the world record for high schoolers. He was a star runner at the University of Kansas, and ran in the Olympics of 1964, 1968 and 1972, winning a silver medal and setting world records for the 880-yard dash and the 1500-meter run. After his competitive athletic career, he operated a sports camp, was a motivational speaker for corporations and Christian groups, wrote two books, started a sports management firm and worked with a hearing aid company that produced a "Sounds of Success" program to help hearing-impaired children achieve their potential.

In May 1996, when 2d District freshman Sam Brownback decided to run for the Senate seat suddenly vacated by Bob Dole, Ryun decided to run for Congress. He was opposed by former Topeka Mayor Douglas Wright and Cheryl Brown Henderson, whose father was the plaintiff in *Brown v. Board*. Wright called Ryun an "extremist" and proclaimed, "This is clearly a battle over the direction of the Republican Party in Kansas," predicting that Ryun couldn't win the general. Ryun campaigned for tax cuts and opposed abortion rights. While the press treated Ryun as something of an oddity, Republican primary voters didn't: he won 62%, to 25% for Wright and 14% for Henderson.

In the general, Ryun was outspent by trial lawyer John Frieden. Frieden was pro-choice, opposed to the Dole-Kemp tax cut; he berated Gingrich and Republican Medicare "cuts." He sounded just a bit condescending when he said, "Ryun clearly falls short of being the kind of person we should send to the United States Congress." Ryun replied that Frieden was lying about his record, maligning his character and trying to buy the office. To charges that his strong religious views made him "extreme," Ryun replied, "I go to church once a week. I do pray over my meals, and so do a lot of people in my district. I don't think that's extreme . . . our family prayed about my decision to run for office. Maybe that makes me an extremist."

In the fall, Democrats circulated "Courtship Makes a Comeback," written by Ryun and his wife for Focus on the Family. It recounted their practice that any young man wanting to date Ryun's daughters has to call him and ask permission. "At this very first meeting or phone call, the father explains that the family believes in courtship, which means that the young man must be spiritually and financially prepared to marry her if they fall in love. Otherwise, don't even bother starting a relationship." Again there was ridicule, with the press calling Dr. Ruth to mock the Ryuns' practices. However absurd the Ryuns' beliefs may seem to Manhattan or Malibu sophisticates, they were not political poison in Kansas. Ryun won 52%–45%, losing Topeka and Shawnee County 52%–46%, but carrying the rest of the district 55%–43%.

In the House, Ryun has a very conservative voting record. He claimed credit for the $500 per child tax credit and reducing capital gains and estate taxes. "Those were the kinds of things we talked about during the campaign, and we've followed through," he said. On the National Security Committee, he backed increased military spending and was pleased that an Army National Guard division moved its headquarters to Fort Riley. He sponsored a bill to give the National Surface Transportation Board control of rails-to-trails conversions, to prevent people getting free land they don't deserve and to foster responsible trail development. He was not immune to funneling federal money to local projects: $500,000 to solve Topeka's red water problem by replacing rusty pipes.

In late 1997 Frieden declined to run again. Democrat Jim Clark ran as a Vietnam veteran who said Ryun did not favor doing enough for Vietnam veterans' health care and criticized Ryun's plan for using 10% of the Social Security fund to cut taxes or pay down the national debt. Ryun opposed Clark's proposal to take troops from Korea and station them in Fort Riley. Ryun won with a solid 61% of the vote, including 54% in Shawnee County and 64% in the rest of the district.

Cook's Call. *Safe.* Ryun's solid victory in 1998 over a rather lackluster candidate does not make him invincible, but it does show that this district, which has elected Democrats in the past, is quite comfortable with a conservative Republican congressman.

The People: Pop. 1990: 619,385; 40.8% rural; 14.9% age 65 + ; 90.2% White, 6.2% Black, 1.1% Asian, 1.2% Amer. Indian, 1.3% Other; 2.8% Hispanic Origin. Households: 58.9% married couple families; 28.6% married couple fams. w. children; 44% college educ.; median household income: $24,903; per capita income: $11,662; median house value: $44,500; median gross rent: $262.

1996 Presidential Vote

Dole (R)	125,087	(49%)
Clinton (D)	100,110	(39%)
Perot (I)	27,748	(11%)

1992 Presidential Vote

Bush (R)	98,884	(36%)
Clinton (D)	98,457	(36%)
Perot (I)	75,549	(28%)

Rep. Jim Ryun (R)

Elected 1996; b. May 29, 1947, Wichita; home, Topeka; U. of KS, B.A. 1970; Presbyterian; married (Anne).

Professional Career: U.S. Olympian, Track & Field, 1964, 1968, 1972; Founder & Dir., Jim Ryun Running Camps, 1976–present; Rancher, 1983–present.

DC Office: 330 CHOB 20515, 202-225-6601; Fax: 202-225-7986; Web site: www.house.gov/ryun.

District Offices: Pittsburg, 316-232-6100; Topeka, 785-232-4500.

Committees: *Armed Services* (25th of 32 R): Military Personnel; Military Procurement. *Banking & Financial Services* (19th of 32 R): Domestic & International Monetary Policy; Financial Institutions & Consumer Credit. *Budget* (17th of 24 R).

Group Ratings

	ADA	ACLU	AFS	LCV	CON	NTU	NFIB	COC	ACU	NTLC	CHC
1998	0	6	0	0	13	54	100	100	100	100	100
1997	5	—	13	—	24	64	—	100	100	—	—

National Journal Ratings

	1997 LIB — 1997 CONS		1998 LIB — 1998 CONS	
Economic	0%	— 90%	0%	— 88%
Social	20%	— 71%	0%	— 97%
Foreign	0%	— 88%	19%	— 75%

Key Votes of the 105th Congress

1. Clinton Budget Deal	Y	5. Puerto Rico Sthood. Ref.	N	9. Cut $ for B-2 Bombers	N
2. Education IRAs	Y	6. End Highway Set-asides	Y	10. Human Rights in China	N
3. Req. 2/3 to Raise Taxes	Y	7. School Prayer Amend.	Y	11. Withdraw Bosnia Troops	Y
4. Fast-track Trade	Y	8. Ovrd. Part. Birth Veto	Y	12. End Cuban TV-Marti	N

Election Results

1998 general	Jim Ryun (R)	108,527	(61%)	($540,653)
	Jim Clark (D)	69,521	(39%)	($116,031)
1998 primary	Jim Ryun (R)	53,401	(78%)	
	Tom Little (R)	14,840	(22%)	
1996 general	Jim Ryun (R)	131,592	(52%)	($415,606)
	John Frieden (D)	114,644	(45%)	($757,637)
	Others	5,928	(2%)	

THIRD DISTRICT

Though the central city is in Missouri, one-third of metropolitan Kansas City's residents now live west of the state line in Kansas. Some are in Kansas City, Kansas, where the low-lying land near the Missouri River used to house one of the nation's largest stockyards. This is still a working-class town with a few dilapidated looking streets and lots of modest frame houses, the largest black neighborhood and oldest Catholic ethnic neighborhoods in Kansas, and an old Democratic machine politics. But Kansas City is losing population, while Johnson County, just to the south, is gaining rapidly, and now casts four times as many votes. Its older neighborhoods are separated from the affluent Kansas City, Missouri, neighborhood around the old Country

Club Plaza shopping center by just a single small street; the newer neighborhoods are arrayed along the interstates, and have grown to the point that Overland Park, Olathe, Shawnee and Lenexa—unfamiliar names to most Kansans—are among the largest municipalities in the state. These suburbs are not just residential; Sprint's headquarters is in Johnson County, and a J.C. Penney catalogue center, as well as lots of thriving small businesses, are located there. Politically, Johnson County has long been heavily Republican, but with plenty of voters moderate or even liberal on cultural issues.

The 3d Congressional District consists of Johnson County, Kansas City and surrounding Wyandotte County, the town of Lawrence, which is the home of University of Kansas and one rural county to the south. But two-thirds of the vote are cast in Johnson County. The most hard-fought struggle in the mid-1990s has been between conservative and moderate Republicans. At first the conservatives made great strides, taking over the Republican Party apparatus and leadership positions in the legislature in 1994. In 1996 they showed across-the-board strength in Kansas, electing three conservative freshmen congressmen as well as Senator Sam Brownback. But in 1998 the moderates held sway. A conservative challenge to Republican Governor Bill Graves was beaten nearly 3–1 in the Republican primary, and in the 3d District conservative freshman Congressman Vince Snowbarger was one of six incumbent House members defeated for re-election.

The congressman from the 3d now is Dennis Moore, a Democrat with a long political pedigree who developed an appeal across party lines. Moore grew up in Wichita, and his father Warner Moore ran for Congress in the 4th District and lost the general by only 50.3%–49.7% in 1958—which was also the last year a Democrat won in the 3d. Moore went to college and law school in Kansas, served in the Army and practiced law in Johnson County. In 1976, at 31, he was elected Johnson County district attorney and re-elected in 1980 and 1984. There he claims credit for starting a Consumers Protection Division and a Victims Assistance Unit and for prosecuting a national oil company. He went into private law practice in 1993 and was elected to the local community college board in 1997. These five Johnson County elections made Moore a natural when national Democrats were recruiting a candidate to oppose an apparently vulnerable Snowbarger.

Snowbarger had earned a reputation as a strong conservative in 12 years as a legislator, the last four as state House majority leader. He strongly supported tax cuts and strongly opposed abortion. In 1995 he decided to run for Congress, before incumbent moderate Republican Jan Meyers announced her retirement, and he won the Republican primary 44%–40% over Overland Park Mayor Ed Eilert, who attacked him for his high rating from the Christian Coalition. In the general, Snowbarger faced Judy Hancock, who outraised and outspent him and criticized him on abortion and gun control. Hancock ran ahead in some polls, but behind on election day. In 1994 she had lost to Meyers 57%–43%; in 1996 she lost to Snowbarger by 50%–45%.

Though Snowbarger had no primary opposition in 1998, Moore took advantage of the turbulence between conservative and moderate Republicans. He got the support of a local Mainstream Coalition formed, it seems, to do in Snowbarger and his like. Moore easily beat token primary opposition, 74%–26%, and started raising money, staying ahead of Snowbarger in every quarter. Both campaigns ran no TV spots until after the August primary; some of the spots each ran came close to or crossed the line. Snowbarger said Moore was "soft on violent criminals" because on a Project Vote Smart questionnaire he did not check the alternative "impose truth in sentencing for violent criminals so they serve full sentences with no chance of parole." But the questionnaire instructed candidates that a failure to check one of many alternatives did not imply opposition. Moore portrayed Snowbarger as a threat to Social Security. But what Snowbarger proposed was allowing workers to put part of their payroll taxes in individual accounts. Moore ran ad suggesting that Snowbarger voted against allowing doctors to discuss all treatment options with patients; Snowbarger said he voted for a Republican "patients' rights" bill which included a provision to prohibit this gag rule. Snowbarger made "trust" his major theme, but ran few if any ads on what he'd done positively.

The 3d District attracted big independent expenditure campaigns in both 1996 and 1998. In 1996 Triad Management spent lavishly on Snowbarger's behalf, helping balance his financial disadvantage. In 1998 he sent a letter to Triad asking them to stay out, and called on Moore to renounce such campaigns as well. But the Sierra Club and the AFL-CIO both spent heavily on TV ads, mailings and phone banks to elect Moore. Interestingly, after the campaign Moore said that the campaign alerted him to the problem of anonymous third party expenditures, and said he'd back a reform requiring disclosure of independent expenditure groups' contributions.

On election day Moore won 52%–48%. He carried Kansas City and Lawrence by wide margins, but his key wins came in northeast Johnson County, in the affluent, long-settled, elderly suburbs around Mission Hills, Roeland Park, Merriam and the north half of Overland Park. That was enough to hold Snowbarger to a 53%–47% margin in Johnson County. Snowbarger was deserted by Jan Meyers and state Senate President Dick Bond; Johnson County lawns sprouted signs for Moore next to those for popular Governor Bill Graves; at the same time conservative groups, dispirited by their primary losses, were not active. "I got hit by the revenge factor from both ends of the party," Snowbarger said. But it also must be said that Moore showed considerable popularity and great fundraising skills. Democrats hope he is the kind of competent and attractive incumbent who held so many Republican-leaning seats for them in the 1970s and 1980s. He may certainly be helped if Republican splits continue. Snowbarger, stunned by his loss, still did not rule out running again.

Cook's Call. *Highly Competitive.* Moore will be a top Republican target in 2000, but whether Republicans will put the right candidate forward to challenge him is the question. A bloody primary battle between the conservative and more moderate wings of the party could leave the nominee badly bruised for the general; a very conservative candidate could have problems drawing votes from rather socially moderate Johnson County. Still, Moore likely will have his hands full holding onto this Republican-leaning district.

The People: Pop. 1990: 619,445; 7.2% rural; 10.8% age 65 + ; 87.3% White, 8.9% Black, 1.6% Asian, 0.8% Amer. Indian, 1.4% Other; 3.2% Hispanic Origin. Households: 56.6% married couple families; 28.4% married couple fams. w. children; 59.5% college educ.; median household income: $34,275; per capita income: $16,585; median house value: $75,800; median gross rent: $377.

1996 Presidential Vote		1992 Presidential Vote	
Dole (R)	144,924 (50%)	Clinton (D)	116,396 (38%)
Clinton (D)	121,152 (42%)	Bush (R)	113,963 (37%)
Perot (I)	18,176 (6%)	Perot (I)	75,413 (25%)

Rep. Dennis Moore (D)

Elected 1998; b. Nov. 8, 1945, Anthony; home, Lenexa; U. of KS, B.A. 1967; Washburn U. Law Schl., J.D. 1970; Protestant; married (Stephene).

Military Career: Army, 1970; Army Reserves, 1971–73.

Elected Office: Johnson Cnty. Dist. Atty., 1976–88.

Professional Career: Asst. KS Atty. Gen., 1971–73; Practicing atty., 1973–76, 1989–98.

DC Office: 506 CHOB 20515, 202-225-2865; Fax: 202-225-2807; Web site: www.house.gov/moore.

District Offices: Kansas City, 913-621-0832; Lawrence, 785-842-9313; Overland Park, 913-383-2013.

Committees: *Banking & Financial Services* (24th of 27 D): Domestic & International Monetary Policy; Financial Institutions & Consumer Credit. *Small Business* (10th of 17 D): Empowerment; Regulatory Reform & Paperwork Reduction.

Group Ratings and Key Votes: Newly Elected

Election Results

1998 general	Dennis Moore (D)	103,376	(52%)	($986,688)
	Vince Snowbarger (R)	93,938	(48%)	($1,003,694)
1998 primary	Dennis Moore (D)	18,428	(74%)	
	Dan Dana (D)	6,388	(26%)	
1996 general	Vince Snowbarger (R)	139,169	(50%)	($465,869)
	Judy Hancock (D)	126,848	(45%)	($840,595)
	Others	13,296	(5%)	

FOURTH DISTRICT

Wichita is the largest Kansas-only metropolitan area, smaller than million-plus metro Kansas City, but a Great Plains metropolis of the magnitude of Omaha or Tulsa. It began as a farm market town and grew with local oil and gas discoveries in the 1920s. But its real impetus came during World War II and the years just after, when aircraft factories sprouted up here on the Kansas plains and Wichita suddenly became the nation's major producer of small planes. Today the big three—Cessna, Raytheon Aircraft (formerly Beechcraft), Learjet—are all located here. Wichita has also become a regional health center in the common Great Plains pattern, as rural counties are unable to attract new doctors or maintain hospitals, and people from miles around come to the metropolis for treatment. Wichita has also become home to franchising and telemarketing companies. In the early 1990s, general aviation was hurt by the recession and by suits which held manufacturers liable for planes they had produced years, even decades, before. But now Wichita has recovered: the demand for small planes is robust, and a federal limit on liability pushed through by, among others, former Wichita area Congressman Dan Glickman, has enlivened the industry.

Kansas's 4th Congressional District is centered around Wichita, covering wheat-growing areas to the east and west, but with most of its people in Wichita and Sedgwick County. Politically, it has voted Republican most years; in 1992 and 1996 it voted for George Bush and Bob Dole. But in the middle 1990s the 4th saw two seriously contested House races.

The congressman from the 4th District is Todd Tiahrt, a Republican first elected in 1994. He grew up on a farm in South Dakota, went to the same high school as South Dakota Senator Tim Johnson, played football for the South Dakota School of Mines and Technology and graduated from Evangel College. In 1976 he moved to the Wichita area to be closer to his wife's family and worked at Zenith as a project engineer and at Boeing as a proposal manager on the Space Station, Air Force One, KC-135, B-52, B-1, B-2, A-67, YF-22 and Comanche helicopter programs. In 1990, he went to the courthouse to file to run for the Kansas House, and decided he was a Republican; he lost that race by only eight votes. His grandfather had raised him to be a Democrat, but he found his strong religious views—"to me, liberty is the freedom to do the right thing, not the freedom to do anything"—were more in line with Republicans. In 1992 he was elected to the Kansas Senate, where his great cause was a concealed weapons law allowing citizens on application to carry firearms.

In 1994, Tiahrt got it into his head to run against Dan Glickman, a task all the more daunting because Glickman seemed to be having a good ninth term: he was chairman of the House Intelligence Committee and, with Senator Nancy Kassebaum, passed legislation reducing the product liability of general aviation manufacturers in 1994. Tiahrt ran ads showing Glickman's face morphing into Clinton's, and attacked him for voting for gun control in the 1994 crime bill. Tiahrt's base was among Wichita's numerous religious conservatives, who had taken over the local Republican party. Tiahrt assembled a corps of 1,800 volunteers, many from church contacts. "I moved below radar and stayed low-key, so my opponent wouldn't start raising lots of money," he said. Even so, Glickman spent $694,000 to Tiahrt's $200,000. On election day

Glickman ran relatively well, as he had for years, in high-income Republican precincts; but he suffered serious losses in middle-income areas in Wichita and Sedgwick County. Tiahrt won a solid 53%–47% victory, and Glickman went on to become secretary of Agriculture.

In the House, Tiahrt was an enthusiastic supporter of the Contract with America and boasted that he voted with Newt Gingrich 97% of the time. He proposed eliminating the Department of Energy and transferring nuclear weapons storage and waste disposal to the Pentagon, to no effect. In his first term he tried to zero out AmeriCorps, as "largely inefficient and ineffective," and in his second to cut its appropriation in half, again with little success. He was more successful in introducing the Adoption Promotion and Stability Act of 1996, which gives tax breaks for adoptive parents and ends the ban on transracial adoptions; introduced by Republicans, it was embraced by Clinton and passed nearly unanimously. For a solid economic conservative, Tiahrt did keep his eye on local economic issues, sponsoring an amendment to allow USDA money to be used for value-added products like wheat flour, and building up the Winfield and Arkansas City levees.

Not surprisingly, Tiahrt was targeted by Democrats in 1996. Starting that March, the AFL-CIO spent upwards of $500,000 on ads against Tiahrt, charging him with favoring "cuts" in Medicare and student loans and complicity in raids on union pensions funds. Some TV stations refused to run these and they were ridiculed in the *Wichita Eagle*. Tiahrt attacked Democratic candidate Randy Rathbun as a liberal, a big spender, a bumbling prosecutor, a pawn of Democratic special interests, and turned the huge AFL-CIO ad campaign against him with a late ad attacking Rathbun as "in the pocket" of organized labor infiltrated by organized crime—a reference to the Laborers' Union, which the Clinton Justice Department found to be mob-ridden while allowing its leader Arthur Coia, a big Democratic contributor, to stay in office. Tiahrt won 50%–47%, a downtick from the 1994 result.

In 1997 Tiahrt got a seat on Appropriations. On the D.C. Subcommittee he sponsored the ban on needle exchanges and called for a felony investigation of District officials who continued to fund abortions after Congress banned that in 1995. He also sponsored a law to allow parents access to their children's school files. And he amended a foreign aid bill to block funding to governments that force women to be sterilized, have abortions or use contraceptives. In 1998 Democrats failed to come up with a strong candidate; their nominee had once headed the Kansas ACLU and as a legislator authored a bill to ban pay toilets. Tiahrt won comfortably, 58%–39%. "Two years ago I was the main target of Democrats' wrath, and I barely survived by three percentage points. This year, it was Vince," he said, referring to the 3d District's Vince Snowbarger, who lost. But this is no guarantee that Tiahrt will not get serious opposition in 2000. In a signal that he may be interested in higher office, he plans to set up his own statewide fundraising committee.

Cook's Call. *Probably Safe.* Like the 2d District, this Witchita-based seat has become more Republican and conservative over the past few years. Given that Democrats were unable to find a strong candidate to run against Tiahrt in 1998, when he was a much more vulnerable target, it is hard to see how a Democrat could unseat him in 2000.

The People: Pop. 1990: 619,373; 24.2% rural; 14.1% age 65 +; 88.9% White, 6.5% Black, 1.5% Asian, 1.3% Amer. Indian, 1.8% Other; 3.4% Hispanic Origin. Households: 57.6% married couple families; 27.9% married couple fams. w. children; 47.6% college educ.; median household income: $28,308; per capita income: $13,623; median house value: $52,500; median gross rent: $278.

1996 Presidential Vote			1992 Presidential Vote		
Dole (R)	145,997	(56%)	Bush (R)	114,001	(40%)
Clinton (D)	90,557	(35%)	Clinton (D)	93,428	(33%)
Perot (I)	21,660	(8%)	Perot (I)	75,350	(27%)

Rep. Todd Tiahrt (R)

Elected 1994; b. June 15, 1951, Vermillion, SD; home, Goddard; Evangel Col., B.A. 1975; SW MO St. U., M.B.A. 1989; Assembly of God; married (Vicki).

Elected Office: KS Senate, 1992–94.

Professional Career: Project Engineer, Zenith Corp., 1976–84; Proposal Mgr., Boeing Co., 1985–94.

DC Office: 428 CHOB 20515, 202-225-6216; Fax: 202-225-3489; Web site: www.house.gov/tiahrt.

District Office: Wichita, 316-262-8992.

Committees: *Appropriations* (26th of 34 R): District of Columbia; Military Construction; Transportation.

Group Ratings

	ADA	ACLU	AFS	LCV	CON	NTU	NFIB	COC	ACU	NTLC	CHC
1998	0	6	0	0	2	57	100	94	100	97	100
1997	5	—	13	—	27	63	—	90	100	—	—

National Journal Ratings

	1997 LIB — 1997 CONS	1998 LIB — 1998 CONS
Economic	19% — 76%	0% — 88%
Social	20% — 71%	0% — 97%
Foreign	0% — 88%	19% — 75%

Key Votes of the 105th Congress

1. Clinton Budget Deal	Y	5. Puerto Rico Sthood. Ref.	N	9. Cut $ for B-2 Bombers	N
2. Education IRAs	Y	6. End Highway Set-asides	Y	10. Human Rights in China	N
3. Req. 2/3 to Raise Taxes	Y	7. School Prayer Amend.	Y	11. Withdraw Bosnia Troops	N
4. Fast-track Trade	Y	8. Ovrd. Part. Birth Veto	Y	12. End Cuban TV-Marti	N

Election Results

1998 general	Todd Tiahrt (R)	94,785	(58%)	($635,508)
	Jim Lawing (D)	62,737	(39%)	($28,869)
	Others	5,171	(3%)	
1998 primary	Todd Tiahrt (R)	unopposed		
1996 general	Todd Tiahrt (R)	128,486	(50%)	($903,348)
	Randy Rathbun (D)	119,544	(47%)	($608,355)
	Others	8,361	(3%)	

KENTUCKY

Kentucky today remains very much what it was at its beginning—a Jeffersonian common-wealth. Literally: it is one of four commonwealths (the others are Virginia, Pennsylvania and Massachusetts) and when the first settlers came here, in the years when Thomas Jefferson was writing his *Notes on Virginia*, it was part of Virginia. Kentucky was admitted to the Union in 1792, when Jefferson was secretary of state; and when Jefferson was aroused at the Federalists' anti-sedition acts, he ghost-wrote the Kentucky Resolutions in 1798. Kentucky's one large county is named after Jefferson and its one large city after the monarch to whom he was credentialed as ambassador to France, Louis XVI. To this day, Kentucky still has a constitution informed by a Jeffersonian jealousy of power. Its one-term limit on governors was raised to two only in 1995, and the current governor, Paul E. Patton, is the first eligible for a second consecutive term; it has strict limits on when the legislature can meet, so that much important business gets done in special sessions; every governor must swear that he or she has not participated in a duel (remember what Jefferson thought of Aaron Burr). Kentucky also has long favored the Democratic Party, which can trace its ancestry at least tenuously back to Jefferson; Republicans have had recent success in congressional elections, but the state voted twice, though by diminishing margins, for William Jefferson Clinton.

The agrarian Jefferson would approve of Kentucky's demography, which is still largely rural, with well under half its population in the big metropolitan areas of Louisville, Lexington and the towns across the Ohio River from Cincinnati. And the tobacco planters who once presided over what one historian called "the alcoholic republic" might not entirely disapprove of a Kentucky economy that remains heavily dependent on century-old industries such as tobacco (Kentucky is the nation's number two producer after North Carolina, and it has the largest number of tobacco farms), whiskey (Bourbon County is in Kentucky) and coal. Many of the buildings here are old: the small-town 19th Century courthouses, the cabins in the coal mining Appalachians, the unpainted houses in the soggy lowlands beneath the levees by the Mississippi River.

Satellite dishes and four-lane highways have brought modern civilization into hollows and lowland farms that lacked indoor plumbing and electricity within living memory, but people in this state still have a strong attachment to place and family. The continuity is real. Kentucky's population has grown just over 30% in the past 50 years; few outsiders have moved in, so today's Kentuckians are mostly descendants of settlers who poured over the mountains in the 40 years after Daniel Boone made his way through the Cumberland Gap in 1775, when Kentucky's population rose from 73,000 in the Census of 1790 to 564,000 in 1820.

There has long been hearty, though lopsided, political competition here, with most of the 120 counties voting today as they did in the Civil War era. The eastern mountains were pro-Union and remain Republican, except for counties where coal miners were organized by the United Mine Workers in the 1930s; the Bluegrass region and the western end of the state were slaveholding territory and Democratic. Louisville, with many German immigrants, was an anti-slavery town, and for years flirted with Republicans, though now it mostly supports Democrats. These patterns, which have more or less prevailed for more than 100 years, were apparent in the returns for governor in 1995, senator in 1996 and 1998, and president in 1992 and 1996.

For years, all this meant control by the Democratic Party, with the real battle in the primary. For nearly half a century there was almost a two-party system within the dominant party, with factions going back to the 1938 primary when Senate Majority Leader (and later Vice President) Alben Barkley was challenged by Governor (and later Senator and Baseball Commissioner) Happy Chandler. Barkley's faction was later led by Governor (1959–63) Bert Combs and

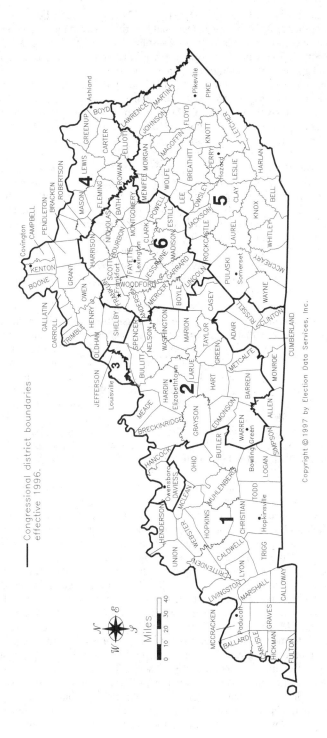

— Congressional district boundaries
effective 1996.

Copyright © 1997 by Election Data Services, Inc.

Chandler's by Governor (1971–74) and Senator (1974–99) Wendell Ford. But as Louisville *Courier-Journal* reporter Al Cross notes, factional has given way to money, with rich candidates elected governor over most of the last 20 years—John Y. Brown Jr. in 1979, Wallace Wilkinson in 1987 and Brereton Jones in 1991. But lineage still has its claims: Ben Chandler, Happy Chandler's grandson, was elected attorney general in 1995.

The 1990s have seen strong two-party competition, with uneven results. Republicans have been winning most congressional races, but often by narrow margins. Senator Mitch McConnell won his third term decisively in 1996, but Senator Jim Bunning won by only 6,766 votes in 1998; Republicans won five of Kentucky's six House seats in 1996 and 1998, but their margins in the 1st and 3d districts have been narrow, and in 1998, after both incumbents ran for the Senate, they traded the 4th and 6th districts. Meanwhile, at the state level, Democrats have held on. Patton was elected governor in 1995 by only 51%–49%, and has aroused much opposition, but mostly in his own party; his overall job ratings were high as he looked ahead in 1998 to the 1999 election. The legislature remains Democratic, but the state Senate by just a 20–18 margin, and in 1997 a coalition of Republicans and conservative Democrats took control and elected the Senate president. But party does not mean everything. The major issues Kentucky government has tackled in the 1990s—education reform, health insurance, workmen's compensation, higher education—have cut across party lines, as politicians found themselves confronted with the unintended consequences of entrenched systems and well-intentioned reforms, and grappled with the task of adapting this commonwealth with its roots in Jefferson's 18th Century to the challenges of the 21st.

Governor. There is no question who stands at the apex of Kentucky politics: the governor. The governor's appointment powers are wide: the legislature meets in regular session only 60 days every two years; after that the governor can shift around line items in the state budget and call special sessions. Kentucky's governor, elected in 1995, is Paul E. Patton, a Democrat from the eastern Kentucky coal fields. He grew up in Lawrence County on the West Virginia border in a house converted from a silo. He was a 1959 graduate of the University of Kentucky's College of Engineering, and ran a coal company from 1962 to 1978. He began his public service career as deputy state Transportation secretary from 1979–80, chaired the state Democratic Party and in 1982 was elected judge-executive of Pike County, at the far eastern extremity of the state. In 1991 he was elected lieutenant governor and worked on a law granting tax credits to firms that create jobs. The 1995 gubernatorial race was an uphill battle. In the Democratic primary, Patton won 45%, with 24% for Secretary of State Bob Babbage, and 21% for legislator John "Eck" Rose.

In the general, Patton faced Larry Forgy, who campaigned hard against the Kentucky Education Reform Act, which passed in 1990 after the state Supreme Court outlawed school finance laws. KERA vastly raised per pupil spending, moved toward equalizing spending in districts, mandated ungraded classes for kindergarten through third grade, and a teacher assessment system based on written portfolios. Unfortunately test scores have not risen, though supporters claim other benefits. On other issues Forgy sounded conservative notes and Patton often echoed them, calling for school prayer and boot camps. Patton won 51%–49%, a fair omen of Clinton's 1% victory the next year. It was the first major Democratic success in stalling Republican advances since Clinton took office, and Democrats all over the country took heart. Patton continued his strong partisan tack, working for the Clinton-Gore ticket, backing the Democratic opponent of Senator Mitch McConnell, and trying to win back congressional and legislative seats—but with little success. But when the Clinton Administration threatened to regulate tobacco as a drug, Patton supported a lawsuit opposing the FDA rules, lit up a cigarette, and said he wouldn't support Clinton in 1996 if the FDA acted.

On state policy, Patton has taken a less partisan—some critics say, not very Democratic—stance on issues. He backed tougher penalties for crime, appointed a task force to review education reform and helped construction unions get higher wages. But his first major initiative in December 1996 was workmens' compensation reform. After extensive research, Patton decided workmens' comp rates were 20% above other states and were hurting Kentucky business. Coal miners were receiving 55% of benefits, black lung sufferers nearly 30%. Patton mastered the details, worked hard and assembled a bipartisan majority for his reform: a four-year limit on re-opening cases, evaluation by state-paid doctors with American Medical Association guidelines on disability, and lower attorney's fees. This stirred great opposition in Patton's eastern Kentucky base and among the unions who had supported him strongly in 1995; it was strongly opposed by Greg Stumbo, House majority leader since 1985 and the dominant figure there, whose legal practice included workmens' comp claims. But it passed anyway. Costs fell and the numbers qualifying for black lung benefits fell toward zero; Stumbo, unions and former Governor Brereton Jones called for a special session to change the law in 1997 and 1998, but Patton refused.

Patton's next big cause was higher education reform, splitting 13 junior colleges from the University of Kentucky and making the latter a major research university. He argued that the community colleges were sending few students to the university and were not training students for jobs; he wanted more concrete goals together with deregulation and decentralization of the schools. Again, he immersed himself in detail and amassed a coalition, and overcame powerful lobbies. In October 1997, he tried another session, this time on health care. Patton argued that the system, led by Jones and passed by the legislature in 1994, was unworkable because all but one private insurer had fled Kentucky. Patton came up with a compromise, creating a high-risk pool with premiums up to 150% of the market standard, in order to preserve guaranteed portability. But Stumbo and the House opposed his plan, with many backing a play-or-pay plan in which insurers would be obliged to cover high-risk people or pay an assessment to companies who would. None of the bills passed. Patton blamed Stumbo, saying he "blindly opposed me" because workmens comp reform hurt Stumbo's law practice and saying he had "no philosophical compass on this and several other issues." Stumbo responded in kind: "I've known Paul Patton for 20 years. I've supported him. But since he's become governor, I've lost confidence in his character."

Patton had more troubles in 1998. His budget passed, and so did federally subsidized health insurance for children of the working poor. But he antagonized state employee unions in September when he forced them to switch to managed care in 1999. And in September, Patton's chief of staff and another staffer plus two Teamster officials were indicted after an investigation by Attorney General Ben Chandler for breaking Kentucky's campaign finance laws. Patton said he was perplexed by the charges and kept the staffers on. One might assume Patton was beleaguered heading into the 1999 campaign year. His home region, his former allies in labor, and Stumbo were angry with him. And Republicans had been airing charges of campaign shenanigans for years. Yet Patton's job approval rating was in the 65% range, the highest of any recent Kentucky governor. And opposition seemed to be vanishing. Right after the November election Congressman Hal Rogers said he had no interest in running; at the end of the month, Forgy said he would not run; on December 1, Brereton Jones said he would not; later in December, Mike Duncan, chairman of Jim Bunning's 1998 Senate campaign, said he wouldn't either. In the May 1999 Republican primary, publicist Peppy Martin barely beat former Democratic Senate candidate David Williams in a race with the lowest local turnout ever. With only 3–4% turnout in some counties, Martin won by 51%–49%, proclaiming a "win is a win." Patton now seems well-positioned, thanks to his legislative skills, hard work and his mostly moderate policies, to be the first Kentucky governor to win a second term.

Cook's Call. *Safe.* Republicans have failed to produce a first-tier challenger to Patton. With the state constitution now amended, he looks like a safe bet to become the first governor in 200 years in the Bluegrass State to be re-elected.

Senior Senator. Mitch McConnell is Kentucky's senior senator, the architect of its 6–1 Republican congressional delegation and a major leader on several national issues. Yet his origins were modest and his rise anything but inevitable. He grew up in Alabama, where he overcame polio, and after age 13 moved to Louisville. He has been in politics almost his whole career: he was an intern for Senator John Sherman Cooper in 1964 and, after finishing law school, became a staffer for Senator Marlow Cook. He moved back to Louisville and in 1977, at 35, won by a narrow margin the office that had been Cook's political stepping stone, Jefferson County judge-executive. In 1981 he was re-elected, again narrowly. In 1984 he ran for the Senate, against incumbent Dee Huddleston. McConnell ran ads showing bloodhounds sniffing for Huddleston in vacation locales where he had collected fees for speeches while the Senate was in session. McConnell won by 5,169 votes of 1.2 million cast, the only challenger to beat an incumbent that year.

In the Senate, McConnell has a mostly conservative record and high party loyalty. Yet he was willing to penalize a fellow Republican when as Ethics Committee chairman in 1995 he led the investigation of Bob Packwood for sexual harassment; the committee recommended expulsion, and Packwood ultimately resigned. McConnell has been a strong backer of product liability and medical malpractice reform, and is a lead sponsor of the auto choice plan that would let car owners pay less for insurance by disclaiming pain and suffering damages. He is the Senate sponsor of so-far unsuccessful measures to ban racial quotas and preferences. He successfully kept horse shows operating despite criticism by animal rights activists—an issue he used in his 1990 campaign. He split with other Republicans and opposed term limits. McConnell served on Foreign Relations until 1992, then switched to Appropriations and in 1994 became chairman of the Foreign Operations Subcommittee. He has strongly supported aid to Israel and has been skeptical about aid to Russia.

McConnell's greatest expertise is on campaigns and elections. He has fought one battle after another against campaign finance bills that in his view limit free speech and vigorous electoral competition. "Spending is speech," he says. "The First Amendment denies government the power to determine that spending to promote one's political views is wasteful, excessive or unwise." He disputes the notions that campaign ads are some kind of pollution and that too much is spent on them. He noted that for the 1995–96 cycle, "we spent roughly what the cosmetic industry did promoting its product, a little more than the public consumed on yogurt, and about twice as much as the public consumed on bubble gum." He has been the lead opponent of the various McCain-Feingold bills to abolish soft money and prohibit issue advocacy ads during campaigns, and has led filibusters in 1994 and 1997. His own proposals are for enforcing the Supreme Court *Beck* decision banning unions from using mandatory dues for politics and indexing contribution limits to inflation.

McConnell ran for chairman of the National Republican Senatorial Committee and lost to Phil Gramm in 1990 and in 1992 by one vote; he won the post in November 1996. But he was not able to get Republican senators to contribute as much to campaigns as Democratic senators for 1998, and he was criticized for contributing heavily to Mark Neumann of Wisconsin, who ran against Russ Feingold, and for giving Washington state's Linda Smith, a McCain-Feingold backer, only $22,500 of a possible $570,000. He responded that polls showed Neumann's chances were better, and indeed Neumann won a higher percentage, but both lost. So did enough Republican hopefuls that the party gained no seats. McConnell blamed better Democratic turnout and a lack of "edge" issues. Evidently colleagues didn't blame him much. Freshman Chuck Hagel of Nebraska ran for the post in December 1998, but McConnell won 39–13. His challenge now will be to hold the Republicans' 55–45 edge in 2000, as 19 Republican and only 14 Democratic seats are up.

McConnell has worked hard to build up Kentucky's chronically ailing Republican Party, with considerable success. He oversaw Ron Lewis's capture of the 2d District House seat in a May 1994 special election. He helped Ed Whitfield pick up the 1st District and Republican legislative candidates win in western Kentucky in 1994. He backed Anne Northup in her win in Louisville's 3d District in 1996. But when Democrat Paul Patton was narrowly elected governor in November 1995, Democrats sensed McConnell might be in trouble. He had won a second term in 1990 over former Louisville Mayor Harvey Sloane 52%–48%. The 1996 Democratic nominee, former Lieutenant Governor Steve Beshear, attacked McConnell for stopping campaign finance reform, for refusing to release his tax returns, for seeking to delay voting on the minimum wage increase and for supporting NAFTA. McConnell charged that Beshear was a lobbyist, a political insider and, worst, a fox hunter; on the campaign trail Beshear was followed by a character dressed in fox-hunting regalia. McConnell put Beshear on the defensive when Bill Clinton proposed that the FDA regulate tobacco as a drug. And he ran an ad showing sheep and saying that voters should not allow themselves to be "Besheared." McConnell spent $5 million to Beshear's $2 million and, after early polls showed a close race, won 55%–43%. He carried the Louisville and Lexington areas, won 2–1 in northern Kentucky, and lost only handfuls of counties in the eastern mountains and in the far western end of the state.

In 1998 McConnell strongly backed Jim Bunning's candidacy for the Senate, but remained in controversy himself. In June 1998 he split with retiring Democrat Wendell Ford and backed an $18 billion tobacco program that would end price supports and provide mandatory buyouts of tobacco farmers. Ford and Bunning backed a $28 billion bailout with voluntary buyouts and continuing price supports. It was the first time in 60 years, Ford said, that Kentucky senators disagreed on tobacco. Later that month, the tobacco settlement bill died in the Senate, and McConnell, stung by criticism from tobacco farmers, reversed his previous desire to end price supports. In September he persuaded conferees to drop a provision that would have required tobacco companies to pay for tobacco price supports; they would take it out of the hide of farmers, he said. And he was fortunate indeed when Bunning beat Democrat Scott Baesler by 6,766 votes, just a few more than McConnell's own margin in 1984. Still, Democrats were already looking forward to running against McConnell in 2002. The obvious candidate would be Governor Patton; other possibilities are 1998 Senate candidates Charlie Owen and Lieutenant Governor Steve Henry.

Junior Senator. Jim Bunning, a Republican elected in 1998 in the second closest race in the country, is the first and so far only member of the Baseball Hall of Fame to serve in Congress. Bunning grew up in northern Kentucky, just across the Ohio River from Cincinnati. He started in minor league baseball in 1950, but at his father's insistence finished high school and college. He made the majors in 1956 and the next year became the only pitcher to strike out Ted Williams three times in one game. Bunning threw a no-hitter for the Detroit Tigers in 1958 and pitched a perfect game for the Philadelphia Phillies in 1964; he also played for the Pittsburgh Pirates and the Los Angeles Dodgers and retired in 1971 with a 224–184 record, a 3.24 ERA, 2,855 strikeouts and one of the highest totals in baseball history for hitting batters. He was inducted into the Baseball Hall of Fame in August 1996. He is a family man, with nine children (two sets of twins) and at last count 32 grandchildren. The skill, energy and aggressiveness he showed in baseball he brought to politics in his native northern Kentucky. He was elected to the Fort Thomas City Council in 1977, to the state Senate in 1979, and won a respectable 44% against Martha Layne Collins in the 1983 race for governor (the best showing for a Republican gubernatorial candidate between 1971 and 1995). When incumbent 4th District Congressman Gene Snyder retired in 1986, Bunning won the seat with 55%.

At first, Bunning showed great impatience with ways of doing business in the Democratic House. He served six years on the ethics committee, starting off in March 1992 by leading the charge against the House bank overdraft scandal, and ending in January 1997 by resigning from the committee out of disgust with the partisanship of ranking Democrat Jim McDermott. Nor is he a respecter of Bill Clinton, whom he called in September 1993 "the most corrupt, the most amoral, the most despicable person I've ever seen in the presidency." As Republicans became the majority, Bunning had achievements as a legislator. He chaired the Finance Social Security Subcommittee for two terms, and sponsored two major changes—raising the earnings limit for Social Security recipients up to $30,000 by 2002, and the 1994 law making the Social Security Administration an independent agency. He was the principal House sponsor of the adoption tax credit and the law to stop the ban on transracial adoptions. He sponsored a disability reform, which would make it easier for recipients to return to work by granting them two years of Medicare benefits; it passed the House 410–1 in June 1998 but was not taken up in the Senate. Another Bunning bill, to require 90% of the budget surplus to be used for Social Security, also passed the House but not the Senate. He is, incidentally, in favor of repealing the antitrust exemption for baseball.

Bunning was re-elected to the House easily, even after redistricting added Democratic territory. By early 1997, Bunning was already making plans to run for the Senate seat held by four-term Democrat Wendell Ford; in February 1997, Ford announced he would retire. Three Democrats ran serious campaigns for the nomination. Louisville businessman Charlie Owen spent $7 million of his own money and ran ads attacking the other two. Lieutenant Governor Steve Henry spent $500,000 of his own money and counted on his Louisville base and Owensboro roots; Governor Paul Patton said he would support him but would not urge his supporters to do so. The third candidate was Lexington Congressman Scott Baesler, who had less money but other advantages: he was popular in his Republican-leaning 6th District, he is a tobacco farmer and he was still known as a star on one of Adolph Rupp's University of Kentucky basketball teams in the early 1960s. Baesler won big in the Lexington media market, where a spirited House primary also brought out voters. Henry carried Louisville and much of western Kentucky. Owen carried northern and eastern Kentucky, where neither of the other two had local bases. Overall, Baesler won the May primary with 34% of the vote, to 29% for Owen and 28% for Henry.

Baesler emerged from the primary ahead of Bunning in the polls but out of money; Bunning, with extensive help from Senator Mitch McConnell, had plenty. Baesler tried to take advantage of McConnell's support for an end to tobacco price supports, but Bunning opposed McConnell's stand, and both candidates had to agree there were no differences between them on tobacco. Bunning went on the air first and evened up the polls. Skillfully he played to the consensus-mindedness of voters. Ads paid for by McConnell's senatorial campaign committee highlighted Bunning's role as chairman of the Social Security Subcommittee. "My ideas," he said, "are not far right or far left. They're right down the middle, like most Kentuckians'—safer schools, lower taxes, balanced budgets." A late September ad showed Baesler's frenzied speechifying at the traditional Fancy Farm gathering in August, to the music of Wagner's "Ride of the Valkyries"; Democrats said this was to suggest that Baesler was a Nazi, while Bunning replied that the same music was used for Elmer Fudd. Bunning ran an ad showing actors thanking Baesler, in Spanish and (with subtitles) Chinese, for voting for NAFTA and MFN status for China. Baesler ads stressed campaign finance reform—a dig at McConnell, its leading opponent—and went back and attacked Bunning votes not only in the House but in the Kentucky legislature. Baesler stressed that he was a Blue Dog Democrat in the House, with a moderate record, and that he supported welfare reform in 1996 and the balanced budget agreement in 1997. He added that he wanted to save 100% of the surplus for Social Security, more than Bunning's 90%. And he criticized Bunning for criticizing UK basketball coach Rick Pitino for welcoming Bill Clinton to Lexington in the last days of the 1996 campaign—an appearance that may have swung Kentucky's eight electoral votes.

This was perhaps the country's closest race for months. And, despite Kentucky's early poll closing times and rapid count, it was not until late in the evening that Bunning was declared the winner. His margin was 49.7%–49.2%, or 6,766 votes. Baesler carried normally Republican Lexington, but only by 54%–46%. Bunning carried the three counties of northern Kentucky by 70%–29%; his margin there was 34,791 votes, more than five times his statewide margin, and more than Baesler's Lexington and Louisville margins put together. "The message from the elections of 1998," Bunning said, "is that Social Security must be strengthened and reformed. We need to take it out of politics, stop the distortion and get down to work."

Presidential politics. In presidential elections, Kentucky is competitive when Democrats run a Southerner or two, as it was in such widely separated years as 1952, 1976, 1980, 1992 and 1996; otherwise it has gone pretty solidly Republican. Bill Clinton and Al Gore carried the state 45%–41% in 1992. In 1996, Clinton lost votes on the tobacco issue and his margin shrunk in most rural counties; he ended up carrying the state 46%–45% only by improving his vote in Lexington, the Bluegrass and the Louisville and northern Kentucky suburbs. Was the difference made by the appearance at a November 4 Clinton-Gore rally in Lexington of University of Kentucky basketball coach Rick Pitino? Maybe so: Kentucky takes basketball very seriously, and under Pitino, UK won its first national championship in two decades in 1996.

Kentucky was part of the Super Tuesday primary in March 1988, but switched back to a May date in 1992, so that state and presidential contests can be held on the same day. It has had no effect on the outcome of the presidential contest.

Congressional districting. Kentucky lost one district in the 1990 Census. Redistricting moved the 4th District out of the Jefferson County suburbs and east into the mountains and merged most of the old 5th and 7th mountain districts, one very Republican and the other very Democratic, into a new 5th. Scandal, death, retirement and political upheaval have produced great turnover in what in the 1980s was one of the House's most stable delegations: Kentucky's six districts have been represented by 14 congressmen in the 1990s.

The People: Est. Pop. 1998: 3,936,499; Pop. 1990: 3,685,296, up 6.8% 1990–1998. 1.5% of U.S. total, 25th largest; 48.2% rural. Median age: 35.1 years. 13.2% 65 years and over. 92.1% White, 7.1% Black, 0.5% Asian, 0.2% Amer. Indian, 0.2% Other; 0.6% Hispanic Origin. Households: 59.2% married couple families; 29.6% married couple fams. w. children; 32.9% college educ.; median household income: $22,534; per capita income: $11,153; 69.6% owner occupied housing; median house value: $50,500; median monthly rent: $250. 4.6% Unemployment. 1998 Voting age pop.: 2,990,000. 1998 Turnout: 1,215,053; 41% of VAP. Registered voters (1998): 2,590,339; 1,570,461 D (61%), 835,465 R (32%), 184,413 unaffiliated and minor parties (7%).

Political Lineup: Governor, Paul E. Patton (D); Lt. Gov., Steven Henry (D); Secy. of State, John Y. Brown III (D); Atty. Gen., Albert B. (Ben) Chandler III (D); Treasurer, John Kennedy Hamilton (D); State Senate, 38 (20 D, 18 R); Majority Leader, David Karem (D); State House, 100 (65 D, 35 R); House Speaker, Jody Richards (D). Senators, Mitch McConnell (R) and Jim Bunning (R). Representatives, 6 (1 D, 5 R).

Elections Division: 502-573-7100; **Filing Deadline for U.S. Congress:** January 25, 2000.

1996 Presidential Vote

Clinton (D)	636,614	(46%)
Dole (R)	623,283	(45%)
Perot (I)	120,396	(9%)

1996 Republican Presidential Primary

Dole (R)	76,669	(74%)
Buchanan (R)	8,526	(8%)
Keyes (R)	3,822	(4%)
Others	14,822	(14%)

1992 Presidential Vote

Clinton (D)	665,095	(45%)
Bush (R)	617,196	(41%)
Perot (I)	203,968	(14%)

GOVERNOR

Gov. Paul E. Patton (D)

Elected 1995, term expires Dec. 1999; b. May 26, 1937, Fallsburg; home, Pikeville; U. of KY, B.S. 1959; Presbyterian; married (Judi).

Elected Office: Pike Cnty. Judge Exec., 1982–91; KY Lt. Gov., 1991–95.

Professional Career: Coal Co. Exec., 1959–79; KY Dpty. Transportation Secy., 1979–80; KY Dem. Party Chmn., 1981–83; KY Economic Develop. Secy., 1991–95.

Office: Office of the Governor, State Capitol, Frankfort, 40601, 502-564-2611; Fax: 502-564-2735; Web site: www.state.ky.us.

Election Results

1995 gen.	Paul E. Patton (D)	500,787	(51%)
	Larry Forgy (R)	479,227	(49%)
1995 prim.	Paul E. Patton (D)	152,203	(45%)
	Bob Babbage (D)	81,352	(24%)
	John (Eck) Rose (D)	71,740	(21%)
	Gatewood Galbraith (D)	29,039	(9%)
1991 gen.	Brereton C. Jones (D)	540,648	(65%)
	Larry J. Hopkins (R)	294,452	(35%)

SENATORS

Sen. Mitch McConnell (R)

Elected 1984, seat up 2002; b. Feb. 20, 1942, Sheffield, AL; home, Louisville; U. of Louisville, B.A. 1964, U. of KY, J.D. 1967; Baptist; married (Elaine).

Elected Office: Jefferson Cnty. Judge Exec., 1977–84.

Professional Career: Chief Legis. Asst., U.S. Sen. Marlow Cook, 1967–70; Dpty. Asst. U.S. Atty. Gen., 1974–75.

DC Office: 361-A RSOB, 20510, 202-224-2541; Fax: 202-224-2499; Web site: www.senate.gov/~mcconnell.

State Offices: Bowling Green, 502-781-1673; Ft. Wright, 606-578-0188; Lexington, 606-224-8286; London, 606-864-2026; Louisville, 502-582-6304; Paducah, 502-442-4554.

Committees: *NRSC Chairman. Agriculture, Nutrition & Forestry* (4th of 10 R): Marketing, Inspection & Product Promotion; Research, Nutrition & General Legislation. *Appropriations* (7th of 15 R): Agriculture & Rural Development; Commerce, Justice, State & the Judiciary; Defense; Energy & Water Development; Foreign Operations & Export Financing (Chmn.). *Rules & Administration* (Chmn. of 9 R). *Joint Committee on Printing* (1st of 5 Sens.). *Joint Committee on the Library of Congress* (2d of 5 Sens.).

Group Ratings

	ADA	ACLU	AFS	LCV	CON	NTU	NFIB	COC	ACU	NTLC	CHC
1998	0	14	0	0	14	63	100	94	92	93	91
1997	5	—	0	—	71	84	—	100	88	—	—

National Journal Ratings

	1997 LIB — 1997 CONS			1998 LIB — 1998 CONS		
Economic	0%	—	89%	18%	—	72%
Social	0%	—	83%	0%	—	88%
Foreign	24%	—	72%	29%	—	58%

Key Votes of the 105th Congress

1. Bal. Budget Amend.	Y	5. Satcher for Surgeon Gen.	N	9. Chem. Weapons Treaty	Y
2. Clinton Budget Deal	Y	6. Highway Set-asides	N	10. Cuban Humanitarian Aid	N
3. Cloture on Tobacco	N	7. Table Child Gun locks	Y	11. Table Bosnia Troops	Y
4. Education IRAs	Y	8. Ovrd. Part. Birth Veto	Y	12. $ for Test-ban Treaty	N

Election Results

1996 general	Mitch McConnell (R)	724,794	(55%)	($5,031,293)
	Steven L. Beshear (D)	560,012	(43%)	($2,073,794)
	Others	22,240	(2%)	
1996 primary	Mitch McConnell (R)	88,620	(89%)	
	Tommy Klein (R)	11,410	(11%)	
1990 general	Mitch McConnell (R)	478,034	(52%)	($5,229,296)
	G. Harvey I. Sloane (D)	437,976	(48%)	($2,929,641)

Sen. Jim Bunning (R)

Elected 1998, seat up 2004; b. Oct. 23, 1931, Campbell Cnty.; home, Southgate; Xavier U., B.S. 1953; Catholic; married (Mary).

Elected Office: Ft. Thomas City Cncl., 1977–79; KY Senate, 1979–83; U.S. House of Reps., 1986–98.

Professional Career: Pro baseball player, 1950–71; Investment broker & agent, 1960–86.

DC Office: 502 HSOB, 20510, 202-224-4343; Fax: 202-228-1373; Web site: www.senate.gov/~bunning.

State Offices: Ft. Wright, 606-341-2602; Hopkinsville, 270-885-1212; Lexington, 606-219-2239; Owensboro, 270-689-9085.

Committees: *Aging (Special)* (10th of 11 R). *Banking, Housing & Urban Affairs* (10th of 11 R): Economic Policy; Financial Institutions; Securities (Vice Chmn.). *Energy & Natural Resources* (8th of 11 R): Energy, Research, Development, Production & Regulation; National Parks, Historic Preservation & Recreation; Water & Power.

Group Ratings (as Member of U.S. House of Representatives)

	ADA	ACLU	AFS	LCV	CON	NTU	NFIB	COC	ACU	NTLC	CHC
1998	0	7	0	8	2	46	100	94	92	92	100
1997	0	—	13	—	42	49	—	90	92	—	—

National Journal Ratings (as Member of U.S. House of Representatives)

	1997 LIB — 1997 CONS			1998 LIB — 1998 CONS		
Economic	24%	—	73%	19%	—	79%
Social	10%	—	82%	3%	—	90%
Foreign	12%	—	81%	7%	—	83%

Key Votes of the 105th Congress (as Member of U.S. House of Representatives)

1. Clinton Budget Deal	Y	5. Puerto Rico Sthood. Ref.	N	9. Cut $ for B-2 Bombers	N
2. Education IRAs	Y	6. End Highway Set-asides	Y	10. Human Rights in China	Y
3. Req. 2/3 to Raise Taxes	Y	7. School Prayer Amend.	Y	11. Withdraw Bosnia Troops	Y
4. Fast-track Trade	Y	8. Ovrd. Part. Birth Veto	Y	12. End Cuban TV-Marti	N

Election Results

1998 general	Jim Bunning (R)	569,817	(50%)	($3,746,540)
	Scotty Baesler (D)	563,051	(49%)	($3,841,950)
	Others	12,546	(1%)	
1998 primary	Jim Bunning (R)	152,493	(74%)	
	Barry Metcalf (R)	52,798	(26%)	
1992 general	Wendell H. Ford (D)	836,888	(63%)	($2,321,131)
	David L. Williams (R)	476,604	(36%)	($335,304)

FIRST DISTRICT

The point where the Ohio River flows into the Mississippi—the intersection Huckleberry Finn and Jim missed in the fog—must have struck early settlers as a site for a great city. But no Pittsburgh or St. Louis grew up on this fertile black soil. Instead, the Kentucky land west of the dammed-up Tennessee and Cumberland rivers, bought from the Chickasaw Indians by General Andrew Jackson and Governor Isaac Shelby in 1818—the Jackson Purchase, it is still called—was settled by farmers. Most people here today are the descendants of these farmers, with memories of earlier generations living in family lore. Just to the east of the Tennessee and the Cumberland rivers is the Pennyrile (after pennyroyal, a common variety of local wild mint), a land of low hills and small farms, where you find the west Kentucky coal fields, the site of much strip mining in recent years. Here is Lyon County, founded by Matthew "Spitting" Lyon, who earned his epithet while a congressman from Vermont, and who later represented western Kentucky from 1803–1811.

The 1st Congressional District is made up of the Jackson Purchase and much of the Pennyrile, plus a line of counties stretching some 200 miles east of the Mississippi along the Tennessee border. There is a distinctive Southern atmosphere here—in the crops that are grown, in historically low wage levels, and in the fact that the big city people look to is more often Nashville than Louisville. The Jackson Purchase and the Pennyrile have long been Democratic; Paducah, the district's largest city, produced one of the most enduring Democratic politicians of this century, Alben Barkley, whose career from 1912–56 included 14 years in the House, 24 in the Senate and four as vice president; he was Senate majority and minority leader, keynoted four Democratic National Conventions, and died while delivering the peroration at Washington and Lee University's mock political convention in 1956. But the hills far from the Mississippi are Republican country and this, combined with the Republican trend that reached north from Dixie to Paducah in 1994, has made the 1st District seriously contested territory, a district that in the angry climate of the early 1990s elected three different congressmen in three elections.

The congressman now is Edward Whitfield, a longtime Democrat who turned Republican. He grew up in Hopkinsville and Madisonville, in a family with Pennyrile roots going back before 1800. He served in the Army, practiced law in Hopkinsville, and was elected to the legislature in 1973 as a Democrat where he was something of an insider; former Governor (1963–67) Edward Breathitt was best man at his wedding. After one term in Frankfort, Whitfield ran an oil distributorship in the west Kentucky coal fields, then in 1979 moved to Washington to become an executive for the Seaboard and CSX railroads. He was legal counsel to the chairman of the then-Interstate Commerce Commission from 1991–93, when he returned to west Kentucky and ran for Congress as a Republican.

He was returning to a district that since Barkley's time had been represented by quiet, long-serving, conservative Democrats. But the incumbent, Tom Barlow, elected in 1992 after beating scandal-tarred incumbent Carroll Hubbard in the Democratic primary, was a free-spirited supporter of the Clinton Administration. In the May 1994 primary, Whitfield beat Barlow's 1992 opponent by only 53%–47%. Then, with help from Senator Mitch McConnell, Whitfield raised enough money to put on a serious campaign and attacked Barlow's 1993 vote for the Clinton budget and tax increase. He won 70% in the counties added after redistricting, but also carried traditionally Democratic areas around Hopkinsville in the Pennyrile, and Murray in the Jackson Purchase, for a 51%–49% victory.

In the House, Whitfield has a moderate-to-conservative voting record and got a seat on the Commerce Committee. In his first term he sponsored the "lock box" amendment on Medicare, prohibiting savings from being used for other purposes; this was to blunt Democratic attacks on Republican Medicare "cuts." In 1996 Whitfield was opposed by Dennis Null, a former law partner of Carroll Hubbard, who traveled around the district in Old Blue, an aging Lincoln Town car; the AFL-CIO ran a barrage of TV ads attacking Whitfield on tax cuts, pension security, and Medicare. But Whitfield had nearly a 2–1 money advantage and he attacked the Clinton Administration proposal for FDA regulation of tobacco. Whitfield carried 18 of the district's 31 counties, including Paducah, which he lost in 1994, and won overall 54%–46%.

In his second term, Whitfield's big issue was TVA's Land Between the Lakes recreation area. In the 1998 omnibus bill, Whitfield and McConnell got $7 million for TVA to administer the area, plus a proviso that the Forest Service would take it over if TVA ever got less than $6 million for it; Congress has threatened to sell off TVA's land management functions. Whitfield also regained funding for the Kentucky Lock on the Tennessee River, opposed a Clinton line-item veto of a vehicle maintenance depot at Fort Campbell and intervened against an effort to deport a Canadian doctor running a clinic in Carlisle County.

Running again in 1998 was Tom Barlow, this time with a "grass roots" campaign that was at a huge money disadvantage. Barlow had union support, but no AFL-CIO ads; he argued that Whitfield's Land Between the Lakes agreement did not have safeguards against commercial development and did not provide money for the Forest Service to manage the area. The result was almost a mirror image of 1996. Whitfield carried 18 counties including Paducah and won 55%–45%.

Cook's Call. *Potentially Competitive.* While this sprawling western Kentucky district still has deep Democratic roots, it has elected Whitfield by increasing margins since his first victory in 1994. A strong Democrat who can raise money could make this a competitive race, but Whitfield has established himself quite well here and will be hard to knock off.

The People: Pop. 1990: 614,265; 61.4% rural; 15.9% age 65 + ; 91.4% White, 7.8% Black, 0.3% Asian, 0.2% Amer. Indian, 0.3% Other; 0.7% Hispanic Origin. Households: 61.6% married couple families; 29.2% married couple fams. w. children; 27.7% college educ.; median household income: $20,331; per capita income: $10,238; median house value: $40,500; median gross rent: $196.

1996 Presidential Vote			1992 Presidential Vote		
Clinton (D)	105,150	(47%)	Clinton (D)	116,648	(48%)
Dole (R)	96,356	(43%)	Bush (R)	96,605	(39%)
Perot (I)	22,727	(10%)	Perot (I)	30,871	(13%)

Rep. Edward Whitfield (R)

Elected 1994; b. May 25, 1943, Hopkinsville; home, Hopkinsville; U. of KY, B.S. 1965, J.D. 1969; Methodist; married (Connie).

Military Career: Army Reserves, 1967–73.

Elected Office: KY House of Reps., 1973–75.

Professional Career: Practicing atty., 1969–79; Owner, Rhodes Oil Co., 1975–79; Cnsl., Seaboard System Railroad, 1979–83; V.P., CSX, 1983–91; Cnsl., Interstate Commerce Comm., 1991–93.

DC Office: 236 CHOB 20515, 202-225-3115; Fax: 202-225-3547; Web site: www.house.gov/whitfield.

District Offices: Henderson, 502-826-4180; Hopkinsville, 502-885-8079; Paducah, 502-442-6901; Tompkinsville, 502-487-9509.

Committees: *Commerce* (15th of 29 R): Energy & Power; Health and Environment; Oversight & Investigations.

Group Ratings

	ADA	ACLU	AFS	LCV	CON	NTU	NFIB	COC	ACU	NTLC	CHC
1998	5	13	22	23	32	47	100	88	96	92	100
1997	0	—	25	—	42	56	—	100	96	—	—

National Journal Ratings

	1997 LIB — 1997 CONS	1998 LIB — 1998 CONS
Economic	28% — 67%	30% — 67%
Social	10% — 82%	32% — 67%
Foreign	30% — 68%	27% — 68%

Key Votes of the 105th Congress

1. Clinton Budget Deal	Y	5. Puerto Rico Sthood. Ref.	N	9. Cut $ for B-2 Bombers	N
2. Education IRAs	Y	6. End Highway Set-asides	Y	10. Human Rights in China	N
3. Req. 2/3 to Raise Taxes	Y	7. School Prayer Amend.	Y	11. Withdraw Bosnia Troops	Y
4. Fast-track Trade	N	8. Ovrd. Part. Birth Veto	Y	12. End Cuban TV-Marti	N

Election Results

1998 general	Edward Whitfield (R)	95,308	(55%)	($608,491)
	Tom Barlow (D)	77,402	(45%)	($144,088)
1998 primary	Edward Whitfield (R)	unopposed		
1996 general	Edward Whitfield (R)	111,473	(54%)	($897,338)
	Dennis L. Null (D)	96,684	(46%)	($479,210)

SECOND DISTRICT

In the 1770s and 1780s, Americans began settling the limestone-soiled country of central Kentucky, staking out towns like Bardstown and Elizabethtown and starting academies and colleges; they were well-settled when Stephen Foster wrote "My Old Kentucky Home" just before the Civil War. That conflict tore deeply here: this part of Kentucky gave birth to both Abraham Lincoln and Jefferson Davis, and in the Civil War it lost thousands of soldiers, Union and Confederate, and would suffer disproportionate casualties in the wars of the 20th Century as well. This area is also the home of several Kentucky landmarks—Fort Knox, the nation's gold depository; some of the nation's largest bourbon distilleries; and Mammoth Cave, the world's largest accessible cavern, in the south near Bowling Green.

The 2d Congressional District consists of much of the territory south and southwest of Louisville, starting with the southern Jefferson County suburbs and proceeding south to Bowling Green and west along the Ohio River to Owensboro. This is rural and small-town country, where most people have family roots that go back generations and a connection with the past not often found in big metropolitan areas. Civil War loyalties are reflected in the election returns here; Kentucky was deeply split on secession, and a color-coded map of the current 2d District would show various splotches of counties pro-South and splotches pro-Union. But the bits of color would only hint at the deep and often bitter feelings caused by the splits over the War— feelings of which current partisan preferences are a persistent reflection, but growing dimmer. In the 1990s, opinion has moved toward the Republicans in what was for 129 years a Democratic district.

The congressman from the 2d District is Ron Lewis, a Republican first elected in a May 1994 special election that had national implications. Lewis was born in a log cabin and raised in eastern Kentucky; he worked his way through Morehead State as a laborer at Armco Steel. He worked in the highway department, at a state hospital, then served in the Navy. He worked in sales, and in 1980 became a Baptist minister; in 1985 he started a Christian book store in Elizabethtown, two counties south of Louisville; he was the opposite of a political insider.

Then, in March 1994, Democratic Congressman William Natcher died. He was chairman of the Appropriations Committee and a politician of a very old school, so hard-working and conscientious that he never missed a roll call vote in 41 years. Though the district voted for George Bush in 1992, Democratic leaders assumed they would win: they hand-picked former state Senate President Joe Prather, who had managed Governor Brereton Jones's campaign; before the election, Prather even flew to Washington to go apartment hunting. But this failed to account for the national and local conservative trend. Lewis ran for the open seat, and the National Republican Congressional Committee contributed $200,000 for the May 1994 special. Lewis ran ads showing Prather's face morphing into Bill Clinton's, and saying that Prather had increased taxes and fees 40 times in the Kentucky legislature. Prather only belatedly raised campaign money and asserted that he was quite a different sort of Democrat than Clinton. Lewis won a solid 55%–45% victory, carrying Bowling Green heavily and running ahead in Owensboro and outside Louisville.

In the House, Lewis made news in August 1994 when he attended a smokers' rights rally where Hillary Rodham Clinton was burned in effigy—"inappropriate," he said, but "kind of a desperate act to get some attention to their cause." Many Democrats assumed that Lewis's victory was aberrational and that Democratic Owensboro Mayor David Adkisson, a protege of Senator Wendell Ford, would win in November. But Lewis projected sincerity, and his strong religious views and opposition to the Clinton tax increase and health care plan were pluses. Lewis won by a resounding 60%–40% margin, even carrying Owensboro's Daviess County.

In 1996, Lewis had another opponent with strong political credentials, former state Senate Majority Leader Joe Wright, who retired from office in 1992 and became head of the Burley Tobacco Growers Association. While President Clinton was proposing that the FDA regulate tobacco as a drug, Wright was taking his cutting knife around the district and helping farmers cut tobacco. Lewis's theme was "promises made, promises kept"; he campaigned hard against Clinton on tobacco issues and called on him to spend more time fighting illegal drugs than legal ones. Lewis won 58%–42%, carrying all but three counties.

Lewis has a solidly conservative voting record. In his second full term, he co-sponsored the 1998 emergency farm relief act and pushed for precision agriculture research; he co-sponsored with Bernie Sanders a 17% increase in federal payments in lieu of taxes. In June 1998 he backed the Lugar tobacco buyout plan, phasing out tobacco price supports and providing a mandatory buyout of tobacco farmers' entitlements. This put him on the same side as Senator Mitch McConnell, and against retiring Senator Wendell Ford and the two nominees to succeed him, Republican Jim Bunning and Democrat Scott Baesler. "The best deal for our farmers is a buyout that preserves our right to continue to grow this legal crop," Lewis argued. "While the money is on the table, we had better get as much money for the farmer as we can and get it to them as quickly as possible.''

Evidently this stand was not as politically perilous as many assumed. Lewis faced only weak opposition: when Hardin County Clerk David Logsdon was going in to file, he saw that he would have a Democratic primary opponent, tobacco farmer Bob Evans, and he decided not to run. The only major surprise was that Lewis, who in 1994 pledged to serve no more than four full terms, announced in October he had changed his mind. "I came to believe that if those of us who believe in term limits limit ourselves, then we're a dying breed." But he said he would still vote for term limits. He won 64%–35%, losing only one county.

In November 1998 Lewis won a seat on the Ways and Means Committee. He seems headed for a long career in the House, where he can work on his promises to cut the capital gains tax to 15%, end the marriage penalty and set aside the budget surplus for Social Security.

Cook's Call. *Safe.* Lewis, who sits in the second most Republican district in the state, has not come close to losing this district in three elections, and probably never will.

The People: Pop. 1990: 615,131; 55.8% rural; 11.9% age 65 + ; 93.5% White, 5.4% Black, 0.6% Asian, 0.2% Amer. Indian, 0.3% Other; 0.7% Hispanic Origin. Households: 63.8% married couple families; 33% married couple fams. w. children; 29.9% college educ.; median household income: $23,212; per capita income: $10,609; median house value: $48,200; median gross rent: $240.

1996 Presidential Vote

Dole (R) 113,923 (49%)
Clinton (D) 95,530 (41%)
Perot (I) 22,021 (9%)

1992 Presidential Vote

Bush (R) 107,401 (45%)
Clinton (D) 98,999 (41%)
Perot (I) 33,232 (14%)

Rep. Ron Lewis (R)

Elected May 1994; b. Sept. 14, 1946, McKell; home, Cecilia; U. of KY, B.A. 1969, Morehead St. U., M.A. 1981; Baptist; married (Kayi).

Military Career: Navy OCS, 1972.

Professional Career: Heavy Equip. Sales Rep., 1975–80; Baptist Minister, 1980–present; Prof., Watterson Col., 1980–85; Owner, Alpha Christian Bookstore, 1985–94.

DC Office: 223 CHOB 20515, 202-225-3501; Web site: www.house.gov/ronlewis.

District Offices: Bowling Green, 502-842-9896; Elizabethtown, 502-765-4360; Owensboro, 502-688-8858.

Committees: *Ways & Means* (22d of 23 R): Human Resources.

Group Ratings

	ADA	ACLU	AFS	LCV	CON	NTU	NFIB	COC	ACU	NTLC	CHC
1998	0	6	0	0	2	51	100	100	100	100	100
1997	0	—	13	—	42	56	—	78	95	—	—

National Journal Ratings

	1997 LIB — 1997 CONS		1998 LIB — 1998 CONS	
Economic	14%	— 85%	15%	— 81%
Social	19%	— 80%	3%	— 90%
Foreign	0%	— 88%	0%	— 93%

Key Votes of the 105th Congress

1. Clinton Budget Deal	Y	5. Puerto Rico Sthood. Ref.	N	9. Cut $ for B-2 Bombers	N
2. Education IRAs	Y	6. End Highway Set-asides	Y	10. Human Rights in China	N
3. Req. 2/3 to Raise Taxes	Y	7. School Prayer Amend.	Y	11. Withdraw Bosnia Troops	Y
4. Fast-track Trade	Y	8. Ovrd. Part. Birth Veto	Y	12. End Cuban TV-Marti	N

Election Results

1998 general	Ron Lewis (R)	113,285	(64%)	($335,500)
	Bob Evans (D)	62,848	(35%)	
	Others	1,833	(1%)	
1998 primary	Ron Lewis (R)	unopposed		
1996 general	Ron Lewis (R)	125,433	(58%)	($639,397)
	Joe Wright (D)	90,483	(42%)	($480,101)

THIRD DISTRICT

At the falls of the Ohio River, Americans more than 200 years ago founded one of their first inland metropolises, the river port and industrial city of Louisville (pronounced *LOOuhv'l*). It is one of the few major American cities today named for a man who was executed, King Louis XVI of France (others are St. Paul and Raleigh). Louisville has always retained an air of the South; when Kentucky decided not to secede in 1861, the decision was not unanimous, and the culture of tidewater Virginia is still visible in the Louisville lawn party. Steamboats are tied up in front of Louisville's downtown, primed to follow the channel around the falls of the Ohio that prompted George Rogers Clark to found the town in 1778. Mint juleps are served on the verandas of mansions, especially (but not only) during Kentucky Derby week in May; horse racing is a preoccupation throughout the year. Although the Ohio River is crossed with many bridges and the accent across the river in Indiana may sound the same to outsiders, Louisville partakes of the cavalier culture that second sons of big landowners from England brought to Virginia in the 17th Century and their heirs brought over the Appalachians to the valleys of Kentucky in the 18th Century.

Though Louisville's economy is not particularly Southern, tobacco and cigarettes are a major business here, and so is distilling whiskey. Louisville still specializes in assembling large, clunky things like appliances and automobiles, and Louisville airport is the hub for UPS. Politically, Louisville has always had some un-Southern aspects and has often voted against the rest of Kentucky; if its elite were Virginia cavaliers, many of its burghers were Germans and Pennsylvanians who made this river town a Republican and anti-slavery island in a secessionist and pro-slavery sea. But Louisville and Jefferson County's two-party politics, which propelled Republican County Judge-Executive Mitch McConnell into the U.S. Senate in 1984, has gone more Democratic lately, though not always by wide margins.

The 3d Congressional District includes all of Louisville and almost all of the Jefferson County suburbs—the strip highway zone running south toward Fort Knox, then blue-collar factory zones south of Churchill Downs and the affluent suburbs in the hills to the east heading out toward Bluegrass country. Louisville's historic Republican tradition made this a closely contested district back in 1958–64 and again in 1970; today it votes for Democrats for most offices and was Bill Clinton's strongest district in Kentucky, but in 1996 and 1998 it elected, albeit by narrow margins, a Republican to the House.

The congresswoman from the 3d District is Anne Northup. She grew up in a large Catholic family in Louisville—she has nine sisters and one brother—and has raised six children of her own. Her husband is a small business owner and she volunteered and served on the boards of many charities and associations. In 1986 she was elected to the Kentucky House, where she worked for holding down taxes and also for Kentucky's 1990 education reform, and where she became the number one critic of tobacco in the capital of the nation's number two tobacco state.

In 1996 she decided to run for Congress, against freshman Democrat Mike Ward, an "old Democrat" who won the seat by 425 votes in 1994, when 12% voted for an anti-abortion third candidate. In a year when almost all Democrats and most Republicans ran cookie-cutter campaigns, Northup showed originality in strategy and tactics. First, she outraised the incumbent, with an amazing $868,000 coming from individuals; she spent $1,182,000 to Ward's $880,000. Second, she started TV spots in August three weeks before Ward got on the air. Third, she used unusual issues, such as Ward's vote against making English the official language. Both candidates opposed FDA regulation of tobacco, but her criticisms of tobacco companies— "I'm very disappointed that the Republicans have not been more forthcoming about kids not smoking"—moderated her image. She argued that government should handle money like the family checkbook: "Hey, if you can't afford it, you can't afford it." Ward ran behind his party ticket and Northup won 50.3%–49.7%, a margin of 1,299 votes.

In Washington, Northup was singled out by the leadership and was one of two Republican freshmen to get a seat on Appropriations. Her voting record is somewhat moderate on economic and foreign issues and conservative on cultural issues. She voted with Transportation Chairman Bud Shuster on the highway bill and got $40 million for two interstate bridges over the Ohio River. She staunchly defended the Republicans' $500 per child tax credit and voted against the Religious Freedom Act. At home she formed an association with two black ministers and got $3 million in funding for their projects. When the Lewinsky scandal broke, Northup appeared on "Meet the Press" and criticized feminists for their silence on Clinton's behavior: "This isn't his private life. This is his workplace."

With her narrow margin and her Democratic-leaning constituency Northup was an obvious target for 1998. But Louisville Mayor Jerry Abramson, ex-Mayor Harvey Sloane and County Judge-Executive Dave Armstrong declined to run, and until nearly filing day her only opponent was Virginia Woodward, director of the Kentucky Commission on Women. Then Governor Paul Patton persuaded former Attorney General and County Commissioner Chris Gorman to run. Gorman was almost born into politics; his mother was secretary to Governors Bert Combs and Edward Breathitt and he has spent almost all his life in the public sector. Gorman attacked Northup for voting with Newt Gingrich 95% of the time and attacked her vote for the Republican version of managed care reform. Northup said the Democratic version would raise insurance rates sharply and she campaigned on education, Social Security and local projects. Gorman was one of the few Democrats to run ads criticizing the Republicans' handling of impeachment. Northup once again showed her fundraising prowess, and was aided by many House colleagues: she raised over $1.6 million, almost three times as much as Gorman. She won 52%–48%, with a margin of 7,825 votes, not much, but more than four times the combined margins in the district in 1994 and 1996.

After the election Northup ran for vice chairman of the House Republican Conference, but lost to Tillie Fowler. She was named by Republican Congressional Campaign Committee Chairman Tom Davis as one of his six vice-chairmen.

Cook's Call. *Competitive.* This Democratic-leaning district will never be entirely safe Republican territory, but Northup's phenomenal fundraising ability and strong political skills have helped her to keep a hold on this Louisville-based seat. Northup's visible role in impeachment undoubtedly hurt her in 1998. While certainly vulnerable to a poor political climate and to a strong Democratic challenge, Northup will still be tough to unseat.

The People: Pop. 1990: 613,266; 1.8% rural; 14.5% age 65 +; 80.6% White, 18.3% Black, 0.7% Asian, 0.2% Amer. Indian, 0.2% Other; 0.6% Hispanic Origin. Households: 49.1% married couple families; 22.2% married couple fams. w. children; 44.4% college educ.; median household income: $26,614; per capita income: $14,072; median house value: $57,000; median gross rent: $280.

1996 Presidential Vote

Clinton (D)	134,975	(53%)
Dole (R)	101,977	(40%)
Perot (I)	17,230	(7%)

1992 Presidential Vote

Clinton (D)	143,824	(50%)
Bush (R)	105,520	(37%)
Perot (I)	35,902	(13%)

Rep. Anne Northup (R)

Elected 1996; b. Jan. 22, 1948, Louisville; home, Louisville; St. Mary's Col., B.A. 1970; Catholic; married (Robert).

Elected Office: KY House of Reps., 1986–96.

DC Office: 1004 LHOB 20515, 202-225-5401; Fax: 202-225-5776; Web site: www.house.gov/northup.

District Office: Louisville, 502-582-5129.

Committees: *Appropriations* (29th of 34 R): Labor, HHS & Education; Treasury, Postal Service & General Government; VA, HUD & Independent Agencies.

Group Ratings

	ADA	ACLU	AFS	LCV	CON	NTU	NFIB	COC	ACU	NTLC	CHC
1998	0	13	11	8	13	47	100	100	88	87	100
1997	5	—	25	—	29	47	—	100	88	—	—

National Journal Ratings

	1997 LIB — 1997 CONS			1998 LIB — 1998 CONS		
Economic	35%	—	63%	28%	—	70%
Social	10%	—	82%	29%	—	69%
Foreign	30%	—	68%	39%	—	58%

Key Votes of the 105th Congress

1. Clinton Budget Deal	Y	5. Puerto Rico Sthood. Ref.	N	9. Cut $ for B-2 Bombers	N
2. Education IRAs	Y	6. End Highway Set-asides	Y	10. Human Rights in China	N
3. Req. 2/3 to Raise Taxes	Y	7. School Prayer Amend.	N	11. Withdraw Bosnia Troops	N
4. Fast-track Trade	Y	8. Ovrd. Part. Birth Veto	Y	12. End Cuban TV-Marti	N

Election Results

1998 general	Anne Northup (R)	100,690	(52%)	($1,772,613)
	Chris Gorman (D)	92,865	(48%)	($702,866)
	Others	1,881	(1%)	
1998 primary	Anne Northup (R)	unopposed		
1996 general	Anne Northup (R)	126,625	(50%)	($1,181,546)
	Mike Ward (D)	125,326	(50%)	($880,073)

FOURTH DISTRICT

The commonwealth of Kentucky has gone to court more than once to assert its claim to all of the Ohio River up to its northern bank: this is one of the northernmost extensions of the South. The Ohio sees many different parts of Kentucky. Ashland, near the West Virginia border, is industrial, the home of Ashland Oil; the river here is bound in by tight hills that hold smoke and soot close in the air. Farther down the river, the country is more bucolic: here Eliza fled across the ice floes in Harriet Beecher Stowe's *Uncle Tom's Cabin*. Farther west, between Louisville and Cincinnati, are counties that still look like they're in the 19th Century. But metropolitan growth obtrudes. Oldham County, just upriver from Louisville, has some of Kentucky's oldest homes, but the horse country is also sprouting affluent subdivisions. And the three northern Kentucky counties across the river from Cincinnati saw rapid population growth and a sharp rise in incomes in the 1990s. Overlooking the suspension bridge built by John Roebling 16 years before the Brooklyn Bridge, new buildings on the Covington waterfront rise while Newport, once known for its gambling, is sprucing up and office buildings and new subdivisions are rising on the hills above.

The 4th Congressional District spans all these variations of Ohio River country; it also includes lightly populated counties just inland. Economically, it runs the gamut from coal mining towns to rich suburbs. Politically, it has some of the most Democratic counties in America, like mountain-bound Elliott County (65%–21% for Bill Clinton in 1996), and some of the most Republican territory in Kentucky, like Oldham County with its new affluent migrants from Louisville (57%–34% for Bob Dole). The three northern Kentucky counties across the river from Cincinnati cast nearly half the district's votes, and in the 1990s have become very heavily Republican.

The congressman from the 4th District is Ken Lucas, a conservative Democrat elected in 1998. Lucas grew up on a farm in northern Kentucky, worked his way through the University of Kentucky on a tobacco farm, and became a financial planner. In the manner of local businessmen, he served two terms on the Florence Council and two years on the Boone County Board of Commissioners in the 1970s and 1980s. In 1992 he was appointed Boone County judge-executive, and was re-elected twice; in this heavily Republican county, Democrats hold most of the courthouse offices. But Lucas, running for the House, stressed that he was a very conservative Democrat, a "common sense conservative, pro-life, pro-gun and pro-business." He pledged to fight crime, Internet pornography and welfare fraud, and said he would limit himself to three terms. He backed NAFTA and the Religious Freedom Act.

Lucas was not the favorite when the campaign started; it looked like the race would be determined in the Republican primary. The contenders were state Senator Gex (pronounced *jay*) Williams and lawyer Rick Robinson, a longtime supporter of 4th District Congressman Jim Bunning, who was running for the Senate. Williams was backed by James Dobson, Pat Robertson, northern Kentucky native Gary Bauer, William Bennett and Steve Forbes; his political consultant was former Christian Coalition head Ralph Reed. Robinson as backed by almost all local Republican politicians, especially Bunning, and was funded by AT&T, Citicorp, the American Bankers Association, Goldman Sachs and Harrah's. Ironically, it was the outsider Williams, a computer consultant, who showed the greater political skills. Robinson proclaimed himself a strong right-to-lifer like Bunning, but Williams seized on the early 1998 effort to deny Republican Party funding to the very few Republicans who oppose the partial-birth abortion ban, and made that the difference between them. Williams won the primary 51%–41%, and leaders of the religious right across the nation pointed to him as one of their future leaders.

But in the general everything started going wrong for Williams and right for Lucas. In July, Williams was accused of making campaign phone calls from the Kentucky Statehouse; an investigation found no significant violation, but only after the election. Also in July, another ethics complaint was filed, alleging Williams sold farmland to a supporter for $60,000, to support his family; the land was donated in turn to an anti-abortion organization. The price was market value and Williams was ultimately cleared by the state legislative ethics committee, but this also looked fishy. So did the fact that his legislative resume listed his two degrees immediately after the U.S. Naval Academy, though he dropped out after 18 months and earned his degrees at the University of Florida. Lucas raised more money and ran hard-hitting ads on the ethics investigations and misleading resume. Williams, whose campaign became increasingly disorganized, raised very little money and put no ads on the air until October. He had always relied on grass-roots campaigns in small constituencies, as he had in the primary, in which 34,000 Republicans voted. But for all the Republican lean of the 4th in general elections, many more vote in the Democratic primary, in 1998 some 70,000; Williams's 51% in the primary was only 17% of all votes cast. Volunteers could help produce the 17,000 votes he needed to win the primary; they could not produce the 88,000 he needed in the general. That could only be done on TV, but in late September, Cincinnati stations refused to run Republican campaign committee ads arguing that when Lucas was county judge-executive, overhead spending rose 85% and Lucas was given a 25% raise and an $18,000 car; Lucas lawyers convinced stations the charges were untrue. And Lucas, staying true to his conservative themes, refused to appear at the Cincinnati airport, which is in Boone County, when Clinton came there September 27.

The result was a stunning 53%–47% victory for Lucas. Williams carried northern Kentucky by only 52%–48%, while Bunning was carrying the area 70%–29%. The state Republican party's executive director said of the 4th District, "that one, on paper, is certainly the best of them as far as Republican and Democrat split." But it is now the only Kentucky district that sends a Democrat to Congress, and keeps alive Kentucky's string of electing at least one Democrat every year since the party was founded by Andrew Jackson in 1828.

Cook's Call. *Highly Competitive.* Lucas is a top Republican target for 2000. He may not be that easy to defeat however, since his conservative views and penchant for bucking the Democratic leadership will help keep him in good stead. Plus, Republicans have had a great deal of trouble trying to convince a top-tier candidate to jump in the race.

The People: Pop. 1990: 602,896; 45.1% rural; 12.6% age 65 + ; 97.3% White, 2.1% Black, 0.3% Asian, 0.2% Amer. Indian, 0.1% Other; 0.4% Hispanic Origin. Households: 61.2% married couple families; 31.5% married couple fams. w. children; 34.1% college educ.; median household income: $26,569; per capita income: $11,935; median house value: $57,300; median gross rent: $263.

1996 Presidential Vote			1992 Presidential Vote		
Dole (R)	115,187	(49%)	Bush (R)	105,023	(44%)
Clinton (D)	95,070	(41%)	Clinton (D)	92,207	(39%)
Perot (I)	20,733	(9%)	Perot (I)	39,900	(17%)

Rep. Ken Lucas (D)

Elected 1998; b. Aug. 22, 1933, Kenton Cnty.; home, Richwood; U. of KY, B.S. 1955, Xavier U., M.B.A. 1970; Christian; married (Mary).

Military Career: Air Force, 1955–57; Air Natl. Guard, 1957–67.

Elected Office: Florence City Cncl., 1967–74; Boone Cnty. Commissioner, 1974–82; Boone Cnty. Judge Exec., 1992–98.

Professional Career: Financial planner, Sagemark Consulting, 1967–98; Pres., Boone St. Bank, 1971–86; Dir., Drees Co., 1980–present; Chmn., Fifth Third Bank, 1986–97.

DC Office: 1237 LHOB 20515, 202-225-3465; Fax: 202-225-0003; Web site: www.house.gov/kenlucas.

District Offices: Ashland, 606-324-9898; Ft. Mitchell, 606-426-0080.

Committees: *Agriculture* (22d of 24 D): Livestock & Horticulture; Risk Management, Research & Specialty Crops. *Budget* (16th of 19 D).

Group Ratings and Key Votes: Newly Elected

Election Results

1998 general	Ken Lucas (D)	93,485	(53%)	($1,065,956)
	Gex Williams (R)	81,547	(47%)	($874,701)
1998 primary	Ken Lucas (D)	46,293	(66%)	
	Howard Feinberg (D)	24,154	(34%)	
1996 general	Jim Bunning (R)	149,135	(68%)	($886,717)
	Denny Bowman (D)	68,939	(32%)	($55,239)

FIFTH DISTRICT

The mountains of eastern Kentucky have been a special place since Daniel Boone came through the Cumberland Gap in 1775. As Virginians poured through and created their version of a Tidewater civilization in the Bluegrass country, the people who settled the mountain counties and the Cumberland Plateau, most of them of Irish Protestant or Border Scot descent, brought different values—an assertive egalitarianism, loyalty to family and community, and passionate willingness to settle differences by feuds or violence. Most of the people in the mountains today are descendants of families who settled there in the two or three generations after Boone. Handed down are living memories of the old ways of doing things from the time not so far distant when there was little contact here with the outside world and the ties to the rest of American civilization were secured mainly by school primers and the King James Bible.

Only when people's lives have been changed and uprooted by outside events and institutions have their basic political attitudes been changed—and with a lasting imprint. The first agent of such change here was the Civil War; the second was the great United Mine Workers organizing drives in the coal mines around the 1930s. The Civil War made the mountains and the Cumberland Plateau a stronghold of the Republican Party. This was never slave territory—hardly any blacks have ever lived here, yet communities and families were riven by the rebellion of the South. People have not forgotten: the counties around Somerset and Corbin in south central Kentucky cast some of the highest Republican percentages in the nation, election after election.

Then came coal. Early in this century, vast seams of coal were discovered under the Kentucky mountains; representatives of eastern capitalists began prowling through these hills, hiring town lawyers to buy up mineral rights from unsuspecting farmers, building industrial slum towns in hollows and creek beds beneath glowering, heavily forested mountainsides. Coal mining was harsh and deadly work: mine accidents, black lung disease and simple exhaustion killed tens of thousands of miners, while low wages and company stores kept them poor. Then John L. Lewis's United Mine Workers came in and something like open warfare followed, with neither mine operators nor union organizers loath to use violence and threats. The union mostly won in eastern Kentucky and in the short run raised wages and built hospitals for miners and their families; in the longer run, the UMW phased out many jobs in the mines in return for job security and health benefits, as use of oil expanded. Politically, the UMW counties in the eastern part of the state became heavily Democratic and have remained so even as underground mine jobs lost out to the strip mining boom of the 1970s, and as UMW membership declined in the 1980s and 1990s.

The 5th Congressional District includes much of the Cumberland Plateau and most of the eastern mountains, a mixture of heavily Republican and heavily Democratic territory. It basically split its vote between Bill Clinton and Bob Dole in 1996, but with huge internal differences. The eastern mountain counties, with diminished turnout, were heavily for Clinton; Knott County gave him a 73%–18% margin. The Cumberland Plateau counties to the west were heavily Republican; Jackson County, a few mountain ridges away from Knott, voted 70%–22% for Dole. The current 5th District was created in 1991 by combining most of the old 5th, long one of the most Republican districts in the nation even though it also has had some of the lowest income levels, and the old 7th, reliably Democratic and represented for 35 years by Carl Perkins, chairman of the Education and Labor Committee from 1967–84.

The congressman from the 5th District is Harold Rogers, a Republican elected in the old 5th in 1980. He grew up in Wayne County, went off to the University of Kentucky and served in the National Guard, then practiced law in Somerset; in 1969, at 34, he was elected Pulaski-Rockcastle commonwealth's attorney. In 1979 he was the Republican nominee for lieutenant governor. In 1980, when the 5th District congressman retired, he was one of 11 Republicans in the primary; he won 23% in the primary and then easily in November. His toughest race came in 1992, with redistricting. At first his likely opponent was 7th District incumbent Chris Perkins, Carl Perkins's son; but then Perkins retired at 37, before it was revealed he had 514 overdrafts on the House bank. Rogers ended up facing state Senator John Doug Hays of Pike County, whose grandfather Doug "Sawloggin" Hays was state senator before him. Hays attacked Rogers for supporting trickle-down economics and argued that as a Democrat he could get more money for the district. Rogers countered by pointing to his ongoing efforts to build the $250 million Cumberland Gap twin tunnels and Harlan County flood projects. Rogers won with 55%. He had 71% in his old 5th District, which cast 52% of the new district's votes; he had 36% in the old 7th District. The returns show the strength of partisan feelings in eastern Kentucky: Owsley County was 78% for Rogers; next-door Breathitt County was 68% for Hays.

Rogers is now the fifth ranking Republican on the Appropriations Committee and chairman of its Commerce-Justice-State-Judiciary Subcommittee as well as number two on Appropriations Energy and Water Development Subcommittee. His voting record is mostly, but not always, conservative. Representing a low-income district, he is sympathetic to some spending bills; he was one of three Republicans to vote for the Clinton stimulus package in March 1993. Rogers's subcommittee spends a small percentage of the federal budget but must deal with many controversial issues. Through the State Department, it provides U.S. funds for international organizations. He has long insisted on budget reforms at the United Nations; he has said its payroll is "bloated and patronage-ridden" and was a severe critic of Secretary General Boutros Boutros-Ghali.

On domestic issues, Rogers was not a Republican revolutionary, though he supported all of the Contract with America except the tax cuts. He prevented the zeroing out of several programs by straightforwardly negotiating deals, then sticking to them. He unsurprisingly opposed abolition of the Appalachian Regional Commission; the ARC lives. When some Republicans wanted to zero out the Legal Services Corporation, Rogers negotiated a cut from $400 million to $278 million; when the Senate put in a higher number, Rogers stuck to his $278 million. Rogers resisted dismantling the Commerce Department, but he agreed to a cut of more than $500 million.

More recently, he has come out fighting against some parts of the Clinton Administration. In March 1997 he confronted Attorney General Janet Reno: "Agencies under your command have been guilty of gross violations of the public trust"—citing the speedy dispatch of FBI files to the Clinton White House, sloppy procedures at the FBI's forensic labs and the naturalization of criminals in time for the 1996 election. In 1998 he introduced a bill to split the Immigration and Naturalization Service between the Justice, Labor and State departments. Rogers's bill went through the Judiciary Committee in July 1998, but the committee was soon occupied with the Starr report. Rogers is more sympathetic to the State Department, but is skeptical about its plan to keep $595 million in passport and visa fees, which currently goes to Treasury. He opposes sampling in the 2000 Census, and held back all but $100 million of the 1998 appropriations until the authorizing committee could rule on the issue. In March 1998 he demanded a Census sampling plan from Commerce Secretary William Daley. The 1999 appropriation funds the agency only until March 31, with money available only when the president requests and the Congress votes; the aim is to force the Clinton Administration to follow court decisions that outlaw sampling. Rogers has labored hard on federal projects in eastern Kentucky. He has worked on flood-control projects and highway construction; he promoted the Center for Rural Development in Somerset and the musical arts center in Prestonburg. In 1997, Rogers and Kentucky state officials set up PRIDE, a long-term project to clean up rivers and streams of sewage and garbage and to end illegal trash dumps; he got $8.7 million for sewage projects in 1998. He got I-66 authorized in 1995, the Cumberland Gap Tunnel completed in 1996, and has helped build two federal prisons in the district, with a third perhaps to come.

Since 1992, Rogers has been re-elected by overwhelming margins, carrying even the most Democratic counties. In November 1998 he announced he would not run for governor in 1999.

Cook's Call. *Safe.* Rogers does not represent the most Republican district in the state, but he is surely the safest member of the Kentucky delegation. He should have no problem winning his 11th election in 2000.

The People: Pop. 1990: 624,837; 87.1% rural; 12.5% age 65 + ; 98.7% White, 0.9% Black, 0.1% Asian, 0.2% Amer. Indian; 0.2% Hispanic Origin. Households: 63.7% married couple families; 34.6% married couple fams. w. children; 19.8% college educ.; median household income: $15,061; per capita income: $7,725; median house value: $35,500; median gross rent: $172.

1996 Presidential Vote

Clinton (D) 95,633 (47%)
Dole (R) 87,692 (43%)
Perot (I) 18,260   (9%)

1992 Presidential Vote

Clinton (D) 111,600 (48%)
Bush (R) 97,432 (42%)
Perot (I) 24,344 (10%)

Rep. Harold Rogers (R)

Elected 1980; b. Dec. 31, 1937, Barrier; home, Somerset; U. of KY, B.A. 1962, J.D. 1964; Baptist; married (Cynthia).

Military Career: Army Natl. Guard, 1957–64.

Professional Career: Practicing atty., 1964–69; Pulaski-Rockcastle Commonwealth's Atty., 1969–80.

DC Office: 2470 RHOB 20515, 202-225-4601; Fax: 202-225-0940; Web site: www.house.gov/rogers.

District Offices: Hazard, 606-439-0794; Pikeville, 606-432-4388; Somerset, 606-679-8346.

Committees: *Appropriations* (5th of 34 R): Commerce, Justice, State & the Judiciary (Chmn.); Energy & Water Development; Transportation.

Group Ratings

	ADA	ACLU	AFS	LCV	CON	NTU	NFIB	COC	ACU	NTLC	CHC
1998	5	6	13	15	13	46	100	88	92	95	100
1997	5	—	25	—	26	44	—	90	80	—	—

National Journal Ratings

	1997 LIB — 1997 CONS		1998 LIB — 1998 CONS	
Economic	19%	76%	26%	72%
Social	10%	82%	21%	76%
Foreign	38%	60%	27%	68%

Key Votes of the 105th Congress

1. Clinton Budget Deal	Y	5. Puerto Rico Sthood. Ref.	N	9. Cut $ for B-2 Bombers	N
2. Education IRAs	Y	6. End Highway Set-asides	Y	10. Human Rights in China	N
3. Req. 2/3 to Raise Taxes	Y	7. School Prayer Amend.	Y	11. Withdraw Bosnia Troops	Y
4. Fast-track Trade	N	8. Ovrd. Part. Birth Veto	Y	12. End Cuban TV-Marti	N

Election Results

1998 general	Harold Rogers (R) 142,215	(78%)	($377,729)
	Sidney Bailey-Bamer (D) 39,585	(22%)	
1998 primary	Harold Rogers (R) .... unopposed		
1996 general	Harold Rogers (R) .... unopposed		($132,717)

SIXTH DISTRICT

With its white picket fences, horse farms and Georgian brick house-filled small towns, the Bluegrass country almost plumb in the middle of Kentucky is the part of interior America longest settled by English speakers: Lexington was founded in 1775; the town of Hopewell was renamed Paris in 1789 out of gratitude for French help during our Revolution and in a salute to theirs (though the county name remained Bourbon even after Louis XVI was guillotined). Tobacco farming started here in the 1770s, horse racing in 1787, and the first whiskey distillery, in Bourbon County, was built in 1790. Tobacco, whiskey and race horses remained the staples of the Bluegrass economy for six generations until 1956, when IBM built its typewriter plant and headquarters in Lexington. IBM's arrival "really was the beginning of Lexington's industrial revolution," as University of Kentucky historian Carl Cone put it. You imagine a Kentucky colonel sitting on the porch, dressed in a white suit and string tie sipping a mint julep, as IBM engineers in their dark suits and white shirts file into their offices. But capitalism, as Joseph Schumpeter wrote, is a process of creative destruction. The typewriter was eventually outclassed by the PC, and the IBM plant put on the block. Meanwhile, in the 1980s, Toyota, lured by generous subsidies, built a $2 billion assembly plant in Georgetown, a town with early 19th Century houses and lush countryside, just one county north of Lexington and west of Paris. Some of the most famous horse farms—Spendthrift, Calumet—went bankrupt or were sold; Toyota doubled the size of its plant. From IBM to Toyota, Lexington seems to be a focus of innovation and certainly of economic growth.

Lexington was the home base of the Whig Party's great leader Henry Clay, but in the 150 years since his death, the Bluegrass country has been mostly Democratic. Bush edged out Clinton here in 1992 (there was a strong Perot vote), but Clinton picked up the 6th in 1996. He bought more time on Lexington TV than in just about any other media market in America, and raised his percentages 2% to 8% in Lexington and Bluegrass counties; the last day of the campaign he came here and appeared with University of Kentucky basketball coach Rick Pitino. All of which was just enough to give him a 46%–45% victory over Bob Dole in the 6th and in Kentucky, despite the president's proposal that the FDA regulate tobacco as a drug.

The 6th Congressional District includes Lexington and the counties all around—a natural unit, unlike some other Kentucky districts. Lexington casts about one-third of the votes. It is closely divided between the parties in national and statewide elections and, in 1998, the congressional race as well.

The congressman from the 6th District is Ernie Fletcher, a Republican elected in a close race in 1998. Fletcher grew up in Mount Sterling, got an engineering degree from the University of Kentucky, was an Air Force pilot for five years, intercepting Soviet aircraft; then he went to medical school, practiced medicine, and was CEO of a company that managed medical practices. He did volunteer medical work in India and was a lay minister. In 1994 he was elected to the Kentucky House. In 1996 he won the Republican primary, by exactly four votes, and ran against Democratic Congressman Scott Baesler, a tobacco farmer and onetime University of Kentucky basketball star. With help from national Republicans, Fletcher raised and spent nearly as much as the incumbent and ran a spirited campaign. He lost 56%–44%, but kept his taste for campaigning. When Baesler announced he was running for the Senate in spring 1997, Fletcher decided to run for the House again, and this time had no serious primary competition.

Seven candidates entered the Democratic primary, which attracted 111,000 voters, compared to 25,000 in the Republican contest—a reminder of the district's ancestral allegiance. The best-known candidate was state Senator John "Eck" Rose, contender in the 1995 governor primary and president of the state Senate until his ouster by a Republican-Democrat coup in January 1997. Rose was described by backers as "pro-business, pro-gun, pro-choice." But he startled voters by running ads featuring his young, very pregnant third wife, and he had competition from several candidates based in small counties. One, Bobby Russell, ran ads attacking Ken Starr; another, Jim Newberry, attacked the eventual winner, Ernesto Scorsone, for defending drug dealers. Scorsone, a criminal defense lawyer, had represented Lexington in the legislature since 1984; he was born in Sicily, the son of professors, and moved to Lexington as a teenager in 1965. Scorsone claimed credit for managing Governor Paul Patton's tough anti-crime bill and he supported the partial-birth abortion ban; but overall his record was liberal, including a vote against a ban on same-sex marriages and sponsorship of living wills. Scorsone took 41% of the vote in Lexington and overall led Rose 24%–21%; Lexington Vice Mayor Teresa Isaac had 16%, Russell 15%, Newberry 12% and former Al Gore aide Jonathan Miller 11%.

Kentucky politics often features races between two moderates; this one was a contest between a liberal criminal lawyer and a culturally conservative doctor. Fletcher called for a "flatter, fairer" tax, Scorsone for more progressiveness. On health care, which turned out to be a major issue, Scorsone said that Fletcher was carrying water for insurance companies; Fletcher said Scorsone played a key role in the health care reform that drove companies from the state and increased insurance premiums and favored trial lawyers, and said that as a physician he could better handle the issue. In TV ads in late September and October, Scorsone talked of the Patton crime bill, his safe schools law and his endorsement by the Fraternal Order of Police. Fletcher ran one ad showing a woman whose breast cancer he had treated and another featuring a rape victim who said Scorsone represented her assailant and helped him avoid prison time. When Scorsone, who is single, ran an ad showing him with his sister and her children, Fletcher on the stump took to introducing his "real wife." Fletcher backed the Republicans' managed care bill and said Scorsone was backing the trial lawyers' bill.

Fletcher spent about $1.3 million to Scorsone's $1 million: much more than was spent in the 6th in 1996. Given Scorsone's liberal record, this was long expected to be a Republican pickup. But Fletcher won by just 53%–46%; he won Lexington 50%–49% and carried all but two counties in the rest of the district. Despite the wide differences between the candidates, Fletcher interpreted his victory to moderation: "Most of us ran on some very centrist themes—mainstream issues that will engender bipartisanship," such as education and Social Security reform. He was named a freshman representative to the party leadership and won seats on the Agriculture, Budget and Education committees. In early 1999, Baesler said he might run for his old seat; given the close margin of the 1998 race and the plethora of Democratic politicians in the Bluegrass, this could be a seriously contested district in 2000.

Cook's Call. *Highly Competitive.* This marginal, but conservative district is never going to be a slam-dunk for either party. But Fletcher may have his hands full here in 2000 if Baesler decides to run for his old seat, which would make this race one of the most hotly contested (and potentially nasty) races in the country.

The People: Pop. 1990: 614,901; 37% rural; 12.1% age 65 +; 90.8% White, 8.1% Black, 0.7% Asian, 0.2% Amer. Indian, 0.2% Other; 0.7% Hispanic Origin. Households: 56.7% married couple families; 27.8% married couple fams. w. children; 40.7% college educ.; median household income: $25,364; per capita income: $12,413; median house value: $61,900; median gross rent: $293.

1996 Presidential Vote			1992 Presidential Vote		
Clinton (D)	110,256	(46%)	Bush (R)	105,215	(42%)
Dole (R)	108,148	(45%)	Clinton (D)	101,817	(41%)
Perot (I)	19,425	(8%)	Perot (I)	39,719	(16%)

Rep. Ernie Fletcher (R)

Elected 1998; b. Nov. 12, 1952, Mt. Sterling; home, Lexington; U. of KY, B.S. 1974, M.D. 1984; Baptist; married (Glenna).

Military Career: Air Force, 1974–80.

Elected Office: KY House of Reps., 1994–96.

Professional Career: Practicing physician, 1984-present; CEO, St. Joseph Medical Foundation, 1997–99.

DC Office: 1117 LHOB 20515, 202-225-4706; Fax: 202-225-2122; Web site: www.house.gov/fletcher.

District Office: Lexington, 606-219-1366.

Committees: *Agriculture* (27th of 27 R): Risk Management, Research & Specialty Crops. *Budget* (21st of 24 R). *Education & the Workforce* (25th of 27 R): Employer-Employee Relations (Vice Chmn.); Oversight & Investigations.

Group Ratings and Key Votes: Newly Elected

Election Results

1998 general	Ernie Fletcher (R)	104,046	(53%)	($1,285,412)
	Ernesto Scorsone (D)	90,033	(46%)	($1,025,395)
	Others	1,839	(1%)	
1998 primary	Ernie Fletcher (R)	18,782	(76%)	
	Jay L. Whitehead (R)	5,961	(24%)	
1996 general	Scotty Baesler (D)	125,999	(56%)	($574,074)
	Ernie Fletcher (R)	100,231	(44%)	($435,065)

LOUISIANA

Louisiana often seems to be America's banana republic, with its charm and inefficiency, its communities interlaced by family ties and its public sector laced with corruption, with its own indigenous culture and its tradition of fine distinctions of class and caste. It is a state with an economy uncomfortably like that of an underdeveloped country, based on pumping minerals out of soggy ground, shipping grain produced in the vast hinterland drained by its great river, and increasingly dependent in recent years on businesses typical of picturesque Third World countries—tourism and gambling. Its politics too has a Third World quality, with its own peculiar election laws and a heritage of no-holds-barred conflict and demagoguery no other state can match: what other state has produced a Huey Long or an Edwin Edwards? Louisiana has a hereditary rich class and a large low-wage working class. It has conservative cultural attitudes: Louisiana and Utah have the most restrictive abortion laws in the U.S. and Louisiana in 1997 became the first state to offer covenant marriages, in which spouses would agree not to be covered by no-fault divorce laws. But Louisiana also has a lazy tolerance of rule-breaking, and feels more like the Caribbean or the Mediterranean than the North Atlantic or the Pacific Rim. This is not an entirely original observation. Four decades ago, A. J. Liebling described Louisiana as an outpost of the Levant along the Gulf of Mexico. Most of the United States faces east toward the vast Atlantic Ocean or west toward the vast Pacific; Louisiana faces south, to the Gulf of Mexico and the steamy heat and volatile societies of Latin America.

New Orleans preserves the look and feel it had as a French and Spanish outpost in the New World. Traditions of centralized control and easygoing corruption—classic traits of colonialism—are part of this heritage. The *dirigiste* tradition comes from the fact that Louisiana is the only state that operates on the Napoleonic Code of France (which until 1990 required parents to leave a large percentage of their estates to their children), not the common law of England; the concept of civil liberties has shallower roots in Louisiana than in the other 49 states. Here abstract ideals have been overshadowed by the practical need for centralized action. This Delta land—much of it below sea level, soggy, swampy, laced with tributaries and offshoots of the Mississippi and other major rivers like the Atchafalaya—requires vast capital expenditures for levees and drainage and causeways. Even today, houses in New Orleans don't have basements, people are buried in above-ground cemeteries in grandiose crypts, and swamp lands begin abruptly at the edges of subdivisions where people find alligators in their backyards.

The economy that grew up in these rich Delta lands has always been based on raw materials. Antebellum Louisiana produced and exported sugar, rice and cotton in enough abundance to generate the wealth which built grand plantation houses behind alleys of oaks running in from the Mississippi, and to make New Orleans the nation's fifth largest city by the time of the Civil War. Then came oil, found in the great Spindletop strike just over the Texas line in 1901 and in salt domes in Louisiana not long after; Jersey Standard (now Exxon) built the huge Baton Rouge refinery that became the training ground for generations of its top executives. When energy prices boomed after the oil shocks of 1973 and 1981, Louisiana, like an oil-rich Third World country, boomed too, reaching up toward national income levels, generating 500,000 new jobs between 1972 and 1981. But it lost 150,000 jobs in the next six years as oil prices crashed and the rig count dropped by two-thirds and energy taxes fell from 41% of state government revenues in 1982 to 9% in 1996. Louisiana's economy has never regained much forward momentum. Gambling, legalized in 1991, has produced less revenue than expected, and nothing like the boom that some promised.

Louisiana has high rates of cancer, early death rates, a high incidence of AIDS; in 1998 the Center for Disease Control declared that New Orleanians were the fattest Americans. In the early 1990s New Orleans had horrendus crime rates; happily, they have been falling after a new police superintendent was appointed, the force was beefed up and New York's crime-fighting tactics were copied. The income disparities here are greater than almost anywhere else in the United States. New Orleans's rich are notoriously unventuresome and tight-knit, determined to hold on to their wealth against the grasp of the impecunious and unlearned masses.

The most enduringly famous, and by far the most talented, was Huey P. Long, who in less than a single term each as governor (1928–32) and senator (1932–35), left an imprint on the state's public life and imposed an organization to its politics that have faded into history only in the last decade. Long's genius was not that he promised to tax the rich to help the poor—hundreds of idealists and demagogues in America have done that—but that, to an amazing extent, he actually delivered. He dominated the legislature so thoroughly that, as governor, he roamed the floors of both chambers at will, bringing to the podium bills he insisted be passed without changing a comma—and they were. He was ready to use bribery, intimidation and physical violence. He built a new skyscraper Capitol, a new Louisiana State University, and more miles of roads than any state but rich New York and huge Texas. He also built a national following, and by 1935, he was planning to run for president on the platform of "Share the wealth, every man a king," when he was assassinated at age 42 in the hallway of the Capitol, where the bullet holes can still be seen in the marble.

For America, the Long threat may have moved Franklin Roosevelt to embrace the liberal programs—the Wagner Labor Act, social security, steeply graduated taxes—of the second New Deal. For Louisiana, Long delivered a political structure that revolved around him even after he was dead—and a class of political leaders who, lacking his talents, treated the state as Long's incompetent doctors had treated his fatal wound, leaving Louisiana without either a fully developed economy or a fully competent public sector. For 50 years, until Huey's son Senator

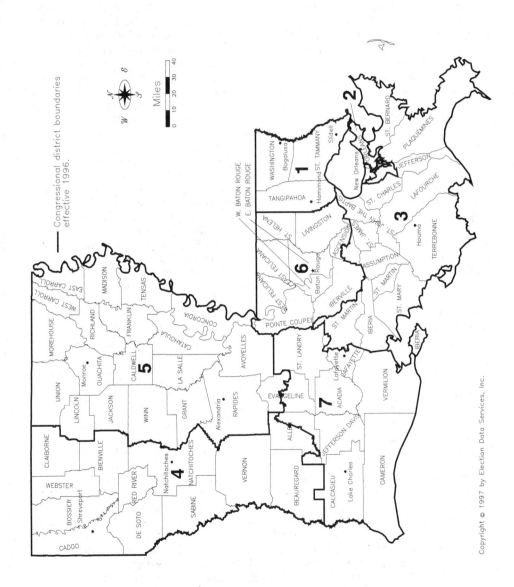

Congressional district boundaries
effective 1996.

Russell Long retired in 1986, Longs and Long proteges held high political office in Louisiana and elections were run along pro- and anti-Long lines. The Long experience has strengthened Louisiana's already strong predispositions—tolerance of corruption, disinterest in abstract reform, and taste for colorful extremists regardless of their short-term means or long-term ends—in a way that helps explain the rise and fall of such unlikely politicians as the four-term Governor Edwin Edwards and the onetime Ku Klux Klan leader and state legislator David Duke.

Louisiana has natural political divides. One divide is by religion: Catholic Cajun parishes cast about 30% of the state's vote, the New Orleans area casts around 25% or so, and about 45% are cast in Protestant parishes from Baton Rouge on north. White Protestants for years have wanted nothing to do with national Democrats, while Cajuns tend to mull it over. Another divide is by race: blacks are overwhelmingly Democratic, whites split in seriously contested elections. A third divide is by income: low- and high-income whites vote very differently and are much less influenced than voters in most other states by candidates' cultural values, marital status, lifestyles and the like. As a result, Louisiana politics since Huey P. Long's time has often been a struggle between reformist and conservative forces on one side and roguish populists on the other, a struggle waged in lavishly financed campaigns and with grandiloquent rhetoric.

For a quarter century, the lead role was played by Edwin Edwards as the roguish populist, with a number of Republican rivals as reformist conservatives. Edwards was elected governor in 1971 and 1975 and was not eligible to run in 1979. In 1983 he beat incumbent Republican David Treen; in 1987 he lost to Buddy Roemer, a Democratic congressman who later switched parties. For much of this third term, he faced corruption charges, until he was acquitted by a jury in 1986. In 1991 he ran again, and this time an even odder character surfaced. David Duke, as Tyler Bridges documented in the New Orleans *Times-Picayune* and his book *The Rise of David Duke*, was an active Nazi sympathizer up through 1989, but he also had a knack for speaking to mainstream political issues in attractive political language. In 1989 he was narrowly elected to the state legislature from a district in suburban Jefferson Parish as a nominal Republican—a victory that got enormous publicity. Immediately he ran for senator in 1990 against incumbent Bennett Johnston, and lost by the unnervingly narrow margin of 54%–44%, making major inroads into the non-affluent white vote, both Cajun and Protestant. Then in 1991, Duke ran for governor, against Roemer and Edwards. (Louisiana has a unique primary system, invented by Edwards: candidates of all parties run in a single primary; any candidate who gets 50% is elected; otherwise, the top two finishers, regardless of party, have a runoff. In December 1997 the Supreme Court ruled that this system violates a federal law requiring all congressional elections to be held on the same day in November; as a result in 1998 the first primary was held on November 3, with runoffs, which proved unnecessary, scheduled for December 5.) Roemer, now a Republican, was unpopular for raising taxes after promising not to do so, and finished third with 27%; Edwards was unpopular because many thought he was a crook, and he had few voters except blacks faithful to his populism, receiving 34%; Duke made the runoff by finishing second with 32%. All articulate opinion in Louisiana moved to Edwards's side, and Republicans from President Bush to Governor Roemer endorsed Edwards, who won 61%–39%. But Duke won enormous attention, even as his electoral career spun into decline; he ran for president in 1992, and got only 9% in the Louisiana primary.

Just before Edwards won his fourth term, Louisiana approved casino gambling, limited to 15 riverboats and one land-based site in New Orleans. But in 1995 the big temporary casino in New Orleans went bankrupt, and the huge new casino under construction at the little-used Rivergate Convention Center at the foot of Canal Street was left partly finished—with something of the shabby grandeur of the French Quarter's many unrenovated houses; construction has since resumed and approval to open secured in October 1998. In 1995 conservative Republican Mike Foster zoomed out of nowhere to win the governorship, on an anti-gambling, anti-tax platform; yet in office the local-option gambling referenda that he promised resulted in approval of riverboat gambling in most parishes. In 1996, with those referenda on the ballot and pro-gambling forces boosting turnout in black precincts, Democrat Mary Landrieu narrowly defeated Republican Woody Jenkins for the Senate—although Jenkins claimed the results were tainted by vote fraud. And in November 1998, Edwards, his son and four associates were indicted for conspiracy to extort millions from businesses seeking riverboat casino licenses, after several defendants turned state's evidence. The prosecution argued that Edwards could control or influence decisions of the state gaming board, even though it was part of Foster's administration; Edwards pointed out that he was charged with taking nothing while in office, and argued that he was paid legitimate consulting fees when he was a private citizen.

Governor. Louisiana's governor is Mike Foster, a Republican elected in November 1995. Foster grew up in Franklin, in St. Mary Parish, in the Cajun country near the Gulf; he served in the Air Force and founded a contracting firm and served as president of Sterling Sugars. He is a large landowner who loves duck hunting, piloting helicopters and riding tractors. He was elected to the state Senate in 1987, and in 1991 was appointed chairman of the Commerce Committee. He portrays himself as an amateur in politics, convincingly, given his penchant for blunt, impolitic statements; bald, with a mustache, he campaigned as "not just another pretty face." But he had a political pedigree: his grandfather Murphy Foster was governor from 1892–1900 and played a part in abolishing Louisiana's graft-ridden lottery.

Foster ran in 1995 as a not very well-known candidate in a large field; he switched parties in mid-campaign. A gambling opponent, he pledged to hold a referendum on video poker (operators had been caught bribing legislators), riverboat gambling (allowed in many parishes) and the New Orleans land-based casino. At first he attracted little attention. Former Governor Buddy Roemer seemed to be the leading Republican, brandishing a Contract with Louisiana, criticizing New Orleans as "Cape Fear" and calling for chain gangs. Congressman Cleo Fields was the one well-known black candidate, as Congressman Bill Jefferson decided not to run, but Fields did not have unequivocal support: New Orleans Mayor Marc Morial, who is black, endorsed both Fields and Democratic State Treasurer Mary Landrieu. Landrieu, whose father was once mayor of New Orleans, called for cleaning up Louisiana; she was running ahead of Lieutenant Governor Melinda Schwegmann, whose family owned New Orleans's biggest supermarket chain. (The business was sold in 1997.) Foster surged ahead in fall campaigning, and in the October 21 primary led with 26%. There was almost a three-way tie for second place. Fields edged into second place with 19%, to 18.4% for Landrieu (who ran for the Senate in 1996 and won) and 17.8% for Roemer. In the runoff against Fields, Foster called for a vast consolidation of state agencies and reform of state education and welfare. Fields said he would get tough on juvenile crime and accused Foster of "race baiting" after Foster referred to "that jungle in New Orleans." Foster won 64% to Fields's 37% and took 84% of the white vote, while Fields took 96% of the black vote.

In office, Foster pushed through a food tax cut and a $25 per child tax credit; he increased teacher salaries and initiated a school-based accountability system. He supported a program to provide free public college tuition for students who finished at or above the statewide level on the ACT. In 1998 he called for selling off the state's share of the tobacco settlement and using the cash to pay off debt and raise teacher salaries some more. He supported building a Shintech polyvinyl chloride plant in both St. James Parish and Westlake near Lake Charles, both attacked by some as environmental racism; but after protests the company dropped its plans and built a smaller plant near Plaquemine. He backed random drug testing of state officials (overturned in court) and resisted efforts to allow the legislature to meet in even-numbered years 60 days (as it did before 1993) rather than 30. He banned racial quotas and preferences in state government and obtained some changes in civil tort law opposed by trial lawyers.

Foster's job rating for three years hovered around 75%, and he has taken his own political course at every turn. He has pushed for initiatives and referenda, unpopular with just about every other Louisiana official. Endorsed by Patrick Buchanan in October 1995, he announced he was voting for Buchanan just before the February 1996 caucus, in which Buchanan won his upset victory. Foster declined in 1995 to disclaim his endorsement by David Duke; when Duke started running for Bob Livingston's House seat Foster pointedly said he would support any

Republican in the runoff—a very different response from the repudiation of Duke by national and local Republicans in 1991. Foster's actions do not always produce the results he wants: the gambling referenda he sponsored in November 1996 resulted in approval of all proposed casinos and a big New Orleans turnout which may have elected Landrieu to the Senate. In 1998 he made it no secret he favored Senator John Breaux over a weak Republican challenger.

Foster entered election year 1999 an overwhelming favorite for re-election. On January 28 he convened in the Governor's Mansion a meeting of the eight statewide elective officials, only one other of whom is a Republican, and they all pledged not to campaign against each other. A display of high-minded nonpartisanship, they said; a conspiracy of political insiders, said others. One such was New Orleans Congressman Bill Jefferson, who announced that he intended to run for governor. But as a black, liberal, city-based Democrat, Jefferson seemed to have little chance against the popular Foster in the October primary. In May 1999, Foster admitted that he had paid Duke $150,000 for his 80,000-name supporter list to use in his own 1995 and 1999 campaigns, after a New Orleans grand jury investigated the purchase, which was not reported on his state campaign finance reports. Foster said he kept his dealings with Duke private because of Duke's political baggage and that his failure to report the transactions was "an honest mistake."

Cook's Call. *Safe.* Foster looked to be cruising toward re-election until his gentleman's agreement with the eight statewide elective officials to not run against each other prompted Representative Bill Jefferson to mount a challenge. Despite the anger that Foster created, his financial advantage and high favorable ratings likely will insulate him. The Harvard Law-educated Jefferson has shown considerable legislative talents, but there is little evidence that his support is likely to extend far beyond the black community, and other Democrats may run.

Senior Senator. John Breaux grew up in the politically fertile soil of the Acadia Parish seat of Crowley in Cajun country, the home town also of Edwin Edwards. After law school and a year of law practice, he worked four years for Edwards, then a junior congressman. When Edwards was elected governor in 1972, Breaux ran for Congress and won the seat, at 28. Quietly in the House, more publicly in the Senate, he has become a natural dealmaker, with contacts developed everywhere from the tennis court (he is one of Congress's best players) to the Democratic Leadership Council (where he followed Bill Clinton as chairman in 1992). His views on issues have a Louisiana Cajun accent: market-oriented with populist twists on economics, rather conservative on cultural issues. But he is not heavily encumbered with narrow principles. As he told the *Los Angeles Times*, "I see myself not as a philosopher, but somebody who is interested in making government work. More and more people in Congress . . . have an all-or-nothing attitude. All-or-nothing attitudes generally wind up getting nothing." Yet at the same time he has shown a mastery of substantive issues and has been willing to take political risks to get results.

Breaux used his committee seats in the House to get money to battle coastal wetlands erosion and defeat the Law of the Sea Treaty; to get sugar and natural gas concessions for Louisiana in the 1981 tax bill he uttered his famed statement that his vote was not for sale "but it is available for rent." He ran for the Senate in 1986, initially trailing his Republican House colleague Henson Moore, but holding him to under 50% in the primary and then overtaking him in the general.

In the Senate, Breaux has a middle-of-the-road voting record and a bent toward bipartisan coalitions. He was active in national campaigns, as head of the Democratic Senatorial Campaign Committee in 1990 (the last time Democrats ended up with more seats than they started) and the Democratic Leadership Council. He was chosen chief deputy whip in 1993 and was mentioned as a candidate for majority leader when George Mitchell retired in 1994; instead he supported Tom Daschle. On the Commerce Committee he worked on issues with local impact: creating in 1990 the $50 million per year Breaux Fund to protect wetlands, and phasing out by 1995 the recreational boat user fee. He worked with Bennett Johnston to get a $2.5 billion royalty relief package as an incentive to offshore drilling, which once again is booming off Louisiana's coast.

He has been less successful in influencing Clinton Administration policy on major issues. He opposed the 1993 Clinton stimulus package and the Btu tax, and helped defeat both. In 1994 he was the chief Senate sponsor of Tennessee Congressman Jim Cooper's managed care health care bill and struggled to come up with bipartisan compromises. As the administration moved to the center after the 1994 elections, Breaux had more successes. He helped shape key compromises on the 1996 health care and welfare reform bills. With John Chafee he devised an alternative budget, with smaller tax cuts and smaller adjustments to Medicare than the Republican plan and an adjustment to the Consumer Price Index; it lost by only 53–46, winning the votes of 24 Democrats and 22 Republicans. On Louisiana issues he won continuation of rice subsidies in the Freedom to Farm Act and successfully opposed shipping deregulation.

In 1998 Breaux became a major force for reform of entitlements and health care. He and Charles Grassley sponsored a bill to reduce home health care costs. With Judd Gregg he introduced the CSIS Social Security reform, with 2% of income in individual investment accounts. In January 1998 he was named chairman of the bipartisan commission on Medicare, and labored for more than a year with Republican Bill Thomas and others to come up with a bipartisan plan. Breaux pushed for premium support, with a choice of eligible plans and government payment for at least a minimum plan or the current Medicare system; he struggled to come up with a plan for a pharmaceutical benefit. He got bipartisan support, from the Republican appointees and Senator Bob Kerrey, but was one vote short of the 11 required for an official recommendation to Congress. Still he persevered in March 1999 and tried to round up support in Senate and House, despite the indifference or veiled opposition from the Clinton Administration. He argued that the problem was urgent because of the pending deficits in Medicare and the moment for bipartisan action was propitious.

Breaux has been re-elected twice without serious opposition. In 1992 he won 73% in the September primary. The 1998 race was pretty much over by August 1997, when Congressman Richard Baker declined to run and Congressman Billy Tauzin, a Democrat-turned-Republican, said "I don't think John can be defeated. I'll never say a bad thing about John Breaux." (They were roommates at LSU Law School and godfathers of each other's children.) Governor Mike Foster made it known he wouldn't oppose Breaux either. Breaux outspent his Republican opponent Jim Donelon by more than 10–1 and after the campaign still had $1.5 million cash on hand. In the November primary Breaux beat Donelon 64%–32%, carrying every parish but one (St. Tammany, the New Orleans suburbs north of Lake Pontchartrain).

Junior Senator. Mary Landrieu is a Democrat elected in 1996; she and John Breaux are the last all-Democratic Senate delegation from Dixie. Landrieu grew up in New Orleans, the oldest of nine children of Moon Landrieu (all with names starting with M), mayor of New Orleans in the 1970s. She was educated at Ursuline Academy and LSU and in 1979, at 23, became the youngest woman ever elected to the Louisiana state legislature, where she was sometimes the object of undue ridicule. In 1987 she was elected state treasurer; she opened bond contracts for bid and restructured the state investment portfolio; she was a sharp critic of Governor Edwin Edwards and opposed gambling. In 1995 she ran for governor, and in the September primary finished third, just 1% and 8,983 votes behind second-place finisher Congressman Cleo Fields. She immediately started running for the Senate seat held by Bennett Johnston, who was retiring 24 years after he was elected to the Senate after a narrow loss in a governor's race.

With a well-known name and a moderate platform—for a balanced budget amendment and capital gains tax cut, promising to make education a top priority—Landrieu shared a lead in the polls with Attorney General Richard Ieyoub, also a Democrat; under Louisiana law if they finished in the top two in the September primary, they would meet in a November runoff, and Democrats would be guaranteed a win no matter what. This was an alarming situation for Republicans, who had no such well-known candidate and who believed, reasonably, that they could win the seat if they could get someone into the runoff. Stepping forward to fill the gap was Woody Jenkins, a 25-year state legislator and strong abortion opponent, who had run twice for the Senate as a Democrat, losing in primaries to Bennett Johnston in 1978 by 59%–41% and to Russell Long in 1980 by 58%–39%. In August he claimed the party endorsement, but Congressman Jimmy Hayes from the Cajun country argued that he was more electable and should have party support. In early September Congressman Bob Livingston, worried that a runoff might include two Democrats or David Duke, rallied other Republicans around Jenkins and abandoned Hayes, who had not raised enough money to get statewide name recognition. Meanwhile, the National Republican Senatorial Committee started running ads attacking Ieyoub on ethics charges for past campaign spending practices. Jenkins surged in the polls, and led the September 21 primary with 26%, to 22% for Landrieu and 20% for Ieyoub; Duke got 12%.

At this point Jenkins looked like the favorite; Republican candidates had won 55% of the total votes and Democrats only 44%. But he had little money left, and Landrieu, who ultimately outspent him, ran ads attacking him as an extremist. Jenkins was a strong conservative, totally against abortion and called for elimination of the IRS; he attacked her for opposing abortion restrictions and supporting gay rights, while she attacked him for never voting for a tax in 25 years. Landrieu had to spend much time getting support from blacks, since many were unhappy that she had given only nominal support to Cleo Fields for governor in 1995. Gambling interests, who were busy trying to increase black turnout in New Orleans and elsewhere for their gambling referenda, also threw their support to Landrieu. At the end of October—in uncustomary fashion—Archbishop Philip Hannan basically came out for Jenkins, saying if "a person actually believes in Catholic doctrine, then I don't see how they can vote for Landrieu without a feeling of sin."

The result was an exceedingly close election. Landrieu carried New Orleans by more than 100,000 votes and heavily Protestant northwest Louisiana around Shreveport; Jenkins carried his home base around Baton Rouge only narrowly, but also won in the heavily Catholic but often Democratic Cajun country. The official results showed Landrieu ahead by 5,788 votes, 50.2%–49.8%. Jenkins filed a lawsuit claiming vote fraud, but withdrew it, and submitted his case to the Senate. At the behest of Majority Leader Trent Lott, whose Mississippi home town is just east of New Orleans, the Senate seated Landrieu "without prejudice" to Jenkins's challenge. To the Senate Rules Committee Jenkins submitted evidence that more votes were counted in many New Orleans precincts than the number of voters who signed in, and that campaign operatives, apparently from New Orleans Mayor Marc Morial's L.I.F.E. organization, ferried. But in June, it was revealed that one of Jenkins's witnesses was a convicted felon, and several others retracted their testimony. Rules Democrats walked out in protest, and the committee's bipartisan two-lawyer team said Jenkins had not met the burden of proof. But Rules Chairman John Warner insisted on conducting the investigation to the end; in September Democrats returned from recess vowing to hold up all Senate business. Landrieu was bitter: "Not only do you run and win your race, now you have to spend the first year defending your race. They've moved the goal posts!" Finally in October 1997 the committee voted unanimously to end the inquiry. While concluding that "isolated instances" of voter fraud did occur, Warner said there was no evidence to prove that there was a "widespread effort to illegally affect the outcome of this election," or that Landrieu had any involvement in the violation of election laws.

In the Senate, Landrieu has a rather liberal voting record on economics, but is more moderate on other issues. Her first bill was for a $5 million block grant for adoption services; her two children are adopted. She cast a key vote for the balanced budget amendment in February 1997; it failed only because Bob Torricelli broke his campaign promise and switched to oppose it. She called for a "fair share" diversion of offshore oil revenues to the states, which would net Louisiana some $200 million annually, and opposed naming two non-polluting Mississippi River parishes as EPA non-compliance areas because EPA yoked them with three other parishes that were out of compliance. Her seat does not come up until 2002.

Presidential politics. Louisiana has become arguably the Southern state most Democratic in presidential politics. It was Michael Dukakis's strongest Southern state in 1988, ranked behind only Bill Clinton's Arkansas and Al Gore's Tennessee in 1992, and behind only Arkansas in 1996 in support of the Democratic ticket. Clinton's 1996 margin of 52%–40% was especially impressive.

Louisiana's presidential primaries in 1992, producing big victories for Clinton and George Bush, got lost in the Super Tuesday shuffle. Not so the February 6 Republican caucuses in 1996. These had been set up by allies of Phil Gramm, who was seeking here as elsewhere early victories that he hoped would strengthen him regardless of what Iowa and New Hampshire did. Instead Louisiana destroyed his campaign. Gramm, relying on polls of active Republicans, was cocksure that he would win. But Pat Buchanan crisscrossed the bayous and upcountry parishes, meeting with voters, talking on cell-phones with any radio show that would have him, dropping in on editorial boards of weekly newspapers. He talked issues national and local, emphasizing his opposition to NAFTA and the need to block imports of Chinese crawfish. It paid off handsomely. Buchanan won more votes than Gramm and took 13 of the 21 delegates. Gramm's campaign in Iowa faltered, and after his poor finish there he had to leave the race without even contesting New Hampshire. Buchanan surged into the public eye, finishing second in Iowa and first in New Hampshire, and surviving long past his loss to Bob Dole in the Super Tuesday Louisiana primary.

In January 1999 Republican party leaders voted to conduct another pre-Iowa caucus. They promised to do it better this time: in 1996 the caucus attracted only 20,000 Republicans to 42 precincts, compared to 100,000 at 2,000 sites in smaller Iowa. Iowa Republicans promised to advise their constituents to shun candidates who campaign in Louisiana.

Congressional districting. Louisiana is the only state to have had three sets of congressional district lines following the 1990 Census. For 1992, the state, under pressure from the Bush Justice Department and a federal court, produced a plan with two black-majority districts, one compact enough in New Orleans, the other a Z-shaped monstrosity trekking from the Atchafalaya swamp to the northern edge of the state and black precincts in Shreveport. That plan was ruled unconstitutional in federal court in December 1993. In April 1994 the legislature passed a plan with a new 4th extending from the Mississippi River parishes south of Baton Rouge northwest to Shreveport. In July 1994 that new plan was disallowed by a federal court, but the Supreme Court kept it in effect for the 1994 elections. In January 1996 a federal court came up with a new plan, then adopted by the legislature, that cut through few parish boundaries and had much more regular lines; it was upheld by the Supreme Court in June 1996. As a result, Louisiana is left with only one black-majority district, the 2d in New Orleans. Congressman Cleo Fields, having lost a bid for governor in 1995 against Mike Foster, announced he would not seek a third term in the newly drawn 4th which dropped from about 55% to 28% black.

The People: Est. Pop. 1998: 4,368,967; Pop. 1990: 4,219,973, up 3.5% 1990–1998. 1.6% of U.S. total, 22d largest; 31.9% rural. Median age: 33 years. 11.6% 65 years and over. 67.3% White, 30.8% Black, 0.9% Asian, 0.5% Amer. Indian, 0.5% Other; 2.1% Hispanic Origin. Households: 53.6% married couple families; 28.5% married couple fams. w. children; 36.6% college educ.; median household income: $21,949; per capita income: $10,635; 65.9% owner occupied housing; median house value: $58,500; median monthly rent: $260. 5.7% Unemployment. 1998 Voting age pop.: 3,149,000. 1998 Turnout: 968,487; 31% of VAP. Registered voters (1998): 2,633,626; 1,638,701 D (62%), 565,047 R (21%), 429,878 unaffiliated and minor parties (16%).

Political Lineup: Governor, Murphy J. (Mike) Foster (R); Lt. Gov., Kathleen B. Blanco (D); Secy. of State, W. Fox McKeithen (R); Atty. Gen., Richard P. Ieyoub (D); Treasurer, Ken Duncan (D); State Senate, 39 (25 D, 14 R); Senate President, Randy Ewing (D); State House, 105 (78 D, 27 R); House Speaker, Hunt Downer Jr. (D). Senators, John Breaux (D) and Mary L. Landrieu (D). Representatives, 7 (2 D, 5 R).

Elections Division: 225-925-7885; **Filing Deadline for U.S. Congress:** August 18, 2000.

1996 Presidential Vote

Clinton (D) 927,836 (53%)
Dole (R) 712,586 (40%)
Perot (I) 123,292   (7%)

1996 Republican Presidential Primary

Dole (R) 37,170 (48%)
Buchanan (R) 25,757 (33%)
Forbes (R) 10,265 (12%)
Others 4,597   (6%)

1992 Presidential Vote

Clinton (D) 815,971 (46%)
Bush (R) 733,386 (42%)
Perot (I) 211,478 (12%)

GOVERNOR

Gov. Murphy J. (Mike) Foster (R)

Elected 1995, term expires Jan. 2000; b. July 11, 1930, Shreveport; home, Franklin; LA St. U., B.S. 1951; Episcopalian; married (Alice).

Military Career: Air Force, 1952–55 (Korea), Air Force Reserves, 1955–59.

Elected Office: LA Senate, 1987–95.

Professional Career: Farmer; Pres., M.J. Foster Inc.; Pres., Sterling Sugars, Inc.; Partner, Maryland Corp.; Owner, Oaklawn Manor.

Office: State Capitol, P.O. Box 94004, Baton Rouge, 70804, 504-342-7015; Fax: 504-342-7099; Web site: www.state.la.us.

Election Results

1995 gen.	Murphy J. (Mike) Foster (R)	984,499	(64%)
	Cleo Fields (D)	565,861	(37%)
1995 prim.	Murphy J. (Mike) Foster (R)	385,267	(26%)
	Cleo Fields (D)	280,921	(19%)
	Mary L. Landrieu (D)	271,938	(18%)
	Buddy Roemer (R)	263,330	(18%)
	Phil Preis (D)	133,271	(9%)
	Melinda Schwegmann (D)	71,288	(5%)
	Others	69,881	(5%)
1991 gen.	Edwin W. Edwards (D)	1,057,031	(61%)
	David Duke (R)	671,009	(39%)

SENATORS

Sen. John Breaux (D)

Elected 1986, seat up 2004; b. Mar. 1, 1944, Crowley; home, Lafayette; U. of SW LA, B.A. 1964, LA St. U., J.D. 1967; Catholic; married (Lois).

Elected Office: U.S. House of Reps., 1972–87.

Professional Career: Practicing atty., 1967–68; Legis. Asst. & Dist. Mgr., U.S. Rep. Edwin W. Edwards, 1968–72.

DC Office: 503 HSOB, 20510, 202-224-4623; Fax: 202-228-2577; Web site: www.senate.gov/~breaux.

State Offices: Baton Rouge, 504-382-2050; Lafayette, 318-262-6871; Monroe, 318-325-3320; New Orleans, 504-589-2531.

Committees: *Aging (Special)* (RMM of 9 D). *Commerce, Science & Transportation* (5th of 9 D): Aviation; Communications; Consumer Affairs, Foreign Commerce & Tourism; Oceans & Fisheries; Science, Technology & Space (RMM); Surface Transportation & Merchant Marine. *Finance* (4th of 9 D): Health Care; International Trade; Social Security & Family Policy (RMM).

Group Ratings

	ADA	ACLU	AFS	LCV	CON	NTU	NFIB	COC	ACU	NTLC	CHC
1998	75	57	89	50	30	15	44	59	20	29	36
1997	55	—	56	—	77	46	—	70	20	—	—

National Journal Ratings

	1997 LIB	—	1997 CONS	1998 LIB	—	1998 CONS
Economic	54%	—	45%	57%	—	42%
Social	39%	—	55%	52%	—	46%
Foreign	62%	—	32%	51%	—	36%

Key Votes of the 105th Congress

1. Bal. Budget Amend.	Y	5. Satcher for Surgeon Gen.	Y	9. Chem. Weapons Treaty	Y
2. Clinton Budget Deal	Y	6. Highway Set-asides	Y	10. Cuban Humanitarian Aid	Y
3. Cloture on Tobacco	Y	7. Table Child Gun locks	Y	11. Table Bosnia Troops	Y
4. Education IRAs	Y	8. Ovrd. Part. Birth Veto	Y	12. $ for Test-ban Treaty	Y

Election Results

1998 primary	John Breaux (D)	620,502	(64%)	($3,858,472)
	Jim Donelon (R)	306,616	(32%)	($364,073)
	Others	42,047	(4%)	
1992 primary	John Breaux (D)	616,021	(73%)	($2,007,675)
	Jon Khachaturian (I)	74,785	(9%)	($94,919)
	Lyle Stockstill (R)	69,986	(8%)	($34,711)
	Nick Accardo (D)	45,839	(6%)	
	Fred Clegg Strong (R)	36,406	(4%)	

Sen. Mary L. Landrieu (D)

Elected 1996, seat up 2002; b. Nov. 23, 1955, Arlington, VA; home, New Orleans; LA St. U., B.A. 1977; Catholic; married (Frank Snellings).

Elected Office: LA House of Reps., 1979–88; LA Treasurer, 1987–96.

DC Office: 702 HSOB, 20510, 202-224-5824; Fax: 202-224-9735; Web site: www.senate.gov/~landrieu.

State Offices: Baton Rouge, 225-389-0395; Lake Charles, 318-436-6650; New Orleans, 504-589-2427; Shreveport, 318-676-3085.

Committees: *Armed Services* (8th of 9 D): Airland Forces; Readiness & Management Support; Strategic Forces (RMM). *Energy & Natural Resources* (7th of 9 D): Energy, Research, Development, Production & Regulation; Forests & Public Land Management; National Parks, Historic Preservation & Recreation. *Small Business* (7th of 8 D).

Group Ratings

	ADA	ACLU	AFS	LCV	CON	NTU	NFIB	COC	ACU	NTLC	CHC
1998	90	57	100	88	42	9	44	67	8	21	18
1997	70	—	67	—	56	39	—	70	16	—	—

National Journal Ratings

	1997 LIB — 1997 CONS	1998 LIB — 1998 CONS
Economic	57% — 40%	72% — 25%
Social	55% — 37%	63% — 26%
Foreign	82% — 17%	51% — 36%

Key Votes of the 105th Congress

1. Bal. Budget Amend.	Y	5. Satcher for Surgeon Gen.	Y	9. Chem. Weapons Treaty	Y
2. Clinton Budget Deal	Y	6. Highway Set-asides	Y	10. Cuban Humanitarian Aid	Y
3. Cloture on Tobacco	Y	7. Table Child Gun locks	N	11. Table Bosnia Troops	Y
4. Education IRAs	N	8. Ovrd. Part. Birth Veto	Y	12. $ for Test-ban Treaty	Y

Election Results

1996 general	Mary L. Landrieu (D)	852,945	(50%)	($2,504,815)
	Louis (Woody) Jenkins (R)	847,157	(50%)	($1,878,242)
1996 primary	Louis (Woody) Jenkins (R)	322,244	(26%)	
	Mary L. Landrieu (D)	264,268	(22%)	
	Richard P. Ieyoub (D)	250,682	(20%)	
	David Duke (R)	141,489	(12%)	
	Jimmy Hayes (R)	71,699	(6%)	
	Bill Linder (R)	58,243	(5%)	
	Others	119,934	(10%)	
1990 primary	J. Bennett Johnston (D)	752,902	(54%)	($5,389,624)
	David Duke (R)	607,391	(44%)	($2,615,267)
	Others	35,820	(3%)	

FIRST DISTRICT

New Orleans, founded in 1718, the nation's fifth largest city at the outbreak of the Civil War, is ancient for an American metropolis; yet it is still closely girded by the peculiar wilderness of the mushy Delta lands of the sluggish Mississippi River. Climb the levee overlooking the

Mississippi and you will see an expanse of water with untidy clumps of trees and disorganized-looking, seemingly abandoned docks—what Mark Twain had in his mind's eye while writing *Life on the Mississippi* in the 1870s. Or drive just past the last block of a suburban subdivision, and you are in unreclaimed swamp, vegetation and wetness, thick with herons and alligators, flat as far as the eye can see. For years the river funneled the products of half a continent down to a single port with an international heritage and flair; the New Orleans metropolitan area is still living off that geography and history, with an inward-looking elite preoccupied with who is in which Mardi Gras krewe and interested more in old families' genealogy than in Oil Patch geology. The old buildings of New Orleans are finely proportioned and its old neighborhoods charming, like those in France; and its early 20th Century improvements, like Olmstead's City Park, are grand. But its middle and late 20th Century streetscapes and subdivisions, like those of France, are without ornament or charm, utilitarian works of man made to master the below-sea-level environment.

The 1st Congressional District includes much of the newer part of the New Orleans metropolitan area, spread over the soggy lands of the lower Mississippi and Lake Pontchartrain. Most of its people live in affluent white neighborhoods in New Orleans and the vast suburb of Metairie in Jefferson Parish, divided by slanting grids and elevated only where bridges jut out over the many canals. The 1st extends across the 26-mile Lake Pontchartrain Causeway to include fast-growing St. Tammany Parish, with old towns lush with trees and clusters of new growth around giant intersections, and north and west to Washington and Tangipahoa parishes, still mostly rural country. This is the most upscale, affluent, highly educated district in Louisiana, and also the most Republican, supportive of political reform and against economic redistribution.

The congressman from the 1st District is Republican David Vitter. He received an economics degree from Harvard, was a Rhodes scholar at Oxford University, and earned his law degree from Tulane Law School. Vitter was elected in 1991 to the first of two terms in the state House, where he became prominent for passing a term limits bill through a reluctant state legislature in 1995.

The chance to run for Congress came suddenly, though not entirely without warning. Congressman Bob Livingston, first elected in a 1977 special after his predecessor was forced to resign because of corruption charges, had become chairman of the Appropriations Committee, installed over three more senior members by incoming Speaker Newt Gingrich in November 1994. After five years of considerable success and tempestuous frustration, Livingston let it be known in early 1998 that he was thinking of retiring, to make money, and would stay only if he were to run for speaker; Gingrich persuaded Livingston to stay and let many Republicans think he would run for president. When Gingrich was forced to announce his retirement three days after the 1998 election, Livingston immediately became a candidate for speaker and, with an active campaign organization already corralling votes, quickly had a majority and became known as speaker-designate after he unanimously won the nomination of the Republican Conference. On December 17, as the House was approaching the impeachment vote, Livingston disquieted some colleagues by confessing that he had had affairs; on December 19, while speaking in the debate on impeachment, he stunned everyone by announcing that he was resigning, even as he called on Clinton to do so. His official date of retirement was February 28, 1999; Governor Mike Foster set the special election for May 1, with a runoff, if no candidate received a majority, May 29: two Saturdays, one when Jazz Fest begins, the other in the Memorial Day weekend, likely to produce low turnout.

The chief preoccupation of the national press, and the chief fear of Louisiana and national Republicans, was that former Ku Klux Klansman and Hitler sympathizer David Duke would run and make it into the runoff. This seemed a bit farfetched, for Duke's career seemed to have peaked almost a decade ago. He achieved some electoral success running against Senator Bennett Johnston in 1990 with 44%, and 39% in the runoff against Edwin Edwards in 1991.

Then he thudded, winning only 9% in the 1992 Louisiana presidential primary. In 1998 he raised some $40,000 by selling his book *My Awakening* and asserted that "belief in racial equality is the modern equivalent of believing the earth is flat." To charges that his appeal had shrunk, he said, "I fly below the radar screen in polls." He was renounced by Republicans from national chairman Jim Nicholson on down, though Governor Mike Foster did not do so.

Jumping into the race just as quickly were several other Republicans. The establishment choice was David Treen, who ran for the House as long ago as 1962 (and gave Democrat Hale Boggs a scare in 1964) and was elected to the House from 1972–78. In 1979 he was elected governor in a year when Edwin Edwards was term-limited from running; four years later Edwards won. Treen called for repealing federal tobacco and alcohol taxes and allowing the states to raise theirs to pay for education. He pledged to serve only the short term and one more and argued that his experience in the House would help the district. In contrast, Vitter said, "We need a younger congressman like me, so we can start building up the seniority we lost when Bob Livingston resigned." Perhaps the most attention-grabbing candidate was Monica Monica, an ophthalmologist, who spent more than $1.2 million including at least $900,000 of her own money, and in mid-February became the first candidate to go up with TV ads. She was encouraged to run by the 5th District's John Cooksey, also an ophthalmologist, whose chief of staff took a leave of absence to run the Monica campaign. Her ads talked of health care, term limits, paying down the national debt; she called herself the Jesse Ventura of the Bayous. Also up on TV before the end of February was Rob Couhig, owner of a family pest control firm and the New Orleans Zephyrs baseball team. He was dogged by some bad publicity about disputes with a contractor over bills for building a stadium, but spent about $500,000, including more than $330,000 of his own money. In 1980 he ran against Democratic Congresswoman Lindy Boggs, and won 34% of the vote. On the Democratic side was Bill Strain, the second-most senior member of the Louisiana House (first elected in 1972), from a district including parts of St. Tammany, Tangipahoa and Washington parishes.

Treen, with 25%, and Vitter, with 22%, advanced to the runoff. Duke came unnervingly close to making the runoff, but finished third with 19%, followed by Monica with 16%, Strain with 11%, and Couhig with 6%. Duke asserted he would have advanced to the runoff if Strain, the conservative Democrat, had not been in the race. "People over the years have asked me what percentage of the vote in . . . a district like the 1st is hard-core racist, and I never knew what to say," University of New Orleans political scientist Susan Howell told Kevin Sack of *The New York Times*. "Now we know, and it's one out of five."

Subtle differences emerged between Vitter and Treen during the runoff: Vitter denounced all forms of gun control; Treen said he supported some restrictions on more sophisticated automatic or semiautomatic weapons, and would require dealers at gun shows to perform background checks. Both opposed racial quotas and preferences but Treen also said the federal government should not prevent colleges and universities from deciding their own racial admission policies. Treen was endorsed by Livingston, Foster and several prominent local politicians, but may have been hurt when he stopped campaigning in the final week to help search for his grandson, who disappeared while hiking in Oregon—he was found three days before the election. But low turnout was probably a bigger factor, as Vitter rallied his troops and won the seat, 51%–49%. Treen carried his home base of St. Tammany Parish north of Lake Pontchartrain, but not enough to overcome Vitter's home advantage in Jefferson Parish.

Slim and boyish-looking, Vitter, 38, is noted for his ability to irritate other politicians; a popular suburban sheriff whose ethics Vitter criticized sued him three separate times. He will have to be more pliant in Washington than he was in Baton Rouge to take care of this district as well as Livingston did.

Cook's Call. *Probably Safe.* Although this is one of the most Republican districts in the state, Vitter should not yet be considered safe. If he steps on as many toes in Congress as he did in the state legislature, a serious candidate from either party could emerge to challenge him.

The People: Pop. 1990: 602,867; 25.6% rural; 12.5% age 65+; 85.5% White, 12.1% Black, 1.1% Asian, 0.3% Amer. Indian, 1% Other; 4.3% Hispanic Origin. Households: 55.4% married couple families; 27.6% married couple fams. w. children; 46.1% college educ.; median household income: $27,413; per capita income: $13,755; median house value: $75,500; median gross rent: $331.

1996 Presidential Vote			1992 Presidential Vote		
Dole (R)	152,655	(57%)	Bush (R)	154,584	(56%)
Clinton (D)	100,655	(37%)	Clinton (D)	87,429	(32%)
Perot (I)	16,325	(6%)	Perot (I)	34,402	(12%)

Rep. David Vitter (R)

Elected May 1999; b. May 3, 1961, New Orleans; home, Metairie; Harvard U., A.B. 1983, Rhodes Scholar, Oxford U., B.A. 1985, Tulane Law Schl., J.D. 1988; Catholic; married (Wendy).

Elected Office: LA House of Reps., 1991–99.

Professional Career: Practicing atty., 1988–99; Adjunct Law Prof., Tulane U. & Loyola U., 1995–98.

DC Office: 2406 RHOB 20515, 202-225-3015; Fax: 202-225-0739; Web site: www.house.gov/vitter.

District Offices: Hammond, 504-542-9616; Metairie, 504-589-2753.

Committees: not assigned as of June 1, 1999

Group Ratings and Key Votes: Newly Elected

Election Results

1999 runoff	David Vitter (R)	61,661	(51%)	($807,505)
	David Treen (R)	59,849	(49%)	($494,789)
1999 primary	David Treen (R)	36,719	(25%)	
	David Vitter (R)	31,741	(22%)	
	David Duke (R)	28,059	(19%)	
	Monica Monica (R)	22,928	(16%)	
	Bill Strain (D)	16,446	(11%)	
	Rob Couhig (R)	9,295	(6%)	
1998 primary	Robert L. Livingston (R)	unopposed		($1,021,235)
1996 primary	Robert L. Livingston (R)	unopposed		($1,042,853)

SECOND DISTRICT

Founded by the French in 1718, ruled by the Spanish from 1763 to just days before the French took over to sell it to the United States in 1803, New Orleans was a Creole city—part French, a bit Spanish, more than a touch Caribbean—when the American flag was raised over what is now Jackson Square. The statue of Andrew Jackson still seems an alien intrusion in a square set off by a French Market, the Cabildo, the Presbytere, the Pontalba apartments and Cathedral St. Louis. New Orleans was the fifth largest American city from 1840 until the Civil War and the only sizable city in the South; yet even as it was sending southern cotton out to the mills of Lancashire, it was an alien cultural force in both the nation and region. Urbanized, yet poor and in many ways primitive, New Orleans had yellow fever epidemics late in the 19th Century, even as it was installing electric lights; it had a riot in which Italian immigrants were massacred, even as it was laying streetcar tracks and telephone lines. This was one of the most corrupt American cities during Reconstruction and the Gilded Age, when its votes were regularly bid for and bought; like other Southern cities, it became rigidly segregated after 1890.

For a time during the 1970s oil boom, New Orleans seemed to be a fast-growing Sun Belt city; then starting in the middle 1980s it reverted to its rougher traditions. Its port lost business—oil to Houston and Latin American trade to Miami. The city was beset by woes big and small, from grotesquely potholed streets to out-of-control crime, sometimes abetted by a notoriously corrupt police force. But in the mid-1990s New Orleans took a turn for the better. Under Mayor Marc Morial, the police force was cleaned up, was increased in size and adopted New York's crime-fighting methods. Crime plummeted, and no longer depressed the tourism business, which today is the city's largest. The city's land-based casino went broke in 1995 even before the permanent building was finished, and though it was licensed again, seems likely to produce disappointing revenues. But that is because people come to New Orleans for other things than gambling. They want to see the gaudy bars of Bourbon Street and the restored houses there and in the Garden District. They want to see Mardi Gras and the Krewes that parade for weeks before. And they want to dine in New Orleans's array of restaurants, with a cuisine all New Orleans's own, spicy and rich and unaffected by today's taste for low-fat food. In 1998, *The Wall Street Journal* reported that the federal government had determined that New Orleanians "are the fattest people in America, the most likely to contract lung cancer and among the shortest lived, with an average lifespan roughly equal to the citizens of Mauritius, North Korea and Uzbekistan."

The 2d Congressional District includes almost all of the city of New Orleans, everything except a few affluent white neighborhoods, plus the west bank towns of Jefferson Parish—Gretna, Harvey, Westwego, Waggaman—industrial enclosures between levee and swamp. Here is the French Quarter—the *Vieux Carre*—its 19th Century homes still intact because the Americans who moved here after 1803 wanted to stay away from the snobbish Creoles and then built a new downtown across Canal Street. North of the Quarter is the site of Storyville, where prostitution was legal until 1918 and where jazz was probably first played; the old frame houses have long since been torn down and replaced by half-empty and crime-ridden housing projects. But many similar neighborhoods remain, where blacks and some working-class whites live in rickety frame houses which are not always strong enough to keep the rain out and never tight enough to protect against the summer humidity or the damp winter chill, along the vividly named streets—Elysian Fields, Spain, Desire, Arts—that go north from the river wharves. But some 37,000 houses stand empty. South of the quarter is the downtown flecked with skyscrapers and the ominous Superdome, and to the east is the old slum known as the Irish Channel—a reminder that New Orleans had more foreign immigrants than any other part of the South. Up St. Charles Avenue is the Garden District. This was the home of the rich, early American settlers, and its antebellum homes are still covered with vines and Spanish moss. Quaintly named trolley cars still roll out St. Charles to Tulane University and Audubon Park. New Orleans, for many years a speckled black-and-white city, now has a solid black majority, and the 2d District is overwhelmingly Democratic.

The congressman from the 2d District is Bill Jefferson, a Democrat first elected in 1990 after the retirement of Lindy Boggs, a charming Louisiana lady with perfect political pitch, who won majorities from blacks and whites alike. Jefferson grew up in the northeast corner of Louisiana in Lake Providence. After attending Southern University, he went to Harvard Law, clerked for a respected federal judge, worked for Senator Bennett Johnston and finally settled in New Orleans to set up what became the largest black law firm in the South; he received an LL.M. from Georgetown in February 1996 while serving in Congress. Jefferson was elected to the state Senate in 1979; he twice ran for mayor and lost. In 1990, when Boggs retired, Jefferson was endorsed by then-Mayor Sidney Barthelemy, and in the primary won 25% of the vote to 22% for Marc Morial, whose father was New Orleans's first black mayor and who was elected mayor himself in March 1994. In the November runoff, charges flew: Jefferson was dogged by reports of defaults on outstanding loans and mortgages, while Morial admitted he was the father of an eight-year-old girl living in the Ivory Coast. Jefferson won with 52% and became the first Louisiana black elected to Congress since Reconstruction.

In the House Jefferson has shown impressive political skills. He was active in the Democratic Leadership Council and got to know its chairman, a young southern governor named Bill Clinton. In November 1991, Jefferson and Mississippi Congressman Mike Espy endorsed Clinton and provided early, and crucial, black support. In December 1992, Jefferson won a seat on the Ways and Means Committee. The Republican majority in 1995 downsized Ways and Means, and Jefferson lost his seat, but only temporarily. He has expressed doubts about Social Security individual investment accounts and has also questioned reliance on the payroll tax: "We know it is regressive. I wonder if it's a good idea to have the payroll tax as the only thing to rely on" for Social Security's financial base. He opposed the proposed Shintech polyvinyl chloride plant farther up the Mississippi River because it was sited near a black community; the company decided to build a smaller plant near Baton Rouge instead. He has backed the Africa free trade bill which passed the House in 1998, and made several trips to Africa himself in 1997 and 1998. In a speech he advised African leaders to reform their often corrupt legal systems because businesses would shun them unless they were confident they would be treated fairly. "I talked about the importance of predictability in investing and the need to be able to resolve disputes fairly." He also supports the Zimbabwe program to encourage trophy hunting for elepants, arguing that giving Africans a stake in maintaining a supply of elephants does more to preserve them than a ban on the ivory trade.

Jefferson has recalled that on election night 1990 he was standing next to Lindy Boggs. "I said, 'Lindy, I'm so glad this is over; I can stop running.' She looked at me and said, 'Honey, in this job you never stop running.'" Evidently he has run well: He won re-election against two opponents in November 1998 with 86% of the vote. But he has also eyed other office. In 1991, he had filed to run for governor, but withdrew; in 1995, he began running for governor again, but withdrew in favor of Cleo Fields, and said he would run for Senate; in May 1996 he bowed out of that race. In January 1999 Republican Mike Foster and other statewide officials met at the Governor's Mansion and promised not to oppose each other regardless of party. Jefferson was evidently peeved and days later circulated a letter of protest and said he was running for governor. Certainly he can capitalize on black resentment of Foster, who scrapped racial quotas and preferences in state government, and refused to denounce former Ku Klux Klan leader David Duke, first when Duke endorsed Foster for governor in 1995, then in 1999 as Duke ran for the 1st District House seat left vacant by the resignation of Bob Livingston. But Jefferson will need more votes to win: black turnout surged in 1998, but still amounted to only 32% of the total, and Foster's job rating has been 70% or more positive. Louisiana's staggered election cycle means he will not have to give up his seat to run, and one statewide campaign might lead to another, with better prospects for success.

Cook's Call. *Safe.* As the most heavily minority and strongest Democratic district in the state, Jefferson is totally safe.

The People: Pop. 1990: 602,830; 0.2% rural; 11.4% age 65 +; 35.7% White, 60.8% Black, 2.2% Asian, 0.3% Amer. Indian, 1.1% Other; 3.3% Hispanic Origin. Households: 37.7% married couple families; 20.1% married couple fams. w. children; 39.7% college educ.; median household income: $18,585; per capita income: $9,918; median house value: $62,400; median gross rent: $274.

1996 Presidential Vote

Clinton (D)	169,930	(79%)
Dole (R)	40,739	(19%)
Perot (I)	5,400	(2%)

1992 Presidential Vote

Clinton (D)	153,134	(69%)
Bush (R)	55,362	(25%)
Perot (I)	13,895	(6%)

Rep. William J. Jefferson (D)

Elected 1990; b. Mar. 14, 1947, Lake Providence; home, New Orleans; Southern U., B.A. 1969, Harvard U., J.D. 1972, Georgetown U., LL.M. 1996; Baptist; married (Andrea).

Military Career: Army Reserves, 1969–78, Army Judge Advocate Corps, 1975.

Elected Office: LA Senate, 1979–90.

Professional Career: Law clerk, U.S. Dist. Judge Alvin Rubin, 1972–73; Legis. aide, U.S. Sen. Bennett Johnston, 1973–75; Practicing atty., 1975–90.

DC Office: 240 CHOB 20515, 202-225-6636; Fax: 202-225-1988; Web site: www.house.gov/jefferson.

District Office: New Orleans, 504-589-2274.

Committees: *Ways & Means* (12th of 16 D): Human Resources; Trade.

Group Ratings

	ADA	ACLU	AFS	LCV	CON	NTU	NFIB	COC	ACU	NTLC	CHC
1998	80	67	100	62	64	14	10	43	13	9	8
1997	75	—	100	—	23	14	—	50	17	—	—

National Journal Ratings

	1997 LIB — 1997 CONS	1998 LIB — 1998 CONS
Economic	68% — 31%	79% — 0%
Social	73% — 24%	67% — 33%
Foreign	62% — 37%	73% — 26%

Key Votes of the 105th Congress

1. Clinton Budget Deal	N	5. Puerto Rico Sthood. Ref.	Y	9. Cut $ for B-2 Bombers	N
2. Education IRAs	N	6. End Highway Set-asides	*	10. Human Rights in China	Y
3. Req. 2/3 to Raise Taxes	N	7. School Prayer Amend.	N	11. Withdraw Bosnia Troops	N
4. Fast-track Trade	*	8. Ovrd. Part. Birth Veto	Y	12. End Cuban TV-Marti	Y

Election Results

1998 primary	William J. Jefferson (D)	102,247	(86%)	($495,522)
	David Reed (D)	10,803	(9%)	
	Don-Terry Veal (D)	5,899	(5%)	($1,609)
1996 primary	William J. Jefferson (D)	unopposed		($301,082)

THIRD DISTRICT

Below sea level, veined with bayous and creeks and wide streams of water, crossed by only an occasional road or railroad, the wetlands of southern Louisiana are one of America's unique landscapes. Technically, most of this waterlogged land rests on islands in a broad river mouth, through which the waters of the Mississippi and its tributaries drain into the Gulf of Mexico. It is rich with animal life, herons and egrets, shrimp and crawfish, muskrats and alligators. Yet it supports more people than one might think, in surprisingly sturdy small towns, with shopping malls on high ground, and in cabins along the bayous and crossroad towns where Cajun French remains the first language and roadside diners feature crawfish etouffe. But the steep-roofed Cajun houses are not the only structures: here and there, jutting out of the swampy land, are huge elaborate metal sculptures—refineries and petrochemical plants, processing the oil and natural gas trapped under these wetlands and the shallow continental shelf of the Gulf, and released through 20th Century oil rig technology. In the 1960s and 1970s, the oil industry, by providing good jobs for young people here, helped preserve Cajun culture and built a Cajun pride that was seldom articulated a generation ago. Then oil payrolls plummeted and the wetlands were threatened by coastal erosion and battered by Hurricane Andrew in August 1992. But now offshore drilling is booming again, unemployment is low, and the outlook for the Cajun country looks good.

The 3d Congressional District includes about half the Cajun country, plus St. Bernard and Plaquemines parishes downriver from New Orleans. It then spreads west over the swamplands, covering Houma, where seven bayous converge; St. Charles, St. John the Baptist, St. James and Ascension parishes on both sides of the Mississippi, once the greatest sugar producers in America, now studded with refineries and petrochemical plants and the site of the proposed Shintech plan which was blocked by charges of "environmental racism"; roughneck Morgan City, which services many offshore oil rigs; and Iberia Parish, the home of McIlhenny's Tabasco sauce. Behind the Mississippi's western levee, hunkered side by side in Vacherie in St. James Parish, are twin reminders of the region's grandeur and pain: the stately Oak Alley plantation, whose stunning vista stood in for the home of a fictional, aristocratic governor in the 1998 movie *Primary Colors*, and the Laura Plantation, believed to be the original home of the famous Br'er Rabbit stories, and whose current owners are preserving and displaying the plantation's slave cabins to remind visitors of the facts many would prefer to forget. The ancestral language here is French, mainly Cajun but also Creole; the ancestral religion is Roman Catholic and the ancestral politics Democratic, though very conservative. In 1996 the 3d District voted for Bill Clinton and for Republican Senate candidate Woody Jenkins.

The congressman from the 3d District is Billy Tauzin, first elected as a Democrat and now a Republican, who brings Cajun caginess and charm to his work. Tauzin grew up in Chackbay, worked on an oil rig to put himself through Nicholls State University and LSU Law School. He was first elected to the legislature in 1971, at 28; he won the 3d District seat in a May 1980 special election. Tauzin ran for governor in 1987, but was doomed when Edwin Edwards entered the race, squeezing him out in Cajun country; he finished fourth, with 10%. In 1989, Tauzin inherited a Merchant Marine subcommittee chairmanship, just in time to handle legislation inspired by the Exxon *Valdez* oil spill in Alaska. In 1990 he drew up plans to allow a drawdown of the Strategic Petroleum Reserve in southern Louisiana to help pay for the Gulf war and then got the reserve built back up afterward. Tauzin is both knowledgeable and eloquent. His floor speech for a 1992 Cable Act amendment allowing wireless cable companies access to cable-originated programming carried 338–68 over the opposition of Democratic leaders and the Bush White House. He was a co-sponsor of the securities litigation reform which was passed in 1996 over Bill Clinton's veto. He can also be wily. Defeated in the committee and on the House floor, he and Senator Bennett Johnston inserted in conference committee on the Alaska Oil Export Act of 1995 a provision for royalty relief for deep-water oil drilling; that, plus advances in technology, led to the resurgence in offshore drilling in 1996.

Tauzin's party switch was not a complete surprise. He was one of two Democrats who supported all provisions of the Contract with America and in February 1995 he and 22 other Democrats formed The Coalition, a conservative group. He was the lead Democrat in pushing property rights legislation, requiring the government to compensate landowners if the value of their property was reduced by 20% by the wetlands laws or the Endangered Species Act; that did not become law, but remains a major Tauzin cause. In August 1995 he finally became a Republican. He was expected to run for Johnston's Senate seat in 1996, but Tauzin bowed out after being promised by the Republican leadership Jack Fields's spot as chairman of the Telecommunications and Finance Subcommittee. Mike Oxley, the next Republican in line, objected, and, as a compromise, Telecommunications lost its Finance jurisdiction to Oxley's subcommittee, and in return received the less important Trade and Consumer Protection portfolios.

Tauzin strongly supported the Telecommunications Act of 1996 and has since criticized the

FCC for blocking the regional Bells from the long-distance business. He opposes giving law enforcement agencies the key to encryption codes and all taxes on e-commerce; he wants to eliminate the long-distance tax. He wants cable companies to give consumers a wider range of options (including low-cost service with few channels) and has passed an anti-slamming bill through the House. He and his Senate counterpart John McCain want to allow satellite TV to broadcast local stations and compete with cable. His bill to ban taping of cell phones and other wireless communications passed with one vote against in 1998. Tauzin opposes auctioning the digital TV spectrum, regulating liquor advertising and any campaign finance bill giving free or discounted air time to candidates (in his view, unconstitutional, unfair and ineffective). On some telecommunications issues Tauzin has taken positions opposite full committee chairman Thomas Bliley; certainly he hopes to replace Bliley after the 2000 election, when the Republicans' three-term limit on chairmen kicks in. Tauzin and Democrat James Traficant of Ohio have proposed a national sales tax to replace federal income tax.

Since becoming subcommittee chairman, Tauzin has been re-elected easily—and has shown no interest in statewide office. In September 1997 he became the only party-switcher to be re-elected without opposition; he had no opposition in 1998 either. Nor is he likely to have serious opposition in the future: He had $825,000 in his treasury at the end of 1998 and with his chairmanship could easily raise hundreds of thousands more.

Cook's Call. *Safe.* Switching parties in 1994 clearly has not caused Tauzin any political fall-out; he has racked up big winning margins ever since.

The People: Pop. 1990: 602,814; 33.5% rural; 9.6% age 65 + ; 73.7% White, 23.5% Black, 0.9% Asian, 1.5% Amer. Indian, 0.4% Other; 2.3% Hispanic Origin. Households: 61.4% married couple families; 35.4% married couple fams. w. children; 25.9% college educ.; median household income: $22,948; per capita income: $9,614; median house value: $56,700; median gross rent: $232.

1996 Presidential Vote			1992 Presidential Vote		
Clinton (D)	153,925	(52%)	Clinton (D)	115,063	(45%)
Dole (R)	120,605	(41%)	Bush (R)	105,982	(41%)
Perot (I)	22,182	(7%)	Perot (I)	36,193	(14%)

Rep. W. J. (Billy) Tauzin (R)

Elected May 1980; b. June 14, 1943, Chackbay; home, Chackbay; Nicholls St. U., B.A. 1964, LA St. U., J.D. 1967; Catholic; married (Cecile).

Elected Office: LA House of Reps., 1971–79.

Professional Career: Practicing atty., 1968–70.

DC Office: 2183 RHOB 20515, 202-225-4031; Fax: 202-225-0563; Web site: www.house.gov/tauzin.

District Offices: Chalmette, 504-271-1707; Gonzales, 504-621-8490; Houma, 504-876-3033; New Iberia, 318-367-8231.

Committees: *Commerce* (2d of 29 R): Finance & Hazardous Materials (Vice Chmn.); Telecommunications, Trade & Consumer Protection (Chmn.). *Resources* (2d of 28 R): Energy & Mineral Resources; Fisheries Conservation, Wildlife & Oceans.

Group Ratings

	ADA	ACLU	AFS	LCV	CON	NTU	NFIB	COC	ACU	NTLC	CHC
1998	5	7	0	8	13	47	100	100	88	89	92
1997	15	—	0	—	49	51	—	100	83	—	—

National Journal Ratings

	1997 LIB — 1997 CONS	1998 LIB — 1998 CONS
Economic	35% — 63%	33% — 67%
Social	39% — 59%	31% — 69%
Foreign	0% — 88%	7% — 83%

Key Votes of the 105th Congress

1. Clinton Budget Deal	Y	5. Puerto Rico Sthood. Ref.	Y	9. Cut $ for B-2 Bombers	N
2. Education IRAs	Y	6. End Highway Set-asides	Y	10. Human Rights in China	N
3. Req. 2/3 to Raise Taxes	Y	7. School Prayer Amend.	Y	11. Withdraw Bosnia Troops	Y
4. Fast-track Trade	Y	8. Ovrd. Part. Birth Veto	Y	12. End Cuban TV-Marti	N

Election Results

1998 primary	W. J. (Billy) Tauzin (R) .... unopposed	($770,827)
1996 primary	W. J. (Billy) Tauzin (R) .... unopposed	($612,332)

FOURTH DISTRICT

Northwestern Louisiana, south of Arkansas and just east of Texas, is part of the Deep South. Most people here are Protestants, not Catholics, often very tradition-minded, with names that are English or Scottish, not French. The tone is set not by wide-open New Orleans—which was not accessible by interstate route until 1996, when the last chunk of I-49 was completed—but by the much smaller Shreveport, which could be just another East Texas oil town. The countryside is agricultural, though there are few vestiges of large riverfront plantations and backward farm country. Oil provided the basis for much of the economic growth of the 20th Century; defense facilities also helped; more recently there has been some high-tech and local entrepreneurship. Politically, northern Louisiana voters, for more than 100 years, have been voting against cosmopolitan New Orleans and the Catholic Cajun south, sometimes for riproaring populists, and more often, as the economy grows more sophisticated, for market-oriented Republicans.

The 4th Congressional District consists of the northwest quadrant of the state. More than half the votes here are cast in Caddo and Bossier parishes around Shreveport, with the rest scattered around rural areas, picturesque old towns like Natchitoches and strip-highway towns like Leesville near the Army's giant Fort Polk. This area seemed to be trending Republican in the 1980s, but in the 1990s it has gone the other way. Black voters, about one-quarter of the vote, are heavily Democratic, but more than one-third of whites have been voting for Democrats, at least at the top of the ticket. Bill Clinton carried the district in 1992 and 1996, and Democrat Mary Landrieu also carried the 4th, a critical factor in her narrow 5,788-vote statewide margin.

The congressman is Jim McCrery, a Republican first elected in April 1988. McCrery grew up in Leesville, graduated from Louisiana Tech in Ruston (next door to Grambling, site of the football-famous, historically black college) and LSU Law School, and practiced law in Leesville and Shreveport. In 1981 he went to work for Congressman Buddy Roemer, then a Democrat; later he worked for Georgia Pacific in Louisiana. When Roemer was elected governor in 1987, McCrery ran as a Republican and won the special election 51%–49%; that fall he won with 68% beating Roemer's mother. McCrery's toughest re-election race was in 1992, when the creation of the new black-majority 4th District put him in the 5th District with 16-year incumbent Jerry Huckaby, a conservative Democrat. But the district, with few black voters, was heavily Republican and Huckaby had 88 overdrafts on the House bank. McCrery weathered some negative personal attacks, led in the October primary 44%–29% and won the November runoff 63%–37%.

McCrery has compiled a mostly conservative voting record and has worked on major legislation from his seat on the Ways and Means Committee. Armed with the intuition that made him one of only 72 House members to vote against the disastrous 1988 catastrophic health care bill, he advanced a Republican alternative to the Clinton health care plan in 1994, capping deductibility of health insurance, opposing the Democrats' cost control measures, limiting medical malpractice and instituting medical savings accounts. Prompted by complaints from constituents that parents were coaching kids to act out in order to qualify for Supplemental Security Income payments for disabled children, he put together a 1996 law that replaced the SSI cash benefit with vouchers. He worked on the Republicans' Medicare proposals in 1996 and defended them against attack when most applicants were rejected. He worked on the Republican task force to craft the HMO reform which passed the House in July 1998. He favors individual investment accounts for Social Security. McCrery serves on the ethics committee and was one of four members appointed to consider the proposal for outside counsel on complaints about Transportation Chairman Bud Shuster. He has worked on local projects like completing I-49 and promoting I-69, the proposed Michigan-to-Mexico interstate, which is supposed to come through the northwest corner of Louisiana. In 1997 he got $28 million for projects on the Red River.

In the 1990s McCrery has run in four different districts—the 1980s plan in 1990 and three different plans in 1992, 1994 and 1996. In that last year, although the black percentage was raised to 28%, he beat a Democrat 71%–29% in the September primary; he was unopposed in 1998. McCrery has served as a vice chairman of the National Republican Congressional Committee, and in 1998 considered running for chairman, but decided against it.

Cook's Call. *Safe.* On paper, this Shreveport-based district looks like it could be fertile ground for Democrats, as Clinton rolled up large margins here in 1992 and 1996. But McCrery has a solid hold on this district and will be extremely difficult to dislodge, barring Democratic redistricting changes.

The People: Pop. 1990: 602,692; 40.5% rural; 13% age 65 + ; 65.9% White, 32.5% Black, 0.6% Asian, 0.5% Amer. Indian, 0.4% Other; 1.7% Hispanic Origin. Households: 54.5% married couple families; 28% married couple fams. w. children; 37.4% college educ.; median household income: $20,920; per capita income: $10,218; median house value: $51,000; median gross rent: $246.

1996 Presidential Vote

Clinton (D)	122,729	(53%)
Dole (R)	92,741	(40%)
Perot (I)	17,525	(8%)

1992 Presidential Vote

Clinton (D)	150,800	(67%)
Bush (R)	57,286	(25%)
Perot (I)	17,298	(8%)

Rep. Jim McCrery (R)

Elected Apr. 1988; b. Sept. 18, 1949, Shreveport; home, Shreveport; LA Tech. U., B.A. 1971, LA St. U., J.D. 1975; Methodist; married (Johnette).

Professional Career: Practicing atty. 1975–78; Asst. Shreveport City Atty., 1979–80; Legis. Dir., U.S. Rep. Buddy Roemer, 1981–84; Regional Mgr., Georgia-Pacific Corp., 1984–88.

DC Office: 2104 RHOB 20515, 202-225-2777; Fax: 202-225-8039; Web site: www.house.gov/mccrery.

District Offices: Leesville, 318-238-0778; Shreveport, 318-798-2254.

Committees: *Ways & Means* (8th of 23 R): Health; Human Resources; Social Security.

Group Ratings

	ADA	ACLU	AFS	LCV	CON	NTU	NFIB	COC	ACU	NTLC	CHC
1998	5	21	11	8	6	60	100	100	96	86	83
1997	20	—	13	—	49	48	—	100	83	—	—

National Journal Ratings

	1997 LIB — 1997 CONS		1998 LIB — 1998 CONS	
Economic	37% —	63%	30% —	67%
Social	45% —	55%	33% —	66%
Foreign	32% —	68%	19% —	75%

Key Votes of the 105th Congress

1. Clinton Budget Deal	Y	5. Puerto Rico Sthood. Ref.	N	9. Cut $ for B-2 Bombers	N
2. Education IRAs	Y	6. End Highway Set-asides	Y	10. Human Rights in China	N
3. Req. 2/3 to Raise Taxes	Y	7. School Prayer Amend.	Y	11. Withdraw Bosnia Troops	Y
4. Fast-track Trade	Y	8. Ovrd. Part. Birth Veto	Y	12. End Cuban TV-Marti	N

Election Results

1998 primary	Jim McCrery (R)	.... unopposed		($666,860)
1996 primary	Jim McCrery (R)	 94,822	(71%)	($823,121)
	Paul M. Chachere (D)	 38,015	(29%)	

FIFTH DISTRICT

Northeast Louisiana is perhaps the least known part of the state. Along the Mississippi River and the Red River and their dozens of tributaries, it was plantation country before the Civil War, with black majorities still in many parishes. Away from the larger rivers, it is hill country, places where small farmers scratched out a living on land connected to parish courthouses by dusty lanes. Such was Winn Parish, where Huey P. Long, the pivotal figure in modern Louisiana politics, was born in 1893, and from which he began his meteoric political career—elected governor in 1928, senator in 1932, a national figure threatening both parties when he was assassinated in his new high-rise Capitol in Baton Rouge in 1935.

The 5th Congressional District contains much of this country, from the river parishes to the hills of Winn Parish. The biggest urban areas here, with under 100,000 people each, are Monroe in the north and Alexandria in the south. Alexandria in Rapides Parish sits at the northernmost extension of Cajun, Catholic Louisiana, while Monroe is heavily WASP and Baptist; it is home to one of the world's leading Bible collections, assembled by an heir to an early Coca-Cola bottler. The district also includes East Carroll Parish, which is hemmed in by the Arkansas border to the north and the Mississippi River to the east; in 1996, *USA Today* reported that an astonishing 55% of parish residents lived in poverty, with even an higher rate in the parish's biggest town, Lake Providence.

This district was newly created for the 1996 election; the 1992 and 1994 districting plans each had a black-majority 4th District whose boundaries jutted here and there throughout northern Louisiana. This new 5th district has geographically regular boundaries and a black population in 1990 of 31%. Politically, it has trended Republican in the 1980s, but there are pockets of Democratic strength in rural as well as urban areas. In 1996 it produced a small margin for Bill Clinton while voting for Republican Woody Jenkins in the close Senate race.

The congressman from the 5th District is John Cooksey, a Republican elected in 1996. Cooksey grew up next to his father's sawmill in Olla, and claims to have lived all his life within a mile of U.S. 165, which runs north and south through the district. He attended LSU and medical school, served in the Air Force and was sent to northern Thailand during the Vietnam war. After a year of medical residency in New Orleans, he moved to Monroe in 1972 and practiced as an ophthalmologist. He also traveled on medical missions five times to Kenya and raised money to set up an eye clinic there. He was a politically active Republican for years, but never ran for office until the new 5th District was created in 1996. It had no incumbent: Jim McCrery chose to run in the 4th, and Cleo Fields, at one time Louisiana's youngest legislator and the youngest member of Congress when he was elected in 1992, decided not to run; Fields had won twice in two black-majority districts but the odds against him seemed strong in this 31% black district. Two other serious candidates ran. Clyde Holloway, a Republican elected narrowly in an Alexandria-based district in 1986, 1988 and 1990, carried the area around Alexandria in the September 1996 primary, and got 27% of the vote. Veteran state Representative Francis Thompson, a Democrat, carried the heavily black Mississippi River parishes, and got 28%; Cooksey carried Monroe and the northern parishes inland from the river, and won 34%. With two-thirds of the primary vote going to Republicans, Cooksey was obviously the favorite in the November runoff. While supporting most conservative positions, he took some original stands—tax credits to encourage people to buy American-made products, business tax credits for developing and creating vocational and technical training programs. Cooksey attacked Thompson for voting for tax increases; Thompson called Cooksey a "rich doctor" out of touch with the people. Cooksey spent $107,000 of his own money and won 58%–42%, carrying every parish except those near the river and winning especially big margins in Monroe and Alexandria.

In the House, Cooksey has a mostly conservative voting record, though rather moderate on cultural issues; his distinctive stands often reflect his background as a physician. He refused to support the tobacco industry settlement and rejected the argument that Louisiana must support tobacco to get others to help sugar and rice: "I think that tobacco and trial lawyers are bad for the country. Tobacco is damaging to people's health, and there's no question about that." Although he called for cutting spending generally, he was not bashful about widening U.S. 165. He disliked the partisan tone of the House: "There's always going to be some partisan politics. . . . But some of the partisan politics has become too aggressive, too vindictive and too mean." In 1996 Cooksey pledged to limit his own terms to three. But in 1998 he formed a leadership PAC, to give money especially to Republican physicians. In early 1999 he actively recruited New Orleans area ophthalmologist Monica Monica to run for Bob Livingston's House seat.

Cook's Call. *Safe.* While Cooksey has not been seriously battle tested in this rather new district, it is hard to see how a Democrat could make inroads in this conservative, Republican trending district. Should he leave to run against Senator Landrieu in 2002, this would be a competitive though Republican-leaning race.

The People: Pop. 1990: 602,928; 49.5% rural; 13.7% age 65 +; 68.1% White, 31% Black, 0.4% Asian, 0.3% Amer. Indian, 0.2% Other; 0.8% Hispanic Origin. Households: 55% married couple families; 28.3% married couple fams. w. children; 31.9% college educ.; median household income: $18,258; per capita income: $9,153; median house value: $44,100; median gross rent: $197.

1996 Presidential Vote

Clinton (D)	132,407	(49%)
Dole (R)	113,846	(42%)
Perot (I)	22,994	(9%)

1992 Presidential Vote

Bush (R)	125,965	(49%)
Clinton (D)	94,936	(37%)
Perot (I)	36,121	(14%)

Rep. John Cooksey (R)

Elected 1996; b. Aug. 20, 1941, Alexandria; home, Monroe; LA St. U., B.S. 1962, M.D. 1966, U. of TX, M.B.A. 1994; Methodist; married (Ann).

Military Career: Air Force, 1967–69 (Vietnam); Air Natl. Guard, 1969–72.

Professional Career: Ophthalmologist, 1972–96.

DC Office: 317 CHOB 20515, 202-225-8490; Fax: 202-225-5639; Web site: www.house.gov/cooksey.

District Offices: Alexandria, 318-448-1777; Monroe, 318-330-9998.

Committees: *Agriculture* (19th of 27 R): Department Operations, Oversight, Nutrition & Forestry. *International Relations* (25th of 26 R): Asia & the Pacific; International Economic Policy & Trade. *Transportation & Infrastructure* (27th of 41 R): Aviation; Economic Development, Public Buildings, Hazardous Materials & Pipeline Transportation (Vice Chmn.).

Group Ratings

	ADA	ACLU	AFS	LCV	CON	NTU	NFIB	COC	ACU	NTLC	CHC
1998	0	14	17	8	13	48	100	100	96	89	91
1997	10	—	14	—	26	52	—	100	91	—	—

National Journal Ratings

	1997 LIB — 1997 CONS		1998 LIB — 1998 CONS	
Economic	19%	— 76%	0%	— 88%
Social	43%	— 56%	42%	— 58%
Foreign	21%	— 79%	7%	— 83%

Key Votes of the 105th Congress

1. Clinton Budget Deal	Y	5. Puerto Rico Sthood. Ref.	Y	9. Cut $ for B-2 Bombers	N
2. Education IRAs	Y	6. End Highway Set-asides	Y	10. Human Rights in China	N
3. Req. 2/3 to Raise Taxes	Y	7. School Prayer Amend.	Y	11. Withdraw Bosnia Troops	Y
4. Fast-track Trade	Y	8. Ovrd. Part. Birth Veto	Y	12. End Cuban TV-Marti	N

Election Results

1998 primary	John Cooksey (R)	unopposed		($537,985)
1996 general	John Cooksey (R)	135,990	(58%)	($898,479)
	Francis D. Thompson (D)	97,363	(42%)	($511,183)

SIXTH DISTRICT

Baton Rouge is the central node of Louisiana, on the boundary between the French-speaking, Catholic Cajun country and the heavily Baptist Deep South, its skyscraper Capitol and Exxon (formerly Jersey Standard) refinery sitting just beyond the levees that line the Mississippi River. Baton Rouge still bears the impress of the man who dominated Louisiana politics for much of the 20th Century, Huey P. Long. Here Long became governor at 36 in the old (and still-standing) Gothic Capitol, when Baton Rouge had only 30,000 people, and was assassinated in 1935 in the hallway of the 34-story Art Deco Capitol he built. To the south are the buildings of Louisiana State University, much of which he built, in an amazingly short time. Today Baton Rouge is the center of a metro area of half a million, almost all on the east bank of the Mississippi, and reaching far inland to Livingston Parish. Baton Rouge tries to maintain all of Louisiana's traditions; according to Clinton adviser James Carville, who comes from nearby Carville in Iberville Parish, it has "the best restaurants per capita of any city in the United States."

The 6th Congressional District is centered on Baton Rouge, running south to the "petroleum alley" parishes along the Mississippi and east to the Florida parishes—so called because, even after the United States purchased Louisiana, they were part of the West Florida colony retained by Spain until it was annexed in 1810. And it includes plantation parishes north along the Mississippi, with high black populations. Historically, all of this territory was Democratic. Baton Rouge in the 1980s moved toward the Republicans, and the Baton Rouge area has been politically marginal in the middle 1990s; in 1996 it gave a comfortable margin to Bill Clinton and to Republican Senate candidate Woody Jenkins.

The congressman from the 6th District is Richard Baker, a Republican first elected in 1986 who survived, barely, a close race in 1998. Baker has spent most of his adult life in public office; he came to Baton Rouge to attend LSU, then in 1972, at 23, was elected as a Democrat to the Louisiana House from a blue-collar district in Baton Rouge. He became a Republican in 1985, and in 1986, when Baton Rouge Republican Congressman Henson Moore ran for the Senate, Baker ran for the House and beat a Democratic state senator 51%–46%. In 1992 he was redistricted in the same district with Republican Congressman Clyde Holloway and was opposed as well by the Democratic mayor of Alexandria. The new district lines put Baker at a disadvantage, and he trailed 37%–33% in the September primary. But he won the November runoff 51%–49%, with 71% in his home territory of East Baton Rouge and Livingston parishes.

Baker has a conservative voting record and is chairman of the Banking Subcommittee on Capital Markets, Securities and Government Sponsored Enterprises. He favors financial services deregulation, including repeal of the Glass-Steagall Act of 1933, which separates banks and other financial institutions. That reform has been stalled for several years. Baker's 1995 amendment, allowing banks and insurance companies to merge, was withdrawn in October 1995 because of opposition from insurance agents. In March 1996 the Supreme Court ruled that national banks can sell insurance in small towns despite state laws; that gave impetus to deregulation, in 1997 and 1998. But action was blocked in the Senate by Phil Gramm because of his qualms about the Community Reinvestment Act as the 1998 session closed. The 1998 merger of Travelers and Citicorp was based on the assumption that Congress would scrap Glass-Steagall; but in early 1999 it was not clear whether Baker and his allies on House Banking could reach agreement with Gramm, now chairman of the Senate Banking Committee. On other banking issues, Baker favored raising the Federal Housing Administration home mortgage loan limit and opposed the requirement that public housing units be replaced one-for-one. He called for disclosure of exposure to risk by banks investing in hedge funds, but no direct regulation. He favored the bankruptcy reform bill. In 1998 he and Democrat Carolyn Maloney sponsored "Kiddie Mac," a $10 million fund to guarantee loans to child care centers.

Baker has tended to local interests. On Agriculture in 1995 he worked successfully to prevent changes in the cotton, sugar and rice programs—the price Republican leaders had to pay for passage of the Freedom to Farm Act. On Transportation in 1998 he worked for local projects in the giant transportation bill. He has also worked on the Carville Academy (in a former leprosarium) and the Comite River Diversion Canal project.

It seems that every six years Baker has a tough challenge, after redistricting in 1992 and from Democrat Marjorie McKeithen in 1998. She is the granddaughter of former Governor (1964–72) John McKeithen, whom she joined in law practice in 1995, and daughter of Secretary of State Fox McKeithen, whose first campaign she managed at 20 in 1986; he has since switched to become a Republican, but supported her because "blood is thicker than political parties." Strongly opposed to gun control and abortion, McKeithen knocked on 40,000 doors and charmed voters with her north Louisiana accent. She attacked Baker as "the number one voice in Congress for the New York banks" and said he favored special interests over consumers, community banks and credit unions. She criticized him for voting to raise his own pay $30,000 while voting against increases in the minimum wage. "He got his own daughter a free legislative scholarship to Tulane,"—a perk for many Louisiana politicians, "but voted to cut the student loan program for the rest of us." Against this barrage Baker attacked her for being a trial lawyer and for not voting consistently in local elections. He called her a tax-and-spend liberal and attacked her close alliance with former Congressman Cleo Fields, who was working to increase black turnout—an attempt to "play the race card," Fields said. Baker raised $1.4 million, with $702,000 from party committees and PACs, many of them in banking. McKeithen attacked him for that, but she was no slouch in raising money, and ultimately spent more than $664,000.

In the end, Baker squeaked by, winning 50.7%–49.3%. He lost the outlying parishes, with their large black percentages, but carried East Baton Rouge and Livingston parishes with 53% and 57%. McKeithen's percentages parish by parish were almost identical to Clinton's two years earlier—an unusual example of a Democratic challenger putting together a Clinton coalition. Baker proclaimed, "This is a landslide for me," and McKeithen quickly let it be known she would probably run again. Indeed she has no other place to take her obvious political skills: Both Senate seats are held by her fellow Democrats, and neither is up until 2002; the only Republican statewide officials she might have challenged in 1999 are the highly popular Governor Mike Foster and her own father.

Cook's Call. *Highly Competitive.* It is highly likely that this district will see a rematch of the very tight 1998 contest between Democratic nominee Marjorie McKeithen and Baker. To survive, Baker must run a better campaign than he did in 1998. He must also be wary of a possible increase in turn-out among black voters, and a better-funded McKeithen. Look for a tight contest.

The People: Pop. 1990: 602,764; 35.9% rural; 9.7% age 65 + ; 66.9% White, 31.7% Black, 0.9% Asian, 0.2% Amer. Indian, 0.3% Other; 1.3% Hispanic Origin. Households: 54.5% married couple families; 29.8% married couple fams. w. children; 42.3% college educ.; median household income: $26,001; per capita income: $11,790; median house value: $65,000; median gross rent: $274.

1996 Presidential Vote			1992 Presidential Vote		
Clinton (D)	142,156	(50%)	Bush (R)	134,222	(51%)
Dole (R)	121,851	(43%)	Clinton (D)	91,273	(35%)
Perot (I)	19,222	(7%)	Perot (I)	35,325	(14%)

Rep. Richard H. Baker (R)

Elected 1986; b. May 22, 1948, New Orleans; home, Baton Rouge; LA St. U., B.A. 1971; United Methodist; married (Kay).

Elected Office: LA House of Reps., 1972–86.

Professional Career: Real estate developer, 1972–86.

DC Office: 434 CHOB 20515, 202-225-3901; Fax: 202-225-7313; Web site: www.house.gov/baker.

District Office: Baton Rouge, 225-929-7711.

Committees: *Banking & Financial Services* (5th of 32 R): Capital Markets, Securities & Government Sponsored Enterprises (Chmn.); Housing & Community Opportunity. *Transportation & Infrastructure* (20th of 41 R): Ground Transportation; Water Resources & Environment. *Veterans' Affairs* (17th of 17 R).

Group Ratings

	ADA	ACLU	AFS	LCV	CON	NTU	NFIB	COC	ACU	NTLC	CHC
1998	0	6	0	8	21	51	100	100	100	95	100
1997	0	—	14	—	29	47	—	100	92	—	—

National Journal Ratings

	1997 LIB — 1997 CONS		1998 LIB — 1998 CONS	
Economic	24% —	73%	0% —	88%
Social	19% —	80%	21% —	76%
Foreign	0% —	88%	7% —	83%

Key Votes of the 105th Congress

1. Clinton Budget Deal	Y	5. Puerto Rico Sthood. Ref.	N	9. Cut $ for B-2 Bombers	N
2. Education IRAs	Y	6. End Highway Set-asides	Y	10. Human Rights in China	N
3. Req. 2/3 to Raise Taxes	Y	7. School Prayer Amend.	Y	11. Withdraw Bosnia Troops	Y
4. Fast-track Trade	Y	8. Ovrd. Part. Birth Veto	Y	12. End Cuban TV-Marti	N

Election Results

1998 primary	Richard H. Baker (R)	97,044	(51%)	($1,444,171)
	Marjorie McKeithen (D)	94,201	(49%)	($664,611)
1996 primary	Richard H. Baker (R)	117,598	(69%)	($554,968)
	Steve Myers (D)	52,092	(31%)	

SEVENTH DISTRICT

More than 200 years ago, French-speaking settlers were forced to leave their land of Acadie, which the British had taken over and renamed Nova Scotia, and make their way to the wetlands of southern Louisiana. Here, without much notice, they built steep-roofed houses to slough off nonexistent snow and adapted French cuisine to the crawfish and muskrat they found in abundance in the pelican-tended swamps. The heart of the Cajun country is around Lafayette, just west of the Atchafalaya Basin, where Mississippi waters pour through bayous and canals, with only occasional bits of solid land visible on the 30-mile section of Interstate 10 built on elevated stilts. For half a century the Cajun country thrived, thanks to the oil and gas plentiful here and just off shore in the Gulf of Mexico; oil rigs are common, and every once in a while the swampy foliage parts to reveal a giant refinery or petrochemical plant. In the past two decades, Cajun pride has grown: Cajun French is surviving decades of efforts to eliminate it, Cajun music (and its black-influenced variant, zydeco) are popular here and nationally, while spicy Cajun cooking has become a tourist attraction here and, in watered-down form, familiar all over the United States. Both Cajun culture and the oil business are particularly evident in Lafayette, with its Acadian Village and plethora of oil exploration firms.

The oil price crash of the middle 1980s hit the Cajun country hard. Rising expectations, and the giddy sense that the oil industry promised lasting prosperity, suddenly collapsed, leaving borrowers overextended and ordinary homeowners unable to maintain the standard of living they expected. Politically, the Cajun country seemed to move then toward national Democrats, whom it had shunned because their cultural liberalism seemed alien to the Cajun tradition of respecting the authority of Church and state while tolerating a certain amount of *laissez les bons temps rouler* spirit. The Cajun country voted for Bill Clinton in 1992 and 1996, as it had voted for Louisiana's foremost Cajun politician, Edwin Edwards, who was elected governor in 1972, 1975, 1983 and 1991.

The 7th Congressional District covers much of the Cajun country, from Lafayette and the Atchafalaya west along I-10 to Lake Charles and the Texas border. Redistricted three times in the 1990s, its boundaries have now smoothed out. It is the descendant of the district represented from 1965–72 by Edwin Edwards and from 1972–86 by John Breaux, both from the small city of Crowley in Acadia Parish, who became governor and senator respectively.

The congressman from the 7th District now is Chris John, a Democrat elected in 1996. John grew up in Crowley, which may be producing more prominent politicians per capita than any other place in America. After graduating from LSU he went into the family trucking business.

In 1987, at 27, he was elected to the seat in the Louisiana House his father had once held, and served two four-year terms, chairing the Acadiana delegation. In 1996 the 7th District seat came open when Jimmy Hayes, a 10-year incumbent who had switched to the Republican Party in December 1995, ran for the Senate; he ended up finishing a distant fifth in the 1996 primary.

A field of eight candidates ran in the September 21 open primary to replace Hayes. John's chief opponents turned out to be Republican David Thibodaux, an English professor at the University of Southwestern Louisiana who called for abolishing the Internal Revenue Service and the Department of Education, and Democrat Hunter Lundy, a maritime lawyer from Lake Charles and an anti-abortion religious conservative. John campaigned as tough on crime and someone who wanted to prepare children to get jobs in the global economy. On September 21 he led with 26% of the vote, and Thibodaux seemed to come in second, 29 votes ahead of Lundy. But a recount gave second place to Lundy by 8 votes; Thibodaux protested and filed suit, to no avail. This meant that Democrats knew they had picked up one House seat even before the voters went to the polls in November—and in a district that would vote for Republican Woody Jenkins over Democrat Mary Landrieu in the Senate race.

Neither candidate showed much endorsement of national Democratic principles. Lundy attacked John for supporting legislative pensions and his vote on an abortion amendment; John said he would not benefit from the pension and was described as "pro-life, unequivocally." John was endorsed in October by the House Blue Dog Democrats and in the closing days by Congressmen Jimmy Hayes and Billy Tauzin. The result came down to geography. Lundy led 63%–37% in the parishes west of the Mermenteau River, but they cast only 36% of the district's votes, and John led 62%–38% in the parishes to the east, for a 53%–47% win.

John has been a Blue Dog Democrat with a moderate voting record. On the Agriculture Committee he sought to encourage exports and looked after rice farmers (his family owns two rice farms), on Resources he was a member of the Congressional Sportsmen's Caucus, he worked to protect estuaries, fishlands and marshlands. He sponsored Outer Continental Shelf revenue-sharing, soon backed by the entire Louisiana delegation; to get more support it included the Great Lakes. He opposed fast track in November 1997, months after Fruit of the Loom closed some local plants and moved production abroad. Undeclared till late, he opposed impeachment because he believed Clinton "had not breached national security," and added that "the 7th District is a mixed bag of philosophic thought." John sought a seat on the Commerce Committee, and in January 1999 Republicans offered him one if he switched parties, but he declined, saying he "had some nice offers . . . but the fact is philosophically I'm a Democrat and will always be one." As one of only two Democratic congressmen in Louisiana, he has been mentioned as a candidate for governor in 2003 or, if John Breaux retires, for senator in 2004.

Cook's Call. *Safe.* Though certainly not as Democratic as the New Orleans-based 2d, the 7th retains a Democratic edge. John is a good match for the district and will be tough to beat. When the seat opens up, however, it will certainly be heavily contested.

The People: Pop. 1990: 603,078; 38.5% rural; 11.3% age 65 + ; 75.1% White, 23.8% Black, 0.5% Asian, 0.3% Amer. Indian, 0.3% Other; 1.2% Hispanic Origin. Households: 57.3% married couple families; 31.1% married couple fams. w. children; 32.3% college educ.; median household income: $20,595; per capita income: $9,999; median house value: $49,400; median gross rent: $210.

1996 Presidential Vote		
Clinton (D)	106,034	(54%)
Dole (R)	70,149	(36%)
Perot (I)	19,644	(10%)

1992 Presidential Vote		
Clinton (D)	123,336	(47%)
Bush (R)	99,985	(38%)
Perot (I)	38,244	(15%)

Rep. Chris John (D)

Elected 1996; b. Jan. 5, 1960, Crowley; home, Crowley; LA St. U., B.A. 1982; Catholic; married (Payton).

Elected Office: Crowley City Cncl., 1983–87; LA House of Reps., 1987–95.

Professional Career: Co-owner, John N. John Truckline, 1983–96.

DC Office: 1504 LHOB 20515, 202-225-2031; Fax: 202-225-5724; Web site: www.house.gov/john.

District Offices: Lafayette, 318-235-6322; Lake Charles, 318-433-1747.

Committees: *Agriculture* (19th of 24 D): Risk Management, Research & Specialty Crops. *Resources* (16th of 24 D): Energy & Mineral Resources.

Group Ratings

	ADA	ACLU	AFS	LCV	CON	NTU	NFIB	COC	ACU	NTLC	CHC
1998	50	27	67	8	44	24	71	76	45	46	58
1997	40	—	25	—	49	40	—	100	64	—	—

National Journal Ratings

	1997 LIB — 1997 CONS		1998 LIB — 1998 CONS	
Economic	51%	48%	53%	47%
Social	50%	48%	41%	59%
Foreign	51%	46%	64%	31%

Key Votes of the 105th Congress

1. Clinton Budget Deal	Y	5. Puerto Rico Sthood. Ref.	Y	9. Cut $ for B-2 Bombers	N
2. Education IRAs	N	6. End Highway Set-asides	N	10. Human Rights in China	N
3. Req. 2/3 to Raise Taxes	Y	7. School Prayer Amend.	Y	11. Withdraw Bosnia Troops	N
4. Fast-track Trade	N	8. Ovrd. Part. Birth Veto	Y	12. End Cuban TV-Marti	N

Election Results

1998 primary	Chris John (D)	unopposed		($287,732)
1996 general	Chris John (D)	128,449	(53%)	($604,865)
	Hunter Lundy (D)	113,351	(47%)	($513,344)
1996 primary	Chris John (D)	45,398	(26%)	
	Hunter Lundy (D)	38,598	(22%)	
	David Thibodaux (R)	38,590	(22%)	
	Tyron Picard (D)	25,914	(15%)	
	Jim Slatten (R)	12,466	(7%)	
	Charlie Buckels (R)	8,301	(5%)	
	Other	7,792	(4%)	

MAINE

Maine is a state with a distinctive personality—ornery, contrary-minded, almost bullheaded, rough-hewn. It is the state closest geographically to Europe, but it was not heavily settled until the mid-19th Century, and then by people coming from the south and west—the opposite of America's usual pattern. In an urbanizing and rapidly changing country, Maine was famous for its pointed firs and steady habits, with a few dozen small factory and mill towns but nothing like a major metropolis. Maine grew in a rush and then mostly stopped: there were 600,000 people here in 1860 and its population did not top 1 million until the 1970s. Then, the tremors of the New England high-tech booms of the 1980s and 1990s—and the recession of the early 1990s—reverberated up I-95 and shook Maine. The simple, back-to-nature Yankee style came into vogue. The antique dockside buildings on Portland's waterfront were restored and an old-style Public Market was constructed; the Maine Mall expanded and saw office parks spring up nearby, a miniature edge city; real estate prices rose by hundreds of percents, not just in vacation coves, but in Portland and small towns that had never considered themselves picturesque. The L.L. Bean headquarters in Freeport, open 24 hours a day, 365 days a year, symbolized the boom: the two chaste initials and the Anglo-Saxon monosyllable suggesting the dry understatement of Down East Yankees; the 24-hour-a-day schedule recalling the hard work needed to eke out a living from the cold waters of the North Atlantic to the pine-covered north woods; the commercial success of the enterprise a prime example of Maine's unexpected 1980s boom.

But that boom didn't help everyone, and the early 1990s bust hurt many. Now, as the economy has recovered and the boom has begun once again, Maine has emerged with an economy transformed. The manufacturing sector withered and service jobs have increased: shoe factory employment fell from 17,000 to 6,000 from 1983 to 1999, while telephone call center employment rose from zero to 10,000. The Grand Banks and lobster grounds have been overfished, and scratching small Maine boiling potatoes out of the soil of Aroostook County has become harder: the nation's top potato producer 50 years ago, Maine fell to eighth place in the 1990s, even as national consumption rose by 15%. By the late 1990s biotech outproduced lobster fishing and potato harvesting combined. Paper mill towns like Millinocket now stand half empty, while intersections around Portland are jammed with cars waiting for the green arrow so they can turn into the mall. Tourism continues to be the biggest business here, and Bath Iron Works, long the state's largest private employer, has a long-term contract to build 21 *Arleigh Burke* Class Naval destroyers, the work partly of former Senator (and Armed Services Committee member) and now Defense Secretary William Cohen. But it is the new economy that undergirds Maine's flannel-shirt lifestyle and its fierce pride.

Up through 1958, it held state elections in September, a date originally chosen because it followed the state's early harvest; in the days before polls, the results here were taken as a gauge of national partisan movement—hence the saying, "As Maine goes, so goes the nation." However, in September 1936, Maine voted 56% for Republican Governor Lewis Barrows and in November only Maine and Vermont voted for Alf Landon over Franklin Roosevelt, prompting Roosevelt's campaign manager to observe, "As Maine goes, so goes Vermont." Maine's adherence to flinty Yankee Republicanism and Prohibition was echoed almost nowhere else in the nation. Since then, it has voted for the loser in the close presidential elections of 1948, 1960, 1968 and 1976, and nearly again in 1980—a record equalled by no other state. In the recession years, Maine distinguished itself by casting the nation's highest percentage for Ross Perot, 30% in 1992, and in 1994 it elected independent (and former Democrat) Angus King governor. This was not without precedent: Maine elected another independent governor, James Longley, in 1974.

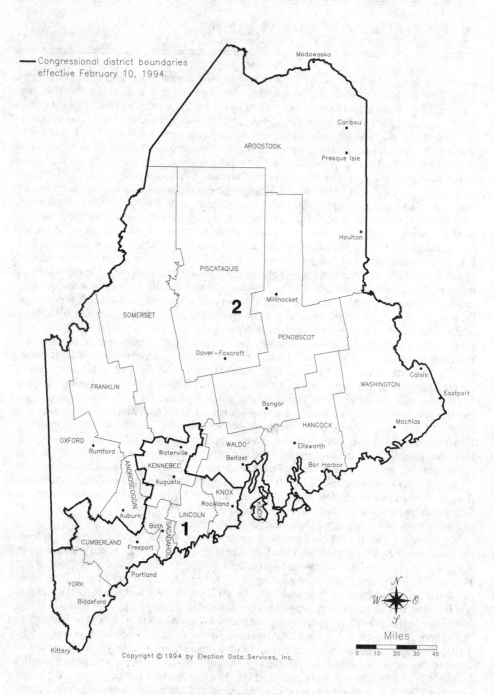

Congressional district boundaries
effective February 10, 1994.

MADAWASKA

AROOSTOOK

Caribou

Presque Isle

Houlton

PISCATAQUIS

SOMERSET

Millinocket

PENOBSCOT

Dover—Foxcroft

FRANKLIN

Bangor

WASHINGTON

Calais

Eastport

2

OXFORD

Rumford

Waterville

KENNEBEC

Augusta

ANDROSCOGGIN

Auburn

WALDO

Belfast

KNOX

Rockland

HANCOCK

Ellsworth

Bar Harbor

Machias

KNOX

LINCOLN

Bath

SAGADAHOC

1

CUMBERLAND

Freeport

Portland

YORK

Biddeford

Kittery

N
W E
S

Miles

0   10   20   30   40

Copyright © 1994 by Election Data Services, Inc.

If Maine's tradition-minded Yankees kept the state Republican long after the nation embraced the New Deal, the sons and daughters of its ethnics—Irish, French Canadian, Greek and Arab immigrants have come to equal the numbers of pure WASPs (though these new Mainers in many ways share traditional Yankee traits and values)—made the Democrats competitive, perhaps even dominant, here in the 1980s as they were losing ground in the rest of the nation. As the economy revived in the middle 1990s, those differences became less important. In 1996, Ross Perot again won his highest percentage here, but it was only 14% this time; what was striking was that all three candidates won percentages within a narrow range in every county: Bill Clinton won between 46% and 54%, Bob Dole between 26% and 37%, Perot between 10% and 19%. These uniform results suggest that ethnic differences and partisan traditions matter less than a Maine consensus, shared by most of those who were raised in Maine or chose to move here. The Maine consensus was even more apparent in 1998, when Angus King was resoundingly re-elected with 59% of the vote; the percentages of the Republican (19%) and Democratic (12%) nominees were closer to those of the Green (7%) and Taxpayers (4%) candidates than to King's. South and west of Augusta, King won between 61% and 65% in each county, north and east between 45% and 54%. Contentment, incidentally, produced not higher but lower turnout, down nearly 20% from 1994 and 1990. So content with King were the voters (his job approval ranged up to 86%) that only 45,000 voted in the Democratic primary and 57,000 in the Republican, compared to 101,000 and 90,000 four years earlier.

This consensus result reflects satisfaction with King's efforts to bolster economic development and with the interested consensus, developed partly by King but also by many others, over how to balance environmental concerns with economic needs. Maine's environment-conscious newcomers have made this a good market for natural toothpaste, organic baby food and canvas bags rather than paper or plastic at the supermarket. It was the first state to ban the juicebox as insufficiently biodegradable; it now recycles liquor bottles; above the Ben and Jerry's in Brunswick is the Buddhist Dharma Study Center. But Maine's old economy depended heavily on polluting paper mills and clearcut logging. The voters are seeking a balance: in 1996 they rejected Proposition 2A, a ban on clearcutting; in 1997 they narrowly rejected an alternative, proposed by the paper industry and supported by King and some environmentalists, to reduce clearcutting zones from 250 to 75 acres and set aside 10,000 acres of public land for conservation. But private interests have moved as the political process stumbled. In December 1998 the Nature Conservancy bought 185,000 acres from International Paper for $35 million, just a week after conservationists purchased 300,000 acres in New Hampshire, Vermont and northern New York: moves to protect the Northern Appalachian Boreal Forest. In March 1999 the Pingree family agreed to sell conservation easements on 755,000 acres (more land than Rhode Island) to the New England Forestry Foundation for $28 million; King proposed a $50 million bond issue to buy land. Many environmentalists, though not Green Party leaders, cheered. Maine had already produced, in December 1997, a salmon conservation plan, put together by state officials, scientists, academics, Indians, anglers, citizens and conservationists, to stock more fish, improve upland habitat and build fish weirs on even rivers; federal agencies agreed to let Maine handle the issue. And in November 1997 the tiny Edwards Dam on the Kennebec River was ordered removed, one of the first decisions to dismantle a hydroelectric dam to protect fish. Local decision-making and private initiative to protect the environment is a Maine tradition: back in the 1920s Governor Percival Baxter bought and donated a giant state park, including the nearly-mile-high Mount Katahdin. The evidence of the 1990s is that Maine is doing a better job of balancing the environment and the economy than the federal government is doing in so many other states: not a bad sort of quirkiness.

Governor. Angus King, elected governor of Maine in 1994 and 1998, grew up in Virginia, moved to Maine after law school to work for Pine Tree Legal Assistance in Skowhegan, then worked for Senator William Hathaway, practiced law, and started his own energy conservation business, which he sold for $20 million in January 1994. For 18 years he hosted Maine Public

Television's "MaineWatch." So he was as well-positioned to run as any independent could be: familiar with issues, capable of heavily self-financing a campaign, experienced at projecting his message over television. For several years Maine politics centered on deadlocks between Republican Governor John McKernan and Democratic legislators, arguing over how to cut spending and whether to raise taxes. King, originally a Democrat, had come to believe that "sometimes the best thing the government can do is get out of the way." He attacked high taxes, clumsy government meddling in business, astonishing inefficiency, and called for specific cuts. He spent $750,000 of his own money and raised about as much from others. He overshadowed Republican nominee (now Senator) Susan Collins, a former aide to then-Senator William Cohen, and he contrasted sharply with the traditionally partisan Democrat, former Governor Joseph Brennan, who won in 1978 and 1982 and lost 47%–44% to McKernan in 1990. King pulled even in the polls and won with 35% to Brennan's 34%, Collins's 23% and 6% for a Green Party candidate. King ran stronger with Republicans than Democrats and did well among Perot voters; he ran his best with high-education and high-income voters.

King is a high-energy, high-tech governor, wearing a beeper and writing a book on his laptop while on the road. He says he spends 50% to 75% of his time on economic development: "That's why I ran. I saw the Maine economy going down the tubes. And I didn't think traditional political solutions were going to fix it." He calls for more infrastructure and lower taxes, better education and no new forms of gambling: "It's a tax on the poor. It sucks money out of the economy." He cut the state budget and work force, reduced the cost of workmen's compensation and reduced environmental permit delays from nine months to 45 days, helping to attract employers like National Semiconductor. He accepted Republicans' future income tax cut in return for a property tax exemption for business machinery and equipment. He vetoed labor-backed bills on workmen's comp and striker replacements. King also vetoed bills to increase the minimum wage and provide health insurance to poor children in 1997, though he supported another version of the latter in 1998. On education, he called for measuring outputs (statewide achievement standards) rather than inputs (spending, teachers' salaries), and got a learning standards bill passed in 1997. He opposed a plan for free tuition for freshmen in state colleges and backed cheaper college loans from the non-profit Maine Education Services.

On the environment, King staked out positions between extremes with varying success. He opposed the ban on clearcutting, but his attempts in 1997 and 1998 to bring experts together on compromise measures were rejected 53%–47%, by a coalition of Greens and property rights advocates. In June 1997 he signed a bill imposing tight controls on paper mills' dioxin discharges into rivers and celebrated by jumping fully clothed into the Kennebec River. He opted out of an EPA plan for reducing vehicle emissions and created his own tougher approach. He backed electric deregulation and was supportive when Florida Power and Light bought all the electric plants of troubled Central Maine Power. He backed a big increase giving Maine the nation's fourth-highest cigarette tax. He signed a bill banning discrimination against gays in May 1997; it was overturned 52%–48% by voters in February 1998.

In 1998 King campaigned for "The Maine Agenda" including a community college system and $25 million a year for research and development; he said one major goal was to reduce the disparity between booming southern Maine and troubled northern Maine, but he opposed the east-west highway from New Brunswick to Quebec backed by other candidates. His victory in November was widely expected. He won among every demographic group, beating former Congressman Jim Longley (son of the late independent governor) among Republicans and attorney Thomas Connolly among Democrats. He ran better among Democrats, contrary to 1994, and better among older than younger voters; he ran similarly among upscale and downscale Mainers. In February 1999 he proposed cutting the sales tax from 5.5% to 5% and proposed a five cent per gallon increase in the gas tax. King has said he will serve no more than two terms and has no interest in other office. It is widely expected that 2d District Congressman John Baldacci, a highly popular Democrat, will run for governor in 2002.

Senior Senator. Maine's senior senator is Olympia Snowe, elected in 1994 to replace then-

Senate Majority Leader George Mitchell. Snowe grew up in Auburn and worked as a legislative staffer after college; in 1973, after her husband, state Representative Peter Snowe, died in an auto accident, she was elected to his seat. In 1978, when then-Congressman William Cohen ran for the Senate, she ran for the House in the northern 2d District, and won handily. She made a moderate record on issues and won by large margins in the 1980s but more narrowly in the 1990s; in 1989 she married Governor John McKernan, her former House colleague. Her voting record has been fairly conservative on economics, rather liberal on cultural issues. A tough partisan on many Republican issues, she is energetic, sometimes even brash, and politically savvy.

Snowe decided instantly to run for the Senate when George Mitchell announced his retirement in March 1994. Immediately she went on the attack against her obvious Democratic opponent, 1st District Congressman Tom Andrews. Two years before, Andrews's margin had been 107,000 votes and hers only 22,000. Snowe attacked him hard for voting for the bill that closed Loring Air Force Base in northern Maine and for opposing the balanced budget amendment. She won 60%–36%, carrying every county, losing only Portland, Lewiston and a few mill towns.

In the Senate she was the least conservative of the 11 freshman Republicans elected in 1994. She has supported Republican positions on most economic issues, calling for a balanced budget, but also has backed abortion rights and family leave. Her record on foreign and defense issues has been solidly conservative. But she was one of the few Republicans to support the Clinton Administration EPA's air-quality standards. She dissented on some other party positions; she was one of eight Republicans to vote for cloture on the Republican filibuster of a campaign finance reform bill in June 1996, and in March 1998 she advanced a proposal to regulate ads that mention a candidate's name 60 days before a general election, but she insisted on the provision, anathema to Democrats, to ban unions from spending their members' dues money on politics without their permission. With five other Republicans, she sponsored in January 1998 a child care tax credit as an alternative to Clinton's. With Harry Reid, in 1998, she supported a bill that would require insurance companies to pay for women's contraceptives.

She has worked on many local issues, establishing a pilot $25 million fishing vessel buyback, passing a "Maine Lights" program to preserve historic Maine lighthouses, working to ban lobster dragging. To the telecommunications bill she and Nebraska's two senators added an amendment for affordable access to telecommunications for rural hospitals and health clinics. She urged extra aid in the transportation bill for short-line railroads and sponsored an amendment to require big airlines at hubs to interconnect with small regional airlines. She opposed the Organization on Economic Development shipyard subsidy termination agreement, concerned about its effect on Bath Iron Works.

Child support enforcement is one of Snowe's major causes, and on the welfare bill she called for retaining some federal role in Medicaid, and helped insert a provision requiring states to spend at least 80% of their old budgets and some $3 billion for child care programs. She called for public Ethics Committee hearings on Bob Packwood in July 1995. At the 1996 Republican National Convention she was one of the most outspoken opponents of the party's anti-abortion plank. On impeachment, she supported Republican positions on most issues, and worked with Democrats to come up with a compromise; she and Susan Collins proposed that the Senate vote first on a "finding of fact" describing Clinton's conduct and then separately on whether he should be removed from office. It was not successful, and Snowe voted against impeachment.

Since 1997 Snowe has served on Armed Services. She took the lead in opposing the recommendation of the commission headed by former Senator Nancy Kassebaum Baker to end gender-integrated basic training. She has been a backer of missile defense and the resolution she introduced with Democrat Mary Landrieu declaring it U.S. policy to deploy a ballistic missile system as soon as "technologically possible" was passed 99–0 in March 1999.

Snowe comes up for re-election in 2000. Her poll numbers have been high and in early

1999 she seemed a strong favorite. But she may have serious opposition, and Maine has not backed a Republican for president since 1988. State Senate President Mark Lawrence will run.

Cook's Call. *Safe.* State term limits have led a number of state legislative leaders to look at challenging Snowe, with Senate President Mark Lawrence announcing his candidacy in May. Most expect that any Senate race by these legislators would simply be to lay the groundwork for a statewide bid in 2002.

Junior Senator. Susan Collins, Maine's junior Republican senator, was elected in 1996, the first time she won elective office. She grew up in Caribou, in potato-growing Aroostook County, about as far northeast as you can get in the United States, closer to the capitals of New Brunswick and Quebec than to the capital of Maine. Her family is in the lumber business, and also in politics: her father was a state senator, her mother a mayor and her uncle a state Supreme Court justice. Right after college, she got a job as an intern with William Cohen, then a congressman on the Judiciary Committee who voted to impeach Richard Nixon. She was a Cohen staffer for 12 years and served as the staff director for the Senate Subcommittee on Oversight of Government Management on Governmental Affairs, which Cohen chaired from 1981–87. After Republicans lost their majority, Collins returned to Maine to work five years for Governor John McKernan as a financial regulation commissioner. In 1992 she was New England administrator of the Small Business Administration, and by 1994 she had announced her candidacy for governor. It was a disastrous campaign: She won the Republican nomination, but was overshadowed by independent Angus King, and ran third, with only 23% of the vote. She then became the executive director of the Husson College Center for Family Business.

Then in January 1996 Cohen surprised almost everybody by announcing he would retire from the Senate—almost as big a surprise as his selection as Defense secretary by Bill Clinton a year later. But there is a precedent in Maine for a third-place gubernatorial finisher to be elected senator: George Mitchell was similarly humiliated in 1974, then, after being appointed senator in 1980, won smashing victories in 1982 and 1988. Collins was running against more familiar faces though. The most visible candidate in the Republican primary was Robert Monks, an entrepreneur and business owner who had run against two senators, Margaret Chase Smith in the 1972 primary and Edmund Muskie in the 1976 general; he lost with 67%–33% and 60%–40% respectively. In 1996 he spent $2.1 million—a huge sum for a Maine primary—but got nowhere. Collins promoted her similarity to Olympia Snowe and Cohen, and called for a balanced budget amendment, line-item veto, term limits (and pledged to serve no more than two terms), welfare run by the states (this was before Clinton signed the 1996 welfare reform). She also supported abortion rights. She won the primary with 56%, carrying at least 50% in every county, to 31% for Hathaway and only 13% for Monks.

The other familiar face belonged to Democrat Joseph Brennan, a product of working class Portland, first elected to the legislature in 1964, elected governor in 1978 and 1982, then to Congress in 1986 and 1988. But he lost races for governor in 1990 and 1994, with 44% and 34% of the vote, and he was called, somewhat unfairly, "an old-time, backroom Democratic politician" by a Democratic activist. He argued that he was a fiscal conservative, backing the balanced budget amendment, the line-item veto and term limits. But he found the going uphill. More votes were cast in the Republican primary than the Democratic for the first time since 1982; Democrats had topped 50% in governor races only once since 1966; Governor Angus King's independent platform in 1994 was much more Republican than Democratic. Brennan attacked Collins for backing only a 50-cent minimum wage increase, wanting to increase estate tax exemptions from $600,000 to $1 million, and for favoring repeal of the assault weapons ban; he charged that Collins was supported by, and her position at Husson College endowed by, a principal in a firm manufacturing assault weapons. Collins responded by reiterating her stands and citing her experience, and added, "The next time you hear Joe speak, just close your eyes and ask yourself what year you're in. It could be 1964, the year he first ran. The world has changed, but Joe Brennan's ideas haven't." Collins raised much more money and won 49%–44%, losing very narrowly the counties around Portland, Lewiston, and Augusta, and carrying everything else. Interestingly, she led among men and he led among women; Brennan ran strongly among the elderly, Collins among college graduates—suggesting that she was more the wave of the future.

Collins has a middle-of-the-Senate voting record; she is quieter, more deliberate than Olympia Snowe, but their records are much the same, and they worked together on many issues, including campaign finance reform, the military pay raise, fisheries, tax cuts (they thought the House's were too much in 1998) and impeachment. Her first great cause in the Senate was campaign finance reform; she was beaten by a millionaire in 1994, faced two of them in the 1996 primary and had only meager finances herself "When I ran for the Senate, I seriously debated whether I could afford to keep my $160-a-month health insurance," she said. "I considered borrowing from my parents, but I was 43 and didn't want to unless I was desperate." She said that limitations on self-financing candidates were a "cornerstone" of any reform for her. These limits weren't included in the bill (they are plainly unconstitutional under *Buckley v. Valeo*), but Russ Feingold persuaded her to sign on to the campaign finance bill he was sponsoring with John McCain, despite heavy pressure from Majority Leader Trent Lott. "I do consider myself to be a good Republican," she said at one point. "I'm just one of those troublesome New England Republicans."

Troublesome to the tobacco industry, at least: in 1997 she and Richard Durbin sponsored an amendment that made settlement costs non-deductible, costing the industry $50 billion. And troublesome to both parties: she insisted that investigations of campaign finances should look at misdeeds of both parties, though there was evidence of far more violations by the Clinton-Gore campaign; at the Fred Thompson hearings on campaign finance, she also probed deftly at some of those, spotlighting the Buddhist temple fundraiser. Right off she became chairwoman of Governmental Affairs' Permanent Subcommittee on Investigations and probed into Medicare fraud, investment scams, unsafe food, Internet ripoffs and fraudulent telephone billing—slamming and cramming.

Collins is one of four Republican senators who voted against the partial-birth abortion ban; she sponsored with Jay Rockefeller a bill for better counseling and communication for patients in advanced stages of disease, endorsed by Rosalynn Carter. Her proposal for deductions for the first $2,700 of interest paid on college loans made it, in modified form, into the 1997 tax cut. In December 1998 she and Republican Thad Cochran moved to investigate sweepstakes. On economic issues, she was not afraid to buck labor unions, still something of a power in Maine; she co-sponsored the Teamwork for Employees and Managers Act and the flextime bill; she backed the Republican version of HMO reform, arguing for leaving "treatment decisions in the hands of doctors, not lawyers."

Collins's approach to impeachment was as earnest as any senator's. She read history and constitutional law, coming up with an obscure article that argued the Senate could vote on findings of fact separately from removal; she and Olympia Snowe pushed a plan to have such separate votes, to no avail. She kept a diary of the trial and voted for Tom Harkin's proposal to make the hearings open to the public. She said that much of the evidence weighed against Clinton, but in the end voted against removal.

Collins has worked on local issues—for limiting giant trawlers from fishing for herring and mackerel, for national weather bouys, for low-income heating assistance, against Canadian potato easements and Chilean salmon trade restrictions. She sought a National Weather Service office for Caribou, pointing out that since it is surrounded by Canada it does not receive weather warnings from adjacent Weather Service offices as most other American communities do. Collins comes up for re-election in 2002.

Presidential politics. Bill Clinton has carried Maine twice, the second time with 52%; it seems that many of the 1980s Republican voters Ross Perot chipped away from George Bush became Clinton Democrats. Or it may be that Maine, like the rest of the Northeast, simply doesn't like the southernness of the post-1994 Republican Party. After all, it inflicted the humiliation on George Bush of having him finish third in 1992 in the state where he has spent every summer of his life. Yet in races for governor and senator Maine is arguably trending Republican. It is obviously risky to predict anything about the state which twice has been Ross Perot's best state in the nation.

Maine held its first-ever presidential primary on March 5, 1996, in an attempt to generate an early contest to which candidates would pay attention. But they didn't much. Clinton had no competition and Bob Dole had clinched the Republican nomination three days earlier in South Carolina; he beat Pat Buchanan here 46%–24%.

Congressional districting. Maine waited until 1994 to redistrict for the 1990s. It hardly mattered: the lines have been almost exactly the same since the state lost its 3d District in the 1960 Census. The Republican legislature then wanted to split areas of Democratic strength; the result is that there is not much partisan difference between the southern 1st District and the northern 2d. Maine is one of two states (Nebraska is the other) where the electoral vote can be divided if one congressional district votes for a candidate who loses statewide; it hasn't happened lately.

The People: Est. Pop. 1998: 1,244,250; Pop. 1990: 1,227,928, up 1.3% 1990–1998. 0.5% of U.S. total, 39th largest; 55.4% rural. Median age: 36.6 years. 13.8% 65 years and over. 98.4% White, 0.4% Black, 0.6% Asian, 0.5% Amer. Indian, 0.1% Other; 0.6% Hispanic Origin. Households: 58.1% married couple families; 27.9% married couple fams. w. children; 41.7% college educ.; median household income: $27,854; per capita income: $12,957; 70.5% owner occupied housing; median house value: $87,400; median monthly rent: $358. 4.4% Unemployment. 1998 Voting age pop.: 957,000. 1998 Turnout: 421,009; 44% of VAP. Registered voters (1998): 933,753; 296,970 D (32%), 268,276 R (29%), 368,507 unaffiliated and minor parties (39%).

Political Lineup: Governor, Angus S. King Jr. (I); Secy. of State, Dan A. Gwadosky (D); Atty. Gen., Andrew Ketterer (D); Treasurer, Dale McCormick (D); State Senate, 35 (20 D, 14 R, 1 I); Majority Leader, Chellie Pingree (D); State House, 151 (79 D, 71 R, 1 I); House Speaker, G. Steven Rowe (D). Senators, Olympia Snowe (R) and Susan Collins (R). Representatives, 2 (2 D).

Elections Division: 207-287-4189; **Filing Deadline for U.S. Congress:** March 15, 2000.

1996 Presidential Vote

Clinton (D)	312,788	(53%)
Dole (R)	186,378	(32%)
Perot (I)	85,970	(15%)

1996 Republican Presidential Primary

Dole (R)	31,147	(46%)
Buchanan (R)	16,478	(24%)
Forbes (R)	9,991	(15%)
Alexander (R)	4,450	(7%)
Others	5,214	(8%)

1992 Presidential Vote

Clinton (D)	263,420	(39%)
Perot (I)	206,820	(31%)
Bush (R)	206,504	(31%)

GOVERNOR

Gov. Angus S. King, Jr. (I)

Elected 1994, term expires Jan. 2003; b. Mar. 31, 1944, Alexandria, VA; home, Brunswick; Dartmouth Col., A.B. 1966, U. of VA Law Schl., J.D. 1969; Episcopalian; married (Mary).

Professional Career: Staff Atty., Pine Tree Legal Assistance, 1969–72; Chief Cnsl., U.S. Sen. William Hathaway, 1972–75; Practicing atty., 1975–83; TV talk show host, 1975–93; Vice Pres. & Gen. Cnsl., Swift River/Hafslund Co., 1983–89; Founder & Pres., Northeast Energy Management Inc., 1989–94.

Office: State House, Sta. 1, Augusta, 04333, 207-287-3531; Fax: 207-287-1034; Web site: www.state.me.us.

Election Results

1998 gen.	Angus S. King Jr. (I)	246,772	(59%)
	James B. Longley Jr. (R)	79,716	(19%)
	Thomas J. Connolly (D)	50,506	(12%)
	Patricia H. Lamarche (I)	28,722	(7%)
	Others	15,293	(4%)
1998 prim.	Angus S. King Jr. (I)	unopposed	
1994 gen.	Angus S. King Jr. (I)	180,829	(35%)
	Joseph E. Brennan (D)	172,951	(34%)
	Susan M. Collins (R)	117,990	(23%)
	Jonathan K. Carter (Green)	32,695	(6%)

SENATORS

Sen. Olympia Snowe (R)

Elected 1994, seat up 2000; b. Feb. 21, 1947, Augusta; home, Auburn; U. of ME, B.A. 1969; Greek Orthodox; married (John McKernan).

Elected Office: ME House of Reps., 1973–76; ME Senate, 1976–78; U.S. House of Reps., 1978–94.

Professional Career: Dir., Superior Concrete Co., 1969–78; Auburn Bd. of Voter Registration, 1971–73.

DC Office: 250 RSOB, 20510, 202-224-5344; Fax: 202-224-1946; Web site: www.senate.gov/~snowe.

State Offices: Auburn, 207-786-2451; Augusta, 207-622-8292; Bangor, 207-945-0432; Biddeford, 207-282-4144; Portland, 207-874-0833; Presque Isle, 207-764-5124.

Committees: *Armed Services* (7th of 11 R): Emerging Threats & Capabilities; Personnel; Seapower (Chmn.). *Budget* (8th of 12 R). *Commerce, Science & Transportation* (7th of 11 R): Aviation; Manufacturing & Competitiveness; Oceans & Fisheries (Chmn.); Surface Transportation & Merchant Marine. *Small Business* (5th of 10 R).

Group Ratings

	ADA	ACLU	AFS	LCV	CON	NTU	NFIB	COC	ACU	NTLC	CHC
1998	35	57	56	50	59	49	89	78	40	36	36
1997	55	—	33	—	45	61	—	70	44	—	—

National Journal Ratings

	1997 LIB — 1997 CONS		1998 LIB — 1998 CONS	
Economic	52% —	46%	50% —	49%
Social	55% —	37%	50% —	48%
Foreign	43% —	50%	12% —	75%

Key Votes of the 105th Congress

1. Bal. Budget Amend.	Y	5. Satcher for Surgeon Gen.	Y	9. Chem. Weapons Treaty	Y
2. Clinton Budget Deal	Y	6. Highway Set-asides	Y	10. Cuban Humanitarian Aid	N
3. Cloture on Tobacco	Y	7. Table Child Gun locks	Y	11. Table Bosnia Troops	N
4. Education IRAs	Y	8. Ovrd. Part. Birth Veto	N	12. $ for Test-ban Treaty	N

Election Results

1994 general	Olympia Snowe (R) 308,244	(60%)	($2,041,834)
	Thomas H. Andrews (D) 186,042	(36%)	($1,482,060)
	Others 17,447	(3%)	
1994 primary	Olympia Snowe (R) .... unopposed		
1988 general	George J. Mitchell (D) 452,590	(81%)	($1,471,426)
	Jasper S. Wyman (R) 104,758	(19%)	($147,760)

Sen. Susan Collins (R)

Elected 1996, seat up 2002; b. Dec. 7, 1952, Caribou; home, Bangor; St. Lawrence U., B.A. 1975; Catholic; single.

Professional Career: Legis. Aide, U.S. Sen. Bill Cohen, 1975–87; Staff Dir., Oversight of Gov. Mgmt. Subcmte., 1981–87; Professional & Financial Regulation Comm., 1987–92; New England Regional Dir., U.S. Small Business Admin., 1992; ME Dpty. Treas., 1993; Exec. Dir., Ctr. for Family Business, Husson Col., 1994–96.

DC Office: 172 RSOB, 20510, 202-224-2523; Fax: 202-224-2693; Web site: www.senate.gov/~collins.

State Offices: Augusta, 207-622-8414; Bangor, 207-945-0417; Biddeford, 207-283-1101; Caribou, 207-493-7873; Lewiston, 207-784-6969; Portland, 207-780-3575.

Committees: *Aging (Special)* (8th of 11 R). *Governmental Affairs* (4th of 9 R): International Security, Proliferation & Federal Services; Investigations (Permanent) (Chmn.). *Health, Education, Labor & Pensions* (7th of 10 R): Children & Families; Public Health.

Group Ratings

	ADA	ACLU	AFS	LCV	CON	NTU	NFIB	COC	ACU	NTLC	CHC
1998	35	57	44	50	59	53	100	78	36	50	36
1997	50	—	11	—	45	62	—	80	48	—	—

National Journal Ratings

	1997 LIB — 1997 CONS		1998 LIB — 1998 CONS	
Economic	51% —	48%	49% —	50%
Social	55% —	37%	57% —	41%
Foreign	43% —	50%	29% —	58%

Key Votes of the 105th Congress

1. Bal. Budget Amend.	Y	5. Satcher for Surgeon Gen.	Y	9. Chem. Weapons Treaty	Y
2. Clinton Budget Deal	Y	6. Highway Set-asides	Y	10. Cuban Humanitarian Aid	N
3. Cloture on Tobacco	Y	7. Table Child Gun locks	Y	11. Table Bosnia Troops	Y
4. Education IRAs	Y	8. Ovrd. Part. Birth Veto	N	12. $ for Test-ban Treaty	N

Election Results

1996 general	Susan Collins (R)	298,422	(49%)	($1,621,475)
	Joseph E. Brennan (D)	266,226	(44%)	($976,805)
	Others	42,129	(7%)	
1996 primary	Susan Collins (R)	53,339	(56%)	
	W. John Hathaway (R)	29,792	(31%)	
	Robert A.G. Monks (R)	12,943	(13%)	
1990 general	William S. Cohen (R)	319,167	(61%)	($1,628,292)
	Neil Rolde (D)	201,053	(39%)	($1,630,894)

FIRST DISTRICT

The 1st District stretches from southernmost Kittery and nearby Kennebunkport to the craggy-shored ancestrally Republican counties to the east. The historic center is Portland, Maine's largest city, home to the yuppies and lawyers that have revived and renovated its downtown landmarks. Most voters in the 1st District, except those far Down East, live within a couple hours drive of the Maine Mall—just off the Maine Turnpike and I-295 and near the airport—the state's heaviest concentration of retail and office space. Politically, the 1st votes very much like the state as a whole, quirkily, often for independents, splitting tickets with abandon. From 1968–94 it elected three Democrats and three Republicans, with each side serving 14 years.

The congressman from the 1st District now is Tom Allen, a Democrat, first elected in 1996. Allen is a native of Portland, where his grandfather and father served on the city council. He was class president in high school and college, and at Bowdoin was captain of the football team and challenged fraternities because they wouldn't admit blacks. He was a Rhodes Scholar in Oxford the same years as Bill Clinton (who struck him as "one of the nicest, warmest people I ever knew"), Robert Reich and Strobe Talbott, and when he returned he got a job on the staff of Edmund Muskie. But he dropped out of politics, went to law school, practiced in Portland, and worked on charities and community service. In 1989 he was elected to the Portland City Council, and in 1991 rotated into the position of mayor; he started a program of low-interest loans to businesses locating downtown. In 1994 he ran for governor, and ran a distant second to Joseph Brennan in the Democratic primary, with 24%.

The 1st District race was an obvious next step, and an attractive opportunity. Freshman Republican James Longley had a well-known name as son of the independent elected governor in 1974, and he had won the 1994 race 52%–48%, though heavily outspent. But Longley's moderate record was overshadowed by his support for the Contract with America and more than $1 million in ads run by the AFL-CIO. The League of Conservation Voters, which gave him a 31% rating, named him as one of their "Dirty Dozen." Allen, with heavy support from Portland, won a 52%–48% primary victory over state Senator Dale McCormick, who is openly lesbian and brought her partner and their daughter to the podium at the state Democratic convention. Allen called for "incremental steps" toward a single-payer health care finance system. He charged that the Republican followed Newt Gingrich rather than people in Maine, that Longley would cut college loans and education funding. The candidates disagreed on capital punishment, partial-birth abortions, term limits and the balanced budget amendment. Allen called for scaling back a Republican $10 billion increase in defense spending; Longley pointed out it included a Navy destroyer to be built at the Bath Iron Works, and Allen back-tracked and said he would of course support Maine defense contracts. In November Allen won 55%–45%.

Allen has a very liberal voting record, with some exceptions on economic issues. His major initiative in his first year was the freshman campaign finance bill, co-sponsored by Republican Asa Hutchinson. A group of a dozen freshmen agreed on a pared-down approach, to minimize partisan objections. Their bill, introduced in July 1997, would ban soft money contributions by unions and corporations, index contribution limits (the $1,000 limit was enacted in 1974) and require disclosure by groups spending more than $25,000. In April 1998, after Allen launched a discharge petition, Speaker Newt Gingrich switched and allowed the freshman bill to come to the floor as the vehicle for campaign finance bills; Allen was pleased when the more stringent Shays-Meehan bill passed the House in August 1998, though the Senate never acted on it.

Other Allen proposals included a bill, co-sponsored by Henry Waxman, that would make prescription drugs available to seniors at the lowest price paid by federal government (the government would end up controlling the price of 40% of the prescription drug market) and a bill, co-sponsored by Olympia Snowe, that would expand tax credits for people taking care of family members. He sought to grant states money for day care centers if they agree to certain inspections, staff ratios and training requirements. He pushed to require power plants and trash incinerators to cut mercury emissions 95% and sponsored the compact to allow Maine and Vermont to dump nuclear waste in Sierra Blanca, Texas, near the Mexico border, a measure Paul Wellstone called "environmental racism." Allen's priorities have on occasion caused scheduling problems. He angered some state Democrats when he insisted on keeping a commitment to visit Maine defense facilities with Ike Skelton, ranking Democrat on Armed Services, instead of joining Al Gore on a campaign trip to the state; Gore cancelled the visit. And Allen said he might have to skip the vote on impeachment on December 19, 1998 in order to attend his daughter's wedding, but ended up chartering a plane to meet both obligations.

Bowdoin political scientist Chris Potholm describes the swing voters in this district as "cruel yuppies," attracted to candidates who reflect their trendy values and negativity toward taxes. Allen seems to have won their allegiance. In 1998 he was opposed by Ross Connelly, a former Bechtel executive who moved to Maine, where his family had roots, in 1996; he spent $120,000 of his own money and came close to matching Allen's spending. But his strong views on abortion and his demand that Bill Clinton resign evidently didn't sell well. Allen won 60%–36%, winning more than 50% in each county; he carried Portland 75%–23% and the "cruel yuppie" suburbs 63%–35%.

Cook's Call. *Probably Safe.* While this Portland- and Augusta-based district has deep blue-collar (read: Democratic) roots, it also has a serious independent streak which makes it competitive. But this district likes its incumbents, and Tom Allen has avoided high-profile controversy that might put him in political danger. A strong candidate could give Allen a run for his money.

The People: Pop. 1990: 613,960; 49.3% rural; 13.9% age 65 + ; 98.4% White, 0.5% Black, 0.7% Asian, 0.3% Amer. Indian, 0.1% Other; 0.6% Hispanic Origin. Households: 57.2% married couple families; 27.5% married couple fams. w. children; 47.2% college educ.; median household income: $31,124; per capita income: $14,453; median house value: $107,700; median gross rent: $413.

1996 Presidential Vote			1992 Presidential Vote		
Clinton (D)	165,053	(54%)	Clinton (D)	145,191	(40%)
Dole (R)	100,851	(33%)	Bush (R)	115,697	(32%)
Perot (I)	39,845	(13%)	Perot (I)	102,828	(28%)

Rep. Tom Allen (D)

Elected 1996; b. Apr. 16, 1945, Portland; home, Portland; Bowdoin Col., B.A. 1967, Rhodes Scholar, Oxford U., B. Phil. 1970; Harvard J.D. 1974; Protestant; married (Diana).

Elected Office: Portland City Cncl., 1989–95; Portland Mayor, 1991.

Professional Career: Staff, U.S. Sen. Edmund Muskie, 1970–71; Practicing atty., 1974–94; Chmn., ME Clinton-Gore Campaign, 1992; Public Policy Consultant, 1995.

DC Office: 1717 LHOB 20515, 202-225-6116; Fax: 202-225-5590; Web site: www.house.gov/allen.

District Office: Portland, 207-774-5019.

Committees: *Armed Services* (14th of 28 D): Military Procurement; Military Research & Development; Special Oversight Panel on the Merchant Marine. *Government Reform* (17th of 19 D): Civil Service; National Security, Veterans' Affairs & Intl. Relations.

Group Ratings

	ADA	ACLU	AFS	LCV	CON	NTU	NFIB	COC	ACU	NTLC	CHC
1998	100	81	100	100	55	12	14	39	0	13	0
1997	95	—	88	—	70	28	—	50	8	—	—

National Journal Ratings

	1997 LIB — 1997 CONS		1998 LIB — 1998 CONS	
Economic	79%	— 18%	72%	— 23%
Social	79%	— 21%	90%	— 7%
Foreign	85%	— 13%	96%	— 2%

Key Votes of the 105th Congress

1. Clinton Budget Deal	N	5. Puerto Rico Sthood. Ref.	Y	9. Cut $ for B-2 Bombers	Y
2. Education IRAs	N	6. End Highway Set-asides	N	10. Human Rights in China	Y
3. Req. 2/3 to Raise Taxes	N	7. School Prayer Amend.	N	11. Withdraw Bosnia Troops	N
4. Fast-track Trade	N	8. Ovrd. Part. Birth Veto	N	12. End Cuban TV-Marti	Y

Election Results

1998 general	Tom Allen (D)	134,335	(60%)	($689,694)
	Ross J. Connelly (R)	79,160	(36%)	($527,330)
	Eric R. Greiner (I)	9,182	(4%)	
1998 primary	Tom Allen (D)	unopposed		
1996 general	Tom Allen (D)	173,745	(55%)	($933,425)
	James B. Longley Jr. (R)	140,354	(45%)	($906,432)

SECOND DISTRICT

The 2d District covers the northern three-quarters of the acreage of Maine. The population is not evenly distributed, however: the district dips south to include the heavily Democratic mill town of Lewiston and reaches to Belfast on Penobscot Bay. There are several different Maines here: the bays of coastal Maine, with their small fishing towns; the potato fields of far northern Aroostook County; the mill towns on the fast-running streams of western Maine, penned in between mountains. This was one of America's frontiers in the 1850s, when Bangor on the Penobscot River was the lumber capital of the world; today it is the largest city in the district. This part of Maine has had its economic troubles: potato production is only half what it was in 1980; Loring Air Force Base was closed in 1994, though new businesses have sprouted to replace its civilian jobs. Politically this is protest country. This was Ross Perot's strongest district in the United States in 1992 and 1996: he finished a solid second here in 1992, with 33%, and got 16% in 1996.

The congressman from the 2d District is John Baldacci, a Democrat elected in 1994, indeed one of only four Democrats elected to replace a Republican that year (in his case, Olympia Snowe, who was elected to the Senate). Baldacci has deep local roots. He grew up in Bangor, where his family ran Momma Baldacci's, a restaurant started by his grandparents in 1933; he is of Italian and Lebanese descent, distantly related to former Senator George Mitchell, and the family restaurant used to get a daily delivery of rolls from former Senator William Cohen's father's bakery. Baldacci followed his father on the Bangor City Council in 1978, at 23; in 1982, he was elected to the state Senate, where he often dissented from Democrats, chairing the tax committee. He is unassuming, unbombastic, earnest; he campaigned for the House seat in 1994 by holding spaghetti dinners at $2 a head (children under 12 free) around the district. In a seven-candidate primary, with lots of support around Bangor, Baldacci won with 27% to 23% for former Democratic state chairman James Mitchell, George Mitchell's nephew. The Republican nominee was Richard Bennett, who won 30% in a four-way primary with a base in western Maine. Baldacci opposed the Clinton health care plan; Bennett was iffy about the Contract With America's defense spending increase; both were pressed by Green Party and independent candidates, who ended up winning 5% and 9% respectively. Baldacci ran ads showing himself as manager of the restaurant and calling for more jobs ("I'm not going to skimp on the sauce or jobs for Maine."); he pledged to oppose any new taxes and was proud of running no negative ads. Baldacci won with 46% to Bennett's 41%. Bennett carried the western area and much of the coast, but Baldacci won solidly in Aroostook and carried the Bangor area as well.

In the House, Baldacci has compiled a mostly but not entirely, liberal record, though he voted for versions of the balanced budget amendment, line-item veto and term limits. He helped lead the effort to retain the "e-rate," the FCC-ordered tax on telephone calls to finance the wiring of schools and libraries for the Internet. He sponsored bills for Rural Enterprise Communities and improved rural health care. He has a bill that would require insurance companies to make co-payments and length of hospital stays the same for mental health as for other conditions. With Olympia Snowe, he pushed to get Canadian drilled lumber reclassified under the U.S.-Canadian Softwood Lumber Agreement; previously, even a tiny drilled hole removed the lumber from the agreement's quota. He worked on local projects: a second pier for Eastport, the Bates Complex in Lewiston, a magnet school at Loring. He brought the Agriculture Committee to Aroostook County for a hearing after Maine farmers were blocking the border to protest subsidized Canadian potato exports.

Baldacci has been re-elected twice by very large margins. In 1998 he won overall by 76%–24%, and carried all but five of the district's 402 cities, towns, plantations and gores. In 1994 Baldacci promised to serve only four terms. He is expected to run for governor in 2002, and his large majorities suggest he would be a very strong candidate.

Cook's Call. *Safe.* Baldacci has had little to worry about in his two re-election contests and should have little to fear in 2000. Come 2002, however, when Baldacci is expected to run for governor, this district should produce a very competitive race.

The People: Pop. 1990: 613,968; 61.5% rural; 13.8% age 65 + ; 98.3% White, 0.4% Black, 0.4% Asian, 0.7% Amer. Indian, 0.1% Other; 0.5% Hispanic Origin. Households: 59.1% married couple families; 28.4% married couple fams. w. children; 36.2% college educ.; median household income: $24,718; per capita income: $11,462; median house value: $66,700; median gross rent: $308.

1996 Presidential Vote

Clinton (D) 147,735 (53%)
Dole (R) 85,527 (31%)
Perot (I) 46,125 (17%)

1992 Presidential Vote

Clinton (D) 118,229 (38%)
Perot (I) 103,992 (33%)
Bush (R) 90,807 (29%)

Rep. John Baldacci (D)

Elected 1994; b. Jan. 30, 1955, Bangor; home, Bangor; U. of ME, B.A. 1986; Catholic; married (Karen).

Elected Office: Bangor City Cncl., 1978–81; ME Senate, 1982–94.

Professional Career: Restaurateur.

DC Office: 1740 LHOB 20515, 202-225-6306; Fax: 202-225-2943; Web site: www.house.gov/baldacci.

District Offices: Bangor, 207-942-6935; Lewiston, 207-782-3704; Madawaska, 207-728-6160; Presque Isle, 207-764-1036.

Committees: *Agriculture* (13th of 24 D): General Farm Commodities, Resource Conservation & Credit; Risk Management, Research & Specialty Crops. *Transportation & Infrastructure* (30th of 34 D): Aviation; Water Resources & Environment.

Group Ratings

	ADA	ACLU	AFS	LCV	CON	NTU	NFIB	COC	ACU	NTLC	CHC
1998	95	81	100	100	55	13	21	39	4	16	0
1997	95	—	88	—	84	33	—	60	8	—	—

National Journal Ratings

	1997 LIB — 1997 CONS		1998 LIB — 1998 CONS	
Economic	71%	— 28%	71%	— 28%
Social	80%	— 19%	73%	— 25%
Foreign	94%	— 3%	78%	— 19%

Key Votes of the 105th Congress

1. Clinton Budget Deal	N	5. Puerto Rico Sthood. Ref.	Y	9. Cut $ for B-2 Bombers	Y
2. Education IRAs	N	6. End Highway Set-asides	N	10. Human Rights in China	Y
3. Req. 2/3 to Raise Taxes	N	7. School Prayer Amend.	N	11. Withdraw Bosnia Troops	N
4. Fast-track Trade	N	8. Ovrd. Part. Birth Veto	N	12. End Cuban TV-Marti	N

Election Results

1998 general	John Baldacci (D) 146,202	(76%)	($437,247)
	Jonathan Reisman (R) 45,674	(24%)	($14,455)
1998 primary	John Baldacci (D) .... unopposed		
1996 general	John Baldacci (D) 205,439	(72%)	($581,219)
	Paul R. Young (R) 70,856	(25%)	($154,653)
	Others 9,341	(3%)	

MARYLAND

Maryland has always been betwixt and between, the midpoint of the 13 Colonies, just south of the Mason-Dixon Line and just north of the line between Union and Confederacy. It has a claim to be the typical American state, yet stands out for its particularities. This was the only one of the 13 colonies founded by Roman Catholics—the Calvert family—and its embrace of religious tolerance came less from abstract principle than from the Calverts' desire to protect their property from Protestant monarchs: a harbinger of Maryland's practical-mindedness. Similarly, although hot-blooded Baltimoreans wanted to secede in 1861 ("Maryland, My Maryland" condemns Abraham Lincoln's suppression of pro-Confederate rioters), practical heads prevailed.

The puritan impulse was never lively here: Prohibition was enforced only laxly in Baltimore, to the delight of its great journalist-cum-lexicographer H.L. Mencken; slot machines were legal in the rural counties of the Western Shore; horse-racing has long thrived here. The state's law guaranteeing blacks equal access to public accommodations specifically excluded the Eastern Shore. By not pursuing any one course rigorously, Maryland could be many things at once: Northern as well as Southern, moralistic as well as libertine, industrial as well as rural, leaving people to their own devices yet with a heavy government presence. Perhaps as a result, much of Maryland's political history reads like a chronicle of rogues, from Luther Martin, the drunken haranguer at the Constitutional Convention, to Spiro Agnew, who took cash bribes as governor and vice president and resigned in 1973.

Maryland's genial tolerance may have given it a little too savory a history, but this state cherishes its sense of uniqueness. The Chesapeake Bay, for example, is the nation's largest estuary, with water saltier than a river but fresher than the ocean and with unique watermen and shellfish. The terrapin and Chesapeake oyster are rare today, but Maryland blue crabs and rockfish are plentiful, though always threatened; it was big news in September 1997 when the Pocomoke River was infested with the toxic microbe Pfiesteria piscicida, which was responsible for fish kills. Maryland delights in its state bird (the Baltimore oriole), state flower (the black-eyed Susan), state dog (the Chesapeake Bay retriever), even if today's political correctness has made it convenient to forget the words to "Maryland, My Maryland."

Maryland also has some reason to be proud of the economy, or economies, it has built over the years. Half a century ago, half the state's population lived in the city of Baltimore and only one-fifth in the suburbs. Now the proportions are the other way around, and then some: 15% Baltimore, 65% suburbs. The Washington-Baltimore area as defined by the Census Bureau is the fourth largest consolidated metropolitan area in the country, with more than 6 million people. But statistical definition is at odds with practical reality: Baltimore and Washington are not fraternal twins like Dallas and Fort Worth or Minneapolis and St. Paul; they are two quite separate cities, with different economic bases and different attitudes toward public life. Baltimore started off as a port and an industrial city, and has managed to stay diversified and successful as it spread out into the countryside from its new central core at the Inner Harbor and the solidly built edifices of its downtown grid streets. Baltimore has raised private money to rebuild the 146-year-old *U.S.S. Constellation*; it makes spices and writes insurance; it is home to the power-tool maker Black & Decker and the investment bank Alex. Brown & Sons. It has big government offices, the headquarters of the Social Security Administration and, quietly down the road, the National Security Agency. It is home to the Orioles in their popular Oriole Park at Camden Yards, the first of the new-old ballparks of the 1990s, and to Johns Hopkins University, with its Georgian buildings along the affluent corridor that runs directly north from downtown all the way to the developing edge city of Hunt Valley. "Bawlmer"

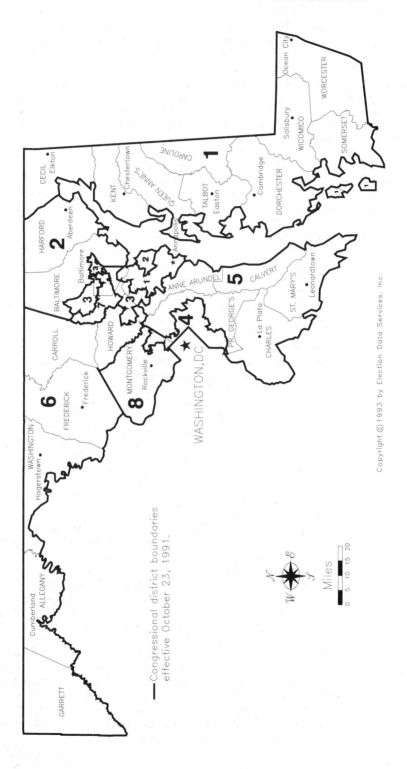

Congressional district boundaries
effective October 23, 1991.

Copyright © 1993 by Election Data Services, Inc.

retains its local accent and a fierce local pride, and is celebrated by artists as vivid in their own ways as Mencken was in his: The novelist Anne Tyler and moviemaker Barry Levinson, who brings to life a Baltimore of the 1950s and 1960s that is at once both unique and universal—the Calverts' achievement all over again.

Baltimore remains the focus of Maryland's public life, for 49% of Marylanders still live in its metropolitan area, and its influence is far greater than Washington's on the Eastern Shore or on the western counties. For years most of Maryland's successful statewide politicians came from Baltimore; today both senators live in Baltimore City and commute to Washington. But Governor Parris Glendening is a notable exception, something of a distrusted stranger in Baltimore; he grew up in Florida, and, in a political culture that loves gambling, he loathes it. But he is from the Washington suburbs, without whose votes he would not have been elected in 1994 nor re-elected in 1998, and many residents there have their focus elsewhere. Montgomery County has a very large percentage of people from all over the nation, who moved there to be near the nation's capital and for whom residence in Maryland is a convenience, not a commitment; Prince George's County has more black high-income residents than any other county in America, most with roots in Washington. The Eastern Shore and the counties south of Annapolis, in contrast, remain as fixated on things Maryland-ish as they are addicted to steamed crabs with characteristic Chesapeake spices: The Chesapeake origins of Maryland are never very far away. The uplands of the western counties, in contrast, are becoming difficult to distinguish from adjacent parts of Pennsylvania, Virginia and West Virginia.

Maryland is by most measures one of the nation's most Democratic states. It was one of Bill Clinton's very best states, as he beat George Bush 50%–36% and Bob Dole 54%–38%, and Maryland came close to going Democratic in the three presidential elections of the 1980s. In statewide elections, Democrats have not lost a contest for senator or governor since liberal Republican Senator Charles Mathias won his last race in 1980. One reason for this is that some 25% of Marylanders are black, the highest percentage in any state outside the Deep South; even the prosperous blacks of Prince George's County still vote overwhelmingly Democratic. Another, overlapping reason is that this state and neighboring Virginia have by far the two highest percentages of federal and public employees, natural backers of the party of government. They help to keep the Washington suburbs solidly Democratic. The Eastern Shore and the western counties may go Republican, whites in the Baltimore metropolitan area may often favor Republicans, but the Democratic margins among blacks and in the Washington suburbs have been big enough to put Maryland in the Democratic column. Inklings of a Republican revival, apparent in Ellen Sauerbrey's near-win for governor in 1994 and Republican gains in upper Montgomery County and other fast-growing suburban areas in 1994 and 1996, were dimmed by the sweeping Democratic victory of 1998. Glendening raised his victory margin from 50.2%–49.8% in 1994 to 55%–45% in 1998, with turnout up 9%, and Republicans, already heavily outnumbered, lost seats in the state House. In no other state but Hawaii are Democrats as surely, if not serenely, in control.

Governor. Parris Glendening grew up in Florida in an impoverished, dysfunctional household—his mother sometimes using food money to play bingo. He worked his way up by studying hard, got a Ph.D. in political science in 1967 at Florida State University, and began teaching at the University of Maryland in College Park. He married a former graduate student whose father was a state senator (after an earlier marriage that he concealed for many years). In 1974 he was elected to the Prince George's Council; in 1982 he was elected Prince George's County executive. Prince George's grew during these years, developed a strong economy, and dealt with school busing by developing an innovative magnet school plan.

Glendening ran for governor in 1994 in a crowded field. Governor William Donald Schaefer had been a dominant figure in Maryland politics, starting as mayor of Baltimore in 1971; his work upgrading city services and building the Inner Harbor earned him great popularity, though that was dimmed by a tax increase in his second term. Glendening won the ordinarily dispositive Democratic primary with 54% of the vote to 18% for his closest rival; he won 75% of the vote in the Washington suburbs and 44% elsewhere. His opponent was a surprise. Schaefer's favorite was probably Congresswoman Helen Delich Bentley, a longtime reporter who covered the Baltimore docks, tough as nails and something of a liberal on economic issues. But Bentley lost the Republican primary 52%–38% to Ellen Sauerbrey, House of Delegates minority leader for eight years.

Sauerbrey had a Newt Gingrich-like program: a 24% income tax cut, limiting state spending growth to the growth rate of the state's economy, and requiring a two-thirds vote to approve a sales or income tax increase. For four years she had built support around the state; in October she and Republican legislative candidates endorsed a Contract With Maryland. Sauerbrey surged in October, and was beaten only after some extraordinary—some say illegal—acts by Democrats: a purging of affluent white voters from the rolls in Baltimore City and a suspiciously timed reporting of 9,000 votes in Baltimore on election night. Sauerbrey cried foul, but state and federal investigations found no evidence of orchestrated wrongdoing, and her criticism of the probes may have harmed her image. Glendening won with 50.2% of the vote, winning 63% in the Washington suburbs while losing metro Baltimore and the rest of the state.

In office Glendening has puzzled voters and infuriated fellow politicians by changing positions and welshing on commitments. After harshly criticizing Sauerbrey's tax cut, he backed a 10% income tax cut in 1997 stretched over five years, then in early 1998 increased it to 5% that year, and in October 1998 proposed to install the other 5% the next. He went back and forth on the intercounty connector proposed for the Washington suburbs. When longtime Controller Louis Goldstein died in summer 1998, he at first said he would appoint former Congressman Michael Barnes, then backed down and appointed former Governor Schaefer, who at 76 was eager to get back into office. He pointedly refused to appear with Bill Clinton at a September 1998 Montgomery County event, then eagerly appeared with him in October.

What infuriated Glendening's fellow politicians the most was his back-and-forth on gambling. In 1995, neighboring Delaware introduced slots machines into racetracks, and Maryland track owner Joseph DeFrancis, a big Glendening backer in 1994, wanted them in Maryland too. In February 1996 Glendening said he was opposed. Weeks later he met with DeFrancis and wrote that he would review the alternatives if Delaware slots hurt Maryland tracks. In a July meeting, Baltimore Mayor Kurt Schmoke, another key 1994 backer, said that he would support the slots and give the revenue to Baltimore schools. Then in August, Glendening said, "No bill that authorizes slots will pass my desk."

On other issues Glendening was steadier. In 1995 he proposed a ban on all workplace smoking; this passed but the legislature carved out an exemption to allow smoking in restaurants—though in March 1999 Montgomery County banned smoking in all restaurants and bars. Glendening passed a bill limiting gun purchases to one per month and called for childproof locks on guns. He backed a $170 million Rural Legacy program to buy up open space. He closed fishing on the Pockomoke River and other Chesapeake Bay tributaries when nutrient-fed Pfiesteria was found to be killing fish in September 1997; the legislature in April 1998 passed a scaled-down version of his proposal to limit the use of farm fertilizers and improve monitoring of poultry operations. He provided state financing for the Ravens football stadium in Baltimore and the Redskins stadium in Prince George's County. But not all these actions were popular. Many on the Eastern Shore thought he was overreacting to Pfiesteria, and chicken magnate Frank Perdue gave $32,000 to Sauerbrey in 1998. Many in Montgomery County and elsewhere thought the stadium money should have gone to education.

Glendening, unusually for an incumbent governor, attracted spirited primary opposition. Former Redskin Ray Schoenke promised to spend $2 million on his race, and Harford County Executive Eileen Rehrmann entered with the support of Kurt Schmoke, still eager for slot machine revenue. But both dropped out in July, well before the September primary. Meanwhile, Ellen Sauerbrey had never stopped campaigning after losing in 1994. This time she was running a softer-line campaign. In ads she talked of growing up in a Baltimore rowhouse, the daughter of a steelworker, and of her work as a biology teacher. Her tax cut message partially adopted by Glendening, she now emphasized cutting taxes on seniors. For most of the fall she ran about even with Glendening in the polls; both had high negatives. The pols still shunned Glendening; Schmoke and Prince George's County Executive Wayne Curry endorsed him October 8, but grudgingly and without notifying him. Former Lieutenant Governor Melvin Steinberg endorsed Sauerbrey. But in late October Glendening pulled ahead. Responsible apparently were ads he ran accusing Sauerbrey of "a civil rights record to be ashamed of." In vain Sauerbrey argued that the votes were cast on bills that were killed by Democrats in the state Senate.

The result was a solid, but not overwhelming, 55%–45% victory for Glendening. The black vote was consolidated by Glendening, and the young vote, targeted by Republicans, went more than 60% for Glendening. Turnout was up 9% statewide: 10% in Baltimore City, 5% in black-majority Prince George's County. Glendening had a huge 71% from those with graduate degrees—teachers, social workers, lawyers, government employees. Also helping was Lieutenant Governor Kathleen Kennedy Townsend, the oldest grandchild of Joseph P. Kennedy, who accompanied Glendening on the campaign trail. Sauerbrey seems likely to leave politics, but Maryland may have a woman governor next time; Townsend, thoughtful and congenial, will likely start with a big advantage.

Senior Senator. Paul Sarbanes was first elected to the Maryland House of Delegates in 1966, to the House in 1970, and to the Senate in 1976: He is in his fourth decade as a legislator. His liberalism is rooted in his experience growing up in Salisbury on the Eastern Shore, the son of a Greek immigrant who owned the Mayflower Grill and taught himself enough on the side to discuss philosophy with his son's Princeton professors. As a big-firm lawyer in Baltimore, Sarbanes got started in local politics campaigning in small groups, talking to voters and leaders, listening gravely to what they had to say. Tabbed early as a reformer, in the state legislature he voted against Marvin Mandel to replace Spiro Agnew as governor in 1969—not the most politic move. He beat a long-time incumbent in the primary to win a House seat in 1970 and in 1976 defeated former Senator Joseph Tydings in the primary and incumbent Senator Glenn Beall in the general by 59%–41%.

Since then Sarbanes has been one of the most durable champions of liberal politics: on the Banking Committee, of which he would have become chairman in 1995 if Democrats had not lost their majority in the Senate; on the Joint Economic Committee, which he did chair from 1991–95; and on Foreign Relations. On economics, he argued that the growth of the 1980s was illusory or confined to the rich; he is one Democrat who still seems more concerned about low growth than high inflation. He was one of just 21 senators who voted against the 1996 Welfare Reform Act. He put a hold on the nomination of John Hawke to be comptroller of the currency because Hawke once opposed the Community Reinvestment Act and as point man for the Treasury wouldn't cooperate on financial services reform. On that issue Sarbanes is against letting non-financial corporations own banks. He does not always take left-wing positions. He has worked on bipartisan financial services reform and, with Connie Mack, on the 1998 public housing reform legislation. In the 105th Congress he worked for approval of $18 billion for the IMF, on the mass transit portion of the federal transportation bill and for a Credit Union Membership Act.

On foreign policy Sarbanes has been skeptical of U.S. military involvement and eager for nuclear disarmament. He is the second ranking Democrat on the Foreign Relations Committee, where he has tilted toward aid for Greece and away from Turkey. He worked successfully to prevent elimination of AID as a separate agency and opposes weapons sales to countries with poor human rights records. With Michael DeWine, he has pressed for aid to small-scale agriculture in Africa. Sarbanes was dismayed after reading a *Washington Post* article on how the Army occasionally denies full military honors at funerals due to staffing cutbacks and asked Defense Secretary William Cohen to review the matter; Sarbanes also sponsored repairs to the Korean War Memorial in Washington, DC.

Closer to home, Sarbanes has sponsored projects like the Chesapeake Bay Gateways and Watertrails Network, a special conservation reserve for buffer zones along Chesapeake Bay, and a project to restore the eroding Poplar Island using material dredged from the port of Baltimore's shipping channels. For many years, Sarbanes seemed to be, in Republicans' words, a "stealth senator," sponsoring few bills and sending out few press releases. But he has always lived in Baltimore and makes a point of attending civic and political events throughout Maryland. He was re-elected easily in 1982 with 63% and in 1988 with 62%, carrying the Baltimore area, and showing best around his boyhood home of Salisbury. In 1994 he had an experienced opponent in former Senator Bill Brock, elected to the House in 1962 and the Senate in 1970 from Tennessee, later Republican National Committee chairman and U.S. trade representative. But Brock won his primary unimpressively over Ruthann Aron (who in 1998 was convicted of hiring someone to kill her husband) and had to dodge charges of being a carpetbagger (he moved to Annapolis in 1988 and started paying Maryland taxes in 1990). Sarbanes won 59%–41%, slightly less than in the 1980s, but still convincingly. His 1994 margin was greatest in metro Washington, and he carried metro Baltimore as well.

Sarbanes said he will run again, which will make him the longest serving Maryland senator by November 2000. Republican Congressman Bob Ehrlich from suburban Baltimore seemed likely to run, but his enthusiasm was somewhat deflated by Ellen Sauerbrey's defeat in her rematch with Governor Parris Glendening. In early 1999, Connie Morella was mentioned as a possible opponent. If Sarbanes does not run, Baltimore Mayor Kurt Schmoke seems likely to, though some of his positions could be controversial. Other possible Democrats include House members Steny Hoyer and Ben Cardin, and Lieutenant Governor Kathleen Kennedy Townsend.

Cook's Call. *Probably Safe.* Sarbanes has been in the Senate since 1977, is overshadowed by his more feisty and aggressive colleague, Barbara Mikulski, and many voters are unfamiliar with his accomplishments. Other Democrats in the state acknowledge that while Sarbanes is very attentive to the Democratic base in the state, he does little to reach out to moderate Democrats or independents and is therefore potentially vulnerable in a general election. But it does not appear that either of the candidates who really could give Sarbanes a competitive challenge-Representatives Bob Ehrlich and Connie Morella-will run. If the Republicans come up with a credible candidate, this could become an interesting race, but it is more likely that Sarbanes will get an easy ride to another term.

Junior Senator. Barbara Mikulski is a senator with deep roots in immigrant, urban America and with a fascination for the new technology and jobs growing in edge cities and beyond, a person who doesn't look anything like a traditional politician but who has become a savvy Senate insider. Her roots are in east Baltimore, where her Polish immigrant parents ran a bakery, and she still lives in the city and commutes to Washington. Mikulski got her start in politics as a social worker, organizing to stop a highway from going through Highlandtown. She won, and in the process was elected to the Baltimore City Council in 1971. As a local official with genuine ethnic roots and a woman with genuine liberal impulses, she was chosen head of the Democratic National Committee's Commission on Delegate Selection in 1972. She ran for the Senate in 1974, and got a respectable 43% against incumbent Charles Mathias; when Paul Sarbanes ran for the other Senate seat in 1976, Mikulski ran for his 3d District House seat and won. Ten years later, she gave up that seat for what seemed like a chancy Senate race, and won handily, with 50% in the primary to 31% for Montgomery County Congressman Michael Barnes and 14% for Governor Harry Hughes. In the general, she beat former White House aide Linda Chavez, 61%–39%.

Mikulski is loud and brash, humorous and warm, brusque and aggressive when she feels it is necessary, curious and thoughtful when encountering another new part of the world. One such world was the Senate. "The House is a scrappy body, and I was scrappy in the body," she explained later. "I knew the Senate was a different institution. I needed to know the rules." And she did; as the Baltimore *Sun*'s David Folkenflik writes, "Mikulski doesn't fight the system. Mikulski works the system." In her first term she won a seat on the Appropriations Committee; within two years she was chairman of a subcommittee, handling housing, space and veterans' programs; she was elected Democratic Caucus secretary in 1994. Today she is the subcommittee's ranking Democrat, and often works closely with Chairman Christopher Bond. She is also the Senate's chief superintendent of the space program and an enthusiast for space exploration. An ardent backer of the manned space station *Freedom* (often attacked by other liberals), she has battled to keep it alive despite her sympathy for veterans' and housing programs also funded by her subcommittee, which tend to compete for funds. She has also strongly supported the Hubble space telescope. It does not hurt that some NASA facilities are in Maryland—the Goddard Space Center in Greenbelt and the Wallops Island flight facility— but she also keeps an eye on others. On defense and foreign policy, Mikulski's voting record is more moderate than that of many Democrats; as a Polish-American, she was never taken with the idea that the United States and the Soviet Union were morally equivalent. She has worked to fund Maryland defense spending, including the Patuxent River Naval Air Station, Curtis Bay Coast Guard Yard and an anti-missile jamming system assembled in Linthicum.

On domestic policy, Mikulski is a liberal who insists that "where there are rights there are responsibilities" and has criticized fellow Democrats for being "angst-addicted." With Sam Nunn she was the major backer of the national service bill that produced AmeriCorps in 1993. She supported workfare in the 1980s and voted for the Welfare Reform Act of 1996. She voted for the Defense of Marriage Act. She sponsored an FBI initiative against online child pornography. She also worked for the 1997 FDA reform, which updated and streamlined the approval process for drugs and medical devices and encouraged safety and efficacy testing on children. It also reauthorized a Mikulski favorite, the prescription drug user fee, which provides money for more FDA personnel to expedite the drug approval process. She has proposed that the FDA bar import of food not prepared, packed and held under conditions that meet U.S. safety standards. And she would ban export of ships to foreign shipbreaking yards unless they meet U.S. safety requirements.

Mikulski is the senior woman in the Senate and convenes meetings of women senators. She has pushed many of what might be called women's issues—mammography clinic standards, an Office of Women's Health Research, homemaker IRAs, and a 1989 law to protect the savings of elderly couples from impoverishment by nursing homes. She defended Anita Hill, opposed the retirement of a four-star admiral because of the Tailhook scandal, blocked reappointment of the architect of the Capitol, condemned former Oregon Senator Bob Packwood as a member of the Ethics Committee, and journeyed to Aberdeen Proving Grounds—in each case pursuing charges of sexual harassment. But she had little to say about Bill Clinton's treatment of White House intern Monica Lewinsky until in late August 1998, when she called his behavior "very disappointing" and his actions "wrong."

Mikulski's skills are not just political. She co-authored *Capitol Offense* and *Capitol Virtues* with Marylouise Oates, mystery novels describing freshman Senator Eleanor Gorzack of Pennsylvania, who is "somewhat younger, somewhat slimmer, but no less politically savvy than I am"—and also 5'4", five inches taller than the 4'11" Mikulski. Mikulski and Oates sold movie rights to CBS.

Mikulski's toughest Senate election was her first, which she won fairly easily after strong initial competition. In 1992 and 1998 she was re-elected with 71%, first against Alan Keyes, a former Reagan appointee who ran for president in 1996, and then against Ross Pierpont, a genial 81-year-old physician who had run for office and lost 14 times.

Presidential politics. Maryland is one of the most Democratic states in presidential elections. It voted for Jimmy Carter in 1980, came close to voting for Walter Mondale and Michael Dukakis in 1984 and 1988 and was one of Bill Clinton's best states in the 1990s. In 1992 it was his third-best state, after Arkansas and New York; in 1996, his fifth-best, tied with Illinois at 54%.

In the 1990s Maryland has held its presidential primaries a week before Super Tuesday to try to get noticed; achieving partial success. In 1992, Paul Tsongas beat Bill Clinton 41%–33%, with all his margin and more coming from suburban Baltimore and Montgomery County. In 1996, Republicans gave Bob Dole a 53%–21% victory over Patrick Buchanan.

Congressional districting. Maryland's convoluted district lines result from an attempt to protect most incumbents and also to create a new black-majority district in the Washington suburbs for 1992. They have mostly succeeded. In the one contest between incumbents, Republican Wayne Gilchrest beat Democrat Tom McMillen; the black-majority 4th has regularly re-elected Democrat Albert Wynn. As for redistricting after the 2000 Census, Democrats will have complete partisan control, but not all Democrats have strong partisan instincts; the new lines may end up looking a lot like the old.

The People: Est. Pop. 1998: 5,134,808; Pop. 1990: 4,781,468, up 7.4% 1990–1998. 1.9% of U.S. total, 19th largest; 18.7% rural. Median age: 34.9 years. 11.3% 65 years and over. 71% White, 24.9% Black, 2.9% Asian, 0.3% Amer. Indian, 0.9% Other; 2.5% Hispanic Origin. Households: 54.2% married couple families; 26.4% married couple fams. w. children; 50.3% college educ.; median household income: $39,386; per capita income: $17,730; 65% owner occupied housing; median house value: $116,500; median monthly rent: $473. 4.6% Unemployment. 1998 Voting age pop.: 3,824,000. 1998 Turnout: 1,567,994; 41% of VAP. Registered voters (1998): 2,569,649; 1,479,530 D (58%), 778,245 R (20%), 311,874 unaffiliated and minor parties (12%).

Political Lineup: Governor, Parris N. Glendening (D); Lt. Gov., Kathleen Kennedy Townsend (D); Secy. of State, John T. Willis (D); Atty. Gen., J. Joseph Curran, Jr. (D); Comptroller, William Schaefer (D); State Senate, 47 (32 D, 15 R); Majority Leader, Clarence Blount (D); State House, 141 (100 D, 41 R); House Speaker, Casper R. Taylor Jr. (D). Senators, Paul S. Sarbanes (D) and Barbara A. Mikulski (D). Representatives, 8 (4 D, 4 R).

Elections Division: 410-974-3711; **Filing Deadline for U.S. Congress:** December 27, 1999.

1996 Presidential Vote

Clinton (D)	966,208	(54%)
Dole (R)	681,530	(39%)
Perot (I)	115,812	(7%)

1996 Republican Presidential Primary

Dole (R)	135,522	(53%)
Buchanan (R)	53,585	(21%)
Forbes (R)	32,207	(13%)
Alexander (R)	14,061	(6%)
Keyes (R)	13,718	(5%)
Others	5,153	(2%)

1992 Presidential Vote

Clinton (D)	988,571	(50%)
Bush (R)	707,094	(36%)
Perot (I)	281,414	(14%)

GOVERNOR

Gov. Parris N. Glendening (D)

Elected 1994, term expires Jan. 2003; b. June 11, 1942, Bronx, NY; home, University Park; FL St. U., B.A. 1964, M.A. 1965, Ph.D. 1967; Catholic; married (Frances).

Elected Office: Hyattsville City Cncl., 1973–74; Prince George's Cnty. Cncl., 1974–82; Prince George's Cnty. Exec., 1982–94.

Professional Career: Prof., U. of MD, 1967–94.

Office: State House, Annapolis, 21401, 410-974-3901; Fax: 410-974-2542; Web site: www.mec.state.md.us/mec.

Election Results

1998 gen.	Parris N. Glendening (D)	846,972	(55%)
	Ellen Sauerbrey (R)	688,357	(45%)
1998 prim.	Parris N. Glendening (D)	296,863	(70%)
	Eileen M. Rehrmann (D)	56,806	(13%)
	Terence McGuire (D)	46,124	(11%)
	Lawrence K. Freeman (D)	23,752	(6%)
1994 gen.	Parris N. Glendening (D)	708,094	(50%)
	Ellen Sauerbrey (R)	702,101	(50%)

SENATORS

Sen. Paul S. Sarbanes (D)

Elected 1976, seat up 2000; b. Feb. 3, 1933, Salisbury; home, Baltimore; Princeton, A.B. 1954, Rhodes Scholar, Oxford U., B.A. 1957, Harvard, LL.B. 1960; Greek Orthodox; married (Christine).

Elected Office: MD House of Delegates, 1966–70; U.S. House of Reps., 1970–76.

Professional Career: Law Clerk, Judge Morris A. Soper, U.S. 4th Circuit Crt. of Appeals, 1960–61; Practicing atty., 1961–62, 1965–70; A.A., Pres. Kennedy's Cncl. of Econ. Advisers, 1962–63; Exec. Dir., Baltimore Charter Revision Comm., 1963–64.

DC Office: 309 HSOB, 20510, 202-224-4524; Fax: 202-224-1651; Web site: www.senate.gov/~sarbanes.

State Offices: Baltimore, 410-962-4436; Cobb Island, 301-259-2404; Cumberland, 301-724-0695; Salisbury, 410-860-2131; Silver Spring, 301-589-0797.

Committees: *Banking, Housing & Urban Affairs* (RMM of 9 D): Financial Institutions. *Budget* (4th of 10 D). *Foreign Relations* (2d of 8 D): African Affairs; European Affairs; International Economic Policy, Export & Trade Promotion (RMM); Near Eastern & South Asian Affairs. *Joint Economic Committee* (8th of 10 Sens.).

Group Ratings

	ADA	ACLU	AFS	LCV	CON	NTU	NFIB	COC	ACU	NTLC	CHC
1998	95	86	100	100	7	7	11	44	4	0	0
1997	100	—	100	—	2	6	—	30	0	—	—

National Journal Ratings

	1997 LIB — 1997 CONS			1998 LIB — 1998 CONS		
Economic	96%	—	0%	90%	—	0%
Social	71%	—	0%	74%	—	0%
Foreign	87%	—	8%	79%	—	15%

Key Votes of the 105th Congress

1. Bal. Budget Amend.	N	5. Satcher for Surgeon Gen.	Y	9. Chem. Weapons Treaty	Y
2. Clinton Budget Deal	N	6. Highway Set-asides	Y	10. Cuban Humanitarian Aid	Y
3. Cloture on Tobacco	Y	7. Table Child Gun locks	N	11. Table Bosnia Troops	Y
4. Education IRAs	N	8. Ovrd. Part. Birth Veto	N	12. $ for Test-ban Treaty	Y

Election Results

1994 general	Paul S. Sarbanes (D)	809,125	(59%)	($2,767,187)
	William Brock (R)	559,908	(41%)	($3,201,650)
1994 primary	Paul S. Sarbanes (D)	382,115	(79%)	
	John B. Liston (D)	52,031	(11%)	
	Dennard A. Gayle (D)	30,665	(6%)	
	Leonard E. Trout (D)	19,393	(4%)	
1988 general	Paul S. Sarbanes (D)	999,166	(62%)	($1,466,477)
	Alan L. Keyes (R)	617,537	(38%)	($662,651)

Sen. Barbara A. Mikulski (D)

Elected 1986, seat up 2004; b. July 20, 1936, Baltimore; home, Baltimore; Mt. St. Agnes Col., B.A. 1958, U. of MD, M.S.W. 1965; Catholic; single.

Elected Office: Baltimore City Cncl., 1971–76; U.S. House of Reps., 1976–86.

Professional Career: Social worker, Baltimore Dept. of Social Svcs., 1965–70; Chmn., DNC Delegate Selection Comm., 1972; Adjunct prof., Loyola Col., 1972–76.

DC Office: 709 HSOB, 20510, 202-224-4654; Fax: 202-224-8858; Web site: www.senate.gov/~mikulski.

State Offices: Annapolis, 410-263-1805; Baltimore, 410-962-4510; College Park, 301-345-5517; Hagerstown, 301-797-2826; Highlandtown, 410-563-4000; Salisbury, 410-546-7711.

Committees: *Appropriations* (7th of 13 D): Commerce, Justice, State & the Judiciary; Foreign Operations & Export Financing; Transportation; Treasury & General Government; VA, HUD & Independent Agencies (RMM). *Health, Education, Labor & Pensions* (4th of 8 D): Aging (RMM); Public Health.

Group Ratings

	ADA	ACLU	AFS	LCV	CON	NTU	NFIB	COC	ACU	NTLC	CHC
1998	90	86	100	88	22	10	38	53	4	12	0
1997	95	—	89	—	4	18	—	44	4	—	—

National Journal Ratings

	1997 LIB — 1997 CONS			1998 LIB — 1998 CONS		
Economic	90%	—	6%	75%	—	20%
Social	71%	—	0%	74%	—	0%
Foreign	54%	—	45%	79%	—	15%

Key Votes of the 105th Congress

1. Bal. Budget Amend.	N	5. Satcher for Surgeon Gen.	Y	9. Chem. Weapons Treaty	Y
2. Clinton Budget Deal	N	6. Highway Set-asides	Y	10. Cuban Humanitarian Aid	N
3. Cloture on Tobacco	Y	7. Table Child Gun locks	N	11. Table Bosnia Troops	Y
4. Education IRAs	N	8. Ovrd. Part. Birth Veto	N	12. $ for Test-ban Treaty	Y

Election Results

1998 general	Barbara A. Mikulski (D)	1,062,810	(71%)	($3,014,312)
	Ross Z. Pierpont (R)	444,637	(30%)	($297,768)
1998 primary	Barbara A. Mikulski (D)	349,382	(84%)	
	Ann L. Mallory (D)	43,120	(10%)	
	Kauko H. Kokkonen (D)	21,658	(5%)	
1992 general	Barbara A. Mikulski (D)	1,307,610	(71%)	($3,623,974)
	Alan L. Keyes (R)	533,688	(29%)	($1,175,682)

FIRST DISTRICT

Chesapeake Bay, technically not a bay but an estuary, was the central focus of the most thickly settled of the 13 colonies, and today remains a central focus for much of modern Maryland— and a backwater where remnants of an older civilization live on. The first British here were amazed at the Chesapeake's oysters and terrapin turtles and crabs and rockfish; despite pollution, and outbreaks of the toxic Pfiesteria microbe in 1997, watermen still make hardy livings bringing them to shore. This was an estuary civilization in colonial days, with every little hamlet tied together by the highways of bays and creeks and inlets off the Chesapeake. Old settlements like Chestertown, Oxford, St. Michaels and Cambridge don't look all that much different from when George Washington slept there. On the Western Shore, Annapolis was laid out as a capital in 1694, with one circle planned for the Statehouse and one for the Church; the marble-halled Statehouse, built in 1772, where the Continental Congress ratified the Treaty of Paris, is the oldest state capitol in continuous use. Annapolis is the home of the United States Naval Academy and its waterfront, though gentrified, is a waterman's as well as a yachter's port.

In post-colonial times, when most Americans were caught up in the romance of westward movement, these estuaries and peninsulas were mostly forgotten, off the main lines of railroads and highways, left behind by thousands moving west. In the 160 years between 1790 and 1950, the Eastern Shore counties of Maryland only doubled in population, perhaps the slowest growth rate on the Eastern Seaboard. Today much of the Chesapeake has changed beyond recognition. But the antique centers of the Eastern Shore towns and even downtown Annapolis would not be unrecognizable to a time traveler from say, the 1840s. Annapolis is now just one part of the mostly booming Baltimore metropolitan area, and the Eastern Shore has been growing vigorously in the 1980s and 1990s as more Americans are able to choose the small-town environment they prefer, even if that choice means a newly minted subdivision house or condominium near burgeoning shopping centers and small factory buildings. This is a land of genteel estates fronting the water and of Frank Perdue's chicken empire around Salisbury, of Easton's Waterfowl Festival and the swarms of motorboats and sailing ships making their way up and down the inlets or under the twin spans of the Bay Bridge. But one of the things that attracts people is its continuity with the past and closeness to nature.

The 1st Congressional District of Maryland includes all of the Eastern Shore and, across the Bay, Annapolis and a strip of four-lane highway suburbs up to the southern tip of Baltimore. In national elections, this is a solidly Republican area, voting against Bill Clinton in both 1992 and 1996.

The congressman from the 1st District is Wayne Gilchrest, a Republican with an unusual political history and some unusual political views. Gilchrest served in the Marine Corps in Vietnam, taught high school for 13 years and painted houses in the summer. In 1988 he ran for Congress and lost to incumbent Democrat Roy Dyson 50.4%–49.6%; Dyson spent vastly more money but was embarrassed by a *Washington Post* story on his personnel practices. In 1990, Gilchrest ran again, was again vastly outspent, but won 57%–43%. In 1992 redistricting placed him in the same district with Democratic incumbent Tom McMillen, former Rhodes Scholar and Maryland and Washington basketball player. McMillen raised vastly more money, but Gilchrest represented 53% of the new district and stood to benefit from Eastern Shore loyalties. Gilchrest won 52%–48%, carrying 60% on the Eastern Shore.

Gilchrest's voting record is almost precisely at the midpoint of the House, making him a crucial vote on many issues. His specialty, helpfully in a district centered on the Chesapeake Bay, is the environment. His committee assignments—Resources and Transportation, with the chairmanship of the Coast Guard and Maritime Transportation Subcommittee—give him some leverage on these issues. In 1995 he took issue with Western Republicans when they sought to relax the Endangered Species Act, even threatening to resign his committee post when a sub-committee chairman wouldn't let him invite scientists to testify in favor of the law at field hearings in the 1st District. He opposed the new majority's revisions of the Clean Water Act. After a Baltimore *Sun* series on the shipbreaking industry, he criticized the industry for allowing polluting and unsafe working conditions and called for an end to selling ships to be disassembled in foreign countries. He braved local opinion by calling for Ocean City to pay some of the cost of rebuilding Assateague Island, which has eroded because of ocean movements caused by a jetty that protects the Ocean City beach. He was the only Maryland member to vote for D.C. statehood, and he voted for the assault weapons ban—in a district assumed to be strongly opposed to gun control.

In recent years Gilchrest's most vehement opposition has come from conservative Republicans. But he has prevailed; against five primary opponents in 1996, he won with 65%. Gilchrest does not accept PAC contributions, but even so he managed to outspend his Democratic opponents in 1994, 1996 and 1998. He also had the endorsements of the Sierra Club and League of Conservation Voters. In 1998 he said his biggest issues were education (he wants to improve secondary schools), health care (he wants the same reimbursement rate for rural and urban patients) and Social Security ("If you're going to have a Social Security system, it will have to . . . in some way mimic existing private-sector investment."). In September 1998 he called on Bill Clinton to resign. Gilchrest seems to have a solid hold on the district: He won with 68% in 1994, 62% in 1996 and 69% in 1998.

Cook's Call. *Safe.* While at least one Democratic State House member is making noise about challenging Gilchrest, he is pretty well entrenched here. His pro-environment record not only makes sense in this Chesapeake Bay district, but it also makes it difficult for Democrats to paint him as too extreme.

The People: Pop. 1990: 597,821; 45.9% rural; 13% age 65 + ; 83.3% White, 15.1% Black, 1% Asian, 0.3% Amer. Indian, 0.3% Other; 1.1% Hispanic Origin. Households: 57.7% married couple families; 26.6% married couple fams. w. children; 41.7% college educ.; median household income: $35,115; per capita income: $16,104; median house value: $101,300; median gross rent: $390.

1996 Presidential Vote

Dole (R)	107,122	(48%)
Clinton (D)	97,338	(43%)
Perot (I)	20,779	(9%)

1992 Presidential Vote

Bush (R)	109,039	(44%)
Clinton (D)	93,165	(37%)
Perot (I)	47,188	(19%)

Rep. Wayne T. Gilchrest (R)

Elected 1990; b. Apr. 15, 1946, Rahway, NJ; home, Kennedyville; Wesley Col., A.A. 1971, DE St. Col., B.A. 1973, Loyola Col., 1984; Methodist; married (Barbara).

Military Career: Marine Corps, 1964–68 (Vietnam).

Professional Career: High schl. teacher, 1973–86; Natl. Forest Service worker, Bitterroot Natl. Forest, 1986.

DC Office: 2245 RHOB 20515, 202-225-5311; Fax: 202-225-0254; Web site: www.house.gov/gilchrest.

District Offices: Annapolis, 410-263-6321; Chestertown, 410-778-9407; Salisbury, 410-749-3184.

Committees: *Resources* (9th of 28 R): Fisheries Conservation, Wildlife & Oceans; Forests & Forest Health. *Transportation & Infrastructure* (9th of 41 R): Coast Guard & Maritime Transportation (Chmn.); Water Resources & Environment.

Group Ratings

	ADA	ACLU	AFS	LCV	CON	NTU	NFIB	COC	ACU	NTLC	CHC
1998	35	44	22	62	13	42	77	89	44	66	64
1997	20	—	25	—	74	44	—	90	71	—	—

National Journal Ratings

	1997 LIB — 1997 CONS		1998 LIB — 1998 CONS	
Economic	42%	— 57%	43%	— 56%
Social	50%	— 48%	59%	— 40%
Foreign	51%	— 46%	56%	— 42%

Key Votes of the 105th Congress

1. Clinton Budget Deal	Y	5. Puerto Rico Sthood. Ref.	Y	9. Cut $ for B-2 Bombers	N
2. Education IRAs	Y	6. End Highway Set-asides	N	10. Human Rights in China	Y
3. Req. 2/3 to Raise Taxes	Y	7. School Prayer Amend.	N	11. Withdraw Bosnia Troops	N
4. Fast-track Trade	Y	8. Ovrd. Part. Birth Veto	Y	12. End Cuban TV-Marti	Y

Election Results

1998 general	Wayne T. Gilchrest (R)	135,771	(69%)	($266,395)
	Irving Pinder (D)	60,450	(31%)	($68,504)
1998 primary	Wayne T. Gilchrest (R)	unopposed		
1996 general	Wayne T. Gilchrest (R)	131,033	(62%)	($259,366)
	Steven R. Eastaugh (D)	81,825	(38%)	($229,073)

SECOND DISTRICT

The spokes of Baltimore's avenues spread out in all directions, from the downtown centered on the Inner Harbor, connecting the central city with the suburbs where most residents of metropolitan Baltimore now live. The streets reach east to Dundalk and Essex, industrial suburbs where the tone of life was set for years by the giant Sparrows Point steel mill, long the biggest in the country. Northeast they extend to modest working class suburbs and the small towns of the Baltimore and Harford County countryside which are now speckled with suburban developments: Bel Air, Joppatowne, Aberdeen, Edgewood; the last two near the Aberdeen Proving Grounds and Edgewood Arsenal military installations. Straight north from downtown are higher-income suburbs, the pleasant county seat of Towson; farther north are Lutherville, Timonium, Cockeysville, Hunt Valley, all flanked by the Baltimore County hunt country.

The 2d Congressional District takes up most of this territory. The Sparrows Point area political tradition is union-Democratic, but that has been tempered lately. The northeast suburbs are ancestrally Democratic, but culturally rather conservative; the suburbs to the north are as solidly Republican as any part of Maryland.

The congressman from the 2d District is Bob Ehrlich, a Republican first elected in 1994. Ehrlich grew up in a rowhouse in the modest suburb of Arbutus, the son of a car salesman. A six-footer at 13, he got a football scholarship to the elite Gilman School in Baltimore and then to Princeton, where he was a linebacker; he went to law school at Wake Forest, working part-time as assistant football coach, then practiced law in Baltimore. Ehrlich volunteered in Republican campaigns and in 1986, at 28, was elected to the Maryland House of Delegates. There he worked on tough sentencing and child pornography laws, but also opposed some bills as unneeded or unconstitutional. When 2d District Congresswoman Helen Delich Bentley ran for governor in 1994 (only to be upset in the primary by anti-tax legislator Ellen Sauerbrey), Ehrlich ran for the House. He campaigned as an opponent of over-regulation, as a military hawk and a libertarian, and beat an anti-abortion candidate in the primary, 57%–38%.

The Democratic nominee was Gerry Brewster, the son of former Congressman and Senator Daniel Brewster, who narrowly won his primary over a labor-backed candidate. It looked to be a close race and there were alluring symmetries between the candidates: They were classmates at Gilman and Princeton, served together in the House of Delegates and on the Judiciary Committee, and spent almost identical amounts in the campaign; interestingly, it was the Democrat who was the aristocrat and the Republican who grew up in a rowhouse. Ehrlich campaigned against the House Democratic leadership and signed the Contract With America, though he opposed term limits. He was enthusiastic about tax cuts. He ran ads showing the rowhouse where he grew up and said the most important lessons he learned were around the dining room table. The result was a solid 63%–37% Ehrlich victory.

Ehrlich began the 104th Congress on Newt Gingrich's "corrections day" panel, producing the Reports Elimination Act that identified 200 federal reports as unnecessary. He showed a willingness to cast tough votes, as when he opposed the minimum wage and argued that it "will make some marginal workers happier and put a little money in their pockets, but you cost the other marginal workers their jobs. That's not the group we should do harm to." He opposed gun control and supported property rights. He tried to block lobbying by nonprofits. He supported the partial-birth abortion ban, though he does not back a ban on all abortions. He broke with the Republican leadership on term limits, loser-pays legal reform and trade sanctions against China. He worked on local projects like protecting Baltimore's Home Port status and financing Harford County sewers.

Ehrlich was outraged by a 1995 desegregation settlement between Baltimore and HUD that would have given 1,342 poor families living in housing projects vouchers to rent private apartments or houses, but only in non-poor or non-minority neighborhoods. To Ehrlich this set constitutionally suspect limits on where the project residents could live and elevated racial criteria improperly. He sponsored a provision in the Public Housing Reform Bill, which passed in 1998, requiring federal officials to inform local governments about impending settlements of housing lawsuits.

"I'm right of center, not on the far right of the party," Ehrlich has said. He has worked with Democrats on some issues, like the Credit Union Membership Act. He has been a champion of the blind, working to restore the earnings link between the blind and senior citizens. He seeks to streamline regulations on nursing facilities and wants to do more to bar access to alcohol by minors. In June 1998 he got a majority of Republican members to sign his letter requesting the Steering Committee to take into account votes on procedural issues when determining committee assignments and naming committee and subcommittee chairmen—an idea obnoxious to (and perhaps aimed at) his 1st District neighbor Wayne Gilchrest.

In 1996 Ehrlich was easily re-elected against the loser of the 1994 Democratic primary, Connie Galiazzo DeJuliis, who had strong labor backing. In 1998 he beat Democrat Kenneth

Bosley, a dairy farmer, by the impressive margin of 69%–31%. Ehrlich has made hundreds of appearances across Maryland and set up a PAC to contribute to Republicans running for the House of Delegates. But Ehrlich was quite deflated by Ellen Sauerbrey's 1998 defeat to Governor Parris Glendening, afterwards expressing doubts about the state Republican organization, and has stepped down from taking on Sarbanes in 2000.

Cook's Call. *Safe.* The 2d District has been quite friendly to Republicans and Ehrlich should be safe here in 2000. Ehrlich made no secret of his interest in running for statewide office, but he was disheartened by the drubbing gubernatorial nominee Ellen Sauerbrey took from Democratic Governor Parris Glendening in the 1998 elections.

The People: Pop. 1990: 597,450; 17.6% rural; 12.6% age 65 + ; 91.8% White, 5.8% Black, 1.8% Asian, 0.3% Amer. Indian, 0.3% Other; 1.1% Hispanic Origin. Households: 61.1% married couple families; 28.5% married couple fams. w. children; 47.3% college educ.; median household income: $40,120; per capita income: $17,931; median house value: $110,900; median gross rent: $432.

1996 Presidential Vote				1992 Presidential Vote			
Dole (R)		119,178	(50%)	Bush (R)		121,087	(44%)
Clinton (D)		95,112	(40%)	Clinton (D)		98,267	(36%)
Perot (I)		22,412	(9%)	Perot (I)		52,668	(19%)

Rep. Robert L. Ehrlich, Jr. (R)

Elected 1994; b. Nov. 25, 1957, Arbutus; home, Timonium; Princeton U., B.A. 1979, Wake Forest U., J.D. 1982; Methodist; married (Kendel).

Elected Office: MD House of Delegates, 1986–94.

Professional Career: Practicing atty., 1982–94.

DC Office: 315 CHOB 20515, 202-225-3061; Fax: 202-225-3094; Web site: www.house.gov/ehrlich.

District Offices: Bel Air, 410-838-2517; Lutherville, 410-337-7222.

Committees: *Commerce* (29th of 29 R): Energy & Power; Finance & Hazardous Materials; Telecommunications, Trade & Consumer Protection.

Group Ratings

	ADA	ACLU	AFS	LCV	CON	NTU	NFIB	COC	ACU	NTLC	CHC
1998	5	25	11	15	42	55	93	94	92	95	75
1997	0	—	13	—	62	58	—	90	72	—	—

National Journal Ratings

	1997 LIB — 1997 CONS			1998 LIB — 1998 CONS		
Economic	19%	—	76%	26%	—	74%
Social	44%	—	55%	49%	—	50%
Foreign	32%	—	65%	27%	—	68%

Key Votes of the 105th Congress

1. Clinton Budget Deal	Y	5. Puerto Rico Sthood. Ref.	N	9. Cut $ for B-2 Bombers	N		
2. Education IRAs	Y	6. End Highway Set-asides	Y	10. Human Rights in China	N		
3. Req. 2/3 to Raise Taxes	Y	7. School Prayer Amend.	Y	11. Withdraw Bosnia Troops	Y		
4. Fast-track Trade	Y	8. Ovrd. Part. Birth Veto	Y	12. End Cuban TV-Marti	N		

Election Results

1998 general	Robert L. Ehrlich Jr. (R) 145,711	(69%)	($487,110)
	Kenneth T. Bosley (D) 64,474	(31%)	
1998 primary	Robert L. Ehrlich Jr. (R) .... unopposed		
1996 general	Robert L. Ehrlich Jr. (R) 143,075	(62%)	($844,918)
	Connie Galiazzo DeJuliis (D) 88,344	(38%)	($641,618)

THIRD DISTRICT

Baltimore, one of America's major cities since the Revolution, in the 1990s suddenly became one of America's star cities. Its Inner Harbor and new ballpark at Camden Yards became national models. Its cuisine—steamed crabs with Chesapeake spices, crab cakes—became known beyond the watershed of the Chesapeake Bay. The central city of Baltimore certainly has its problems—high crime, poor schools—but the greater Baltimore that has grown far beyond the Baltimore City and County lines retains a distinctive character. There is a patina of age, as on its 1829 Washington Monument and the townhouses of Mount Vernon Square, and an atmosphere of tolerance and diversity nurtured by Maryland's founding Catholics in search of liberty; the nation's first Catholic diocese and cathedral were built here when America was overwhelmingly and militantly Protestant. This is a city built solidly on commerce, and one that has always known how to reap its pleasures.

The 3d Congressional District of Maryland is centered on Baltimore and consists of three portions that extend outward like spokes of a wheel from the focus of the Inner Harbor. The three spokes are connected by narrow bridges of land, with boundaries designed to build a black-majority 7th District next door. One spoke extends northeast out into the Polish Highlandtown neighborhood and the mostly white Catholic northeast precincts and close-in suburbs of Overlea and Parkville. Another extends northwest to the heavily Jewish suburbs of Pikesville and Owings Mills, past the array of temples and synagogues on Park Heights Avenue to the open subdivisions where the newest Jewish neighborhoods are being built. A third spoke extends southwest, past the old rowhouse neighborhoods overlooking Fort McHenry, where Francis Scott Key saw by the dawn's early light the star-spangled banner still waving, and out past Arbutus and Lansdowne into Linthicum and Fort Meade in Anne Arundel County and Elkridge and Columbia in Howard County, at the cusp of the invisible boundary between metro Baltimore and metro Washington. The 3d District is ancestrally Democratic and remains loyal to Democrats in most elections. Pikesville and Columbia are solidly liberal on most issues; the northeast and close-in southeast areas are culturally more conservative.

The congressman from the 3d is Benjamin Cardin, former speaker of the Maryland House of Delegates and one of the many bright politicos produced by the Jewish neighborhoods of northwest Baltimore. He was elected to the House of Delegates in 1966, at 23, the first time he was eligible to run; he became speaker in 1979, at 35; and was easily elected to Congress in 1986 when Barbara Mikulski ran for the Senate. In the House, Cardin got a seat on Ways and Means in his second term and has been a productive and creative legislator. His record is generally liberal, but by no means on the left of the Democratic Party: He supported NAFTA despite union opposition and backed a cap on medical malpractice damages despite opposition by trial lawyers.

"Being a member of Congress is about working with Democrats and Republicans and crafting legislation. From reforming the IRS to protecting pensions, members need to work together," Cardin said in 1998. Such has been his record. His bill to restore the tax deduction for health insurance for the self-employed was quickly passed in the Republican Congress in 1995. He was co-sponsor with Rob Portman of the IRS reform law that passed in 1998, the first IRS reform in four decades, which shifts the burden of proof away from the taxpayer and to the government, establishes greater oversight of the agency, and encourages electronic filing and updated technology. He is an expert on 401(k) savings plans and in 1998 with Portman sponsored a bill to allow more contributions to plans and to make it easier to roll them over when taking new jobs. On Social Security he has said, "Ultimately we should look carefully at the possibility of permitting younger working Americans to direct some part of their FICA taxes into private retirement-saving accounts."

Cardin has also been a workhorse on health care. He helped draft the Democrats' version of managed care reform in 1998, and is proud of the provision that guarantees patients the right to an external process to appeal adverse health insurance decisions; he was angry when Republicans dropped a provision allowing patients emergency treatment without pre-approval. In 1996 he supported allowing Medicare recipients to voluntarily participate in managed-care options. In 1998, when three of six Maryland Medicare HMOs dropped coverage, he proposed expanding supplemental coverage options, especially for prescription drugs. To support beleaguered teaching hospitals, like Baltimore's Johns Hopkins and the University of Maryland, he proposed a 1% fee on health insurance premiums to finance medical education.

Now in his fourth decade as a legislator, Cardin takes an institutional focus. In 1998, he and Jim Nussle proposed a budget process reform to encourage accrual accounting, force earlier agreement between the president and Congress, and create an automatic continuing resolution to prevent government shutdowns. He served on the ethics committee for the first half of the 1990s and was ranking Democrat on the subcommittee that painstakingly investigated the charges against Newt Gingrich; in 1998 Maryland legislators named him to head a panel to recommend changes in state ethics laws. He has worked with Republican Wayne Gilchrest on laws to protect key sites on the Chesapeake Bay.

Cardin has been mentioned many times as a candidate for governor, and in 1997 canvassed support. But few politicians were willing to back him publicly, and in September 1997 he announced he wasn't running. He could conceivably be a candidate for senator in 2000 or governor in 2002; but he already can take satisfaction from being a major policy-maker even as a mid-seniority member of the minority party. Cardin has been re-elected easily.

Cook's Call. *Safe.* Cardin is well-entrenched in this heavily Democratic Baltimore-based district. Baltimore's big population loss, however, could mean that this district is altered in 2001 redistricting.

The People: Pop. 1990: 597,712; 1.9% rural; 13.9% age 65 + ; 79.7% White, 17.3% Black, 2.2% Asian, 0.3% Amer. Indian, 0.5% Other; 1.7% Hispanic Origin. Households: 50.8% married couple families; 23.6% married couple fams. w. children; 49.1% college educ.; median household income: $35,970; per capita income: $17,779; median house value: $91,000; median gross rent: $428.

1996 Presidential Vote

Clinton (D) 123,532 (58%)
Dole (R) 72,017 (34%)
Perot (I) 13,872   (7%)

1992 Presidential Vote

Clinton (D) 136,829 (54%)
Bush (R) 82,494 (32%)
Perot (I) 34,973 (14%)

Rep. Benjamin Cardin (D)

Elected 1986; b. Oct. 5, 1943, Baltimore; home, Baltimore; U. of Pittsburgh, B.A. 1964, U. of MD, LL.B., J.D. 1967; Jewish; married (Myrna).

Elected Office: MD House of Delegates, 1966–86, Speaker, 1979–86.

Professional Career: Practicing atty., 1967–86.

DC Office: 104 CHOB 20515, 202-225-4016; Fax: 202-225-9219; Web site: www.house.gov/cardin.

District Office: Baltimore, 410-433-8886.

Committees: *Ways & Means* (6th of 16 D): Human Resources (RMM); Social Security.

Group Ratings

	ADA	ACLU	AFS	LCV	CON	NTU	NFIB	COC	ACU	NTLC	CHC
1998	95	81	100	77	97	27	18	25	8	14	0
1997	85	—	88	—	88	30	—	40	12	—	—

National Journal Ratings

	1997 LIB — 1997 CONS		1998 LIB — 1998 CONS	
Economic	64% —	35%	79% —	0%
Social	79% —	21%	75% —	24%
Foreign	82% —	16%	64% —	31%

Key Votes of the 105th Congress

1. Clinton Budget Deal	N	5. Puerto Rico Sthood. Ref.	Y	9. Cut $ for B-2 Bombers	Y
2. Education IRAs	N	6. End Highway Set-asides	N	10. Human Rights in China	Y
3. Req. 2/3 to Raise Taxes	N	7. School Prayer Amend.	N	11. Withdraw Bosnia Troops	N
4. Fast-track Trade	N	8. Ovrd. Part. Birth Veto	N	12. End Cuban TV-Marti	N

Election Results

1998 general	Benjamin Cardin (D)	137,501	(78%)	($441,950)
	Colin Felix Harby (R)	39,667	(22%)	
1998 primary	Benjamin Cardin (D)	50,240	(90%)	
	Dan Hiegel (D)	5,856	(10%)	
1996 general	Benjamin Cardin (D)	130,204	(67%)	($577,270)
	Patrick L. McDonough (R)	63,229	(33%)	($49,459)

FOURTH DISTRICT

In 1696 the proprietors of the colony of Maryland created a new county between the Potomac and Patuxent Rivers and named it after the husband of the heir to the throne, Prince George of Denmark. For 300 years Prince George's County has not often won national fame—maybe briefly when investigators chased the plotters of Abraham Lincoln's murder here—but it should now. Historically Prince George's was tobacco country, rural and heavily settled, with blacks and Catholics and big property-owners who pretty much ran things. Today Prince George's is—or should be known as—the home of America's largest black middle class, a place that gives a hopeful glimpse of the future. Prince George's is affluent by national standards, with one of the highest percentages of women in the work force in the nation (over 70%); if it has not had as much office and shopping mall growth as northern Virginia or next-door Montgomery County, it has proved itself a far more commercially vibrant and culturally constructive community than adjacent parts of the District of Columbia. Prince George's has always had many black residents, since the first tobacco crop was planted, but that population grew as middle-class blacks moved out of Washington into modest suburbs at the county's edge and affluent subdivisions far to the east. The black percentage here increased from 14% in 1970 to 37% in 1980, and reached 50% by the early 1990s.

The 4th Congressional District of Maryland includes most of Prince George's County and a portion of Montgomery County to the west; it is mostly, but not entirely, inside the Capital Beltway. The biggest industry here is still government: In 1990, 21.5% of its workers were employed by the federal government, the highest percentage of any congressional district in the nation. The district is 58% black and also 6% Hispanic; it is overwhelmingly Democratic.

The congressman from the 4th District is Albert Wynn, a Democrat effectively chosen in the 1992 primary. Wynn grew up in Prince George's County, attending all-black schools there until integration began in his sophomore year. He went to the University of Pittsburgh on a debate team scholarship and received a law degree from Georgetown University. He served a decade in the Maryland legislature, first as a member of the House and later the Senate, where he was deputy majority whip. Twenty candidates—13 Democrats and seven Republicans—ran for the seat when it was created in 1992; the two best known were Wynn and Prince George's State's Attorney Alex Williams. But Wynn was better funded, and his "put America first" platform, emphasizing domestic issues and attacks on George Bush, overshadowed Williams's proclamation that he would be "a strong, independent voice for Congress." Wynn spent much effort in Montgomery County, while Williams seemed to be targeting primarily Prince George's blacks. Wynn was endorsed by the *Prince George's Journal* and *The Washington Post* and won the primary with 28% of the vote; Williams had 26%, Montgomery Delegate Dana Dembrow 15%, almost all from Montgomery; and Prince George's Councilwoman Hilda Pemberton 13%. Wynn won the general election with 75%.

"I consider myself a team player," Wynn has said, a loyal member of the Democratic Caucus who campaigned heartily for Bill Clinton and Governor Parris Glendening when they were beleaguered, and for a time at odds, in fall 1998. One of his causes has been racial discrimination in the federal government. Since 1993 he has alleged bias at the National Institutes of Health, and by 1998 was also focusing on the Library of Congress and the Voice of America. He worked on a subcommittee with Republican John Mica to streamline the Equal Employment Opportunity complaint process and reduce the backlog of EEO cases. He has pushed for more federal contracting with small businesses, raising the goal from 20% to 23% and trying to restrict bundling (contract consolidation), which he says put contracts beyond the reach of small businesses; he received the SBA's first "Administrator's Leadership Award" in 1998. In 1997 he tried unsuccessfully to get the federal government to allow Maryland HMOs to offer cheap bare-bones policies, to avoid the expensive benefits mandated by Maryland law.

Wynn prides himself on being a loyal Democrat, and in the 105th Congress served as a party whip. He lost the race for caucus vice chairman in November 1998 but continues to serve as a deputy whip and represents the Congressional Black Caucus in the Democratic Leadership Council. At home Wynn sponsors an annual jobs fair, bringing together 9,000 jobseekers and over 200 employers. He has won re-election without significant opposition. In October 1996 the Republican nominee, John Kimble, offered to pose naked for *Playgirl* magazine, saying "I'll do whatever it takes to win the election." Wynn won with 85%. In 1998 Kimble rescinded the offer, saying he had gained 40 pounds. Wynn won again, with 86%.

Cook's Call. *Safe.* Don't look for a competitive general election in this overwhelmingly Democratic district. Wynn has one of the safest Democratic seats in the country.

The People: Pop. 1990: 597,791; 0.6% rural; 7.7% age 65 + ; 33.5% White, 58.4% Black, 4.5% Asian, 0.4% Amer. Indian, 3.2% Other; 6.2% Hispanic Origin. Households: 46.1% married couple families; 24.6% married couple fams. w. children; 55.5% college educ.; median household income: $41,081; per capita income: $17,251; median house value: $124,000; median gross rent: $610.

1996 Presidential Vote

Clinton (D) 152,396 (81%)
Dole (R) 30,071 (16%)
Perot (I) 5,591 (3%)

1992 Presidential Vote

Clinton (D) 149,262 (74%)
Bush (R) 37,716 (19%)
Perot (I) 14,160 (7%)

Rep. Albert Wynn (D)

Elected 1992; b. Sept. 10, 1951, Philadelphia, PA; home, Largo; U. of Pittsburgh, B.S. 1973, Howard U., 1973–74, Georgetown U. Law Schl., J.D. 1977; Baptist; separated.

Elected Office: MD House of Delegates, 1982–87; MD Senate 1987–92.

Professional Career: Exec. Dir., Prince Georges Cnty. Consumer Protection Comm., 1977–81; Chmn., Metro Wash. Cncl. of Consumer Agencies, 1980–81; Practicing atty., 1981–92.

DC Office: 407 CHOB 20515, 202-225-8699; Fax: 202-225-8714; Web site: www.house.gov/wynn.

District Offices: Landover, 301-773-4094; Oxon Hill, 301-839-5570; Silver Spring, 301-588-7328.

Committees: *Commerce* (17th of 24 D): Energy & Power; Telecommunications, Trade & Consumer Protection.

Group Ratings

	ADA	ACLU	AFS	LCV	CON	NTU	NFIB	COC	ACU	NTLC	CHC
1998	100	75	100	100	41	13	29	33	4	8	0
1997	90	—	88	—	56	21	—	40	4	—	—

National Journal Ratings

	1997 LIB	—	1997 CONS	1998 LIB	—	1998 CONS
Economic	85%	—	10%	72%	—	23%
Social	73%	—	24%	79%	—	20%
Foreign	69%	—	28%	84%	—	11%

Key Votes of the 105th Congress

1. Clinton Budget Deal	N	5. Puerto Rico Sthood. Ref.	Y	9. Cut $ for B-2 Bombers	Y
2. Education IRAs	N	6. End Highway Set-asides	N	10. Human Rights in China	Y
3. Req. 2/3 to Raise Taxes	N	7. School Prayer Amend.	N	11. Withdraw Bosnia Troops	N
4. Fast-track Trade	N	8. Ovrd. Part. Birth Veto	N	12. End Cuban TV-Marti	Y

Election Results

1998 general	Albert Wynn (D)	129,139	(86%)	($529,177)
	John B. Kimble (R)	21,518	(14%)	
1998 primary	Albert Wynn (D)	46,867	(87%)	
	E. Richard Rosenthal (D)	4,812	(9%)	
	Krisnan Persaud (D)	2,394	(4%)	
1996 general	Albert Wynn (D)	142,094	(85%)	($343,875)
	John B. Kimble (R)	24,700	(15%)	

FIFTH DISTRICT

Southern Maryland was first settled by Catholics, the Calvert family of the Lords Baltimore, who founded their capital of St. Marys in 1634, not long after Jamestown and Plymouth Rock. Maryland became one of the two great tobacco colonies, and plantation houses were built on every inlet off the broad Potomac and Patuxent Rivers, with docks where ships tied up straight from London. For years, none of these towns grew much, and even today many people here are directly descended from the old families. The biggest growth came from government installations like the Civil War Point Lookout prisoner-of-war camp and the Patuxent River Naval Complex, where many astronauts got their first training. This was never puritanical country: Liquor flowed even during Prohibition and slot machines were specifically allowed by Maryland law until the 1940s.

The 5th Congressional District includes the three counties of southern Maryland, now attracting people who grew up in metro Washington and Baltimore, plus large slices of suburban Prince George's and Anne Arundel counties between Washington and Annapolis. Its lines were drawn to make the adjacent 4th District in Prince George's majority-black, though with blacks moving outward in Prince George's and southern Maryland's historic black population, the 5th was 19% black in 1990. Many of its people live north of Washington, in College Park, home of the University of Maryland, and in Hyattsville, Greenbelt, Beltsville and Laurel. The 5th also includes southern Prince George's, from Clinton south, and the suburbs of Bowie, Crofton and Davidsonville just west of Annapolis. Historically, this is a Democratic area. Nearly half the votes are cast in Prince George's, which is heavily Democratic; another 40% in southern Maryland, historically Democratic but culturally conservative; another 16% in Anne Arundel, whose new communities lean Republican.

The congressman from the 5th District is Steny Hoyer, a veteran Democrat and one of his party's leaders in the House, who in 1981 won a seat with a large black percentage based in Prince George's and then relocated following redistricting to this south Maryland seat. Hoyer was elected to the Maryland Senate in 1966, at 27, just after graduating from law school. He was Senate president from 1975–78; he made a misstep running for lieutenant governor on a losing ticket in 1978. But when the 5th District, then entirely in Prince George's, was declared vacant in 1981—after Representative Gladys Spellman went into an irreversible coma—Hoyer won the special election by edging out Spellman's husband and several other Democrats in the primary and beating a well-financed, competent Republican candidate in the general.

Interestingly, Hoyer is of Danish descent, like the original Prince George. He has fine political instincts, works hard and can speak in an old-fashioned patriotic style that is genuinely moving. A fast riser in Maryland politics, he was also a fast riser in Congress. He excelled at constituency service and won a seat on the Appropriations Committee, where he became a key player not only for Prince George's County but for Maryland and the overall D.C. metropolitan area. When Democrats had control, Hoyer chaired the Treasury, Postal Service and General Government Appropriations Subcommittee, which oversees several major components of the federal work force—17% of 5th District workers are federal employees—and the White House budget. He used the panel to prohibit changes in federal workers' health plans, to get $6 million for flexiplace telecommuting centers, to encourage buyouts when payrolls are reduced, to guarantee pay comparable to the private sector, and to kill a Republican proposal to require federal employees to pay fair market value for parking. He has pushed for the completion of Washington's Metro subway system, to maintain 3,300 civil service and 8,000 contract personnel jobs at the Goddard Space Flight Center, to fund Chesapeake Bay cleanup, to require the District of Columbia to spend more on the Blue Plains wastewater treatment plant, and to fund ship self-defense work at St. Inigoes. Hoyer has worked hard to maintain local military bases through the base-closing procedure: He boasts of keeping 5,000 jobs at the Patuxent River Naval Air Station and adding 5,000 more ("If you're not growing, you're going"), saving 3,000 jobs at the Naval Surface Warfare Center at Indian Head, and 200 federal and 1,400 private jobs at

St. Inigoes. He is active on many local issues, getting $10 million for Pfiesteria research in 1997, starting the Chesapeake Bay Oyster Recovery Project, adding acreage to the Patuxent wildlife reserve, and funding Baltimore harbor dredging.

Hoyer's voting record is fairly liberal, though less so than when he represented a near-black-majority district in the late 1980s. He broke with party lines by supporting the balanced budget amendment in 1995, but worked hard in 1996 to support Democratic stands on the minimum wage and health insurance portability; he backed NAFTA, GATT and fast track. He was the chief House sponsor of the Americans with Disabilities Act of 1990 and of the Deadbeat Parents Punishment Act of 1998. He was a sponsor of the "three-strikes-you're-out" provision of the 1994 crime bill. Opposed to the partial-birth abortion ban, he favors Tom Daschle's ban on late-term abortions except in cases of "serious adverse health consequences." Hoyer is capable of asserting principle as well as playing team ball: He was one of four members to vote against IRS reform in 1997, fearing the consequences of shifting the burden of proof from taxpayer to government.

In 1989 Hoyer was elected chairman of the Democratic Caucus, a term-limited position. But when he tried to move up again in June 1991, he was beaten for majority whip by David Bonior, who had the support of liberals and committee chairmen, 160–109. Now Hoyer is chairman of the Democratic Steering Committee. If Democrats regain a majority, Hoyer might be a strong candidate for majority whip or even majority leader.

Before the 1992 redistricting, Hoyer's main contest was in the Democratic primary; now it comes at the general election. In 1992 he had a serious challenge from Lawrence Hogan Jr., whose father was a Prince George's congressman from 1968–74. Hogan won 50%–45% in the half of the district outside Prince George's, but Hoyer's 60%–38% margin in Prince George's gave him a 53%–44% win, as Bill Clinton was carrying the district 45%–39%, and Hoyer was spending $1.6 million. He spent $1.3 million in 1994 to defeat Donald Devine, director of the Office of Personnel Management in the first Reagan term, 59%–41%. Against less well-funded opponents, he won with 57% in 1996 and 65% in 1998. In the latter year he won 72% of the vote in Prince George's, 63% in southern Maryland and 51% in Anne Arundel County.

Cook's Call. *Safe.* After a close call in 1992, Hoyer has had little trouble winning re-election. And, with Democrats controlling the redistricting process in Maryland, Hoyer could benefit from a plan that adds more Democratic areas to his district. Consider Hoyer safe for 2000.

The People: Pop. 1990: 597,573; 30% rural; 8% age 65 + ; 77.3% White, 18.5% Black, 3% Asian, 0.5% Amer. Indian, 0.8% Other; 2.3% Hispanic Origin. Households: 60.6% married couple families; 31.5% married couple fams. w. children; 52.5% college educ.; median household income: $46,936; per capita income: $18,178; median house value: $132,100; median gross rent: $620.

1996 Presidential Vote		1992 Presidential Vote	
Clinton (D)	117,345 (51%)	Clinton (D)	107,618 (45%)
Dole (R)	95,737 (42%)	Bush (R)	95,356 (39%)
Perot (I)	14,546 (6%)	Perot (I)	37,441 (15%)

Rep. Steny H. Hoyer (D)

Elected May 1981; b. June 14, 1939, New York, NY; home, Mitchellville; U. of MD, B.S. 1963, Georgetown U., J.D. 1966; Baptist; widowed.

Elected Office: MD Senate, 1966–78, Pres., 1975–78.

Professional Career: Practicing atty., 1966–80; MD Bd. of Higher Educ., 1978–81.

DC Office: 1705 LHOB 20515, 202-225-4131; Fax: 202-225-4300; Web site: www.house.gov/hoyer.

District Offices: Greenbelt, 301-474-0119; Waldorf, 301-843-1577.

Committees: *Appropriations* (6th of 27 D): Labor, HHS & Education; The Legislative Branch; Treasury, Postal Service & General Government (RMM). *House Administration* (RMM of 3 D). *Joint Committee on Printing* (4th of 5 Reps.). *Joint Committee on the Library of Congress* (4th of 6 Reps.).

Group Ratings

	ADA	ACLU	AFS	LCV	CON	NTU	NFIB	COC	ACU	NTLC	CHC
1998	95	81	100	100	89	22	14	28	4	16	0
1997	85	—	88	—	49	23	—	40	12	—	—

National Journal Ratings

	1997 LIB — 1997 CONS	1998 LIB — 1998 CONS
Economic	73% — 26%	72% — 23%
Social	79% — 21%	76% — 23%
Foreign	64% — 33%	84% — 11%

Key Votes of the 105th Congress

1. Clinton Budget Deal	N	5. Puerto Rico Sthood. Ref.	Y	9. Cut $ for B-2 Bombers	N
2. Education IRAs	N	6. End Highway Set-asides	N	10. Human Rights in China	Y
3. Req. 2/3 to Raise Taxes	N	7. School Prayer Amend.	N	11. Withdraw Bosnia Troops	N
4. Fast-track Trade	N	8. Ovrd. Part. Birth Veto	N	12. End Cuban TV-Marti	Y

Election Results

1998 general	Steny H. Hoyer (D)	126,792	(65%)	($916,632)
	Robert B. Ostrom (R)	67,176	(35%)	($235,004)
1998 primary	Steny H. Hoyer (D)	40,485	(86%)	
	Orville Arnett (D)	6,625	(14%)	
1996 general	Steny H. Hoyer (D)	121,288	(57%)	($1,155,840)
	John S. Morgan (R)	91,806	(43%)	($236,483)

SIXTH DISTRICT

America's first frontier was in western Maryland, where the long green sloping fields are cut through by the Appalachian ridges that cross the state diagonally from northeast to southwest. These wheat fields were settled first by Pennsylvania Dutch and Scots-Irish hill people, not Chesapeake Bay tobacco growers. Maryland is where the fall line comes closest to an ocean port, where the 19th Century's great paths to the interior were staked out: the National Road, and then the nation's first railroad, the Baltimore & Ohio, crossed the wide valleys of bounteous farms and climbed over the Catoctin Mountains. Towns grew up on narrow streets lined with rowhouses that today are overhung with telephone and streetcar wires, overlooking long vistas of cornfields, pasturelands and mountains of ancient stone rising above the plains. Across this placid land moved vast armies during the Civil War. In Frederick, city officials paid Confederates $200,000 not to burn down the town, and near Sharpsburg, blue- and gray-clad soldiers fought the Battle of Antietam, on the bloodiest day in American military history. Today, there is a new rush of settlement in Carroll and Howard Counties, long parts of metro Baltimore, and Frederick County, which grew 31% in the 1980s and is now classified as part of metro Washington; growth remains slow west of the Catoctins.

The 6th Congressional District of Maryland includes all of western Maryland, to mountainous Cumberland and Garrett counties, and runs east to Carroll County northwest of Baltimore and the old town of Ellicott City in Howard County. The political tradition in most of this area, unlike the rest of Maryland, is Republican: This was Union country in the Civil War and has been mostly Republican ever since. The new rush of settlement seems to come from those seeking respite from metropolitan crime, strengthening the area's already conservative leanings. The 6th voted for Republican Ellen Sauerbrey in 1994 and 1998 and for Bob Dole in 1996.

The congressman from the 6th District is a Republican who matches its current mood, Roscoe Bartlett. "I represent my district well. I essentially never have to vote to violate my conscience," he says. He is an interesting character, a descendant of a signer of the Declaration of Independence and a Seventh Day Adventist with 10 children; he grew up in poverty in Pennsylvania, but his family would not take welfare. He invented life-support equipment for pilots, astronauts and fire fighters, ran his own business and taught at Frederick Community College. When Bartlett first ran for Congress in 1992, he was a 65-year-old retired University of Maryland physiology professor who seemed to have no chance of winning. Democrat Beverly Byron had represented the district for 14 years, had a conservative voting record, and chaired a subcommittee on National Security. But Byron was upset in the primary by Delegate Thomas Hattery, 56%–44%, who called for national health insurance and was pro-choice. Bartlett won his primary by only 42%–41%. But his conservative views, campaign help from Oliver North and Tom Clancy, and his attacks on Hattery for legislative perks won him a 54%–46% victory.

Bartlett has proved a surprisingly durable politician. He has as conservative a voting record as any House member and was the only Marylander to vote for all 10 provisions of the Contract With America. Camp David is in the 6th District, and in May 1994 it was Bartlett who drew attention to a local newspaper photograph showing Clinton aide David Watkins boarding a helicopter at a Frederick County golf course: "The photo of two Marine guards saluting a golf bag as it was carried up the helicopter stairs is truly a picture that is worth a thousand words," Bartlett said. He carries a copy of the Constitution and consults it frequently; he voted against fast track in 1997 because he believes Congress can't give away the power of regulating trade. He switched to vote against MFN for China in 1997 because of its threatening military actions and human rights violations. He voted no on the monstrous October 1998 budget bill.

Bartlett's Military Honor and Decency Act bans the sale or rental of sexually explicit material in military facilities; *Penthouse* sued, but the law was upheld by the courts. Another Bartlett measure banned after-hours visits by military men or women to the other sex's barracks. He was less successful in pushing the recommendation of a commission headed by former Senator Nancy Kassebaum-Baker that men and women should be separated for basic training; he could not even get a roll call on this politically incorrect proposal. Bartlett has another perhaps quixotic cause: He believes the $14 billion the U.S. has spent on peacekeeping exercises should be credited toward our unpaid United Nations dues; since those are only $1.3 billion, he would have Congress say we owe no money at all. Possibly inconsistent with his principles, Bartlett approved of the government paying for 30% of winter feed for western Maryland farmers with 35% crop loss due to drought; but he says they should buy crop insurance.

Bartlett has been re-elected by solid margins. In 1996 he was opposed by a Democrat who outspent him significantly and conducted "smear polls" saying he was part of a "secret militia group." Bartlett bragged he had voted to repeal the assault weapons ban and charged the

Democrat with taking $40,000 from labor groups linked to organized crime. Bartlett won with 57% that year, and with 63% in 1998.

Cook's Call. *Safe.* This western Maryland district is the most Republican in the state. Even though this once rural district is experiencing a tremendous amount of suburban growth—especially along the I-270 corridor—that could impact its politics, Bartlett is quite safe for now.

The People: Pop. 1990: 597,660; 47% rural; 11.9% age 65 +; 94% White, 4.5% Black, 1.2% Asian, 0.2% Amer. Indian, 0.2% Other; 0.8% Hispanic Origin. Households: 63.9% married couple families; 31.7% married couple fams. w. children; 43.8% college educ.; median household income: $36,883; per capita income: $15,979; median house value: $113,700; median gross rent: $369.

1996 Presidential Vote				1992 Presidential Vote			
Dole (R)		130,321	(52%)	Bush (R)		125,494	(48%)
Clinton (D)		96,185	(38%)	Clinton (D)		88,196	(34%)
Perot (I)		21,205	(8%)	Perot (I)		46,376	(18%)

Rep. Roscoe G. Bartlett (R)

Elected 1992; b. June 3, 1926, Moreland, KY; home, Frederick; Columbia Union Col., B.A. 1947, U. of MD, M.S. 1949, Ph.D. 1952; Seventh Day Adventist; married (Ellen).

Professional Career: Farmer; Prof., U. of MD, 1948–52; Asst. Prof., Loma Linda Schl. of Medicine, 1952–54; Asst. Prof., Howard U. Medical Schl., 1954–56; Research scientist, N.I.H., 1956–58; Research scientist, U.S. Naval Aerospace Medical Inst., 1958–62; Research scientist, Johns Hopkins U., 1962–67; Research Mgr., IBM, 1967–74; Pres., Roscoe Bartlett & Assoc., 1974–86.

DC Office: 2412 RHOB 20515, 202-225-2721; Fax: 202-225-2193; Web site: www.house.gov/bartlett.

District Offices: Frederick, 301-694-3030; Frostburg, 301-689-0034; Hagerstown, 301-797-6043; Westminster, 410-857-1115.

Committees: *Armed Services* (15th of 32 R): Military Personnel; Military Research & Development; Special Oversight Panel on Morale, Welfare and Recreation. *Science* (10th of 25 R): Space & Aeronautics; Technology. *Small Business* (5th of 19 R): Government Programs & Oversight (Chmn.).

Group Ratings

	ADA	ACLU	AFS	LCV	CON	NTU	NFIB	COC	ACU	NTLC	CHC
1998	5	6	11	0	77	66	100	78	100	97	100
1997	5	—	13	—	49	64	—	90	100	—	—

National Journal Ratings

	1997 LIB — 1997 CONS			1998 LIB — 1998 CONS		
Economic	10%	—	86%	12%	—	85%
Social	20%	—	71%	26%	—	72%
Foreign	12%	—	81%	0%	—	93%

Key Votes of the 105th Congress

1. Clinton Budget Deal	Y	5. Puerto Rico Sthood. Ref.	N	9. Cut $ for B-2 Bombers	N
2. Education IRAs	Y	6. End Highway Set-asides	Y	10. Human Rights in China	N
3. Req. 2/3 to Raise Taxes	Y	7. School Prayer Amend.	Y	11. Withdraw Bosnia Troops	Y
4. Fast-track Trade	N	8. Ovrd. Part. Birth Veto	Y	12. End Cuban TV-Marti	N

Election Results

1998 general	Roscoe G. Bartlett (R)	127,802	(63%)	($300,077)
	Timothy D. McCown (D)	73,728	(37%)	($3,427)
1998 primary	Roscoe G. Bartlett (R)	unopposed		
1996 general	Roscoe G. Bartlett (R)	132,853	(57%)	($253,966)
	Stephen Crawford (D)	100,910	(43%)	($383,127)

SEVENTH DISTRICT

At the junction of North and South, terminus of America's first railroad and the East Coast port closest to the great West, Baltimore is one of the few American cities to have had large numbers of both blacks and European immigrants throughout its history. Its black community has a notable history: The *Afro-American* newspaper has been published here for more than 100 years, there was once a black symphony orchestra, and the city's black neighborhood west of downtown had a vital shopping district before World War II. Eubie Blake, the famous black musician and one of the founders of ragtime music, grew up here and now has a museum to honor him on Charles Street. Near downtown on the west side is the childhood home of Babe Ruth and the home of H.L. Mencken, two great white westside Baltimoreans. For years this side of town had a biracial, bipartisan politics in which Democrats like Governor Albert Ritchie and Republicans like Mayor and Governor Theodore McKeldin competed zestfully for black and white votes.

Baltimore has been a black-majority city since the late 1970s, and most of its westside neighborhoods are heavily black. Black Republicanism has long since died out, and William Donald Schaefer, who carried west Baltimore for mayor as late as 1983, was elected governor in 1986. Black Democrats are the key politicians here, notably Mayor Kurt Schmoke, first elected in 1987. Schmoke's abilities—he is a Rhodes Scholar—and good intentions sparked hopes he could help Baltimore lessen the pathologies of violent crime, single parenthood and labor force non-participation that plague cities elsewhere. But results are at best mixed. Crime is still high, though it has been reduced in other cities, and while public housing towers have been pulled down, housing values in rowhouse neighborhoods are still dismally low. But it is not clear what effect these had on behaviors, nor is it clear whether Schmoke's recent efforts to improve public schools have had results.

Maryland's 7th Congressional District includes almost all of Baltimore City's black neighborhoods and extends into the heavily black suburbs running west from the city, Catonsville along the old Baltimore National Pike and Randallstown out Liberty Heights Avenue: 79% of the people and 69% of the votes are in the city. From 1987 to February 1996 the congressman here was Kweisi Mfume, former councilman and radio talk show host, who won the seat in 1986, became chairman of the Congressional Black Caucus in 1992, then resigned in February 1996 to become president of the troubled NAACP. The current congressman is Elijah Cummings, who was effectively chosen in a March 1996 primary.

Cummings grew up in Baltimore, graduated from Howard University and the University of Maryland Law School, practiced law in Baltimore, and in 1982, at 31, was elected to the Maryland House of Delegates. Two years later he was chairman of the Legislative Caucus, the youngest in its history, and he became known as a consensus builder and effective speaker. He chaired the governor's Commission on Black Males and founded the Maryland Bootcamp Aftercare program to address the self-sufficiency of former youth offenders. Cummings was one of 27 Democrats to jump into the race to succeed Mfume; there were five Republicans as well—probably one of the largest congressional fields in history—but only two or three turned out to have much backing. Cummings's main competition came from the Reverend Frank Reid III, step-brother of Mayor Schmoke, who raised $255,000; Reid won 24% of the vote. Cummings had support from community development organizations and from businessmen, lobbyists and state House Speaker Casper Taylor. He raised $450,000 and won 37% of the vote. His victories in the April special and November general elections were anticlimactic.

Cummings still lives in west Baltimore, where in a two-year period he was robbed at shotgun point, had his home burglarized four times and his car broken into seven times. As a witness to the effects of crime and drugs—he says he attends about 50 funerals a year for youths murdered or killed by overdoses—he favors strict gun control and has introduced a bill to establish a Commission on National Drug Policy. His voting record is very liberal; he was the only Marylander to oppose the 1996 Welfare Reform Act. He filed a bill to impose economic sanctions on countries that invoke diplomatic immunity to protect those who harm American citizens; this came after a tragic traffic accident in Washington, DC, when a teenager was killed by a drunk Georgian diplomat.

Surprised at the degree of partisanship in the House, Cummings has gotten into committee work. He lost a seat on the Government Reform subcommittee he wanted to Vermont Socialist Bernard Sanders, after a protest, but party leaders gave him two other subcommittee spots, covering civil service and national security. He also has a seat on Transportation and Infrastructure, where he supported Chairman Bud Shuster's big spending bill and got three highway projects worth $40 million.

Cummings has a safe seat and can only be threatened in the primary.

Cook's Call. *Safe.* Taking in inner-city Baltimore and western Baltimore County, the 7th is a solid Democratic seat. Cummings will have no problem winning here in 2000.

The People: Pop. 1990: 597,701; 0.8% rural; 12.7% age 65 +; 27.2% White, 71% Black, 1.3% Asian, 0.3% Amer. Indian, 0.2% Other; 0.8% Hispanic Origin. Households: 33.5% married couple families; 15.4% married couple fams. w. children; 36.6% college educ.; median household income: $25,684; per capita income: $11,718; median house value: $60,100; median gross rent: $329.

1996 Presidential Vote

Clinton (D)	127,850	(81%)
Dole (R)	23,757	(15%)
Perot (I)	5,207	(3%)

1992 Presidential Vote

Clinton (D)	159,191	(77%)
Bush (R)	32,431	(16%)
Perot (I)	13,009	(6%)

Rep. Elijah Cummings (D)

Elected April 1996; b. Jan. 18, 1951, Baltimore; home, Baltimore; Howard U., B.S. 1973, U. of MD, J.D. 1976; Baptist; separated.

Elected Office: MD House of Delegates, 1982–96, Speaker Pro-Tem, 1995–96.

Professional Career: Practicing atty., 1976–96.

DC Office: 1632 LHOB 20515, 202-225-4741; Fax: 202-225-3178; Web site: www.house.gov/cummings.

District Offices: Baltimore, 410-496-2010; Catonsville, 410-719-8777.

Committees: *Government Reform* (11th of 19 D): Civil Service (RMM); Criminal Justice, Drug Policy & Human Resources. *Transportation & Infrastructure* (21st of 34 D): Aviation; Ground Transportation.

Group Ratings

	ADA	ACLU	AFS	LCV	CON	NTU	NFIB	COC	ACU	NTLC	CHC
1998	100	88	100	100	55	14	14	28	4	3	0
1997	100	—	88	—	53	29	—	30	4	—	—

National Journal Ratings

	1997 LIB	—	1997 CONS	1998 LIB	—	1998 CONS
Economic	75%	—	22%	79%	—	0%
Social	85%	—	0%	73%	—	25%
Foreign	97%	—	0%	90%	—	5%

Key Votes of the 105th Congress

1. Clinton Budget Deal	N	5. Puerto Rico Sthood. Ref.	Y	9. Cut $ for B-2 Bombers	Y
2. Education IRAs	N	6. End Highway Set-asides	N	10. Human Rights in China	Y
3. Req. 2/3 to Raise Taxes	N	7. School Prayer Amend.	N	11. Withdraw Bosnia Troops	N
4. Fast-track Trade	N	8. Ovrd. Part. Birth Veto	N	12. End Cuban TV-Marti	Y

Election Results

1998 general	Elijah Cummings (D)	112,699	(86%)	($339,883)
	Kenneth Kondner (R)	18,742	(14%)	
1998 primary	Elijah Cummings (D)	47,293	(91%)	
	Joseph E. Ward (D)	4,433	(9%)	
1996 general	Elijah Cummings (D)	115,764	(83%)	($248,070)
	Kenneth Kondner (R)	22,929	(17%)	

EIGHTH DISTRICT

Along an old road, down which colonial farmers rolled barrels of tobacco to the port of Georgetown 200 years ago, has grown one of America's most affluent and best-educated communities. The old road, now called Wisconsin Avenue and Rockville Pike, is the commercial spine of Montgomery County. And this suburban jurisdiction just northwest of Washington, D.C., has for several decades ranked at or near the top of the list of counties in income and education. Today's Montgomery County is in large part a creation of the federal government, which has put huge facilities there—Bethesda Naval Hospital, the National Institutes of Health, the Food and Drug Administration, the National Institute of Standards and Technology—to make it the center of America's fast-growing health research industry. But the percentage of workers employed by the government has been declining markedly, to about one in six in the mid-1990s—a figure only a percentage point or two above the national average. In the late 1970s and early 1980s, Montgomery seemed to have reached a critical mass and started generating thousands of private sector health, high-tech, defense and service-industry jobs.

Wisconsin Avenue and Rockville Pike have become strip highways, with 1950s commercial development and 1960s shopping centers like so many in the country. But the stores are upscale, some *very* upscale, and the new skyscrapers of downtown Bethesda and the office parks-cum-fitness centers of farther-out Gaithersburg are genuinely impressive. Not all of Montgomery County is exclusively high-income: There are some modest neighborhoods in Silver Spring and Wheaton. The 1980s saw a significant increase in foreign migration here, with the Asian population up 172% in the 1980s. Historically, the typical Montgomery County voter was a high-ranking civil servant, but as private employment outpaces government work, the picture has changed. The fastest-growing parts of the county, out past Rockville in Gaithersburg and Germantown, are filling up with Republicans and conservatives as much as Democrats and liberals.

The congresswoman from the 8th District is Connie Morella, a Republican first elected in 1986 when incumbent Democrat Michael Barnes ran for the Senate. Morella grew up in Massachusetts and taught school in Montgomery County in the 1950s. She raised nine children, six of them her late sister's, and at the same time earned a master's degree and taught English at American University and Montgomery College. In 1978, she was elected to the Maryland House of Delegates; after two four-year terms, she ran for Congress, and won with 53% against nursing home millionaire Stewart Bainum, who spent $1.5 million of his own money. She is

762   MARYLAND

hard-working, cooperative with colleagues, congenial with constituents, energetic enough to tend to 600,000 constituents who are a local phone call and a few miles away.

Morella is by any measure the most liberal Republican in the House. She voted against seven of 10 items in the Contract With America in 1995 and in 1998 was more liberal on cultural and foreign issues than the average Democrat. On abortion rights, gun control, campaign finance reform, Legal Services, and the environment, she has voted against most Republicans and with most Democrats. She was one of two Republicans to vote to open the government in January 1996. On economics she votes near the midpoint of the House. She chairs the Science subcommittee on technology and claims credit for funding of two new NIST labs and increases in NIH funding, which has thrived under Republicans. On the Government Reform Committee she looks out for federal workers. In the 105th Congress she passed laws on violence against women, pushed the government to pay child-care costs for low-income federal employees, and set up a commission to review roadblocks to women and minorities in the sciences.

But her party loyalty often has come under attack, and for 1998 that brought serious competition from Democrat Ralph Neas, an aide to Republican Senators Edward Brooke and David Durenberger, and head of the Leadership Conference on Civil Rights from 1981 to 1995. Neas switched to become a Democrat in 1996, and his legislative work and his valiant recovery from Guillain-Barre syndrome (he was paralyzed for three months in 1981) won him many friends in Washington and he was able to raise almost as much money as Morella. He criticized her for voting against the 1993 Clinton budget and tax increase and for voting "present" rather than opposing Newt Gingrich for speaker in January 1997. He charged that she voted much more often with the Republican leadership after the 1994 election than before. He questioned her for voting on the Government Reform Committee to hold Attorney General Janet Reno in contempt in August 1998 (Morella said it was "the only legal remedy") and for voting for the Republicans' impeachment inquiry resolution in October 1998. Morella, who had always been aggressive in investigating charges of sexual harassment, could claim consistency and attention to possible wrongdoing.

Morella's refusal to discount charges against Clinton carried some risk in a district he carried 57%–38% in 1996. Indeed her percentage fell from 70% in 1994 to 61% in 1996. If her standing was worse with the NAACP and the Children's Defense Fund, and if the Montgomery Education Association failed to endorse her, she was still strongly endorsed by the Sierra Club, Handgun Control, Inc., and the *Washington Post*. Morella was re-elected by a solid 60%–40%. That is a sign that her hard work and effervescence is widely appreciated—but not a guarantee that she will not have serious opposition again. In early 1999, she was mentioned as a possible challenger to Senator Paul Sarbanes.

Cook's Call. *Probably Safe.* Although this district has strong Democratic underpinnings, Democrats have not had much luck trying to oust Morella. If she takes on Democratic Senator Paul Sarbanes in 2000, this seat will most likely fall into Democratic hands. If, however, Morella decides to remain in the House, she may face a challenge by her 1998 opponent. But Morella has proven time and again that she is a good fit for this suburban district, and she will be tough to defeat.

The People: Pop. 1990: 597,760; 5.7% rural; 10.8% age 65+; 81.6% White, 8.2% Black, 8% Asian, 0.2% Amer. Indian, 1.9% Other; 6.1% Hispanic Origin. Households: 60.5% married couple families; 29.8% married couple fams. w. children; 74.7% college educ.; median household income: $56,789; per capita income: $26,900; median house value: $207,200; median gross rent: $721.

1996 Presidential Vote

Clinton (D) 156,450 (57%)
Dole (R) 103,327 (38%)
Perot (I) 12,200   (4%)

1992 Presidential Vote

Clinton (D) 156,043 (53%)
Bush (R) 103,477 (35%)
Perot (I) 35,599   (12%)

Rep. Constance A. Morella (R)

Elected 1986; b. Feb. 12, 1931, Somerville, MA; home, Bethesda; Boston U., A.B. 1954, American U., M.A. 1967; Catholic; married (Anthony).

Elected Office: MD House of Delegates, 1978–86.

Professional Career: Teacher, Montgomery Cnty. Pub. Schls., 1956–60; Instructor, American U., 1968–70; Prof., Montgomery Col., 1970–86.

DC Office: 2228 RHOB 20515, 202-225-5341; Fax: 202-225-1389; Web site: www.house.gov/morella.

District Office: Rockville, 301-424-3501.

Committees: *Government Reform* (3d of 24 R): Civil Service; District of Columbia (Vice Chmn.). *Science* (4th of 25 R): Basic Research; Technology (Chmn.).

Group Ratings

	ADA	ACLU	AFS	LCV	CON	NTU	NFIB	COC	ACU	NTLC	CHC
1998	65	81	78	92	85	40	36	56	20	34	17
1997	65	—	38	—	98	53	—	90	20	—	—

National Journal Ratings

	1997 LIB — 1997 CONS		1998 LIB — 1998 CONS	
Economic	49%	— 50%	55%	— 45%
Social	82%	— 15%	73%	— 25%
Foreign	76%	— 22%	82%	— 18%

Key Votes of the 105th Congress

1. Clinton Budget Deal	Y	5. Puerto Rico Sthood. Ref.	Y	9. Cut $ for B-2 Bombers	Y
2. Education IRAs	N	6. End Highway Set-asides	N	10. Human Rights in China	N
3. Req. 2/3 to Raise Taxes	N	7. School Prayer Amend.	N	11. Withdraw Bosnia Troops	N
4. Fast-track Trade	Y	8. Ovrd. Part. Birth Veto	N	12. End Cuban TV-Marti	Y

Election Results

1998 general	Constance A. Morella (R)	133,145	(60%)	($884,238)
	Ralph G. Neas (D)	87,497	(40%)	($810,258)
1998 primary	Constance A. Morella (R)	20,687	(77%)	
	Luis F. Columba (R)	6,009	(23%)	
1996 general	Constance A. Morella (R)	152,538	(61%)	($559,807)
	Donald Mooers (D)	96,229	(39%)	($196,858)

MASSACHUSETTS

It would be a city on a hill, John Winthrop wrote of the Massachusetts Bay colony his Puritans were building, an example to the entire world. And Massachusetts, in the nearly four centuries since, has always assumed it has a lot to teach others. The New World Puritans' austere creed taught that only the select would be saved and that they must extirpate the forces of Satan—Indians, Papists, tolerationists. For 150 years, New England was partial to learning, but also insular, hostile to outsiders and economically stagnant. Then, after the American Revolution, the international war between royal Britain and revolutionary and Napoleonic France allowed New England ship owners to cross enemy lines to become the world's leading merchants. They made vast profits in just a few brief years and plowed the money into textile mills, then railroads, then coal mining and steel-making: This was the capital that made industrial America.

Massachusetts made a new America in other ways. Intellectually, New England flowered in the 19th Century: A few writers from Boston and Concord—Ralph Waldo Emerson, Henry Wadsworth Longfellow, Henry David Thoreau, John Greenleaf Whittier, Nathaniel Hawthorne—created an American literary genre and popularized an American philosophy, more than 200 years after Plymouth Rock. Demographically, New England Yankees surged across the continent: Long blocked from Upstate New York by mountains and the British-Iroquois alliance, they only reached Syracuse in the 1820s; by the 1850s they were in Iowa and Kansas and Oregon's Willamette Valley; by the 1880s they had settled Los Angeles. They built new cities in the wilderness. They helped start the Republican Party and did much to start—and win—the Civil War. They planted their economic system and their values, articulated in the *McGuffey Readers*, across the continent.

In the meantime, Massachusetts itself and Boston, the hub of the universe, were being remade. The potato famine of the 1840s and an economy that continued imploding for decades sent Irishmen across the Atlantic, and many came to Boston, looking for work in the mills, docks and factories. Yankee Protestants had seen Catholics as their great political and cultural enemy for 200 years and felt their commonwealth was under siege. As the Irish became a majority, first in Boston and then statewide, Protestants feared the Irish would use their political clout to ladle out government jobs and benefits to their own. And the Irish had a much better flair for politics than instinct for commerce; they yearned for the security of a government job. But they encountered such bigotry and rejection by the Yankees that even as successful an Irish Catholic as Joseph Kennedy felt obliged to move from Boston to New York in 1927. Politics in Massachusetts for years was a kind of culture war between Yankee Republicans and Irish Democrats, an argument not so much over the distribution of income or the provision of services as over whose vision of Massachusetts should be honored, and whose version of history should be taught—not unlike battles being fought between liberals and conservatives today.

Sometimes, the stakes were concrete—control of patronage jobs, command of the Boston Police Department—but more often they were symbolic. Yankee Republicans tended to back activist government programs: public works and protective tariffs to help business, the Civil War and Reconstruction to help suitably distant oppressed people like Southern blacks, uplifting (and productivity-enhancing) social movements like temperance. The Irish found 19th Century Democrats—a party promoting *laissez-faire*—more congenial. The Irish had come from a place where the government was the enemy and didn't want government spending money to help the rich or to stimulate commerce. They also didn't want government to restrict immigration, to advance blacks, who might compete with them in the labor market, or to prohibit liquor.

The Irish and Catholic populations slowly rose over the years. Yankees had smaller families, moved west, intermarried with people of immigrant stock and lost their Yankee identity. The

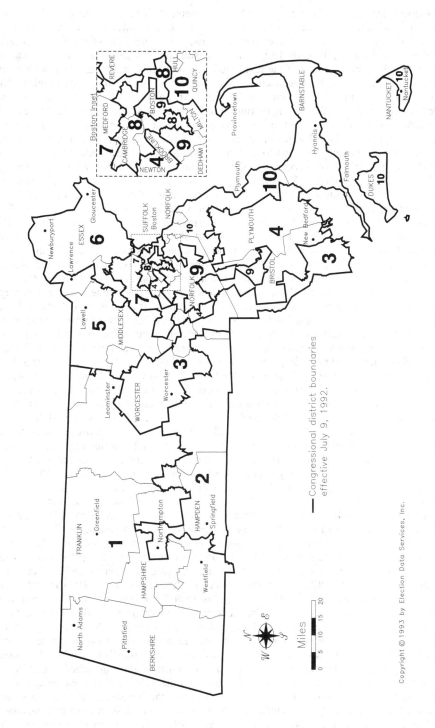

—Congressional district boundaries
effective July 9, 1992.

Copyright © 1993 by Election Data Services, Inc.

Irish mostly stayed put, raising large families, and eventually Massachusetts moved from being one of the most Republican states to one of the most Democratic. Economically, early 20th Century Massachusetts did not make much progress. The descendants of the Yankees who had been so venturesome in the early 19th Century became the most cautious investors in the early 20th, while the predominance of the textile mills in their home state meant that for a century beginning in the 1820s, Massachusetts imported low-skill labor and exported highly skilled people. As textile mills moved south in the 1920s, Massachusetts started exporting low-skill people as well; and from the waning of Yankee authority until the national rise of the Kennedys, Massachusetts seemed to run out of things to teach the rest of the nation. The state's Yankee Republicans were backward-looking, out of power in Washington, on the defensive at home, without a cause to champion. The Irish Democrats were hostile to Franklin Roosevelt's pro-British internationalism and receptive to the anti-Communism of the very Irish Joe McCarthy.

Then came the Kennedys. Rose Kennedy was born in 1890 (and died in 1995 after a remarkable life that spanned nearly half this country's history), the daughter of John "Honey Fitz" Fitzgerald, who was elected to Congress at 31 and mayor of Boston in 1906–07 and 1910–14; her husband Joseph Kennedy, first chairman of the Securities and Exchange Commission in the 1930s and ambassador to the Court of St. James from 1937–40, was perhaps the richest Catholic in the world and a shrewd and ruthless political operator. Their only residence in Massachusetts after 1927 was their summer home in Hyannis Port. Joseph Kennedy moved his oldest surviving son, John, to Massachusetts, and engineered his election to the House in 1946, the Senate in 1952 and the presidency in 1960. The Kennedys, with their elegant manners and great achievements, seemed like royalty to the Irish Catholics of Massachusetts, and John Kennedy's election in 1960 certified to U.S. Catholics, 78% of whom voted for him, that they too were Americans. Joseph and John Kennedy were, on many issues, conservative or skeptical. But Kennedy's Administration was increasingly, even before his untimely death, identified as liberal, and his example and that of his brother, Edward, elected to the U.S. Senate in 1962, moved Massachusetts Catholics to the left. At the same time, Massachusetts Protestants were influenced by the leftward direction on the state's great campuses in the 1960s. The universities also provided the basis for a surging high-tech economy, to the point that Massachusetts started importing high-skill people even as it exported those with low skills.

In the 1970s and 1980s, Massachusetts, with one interval, had the most liberal governance and national politics of any state in the country. Massachusetts was the only state to vote for George McGovern in 1972 and, although it voted twice for Ronald Reagan, the son of an Irish Catholic, its Democratic percentage in presidential contests from 1968–88 was 53%, just 0.4% behind Rhode Island and well ahead of every other state. The state's senators included Edward Kennedy, liberal Republican Edward Brooke, and Democrats Paul Tsongas and John Kerry. Liberal governors such as Republican Francis Sargent and Democrat Michael Dukakis vastly increased spending and endorsed the inexplicable policies that sunk Dukakis's 1988 presidential campaign: prisoners sentenced to life without parole being given weekend furloughs—a policy that liberals in the press said was racist to oppose, prisoners allowed to vote and be registered by state employees sent into prisons for that purpose, and government spending that rose 9% a year in the 1980s. Rebellion against this resulted in Dukakis's defeat in 1978 and the election of conservative Democrat Edward King. As historian David Hackett Fischer points out in *Albion's Seed*, the mindset of the original settlers remains strong even when the ethnic origin of current residents is far different, and the spirit of the Puritans, the faith that they had much to teach the rest of the world, is strong in Massachusetts liberals: in both the quietly smug liberalism of Michael Dukakis and the hearty and combative liberalism of Edward Kennedy.

In 1990, Massachusetts rejected these politics, with a suddenness matched in its history by its merchants' sudden emergence as world traders in the 1790s and the appearance of Irish immigrants on Boston docks in the 1840s. It was a juddering shift: just two years earlier, Dukakis was touting "the Massachusetts miracle" and leading George Bush by wide margins in the polls. But after Bush seized the lead in August 1988, Massachusetts's financial problems silently worsened as Dukakis campaigned across the country; he won just 53% of the vote in Massachusetts, running strong in the Berkshires and the Pioneer Valley in the west, but only running even in the Boston media market (which includes New Hampshire, a low-tax haven from high-tax Massachusetts since colonial times). Right after the election the state economy sagged badly: The slump in minicomputers hurt Massachusetts-based Wang and Digital; Cambridge's Lotus software was outflanked by Seattle's Microsoft; defense spending cutbacks, long sought by Massachusetts politicians, produced big job losses. More spectacular was the bursting of the Northeast real estate bubble and the resultant collapse of major New England banks. The state government essentially went bankrupt, and Dukakis retired from office.

In the decade since, Massachusetts has learned some lessons and gone some distance toward forming a new consensus. It is a combination of fiscal austerity and cultural liberalism, best personified by Republican Governor William Weld, a Republican elected in 1990, who envisioned a government that taxes and spends lightly, that is friendly to feminism and gay rights, that exerts some effort to protect the environment and that is tough on crime. This combination also produced overwhelming majorities for some Democrats. In 1992, Massachusetts, after backing native son Paul Tsongas in the Democratic primary, delivered a 48%–29% margin for Bill Clinton in November and elected veto-proof Democratic majorities in the legislature, while Democrats won the total vote cast for Congress by 57%–35%. In 1994, Edward Kennedy seemed momentarily threatened by businessman Mitt Romney. But Kennedy rallied and won by a solid 58%–41%; Weld was re-elected 71%–28%, but Democrats held all statewide offices except treasurer and led by 72%–28% in popular votes in House races.

Clinton, even in his 1994 national nadir, proved widely popular in Massachusetts. He had been careful to maintain close ties to the Kennedys, attending their commemorations and remembering his Rose Garden handshake with President Kennedy, appointing Jean Kennedy Smith ambassador to Ireland and subcontracting Northern Ireland policy to her and former Edward Kennedy aide Nancy Soderberg. Clinton evidently calculated early on that a leftish Democratic challenge in the 1996 primaries would not prosper if he could hold on to the Kennedys' support. They and other Massachusetts politicians like Barney Frank stuck with Clinton solidly in 1995 when others on the left were muttering curses and plotting mutiny. (There is a vivid contrast here with Jimmy Carter, who went out of his way to antagonize the Kennedys, and whose re-election campaign was gravely weakened by Edward Kennedy's 1980 primary challenge.) At the same time, liberal campuses continued generating talented young Democratic politicos in Massachusetts. For his part, Weld was so desultory in building a Republican Party that there were fewer Republicans in the legislature after his big win in 1994 than there had been four years before; he declined to run for president and watched wanly as the candidacy of his first choice, Pete Wilson, imploded.

By the beginning of 1996, Clinton's popularity was so high in Massachusetts that it spread throughout New England, even into usually Massachusetts-hating New Hampshire. In November 1996, Massachusetts voted 61%–28% for Clinton, his best showing in the country; in the political dialogue that goes on endlessly in the state, it was taken for granted there was nothing to say for or even about the Republicans and Bob Dole. However, the Senate contest between incumbent John Kerry and William Weld endlessly fascinated Boston writers and got probably as much coverage in the national press as all other Senate races that year combined. But it ended predictably: This Democratic state, however much it approved Weld as governor, decided it wanted to keep two Democratic senators, and it voted 52%–45% for Kerry. As for Weld, he grew bored with the governorship and eventually resigned it in July 1997 to his Lieutenant Governor Paul Cellucci, to seek the ambassadorship to Mexico which was denied him by Jesse Helms. Massachusetts's lesson was not absorbed everywhere, but it was followed in New England and in the Metroliner corridor from New York to Washington, where Clinton ran strongly and Democrats walloped even Republican candidates who had previously run well. Clinton carried this part of the country by a whopping 55%–34%, compared to only 47%–43% in the rest of the country; Democratic House candidates won here 55%–43%, while losing

51%–47% in the rest of America. Why were Clinton and the Democrats so strong in Massachusetts and the Northeast? With tax increases now unthinkable, it was safe to vote on other issues, and on those this greater Massachusetts seemed to be closer to Western Europe than to the South, the Great Plains and the Rocky Mountains.

The Massachusetts consensus continued into 1998. The state was once again bathed in great prosperity; if it had lost high-tech supremacy to the San Francisco Bay Area and Seattle, its financial sector was surging. Government helped: The Big Dig, an $11 billion project to move Boston's unsightly Central Artery underground, moved toward completion—one of the most expensive public works project in history, and a bequest of the late Speaker Tip O'Neill; Logan Airport was updated to the tune of $1 billion; a cleanup of Boston Harbor, which Michael Dukakis let drop low on his priority list to his discomfort in the 1988 campaign, was finished with a price tag of $4.6 billion. Massachusetts looked forward to hosting the Tall Ships, baseball's All-Star Game and the Ryder Cup in 2000, though it was saddened to lose the Democratic National Convention to Los Angeles.

Massachusetts had its characteristic political scuffles, and at the Parker House bar you might suppose that politics was the great preoccupation of Bay Staters as it had been during the Yankee-Irish culture wars and the ascendancy of the Kennedys. But not many voters seemed interested. Cellucci was challenged in the Republican primary by Treasurer Joe Malone, and won 59%–41%; but only 232,000 voted in the Republican primary, compared to 600,000 in the Democrats' contest. The general was a sharp contest between Cellucci and Attorney General Scott Harshbarger. Cellucci won by 51%–47%, a kind of retrospective endorsement of Weld. But turnout was just 1.9 million, lower than in every non-presidential year but one (1986) in the last 50 years. Democrats, as usual, won just about everything else; but Massachusetts was not quite ready for full-throated liberalism. Faith in the public sector was at least jarred a bit when, in spring 1998, fully 59% of public school teaching applicants flunked a simple entrance exam—a sharp contrast with the excellence of Massachusetts's private sector. In all, Massachusetts seems a bit weary of using politics to teach lessons to the rest of America and more interested in enjoying the fruits of its own achievements and cultivating its own gardens.

Governor. Paul Cellucci, a Republican, became governor when William Weld resigned in July 1997; he was elected in his own right in November 1998. He is in many ways the personification of Massachusetts's middle class. He grew up in Hudson, a small town halfway between Boston and Worcester, where his family owned an auto dealership. He graduated from Boston College and its law school, and served in the Army Reserves: a Catholic, not an Ivy League, education. After school he worked in the auto dealership and practiced law in Hudson. In 1970, at 22, he was elected to the Hudson Charter Commission, and in 1971, to the Hudson Board of Selectmen. In 1976 he was elected to the state House, where he served four terms and in 1984, he was elected to the state Senate; in each he was part of a small Republican minority. In 1990, William Weld, from a rich Yankee family and a graduate of Harvard College and Law School, chose Cellucci as his running mate; their ticket won narrowly in 1990 and by a landslide in 1994. Weld constantly referred to the Weld-Cellucci relationship, mentioning Cellucci in every press release and official sign, and insisting that Cellucci play an important role in making policy on downsizing government, attracting jobs and supervising the Big Dig. This was not the usual gubernatorial practice, and it associated Cellucci with Weld's popular record of cutting taxes, holding down spending, reforming welfare and endorsing liberal positions on cultural issues and the environment. Weld's resignation was an act of generosity as well, enabling Cellucci to demonstrate gubernatorial stature before facing the voters in 1998.

Cellucci promised to continue Weld's policies while putting his own stamp on the office: Off the wall went Weld's portrait of the raffish former Governor James Michael Curley, and up went former Governor John Volpe; out went Weld's stuffed armadillo, to be replaced by Republican wood elephants. Cellucci's first acts were to call for a $1 billion tax cut, eliminating Michael Dukakis's .95% "temporary" increase, and to sign the 20th and 21st tax cuts of the Weld-Cellucci years, ending the sales tax on internet services and exempting veterans' pensions from income taxes. He also called for cutting in half the state tax on interest and dividend income; two-thirds of the net outflow from Massachusetts over the previous decade had gone to New Hampshire and Florida, which have no income tax. Massachusetts's economy was in fine shape, and voters seemed content.

Nevertheless, Cellucci had spirited competition in 1998, though not from the expected quarter. Congressman Joe Kennedy, in his sixth term in the House, was gearing up to run, and if his impulsiveness seemed ungubernatorial, no Kennedy had ever been defeated in Massachusetts. But in August 1997 Kennedy abruptly withdrew after negative personal publicity: his former wife's book detailed their annulment and his verbal abuse, his brother Michael was alleged to have had an affair with an underage babysitter (Michael died in a skiing accident in December). Left in the lead for the Democratic nomination was Scott Harshbarger, a Pennsylvania minister's son who was a halfback at Harvard, a lawyer who was counsel to the state ethics commission and was elected Middlesex County district attorney in 1982 and attorney general in 1990. In those high-visibility offices, Harshbarger pursued popular liberal causes: anti-stalking laws, prosecutions of child molesters, a student mediation program, opposition to the death penalty. For a while it seemed Harshbarger would be opposed by Raymond Flynn, who resigned as ambassador to the Vatican and returned to Boston, where he had been mayor from 1983 to 1993; but Flynn instead decided to run for Kennedy's House seat when the incumbent opted to retire.

Harshbarger's opponents were former state Senator Patricia McGovern, who was even more liberal, and former Congressman Brian Donnelly, who refused to use $300,000 left in his congressional campaign treasury; Harshbarger favored the $1 billion tax cut, while the others said it was too much. Harshbarger won with 51% of the vote, to 31% for McGovern and 17% for Donnelly. But turnout was low, just less than 600,000, far below the 1,052,000 in the spirited Democratic primary of 1990. Republican turnout was far lower, 232,000, compared to 446,000 in 1990, even though Cellucci had spirited and abrasive opposition from state Treasurer Joe Malone. Malone attacked him for not cutting taxes more, for overruns on the Big Dig, and for proposing bonuses for polite toll-takers. Cellucci was also hurt by the the fact that he had $750,000 in personal debt and had received $100,000 in loans without collateral from a Hudson bank on whose board his father served; Cellucci said he needed to finance his daughters' college educations and that his assets exceeded his liabilities. Cellucci won the primary, but by just 59%–41%.

But party unity was more of a problem for the Democrats. Harshbarger was seen by many as an elitist liberal, representing the graduate-school-educated professionals who are now a large part of the core Democratic constituency, but deaf to the values of the middle-income, middle-class Catholics who are the descendants of the party's historic constituency. At a party unity breakfast after the primary, state House Speaker Thomas Finneran worried that Harshbarger might go "loony left." The state Senate majority leader endorsed Cellucci, as did Flynn; the Democratic state chairman had no difficulty restraining his enthusiasm for his party's nominee. Cellucci was invited to a big celebration for Edward McCormack, a long-ago attorney general who lost to Edward Kennedy in the 1962 Senate primary; Harshbarger was not. The failure of 59% of teacher applicants on a simple entrance exam the preceding spring made teacher quality an issue; Cellucci called for a $20,000 signing bonus for qualified teachers and for testing of all current teachers; Harshbarger, evidently obedient to the teachers' unions, opposed the latter. Cellucci spent some $6.9 million and wisely targeted Harshbarger's vulnerability. An October ad noted that Harshbarger had prohibited Christmas decorations in his agency's offices; it also showed pictures of black-hatted, green-faced crones and noted that Harshbarger had threatened in June 1992 to prosecute a group for harassing witches. The North Shore and Salem, site of the 1692 witch trials, now has some 2,000 Wiccans; they staged a demonstration in Boston during one of the candidates' acerbic debates. This colorful episode vividly made the point that putting Democrats in total control of state government could lead to the kind of loopy left excesses that characterized the Dukakis years, and middle-class voters concluded they didn't want to be governed by the graduate student elite.

Still, the graduate student elite is large enough in Massachusetts—28% of the electorate in 1998—to have made the election close. Cellucci won 51%–47% in a turnout that was 19% below that of 1990. Turnout declined since 1990 by as much as one-third in the mill and factory towns that were, three or four decades ago, the Democratic base: Lawrence, Lowell, Brockton, Holyoke, Framingham, Fitchburg, Malden, Lynn, Chelsea. Harshbarger's base was in the university and college towns, where turnout was down less. He carried Cambridge 74%–24%, Amherst 76%–23% and Northampton 66%–32% and carried the string of academic-heavy towns running out Route 2 from Cambridge to Concord; he won in the college-heavy Pioneer Valley and in the left-leaning towns at the tip of Cape Cod. He also carried towns with large Jewish communities: Brookline, Newton, Swampscott, Sharon. But Cellucci, with his broad Massachusetts accent, conciliatory manner and record of tax cuts, carried middle-income and working-class towns, which have many more votes and which had been the heart of the Democratic constituency since John Kennedy beat Henry Cabot Lodge Jr. in 1952: Quincy and Weymouth, Everett and Revere, Lowell and Peabody, Woburn and Medford. Harshbarger carried 59% of those with graduate school educations, but Cellucci won 55%–57% among high school grads, those with some college and those with college degrees. In a state long divided on religious lines, Cellucci carried Catholics (53%–45%) as well as Protestants (57%–41%), while losing by more than 2–1 Jews and those with no religion.

In early 1999, Cellucci continued to press for more tax cuts, against concurrent sentences for violent crimes and for the death penalty, for testing of current teachers and against increased tolls to pay for the Big Dig. He spoke consensus language, quoting Robert Kennedy and Calvin Coolidge in the same speech, calling for "exceptional" schools, access to affordable health care, and an end to "unyielding partisanship." With almost no Republicans in the legislature—not enough even to force roll call votes in the Senate—he nevertheless seemed to work well with Speaker Thomas Finneran and Senate President Thomas Birmingham, who share some if not all of his goals. He visited Israel with Texas Governor George W. Bush after the election, and said he would endorse Bush if he runs for president. He showed every sign of wanting to run again in 2002, but added, "I should probably check with my wife."

Senior Senator. Edward Kennedy is now well into his fourth decade as a national celebrity and politician. He has had the highs and lows of his personal life followed by millions and criticized vitriolically by many; he has been a presidential candidate and, while still in his 30s, was widely assumed to be the next president. He is third in seniority in the Senate, behind Strom Thurmond and Robert Byrd. His reputation as an idealistic champion of the poor has been burnished by the praise of first-rate celebrators that no American political family has attracted before. To others, he is a symbol of personal immorality and unpunished criminal behavior, a man who has gotten away with things that would have ended the public career of almost anyone else. There is some basis for both views, but neither is an entirely fair picture of this politician, who was re-elected by a smart margin in 1994 in a race whose outcome seemed by no means certain; Kennedy has been paid more attention in the 1990s as a scandal-beset celebrity than as a consistent and often effective advocate of public policy.

The luster of the Kennedys has worn off, in America and even in Massachusetts, and the percentage of Americans who look to the Kennedys for political leadership has grown small; most voters can't remember, or never knew, what made the Kennedys so exciting. Still, there was little in the early life of this youngest of the Kennedy siblings to suggest he would be a major politician, much less for so long. He grew up in Bronxville, New York, a rich suburb with many other rich Catholics, was thrown out of Harvard for cheating on a Spanish exam and served in the Army, returned to earn degrees at Harvard and Virginia Law School, and married a Bronxville girl who never developed a taste for politics. Then his brother was elected President of the United States at 43, and the 28-year-old Edward Kennedy was a national celebrity. His father insisted that he run for the Senate; a JFK college roommate was found to hold the seat until he reached the constitutional age of 30, in 1962. His family money and the enthusiasm among Massachusetts Catholics for this seeming royalty enabled him to beat strong candidates with good political names: Attorney General Edward McCormack, nephew of Speaker John McCormack, in the Democratic primary; George Cabot Lodge, son and great-grandson of senators, in the general. "He can do more for Massachusetts" was his slogan, as had been John Kennedy's 10 years before.

After his brothers' assassinations, Edward Kennedy was seen by many as their natural heir, and he could have been nominated for president in 1968, at 36, or in 1972 had he chosen to run. Instead, in the latter year, he gave the first of several stirring convention speeches promoting his trademark liberalism. In 1979 he did run for president, and began the race against incumbent Jimmy Carter far ahead in the polls. But he was unable to articulate his reasons for running, and his candidacy was greeted with adverse reaction to him personally as well as to his policies. It ended in a crushing defeat, relieved only by another stirring convention speech, after which he pointedly refused to raise Carter's hand on the podium. In retrospect, it is plain that Edward Kennedy's presidential chances were ended in July 1969, with the accident at Chappaquiddick, even though the Kennedy family retainers managed to cast a cloud over the specifics. And after the Good Friday 1991 bar-hopping in Palm Beach and his nephew William Kennedy Smith's subsequent trial and acquittal for rape, Kennedy had to fight hard, with some low punches as well as fair hard lefts, to win re-election to the Senate.

Kennedy has been a hardworking and practical politician who, after his brothers' deaths, took up the liberal causes and attention to the poor, which had been the focus of Robert Kennedy in the last years of his life. He has worked hard for a quarter century on their behalf without the friendship of a Democratic administration, until the election of Bill Clinton, and since 1994 without the backing of a Democratic majority. As chairman of the Health, Education, Labor and Pensions Committee from 1987–94, Kennedy supported teachers' unions; on the Judiciary Committee, he supported pro-choice and feminist groups with energy and enthusiasm. He immediately pounced on Judge Robert Bork's nomination in 1987, but was precluded from a similarly loud role in the Clarence Thomas hearings in October 1991 because of the Palm Beach incident.

In 1992 Kennedy supported Bill Clinton happily and basked as Clinton gave repeated homage to the Kennedy family; he was also delighted when Clinton appointed his sister Jean Kennedy Smith ambassador to Ireland. Legislatively, Kennedy was productive, though not as much as he wished. He worked to pass direct student loans, AmeriCorps, Goals 2000 and the School-to-Work Opportunity Act. He again sponsored the Family and Medical Leave Act which George Bush had vetoed and which was the first law Bill Clinton signed. He also passed a bill making it illegal to block access to abortion clinics. But he was gravely frustrated on other issues. He sought to prevent states from regulating abortions and to ban the death penalty when imposed disproportionately on criminals of different races; both efforts failed. On health care, a longtime Kennedy cause, he backed a Canadian-style single-payer system. In May 1994 he got a health care bill resembling Clinton's through committee, but that was as far as it went. Kennedy smelled the possibility of a bipartisan compromise, but the Clinton White House insisted on standing firm and trying to push a Democratic bill through and got no result at all.

Kennedy entered the 1994 campaign popular, but appeared tired and overweight. His opponent was businessman Mitt Romney, whose father was governor of Michigan and a presidential candidate in the 1960s; Romney fit the Massachusetts profile on issues: against 1960s-style big government, pro-choice on abortion, for the death penalty, for Clinton's don't-ask-don't-tell policy on gays in the military. This was the second most expensive campaign in the country—Kennedy spent $11.5 million, Romney $7.6 million, both dipping into their own money—and among the most sharply contested. A Romney ad showed Kennedy painfully sitting down, and Romney had a 43%–42% lead in a September poll. Astonishingly for a man whose brother won the presidency while appealing against religious bigotry, Kennedy echoed questions, first raised by his nephew Joe Kennedy, about Romney's Mormon faith, asking whether he had challenged that church's racially discriminatory beliefs before they were changed in 1978. *The Boston Globe* responded, "That line of attack makes no more sense than asking Kennedy how many times he has written to Rome demanding that the church change its stand on abortion." More damaging were Kennedy ads attacking Romney's business practices. Romney claimed his work at Bain Capital produced 10,000 jobs, but Kennedy private detectives found an Indiana factory where 350 workers had gone on strike after their pay and benefits were cut when it was bought by Bain Capital. Romney claimed he severed his ties with Bain before the purchase was complete, but the damage was palpable. Also, Kennedy performed above expectations in debate. By late October, a *Boston Herald* poll had Kennedy ahead 50%–32%; he won 58%–41%.

Kennedy returned to a Republican Senate and shifted his focus from expanding government to protecting it from downsizing. In 1995 he defended Medicare and Medicaid from reductions and opposed changes in labor laws—Davis-Bacon repeal, the Teamwork for Employees and Management Act and the flex-time bill. He led the effort to block a limited school choice experiment in Washington, D.C.—taking the side of teachers' unions and the wretched D.C. school system. On immigration, he successfully opposed an amendment to give states authority to expel children of illegal immigrants. In 1996 he went on the offensive. He pushed the minimum wage issue, ignored by Clinton and Kennedy when the Democrats were in control, and split the Republicans while developing a campaign issue. He pushed the Kassebaum-Kennedy health care bill, an incremental measure to provide portability of health insurance and to limit exclusions for pre-existing conditions; he worked to keep Medical Savings Accounts out. He tried to add to the Defense of Marriage Act a provision to prohibit job discrimination against gays; this was rejected by only a narrow margin, indicating there may be a majority in the Senate for a gay rights bill some time soon. In 1996, Kennedy strongly supported Clinton, even after the president embraced a balanced budget and signed the Welfare Reform Act, and Kennedy had the pleasure of watching Clinton win and run strongest in Massachusetts.

In 1997, Kennedy, a longtime cigar smoker, worked with Orrin Hatch on a tobacco bill, with a $1.50 per pack cigarette tax; it was shunted aside in May 1998 favor of John McCain's bill. Kennedy filibustered a bipartisan bill to streamline FDA regulation of medical devices. But in 1998 he worked on several bipartisan measures that passed without much dissent, including a higher education reauthorization that reduced student loan interest rates, reauthorization of the IDEA bill for educating disabled students and a job training reauthorization. He sponsored an anti-gay discrimination bill, a hate crimes bill and a bill to reduce the Social Security payroll tax and remove the cap on earnings that are taxed. He also sponsored a bipartisan bill to allow disabled people to work without jeopardizing their health care benefits. He moved in January 1999 to oppose John Breaux's Medicare reforms. In the debate on impeachment procedures in early January 1999, he took up Phil Gramm's suggestion to agree on most procedures and leave the issue of witnesses aside, since any deal could be overturned by the Republican majority. But Kennedy was steadfast in his defense of Clinton. On local issues, Kennedy produced $70 million for the Big Dig in the October 1998 omnibus budget and also secured funding for dredging Boston Harbor and building a new Springfield courthouse. In late 1998, he sought aid for Massachusetts's beleaguered fishing ports.

Kennedy's seat comes up again in 2000, and he left no doubt he intended to run and said he would not pledge to take no PAC money as he did in 1994; the talk some years ago that he would leave the seat for his nephew Joe or some other relative has not been heard since Joe left the governor's race in August 1997. In early 1999, former Governor William Weld said he would not run, and former Treasurer and 1988 Kennedy opponent Joe Malone seemed unlikely to (and would presumably have little help from Governor Paul Cellucci, who beat him in the 1998 primary). Mitt Romney moved to Utah for a three-year stint heading the troubled Salt Lake Olympic Organizing Committee; a former colleague of Romney's at Bain, Geoffrey Rehnert, said he might run. Kennedy's poll ratings are high, and it seems unlikely this will be a seriously contested race.

Cook's Call. *Safe.* Republicans do not seem that anxious to try to defeat Kennedy after losing in 1994, and first-tier potential candidates like former Governor Bill Weld have said they will not run. Kennedy should have an easy time winning re-election in 2000.

Junior Senator. John Kerry has been a national political figure since he was one of the organizers of Vietnam Veterans Against the War in 1971. He attracted attention then because of his background, unusual for a Vietnam veteran (he went to Yale, and his mother is from the Brahmin Forbes family) and because of his record of genuine heroism in combat. "How do you ask a man to be the last to die for a mistake?" he asked in congressional testimony—a good question, and one which also suggested his future political ambitions. Yet his political career did not proceed straight ahead. He ran for Congress in 1972, after some widely observed district-shopping, and lost in a district carried by George McGovern. Chastened, Kerry went to law school, worked for a prosecutor, was elected lieutenant governor on the Dukakis ticket in 1982, and ran for senator in 1984; in both races, he upset a favored rival for the Democratic nomination. In 1982, Kerry won the general as part of a tied ticket with Dukakis; in the 1984 general, he beat Raymond Shamie, a businessman and state Republican chairman, 55%–45%.

Kerry came to the Senate with a reputation as a strong liberal. He has a similar voting record to fellow Senator Edward Kennedy, but there have been differences of nuance and interest: Kerry has been more respectful of economic free markets and moved earlier than Kennedy toward supporting an expansive U.S. foreign and military policy. In the majority, Kerry made a name as an investigator, spending some time up blind alleys with klieg lights but also producing some important information regardless of political fallout. He used his Foreign Relations Western Hemisphere, Peace Corps, Narcotics and Terrorism Subcommittee chairmanship to investigate the infamous Bank of Credit & Commerce International scandal; his October 1992 report accused the Justice Department, British banking regulators and especially the CIA of "institutional failure" in recognizing the fraudulent nature of BCCI's operations. But the subcommittee also spent much time trying to pin drug-running charges on Central American rightists—convenient for American politicians supportive of Central American left-wingers. Kerry was on more solid ground, as later events made clear, in charging Manuel Noriega of Panama with drug-dealing.

Kerry's other great investigation was as chairman of the Select Committee on POW/MIA Affairs, on whether Americans were left behind in Vietnamese hands in 1973. Kerry and Republican Bob Smith of New Hampshire went to Vietnam and attempted to dig up new evidence. Kerry grilled former Secretary of State Henry Kissinger, a bit unfairly, but overall this was a serious effort, with a hedged conclusion: There is evidence "that indicates the possibility of survival, at least for a small number," after 1973, but also said, "There is at this time no compelling evidence that any American remains alive in captivity in southeast Asia." By May 1995, Kerry and fellow Vietnam veteran Senator John McCain's efforts in this area had convinced them that Hanoi was fully cooperating and, aware they had standing on this issue that Bill Clinton conspicuously lacked, they got him to normalize relations with Vietnam. Kerry has traveled a number of times to Vietnam, and he and McCain have supported normal trade relations and the appointment of the first U.S. ambassador there, former Congressman and Vietnam POW Pete Peterson.

On other issues, Kerry successfully worked with Richard Bryan of Nevada to eliminate the wool and mohair subsidy in 1993, and he won a fight to eliminate the Advanced Liquid Metal Reactor nuclear disposal in 1994. He has long called for campaign finance reform and has refused to take PAC contributions. In 1990, when Massachusetts was in revolt against Michael Dukakis, Kerry had a self-financed opponent who ran what is probably the first "morph spot" ever, showing Kerry changing into Dukakis. But Kerry won by a convincing 57%–43% margin.

Even as the Senate was captured by the Republicans in 1994, Massachusetts seemed to be moving toward the Democrats, and Kerry was in a secure political position, with a mostly liberal voting record and a mostly liberal constituency. In May 1995 he married Teresa Heinz, widow of Republican Senator John Heinz of Pennsylvania, who inherited his fortune of more than $600 million; *Roll Call* in 1999 rated Kerry the richest member of Congress, with $675 million, but he said he would not spend it on a presidential campaign when he was considering one: "It's my wife's money, not mine." But he did spend $1.9 million of personal funds on his 1996 Senate race. It was needed: Kerry was faced with the one opponent who could give him real trouble, Governor William Weld. Weld had just been re-elected with 71% of the vote, his job rating was as positive as Kerry's or more so and he was much more familiar to voters in Massachusetts.

Earlier, the two had worked together on some state problems and emphasized the similarity of their views: They were both pro-choice on abortion, even against the partial-birth abortion ban; they were both for gay rights; they both supported the deployment of U.S. troops in Bosnia. But the campaign inevitably produced disagreements and some gentlemanly acrimony. Weld called Kerry a "tax-and-spend liberal who is soft on crime." Kerry charged that Weld would vote for budget cuts that would hurt Medicare, Medicaid, education and the environment. Weld tied Kerry to Michael Dukakis; Kerry tied Weld to Jesse Helms. Weld said he would change Washington; Kerry said Weld would tear down government. They held seven debates altogether, literate rounds of accusations and one-liners. They both spent liberally—Kerry, $12.6 million, the second highest of any Senate candidate for 1996; Weld, $8 million.

This battle of bluebloods was a race beloved of reporters, and was reported extensively. Most polls showed Kerry ahead, some showed Weld leading, but most were within the margin of error, with both candidates usually between 40% and 45%. Kerry was hurt a bit by the revelation in mid-October that he had accepted free lodging at lobbyist and Democratic fundraiser Robert Farmer's Washington apartment in the late 1980s. But in the last debate, Kerry framed the issues his way by asking Weld what programs he would cut; Weld declined to answer. The VNS exit poll suggested that most voters making up their minds in the last week chose Kerry. In heavily Republican states, extremely popular Democratic governors were beaten in Senate races, in Wyoming in 1994 and Nebraska in 1996; in heavily Democratic Massachusetts, 61%–28% for Bill Clinton in 1996, an extremely popular Republican lost to a competent and popular Democrat by 52%–45%. The electorate was not split along historic lines: Catholics voted only 56%–40% for Kerry, Protestants by only 53%–42% for Weld, numbers a world away from what exit polls would have shown when John Kennedy beat Henry Cabot Lodge Jr. in 1952, or when Kennedy's grandfather John Fitzgerald lost to Lodge's grandfather in 1916. Income didn't make much difference: Weld carried only the top bracket, and not by much. The real split was along cultural lines. Jews and those voters with no religion voted about 75% for Kerry; and there was no significant bloc of conservative Protestants to balance them off. Kerry's biggest margins among education groups was among those with graduate degrees, who gave him a 62%–35% margin: teachers, social workers, lawyers, doctors and other credentialed professionals. Kerry got his biggest percentages in Boston and university towns like Cambridge and Amherst, and he carried—but not by large margins—old mill towns like Lowell and Lawrence.

With a safe seat, Kerry began to ponder running for president—and in the process came up with interesting public policy positions. He raised money spasmodically to cut down his $2.1 million campaign debt, and made trips to New Hampshire (though he never got to Iowa). In June 1998 he decried the "implosion" of public education and said it was caused not just by overcrowded classrooms (Edward Kennedy was backing Bill Clinton's call for classroom construction) but also by the "stifling bureaucracy" of school systems. Typically, he placed himself in the middle of the spectrum, between those who wanted to divert money to private schools through vouchers and those who wanted to pump more money into public schools that weren't working. He drew up a list of 10 reforms, some unexceptionable and some strongly opposed by the teachers' unions—important backers of the Democratic Party. "We should end tenure as we know it," he said, and "we should change certification requirements" to end the teacher college monopoly and allow competent professionals lateral entry into teaching jobs. Edward Kennedy refused to co-sponsor his bill, because of the lack of construction money, he said, but more likely because he has always followed the unions on education policy; Kerry signed up Oregon Republican Gordon Smith as a co-sponsor instead. Some saw this as a ploy for a presidential campaign, but it was guaranteed to arouse vehement opposition from teachers' unions in Democratic primaries; one must conclude that this Democrat, unlike so many others, was more interested in helping children learn than in paying off political allies, and was willing to take some political risks in that cause.

In any case, Kerry's presidential campaign came to nothing. The impeachment issue took much of his time, causing him to cancel trips to Iowa and postpone setting up an exploratory committee. Kerry, like most northeast Democrats, thought it was frivolous to remove Clinton from office for his offenses. In September 1998 he proposed that Clinton testify voluntarily before the House Judiciary Committee in return for an expedited vote; but neither Clinton nor House Republican leaders were interested. In February 1999, just days after the Senate acquitted Clinton, he announced he would not run for president: "I have concluded that to raise the necessary amount of money, with only 10 months to do so, compounded by the newly accelerated primary schedule, simply isn't possible at this time."

In the meantime, Kerry has continued to work on various issues, working with John McCain to get more children on Medicaid, seeking to repeal the tax that bars computer consultants from claiming contract worker status and seeking aid for the ailing fishing industry in Massachusetts. It is not likely he will have serious opposition for re-election in 2002; Governor Paul Cellucci has shown no interest in the office.

Presidential politics. Massachusetts is the most Democratic state in presidential elections with the arguable exceptions of Rhode Island and Hawaii. In 1996 it gave Bill Clinton his largest percentage and largest margin of victory (with the exception of the District of Columbia); in 1992 it also gave him his largest percentage margin. There was something approaching unanimity for Clinton in 1996 among many groups: He carried women 69%–22% and those with graduate school educations 67%–25%.

Massachusetts's presidential primary has long been in early March and is the leading northern Super Tuesday contest. In 1988 and 1992, victory in Massachusetts went to its native sons: Democrats Michael Dukakis and Paul Tsongas and Republican George Bush. In 1996, the primary was held on Junior Tuesday, March 5; Bob Dole won over Pat Buchanan 48%–25%. Candidates contesting New Hampshire always buy time on Boston TV stations, which reach much of the Granite State and the cost of which does not have to be charged against the low limit on spending in New Hampshire, but don't expect a lot of personal campaigning here.

Congressional districting. Massachusetts's convoluted congressional district lines deserve their own biographer, someone with a sure political instinct and a touch of whimsy. The state lost one seat in each of the last two reapportionments. It may lose another after the 2000 Census, which would be bad news for Democrats, who currently hold all 10 seats. Some members asked the 5th District's Martin Meehan to keep his 1992 campaign promise and retire after four terms, but Meehan decided to run again. In any case, the district lines' biographer will be kept busy watching the maneuvering in the Capitol and on Beacon Hill.

The People: Est. Pop. 1998: 6,147,132; Pop. 1990: 6,016,425, up 2.2% 1990–1998. 2.3% of U.S. total, 13th largest; 15.7% rural. Median age: 35.6 years. 14.3% 65 years and over. 90% White, 4.9% Black, 2.3% Asian, 0.2% Amer. Indian, 2.6% Other; 4.6% Hispanic Origin. Households: 52.1% married couple families; 24.1% married couple fams. w. children; 50.3% college educ.; median household income: $36,952; per capita income: $17,224; 59.3% owner occupied housing; median house value: $162,800; median monthly rent: $506. 3.3% Unemployment. 1998 Voting age pop.: 4,731,000. 1998 Turnout: 1,935,277; 41% of VAP. Registered voters (1998): 3,718,528; 1,388,177 D (37%), 485,961 R (13%), 1,844,390 unaffiliated and minor parties (50%).

Political Lineup: Governor, Paul Cellucci (R); Lt. Gov., Jane Swift (R); Secy. of the Commonwealth, William Galvin (D); Atty. Gen., Scott Harshbarger (D); Treasurer, Shannon O'Brien (D); State Senate, 40 (33 D, 7 R); Majority Leader, Linda Melconian (D); State House, 160 (130 D, 27 R, 1 I, 2 vacancies); House Speaker, Thomas Finneran (D). Senators, Edward Kennedy (D) and John F. Kerry (D). Representatives, 10 (10 D).

Elections Division: 617-727-2828; **Filing Deadline for U.S. Congress:** June 6, 2000.

1996 Presidential Vote

Clinton (D)	1,571,755	(61%)
Dole (R)	718,104	(28%)
Perot (I)	226,787	(9%)
Others	39,347	(2%)

1992 Presidential Vote

Clinton (D)	1,318,639	(48%)
Bush (R)	805,039	(29%)
Perot (I)	630,731	(22%)

1996 Republican Presidential Primary

Dole (R)	135,946	(48%)
Buchanan (R)	71,688	(25%)
Forbes (R)	39,605	(14%)
Alexander (R)	21,456	(8%)
Others	16,138	(6%)

GOVERNOR

Gov. Paul Cellucci (R)

Assumed office, July 1997, term expires Jan. 2003; b. Apr. 24, 1948, Marlborough; home, Hudson; Boston Col., B.A. 1970, J.D. 1973; Catholic; married (Jan).

Military Career: Army Reserves, 1970–78.

Elected Office: Hudson Charter Comm., 1970–71; Hudson Bd. of Selectmen, 1971–77; MA House of Reps., 1976–84; MA Senate, 1984–90; MA Lt. Gov., 1990–97.

Professional Career: Family-owned auto dealership; Practicing atty., 1973–90.

Office: State House, Boston, 02133, 617-727-3600; Fax: 617-727-9725; Web site: www.state.ma.us.

Election Results

1998 gen.	Paul Cellucci (R)	967,160	(51%)
	Scott Harshbarger (D)	901,843	(47%)
	Others	34,333	(2%)
1998 prim.	Paul Cellucci (R)	136,258	(59%)
	Joseph D. Malone (R)	95,963	(41%)
1994 gen.	William Weld (R)	1,533,380	(71%)
	Mark Roosevelt (D)	611,641	(28%)

SENATORS

Elected 1962, seat up 2000; b. Feb █████
Port; Harvard U., B.A. 1956, The █████
VA, LL.B. 1959; Catholic; marrie█████

Military Career: Army, 1951–5█

Professional Career: Western st█████
Campaign, 1960; Asst. Dist. Atty█████

DC Office: 315 RSOB, 20510, █████
Web site: www.senate.gov/~kenn█████

State Office: Boston, 617-565-█

Committees: *Armed Services* (█████
Capabilities; Personnel; Seapower █████
& Pensions (RMM of 8 D): Empl█████
Health (RMM). *Judiciary* (2d of 8 D): Immigration (RMM); The
Constitution, Federalism & Property Rights. *Joint Economic Committee* (9th of 10 Sens.).

Group Ratings

	ADA	ACLU	AFS	LCV	CON	NTU	NFIB	COC	ACU	NTLC	CHC
1998	95	86	100	100	46	9	22	47	0	3	0
1997	100	—	100	—	8	10	—	40	4	—	—

National Journal Ratings

	1997 LIB — 1997 CONS			1998 LIB — 1998 CONS		
Economic	90%	—	6%	83%	—	10%
Social	71%	—	0%	74%	—	0%
Foreign	87%	—	8%	95%	—	0%

Key Votes of the 105th Congress

1. Bal. Budget Amend.	N	5. Satcher for Surgeon Gen.	Y	9. Chem. Weapons Treaty	Y
2. Clinton Budget Deal	N	6. Highway Set-asides	Y	10. Cuban Humanitarian Aid	Y
3. Cloture on Tobacco	Y	7. Table Child Gun locks	N	11. Table Bosnia Troops	Y
4. Education IRAs	N	8. Ovrd. Part. Birth Veto	N	12. $ for Test-ban Treaty	Y

Election Results

1994 general	Edward Kennedy (D)	1,265,997	(58%)	($11,493,735)
	W. Mitt Romney (R)	894,000	(41%)	($7,624,491)
1994 primary	Edward Kennedy (D)	unopposed		
1988 general	Edward Kennedy (D)	1,693,344	(65%)	($2,702,865)
	Joseph D. Malone (R)	884,267	(34%)	($587,323)

Elected 1984, seat up 2002; b. █
Boston; Yale U., A.B. 1966, Bost█
ried (Teresa Heinz).

Military Career: Navy, 1966–█
1972–78.

Elected Office: MA Lt. Gov., 19█

Professional Career: Organizer,█
Asst. Dist. Atty., Middlesex █
1981–82.

DC Office: 304 RSOB, 20510,█
Web site: www.senate.gov/~kerry█

State Offices: Boston, 617-56█
Springfield, 413-785-4610; Worc█

Committees: *Banking, Housing█*
nomic Policy; Housing & Transportation (RMM); International Trade █████ ████████ ████████ █
Transportation (4th of 9 D): Communications; Oceans & Fisheries (RMM); Science, Technology & Space.
Foreign Relations (4th of 8 D): East Asian & Pacific Affairs (RMM); International Economic Policy,
Export & Trade Promotion; International Operations. *Intelligence* (4th of 8 D). *Small Business* (RMM of
8 D).

Group Ratings

	ADA	ACLU	AFS	LCV	CON	NTU	NFIB	COC	ACU	NTLC	CHC
1998	95	86	100	100	42	13	22	50	4	3	0
1997	95	—	100	—	10	16	—	50	0	—	—

National Journal Ratings

	1997 LIB — 1997 CONS			1998 LIB — 1998 CONS		
Economic	79%	—	18%	83%	—	10%
Social	71%	—	0%	74%	—	0%
Foreign	87%	—	8%	86%	—	12%

Key Votes of the 105th Congress

1. Bal. Budget Amend.	N	5. Satcher for Surgeon Gen.	Y	9. Chem. Weapons Treaty	Y
2. Clinton Budget Deal	N	6. Highway Set-asides	Y	10. Cuban Humanitarian Aid	Y
3. Cloture on Tobacco	Y	7. Table Child Gun locks	N	11. Table Bosnia Troops	Y
4. Education IRAs	N	8. Ovrd. Part. Birth Veto	N	12. $ for Test-ban Treaty	Y

Election Results

1996 general	John F. Kerry (D)	1,334,135	(52%)	($12,619,152)
	William Weld (R)	1,143,120	(45%)	($8,002,123)
	Others	78,687	(3%)	
1996 primary	John F. Kerry (D)	unopposed		
1990 general	John F. Kerry (D)	1,321,712	(57%)	($8,040,970)
	Jim Rappaport (R)	992,917	(43%)	($5,177,801)

FIRST DISTRICT

The stony hills and green-clad mountains of western Massachusetts, with more trees today than
when Henry David Thoreau was writing in the 1840s, where stone wall fencing once bounded
one working farm from another, probably does not look much different from 300 years ago.
This was the frontier in the 17th Century, where Puritan preachers formed new towns in the

wilderness, farming the stony soil and preaching against declension. It was dangerous here as well—this was the site of the Indian uprising known as King Philip's War in 1676, and the Indian raid, supported by the French from Quebec, at Deerfield in 1704. This was Yankee New England's western frontier for nearly 200 years. In the 19th Century, western New England was the home of writers and artists, Emily Dickinson lived quietly in Amherst, Edith Wharton grandly on her estate in Lenox, "The Mount," and the sculptor Augustus Saint Gaudens lived not far from where the Boston Symphony plays at the Tanglewood Festival each summer. There were mill towns here as well, jammed in mountain crevasses or along the wide Connecticut River; but as the 20th Century went on, and trees grew up on stony land once farmed, western Massachusetts came to look less settled, except near giant factories like General Electric's now-closed electric transformer plant in Pittsfield and the Crane paper factory in nearby Dalton.

Western Massachusetts has also changed politically. For many years it was one of the heart-lands of the Republican Party—flinty, thrifty and chilly just like the area's most famous politician, Calvin Coolidge, who worked his way up from mayor of Northampton to governor and president by lowering taxes and saying no to pleas for government action. But by the 1980s, western Massachusetts contained some of the most left-wing parts of America. Stockbridge attracted liberal artist Norman Rockwell (a solid New Dealer and peacenik) and baby boom radical Arlo Guthrie, whose Alice's Restaurant was there. The concentration of colleges and universities in the Pioneer Valley, around Amherst, Northampton and South Hadley, brought together a critical mass of liberal scholars and an even more leftish graduate student proletariat. The results show up in the election returns: Hampshire County, dominated by Pioneer Valley college towns, voted 64%–23% for Bill Clinton in 1996; he carried Amherst, home of the University of Massachusetts, 75%–15%.

The 1st Congressional District, like all the Massachusetts districts, has convoluted boundaries that defy easy description. It covers much but not all of western Massachusetts and stretches far to the northeast. It includes all of Berkshire and Franklin Counties and much of the Pioneer Valley: Amherst is in the 1st and so is the mill town of Holyoke on the Connecticut River, but the college towns of Northampton and South Hadley are in the 2d District. It includes New Braintree and Westfield, but not Springfield; it includes Fitchburg and Gardner, north of Worcester, but not Worcester itself. This is a Democratic district in most elections, but not overwhelmingly so. The Democratic base is split among the Amherst radicals, low-income factory workers of Holyoke and the descendants of ethnic mill and blue-collar workers in places like Pittsfield and Fitchburg. The Republican base is even more scattered, among the small towns in the hills.

The congressman from the 1st is John Olver, a Democrat chosen in a special election in June 1991. Olver was educated at Tufts and MIT and came to UMass as a chemistry professor in 1961, at 25; his wife Rose is a professor of psychology and women's and gender studies at Amherst College. Olver does not seem a natural politico: He likes to rock climb, a solitary and meticulous business, and as late as November 1998 admitted he doesn't use the Internet. In 1968, he was elected to the state House; he was elected to the state Senate in 1972. When longtime Republican Congressman Silvio Conte died in 1991, Olver ran for the seat, and his Pioneer Valley base helped him win 31% in the fragmented Democratic primary. In the June 1991 general he faced Steven Pierce, former state House Republican leader, Governor William Weld's conservative opponent in the 1990 primary and a Weld cabinet appointee. With Massachusetts liberalism in grave disrepute, the race was close; the election was scheduled after students' summer vacation began. But Olver was able to eke out a 50%–48% win.

Olver has had one of the most liberal voting records in the House. He sees his job as encouraging economic development and making the "federal government more responsive to people's needs by extending unemployment benefits, helping to ease the credit crunch on businesses and fighting to control the cost of health care." He was against NAFTA and for Canadian-style single-payer health insurance. He has attacked the IRS for not collecting enough of taxes owed. He told a local labor group, "We need a positive program, a jobs strategy, a national minimum wage, a guarantee of jobs, increased money for research and development, universal health care and portability of health insurance."

But Olver has had little opening to pursue these social democratic goals in the Republican House. Instead he has worked to fund local projects on the Appropriations Committee, on which he got a seat in January 1993, which he lost after the Democrats lost control in January 1995, then got back in January 1997. He started off passing a bill creating a network of Manufacturing Outreach Centers to help businesses tap into university resources and securing two-year funding for the Low-Income Home Energy Assistance Program. More recently he has pushed successfully for a new $3 million dining facility and fitness center for Barnes Air National Guard Base, a $490,000 helicopter flight simulator at Westover Air Reserve Base, renewal of the Northeast Dairy Compact, $400,000 for a venture incubator center in North Adams, a plastics technology center in Leominster, and planning money for a UMass medical center in Franklin County. He gets involved in lots of details, like cleaning up Parkers Pond in Gardner, a new veterans' cemetery in Winchendon, and opposing a for-profit company buying HealthAlliance in Fitchburg and Leominster.

On the Transportation Subcommittee he worked to prevent cost overruns on Boston's Big Dig from gobbling up all the state's transportation money. But some Massachusetts Democrats have said that as the state's only Appropriations member, he hasn't done much for their districts. In May 1997 he helped stop an Appropriations rider which would have subjected Crane Paper, which gets one-third of its revenues from printing the paper for U.S. paper currency, to competition; its monopoly will continue through at least 2002, though it is still subject to competition from plastic (they use plastic bills in Australia) and coins. Now he is the ranking Democrat on the subcommittee.

For a conscientious Democrat in a basically Democratic district, Olver has not always had dazzling electoral performance. In 1992, he won 52%–43%, carrying Pittsfield and other Berkshire towns narrowly, winning big in the Pioneer Valley and carrying a plurality around Fitchburg. In 1994 he was unopposed. In 1996 he faced state Representative Jane Swift, a 31-year-old moderate, who spent an impressive sum ($693,000). Olver won by only 53%–47%, and Swift has moved up: She was elected lieutenant governor in 1998. His 1998 Republican opponent called him a "leftist liberal"; Olver won 72%–28%, his first big margin. The position of the 1st District, at one end of the state, means that redistricting will probably be no great problem for him.

Cook's Call. *Probably Safe.* Olver has held this western Massachusetts district for eight years, but his tenure has been a little schizophrenic, winning by narrow margins one year, only to be unopposed the next. Olver's less than definitive victories in the past certainly make him an intriguing target, but the Democratic base here still gives Olver the advantage.

The People: Pop. 1990: 601,721; 36% rural; 14.7% age 65 +; 94.2% White, 1.6% Black, 1.3% Asian, 0.2% Amer. Indian, 2.7% Other; 4.7% Hispanic Origin. Households: 54.1% married couple families; 25.4% married couple fams. w. children; 45% college educ.; median household income: $31,903; per capita income: $14,200; median house value: $123,700; median gross rent: $412.

1996 Presidential Vote

Clinton (D)	151,531	(61%)
Dole (R)	63,998	(26%)
Perot (I)	29,116	(12%)
Others	4,718	(2%)

1992 Presidential Vote

Clinton (D)	130,308	(48%)
Bush (R)	72,238	(26%)
Perot (I)	68,545	(25%)

Rep. John W. Olver (D)

Elected June 1991; b. Sept. 3, 1936, Honesdale, PA; home, Amherst; Rensselaer Polytechnic Inst., B.S. 1955, Tufts U., M.S. 1956, M.I.T., Ph.D. 1961; no religious affiliation; married (Rose).

Elected Office: MA House of Reps., 1968–72; MA Senate, 1972–91.

Professional Career: Prof., U. of MA, Amherst, 1961–69.

DC Office: 1027 LHOB 20515, 202-225-5335; Fax: 202-226-1224; Web site: www.house.gov/olver.

District Offices: Fitchburg, 978-342-8722; Holyoke, 413-532-7010; Pittsfield, 413-442-0946.

Committees: *Appropriations* (15th of 27 D): Military Construction (RMM); Transportation.

Group Ratings

	ADA	ACLU	AFS	LCV	CON	NTU	NFIB	COC	ACU	NTLC	CHC
1998	95	94	100	100	36	16	8	24	0	8	0
1997	100	—	100	—	24	28	—	30	4	—	—

National Journal Ratings

	1997 LIB — 1997 CONS		1998 LIB — 1998 CONS	
Economic	91%	— 7%	79%	— 0%
Social	85%	— 0%	93%	— 0%
Foreign	90%	— 8%	98%	— 0%

Key Votes of the 105th Congress

1. Clinton Budget Deal	N	5. Puerto Rico Sthood. Ref.	Y	9. Cut $ for B-2 Bombers	Y
2. Education IRAs	N	6. End Highway Set-asides	N	10. Human Rights in China	Y
3. Req. 2/3 to Raise Taxes	N	7. School Prayer Amend.	N	11. Withdraw Bosnia Troops	N
4. Fast-track Trade	N	8. Ovrd. Part. Birth Veto	N	12. End Cuban TV-Marti	Y

Election Results

1998 general	John W. Olver (D)	121,863	(72%)	($569,967)
	Gregory L. Morgan (R)	48,055	(28%)	($28,828)
1998 primary	John W. Olver (D)	unopposed		
1996 general	John W. Olver (D)	129,232	(53%)	($1,005,595)
	Jane Swift (R)	115,801	(47%)	($693,538)

SECOND DISTRICT

As American as apple pie, the place where basketball was invented, the city where the Webster's unabridged dictionaries (2d and 3d editions) were edited and published, the site of the armory where M-1 rifles were manufactured in World War II, the city with the highest percentage of Puerto Ricans: This is Springfield, Massachusetts. Springfield is the third largest city in the Bay State, but far from Boston; the second-largest city in the Connecticut River Valley, but overshadowed by Hartford; a medium-sized American city built by New England Yankees, where immigrants from a dozen different countries have worked their way up.

Springfield is the largest city in the 2d Congressional District, whose irregular boundaries stretch north to South Hadley and Northampton, college towns of the Pioneer Valley, and east across stony hills and the antique center of Brimfield to the factory towns of the Blackstone

Valley just north of Woonsocket, Rhode Island. Historically, this was a Yankee Republican district for much of the 20th Century, then a solidly Catholic Democratic district; now it is more marginal but still leans Democratic.

The congressman from the 2d District is Richard Neal, mayor of Springfield from 1984–88. Neal grew up in Springfield, went to work for the mayor in 1973, was elected to the Council in 1978, while teaching high school and college history. As mayor himself, Neal boasted of both downtown rehabilitation and neighborhood revitalization. He was essentially bequeathed the seat by his predecessor, 36-year incumbent Edward Boland, a longtime friend of Tip O'Neill. In 1988, Boland announced his retirement just before the filing deadline, and after Neal had been making the rounds of the district for a year. Unopposed in the Democratic primary, Neal won 80% in the general.

Neal has a generally liberal voting record, with some exceptions; he voted for the final version of welfare reform, the partial birth abortion ban and the Defense of Marriage Act and refused to support the Clinton health care plan. He voted for NAFTA and GATT but against fast track in 1997. He serves on Ways and Means, where he decries the complication of the tax code and has a bill that would allow taxpayers to claim the child tax credit without calculating the alternative minimum tax; to pay for this, he would phase out the child credit at lower incomes. He also has a bill, with Republican Phil English, to eliminate the 1991 $18 per barrel beer tax. No action was taken on either. With Barney Frank and Jim McGovern, he sought to preserve a state drug mandate for Medicare patients by repealing a federal exemption.

Neal tends to local matters, hailing extension of the Quinebaug-Shetucket River Valley Heritage Corridor from Connecticut to Massachusetts and pushing the Defense Center for Financial Management and Training at Southbridge. He has long had an interest in Ireland; in 1980, when he was a city council member, he sponsored a plank at the Democratic National Convention for the unification of Ireland. In 1993 he started one-hour special orders sessions on Irish issues; in 1994 he personally lobbied Bill Clinton to grant a visa for Gerry Adams of Sinn Fein to visit the United States, though Adams would not condemn IRA bombing; in April 1998 Neal attended Sinn Fein's convention in Ireland.

Neal had serious primary challenges in 1990 and 1992, but won by satisfactory margins; his 1996 Republican opponent had been convicted of arson in 1991 (Massachusetts is the only state that allows convicted felons to run for office); in 1998 he had no opposition at all. He took a partisan Democratic stand on impeachment; after release of the Starr report, he said, "I think there's a major bloodbath coming inside the institution. You have this level of intensity now that's difficult to put back in the box." Neal was distinctly unenthusiastic about Democratic gubernatorial nominee Scott Harshbarger, who did not carry the district.

Cook's Call. *Safe.* During his 10 terms, Neal has won re-election rather easily, but had a bumpy road early in his career, due to self-inflicted political troubles. Barring any further blunders, Neal remains a safe incumbent.

The People: Pop. 1990: 601,490; 20.7% rural; 14.7% age 65 + ; 89.7% White, 5.7% Black, 0.9% Asian, 0.2% Amer. Indian, 3.5% Other; 5.8% Hispanic Origin. Households: 54.6% married couple families; 25.4% married couple fams. w. children; 42% college educ.; median household income: $33,401; per capita income: $14,652; median house value: $129,100; median gross rent: $422.

1996 Presidential Vote		
Clinton (D)	147,670	(61%)
Dole (R)	66,344	(27%)
Perot (I)	25,252	(10%)

1992 Presidential Vote		
Clinton (D)	121,759	(46%)
Bush (R)	76,277	(29%)
Perot (I)	65,935	(25%)

Rep. Richard E. Neal (D)

Elected 1988; b. Feb. 14, 1949, Springfield; home, Springfield; Amer. Intl. Col., B.A. 1972, U. of Hartford, M.A. 1976; Catholic; married (Maureen).

Elected Office: Springfield City Cncl., 1978–83; Springfield Mayor, 1984–88.

Professional Career: Staff Asst., Springfield Mayor William C. Sullivan, 1973–78; High Schl. & Col. teacher, 1978–83.

DC Office: 2236 RHOB 20515, 202-225-5601; Fax: 202-225-8112; Web site: www.house.gov/neal.

District Offices: Milford, 508-634-8198; Springfield, 413-785-0325.

Committees: *Ways & Means* (10th of 16 D): Oversight; Trade.

Group Ratings

	ADA	ACLU	AFS	LCV	CON	NTU	NFIB	COC	ACU	NTLC	CHC
1998	95	69	100	100	51	10	21	35	12	8	8
1997	90	—	88	—	62	32	—	50	25	—	—

National Journal Ratings

	1997 LIB — 1997 CONS		1998 LIB — 1998 CONS	
Economic	85% —	15%	79% —	0%
Social	69% —	30%	68% —	32%
Foreign	69% —	28%	90% —	10%

Key Votes of the 105th Congress

1. Clinton Budget Deal	N	5. Puerto Rico Sthood. Ref.	Y	9. Cut $ for B-2 Bombers	Y
2. Education IRAs	N	6. End Highway Set-asides	N	10. Human Rights in China	Y
3. Req. 2/3 to Raise Taxes	N	7. School Prayer Amend.	N	11. Withdraw Bosnia Troops	N
4. Fast-track Trade	N	8. Ovrd. Part. Birth Veto	Y	12. End Cuban TV-Marti	Y

Election Results

1998 general	Richard E. Neal (D) .... unopposed			($250,407)
1998 primary	Richard E. Neal (D) .... unopposed			
1996 general	Richard E. Neal (D)	162,995	(72%)	($227,105)
	Mark Steele (R)	49,885	(22%)	($1,358)
	Scott Andrichak (I)	9,181	(4%)	
	Others	5,350	(2%)	

THIRD DISTRICT

Worcester (its name still pronounced with a particularly pungent Massachusetts accent making it sound as if it had no *R*s), although technically the second-largest city in Massachusetts, is often overlooked. People may drive in for concerts at the Centrum, but otherwise they zoom by on I-495 or the Turnpike. Worcester is one of the few major industrial cities not located on a river, lake or sea coast, and it is far from a major airport. A high-tech manufacturing haven before the term was invented, for 200 years the city has been one of the nation's centers of tinkering, contriving and inventing. But it hasn't always been smooth going; 50 years ago, Worcester's biggest industries were wire-making, textiles, grinding wheels and envelopes: not on the cutting edge then and certainly not now. But in the 1970s and 1980s, electronics and computer firms sprouted along I-495—the circumferential highway located 20 miles east of Worcester, as they had earlier around Route 128, closer to Boston. The high-tech boom brought prosperity, labor shortages, new residents and higher housing prices to central Massachusetts. Then, in the early 1990s, the minicomputer industry slumped, bringing recession and a collapse of real estate values. But Worcester's ingenious entrepreneurs and skilled labor force have hustled, local leaders have set up a Biotechnology Research Institute and the local economy again is perking up.

The 3d Congressional District, grotesquely shaped, has Worcester as its largest city though not its geographic center. A little more than half its people live in Worcester and a cluster of towns all around. The other cluster of population is far away, in and around the old textile mill town of Fall River, east of Rhode Island, and Dartmouth and Westport on Buzzards Bay. The two are connected by a string of towns in some places only a few miles wide. Thus has the 3d District, if not quite Worcester, been made a seaport. The I-495 corridor and the towns around Worcester are Republican; Worcester itself is Democratic and Fall River and the area around it even more so.

The congressman from the 3d District is Jim McGovern, a Democrat elected in 1996. McGovern grew up in Worcester, where his parents owned a package store on West Boylston Street; he went to American University in Washington, and while in graduate school worked in the office of former South Dakota Senator George McGovern, who is of no relation. He ran McGovern's 1984 campaign in the Massachusetts presidential primary, where he finished third with 21% of the vote, and nominated him at the San Francisco convention. After that he got a job in Boston Congressman Joe Moakley's office and moved up to chief of staff as Moakley moved up to Rules Committee chairman. McGovern then got into the spotlight himself, leading a 1989 investigation of the murders of six Jesuits and two lay women in El Salvador, which led to a cutoff of aid. In 1994 he ran for the House and lost in the Democratic primary 38%–30% to Kevin O'Sullivan, who in turn lost to incumbent Republican Peter Blute. In 1996 McGovern ran again, this time with no primary opposition.

The 1996 campaign was targeted by both sides. Blute, a state representative and sports promoter, had won the seat 50%–44% in 1992 thanks to the House bank problems of incumbent Democrat Joe Early. In 1994 Blute beat O'Sullivan 55%–44%. In 1996 Blute stressed his "independence" from the House leadership and attacked McGovern for liberal stands on abortion and Cuba. The AFL-CIO targeted the district with TV ads, and McGovern ran a humorous spot that asked, "If you wouldn't vote for Newt, why would you ever vote for Blute?" Blute spent more than McGovern, but McGovern outraised him among PACs—an example of how well Democratic Hill denizens can use the PAC system. Blute ran slightly behind, 50%–45%, in the area around Worcester, and was clobbered 56%–45% in the Fall River area and the rest of the district, as McGovern won 53%–45%.

McGovern got some negative publicity in early 1997 for hiring a Philip Morris lobbyist as his chief aide after criticizing Blute for accepting tobacco PAC money. He made several visits to Cuba and has called for easing sanctions against Fidel Castro's regime. But despite his liberal voting record, he worked on a bipartisan basis on some issues. With Republican Tom Coburn, he worked on a home health care bill to restore some of the benefits cuts in the Balanced Budget Act of 1997; it passed in the October 1998 Omnibus Appropriations Act. He introduced several other bipartisan home care bills that did not pass. He called for increasing grant awards for college freshmen and sophomores who were in the top 10% of their high school classes. He got a seat on the Transportation and Infrastructure Committee and its Surface Transportation Subcommittee in time to work on the big 1998 transportation reauthorization bill, the only New England House member on the conference committee. In the bill, Worcester got $11.5 million for Union Station, $6 million for the Blackstone Valley bike path and $1.8 million for Main Street. He got the Blackstone and Woonasquatucket Rivers declared American Heritage Rivers. In August 1998 he made headlines when he invited Bill Clinton to interrupt his vacation for a carefully controlled appearance in Worcester, just 10 days after Clinton admitted he lied about

Monica Lewinsky. "Worcester is not a city of fair-weather friends . . . and you, Mr. President, through your policies, have been a true friend to Worcester," he proclaimed.

At that point McGovern was facing a serious challenge from Matt Amorello, who had won a Democratic state Senate seat in 1990. Amorello attacked McGovern for voting against the balanced budget amendment, the partial-birth abortion ban and supporting the ban on needle exchanges. McGovern attacked Amorello for favoring privatization of Social Security and for his support from conservative Republican leaders. In this pro-incumbent year, the result was not particularly close: McGovern won 57%–41%. In the new spirit of bipartisanship, McGovern invited Speaker Dennis Hastert to Worcester in January 1999; he did not immediately accept.

Cook's Call. *Probably Safe.* McGovern's strong showing in 1998 indicates that he may have found a way to hold onto this Democratic leaning but culturally conservative district. McGovern's liberal voting record could still cause him some problems, but he is a savvy politician who has used his position on the Transportation Committee to bring federal highway dollars home to this economically struggling district.

The People: Pop. 1990: 601,852; 18.5% rural; 14.3% age 65 + ; 94.6% White, 1.8% Black, 1.6% Asian, 0.2% Amer. Indian, 1.8% Other; 3.7% Hispanic Origin. Households: 56.8% married couple families; 27.1% married couple fams. w. children; 47.9% college educ.; median household income: $36,873; per capita income: $15,917; median house value: $150,800; median gross rent: $440.

1996 Presidential Vote

Clinton (D)	154,915	(60%)
Dole (R)	76,413	(29%)
Perot (I)	24,690	(9%)
Others	4,096	(2%)

1992 Presidential Vote

Clinton (D)	123,724	(45%)
Bush (R)	85,047	(31%)
Perot (I)	62,667	(23%)

Rep. James McGovern (D)

Elected 1996; b. Nov. 20, 1959, Worcester; home, Worcester; American U., B.A. 1981, M.P.A. 1984; Catholic; married (Lisa).

Professional Career: Aide, U.S. Sen. George McGovern, 1977–80; Sr. Aide, U.S. Rep. John Joseph Moakley, 1982–96.

DC Office: 416 CHOB 20515, 202-225-6101; Fax: 202-225-5759; Web site: www.house.gov/mcgovern.

District Offices: Attleboro, 508-431-8025; Fall River, 508-677-0140; Worcester, 508-831-7356.

Committees: *Transportation & Infrastructure* (27th of 34 D): Aviation; Water Resources & Environment.

Group Ratings

	ADA	ACLU	AFS	LCV	CON	NTU	NFIB	COC	ACU	NTLC	CHC
1998	100	81	100	100	38	16	7	39	4	5	0
1997	100	—	100	—	3	26	—	30	4	—	—

National Journal Ratings

	1997 LIB — 1997 CONS			1998 LIB — 1998 CONS		
Economic	93%	—	0%	79%	—	0%
Social	82%	—	15%	90%	—	7%
Foreign	97%	—	0%	90%	—	5%

Key Votes of the 105th Congress

1. Clinton Budget Deal	N	5. Puerto Rico Sthood. Ref.	Y	9. Cut $ for B-2 Bombers	Y
2. Education IRAs	N	6. End Highway Set-asides	N	10. Human Rights in China	Y
3. Req. 2/3 to Raise Taxes	N	7. School Prayer Amend.	N	11. Withdraw Bosnia Troops	N
4. Fast-track Trade	N	8. Ovrd. Part. Birth Veto	N	12. End Cuban TV-Marti	Y

Election Results

1998 general	James McGovern (D)	108,613	(57%)	($1,312,181)
	Matthew Amorello (R)	79,174	(41%)	($680,809)
	Others	3,091	(2%)	
1998 primary	James McGovern (D)	unopposed		
1996 general	James McGovern (D)	135,044	(53%)	($806,939)
	Peter I. Blute (R)	115,694	(45%)	($1,144,540)
	Others	4,359	(2%)	

FOURTH DISTRICT

The political transformation of Massachusetts is nowhere better illustrated than in the Boston suburbs of Brookline and Newton. These were Yankee enclaves a century ago, with avenues built to resemble the sweep of Haussmann's Grand Boulevards in Paris, and villages of giant clapboard houses clustered within a few blocks of commuter railroad stations. Brookline was where The Country Club (the very first one) was established in 1882, and where Joseph Kennedy, an Irish Catholic 20-something banker seeking respectability, moved his family in 1914. Brookline and Newton then were solidly Republican in politics, the political base of leading politicians like Christian Herter, governor of Massachusetts and U.S. secretary of state in the 1950s; as late as 1960, Brookline and Newton and adjacent wards of Boston were electing a Republican congressman. Then came the transformation, personified by the election in 1962 of Michael Dukakis at 29 to the Great and General Court (the legislature). As Massachusetts's university-educated classes became more liberal, and as Brookline's and Newton's Jewish populations grew, and as young liberal-minded families refurbished the graceful old houses, these towns became Democratic bastions. By the 1970s, the Brookline Town Meeting was opening each year with debates over whether they should recite the "Pledge of Allegiance." Brookline and Newton, more than Boston, are the liberal heart of Massachusetts: They voted 69%–29% for Dukakis in 1988, 68%–20% for Bill Clinton in 1992 and again for Clinton 75%–20% in 1996, 65%–34% for Democrat Scott Harshbarger over Governor Paul Cellucci in 1998.

The 4th Congressional District includes Brookline and Newton, which are the political home bases for its congressman, Barney Frank. But they cast only 25% of the district's votes, and this grotesquely shaped district is not all of one piece: Indeed, one setting out to canvass entirely the district's bounds might have to get off the road and step over fences and trudge through marshes. The shape results from successive redistrictings: In 1982, Frank's district was extended south to the old textile mill city of Fall River; in 1992, it lost much of Fall River and gained New Bedford, a great 19th Century whaling port and still home to one of the largest fishing fleets in the United States, with the largest percentage of Portuguese-Americans in the nation. The 4th also curves north to the interior of Plymouth County around old towns like Bridgewater. This is a Democratic district in national politics, but not nearly so Democratic nor as uniformly culturally liberal as Brookline and Newton. There is a bit of most kinds of America here: high-income WASPy Wellesley, French-Canadian mill-worker Fall River, Foxboro with its football stadium, Sharon with a middle-income Jewish population and countrified Dover.

Barney Frank, elected in 1980, is one of the intellectual and political leaders of the Democratic Party in the House—political theorist and pit bull all at the same time. Frank grew up in Bayonne, New Jersey, and went to Harvard, where he got to know local politicians as well as political scientists. In 1967, he went to work for newly elected Boston Mayor Kevin White;

in 1971, he went to Washington to work for Congressman Michael Harrington. In 1972, Frank was elected to the Massachusetts House from the Back Bay of Boston, then just starting to be a liberal singles neighborhood. In 1980, when Congressman Robert Drinan retired after Pope John Paul II commanded Jesuits to leave elective office, Frank moved to Brookline and ran in the 4th District. With a strong base in Brookline and Newton, he won; keeping them together as redistricting moved the seat down to Fall River; he beat Republican Margaret Heckler 60%–40% in 1982. He has been re-elected by wide margins since.

In the House, Frank soon gained a reputation as one of the smartest talkers and best debaters in the chamber—may be one of the best of all time. At a time when so many members seem to rely on canned speeches produced by staffers and letterhead interest groups, debaters Frank listens to others' arguments and engages them in his inimitable rapid-fire delivery. While he stands at the left end of the American electoral spectrum, there is an element of solid small-c conservatism beneath him. "Democratic positions are fully consistent with the values of patriotism, free enterprise, working hard for one's self and one's family, and holding people to a standard of behavior fully respectful of the person and property of others," he wrote in his 1992 book *Speaking Frankly*. More recently he said he is for "capitalism plus," that is, market capitalism with welfare state protections, and he has expressed unease at what he considers increasing isolationism in Congress, though he also believes in "tens of billions" in cuts for defense spending and has tried to tear down the firewalls around defense and domestic spending, arguing that defense should not be exempt from cuts.

Frank has worked hard, often behind the scenes, on many substantive issues. He took over the subcommittee handling the bill to provide redress to Japanese Americans interned in World War II and got it through the House and signed into law. He has shaped immigration acts from 1986–96: to expand legal immigration, to allow HIV-positive people to enter the country, and to bar states from excluding children of illegal aliens from school. As ranking Democrat on the Courts and Intellectual Property Subcommittee of Judiciary, he helped build a bipartisan coalition that in the 105th Congress linked two related issues, the World Intellectual Property Organization treaties and the protection of intellectual property on the Internet. The result, he said, was "one bill which preserved the protection of intellectual property without impinging on the freedom necessary to the Internet." In addition, the term of copyright was extended by 20 years. After the 1998 election Frank left the ranking position on Intellectual Property and took the ranking position on Banking's Housing Subcommittee. There he worked with Joe Kennedy and HUD Secretary Andrew Cuomo to resist Republican initiatives that they believe would gut housing programs. In previous years he worked to create the HOME program of housing block grants to the states, shaping the RTC program that sold low-end housing units acquired by bankrupt S&Ls to low- and moderate-income people, barring housing discrimination against people with AIDS, and blocking a Republican attempt to raise the 30% income cap on public housing rents.

He has also had some bipartisan successes. With Republican Charles Canady, he managed the Lobbying Disclosure Act, barring all amendments so that the House would pass the Senate bill and no conference committee would be necessary. With Bob Dole, he was a lonely voice for auctioning off the digital TV spectrum rather than giving it away free, as most in Congress and the Clinton Administration favored. He also passed a law, vital for the biotech industry, allowing companies to receive patents for processes for artificially manufacturing substances which exist naturally. He and Daniel Patrick Moynihan are co-sponsors of a bill to block the use of tax-exempt municipal bonds for new sports facilities. In 1998, after years of trying, he got passed an amendment limiting the American financial contribution for the expansion of NATO; in celebration, he voted for the defense bill for the first time in years. He and David Bonior secured compromise language on the 1998 IMF funding bill committing the U.S. to do more for workers' rights in countries receiving financial bailouts.

But not until the impeachment hearings of 1998 was Frank able to overshadow another aspect of his career. In May 1987, in a seemingly casual answer to a reporter's question, Frank said he is gay. Then in August 1989, the conservative *Washington Times* reported that Frank had employed as a personal aide a male prostitute and convicted drug possessor, Steve Gobie, and let him live in his apartment, where the man allegedly carried on his trade. Frank admitted to paying Gobie, but was careful never to use official or campaign funds; he denied that he tolerated prostitution in his apartment and said he had thrown the man out when he suspected it was going on. *The Boston Globe* called on Frank to resign; his picture appeared on the cover of *Newsweek*; he called on the ethics committee to investigate. It did and dismissed all but two minor charges (Frank made a few mistakes in declaring which of several parking tickets were entitled to be dismissed because they were incurred in the line of official business). The committee recommended a reprimand but not censure; Frank agreed in a contrite appearance before the House in July 1990; the House voted 287–141 against censure (moved by Newt Gingrich); the vote for reprimand was 408–18. "I think members will agree that I have always had a reputation for honesty, not always tact or tolerance," Frank said to the House. That reputation was one reason he survived and has thrived in the House; his brains, liberal stands, hard work and constituency service helped him not only survive but be overwhelmingly popular in the 4th District.

His admission did cost him any chance of a House leadership position; Tip O'Neill thought it cost him a chance to be the first Jewish speaker. It also made him a leading spokesman on gay rights issues. One was the issue, raised in the 1992 campaign by Bill Clinton and not by Frank or by gay advocacy groups, of gays in the military. To the disappointment of many in the gay community, Frank admitted that allowing open homosexuals to serve in the military would not be accepted by most in Congress or the Pentagon. Taking Senator Sam Nunn's "Don't Ask, Don't Tell" compromise a step further, Frank suggested that gays be allowed to conduct an openly gay lifestyle when off-base without fear of reprisal; but Clinton eventually declined to go so far. In the years since, Frank has criticized the administration and the military because the number of service members discharged for homosexuality has actually increased. Frank and Republican Christopher Shays have sponsored a bill to prohibit employment discrimination on account of sexuality; it has not passed, but the success of Frank and Republican Jim Kolbe in blocking Republican Joel Hefley's amendment to overturn a Clinton executive order prohibiting such discrimination in the civil service suggests there may be, even in a Republican House, a majority for the concept. Frank is also the sponsor of a bill to make domestic partners of federal employees eligible for health insurance and of the bill which would provide federal penalties for hate crimes.

After the Republican victory in November 1994, Minority Whip David Bonior asked Frank to be the Democrats' point man in floor debates; Frank asked whether Bonior wanted him to be such a visible symbol of the party, and Bonior said yes. During the Contract With America debate, Frank prowled the floor, ready to take up a microphone and deliver stinging attacks on Republicans' hypocrisy or cross-examine a freshman with all the mercy of a Harvard Law professor questioning a not-quite-prepared first-year student. His strong and orderly mind, his ability to argue abstract principles in rapid-fire but comprehensible words, were on display— and made him the most feared adversary by the Republican side. But his belief that the Republicans' positions would prove unpopular and cost them their majority has not, or at least not yet, proven true.

Frank also emerged, well before the impeachment crisis, as a defender of Bill Clinton against charges of scandal. He came at these issues as a civil libertarian who is attentive to defendants' rights, and perhaps to memories of the time his father, a truck stop owner, was jailed for contempt of court for refusing to answer questions about his brother in a Hudson County investigation; "he was the Susan McDougal of his day," Frank once said. On the Banking Committee in 1994 he defended Clinton with attack-dog intensity against Whitewater charges; on the Judiciary Committee in October 1997 he and William Delahunt peppered Janet Reno with questions and made tough arguments when Republicans were trying to pressure her to appoint more independent counsels. In those cases, and in impeachment, his goal was clear and, he and many other believe, achieved. After impeachment was voted he said, "I think we effectively demonstrated the partisan and unfair nature of the House proceedings." He did so despite a liking for his chief adversary, Judiciary Committee Chairman Henry Hyde. They seem to have a genuine appreciation and regard for each other.

Frank acknowledged that Clinton lied in his deposition in the Paula Jones case and said, "He screwed up. Bill Clinton is entitled to fairness but not indignation on his behalf. He's not a purely innocent person having suddenly been mugged." But Frank also ridiculed the case against him, saying it boiled down to the question: "What did the president touch and why did he touch it?" When Republicans argued that Frank's preferred result, censure, would be trivial, he seized on his own experience and said, "I am struck by those who argued that censure is somehow an irrelevancy, a triviality, something of no weight. I would tell you that having been reprimanded by this House of Representatives, where I'm so proud to serve, was no triviality." But in making this valid political point he did himself a personal injustice: The misstatements he made were of the most trivial sort, mere bookkeeping errors; and on the main charges, he stood up, faced the facts and told the truth, however embarrassing, with no assurance that his political career would survive.

Through all his work on national issues, Frank has not neglected the home front. He has worked especially hard on projects in Fall River and, after it was added to the district after the 1990 Census, New Bedford, for which he obtained the creation of a national park commemorating the whaling industry, the funding for a new Route 18 and assistance to the fishing industry. He got Portugal, from which many in New Bedford have emigrated, added to the list of countries for which the United States does not require visas for visitors, in the face of opposition from the Judiciary Committee's leadership and the Clinton Administration. Frank has been re-elected by very wide margins and in 1998 was unopposed.

Cook's Call. *Safe.* A well-known fixture in the Washington political scene, Frank is securely entrenched in this heavily Democratic suburban Boston district. Not even a scandal in 1989 put a dent in his re-election percentage; he is about as safe as they come.

The People: Pop. 1990: 601,392; 26.9% rural; 14.4% age 65 + ; 93.6% White, 2.1% Black, 2.1% Asian, 0.2% Amer. Indian, 2% Other; 2.3% Hispanic Origin. Households: 56.3% married couple families; 27.4% married couple fams. w. children; 51.4% college educ.; median household income: $39,005; per capita income: $18,963; median house value: $170,600; median gross rent: $434.

1996 Presidential Vote

Clinton (D)	169,078	(64%)
Dole (R)	69,548	(26%)
Perot (I)	22,782	(9%)

1992 Presidential Vote

Clinton (D)	143,595	(51%)
Bush (R)	74,769	(26%)
Perot (I)	62,746	(22%)

Rep. Barney Frank (D)

Elected 1980; b. Mar. 31, 1940, Bayonne, NJ; home, Newton; Harvard U., B.A. 1962, J.D. 1977; Jewish; single.

Elected Office: MA House of Reps., 1972–80.

Professional Career: Exec. Asst., Boston Mayor Kevin White, 1967–71; A.A., U.S. Rep. Michael Harrington, 1971–72; Lecturer, Harvard JFK Schl. of Govt., 1978–80.

DC Office: 2210 RHOB 20515, 202-225-5931; Fax: 202-225-0182; Web site: www.house.gov/frank.

District Offices: Bridgewater, 508-697-9403; Fall River, 508-674-3551; New Bedford, 508-999-6462; Newton, 617-332-3920.

Committees: *Banking & Financial Services* (3d of 27 D): Domestic & International Monetary Policy; Housing & Community Opportunity (RMM). *Judiciary* (2d of 16 D): Immigration & Claims; The Constitution.

Group Ratings

	ADA	ACLU	AFS	LCV	CON	NTU	NFIB	COC	ACU	NTLC	CHC
1998	100	94	100	92	76	18	0	33	4	3	0
1997	100	—	100	—	14	27	—	30	4	—	—

National Journal Ratings

	1997 LIB — 1997 CONS		1998 LIB — 1998 CONS	
Economic	91%	— 7%	72%	— 23%
Social	85%	— 0%	90%	— 7%
Foreign	85%	— 13%	82%	— 16%

Key Votes of the 105th Congress

1. Clinton Budget Deal	N	5. Puerto Rico Sthood. Ref.	Y	9. Cut $ for B-2 Bombers	Y
2. Education IRAs	N	6. End Highway Set-asides	N	10. Human Rights in China	Y
3. Req. 2/3 to Raise Taxes	N	7. School Prayer Amend.	N	11. Withdraw Bosnia Troops	Y
4. Fast-track Trade	N	8. Ovrd. Part. Birth Veto	N	12. End Cuban TV-Marti	Y

Election Results

1998 general	Barney Frank (D)	.... unopposed		($345,272)
1998 primary	Barney Frank (D)	.... unopposed		
1996 general	Barney Frank (D)	 183,844	(72%)	($334,002)
	Jonathan Raymond (R)	 72,701	(28%)	($108,348)

FIFTH DISTRICT

The Merrimack River Valley at the northern edge of Massachusetts has had an erratic history: high-tech boom, bust, boom, bust, boom. When Massachusetts was a kind of maritime republic in the 19th Century, with a few farmers struggling to scratch out a living from the stony soil, a few clever Yankees used their profits from the sea trade to try to tame the rapidly flowing Merrimack and build cotton spinning mills. Creating the cities of Lowell and Lawrence, they built model dormitories and recreation programs for their women workers. This was the center of America's textile industry for more than a century, long after the maritime industry faded. But in the 1920s, the price of labor rose and newly built mills in the Carolinas—much closer to the cotton supply—decimated the industry that Lawrence and Lowell built. Many residents— by then rather elderly—waited forlornly for an upturn in the local economy.

It came eventually, largely due to an unexpected source. High-tech industry drove the growth, beginning in the 1960s around MIT, then moving out to the Route 128 ring road and then I-495, which passes through Lowell and Lawrence. Wang, headquartered in Lowell, grew spectacularly, and former Congressman and Senator Paul Tsongas spearheaded a national historical restoration of the old mill area. This was the Massachusetts miracle of the early 1980s. Then came the bust: Wang's word processors and minicomputers slumped as businesses purchased personal computers and hooked them together in networks. But Lowell revived again. Its new immigrants—mostly from Cambodia and Puerto Rico—provide vitality and entrepreneur creativity; the old Wang buildings are filled with health care, banking, telecommunications and Internet companies. Paul Tsongas died in January 1997, but lived long enough to see Lowell on the move again, rehabbing the River Place Towers, renovating the Bon Marche and building the Paul Tsongas Arena. And high-tech growth boomed in the smaller towns all around.

The 5th Congressional District includes Lawrence and Lowell, which along with next-door towns account for about half the district's population. The remainder of the district includes the high-tech corridor further south on I-495, running from the stony hills of Lawrence and Lowell to Maynard and Marlborough. The district also includes fancy suburbs like Concord, aging mill towns like Ayer and the mountains along the New Hampshire state line. Except for Lowell and Lawrence, it is ancestrally Yankee Republican. It is culturally liberal and trended toward the Democrats in the early 1970s. But in the 1980s and 1990s, amid the high-tech boom, it went Republican in national and even statewide elections: a kind of Baja New Hampshire. In 1992 it gave Bill Clinton his lowest percentage in the state, while a big vote went to high-tech pioneer Ross Perot; in 1996, unnerved by the Republican revolutionaries, it went heavily Democratic.

The congressman from the 5th District is Martin Meehan, a Democrat elected in 1992. Meehan grew up in Lowell, one of seven children of a Lowell *Sun* typesetter. As a child, he memorized President Kennedy's speeches from long-playing records, kept a scrapbook on Robert Kennedy, and idolized Edward Kennedy, who was elected to the Senate when Meehan was 5. He is a lifelong politico: he was an aide to Congressman James Shannon while working on his masters degree, worked in the Massachusetts secretary of state's office after law school, and was first assistant district attorney in Middlesex County from 1990 until he ran for Congress in 1992. He took on eight-year incumbent Democrat Chester Atkins, who was hurt when he alienated an old ally, state Senate President Billy Bulger, who with Governor William Weld kept Lawrence and Lowell, where Atkins was highly unpopular, in the district. Meehan beat Atkins by the astonishing margin of 65%–35%, winning the Lowell-Lawrence area 75%–25%. In the general, Meehan faced former Congressman Paul Cronin, who beat John Kerry in 1972 (the only open seat carried by George McGovern to also elect a Republican to the House), but lost to Paul Tsongas in 1974. Meehan called for a 50% defense cut, targeted capital gains tax cuts, income tax increases, and backed the balanced budget amendment and term limits—he won 52%–38%.

Meehan combines a mostly liberal voting record with distinctive stands on issues; this has gotten him labeled a maverick. One of his crusades is against tobacco; his father, a smoker, had heart surgery when Marty was 11. In his first term he worked with Henry Waxman when he was conducting hearings with tobacco company heads and called for more prominent warnings on cigarette packages. After the 1994 election, Meehan prepared a 111-page memo urging prosecution of tobacco companies, and later joined with Utah Republican James Hansen to sponsor a bill with a $1.50 a pack tax and a target of cutting youth smoking by 80%.

His other great cause is campaign finance reform. In 1997, with Christopher Shays and Senators Russ Feingold and John McCain, Meehan co-sponsored the campaign finance plan whose eventual final version would outlaw soft money and foreign money, subject non-candidate ads to disclosure and contribution limit requirements, strengthen FEC enforcement powers, require posting of forms on the Internet, and create a commission to recommend more reforms. When House Republican leaders refused to let the measure come to the floor, Meehan and others gathered signatures on a discharge petition; under such pressure, the leadership finally allowed a vote in August 1998, and it passed 252–179, with 61 Republican votes. But no vote was taken in the Senate, and in early 1999, Meehan again was trying to get a House vote to put more pressure on the Senate to act.

Meehan serves on the Armed Services Committee and has generally moved to cut defense spending, but boosts Raytheon and its upgrades of the Patriot missile. Over the years, his voting record seems to have drifted left: He voted for NAFTA in 1993 and against fast track in 1997. He was staunchly against impeachment and peppered the House deliberations with remarks assailing Republicans for partisanship. He has worked on local projects, getting $11.9 million in highway projects in 1998, working for a Lowell baseball stadium and preservation of O'Rourke's farm in Carlisle.

When Meehan ran in 1992, he pledged to serve no more than four terms. In January 1999 he appeared to change his mind. For this he was attacked by Massachusetts colleagues, who were irritated by his support of campaign finance reform (though on the record they're for it) and for other maverick tendencies, such as introducing Republican Paul Cellucci as "a friend" at a women's issues forum he hosted for Hillary Rodham Clinton in Lowell in May 1998. As Meehan has explained, "I didn't like being a backbencher until the Democrats took back Congress. That made some—Moakley and Barney Frank—question my loyalty. But I got elected at a different time than they did, and my view of what Democrats need to learn to be an effective minority party is different, too." In a May 1999 letter to his constituents, Meehan finally declared he would seek a fifth term, saying "I have come to realize over the past seven years that, with the failure of term limits nationally, to arbitrarily limit my own service puts the people I represent at a disadvantage." He had more than $1 million in campaign finances left over from the 1998 election.

Cook's Call. *Probably Safe.* Meehan, who pledged to serve only four terms during his 1992 race, announced in spring 1999 that he will run for re-election in 2000. While this has raised the ire of national term limits proponents, it is unlikely to cause Meehan to lose the election in the heavily Democratic district.

The People: Pop. 1990: 601,527; 16% rural; 11% age 65 + ; 89.6% White, 2.2% Black, 3.5% Asian, 0.2% Amer. Indian, 4.5% Other; 8% Hispanic Origin. Households: 58.4% married couple families; 29.8% married couple fams. w. children; 51.7% college educ.; median household income: $42,701; per capita income: $18,293; median house value: $174,200; median gross rent: $526.

1996 Presidential Vote		
Clinton (D)	143,122	(58%)
Dole (R)	76,605	(31%)
Perot (I)	24,079	(10%)
Others	4,070	(2%)

1992 Presidential Vote		
Clinton (D)	113,073	(42%)
Bush (R)	85,366	(32%)
Perot (I)	70,474	(26%)

Rep. Martin T. Meehan (D)

Elected 1992; b. Dec. 30, 1956, Lowell; home, Lowell; U. of MA, B.S. 1978, Suffolk U., M.A. 1981, J.D. 1986; Catholic; married (Ellen Murphy).

Professional Career: Staff Asst., U.S. Rep. James Shannon, 1979–81; Research analyst, MA Legislature's Joint Cmte. on Elections, 1982–84; MA Dpty. Secy. of State for Securities & Corps., 1985–90; Middlesex Cnty. 1st Asst. Dist. Atty., 1990–92.

DC Office: 2434 RHOB 20515, 202-225-3411; Fax: 202-226-0771; Web site: www.house.gov/meehan.

District Offices: Lawrence, 978-681-6200; Lowell, 978-459-0101; Marlborough, 508-460-9292.

Committees: *Armed Services* (9th of 28 D): Military Personnel; Military Research & Development; Special Oversight Panel on Morale, Welfare and Recreation (RMM). *Judiciary* (11th of 16 D): Crime; Immigration & Claims.

Group Ratings

	ADA	ACLU	AFS	LCV	CON	NTU	NFIB	COC	ACU	NTLC	CHC
1998	100	94	100	92	93	18	15	31	4	5	0
1997	90	—	71	—	100	43	—	44	20	—	—

National Journal Ratings

	1997 LIB — 1997 CONS			1998 LIB — 1998 CONS		
Economic	90%	—	9%	72%	—	23%
Social	85%	—	0%	93%	—	0%
Foreign	76%	—	22%	78%	—	19%

Key Votes of the 105th Congress

1. Clinton Budget Deal	*	5. Puerto Rico Sthood. Ref.	Y	9. Cut $ for B-2 Bombers	Y
2. Education IRAs	N	6. End Highway Set-asides	N	10. Human Rights in China	Y
3. Req. 2/3 to Raise Taxes	N	7. School Prayer Amend.	N	11. Withdraw Bosnia Troops	N
4. Fast-track Trade	N	8. Ovrd. Part. Birth Veto	N	12. End Cuban TV-Marti	Y

Election Results

1998 general	Martin T. Meehan (D)	127,418	(71%)	($283,239)
	David E. Coleman (R)	52,725	(29%)	
1998 primary	Martin T. Meehan (D)	unopposed		
1996 general	Martin T. Meehan (D)	unopposed		($308,067)

SIXTH DISTRICT

The North Shore of Massachusetts Bay has a number of times been at the leading edge of the nation's economy. In 1640, the Saugus Iron Works was built here—the beginning of American heavy industry. When Europe's great powers were convulsed in international war from 1792 to 1815, American ship owners suddenly became the richest in the world and traders from Boston accumulated the capital needed to build textile mills and railroads and to finance much of the American industrial revolution. From the small port of Salem, ships left for China, bringing back porcelain and artifacts, which helped change American styles forever. Salem, first settled in 1626, had the nation's first millionaire, Elias Hasket Derby; in 1900 it was the richest city per capita in the nation. But the North Shore is a quiet place, from Boston harbor north to the mouth of the Merrimack River, a collection of ethnic factory towns from Lynn on up through next-door Peabody to Newburyport, alternating with the high-income enclaves of Marblehead with its yachts and Beverly with its estates, artsy Rockport and the fishing port of Gloucester—hard hit by overfishing of mackerel and herring in the 1970s and cod in the 1990s. Lynn is the largest town and its General Electric jet engine plant is the largest employer, though with far fewer jobs than during the defense buildup of the 1980s and with payrolls threatened by offset deals to produce some engines in the countries purchasing them.

The 6th Congressional District includes the North Shore from Lynn onward, plus towns and cities several miles inland. It is a varied area demographically and politically: its high-income Yankee towns are liberal Republican, while Lynn, Salem, Peabody and the Merrimack mill towns are still Irish working-class Democratic. The 6th has been a Democratic district on balance since the 1960s; but in the 1980s and in the 1990s only marginally so. While this district is the site of the original gerrymander—named after Elbridge Gerry—the current 6th District boundaries are less grotesque and politically determined than those of any other Massachusetts district.

The congressman from the 6th District is John Tierney, a Democrat elected in 1996 after coming close in 1994. Tierney grew up in Salem in modest circumstances; he worked his way through Salem State College and Suffolk University Law School as a janitor on the night shift. For nearly 20 years he practiced law in his family's firm in Salem. In 1994 he spied a political opening and ran for Congress. The incumbent, Peter Torkildsen, was a Republican elected in 1992 by beating incumbent Nicholas Mavroulas, who had been indicted for tax evasion and bribery (he pled guilty in 1993); the district had otherwise been safely Democratic since liberal Michael Harrington won a special election in 1969. In 1994, Tierney won a closely contested primary with 34% over two other Democrats with 33% and 25%; he called for a single-payer health insurance plan and a ban on all handgun sales, and attacked Torkildsen for voting against the crime bill. But in a Republican year, Torkildsen won 51%–47%.

In 1996 Tierney ran again. His ads, along with the AFL-CIO's, assailed Newt Gingrich and Republican Medicare "cuts." He called for "greater educational opportunities," government health care insurance for children, aid to college students and criticized Torkildsen for not bringing enough defense dollars to the district. Torkildsen raised and spent $1.1 million, while keeping his promise to accept no PAC money, and led in early polls. Tierney held his spending—$776,000 in total—mostly until the end. The result was one of the closest races in the country. Tierney came out slightly ahead in initial returns and after several recounts, which stretched into December, Tierney won by only 372 votes.

In the House, Tierney got a seat on Education and the Workforce, where he voted down the line for the unions. He made a splash early by calling for combining the Senate and House investigations of Clinton-Gore campaign finances and attacked Republicans for subpoenaing the wrong Dr. Chi Wang, a Georgetown professor rather than the participant in the infamous Buddhist temple fundraiser. To promote the Shays-Meehan campaign finance bill, he started forcing roll calls on the previous day's record in September 1997. But he worked with Republicans to get aid for the district—with Jerry Lewis to get $2 million for sewer aid for Essex County, with Frank Wolf to get $1 million to study an extension of the Blue Line T from East Boston to Beverly (opposed by the MBTA as too expensive). After some hesitation, he joined with William Delahunt and New Jersey Republican Jim Saxton to support a ban on big fishing trawlers from Georges Bank.

The 1998 campaign was another rematch. Tierney attacked Torkildsen on old themes: "Whenever Newt Gingrich needed him to cut an education program, he was there." Tierney emphasized his fight against Republican efforts to cut funding for summer jobs and literacy programs, and said Torkildsen would vote for measures that would endanger Social Security. Torkildsen said Tierney is "not doing a good job of bringing tax dollars back home," and noted that Tierney had not taken seats on Armed Services (to help the GE plant in Lynn) and the fisheries and national parks subcommittees. He also hit Tierney for opposing the Republicans' $80 billion tax cut and for blocking a probe of the Teamsters Union after taking $30,000 from them in campaign contributions. But this was the first time that Tierney, with help from PAC money, outspent the Republicans. Even as Republican Governor Paul Cellucci easily carried the district, Tierney won 55%–42%, a marked improvement over 1996. It is not clear whether this district, in play for most of the 1990s, will be seriously contested in 2000.

Cook's Call. *Potentially Competitive.* Tierney had a good showing in 1998, but the demographics of this district can still prove tricky for him. Although the 6th has a solid working-class Democratic foundation, the wealthier Boston suburbs give it a significant Republican base; there is also a substantial independent vote here. A top-flight Republican candidate could make this a good race in 2000.

The People: Pop. 1990: 601,811; 10% rural; 14.4% age 65 + ; 95.4% White, 1.8% Black, 1.4% Asian, 0.2% Amer. Indian, 1.3% Other; 2.7% Hispanic Origin. Households: 56.2% married couple families; 25.6% married couple fams. w. children; 53.5% college educ.; median household income: $40,836; per capita income: $18,549; median house value: $181,100; median gross rent: $542.

1996 Presidential Vote		
Clinton (D)	166,037	(59%)
Dole (R)	86,306	(31%)
Perot (I)	26,273	(9%)

1992 Presidential Vote		
Clinton (D)	134,424	(43%)
Bush (R)	96,857	(31%)
Perot (I)	75,893	(25%)

Rep. John F. Tierney (D)

Elected 1996; b. Sept. 18, 1951, Salem; home, Salem; Salem St. U., B.A. 1973, Suffolk U., J.D. 1976; no religious affiliation; married (Patrice).

Professional Career: Practicing atty., 1976–96.

DC Office: 120 CHOB 20515, 202-225-8020; Fax: 202-225-5915; Web site: www.house.gov/tierney.

District Offices: Haverhill, 978-469-1942; Lynn, 781-595-7375; Peabody, 978-531-1669.

Committees: *Education & the Workforce* (16th of 22 D): Employer-Employee Relations; Postsecondary Education, Training & Life-Long Learning. *Government Reform* (15th of 19 D): Criminal Justice, Drug Policy & Human Resources; National Security, Veterans' Affairs & Intl. Relations.

Group Ratings

	ADA	ACLU	AFS	LCV	CON	NTU	NFIB	COC	ACU	NTLC	CHC
1998	100	94	100	100	48	21	7	22	4	5	0
1997	100	—	100	—	24	28	—	20	12	—	—

National Journal Ratings

	1997 LIB — 1997 CONS			1998 LIB — 1998 CONS		
Economic	93%	—	0%	79%	—	0%
Social	85%	—	0%	93%	—	0%
Foreign	72%	—	26%	89%	—	10%

Key Votes of the 105th Congress

1. Clinton Budget Deal	N	5. Puerto Rico Sthood. Ref.	Y	9. Cut $ for B-2 Bombers	Y
2. Education IRAs	N	6. End Highway Set-asides	N	10. Human Rights in China	Y
3. Req. 2/3 to Raise Taxes	N	7. School Prayer Amend.	N	11. Withdraw Bosnia Troops	*
4. Fast-track Trade	N	8. Ovrd. Part. Birth Veto	N	12. End Cuban TV-Marti	Y

Election Results

1998 general	John F. Tierney (D) 117,132	(55%)	($998,475)
	Peter G. Torkildsen (R) 90,986	(42%)	($882,595)
	Others 6,588	(3%)	
1998 primary	John F. Tierney (D) 45,951	(87%)	
	David A. Francoeur (D) 6,819	(13%)	
1996 general	John F. Tierney (D) 133,002	(48%)	($776,359)
	Peter G. Torkildsen (R) 132,642	(48%)	($1,120,913)
	Others 10,735	(4%)	

SEVENTH DISTRICT

The Yankee Protestants and Irish Catholics who settled Massachusetts arrived by boat, the Yankees to a cold stony land with a few Indians, the Irish to a crowded city with Yankees who seemed even less welcoming. The Yankees whose ancestors once farmed the soil had, by the early 20th Century, founded suburbs filled with solid brick and white frame houses, furnished in Early American furniture. As the years went on, their local public schools were emptied as young people with children moved out, and attendance at Protestant churches went down. The Irish, for decades heavily concentrated in the crowded wards of Boston, started moving out into the Yankee suburbs 50 years ago. There were other ethnic groups here and there (Jews, Italians, French-Canadians) but the major conflict—fought out in neighborhood playgrounds, in school committee meetings and not least in political campaigns—was between Protestant Yankee Republicans and Catholic Irish Democrats.

The 7th Congressional District is made up of Boston's northern and western suburbs, where vestiges of this conflict can still be seen. Geographically, it forms an arc around Boston, starting with the clapboard beach towns of Winthrop and Revere just beyond Logan Airport, going north as far as Wakefield, west past working-class Woburn and Medford, home of Tufts University, to the patriot town of Lexington, and Waltham, home of Brandeis University, through high-income Lincoln and Weston to modest-income Natick and Framingham. Most of these towns were Yankee Republican through the 1950s, but by the late 1960s they were solidly Democratic; the high-tech suburbs trended Republican again in the 1980s but swung against George Bush in 1992. The highest income areas seem to run across the grain of their ethnic experience: Weston, with many Catholics, is pretty solidly Republican; Lincoln, with Yankees like Thomas Boylston Adams and George Bush's sister Nancy Ellis, has been liberal Democratic since it voted for George McGovern in 1972.

The congressman in the 7th District is Edward Markey, elected in 1976 at age 30, and now one of the most powerful Democrats in the House. He grew up in Malden, where his father was a milkman; he went to Malden Catholic High, Boston College and Boston College Law, then immediately to the state House, at 26. In 1976, he ran for the House and won a 12-candidate primary with 22% of the vote; he had never been to Washington. Markey first made a name as a fierce opponent of nuclear power. In 1983 he was the leading political organizer for the nuclear freeze, which would have given away America's technological edge just as the defense buildup was starting to destabilize the Soviets' evil empire. Markey's enthusiastic certainty and his thirst for publicity infuriated many colleagues, who saw him as a self-righteous grandstander.

But seniority and events put Markey in position to be a serious legislator, and he has long since become one of the most legislatively productive and creative members of the House. He is one of those lucky House members for whom the seniority system has clicked. With help from Tip O'Neill, he got on the Commerce Committee; impressed by the high-tech boom around Route 128, he got on the old Communications Subcommittee early. He flirted with running for the Senate in 1984, when Paul Tsongas retired, but when faced with a three-person primary, he jumped back into the 7th District race and scrambled to win. Then, after only eight years in the House, he became chairman of the Energy Conservation and Power Subcommittee; after the 1986 election, with help from Chairman John Dingell, who liked aggressive and loyal younger Democrats, Markey became chairman of the Telecommunications Subcommittee. This is one of the plum positions in the House, with fabulous possibilities for campaign fundraising (Markey doesn't take PAC money, but owners and executives of regulated companies can and do contribute), and with subject matter that is intellectually more demanding (and in lobbying terms more fiercely contested) than almost anything else in Congress. Markey raised $455,000 in the 1998 cycle and could easily raise four times that if he wanted.

As chairman and ranking Democrat since 1994, Markey has been a major shaper of public policy, often working with Republicans, often coming up with original initiatives, knowledgeable about the workings of these industries and inclined often toward deregulation, but also casting himself as the defender of consumers. His 1990 law responding to the 1987 market crash increased the power of the SEC to shut down markets or limit computer programs in emergencies. On derivatives, Markey has sought not to shut the markets down but to provide more disclosure. In communications, Markey passed bills limiting dial-a-porn services and requiring TVs to include decoder circuitry for close-captioned signals for the deaf. In 1992, he combined his penchant for regulation with political shrewdness to produce the cable TV reregulation bill on which both houses overrode President Bush's veto—the only bill passed over his veto in his four-year term. Another Markey achievement in 1993 was the law reallocating from the public to the private sector 200 megahertz of the radio frequency spectrum, four times as much as created the entire cellular phone industry, allocated by the most lucrative auction in history.

Markey's influence was not greatly reduced when he became ranking minority member; bills in these areas are hard to pass without bipartisan consensus, and he was in a key position to create or withhold it. For four years, in the minority and out, he was a major player on telecommunications deregulation. A bill Markey co-sponsored with then ranking Republican Jack Fields passed the House in 1994 but was killed by Bob Dole in the Senate. In 1995, Markey amended Fields's bill to restrict cross-ownership of broadcast and cable outlets in the same market and to establish the V-chip. These provisions stayed in the bill passed in 1996; afterward, Markey objected to the networks' coding and succeeded in getting new codes, written with input from parents, with specific references to sex, violence and language—V-chips must be placed in 50% of TV sets sold in 1999 and 100% in 2000.

After the 1996 election, the subcommittee's jurisdiction was altered; it lost securities and gained consumer protection laws and was renamed Telecommunications, Trade and Consumer Protection. Markey continued to be active. With Senator Richard Bryan, he passed a bill protecting the Internet privacy rights of children under 13 into the October 1998 omnibus bill; in the 106th Congress he proposed an Internet privacy bill of rights for everyone; he is particularly concerned about the transmittal of financial and health information. Markey and Commerce Chairman Tom Bliley passed through the House a resolution to demonopolize the satellite communications industry. Markey and Republican Rick White won a key battle on encryption, by beating the FBI-NSA plan to require a "techno-backdoor" to all computer communications. Markey and Republican Mike Oxley moved a bill to stop stock exchanges from denominating prices in 1/8s and to use dollars and cents instead; when it passed, the exchanges decided to do this on their own. Markey and Lindsey Graham stopped the Clinton administration plan to bail out the Bellefonte nuclear reactor by producing tritium for nuclear bombs.

Among Markey's goals for the 106th Congress is to demonopolize the electric power industry; he has co-sponsored a bill with none other than Tom DeLay and seeks "robust incentives . . . to break up each local monopoly." But Markey admits electric deregulation is "a multidimensional chess game, with many parties on different sides taking different stands on different issues." Many states have taken action on their own, and industry groups are leery of a national bill; Markey assures them that he would let states rule on the recovery of stranded costs—the cost of huge unprofitable plants which utilities say regulators forced on them. Other Markey proposals: a spam ban (unsolicited e-mail senders could be liable for $50 per customer to e-mail service providers), hedge fund regulations, a withdrawal of normal trading status for India in textiles and apparel in retaliation for its nuclear bomb tests.

On non-commerce issues, Markey has one of the most liberal voting records in the House. He co-sponsored Greg Ganske's bill to ban "gag rules" implemented by HMOs that prohibit doctors from disclosing all options. He has also backed sanctions on China for ignoring nuclear export controls and opposes normal trade status for China. He backs the Clinton administration proposal for the government to invest Social Security revenues in index funds. He argued stoutly against impeachment.

The 7th District is not quite as safely Democratic as it once was: Governor Paul Cellucci failed to carry it over Democrat Scott Harshbarger by only 300 votes in 1998. But Markey has been easily re-elected, without serious opposition since 1984.

Cook's Call. *Safe.* The Democratic nature of the district, combined with Markey's high-profile role in telecommunications and high-tech issues (key in a district that boasts a substantial high-tech corridor), helps keep him safely ensconced.

The People: Pop. 1990: 601,476; 0.9% rural; 16% age 65 +; 93.9% White, 2.3% Black, 2.7% Asian, 0.1% Amer. Indian, 0.9% Other; 2.8% Hispanic Origin. Households: 51.7% married couple families; 21.8% married couple fams. w. children; 52.7% college educ.; median household income: $41,318; per capita income: $19,825; median house value: $193,600; median gross rent: $613.

1996 Presidential Vote		
Clinton (D)	171,125	(64%)
Dole (R)	72,823	(27%)
Perot (I)	19,374	(7%)

1992 Presidential Vote		
Clinton (D)	150,073	(50%)
Bush (R)	87,418	(29%)
Perot (I)	61,963	(21%)

Rep. Edward J. Markey (D)

Elected 1976; b. July 11, 1946, Malden; home, Malden; Boston Col., B.A. 1968, J.D. 1972; Catholic; married (Susan Blumenthal).

Military Career: Army Reserves, 1968–73.

Elected Office: MA House of Reps., 1973–76.

DC Office: 2108 RHOB 20515, 202-225-2836; Web site: www.house.gov/markey.

District Offices: Framingham, 508-875-2900; Medford, 781-396-2900.

Committees: *Budget* (11th of 19 D). *Commerce* (3d of 24 D): Energy & Power; Finance & Hazardous Materials; Telecommunications, Trade & Consumer Protection (RMM).

Group Ratings

	ADA	ACLU	AFS	LCV	CON	NTU	NFIB	COC	ACU	NTLC	CHC
1998	90	87	100	62	73	14	0	31	4	3	0
1997	100	—	100	—	16	30	—	20	8	—	—

National Journal Ratings

	1997 LIB — 1997 CONS			1998 LIB — 1998 CONS		
Economic	93%	—	0%	79%	—	0%
Social	85%	—	0%	87%	—	13%
Foreign	79%	—	19%	84%	—	16%

Key Votes of the 105th Congress

1. Clinton Budget Deal	N	5. Puerto Rico Sthood. Ref.	Y	9. Cut $ for B-2 Bombers	Y
2. Education IRAs	N	6. End Highway Set-asides	N	10. Human Rights in China	Y
3. Req. 2/3 to Raise Taxes	N	7. School Prayer Amend.	N	11. Withdraw Bosnia Troops	Y
4. Fast-track Trade	N	8. Ovrd. Part. Birth Veto	*	12. End Cuban TV-Marti	Y

Election Results

1998 general	Edward J. Markey (D)	137,178	(71%)	($390,660)
	Patricia H. Long (R)	56,977	(29%)	($5,262)
1998 primary	Edward J. Markey (D) .... unopposed			
1996 general	Edward J. Markey (D)	177,053	(70%)	($351,683)
	Patricia H. Long (R)	76,407	(30%)	($3,033)

EIGHTH DISTRICT

A long generation ago, Cambridge, Massachusetts, was a plainly aging city, with a grayness in the air matching its gray winter skies. Its two great universities, Harvard and MIT, were closely hemmed in by a not very friendly town of Irish Catholics, Italians and a few Portuguese, living generation after generation in three-decker houses with cracked walls letting in the cold in the long winters. Boston was the nation's slowest-growing metropolitan area, economically stagnant, still caught in a 17th Century Puritan-Papist rivalry. Students from suburbs across the country, exploring Boston from their dormitories and campuses, felt they were pawing through the living remnants of 1920s America, a quaint place where people called traffic circles "rotaries" and milk shakes "frappes." Massachusetts has since changed, and nowhere more than in Cambridge. As universities and high tech have become driving forces of economic growth, Cambridge has gone glitzy, with trendy restaurants and high-priced hotels, boutiques and upscale condominiums. Greater Boston may well have the heaviest concentration of graduate students and post-graduate hangers-on of any major city, and this graduate student proletariat's world is centered on Cambridge, with outposts in lower-income Somerville, tenured-faculty haven Belmont, Boston's Back Bay, and Allston and Brighton near the Harvard Business School.

Cambridge is the center, and the rest of these communities are part, of Massachusetts's 8th Congressional District, a district with great historic sites, from the gold dome of the State House on Beacon Hill to the frigate *U.S.S. Constitution* in the Charlestown docks; the district, with MIT and the software concentration in Cambridge's once downscale Lechmere Square, is one of the high-tech capitals of America. The 8th also includes the impoverished suburb of Chelsea and much of the Roxbury black ghetto in Boston, now with many Puerto Rican and other Hispanic residents as well. This is by far the most Democratic district in Massachusetts.

The congressman from the 8th District is Michael Capuano, the winner of a 10-candidate primary in 1998. It could be said that over the last 50-odd years this district has been represented alternatively by townies and Kennedys: James Michael Curley, the scampish-five-term mayor of Boston and one-term governor; followed by John F. Kennedy in 1946, then from 1952, Tip O'Neill, the most successful House speaker of this half-century; succeeded on his retirement in 1986 by Joe Kennedy; and now Capuano. Capuano was born and raised in Somerville; his paternal grandfather immigrated from Italy, and his father was the first Italian-American elected official in Somerville; his mother is the granddaughter of Irish immigrants. Capuano graduated from Dartmouth and Boston College Law School. He returned to Somerville to raise his family, practice law and get into politics. By day, he worked for the legislature's Joint Committee on Taxation and practiced law; in off-hours, he served as alderman in the 5th Ward, like his father before him; he was elected alderman-at-large from 1985–89. In November 1989 he was elected mayor of Somerville in the city's closest race; he was re-elected five times.

Somerville is packed with three-deckers, giving it the densest population in the United States outside Manhattan and Hudson County, New Jersey; for years an Irish and Italian town, in the 1990s it has attracted many grad students and yuppies. Capuano seems to have been the right politician for this mix, with deep Somerville roots and a penchant for innovation and reform. He got the city's fiscal house in order, promoted recycling and created nine new parks, increasing open space by more than 15 acres (a big deal here); he made Somerville the first city in Massachusetts to offer residents a choice in cable TV, and required cable operators to build a fiber-optic network for all city buildings, including schools. He built new schools and boasted the smallest class-size (19) in the Boston area; he authored a tough ethics code. So, Capuano had a solid base to run for the 8th District seat in 1998 when, everyone expected, Joe Kennedy would run for governor. But after Kennedy's former wife wrote a book detailing their annulment and his verbal abuse, and after his brother Michael Kennedy was alleged to have had an affair with his family's 14-year-old babysitter, Joe Kennedy announced at the end of August 1997 that he wasn't running for governor and would run for re-election; sadly, Michael Kennedy died in a skiing accident in December 1997. Then, in March 1998, Joe Kennedy said he wouldn't run for re-election after all. This gave Capuano, and many others, a chance to prepare for the September 1998 primary that would determine who would represent this safe Democratic seat, probably for many years to come.

There was no lack of competitors: Ten in all ran for the Democratic nomination. Six were far out on the left wing of the Democratic party, and between them won 49% of the votes. George Bachrach, a former state senator who finished second to Joe Kennedy in the 1986 primary, ran as "an unabashed, unrepentant, unreconstructed liberal." More recently a lawyer, lobbyist and political consultant, he spent more than $350,000 of his own money, and finished third with 14%. Environmental activist John O'Connor, married to a supermarket heiress, spent even more, $2 million; he called for repealing Massachusetts's electric deregulation and was endorsed by Ralph Nader. O'Connor ran fourth, with 13%. Then there was Marjorie Clapprood, a former state legislator and radio talk show host, who promised exuberantly to go to Washington to "kick butt." She finished fifth, with 12%. Three other liberals, one black, one lesbian, one Hispanic, won 5% or less.

The four more moderate candidates split 51%, and Capuano got a near-majority of that. High-tech entrepreneur Chris Gabrieli, who called for education reform, charter schools and freer trade, spent $5 million on his campaign. But he won only 7%, and became better known in April 1999 when his nanny won $70 million in the lottery. Boston City Councilman Thomas Keane, a protege of the late Senator Paul Tsongas, won only 3%. But the real competition, as it turned out, was between Capuano and former Boston Mayor (1983–93) Ray Flynn. Flynn had returned from a tempestuous tour as ambassador to the Vatican, where he became involved in out-of-country issues, amid speculation that he might run for governor. Athletic, with deep roots in South Boston (which is outside the district), he is a Democrat who favors old-fashioned liberal economic programs and is opposed to abortion—the dominant Democratic politics here up through the 1960s. But at candidate forums and public appearances, he was attacked by supporters of abortion rights and pilloried as a troglodyte. In early polls he was in the low 20s, but he ended up with just 17% of the vote, for second place in the primary. "The climate has changed," he explained. "People are just turned off. They don't believe either party represents them. . . . I stand for the poor people who have a need for someone to speak for them in government. But when times are good . . . most people could care less. They don't need me and they don't need government." Meanwhile, Capuano, with his solid Somerville base, was running first or second in polls; among the 85,000 Democratic primary voters, he came in first with 23%. "This wasn't done the electronic way or the fancy way," he said of his victory. "This was done with shoe leather and knuckles knocking on doors."

Capuano is still well to the left on the national political spectrum: for gay marriage, against the partial-birth abortion ban and opposed to the flag-burning amendment. Coming to Washington, he said he wants to reform Social Security, spend more on public schools and somehow secure affordable housing for districts whose housing values have been rising rapidly: "I'm not a Kennedy, I'm a Capuano. I know I don't bring the notoriety to issues like a Kennedy would, but I want to do my job and deliver the things that I have promised to people." It is possible he could have serious competition in the 2000 primary, but the 1998 figures suggest a leftist candidate could not count on a majority in a two-candidate race.

Cook's Call. *Safe.* Arguably the most liberal district in the state, this area is so heavily Democratic that Capuano should never have problems in a general election. There are some rumblings, however, that Capuano could face a challenge in the Democratic primary. Unless Capuano trips himself up, he will be hard to dislodge.

The People: Pop. 1990: 602,396; 11.8% age 65 + ; 65.6% White, 23.3% Black, 5.6% Asian, 0.3% Amer. Indian, 5.2% Other; 10.1% Hispanic Origin. Households: 30.3% married couple families; 13% married couple fams. w. children; 53.4% college educ.; median household income: $30,417; per capita income: $16,327; median house value: $189,700; median gross rent: $560.

1996 Presidential Vote			1992 Presidential Vote		
Clinton (D)	139,383	(77%)	Clinton (D)	136,438	(67%)
Dole (R)	28,253	(16%)	Bush (R)	39,368	(19%)
Perot (I)	7,928	(4%)	Perot (I)	25,423	(13%)
Others	4,557	(3%)			

Rep. Michael Capuano (D)

Elected 1998; b. Jan. 9, 1952, Somerville; home, Somerville; Dartmouth Col., B.A. 1973, Boston Col., J.D. 1977; Catholic; married (Barbara).

Elected Office: Somerville Alderman Ward 5, 1977–79; Somerville Alderman-At-Large, 1985–89; Somerville Mayor, 1989–98.

Professional Career: Chief Legal. Cnsl., MA Legislature Taxation Cmte., 1978–84; Practicing atty., 1984–90.

DC Office: 1232 LHOB , 202-225-5111; Fax: 202-225-9322; Web site: www.house.gov/capuano.

District Office: Cambridge, 617-621-6208.

Committees: *Banking & Financial Services* (27th of 27 D): Capital Markets, Securities & Government Sponsored Enterprises; Housing & Community Opportunity. *Science* (18th of 22 D): Technology.

Group Ratings and Key Votes: Newly Elected

Election Results

1998 general	Michael Capuano (D)	99,603	(82%)	($633,746)
	Philip Hyde (R)	14,125	(12%)	
	Others	8,159	(7%)	
1998 primary	Michael Capuano (D)	19,446	(23%)	
	Ray Flynn (D)	14,839	(17%)	
	George Bachrach (D)	12,157	(14%)	
	John O'Connor (D)	11,092	(13%)	
	Marjorie Clapprood (D)	10,446	(12%)	
	Chris Gabrieli (D)	5,740	(7%)	
	Charles Yancey (D)	4,437	(5%)	
	Others	6,831	(8%)	
1996 general	Joseph Kennedy II (D)	147,126	(84%)	($1,952,906)
	Philip Hyde (R)	27,303	(16%)	

NINTH DISTRICT

The "Hub of the Universe," is what the elder Oliver Wendell Holmes called Boston in the 19th Century, and so it seems again sometimes: When you reflect that Fidelity mutual funds and so many other big financial outfits are headquartered in modern towers built on streets originally laid out as 17th Century cowpaths; when you walk on the streets where Samuel Adams and Paul Revere plotted revolution or track down the sites of rallies and headquarters of the various Kennedy campaigns; when you walk on Beacon Street past the Bull and Finch Pub, the original setting for the TV show *Cheers* (and whose name is a play on the architect of the state House, Thomas Bulfinch). Today's Boston is a different city from the Boston of John Kennedy's time. Boston then was a gray city with no new buildings and dust on every windowsill; the sky was dark with pollution and the air was thick with ancient Yankee and Irish animosity. The old office buildings were full of Yankees seeking safe investments for their antique family fortunes; the State House and City Hall were full of Irishmen, scampering after good patronage jobs and regaling each other with political battle stories. Today that Boston is mostly gone. The new skyscrapers are full of venture capitalists, lawyers and management consultants, many working for high-tech companies radiating from Cambridge out into the countryside; the advertising slogans crackle with a sauciness and *double entendre* you can find only here and maybe in New York and London.

Most of Boston's neighborhoods have changed. There are still vestiges of the old Irish neighborhoods, but even South Boston, long the center of Irish Boston, is starting to gentrify, and the central city is increasingly populated by blacks and young singles; its population is down from 801,000 in 1950 to 575,000 in 1998; more than 80% of the metropolitan area is in the suburbs. The 9th Congressional District, historically anchored in Boston, has followed the move, and today only one-third of its residents are in Boston, mostly in still-Irish areas of South Boston, Hyde Park and West Roxbury. From there, the 9th heads southwest to Easton and the old Patriots Stadium, southeast to Braintree, ancestral home of the presidential Adamses, Brockton, the old shoe manufacturing town, and the old textile mill town of Taunton. Ethnically, it is probably the most heavily Irish congressional district in the nation; politically, it has been represented by only three members, all of them Democrats, for the last 70-plus years, and one served only a single term.

The congressman from the 9th is Joe Moakley, elected in 1972 as an independent, but very much a Democrat. Moakley is a son of South Boston who has lived in the 7th Ward all his life. "Growing up in Southie is absolutely responsible for who I am," he has said. "You're equipped to face the world because you've had every kind of shot taken at you." He was a high school football star who volunteered for the Navy in 1943, at 15, went to college in Miami after the war, then went to law school in Boston; in 1952, at 25, he was elected to the Massachusetts House. He was elected to the state Senate in the splendidly Democratic year of 1964, then to the Boston Council in 1971. He ran for the House when Speaker John McCormack retired in 1970 after 45 years of service, and lost the primary to Louise Day Hicks, the anti-busing chairman of the Boston School Committee. In 1972 he ran again, this time as an independent; in the six-candidate primary, opposition to Hicks was split, and she won with 37%, but Moakley won the general by 5,000 votes.

In the House, Moakley got a seat on the Rules Committee in his second term. On the back benches in the 1970s, he moved up quickly in seniority and became chairman when Claude Pepper died in June 1989. As chairman of the Rules Committee, Moakley worked closely with Speaker Thomas Foley and Majority Leader Dick Gephardt; he helped David Bonior, another Catholic deeply opposed to U.S. Central American policy, win his party whip leadership post. Under their lead, Rules increasingly passed closed rules, limiting amendments and debate, to the fury of the Republicans. Moakley's one headline cause was El Salvador. Acquainted with several nuns and priests murdered there in 1989, he sponsored a commission to look into their deaths; its top staffer was James McGovern, now congressman from the 3rd District. It found that high-ranking Salvadoran military officials were involved, and Moakley led a fight for cutoff of U.S. aid and claims credit today for El Salvador's transition to democracy.

Growing up in South Boston, politicians were the providers, says Moakley: "They made sure you had a job. That you had heat for your home." Today he believes that "government is to help the vulnerable in society." He has made sure to keep flowing the federal funds which have made Boston's Big Dig—the relocation of the Central Artery expressway to a tunnel—one of the biggest public works projects in American history, and for financing the Ted Williams Tunnel under the harbor as well. In the 105th Congress he got $54 million for the South Boston Piers Transitway and $50 million for Boston Harbor cleanup; he worked to continue the $1.1 billion Low-Income Heating Assistance Program. He helped create the Boston Harbor Islands National Recreation Area and got conservation easement for Thompson Island, where he played as a boy.

Moakley, usually a humorous and gentle man, loathed Newt Gingrich and his Republican revolutionaries, whose rise he dated from the mid-1980s: "When [former speaker Tip] O'Neill left [in 1986], the fun went out of this business, and the walls started to be built in that middle aisle." Since 1995, he has often found himself criticizing Republicans for their restrictions on House debate, though arguably not as tight as the ones that he had backed—"I don't say we were fair and open all the way," he conceded. After 40 years in the majority, that must have hurt. Personal problems also struck. In June 1995 he stayed in South Boston to care for his wife, who was ill with a brain tumor; in July 1995 he had a liver transplant. In September 1995 he was about to announce his retirement but decided to run instead.

Moakley returned to the House, his health sharply improved and he got involved in other projects. In 1996 he visited Cuba for an audience with Fidel Castro; in January 1998 he was there for the Pope's visit; he has called for ending the embargo on trade with Cuba. In February 1997 he blocked New England Patriots' owner Robert Kraft's plans for a stadium in South Boston by talking the Army into refusing to turn over a key land parcel; he pressured Ocean Spray to make sure the Tall Ships visit Boston in 2000, and opposed Rhode Island Senator John Chafee's proposal to sail the 200-year-old *U.S.S. Constitution*—Old Ironsides—from its pier in Charlestown 70 miles down to Newport. Capitol Police Officer John Gibson, murdered in July 1998, was married to his niece; Moakley said, "John was a hero in life, as well as a hero in death. He was my idea of what a model police officer should be." Of retirement, he has said, "As long as I'm in good health I will continue to serve. . . . I've been in the political business for over 40 years. And to be totally truthful, I have loved every minute of it."

Cook's Call. *Safe.* The dean of the Massachusetts delegation, the only thing that will ultimately get Moakley out of office may be his health problems or his age. Even when he does retire, this heavily Democratic district is not likely to fall into Republican hands.

The People: Pop. 1990: 601,250; 1.5% rural; 15.4% age 65 + ; 87.7% White, 6.6% Black, 2.8% Asian, 0.2% Amer. Indian, 2.7% Other; 4.5% Hispanic Origin. Households: 49.2% married couple families; 22.3% married couple fams. w. children; 50.2% college educ.; median household income: $38,646; per capita income: $17,980; median house value: $172,800; median gross rent: $532.

1996 Presidential Vote			1992 Presidential Vote		
Clinton (D)	158,967	(62%)	Clinton (D)	131,644	(48%)
Dole (R)	76,202	(30%)	Bush (R)	85,901	(31%)
Perot (I)	19,168	(7%)	Perot (I)	56,431	(21%)

Rep. Joe Moakley (D)

Elected 1972; b. Apr. 27, 1927, Boston; home, Boston; U. of Miami, Suffolk U., LL.B. 1956; Catholic; widowed.

Military Career: Navy, 1943–46 (WWII).

Elected Office: MA House of Reps., 1952–62, Majority Whip, 1957; MA Senate, 1964–70; Boston City Cncl., 1971–72.

Professional Career: Practicing atty., 1957–72.

DC Office: 235 CHOB 20515, 202-225-8273; Fax: 202-225-3984; Web site: www.house.gov/moakley.

District Offices: Boston, 617-565-2920; Brockton, 508-586-5555; Taunton, 508-824-6676.

Committees: *Rules* (RMM of 4 D): The Legislative & Budget Process.

Group Ratings

	ADA	ACLU	AFS	LCV	CON	NTU	NFIB	COC	ACU	NTLC	CHC
1998	65	55	100	85	28	10	7	33	13	6	17
1997	85	—	100	—	3	20	—	30	8	—	—

National Journal Ratings

	1997 LIB — 1997 CONS	1998 LIB — 1998 CONS
Economic	93% — 0%	79% — 0%
Social	63% — 37%	66% — 34%
Foreign	90% — 8%	78% — 19%

Key Votes of the 105th Congress

1. Clinton Budget Deal	N	5. Puerto Rico Sthood. Ref.	Y	9. Cut $ for B-2 Bombers	Y
2. Education IRAs	N	6. End Highway Set-asides	N	10. Human Rights in China	Y
3. Req. 2/3 to Raise Taxes	N	7. School Prayer Amend.	N	11. Withdraw Bosnia Troops	N
4. Fast-track Trade	N	8. Ovrd. Part. Birth Veto	Y	12. End Cuban TV-Marti	Y

Election Results

1998 general	Joe Moakley (D)	.... unopposed		($919,465)
1998 primary	Joe Moakley (D)	.... unopposed		
1996 general	Joe Moakley (D)	 172,009	(72%)	($769,122)
	Paul V. Gryska (R)	 66,079	(28%)	($232,527)

TENTH DISTRICT

The South Shore of Massachusetts Bay, from Boston southward to Plymouth and then down Cape Cod (there is a lot of dispute about which way is up and down on the Cape), is Massachusetts's oldest-settled territory. The Pilgrims landed here at Plymouth Rock in 1620; this stony land was farmed by John Adams's father, who was anything but the aristocrat some later members of the Adams family would have you believe. Daniel Webster lived in the South Shore town of Marshfield, today a high-income suburb of Boston far out on the usually clogged Southeast Expressway; Joseph P. Kennedy used to summer with his young family on Nantasket Beach in Hull, before moving out of Massachusetts when the Yankees wouldn't let them into their beach club in Cohasset in the 1920s; but the Kennedy family continues to summer at their Hyannisport compound. The Plymouth area and Cape Cod were originally farming country, with some industry; a railroad, now long-gone, steamed along the middle of the Cape. Provincetown, at the tip of the Cape, is still a fishing port, and also one of the major gay vacation areas in the country; the islands of Martha's Vineyard and Nantucket, rich whaling ports in the early 19th Century, are now favored summer resorts for the trendy liberal rich of New York and Washington. Cape Cod is the site of the bogs that still produce half of America's cranberries, but it is also filled increasingly with retirees and, to the dismay of some, is the fastest-growing part of Massachusetts.

The 10th Congressional District, with grotesque boundaries like most other Bay State districts, follows the South Shore from Quincy to the Cape, jutting inland near Brockton, and including Martha's Vineyard and Nantucket. The South Shore and the Cape were once exclusively Protestant and Yankee, but in the Massachusetts way they have changed over the years, with Irish and Italian surnames as common as Yankee ones, and the descendants of Portuguese-Azorean fishermen have fanned out into the countryside. Trendy liberal politics, well-established on the Vineyard and Nantucket, have spread inland as well.

The congressman from the 10th District is William Delahunt, a Democrat elected in 1996. Delahunt is a lifelong resident of Quincy, who went to college at Middlebury and Boston College Law School and served in the Coast Guard. He practiced law and was elected to the Quincy Council. In 1972 he was elected to the state House; in 1975 Governor Michael Dukakis appointed him district attorney of Norfolk County, which extends from Cohasset to Rhode Island and also includes non-contiguous Brookline. He was prompted to run for Congress in 1996 by the retirement of 12-term Congressman Gerry Studds. Delahunt had serious primary competition from former state Representative Philip Johnston and self-financed environmentalist Ian Bowles. Delahunt was the favorite; Johnston and Bowles attacked him for refusing to release his income tax returns and spending $100,000 of campaign money on meals. Johnston carried most of the Cape and Plymouth County; Bowles carried Martha's Vineyard and Falmouth, where you catch the ferry; Delahunt won nearly half his votes, and very big margins, in Quincy and next-door Weymouth.

The initial results of the September 17 primary showed 38% each for Delahunt and Johnston and 22% for Bowles, with Johnston ahead by 266 votes. A recount declared Johnston still ahead by 175 votes. But Delahunt sued, and on October 4, a judge ruled that more than 900 punch card votes in Weymouth had not been properly tabulated and proceeded to order a recount of every ballot with an indentation, dimple or other mark. On October 10, Delahunt was declared the winner by 108 votes, even as Johnston was being hailed at a Quincy rally by Edward Kennedy and Hillary Rodham Clinton. Johnston called the result a "travesty," and Delahunt had less than a month to campaign for the general. The Republican primary had been won by conservative state House Minority Leader Edward Teague. Both ran million dollar campaigns, but Teague had been running ads against Johnston, and Delahunt's campaign was dormant. Eight years earlier, George Bush carried this district over Michael Dukakis, but reaction here to the new Republican majority in the House was hostile, and Delahunt won 54%–42%. Teague ran only about even on Cape Cod, a bit behind in Plymouth County, and lost the rest of the district by wide margins.

Delahunt pledged to wear Cape Cod ties in the House and has handed them out to colleagues of both parties. With Roy Blunt, he convened a bipartisan freshman task force on Social Security. On the Judiciary Committee, he worked for the Citizens Protection Act, which binds federal prosecutors to the same ethical standards as members of the bar. He opposed bankruptcy reform and worked on the successful copyright and patent bill. He supported House approval of cameras in federal courtrooms and a moratorium on Internet taxes. He sponsored a law to curb overzealous use of Medicare anti-fraud statutes against hospitals and physicians, and he wrote laws to ease international adoptions and to provide compensation from Germany for former U.S. servicemen interned in concentration camps. His positions on abortion are part of the story of Massachusetts's move to the left: In 1974 as a state legislator he called *Roe v. Wade* "a tragic decision," but switched to a pro-abortion rights position around 1992 and in 1997 voted against the partial-birth abortion ban.

Delahunt also served on the Resources Committee and supported the Cape Cod land bank, the Mashpee Refuge and conversion of the former Camp Edwards National Guard training site to a federal wildlife refuge, a project resisted by the Army National Guard. He passed laws to enhance the Cape Cod National Seashore, the Adams National Historic Site, and the Boston Harbor Islands National Recreation Area. He helped pass a moratorium on giant trawlers fishing for herring and mackerel. He got approval, after nearly five years, of a land transfer to Provincetown for solid waste disposal. He wrote a law requiring large ships entering Massachusetts waters to notify the Coast Guard, so they could be warned away from endangered right whales; the International Maritime Organization approved this in December 1998.

But Delahunt's greatest visibility came on impeachment. On the polarized Judiciary Committee he was one of the few members who sat down in bipartisan breakfasts to discuss procedures, with Howard Berman, Asa Hutchinson and Lindsey Graham. But he ended up siding completely with impeachment opponents—not too much of a surprise, since in October 1997 he joined Barney Frank in a hearing questioning Attorney General Janet Reno so as to discredit the case for another independent counsel. He took the lead in framing a Democratic motion to censure Clinton and protested bitterly when Judiciary Chairman Henry Hyde would not allow it to be heard: "I think there is a fundamental unease out in the land right now about those who would tell us what is right and what is wrong. There's overtones of the Inquisition." After impeachment, he said, "I think it is clearly money-driven. I don't think most people are aware of the fact that [Republicans'] financial resources come from the religious conservatives"— not quite an accurate view, though it could be said that both parties' big financial contributors strongly backed their stands on the issue.

In 1998, Delahunt was re-elected easily; Johnston bowed out of the race early in the year. In January 1999, Delhunt switched from Resources to International Relations. He promised to work to protect the endangered right whales, encourage democracy in Haiti, support microcredit investment and Central American disaster relief and oppose abusive child-labor practices.

Cook's Call. *Probably Safe.* Based on Delahunt's strong showing in 1998, it is hard to believe that this is one of the most marginal seats in the state. Though the district does have a Democratic leaning, a strong Republican candidate in the right political environment could spell trouble for Delahunt.

The People: Pop. 1990: 601,510; 27% rural; 16.7% age 65 +; 95.3% White, 2% Black, 1.4% Asian, 0.4% Amer. Indian, 0.9% Other; 1.2% Hispanic Origin. Households: 55% married couple families; 24.3% married couple fams. w. children; 54.1% college educ.; median household income: $37,489; per capita income: $17,535; median house value: $163,700; median gross rent: $571.

1996 Presidential Vote

Clinton (D)	169,927	(56%)
Dole (R)	101,612	(33%)
Perot (I)	28,125	(9%)

1992 Presidential Vote

Clinton (D)	133,601	(42%)
Bush (R)	101,798	(32%)
Perot (I)	80,654	(25%)

Rep. William D. Delahunt (D)

Elected 1996; b. July 18, 1941, Quincy; home, Quincy; Middlebury Col., B.A. 1963, Boston Col., J.D. 1967; Catholic; divorced.

Military Career: Coast Guard, 1963; Coast Guard Reserves, 1963–71.

Elected Office: Quincy City Cncl., 1971; MA House of Reps., 1972–75.

Professional Career: Practicing atty., 1967–75; Asst. Clerk, Norfolk Superior Court, 1969–71; Norfolk Cnty. Dist. Atty., 1975–96.

DC Office: 1317 LHOB 20515, 202-225-3111; Fax: 202-225-5658; Web site: www.house.gov/delahunt.

District Offices: Hyannis, 508-771-0666; Quincy, 617-770-3700.

Committees: *International Relations* (19th of 23 D): International Economic Policy & Trade; International Operations and Human Rights. *Judiciary* (12th of 16 D): Commercial & Administrative Law; Courts & Intellectual Property.

Group Ratings

	ADA	ACLU	AFS	LCV	CON	NTU	NFIB	COC	ACU	NTLC	CHC
1998	100	88	100	92	38	18	0	28	8	5	0
1997	95	—	100	—	19	27	—	20	0	—	—

National Journal Ratings

	1997 LIB	—	1997 CONS	1998 LIB	—	1998 CONS
Economic	91%	—	7%	79%	—	0%
Social	80%	—	19%	93%	—	0%
Foreign	90%	—	8%	84%	—	11%

Key Votes of the 105th Congress

1. Clinton Budget Deal	N	5. Puerto Rico Sthood. Ref.	Y	9. Cut $ for B-2 Bombers	Y
2. Education IRAs	N	6. End Highway Set-asides	N	10. Human Rights in China	Y
3. Req. 2/3 to Raise Taxes	N	7. School Prayer Amend.	N	11. Withdraw Bosnia Troops	N
4. Fast-track Trade	N	8. Ovrd. Part. Birth Veto	N	12. End Cuban TV-Marti	Y

Election Results

1998 general	William D. Delahunt (D)	164,917	(70%)	($242,576)
	Eric V. Bleicken (R)	70,466	(30%)	($7,286)
1998 primary	William D. Delahunt (D)	unopposed		
1996 general	William D. Delahunt (D)	160,745	(54%)	($1,072,986)
	Edward B. Teague (R)	123,520	(42%)	($1,391,148)
	Others	11,658	(4%)	

MICHIGAN

Michigan is surging into the 21st Century much as it surged into the 20th: a state transformed in a few years by a creative, dynamic economy and a burst of political reform. Today, Michigan is one of America's premier laboratories of innovation, busy expanding high-skill manufacturing while rethinking and downsizing government programs, just as it was once busy inventing the mass-production factory economy and then developing the giant industrial labor union and its version of the American welfare state. The latest experiment, like the earlier one, seems to be a success: the unemployment rate here is below the national average, the number of new factories leads the nation and the quality of Michigan products is vastly better than that of a generation ago. Michigan's achievement since the Big Three auto companies collapsed in the late 1970s has been to move from an industrial to a post-industrial economy, from domination by big units—big business, big labor, big government—to growth increasingly driven by small units—small businesses, individual workers, flexible government.

Michigan is arguably going back to its roots in the Tocquevillian decade of the 1830s. These two peninsulas, explored and named by French explorers (which explains why Mackinac is pronounced with a silent final *c* and Michigan with a *ch* pronounced like *sh*), were settled in a rush by Yankee migrants from Upstate New York, who cut down trees and built farms and neat New Englandish towns complete with schools and colleges. Politically, Michigan was full of reformers who hated slavery, manned the Underground Railroad, promoted temperance and in 1855 gave Michigan a constitution that banned (as it does to this day) capital punishment. Michigan was one of the birthplaces of the Republican Party, which was founded in Jackson in 1854 (Ripon, Wisconsin, also stakes a claim as the party's birthplace) and swept the state in the elections later that year. Until 1929, Michigan was one of the most Republican states in the nation.

Michigan also developed an industrial economy. Its Lower Peninsula was mostly covered with trees, and lumber was the first boom industry on which Michigan over-relied; forests were clear-cut or swept by blazes like the 1881 fire that burned out half the Thumb. In the late 1800s, huge copper deposits were discovered on the Keweenaw Peninsula, which juts from the Upper Peninsula into icy Lake Superior; immigrants from Italy and Finland, Cornwall and Croatia came to work in the mines. Then came the auto industry. A combination of accident and shrewdness, of bankers willing to finance auto startups and the prickly genius of Henry Ford, ensured that America's fastest-growing industry of the first 30 years of the 20th Century was centered in Michigan. Detroit became a boom town—the nation's fastest-growing metropolitan area after Los Angeles—zooming from 426,000 in 1900 to 2.2 million in 1930. The auto industry drew labor from the Outstate Michigan areas beyond Detroit, from southern Ontario and from the farms of Ohio and Indiana. During World War II and after, it brought whites from the Kentucky and Tennessee mountains and blacks from Alabama and Mississippi. It attracted Poles and Italians, Hungarians and Belgians, Greeks and Jews. This influx of a polyglot proletariat eventually changed Michigan's politics. The catalyst was the Great Depression of the 1930s and the company managers' desire to use machines efficiently, treating employees as extensions of machines and with great distrust. The results were the 1937 sit-down strikes organized by the new United Auto Workers (UAW); management and labor fought, sometimes literally, for pieces of what both sides feared was a shrinking pie. The UAW won and organized most of the companies after Democratic Governor Frank Murphy refused to send in troops to break the illegal strikes. In the years that followed, auto workers became a heavily Democratic voting bloc.

Michigan politics became a species of class warfare, conducted with a bitterness that split

Congressional district boundaries
effective April 6, 1992.

Miles
0 10 20 30 40

families and neighbors. The union mostly won, because demographics benefited the Democrats: auto workers and post-1900 immigrants produced more children than did Outstate Yankees or management. After Walter Reuther's election as UAW president in 1947, voters elected young, liberal G. Mennen Williams governor in 1948. By 1954, the Democrats, closely tied to the UAW, seemed to have become the natural majority in the state. And as growth continued, economic issues became less bitter; by the early 1960s, the class-warfare atmosphere had dissipated. A Republican former auto executive, George Romney, was narrowly elected governor in 1962, and Henry Ford II joined Reuther in backing Lyndon Johnson in 1964. Romney and his successor, William Milliken, accepted the welfare-state policies endorsed by the UAW leadership and the Democrats. The state government was one of the nation's most generous, and not just to the poor and the unemployed: it supported one of the nation's most distinguished and extensive higher education systems, built state parks and recreation areas, and pioneered efforts to end racial discrimination.

This system, which had seemed eternal, came crashing down with the collapse of the domestic auto industry after the oil shock of 1973. Union-management relations had been static since 1941, and there had been no major technological changes in American autos since the automatic transmission in 1940. Michigan incomes had grown as Americans grew more affluent; the one-car household became the two-car household, and consumers enjoyed the tail fins and chrome of new car styling. Michigan was the fastest-growing state in the Midwest from 1940 to 1965; except for Illinois, with its big white-collar job base in Chicago, Michigan had the highest incomes in the Midwest. But in 1979, this big-unit economy went bust. It became startlingly clear that the Big Three and the UAW did not have a captive market, Americans did not have to buy a new full-sized American-made car every two or three years, and foreign competitors were producing better and cheaper cars more responsive to changes in gas prices and consumer preference. Big business and labor, so well adapted for growth in the quarter century after World War II started, proved poorly adapted for the quarter century that followed. Auto employment in Michigan fell from 437,000 in October 1978 to 289,000 in October 1982. Chrysler nearly went bankrupt, Ford was in financial distress, General Motors had its first losses in years. As the recession passed, auto employment settled at 280,000, and wages and fringe benefits declined.

The collapse of the big-unit economy after 1979 forced the state to experiment. The first to try was Governor James Blanchard, a Democrat elected in 1982 with a record of supporting big units. His major achievement in eight years in Congress was managing the Chrysler bailout in the House. Blanchard worked to build a small-unit economy; he was proud of his efforts to stimulate high-skill, capital-intensive, flexible manufacturing, and he used $750 million of state pension funds as venture capital for manufacturers of items from tape drives for microcomputers to fiberglass coffins. Dodging his traditional labor allies, Blanchard made it clear that Michigan must learn how to nurture growth and that workers, instead of seeking more vacation and earlier retirement, would have to hustle and work harder than ever before. The second, and for the moment more successful, experiment came from John Engler, the Republican who beat Blanchard in 1990 and was resoundingly re-elected in 1994 and 1998. Engler believes in less government activism and industrial policy; he cut or held the line on every state program but education. He zeroed out general assistance to nonworkers without children, cut off funding for the museums and arts, and closed a state mental clinic—all actions that sparked fierce protest and hostile media coverage. In 1993, while Republicans controlled the legislature, Engler reduced the powers of his great adversaries, the teachers' unions; in 1994 he pushed through a tax reform, approved in a March referendum, cutting property taxes by raising sales taxes and prodding school districts to reform.

In 1992 Republicans beat the incumbent House speaker and won a 55–55 tie in the state House; in 1994, Engler was re-elected 61%–38% and Republicans won both houses of the legislature. Engler pressed for more reforms: public school choice and charter schools, changing state pensions from defined benefits (which produce huge liabilities for the state and a sense of entitlement in employees) to defined contributions (which reduce the state's future expenses and empower employees to act as investors). In 1996, as Bill Clinton carried Michigan 52%–38%, Engler's Republicans were set back, losing control of the state House. In 1998 they won back the House as Engler was re-elected over Dr. Jack Kevorkian's lawyer Geoffrey Fieger.

Historically, politics divided Michigan between labor and management, and between the Detroit metro area and Outstate: in 1960, John Kennedy carried metro Detroit 62%–38% and Richard Nixon carried Outstate 60%–39%. Now that difference has diminished: George Bush in 1988 and then Bill Clinton in 1992 and 1996 carried both regions. New divisions have been created. In the Detroit metro area, the economically growing regions usually vote Republican—almost all of Oakland County, much of western Wayne County and about half of Macomb County, which is no longer as blue-collar as its reputation. Though it voted 63%–37% for Kennedy, Macomb County was carried by Bush in 1988 and 1992; it voted 49%–39% for Clinton in 1996 but 67%–33% for Engler two years later. Central city Detroit, 70% black and with a population half of its peak, and some close-in working class suburbs are solidly Democratic. Outstate, Democrats still run well in the old auto factory corridor from Flint through Saginaw and Bay City, in the university town of Ann Arbor, in the capital town of Lansing, and in the Upper Peninsula. Republicans run far ahead in the fast-growing western Michigan areas around Grand Rapids and Traverse City.

The success of Michigan's experiments can not be evaluated until the nation undergoes a serious recession. But its economy seems more vigorous and supple now that it is bolstered by so many more small units than it did when it depended so heavily on the Big Three. It is worth noting that the recovery has even reached Michigan's hard-hit central cities. Detroit, devastated by riots in 1967 and by vast crime during the administration of liberal Mayor Coleman Young from 1973 to 1993, is now seeing new businesses and new development under Mayor Dennis Archer; even Pontiac, 30 miles north, with new stores and shops is partaking in the economic growth of surrounding Oakland County. Across the state, welfare rolls are on the decline, charter schools proliferate, once empty old factories are full of new machine tools and high-skill workers, and Detroit's airport sends out 747s every day direct to London, Tokyo and Beijing.

Governor. John Engler sits astride Michigan politics and government like a colossus, the last governor to win a third term (term limits go into effect after him), with a clear agenda for reform and a cooperative Republican-controlled legislature. Engler grew up on a farm near Mount Pleasant, drove 60 miles south to go to Michigan State in East Lansing, then was elected to the state legislature in 1970, at 22, and remained there for 20 years: this downsizer of government has spent all his adult life in the public sector. He came to the fore in 1983, when Republicans, reacting to Jim Blanchard's tax increase, used recalls to seize control of the state Senate; at 33 Engler became the state's most visible Republican. In a climate where liberals controlled most institutions, Engler was a skillful political player, capable of keeping on civil terms with opponents even as he gathered ideas from conservative think tanks and marshalled a fine political organization run by Spencer Abraham, now Senator, and Pete Secchia, George Bush's ambassador to Italy. In 1990 Engler ran for governor and lagged behind Blanchard in the polls. But his call for increasing education spending and cutting property taxes was popular, and he won 50%–49%.

From that narrow margin Engler has become one of the major policy innovators in the United States. In his first years in office Engler challenged liberal conventional wisdom and ploughed ahead despite vitriolic criticism, and eventually succeeded in moving the fulcrum point of the political balance. He ended general assistance (welfare for able-bodied non-parents) and aid to the arts; he privatized services and started seeking federal waivers for welfare reform. Democrats and the *Detroit Free Press* habitually called him "mean-spirited." His crucial first-term victory was cutting property taxes; when Democratic state Senator Debbie Stabenow moved to zero out the current system of financing schools, Engler accepted the dare and pushed through his own plan—a major cut in property taxes plus a sales tax increase—to a 70%–30% victory in a March 1994 referendum, with help from Detroit Mayor Dennis Archer. By 1994,

Michigan's new small-unit economy was growing faster than the nation's, and Engler campaigned on the theme, "Promises made, promises kept." The Democratic primary was won by former Congressman Howard Wolpe, backed by the AFL-CIO, with 35%, over Stabenow, running as a Blanchard Democrat, with 30%, and Larry Owen, backed by the teachers' union, with 26%. Wolpe's earnest liberalism was no match for Engler's record, and Engler won 61%–38%.

In his second term, with a Republican legislature, Engler stepped up the pace of reform. More taxes were cut or abolished, education spending rose and charter schools were authorized, and a welfare reform requiring work was passed; by 1998, welfare rolls were down to their lowest level in 29 years. His Project Zero program to require work succeeded in Ottawa County, heavily Dutch-American and just west of Grand Rapids, where by 1998 every welfare recipient was working, helped by child care services and personal mentoring often provided by the area's many churches. Engler also sponsored a Clean Michigan Initiative—a bond issue to spend money on environmental cleanup, especially on lakefronts and riverfronts, improving water quality and building infrastructure in state parks. As head of the Republican Governors Association, Engler helped write the Republican welfare reform bill, which was passed on its third attempt in August 1996. But Engler did have some setbacks. He was mentioned as a candidate for vice president in 1996, but was subject to some ridicule when it was revealed he had been deferred from the draft for being two pounds overweight. Democrats won control of the state House in 1996 and jettisoned Engler's call for state takeover of failing school districts and a three-fifths supermajority for raising taxes. Responding to road conditions so bad that some called him "the prince of potholes," Engler sponsored a 4-cent gas tax increase and $570 million roadbuilding program in 1997.

In early 1997 it was not clear whether Engler would run or who the Democratic nominee would be, but after the August 1998 primary Engler was in a commanding position. The Democratic primary was originally a contest between Larry Owen, backed by the unions, and former state Senator and Clinton appointee Doug Ross, a New Democrat in the Blanchard mold: a straightforward choice between two breeds of Democrat. But then a surprise candidate entered: Geoffrey Fieger, a very successful trial lawyer with family roots in the left wing of the Democratic Party, known best for defending assisted-suicide advocate and practitioner Dr. Jack Kevorkian in four widely-publicized trials. Fieger is brash, self-assured, shrewd in manipulating juries; but his controversial statements and vitriol ultimately worked against him. He won a surprise victory in the Democratic primary, winning 41% of the vote, to 37% for Owen and 22% for Ross. It was widely said that Fieger owed his victory to black voters in Detroit, and he did carry it; but his margin there was not as one-sided as those for some primary candidates, and he carried all the counties in the Detroit, Grand Rapids and Traverse City media markets, suggesting that he simply outbought the competition on those TV stations.

Suddenly the spotlight was on Fieger, and it was not an attractive sight. Engler, he said, was "fat," a "moron," a "racist," the product of barnyard miscegenation. He criticized his fellow Democrats as well. At a unity breakfast, he said they were "a party of wimps and oatmeal"; he called Dennis Archer "a slow learner." He called Catholic Archbishop Adam Maida a "nut" and when Council of Orthodox Rabbis called assisted suicide murder, he said "They are closer to Nazis than they think they are." Congressmen Bart Stupak and Sander Levin declined to endorse him; when Al Gore appeared at a Democratic rally, Fieger was not present and Gore did not refer to him. Fieger did have a program—cutting the sales tax and property taxes and repealing the gas tax and single-business tax—and spent $5.7 million of his own money on his campaign, but, despite his contempt for others' intelligence, showed no mastery of state issues. Engler refused to debate Fieger and ran ads calling for drug tests of welfare recipients and attacking Fieger's ethical lapses. The outcome was never in doubt. Assisted suicide was on the ballot, and lost 71%–29%. Engler won 62%–38%, winning 27% of an expanded black voter turnout; Republicans regained control of the state House.

Starting his third term with a Republican legislature, Engler called for a raft of new programs and polices, many previously stopped by Democrats—an income tax cut from 4.4% to 3.9%, drug tests for welfare recipients, turning over control of troubled schools (including Detroit's) to mayors, $2,500 Michigan Merit Awards for tuition for students who test well, more charter schools, juvenile drug testing and expulsion of students who assault teachers, a ban on genetic testing for health care or employment. He has said he is not interested in national office or in running for the Senate.

Senior Senator. Carl Levin, first elected in 1978, is a durable and likable liberal Democrat, a member of one of Michigan's most respected political families. He is rumpled, unfashionable, speaks articulately but without apparent political artifice and takes unpopular stands on issues he cares about, although conservative columnist Robert Novak referred to "his reputation as one of the toughest, smartest and most partisan senators." He grew up in Detroit, worked for the state civil rights commissioner and the appellate public defender's office, and was elected to Detroit's city council in 1969 and 1973, practically the only member with substantial support from both blacks and whites. In 1978 he ran for the Senate and was helped when incumbent Robert Griffin got out of the race and then back in; Levin won 52%–48%. In 1984 he won by a similar margin against a former astronaut who had given a public testimonial for his Japanese car; in 1990 and 1996 he was re-elected by wide margins.

Since the retirement of Sam Nunn in 1996, Levin has been the ranking Democrat on Armed Services. Levin brought to the Senate the skepticism about defense spending and military involvements common among Democrats in the 1970s, an attitude that seldom has a majority on Armed Services. He characterizes his approach as supportive of basic, reliable weapons systems and conventional forces and skeptical of strategic weapons systems. He has strongly opposed acceleration of missile defense systems, leading the September 1998 filibuster in the Senate that prevailed by just one vote a week after North Korea launched its three-stage Taepo Dong 1 missile over Japan; he argued that missile defense would undermine chances of Russian approval of the 1993 START II treaty and that the nature of the missile threat was not clear. He supports full funding of the Nunn-Lugar program for buying up and disassembling nuclear weapons from the former Soviet Union. He sponsored a June 30, 1998, date for U.S. withdrawal from Bosnia; in January 1998, he said another two years would be reasonable. He joined John McCain in seeking a new round of base closures; that failed amid widespread distrust after the Clinton Administration paid special attention to preserving jobs at bases in states with more electoral votes.

Levin has spent much of his time on process issues. He was chief sponsor of the lobbying disclosure bill that passed the Senate in 1993 and, after Republicans took control of Congress, the House in 1995. Levin also was the chief sponsor of the Senate gift rule, setting a limit of $50 on gifts to senators and staffers. He was the prime mover in re-enacting in 1994 the independent counsel law, opposed by many Republicans and signed, perhaps to his later regret, by President Clinton. But he was very displeased with Independent Counsel Kenneth Starr. He tried to get Starr disqualified when he was first appointed, and in October 1998 he charged that Starr violated the law by failing to follow Justice Department guidelines, failing to disclose conflicts of interest and advocating impeachment. The law expires in June 1999; now that it has stung Democrats as well as Republicans it seems unlikely to be renewed, but Levin has promised to try, with modifications. Levin fought hard against the Contract With America proposals on unfunded mandates and regulatory reform. But more recently he has joined with Republican Fred Thompson in co-sponsoring a milder regulatory reform bill that would require cost-benefit analyses so that government regulations would be "sensible and cost-effective."

Levin generally has one of the most liberal records in the Senate. He opposed NAFTA and got Trade Representative Mickey Kantor to bring a Section 301 case against Japanese auto-parts trade practices. One issue on which he is passionate is capital punishment, and he has often led the fight against it: His legal practice was mostly in criminal defense and Michigan has not had capital punishment since 1855. He has worked on Michigan projects like refurbishing Metro airport; he personally lobbied Bill Clinton in March 1996 to get approval of

Northwest flights from Detroit non-stop to Beijing. Earlier he worked successfully to freeze CAFE car fuel-mileage standards and to get a marketing order for tart cherry producers (Michigan is the nation's largest producer of tart cherries).

Levin's reputation for candor and hard work, his rumpled persona and the strength of Bill Clinton in Michigan helped Levin easily win re-election in 1996. Republicans had a spirited primary out of which the 52%–48% winner, Ronna Romney, emerged with little money. Levin spent $6.2 million and in July started talking to *Detroit News* and *Free Press* reporters; most Democrats have boycotted them because of an extended strike. The result was not in doubt: Levin won 58%–40%, a bit better than his 57%–41% margin in 1990; he carried Outstate Michigan as well as the Detroit metro area.

Junior Senator. Spencer Abraham, first elected in 1994, is the first Republican elected to the Senate from Michigan in more than 20 years. He grew up in Lansing, the son of an auto worker who opened a "mom and pop" store, and grandson of Lebanese immigrants. He got the political bug early: while at Michigan State in 1974 he ran Clifford Taylor's nearly successful campaign against Democratic Congressman Bob Carr, and he became allies with a 26-year-old state legislator named John Engler. At Harvard Law School Abraham founded the Federalist Society and a conservative law review; in 1982, at 30, he became state Republican chairman. The party was then out of power throughout the state, but helped it regain the state Senate in 1983 and the governorship in 1990. Abraham's efforts to make Michigan an early presidential-caucus state in 1988 backfired when Pat Robertson's forces won a plurality of delegates.

In 1990 he joined Vice President Dan Quayle's staff and worked on the National Republican Congressional Committee. In 1993 he returned to Michigan and started running for the Senate, where he had anything but a clear field and trailed in initial polls for both the primary and general. But incumbent Donald Riegle, originally a young Republican and then a fiery liberal Democrat, retired after three terms and a brush with the Keating Five affair. In the primary Abraham faced Ronna Romney, also a Republican Party official; Abraham accused her of being less than strongly opposed to abortion and boasted of his endorsement by former Governor George Romney (made before Ronna, his former daughter-in-law, entered the race). Abraham won 52%–48%, trailing in metro Detroit but running far ahead in western Michigan. In the general Abraham faced Lansing Congressman Bob Carr, the narrow winner of a primary with six serious candidates. This was at the peak of Bill Clinton's unpopularity: an Abraham ad showed footage of Clinton saying he couldn't have gotten his budget and tax package through without Carr; Carr sheepishly sat deep in the audience, not on the platform, at a Clinton appearance in Dearborn in October. Abraham ran a straightforward conservative candidacy, refusing even to rule out cuts in entitlements, opposing abortion, and favoring NAFTA and GATT, and won by a solid 52%–43% margin.

Abraham's voting record in the Senate has not been entirely conservative, and he has had unusual successes for a freshman senator. His greatest impact has come on immigration. As a grandson of immigrants, his stance is not in doubt: "I really believe America was built, much of it, on the contributions of immigrants." Yet in the new Republican Congress both immigration subcommittees had chairmen—Lamar Smith in the House and Al Simpson in the Senate—who wanted to clamp down on illegal immigrants and reduce the number of legal immigrants. Abraham put together an unlikely coalition of liberal Democrats, business interests (notably Silicon Valley) and market and family-minded conservatives. He took on the popular Simpson in his final year in the Senate, who was determined to leave a legacy on an issue he had worked on for nearly 20 years. Abraham's coalition was strong enough that Simpson in March 1996 made concessions in the Judiciary Committee—removing provisions on verification and barring high-skill workers. But a week later Abraham moved to split the bill, keeping its provisions on illegal immigration, which seemed sure to pass, from its provisions reducing legal immigration, which on their own seemed likely to go nowhere. Abraham's coalition held and his motion passed 12–6. It was a major decision on a policy that will shape the nation in the 21st Century, which probably wouldn't have happened but for this junior senator.

After Simpson's retirement Abraham became chairman of the Immigration subcommittee. There his major project was to raise the limit on H1-B visas for skilled workers from 65,000; its main backers were Silicon Valley interests, its main opponents, labor unions. The change seemed to be beaten in September 1998. But Abraham compromised on numbers and got it included in the October 1998 omnibus budget bill: 115,000 would be issued in 1999 and 2000, 107,500 in 2001. Also, Abraham sponsored an amendment to allow the entry of certain religious workers; this was supported by Mother Theresa and the Christian Reform Church, which is strong in western Michigan. And he got a two-year delay of a law which he said would cause gridlock at border crossings; Detroit has one of the busiest in the world.

Abraham has relentlessly sought tax cuts. It was at a May 1996 dinner that he first suggested the 15% across-the-board tax cut which became part of Bob Dole's campaign in 1996; in 1997 he proposed giving taxpayers the option of paying a 25% flat tax; in 1998 he was holding out for a $100 billion tax cut. He helped pass laws attempting to bar frivolous civil lawsuits by prison inmates and pushed for stiffer sentences for powdered cocaine. He was the chief sponsor of the ban on interstate travel to help minors evade parental consent requirements for abortions; it passed the House but was blocked in the Senate in September 1998. He was chief Senate sponsor, with Joseph Lieberman, of the American Community Renewal Act. He sought to require a separate vote on unfunded mandates on business of $100 million or more. He worked successfully to lift the travel ban on Lebanon.

Some of his work was clearly done with Michigan in mind. He blocked Patrick Leahy's attempt to declare Vermont's Lake Champlain a Great Lake. Abraham sponsored a law to make brownfield cleanup expenses more quickly deductible. He saved the ELF submarine transmitter facility in northern Michigan from elimination. He placed in the omnibus bill provisions for 10,000 college scholarships for low-income students in engineering and computer science, replacement of the 54-year-old icebreaker *Mackinaw*, a ban on Coast Guard user fees in the Great Lakes, encouragement of on-line government forms. He supported the transportation bill, which increased spending in pothole-plagued Michigan from $512 million to $825 million. He emphasized environmental issues, co-sponsoring the National Parks Restoration Act and pushing a migratory birds bill through the Senate.

In 1998 Governor Engler named Abraham the head of the campaign to pass his Clean Michigan environmental bond issue. This passed easily, and was widely seen as an attempt to boost Abraham's not dazzling poll ratings. It seems to have done so, but Abraham will surely be targeted by Democrats in 2000. Detroit Mayor Dennis Archer and former Governor James Blanchard, who has maintained close involvement in Michigan politics after serving two years as ambassador to Canada, both said they would not run. But Congresswoman Debbie Stabenow announced her candidacy in March 1999, and Geoffrey Fieger, the Democrats' spectacularly unsuccessful gubernatorial nominee in 1998, said he intends to run as an independent.

Cook's Call. *Competitive.* Abraham has pulled a very competitive challenge from Democratic Representative Debbie Stabenow. The race will focus on Abrahams conservative ideology and both candidates records in Congress. A consistent theme will be which candidate stands for middle-class families. As long as Stabenow can raise the money needed to compete with Abraham, this should be a very competitive race until the finish.

Presidential politics. In 1984, 1988 and 1992 Michigan voted within 1% of the national average for all major presidential candidates. But it lost its bellwether status in 1996, when it voted 52%–38% for Bill Clinton, 3% more Democratic and less Republican than the nation. Clinton targeted the state early, appeared there often, and clearly benefited from the good feeling about Michigan's economic prospects, which also contributed to Republican Governor John Engler's victories in 1994 and 1998. Special attention was devoted to Macomb County, where most voters have blue-collar roots and Democratic traditions but who now have more upscale jobs and weaker party ties. Macomb turned sharply Republican in the 1970s and 1980s, prompting 1992 Clinton pollster Stan Greenberg to study it closely; Clinton lost Macomb 42%–38% in 1992 but carried it 49%–39% in 1996, one of his biggest gains in the state. He turned around more upscale Oakland County next door as well, from a 44%–39% loss to a 48%–43% win. In general Clinton gained most in cities with long-established blue-collar populations—Muskegon, Saginaw—or areas with blue-collar migration fanning out from Detroit or other metro areas—the Thumb, central Michigan north of Lansing, downscale lake counties. These are signs of a hesitant emergence from slumber of the old blue collar, unionized Democratic voting bloc—not anything major yet, but enough to cheer Democrats and bother Republicans.

In presidential primary races, Michigan has become a state where outsiders enter hoping support from disgruntled auto workers or some other constituency will give them victory—hopes that so far have been disappointed. Their hopes are further kindled because Michigan has kept switching from one defective selection system to another. In 1992 Michigan scheduled a regular primary for March 17, the same day as Illinois and a week after Super Tuesday. But the Illinois contest proved more crucial. Jerry Brown donned a UAW jacket and hoped to tap union activists who had been backing Tom Harkin, who had already withdrawn. But Clinton beat Brown 51%–26%. Meanwhile, Pat Buchanan had discovered the trade issue and on the Sunday before the primary motorcaded from Bay City to Saginaw and then to Flint, where he was jeered outside UAW Local 599. He lost to Bush 67%–25%. Undaunted, Buchanan was back again in 1996 for the March 19 primary, and took 34%. It was his best showing except for Wisconsin, and he seemed to be cracking that blue-collar vote at least a little (it helped that Michigan does not have party registration). But he still lost to Bob Dole 51%–34%.

Democrats in 2000 will choose delegates in caucuses which Al Gore seems likely to dominate easily. But at least one question mark about Gore is raised by his advocacy in *Earth in the Balance* of getting rid of the internal combustion engine; Gore may be accused of seeking to shut down the high-skill manufacturing which has revived Michigan's economy.

Congressional districting. Michigan lost one seat after the 1980 Census, two after the 1990 Census, and seems likely to lose one after the 2000 Census. The 1990s districting plan, drawn by a nonpartisan court with rather regular lines, has worked well for Democrats; they have fewer utterly safe districts, but have held onto marginal districts in tough contests and hold two Outstate seats thanks to popular incumbents who run well ahead of party lines. The plan for 2000 will depend on the results for elections to the state House in 2000. If Republicans hold onto their current narrow majority, they can control the process, and they will likely redraw the suburban Detroit districts to eliminate one Democrat and substantially weaken one or two others. One incumbent at risk: House Minority Whip David Bonior. If Democrats retake the state House, the result will either be a compromise or a court-drawn plan, with less dire political effects on Democrats.

The People: Est. Pop. 1998: 9,817,242; Pop. 1990: 9,295,297, up 5.6% 1990–1998. 3.6% of U.S. total, 8th largest; 29.5% rural. Median age: 34.6 years. 12.5% 65 years and over. 83.5% White, 13.9% Black, 1.1% Asian, 0.6% Amer. Indian, 0.9% Other; 2% Hispanic Origin. Households: 55.1% married couple families; 26.6% married couple fams. w. children; 44.5% college educ.; median household income: $31,020; per capita income: $14,154; 71% owner occupied housing; median house value: $60,600; median monthly rent: $343. 3.9% Unemployment. 1998 Voting age pop.: 7,266,000. 1998 Turnout: 3,143,432; 43% of VAP. Registered voters (1998): 6,915,613; no party registration.

Political Lineup: Governor, John M. Engler (R); Lt. Gov., Dick Posthumus (R); Secy. of State, Candice Miller (R); Atty. Gen., Jennifer Granholm (D); Treasurer, Mark Murray; State Senate, 38 (15 D, 23 R); Majority Leader, Dan DeGrow (R); State House, 110 (52 D, 58 R); House Speaker, Charles Perricone (R). Senators, Carl Levin (D) and Spencer Abraham (R). Representatives, 16 (10 D, 6 R).

Elections Division: 517-373-2540; **Filing Deadline for U.S. Congress:** May 16, 2000.

1996 Presidential Vote

Clinton (D) 1,989,683 (52%)
Dole (R) 1,481,572 (39%)
Perot (I) 336,681 (9%)

1992 Presidential Vote

Clinton (D) 1,871,182 (44%)
Bush (R) 1,554,940 (36%)
Perot (I) 824,813 (19%)

1996 Republican Presidential Primary

Dole (R) 265,425 (51%)
Buchanan (R) 177,562 (34%)
Forbes (R) 26,610 (5%)
Others 54,564 (11%)

GOVERNOR

Gov. John M. Engler (R)

Elected 1990, term expires Jan. 2003; b. Oct. 12, 1948, Mt. Pleasant; home, Mt. Pleasant; MI St. U., B.A. 1971, Cooley Law Schl., J.D. 1981; Catholic; married (Michelle).

Elected Office: MI House of Reps., 1970–76; MI Senate, 1978–90, Majority Ldr. 1984–90.

Office: Olds Plaza, 111 S. Capitol, Lansing, 48933, 517-373-3400; Fax: 517-335-6863; Web site: www.state.mi.us.

Election Results

1998 gen.	John M. Engler (R)	 1,883,005	(62%)
	Geoffrey Fieger (D)	 1,143,574	(38%)
1998 prim.	John M. Engler (R)	 477,628	(90%)
	Gary Artinian (R)	 55,453	(10%)
1994 gen.	John M. Engler (R)	 1,899,101	(61%)
	Howard Wolpe (D)	 1,188,438	(38%)

SENATORS

Sen. Carl Levin (D)

Elected 1978, seat up 2002; b. June 28, 1934, Detroit; home, Detroit; Swarthmore Col., B.A. 1956, Harvard U., LL.B. 1959; Jewish; married (Barbara).

Elected Office: Detroit City Cncl., 1969–77, Pres., 1973–77.

Professional Career: Practicing atty., 1959–64, 1971–73, 1978–79; MI Asst. Atty. Gen. & Gen. Cnsl., MI Civil Rights Comm., 1964–67; Detroit Chief Appellate Defender, 1967–69.

DC Office: 459 RSOB, 20510, 202-224-6221; Fax: 202-224-1388; Web site: www.senate.gov/~levin.

State Offices: Alpena, 517-354-5520; Detroit, 313-226-6020; Escanaba, 906-789-0052; Grand Rapids, 616-456-2531; Lansing, 517-377-1508; Saginaw, 517-754-2494; Southgate, 313-285-8596; Traverse City, 616-947-9569; Warren, 810-573-9145.

Committees: *Armed Services* (RMM of 9 D). *Governmental Affairs* (2d of 7 D): International Security, Proliferation & Federal Services; Investigations (Permanent) (RMM). *Intelligence* (8th of 8 D). *Small Business* (2d of 8 D).

Group Ratings

	ADA	ACLU	AFS	LCV	CON	NTU	NFIB	COC	ACU	NTLC	CHC
1998	90	86	100	88	79	16	33	44	0	3	0
1997	95	—	100	—	40	13	—	50	0	—	—

National Journal Ratings

	1997 LIB — 1997 CONS			1998 LIB — 1998 CONS		
Economic	88%	—	10%	90%	—	0%
Social	71%	—	0%	74%	—	0%
Foreign	73%	—	19%	73%	—	21%

Key Votes of the 105th Congress

1. Bal. Budget Amend.	N	5. Satcher for Surgeon Gen.	*	9. Chem. Weapons Treaty	Y
2. Clinton Budget Deal	N	6. Highway Set-asides	Y	10. Cuban Humanitarian Aid	Y
3. Cloture on Tobacco	Y	7. Table Child Gun locks	N	11. Table Bosnia Troops	Y
4. Education IRAs	N	8. Ovrd. Part. Birth Veto	N	12. $ for Test-ban Treaty	Y

Election Results

1996 general	Carl Levin (D)	2,195,738	(58%)	($6,223,409)
	Ronna Romney (R)	1,500,106	(40%)	($3,208,968)
	Others	66,731	(2%)	
1996 primary	Carl Levin (D)	unopposed		
1990 general	Carl Levin (D)	1,471,753	(57%)	($7,066,832)
	Bill Schuette (R)	1,055,695	(41%)	($2,417,705)

Sen. Spencer Abraham (R)

Elected 1994, seat up 2000; b. June 12, 1952, East Lansing; home, Auburn Hills; MI St. U., B.A. 1974, Harvard U., J.D. 1979; Eastern Orthodox; married (Jane).

Professional Career: Practicing atty.; Asst. Prof., Thomas Cooley Law Schl., 1981–83; MI Repub. Party Chmn., 1982–90; Dep. Chief of Staff, V.P. Dan Quayle, 1990–91; Co-Chair, Natl. Repub. Cong. Cmte., 1991–92.

DC Office: 329 DSOB, 20510, 202-224-4822; Fax: 202-224-8834; Web site: www.senate.gov/~abraham.

State Offices: Detroit, 313-961-2349; Grand Rapids, 616-975-1112; Lansing, 517-484-1984; Marquette, 906-226-9466; Saginaw, 517-752-4400; Southfield, 810-350-0510; Traverse City, 616-922-0915.

Committees: *Budget* (9th of 12 R). *Commerce, Science & Transportation* (10th of 11 R): Aviation; Communications; Consumer Affairs, Foreign Commerce & Tourism; Manufacturing & Competitiveness (Chmn.); Science, Technology & Space; Surface Transportation & Merchant Marine. *Judiciary* (8th of 10 R): Administrative Oversight & the Courts; Criminal Justice Oversight; Immigration (Chmn.). *Small Business* (10th of 10 R).

Group Ratings

	ADA	ACLU	AFS	LCV	CON	NTU	NFIB	COC	ACU	NTLC	CHC
1998	5	14	22	13	67	65	100	83	76	89	91
1997	15	—	0	—	82	80	—	90	76	—	—

National Journal Ratings

	1997 LIB — 1997 CONS			1998 LIB — 1998 CONS	
Economic	36%	—	63%	30%	—	69%
Social	28%	—	62%	12%	—	79%
Foreign	30%	—	66%	29%	—	58%

Key Votes of the 105th Congress

1. Bal. Budget Amend.	Y	5. Satcher for Surgeon Gen.	N	9. Chem. Weapons Treaty	Y
2. Clinton Budget Deal	Y	6. Highway Set-asides	N	10. Cuban Humanitarian Aid	N
3. Cloture on Tobacco	Y	7. Table Child Gun locks	Y	11. Table Bosnia Troops	Y
4. Education IRAs	Y	8. Ovrd. Part. Birth Veto	Y	12. $ for Test-ban Treaty	N

Election Results

1994 general	Spencer Abraham (R) 1,578,770	(52%)	($4,437,038)
	Bob Carr (D) 1,300,960	(43%)	($3,040,416)
	Jon Coon (Lib) 128,393	(4%)	($303,369)
1994 primary	Spencer Abraham (R) 292,399	(52%)	
	Ronna Romney (R) 270,304	(48%)	
1988 general	Donald W. Riegle Jr. (D) 2,116,865	(60%)	($3,383,849)
	Jim Dunn (R) 1,348,216	(39%)	($442,693)

FIRST DISTRICT

Michigan's Upper Peninsula, commonly known as the UP, is a land apart. Surrounded on three sides by frigid Lake Superior and Lake Michigan, it has its own flora, including the world's largest known-living object, a giant fungus that lives under 37 acres of a forest floor and is 1,500 years old. Although the UP is no farther north than Montreal or Seattle, it has one of the coldest climates in settled parts of North America. "In October, usually, the first snow falls steady on the northland," writes Dixie Lee Franklin in *A Most Superior Land*, "whispering teasing promises of more to come"—for seven months or more. Far away from any major city, with ground too frozen and a growing season too short for most crops, the Upper Peninsula was explored by French voyagers more than 300 years ago but was never thickly settled until prospectors found rich veins of ore here. The mineral veins of the Keweenaw Peninsula produced 13.3 billion pounds of copper; the Marquette, Menominee and Gogebic iron ranges have more than one billion tons of iron ore. Starting in the 1880s, immigrants flocked here to work the mines: Irish, Italians, Swedes, Norwegians, miners' sons from Wales and Cornwall, and most prominently Finns, who must have found this cold land with its lakes and hills much like their home. By 1900, the UP was a northern industrial belt, with a few bosses and some absentee overlords and a work force disposed to radical ideas and union movements.

A major strike in 1913–14 and falling ore prices after World War I—events that would be long forgotten elsewhere—are remembered in the UP as the beginning of its decline: The UP's population peaked at 332,000 in 1920. The copper veins were mostly depleted by then, mining iron ore became less labor-intensive, and lumber and farming provided only a few thousand jobs. In the last half century, there has been great migration to Detroit, Chicago and the West Coast; the UP's population has hovered around 300,000, rising to 318,000 in 1980 and dropping back to 313,000 in 1990. But "Yoopers" who some say have their own dialect, "Yoopanese," remain devoted to their land.

The 1st Congressional District of Michigan includes the Upper Peninsula and most of the three northern-tier counties in the Lower Peninsula. About half the people live in the UP; the other half live south of the breathtaking Mackinac Bridge. This is a vast area, geographically the second-largest district east of the Mississippi and smaller than only 26 farther west; it is a 450-mile drive from Ironwood at the western end of the UP to the Sleeping Bear Dunes towering over Lake Michigan. The Lower Peninsula counties have two different personalities. On Lake

Huron—the sunrise side—are smaller industrial towns and resorts that have been growing in the 1990s. On Lake Michigan are affluent resort areas around Petoskey and Charlevoix, long summer places for people from Chicago (this is Ernest Hemingway's "up in Michigan"), and the boom area around Traverse City, with its burgeoning condominiums and resorts. Politically, the UP has long been Democratic, some parts more than others; the Lake Michigan shore of the Lower Peninsula is heavily Republican, the sunrise side marginal.

The congressman from the 1st District is Bart Stupak, a Democrat and a "Yooper" from Menominee on the Wisconsin border. He was a police officer in Escanaba, then became a Michigan state trooper in 1974 and also earned a law degree; in 1984 he was injured in the line of duty and retired from the force. In 1988 he was elected to the Michigan House; in 1990 he lost a race for the state Senate. Stupak got into the 1992 House race when incumbent Republican Bob Davis, with 878 overdrafts on the House bank, decided to drop out in May 1992. Stupak won the three-way primary with 58% in the UP, which cast 70% of Democratic primary votes; overall he beat restauranteur Mike McElroy 49%–43%. In the general he beat Republican Philip Ruppe, who had represented the district from 1966–78, by 54%–44%.

In the House Stupak has paid great attention to local issues. Angered by the closing of K.I. Sawyer Air Force Base, the biggest employer in Marquette County in the UP, he threatened to vote against the Clinton budget and tax package; after some muscling, he voted for it. He bucked Clinton by opposing NAFTA and the 1994 crime bill. He formed the Law Enforcement Caucus and has sought to ban mail-order sales of body armor and to exempt those persons needing a gun for their job (police and military personnel) from the law banning gun-carrying by those convicted of abusing spouse or child. He passed a law requiring a study of whether auto makers should install interior releases in car trunks. He sponsored a bill to hold landowners not responsible under Superfund for past pollution. When a Sault Ste. Marie, Ontario, firm tried to sell Lake Superior water to China, he sponsored a resolution to prevent sale of any Great Lake water to a foreign country. He has a bill to ban directional drilling for oil and gas under the Great Lakes. He worked to find new uses for two closed UP Air Force bases and for northern Michigan Coast Guard properties—giving land to the Great Lakes Shipwreck Historical Society near the wreck of the *Edmund Fitzgerald* to the Michigan Audubon Society and to the Traverse City schools for a soccer field. He is strongly opposed to abortion, and was one of the few Democrats to speak out against it at the 1996 Democratic National Convention.

Stupak has become well known in the House for his unpredictability and for taking his time making decisions on issues. "Stupak is a good dancer, a notoriously good dancer," wrote Kevin Merida of the *Washington Post*. "He studies, he frets, he waits. He is a methodical hedger." His own press secretary puts it differently, "If you're looking at something that, for example, is a Republican issue in the normal course of voting, he wants to be able to explain to his Democratic constituents why he voted a certain way. It's what makes him the best person for the district."

This modus operandi has served him well in elections. In 1994 he was opposed by an auto-components manufacturer who spent $529,000 of his own money and attacked Stupak on the 1993 tax vote and on abortion. Stupak raised over $500,000 from PACs, and carried the UP and the sunrise side by large margins, for a solid 57%–42% victory. In 1996, he was helped when Governor John Engler's choice lost the Republican primary to a candidate who spent all of $5,800. Stupak won 71%–27%. In June 1997 he said he was exploring running for governor; he pondered for a while and bowed out of the race three months later.

In 1998 he had vigorous and well-financed opposition from Traverse City area state Representative Michelle McManus, whose uncle is a state Senator representing 11 of the district's 28 counties. She was also the recipient of major spending by the national Republican Party. McManus's strategy after the August primary was to associate Stupak with two presumably unpopular figures, Bill Clinton and Geoffrey Fieger. Stupak's indecision on both lured her into what turned out to be a trap. Clinton's numbers went down after his August 17 speech, and Stupak typically delayed deciding on whether he favored an impeachment investigation until the last days before the October vote. In that time Stupak said that Clinton's behavior was "immoral and unacceptable and he should be held accountable." Then Clinton's numbers rose after the release of the Starr report. Stupak supported the Democratic version of the investigation, and suddenly the Clinton card was working for him. (In her October 1998 speech to the House Democratic freshmen, Hillary Rodham Clinton cited Stupak's courage in defending his vote for the 1993 tax increase in the 1994 election; Stupak, the last one in the Michigan delegation to announce his decision, voted against impeachment.) As for Fieger, Stupak was obviously disturbed by many of his statements, and refused for six weeks after the primary to say whether he would support him or not. McManus ran spots attacking Stupak and asked Michigan Right to Life to withdraw its endorsement. Then on September 23, Stupak said he would not endorse Fieger; McManus had lost the Fieger card as well. Meanwhile, she was peppered with criticism by state Democratic Party leaders for handing in faulty filing petitions. Stupak won 59%–40%, carrying the UP by 2–1 and losing just two small counties; he even carried, narrowly, McManus's base around Traverse City.

Cook's Call. *Probably Safe.* Michigan Republicans continue to be stymied by Stupak's resilience in this conservative, rather marginal district. Stupak has racked up solid margins even against strong opponents with lots of money. His pro-labor, pro-life and pro-gun record fits this district well and he has proven that he can weather difficult political environments.

The People: Pop. 1990: 581,006; 69.3% rural; 16.3% age 65 +; 96.1% White, 0.8% Black, 0.5% Asian, 2.4% Amer. Indian, 0.2% Other; 0.6% Hispanic Origin. Households: 59.4% married couple families; 27.3% married couple fams. w. children; 38.8% college educ.; median household income: $22,788; per capita income: $10,846; median house value: $44,900; median gross rent: $259.

1996 Presidential Vote		
Clinton (D)	125,135	(47%)
Dole (R)	107,577	(40%)
Perot (I)	31,184	(12%)

1992 Presidential Vote		
Clinton (D)	118,983	(41%)
Bush (R)	101,110	(35%)
Perot (I)	65,402	(23%)

Rep. Bart Stupak (D)

Elected 1992; b. Feb. 29, 1952, Milwaukee, WI; home, Menominee; NW MI Comm. Col., A.A. 1972, Saginaw Valley St. Col., B.S. 1977, Thomas Cooley Law Schl., J.D. 1981; Catholic; married (Laurie).

Elected Office: MI House of Reps., 1988–90.

Professional Career: Escanaba Police Officer, 1972–73; MI St. Trooper, 1974–84; Practicing atty., 1981–1992.

DC Office: 2348 RHOB 20515, 202-225-4735; Fax: 202-225-4744; Web site: www.house.gov/stupak.

District Offices: Alpena, 517-356-0690; Crystal Falls, 906-875-3751; Escanaba, 906-786-4504; Houghton, 906-482-1371; Marquette, 906-228-3700; Traverse City, 616-929-4711.

Committees: *Commerce* (14th of 24 D): Finance & Hazardous Materials; Health and Environment; Oversight & Investigations.

Group Ratings

	ADA	ACLU	AFS	LCV	CON	NTU	NFIB	COC	ACU	NTLC	CHC
1998	90	63	100	69	78	22	14	17	20	16	33
1997	80	—	888	—	88	34	—	40	20	—	—

National Journal Ratings

	1997 LIB — 1997 CONS			1998 LIB — 1998 CONS		
Economic	66%	—	33%	72%	—	23%
Social	54%	—	46%	53%	—	46%
Foreign	88%	—	10%	82%	—	18%

Key Votes of the 105th Congress

1. Clinton Budget Deal	N	5. Puerto Rico Sthood. Ref.	Y	9. Cut $ for B-2 Bombers	Y
2. Education IRAs	N	6. End Highway Set-asides	N	10. Human Rights in China	Y
3. Req. 2/3 to Raise Taxes	N	7. School Prayer Amend.	N	11. Withdraw Bosnia Troops	*
4. Fast-track Trade	N	8. Ovrd. Part. Birth Veto	Y	12. End Cuban TV-Marti	Y

Election Results

1998 general	Bart Stupak (D)	130,129	(59%)	($672,773)
	Michelle McManus (R)	87,630	(40%)	($474,199)
	Others	4,037	(2%)	
1998 primary	Bart Stupak (D)	unopposed		
1996 general	Bart Stupak (D)	181,486	(71%)	($458,509)
	Bob Carr (R)	69,957	(27%)	($5,834)
	Others	5,348	(2%)	

SECOND DISTRICT

Lining the eastern shoreline of Lake Michigan, where the lake winds temper the frigid Michigan winters, are some of the nation's longest and highest sand dunes. In the late 19th Century, this shoreline was America's greatest lumber country; the ports on the small rivers were choked with logs and full of lumbermen from Norway and Sweden, Ireland and Scotland, Quebec and New England. During the lumber boom, the shoreline just to the south was the locus of America's largest migration from the Netherlands and still has the nation's largest concentration of Dutch-Americans. Wooden shoes are now seen only in the Tulip Festival in Holland, but here conscientious Dutch work habits have produced some of the most highly skilled workers in America, and major companies have grown up, like Gerber Foods in Fremont and Herman Miller furniture in Zeeland.

The 2d Congressional District of Michigan occupies the Lake Michigan shoreline counties, plus a tier of counties inland, from the lumber country around Manistee south to Holland and the resort town of Saugatuck. Some 25% of people here claim Dutch ancestry. Politically, the district is one of Michigan's two most Republican (the other is the Grand Rapids 3d). Its first Yankee settlers were part of the original Republican Party, and Dutch-Americans with their innate conservatism vie with Cuban-Americans for the title of America's most heavily Republican ethnic group. Holland and surrounding Ottawa County voted 85% for Governor John Engler in 1998.

The congressman from the 2d is Peter Hoekstra (pronounced *HOOKstra*), who immigrated from the Netherlands at 3, graduated from Hope College in Holland (with a semester in Washington during Watergate) and got an MBA at the University of Michigan. Hoekstra went to work at Herman Miller, where he helped develop the "Equa Chair" seat in the early 1980s and became a vice president. In 1992, he decided to run what seemed an improbable campaign for Congress against Guy Vander Jagt, 26-year incumbent and chairman of the National Republican Congressional Committee since 1975. Hoekstra saved up vacation time and in 1992 took a county-by-county bicycle tour of the district. With an earnestness that rang true, Hoekstra called for citizen, not career, politicians, refused PAC money and supported abolishing PACs, advocated 12-year term limits, and promised to uphold family values and to oppose abortion. He advocated balancing the budget, protecting the environment and upholding the Second

Amendment. Hoekstra spent only $55,600 to Vander Jagt's $725,000. But on primary day, Hoekstra carried the heavily Dutch Ottawa and Allegan Counties, which were newly added to the district, 53%–31%; they cast 59% of the primary vote, and so Hoekstra won 46%–40%. He won the general election easily.

Hoekstra brought to Washington a mistrust of government—he says he is "working to re-establish a rational federal government"—and a desire to apply the participatory management ideas he had developed at Herman Miller. In early 1994 he was asked by Newt Gingrich to plan how to manage a Republican House—something few others thought they would live to see. In October 1995 he gave up his seat on Budget to Mark Neumann, who had been bounced from Appropriations by Chairman Bob Livingston. In return Hoekstra got to chair a task force on reform. After his proposals were stalled in March 1996, he had an angry confrontation with Gingrich. Only a few of his reforms were adopted: the House barred former members from lobbying on the floor and it passed (though the Senate didn't) a ban on pensions to former members convicted of a felony. Hoekstra backed Gingrich for re-election only after much mulling in January 1997 and he opposed Gingrich's committee funding bill in March 1997. But he walked out of an anti-Gingrich coup meeting.

Hoekstra was the only one of the 1992 Republican freshmen who requested a seat on the Education and Workforce Committee; he got one, plus the chair of the Oversight and Investigations Subcommittee in 1995. In summer 1997 he started on two major assignments from the leadership, with a special $1.4 million budget. The first was an investigation of labor law. Republican leaders hoped he would investigate the role of unions in the 1996 campaigns, but instead he conducted what he called the American Worker at a Crossroads project. Eschewing spectacular hearings, except for a look at garment industry and union oppression of workers in April 1998, he held closed-door meetings with executives from companies like Boeing and Microsoft and later with some union leaders as well. He argued that the workplace has changed since federal labor laws were written and that they stifle cooperation, innovation and employee participation—themes Republicans had already addressed in their TEAM Act, passed by the 104th Congress but vetoed by President Clinton. Democrats charged that Hoekstra had a preset agenda and was not holding open hearings; Republicans grumbled that he was missing a chance to publicize union abuses and had no clear legislative focus.

Hoekstra's other assignment was investigating the Teamsters Union. An investigation of the Teamsters in the 1950s helped make John Kennedy a presidential candidate and James Hoffa and Robert Kennedy national figures, and provided the impetus for the last major revision of labor laws in 1959. Once again there were clear abuses: The 1996 election of Teamsters president Ron Carey had to be set aside in August 1997 and the union treasury was found depleted of $150 million. But the Teamsters were unforthcoming with evidence and subpoena problems delayed the probe until July 1998 when the requirement of subcommittee approval for every deposition and subpoena was dropped. Hoekstra would not hold publicized hearings: "I don't want to grandstand. It's the wrong thing to do." In early 1999 the leadership moved to take the issue away from Hoekstra and give it to full committee chairman William Goodling.

One of Hoekstra's other causes is abolishing the National Endowment for the Arts. "We have to learn how to eliminate agencies. We have to build the case and shame the proponents into acknowledging they are wasting taxpayers' money." Hoekstra was more successful in sponsoring a law to insure federal funding for medical schools that refuse to teach abortion. On foreign policy, Hoekstra sometimes tends toward the liberal: He was one of 24 Republicans who voted against the Contract With America missile defense bill. Some of his proposals are quixotic: He has proposed a constitutional amendment to establish recall for members of Congress, nonbinding national referenda on issues and a "none of the above" choice on federal elections. Some are more practical-minded: He wants to end the requirement that government shop for furniture with prison industries. In November 1998 he ran for vice chairman of the House Republican Conference. This spot had been held by Jennifer Dunn, who ran for majority leader; after she lost, many Republicans wanted to have a woman in a leadership position, and

Hoekstra's chances evaporated. He was eliminated on the second ballot, with 42 votes, to 108 for Tillie Fowler and 58 for Anne Northup.

Cook's Call. *Safe.* As one of the most Republican districts in the state, there is little competition for this seat from Democrats.

The People: Pop. 1990: 581,017; 52.2% rural; 12.8% age 65 + ; 92.9% White, 4.3% Black, 0.7% Asian, 0.7% Amer. Indian, 1.5% Other; 2.9% Hispanic Origin. Households: 63.4% married couple families; 31.5% married couple fams. w. children; 39.4% college educ.; median household income: $28,905; per capita income: $12,305; median house value: $58,400; median gross rent: $309.

1996 Presidential Vote		
Dole (R)	133,022	(50%)
Clinton (D)	108,242	(41%)
Perot (I)	23,512	(9%)

1992 Presidential Vote		
Bush (R)	126,969	(45%)
Clinton (D)	95,351	(34%)
Perot (I)	58,238	(21%)

Rep. Pete Hoekstra (R)

Elected 1992; b. Oct. 30, 1953, Groningen, Netherlands; home, Holland; Hope Col., B.A. 1975, U. of MI, M.B.A. 1977; Reformed Church of America; married (Diane).

Professional Career: Furniture Exec., Herman Miller Co., 1977–92.

DC Office: 1122 LHOB 20515, 202-225-4401; Fax: 202-226-0779; Web site: www.house.gov/hoekstra.

District Offices: Cadillac, 616-775-0050; Holland, 616-395-0030; Muskegon, 616-722-8386.

Committees: *Budget* (8th of 24 R). *Education & the Workforce* (7th of 27 R): Employer-Employee Relations; Oversight & Investigations (Chmn.); Workforce Protections.

Group Ratings

	ADA	ACLU	AFS	LCV	CON	NTU	NFIB	COC	ACU	NTLC	CHC
1998	5	13	11	15	74	83	100	82	100	97	100
1997	15	—	0	—	92	78	—	100	88	—	—

National Journal Ratings

	1997 LIB — 1997 CONS		1998 LIB — 1998 CONS	
Economic	14% —	85%	12% —	85%
Social	30% —	64%	29% —	69%
Foreign	38% —	60%	34% —	62%

Key Votes of the 105th Congress

1. Clinton Budget Deal	Y	5. Puerto Rico Sthood. Ref.	N	9. Cut $ for B-2 Bombers	Y
2. Education IRAs	Y	6. End Highway Set-asides	Y	10. Human Rights in China	N
3. Req. 2/3 to Raise Taxes	Y	7. School Prayer Amend.	Y	11. Withdraw Bosnia Troops	Y
4. Fast-track Trade	N	8. Ovrd. Part. Birth Veto	Y	12. End Cuban TV-Marti	Y

Election Results

1998 general	Pete Hoekstra (R) 146,854	(69%)	($210,118)
	Bob Shrauger (D) 63,573	(30%)	($98,380)
	Others 3,195	(2%)	
1998 primary	Pete Hoekstra (R) .... unopposed		
1996 general	Pete Hoekstra (R) 165,608	(65%)	($185,831)
	Dan Kruszynski (D) 83,603	(33%)	($30,962)
	Others 4,488	(2%)	

THIRD DISTRICT

Grand Rapids is Michigan's second-largest city, the center of its most prosperous and confident metropolitan area. The city's roots are in trees: It grew as a center for processing and turning into furniture the hardwood forests of northern Michigan. By the early 20th Century, Grand Rapids was the leading furniture manufacturer in the nation. But the Depression of the 1930s knocked the bottom out of the residential furniture market, and many manufacturers moved to cheaper-labor North Carolina. So Grand Rapids had to reinvent itself, and did. It went into office furniture, and today, three of the nation's largest office furniture manufacturers (Steelcase, Haworth and Herman Miller) are located in or near here. It capitalized also on a knack for retailing. Rich DeVos and Jay Van Andel started Amway, the direct sales empire, which now has half of its sales abroad, and Frederik and Hendrik Meijer started Meijer's Thrifty Acres, combining supermarkets with discount stores in a way that even Wal-Mart has not been able to equal. Lumber is still important: Peter Secchia, ambassador to Italy during the Bush Administration, made his fortune in that business. Grand Rapids is also the center of a machine tool empire. Fifty years ago Grand Rapids and its up-and-coming businesses were outshined by Detroit and the auto industry. Today, the western Michigan region centered on Grand Rapids has been growing rapidly and has been a major engine in the surging growth in Michigan's economy in the 1990s.

One ingredient in Grand Rapids' success is its unique ethnic mix. It was founded by New England Yankees, but much of its character was set by the Dutch immigrants who began arriving in western Michigan in the 1870s, and are still coming today; 23% of people here claim Dutch ancestry (probably no other city has as high a proportion of "V" pages in the phone book). The Dutch brought with them a piety witnessed in their Reform and Christian Reform churches, and a culture of hard work and precision craftsmanship. Politically, Dutch-Americans have been the nation's most heavily Republican identifiable ethnic group, except perhaps for Cuban-Americans; their cultural conservatism and belief in market economics runs deep. Dutch tradition and entrepreneurial success have been the ingredients of a civic activism that has given Grand Rapids a host of creative civic institutions that are the match of any city in the country.

Politically, Grand Rapids has been the center of Michigan Republicanism for most of the century. It has also produced national Republican leaders. One was Arthur Vandenberg, a newspaper editor who was U.S. senator from 1928–51; a one-time isolationist, he provided key support for the bipartisan internationalist foreign policies of Franklin Roosevelt and Harry Truman. Another was Gerald Ford, backed by Vandenberg in the 1948 House primary, who rose to become House Republican leader in 1965, vice president in 1973, and then president after Richard Nixon resigned in 1974. Nixon got a bit of a nudge from the Grand Rapids district when, in an early 1974 special election, it voted to replace Vice President Ford with a Democrat, a clear sign that the Republican heartland was turning on the president. In the 1980s and 1990s, however, Grand Rapids became more Republican than ever; in 1998 Grand Rapids and Kent County voted 77% for Republican Governor John Engler.

The 3d Congressional District of Michigan includes all of Grand Rapids and Kent County, plus one and a half smaller counties east and southeast. It is the most Republican district in Michigan, indeed one of the most Republican in all the Midwest, and has produced many

Michigan Republican leaders—Lieutenant Governor Dick Posthumus, former state House Majority Leader Ken Sikkema, National Committeeman Chuck Yob and Betsy DeVos, a national committeewoman and state party chairwoman.

The congressman from the 3d District is Vern Ehlers, chosen in a December 1993 special election. Ehlers grew up in small-town Minnesota, the son of a Christian Reform minister, attended Calvin College in Grand Rapids, got a Ph.D. in physics at Berkeley and then returned to Calvin to teach for 17 years; he is the first research physicist in Congress. In 1974, concerned about local waste management, he ran for Kent County commissioner; in 1982 he was elected to the state House and in 1986 the state Senate. After Congressman Paul Henry died in July 1993, Ehlers ran to succeed him, as he had in both houses of the legislature. In the November 1993 primary, Ehlers led with 33%, followed by 25% for Ken Sikkema, 19% for state commerce official Marge Byington, and 16% for a furniture manufacturer. A month later Ehlers whipped the Democrat 67%–23%.

Ehlers brought to House Republicans, then entering their 40th year in the minority, a majority mindset, which brought him to the attention of Newt Gingrich, who named him to his transition team after the 1994 election. He also assigned Ehlers to lead efforts to revamp the House's computer system. In 1995 Ehlers responded with a system making available to anyone vote tallies, public hearing transcripts and texts of amendments and bills.

Ehlers brings to his work a religious faith and scientific training that have left him with a middle-of-the-House voting record. "I want to be a voice for justice. I try to analyze every piece of legislation from a Christian framework." He is the author of *Earthkeeping in the '90s: Stewardship of Creation* and *Earthkeeping: Christian Stewardship of Natural Resources*, and his record on environmental issues won him support from both the Sierra Club and Consumers Power Company. In the House, he opposed Republicans' EPA riders on appropriations bills, supported the National Biological Survey, and opposed setting aside part of the Mojave National Reserve for hunting. He opposes the auto companies' proposal to freeze CAFE standards. His amendment converted from voluntary to mandatory the Great Lakes Water Quality Initiative standards in the 1996 Safe Drinking Water Act. He has introduced legislation to make permanent the ban on human cloning. As vice chairman of the Science Committee, he produced in September 1998 "Unlocking Our Future," the first major report on federal support of science in half a century, calling for "substantial and stable" science funding. He was the only republican member to vote against Star Wars in May 1999.

Ehlers has a penchant for compromise. He has proposed block-granting NEA funding. As head of a three-member task force on Robert Dornan's challenge to his 984-vote defeat in 1996, Ehlers looked over the evidence and in February 1998 announced that it showed "a large amount" of vote fraud but not enough to vacate the seat. On the Transportation Committee, he worked with Michigan Democrat James Barcia to change the funding formula and increase Michigan's funding from $512 million to $825 million. He also looked after the long-stalled M-6 South Beltline project and preserved money for Great Lakes research.

Ehlers refuses to take more than 30% of his campaign money from outside the district. He has been re-elected by very wide margins.

Cook's Call. *Safe.* This Grand Rapids-based district, once represented by President Gerald Ford, has been staunchly Republican for years. This seat is about the safest in the state—if not the country—for a Republican.

The People: Pop. 1990: 580,874; 24.5% rural; 11.3% age 65 +; 89.7% White, 7.4% Black, 0.9% Asian, 0.6% Amer. Indian, 1.4% Other; 2.5% Hispanic Origin. Households: 57.7% married couple families; 29.6% married couple fams. w. children; 47.3% college educ.; median household income: $31,917; per capita income: $13,924; median house value: $66,000; median gross rent: $372.

1996 Presidential Vote

Dole (R) 135,759 (53%)
Clinton (D) 99,698 (39%)
Perot (I) 17,583 (7%)

1992 Presidential Vote

Bush (R) 128,670 (46%)
Clinton (D) 94,715 (34%)
Perot (I) 52,773 (19%)

Rep. Vernon J. Ehlers (R)

Elected Dec. 1993; b. Feb. 6, 1934, Pipestone, MN; home, Grand Rapids; Calvin Col., 1952–55; U. of CA at Berkeley, A.B. 1956, Ph.D. 1960, U. of Heidelberg, Germany, 1961–62; Christian Reformed; married (Johanna).

Elected Office: Kent Cnty. Comm., 1975–82, Chmn., 1978–81; MI House of Reps., 1982–86; MI Senate, 1986–93, Pres. Pro Tem, 1990–93.

Professional Career: Prof., Calvin Col., 1966–82.

DC Office: 1714 LHOB 20515, 202-225-3831; Fax: 202-225-5144; Web site: www.house.gov/ehlers.

District Office: Grand Rapids, 616-451-8383.

Committees: *Education & the Workforce* (22d of 27 R): Postsecondary Education, Training & Life-Long Learning. *House Administration* (3d of 6 R). *Science* (Vice Chmn. of 25 R): Energy & Environment; Space & Aeronautics. *Transportation & Infrastructure* (15th of 41 R): Aviation; Water Resources & Environment. *Joint Committee on the Library of Congress* (3d of 6 Reps.).

Group Ratings

	ADA	ACLU	AFS	LCV	CON	NTU	NFIB	COC	ACU	NTLC	CHC
1998	25	31	33	69	50	51	100	89	56	58	92
1997	35	—	13	—	84	58	—	90	67	—	—

National Journal Ratings

	1997 LIB — 1997 CONS		1998 LIB — 1998 CONS	
Economic	41%	— 58%	42%	— 58%
Social	43%	— 57%	46%	— 53%
Foreign	63%	— 37%	61%	— 37%

Key Votes of the 105th Congress

1. Clinton Budget Deal	Y	5. Puerto Rico Sthood. Ref.	Y
2. Education IRAs	Y	6. End Highway Set-asides	N
3. Req. 2/3 to Raise Taxes	Y	7. School Prayer Amend.	Y
4. Fast-track Trade	Y	8. Ovrd. Part. Birth Veto	Y

9. Cut $ for B-2 Bombers	Y
10. Human Rights in China	Y
11. Withdraw Bosnia Troops	Y
12. End Cuban TV-Marti	Y

Election Results

1998 general	Vernon J. Ehlers (R) 146,364	(73%)	($346,312)
	John Ferguson Jr. (D) 49,489	(25%)	($10,406)
	Others 4,398	(2%)	
1998 primary	Vernon J. Ehlers (R) .... unopposed		
1996 general	Vernon J. Ehlers (R) 169,466	(69%)	($265,960)
	Betsy J. Flory (D) 72,791	(29%)	($13,042)
	Others 4,786	(2%)	

FOURTH DISTRICT

Flat and treeless for miles, the central reaches of Michigan's Lower Peninsula are farm country, exposed to bitter winds and snow drifts in winter and shining sun for precious weeks in summer.

Like the steppes of Eastern Europe, these are farmlands that produce hearty crops: potatoes, navy beans, sugar beets. The little cities here are often small factory towns, with neat tree-lined streets on a grid layout that suddenly end and turn to bare fields. Each city has some distinction. Midland in 1891 was a declining lumber town when Herbert Dow perfected an electrolytic process to extract chemicals from northern Michigan's extensive brine wells; that was the start of Dow Chemical, still headquartered in this now upscale town. Owosso in 1902 was the birthplace of Thomas E. Dewey, later New York governor and Republican candidate for president in 1944 and 1948. It was also the home of novelist James Oliver Curwood and his Curwood Castle writing studio; today it hosts the Curwood Festival, lovingly chronicled by Thomas Mallon in *Rockets and Rodeos*, and is the site of Mallon's novel *Dewey Defeats Truman*. Mount Pleasant, to the north, is the site of Central Michigan University, where parka-clad students stomp through snow to class; it is the home base of Governor John Engler.

The 4th Congressional District of Michigan includes much of this territory north of Lansing and Grand Rapids and west of Flint and Saginaw. It stretches north up the freeways, where thousands drive in fall to hunt and in winter to ski, into the rolling country around Houghton Lake, once lumber country and now a retirement and resort area, with trailers and condominiums between knotty-pine cottages clustered around icy green lakes. Politically, it remains mostly Republican territory, though retirees from the Detroit area and commuters to Flint and Saginaw have brought in some Democratic tendencies. The area gave small pluralities to Bill Clinton in 1992 and 1996.

The congressman from the 4th District is Dave Camp, a Republican first elected in 1990. Camp grew up in Midland and returned there after school to practice law; he has reported owning more than $500,000 in Dow stock. In 1984 he managed the successful congressional campaign of his boyhood friend Bill Schuette; in 1990 Schuette (now a state senator) unsuccessfully ran against Senator Carl Levin, and Camp ran for Congress. Camp's key victory was in the Republican primary, where with 62% in Midland County he beat former legislator and Pat Robertson supporter Al Cropsey, 33%–30%. He has won since without difficulty.

Camp has a generally conservative voting record and has attained some seniority on the Ways and Means Committee. There he played a key role in passing welfare reform in 1996. As the number two Republican on the Human Resources Subcommittee, he helped write the two welfare reform bills vetoed by Bill Clinton. In July 1996 he and Nevada freshman John Ensign circulated a letter signed ultimately by about 100 Republicans urging that they separate their welfare and Medicaid reforms, which had been passed as one bill, and vote on welfare reform alone, daring Bill Clinton to sign it and make history, or veto it and make it a campaign issue. Newt Gingrich and the Republican leadership decided to do this in July 1996, essentially disengaging House Republicans from the fate of the flagging Bob Dole presidential campaign. The bill passed, Clinton signed it, and the incumbent president and incumbent congressional Republicans got credit in November.

Camp has worked on other issues. He co-sponsored the 1996 Adoption and Safe Families Act, making the safety and best interests of the child paramount to family preservation, and helping foster children become adopted. He also authored the 1996 Organ Donor Card Insert Act, under which 70 million taxpayers received organ donor information with their income tax refunds. He pushed for tax breaks for electric cars and against the designation of Lake Champlain as a Great Lake. With Democrat Tim Roemer, he has led unsuccessful efforts to defund the space station: "The space station is simply a floating lemon that will cost 24 times its weight in pure gold." He wants duty-free stores at borders to be able to sell gas without the 18.3-cent federal tax. Since 1997 he has chaired the Corrections Day advisory group, which decides which regulations the Republicans will try to get the House to abolish as absurd.

Camp has had minimal opposition in the 4th District. In 1998 his Democratic opponent fell 12 signatures short of getting his name on the ballot.

Cook's Call. *Safe.* While not the most Republican district in the state, Camp has had little trouble racking up big margins of victory here. He is a sure bet for 2000.

The People: Pop. 1990: 580,890; 71.9% rural; 12.8% age 65 + ; 97.1% White, 1.1% Black, 0.4% Asian, 0.8% Amer. Indian, 0.7% Other; 1.6% Hispanic Origin. Households: 63% married couple families; 29.8% married couple fams. w. children; 38.3% college educ.; median household income: $25,898; per capita income: $11,549; median house value: $49,300; median gross rent: $282.

1996 Presidential Vote

Clinton (D)	112,625	(47%)
Dole (R)	98,215	(41%)
Perot (I)	28,350	(12%)

1992 Presidential Vote

Clinton (D)	104,228	(38%)
Bush (R)	102,284	(37%)
Perot (I)	67,263	(24%)

Rep. Dave Camp (R)

Elected 1990; b. July 9, 1953, Midland; home, Midland; Albion Col., B.A. 1975, U. of San Diego Law Schl., J.D. 1978; Catholic; married (Nancy).

Elected Office: MI House of Reps., 1988–90.

Professional Career: Practicing atty., 1978–90; MI Special Asst. Atty. Gen., 1980–84; A.A., U.S. Rep. Bill Schuette, 1984–87.

DC Office: 137 CHOB 20515, 202-225-3561; Fax: 202-225-9679; Web site: www.house.gov/camp.

District Offices: Houghton Lake, 517-366-4922; Midland, 517-631-2552; Owosso, 517-723-6759.

Committees: *Standards of Official Conduct* (4th of 5 R). *Ways & Means* (9th of 23 R): Health; Human Resources; Trade.

Group Ratings

	ADA	ACLU	AFS	LCV	CON	NTU	NFIB	COC	ACU	NTLC	CHC
1998	10	13	0	23	13	50	100	100	96	87	92
1997	20	—	25	—	70	58	—	100	84	—	—

National Journal Ratings

	1997 LIB	—	1997 CONS		1998 LIB	—	1998 CONS
Economic	28%	—	67%		23%	—	74%
Social	10%	—	82%		32%	—	67%
Foreign	32%	—	65%		39%	—	58%

Key Votes of the 105th Congress

1. Clinton Budget Deal	Y	5. Puerto Rico Sthood. Ref.	N	9. Cut $ for B-2 Bombers	Y
2. Education IRAs	Y	6. End Highway Set-asides	Y	10. Human Rights in China	N
3. Req. 2/3 to Raise Taxes	Y	7. School Prayer Amend.	Y	11. Withdraw Bosnia Troops	Y
4. Fast-track Trade	Y	8. Ovrd. Part. Birth Veto	Y	12. End Cuban TV-Marti	Y

Election Results

1998 general	Dave Camp (R)	155,343	(91%)	($654,061)
	Dan Marsh (Lib)	10,404	(6%)	
	Others	4,362	(3%)	
1998 primary	Dave Camp (R)	unopposed		
1996 general	Dave Camp (R)	159,561	(65%)	($555,815)
	Lisa Donaldson (D)	79,691	(33%)	($13,284)
	Others	4,393	(2%)	

FIFTH DISTRICT

Saginaw Bay, the inlet of Lake Huron that separates Michigan's Thumb (people really call it that) from the mitten of its Lower Peninsula, was for a moment in the 1870s the site of the greatest flow of lumber in the United States. There were 36 sawmills in Bay City then, and logs were piled high along both banks of the Saginaw River for miles. Bay City and Saginaw, 15 miles upstream, handled logs from the wide area on both sides of Saginaw Bay drained by the Saginaw River and its tributaries. Saginaw was also a center of precision machinery manufacturing, one reason General Motors put its huge power steering plants here. But starting in 1979 GM payrolls fell, and for a while the Saginaw area foundered. More recently, small high-skill manufacturing operations have grown up in old factory buildings once considered worthless; this is part of the southern Michigan industrial belt with expertise needed to sustain just-in-time manufacturing. There also is agriculture here: The flat, broad fields around Saginaw Bay that once held so many trees are now the nation's leading producer of navy beans and among the leaders in sugar beets.

The 5th Congressional District of Michigan includes Saginaw and Bay City and lands on both sides of Saginaw Bay. To the north it goes up past Oscoda on Lake Huron, where the 1993 closing of Wurtsmith Air Force Base resulted in a local economic boom rather than a bust as new employers were attracted and property sold readily. To the east it includes most of the Thumb. To the south it reaches to the city limits of Flint, including both black and white working-class townships just north of the city. Bay City, with its large Polish population, has long been Democratic and, since the auto industry woes of the 1980s, so are Saginaw and the Flint suburbs. While the Thumb historically is among the most Republican parts of Michigan, and the Oscoda area is Republican as well, both seem to be trending Democratic.

The congressman from the 5th District is Jim Barcia, a Democrat elected in 1992. Barcia grew up in Bay City, went to Saginaw Valley State College, and has always lived in the area. He held political staff jobs until being elected to the state House in 1976, at age 24, and the state Senate in 1982. Barcia was known in the legislature for his whistleblower protection law, and he was not an automatic vote for unions or management; he bucked organized labor by backing a measure to cut the cost of workers' compensation and bucked others in his party by voting against abortion rights. In 1992 he had opposition from state Senator John Cherry of Saginaw, who had strong backing from organized labor, and from Don Hare, district staffer for incumbent Bob Traxler. Barcia, with 72% in Bay County, won overall with 46%, to 29% for Cherry and 25% for Hare. Barcia won the general 60%–38%.

Barcia has a moderate, middle-of-the-House voting record. He supported the balanced budget constitutional amendment and the line-item veto; he opposed the 1994 Clinton health care plan and NAFTA (this has long been a protectionist area: Saginaw Congressman "Sugar Beet Joe" Fordney sponsored the nation's highest tariffs ever in 1922).

Barcia serves on Transportation and supported the huge transportation bill of 1998; he worked with Grand Rapids Republican Vern Ehlers to change the funding formula and increase Michigan's funding from $512 million to $825 million. He included water supply infrastructure earmarks for the town of Bad Axe, defending against charges of pork barrel spending by saying, "If this is pork, pass the platter." In October 1997 Barcia introduced a compromise Superfund reform to let small companies out of liability; but no bill passed. In September 1998 he attacked EPA for giving grants to a Flint group that also was trying to stop a new 200-job steel mill. Outraged by attacks on constituents, he got approval in June 1998 of a resolution urging all states to keep violent offenders in prison for at least 85% of their sentences.

Barcia has been re-elected by wide margins; in 1998 he won 81% of the vote in Bay County.

Cook's Call. *Safe.* This Saginaw-based district, heavily populated with union members and retirees, is solidly Democratic. Barcia, who has never been elected with less than 60% of the vote, is a sure bet for re-election in 2000.

The People: Pop. 1990: 580,981; 50.5% rural; 13.4% age 65 + ; 88.9% White, 8.4% Black, 0.4% Asian, 0.6% Amer. Indian, 1.7% Other; 3.2% Hispanic Origin. Households: 58.8% married couple families; 28% married couple fams. w. children; 36% college educ.; median household income: $26,312; per capita income: $11,891; median house value: $47,400; median gross rent: $290.

1996 Presidential Vote

Clinton (D)	155,995	(57%)
Dole (R)	90,107	(33%)
Perot (I)	27,477	(10%)

1992 Presidential Vote

Clinton (D)	119,086	(45%)
Bush (R)	85,603	(32%)
Perot (I)	61,544	(23%)

Rep. Jim Barcia (D)

Elected 1992; b. Feb. 25, 1952, Bay City; home, Bay City; Saginaw Valley St. U., B.A. 1974; Catholic; married (Vicki).

Elected Office: MI House of Reps., 1976–82, Majority Whip, 1979–82; MI Senate, 1982–92.

Professional Career: Staff Asst., U.S. Sen. Philip Hart, 1971; Comm. Svc. Coord., MI Comm. Blood Ctr., 1974–75; A.A., MI Rep. Donald Albosta, 1975–76.

DC Office: 2419 RHOB 20515, 202-225-8171; Fax: 202-225-2168; Web site: www.house.gov/barcia.

District Offices: Bay City, 517-667-0003; Flushing, 810-732-7501; Saginaw, 517-754-6075.

Committees: *Science* (5th of 22 D): Energy & Environment; Technology (RMM). *Transportation & Infrastructure* (15th of 34 D): Ground Transportation; Water Resources & Environment.

Group Ratings

	ADA	ACLU	AFS	LCV	CON	NTU	NFIB	COC	ACU	NTLC	CHC
1998	90	31	89	46	13	24	50	50	40	38	50
1997	50	—	63	—	62	39	—	60	64	—	—

National Journal Ratings

	1997 LIB — 1997 CONS			1998 LIB — 1998 CONS		
Economic	55%	—	44%	64%	—	34%
Social	48%	—	51%	48%	—	51%
Foreign	43%	—	55%	39%	—	58%

Key Votes of the 105th Congress

1. Clinton Budget Deal	N	5. Puerto Rico Sthood. Ref.	Y	9. Cut $ for B-2 Bombers	N
2. Education IRAs	N	6. End Highway Set-asides	N	10. Human Rights in China	Y
3. Req. 2/3 to Raise Taxes	Y	7. School Prayer Amend.	Y	11. Withdraw Bosnia Troops	N
4. Fast-track Trade	N	8. Ovrd. Part. Birth Veto	Y	12. End Cuban TV-Marti	N

Election Results

1998 general	Jim Barcia (D)	135,254	(71%)	($183,629)
	Donald Brewster (R)	51,442	(27%)	($7,220)
	Others	3,275	(2%)	
1998 primary	Jim Barcia (D)	unopposed		
1996 general	Jim Barcia (D)	162,675	(70%)	($200,556)
	Lawrence Sims (R)	65,542	(28%)	($162,739)
	Others	4,234	(2%)	

832   MICHIGAN

SIXTH DISTRICT

The southwest corner of Michigan is at the western end of the overland trail from Detroit, where the state's two southern tiers of counties were settled by New England Yankees and Upstate New Yorkers in the 1830s and 1840s. They built small towns with schools and churches and colleges, supported temperance and opposed capital punishment, and in 1854 started the Republican Party. There are towns in southwest Michigan that still recall proudly their past as termini of the Underground Railroad, and black families with ancestors who made their way north out of slavery to freedom (Detroit Mayor Dennis Archer grew up here). Later, big industries transformed some of the small towns into significant cities: Kalamazoo, started by Dutch-Americans who introduced celery to this country, became the home of Upjohn pharmaceuticals; Benton Harbor and St. Joseph, twin towns on Lake Michigan originally known for cherry and peach orchards, became the home of Whirlpool appliances. But this southwest corner is also where the influence of Michigan recedes: People here watch Chicago television and root for the Cubs or White Sox rather than the Tigers.

The 6th Congressional District of Michigan occupies this southwest corner of the state, with Kalamazoo and Benton Harbor-St. Joseph its two major urban areas, and three smaller counties besides. It was for many years arch-Republican territory, represented by a succession of congressmen who deplored federal spending and welfare state measures: New Deal opponent Clare Hoffman (1935–63), Nixon defender Edward Hutchinson (1963–77), and pork barrel critic and later Reagan Office of Management and Budget Director David Stockman (1977–81). More recently, Kalamazoo has trended toward the Democrats, and the 6th cast small pluralities for Bill Clinton in 1992 and 1996.

The current congressman from the 6th District is Fred Upton. The grandson of one of the founders of Whirlpool, Upton grew up in St. Joseph, attended the University of Michigan and worked for David Stockman, first on his House staff, then from 1981–85 at OMB. He returned home and challenged Congressman Mark Siljander, a conservative and evangelical Christian, in the 1986 Republican primary, and won 55%–45%. Upton is less like the congressional David Stockman, a scourge of federal spending, and more like the OMB Stockman, who rued the Reagan tax cuts. He has a moderate voting record and an impulse toward bipartisanship. He voted for the Brady bill and the national service bill, and in January 1993 resigned as deputy whip. He worked on the Commerce Committee for bipartisan bills on interstate waste shipments, Superfund and health care. He has worked with Democrat John Dingell on nuclear waste; their bill for an interim central waste disposal site in Nevada passed the House and Senate in 1997, but the threat of a presidential veto prevented it from reaching Clinton's desk; he reintroduced the bill in 1999.

Upton has been anything but a team player in the Republican House. He kept trying to lower the income limit for the $500 per-child tax credit, to as low as $50,000. He voted against some Republican environmental bills and called for a lifetime ban on members' lobbying for foreign governments. He called for making Republican tax cuts contingent on certification by the (Clinton) OMB that the budget was on a realistic path toward being balanced in 2002. Looking back at his experience with Stockman, Upton said, "We don't want to make the historic mistake we made in the '80s." In 1995 he became part of the Tuesday Lunch Bunch, now called the Tuesday Group, a band of 40 or so Republican moderates. In January 1996 he worked in vain with Democrat Tim Roemer of nearby Indiana to construct a bipartisan budget even as the government was shut down. He was successful later in 1996 with bipartisan action on welfare reform and the Safe Drinking Water Act. "Our group" he said, referring to the Tuesday Lunch Bunch, "was responsible for the positive agenda at the end of the Congress."

After the 1996 election, Upton decried the "shut-down, dark ages" approach taken by Republicans and said his party had come to be seen as "narrow" and "intolerant." He spoke out against John Kasich's proposed budget cuts in May 1998. He backed the Udall bill earmarking $100 million for Parkinson's disease research; Muhammad Ali, who testified for it, has lived in Berrien Springs in the district. He supported the Shays-Meehan campaign finance bill. He worked to arrange the two-year delay in a tougher border crossing law, which he said would cause gridlock at Michigan-Ontario border crossings, and to have Lake Champlain not declared a Great Lake. He got money for dredging the St. Joseph River and, showing an old "I drive U.S. 31—pray for me" bumper sticker, money for completing the U.S. 31 freeway in Berrien County. In December 1998 many in the Clinton White House hoped Upton would vote against impeachment, but on December 15 he announced he would vote for it.

Upton considered running for the Senate in 1994 and 1996, but both times decided not to. He had one serious primary challenge from a conservative in 1990, but otherwise has won re-election easily.

Cook's Call. *Safe.* This district has elected a Republican to the House since the 1930s, and Upton should have no trouble here in 2000.

The People: Pop. 1990: 580,973; 50% rural; 12.7% age 65 + ; 88.1% White, 9.5% Black, 1% Asian, 0.6% Amer. Indian, 0.8% Other; 1.7% Hispanic Origin. Households: 56.2% married couple families; 26.5% married couple fams. w. children; 45.2% college educ.; median household income: $28,453; per capita income: $13,043; median house value: $54,600; median gross rent: $322.

1996 Presidential Vote			1992 Presidential Vote		
Clinton (D)	103,454	(46%)	Clinton (D)	100,677	(39%)
Dole (R)	99,975	(44%)	Bush (R)	97,234	(38%)
Perot (I)	19,967	(9%)	Perot (I)	55,682	(22%)

Rep. Fred Upton (R)

Elected 1986; b. Apr. 23, 1953, St. Joseph; home, St. Joseph; U. of MI, B.A. 1975; Protestant; married (Amey).

Professional Career: Project coord., U.S. Rep. David Stockman, 1975–80; Legis. Affairs, O.M.B., 1981–83, Dir., 1984–85.

DC Office: 2333 RHOB 20515, 202-225-3761; Fax: 202-225-4986; Web site: www.house.gov/upton.

District Offices: Kalamazoo, 616-385-0039; St. Joseph, 616-982-1986.

Committees: *Commerce* (6th of 29 R): Health and Environment; Oversight & Investigations (Chmn.). *Education & the Workforce* (19th of 27 R): Early Childhood, Youth & Families.

Group Ratings

	ADA	ACLU	AFS	LCV	CON	NTU	NFIB	COC	ACU	NTLC	CHC
1998	15	19	22	46	50	51	93	89	56	71	75
1997	25	—	0	—	93	67	—	90	80	—	—

National Journal Ratings

	1997 LIB — 1997 CONS			1998 LIB — 1998 CONS		
Economic	38%	—	61%	46%	—	53%
Social	46%	—	53%	47%	—	52%
Foreign	43%	—	55%	47%	—	51%

Key Votes of the 105th Congress

1. Clinton Budget Deal	Y	5. Puerto Rico Sthood. Ref.	N	9. Cut $ for B-2 Bombers	Y
2. Education IRAs	Y	6. End Highway Set-asides	Y	10. Human Rights in China	Y
3. Req. 2/3 to Raise Taxes	Y	7. School Prayer Amend.	Y	11. Withdraw Bosnia Troops	Y
4. Fast-track Trade	Y	8. Ovrd. Part. Birth Veto	Y	12. End Cuban TV-Marti	Y

Election Results

1998 general	Fred Upton (R) 113,292	(70%)	($600,617)
	Clarence J. Annen (D) 45,358	(28%)	($14,943)
	Others 2,977	(2%)	
1998 primary	Fred Upton (R) .... unopposed		
1996 general	Fred Upton (R) 146,170	(68%)	($399,520)
	Clarence J. Annen (D) 66,243	(31%)	($12,089)
	Others 3,421	(2%)	

SEVENTH DISTRICT

The small cities and towns spotting the southern-tier farmland counties of Michigan have been incubators of innovation since they were settled by Yankees from New England 150 years ago. The state's public school system was established by two politicians from Marshall, whose dashed hopes to make it the state capital resulted in the preservation of many of its 19th Century structures whose counterparts in Lansing, which won the contest, have long since been demolished. A few miles away, in Battle Creek, sanitarium operator W.K. Kellogg invented corn flakes as a health food; he and his one-time patient, C.W. Post, both established factories in the late 19th Century and created the American breakfast cereal industry. To the south is Hillsdale, where Hillsdale College has been proudly admitting blacks and women since the 1850s and refusing all federal aid. Politically, this area has been Republican territory since 1854, when the party was founded in the manufacturing and prison town of Jackson as a kind of reformist institution out of the same activist impulse that produced local support for women's rights and Prohibition and opposition to the death penalty. Southern Michigan mostly rejected New Deal tinkering and was hostile to the UAW, but the people here were receptive to moral claims made by later 20th Century reformers challenging racial segregation, the Vietnam war and the Watergate coverup.

The 7th Congressional District of Michigan covers all of six counties and parts of two others in Michigan's southern tier. It typically votes Republican, but not always: Bill Clinton carried the district by small pluralities in 1992 and 1996.

The congressman from the 7th District is Nick Smith, a Republican who won the seat in 1992 after it was greatly altered by redistricting. Smith is a dairy farmer in Hillsdale County who was elected to the Somerset Township Board in 1962 after his wife "told me to get involved or stop complaining." He was elected to the state House in 1978 and state Senate in 1982. In 1992 the new 7th District included much territory formerly represented by Republican Carl Pursell and Democrat Howard Wolpe. But Pursell's base was far distant and Wolpe found the district dauntingly Republican, and both retired from Congress. The 7th then had a brawling primary between Smith and fellow state Senator John Schwarz of Battle Creek, a physician accused by a third candidate of backing his car into a hospital security officer who had written him a ticket. Smith boasted of his 1992 property tax freeze and anti-abortion record and attacked Schwarz for raising money in Washington and from PACs while he took no PAC money. Smith won 43%–36%.

In the House Smith has worked on agriculture and local issues but has been most prominent as an advocate of Social Security reform. He backed the Freedom to Farm Act and supported a bipartisan agriculture research program in 1998; he looked into an outbreak of hepatitis A in Calhoun County from imported frozen strawberries and got the county reimbursed for treating it; he wants research on the apple fireblight which hit Michigan in the 1990s. He is for the balanced budget amendment and tight budgets, but fought to save the Battle Creek Federal Center from the base-closing commission. He got funding for I-94 earmarked in the 1998 transportation bill. In 1997 he got a reprieve in a funding formula change which would have cost Michigan money for drug abuse treatment and mental health grants; in 1998 he co-sponsored the House effort to repeal the law requiring record-keeping at border crossings. In the bankruptcy reform bill he put a provision preventing parents from evading their child support debts to governments. He got some notice in July 1997 when his piercing whistle attracted Capitol Police to nab a purse-snatcher; he says he used to whistle so loudly on the farm his children could hear him a half-mile away.

But it is on Social Security that Smith has made his biggest mark. Back in 1995 he came forward, a self-starter, with a plan to allow workers to put 2.3% of their 12.4% payroll tax into a private account that could be invested in stocks, to raise the retirement age in steps to 69. Around his district and to anyone in Washington who would listen, Smith showed his Social Security proposal charts. All this despite the conventional wisdom that Social Security is the third rail of American politics, touch it and you die.

That conventional wisdom was tested in the 1996 and 1998 elections. In October 1996 Democrat Kim Tunnicliff started campaigning vigorously, running ads attacking Smith for Medicare "cuts" and for accepting $750,000 in farm subsidy payments. Smith, who still takes no PAC money, was outspent on the air, and won by just 55%–43%, much less than expected. That made Smith an obvious Democratic target for 1998. The Democratic nominee was Jim Berryman, a state Senator from a Republican-leaning district including Adrian and (not in the 7th District) Monroe with a solid liberal record, who was thinking about running for governor but decided to run for Congress instead.

"This campaign comes down to Social Security," Berryman said. "Do we want to strengthen a system that never broke a promise, or do we want to make it a system of winners and losers?" Joining in the chorus were AFL-CIO ads calling for saving Social Security first, before any tax cuts. Berryman also attacked Smith for "feasting at the public trough" for taking money from the Conservation Reserve Program and the Production Flexibility Program, the latter created in the 1996 farm bill he voted for. Smith hit Berryman for taking PAC and union money. Interestingly, both candidates said Bill Clinton should resign. Polls showed Smith hovering around 50%, but he benefited from the pro-incumbent climate. Smith won 57%–40%, a better showing than in 1996, and carried every county including, by a narrow margin, Berryman's home base. After the election Smith said, "Clearly, it's going to send a message that dirty politics and not telling the truth doesn't work with voters of our rural southern Michigan area." But even more the message was that Social Security reform is no longer politically fatal.

Cook's Call. *Probably Safe.* While this conservative district is about as Republican as the neighboring 6th, Smith has not racked up Fred Upton's large margins of victory. Still, he has never come all that close to losing and remains the favorite in 2000.

The People: Pop. 1990: 581,005; 51.9% rural; 12.6% age 65 + ; 92.3% White, 5.6% Black, 0.5% Asian, 0.5% Amer. Indian, 1.1% Other; 2.2% Hispanic Origin. Households: 59.4% married couple families; 28.6% married couple fams. w. children; 42.5% college educ.; median household income: $29,976; per capita income: $12,900; median house value: $50,700; median gross rent: $313.

1996 Presidential Vote			1992 Presidential Vote		
Clinton (D)	105,185	(46%)	Clinton (D)	96,872	(38%)
Dole (R)	99,518	(43%)	Bush (R)	96,253	(37%)
Perot (I)	24,501	(11%)	Perot (I)	62,657	(24%)

Rep. Nick Smith (R)

Elected 1992; b. Nov. 5, 1934, Addison; home, Addison; MI St. U., B.A. 1957, U. of DE, M.S. 1959; Congregationalist; married (Bonnalyn).

Military Career: Air Force, 1959–61.

Elected Office: Somerset Township Trustee, 1962–68, Supervisor, 1966–68; Hillsdale Cnty. Bd. of Supervisors, 1966–68; MI House of Reps., 1978–82; MI Senate, 1982–92, Pres. Pro-Tem, 1983–90.

Professional Career: Businessman, farmer; Hillsdale Cnty. Repub. Chmn., 1966–68; MI Chmn., Agricultural Stabilization and Conservation Svc., 1969–72; Natl. Energy Dir., U.S. Dept. of Agriculture, 1972–74; MI Occup. Safety Standards Comm., 1975.

DC Office: 306 CHOB 20515, 202-225-6276; Fax: 202-225-6281; Web site: www.house.gov/nicksmith.

District Offices: Battle Creek, 616-965-9066; Jackson, 517-783-4486.

Committees: *Agriculture* (8th of 27 R): General Farm Commodities, Resource Conservation & Credit; Risk Management, Research & Specialty Crops. *Budget* (6th of 24 R). *Science* (9th of 25 R): Basic Research (Chmn.).

Group Ratings

	ADA	ACLU	AFS	LCV	CON	NTU	NFIB	COC	ACU	NTLC	CHC
1998	20	14	33	31	60	62	100	83	76	89	100
1997	15	—	13	—	92	72	—	90	88	—	—

National Journal Ratings

	1997 LIB — 1997 CONS	1998 LIB — 1998 CONS
Economic	0% — 90%	26% — 72%
Social	18% — 81%	38% — 60%
Foreign	42% — 57%	7% — 83%

Key Votes of the 105th Congress

1. Clinton Budget Deal	Y	5. Puerto Rico Sthood. Ref.	N	9. Cut $ for B-2 Bombers	Y
2. Education IRAs	Y	6. End Highway Set-asides	Y	10. Human Rights in China	Y
3. Req. 2/3 to Raise Taxes	Y	7. School Prayer Amend.	Y	11. Withdraw Bosnia Troops	Y
4. Fast-track Trade	N	8. Ovrd. Part. Birth Veto	Y	12. End Cuban TV-Marti	N

Election Results

1998 general	Nick Smith (R)	104,656	(57%)	($605,528)
	Jim Berryman (D)	72,998	(40%)	($458,229)
	Others	4,473	(2%)	
1998 primary	Nick Smith (R)	unopposed		
1996 general	Nick Smith (R)	120,227	(55%)	($263,739)
	Kim Tunnicliff (D)	93,725	(43%)	($145,511)
	Others	4,592	(2%)	

EIGHTH DISTRICT

Lansing is Michigan's state capital, chosen in 1847 because of its geographic position halfway between Lake Huron and Lake Michigan and in ignorance of the fact that it has fewer days with sunshine than any place else in the state. But it is a tidy and pleasant city with more than its share of amenities. It has a beautifully restored Capitol and a fine state history museum and is neighbor to Michigan State University in East Lansing, started in 1855 as America's first land-grant college. Its Oldsmobile plant stimulated growth in the first half of this century, and state government has done the same in the second half. Lansing has tended to go with the party controlling state government. When the legislature was apportioned to stay Republican, as it was until 1964, the Lansing area was usually Republican; Democrats have had majorities in the state House in 28 of the 36 years since and Lansing has voted mostly Democratic.

The 8th Congressional District of Michigan includes Lansing and Ingham County but not the Lansing suburbs just across the line in Clinton and Eaton Counties, which are, respectively, in the 4th and 7th Districts. The 8th has two other very different population centers. One is the suburban fringe southwest of Flint, an area long Democratic and in deep trouble in the past two decades with the shutdown of General Motors operations there. The other is Livingston County, where I-96 crosses U.S. 23. Strewn with lakes and hills, this has been one of the fastest-growing counties in Michigan; its many new residents left the Detroit area because they disliked the crime, high taxes and liberal politics they found there. Livingston is very conservative and Republican; in 1992 and 1996 it was Clinton's second and third worst county in Michigan, one of only five to give Dole an absolute majority of the vote. Such politically disparate areas leave the 8th District closely balanced, and it switched parties in two of the last three elections.

The congresswoman from the 8th District is Debbie Stabenow, a Democrat elected in 1996. She grew up in the small Outstate town of Clare and went to Michigan State, where she got a master's degree in social work. Almost all her adult life Stabenow has been in politics. She was elected county commissioner before she finished her graduate degree; she was elected to the state House in 1978, at 28, making a record in family law and child abuse; she was elected to the state Senate in 1990. In 1994, while running for governor, she was at the storm center of state politics and policy. In response to Republican Governor John Engler's call for education finance reform, she proposed to zero out the existing property tax and start over, apparently calculating he would reject such a tax cut. Instead he accepted her proposal and passed a plan reducing property taxes vastly and increasing the sales tax, which was approved by voters 70%–30% in March 1994. In the August primary for governor, Stabenow was opposed by the two major forces in the Democratic Party, the Michigan Education Association, which backed Larry Owen, and the AFL-CIO and UAW, which backed former Congressman Howard Wolpe. Stabenow, comparing her politics to that of former Governor James Blanchard, won 30% of the vote, ahead of Owen's 26% but behind Wolpe's 35%. Eventually Wolpe chose her as his running mate, but the ticket lost to Engler 61%–38%.

Undaunted, Stabenow almost immediately started running for Congress. Her target in the 8th District was Dick Chrysler, a self-made millionaire (car customizing) who spent $1.6 million of his own money in 1992 and narrowly lost to Democratic incumbent Democrat Bob Carr, 48%–46%. Carr ran, unsuccessfully, for Senate in 1994 and Chrysler won the House seat 52%–45%. In the 1996 cycle, Chrysler refused to self-finance, and Stabenow outraised him from the start, getting more than $1 million in individual contributions, a tribute to her industriousness and the fundraising prowess of the feminist left; in mid-1995, when many potentially strong Democrats were declining to challenge Republican freshmen, she was already leading in public polls. Overall each spent $1.5 million. Stabenow was helped by AFL-CIO ads charging Chrysler "cut" Medicare, and Sierra Club ads attacking his votes on the environment. Chrysler fought back by charging Stabenow voted to raise taxes 79 times in the state House, a number that turned out to be imprecise; she attacked his proposal for a 15% sales tax to replace the income tax and took credit for the property tax decrease resulting from Engler's referendum. On national issues Stabenow struck a thematic note similar to Bill Clinton, calling for "balancing the budget in a way that does not shift the burden to middle-class families," equipping schools with computers, and encouraging job creation by new-tech small businesses. She won impressively, 54%–44%.

In the House, Stabenow has a fairly liberal voting record; she was sought out by the moderate Democratic Blue Dogs but did not join. She has spent much energy encouraging unions and businesses to donate labor and old computers so that every local school can have access to the Internet. "From a job standpoint, it's absolutely critical that we are wiring our schools, giving our children access to technologies they will face in the workplace." She got some tax breaks to that end in the 1997 tax law, and she has proposed a three-year tax credit for new small businesses. After Michigan schoolchildren contracted hepatitis A from imported frozen straw-berries, she and Senator Carl Levin introduced a food safety bill in 1998, to create rapid response teams for crisis and develop better tests for E. coli and salmonella. She called for a study of the impact on women of Social Security reform, while conceding that the current program on average gives women smaller monthly checks than men. She opposed fast track and the partial-birth abortion ban.

Stabenow did not have serious competition in the 1998 election. A ten-year state House member ran, but raised little money and was not on Republicans' priority list. Stabenow won 57%–39%. Back in Washington she was passed over for a Ways and Means seat in favor of Lloyd Doggett of Texas. In March 1999 Stabenow announced her intention to run for Spencer Abraham's senate seat in 2000; that same day Abraham ran full-page ads calling her a liberal. Stabenow voiced support for State Senator Dianne Byrum to succeed her in the House, but Byrum may have to face fellow state senator Republican Mike Rogers who was leaning towards a run in 1999.

Cook's Call. *Highly Competitive.* Clinton's strong showing here in 1996 and Stabenow's solid win against a lackluster opponent in 1998 belies the competitiveness of the district. From 1992–96, no candidate had won here with more than 54% of the vote. Stabenow's decision to run for the Senate in 2000 creates some problems for Democrats. Democratic State Senator Dianne Byrum announced her candidacy in early April 1999 and it looks likely that state senator and former FBI agent Mike Rogers will be the Republican nominee. This race will be one of the most closely watched and competitive in the country.

The People: Pop. 1990: 581,072; 39.7% rural; 9.5% age 65 + ; 90.4% White, 5.7% Black, 1.6% Asian, 0.7% Amer. Indian, 1.5% Other; 2.9% Hispanic Origin. Households: 57.4% married couple families; 29% married couple fams. w. children; 55.6% college educ.; median household income: $35,911; per capita income: $15,455; median house value: $72,100; median gross rent: $382.

1996 Presidential Vote		
Clinton (D)	135,653	(49%)
Dole (R)	111,811	(40%)
Perot (I)	25,949	(9%)

1992 Presidential Vote		
Clinton (D)	118,391	(40%)
Bush (R)	104,437	(36%)
Perot (I)	68,340	(23%)

Rep. Deborah Ann Stabenow (D)

Elected 1996; b. Apr. 29, 1950, Clare; home, Lansing; MI St. U., B.A. 1972, M.S.W. 1985; United Methodist; divorced.

Elected Office: Ingham Cnty. Comm., 1975–78, Chair, 1976–78; MI House of Reps., 1978–90; MI Senate, 1990–94.

Professional Career: Consultant & Co-founder, MI Leadership Inst., 1995–96.

DC Office: 1039 LHOB 20515, 202-225-4872; Fax: 202-225-5820; Web site: www.house.gov/stabenow.

District Offices: Flint, 810-230-8275; Howell, 517-545-2195.

Committees: *Agriculture* (17th of 24 D): Livestock & Horticul-ture; Risk Management, Research & Specialty Crops. *Science* (12th of 22 D): Space & Aeronautics; Technology.

Group Ratings

	ADA	ACLU	AFS	LCV	CON	NTU	NFIB	COC	ACU	NTLC	CHC
1998	100	69	100	85	38	14	36	61	9	13	0
1997	95	—	88	—	76	33	—	50	12	—	—

National Journal Ratings

	1997 LIB — 1997 CONS		1998 LIB — 1998 CONS	
Economic	67% —	32%	64% —	34%
Social	70% —	30%	75% —	25%
Foreign	82% —	16%	70% —	29%

Key Votes of the 105th Congress

1. Clinton Budget Deal	N	5. Puerto Rico Sthood. Ref.	N	9. Cut $ for B-2 Bombers	Y
2. Education IRAs	N	6. End Highway Set-asides	N	10. Human Rights in China	Y
3. Req. 2/3 to Raise Taxes	N	7. School Prayer Amend.	N	11. Withdraw Bosnia Troops	N
4. Fast-track Trade	N	8. Ovrd. Part. Birth Veto	N	12. End Cuban TV-Marti	Y

Election Results

1998 general	Deborah Ann Stabenow (D)	125,169	(57%)	($996,148)
	Susan Grimes Munsell (R)	84,254	(39%)	($125,971)
	Others	8,617	(4%)	
1998 primary	Deborah Ann Stabenow (D)	unopposed		
1996 general	Deborah Ann Stabenow (D)	141,086	(54%)	($1,497,300)
	Dick Chrysler (R)	115,836	(44%)	($1,515,307)
	Others	5,499	(2%)	

NINTH DISTRICT

General Motors was formed in 1918 as a merger of several smaller car companies; headquartered in Detroit, it had plants in small cities in Michigan and Ohio. Foremost among these cities were Flint and Pontiac, two industrial county seats on the old Woodward Avenue route that led northwest from Detroit. Pontiac, named for the 18th Century Indian chief who sparked a rebellion that spread all the way to what is now Pittsburgh, produced Pontiacs and GMC Trucks; Flint, named for the flint from which Indians made arrowheads, produced Buicks and Chevrolets. For five decades after 1918, Flint and Pontiac grew lustily, attracting new workers from the mountains of Kentucky and Tennessee and the Black Belt of Alabama; country and black music and Southern accents became common in towns originally settled by Yankees. There was turmoil, too. Flint was the scene in January 1937 of the great sitdown strike that, when Governor Frank Murphy refused to send the National Guard to enforce a court order, forced GM to recognize the United Auto Workers as the bargaining agent for all its workers. Yet in many ways these GM company towns built good lives for their citizens. The UAW-GM contracts produced the world's highest wages for industrial workers and lavish fringe benefits, including a generous health care plan. The Mott Foundation, started by GM's largest shareholder, Charles Stewart Mott, funded schools, including a university branch in Flint, and historical exhibitions—an exemplary plowing-back of money into a one-industry town.

Then disaster struck starting in the late 1970s. Auto sales plummeted with the oil shock of 1979, and imports, especially from Japan, that were higher in quality and cheaper in price than American cars, were taking an increasing share of the market. GM managers and UAW leaders assumed that increased labor costs could be passed along to consumers, that buyers were indifferent to quality and eager for new models. Those assumptions proved vitally wrong: not even the cleverest advertising could persuade Americans to buy a new American car every two years. In 1979 GM employed more than 70,000 workers in its Flint plants, a huge share of the labor force in a metro area of 430,000 people; by the early 1990s GM employment was down significantly and the old Buick City assembly plant was closed in summer 1999. Over the years thousands left Flint. Those who stayed found their real estate values—the store of wealth for most Americans—stagnant, and government attempts to develop an upscale shopping mall, a Hyatt hotel and the AutoWorld theme park went bankrupt.

Pontiac was also hurt in the late 1980s and early 1990s when GM closed plants there, but Pontiac has some advantages. The Detroit metro area has expanded, and surrounding Oakland County gained over 140,000 jobs in the 1980s, mainly in services and retail. Chrysler built its new headquarters along I-75 in Auburn Hills just east of Pontiac, and the freeway became the main street for a newly lean and efficient auto industry and its nimble just-in-time suppliers.

The 9th Congressional District of Michigan runs from Flint to Pontiac and takes in some diverse political territory. It includes the city of Flint and some of its suburbs to the southeast; this Genesee County portion has about one-third of the district's people and is heavily Democratic. Pontiac, about half black, is heavily Democratic but is only 12% of the district. Lake-strewn Waterford Township to the west, where many Pontiac whites moved when a school busing plan was ordered in the 1970s, is larger now and leans Republican. Auburn Hills and Rochester Hills east of Pontiac are high-income and heavily Republican. Clarkston and other burgeoning communities to the north, are heavily Republican. Similarly, Lapeer County, north of Pontiac and east of Flint, has been growing and has long been Republican. That means that about half the district is solidly Democratic, with a long union heritage; the other half is Republican, in some places very much so.

The congressman from the 9th District is Dale Kildee, a Democrat first elected in 1976, whose district until 1992 clustered closely around Flint. Kildee grew up in Flint, studied for the priesthood, taught at a Catholic high school in Detroit and at Flint Central. His door-to-door campaigning got him elected to a newly created state legislative seat in 1964, at 35, and enabled him to beat a 26-year veteran of the state Senate in 1974. He won the House seat in 1976, when it was solidly Democratic, without a primary opponent and held it easily for 16 years. Kildee brings to politics an intensity of conviction derived from the liberal tradition lively in the American Catholic church—a tradition with little regard for market economics and a strong obligation to care for the needy. He is solidly liberal on economics and always pro-union; he is against abortion and is something of a stickler on ethics and attendance. In December 1998 he cast his 6,961st consecutive vote, the longest in the House; the last one he missed was in October 1985 when he had a bleeding ulcer.

Kildee is now a senior member of the Education and the Workforce and Resources Committees. He is a strong ally of teachers' unions, a backer of increased federal aid for education and an opponent of school choice. He worked on the 1994 elementary and secondary education reauthorization, downplaying President Clinton's proposal for national testing standards and promoting the "Opportunity to Learn" standards designed to ensure adequate learning resources. As ranking Democrat on the Postsecondary Education, Training and Lifelong Learning Subcommittee, he sponsored Goals 2000, the Star Schools Program and Head Start, and backed the Schools-to-Work Act of 1994 and magnet schools. He and Chairman Buck McKeon have cooperated in lowering interest rates on student loans; in 1998 they agreed on a plan to lower the 7.8% to 7% for students and 7.5% for banks, with the government making up the difference. Kildee sponsored the first federal law against child pornography and backs stipends for Senior Companions and Foster Grandparents. He has fought against reducing federal standards on special education students.

On other issues, Kildee was the first House member to argue imported minivans should be subject not to the 2.5% tariff for cars but to the 25% tariff for trucks, and was a strong opponent of NAFTA. He pressured Puerto Rico to stop taxing cars on weight: Sales of hefty Flint-assembled cars went up. With John Dingell he opposed the FTC proposal to reduce to 75% the American content required for a Made in U.S.A. label. In 1998 he got $26 million in highway projects, much more than most other Michigan districts; he is close to James Oberstar, ranking Democrat on Transportation, and his Rayburn Building office is next door to that of Chairman Bud Shuster.

On Resources he has concentrated on Indian issues. Kildee can remember as a child traveling to the Grand Traverse reservation, where his grandfather had traded with Indians, and hearing his father talk of the Indians' plight. In the Michigan legislature he set up a state Commission on Indian Affairs and passed a law waiving tuition for Indians at state colleges. As a congressman he took to visiting reservations and noting how the Bureau of Indian Affairs spruced them up for his visits; Kildee carries with his copy of the Constitution a copy of the 1832 Supreme Court decision that recognized Indian sovereignty. In 1997 he set up a Native American Caucus with J.D. Hayworth of Arizona. As a backer of Indian sovereignty, Kildee has generally supported Indian gaming, and in 1997 he received some $50,000 in contributions from Indian groups. But he points out that he backed sovereignty long before Indians had money to give, and he remains a stickler for the rules. In 1997 he opposed the Bay Mills tribe's attempt to build a casino in Auburn Hills because "the land is so far removed from the reservation." In 1998 he opposed Joe Knollenberg's bill to recognize the Swan Creek Black River Confederated Ojibwa as a tribe separate from the Saginaw Chippewa tribe of which they had long been a part; the Swan Creek's wanted to build a casino at Hazel Park Harness Raceway in southern Oakland County.

Kildee fit his old Flint-area district like a glove, but has had serious challenges in the 9th District, in which 60% of the votes are cast in Oakland County. Against former Bush/Quayle advance staffer Megan O'Neill, whom he vastly outspent, Kildee won by just 54%–45% in 1992 and 51%–47% in 1994. In 1996, he was opposed by former state Transportation Director Patrick Nowak; but Michigan roads were in notoriously bad shape and Kildee used his experience against him by calling him "Pothole Pat" and running a radio ad commending Nowak for making money for auto repair shops. This time Kildee won 59%–39% and led for the first time in Oakland, 49%–48%. The 1998 contest proved a bit tougher, even though well-known Republicans—state Representative Greg Kaza and former Detroit Piston Bill Laimbeer—declined to run. The Republican nominee, Tom McMillin, Auburn Hills Council member and onetime field director for the Michigan Christian Coalition, raised relatively little money. This year, when most incumbents of both parties improved their showing, Kildee won by the reduced margin of 56%–42%, winning Genesee County 77%–22%, but losing Oakland, which has been voting more Republican, 52%–45%.

Cook's Call. *Probably Safe.* After a number of close calls following 1991 redistricting, Kildee looks to have solidified his hold on this district. If the 70-year old Kildee decides to retire, however, Democrats would have a hard time holding onto this very marginal seat. Kildee's biggest threat should he remain in Congress, is likely to come from the next round of redistricting. Republicans may control the process in the state and if so, may want to boost their strength here.

The People: Pop. 1990: 580,908; 20.2% rural; 9.5% age 65+; 79.4% White, 17.7% Black, 1% Asian, 0.6% Amer. Indian, 1.3% Other; 2.7% Hispanic Origin. Households: 52.4% married couple families; 26.3% married couple fams. w. children; 47.1% college educ.; median household income: $34,737; per capita income: $15,132; median house value: $65,200; median gross rent: $365.

1996 Presidential Vote

Clinton (D) 95,473 (46%)
Dole (R) 89,538 (43%)
Perot (I) 21,567 (10%)

1992 Presidential Vote

Clinton (D) 117,872 (44%)
Bush (R) 92,262 (35%)
Perot (I) 55,077 (21%)

Rep. Dale E. Kildee (D)

Elected 1976; b. Sept. 16, 1929, Flint; home, Flint; Sacred Heart Seminary, B.A. 1952, U. of MI, M.A. 1961, Rotary Fellow, U. of Peshawar, Pakistan; Catholic; married (Gayle).

Elected Office: MI House of Reps., 1964–74; MI Senate, 1974–75.

Professional Career: High schl. teacher, 1954–64.

DC Office: 2187 RHOB 20515, 202-225-3611; Fax: 202-225-6393; Web site: www.house.gov/kildee.

District Offices: Flint, 810-239-1437; Pontiac, 248-373-9337.

Committees: *Education & the Workforce* (3d of 22 D): Early Childhood, Youth & Families (RMM); Employer-Employee Relations. *Resources* (4th of 24 D): Forests & Forest Health; National Parks & Public Lands.

Group Ratings

	ADA	ACLU	AFS	LCV	CON	NTU	NFIB	COC	ACU	NTLC	CHC
1998	95	50	100	92	38	14	21	33	16	11	42
1997	80	—	88	—	70	26	—	40	24	—	—

National Journal Ratings

	1997 LIB — 1997 CONS		1998 LIB — 1998 CONS	
Economic	75%	— 22%	77%	— 22%
Social	50%	— 48%	56%	— 44%
Foreign	64%	— 33%	61%	— 37%

Key Votes of the 105th Congress

1. Clinton Budget Deal	N	5. Puerto Rico Sthood. Ref.	Y	9. Cut $ for B-2 Bombers	Y
2. Education IRAs	N	6. End Highway Set-asides	N	10. Human Rights in China	Y
3. Req. 2/3 to Raise Taxes	N	7. School Prayer Amend.	N	11. Withdraw Bosnia Troops	N
4. Fast-track Trade	N	8. Ovrd. Part. Birth Veto	Y	12. End Cuban TV-Marti	Y

Election Results

1998 general	Dale E. Kildee (D)	105,457	(56%)	($394,037)
	Tom McMillin (R)	79,062	(42%)	($209,050)
	Others	4,006	(2%)	
1998 primary	Dale E. Kildee (D)	unopposed		
1996 general	Dale E. Kildee (D)	136,856	(59%)	($816,337)
	Patrick Nowak (R)	89,733	(39%)	($443,415)
	Others	4,611	(2%)	

TENTH DISTRICT

Macomb County, Michigan, on the billiard-table-flat shore of Lake St. Clair just northeast of Detroit, has become one of the nation's most closely watched political battlegrounds, a place where the electoral fate of Michigan and even the entire country may be determined. Its reputation is not quite accurate: more people hold white-collar jobs than blue-collar these days and far fewer work in auto plants than in earlier generations; there are plenty of affluent subdivisions and boat ownership may well be the highest in the country. Macomb County is the product of the post-World War II boom: With just over 107,000 people in 1940, many in the old sulphur-water spa town of Mount Clemens, Macomb passed the 400,000 mark in 1960 and 600,000 by 1970; in 1990 it reached 717,000. Most people came here from Detroit: Polish-Americans marching out Van Dyke from Hamtramck to Warren; Italian-Americans heading out Gratiot from Detroit's east side to Roseville and Clinton Township; Belgian-Americans from the Mack corridor moving out farther to St. Clair Shores. These new suburbanites were heavily Catholic, often blue-collar, at least modestly affluent and ancestrally Democratic. They accepted the New Deal as part of their natural heritage but resented the efforts of Detroit politicians to tax them to pay for welfare, and they were fearful of the high crime rates in Detroit's black neighborhoods. Indeed, the suburb of East Detroit voted to change its name to Eastpointe to avoid any implication it was part of the central city.

In 1960, Macomb County was the most Democratic major suburban county in the United States, voting 63% for America's first Catholic president, John F. Kennedy. For three decades afterwards Macomb was moving away from the national Democrats—in 1962 because they would let Detroit tax suburbanites, in 1972 because they didn't vehemently oppose a metropolitan school busing plan. From 1976 through 1992, no Democratic presidential candidate got more than 40% of the vote here; in 1996, after great effort and with the advice of his sometime pollster Stan Greenberg, who has studied Macomb closely, Bill Clinton carried Macomb County by a 49%–39% margin. It was a solid win, but not as impressive as the 1994 margins for Republican Governor John Engler (70%–30%) or Senator Spencer Abraham (56%–36%). Democrats still hold most county and legislative offices in Macomb, but not all, and Republicans have one Macomb statewide officeholder, Secretary of State Candice Miller.

The 10th Congressional District of Michigan includes most of Macomb County (all but the southwest corner) and takes in Port Huron and St. Clair County to the northeast. In the House it has been represented for nearly a quarter-century by David Bonior, now the Democratic whip. Bonior grew up in East Detroit (as it then was called), the grandson of Polish and Ukrainian immigrants; he became a seminarian in high school, had an athletic scholarship to the University of Iowa where he played football, worked as a probation officer and social worker in Mount Clemens and served in the Air Force stateside in the Vietnam era (he came to oppose the war). His father was a printer and auto worker who became mayor of East Detroit; it is his loss of that office in 1967 which Bonior refers to as his family's brush with unemployment. Bonior never became a priest, but he remains in accord with liberal strains of Catholic thought and liberation theology; he is against abortion, though he has voted with most Democrats against the anti-abortion "gag rule" and for fetal tissue research. In 1972 he was elected to the Michigan House, and in 1976, when Congressman James O'Hara ran for the Senate, Bonior ran for the U.S. House. He had a knack for symbolism: that winter an ice storm killed many Macomb County trees, and in response he gave out thousands of pine seedlings as a campaign gimmick. This struck a chord with gun-toting sportsmen and baby-boomer environmentalists alike, and by now he has handed out more than 400,000 seedlings and featured them in his TV ads. He has done conspicuous work on local environmental problems—securing funds to study replacing the environmentally unsound Clinton River dam, taking credit for provisions in the Oil Spill Liability Act that subject foreign tanker pilots to the same standards as U.S. pilots.

Bonior brings to his work a great intensity and passion. "I think God's work should also be an expression of what you do on earth as much as what you strive for in heaven." Like many Catholic admirers of liberation theology, he opposed aid to the Nicaraguan Contras and El Salvador government. It was Bonior's deep convictions and determination that probably commended him to Speaker Jim Wright, who appointed him chief deputy whip in 1986. He did not move up the leadership ladder immediately: William Gray beat him for whip in June 1989, 134–97, after Wright and Whip Tony Coelho resigned. But when Gray retired in June 1991, Bonior beat Maryland's Steny Hoyer 160–109. And after Speaker Thomas Foley lost his

House seat in 1994, Dick Gephardt became minority leader and Bonior won the minority whip post by 145–60 over Charles Stenholm. One of Bonior's great crusades was against Newt Gingrich. He led Democrats to file over 70 ethics charges against Gingrich, some arguably serious, many entirely without merit.

Bonior sees himself representing a forgotten and scorned blue-collar working class at home. With Marcy Kaptur of Ohio, he was one of the most passionate opponents of NAFTA, arguing it was "basically the sellout of [American] workers" and that "we can't let jobs be our number one export." He opposed fast-track trade authority despite the pleadings of Bill Clinton, and called for more labor and environmental protections in trade agreements. He has also opposed Most Favored Nation status for China because of its human rights violations.

Bonior's principled stands and political crusades have put him at risk in a district which has often voted Republican for other offices. In 1988 and 1992 he beat state Senator Doug Carl, a religious conservative, by 54%–45% and 53%–44%, after spending immense sums—$1.34 million in 1992, with $934,000 from PACs—mostly on Detroit TV. In 1994, against nuisance opposition, he spent $1.12 million. In 1996, Republican Governor John Engler recruited Republican state Chairman Susy Heintz, who attacked Bonior as a "whiny, wacky, wimpy, wasteful, worn-out, washed-up, windbag whip." Bonior attacked Heintz for paying taxes late in 1991–93; she claimed it happened because of a disputed divorce. Once again Bonior had a huge financial advantage. He raised $862,000 from PACs and spent a total of $1.51 million; Bill Clinton was leading in Macomb and St. Clair Counties and by mid-October Bonior was leading 56%–30% in a public poll. But Heintz raised enough to become the first Bonior opponent to run TV ads. "Too liberal too long," her campaign said, and attacked him for his courageous vote against the 1996 welfare reform act (he was one of only three Michigan Democrats to vote against it, with the other two being from Detroit). The final result was a 54%–44% Bonior victory, almost identical to his wins in 1992 and 1988.

His 1998 opponent was Brian Palmer, a self-made businessman and Bruce Township Trustee. He called for a part-time citizen legislature and said he was concerned about pollution in Lake St. Clair. But much of the campaign was taken up with silly charges, from both sides. Democrats accused Palmer of late payment of property taxes and of not properly filing parties on a charitable foundation. Republicans attacked Bonior for fixing D.C. parking tickets (a perfectly legitimate practice) and for supposed tax fraud in claiming his $318,000 Maryland residence as a chief residence while claiming a homestead exemption on his $38,000 condominium in Mount Clemens. There was not much to any of these charges. Bonior raised and spent more than $1.4 million. Palmer contributed $360,000 to his own campaign but spent only $734,000, not the $1 million he had expected. Bonior won by 52%–45%, a scarcely overwhelming—but decisive—victory.

On impeachment Bonior steadfastly defended Clinton, despite their past disagreements on policy, and despite his own eloquent statements after Gingrich was reprimanded. "Every time we look the other way when somebody breaks the rules, we don't just damage the integrity of the House, we send a message to every kid in Michigan and California and Georgia that lying pays, that cheating works and that wrongdoing goes unpunished. And sometimes saying you're sorry just isn't enough." Given Democrats' upbeat mood, Bonior clearly looks forward to a Democratic majority after the 2000 election and to becoming majority leader. Yet he will continue to have to work hard to win in the 10th District. And if Republicans should hold the state House and control the redistricting process, he will surely be a target of Engler's wrath; the obvious thing for Republicans would be to attach the more Democratic southern part of his district to one of the black-majority Detroit seats and stretch Bonior's district into the heavily Republican and unfamiliar counties north of Port Huron in the Thumb.

Cook's Call. *Potentially Competitive.* Bonior has survived a number of all out assualts by Republicans over the last few years, but is likely to face his most serious challenge in years from popular Republican Secretary of State Candace Miller. Bonior rarely racks up big margins of victory, but his political savvy and strong fundraising skills do make him formidable.

The People: Pop. 1990: 580,974; 16.7% rural; 12.6% age 65 + ; 96.6% White, 2% Black, 0.7% Asian, 0.4% Amer. Indian, 0.3% Other; 1.1% Hispanic Origin. Households: 60.5% married couple families; 29.4% married couple fams. w. children; 42.2% college educ.; median household income: $36,536; per capita income: $15,603; median house value: $71,500; median gross rent: $408.

1996 Presidential Vote			1992 Presidential Vote		
Clinton (D)	120,921	(49%)	Bush (R)	115,849	(41%)
Dole (R)	96,592	(39%)	Clinton (D)	100,587	(36%)
Perot (I)	27,083	(11%)	Perot (I)	60,927	(22%)

Rep. David E. Bonior (D)

Elected 1976; b. June 6, 1945, Detroit; home, Mt. Clemens; U. of IA, B.A. 1967, Chapman Col., M.A. 1972; Catholic; married (Judy).

Military Career: Air Force, 1968–72.

Elected Office: MI House of Reps., 1972–76.

Professional Career: Probation officer, adoption caseworker, 1967–68.

DC Office: 2207 RHOB 20515, 202-225-2106; Fax: 202-226-1169; Web site: www.house.gov/bonior.

District Offices: Mt. Clemens, 810-469-3232; Port Huron, 810-987-8889.

Committees: *Minority Whip.*

Group Ratings

	ADA	ACLU	AFS	LCV	CON	NTU	NFIB	COC	ACU	NTLC	CHC
1998	95	81	100	92	55	16	14	22	16	11	8
1997	85	—	88	—	39	31	—	40	12	—	—

National Journal Ratings

	1997 LIB — 1997 CONS			1998 LIB — 1998 CONS		
Economic	79%	—	21%	79%	—	0%
Social	68%	—	32%	68%	—	32%
Foreign	97%	—	0%	74%	—	25%

Key Votes of the 105th Congress

1. Clinton Budget Deal	N	5. Puerto Rico Sthood. Ref.	Y	9. Cut $ for B-2 Bombers	Y
2. Education IRAs	N	6. End Highway Set-asides	N	10. Human Rights in China	Y
3. Req. 2/3 to Raise Taxes	N	7. School Prayer Amend.	N	11. Withdraw Bosnia Troops	N
4. Fast-track Trade	N	8. Ovrd. Part. Birth Veto	Y	12. End Cuban TV-Marti	Y

Election Results

1998 general	David E. Bonior (D)	108,770	(52%)	($1,477,749)
	Brian Palmer (R)	94,027	(45%)	($734,291)
	Others	4,727	(2%)	
1998 primary	David E. Bonior (D)	unopposed		
1996 general	David E. Bonior (D)	132,829	(54%)	($1,513,432)
	Susy Heintz (R)	106,444	(44%)	($673,996)
	Others	5,008	(2%)	

ELEVENTH DISTRICT

Oakland County, Michigan, long considered just a suburban adjunct of Detroit, is now the center of a giant, spread-out, affluent urban area. It is only minutes on the Lodge Freeway from the empty, abandoned blocks of inner-city Detroit; but suddenly, north of the Eight Mile Road boundary, there are giant office buildings and multiplying small businesses, expensive houses on large lots and one shopping mall after another, high education levels and low crime rates. Even physically there is a distinction between the two areas: Detroit is on almost perfectly flat land, while many of the Oakland County suburbs run along a line of hills and lakes that marks the southernmost advance of an Ice Age glacier. Southfield, in southern Oakland County, is Michigan's largest office space center, far ahead of Detroit; Troy is another big office center, with upscale malls that compete with high-income Birmingham; new development proliferates around Novi and Northville, north of Eight Mile Road; Bloomfield Hills has Michigan's highest incomes. Forty years ago, Detroit had 1.9 million people and Oakland County 396,000. In 1990 Oakland had over one million, while Detroit topped that mark only after a recanvass.

The 11th Congressional District of Michigan includes almost half of Oakland County plus the comfortable Wayne County suburbs of Redford Township and Livonia, west of Detroit. This is mostly high-income Republican territory, where people generally believe in free market economics and fiercely oppose higher taxes. It is also home to most of the Detroit area's Jewish community, which has moved out the Lodge first to Southfield and then to West Bloomfield and scattered in most of these suburbs. Jewish voters and affluent blacks who have moved to Southfield and other suburbs, form the district's chief Democratic bloc and hold down the Republican percentages—enough that Bill Clinton carried the district narrowly in 1996.

The congressman from the 11th District is Joe Knollenberg, a Republican first elected in 1992. Knollenberg grew up the fifth child in a family of 13 on a farm in Downstate Illinois, went to college in Illinois and became an insurance agent. He moved to Oakland County in 1967 and became involved in civic affairs and Republican politics. When Republican William Broomfield retired in 1992 after 36 years in office—all in the minority—Knollenberg ran. He had two colorful opponents in the Republican primary, David Honigman, a young and wealthy state Senator, and Alice Gilbert, a pro-choice former judge. But they attacked one another, while Knollenberg, pro-life and supported by Broomfield, won with 43% to 30% for Honigman and 27% for Gilbert. He won the general election easily.

Knollenberg entered the House as a junior member of the minority with a prosaic background. But in two years, with a change in control, he became a member of Appropriations advancing some cutting-edge ideas. He moved to zero out funding for the statistics required for CAFE standards and to zero out funding for implementation of the 1997 Kyoto treaty until it is ratified by the Senate. He argues that the treaty is "fatally flawed" and based on "immature science," and notes that the exemption for developing nations will put Michigan at a disadvantage in trade; he and Michigan Democrat John Dingell are leading the fight against Kyoto in the House. Knollenberg, unlike most Michigan colleagues, has been a strong supporter of NAFTA and fast track; Michigan is the fourth-largest exporter among states. He proposed a $500 tax credit for donations to charities which spend 75% of their money on relieving poverty; a privatization of antipoverty programs. He calls for Social Security reform, by using a portion of the budget surplus to establish individual investment accounts.

Knollenberg is chief sponsor of the Plumbing Standards Improvement Act, to repeal the 1992 law which reduced the waterflow in toilets from 3.5 to 1.6 gallons per flush; toilet makers, eager for more sales and uniformity among states, supported that law, but Knollenberg points out that the new toilets often do not perform adequately.

With his seat on Appropriations, Knollenberg has been involved in local projects. He and Dingell co-sponsored the $10 million National Automobile Heritage Area in southeast Michigan. He got money to establish regular customs service for Oakland Airport, the nation's fourth busiest in corporate jets. In 1998 he sponsored a bill to recognize the Swan Creek Black River

Confederated Ojibwa Indians as a tribe separate from the Saginaw Chippewa tribe, which owns a big casino. "This bill is about justice that has been put off for over 100 years," he said, although opponents argue that its goal is to set up a casino in Hazel Park Harness Raceway in southern Oakland County.

Knollenberg has been re-elected without difficulty; he won 64%–34% in 1998 against a 25-year-old lawyer. In December 1998, after he voted for impeachment, there was a fire at his Farmington Hills campaign headquarters. "They targeted my sign, they targeted my name, the only deduction I can come to is there is a connection," he said.

Cook's Call. *Safe.* It will be very hard to dislodge Knollenberg from this strongly Republican district. He is a sure thing in 2000.

The People: Pop. 1990: 580,934; 5% rural; 12.8% age 65+; 93% White, 4.1% Black, 2.3% Asian, 0.3% Amer. Indian, 0.3% Other; 1.1% Hispanic Origin. Households: 62.7% married couple families; 28.5% married couple fams. w. children; 63.2% college educ.; median household income: $49,021; per capita income: $24,466; median house value: $111,100; median gross rent: $574.

1996 Presidential Vote

Clinton (D)	134,344	(46%)
Dole (R)	131,571	(46%)
Perot (I)	19,322	(7%)

1992 Presidential Vote

Bush (R)	147,786	(47%)
Clinton (D)	116,266	(37%)
Perot (I)	50,385	(16%)

Rep. Joseph Knollenberg (R)

Elected 1992; b. Nov. 28, 1933, Mattoon, IL; home, Bloomfield Township; E. IL U., B.S. 1955; Catholic; married (Sandie).

Military Career: Army, 1955–57.

Professional Career: Insurance agent, 1958–92.

DC Office: 2349 RHOB 20515, 202-225-5802; Fax: 202-226-2356; Web site: www.house.gov/knollenberg.

District Offices: Farmington Hills, 248-851-1366; Livonia, 734-425-7557.

Committees: *Appropriations* (17th of 34 R): Energy & Water Development; Foreign Operations & Export Financing; VA, HUD & Independent Agencies. *Budget* (15th of 24 R). *Standards of Official Conduct* (3d of 5 R).

Group Ratings

	ADA	ACLU	AFS	LCV	CON	NTU	NFIB	COC	ACU	NTLC	CHC
1998	0	13	11	8	13	50	100	100	96	95	100
1997	10	—	25	—	34	45	—	100	76	—	—

National Journal Ratings

	1997 LIB — 1997 CONS		1998 LIB — 1998 CONS	
Economic	28% —	67%	15% —	81%
Social	30% —	64%	29% —	69%
Foreign	46% —	53%	43% —	53%

Key Votes of the 105th Congress

1. Clinton Budget Deal	Y	5. Puerto Rico Sthood. Ref.	N	9. Cut $ for B-2 Bombers	N
2. Education IRAs	Y	6. End Highway Set-asides	Y	10. Human Rights in China	N
3. Req. 2/3 to Raise Taxes	Y	7. School Prayer Amend.	Y	11. Withdraw Bosnia Troops	N
4. Fast-track Trade	Y	8. Ovrd. Part. Birth Veto	Y	12. End Cuban TV-Marti	N

Election Results

1998 general	Joseph Knollenberg (R) 144,264	(64%)	($992,746)
	Travis M. Reeds (D) 76,107	(34%)	($16,294)
	Others 5,433	(2%)	
1998 primary	Joseph Knollenberg (R) .... unopposed		
1996 general	Joseph Knollenberg (R) 169,165	(61%)	($608,882)
	Morris Frumin (D) 99,303	(36%)	($31,796)
	Others 8,150	(3%)	

TWELFTH DISTRICT

The flat expanse of land just north of Eight Mile Road, Detroit's northern city limit, was mostly vacant in the years just after World War II. A string of suburbs in Oakland County ran along Woodward Avenue, Detroit's main street, already eight lanes wide, which led to the Shrine of the Little Flower church in Royal Oak. There, in the 1930s, Father Charles Coughlin made his radio broadcasts backing and then opposing Franklin Roosevelt and denouncing bankers and Jews. To the east in Macomb County was some industrial development along Van Dyke, but this was mostly empty land, too; Detroit's population was heading toward two million. Today, these areas are well-settled suburbs, long since built up, a few neighborhoods edging toward seediness, many others continually renovated and restored. Almost half of metro Detroit's population is now north of Eight Mile, in communities drawing on old traditions but crackling with economic creativity.

The 12th Congressional District of Michigan is in this suburban territory, with about half its population in the two suburban counties. On the Oakland County side are Royal Oak and other Woodward Avenue suburbs, now attracting singles and gays as well as families; Oak Park, heavily Jewish in the 1950s and now perhaps the only small city in America with sizable numbers of Jews, Arabs and blacks; Hazel Park and Madison Heights, mostly peopled with descendants of the Appalachian migrants of a few decades ago; and Troy, once barren fields and now a major office center, with the Kmart world headquarters across from the upscale Somerset Malls on Big Beaver Road. On the Macomb County side are Warren and Sterling Heights, the destination often of Polish-Americans moving out from Hamtramck and the East Side of Detroit, and site of the General Motors Technical Center, a big Chrysler plant and the M-1 tank plant where Michael Dukakis took his famous ride in the 1988 campaign. Historically, Macomb County is Democratic, and Oakland Republican, but Oak Park and Hazel Park have long been very Democratic, and Macomb has been trending Republican for years; both voted by similar percentages for George Bush in 1992 and Bill Clinton in 1996 and for Republican Governor John Engler in 1994 and 1998.

The congressman from the 12th District is Sander Levin, a Democrat first elected in 1982 and a member of one of Michigan's most respected political families; he is the brother of Senator Carl Levin, and they are one of two House-Senate brother combinations (the others are the Hutchinsons of Arkansas). Levin grew up in Detroit, settled in the Woodward Avenue suburb of Berkley after school and was elected state senator in 1964; in 1970 and 1974 he ran for governor and lost narrowly each time to Republican William Milliken. In the Carter Administration he was a top appointee at the Agency for International Development. In 1982 a House seat suddenly opened up, even though Michigan lost a seat in redistricting, when incumbent James Blanchard ran for governor and incumbent William Brodhead retired. Levin won a spirited primary and held the seat without difficulty through 1990. The 1992 redistricting moved him east, into Macomb County, and placed him in the same district with Democrat Dennis Hertel, who decided to retire, and Levin easily won the Democratic nomination.

Levin is a hard worker, a details man, willing to spend endless hours with others working out solutions. He seems always to be seeking the mean between two extremes; he likes negotiations and dislikes issues that divide opponents on stark lines of principle. He is the fifth-ranking Democrat on Ways and Means, where he has played an important role on major issues in the 1990s. On the Health Subcommittee in 1994 he withheld his vote for the Democrats' health care bill until they agreed to remove Chairman Pete Stark's payroll tax increase and substituted a mix of smaller, health-related levies. On welfare reform, Levin opposed the 1995 bills passed by Republicans but helped shape and supported the bill passed in August 1996. He was willing to end the welfare entitlement but supported guarantees of continuing health insurance and child care support for welfare recipients who go to work. In 1997 he opposed Republican attempts to ban benefits for welfare recipients who take public service jobs.

Levin has also weighed in on trade issues. He favored the Free Trade Agreement with Canada, which was shaped in large party by auto manufacturers and the United Auto Workers. But he was wary of Japanese trade barriers and pushed unsuccessfully for stringent measures—limits on Japanese car and truck sales, including those manufactured in U.S. plants, and a 25% rather than a 2.5% tariff on Japanese minivans. In 1990 he published in the *Congressional Record* the controversial anti-American article, *The Japan That Can Say No*, by Akio Morita and Shintaro Ishihara, when the Japanese authors refused to allow it to appear in translation. He was a strong opponent of NAFTA in 1993, arguing that Mexican environmental and labor standards were so far below those of the United States that the side agreements did not make sense. But after NAFTA passed, he was one of the few House Democrats to back the original Mexican peso bailout proposed in early 1995 by the Clinton Administration. He supported GATT but opposed fast track. In January 1999 he replaced the pro-NAFTA Robert Matsui as ranking Democrat on the Trade Subcommittee. He wants trade agreements to contain provisions on workers' rights, fair ways of settling workers' disagreements and environmental provisions: "I think the issue in the United States is whether and to what extent we shape globalization." He has continued to try to outlaw Japan's informal trade barriers. Back home, he worked successfully to allow communities to collaborate in applications for community policing funds, a help in this area of many small municipalities; he introduced a bill for federal matching funds for local anti-drug drives.

The 1992 redistricting removed much of metro Detroit's Jewish community from Levin's district and added unfamiliar territory in Macomb County, and he has had serious competition ever since. He has raised more than $1 million every two years, and prevailed. In three elections he faced Republican John Pappageorge, a retired Army colonel and M-1 tank executive who later was elected to the Oakland County Commission. In the anti-incumbent atmosphere of 1992, when Bill Clinton was losing the district, Levin outspent Pappageorge by $1.18 million to $190,000 and won by just 53%–46%. In 1994, when Clinton was affirmatively unpopular and John Engler was running strong in both Oakland and Macomb, Levin again outspent the competition, $1.5 million to $470,000, emphasizing his work helping local law enforcement, and won by 52%–47%. In the much more pro-incumbent environment of 1996, Levin emphasized his work on welfare reform and making college tuition deductible; he again outspent Pappageorge, $1.3 million to $433,000, and won by a significantly larger 57%–41%.

In 1998 the pro-incumbent feeling continued, but this time Engler was at the top of the ticket, and Levin was embarrassed by the Democratic governor nominee, Geoffrey Fieger, who called Detroit Archbishop Adam Maida a "nut" and said that Orthodox rabbis are "closer to Nazis than they think they are." Levin shied away from endorsing Fieger. Republicans recruited Leslie Touma, a former Engler and Pentagon aide who ran a Michigan coalition for NAFTA and worked for the Southfield defense contractor Lear Corporation; she raised more money than any other of Levin's 1990s challenger and became the first Republican to buy Detroit TV against him. But Levin still outspent her by $700,000.

Much of the campaign consisted of a solid clash on issues. Touma's theme was, "We don't make '60s era cars any more, and we should stop electing '60s style politicians." She called for big tax cuts, a better awareness of business's needs; Levin countered by stressing his support of community policing and anti-drug drives, and his work on the Warren tank plant and welfare reform. She was pro-choice on abortion, eliminating an issue Levin used against Pappageorge.

She backed Social Security individual investment accounts; he accused her of wanting to "let Wall Street investors gamble your retirement, eliminating the guarantee of a Social Security check." He held a fundraiser with Al Gore which raised $60,000; she said Gore was "Michigan's biggest enemy" because of his stands on auto issues and pledged that 70% of her money would be raised in Michigan. Democrats attacked Touma, who grew up in the district, of having moved back in to run. They argued that she didn't pay property taxes in the district; Republicans countered, "Where does Congressman Levin pay most of his property taxes? Not in Michigan, but at Martha's Vineyard, Massachusetts." But Levin has lived in the district for 36 of the last 41 years. In November, Levin won 56%–42%—by 57%–41% in Oakland, 54%–44% in Macomb—calling it "the sweetest victory of my career." This district could be seriously contested again. Touma said she "would not rule out another run." If Republicans hold the state House in 2000, they would have control of redistricting, and could weaken Levin significantly.

Cook's Call. *Potentially Competitive.* Levin was hurt by the 1991 redistricting that took away some of the most Democratic parts of his district, but, a strong fundraiser and good campaigner, he has managed to solidify himself here. Levin looks well-positioned for 2000, though he could find himself in danger again after the next round of redistricting in 2001.

The People: Pop. 1990: 580,987; 13.3% age 65 + ; 93.3% White, 3.8% Black, 2.3% Asian, 0.5% Amer. Indian, 0.2% Other; 0.9% Hispanic Origin. Households: 57% married couple families; 26.9% married couple fams. w. children; 48.1% college educ.; median household income: $38,760; per capita income: $16,796; median house value: $76,200; median gross rent: $458.

1996 Presidential Vote		
Clinton (D)	128,820	(52%)
Dole (R)	95,071	(38%)
Perot (I)	20,612	(8%)

1992 Presidential Vote		
Clinton (D)	119,055	(42%)
Bush (R)	115,065	(40%)
Perot (I)	49,519	(17%)

Rep. Sander M. Levin (D)

Elected 1982; b. Sept. 6, 1931, Detroit; home, Royal Oak; U. of Chicago, B.A. 1952, Columbia U., M.A. 1954, Harvard U., LL.B. 1957; Jewish; married (Vicki).

Elected Office: Oakland Bd. of Supervisors, 1961–64; MI Senate, 1964–70.

Professional Career: Practicing atty., 1957–64, 1970–76; Fellow, Harvard JFK Schl. of Govt., 1975; A.A., Agency for Intl. Devel., 1977–81.

DC Office: 2268 RHOB 20515, 202-225-4961; Fax: 202-226-1033; Web site: www.house.gov/levin.

District Office: Sterling Heights, 810-268-4444.

Committees: *Ways & Means* (5th of 16 D): Social Security; Trade (RMM).

Group Ratings

	ADA	ACLU	AFS	LCV	CON	NTU	NFIB	COC	ACU	NTLC	CHC
1998	100	88	100	100	76	15	14	33	8	11	0
1997	100	—	88	—	80	33	—	50	4	—	—

National Journal Ratings

	1997 LIB — 1997 CONS			1998 LIB — 1998 CONS		
Economic	75%	—	22%	79%	—	0%
Social	85%	—	0%	81%	—	16%
Foreign	85%	—	13%	64%	—	31%

Key Votes of the 105th Congress

1. Clinton Budget Deal	N	5. Puerto Rico Sthood. Ref.	Y	9. Cut $ for B-2 Bombers	Y
2. Education IRAs	N	6. End Highway Set-asides	N	10. Human Rights in China	Y
3. Req. 2/3 to Raise Taxes	N	7. School Prayer Amend.	N	11. Withdraw Bosnia Troops	N
4. Fast-track Trade	N	8. Ovrd. Part. Birth Veto	N	12. End Cuban TV-Marti	Y

Election Results

1998 general	Sander M. Levin (D)	105,824	(56%)	($1,638,901)
	Leslie A. Touma (R)	79,619	(42%)	($1,188,234)
	Others	3,985	(2%)	
1998 primary	Sander M. Levin (D)	unopposed		
1996 general	Sander M. Levin (D)	133,436	(57%)	($1,313,913)
	John Pappageorge (R)	94,235	(41%)	($432,894)
	Others	4,804	(2%)	

THIRTEENTH DISTRICT

From Detroit's Metro Airport west to Ann Arbor runs what was once a key artery in the "arsenal of democracy." Now the I-94 expressway, it was built in 1942 so workers from Detroit could drive to the huge Willow Run bomber plant 30 miles west; later it was known by travelers for its pothole-pocked pavement and the giant Goodyear tire over the billboard with the digital counter showing the year's (American) car production. Today, it is still a key link between factories and suppliers, workers and workplaces, between the blue-collar neighborhoods of southwest Wayne County and Ann Arbor, home of the University of Michigan. But over the past two decades I-94 has seen a profound shift in Michigan's industrial economy: from that of many low-skill jobs assembling high-style but low-tech cars, to one with fewer but higher-skill jobs in higher-tech manufacturing, requiring precision work and computerized tools.

The 13th Congressional District of Michigan covers much of this unpicturesque landscape from the airport to Ann Arbor. A few of its suburbs are distinctly downscale, like Romulus, where poorer residents have worked a little at a time to build their own houses, on land so flat it oozes water after a rain. Others are proudly middle-income, like Westland, which was named after a shopping center, and Canton Township, which has been robust in recent years; Plymouth and Northville just to the north are high-income and fast-growing. Southwest Wayne County has been Democratic since the UAW forced an unwilling Henry Ford to sign a collective bargaining contract in 1941, but as working-class wages went up and working-class conscious-ness declined it has become less so. In Washtenaw County, the district's largest city, Ann Arbor, has a Republican history going back to its beginnings as a haven for German veterans of the failed revolutions of 1848, but undergraduates in the 1970s and graduate students in the 1980s swung it sharply to the left, making it one of the most dependably Democratic parts of Michigan. Ypsilanti, working class and home to Eastern Michigan University, is also Democratic. On balance the 13th leans Democratic but with pockets of Republican strength.

The congresswoman from the 13th District is Lynn Rivers, a Democrat first elected in 1994. Her story is an unusual one for an American politician. She was married and became a mother at 18; her husband is an auto worker and UAW member; she worked her way through school as her kids grew and got a bachelor's degree at University of Michigan in 1987 and a law degree in 1992. "I understand what families are struggling with," she says now. "I know what it's like to go without health insurance, not to be able to buy a home, and to have more bills than money." She entered politics as "a mom who got mad at the system" and was elected to the Ann Arbor school board in 1984. In 1992 she was elected to the state House. In 1994, 13th District incumbent William Ford decided to retire after 30 years in the House and a close call in 1992. Rivers, with strong support from the liberal Democrats who dominate politics in Ann Arbor, easily won the Democratic primary. In the general election, with generous support from local and national unions as well as feminists, she outraised her Republican opponent, a Bush Administration appointee, and won 52%–45%.

In a House with 73 mostly conservative Republican freshmen, Rivers stood out; her voting record has been one of the most liberal. She spoke out strongly against the partial birth abortion ban. She served on the Budget Committee and on the Science Committee, where she promised to expose "junk science" used to justify repeal of environmental protections. But she also worked with Republicans on some issues. With Ohio Republican Steve LaTourette she restored funding for the Great Lakes Environmental Research Laboratory in Ann Arbor and supported more research in ridding the Great Lakes of the zebra mussel. She sought tougher gift bans, wanted to abolish many congressional perks, including pensions and automatic pay raises, and sought to require members of Congress to pay out of their office allowance for special orders speeches—the last an odd position for one whose politics has long been associated with vigorous defense of free expression. She is one of the members who has sent her pay raise back to the Treasury and she opposed a measure to pay legal fees of congressmen who are cleared by juries. She favors immediate disclosure of campaign contributions.

Rivers has done well against spirited challenges in 1996 and 1998. In 1996 Ann Arbor businessman Joe Fitzsimmons spent $566,000 of his own money on the race. But in that pro-incumbent year Bill Clinton was carrying the district 58%–33%, and Rivers won 57%–41%, with 65%–33% in Washtenaw and 51%–47% in Wayne. In 1998 she was opposed by Thomas Hickey, a pro-life businessman in what turned out to be a low-spending contest. The results were almost exactly the same: Rivers won 58%–40%, with 67%–31% in Washtenaw and 53%–45% in Wayne. Redistricting could change the boundaries here in 2002, but Rivers presumably will stick with her strong base in Ann Arbor.

Cook's Call. *Probably Safe.* After solid victories in 1996 and 1998, Rivers may finally find herself off the Republican target list in 2000. This district has a good Democratic core (thanks to liberal Ann Arbor), but is not entirely safe Democratic territory.

The People: Pop. 1990: 580,882; 6.6% rural; 9.1% age 65 + ; 85.4% White, 11% Black, 2.8% Asian, 0.4% Amer. Indian, 0.4% Other; 1.6% Hispanic Origin. Households: 51.9% married couple families; 25.9% married couple fams. w. children; 54.7% college educ.; median household income: $36,596; per capita income: $16,267; median house value: $77,500; median gross rent: $467.

1996 Presidential Vote			1992 Presidential Vote		
Clinton (D)	135,250	(58%)	Clinton (D)	129,113	(49%)
Dole (R)	76,165	(33%)	Bush (R)	89,040	(34%)
Perot (I)	16,954	(7%)	Perot (I)	43,946	(17%)
Others	3,990	(2%)			

Rep. Lynn Rivers (D)

Elected 1994; b. Dec. 19, 1956, Au Gres; home, Ann Arbor; U. of MI, B.A. 1987, Wayne St. U., J.D. 1992; Protestant; married (Joseph).

Elected Office: Ann Arbor Schl. Bd., 1984–92; MI House of Reps., 1992–94.

DC Office: 1724 LHOB 20515, 202-225-6261; Fax: 202-225-3404; Web site: www.house.gov/rivers.

District Office: Ypsilanti, 734-485-3741.

Committees: *Budget* (3d of 19 D). *Science* (7th of 22 D): Basic Research; Technology.

Group Ratings

	ADA	ACLU	AFS	LCV	CON	NTU	NFIB	COC	ACU	NTLC	CHC
1998	100	88	100	92	93	27	21	33	12	5	0
1997	100	—	88	—	93	39	—	30	12	—	—

National Journal Ratings

	1997 LIB	—	1997 CONS	1998 LIB	—	1998 CONS
Economic	91%	—	7%	68%	—	30%
Social	85%	—	0%	81%	—	16%
Foreign	76%	—	22%	64%	—	31%

Key Votes of the 105th Congress

1. Clinton Budget Deal	N	5. Puerto Rico Sthood. Ref.	N	9. Cut $ for B-2 Bombers	Y
2. Education IRAs	N	6. End Highway Set-asides	N	10. Human Rights in China	Y
3. Req. 2/3 to Raise Taxes	N	7. School Prayer Amend.	N	11. Withdraw Bosnia Troops	N
4. Fast-track Trade	N	8. Ovrd. Part. Birth Veto	N	12. End Cuban TV-Marti	Y

Election Results

1998 general	Lynn Rivers (D)	99,935	(58%)	($432,084)
	Thomas Hickey (R)	68,328	(40%)	($308,030)
	Others	3,624	(2%)	
1998 primary	Lynn Rivers (D)	unopposed		
1996 general	Lynn Rivers (D)	123,133	(57%)	($1,099,549)
	Joe Fitzsimmons (R)	89,907	(41%)	($1,223,433)
	Others	4,618	(2%)	

FOURTEENTH DISTRICT

Detroit's early auto factories—Packard, Hudson, Ford Highland Park, Dodge Main, Briggs, Ford Rouge, Cadillac, Kelsey-Hayes, Chrysler, Plymouth, DeSoto—were built between 1905 and 1925 in an arc about five miles from the city's center, in green fields at what was then the edge of urban development. Almost instantly the flat farmlands all around were platted in grid streets and filled with wooden bungalows and brick prairie-style houses, often with a driveway at the side and a single elm in front. Commercial strips lined the mile-square and radial main streets, stretching straight as far as the eye could see. Detroit was the nation's second fastest growing big city in those years, after Los Angeles, and like LA was built to automobile scale. Its neighborhoods filled up with factory workers and civil servants, professionals and maintenance men, corner store owners and management personnel, Catholics and Protestants and Jews: a middle-class melting pot. With one exception: Detroit in those days had few blacks, who did not begin their big migrations here from the South, especially Alabama, until around 1940, when defense plants began hiring in large numbers.

The history of black Detroit is one of conflict and uplift, inspiration and tragedy. The wartime mixture of Appalachian mountain whites and Deep South blacks proved volatile: there was a violent race riot in June 1943. During the war years, blacks were pent up in a few severely overcrowded neighborhoods like the Black Bottom, which is now the Chrysler Freeway. After 1945, when blacks began moving outward, real estate agents played on racial fears, and in the 1950s whole square miles of Detroit changed racial composition in months. In the 1960s there was hope that the civil rights movement, encouraged by Walter Reuther's UAW, and antipoverty programs would improve blacks' lot, and in fact many black Detroiters found good jobs and made good incomes, bought their own homes and built community institutions. Then came the riot of July 1967, followed by extensive white flight and terrible increases in crime. Detroit's first black mayor, Coleman Young, elected in 1973, responded with policies that may have seemed appropriate in the 1960s but had disastrous results in the 1970s and 1980s: He pressured major employers like the Big Three auto companies to build facilities in Detroit, raised taxes to support a vast army of city employees, and attributed city problems to white racism. Violent crime became a part of everyday life and arson became common, especially on "devil's night" before Halloween. In Young's view, to criticize blacks who commit crimes would have been blaming the victim and playing into the hands of white racists.

Detroit took on a garrison atmosphere. Crime reduced the value of residential real estate to near zero, and the city's population dropped from 1.7 million in 1960 to an estimated 992,000 in 1994. Thousands of houses were abandoned to arsonists and drug dealers; in early 1993, the city's ombudsman proposed large stretches of property be purchased by the city, fenced off and abandoned. In political dialogue, most black politicians called for, and most black voters seemed to support, an ever-increasing public sector. Yet the existing public sector, which takes a larger share of residents' income than almost anywhere else in the country, serves citizens very poorly.

Turnaround has come agonizingly late in the 1990s, as Mayor Dennis Archer, elected in 1993, worked to fight crime and encourage private-sector growth. Detroit made headlines when General Motors bought the Renaissance Center downtown for its headquarters. But more important is that crime rates are falling, housing values are rising and commercial activity is starting to pick up.

The 14th Congressional District of Michigan consists of the northern half of Detroit, including most neighborhoods just beyond the auto plants. It includes adjacent suburbs from high-income Grosse Pointe Woods and more modest Dearborn Heights to Highland Park, an enclave within the city, which had 52,000 people and fine city services in 1930 and 20,000 people and an essentially defunct government in 1990. There are some solid neighborhoods here, including high-income Palmer Woods and Sherwood Forest, and Rosedale Park. On many blocks homeowners bravely install the big front-lawn lights Detroit Edison sells and patrol their streets, trying to discourage thugs that have dominion over most blocks nearby. Politically, this is one of the most Democratic areas in the nation, with many precincts turning in percentages between 90% and 98%.

The congressman from the 14th District is John Conyers, senior member (and one of the founders) of the Congressional Black Caucus, ranking Democrat on the House Judiciary Committee. The son of a left-wing operative in the UAW, he grew up in Detroit, served in the Army in Korea, practiced law and worked as a staffer for a young congressman named John Dingell. Conyers was first elected to Congress in 1964—one of six blacks in the House at the time and the only one to take a militant approach to politics; he won his primary, in which 60,000 votes were cast, by less than 150 votes. "Jobs, justice and peace" was his slogan, and he distanced himself from the Johnson Administration, criticizing the Vietnam war from the beginning and charging liberals were not doing enough for the poor. His response to the 1967 riots was to introduce the first bill for a guaranteed annual income. He supported reparations for the descendants of slaves. He stood by in disgust as his white Michigan Democratic colleagues opposed metropolitan school busing, and he opposed most of the controversial parts of the crime bills of the 1970s, 1980s and 1990s. He has one of the most liberal voting records in the House, calling for single-payer health plans and massive public works projects.

Conyers remains alert to evidence of racism. He pushed through the House a bill to collect statistics on traffic stops, in the belief that many blacks are stopped for DWB (driving while black). In 1998 he criticized the tobacco companies for targeting blacks, and he joined the criticism on a proposed plastics plant in Louisiana as environmental racism. He criticizes Republicans bitterly, but not only Republicans. He criticized the Clinton Administration on Haiti until it weighed in on the side of Jean-Bertrand Aristide, and in an investigation of the Branch Davidian deaths in Waco he told Attorney General Janet Reno she did "the right thing" by offering to resign.

On Judiciary Conyers led the defense of Bill Clinton in the 1998 hearings on impeachment. He is no stranger to the subject. In May 1972 he called for impeaching Richard Nixon because of his conduct of the Vietnam war. He was a member of the committee when it voted to impeach

Nixon in July 1974—the only member of Congress ever to serve on two committees handling presidential impeachment. In 1988 and 1989 he led the fight to impeach Alcee Hastings, then federal judge, now a congressman from Florida; in 1997, when an investigation found that an agent lied in that case, he moved to reopen it. As impeachment hearings started in 1998, some Democrats were queasy about Conyers, sharing the judgment of Judiciary Republican George Gekas that he was "predictably unpredictable." But Conyers performed ably. He had long been criticizing independent counsel Kenneth Starr; in January he questioned "the integrity and independence of Mr. Starr's investigation" and in August called Starr one of the "enemies of the nation." For all his criticisms of Clinton, Conyers rallied behind him, following the Democrats' strategy of partisanizing the investigation and then claiming it was partisan; he managed to craft an alternative investigation resolution which Republicans wouldn't accept, the start of partisan divisions on the issue. His own speeches and interventions were competent, and he kept some sense of humor; at one point he said, "This is my 15 minutes of fame. I have about six minutes left." But he is still ranking member and has hopes of becoming chairman one day soon. It will be interesting to see whether he votes to reauthorize the independent counsel law, which he strongly supported in 1994.

Over the years, Conyers has mostly been re-elected without difficulty. He made two runs for mayor of Detroit, in 1989 and 1993. But he ran a desultory campaign the first time and almost no campaign the second, and came in far behind. Perhaps because of that he had two serious primary opponents in 1994, but finished well ahead of both with 51% of the vote. In 1996 and 1997, he had serious cost overruns in his office, and had to cut back staff salaries sharply. His defenders argue that he keeps large staffs to keep in touch with Detroit's problems; one of his staffers for many years has been civil rights pioneer Rosa Parks.

Cook's Call. *Safe.* Sitting in an extremely Democratic district, Conyers has little fear of losing in 2000, but could have some real problems in 2001 redistricting. Detroit has been steadily losing population and, with Michigan slated to lose one seat, this district could be drastically altered.

The People: Pop. 1990: 580,977; 12% age 65 + ; 29.2% White, 69.1% Black, 1% Asian, 0.2% Amer. Indian, 0.4% Other; 1% Hispanic Origin. Households: 37.1% married couple families; 18.4% married couple fams. w. children; 40.1% college educ.; median household income: $25,079; per capita income: $11,462; median house value: $29,800; median gross rent: $307.

1996 Presidential Vote			1992 Presidential Vote		
Clinton (D)	160,009	(86%)	Clinton (D)	165,363	(79%)
Dole (R)	20,915	(11%)	Bush (R)	31,360	(15%)
Perot (I)	4,772	(3%)	Perot (I)	11,992	(6%)

Rep. John Conyers, Jr. (D)

Elected 1964; b. May 16, 1929, Detroit; home, Detroit; Wayne St. U., B.A. 1957, LL.B. 1958; Baptist; married (Monica).

Military Career: National Guard, 1948–50; Army, 1950–54 (Korea), Army Reserves, 1954–57.

Professional Career: Legis. Asst., U.S. Rep. John Dingell, 1958–61; Practicing atty., 1959–61; Referee, MI Workmen's Comp. Dept., 1961–63.

DC Office: 2426 RHOB 20515, 202-225-5126; Fax: 202-225-0072; Web site: www.house.gov/conyers.

District Office: Detroit, 313-961-5670.

Committees: *Judiciary* (RMM of 16 D): Courts & Intellectual Property; The Constitution.

Group Ratings

	ADA	ACLU	AFS	LCV	CON	NTU	NFIB	COC	ACU	NTLC	CHC
1998	80	100	100	69	51	22	0	20	0	1	0
1997	95	—	100	—	25	27	—	30	4	—	—

National Journal Ratings

	1997 LIB — 1997 CONS			1998 LIB — 1998 CONS		
Economic	85%	—	15%	79%	—	0%
Social	85%	—	0%	93%	—	0%
Foreign	97%	—	0%	82%	—	16%

Key Votes of the 105th Congress

1. Clinton Budget Deal	N	5. Puerto Rico Sthood. Ref.	Y	9. Cut $ for B-2 Bombers	Y
2. Education IRAs	N	6. End Highway Set-asides	N	10. Human Rights in China	Y
3. Req. 2/3 to Raise Taxes	N	7. School Prayer Amend.	N	11. Withdraw Bosnia Troops	N
4. Fast-track Trade	N	8. Ovrd. Part. Birth Veto	N	12. End Cuban TV-Marti	*

Election Results

1998 general	John Conyers Jr. (D)	126,321	(87%)	($256,651)
	Vendella M. Collins (R)	16,140	(11%)	
	Others	2,844	(2%)	
1998 primary	John Conyers Jr. (D)	unopposed		
1996 general	John Conyers Jr. (D)	157,722	(86%)	($267,039)
	William Ashe (R)	22,152	(12%)	
	Others	3,821	(2%)	

FIFTEENTH DISTRICT

Few central cities in America have as vibrant a 20th Century history, and as sad a recent past, as Detroit. This was America's first automobile city, not just because it manufactured so many of the nation's cars but also because it was built to automobile scale. Detroit started the century as a second-rank city, no bigger than Milwaukee, with less than half a million people and extending no farther than four or five miles out from the site where the French built Fort Pontchartrain on the Detroit River in 1701. As the Motor City boomed, it grew outward along wide avenues and freeways; the auto companies put their factories and headquarters near the edge of urban settlement. As early as 1954, the nation's first big suburban shopping center, with parking for 10,000 cars, was drawing retail trade from downtown. Metro Detroit expanded to four million people, each generation moving out the roadways rapidly in many directions, leaving behind the previous generation's neighborhoods and civic institutions.

Today, that rapid movement has left large parts of Detroit literally empty. The central city, which had nearly 1.9 million people in 1950, was down to just over 1 million in 1990, and then only with the help of a city bureaucracy detailed to round up uncounted residents. It had the biggest rate of population loss of any 100,000-plus city in the 1980s except for Gary and Newark. The reason is obvious: crime. For 30 years Detroit had a murder rate drastically higher than in the suburbs, and naturally those who could afford to leave did so. Downtown, the giant Hudson's department store has been torn down and several skyscrapers are all but empty; GM bought the 70-story Renaissance Center, built in the 1970s for $350 million, for $72 million. Beyond downtown, some of the city's jewels have been maintained: the Detroit Institute of Arts, the hospital center, the old Fox Theater. New residential and commercial projects have risen on the once-neglected riverfront. And new development, initiated by Mayor Dennis

Archer, is promised: new baseball and football stadiums, three casinos. But beyond these well-policed enclaves lie acres of vacant fields and half-empty blocks where there were once five-story apartments or brick houses; once vital neighborhoods are now home to pheasants.

Detroit's fate is all the more tragic because it comes in a city where liberal reformers hoped to create model anti-poverty and anti-discrimination programs. Instead, they seem to have undermined the sense of individual responsibility and confidence in the legitimacy of institutions. Metro area jobs rose from 1.5 million at the trough of the 1980s to over 2 million in the 1990s; the problem is not so much a lack of jobs as the fact that too many people lived by crime instead. Detroit's mayor for 20 years from 1973 to 1993, Coleman Young, spent his energy on courting the Big Three, bulldozing the viable Poletown neighborhood for a new Cadillac plant. Meanwhile, high taxes and high crime meant thousands of small-business jobs vanished. Dennis Archer, elected mayor in 1993, takes a more intelligent and judicious approach, and the city is now turning around, with lower crime, more jobs, new housing permits and a start at a growing private sector. But much of Detroit is still achingly vacant.

The 15th Congressional District of Michigan includes the southern half of Detroit, plus a few adjacent suburbs, from affluent Grosse Pointe Farms on Lake St. Clair to the Downriver industrial town of Ecorse. The district also includes Hamtramck, America's fastest-growing city between 1910–20, the Polish-American enclave around the now demolished Dodge Main plant. The district leads the nation in infant mortality and welfare dependency, and is among the top in crime and unemployment. Its 1990 median household income, at $15,264, is lower than in all but three other districts nationwide. Politically, the 15th is overwhelmingly Democratic, but voter turnout is low—162,000 in 1996, compared with 276,000 in the high-income 11th District.

The congresswoman from the 15th District is Carolyn Cheeks Kilpatrick, a Democrat elected in 1996. She was raised in Detroit, became a teacher in Detroit public schools, and was elected to the state House in 1978. There she got a seat on the Appropriations Committee and worked on local projects, notably the highly successful River Place hotel and office complex in the old Stroh headquarters. She was a strong party loyalist, seeking the recall of Mayor Dennis Archer in March 1994 when he supported Governor John Engler's Proposition A to change school financing. Kilpatrick lost a race for the Detroit City Council, but won the 15th seat in the August 1996 Democratic primary by a solid 51%–31% margin against her one-time political ally, incumbent Barbara-Rose Collins. Collins, an ally of Coleman Young, was accused of campaign finance violations and misuse of campaign and office funds and had the third highest absentee rate in 1995.

In her first term, Kilpatrick served on the Banking and House Administration committees. She passed amendments allowing public housing tenants to arbitrate some disputes with agencies and to require insurance providers to take ethics courses. She made a point of visiting the suburbs in her district, meeting local officials and assigning staffers to work with them—a contrast with Collins. She got an $8 million earmark in the Transportation bill for an intermodal freight terminal. She started studying the advertising industry and encouraging more contracts for minority ad agencies. She opposed the 1997 budget agreement because of Medicare and Medicaid cuts and said that Congress should monitor bank mergers and make sure there were low fees for recipients of federal electronic funds transfers. She fought the elimination of the Low Income Heating Assistance Program and called for lifting of sanctions on Iraq. She was one of 16 members to vote against a ban on federal funds for assisted suicides.

Kilpatrick was easily re-elected in 1998; her Republican opponent tried to drop out of the race before the primary. In December, with help from Michigan's David Bonior and John Dingell, she got a seat on Appropriations. There has been speculation that she might run for mayor of Detroit in 2001.

Cook's Call. *Safe.* Kilpatrick is another member without a care in the world in 2000. But, Detroit has lost more population than another area of the state and this district could be severely altered in the 2001 redistricting, though the Voting Rights Act could well protect her.

858   MICHIGAN

The People: Pop. 1990: 580,933; 14.7% age 65 + ; 26.4% White, 70.1% Black, 0.7% Asian, 0.4% Amer. Indian, 2.4% Other; 4.1% Hispanic Origin. Households: 26.1% married couple families; 12.1% married couple fams. w. children; 32.7% college educ.; median household income: $15,264; per capita income: $9,650; median house value: $23,200; median gross rent: $242.

1996 Presidential Vote			
Clinton (D)	146,357	(87%)	
Dole (R)	17,275	(10%)	
Perot (I)	3,723	(2%)	

1992 Presidential Vote			
Clinton (D)	159,284	(82%)	
Bush (R)	24,552	(13%)	
Perot (I)	8,998	(5%)	

Rep. Carolyn C. Kilpatrick (D)

Elected 1996; b. June 25, 1945, Detroit; home, Detroit; Ferris St. U., 1968–70, W. MI U., B.S. 1972, U. of MI, M.S. 1977; African Methodist Episcopal; divorced.

Elected Office: MI House of Reps., 1978–96.

Professional Career: Teacher, Detroit public schls., 1970–78.

DC Office: 503 CHOB 20515, 202-225-2261; Fax: 202-225-5730; Web site: www.house.gov/kilpatrick.

District Office: Detroit, 313-965-9004.

Committees: *Appropriations* (26th of 27 D): Foreign Operations & Export Financing; Transportation.

Group Ratings

	ADA	ACLU	AFS	LCV	CON	NTU	NFIB	COC	ACU	NTLC	CHC
1998	90	100	100	92	55	15	0	28	0	8	0
1997	100	—	100	—	4	23	—	30	12	—	—

National Journal Ratings

	1997 LIB — 1997 CONS		1998 LIB — 1998 CONS	
Economic	73% —	26%	79% —	0%
Social	85% —	0%	93% —	0%
Foreign	97% —	0%	95% —	4%

Key Votes of the 105th Congress

1. Clinton Budget Deal	N	5. Puerto Rico Sthood. Ref.	*	9. Cut $ for B-2 Bombers	Y
2. Education IRAs	N	6. End Highway Set-asides	N	10. Human Rights in China	Y
3. Req. 2/3 to Raise Taxes	N	7. School Prayer Amend.	N	11. Withdraw Bosnia Troops	N
4. Fast-track Trade	N	8. Ovrd. Part. Birth Veto	N	12. End Cuban TV-Marti	*

Election Results

1998 general	Carolyn C. Kilpatrick (D)	108,582	(87%)	($328,037)
	Chrysanthea Boyd-Fields (R)	12,887	(10%)	
	Others	3,391	(3%)	
1998 primary	Carolyn C. Kilpatrick (D)	72,860	(89%)	
	Godfrey Dillard (D)	8,600	(11%)	
1996 general	Carolyn C. Kilpatrick (D)	143,683	(88%)	($174,457)
	Stephen Hume (R)	16,009	(10%)	
	Others	2,908	(2%)	

SIXTEENTH DISTRICT

One of America's great heavy-industry corridors is along the Detroit River, the choke point of the Great Lakes, in the Downriver communities below Detroit. Steel and chemical plants line the water, their dark and rusted hulks glaring across at Canada. A little ways up the sluggish Rouge River stands the giant Rouge complex, built by Henry Ford for $1 billion in the 1910s to take loads of iron ore, coal, limestone, and sand from Great Lake freighters and railroad cars and convert them into automobiles in 48 hours. This swampy, low-lying land, along the nation's most heavily trafficked waterway and within easy reach of the great East-West rail lines, was a natural place for industry in the early 20th Century. Around the older factories and well within range of their sulfurous odors, residential neighborhoods with neat, tightly packed houses were home to migrants who came for work—Polish, Hungarian, black, Italian, and more recently Mexican and Arab (the area has America's largest concentration of Arab-Americans). This industrial region has had some rough times: many factories have closed, and neighborhoods have emptied out. But there are also new factories, like Mazda's in Flat Rock, and smaller manufacturers are picking up the slack resulting from layoffs by corporate giants.

The 16th Congressional District of Michigan covers Dearborn and the Downriver communities, plus Monroe County directly to the south. The political tradition has been Democratic since the New Deal days, and while there is some cultural conservatism seen in top-of-the-ticket races, the basic preference remains much more Democratic here than in increasingly upscale Macomb County.

The congressman is John Dingell, the senior member of the House of Representatives. His father, John Dingell, Sr., was elected to the House in 1932, from a district created as a result of the Detroit area's auto boom. The first Congressman Dingell was one of the most productive urban liberals of his day, a sponsor of Social Security and, starting in 1943, of national health insurance. John Dingell Jr. has been around Capitol Hill almost as long: He was a House page from 1938–43. After his father died, Dingell was elected to succeed him in December 1955, at 29, from a district with large Polish, black and Jewish populations. He is the only member of the House who served in the 1950s; indeed only six served in the 1960s (George Brown, John Conyers, Patsy Mink, Bill Clay, Philip Crane and David Obey, none of whom is a committee chairman) and one of them, Conyers, was a Dingell staffer before he was elected. Dingell has had one really serious contest, because of redistricting, in 1964, against a fellow Democrat who opposed the Civil Rights Act. Although most of the district was new to Dingell, he won, and has been re-elected easily since. He has an interesting personal life, raising his children after his divorce (his son Christopher was elected to the Michigan Senate in 1986) and marrying in 1981 a granddaughter of one of General Motors' Fisher brothers. Debbie Dingell is head of the General Motors Foundation and a Democratic National Committeewoman, and an encourager of bipartisan amity as well; they are "a real power couple in Michigan," writes the *Detroit News*'s George Weeks, and in Washington as well.

From 1981–95 Dingell was chairman of the Energy and Commerce Committee and of its Investigative and Oversight Subcommittee, one of the most powerful and effective chairmen ever. It had wide jurisdiction and handled up to 40% of all House bills, had the largest budget and staff of any House committee and for a decade was the House's most sought-after committee assignment. As institutions will, the committee took on the character of its leader, widely known as "the truck": bright, aggressive, domineering, determined. Dingell and his committee superintended the breakup of AT&T and the sale of Conrail by public offering; Commerce's cable reregulation law of 1992 was the only bill on which Congress overrode George Bush's presidential veto. After a decade of sparring with Health Subcommittee Chairman Henry Waxman over clean air legislation, Dingell and Waxman worked together to produce the 1990 Clean Air Act. These were complex, heavily lobbied matters on which Dingell often had jurisdictional fights with Jack Brooks of Judiciary and Henry Gonzalez of Banking.

On other issues, Dingell backed organized labor's agenda against NAFTA and other trade agreements. A well-known sportsman, he long opposed gun control but voted for the 1994 crime bill and resigned from the National Rifle Association board. In many ways, he is an old-fashioned Franklin Roosevelt Democrat, supporting big government and strenuous regulation, taking a conservative line on some cultural issues and backing an assertive foreign policy; he was the only Michigan Democrat to vote for the Gulf war resolution.

But in the early 1990s the same forces that produced the Republican majority in 1994 frustrated Dingell's efforts. For years he had introduced his father's national health care bill at the beginning of each session, and looked forward to passing some version of the Clinton health care plan. But for all his efforts he could not put together a majority on the committee for a bill with an employer mandate, and in June 1994 conceded that Commerce was hopelessly deadlocked on health care. Similarly, he was stymied in October 1994 when Superfund reform was killed under time pressure and House-passed telecommunications reform went down in the Senate.

When the Republican majority took over, many expected Dingell to sulk or to launch bitter attacks on the other side. But he did neither. As the senior House member, he swore in Newt Gingrich with good grace and proceeded to work with Republicans and produce legislation. In 1995 and 1996 he successfully opposed repeal of the Glass-Steagall Act separating commercial and investment banking; in 1997 he worked on compromise language acceptable to insurance agents. He worked with new Commerce Chairman Thomas Bliley to pass the Safe Drinking Water Act of 1996—though he voted against it to protest the addition of too much pork—and to work out provisions in the pesticide regulation bill repealing the Delaney clause. With Bliley he opposed auctions of certain broadcast frequencies in 1996 and opposed the radio spectrum auction in June 1997 as "short-sighted, unwise, counterproductive and stupid"; as he predicted, it brought in less than projected. In 1997 he helped build consensus on the FDA. bill. Years before, on the old Merchant Marine and Fisheries Committee, he had pushed wildlife refuge legislation; he worked with Resources Chairman Don Young and ranking Democrat George Miller to produce a revision that protected wildlife and recognized hunting and recreation as a priority and which passed in June 1997 by a 407–1 vote.

Dingell was also successful in forging Democratic positions that prevailed in the Republican House. He proposed the health care portability pre-existing conditions legislation that in some-what different form was passed into law in August 1996. He introduced a patient's bill of rights to regulate HMOs in February 1998 and then joined with Republican Greg Ganske; they threat-ened a discharge petition in June and got a vote on their measure in July. It lost 217–212 and a Republican alternative passed 216–210. But the Senate never acted and, with five more Democrats in the House, a version seemed likely to pass in 1999. On campaign finance, he proposed a base-closing-type solution, in which a bipartisan panel would recommend changes that Congress would have to accept or reject as a package. But in June 1998, he switched to the Shays-Meehan bill, which gathered Republican support and passed the House in August.

Dingell also was unafraid to take on the Clinton Administration. He compared the 5% tax imposed by the FCC on long distance calls to finance Internet access for schools, widely known as "the Gore tax," to the taxes of George III. He opposed EPA's 1997 attempt to tighten requirements on ozone and particulate emissions as environmentally unnecessary and eco-nomically disastrous. And in 1998 he opposed the Kyoto global warming treaty, calling it "the most asinine treaty I've ever seen." He pointed out that the burdens were on the United States, because Europeans dependent on nuclear power or natural gas would not have to shut down plants and China, India and underdeveloped countries refused to be bound. In between these fights, he tended to locally important issues. Working with Republicans, he got the FTC to drop the rule reducing to 75% the amount of American content required for the Made in U.S.A. label. He got the administration to create the Southeast Michigan Auto National Heritage label. The new veterans' hospital in Detroit was named after him.

In the anti-incumbent early 1990s Dingell seemed to be under some political threat. In 1994 he spent $1.07 million against his opponent's $8,000 and was re-elected by 59%–40%, less than many expected. For 1996 Republicans recruited James DeSana, former Democratic legislator and mayor of Downriver Wyandotte. Dingell did not stint on fundraising, and spent $1.9 million to DeSana's $259,000. It paid off: Dingell improved on his 1994 showing and beat DeSana 62%–36%. To rumors that he might retire, Dingell said, "There's an old Polish saying: 'Before you sell the bearskin, you first have to shoot the bear.' This bear is still doing just fine." Republicans called on Gibraltar Mayor Scott Denison to run for the seat, but in May 1998 Denison said, "I'd have to compliment John so much, I don't know what I'd run on. He's done a great job for the last 40 years." Actually, Dingell had served 42 years, but Denison was only 40 and so would not remember the first two. Dingell raised more than $1 million and won 67%–31%. No one should bet too heavily against him.

Cook's Call. *Safe.* Dean of the Michigan delegation, John Dingell can keep a hold of this seat for as long as he wants. But, when the 73-year-old Dingell decides to retire, there will be a spirited contest for this Democratic leaning but conservative district.

The People: Pop. 1990: 580,884; 13.2% rural; 13.5% age 65 + ; 96.7% White, 1.3% Black, 0.9% Asian, 0.5% Amer. Indian, 0.6% Other; 2.4% Hispanic Origin. Households: 58.7% married couple families; 27.9% married couple fams. w. children; 39.3% college educ.; median household income: $35,315; per capita income: $15,175; median house value: $62,400; median gross rent: $389.

1996 Presidential Vote		
Clinton (D)	122,522	(54%)
Dole (R)	78,461	(34%)
Perot (I)	24,125	(11%)

1992 Presidential Vote		
Clinton (D)	115,339	(43%)
Bush (R)	96,466	(36%)
Perot (I)	52,070	(20%)

Rep. John D. Dingell (D)

Elected Dec. 1955; b. July 8, 1926, Colorado Springs, CO; home, Dearborn; Georgetown U., B.S. 1949, J.D. 1952; Catholic; married (Deborah).

Military Career: Army, 1944–46 (WWII).

Professional Career: Practicing atty., 1952–55; Wayne Cnty. Asst. Prosecuting Atty., 1953–55.

DC Office: 2328 RHOB 20515, 202-225-4071; Web site: www.house.gov/dingell.

District Offices: Dearborn, 313-846-1276; Monroe, 313-243-1849.

Committees: *Commerce* (RMM of 24 D).

Group Ratings

	ADA	ACLU	AFS	LCV	CON	NTU	NFIB	COC	ACU	NTLC	CHC
1998	85	80	100	69	61	12	14	28	8	5	8
1997	80	—	88	—	33	29	—	50	8	—	—

National Journal Ratings

	1997 LIB — 1997 CONS			1998 LIB — 1998 CONS		
Economic	70%	—	30%	72%	—	23%
Social	70%	—	30%	69%	—	31%
Foreign	87%	—	13%	95%	—	4%

Key Votes of the 105th Congress

1. Clinton Budget Deal	N	5. Puerto Rico Sthood. Ref.	Y	9. Cut $ for B-2 Bombers	Y
2. Education IRAs	N	6. End Highway Set-asides	N	10. Human Rights in China	Y
3. Req. 2/3 to Raise Taxes	N	7. School Prayer Amend.	N	11. Withdraw Bosnia Troops	N
4. Fast-track Trade	N	8. Ovrd. Part. Birth Veto	Y	12. End Cuban TV-Marti	Y

Election Results

1998 general	John D. Dingell (D) 116,145	(67%)	($867,718)	
	William Morse (R) 54,121	(31%)		
	Others 4,091	(2%)		
1998 primary	John D. Dingell (D) .... unopposed			
1996 general	John D. Dingell (D) 136,854	(62%)	($1,854,280)	
	James DeSana (R) 78,723	(36%)	($259,035)	
	Others 5,035	(2%)		

MINNESOTA

Minnesota has long been a distinctive commonwealth, set far in America's frozen North, a state which in commerce, culture and politics has set one example after another for the rest of the nation. It is the node of transcontinental railroads that linked the winter wheat fields of the northern prairies to the greatest grain milling center in the world and the great Pacific ports of Puget Sound. It is also the birthplace of Scotch Tape, Betty Crocker, Target and the Mall of America, the home base of chroniclers of small town America from Sinclair Lewis to Garrison Keillor. Politically, Minnesota over the last half century provided the nation with some of its most articulate and honorable leaders—Harold Stassen, Hubert Humphrey, Eugene McCarthy, Walter Mondale—and with traditions of probity, civic-mindedness and innovation which are second to none. Yet while commercially and culturally Minnesota has never been stronger, its recent political history often seems to be one antic episode after another. Its two political parties, with their distinctive names—Democratic-Farmer-Labor and (from 1975 until 1995) Independent Republican—have been dominated by activists of left and right stubbornly out of touch with ordinary voters. Minnesota's two senators come from the extreme wings of their respective parties, former Carleton College political science professor Paul Wellstone on the Democratic-Farmer-Labor left and former KMSP-TV news anchor Rod Grams on the Independent-Republican right. And in 1998, Minnesota elected a former professional wrestler and suburban mayor, Jesse "The Body" Ventura, as governor. The completely bald, blunt-spoken Ventura, with his strong Midwestern accent and gift for pithy phrases, quickly became a national celebrity, a possible national trend-setter as a political libertarian on most cultural issues and market-oriented on economics. But his election may simply be an indication that when a competent state lets its ideological party activists have too much influence over its politics, voters will recoil against party politicians altogether, in a Lake Wobegon backlash against foolishness and toward common sense.

Minnesota's distinctive traditions come from a distinctive history. The far northern states were ignored by most Yankee immigrants, who headed straight west into Iowa, Nebraska and Kansas. But others saw opportunity in Minnesota's icy lakes and ferocious winters. James J. Hill, the builder of the Great Northern Railroad ("You can't interest me in any proposition in any place where it doesn't snow."), and others operating out of Minneapolis and St. Paul—already twin cities by 1860—worked to attract Norwegian, Swedish and German migrants who would find the terrain and climate congenial. By 1890, the Twin Cities—rivals that year in a

Census competition—were the nerve center of a sprawling and rich agricultural empire stretching west from Minnesota through the Dakotas and into Montana and beyond. Minneapolis and St. Paul became the termini of its rail lines and the site of its grain-milling companies.

The Twin Cities also became the center of a three-party politics and an economic radicalism reminiscent of the politics of Scandinavia. For our American regions seem a mirror image of the geography of Europe, with the East Coast resembling the British Isles and France, the industrial Midwest reminiscent of Germany and Poland, the relatively poor and always hawkish South a Baptist Mediterranean, and the Upper Midwest of Minnesota, Wisconsin and North Dakota as North American versions of Scandinavia. Like Scandinavia, these Upper Midwestern commonwealths pioneered their continent's welfare states, with an effect on public policy far out of proportion to their numbers. Alarmed by the unprecedented concentration of economic power and wealth into the hands of just a few identifiable millionaires who lived on St. Paul's Summit Avenue or the hill above Minneapolis's Hennepin Avenue, the immigrants drew on their native traditions of cooperative activity and bureaucratic socialism.

As in Wisconsin and North Dakota, a strong third party developed here in the years after the Populist era. This Farmer-Labor Party elected senators in the 1920s and dominated state politics in the 1930s. Hurt by their ties to Communists, the Farmer-Laborites were beaten by Harold Stassen's Republicans in 1938. But this was still a New Deal state and by 1944 the bedraggled local Democrats were merged with the anti-Communist faction of Farmer-Laborites to form the Democratic-Farmer-Labor Party. A key role was played by Hubert Humphrey—mayor of Minneapolis in 1945, and the dazzling advocate of the civil rights plank at the 1948 Democratic National Convention. Humphrey's DFL—clean, idealistic, closely tied to labor, backed by many farmers—attracted dozens of talented politicians, including Eugene McCarthy, Orville Freeman and Walter Mondale. In 1948, Humphrey's speech helped put the Democrats on record for civil rights, and he was elected to the Senate at age 37.

In the years following, the DFL dominated Minnesota politics, while a series of progressive companies led the development of a strong, diversified economy. The DFL stood for a generous, compassionate federal government, for strong labor unions and high wages, for an expansionist fiscal policy to encourage consumer-led economic growth, for civil rights, and for an anti-Communist, but not bombastic, foreign policy. Its base was among blue-collar workers in the Twin Cities, in Duluth and the Iron Range, and among farmers of Scandinavian origin. Minnesota's business leaders were conservative politically and innovation-minded in their work: Control Data was an early high-tech pioneer; 3M was famous as an inventor of new products from Scotch tape to Post-Its; IDS was one of the first mass-marketers of mutual funds; the Dayton family retail empire helped invent the indoor shopping mall, the discount store, and the national bookstore chain. Not all continue to dazzle: Control Data and IDS are no longer cutting-edge, 3M profits dipped in the late 1990s, B. Dalton has given way to Borders and Barnes & Noble. Some great Minnesota firms, like the grain-trading Cargill, are privately held and secretive. But the economy hums along, growing robustly in prosperous years and not falling behind in recessions, and squeaky-clean if sometimes eccentric Minnesota has levels of crime, divorce and aberrant behavior most states should envy.

On this solid economic base Minnesota has innovated in public policy. It produced the nation's first anti-smoking bill, one of the first public campaign financing schemes, and the nation's first statewide educational choice plan and authorized charter schools. It was one of the first states to establish HMOs and boasts of its MinnesotaCare plan intended to hold down costs and provide health care coverage for the poor. It has tried industrial policy, pledging $840 million in credit and loan guarantees to Northwest Airlines in 1991, which in turn kept its Twin Cities hub and built a repair facility in the Iron Range. In 1995 it passed a generous welfare reform, which raised spending even as more recipients got jobs. In 1997, at the insistence of Governor Arne Carlson and over the furious opposition of the teachers' unions, it instituted a form of school choice.

Not very much of this was the product of the activists who dominate both Minnesota parties'

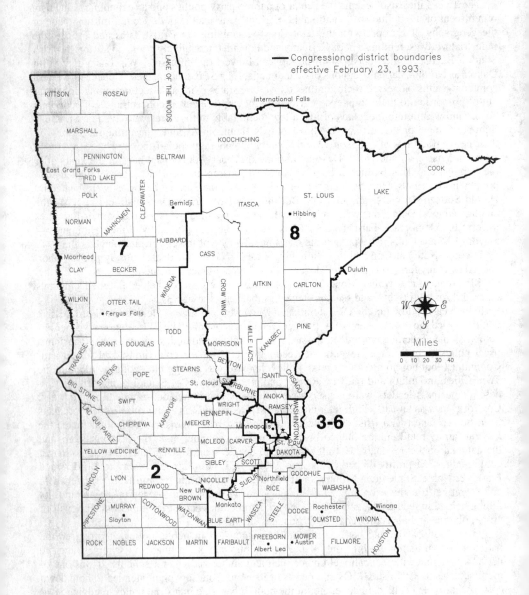

Congressional district boundaries
effective February 23, 1993.

KITTSON
ROSEAU
LAKE OF THE WOODS
International Falls
MARSHALL
KOOCHICHING
PENNINGTON
BELTRAMI
East Grand Forks
RED LAKE
POLK
CLEARWATER
Bemidji
ITASCA
ST. LOUIS
COOK
LAKE
Hibbing
NORMAN
MAHNOMEN
HUBBARD
8
Moorhead
CLAY
7
BECKER
CASS
CROW WING
AITKIN
CARLTON
Duluth
WILKIN
OTTER TAIL
Fergus Falls
WADENA
MILLE LACS
PINE
TRAVERSE
GRANT
DOUGLAS
TODD
MORRISON
KANABEC
BENTON
CHISAGO
BIG STONE
STEVENS
POPE
STEARNS
ISANTI
WASHINGTON
St. Cloud
SHERBURNE
ANOKA
SWIFT
KANDIYOHI
WRIGHT
RAMSEY
3-6
LAC QUI PARLE
CHIPPEWA
MEEKER
HENNEPIN
Minneapolis
YELLOW MEDICINE
RENVILLE
MCLEOD
CARVER
St. Paul
DAKOTA
LINCOLN
LYON
REDWOOD
SIBLEY
SCOTT
2
NICOLLET
LE SUEUR
RICE
GOODHUE
New Ulm
Northfield
1
WABASHA
PIPESTONE
MURRAY
COTTONWOOD
BROWN
WATONWAN
Mankato
WASECA
STEELE
DODGE
Rochester
OLMSTED
WINONA
Winona
Slayton
BLUE EARTH
MOWER
ROCK
NOBLES
JACKSON
MARTIN
FARIBAULT
FREEBORN
Albert Lea
Austin
FILLMORE
HOUSTON

N
W   E
S

Miles
0 10 20 30 40

caucuses and nominating conventions. The early DFLers were proud of this system, which allowed plenty of political participation and ended control by party bosses. But in time the conventions came to be dominated not by laborite Humphrey followers or the wives of management Republicans, but by left-wingers and counterculturites and right-wing abortion opponents and religious hardliners.

As Carleton College political scientist Steven Schier says, "Each party's endorsing convention has become an outpost of exotic and extreme politics." Much press attention was focused in 1994 on the supposedly fatal capture of the Republican Party by the religious right. But the party that was really hurt that year was the DFL, whose left-wing candidates lost races for governor and senator. The left has had one success, the election of liberal Senator Paul Wellstone in 1990 and 1996, but he won with just 50% both times: Neither of Minnesota's wings has shown itself able to win more than a bare majority. Party-endorsed candidates have seldom won primaries, but they and the issues which produce them dominate most of the campaign period, since primaries are not held until September. Never was that clearer than in 1998. At the beginning of the year, the major questions were which of the three sons of DFL heroes—Attorney General Skip Humphrey, former state Senator Mike Freeman or former state Senator Ted Mondale—would be the DFL governor nominee, and whether DFLer-turned-Republican Norm Coleman, the mayor of St. Paul—would be accepted by the Republican Party. But the real gainer was Jesse Ventura, who scored in the low teens in most polls but who produced a turnout surge in November and won with 37% of the vote to 34% for Coleman and only 28% for Humphrey—less than half the 60% his father won in his first electrifying election for senator exactly 50 years earlier.

It was, literally, a new Minnesota that elected Ventura. In the Twin Cities core, Hennepin and Ramsey counties, with one-third of the vote, it was an almost even three-way race, with Ventura leading narrowly with 36% of the vote to 32% for Coleman and 31% for Humphrey. In the one-third of Minnesota beyond the range of Minneapolis-St. Paul TV stations on which Ventura concentrated his meager TV buy, Ventura finished third, with 29%, to 37% for Coleman and 33% for Humphrey. Coleman carried the ancestral Republican base—heavily German counties in southern Minnesota and the heavily Norwegian counties north and west of St. Cloud—and Humphrey carried the far north with pluralities plus Austin, site of the bitter Hormel strike. Humphrey carried only one county with more than 50%, Coleman none—a sign of the erosion of the old party base. Ventura's breakout came in the counties outside the Twin Cities core but within the Twin Cities media market. In this one-third of the state, turnout was actually up 2% from the presidential year of 1996, and up a whopping 31% from the last off year of 1994. This is the youngest part of Minnesota, with many young families moving out from the twin metropolis; Minnesota allows Election Day registration, and the bulk of the new voters went for Ventura. He carried absolute majorities in six of these counties, and above 40% in all but two others.

Governor. Jesse Ventura, elected in 1998, is America's most distinctive governor: 6'4", bald, a former professional wrestler who won as the candidate of the Reform Party. Ventura grew up in Minneapolis, the son of a steamfitter and a nurse-anesthetist; his legal name is still James George Janos, and he is one of two governors of Hungarian descent (the other is George Pataki of New York). On graduating from high school, he joined the Navy, and served as a SEAL in Vietnam. On returning home he went to community college and for 11 years was a professional wrestler—essentially a form of acting, but one that requires a good physique and some considerable athletic skill; he picked the name Ventura from a map of California (wisely rejecting nearby Oxnard and Santa Barbara). He also worked as a bodyguard for the Rolling Stones. In the mid-1980s he became a broadcaster, later a talk radio host and a movie actor; he appeared in *Predator* with Arnold Schwarzenegger and uttered the line, "I ain't got time to bleed." He entered politics by getting elected mayor of Brooklyn Park, a middle-income suburb northwest of Minneapolis and served from 1991–95.

Sometime in 1995 Ventura got into his head the improbable idea of running for governor, as a candidate for Ross Perot's Reform Party. There was a certain shrewdness here. He knew that both parties' endorsing conventions were dominated by extremists; as he put it later, "I believe the Republicans and the Democrats have reached levels of extreme, where they're out there representing 15% extreme left and 15% extreme right. And the 70% of us who are more centrist have to then choose the lesser of two evils." The endorsement conventions and primaries would keep the two major parties busy until September, while Ventura, well known from talk radio, could set out his platform. Moreover, Minnesota's high-minded public finance system would limit the major party nominees to $2.1 million each, giving Ventura the opportunity to raise enough money to get matching funds and be reasonably competitive in spending.

In the meantime, candidates of the two major parties tried to set forth their competing visions; it was as if each represented a ring on a tree, representing a decade of Minnesota politics. They included "my three sons," the sons of revered DFL politicians. Former legislator Mike Freeman was a kind of 1940s liberal, a strong backer of labor unions, who relied on union support and won the party endorsement at the June convention. Attorney General Hubert Humphrey III, universally known as Skip, was mostly famous for the large settlement he reached with the tobacco companies; otherwise, he was a 1950s liberal, recalling his father's ebullience. Former state Senator Ted Mondale, who antagonized unions by supporting workmen's comp reform and called for a program of HOPE scholarships, was a 1980s New Democrat. A fourth Democrat, department store heir and former auditor Mark Dayton, recalled the era of 1960s liberalism, opposed to the Vietnam war and inspired by the civil rights movement. Competing for the Republican nomination were Lieutenant Governor Joanne Benson, a 1970s Gerald Ford moderate; Allen Quist, a 1980s abortion opponent; and St. Paul Mayor Norm Coleman, a 1990s party-switcher. Coleman, an abortion opponent himself, had tangled with public employee unions and left the Democratic Party in 1996; after a battle at the Republican party convention, he won its endorsement and faced only token primary opposition. In the September primary, Humphrey's name-identification prevailed: He won with 37% of the vote, to 19% for Freeman, 19% for pro-life Iron Range state Senator Doug Johnson, 18% for Dayton and 7% for Mondale.

Post-primary polls showed Humphrey leading with about half the vote, with Ventura around 10%; taking note, Humphrey insisted that Ventura be included in all debates. But Ventura used his limited budget and his unique persona to forge ahead. He hired the admaker who produced the humorous spots that helped elect Paul Wellstone senator in 1990. This time, the ads used the sound track from the movie *Shaft*, showed Ventura in the pose of Rodin's "The Thinker," and pitted a Jesse Ventura action figure fighting "Evil Special Interest Man"; Ventura made a virtue of necessity by renouncing PAC contributions. He put together an especially winsome Web site. There was also substance. Ventura is solidly pro-choice on abortion and said that he would consider legalization of drugs and prostitution. But he was also for cutting taxes: He was irked at the state's $50 tax for personal watercraft (he owns five) and proposed a rebate of the state budget surplus. "I'll fight to get those Democrats and Republicans to return the $4 billion in excess taxes they took from you. That's $1,000 for every person in Minnesota." His running mate, 36-year teacher Mae Schunk, called for reducing class size, a classical curriculum and competency tests for teachers. Ventura called for restricting college loans to two years, on the grounds that many students do nothing but drink beer and party. By mid-October, the polls showed Humphrey and Coleman even at around 35%, and Ventura with a promising 21%. His advertising, concentrated in the Twin Cities media market that covers two-thirds of the state, won over many young voters and erstwhile non-voters.

In a year when turnout nationally mostly sagged, turnout surged in Minnesota, especially in the outer counties of the Twin Cities media market; in many counties turnout rose 40% or more from the last off-year election, and was even above the presidential year of 1996. This was the area where Ventura ran best, with 45% of the vote, to 34% for Coleman and only 21% for Humphrey. Interestingly, the new voters seemed to go heavily Republican in legislative races, enabling the Republicans to win control of the state House. Ventura also carried the Twin

Cities core counties of Hennepin and Ramsey narrowly over Coleman and Humphrey, and ran behind, but not by much, in the rest of the state, where his exposure was much less. Overall, Ventura won with 37% of the vote; Coleman, holding much of the Republican core despite switching parties, won 34%; Humphrey, with the old DFL constituency atrophying far more than almost anyone expected, had 28%. As Minnesota political observer Barry Casselman said, "Ventura exploited the state's historic populism, which in the past has had both a right-wing and a left-wing character." Ventura won largely because of his support from young voters, and from young men in particular. The VNS exit poll showed Ventura running 39%–39% with Coleman among men, while Humphrey edged Ventura 36%–34% among women. Ventura led Coleman 46%–36% with voters under 30, with only 16% for Humphrey; among voters 30 to 44, Ventura led Coleman 43%–33%. Only among the elderly, many with fond memories of his father's career, did Humphrey lead, 40%–39% over Coleman, with 21% for Ventura. Ventura's was not an elite coalition: Voters with $100,000-plus incomes widely favored Coleman, and those with graduate school degrees narrowly favored Humphrey; Ventura's best income group was $50,000-$75,000 and his best education groups were high school graduates and those with some college.

Ventura charmed almost everyone on election night by saying that his wife would continue running her riding school on their Maple Grove horse farm and he would continue as volunteer football coach, as he had for 11 years, at Champlain High School. As chief of staff, he chose a longtime top aide to former Congressman Tim Penny, a fiscally conservative Democrat. Republican Congressman Jim Ramstad's sister became commissioner of Corrections. His choice for Natural Resources commissioner dropped out when it became known he had numerous fish and game license violations; his choice for the Department of Education, Children and Families surprised everyone (including her daughters) when she revealed she had had an abortion. Ventura struck a few false notes at first, suggesting that his wife be paid $25,000 a year and obtaining a permit to carry a handgun. But his dramatic inauguration and State of the State speech were well received. "I stand before you as governor willing to say what too many politicians at all levels of government have been scared to say: The free ride is over." He proposed a $1.1 billion sales tax rebate, or $775 to the average family; that was less than he had promised during the campaign, but he said, "That's a would-have-been, if we had not spent the surplus." He also proposed a $1.6 billion income tax cut over four years, and called for revenue from the tobacco lawsuit to finance endowments for medical education and research and health and welfare-to-work programs. After beating his budget proposal deadline by two weeks, Ventura complained about the legislature's failure to expeditiously pass the state budget: "They cock-a-doodle-do and act real tough, and posture around at the people's expense." But the DFL-controlled state Senate agreed with Ventura that tax cuts should be held down and backed his stance on using tobacco money for health-related purposes. Meanwhile, the Republican-controlled state House dropped its longtime push for private school vouchers, switching to the governor's position.

Ventura was mobbed at the National Governors' Association meeting and appeared on the Tom Snyder, David Letterman and Jay Leno shows. But he insisted he would not run for president. Even so, he is an important national political figure.

Senior Senator. Paul Wellstone was first elected in 1990 in one of the great upsets of the decade. He grew up in northern Virginia, the son of Russian immigrants, more interested in wrestling than politics. He married young, quickly earned a Ph.D. at North Carolina, then went to teach at Carleton College in Minnesota in 1969. He was a "rock-the-boat professor" at Carleton, where he published little and taught the politics of protest. He made a name for himself in local politics by leading protesters in sympathy with Hormel meatpacker strikers in Austin and getting arrested while picketing a bank that had foreclosed on local farmers; he ran for state auditor and co-chaired Jesse Jackson's 1988 presidential campaign in Minnesota.

Then in 1990 Wellstone ran for the Senate seat held by Republican Rudy Boschwitz. In the primary Wellstone beat Agriculture Commissioner Jim Nichols, a populist on economics but anti-abortion, 60%–34%. In the general, he traveled around the state in a green bus and ran shrewd and humorous TV ads proclaiming that viewers wouldn't be seeing him as often as they saw Boschwitz (because he didn't accept PAC money) and made cute appeals ("I'm better looking"). In a takeoff on the film *Roger and Me*, one ad showed Wellstone in pursuit of a confrontation-shy Boschwitz; like the film, this was not entirely honest, since Boschwitz had agreed to debate. But the ad's cleverness and the candidate's charm created an almost cuddly impression, while Boschwitz responded hamhandedly, needlessly involving himself in controversy over the Republican gubernatorial nominee, switching his stand on the voting rights renewal, sending out a letter to Jewish voters suggesting that in this first Senate race between two Jewish candidates, Boschwitz was the better Jew because Wellstone took no part in Jewish affairs and had not raised his children as Jews. Wellstone won 50%–48%, carrying metro Twin Cities 54%–45% while losing outstate Minnesota 51%–47%. This happy warrior of the campus left became "the first 1960s radical elected to the U.S. Senate," in *Mother Jones*'s words.

Wellstone has one of the most liberal voting records in Congress. "I still believe that government can be a force for good in people's lives." At first he seemed awkward in the Senate, demanding roll call votes on all appropriations. But in time he learned to use Senate rules to achieve results. He successfully led opposition to the 1991 energy bill that would have opened the Arctic National Wildlife Refuge to oil drilling. He worked hard on lobbying reform and the gift ban, then finally got a vote on them in 1996 by threatening to attach the issue to telecommunications reform. He opposed U.S. military action in the Gulf war and, showing consistency, he criticized President Clinton for sending troops to Haiti without the consent of Congress. He and Pete Domenici pushed successfully in 1996 for mental health coverage in health insurance. And in March 1996 he seized an opportune parliamentary moment to force a vote on a minimum wage increase.

In 1996 Wellstone once again faced Boschwitz, who seemed interested in revenge and won the Republican primary easily. Republican ads called him "embarrassingly liberal and decades out of touch" and "Senator Welfare" for his vote against the 1996 Welfare Reform Act. Wellstone responded exuberantly, invoking Minnesota DFL tradition: "I am a Hubert Humphrey senator. I go to the floor of the Senate, and I fight for children, I fight for senior citizens, I fight for health care. I'm a Minnesota senator!" Unlike 1990, he did not limit himself to $100 contributions, but proved himself a master of the current campaign finance system even as he denounced it, raising and spending $7.4 million, far more than Boschwitz's $4.3 million. His welfare vote proved not to be disabling; he received more flak from his own supporters for voting for the Defense of Marriage Act. Boschwitz, evidently in desperation, ran ads citing issues on which he agreed with Bill Clinton, who was cruising to an easy victory in Minnesota; on the day before the election, without evidence, Boschwitz accused Wellstone of burning an American flag in the 1960s. Wellstone won 50%–41%, carrying the Twin Cities heavily, 52%–39%, and running a bit ahead in the rest of the state, 49%–45%. Reform Party candidate Dean Barkley, who helped manage Jesse Ventura's campaign in 1998, took 7%. Wellstone has said that he is limiting himself to two terms.

Wellstone's focus has become increasingly national. In 1997 he embarked on a trip to the poorest parts of America, like Tunica County, Mississippi (full of poor farmers but also gleaming casinos), echoing a trip Robert Kennedy took in 1967. "The Democratic Party has lost some of its soul," he proclaimed. He continued to campaign against low hog prices and Disney's lockout of union workers, against a radioactive waste storage facility in Sierra Blanca, Texas (he lost in the Senate, 78–15) and against fraudulent black lung testing. He opposed a ban on human cloning, for fear it would stop useful medical research, and called on the Clinton Administration to criticize China's human rights record (which was opposed by his Minnesota colleague Rod Grams). "We need more strong, authentic populist candidates to fight back against big money and their friends in Congress and focus on the kitchen table issues central to the lives of working families," he said and prepared to run for president himself. In July 1998 he said he was almost certain to run; Wellstone for President paraphernalia appeared at a coffee shop in the self-declared nuclear-free zone of Takoma Park, Maryland. He became the first to set up an exploratory committee. But in January 1999 he surprised and disappointed a crowd at the Capitol in St. Paul by announcing that he would not run because his injured back couldn't sustain the trauma of campaigning. As he told *USA Today*'s Walter Shapiro, "It was a crusade that I wanted to carry on. I wanted to galvanize the political debate. But I had a ruptured disc in my lower back." Wryly, he added to supporters, "I apologize for all the cabinet positions I promised" and vowed to continue to restore "the Democratic wing of the Democratic Party."

He saw Jesse Ventura's election as a rejection of candidates backed by big money. "Many voters yearn for populist voices, and they're willing to look outside the box to find them." He promised to plug away for national health insurance, with coverage for mental illness and alcohol and drug addiction. He was a defender of Bill Clinton from impeachment, and with Tom Harkin moved to make Senate deliberations open; he was one of three senators to oppose national missile defense legislation in March 1999. He continued to argue that "government pays too little attention to the kitchen-table issues of working families—a living wage, affordable housing, their children's future and having enough to live the American dream."

Junior Senator. Rod Grams, a Republican elected in 1994, has one of the most conservative voting records in the Senate. He grew up on a dairy farm 50 miles north of the Twin Cities, graduated from high school and went to "the Cities" to work as an electrical technician for $300 a month. He tried to enlist in the military, but was rejected three times because of a heart problem (for which he had surgery in December 1998). He was not political but was always a Republican: "We never had a lot of money. My major conservatism comes as fiscal conservatism." He went into broadcasting, and with his good looks and smooth delivery worked his way up as a TV reporter through small markets in Great Falls, Montana; Wausau, Wisconsin; and Rockford, Illinois to become an anchor on Channel 9 in Minneapolis-St. Paul in 1982. In 1985 he started a home building and land development business. Unlike most reporters, he was solidly conservative, a fervent opponent of abortion, an angry critic of government regulation, staunchly against higher taxes. "Families are under attack from all angles—the media, in schools and from all levels of government," he said. In 1991, Grams left his broadcast job and ran for Congress in the 6th District in the northern suburbs. The incumbent, Democrat Gerry Sikorski, had 697 overdrafts on the House bank and had just shifted from pro-life to pro-choice; an Independent calling for a national sales tax was also running. Grams was elected by 44%–33%–16%. In the House he pushed for the $500 per-child tax credit that became part of the Contract With America; he backed term limits and proposed sunset amendments to dozens of laws.

A 1993 redistricting made the 6th District more Democratic, and Grams decided to run for the Senate. The seat was being vacated by David Durenberger, a moderate Republican who was denounced by the Senate for ethics violations. Grams won a robust, multi-ballot fight at the Republican convention for the party endorsement. He was challenged in the primary by pro-choice Lieutenant Governor Joanell Dyrstad, but the same voters who chose Governor Arne Carlson 2–1 over anti-abortion Allen Quist gave the anti-abortion Grams a 58%–35% victory. DFL leaders endorsed Ann Wynia, a serious-minded St. Paul liberal, teacher at a community college and longtime state representative from 1976–90. In the primary she beat Ramsey County Attorney Tom Foley, local head of the moderate Democratic Leadership Council, by 62%–33%. The general election was a battle of extremes. Grams attacked Wynia for voting 300 times for tax increases; she attacked him for opposing the Brady bill, family leave and single-payer health care reform. Wynia was embarrassed at a press conference with retiring Congressman Tim Penny, when she admitted she would not have backed the Penny-Kasich budget cuts; Grams brandished a note from Penny thanking him for his vote and saying, "We did Minnesota proud!" At the beginning of the cycle this looked like a sure Democratic pickup. But Wynia's liberalism was more of a handicap than Grams's conservatism. Wynia carried the

Twin Cities area by only 46.4%–45.5%, while Grams carried the rest of the state 53%–42%, winning all but seven counties there, and won 49%–44%.

One of the causes Grams has staked out in the Senate is nuclear waste disposal. Minnesota gets nearly 30% of its energy from nuclear plants, yet the legislature has limited on-site storage of nuclear waste: something has to give. Grams supports permanent and temporary nuclear waste depositories in Nevada and has attacked the Energy Department, and even proposed its abolition, for not meeting a January 1998 deadline for a new waste facility. He opposes the Kyoto Treaty on global warming and hailed passage of a compromise wetlands bill in September 1998. He opposed western Republicans when they tried to block a compromise expanding a runway at the Minneapolis-St. Paul International Airport and urged them to protect the Minnesota Valley National Wildlife Preserve. He obtained $3 million for wheat and barley scab research.

Grams is not afraid of challenging sacred cows. He has called for individual investment accounts as part of Social Security. And for some weeks he supported Republican tactics to hold up a flood relief bill after the terrible floods along the Red River of the North in northwest Minnesota, in order to push other issues. He was the most prominent critic of the decision to close Pennsylvania Avenue in front of the White House and has questioned the intrusive security measures in federal buildings. He is a strong believer in free trade, which could be helpful in this export-producing state. He opposed Paul Wellstone's resolution calling for criticism of China at a U.N. Human Rights Commission conference. "This kind of demagoguery is the easy way out," he said, as he was outvoted 16–1 on the Foreign Relations Committee. He favored IMF funding and proposed a review of the U.S. policy toward Cuba—issues which could irritate many conservatives. He worked to revise the International Religious Freedom Act, and also for a December 1998 agreement that let U.S. wheat farmers use Canadian railroads to export grain. He asked for an investigation of Interior Department officials who were probing allegations of worker mistreatment in the Commonwealth of the Northern Mariana Islands.

Grams is reserved, even shy, by no means always available to the press; if he refused to comment outside the Senate on impeachment, that was not atypical. As a conservative Republican in a historically liberal Democratic state, he is an obvious Democratic target for 2000; by late 1998 he had raised little money, and he has never won more than 50% in an election. On the other hand, he holds his ground steadily and without fear—like his liberal colleague Paul Wellstone, who has never won more than 50% either—and has never lost. The Minnesota Reform Party is uncomfortable with him and would love to run former Democratic Congressman Tim Penny, who served on Governor Jesse Ventura's transition team; Penny in early 1999 said he will run only as a Democrat, and probably not at all, but any Reform candidate would split the anti-Grams vote, and the 1998 governor race showed that a strong Reform candidate erodes the DFL base more than the Republican. The first declared candidate, in March 1999, was David Lillehaug, second-place finisher in the 1998 primary for attorney general and former U.S. attorney, and longtime strategist for Wellstone, who calls Grams's record "strange and inappropriate." Moderate David Minge of the 2nd District in April 1999 said he was forming an exploratory committee. Another possibility is 7th District Congressman Collin Peterson, a moderate who differs with Twin Cities liberals on many issues. Congressman Bill Luther got out of the race after winning only narrowly in 1998 and then getting a seat on the Commerce Committee. Democrats' attempts in early 1999 to get state Supreme Court Justice Alan Page, a big vote-winner and one-time Minnesota Viking, to run evidently failed. A wild card: Minneapolis lawyer Michael Ciresi, who led the state's lawsuit against the tobacco industry, might run on the DFL or perhaps on the Reform Party line.

Cook's Call. *Competitive.* Grams is arguably the most vulnerable incumbent of either party up for re-election in 2000. His strong conservative bent puts him out of step with the majority of the fairly moderate Minnesota electorate, and he had raised little money by the end of 1998. But Democrats are still reeling from their unexpected loss in the 1998 gubernatorial race and, although there is a long list of potential candidates, the only people seriously looking at the

Senate race are Representative David Minge and former U.S. Attorney David Lillehaug. The bottom line is that almost any credible candidate will give Grams a tough race.

Presidential politics. Minnesota has the longest consecutive streak going of voting Democratic for president of any state: the last time it voted Republican was in 1972, and even then it gave Richard Nixon his lowest percentage margin over George McGovern. So it is scarcely surprising that it gave large margins to Bill Clinton, 44%–32% in 1992 and 51%–35% in 1996. But Clinton's percentages were not especially high. Minnesota voted 24% for Ross Perot in 1992, 12% in 1996, among his best showings in the country: a precursor perhaps of Jesse Ventura's 37% victory for governor in 1998.

Minnesota has a tradition of selecting national convention delegates in caucuses. But, reeling from its third-place finish in the 1998 gubernatorial race, the DFL in April 199 abandoned its precinct-based system—which had been sparsely attended in recent years—replacing it with a mid-March 2000 event at which participants will cast a presidential preference ballot.

Congressional districting. Minnesota redistricted twice in the 1990s. A federal court set the lines for 1992; in 1993 the Supreme Court ruled that it should have deferred to a state court, whose plan was put into effect. That made for significant differences in the Twin Cities' suburban 3d and 6th districts, making the 3d even more heavily Republican and tilting the 6th toward the DFL; and in 1994 the DFL's Bill Luther captured the 6th, which had been represented by Republican Rod Grams.

The People: Est. Pop. 1998: 4,725,419; Pop. 1990: 4,375,099, up 8% 1990–1998. 1.7% of U.S. total, 20th largest; 30.2% rural. Median age: 34.6 years. 13% 65 years and over. 94.5% White, 2.2% Black, 1.8% Asian, 1.1% Amer. Indian, 0.5% Other; 1.1% Hispanic Origin. Households: 57.2% married couple families; 28.4% married couple fams. w. children; 49.4% college educ.; median household income: $30,909; per capita income: $14,389; 71.8% owner occupied housing; median house value: $74,000; median monthly rent: $384. 2.5% Unemployment. 1998 Voting age pop.: 3,483,000. 1998 Turnout: 2,105,377; 60% of VAP. Registered voters (1998): 3,000,412; no party registration.

Political Lineup: Governor, Jesse Ventura (Ref); Lt. Gov., Mae Schunk (Ref); Secy. of State, Mary Kiffmeyer (R); Atty. Gen., Mike Hatch (DFL); Treasurer, Carol Johnson (DFL); State Senate, 67 (40 DFL, 26 R, 1 I); Majority Leader, Roger Moe (DFL); State House, 134 (63 DFL, 71 R); House Speaker, Steve Sviggum (R). Senators, Paul Wellstone (DFL) and Rod Grams (R). Representatives, 8 (6 DFL, 2 R).

Elections Division: 651-215-1440; **Filing Deadline for U.S. Congress:** July 4, 2000.

1996 Presidential Vote

Clinton (D)	1,120,279	(51%)
Dole (R)	766,476	(35%)
Perot (I)	257,704	(12%)
Others	48,425	(2%)

1992 Presidential Vote

Clinton (D)	1,020,997	(44%)
Bush (R)	747,841	(32%)
Perot (I)	562,506	(24%)

GOVERNOR

Gov. Jesse Ventura (Ref)

Elected 1998, term expires Jan. 2003; b. July 15, 1951, Minneapolis; home, Maple Grove; N. Hennepin Commun. Col., 1975.; Lutheran; married (Terry).

Military Career: Navy, 1969–73 (Vietnam), Naval Reserves, 1973–75.

Elected Office: Brooklyn Park Mayor, 1990–95.

Professional Career: Professional wrestler, 1973–84; Actor, 1984–97; Radio talk show host, 1995–98.

Office: 130 State Capitol Bldg., Aurora Ave., St. Paul, 55155, 651-296-3391; Fax: 651-296-0039; Web site: www.state.mn.us.

Election Results

1998 gen.	Jesse Ventura (Ref)	773,713	(37%)
	Norm Coleman (R)	717,350	(34%)
	Hubert Humphrey III (DFL)	587,528	(28%)
	Others	13,175	(1%)
1998 prim.	Jesse Ventura (Ref)	unopposed	
1994 gen.	Arne H. Carlson (IR)	1,094,165	(62%)
	John Marty (DFL)	589,344	(33%)
	Others	82,081	(5%)

SENATORS

Sen. Paul Wellstone (DFL)

Elected 1990, seat up 2002; b. July 21, 1944, Washington, D.C.; home, St. Paul; U. of NC, B.A. 1965, Ph.D. 1969; Jewish; married (Sheila).

Professional Career: Prof., Carleton Col., 1969–90.

DC Office: 136 HSOB, 20510, 202-224-5641; Fax: 202-224-8438; Web site: www.senate.gov/~wellstone.

State Offices: St. Paul, 651-645-0323; Virginia, 218-741-1074; Wilmar, 320-231-0001.

Committees: *Foreign Relations* (6th of 8 D): East Asian & Pacific Affairs; European Affairs; Near Eastern & South Asian Affairs (RMM). *Health, Education, Labor & Pensions* (6th of 8 D): Children & Families; Employment, Safety & Training (RMM). *Indian Affairs* (5th of 6 D). *Small Business* (5th of 8 D). *Veterans' Affairs* (4th of 5 D).

Group Ratings

	ADA	ACLU	AFS	LCV	CON	NTU	NFIB	COC	ACU	NTLC	CHC
1998	100	86	100	100	83	18	11	22	4	0	0
1997	100	—	100	—	0	13	—	10	4	—	—

National Journal Ratings

	1997 LIB — 1997 CONS			1998 LIB — 1998 CONS		
Economic	96%	—	0%	90%	—	0%
Social	71%	—	0%	74%	—	0%
Foreign	92%	—	0%	95%	—	0%

Key Votes of the 105th Congress

1. Bal. Budget Amend.	N	5. Satcher for Surgeon Gen.	Y	9. Chem. Weapons Treaty	Y
2. Clinton Budget Deal	N	6. Highway Set-asides	Y	10. Cuban Humanitarian Aid	Y
3. Cloture on Tobacco	Y	7. Table Child Gun locks	N	11. Table Bosnia Troops	Y
4. Education IRAs	N	8. Ovrd. Part. Birth Veto	N	12. $ for Test-ban Treaty	Y

Election Results

1996 general	Paul Wellstone (DFL)	1,098,493	(50%)	($7,459,878)
	Rudy Boschwitz (R)	901,282	(41%)	($4,385,982)
	Dean Barkley (Ref)	152,333	(7%)	($37,240)
1996 primary	Paul Wellstone (DFL)	194,699	(86%)	
	Dick Franson (DFL)	16,465	(7%)	
	Ed Hansen (DFL)	9,990	(4%)	
	Others	4,180	(2%)	
1990 general	Paul Wellstone (DFL)	911,999	(50%)	($1,338,708)
	Rudy Boschwitz (IR)	864,375	(48%)	($6,221,133)
	Others	29,820	(2%)	

Sen. Rod Grams (R)

Elected 1994, seat up 2000; b. Feb. 4, 1948, Princeton; home, Ramsey; Brown Inst., 1966–68, Anoka-Ramsey Jr. Col., 1970–72, Carroll Col., 1974–75; Lutheran; divorced.

Elected Office: U.S. House of Reps., 1992–94.

Professional Career: Engineering consultant, 1966–68, 1970–73; News Anchor: KFBB-TV, Great Falls, MT, 1976–78; WSAU-TV, Wausau, WI, 1978–81; WIFR-TV, Rockford, IL, 1981–83; Sr. News Anchor, KMSP-TV, Minneapolis, 1982–91; Pres. & CEO, Sun Ridge Builders, 1985–present.

DC Office: 257 DSOB, 20510, 202-224-3244; Fax: 202-228-0956; Web site: www.senate.gov/~grams.

State Office: Anoka, 612-427-5921.

Committees: *Banking, Housing & Urban Affairs* (5th of 11 R): Housing & Transportation; International Trade & Finance; Securities (Chmn.). *Budget* (11th of 12 R). *Foreign Relations* (6th of 10 R): African Affairs; International Operations (Chmn.); Near Eastern & South Asian Affairs. *Joint Economic Committee* (4th of 10 Sens.).

Group Ratings

	ADA	ACLU	AFS	LCV	CON	NTU	NFIB	COC	ACU	NTLC	CHC
1998	0	14	0	0	95	73	89	94	88	96	100
1997	0	—	22	—	22	77	—	80	100	—	—

National Journal Ratings

	1997 LIB	—	1997 CONS	1998 LIB	—	1998 CONS
Economic	11%	—	76%	12%	—	85%
Social	0%	—	83%	12%	—	79%
Foreign	0%	—	77%	29%	—	58%

Key Votes of the 105th Congress

1. Bal. Budget Amend.	Y	5. Satcher for Surgeon Gen.	N	9. Chem. Weapons Treaty	N
2. Clinton Budget Deal	N	6. Highway Set-asides	N	10. Cuban Humanitarian Aid	N
3. Cloture on Tobacco	N	7. Table Child Gun locks	Y	11. Table Bosnia Troops	N
4. Education IRAs	Y	8. Ovrd. Part. Birth Veto	Y	12. $ for Test-ban Treaty	N

Election Results

1994 general				
	Rod Grams (IR)	869,653	(49%)	($2,439,798)
	Ann Wynia (DFL)	781,860	(44%)	($2,659,423)
	Dean M. Barkley (I)	95,400	(5%)	($24,266)
1994 primary	Rod Grams (IR)	269,931	(58%)	
	Joanell M. Dyrstad (IR)	163,205	(35%)	
	Harold Edward Stassen (IR)	22,430	(5%)	
	Others	8,467	(2%)	
1988 general	Dave Durenberger (IR)	1,176,210	(56%)	($5,410,783)
	Hubert H. Humphrey, III (DFL)	856,694	(41%)	($2,477,068)

FIRST DISTRICT

The Mississippi River runs majestically southeast from Minneapolis and St. Paul, cutting a path through rolling hills and, where it widens, forming calm lakes lapping at the bottomlands: one of the finest river landscapes of North America. This far north, the westward tide of Yankee migrants thinned out. After the Civil War, most settlers following the railroads on the flood plains west of the river were Germans and Scandinavians, bringing their families to this terrain so much like the Rhine, and to the rolling uplands beyond which resemble the northern European plain. Southeastern Minnesota is a borderland between Yankee and German settlements—politically, between Civil War Republicans and Farmer-Laborites favoring interventionist economic and isolationist foreign policies.

The 1st Congressional District occupies the state's southeastern corner. Within its compact bounds is considerable diversity. Rochester has been home of the Mayo Clinic since it was founded in 1863, when English-born physician William Mayo set up a practice to examine inductees into the Union Army—early government involvement in medicine. Today, Rochester, with its large professional population, is prosperous and growing. Austin, a county away, is headquarters of the Hormel meatpacking firm that beat a bitter strike in the 1980s; the huge meatpacking plant here produces Spam, Hormel chili, Dinty Moore stew and, say critics, too much ammonia-loaded waste; this is one place where class warfare politics seems alive. Rochester is a Republican stronghold; Austin is solidly DFL, the only southeastern Minnesota county to vote for Skip Humphrey for governor in 1998. The 1st District extends north to new subdivisions spreading out from the Twin Cities, the stomping grounds of Jesse Ventura and his Reform Party candidacy in 1998, and to Northfield, home of former Carleton College professor Paul Wellstone, now senator. The 1st also includes the river towns of Red Wing, Wabasha and Winona, with their 19th Century stone storefronts and mountain-like rock outcroppings that overlook the river; this is dairy farming and small industrial country.

The congressman from the 1st District is Gil Gutknecht, a Republican elected in 1994. The name, he likes to explain, means "good hired hand," though "good indentured servant" might be closer to the mark. He grew up in Iowa, son of a union member, worked nine years as a school supply salesman, then became an auctioneer, eventually handling large real estate auctions. He was elected to the legislature in 1982 from Rochester and became Republican floor leader. Partisan, ebullient, he once told Iron Range DFLers that the state motto *L'etoile du Nord* did not mean "send the money north." His legislation includes a whistleblowing law, ethics reforms and the 21-year-old drinking age. He had intended to run for the Senate in 1994, but 1st District Congressman Tim Penny, the very popular moderate Democrat who co-sponsored the Penny-Kasich budget cuts of 1993 and 1994, decided to retire, and Gutknecht instead ran for the House.

In the Republican primary, Gutknecht argued that he was the more conservative candidate and beat former two-term Congressman Arlen Erdahl, 57%–36%. In the general against Mankato state Senator John Hottinger, who backed a single-payer health care system, Gutknecht called himself "the Minnesota equivalent of Newt Gingrich." Hottinger carried Austin and ran even in Mankato. But Gutknecht won big in Rochester and in the river counties, for a 55%–45% victory.

Gutknecht was an enthusiastic member of the new House majority and has a mostly conservative voting record. He supported the Freedom to Farm Act, despite some concerns about its dairy provisions. He was one of several Minnesota members to oppose the IRS ruling taxing in the current year income from futures contracts payable in the next. He paid heed to district interests, sponsoring a Medicare formula that would pay more to rural hospitals and opposing changes in the sugar program (Minnesota is sugar beet country). He sponsored and went on the talk radio circuit to boost a 12-year limit on congressional pension accrual—a pension term limit. He supported fast track and sought to increase farm exports. For months he was a scathing critic of the stationing of U.S. troops in Bosnia. But a February 1998 visit there—his first trip abroad—changed his mind. Seeing how American troops were enabling Bosnians to live in freedom and peace, he said, "My views were changed" by "one of the most powerful experiences" of his life.

Gutknecht's ebullient conservatism has attracted active opposition in a district with a strong DFL base. In 1996 he was targeted by AFL-CIO ads and had serious competition from Winona State economics professor Mary Rieder. She said she was a fiscal conservative like Penny, and she raised enough money to be competitive. Bill Clinton carried the district with a plurality and Reider's vote tracked his closely. But that left the Democrat with 47% to Gutknecht's 53%. Again Gutknecht he won Rochester and lost Austin; he carried Mankato and the river counties but racked up high percentages nowhere. In 1998 state Senator Tracy Beckman, with Tim Penny as his campaign chairman, focused on Gutknecht's support for the Freedom to Farm Act together with the year's sharp drop in crop prices. Gutknecht wobbled a bit, voting against a Republican tax cut, and running ads with a former Agriculture commissioner saying he "listens to farmers" and "has been pushing the administration to enforce our trade agreements." Gutknecht had a big money advantage, and won 55%–45%; in the now familiar pattern, he lost Austin and carried Rochester big; in the counties closer to the Twin Cities, where turnout zoomed and which Jesse Ventura carried, Gutknecht got good margins. After the election he got a seat on the Agriculture Committee, where he sponsored a bill requiring that packers disclose the prices they pay to hog farmers and promised to "push for a better 'shock absorber' that protects farm income."

Cook's Call. *Potentially Competitive.* After a couple of close races, it looks like Gutknecht may finally have established a foothold in this district. A good conservative and well-funded Democrat could give Gutknecht some fits, but he seems well-entrenched enough to survive.

The People: Pop. 1990: 546,881; 46.9% rural; 14.7% age 65 + ; 97.9% White, 0.3% Black, 1.1% Asian, 0.2% Amer. Indian, 0.4% Other; 0.9% Hispanic Origin. Households: 60.9% married couple families; 30.2% married couple fams. w. children; 44% college educ.; median household income: $28,403; per capita income: $12,688; median house value: $58,800; median gross rent: $294.

1996 Presidential Vote

Clinton (D)	127,730	(48%)
Dole (R)	97,050	(37%)
Perot (I)	35,408	(13%)

1992 Presidential Vote

Clinton (D)	109,829	(38%)
Bush (R)	98,384	(34%)
Perot (I)	75,227	(26%)

Rep. Gil Gutknecht (R)

Elected 1994; b. Mar. 20, 1951, Cedar Falls, IA; home, Rochester; U. of N. IA, B.A. 1973; Catholic; married (Mary).

Elected Office: MN House of Reps. 1982–94.

Professional Career: Sales Rep., Latta School Supply Co., 1973–82; Real Estate Auctioneer, 1979–94.

DC Office: 425 CHOB 20515, 202-225-2472; Fax: 202-225-3246; Web site: www.house.gov/gutknecht.

District Office: Rochester, 507-252-9841.

Committees: *Agriculture* (21st of 27 R): Livestock & Horticulture; Risk Management, Research & Specialty Crops. *Budget* (11th of 24 R). *Science* (13th of 25 R): Basic Research; Technology (Vice Chmn.).

Group Ratings

	ADA	ACLU	AFS	LCV	CON	NTU	NFIB	COC	ACU	NTLC	CHC
1998	5	6	11	8	31	48	93	94	92	92	100
1997	15	—	0	—	95	60	—	100	92	—	—

National Journal Ratings

	1997 LIB — 1997 CONS	1998 LIB — 1998 CONS
Economic	16% — 82%	37% — 61%
Social	0% — 90%	21% — 76%
Foreign	32% — 65%	19% — 75%

Key Votes of the 105th Congress

1. Clinton Budget Deal	Y	5. Puerto Rico Sthood. Ref.	N	9. Cut $ for B-2 Bombers	Y
2. Education IRAs	Y	6. End Highway Set-asides	Y	10. Human Rights in China	N
3. Req. 2/3 to Raise Taxes	Y	7. School Prayer Amend.	Y	11. Withdraw Bosnia Troops	Y
4. Fast-track Trade	Y	8. Ovrd. Part. Birth Veto	Y	12. End Cuban TV-Marti	N

Election Results

1998 general	Gil Gutknecht (R)	131,233	(55%)	($948,385)
	Tracy L. Beckman (DFL)	108,420	(45%)	($323,895)
1998 primary	Gil Gutknecht (R)	unopposed		
1996 general	Gil Gutknecht (R)	137,545	(53%)	($927,715)
	Mary Rieder (DFL)	123,188	(47%)	($625,244)

SECOND DISTRICT

West of the Mississippi and Minnesota rivers, where the plains rise above the gorges that the rivers have cut through them, is the great farming country of southwestern Minnesota. This is where Laura Ingalls Wilder's family came on the way west from their little house in the big woods in Wisconsin to the "Little House on the Prairie" in South Dakota, and stopped by the shores of Plum Creek, near Walnut Grove, Minnesota, not long after the Indians were forced out by U.S. troops following the Dakota rebellion of 1862. The creeks and rivers cut crevasses into these plains, spotted with occasional hills and towns settled more than 100 years ago by Yankee, German and Scandinavian farmers. This is a hard place to make a living; Laura's family, after all their struggles, left the farm for town as soon as they could. Even in the 1990s, farmers still toil against the elements to make a profitable living, and even their successes hurt; with higher productivity, fewer people live on the land or even in town.

The 2d Congressional District takes in roughly the southwestern quadrant of the state. The farm counties slowly have become depopulated, as young people move off farms into small towns and, more often, to the Twin Cities or other big metro areas. The 2d District's boundaries were shifted eastward after the 1990 Census and now take in outlying counties and townships of the Twin Cities metro area. Some, around Chanhassen and Shakopee, southwest of Minneapolis, are relatively high income areas. Others, farther out, like Waverly where Hubert Humphrey had his lakeside home, are more humble—places where modest-income young families are moving into what was once open countryside punctuated by small villages. This outlying part of the Twin Cities metro area and media market was the heartland of support for Jesse Ventura's Reform Party candidacy for governor in 1998 and, with turnout sharply rising, cast 48% of the district's votes that year.

The congressman from the 2d District is David Minge (pronounced with a hard *G*), a "common sense Democrat," as he puts it, first elected in 1992. Minge is close to a personification of "Minnesota nice," a Norwegian-American with the quiet earnestness and pleasantness which permeate life in Minnesota. He grew up in Worthington, the son of a doctor who became a medical missionary, practiced law in Minneapolis, taught law for seven years in Wyoming and worked briefly on Capitol Hill. Then he returned to Minnesota to practice law in Montevideo, the town where Walter Mondale grew up, where he worked with community organizations to clean up the Minnesota River and resettle Vietnamese refugees and served on the school board.

In 1992, Minge decided to run against Congressman Vin Weber, one of the leading-edge Republican conservatives in the House. But Weber had overdrafts on the House bank and decided to retire. Against conservative state legislator Cal Ludeman, the Republican nominee for governor in 1986, Minge campaigned with less money but more energy, riding 500 miles on his bicycle and stopping in 47 towns in nine days. He attacked Ludeman for voting against minimum wages, drug abuse programs, and federal disaster relief, and called for handling the deficit with a commission like the one Congress used for military base closings, and for a "unified" national health care plan. Bill Clinton carried the district 37%–35%, and Minge won 47.9%–47.7%. Ludeman was proclaimed the winner on election night, but Minge, with Norwegian stoicism, went to sleep and woke up to find out he had won by 569 votes.

Minge was one of the founders of the conservative Blue Dog Democrats and is a co-chairman of the House Porkbusters Coalition; he voted against the 1998 transportation bill though it funded projects in his district. His middle-of-the-House voting record includes support for early unpopular Clinton bills, but his energy seemed directed more at budget issues; he supported the balanced budget amendment, line-item veto and, on the Budget Committee since 1997, the Blue Dog budget which was a model for the 1997 balanced budget agreement. He brags about returning $620,000 in salary increases and office allowances to the Treasury and promised to serve no more than six terms. When the balanced budget was achieved in 1998, he responded with Minnesota-nice caution (though with metaphors more effusive than Minnesota), "The victory party had best be modest. We need to redouble our efforts to build a much sturdier financial structure. The El Nino of baby boom retirements is about to hit, and we are living in a sod house on the prairie."

Minge supported the 1996 Freedom to Farm Act, but with enough reservations to vote against the House version. As corn, soybean and hog prices slumped in 1998, he moved to reopen the law from his post as ranking Democrat on the General Farm Commodities Subcommittee. He wanted improved marketing loan and crop insurance programs to help farmers manage risks. He strongly backs the Conservation Reserve Program, and helped write a CRP Enhancement program to pay farmers to idle environmentally-sensitive land along rivers to prevent topsoil erosion and other runoff. Like many farm state Republicans, he called for expanding trade and supported the IMF funding bill. He also supported Republicans' bill for early payment of $5.5 billion in phase-out payments for farmers, but added, "It's more like offering chicken soup when you are sick. It can't hurt. It may make you feel better." In tones redolent of the prairie politicians of 100 years ago, he expressed unease about corporate mergers, citing the big delays getting wheat to market after Union Pacific bought two other lines, the purchase by grain-trader Cargill of Continental, and the smaller number of meat-packers ready to buy livestock. He met with antitrust and agriculture officials to see if something could be done, but tried not to demagogue constituents in town meetings: "People shouldn't lose faith, even if they look at prices that seem so blatantly wrong."

Minge has continued to ride his bicycle through the district every year, and has won re-election with increasing margins every two years. In 1994 he won 52%–45% and in 1996, against the same candidate, 55%–41%. In 1998, he faced a challenge from a retired Air Force colonel who accused him of not being conservative enough, and a challenge from Jesse Ventura's Reform party, which fielded a candidate here and whose new voters in the Twin Cities media market showed little affection for the old DFL. Outside the Twin Cities media market, Minge ran far ahead, 63%–34%. Inside, it was closer, but he still prevailed, 51%–42%, for a 57%–38% victory overall—his best yet.

In April 1999, Minge announced he was forming an exploratory committee to challenge Senator Rod Grams in 2000. He began his campaign by denouncing "extremism of every type" and said he would focus on the debt, Social Security, health insurance and education.

Cook's Call. *Potentially Competitive.* This very marginal district gave Minge some trouble in the early 1990's, but his middle of the road voting record and down-home style have helped him to gain a pretty solid foundation here. A down year for Democrats could make Minge vulnerable, but, after surviving the 1994 election and an onslaught of Republican money in 1998, he looks good for 2000. If Minge runs for Senate in 2000, holding onto this district could be a real problem for Democrats.

The People: Pop. 1990: 546,890; 59.6% rural; 16.2% age 65 + ; 98.6% White, 0.1% Black, 0.5% Asian, 0.4% Amer. Indian, 0.5% Other; 0.9% Hispanic Origin. Households: 64.4% married couple families; 32.3% married couple fams. w. children; 36.9% college educ.; median household income: $26,937; per capita income: $12,043; median house value: $54,700; median gross rent: $247.

1996 Presidential Vote			1992 Presidential Vote		
Clinton (D)	120,652	(45%)	Clinton (D)	103,246	(37%)
Dole (R)	105,205	(39%)	Bush (R)	97,867	(35%)
Perot (I)	38,117	(14%)	Perot (I)	79,442	(28%)

Rep. David Minge (DFL)

Elected 1992; b. Mar. 19, 1942, Clarkfield; home, Montevideo; St. Olaf Col., B.A. 1964, U. of Chicago, J.D. 1967; Lutheran; married (Karen).

Elected Office: Montevideo Schl. Bd., 1990–92.

Professional Career: Practicing atty., 1967–70, 1977–92; Prof., U. of WY Law Schl., 1970–77.

DC Office: 1415 LHOB 20515, 202-225-2331; Fax: 202-226-0836; Web site: www.house.gov/minge.

District Offices: Chaska, 612-448-6567; Montevideo, 320-269-9311; Windom, 507-831-0115.

Committees: *Agriculture* (7th of 24 D): Department Operations, Oversight, Nutrition & Forestry; General Farm Commodities, Resource Conservation & Credit (RMM). *Budget* (5th of 19 D).

Group Ratings

	ADA	ACLU	AFS	LCV	CON	NTU	NFIB	COC	ACU	NTLC	CHC
1998	85	56	89	62	99	41	50	56	24	18	17
1997	70	—	50	—	99	52	—	70	28	—	—

National Journal Ratings

	1997 LIB — 1997 CONS			1998 LIB — 1998 CONS		
Economic	59%	—	40%	60%	—	39%
Social	66%	—	33%	64%	—	35%
Foreign	82%	—	16%	84%	—	11%

Key Votes of the 105th Congress

1. Clinton Budget Deal	N	5. Puerto Rico Sthood. Ref.	Y	9. Cut $ for B-2 Bombers	Y
2. Education IRAs	N	6. End Highway Set-asides	N	10. Human Rights in China	Y
3. Req. 2/3 to Raise Taxes	N	7. School Prayer Amend.	N	11. Withdraw Bosnia Troops	N
4. Fast-track Trade	Y	8. Ovrd. Part. Birth Veto	Y	12. End Cuban TV-Marti	Y

Election Results

1998 general	David Minge (DFL)	148,933	(57%)	($631,766)
	Craig Duehring (R)	99,490	(38%)	($291,322)
	Stan Bentz (Ref)	12,319	(5%)	
1998 primary	David Minge (DFL)	unopposed		
1996 general	David Minge (DFL)	144,083	(55%)	($616,673)
	Gary B. Revier (R)	107,807	(41%)	($284,943)
	Others	10,463	(4%)	

THIRD DISTRICT

Over the past half century, Minnesota's great twin metropolis has spread out from the neat streets inside the city limits of Minneapolis and St. Paul into the countryside all around. People have sorted themselves out geographically. In the lower lands along the Mississippi and Minnesota rivers, where rail lines fan out from the Twin Cities heading toward the great farmlands of America, are the blue-collar suburbs, with neat modest houses on grid streets and warehouses and factories near the tracks. Inland, around the lakes Minnesota is so proud of, in subdivisions with curved streets hugging the hills, are the Twin Cities' more affluent neighborhoods, quiet and unflashy in the Minnesota way, but comfortable whether blanketed with snow or when the lake is glinting in the summer sun. In between are the freeway interchanges where some of the Twin Cities' great innovations can be seen—Southdale Shopping Center in Edina, the first enclosed mall and site of the first B. Dalton store, the beginning of national book chains; and now the giant Mall of America, with its 4.2 million square feet, 500 stores, 49 restaurants, 14 theaters and 12,000 employees.

The 3d Congressional District takes in Hennepin County suburbs north, south and west of Minneapolis. On the northside is working-class Brooklyn Park, long a DFL stronghold but more famous now for its former mayor, Governor Jesse Ventura; on the south is middle-income Bloomington, home of the Mall of America; to the west are Edina, Plymouth, Wayzata and other towns around Lake Minnetonka, all heavily Republican. This is the largest lake and these are the most affluent communities in the Twin Cities area. The area is home to the headquarters of such diverse companies as Cargill and Radisson Hotels. The 3d also takes in fast-growing Burnsville across the Minnesota River from the airport and still vacant land northwest of Minneapolis. This is a district that usually votes Republican, though it gave pluralities to Bill Clinton in 1992 and 1996.

The congressman from the 3d District is Jim Ramstad, a Republican elected in 1990. He has been in politics since childhood: Raised in North Dakota, he used to go with his grandfather to visit Republican Senator Milton Young. He saw President Eisenhower in 1956 and met President Kennedy in 1963 at the same Rose Garden ceremony where a young Bill Clinton was photographed shaking Kennedy's hand (Ramstad is in the background of the now-famous photo). He worked as an intern to Young and a staffer to Congressman Tom Kleppe while in his 20s. In 1980, at 34, he beat a Democratic state senator (spending the then record-breaking sum of $77,932) and worked on issues like chemical dependency in young people, crack babies and the handicapped, while favoring mandatory minimum sentences for drug dealers and boot camps for drug offenders. He used to spend time with police on all-night rounds.

In 1990, when 3d District Congressman Bill Frenzel retired after 20 years, Ramstad ran for the House. The crucial contest was the Republican convention. Ramstad was pro-choice on abortion while most delegates were anti-abortion, but he had good endorsements, from Senator Rudy Boschwitz and Congressman Vin Weber, both anti-abortion, and won on the eighth ballot.

Ramstad's voting record has been squarely in the middle of the House. He has taken on some environmental causes—trying to stop the Advanced Liquid Metal Reactor and scale down the proposed bridge over the St. Croix River—and voted against some appropriations riders weakening environmental regulations. He has attacked the FDA for stifling innovation and backs tort reform; his task force on legal reforms helped produce the securities litigation bill that was passed over Bill Clinton's veto.

Ramstad has taken his market economics to the Ways and Means Committee, on which he has served since 1995. He sponsored two planks in the Republicans' 1995 House rules reforms, one requiring proposed spending to be compared to actual spending the year before, not to a "current services" figure based on the assumption that government has become as efficient as it ever could, and the other a ban on retroactive tax increases. He has backed 401(k)-type pensions for public employees, employee stock ownership plans and exemptions for state health insurance risk pools; he sponsored an exemption for survivor benefits for spouses of police and fire officers killed in the line of duty. He worked on the Taxpayer Bill of Rights and on Medicare and hospital funding formulas. He argues that the current tax system is too complex, too costly and too invasive, but doesn't see reform as likely before 2000. He has been a strong supporter of free trade, whipping votes for NAFTA and fast track.

Ramstad is a recovering alcoholic and has backed measures for both discipline and therapy for substance abusers. He opposed SSI cash benefits for alcoholics ("Cash benefits only make the problem of alcoholism worse") and drug tests for released federal prisoners. In 1997, with Senator Paul Wellstone, he sponsored a bill to require insurance coverage for alcohol and drug addiction programs; they got the backing of Gerald and Betty Ford. Ramstad argues that alcoholism costs society $90 billion a year, and that his program would save $7 for every dollar spent; the increase in premiums, he says, would be no more than the price of a cup of coffee. In September 1998 he charged that the bill was being "held hostage by the president's scandal." On other issues, Ramstad co-sponsored with St. Paul neighbor Bruce Vento a bill to waive English language and residency requirements for US citizenship for Hmong and Laotians recruited into pro-U.S. guerrilla units between 1961–75. He opposed Vento's and James Oberstar's bill to relax limits on motorboats in the Boundary Waters Canoe Area Wilderness. Ramstad was one of the Republicans the Clinton White House hoped would vote against impeachment; he opposed holding the impeachment debate while U.S. planes were bombing Iraq, but voted for impeachment.

Ramstad has been easily re-elected every two years, and in this high-turnout district in high-turnout Minnesota in 1998, he won 203,000 votes, more than any other House member with major-party opposition. (Just behind was Jim Gibbons, of the Nevada 2d, with 201,000.)

Cook's Call. *Safe.* Ramstad has proved to be a good fit for this wealthy suburban Minneapolis district. He is well positioned for 2000 and beyond.

The People: Pop. 1990: 546,796; 1.9% rural; 7.7% age 65 +; 95.5% White, 1.8% Black, 2.1% Asian, 0.3% Amer. Indian, 0.3% Other; 0.8% Hispanic Origin. Households: 61.3% married couple families; 31.4% married couple fams. w. children; 66.1% college educ.; median household income: $44,329; per capita income: $20,805; median house value: $102,900; median gross rent: $535.

1996 Presidential Vote

Clinton (D)	141,109	(47%)
Dole (R)	125,019	(41%)
Perot (I)	31,021	(10%)
Others	5,532	(2%)

1992 Presidential Vote

Clinton (D)	129,171	(39%)
Bush (R)	117,975	(36%)
Perot (I)	79,877	(24%)

Rep. Jim Ramstad (R)

Elected 1990; b. May 6, 1946, Jamestown, ND; home, Minnetonka; U. of MN, B.A. 1968, George Washington U., J.D. 1973; Protestant; single.

Military Career: Army Reserves, 1968–74.

Elected Office: MN Senate, 1980–90.

Professional Career: Special Asst., U.S. Rep. Tom Kleppe, 1970; Practicing atty., 1973–80; Adjunct Prof., American U., 1975–78.

DC Office: 103 CHOB 20515, 202-225-2871; Fax: 202-225-6351; Web site: www.house.gov/ramstad.

District Office: Bloomington, 612-881-4600.

Committees: *Ways & Means* (10th of 23 R): Health; Trade.

Group Ratings

	ADA	ACLU	AFS	LCV	CON	NTU	NFIB	COC	ACU	NTLC	CHC
1998	20	13	0	85	33	48	93	94	60	50	42
1997	40	—	13	—	98	64	—	90	64	—	—

National Journal Ratings

	1997 LIB	—	1997 CONS	1998 LIB	—	1998 CONS
Economic	44%	—	55%	48%	—	51%
Social	55%	—	45%	48%	—	51%
Foreign	49%	—	49%	49%	—	48%

Key Votes of the 105th Congress

1. Clinton Budget Deal	Y	5. Puerto Rico Sthood. Ref.	N
2. Education IRAs	Y	6. End Highway Set-asides	Y
3. Req. 2/3 to Raise Taxes	Y	7. School Prayer Amend.	Y
4. Fast-track Trade	Y	8. Ovrd. Part. Birth Veto	Y

9. Cut $ for B-2 Bombers	Y
10. Human Rights in China	N
11. Withdraw Bosnia Troops	Y
12. End Cuban TV-Marti	Y

Election Results

1998 general	Jim Ramstad (R)	203,731	(72%)	($766,951)
	Stan J. Leino (DFL)	66,505	(23%)	($13,098)
	Derek W. Schramm (TXP)	12,823	(5%)	
1998 primary	Jim Ramstad (R)	unopposed		
1996 general	Jim Ramstad (R)	205,845	(70%)	($494,908)
	Stan J. Leino (DFL)	87,359	(30%)	($22,600)

FOURTH DISTRICT

Above the Mississippi River bluffs, forested when the first settlers arrived in the 1850s and one of America's great urban vistas today, stand the two great landmarks of St. Paul: the

Minnesota Capitol and Archbishop Ireland's Cathedral. This is the older and smaller of the Twin Cities, settled mainly by Catholic Irish and German immigrants, while Minneapolis was attracting Protestant Swedes and Yankees. St. Paul became a major transportation hub, a railroad center and river port, while Minneapolis, farther up river at the Falls of St. Anthony, became the nation's largest grain milling center. St. Paul has a vibrant core. Beneath the Capitol and the cathedral, its skywalk-linked downtown is home to the Ordway Music Theater, the headquarters of Minnesota Public Radio and an active pop music industry. Beyond the cathedral is Summit Avenue, on which capitalists like the Great Northern Railway's James J. Hill built grandiose Romanesque houses, and which, with Monument Avenue in Richmond and Meridian Street in Indianapolis, remains one of America's grand residential boulevards. In more modest neighborhoods are sturdy houses lined up on grid streets, and beyond are the close-in suburbs with more irregular street patterns and shopping nodes.

Minnesota's 4th Congressional District is made up of St. Paul, the Ramsey County suburbs to the north, West St. Paul and South St. Paul (which are right next to each other) to the south, and Lake Elmo and Woodbury to the east. St. Paul was one of the most Democratic parts of Minnesota even before the Democratic-Farmer-Labor Party was formed in 1944, and it remained proudly DFL for a half-century. The 4th District has been held by the DFL since 1948, when it elected Eugene McCarthy.

The congressman from the 4th District is Bruce Vento, who was elected in 1976. Vento grew up on the east side of St. Paul, where his father was an officer in the Machinist's Union. While in college, he worked in the St. Paul Hotel restaurant and in the Hamm's Brewery and was a machinist steward at Minnesota Plastics. He taught science and social studies in Minneapolis schools for 11 years and was elected to the state House in 1970, at 30, where he became a committee chairman. When the incumbent retired in 1976, Vento ran for the House and won the party endorsement at the DFL convention with union support, then won the primary and general elections easily.

In the House, Vento has an almost perfectly liberal voting record. He is the second ranking Democrat on the Banking Committee, and ranking Democrat on the subcommittee handling financial services deregulation. Vento is a strong backer of the Community Reinvestment Act and has sponsored amendments to increase its coverage; he has not always been sympathetic to repealing the Glass-Steagall Act, which prohibits banks from investing in other businesses, but he has worked on the details of bills that purport to do so. In April 1998 he urged Congress to stop bank "megamergers," for fear they will not serve community needs. He worked on the bipartisan Credit Union Membership Access Act. He worked to pass the bill that automatically cancels mortgage insurance when a buyer's equity reaches 25%. He passed an amendment prohibiting the Export-Import Bank from assisting companies that violate U.S. child labor laws.

Vento has tried twice to become the top-ranking Democrat on Banking. In December 1990 he challenged Chairman Henry B. Gonzalez and lost in the Democratic Caucus 163–89. In November 1996 the Democratic Steering Committee voted 29–12 to oust Gonzalez, and Banking Committee Democrats voted 22–19 for the more senior John LaFalce over Vento. The three squared off in the December 1996 Democratic Caucus, where the 80-year-old Gonzalez made an impassioned speech, promising to give up the post after two years. Gonzalez led with 82 votes, to 62 for LaFalce and 47 for Vento; at that point LaFalce unexpectedly quit the race and let Gonzalez win. But in 1997 Gonzalez returned to San Antonio (to come back only to vote against impeachment in December 1998), and LaFalce was named acting ranking member; in February 1998, with Gonzalez's consent, he was unanimously elected ranking member. This means that LaFalce, not Vento, will likely chair Banking if Democrats win a majority in the House.

Vento has already been a chairman, of the subcommittee on National Parks, Forests and Lands from 1985–94. This is the body which sorts through proposals for wilderness areas and national parks, national seashores, lakeshores and historic sites, wild and scenic rivers—attractive political plums for many members. Vento is a solid backer of environmental groups, favoring restrictions on logging to protect the spotted owl in the Pacific Northwest, higher grazing fees on public lands and more money for urban parks. But since the Republicans took over, he has mostly been confined to inveigh against Republican environmental riders on appropriations bills, voting against them in committee. On a Minnesota issue, he compromised with James Oberstar of the 8th District and backed two motorized portages in the Boundary Waters Canoe Area Wilderness. The creation of this park in 1978 was opposed by many locals, who were incensed when trucks were removed from the portages in 1993; Oberstar supported their return, as did Senators Paul Wellstone and Rod Grams; Vento felt they had the votes, and for his concession got them to drop their proposal for motorboats on Seagull Lake.

On other issues, Vento pushed a bill to waive the English language test for U.S. citizenship for Hmong and Laotians who served in guerrilla forces in Laos alongside U.S. soldiers. He has worked to allow development of St. Paul brownfields and got a Eugene J. McCarthy Post Office Building approved. He has opposed normal trading status with China. He has a bill to require written permission before Internet service providers can disclose a user's personal information to third parties.

In the 1990s, St. Paul has moved somewhat to the right and Vento has won re-election by less than dazzling margins. An easy winner in the 1980s, Vento slipped below 60% in 1992 and has not risen above it since. Against underfunded opponents, he won with 57% in 1992 and 55% in 1994. Against better-funded Republican Dennis Newinski, who assailed him for backing "the six largest tax hikes in history," Vento won 57%–37% in 1996, running even with Bill Clinton's showing in the district, and 54%–40% in 1998, a decline in a year in which most incumbents of both parties improved their percentages. Vento may find his way onto the Republican target lists in 2000.

Cook's Call. *Probably Safe.* This St. Paul-based district has a Democratic core, but is certainly more conservative than the neighboring Minneapolis-based 5th (St. Paul even has a Republican mayor). Vento's winning margins over the past four cycles have been less than impressive, but it will still be very hard for a Republican to dislodge this 12 term-incumbent. Once this seat opens up, it could be rather competitive.

The People: Pop. 1990: 547,061; 0.1% rural; 13.4% age 65+; 89.1% White, 4.2% Black, 4.7% Asian, 0.8% Amer. Indian, 1.2% Other; 2.5% Hispanic Origin. Households: 49.4% married couple families; 23.1% married couple fams. w. children; 54.8% college educ.; median household income: $32,287; per capita income: $15,937; median house value: $84,100; median gross rent: $423.

1996 Presidential Vote

Clinton (D)	152,555	(58%)
Dole (R)	77,704	(30%)
Perot (I)	23,566	(9%)
Others	7,688	(3%)

1992 Presidential Vote

Clinton (D)	147,266	(51%)
Bush (R)	79,137	(28%)
Perot (I)	58,850	(21%)

Rep. Bruce F. Vento (DFL)

Elected 1976; b. Oct. 7, 1940, St. Paul; home, St. Paul; U. of MN, A.A. 1961, WI St. U., B.S. 1965; Catholic; divorced.

Elected Office: MN House of Reps., 1970–76, Asst. Majority Ldr., 1974–76.

Professional Career: Teacher, 1965–76.

DC Office: 2413 RHOB 20515, 202-225-6631; Fax: 202-225-1968; Web site: www.house.gov/vento.

District Office: St. Paul, 651-224-4503.

Committees: *Banking & Financial Services* (2d of 27 D): Financial Institutions & Consumer Credit (RMM); Housing & Community Opportunity. *Resources* (3d of 24 D): Fisheries Conservation, Wildlife & Oceans; National Parks & Public Lands.

Group Ratings

	ADA	ACLU	AFS	LCV	CON	NTU	NFIB	COC	ACU	NTLC	CHC
1998	100	81	100	100	76	21	14	33	8	8	0
1997	100	—	88	—	93	34	—	40	4	—	—

National Journal Ratings

	1997 LIB	—	1997 CONS		1998 LIB	—	1998 CONS
Economic	85%	—	10%		79%	—	0%
Social	85%	—	0%		78%	—	21%
Foreign	94%	—	3%		90%	—	5%

Key Votes of the 105th Congress

1. Clinton Budget Deal	N	5. Puerto Rico Sthood. Ref.	Y	9. Cut $ for B-2 Bombers	Y
2. Education IRAs	N	6. End Highway Set-asides	N	10. Human Rights in China	Y
3. Req. 2/3 to Raise Taxes	N	7. School Prayer Amend.	N	11. Withdraw Bosnia Troops	N
4. Fast-track Trade	N	8. Ovrd. Part. Birth Veto	N	12. End Cuban TV-Marti	Y

Election Results

1998 general	Bruce F. Vento (DFL)	128,726	(54%)	($599,905)
	Dennis Newinski (R)	95,388	(40%)	($370,060)
	Others	15,632	(7%)	
1998 primary	Bruce F. Vento (DFL)	unopposed		
1996 general	Bruce F. Vento (DFL)	145,831	(57%)	($559,370)
	Dennis Newinski (R)	94,110	(37%)	($315,410)
	Others	15,818	(6%)	

FIFTH DISTRICT

From almost nowhere in Minneapolis today can you see the geographic feature that put the city here—the Falls of St. Anthony, the head of navigation on the Mississippi River, where waters rush in rapids beneath low downtown bridges. In olden days, every riverboat had to stop here, and the waterpower generated by the falls was the energy source first for pioneers' grist mills and then for the giant grain mills that processed the wheat of the northern Great Plains into food for the United States and the world. By 1890, Minneapolis and St. Paul made up one of America's largest urban areas, living mainly off grain. Today, Minneapolis is a center of high-tech industry, banking and finance. It is a regional railroad center, and the headquarters of Northwest Airlines; it is also the nerve center of an economic area that extends almost 1,000 miles west to the Rocky Mountains in Montana.

All of the city of Minneapolis, plus a few of its older suburbs directly west and south, make up the 5th District. In the southwest corner are part of the suburb of Edina and the gracefully aged Minneapolis neighborhoods around Lake Calhoun and Lake Harriet—affluent areas, long built-up and proudly maintained, not far from Minneapolis's skywalk-laced downtown skyscrapers and museum quarter up on the hill above Hennepin Avenue. But most of the 5th District is lower on the income scale. There are few blocks here as abandoned and ruined by crime as are some square miles of Chicago or Detroit. But many of the working-class neighborhoods of small frame houses on grid streets are now kept up by elderly homeowners, while new immigrants have built small communities of their own. North of the Mississippi is the University of Minnesota; to the northeast, behind the railroad and warehouse district along the Mississippi, is the home of many Hmongs from Laos. The 5th District is solidly Democratic. Minneapolis's political liberalism is drawn from the Yankee tradition of clean government, the Scandinavian tradition of cooperative enterprise and the industrial labor tradition of economic redistribution. To this has been added in recent years, by feminists and the graduate student proletariat, an antic cultural liberalism notable for its ignorance not only of any conservative heritage but of many of the liberal traditions here as well.

The congressman from the 5th District is Martin Olav Sabo, son of Norwegian immigrants, a DFL leader who has spent all his adult life in politics. He was elected to the Minnesota legislature in 1960 at age 22, was the minority leader at 30, and speaker at 34. In 1978, he was elected to the House and in his first year got a seat on the Appropriations Committee. It began as a quiet career: Sabo can be articulate, even humorous, and certainly is knowledgeable and averse to the cheap shot. But he pursued his career with a certain Scandinavian reticence and aversion to national publicity—except perhaps for his role as coach and second baseman for the Democrats in the annual House baseball game. Sabo also served on the Budget Committee, where he wrote the 1990 budget summit agreement's "firewalls" between defense and domestic spending, intended by liberals as an attempt to save domestic programs and by conservatives as a way of protecting the Pentagon. After Leon Panetta was appointed OMB director in January 1993, Sabo ran for Budget chairman, and won by 149–112 over the more moderate John Spratt of South Carolina. In that position it fell to Sabo to defend the first Clinton budget, which eventually passed by 218–216. Sabo then fought against the spending cut packages proposed by his Minnesota colleague Tim Penny and Budget ranking Republican John Kasich in late 1993 and early 1994. After Republicans won their majority in 1994, Kasich became chairman and Sabo ranking Democrat.

After the 1996 election Sabo rotated off Budget (Spratt was elected to succeed him) and concentrated more on Appropriations, where he is an ally of ranking Democrat David Obey. Sabo is ranking member on the Transportation Subcommittee, which puts him at odds with Bud Shuster, chairman of the authorizing Transportation and Infrastructure Committee, one of the great power-grabbers in the House. Sabo nevertheless came out in the April 1998 transportation bill with $37.2 million in projects for the Twin Cities, including $12 million for a transitway along Hiawatha Avenue (the direct route from downtown to the airport), $10.5 million for new buses on I-35W, $7.7 million for bus stops and other facilities on University Avenue (the direct route from downtown Minneapolis to downtown St. Paul) and $6 million for the Minnesota Guidestar: a reflection of Sabo's penchant for mass transit. He also got $15 million for noise protection at houses near the Minneapolis-St. Paul International Airport (at $28,000 per house).

On other issues Sabo pursues goals both practical and visionary. He endorsed the 1997 Blue Dog Medicare plan, partly because he believed the current formula short-changed Minnesota, which had already cut costs through HMOs. He joined then Democratic Congressional Campaign Committee Chairman Martin Frost in defending soft money in September 1997. But he has a bill, not likely to pass soon, limiting CEO pay to 25 times the pay of the lowest-paid full-time worker or taxing the corporation at a higher rate. He has another bill for public financing of House general election campaigns. He wants to guarantee Medicare benefits for divorcees and is against raising the Medicare age, as the Social Security age is scheduled to be raised, to 67. He opposes normal trade relations with China, despite the importunings of Minnesota's 3M, Honeywell and Cargill.

Sabo has been re-elected by wide margins of 2–1 or more. He once had a noisy challenge from the left, in 1992 when Lisa Niebauer-Stall kept him from winning the party endorsement at the convention until the sixth ballot; he did better with voters than DFL activists and won the primary 67%–28%. He has a solid hold on this seat.

Cook's Call. *Safe.* This Minneapolis-based seat is the most Democratic district in the state. Ten-term incumbent Martin Olav Sabo will have no trouble winning another term.

The People: Pop. 1990: 546,858; 15% age 65 + ; 84% White, 9.4% Black, 3.6% Asian, 2.4% Amer. Indian, 0.7% Other; 1.6% Hispanic Origin. Households: 38.8% married couple families; 16% married couple fams. w. children; 58.4% college educ.; median household income: $28,880; per capita income: $16,099; median house value: $80,100; median gross rent: $414.

1996 Presidential Vote			1992 Presidential Vote		
Clinton (D)	159,018	(62%)	Clinton (D)	167,941	(58%)
Dole (R)	62,507	(25%)	Bush (R)	68,072	(23%)
Perot (I)	20,499	(8%)	Perot (I)	52,374	(18%)
Others	12,636	(5%)			

Rep. Martin Olav Sabo (DFL)

Elected 1978; b. Feb. 28, 1938, Crosby, ND; home, Minneapolis; Augsburg Col., B.A. 1959; Lutheran; married (Sylvia).

Elected Office: MN House of Reps., 1961–78, Minority Ldr., 1969–73, Speaker, 1973–78.

DC Office: 2336 RHOB 20515, 202-225-4755; Fax: 202-225-4886; Web site: www.house.gov/sabo.

District Office: Minneapolis, 612-664-8000.

Committees: *Appropriations* (4th of 27 D): Defense; Foreign Operations & Export Financing; Transportation (RMM). *Standards of Official Conduct* (2d of 5 D).

Group Ratings

	ADA	ACLU	AFS	LCV	CON	NTU	NFIB	COC	ACU	NTLC	CHC
1998	90	94	100	100	78	24	14	24	0	5	0
1997	100	—	88	—	62	32	—	30	4	—	—

National Journal Ratings

	1997 LIB — 1997 CONS			1998 LIB — 1998 CONS		
Economic	85%	—	10%	79%	—	0%
Social	85%	—	0%	78%	—	21%
Foreign	90%	—	8%	90%	—	5%

Key Votes of the 105th Congress

1. Clinton Budget Deal	N	5. Puerto Rico Sthood. Ref.	Y	9. Cut $ for B-2 Bombers	Y
2. Education IRAs	N	6. End Highway Set-asides	N	10. Human Rights in China	Y
3. Req. 2/3 to Raise Taxes	N	7. School Prayer Amend.	N	11. Withdraw Bosnia Troops	N
4. Fast-track Trade	N	8. Ovrd. Part. Birth Veto	N	12. End Cuban TV-Marti	Y

Election Results

1998 general	Martin Olav Sabo (DFL) 145,535	(67%)	($414,554)
	Frank Taylor (R) 60,035	(28%)	($14,788)
	Others 12,042	(6%)	
1998 primary	Martin Olav Sabo (DFL) .... unopposed		
1996 general	Martin Olav Sabo (DFL) 158,272	(64%)	($515,970)
	Jack Uldrich (R) 70,115	(29%)	($66,821)
	Erika Anderson (GRT) 13,102	(5%)	
	Others 4,569	(2%)	

SIXTH DISTRICT

The earliest settlers to the Twin Cities of Minneapolis and St. Paul came up the Mississippi River, or up the rail lines which were soon built on the bottomlands beside. They lived within walking distance of the mills and factories and railyards; as first streetcars and then automobiles allowed them to live farther from work, they spread out in St. Paul and Minneapolis and then over the lake-strewn countryside all around. The flatlands are bleak here when the winter sun struggles to shine through gray clouds. The lakes are often surrounded by, sometimes indistinguishable from, swamps. The old lumber mill towns which pioneers built, like Stillwater on the St. Croix, were for years economic backwaters, their antique structures ill-tended. But the creativity and productivity of Minnesotans have turned this not especially attractive environment into some of the most pleasant suburbs in the world. They have taken maximum advantage of their lakes and have refurbished old towns and farmhouses and have built comfortable homes in new subdivisions. Here live today's typical American families. Busy at home and at the workplace, communicating with each other by Post-it notes (invented at St. Paul's 3M), exhausted at the end of each day, winning through their efforts a material standard of living that would have dazzled their grandparents but at a price that might well have appalled them.

The 6th Congressional District includes much of the Twin Cities metropolitan area, suburbs and townships north, east and south of St. Paul and Minneapolis. To the northwest, the Anoka County suburbs along the Mississippi River have attracted blue collar families. Incomes are below the high metro average, and politically this has long been a DFL area. Stillwater, facing Wisconsin on hills above the St. Croix River, with Victorian buildings from its days as a lumber port when it nearly became Minnesota's capital, and surrounding Washington County have attracted a mix of people and are politically marginal. South of St. Paul, the Dakota County towns along the Mississippi are blue collar and DFL; the newer, fast-growing Eagan and Apple Valley to the southwest are quite affluent and tend to vote Republican. Altogether, this is perhaps Minnesota's most volatile district. And never more so than in 1998, for it was in the 6th District, more than any other, that former professional wrestler Jesse Ventura, running as the Reform Party candidate, was elected governor of Minnesota. Ventura's home town is just across the Mississippi River west of Anoka, and he clearly appealed to the hard-working young families of these suburbs. Turnout in the 6th District was up 31% from 1994, and was even up 1% over the presidential year of 1996. Ventura carried the district solidly, with 44% of the vote, to 34% for Democrat-turned-Republican Norm Coleman, the mayor of St. Paul, and only 21% for the DFL nominee, Skip Humphrey, the attorney general who produced Minnesota's huge tobacco settlement. The DFL was reduced to its left-wing core, the Republicans did not do much better than their 1990s presidential nominees, and Ventura not only carried the vote but carried new voters to the polls.

The congressman from the 6th District is Bill Luther, a Democrat elected in 1994. He grew up near Fergus Falls on a dairy farm owned by his family since 1882, went to college and law school at the University of Michigan, then was elected to the state House in 1974 at 29, and to the state Senate in 1976; his wife has been a member of the state House since 1992. He ran once before for Congress, in 1982, and lost the DFL endorsement to fellow legislator Gerry

Sikorski, whose 697 overdrafts on the House bank ended his career in 1992. The seat was then won by Republican newscaster Rod Grams; when the district lines were altered for 1994, making it less Republican, Grams ran for the Senate and won. In his 20 years in the legislature, Luther worked hard, kept a low profile, developed shrewd strategies and was strongly partisan. He was assistant majority leader in the state Senate, wrote the state's campaign finance laws, promoted an anti-drug initiative for children. He had been eyeing the 6th District since Grams won it, and when the boundaries changed he moved his residence from Brooklyn Park (of which Jesse Ventura was then mayor) to Stillwater. His Republican opponent, Tad Jude, was another career politician with a residence outside the new district lines. Jude was elected to the state House as a DFLer in 1972, at 20, ran for the 6th District as a pro-lifer and lost the DFL endorsement in 1980, was elected to the state Senate in 1982, then lost the 1992 congressional primary to Sikorski 49%–46%. The Luther-Jude matchup was an expensive and fierce campaign: Luther spent $1.1 million and Jude $699,000. Luther painted Jude as an extremist on abortion; Jude attacked Luther for voting against longer sentences for violent rapists and criminals who attacked seniors. Luther won by 550 votes, carrying Washington and Anoka counties and losing Dakota.

In the House, Luther has a moderate record on economics and is more liberal on cultural and foreign issues. He supported the Blue Dog budget in 1996 and was a co-founder of the New Democrat Coalition in 1997. The latter year, he was rated number two in the House by Taxpayers for Common Sense, which tends to give Democrats higher ratings than Republicans, and number one among Democrats by the National Taxpayers Union, which tends to give Republicans higher ratings; NTU noted that bills he sponsored would reduce federal spending by $23 billion. With Jim Ramstad, he successfully moved to cut $65 million from the Trident D-5 submarine-launched missile program, and with Jack Metcalf and Todd Tiahrt, he moved successfully to deny the Cost of Living Adjustment to members of Congress. He voted against fast track and school vouchers, for welfare reform in 1996 and the balanced budget agreement in 1997; he opposed the omnibus budget in 1998. Prompted by a letter from 14-year-old Alicia Sarrazin of Hastings, he sponsored a resolution to urge Hollywood to stop portraying cigarette smoking as glamorous; he sponsored another to make the export and advertising of tobacco products abroad subject to U.S. restrictions.

Luther has also worked the district hard, holding more than 145 "listening sessions." Although not on the Transportation Committee, he got involved in transportation projects. In 1997 he worked with other Twin Cities area members of both parties to back the 610–10 North Metro Crosstown corridor and a number of "Transitways" connecting the downtowns of Minneapolis and St. Paul with the airport, the Mall of America and the Northtown transit hub, plus a plan for bike trails and commuter trains paralleling U.S. 10 through Anoka County to St. Cloud. The 1998 transportation bill included $14.2 million for reconstructing the I-494 Wakota Bridge southeast of St. Paul and also preliminary design and engineering for the Red Rock rail line from St. Paul to Hastings. He attempted to break the great impasse between transportation plans and the riverway protections of the Wild and Scenic Rivers Act; he successfully opposed exempting it from the latter, but urged all parties to get together and negotiate a solution—not forthcoming yet in early 1999.

Luther is a critic of the federal campaign finance laws and an admirer of the Minnesota laws, which he helped write, which limit total spending; but he is also a prodigious fundraiser, able and willing to raise more than $1 million each cycle under the federal rules he dislikes. In 1996, again facing Tad Jude, he raised $1.3 million and spent $851,000, more than twice as much as the Republican. Luther won 56%–44%, running well ahead of Bill Clinton. In 1998 he was expected to face state Senator Linda Runbeck, who raised $204,000 in 1997. But she was upset in the Republican endorsement convention in May 1998, by John Kline, who went door-to-door to contact all 309 delegates while she toiled in the Capitol in St. Paul. Kline is a retired Marine colonel, who served in Vietnam and Somalia and who was one of the military aides holding the nuclear "football" for Presidents Carter and Reagan. Kline campaigned for tax cuts and against abortion, for more military spending and the resignation of Bill Clinton. He spent only $278,000 in all; but Luther, who raised $1.1 million in the cycle, spent only $412,000. That may have been a mistake. In a turnout swelled with new voters supporting Jesse Ventura, Republicans did well in these suburban counties, electing Republican legislators who helped their party win control of the state House. Luther won by only 50%–46%, winning Anoka County 52%–43% and Washington 50%–46%, while losing Dakota 50%–46%.

Before the election, Luther was thinking about challenging Rod Grams in 2000, and he had $1.3 million cash on hand after the campaign. After, he finally won the Commerce Committee seat he had been seeking for four years, and announced in December 1998 that he wouldn't run for the Senate after all. His anemic 1998 showing, in a year when most incumbents improved their percentages, makes him an obvious target for Republicans in 2000. But the fact that he had more than $1 million on hand, a seat on Commerce from which it will be easy to raise even more, plus his capacity for hard work, suggests he will not be an easy mark.

Cook's Call. *Potentially Competitive.* If Luther learned any lesson from his brush with defeat in 1998, it was that he cannot afford to take any challenge lightly in this very marginal district. As one of the best fundraisers in the House, Luther is not an easy target. But, a down turn for Democrats on the national level could be felt in this swing seat.

The People: Pop. 1990: 546,807; 10.7% rural; 5.5% age 65 + ; 96.9% White, 0.9% Black, 1.3% Asian, 0.5% Amer. Indian, 0.3% Other; 1% Hispanic Origin. Households: 67.2% married couple families; 39.4% married couple fams. w. children; 54.5% college educ.; median household income: $42,161; per capita income: $15,922; median house value: $89,500; median gross rent: $473.

1996 Presidential Vote

Clinton (D)	154,333	(51%)
Dole (R)	107,560	(35%)
Perot (I)	37,111	(12%)
Others	5,201	(2%)

1992 Presidential Vote

Clinton (D)	120,759	(39%)
Bush (R)	102,265	(33%)
Perot (I)	82,587	(27%)

Rep. William P. (Bill) Luther (DFL)

Elected 1994; b. June 27, 1945, Fergus Falls; home, Stillwater; U. of MN, B.S. 1967, J.D. 1970; Catholic; married (Darlene).

Elected Office: MN House of Reps., 1974–76; MN Senate, 1976–94.

Professional Career: Clerk, 8th Circuit U.S. Court of Appeals, 1970–71; Practicing atty., 1971–92.

DC Office: 117 CHOB 20515, 202-225-2271; Fax: 202-225-3368; Web site: www.house.gov/luther.

District Office: Woodbury, 651-730-4949.

Committees: *Commerce* (23d of 24 D): Finance & Hazardous Materials; Telecommunications, Trade & Consumer Protection.

Group Ratings

	ADA	ACLU	AFS	LCV	CON	NTU	NFIB	COC	ACU	NTLC	CHC
1998	90	69	100	85	99	27	21	56	4	13	8
1997	85	—	63	—	99	49	—	60	24	—	—

National Journal Ratings

	1997 LIB — 1997 CONS			1998 LIB — 1998 CONS		
Economic	62%	—	37%	61%	—	37%
Social	71%	—	29%	77%	—	23%
Foreign	82%	—	16%	84%	—	11%

Key Votes of the 105th Congress

1. Clinton Budget Deal	N	5. Puerto Rico Sthood. Ref.	*	9. Cut $ for B-2 Bombers	Y
2. Education IRAs	N	6. End Highway Set-asides	N	10. Human Rights in China	Y
3. Req. 2/3 to Raise Taxes	N	7. School Prayer Amend.	N	11. Withdraw Bosnia Troops	N
4. Fast-track Trade	N	8. Ovrd. Part. Birth Veto	N	12. End Cuban TV-Marti	Y

Election Results

1998 general	William P. (Bill) Luther (DFL) 148,728	(50%)	($412,541)
	John Kline (R) 136,866	(46%)	($283,348)
	Others 12,107	(4%)	
1998 primary	William P. (Bill) Luther (DFL) .... unopposed		
1996 general	William P. (Bill) Luther (DFL) 164,921	(56%)	($850,638)
	Tad Jude (R) 129,989	(44%)	($392,953)

SEVENTH DISTRICT

The lake-strewn country along the upper stretches of the Mississippi River, settled by Norwegian and German immigrants, is the source of some prime American literary and political traditions. Here a century ago in the town of Sauk Centre grew up Sinclair Lewis, whose *Main Street* and *Babbitt* were greeted as the definitive satires of small-town life, though on rereading they show surprising affection for their subjects. Not far north of Sauk Centre is Little Falls, the boyhood home of Charles Lindbergh, whose father was a progressive and isolationist congressman who opposed declaring war on Germany in 1917. In those years this seemingly placid country was seething with rage, as WASPy nationalists banned German from schools, renamed sauerkraut liberty cabbage, and boycotted German-American businesses. The rage simmered and became the source of the bitter isolationism of the 1930s and 1940s, of which Lindbergh was a national leader, and of the bitter anti-Communism of the 1950s. This part of Minnesota is probably also the home—though the actual location has somehow disappeared from the map—of Garrison Keillor's Lake Wobegon, whose history has an authentic ring: founded by New England Yankees as New Albion in 1852, renamed when Norwegians got a majority on the council in 1880, where the Norwegian flag still flies on holidays but where no one has seen a German flag fly since 1917.

The 7th Congressional District, covering the northwest corner of Minnesota, includes just about all this territory. It takes in the wheat-farming plains up near North Dakota and the German Catholic country, strewn with farm villages named for saints, around Sauk Centre and St. Cloud. There are many political traditions here: Some wheat counties are heavily DFL; heavily Norwegian Otter Tail County leans Republican; St. Cloud and Stearns County are volatile, dovish and anti-abortion. The 7th's political history reads like something out of *Lake Wobegon Days*. Back in 1958, Congresswoman Coya Knutson lost re-election when her husband Andy issued a plaintive statement urging her to come home and make his breakfast again; she was the only incumbent Democrat to lose in heavily Democratic 1958. Other Scandinavian names followed: Odin Langen, Bob Bergland (later Jimmy Carter's secretary of Agriculture) Arlan Stangeland. None except Bergland won by any great margin. For most of the last 40 years this has been one of America's prime marginal districts.

The congressman from the 7th District today is Collin Peterson, who has run for this seat nine times and won five times, and has convincingly removed the 7th from the marginal column. Peterson grew up here, went to Moorhead State College across the Red River of the North from Fargo, North Dakota, then started a CPA office in Detroit Lakes. In 1976 he was elected to the state Senate, where he served 10 years, passing a 16% farm property tax reduction in 1985 and starting the Chickadee Checkoff, which raises $900,000 a year for a non-game wildlife fund. He also started running for the House. He lost a DFL caucus in 1982; he lost to Stangeland in 1984 and 1986 (by only 121 votes the second time; he declared victory and went to Washington to set up an office); he lost the DFL primary again in 1988. But in 1990, when the *St. Cloud Times* reported that Stangeland made 341 credit card calls to a woman not his wife, Peterson won with a robust 54%. In office, he continued to do things his way, wearing cowboy boots and playing guitar in a country rock band called the Recess Renegades, acting as his own press secretary, campaign consultant and pilot on flights within the district. He has a small staff, with community economic development professionals rather than Washington policy wonks. He opposes abortion and gun control, backs farm subsidies and labor unions, and opposed the 1993 Clinton budget and NAFTA.

Peterson's political fortune has been made by the event that ruined the fortunes of so many Democrats, the Republican victory of 1994, which has made him a nationally important figure in the House and a visibly different kind of Democrat in the 7th District. In February 1995, while voting for some parts of the Contract with America, Peterson and Gary Condit founded the Blue Dog Democrats for "common sense legislation that embraces the ideas and values of mainstream America." He helped produce Blue Dog budgets which, though not passing, provided a road map to the 1997 balanced budget agreement. Peterson is the opposite of many middle-of-the-House Republicans, who favor market economics and heavy environmental restrictions; he takes the view of his constituents, who hunt and fish in great numbers and sees environmentalists' policies as hindrances. Peterson once said, presumably with a sigh, "City people have no understanding of the rural way of life. Still, they always come up there and try to tell us how to live." He is co-chairman of the Congressional Sportsmen's Caucus and wants to require that federal lands be open to hunting and fishing except when there is a good reason not to (as in national parks).

In March 1998, Peterson attracted attention when he proposed a constitutional amendment to allow residents of Minnesota's Northwest Angle to secede from the United States and join Canada. The 120-square-mile Northwest Angle is the swampy land across Lake of the Woods, the northernmost point of the continental 48 states, included in Minnesota because Benjamin Franklin and John Jay, negotiating the Treaty of Paris in 1783, were ignorant of local geography; Peterson's ire was aroused because Ontario authorities were not allowing Americans to keep their catch of walleye unless they stayed in Canadian resorts. But Peterson didn't tell the Red Lake Band of Chippewas, who own the Northwest Angle, or then-Governor Arne Carlson of his amendment; he apologized to Tribal Chairman Bobby Whitefeather and assured Carlson and others that he was only trying to draw attention to the Canadians' unfairness, and indeed Ontario officials did agree to discuss the issue.

This was not the only example of border trouble in the area. In 1998, Minnesota farmers dumped wheat and attempted to blockade the border, charging that under NAFTA, Canadian-subsidized wheat had an unfair advantage over U.S. wheat. Five years of wet weather and plummeting world wheat prices have marginalized the value of farm property in northwest Minnesota, and Peterson has struggled to respond. The Red River floods that devastated Grand Forks, North Dakota, also affected the east bank of the river in Minnesota; Peterson pushed for federal aid, and in July 1997 Speaker Newt Gingrich included his amendment for greater local reimbursement into the balanced budget act. As for wheat prices, Peterson had expressed reservations about the 1996 Freedom to Farm Act and predicted low prices. "Farmers are going to be in Washington asking for help. And we'll help them. We always do." Not exactly, it turned out. In summer 1998 he pushed for raising the commodity loan rate, but it lost in the Senate. He worked to persuade Agriculture Secretary Dan Glickman to let farmers buy more crop insurance, and to allow scab-infested land to be put in the Conservation Reserve Program for 10 years. But the number of farmers in northwest Minnesota seems to be continuing its historic decline, as commodity prices continue their historic trend downward. "I don't know how to fix it. We're in a box. The world is awash in wheat. There's too much barley. Commodity prices show it," Peterson admitted. "I'm tired of going to meetings and hearing grown men cry because they have lost what they have worked a lifetime for, and I have no answers."

Peterson's politics have been a smash hit with 7th District voters and an irritant to local DFL activists. In 1992 and 1994, he beat a young Republican legislator from Stearns County 51%–49% each time. In 1996, against the communications director of the Minnesota Family Council, he won 68%–32%, carrying every county: a stirring endorsement of his independent course. At the May 1998 DFL convention, he was opposed by a former staffer he had fired, and led on the first ballot by only 52%–40%, short of the 60% needed for endorsement; he won 73% on the second ballot. But in November Peterson won 72%–28%. Stearns County, fast-growing and supposedly out of joint because Peterson spent so much time on the floods and farmers in the northwest, voted for him 68%–32%. In January 1999, Peterson was mentioned as a candidate for state natural resources director and had an interview with Governor Jesse Ventura. But "I did not get the vibes I would have needed to even consider" the job: Not all mavericks are alike. He is considering challenging Senator Rod Grams in 2000.

Cook's Call. *Probably Safe.* After some very close races in the early 1990s, the fact that Peterson had only nominal opposition in 1998 is a pretty good sign that he has solidified himself in this conservative swing district. If Peterson decides to challenge Rod Grams, this very marginal district will be heavily contested in 2000.

The People: Pop. 1990: 547,011; 62.4% rural; 15.7% age 65 + ; 96.8% White, 0.2% Black, 0.4% Asian, 2.3% Amer. Indian, 0.3% Other; 0.7% Hispanic Origin. Households: 60.4% married couple families; 30% married couple fams. w. children; 40% college educ.; median household income: $23,146; per capita income: $10,341; median house value: $50,900; median gross rent: $267.

1996 Presidential Vote			1992 Presidential Vote		
Clinton (D)	115,996	(45%)	Clinton (D)	104,359	(38%)
Dole (R)	103,336	(40%)	Bush (R)	103,624	(38%)
Perot (I)	33,577	(13%)	Perot (I)	63,610	(23%)
Others	4,079	(2%)			

Rep. Collin C. Peterson (DFL)

Elected 1990; b. June 29, 1944, Fargo, ND; home, Detroit Lakes; Moorhead St. U., B.A. 1966; Lutheran; divorced.

Military Career: Army Natl. Guard, 1963–69.

Elected Office: MN Senate, 1976–86.

Professional Career: Accountant, 1966–90.

DC Office: 2159 RHOB 20515, 202-225-2165; Fax: 202-225-1593; Web site: www.house.gov/collinpeterson.

District Offices: Detroit Lakes, 218-847-5056; Red Lake Falls, 218-253-4356; Waite Park, 320-259-0559.

Committees: *Agriculture* (4th of 24 D): Livestock & Horticulture (RMM). *Veterans' Affairs* (6th of 14 D): Health.

Group Ratings

	ADA	ACLU	AFS	LCV	CON	NTU	NFIB	COC	ACU	NTLC	CHC
1998	60	25	89	23	94	28	71	56	56	37	58
1997	65	—	63	—	76	44	—	70	52	—	—

National Journal Ratings

	1997 LIB — 1997 CONS			1998 LIB — 1998 CONS		
Economic	54%	—	45%	56%	—	44%
Social	48%	—	51%	42%	—	57%
Foreign	49%	—	49%	47%	—	51%

Key Votes of the 105th Congress

1. Clinton Budget Deal	N	5. Puerto Rico Sthood. Ref.	N	9. Cut $ for B-2 Bombers	Y
2. Education IRAs	N	6. End Highway Set-asides	N	10. Human Rights in China	N
3. Req. 2/3 to Raise Taxes	N	7. School Prayer Amend.	Y	11. Withdraw Bosnia Troops	Y
4. Fast-track Trade	N	8. Ovrd. Part. Birth Veto	Y	12. End Cuban TV-Marti	Y

Election Results

1998 general	Collin C. Peterson (DFL)	169,907	(72%)	($271,794)
	Aleta Edin (R)	66,562	(28%)	($35,751)
1998 primary	Collin C. Peterson (DFL)	unopposed		
1996 general	Collin C. Peterson (DFL)	170,936	(68%)	($532,229)
	Darrell McKigney (R)	80,132	(32%)	($181,026)

EIGHTH DISTRICT

In the 1860s, prospectors in the Arrowhead region of the new state of Minnesota, northwest of Lake Superior in the low hills of the Mesabi Range, happened upon the nation's largest veins of iron ore; they moved on, looking for gold. But in the 1880s, Duluth banker George Stone and Philadelphia financier Charlemagne Tower started mining the Iron Range and created the northern end of the lifeline of American heavy industry. The range runs south alongside rail lines to the port of Duluth nestled on dramatic bluffs over the always cold and, every winter, frozen waters of Lake Superior—one of the most beautiful settings for a city in North America. Duluth was a grain-shipping rival of Chicago and the premier iron-ore port. Its city plan was drawn up by Daniel Burnham and its splendid turn-of-the-century buildings still celebrate the triumph of technology and civilization over wilderness and the elements. Millions of tons of ore have been dug out of the Range, loaded into rail cars for the ride to Duluth, and into Great Lakes freighters for shipment to Cleveland, Gary, Detroit, Chicago, Pittsburgh and Buffalo.

For most of this century, in this land where the Arctic winds blow down over the Canadian Shield's thousands of inland lakes, about 100,000 people have lived on the Iron Range and another 100,000 in Duluth, most of them the products of America's 1880–1924 wave of immigration—Italians, Poles, Serbs and Croats, Jews, Swedes and Finns. In this punishing environment, they worked to the point of exhaustion, built solid houses with staunch central heating, and wore layers of warm clothing to survive the winter. Life was rough: The work was hard, the hours long, and the pay low. The churches, a separate one for each ethnic group, were the main community institutions. Living conditions improved vastly in the decades of great economic growth after World War II, but life remains rough-hewn today, and there is still economic distress. As iron mines and steel factories got more efficient, they needed fewer workers; employment is still well below its 1970s peak. As water fills abandoned open-pit mines and factories close, the Iron Range looks bleaker. But all is not moribund. Northwest Airlines, with an $840 million investment from state government in 1993, has built a repair facility in Duluth and a reservations center in the Iron Range. Fiber-optic cable is being laid all over the Range. And though steel prices fell sharply with imports in 1998, the port of Duluth had a fine year shipping grain, and Minnesota Iron & Steel prepared to build a $1.3 billion taconite and steelmaking factory on the Range that will employ 1,000 workers—the first big new plant in more than 20 years.

The 8th Congressional District includes Duluth and the Iron Range, plus much of the north woods and lake country to the west and south; it moves all the way south to the boundaries of the Twin Cities metro area, to Isanti and Chisago counties where young families are building new homes near pleasant old lakeside towns. This district has been the bulwark of Minnesota's Democratic-Farmer-Labor Party since it was formed in 1944, and is ordinarily safe Democratic today; but with big turnout increases in the southern counties, which are in the Twin Cities media market, Jesse Ventura actually carried the 8th in 1998, with 34% of the vote to 33% for the DFL's Skip Humphrey and 32% for Republican Norm Coleman.

The congressman from the 8th District is Jim Oberstar, a Democrat first elected in 1974—"part scholar and part Iron Range street fighter, part pothole-filling ward healer and part work-aholic," as the *St. Paul Pioneer Press* called him. Oberstar grew up in Chisholm in the Iron Range, where his father was an iron miner and union official, who sent him off to St. Thomas College with $2,500 saved in quarters at the Slovenian National Benefit Society. He studied French there and in Belgium; for four years he was a civilian employee of the U.S. Naval Mission to Haiti, teaching French and Creole to Marines, and French and English to Haitians (he also speaks Serbo-Croatian, Italian and Spanish). Then, in 1963, at 29, he landed a job as chief of staff to Congressman John Blatnik in Washington: He has been working for the 8th District for going on four decades. When Blatnik retired in 1974, Oberstar won the seat, by winning a primary over Tony Perpich, brother of Governor Rudy Perpich. He won tough primaries in 1980 and 1984, the latter after briefly running for the Senate. His views are in the liberal Catholic tradition: "I believe you will be measured by how you respond to the neediest among you," he says. He believes in an economically active government and has little faith in economic markets. He was long dubious about American military involvement abroad, espe-cially in Central America, but favored the 1994 deployment in Haiti. He is an opponent of abortion and a backer of adoption, sponsoring bills to insure family and medical leave and dependent deductions for families in the process of adopting. With Henry Hyde, he sponsored a bill to ban the use of drugs in assisted suicides.

From this North Country district, Oberstar has been a supporter of local hunting and fishing activities and of the steel industry. He proposed making the Boundary Waters Canoe Area Wilderness—a raging issue in these parts—and after a 1993 ruling outlawed motorized portage (using trucks to take boats between lakes) he pushed to reinstate it. In a 1998 compromise with St. Paul's Bruce Vento he got motorized portages restored at the Moose Lake-Basswood portage and between Vermilion and Trout lakes; in return, he acceded to a ban on motorboats in Seagull Lake and two smaller lakes. On steel, he favored retaliation against what he considered dumping by Russia and East Asian countries in 1998. When Treasury Secretary Robert Rubin proposed a tax break as the administration's answer in January 1999, Oberstar wrote Bill Clinton thusly: "Your response is, 'Here's $300 million, go play in traffic,' and that's an outrage. It shows that your vaunted Mr. Rubin doesn't understand a damned thing about jobs in the real world."

Since October 1995 Oberstar has been ranking Democrat on Transportation and Infrastruc-ture—a position of real power, even in a Republican Congress. This committee (Public Works) has a long tradition of bipartisanship, and of sponsoring members' roads (and, since 1994, other transportation) projects; it has 75 members, the largest in the House, and Chairman Bud Shuster and Oberstar have worked to make it more powerful than ever. Their great monument was the May 1998 transportation bill, with $217 billion in spending, including $10 billion in projects earmarked by members. This came just a year after the Republican leadership managed to stop, by only 216–214, Shuster's and Oberstar's attempt to take transportation spending off budget; and they had to break through projected budget limits to win. Earmarking was done by formula: Committee members received $40 million for specific projects in their districts, with more for high-seniority members; other members of the House received $15 million. Shuster, Oberstar, and the chairman and ranking member of the Surface Transportation Subcommittee, Tom Petri and Nick Rahall, each can veto anyone's earmark. Back when Oberstar's boss John Blatnik was chairman, the committee's power was threatened by an alliance of environmentalists and fiscal conservatives; by 1998 it was carrying all before it. Another reason: the 1991 ISTEA, of which 1998's TEA-21 was the reauthorization, included spending for mass transit, bicycle trails and pollution control research, at the option of states or House members. This has helped win the support of many liberals; Oberstar himself is a bicycling enthusiast, proud of logging 2,000 miles a year in Washington, Duluth, on the Range and in the Tour de Frog in St. Cloud. The 8th District got some $80 million from the 1998 bill, including a bridge overpass on U.S. 53 between Virginia and Cook where seven people died in an accident, and improvements on U.S. 8 in Chisago County where 57 have died during the last 15 years.

Oberstar once chaired Transportation's Aviation Subcommittee and remains involved in aviation issues. He worked hard for the state investment in Northwest Airlines, but in recent years has criticized the company harshly, opposing presidential intervention in the summer 1998 pilots' strike and criticizing Northwest for opposing regulations intended to help small startup airlines. As if in response to pressure, the airline instituted jet service from its Detroit hub to Duluth in October 1998. In 1999, Oberstar and Shuster once again pressed to take the airport trust fund off-budget.

Oberstar's one political setback came in 1984, when he ran for the Senate but was denied endorsement by the liberal DFL convention. In the 8th District he has been re-elected by very wide margins. He won 66%–26% in 1998, almost double the percentage of his party's governor candidate.

Cook's Call. *Safe.* Not quite as Democratic as the Minneapolis-St. Paul districts, this rural Iron Range district still has deep DFL roots and has elected Oberstar to Congress without much fanfare for the last 24 years. Don't look for that to change in 2000.

The People: Pop. 1990: 546,795; 59.7% rural; 16.2% age 65 + ; 97% White, 0.4% Black, 0.4% Asian, 2.1% Amer. Indian, 0.2% Other; 0.5% Hispanic Origin. Households: 59.7% married couple families; 28.2% married couple fams. w. children; 39.4% college educ.; median household income: $24,472; per capita income: $11,279; median house value: $49,000; median gross rent: $256.

1996 Presidential Vote			1992 Presidential Vote		
Clinton (D)	148,886	(53%)	Clinton (D)	138,426	(48%)
Dole (R)	88,095	(31%)	Bush (R)	80,517	(28%)
Perot (I)	38,405	(14%)	Perot (I)	70,539	(24%)
Others	6,147	(2%)			

Rep. James L. Oberstar (DFL)

Elected 1974; b. Sept. 10, 1934, Chisholm; home, Chisholm; St. Thomas Col., B.A. 1956, Col. of Europe, Bruges, Belgium, M.A. 1957; Catholic; married (Jean).

Professional Career: Navy civilian language teacher, Haiti, 1959–63; A.A., U.S. Rep. John Blatnik, 1963–74; A.A., U.S. House Public Works Cmte., 1971–74.

DC Office: 2365 RHOB 20515, 202-225-6211; Fax: 202-225-0699; Web site: www.house.gov/oberstar.

District Offices: Brainerd, 218-828-4400; Chisholm, 218-254-5761; Duluth, 218-727-7474; Elk River, 612-241-0188; Fojo, 218-723-8813.

Committees: *Transportation & Infrastructure* (RMM of 34 D).

Group Ratings

	ADA	ACLU	AFS	LCV	CON	NTU	NFIB	COC	ACU	NTLC	CHC
1998	95	87	100	69	55	19	0	24	13	18	36
1997	80	—	100	—	1	18	—	40	17	—	—

National Journal Ratings

	1997 LIB — 1997 CONS			1998 LIB — 1998 CONS		
Economic	90%	—	9%	79%	—	0%
Social	61%	—	39%	65%	—	35%
Foreign	93%	—	6%	96%	—	2%

Key Votes of the 105th Congress

1. Clinton Budget Deal	N	5. Puerto Rico Sthood. Ref.	Y	9. Cut $ for B-2 Bombers	Y
2. Education IRAs	N	6. End Highway Set-asides	N	10. Human Rights in China	Y
3. Req. 2/3 to Raise Taxes	N	7. School Prayer Amend.	N	11. Withdraw Bosnia Troops	N
4. Fast-track Trade	N	8. Ovrd. Part. Birth Veto	Y	12. End Cuban TV-Marti	Y

Election Results

1998 general	James L. Oberstar (DFL)	173,734	(66%)	($696,670)
	Jerry Shuster (R)	69,667	(26%)	($7,616)
	Stan (The Man) Estes (Ref)	15,137	(6%)	($3,588)
	Others	4,725	(2%)	
1998 primary	James L. Oberstar (DFL)	unopposed		
1996 general	James L. Oberstar (DFL)	185,333	(67%)	($538,159)
	Andy Larson (R)	69,460	(25%)	($26,951)
	Stan (The Man) Estes (Ref)	16,639	(6%)	

MISSISSIPPI

Mississippi carries the weight of a tragic history as it takes hurried steps toward the future. This green land was settled in a rush in Jacksonian America, mostly by small farmers heading west from Georgia and south from Tennessee—and also by a small number of big planters, who made vast gains and great losses, built grand mansions and sent their sons to fight in the Civil War. For a century afterward, even as industrial farmers drained the Delta lands, Mississippi with its racial segregation, subsistence farmers and sharecroppers and low wages, lived apart from most of America. Faulkner's Mississippi never knew the Homestead Act, the giant factories, the rushes of immigration, the rise of suburbs that are the indispensable backdrop of most of 20th Century American life. Mississippi never developed great cities—its two commercial metropolises are Memphis and New Orleans. But if it did not excel at commerce, it did produce great art. Mississippi gave us the music of the blues and Elvis Presley. It gave the world William Faulkner and Eudora Welty, Walker Percy and Shelby Foote. Their work was informed by a sense of the tragic missing or forgotten in most of America, where life is a triumphant sales pitch or a labor-saving invention. As Anthony Walton, born in Illinois to Mississippi-born parents, put it, "In Mississippi I have learned to stop trying to evade and forget what I have seen and heard and understood and now must know, but rather to embrace the ghosts and cradle the bones and call them my own."

Mississippi has made much progress in the last three decades, but the past still hangs heavy. For years no other state had such a painful contrast between image and reality, between an ideal sincerely strived for and the tawdry facts of everyday life. Magnolia trees on the lawns of antebellum mansions, golden-haired young women in white dresses on the veranda, faithful black servants and retainers: this was once the ideal. And behind it stood loose-jointed frame houses and unpainted back-country stores, cabins without indoor plumbing and poor white crossroads clustered with askew advertising signs. This is a state, writes David Sansing, with "two souls, two hearts, two minds. We have the highest rate of illiteracy and the largest number of Pulitzer Prize winners in literature. We at one time have the scent of magnolias and the smell of burning crosses." Mississippi for years ranked 50th, and a very low 50th, among states in income, literacy, health and education levels, despite the best efforts of civic, political and business leaders. As William Faulkner said of his state, "You don't love because: you love despite."

Today Mississippi still ranks 50th on many scales; it is the poorest state with more than one in five people living in poverty. But the gulf between Mississippi and the rest of America has narrowed enormously in the last half-century. In 1940, Mississippi had an economy based on low-wage, subsistence or sharecropper agriculture and a system of racial segregation enforced often by violence. If history is, as Frederic Maitland wrote, the story of the progress from status to contract, then old Mississippi was still at the beginning, for status—race—meant just about everything. In the years since, Mississippi has moved, not always willingly, from status to contract, in its economy and in race relations. Per capita income in Mississippi was 36% of the national average in 1940; in 1995, it was 73%, well below average but, given the lower cost of living here, a level recognizably American. Mississippi is even home to a giant corporation, WorldCom, which bought MCI in 1997. Daily life, thanks to cheap gas and air conditioning, national brands and the mechanization of farming, has changed drastically: Most Mississippians of 50 years ago would be astonished by the physical comforts and mechanical marvels their grandchildren take for granted today. They would be astonished as well by relations between blacks and whites. As *The Washington Post's* William Raspberry, a Mississippi native, wrote, "There is an easiness to relationships, a mutual respect and a willingness to move beyond race that, quite frankly, didn't exist during my years in the state. Mississippi is finally a good place to be."

But everyone knows it should be better. The question is how. One answer, put forward by Democratic Governors William Winter and Ray Mabus in the 1980s, can be summarized by the single word "education." Winter finally made kindergarten mandatory and raised the drop-out age to 14; Mabus proposed a major school reform policy. But the uncomfortable fact is that most high taxpayers are white and most public school children are black (Jackson's student body is 88% black), because many white children attend private academies. About 40% of state spending goes to education, but those who oppose higher spending or taxes can point to the fact that there is no demonstrated correlation between higher spending and improved test scores and learning. The other view, expressed in blunt terms by Governor Kirk Fordice, who beat Mabus in 1991 and was re-elected in 1995, is that it is better to encourage private sector growth by holding down taxes and cutting regulation, by tort reform and by getting tough on crime and prisoners, and by boosting Mississippi's reputation: "Only positive Mississippi spoken here," say the signs Fordice has ordered put up on highways at the state line. Also important is encouraging traditional values, widely shared by blacks as well as whites. Fordice applauded when black Jackson high school principal Bishop Knox instituted school prayer; when Knox was fired by administrators, Mississippi passed a law authorizing student-initiated prayer in schools—which was promptly overturned in federal court. Fordice also cheered when Jackson TV station owner Frank Melton, also black, went on the air and put up billboards calling on police to arrest certain named drug dealers; arrests were made and convictions followed.

The division between these views is rather close. Fordice won re-election by just 56%–44% in 1995, and in 1996 Bob Dole carried the state by just 49%–44%. Mississippi has two Republican senators, but Democrats hold three of the five House seats and still have solid legislative majorities in the legislature. The points of view of both sides are plausible. But both are in danger of being undercut by the culture. Greenville, which produced authors Hodding Carter (*Main Street Meets the River*) and William Alexander Percy (*Lanterns on the Levee*), and where Shelby Foote and Walker Percy went to high school together, is now the nation's top media market in which people watch television more hours a day than any other. And, as Fordice does not like to mention, the biggest driver of economic growth in Mississippi is gambling.

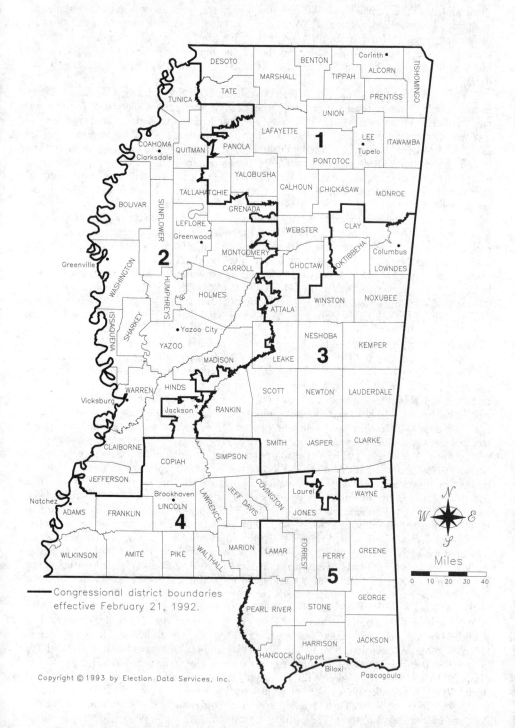

Congressional district boundaries
effective February 21, 1992.

Mississippi approved riverboat gambling in 1989, when Mabus was governor, and Mississippi now has 29 casinos, 10 in Harrison County and nine in once-impoverished Tunica County, just south of Memphis, and the rest scattered along the Mississippi River border. In Tunica, once plantation country and now with four-lane roads jammed with casinogoers, few locals have been able to hold jobs at the casinos. But Fordice, who opposed gambling in his home town of Vicksburg and says it has turned it "into a rather tawdry little gambling town," also opposes abolishing it: "you'd be confiscating all that property and that's totally wrong." And gambling is booming: In 1998 Mississippi was number three in gambling revenues, behind only Nevada and New Jersey. The original riverboats Mark Twain described in *Life on the Mississippi* were working vehicles, sooty and dangerous, taking chances on the treacherous river; but their captains showed how hard work could get people ahead. Mississippi's riverboat casinos are a form of entertainment, a diversion from gainful economic activity, which teach the lesson that getting ahead depends on luck rather than talent and hard work. Is this really the lesson Mississippi wants to teach the nation?

Governor. Mississippi Governor Kirk Fordice, a businessman not entirely new to politics, is the first Republican governor elected here since 1874. He has the bluntness of an engineer and the self-assurance of a self-made man; he started his own construction company in Vicksburg at age 28 and in 1990 became head of the Associated General Contractors of America. In 1995, while running for re-election, he said, "I'll tell you this. I don't believe we need to keep running this state by *Mississippi Burning* and apologizing for what happened 30 years ago. This is the '90s. This is now. We are on a roll. We've got the best race relations in all the United States of America." He won the governorship in 1991 by beating tough opponents, topping Auditor Pete Johnson, the grandson and nephew of governors, in the Republican primary, then beating incumbent Ray Mabus in the general. Fordice campaigned against welfare abusers and racial quotas—veiled racism, Mabus supporters said. Fordice trailed in polls but won 51%–48%.

Fordice's "relationship with the legislature ranges from strained to confrontational," wrote the Memphis *Commercial Appeal.* But he has had some successes—a capital gains tax cut, tort reform, eliminating air conditioning and television from prisons, requiring prisoners to wear stripes and to work more hours. Welfare rolls peaked in 1992, his first year in office, at 61,000; they were cut to 46,000 in August 1996 and 20,800 in June 1998. But he also had setbacks. A 1% increase in the sales tax was passed over his veto, and he opposed the successful tobacco lawsuit seeking reimbursement for Medicaid spending pressed by Attorney General Mike Moore and argued by Pascagoula lawyer Richard Scruggs (who is Senator Trent Lott's brother-in-law).

Fordice was re-elected in 1995 after a bitter campaign against Secretary of State Dick Molpus, one of the young moderate liberals associated with former Governors Winter and Mabus. It was a clear contrast in philosophies, and Fordice won 56%–44%, carrying the Gulf Coast and the Jackson area as well as most rural counties, posting respectable percentages in black-majority counties while Molpus carried some nearly all-white counties in the northeast.

Fordice is term-limited, and Mississippi elects a new governor in November 1999. The initial favorite was Mike Moore, probably Mississippi's best known politician; he was the first state attorney general to file a lawsuit against tobacco companies to recover damages for Medicaid expenses, and Mississippi netted $3.3 billion over 25 years. Around Christmas time 1998, Moore was talking like a candidate; but in early January 1999 said he could accomplish more in a fourth term as attorney general—and, considering the huge transfer of corporate assets he had done so much to engineer, that may well be true. So the single well-known Democrat left was Lieutenant Governor Ronnie Musgrove, who called for education reform, more jobs, less crime. Several well-known Republicans have announced, a reversal of the old days when all the competition was in the Democratic primary. One was former Lieutenant Governor Eddie Briggs, a lawyer and car dealer, who admitted he ran a poor campaign when he lost to Musgrove in 1995; he called for making sure that all children can read by second or third grade. Another was former Congressman Mike Parker, originally a funeral home owner, who retired from the House in 1998, who had switched from the Democratic to the Republican Party in November 1995. Other lesser-known Republicans in the race are state House Republican leader Charlie Williams and Crystal Springs Mayor Dan Gibson.

Cook's Call. *Highly Competitive.* With the governor's mansion vacant for the first time in 8 years, both parties expect to field several strong candidates in a very competitive battle.

Senior Senator. Thad Cochran, Mississippi's senior senator, was elected to the House in 1972 and the Senate in 1978. He grew up in small towns in northern Mississippi, the son of a principal and a teacher, graduated with high grades from Ole Miss (where he was a cheerleader, which was a very big deal) and its Law School, served in the Navy, spent a year abroad and practiced law in Jackson. In 1972, as Richard Nixon was sweeping Mississippi, he was elected as a Republican to the House from the Jackson-area district with a plurality against a white Democrat and black independent. After three terms, he was ready to step down, when Senator James Eastland retired; Cochran ran, and once again won with a plurality over a white Democrat and a black independent. In the House and in the Senate he has managed to amass a solidly conservative record with little controversy or acrimony. His pleasant personal demeanor, his refusal to engage in racial politics and his Republican Party label, in a state where most whites have been voting Republican for president for three decades, have made him broadly acceptable to voters. His toughest race came in 1984, when he was opposed by popular former Governor William Winter. Winter could make a case for himself but not against Cochran; Cochran out-raised him $2.7 million to $738,000, and won 61%–39%.

One Cochran specialty is farm policy: He serves on the Agriculture Committee and chairs the Appropriations Subcommittee on Agriculture and Rural Development. In 1996 he played a major role on the Freedom to Farm Act. He supported the move to phase out most crop subsidies over seven years, but insisted on maintaining the cotton marketing loan plan which he largely wrote in 1985, with farmers allowed to pay back loans at lower than the nominal interest rate if world prices drop below specified levels. He also pushed for open markets for farm exports and resisted demands for money to combat food-borne diseases. He worked with Vermont's James Jeffords on the complex dairy program. And he wrote the Senate version of the Wildlife Habitat Incentives Program, to give farmers an incentive to preserve habitat.

On other issues, he authored the Mississippi Wilderness Act and worked for grants for historically black colleges and for vocational training for the disabled; he sponsored a bill to bring the latest computer technologies to the nation's schools. His voting record is tempered with respect for Mississippi interests. "I always voted against subsidies for the maritime industry," he explained in 1993. "It was the conservative position to take. Then I was campaigning for re-election at the gates of the Ingalls shipyard in Pascagoula. I was handing out my leaflets and the union guys showed up with their leaflets, saying 'A vote for Cochran is a vote against your job.' Ever since then, I've voted for maritime subsidies." He serves on Defense Appropriations, and the 1998 appropriation included $2.6 billion for three additional DDG-51 Aegis destroyers, two of them to be built at Ingalls. He has been the Senate's leading proponent of missile defense. Republicans twice failed to get the 60 votes needed to block filibusters and the bill was dropped in September 1998, but in March 1999, after the implications of the July 1998 Rumsfeld report and the August 1998 North Korean three-stage missile launching sunk in, his missile defense resolution passed by 97–3.

Cochran's relations with his Senate colleague Trent Lott, with whom he has served in Congress now for nearly 30 years, have not always been harmonious. They clashed over judgeships and vied for White House favor in the 1980s and mixed it up in leadership fights in the 1990s. In 1990 Cochran challenged the more moderate John Chafee of Rhode Island for the chairmanship of the Senate Republican Conference, the number three leadership position, and won 22–21. When Trent Lott challenged Al Simpson for majority whip, the number two position, Cochran pointedly endorsed Simpson; Lott won anyway, with the support of junior conservatives, and thus leapfrogged Cochran. When Bob Dole announced in May 1996 that he would resign from the Senate in June, Cochran and Lott both entered the race for majority leader; Lott had the contest sewed up, but Cochran stayed in and lost 44–8. He has fared much better at the polls in Mississippi. In 1990 he was unopposed and for 1996 he was re-elected 71%–27% over a Democrat who spent half of his $4,700 on gas for a borrowed car.

Junior Senator. Trent Lott, elected to the Senate in 1988, has been majority leader since June 1996, a post he achieved after less than a decade in the Senate (as did Lyndon Johnson in 1955 and Mike Mansfield in 1961). Lott grew up in Pascagoula, the son of a shipyard worker and a teacher, went to Ole Miss (where he was a cheerleader, like his Mississippi colleague Thad Cochran) and worked his way through law school by running the Ole Miss alumni affairs office, accumulating good contacts along the way. After just a year of law practice, he got a job with Democratic Gulf Coast Congressman William Colmer, chairman of the Rules Committee. When Colmer retired in 1972, Lott ran for the House seat with Colmer's encouragement and endorsement—as a Republican. He was elected with 55% in what was the strongest Nixon district in the country that year. In 1974, Lott was the youngest member of the Judiciary Committee, loyally defending Richard Nixon in the impeachment hearings. In 1980, he was elected Republican whip, and he ran the Republican National Convention's platform committees in 1980 and 1984. In the House he was an ally of Jack Kemp and the young Newt Gingrich. He supported Kemp for president in 1988, and his decision to run for the Senate that year opened the way for Gingrich's rise: Lott was succeeded as whip by Dick Cheney; when Cheney became Defense secretary in March 1989, Gingrich was elected whip 87–85. Six years and three months later those two conservatives who were out on one wing of the minority party had become the leaders of the majority party in both houses of Congress.

Lott gave up a safe seat and a chance at being speaker to run for the Senate in 1988, and he had something of a fight for it. Congressman Wayne Dowdy, who beat Secretary of State Dick Molpus in the primary 54%–42%, voiced populist themes and criticized Lott for having a chauffeur. Lott responded with an ad showing the employee in question, a black law enforcement professional named George Awkward, who explained he was guarding Lott because he was a member of the leadership: "I'm nobody's chauffeur, Mr. Dowdy." Lott outraised Dowdy and won a 61%–39% margin in the Jackson area, the Gulf Coast and other counties where turnout had increased 10% since 1980; in the rest of the state, Dowdy won only 51%–49%, giving Lott a 54%–46% win overall.

There is a discernible hard core of beliefs in Lott's career, and yet he is less the hard-edged ideologue that Washington insiders presumed than he is an instinctive deal-maker, not much interested in quixotic gestures, an orderly and well-organized man who is dismayed by the dilatoriness of others. His beliefs are reminiscent of the mostly unarticulated beliefs of the coalition of Southern conservative Democrats and small-town conservative Northerners which had controlled the House for most of the 35 years when he came to work for Colmer and of which Colmer was one of the leaders: against increased taxes, hostile to federal regulation of business and local government, for an assertive foreign policy and strong defense, for the traditional rules of moral conduct which were seldom the subject of political debate back then; on one issue, civil rights, he moved as seamlessly as he changed parties, from Colmer's support for racial segregation to the small town Republicans backing for civil rights. He can be sharp in debate, aggressively partisan and combative, but he is gregarious and personable, on good terms with most other members and careful to cultivate those whose support he needs.

In the Senate Lott moved quickly into the leadership. After the 1992 election, he ran for Conference secretary, the number four leadership post, and won, with 20 votes to 14 for Christopher Bond and five for Frank Murkowski. In 1993 he was chosen the Republican point man on Clinton appointments, but he mostly avoided confrontations; with the largest percentage of black constituents of any senator, he did not raise ethical questions against the nominations of Ron Brown for Commerce Secretary in 1993 or Alexis Herman (who once worked in Pascagoula) for Labor Secretary in 1997. In 1994, after he had been re-elected 69%–31%, he challenged Republican Whip Al Simpson. Majority Leader Bob Dole and most Republican moderates backed Simpson, but Lott won most of the younger conservatives elected in 1992 and 1994 and won 27–26—the first Republican ever elected whip in both houses. In the process he leapfrogged over his Mississippi colleague Thad Cochran, who held the number three leadership position. Lott's comment was typically unsentimental. "There comes a time in life, in politics as in baseball, when you seize the moment or it's gone forever. I ran and he didn't."

As whip for 17 months, Lott was careful not to usurp the prerogatives of Dole, who kept many decisions close to the chest. Then in May 1996 Dole surprised almost everyone when he announced he would resign from the Senate in June. Lott immediately began canvassing for votes for majority leader and found himself far ahead of Cochran, who ran anyway and lost 44–8. During the summer, Lott moved adroitly, pushing for a vote on welfare reform, disposing of the minimum wage issue, pushing for the compromise health care bill and the Safe Drinking Water Act. He gave Republicans a solid record to run on—but left Dole with fewer issues on which to attack Clinton. He kept a back channel to the Clinton White House through pollster Dick Morris, who had worked for him as well as for Clinton in the past. He was solicitous to the new whip, Don Nickles, to freshmen and to party moderates and established a smooth working relationship with Democratic Leader Tom Daschle.

After Dole lost and Gingrich faced ethics charges that threatened to topple him, Lott was suddenly the most visible Republican leader in Congress—called on often to repeat that he had no interest in running for president. After sending conciliatory signals that he would wait for President Clinton to come forward with a budget in early 1997, he moved relentlessly in closed-door negotiations that led to the May bipartisan agreement to balance the budget and passage of the budget in July. But from time to time he angered colleagues. His insistence on investigating the Louisiana Senate race results infuriated Democrats. Conservatives were angry when he worked with the Clinton Administration, and against Foreign Relations Chairman Jesse Helms, to secure ratification of the Chemical Weapons Treaty in April 1997, and when he spoke out against cashiered Air Force flier Kelly Flinn. Democrats were furious that he sidelined their campaign finance bill in October 1997 by presenting an amendment to require union members to give their authorization before union leaders could use their dues money for political purposes. Lott's response to complaints: "I'm not a free agent any more. I don't have the luxury of just standing on the back row throwing bombs. I'm the Leader. I have to consider the institution of the Senate. I have to consider the Republican Party. And I have to consider my country, not to mention my children and my constituents."

Lott encountered—or engendered—more controversy in 1998. After urging Commerce Chairman John McCain to get a committee consensus on a tobacco bill; McCain did in March, and Lott brought the bill forward. The measure aroused fierce opposition from Republicans as a tax bill, and Lott ordered it pulled from the calendar in June 1998. He had avoided working on the specifics, because his brother-in-law Richard Scruggs was one of the chief lawyers for Mississippi Attorney General's case against the companies, and stood to make nearly a billion dollars in fees. "The bill has grown and grown and grown, and what has happened is that greed has just taken over," Lott said. "It's a spending bill, and it should be pulled." That same month he aroused catcalls when he said that homosexuality was an illness akin to alcoholism, kleptomania and "sex addiction" and in his view a sin; gay rights groups and others were angry when he honored other senators' holds and refused to bring to the floor the nomination of openly gay James Hormel to be Ambassador to Luxembourg. In July 1998 he made a speech charging that China's missile program had been improved by the Clinton Administration's easing of export controls. He continued to pursue other pet causes: more contracts for the Ingalls shipyard in Pascagoula, extending the duck hunting season 11 days in Mississippi (that got into the October 1998 omnibus bill), objecting to a visitors' complex at Gettysburg as overly commercial, singing in the Singing Senators group with John Ashcroft, Larry Craig and Jim Jeffords.

Then came impeachment, which tested his influence among Republican senators and his close working relationship (probably the best since Lyndon Johnson and Everett Dirksen in

1959–60) with Daschle. In December 1998, as the House was considering impeachment, Clinton ordered the bombing of Iraq, and Lott quickly said, "I cannot support this military action in the Persian Gulf at this time. Both the timing and the policy are subject to question." Then, after Congressman Bob Barr was attacked for speaking before the Council of Conservative Citizens, Lott was attacked for speaking to the group's semi-annual board meeting in 1992. Much of the group's platform is standard conservative fare, but a search of its Website and reading of its literature shows a preoccupation with race and an assumption that whites are racially superior to blacks; liberals called the group "the re-incarnation" of the pro-segregation White Citizens' Councils of the 1950s and 1960s, though there is no direct organizational linkage. Lott renounced the group and said he was not aware of its repugnant views.

After the House voted, Lott encouraged the Gorton-Lieberman plan to allow four days of argument in the impeachment trial, to be followed by a vote on whether the charges, if true, would justify impeachment; if that fell short of the two-thirds required for removal, as everyone assumed it would, the trial would be adjourned. House Judiciary Chairman Henry Hyde, the leader of the House managers, wrote an angry letter and Senate conservatives howled; Lott retreated. Democrats remained furious about the prospect of a lengthy, salacious trial, and raised the specter of partisanship which most senators, after the House debate and in line with Senate tradition, wanted to avoid. On January 7, Lott tagged along with Daschle for a scheduled press conference, and they agreed to an all-senators closed caucus the next day. In that extraordinary meeting, senators agreed to a suggestion by Phil Gramm and Edward Kennedy to postpone the issue of calling witnesses and go on with the trial. There was giddy delight at this demonstration of senatorial comity, though the House managers were furious and the Clinton defense team still wary. The trial proceeded in orderly fashion; ultimately, few witnesses were called; the verdict went as expected, mostly along partisan lines, with Lott and most Republicans preventing a vote on censure until after the verdict, at which point Democrats weren't much interested.

Lott comes up for re-election in Mississippi in 2000. His fundraising capacities are great, as shown by his $4.5 million-plus New Republican Majority Fund leadership PAC, and in early 1998 big-name Democrats in Mississippi—former Governor Ray Mabus, Attorney General Mike Moore, former Congressman and Agriculture Secretary Mike Espy—seemed disinclined to run.

Cook's Call. *Safe.* While Lott might be a tempting target, Democrats know how difficult it is to unseat a majority leader. They harbor hope that Attorney General Mike Moore, might be lured into the race, but this looks very unlikely, and the chances are that Lott won't get much of a challenge.

Presidential politics. Mississippi voted 50%–41% for George Bush in 1992, his best percentage in the country; it was 49%–44% for Bob Dole in 1996, suggesting a tilt toward Democrats, or perhaps higher black turnout. On balance it is a Republican state, but not because of race; it is other issues—defense, crime, cultural attitudes, taxes—on which majorities here shunned Walter Mondale, Michael Dukakis and Bill Clinton. Mississippi held its primary on Super Tuesday in 1996; Dole easily beat Pat Buchanan.

Congressional districting. In 1984, Mississippi was the first state to get a redistricting plan dictated by the dominant interpretation of the 1982 Voting Rights Amendments. The result was the black-majority 2d District, which elected Mike Espy in 1986; he went on to become Bill Clinton's Agriculture secretary from 1993–94. Ironically, Espy wanted to hold down the black percentage in the 2d in the 1991 plan, because he was winning white votes and he wanted more black influence in other districts. But civil rights organizations said no. The result is that the other four districts vote heavily Republican in national politics. Democrats elected four congressmen here as recently as 1992. But one retired in 1994, one switched parties in 1995 and another retired in 1996; but Democrats picked up party-switcher Mike Parker's seat when he left it open in 1998.

Reapportionment threatens to cost Mississippi a seat after the 2000 Census. Since the black-majority 2d is likely to remain in much its present shape, maneuvering is limited: the Gulf Coast district may include the southern part of the current 4th, the current 3d may take the current 4th's white Jackson neighborhoods, and the northeast 1st will probably stay the same. Such a plan, applied to today's members, would put Democrat Ronnie Shows in the same district as either Democrat Gene Taylor or Republican Chip Pickering.

The People: Est. Pop. 1998: 2,752,092; Pop. 1990: 2,573,216, up 6.9% 1990–1998. 1% of U.S. total, 31st largest; 52.9% rural. Median age: 32.9 years. 13% 65 years and over. 63.5% White, 35.6% Black, 0.5% Asian, 0.3% Amer. Indian, 0.1% Other; 0.6% Hispanic Origin. Households: 54.7% married couple families; 28.2% married couple fams. w. children; 36.8% college educ.; median household income: $20,136; per capita income: $9,648; 71.5% owner occupied housing; median house value: $45,600; median monthly rent: $215. 5.4% Unemployment. 1998 Voting age pop.: 2,014,000. 1998 Turnout: 550,917; 27% of VAP. Registered voters (1998): 1,779,932; no party registration.

Political Lineup: Governor, Kirk Fordice (R); Lt. Gov., Ronnie Musgrove (D); Secy. of State, Eric Clark (D); Atty. Gen., Mike Moore (D); Treasurer, Marshall Bennett (D); State Senate, 52 (34 D, 18 R); Senate President, Ronnie Musgrove (D); State House, 122 (83 D, 37 R, 2 I); House Speaker, Tim Ford (D). Senators, Thad Cochran (R) and Trent Lott (R). Representatives, 5 (3 D, 2 R).

Elections Division: 601-359-6357; **Filing Deadline for U.S. Congress:** January 14, 2000.

1996 Presidential Vote

Dole (R)	439,833	(49%)
Clinton (D)	394,020	(44%)
Perot (I)	52,221	(6%)

1992 Presidential Vote

Bush (R)	487,793	(50%)
Clinton (D)	400,258	(41%)
Perot (I)	85,626	(9%)

1996 Republican Presidential Primary

Dole (R)	91,639	(60%)
Buchanan (R)	39,324	(26%)
Forbes (R)	12,119	(8%)
Others	8,843	(7%)

GOVERNOR

Gov. Kirk Fordice (R)

Elected 1991, term expires Jan. 2000; b. Feb. 10, 1934, Memphis, TN; home, Vicksburg; Purdue U., B.S. 1956, M.S. 1957; Methodist; married (Pat).

Military Career: Army, 1957–59, Army Reserves, 1959–77.

Professional Career: Engineer, Exxon Corp., 1956, 1959–62; Exec., Fordice Construction Co., 1962–92; Pres., Assoc. General Contractors of Amer., 1989–91.

Office: State Capitol, P.O. Box 139, Jackson, 39205, 601-359-3100; Fax: 601-359-3150; Web site: www.state.ms.us.

Election Results

1995 gen.	Kirk Fordice (R)	455,261	(56%)
	Dick Molpus (D)	364,210	(44%)
1995 prim.	Kirk Fordice (R)	117,907	(94%)
	George (Wagon Wheel) Blair (R)	4,919	(4%)
	Others	2,956	(2%)
1991 gen.	Kirk Fordice (R)	361,500	(51%)
	Ray Mabus (D)	338,459	(48%)
	Others	11,253	(2%)

SENATORS

Sen. Thad Cochran (R)

Elected 1978, seat up 2002; b. Dec. 7, 1937, Pontotoc; home, Jackson; U. of MS, B.A. 1959, J.D. 1965, Rotary Fellow, Trinity Col., Ireland, 1963–64; Baptist; married (Rose).

Military Career: Navy, 1959–61.

Elected Office: U.S. House of Reps., 1972–78.

Professional Career: Practicing atty., 1965–72.

DC Office: 326 RSOB, 20510, 202-224-5054; Fax: 202-224-9450; Web site: www.senate.gov/~cochran.

State Offices: Jackson, 601-965-4459; Oxford, 601-236-1018.

Committees: *Agriculture, Nutrition & Forestry* (3d of 10 R): Marketing, Inspection & Product Promotion; Production & Price Competitiveness. *Appropriations* (2d of 15 R): Agriculture & Rural Development (Chmn.); Defense; Energy & Water Development; Interior; Labor & HHS. *Governmental Affairs* (7th of 9 R): International Security, Proliferation & Federal Services (Chmn.); Investigations (Permanent). *Rules & Administration* (5th of 9 R). *Joint Committee on Printing* (2d of 5 Sens.). *Joint Committee on the Library of Congress* (3d of 5 Sens.).

Group Ratings

	ADA	ACLU	AFS	LCV	CON	NTU	NFIB	COC	ACU	NTLC	CHC
1998	0	29	0	0	67	57	89	100	81	63	73
1997	15	—	0	—	74	68	—	90	56	—	—

National Journal Ratings

	1997 LIB — 1997 CONS		1998 LIB — 1998 CONS	
Economic	44%	— 52%	31%	— 63%
Social	39%	— 55%	39%	— 58%
Foreign	43%	— 50%	29%	— 58%

Key Votes of the 105th Congress

1. Bal. Budget Amend.	Y	5. Satcher for Surgeon Gen.	Y	9. Chem. Weapons Treaty	Y
2. Clinton Budget Deal	Y	6. Highway Set-asides	N	10. Cuban Humanitarian Aid	N
3. Cloture on Tobacco	N	7. Table Child Gun locks	Y	11. Table Bosnia Troops	Y
4. Education IRAs	Y	8. Ovrd. Part. Birth Veto	Y	12. $ for Test-ban Treaty	N

Election Results

1996 general	Thad Cochran (R)	624,154	(71%)	($1,305,680)
	James W. Hunt (D)	240,647	(27%)	
	Others	13,861	(2%)	
1996 primary	Thad Cochran (R)	138,813	(95%)	
	Richard O'Hara (R)	6,762	(5%)	
1990 general	Thad Cochran (R)	unopposed		($691,865)

Sen. Trent Lott (R)

Elected 1988, seat up 2000; b. Oct. 9, 1941, Grenada; home, Pascagoula; U. of MS, B.A. 1963, J.D. 1967; Baptist; married (Tricia).

Elected Office: U.S. House of Reps., 1972–88.

Professional Career: Practicing atty., 1967–68; A.A., U.S. Rep. William Colmer, 1968–72.

DC Office: 487 RSOB, 20510, 202-224-6253; Fax: 202-224-2262; Web site: www.senate.gov/~lott.

State Offices: Greenwood, 601-453-5681; Gulfport, 601-863-1988; Jackson, 601-965-4644; Oxford, 601-234-3774; Pascagoula, 601-762-5400.

Committees: *Majority Leader. Commerce, Science & Transportation* (5th of 11 R): Aviation; Communications. *Finance* (8th of 11 R): International Trade; Social Security & Family Policy; Taxation & IRS Oversight. *Rules & Administration* (8th of 9 R).

Group Ratings

	ADA	ACLU	AFS	LCV	CON	NTU	NFIB	COC	ACU	NTLC	CHC
1998	0	14	0	0	14	61	100	94	92	82	100
1997	5	—	0	—	81	73	—	90	72	—	—

National Journal Ratings

	1997 LIB — 1997 CONS	1998 LIB — 1998 CONS
Economic	11% — 76%	16% — 83%
Social	0% — 83%	0% — 88%
Foreign	24% — 72%	12% — 75%

Key Votes of the 105th Congress

1. Bal. Budget Amend.	Y	5. Satcher for Surgeon Gen.	N	9. Chem. Weapons Treaty	Y
2. Clinton Budget Deal	Y	6. Highway Set-asides	N	10. Cuban Humanitarian Aid	N
3. Cloture on Tobacco	N	7. Table Child Gun locks	Y	11. Table Bosnia Troops	N
4. Education IRAs	Y	8. Ovrd. Part. Birth Veto	Y	12. $ for Test-ban Treaty	N

Election Results

1994 general	Trent Lott (R)	418,333	(69%)	($2,516,189)
	Ken Harper (D)	189,752	(31%)	($345,379)
1994 primary	Trent Lott (R)	72,543	(95%)	
	Others	3,476	(5%)	
1988 general	Trent Lott (R)	510,380	(54%)	($3,405,242)
	Wayne Dowdy (D)	436,339	(46%)	($2,355,957)

FIRST DISTRICT

The university town of Oxford, the center of William Faulkner's fictional Yoknapatawpha County, sits on a divide between the hill country of Mississippi and the flat farmlands of the Mississippi Delta. The mostly white-hill counties run up to where the Tennessee River nicks the northeast corner of Tishomingo County. The Tennessee Valley Authority brought electricity here, the Tennessee-Tombigbee Waterway provided construction jobs for years and a new shipping canal when it was completed in 1985. The focus, though, is different in the hill-country metropolis, Tupelo, which is a stronghold of private enterprise and traditional values. It excels at corporate recruitment, attracting new jobs without giving away the store—"probably the best small city in the South" at it, says one corporate recruiter—and calls itself the nation's leading producer of upholstered furniture. Tupelo is also the home of the Reverend Donald Wildmon, who organizes boycotts of products advertised on television shows that he thinks have excessive sex or violence. West of Oxford is Mississippi's Delta, the swampy land pioneered by large planters around the turn of the century, with large black work forces little removed—in the conditions of their daily lives or long-term economic chances—from slavery. Oxford, home of Ole Miss, is also the home today of the Center for the Study of Southern Culture.

The 1st Congressional District includes most of the hill country and a little bit of the Delta plus the Memphis suburban fringe that has run over the Mississippi line. This was the district represented by Jamie Whitten, the longest-serving House member in history, from his special election victory in November 1941 until January 1995: 53 years and two months. Whitten served as chairman of the Agriculture Appropriations Subcommittee for 42 years and was Appropriations chairman from 1979–93.

The congressman from the 1st District now is Roger Wicker, a Republican elected in 1994. He grew up in Pontotoc, 20 miles from Tupelo, the son of a state senator and circuit judge, attended public schools and was a House page in 1967: the first of the 1994 freshmen to get on the floor of the House. He is a fifth cousin once removed of Senator Fred Thompson, who grew up not far across the state line in Lawrenceburg, Tennessee; Thompson was an actor in many movies and Wicker appeared in a Tupelo production of *Bye Bye, Birdie* and in a 1997 benefit production of *State of the Union* at Washington's Arena Stage. Wicker went to college and law school at Ole Miss, where he was student body president, served in the Air Force, and in 1980 became a staffer to Trent Lott on the House Rules Committee. In 1987, at 36, he was elected as a Republican to the state Senate and chaired the Elections, and Public Health and Welfare committees, where he sponsored a 24-hour waiting period for abortions. In 1994, when Whitten retired, Wicker was one of six Republicans and three Democrats to run for the seat.

Wicker, carrying his home base around Tupelo, led in the first primary 27%–19% over Grant Fox, former aide to Senator Thad Cochran. In the runoff, Wicker campaigned as a conservative, but Fox, just 27, hit him hard for voting to override Governor Fordice's sales tax increase veto. Wicker won by just 53%–47%. In the Democratic primary, state Representative Bill Wheeler, who walked across the district, upset House Speaker Tim Ford. But the big news was that Democratic turnout was not much higher than Republican in the primary (33,766 versus 26,607) or in the runoff (29,871 versus 22,268). Wheeler had support from blacks, unions and teachers' unions, an advantage in the primary but not the general. "If you want more Bill Clinton, maybe you should vote for my opponent," Wicker said, while Wheeler campaigned as the candidate of working people against a "country club Republican." The result wasn't even close: a district held for 53 years by a Democratic leader voted 63%–37% for the Republican.

In the House Wicker was elected president of the 73-member freshman class, one of the largest in the 20th Century. He also won Whitten's old seat on the Appropriations Committee. Wicker had a very conservative voting record, and rallied the freshman to support the budget even after Newt Gingrich capitulated to Clinton in January 1996. "We have fundamentally changed the debate in Washington," he said; even Clinton "is talking like a Republican." Yet in some ways Wicker has acted like an old-style Democrat. He did co-sponsor the amendment which outlawed fetal tissue research and worked without success to allow voluntary school prayer, but he also worked on local projects and backed measures which helped local industries. He worked to preserve the Appalachian Regional Commission and the Economic Development Administration, to support funding of the Natchez Trace Parkway, started in the 1930s but never completed, and for Yalobusha River flood control. He got TVA to agree to buy power from a proposed lignite-burning plant in Choctaw County which will be one of the largest construction projects in Mississippi history, with 9,000 jobs. In 1997 he sponsored a resolution of disapproval of OSHA regulations which would restrict the use of methylene chloride, used in foam on the seatbacks of chairs and to cleanse antique furniture, and in 1998 he passed an Appropriations rider to prevent the Consumer Product Safety Commission from mandating flame-retardant chemicals in upholstered furniture until scientists found that they were not harmful to workers or consumers.

Wicker was re-elected by better than 2–1 in 1996 and 1998. The nation's consensus-minded mood has even reached the rebel hills of northern Mississippi; after winning in 1998 he said, "There's too much partisanship in Congress. I served in the Mississippi legislature where we had to work with people from both sides of the aisle. It's far different in Washington."

Cook's Call. *Safe.* While not as Republican as some of the other districts in the state, the 1st is still conservative territory. Wicker has had little trouble, or little competition, since winning it in 1994. He is a sure bet for 2000.

The People: Pop. 1990: 515,196; 67.1% rural; 13.8% age 65+; 76.7% White, 22.8% Black, 0.3% Asian, 0.1% Amer. Indian, 0.1% Other; 0.5% Hispanic Origin. Households: 60% married couple families; 30.2% married couple fams. w. children; 30% college educ.; median household income: $20,867; per capita income: $9,639; median house value: $43,900; median gross rent: $187.

1996 Presidential Vote

Dole (R)	90,604	(48%)
Clinton (D)	78,894	(42%)
Perot (I)	13,695	(7%)
Others	3,864	(2%)

1992 Presidential Vote

Bush (R)	101,252	(50%)
Clinton (D)	84,765	(42%)
Perot (I)	17,984	(9%)

Rep. Roger Wicker (R)

Elected 1994; b. July 5, 1951, Pontotoc; home, Tupelo; U. of MS, B.A. 1973, J.D. 1975; Baptist; married (Gayle).

Military Career: Air Force, 1976–80; Air Force Reserves, 1980–present.

Elected Office: Tupelo City Judge Pro Tem, 1986–87; MS Senate, 1987–94.

Professional Career: Staff, U.S. House Rules Cmte., 1980–82; Practicing atty., 1982–94; Lee Cnty. Public Defender, 1984–87.

DC Office: 206 CHOB 20515, 202-225-4306; Fax: 202-225-3549; Web site: www.house.gov/wicker.

District Offices: Southaven, 601-342-3942; Tupelo, 601-844-5437.

Committees: *Appropriations* (22d of 34 R): Labor, HHS & Education; Military Construction; VA, HUD & Independent Agencies.

Group Ratings

	ADA	ACLU	AFS	LCV	CON	NTU	NFIB	COC	ACU	NTLC	CHC
1998	0	6	0	8	4	53	100	100	96	97	100
1997	0	—	13	—	42	46	—	100	80	—	—

National Journal Ratings

	1997 LIB — 1997 CONS		1998 LIB — 1998 CONS	
Economic	19% —	76%	0% —	88%
Social	10% —	82%	3% —	90%
Foreign	12% —	81%	47% —	53%

Key Votes of the 105th Congress

1. Clinton Budget Deal	Y	5. Puerto Rico Sthood. Ref.	N	9. Cut $ for B-2 Bombers	N
2. Education IRAs	Y	6. End Highway Set-asides	Y	10. Human Rights in China	N
3. Req. 2/3 to Raise Taxes	Y	7. School Prayer Amend.	Y	11. Withdraw Bosnia Troops	N
4. Fast-track Trade	Y	8. Ovrd. Part. Birth Veto	Y	12. End Cuban TV-Marti	N

Election Results

1998 general	Roger Wicker (R)	66,738	(67%)	($288,354)
	Rex N. Weathers (D)	30,438	(31%)	
	Others	2,157	(2%)	
1998 primary	Roger Wicker (R)	unopposed		
1996 general	Roger Wicker (R)	123,724	(68%)	($524,101)
	Henry Boyd Jr. (D)	55,998	(31%)	
	Others	3,244	(2%)	

SECOND DISTRICT

"The Mississippi Delta," wrote Delta native David Cohn, "begins in the lobby of the Peabody Hotel in Memphis and ends on Catfish Row in Vicksburg." For centuries, the flooding Mississippi and Yazoo Rivers left their sediments here, producing a fertile dark soil. Ironically, what may well be America's richest agricultural land has been home for more than a century to many of its poorest people. The Delta, criss-crossed by rivers and famously disease-ridden, wasn't much settled until after the Civil War; the tradition here is not of paternal masters and gracious mansions, but of sharp, profit-seeking operators who used 19th Century technology to drain the land, line the river with levees and build railroads on tracks above the rise of the river. Black sharecroppers and field hands worked here in conditions almost of bondage. From this episode of industrial farming came both great misery and great art: Clarksdale in Coahoma County was the home of W.C. Handy and Muddy Waters, the real birthplace of blues music; Greenville on the Mississippi has produced writers of the caliber of Walker Percy and Shelby Foote. Now Vicksburg's antebellum mansions, battlefield monuments and riverboat gambling bring in 1.5 million tourists annually from around the country.

Then 20th Century technology changed life in the Delta once again. The mechanical cotton-picking machine, invented in 1944, came along just as northern factories were seeking low-wage workers; the great exodus to Chicago and Memphis began, and the Delta's population has been declining ever since. Income levels remain very low, poverty is over 50% in some areas and infant mortality is at Third World levels; the crime and drugs of urban Chicago have been brought back by Delta migrants returning home. There are signs of hope: soybeans have become a big dollar crop here, although there is more acreage still in cotton; poultry farms have become a major enterprise, and the Delta produces 75% of the nation's catfish. Riverboat gambling was approved in 1992 in Tunica County, by some measures the nation's poorest county; in 1993 1.7 million people came in and spent $140 million in the casinos, which now have more square footage than Atlantic City's. There is still a gulf between the races, culturally and economically, but also positive signs: by 1990 a former state NAACP head was elected by a margin of 2–1 the mayor of Vicksburg, which is about half black; when Ku Klux Klansmen demonstrated in Greenwood and Clarksdale in 1994, they were promptly arrested and attracted no support. Still, the Delta has been unable to develop the self-propelling market economy that has brought growth to most of the nation.

The 2d Congressional District occupies the entire Mississippi Delta region, indeed the whole riverfront from Tunica almost to Natchez, plus black neighborhoods of Jackson. It is Mississippi's one black-majority (63%) district, first created as such in 1984, with modest changes in boundaries for 1992. Thirty years ago, when blacks were not allowed to vote in Mississippi, politics here was the domain of the big plantation owners, symbolized by James Eastland, U.S. senator from 1941–79, Judiciary chairman from 1955–79, an unyielding segregationist and conservative. Even after blacks got the vote, black registration was low and habits of deference in some places prevailed; voting was very racially polarized. In 1986, the district elected its first black congressman since Reconstruction, Mike Espy, whose grandfather and father built a chain of funeral homes and were among the biggest landowners in the state. He won narrowly, worked on farm issues, opposed gun control and courted white voters; he won re-election with

65%, 84% and 76% and in 1993 became secretary of Agriculture. In October 1994 he resigned amid charges that he accepted Superbowl tickets from Tyson Foods; an independent counsel prosecuted, but he was acquitted by a Washington jury in December 1998.

The congressman from the 2d District is Bennie Thompson, who grew up in Bolton, in Hinds County outside Jackson, graduated from Tougaloo College and received a masters from Jackson State. He was elected alderman in Bolton in 1969, at 21, and mayor four years later; he was the first person in Mississippi to have a street named after Martin Luther King Jr. In 1980 he became a Hinds County supervisor. He worked to encourage other blacks to run for office; Mississippi now has more than 800 black officeholders; he was lead plaintiff in a suit charging that the state underfunded historically black state colleges. When Espy was appointed to the Cabinet, Thompson ran in the 2d District. In the March 1993 all-party primary, he won 28% to 20% for Henry Espy, Mike Espy's brother and mayor of Clarksdale. But the leader, with 34%, was Republican Hayes Dent, a 31-year-old aide to Governor Kirk Fordice. In the April runoff, voting was mostly along racial lines, and Thompson won 55%–45%. Most of his margin came from Jackson and Hinds County; elsewhere he led only 51%–49%.

Thompson, unlike Espy, made no particular attempt to win white votes and had a solidly liberal voting record, making as few concessions across the racial divide as had Eastland in day. He likes to quote Deuteronomy: "Thou shalt not harden thine heart, nor shut thine hand from thy poor brother: But thou shalt open thine hand unto him, and shalt surely lend him sufficient for his need." He worked for the empowerment zone which Bill Clinton established in six Delta counties; he got money for restoring buildings at Tougaloo and Rust colleges; he got the Jackson and Ruleville post offices named for Medgar Evers and Fannie Lou Hamer; he got an exemption from EPA for a pesticide to kill the beet armyworm threatening cotton crops. He successfully sought restitution for black farmers who lost land because of Agriculture Department discrimination.

Thompson chaired the Black Caucus's Tobacco Working Group, which worked to make sure minority groups got a share of public health spending in the tobacco settlement. In 1998 he asked the FBI and ATF to investigate the fire-bombing of the black-owned *Jackson Advocate* as a hate crime, and attacked the indictment of two black Jackson businessmen for extortion of $150,000 in cash payments from Time Warner to influence a cable TV franchise; cash payments are common in business, he said, but, "When the complexion changes, that's extortion." In 1999 he sponsored the law to award the Congressional Gold Medal to the nine students who integrated Little Rock's Central High School.

In 1994 and 1996, against black Republicans, Thompson won 54%–39% and 60%–38%. In 1998 against a Libertarian candidate he was re-elected with 71%.

Cook's Call. *Safe.* This majority-black district is the safest Democratic seat in the state. Thompson has done little to reach out to white voters, but the black percentage is high enough to sustain him.

The People: Pop. 1990: 514,469; 54.7% rural; 13.5% age 65 + ; 36.5% White, 63% Black, 0.2% Asian, 0.1% Amer. Indian, 0.1% Other; 0.4% Hispanic Origin. Households: 46.2% married couple families; 24.9% married couple fams. w. children; 32.5% college educ.; median household income: $15,530; per capita income: $7,771; median house value: $40,200; median gross rent: $154.

1996 Presidential Vote

Clinton (D)	104,639	(62%)
Dole (R)	58,177	(34%)
Perot (I)	5,714	(3%)

1992 Presidential Vote

Clinton (D)	105,185	(58%)
Bush (R)	66,905	(37%)
Perot (I)	9,879	(5%)

Rep. Bennie G. Thompson (D)

Elected Apr., 1993; b. Jan. 28, 1948, Bolton; home, Bolton; Tougaloo Col., B.A. 1968, Jackson St. U., M.S. 1972; Methodist; married (London).

Elected Office: Bolton Bd. of Aldermen, 1969–73; Bolton Mayor, 1973–79; Hinds Cnty. Supervisor, 1980–93.

DC Office: 1408 LHOB 20515, 202-225-5876; Fax: 202-225-5898; Web site: www.house.gov/thompson.

District Offices: Bolton, 601-866-9003; Greenville, 601-335-9003; Greenwood, 601-455-9003; Marks, 601-326-9003; Mound Bayou, 601-741-9003.

Committees: *Agriculture* (12th of 24 D): Department Operations, Oversight, Nutrition & Forestry; General Farm Commodities, Resource Conservation & Credit. *Budget* (4th of 19 D).

Group Ratings

	ADA	ACLU	AFS	LCV	CON	NTU	NFIB	COC	ACU	NTLC	CHC
1998	95	79	100	85	38	12	21	18	13	16	0
1997	80	—	100	—	17	16	—	40	16	—	—

National Journal Ratings

	1997 LIB	—	1997 CONS		1998 LIB	—	1998 CONS
Economic	64%	—	35%		79%	—	0%
Social	82%	—	15%		69%	—	30%
Foreign	64%	—	33%		64%	—	31%

Key Votes of the 105th Congress

1. Clinton Budget Deal	N	5. Puerto Rico Sthood. Ref.	Y	9. Cut $ for B-2 Bombers	N
2. Education IRAs	N	6. End Highway Set-asides	N	10. Human Rights in China	Y
3. Req. 2/3 to Raise Taxes	N	7. School Prayer Amend.	Y	11. Withdraw Bosnia Troops	N
4. Fast-track Trade	N	8. Ovrd. Part. Birth Veto	N	12. End Cuban TV-Marti	Y

Election Results

1998 general	Bennie G. Thompson (D)	80,284	(71%)	($281,858)
	William G. Chipman (Lib)	32,533	(29%)	
1998 primary	Bennie G. Thompson (D)	unopposed		
1996 general	Bennie G. Thompson (D)	102,503	(60%)	($361,452)
	Danny Covington (R)	65,263	(38%)	($215,943)
	Others	4,167	(2%)	

THIRD DISTRICT

Mississippi, old and new: the old Mississippi is the Neshoba County fair, held every August since 1892 in the town of Philadelphia. This is traditionally the place where Mississippi politicians announce their candidacies, with the crowds watching to take their measure. When Ronald Reagan came here in 1980 and Michael Dukakis in 1988, neither mentioned what Philadelphia and Neshoba County are best known for in history, nor is there any memorial except engraved stones at two black churches: It was here during the "Freedom Summer" of 1964 that three civil rights workers, two white and one black, were murdered for the crime of urging black American citizens to register and vote. The new Mississippi is some 80 miles away, in Rankin and Madison County east and north of Jackson, where subdivisions and shopping centers are sprouting up on lands which only a few years ago seemed out in the country.

The 3d Congressional District includes the Rankin and the Madison County suburbs of Jackson and Neshoba County. It stretches north to Starkville, home of Mississippi State University, and south to Laurel, an hour's drive from the Gulf Coast. In the middle is Meridian, a small city that may go down in history as the site of departures of White House chiefs of staff: On the last two presidential trips here, President Nixon informed Bob Haldeman that he was out as chief of staff in April 1973 and in December 1991 John Sununu penned his letter of resignation to President Bush. The political tradition here is Southern Democratic, but the area's recent preference has been Republican: Mississippi, old and new.

The congressman from the 3d District is Chip Pickering, a Republican elected in 1996. He grew up in Laurel where he worked on the family dairy and catfish farm and attended public schools; his father was a state senator and state Republican chairman and is now a federal judge. But Pickering was more interested in football than politics at college, and afterwards he spent 17 months as a Southern Baptist missionary in then-Communist Hungary. He then was at the Agriculture Department in the Bush Administration, and as a staffer for Senator Trent Lott, working primarily on telecommunications issues. In fall 1995, Sonny Montgomery, congressman from the 3d District since 1966, a Democrat who mostly voted with Republicans, announced that he would retire after 30 years, and Pickering returned to Mississippi and started running for Congress.

He was not without competition; nine Republicans and three Democrats ran. Pickering used his old party ties: His father's executive director at the state party had been Haley Barbour, Republican National Committee chairman from 1993–97, and Pickering's campaign manager was his brother Henry Barbour. In the primary there was tough competition from candidates with regional bases in Meridian and in the Jackson suburbs; Pickering ran first in 13 of 19 counties, though in neither of the big population centers, and won 27% of the vote. In second was former state Representative Bill Crawford from Meridian, with 24%. Crawford had worked to save Meridian Naval Air Station and was vice president of the local community college, and attacked Pickering for having worked most of his adult life outside Mississippi. But Pickering attacked him strongly for resigning from the Republican state committee and supporting Democratic gubernatorial candidate Ray Mabus in 1987, and won the runoff 56%–44%; big margins in the Jackson suburbs were the key.

The general election was a battle between the 32-year-old Pickering and 29-year-old John Arthur Eaves Jr., son of a well-known lawyer and Democratic politician. Eaves spent $542,000 of his own money, and stressed his opposition to abortion and gun control and support of school prayer. But Pickering raised and spent more than $1 million. Boasting of his Republican label ("I consider politics a team sport"), he won in this heavily Republican district 61%–36%.

In the House, Pickering has a very conservative voting record and with his Capitol Hill contacts picked up key assignments. He was named vice chairman of a Science subcommittee chaired by Stephen Schiff, who was at home in New Mexico battling cancer; he presided over hearings on who should control domain-registration names after the current contractor's writ expires. He was also named vice chairman of the Surface Transportation Subcommittee as it presided over the huge 1998 transportation bill; he worked on completing Montgomery projects like improving Columbus Air Force Base and completing construction of the third floor of a VA hospital in Jackson. In November 1998, after he easily won re-election over a Libertarian candidate, he was named to the Commerce Committee, which has huge regulatory jurisdiction; he had already chaired a pro-electric deregulation caucus with Commerce Chairman Thomas Bliley. He seems headed for a long and influential House career—unless he runs for the Senate if Thad Cochran or Trent Lott should choose to retire.

Cook's Call. *Safe.* Like so many southern districts, the 3d, once a safe haven for conservative Democrats, has trended strongly Republican over the last few years. Pickering has little to worry about in a general election, but with Mississippi scheduled to lose one district after 2000, this district could be severly altered or could be thrown in with the 4th District.

The People: Pop. 1990: 515,225; 60.7% rural; 12.8% age 65 +; 66.9% White, 31.4% Black, 0.5% Asian, 1.1% Amer. Indian, 0.1% Other; 0.5% Hispanic Origin. Households: 56.6% married couple families; 29.2% married couple fams. w. children; 38.6% college educ.; median household income: $21,625; per capita income: $10,303; median house value: $47,100; median gross rent: $235.

1996 Presidential Vote

Dole (R)	107,292	(58%)
Clinton (D)	66,027	(36%)
Perot (I)	9,733	(5%)

1992 Presidential Vote

Bush (R)	116,973	(58%)
Clinton (D)	67,411	(34%)
Perot (I)	16,049	(8%)

Rep. Charles (Chip) Pickering (R)

Elected 1996; b. Aug. 10, 1963, Laurel; home, Laurel; MS Col., 1981–82, U. of MS, B.A. 1986, Baylor U., M.B.A. 1988; Baptist; married (Leisha).

Professional Career: Baptist missionary, Budapest, Hungary, 1986–87; Spec. Asst. to the Admin. & Asst. Coord., East European & Soviet Secretariat, U.S. Dept. of Agriculture, 1989–90; Legis. Aide, U.S. Sen. Trent Lott, 1990–94.

DC Office: 427 CHOB 20515, 202-225-5031; Fax: 202-225-5797; Web site: www.house.gov/pickering.

District Offices: Golden Triangle, 601-327-2766; Meridian, 601-693-6681; Pearl, 601-932-2410.

Committees: *Commerce* (25th of 29 R): Energy & Power; Health and Environment; Telecommunications, Trade & Consumer Protection.

Group Ratings

	ADA	ACLU	AFS	LCV	CON	NTU	NFIB	COC	ACU	NTLC	CHC
1998	0	7	0	8	13	52	100	94	100	100	100
1997	0	—	13	—	42	54	—	90	92	—	—

National Journal Ratings

	1997 LIB — 1997 CONS			1998 LIB — 1998 CONS		
Economic	0%	—	90%	0%	—	88%
Social	18%	—	81%	0%	—	97%
Foreign	0%	—	88%	26%	—	73%

Key Votes of the 105th Congress

1. Clinton Budget Deal	Y	5. Puerto Rico Sthood. Ref.	N	9. Cut $ for B-2 Bombers	N
2. Education IRAs	Y	6. End Highway Set-asides	Y	10. Human Rights in China	N
3. Req. 2/3 to Raise Taxes	Y	7. School Prayer Amend.	Y	11. Withdraw Bosnia Troops	Y
4. Fast-track Trade	Y	8. Ovrd. Part. Birth Veto	Y	12. End Cuban TV-Marti	N

Election Results

1998 general	Charles (Chip) Pickering (R)	84,785	(85%)	($517,249)
	Charles T. Scarborough Jr (Lib)	15,465	(15%)	
1998 primary	Charles (Chip) Pickering (R)	unopposed		
1996 general	Charles (Chip) Pickering (R)	115,443	(61%)	($1,167,906)
	John Arthur Eaves, Jr. (D)	68,658	(36%)	($667,567)
	Others	4,043	(2%)	

FOURTH DISTRICT

A few decades ago, Jackson was a small town centered on the grand Beaux Arts 1901 state Capitol. Today, Jackson is clearly the metropolis of Mississippi, the pivot point between the Delta and the hills, the rivers flowing sluggishly to New Orleans and the Gulf of Mexico and the highways running north to Memphis and Chicago. Like Mississippi generally, it is racially divided, with a black, not-so-affluent south side and a white affluent north side; in its new subdivisions of pleasant, large colonial houses under huge, overhanging trees, you can get a sense of what growth has meant to Jackson—especially when you consider that at least some of the people in these neighborhoods came from humble, rural Mississippi beginnings. This newer Mississippi contrasts with Natchez, where the finest collection of antebellum mansions sit on the bluffs overlooking the Mississippi River. Natchez had white millionaires and half the state's free blacks before the Civil War; it was content enough to oppose secession, and was spared major damage in the war because it was of no military importance. Both Jackson and Natchez went through an ugly decade during the civil rights revolution: Mississippi blacks were murdered for registering to vote or for seeking higher-paying jobs; today, the cities are more open, with more social contact between the races than in most northern metropolitan areas, but there is still yearning for economic growth and high-skill jobs.

The 4th Congressional District includes most of Jackson (excluding most black areas, which are in the black-majority 2d) and all of Natchez; it extends east to Laurel and south to the Louisiana line. This is an area that has trended Republican in national and state-wide elections, as newly affluent white Mississippians vote for a party they associate with economic growth and assertive foreign policy, while blacks remain pretty solidly Democratic. But in local contests, Democrats still win many races.

Indeed, the congressman from the 4th District, Ronnie Shows, is a Democrat elected in 1998. Shows grew up on a farm in Jones County, went to two junior colleges and graduated from the University of Southern Mississippi—the first college graduate in his family. As he puts it, "I started my way on the bottom and worked up. I started as a teacher and coach. I worked on a farm, washed dishes in a restaurant." He taught in junior high and elementary schools and two private academies. In 1976, at 29, he was elected Jefferson Davis County Clerk; he moved up twice by winning elections to fill vacancies, to the state Senate in 1980 and as southern district transportation commissioner in 1988. He was re-elected twice without opposition, but the job gave him lots of opportunity to make friends throughout an area that covers 13 of the 15 counties of the 4th District, even as he stayed in his two-bedroom house in tiny Bassfield. He was as well positioned as anyone to run when in January 1998 4th District Congressman Mike Parker, elected as a Democrat in 1988 and a switcher to the Republicans in 1995, announced he would not run again, and would probably run for governor in 1999.

Republicans were favored to hold this district, which voted twice against Bill Clinton, and the Republican primary outdrew the Democrats, with nine candidates rather than three and 59% of the primary votes. But just as Democrats in the old days bruised themselves and sapped their energy in vigorously contested primaries and runoffs, so did Republicans here. Shows won the primary in June, topping the 50% mark with 54% against two black candidates, attorney Carroll Rhodes and Natchez Councilwoman and high school teacher Joyce Arceneaux. The initial favorite for the Republican nod was Art Rhodes, Parker's chief of staff, whom he endorsed in January, but Rhodes had little backing in Jackson and Hinds County, which cast 39% of the votes. The leader there was Delbert Hosemann, a tax lawyer with a 225-lawyer law firm, Jackson's largest, who had served on many civic boards but had not run for office before. Also competitive were Phil Davis, from Simpson County, who won 14% of the vote in the 1988 primary (when only 25% of all voters voted in the Republican primary, versus 59% in 1998); Pike County District Attorney Dunn Lampton; and Heath Hall, former press secretary to Governor Kirk Fordice.

All five were running within close range of each other, when odd mailings started to appear in the last days before the primary—what looked like a letter from the ACLU endorsing Rhodes because he was against school prayer and what looked like a letter from Hall promising to move into the district if he was elected. Hosemann, with the gimlet eye of a tax lawyer, noticed that misspellings on Davis's campaign mailing labels matched those on the fake ACLU brochure (Rhodes, like just about every politician in Mississippi, is in favor of school prayer) and accused Davis of violating federal law; the FBI started investigating. Hosemann ran first in the June 2 primary, with 37% of the vote in Hinds County and 21% overall. Davis was second, with 18.0%, just 87 votes ahead of Rhodes's 17.7%; Lampton had 15% and Hall 12%. In the three weeks before the runoff, Hosemann ran an ad on the subject: "Dirty tricks, negative phone calls, false mailings and an FBI investigation. Mr. Davis, we deserve better. We demand an answer." Hosemann won the June 23 runoff 56%–44%, chiefly because of his 62%–38% margin in Hinds County, which cast 47% of the votes; in the rest of the district Hosemann led by just 58 votes. Nine months later, in March 1999, Davis was indicted by U.S. Attorney Brad Pigott (who lost to Parker in the 1988 Democratic runoff) for violating the Watergate-era law, apparently never before used in a prosecution, banning misidentifying the source of a campaign mailing. The tantalizing question is whether the mailing changed the outcome in November. It probably enabled Davis to overtake Rhodes and get into the runoff. Would Rhodes have been able to beat Hosemann in the runoff? If so, would he have run better than the citified Hosemann ran against Shows in the general? No one can know for sure.

Certainly in the general Shows displayed greater political skills and strength. From his work as highway commissioner, he started off with more name identification. He was heavily outspent, and Hosemann started off early with ads that attacked him for liberal votes in the legislature on taxes and education and charged him with weakness on gun owners' rights. Shows campaigned in his good ole boy manner, and charged that Hosemann was a wealthy big city lawyer out of touch with rural areas and unable to relate to the problems of ordinary people. He opposed abortion rights and supported gun owners' rights. He was endorsed by the Blue Dog Democrats in Washington, and he compared himself to the highly popular Gene Taylor, Democratic congressman in the 5th District. In a 41% black district, he did not take black voters for granted, but appeared constantly in black churches and sought to capitalize on black voters' continuing bitterness over Parker's 1995 party-switch. "In every race I've ever run in, I've always gotten a good African American vote. The reason is I've always been fair. Black or white, Asian, Hispanic, it just doesn't make any difference to us. People are people and want to be treated with respect."

When Hurricane Georges struck Mississippi in September 1998, Shows took advantage of his office by donning blue jeans and going out in a highway department truck talking to people and monitoring the damage; Hosemann stuck to his schedule and made phone calls and attended a Farm Bureau luncheon. And when it came time to go up with the ads he could afford, Shows hit target. One ad featured his gravelly-voiced father, a World War II veteran who talked of his military experiences at the Battle of the Bulge and his pride in his son who got an education and worked to help people; at the end Shows said, "Thanks, Dad." Another accused Hosemann's law firm of freeing a murderer (actually, in a pro bono case it got a sentence reduced from death to life). Another tactic, Republicans charged, were phone calls to seniors saying that Hosemann would cut Social Security.

Shows won a solid 53%–45% victory, all the more impressive because he was outspent more than 2–1. Shows joined the Blue Dog Democrats in the House and won seats on the Transportation and Veterans' Affairs Committees. He will probably be targeted by Republicans in 2000, but they will have to show more political acumen if they want to beat him. Another threat could be redistricting. Mississippi is likely to lose a district and, under prevailing interpretations of the Voting Rights Act, must have at least one black-majority district. That means the legislature must add black voters to the population-losing 2d District, and they will have to come from the 4th, which would obviously hurt Shows. But that is some distance down the road.

Cook's Call. *Potentially Competitive.* Shows' 1998 victory here was the first positive thing to happen for Democrats in the South in quite a while. While this conservative, Republican-leaning district is not easy for any Democrat to hold onto, Shows' conservative voting record and down-home, good-old-boy style make him a solid fit for this mostly rural district. He will be tough to beat in 2000.

The People: Pop. 1990: 513,715; 47.3% rural; 13.7% age 65+; 58.8% White, 40.7% Black, 0.3% Asian, 0.1% Amer. Indian, 0.1% Other; 0.4% Hispanic Origin. Households: 52.5% married couple families; 26.5% married couple fams. w. children; 41.5% college educ.; median household income: $20,234; per capita income: $10,411; median house value: $47,900; median gross rent: $243.

1996 Presidential Vote			**1992 Presidential Vote**		
Dole (R)	86,880	(48%)	Bush (R)	102,666	(50%)
Clinton (D)	83,425	(46%)	Clinton (D)	84,089	(41%)
Perot (I)	9,648	(5%)	Perot (I)	16,758	(8%)

Rep. Ronnie Shows (D)

Elected 1988; b. Jan. 26, 1947, Moselle; home, Bassfield; Jones Cnty. Jr. Col., SE Baptist Col., U. of S. MS, B. A. 1971; Baptist; married (Johnnie Ruth).

Elected Office: Jefferson Davis Cnty. Circuit Clerk, 1976–80; MS Senate, 1980–88; MS Southern Dist. Transportation Comm., 1988–98.

Professional Career: High schl. teacher & coach, 1971–76.

DC Office: 509 CHOB 20515, 202-225-5865; Fax: 202-225-5886; Web site: www.house.gov/shows.

District Offices: Jackson, 601-352-1355; Laurel, 601-425-4999; Natches, 601-446-8825.

Committees: *Transportation & Infrastructure* (32d of 34 D): Economic Development, Public Buildings, Hazardous Materials & Pipeline Transportation; Ground Transportation. *Veterans' Affairs* (11th of 14 D): Health.

Group Ratings and Key Votes: Newly Elected

Election Results

1998 general	Ronnie Shows (D)	73,252	(53%)	($654,887)
	Delbert Hosemann (R)	61,551	(45%)	($1,462,310)
	Others	2,396	(2%)	
1998 primary	Ronnie Shows (D)	12,377	(57%)	
	Carroll Rhodes (D)	5,104	(23%)	
	Joyce Arcenueaux (D)	4,300	(20%)	
1996 general	Mike Parker (R)	112,444	(61%)	($288,719)
	Kevin Antoine (D)	66,836	(36%)	($44,420)
	Others	4,383	(2%)	

FIFTH DISTRICT

The strand where Mississippi faces the Gulf of Mexico has gone through several transformations. French explorers here founded Biloxi in 1699, before New Orleans or St. Louis, and made it the capital of an empire extending to Yellowstone Park. In later decades, rich people from New Orleans came to this Gulf Coast in summer to get away from yellow fever and to rest on Victorian verandas; six American presidents have vacationed here. More recently the Gulf Coast, with the help of riverboat casinos, has been growing more than any other part of Mississippi; along much of the strand, new 1,000-room hotels are rising as part of Mississippi's boom. And Biloxi's Keesler Air Force Base is one of the four largest bases in the country. Pascagoula, once a small town, is now home of the 11,000-worker Ingalls Shipyard, whose gray hangar-like buildings and skeletons of ships under construction loom over the flat landscape. To the west is the Stennis Space Center named for longtime (1947–88) Senator John Stennis, who died in 1995.

This is the heart of the 5th Congressional District, some 60% of whose people live on the Gulf Coast; the rest are inland, in farm counties or around Hattiesburg. This was mostly scrub land, not much good for plantations, and thus has never had many black residents. With its low black percentage and mostly booming economy, the 5th District has become prime Republican territory. It gave Richard Nixon his highest percentage in all 435 districts in 1972, it voted twice against fellow Southerners Jimmy Carter and Bill Clinton, and it was represented for 16 years in the House by Trent Lott until he was elected to the Senate in 1988.

The congressman from the 5th District is Gene Taylor, a Democrat first chosen in an October 1989 special election. Taylor graduated from Tulane, served in the Coast Guard Reserves, as skipper of a search and rescue boat for 10 years. He was elected to the Bay St. Louis Council in 1981 and in 1983, at 30, was elected to the state Senate. In 1988, when Lott left the House to run for the Senate, Taylor ran for Congress, won the Democratic primary, but lost to Republican Larkin Smith 55%–45%. Smith died in an August 1989 plane crash, and Lott brushed aside Smith's widow and backed his own longtime aide Tom Anderson, who had spent little time in the district and proved to be an abrasive candidate. Taylor, combining a barely reined-in aggressiveness with a down-home manner, won the special 65%–35%.

In the House, Taylor has a conservative voting record and has criticized the leadership of his own party and the Republicans. When asked to vote for the October 1998 omnibus bill, he characteristically remarked, "One of the people who is asking us to trust him is now being studied to see if he committed perjury. Another of the people who says trust us admitted lying to the ethics committee. That's not a very good place to start." Taylor is a peppery populist ("what Mississippians think is usually the right answer") with a reasonably consistent view on issues. He is against abortion, gun control, free trade and foreign aid. He is strongly pro-defense and boasts of bringing defense contracts to the area: When the Navy announced a new human resources center with 300 civilian jobs near Bay St. Louis, Taylor said he had just the buildings in mind. As ranking Democrat on an Armed Services subcommittee, he is a firm believer in improving the pay and benefits of military personnel and health care for military retirees.

Feisty to the point of being belligerent, he is opposed to any U.S. military commitment that stops short of assured and total victory: He opposed the Gulf war resolution, lifting the arms embargo on Bosnia, sending troops to Haiti. But when faced with apparently ineffective American military involvement in Serbia in April 1999, he called for a declaration of war: "The best course of action for this nation is to use the overwhelming military might that we have at our disposal to end this war swiftly and quickly." He is a protectionist, loudly opposing NAFTA and GATT. He gives away his pay raise in local scholarships and cheers on lobbying reform. If there is anything that holds his record together, it is boats. He promotes Ingalls and other shipyards, he succeeded in widening and deepening the Gulfport shipping channel, he champions the seafood industry, and he wants to prohibit foreign-flag ships from conducting passenger "voyages to nowhere" from U.S. ports. He supported the 1993 federal shipbuilding program and the 1995 act to revitalize the U.S. Merchant Marines; he objects to waivers to the Jones Act, which requires coastal shipping to be conducted in U.S.-made ships. His Washington residence is a 34-foot boat on the Anacostia River.

Taylor voted "present" rather than vote for Dick Gephardt for speaker in January 1995 and in 1996 announced he would not vote for Clinton. He voted against disciplining Gingrich in January 1997, because he opposed the $300,000 "penalty" the ethics committee had concocted. There was little doubt about his vote for impeachment. When White House chief of staff Erskine Bowles asked a group of Blue Dog Democrats what they thought the president should do, Taylor's hand shot up first. "I think he should resign." He was one of five Democrats to vote for two counts of impeachment. The Campaign for Working Families, a PAC run by Republican presidential candidate Gary Bauer, gave $2,000 to Taylor because of his stands on taxes, abortion and trade. But Taylor has rebuffed all importunings to switch parties. "I personally would feel like a prostitute. I still believe the average working person's best interest is best served by the Democratic Party." When Republican National Chairman Haley Barbour offered a $1 million reward to anyone who could prove Republicans had "cut" Medicare, Taylor laid claim to it. He voted for welfare reform: "It's this or nothing. And this is better than nothing." He wants to expand random drug testing from the Defense Department to the entire federal government. Evidently this aggressive Mississippian sees that House Republicans are more cohesive and disciplined than Democrats, and finds it more congenial to captain his own ship in the less disciplined fleet of the Democratic Party.

Taylor has seldom had much in the way of serious opposition, except in 1996, when he was opposed by Republican Dennis Dollar, a party-switcher himself in the legislature, who matched Taylor's spending. But Taylor won with a solid 58%–40%, even as Bob Dole was carrying the district by a similar margin. In 1998 less than 4,000 people bothered to vote in the Republican primary; Taylor won in November 78%–19%.

Cook's Call. *Safe.* Although this conservative district votes for Republicans on the national level, they are also quite comfortable electing Democrat Gene Taylor year after year. Once Taylor decides to leave the House, the district will likely fall into Republican hands. Until then, Taylor remains secure.

The People: Pop. 1990: 514,611; 34.9% rural; 11.5% age 65 +; 78.3% White, 20% Black, 1.2% Asian, 0.3% Amer. Indian, 0.2% Other; 1.2% Hispanic Origin. Households: 57.4% married couple families; 30% married couple fams. w. children; 40.9% college educ.; median household income: $21,702; per capita income: $10,116; median house value: $49,700; median gross rent: $261.

1996 Presidential Vote		
Dole (R)	96,880	(56%)
Clinton (D)	61,035	(35%)
Perot (I)	13,431	(8%)

1992 Presidential Vote		
Bush (R)	99,997	(54%)
Clinton (D)	58,808	(32%)
Perot (I)	24,956	(14%)

Rep. Gene Taylor (D)

Elected Oct., 1989; b. Sept. 17, 1953, New Orleans, LA; home, Bay St. Louis; Tulane U., B.A. 1974; Catholic; married (Margaret).

Military Career: Coast Guard Reserves, 1971–84.

Elected Office: Bay St. Louis City Cncl., 1981–83; MS Senate, 1983–89.

Professional Career: Sales rep., Stone Container Corp., 1977–89.

DC Office: 2311 RHOB 20515, 202-225-5772; Fax: 202-225-7074; Web site: www.house.gov/genetaylor.

District Offices: Gulfport, 601-864-7670; Hattiesburg, 601-582-3246; Ocean Spring, 601-872-7950.

Committees: *Armed Services* (7th of 28 D): Military Installations & Facilities (RMM); Military Research & Development; Special Oversight Panel on the Merchant Marine. *Transportation & Infrastructure* (19th of 34 D): Coast Guard & Maritime Transportation; Water Resources & Environment.

Group Ratings

	ADA	ACLU	AFS	LCV	CON	NTU	NFIB	COC	ACU	NTLC	CHC
1998	30	0	38	23	95	53	85	41	79	79	83
1997	20	—	13	—	24	50	—	80	80	—	—

National Journal Ratings

	1997 LIB — 1997 CONS		1998 LIB — 1998 CONS	
Economic	34% —	66%	44% —	55%
Social	20% —	71%	32% —	67%
Foreign	41% —	58%	43% —	53%

Key Votes of the 105th Congress

1. Clinton Budget Deal	Y	5. Puerto Rico Sthood. Ref.	Y	9. Cut $ for B-2 Bombers	N
2. Education IRAs	Y	6. End Highway Set-asides	Y	10. Human Rights in China	Y
3. Req. 2/3 to Raise Taxes	Y	7. School Prayer Amend.	Y	11. Withdraw Bosnia Troops	N
4. Fast-track Trade	N	8. Ovrd. Part. Birth Veto	Y	12. End Cuban TV-Marti	Y

Election Results

1998 general	Gene Taylor (D)	78,661	(78%)	($233,630)
	Randy McDonnell (R)	19,341	(19%)	($7,980)
	Others	3,093	(3%)	
1998 primary	Gene Taylor (D)	unopposed		
1996 general	Gene Taylor (D)	103,415	(58%)	($451,833)
	Dennis Dollar (R)	71,114	(40%)	($462,252)
	Others	2,916	(2%)	

MISSOURI

When Meriwether Lewis and William Clark set out on their expedition to the Pacific, they embarked from St. Louis in 1804. On high ground just below the point where the Missouri River swirls into the Mississippi, St. Louis was at the time the one well-established city in America's interior, with an aristocracy of French merchants, a brawling bourgeoisie of Yankee and Southern frontiersmen and fur traders and a proletariat of black slaves. Part of the Louisiana Purchase in 1803, St. Louis by 1821 was part of the new state of Missouri, and for decades St. Louis and Missouri were the gateways to the frontier. In Missouri, Daniel Boone finally found elbow room. Here were the eastern termini of the Pony Express, in St. Joseph, and the Santa Fe Trail, in Westport, now part of Kansas City; here were railroads reaching across the continent, connecting the farmers of vast prairies with their markets. Here also were the Mississippi River steamboats, and here grew up their great chronicler, Mark Twain.

For Missouri was not just the gateway to the frontier; it was also the focus of the furious battle over slavery. Missouri was the northernmost slave state at mid-century; it was Missouri ruffians crossing the border and killing antislavery settlers in the Kansas Territory that led proximately to the Civil War. In the 1860s, Missouri had its own mini civil war in the hilly counties along the Missouri River. Throughout the 19th Century, both before and after the Civil War, Americans turned away from their oceans and headed inward to settle the great interior of the continent. They found Missouri at its heart, with farmland and mines, rivers and railroads, a major manufacturing state—and in the days before tractors, the nation's leading breeder and trader of mules. In 1874 the Eads Bridge opened, one of very few across the Mississippi, and

St. Louis's Cupples Station was the largest rail hub in the world. At the turn of the 20th Century, Missouri was the fifth-largest state. St. Louis was the fourth-largest city, site of the 1904 World's Fair, and one of the few cities with two major league baseball teams, the Cardinals and the Browns; Missouri after the 1900 Census had 16 congressional districts.

Today Missouri does not loom as large in the national consciousness, yet it is in some sense still central. In the 20th Century, Americans—like the Browns who moved to Baltimore in the '50s and the football Cardinals who moved to Phoenix in the '80s—increasingly headed to the coasts, to the big cities of the East and to California, and eventually to Florida and Texas. Missouri has had below-average population growth since 1900, and today it is the 16th largest state, with just nine congressional districts. But Missouri is the geographic center of the nation's population. Its airport is TWA's hub; next door is the former headquarters of McDonnell Douglas, which was bought by Boeing in December 1996. Its Anheuser-Busch is the world's largest beer producer. And Missouri has again captured Americans' imaginations: if Americans in 1904 flocked to St. Louis on the banks of the Mississippi, in the 1990s their vans and buses were jamming the two-lane road through the Ozarks to Branson, population 4,400, now America's number two tourist destination (with 6 million visitors a year), with country music stars and soft rock veterans, country violinist Shoji Tabuchi, more theater seats than Broadway, and more seats for regularly scheduled music concerts than anywhere else in America.

Politically, Missouri has remained the nation's best bellwether state: it has voted for every presidential winner but one (Eisenhower in 1956) in the 20th Century. From the 1960s to the 1980s it mirrored national trends by moving its congressional politics from pretty solidly Democratic to leaning Republican. It votes for governor in presidential years and, since 1972, has voted for the same party for governor as the nation has for president. Missouri's ancient Civil War political divisions still hold in most rural areas: Little Dixie in the northeast, first settled by Virginians, and the northwest, settled by Southerners, lean Democratic; the Ozarks in the southwest, which was pro-Union, is Republican; the southeast is split, like next-door Downstate Illinois. About one-third of the state's votes are cast in metro St. Louis, which is typically more Democratic than the state as a whole. About one-sixth are cast in metro Kansas City, which has been volatile in the 1980s and 1990s; it voted 25% for Ross Perot in 1992, giving him nearly as many votes as George Bush, and tilted Democratic in 1996, voting 66% for Governor Mel Carnahan, and Republican in 1998, with a small majority for Senator Christopher Bond. The rest of the state, which casts almost half the votes, went 41%–38% for Bill Clinton in 1992 and 45%–43% for Bob Dole in 1996—similar to trends in Downstate Illinois and rural Iowa.

Culturally, Missouri remains more conservative than most bigger states. The state's relatively slow-growing metro areas have not overwhelmed the countryside; 44% of the votes are cast outside metro St. Louis and Kansas City. This rest of Missouri is a land of farms and small towns, thick with churches and free of glitzy shopping centers, laced with man-made lakes and boat launches, with only one town over 100,000 (Springfield) and 102 counties where life—and politics—seem not to have changed much over the past half-century. Some 29% of Missourians smoke, second only to Kentucky. To adapt to rural Missouri, Democrats have nominated moderates with rural backgrounds, like Governor Mel Carnahan, while Republicans have nominated strong cultural conservatives, like Senator and former Governor John Ashcroft. It was Missouri's restrictions on abortion that were upheld by the Supreme Court in the 1989 *Webster* case. Even on economic issues it does not have an easy liberalism: Voters in 1996 rejected a ballot initiative to raise the minimum wage to $6.25. It took a $10 million campaign to persuade Missouri voters in 1998 to approve "boats in moats"—to allow gambling casinos located on ponds to be treated as if they were on rivers, as required by state law. Another issue on the ballot that year was cockfighting: Voters outlawed it and other animal fights, such as bear wrestling, by 63%–37%. But sometimes the urban areas outvote the countryside: in an April 1999 referendum Missouri rejected 52%–48% a proposal to allow issuance of concealed weapons permits to law-abiding citizens, as more than 70% in metro St. Louis voted no. But all of Missouri (or everyone outside the Kansas City area) joined the cheers when the St. Louis

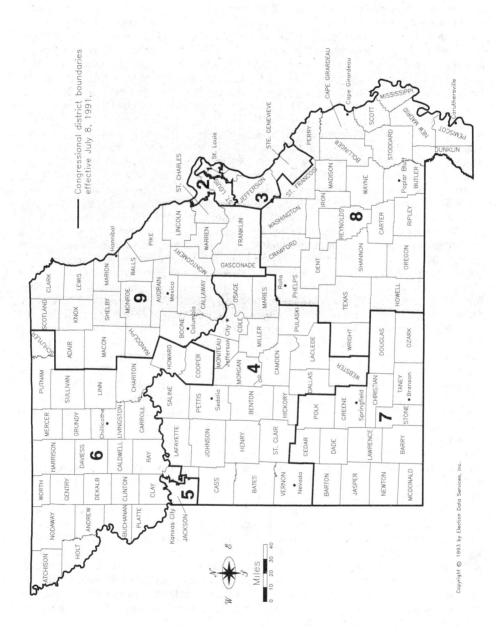

Congressional district boundaries effective July 8, 1991.

Cardinals' Mark McGwire hit home runs 62 through 70 in summer 1998; and people here, and around the country as well, were awed when Pope John Paul II visited St. Louis on his way home from Mexico in January 1999.

Governor. The governorship is central to Missouri politics, and Missourians have been partial to most recent governors: Republican Senators Christopher Bond and John Ashcroft both won two terms as governors, and Democratic Governor Mel Carnahan won in 1992 and 1996 with the biggest percentages any Democrat has won here since 1968. Carnahan grew up in Shannon and Carter counties, in the midst of politics; his father, A.S.J. Carnahan, was a U.S. congressman (1945–47, 1949–61) and ambassador to Sierra Leone in the 1960s. After the Air Force and law school, Mel Carnahan was elected municipal judge in 1960 at age 26; he was elected to the legislature in 1962, then became majority leader in his second term, and returned to full-time law practice in Rolla two years later. In 1980, he was elected state treasurer and served four years; in 1988, he was elected lieutenant governor even while Republican Governor John Ashcroft was re-elected by a wide margin—the beginning of a relationship of mutual loathing. In 1992 Carnahan ran for governor and won the Democratic primary over then-Mayor Vince Schoemehl of St. Louis, 55%–34%. He focused on education and went on to defeat Attorney General William Webster, 59%–41%, with 63% in the metro areas and 53% outside.

In his first term Carnahan got the legislature to act on his platform. In 1993, his Outstanding Schools Act was passed, complete with a $310 million tax increase: It sought to reduce class sizes in lower grades, raise state aid to low-revenue school districts, finance careers programs and apprenticeships for non-college-bound high schoolers, and fund a Parents as Teachers program. He had one major defeat: in 1994 the legislature rejected his attempt to require health insurers to disregard pre-existing conditions and make policies portable between jobs. But he claimed credit for a welfare program emphasizing work, for reorganizing state government and for lifetime sentences for sexual predators. He vetoed a concealed weapons law and a bill to further restrict abortion. He backed an initiative requiring voter approval of tax increases of more than $50 million, which passed in August 1996.

In 1996 the Missouri economy was humming and Carnahan, like Bill Clinton, steamed ahead to re-election. Republican Auditor Margaret Kelly attacked Carnahan for his education tax increase and called for a $640 million tax cut. Carnahan called for a $1,500-a-year college tuition tax credit and elimination of the sales tax on food. At the polls Carnahan won almost as many votes as Clinton and Ross Perot combined, leading Kelly 57%–40%—a solid margin, though a bit under his 1992 mark. He ran very far ahead, 66%–32%, in the volatile Kansas City area, and won non-metro Missouri with 55%, the best for a Democrat in some time.

In his second term, he was obliged by the 1980 Hancock Amendment, sponsored by a conservative Republican, to refund taxes when spending reached a certain level; more than $1 billion is going back to taxpayers over five budget years. The food sales tax was eliminated in 1997; welfare rolls continued to fall and Clinton praised Carnahan's welfare-to-work program; in 1997 the legislature failed to override Carnahan's veto of a partial-birth abortion ban by one vote. Carnahan pushed through a children's health insurance plan with coverage wider than all but a few other states. In 1998 he was able to combine tax refunds with stepped-up spending for early childhood education and school aid. In 1999 he and Republicans argued about the amount of tax cuts. Carnahan favors the death penalty and let most executions go ahead, though like most governors he examines the cases conscientiously and commuted at least one sentence. Then on his January 1999 visit to St. Louis Pope, John Paul II asked him to spare the life of a man convicted of murdering two grandparents and their paraplegic grandson. After mulling the request, Carnahan agreed. "I'll have to say I was moved by his concern for this prisoner. I continue to support capital punishment."

Days after the November 1998 election Carnahan announced he would run for Senate and stepped up his criticisms of John Ashcroft. Their loathing goes back a decade; Ashcroft as governor brought a lawsuit to clarify Carnahan's lack of power as lieutenant governor when he left the state. In November 1998 Carnahan said of Ashcroft, "He's a voice of the far right—

he would rather spout his ideology than solve something," and that he left the state "stagnant, not going anywhere." He argued that Ashcroft posed as a tax-cutter while as governor he had pressed for tax increases; indeed, Ashcroft had backed a $385 million tax increase for education that lost in a referendum in 1991—a bit larger than the increase Carnahan got two years later. Carnahan criticized Ashcroft for taking an anti-government line while he had spent most of his adult life in politics and government. Ashcroft had spent much of 1998 going around the country, looking to run for president; he left the race abruptly in January 1999, and Carnahan allies crowed that Carnahan was leading him in polls for the Senate race. When Carnahan commuted the death sentence at the Pope's request, Ashcroft said he had no comment but his staff faxed reporters 12 pages from Ashcroft's book, *Lessons from a Father to His Son*, on the death penalty. Even the liberal *St. Louis Post-Dispatch* criticized Carnahan after the Democratic Party charged that praise by the head of the Council of Conservative Citizens "proves [Ashcroft's] base of support is from the extreme right." (The party can be considered Carnahan's instrument; parties in Missouri have been the main recipients of campaign dollars since a limit on contributions to candidates was upheld in 1995.)

Much argument revolved around assessments of their governorships. Carnahan said that state spending was up 72% in Ashcroft's years and 51% in his and cited census figures that Missouri was one of the lowest states in per capita spending and tax revenues. Ashcroft cited a Tax Foundation analysis that said Missouri had the 16th highest tax burden and a Cato Institute study that Missouri was number one in average annual change in tax revenue per $1,000 of income in Carnahan's terms. The *Post-Dispatch* argued that there was less difference than meets the eye, that both had emphasized education and both were scandal-free, that both balanced budgets and the larger percentage increase in spending in Ashcroft's term reflected higher inflation and the tax refunds in Carnahan's reflected the state's stronger economy in the 1990s.

Who will be elected governor in 2000? In March 1998 Carnahan endorsed state Treasurer Bob Holden; they both grew up in the same small town, Birch Tree, and Holden, responding to Republican Jim Talent's criticisms of the status quo, said it was pretty good: "300,000 new jobs, 120,000 people taken off welfare, $400 million returned to the taxpayers and our schools are improving. What doesn't he like?" By February 1999 he had raised over $1 million for the governor race. Lieutenant Governor Roger Wilson, an inspiring orator and 20-year political veteran, took himself out of the race the same month Carnahan endorsed Holden.

The Republican candidate seemed sure to be Congressman Jim Talent, from suburban St. Louis County; if elected, he would be the first St. Louis area resident elected governor since Forrest Donnell in 1940. He announced for governor in February 1999, just after winning a leadership post in Washington, and said, "There's a status quo in Jefferson City; that's what I'm going to run against. . . . Taxes have shot up, while the quality of public education and highways have remained a mess." Starting with a transferable $500,000 in his federal campaign account, he is also likely to be well-financed.

Cook's Call. *Highly Competitive.* Although this race will likely be overshadowed by the Ashcroft-Carnahan Senate fight, it looks to be interesting in its own right. Both parties seem to have recruited the candidate they wanted: the Democratic banner will likely be carried by state Treasurer Bob Holden, while the Republican favorite for the nomination is Representative Jim Talent.

Senior Senator. Christopher Bond grew up in the town of Mexico, Missouri, where his family were part owners of the largest business, A.P. Green, makers of heat-resistant bricks, which was sold to another firm in 1998. He graduated from Princeton and the University of Virginia Law School, then ran for Congress in 1968, at age 29, and narrowly lost. He was elected state auditor in 1970, was elected governor at 33 in 1972, then lost in an upset to Democrat Joseph Teasdale in 1976 and won a comeback victory against Teasdale in 1980. As governor, Bond pushed reorganization, open meetings, merit hiring and campaign finance in his first term; he wrestled with fiscal problems, crime control and early childhood education in his second term. He still touts his Parents As Teachers program, and made it the basis of a federal law. After two years in private life, he ran for the Senate against Harriett Woods, who had come close to beating Bond's longtime ally, then-Senator John Danforth, in 1982. Woods ran a three-part ad showing a farmer breaking into tears as he and his wife told Woods about their foreclosure and named Bond as a board member of the insurance company that foreclosed; evidently this struck voters as either demagoguery or an invasion of privacy, and Woods fell in the polls. Bond won, 53%–47%.

Bond has a moderate voting record in the Senate. He has usually worked behind the scenes, trying to forge bipartisan consensus; "he works hard even when no one's looking," his colleague John Ashcroft once said. He was the chief Republican sponsor of the Family and Medical Leave Act, vetoed by George Bush and signed by Bill Clinton. He has been the lead Republican senator on housing, starting on the Banking Committee and now as chairman of the VA-HUD Appropriations Subcommittee. He supervised Henry Cisneros's downsizing and decentralizing of HUD, passed legislation to allow demolition of public housing projects, worked to reduce looming Section 8 multi-family housing program costs, supported locally-based community development organizations that build housing and fought to allow elderly housing that excludes youngsters. He has used his post as chairman of the Small Business Committee to push for regulatory reform, health insurance deductibility for the self-employed, IRS reform and to oppose raising the minimum wage. He used the appropriations process to zero out the White House's Office of Consumer Affairs. He worked to pass a law with $2 billion in preferences for small businesses located in poor neighborhoods that hire local residents. He has ranged afield on other issues, co-sponsoring a ban on human cloning in early 1998, funding research on the plant genome process and passing a law on birth defect prevention. He called for ending the ban on foreign assassinations and wants to ban triple-trailer trucks nationwide.

Bond has been harshly attacked by environmentalists for urging relaxation of Superfund regulations and opposing the EPA's new air-quality standards; he has called them "wackos" and "green socialists." He sponsored a Good Samaritan Food Donation Act and a new Cape Girardeau Bridge, both named after the late Congressman Bill Emerson. In October 1998 he tried to get part of I-70 named after Mark McGwire and got $2 million for restoring the Old Chain of Rocks Bridge for bicyclists and hikers. He has called himself the "best friend" of McDonnell Douglas, and promotes the F/A-18 Hornet to the point of denouncing U.S. Embassy personnel in Prague for recommending another fighter to the Czechs. He blocked funding an outlet for swollen Devils Lake in North Dakota for fear it would take water from the Missouri River. He promotes barge traffic on the Mississippi and Missouri rivers and brought together the barge industry and the anti-barge American Rivers organization to agree on a $50 million program for the rivers. He has had some embarrassments: in 1994 he got in a shoving match with an *Inside Edition* reporter taping members at a charity ski trip in Utah.

Bond can be a strong partisan on occasion. After Missouri Republicans lost every major race but his in 1992—he beat Democrat Geri Rothman-Serot 52%–45%—he spent two years raising $750,000 for the party. In 1998 Bond's opponent was Jay Nixon, who had lost 68%–32% to Senator John Danforth in 1988 but had been elected attorney general in 1992 (after canoeing the length of the Missouri River) and was re-elected 57%–39% in 1996. Nixon had earned considerable publicity for cleaning up the second injury fund and prosecuting consumer fraud and attacking telecom and insurance fraud. Nixon pledged to serve only two terms and opposed Bond's stands on tobacco, the minimum wage and HMO reform. But before he could get started, he was dogged by controversy over his actions on the St. Louis school desegregation cases. Both St. Louis and Kansas City schools have labored under court orders since the 1970s which required massive busing and ordered the state government to spend large sums. There was widespread support for ending the cases, but when Nixon opposed a bipartisan legislative plan and, like previous Republican attorneys general, moved for a settlement with sharply reduced state payments, black leaders protested vehemently. St. Louis Congressman Bill Clay denounced Nixon in vitriolic terms and the NAACP threatened to mount a picket line when President Clinton came in for a Nixon fundraiser, which was then postponed. In the meantime

Bond built on the ties he had developed with black leaders over many years of working on housing programs and sought their support or neutrality. "I'm not saying [black leaders] will endorse me publically, but I'm very comfortable with what they've said to me one-on-one." The result was that Nixon had to spend much of his energy and time in the spotlight mollifying black Democrats to simply get votes most Democrats can take for granted.

Nixon made other mistakes. Early attacks on Bond turned out to be based on simple factual errors—which didn't impress potential money-givers. His attacks on Bond for commuting sentences of violent criminals when he was governor and his ad replaying the *Inside Edition* footage seemed to be dredging up the past for voters who were in an optimistic, pro-incumbent mood. Bond campaigned hard, traveling across the state pointing to projects he had funded and raising nearly $6 million, while Nixon spent $2.6 million. He attacked Nixon for paying private trial lawyers a fee on the order of $350 million in the state's tobacco suit, and for opposing Auditor Margaret Kelly's lawsuit seeking an additional $120 million tax refund from state revenues from riverboat admission fees. Bond won 53%–44%, a slight improvement on 1992. He ran better in the Kansas City area, a little worse in the St. Louis area and far ahead of Nixon in the rest of the state: outside the two big metro areas, Nixon carried only 11 of 102 counties. Bond carried 33% of blacks' votes—an enormous percentage for a Republican—and ran almost as well among women as men.

Junior Senator. John Ashcroft was first elected in 1994. He grew up in Springfield, the son and grandson of Assemblies of God ministers; the fast-growing church is headquartered in Springfield, and the senior Ashcroft was president of one of its universities. John Ashcroft graduated from Yale and met his wife when they were students at the University of Chicago Law School; they practiced law and wrote books together, raised a family and were active church members. Ashcroft is serious, hard-working, abstemious; he sings gospel hymns, plays the piano and is one of the four Singing Senators. He ran for Congress in 1972, at age 30, and lost the Republican primary 50%–45%; he was appointed state auditor in 1973, succeeding Christopher Bond when he became governor. Ashcroft went on to be elected attorney general in 1976 and 1980, succeeding John Danforth, and governor in 1984 and 1988, succeeding Bond. As governor he held tax rates down and concentrated on creating a favorable job environment, establishing 50 enterprise zones, building new prison cells and championing a Learnfare program and education reform. Tax revenues per capita were among the lowest in the nation when he left office, though he had sought a tax increase for education in 1991.

For two years Ashcroft practiced law in St. Louis, but when Danforth surprised everyone by announcing his retirement from the Senate, Ashcroft was the obvious and best-known Republican to succeed him. He raised large sums and his conservative stands seemed increasingly in line with voters' views as the year went on. Democrats had a close primary between Kansas City Congressman Alan Wheat and Jackson County Executive Marsha Murphy, which Wheat eventually won 41%–38%. Wheat is black, and some speculated that his race hurt him against Ashcroft; a bigger problem was Wheat's solidly liberal voting record. Ashcroft ran ads against Wheat's votes on crime and welfare and about the House bank; Wheat had to pull one ad because it contained inaccuracies. Wheat nearly equalled Ashcroft in spending, but Ashcroft won easily, 60%–36%, losing St. Louis City and Kansas City, but carrying all 114 counties.

In the Senate, Ashcroft soon established himself as a conservative activist with a very conservative voting record and a knack for original proposals. He sponsored the first term limits bill to reach the Senate floor in October 1995—the first in 50 years; he sponsored a constitutional amendment to reverse the Supreme Court decision overturning term limits. While welfare reform languished, he proposed Charitable Choice, block grants specifically allowing states to use charities or faith-based organizations to provide services; that provision was included in the August 1996 Welfare Reform Act. But Ashcroft tried unsuccessfully to pass amendments in the welfare reform bill requiring recipients to work toward obtaining high school degrees and giving states the authority to deny benefits to recipients who test positive for drugs. He has supported the flextime bill, opposed by labor unions, which would allow employers to give employees the option of compensatory time in place of overtime pay, and the Teamwork for Employees and Managers Act, also opposed by labor and vetoed by Clinton, which would allow more worker-management cooperation in non-union shops. Ashcroft is an Internet enthusiast and was one of the first senators with a home page; he developed a "Gateways to Government" program for students and responds to constituents' questions via e-mail.

In January 1998 Ashcroft began to prepare to run for president; at the same time the Lewinsky scandal broke, and Ashcroft was one of the first to say that the charges might warrant impeachment. In the Senate he became a gadfly not only to Clinton but to the Republican leadership. In March 1998 he moved adroitly to revive proposals for a tax cut; he has long sought to end the marriage penalty (which he got a majority of the Senate to vote to do in August 1998) and the Social Security earnings tax. He cast the only vote in the Commerce Committee against John McCain's tobacco bill in April 1998; he opposed it as a giant tax increase, and in two months most Republicans swung over to his view and the tobacco bill was dead. Ashcroft opposed Surgeon General David Satcher because Satcher opposed the partial-birth abortion ban, and he sponsored a bill to require parental consent for abortion referrals or contraceptives. He pushed for longer terms for sellers of meth, a popular drug in Missouri, and co-sponsored with Tom Harkin a bill giving Congress more power over food embargoes, a popular stand among Missouri farmers. He opposed the Clinton national educational testing program and sponsored bills requiring that discipline records be transmitted to new schools and that charitable volunteers be immune from frivolous lawsuits. He opposed the October 1998 omnibus budget: "eight of the 13 appropriations bills have been tossed into one enormous, rotting heap of spending." He wrote a book, *Lessons from a Father to His Son*, about his father, who died while returning to Missouri from his swearing-in at the Senate.

All the while, he was traveling to Iowa and New Hampshire, raising money, expounding a new tax program to help what he called the working middle class. He sought and gained support from Christian conservatives, and James Dobson and others spoke well of him. At the same time, he said he was an economic conservative. And he was one of the most caustic critics of Clinton. But the November 1998 election did not go his way. Republicans' failure to make gains and the fact that only 34% of Missouri voters said he would be a good president in the VNS exit poll tended to undercut his candidacy. Ashcroft, one of the first Republicans to call for Clinton's resignation, suddenly had little to say about impeachment. Then came volleys of attacks from Governor Mel Carnahan, a Democrat who was lieutenant governor in Ashcroft's second term; the two men obviously loathe each other. Carnahan, prevented by term limits from seeking a third term, announced he would run for the Senate. He argued that Ashcroft posed as a tax-cutter, while as governor he had pressed for tax increases, and criticized him for taking an anti-government line while he had spent most of his adult life in politics and government; Carnahan aides boasted that he was leading Ashcroft in their polls. The implication was that Ashcroft's presidential campaigning and his opposition to Clinton were hurting his ability to win re-election in Missouri. In November 1998 Ashcroft, before the Detroit Economic Club, put forward an economic conservative plank; he still sounded like he was running for president. But on January 5, 1999, he abruptly pulled out of the presidential race.

This left a Senate race between two men who have twice been elected governor and have nine statewide victories between them. As a Democratic consultant said, "This will be like the 1985 World Series between the St. Louis Cardinals and the Kansas City Royals. Everybody in the state took sides." Ashcroft voted for Clinton's removal in February, but would have no part of censure after his side lost: "In my view, one more day spent on Bill Clinton's misdeeds is time wasted." Then it was Carnahan's turn on the defensive. Pope John Paul II in his January 1999 visit to St. Louis asked Carnahan to commute the death sentence of a Missouri inmate. After hesitation, in February 1999 Carnahan did so. In March, Ashcroft held hearings in St. Louis on his amendment to the victim's rights bill which would give victims or their relatives two months' notice of a decision to commute a death sentence; the parents of the 19-year old paraplegic whom the pardoned convict killed had learned about his commutation from the newspapers. In another February controversy, even the liberal *St. Louis Post-Dispatch* criticized Carnahan after the Democratic Party charged that praise by the head of the Council of Conservative Citizens "proves [Ashcroft's] base of support is from the extreme right."

Cook's Call. *Highly Competitive.* This will be one of a handful of marquee Senate races in the country. Democratic Governor Mel Carnahan is challenging Ashcroft. Although Ashcroft won the open seat easily in 1994, Carnahan will prove to be a much more difficult opponent. Early surveys suggest a nip-and-tuck race that is likely to remain very close to the finish. There is no love lost between the two candidates and the race is likely to be bitter, bloody and very expensive.

Presidential politics. Missouri's peculiar balance of northern and southern, urban and rural, has helped to make it a presidential bellwether and explains its one deviation in the 20th Century: it voted for Adlai Stevenson in 1956, who capitalized on farmer discontent and whose lukewarmness about civil rights helped him carry traditional Southern Democrats. In 1992, the economically hard-pressed northern part of the state trended to the Democrats, and Bill Clinton won 44%–34%. In 1996, although the Dole campaign never targeted the state, rural Missouri moved toward Republicans while the Kansas City area moved toward Democrats, and Clinton's margin was a bit smaller, 48%–41%. This is likely to be a very seriously contested state in 2000.

Missouri joined the Super Tuesday primary for 1988, then went back to multi-tiered caucuses to elect delegates. In 1992 the winners were Clinton and George Bush. In 1996 Pat Buchanan won the March 9 Republican caucuses, thanks to support from many religious conservatives, including Phyllis Schlafly, longtime conservative networker, who had moved from Alton, Illinois, across the river to Missouri. After district caucuses and state conventions, the final delegation had 19 Dole, 11 Buchanan and 6 Alan Keyes delegates, the strongest anti-Dole and pro-Buchanan delegation beyond New Hampshire.

Congressional districting. Missouri did not lose any seats in the 1990 Census, but the loss of population in heavily Democratic areas forced new lines which in turn have helped Republicans, who are now down only 5–4 in the delegation. Demographics will make it difficult for Democrats to improve their position even if they control the process after the 2000 election and Census.

The People: Est. Pop. 1998: 5,438,559; Pop. 1990: 5,117,073, up 6.3% 1990–1998. 2% of U.S. total, 16th largest; 31.3% rural. Median age: 35.2 years. 14.6% 65 years and over. 87.7% White, 10.7% Black, 0.8% Asian, 0.4% Amer. Indian, 0.4% Other; 1.2% Hispanic Origin. Households: 56.3% married couple families; 26.6% married couple fams. w. children; 40.8% college educ.; median household income: $26,362; per capita income: $12,989; 68.8% owner occupied housing; median house value: $59,800; median monthly rent: $282. 4.2% Unemployment. 1998 Voting age pop.: 4,042,000. 1998 Turnout: 1,756,857; 39% of VAP. Registered voters (1998): 3,635,991; no party registration.

Political Lineup: Governor, Mel Carnahan (D); Lt. Gov., Roger B. Wilson (D); Secy. of State, Rebecca McDowell Cook (D); Atty. Gen., Jay Nixon (D); Treasurer, Bob Holden (D); State Senate, 34 (18 D, 16 R); Majority Leader, Ronnie DePasco (D); State House, 163 (85 D, 76 R, 1 I, 1 vacancy); House Speaker, Steve Gaw (D). Senators, Christopher S. Bond (R) and John Ashcroft (R). Representatives, 9 (5 D, 4 R).

Elections Division: 573-751-2301; **Filing Deadline for U.S. Congress:** March 28, 2000.

1996 Presidential Vote

Clinton (D) 1,025,935 (48%)
Dole (R) 890,014 (41%)
Perot (I) 217,219 (10%)

1992 Presidential Vote

Clinton (D) 1,053,873 (44%)
Bush (R) 811,159 (34%)
Perot (I) 518,741 (22%)

GOVERNOR

Gov. Mel Carnahan (D)

Elected 1992, term expires Jan. 2001; b. Feb. 11, 1934, Birchtree; home, Rolla; George Washington U., B.A. 1954, U. of MO, J.D. 1959; Baptist; married (Jean).

Military Career: Air Force, 1954–56.

Elected Office: Rolla Municipal Judge, 1960–62; MO House of Reps., 1962–66, Majority Ldr., 1964–66; MO Treasurer, 1980–84; MO Lt. Gov., 1988–92.

Professional Career: Practicing atty., 1959–61, 1962–80, 1984–88.

Office: State Capitol Bldg., Jefferson City, 65101, 573-751-3222; Fax: 573-751-1495; Web site: www.state.mo.us.

Election Results

1996 gen.	Mel Carnahan (D)	1,224,801	(57%)
	Margaret Kelly (R)	866,268	(40%)
	Others	51,449	(2%)
1996 prim.	Mel Carnahan (D)	347,488	(82%)
	Ruth Redel (D)	33,452	(8%)
	Edwin W. Howald (D)	29,890	(7%)
	Nicholas Clement (D)	14,940	(4%)
1992 gen.	Mel Carnahan (D)	1,375,425	(59%)
	William B. Webster (R)	968,574	(41%)

SENATORS

Sen. Christopher S. Bond (R)

Elected 1986, seat up 2004; b. Mar. 6, 1939, St. Louis; home, Mexico; Princeton U., B.A. 1960, U. of VA, LL.B. 1963; Presbyterian; divorced.

Elected Office: MO Auditor, 1970–72; MO Gov., 1972–76, 1980–84.

Professional Career: Practicing atty., 1964–69, 1977–80; MO Asst. Atty. Gen., 1969–70.

DC Office: 274 RSOB, 20510, 202-224-5721; Fax: 202-224-8149; Web site: www.senate.gov/~bond.

State Offices: Cape Girardeau, 573-334-7044; Jefferson City, 573-634-2488; Kansas City, 816-471-7141; Springfield, 417-881-7068; St. Louis, 314-725-4484.

Committees: *Appropriations* (5th of 15 R): Agriculture & Rural Development; Defense; Foreign Operations & Export Financing; Transportation; VA, HUD & Independent Agencies (Chmn.). *Budget* (5th of 12 R). *Environment & Public Works* (6th of 10 R): Fisheries, Wildlife & Drinking Water; Transportation & Infrastructure. *Small Business* (Chmn. of 10 R).

Group Ratings

	ADA	ACLU	AFS	LCV	CON	NTU	NFIB	COC	ACU	NTLC	CHC
1998	15	29	11	0	25	53	100	89	72	68	82
1997	15	—	0	—	54	71	—	100	76	—	—

National Journal Ratings

	1997 LIB — 1997 CONS			1998 LIB — 1998 CONS		
Economic	25%	—	67%	43%	—	56%
Social	28%	—	62%	38%	—	61%
Foreign	30%	—	66%	0%	—	88%

Key Votes of the 105th Congress

1. Bal. Budget Amend.	Y	5. Satcher for Surgeon Gen.	Y	9. Chem. Weapons Treaty	N
2. Clinton Budget Deal	Y	6. Highway Set-asides	Y	10. Cuban Humanitarian Aid	Y
3. Cloture on Tobacco	N	7. Table Child Gun locks	Y	11. Table Bosnia Troops	N
4. Education IRAs	Y	8. Ovrd. Part. Birth Veto	Y	12. $ for Test-ban Treaty	N

Election Results

1998 general	Christopher S. Bond (R)	830,625	(53%)	($6,229,649)
	Jay Nixon (D)	690,208	(44%)	($2,568,879)
	Others	56,024	(4%)	
1998 primary	Christopher S. Bond (R)	213,569	(87%)	
	Others	32,274	(13%)	
1992 general	Christopher S. Bond (R)	1,221,901	(52%)	($5,048,333)
	Geri Rothman-Serot (D)	1,057,967	(45%)	($1,112,187)
	Others	75,048	(3%)	

Sen. John Ashcroft (R)

Elected 1994, seat up 2000; b. May 9, 1942, Chicago, IL; home, Springfield; Yale U., B.A. 1964, U. of Chicago, J.D. 1967; Assembly of God; married (Janet).

Elected Office: MO Auditor, 1973–75; MO Gov., 1984–92.

Professional Career: Practicing atty; Prof., SW MO St. U., 1968–73; Asst. Atty. Gen. of MO. 1975–76; Atty Gen. of MO, 1976–84.

DC Office: 316 HSOB, 20510, 202-224-6154; Fax: 202-228-0998; Web site: www.senate.gov/~ashcroft.

State Offices: Cape Girardeau, 573-334-7044; Jefferson City, 573-634-2488; Kansas City, 816-471-7141; Springfield, 417-881-7068; St. Louis, 314-725-4484.

Committees: *Commerce, Science & Transportation* (8th of 11 R): Aviation; Communications; Consumer Affairs, Foreign Commerce & Tourism (Chmn.); Manufacturing & Competitiveness; Surface Transportation & Merchant Marine. *Foreign Relations* (9th of 10 R): European Affairs; Near Eastern & South Asian Affairs; Western Hemisphere, Peace Corps, Narcotics & Terrorism. *Judiciary* (7th of 10 R): Criminal Justice Oversight; The Constitution, Federalism & Property Rights (Chmn.); Youth Violence.

Group Ratings

	ADA	ACLU	AFS	LCV	CON	NTU	NFIB	COC	ACU	NTLC	CHC
1998	5	14	0	0	89	80	89	78	100	100	100
1997	0	—	0	—	29	85	—	70	100	—	—

National Journal Ratings

	1997 LIB — 1997 CONS			1998 LIB — 1998 CONS		
Economic	0%	—	89%	0%	—	88%
Social	0%	—	83%	0%	—	88%
Foreign	0%	—	77%	0%	—	88%

Key Votes of the 105th Congress

1. Bal. Budget Amend.	Y	5. Satcher for Surgeon Gen.	N	9. Chem. Weapons Treaty	N
2. Clinton Budget Deal	Y	6. Highway Set-asides	N	10. Cuban Humanitarian Aid	N
3. Cloture on Tobacco	N	7. Table Child Gun locks	Y	11. Table Bosnia Troops	N
4. Education IRAs	Y	8. Ovrd. Part. Birth Veto	Y	12. $ for Test-ban Treaty	N

Election Results

1994 general	John Ashcroft (R)	1,060,149	(60%)	($4,063,927)
	Alan Wheat (D)	633,697	(36%)	($3,505,701)
	Bill Johnson (Lib)	81,264	(5%)	
1994 primary	John Ashcroft (R)	260,065	(83%)	
	Joyce Lea (R)	15,228	(5%)	
	Joseph A. Schwan (R)	14,713	(5%)	
	Others	22,642	(7%)	
1988 general	John C. Danforth (R)	1,407,416	(68%)	($4,060,441)
	Jay Nixon (D)	660,045	(32%)	($880,160)

FIRST DISTRICT

For a century or more, St. Louis seemed the center of America: the starting point for the Lewis and Clark expedition in 1804; the locus half a century later of the Dred Scott case, which produced a Supreme Court ruling that helped split the nation; the site of the 1904 World's Fair that introduced the hot dog and the ice cream cone and got 19 million people to *Meet Me in St. Louis*. Its 630-foot-high Gateway Arch is just below the point where the waters of the Missouri surge into the Mississippi, about halfway between New Orleans and Lake Superior, the Atlantic and the Pacific. St. Louis was once again a great gathering place in January 1999, when Pope John Paul II visited here, recalling the *Dred Scott* decision and speaking out for life and against abortion and capital punishment.

This first major American city west of the Mississippi River was the final resting place of Daniel Boone and for many years was Chicago's rival as the transportation hub of America. In 1904, St. Louis already had the Wainwright Building, one of Louis Sullivan's first skyscrapers, and Union Station, the world's largest passenger train station when it opened in 1894; some 600,000 people lived in densely-packed brick houses on old street grids radiating outward from downtown. This was a heavily German city, with a Teutonic solidity and orderliness which distinguished it from the surrounding Southern-accented rural terrain; and from Mitteleuropa came the founders of St. Louis's great businesses—the Anheuser-Busch brewery, May Company department stores, Joseph Pulitzer's *St. Louis Post-Dispatch*—and its first great politician and a friend of Abraham Lincoln, Senator and Interior Secretary Carl Schurz. And there is almost a European aura to Forest Park, the site of the 1904 fair, and the dozen mansion-lined private streets nearby, like Portland Place.

St. Louis is still one of the nation's 20 largest metro areas, but today does not occupy as central a place in the national consciousness, and the central city itself has largely emptied out. The German order that made so many people comfortable living in close quarters and commuting by streetcar seems to have yielded to an American desire for Daniel Boone's wide open (suburban) spaces and the less restrictive automobile. St. Louis's population peaked at 856,000 in 1950; in 1990, it was 396,000, dwarfed by the one million in suburban St. Louis County. Downtown St. Louis has been spruced up admirably: the Gateway Arch was finished in 1965; Union Station has been redeveloped; Laclede's Landing is stocked with shops. But most of St. Louis's old factories have closed and many of its once tight neighborhoods are only a memory.

Missouri's congressional districts have followed the people out of St. Louis. The 1st District, historically based on the north side of the city, in 1971 had 71% of its votes cast in suburban St. Louis County. It includes most of central and north St. Louis, the affluent and racially integrated suburbs of University City and Clayton just west of Forest Park, and the mostly black and mixed-race suburbs from the city limits north to Bellefontaine Neighbors, Florissant and the airport. In 1990, this district was 52% black, a figure increasing since. This is easily Missouri's most Democratic district.

The congressman from the 1st District is the dean of the Missouri delegation and third most senior member of the House, Bill Clay. He grew up in St. Louis and sold real estate and life insurance. In the 1960s he was a union staffer and firebrand civil rights activist known as "Wild Bill" (he served 105 days in jail in 1963 for participating in a civil rights demonstration). He was a House leader when Democrats were in control, and is now one of the angriest opponents of the fiery, conservative Republicans. Clay was first elected to the House in 1968, when the black members could be counted on two hands. He weathered some serious ethical charges in the 1970s, when he billed the government for numerous auto trips home though he was apparently traveling on cheaper airline tickets. In 1992 it was revealed he had 328 overdrafts on the House bank. Though there is a stubborn bloc against him in the suburbs, he has always won re-election easily.

Clay has just about a perfectly liberal voting record and is an especially strong supporter of labor unions—"workers' rights," he says. Before the Republicans won control in 1994, he was chairman of the now-abolished Post Office and Civil Service Committee and heir apparent to the then-Education and Labor Committee. One major Clay achievement was the Family and Medical Leave Act, vetoed by President Bush but signed by President Clinton in February 1993 as his first law. Hatch Act reform—allowing federal employees to be involved in politics—took only a bit longer; it passed the House in March 1993 and was signed by Clinton in October 1993. Less controversial was a Clay measure authorizing buyouts of senior federal employees, which passed the House 391–17 in February 1994 and became law in March. But Clay was not as successful in pushing striker replacement, which would revise the 1935 Wagner Act and give more leverage to unions; the bill passed the House in 1994, but in the Senate could not get the 60 votes required to break a promised Republican filibuster.

Since 1995 Clay, now ranking member of the renamed Education and the Workforce Committee, has been mostly frustrated on the legislative front. He opposed the Republicans' welfare reform plans vitriolically, predicting they would "potentially starve hundreds of thousands of children and impair the health of their mothers. This bill is not about welfare reform. . . . It's about writing blank checks to governors while imposing no standards or accountability." Despite his support of family and medical leave, he opposed the Republican bill to allow employees to choose between overtime pay and compensatory time on the grounds that the choice can never be really voluntary. The one major bill he joined Republicans in supporting, Howard McKeon's CAREERS Act, which consolidated job training programs, was passed in different forms in both chambers; but the conference committee was unable to produce a version that made it back to the House floor. His biggest success was the bill increasing the minimum wage. He also succeeded in preventing students from having higher education aid reduced on up to $1,500 in HOPE scholarships and increasing the amount of income excluded in calculating Pell grant eligibility. He bitterly opposed school vouchers, and prevailed. He sponsored the class reduction size bill included in the October 1998 omnibus budget and sponsored several Clinton education bills. He asked for a review of a National Science Foundation grant of $175,000 to political scientists for a study of why qualified candidates don't run for Congress. And he was even criticized by a union, the American Federation of Government Employees, for his support of military depots.

Clay expresses his views with great vehemence. He is the author of two books, *To Kill or Not to Kill*, on capital punishment, and *Just Permanent Interests*, on black members of Congress. And, for more than 50 years Clay has been a political force in St. Louis; as the *St. Louis Post-Dispatch* wrote, "Strong Clay opposition can often spell defeat." In 1992 he opposed the gubernatorial candidacy of former Mayor Vince Schoemehl; Schoemehl lost 27 of 28 St. Louis wards to Governor Mel Carnahan. In 1997 and 1998 Clay raised strong objections to gubernatorial nominee Jay Nixon, who as attorney general pushed to close the decades-long St. Louis school desegregation case and cut off the flow of state funds to the school system. Clay called Nixon a racist and said he was conducting "unremitting warfare" against court decisions. In October 1998 he wrote a letter to Bill Clinton asking him not to attend a November Nixon fundraiser. "I am certain that if Orval Faubus had sought your support for a Senate campaign, you would not have given it. You should not give it to Jay Nixon today." Clinton did not show. (The school case was tentatively settled in January 1999.) In the 1996 and 1998 campaigns there were charges that Clay would retire and try to hand the seat on to his son, state Senator Lacy Clay (would he be the first member of Congress whose names are anagrams of each other?). The younger Clay was elected to the state House in 1984 and, after state Senator John Bass was given a $100,000 staff job with the elder Clay in Washington, won his state Senate seat in 1991. In May 1999 Clay announced that he would not run again in 2000. Lacy Clay, with his father's support, started running. Other likely candidates include St. Louis County Councilman Charles Dooley, state Representative Tim Green of Spanish Lake and attorney Eric Vickers. Mentioned as possible candidates are former St. Louis Mayor Freeman Bosley Jr. and former Deputy City Comptroller Z. Dwight Billingsly, a Republican who ran against Lacy Clay in 1998.

Cook's Call. *Safe.* While there may be a competitive primary to replace Clay, there is no hope for a Republican in this heavily Democratic district. However, St. Louis has been losing population and could therefore face some serious alterations in the 2001 redistricting.

The People: Pop. 1990: 568,472; 0.8% rural; 14.6% age 65 +; 46.3% White, 52.2% Black, 0.9% Asian, 0.2% Amer. Indian, 0.3% Other; 0.8% Hispanic Origin. Households: 38.8% married couple families; 17.8% married couple fams. w. children; 43.5% college educ.; median household income: $24,963; per capita income: $12,632; median house value: $55,800; median gross rent: $299.

1996 Presidential Vote

Clinton (D)	145,586	(74%)
Dole (R)	38,505	(20%)
Perot (I)	9,721	(5%)

1992 Presidential Vote

Clinton (D)	161,447	(68%)
Bush (R)	45,231	(19%)
Perot (I)	29,682	(13%)

Rep. William (Bill) Clay (D)

Elected 1968; b. Apr. 30, 1931, St. Louis; home, St. Louis; St. Louis U., B.S. 1953; Catholic; married (Carol).

Military Career: Army, 1953–55.

Elected Office: St. Louis City Alderman, 1959–64.

Professional Career: Real estate broker; Life insurance business, 1959–61.

DC Office: 2306 RHOB 20515, 202-225-2406; Fax: 202-225-1725; Web site: www.house.gov/clay.

District Offices: Florissant, 314-839-9148; St. Louis, 314-367-1970.

Committees: *Education & the Workforce* (RMM of 22 D).

Group Ratings

	ADA	ACLU	AFS	LCV	CON	NTU	NFIB	COC	ACU	NTLC	CHC
1998	85	93	100	54	55	12	0	19	5	3	0
1997	95	—	100	—	1	21	—	20	9	—	—

National Journal Ratings

	1997 LIB	—	1997 CONS	1998 LIB	—	1998 CONS
Economic	75%	—	25%	79%	—	0%
Social	85%	—	0%	93%	—	0%
Foreign	97%	—	0%	69%	—	30%

Key Votes of the 105th Congress

1. Clinton Budget Deal	N	5. Puerto Rico Sthood. Ref.	Y	9. Cut $ for B-2 Bombers	Y
2. Education IRAs	N	6. End Highway Set-asides	N	10. Human Rights in China	Y
3. Req. 2/3 to Raise Taxes	N	7. School Prayer Amend.	N	11. Withdraw Bosnia Troops	N
4. Fast-track Trade	N	8. Ovrd. Part. Birth Veto	N	12. End Cuban TV-Marti	*

Election Results

1998 general	William (Bill) Clay (D)	90,840	(73%)	($270,118)
	Richmond A. Soluade Sr. (R)	30,635	(25%)	
	Others	3,576	(3%)	
1998 primary	William (Bill) Clay (D)	unopposed		
1996 general	William (Bill) Clay (D)	131,659	(70%)	($366,550)
	Daniel F. O'Sullivan Jr. (R)	51,857	(28%)	($77,978)
	Others	4,137	(2%)	

SECOND DISTRICT

Just as the U.S. population's geographic center has slowly crept westward into Missouri (the 1990 Census placed the point just outside tiny Steelville), the greater St. Louis area continues to move farther west from the Gateway Arch on the Mississippi River. The fulcrum now rests in St. Louis County, established in 1876 when the city, tired of paying for dusty back roads, separated itself from the sticks. There were then about 350,000 people in the city and 31,000 in the county. In 1990, the city, which once had 856,000 people, was down to 396,000, while the county was about 1 million. By the 1960s, the center of office employment had moved from downtown across the county line to Clayton; now even many Clayton office buildings seem half-empty, and the focus is fast moving out the Daniel Boone Expressway (U.S. 40) to Chesterfield, west of the I-270 ring road.

The 2d Congressional District is made up of central and western St. Louis County, plus some St. Charles County suburbs northwest across the Missouri River. It includes the blue-collar areas around the Ford plant, the airport and Boeing's McDonnell Douglas in North County and the Chrysler plant in South County; these are mostly Democratic areas. It has fast-growing suburbs in and beyond St. Charles and historic suburbs like Webster Groves and Kirkwood; these are pretty solidly Republican. And in the center of St. Louis County, along the Daniel Boone Expressway, are elite Ladue and high-income Creve Coeur, Town and Country, Manchester and Chesterfield: all Republican, even more so in the newer family-oriented subdivisions than in the leafy precincts of the old rich.

The congressman from the 2d District is Jim Talent, a Republican who first won the seat in 1992. Talent grew up in Des Peres and lives in Chesterfield; he was a law clerk to Judge Richard Posner, one of the great free market legal minds, and was a management lawyer in St. Louis. In 1984, at age 28, he was elected to the state House, where he opposed taxes and backed reform of House rules. He was House minority leader from 1989 to 1992. In 1992, Talent ran for the U.S. House, and in the primary beat George Bush's cousin, George Herbert Walker, by the unambiguous margin of 58%–32%. In the general, Talent faced incumbent Democrat Joan Kelly Horn, who in 1990 defeated Republican Jack Buechner by a grand total of 54 votes. But redistricting had made the district more Republican, and even in a Democratic year in Missouri, Talent won 50%–48%.

Talent has compiled a solidly conservative voting record and has emerged as a leader on conservative causes. In his first term he got a seat on Armed Services and formed an ad hoc hollow forces committee in the 103d Congress; he focused on military readiness and decried Clinton Administration defense budget cuts. "We have shrunk and starved our services to the breaking point." In 1997, when Procurement Subcommittee Chairman Duncan Hunter moved against the F-18 C/D Hornet, Talent fought and managed to save it; in 1998 he helped get eight F-18s, originally scheduled for Thailand, to be built for the Marines instead following the Asian economic crisis. In his first term Talent introduced his own welfare reform bill; in 1996 he teamed with freshman J.C. Watts to sponsor the American Community Renewal Act, to encourage enterprise zones, capital gains tax cuts, reduction of red tape, and public-private partnerships in central cities; some of its tax provisions were included in the Republicans' September 1998 tax cut.

In 1997 Talent became chairman of the Small Business Committee, which Republicans spared from abolition in 1994 because it was the only committee headed by a woman (Jan Meyers); she retired in 1996, but it survives. He managed to insert tax relief for businesses in poor communities in the 1998 tax cut bill, and worked, often in tandem with Christopher Bond, who chairs the Senate Small Business Committee, to make it harder for the IRS to penalize misclassification of employees as independent contractors, to provide full deductibility of health insurance for the self-employed, and to give employers who hire third-party consultants to inspect their businesses a partial break when facing OSHA inspections. He proposed family development accounts, to allow businesses to deduct donations made to match the savings of low-income families. In February 1999 the House passed his bill to increase the venture capital program from $300 million to $1.2 billion.

Other Talent bills include one to make private contracting an option in Medicare and another to restore the policy of not funding abortions abroad. He sharply criticized the Clinton Administration for cutting in half funding for the Army Corps of Engineers in 1998, pointing to Missouri communities at risk in floods. Talent has supported the Page Avenue extension, a new freeway over the Missouri River to St. Charles County. He opposed the $2.6 billion W1-W plan to expand Lambert Field, questioning the capacity and safety of the proposed new runway in bad weather.

Talent has been re-elected three times by better than 2–1, in 1998 against a Democrat who reported spending nothing. He also contributed to Republican legislative candidates around the state, though the party did not make gains. Talent said throughout 1998 that he was thinking of running for governor in 2000. When Speaker Newt Gingrich announced his resignation, Talent started running for speaker, despite his low seniority; after Whip Tom DeLay endorsed Bob Livingston, Talent withdrew from the race. He was later named as an assistant majority leader by Dick Armey, not an official leadership position.

In February 1999 Talent surprised few when he announced for governor. "We made this a family decision of where I could serve best," he said. He promised to concentrate on education, tax cuts and the highway program. A November 1998 federal appeals court decision wiping out the state's $1,075 limit on contributions probably helps him; Democratic candidate and state Treasurer Bob Holden said he would abide by the limit but Talent declined to do so.

Very quickly an army of likely candidates to succeed Talent rose from the soil of the 2d District—seven Republicans and two Democrats. They included Republicans, state Senate Minority Leader Steve Ehlmann of St. Charles ("Philosophically, I'm very close to Jim Talent"); state Senator David Klarich of Chesterfield (whose mother founded the West County Republican Organization); state Senator Franc Flotron of Chesterfield ("I'm an effective conservative who tries to figure out how to solve problems"); Talent district office director Barbara Cooper of Ballwin ("Nobody knows the people in this district or the policies in this district better than I do"); state Representative Todd Akin of Town and Country (who challenged in court the 1993 state tax increase and the 1998 gambling referendum legalizing "boats in moats"); state Representative Brent Evans of Manchester (a job-training firm head and longtime Talent ally); and former 15-year St. Louis County Executive Gene McNary (who lost races for governor in

1972 and 1984 and for senator in 1980 and was George Bush's INS commissioner). The two Democrats were state Senator Ted House of St. Charles ("I am as ideologically compatible with this district as any one person can be") and Webster University Business School Dean and TV commentator David Harpool of Rock Hill ("I'm someone who's willing to take the wrath from both sides—from left-wing liberals in my own party and right-wing Republican conservatives").

Cook's Call. *Probably Safe.* Talent's decision to run for governor in 2000 has set off a scramble for this open seat. A solid Democratic candidate could make this race competitive, but it will be hard for any Democrat to wrest this wealthy and reliably Republican seat from Republican control.

The People: Pop. 1990: 568,449; 3.2% rural; 10.7% age 65 + ; 94.3% White, 3.7% Black, 1.6% Asian, 0.2% Amer. Indian, 0.2% Other; 1.1% Hispanic Origin. Households: 63.8% married couple families; 31.7% married couple fams. w. children; 61.4% college educ.; median household income: $43,957; per capita income: $20,654; median house value: $95,300; median gross rent: $434.

1996 Presidential Vote			1992 Presidential Vote		
Dole (R)	138,401	(49%)	Bush (R)	126,621	(40%)
Clinton (D)	115,698	(41%)	Clinton (D)	114,612	(36%)
Perot (I)	22,791	(8%)	Perot (I)	72,885	(23%)

Rep. James M. Talent (R)

Elected 1992; b. Oct. 18, 1956, Des Peres; home, Chesterfield; Washington U., B.S. 1978, U. of Chicago Law Schl., J.D. 1981; Presbyterian; married (Brenda).

Elected Office: MO House of Reps., 1984–92, Minority Ldr., 1989–92.

Professional Career: Practicing atty., 1981–92; Law Clerk, 7th Circuit Court of Appeals Judge Richard Posner, 1982–83.

DC Office: 1022 LHOB 20515, 202-225-2561; Fax: 202-225-2563; Web site: www.house.gov/talent.

District Offices: St. Charles, 314-949-6826; St. Louis, 314-872-9561.

Committees: *Armed Services* (13th of 32 R): Military Procurement; Military Readiness. *Education & the Workforce* (11th of 27 R): Employer-Employee Relations. *Small Business* (Chmn. of 19 R).

Group Ratings

	ADA	ACLU	AFS	LCV	CON	NTU	NFIB	COC	ACU	NTLC	CHC
1998	5	6	0	15	2	51	100	100	96	95	100
1997	5	—	13	—	49	62	—	80	100	—	—

National Journal Ratings

	1997 LIB — 1997 CONS		1998 LIB — 1998 CONS	
Economic	18% —	82%	0% —	88%
Social	20% —	71%	26% —	72%
Foreign	19% —	80%	7% —	83%

Key Votes of the 105th Congress

1. Clinton Budget Deal	Y	5. Puerto Rico Sthood. Ref.	N	9. Cut $ for B-2 Bombers	N
2. Education IRAs	Y	6. End Highway Set-asides	Y	10. Human Rights in China	Y
3. Req. 2/3 to Raise Taxes	Y	7. School Prayer Amend.	Y	11. Withdraw Bosnia Troops	Y
4. Fast-track Trade	Y	8. Ovrd. Part. Birth Veto	Y	12. End Cuban TV-Marti	N

Election Results

1998 general	James M. Talent (R) 142,313	(70%)	($926,361)
	John Ross (D) 57,565	(28%)	
	Others 3,381	(2%)	
1998 primary	James M. Talent (R) 26,908	(90%)	
	John A. Holmes Jr. (R) 2,982	(10%)	
1996 general	James M. Talent (R) 165,999	(61%)	($1,165,814)
	Joan Kelly Horn (D) 100,372	(37%)	($381,873)
	Others 4,355	(2%)	

THIRD DISTRICT

Middle America, it could be said, lies somewhere on the south side of metropolitan St. Louis. The geographical center of the country's population was here in 1980, just south of St. Louis in once rural and now mostly suburban Jefferson County; and while that point has moved a few miles southwest, St. Louis is still the metro area nearest the midpoint of a country most of whose people live in million-plus metro areas. Geographically, this is a node where some of the nation's main arteries come together. The Missouri River flows into the Mississippi a few miles north of St. Louis's Gateway Arch; the National Road and its successors, U.S. 40 and Interstate 70, cross the Mississippi just below the Arch. And the great tides of Southerners migrating west up the Mississippi and Germans migrating overland met here to create one of the nation's largest and most bustling cities out of a town founded by the French before the Revolutionary War. The south side of St. Louis is famous for its tight-knit, neat neighborhoods and pleasant parks; its most famous symbols are the Anheuser-Busch brewery just south of downtown and Grant's Farm, where Ulysses S. Grant lived in the 1850s and where Anheuser-Busch now keeps the Budweiser Clydesdales. But many more people now live in the suburbs heading out all directions, well into Jefferson County to the south.

The 3d Congressional District consists of the south side of St. Louis City, the southern St. Louis County suburbs, Jefferson County, and rural Ste. Genevieve County on the Mississippi to the south, the site of Missouri's oldest permanent settlement, founded near a salt mine in 1730. It is the descendant of districts dominated by St. Louis voters, but now the city casts less than 25% of its votes, fewer than Jefferson County; almost half are cast in St. Louis County. Ethnically, this has been a heavily German-American area since the mid-19th Century. Politically, it has been Democratic since the New Deal of the 1930s.

The congressman from the 3d District is Dick Gephardt, first elected in 1976, the leader of the Democratic Party in the House, presidential candidate in 1988 and, he hopes, speaker of the House in January 2001. Gephardt grew up on the south side of St. Louis, the son of a milk truck driver who worked himself up into the middle class. A bit too old to be part of the generation of Vietnam-era student rebels, Gephardt returned home from law school in 1965 to work in a large downtown law firm, but was clearly intent on a traditional political career; he moved to the south side and was elected alderman in 1971. In 1976, when 3d District Congresswoman Leonor Sullivan announced her retirement, Gephardt jumped into the race as an anti-establishment candidate. He beat a labor union official in the primary and a former board of aldermen president in the general. Gephardt started off in the House as one of the newer breed of Democrats who did not automatically favor big government and higher taxes. With the help of Missouri's Richard Bolling, Gephardt got a seat on the Ways and Means Committee—rare for a freshman. He voted for the 1981 Reagan tax cut and was the House co-sponsor of New Jersey Senator Bill Bradley's bill that was the basis of the 1986 tax reform. Gephardt was one of the founders of the moderate Democratic Leadership Council and opposed many popular Democratic causes such as abortion, busing and raising the minimum wage.

But around the mid-1980s he began to shift, perhaps reflecting the increasingly liberal tenor of the Democratic Caucus, of which he was elected chairman over David Obey in 1984. Gephardt has always been a superb caucus politician and a good listener. He is a hard-working detail man, eager to absorb information, with a gift for molding compromises, and for coming up with positions that hold together the often unruly and fissiparous Democratic Caucus. When Gephardt started running for president in 1986, he had the enthusiastic support of dozens of House colleagues as he spent 144 days in Iowa campaigning for the February 1988 caucuses.

Gephardt adjusted to this new arena, sometimes to the dismay of his former allies. He played little role in the 1986 tax reform he had originally co-sponsored; he changed his stand on abortion to pro-choice. In Iowa, he supported mandatory agricultural production controls, a non-starter even in a Democratic Congress. Even more prominently, he went on the offensive on trade issues. The United Auto Workers is a major factor in Iowa caucuses, and Gephardt, who had opposed the UAW's domestic content bill, came up with his amendment requiring retaliation against countries (read: Japan) running large trade surpluses with the United States. Gephardt won the Iowa caucuses with 31% of the vote, to 27% for Paul Simon and 22% for Michael Dukakis. In New Hampshire, Gephardt found himself under attack for switching positions in a fast-growing and prosperous state that hates taxes and government regulation; he finished second with 20% to Dukakis's 36%. On Super Tuesday, Gephardt had run out of money, won only Missouri and was out of the race.

In the House Gephardt rebounded when another leadership position came his way. In June 1989 Speaker Jim Wright and Majority Whip Tony Coelho resigned, and as Thomas Foley was elected speaker, Gephardt ran for majority leader and defeated Georgian Ed Jenkins 181–76. Gephardt went to work creating a sense of camaraderie in a dispirited caucus. In the 1990 budget summit talks, Gephardt used OMB Director Richard Darman's desire for agreement to frame the issue as a choice between the Democrats' plan to tax the rich more and Bush's refusal to do so—a contrast that at least momentarily hurt Republican candidates and prevented them from making gains in the November 1990 elections. In September 1990, Gephardt supported Bush's dispatch of troops to the Persian Gulf, but in January 1991, he led the opposition to the Gulf war resolution and uncharacteristically stumbled by threatening to cut off funds for U.S. troops there.

In the first Clinton years, Gephardt combined ardent support for the administration on most issues with carefully calibrated dissent on others. He fought for the Clinton economic stimulus plan and for the spending cuts and tax increase package which passed with exactly 218 votes in August 1993. His major dissent was on trade. He held off opposing NAFTA for several months as he sought more concessions from administration officials and he eventually came out against it. In December 1993, Gephardt endorsed GATT; in February 1994, he came up with his own plan to force Japan to meet numerical goals in opening its markets or face retaliation. Gephardt vigorously supported the Clinton health care plan in 1994, and tried to put together his own bill combining the Clinton and Ways and Means plans; but it was tough slogging and no bill came to the floor. Then in August 1994 the leadership lost the vote on the crime bill rule. To hold together the caucus, gun control amendments as well as tougher penalties were included; but gun control repelled too many moderate Democrats and Chairman Jack Brooks's high-handedness antagonized many moderate Republicans, and the rule failed.

Clinton had shaped his two major initiatives—the 1993 budget and tax increase and the 1994 health care bill—along the lines recommended by House Democratic leaders. In November 1994 they were all stunningly repudiated. Democrats lost 52 seats and control of the House. Speaker Thomas Foley was defeated, and Gephardt lost his post as majority leader and became minority leader instead. The strategy followed by Speakers Tip O'Neill, Jim Wright and Foley—hold the Democratic Caucus together enough to produce 218 votes—was now obsolete: There weren't 218 Democrats any more. Gephardt pushed aside a challenge by North Carolina's Charlie Rose for the party leadership, 150–58. But the day he handed over the gavel to Speaker Newt Gingrich, Gephardt later said, "was one of the worst days of my life." In December 1994 Gephardt proposed a tax cut just days before Clinton was set to do the same. In the debates on the Contract with America, Gephardt was far less visible than the rabidly anti-Gingrich Democratic Whip David Bonior. In June 1995 Gephardt and other Democrats were stunned when Clinton accepted the Republican goal of a balanced budget by 2002. Gephardt produced a "flat tax" plan in July 1995 under which most taxpayers would pay 10% and most deductions—except for mortgage interest—be abolished, and higher brackets ranging up to 34%; but it got just 119 votes on the floor.

Times got better for Democrats as support for Republicans and Gingrich plummeted during the government shutdown. Gephardt created a House Democratic Policy Committee to serve as a forum for developing a Democratic alternative to the Contract. By June 1996 Gephardt and Senate Minority Leader Tom Daschle came up with a united Democratic "Families First" platform, including tax deductions for child care, health insurance and higher education, a balanced budget and tough anti-crime measures. And House Democrats scored a rousing success when they forced a vote on, and passage of, a minimum-wage increase in summer 1996. But the surging Clinton-Gore campaign ignored Gephardt and, though most polls started showing Democrats ahead of Republicans in the generic vote, ignored Democrats' efforts to win a majority in the House. Clinton never mentioned Families First, but instead unveiled a package of "little things" himself. When Gephardt spoke to the Democratic National Convention in August, the obedient crowd chanted "Four more years!" Clinton and Gore each devoted one sentence in their acceptance speeches to the need for Democratic majorities in Congress. Gephardt's hopes to become speaker came crashing down in November 1996, as Democrats won only 207 House seats and Republicans 227, despite Gingrich's unpopularity, despite the AFL-CIO $35 million ad campaign, and despite Clinton's victory.

Over the next two years Gephardt's fortunes and strategies oscillated widely. Forging majorities with moderate Republicans was difficult because Democratic leaders had mostly refused to deal with them when they had a majority. Holding together the Democrats is always hard; they have always tended to be a divided party, an uneasy alliance of disparate elements. Most of the Black Caucus and perhaps 40 other members are dedicated social democrats, dismayed at the acceptance of the goal of a balanced budget, frustrated with downward pressure in discretionary spending, and determined not to give up the fading strength of the Medicare or Social Security issues. And then there are the 29 Blue Dogs, moderate on cultural issues, generally conservative and budget-balancing on economics, supportive of some Republican stands. And there are the many Democrats motivated most strongly by liberal views on cultural issues like abortion. One issue on which Gephardt managed to unite them and add some Republicans was campaign finance. He favors amending the First Amendment to allow limits on campaign spending: "What we have here is two important values in direct conflict: freedom of speech and our desire for healthy campaigns in a healthy democracy. You can't have both." In August 1998, after months of maneuvering advocates of the Shays-Meehan bill, Gephardt forced a vote and won a large majority. But it was too late for action in the Senate, where advocates were far short of the votes needed to overcome a filibuster.

Meanwhile, major budget issues had been settled by negotiations between House Republicans and the White House, from which Gephardt was ostentatiously shut out. He opposed the balanced budget agreement ("a budget of many deficits—a deficit of principle, a deficit of fairness, a deficit of tax justice and, worst of all, a deficit of dollars") reached in principle in May 1997 and sealed in legislation in August; even then 132 House Democrats supported it anyway. House Democrats looked to be as split and fornlorn as House Republicans were after the budget deal of 1990. In December 1997 Gephardt made a speech at Harvard's Kennedy School, celebrating "core Democratic values," calling for the party to reject small-bore ideas and speak boldly to the needs of working people in the United States and around the world: cri de coeur against the Clinton Administration. For that Gephardt was criticized by many House Democrats. He continued to receive great applause from AFL-CIO audiences, happy with his opposition to NAFTA and normal trade relations status with China, and angry at Al Gore's stands in favor.

Then came the Lewinsky scandal. Suddenly Clinton was finding his strongest defenders among the left wing of the congressional party; he began making concessions with them and, as his poll numbers stayed high, confronting them on budget issues. After Clinton's disastrous August 17 speech, Gephardt, whose personal life is exemplary, called his conduct "reprehensible" and said impeachment was possible. He said he would decline to take a partisan role in defending Clinton, and began the impeachment inquiry process in a statesmanlike joint appearance with Gingrich. But he still saw no tension between that stance and with relying on Clinton to raise money for Democratic candidates: "We don't have a choice. We have to have the money." Clinton was more than happy to put Democrats in his debt and raised funds for them as never before.

October, usually a good month for Republicans, proved to be a good month for Democrats in 1998. Republican core voters were turned off by the tepid compromises the party's leaders accepted in the October 1998 omnibus budget. Democratic core voters were turned on by a desire to save their president. "We won!" proclaimed Gephardt on election night, as Democrats gained five House seats, the first such gain for a president's party in off-year elections since 1934. "Their problem is that the far right dominates their party," he said. "What I see is a unified Democratic Party that can work with moderate Republicans to get a lot of things done." This was overly optimistic, or an attempt to exhort a divided army to unity: House Democrats are split down the middle on major issues like Social Security reform, Medicare reform and trade. But Gephardt's gift is holding a caucus together, and House Democrats in late 1998 and early 1999 seemed absolutely convinced that they would win the six seats they needed for control, and more, in the 2000 elections. Actually the 1998 elections were a defeat for both parties and a victory for Clinton. House Republicans failed to make the gains that in the fall they had with good reason expected to make. House Democrats failed to gain the majority that in the spring they had with good reason expected to win. But Clinton, it was clear, was not going to be removed from office. On December 13 Gephardt assailed Clinton's character and reliance on polls—and said he would vote against impeachment. On the day of the vote, December 19, speaking just after Bob Livingston made his breathtaking announcement that he would step down, Gephardt junked his previous draft and made an eloquent speech. "The politics of slash and burn must end," he said. "We need to stop destroying imperfect people at the altar of an unobtainable majority." Yet, after Clinton was impeached, he joined the Democratic members that bused over to the White House for a kind of celebration of the president almost all of them had agreed had dishonored his office.

There still remained the question of whether Gephardt would run for president against Gore, Clinton's choice. Before the election there were many signs he would. His campaign schedule took him six times to Iowa, scene of his 1988 triumph in a contest Gore bypassed; his principled disagreements with Clinton and Gore on NAFTA, fast track, relations with China, welfare reform and the 1997 budget agreement provided a rationale for running. But in February 1999 Gephardt announced he would not run for president in a press conference emblazoned with "Speaker Gephardt" signs. "I want to take this House back to what really matters," he said. As the year went on, the Clinton-Gore team took stands in line with Gephardt's, in rejecting Social Security reform, which obviously had a latent majority in the Congress, in rejecting the Medicare reform worked out by Democrats John Breaux and Bob Kerrey, in resisting broad-based tax cuts for the targeted tax cuts favored by Clinton (though those are very much in tension with Gephardt's "flat tax" as modified in January 1998). In the meantime, Gephardt's strategy of trying to build coalitions with moderate Republicans was frustrated by the fact that House rules allow the majority party, if it stays together, to schedule issues and set the terms of debate. Speaker Denny Hastert instead reached across the lines to propitiate enough Democrats to win large bipartisan majorities on issues like EdFlex, missile defense, bankruptcy reform and Y2K liability. In the spring, Gephardt and Democratic leaders tried to put campaign finance on the schedule by threatening a discharge petition, and in May threatened to do the same on five other issues. In June 1999 Gephardt seemed to set out another agenda, when he told Philadelphia Democrats he backed major spending increases in education and set out how he would get the money: "You've got to have a combination of taking it out of defense cuts and raising revenue. We can argue about how to do that, closing loopholes or even raising taxes to do it." This apparent return to the Democratic agenda of the early 1990s startled and delighted Republicans, who argued that it made the Democrats a party of defense cuts and tax increases.

Little noticed on election night was the fact that, in a pro-incumbent year, Gephardt won re-election in the 3d District by only 56%–42% over an opponent who had only lived in Missouri for two years and spent only $196,000 to Gephardt's $3.3 million. This was not because of any neglect by Gephardt of local issues. He had worked hard to keep the National Imagery and Mapping Agency in Jefferson County, he earmarked $30 million for rebuilding Route 21 (the most dangerous road in Missouri, he said), he pumped in money to keep the Ste. Genevieve levee on schedule instead of ten years behind as the Army Corps of Engineers proposed, he got money for a new sewage treatment plant at the confluence of the Meramec and Mississippi Rivers and for a levee between Festus and Crystal City (Bill Bradley's home town: the 3d District produced at least one 2000 presidential candidate). In busy October 1998, he convened a meeting of Missouri and Illinois officials to get a move on the projected third runway at St. Louis's Lambert Airport. But the trend of opinion in the 3d District seems to be moving toward the Republicans. In 1992, 1994 and 1996 Gephardt spent $3.3 million, $2.6 million and $3.1 million, and won 64%–33%, 58%–40% and 59%–39%—nothing like as close a margins as Gingrich won by in Georgia in 1990 and 1992, but not entirely comforting either. No one expects him to lose in 2000, but amid all his other work he will have to tend to his district closely. Footnote: Gephardt may be joined in Congress by his cousin, Florida state Senator Patsy Gephardt Kurth, who in early 1999 was term-limited and said to be considering a race against 15th District Republican Dave Weldon.

Cook's Call. *Safe.* While it is exceedingly unlikely that a Republican could knock off Minority Leader Gephardt, it is not that hard for a Republican to keep Gephardt under 60%. This district is Democratic leaning, but not overwhelmingly so, which means that once this seat does open up, it will be very competitive.

The People: Pop. 1990: 568,105; 15.9% rural; 15.4% age 65 + ; 96.4% White, 2.3% Black, 0.8% Asian, 0.3% Amer. Indian, 0.2% Other; 1.1% Hispanic Origin. Households: 54.9% married couple families; 25.9% married couple fams. w. children; 40.8% college educ.; median household income: $30,863; per capita income: $14,272; median house value: $72,100; median gross rent: $301.

1996 Presidential Vote

Clinton (D)	115,141	(48%)
Dole (R)	93,190	(39%)
Perot (I)	25,643	(11%)
Others	3,604	(2%)

1992 Presidential Vote

Clinton (D)	121,213	(44%)
Bush (R)	87,155	(32%)
Perot (I)	64,415	(24%)

Rep. Richard A. Gephardt (D)

Elected 1976; b. Jan. 31, 1941, St. Louis; home, St. Louis; Northwestern U., B.S. 1962, U. of MI, J.D. 1965; Baptist; married (Jane).

Military Career: Air Natl. Guard, 1965–71.

Elected Office: St. Louis City Alderman, 1971–76; Dem. Presidential Candidate, 1988.

Professional Career: Practicing atty., 1965–77.

DC Office: 1226 LHOB 20515, 202-225-2671; Fax: 202-225-7452; Web site: www.house.gov/gephardt.

District Office: St. Louis, 314-894-3400.

Committees: *Minority Leader.*

Group Ratings

	ADA	ACLU	AFS	LCV	CON	NTU	NFIB	COC	ACU	NTLC	CHC
1998	90	75	100	92	70	14	0	24	12	11	0
1997	80	—	100	—	1	16	—	11	14	—	—

National Journal Ratings

	1997 LIB	—	1997 CONS	1998 LIB	—	1998 CONS
Economic	93%	—	0%	79%	—	0%
Social	68%	—	31%	69%	—	31%
Foreign	85%	—	15%	58%	—	41%

Key Votes of the 105th Congress

1. Clinton Budget Deal	N	5. Puerto Rico Sthood. Ref.	Y	9. Cut $ for B-2 Bombers	Y
2. Education IRAs	N	6. End Highway Set-asides	N	10. Human Rights in China	Y
3. Req. 2/3 to Raise Taxes	N	7. School Prayer Amend.	N	11. Withdraw Bosnia Troops	*
4. Fast-track Trade	N	8. Ovrd. Part. Birth Veto	Y	12. End Cuban TV-Marti	N

Election Results

1998 general	Richard A. Gephardt (D)	98,287	(56%)	($3,340,959)
	William J. Federer (R)	74,005	(42%)	($196,061)
	Others	3,807	(2%)	
1998 primary	Richard A. Gephardt (D)	28,440	(74%)	
	Steven G. Balley (D)	10,070	(26%)	
1996 general	Richard A. Gephardt (D)	137,300	(59%)	($3,110,509)
	Deborah Lynn Wheelehan (R)	90,202	(39%)	($62,504)
	Others	5,253	(2%)	

FOURTH DISTRICT

Missouri was the first state settled west of the Mississippi, and the folks who settled it were a picture of pioneer diversity. Virginians and other Southerners made their way to counties north of the Missouri River, while Germans settled around the still small capital city of Jefferson City. A taste of that diversity can be found in the Capitol, with its mural by Thomas Hart Benton, great-grandnephew and eponym of Missouri's first senator, who championed hard money and westward expansion for 30 years and lost his seat for opposing the expansion of slavery. The painting shows dance hall girls, black coal miners and a mother diapering an infant—all reminders that pioneer life was less homogeneous than many imagine.

The 4th Congressional District occupies much of this early-settled part of central and western Missouri. It penetrates Kansas City's Jackson County and its metro overflow in Cass County, but the overall atmosphere here is rural and small town, with political traditions dating back to the community's early days. The rural counties around Kansas City were full of pro-slavery-expansion Bushwhackers who rode across the Kansas line to thwart the Yankee Jayhawks, and these areas today vote Democratic. The German area around Jefferson City was anti-slavery and remains among the most Republican parts of Missouri, and the new resort areas around Lake of the Ozarks are mixed. Party Cove, at the lake's western end, is an archetypical example of deregulation—no curfew, speed or size limits for boats on the water. Growth in the Lake of the Ozarks area has been rapid in the 1990s. Much of this region is Truman country: Harry Truman was born just south of the district and lived just northwest of it, spanning the gaps between country and city, South and North; Truman's mother could remember her house being attacked by Yankee soldiers, and she remained pro-Confederate even when her son was in the White House.

The congressman from the 4th District is Ike Skelton, who in many ways can be called a Truman Democrat; his father met Truman in 1928, when he was Lafayette County prosecutor and the future president was Jackson County judge, and they remained friends for life. Ike Skelton grew up in Lexington, where he returned after college and law school to practice law; he became county prosecutor in 1957, at 25, and was elected to the Missouri Senate in 1970. In 1976 Skelton ran for Congress and won rather easily. Skelton looks and votes like an old-fashioned rural Missouri Democrat: his voting record puts him near the midpoint of this Republican House on economics and foreign issues, slightly to the right on cultural issues. He supports the same expansive, assertive foreign and defense policies the preponderance of Democrats supported in the days of Truman.

Skelton is the ranking Democrat on the Armed Services Committee where he has made great contributions to policy. He has long called for better strategic training in the armed services, particularly in the war colleges, and for improving the higher-level military educational programs. Since the end of the Cold War, he has warned of the perils of further cuts in military spending. "If our nation, as the world's only superpower, chooses to go without a strong military, we are inviting global instability and conflict," he said in 1997. In April 1997, after the administration announced a new strategy, Skelton said, "The new strategy, it seems very clear, requires forces perhaps larger and certainly more flexible. It cannot be done with less." Armed Services is one of the House's least partisan committees; most members are strong defense supporters, and it has generally voted for more spending than the Clinton Administration has requested. It usually reports bills with bipartisan support, and Skelton is greatly respected by Republicans as well as Democrats on the committee. But the House as a whole is quite different. As Skelton noted in November 1997, "I have detected a growing cultural gap between military and civilian America. Fewer people today have direct contact with the military. I can tell you that as fewer sons and daughters wear the uniforms of our country, members of Congress receive less encouragement from voters in their districts to support a substantial military for our nation." Skelton's work over the years has helped transform the American military into the high-performance force evident in the Gulf war. But he has remained cautious about military engagement and wary of the strain the stepped-up operational tempo of the Clinton years has put on the military. He was reluctant to support sending troops to Bosnia in September 1995, and passed a resolution in the House, 287–141, which called for strict neutrality in the peacekeeping effort. He also warned against arming the Bosnian Muslims. He has been critical of applying too little force as well. He supported the air war in the former Yugoslavia in March 1999, and backed the May 1999 supplemental appropriation which was double the administration's request. He promises to concentrate on improving the quality of life for service personnel.

Some military personnel live in the 4th District, which includes the Army's giant Fort Leonard Wood and, in Skelton's home county, Whiteman Air Force Base, from which B-2s took off to bomb Serbia and Kosovo and returned the same day. Skelton worked to see that Leonard Wood was expanded rather than cut back in the 1995 base closing bill and convinced Bill Clinton to upgrade the B-2 as a deployable bomber. He worked hard on the counter-terrorism program and suggested stationing a National Guard anti-terrorism unit at Fort Leonard Wood. He also worked for 10 years for the aircraft carrier the *U.S.S. Harry S Truman*, which was commissioned in July 1998.

Skelton voted for some but not all of the Republicans' Contract with America, notably for the balanced budget amendment and the 1996 welfare reform. But he criticized Republican proposals for Medicare and tax cuts. In October 1998 he was one of 31 Democrats who voted for the Republican impeachment inquiry resolution. But he strongly criticized the Republicans for going ahead with the impeachment vote while Clinton's bombing of Iraq was going on, and voted against impeachment after being one of the last Democrats to announce his position.

Skelton's toughest race came in 1982, when he was redistricted in with a Republican incumbent; he won 55%–45%. In 1996 he was opposed by a former lieutenant governor who ran an aggressive campaign, but Skelton won 64%–34%. In 1998 he was re-elected 71%–27%, carrying every county, even those with strong Republican traditions. In 1997, Skelton left his seat on Small Business when he was appointed to the Select Committee on Intelligence. His goal is to become Armed Services chairman—"That's what I have been working toward for years"—which he will achieve if Democrats win control of the House in 2000.

Cook's Call. *Safe.* Skelton's solid winning margins here over the past 22 years belie the fact that this is a rather marginal district. Like the 3d, this district could be a real trouble spot for Democrats once it opens up.

The People: Pop. 1990: 569,295; 61% rural; 15.2% age 65 + ; 95.4% White, 3.2% Black, 0.5% Asian, 0.5% Amer. Indian, 0.4% Other; 1.1% Hispanic Origin. Households: 62.9% married couple families; 29.9% married couple fams. w. children; 33.7% college educ.; median household income: $23,064; per capita income: $10,984; median house value: $49,600; median gross rent: $230.

1996 Presidential Vote			1992 Presidential Vote		
Dole (R)	111,172	(46%)	Bush (R)	96,770	(38%)
Clinton (D)	99,975	(41%)	Clinton (D)	94,948	(37%)
Perot (I)	29,011	(12%)	Perot (I)	65,233	(25%)

Rep. Ike Skelton (D)

Elected 1976; b. Dec. 20, 1931, Lexington; home, Lexington; Wentworth Military Academy Jr. Col., 1949–51, U. of MO, A.B. 1953, LL.B. 1956; Disciples of Christ; married (Susie).

Elected Office: MO Senate, 1971–76.

Professional Career: Lafayette Cnty. Prosecuting atty., 1957–60; MO Special Asst. Atty. Gen., 1961–63; Practicing atty., 1963–76.

DC Office: 2206 RHOB 20515, 202-225-2876; Web site: www.house.gov/skelton.

District Offices: Blue Springs, 816-228-4242; Jefferson City, 573-635-3499; Lebanon, 417-532-7964; Sedalia, 660-826-2675.

Committees: *Armed Services* (RMM of 28 D): Military Procurement.

Group Ratings

	ADA	ACLU	AFS	LCV	CON	NTU	NFIB	COC	ACU	NTLC	CHC
1998	65	25	89	23	44	24	57	65	36	42	50
1997	40	—	63	—	54	38	—	78	52	—	—

National Journal Ratings

	1997 LIB — 1997 CONS		1998 LIB — 1998 CONS	
Economic	56% —	44%	59% —	41%
Social	48% —	51%	42% —	57%
Foreign	51% —	46%	64% —	31%

Key Votes of the 105th Congress

1. Clinton Budget Deal	Y	5. Puerto Rico Sthood. Ref.	N	9. Cut $ for B-2 Bombers	N
2. Education IRAs	N	6. End Highway Set-asides	N	10. Human Rights in China	Y
3. Req. 2/3 to Raise Taxes	Y	7. School Prayer Amend.	Y	11. Withdraw Bosnia Troops	N
4. Fast-track Trade	Y	8. Ovrd. Part. Birth Veto	Y	12. End Cuban TV-Marti	N

Election Results

1998 general	Ike Skelton (D)	133,173	(71%)	($333,525)
	Cecilia D. Noland (R)	51,005	(27%)	($22,762)
	Others	3,438	(2%)	
1998 primary	Ike Skelton (D)	unopposed		
1996 general	Ike Skelton (D)	153,566	(64%)	($770,607)
	Bill Phelps (R)	81,650	(34%)	($316,989)
	Others	5,573	(2%)	

FIFTH DISTRICT

Kansas City, Missouri, named after a state it isn't in and a river that doesn't touch it, is the center of one of America's large metro areas, the biggest on the central Great Plains. The first pioneers here started little towns on the bluffs above the Missouri River—Independence, Kansas City, Westport—which coalesced a few decades later. Here the Santa Fe Trail set out to cross the Sand Hills of Kansas and reach Mexican territory; here Jayhawks and Bushwhackers set out to fight for control of Bleeding Kansas. It was a rail center and had one of the largest stockyards in the country, a major commercial center with lean skyscrapers and the Country Club Plaza, the first shopping center in America, in the 1920s. It is famous for Harry Truman, who grew up on a farm now in the suburb of Grandview and who lived in his wife's family's house in Independence, the old county seat just to the east. It is famous also for its black community, and jazz musicians like Scott Joplin, Charlie Parker and Count Basie, and for its much-praised barbecue.

The 5th Congressional District includes most of Kansas City in Jackson County, plus Grandview and the bulk of Independence; most of the city's landmarks, including the Truman home, are here. It includes all of Kansas City's black neighborhoods and was 24% black in 1990. About half its voters are in Kansas City, half in the suburbs. Politically, it is solidly Democratic.

The congresswoman from the 5th is Karen McCarthy, a Democrat first elected in 1994. She moved to Kansas City to teach school, and shortly thereafter, in 1976, at 29, was elected to the Missouri House. She served there 18 years, rising to become chairman of Ways and Means in 1983 and president of the National Conference of State Legislators in 1994, working also as a government affairs consultant. In 1994 the 5th District congressman, Alan Wheat, ran for the Senate, and ultimately lost to John Ashcroft. McCarthy ran for the House seat and managed the not inconsiderable feat of winning 41% in an 11-candidate primary; the next two finishers also were women. McCarthy was supported by unions, environmentalists, black organizations and Kansas City Mayor Emanuel Cleaver; she raised more than $350,000 for the primary. The Republicans had a serious candidate, Ron Freeman, a black who played professional football in the short-lived United States Football League and then worked with the Fellowship of Christian Athletes, and who attacked "a government which has refused to be accountable to the citizenship." McCarthy stressed her conciliatory skills. She was supported by business leaders and had a $250,000 edge in PAC money. She won 57%–43%, carrying Kansas City 2–1 but losing the suburban half of the district.

McCarthy calls herself a New Democrat and supported the balanced budget amendment, a capital gains tax cut and opposed unfunded federal mandates. But overall she has a mostly liberal voting record—pro-gun control, pro-choice on abortion, against the flat tax and school vouchers. She lobbied successfully for a seat on Transportation and met with then-White House Chief of Staff Leon Panetta to restore funding for a $100 million courthouse in Kansas City. In the Missouri House she sponsored an energy policy act that encouraged alternative fuels; in Kansas City buses she supported mixing diesel fuel with beef tallow. "This is the fuel of the future, and we're going to prove it right here in our community," she said, though she might have said the same of the soybean oil used before. She attended the Kyoto conference and praised Al Gore's speech there as "a shot in the arm" that "resuscitated" the talks.

McCarthy favors a simplified but progressive tax. But her greatest legislative accomplishment was a tax credit for cleaning up central city "brownfield" sites in the August 1997 budget bill. In October 1997 she was lobbied hard by business and labor for and against fast track, and finally decided to oppose it; union PACs had given her more than $130,000, some 46% of her PAC money. McCarthy has promoted many other projects beyond the courthouse—$5 million to replace the 110-year-old Chouteau Bridge, $5 million in high-tech grants to local schools to use computers to study the Santa Fe Trail and put Truman Library documents online, $500,000 for the Discovery Nature Center in the Brush Creek Corridor, $12 million in the 1998 transportation bill for Jackson County Roadway, Strother Road in Lee's Summit and Missouri 150.

McCarthy has been re-elected by margins better than 2–1 in 1996 and 1998 against a lightly funded opponent.

Cook's Call. *Safe.* This Kansas City-based district is the second most Democratic in the state. McCarthy should have no problem winning her fourth term in 2000.

The People: Pop. 1990: 569,289; 1.2% rural; 14.3% age 65 + ; 73.3% White, 23.7% Black, 0.9% Asian, 0.6% Amer. Indian, 1.6% Other; 3.1% Hispanic Origin. Households: 46.2% married couple families; 20.7% married couple fams. w. children; 46.4% college educ.; median household income: $26,968; per capita income: $13,650; median house value: $56,700; median gross rent: $318.

1996 Presidential Vote			1992 Presidential Vote		
Clinton (D)	127,691	(58%)	Clinton (D)	134,862	(52%)
Dole (R)	71,453	(33%)	Bush (R)	67,511	(26%)
Perot (I)	17,489	(8%)	Perot (I)	55,799	(22%)

Rep. Karen McCarthy (D)

Elected 1994; b. Mar. 18, 1947, Haverhill, MA; home, Kansas City; U. of KS, B.A. 1969, M.B.A. 1986, U. of MO, M.A. 1976; Catholic; divorced.

Elected Office: MO House of Reps., 1976–94.

Professional Career: High schl. teacher, 1969–76; Financial analyst, 1984–86; Govt. affairs consultant, Marion Merrill Dow, 1986–94; Pres., Natl. Conf. of State Legislatures, 1994.

DC Office: 1330 LHOB 20515, 202-225-4535; Fax: 202-225-4403; Web site: www.house.gov/karenmccarthy.

District Offices: Independence, 816-833-4545; Kansas City, 816-842-4545.

Committees: *Commerce* (19th of 24 D): Energy & Power; Oversight & Investigations; Telecommunications, Trade & Consumer Protection.

Group Ratings

	ADA	ACLU	AFS	LCV	CON	NTU	NFIB	COC	ACU	NTLC	CHC
1998	100	81	100	92	72	20	21	56	0	11	8
1997	80	—	75	—	88	44	—	60	16	—	—

National Journal Ratings

	1997 LIB — 1997 CONS		1998 LIB — 1998 CONS	
Economic	62%	37%	68%	32%
Social	73%	27%	77%	22%
Foreign	82%	16%	82%	16%

Key Votes of the 105th Congress

1. Clinton Budget Deal	N	5. Puerto Rico Sthood. Ref.	Y	9. Cut $ for B-2 Bombers	Y
2. Education IRAs	N	6. End Highway Set-asides	N	10. Human Rights in China	Y
3. Req. 2/3 to Raise Taxes	N	7. School Prayer Amend.	N	11. Withdraw Bosnia Troops	N
4. Fast-track Trade	N	8. Ovrd. Part. Birth Veto	N	12. End Cuban TV-Marti	*

Election Results

1998 general	Karen McCarthy (D)	101,313	(66%)	($316,001)
	Penny Bennett (R)	47,582	(31%)	($29,620)
	Others	4,790	(3%)	
1998 primary	Karen McCarthy (D)	33,682	(79%)	
	Walter Wright (D)	8,916	(21%)	
1996 general	Karen McCarthy (D)	144,223	(67%)	($220,339)
	Penny Bennett (R)	61,803	(29%)	
	Others	7,945	(4%)	

SIXTH DISTRICT

The rolling, surging fields along the Missouri River in northwest Missouri were settled in a rush in the late 19th Century and have been losing people ever since. Fewer hands are needed on farms than half a century ago, far fewer than at the turn of the century. In 1940, this area had the fifth largest meatpacking operation in the world, but the meatpacking business has generated no more new jobs than farming, and St. Joseph, the biggest town here, has fewer people than in 1900. The counties of northwest Missouri, aside from those in the Kansas City metro area, had 508,000 people in 1900, 452,000 in 1940 and under 300,000 in 1990.

All these counties plus part of metro Kansas City—Clay and Platte counties and a small portion of Jackson County east of Independence—make up Missouri's 6th Congressional District: Greater Kansas City has gained people almost precisely to the extent that northwest Missouri has lost them. The Kansas City area casts a little more than half the district's votes. The historic political tradition here is mostly Democratic, tempered by dislike for national Democrats' cultural liberalism, but strengthened in the 1980s by anger at what people regarded as neglect of this salt-of-the-earth farming area—an attitude similar to that found across the border in Iowa. This was strong Perot country in 1992: He got 27% of the vote in the 6th District, and Bill Clinton carried it with a solid 40%–32% plurality in 1992 and a narrower 46%–42% in 1996.

The congresswoman from the 6th District is Pat Danner, a Democrat first elected in 1992. Danner has been in politics much of her adult life. In the 1970s she was a staffer for 6th District Congressman Jerry Litton, who died in a plane crash the night he won the 1976 Democratic Senate nomination. Danner ran to succeed Litton that year, but placed second in the Democratic primary to Morgan Maxfield, who lost to Republican Tom Coleman when it was discovered Maxfield had falsified his life story. Following her defeat, Danner became co-chair of the Ozark Regional Planning Commission under President Carter; in 1982 she was elected to the state

Senate. In 1990, her son Stephen was elected in an adjoining district, and they became the only mother-son team in a state Senate in America; he ran for state auditor in 1994, and lost 58%–39%. Things went better for Pat Danner in 1992, when she won an eight-candidate Democratic primary with 52% of the vote, and defeated 16-year incumbent Republican Coleman, 55%–45%, in a spirited campaign.

Danner has a moderate, almost middle-of-the-House voting record; she also works assiduously on local projects. She opposed the Clinton budget and tax increase in 1993 and pushed strongly for flood relief after the disastrous 1993 floods. She opposed nationalized health care, and, having voted for the Missouri abortion law upheld in the 1989 *Webster* case, she balked at the House version of the Freedom of Choice Act which gave states less leeway than the Senate version. She voted against NAFTA and GATT. She had attacked Coleman for sending out too much franked mail, and she spent far less, returning $100,000 of her office franking allowance to the Treasury. She contributed her pay raise to fund Danner Youth Awards for 6th District high school seniors.

She did not seem out of place in 1995 serving for the first time in a Republican-controlled legislative chamber. She joined the Blue Dog Democrats, seeking bipartisan solutions for tough problems. She argued for restricting members' personal use of frequent flier miles, which Republicans balked at. And she was one of the first members to use Speaker Newt Gingrich's Corrections Day procedure to get rid of outmoded or foolish regulations: she sponsored the Edible Oils Regulatory Reform Act, to require federal agencies to distinguish between petroleum and vegetable oils; 1970s legislation had mindlessly treated them the same. Danner formed a Missouri/Mississippi River Task Force and convinced the Army Corps of Engineers to revise its flood control plans for the Missouri. Prompted by Harold Martin of the Patee Park Baptist Church Pantry in St. Joseph, she sponsored a uniform national law to protect good-faith donors of unused food; it was signed as the Bill Emerson Good Samaritan Food Donation Act in October 1996. She is working for a national cell phone number for stranded motorists.

Danner was one of the swing votes on impeachment. She was one of 31 Democrats who voted for the Republican impeachment inquiry in October 1998. Thereafter she was lobbied heavily—she was seated next to Clinton at the White House dinner for Czech President Vaclav Havel—but did not announce a position until the day of the vote, when she voted no. "The president's actions, while worthy of contempt, do not meet this threshold," she said.

Danner has been re-elected by wide margins. Her 1998 opponent had run for the seat four times; he got 4% in the Democratic primary in 1992, then lost the Republican primary in 1994; in 1996 and 1998 he lost to Danner by 69%–29% and 71%–27%. Danner spent only $54,000 on her 1998 campaign and left her campaign treasury with $553,000 cash on hand; she is not likely to have serious competition soon.

Cook's Call. *Safe.* Danner's solid victories here help to hide the fact that this sprawling rural district is quite marginal. While Danner should have no problems here in 2000, this seat could be a problem for Democrats when Danner leaves.

The People: Pop. 1990: 568,823; 37.5% rural; 14.9% age 65 + ; 96.5% White, 2.1% Black, 0.5% Asian, 0.3% Amer. Indian, 0.5% Other; 1.5% Hispanic Origin. Households: 61.1% married couple families; 29.2% married couple fams. w. children; 40.1% college educ.; median household income: $27,165; per capita income: $12,641; median house value: $55,300; median gross rent: $281.

1996 Presidential Vote		1992 Presidential Vote	
Clinton (D)	115,342 (46%)	Clinton (D)	110,137 (40%)
Dole (R)	105,084 (42%)	Bush (R)	88,980 (32%)
Perot (I)	29,302 (12%)	Perot (I)	75,150 (27%)

Rep. Pat Danner (D)

Elected 1992; b. Jan. 13, 1934, Louisville, KY; home, Smithville; NE MO St. U., B.A. 1973; Catholic; married (Markt Meyer).

Elected Office: MO Senate, 1982–92.

Professional Career: Dist. Asst., U.S. Rep. Jerry Litton, 1973–76; Co-Chmn., Ozarks Regional Plng. Comm., 1977–81.

DC Office: 2262 RHOB 20515, 202-225-7041; Fax: 202-225-8221.

District Offices: Kansas City, 816-455-2256; St. Joseph, 816-233-9818.

Committees: *International Relations* (12th of 23 D): International Economic Policy & Trade. *Transportation & Infrastructure* (12th of 34 D): Aviation; Ground Transportation.

Group Ratings

	ADA	ACLU	AFS	LCV	CON	NTU	NFIB	COC	ACU	NTLC	CHC
1998	60	38	78	15	13	34	71	67	52	55	50
1997	50	—	63	—	32	51	—	70	56	—	—

National Journal Ratings

	1997 LIB — 1997 CONS	1998 LIB — 1998 CONS
Economic	54% — 46%	52% — 48%
Social	53% — 46%	55% — 45%
Foreign	51% — 46%	39% — 58%

Key Votes of the 105th Congress

1. Clinton Budget Deal	Y	5. Puerto Rico Sthood. Ref.	N	9. Cut $ for B-2 Bombers	Y
2. Education IRAs	Y	6. End Highway Set-asides	N	10. Human Rights in China	Y
3. Req. 2/3 to Raise Taxes	Y	7. School Prayer Amend.	Y	11. Withdraw Bosnia Troops	Y
4. Fast-track Trade	N	8. Ovrd. Part. Birth Veto	Y	12. End Cuban TV-Marti	Y

Election Results

1998 general	Pat Danner (D)	136,774	(71%)	($53,708)
	Jeff Bailey (R)	51,679	(27%)	
	Others	4,324	(2%)	
1998 primary	Pat Danner (D)	unopposed		
1996 general	Pat Danner (D)	169,006	(69%)	($112,970)
	Jeff Bailey (R)	72,064	(29%)	
	Others	5,212	(2%)	

SEVENTH DISTRICT

The second biggest tourist destination in America today, after Orlando, Florida, is Branson, Missouri—a fact almost no one predicted 20 years ago. Even today Branson has only 4,400 residents, is served by two-lane roads, is nowhere near a major airport; but it thrives, paralleling the surging popularity of Country and Western music. Branson was put on the map early in the century by Harold Bell Wright's novel, *The Shepherd of the Hills*, about the hardy people of the mountains, hills and meadows of southwest Missouri, just north of Arkansas. More tourists came in with completion of the Ozark Beach Dam which created Bull Shoals Lake in 1913, lured by the native bass and stocked trout. Then in the 1960s, new lakes were formed, a Shepherd of the Hills pageant and Silver Dollar City were started, and entertainers—the five Maybe brothers performing as "The Baldknobbers" and Box Car Willie from the Grand Ole Opry—started performing. They were followed by others—Roy Clark, Glen Campbell, Charlie Pride, Mel Tillis, Louise Mandrell and the violinist Shoji Tabuchi. Today Branson has 6 million visitors a year and more than two dozen theaters with 55,000 seats—more than Broadway. Workers come in from as far away as Springfield, the biggest city in southwest Missouri, and headquarters of such middle American institutions as the Mid-America Dairymen, the nation's largest milk producers' cooperative; the Bass Pro Shops Outdoor World, probably the nation's largest fishing equipment store; and the Assemblies of God, one of the nation's largest and fastest-growing Protestant denominations. What do people like about Branson? The nonstop entertainment and fishing and boating; country music and family style entertainment; plenty of shopping and a safe atmosphere. These are also things that have made southwest Missouri the fastest growing part of the state in the last 20 years, generating new businesses and attracting retirees as well as vacationers.

The 7th Congressional District includes Branson and Springfield and most of southwest Missouri. Historically, southwestern Missouri has been Republican—against secession in 1861: pro-Union Springfield changed hands several times during Missouri's own civil war. Its conservative response to the big-spending government of the 1960s and cultural liberalism of the 1970s reinforced its allegiance, and now this is the most Republican part of Missouri.

The congressman from the 7th District is Roy Blunt, a Republican first elected in 1996. Blunt grew up in southwest Missouri, in a political family; his father was a state representative from a district near Springfield. He taught high school and college history and government, and in 1973, at 23, became Greene County (Springfield) clerk. In 1984, at 34, he was elected Missouri secretary of State and was re-elected with 60% in 1988. In 1992 he ran for governor, and lost the Republican primary to William Webster, 44%–39%. (Webster was defeated and disgraced, sent to jail because of his improper administration of the Second Injury Fund.) Blunt became president of his alma mater, Southwest Baptist University in Bolivar. In 1996 Congressman Mel Hancock, author of Missouri ballot initiatives requiring voter approval of tax increases, kept his pledge to serve only four terms and retired. In the primary Blunt faced Gary Nodler, businessman and one-time staffer to Congressman Gene Taylor. Nodler carried his (and Webster's) home area around Joplin and Carthage, but Blunt carried everything else and won 56%–44%. There were 75,000 votes cast in the Republican primary and only 16,000 in the Democratic primary: a harbinger of the general election, which Blunt won 65%–32%, running ahead of the Republican ticket and carrying every county with at least 62% of the vote.

Blunt has a solidly conservative voting record. His political adeptness was apparent in his committee assignments: Agriculture, International Relations, Transportation and Infrastructure. On Agriculture he supported the Clinton Administration's proposal to reduce the number of federal milk marketing orders from 31 to 11 and to include southern Missouri in the southeast region—a position also supported by Mid-America Dairymen—and he opposed food embargoes. On International Relations, he supported the bill to penalize countries that practice or allow religious persecution—a concern of denominations like the Assemblies of God, which has more members abroad than in the United States. He was on Transportation in time for the 1998 transportation bill, which increased Missouri's funding $213 million. He and Asa Hutchinson from the adjoining Arkansas district made U.S. 71 from Kansas City to Shreveport a "high priority corridor," a step on the way to upgrading it to interstate status.

Blunt also took up important conservative causes. He co-sponsored the bill to zero out the tax code by December 2000. He opposed normal trade relations status with China ("America should place her political principles above commerce"). When tobacco became a headline issue, he proposed to yank teenagers' driver's licenses for 60 days if they were caught with tobacco, and with Hutchinson he moved to earmark tobacco settlement funds not used for anti-smoking programs for debt reduction and tax cuts. He was part of Majority Whip Tom DeLay's "free speech" team proposing bills to undermine the Shays-Meehan campaign finance bill. He was not inattentive to his fellow members. He supported a cost-of-living pay increase for House members in 1997, despite local flak. With Bob Clement of Tennessee, he formed an Education Caucus in May 1997, open to former teachers and administrators in schools and colleges. In the 1998 campaign cycle he raised and contributed $250,000 to other incumbent Republicans.

This record strengthened him at home and brought considerable rewards in the House. His Democratic opponent was an advocate of legalized prostitution and author of works like *Nerds' Guide to Better Sex* whose Website included pictures of scantily clad women. The Missouri Democratic party wanted nothing to do with him, and Blunt won 73%–24%; the same day his son Matt Blunt was elected to the Missouri House. Three weeks after the election Blunt won a seat on the Commerce Committee. In January 1999 DeLay appointed Blunt chief deputy whip, the position Denny Hastert held until his astonishing elevation to speaker. Blunt promised to try to emulate him: "Denny did a great job defining the deputy whip job: open door, never overpromise, always try to overperform." Some weeks later he became George W. Bush's chief liaison to House Republicans. Blunt, wrote the *Weekly Standard*'s Matthew Rees, "may be the most influential Republican no one's ever heard of." Yet.

Cook's Call. *Safe.* Blunt should have no trouble winning a third term in this strongly Republican district.

The People: Pop. 1990: 568,017; 48% rural; 16.3% age 65 + ; 97.3% White, 0.9% Black, 0.5% Asian, 1.1% Amer. Indian, 0.2% Other; 0.7% Hispanic Origin. Households: 59.9% married couple families; 26.7% married couple fams. w. children; 37.6% college educ.; median household income: $21,712; per capita income: $11,029; median house value: $48,400; median gross rent: $244.

1996 Presidential Vote			1992 Presidential Vote		
Dole (R)	129,249	(51%)	Bush (R)	118,817	(45%)
Clinton (D)	93,537	(37%)	Clinton (D)	96,621	(36%)
Perot (I)	27,580	(11%)	Perot (I)	48,824	(18%)

Rep. Roy Blunt (R)

Elected 1996; b. Jan. 10, 1950, Niangua; home, Strafford; SW Baptist U., B.A. 1970, SW MO St. U., M.A. 1972; Baptist; married (Roseann).

Elected Office: MO Secy. of State, 1984–93.

Professional Career: High schl. teacher, 1970–73; Greene Cnty. Clerk, 1973–85; Adjunct Instructor, Drury Col., 1976–82; Pres., SW Baptist U., 1993–96.

DC Office: 217 CHOB 20515, 202-225-6536; Fax: 202-225-5604; Web site: www.house.gov/blunt.

District Offices: Joplin, 417-781-1041; Springfield, 417-889-1800.

Committees: *Chief Deputy Majority Whip. Commerce* (27th of 29 R): Finance & Hazardous Materials; Oversight & Investigations; Telecommunications, Trade & Consumer Protection.

Group Ratings

	ADA	ACLU	AFS	LCV	CON	NTU	NFIB	COC	ACU	NTLC	CHC
1998	0	6	0	8	4	54	100	82	100	95	92
1997	10	—	13	—	22	57	—	90	80	—	—

National Journal Ratings

	1997 LIB — 1997 CONS		1998 LIB — 1998 CONS	
Economic	0%	— 90%	28%	— 70%
Social	30%	— 64%	28%	— 72%
Foreign	21%	— 78%	7%	— 83%

Key Votes of the 105th Congress

1. Clinton Budget Deal	Y	5. Puerto Rico Sthood. Ref.	N	9. Cut $ for B-2 Bombers	*
2. Education IRAs	Y	6. End Highway Set-asides	Y	10. Human Rights in China	N
3. Req. 2/3 to Raise Taxes	Y	7. School Prayer Amend.	Y	11. Withdraw Bosnia Troops	Y
4. Fast-track Trade	Y	8. Ovrd. Part. Birth Veto	Y	12. End Cuban TV-Marti	N

Election Results

1998 general	Roy Blunt (R)	129,746	(73%)	($567,315)
	Marc Perkel (D)	43,416	(24%)	
	Others	5,639	(3%)	
1998 primary	Roy Blunt (R)	unopposed		
1996 general	Roy Blunt (R)	162,558	(65%)	($985,764)
	Ruth Bamberger (D)	79,306	(32%)	($103,747)
	Others	8,720	(3%)	

EIGHTH DISTRICT

Mark Twain might not recognize life on the Mississippi below St. Louis today, where the land flattens out and the river is hidden behind levees, which ordinarily—except during the terrible flood of 1993—screen small towns and river roads from the sight of rows of barges tethered together, full of coal or soybeans. The Mississippi today is an industrial waterway. But it was never really all that romantic, for Twain's steamboats, as he was at pains to point out, were dangerous, noisy contraptions, forever blowing up or getting embedded in roots and branches in the swirling river currents. This is one of the older-settled parts of the United States: French settlers founded Missouri towns like Cape Girardeau in the late 1700s. But the big influx started just a few years after the 1811 earthquake centered on New Madrid; the spongy Mississippi valley land is also seismically very active, and this was the site of one of the most devastating earthquakes in U.S. history.

Outwardly, the southeast quadrant of Missouri—the river valley and the hills to the west, with coal and lead mines (the area produces most of the world's lead) with their miles of tunnels, plus the Bootheel that hangs down in the far southeast—hasn't changed much in 50 years. For years there has been a big population outflow from the Bootheel, as machines replace low-wage farm workers, and the only big growth here has been around Cape Girardeau and along the route of I-44; in the 1990s growth rates are picking up, as people seek lives in small communities.

The 8th Congressional District covers this southeast quadrant of Missouri. The political heritage is mixed. The Bootheel was as solidly Democratic as the Mississippi Valley around Memphis used to be, and some of the mining counties are Democratic. Cape Girardeau, the boyhood home of Rush Limbaugh and also the starting point of the 1996 Clinton-Gore bus tour, votes solidly Republican, as do surrounding counties. For many years this was a safe Democratic district; since 1980, it has been represented by Republicans.

The congresswoman from the 8th District is Jo Ann Emerson, elected in 1996 to replace her husband Bill Emerson, who was first elected in 1980 and died in June 1996. Jo Ann Emerson grew up in the Washington suburb of Bethesda, Maryland, in a Republican family (her father was executive director of the Republican National Committee) but next door to Democrats Hale and Lindy Boggs, who served in Congress over a period of 50 years; their daughter, Cokie Roberts, babysat for Jo Ann. In 1975 she married Republican Bill Emerson, then a Washington lobbyist with Capitol Hill experience; as a congressional page in 1954, he was on the House floor when it was fired upon by Puerto Rican terrorists. In 1979, spotting the personal vulnerability of the Democratic incumbent, Bill Emerson went back home to Missouri to run, and won with 55%. In 1995 he was diagnosed with cancer, but missed few votes during radiation therapy. Two pieces of legislation passed in 1996 memorialize him: the Bill Emerson Good

Samaritan Food Donation Act, setting national standards to encourage donations of unused food, and the Bill Emerson Bridge across the Mississippi at Cape Girardeau.

After Bill's death on June 22, Jo Ann Emerson decided to run and announced on July 10. "I was so totally focused on a mission to keep the seat and make it a living memorial to Bill," she said. She had political experience of her own: she worked for the American Insurance Association and National Restaurant Association and had been a press aide at the National Republican Congressional Committee. Her views are conservative—for the balanced budget amendment, against gun control, for abortion restrictions, for property rights—and she was immediately endorsed by Senators Christopher Bond and John Ashcroft. But while she was named the Republican nominee in the contest for the remainder of her husband's term, to be held also on November 5, she could not run for the Republican nomination in the August 6 primary: Missouri law bars reopening filing for new candidates if an incumbent dies less than 11 weeks before the August primary, so Emerson ran as an independent in the general. Democrats had a serious candidate, Emily Firebaugh, a timber company owner and lifelong area resident, who attacked Emerson as a product of the Washington suburbs. Firebaugh eventually spent the impressive sum of $831,000, more than Emerson's $806,000. The Republican nominee was less trouble: Richard Kline, who in 1995 had used pepper spray to try to place a Veterans Administration doctor under citizen's arrest. Bill Emerson's record, Jo Ann Emerson's conservative views on issues, and the poignancy of the situation all worked in the same direction: toward an Emerson victory. For the full term she received 50% of the votes, with 37% for Firebaugh and 11% for Kline. A better gauge of opinion may have been the two-way contest for the short term, in which Emerson won 63%.

Emerson was given her husband's seats on Agriculture, and Transportation and Infrastructure. On Transportation she secured funding for local projects, including $8 million for the Bill Emerson Bridge, but voted against the final version of the transportation bill in May 1998, because of what she considered a potential reduction in veterans' disability benefits. Amid the argument over the tobacco bill, she co-sponsored a bill for full funding of benefits for veterans with tobacco-related illnesses. Emerson traveled to Kyoto for the November 1997 climate change conference, starting off with a skeptical attituded toward the theory of global warming. "You're setting policy for 78 years. It's daunting," she said. Returning home, she said the treaty would impose high costs on farmers in the United States and would put them under a competitive disadvantage with countries like China, which the treaty exempted: "If this gets implemented, this decimates the 8th District of Missouri." Emerson worked to help pass the Birth Defects Prevention Act in March 1998; southern Missouri has one of the nation's highest rates of birth defects. A property rights supporter, she got her portion of the district excluded from the American Heritage Rivers project. She opposed the Republican delays of the flood relief bill in spring 1998 and secured an $8 million flood control project while holding out on supporting the leadership on the budget in June 1998. She conducted an interactive drug summit in the district in November 1997, and worked to get money for district projects—$475,000 for soybean cyst nematode research and the University of Missouri Delta Center in Portageville, a $4 million guaranteed loan to Interlochen, a cement block producer in Sikeston. She supported the farm aid package in October 1998.

The 1998 Democratic candidate, former Circuit Judge Tony "Hang 'Em High" Heckemeyer, attacked her for backing a Superfund bill that he said would save legal fees for insurance companies and small business; Emerson charged that 80% of his contributions were from lawyers. She outspent him almost 3–1 and won 63%, the same as her win for the short term in 1996. In November 1998 Emerson moved to the Appropriations Committee and its Agriculture Subcommittee. Her first priority seemed to be doing something about low prices for farm commodities. In February 1999 she complained that with $4.99 beans, $2.15 corn, $2.60 wheat and 58 cent cotton, farmers can't get production loans: "Producers simply cannot afford the continuation of these tough market conditions, and I believe that Congress must continue to aggressively look for solutions to the problems in our farm economy."

Cook's Call. *Safe.* After a competitive 1996 contest, Emerson performed better in 1998, a sign that Democrats may be conceding this marginal district to her.

The People: Pop. 1990: 568,385; 62.7% rural; 16.8% age 65 + ; 94.7% White, 4.4% Black, 0.3% Asian, 0.4% Amer. Indian, 0.1% Other; 0.5% Hispanic Origin. Households: 60.1% married couple families; 28.3% married couple fams. w. children; 24.9% college educ.; median household income: $18,207; per capita income: $9,300; median house value: $37,900; median gross rent: $179.

1996 Presidential Vote		
Clinton (D)	101,339	(45%)
Dole (R)	96,457	(43%)
Perot (I)	25,089	(11%)

1992 Presidential Vote		
Clinton (D)	109,858	(46%)
Bush (R)	89,238	(37%)
Perot (I)	41,558	(17%)

Rep. Jo Ann Emerson (R)

Elected 1996; b. Sept. 16, 1950, Washington, DC; home, Cape Girardeau; Ohio Wesleyan U., B.A. 1972; Presbyterian; widowed.

Professional Career: Deputy Communications Dir., Natl. Repub. Cong. Cmte., 1984–91; Dir., State Relations & Grassroot Programs, Natl. Restaurant Assn., 1991–94; Sr. Vice Pres., Pub. Affairs, American Insurance Assn., 1994–96.

DC Office: 132 CHOB 20515, 202-225-4404; Web site: www.house.gov/emerson.

District Offices: Cape Girardeau, 573-335-0101; Farmington, 573-756-9755; Rolla, 573-364-2455.

Committees: *Appropriations* (31st of 34 R): Agriculture, Rural Development, & FDA; District of Columbia; Treasury, Postal Service & General Government.

Group Ratings

	ADA	ACLU	AFS	LCV	CON	NTU	NFIB	COC	ACU	NTLC	CHC
1998	5	6	11	8	33	51	93	83	92	89	100
1997	5	—	13	—	29	52	—	90	88	—	—

National Journal Ratings

	1997 LIB	—	1997 CONS		1998 LIB	—	1998 CONS
Economic	16%	—	82%		34%	—	64%
Social	20%	—	71%		3%	—	90%
Foreign	12%	—	81%		0%	—	93%

Key Votes of the 105th Congress

1. Clinton Budget Deal	Y	5. Puerto Rico Sthood. Ref.	N	9. Cut $ for B-2 Bombers	N
2. Education IRAs	Y	6. End Highway Set-asides	Y	10. Human Rights in China	N
3. Req. 2/3 to Raise Taxes	Y	7. School Prayer Amend.	Y	11. Withdraw Bosnia Troops	Y
4. Fast-track Trade	Y	8. Ovrd. Part. Birth Veto	Y	12. End Cuban TV-Marti	N

Election Results

1998 general	Jo Ann Emerson (R) 104,271	(63%)	($1,084,449)
	Anthony J. (Tony) Heckemeyer (D) 59,426	(36%)	($375,093)
	Others 2,827	(2%)	
1998 primary	Jo Ann Emerson (R) .... unopposed		
1996 general	Jo Ann Emerson (I) 112,472	(50%)	($806,205)
	Emily Firebaugh (D) 83,084	(37%)	($831,533)
	Richard Kline (R) 23,477	(11%)	
	Others 3,821	(2%)	

NINTH DISTRICT

Little Dixie, the swath of northeast Missouri along the Mississippi River, was settled by South-erners from Kentucky and Virginia. Its most famous native son is Mark Twain, born Sam Clemens in Hannibal, then as now a little town on bluffs overlooking the river. Hannibal was the thinly disguised St. Petersburg of Tom Sawyer and Huckleberry Finn, lovingly created years later complete with Pike County and other dialect by Twain, then living in New England. Little Dixie has always been Democratic politically and was pro-Confederate during the Civil War; Callaway County declared its independence from the Union. Twain's view of politics was different, both darker and more optimistic: he created a vision of America that transcended region and a view of antebellum society that identified slavery as an evil without ever saying so; Twain himself was a Republican and close friend of Union General and President Ulysses S. Grant. But whatever the author's feelings for his birthplace, Hannibal loves Twain; some quarter-million tourists pour in to visit his boyhood home each year.

Long faithfully Democratic, Little Dixie has reared some notable politicians as well. One was Champ Clark, speaker of the House from 1911–19 and presidential candidate in 1912; another was Clarence Cannon, author of the definitive text on the House's parliamentary pro-cedures and chairman of the House Appropriations Committee until his death in 1964.

The 9th Congressional District is the descendant of the Little Dixie districts that elected Clark and Cannon, but declining population has required that it be expanded far to the south. Now it extends south to Columbia, home of the University of Missouri, and Fulton, home of Westminster College, where in 1946 Winston Churchill, accompanied by President Harry Tru-man, told the world that "from Stettin on the Baltic to Trieste on the Adriatic, an iron curtain has descended across the continent." To the east the 9th includes Franklin County and half of St. Charles County, formerly rural territory but now increasingly suburbanized, with population up more than 20% in the 1990s. These suburban areas, which lean Republican, now cast one-third of the district's votes, and another one-third are cast in Columbia and adjoining counties, leaving only one-third for the formerly dominant and still usually Democratic Little Dixie.

The congressman from the 9th District is Kenny Hulshof, a Republican first elected in 1996. Hulshof grew up on a farm in far southeast Missouri, near the confluence of the Mississippi and Ohio rivers. After college and law school he joined the public defender's office in Cape Girardeau. In 1989 he became a special prosecutor for the Missouri Attorney General's office, and from his home in Columbia traveled to 53 Missouri counties, getting 60 violent felony convictions and seven death sentences. In the midst of this, in 1994, he became the Republican nominee for Congress in the 9th District. This was a surprise: challenger Rick Hardy had held Democratic Congressman Harold Volkmer to a 48%–46% victory in 1992 and was running again; but after the primary filing deadline, he withdrew from the race due to depression and exhaustion. In August, party leaders named Hulshof as Hardy's replacement. He was far out-spent, but even so made a respectable showing, carrying Columbia and Boone County, where the Libertarian candidate won 10% of the vote, and trailing 50%–45% overall.

In January 1996 Hulshof resigned as special prosecutor and started to run again. First elected in 1976, Volkmer had been known mainly as the House's leading opponent of gun control. But in 1995 his combative temperament and irritation with the new Republican majority made him one of its most persistent antagonists on the floor. His close showings, and the fact that a LaRouche follower got 28% in the primary against him, suggested weakness. But Hulshof had competition in the primary. Ophthalmologist Harry Eggleston moved to St. Charles County, spent $806,000, and carried St. Charles and Franklin counties with big margins and ran slightly ahead in Little Dixie. But Hulshof won big in and around Columbia. Hulshof won by only 168 votes out of 38,000 cast.

This also was a sharply contested general election. Volkmer ran an ad showing Hulshof in a Porsche driven by Newt Gingrich, attacking him for signing away his independence in the Contract with America. Hulshof replied that his Porsche was a used car sitting under a tarp in his yard. Hulshof charged Volkmer had voted to raise taxes 20 times in 20 years and had voted for 40% pay raises. Hulshof actually outspent the incumbent, though much of his money was spent in the primary. The key moment came in October, when Volkmer, in response to a question, said voters were not overtaxed and that he would not mind paying $1 million in taxes. Hulshof ran radio ads quoting Volkmer all over the district. Volkmer still carried Little Dixie 53%–46%, but Hulshof carried the Columbia area 54%–39% and St. Charles and Franklin counties 49%–48%, for an overall 49%–47% margin.

In the House, Hulshof was elected president of the Republican freshman class and quickly sounded the note of consensus voters yearned for: he decried "partisan bickering" 15 days after taking office, helped organize the civility retreat in Hershey, Pennsylvania, bemoaned the partisanship of AFL-CIO TV ads against him in April 1997, and, with Democratic freshman president Jim Davis, supported the 1997 balanced budget agreement. The Republican leadership gave him a prized seat on Ways and Means. This gave him a platform for backing proposals like repeal of the death tax, exemption of the first $400 of dividend and interest income from the income tax (which would benefit 68 million filers) and FARRM accounts which would allow farmers to income-average over five years; it also gave him a fine base for fundraising, and before the end of the year he had raised $220,000. But Ways and Means also presented perils. One of Hulshof's major causes was preserving the favorable tax treatment of ethanol. But after his amendment was defeated in committee, he voted for the Republican tax bill immediately. Missouri Democrats quickly charged, "Hulshof abandons support of ethanol." To his rescue eventually came Speaker Gingrich, who in May 1998 put Hulshof and Iowa's Jim Nussle on the transportation conference committee, on which their votes guaranteed that the House side would favor the ethanol credit.

Hulshof got more publicity than he must have expected on a successful amendment to cut the capital gains tax on taxpayers selling businesses to farm cooperatives. It was suggested to him, he said, by co-op leaders, but the Joint Tax Committee singled it out as a provision that would affect only a few taxpayers—including an $80 million break for $1 million Republican contributor Harold Simmons. Simmons said the transaction occurred before the starting date of the provision and that it was structured so that he would pay no tax anyway, but Bill Clinton singled it out as one of his first three line-item vetoes in August 1997. Efforts to override the veto were unsuccessful, but the Supreme Court declared the line-item veto unconstitutional in June 1998 and restored the provision.

Hulshof sits on the Social Security Subcommittee, and has approached reform gingerly. Though he stuck with the leadership on many tough votes, he voted for the Shays-Meehan campaign finance bill. He worked for highway funds for U.S. 63 and U.S. 36 and on the Jefferson Institute for Crop Diversity, a USDA initiative likely to be located in Columbia.

When Hulshof was elected, Democrats looked forward to giving him a tough challenge in 1998. But his success at fundraising, his shrewdness at spotting issues and the general pro-incumbent trend of opinion led one Democrat after another to decide not to run. The list is long: state House Speaker Steve Gaw, House Majority Leader Gracia Backer, former Volkmer aide Lee Viorel, state Representative Steve Carroll, state Senator Ted House and state Senator Ken Jackob. The Democratic nominee, Boone County Commissioner Linda Vogt, spent only

$158,000; Hulshof raised more than $1 million and spent $964,000. He won impressively, carrying every county and with an overall margin of 62%–36%, the biggest margin in the 9th District since 1988. His prospects for 2000 look good, and some are talking of him as a statewide candidate some day.

Cook's Call. *Probably Safe.* This district was the site of one of the Democrats' biggest recruiting failures in 1998, as they were unable to find a top-tier candidate to challenge freshman Hulshof in this marginal, but previously Democratic-held district. There are rumors that Hulshof is looking to run for statewide office someday, which means that this seat could be in play soon. For now, however, Hulshof looks to be in good shape.

The People: Pop. 1990: 568,238; 51.4% rural; 13.4% age 65 +; 95.1% White, 3.7% Black, 0.8% Asian, 0.3% Amer. Indian, 0.2% Other; 0.7% Hispanic Origin. Households: 60.9% married couple families; 30.6% married couple fams. w. children; 37.9% college educ.; median household income: $26,055; per capita income: $11,741; median house value: $55,400; median gross rent: $248.

1996 Presidential Vote

Clinton (D)	111,626	(44%)
Dole (R)	106,503	(42%)
Perot (I)	30,593	(12%)

1992 Presidential Vote

Clinton (D)	110,175	(41%)
Bush (R)	90,836	(34%)
Perot (I)	65,195	(24%)

Rep. Kenny Hulshof (R)

Elected 1996; b. May 22, 1958, Sikeston; home, Columbia; U. of MO, B.S. 1980, U. of MS, J.D. 1983; Catholic; married (Renee).

Professional Career: Asst. Pub. Defender, 32nd Judicial Circuit, 1983–86; Asst. Prosecuting Atty., Cape Girardeau, 1986–89; Special Prosecutor, MO Atty. General, 1989–96.

DC Office: 412 CHOB 20515, 202-225-2956; Fax: 202-225-5712; Web site: www.house.gov/hulshof.

District Offices: Columbia, 573-449-5111; Hannibal, 573-221-1200; Washington, 314-239-4001.

Committees: *Ways & Means* (20th of 23 R): Oversight; Social Security.

Group Ratings

	ADA	ACLU	AFS	LCV	CON	NTU	NFIB	COC	ACU	NTLC	CHC
1998	15	6	0	38	21	48	100	100	88	84	92
1997	15	—	13	—	80	56	—	90	92	—	—

National Journal Ratings

	1997 LIB — 1997 CONS			1998 LIB — 1998 CONS		
Economic	39%	—	60%	23%	—	74%
Social	39%	—	59%	14%	—	81%
Foreign	0%	—	88%	19%	—	75%

Key Votes of the 105th Congress

1. Clinton Budget Deal	Y	5. Puerto Rico Sthood. Ref.	N	9. Cut $ for B-2 Bombers	N
2. Education IRAs	Y	6. End Highway Set-asides	Y	10. Human Rights in China	N
3. Req. 2/3 to Raise Taxes	Y	7. School Prayer Amend.	Y	11. Withdraw Bosnia Troops	Y
4. Fast-track Trade	Y	8. Ovrd. Part. Birth Veto	Y	12. End Cuban TV-Marti	N

Election Results

1998 general	Kenny Hulshof (R) 117,196	(62%)	($963,984)
	Linda Vogt (D) 66,861	(36%)	($157,869)
	Others 4,248	(2%)	
1998 primary	Kenny Hulshof (R) .... unopposed		
1996 general	Kenny Hulshof (R) 123,580	(49%)	($686,450)
	Harold L. Volkmer (D) 117,685	(47%)	($542,368)
	Others 8,965	(4%)	

MONTANA

"Montana is what America used to be," says Governor Marc Racicot. Physically, it is America's Big Sky Country, a land of great empty vistas, with mountains in the west and vast expanses of plateaus and plains in the east—the 4th largest state in area and 44th in population. To the casual observer, Montana still seems mostly empty yet is growing lustily once again, a place where you'll come across the Old West of 19th Century cowboys but whose recent growth owes much to 21st Century electronic communications—a financial advisor with a modem can live here as easily as in Los Angeles.

Montana sits atop America, spanning the Rockies so that on Interstate 15 you can cross the Continental Divide three times. Here in the mountains are the headwaters of the Missouri, from its source in Beaverhead County to its mouth in the Gulf of Mexico the longest river in North America, and of the Clark Fork which flows into the Columbia and eventually the Pacific. Not far away, at Egg Mountain near Choteau on the Deep Teton River, is the world's most plenteous source of dinosaur remains. But Montana's recorded history is recent: at its 1989 centennial, the son of one of its original cattleman-settlers watched 105 cowboys drive 4,000 cattle with 300 covered wagons trailing behind.

Statehood came less than a century after the first white Americans came here as agents of the government—the Lewis and Clark expedition in 1805. Next came the mountain men, seeking fur, and then came the miners seeking gold, silver, copper—sudden riches that would make them kings not of this barren land but of the metropolises back East. Raucous mining towns sprang up, complete with outlaws and vigilantes. The mining economy gave Montana a radical, class warfare politics. On one side was the Anaconda Mining Company, which until 1959 owned five of Montana's six daily newspapers, many of its utilities, and many of its politicians, and had strong allies in the Stockmen's Association and the Farm Bureau. On the other side were progressives like Senators Thomas Walsh, who exposed the Teapot Dome scandal, and Burton Wheeler, a New Dealer who broke with Franklin Roosevelt over court packing and isolationism, the labor unions (Montana has no right-to-work law and is the most pro-union state in the Rockies), and pork barrel beneficiaries (for a while in the 1930s, Montana received more federal money per capita than almost any other state). The locus of all this was Butte, with its gold and copper mines on "The Richest Hill on Earth," with its gamblers and bootleggers, company goons and union thugs, IWW organizers and Socialist mayor and millionaires who bought seats in the U.S. Senate. Today the mines are closed, the ore depleted, and the stone temples of commerce and grim, looming mineheads are being restored to a cleanliness they never enjoyed in the boom days.

Slowly Montana has changed. Butte's population peaked in 1920, mines gradually closed all over the state, and agriculture—wheat growing and cattle grazing—became the mainstays of the economy and class warfare died down. Other towns grew, though none is over 100,000 yet: Billings with its agricultural marketing in the east; the university town of Missoula, Great Falls just east of the Rockies; Kalispell near Lake Flathead; the university and resort town of Bozeman; and the state capital of Helena. The muscular tone of a land settled by ranch hands, miners and railroad workers, of cowboy hats, boots and blue jeans, of men who do hard physical work and relax hard afterwards, remains a link with Montanans going back to the mountain men, miners and cowboys who drove herds of Texas longhorns across the open range. And there is still the sense of space. Hunting and fishing are never far away; development in the small cities and resort areas has not been enough to drive the game away.

In the late 1970s, Montana started attracting affluent second home buyers, and by the mid-1990s they came in a rush, movie stars and Wall Street magnates but also just ordinary people buying small spreads near Big Sky or McLeod, near Bozeman, or around Flathead Lake or Big Timber or the Big Mountain ski resort in Whitefish, where grizzlies come down to forage and the bars hold mouse races. And many newcomers, from California and other urban states, set down roots here, as computers, modems and fax machines make it possible for small businessmen and entrepreneurs to work in Montana, far from their customers and clients, but in an environment they love. These new Montanans have added a spark of energy and inventiveness to a state much of which consisted of those left behind when others moved elsewhere; at the same time they do not want to change the character of the place that attracted them. In the 1990s Montana's population grew rapidly, even though the eastern plains lost population, like neighboring parts of the Dakotas and Wyoming. But where you can see the mountains, population has spiked upwards, especially around Bozeman, Missoula and Kalispell.

Politically, Montana is the most Democratic of the Rocky Mountain states—which means pretty Republican by national standards. There are still Democratic strongholds—Butte with its union heritage, Missoula with its large university and various Indian reservations. But Billings and the grazing counties are Republican, and Montana, after voting 38%–35% for Bill Clinton over George Bush in 1992, with 26% for Ross Perot, swung to the right and voted 44%–41% for Bob Dole over Clinton in 1996. Most voters here seem part of what conservative activist Grover Norquist calls the "Leave-Us-Alone Coalition." Montana was the only state without a daytime speed limit from 1995–99, when a state Supreme Court decision forced the legislature to pass one: 75 miles per hour. A 1998 initiative requiring voter approval for tax increases was also overturned by the courts, but legislators seemed unlikely to pass one in their 90-day session. Many issues arise out of the intersection of wilderness and civilization: what should be done about diseased bison migrating from Yellowstone National Park into Montana (they are shot by the state Livestock Department), whether to allow new gold and silver mines that use cyanide (voters outlawed that in referendum, but some state legislators want to allow it), whether to build a railroad on the Tongue River to ship coal (proposal still pending since 1986), whether to allow gas drilling in the Rocky Mountain Front (the Forest Service banned that in 1997).

Governor. Marc Racicot (pronounced *roscoe*) is probably the nation's most popular governor; in October 1998 his job approval was 87%, about as high as you can go. He grew up in the logging town of Libby, the son of a basketball coach. Racicot is famously unassuming, lobbying legislators himself, speaking at a high school commencement with just one graduate, corresponding with an 11-year-old concerned about guns in schools, keeping his home phone number listed and driving his own car. Educated in Montana, he worked as a statewide prosecutor for 12 years, lost a couple of races for judge, then in 1988 ran for attorney general, startling his father and friends by doing so as a Republican. He ran for governor in 1992 after incumbent Republican Stan Stephens retired after a mild stroke, and as the state was about to face a $200 million budget gap. He and Democrat Dorothy Bradley waged an unusually civil and specific campaign, both calling for a 4% sales tax to be voted on by referendum, but Bradley

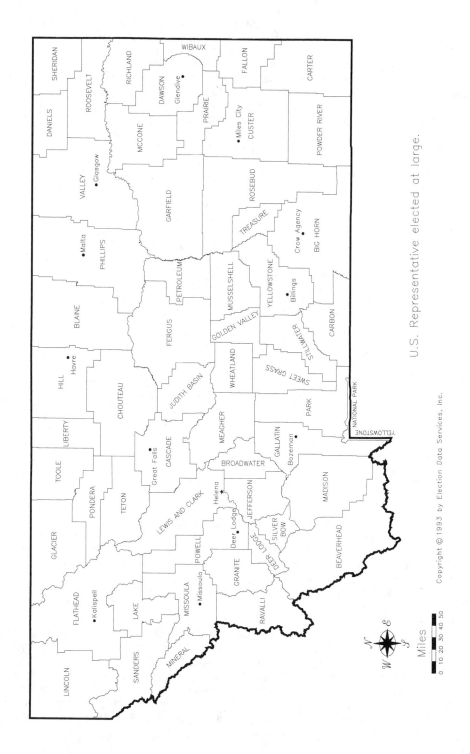

U.S. Representative elected at large.

favored more government while Racicot called for downsizing. Racicot won 51%–49%, and Republicans captured the state House.

The sales tax was rejected by the voters 3–1, after which Racicot cut spending and produced a $22 million surplus, which he turned back to the voters as a 7% income tax rebate. "No one told us to keep the change." He got the state workmen's compensation law revised and inspired voters to elect large Republican majorities to both houses in 1994. In his second two years he signed abortion restrictions, worked to soften state water discharge laws, opposed an initiative to regulate mining and got the legislature to approve a $45 million tax cut. His 1995 welfare reform plan led to sharp drops in the welfare rolls in 1996. His job approval rating hovered around 75%, but with his kids still in school he declined to run against Senator Max Baucus. In his 1996 race, he was endorsed by the teachers' unions and was opposed by a 71-year-old former legislator Chet Blaylock, who died suddenly on October 21; Blaylock's running mate became the Democratic candidate. Racicot won with 79% of the vote.

In his second term Racicot addressed the fact that Montana's wages and incomes are the lowest in the nation. He sought to create more irrigated farmland to produce specialty crops and competed for the Lockheed Martin VentureStar spaceport. He opposed the 1998 referendum requiring a popular vote for tax increases and, when it narrowly won, successfully argued against it in the Montana Supreme Court. In his 1999 State of the State speech he called for overhaul of "a decrepit tax system which causes too many Montanans to pay too much and too few visitors to pay too little." The legislature didn't agree to his value-added tax, but did cut the residential property tax, halved the business equipment tax (with the possibility of abolishing it in 2006), phased out the livestock tax, cut taxes on electricity, telecommunications and oil and gas. He got a $40 million increase for public education and $23 million more for the university, including permanent research and development funding. He passed a children's health insurance plan and open space easements for agricultural lands; bonding authority for irrigation, a 75-mile-per-hour speed limit and funding for highways and restoration of the state Capitol. After farmers blockaded the border in protest of Canadian grain marketing practices, he started a series of meetings with Alberta Premier Ralph Klein. On environment issues, he supported the killing of roaming bison with brucellosis, opposed the ban on cyanide mining of gold and silver, favored reintroduction of grizzly bears in the Selway-Bitterroot Wilderness. "We really need no lectures about valuing wildlife; it was Montanans 60 years ago who saved grizzly bears when the federal policy was extinction."

At a time when Americans are eager for consensus and agreement, Racicot has spoken often about the need for civility and listening to others. In his 1999 State of the State speech, he said, "Montanans could become the nation's pioneers again, showing the other world the power and achievements possible when a people share a humility, a respect for others and a stubborn sense of civility." At a meeting of Republican leaders in Washington, he urged national Chairman Jim Nicholson to hold a series of "Listening to America" hearings around the country. He was unenthusiastic about impeachment in December 1998. "It appears to me that there ought to be some sort of inquiry made as to whether the president is willing to accept some responsibility without a trial. Removal from office is disproportionate to the offense committed."

As early as 1997 he was urging George W. Bush to run for president; he traveled with Bush and two other governors to Israel after the November 1998 election. In February 1999 Racicot helped round up commitments at the National Governors' Association conference at which half the Republican governors endorsed Bush. Racicot is ineligible for a third term in 2000 and seems utterly uninterested in running for the Senate. He has been mentioned as a possible attorney general or Interior secretary in a Bush Administration.

Cook's Call. *Highly Competitive.* The departure of the wildly popular Racicot immediately brought a number of potentially strong candidates out of the woodwork. The Democratic primary will feature Secretary of State Mike Cooney, state Auditor Mark O'Keefe and Attorney General Joseph Mazurek. On the Republican side, Lieutenant Governor Judy Martz and Senate Majority Leader John Harp are likely to run.

Senior Senator. Max Baucus, now in his fourth term, is from a well-known Montana ranching family; his great-grandfather Henry Sieben started the huge Sieben Ranch in 1897, which includes the land seen in *A River Runs Through It*. Baucus grew up on a 125,000-acre ranch near Helena, graduated from college and law school at Stanford, then worked at the SEC in Washington and returned home in 1971 and was executive director of the state constitutional convention in 1972. In 1973 he served in the state House. In 1974, at 32, he won the western House seat (Montana had two House seats until 1992) by walking 600 miles along highways through the district and beating three past or future holders of it (Democrats Pat Williams and Arnold Olsen in the primary and Republican Richard Shoup in the general). He won his Senate seat in 1978 by easily beating an appointed senator in the primary and a conservative Republican investment adviser in the general. He has had a moderate to liberal voting record.

With seniority, he has reached powerful positions: he chaired the Environment and Public Works Committee in 1993–94 and ranks just behind Daniel Patrick Moynihan on Finance, and he chaired its Trade Subcommittee when Democrats held the majority. He worked for greater use of low-sulfur coal in the Clean Air Act of 1990, and worked on the bipartisan Safe Drinking Water Act of 1996. On the 1998 transportation bill, he worked for a funding formula much more favorable to Montana than the House version; it gave Montana $260 million a year, a 60% increase. Baucus makes a practice of working a full day at a different job every month, and worked on a road crew on the Beartooth Highway leading to Yellowstone National Park. He supported the Clinton Administration moratorium on mining in the Rocky Mountain Front north of Helena. He has worked on Superfund reform, and opposes Republican attempts to limit claims of natural resource damages. Another Baucus cause is stopping the construction of expensive federal courthouses.

On trade issues Baucus has followed Montana interests. He has been a leading advocate of normal trade relations status (formerly MFN) with China, a potentially huge market for Montana wheat. "U.S.-China relationships are in large measure going to determine our lives in the next century," he said. He traveled with Bill Clinton to China in June 1998 and has also led Montana trade missions to China, South Korea, Japan, Mexico and South America. He stresses that Montana does business all over the world: Corporate Air in Billings contracts for FedEx in the Philippines; Montana State University's TechLink is selling locust control product for plague in Madagascar. He is a strong supporter of fast-track legislation. But he has complained much about Canadian restrictions on Montana exports and in December 1998 traveled to Ottawa to work on a multi-commodity step trade agreement. In the meantime, he has worked against reductions in the wool tariff and for labeling of imported meat. He calls for a safety net for the Freedom to Farm Act and worked for speeding up transition payments to farmers in 1998. He also worked for the bill to allow farmers to income-average by putting income into tax-deferred FARRM accounts for five years.

In March 1993, he opposed the Clinton proposal to raise grazing fees and impose a 12.5% mining royalty on federal land and Clinton eventually buckeled. He pondered voting for the Clinton health care plan in 1994, but then withdrew from a bipartisan group seeking a compromise, because he opposed new taxes. After initial qualms, he supported the Republican welfare reform in 1996. In the runup to the 1996 election, he switched and supported the balanced budget amendment. He worked successfully for education tax credits in 1998, for the first $1,000 and half the second $1,000 of college costs. In 1998 he and four other moderates proposed their own HMO bill, to allow lawsuits but not pain and suffering damages. In 1999 he opposed the Clinton government-invested USA accounts and proposed his own Y2Save private accounts instead. He favors the e-rate tax to wire schools for the Internet and a tripling of funding for 21st Century Learning Centers for after-school and summer-school programs. As an end run against Foreign Relations Chairman Jesse Helms, Baucus and Republican Chuck Hagel convened bipartisan meetings on foreign policy.

Baucus was re-elected by wide margins in 1984 and 1990, but in 1996, as the state seemed to be moving right, he was targeted by Republicans. In 1995 and 1996 he walked 820 miles across the state and shook thousands of hands. His opponent, Lieutenant Governor Dennis Rehberg, backed term limits and promised to forego pay increases and pensions. Rehberg attacked him for his 1993 tax increase vote and for changing his stand on the balanced budget amendment, the assault weapons ban (he voted for the 1994 crime bill), and welfare reform. "Max takes three sides of a two-sided issue," he said. Criticism was also volleyed by environmentalists on the left, who were angry that the $1.4 billion McDonald mine was prospecting for gold on land along the Blackfoot River owned by the Sieben Ranch.

Baucus responded that Rehberg was a "special interest" candidate backing billions in tax breaks for the rich and that the Republican balanced budget would produce "cuts" in Medicare and student loans. Polls showed Baucus in the lead throughout, hovering around 50%, and he benefited from a huge money advantage: $4.2 million to Rehberg's $1.3. But in the end Baucus won by just 50%–45%, his closest showing ever. Baucus comes up for re-election in 2002. By then, with Daniel Patrick Moynihan's retirement, he will have become ranking Democrat on or, possibly, chairman of the Finance Committee, surely a helpful credential. But he may also encounter serious opposition: Republicans trailed by only 51%–47% in the last four Senate races here as compared to 57%–42% in the nine Senate races before that. One possible opponent is Congressman-at-Large Rick Hill, who first won in 1996 and pledged to serve only three terms in the House.

Junior Senator. Conrad Burns is almost a stereotypical Westerner, picking his teeth with a pocketknife, chewing tobacco, sporting pellets in his arm from a hunting accident, forever telling deadpan jokes. He grew up in northwest Missouri, joined the Marines after two years of college, worked for two airlines, then became a livestock fieldman and auctioneer and field representative of the *Polled Hereford World* and moved to Billings; when he was reassigned back east (to Des Moines), he quit so he could stay in Billings where he set up a farm news radio network, which grew from four radio stations in 1975 to 29 radio and six TV stations in 1988. Piqued at a local politician, Burns ran for Yellowstone County Commissioner in 1986 and won; two years later, he ran against Democratic Senator John Melcher. Melcher had been in Congress for 19 years and Burns attacked him as "a liberal who is soft on drugs, soft on defense and very high on social programs." Melcher was hurt by a Reagan veto of a Melcher wilderness bill and by public opposition to the "let-it-burn" policy that resulted in the Yellowstone fires of summer 1988. Burns, who ended every speech with a Western "You bet!" won 52%–48%. In 1994 he faced law professor Jack Mudd, who beat Melcher, freshly returned from Washington, in the Democratic primary. Mudd was poorly funded and his support of the 1993 Clinton tax increase and the 1994 crime bill with its gun control provisions were highly unpopular. Burns won 62%–38%, the first time Montana voters have ever re-elected a Republican senator.

Burns has a mostly conservative voting record in the Senate and has risen enough in seniority on the Commerce Committee to be chairman of the Communications Subcommittee, one of the key regulatory posts in Congress. There this former broadcaster has generally favored deregulation and encouragement of Internet commerce. He favored allowing the regional Bells into long-distance service, a key feature of the 1996 Telecommunications Act. He wrote its Section 706, providing incentives for broadband data networks. He supported the Children's Online Privacy Protection Act included in the October 1998 omnibus budget, and wants to expand it to protect the privacy of adults. He has sponsored bills encouraging encryption, with Patrick Leahy and John Ashcroft, that have been called successively Pro-CODE and E-Privacy (Burns or some staffer has a penchant for snappy names); the aim is to allow commerce to be conducted in secret, to compete with other countries which already do. He is also working on a bill to provide for electronic authentication of online contracts and user identities. He has a bill to require privatization of Intelsat by January 2002, to provide competition in the satellite business. He favors allowing satellite TV to broadcast local channels; 30% of Montanan TV households are satellite subscribers, the highest in the nation. In 1996 he conducted the first congressional hearing on the Internet, with cybersurfers able to ask questions of witnesses and chat with subcommittee staffers. He wants to cut the 3% telephone tax to 1% and dedicate it to the e-rate program for wiring schools and libraries to the Internet, but he wants to take the e-rate away from the FCC. He is working for a national 911 emergency number. He wants Class A status for low-power broadcasters. He is against requiring free air time to be given to political candidates and against banning liquor ads on broadcasts, though he wants broadcasters to continue not to run them voluntarily. He held up the nomination of Antitrust head Joel Klein, to learn his views on telecommunications issues and on Microsoft, and applauded the case Klein brought against it; he sought a field hearing in Montana on the proposed Cargill-Continental grain merger and attacked high airline fares to Montana.

On Montana issues Burns is often critical of environmentalists. He opposed reintroduction of grey wolves into Yellowstone National Park, estimating the cost at $1.8 million per wolf. He criticized the Clinton Administration and Max Baucus for short-circuiting the legal process when they reached agreement limiting the Crown Butte New World gold mine near Yellowstone, and later attacked Clinton line-item vetoes of mineral rights there and of NTIS money for Montana State University's "green" buildings. He has blocked Democrats' plans for a Montana wilderness bill and they have blocked his. He co-sponsored Orrin Hatch's property rights bill and with Richard Shelby sponsored a sportsmen's bill of rights; he favors ending tribal jurisdiction over non-Indians. He attacked the listing of the mountain plover as a threatened species as a back-door means of listing the black-tailed prairie dog. On farm issues, he favors expanded exports, including a $500 million grain sale to Iran, and meat import labels. He has criticized Canada's trade policies and called the December 1998 agreement "a small first step." He opposed fast track in September 1997 because "I do not have faith in the administration's ability to look out for the needs of Montana's farmers and ranchers." He favors repealing the estate tax and in early 1999 said his top goal was raising the incomes of Montana farmers and ranchers.

Burns is often ready—sometimes too ready—with a quip. When the tobacco bill was brought to the floor with assurances it could be improved, he said, "If you bring a bucket of manure to the floor, it's not going to get any better." But sometimes he speaks faster than he thinks. In 1994 he repeated an ethnic slur made, he said, by an elderly Montana rancher and said that living in the District of Columbia was "a hell of a challenge"; he apologized the next day. In February 1999, speaking before a Montana group, he referred to Arabs as "ragheads"; again a quick apology.

Burns has not apologized for changing his mind about his 1988 pledge to seek only two terms. In February 1999 he announced he was running for a third, and said that he had risen to positions where he still had much to do. "I still support the idea of term limits, but I don't want to risk the position of Montana," he said. He intends to raise $5 million for the race and it would be astonishing if a Communications Subcommittee chairman were not able to do so. Democrats were fairly optimistic about the race in early 1999, despite Montana's rightward trend. In March Brian Schweitzer, a Whitefish rancher-farmer millionaire who raises mint, cattle and alfalfa, announced he was running and said the major problem was Montana's low-income economy.

Cook's Call. *Probably Safe.* Democrats seem focused more on taking the open governorship in 2000 than trying to topple Burns. His dark horse victory in 1988 always lands Burns on the Democratic target list, but there isn't a long line of Democratic elected officials waiting to take him on. Burns is prone to verbal missteps that could provide fodder for a challenger, but he has a clear advantage in the race.

Representative-At-Large. The congressman-at-large from Montana is Rick Hill, a Republican elected in 1996. Hill grew up in northern Minnesota, where his father ran a tire repair shop, battled polio successfully as a child, went to college in Minnesota and worked in the insurance business for five years, then moved to Montana. In Helena he worked in insurance and became active in Republican politics. Governor Marc Racicot made him head of the state workmen's compensation agency, and his reforms, with more attention to workplace safety and aggressive investigation of fraudulent claims, brought rates way down. In 1996, he was one of four serious candidates who ran for the at-large seat when the state was surprised by the retirement announcement of 18-year incumbent Democrat Pat Williams, a feisty, old-fashioned Montana liberal.

Williams pushed the candidacy of Bill Yellowtail, former state senator and regional EPA administrator in Denver, who grew up on and still lives on the Crow Indian reservation. But the month before the primary, it was revealed that Yellowtail two decades ago had hit his wife hard enough to break her glasses and send her to the hospital, that he had failed to pay child support for five years in the mid-1980s and that his state legislative paycheck had been garnished. Also, he had burglarized a camera store while a sophomore at Dartmouth and had been found guilty of two felony counts. "I didn't have any money. I guess I wanted some camera stuff," he explained. Yellowtail held a press conference, complete with former wife, confessing error, expressing contrition, and concluding, "All I ask for is forgiveness." He seems to have gotten it all along, and in June 1996 he won the four-way Democratic primary with 56%, far ahead of the next highest candidate with 22%.

Meanwhile, the three little-known Republican candidates were working for recognition. Hill, in something of an upset, won the primary with 44% to 36% for former Conrad Burns staffer Dwight MacKay and 20% for businessman Alan Mikkelsen. Yellowtail led Hill consistently in polls; the AFL-CIO came in with anti-Hill ads; Hill ran ads asking delphically, "Congressman Bill Yellowtail: Can we really afford to take the risk?" Hill turned out to have problems of his own. He had appeared at a militia gathering in spring 1996. "I believe in the politics of inclusion rather than exclusion," he said. And he had left his first wife after an affair with a cocktail waitress and had an eight-year battle over finances and child custody. But he had paid his child support: "I lived up to my responsibilities every step of the way." The final outcome was not terribly close. Hill won 52%–43%, carrying all but nine counties—the old mining towns of Butte and Anaconda, the university town of Missoula, and the Indian reservations.

In the House, Hill's voting record is moderate on economics and conservative on cultural and foreign issues. He paid considerable attention to farm issues, supporting a speedup of transition payments due under the Freedom to Farm Act and criticizing Canadian restrictions on imports of U.S. grain and meat. He voted against fast track and supported labeling of meat imports. He voted for the October 1998 agriculture appropriation, though he said it wasn't enough money. He voted against the House version of the transportation bill, despite a promise of $65 million in demonstration projects; he did vote for the final version, which was much more generous to Montana. He was against the September 1998 tax cut because he wanted to save the money for Social Security. Hill worked on the buyout of the proposed Crown Butte gold mine near Yellowstone National Park and insisted on federal coal reserves to compensate Montana and a commitment to repair the Beartooth Highway. He worked to let Canyon Ferry cabin owners buy their leased land and for land swaps to obtain Lindbergh Lake. He supported the $1,000 charitable tax credit in the Project for American Renewal, and said the nation's problems will not be solved "until the hearts of parents are turned toward their children, until respect is restored for human life and property, until a commitment is renewed to care about our neighbor."

Hill had strong opposition in 1998 from Dusty Deschamps (pronounced DAYshaw), for 27 years the prosecutor in Missoula County. Deschamps opposed school vouchers (Hill favored them for Washington, D.C.) and Social Security privatization (Hill came out for individual retirement accounts). He said the Freedom to Farm Act ought to be revised, and boasted that Minority Leader Dick Gephardt promised him a seat on Agriculture. He decried "Depression-era" farm prices and based much of his campaign on farm issues; Hill replied that many of the farm groups were supporting him. Deschamps, who decried the glut of guns in 1996, said he supported the Brady bill waiting period for gun purchases but opposed its assault weapons ban. He criticized Hill for voting against the National Endowment for the Arts.

Deschamps was an attractive candidate, well-thought of after many years as prosecutor and also as a cattle rancher; he raised substantial money, though not as much as Hill. The candidates agreed on some issues: overhaul of the 1872 Mining Act, tough trade positions against Canada, the flag burning amendment, opposition to reintroduction of wolves and the marriage penalty. In March 1998 Montana Democrats charged that Hill in 1996 had colluded with Triad Management Group, which ran ads in the fall attacking Yellowtail's personal life; Hill denied the charges. In September Deschamps accused Hill of running an automated telephone survey, outlawed in Montana; Hill sued for libel.

Some fall polls showed Hill far ahead; these may well have been wrong. Hill won 53%–44%, just a bit better than his 1996 margin. Hill carried all but nine counties this time. Hill was evidently correct when he said Deschamps's attempt to use farm issues "never got any traction in farm country because they know my record, that I worked very hard for agriculture."

In January 1999 Hill said he would not run for governor in 2000; many think he will run against Senator Max Baucus in 2002, when if he keeps his three-term-limit pledge he will not run for the House. Democratic Superintendent of Public Instruction Nancy Keenan announced in May 1999 she will run against him in 2000, and another possible Democratic candidate is attorney-author John Morrison, whose grandfather was governor of Nebraska in the 1960s.

Cook's Call. *Potentially Competitive.* Hill's mediocre winning margins in the past two elections certainly make him an intriguing target, but challengers have a very difficult (and expensive) time trying to campaign across this huge district. Hill is likely to face a serious challenge in 2000 from Superintendent of Public Instruction Nancy Keenan, but Hill's political savvy and the increasingly conservative bent of the state make it tough to dislodge him.

Presidential politics. Montana, with only three electoral votes, can't expect to see much of presidential candidates, particularly because its presidential primary is in early June, the same day as New Jersey's. In the 1980s only Alaska, Idaho, Utah and North Dakota were farther out of the national political jetlanes. But in 1992 and 1996 Montana was closely divided and was visited by national candidates, though if it continues its Republican trend, and if environmentalist-friendly Al Gore is the Democratic nominee, it might not be in 2000. Ross Perot won 26% of the vote here in 1992, and as high as 36% in Phillips County up on the Canadian border; and he won 13.6% in Montana in 1996, just under Maine's 14.2% for his best showing. The move to put Montana in a Western states primary on March 10, 2000 failed in the 1999 session of the legislature.

Congressional districting. Montana lost its second congressional district after the 1990 Census, and is now the nation's largest district in population and second largest (after Alaska) in size. But Montana has grown smartly in the 1990s, and most projections show it gaining the second seat back. It is generally expected that the lines will resemble those up to 1990, with an eastern district covering most of the plains and a western district in the mountains; the two areas cast almost exactly the same percentages in the 1998 House race.

The People: Est. Pop. 1998: 880,453; Pop. 1990: 799,065, up 10.2% 1990–1998. 0.3% of U.S. total, 44th largest; 47.4% rural. Median age: 36.5 years. 13.8% 65 years and over. 92.8% White, 0.3% Black, 0.5% Asian, 6% Amer. Indian, 0.5% Other; 1.5% Hispanic Origin. Households: 57.7% married couple families; 28% married couple fams. w. children; 47.5% college educ.; median household income: $22,988; per capita income: $11,213; 67.3% owner occupied housing; median house value: $56,600; median monthly rent: $251. 5.6% Unemployment. 1998 Voting age pop.: 658,000. 1998 Turnout: 338,733; 51% of VAP. Registered voters (1998): 639,241; no party registration.

966 MONTANA

Political Lineup: Governor, Marc Racicot (R); Lt. Gov., Judy Martz (R); Secy. of State, Mike Cooney (D); Atty. Gen., Joseph P. Mazurek (D); Auditor, Mark O'Keefe (D); State Senate, 50 (18 D, 32 R); Majority Leader, John G. Harp (R); State House, 100 (41 D, 59 R); House Speaker, John Mercer (R). Senators, Max Baucus (D) and Conrad Burns (R). Representative, 1 R at-large.

Elections Division: 406-444-2034; **Filing Deadline for U.S. Congress:** March 23, 2000.

1996 Presidential Vote

Dole (R)	179,652	(44%)
Clinton (D)	167,922	(41%)
Perot (I)	55,229	(14%)

1992 Presidential Vote

Clinton (D)	154,507	(38%)
Bush (R)	144,207	(35%)
Perot (I)	107,225	(26%)

1996 Republican Presidential Primary

Dole (R)	72,176	(61%)
Buchanan (R)	28,581	(24%)
Forbes (R)	8,456	(7%)
Others	8,533	(7%)

GOVERNOR

Gov. Marc Racicot (R)

Elected 1992, term expires Jan. 2001; b. July 24, 1948, Thompson Falls; home, Helena; Carroll Col., B.A. 1970, U. of MT, J.D. 1973; Catholic; married (Theresa).

Military Career: Army Judge Advocate Corps, 1973–76.

Elected Office: MT Atty. Gen., 1988–92.

Professional Career: Dep. Missoula Cnty. Atty., 1976–77; MT Asst. Atty. Gen., 1977–88.

Office: Office of the Governor, State Capitol, Helena, 59620, 406-444-3111; Fax: 406-444-4151; Web site: www.state.mt.us.

Election Results

1996 gen.	Marc Racicot (R)	320,768	(79%)
	Judy Jacobson (D)	76,471	(19%)
	Others	7,936	(2%)
1996 prim.	Marc Racicot (R)	92,644	(76%)
	Rob Natelson (R)	28,672	(24%)
1992 gen.	Marc Racicot (R)	209,401	(51%)
	Dorothy Bradley (D)	198,421	(49%)

SENATORS

Sen. Max Baucus (D)

Elected 1978, seat up 2002; b. Dec. 11, 1941, Helena; home, Helena; Stanford U., B.A. 1964, LL.B. 1967; Protestant; married (Wanda).

Elected Office: MT House of Reps., 1973–74; U.S. House of Reps., 1974–78.

Professional Career: Staff atty., Civil Aeronautics Bd., 1967–69; Legal Asst., Securities & Exchange Comm., 1969–71; Practicing atty., 1971–74.

DC Office: 511 HSOB, 20510, 202-224-2651; Fax: 202-224-1974; Web site: www.senate.gov/~baucus.

State Offices: Billings, 406-657-6790; Bozeman, 406-586-6104; Butte, 406-782-8700; Great Falls, 406-761-1574; Helena, 406-449-5480; Kalispell, 406-756-1150; Missoula, 406-329-3123.

Committees: *Agriculture, Nutrition & Forestry* (5th of 8 D): Forestry, Conservation & Rural Revitalization; Marketing, Inspection & Product Promotion (RMM). *Environment & Public Works* (RMM of 8 D): Transportation & Infrastructure (RMM). *Finance* (2d of 9 D): Health Care; International Trade; Taxation & IRS Oversight (RMM). *Intelligence* (5th of 8 D). *Joint Committee on Taxation* (5th of 5 Sens.).

Group Ratings

	ADA	ACLU	AFS	LCV	CON	NTU	NFIB	COC	ACU	NTLC	CHC
1998	80	83	100	63	85	22	44	56	5	11	10
1997	65	—	44	—	49	48	—	70	4	—	—

National Journal Ratings

	1997 LIB — 1997 CONS		1998 LIB — 1998 CONS	
Economic	60%	— 36%	69%	— 28%
Social	71%	— 0%	62%	— 37%
Foreign	73%	— 19%	65%	— 27%

Key Votes of the 105th Congress

1. Bal. Budget Amend.	Y	5. Satcher for Surgeon Gen.	Y	9. Chem. Weapons Treaty	Y
2. Clinton Budget Deal	Y	6. Highway Set-asides	Y	10. Cuban Humanitarian Aid	Y
3. Cloture on Tobacco	Y	7. Table Child Gun locks	Y	11. Table Bosnia Troops	*
4. Education IRAs	*	8. Ovrd. Part. Birth Veto	N	12. $ for Test-ban Treaty	Y

Election Results

1996 general	Max Baucus (D)	201,935	(50%)	($4,280,747)
	Dennis Rehberg (R)	182,111	(45%)	($1,358,165)
	Becky Shaw (Reform)	19,276	(5%)	
1996 primary	Max Baucus (D)	unopposed		
1990 general	Max Baucus (D)	217,563	(68%)	($2,568,899)
	Allen C. Kolstad (R)	93,836	(29%)	($747,661)
	Others	7,937	(2%)	

Sen. Conrad Burns (R)

Elected 1988, seat up 2000; b. Jan. 25, 1935, Gallatin, MO; home, Billings; U. of MO, 1952–54; Lutheran; married (Phyllis).

Military Career: Marine Corps, 1955–57.

Elected Office: Yellowstone Cnty. Comm., 1986–88.

Professional Career: TWA and Ozark Airlines, 1958–61; Field rep., *Polled Hereford World*, 1962; Mgr., Billings Livestock Show, 1968; Radio & TV broadcaster, 1968–86.

DC Office: 187 DSOB, 20510, 202-224-2644; Fax: 202-224-8594; Web site: www.senate.gov/~burns.

State Offices: Billings, 406-252-0550; Bozeman, 406-586-4450; Butte, 406-723-3277; Glendive, 406-365-2391; Great Falls, 406-452-9585; Helena, 406-449-5401; Kalispell, 406-257-3360; Missoula, 406-329-3528.

Committees: *Aging (Special)* (4th of 11 R). *Appropriations* (8th of 15 R): Agriculture & Rural Development; Energy & Water Development; Interior; Military Construction (Chmn.); VA, HUD & Independent Agencies. *Commerce, Science & Transportation* (3d of 11 R): Aviation; Communications (Chmn.); Consumer Affairs, Foreign Commerce & Tourism; Science, Technology & Space; Surface Transportation & Merchant Marine. *Energy & Natural Resources* (11th of 11 R): Forests & Public Land Management (Vice Chmn.); National Parks, Historic Preservation & Recreation. *Small Business* (2d of 10 R).

Group Ratings

	ADA	ACLU	AFS	LCV	CON	NTU	NFIB	COC	ACU	NTLC	CHC
1998	0	29	11	0	14	64	100	100	84	81	91
1997	15	—	0	—	71	78	—	78	88	—	—

National Journal Ratings

	1997 LIB — 1997 CONS		1998 LIB — 1998 CONS	
Economic	11%	— 76%	18%	— 72%
Social	17%	— 72%	24%	— 73%
Foreign	0%	— 77%	12%	— 75%

Key Votes of the 105th Congress

1. Bal. Budget Amend.	Y	5. Satcher for Surgeon Gen.	N	9. Chem. Weapons Treaty	N
2. Clinton Budget Deal	Y	6. Highway Set-asides	N	10. Cuban Humanitarian Aid	*
3. Cloture on Tobacco	N	7. Table Child Gun locks	Y	11. Table Bosnia Troops	N
4. Education IRAs	Y	8. Ovrd. Part. Birth Veto	Y	12. $ for Test-ban Treaty	N

Election Results

1994 general	Conrad Burns (R)	218,542	(62%)	($3,518,574)
	Jack Mudd (D)	131,845	(38%)	($1,107,591)
1994 primary	Conrad Burns (R)	unopposed		
1988 general	Conrad Burns (R)	189,445	(52%)	($1,076,010)
	John Melcher (D)	175,809	(48%)	($1,338,622)

REPRESENTATIVE

Rep. Rick Hill (R)

Elected 1996; b. Dec. 30, 1946, Grand Rapids, MN; home, Helena; St. Cloud St. U., B.A. 1968; Assembly of God; married (Betti).

Professional Career: Businessman; Pres., InsureWest Inc., 1984–96; Managing Partner, Hill Properties, 1988–present; Chmn., MT Republican Party, 1991–1992; Chmn., MT Mutual Compensation Insurance Fund, 1993–96.

DC Office: 1609 LHOB, 20515, 202-225-3211; Fax: 202-225-5687; Web site: www.house.gov/hill.

District Offices: Billings, 406-256-1019; Great Falls, 406-454-1066; Helena, 406-443-7878; Missoula, 406-543-9550.

Committees: *Banking & Financial Services* (22d of 32 R): Financial Institutions & Consumer Credit; Housing & Community Opportunity. *Resources* (20th of 28 R): Forests & Forest Health; National Parks & Public Lands. *Small Business* (11th of 19 R): Government Programs & Oversight; Rural Enterprise, Business Opportunities & Special Small Business Problems (Vice Chmn.).

Group Ratings

	ADA	ACLU	AFS	LCV	CON	NTU	NFIB	COC	ACU	NTLC	CHC
1998	10	7	24	8	89	46	79	83	79	78	92
1997	0	—	25	—	24	49	—	80	92	—	—

National Journal Ratings

	1997 LIB — 1997 CONS		1998 LIB — 1998 CONS	
Economic	38%	— 61%	43%	— 57%
Social	10%	— 82%	13%	— 86%
Foreign	12%	— 88%	19%	— 75%

Key Votes of the 105th Congress

1. Clinton Budget Deal	Y	5. Puerto Rico Sthood. Ref.	N	9. Cut $ for B-2 Bombers	N
2. Education IRAs	Y	6. End Highway Set-asides	Y	10. Human Rights in China	N
3. Req. 2/3 to Raise Taxes	N	7. School Prayer Amend.	Y	11. Withdraw Bosnia Troops	Y
4. Fast-track Trade	N	8. Ovrd. Part. Birth Veto	Y	12. End Cuban TV-Marti	N

Election Results

1998 general	Rick Hill (R)	175,748	(53%)	($1,228,097)
	Dusty Deschamps (D)	147,073	(44%)	($705,914)
	Others	8,730	(3%)	
1998 primary	Rick Hill (R)	unopposed		
1996 general	Rick Hill (R)	211,975	(52%)	($943,062)
	Bill Yellowtail (D)	174,516	(43%)	($635,282)
	Jim Brooks (NL)	17,935	(4%)	

NEBRASKA

"The sea of Nebraska" is what the first settlers coming west called the Platte River—not actually a single river but a braid of streams that weaves a silver chain around sandbars and islands, flooding the level floor of the great plain—a mile wide, as the saying goes, and six inches deep. Nebraska was formed in one rush of settlement in the 1880s, when its population increased from 452,000 to 1,062,000, more than in the century since (it was 1,652,000 in 1998). In the 1880s Omaha became a major railroad center, Lincoln the state capital, and farming and food products the main businesses. And for about 100 years, Nebraska remained pretty much that way. This is not what its founders intended: they hoped Nebraska would develop a diversified farming, industrial and commercial economy like Ohio, Illinois, Missouri or Minnesota. But while the 1880s were a time of plentiful rain here, the 1890s were a decade of drought, and Nebraska stopped growing. Many rural counties, and even Omaha, lost population and Nebraska has exported people ever since: 48% of Nebraskans in 1890 were children; in 1990, only 27% were. The creative energies in the economy seem to have skipped over the Great Plains and moved far to the West.

The sudden boom of the 1880s and the bust of the 1890s produced the most colorful—and atypical—politics of Nebraska's history: the populist movement and William Jennings Bryan, the "silver tongued orator of the Platte." Bryan was only 36 when he delivered the famous Cross of Gold speech at the 1896 Democratic National Convention and was swept to the Democratic nomination. He was thought so radical that Democratic President Grover Cleveland wouldn't support him, but he still won 47% of the popular vote in the first of three attempts at the presidency. Nebraskans supported Bryan, whose program may have been forward-looking, but whose purpose was retrograde: to restore Nebraska to the prosperity it had enjoyed a few years before. Since Bryan's time, Nebraska's most notable politician has been George Norris, who led the House rebellion against Speaker Joseph Cannon in 1911, and in the 1930s pushed through the Norris-LaGuardia Anti-Injunction Act, the first national pro-union legislation, and the Tennessee Valley Authority. But most Nebraskans were repelled by the New Deal, which seemed to threaten their way of life. Although it often elects Democratic governors and senators, Nebraska for half a century has been among the most Republican of states in national elections.

Now in the 1990s Nebraska seems to be growing and changing after a century's pause. Omaha is the home base of the fast-growing ConAgra food combine, of the giant Peter Kiewit construction company and of mega-investor Warren Buffett, whose down-home wit complements his knack for picking stocks that go up hundreds of percents. The nearby Strategic Air Command base brought the world's most advanced phone system to the Omaha area 40-odd years ago; starting in the 1980s hotel chains, credit card companies and telemarketers set up operations, making this the world's leading place to make a living by talking on the phone. Computers and fiber optics have made Nebraska, as one mayor said, "just another suburb of Chicago." Nebraska has also become a major exporter of farm produce and of machinery and equipment. In 1997 it exported $2.5 billion worth of goods, $1.1 billion to Japan, but the Asian economic crisis lowered Japanese exports to only $560 million in 1998.

Unemployment in Nebraska has been the lowest in the nation, only 1.6% in 1998, and Nebraska businesses have recruited high-skill workers from out of state while meatpackers have attracted workers from the Mexican border; for the first time in a century there is in-migration into the state. Businesses and the state spent $70 million to create the Peter Kiewit Institute of Information Sciences, Technology and Engineering; First Data donated the old Ak-Sar-Ben (try spelling it backward) race track as the site for the new building. Businesses were donating generous scholarships to keep smart high school graduates in Nebraska; in 1998 the

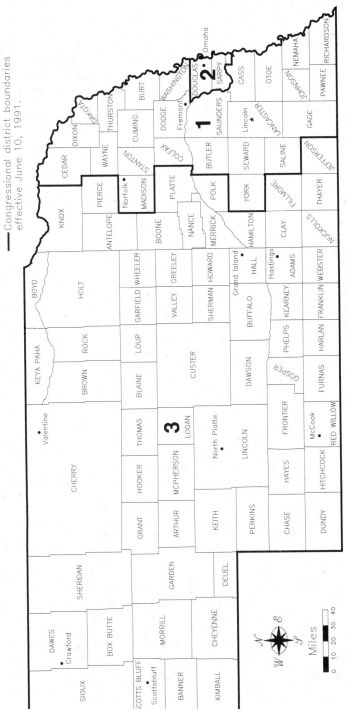

—Congressional district boundaries
effective June 10, 1991.

Copyright ©1993 by Election Data Services, Inc.

legislature was considering a bill to create $5,000-a-year Brain Gain scholarships for high-achieving students at Nebraska colleges, but state lawmakers killed the $2 million program. Growth is concentrated: The rural population dropped 15% between 1970 and 1997, while greater Omaha and Lincoln and Beatrice and the towns along I-80 and the Platte are growing rapidly. Demographically, this makes Nebraska more like a Rocky Mountain state, with population concentrated in two cities and several smaller towns, not spread over farmlands as it was for most of the 20th century. The atmosphere has visibly changed. "If someone doesn't have a job in Omaha," said one Nebraskan with two jobs, "they don't want one."

Politically, Nebraska has remained a heavily Republican state with a proclivity for Democratic governors. Its senior senator, Democrat Bob Kerrey, served as governor from 1983–87 and was a candidate for president in 1992. For most of the 1990s, its governor, Democrat Ben Nelson, had one of the highest job ratings in the nation. But Nebraska cast the third-highest percentage for Bob Dole (after Kansas and Utah) and the second highest Dole-Clinton margin. And as in the Rocky Mountain states, Republicans have been winning big elections over popular Democrats in the late 1990s. In 1996 Nelson ran for the Senate seat vacated by Democrat Jim Exon (another former governor), but lost all but five counties to Republican Chuck Hagel; his victory made Nebraska the only state represented in the Senate by two decorated Vietnam combat veterans. In 1998 Democrats had a strong governor candidate, Bill Hoppner, who worked for Kerrey and lost the 1990 governor primary to Nelson by 42 votes, but lost 54%–46% to Mike Johanns, despite a fractious Republican primary. Interesting also is what didn't happen: despite low commodity prices and the economic woes facing farmers, there was no move toward the Democrats, as in the past. Nebraska is not just a farm state any more.

Governor. Mike Johanns was born in Iowa, grew up on a dairy farm, went to college in Minnesota, then got a law degree at Creighton University in Omaha and clerked there for one year. He practiced law in O'Neill, in the vast plains of Holt County, then in Lincoln; he was elected to the Lancaster County Board of Commissioners in 1982 and to the Lincoln City Council in 1989. These were nonpartisan offices; Johanns was a Democrat until 1988. He was elected Lincoln mayor in 1991 and re-elected without opposition in 1995; his wife is a former state senator (a nonpartisan office in Nebraska, which is unicameral). He helped establish a work empowerment program for Lancaster County inmates and a Handi-Van service for seniors in rural Lancaster County. In 1995 he began his campaign for governor and traveled all over the state, ultimately visiting all 93 counties (some with only a few hundred voters).

Johanns was not without competition for the Republican nomination. State Auditor John Breslow was running and spending his own money, ultimately $2.5 million of it. After 20-year Lincoln Congressman Doug Bereuter announced he was not running for governor, Omaha Congressman Jon Christensen announced in August 1997 he would, even though he had gotten much publicity for winning a seat on Ways and Means as a freshman; he had promised to limit himself to three or four terms and had already been elected to two. Christensen is a conservative with much backing from the Christian right, who startled people with his own life; during the 1994 campaign he sought a divorce, and his then-wife admitted to adultery; in 1998 he announced he was marrying a former Miss America and that she had been "saving herself for marriage"—a statement that was a little too much information for Nebraskans. He was also criticized, and opposed by Johanns, when he said he would not knowingly hire a homosexual. This was a high-spending contest—Breslow spent $3.8 million altogether, Christensen $1.8 million, Johanns $1.7 million—and one in which the candidates agreed on many issues. All supported Initiative 413, which would limit state spending increases based on the rate of inflation plus population growth; all favored property tax relief—25%, Breslow promised.

Polls showed Christensen ahead, but in a tight three-way race. Then came a rush of negative ads. Breslow ran a spot showing animated peas (I am not making this up) saying that Johanns and Christensen were both tax-and-spend liberals. Then Christensen ran an ad attacking Johanns for opposing Ronald Reagan in the 1980s (he did; he was a Democrat then) and for supporting Bill Clinton's 1993 budget package and tax increase. "Fact. Mike Johanns did endorse the

Clinton tax increase," the ad said. "In fact, Mike Johanns felt so strongly he flew to Washington to help sign the tax increase into law." Not exactly. Johanns had traveled with other mayors to endorse the outline of Clinton's soon-dead stimulus package and budget resolution in March 1993, but he had not been present at the bill signing in August 1993. A week before the May primary, Christensen's campaign distributed flyers attacking Johanns for allowing obscene and racist broadcasts to air on Lincoln's public access cable channel. Senator Chuck Hagel had called on all three campaigns to eschew negative ads, and they were in the habit of sending him copies of all ads and literature. On the Saturday before the primary, Hagel called the flyer "absolute trash" and said, "Nobody in the Republican Party of Nebraska can be proud of Jon Christensen's conduct. I hope the people of the state will get out and vote and register their feelings on the conduct of this campaign." Christensen's two colleagues in the House, Bereuter and Bill Barrett, made similar statements. Johanns had in fact tried to take the public access channel off the air, losing in the Council, and could not override federal regulations ensuring the public access broadcast.

With turnout up a robust 14% from the last serious Republican gubernatorial primary, Johanns won with 40% of the vote, to 30% for Breslow and 28% for Christensen. Christensen carried his congressional district by only 36%–34% over Johanns, while Johanns won with 61% in Lincoln's Lancaster County and his travels to all 93 counties paid off in rural areas. Meanwhile, the winner in the much quieter Democratic primary was Bill Hoppner, longtime aide to former Governor and Senator Jim Exon and former Governor and current Senator Bob Kerrey, who had lost the 1990 primary to Ben Nelson by only 42 votes. This time he faced a former state senator and University of Nebraska and pro football player, James McFarland, who admitted he had beaten his first wife and son; Hoppner won 65%–30%.

Hoppner based much of his campaign on the plausible charge that Initiative 413, which Johanns supported, would make property tax relief impossible. But in early July Johanns, after working on the Lincoln budget, switched and came out against 413. Hoppner argued that Johanns couldn't be trusted to keep his word. Hagel again came to his rescue, saying Johanns "gave good, solid reasons for his decision and showed leadership by being willing to change his position." The campaign was conducted civilly, but with major differences on issues, with Johanns taking crisp conservative positions. Hoppner was for reducing class sizes; Johanns was opposed. Hoppner called for amending the Freedom to Farm Act and reviving farm subsidies; Johanns was against, saying, "Markets solve this problem." Hoppner was for trade restrictions; Johanns said he was for free trade so Nebraska farmers could increase sales abroad. Hoppner favored environmental regulation of large hog lots; Johanns was opposed. Hoppner was for state spending on the $275 million Omaha convention center; Johanns was against. Hoppner was against carrying concealed weapons law; Johanns was in favor. Hoppner accused Johanns of raising property taxes in Lincoln; Johanns said that Hoppner got his numbers wrong and that he had actually made cuts.

Johanns won 54%–46%; his primary victory was hailed in the national press as a victory for moderates, but this one was a victory for conservatives. Hoppner carried Lancaster County (always an opponent of state spending cuts) but Johanns carried the Omaha area and got nearly 60% in central and western Nebraska; that regional split helps to explain why Johanns carried lower-income voters and the Democrat carried higher-income voters. At the same time, Initiative 413 lost by a wide margin.

One of Johann's first acts as governor in January 1999 was to propose a state refund of 11% of property tax bills for that year. He decided to continue distribution of 300,000 state road maps with Ben Nelson's picture: "I'm just hopelessly cheap. I can't bring myself to throw away boxes of good maps."

Senior Senator. Bob Kerrey was elected governor in 1982 and senator in 1988. The achievement for which he is best known he is appealingly modest about: when asked which medals he won during his service in Vietnam, he has been known to answer, "One Purple Heart, one Bronze Star, one whatever." "Whatever" is the Congressional Medal of Honor, the nation's highest decoration; Kerrey is only the fifth Medal of Honor winner to serve in the Senate, and the other four won theirs in the Civil War. He is a man of determination and charm. He grew up in Lincoln, and after graduating from the University of Nebraska with a pharmacy degree in 1966 he volunteered for the Navy SEALs. In March 1969, after three months in Vietnam, a grenade exploded at his feet, and he lost his right leg below the knee. But he kept directing his platoon's fire until his men were able to escape. He was awarded the Medal of Honor by President Nixon and later became an avid opponent of the war in which he so honorably served. Back in Lincoln, he started a chain of restaurants and health clubs, then ran for governor in 1982 as a Democrat, though he had been a Republican not long before, and defeated incumbent Charles Thone. In office, he made some tough budget cuts and settled water rights disputes. In 1986, Kerrey shocked most politicians by deciding not to seek re-election, despite 70%-plus job approval ratings; in 1988, he surprised very few by winning 57%–42% the Senate seat held by Republican appointee David Karnes after the death of Democrat Edward Zorinsky.

In the Senate, Kerrey attracted more attention than most freshmen, with varying results. On the Agriculture Committee, he set for himself the task of increasing farm price supports, without success; they are being phased out by the Freedom to Farm Act. He had more success when he spoke out against the flag burning amendment. His campaign against the Gulf war was less successful. Although he supported the initial deployment of troops to the Gulf, he vocally opposed military action, taking to the floor often with Terry Sanford of North Carolina to predict that there would be many casualties and that Bush's threats to Saddam Hussein were more the language of "a little league football coach than a commander in chief"—not prognostications of great foresight.

In September 1991 Kerrey abruptly decided to run for president. His great issue was national health insurance reform. In July 1991, with little publicity, he had introduced a health care bill that would have created a publicly financed system under which the federal government would determine total spending and minimum benefits. He presented his case articulately and in detail, but he won only 11% in New Hampshire, finishing third, barely ahead of Tom Harkin and Jerry Brown. Then, despite his 40%–25% win over Harkin in South Dakota and his harsh attacks in Georgia on Bill Clinton's lack of candor on his experiences with the draft, Kerrey finished fourth or fifth in five states a week later, and said, "I just woke up Wednesday and said it was over." Unlike Tom Harkin, Kerrey did not endorse Clinton or campaign for him.

In 1993 Kerrey continued to tussle with Clinton. He abandoned his own government health care plan just as Hillary Rodham Clinton was designing hers. And he balked at supporting the Clinton budget and tax package. In August 1993 he turned out to be the deciding vote in the Senate—the man who could make the administration fail, some said—and he had an angry shouting session with Clinton. Finally Elizabeth Moynihan, wife of Daniel Patrick Moynihan, who had supported Kerrey's presidential candidacy, persuaded him to vote yes. Kerrey's quid pro quo was creation of a bipartisan commission, headed by himself and retiring Republican Senator John Danforth, on cutting federal spending for entitlements. In 1994 Kerrey and Danforth tried to persuade their fellow commissioners to recommend cuts in Social Security and Medicare. But their January 1995 report was attacked by organized labor and liberal Democrats, and its calls for Social Security cuts were spurned by both Clinton and incoming House Speaker Newt Gingrich.

Kerrey, writes George Will, "the most interesting senator not named Moynihan, has a flair for public-spirited impudence, uttering indiscreet facts." Kerrey once said, "Clinton is an unusually good liar. Unusually good." And he predicted that Clinton's much-ballyhooed tax credits for college tuition "will do for higher education what health care deductibility did for health care"—increase inflation. Kerrey has been willing to change positions when he changes his mind—on party identification, health care, gun control, abortion—and he sees no reason not to speak his mind when he sees a reason for a change in position. Kerrey has continued to question entitlements. In 1996 he and Wyoming Senator Alan Simpson proposed a Social Security reform—raising the retirement age to 70, adjusting the COLA downward and allowing workers to invest 2% of Social Security payments in personal investment accounts. In March 1998 he and Moynihan supported a Social Security reform proposal that would have taken 2% of payroll taxes to finance individual investment accounts and placed a higher cap on the payroll tax. In June 1998 he rolled out KidSave, a proposal that would provide every child with $1,000 at birth and $500 in each of the first five years for a personal investment income, co-sponsored by Moynihan, Joseph Lieberman and John Breaux. But the Clinton Administration gave it no support, even though some Republicans pushing for reform acknowledged that Kidsave would address some future problems. Kerrey also served on the bipartisan Medicare commission, and was the only Democrat to side with co-chairman Breaux on his bipartisan reform package, which was brushed aside by the Clinton Administration.

Kerrey had more success in reforming the Internal Revenue Service. In a 1996 appropriation, Kerrey created a National Commission on Restructuring the IRS; he was co-chairman with Congressman Rob Portman. The IRS, he argued, should treat taxpayers like customers; he attacked then-Deputy Treasury Secretary Lawrence Summers for "misrepresenting if not falsifying" the recommended independent citizens's board as a bunch of "corporate CEOs." He took the commission's report to the Finance Committee and, with Republican Charles Grassley, got an IRS reform bill through which was signed, despite the administration's earlier hostility, in July 1998.

Kerrey has a mostly, but not always predictably, liberal voting record, but his instinct is often toward the center. He serves on Agriculture and Finance, for which he left Appropriations in 1997, and is ranking minority member of Intelligence. He called for a determination in September 1995 of whether CIA employees broke the law when they withheld information from Congress about the murder of an American in Guatemala. Kerrey was clearly troubled by Chairman Richard Shelby's delays and overbearing questions of CIA nominee Anthony Lake in early 1997. But Kerrey questioned whether Lake was properly in control of the National Security Council when it was pestered for White House invitations for a big Democratic contributor, and Lake promptly withdrew his nomination. Kerrey has worked on encryption, and with John McCain produced a bill that would include key recovery, but only allow the government to exercise it under conditions similar to a search warrant and allow businesses the option of private key recovery. It would set up an advisory board to approve software exports, subject to a presidential veto when national security is at stake.

In 1994 Kerrey had a serious challenge from Republican Jan Stoney, a USWest executive, who attacked him for his 1993 budget and tax vote and for switching to favor the assault weapons ban. One summer poll showed her trailing by only 48%–40%. Kerrey cited his attempts to cut Clinton budgets, and ran an ad showing himself at a target range picking up an AK-47 and saying, "Twenty-five years ago, in the war in Vietnam, people hunted me. They needed a good weapon, like this AK-47. But you don't need one of these to hunt birds." He outspent her 2–1 and won 55%–45%, less than in 1988; he carried eastern Nebraska and the southern tier of the state, ran the strongest around Lincoln, and won 56% in greater Omaha. The Clinton White House, perhaps to forestall a Kerrey primary challenge in 1996, urged him to chair the Democratic Senatorial Campaign Committee in 1995. It was a tough assignment: by April 1995 five Democratic incumbents announced their retirements and Republicans had several more plausible targets. Kerrey's strategy was to recruit candidates rich enough to help finance their campaigns and moderate enough to appeal to voters. He did so in five states, but Republicans gained a net two seats. He stayed on in 1997, and his task seemed even harder, with half a dozen Democratic seats in jeopardy; some thought Republicans might gain the five seats they needed for a filibuster-proof 60–40 majority. But by cultivating contributors and targeting money shrewdly, Kerrey held Republicans to zero net gain—and stayed within sight of a Senate majority. After the election, he vowed to conduct a bipartisan investigation on Intelligence on whether contractors who contributed heavily to Democrats divulged secrets to the Chinese. He acknowledged that he had raised money from some, but insisted he would investigate fairly: "I love my country a whole lot more than I love the DSCC." On impeachment, he joined Lieberman and Moynihan in decrying Clinton's conduct and opposed negotiations with the White House over a lesser penalty. But in the end he voted against removal.

In summer 1998 Kerrey appointed a national political director and opened an office in New Hampshire; many expected him to run for president. But in December 1998 he announced in Omaha that he would run for re-election in 2000 instead. Pizza entrepreneur Herman Cain and state Treasurer Dave Heineman quickly said they wouldn't run; a few months later Omaha Mayor Hal Daub, loser in the 1990 Senate race, said the same. There were rumors that outgoing Governor Ben Nelson would become a Republican and run, but he showed up at the April 1999 Jeff-Jack Day Dinner praising Kerrey. One Republican in the race in early 1999 was state Attorney General Don Stenberg, who lost the 1996 Senate primary 62%–37% to Chuck Hagel. Another Republican George Grogan, who helped support the campaigns of Mike Johann and Chuck Hagel, announced in May 1999 that he would run. Stenberg said Kerrey had "a liberal Democratic view," and attacked him for stands on the 1993 budget, the flag burning amendment, impeachment and the partial-birth abortion ban. The other was former Millard school board member Mary Beth Heawin, who promised to give half of every campaign contribution to charity. The Republican registration edge in Nebraska has been growing, but Kerrey's popularity is great, and the Republican nominee is not likely to get the aid from Hagel, which proved crucial for Governor Mike Johanns in 1998. Kerrey has acknowledged Nebraska's Republican trend, but has also said that he would concentrate his national ambitions on 2004, when he won't be up for re-election.

Cook's Call. *Safe.* Republicans have Kerrey on their target list, but defeating him is a long shot. Republican Attorney General Don Stenberg and businessman George Grogan are running, and rumors abound that former Governor Ben Nelson may switch to the Republican Party for a shot at Kerrey. A Kerrey-Nelson match-up would indeed be competitive, although rank and file Republicans may be reticent to embrace a party switcher, raising the question of whether Nelson could win a primary.

Junior Senator. Chuck Hagel, elected in 1996, was the first Republican senator elected from Nebraska since 1972. It was an upset victory over popular Governor Ben Nelson, but he was not phased by the rigors of the campaign. "I used to kid people, saying, 'What are you going to do? Send me to Vietnam?' I mean, I've been to hell, so I never saw anything I've done as a risk." Hagel grew up in the Sand Hills and small towns of Nebraska; his father died when he was 16; he became a radio DJ, then with his younger brother Tom volunteered for service in Vietnam. Promoted to sergeant because so many were dying, Chuck and Tom served together; when their armored personnel carrier was hit by a mine, Chuck, his body on fire, dragged Tom from the APC to safety. Chuck Hagel returned home, worked his way through the University of Nebraska, then got a job in Omaha Congressman John McCollister's office. He rose to administrative assistant; after McCollister lost a Senate race in 1976, Hagel became a lobbyist for Firestone. He got the number two position in the Reagan Veterans' Affairs Administration, but resigned after only one year. He was one of two main speakers at the 1982 groundbreaking of the Vietnam Veterans' Memorial. Then he made his great break, using all of his savings—$5,000—and starting Vanguard Cellular Systems, which became the second largest independent cell phone company in the nation; Hagel traveled on business to 60 countries and installed cell phone systems in Costa Rica, Saudi Arabia and Britain. Then he went back into government, as head of World USO and then deputy director of the 1990 G-7 Summit. In 1992 he returned to Omaha, to work in investment banking—and to prepare to run for the Senate.

In 1995 he started running, very much the underdog. In his first ad in January 1996, he said, "I fought in Vietnam where my brother and I were wounded. I served President Reagan. I started my own business, creating hundreds of new jobs. Now I'm running for the United States Senate because we don't need more career politicians in Washington. We need lower taxes, less government, a balanced budget and more personal responsibility." His platform was solidly conservative, sometimes riskily so: he backed school choice, opposed racial quotas and preferences, backed the Freedom to Farm Act ("less government and more open markets"), opposed the estate tax. In the primary he called state Attorney General Don Stenberg a "career politician"; Stenberg hit him for living 20 years in Virginia and for contributing to Bob Kerrey's 1992 presidential campaign. Hagel won the May primary 62%–37%, losing only seven counties and tying Stenberg in four.

Ben Nelson was an even tougher opponent, a popular governor who held down spending and supported the balanced budget amendment and other conservative causes. He had just been re-elected 73%–26%. But in the process he had pledged to serve his full term, and Hagel hammered him for that and for not cutting property taxes as much as he had promised. Nelson led consistently in polls, though by lower margins in the fall. Nelson raised far more PAC money—$909,000, nearly half of his campaign funds—but Hagel spent $1 million of his own money and $3.5 million altogether. Hagel resisted advice from Republican campaign committee head Alfonse D'Amato to go negative; Nelson in the last weeks charged that Hagel had engaged in fraudulent franchising practices with Vanguard. Newspapers hit Nelson, and Hagel responded, "This is a guy who lies. This is a guy who cheats. This is a guy who will do anything."

The result was not even close. Hagel won 56%–42%, carrying all but five counties. In the Senate Hagel got seats on Banking and, because no one else wanted it, Foreign Relations. He quickly became, in David Broder's words, "the freshman who probably has made the deepest impression on his colleagues of both parties." From a historically isolationist state, but one now heavily dependent on exports, Hagel has become a leading internationalist. "We are living in a global village, undergirded by a global economy," he said. "When the markets go down in Asia, it's not good for the United States and it's not good for Nebraska. They can't buy your beef, pork and feed grains." He argues that he finds Nebraska voters far more interested in foreign policy than most senators. Trent Lott made him the lead man on the $18 billion IMF funding. Hagel negotiated with Treasury Secretary Robert Rubin and Federal Reserve Chairman Alan Greenspan and came up with conditions that were widely acceptable; in March 1998 the Senate passed his IMF measure 84–16. In September he beat back even tougher conditions, which would have lost the bill many votes, and saw his measure passed 74–19.

Hagel also took the lead among Republicans against the global warming treaty. In July 1997 he and Democrat Robert Byrd sponsored a resolution requiring that all nations be included in the treaty, even though the treaty would exclude developing nations like China and India—soon likely to be the world's biggest polluters; it passed 95–0, effectively preventing ratification. In December 1997 he attended the Kyoto treaty sessions and denounced the version to which U.S. negotiators agreed. Hagel called on his military experience in 1997 to support the treaty against land mines, opposed by the Clinton Administration; he also spoke for the chemical weapons treaty ratified by the Senate over the objections of Foreign Relations Chairman Jesse Helms. On Clinton's foreign policy, he said in 1998, "I'm not sure the president has ever had a philosophy about foreign policy or thought through what role the United States should have in the world. The administration's foreign policy has been to ricochet from crisis to crisis." Even so, he supported the bombing of Serbia in March 1999. "Peace cannot exist in a Europe where genocide is tolerated." But he insisted that "we must be prepared to do what is necessary to achieve our objectives and ensure victory, including the option of ground troops. If we show weakness or fail, then our adversaries around the world—Iraq, North Korea, terrorist groups—will challenge us in other areas at other times."

On other issues, Hagel's first law passed, in October 1998, providing greater veterans' preferences in federal jobs. The Senate approved a Hagel motion to exclude farm products from U.S. sanctions in July 1998. He has a bill that would allow farmers to defer up to 20% of their income in tax-free accounts and withdraw money in rough years: a form of income-averaging. And he would replace the current military health care system with something more like the Federal Employees Health Benefit Program.

In his first 20 months in the Senate, Hagel was a great favorite of Lott and other Republican leaders. But in November 1998 he criticized the leadership in a letter calling for biennial budgets and a mechanism to cut pork barrel spending. After the 1998 elections he launched a campaign to head the Senate Republican campaign committee; remembering his resistance to D'Amato's negative campaign advice, he was scathing about "demonizing" ads and called for a more "positive" focus. Good advice, perhaps, but incumbent Chairman Mitch McConnell had the votes and won 39–13—Hagel's first major setback in the Senate. Still, he seems a very strong candidate for re-election in 2002, and when Nebraska schoolchildren asked him if he would like to be president, he said, "Maybe." In March 1999 he endorsed the presidential candidacy of John McCain, though in August 1998 he had endorsed George W. Bush.

Presidential politics. Over the last 50 years, Nebraska has voted more Republican in presidential elections than any other state—61% to Kansas' second-place 57%. It was George Bush's best state outside the South in 1992, and Bob Dole's best state in 1996 except for Utah and his home state of Kansas. Greater Omaha usually goes Republican, Lincoln a few points less so, while the western counties are heavily Republican, much like neighboring Wyoming and eastern Colorado. In the 1996 exit polls, elderly voters were for Bill Clinton, voters under 60 heavily for Dole: an indicator of future trends.

Nebraska has a presidential primary in May which once attracted attention; the whole national press followed Robert Kennedy and Eugene McCarthy out here in 1968 and took note when Frank Church won in 1976. No more: nominations are now sewn up long before May, and Nebraska votes unnoticed.

Congressional districting. Nebraska has had three congressional districts since the 1960s. Redistricting made only marginal changes for the 1990s, and is not likely to make significant changes after the 2000 Census. No Democrat has been elected from a Nebraska district since 1992.

The People: Est. Pop. 1998: 1,662,719; Pop. 1990: 1,578,385, up 5.3% 1990–1998. 0.6% of U.S. total, 38th largest; 33.9% rural. Median age: 34.9 years. 14.7% 65 years and over. 93.8% White, 3.6% Black, 0.8% Asian, 0.8% Amer. Indian, 1% Other; 2.2% Hispanic Origin. Households: 58.2% married couple families; 28.5% married couple fams. w. children; 47.1% college educ.; median household income: $26,016; per capita income: $12,452; 66.5% owner occupied housing; median house value: $50,400; median monthly rent: $282. 2.7% Unemployment. 1998 Voting age pop.: 1,231,000. 1998 Turnout: 581,775; 47% of VAP. Registered voters (1998): 1,056,351; 390,776 D (37%), 521,137 R (49%), 144,438 unaffiliated and minor parties (14%).

Political Lineup: Governor, Mike Johanns (R); Lt. Gov., Dave Maurstad (R); Secy. of State, Scott Moore (R); Atty. Gen., Donald Stenberg (R); Treasurer, David Heineman (R); Unicameral Legislature, 49 (no party affiliation); Legislature Speaker, Doug Kristensen (R). Senators, Bob Kerrey (D) and Chuck Hagel (R). Representatives, 3 (3 R).

Elections Division: 402-471-3229; **Filing Deadline for U.S. Congress:** March 1, 2000.

1996 Presidential Vote
Dole (R) 363,467 (54%)
Clinton (D) 236,761 (35%)
Perot (I) 71,278 (11%)

1996 Republican Presidential Primary
Dole (R) 129,131 (76%)
Buchanan (R) 17,741 (10%)
Forbes (R) 10,612 (6%)
Others 13,107 (9%)

1992 Presidential Vote
Bush (R) 343,678 (47%)
Clinton (D) 216,864 (29%)
Perot (I) 174,104 (24%)

GOVERNOR
Gov. Mike Johanns (R)

Elected 1998, term expires Jan. 2003; b. June 18, 1950, Osage, IA; home, Lincoln; St. Mary's Col., B.A. 1971; Creighton U., J.D. 1974; Catholic; married (Stephanie).

Elected Office: Lancaster Cnty. Bd. of Comm., 1982–88; Lincoln City Cncl., 1989–90; Lincoln Mayor, 1991–98.

Professional Career: Law clerk, Hon. Hale McCown, 1974–75; Practicing atty., 1975–91.

Office: State Capitol, P.O. Box 94848, Lincoln, 68509, 402-471-2244; Fax: 402-471-6031; Web site: www.state.ne.us.

Election Results

1998 gen.	Mike Johanns (R)	293,910	(54%)
	Bill Hoppner (D)	250,678	(46%)
1998 prim.	Mike Johanns (R)	88,173	(40%)
	John Breslow (R)	65,806	(30%)
	Jon Christensen (R)	62,107	(28%)
	Others	4,229	(2%)
1994 gen.	Benjamin Nelson (D)	423,270	(73%)
	Gene Spence (R)	148,230	(26%)

SENATORS
Sen. Bob Kerrey (D)

Elected 1988, seat up 2000; b. Aug. 27, 1943, Lincoln; home, Omaha; U. of NE, M.S. 1966; Congregationalist; divorced.

Military Career: Navy, 1966–69 (Vietnam).

Elected Office: NE Gov., 1982–87.

Professional Career: Businessman, Restaurateur, 1972–81.

DC Office: 141 HSOB, 20510, 202-224-6551; Fax: 202-224-7645; Web site: www.senate.gov/~kerrey.

State Offices: Lincoln, 402-437-5246; Omaha, 402-391-3411; Scottsbluff, 308-632-3595.

Committees: *Agriculture, Nutrition & Forestry* (6th of 8 D): Marketing, Inspection & Product Promotion; Production & Price Competitiveness (RMM). *Finance* (8th of 9 D): Health Care; International Trade; Social Security & Family Policy. *Intelligence* (RMM of 8 D).

Group Ratings

	ADA	ACLU	AFS	LCV	CON	NTU	NFIB	COC	ACU	NTLC	CHC
1998	95	86	100	100	86	22	33	56	0	21	0
1997	75	—	67	—	51	39	—	60	4	—	—

National Journal Ratings

	1997 LIB — 1997 CONS			1998 LIB — 1998 CONS		
Economic	71%	—	25%	75%	—	20%
Social	71%	—	0%	74%	—	0%
Foreign	92%	—	0%	65%	—	27%

Key Votes of the 105th Congress

1. Bal. Budget Amend.	N	5. Satcher for Surgeon Gen.	Y	9. Chem. Weapons Treaty	Y
2. Clinton Budget Deal	Y	6. Highway Set-asides	Y	10. Cuban Humanitarian Aid	Y
3. Cloture on Tobacco	Y	7. Table Child Gun locks	N	11. Table Bosnia Troops	Y
4. Education IRAs	N	8. Ovrd. Part. Birth Veto	N	12. $ for Test-ban Treaty	Y

Election Results

1994 general	Bob Kerrey (D)	317,297	(55%)	($5,009,792)
	Jan Stoney (R)	260,668	(45%)	($1,821,778)
1994 primary	Bob Kerrey (D)	unopposed		
1988 general	Bob Kerrey (D)	378,717	(57%)	($3,461,148)
	David Karnes (R)	278,250	(42%)	($3,411,361)

Sen. Chuck Hagel (R)

Elected 1996, seat up 2002; b. Oct. 4, 1946, North Platte; home, Omaha; U. of NE, B.A. 1971; Episcopalian; married (Lilibet).

Military Career: Army, 1967–68 (Vietnam).

Professional Career: Newscaster & Talk Show Host, KBON & KLNG Radio, 1969–71; Admin. Asst., U.S. Rep. John Y. McCollister, 1971–77; Mgr., Govt. Affairs, Firestone Tire & Rubber Co., 1977–80; Dpty. Admin., Veterans' Admin., 1981; U.S. Dpty. Commissioner General, World's Fair, 1982; Pres., Collins, Hagel & Clarke Inc., 1983–84; Co-founder, Dir. & Exec. V.P.., Vanguard Cellular Systems Inc., 1984–87; Pres. & CEO, World USO, 1987–90; Pres. & CEO, Priv. Sector Cncl., 1990–92; Pres., McCarth & Co., 1992–95.

DC Office: 346 RSOB, 20510, 202-224-4224; Fax: 202-224-5213; Web site: www.senate.gov/~hagel.

State Offices: Kearney, 308-237-5145; Lincoln, 402-476-1400; Omaha, 402-758-8981; Scottsbluff, 308-632-6295.

Committees: *Aging (Special)* (7th of 11 R). *Banking, Housing & Urban Affairs* (8th of 11 R): Financial Institutions (Vice Chmn.); International Trade & Finance; Securities. *Foreign Relations* (4th of 10 R): East Asian & Pacific Affairs; European Affairs; International Economic Policy, Export & Trade Promotion (Chmn.). *Health, Education, Labor & Pensions* (9th of 10 R): Children & Families; Employment, Safety & Training.

Group Ratings

	ADA	ACLU	AFS	LCV	CON	NTU	NFIB	COC	ACU	NTLC	CHC
1998	0	29	0	0	78	66	89	94	72	86	100
1997	5	—	0	—	77	74	—	100	80	—	—

National Journal Ratings

	1997 LIB — 1997 CONS		1998 LIB — 1998 CONS	
Economic	25% —	67%	31% —	63%
Social	0% —	83%	12% —	79%
Foreign	34% —	57%	45% —	52%

Key Votes of the 105th Congress

1. Bal. Budget Amend.	Y	5. Satcher for Surgeon Gen.	N	9. Chem. Weapons Treaty	Y
2. Clinton Budget Deal	Y	6. Highway Set-asides	N	10. Cuban Humanitarian Aid	N
3. Cloture on Tobacco	N	7. Table Child Gun locks	Y	11. Table Bosnia Troops	Y
4. Education IRAs	Y	8. Ovrd. Part. Birth Veto	Y	12. $ for Test-ban Treaty	N

Election Results

1996 general	Chuck Hagel (R)	379,933	(56%)	($3,564,316)
	Benjamin Nelson (D)	281,904	(42%)	($2,159,653)
	Others	14,952	(2%)	
1996 primary	Chuck Hagel (R)	112,953	(62%)	
	Don Stenberg (R)	67,974	(37%)	
1990 general	James Exon (D)	349,779	(59%)	($2,410,097)
	Hal Daub (R)	243,013	(41%)	($1,452,681)

FIRST DISTRICT

The eastern half of Nebraska, between the Missouri River and the 98th parallel, was laid out in relentless Midwestern mile-square grids and became some of America's prime farmland in the single decade of the 1880s. The land here has contours just regular enough and weather just favorable enough to make farming economically viable. The plains here have completed most of their gentle decline from the Rockies to sea level; above the river bottoms the land is open to the winds. This land was settled by Yankee-descended Midwestern farmers and German immigrants. Politically it has long been Republican in national elections, but votes Democratic in seriously contested state races.

The 1st Congressional District includes 25 counties in eastern Nebraska. It does not include Omaha or its suburbs, which form the 2d District, but does take in Lincoln, the state capital and home of the University of Nebraska Cornhuskers. Lincoln, with the state government, the university and telemarketing, has been growing rapidly; big meatpacking operations have kept the population steady in smaller counties. Politically, Lincoln is fond of moderate-toned Republicans, and is more hospitable to Democrats than other parts of the state; Lincoln's Lancaster County stopped just short of giving Bill Clinton pluralities in 1992 and 1996, while almost every other Nebraska county voted more than 50% Republican.

The congressman from the 1st District is Douglas Bereuter (pronounced *BEEwriter*), a Republican first elected in 1978. He grew up in Utica, in Seward County, graduated from the University of Nebraska, served in the Army, then got degrees in planning and public policy from Harvard and worked as a planning consultant and part-time professor in Lincoln in the 1970s. He was elected to the Nebraska legislature in 1974, and when Congressman Charles Thone was elected governor in 1978, Bereuter ran for the House, winning the primary 52%–48% and the general 58%–42% in what was then an expensive campaign ($167,000). He was elected the same year as Newt Gingrich, but his approach was different. "Partisanship is not a compelling motive for service for me. I'm more interested in legislation." He has a rather moderate voting record and has done much of his work on the International Relations Committee, where he is chair of the Asian and Pacific Subcommittee.

Bereuter's main cause has been eliminating trade barriers and opening up more markets for agricultural exports. He has led the fight for renewing Most Favored Nation status for China, and for renaming the designation to the more accurate Normal Trade Relations; in 1997 he proposed granting permanent NTR to China as soon as it is admitted to the World Trade Organization. He worked on the China Policy Act of 1995 and in March 1996 toned down the resolution committing U.S. troops to defend Taiwan if attacked. "We don't need to make an enemy of China. I'm concerned we're pushing ourselves into an adversary relationship," he said. He has called for repealing the Jackson-Vanik law. He wrote the export promotion and food assistance sections of the 1996 Freedom to Farm Act. In January 1997 he introduced a fair trade opportunities bill, which would give the president leverage by authorizing modest "snap-back" tariffs on countries not in the WTO, notably Russia and China. He wants to reform U.S. sanctions to exclude agricultural products. On other foreign issues, he supported expanding of NATO, has worked for aid programs that encourage sustainable agriculture in the poor countries of Africa, has written amendments to set up a commission to study the IMF and cutting off aid to Cambodia after the coup there. He has been a strong critic of stationing ground forces in the former Yugoslavia, expressed deep skepticism on the 1998 air strikes against Iraq and was opposed to the bombing campaign against Serbia.

On the Banking Committee he has backed regulatory relief and passed a loan guarantee program for developers and non-profits to construct low-cost rental housing. One of his favorite projects has been promoting hiking trails, notably the 6,357-mile American Discovery Trail from Cape Henlopen, Delaware, to Point Reyes, California, running from Omaha west along the Platte River Valley through Nebraska. For more than a decade he has been getting money for the Lewis & Clark National Historic Trail along the Missouri River and an interpretive center in Nebraska City. He has also promoted bridges across the Missouri, including the Standing Bear Bridge, named after a Ponca chief, connecting Niobrara and Springfield, South Dakota, criticized by South Dakota native Tom Brokaw in a "fleecing of America" report because it was projected to carry only 340 vehicles a day but necessary for Indians to reach a South Dakota health center. When Bellevue, just south of Omaha and Plattsmouth both wanted new Missouri River bridges, he and the 2d District's Jon Christensen came up with a compromise: build both. He has voted to take the transportation trust fund off-budget, and for 1999 the leadership gave him a seat on Transportation and Infrastructure.

Bereuter has been re-elected easily—in 1998 he ran no ads—but has waded into political controversy in Nebraska. In May 1998 he joined Senator Chuck Hagel in denouncing a Christensen flyer that was critical of Mike Johanns, which helped doom his colleague's candidacy for governor. At the July 1998 Republican state convention Bereuter warned against becoming an anti-public school party. "It is now the Republican party that is being 'McGovernized.'" He went on, in a thinly veiled jab at Christensen, "I question no man or woman's religious sincerity, but I will say, though, a lot of people got religion lately when it seemed to be especially good politics with certain voting blocs." This was denounced by many Republican activists; the county chairman in Lincoln invited him to register as a Democrat, and others were not so polite. He has resisted the temptation to run for statewide office. He considered running for the open Senate seat in 1996, but decided not to. In July 1997 he told his staff he would run for governor; in September 1997, after talking to Gingrich and Dick Armey about succeeding to the International Relations chairmanship, he announced he would not run, and in December 1998 he said he would not run against Senator Bob Kerrey. The Republican Conference rule limiting chairmen's terms would force Benjamin Gilman to step aside at International Relations, and the next three most senior Republicans—Bill Goodling, Jim Leach, Henry Hyde—are now chairmen of other committees and are considered unlikely to play musical chairmanships with this one. Of course, Republicans might not have a majority after 2000, and Gingrich is in no position to deliver on any promises, but Bereuter's chances of chairing International Relations still seem good.

Cook's Call. *Safe.* While by presidential voting standards this district is the least Republican in the state, it is still safe for Bereuter.

The People: Pop. 1990: 526,291; 39.3% rural; 15.4% age 65 +; 96.5% White, 1.1% Black, 0.8% Asian, 1.1% Amer. Indian, 0.5% Other; 1.2% Hispanic Origin. Households: 58.4% married couple families; 28% married couple fams. w. children; 45.9% college educ.; median household income: $25,763; per capita income: $12,088; median house value: $50,100; median gross rent: $274.

1996 Presidential Vote

Dole (R) 114,563 (50%)
Clinton (D) 87,712 (38%)
Perot (I) 25,974 (11%)

1992 Presidential Vote

Bush (R) 107,081 (43%)
Clinton (D) 80,696 (32%)
Perot (I) 59,974 (24%)

Rep. Douglas K. Bereuter (R)

Elected 1978; b. Oct. 6, 1939, York; home, Cedar Bluffs; U. of NE, B.A. 1961, Harvard U., M.C.P. 1966, M.P.A. 1973; Lutheran; married (Louise).

Military Career: Army, 1963–65.

Elected Office: NE Legislature, 1974–78.

Professional Career: Urban planner, U.S. Dept. of HUD, 1965–66; Div. Dir., NE Econ. Devel. Dept., 1967–68; Dir., NE Office of Planning, 1968–70.

DC Office: 2184 RHOB 20515, 202-225-4806; Web site: www.house.gov/bereuter.

District Offices: Fremont, 402-727-0888; Lincoln, 402-438-1598.

Committees: *Banking & Financial Services* (4th of 32 R): Financial Institutions & Consumer Credit; Housing & Community Opportunity. *International Relations* (5th of 26 R): Asia & the Pacific (Chmn.); International Economic Policy & Trade. *Transportation & Infrastructure* (38th of 41 R): Ground Transportation; Water Resources & Environment.

Group Ratings

	ADA	ACLU	AFS	LCV	CON	NTU	NFIB	COC	ACU	NTLC	CHC
1998	5	6	0	15	26	33	79	100	64	67	83
1997	20	—	25	—	76	44	—	90	68	—	—

National Journal Ratings

	1997 LIB — 1997 CONS			1998 LIB — 1998 CONS		
Economic	44%	—	56%	43%	—	56%
Social	37%	—	61%	41%	—	58%
Foreign	46%	—	53%	47%	—	51%

Key Votes of the 105th Congress

1. Clinton Budget Deal	Y	5. Puerto Rico Sthood. Ref.	N	9. Cut $ for B-2 Bombers	Y
2. Education IRAs	Y	6. End Highway Set-asides	Y	10. Human Rights in China	N
3. Req. 2/3 to Raise Taxes	N	7. School Prayer Amend.	Y	11. Withdraw Bosnia Troops	Y
4. Fast-track Trade	Y	8. Ovrd. Part. Birth Veto	Y	12. End Cuban TV-Marti	N

Election Results

1998 general	Douglas K. Bereuter (R)	136,058	(73%)	($214,449)
	Don Eret (D)	48,826	(26%)	($14,746)
1998 primary	Douglas K. Bereuter (R)	66,033	(99%)	
	Others	460	(1%)	
1996 general	Douglas K. Bereuter (R)	157,108	(70%)	($394,292)
	Patrick J. Combs (D)	67,152	(30%)	($59,666)

SECOND DISTRICT

Omaha, the commercial metropolis of Nebraska, the largest city on the Great Plains north of Kansas City and west of Minneapolis, the city that still produces one out of five American steaks, got its start from government: Abraham Lincoln picked it as the eastern terminus of the Union Pacific railroad, from which emerged the stockyards and livestock exchange that made it a top livestock town. Over the years, Omaha filled up with cattle hands from the West and European immigrants, especially Germans and Czechs; it developed fine civic institutions from the Joslyn Art Museum and the Ak-Sar-Ben (spell it backwards) Exhibition to the Boys Town, founded by Father Flanagan in 1917, the subject of a 1938 movie and today still innovative and thriving in its promotion of traditional values. Though a major city by the 1880s, Omaha has remained small enough (and famous on Wall Street as the place where Warren Buffett lives and works) to be readily comprehensible; you don't feel distant, physically or psychologically, from the other side of town, and you usually know people from a broader range of backgrounds than you would in a large homogeneous neighborhood within a big metropolitan area. The older, less affluent part of Omaha is near the river and Iowa; to the west, the city has been quietly booming, with affluent neighborhoods and new shopping malls. All over, Omaha's economy has been changing. It still has many processors of food products, like the hard-charging ConAgra company, and the giant Peter Kiewit construction firm; but it is also the nation's telecommunications center, handling 100 million '800' and '900' calls annually and employing more than 10,000 people in 24 telemarketing centers. Its civic institutions are thriving as well: an opera company, museums, a children's theater, a zoo with the country's largest indoor jungle west of Chicago.

The 2d Congressional District is metropolitan Omaha: Douglas County with Omaha and its western suburbs; Sarpy County with suburbs to the south and the old Strategic Air Command headquarters at Offutt Air Force Base; and a sliver of Cass County just to the south. Politically, Omaha has long had competitive politics, with Democrats strong on the south side around the stockyards and the northeast and Republicans strong in the area west of 72d Street. But as Omaha and Nebraska have boomed, they have become more Republican, and increasingly it is the Republican primary that decides elections here.

The congressman from the 2d District is Lee Terry, a Republican elected in 1998. Terry grew up in Omaha, and became interested in politics at 14 when his father, TV anchor Lee Terry Sr., ran for the House in 1976; a confrontational conservative, he lost 55%–45% to 31-year-old Democrat John Cavanaugh. Terry Sr. remained a prominent local commentator on politics; Terry Jr. went off to college and law school, practiced law, and was elected to the Omaha Council from an affluent west side district in 1991, at 29. There he worked to stop teenage cruising on Dodge Street and collaborated with private enterprise to build the Moylan-Tranquillity IcePlex skating rink at 125th Street and West Maple Road. He contemplated not running for a Council seat again in 1997, but stayed on.

Then in September 1997, 2d District Congressman Jon Christensen announced he was running for governor—a surprise, since he had touted his seat on Ways and Means and had been appointed the National Republican Congressional Committee's recruiting director. Christensen had strong support from Christian conservatives and a record of odd political utterances and bizarre controversy; he ended up finishing third in the May 1998 primary after a last-minute flyer critical of Mike Johanns was attacked as unfair by Senator Chuck Hagel and his two House colleagues. His former wife, fundraiser Meredith Christensen, well known for admitting adultery in their 1994 divorce; entered the race, but withdrew in November. A few days after her announcement, Terry announced at the IcePlex. He decried frivolous lawsuits, the Department of Education and "corporate welfare," and said he would apply the lessons he learned in city government and devolve power to local government.

Terry had primary competition from Brad Kuiper, owner of a pest control business in west Douglas County, and Steve Kupka, former chief of staff to Mayor Hal Daub (who served four terms in the House in the 1980s) and an official in the Reagan-David Stockman OMB. The contrast between the three was less on issues—they were all for lower taxes and against abortion, for example—than on style and approach. Kuiper, with less money than the other two, targeted religious conservatives and emphasized cultural issues—much as Christensen had done here and was doing in the governor primary. Kupka assembled Washington endorsements (Congressman Fred Upton, former Attorney General Edwin Meese, former OMB Director Jim Miller) and, spending the most money, went on the attack. He argued that Terry's elevation would give Democrats control of the Council. He criticized Terry for not opposing a 1991 garbage fee (actually, Terry favored the legislature giving the city authority to impose the fee, but voted against it) and said Terry had added $1 million to the city budget over two years.

Terry's approach was more in line with the consensus-minded mood that pervaded the country in 1998. As his rather partisan father said, "I see him as passionate, but not as angry and stubborn as his old man." He stressed his work building consensus on the Council, and his ads trumpeted that and his support of lower taxes, including a flat tax with mortgage and charity deductions. He bristled at Kupka's ads and called them dishonest, but resisted consultants' advice to go up with negative ads of his own. "I told them I would rather lose than lose my reputation," he said. He counted on strong support from his council district, which included 20% of Republican primary voters, and from his greater name identification. The dynamic was much the same as in the governor's race, in which Mike Johanns, who declined to run negative ads, won with 40% to 30% for John Breslow, who ran confrontational conservative ads, and 28% for Christensen. The results in the 2d District primary were almost identical: 40% for Terry, 30% for Kupka and 26% for Kuiper.

The general election was anticlimactic. Democrat Michael Scott had appeared on Omaha TV off an on since 1982 (his signoff: "Take care of one another"), but he raised less than $100,000, while Terry spent $824,000 in all. Democrats were competitive in this district the last four times it has been open, in 1970, 1974, 1980 and 1988; they won in 1974 and 1988. Now, as Nebraska has moved to the right, they have not been competitive at all. Terry won 66%–34%, a much wider margin than Christensen's 57%–40% in 1996 when his opponent was hobbled by family tragedy. In Washington, Terry got seats on the Transportation, Banking and Government Reform committees. Unlike many of the 1994 Republican revolutionaries, he sold his house in the district and moved his family to Washington; in April 1999 he backed off his pledge to serve only three terms.

Cook's Call. *Safe.* Terry should have little concern about losing this very Republican district to a Democrat in 2000. However, after recently denouncing his pledge to serve only three terms, Terry's toughest opponent may be national term limit proponents, who have launched all-out assaults on potential term limit breakers this cycle.

The People: Pop. 1990: 526,573; 6.3% rural; 10.6% age 65 +; 87.4% White, 9.6% Black, 1.3% Asian, 0.6% Amer. Indian, 1.1% Other; 2.6% Hispanic Origin. Households: 54.5% married couple families; 28.4% married couple fams. w. children; 55.6% college educ.; median household income: $30,889; per capita income: $14,322; median house value: $61,300; median gross rent: $345.

1996 Presidential Vote

Dole (R) 116,889 (52%)
Clinton (D) 84,667 (38%)
Perot (I) 18,934 (9%)

1992 Presidential Vote

Bush (R) 115,255 (47%)
Clinton (D) 78,701 (32%)
Perot (I) 48,657 (20%)

Rep. Lee Terry (R)

Elected 1998; b. Jan. 29, 1962, Omaha; home, Omaha; U. of NE at Lincoln, B.A. 1984; Creighton U., J.D. 1987; Methodist; married (Robyn).

Elected Office: Omaha City Cncl., 1990–98, Pres., 1995–96.

Professional Career: Practicing atty., 1988–98.

DC Office: 1728 LHOB 20515, 202-225-4155; Fax: 202-226-5452; Web site: www.house.gov/terry.

District Office: Omaha, 402-397-9944.

Committees: *Banking & Financial Services* (30th of 32 R): Capital Markets, Securities & Government Sponsored Enterprises; Housing & Community Opportunity. *Government Reform* (18th of 24 R): National Economic Growth, Natural Resources & Regulatory Affairs; National Security, Veterans' Affairs & Intl. Relations. *Transportation & Infrastructure* (33d of 41 R): Ground Transportation; Oversight, Investigations & Emergency Management (Vice Chmn.).

Group Ratings and Key Votes: Newly Elected

Election Results

1998 general	Lee Terry (R)	106,782	(66%)	($868,153)
	Michael Scott (D)	55,722	(34%)	($94,939)
1998 primary	Lee Terry (R)	23,769	(40%)	
	Steve Kupka (R)	17,673	(30%)	
	Brad Kuiper (R)	15,569	(26%)	
	Others	2,181	(4%)	
1996 general	Jon Christensen (R)	125,201	(57%)	($1,722,490)
	James Martin Davis (D)	88,447	(40%)	($384,582)
	Others	6,676	(3%)	

THIRD DISTRICT

West of Grand Island, Nebraska is wheat and livestock country. For miles on end you can see nothing but rolling brown fields, sectioned off here and there by barbed wire fences, and in the distance a grain elevator towering over a tiny town and its miniature railroad depot. The winds and rain and tornadoes that come suddenly out of the sky remind you that the original settlers likened this part of the country to an ocean and thought themselves in their wooden wagons almost as helpless as passengers at sea in a rowboat. Settlers passed through here on the Oregon Trail in the 1840s, then set down roots in the 1880s, but the rain they hoped for fell too unreliably, and wheatlands gave way to pasture and open range. It is a beautiful but hard land, exacting much from its people, as the novels of western Nebraska's Willa Cather make poignantly clear.

The 3d Congressional District has 33% of the state's people spread out over 82% of its acreage. And the land is emptying out: except along the interstate and around Scottsbluff, the 3d has been losing population for decades; these 66 counties had 608,000 people in 1940, 525,000 in 1990. Geographically and politically, the 3d District is where the Midwest becomes the West. For years people here welcomed farm subsidies even as they angrily opposed federal interference. Politically, it is heavily Republican and sometimes ornery: George Bush and Bob Dole easily carried the district in the 1990s, and in 1992 Ross Perot got more votes than Bill Clinton.

The congressman from the 3d District is Bill Barrett, a Republican elected in 1990. He has lived all his life in Lexington, where he ran the insurance and real estate firm founded by his grandfather in 1924. He was Republican state chairman from 1973–75 and in 1978 he was elected to Nebraska's unicameral legislature. In 1987 he became speaker. In 1990 he ran for the House and won a five-candidate Republican primary with 30%, running well in his home area and in the eastern end of the district, in the Lincoln media market. In the general he had an unaccustomed hard time, as he was hammered for supporting Governor Kay Orr's 1987 tax package and for opposing abortion. Barrett won with 51% in a friends-and-neighbors contest, losing most of the western counties and carrying his home area.

In the House Barrett has compiled a solidly conservative voting record. He serves on the Agriculture Committee and after just four years became chairman of the General Farm Commodities Subcommittee. In 1995 and 1996 he worked with former House Agriculture Chairman Pat Roberts to write the Freedom to Farm Act, which phases out most farm subsidies over seven years. Barrett said it would "unleash our nation's single largest industry from antiquated programs and overbearing federal intrusion [by] allowing producers to plant for the market, to make choices, to weigh risk, and to be in charge of their farms and their future." In 1998 he called falling grain prices a "blip"—a remark taken out of context, he says. In June 1998 he hailed the farm bill for its $470 million for crop insurance and $600 for research, and was part of negotiations with the Senate to settle the issue of food stamps for legal immigrants. He opposed gutting the Freedom to Farm Act and supported the Republican provision allowing farmers to collect 1999 transition payments any time after October 1, 1998. In September 1998 he sponsored another $2.3 billion in payments to farmers.

In past decades such a fall in farm prices might have produced demands for much higher supports and would have shifted votes to the Democrats. Not so in the late 1990s, as the number of actual farmers continues to decline and Republicans like Barrett emphasize the growth of farm exports. Barrett, used to easy re-election, had no problems in 1998. A former aide threatened to run in the primary, but didn't. No Democrat filed, and Barrett won enough write-in votes to have become the Democratic nominee had he wanted to, as in 1996; he declined again to switch parties, and easily beat Democrat John Webster 77%–23%. Barrett announced in March 1999, after two top aides left his staff, that he would run again in 2000.

Cook's Call. *Safe.* Barrett, or any Republican for that matter, will have no trouble holding on to the 3d District, the most Republican in the state, and one of the most Republican in the country.

The People: Pop. 1990: 525,521; 56% rural; 18.1% age 65 +; 97.6% White, 0.2% Black, 0.3% Asian, 0.7% Amer. Indian, 1.2% Other; 2.8% Hispanic Origin. Households: 61.5% married couple families; 29% married couple fams. w. children; 40.2% college educ.; median household income: $22,344; per capita income: $10,942; median house value: $38,300; median gross rent: $209.

1996 Presidential Vote		
Dole (R)	132,015	(59%)
Clinton (D)	64,382	(29%)
Perot (I)	26,370	(12%)

1992 Presidential Vote		
Bush (R)	121,342	(49%)
Perot (I)	65,473	(27%)
Clinton (D)	57,467	(23%)

Rep. Bill Barrett (R)

Elected 1990; b. Feb. 9, 1929, Lexington; home, Lexington; Hastings Col., B.A. 1951; Presbyterian; married (Elsie).

Military Career: Navy, 1951–52.

Elected Office: NE Legislature, 1978–90, Speaker, 1987–90.

Professional Career: Real estate & insurance exec., 1956–90; Chmn., NE Repub. Party, 1973–75.

DC Office: 2458 RHOB 20515, 202-225-6435; Fax: 202-225-0207; Web site: www.house.gov/billbarrett.

District Offices: Grand Island, 308-381-5555; Scottsbluff, 308-632-3333.

Committees: *Agriculture* (Vice Chmn. of 27 R): General Farm Commodities, Resource Conservation & Credit (Chmn.); Risk Management, Research & Specialty Crops. *Education & the Workforce* (5th of 27 R): Postsecondary Education, Training & Life-Long Learning; Workforce Protections (Vice Chmn.).

Group Ratings

	ADA	ACLU	AFS	LCV	CON	NTU	NFIB	COC	ACU	NTLC	CHC
1998	15	6	22	8	60	61	100	89	76	82	83
1997	5	—	25	—	42	43	—	100	79	—	—

National Journal Ratings

	1997 LIB — 1997 CONS		1998 LIB — 1998 CONS	
Economic	40%	— 59%	37%	— 61%
Social	10%	— 82%	34%	— 64%
Foreign	24%	— 76%	49%	— 51%

Key Votes of the 105th Congress

1. Clinton Budget Deal	Y	5. Puerto Rico Sthood. Ref.	N	9. Cut $ for B-2 Bombers	N
2. Education IRAs	N	6. End Highway Set-asides	Y	10. Human Rights in China	N
3. Req. 2/3 to Raise Taxes	Y	7. School Prayer Amend.	Y	11. Withdraw Bosnia Troops	Y
4. Fast-track Trade	Y	8. Ovrd. Part. Birth Veto	Y	12. End Cuban TV-Marti	Y

Election Results

1998 general	Bill Barrett (R)	149,896	(84%)	($160,275)
	Jerry Hickman (Lib)	27,278	(15%)	
1998 primary	Bill Barrett (R)	unopposed		
1996 general	Bill Barrett (R)	167,758	(77%)	($203,582)
	John Webster (D)	48,833	(23%)	($15,190)

NEVADA

Giant plinths, New York skyscrapers across the street from the sphinx-like lion, a flaming pirate ship next door to Roman ruins, a pyramid and obelisk, all rising in a bowl-shaped desert valley rimmed by barren peaks: welcome to Nevada! Nature left little here to encourage human settlement—lodes of gold and silver which attracted sudden agglomerations of miners and hangers-on for brief years, but almost no water or arable land. So Nevada is wholly the creation of post-industrial man. Its existence as a state is happenstance: the discovery of the Comstock Lode silver mine in 1859—$500 million worth was taken out in 20 years—brought settlers, and Abraham Lincoln's Republicans made it a state in 1864 even though Nevada did not meet the population requirement for statehood because Republicans thought they needed its three electoral votes. But Nevada's population dropped by the early 20th Century; in the early 1930s, there were only 91,000 Nevadans and the state government was about to go bankrupt. So Nevada decided to roll the dice. The state reduced its residency requirement for divorce to six weeks and legalized gambling. Catering to what most Americans considered sin—casinos, pawnshops, divorce mills, quick wedding chapels, even legal brothels—turned out to be good business. Nevada has been America's fastest growing state since 1960; in the 1980s its population rose 50%, from 800,000 to 1.6 million, adding 6,000 new residents every week; from 1990–98, it added another 545,000, growing 45% in just six years, to 1.75 million. Growth slowed a bit in the late 1990s, as California's economy recovered and fewer Californians moved east, but Nevada's 1997–98 growth rate of 4.1% was still easily the highest in the country.

Las Vegas, a mere spot on the map when gambling was legalized, is now a metro area of 1.1 million and Reno, in the 1940s the divorce capital of America, is pressing 400,000. Gaming—the Nevada word for gambling—generates most of this growth: Las Vegas's 106,000 hotel rooms (as of early 1999) house more than 30 million tourists who spend $24.6 billion a year, Reno's nearly 5 million tourists spend almost $4 billion, and not just in casinos and hotels but in increasingly upscale malls and restaurants. Almost half of Nevada's jobs are in services some way related to gaming or tourism. Las Vegas is especially attractive to Japanese tourists, whose numbers doubled in 1994–98 despite the recession in Japan. The 6.4% gambling receipts tax generates enough revenue so that Nevada has no income, corporate or inheritance tax, and the cost of living is low; half the houses in Las Vegas are valued at under $100,000 and many migrants from California cannot find a house that costs as much as the one they sold.

From mining to gaming, Nevada has been a second chance state, a place for outcasts to succeed and misfits to rebound. Some 11% of its adults are divorced, the highest rate in the nation. It has been an avenue of success for ethnic groups who faced roadblocks elsewhere. The four owners of the Comstock Lode—MacKay, Fair, Flood, O'Brien—were Irishmen; the first big hotel on the Las Vegas strip, the Flamingo, was built in 1946 by Jewish gangster Bugsy Siegel, later gunned down in his Beverly Hills home; most of the big casinos were owned by mobsters until Howard Hughes—a different kind of outcast—bought them up in the late 1960s. For years, the casinos catered to older tastes in entertainment, from Frank Sinatra to girlie shows, and depended on gamblers for all their trade. But in the early 1990s, as riverboat and Indian casinos opened in many states, Las Vegas became a family-friendly destination resort. Its huge and flashy hotels have glittering attractions: the 3,000-room Mirage with its tropical rainforest lobby has Siegfried and Roy's tiger-taming extravaganza; the MGM Grand, its lion entry-hall, hosted Barbra Streisand's first live performance in decades in 1994 and wooed her with $13 million for New Year's Eve 1999; Caesars Palace has an upscale shopping center with Roman-style storefronts; the pyramid-shaped Luxor that looms over this desert has an amusement park and huge obelisk inside; New York New York imitates Gotham and the Bel-

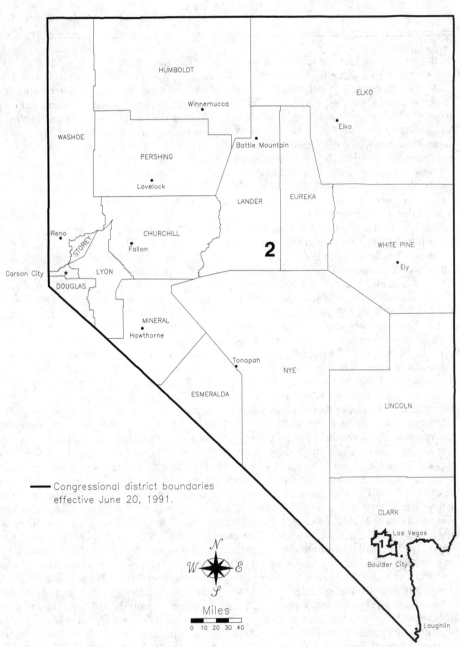

Congressional district boundaries
effective June 20, 1991.

Miles
0 10 20 30 40

lagio has a museum-class art gallery and an eleven-acre lake with 1,000 fountains. Slot machines no longer line every hallway, because that would mean keeping children out; Las Vegas has become decorous enough to attract the American Booksellers and Southern Baptist conventions. Will either political party ever dare to hold its national convention here?

There are other things going on in Nevada besides gambling and other places besides Las Vegas (though Clark County contains more than 65% of Nevadans). The state's low taxes have made it a regional distribution and credit card operations center and it has attracted warehouses and factories from California. There is still some mining, a little gold and silver, plus less glamorous diatomaceous earth, used for swimming pool filters and kitty litter. And the Wild West atmosphere remains, especially in the "Cow Counties" beyond Las Vegas and Reno. Near Elko, a Canadian company's subsidiary in 1995 paid the federal government $9,765 for title to 1,949 acres of public lands with 30 million ounces of gold—all legal under the Mining Act of 1872. In Tonopah the federal government sued Nye County for claiming to own public lands and prosecuting federal officers enforcing federal land management laws.

For the past two decades, Nevada has had a volatile politics. Historically, it was Democratic, sending politically shrewd Democrats to Washington to protect the interests of a state always heavily dependent on the federal government. The most powerful were Key Pittman, chairman of the Senate Foreign Relations Committee, who backed FDR's foreign policy only after Roosevelt agreed to buy absurdly large amounts of silver, and penny-pinching Pat McCarran, author of the repressive McCarran Act, who shamelessly pushed aid for Reno and Las Vegas (the airport there is named for him) and became suddenly solicitous of civil liberties when mobsters and casino owners were called to testify before the Kefauver committee investigating crime and racketeering. In the 1980s Nevada trended sharply Republican, primarily because of newcomers. This came not out of devotion to family values, for Nevada is the least family-oriented state, with the nation's largest percentage of non-family households, but from people who think they are sharper than others, have a special angle, are a step ahead of the market, and can and will beat the odds.

In the 1990s the dice have rolled both ways. Republicans now hold a narrow 42%–41% edge in party registration, and Republican Kenny Guinn was elected governor in 1998. But Bill Clinton, to the surprise of managers on both sides, carried Nevada twice, by 37%–35% in 1992 and 44%–43% in 1996, after promising to veto any bill that furthers the nuclear waste depository proposed for Yucca Mountain, some 90 miles north of Las Vegas. Nevada has elected and re-elected two Democratic senators, but Harry Reid won by only 428 votes in 1998 and Richard Bryan announced in 1999 that he would not run again in 2000. In the state's two congressional districts, Republicans won 7 of 10 contests in the 1990s. Republicans control five of six statewide offices and the state Senate. Nevada may be vastly more populous than it used to be, but a few votes can still make a difference. Another unique feature of Nevada politics: since 1975 voters can vote for "none of these candidates." "None" finished second in the 1998 Democratic primary for lieutenant governor and has occasionally finished first in races for minor offices; but even then the top-running candidate wins.

But special issues are often more important in Nevada than political parties. Guinn was elected more because of his support from the gaming industry than for partisan reasons. And since unions have successfully organized Las Vegas's casinos and hotels, Guinn was no more interested than the Democrats in curbing union power; a payroll protection initiative, to require that union members give written permission before their dues money is used for political purposes, was ruled off the ballot by a judge and then withdrawn when unions threatened a retaliatory ballot measure. The federal gambling commission sponsored by gambling opponents was feared here; the Nevada delegation worked to make its mandate less anti-gaming and to narrow its subpoena power; its report is expected by June 1999. The American Gaming Commission has Nevadan Frank Fahrenkopf, former Republican national chairman, to represent the industry and in the 1998 cycle it contributed a total of $5 million to the two major parties.

The other raging Nevada issue is the proposed Yucca Mountain nuclear depository. It was chosen by Congress in 1987, when the Nevada delegation was unusually weak: Harry Reid was in his first year in the Senate and Republican Chic Hecht seemed to be facing sure defeat. The plan is to bury the waste deep within the mountain, 1,300 feet above the water table, in reinforced steel containers in a 1,400-acre maze with 100 miles of storage tunnels. Many in Nevada argue that rainwater will flush the radioactive material out of the depository and into the water table; a December 1998 Energy Department study found no evidence that would happen. But Nevada opinion is strongly opposed and Nevadans in Congress have tried to stop the project and have succeeded in delaying it. But support for Yucca Mountain has accumulated as nuclear waste has piled up in more than 70 sites in other states, and the key issue now is whether to build a temporary depository at the Nevada Test Site, next to Yucca Mountain; the expectation is that once the waste is in Nevada, Congress will never vote to ship it elsewhere. Idaho Senator Larry Craig, whose state agreed to temporarily take government nuclear waste, got 63 votes in 1995 and 65 in 1997—just two votes short of a veto-proof for the temporary site, and similar measures have won veto-proof margins in the House. But in June 1998 the temporary site bills were withdrawn, as Senators Harry Reid and Richard Bryan brandished a Clinton veto threat and Speaker Newt Gingrich pulled it off the calendar to help the Senate candidacy of Congressman John Ensign. The Clinton Administration EPA has stalled in providing data on the local geology, and the DOE missed the February 1998 deadline to begin receiving waste from other sites. But proponents of Yucca Mountain were preparing to fight again in early 1999, arguing that $3 billion has already been spent on Yucca Mountain and that waste would be far safer there than where it is accumulating now. The mayor of tiny Caliente has offered his town as a site for offloading the waste from trains for delivery to the depository. Existing law says the permanent depository is supposed to open in 2010, but the political battles are far from over.

Then there is the issue of water, vital everywhere in the West, but especially so in parched Nevada. Bill Clinton and Al Gore made a big point in appearing at Lake Tahoe in July 1997, pledging to double federal spending to prevent buildup of nitrogen and growth of algae. The Interior Department is working to buy out farmers along the Truckee River, site of the first federal irrigation project in 1914, to increase the flow to Pyramid Lake, sacred to the Paiute tribe. And in December 1997 Interior Secretary Bruce Babbitt allowed interstate water sales of Colorado River water; Arizona has offered to sell stored water to Nevada.

Governor. Kenny Guinn was elected governor of Nevada in 1998 in his first race for elective office. But he was not inexperienced in civic affairs. He grew up in the Central Valley of California, due west of Las Vegas but separated by Death Valley and Mount Whitney; he majored in physical education at Fresno State and got an education doctorate at Utah State. In 1964 he moved to Las Vegas to work for the Clark County School District; he became school superintendent in 1969. Later he went to work for the S&L that became PriMerit Bank and became chairman in 1987; then he went to Southwest Gas Corporation and became chairman in 1993; in 1994 he spent a year as interim president of the University of Nevada at Las Vegas, then recovering from a basketball scandal, and donating his salary to the schools scholarship fund. In the process he accumulated much civic renown. In February 1996 he started running to replace term-limited Governor Bob Miller; immediately he picked up much of the support from the gaming industry Miller had, though he is a Republican and Miller a Democrat. "The Anointed One" he was christened by the *Las Vegas Review-Journal*'s Jon Ralston.

But if the Anointed One had widespread support, he also had opposition. In the September 1998 primary he faced Aaron Russo, a former Hollywood producer who moved to Las Vegas in 1996. Russo refused casino money, leaving a $1,000 check from Donald Trump on his desk ostentatiously uncashed, and called for increasing the 6.25% tax on casinos' gross. Guinn retaliated by playing in his ads a video Russo had made in 1994 when he formed a Ross Perot-like Constitution Party; it showed Russo in long hair and a dangling earring ranting in protest at politicians. "It's overturned the rock a little bit to show what he's really all about," Guinn said. Russo got within 7% in an August poll, but Guinn won handily, 58%–26%.

The Democratic nominee was Las Vegas Mayor Jan Laverty Jones. She had become locally famous in the 1980s as a costumed pitchman in television commercials for her then-husband's car dealerships; then she ran for mayor in 1991, and won. "Politics was the only job I could have found where I didn't step down from selling cars." Jones announced on filing day, only a few months after breast cancer surgery, and while still undergoing chemotherapy and radiation; she was utterly open about this and showed great vigor. In 1994 she ran against Governor Bob Miller in the primary, and lost 63%–28%. In 1998 her main primary opponent was state Senator Joe Neal, who campaigned against the casinos and called for an 8% gaming tax. Jones boasted of hiring hundreds more policemen and a 9% property tax rebate in 1997, and creating a MASH homeless shelter and the Fremont Street Experience. In July 1998 she was brought before the state ethics committee on charges of favoring political allies in a zoning dispute, her seventh such charge since 1994; in August 1998, she was absolved, as she had been in each case before. In September she beat Neal 60%–16%, with 14% for "none of these candidates."

The general election campaign was not very eventful. Guinn charged Jones with raising property taxes; Jones charged Guinn with raising gas rates. Aaron Russo endorsed Jones. Guinn won 52%–42%, carrying the Las Vegas and Reno areas by almost identical majorities and, the product of much early campaigning, winning by 59%–34% in the Cow Counties. On taking office he was promptly confronted by a budget shortfall; hotel occupancies had been sagging and growth slowing down. He proceeded confidently to pare down spending. In February 1999, despite his low seniority, he was a visible figure at the National Governors Association conference in Washington, urging Bill Clinton to cover more of the cost of federally-mandated special education programs. Jan Jones, after a brief flurry, announced in December 1998 she wouldn't seek to become Democratic national chairman; she said she would run for a third term as mayor and wouldn't seek other office.

Senior Senator. Harry Reid, a Democrat first elected in 1986, has held high office in Nevada for most of the last 30 years. He grew up in Searchlight, Nevada, in the scorching desert south of Las Vegas, and hitchhiked 40 miles to high school in Henderson, where his civics teacher and boxing coach Mike O'Callaghan became his political mentor. Reid was elected to the Assembly in 1968, at age 28; in 1970 Callaghan was elected governor and Reid, running separately, was elected lieutenant governor. In 1974, he came within 624 votes of beating Paul Laxalt in the race for senator, lost for mayor of Las Vegas in 1976, and then became head of the Gaming Commission from 1977–81—as sensitive a post as any in Nevada. In 1982, when Nevada got two House seats for the first time and Congressman-at-Large Jim Santini ran for the Senate, Reid ran for the Las Vegas 1st District seat and won. Laxalt retired in 1986, and Reid ran for the Senate again; his opponent turned out to be Santini, who had switched parties at the last minute and was running as a Republican. Reid's ads depicted him as David to Santini's Goliath, and he won 50%–45%.

Reid is an unprepossessing figure and an awkward debater, but is also tough and persevering, a moderate Democrat who is his party's whip in the Senate. He is conservative on some issues: against abortion, for the Gulf war resolution, against environmental groups' proposals to change the Mining Act of 1872, for revision of the Endangered Species Act. But he is also a party man: for the 1993 budget and tax increase, for the 1994 crime bill with its gun control provisions, casting a decisive vote against the balanced budget amendment in 1993. He took on Ross Perot, then still highly popular, when he appeared before the Joint Committee on the Organization of Congress: "I think you should start checking your facts a little more and stop listening to the applause as much." After the 1994 election, he said, "We have to all swallow a little bit of our pride and go toward the middle." In December 1998, after months of rounding up votes, he was elected minority whip, even after winning re-election by only 428 votes.

In his 1998 campaign Reid boasted that he had accomplished more for Nevada than any other senator. He pushed through a "source tax" amendment barring states from taxing the state pensions of retirees who move to another state—as many have to Nevada. Through two years of negotiation he produced an agreement on allocating water from Lake Tahoe and the

Truckee River between Nevada and California; Reid got the Pyramid Lake Paiute Indians to agree to return their fisheries to the state for $25 million, plus $40 million in economic aid. He pushed through a Nevada Wilderness Protection Act in 1990, over the objections of Republican Congresswoman Barbara Vucanovich. He has used his seat on Appropriations to bring in highway money, especially to the growing Las Vegas area. He got a grant for a Suicide Prevention Center at the University of Nevada's medical school—Nevada's suicide rate is the nation's highest—and opposed lowering the blood alcohol level for DWIs—a measure disliked by owners of hotels and bars. He has led the fight to block creation of a temporary nuclear waste depository at the Nevada Test Site, next to Yucca Mountain which Congress designated in 1987 as the nation's permanent waste depository. Armed with a veto threat from Bill Clinton, he and Nevada colleague Richard Bryan were able to avoid a vote on the temporary site in 1998; proponents promise to bring it up again in 1999. The week before the 1998 election he was able to announce a $14.6 million grant to design a new Hoover Dam bypass bridge and $10 million for projects around Lake Tahoe.

On national issues Reid has taken some distinctive positions. He worked for the Taxpayers Bill of Rights in 1988 and the IRS reform of 1998; he has demanded prosecution of IRS officials who encouraged or tolerated collection quotas. He has said he favors a consumption tax and has voted for the Republican initiative of sunsetting the current Internal Revenue Code in 2002 so as to require reform. He wants to remove J. Edgar Hoover's name from the FBI Building in Washington. He opposed the omnibus budget in October 1998 and in that same month stalled the adjournment-hungry Senate to protest the killing of an amendment that would provide prescription contraceptives for federal workers.

Despite this record, Reid has not won by large margins. Part of the problem is that Nevada is changing rapidly. Rapid population growth may bespeak a strong economy, but it also brings in people totally unfamiliar with existing officeholders: About 125,000 people moved into Nevada in each of the six years of Reid's second term. In 1992 Reid won by unimpressive margins over nonoverwhelming opponents: In the primary he won 53%–39% over Charles Woods, a businessman badly wounded and scarred in World War II; in the general he beat rancher Demar Dahl 51%–40%. In the 1998 race his opponent was 1st District Congressman John Ensign, who had run and won high-spending races in the Las Vegas area in 1994 and 1996. Ensign is a veterinarian and son of a casino owner, with good connections in Las Vegas; he is tall, charming and articulate. In the House he and colleague David Camp were the ones who persuaded Newt Gingrich in summer 1996 to separate the welfare and Medicaid issues and present President Clinton with a welfare bill, which he signed 14 weeks before the election; he can reasonably claim to be one of the fathers of the 1996 welfare reform.

Reid in his feisty way attacked Ensign harshly as an "extremist" who called environmentalists "socialists," and would gut Social Security. "You send Ensign to the Senate, you send nuclear waste to Nevada," he proclaimed. Ensign responded, "Does Reid think that Dick Bryan is going to give up the fight? Bryan's a Democrat who works with Republicans, and I'm a Republican who works with Democrats." He argued that Reid always favors tax cuts in Nevada but votes for higher taxes in the Senate. Reid called Clinton's conduct "immoral"; Ensign called on Clinton to resign. But Reid, father of five and grandfather of six, was able to build on this issue with an ad showing his wife saying, "For me, Harry Reid's greatest accomplishment is being a devoted husband and father who helped raise five exceptional children. His being a senator is great, but having the love and respect of your family is the ultimate accomplishment."

This was Nevada's most expensive Senate campaign ever. Reid put ads up on the air in April 1998, Ensign in May. Eventually they spent $4.9 million and $3.5 million respectively; both were supported by the gaming and mining industries. The League of Conservation Voters and the Sierra Club spent $400,000 on ads to help Reid. The Foundation for Government spent $300,000 against Reid because of his opposition to triple-trailer trucks. The AFL-CIO ran a "ground war" campaign costing perhaps $300,000. That in many observers' views made the difference; but anything makes the difference in such a close race: Reid believes he won because of his inroads into Republican votes in Reno and Washoe County, because of his work on local projects; he lost the usually Republican area by only 48%–46%. Ensign did better in the Cow Counties, winning 59%–36%. In Las Vegas's Clark County, both candidates' home base, Reid won 53%–44%. The election night tally showed Reid ahead by 459 votes; Ensign called for a recount, and it turned out that the Washoe County ballots had been misprinted, preventing some from being read by machines. The hand count there took weeks, and Ensign finally conceded December 9, with Reid ahead by 428 votes. Whether Reid will have another tough race in 2004 is anyone's guess: Nevada will probably have changed again, in ways that aren't predictable. In the meantime he remains a formidable member of the Senate.

Junior Senator. Senator Richard Bryan was first elected in 1988 and has held elective office most of his adult life. He grew up in Las Vegas, was a deputy district attorney in Clark County; in 1964, at 27, he became the county's first public defender. In 1968 he was elected to the Assembly (the same year as Harry Reid), in 1972 to the state Senate. In 1978 he was elected attorney general; in 1982 he defeated incumbent Governor Robert List, and in 1986 was re-elected. In 1988 he defeated Senator Chic Hecht by 50%–46% after Hecht had failed to stop the law declaring Yucca Mountain as the nation's permanent nuclear waste disposal site.

Bryan combines a moderate-to-liberal voting record with an aggressive pursuit of particular causes. He has dissented from other Democrats on key issues, like the Gulf war resolution in 1991 and the Clinton budget and tax increase in 1993. His special causes include telemarketing fraud, on which he sponsored a law in his first term, and auto safety; his amendment required air bags in every new car. He was not able to raise the CAFE (Corporate Average Fuel Economy) standards on automakers to 40 miles per gallon by 2001. He was successful in eliminating the mohair subsidy and NASA's Search for Extraterrestrial Intelligence. He has sponsored fair credit reporting and toy labeling legislation; he proposed killing ATM surcharges on non-depositors. In contrast to most intermountain senators, he opposes building new logging roads in national forests and struggled to cut or eliminate them several times; he was moved to do so by observing the continuing damage of logging roads from the clear-cutting in forests around Lake Tahoe of the 19th Century. With John McCain, he co-sponsored a bill to regulate boxer-promoter relations in boxing. Perhaps his most visible moment was as chairman of the Ethics Committee in 1993 and 1994, when he conducted the investigation of Bob Packwood and led the successful fight for access to his diaries; Packwood resigned in fall 1995.

Bryan naturally looks out for Nevada interests. He is opposed to any further federal regulation of gaming, and has been a constant critic of the federal commission on gambling, demanding a GAO audit in October 1998: "There has been an exodus of personnel, and now the commission is changing policy and saying it does not have to comply with the open meeting law." He has called for reform of the Indian Gaming Act and co-sponsored the 1998 law that outlawed Internet gambling. Also in October 1998 he placed in the omnibus budget a measure giving jackpot or lottery winners the option of taking their winnings in a lump sum; this would save casinos and states the administrative costs of long payoffs and would give the federal government $1.3 billion extra revenue in four years. In February 1998, on the Aviation Subcommittee, he called for hearings on why Las Vegas Airport was not getting more flights when the number of hotel rooms was shooting up. In October 1998 he pushed through the Senate a law requiring the Bureau of Land Management to auction off 20,000 acres in the Las Vegas Valley; this will provide land for development in North Las Vegas and a cargo airport near the California line, and 10% of the proceeds will go to local pipelines and water treatment plants and 5% to Clark County schools.

But most important, he strongly opposes any nuclear waste disposal site, permanent or temporary, at Yucca Mountain or at the Nevada Test Site. "They want a toilet to flush their nuclear waste down," he says of the opposition. "And that toilet is Nevada." In July 1996 Bryan and Harry Reid filibustered the bill for a temporary disposal site; although cloture was voted, 65–34, and the bill passed, 63–37, it lacked the two-thirds vote necessary to overcome a promised Clinton veto, and it was not voted on in the House. The battle continued, as the Senate in April 1997 mandated the temporary depository at the Nevada Test Site, next to Yucca Mountain. But that bill got 65 votes, two short of a veto override, and Speaker Newt Gingrich pulled it from the calendar in June 1998 to help the Senate campaign of Congressman John Ensign. The battle is sure to continue into 1999 and perhaps 2000.

Bryan was re-elected in 1994 by the comfortable but not overwhelming margin of 51%–41%. He entered the 2000 cycle as the clear favorite; Ensign, the loser by just 428 votes in his 1998 race against Reid, seemed uninterested in a race against Bryan, whom he counted as a friend. But in February 1999 Bryan announced that he would not run in 2000: "It's time to come home." "This is like a funeral to me," Reid said. But not to Ensign: 25 hours after Bryan's announcement he was in the race. He said that the Republican Senate campaign committee would support him, even against primary opponents. Even so, 2d District Congressman Jim Gibbons and Secretary of State Dean Heller said they might run. On the Democratic side, former Governor Bob Miller, clearly the party's strongest contender, announced in March 1999 that he would not run. Attorney General Frankie Sue Del Papa entered the race in June 1999. Another possibility is Las Vegas Sun publisher Brian Greenspun, a college roommate of Bill Clinton, though he is a registered Republican.

Cook's Call. *Highly Competitive.* When Bryan made his surprising retirement announcement, former Representative John Ensign immediately jumped in the race and was quickly anointed as the Republican favorite. Representative Jim Gibbons has talked about running, but that seems unlikely. On the Democratic side, former Governor Bob Miller passed up the opportunity and attention has turned to Attorney General Frankie Sue Del Papa. Del Papa has some serious problems with organized labor in the state, which gives Ensign a slight edge going into the race.

Presidential politics. In the 1940s, Nevada was a Democratic state; in the 1960s, it was divided much as the nation was, voting narrowly for John Kennedy in 1960 and Richard Nixon in 1968. In the 1980s, it was heavily Republican, over 60% for Ronald Reagan and 59%–38% for George Bush in 1988. If it were bigger, it would have been a key battleground. In the 1990s it voted twice, to the surprise of both sides, for Bill Clinton, 37%–35% in 1992 and 44%–43% in 1996. Undoubtedly his pledge to veto the bill to create a temporary nuclear waste disposal site at the Nevada Test Site made the difference, and could again in 2000.

Nevada's late March presidential primary has attracted little attention; it hopes for more in the Western states primary Friday, March 10.

Congressional districting. Nevada has two congressional districts after the 1980 and 1990 Censuses; the 1st has consisted of most of Clark County, the 2d is the rest of the state. With its rapid growth, Nevada is expected to gain a third seat after the 2000 Census. Clark County would have enough population for two districts, the rest of the state enough for one. One likely scenario is the creation of two safe Clark County seats, one safe Republican and one safe Democratic; the current 1st District changed party hands twice in the 1990s.

The People: Est. Pop. 1998: 1,746,898; Pop. 1990: 1,201,833, up 45.4% 1990–1998. 0.6% of U.S. total, 36th largest; 11.7% rural. Median age: 34.8 years. 11.1% 65 years and over. 84.3% White, 6.5% Black, 3.2% Asian, 1.7% Amer. Indian, 4.3% Other; 10.1% Hispanic Origin. Households: 51.4% married couple families; 23.8% married couple fams. w. children; 47.2% college educ.; median household income: $31,011; per capita income: $15,214; 54.8% owner occupied housing; median house value: $95,700; median monthly rent: $445. 4.3% Unemployment. 1998 Voting age pop.: 1,314,000. 1998 Turnout: 440,042; 33% of VAP. Registered voters (1998): 897,865; 372,219 D (41%), 375,469 R (42%), 150,177 unaffiliated and minor parties (17%).

Political Lineup: Governor, Kenny Guinn (R); Lt. Gov., Lorraine Hunt (R); Secy. of State, Dean Heller (R); Atty. Gen., Frankie Sue Del Papa (D); Controller, Kathy Augustine (R); State Senate, 21 (9 D, 12 R); Majority Leader, William Raggio (R); State Assembly, 42 (28 D, 14 R); Assembly Speaker, Joe Dini (D). Senators, Harry Reid (D) and Richard H. Bryan (D). Representatives, 2 (1 D, 1 R).

Elections Division: 775-684-5705; **Filing Deadline for U.S. Congress:** May 15, 2000.

1996 Presidential Vote

Clinton (D) 203,974 (44%)
Dole (R) 199,244 (43%)
Perot (I) 43,986   (9%)
Others 17,130   (4%)

1996 Republican Presidential Primary

Dole (R) 72,932 (52%)
Forbes (R) 27,063 (19%)
Buchanan (R) 21,321 (15%)
Others 19,321 (15%)

1992 Presidential Vote

Clinton (D) 189,148 (37%)
Bush (R) 175,828 (35%)
Perot (I) 132,580 (26%)

GOVERNOR

Gov. Kenny Guinn (R)

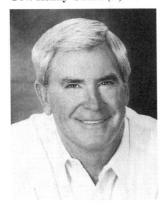

Elected 1998, term expires Jan. 2003; b. Aug. 24, 1936, Garland, TX; home, Las Vegas; Fresno St. U, B.A. 1957, M.A. 1958; Utah St. U., Ph.D. 1970; Non-denominational; married (Dema).

Professional Career: Planning Specialist, Clark Cnty. Schl. Dist., 1964–69; Superintendent, Clark Cnty. Schl. Dist., 1969–78; Nevada Savings & Loan, 1978–80; Pres. & COO, PriMerit Bank, 1980–85; CEO, 1985–87; Pres. & COO Southwest Gas Corp., 1987–93; Chairman & CEO 1988–93; Interim Pres., U.N.L.V., 1994–95.

Office: Executive Chambers, Capitol Bldg., Carson City, 89710, 775-687-5670; Web site: www.state.nv.us.

Election Results

1998 gen.	Kenny Guinn (R)	223,892	(52%)
	Jan Laverty Jones (D)	182,281	(42%)
	Others	27,457	(6%)
1998 prim.	Kenny Guinn (R)	76,953	(58%)
	Aaron Russo (R)	34,251	(26%)
	Lonnie Hammargren (R)	13,410	(10%)
	Others	1,956	(1%)
1994 gen.	Bob Miller (D)	200,026	(53%)
	Jim Gibbons (R)	156,875	(41%)
	Others	22,775	(6%)

SENATORS

Sen. Harry Reid (D)

Elected 1986, seat up 2004; b. Dec. 2, 1939, Searchlight; home, Searchlight; S. UT St. Col., A.S. 1959, UT St. U., B.S. 1961, George Washington U., J.D. 1964, U. of NV, 1969–70; Mormon; married (Landra).

Elected Office: NV Assembly, 1968–70; NV Lt. Gov., 1970–74; U.S. House of Reps., 1982–86.

Professional Career: Practicing atty., 1969–82; Henderson City Atty., 1964–66; Chmn., NV Gaming Comm., 1977–81.

DC Office: 528 HSOB, 20510, 202-224-3542; Fax: 202-224-7327; Web site: www.senate.gov/~reid.

State Offices: Carson City, 775-882-7343; Las Vegas, 702-474-0041; Reno, 775-686-5750.

Committees: *Minority Whip. Aging (Special)* (2d of 9 D). *Appropriations* (8th of 13 D): Energy & Water Development (RMM); Interior; Labor & HHS; Military Construction; Transportation. *Environment & Public Works* (4th of 8 D): Fisheries, Wildlife & Drinking Water (RMM); Transportation & Infrastructure. *Ethics (Select)* (Vice Chmn. of 3 D). *Indian Affairs* (3d of 6 D).

Group Ratings

	ADA	ACLU	AFS	LCV	CON	NTU	NFIB	COC	ACU	NTLC	CHC
1998	90	57	100	63	75	24	44	56	20	11	9
1997	85	—	78	—	32	21	—	50	8	—	—

National Journal Ratings

	1997 LIB — 1997 CONS		1998 LIB — 1998 CONS	
Economic	82% —	12%	65% —	33%
Social	50% —	49%	50% —	48%
Foreign	68% —	27%	73% —	21%

Key Votes of the 105th Congress

1. Bal. Budget Amend.	N	5. Satcher for Surgeon Gen.	Y	9. Chem. Weapons Treaty	Y
2. Clinton Budget Deal	N	6. Highway Set-asides	Y	10. Cuban Humanitarian Aid	N
3. Cloture on Tobacco	Y	7. Table Child Gun locks	Y	11. Table Bosnia Troops	Y
4. Education IRAs	N	8. Ovrd. Part. Birth Veto	Y	12. $ for Test-ban Treaty	Y

Election Results

1998 general	Harry Reid (D)	208,650	(48%)	($4,939,010)
	John Ensign (R)	208,222	(48%)	($3,490,256)
	Others	18,918	(4%)	
1998 primary	Harry Reid (D)	unopposed		
1992 general	Harry Reid (D)	253,150	(51%)	($3,259,802)
	Demar Dahl (R)	199,413	(40%)	($471,371)
	Others	43,333	(9%)	

Sen. Richard H. Bryan (D)

Elected 1988, seat up 2000; b. July 16, 1937, Washington, D.C.; home, Carson City; U. of NV, B.A. 1959; U. of CA Hastings Col. of Law., LL.B. 1963; Episcopalian; married (Bonnie).

Military Career: Army, 1959–60.

Elected Office: NV Assembly, 1968–72; NV Senate, 1972–78; NV Atty. Gen., 1978–82; NV Gov., 1982–88.

Professional Career: Clark Cnty. Dpty. Dist. Atty., 1964–66; Clark Cnty. Public Defender, 1966–68; Cnsl., Clark Cnty. Juvenile Court, 1968–69.

DC Office: 269 RSOB, 20510, 202-224-6244; Fax: 202-224-1867; Web site: www.senate.gov/~bryan.

State Offices: Carson City, 775-885-9111; Las Vegas, 702-388-6605; Reno, 775-686-5770.

Committees: *Aging (Special)* (7th of 9 D). *Banking, Housing & Urban Affairs* (4th of 9 D): Financial Institutions (RMM); Housing & Transportation; Securities. *Commerce, Science & Transportation* (6th of 9 D): Aviation; Consumer Affairs, Foreign Commerce & Tourism (RMM); Manufacturing & Competitiveness; Surface Transportation & Merchant Marine. *Finance* (7th of 9 D): Health Care; Long-Term Growth & Debt Reduction; Taxation & IRS Oversight. *Intelligence* (2d of 8 D).

Group Ratings

	ADA	ACLU	AFS	LCV	CON	NTU	NFIB	COC	ACU	NTLC	CHC
1998	95	86	100	75	42	13	44	50	8	11	9
1997	70	—	44	—	93	48	—	70	4	—	—

National Journal Ratings

	1997 LIB — 1997 CONS			1998 LIB — 1998 CONS		
Economic	60%	—	36%	90%	—	0%
Social	71%	—	0%	63%	—	26%
Foreign	68%	—	27%	91%	—	5%

Key Votes of the 105th Congress

1. Bal. Budget Amend.	Y	5. Satcher for Surgeon Gen.	Y	9. Chem. Weapons Treaty	Y
2. Clinton Budget Deal	Y	6. Highway Set-asides	Y	10. Cuban Humanitarian Aid	N
3. Cloture on Tobacco	Y	7. Table Child Gun locks	Y	11. Table Bosnia Troops	Y
4. Education IRAs	N	8. Ovrd. Part. Birth Veto	N	12. $ for Test-ban Treaty	Y

Election Results

1994 general	Richard H. Bryan (D)	193,804	(51%)	($3,021,834)
	Hal Furman (R)	156,020	(41%)	($845,340)
	Others	30,706	(8%)	
1994 primary	Richard H. Bryan (D)	unopposed		
1988 general	Richard H. Bryan (D)	175,548	(50%)	($2,957,789)
	Jacob (Chic) Hecht (R)	161,336	(46%)	($3,007,864)

FIRST DISTRICT

Nevada's congressional districts, nearly identical in 1990 population, differ vastly in physical size; the 1st consists of Las Vegas and its close-in suburbs; the 2d covers everything else, the other 99.8% of Nevada's land mass. The 1st, something like a nervously drawn circle in the center of Clark County, takes in all of Las Vegas, most of Henderson, part of heavily black

North Las Vegas and just a bit of the Las Vegas Colony Indian Reservation. It also includes most of the Democratic precincts in the state.

The congresswoman from the 1st District is Shelley Berkley, a Democrat elected by a narrower than expected margin in 1998. Berkley moved to Las Vegas at 11; her father worked at the Sands, and rose to maitre d'; she waited tables and was a keno runner as she made her way through University of Nevada at Las Vegas, where she was student body president, and the University of San Diego Law School. "My roots in this community run very, very deep," she says, and she has worked for many of its major institutions. She was chairman of the Nevada Hotel and Motel Associations, government and business affairs vice president at the Sands, in-house counsel at Southwest Gas (of which Governor Kenny Guinn was once chief executive). She was elected to one term in the state House, in 1982, and in 1990 was appointed to the University of Nevada Board of Regents by Governor Bob Miller. After Republican Congressman John Ensign was re-elected in 1996 by only 50%–44% after spending $1.9 million (he has lots of local connections too), she decided to run for the 1st District seat. In September 1997 House Democratic Leader Dick Gephardt endorsed her and promised her a seat on Ways and Means. Brassy, direct, effusive, she seemed headed for victory after Ensign decided to run against Senator Harry Reid.

Indeed, Republicans lacked a serious candidate until filing day in May 1998. Then Lieutenant Governor Lonnie Hammargren ran for governor instead of Congress (he got 10% in the Republican primary), and 15 minutes before the deadline Judge Donald Chairez, who had switched his registration to Republican, resigned his post and filed for the seat. A newcomer to Nevada (he moved there in 1990), he was known for ruling that smut peddlers on the Strip were trespassing and for stopping the redevelopment agency from seizing a small business to turn it over to a big casino. He quit in the middle of the high-profile trial of Jeremy Strohmeyer, accused of killing a seven-year-old, in which he excluded illegally seized evidence from the man's personal computer. Then in June 1998 came a bombshell. The *Las Vegas Review-Journal* reported on tapes of Berkley's May 1997 telephone conversations to a friend and texts of a memo Berkley sent the Sands' owner, Sheldon Adelson in 1996, when he was seeking approvals for his Venetian mega-hotel. They showed her advising him to make campaign contributions to local judges to curry favor, to grant Clark County Commissioner Yvonne Atkinson Gates a daiquiri concession and to hire the uncle of County Commissioner Erin Kenny in the hopes of getting their votes for approval. "Those suggestions were at best unethical and at worst illegal," said the Sands' President Bill Weidner, and Adelson fired Berkley in May 1997. Berkley quickly apologized, and the Clark County District Attorney saw no cause for prosecution. But Chairez made his slogan, "Fairness not favors!" And the Republicans' campaign committee eventually ran six ads featuring the charges. Both candidates easily won their primaries. But Berkley's margins in public polls slipped from 41%–27% in June to 44%–40% in mid-October.

Berkley raised other issues, arguing for affordable college tuition, adequate classrooms and computers; both candidates supported the gaming industry and opposed the temporary nuclear depository near Yucca Mountain. The Democrats' campaign committees, ran ads criticizing Chairez's exclusionary ruling in the Strohmeyer case and in a second case; on the first Chairez said he was bound by the law, and on the second many lawyers said he was bound by a plea bargain agreement. Berkley also hit him for being subject to liens for not paying taxes more than ten years ago. With strong support from the gaming industry, she outspent him by $1.2 million to $554,000. She won more narrowly, by 49%–46%.

In Washington Berkley was elected vice president of the Democratic freshman class. But she did not get the promised seat on Ways and Means; Democrats had only one vacancy and it went to Lloyd Doggett of Texas. She serves on the Transportation and Infrastructure, Veterans' Affairs, and Small Business committees. In March 1999, Berkley married Larry Lehrner.

Cook's Call. *Highly Competitive.* Berkley's narrow win in 1998, and the fact that Republicans are likely to put up a top tier challenger to face her in 2000, virtually guarantees that this district will be on top of the Republican target list. But, after a shaky 1998, Berkley looks to have shored herself up well. Her proven fundraising ability and the Democratic lean of this district will also help to give her an edge in 2000.

The People: Pop. 1990: 601,042; 0.1% rural; 11.5% age 65 + ; 79.6% White, 10.5% Black, 3.7% Asian, 0.9% Amer. Indian, 5.3% Other; 11.8% Hispanic Origin. Households: 47.6% married couple families; 21.4% married couple fams. w. children; 43.7% college educ.; median household income: $29,611; per capita income: $14,837; median house value: $89,300; median gross rent: $449.

1996 Presidential Vote			1992 Presidential Vote		
Clinton (D)	91,307	(51%)	Clinton (D)	98,700	(43%)
Dole (R)	65,990	(37%)	Bush (R)	70,440	(31%)
Perot (I)	15,949	(9%)	Perot (I)	55,964	(24%)
Others	5,811	(3%)			

Rep. Shelley Berkley (D)

Elected 1998; b. Jan. 20, 1951, South Fallsburg, NY; home, Las Vegas; U.N.L.V., B.A. 1972; U. of San Diego Law Schl., J.D. 1976; Jewish; married (Larry Lehrner).

Elected Office: NV Assembly, 1982–84; Regent, U. Commun. Col. System of NV, 1990–98.

Professional Career: Cnsl., SW Gas Corp., 1977–82; VP, Sands Hotel, 1989–98; Chair, NV Hotel & Motel Assn., 1994.

DC Office: 1505 LHOB 20515, 202-225-5965; Fax: 202-225-3119; Web site: www.house.gov/berkley.

District Office: Las Vegas, 702-220-9823.

Committees: *Small Business* (17th of 17 D). *Transportation & Infrastructure* (34th of 34 D): Ground Transportation; Oversight, Investigations & Emergency Management. *Veterans' Affairs* (12th of 14 D): Benefits.

Group Ratings and Key Votes: Newly Elected

Election Results

1998 general	Shelley Berkley (D)	79,315	(49%)	($1,295,091)
	Don Chairez (R)	73,540	(46%)	($554,983)
	Others	8,227	(5%)	
1998 primary	Shelley Berkley (D)	34,120	(81%)	
	Clay Baty (D)	7,758	(19%)	
1996 general	John Ensign (R)	86,472	(50%)	($1,904,413)
	Bob Coffin (D)	75,081	(44%)	($592,726)
	Others	11,040	(6%)	

SECOND DISTRICT

Nevada's 2d Congressional District is the more Republican of Nevada's two districts. It includes all of the state except the urban core of Las Vegas. With 99.8% of the state's land area, it is the nation's third largest district in area; with 1.1 million people, it is one of the nation's most populous. Since the 1990 Census, Las Vegas area subdivisions have been sprouting up in what was desert land in the 2d District's portion of Clark County; there may be more people (though there are not yet more voters) in the 2d District's portion of Clark County than in all of Reno's Washoe County. Reno itself is growing, though not so rapidly; historically, it was the more

Republican of Nevada's two cities, though today in some races it votes much the same. The Cow Counties, sparsely populated, with more than 80% of their land owned by the federal government, are heavily Republican.

The congressman from the 2d District is Jim Gibbons, a Republican elected in 1996. Gibbons grew up near Reno, went to the University of Nevada and served in the Air Force in Vietnam. He went to law school and has practiced law, but he also was a mining geologist, a hydrologist and a pilot for Delta and Western Airlines and became vice commander of the Nevada Air National Guard. In 1988 he was elected to the Assembly; in 1990 he was called up to active duty in the Gulf war. While he was flying unarmed air reconnaissance missions, his wife was taking his place in the legislature. After his celebrated return, he proposed a tax initiative to require a two-thirds supermajority to raise any state tax; it passed with more than 70% of the votes in 1994 and by 1996 became law. In 1994 Gibbons ran for governor. He beat Secretary of State Cheryl Lau 52%–32% in the primary, but lost the general to Bob Miller, 53%–41%.

In 1996, after Congresswoman Barbara Vucanovich retired, Gibbons ran for the seat. He had serious competition in the primary from Lau, who returned from more than a year as counsel to the U.S. House, and Patty Cafferata, former state treasurer and Vucanovich's daughter. Gibbons carried the Reno area and Las Vegas suburbs to win with 42%, to 24% each for Lau and Cafferata. Meanwhile, in the Democratic primary, former state senator and former head of the state Ethics Commission Spike Wilson beat former Mustang Ranch brothel worker Jessi Winchester 62%–21%. In the general Gibbons won solidly, 59%–35%.

Gibbons has said, "Nevadans are a fiercely proud citizenry who believe they know more about the education of their children than Washington does, that they know how to solve their problems, whether it's crime, pollution or what have you, than Washington." He serves on the Resources Committee, where he opposes what he regards as federal intrusion on local rights. He has sponsored bills to allow Clark County to buy two different sites, one near Jean and the other near Mesquite, to build a new cargo airport, and he has tried to allow Elko and Winnemucca to buy surrounding federal lands. He strongly opposes the permanent nuclear depository at Yucca Mountain and the proposed temporary depository next door at the Nevada Test Site—both in the district. He strongly supports the gaming industry, and with John Ensign proposed a bill to stop the IRS from taxing free meals eaten by gaming employees, and he opposed the Interior Department plan to allow the Interior secretary to approve Indian casinos without the consent of the states. When an investigation of gaming contributions was threatened, he said, "The gaming industry has been wrongfully targeted as a scapegoat for the debate on campaign finance reform. These accusations are personally biased—and they are dead wrong."

In 1998 Gibbons was re-elected with no Democratic opposition, even as his wife Dawn Gibbons was again elected to the legislature. But his campaign to win a seat on Ways and Means did not succeed. In 1997 he was mentioned as a candidate for senator or governor in 1998, but he ran for neither office; the 1st District's John Ensign ran against Senator Harry Reid and lost by 428 votes. In early 1999, even after Ensign announced for the Senate seat Richard Bryan is vacating, Gibbons reserved the possibility of running for senator this time. Redistricting will change this seat considerably after the 2002 Census; Nevada is likely to gain a seat, and most likely Clark County will have two seats and the rest of the state will make up one.

Cook's Call. *Safe.* There are rumblings that Gibbons may give up the 2d District in a quest for the open Senate seat of Richard Bryan. Whether or not Gibbons ultimately takes that step, this district will stay in Republican hands.

The People: Pop. 1990: 600,791; 23.2% rural; 10.6% age 65 +; 89% White, 2.6% Black, 2.6% Asian, 2.5% Amer. Indian, 3.4% Other; 8.4% Hispanic Origin. Households: 55.2% married couple families; 26.2% married couple fams. w. children; 50.9% college educ.; median household income: $32,413; per capita income: $15,592; median house value: $104,100; median gross rent: $439.

1996 Presidential Vote

Dole (R)	133,254	(47%)
Clinton (D)	112,667	(39%)
Perot (I)	28,037	(10%)
Others	11,319	(4%)

1992 Presidential Vote

Bush (R)	105,388	(38%)
Clinton (D)	90,448	(33%)
Perot (I)	76,616	(28%)

Rep. Jim Gibbons (R)

Elected 1996; b. Dec. 16, 1944, Sparks; home, Reno; U. of NV, B.S. 1967, M.S. 1973, Southwestern U., J.D. 1979; Protestant; married (Dawn).

Military Career: Air Force, 1967–71 (Vietnam), NV Air Natl. Guard, 1975–95 (Persian Gulf).

Elected Office: NV Assembly, 1988–94.

Professional Career: Pilot, Western Airlines, 1979–87, Delta Airlines, 1987–96.

DC Office: 100 CHOB 20515, 202-225-6155; Fax: 202-225-5679; Web site: www.house.gov/gibbons.

District Offices: Elko, 775-777-7920; Las Vegas, 702-255-1615; Reno, 775-686-5760.

Committees: *Armed Services* (27th of 32 R): Military Procurement; Military Readiness. *Permanent Select Committee on Intelligence* (7th of 9 R): Human Intelligence, Analysis & Counterintelligence; Technical & Tactical Intelligence. *Resources* (22d of 28 R): Energy & Mineral Resources; National Parks & Public Lands. *Veterans' Affairs* (15th of 17 R): Benefits.

Group Ratings

	ADA	ACLU	AFS	LCV	CON	NTU	NFIB	COC	ACU	NTLC	CHC
1998	20	19	22	8	2	52	100	89	92	92	82
1997	0	—	14	—	42	61	—	80	91	—	—

National Journal Ratings

	1997 LIB — 1997 CONS			1998 LIB — 1998 CONS		
Economic	33%	—	67%	23%	—	74%
Social	43%	—	57%	38%	—	60%
Foreign	20%	—	79%	27%	—	68%

Key Votes of the 105th Congress

1. Clinton Budget Deal	Y	5. Puerto Rico Sthood. Ref.	N	9. Cut $ for B-2 Bombers	N
2. Education IRAs	Y	6. End Highway Set-asides	N	10. Human Rights in China	Y
3. Req. 2/3 to Raise Taxes	Y	7. School Prayer Amend.	Y	11. Withdraw Bosnia Troops	Y
4. Fast-track Trade	N	8. Ovrd. Part. Birth Veto	Y	12. End Cuban TV-Marti	Y

Election Results

1998 general	Jim Gibbons (R)	201,623	(81%)	($236,465)
	Christopher Horne (AI)	20,738	(8%)	
	Louis R. Tomburello (Lib)	18,561	(7%)	
	Others	7,841	(3%)	
1998 primary	Jim Gibbons (R)	unopposed		
1996 general	Jim Gibbons (R)	162,310	(59%)	($724,036)
	Thomas (Spike) Wilson (D)	97,742	(35%)	($606,227)
	Others	17,140	(6%)	

NEW HAMPSHIRE

New Hampshire, in an odd corner of the country, with four-tenths of 1% of the nation's population, with unusual public policies—now in flux—has done more to change the political course of the country, perhaps even the world, over the last 20 years than any similarly-sized unit anywhere. The lever by which this small state moves the world is New Hampshire's first-in-the-nation presidential primary, a device first contested in the 1950s, then sanctioned by Democratic reformers in the 1970s, and exploited by Republicans in the 1980s. For good reason, George Bush ended his victory speech in November 1988 by saying, "Thank you, New Hampshire." But New Hampshire did not say, "You're welcome," when the recession of 1990–91 sent real estate values plunging and unemployment rising: Bush saw Pat Buchanan win 38% against him in the primary and then saw his vote fall from 63% in 1988 to 37% in November 1992—his biggest drop in the nation. Bill Clinton, who treated his 1992 second-place primary finish here as a victory ("the comeback kid!"), solidified his hold on New Hampshire in 1996, as Democrat Jeanne Shaheen was elected governor and, two years later, Democrats won control of the state Senate. New Hampshire, long a leader in the move against taxes and for less government, now seems to be moving in a different direction—or is it?

In a country that prides itself on its feistiness and freedom from outside direction, New Hampshire has always been even feistier and less fettered by authority. Before the Revolutionary War, New Hampshire was almost an outlaw colony, its great fortunes made by poachers in the king's forests and smugglers avoiding taxes. It was the first colony with an independent government and was fighting the British before the Minutemen stood at Lexington and Concord. In this environment, 19th Century entrepreneurs built textile mills along fast-flowing rivers; the Amoskeag Mills in Manchester, lining the Merrimack River for a mile, were once the largest cotton mills on the globe, employing 17,000 people and producing enough cloth every two months to put a band around the world. Around the mills grew a city of red brick dormitories and three-family frame houses filled with immigrants from Quebec, Ireland, Poland and Greece, set down amid dirt-roaded villages of flinty Yankee farmers and mechanics. New Hampshire held to its traditions of local government and little external control, and for years its refusal to join most other states and enact an income or sales tax, or to provide statewide guidance of schools and social services, seemed to doom it to continued backwardness.

Low taxes proved to be New Hampshire's fortune. Starting in the 1960s, New Hampshire has had the fastest growth on the East Coast, attracting businesses from Massachusetts and other high-tax states. It became a location of choice for entrepreneurs and high-tech innovators, attracting an increasing number of people skeptical of government programs. From 1965–97, Massachusetts grew from 5.5 million to 6.1 million, up 11%; New Hampshire grew from 676,000 to 1,173,000, up 742%. The bedraggled New Hampshire of 50 years ago, of poor Yankee farmers and French Canadian mill hands, has largely disappeared, and in its place one of the nation's most prosperous economic communities has arisen. This "Nouvelle Hampshire," to use *Washington Post* writer Henry Allen's term, has none of the architectural purity of Amoskeag: its shopping centers and new subdivisions have a slap-dash, half-built look, as if there were no time for details in the hurry to build.

In the late 1980s, New Hampshire was producing more jobs per capita than any other state and fabulous increases in real estate value; descendants of Amoskeag mill hands and stone-poor farmers found themselves with high-income jobs and perhaps even substantial wealth, property and interests in businesses worth hundreds of thousands of dollars. Then the recession of the early 1990s hit New Hampshire especially hard. In retrospect, it seems plain that New Hampshire priced itself out of the growth market: its giddily high real estate prices kept out

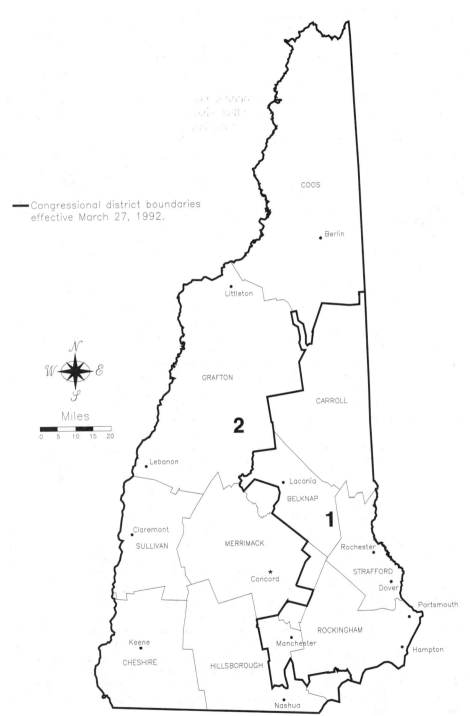

Congressional district boundaries
effective March 27, 1992.

COOS

• Berlin

Littleton

GRAFTON

N
W · E
S

Miles
0   5   10 15 20

2

• Lebanon

CARROLL

• Laconia
BELKNAP

1

• Claremont
SULLIVAN

MERRIMACK

Rochester

STRAFFORD

Dover

★
Concord

Portsmouth

Keene •

ROCKINGHAM

Manchester

Hampton

CHESHIRE

HILLSBOROUGH

Nashua

the new workers its businesses needed to continue expanding. For a moment New Hampshire led the nation in new welfare cases and personal bankruptcies. Property taxes doubled over four years, and the state government faced a fiscal crunch relieved only by Medicaid accounting legerdemain. Thousands of jobs disappeared; real estate prices crashed so that ordinary people lost not only short-term income but long-term wealth. But by the mid-1990s growth returned again, though not as frenzied as in the decades before. Jobs grew by 2.6% in 1996 and 1997; unemployment in fall 1998 was 2.4%. New Hampshire has the smallest percentage of people living in poverty out of any state, 6.9% in 1995, according to a Census study released in 1999; the national average is 13.8%.

The low taxes that spurred New Hampshire's growth would probably have been raised in the late 1960s or early 1970s, as they were in so many states at the time, but for the far from gentle advocacy of the Manchester *Union Leader* and its owner William Loeb. The *Union Leader* insisted that governors and legislators "take the pledge" to vote for no sales or income tax and, from 1972 on, almost all did. That meant keeping education and welfare as local responsibilities and holding down spending. At the same time, New Hampshire boasted the highest SAT scores in the country and had the brainpower to participate fully in New England's high-tech boom for most of the 1980s: The old Amoskeag Mills were converted to offices, and once grimy Manchester is now a high-tech center. The state also ranked 48th in violent crime and 49th in births to teenage mothers. New Hampshire is an anomaly in another fashion: In May 1999, it was the last state to approve a holiday in honor of Martin Luther King, Jr.

Translating New Hampshire's penchant for low taxes into a national political force was its presidential primary. First in the nation since 1920, it first listed candidates' names in 1952, at which point it started attracting the nation's eye—and has never lost it. That year Estes Kefauver beat Harry Truman, who promptly announced he would not run again, and Dwight Eisenhower beat "Mr. Republican," Robert Taft. For the next 40 years, no one won a presidential election without winning the New Hampshire primary first—until Bill Clinton lost to Paul Tsongas in 1992. The New Hampshire primary has played other roles, hurting front-runners by giving them fewer votes than expected (Barry Goldwater in 1964, Lyndon Johnson in 1968, Edmund Muskie in 1972, Walter Mondale in 1984, Bob Dole in 1996) and propelling little-known or little-considered candidates into the national spotlight (Henry Cabot Lodge in 1964, Eugene McCarthy in 1968, George McGovern in 1972, Gary Hart in 1984, Paul Tsongas and Pat Buchanan in 1992). But a common motif in most of these surprises was an aversion to high-tax candidates. Ronald Reagan won his smashing victory here in 1980 not just by one-upping the other candidates at a debate, by saying "I paid for this microphone," but because he favored the Kemp-Roth tax cut; George Bush won in 1988 when Bob Dole refused to take the pledge not to raise taxes. By 1996 all serious candidates were abjuring any tax increase: New Hampshire had won its battle against 20th Century statism.

But in the 1990s New Hampshire's political influence has become less unidirectional. In 1992, feeling the full force of the recession, New Hampshire was an island of angry discontent. George Bush, by breaking his "read my lips" pledge and joining Democrats to raise taxes just as the economy was about to decline, seemed to have betrayed his promise to New Hampshire. When he returned to the state in January 1992 to read off a card, "Message: I care," he was in deep trouble. Pat Buchanan challenged Bush in the primary, with full-throated support from the *Union Leader*, attacking him for raising taxes and (after he was moved by meeting unemployed workers) not putting up trade barriers to protect American jobs. Buchanan held him to an unimpressive 53%–37% win, then harried him for months; Ross Perot joined the attack and Bill Clinton overcame his scandal problems enough to be a serious challenger. New Hampshire Republicans rallied to hold other offices: Judd Gregg was elected senator by 48%–45% and Steven Merrill beat pro-tax-increase Deborah "Arnie" Arnesen 56%–40%. But New Hampshire had shown that it preferred a Democrat who would tinker and experiment with the economy to a Republican who would not.

That mood was not evanescent. In 1994 New Hampshire seemed to return to normal Republicanism, with a strong re-election win for Merrill (this state and next-door Vermont are the last with two-year terms for governors) and increasing Republican majorities in the legislature (the state House, with 400 members, is the world's largest legislature after the British House of Commons, the Indian Lok Sabha and the U.S. House of Representatives and legislators are paid only $100 a year). But in 1996, as Republican candidates were debating in the studio of Manchester's Channel 9, the state's only commercial TV station, George Stephanopoulos was spinning the press in a side room ("the President has kept the promises he meant to keep") and Clinton was running way ahead in New Hampshire polls. In November Clinton easily carried the state and Senator Bob Smith and Republicans in the two congressional districts came very close to losing (indeed, Smith was behind in the VNS exit poll). Democrat Jeanne Shaheen was easily elected as governor—after taking the pledge early on. Two years later Republicans did better in congressional elections, but Shaheen won resoundingly and Democrats won control of the state Senate. New Hampshire, having made the politics of Ronald Reagan possible in the 1980s, made the politics of Bill Clinton possible in the 1990s, across the country and at home.

The state Supreme Court in December 1997 ruled New Hampshire's school financing system unconstitutional because it leaves some districts with less taxable resources than others (the state provides only 10% of funding) and gave the state an April 1, 1999, deadline for coming up with a new system—a decision that ignores educational results and accepts the assumption that fairness in education can be determined solely by the amount of dollars spent. Though Shaheen struggled to keep her pledge, the need for much larger state funding moved reluctant politicians toward a statewide income, sales or property tax, or some combination thereof. Both the House and Senate dickered over different versions of an income tax as the April deadline passed. Finally on April 29, both houses of the legislature passed a compromise plan calling for $825 million in school funding based on a statewide property tax, and increases in business, cigarette and property sales taxes, and a new tax on rental cars. While this may have broken her pledge of no new broad-based tax, it did not include an income tax, and she thus signed the bill.

Governor. Like many in New Hampshire politics, Governor Jeanne Shaheen, elected in 1996 and 1998, is from somewhere else: She was born in Missouri, went to college in Pennsylvania and graduate school in Mississippi. She moved to New Hampshire in 1973, taught school, ran a silver and leather business with her husband and got into politics. She worked in Jimmy Carter's campaigns in 1976 and 1980 and managed Gary Hart's campaign here in 1984—three winners in a row. In 1990 she ran for the state Senate and served three terms. There she worked on New Hampshire's pioneering effort to open up electric utilities to competition and sponsored health care laws—stabilizing insurance rates, barring rejection for pre-existing conditions, and trying to stop managed care insurers from denying access to physicians of choice. She sought to spend more on higher education and fought to create the first state-sponsored industrial research center.

In April 1996 Republican Governor Steve Merrill announced he was not running, and Shaheen decided to seek the office. Up through the September primary, most eyes were on rival Republicans—1st District Congressman Bill Zeliff, an economic-issues conservative, and state Board of Education Chairman Ovide Lamontagne, strongly against abortion and endorsed by the Manchester *Union Leader*. They were old rivals: four years before Zeliff beat Lamontagne 50%–35% in a House primary. But this time, after a petition-signature dispute knocked Zeliff off the ballot temporarily, Lamontagne won 47%–43%, largely from his margin in Manchester.

Shaheen suited much better the mood of a contented, pro-incumbent year. "I think most people would agree I'm less confrontational than some of my predecessors have been." She took the anti-tax pledge and campaigned for expanding kindergarten (only 119 of 154 New Hampshire school districts have them), cutting electric rates through deregulation and promoting tourism. As Clinton was carrying the state 49%–39%, Shaheen won 57%–40%.

New Hampshire now has a woman governor, plus a woman speaker, Republican Donna

Sytek; altogether 32% of the state's legislators are women. In 1997 Shaheen bargained with the legislature and increased kindergarten aid from $500 to $750 per pupil; she also signed a needle exchange pilot program (but no community asked for the money) and a gay rights measure; she pleased teachers' unions by vetoing teacher tenure reform and limited school vouchers.

Shaheen's greatest problem was the state Supreme Court decision in the Claremont cases outlawing local-based school financing. The court in December 1993 and again in December 1997 ruled against the state. The next month Shaheen proposed an "ABC" funding reform, with a statewide property tax rate and supplemental aid for districts unable to meet state-determined minimum costs from their own tax bases; the money would come from taxes on video slot machines at race tracks and a 23 cent tobacco tax increase. Most Republicans were opposed and called for a constitutional amendment to overturn the Claremont ruling; but they could never get the three-fifths necessary in the state House to get the issue on the ballot. Speaker Sytek proposed to delay ABC a year and temporarily increase state aid by $50 million; Shaheen accepted a delay for a $95 million figure. In May the state Senate requested an advisory opinion from the state Supreme Court and in June the court said ABC was unconstitutional. In November 1998, after Shaheen was re-elected, the Supreme Court restated its April 1, 1999 deadline for legislative change and said that local school property taxes would afterwards be illegal. The obvious effect, and perhaps the intent, was to force a statewide tax, although at least 60% of voters oppose any of the three proposed—income, sales, property. But Shaheen had taken the pledge again in 1998, and in March 1999 promised to veto any plan that included a state income tax. In late April 1999 the state House and Senate finally agreed on a compromise plan which did include a statewide property tax and other tax increases—but no income tax—and Shaheen signed it within hours.

New Hampshire Republicans had a typically vigorously contested primary, as if the nomination were as tantamount to victory as it once was. Jay Lucas, a management consultant with an impressive resume and considerable wealth, spent $941,000 to win the primary by 34%–31%, over state Senator James Rubens, the prime sponsor of the teacher tenure and school voucher bills Shaheen vetoed. Lucas called for major tax and spending cuts and said Shaheen had broken her promise on electric deregulation. She replied that his economic plan was "reckless" and would require cuts in Meals on Wheels, while claiming credit for "16,000 new jobs, more public kindergarten, new protections from HMOs . . . and no broad-based taxes." All of this was partly financed by putative presidential candidates, who are happy to contribute to New Hampshire campaigns at all levels. In happy, prosperous times, with a consensus-minded governor who said things like, "no one party has a lock on the best answers," this was no contest. Shaheen won 66%–31%.

Democrats also converted a 9–15 deficit in the state Senate to a 13–11 majority, although incoming Senate President Clesson Blaisdell promised to maintain bipartisan traditions. On the House side, it took Sytek four ballots to be re-elected. All looks sunny for Shaheen, except the school finance issue. Beyond that, she has good choices for continued service: she could run for governor again in 2000; she could play a major role in Al Gore's campaign (her husband is organizing Gore's New Hampshire effort) and get a plum job if he wins; she could run for Senator Bob Smith's seat in 2002.

Cook's Call. *Probably Safe.* Shaheen had been riding an unprecedented wave of popularity until the state Supreme Court ruled unconstitutional the Granite State's property tax-based method of financing schools. No major Republican challenger has stepped in as of yet to challenge her, but she could be vulnerable because of the school funding issue.

Senior Senator. Senator Bob Smith grew up in New Jersey, worked his way through college, then served in the Navy, including a year in the Gulf of Tonkin. He moved to Wolfeboro, New Hampshire, taught high school history and coached baseball, then managed Yankee Pedlar Real Estate. In 1980 he ran for the House and lost the primary; in 1982 he ran and lost the general 55%–45%; in 1984 he ran again, won the four-candidate primary with 42% and beat Democrat

Dudley Dudley 59%–40%. In 1990, when Senator Gordon Humphrey honored a promise to retire after 12 years, Smith won the Republican nomination over a pro-choicer, 65%–29%, and in the general beat feisty former (1975–80) Senator John Durkin, who attacked the big oil companies as he had in the 1970s and called for $10 billion in new spending programs. Smith won 65%–32%.

In the Senate Smith has one of the most conservative voting records and has taken on a variety of issues. In 1991 he became vice chairman of the Select Committee on POW/MIA Affairs, chaired by Massachusetts Senator John Kerry, also a Vietnam veteran; in 1993 Smith signed the final report concluding that there was "no compelling evidence" that POWs or MIAs left behind in Vietnam are now in Southeast Asia, but the investigation brought to light disturbing evidence that some may have been left behind and could not rule out the possibility that some are still there against their will. In 1994, he opposed the Clinton Administration's lifting of the economic embargo against Vietnam.

Smith chairs the Superfund subcommittee and has worked on a reauthorization bill for years. He sought to repeal retroactive liability but abandoned that in search of bipartisan compromise. His version in the 105th Congress would have exempted small businesses and municipalities and eliminated joint and several liability for what Smith calls proportional orphan share (you pay for your own pollution, not for that of someone else who once owned the property). But he did not report a bill to the floor until March 1998 and it did not pass. On the Environment Committee, he worked on the Safe Drinking Water Act and the Solid Waste Disposal Act. He sought full funding for the Land and Water Conservation Fund and was a lead sponsor of the North American Wetlands Conservation Act. In the House, Smith founded an Animal Rights Caucus with Tom Lantos. He protested the treatment of elephants at a circus production in front of the Capitol in 1995 and tried to block the NASA project to send Russian monkeys into space in 1996.

Smith is a strong opponent of abortion—"My life's goal is to protect all unborn children," he has said—and once used an anatomically correct doll to explain partial-birth abortion on the Senate floor; he sponsored the first ban on the procedure in 1994. Many of Smith's other projects also are clearly conservative, such as missile defense and confidentiality for the advice of authorized tax preparers. But he has also investigated Gulf war syndrome and opposed putting U.S. troops in Bosnia in 1995 and Kosovo in 1998. His conservatism did not prevent him from seeking highway projects for New Hampshire in the 1998 transportation bill, including $10 million to preserve covered bridges, funding for an airport access road, plus an exemption for New Hampshire until 2000 from the national seat belt mandates. He is chairman of the Senate Ethics Committee and in September 1998 called on Bill Clinton to resign.

In an amazing sequence, Smith was re-elected with the narrowest of margins in New Hampshire in 1996 and promptly started preparing a run for president in 1997. His Senate opponent was Dick Swett, elected to the 2d District House seat in 1990 and 1992 and defeated 51%–46% in 1994. Swett only narrowly won the primary, but ultimately spent more than $1.5 million, much of it raised with the help of his father-in-law Tom Lantos. Swett hit Smith for voting for the congressional pay raise and moving his family to Washington. Smith attacked Swett as a liberal and for raising 90% of his money out of state. Smith had only a narrow lead in most polls and was behind in some; he perhaps suffered from his heavy campaigning for Phil Gramm, who ended up withdrawing from the presidential campaign before he got to New Hampshire. In the end, Smith won by just 49%–46%; he had a near-political-death experience on election night when the VNS exit poll declared him the loser (New Hampshire exit polls have leaned Democratic since 1988). He was later fined $95,000 for exceeding by $130,000 the state's voluntary campaign spending limit.

Not many months later Smith was traveling to Iowa (where he spent 42 days in 1997) and Louisiana, exploring a presidential race. What in his career prompted him to think he would make a plausible candidate is not clear: he has had no executive experience since his real estate days, he is out on one end of the political spectrum, and he has no major legislative achievement.

But he has formed a Live Free or Die PAC and gone on the circuit to belt out, with impressive articulateness, his message of strong conviction and steadiness under pressure. Smith became the first candidate to formally announce for the presidency in February 1999. Much of the buzz in New Hampshire was hostile, and many feared his presence would drive out (or give a good excuse to pretend to be driven out to) other presidential contenders, and thus reduce the importance of New Hampshire's first-in-the-nation primary. The liberal *Concord Monitor* wondered, "Where did this down-home guy get this goofy idea?" The conservative Manchester *Union Leader* worried, "A Smith candidacy would pretty much drive a stake through the heart of the GOP primary in the Granite State." And a Channel 9 poll on whether he should run came out 59%–25% against. But perhaps the Smith campaign will not reach New Hampshire at all. In November 1998, he said, "If I don't do well or win in Iowa, to run in New Hampshire would not be the right thing to do."

If Smith runs for re-election to the Senate in 2002, one strong opponent might be Governor Jeanne Shaheen. But New Hampshire senators have a habit of retiring after two terms; the last to win a third full term was Norris Cotton, in 1968.

Junior Senator. Judd Gregg grew up in Nashua and in politics: His father, Hugh Gregg, was elected governor in 1952 and was a power in presidential primary politics up through 1988, when he backed George Bush. Judd Gregg was a student at Columbia during the student riots of 1968, but stayed true to New Hampshire Republicanism; after law school, he returned to Nashua and practiced law. In 1978 he was elected to the Executive Council, which dates to the colonial era and approves state appointments and expenditures. In 1980 he was elected to the House, where he was an eager participant in the Reagan revolution. In 1988, he ran for governor and won handily; he was easily re-elected in 1990.

In 1992, Gregg ran for the Senate when Warren Rudman retired, and in his taciturn way seemed sure he would win. But the New Hampshire economy had turned sour, and the race turned close. In the September primary he beat a construction company owner by only 50%–38%. In the general, he faced retired businessman John Rauh, who backed the line-item veto and balanced budget amendment and attacked Gregg for opposing abortion. Gregg was also attacked for having received a draft deferment in 1969 for bad knees, sleepwalking and severe acne. He won by an unimpressive 48%–45% margin.

In the Senate Gregg has a moderate to conservative voting record. He has been chief deputy majority whip since June 1996 and became an Appropriations subcommittee chairman in 1999, but has made his greatest impression by taking the lead on some controversial issues. He served on the 1994 Entitlements Commission and in 1995 headed the Senate Republicans' working group on entitlement reform; he drafted a Medicare reform to give seniors more choices, including the current system. In 1998 he served on the CSIS National Commission on Retirement Policy and co-sponsored its Social Security reform, which would put 2% of payroll taxes into mandatory investment accounts, lift minimum benefits levels, raise the retirement age and means-test affluent workers. It had bipartisan support and, said Gregg, referring to other Social Security reforms, is "in concert with those who are moving in the same direction."

On environmental issues Gregg backed reform of the 1872 Mining Act, higher grazing fees and fewer logging roads on federal lands. He worked to preserve Great Bay in Portsmouth and for land purchases in Bretton Woods, and backed the Green Scissors movement to stop spending on projects that harm the environment. In 1998 he and Vermont's Patrick Leahy sponsored the Northern Forest Stewardship Act, to preserve mostly privately owned forests from Maine west to Upstate New York. Gregg and Leahy also combined in May 1998 to pass by 61–37 an amendment removing tobacco companies' exemption from civil liability in John McCain's tobacco bill. Gregg wants the federal government to fund 40% rather than 7% of special education. He passed an amendment barring states from regulating over-the-counter drugs without FDA permission. He proposed a ban on cloning of human beings in January 1998. He also proposed a law to allow homemakers to contribute to IRAs and workers who take leave to make catchup payments toward their pensions.

Gregg's work on local issues prompted Democratic Governor Jeanne Shaheen to give him credit in 1997 for getting federal money to preserve Lake Tarleton, expand special education and pay for the Medicaid hospital program. Gregg's close margin in 1992 might appear enticing to challengers, but much had changed in New Hampshire and by 1998 the state was in a euphoric pro-incumbent mood. Possible serious challengers—Dick Swett, John Rauh and his wife Mary—declined to run against Gregg, and his opponent was George Condodemetraky, who spent all of $25,000 and called Gregg a "draft dodger" and a "wimp." At one rally he said he would like to get Gregg between a dog and a fire hydrant. One thing he didn't get Gregg into was a debate: The incumbent said he wasn't interested in such abuse. Gregg won 68%–28%.

Presidential politics. Since 1920, New Hampshire has had the first-in-the-nation primary, and since 1952, when candidates' names were first put on the ballot, it has had extraordinary influence on the presidential selection process—a fact that will surely strike future political scientists as bizarre. To be sure, there are arguments for having early contests in small states which provide a venue for "retail politics," in which candidates meet voters in person, listen and talk to them, exchange ideas and allow them to gauge their character. In-person contact was one of the things that saved Bill Clinton in 1992, after the Gennifer Flowers charges; exit polls showed he did much better than average with voters who had personally met one or more of the candidates. But New Hampshire is becoming large and metropolitan enough that the primary is increasingly fought out on television, in ads and on Channel 9's newscasts. And New Hampshire is one of the last states you would pick as typical.

In any case, New Hampshire retains its first-in-the-nation status not on its merits but because of threats. Democrats tried in the 1970s to confine primaries to a "window" period in which New Hampshire would have competition. But New Hampshire, with its outlaw tradition, in- sisted it would hold its primary before the window if necessary, confident that candidates and reporters would pay it heed even if its tiny delegation were threatened with not being seated at the national convention. Republicans made no such rules, but in 1996 let Iowa Governor Terry Branstad and New Hampshire Governor Steve Merrill, both Republicans, threaten voter retaliation against candidates who took part in caucuses or primaries held before their states' or even during the week afterwards. Democratic Governor Jeanne Shaheen continued the tra- dition in December 1998, demanding candidates take a pledge not to participate in such con- tests. This has not been entirely successful. New Hampshire considers it an affront that Dela- ware holds its primary four days *after* New Hampshire, and threatens to shun candidates who campaign in Delaware. That threat became moot in 1996 in the case of Phil Gramm, whose campaign imploded after Iowa; it seemed weak enough to be ignored in late 1998 by Steve Forbes and Lamar Alexander, who spoke in Delaware and still insisted they would contest New Hampshire. But that is as far as the rebellion against New Hampshire has gone.

A word should be said about New Hampshire media. The Manchester *Union Leader* has one of the nation's sharpest conservative tongues. Its owner Nackey Loeb (the widow of Wil- liam) and its editorials scold Republicans who stray from its gospel, which these days includes Pat Buchanan's opposition to free trade. Its insistence that politicians take the anti-tax pledge has set the course for New Hampshire state politics and government. But the *Union Leader* cannot automatically deliver votes on primary day—Buchanan won in 1996, but with just 27% of the votes—and its news coverage is more objective than that of many left-leaning national media outlets. New Hampshire's other great medium is Manchester's WMUR-TV, Channel 9, which also provides tons of information to a winter-bound audience. Channel 9's rule is to cover every candidate every day he or she is in New Hampshire, allowing each to present views and make arguments without the overlay of opinionated commentary that national network reporters use.

Despite Democrats' recent successes here, New Hampshire is one of the few states with substantially more registered Republicans than Democrats—just another way in which it is not typical of the nation. The Republican heart of the state is the Merrimack Valley, with the two biggest cities of Manchester and Nashua. Old Yankee towns farther north are also heavily Republican, and so are the suburbs just north of the Massachusetts line. More Democratic is the western edge of the state along the Connecticut River, which partakes a bit of the Ben & Jerry's Vermont liberalism, and Portsmouth and smaller old mill towns along the Maine border. The highest Democratic percentages in New Hampshire often come from Hanover, home of Dartmouth College; the highest Republican percentages from Dixville Notch in the far north, whose 29 voters troop in at one minute after midnight and cast the nation's first recorded votes every presidential year.

It is not so clear that contesting New Hampshire is as crucial as it used to be. It is unlikely that New Hampshire's motel rooms will go empty or its diners unpatrolled by TV camera crews. Al Gore will surely be opposed by Bill Bradley or someone else on the Democratic side. And there will be something like a mob scene on the Republican side. New Hampshire still has the capacity to make a contender out of an unknown and to convert a favorite into an also-ran. But it is no longer an essential win in a presidential campaign.

Congressional districting. With only slight changes, New Hampshire's two congressional districts basically have had the same boundaries since 1881, neatly separating the Merrimack River mill towns of Manchester and Nashua, the state's largest cities. That was done originally to split the Catholic Democratic vote, but now both cities are high-tech Republican towns. The split now gives Democrats a chance for upset victories in either seat. Incidentally, both of New Hampshire's congressmen and one of its senators are the son or grandson of governors.

The People: Est. Pop. 1998: 1,185,048; Pop. 1990: 1,109,252, up 6.8% 1990–1998. 0.4% of U.S. total, 42d largest; 49% rural. Median age: 35.1 years. 11.8% 65 years and over. 98% White, 0.6% Black, 0.8% Asian, 0.2% Amer. Indian, 0.3% Other; 1% Hispanic Origin. Households: 59.7% married couple families; 29.8% married couple fams. w. children; 50.5% college educ.; median household income: $36,329; per capita income: $15,959; 68.2% owner occupied housing; median house value: $129,400; median monthly rent: $479. 2.9% Unemployment. 1998 Voting age pop.: 890,000. 1998 Turnout: 330,555; 37% of VAP. Registered voters (1998): 747,608; 203,257 D (27%), 272,217 R (36%), 272,134 unaffiliated and minor parties (36%).

Political Lineup: Governor, Jeanne Shaheen (D); Secy. of State, William M. Gardner (D); Atty. Gen., Philip McLaughlin (D); Treasurer, Georgie A. Thomas (R); State Senate, 24 (13 D, 11 R); Majority Leader, Burton Cohen (D); State House, 400 (154 D, 244 R, 1 I, 1 vacancy); House Speaker, Donna Sytek (R). Senators, Bob Smith (R) and Judd Gregg (R). Representatives, 2 (2 R).

Elections Division: 603-271-3242; **Filing Deadline for U.S. Congress:** June 16, 2000.

1996 Presidential Vote

Clinton (D)	246,166	(49%)
Dole (R)	196,486	(39%)
Perot (I)	48,387	(10%)
Others	8,014	(2%)

1996 Republican Presidential Primary

Buchanan (R)	56,921	(27%)
Dole (R)	54,840	(26%)
Alexander (R)	47,216	(23%)
Forbes (R)	25,535	(12%)
Lugar (R)	10,862	(5%)
Others	13,923	(8%)

1992 Presidential Vote

Clinton (D)	209,040	(39%)
Bush (R)	202,484	(38%)
Perot (I)	121,337	(23%)

GOVERNOR
Gov. Jeanne Shaheen (D)

Elected 1996, term expires Jan. 2001; b. Jan. 28, 1947, St. Charles, MO; home, Madbury; Shippensburg U., B.A. 1969, U. of MS, M.A. 1973; Protestant; married (William).

Elected Office: NH Senate, 1990–96.

Professional Career: Teacher, 1969–71; A.A., U. of NH, 1973–74, Parents' Assoc. Program Coord., 1982–86; Mgr., seasonal retail business, 1973–76; Campaign Mgr., Carter/Mondale NH Pres. Campaign, 1979–80; Hart NH Pres. Campaign, 1983–84; McEachern NH Gov. Campaign, 1986–88.

Office: State House, Concord, 03301, 603-271-2121; Fax: 603-271-2130; Web site: www.state.nh.us.

Election Results

1998 gen.	Jeanne Shaheen (D)	210,769	(66%)
	Jay Lucas (R)	98,473	(31%)
	Others	9,698	(3%)
1998 prim.	Jeanne Shaheen (D)	unopposed	
1996 gen.	Jeanne Shaheen (D)	284,131	(57%)
	Ovide Lamontagne (R)	196,278	(40%)
	Others	16,514	(3%)

SENATORS
Sen. Bob Smith (R)

Elected 1990, seat up 2002; b. Mar. 30, 1941, Trenton, NJ; home, Tuftonboro; Trenton Jr. Col., A.A. 1963, Lafayette Col., B.A. 1965, Long Beach St. Col., 1968–69; Catholic; married (Mary Jo).

Military Career: Navy, 1965–67 (Vietnam); Naval Reserves, 1962–65, 1967–69.

Elected Office: Chmn., Gov. Wentworth Schl. Bd., 1978–83; U.S. House of Reps., 1984–90.

Professional Career: High schl. teacher, 1975–84; Real estate agent, 1975–84.

DC Office: 307 DSOB, 20510, 202-224-2841; Fax: 202-224-1353; Web site: www.senate.gov/~smith.

State Offices: Berlin, 603-752-2600; Manchester, 603-634-5000; Portsmouth, 603-433-1667.

Committees: *Armed Services* (4th of 11 R): Emerging Threats & Capabilities; Seapower; Strategic Forces (Chmn.). *Environment & Public Works* (3d of 10 R): Superfund, Waste Control & Risk Assessment (Chmn.); Transportation & Infrastructure. *Ethics (Select)* (Chmn. of 3 R). *Judiciary* (10th of 10 R): The Constitution, Federalism & Property Rights; Youth Violence.

Group Ratings

	ADA	ACLU	AFS	LCV	CON	NTU	NFIB	COC	ACU	NTLC	CHC
1998	5	14	0	0	81	81	89	78	100	100	100
1997	5	—	0	—	32	84	—	50	96	—	—

National Journal Ratings

	1997 LIB — 1997 CONS	1998 LIB — 1998 CONS
Economic	11% — 76%	0% — 88%
Social	17% — 72%	0% — 88%
Foreign	0% — 77%	0% — 88%

Key Votes of the 105th Congress

1. Bal. Budget Amend.	Y	5. Satcher for Surgeon Gen.	N	9. Chem. Weapons Treaty	N
2. Clinton Budget Deal	Y	6. Highway Set-asides	N	10. Cuban Humanitarian Aid	N
3. Cloture on Tobacco	N	7. Table Child Gun locks	Y	11. Table Bosnia Troops	N
4. Education IRAs	Y	8. Ovrd. Part. Birth Veto	Y	12. $ for Test-ban Treaty	N

Election Results

1996 general	Bob Smith (R) 242,257	(49%)	($1,929,468)
	Dick Swett (D) 227,355	(46%)	($1,558,563)
	Ken Blevens (Lib) 22,261	(5%)	
1996 primary	Bob Smith (R) 85,223	(97%)	
	Others 2,354	(3%)	
1990 general	Bob Smith (R) 189,792	(65%)	($1,419,127)
	John A. Durkin (D) 91,299	(32%)	($319,879)
	Others 10,302	(3%)	

Sen. Judd Gregg (R)

Elected 1992, seat up 2004; b. Feb. 14, 1947, Nashua; home, Rye; Columbia U., A.B. 1969, Boston U., J.D. 1972, LL.M. 1975; Protestant; married (Kathleen).

Elected Office: NH Exec. Cncl., 1978–80; U.S. House of Reps., 1980–88; NH Gov., 1988–92.

Professional Career: Practicing atty., 1976–80.

DC Office: 393 RSOB, 20510, 202-224-3324; Fax: 202-224-4952; Web site: www.senate.gov/~gregg.

State Offices: Berlin, 603-752-2604; Concord, 603-225-7115; Manchester, 603-622-7979; Portsmouth, 603-431-2171.

Committees: *Appropriations* (10th of 15 R): Commerce, Justice, State & the Judiciary (Chmn.); Defense; Foreign Operations & Export Financing; Interior; Labor & HHS. *Budget* (7th of 12 R). *Governmental Affairs* (9th of 9 R): Government Management, Restructuring and the District of Columbia; International Security, Proliferation & Federal Services. *Health, Education, Labor & Pensions* (2d of 10 R): Aging; Children & Families (Chmn.); Public Health.

Group Ratings

	ADA	ACLU	AFS	LCV	CON	NTU	NFIB	COC	ACU	NTLC	CHC
1998	5	29	11	50	52	63	100	89	76	86	91
1997	10	—	0	—	95	86	—	100	76	—	—

National Journal Ratings

	1997 LIB — 1997 CONS	1998 LIB — 1998 CONS
Economic	25% — 67%	31% — 63%
Social	38% — 61%	29% — 69%
Foreign	30% — 66%	12% — 75%

Key Votes of the 105th Congress

1. Bal. Budget Amend.	Y	5. Satcher for Surgeon Gen.	N	9. Chem. Weapons Treaty	Y
2. Clinton Budget Deal	Y	6. Highway Set-asides	N	10. Cuban Humanitarian Aid	N
3. Cloture on Tobacco	Y	7. Table Child Gun locks	Y	11. Table Bosnia Troops	N
4. Education IRAs	Y	8. Ovrd. Part. Birth Veto	Y	12. $ for Test-ban Treaty	N

Election Results

1998 general	Judd Gregg (R)	213,477	(68%)	($904,448)
	George Condodemetraky (D)	88,883	(28%)	($28,547)
	Others	12,596	(4%)	
1998 primary	Judd Gregg (R)	63,729	(86%)	
	Phil Weber (R)	10,784	(14%)	
1992 general	Judd Gregg (R)	249,591	(48%)	($875,675)
	John Rauh (D)	234,982	(45%)	($1,109,467)
	Katherine Alexander (Lib)	18,214	(4%)	
	Others	15,629	(3%)	

FIRST DISTRICT

The 1st Congressional District of New Hampshire includes Manchester, its suburbs and the seacoast. Manchester was once a heavily French Canadian textile mill town, which also had the nation's largest percentage of Greek-Americans; in the 1980s it became a fast-growing, high-tech city. There are new shopping malls here and in towns on the Massachusetts border. Portsmouth has restored its downtown to some of its historic splendor; and the successful redevelopment of Pease Air Force Base (it was the first base in the nation to be closed) into the Pease International Tradeport is driving the seacoast economy with new jobs. There is a Democratic heritage, especially in Manchester, but in general elections this is usually Republican territory.

The congressman from the 1st District is John E. Sununu, a Republican elected in 1996, one of eight children of former New Hampshire Governor and White House Chief of Staff John H. Sununu. The younger Sununu grew up in Salem, became an engineer, worked for a microwave manufacturer, a high-tech consulting firm, the building automation manufacturer Teletrol and as a consultant for JHS Associates. In April 1996, when Congressman Bill Zeliff announced for governor, Sununu and seven other Republicans got into the House race. The best known was four-term Manchester Mayor Raymond "The Wiz" Wieczorek, builder of the new airport and endorsee of the Manchester *Union Leader*. But Wieczorek was 67 and did not carry much punch outside of Manchester. Sununu called for tax simplification and a capital gains tax cut and a devolution of education programs to the states. This was an exceedingly close race: Sununu won with 28%, Wieczorek had 27% and Jack Heath, news director of WMUR-TV, took 26%. In the general Sununu faced Joe Keefe, former Democratic state chairman, who had run twice before in the district and who, with help from PACs, raised more money than Sununu. This also was a close race: Keefe carried the eastern part of the district around Portsmouth, Rochester and Durham, and also won in Manchester, but Sununu won big in the Manchester suburbs and the north country, winning overall 50%–47%.

In the House Sununu got a seat on the Budget Committee and worked on local projects—the Portsmouth Naval Shipyard, the Manchester Airport Access Road. He was the only Republican in New England not to support the Shays-Meehan campaign finance measure. With other Republican freshmen, he offered his own tax cut in January 1998. Despite the close result in 1996, Democrats had a tough time coming up with a candidate. Keefe opted out of the race in March. Another Democrat got out just before the filing deadline. Former state Representative Cynthia McGovern did file, but shortly afterward it was reported she had been arrested for assaulting a policeman in 1987; she got off the ballot by moving to Massachusetts. The final nominee, a 65-year-old real estate salesman, had no chance. Sununu won 67%–33%, carrying every city and town except Portsmouth (by 23 votes) and Durham (by 79). Later that month in Washington, then-Speaker-designate Bob Livingston helped Sununu get a seat on Appropriations; he remains on Budget.

Cook's Call. *Safe.* Based on the trouble Democrats had in recruiting a candidate to run here in 1998, when Sununu was a much more obvious target, it is pretty safe to say that he will again avoid a top-tier challenge in 2000. The state has been trending away from Republicans in recent years, at some point this could become a competitive district.

The People: Pop. 1990: 554,303; 45% rural; 11.6% age 65 + ; 98% White, 0.7% Black, 0.8% Asian, 0.2% Amer. Indian, 0.3% Other; 1.1% Hispanic Origin. Households: 59% married couple families; 29.6% married couple fams. w. children; 51.1% college educ.; median household income: $36,511; per capita income: $16,044; median house value: $132,500; median gross rent: $484.

1996 Presidential Vote		1992 Presidential Vote	
Clinton (D)	121,602 (48%)	Bush (R)	104,653 (39%)
Dole (R)	101,295 (40%)	Clinton (D)	101,415 (38%)
Perot (I)	23,898 (10%)	Perot (I)	61,571 (23%)
Others	3,937 (2%)		

Rep. John E. Sununu (R)

Elected 1996; b. Sept. 10, 1964, Boston, MA; home, Bedford; M.I.T., B.S. 1986, M.S. 1987, Harvard U., M.B.A. 1991; Catholic; married (Kitty).

Professional Career: Design Engineer, Remec Inc., 1987–89; Mgr. & Operations Specialist, Pittiglio, Rabin, Todd & McGrath, 1990–92; C.F.O. & Dir. of Operations, Teletrol Systems Inc., 1993–95; Consultant, JHS Associates, 1995–96.

DC Office: 316 CHOB 20515, 202-225-5456; Fax: 202-225-5822; Web site: www.house.gov/sununu.

District Offices: Dover, 603-743-4813; Manchester, 603-641-9536.

Committees: *Appropriations* (32d of 34 R): District of Columbia; Treasury, Postal Service & General Government; VA, HUD & Independent Agencies. *Budget* (13th of 24 R).

Group Ratings

	ADA	ACLU	AFS	LCV	CON	NTU	NFIB	COC	ACU	NTLC	CHC
1998	0	6	0	31	74	56	100	94	92	89	100
1997	5	—	13	—	88	57	—	100	92	—	—

National Journal Ratings

	1997 LIB — 1997 CONS		1998 LIB — 1998 CONS	
Economic	28% —	67%	0% —	88%
Social	30% —	64%	26% —	72%
Foreign	12% —	81%	43% —	53%

Key Votes of the 105th Congress

1. Clinton Budget Deal	Y	5. Puerto Rico Sthood. Ref.	N	9. Cut $ for B-2 Bombers	Y
2. Education IRAs	Y	6. End Highway Set-asides	Y	10. Human Rights in China	N
3. Req. 2/3 to Raise Taxes	Y	7. School Prayer Amend.	Y	11. Withdraw Bosnia Troops	Y
4. Fast-track Trade	Y	8. Ovrd. Part. Birth Veto	Y	12. End Cuban TV-Marti	Y

Election Results

1998 general	John E. Sununu (R)	104,430	(67%)	($536,509)
	Peter Flood (D)	51,783	(33%)	($26,812)
1998 primary	John E. Sununu (R)	unopposed		
1996 general	John E. Sununu (R)	123,939	(50%)	($545,865)
	Joseph F. Keefe (D)	115,462	(47%)	($580,749)
	Others	8,335	(3%)	

SECOND DISTRICT

The 2d Congressional District includes Nashua, the state's second largest city, and Salem, both right on the Massachusetts line and solidly conservative: people came here to get away from "Taxachusetts." It also includes, farther from Boston and readier for taxes and government services, the state capital of Concord and towns in the Connecticut River Valley, from Keene near Mount Monadnock north to Hanover, home of Dartmouth College, an area of artists' retreats: from sculptor August Saint Gaudens a century ago to writer J.D. Salinger today. The 2d runs to the farthest north country: Dixville Notch and the paper mill town of Berlin, the Mount Washington Hotel and cog railway and the resort of Bretton Woods where the world monetary system, and the basis for post-World War II prosperity, was established in a conference in 1944.

The congressman from the 2d District is Charles Bass, who has a long political pedigree: His grandfather Robert Bass was elected governor in 1910 and his father Perkins Bass served in the House from 1955–63. Charles Bass, after graduating from Dartmouth, worked for Maine Congressmen William Cohen and David Emery, then returned to New Hampshire to run for Congress in 1980; he finished third in the primary, with 22%, to 34% for now-Senator Judd Gregg and 25% for liberal Susan McLane. He ran a factory making architectural products with his two brothers and served in the state legislature—in the House from 1982 and the Senate from 1988—where he wrote the state's voluntary campaign spending law, which called on U.S. House candidates to observe the $500,000 total limit for both primary and general elections.

In 1994 Bass ran in the Republican primary for the right to oppose two-term Democratic Congressman Dick Swett. Bass ran as a moderate—pro-choice on abortion, but also as a fiscal conservative, a supporter of welfare cuts and tougher sentencing. Bass ran only a few points better in the primary than in 1980, but his 29% this time was enough to beat former NRA consultant Mike Hammond, who had 24%. Bass attacked Swett for voting with Bill Clinton 90% of the time and ran a TV spot of Swett and Clinton embracing. He also attacked Swett for switching on gun control and for raising most of his money out of state, much of it generated by his father-in-law, California Congressman Tom Lantos. Swett spent over $1 million, while Bass adhered to the voluntary spending limits and spent $448,000; Bass won 51%–46%. Swett carried Concord, Hanover and other towns on the Connecticut River, the Keene area and the mill town of Berlin, but Bass carried practically everything else.

In the House Bass has a conservative record on economics and a moderate record on cultural and foreign issues; he has emphasized environmental issues. He is a sponsor of the Northern Forest Stewardship Act, which encourages states and private owners to preserve the massive forests from Maine west to Upstate New York. He also backed the Conte Refuge Eminent Domain Protection Act, the Androscoggin River Valley Heritage Act and protecting the area around Lake Tarleton. The House passed his amendment for an inspector general in the White House, which would in effect hold the highest office to the same laws and regulations by which ordinary American people, and now also Congress, must abide. On the Budget Committee he supported Republican moves to hold down spending and cut taxes.

In 1996 Bass had spirited opposition in both the primary and general elections. He again faced Mike Hammond, who had chaired Pat Buchanan's New Hampshire campaign and attacked Bass on abortion, the environment and gun control. But Senator Bob Smith and Majority

Leader Dick Armey endorsed Bass, and he won by a solid 66%–27%. In the general election he was pressed hard by Deborah "Arnie" Arnesen, the Democratic gubernatorial candidate in 1992. She spent more money and September polls showed the race even. Bass recalled how she backed a 6% state income tax four years before; she said Bass was no longer the moderate that used to vote with her in the state Senate. Bass won 51%–43%.

In the House Bass got seats on Intelligence and Transportation. He got $810 million for New Hampshire in the 1998 transportation bill, plus $9 million for winter ice storm cleanup and Superfund money to clean up the Nashua Manville asbestos site. He supported the Shays-Meehan campaign finance bill and sponsored a bill against "slamming"—the switching of long-distance phone carriers without customer notice. He also pushed for federal funds to help implement Megan's Law, support special education and promote breast cancer research.

But his moderate record continued to irritate both Democrats and conservative Republicans. He had little enough trouble winning the 1998 primary, with 83% against two candidates. The general was more of a contest. His opponent was Mary Rauh, former head of New England Planned Parenthood, wife of 1992 and 1996 Senate candidate John Rauh. She took no PAC money and limited her contributions to $250, a more stringent regimen than that of Bass, who kept to his New Hampshire law and, for the first time, outspent his Democratic opponent. Bass bragged about the balanced budget, tax cuts for small businesses and welfare reform, and said he wanted to use some of the budget surplus for special education. Rauh talked about the environment, education; interestingly, she favored public school choice and charter schools. Polls from February to September showed Bass with well under 50%, a danger sign for an incumbent. But he pulled away to lead by early October and won 53%–45%—for the third time, he lost Concord and several towns in the Connecticut Valley, but carried southern New Hampshire around Nashua and Salem—not a landslide but his best showing yet.

Cook's Call. *Competitive.* Bass's lackluster wins here for the past three cycles, even against rather marginal candidates, shows that he has not yet put down deep roots in this swing district. But, for all Bass's perceived vulnerabilities, Democrats have had problems the last couple of years finding top-notch nominees. Given the growing strength of Democrats here, this would be the first district to fall. Bass doesn't seem as aggressive as Sununu, this is a district to watch.

The People: Pop. 1990: 554,949; 53% rural; 12% age 65 +; 98.1% White, 0.6% Black, 0.9% Asian, 0.2% Amer. Indian, 0.3% Other; 1% Hispanic Origin. Households: 60.3% married couple families; 30% married couple fams. w. children; 49.9% college educ.; median household income: $36,145; per capita income: $15,874; median house value: $125,800; median gross rent: $471.

1996 Presidential Vote

Clinton (D)	124,564	(50%)
Dole (R)	95,191	(38%)
Perot (I)	24,489	(10%)
Others	4,077	(2%)

1992 Presidential Vote

Clinton (D)	107,625	(40%)
Bush (R)	97,831	(37%)
Perot (I)	59,766	(22%)

Rep. Charles Bass (R)

Elected 1994; b. Jan. 8, 1952, Boston, MA; home, Peterborough; Dartmouth Col., A.B. 1974; Episcopalian; married (Lisa).

Elected Office: NH House of Reps., 1982–88; NH Senate, 1988–92.

Professional Career: Field worker, U.S. Rep. William Cohen, 1974; Legis. Asst., U.S. Rep. David Emery, 1975–76, Chief of Staff, 1976–79; Vice Pres., High Standard Inc., 1980–93; Chmn., Columbia Architectural Products, 1980–93.

DC Office: 218 CHOB 20515, 202-225-5206; Fax: 202-225-2946; Web site: www.house.gov/bass.

District Offices: Concord, 603-226-0249; Keene, 603-358-4094; Littleton, 603-444-1271; Nashua, 603-889-8772.

Committees: *Budget* (10th of 24 R). *Permanent Select Committee on Intelligence* (6th of 9 R): Human Intelligence, Analysis & Counterintelligence (Vice Chmn.); Technical & Tactical Intelligence. *Transportation & Infrastructure* (21st of 41 R): Aviation; Ground Transportation.

Group Ratings

	ADA	ACLU	AFS	LCV	CON	NTU	NFIB	COC	ACU	NTLC	CHC
1998	10	25	11	54	26	47	100	94	63	68	75
1997	15	—	0	—	93	62	—	90	80	—	—

National Journal Ratings

	1997 LIB — 1997 CONS			1998 LIB — 1998 CONS		
Economic	35%	—	63%	42%	—	58%
Social	48%	—	51%	52%	—	48%
Foreign	36%	—	63%	38%	—	61%

Key Votes of the 105th Congress

1. Clinton Budget Deal	Y	5. Puerto Rico Sthood. Ref.	N	9. Cut $ for B-2 Bombers	Y
2. Education IRAs	Y	6. End Highway Set-asides	Y	10. Human Rights in China	N
3. Req. 2/3 to Raise Taxes	Y	7. School Prayer Amend.	Y	11. Withdraw Bosnia Troops	Y
4. Fast-track Trade	Y	8. Ovrd. Part. Birth Veto	Y	12. End Cuban TV-Marti	N

Election Results

1998 general	Charles Bass (R)	85,740	(53%)	($547,937)
	Mary Rauh (D)	72,217	(45%)	($330,690)
	Others	3,419	(2%)	
1998 primary	Charles Bass (R)	30,601	(83%)	
	Phil Cobbin (R)	4,023	(11%)	
	Robert J. Kulak (R)	2,457	(7%)	
1996 general	Charles Bass (R)	122,957	(51%)	($625,147)
	Deborah (Arnie) Arnesen (D)	105,824	(43%)	($706,623)
	Carole Lamirande (I)	10,753	(4%)	($7,091)
	Others	3,961	(2%)	

NEW JERSEY

New Jersey has spent much of its history betwixt and between. It was named by King James II, then Duke of York, for the Channel Island on which he was sheltered during the English Civil War. It was plagued in its early years by rival claims from its neighbors and has taken to the Supreme Court its argument with New York over who owns the Statue of Liberty and Ellis Island; in May 1997 an arbitrator recommended giving New York Ellis Island's original three acres of bedrock and New Jersey the 24 acres of fill land. New Jersey's largest cities lie on the swampy sides of America's two greatest harbor rivers, overshadowed for years by the metropolises of New York and Philadelphia—"a valley of humility between two mountains of conceit," its neighbor Benjamin Franklin called it. But New Jersey has much to say for itself. It is "a sort of laboratory in which the best blood is prepared for other communities to thrive on," Woodrow Wilson said when he was governor, just a tad defensively; it is "the fighting center of the most important social questions of our time."

Today, New Jersey is the nation's ninth most populous state: It boomed in the 1980s, suffered sharply in the early 1990s recession, and now has come back more strongly than its neighbors. High-tech has led the resurgence: New Jersey's pharmaceutical firms, like Merck and Johnson & Johnson, anchor the "Jersey Research Corridor," while AT&T and Lucent also help make the state a leader in telecommunications. Within its close boundaries is great diversity, geographically from beaches to mountains, demographically from old Quaker stock to new Hispanics, economically from inner city slums to hunt country mansions. Though New York writers are inclined to look on New Jersey as a land of 1940s diners and 1950s pizza parlors, this state much more closely resembles the rest of America than does Manhattan, even if some of its traffic signals are arrayed horizontally rather than vertically and its accents can sometimes be incomprehensible to outsiders. The Jersey City row houses seen on emerging from the Holland Tunnel, many renovated by Wall Street commuters and Latin immigrants, give way within a few miles to the lonely skyscrapers of Newark and comfortably packed middle-income suburbs. Nearby are the horse country around Far Hills, the university town of Princeton, old industrial cities like Paterson, and dozens of suburban towns and small factory cities where people work and raise families over generations; an hour from Philadelphia and two hours from Manhattan is Atlantic City, with more gambling revenues in 1998 ($4 billion) than the Las Vegas strip.

In the last 20 years, a new New Jersey has sprouted. The oil tank farms and swamplands of the Jersey Meadows have become sports palaces and office complexes; the intersection of I-78 and I-287 has become a major shopping and office edge city; U.S. 1 north from Princeton to North Brunswick has become one of the nation's high-tech centers; the flat vegetable fields once dotted with gas station junctions now have tourist attractions like Great Adventure amusement park. For the first census year since 1840, New Jersey in 1990 had more people (7.7 million) than New York City (7.3 million); it had far more than metropolitan Philadelphia (5.9 million), and it has been generating more new jobs than either New York or Pennsylvania. Growth is strongest in the interior away from New York City and Philadelphia, and New Jersey increasingly has an identity of its own. It is the home of Bruce Springsteen, and of big league football, basketball and hockey franchises and of the world's longest expanse of boardwalks on the Jersey Shore from Cape May to Sandy Hook.

State government played an important role in building New Jersey identity and pride. Governor Brendan Byrne in the 1970s started the Meadowlands sports complex and got casino gambling legalized in Atlantic City. In the 1980s, Governor Tom Kean started education reforms and promoted the state shamelessly. The revolt against Governor Jim Florio's tax increase in 1990 was led by the first all-New Jersey talk radio station and took on national significance,

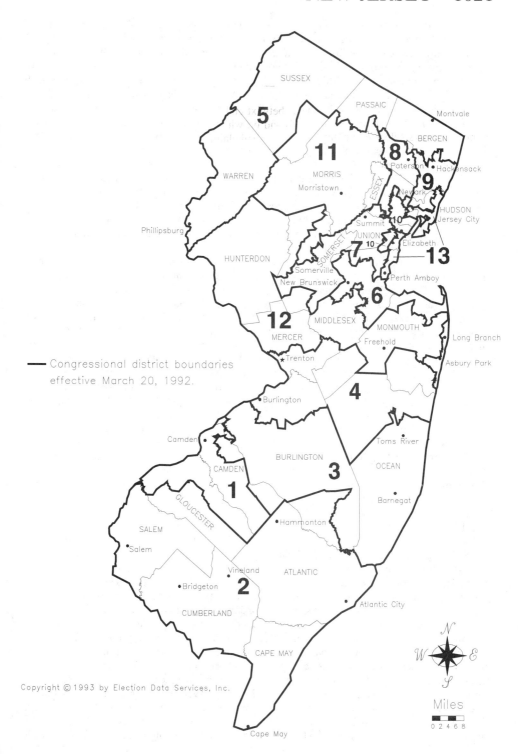

Congressional district boundaries
effective March 20, 1992.

Miles
0 2 4 6 8

and for the first time since Wilson, New Jersey has produced politicians of national stature—Bill Bradley, who retired from the Senate in 1996 after three terms and started running for president in 1998; Christine Todd Whitman, who gave Bradley a scare in 1990 and became governor by beating Florio in 1993 and is now running for the Senate in 2000; publisher Steve Forbes, who helped prepare Whitman's tax cut package in 1993 and then ran for president himself in 1996 and seems certain to run again. Whitman's election was a harbinger of the national rejection of tax increases and of the Republican trend of 1994, which in turn sparked the New Jersey and Northeastern countertrend of 1996: With tax increases ruled out, many Republican voters decided on other issues and voted Democratic. Bill Clinton carried the state 54%–36% and Democrat Bob Torricelli won the Senate race over Dick Zimmer 53%–43%. These were the largest margins of any statewide races here in the 1990s and, except in candidates' home areas, Torricelli's percentage tracked closely to Clinton's. Republicans still won the popular vote here for the U.S. House in 1996 and 1998, in part because New Jersey's moderate Republicans have made records that enable them to run ahead of their national party. White Catholics, among whom Republicans elsewhere have made inroads, voted almost evenly in the presidential races, as did white Protestants, while blacks, Jews and those with no religion produced huge Democratic majorities.

These political experiments have been carried on in a laboratory that, if it does not meet the standards of New Jersey's pharmaceutical or telecommunications labs, is in some ways exemplary. The state's public financing of gubernatorial campaigns has, at last, made New Jersey politicians personally known statewide through TV ads in what is the second most expensive state in which to campaign (you must buy both New York and Philadelphia TV). New Jersey has had a string of strong and distinctive governors—Byrne, Kean, Florio, Whitman—not beholden, as so many of their predecessors were, to county political bosses, a few of whom were shrewd political leaders but many of whom were hacks and crooks. New Jersey, once corrupt, is now pretty well cleaned up. It also gives its governors more real power than any other state. They are the only statewide elected officials with power to appoint all county prosecutors and judges and have great clout in the budgetary process. This does insulate governors from pressure, which Florio's critics bemoaned in the early 1990s. But it makes them accountable, as Florio's backers found in November 1993; in 1995 the New Jersey legislature enacted a constitutional amendment subjecting the governor to recall.

Governor. Christine Todd Whitman grew up in a political family, on the same estate in the New Jersey horse country where she now lives. Her father, Webster Todd, was state Republican chairman in 1964 and again in 1977; her mother was vice chairwoman of the Republican National Committee. Christie attended her first Republican National Convention in San Francisco in 1956, at age 9; her husband's grandfather was elected governor of New York in 1914 and 1916. She served five years on the Somerset County Board of Chosen Freeholders in the 1980s and was appointed president of the Board of Public Utilities by Governor Tom Kean in 1988. In 1990 she took on the task of running against Senator Bill Bradley; it was just after Governor Jim Florio's big tax increases, and she attacked Bradley for taking no position on them. The result was a near-upset: Bradley won by only 50%–47%. In 1993 Whitman ran for governor, winning the June primary with 40% of the vote to 33% for former Attorney General Cary Edwards and 24% for former state Senator James Wallwork.

The race between Florio and Whitman had national implications. Florio's 1990 tax package was marketed by Clinton advisers James Carville and Paul Begala, very much like Clinton's 1993 package, as an attempt to soak the rich and as the only way to pay for necessary government services. The two candidates' backgrounds echoed the class warfare theme: Florio grew up in working class Brooklyn, joined the Navy and became a boxer, practiced law and worked his way up in Camden County politics to the legislature in 1970 and Congress in 1974; Whitman lives on her family estate, and in debate matter-of-factly noted she and her husband paid more than $1 million in taxes the year before. But the tax issue worked Whitman's way. Florio's tax on the "rich" hit couples with $70,000 incomes who felt anything but rich, and Whitman's promise of a 30% across-the-board income tax cut trumped class warfare. Under New Jersey's public finance law, each candidate has the same amount of money to spend; Whitman husbanded hers, withstanding pressure even as Florio built up a lead in polls, and then outspent him heavily the last two weeks. Carville and New Jersey media were ready to hail a Florio triumph as evidence that voters could be sold on higher taxes; instead they floundered to explain Whitman's 49%–48% victory.

As governor, Whitman delivered on her tax cuts a year ahead of schedule. Democrats charged that local governments would increase property taxes to make up for drops in state aid. Whitman argued that property taxes rose by an average of 4.2% in her first three years as compared to 5.4% in Florio's, and said she and the legislature made property taxes deductible on the state income tax and were sending local governments more in state aid. Neutral critics said that the main reason for rising property taxes was high-spending local governments, dominated, one suspects, by public employees who are often much more alert and involved in local elections than ordinary citizens who are trying to hold down two jobs and pick up their children after work. Critics also charged Whitman was underfunding state pensions; she said they were overfunded, and in February 1997 proposed a $2.9 billion bond issue—the largest in state history—to fund them to 2056 and offset lost tax revenues. On crime issues, Whitman signed the first Megan's Law—inspired by the case of a New Jersey girl murdered by a released sexual offender—plus the "three strikes and you're in" law, which mandates a life sentence for any violent criminal convicted for the third time. She set up boot camps for juvenile offenders. She privatized health care for prison medical centers. On the environment she got dredging and environmental bond issues passed, as well as legislation providing $10 million for the preservation of Sterling Forest. Her 1996 Work First welfare reform bill limits benefits to five years and exacts tougher work requirements; it stalled in the legislature, which wanted to preserve local control of welfare programs, but was finally signed into law in March 1997. On education, Whitman opened charter schools and worked to satisfy a state Supreme Court ruling requiring equalized school funding by pushing through a plan that emphasized stricter curriculum standards. On cultural issues Whitman is liberal. She supports affirmative action programs and is outspokenly in favor of abortion rights. When the legislature voted to ban partial-birth abortions, Whitman proudly vetoed the bill; the legislature promptly passed it over her veto. But her abortion-rights stance softened a bit in May 1999 when she agreed to legislation requiring parental notification for a teenager to have an abortion.

In the process Whitman became a national figure, looked to by many who were frustrated by the dominance of cultural conservatives in the Republican Party; but she did not become much more popular, indeed may even have become less so, in New Jersey. In January 1995 she delivered the Republican response to the President's State of the Union message—the first time a governor has done so—and in 1996 there was speculation she might be the vice presidential nominee, or even run for president in 2000. But as she ran for re-election in 1997, her job rating hovered at no more than 50%, in a state that had shiftly sharply to Democrats the year before. Her opponent was James McGreevey, Middlesex County state senator and mayor of Woodbridge, who edged out 1st District Congressman Rob Andrews and Morris County Prosecutor Michael Murphy in the June 1997 primary. McGreevey concentrated his attacks on property taxes and auto insurance rates. He blamed Whitman's tax cuts for the property tax hikes (they went up 9% in his own town of Woodbridge) and charges, with more basis, that Whitman's budgets were balanced by more than usual borrowing and reliance on public pension funds. As for auto insurance, New Jersey has tight regulation and high requirements for coverage, as well as a high accident rate, and its insurance premiums have been highest in the nation for years. Whitman tried to push an auto choice plan, which would allow policyholders to relinquish "pain and suffering" damages and pay accordingly lower premiums; but it did not get through the legislature.

The 1997 result may have come down to the same issue as 1993, the Florio tax increase, for which McGreevey had voted. The race tightened in October, and Whitman won by only a

47%–46% margin, with 5% of the vote for Libertarian Murray Sabrin. Whitman's percentage was down in Republican counties with high property tax increases (Hunterdon, Warren, Sussex), and in middle-income counties as well (Passaic, Middlesex); she gained ground in affluent Bergen and Morris counties, and on the Jersey Shore. In 1998 she pushed through $1 billion in property tax rebates over five years, direct to taxpayers rather than through the voracious local governments. She advanced a proposal for a 13% rate cut in auto insurance. She pushed for electricity deregulation in 1999. And she got the legislature to pass new laws extending the protection of open space.

After Senator Frank Lautenberg announced in February 1999 that he would retire in 2000, Whitman gave close consideration to the race and in April 1999 announced she would run. Initial polls presented a mixed picture, but most showed she started with a significant lead—a strong position for a candidate who has not won more than 49% of the vote in three statewide races. The best-known Democrat to express an interest in the Senate race was none other than Jim Florio; Congressman Frank Pallone, staring at his chances in a Republican redistricting, expressed interest as well. If Whitman wins the Senate seat, the new governor will be state Senate President Donald DiFrancesco, generally considered consensus-minded and a skeptic about far-reaching reforms, like the school vouchers sought by Jersey City Mayor Bret Schundler. DiFrancesco sponsored the state's family leave act and a catastrophic illness insurance fund for children. "People have told me I've got to be more aggressive. I ask them, 'What would that get me? Would it get me where I am today?' " Schundler could also be a governor candidate in 2001. On the Democratic side, Jim McGreevey will almost surely run; Congressman Rob Andrews will likely run as well.

Senior Senator. Frank Lautenberg is one of a species common in the late 19th Century and the late 20th Century as well—the millionaire who becomes a senator. In 1980 he was a Democratic moneygiver and member of the board of the New York and New Jersey Port Authority; in 1994 he was re-elected to a third term in the Senate at 70. He has shown he knows how to play the game—and that it helps to come in with a large pile of chips. Lautenberg grew up poor, the son of an immigrant silk worker in Paterson. He served in the Army Signal Corps in World War II and says he would never have gone to college without the G.I. Bill of Rights. In 1952, he started a company called Automatic Data Processing, which by the mid-1990s had almost 30,000 employees and processed the payroll for nearly 10% of private sector jobs in the United States—a brilliant success story. When an open Senate seat came up in 1982, Lautenberg ran, starting off as an unknown, but willing to spend $5 million of his own money spotlighting his high-tech experience. He beat several professional politicians in the primary and upset Republican Congresswoman Millicent Fenwick, 51%–48%, in the general.

Lautenberg believes government helped him and many others work their way up, and he has a very liberal voting record. He has bucked party lines on occasion; when Governor Jim Florio's tax increase was blazingly unpopular, Lautenberg obdurately refused to vote for the Clinton tax increase in 1993. As chairman (now ranking minority member) of the Transportation Appropriations Subcommittee, he sponsored the laws that banned smoking first on two-hour, then on all domestic flights. He has been sponsoring anti-tobacco legislation ever since. In 1994 he passed a bill banning smoking in all federally funded children's facilities and sponsored legislation that would force the tobacco industry to pay for states' costs associated with tobacco-caused illnesses—the theory behind the states' anti-tobacco lawsuits. After the tobacco settlement was announced in summer 1997, he pushed for an immediate $1.50 tax and other anti-tobacco provisions without the settlement's protection against liability for the companies. He pressed for the FTC investigation which in 1997 ended the career of "Joe Camel." He even called for banning smokeless tobacco at baseball's 1997 All-Star Game. He was the author of the law pushing states to adopt the 21-year-old drinking age, and in 1998 pushed unsuccessfully to impose the 0.08% blood-alcohol level on states through the transportation bill. He is a strong backer of gun control and author of the 1996 law barring those convicted of domestic abuse from possessing firearms. Along with five other Democratic Senators, he proposed a number of gun control initiatives in the wake of the Littleton, Colorado, shooting. In May 1999 the Senate approved his proposal, sponsored with Bob Kerrey, to require background checks for sales at gun shows and for persons who seek to sell their guns at pawn shops, by 51–50, with Al Gore casting the deciding vote; an earlier version had failed 51–47 a week earlier.

As ranking Democrat on the Environment subcommittee on Superfund, Lautenberg has resisted Republican attempts at reforming the law; he pushed instead to pass separately a bill designed to allow development of brownfields, of which there are many in New Jersey. He opposed the Republicans' 1996 bill limiting retroactive liability; he also worked on the Clean Air and Safe Drinking Water Acts. He wants to amend the Safe Water Act to screen for more chemicals, like the styrene acrylonitrile trimer found in Toms River water. On the Budget Committee he has often taken an adversarial role but was party to the 1997 balanced budget agreement. With Republicans William Roth and John Chafee, he played a critical role in saving Amtrak funding in 1998. In February 1996, when four F-16s nearly collided with civilian planes off New Jersey, he called two Air Force generals into his office and got them to change the Air Force flight patterns.

Lautenberg's willingness to spend large amounts of his own money helped him win re-election in 1988 over former General Peter Dawkins and in 1994 over state House Speaker Chuck Haytaian. In late 1998 he seemed primed to run again, and no well-known Republican seemed eager to challenge him. But in February 1999 he surprised many when he announced he would retire. Evidently he decided not to self-finance this time; he said, "A powerful factor in my decision was the searing reality that I would have to spend half of every day between now and the next election fundraising." The state's two most recent governors immediately seemed the likeliest candidates. Governor Christie Whitman pondered the race, then in April 1999 said she thought she could achieve her goals by the end of 2000 and announced she was running. The best-known Democratic possibility was former Governor Jim Florio, and polls showed him well ahead in primary pairings. But many Democrats worried that Florio's 1990 tax increase would make it difficult or impossible for him to win. Congressman Bob Menendez, the choice of many insiders, decided to stay in the House, where he won a leadership position in November 1998; Congressman Frank Pallone, threatened with a Republican redistricting in 2001, seemed likely to run. Other possible Democrats included retiring Goldman Sachs chairman Jon Corzine and Thomas Byrne, former state Democratic Chairman and son of former Governor Brendan Byrne.

Conventional wisdom seemed to assume that Whitman would win, and she certainly would be a strong candidate. But she hasn't won more than 49% in a statewide race yet, and New Jersey's proliferation of minor party candidates raises the possibility of a third party conservative costing her votes; the Libertarian candidate for governor in 1997 won 5%, which Whitman could certainly have used. In May radio talk show host Bob Grant announced he was considering a run as a third-party candidate. Grant would appeal to social conservatives unhappy with some of Whitman's stands. This is likely to be one of the country's most seriously and expensively contested Senate elections in 2000; the New York media market, with ads for this race and the race to succeed Daniel Patrick Moynihan in New York, should be a fine place for ad-watching.

Cook's Call. *Highly Competitive.* This seat was safely in Democratic hands until Lautenberg decided not to seek another term; now it leans a bit Republican. Whitman will be the Republican standard bearer, while Democrats look likely to slug it out for their nomination. Florio has been amassing support in the southern part of the state, but he remains unpopular with many voters making it difficult to see how he can win the general election. Pallone's backing is mostly in the north, but there are questions whether he can raise the money necessary to be competitive. Corzine would be able to self-fund his race, making him a very attractive potential candidate in the early going. Whitman has the advantage, but this is a fairly Democratic state; her track record of narrow victories guarantees a competitive contest.

Junior Senator. Bob Torricelli, a Democrat elected in 1996, grew up in Franklin Lakes in north Jersey, graduated from Rutgers and the Kennedy School at Harvard and in 1975, at 24, became an aide to New Jersey Governor Brendan Byrne. Three years later he was working for Vice President Walter Mondale; he managed the decisive Carter-Mondale victory over Edward Kennedy in the 1980 Illinois primary and argued party rules with Kennedy's Harold Ickes at the convention. He is aggressive, adversarial, articulate and politically savvy. In 1982, at 31, he returned home to New Jersey, raised lots of money and beat an incumbent Republican congressman in the 9th District. In the House, he took politically beneficial committee assignments: International Relations (many of his ethnic constituents had particular interests in Israel, Greece, Korea, the Philippines and Cuba) and Science (North Jersey is one of the biggest high-tech areas in the country). He is a tough party loyalist: He was one of Speaker Jim Wright's most outspoken defenders in 1989 and one of Bill Clinton's most outspoken defenders in 1998. But he can also take an independent stand: He was one of the most vocal supporters of the Gulf war resolution in 1991 and he sharply criticized Clinton's Kosovo policy in 1999. He can seize a leadership role, as he did on the 1992 Cuban Democracy Act that tightened trade restrictions on Cuba. His ambitiousness caused him to be passed over for head of the Democratic Congressional Campaign Committee in 1990 and Democratic national chairman in 1995, but it also caused him to be chosen head of the Democratic Senatorial Campaign Committee after the 1998 election.

Torricelli has kept a high profile on foreign issues. On Haiti he favored tough sanctions, as on Cuba, the course Bill Clinton eventually took. He sought better protection of Taiwan from potential Chinese aggression; he challenged the labeling of the Iranian Mujahedin as "terrorist;" he opposed Clinton's 1995 agreement with Fidel Castro to restrict admission of Cuban refugees. On the House Intelligence Committee in 1995, he made national headlines when he announced that a Guatemalan military officer on the CIA payroll had been linked to the killings of an American innkeeper and a guerrilla leader in Guatemala. Colleagues charged that he broke his oath not to disclose confidential material; he said he got the information from outside sources, and in any case had an obligation to disclose a crime.

In August 1995 Bill Bradley announced he would not run for re-election in 1996, and Torricelli rushed into the race for Senate. He cleared away any Democratic opposition and raised money at a record-setting pace: $6.8 million by July 1996, spending $9 million in all, the most of any non-self-financing candidate in 1996. He had sponsored popular bills in the House: a handgun ban on those convicted of domestic violence, a deal to end ocean dumping in the New Jersey Mud Dump Site, a mandated 48-hour hospital stay for childbirth, welfare reform requiring community service after two years of benefits. Torricelli had serious opposition from 12th District Republican Congressman Dick Zimmer, who maneuvered former Governor Tom Kean out of the race and spent $8 million. Zimmer was solidly conservative on taxes, more moderate on cultural issues—pro-choice on abortion, for environmental protection of undeveloped land. He was chief sponsor of Megan's Law, requiring the disclosure of the whereabouts of released sexual offenders like the one who killed seven-year-old Megan Kanka in New Jersey.

The campaign was classically hard-hitting. Torricelli hit Zimmer for supporting the assault weapons ban, Medicare "cuts," changes in student loans, renewal of ocean dumping and constantly brought up Newt Gingrich. Zimmer attacked Torricelli for missing many votes, for liberal votes on crime, for increasing taxes; Zimmer ran ads showing Whitman endorsing him. An odd story came forward, that Torricelli in the 1980s provided a home for a teenager whose father was a fugitive on charges of stealing $34 million from banks in California. Editorialists and commentators bemoaned all the attack ads, and in fact the ads were not terribly effective. Torricelli was going with the flow: Opinion in New Jersey was clearly hostile to the Gingrich Republicans, and moving sharply toward Bill Clinton, who got 43% of the vote here in 1992 and 54% in 1996. Torricelli won 53%–43%, losing the western suburbs and the Jersey Shore, but piling up large margins in the counties within an hour's drive of New York and Philadelphia.

Torricelli's aggressiveness became immediately apparent in the Senate. He gave a rousing speech in the December 1996 Democratic Caucus, and was named vice chairman of the Democratic Senatorial Campaign Committee. His maiden speech, in which he decided to cast the decisive vote against the balanced budget amendment even though he had campaigned for it, attracted much attention. His voting record was fairly moderate on economic and foreign issues, but his partisanship was high: He leaped to the defense of Mary Landrieu when her election was challenged and Bill Clinton when charged with fundraising abuses. He attracted some negative attention when he said that hearings on Asian-American contributors roused the same kind of ethnic prejudice he remembered being roused against Italian-Americans by Estes Kefauver's hearings in the 1950s (the Kefauver committee disbanded when Torricelli was five days old). He reveled in occupying Robert Kennedy's old Senate office ("I admire Robert Kennedy not only for the passionate and thoughtful manner in which he addressed issues, but the practical ability to use power") and in the wide range the Senate gave him to explore issues: "I've found being in the Senate to be a very liberating experience. The House is so structured by its rules, and members are so compartmentalized by ideologies or interests. Sometimes it's hard to make an impact."

Torricelli's legislative initiatives seem well chosen for New Jersey. He added a provision to the hate crimes bill to require reporting of harassments, vandalism and assaults on campus. He backed raising the threshold for the inheritance tax from $600,000 to $1.275 million—New Jersey is a high-income state. He thwarted proposed national organ donor guidelines in October 1998; the waiting time for organs is much lower in New Jersey than nationally. With Republican Paul Coverdell he sponsored the bill for tax-free savings accounts for children's education, which could be used for private schools, colleges or trade schools. It passed the Senate 59–36 in June 1998, with only eight Democratic votes, and was vetoed in July by Bill Clinton. To Democrats who said this was unprogressive, Torricelli said, "Nobody told me when I became a Democrat that that involved opposition to lower taxes."

On impeachment, Torricelli was a steadfast Clinton supporter, dismissing the case for conviction as unserious, racing fellow New York area freshman Charles Schumer to the microphones at every recess in the Senate trial. It was a role to be expected from one just named head of the DSCC; no one else wanted the job, and Torricelli sniffed the prospect of gains. "The difference between 1998 and 2000 is the difference between defense and offense." It was Torricelli who on *Meet the Press* in January 1999 first mentioned, without asking her permission, that Hillary Rodham Clinton was thinking about running for the Senate in New York. This ignited a firestorm of speculation, and put in the shade the likely nominee otherwise, Congresswoman Nita Lowey; to criticism, Torricelli blandly replied that he was trying to prod Clinton into running. Meanwhile, after New Jersey colleague Frank Lautenberg announced his retirement in February 1999, Torricelli's maneuverings prompted backers of two potential candidates (Congressman Frank Pallone and Goldman Sachs chairman Jon Corzine) to claim they had his support, while a potential candidate who dropped out of the race, Congressman Robert Menendez, said Torricelli reneged on a pledge of support. In March 1999, when Torricelli was briefing Democratic senators on the races, Lautenberg accused Torricelli of being too friendly with the Republican candidate, Governor Christie Whitman; Torricelli was enraged and in full view after the meeting approached Lautenberg and, as *The New York Times* daintily put it, "made a vulgar threat on his manhood." It is a common thing for senators of the same party and the same state to have a frayed, even acrimonious relationship; the relationship between Lautenberg and Torricelli, both aggressive men quick to take offense, may set the all-time record in this regard, at least since 1859, when California Senator David Broderick was killed in a duel by David Terry.

In December 1998 Torricelli got a seat on Foreign Relations. In March and April 1999 he harshly criticized the Clinton policy in Kosovo, especially the ruling out of ground troops; he said that Clinton had no clear strategy and that the White House advisers were terrible. He has evidently given the White House some thought himself, and has said he expects to seek one more term in the Senate and then run for president in 2008. As he told *The New York Times*'s

James Dao, "I do not want to spend 18 years rising through the committee ranks in order to exercise some influence over education and tax policies, law enforcement issues and others. I've wanted to do this all my life, but I'm not going to do this the rest of my life."

Presidential politics. New Jersey has been a close state in close presidential elections most of this century, and has usually supported the winner—Kennedy in 1960, Nixon in 1968, Reagan in 1980, Bush in 1988—and only occasionally backing the loser—Dewey in 1948, Ford in 1976. Its demographic makeup is similar to New York's, but there is no huge central city here, and a lower percentage of Jews and fewer singles; hence New Jersey was closer to the national average. But in 1996 New Jersey seemed to move noticeably to the left of the nation, voting 54%–36% for Clinton. One reason is the relative absence of the new Republican base of the religious right; such voters are numerous in the vast interior of the country from the Appalachians to the Sierra Nevada and in the South Atlantic states as well, but not in the Northeast and New Jersey. Absent a change in the face of the national Republican Party, New Jersey may find itself no longer the host of dozens of visits of presidential and vice presidential candidates—the more so if New Jersey's Bill Bradley is the Democratic presidential nominee.

For years, New Jersey's June presidential primary was overshadowed by California's on the same day. In 1996 California voted in March, and New Jersey did not get to the polls until two months after the nominations were sewed up. The last time New Jersey mattered much was 1984, when Walter Mondale seized on a quip by Gary Hart and took most of the state's delegates. In 1998 the Assembly voted to move the primary to March 7, 2000, but the Senate never followed suit; there was argument between those who wanted to keep the state primary in June and those who thought that was too expensive and wanted one primary for both. It might be assumed that Bill Bradley will carry his own state in the Democratic contest, and indeed his numbers are good; but most of New Jersey's Democratic establishment in early 1999 was supporting Al Gore, and an early primary would give them a chance to demolish Bradley's candidacy.

Congressional districting. New Jersey lost a seat in the 1990 Census and the Democrats, in control of the legislature and governor in 1991, fumbled the chance to draw new district lines before the Republicans unexpectedly won a veto-proof margin in both chambers in November 1991. The current plan, with its grotesquely-shaped districts, is the product of a bipartisan commission—proof that bipartisanship doesn't always produce neat and orderly outcomes. Republicans will have complete control in 2001 and, with the example of a decade ago before them, presumably won't fritter it away. The districts most likely to be squeezed are the 12th and the 6th, in the center of the state, both now held by Democrats.

The People: Est. Pop. 1998: 8,115,011; Pop. 1990: 7,730,188, up 4.7% 1990–1998. 3% of U.S. total, 9th largest; 10.6% rural. Median age: 36 years. 13.9% 65 years and over. 79.4% White, 13.4% Black, 3.5% Asian, 0.2% Amer. Indian, 3.6% Other; 9.3% Hispanic Origin. Households: 56.5% married couple families; 26.5% married couple fams. w. children; 45.6% college educ.; median household income: $40,927; per capita income: $18,714; 64.9% owner occupied housing; median house value: $162,300; median monthly rent: $521. 4.6% Unemployment. 1998 Voting age pop.: 6,075,000. 1998 Turnout: 1,894,496; 31% of VAP. Registered voters (1998): 4,538,944; 1,141,593 D (25%), 872,349 R (19%), 2,525,002 unaffiliated and minor parties (56%).

Political Lineup: Governor, Christine Todd Whitman (R); Secy. of State, DeForest B. Soaries Jr. (I); Atty. Gen., Peter Verniero (R); Treasurer, James A. DiEleuterio Jr. (R); State Senate, 40 (16 D, 24 R); Majority Leader, John Bennett (R); State Assembly, 80 (32 D, 48 R); Assembly Speaker, Jack Collins (R). Senators, Frank Lautenberg (D) and Robert G. Torricelli (D). Representatives, 13 (7 D, 6 R).

Elections Division: 609-292-3760; **Filing Deadline for U.S. Congress:** April 13, 2000.

1996 Presidential Vote

Clinton (D) 1,651,019 (54%)
Dole (R) 1,102,577 (36%)
Perot (I) 261,932 (9%)
Others 59,424 (2%)

1996 Republican Presidential Primary

Dole (R) 180,412 (82%)
Buchanan (R) 23,789 (11%)
Keyes (R) 14,611 (7%)

1992 Presidential Vote

Clinton (D) 1,436,206 (43%)
Bush (R) 1,356,865 (41%)
Perot (I) 521,829 (16%)

GOVERNOR

Gov. Christine Todd Whitman (R)

Elected 1993, term expires Jan. 2002; b. Sept. 26, 1946, New York City, NY; home, Oldwick; Wheaton Col., B.A. 1968; Presbyterian; married (John).

Elected Office: Somerset Cnty. Bd. of Chosen Freeholders, 1983–88; Repub. nominee, U.S. Senate, 1990.

Professional Career: Staff Asst., Repub. Natl. Cmte., 1969–71; Pres., Bd. of Public Utilities, 1988–1990.

Office: State House, 125 W. State St., #CN-001, Trenton, 08625, 609-292-6000; Fax: 609-292-3454; Web site: www.state.nj.us.

Election Results

1997 gen.	Christine Todd Whitman (R)	1,133,394	(47%)
	Jim McGreevey (D)	1,107,968	(46%)
	Murray Sabrin (L)	114,172	(5%)
	Others	65,099	(2%)
1997 prim.	Christine Todd Whitman (R)	unopposed	
1993 gen.	Christine Todd Whitman (R)	1,236,124	(49%)
	Jim Florio (D)	1,210,031	(48%)
	Others	59,809	(2%)

SENATORS

Sen. Frank Lautenberg (D)

Elected 1982, seat up 2000; b. Jan. 23, 1924, Paterson; home, Montclair; Columbia U., B.S. 1949; Jewish; divorced.

Military Career: Army Signal Corps, 1942–46 (WWII).

Professional Career: Co-founder, Automatic Data Processing, 1952–82; NY & NJ Port Authority Comm., 1978–82.

DC Office: 506 HSOB, 20510, 202-224-4744; Fax: 202-224-9707; Web site: www.senate.gov/~lautenberg.

State Offices: Barrington, 609-757-5353; Newark, 973-645-3030.

Committees: *Appropriations* (5th of 13 D): Commerce, Justice, State & the Judiciary; Defense; Foreign Operations & Export Financing; Transportation (RMM); VA, HUD & Independent Agencies. *Budget* (RMM of 10 D). *Environment & Public Works* (3d of 8 D): Fisheries, Wildlife & Drinking Water; Superfund, Waste Control & Risk Assessment (RMM). *Intelligence* (7th of 8 D).

Group Ratings

	ADA	ACLU	AFS	LCV	CON	NTU	NFIB	COC	ACU	NTLC	CHC
1998	95	86	100	100	22	13	33	50	4	0	0
1997	95	—	89	—	29	20	—	60	0	—	—

National Journal Ratings

	1997 LIB	—	1997 CONS	1998 LIB	—	1998 CONS
Economic	82%	—	12%	90%	—	0%
Social	71%	—	0%	74%	—	0%
Foreign	83%	—	14%	91%	—	5%

Key Votes of the 105th Congress

1. Bal. Budget Amend.	N	5. Satcher for Surgeon Gen.	Y	9. Chem. Weapons Treaty	Y
2. Clinton Budget Deal	N	6. Highway Set-asides	Y	10. Cuban Humanitarian Aid	Y
3. Cloture on Tobacco	Y	7. Table Child Gun locks	N	11. Table Bosnia Troops	Y
4. Education IRAs	N	8. Ovrd. Part. Birth Veto	N	12. $ for Test-ban Treaty	Y

Election Results

1994 general	Frank Lautenberg (D)	1,033,487	(50%)	($8,217,716)
	Garabed (Chuck) Haytaian (R)	966,244	(47%)	($5,110,378)
	Others	55,156	(3%)	
1994 primary	Frank Lautenberg (D)	151,416	(81%)	
	Bill Campbell (D)	26,066	(14%)	
	Lynne A. Speed (D)	9,563	(5%)	
1988 general	Frank Lautenberg (D)	1,599,905	(54%)	($7,298,663)
	Peter M. Dawkins (R)	1,349,937	(46%)	($7,616,249)

Sen. Robert G. Torricelli (D)

Elected 1996, seat up 2002; b. Aug. 26, 1951, Paterson; home, Englewood; Rutgers U., B.A. 1974, J.D. 1977, Harvard JFK Schl. of Govt., M.P.A. 1980; United Methodist; divorced.

Elected Office: U.S. House of Reps., 1982–96.

Professional Career: Asst., NJ Gov. Brendan Byrne, 1975–77; Cnsl., Vice Pres. Walter Mondale, 1978–81; Practicing atty., 1981–82.

DC Office: 113 DSOB, 20510, 202-224-3224; Fax: 202-224-8567; Web site: www.senate.gov/~torricelli.

State Offices: Bellmawr, 609-933-2245; Newark, 973-624-5555.

Committees: *DSCC Chairman. Foreign Relations* (8th of 8 D): East Asian & Pacific Affairs; Near Eastern & South Asian Affairs; Western Hemisphere, Peace Corps, Narcotics & Terrorism. *Governmental Affairs* (5th of 7 D): Government Management, Restructuring and the District of Columbia; International Security, Proliferation & Federal Services. *Judiciary* (7th of 8 D): Administrative Oversight & the Courts (RMM); Antitrust, Business Rights & Competition; Criminal Justice Oversight. *Rules & Administration* (6th of 7 D).

Group Ratings

	ADA	ACLU	AFS	LCV	CON	NTU	NFIB	COC	ACU	NTLC	CHC
1998	85	86	88	88	22	18	38	47	8	22	9
1997	80	—	78	—	18	22	—	40	16	—	—

National Journal Ratings

	1997 LIB — 1997 CONS			1998 LIB — 1998 CONS		
Economic	77%	—	22%	67%	—	32%
Social	71%	—	0%	74%	—	0%
Foreign	59%	—	38%	51%	—	36%

Key Votes of the 105th Congress

1. Bal. Budget Amend.	N	5. Satcher for Surgeon Gen.	Y	9. Chem. Weapons Treaty	Y
2. Clinton Budget Deal	N	6. Highway Set-asides	Y	10. Cuban Humanitarian Aid	N
3. Cloture on Tobacco	Y	7. Table Child Gun locks	N	11. Table Bosnia Troops	Y
4. Education IRAs	Y	8. Ovrd. Part. Birth Veto	N	12. $ for Test-ban Treaty	Y

Election Results

1996 general	Robert G. Torricelli (D)	1,519,154	(53%)	($9,134,854)
	Dick Zimmer (R)	1,227,351	(43%)	($8,238,181)
	Others	136,961	(5%)	
1996 primary	Robert G. Torricelli (D)	unopposed		
1990 general	Bill Bradley (D)	977,810	(50%)	($12,444,283)
	Christine Todd Whitman (R)	918,874	(47%)	($801,660)
	Others	41,770	(2%)	

FIRST DISTRICT

There are few urban spaces that have been more ravaged than Camden, New Jersey. Across the Delaware River from Philadelphia's skyline, its closely built streets were jammed with immigrants in the 19th Century, when poet Walt Whitman lived here. In 1894, a Camden machinist named Eldridge Johnson produced the Victor Talking Machine—the birth of the company that became RCA Victor in 1929. In 1897, Camden was the site of the invention of condensed soup, and the Campbell Soup Company was founded soon afterwards. Thus Camden became a major industrial locus on the Jersey side of the Delaware River, not the broadest and certainly not the most picturesque of our Atlantic estuaries, but probably the East Coast's premier industrial waterway, with a concentration of steel factories, chemical plants and oil tank farms equal to any in the country. The flat lands of South Jersey all around, ignored in the 19th Century, had easy access to cheap water transport and plenty of skilled labor from the Philadelphia area. For a quarter-century starting in the 1940s, they became one of the country's fastest-growing industrial areas. Now, Camden has tended to empty out, many of its factories closed, its neighborhoods beset by crime, its local government so incompetent the state was moving toward a takeover. But the local Cooper's Ferry Development Corporation has developed a riverfront park, with the New Jersey Aquarium and the Sony Music/Pace amphitheater, that takes advantage of Camden's site and attracts multiracial crowds; an aerospace complex and a Campbell Soup office tower have gone up. Still, city government and crime remain major impediments to Camden making additional strides.

The 1st Congressional District is, more or less, greater Camden, the Delaware riverfront from Riverton south to a point across from the Delaware state line, and suburbs running southeast to the flat vegetable fields of South Jersey. Its boroughs and townships retain their separate identities; right next to Camden is Collingswood, with its middle-class porches still freshly painted and its shops prosperous. The district includes some underclass poor, but most people here are at some level of upward mobility from the grinding working-class life of 50 years ago, living in comfortable communities, worried that the petrochemical plants which have helped many of them move up may also be poisoning their land, water and air. Politically, this is an area with a Democratic heritage, the most Democratic district in South Jersey.

The 1st District is represented by Rob Andrews, one of the most interesting young Democratic congressmen. Andrews grew up in Bellmawr, the son of a shipyard worker, made a splendid record in college and law school, returned home and with then-Congressman Jim Florio's support was elected to the Camden County Board of Chosen Freeholders (wonderful name!) before he was 30. When Florio left Congress to become governor in January 1990, he postponed the special election to replace him until November; he supported Andrews, though Andrews was silent on his tax increase. Andrews had other help. He spent $541,000 on his campaign, and he had a Republican opponent who switched positions on abortion and claimed to have attended a college he hadn't. Even so, in the anti-Florio climate, Andrews won by only 54%–43%.

Andrews entered the House as its youngest Democrat and has proved to be one of its most aggressive and independent-minded reformers. One big initiative was direct student loans. Andrews felt banks were making college loans inefficiently and that direct government loans would "save money for students, families, schools and the federal treasury." Against strong lobbying opposition, he got the House to approve direct loan demonstration projects, got candidate Bill Clinton to endorse the idea in 1992 and then got it passed into law in 1993. He argues that it is one of the major achievements of the Clinton Administration. He has a rather conservative record on economics and foreign policy but is more liberal on cultural issues. He voted against tax increases, including the Clinton budget package of 1993 and announced early opposition to the Clinton health care program. To some of Andrews's Democratic critics, he is a grandstander who would cut needed government programs. But his record shows that he supports government that is vigorous and serves real needs—but insists on pruning government that isn't working and on not forcing voters to pay more in taxes for the same low level of services they've been getting.

Andrews's other priority that made him stand out in the early Clinton years was the A-to-Z spending cut; its originator, New Hampshire Republican Bill Zeliff, looked for a Democratic co-sponsor whose name started with A and came up with Andrews. The idea was to set aside 56 hours of congressional debate during which any member could propose reducing or zeroing out spending on any program, with a guaranteed roll call vote. Speaker Thomas Foley strongly opposed it, and Andrews and Zeliff, with 228 co-sponsors, sought to come up with 218 signatures on a discharge petition to get it out of committee. This helped trigger the reform making discharge signatures public, but Foley twisted enough arms to keep it from the floor. Interest waned when Republicans took control and Zeliff left to run for governor; instead Speaker Newt Gingrich put his somewhat similar Corrections Day procedure into effect.

In the Republican House Andrews has had less opportunity for such initiatives and perhaps less interest, for his focus has remained on New Jersey. After the November 1996 election he announced he was running for governor; he managed to get the endorsements of Jim Florio and Hudson County Executive Bob Janiszewski, who were both mentioned as candidates themselves. Andrews was initially favored to win the primary, but he ran into stiff competition from state Senator James McGreevey, who had the backing of more-Democratic county organizations plus key elements of organized labor. Former Morris County Prosecutor Michael Murphy was the dark horse of the race, running, he said, as the "un-candidate." Andrews promised never to raise taxes, said he would force auto insurance costs down by requiring companies to lower rates if they wanted to continue issuing other policies, and called for combining the state's three toll road authorities. McGreevey said he would create a new insurance commissioner's office and proposed education referenda. Andrews swept south Jersey and took Hudson County, but McGreevey's big margins in Middlesex, Essex and Union Counties gave him a tight 39%–37% win, with Murphy taking 21%.

Andrews has been re-elected to the House by overwhelming margins and has continued to live in Haddon Heights, commuting by train to the Capitol. In the 105th Congress he helped win passage of a bill ensuring the rights of grandparents to visit grandchildren who moved to states with different custody laws. Despite his split with the Camden County Democratic organization which started in 1995 and widened to open rupture in 1998, his House seat seems safe as long as he wants it. His close loss in the gubernatorial primary does not rule out another race in 2001, when a wide-open contest seems likely. In the House, he joined the Armed Services Committee in 1999, a belated move that left him junior to 17 Democrats who were first elected to the House after Andrews.

Cook's Call. *Safe.* Don't look for a competitive race in this solidly Democratic district.

The People: Pop. 1990: 594,494; 3.9% rural; 12.2% age 65 + ; 78.4% White, 15.8% Black, 1.7% Asian, 0.2% Amer. Indian, 3.9% Other; 5.8% Hispanic Origin. Households: 53.9% married couple families; 27.5% married couple fams. w. children; 37.9% college educ.; median household income: $35,250; per capita income: $14,502; median house value: $94,100; median gross rent: $442.

1996 Presidential Vote			1992 Presidential Vote		
Clinton (D)	132,715	(59%)	Clinton (D)	118,060	(48%)
Dole (R)	61,294	(27%)	Bush (R)	78,095	(32%)
Perot (I)	25,052	(11%)	Perot (I)	48,252	(20%)
Others	5,122	(2%)			

Rep. Robert Andrews (D)

Elected 1990; b. Aug. 4, 1957, Camden; home, Haddon Heights; Bucknell U., B.A. 1979, Cornell U., J.D. 1982; Episcopalian; married (Camille).

Elected Office: Camden Cnty. Bd. of Chosen Freeholders, 1987–90.

Professional Career: Practicing atty., 1982–90; Adjunct Prof., Rutgers Law Schl., 1985–86, 1989–90.

DC Office: 2439 RHOB 20515, 202-225-6501; Fax: 202-225-6583; Web site: www.house.gov/andrews.

District Offices: Haddon Heights, 609-546-5100; Woodbury, 609-848-3900.

Committees: *Armed Services* (25th of 28 D): Military Research & Development; Special Oversight Panel on Morale, Welfare and Recreation. *Education & the Workforce* (8th of 22 D): Employer-Employee Relations (RMM); Postsecondary Education, Training & Life-Long Learning.

Group Ratings

	ADA	ACLU	AFS	LCV	CON	NTU	NFIB	COC	ACU	NTLC	CHC
1998	95	75	100	100	80	27	36	44	12	14	8
1997	85	—	75	—	94	38	—	33	22	—	—

National Journal Ratings

	1997 LIB — 1997 CONS			1998 LIB — 1998 CONS		
Economic	69%	—	31%	63%	—	36%
Social	71%	—	27%	70%	—	28%
Foreign	62%	—	37%	55%	—	44%

Key Votes of the 105th Congress

1. Clinton Budget Deal	N	5. Puerto Rico Sthood. Ref.	Y	9. Cut $ for B-2 Bombers	Y
2. Education IRAs	N	6. End Highway Set-asides	N	10. Human Rights in China	Y
3. Req. 2/3 to Raise Taxes	Y	7. School Prayer Amend.	N	11. Withdraw Bosnia Troops	N
4. Fast-track Trade	N	8. Ovrd. Part. Birth Veto	N	12. End Cuban TV-Marti	N

Election Results

1998 general	Robert Andrews (D)	90,279	(73%)	($332,906)
	Ronald L. Richards (R)	27,855	(23%)	($8,796)
	Others	5,208	(4%)	
1998 primary	Robert Andrews (D)	unopposed		
1996 general	Robert Andrews (D)	160,413	(76%)	($414,266)
	Mel Suplee (R)	44,287	(21%)	($9,010)
	Others	6,034	(3%)	

SECOND DISTRICT

The builders of the Camden & Atlantic Railroad in 1852 may not have known it, but when they extended their line to the little inlet town of Absecon, they were starting America's biggest beach resort, Atlantic City. Like all resorts, it was a product of developments elsewhere: of industrialization and spreading affluence, of railroad technology and the conquest of diseases which used to make summer a time of terror for parents and doctors. In the years after the Civil War, first Atlantic City and then the whole Jersey Shore from Brigantine to Cape May became America's first seaside resort, and Atlantic City developed its characteristic features: the Boardwalk in 1870, the amusement pier in 1882, the rolling chair in 1884, salt water taffy in the 1890s, Miss America in 1921. By 1940, when 16 million Americans visited every summer, Atlantic City was a common man's resort of old traditions; it declined in the years after World War II as people could afford nicer vacations. By the early 1970s, Atlantic City was grim, with a bedraggled convention hall (site of the 1964 Democratic National Convention), empty hotels and bleak streets of rowhouses built in the ugliest Philadelphia style.

Then in 1977, New Jersey voters legalized casino gambling in Atlantic City and gleaming new hotels sprang up, big name entertainers came in and Atlantic City became more glamorous than it had been in 90 years. But not for all of its residents: casino and hotel jobs tend to be low-wage, and the slums begin just feet from the massive parking lots of the casinos. In the 1990s Atlantic City's gambling business was thriving—casinos came out ahead $4 billion in 1998—and huge new casinos were built on both Boardwalk and bayside. Now listed among the top 10 House districts nationwide for tourist economies, Atlantic City is growing into what Las Vegas has become, not just a collection of gaudy casinos but a gaggle of theme parks, with entertainment for the family as well as adults.

The Jersey Shore south of Atlantic City is a string of different resorts. There is the old Methodist town of Ocean City, where Gay Talese grew up the son of Italian immigrants, as he tells movingly in *Unto the Sons*. There is Wildwood, with its gritty boardwalk, and Cape May, with its beautifully preserved Victorian houses. Behind the Shore are swamp and flatland, the Pine Barrens and vegetable fields that gave New Jersey the name "Garden State." Growth has been slow in these small towns and gas station intersections, communities in whose eerie calmness in the summer you can hear mosquitoes whining. In the flatness, you can also find towns clustered around low-wage apparel factories or petrochemical plants on the Delaware estuary; the Northeast high-tech service economy has not reached this far south in Jersey yet.

This part of South Jersey makes up the 2d Congressional District. Politically, it has strong Democratic presences in the chemical industry towns along the Delaware River and in Vineland and a strong Republican presence in Cape May; Atlantic City often votes Democratic but has an antique Republican machine which goes back generations. Democrats have carried the area in all 1990s statewide elections. This is prime marginal territory, off the beaten track of Northeast politics.

The congressman from the 2d District is Frank LoBiondo, a Republican elected in 1994. He grew up in Vineland, went to college in Philadelphia and worked for the family trucking firm, LoBiondo Brothers Motor Express. In 1987 he was elected to the Assembly, where he stoutly opposed new taxes. LoBiondo also opposes gun control, and was backed by the National

Rifle Association. In 1992 LoBiondo ran against Congressman William Hughes, first elected in 1974, a former prosecutor who worked on crime bills. Hughes won 56%–42%, his lowest margin ever, and he decided to retire in 1994. LoBiondo ran again and in the primary faced Atlantic County state Senator William Gormley; LoBiondo attacked him as a taxer and NRA ads called him "a liberal in Republican clothing." To the surprise of many, LoBiondo won 54%–35%. And then easily won the general, 65%–35%.

In the House, LoBiondo has compiled a moderate voting record, especially on economic issues. He was one of six Republicans to vote against Newt Gingrich's Medicare plan in October 1995 (four were from New Jersey); he voted against a veterans' appropriation as having insufficient medical care and against exempting small businesses from the minimum wage. Much of his effort has been devoted to local issues. He is a founder and co-chair of the Congressional Gaming Caucus. In 1996 he hailed passage of the water resources bill with major beach restoration for Atlantic City. In February 1997 he rallied local officials against a study recommending that the FAA's William J. Hughes Technical Center be moved from Egg Harbor Township to Oklahoma. He sponsored the Honesty in Sweepstakes Act of 1998, to require a disclaimer on magazine sweepstakes mailings; he has a bill to ban Internet gambling. The bill he and Peter Visclosky sponsored to provide $25 million in funding for bulletproof vests for police officers passed almost unanimously. In 1997 he won a seat on the Transportation Committee, just as it was poised to consider the big 1998 transportation bill. He continues to promote the New Jersey Coastal Heritage Traii.

LoBiondo was easily re-elected in 1996. In 1998 the only Democrat to challenge him, Derek Hunsberger, said he supported legalizing recreational drugs; local Democratic politicians disavowed him; Hunsberger basically abandoned his campaign in April 1998. LoBiondo was re-elected 66%–31%.

Cook's Call. *Safe.* Based on past Democratic performance here, especially on the Presidential level, one would think that this district would be a prime target for Democrats. But LoBiondo, who has easily won here since 1994, has turned this swing district into rather safe territory for himself.

The People: Pop. 1990: 594,723; 29.7% rural; 15.4% age 65 +; 80.7% White, 14.1% Black, 1.2% Asian, 0.4% Amer. Indian, 3.5% Other; 6.3% Hispanic Origin. Households: 53.2% married couple families; 24.5% married couple fams. w. children; 35.7% college educ.; median household income: $32,410; per capita income: $14,732; median house value: $93,900; median gross rent: $446.

1996 Presidential Vote			1992 Presidential Vote		
Clinton (D)	117,526	(50%)	Clinton (D)	101,718	(40%)
Dole (R)	84,043	(36%)	Bush (R)	97,696	(39%)
Perot (I)	27,589	(12%)	Perot (I)	50,773	(20%)
Others	4,464	(2%)			

Rep. Frank A. LoBiondo (R)

Elected 1994; b. May 12, 1946, Bridgeton; home, Vineland; St. Joseph's U., B.A. 1968; Catholic; married (Jan).

Elected Office: Cumberland Cnty. Bd. of Chosen Freeholders, 1985–88; NJ Assembly, 1987–94.

Professional Career: Operations Mgr., LoBiondo Bros. Motor Express Inc., 1968–94.

DC Office: 222 CHOB 20515, 202-225-6572; Fax: 202-225-3318; Web site: www.house.gov/lobiondo.

District Office: Mays Landing, 609-625-5008.

Committees: *Small Business* (6th of 19 R): Empowerment; Rural Enterprise, Business Opportunities & Special Small Business Problems (Chmn.). *Transportation & Infrastructure* (29th of 41 R): Aviation; Coast Guard & Maritime Transportation (Vice Chmn.); Water Resources & Environment.

Group Ratings

	ADA	ACLU	AFS	LCV	CON	NTU	NFIB	COC	ACU	NTLC	CHC
1998	30	13	44	69	26	46	86	78	68	47	67
1997	35	—	50	—	62	61	—	67	68	—	—

National Journal Ratings

	1997 LIB — 1997 CONS		1998 LIB — 1998 CONS	
Economic	48% —	52%	50% —	50%
Social	30% —	64%	38% —	60%
Foreign	45% —	55%	7% —	83%

Key Votes of the 105th Congress

1. Clinton Budget Deal	Y	5. Puerto Rico Sthood. Ref.	N	9. Cut $ for B-2 Bombers	Y
2. Education IRAs	N	6. End Highway Set-asides	Y	10. Human Rights in China	Y
3. Req. 2/3 to Raise Taxes	Y	7. School Prayer Amend.	Y	11. Withdraw Bosnia Troops	Y
4. Fast-track Trade	N	8. Ovrd. Part. Birth Veto	Y	12. End Cuban TV-Marti	N

Election Results

1998 general	Frank A. LoBiondo (R)	93,248	(66%)	($382,050)
	Derek Hunsberger (D)	43,563	(31%)	
	Others	4,703	(3%)	
1998 primary	Frank A. LoBiondo (R)	unopposed		
1996 general	Frank A. LoBiondo (R)	133,131	(60%)	($890,526)
	Ruth Katz (D)	83,890	(38%)	($806,232)
	Others	3,697	(2%)	

THIRD DISTRICT

The Pine Barrens of New Jersey are one of the last vacant spots on the eastern seaboard; not quite *terra incognita*, but still not thickly populated. Encroached by the Philadelphia suburbs of South Jersey on the west and burgeoning retirement developments of the Jersey Shore on the east, they are crossed even today mostly by narrow two-lane roads; there are only a few small towns here, plus Fort Dix and McGuire Air Force Base. For years, the Barrens were seen as a barrier to civilization; only recently have environment-minded Jerseyites come to see them as a natural treasure.

The 3d Congressional District spans the Pine Barrens. Most of its residents live in the South Jersey suburbs of Philadelphia, in the spread-out suburb of Cherry Hill with its 1960s and 1970s shopping centers, or in the older towns along the Delaware River and newer ones inland toward McGuire. This is comfortable, but not hugely affluent, suburban country. East of the Pine Barrens is Ocean County, including the barrier islands from Normandy Beach south to Little Egg Harbor, with older beachfront communities and larger clusters of new subdivisions and condominium complexes inland. Ocean County grew rapidly in the 1980s, a kind of frost belt Florida, with many retirees from New York and north Jersey eager to leave the big cities' high crime and high taxes, but still jealous of their Social Security benefits and concerned about the local environment. Politically, both the west and east ends of this district are solidly Republican.

The congressman from the 3d District is James Saxton. He grew up in South Jersey, worked as a teacher for three years, then became a real estate broker. In 1975 he was elected to the New Jersey Assembly, when Republicans were struggling to stop Governor Brendan Byrne's income tax. In 1984 he ran to fill a vacancy in the House, won the Republican primary 45%–41%, easily won the general and has not had a serious challenge since then.

In the House he has compiled a moderate to conservative voting record. He co-sponsored the ocean dumping law of 1988, when medical wastes were washing up against the Jersey Shore. In 1995, he was given a seat with seniority on the Resources Committee, and became chairman of the new Fisheries Conservation, Wildlife and Oceans Subcommittee. But unlike most Republicans, he did not want to revise the Endangered Species Act to require compensation of property owners whose land value decreased as a result of federal regulations, and Resources Chairman Don Young turned the issue over to Californian Richard Pombo. With Republican Wayne Gilchrest, Saxton came up with a proposal for tax incentives for landowners who help protect endangered species before they are listed. With memories of the ocean dumping of 1988 still fresh, he opposed House Republican changes to the Clean Water Act, and persuaded all but one New Jersey member to join him in opposing the bill in 1995. He supported a revision of the Safe Drinking Water Act in 1996, and with Democrat Henry Waxman authored a "right to know" provision requiring water utilities to disclose pollutants. He backed legislation to clean up 28 "nationally significant" local estuaries and has won millions of dollars to study high childhood cancer in Toms River. He was one of four New Jersey Republicans to vote against the Republican Medicare plan in October 1995.

Saxton is a supporter of strong anti-terrorism efforts and of aid to Israel. After the 1998 bombings of U.S. embassies in Kenya and Tanzania, he criticized the "lack of determination" to punish terrorists. He sponsored a bill that allowed a local couple to successfully sue Iran for their daughter's death in a 1995 Gaza Strip bombing; that apparently was the first time that a U.S. citizen won damages in federal court from a foreign government in a terrorism case. In April 1999 he went to Belgrade and met with the foreign minister, to the surprise of the White House, but did not secure release of the three soldiers captured by the Serbians or further any negotiations.

On the Joint Economic Committee, he worked with Majority Leader Dick Armey to question the Clinton Administration's request for an additional $18 billion to the IMF. His efforts pressured IMF officials to open their operations to greater public view; after months of delay, the House agreed that some Asian and Latin American nations might go bankrupt and in October 1998 approved the full amount. With a seat on Armed Services he has worked to save local bases. When Fort Dix ended up on the 1991 base closing list, Saxton turned much of it into a federal prison and state police training center. When McGuire Air Force base was on the 1993 list, Saxton convinced the commission the base needed to be expanded as the East Coast air mobility hub for the armed forces.

Cook's Call. *Safe.* Saxton continues to be re-elected easily here election after election. He's a sure favorite in 2000.

The People: Pop. 1990: 594,667; 18.4% rural; 15.6% age 65 + ; 89% White, 8% Black, 2% Asian, 0.2% Amer. Indian, 0.8% Other; 2.5% Hispanic Origin. Households: 64.6% married couple families; 29.6% married couple fams. w. children; 47.5% college educ.; median household income: $41,257; per capita income: $18,138; median house value: $129,200; median gross rent: $568.

1996 Presidential Vote

Clinton (D) 134,326 (50%)
Dole (R) 101,100 (38%)
Perot (I) 28,212 (11%)
Others 4,914 (2%)

1992 Presidential Vote

Clinton (D) 114,503 (40%)
Bush (R) 113,583 (40%)
Perot (I) 54,996 (19%)

Rep. Jim Saxton (R)

Elected 1984; b. Jan. 22, 1943, Nicholson, PA; home, Mt. Holly; E. Stroudsburg St. Col., B.A. 1965, Temple U., 1967–68; United Methodist; divorced.

Elected Office: NJ Assembly, 1975–82; NJ Senate, 1982–84.

Professional Career: Jr. High schl. teacher, 1965–68; Real estate broker, 1968–84.

DC Office: 339 CHOB 20515, 202-225-4765; Fax: 202-225-0778; Web site: www.house.gov/saxton.

District Offices: Cherry Hill, 609-428-0520; Mt. Holly, 609-261-5800; Ocean County, 732-914-2020; Toms River, 908-914-2020.

Committees: *Armed Services* (9th of 32 R): Military Installations & Facilities; Military Procurement; Special Oversight Panel on the Merchant Marine. *Resources* (4th of 28 R): Fisheries Conservation, Wildlife & Oceans (Chmn.). *Joint Economic Committee* (Vice Chmn. of 10 Reps.).

Group Ratings

	ADA	ACLU	AFS	LCV	CON	NTU	NFIB	COC	ACU	NTLC	CHC
1998	25	25	43	69	28	46	85	81	63	58	83
1997	30	—	25	—	56	45	—	80	68	—	—

National Journal Ratings

	1997 LIB — 1997 CONS		1998 LIB — 1998 CONS	
Economic	41%	— 58%	37%	— 63%
Social	30%	— 64%	47%	— 53%
Foreign	38%	— 60%	27%	— 68%

Key Votes of the 105th Congress

1. Clinton Budget Deal	Y	5. Puerto Rico Sthood. Ref.	Y	9. Cut $ for B-2 Bombers	N
2. Education IRAs	Y	6. End Highway Set-asides	Y	10. Human Rights in China	N
3. Req. 2/3 to Raise Taxes	Y	7. School Prayer Amend.	N	11. Withdraw Bosnia Troops	Y
4. Fast-track Trade	*	8. Ovrd. Part. Birth Veto	Y	12. End Cuban TV-Marti	N

Election Results

1998 general	Jim Saxton (R)	97,508	(62%)	($535,528)
	Steven J. Polansky (D)	55,248	(35%)	($2,738)
	Others	4,483	(3%)	
1998 primary	Jim Saxton (R)	unopposed		
1996 general	Jim Saxton (R)	157,503	(64%)	($533,850)
	John Leonardi (D)	81,590	(33%)	($21,957)
	Others	6,185	(3%)	

FOURTH DISTRICT

New Jersey, a state long thought to be split between a North Jersey that is an appendage of New York City and a South Jersey that has the distinctive accent of Philadelphia, is becoming a state with its own identity. In the 1980s, it bubbled over with pride at its growth and new civic institutions; in 1990, it raged with anger at Governor Jim Florio's tax increases. This showed a new unity: for the great medium of protest was the first New Jersey-oriented talk radio station, begun in Trenton in 1989, and the symbolic event was the Hands Across New Jersey demonstration on a route approximating I-195, from the Jersey Shore west to the State House in Trenton overlooking the Delaware River. Trenton, an old manufacturing city ("Trenton Makes, The World Takes," the sign proclaims over the rooftops) where John Roebling of Brooklyn Bridge fame started making wire in 1848, and Walter Scott Lenox started making dishes in 1889. It is now the anomalously gritty capital—the only state capital with no large downtown hotel—of a mostly white-collar state.

The 4th Congressional District covers approximately the same span as Hands Across New Jersey, from Trenton to the Jersey Shore, roughly following I-195 to the Shore communities of Manasquan and Point Pleasant and Mantoloking. It includes the old colonial town of Burlington on the Delaware River and the Great Adventure Safari and Entertainment Park in the Pine Barrens. This is one part of America where population movement has been eastward, from the old neighborhoods of Trenton and its close-in suburbs to the new subdivisions of Ocean County and Wall Township. Trenton has long been a solidly Democratic town, but its suburbs are much less so, with the Jersey Shore parts of the district solidly Republican.

The congressman from the 4th District is Christopher Smith, a youthful-looking Republican with great seniority who has applied strong moral principles to practical politics with impressive results. Smith grew up in the Trenton area, worked in his family's sporting goods business, and was executive director of the New Jersey Right to Life Committee in the 1970s. In 1980 he ran for the House in a more Trenton-centered 4th District and beat 26-year incumbent Frank Thompson, a convicted Abscam defendant. A fluke, it seemed: but Smith proceeded to beat several additional serious Democrats, winning more than 60% each time.

His motivation comes from religion: "Christ said it in Matthew 25: 'Whatsoever you do to the least of my brethren, you do likewise to me.' That was my motivating scripture through all of my years in Right to Life, and it continues to be," he has said. He is concerned about children and about victims of human rights violations. If his anti-abortion stance comes from his Catholicism, his concern for victims also is part of a Catholic tradition.

On abortion, Smith got the House in 1995 to reinstate the ban, overturned by the Clinton Administration, on federal health insurance paying for abortion except when the woman's life is in danger, and he has worked to stop abortions in military hospitals. Smith has sought for years to reinstate the Reagan-era restrictions that would deny federal funds to family planning organizations that promote abortions abroad. The House finally passed his provision in February 1997, but the Senate voted to release international family planning funds without abortion restrictions. What ensued was a struggle that lasted for more than a year, with Smith leveraging his opposition to the family planning money to prevent passage of the Clinton Administration's high-priority efforts to reorganize the State Department, pay U.S. dues to the United Nations and provide $18 billion for the International Monetary Fund. Smith finally was forced to yield in October 1998, when Congress passed the omnibus spending bill. Smith also was a prime mover of legislation to ban partial-birth abortions, which passed the House in 1996 and 1997; the House voted to override Clinton's vetoes, but Smith's side fell a few votes short of the two-thirds needed in the Senate.

As chairman of the International Operations and Human Rights Subcommittee, Smith has criticized China for its forced sterilizations and abortions and its persecution of Christians and other religious minorities, and has opposed normal trade status. He urged Clinton to reverse his June 1998 trip to China because he "must understand the true nature of the tyrants who will be receiving him." He has also pushed for money for pregnant women and neonatal care in the developing world. He has promised to fight slavery in Sudan and has led protests against the military regime in Burma.

On domestic issues, he is a contrast to many anti-abortion Republicans. He has filed legislation to raise the 1996 welfare law's family cap so that states can provide extra benefits to women who have babies while on welfare, with the hope that they will be less likely to seek an abortion. This proposal created an unusual coalition with the National Organization for Women and the American Civil Liberties Union. He cosponsored with socialist Bernie Sanders of Vermont a proposal to kill a Clinton Administration policy that rewards Pentagon contractors that merge—which critics term "payoffs for layoffs."

Smith says he is "fiercely independent" and has a moderate voting record. In 1996 he backed former Congressman Joseph DioGuardi in his primary against New York incumbent Sue Kelly, who is pro-choice; in response, the leadership struck him from a delegation to Bosnia. Back home, some Democrats continue to view him as a target in his independent district, but Smith has a reputation for tending to constituent problems and has been re-elected by impressive margins, 62%–35% in 1998.

Cook's Call. *Safe.* Nineteen-year incumbent Chris Smith is firmly established in this district. He is a sure bet in 2000.

The People: Pop. 1990: 594,673; 15.9% rural; 17.4% age 65+; 83.8% White, 12.5% Black, 1.5% Asian, 0.2% Amer. Indian, 2.1% Other; 5.1% Hispanic Origin. Households: 56.8% married couple families; 26.4% married couple fams. w. children; 41.4% college educ.; median household income: $36,888; per capita income: $16,107; median house value: $130,500; median gross rent: $509.

1996 Presidential Vote

Clinton (D)	127,489	(51%)
Dole (R)	92,845	(37%)
Perot (I)	26,880	(11%)
Others	4,709	(2%)

1992 Presidential Vote

Bush (R)	109,907	(41%)
Clinton (D)	105,335	(39%)
Perot (I)	50,721	(19%)

Rep. Christopher H. Smith (R)

Elected 1980; b. Mar. 4, 1953, Rahway; home, Washington Township; Trenton St. Col., B.S. 1975; Catholic; married (Marie).

Professional Career: Sales exec., family-owned sporting goods business, 1975–80; Exec. Dir., NJ Right to Life, 1976–78.

DC Office: 2370 RHOB 20515, 202-225-3765; Fax: 202-225-7768; Web site: www.house.gov/chrissmith.

District Offices: Hamilton, 609-585-7878; Whiting, 732-350-2300.

Committees: *International Relations* (6th of 26 R): International Operations and Human Rights (Chmn.); Western Hemisphere. *Veterans' Affairs* (Vice Chmn. of 17 R): Health (Vice Chmn.).

Group Ratings

	ADA	ACLU	AFS	LCV	CON	NTU	NFIB	COC	ACU	NTLC	CHC
1998	25	6	33	85	30	48	79	61	72	53	92
1997	30	—	50	—	46	47	—	50	64	—	—

National Journal Ratings

	1997 LIB — 1997 CONS			1998 LIB — 1998 CONS		
Economic	49%	—	51%	50%	—	50%
Social	10%	—	82%	36%	—	64%
Foreign	51%	—	49%	39%	—	58%

Key Votes of the 105th Congress

1. Clinton Budget Deal Y	5. Puerto Rico Sthood. Ref. Y	9. Cut $ for B-2 Bombers N
2. Education IRAs Y	6. End Highway Set-asides Y	10. Human Rights in China Y
3. Req. 2/3 to Raise Taxes Y	7. School Prayer Amend. Y	11. Withdraw Bosnia Troops N
4. Fast-track Trade N	8. Ovrd. Part. Birth Veto Y	12. End Cuban TV-Marti N

Election Results

1998 general	Christopher H. Smith (R)	92,991	(62%)	($317,824)
	Larry Schneider (D)	52,281	(35%)	($37,604)
	Others	4,305	(3%)	
1998 primary	Christopher H. Smith (R)	unopposed		
1996 general	Christopher H. Smith (R)	146,404	(64%)	($284,776)
	Kevin John Meara (D)	77,565	(34%)	
	Others	6,145	(3%)	

FIFTH DISTRICT

The northern edge of New Jersey was first settled three centuries ago by the Dutch, for whom this plateau of land behind the Hudson River Palisades seemed a natural part of Nieuw Amsterdam. The Dutch influence is seen in old steep-roofed farmhouses and in many of the place names—Bergen County, Cresskill, Closter. But overall, northernmost New Jersey has the well-settled look of so many northeastern suburbs, with touches both of affluence and small town hominess, criss-crossed at its edges with limited access highways lined with shopping centers—with five million square feet in Paramus, the headquarters of Toys "R" Us. Not far away are Saddle River, with million-dollar houses on multi-acre lots, and Park Ridge, with office buildings and condominiums, the last two retirement homes of the late President Richard Nixon. This area may look like WASP suburbia on the surface, but in fact it is home to successful people of all ethnic groups, many descended from those who first saw the Statue of Liberty from the steerage deck and passed through the inspection queues at Ellis Island.

The 5th Congressional District consists of most of northern Bergen County, plus a swath of North Jersey stretching west to the hill-enclosed upper reaches of the Delaware, crossing one ridge of mountains after another, running south along I-78. Three-fifths of its population is clustered in Bergen; to the west, little subdivisions set amid the lakes of western Passaic County are filling up with young families; farther west are once rural, now more or less suburban Sussex and Warren counties. Politically, this area is solidly Republican, more so in the west.

Since 1980, the congresswoman from this district has been Marge Roukema, a Republican whose Dutch name and Italian descent tell much of the district's ethnic history. She grew up in West Orange, settled with her psychiatrist husband in Ridgewood. She was a teacher who gave up her job to raise her children and was involved in community activities before becoming a candidate; she brings to politics experience in the actual workings of civic institutions. She has a moderate, middle-of-the-House, but sometimes liberal, voting record and is not shy about frequently dissenting from Republican leadership bills.

Before Republicans won the majority in 1994, Roukema was the lead Republican sponsor of the Family and Medical Leave Act, which President Bush vetoed in 1990 and 1992 and President Clinton signed in February 1993. On student loans, Roukema in 1990 worked to make lenders and borrowers more accountable, and to crack down on for-profit trade schools that were generating many defaulted loans and in effect living off government guarantees; but her reform was superseded by the direct student loan program boosted by New Jersey Democrat Rob Andrews and signed by President Clinton. After Republicans took control of Congress, she frequently opposed items on Speaker Newt Gingrich's agenda, including faster missile defense research, small business exemptions from the minimum wage, term limits and the 1996 Welfare Reform Act, though she sponsored its child support provisions. She was the lead House sponsor of the 1996 health care portability bill to ban insurance rejections for pre-existing conditions, but was the only Republican to vote against it because of leadership-added malpractice liability limitations and Medical Savings Account provisions. She backs the Shays-Meehan campaign finance reform plan. As a senior member of the Banking Committee, she favored more sweeping reform of financial institutions than was prepared by Republican leaders in 1998, including repeal of Glass-Steagall and merger of the three bank insurance funds. If Republicans retain their majority after 2000 and retain term limits for committee chairmen, and now that Bill McCollum is running for the Senate, she is next in line to become chairman of the Banking Committee.

Speaker-designate Bob Livingston in November 1998 named Roukema to co-chair his transition team, presumably to reach out to Republican moderates. But Roukema didn't suffer when Livingston unexpectedly quit in December. During the previous leadership contests, she was among a few members promoting Denny Hastert for majority leader, a move that the new speaker no doubt appreciated after he took control. She also displayed her feisty independence when she was one of the few moderates and the first in the New Jersey delegation, to demand Clinton's resignation, even before the Judiciary Committee debated impeachment.

At a time of few serious re-election challenges to incumbents, Roukema has been kept busy in her district. After several years in which conservatives threatened to run a serious opponent in the Republican primary, Assemblyman E. Scott Garrett, a trial lawyer, gave her a scare in the June 1998 primary. He emphasized his opposition to gun control and abortion; she pointed to her conservative record on economic issues and received financial help from national Republicans, including Gingrich and Maine Senator Olympia Snowe. Roukema won by only 52%–48%, and Garrett did not rule out another try in 2000. In the fall campaign, Roukema faced Mike Schneider, a former Fox News Channel newsman with good name ID but no political experience. He criticized Roukema's reliance on PACs and her call for Clinton's resignation. Despite some national Democrats' encouragement, he was poorly financed and lost 64%–33%.

Cook's Call. *Safe.* The biggest threat to Roukema's tenure in this wealthy and Republican leaning district comes not from Democrats but conservative Republicans who are unhappy with her moderate voting record. She narrowly defeated a conservative Republican in her 1998 primary and should be wary of another challenge from the right in 2000.

The People: Pop. 1990: 594,581; 18.6% rural; 13.1% age 65 + ; 93.7% White, 1.2% Black, 4.5% Asian, 0.2% Amer. Indian, 0.5% Other; 2.7% Hispanic Origin. Households: 68.5% married couple families; 32.9% married couple fams. w. children; 55% college educ.; median household income: $53,433; per capita income: $23,942; median house value: $214,400; median gross rent: $633.

1996 Presidential Vote

Dole (R)	127,286	(47%)
Clinton (D)	115,060	(42%)
Perot (I)	23,642	(9%)
Others	5,090	(2%)

1992 Presidential Vote

Bush (R)	146,004	(49%)
Clinton (D)	99,733	(34%)
Perot (I)	48,661	(16%)

Rep. Marge Roukema (R)

Elected 1980; b. Sept. 19, 1929, W. Orange; home, Ridgewood; Montclair St. Col., B.A. 1951, Rutgers U.; Protestant; married (Richard).

Elected Office: Ridgewood Board of Ed., 1970–73.

Professional Career: High schl. teacher, 1951–55; Co-founder, Ridgewood Sr. Citizens Housing Corp., 1973.

DC Office: 2469 RHOB 20515, 202-225-4465; Fax: 202-225-9048; Web site: www.house.gov/roukema.

District Offices: Hackettstown, 908-850-4747; Ridgewood, 201-447-3900.

Committees: *Banking & Financial Services* (3d of 32 R): Capital Markets, Securities & Government Sponsored Enterprises; Financial Institutions & Consumer Credit (Chmn.). *Education & the Workforce* (3d of 27 R): Early Childhood, Youth & Families; Employer-Employee Relations.

Group Ratings

	ADA	ACLU	AFS	LCV	CON	NTU	NFIB	COC	ACU	NTLC	CHC
1998	20	19	22	69	30	52	71	78	60	50	42
1997	50	—	43	—	98	55	—	80	42	—	—

National Journal Ratings

	1997 LIB — 1997 CONS		1998 LIB — 1998 CONS	
Economic	44%	— 55%	49%	— 51%
Social	56%	— 43%	45%	— 55%
Foreign	51%	— 46%	53%	— 45%

Key Votes of the 105th Congress

1. Clinton Budget Deal	Y	5. Puerto Rico Sthood. Ref.	N	9. Cut $ for B-2 Bombers	Y
2. Education IRAs	Y	6. End Highway Set-asides	Y	10. Human Rights in China	N
3. Req. 2/3 to Raise Taxes	Y	7. School Prayer Amend.	Y	11. Withdraw Bosnia Troops	Y
4. Fast-track Trade	Y	8. Ovrd. Part. Birth Veto	Y	12. End Cuban TV-Marti	Y

Election Results

1998 general	Marge Roukema (R)	106,304	(64%)	($760,098)
	Mike Schneider (D)	55,487	(33%)	($62,440)
	Others	5,027	(3%)	
1998 primary	Marge Roukema (R)	16,215	(53%)	
	Scott Garrett (R)	14,498	(47%)	
1996 general	Marge Roukema (R)	181,323	(71%)	($496,610)
	Bill Auer (D)	62,956	(25%)	($28,002)
	Others	10,054	(4%)	

SIXTH DISTRICT

For generations great transportation arteries have brought people out of the huge central cities of New York and Philadelphia and into the long-empty flatlands and hills of New Jersey—to vacation, to raise families and to work toward affluence and build communities. The railroads of the late 19th Century created the towns of the Jersey Shore, from 1874, when the first train from New York City reached Long Branch, which quickly became the summer home of presidents from Grant to Wilson (Garfield, convalescing after he was shot, died there in 1881) and of New York race horse owners and socialites. The great freight rail lines in the New York-Philadelphia corridor sparked big electrical and chemical industries here—building on the inventions of Thomas Edison, many produced in his Menlo Park laboratory just off the rail lines. The same corridor was the site of America's first cloverleaf intersection, at the junction of U.S. 1 and U.S. 9, and the intersection of two of America's great post-World War II highways, the New Jersey Turnpike and the Garden State Parkway. The Turnpike, now 12 lanes wide, roars past oil tank farms and petrochemical plants, major rail lines and Newark Airport and the oily waters of Raritan Bay; the Parkway links leafy affluent suburbs a dozen miles west of the Hudson with the Jersey Shore.

The 6th Congressional District ties together these great transportation nodes and the upward mobility and economic progress that have taken place around them. It includes the central core of Middlesex County—New Brunswick and Edison Township and the surrounding communities—a heavy industry area that also, since the time of Thomas Edison, has housed some of America's great research and development facilities. Here, immigrant factory workers in modest frame houses have raised their families in small towns that seem as far removed from Manhattan as any place in the Midwest. The 6th District also includes a strip of territory overlooking Lower New York Bay, with spacious estates on highlands above little port towns from Sandy Hook south to Sea Girt: Asbury Park, once the vital center of this beachfront; and Ocean Grove, founded in 1869 as a Methodist resort "free from the dissipation and follies of fashionable watering places," still for teetotalers who throng to its 10,000-seat 1894 Great Hall. The Shore has remained a summer vacation area that attracts millions, but also has year-round communities, with their own upward-striving families, whose teenage energies have been expressed by the Shore's biggest celebrity, musician Bruce Springsteen.

The congressman from the 6th District is Frank Pallone, a Democrat who initially overcame severe challenges to hold the seat. Pallone is the son of a disabled Long Branch policeman; he has been an environmentalist since 1969, when as a college freshman in Vermont he worked for that state's first-in-the-nation bottle deposit law. He was elected to the Long Branch City Council in 1982, at 31, and to the New Jersey Senate in 1983, where he did not always follow party lines and concentrated on environmental issues. When Congressman Jim Howard, chairman of the Transportation and Infrastructure Committee, died in March 1988, Pallone ran for the House. The district leaned Republican, but was angry about untreated sludge, plastic containers and medical waste washing up on the beach in 1987 and 1988. Pallone's bumper sticker, without mentioning his party affiliation, said, "Stop Ocean Dumping." That, combined with his conservative stands on taxes and crime, helped him to a 52% win.

In the House, Pallone continued to be a maverick, distancing himself from Governor Jim Florio's 1990 tax increase. Redistricting nearly ended Pallone's career. For 1992, the new 6th combined much of Pallone's Shore district in Monmouth County with large parts of the former Middlesex County seat; Pallone won the primary with only 55% against a Middlesex opponent. In the general, Pallone depended on a huge money advantage and Bill Clinton's edge in the district to win 52%–45%. In 1994 and 1996 he was re-elected with at least 60% of the vote.

Pallone has continued his moderate-liberal voting record, while adding a more partisan edge after Democrats lost House control. He supported the Clinton Administration on many budget issues but voted against the budget and tax package in August 1993; he was one of nine non-Southern Democrats to vote for the Contract with America's tax cut provision in 1995. Pallone had supported single-payer health insurance in the 1992 campaign, but steered clear of the Clinton health care plan in 1994, helping to stymie its progress through John Dingell's Commerce Committee. In the minority, Pallone opposed repealing retroactive liability in Superfund and worked on the Safe Drinking Water Act. He became an active member of the Democrats' floor team—known as The Message Group—that frequently engaged in late-night attacks that trumpeted his party's latest initiative and dumped on the latest Republican scheme. With many Indian-Americans in the district (the most in the country, he says), he formed the Congressional

Caucus on India and Indian-Americans with Republican Bill McCollum in 1993; but he canceled a trip to India and supported sanctions against India after its nuclear tests in May 1998.

The 1998 campaign was a stormy season for Pallone. His Republican opponent, 28-year-old Michael Ferguson, was an education reformer close to former Governor Thomas Kean and onetime Education Secretary William Bennett; he spent $1 million for this race, matching Pallone. At the same time Pallone got involved in a controversy over the Democratic nomination in the next-door 12th District. Democrats supporting Carl Mayer, who spent nearly $1 million of his own money, charged that Pallone agreed to support Mayer and then turned around and helped physicist Rush Holt win the endorsements of county Democratic parties. When Holt won the June primary 53%–37%, Mayer turned around and filed as an independent in the 6th District—not a violation of the state "sore loser" law, said a court, because it was a different district from where he had run as a Democrat. Also, nearly $2 million was spent in an independent expenditure campaign by an insurance group unhappy with Pallone's support for Clinton's managed-care bill of rights plan. But Mayer evidently did little to campaign, and Ferguson's spending did not help him much in a pro-incumbent year: Pallone beat him 57%–40%.

In 1999, Dick Gephardt named Pallone chairman of the Democrats' Health Care Task Force, and he was also named a co-chairman of the Democratic Congressional Campaign Committee. But when Senator Frank Lautenberg announced his retirement in February 1999, Pallone announced an exploratory committee for a Senate bid. This might pit him in a chancy primary with former Governor Jim Florio (and perhaps others), but there are redistricting risks for him staying in the 6th District.

Cook's Call. *Potentially Competitive.* Pallone's public flirtation with a Senate bid is giving some national Democrats heartburn. Not only would Democrats have to defend a marginal open seat, but Pallone's 1998 opponent—Mike Ferguson, a solid campaigner and proven fundraiser—is already gearing up to run for the seat, regardless of Pallone's decision. If Pallone stays, this race could still turn competitive. But, after some very close wins in his first two terms, Pallone has established a voting record and an image that works well in this district and he won't be easy to beat.

The People: Pop. 1990: 594,650; 0.3% rural; 12.8% age 65 + ; 81.8% White, 11.2% Black, 4.8% Asian, 0.2% Amer. Indian, 2% Other; 5.9% Hispanic Origin. Households: 55.5% married couple families; 26% married couple fams. w. children; 47.3% college educ.; median household income: $42,309; per capita income: $18,135; median house value: $160,600; median gross rent: $587.

1996 Presidential Vote			1992 Presidential Vote		
Clinton (D)	122,851	(54%)	Clinton (D)	110,821	(44%)
Dole (R)	74,937	(33%)	Bush (R)	98,397	(39%)
Perot (I)	22,192	(10%)	Perot (I)	41,867	(17%)
Others	5,968	(3%)			

Rep. Frank E. Pallone (D)

Elected 1988; b. Oct. 30, 1951, Long Branch; home, Long Branch; Middlebury Col., B.A. 1973, Fletcher Schl. of Law & Diplomacy, M.A. 1974, Rutgers U., J.D. 1978; Catholic; married (Sarah).

Elected Office: Long Branch City Cncl., 1982–88; NJ Senate, 1983–88.

Professional Career: Asst. prof., Rutgers U., 1979–80; Practicing atty., 1981–83; Instructor, Monmouth Col., 1984–86.

DC Office: 420 CHOB 20515, 202-225-4671; Fax: 202-225-9665.

District Offices: Hazlet, 908-264-9104; Long Branch, 908-571-1140; New Brunswick, 908-249-8892.

Committees: *Commerce* (7th of 24 D): Energy & Power; Finance & Hazardous Materials; Health and Environment. *Resources* (10th of 24 D): Fisheries Conservation, Wildlife & Oceans.

Group Ratings

	ADA	ACLU	AFS	LCV	CON	NTU	NFIB	COC	ACU	NTLC	CHC
1998	100	81	100	100	44	21	36	28	12	11	8
1997	95	—	86	—	78	34	—	30	12	—	—

National Journal Ratings

	1997 LIB	—	1997 CONS		1998 LIB	—	1998 CONS
Economic	75%	—	22%		72%	—	23%
Social	82%	—	15%		70%	—	28%
Foreign	68%	—	31%		59%	—	40%

Key Votes of the 105th Congress

1. Clinton Budget Deal	N	5. Puerto Rico Sthood. Ref.	Y	9. Cut $ for B-2 Bombers	Y
2. Education IRAs	N	6. End Highway Set-asides	N	10. Human Rights in China	*
3. Req. 2/3 to Raise Taxes	Y	7. School Prayer Amend.	N	11. Withdraw Bosnia Troops	N
4. Fast-track Trade	N	8. Ovrd. Part. Birth Veto	N	12. End Cuban TV-Marti	N

Election Results

1998 general	Frank E. Pallone (D)	78,102	(57%)	($1,144,629)
	Michael Ferguson (R)	55,180	(40%)	($1,069,603)
	Others	3,730	(3%)	
1998 primary	Frank E. Pallone (D)	unopposed		
1996 general	Frank E. Pallone (D)	124,635	(61%)	($658,357)
	Steven J. Corodemus (R)	73,402	(36%)	($319,354)
	Others	5,441	(3%)	

SEVENTH DISTRICT

The transportation arteries beneath the curve of the First Watchung Mountain are one of New Jersey's historic lines of development. The rail lines of the late 19th Century opened up commuter suburbs; in the 1940s the four lanes of U.S. 22 created an automobile civilization; and finally Interstate 78, completed in the mid-1980s, put Newark only an hour's distance from the Pennsylvania line. I-78 stimulated the development of an Edge City called Bridgewater Commons, where a huge shopping mall and office developments that included the new headquarters of AT&T rose up amid horse country around Far Hills and Bernardsville, where the likes of Malcolm Forbes and Charles Engelhard owned huge estates.

The 7th Congressional District covers these several generations of suburban development. It begins just west of Elizabeth, taking in affluent railroad commuter towns like Short Hills and Summit. It also includes more modest suburbs along U.S. 22, like Union and Westfield and the old city of Plainfield, with its large black community, plus the working class suburbs of Woodbridge and South Plainfield in Middlesex County. It then follows I-78 and the Watchung Mountains far into the countryside to the fields of Somerset County. Once this was all solidly Republican; now the closer-in suburbs are more mixed, with Democratic inner cities; the farther-out Edge City areas are, if anything, increasingly Republican. In the House, this area has been represented by Republicans for many years.

The congressman from the 7th is Bob Franks, a Republican first elected in 1992. He grew up in New Jersey, went to DePauw University and earned a law degree from Southern Methodist University, worked as a political consultant, then in 1979, at 28, was elected to the New Jersey Assembly from a district including parts of all four counties now in the 7th. He served as state Republican chairman for all but one year from 1988–92 and was one of the leaders of the revolt against Governor Jim Florio's 1990 tax increase. And he was a political ally of Matthew Rinaldo, the 7th District congressman for 20 years, who had a liberal voting record and a high-ranking spot on the Commerce Committee. When Rinaldo abruptly dropped out of the race in September 1992, after being renominated three months before, the local Republican organization chose Franks to take his place. Franks had serious competition from Democrat Leonard Sendelsky, a well-known local builder active in civic organizations. The two ran even in Middlesex, while Franks won 55% in the rest of the district, for a 53%–43% win.

In the House, Franks has a moderate record on economic and foreign issues and a rather liberal record on cultural issues. He serves on the Budget Committee and on Transportation and Infrastructure, where much of his work has a local angle. After the big pipeline explosion in Edison in March 1994 he worked on pipeline safety; after dredging for the port of New York and New Jersey was stopped because the waste could not be dumped in the ocean, he got a bill passed in October 1996 authorizing and financing an alternative disposal site; after complaints from those under the flight paths to Newark Airport, he proposed creating an FAA ombudsman on airplane noise. After Susan Molinari resigned in mid-term, Franks in 1998 became chairman of the Railroads subcommittee, a useful post for his district. But when the Transportation Committee in 1999 was forced to reorganize and drop a subcommittee, he took over a catch-all panel whose hazardous materials and pipeline jurisdiction could also prove useful for his industrial region. Franks has some interesting causes too. He wants to stop the unrestricted sale of personal information about children by commercial list brokers. He wants a bipartisan commission on campaign finance reform to recommend a package of reform, with Congress getting an up or down vote. He wants the government to stop subsidizing electric power produced by the Tennessee Valley Authority and transmitted by the Power Marketing Administrations.

Franks had his closest race in 1998 against Fanwood Mayor Maryanne Connelly, a retired AT&T human resources executive. Although outspent more than 4-to-1 and receiving little national support, Connelly was a capable foe, and carried the Middlesex County portion of the district. Overall Franks won 53%–44%, a decisive margin but one which may invite more well-financed opposition. Franks has been mentioned as a candidate for governor in 2001, presuming he is re-elected in 2000. But if Governor Christie Whitman is elected to the Senate in 2000, Senate President Donald DiFrancesco will become acting governor, and Franks may not want to challenge an incumbent in the primary.

Cook's Call. *Potentially Competitive.* Franks' unexpectedly close race against an under-funded candidate in 1998 has earned him a place on the watch list for 2000. Franks has never won in this swing district with big margins, but he has survived a well-financed challenger and some particularly bad political climates.

The People: Pop. 1990: 594,844; 4.1% rural; 14.4% age 65 + ; 83.6% White, 10.1% Black, 4.6% Asian, 0.1% Amer. Indian, 1.5% Other; 4.8% Hispanic Origin. Households: 62.6% married couple families; 27.5% married couple fams. w. children; 52.7% college educ.; median household income: $50,996; per capita income: $23,253; median house value: $186,900; median gross rent: $632.

1996 Presidential Vote			1992 Presidential Vote		
Clinton (D)	129,773	(51%)	Bush (R)	125,592	(44%)
Dole (R)	101,538	(40%)	Clinton (D)	115,846	(41%)
Perot (I)	19,769	(8%)	Perot (I)	40,690	(14%)
Others	4,710	(2%)			

Rep. Bob Franks (R)

Elected 1992; b. Sept. 21, 1951, Hackensack; home, New Providence; DePauw U., B.A. 1973, S. Methodist U., J.D. 1976; Methodist; married (Fran).

Elected Office: NJ Assembly, 1979–92.

Professional Career: Political consultant, 1976–79; Med Data Inc., 1979–81; Co-owner, *County News*, 1982–84; NJ Repub. St. Chmn., 1988–89, 1990–92.

DC Office: 225 CHOB 20515, 202-225-5361; Fax: 202-225-9460; Web site: www.house.gov/bobfranks.

District Offices: Union, 908-686-5576; Woodbridge, 732-602-0075.

Committees: *Budget* (5th of 24 R). *Transportation & Infrastructure* (11th of 41 R): Economic Development, Public Buildings, Hazardous Materials & Pipeline Transportation (Chmn.); Ground Transportation (Vice Chmn.); Water Resources & Environment.

Group Ratings

	ADA	ACLU	AFS	LCV	CON	NTU	NFIB	COC	ACU	NTLC	CHC
1998	25	31	33	77	33	50	86	83	52	45	50
1997	40	—	25	—	91	62	—	90	64	—	—

National Journal Ratings

	1997 LIB — 1997 CONS			1998 LIB — 1998 CONS		
Economic	46%	—	54%	45%	—	54%
Social	50%	—	48%	57%	—	43%
Foreign	49%	—	49%	34%	—	62%

Key Votes of the 105th Congress

1. Clinton Budget Deal	Y	5. Puerto Rico Sthood. Ref.	Y	9. Cut $ for B-2 Bombers	Y
2. Education IRAs	Y	6. End Highway Set-asides	Y	10. Human Rights in China	Y
3. Req. 2/3 to Raise Taxes	Y	7. School Prayer Amend.	N	11. Withdraw Bosnia Troops	Y
4. Fast-track Trade	Y	8. Ovrd. Part. Birth Veto	Y	12. End Cuban TV-Marti	N

Election Results

1998 general	Bob Franks (R)	77,751	(53%)	($802,120)
	Maryanne Connelly (D)	65,776	(44%)	($199,576)
	Others	4,515	(3%)	
1998 primary	Bob Franks (R)	unopposed		
1996 general	Bob Franks (R)	128,821	(55%)	($1,305,753)
	Larry Lerner (D)	97,285	(42%)	($801,815)
	Others	6,465	(3%)	

EIGHTH DISTRICT

Paterson, New Jersey, is one of few American cities that has turned out pretty much as planned. The planner was Alexander Hamilton, who in the 1790s journeyed 20 miles from Manhattan into the interior of New Jersey to the Great Falls of the Passaic River. Watching the water surge down 72 feet—the highest falls along the East Coast—he predicted an industrial city would rise on this site. He formed the Society for Establishing Useful Manufactures, which opened a calico factory in 1794, and got Pierre L'Enfant, the designer of Washington, D.C., to design Paterson (named after then-Governor William Paterson). In 1836, Samuel Colt began manufacturing revolvers here; the first locomotive, the Sandusky, was built here in 1837; a walkout of Paterson cotton workers in 1828 was America's first factory strike. Paterson ultimately became America's "Silk City," employing 25,000 silk mill workers before the great strike of 1913 led by the radical Industrial Workers of the World, at a time when the city fathers were erecting imposing public buildings and the narrow streets were buzzing with rumors of anarchist plots. Paterson kept producing locomotives and, after the silk mills started closing down following another unsuccessful strike in 1924, became a cloth-dying center. Throughout, it attracted immigrants from England, Ireland and, after 1890, Italy and Poland. But now Paterson is a kind of misfit in time and place: still a manufacturing center in a service-dominated economy, a blue-collar city set amid dozens of white-collar suburbs.

The 8th Congressional District includes Paterson as its largest city, plus much suburban territory west and south of Paterson and north and west of Newark. It includes the mixed factory and middle-class towns south of Paterson on the Passaic River—Clifton, Passaic, Nutley, Belleville. On higher ground are Bloomfield and, up on a ridge with views of New York City, part of Montclair. An affluent part of the Oranges is also included, as well as Wayne Township west of Paterson. The political heritage of the 8th District is Democratic, partly from its radical past, but more from the allegiances of its immigrant groups. But by the 1980s, the central cities were outvoted by the increasingly Republican suburbs, and the district has been closely divided, though it swung heavily to Bill Clinton in 1996.

The congressman from the 8th District—the fourth the district has chosen in the 1990s—is Bill Pascrell, a Democrat elected in 1996. He grew up in Paterson, the grandson of Italian immigrants, graduated from Fordham, served in the Army, then taught high school for 14 years. From there he went into politics, first on the Paterson Board of Education, then in 1987 to the New Jersey Assembly. In 1990 he was elected mayor of Paterson, but continued to serve in the Assembly—a common practice in New Jersey. In these offices Pascrell showed a flair for innovation. He sponsored a health program with preventive medicine and child immunizations and a housing program with new construction and help for first-time home-buyers. To stop drug dealers, he required permits for new pay phones and personally ripped out phones without permits.

Meanwhile, he watched as the 8th District seat changed hands. After Public Works Committee Democrat Robert Roe retired in 1992, liberal Democrat Herb Klein, who spent $580,000 of his own money, won the seat 47%–41%. Two years later Republican Bill Martini, active in politics in Clifton for years, beat Klein 50%–49%. In the House Martini supported the Contract with America 91% of the time, but also made a liberal record on the environment and other issues. Pascrell nevertheless attacked him strenuously as the puppet of an "extremist" Republican leadership—one ad even showed Martini's face on a puppet operated by Speaker Gingrich. Despite Martini's support from the Sierra Club and some labor unions, Pascrell echoed the soothing tone of the Clinton-Gore campaign. In a district that went 58% for Clinton, Pascrell won 51%–48%.

In the House Pascrell compiled a liberal record on economics, more moderate on cultural and foreign issues; he split with Clinton on protecting military construction projects from line-item vetoes, opposed Clinton's plan for withdrawing U.S. troops in Bosnia and voted for the partial-birth abortion ban. He gave new meaning to the "all politics is local" view by leading a move to give Italy a permanent seat on the United Nations Security Council. In 1998 Pascarell was opposed by Verona Mayor Matthew Kirnan, and benefited by a big fundraising advantage and the pro-incumbent feeling of the year. He won 62%–35%, a margin reminiscent of Robert Roe's in the 1980s.

In early 1999, Pascrell voiced interest in running for governor in 2001, a contest in which he is sure to face significant primary opposition. He may have created problems for such a bid when defeated Passaic County Democratic candidates complained that he did not campaign actively for them when he sought re-election in November 1998.

Cook's Call. *Probably Safe.* Pascrell's win here in 1998 marked the first time since 1990 that this notoriously fickle and unstable district has re-elected an incumbent. Republicans were unable to recruit a top-tier candidate for that race, and 2000 won't be any easier now that Pascrell is a two-term incumbent with a solid win under his belt.

The People: Pop. 1990: 594,912; 15.3% age 65 + ; 74.8% White, 13% Black, 3.5% Asian, 0.2% Amer. Indian, 8.5% Other; 17.4% Hispanic Origin. Households: 54.1% married couple families; 24.6% married couple fams. w. children; 42.1% college educ.; median household income: $39,944; per capita income: $18,527; median house value: $193,600; median gross rent: $517.

1996 Presidential Vote		
Clinton (D)	123,856	(58%)
Dole (R)	73,731	(34%)
Perot (I)	12,864	(6%)
Others	4,095	(2%)

1992 Presidential Vote		
Clinton (D)	107,304	(45%)
Bush (R)	99,974	(42%)
Perot (I)	27,703	(12%)

Rep. Bill Pascrell, Jr. (D)

Elected 1996; b. Jan. 25, 1937, Paterson; home, Paterson; Fordham U., B.A. 1959, M.A. 1961; Catholic; married (Elsie).

Military Career: Army, 1961; Army Reserves, 1962–67.

Elected Office: Pres., Paterson Bd. of Ed., 1979–82; NJ Assembly, 1987–97, Minority Ldr. Pro-Tem; Paterson Mayor, 1990–97.

Professional Career: High Schl. teacher, 1960–74; Dir., Paterson Dept. of Public Works, 1974–77; Dir., Paterson Dept. of Policy, 1977–87.

DC Office: 1722 LHOB 20515, 202-225-5751; Fax: 202-225-5782; Web site: www.house.gov/pascrell.

District Office: Paterson, 973-523-5152.

Committees: *Small Business* (5th of 17 D): Regulatory Reform & Paperwork Reduction (RMM). *Transportation & Infrastructure* (25th of 34 D): Ground Transportation; Water Resources & Environment.

Group Ratings

	ADA	ACLU	AFS	LCV	CON	NTU	NFIB	COC	ACU	NTLC	CHC
1998	95	56	100	100	68	14	21	33	16	8	17
1997	70	—	88	—	76	31	—	40	36	—	—

National Journal Ratings

	1997 LIB — 1997 CONS			1998 LIB — 1998 CONS	
Economic	64%	—	35%	79%	—	0%
Social	64%	—	35%	65%	—	34%
Foreign	54%	—	46%	56%	—	42%

Key Votes of the 105th Congress

1. Clinton Budget Deal	N	5. Puerto Rico Sthood. Ref.	Y	9. Cut $ for B-2 Bombers	Y
2. Education IRAs	N	6. End Highway Set-asides	N	10. Human Rights in China	Y
3. Req. 2/3 to Raise Taxes	N	7. School Prayer Amend.	N	11. Withdraw Bosnia Troops	N
4. Fast-track Trade	N	8. Ovrd. Part. Birth Veto	Y	12. End Cuban TV-Marti	N

Election Results

1998 general	Bill Pascrell Jr. (D)	81,068	(62%)	($968,274)
	Matthew Kirnan (R)	46,289	(35%)	($289,910)
	Others	3,231	(2%)	
1998 primary	Bill Pascrell Jr. (D)	unopposed		
1996 general	Bill Pascrell Jr. (D)	98,861	(51%)	($952,722)
	Bill Martini (R)	92,609	(48%)	($1,393,134)

NINTH DISTRICT

The George Washington Bridge, one of several wondrous suspension bridges completed in America in the 1930s, strides the Hudson, its west tower almost up against the green cliff of New Jersey's Palisades. It is one of the glories of modern engineering, enabling people and goods to be transported through the irregular terrain of metropolitan New York—tidal rivers and cliffs and broad expanses of swamp. For a century the dramatic beauty of the Palisades contrasted with the ugly sprawl of the Hackensack River Valley and the Jersey Meadowlands. This giant swamp was the image of New Jersey for many—a landscape of gas station signs, oil tank farms, truck terminals and 12 lanes of New Jersey Turnpike—a smelly, ugly place that meant you were still not where you wanted to go, full of garbage and pig farms, briefly famous when Secaucus tavern owner Henry Krajewski ran for president in 1956 and commemorated in today's New Jersey Garbage Museum. But the Meadowlands were the largest hunk of empty real estate near such a huge city center, and eventually they were developed. In the 1970s, the state built the Meadowlands Sports Complex—Giants Stadium (where the Giants and Jets play now), the Meadowlands Racetrack, the Brendan Byrne Arena (later Continental Airlines Arena, home of the Nets and Devils). Private development followed—hotels, warehouses, light industry—whole small cities—and the Meadowlands hosted the World Cup, the Final Four, the Stanley Cup and Pope John Paul II.

The 9th Congressional District includes much of the Palisades and the Meadowlands. It runs from the high-rise towers of Fort Lee and Cliffside Park, where apartment houses brag about their views of New York City, west and north to the leafy suburbs of Englewood and Teaneck, and southwest to the high land overlooking the Meadowlands and the Passaic River in old small towns like Rutherford, with Polish-, German- and Italian-Americans. Hackensack, an old industrial town and the Bergen County seat, and much of Fair Lawn, a planned town with a large Jewish population, also are in the 9th. This area grew in the 1950s and 1960s, as New Yorkers moved out of the City; it lost population in the 1970s and 1980s, as young people moved farther out and left empty nesters behind. Now there are new immigrants here: Englewood's schoolchildren are mostly black, Fort Lee's mostly Asian, many of Hackensack's are Hispanic, though most of New Jersey's Cuban-American community is just to the south, around Union City in Hudson County. This was Republican country in the New Deal years, an area of white-collar enclaves. But the conservative families who grew up here are now being replaced by heavily Democratic immigrants and "tower dwellers."

The congressman from the 9th District is Steve Rothman, a Democrat elected in 1996. Rothman grew up in Englewood and Tenafly, went off to school at Syracuse University and Washington University law school in St. Louis, then practiced law. From 1983–89 he was mayor of Englewood, where he claims to have cut taxes, reduced crime and led an economic renaissance. In 1993 he became a judge in the Bergen County Surrogate's Court. When 14-

year Congressman Bob Torricelli ran for the Senate in 1996, Rothman resigned his judgeship and ran for the House. He won the party endorsement, then won 79% against former Fair Lawn Mayor Robert Gordon in the primary. In the general Rothman faced Kathleen Donovan—Bergen County clerk, former assemblywoman, and from 1994–95 chairman of the New York-New Jersey Port Authority. Rothman said he wanted to balance the budget, preserve open parcels of land, build new highways and mass transit. Donovan said much the same. But Rothman took some strong liberal stands, against the welfare reform law and the partial-birth abortion ban. Donovan spotlighted her record on environmental issues and won endorsements from the Sierra Club, New Jersey Education Association and Cuban-American leader Jorge Mas Canosa. She was also endorsed by three northern New Jersey papers: the Newark *Star-Ledger, Bergen Record* and *North Jersey Herald & News*. Republicans had fond hopes for this race, but the district seems to have become too Democratic for a Republican win—after the Newark 10th and Jersey City 13th, the 9th District produced the third highest Clinton percentage in New Jersey. Rothman won by a solid 56%–42%.

In the House Rothman moved to form a juvenile crime task force and called for Israel to be grouped with the Western European bloc at the United Nations so it might have a chance for a Security Council seat. But he first found himself in the spotlight in the Judiciary Committee impeachment hearings. After Independent Counsel Kenneth Starr sent his report to the House, Rothman initially expressed unhappiness with Clinton's behavior and studied the charges intently. Within a few weeks, as public opinion turned against impeachment, so did Rothman. He actively supported Clinton on television talk shows and complained that Republicans were ignoring the few moderate Democrats like himself. The divisive process left him more partisan and, Rothman said, "heartsick."

Rothman raised and spent $1.1 million in his race for re-election. His opponent Bogota Mayor Steven Lonegan, who is legally blind from a rare eye disease, had an appealing personal story, but he raised far less money and his calls for Clinton's resignation fell on stony ears in this Northeastern district. Rothman won 65%–34%, almost as good as Torricelli's best showings, and seems to have a safe seat, at least until redistricting after the 2000 Census.

Cook's Call. *Safe.* One can make the case that Rothman is still vulnerable to a strong Republican challenge since his two wins have coincided with particulary good Democratic years in New Jersey. But this district does have a solid Democratic core and even in a down year for Democrats, Rothman will be hard to beat.

The People: Pop. 1990: 594,790; 16.8% age 65 + ; 83.8% White, 6.4% Black, 6.5% Asian, 0.1% Amer. Indian, 3.2% Other; 11.3% Hispanic Origin. Households: 52.7% married couple families; 22.2% married couple fams. w. children; 43.8% college educ.; median household income: $40,816; per capita income: $20,012; median house value: $195,700; median gross rent: $577.

1996 Presidential Vote			1992 Presidential Vote		
Clinton (D)	138,242	(60%)	Clinton (D)	122,676	(47%)
Dole (R)	71,741	(31%)	Bush (R)	102,578	(40%)
Perot (I)	17,012	(7%)	Perot (I)	31,534	(12%)

Rep. Steven R. Rothman (D)

Elected 1996; b. Oct. 14, 1952, Englewood; home, Fair Lawn; Syracuse U., B.A. 1974, Washington U., J.D. 1977; Jewish; divorced.

Elected Office: Englewood Mayor, 1983–89; Bergen Cnty. Surrogate Court Judge, 1993–96.

Professional Career: Practicing atty., 1977–93.

DC Office: 1607 LHOB 20515; 202-225-5061; Fax: 202-225-5851; Web site: www.house.gov/rothman.

District Offices: Hackensack, 201-646-0808; Jersey City, 201-798-1366.

Committees: *International Relations* (16th of 23 D): International Economic Policy & Trade; Western Hemisphere. *Judiciary* (14th of 16 D): Crime.

Group Ratings

	ADA	ACLU	AFS	LCV	CON	NTU	NFIB	COC	ACU	NTLC	CHC
1998	100	75	100	92	76	18	17	29	8	8	0
1997	90	—	88	—	91	27	—	40	13	—	—

National Journal Ratings

	1997 LIB — 1997 CONS			1998 LIB — 1998 CONS		
Economic	79%	—	18%	72%	—	23%
Social	71%	—	27%	76%	—	23%
Foreign	69%	—	28%	64%	—	31%

Key Votes of the 105th Congress

1. Clinton Budget Deal	N	5. Puerto Rico Sthood. Ref.	Y	9. Cut $ for B-2 Bombers	Y
2. Education IRAs	N	6. End Highway Set-asides	N	10. Human Rights in China	Y
3. Req. 2/3 to Raise Taxes	N	7. School Prayer Amend.	N	11. Withdraw Bosnia Troops	N
4. Fast-track Trade	N	8. Ovrd. Part. Birth Veto	N	12. End Cuban TV-Marti	N

Election Results

1998 general	Steven R. Rothman (D)	91,330	(65%)	($1,120,409)
	Steve Lonegan (R)	47,817	(34%)	($598,958)
	Others	2,312	(2%)	
1998 primary	Steven R. Rothman (D)	unopposed		
1996 general	Steven R. Rothman (D)	117,646	(56%)	($797,632)
	Kathleen A. Donovan (R)	89,005	(42%)	($789,894)
	Others	4,279	(2%)	

TENTH DISTRICT

Newark is the hollow core of New Jersey, the city to which main transportation arteries once led and whose corporate headquarters buildings were the tallest in the state. In 1930, 442,000 people lived here, one of every nine in New Jersey; in 1996, 275,000 did, one of every 28. Downtown Newark still has the Prudential and Public Service Electric & Gas headquarters, there are still factories in the Ironbound district, the area around Newark airport has some industrial development, and the New Jersey Performing Arts Center had its grand opening in October 1997. But big corporate leaders and small businesses alike have put few new jobs here since the 1967 riot. The reason is obvious: high crime. Some neighborhoods of Newark have retained their vitality, but large parts have been dominated by criminals and deserted by most law-abiding residents who can get out. In 1994 the state took over the public schools, abysmally run, while spending per pupil ranks among the nation's highest.

The 10th Congressional District is made up of most of Newark—the Central, South and West Wards—plus Irvington, most of the Oranges and part of Montclair to the west, and much of Elizabeth, Rahway, and Linden to the south. The 10th was 59% black in 1990, and over-whelmingly Democratic; its boundary lines wiggle around to include blacks in Jersey City, Montclair and Elizabeth, and leave Hispanics in the next-door 13th District.

The congressman from the 10th is Donald Payne, a Democrat elected in 1988. He grew up in Newark, was a teacher, worked for Prudential, served on the Essex Board of Chosen Free-holders in the 1970s and was vice president of Urban Data Systems for 13 years. In 1980 and 1986, he ran against Congressman Peter Rodino, chairman of the House Judiciary Committee when it voted to impeach President Richard Nixon; Payne lost, even as an African-American in a district with a black majority. But when Rodino retired in 1988, Payne got 73% in the Democratic primary and easily won the general, and has been re-elected routinely ever since.

Payne has an impeccably liberal voting record. He served as chairman of the Congressional Black Caucus in 1995 and 1996, just as Republicans were defunding the caucuses (the Black Caucus has raised enough money on its own to remain a vigorous force) and just as senior Democrats had to relinquish chairmanships to Republicans. Payne struggled to save affirmative action and racial quota programs as they were under attack, with varying success. He could not stop a law that eliminated race preferences in broadcast licenses nor could he stop the House from passing a bill outlawing "social investments" for pension funds. But he was successful in urging Bill Clinton not to abandon racial quotas and preferences and in urging Newt Gingrich not to bring such measures to the floor.

Payne saved the Africa Subcommittee from abolition, and attacked cuts in aid to African countries; in 1995 he successfully restored $675 million to the Africa Development Fund. But he did not lionize all of Africa's leaders. He sponsored a resolution to cut off new investment in Nigeria because of the human rights abuses of the Abacha regime and in Sudan because of its practice of slavery. In a similar vein, he was one of only two House Democrats to criticize President Clinton for receiving China's General Chi, who suppressed the Tienanmen Square demonstrations in 1989. Nationally, he was a leader in passage of legislation to protect churches and other places of worship from burnings. He worked to drum up money for a revolutionary war memorial for African-Americans on Washington's Mall. He won an apology from Rules Committee chairman Gerald Solomon who had said that U.N. Secretary General Kofi Annan should be "horsewhipped" for his handling of negotiations over weapons inspections with Iraq. Internationally, he led efforts to urge restoration of democracy and human rights. He traveled on Clinton's spring 1998 trip to Africa, which Payne praised as a "sea change" for viewing African issues and leaders as equals to those of other continents. In 1999, he gained from fellow New Jerseyan Robert Menendez the ranking Democratic slot on the Africa Subcommittee.

On local issues, Payne has worked to bring millions of dollars in federal housing grants to his district, supported the Newark Riverfront project and secured grants to hire more police officers in Newark and Jersey City. Payne seems strong at home; in 1998 he felt free to take a bus tour the weekend before the election with other Black Caucus members to urge high black voter turnout in Midwest districts with competitive contests.

Cook's Call. *Safe.* Payne is sitting in the most Democratic district in New Jersey and one of the most Democratic districts in the entire country. He's a slam dunk in 2000.

The People: Pop. 1990: 593,876; 12.2% age 65 + ; 32.6% White, 60.2% Black, 2.4% Asian, 0.2% Amer. Indian, 4.5% Other; 11.7% Hispanic Origin. Households: 37.4% married couple families; 18.6% married couple fams. w. children; 34.3% college educ.; median household income: $28,849; per capita income: $12,833; median house value: $137,600; median gross rent: $455.

1996 Presidential Vote

Clinton (D) 138,128 (82%)
Dole (R) 21,911 (13%)
Perot (I) 5,774 (3%)

1992 Presidential Vote

Clinton (D) 126,415 (70%)
Bush (R) 36,299 (20%)
Perot (I) 14,887 (8%)

Rep. Donald M. Payne (D)

Elected 1988; b. July 16, 1934, Newark; home, Newark; Seton Hall, B.A. 1957; Baptist; widowed.

Elected Office: Essex Cnty. Bd. of Chosen Freeholders, 1972–78, Dir. 1977–78; Newark Municipal Cncl., 1982–89.

Professional Career: Elem. & High Schl. teacher, 1957–64; Exec., Prudential Insurance Co., 1964–72; Pres., YMCAs of the U.S., 1970; Vice Pres., Urban Data Systems Inc., 1975–88.

DC Office: 2209 RHOB 20515, 202-225-3436; Fax: 202-225-4160; Web site: www.house.gov/payne.

District Offices: Elizabeth, 908-629-0222; Newark, 201-645-3213.

Committees: *Education & the Workforce* (6th of 22 D): Early Childhood, Youth & Families; Employer-Employee Relations. *International Relations* (7th of 23 D): Africa (RMM).

Group Ratings

	ADA	ACLU	AFS	LCV	CON	NTU	NFIB	COC	ACU	NTLC	CHC
1998	90	94	100	69	87	24	0	20	9	3	0
1997	85	—	100	—	2	25	—	20	5	—	—

National Journal Ratings

	1997 LIB — 1997 CONS			1998 LIB — 1998 CONS		
Economic	82%	—	18%	79%	—	0%
Social	85%	—	0%	93%	—	0%
Foreign	97%	—	0%	84%	—	11%

Key Votes of the 105th Congress

1. Clinton Budget Deal	N	5. Puerto Rico Sthood. Ref.	Y	9. Cut $ for B-2 Bombers	Y
2. Education IRAs	N	6. End Highway Set-asides	*	10. Human Rights in China	Y
3. Req. 2/3 to Raise Taxes	N	7. School Prayer Amend.	N	11. Withdraw Bosnia Troops	N
4. Fast-track Trade	N	8. Ovrd. Part. Birth Veto	N	12. End Cuban TV-Marti	Y

Election Results

1998 general	Donald M. Payne (D) 82,244	(84%)	($414,705)
	William Stanley Wnuck (R) 10,678	(11%)	
	Others 5,572	(6%)	
1998 primary	Donald M. Payne (D) 24,747	(92%)	
	Dennis H. Speed (D) 2,254	(8%)	
1996 general	Donald M. Payne (D) 127,126	(84%)	($404,017)
	Vanessa Williams (R) 22,086	(15%)	($20,902)

ELEVENTH DISTRICT

New Jersey's Morris County, west of the Watchung Mountain ridges, was one of the first settled parts of the interior United States west of the seaboard. It has long been a place of comparative affluence, the home of skilled craftsmen during the Revolutionary War, with plenty of water mills and iron forges by the 19th Century. But only in the late 20th Century has it come into its own, as one of the wealthiest areas in the United States. And it is not just a collection of country estates with huddled small towns for the servants to live in, but a well-rounded community with all the appurtenances of urbanity except high crime and poverty rates. The very rich have lived here for some time, connected to Manhattan by commuter rail lines, but in the 1970s and 1980s, new residents rushed out the newly completed I-80 and I-280 or the ring road I-287. Bayer was setting up a big operation down the road and hundreds of small businesses were quietly creating jobs more rapidly than highly-publicized big companies (AT&T had huge layoffs here in 1996) were downsizing.

The 11th Congressional District includes all of Morris County plus similar adjacent areas. It is one of the most affluent districts in the country: number one in median household income in 1990, at $57,219, with the highest median housing value in New Jersey, $215,600—exceeded only by four districts in the New York area, 25 in California and one in Hawaii. It is family territory, with relatively few singles; not a strongly cultural conservative area, but not aggressively liberal either. Politically, it is the most Republican district in New Jersey, and one of the most in the Northeast.

The congressman from the 11th District is Rodney Frelinghuysen, a Republican and member of one of New Jersey's most durable political families, which moved from Germany near the Dutch border in 1720 and settled in Rodney's current district. Four Frelinghuysens served as senator from New Jersey, starting in 1793 and as recently as 1923; Theodore Frelinghuysen was Whig presidential nominee Henry Clay's running-mate in 1844 (leading to the memorable slogan, "Hurrah! Hurrah! The country's risin'/ For Henry Clay and Frelinghuysen"); Frederick Frelinghuysen was Chester Arthur's secretary of State; Peter Frelinghuysen, Rodney's father, was elected to the House in 1952 and served until his retirement in 1974. As a child, Rodney Frelinghuysen lived in the large brick house on Georgetown's N Street now owned by former *Washington Post* editor Ben Bradlee and his wife Sally Quinn, and he attended St. Albans school with Al Gore. After college, the congressman's son was drafted in the Army to Vietnam, where he built roads in the Mekong Delta. In 1972 he was appointed an aide by then-Morris County Freeholder (and later 11th District congressman) Dean Gallo; he served as a freeholder himself from 1974–83 and was elected to the Assembly in 1983. There he supported one tax increase by Republican Governor Thomas Kean, but opposed Democratic Governor Jim Florio's 1990 tax increase and, as chairman of the Appropriations Committee, worked to control spending and roll back taxes as an ally of Governor Christie Whitman.

Frelinghuysen ran for Congress in the 12th District in 1990, when its boundaries were different, and lost the primary to Dick Zimmer. In August 1994, after that year's primary, Gallo retired because of illness; he died two days before the election. Frelinghuysen was chosen to be the Republican nominee at a September party convention and was elected with 71% of the vote. He showed his insider skills by winning a seat on the Appropriations Committee, where Gallo had served. On Appropriations Frelinghuysen worked to cut spending on many programs, including the Tennessee Valley Authority, while maintaining a moderate voting record and concentrating on New Jersey projects. He supported funds for "Urban Core" and "Midtown Direct" mass transit lines. He helped push Sterling Forest preservation into the 1996 parks bill President Clinton signed, and got $1 million to expand the Great Swamp National Wildlife Refuge by 79 acres. In 1997, he was one of three House Republicans to switch their vote to support the partial-birth abortion ban; in 1996, he had voted against the attempt to override Clinton's veto of a similar bill. He showed his moderate stripes in 1998 as one of five Appropriations Republicans to join Democrats in preserving the National Endowment for the Arts. When he voted to impeach Clinton, he was the third Frelinghuysen with a similar distinction: his great-great-grandfather Frederick voted to convict Andrew Johnson in 1868, and his father Peter, after the revelations of July 1974, would have voted to impeach Nixon if the president had not resigned.

Frelinghuysen has been easily re-elected. In 1999 he joined the Appropriations subcommittee on Defense.

Cook's Call. *Safe.* Frelinghuysen sits in the most Republican district in the state and has no reason to be worried about his re-election prospects in 2000.

The People: Pop. 1990: 594,526; 12.9% rural; 11.2% age 65 +; 92.5% White, 2.6% Black, 3.9% Asian, 0.1% Amer. Indian, 1% Other; 4.1% Hispanic Origin. Households: 66.1% married couple families; 31.5% married couple fams. w. children; 60.3% college educ.; median household income: $57,219; per capita income: $25,454; median house value: $215,600; median gross rent: $660.

1996 Presidential Vote

Dole (R)	135,972	(49%)
Clinton (D)	116,225	(42%)
Perot (I)	21,376	(8%)
Others	5,240	(2%)

1992 Presidential Vote

Bush (R)	153,731	(51%)
Clinton (D)	97,697	(33%)
Perot (I)	46,407	(16%)

Rep. Rodney Frelinghuysen (R)

Elected 1994; b. Apr. 29, 1946, New York City; home, Morristown; Hobart Col., B.A. 1969; Episcopalian; married (Virginia).

Military Career: Army, 1969–71 (Vietnam).

Elected Office: Morris Cnty. Bd. of Freeholders, 1974–83; NJ Assembly, 1983–94.

Professional Career: Aide, Morris Cnty. Bd. of Freeholders, 1972–74.

DC Office: 228 CHOB 20515, 202-225-5034; Fax: 202-225-3186; Web site: www.house.gov/frelinghuysen.

District Office: Morristown, 973-984-0711.

Committees: *Appropriations* (21st of 34 R): Defense; Energy & Water Development; VA, HUD & Independent Agencies.

Group Ratings

	ADA	ACLU	AFS	LCV	CON	NTU	NFIB	COC	ACU	NTLC	CHC
1998	10	38	11	54	42	57	86	83	52	50	50
1997	40	—	25	—	70	48	—	90	52	—	—

National Journal Ratings

	1997 LIB — 1997 CONS		1998 LIB — 1998 CONS	
Economic	47% —	52%	45% —	54%
Social	55% —	44%	59% —	41%
Foreign	51% —	46%	32% —	67%

Key Votes of the 105th Congress

1. Clinton Budget Deal	Y	5. Puerto Rico Sthood. Ref.	Y	9. Cut $ for B-2 Bombers	N
2. Education IRAs	Y	6. End Highway Set-asides	Y	10. Human Rights in China	N
3. Req. 2/3 to Raise Taxes	Y	7. School Prayer Amend.	N	11. Withdraw Bosnia Troops	Y
4. Fast-track Trade	Y	8. Ovrd. Part. Birth Veto	Y	12. End Cuban TV-Marti	N

Election Results

1998 general	Rodney Frelinghuysen (R) 100,910	(68%)	($418,522)
	John P. Scollo (D) 44,160	(30%)	
	Others 3,901	(3%)	
1998 primary	Rodney Frelinghuysen (R) .... unopposed		
1996 general	Rodney Frelinghuysen (R) 169,091	(66%)	($581,895)
	Chris Evangel (D) 78,742	(31%)	($181,050)
	Others 7,325	(3%)	

TWELFTH DISTRICT

It was once the main East Coast arterial highway, carrying the nation's highest volume of truck traffic. Today it is crowded with cars taking high-salaried workers and clerical help to one of the East Coast's thickest concentrations of office buildings in one of the bigger edge cities spawned in the 1980s. This is U.S. 1, which once just connected the industrial cities of Trenton and New Brunswick on its way from Philadelphia to New York; now it is better thought of around here as connecting the university towns around Princeton and Rutgers, and is a locus of telecommunications and pharmaceutical research. This had been empty bucolic country, looked out on by F. Scott Fitzgerald's undergraduates from their Gothic Princeton towers; now it is filled with postmodern office campuses and hotels and restaurants clamoring for attention.

The 12th Congressional District extends several dozen miles on either side of U.S. 1. To the west, it takes in the rolling country of Hunterdon County, around the old county seat of Flemington, once the site of the Lindbergh kidnapping trial, now an outlet store center with many young families, affluent if not elite, modern but seeking traditional values. On the other side of U.S. 1, the 12th takes in modest-income suburbs like East Brunswick in Middlesex County and much of Monmouth County, almost to the beach resorts of the Jersey Shore. Some of these communities are long-settled, others are spanking new. Politically, the Princeton area and Middlesex County, in the center of the district, lean Democratic. The two ends of the district—Monmouth County near the Shore and Hunterdon County inland—are usually heavily Republican. The balance is usually Republican, though Bill Clinton carried the district in 1996.

The congressman from the 12th District is Rush Holt, a Democrat elected in 1998 with an unusual political pedigree. His father Rush D. Holt—a favorite of United Mine Workers' leader John Lewis—was elected as the "boy senator" from West Virginia in 1934 at 29; he could not take his seat until June 1935 when he turned 30. But he clashed early and often with Franklin Roosevelt and lost the Democratic primary to Harley Kilgore in 1940. After his father died when young Rush was age 6, he grew up in Washington, D.C., where his mother Helen—who had been West Virginia secretary of State—became a top official with the Federal Housing Agency. He went off to Carleton College in Minnesota and to New York University, where he earned master's and doctorate degrees in physics, eventually settling at Princeton as assistant director of its plasma laboratory, which studies fusion. He also was an arms-control expert for the State Department.

Rush Holt entered politics in 1996, when Republican Dick Zimmer's unsuccessful Senate run opened his House seat. Holt finished third in the Democratic primary with 24% of the vote, trailing David Del Vecchio, mayor of Lawrenceville, who had 45%, and Princeton Town Committeeman Carl Mayer with 31%. The Republican primary victory of cultural conservative Mike Pappas gave Democrats an unexpected chance to win the seat. But Pappas insisted that his top goal was cutting taxes, and he won 50%–47%—far closer than Zimmer's 68%–30% in 1994. Del Vecchio carried the Princeton area and Middlesex County, but Pappas won more than 60% in Hunterdon and Somerset.

Pappas immediately became a top Democratic target in 1998. The wealthy and self-financed Mayer—an investment attorney and former Ralph Nader aide—decided to run again, but national and local Democrats favored Holt, who won the endorsements of all five country Democratic organizations plus all of Mayer's former colleagues on the Princeton Town Committee, and took the primary by 64%–36%. Holt decided early in the year that Clinton's State of the Union message gave him an agenda to appeal to suburban voters.

Then, Pappas gave him an additional opportunity that Holt eagerly exploited. When Pappas took to the House floor in July to recite a poem: "Twinkle, Twinkle Kenneth Starr, now we see how brave you are. We could not see which way to go, if you did not lead us so." For Holt that encapsulated the Republican's partisanship and disdain for voter opinion. Pappas's recital gained extensive network coverage; Holt turned it into campaign ads, which he aired extensively across the district. Holt emphasized gun control, abortion rights, the environment and preserving Social Security. Still, the 12th District is Republican enough that Holt's 50%–47% victory was a one of the biggest surprises on election night. Pappas won 60% of the vote in Hunterdon and 59% in Somerset, but barely led in Monmouth County, while Holt won 61%–37% in Mercer and 60%–38% in Middlesex.

Holt barely took his seat before Republicans started lining up for the 2000 campaign. Among others, both the moderate Zimmer and conservative Pappas said that they would seek to regain their old seat, raising the prospect of a divisive primary; Zimmer won early endorsements from county Republican leaders in Mercer and Middlesex plus close allies of Governor Christie Whitman. Holt took seats on the Education and Workforce Committee to work on the Elementary and Secondary Education Act renewal, and on the Budget Committee to focus on national priorities.

Cook's Call. *Highly Competitive.* This Republican leaning district will be a challenge for Holt to hold onto, especially if he faces popular former Representative Dick Zimmer. But, a messy primary between Zimmer and former Representative Mike Pappas, who has also expressed his intention to run, could give Holt a badly needed boost. This will be one of the Republicans' top take-over targets in 2000.

The People: Pop. 1990: 594,577; 34.1% rural; 11.9% age 65 +; 89.7% White, 5.2% Black, 4.4% Asian, 0.1% Amer. Indian, 0.7% Other; 2.6% Hispanic Origin. Households: 66.5% married couple families; 32.1% married couple fams. w. children; 62.2% college educ.; median household income: $54,630; per capita income: $24,615; median house value: $205,700; median gross rent: $628.

1996 Presidential Vote

Clinton (D)	139,252	(48%)
Dole (R)	120,913	(42%)
Perot (I)	23,159	(8%)
Others	6,716	(2%)

1992 Presidential Vote

Bush (R)	130,651	(43%)
Clinton (D)	121,447	(40%)
Perot (I)	50,357	(17%)

Rep. Rush Holt (D)

Elected 1998; b. Oct. 15, 1948, Weston, WV; home, Hopewell Township; Carleton Col., B.S. 1970, N.Y.U., PhD. 1981; Protestant; married (Margaret Lancefield).

Professional Career: Prof., Swarthmore Col., 1981–89; Asst. Dir., Princeton Plasma Physics Lab., 1989–98.

DC Office: 1630 LHOB 20515, 202-225-5801; Fax: 2-2-225-6025; Web site: www.house.gov/rholt.

District Office: Princeton Junction, 609-750-9365.

Committees: *Budget* (17th of 19 D). *Education & the Workforce* (22d of 22 D): Employer-Employee Relations; Postsecondary Education, Training & Life-Long Learning.

Group Ratings and Key Votes: Newly Elected

Election Results

1998 general	Rush Holt (D)	92,528	(50%)	($919,905)
	Michael Pappas (R)	87,221	(47%)	($889,475)
	Others	4,861	(3%)	
1998 primary	Rush Holt (D)	10,177	(64%)	
	Carl J. Mayer (D)	5,830	(36%)	
1996 general	Michael Pappas (R)	135,811	(50%)	($591,536)
	David M. Del Vecchio (D)	125,594	(47%)	($475,370)
	Others	7,816	(3%)	

THIRTEENTH DISTRICT

The Statue of Liberty, standing in New York Harbor since 1886, has been the great symbol of America welcoming immigrants to its shores. Actually, the statue is on the New Jersey side of the harbor, so that is where many immigrants first arrived, and most of Ellis Island, where they were processed, the majority of which has been ruled by the Supreme Court to be in New Jersey as well. The towns sitting on the granite and gneiss ridge of Hudson County, overlooking the harbor, have in particular been immigrant territory. When immigration was shut off by the laws of 1921 and 1924, many children and grandchildren of the Irish and Italian immigrants stayed in Hudson County, living in the same neighborhoods, working on the same docks or factories—Maxwell House and Palmolive were here—and voting the dictates of the same political machine.

Hudson County was the setting of one of America's classic political machines, undisciplined by any metropolitan elite. From 1917–49, the boss of Hudson County was Frank ("I am the law") Hague; his machine chose governors and U.S. Senators, prosecutors and judges, and had influence in the White House of Franklin D. Roosevelt. Hague collected high taxes from industries clustered here—who then passed them on to consumers everywhere—and in return gave them an orderly city, free of most crime and vice, and a work force insulated against racketeers and militant unions. Hague's successor, John V. Kenny, was boss from 1949–71—continuous power for 54 years. But Hudson County began changing again, in ways little noticed by either the local machine or Manhattan sophisticates. New immigrants were coming in—refugees from Castro's Cuba, other Latinos and Asians after the 1965 immigration law changed the rules. Union City became predominantly Cuban, Jersey City neighborhoods became heavily Latino. Upscale young singles looking for lower rents moved into Hoboken's five-story Victorian apartments that sparkle with light off the Hudson, and are a quick commute through the PATH tubes to Wall Street or Greenwich Village. The Jersey City waterfront is the scene of huge new condominium developments—Port Liberte, opposite the Statue of Liberty; Newport, with thousands of housing units and hundreds of thousands of square feet of office space; Liberty Place, on the site of the old Colgate-Palmolive factory. This vibrant private sector contrasted with a somnolent public sector so incompetent and expensive that it gave an opening to Jersey City's Republican mayor, Bret Schundler, a former Wall Streeter elected in 1992 after the incumbent went to jail, elected to a full term in 1993 and re-elected in 1997.

The 13th Congressional District of New Jersey includes most of Hudson County plus most of the immigrant entry ports along the water. It was designed in 1992 to be an "Hispanic influence" district; 41% of its residents in 1990 were Hispanic and 14% were black. With most of Jersey City and all of Union City and West New York and Weehawken, it includes 105,000 people in the old Ironbound area and North Ward of Newark, half of them Hispanic, and takes in the industrial city waterfront areas of Elizabeth, Linden, Carteret and Perth Amboy. It still votes heavily Democratic in most elections.

The congressman from the 13th is Robert Menendez, a Democrat elected in 1992. He is of

Cuban descent and grew up in Union City, America's most densely populated city (in 1990 it had 58,000 people in 1.3 square miles), and got into politics early: He was elected to the school board in 1974, at 20. He worked for Union City Mayor William Musto in the 1970s, but quit and testified against Musto in a corruption trial, and ran against him and lost in 1982. Menendez was elected mayor in 1986 and to the legislature in 1987, serving in both jobs (a common practice in New Jersey) until his 1992 election to Congress. When new district lines were created and incumbent Frank Guarini retired, Menendez won the primary 68%–32% and the general 64%–31%.

In the House, Menendez serves on the International Relations Committee where he is now ranking minority member on the International Economic Policy and Trade Subcommittee. He supported Bob Torricelli's 1992 Cuban Democracy Act, and after the Brothers to the Rescue fliers were shot down in February 1996, he helped broker Clinton Administration acceptance of the Helms-Burton Act. He was disappointed when Clinton twice suspended lawsuits authorized by Helms-Burton against those who take title to expropriated property in Cuba and he opposed Clinton steps to relax the trade embargo, but he plugged on nonetheless. He is an ally of organized labor: he opposed NAFTA and criticized the Republicans' Shipping Act deregulation as cartelization. He helped to secure $733 million to deepen the main channel of Newark Bay from 40 to 45 feet by 2004 to accommodate larger cargo ships to the container port.

Menendez has taken a high-profile role in recent years as a House Democratic leader. In 1997, he was tapped as the Hispanic to fill the chief deputy minority whip post Bill Richardson vacated, which he used to aggressively support Loretta Sanchez in her election challenge from Bob Dornan. In November 1998 Democrats elected him vice chairman of the Caucus; on the second ballot he beat Cal Dooley of California 124–81. When Senator Frank Lautenberg announced his retirement in February 1999, Menendez was widely expected to run for the Senate. But Minority Leader Dick Gephardt urged him to stay in the House, arguing that Democrats would likely win a majority there in 2000 and as a leader of a Democratic House Menendez could accomplish more than as a low-seniority minority-party senator. Menendez evidently agreed, and decided to stay on, and with his considerable political skills could well live up to Gephardt's prophecies.

Cook's Call. *Safe.* While not the most Democratic district in the state, this Jersey City-based district is still solidly Democratic and will not give Menendez any worries in 2000. Redistricting, however, could be a concern since this seat and Payne's Newark-based district have experienced the most population loss in the state.

The People: Pop. 1990: 594,875; 12.8% age 65 + ; 67.5% White, 13.8% Black, 4.5% Asian, 0.2% Amer. Indian, 14.1% Other; 41% Hispanic Origin. Households: 43.8% married couple families; 21.4% married couple fams. w. children; 30.6% college educ.; median household income: $28,721; per capita income: $13,028; median house value: $143,900; median gross rent: $440.

1996 Presidential Vote

Clinton (D)	115,576	(71%)
Dole (R)	35,266	(22%)
Perot (I)	8,411	(5%)
Others	2,764	(2%)

1992 Presidential Vote

Clinton (D)	94,651	(53%)
Bush (R)	64,358	(36%)
Perot (I)	14,981	(8%)

Rep. Robert Menendez (D)

Elected 1992; b. Jan. 1, 1954, New York, NY; home, Union City; St. Peter's Col., B.A. 1976, Rutgers Law Schl., J.D. 1979; Catholic; married (Jane Jacobsen-Menendez).

Elected Office: Union City Board of Ed., 1974–82; Union City Mayor, 1986–92; NJ Assembly, 1987–91; NJ Senate, 1991–92.

Professional Career: Practicing atty., 1980–92.

DC Office: 405 CHOB 20515, 202-225-7919; Fax: 202-226-0792; Web site: www.house.gov/menendez.

District Offices: Bayonne, 201-823-2900; Jersey City, 201-222-2828; Perth Amboy, 908-324-6212.

Committees: *Democratic Caucus Vice Chairman. International Relations* (8th of 23 D): International Economic Policy & Trade (RMM); Western Hemisphere. *Transportation & Infrastructure* (13th of 34 D): Aviation; Water Resources & Environment.

Group Ratings

	ADA	ACLU	AFS	LCV	CON	NTU	NFIB	COC	ACU	NTLC	CHC
1998	95	81	100	100	55	14	14	33	12	8	0
1997	90	—	86	—	76	27	—	40	13	—	—

National Journal Ratings

	1997 LIB	—	1997 CONS		1998 LIB	—	1998 CONS
Economic	75%	—	22%		72%	—	23%
Social	82%	—	15%		72%	—	28%
Foreign	69%	—	28%		61%	—	37%

Key Votes of the 105th Congress

1. Clinton Budget Deal	N	5. Puerto Rico Sthood. Ref.	N	9. Cut $ for B-2 Bombers	Y
2. Education IRAs	N	6. End Highway Set-asides	N	10. Human Rights in China	Y
3. Req. 2/3 to Raise Taxes	N	7. School Prayer Amend.	N	11. Withdraw Bosnia Troops	N
4. Fast-track Trade	N	8. Ovrd. Part. Birth Veto	N	12. End Cuban TV-Marti	N

Election Results

1998 general	Robert Menendez (D)	70,308	(80%)	($964,145)
	Theresa De Leon (R)	14,615	(17%)	($35,252)
	Others	2,900	(3%)	
1998 primary	Robert Menendez (D)	unopposed		
1996 general	Robert Menendez (D)	115,459	(79%)	($379,469)
	Carlos E. Munoz (R)	25,427	(17%)	
	Others	5,587	(4%)	

NEW MEXICO

America's oldest settlements and its newest technologies can be found, in surrealistic proximity, in New Mexico. For the oldest permanently inhabited city in the United States is not Plymouth, Massachusetts, or Jamestown, Virginia, or even St. Augustine, Florida, it is probably Acoma, New Mexico. Probably, because Acoma, inhabited by the Anasazi, "an agricultural, settled and architecturally sophisticated people," wrote historian Roger Kennedy in *Rediscovering America*, had perhaps 1,000 years of unrecorded history before Spanish conquistadors came upon them in 1540. Some 460 years later, much of what makes New Mexico distinctive derives from the people found here by the first European explorers—something true of no other state but Hawaii. While the Pilgrims built flimsy wood houses, the Indians in New Mexico were living in extensive dwellings hundreds of years old, made with the adobe that is still the characteristic building material here.

Other state cultures are generally based on what early white settlers brought to the land; natives have mostly disappeared or been killed off by diseases contracted from the first white settlers. Not in New Mexico. The English-speaking culture here is superimposed, at times rather lightly, on a society whose written history dates back to the Spanish settlement of Santa Fe in 1609, and to centuries long past when the Pueblo Indians set up stable agricultural societies on the sandy, rocky lands of northern New Mexico, using small pebbles as mulch to retain scarce moisture. Pueblo culture is still celebrated in the Indian pottery that commands premium prices in Santa Fe and in the annual Gathering of Nations pow-wow in Albuquerque which attracts 30,000 Indians. Today, a very substantial minority of New Mexicans are descendants of these Indians or the Spanish, or both. New Mexico had the highest percentage of Hispanics (38%) in the U.S. after the 1990 Census. Nearly one-third of the people in this state speak Spanish in everyday life, and relatively few are recent migrants from Mexico. The Hispanic roots go very deep, as witnessed by the recent discovery of Hebrew symbols left on Christian gravestones by the *conversos*, Jews who hid their religion after it was outlawed by the Spanish in 1492; there are families here who have secretly maintained Jewish practices for centuries.

New Mexico is the northernmost salient of the great Indian-Spanish civilizations of the Cordillera, which extend along the mountain chain through Mexico and Central and South America, to the southern tip of Chile and Argentina. Yet New Mexico also is a civilization built on modern technology. It was to a remote mesa called Los Alamos that General Leslie Groves brought his Manhattan Project scientists during World War II to build a secret town and develop a secret weapon that would in two explosions end World War II and change the course of history. Los Alamos, which remains a government high-tech laboratory, made news in early 1999 when it was revealed that Chinese spies had obtained thousands of computer files from there. New Mexico has other high-tech sites as well—the White Sands Missile Range near Alamogordo, where the first atomic bomb was detonated, and the Sandia Laboratories near Albuquerque, run by Lockheed-Martin for the government, a non-nuclear high-tech weapons research facility, with one of the fastest computers in the world, used to simulate nuclear explosions. Near Carlsbad is the federal Waste Isolation Pilot Plant (WIPP), where the Energy Department plans to conduct a seven-year test of radioactive waste storage; after many delays, the first waste from the Idaho National Engineering and Environmental Laboratory arrived here in April 1999.

But the past intrudes on this new high-tech New Mexico. West of Albuquerque, developers and most local politicians want to build a highway through 8.5 acres of the 7,244-acre Petroglyph National Monument, filled with black volcanic rock with ancient mysterious carvings; a proposal to put the road through a nearby golf course was nixed. But Albuquerque Mayor Jim

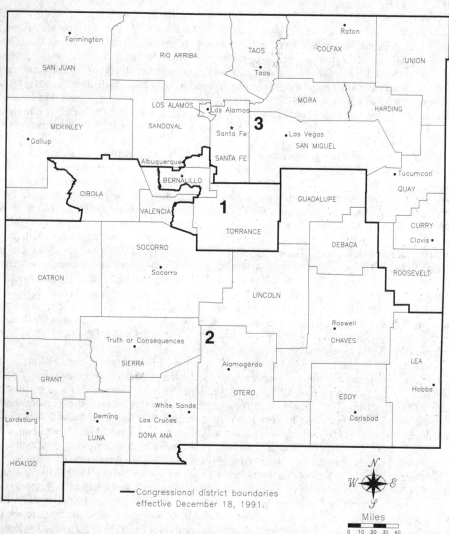

Farmington

SAN JUAN

RIO ARRIBA

TAOS

Taos

COLFAX

Raton

UNION

MCKINLEY

Gallup

SANDOVAL

LOS ALAMOS

Los Alamos

Santa Fe

MORA

HARDING

SANTA FE

3

Las Vegas

SAN MIGUEL

Albuquerque

BERNALILLO

GUADALUPE

Tucumcari

QUAY

CIBOLA

VALENCIA

1

TORRANCE

CURRY

Clovis

SOCORRO

DEBACA

ROOSEVELT

Socorro

CATRON

LINCOLN

Truth or Consequences

2

Roswell

CHAVES

SIERRA

Alamogordo

LEA

GRANT

OTERO

EDDY

Hobbs

Lordsburg

Deming

LUNA

White Sands

Las Cruces

DONA ANA

Carlsbad

HIDALGO

N
W   E
S

Miles

0 10 20 30 40

——Congressional district boundaries
effective December 18, 1991.

Baca is opposed, and perhaps it will occur to others that it is easier to replace a few golf holes than 2,000-year-old pictographs. Golf courses and other resort facilities are also springing up around the Indian casinos operated by 11 of New Mexico's 22 tribes; these employ many Indians, and are an opportunity for many to segue into the mainstream economy and culture; but some wonder whether they are killing off ancient traditions and religious practices. Then there is the question of land ownership: Many Hispanic families claim that they were cheated out of land in the 19th Century contrary to the terms of the Treaty of Guadalupe Hidalgo, which ended the war with Mexico in 1848 and brought what is now the Southwest into the United States. Congressman Bill Redmond, a Republican elected in a special election, and Speaker Newt Gingrich called for a presidential commission to examine their claims and recommend compensation, a cause in which they were joined by many on the left. But environmentalists warned of privatization of land, and Redmond lost in November 1998 and Gingrich resigned soon after. Controversy exists even about the state symbol; it turns out that it is the symbol of the Zia Pueblo, which is suing the state for $73 million for its use.

New and old New Mexico intermingle in varying proportions in this land of majestically vast vistas. The Hispanic-Indian culture predominates north and west of Albuquerque, with picturesque old towns and still-functioning pueblos, backward Indian reservations and lavish casino resorts. "Little Texas," in the south and east, has small cities, plenty of oil wells, vast cattle ranches and desolate military bases, and resembles, economically and culturally, the adjacent west Texas High Plains. Here, as everywhere in New Mexico, government is a prime employer (accounting for 24% of jobs, one of the highest figures in the country) and often the moving force in the local economy. In the middle is Albuquerque which, with the arrival of air conditioning, grew from a small desert town of 35,000 in 1940 into a Sun Belt metropolis of 678,000 today. Albuquerque has a large Hispanic minority, as do many fast-growing U.S. cities. Its economy is based heavily on high tech, especially nuclear power; but it has relatively low income and education levels—the downscale Sun Belt. Each of these three areas has about one-third of the state's population, and their impressionistic boundaries are followed pretty closely by the boundaries of New Mexico's three congressional districts.

For many years, New Mexico politics was a somnolent business. Local bosses—first Republican, later Democratic—controlled the large Hispanic vote. Elections in many counties featured irregularities that would have made a Chicago ward committeeman blush. New Mexico also had for years another feature of boss-controlled politics: the balanced ticket, one Spanish and one Anglo senator, with the offices of governor and lieutenant governor split as well. But for all its distinctiveness, in national politics New Mexico was a bellwether, voting for every winning presidential candidate from 1912, when it became a state, until 1976, when it backed Gerald Ford. In 1988 it voted 52%–47% for George Bush, 1% off the national average; in 1996 it was 49% for Bill Clinton, right on the national mark, and 42% for Bob Dole, just 1% off. In the 1990s, Democrats have a strong base in the north, from Hispanics and from hip newcomers in Santa Fe and Taos. Albuquerque has been politically marginal; its migrants have been conservative culturally but liberal on economics. Southeast New Mexico is as conservative and Republican as west Texas. Southwest New Mexico, around Las Cruces and Silver City, is more Hispanic and marginally Democratic.

Some new patterns have emerged in the 1990s. A Green Party formed, in protest against the practical-minded and sometimes corrupt brand of politics of many Democratic wheelhorses; the Green candidate for governor won 10% of the vote in 1994, and Gary Johnson might well have not been elected otherwise. Johnson is also a new political force—the first strongly conservative Republican to win major office in many years, and one ferociously opposed by the Democrats who control the legislature. But he won re-election without any third party candidacies in 1998, against a strong candidate, former Albuquerque Mayor Martin Chavez, and his Republicans have been steadily closing the Democrats' margin in the legislature. New Mexico continues to have two long-serving senators, Republican Pete Domenici and Democrat Jeff Bingaman. But two of its three House members were first elected in 1998. Meanwhile, former

Congressman Bill Richardson, for two years ambassador to the United Nations and now Energy secretary, has been mentioned as a possible nominee for vice president in 2000. He proved himself a competent practical politician in the House, and in the administration has shown himself to be an able and indefatigable international negotiator, and an administrator with the good sense to get rid of the accused Los Alamos spy as soon as he became aware of the charges.

Governor. The governor of New Mexico is Gary Johnson, a Republican elected in 1994 and 1998. Johnson moved to Albuquerque when he was in junior high. In 1974, at 21, while still a student at the University of New Mexico, he started a construction business, and built a door-to-door solicitation business into Big J Enterprises, one of the largest construction companies in the state with 600 employees. He served on civic boards, sponsored children's athletic events and was himself a competitor: He won the 1993 Bump, Bike and Bolt competition in Taos, completed a triathlon in Hawaii in October 1993, and ran a 100-mile race partly backward after pulling a muscle. In 1994, he ran for governor, on vague slogans—"people before politics," "citizen service"—and on promises to hold the line on government growth and to roll back a six-cent gas tax increase. He won the Republican primary by only 34%–33% over Dick Cheney (not the former Defense secretary), and in the general election faced Governor Bruce King, elected in 1970, 1978, and 1990, and now eligible for the first time for a second consecutive term. But King had won the Democratic primary by only 39%–36% over his lieutenant governor, Casey Luna, with 25% for former Clinton Interior official Jim Baca, now mayor of Albuquerque. And King also had to face a Green Party candidate, former Lieutenant Governor Roberto Mondragon. Mondragon won 10% of the vote, as Johnson beat King 50%–40%. Did the Greens produce victory for Johnson? The combined Green and Democratic vote was slightly larger than Johnson's, but he would have lost a two-candidate race only if Green voters had gone by more than 98% for King—which is not very likely.

In his first term, Johnson faced bitter opposition from Democratic legislative leaders. He vetoed 388 bills, cut the state budget unilaterally, reduced state workforce by 1,200 and limited state budget growth to 4.2% a year, down from nearly 10% in the previous decade. He did not get his proposed income tax cut and prescription tax abolition, but he did get the six-cent gas tax repealed and claimed to reduce taxes by $106 million a year. In 1998 he cut the top personal income tax rate, instituted a low income tax rebate, and a gross receipts tax cut that included prescription drugs. He pushed successfully for two new prisons, to be privately built, used drivers license offices to get unpaid child support, worked to create a launch site for space vehicles and established a tough prison regime—frequent drug tests, mandatory hard labor, deprivation of bodybuilding equipment, and 23-hour solitary confinement for misbehaving gang members. He called for school vouchers, charter schools and testing of students every year, and raised teachers' salaries sharply. He supported Indian gambling and signed a bill banning drive-through alcohol sales.

Johnson was not afraid of a fight. He established a Salud! managed care program in Medicaid. And he fought for welfare reform. He vetoed the legislature's 1997 bill and instituted his own Progress plan, counting federal housing subsidies and incomes of everyone in a house to determine eligibility and instituting tough work requirements. Welfare rolls fell from 34,900 in November 1994 to 16,500 in November 1997. But the Progress plan was rejected by the feds, and Johnson was held in indirect civil contempt by the state Supreme Court and ordered to reinstate the old AFDC system in December 1997. Eventually Johnson got a welfare reform approved—the last in the nation—with a mandatory work requirement, but the rolls rose to 23,700 in September 1998. Meanwhile, Johnson stayed in shape: He competed in the Iron Man Triathlon again in October 1997, hang-glided off a 10,000-foot cliff and rode his bicycle across New Mexico five times.

Johnson's Republicans picked up legislative seats in 1996 even as Bill Clinton carried the state. Still, Democrats had fond hopes of beating Johnson in 1998. They took special care to propitiate the Green Party, to prevent a candidacy like those that hurt them in 1994 and in the May 1997 3d District special election. Their strongest candidate was Martin Chavez, state senator from 1989–93 and mayor of Albuquerque from 1993–97. In the June 1998 primary, Chavez beat state Representative Gary King, son of Bruce King, by 48%–30%. Chavez promised full-time kindergarten and criticized Johnson for not getting along with the legislature. Johnson replied, "I wasn't elected to get along with the legislature." Johnson continued to describe himself as a "nonpolitician," which irritated Chavez, who said he was proud to be in public service.

The two candidates participated, mostly civilly, in 24 debates. Johnson liked to end by holding up his checkbook, saying, "Citizens of New Mexico, guard your checkbook—it is doomed." His argument was that Chavez couldn't fulfill his promises without raising taxes; Chavez said he would go after $432 million of uncollected taxes. Chavez said he could accomplish more as governor because he would avoid confrontation with the legislature. Johnson took some nervy stands—suggesting that state university tuitions were low, and might be raised; opposing laws directed at hate crimes; favoring concealed weapons laws. Johnson led most of the way, and won 55%–45%; he carried the Anglo vote 2–1, while losing Hispanic 2–1, the latter an improvement over his showing in 1994. He won an impressive 58% in Albuquerque and Bernalillo County, and carried Little Texas 2–1. Chavez carried Santa Fe County 2–1, but next-door Sandoval County, once rural, Hispanic and Democratic, was now filling up with suburbanites spreading north from Albuquerque, and Johnson carried it 60%–40%.

Johnson thus became the first New Mexico governor to win a second consecutive four-year term, and his Republicans made more small gains in the state House, but not enough for a majority. He called for an income tax cut, and a repeal of New Mexico's "prevailing wage" law, which makes construction more expensive for state government than for private firms, and for school vouchers which were tabled by the legislature in February 1999. He signed two bills allowing more charter schools in April 1999 and vetoed a budget proposal because it did not include a private school voucher program. He vetoed an extension of the public employees collective bargaining act, which is set to sunset in July 1999, and threatened to veto any other budget that addressed the issue. His big highway-building program, to make every town of 15,000 reachable by four-lane highways, was approved. Johnson is not eligible to run for a third term in 2002.

Senior Senator. Pete Domenici is in his third decade in the Senate and rounding out his second decade as chairman of (or ranking Republican on) the Senate Budget Committee. Certainly he is the giant political figure in New Mexico. Domenici grew up in Albuquerque, the son of Italian immigrants who ran a grocery wholesale business. He played sports, practiced law, was elected to the city commission in 1966; he ran for governor in 1970, and lost to Bruce King. In 1972, when a Senate seat opened up in a Republican year, he ran and won, beating a Democrat named Jack Daniels. Ever since he has been re-elected by wide margins.

Domenici's great work in the Senate is on the budget. He chaired the Budget Committee from 1981–87, was ranking Republican from 1987–95, and now is chairman again: no other Republican need apply. In 1990 he turned down the ranking minority position on Energy and Natural Resources, an important committee for New Mexico, in order to stay on the Budget Committee. For years Domenici was frustrated there: He was genuinely appalled at the deficits of the 1980s and was ready to recommend the bitterest of medicine—entitlement cuts, tax increases. But Democrats fought spending cuts and Republicans fought tax increases, and so Domenici's victories were few and hard won. In May 1985, Domenici and Bob Dole got Republican senators to pass a freeze on Social Security cost-of-living adjustments; then President Reagan dropped the COLA freeze in a compromise with House Speaker Tip O'Neill, and Senate Republicans, left exposed, lost their majority in 1986. Domenici backed the 1987 Gramm-Rudman Act, whose mechanisms, along with Reagan Budget Director Jim Miller's fixation on holding down spending, did in fact cut the deficit by about half; he backed the 1990 budget summit tax increase with its domestic and defense spending caps. Domenici opposed the Clinton budget and tax package in 1993.

Domenici did not get his way after Republicans won majorities in 1994. His own preference was a plan with $476 billion in tax cuts, $1.4 trillion in spending cuts over 10 years and a consumption-based tax to replace the income tax. The pace was set by Speaker Newt Gingrich and House Budget Chairman John Kasich in the 1995–96 confrontation with Bill Clinton. But the tax increase he opposed in 1993 and the spending standstill in the budget eventually passed in early 1996 put the deficit on a downward trajectory. In this setting Domenici was the impresario in the negotiations that produced the 1997 balanced budget agreement. In 1998 he opposed Kasich's and Gingrich's proposal for a large tax cut and effectively scuttled it. In January 1999, with the budget now officially balanced, Domenici took a different tack. He accepted Bill Clinton's proposal to reserve 62% of the surplus for Social Security, but argued that much of the rest should be devoted to tax cuts—he favored eliminating the marriage penalty, providing incentives for education and allowing deductions for business research and development. "Those who have concluded that Pete Domenici does not understand the value of tax cuts have just got me wrong. It's the right thing now." He called also for increased spending on defense and elementary and secondary education.

Generally, Domenici is a passionate moderate, with a middle-of-the-road record. He has argued strongly for including coverage of mental illness in health insurance, and talked of the severe mental illness of one of his daughters. Working with Democrat Paul Wellstone, he got the Senate to include mental illness in the 1996 health care bill and got the conference committee to accept coverage with a low cap. Domenici cited evidence that mental health treatments are increasingly rigorous and efficacious; opponents feared high and uncontrollable costs. This is a cause he is likely to pursue further. On the Governmental Affairs Committee he was a passionate critic of the campaign law violations by the Clinton-Gore campaign, and in 1997 urged that Attorney General Janet Reno be fired for refusing to appoint independent counsels. He fears "the social fabric has broken down," calling on Hollywood and businesses to take responsibility for the morality of their products.

Familiar with New Mexico's research laboratories, Domenici had a bill to double federal spending on basic research over 10 years, and he argued for different nuclear policies—more use of nuclear energy to generate power, opening of an interim nuclear waste storage facility in Nevada, a reduction in nuclear weapons stockpiles and irradiation of food. He waged a successful public battle, with swipes at the White House, to get Kirtland Air Force Base taken off the 1995 list of base closures. Domenici uses his Appropriations seat to help New Mexico projects, generating $18 million for the Hispanic Cultural Center in Albuquerque and lesser sums for the National Center of Genome Research in Santa Fe and a fish hatchery in Mora; of course, he pays close attention to the Sandia and Los Alamos labs. He threatened a filibuster against a proposed 85% increase in grazing fees in October 1993. He has worked to avoid decertifying Mexico as a partner in the drug war, but expressed "concern about ineffective and insufficient progress" by Mexico. He opposed a Clinton proposal for issuing $400 million for Indian schools and said the government should finance them directly instead. Overall, New Mexico gets back more dollars in federal spending than it sends in taxes than any other state; Domenici may take some credit for this, but the larger reason is the location of huge federal research facilities in this still lightly-populated state.

Domenici has remained highly popular and wins re-election by wide margins, most recently in 1996. Ordinarily he does not get involved in local politics, but in the June 1998 special election he campaigned heavily for Heather Wilson, who won.

Junior Senator. Jeff Bingaman, a Democrat first elected in 1982, is New Mexico's junior senator. He has a good political lineage: His father was a professor at Western New Mexico University in Silver City, and his uncle was campaign manager for longtime Senator Clinton Anderson. A year out of law school, Bingaman was counsel to the state constitutional convention; a few years later, he went into law practice in Santa Fe with former Governor Jack Campbell. Bingaman's wife, Anne, started a highly successful law practice of her own that helped finance his first campaigns; she was assistant attorney general for antitrust in the first Clinton term. In a small state, bright young people like Jeff Bingaman rise fast. He ran for attorney general in 1978 and won; in 1982, he ran against Senator Harrison Schmitt, the former astronaut, also from Silver City, and won with 54%, partly because it was a recession year, but also because of Schmitt's misleading and negative ads.

Bingaman has followed a course in the Senate much like that of Clinton Anderson, who used his influence behind the scenes to great effect but shunned national publicity—so much so that one New Mexico magazine called him "the invisible senator." He got seats on two committees of great importance to the state, Armed Services and Energy. On Armed Services he became a protege of Sam Nunn, who created a subcommittee tailored to his interests, now called Acquisition and Technology; in 1997, Bingaman traded his ranking position there for one on the Strategic Forces Subcommittee. From these seats Bingaman has had lots of say over New Mexico's Los Alamos and Sandia labs, which he has encouraged to enter into partnership with private firms. With Pete Domenici, Phil Gramm and Joseph Lieberman, he sponsored a bill to double federal research spending over 10 years. He sponsored a $1.6 billion defense conversion package that passed in 1992 and $100 million in seed money for regional partnerships of small technology firms. Behind the scenes he helped to get Kirtland Air Force Base off the 1995 base-closing list.

On the Energy Committee, he became the top-ranking Democrat in 1999. On grazing fees, he worked to preserve the program, but with higher fees and more restrictions than Domenici favored. He was the Senate sponsor of the 975-acre extension of Bandelier National Monument, backed by Republican Bill Redmond in the House; he worked unsuccessfully to acquire the Baca Ranch near Los Alamos. In July 1998 he proposed spending $420 million to restock the Strategic Petroleum Reserve; he argued that the government had been selling oil to raise cash, and it made more sense to buy oil when the price was low. He sponsored the Radiation Exposure Act of 1990, to compensate uranium miners and workers; in 1998 he worked to expand it.

Bingaman's voting record is moderate to liberal, with efforts at bipartisanship. "There's too heavy a dose of partisanship to a lot of what goes on in Washington these days," he said in 1998. But he has indulged in a bit of it himself: in 1995, just after being re-elected, he was one of six Democrats who switched their votes from a year before and opposed the balanced budget amendment, which lost by one vote. He has been creative in coming up with projects to improve education—grants for technology in schools, grants to encourage education schools to train teachers in the subjects they will teach, grants to enable low-income students to take the SAT for free, a 1997 law to discourage dropouts (the dropout rate is high in New Mexico). He wants to get tribally controlled Indian colleges treated the same as Historically Black Colleges and he pushed for a Marine Junior ROTC program in newly opening Rio Rancho High School near Albuquerque. He tried in 1998 to get the highway bill to ban drive-through sales of liquor (New Mexico passed such a law later that year). He tried to forge a compromise on the Teamwork for Employees and Managers Act in January 1998, but he gave up on the bill when no Democrat would co-sponsor his amendment.

Bingaman had his most serious challenge in 1994, from Republican Colin McMillan, a rancher and former assistant Defense secretary, and sponsor in the legislature of a 1981 "Big Mac" tax cut. McMillan spent over $1 million of his own money and attacked Bingaman's vote for Clinton's 1993 tax increase and for what McMillan said was a vote to increase grazing fees. Bingaman ads boasted of his work on defense conversion, national education standards and education technology. The race tightened up in October, and Bingaman won 54%–46%, decisive but not overwhelming. He carried Albuquerque and won wide margins among Hispanics and Indians, but lost Little Texas. Bill Redmond, who lost the 3rd District to Tom Udall in 1998 after winning it in a 1997 special election, will probably run in 2000. Other possible opponents include state Republican Chairman John Dendahl, who finished third in the 1994 governor primary, and Lieutenant Governor Walter Bradley.

Cook's Call. *Probably Safe.* Republicans would like to build on their recent electoral successes here by knocking off Bingaman, but they are having trouble finding a candidate willing to run. Their continued interest is based primarily on the fact that as Senate seats go, New

Mexico's is fairly cheap, with relatively low statewide advertising costs. Former Representative Bill Redmond, who was unseated in 1998 after winning a special election the previous year, has recently been mentioned as a candidate. Bingaman does not appear all that vulnerable, and Republicans would need a star quality candidate to beat him.

Presidential politics. New Mexico, the most Democratic of the Rocky Mountain states, voted by decisive margins for Bill Clinton in 1992 and 1996. Its bellwether status seems more accidental than anything else; it's hard to think of a state more atypical of the nation. It could easily be seriously contested again in 2000.

The state Senate in March 1999 rejected moving new Mexico's primary to coincide with a proposed eight-state Rocky Mountain primary in March; it will be held instead in June.

Congressional districting. The boundaries of New Mexico's three congressional districts were slightly redesigned for 1992, with the apparent aim of making the Republican-held 1st and 2d both marginally more Democratic; but neither has voted Democratic since. After the 2000 Census, minor adjustments will need to be made, though it's possible that Governor Gary Johnson and the presumably still Democratic legislature will deadlock and force the courts to take over.

The People: Est. Pop. 1998: 1,736,931; Pop. 1990: 1,515,069, up 14.6% 1990–1998. 0.6% of U.S. total, 37th largest; 27.1% rural. Median age: 33.3 years. 11.2% 65 years and over. 75.8% White, 2% Black, 0.9% Asian, 8.8% Amer. Indian, 12.4% Other; 38.1% Hispanic Origin. Households: 56% married couple families; 29.7% married couple fams. w. children; 46.4% college educ.; median household income: $24,087; per capita income: $11,246; 67.4% owner occupied housing; median house value: $70,100; median monthly rent: $312. 6.2% Unemployment. 1998 Voting age pop.: 1,250,000. 1998 Turnout: 517,355; 41% of VAP. Registered voters (1998): 918,711; 493,134 D (54%), 301,729 R (33%), 123,848 unaffiliated and minor parties (13%).

Political Lineup: Governor, Gary E. Johnson (R); Lt. Gov., Walter Bradley (R); Secy. of State, Rebecca Vigil-Giron (D); Atty. Gen., Patricia Madrid (D); Treasurer, Michael A. Montoya (D); State Senate, 42 (25 D, 17 R); Majority Leader, Tim Jennings (D); State House, 70 (40 D, 30 R); House Speaker, Raymond G. Sanchez (D). Senators, Pete V. Domenici (R) and Jeff Bingaman (D). Representatives, 3 (1 D, 2 R).

Elections Division: 505-827-3620; **Filing Deadline for U.S. Congress:** February 8, 2000.

1996 Presidential Vote

Clinton (D)	273,495	(49%)
Dole (R)	232,751	(42%)
Perot (I)	32,271	(6%)
Others	17,566	(3%)

1992 Presidential Vote

Clinton (D)	261,617	(46%)
Bush (R)	212,824	(37%)
Perot (I)	91,895	(16%)

1996 Republican Presidential Primary

Dole (R)	53,300	(76%)
Buchanan (R)	5,679	(8%)
Forbes (R)	3,987	(6%)
Alexander (R)	2,676	(4%)
Others	4,822	(6%)

GOVERNOR

Gov. Gary E. Johnson (R)

Elected 1994, term expires Jan. 2003; b. Jan. 1, 1953, Minot, ND; home, Santa Fe; U. of NM, B.A. 1975; Lutheran; married (Dee).

Professional Career: Pres. & CEO, Big J Enterprises Inc., 1976–present.

Office: State Capitol, #417, Santa Fe, 87503, 505-827-3000; Fax: 505-827-3026; Web site: www.state.nm.us.

Election Results

1998 gen.	Gary E. Johnson (R) 271,948	(55%)
	Martin Chavez (D) 226,755	(45%)
1998 prim.	Gary E. Johnson (R) .... unopposed	
1994 gen.	Gary E. Johnson (R) 232,945	(50%)
	Bruce King (D) 186,686	(40%)
	Roberto Mondragon (Green) 47,990	(10%)

SENATORS

Sen. Pete V. Domenici (R)

Elected 1972, seat up 2002; b. May 7, 1932, Albuquerque; home, Albuquerque; U. of NM, B.S. 1954, Denver U., LL.B. 1958; Catholic; married (Nancy).

Elected Office: Albuquerque City Comm., 1966–70, Mayor Ex-Officio, 1967–70.

Professional Career: Practicing atty., 1958–72.

DC Office: 328 HSOB, 20510, 202-224-6621; Web site: www.senate.gov/~domenici.

State Offices: Albuquerque, 505-766-3481; Las Cruces, 505-526-5475; Roswell, 505-623-6170; Santa Fe, 505-988-6511.

Committees: *Appropriations* (4th of 15 R): Commerce, Justice, State & the Judiciary; Defense; Energy & Water Development (Chmn.); Interior; Transportation. *Budget* (Chmn. of 12 R). *Energy & Natural Resources* (2d of 11 R): Energy, Research, Development, Production & Regulation (Vice Chmn.); Forests & Public Land Management. *Governmental Affairs* (6th of 9 R): International Security, Proliferation & Federal Services; Investigations (Permanent). *Indian Affairs* (5th of 8 R).

Group Ratings

	ADA	ACLU	AFS	LCV	CON	NTU	NFIB	COC	ACU	NTLC	CHC
1998	5	43	13	0	45	58	100	100	70	71	82
1997	25	—	0	—	54	67	—	100	60	—	—

National Journal Ratings

	1997 LIB — 1997 CONS			1998 LIB — 1998 CONS		
Economic	37%	—	57%	44%	—	55%
Social	39%	—	55%	48%	—	51%
Foreign	34%	—	57%	42%	—	56%

Key Votes of the 105th Congress

1. Bal. Budget Amend.	Y	5. Satcher for Surgeon Gen.	Y	9. Chem. Weapons Treaty	Y
2. Clinton Budget Deal	Y	6. Highway Set-asides	Y	10. Cuban Humanitarian Aid	N
3. Cloture on Tobacco	N	7. Table Child Gun locks	Y	11. Table Bosnia Troops	Y
4. Education IRAs	*	8. Ovrd. Part. Birth Veto	Y	12. $ for Test-ban Treaty	*

Election Results

1996 general	Pete V. Domenici (R)	357,171	(65%)	($3,435,164)
	Art Trujillo (D)	164,356	(30%)	($155,213)
	Abraham J. Gutmann (Green)	24,230	(4%)	($12,025)
1996 primary	Pete V. Domenici (R)	unopposed		
1990 general	Pete V. Domenici (R)	296,712	(73%)	($2,250,086)
	Tom R. Benavides (D)	110,033	(27%)	($38,510)

Sen. Jeff Bingaman (D)

Elected 1982, seat up 2000; b. Oct. 3, 1943, El Paso, TX; home, Santa Fe; Harvard U., B.A. 1965, Stanford U., LL.B. 1968; United Methodist; married (Anne).

Military Career: Army Reserves, 1968–74.

Elected Office: NM Atty. Gen., 1979–82.

Professional Career: NM Asst. Atty. Gen., 1969; Practicing atty., 1970–78.

DC Office: 703 HSOB, 20510, 202-224-5521; Fax: 202-224-2852; Web site: www.senate.gov/~bingaman.

State Offices: Albuquerque, 505-346-6601; Las Cruces, 505-523-6561; Las Vegas, 505-454-8824; Roswell, 505-622-7113; Santa Fe, 505-988-6647.

Committees: *Armed Services* (3d of 9 D): Emerging Threats & Capabilities (RMM); Readiness & Management Support; Strategic Forces. *Energy & Natural Resources* (RMM of 9 D). *Health, Education, Labor & Pensions* (5th of 8 D): Children & Families; Public Health. *Joint Economic Committee* (7th of 10 Sens.).

Group Ratings

	ADA	ACLU	AFS	LCV	CON	NTU	NFIB	COC	ACU	NTLC	CHC
1998	85	86	100	63	62	14	33	56	0	11	0
1997	90	—	78	—	16	23	—	60	0	—	—

National Journal Ratings

	1997 LIB — 1997 CONS		1998 LIB — 1998 CONS	
Economic	76% —	23%	69% —	28%
Social	71% —	0%	74% —	0%
Foreign	87% —	8%	64% —	35%

Key Votes of the 105th Congress

1. Bal. Budget Amend.	N	5. Satcher for Surgeon Gen.	Y	9. Chem. Weapons Treaty	Y
2. Clinton Budget Deal	N	6. Highway Set-asides	Y	10. Cuban Humanitarian Aid	Y
3. Cloture on Tobacco	Y	7. Table Child Gun locks	N	11. Table Bosnia Troops	Y
4. Education IRAs	N	8. Ovrd. Part. Birth Veto	N	12. $ for Test-ban Treaty	*

Election Results

1994 general	Jeff Bingaman (D)	249,989	(54%)	($3,652,899)
	Colin R. McMillan (R)	213,025	(46%)	($1,537,563)
1994 primary	Jeff Bingaman (D)	unopposed		
1988 general	Jeff Bingaman (D)	321,983	(63%)	($2,808,659)
	Bill Valentine (R)	186,579	(37%)	($659,624)

FIRST DISTRICT

The future and the past of New Mexico come together in its single metropolis, Albuquerque. Its Spanish and Indian past is memorialized in its name (for a 17th Century Spanish grandee) and age (founded in 1706) and its quaint Old Town; its high-tech future is symbolized by Sandia Laboratories and Kirtland Air Force Base, the government installations that are the city's biggest employers. When rocket scientist Robert Goddard moved here in 1930 and nuclear scientist J. Robert Oppenheimer reconnoitered the site in 1940, Albuquerque was still a town of 35,000 sitting at the junction of the Rio Grande and the old U.S. 66 that paralleled the Santa Fe Railroad—"a dirty red sod-hut tortilla desert highway city," Tom Wolfe wrote. Since then, Albuquerque has grown more than any place in New Mexico and, with a metro population of 678,000, has as many people as all New Mexico did when the scientists first arrived. Albuquerque's prosperous neighborhoods have climbed the gently rising heights to the east; poorer residents have spread north and south along the Rio Grande. Hemmed in by mountains and federal installations, growth is now moving west, across the Rio Grande, to the new town of Rio Rancho, with Intel, Olympus, U.S. Cotton and Pepsico installations. Albuquerque is counted as part of the Sun Belt, but its climate is closer to that of the High Plains of west Texas: hot in the summer, sometimes very cold in the winter, with high winds most of the time. Nor is its economy like that of other Sun Belt cities. It has lower income levels; its recent growth has lagged behind Phoenix, Dallas, and even El Paso. Albuquerque has some white-collar job growth and diversification and has become something of a tourist center (it is home of the International Balloon Fiesta every October), but it still depends heavily on government.

The 1st Congressional District is, for all practical purposes, the city of Albuquerque and its suburbs; it also includes largely empty Torrance County and communities north and south along the Rio Grande. Albuquerque is one Sun Belt city which is not solidly Republican, but not solidly Democratic either; it voted for Ronald Reagan and George Bush in the 1980s and for Bill Clinton in the 1990s. The 1st District in 1990 was 38% Hispanic, with both descendants of longtime New Mexicans and recent immigrants.

The congresswoman from the 1st District is Heather Wilson, a Republican and the winner of two elections in 1998 against the second-highest spender in the history of House campaigns. She grew up in New Hampshire, graduated from the Air Force Academy, then became a Rhodes Scholar, winning an Oxford degree in international relations. After leaving the Air Force, she served in 1989–91 on the National Security Council in charge of NATO and European affairs. In 1991 she moved to New Mexico, to marry her former Air Force Academy law instructor; she started a consulting firm and then Governor Gary Johnson appointed her secretary of the Children, Youth and Families Department.

Then, in January 1998, just 12 days before the filing deadline, Congressman Steven Schiff announced he would not run again. Schiff chaired the Basic Research Subcommittee, critical to Albuquerque, and had helped create the Petroglyph National Monument on the west side of town; he was one of four ethics committee members who found a way to compromise in the case of Newt Gingrich. But after surgery in April 1997 for a form of skin cancer, he did not return to Congress; the cancer recurred, and he died in March 1998. In January, Senator Pete Domenici, usually loath to intervene in local politics, backed Wilson strongly; after the county Republican chairman filled vacancies by appointing Wilson backers, she beat a conservative state senator for the state central committee endorsement by winning 55 votes, the exact minimum required. The Democratic nomination was captured by Phil Maloof, a young state senator from a wealthy family that made its fortune through beer distribution, casinos, banking interests, hotels and professional sports franchises; a statue of his late father stands in Albuquerque's Civic Plaza. Also running was Green Party candidate Bob Anderson; fresh in everyone's mind was the fact that the Green candidate had won 17% in the 3d District special election in May 1997 and helped Republican Bill Redmond to an upset 43%–40% win.

This was a key race for both parties. A Democratic pickup in a House seat held by Republicans for nearly 30 years would help put Democrats on a flight path to a majority; a Republican hold would show the party could still hold marginal seats. Wilson's slogan was "fighting for our families," and her first ad showed her two-year-old daughter running into her arms; she concluded speeches by talking about reading to her four-year-old son on the roof of their house. She called for a dollars-to-classroom program, with less money for bureaucracy, and for a pilot program of school vouchers. She also called for eliminating the marriage penalty and reducing death taxes. Maloof, appointed to the state Senate in 1993 and elected in 1994 and 1996, talked of his work in the legislature on a three-strikes law, the Montano Bridge, and a mobile police unit. He favored raising the minimum wage, opposed school vouchers, and ran soft-focus ads playing on his family's 100-year history in New Mexico (next to Wilson's seven).

But in the short campaign between April 2, when the first ads went up, and the June 23 special, the tone quickly became negative. "A vote for either Heather Wilson or Bob Anderson is a vote for Newt Gingrich and his right-wing Republican agenda," Maloof said. In turn, Wilson said Maloof was "too young," while brandishing a tricycle (he was 30 and she 37) and too inexperienced; claiming that he "doesn't understand the issues" and "is hiding behind his family's money." In fact, Maloof's performance on the stump was poor: He seemed bewildered by a debate question about the Endangered Species Act and replied that camping is "something I really enjoy." Wrote Jack Moczinski in the liberal weekly *Alibi*, "Maloof at times seems to be a political mannequin, placed in the storefront window for voters as this year's political haute couture. He looks good, but what's inside?" The Republican campaign committee started sending out daily "Mal-OOPS" faxes. Meanwhile, the cerebral Wilson got a reputation for being nervous, aloof and arrogant. When Maloof attacked her for supporting a bill for vouchers for at-risk children, she reminded him brusquely that he was a co-sponsor: "I was testifying in favor of your bill. Do your homework."

The toughest ads came when Maloof ran a spot showing footage of a 1996 KOAT-TV report alleging that Wilson, while commissioner of Children, Youth and Families, "abused her position of power" by moving a state foster-family file about her, her husband and their foster son. The charge at first cut into Wilson's small lead in polls; she countered that she ordered the file sequestered, and did not read it herself, to keep it away from those who might use it politically.

Democrats also criticized her for not voting in three elections, though Maloof skipped one of them also. Media coverage of this race bemoaned the negative tone. And certainly it could not be avoided by watchers of Albuquerque TV: Maloof spent $3.1 million, almost all of it his own, up through June 23, and some $5.3 million by November, the third most expensive House campaign in history (after Newt Gingrich's 1996 and 1998 campaigns); Wilson spent $1.1 million by November, with the national Republican Party pouring in another $1 million. Democrats sent in less money but more celebrities: Hillary Rodham Clinton, Dick Gephardt, Patrick Kennedy, Tipper Gore and Loretta Sanchez.

But for all the hoopla and negative charges, issue positions and perceived competence seemed to make the difference. On June 23, Wilson won 45% of the vote, Maloof 40% and Green Party nominee Bob Anderson, though he spent less than $10,000, won 15%. Of Wilson's 11,744-victory margin, 6,564 came from absentees after Republicans conducted a strong absentee drive (predictably Democratic legislators in February 1999 sought to make illegal the mailing out of absentee ballot requests). Local analysts said that the Green vote included not just left-wing environmentalists but also voters disgruntled with the negative campaigns of both major parties. For November, Maloof tried to appeal to environmentalists; he switched to oppose the road proposed to cut through 8.5 acres of the Petroglyph National Monument, and Anderson's former campaign manager endorsed him. But on November 3, the margin was similar: Wilson 48%, Maloof 42%, Anderson 10%.

Wilson thus became the first woman veteran to serve in Congress. Her first vote was cast for IRS reform; she also voted for reducing death taxes and continuing the research and development tax credit. She cast moderate votes on public broadcasting, discrimination against gays, contraceptive coverage for federal employees. She bragged about getting $5 million for realistic hardware testing at Kirtland and $1.4 million to buy remaining Tres Pistolas property in the East Mountains. She has a bill to proclaim the old U.S. 66 as America's Main Street. Wilson was given a seat on the Commerce Committee, a fine perch for legislating and fundraising, in August 1998. Speaker Dennis Hastert also used Wilson as his point person on Kosovo; she lead two Kosovo discussions during conference meetings and gave the Republican response to Clinton's radio address on the situation. Her prospects for re-election seem reasonably good against a less free-spending candidate.

Cook's Call. *Competitive.* Wilson's sub-50% showing in 1998 makes her an intriguing target for 2000. Democrats, however, need to recruit a much stronger candidate than they did in 1998. A credible Green Party candidate could also give the Democratic nominee trouble.

The People: Pop. 1990: 505,329; 7.6% rural; 10.9% age 65 +; 77.8% White, 2.6% Black, 1.5% Asian, 2.7% Amer. Indian, 15.4% Other; 37.8% Hispanic Origin. Households: 51.7% married couple families; 25.9% married couple fams. w. children; 53.6% college educ.; median household income: $27,074; per capita income: $13,373; median house value: $84,600; median gross rent: $350.

1996 Presidential Vote

Clinton (D)	93,178	(48%)
Dole (R)	82,613	(43%)
Perot (I)	9,520	(5%)
Others	7,212	(4%)

1992 Presidential Vote

Clinton (D)	95,754	(45%)
Bush (R)	81,038	(38%)
Perot (I)	33,034	(16%)

Rep. Heather Wilson (R)

Elected June 1998; b. Dec. 30, 1960, Keene, NH; home, Albuquerque; U.S. Air Force Acad., B.S. 1982, Rhodes Scholar, Oxford U., M.A. 1984, Ph.D. 1985; Methodist; married (Jay Hone).

Military Career: Air Force, 1982–89.

Professional Career: Dir., European Defense Policy & Arms Control, White House NSC, 1989–91; Pres. Keystone Intl. Inc., 1991–95; NM Secy. of Children, Youth & Families, 1995–98.

DC Office: 226 CHOB 20515, 202-225-6316; Fax: 202-225-4975; Web site: www.house.gov/wilson.

District Office: Albuquerque, 505-346-6781.

Committees: *Commerce* (23d of 29 R): Energy & Power; Finance & Hazardous Materials; Telecommunications, Trade & Consumer Protection. *Permanent Select Committee on Intelligence* (9th of 9 R): Human Intelligence, Analysis & Counterintelligence; Technical & Tactical Intelligence.

Group Ratings & Key Votes: (Only Served Partial Term)

Election Results

1998 general	Heather A. Wilson (R)	86,784	(48%)	($1,121,676)
	Phillip J. Maloof (D)	75,040	(42%)	($5,379,249)
	Robert L. Anderson (Green)	17,266	(10%)	($14,773)
1998 primary	Heather A. Wilson (R)	18,147	(62%)	
	William F. Davis (R)	8,848	(30%)	
	Others	2,050	(7%)	
1998 special	Heather A. Wilson (R)	54,853	(45%)	($1,415,139)
	Phillip J. Maloof (D)	48,747	(40%)	($3,100,286)
	Robert Anderson (Green)	18,108	(15%)	($8,807)
	Others	1,347	(1%)	
1996 general	Steven H. Schiff (R)	109,290	(57%)	($603,316)
	John Wertheim (D)	71,635	(37%)	($285,999)
	Others	12,153	(6%)	

SECOND DISTRICT

The plains of southern and eastern New Mexico are about as disparate a landscape as can be imagined: miles of sagebrush-strewn acreage, and then, suddenly, 9,000-foot mountain peaks rising in the distance. The eastern part of this region, Little Texas, is an extension of the Texas civilization that filled up empty counties when irrigation was developed. Oil has long been the economic mainstay here; cattle ranching is common; cotton is grown on irrigated land. The little cities are full of people with Texas twangs, not the lilt of northern New Mexico. West from Clovis and Portales, Lovington and Hobbs, the towns become fewer and farming mostly disappears. The scrub land shades into desert, and people are crammed into small cities, protected from an environment that is burning hot in the summer and sometimes deathly cold in winter. Here the major center is Las Cruces, now New Mexico's second largest city, with migrants from Mexico coming up the Rio Grande from million-plus El Paso, Texas, and Juarez, Chihuahua, just 45 miles south.

The 2d Congressional District includes the entire southern half of the state—most of Little Texas, plus the desert on either side of the Rio Grande and the mining territory in the mountains just north of the Mexican border and just short of the Arizona line. These places today vote the opposite of their partisan tradition: Little Texas, settled by Yellow Dog Democrats from the Lone Star state, is now solidly Republican; Las Cruces, long leaning Republican, has moved Democratic. The 2d District usually votes Republican, but Bill Clinton has carried it by 1% twice in a row; increased Indian turnout helped in 1996.

The congressman from the 2d District is Republican Joe Skeen. Skeen has been a sheep rancher for more than 40 years, since he bought his grandmother's ranch. He was elected to the New Mexico Senate in 1960, at 33; he ran for lieutenant governor on a ticket with Pete Domenici and narrowly lost in 1970, and ran for governor in 1974 and 1978, losing by 1% each time. He was elected to the House in 1980, the hard way, as a write-in, with 61,000 votes, when Democratic incumbent Harold "Mud" Runnels died and the Democrats put Governor Bruce King's nephew on the ballot. Skeen got 38% of the vote to 34% for King and 28% for Runnels's widow, also a write-in; in 1986, Skeen beat Runnels's son Mike 63%–37%.

When Skeen became minority leader of the state Senate 30 years ago, there were only three other Republicans there. Since 1994, he has been part of the majority, and he is a member of the House's "college of cardinals" as chairman of the House Appropriations Subcommittee on Agriculture. Skeen is something of an old-fashioned conservative, generally voting against domestic spending, but working to benefit his district: "We're doing the job people tell us they want us to do. Get government out of their lives as much as possible, get good jobs for them and a good place to live in. That's what people want."

He has staunchly opposed efforts to increase grazing fees for livestock producers, so far successfully; he would like to see the Bureau of Land Management turn over its western lands to the states. In July 1998 he attacked secret agreements between the Forest Service and environmental groups engaged in apparently collusive lawsuits to bar cattle from waterways in dozens of national forest grazing allotments. He has worked for a lamb and wool checkoff program to promote sheep products and proposed a uniform national policy for fossil collecting on federal lands. He blocked the designation of the Rio Grande as an American Heritage River. He also blocked defunding of the Animal Damage Control unit (renamed Wildlife Services) in June 1998. He has worked to save the High Energy Laser Systems Test Facility at White Sands Missile Range, where short-range rockets, of the type fired by guerrillas around the world, were shot down with lasers. He has worked for the WIPP nuclear waste disposal site in Carlsbad, finally licensed in May 1998, over the opposition of Attorney General, now Congressman Tom Udall. With Senator Jeff Bingaman he sponsored the October 1998 law that created a National Cave and Karst Research Institute near Carlsbad. With Senator Pete Domenici, he sponsored a June 1998 law to set up a 14-member National Drought Policy Commission.

Skeen has won re-election by varying margins, by just 56%–44% in 1992, then by 63%–32% in 1994. In 1996, against Democrat Shirley Baca, he won by a decisive but not impressive 56%–44%, winning nearly 2–1 in Little Texas but narrowly losing Las Cruces and the Indian areas. Skeen has refused to debate opponents since 1992; he has announced that he has Parkinson's disease, but insists it has not impaired his ability to work. He says, "When the time comes I don't feel like I can give it my very best, I'll pull the plug on it." In 1998 Baca again ran, attacking Skeen for saying, "There's no such thing as the working poor," but her appeals to middle- and lower-income people did not carry as far in 1998 as 1996. This time he carried Little Texas by a 2–1 margin and carried Las Cruces and Dona Ana County as well. Skeen won by 58%–42%, a solid though not overwhelming margin. In February 1999, former Lieutenant Governor Mike Runnels announced plans to challenge Skeen again, setting up a rematch of the 1986 race.

Cook's Call. *Probably Safe.* In an open-seat situation, this marginal district would be up for grabs. But, beating the well-entrenched, 10-term incumbent Skeen will not be very easy, though his frail health and limited endurance could become a problem.

The People: Pop. 1990: 504,767; 33.2% rural; 12.3% age 65 + ; 84.1% White, 2.1% Black, 0.7% Asian, 3.8% Amer. Indian, 9.3% Other; 41.9% Hispanic Origin. Households: 59.9% married couple families; 31.8% married couple fams. w. children; 39.8% college educ.; median household income: $21,456; per capita income: $9,672; median house value: $52,700; median gross rent: $257.

1996 Presidential Vote

Clinton (D)	80,572	(46%)
Dole (R)	77,634	(45%)
Perot (I)	12,149	(7%)
Others	3,149	(2%)

1992 Presidential Vote

Clinton (D)	70,630	(41%)
Bush (R)	68,754	(40%)
Perot (I)	31,780	(18%)

Rep. Joe Skeen (R)

Elected 1980; b. June 30, 1927, Roswell; home, Picacho; TX A&M, B.S. 1950; Catholic; married (Mary).

Military Career: Navy, 1945–46 (WWII), Air Force Reserves, 1949–52.

Elected Office: NM Senate, 1960–70, Minority Ldr., 1965–70.

Professional Career: Sheep rancher; Engineer, Zuni & Ramah Navajo Indian Reservations, 1950–51.

DC Office: 2302 RHOB 20515, 202-225-2365; Fax: 202-225-9599; Web site: www.house.gov/skeen.

District Offices: Las Cruces, 505-527-1771; Roswell, 505-622-0055.

Committees: *Appropriations* (6th of 34 R): Agriculture, Rural Development, & FDA (Chmn.); Defense; Interior.

Group Ratings

	ADA	ACLU	AFS	LCV	CON	NTU	NFIB	COC	ACU	NTLC	CHC
1998	10	13	11	15	13	44	100	100	84	92	83
1997	0	—	13	—	42	45	—	100	95	—	—

National Journal Ratings

	1997 LIB — 1997 CONS	1998 LIB — 1998 CONS
Economic	19% — 76%	37% — 61%
Social	30% — 64%	41% — 58%
Foreign	36% — 63%	39% — 58%

Key Votes of the 105th Congress

1. Clinton Budget Deal	Y	5. Puerto Rico Sthood. Ref.	Y	9. Cut $ for B-2 Bombers	N
2. Education IRAs	Y	6. End Highway Set-asides	Y	10. Human Rights in China	N
3. Req. 2/3 to Raise Taxes	Y	7. School Prayer Amend.	Y	11. Withdraw Bosnia Troops	Y
4. Fast-track Trade	Y	8. Ovrd. Part. Birth Veto	Y	12. End Cuban TV-Marti	N

Election Results

1998 general	Joe Skeen (R)	85,077	(58%)	($557,221)
	E. Shirley Baca (D)	61,796	(42%)	($298,176)
1998 primary	Joe Skeen (R)	unopposed		
1996 general	Joe Skeen (R)	95,091	(56%)	($539,969)
	E. Shirley Baca (D)	74,915	(44%)	($191,794)

THIRD DISTRICT

"The dancing ground of the sun" the Pueblo Indians called the land of northern New Mexico, where the long, empty vistas stretch for miles, the mountains in the distance detailed in pinpoint clarity in the cold light and clear air. For 100 years, artists have been coming here, attracted by the scenery and by a unique civilization that is part Indian, part Spanish, only a little Mexican (northern New Mexico was Mexican only briefly, from 1821–46), part Anglo-American. The Spanish language, Indian pottery and dances, and the adobe pueblos give the impression that life on this rocky desert soil has gone on for centuries in much the same way. Actually, the civilization hasn't been so stable. The pueblos were built in sudden spurts; the Spanish conquistadors and priests brought the Catholic religion, the baroque accents of the adobe buildings and the Spanish language in a rush; successive waves of American settlement have changed New Mexico in different ways. The Indian crafts which thrive today nearly died out in the 1880s, and the Palace of the Governors, built in Santa Fe in 1610, had its Victorian balustrade torn off in 1913 to restore its original appearance. Yet up the back roads in Rio Arriba or Taos counties, one can find a religion that mixes Catholicism with adaptations of Indian festivals, buildings not that much different from the old pueblos, and a standard of living reminiscent of the Indian past—quite a contrast to Santa Fe, with its thousands of affluent, bohemian migrants, its 200-plus restaurants, its local book publishers and the third-largest art market in the country.

The politics of northern New Mexico is a unique blend. For years, debate was conducted and votes bartered in Spanish, not by separatists, but by Republican and Democratic politicos, often cynically, sometimes corruptly; loyalties ran to families and communities more than to principles or parties. In the back country, you can still find more than just vestiges of the old communities and the old politics—though no one is going to let you in on them, even if you speak good Spanish. In Santa Fe and Taos, the affluent and hippie migrants have produced a politics of the cultural and environmental left, while in high-tech havens—the atomic laboratory town of Los Alamos, the mining country around Farmington, the huge new suburb of Rio Rancho, north of Albuquerque and centered on an Intel installation—favor free-market politics.

The 3d Congressional District contains most of the state's historic Spanish-speaking and Indian parts. Its largest and dominant city is Santa Fe, but the district runs from the High Plains along the Texas border, past the haunting Sangre de Cristo Mountains, through the vast ridges and isolated buttes in the center, to the windy and dusty desert-like plains, dotted occasionally by mountains, with Indian reservations in the west. The population is 35% Hispanic origin and 20% Indian (with at least 6% overlap between the categories). Politically, it has long been heavily Democratic, and migrants to Santa Fe and Taos counties in the 1980s made it more so. But it also has its Republican bastions at its east and west ends, in the mineral prospecting country in San Juan County around Farmington in the west, and on the dusty Little Texas plains around Clovis in the east. And Rio Rancho has supplied more conservative voters every year in the 1990s. The congressman from the 3d for 15 years after it was created in 1982 was Bill Richardson, a Democrat of Mexican background, who became a skilled international negotiator and was named ambassador to the United Nations in January 1997 and Energy secretary in August 1998. But changes in the district plus local political machinations produced an upset victory for Republican Bill Redmond in the May 1997 special election to replace Richardson and then a Democratic resurgence in November 1998.

The congressman from the 3d District now is Tom Udall, a Democrat elected in 1998, the son of Arizona Congressman (1955–61) and Interior Secretary (1961–69) Stewart Udall and nephew of Arizona Congressman (1961–91) Morris Udall, first cousin of Colorado Congressman Mark Udall, also elected in 1998, and distant cousin of Oregon Senator Gordon Smith, the only Republican in the bunch. Tom Udall grew up in Tucson and McLean, Virginia, went to college in Arizona, got a degree at Cambridge University in England, and went to law school in New Mexico. He worked as a federal law clerk, then as a counsel in New Mexico state government, and went into private law practice; his father had moved to New Mexico in the meantime. Politics was obviously on his mind: he ran for Congress in 1982 when the 3d District was newly created, and finished last among four candidates, with 13%; in 1988 he ran in the Albuquerque-based 1st District, won the 10-candidate Democratic primary with 25%, and lost the general to Steven Schiff 51%–47%. In 1990 he was elected state attorney general; he was re-elected in 1994. In 1997, when Richardson resigned and opened the 3d District seat, he didn't run—a prudent decision, it now seems.

That election was won in a stunning upset by Republican Bill Redmond, son of a Chicago tool and die maker and a self-styled "blue-collar person," an independent Christian minister from Los Alamos, who had won just 31% against Richardson in November 1996. The Democratic nomination, which was widely considered tantamount to election, was decided by 89 members of the Democratic central committee; in January the Democratic county chairmen in the district's 11 counties declared that Eric Serna, Rio Arriba County politico and member of the state Corporation Commission since 1981, had the votes locked up. This was an unfortunate choice. Charges were well known that Serna had raised money from firms with interests before the Corporation Commission, used a state airplane for unofficial business, applied pressure on Commission employees to buy jewelry at a store he owned and used a state phone for campaign purposes. Redmond attacked his "seamy past" and said it was "no secret that Eric Serna is a corrupt politician." Carol Miller, a public health care consultant and candidate of the Green Party, whose nominee won 10% in the 1994 governor race, seized on these charges and built on a base of support in Santa Fe and Taos counties' feminist communities. But Redmond courted Navajos in McKinley and Cibola counties and ran organizing drives in the high-tech areas. The result was a shocker: Redmond beat Serna 43%–40%, with 17% for Miller. There were great regional splits. The four most heavily Hispanic counties, once the political heart of the district, voted 62%–26% for Serna over Redmond; but they cast only 16% of the district's votes.

Redmond had a sometimes moderate voting record and worked hard to make a record to appeal to the district. Most importantly, he pushed a proposal Richardson had been working on, to create a commission to review the land claims of heirs to Hispanic families to communal land grants which, they claimed, had been extinguished contrary to the terms of the 1848 Treaty of Guadalupe Hidalgo, which ceded most of the Southwest to the United States after the Mexican-American War. This infuriated environmentalists, who realized that recognition of such claims would convert federal lands to private property, and who feared that it would put a wedge between them and the Hispanic constituency they had long taken for granted—which accounts for the fury of their criticisms of Redmond on the Baca Ranch and the Bandelier National Monument, which they would have approved docilely if he had been a Democrat. Speaker Newt Gingrich, who understood these things, made Redmond's issues a high priority, and the land grant commission passed the House 223–187 in July 1998.

In the meantime, Udall had done a good job consolidating the Democratic vote. One weapon was money. Drawing on lawyers, the arts community and friends of the Udall family, he raised daunting sums. In the run up to the June primary, he outspent Eric Serna, his main opponent, by better than 2–1, and won the primary 44%–36%. Though he lost the Hispanic counties, he moved to propitiate the Hispanic constituency, and was helped by the distaste of active politicians for Redmond. The Sierra Club and the League of Conservation Voters criticized Redmond and ran waves of ads against him. Udall's own platform was not much more than a restatement of Clinton-Gore campaign slogans on Social Security, HMOs and education. Udall criticized the campaign finance laws fiercely and at the same time took better advantage of them than the Gingrich-backed Redmond: He spent $1.59 million to Redmond's $1.39 million.

The other problem was the Green Party's Carol Miller. "I intend to make peace with the Greens," Udall said, and set about to reduce Miller's 17% of the vote. In that he was utterly successful. Hispanic politicians had been resentful of what they called the "trust-funder" base of the Greens in Santa Fe; but when confronted with the specter of a Republican congressman who agreed with the religious right on many issues, and presented with the alternative of a Udall who was not a traditional politico like Serna, the trust funders, feminist left and others of similar persuasion decided to vote Democratic this time. Udall won 53% of the vote, Redmond, for all his efforts to attract various constituencies, won the same 43% he had won 18 months before, and Miller saw her 17% evaporate to 4%. Leftish newcomers to Santa Fe and Taos counties rallied to Udall, who carried them 69%–26%; this was 28% of the district's votes. The high-tech counties cast 36%, and Redmond carried them 56%–40%, but this was down from the 60%–28% he had carried them before; evidently many techies found Udall more palatable than Serna. In Little Texas (12% of the vote) his margin was trimmed as well, to 64%–34%. Redmond improved his standing in the Hispanic counties to 34%, but they only cast 15% of the vote. And the Indian counties, with 8% of the vote, were 64%–34% for Udall.

In the House, Udall has a seat on the Resources Committee, which his father served on and his uncle once chaired. He signed up as a co-sponsor of Republican Heather Wilson's bill to declare U.S. 66 a national historic highway and said he would work to purchase the Baca Ranch (unfortunately, the owners withdrew their offer to sell in January 1999). He reintroduced Redmond's bill to create a commission to examine land grants; this is unlikely to be taken up by the new Republican leadership for a Democratic congressman. He chairs the House campaign finance task force and has asked Speaker Dennis Hastert to bring the Shays-Meehan bill to the floor.

Cook's Call. *Probably Safe.* Barring a serious political blunder, Udall should be safe from a tough challenge. This district, while it has some Republican and independent leanings, is the most solidly Democratic in the state.

The People: Pop. 1990: 504,973; 40.5% rural; 10.2% age 65 + ; 65.5% White, 1.1% Black, 0.6% Asian, 20.1% Amer. Indian, 12.6% Other; 34.5% Hispanic Origin. Households: 56.8% married couple families; 31.9% married couple fams. w. children; 45.1% college educ.; median household income: $23,610; per capita income: $10,689; median house value: $68,600; median gross rent: $298.

1996 Presidential Vote			1992 Presidential Vote		
Clinton (D)	99,745	(52%)	Clinton (D)	95,233	(51%)
Dole (R)	72,504	(38%)	Bush (R)	63,032	(34%)
Perot (I)	10,602	(6%)	Perot (I)	27,081	(15%)
Others	7,205	(4%)			

Rep. Tom Udall (D)

Elected 1998; b. May 18, 1948, Tucson, AZ; home, Santa Fe; Prescott Col., B.A. 1970; Cambridge U., B.L. 1975; U. of NM, J.D. 1977; Mormon; married (Jill Cooper).

Elected Office: NM Atty. Gen., 1990–98.

Professional Career: Law clerk, 10th Circuit Court of Appeals, 1977; Asst. U.S. Atty., 1978–81; Practicing atty., 1981–83, 1985–90; Chief Cnsl., NM Health & Environment Dept., 1983–84.

DC Office: 502 CHOB 20515, 202-225-6190; Fax: 202-226-1331; Web site: www.house.gov/tomudall.

District Office: Santa Fe, 505-984-8950.

Committees: *Resources* (21st of 24 D): Forests & Forest Health; National Parks & Public Lands. *Small Business* (9th of 17 D): Empowerment; Rural Enterprise, Business Opportunities & Special Small Business Problems.

Group Ratings and Key Votes: Newly Elected

Election Results

1998 general	Tom Udall (D)	91,248	(53%)	($1,591,017)
	Bill Redmond (R)	74,266	(43%)	($1,390,159)
	Others	6,135	(4%)	
1998 primary	Tom Udall (D)	32,533	(44%)	
	Eric P. Serna (D)	26,340	(36%)	
	Roman M. Maes III (D)	4,382	(6%)	
	Tony Scarborough (D)	3,681	(5%)	
	Others	6,960	(9%)	
1997 special	Bill Redmond (R)	43,472	(43%)	($57,457)
	Eric P. Serna (D)	40,424	(40%)	($265,255)
	Carol A. Miller (Green)	17,079	(17%)	($7,443)
1996 general	Bill Richardson (D)	124,594	(67%)	($526,898)
	Bill Redmond (R)	56,580	(31%)	($56,442)
	Others	4,097	(2%)	

NEW YORK

New York is a place of miracles and disasters—and often both at once. For three decades New York state has had sluggish growth—more people lived here in 1970 than 1997—yet it still has America's largest city, its financial capital, its center of arts and letters and media, and its first (legal) largest immigrant destination. Neither New York's successes nor its sluggishness was inevitable. They happened because New Yorkers—and not least those people from elsewhere who opted to become New Yorkers—worked to make them happen. They did it in a city that has a certain enduring character which goes back to its birth as the 17th Century Dutch colony of Nieuw Amsterdam. Simon Schama's *The Embarrassment of Riches* paints a picture of the old world Amsterdam: the richest city in the world; full of people who work hard all day and stay up late at night, smoke too much tobacco and drink too much coffee and gin, but are dazzlingly smart and shrewd; people who know their way around every corner of the globe and can make fine aesthetic discriminations, but are attached to their uncomfortable, crowded, bad-smelling city; merchants and manipulators with no aristocratic pedigree, welcoming any religious or ethnic group who can achieve and accumulate and show good taste, cherishing education and culture but indifferent to credentials. This could be a portrait of the New York of today, of Tom Wolfe and Tina Brown, or the New York of Alexander Hamilton and Aaron Burr, or the New York of Edith Wharton and Theodore Dreiser, or the New York of Harold Ross's *New Yorker* and Henry Luce's early *Time*. Probably fewer than 2% of today's New Yorkers are descended from the Dutch of Nieuw Amsterdam, but the character of the place endures in daily life and in the workings of its great institutions, and helps explain its miraculous and entirely inevitable growth. Combine Amsterdam and America: Dutch character with British-born political freedoms and American military invulnerability and you have the opportunity to build a city-state that can lead the world.

New York was not always the nation's leader. In 1776 it was the seventh most populous colony. Only in the 19th Century did the descendants of Dutch patroons, Huguenot refugees, British West Indies traders and Yankee farmers become the nation's most successful merchants and capitalists, forging the first routes to the great American interior through the valleys of the Hudson and the Mohawk, over the Finger Lakes and the Great Lakes, and building grand brownstone mansions on broad midtown Manhattan avenues. That early diversity provides one clue to New York's success: if New York has been cynical, ready to cooperate with Loyalists and Revolutionaries, depending on who was ahead, it has also been tolerant, ready to accept anyone smart or rich enough to be counted a success. It has been propelled upward at each stage—forging ahead of London as a financial and manufacturing center by the first World War, and staying ahead of surging Chicago—by incorporating every wave of immigrants and consistently rewarding intelligence and hard work, unconcerned about preserving hierarchies.

New York's success has been a product not only of market economics, but of government—and politics. The Iroquois, the most deeply-rooted and militarily strong Native Americans, kept in place for 100 years by an alliance with British troops, were driven out of New York by the Revolution. The Erie Canal, which connected western New York state with the Hudson River, was the project of Governor DeWitt Clinton's state government. The railroads were subsidized by land grants and favorable laws. And New York led the nation in political innovation: Martin Van Buren's Albany Regency was the first state political machine, an ally of New York City's Tammany Hall, and Van Buren himself invented the Democratic Party, the national convention and the inaugural parade. His adversaries, Thurlow Weed and William Seward, formed the Whig Party and ultimately became Republicans; noting that Van Buren's Democrats were winning large margins from Irish Catholics and other immigrants, they too made bids for the

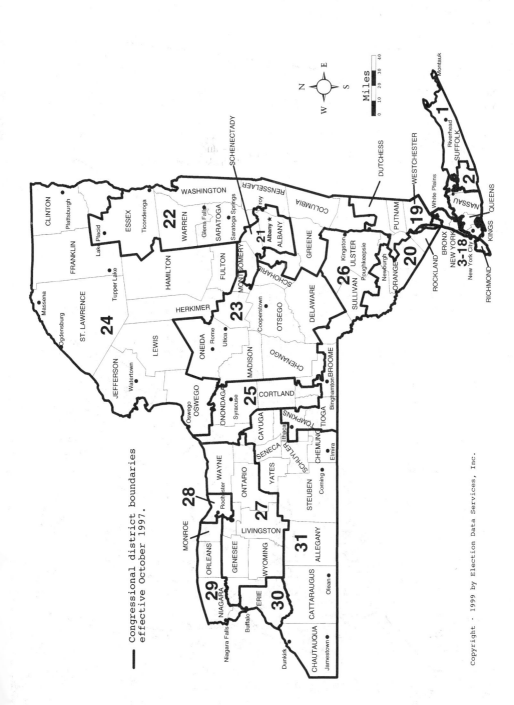

Congressional district boundaries effective October 1997.

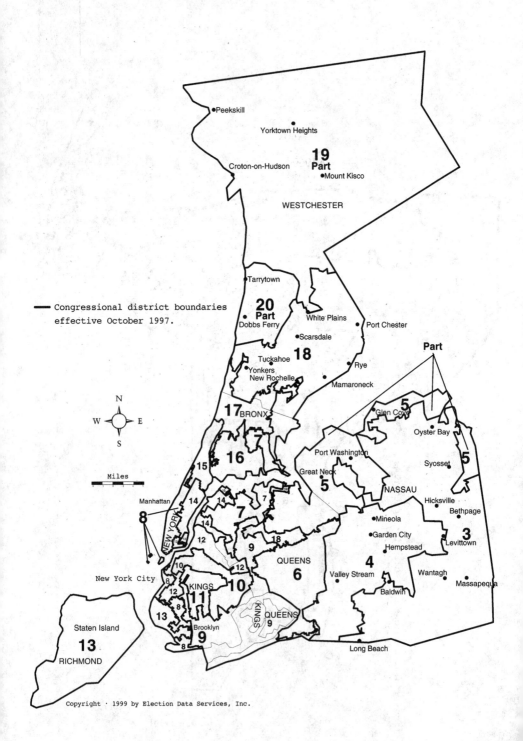

Peekskill

Yorktown Heights

19
Part

Croton-on-Hudson

●Mount Kisco

WESTCHESTER

Tarrytown

20
Part
Dobbs Ferry

White Plains

Port Chester

●Scarsdale

18

Tuckahoe

Rye

Part

Yonkers
New Rochelle

Mamaroneck

17 BRONX

5

Glen Cove

7

Oyster Bay

N
W — E
S

16

Port Washington

5

Syosset

15

Great Neck

5

NASSAU

Miles

Manhattan

14

14

7

Hicksville
Bethpage

8

NEW YORK

14

Mineola

3

12

9

18

Garden City

Levittown

New York City

10

8

12

10

QUEENS
6

Hempstead

4

Valley Stream

Wantagh

KINGS

Baldwin

Massapequa

12

8

11

13

KINGS

QUEENS

Brooklyn

9

9

Staten Island

13

8

Long Beach

RICHMOND

Congressional district boundaries
effective October 1997.

newcomers' votes. Both parties served the function of mediating between the divergent interests of the New York City masses and Upstate New York's farmers and burghers, a conflict still evident in New York between city and country, immigrant and native, Catholic and Protestant, the Big Apple and the apple-knockers.

Both parties also worked to protect New Yorkers against the untrammeled workings of free economic and political markets. Old-line Democrats, embarked on an unprecedented, labor-intensive building of infrastructure, of bridges and tunnels that made Greater New York possible, from the time of Mayor Abram Hewitt, elected in 1886 over the single taxer Henry George and the young Theodore Roosevelt, up through the time of Governor Al Smith in the 1920s and his protege Robert Moses, who built bridges and tunnels and highways and beaches and two World's Fairs up through the 1960s. Mugwump Republicans, from Theodore Roosevelt through Elihu Root and Henry Stimson, worked to create civil service laws and bureaucratized purchasing and spending to protect taxpayers from corrupt party machines. And the Tammany machine led by Charles F. Murphy and the talented young men he advanced, Al Smith and Robert Wagner, responded to the shocking 1911 Triangle Shirtwaist fire (when hundreds of women jumped 11 floors to their death because fire escapes were blocked) by passing labor and safety measures. The results included minimum wages, maximum work hours, working-conditions regulations, encouragement of unions and state-owned electric utilities—the proto-type 20 years later of the New Deal and the first American welfare state. In years after, New York pioneered public housing and fair housing laws, industry-wide unions (in the garment trades), increased minimum wages, rent control and dairy price controls to help both New York City tenants and Upstate farmers.

Statewide elections were exceedingly close, with Democrats carrying the New York City Catholic vote and Republicans winning Protestants Upstate. Swing votes were cast by the 2 million Jewish immigrants and their children, who supported a generous welfare state but mistrusted the Tammany machine and valued civil rights. The politician who combined these appeals most cannily was Fiorello LaGuardia: a nominal Republican but almost a socialist, an Episcopalian who was half-Jewish and half-Italian, and who, as mayor of New York City from 1933–45, built much of the public housing and many of the civic monuments that still stand. But both parties produced politicians whose positions appealed to these swing voters, politicians who became nationally prominent and often presidential candidates at a time when the national media was much more concentrated in Manhattan than today: Democrats Al Smith, Robert Wagner, Franklin Roosevelt and Averell Harriman; Republicans Thomas Dewey, Wendell Willkie, Dwight Eisenhower (a New Yorker as president of Columbia University when he was elected president in 1952) and Nelson Rockefeller.

The polity that these men built was productive, generous, tolerant and closely regulated. In an America where people were becoming used to working in big units—for big corporations, represented by big unions, regulated by big government—this kind of New York was a natural leader. The financial dominance of Wall Street and the big banks was protected by federal regulation. The high-tech thrust of America in the mid-20th Century was directed by big companies headquartered in New York's suburbs or Upstate: General Electric and IBM, Eastman Kodak and Xerox. This New York took for granted the productivity of its thousands of entrepreneurs and the high skills of its largely immigrant-born, public school-educated work force. It was blase about its own miraculous infrastructure—the bridges and subways, electronic cables and electric wires connecting it better than any place else with every corner of the world.

But in the last quarter-century, New York's public strengths have become weaknesses. The state which was clearly the national leader of a big-unit America lost the leadership of a country where growth now occurs in small economic units, and flexibility and adaptability are more important than centralized planning. The institutions and practices and infrastructure which helped produce its successes are now ossified and brittle and likely, unless they are reformed and rebuilt, to lead to further decline. Welfare state benefits became too expensive, measures meant to protect against corruption stifled innovation, and both have failed to achieve their objectives—ghettos throb with the pains of disorganization, and payoffs and rackets are part of the everyday cost of doing business in New York as in no other place in the country. The noble aim of creating a public sector which would guarantee cheap rents, topnotch public schools and colleges, and public hospitals, instead guarantees that none of these will be readily available: rent control keeps housing scarce, school bureaucracies stifle good teaching, public hospitals ration care down toward nothing. The attempt to create a fail-safe government has produced a government that is sure to fail. The government that intended to aid growth seemed to be cutting it off—not completely, but enough to explain why New York state, which grew 32% in population from 1940–65, grew only 2% from 1965–97, while California was growing about 74% and Texas about 87%, making both larger now than New York.

People and businesses started voting with their feet, especially during the terms of Mayor John Lindsay, a liberal Republican hailed when he was elected in 1965 by the powerful New York-based liberal media of the day as the next John Kennedy, though about all he shared with Kennedy was good looks. Lindsay denounced Democrats for being too cozy with municipal unions, but gave up more to them than any mayor before or since. He institutionalized the practice of borrowing against next year's revenues to pay this year's bills, bringing city government to the brink of bankruptcy two years after he left office. He convinced New York's minorities that he cared about them, while allowing the institutions that had taught previous generations' immigrants to embrace middle-class values, to scorn those values. "The confluence of radical spite, absurd legal extrapolations and liberal disdain for white ethnics that led to forced busing, the bloating of welfare rolls and the mau-mauing of white teachers broke the spine of New York's civic culture," writes liberal Jim Sleeper in *The Closest of Strangers*. Antagonized middle-class New Yorkers fled not just to the suburbs, but by the hundreds of thousands to (then) low-tax New Jersey, Connecticut and Florida. In the 1970s, the population of New York, city and state, dropped by one million—an unprecedented hemorrhage of talent and productivity, a flight of the middle class away from a polity that seemed to be dying.

Retrenchment followed the mid-1970s bankruptcy crisis. Private financiers and the state government took control of city government, cut spending and negotiated cutbacks in jobs and salaries with public employees' unions. Wall Street boomed in the 1980s and Manhattan once again brimmed over with confidence. Two highly competent Democrats headed the city and state government, Edward Koch for 12 years after he was first elected mayor in 1977, Mario Cuomo for 12 years after he was first elected governor in 1982. Some taxes were cut, bureaucracy was for a time reined in, rational management installed. But institutional problems remained. New York's legislature—"the worst governmental institution in the western world," writes former city official William Stern—remained unusually tightly controlled by the two chambers' leaders, with the Assembly dominated by New York City Democrats and the state Senate by suburban and Upstate Republicans engaged in classic political logrolling, lavishing taxpayers' dollars on each other's pet projects, with no incentives to hold spending down or deliver services. Public employee unions re-established their stranglehold. New York's old welfare state measures left clever members of the middle class in comfortable niches, on public payrolls protected from accountability, in rent-controlled apartments paying a fraction of market value. These same measures left newcomers and the lower classes out in the cold. The mild recession of the early 1990s struck New York with great force: a private sector that had grown little if at all outside Wall Street could no longer finance the countercyclically growing demands of its oversized welfare state.

In the 1990s New York has adapted and changed. Leading the way to reform are two Republican executives, elected on similar government-cutting platforms, though not at all as political allies, Mayor Rudolph Giuliani, who beat David Dinkins in 1993, and Governor George Pataki, who beat Cuomo in 1994. Both are unsentimental men of little eloquence, without illusions, ambitious politicians who have unhesitatingly elbowed others aside, navigating with a clear eye on a lodestar of principle but willing to maneuver course to avoid political shoals and rapids. Giuliani was elected by just 51%–48%, a reversal of his 50%–48%

defeat in 1989, after Dinkins outraged many New Yorkers by hesitating before denouncing a black boycott of a Korean-owned Brooklyn grocery and visiting relatives of a suspected drug dealer shot by a policeman. Pataki won 49%–45% after falling behind in the polls, watching Giuliani endorse Cuomo, being snubbed by the patronage-rich Nassau County Republicans and being dismissed by most of the media, led by *The New York Times*, which cheered for "our governor." Both victories represented a judgment that what Cuomo and *New York Times* writers called "the New York tradition" was destroying jobs, communities and neighborhoods. The New York version of the welfare state, for all the attractiveness of its champions, was repudiated.

The results are not all in, but plainly policies—and life on the ground—have changed. In New York City, Giuliani and his first police commissioner, William Bratton, employed the police tactics urged by James Q. Wilson and George Kelling: aggressively enforcing and prosecuting perpetrators of small crimes—the graffiti vandals, turnstile jumpers, squeegee men, aggressive panhandlers. Giuliani used computers to keep track of crimes every day and to send in police to stop them, and he used accountability, demoting police precinct commanders whose numbers went up. The result is a department where patrolmen believe the mayor will know if there is a crime increase on their beats; a department that is focused not on making arrests or avoiding complaints but on stopping crime. Between 1993 and 1998 crime was cut 40% in New York City, and murders even more: a result that liberal criminologists had long declared impossible and which even Giuliani declined to predict. Giuliani also succeeded in cutting by more than one-third the city's welfare rolls, swollen since Lindsay's welfare commissioner announced that no applicant's eligibility would be checked. Welfare recipients were put to work and subjected to drug tests and applicants were no longer presumed eligible, despite vehement liberal protests. And Giuliani hacked away at bureaucracy and taxes, with little regard to the log-rolling Democratic majority on the city council or the constantly demonstrating public employee unions; and he cracked down on jaywalkers, speeding cab drivers, horn honkers and street vendors.

Giuliani's reforms had national ramifications. His drive against crime set an example followed in dozens of other cities and destroyed the myth that crime is something city-dwellers just have to endure. This conservative reformer showed that a smaller government, held accountable to the mayor and the voters, could be more vigorous and competent than the flabby, oversized government built by his predecessors. In 1997 he was re-elected by 58%–40% over Manhattan Borough President Ruth Messinger, a competent liberal who wanted to return to the policies of Dinkins.

Yet New York City still has problems. Its surging economy is uncomfortably dependent, even more than in the 1980s, on a surging Wall Street: the securities industry, which supplied 2% of city jobs and 4% of wages in 1975, by 1998 provided 4.5% of jobs and a whopping 17% of wages. As historian Fred Siegel says, "The growth in Wall Street wages has masked the continued weaknesses of most other sectors of the economy." In contrast, as Siegel points out, the outer boroughs are increasingly dependent on public sector jobs—not a growth industry in these cutback times—with one-third of jobs in Brooklyn and half in the Bronx directly dependent on the city or state governments. It took five years of Giuliani to return to New York City the number of jobs it had at the beginning of Dinkins's Administration. New York City's economy has recovered from the recession of the early 1990s, but at an achingly slow rate, in a dangerously unbalanced way, far behind the rest of the nation.

There are indeed signs of revival. Large swaths of the south Bronx are now livable again, and neighborhoods in Brooklyn and Queens have been revived. Immigrants have been streaming into outer borough neighborhoods, creating new businesses, churches and neighborhood institutions—Caribbean blacks in Flatbush, Chinese in Flushing and Borough Park, Colombians in Corona, Pakistanis in Jackson Heights, Greeks in Astoria, Russians in Brighton Beach. For a quick look at the future, go and see the crowds of young people of dozens of ethnic backgrounds studying every day at the main Queens Library in Jamaica. The question is whether the outer boroughs will develop the private sector jobs and housing as New York did in the earlier 20th Century surge of immigration and whether immigrants will be helped to assimilate into American society as they were then or shunted off into multicultural ghettos.

But New York's noble infrastructure is deteriorating after three decades of neglect. Large hunks of the Brooklyn Bridge are crumbling, Brooklyn's Gowanus Expressway is about to be junked as Manhattan's West Side Highway was, efforts to build a Second Avenue subway were abandoned years ago, although Giuliani requested $400 million to restart the program in March 1999. Thirty years ago Governor Nelson Rockefeller and the Port Authority blithely allowed the closedown of the Manhattan and Brooklyn deep-water docks—once one of New York's great sources of jobs and vitality—in favor of a port in New Jersey which requires constant dredging, in order to build the World Trade Center, though the private sector remains quite capable of building skyscrapers. Now there are proposals for a rail connection between the Brooklyn docks and Staten Island or Bayonne, New Jersey, advanced by Congressman Jerrold Nadler and others, which could supply the blue-collar jobs immigrants are ready to fill. But the project is very expensive, and it is not clear whether New York can summon up the energy to rebuild what was once one of its great economic strengths.

In Albany, Governor George Pataki has pushed much of his program through. He got the death penalty reinstated, reformed the workmen's comp system, cut and reformed welfare and halted the growth of state government to nearly zero in 1995 and 1996. He sponsored tax cuts, including the estate and gift taxes. But plans to zero out rent control were frustrated in 1997, and in 1997 and 1998 he accelerated spending to discourage serious Democratic opposition and cinch re-election. Politically his strategy was successful. Congressman Charles Schumer decided in 1997 to run for senator rather than governor and in 1998 Pataki defeated New York Council Majority Leader Peter Vallone by 54%-33%. But Pataki has depended on bonds to maintain levels of public spending that voters have become used to. The state has borrowed $3 billion for State and City University campus improvements, $425 million for sports facilities and cultural projects, $1.75 billion for the 1996 environmental program. Its funded debt was $20 billion in 1991, at the beginning of Cuomo's last term, $27 billion in 1995 when Pataki took office and $35 billion in 1998, the largest debt of any state.

New York state outside New York City continues to face serious problems. Job growth is even slower outside the City than within its limits. Long Island's economy is held down by some of the nation's highest local taxes, to buttress the huge government that Republican political machines have built. This system has been maintained in part because the state Senate is dominated by suburban Republicans, who make cozy deals with the Assembly dominated by City Democrats, all at massive cost to taxpayers. Long Island is also hindered by the nation's highest utility rates. That is a public sector problem as well: Mario Cuomo shut down Lilco's Shoreham nuclear plant, with great harm to the company, which was essentially bought out by the state under Pataki—a reversal of the trend toward privatization around the world. It aroused controversy largely because of a $42 million severance package for Lilco's CEO. And while much of inland industrial America has revived in the 1990s, Upstate New York remains in deep trouble. Upstate no longer has central transportation arteries as in the days of the New York Central's water level route, and so is off the beaten path; its population has not risen much since the 1950s. The largest city, Buffalo, is one of those Great Lakes factory cities where old steel mills have closed and is now growing as a low-wage back-office adjunct to Toronto. Much of the Upstate economy has depended on the benevolent policies of large paternalistic corporations—IBM, Kodak, Xerox, Corning, General Electric. In the 1990s these companies had severe problems and, like Japanese firms, dropped lifetime employment policies and made major layoffs. Despite tax cuts, Upstate New York is still a much more expensive place to do business than its Great Lakes competitors, and has had nothing of the economic revival so apparent in Ohio, Michigan and even western Pennsylvania. As Fred Siegel puts it, "A state economy run into the ground by almost 30 years of Nelson Rockefeller and Mario Cuomo doesn't turn around so quickly."

Almanac 2000 Order Card

✓ **YES!** send me *The Almanac of American Politics 2000.*

_____ Copies of the softcover *Almanac 2000* for $54.95 $ _____
_____ Copies of the hardcover *Almanac 2000* for $72.95 $ _____
Add 10% shipping and handling $ _____
Located in DC or Virginia? Add appropriate sales tax $ _____
TOTAL $ _____

☐ **Check Enclosed**   ☐ **Bill me**   *P.O. #:* _____

☐ **Charge:**   ☐ Visa   ☐ Mastercard   ☐ American Express

_____   _____
Acct. #   *Exp. Date*

_____
Signature

Name: _____ Title: _____
Organization: _____
Address: _____
City/State/Zip: _____
Phone: _____ Fax: _____
E-mail: _____

For even faster service, or special discounts on 10 or more
Call Toll Free 1-800-356-4838

National Journal Subscription Reply Card

✓ **YES!** I want six free issues of **National Journal**

The leading weekly on politics, policy, and government

Name: _____ Title: _____
Organization: _____
Address: _____
City/State/Zip: _____
Phone: _____ Fax: _____
E-mail: _____

Mail this postage-paid card today, or for faster service
Call 1-800-424-2921, ext. 1

BUSINESS REPLY MAIL

FIRST-CLASS MAIL   PERMIT NO. 10574 WASHINGTON, DC

POSTAGE WILL BE PAID BY ADDRESSEE

NATIONAL JOURNAL GROUP INC
DEPT NJ
1501 M ST NW
WASHINGTON DC 20078-2040

BUSINESS REPLY MAIL

FIRST-CLASS MAIL   PERMIT NO. 10574 WASHINGTON, DC

POSTAGE WILL BE PAID BY ADDRESSEE

NATIONAL JOURNAL GROUP INC
DEPT NJ
1501 M ST NW
WASHINGTON DC 20078-2040

For 60 years New York has been counted as a Democratic state, and in presidential politics it certainly is: It was Bill Clinton's second best state in 1992, after Arkansas, and his third best in 1996, after Massachusetts and Rhode Island. Yet in the 1990s New York also seems to have trended Republican in state and local politics, electing Giuliani in 1993 and Pataki in 1994. These divergent trends can perhaps be reconciled. New York is happy to support Clinton, a Democrat who promised tax cuts not tax increases in both of his campaigns, and would keep more federal money flowing here than a Republican; but in state politics, in which the project is cutting back an overlarge and over-expensive welfare state, voters have been trending Republican.

Governor. George Pataki began the 1990s as a politically obscure minority-party assemblyman; he ends the decade as a two-term governor of New York and plausible candidate for national office. He grew up in Peekskill, a small industrial city on the Hudson in northern Westchester County, at the cusp of metropolitan New York City and Upstate New York. His father was the son of Hungarian immigrants, his mother is of Italian and Irish ancestry; his parents had a farm in Peekskill and built it into a business; those years are the primary subject of his autobiography *Pataki*. Pataki went to Yale and Columbia Law School, where he was an unabashed conservative in the late 1960s; he practiced law with a big Wall Street firm, then moved to a Westchester firm in 1974. In 1982 he was elected mayor of Peekskill, where he converted tax-exempt property to taxpaying housing, held taxes down, opened an industrial plant and approved 1,000 new housing units. In 1984 he ran against an incumbent Democratic assemblyman and won. In 1992, after eight years as a member of a powerless minority, he challenged an incumbent Republican state senator and beat her by 558 votes. In the state Senate he chafed at the leadership of Nassau County's Ralph Marino and voted against the budget—an almost unheard of rebellion in lockstep-party-voting Albany. In all this he showed ambition, ruthlessness, a penchant for cutting government; but few were paying attention.

In 1993, the almost unknown Pataki began running for governor, taking on one of America's best-known politicians, Mario Cuomo. For all his national fame, and his feints at running for president in 1987 and 1991, Cuomo was in trouble in New York: he cut the top tax rates but also created other taxes and increased spending robustly; he claimed credit for a workfare program but tended to support the public employee unions; he resolutely opposed capital punishment. Pataki provided a clear contrast on both taxes and capital punishment, and he also showed political skill. He got the support of Senator Alfonse D'Amato, fresh from his triumphant re-election and in control of the Republican Party apparatus. Pataki easily won the May 1994 convention and prevented a primary challenge and a Conservative Party candidacy from 1990 Conservative nominee Herb London, who was nominated instead for comptroller. In the general election, Cuomo attacked Pataki for having raised taxes in Peekskill and Democrats charged that he was a puppet of D'Amato. But Pataki led in polls until New York City Mayor Rudolph Giuliani in late October endorsed Cuomo and bitterly criticized Pataki. Cuomo went into the lead, gaining votes in New York City and in Nassau County, with its revenue-hungry Republican machine. Thomas Golisano, a Rochester businessman, was spending millions as an independent, advised by pro-Perot pollster Gordon Black; Perot endorsed him and polls showed him with 8%. But Golisano's share of the vote fell to 4%, and Cuomo got 45%, about where he was running in polls. Pataki won 49% of the vote, losing New York City 70%–28% but carrying the suburbs 54%–43% and Upstate (where Giuliani's endorsement hurt Cuomo) 59%–32%. It was the best Republican year in recent New York h̶i̶s̶t̶o̶r̶y̶. ̶ Vacco was elected attorney general over Democrat Karen Burstein won 47% of the votes for U.S. House as compared to Democrats Patrick Moynihan's winning margin was reduced to 55%–42%.

As governor, Pataki showed determination and even ruthlessness the election, he declined to take a congratulatory phone call from G engineered a coup ousting Marino as Senate leader that was execute a failing store) while he was on vacation in Florida. Pataki prop spending and, after bruising negotiations with Democratic Assembly Speaker Sheldon Silver, got much of what he wanted. Pataki signed the death penalty into law in March 1995 and transferred back to Oklahoma an inmate scheduled to be executed there. In 1996 he got reform of workmen's comp. With D'Amato and almost all leading New York Republicans except Giuliani, he endorsed Bob Dole for the Republican nomination; but when the Dole campaign went nowhere in New York he coolly said in November, "I wasn't involved in the campaign."

Instead he spent much effort on a $1.75 billion bond issue, citing his longtime admiration for Theodore Roosevelt and gathering support from business, labor and environmental groups. The bond issue passed with large majorities from New York City and the suburbs, where it would help in 1998, and lost in Upstate, which he was sure to carry anyway. He also switched and supported the partial state takeover of Lilco, agreeing in early 1997 to issuing $7 billion in bonds. In early 1997 Pataki unveiled his welfare reform plan, cutting benefits to recipients who do not find work by 45% over four years; he called for a three-year phaseout of estate and gift taxes, which send many affluent New Yorkers to Florida; he pushed his STAR school tax relief plan to rebate taxes and give more aid to schools. He stayed aloof from Senate President Joseph Bruno's crusade to end state-wide rent controls, brokering a compromise which left controls intact in Manhattan.

All these policies, plus the rising tide of pro-incumbent feeling left Pataki in strong shape for re-election even as the Dole-Kemp ticket was overwhelmingly defeated and Republicans receded from their peak of 1994. He had the endorsement of former Mayor Edward Koch and was working in tandem with Giuliani. Pataki's budgets in 1997 and 1998 had above-economic-growth spending increases; he established who was in control, however, by line-item-vetoing $1.6 billion from the legislature's budget in April 1998. In April 1997 he dropped from his ticket Lieutenant Governor Betsy McCaughey Ross; she became a Democrat in September and ran for governor in 1998, losing the Democratic primary and winning 2% on the Liberal line in the general. In her place Pataki picked Mary Donohue, a judge from Rensselaer County, just across the Hudson from Albany. Meanwhile, strong opposition faded away. Congressman Charles Schumer, long eyeing the governorship, announced in April 1997 that he was running against D'Amato instead. State Comptroller Carl McCall, after criticizing Pataki, also decided not to run. The Democratic nomination was won by New York City Council Speaker Peter Vallone, a competent and constructive veteran widely admired in knowledgeable circles. But he was scarcely known outside New York City, and never had a chance against the well-financed Pataki. Pataki won 54%–33%, losing New York City by 60%–33%—a slight improvement over 1994—but carrying the suburbs 62%–29% and Upstate by 64%–19%; 13% of the vote there went to Golisano, again running a third-party candidacy.

In his second term, Pataki again tightened up on spending, which led to sharp protests from Giuliani; they disagreed on Giuliani's plans for a Manhattan baseball stadium. They were also both competing for the national spotlight. Giuliani spent much of 1998 traveling the country and testing the presidential waters; after the November election and Pat Moynihan's announcement that he would retire from the Senate, Giuliani seemed determined to run for that seat in 2000. Pataki's state party chairman had been touting him as presidential contender as early as March 1997, and he made fundraising trips around the country as well. Some of Pataki's stands on issues would surely hurt with Republican core voters—he supports abortion rights and welfare for legal immigrants. Nor is his quiet, almost languid speaking style likely to ignite partisan crowds. He claims to have turned around state government, and to a surprising extent has, yet he cannot claim to have solved all of New York's problems. And his style of closed-mouth, lockstep control of his party may not be attractive under a spotlight harsher than it ⟶eives in Albany. In May 1999 he officially endorsed George W. Bush for president. Yet he ⟶ still come into contention for the vice presidency: His ethnic background could be an ⟶ his party in other, more marginal industrial states from Pennsylvania to Illinois.

Senator. Daniel Patrick Moynihan, the nation's best thinker among politicians since ⟶its best politician among thinkers since Jefferson, now approaches the end of a long career in public office. Even after he announced three days after the 1998 election that he would retire in 2000, he is still New York's senior senator, the ranking Democrat on the Finance Committee, crucially positioned in a still closely balanced Senate to advance major reforms and his own projects. For all his academic credentials, Moynihan has a range of experience in American government as broad as any member of Congress. He worked for Governor Averell Harriman in the 1950s, served as assistant secretary of Labor in the Kennedy and Johnson Administrations, was chief domestic adviser to President Nixon and was ambassador to the United Nations under President Ford—the only person in American history, he likes to note, who has served in the cabinet or subcabinet of four successive presidents. As Finance chairman, he helped shepherd the 1993 budget and tax package to passage by one vote. And he advised Bill and Hillary Rodham Clinton early and often to give priority to welfare reform over health care reform. Had his advice been taken, it might have changed the course of their administration and the fortunes of the Democratic Party.

Moynihan is known rightly for his ability to spot emerging issues long before anyone else, qualities that were apparent at least as early as 1965, when he wrote "The Negro Family: The Case for National Action." The long expanse of his career has underlined the consistency of his ideas and interests and the persistence with which he has kept at his causes. Every summer Moynihan spends several weeks in an old one-room schoolhouse on his farm in Pindars Corners, deep in the hills of Upstate New York, writing in distinctive prose another book on any of a dozen subjects. This is the kind of philosopher-politician who the Founding Fathers hoped would people the Senate—although they would have been surprised to see one spring, as Moynihan did, from the Manhattan slum of Hell's Kitchen.

In the early 1960s, before Ralph Nader, Moynihan was arguing that traffic deaths could be reduced by redesigning car interiors. Later he became almost the nation's transportation czar. As then-chairman of Environment and Public Works Subcommittee on Transportation and Infrastructure, he produced "Ice Tea," insider language for the Intermodal Surface Transportation Efficiency Act of 1991 (ISTEA), which provided vast new sums for transportation and gave states the choice of whether to use money for highways or mass transit. It made funding formulas more favorable to New York—a pet Moynihan cause on which he publishes yearly data to show how New York is shortchanged—and got New York reimbursed for building its Thruway and funded magnetic levitation trains, also a favorite cause. He endorsed the plan for a rail tunnel to connect Brooklyn and Staten Island and Jersey City, with the aim of reviving the Brooklyn waterfront and stimulating small businesses there. ISTEA came up for reauthorization in 1997, and was expanded into the much larger TEA-21, with even more money and more flexibility for states and localities.

In 1993 Moynihan became the first New Yorker to chair the Senate Finance Committee in 155 years. The two major Clinton initiatives, the 1993 budget and tax package and the 1994 health care reform, had to go through Finance, and Moynihan played a pivotal role on each. Initially the Clinton White House was contemptuous. One staffer said to *Time* in early 1993, "He's not one of us. He can't control Finance like Bentsen did. He's cantankerous, but we'll roll right over him if we have to." But Moynihan got the budget and tax package through the Senate and in August when the White House needed one last vote it was Elizabeth Moynihan who persuaded Bob Kerrey (whose presidential candidacy Moynihan supported in 1992) to cast the critical vote. Under Moynihan's guidance, the nanny tax was reformed and the Social Security Administration was made an independent agency.

Health care went differently. In January 1993 Moynihan criticized HHS Secretary Donna Shalala sharply for not mentioning welfare reform in her opening statement to the committee, and for months he pressed the Clintons to emphasize welfare reform, but to no great avail. In January 1994, when the Clintons produced a vast health care bill, Moynihan called their puny efforts on welfare "boob bait for bubbas." On *Meet the Press* he insisted, "We don't have a health care crisis in this country. We do have a welfare crisis." He called the original Clinton financing mechanism "a fantasy," and he threatened to hold health care hostage to a welfare bill. He got Shalala to admit that the "few" who would pay more under the Clinton plan were actually 40% of insured families. Nonetheless Moynihan stood ready to cobble a compromise with Bob Dole, who seemed at the beginning of 1994 to be interested. But the Clintons, backed by Majority Leader George Mitchell and Finance member Jay Rockefeller, said it wasn't time to compromise yet. Finance did produce a bill, and Mitchell got ready to introduce his own version on the floor. But in August 1994 House Democrats lost a crucial procedural vote on the crime bill and had to delay action on health care, and the Mitchell effort ran out of steam. Moynihan's great cause on health care was preserving teaching hospitals, and not just because New York has several of them. For him it was "a sin against the Holy Ghost" to threaten the existence of these institutions. In 1997 he proposed a Medical Education Trust Fund, with $17 billion from Medicare, Medicaid and the private sector to double federal spending on medical schools and teaching hospitals. One of his great causes on the Finance Committee was pre- serving the deductibility of gifts of appreciated property to nonprofit entities such as universities and museums.

Surprisingly, for one whose critique of society can be so radical, Moynihan's approach to some issues can be cautious and conservative. In the 1986 tax reform debate, his great cause was preserving the deductibility of state taxes, worth more in high-tax New York than any other state. In 1991, he got both Democrats and Republicans in a tizzy with his "Moyniplan" to cut the Social Security payroll tax 1%. In December 1996 he and Finance Chairman William Roth sponsored the Boskin Commission of economists who recommended adjusting the Con- sumer Price Index downward by 1.1% on the ground that it overstates inflation. His hope was that entitlement spending would grow more slowly. In March 1998 he came out with his own plan for Social Security reform, an attempt to save it, in his view, from being abolished when it became unsustainable as the welfare entitlement was abolished suddenly at a propitious political moment in August 1996. Moynihan's plan, supported also by Bob Kerrey, would let workers invest 2% of the 12.4% payroll tax in individual investment accounts, which would allow all workers to build up wealth over their lifetimes: "I think that could have more effect on race in this country than anything else we're talking about." It would also raise the retirement age, lower the COLA 1% below the CPI and increase the wage base of the tax from $68,400 to $97,500. Such a plan could be the basis of a bipartisan Social Security reform in Moynihan's last Congress, although in early 1999 the Clinton Administration appeared to be lining up with labor unions to block it.

Welfare reform is the idea with which Moynihan has been most closely associated. He was harshly criticized for years for "blaming the victim"; in fact, he was blaming fatherlessness. Since then, family breakdown among blacks has reached harrowing proportions, and family breakdown overall is now about as common as it was among blacks in 1965. His response was the Welfare Reform Act of 1988, which recognized the responsibilities of fathers to provide for their children and encouraged workfare experiments. But enforcement of child support and work incentives produced disappointing results. The Clinton campaign promised to "end wel- fare as we know it." But the 1996 Welfare Reform Act, in ending the federal entitlement to welfare, in Moynihan's opinion went much too far. He feared that it would leave children hungry in the streets, and spoke out against it more than any other senator. "Shame on the President," he said when Clinton signed the bill, adding that if it had come before Clinton 14 weeks after the election instead of 14 weeks before he would have vetoed it.

Moynihan has also been a force in foreign policy. In 1975 and 1976, as ambassador to the United Nations, he denounced the Soviet Union and some Third World nations, opposing their resolution declaring Zionism as racism. Once considered a foreign policy hawk, in the late 1970s he became convinced that the Soviet Union was not a strong enemy and would come apart through ethnic conflict. Moynihan believes ethnic allegiances and rivalries are more im- portant in politics than economic differences: that is the theme of his and Nathan Glazer's *Beyond the Melting Pot*, a description of New York's ethnic groups that was published in 1963 and still rings true today, and it is the theme of his 1993 book *Pandaemonium*, which describes how ethnic conflicts produce war and genocide. Though he came to be classed with foreign policy doves, there is a great difference between them: most doves believed that the Soviet Union was dangerous but not evil, while Moynihan believed that the Soviet Union was evil but, because it was economically weak and ethnically riven, not dangerous. Today, Moynihan believes the United States should have a far smaller military and should basically abolish the CIA. He opposed NAFTA because of his feeling that Mexico remains a "Leninist" society, but he was very much for GATT and fast-track trade negotiating authority.

Moynihan has on occasion broken with his fellow Democrats. In early 1995 he was the first Democratic senator to call for an independent counsel to investigate Whitewater; in early 1997 he was the first major Democrat to call for an independent counsel to investigate the Clinton-Gore campaign finance violations. He broke with liberals in 1996 when he supported the partial-birth abortion ban; the practice, he said, was too close to infanticide. And he broke with decades of bipartisan practice in 1997 when, as chairman of a Commission on Secrecy, he called for "a new way of thinking about secrecy," arguing that because government tries to keep too much information secret, it often fails to protect adequately the secrets most critical to national security. The unanimous report, supported by Senator Jesse Helms, former CIA Director John Deutsch and House Intelligence Committee Chairman Larry Combest, concluded, "The best way to ensure that secrecy is respected, and that the most important secrets remain secret, is for secrecy to be returned to its limited but necessary role." The commission also released the Venona transcripts, records of Soviet spymasters which showed the penetration of the U.S. government by Soviet spies in the 1940s. This was the subject of Moynihan's 1998 book *Secrecy*, which argued that the evils of McCarthyism could have been avoided if the Venona secrets were less closely held, since the Truman Administration could have argued accurately that there had been some Soviet espionage in the 1940s and that it had been stopped in 1948, well before Joe McCarthy's first speech in early 1950.

Moynihan seems increasingly concerned about constitutional issues. He was one of the members challenging the line-item veto, and was pleased when the Supreme Court ruled it unconstitutional in June 1998. He inveighed against the omnibus budget bill of October 1998, as an evisceration of the legislative process: "Members loudly debate issues on the floor, but the real decisions are made in a closed room by three or four people"—much as they are in Albany, one might add. In September 1998 he said that perjury was an impeachable offensive, but later he concluded that Clinton's acts did not rise to the level justifying removal from office and voted against impeachment. He sought an exemption from federal taxes for the $1 million reward David Kaczynski won for turning in evidence against his brother, the Unabomber, since Kaczynski said he would turn all the money over to the victims and their families; but obdurate Republicans blocked it, and so one-third goes to the Treasury instead.

Electoral politics has proved surprisingly congenial to Moynihan. After beating Bella Abzug in the 1976 primary, he won a party-line victory against incumbent James Buckley in a year when Republicans were hurt by President Ford's opposition to federal loan guarantees for New York City. For 1982, Moynihan's opposition to Reagan programs prevented the emergence of opposition from the left, and he eliminated the main Republican candidate, Bruce Caputo, when it became known that Caputo had falsified his military record. Moynihan won 65%–34% in 1982 and 67%–31% in 1988, both records for New York. In heavily Republican 1994, against Bernadette Castro, heiress of the Castro convertible sofabed fortune, he ran less well, winning 55%–42%, carrying New York City 73%–25%, but winning the suburbs by only 49%–48% and Upstate by 48.2%–48.1%.

On November 6, 1998, Moynihan announced he would not run again in 2000. "It will have been 24 years. . . . I've been very happy, and there was a very positive note to this last election. It's time to make room for others." His only possible regret, he said, was voting against the Gulf war resolution. Not since 1958 has there been an open seat in New York: contenders in large numbers came into view and many vanished. Moynihan endorsed state Controller Carl McCall, but in December he said he would not run. Democrats with prominent names—environmental lawyer Robert Kennedy Jr., HUD Secretary Andrew Cuomo—also declined to run. Congresswoman Nita Lowey and New York City Public Advocate Mark Green (a candidate in 1986 and 1998) said they were interested. Mayor Rudolph Giuliani made it clear that he would like to run, but faced the possibility of a primary with Long Island Congressman Rick Lazio; almost none of New York's Republican primary votes are cast in New York City, and Lazio has a moderate record and penchant for solving local problems that resembles Alfonse D'Amato. Then in January 1999 the name of Hillary Rodham Clinton was floated. In February she said she was giving serious consideration to the race, and led Giuliani in most polls. In June Lowey offered to step aside for the first lady, saying, "she's clearly made the decision to run," but held open the prospect of running herself if Clinton changed her mind. The race for Moynihan's seat could be the most high-profile and sharply contested in the country, but none of the contenders can hope to duplicate the record of the incumbent.

Cook's Call. *Highly Competitive.* Initially, it seemed a battle of the titans was brewing between Hillary Rodham Clinton and Republican New York City Mayor Rudy Giuliani. Clinton will certainly get the Democratic nod, but Representative Rick Lazio, who seems ready to challenge Giuliani, has complicated the situation on the Republican side. Although Giuliani begins with a wide lead, philosophically he is well to the left of most Repubicans. Only 13% of the Republican primary vote comes from New York City which could also leave Lazio an opening. The state's multiple party lines further complicates matters as Lazio could run for both the Republican and Conservative Party nods.

A two-way race between Clinton and either Giuliani or Lazio would be extremely competi- tive, but Clinton would have an edge in a three-way race since the Republican and anti-Clinton vote would be split.

Junior Senator. Charles Schumer is a Democrat elected in 1998 after the most expensive Senate race ever in which neither candidate self-financed his campaign. Schumer grew up in Flatbush, Brooklyn, and graduated first in his class at James Madison High School, alma mater of Justice Ruth Bader Ginsburg and many other notables. He was only slightly derumpled in seven years at Harvard College and Harvard Law School; he graduated from the latter in June 1974 and immediately began running for an open Assembly seat. He won, at 23. In 1980 he was elected to the House from an open Brooklyn seat, just before he turned 30. Through energy, imagination, hard work, good humor and a certain amount of chutzpah, he became a skilled legislator, and one noted—and sometimes resented—for his knack for getting publicity. Im- mediately he raised a campaign treasury of over $1 million, lest he and Brooklyn neighbor Stephen Solarz be redistricted together in 1982, but they weren't and both coexisted for a decade. By 1992 he had $2 million in the bank, again for fear of a primary race against Solarz; but Solarz ran and lost in the neighboring Hispanic-majority 12th District.

From the unlikely venue of the Banking Committee, a panel that most talented members lobby to get off of, Schumer spotted the perverse incentives set up by the combination of deposit insurance and letting S&Ls make risky investments. He fought Banking Chairman Fernand St. Germain, calling early on for higher capital requirements, and helped shape the 1989 S&L bailout bill. He has also worked on housing programs, building on the success of the Nehemiah projects in Brooklyn. On Judiciary and, eventually, as chairman of its Crime Subcommittee, he ranged far afield, contributing key provisions to immigration acts in 1986 and 1990, leading with free marketeer Dick Armey attacks on farm subsidies, and with Florida Republican Dan Miller a nearly-successful assault on sugar programs. He wrote an auto theft law to reduce the market for resale of stolen parts. Other causes include the Violence Against Women Act and a federal law against impeding access to abortion clinics. Schumer sponsored the 1994 crime bill and got the House to pass the Brady bill, with its waiting period for handgun purchases, over strong opposition from the National Rifle Association.

In the Republican House, Schumer had more trouble exerting leverage, and helped crystal- lize opinion in New York and elsewhere against Newt Gingrich and his Republicans, but some- times unfairly, as in his criticism of Christina Jeffrey, whom Gingrich appointed as House historian and then deserted after Schumer's attacks. But he was already thinking statewide. Had Mario Cuomo retired in 1994, Schumer would probably have run for governor, and in 1995 and 1996 he was considering running against Governor George Pataki. But in April 1997 Pataki's strong job rating, and especially his overwhelming strength Upstate, led Schumer to switch and use his $5 million treasury to run for Alfonse D'Amato's senate seat instead.

It was by no means obvious that he would win. D'Amato, often called "Senator Pothole," was known for his assiduous constituent service and for his ability to win the tabloid wars that dominate campaigning in metropolitan New York. Although some of his stands—against abortion and gun control—and his aggressive investigation of Whitewater in 1995 were unpopular in New York, he also achieved results in popular crusades—for breast cancer research, against Swiss banks withholding money from Holocaust survivors, for gay rights. D'Amato was chairman of the Banking Committee and excelled at raising money; his early support did much to make Pataki governor and he cinched New York's Republican delegation for Bob Dole in 1996. Moreover, Schumer started off largely unknown outside his district (which starting in 1992 included part of Queens as well as Brooklyn) and faced serious primary opposition from 1984 vice presidential nominee Geraldine Ferraro and Mark Green, New York City public advocate (the title used to be council chairman) and D'Amato's opponent in 1986. But Ferraro hesitated before running in January 1998, and by July had collected only $2 million for the September primary; and Green was outraised and overshadowed by Schumer, who started running ads in November 1997. For a long time he went nowhere in the polls, but by summer he was leading. In September he won 51% of the primary vote, to 26% for Ferraro and 19% for Green; Schumer won 53% in New York City and 63% in the suburbs; Ferraro carried Upstate by 47%–39%, but it cast only 27% of the Democratic primary vote.

Schumer immediately launched an attack on D'Amato, saying he had told "too many lies for too long"; it echoed D'Amato's attacks on earlier opponents as "too liberal for too long." Schumer claimed he was tougher on crime, citing his support for longer sentences, limiting death row appeals, expanding capital punishment and broadening wiretap authority; he emphasized his support of abortion rights and gun control. D'Amato concentrated heavily on Schumer's missed votes while running for Senate, but the implication that Schumer was lazy was implausible. Still, by mid-October, Schumer's poll leads were mostly less than the statistical margin of error. On October 20, D'Amato scored coups by winning endorsements from the Human Rights Campaign and former Democratic Congressman Floyd Flake of Queens. But in a closed meeting before a Jewish group D'Amato called Schumer a "putzhead"; when that became public, he denied it, then backtracked unconvincingly after his own supporter, former Democratic Mayor Edward Koch, confirmed it. "New Yorkers can't trust Al D'Amato. Eighteen years is too long," Schumer's ad proclaimed; D'Amato lost confidence and momentum, and by early November was sagging in polls.

D'Amato was finally a victim in the tabloid wars in which he had so long excelled; all his support from Pataki, Koch and Mayor Rudolph Giuliani did him little good. Schumer, who announced in October that he would vote against impeachment though he believed Bill Clinton lied under oath, was the beneficiary of two visits from Clinton and no less than four from Hillary Rodham Clinton. Though outspent, Schumer won 55%–44%, winning 74%–25% in a big turnout in New York City, a percentage margin as large as Daniel Patrick Moynihan had won there four years before. Schumer lost the suburbs by only 51%–49% and Upstate by only 53%–45%; he carried only six counties there, but they included Buffalo, Niagara Falls, Rochester and Albany. Jewish voters, about 40% of whom voted for D'Amato in 1986 and 1992, now went 76%–23% for Schumer; voters with graduate degrees, the most heavily Democratic educational group in New York, went 69%–31% for Schumer.

Schumer faces the prospect of a long Senate career: no Democratic incumbent senator has been defeated in New York since direct election of senators began (though seven incumbent Republicans have lost). In some ways his life hasn't changed. He continues to live in a Park Slope apartment, and to room on Capitol Hill with Senator Richard Durbin and Congressmen

George Miller and Sam Gejdenson. He serves on the same major committees as in the House, Banking and Judiciary. But of course he has the potential for vastly more visibility and influence—and mostly Democratic New York, for the first time since 1946, has two Democratic senators.

Presidential politics. For more than 100 years, New York was a pivotal state in presidential politics: it was the nation's largest state and closely divided first between Whigs and Jacksonians, then Democrats and Republicans. But now California, with 54 electoral votes, is much larger than New York, with 33. And over the last several decades California's moods have been more changeable, thus attracting candidates' attention, while New York has typically been the most Democratic large state. Back in the 1960s New York's Democratic margins came from middle-income Jews and Catholics in the outer boroughs of New York City. Today they come primarily from blacks and Puerto Ricans in the outer boroughs and liberal, highly educated whites in Manhattan and elsewhere. Manhattan liberals tend to be young singles, affluent childless couples, feminists, gays and the often underpaid highly-educated people who flock to this center of arts and letters—the nation's prime leftish voting bloc. Bill Clinton won New York state by the onesided margin of 59%–31% in 1996, carrying New York City overwhelmingly (77%–17%) and winning impressively in the suburbs (55%–36%) and Upstate (50%–37%); he carried all 31 congressional districts.

For years New York had bossed politics, and it never had a presidential primary until 1968. Turnout is low—for Democrats 1 million in 1980 and 1992, 1.3 million in 1984 and 1.5 million 1988—and convoluted petition requirements make it hard for candidates to qualify; Pat Buchanan never made it on the ballot here in 1992, and Steve Forbes qualified only after spending $1 million. The rules have been modified since, but one suspects only a little.

Such primaries as do occur have an ethnic cast. Jewish voters, turning out heavily, set the tone of Democratic primaries from 1976–84. Black voters, turning out heavily partly out of enthusiasm for Jesse Jackson but also because of anger at Mayor Edward Koch, set the tone in 1988. In 1992, the local press hyped the New York primary as a make-or-break test of Clinton, when in fact he had clinched the nomination in Illinois and Michigan three weeks before. Paul Tsongas had withdrawn, Jerry Brown was not going to win, Mario Cuomo was not running. Clinton played along with the charade, appearing on Don Imus's syndicated radio program and parrying questions from Gabe Pressman: he won with 41% to 26% for Brown and 29% for the withdrawn Tsongas. New York's Republican primary electorate is made up almost entirely of suburbanites and Upstaters, with a large number of Italian-Americans.

New York's minor parties no longer much matter, except occasionally the Conservatives. The Liberal Party and its predecessor, the American Labor Party, were founded to give Jewish garment workers a line on which to vote for Franklin Roosevelt and against local Tammany Hall candidates; with Betsy McCaughey Ross, the Republican-turned-Democrat lieutenant governor, it won 1.6% of the vote for governor in 1998. But the Liberal Party is more important in city elections, in which it has staunchly backed Mayor Rudolph Giuliani. The Conservative Party was founded to withhold votes from liberal Republicans like Nelson Rockefeller and John Lindsay and encourage the Republican Party to nominate more conservative candidates; now it almost always does, and George Pataki is the first Conservative-backed governor; but withdrawal of the Conservative line locally can hurt.

Congressional districting. When John Kennedy was elected president in 1960, New York elected 43 congressmen and California 30. When Bill Clinton was elected in 1992, New York elected 31 and California 52. This is what happens when one state grows rapidly and another grows not at all. Redistricting is carnage time: New York lost five districts in the 1980 Census and another three in 1990 and is projected to lose two more in 2000. In 1992, New York was the last state to redistrict, in June. The plan has many districts with convoluted lines, all drawn for good political reasons. But after two Supreme Court rulings overturning district lines drawn using race as the predominant factor, a lawsuit was brought challenging New York's Hispanic-majority 12th District that snakes through Brooklyn, Manhattan and Queens, and borders on seven other congressional districts. In February 1997 a federal court ordered redrawing of this "Bullwinkle district," and the legislature complied in August 1997. Congresswoman Nydia Velazquez of the 12th retained her constituencies in lower Manhattan and Brooklyn but lost most voters in Queens. Hispanic percentages in the 12th dropped from about 57% to about 45%, altering five adjoining districts which became even more Democratic.

Redistricting after the 2000 census will probably cost both parties a seat, since the legislature is permanently divided between the parties.

The People: Est. Pop. 1998: 18,175,301; Pop. 1990: 17,990,455, up 1% 1990–1998. 6.7% of U.S. total, 3d largest; 15.7% rural. Median age: 35.3 years. 13.8% 65 years and over. 74.5% White, 15.9% Black, 3.8% Asian, 0.3% Amer. Indian, 5.5% Other; 12% Hispanic Origin. Households: 49.9% married couple families; 23.5% married couple fams. w. children; 45.3% college educ.; median household income: $32,965; per capita income: $16,501; 52.2% owner occupied housing; median house value: $131,600; median monthly rent: $428. 5.6% Unemployment. 1998 Voting age pop.: 13,590,000. 1998 Turnout: 4,985,932; 37% of VAP. Registered voters (1998): 10,740,788; 4,997,773 D (47%), 3,114,832 R (29%), 2,628,183 unaffiliated and minor parties (24%).

Political Lineup: Governor, George E. Pataki (R); Lt. Gov., Mary Donohue (R); Secy. of State, Alexander Treadwell (R); Atty. Gen., Eliot Spitzer (D); Comptroller, H. Carl McCall (D); State Senate, 61 (25 D, 36 R); Majority Leader, Joseph Bruno (R); State Assembly, 150 (98 D, 52 R); Assembly Speaker, Sheldon Silver (D). Senators, Daniel Patrick Moynihan (D) and Charles E. Schumer (D). Representatives, 31 (18 D, 13 R).

Elections Division: 518-474-1953; **Filing Deadline for U.S. Congress:** Date TBA, December 1999.

1996 Presidential Vote

Clinton (D)	3,756,565	(61%)
Dole (R)	1,932,900	(31%)
Perot (I)	503,356	(8%)

1996 Republican Presidential Primary

Dole (R)	599,748	(55%)
Forbes (R)	325,211	(30%)
Buchanan (R)	163,365	(15%)

1992 Presidential Vote

Clinton (D)	3,435,104	(50%)
Bush (R)	2,342,194	(34%)
Perot (I)	1,089,523	(16%)

GOVERNOR

Gov. George E. Pataki (R)

Elected 1994, term expires Jan. 2003; b. June 24, 1945, Peekskill; home, Garrison; Yale U., B.A. 1967, Columbia U. Law Schl., J.D. 1970; Catholic; married (Libby).

Elected Office: Peekskill Mayor, 1982–84; NY Assembly, 1984–92; NY Senate, 1992–94.

Professional Career: Practicing atty., 1970–89.

Office: Executive Chamber, State Capitol, Albany, 12224, 518-474-8390; Web site: www.state.ny.us.

Election Results

1998 gen.	George E. Pataki (R-C)	2,571,991	(54%)
	Peter F. Vallone (D-WF)	1,570,317	(33%)
	B. Thomas Golisano (Ind)	364,056	(8%)
	Others	228,872	(5%)
1998 prim.	George E. Pataki (R)	unopposed	
1994 gen.	George E. Pataki (R-C)	2,538,702	(49%)
	Mario M. Cuomo (D-L)	2,364,904	(45%)
	B. Thomas Golisano (Ind)	217,490	(4%)
	Others	82,666	(2%)

SENATORS

Sen. Daniel Patrick Moynihan (D)

Elected 1976, seat up 2000; b. Mar. 16, 1927, Tulsa, OK; home, Pindars Corners; City Col. of NY, 1943, Tufts U., B.A. 1948, M.A. 1949, Ph.D. 1961; Catholic; married (Elizabeth).

Military Career: Navy, 1944–47; Naval Reserves, 1947–1966.

Professional Career: Aide, NY Gov. Averell Harriman, 1955–58; U.S. Asst. Secy. of Labor, 1963–65; Dir., Joint Ctr. for Urban Studies, MIT & Harvard, 1966–69; Asst. to Pres. Nixon, Urban Affairs, 1969–71; Prof., Harvard, 1971–73; U.S. Ambassador to India, 1973–75; U.N. Ambassador, 1975–76.

DC Office: 464 RSOB, 20510, 202-224-4451; Fax: 202-228-0406; Web site: www.senate.gov/~moynihan.

State Offices: Buffalo, 716-551-4097; Manhattan, 212-661-5150; Oneonta, 607-433-2310.

Committees: *Environment & Public Works* (2d of 8 D): Superfund, Waste Control & Risk Assessment; Transportation & Infrastructure. *Finance* (RMM of 9 D): International Trade (RMM); Social Security & Family Policy; Taxation & IRS Oversight. *Rules & Administration* (4th of 7 D). *Joint Committee on Taxation* (4th of 5 Sens.). *Joint Committee on the Library of Congress* (4th of 5 Sens.).

Group Ratings

	ADA	ACLU	AFS	LCV	CON	NTU	NFIB	COC	ACU	NTLC	CHC
1998	95	43	89	88	97	16	22	44	8	14	9
1997	60	—	67	—	29	32	—	50	12	—	—

National Journal Ratings

	1997 LIB — 1997 CONS			1998 LIB — 1998 CONS		
Economic	57%	—	40%	90%	—	0%
Social	55%	—	37%	63%	—	26%
Foreign	62%	—	32%	65%	—	27%

Key Votes of the 105th Congress

1. Bal. Budget Amend.	N	5. Satcher for Surgeon Gen.	Y	9. Chem. Weapons Treaty	Y
2. Clinton Budget Deal	Y	6. Highway Set-asides	Y	10. Cuban Humanitarian Aid	Y
3. Cloture on Tobacco	Y	7. Table Child Gun locks	N	11. Table Bosnia Troops	Y
4. Education IRAs	N	8. Ovrd. Part. Birth Veto	Y	12. $ for Test-ban Treaty	Y

Election Results

1994 general	Daniel Patrick Moynihan (D-L)	2,646,541	(55%)	($6,705,482)
	Bernadette Castro (R-C)	1,988,308	(42%)	($1,581,901)
	Others	155,487	(3%)	
1994 primary	Daniel Patrick Moynihan (D)	526,766	(75%)	
	Al Sharpton (D)	178,231	(25%)	
1988 general	Daniel Patrick Moynihan (D-L)	4,048,649	(67%)	($4,809,810)
	Robert R. McMillan (R-C)	1,875,784	(31%)	($528,989)

Sen. Charles E. Schumer (D)

Elected 1998, seat up 2004; b. Nov. 23, 1950, Brooklyn; home, Brooklyn; Harvard U., B.A. 1971, J.D. 1974; Jewish; married (Iris).

Elected Office: NY Assembly, 1974–80; U.S. House of Reps., 1980–1998.

DC Office: 313 HSOB, 20510, 202-224-6542; Fax: 202-228-3027; Web site: www.senate.gov/~schumer.

State Offices: Albany, 518-431-4070; Buffalo, 716-846-4545; Manhattan, 212-486-4430; Rochester, 716-263-5866; Syracuse, 315-423-5471.

Committees: *Banking, Housing & Urban Affairs* (7th of 9 D): Financial Institutions; International Trade & Finance; Securities. *Judiciary* (8th of 8 D): Administrative Oversight & the Courts; Criminal Justice Oversight (RMM); Immigration. *Rules & Administration* (7th of 7 D).

Group Ratings (as Member of U.S. House of Representatives)

	ADA	ACLU	AFS	LCV	CON	NTU	NFIB	COC	ACU	NTLC	CHC
1998	85	93	100	85	65	18	17	36	9	3	0
1997	85	—	86	—	84	32	—	40	19	—	—

National Journal Ratings (as Member of U.S. House of Representatives)

	1997 LIB — 1997 CONS			1998 LIB — 1998 CONS		
Economic	91%	—	7%	79%	—	0%
Social	80%	—	20%	84%	—	16%
Foreign	72%	—	28%	71%	—	27%

Key Votes of the 105th Congress (as Member of U.S. House of Representatives)

1. Clinton Budget Deal	N	5. Puerto Rico Sthood. Ref.	Y	9. Cut $ for B-2 Bombers	*
2. Education IRAs	N	6. End Highway Set-asides	N	10. Human Rights in China	Y
3. Req. 2/3 to Raise Taxes	*	7. School Prayer Amend.	N	11. Withdraw Bosnia Troops	N
4. Fast-track Trade	N	8. Ovrd. Part. Birth Veto	N	12. End Cuban TV-Marti	Y

Election Results

1998 general	Charles E. Schumer (D-Ind-L)	2,551,065	(55%)	($16,671,877)
	Al D'Amato (R-C-RTL)	2,058,988	(44%)	($24,195,287)
	Others	60,752	(1%)	
1998 primary	Charles E. Schumer (D)	388,701	(51%)	
	Geraldine A. Ferraro (D)	201,265	(26%)	
	Mark Green (D)	145,819	(19%)	
	Others	28,493	(4%)	
1992 general	Al D'Amato (R-C-RTL)	3,166,994	(49%)	($11,550,958)
	Robert Abrams (D-L)	3,086,200	(48%)	($6,408,981)
	Others	205,632	(3%)	

FIRST DISTRICT

Long Island—the Island to most New Yorkers—is America's largest, most populous and in some ways most troubled island: 103 miles long, 12 to 20 miles wide, with gentle hills and cliffs above Long Island Sound and sandspit beaches fronting the Atlantic Ocean. Nearly 7 million people live here, more than in all but nine states, 4.3 million in the New York City boroughs of Brooklyn and Queens and 2.7 million in the suburban counties of Nassau and Suffolk. Brooklyn, at the western end of the island, is urban and thickly settled, while the Hamptons at the east end are carefully manicured countryside, preserved by a stylish New York elite. The Hamptons and the old whaling village of Sag Harbor, originally settled by New Englanders, were left behind in the rush of westward migration; today they appear more comfortable than grand, a shingled and windmilled portion of middle America kept more pristine than workaday middle America ever was.

But demographically, the Hamptons are only a small (though growing) part of Long Island. More important are the (no longer growing) suburbs created in the rush eastward into what was once farmland after World War II. Developers looked for cheaper land for aircraft factories and shopping centers, subdivisions and office parks, and found them first in Nassau County just east of Queens, and then in Suffolk County. Suffolk attracted young families, of Irish and Italian descent more often than Jewish or black, looking for more ground and trees and less crime and tension than in their city neighborhoods. Politically, Suffolk County was long one of the most conservative parts of New York. It has also become turbulent political territory, as life in Long Island has turned sour in the last decade. Defense plants shut down and jobs evaporated as the defense buildup and then the Cold War ended. Lilco, the local electric utility, had cost overruns on its nuclear plant in Shoreham, and then went into bankruptcy after Governor Mario Cuomo shut the plant down, giving Long Island the nation's highest electric rates. The partial state takeover of Lilco, brokered by Governor George Pataki, was designed to cut rates, but they are still among the nation's highest.

The 1st Congressional District covers eastern Suffolk County, running east from Smithtown on the North Shore and Patchogue on the South Shore. It includes the Hamptons but, more important politically, the Brookhaven National Laboratory and the defense plants in the center of the Island. Politically, this is a Republican area willing in times of discontent to vote for Democrats with some special claim on support.

The congressman from the 1st District is Michael Forbes, a Republican elected in 1994. Forbes has roots in the East End, and a certain theatricalness. His grandfather was part of a vaudeville song and dance team, and founded *The News Review* in Riverhead. Forbes was voted the "most spirited" member of his class at Westhampton Beach High School. Though he grew up in a Democratic household, he got the political bug early, as a Republican. In 1971, at 19, he started working in the Suffolk County legislature; he worked for Speaker Perry Duryea of Montauk in the mid-1970s, then for Senator Alfonse D'Amato, Upstate conservative Democrat Sam Stratton, Florida Congressman (now Senator) Connie Mack, and for the 1988 and 1992

Bush campaigns. He was a Small Business Administration regional director in the Bush Administration, then a New York area staffer for the U.S. Chamber of Commerce.

In 1994 Forbes ran against Democratic Congressman George Hochbrueckner, a four-term member of the Armed Services Committee who tried to save jobs at Grumman and other Long Island contractors. But in September, Grumman announced another 3,500 layoffs, and voters turned to other issues. Forbes called for a balanced budget and tax incentives for small business and jobs. He was heavily outspent, but won 53%–47%, as national issues overcame local.

In the House Forbes has had close relations with Republican leaders but also a middle-of-the-House voting record. His 10-year acquaintance with Newt Gingrich helped him win a seat on Appropriations—unusual for a freshman—where he built a good relationship with Chairman Bob Livingston. But he also voted with Upstate Republican Sherwood Boehlert to strip 17 EPA riders in 1995, and in 1996 he tried to get a vote on the campaign finance bill. In 1996 he was hard pressed as Bill Clinton carried the district. But he heavily outspent his opponent, Suffolk County legislator Nora Bredes, a longtime opponent of the Shoreham nuclear plant whom he called a "sixties liberal" and denied that he was in lockstep with Gingrich. Forbes won 55%–45%. Then came his moment in the spotlight, in December 1996, when he was the first House Republican to announce he would not vote for Gingrich for speaker on January 7. Democrats and the press treated this as the beginning of the end for Gingrich; Republican leaders muttered that it was just personal ambition. Forbes ended up voting for Jim Leach for speaker, and eight other Republicans refused to vote for Gingrich; but he was re-elected nevertheless.

Forbes was shunned by some Republicans but suffered no serious retaliation. Meanwhile, he became close with local union leaders. "He did a 180 and now he's solid with us," said one; Forbes said, "I'm learning that everything isn't black and white," said Forbes. But in fact his overall voting record, already moderate, did not change hugely. He supported switching $20 billion from defense to education, backed Clinton's national testing standards and flew on *Air Force One* when Clinton visited the Hamptons in summer 1998. He also worked on many local issues, often with Senator Alfonse D'Amato. They worked to stop the reopening of Brookhaven National Laboratory after it was revealed in January 1997 that water with radioactive tritium was leaking from the reactor's spent fuel pool. He attacked the Energy Department for advertising its high flux beam nuclear reactor—to the point that some local businessmen started to complain that he was hurting the local economy. He worked in 1998 to get environmental clearance for a closed Navy facility in Calverton, though reopening was partly blocked because the unit's Hangar 6 was being used for the reconstruction of the TWA 800 aircraft that crashed off Long Island in July 1996. He and D'Amato helped acquire the Robinson Duck Farm for the Wertheim National Wildlife Reserve; he sought $19 million for research on algal blooms which hurt local fishing; he located two surplus Navy ships for the town of Brookhaven to use as ferries across Great South Bay to Fire Island. He sought to bar Navy dumping of contaminated sediment from Thames River into Long Island Sound in 1997. He worked to get the Smithsonian to drop the sponsorship of what he termed was an anti-Israel group for a program on Israel and, with John Fox, questioned the appointment of John Roth to a top spot at the Holocaust Museum.

Against an underfunded Democrat in 1998, Forbes was easily re-elected, 64%–36%. In early December, Livingston, then speaker-designate, named him one of his "assistants to the speaker." But both came on hard times. Forbes was attacked by some Republicans for giving money to two Democratic colleagues, New Jersey's Bill Pascrell and California's Loretta Sanchez. And, after being widely mentioned as a Republican vote against impeachment, he came out for it, leaving many Democrats and Hamptons denizens angry. In May 1999 he was one of six House Republicans to sign a Democratic petition to force a floor vote on campaign finance reform. Despite his big margin in 1998, he could have serious opposition in 2000; one possibility is Tony Bullock, chief of staff to retiring Senator Daniel Patrick Moynihan.

Cook's Call. *Safe.* This is the type of marginal district where the right Democratic challenger, in the right year, could give Forbes a race. But Forbes, who took great strides to distance himself from the Gingrich-led House, is hard to demonize as an extremist.

The People: Pop. 1990: 580,076; 7.8% rural; 12.3% age 65 +; 93.2% White, 4.1% Black, 1.7% Asian, 0.3% Amer. Indian, 0.8% Other; 4.4% Hispanic Origin. Households: 65.1% married couple families; 33.7% married couple fams. w. children; 49.5% college educ.; median household income: $45,464; per capita income: $17,614; median house value: $159,000; median gross rent: $674.

1996 Presidential Vote			1992 Presidential Vote		
Clinton (D)	118,187	(52%)	Bush (R)	101,160	(40%)
Dole (R)	83,956	(37%)	Clinton (D)	96,890	(38%)
Perot (I)	25,850	(11%)	Perot (I)	54,128	(21%)

Rep. Michael P. Forbes (R)

Elected 1994; b. July 16, 1952, Riverhead; home, Quogue; S.U.N.Y. Albany, B.A. 1983; Catholic; married (Barbara).

Professional Career: Staff asst., U.S. Sen. Alfonse D'Amato, 1980–83; Staff asst., U.S. Rep. Sam Stratton, 1983–84; A.A., U.S. Rep. Connie Mack, 1984–87; Owner, Forbes & Co. PR firm, 1987–89; Regional Admin., Small Business Admin., 1989–93; Regional Dir., U.S. Chamber of Commerce, 1993–94.

DC Office: 125 CHOB 20515, 202-225-3826; Fax: 202-225-3143; Web site: www.house.gov/forbes.

District Office: Shirley, 516-345-3400.

Committees: *Appropriations* (23d of 34 R): Energy & Water Development; Foreign Operations & Export Financing; Treasury, Postal Service & General Government. *Small Business* (13th of 19 R): Government Programs & Oversight; Tax, Finance & Exports.

Group Ratings

	ADA	ACLU	AFS	LCV	CON	NTU	NFIB	COC	ACU	NTLC	CHC
1998	65	33	67	92	13	38	50	61	46	46	75
1997	30	—	25	—	23	57	—	60	70	—	—

National Journal Ratings

	1997 LIB — 1997 CONS			1998 LIB — 1998 CONS		
Economic	53%	—	46%	52%	—	48%
Social	36%	—	64%	46%	—	54%
Foreign	43%	—	57%	33%	—	66%

Key Votes of the 105th Congress

1. Clinton Budget Deal	Y	5. Puerto Rico Sthood. Ref.	Y	9. Cut $ for B-2 Bombers	N
2. Education IRAs	Y	6. End Highway Set-asides	N	10. Human Rights in China	Y
3. Req. 2/3 to Raise Taxes	Y	7. School Prayer Amend.	Y	11. Withdraw Bosnia Troops	Y
4. Fast-track Trade	N	8. Ovrd. Part. Birth Veto	Y	12. End Cuban TV-Marti	N

Election Results

1998 general	Michael P. Forbes (R-C-Ind-RTL)	99,460	(64%)	($874,633)
	William G. Holst (D-HMO)	55,630	(36%)	($50,454)
1998 primary	Michael P. Forbes (R)	unopposed		
1996 general	Michael P. Forbes (R-C-Ind-RTL)	116,620	(55%)	($918,162)
	Nora L. Bredes (D-SM)	96,496	(45%)	($394,083)

SECOND DISTRICT

Following World War II, hundreds of thousands of New York City residents—people who had trouble imagining they would live anywhere but the close-packed city streets—moved to what had been the potato fields of central Long Island. The highways that Robert Moses built to connect Jones Beach with the city masses were the routes of that migration—and often the daily commuter paths back into New York—as young veterans and their families found they could afford to leave the row-house neighborhoods where they had grown up for the single-family houses of Levittown and other Long Island subdivisions. The first wave of postwar migration moved into Nassau County, and it was largely a cross-section of all but the poorest New Yorkers: about half Catholic, with the other half split almost evenly between Jews and Protestants. As Long Island developed its own employment base, another wave moved farther east into Suffolk County. This group was more Catholic and less Jewish than the first, and more blue-collar. It was ancestrally Democratic, but firmly traditional and culturally conservative.

The 2d Congressional District includes most of western Suffolk County. The bulk of the district's population is concentrated in the South Shore townships of Babylon and Islip, with dozens of suburbs in each. There are some spacious houses with views of the Great South Bay and, across the bay—but still within the district—lie the beaches of Fire Island, where many of the homes are weekend retreats owned by affluent New York City residents. But, for the most part, the 2d is the lower-income part of Long Island, beyond the more fashionable and expensive commuter suburbs to the west and well south of the picturesque North Shore. This area filled up with people in the 1950s and 1960s but has grown little in the past quarter century. However, with some of the lowest-priced housing on the Island, it continues to attract young families. Almost 10% of the 2d is Hispanic, the largest percentage of any of the Long Island districts.

The congressman from the 2d District is Rick Lazio, a Republican elected in 1992. Lazio grew up in West Islip on the South Shore. After Vassar and law school in Washington, he was a prosecutor and, after 1989, a legislator in Suffolk County; he has been in the public sector since age 25. In 1992 he ran against Congressman Thomas Downey, a Democrat elected in 1974 at 25, the kind of natural politician who helped Democrats maintain majorities for 20 years. Lazio attacked Downey as part of the Washington culture out of touch with Long Island, for junketing and for his 151 overdrafts on the House bank. Downey spent $1.4 million to Lazio's $276,000, but Lazio won 53%–47%.

This was a presage of 1994 Republican victories, but Lazio has not been exactly a Contract With America Republican, though he did call for congressional reform and promised to serve no more than six consecutive terms. His voting record has been in the middle of the House: he supported the Brady bill, the assault weapons ban, the striker replacement bill, and family leave. He has worked behind the scenes on some issues, trying to maintain good ties with the leadership; one such is the National Endowment for the Arts, on which he refused to back block grants but instead backed increased federal funding.

Lazio served on the Budget Committee in his first two terms and in 1996 got a waiver from the rules to take a seat on Commerce while retaining the chairmanship of the Banking Subcommittee on Housing and Community Opportunity. For four years he worked on reforming the public housing laws, disagreeing often with the Senate and with HUD Secretary Andrew Cuomo and finally arriving at a compromise that passed nearly unanimously in October 1998. One goal was to reduce the percentage of very poor public housing tenants, which he argues leaves projects too often overwhelmed by crime. The law allows housing authorities to set a minimum of as low as 40% for very poor tenants, to let them charge minimum rents and to set higher income levels for Community Development Block Grants and the HOME low-income home-buying program. To give tenants an incentive to move up the economic ladder, their rent would not increase if they got a job, and they could be required to get a job or perform eight hours of community service. It also increased the number of Section 8 vouchers from 1.4 million by 90,000 in 1999 and 100,000 each in 2000 and 2001. "Who says Republicans don't have an urban policy?" he asked after the law passed the House. "To know that if I do nothing else, I will have helped save some of these parents, helped save some of these children from a life of despair and virtually zero opportunity and give them a chance to make it . . . I'll feel pretty darned satisfied about my contributions here in Congress." He also pushed a bill to protect elderly homeowners from "reverse mortgage" scams and a Homeowners Insurance Availability Act with a fail-safe claims-paying mechanism in cases of natural disaster; Long Island has been hit more than once by hurricanes.

On local issues, he got money for a federal courthouse in Central Islip and for Touro Law Center to move there; he got Weed and Seed money for low-income Suffolk neighborhoods, a toll-free line on medical research on life-threatening illnesses and $5 million for monitoring Fire Island beach erosion. Newt Gingrich let Lazio and not Michael Forbes (who had voted against him for speaker) make the announcement of reimbursement for Long Island agencies who responded to the TWA 800 crash in July 1996. He often worked with Senator Alfonse D'Amato on these projects and after D'Amato was defeated in November 1998 said, "I think it means I'm going to have to work a lot harder for Long Island."

Lazio has been re-elected easily three times and by 1997 was beginning to contemplate running for senator in 2000. The impeachment issue put him on the spot. He was on everyone's list of New York Republicans likely to vote against impeachment in November and December 1998, and was heavily lobbied by voters and activists on both sides. Days before the vote he traveled on *Air Force One* to the Middle East, as a guest of the Republican leadership, and spoke briefly to Clinton. In the end he voted for impeachment—a vote unlikely to hurt him much in the 2d District, but which could hurt in a statewide campaign. But, with nearly $2 million in cash on hand after the 1998 election, and despite the possible candidacies of such big names as Rudolph Giuliani and Hillary Rodham Clinton, he continued to contemplate a Senate run well into 1999. He argued that he could best represent ordinary New Yorkers who want to cut taxes and get better government and had shown he can work with other legislators for sensible compromise solutions—not exactly the style of either Giuliani or Clinton. There was speculation in spring 1999 that he would be supported by George Pataki against his ofttime rival Giuliani, but there is reason to believe that on his own Lazio could be a strong candidate. The overwhelming majority of Republican primary voters are cast outside New York City, very many on Long Island and by Italian-Americans, which fits Lazio's profile exactly. In his moderate voting record and penchant for working of local projects, he resembles D'Amato, who won three Senate races (and beat a New York City-based favorite in the Republican primary) before he lost his fourth. If Lazio should be the nominee against Hillary Rodham Clinton, he will instantly become an important national political figure, lose or (especially) win.

Cook's Call. *Potentially Competitive.* If Lazio does decide to run for the open Senate seat of Democrat Patrick Moynihan, this swing district should be highly contested in 2000. If he stays in the House, the well-entrenched Lazio, who has not had a hotly contested race since he won the seat in 1992, will be safe.

The People: Pop. 1990: 580,303; 0.1% rural; 10% age 65 + ; 85.6% White, 9.7% Black, 1.6% Asian, 0.2% Amer. Indian, 2.8% Other; 9.4% Hispanic Origin. Households: 66.4% married couple families; 33.9% married couple fams. w. children; 45% college educ.; median household income: $50,076; per capita income: $17,515; median house value: $159,600; median gross rent: $717.

1996 Presidential Vote

Clinton (D)	108,598	(55%)
Dole (R)	68,710	(35%)
Perot (I)	20,419	(10%)

1992 Presidential Vote

Bush (R)	92,762	(41%)
Clinton (D)	91,430	(40%)
Perot (I)	44,603	(19%)

Rep. Rick A. Lazio (R)

Elected 1992; b. Mar. 13, 1958, West Islip; home, Brightwaters; Vassar Col., B.A. 1980, American U., J.D. 1983; Catholic; married (Patricia Moriarty).

Elected Office: Suffolk Cnty. legislator, 1989–92.

Professional Career: Asst. Dist. Atty., Suffolk Cnty., 1983–88; Practicing atty., 1989–92.

DC Office: 2444 RHOB 20515, 202-225-3335; Fax: 202-225-4669; Web site: www.house.gov/lazio.

District Office: Babylon, 516-893-9010.

Committees: *Banking & Financial Services* (6th of 32 R): Housing & Community Opportunity (Chmn.). *Commerce* (19th of 29 R): Finance & Hazardous Materials; Health and Environment.

Group Ratings

	ADA	ACLU	AFS	LCV	CON	NTU	NFIB	COC	ACU	NTLC	CHC
1998	40	25	44	77	13	43	79	89	52	50	73
1997	30	—	25	—	88	50	—	80	65	—	—

National Journal Ratings

	1997 LIB — 1997 CONS		1998 LIB — 1998 CONS	
Economic	51% —	49%	46% —	53%
Social	46% —	53%	53% —	47%
Foreign	43% —	57%	49% —	48%

Key Votes of the 105th Congress

1. Clinton Budget Deal	Y	5. Puerto Rico Sthood. Ref.	Y	9. Cut $ for B-2 Bombers	Y
2. Education IRAs	Y	6. End Highway Set-asides	N	10. Human Rights in China	N
3. Req. 2/3 to Raise Taxes	Y	7. School Prayer Amend.	Y	11. Withdraw Bosnia Troops	N
4. Fast-track Trade	Y	8. Ovrd. Part. Birth Veto	Y	12. End Cuban TV-Marti	N

Election Results

1998 general	Rick A. Lazio (R-C)	85,089	(66%)	($1,451,458)
	John C. Bace (D)	37,949	(30%)	
	Others	5,400	(4%)	
1998 primary	Rick A. Lazio (R)	unopposed		
1996 general	Rick A. Lazio (R-C)	112,135	(64%)	($574,460)
	Kenneth J. Herman (D-Ind)	57,953	(33%)	($14,487)
	Others	4,506	(3%)	

THIRD DISTRICT

It was a pivotal moment in American suburban history: in September 1947, families moved into 300 tiny 750-square-foot houses, built in record time by mass production. They sold for $6,990, with no down payment for veterans. This was Levittown, and by the time the last new house was sold for $9,500 in November 1951, the name had become a synonym for rapid suburban development. Developer William Levitt recognized that many young veterans and their families were eager to move out of crowded New York City neighborhoods, so he bought a Nassau County potato field, planted trees, designed floor plans to allow easy additions and built a community of 65,000 people. As Levittown celebrated its 50th anniversary in 1997, few of the original four-room bungalows could be found, but homes are still affordable. And if school enrollment has dropped here, and retiree workshops have cropped up, it only reflects the trend toward empty nesters that can be seen in the rest of Nassau County. In 1940 the county population was 450,000; by 1960 it was 1.3 million and 1.4 million in 1970; then it went back to around 1.3 million by 1990 as youngsters moved out.

Nassau County also is home to what may be the nation's premier county Republican machine. It was the creation of Nassau Republican Chairman J. Russell Sprague before the postwar population boom. Sprague managed to carry the county for Alf Landon in 1936 and that same year persuaded the voters to adopt a county executive form of government in which control of political patronage would center in one man, responsible to the county Republican chairman. The result now is one of the most high-salaried, high-spending local governments in America, and a Republican political machine that vies in size and power with the Democratic big city machines of old.

The 3d Congressional District includes nearly half of Nassau County. Most of the people in the district live in towns strung along either side of Sunrise Highway or just off the Southern or Northern State Parkways from Levittown and Hicksville, east to the county line. The district also includes Bethpage, home to the old Grumman aircraft company, once a big employer here and now part of Northrop Grumman. The northern geographic half of the district, with about one-fifth of the population, includes the old estate areas around Oyster Bay, Old Westbury and Manhasset. Not many of greater New York's wealthiest live in the 3d, but the overall level of affluence is high, and the district has the third highest median income of any in the nation, just behind the New Jersey 11th and Maryland 8th. The 3d tends to be pretty solidly Republican, although Democrats are sometimes competitive here, and Bill Clinton carried the district by a wide margin in 1996.

The congressman from the 3d District is Peter King, a Republican first elected in 1992. King grew up in Sunnyside, Queens; his parents were Irish immigrants and Democrats, his father an NYPD detective. He went to St. Francis College and law school at Notre Dame, and clerked one summer at Richard Nixon's law firm with a Long Islander named Rudolph Giuliani. After school he followed the trek to the suburbs and became part of the Nassau County Republican machine. He started working as a lawyer and staffer in county government in 1972, at 28; in 1981 he became Nassau County comptroller. When 22-year incumbent Republican Norman Lent announced his retirement in June 1992, King ran and won the Republican primary 2–1. In the general he faced a Democrat who spent $700,000 of his own money and ran as a reformer and supporter of abortion rights. King ran as a political insider, fiscal conservative and abortion opponent, and won by just 50%–46%.

King has a middle-of-the-House voting record, more conservative on cultural issues, but with distinctive interests and accents. He came to the House as one of the country's strongest supporters of the Irish Republican Army; within days of his election in 1992 he flew to Belfast to meet with leaders of Sinn Fein, the IRA's political arm. He urged the Clinton Administration to drop travel and fundraising restrictions on Sinn Fein leader Gerry Adams. He insisted that Northern Ireland negotiations include Sinn Fein, and in 1997 when Jesse Helms demanded that the IRA be labeled a terrorist organization, he wrote him, "Your October 20 letter to President Clinton regarding the Irish Republican Army literally reeks of bigotry and ignorance." In the April 1998 negotiations finale, King carried messages between the IRA and the Irish government. In the process he became close to, among others, President Clinton; in August 1998 Clinton took him on *Air Force One* to Russia and Ireland and had a long late-night conversation with him.

King is not so close to Clinton on many other issues. He is against abortion, racial quotas and preferences, bilingual education, gun control and the National Endowment for the Arts. He denounced the hiring of Louis Farrakhan's groups to police public housing projects. He is for English-only laws and against aid to illegal immigrants. He sponsored a bill to deduct from foreign aid 110% of the amount owed by foreign countries on New York City parking tickets.

He is unapologetic about being a machine politician—he wrote a college paper on ousted New York Mayor Jimmy Walker—and seethes against proposals for campaign finance reform. He has come out forthrightly for congressional pay raises.

King often seems more comfortable with Democrats and labor leaders—the kind of people he dealt with in Nassau County, than with Southern or Western Republicans, for whom he seems to have no more affinity than Ulster Protestants. In 1996, when Republican leaders resisted a minimum wage increase, he said they were driving people toward Clinton: "We're going to turn ourselves into a party of barefoot hillbillies who go to revival meetings." In 1997 he criticized Peter Hoekstra's investigation of labor unions. He called for Newt Gingrich to step down after the 1996 elections and in March 1997 wrote in the *Weekly Standard*, "As roadkill on the highway of American politics, Newt Gingrich cannot sell the Republican agenda. So instead of replacing Newt, the Republican leadership has replaced the agenda . . . Congressional Republicans are adrift." But he did not support the July 1997 coup against Gingrich, on the ground that it made no sense to change leaders in mid-term, and in a chance meeting with Gingrich afterward at the Dubliner pub they were persuaded by Senator Alfonse D'Amato (a 3d District resident) to shake hands.

On impeachment King played a visible but not pivotal role. He was torn by party loyalty and his closeness to Clinton and support of his Northern Ireland policy. He voted for an impeachment inquiry in October, but in December worked for a censure with a financial penalty. He contended that the "reform politics," which included the independent counsel law, had produced a situation that made little sense and threatened to make Republicans a minority again. He said publicly that as many as 20 Republicans were prepared to vote against impeachment; in the end only five, including King, did.

What effect did this have on King's electoral prospects? In 1994 and 1996 he was outspent by self-financed Democrats but won 59%–40% and 55%–42%. (The second opponent, owner of a tweezer company, ran as "Mr. Tweezerman" and was fined by the Federal Election Commission in February 1999 for handing out 10,000 tweezers.) In 1998 he faced a hapless Nassau County patronage employee and won 64%–35%. King has been mentioned as a possible Senate candidate in 2000; his anti-impeachment vote might help him in a general election, but could be a liability in a Republican primary; and in early 1999 few expected he would run. In the House, King suffered little visible retribution for his apostasy. "There's a small majority, so the Republicans will have to deal with the cards they're dealt, and I'm one of the cards," he said shortly after the election. "Hope I'm not the joker." Not at first, anyway. In 1997 Republican leaders maneuvered to keep King from getting the Africa Subcommittee chair. But in January 1999 they acquiesced in giving him the chair of the Banking General Oversight and Investigations Subcommittee, a good platform for high-visibility hearings. With his brash good humor, King may take advantage of it.

Cook's Call. *Safe.* The outspoken King made few friends among Republicans during the impeachment hearings, but he is safely ensconced in his Long Island-based seat.

The People: Pop. 1990: 580,468; 0.4% rural; 14.1% age 65 + ; 94.4% White, 2% Black, 2.7% Asian, 0.1% Amer. Indian, 0.9% Other; 4.1% Hispanic Origin. Households: 69.3% married couple families; 30.6% married couple fams. w. children; 54.7% college educ.; median household income: $56,060; per capita income: $23,702; median house value: $205,300; median gross rent: $724.

1996 Presidential Vote			1992 Presidential Vote		
Clinton (D)	136,505	(54%)	Clinton (D)	126,120	(44%)
Dole (R)	97,034	(38%)	Bush (R)	121,167	(42%)
Perot (I)	18,975	(8%)	Perot (I)	40,446	(14%)

Rep. Peter T. King (R)

Elected 1992; b. Apr. 5, 1944, Manhattan; home, Seaford; St. Francis Col., B.A. 1965, U. of Notre Dame, J.D. 1968; Catholic; married (Rosemary).

Military Career: Army Natl. Guard, 1968–73.

Elected Office: Hempstead Town Cncl., 1977–81; Nassau Cnty. Comptroller, 1981–92.

Professional Career: Practicing atty., 1968–72, 1978–81; Dep. Atty., Nassau Cnty., 1972–74; Exec. Asst., Nassau Cnty. Exec., 1974–76, Gen. Cnsl., 1977.

DC Office: 403 CHOB 20515, 202-225-7896; Fax: 202-226-2279; Web site: www.house.gov/king.

District Office: Massapequa Park, 516-541-4225.

Committees: *Banking & Financial Services* (9th of 32 R): Capital Markets, Securities & Government Sponsored Enterprises; General Oversight & Investigations (Chmn.). *International Relations* (14th of 26 R): Asia & the Pacific; International Operations and Human Rights.

Group Ratings

	ADA	ACLU	AFS	LCV	CON	NTU	NFIB	COC	ACU	NTLC	CHC
1998	10	13	33	15	31	52	79	82	76	71	100
1997	25	—	63	—	13	36	—	40	64	—	—

National Journal Ratings

	1997 LIB	—	1997 CONS	1998 LIB	—	1998 CONS
Economic	49%	—	51%	43%	—	56%
Social	20%	—	71%	34%	—	64%
Foreign	56%	—	42%	49%	—	48%

Key Votes of the 105th Congress

1. Clinton Budget Deal	Y	5. Puerto Rico Sthood. Ref.	Y	9. Cut $ for B-2 Bombers	N
2. Education IRAs	Y	6. End Highway Set-asides	Y	10. Human Rights in China	Y
3. Req. 2/3 to Raise Taxes	Y	7. School Prayer Amend.	Y	11. Withdraw Bosnia Troops	N
4. Fast-track Trade	Y	8. Ovrd. Part. Birth Veto	Y	12. End Cuban TV-Marti	N

Election Results

1998 general	Peter T. King (R-C-RTL)	117,258	(64%)	($278,908)
	Kevin N. Langberg (D)	63,628	(35%)	
	Others	1,497	(1%)	
1998 primary	Peter T. King (R)	6,521	(78%)	
	Robert Previdi (R)	1,819	(22%)	
1996 general	Peter T. King (R-C-FR)	127,972	(55%)	($645,951)
	Dal A. LaMagna (D-Ind)	97,518	(42%)	($1,083,576)
	Others	5,936	(3%)	

FOURTH DISTRICT

Garden City is one of America's first suburbs, created more than a century ago by New York retailer A.T. Stewart at a time when reformers wanted to maintain the commercial vitality and social interaction of the city, but in a setting that preserved the healthful openness of the countryside. Garden City's wide avenues and single-family homes, connected to New York City by the Long Island Railroad, were intended to be middle-income territory, but its amenities have made it one of the highest-income parts of Long Island. In the century after its founding, the rest of Nassau County has changed from almost entirely rural to suburban. The big rush came after World War II, as one town ran into another, freeways replaced strip highways, and shopping centers sprang up at intersections. Today, many of the middle- and upper-income residents of the 4th Congressional District still depend on the Long Island Railroad to get them to jobs in New York City. But once-removed Garden City now sits amid Nassau County's civic institutions just south of the county seat of Mineola and the site of Roosevelt Field, where Charles Lindbergh took off for Paris. Almost 60 years later, Roosevelt Field is a large suburban shopping center, with the Nassau Coliseum—home to hockey's New York Islanders—nearby.

The 4th District includes Garden City and the civic center of Nassau County. It includes half of Levittown and the neat and conservative suburbs along the Queens line from New Hyde Park to Valley Stream; it takes in the "Five Towns"—Lawrence, Inwood, Cedarhurst, Hewlett and Woodmere—near Kennedy Airport's flight paths. Nassau County has traditionally been Republican, and Garden City and heavily Catholic suburbs like Elmont and East Meadow are solidly Republican. But about one-quarter of the residents here are either black or Hispanic, and the Five Towns are heavily Democratic. The 4th District has voted mostly Republican in local and state politics, but it has also voted twice for Bill Clinton. And its congressional politics has proved to be a bit quirky, as it has elected four different people to the House in the 1990s.

The congresswoman from the 4th District is Carolyn McCarthy, elected as a Democrat in 1996. She was born in Brooklyn, trained as a nurse, married and raised a family on Long Island; originally, she was a Republican. In 1993 her husband was killed and her son seriously injured in the "Long Island Railroad Massacre," when a black gunman opened fire on passengers as the train crossed the Nassau County line (he said he did not want to kill anyone in New York City lest he embarrass Mayor David Dinkins). McCarthy spoke movingly at Colin Ferguson's trial and her strength in tragedy won her many admirers. "You took away my husband," she said directly to Ferguson. "You took away my best friend." She began campaigning for gun control, and in 1995 lobbied 4th District Congressman Daniel Frisa to vote against the repeal of the assault weapons ban, unsuccessfully.

McCarthy made inquiry about running against Frisa in the primary, but Nassau County Republicans discouraged this. But Democrats had been eyeing the seat for some time and recruited her. McCarthy initially knew little about politics. When she was told that Minority Leader Dick Gephardt wanted to meet her, she reportedly asked, "Who's Dick Gephardt?" But she learned quickly. With the Democratic nomination in hand, she called for gun control and attacked Frisa as too close to Newt Gingrich. The political tide was clearly going her way, and Frisa disappeared in the last week of the campaign, did not show up at his election night party and never made a concession statement. On election day McCarthy won 57%–41%.

In her first term McCarthy compiled a moderately liberal voting record and sponsored gun control measures. She called for childproof locks on handguns, and fines for parents if a child gets a handgun and shows it in public and jail terms if a crime is committed with it. She beat John Murtha's September 1997 amendment to allow import of World War II-era firearms and sought to ban the sale of guns to temporary visitors to the United States. She successfully sponsored a $250 million grant program for teacher training and a $7 million grant for water supply in Hempstead village. She worked hard and surprised people on some votes, opposing the partial-birth abortion ban and backing the Republicans' impeachment investigation resolution. In May 1998 a TV movie of McCarthy's story was broadcast; the National Rifle Association said it was inaccurate and Nassau County Republican Chairman Joseph Mondello said, "That's one hell of a campaign advertisement." But she declined a contract to write a book in time for the movie.

Republicans thrashed around to line up opposition: Frisa ran ads in early 1998 but withdrew from the race in July 1998; Mondello even pondered running. The ultimate Republican nominee was 16-year Assemblyman Gregory Becker, from an ancestral Long Island Republican family; his grandfather moved to Lynbrook in 1905 and served in the House from 1953–65; his father was mayor of Lynbrook; his uncle is a district leader who feuded with Mondello. Becker ran ads saying McCarthy was too liberal for the district and called her a "media star." She replied, "It is mean-spirited, it is extremely hurtful. . . . I certainly didn't choose this path, and if I could change the clock back, I would rather not go through any of it." But Mondello spoke patronizingly about Becker and he was outraised almost 3–1 by McCarthy. She insisted she was not very partisan: "I don't get up in the morning thinking I am a Republican or a Democrat. I am just a person who went into office." But after her impeachment inquiry votes, all registered Democrats got phone calls with a tape of Clinton endorsing her.

This turned out to be a closer election than most expected. McCarthy won in this pro-incumbent year by just 53%–47%. She was the first incumbent since 1990 re-elected to this seat, but it could easily be seriously contested again in 2000.

Cook's Call. *Competitive.* McCarthy's less than impressive win in 1998 highlights just how marginal this district is. Her personal story is her biggest asset, but she can no longer simply rely on her outsider appeal to win races here. Plus, McCarthy could feel the impact of a down year for Democrats nationally in this conservative-minded district.

The People: Pop. 1990: 580,492; 15.4% age 65 + ; 78.5% White, 16.3% Black, 3% Asian, 0.2% Amer. Indian, 2% Other; 7.1% Hispanic Origin. Households: 63.7% married couple families; 29% married couple fams. w. children; 50.1% college educ.; median household income: $50,887; per capita income: $20,349; median house value: $197,800; median gross rent: $639.

1996 Presidential Vote			1992 Presidential Vote		
Clinton (D)	131,825	(57%)	Clinton (D)	119,947	(47%)
Dole (R)	83,750	(36%)	Bush (R)	106,016	(41%)
Perot (I)	14,493	(6%)	Perot (I)	30,476	(12%)

Rep. Carolyn McCarthy (D)

Elected 1996; b. Jan. 5, 1944, Brooklyn; home, Mineola; Glen Cove Nursing Schl., L.P.N. 1964; Catholic; widowed.

Professional Career: Nurse, 1964–93; Gun control activist, 1993–96.

DC Office: 1725 LHOB 20515, 202-225-5516; Fax: 202-225-5758; Web site: www.house.gov/carolynmccarthy.

District Office: Hempstead, 516-489-7066.

Committees: *Education & the Workforce* (15th of 22 D): Early Childhood, Youth & Families; Employer-Employee Relations. *Small Business* (4th of 17 D): Tax, Finance & Exports (RMM).

Group Ratings

	ADA	ACLU	AFS	LCV	CON	NTU	NFIB	COC	ACU	NTLC	CHC
1998	90	75	89	92	26	26	43	61	24	18	8
1997	80	—	75	—	56	35	—	50	16	—	—

National Journal Ratings

	1997 LIB — 1997 CONS		1998 LIB — 1998 CONS	
Economic	64% —	36%	61% —	37%
Social	82% —	15%	73% —	25%
Foreign	76% —	22%	61% —	37%

Key Votes of the 105th Congress

1. Clinton Budget Deal	Y	5. Puerto Rico Sthood. Ref.	Y	9. Cut $ for B-2 Bombers	Y
2. Education IRAs	N	6. End Highway Set-asides	N	10. Human Rights in China	Y
3. Req. 2/3 to Raise Taxes	Y	7. School Prayer Amend.	N	11. Withdraw Bosnia Troops	N
4. Fast-track Trade	N	8. Ovrd. Part. Birth Veto	N	12. End Cuban TV-Marti	Y

Election Results

1998 general	Carolyn McCarthy (D-Ind) 90,256	(53%)	($896,128)
	Gregory R. Becker (R-C-RTL) 79,984	(47%)	($298,760)
	Others 1,343	(1%)	
1998 primary	Carolyn McCarthy (D) .... unopposed		
1996 general	Carolyn McCarthy (D-Ind) 127,060	(57%)	($967,221)
	Dan Frisa (R-C-FR) 89,542	(41%)	($893,147)
	Others 4,414	(2%)	

FIFTH DISTRICT

The North Shore of Long Island is "Gatsby country," where peninsulas jutting out into the Sound are covered with vast green lawns leading to the mansions of America's great capitalists. Nineteenth Century millionaires commuted by steam yacht from Manhattan to their estates in what now is Queens or Nassau County. In the early 20th Century the richest people in business and entertainment spent their leisure time here, playing croquet while their servants unloaded bootleggers' boats at their private docks during Prohibition. Inland, behind the expansive lawns, Long Island was still farm country, with little villages clustered at railroad stations, occasional colonial era houses, and acres of billboard-strewn wasteland on the highways to New York City. But The City grew out. Affluent neighborhoods developed in Douglaston and Bayside on the water, just beyond the middle-class Flushing area of Queens inland. The Great Neck peninsula became a very affluent, mostly Jewish suburb. Farther out, on Sands Point and Oyster Bay, old estates alternated with more modest homes, originally built for servants, and newer subdivision mansions. Further east, in Suffolk County, affluent subdivisions grew up on hilly land above the bays and points.

The 5th Congressional District ties together a disparate collection of New York City neighborhoods and suburbs on or within a few miles of the North Shore. At several points the district is connected across open water, and anyone wishing to traverse its boundaries from one end of it to the other better be a good swimmer. About one-third of its votes are cast in Suffolk County, where the political leanings are conservative on cultural and economic issues. In the middle, with about one-quarter of the votes, are the North Shore communities of Nassau: the Jewish areas Democratic and liberal, the WASPy areas Republican but also culturally liberal. Half the district's population and about 40% of its voters are in the borough of Queens. Here along the Sound are the affluent double-house Bayside neighborhood, and higher-income Douglaston and Little Neck, next to the Nassau border—all Republican territory. A few blocks inland is Flushing, an old Dutch settlement from the 17th Century, with the Queens numbered-street grid superimposed on old Dutch trails; once heavily Jewish, this has become one of the biggest Chinese (mostly Taiwanese) communities in the country. The 5th also goes south almost to the Long Island Expressway, to pleasant homeowner neighborhoods like Fresh Meadows and Oakland Gardens. But even here, far from Manhattan and in relatively affluent areas, there are plenty of high-rises.

The congressman from the 5th District is Gary Ackerman, a Democrat first elected in a March 1983 special election. Ackerman grew up in Flushing, taught junior high school, ran an advertising agency, started the weekly *Queens Tribune* in 1970 and sold it to publisher Jerry Finkelstein in 1978. That same year he was elected to the New York Senate, where Democrats seem permanently in the minority. He won his seat in the House, from a district centered in the heavily Jewish apartment complexes in central Queens. Ackerman is a colorful character, who always wears a white carnation and lives on a houseboat in Washington (the *Unsinkable II*, successor to the *Unsinkable I*, which sunk); he hosts an annual "Taste of New York" fundraiser, featuring pastrami sandwiches and stuffed cabbage, with waiters imported from New York. Acerbic but humorous, he is a pungent speaker, with a humor that makes even opponents smile. On the roll call for speaker in January 1995, when he was second in alphabetical order, after Neil Abercrombie of Hawaii voted for Dick Gephardt, Ackerman said, "Move to close the roll!" During the impeachment inquiry debate, frustrated by time limits, he rose and said, "I move that when the House adjourn, we do so to Salem, a quaint village in the Commonwealth of Massachusetts whose history beckons us thence."

Ackerman has a solidly liberal voting record and a penchant for taking on worthy but usually neglected causes. When Democrats were in control, he was active on the International Relations Committee, devoting much attention to rescuing Ethiopian Jews and relieving government-caused famines in Ethiopia and Sudan. In October 1993 he chaired the Asia and the Pacific Subcommittee and was one of the few Americans ever to meet with North Korean dictator Kim Il Sung. On AIDS issues he has joined with Oklahoma Republican Tom Coburn ("one of the leaders of those people we used to call wackos," he said) to pass the 1996 "Baby AIDS" bill requiring HIV testing of newborns and disclosure of the results to the mother; the bill also bars insurers from terminating coverage because of AIDS test results. This measure had been opposed by Manhattan liberals, although many HIV-positive newborns can be saved if identified in time; it took some courage for Ackerman to brave the wrath of New York's left wing. He and Coburn worked to stop the Center for Disease Control from opposing this and got into the October 1998 omnibus bill $10 million to assist states in AIDS testing.

Ackerman has also looked after North Shore issues. He has opposed the inane postal regulation that requires Queens zip codes to be labeled only Jamaica, Long Island City, Flushing or Far Rockaway rather than the dozens of other community names or simply Queens. He got $5 million for the Glen Cove waterfront, an additional $500,000 for the Merchant Marine Academy in Kings Point, government-financed housing in East Northport (despite some local opposition) and helped to save the 200-year-old Coast Guard station at Easton's Neck from closing. He sought to open PX stores to veterans with disabilities of less than 100% and to keep open the East Garden City INS office. He has opposed the flag-burning amendment, criticized Pete Hoekstra's investigation of labor unions, and sought money to track down whether elderly German immigrants were Nazi war criminals.

The 1992 redistricting switched Ackerman to this less Democratic North Shore district in which two other incumbents also lived. But both retired, and Ackerman has made this a safe district. He won the primary in 1992 by just 60%–40% over consultant Hank Morris's mother and the general by just 52%–45% over a Republican who carried Suffolk County. In 1994 Republican Grant Lally spent heavily and held Ackerman to a 55%–43% victory; in 1998 Lally was fined $280,000 for having used his father's assets as his own. Ackerman beat Lally in 1996 and a retired New York policeman who had been working as "Mr. Mom" in 1998 by nearly 2–1 margins. Redistricting after the 2000 Census may pose a threat, since Ackerman has few friends in Albany and this long, thin district could easily be sliced up among its neighbors; the head of Governor George Pataki's New York City office ostentatiously moved into Great Neck in 1998. But Ackerman has survived tough threats before.

Cook's Call. *Safe.* Although he had a couple of tight races in the early 1990s when his district was heavily altered, Ackerman has made himself a safe seat here, unless, of course, redistricting changes this seat once again in 2002.

The People: Pop. 1990: 581,073; 0.8% rural; 16% age 65 + ; 84.2% White, 3.4% Black, 10.5% Asian, 0.1% Amer. Indian, 1.7% Other; 7% Hispanic Origin. Households: 62.3% married couple families; 26.5% married couple fams. w. children; 57.7% college educ.; median household income: $50,103; per capita income: $24,296; median house value: $256,900; median gross rent: $604.

1996 Presidential Vote

Clinton (D)	132,588	(61%)
Dole (R)	71,194	(33%)
Perot (I)	13,354	(6%)

1992 Presidential Vote

Clinton (D)	130,728	(52%)
Bush (R)	88,375	(35%)
Perot (I)	30,424	(12%)

Rep. Gary L. Ackerman (D)

Elected Mar. 1983; b. Nov. 19, 1942, Brooklyn; home, Jamaica Estates; Queens Col., B.A. 1965; Jewish; married (Rita).

Elected Office: NY Senate, 1978–83.

Professional Career: Jr. High schl. teacher, 1966–70; Editor & publisher, *Queens Tribune*, 1970–78; Pres., advertising agcy., 1972–78.

DC Office: 2243 RHOB 20515, 202-225-2601; Fax: 202-225-1589; Web site: www.house.gov/ackerman.

District Offices: Bayside, 718-423-2154; Huntington, 516-423-2154.

Committees: *Banking & Financial Services* (10th of 27 D): Capital Markets, Securities & Government Sponsored Enterprises; Financial Institutions & Consumer Credit. *International Relations* (4th of 23 D): Asia & the Pacific; Western Hemisphere (RMM).

Group Ratings

	ADA	ACLU	AFS	LCV	CON	NTU	NFIB	COC	ACU	NTLC	CHC
1998	100	88	100	92	68	14	14	35	0	3	0
1997	80	—	86	—	32	27	—	33	13	—	—

National Journal Ratings

	1997 LIB	—	1997 CONS	1998 LIB	—	1998 CONS
Economic	85%	—	10%	79%	—	0%
Social	85%	—	0%	90%	—	7%
Foreign	78%	—	21%	78%	—	19%

Key Votes of the 105th Congress

1. Clinton Budget Deal	N	5. Puerto Rico Sthood. Ref.	Y	9. Cut $ for B-2 Bombers	N
2. Education IRAs	N	6. End Highway Set-asides	N	10. Human Rights in China	Y
3. Req. 2/3 to Raise Taxes	N	7. School Prayer Amend.	N	11. Withdraw Bosnia Troops	N
4. Fast-track Trade	N	8. Ovrd. Part. Birth Veto	N	12. End Cuban TV-Marti	N

Election Results

1998 general	Gary L. Ackerman (D-Ind-L)	97,404	(65%)	($486,401)
	David C. Pinzon (R-C)	49,586	(33%)	($8,918)
	Others	2,872	(2%)	
1998 primary	Gary L. Ackerman (D)	unopposed		
1996 general	Gary L. Ackerman (D-Ind-L)	125,918	(64%)	($1,123,926)
	Grant M. Lally (R-C-FR)	69,244	(35%)	($170,326)

SIXTH DISTRICT

New York City's largest middle-class black neighborhoods are not in Harlem or Brooklyn, but in the southeast corner of Queens. Here, in block on block of frame and brick one- and two-family houses built mostly from the 1920s to the 1950s, are the neighborhoods of Springfield Gardens and Laurelton, St. Albans and Rosedale, Cambria Heights and Queens Village, near Kennedy Airport and the tidal marsh of Jamaica Bay, just west of the Nassau County line. There was a small black community in South Jamaica half a century ago, and since then many black families have bought houses and raised their families in neighborhoods on the streets fanning east from Jamaica. They fought to maintain the relatively spacious streets, relishing unrefracted light in their windows, enjoying safe schools and good neighborhood stores.

The 6th Congressional District contains all of these southeast Queens neighborhoods, plus others less affluent and orderly, in southern Queens, roughly south of the Jackie Robinson and Grand Central parkways, including half of the Rockaway Peninsula across Jamaica Bay. It includes white ethnic Richmond Hill and Ozone Park as well as the heavily black neighborhoods in the southeast. In 1990, 53% of the people here were black, 16% Hispanic, 6% Asian and 23% non-Hispanic white. While there are pockets of poverty, the district is mostly middle-class country: the median income was $36,200, far ahead of the $19,000 to $27,000 of New York's other black-majority districts—indeed ahead of the $30,300 of Queens's white-majority 7th District. Politically, it is heavily Democratic, though one black-majority assembly district voted for Republican Mayor Rudolph Giuliani in 1997.

The congressman from the 6th District is Gregory Meeks, a Democrat elected in February 1998 to replace 11-year incumbent Floyd Flake, who resigned in November 1997 to devote more time to his church. Meeks grew up in Harlem, in public housing projects. After graduating from college and law school, he moved to Far Rockaway, Queens, and pursued a public sector career. He became an assistant district attorney in 1978, a staffer for the Committee on Investigations in 1984, a workmen's comp judge in 1985; after losing a race for City Council in 1991, was elected assemblyman in 1992. Like most members there, he voted along party lines; he voted to help livery cab drivers and against Megan's law, and worked to clean up the Dubos Point Wildlife Sanctuary in Arverne. In the course of his service, he became allied with Flake, an extraordinary minister who built his Allen A.M.E. Church from 1,400 members in 1976 to 11,000 in 1998, built community schools and hundreds of housing units and encouraged private sector investment in the community. Flake dissented from most of his fellow Democrats by backing school choice for central city students and said of his party, "much of our leadership is still mired in the rhetoric of the 1960s and 1970s." He supported Giuliani for mayor in 1997 and Senator Alfonse D'Amato in 1998; some Republicans would like to see him run for mayor in 2001.

Flake supported Meeks to succeed him, though the initial favorite was state Senator Alton Waldon, who lost to Flake in the 1986 Democratic primary. But at the January 9, 1998, endorsement meetings Meeks won a bare majority of committeemen and was the Democratic nominee. Waldon ran on the Conservative and Independence lines, and spent $100,000; Assemblywoman Barbara Clark ran an independent candidacy; Republicans had a candidate as well. But Meeks had support not only from Flake but from City Comptroller Alan Hevesi, Congressman Charles Rangel, Al Sharpton and Jesse Jackson. Meeks won with 57%, to 21% for Waldon and 13% for Republican Celestine Miller.

On winning Meeks said, "My role, as a part of a new generation of African-American leadership, is to take us to the new phase of the civil rights movement, that is, the economic development of our community." He got Flake's seat on the Banking Committee. In his first year he got $500,000 for classes on space technology in York College in Jamaica and $4 million for rebuilding Springfield Boulevard from the Long Island Railroad to Rockaway Boulevard. He was elected to a full term without opposition in November 1998.

Cook's Call. *Safe.* There are more heavily Democratic seats in New York City, but this is still a very safe seat and Meeks is a sure bet here in 2000.

The People: Pop. 1990: 581,812; 11.9% age 65 + ; 29.7% White, 56.1% Black, 6.3% Asian, 0.6% Amer. Indian, 7.4% Other; 16% Hispanic Origin. Households: 49.4% married couple families; 26.3% married couple fams. w. children; 37.9% college educ.; median household income: $36,223; per capita income: $13,150; median house value: $159,600; median gross rent: $515.

1996 Presidential Vote		1992 Presidential Vote	
Clinton (D) 128,166 (86%)		Clinton (D) 115,267 (76%)	
Dole (R) 15,960 (11%)		Bush (R) 27,919 (18%)	
Perot (I) 4,381 (3%)		Perot (I) 9,341 (6%)	

Rep. Gregory Meeks (D)

Elected Feb. 1998; b. Sept. 25, 1953, Harlem; home, Far Rockaway; Adelphi U., B.A., 1975, Howard U., J.D., 1978; Baptist; married (Simone-Marie).

Elected Office: NY Assembly, 1992–98.

Professional Career: Asst. Dist. Atty., Queens Co., NY, 1978–84; NY St. Comm. of Investigations, 1984–85; Judge, NY St. Workers Compensation Bd., 1985–92.

DC Office: 1710 LHOB 20515, 202-225-3461; Fax: 202-226-4169; Web site: www.house.gov/meeks.

District Offices: Far Rockaway, 718-327-9791; St. Albans, 718-949-5600.

Committees: *Banking & Financial Services* (18th of 27 D): Domestic & International Monetary Policy; Financial Institutions & Consumer Credit. *International Relations* (20th of 23 D): Africa; International Operations and Human Rights.

Group Ratings (Only Served Partial Term)

	ADA	ACLU	AFS	LCV	CON	NTU	NFIB	COC	ACU	NTLC	CHC
1998	85	92	100	77	59	18	0	33	5	11	33
1997	*	—	—	—	*	*	—	*	*	—	—

National Journal Ratings (Only Served Partial Term)

	1997 LIB — 1997 CONS			1998 LIB — 1998 CONS	
Economic	*	—	*	70% — 30%	
Social	*	—	*	93% — 0%	
Foreign	*	—	*	77% — 22%	

Key Votes of the 105th Congress (Only Served Partial Term)

1. Clinton Budget Deal	*	5. Puerto Rico Sthood. Ref.	Y	9. Cut $ for B-2 Bombers	*
2. Education IRAs	*	6. End Highway Set-asides	N	10. Human Rights in China	*
3. Req. 2/3 to Raise Taxes	N	7. School Prayer Amend.	N	11. Withdraw Bosnia Troops	N
4. Fast-track Trade	N	8. Ovrd. Part. Birth Veto	N	12. End Cuban TV-Marti	Y

Election Results

1998 general	Gregory Meeks (D-Ind-L) .... unopposed			($43,269)
1998 primary	Gregory Meeks (D) .... unopposed			
1998 special	Gregory Meeks (D) 14,224	(57%)		($51,432)
	Alton R. Waldon Jr. (C) 5,229	(21%)		($88,501)
	Barbara M. Clark (21C) 3,305	(13%)		($35,524)
	Celestine V. Miller (R) 2,209	(9%)		
	Others 206	(1%)		
1996 general	Floyd H. Flake (D) 102,799	(85%)		($165,311)
	Jorawar Misir (R-C-I-FR) 18,348	(15%)		($7,689)

SEVENTH DISTRICT

The borough of Queens, home of Shea Stadium and Forest Hills Stadium, site of the 1939 and 1964 World's Fairs, the home base of national politicians Mario Cuomo and Geraldine Ferraro, doesn't get much attention or respect, even though this two million-person borough on its own would be the nation's fourth-largest city. But Queens does not have well-known history. It started as nondescript farmland in the 17th Century, with villages growing quickly into urban nodes as the subways reached the borough. It has no obvious center, unlike downtown Brooklyn or the Grand Concourse in the Bronx. Even Queens Boulevard is just another arterial street, starting in the industrial mishmash around the Queensborough Bridge (usually referred to by its Manhattan name, 59th Street) and ending near the unimpressive brick Borough Hall, near the Grand Central Parkway overpass, across from the Pastrami King and Crossroads Drugs.

Yet Queens is still growing with great vitality around dozens of small hubs, not from a central point outward or directly from Manhattan. More than any other area of New York City, this is a borough of neighborhoods and of immigrants. It has high-income enclaves, like the old Tudor-mansioned Forest Hills. It has old ethnic communities, like Irish Sunnyside and College Point and German Ridgewood. Astoria, on the tip of Queens near the Triborough Bridge, is Greek-American and effervescently prosperous. Flushing, once mostly Jewish, is now heavily Chinese, the terminus of the Number 7 subway line known as the Orient Express. Indian and Pakistani immigrants own stores and restaurants, Koreans own fruit stands, Colombians and Irish and Dominicans shop in the bustling streets of Jackson Heights and Corona. Sixty years ago the small frame houses and stolid brick apartments of Queens neighborhoods adjacent to subway lines were the homes of the immigrant wave of the early 20th Century; now they are the home again of late 20th Century immigrants. New York's high taxes, its burdensome regulations, its housing shortage created by rent control, all impose burdens on these immigrants that were not borne by their predecessors. But with the aid of public schools, by no means all of which are hopeless, and the entrepreneurial-minded Queens Library with its dozens of branches, they are learning to be successful Americans, not fenced-off "multicultural" groups dependent on government for quotas and welfare.

The 7th Congressional District, loosely connected by narrow corridors, is a collection of Queens neighborhoods plus, over the Bronx-Whitestone Bridge, a salient of land running far into the Bronx, the boundaries of which for the 1992, 1994 and 1996 elections are nearly indescribable. A federal court overturned the boundaries of the adjacent "Bullwinkle" Hispanic-majority 12th District in 1997, and now the lines are somewhat more regular. Major landmarks include the Queensborough Bridge, LaGuardia Airport, Flushing Meadow, site of the still-remembered Trylon and Perisphere rising over the 1939 World's Fair and of Shea Stadium, the graceful Bronx-Whitestone Bridge and the giant Parkchester apartment complex and Yeshiva University in the Bronx. Fifty years ago most residents of Queens referred to Manhattan as "The City," and voted Republican, against the masters of Tammany Hall. Today, many still call Manhattan "The City" and, though they vote heavily Democratic in national elections, also gave a solid margin to Republican Mayor Rudolph Giuliani.

The congressman from the 7th District is Joseph Crowley, a Democrat effectively chosen by one man, his predecessor Tom Manton, in July 1998. Manton is a veteran Queens politician, head of the Queens County Democratic Party, a former Marine and cop elected councilman in 1969 and, after two primary losses in 1972 and 1978, congressman in 1984, when Geraldine Ferraro left to run for vice president. Crowley grew up in Woodside, where his family was involved in politics; his uncle Walter Crowley was elected to succeed Manton on the council in 1984. When Walter Crowley died in 1985, Crowley wanted to succeed him, though he was only 23; Manton chose his chief of staff, Walter McCaffrey, instead. In 1986 Assemblyman Ralph Goldstein from Elmhurst died; Crowley ran and, with support from Manton, won at 24, fresh from Queens College. Since 1993 he chaired the Racing and Waging Committee, working to revive harness racing and to get the city's Off-track Betting Corporation to make a profit (only the New York public sector could produce a bookie that loses money). Crowley was known as interested in Irish affairs and sponsored the law that requires public school students to be taught about the Irish potato famine. He supported legalized casino gambling and higher police pay; he opposed abortion. He played guitar and sang tenor with the Budget Blues Boys, a group of assemblymen who performed on cold Albany nights. Interestingly, his assembly district had high immigrant populations (28% Hispanic, 13% Asian), but Irish made up a disproportionate share of voters.

Crowley's elevation to Congress came suddenly. Manton filed for re-election by the July 16 filing deadline. Then at 11 a.m. on July 21, he convened a meeting of Queens Democratic committeemen, announced he was retiring and got them to vote in Crowley as the Democratic nominee. Other potential candidates were not notified ahead of time and were naturally miffed, but quickly accepted the reality. Manton was unapologetic: "After 29 years of service, I have the right to decide when I'm going to leave." Perhaps remembering the 1972 and 1978 primaries, he went on: "I'm not so sure primaries are a good indication, anyway. I find them expensive and divisive." He argued that Crowley, at 36, was in a good position to accumulate seniority and power in Washington. Crowley was plainly delighted: "What you're hearing is not so much about the process, but sour grapes. What happened here is simply that I was offered an ice cream cone, and I took it."

Local Republicans have long had a pact with Manton and have not run serious candidates in a seat in which their party in some years might have had a chance to win. Their 1998 nominee, a former Democrat who knew the local rules, had no money and no chance. Crowley raised over $200,000 but spent little of it, and won in November 69%–26%. But there are possible threats to his tenure. A number of Queens Democrats, including McCaffrey, Assemblywoman Cathy Nolan and Councilman John Sabini, are threatening to meet later this year and organize behind one of their candidacies to take on Crowley in the 2000 primary. In 2002 redistricting could change or wipe out the seat. In some later year an opponent from one of the many new ethnic groups could arise. And Republicans, if they tire of making judgeship deals with Manton (who remains county Democratic chairman), might seriously contest the seat.

Cook's Call. *Safe.* Crowley's only threat in this heavily Democratic district comes from other Democrats who were upset by the insider/backroom process which enabled him to win this seat in the first place. But this seat will almost certainly remain in Democratic hands.

The People: Pop. 1990: 580,116; 17.6% age 65 + ; 49.6% White, 8.6% Black, 13% Asian, 0.2% Amer. Indian, 0.4% Other; 28.3% Hispanic Origin. Households: 44.4% married couple families; 18.7% married couple fams. w. children; 36.5% college educ.; median household income: $30,324; per capita income: $14,905; median house value: $206,100; median gross rent: $471.

1996 Presidential Vote			1992 Presidential Vote		
Clinton (D)	94,661	(70%)	Clinton (D)	83,849	(56%)
Dole (R)	33,352	(25%)	Bush (R)	51,452	(35%)
Perot (I)	6,601	(5%)	Perot (I)	13,157	(9%)

Rep. Joseph Crowley (D)

Elected 1998; b. Mar. 16, 1962, Elmhurst, NY; home, Elmhurst; C.U.N.Y. Queens College, B.A. 1985; Catholic; married (Kasey).

Elected Office: NY Assembly, 1986–98.

DC Office: 1517 LHOB 20515, 202-225-3965; Fax: 202-225-1909; Web site: www.house.gov/crowley.

District Offices: Bronx, 718-931-1400; Jackson Heights, 718-779-1400.

Committees: *International Relations* (22d of 23 D): International Economic Policy & Trade. *Resources* (23d of 24 D): Forests & Forest Health; National Parks & Public Lands.

Group Ratings and Key Votes: Newly Elected

Election Results

1998 general	Joseph Crowley (D)	50,924	(69%)	($99,776)
	James J. Dillon (R)	18,896	(26%)	
	Richard Retcho (C)	3,960	(5%)	
1998 primary	Joseph Crowley (D) .... nominated by convention			
1996 general	Thomas J. Manton (D)	78,848	(71%)	($374,982)
	Rose Birtley (R-C-Ind)	32,092	(29%)	($62,209)

EIGHTH DISTRICT

For the last 200 years, New York has been a heavily Jewish city. New York's Dutch founders came from the European country most tolerant of Jews, and so Jews settled in Nieuw Amsterdam as they had in old. German Jews came in large numbers in the 19th Century, some insisting they were more German than they were Jewish; some founded great merchant banking dynasties. Around 1890, Ashkenazi Jews from Eastern Europe started coming from what were then the Romanov and Hapsburg empires—now Poland, Lithuania, Belarus, Ukraine, Hungary and Romania. Then, after being persecuted in the years after World War I, as many as 400,000 Jews came past the Statue of Liberty to Ellis Island every year in the early 1920s, until a 1924 law virtually shut down immigration. Had a malapportioned, rural-dominated, nativist Congress not done that, perhaps two million of the six million who perished in the Holocaust would instead have become Americans.

Ashkenazi Jews initially lived on the Lower East Side but moved out to Brooklyn and the Bronx almost as soon as the subways were built. Their children moved up faster than any new group in memorable history, rising despite prejudice to the top of almost every profession that would let them in. They invented new businesses from the rag trade to show biz: second-caste people from third-rate countries almost immediately becoming elite in the world's foremost country. Their descendants live all over the country, but New York remains America's most heavily Jewish city and has the largest Jewish population of any city in the world.

While there are no reliable figures, as the Census does not record religion, the 8th Congressional District of New York may be the most heavily Jewish district in the nation. About three-fifths of its population is in Manhattan, two-fifths in Brooklyn. Bizarre boundaries cordon off blacks and Hispanics in nearby majority-minority districts. One big voting area is the Upper West Side from 59th Street north to Morningside Heights and Columbia University: the venerable apartments along Central Park West and West End Avenue and Riverside Drive, and the brownstones on the cross streets which house some of America's most idealistic and dedicated liberal-to-radical voters. These professional people include the wealthy, as well as the struggling who enjoy the grittiness of the Upper West Side, the almost European atmosphere of boulevarded upper Broadway, and the fierce struggle that is daily life in New York. People on the West Side took up the reform issue in the 1950s and eventually eviscerated the old Tammany Hall Democratic machine; in the 1960s they took up the struggle against the Vietnam war and helped oust a Democratic administration. By the late 1980s their dominant cause was feminism, from the preservation of abortion rights against all erosion to the eradication of gender-incorrect speech. Another big voting area is Greenwich Village, America's original Bohemia in the 1910s, now a neighborhood of expensive apartments and houses interlaced with much cheaper dwellings, and New York's most conspicuous gay community. Politically the Village has long had a taste for what it regards as radical. Then there are new Village-type residential areas to the south: SoHo, where old factory buildings have been refurbished as lofts; TriBeCa, where commercial space now houses artists; Battery Park City, the attractive modern apartments built on a landfill west of the now-crumbled West Side Highway. After many years of decline, Manhattan's population has been rising in the 1990s, briskly in some of these neighborhoods—though it is still far below its peak in 1910, when the subways were just starting to siphon people to the outer boroughs.

The 8th District includes two Brooklyn neighborhoods: Brighton Beach and Coney Island, with the largest concentration of Russian Jewish immigrants in New York; and Borough Park, with many militantly pro-Israel Orthodox Jews. While they are connected to the heavily Jewish Manhattan neighborhoods by a narrow land bridge running along the Brooklyn waterfront and the massive Bush Terminal buildings, these areas are politically very different. The Russians favor free enterprise and are anti-socialist. Borough Park is hostile to racial preferences and favors tough police treatment of crime. Overall this is a very solidly Democratic district.

The congressman from the 8th District is Jerrold Nadler, a West Side liberal Democrat elected in 1992. He was born in Brooklyn and moved around; his father was a chicken farmer in New Jersey, ran a gas station on Long Island and owned a traveling auto parts store. At Stuyvesant High School in Manhattan he met Richard Gottfried (elected to the Assembly in 1970 at 23 and still there) and Dick Morris (pollster for Bill Clinton among others); they helped Nadler get elected student body president. At Columbia he roomed with Morris; they campaigned for Eugene McCarthy and were there during the 1968 campus riots. He worked as a legislative staffer and ran for the Assembly in 1976, at 29; in the primary he beat Ruth Messinger (Democratic nominee for mayor in 1997) by 73 votes. In the Assembly he was known as an expert on mass transit and advocate of rail freight into New York City. He voted there against the big tax cut of 1987.

In 1992 he was suddenly presented with the opportunity to run for Congress. Two incumbents were based in the new 8th District; Stephen Solarz of Brooklyn, a lead backer of the Gulf war resolution, shied away from running in leftish Manhattan and ran and lost in the Hispanic-majority 12th District. That left the 8th to Manhattan's Ted Weiss, long an Upper West Side icon. But he died the day before the September 1992 primary (which he won anyway). The nomination was decided by a convention of almost 1,000 county Democratic committee members, many of them involved in acerbic ideological and personal squabbles for decades. The key vote was procedural, for a system of weighted voting under which Nadler won 62% of the votes and Councilwoman Ronine Eldridge 21%; opponents decried this system (after they lost), perhaps with some reason. Nadler became the Democratic nominee and thus congressman.

Nadler's voting record has been among the most liberal in the House. Over the opposition of John Dingell, he pushed to passage the "Nadler rule" which restricted ranking members on full committees from taking any ranking subcommittee posts on their panels as well. He has opposed bankruptcy reform, saying the 1998 bill was "nothing more than a special interest favor to the big credit card companies and the big banks." He has fought developer Donald Trump's attempts to alter the West Side Highway to accommodate his luxury housing projects.

1120 NEW YORK

He opposed NAFTA in 1993 and welfare reform in 1996. He worked successfully to get Republican leaders not to schedule votes during Jewish holy days. He fought to get more rail competition east of the Hudson as Conrail was being carved up by CSX and the Norfolk Southern, and worked to save Amtrak. Nadler was also in the news in October 1998 when Senator Alfonse D'Amato, in a private meeting, called him "Jerry Waddler" and mimicked his movements. D'Amato later apologized, but Nadler said he considered weight jokes a form of bigotry.

His greatest project is a rail-freight tunnel under the Hudson, from the 65th Street rail yard in Bay Ridge to little-used rail yards in either Bayonne, New Jersey or Staten Island. Lack of a rail-freight line means that New York gets only about 3% of its freight from rails, compared to 30% in the average large city; cheaper freight could help rebuild small manufacturing in New York and could revive the Brooklyn docks, which were abandoned by Governor Nelson Rockefeller in an absent-minded moment in the 1960s. The cost would be huge—an estimated $900 million—but it could provide the manufacturing jobs New York has thoughtlessly cast away which could provide a way upward for the city's economy and its hundreds of thousands of new immigrants. Nadler's proposal was ridiculed for years. But he persisted. In 1997 Mayor Rudolph Giuliani endorsed it, and others have come to appreciate it as well; if it is ever built, it would be an impressive monument for a career.

Nadler achieved more prominence during the impeachment hearings in late 1998. He was one of several Judiciary members who peppered Republicans with questions, objections, high-minded arguments and low-minded ridicule in what Nadler called a "partisan coup d'etat." Nadler seemed to take delight in interjecting comments, and perhaps irritating Chairman Henry Hyde; but they also showed that he has a fine mind, a quick wit, an ability to make strong arguments. Nadler argued that Clinton didn't commit perjury or obstruct justice, and that even if he had those offenses would not be impeachable because they were not "an abuse of presidential power designed to or with the effect of undermining the structure or function of government, or undermining constitutional liberties." He spoke ably but perhaps a bit too smugly: he and, unaccountably, the Republicans, failed to note that the federal courts are part of government, so that undermining them meets Nadler's standard. In any case, Nadler was cheered and feted in Manhattan as never before. His verdict: "It would have been better for the country if this whole thing hadn't happened. But if it had to happen, I'm glad I was on the Judiciary Committee. After all, the reason I got into public life was to be at the center of important things."

Nadler has been re-elected without difficulty. In 1994 he beat Councilman Thomas Duane, openly gay and HIV positive, by 62%–29%; Duane has gone on to a seat in the state Senate.

Cook's Call. *Safe.* Besides being the brunt of a bad joke by former Senator Al D'Amato, Nadler will never be targeted in this heavily Democratic, very liberal district.

The People: Pop. 1990: 581,453; 16% age 65 +; 80.5% White, 8.5% Black, 6.3% Asian, 0.2% Amer. Indian, 4.5% Other; 11.9% Hispanic Origin. Households: 31.3% married couple families; 12.2% married couple fams. w. children; 59.3% college educ.; median household income: $32,784; per capita income: $26,168; median house value: $223,000; median gross rent: $507.

1996 Presidential Vote			1992 Presidential Vote		
Clinton (D)	147,864	(81%)	Clinton (D)	167,491	(77%)
Dole (R)	30,141	(16%)	Bush (R)	37,126	(17%)
Perot (I)	5,142	(3%)	Perot (I)	12,082	(6%)

Rep. Jerrold Nadler (D)

Elected 1992; b. June 13, 1947, Brooklyn; home, Manhattan; Columbia U., B.A. 1970, Fordham U., J.D. 1978; Jewish; married (Joyce Miller).

Elected Office: NY Assembly, 1976–92.

Professional Career: Legis. Asst., NY Assembly, 1972; Law Clerk, 1976.

DC Office: 2334 RHOB 20515, 202-225-5635; Fax: 202-225-6923; Web site: www.house.gov/nadler.

District Offices: Brooklyn, 718-373-3198; Manhattan, 212-334-3207.

Committees: *Judiciary* (5th of 16 D): Commercial & Administrative Law (RMM); The Constitution. *Transportation & Infrastructure* (11th of 34 D): Ground Transportation; Oversight, Investigations & Emergency Management.

Group Ratings

	ADA	ACLU	AFS	LCV	CON	NTU	NFIB	COC	ACU	NTLC	CHC
1998	100	87	100	92	68	20	7	24	8	0	0
1997	100	—	100	—	7	25	—	20	4	—	—

National Journal Ratings

	1997 LIB	—	1997 CONS	1998 LIB	—	1998 CONS
Economic	93%	—	0%	79%	—	0%
Social	85%	—	0%	89%	—	11%
Foreign	93%	—	6%	78%	—	19%

Key Votes of the 105th Congress

1. Clinton Budget Deal	N	5. Puerto Rico Sthood. Ref.	Y	9. Cut $ for B-2 Bombers	Y
2. Education IRAs	N	6. End Highway Set-asides	N	10. Human Rights in China	*
3. Req. 2/3 to Raise Taxes	N	7. School Prayer Amend.	N	11. Withdraw Bosnia Troops	N
4. Fast-track Trade	N	8. Ovrd. Part. Birth Veto	N	12. End Cuban TV-Marti	Y

Election Results

1998 general	Jerrold Nadler (D-L)	112,948	(86%)	($336,133)
	Theodore Howard (R)	18,383	(14%)	
1998 primary	Jerrold Nadler (D)	unopposed		
1996 general	Jerrold Nadler (D-L)	131,943	(82%)	($780,423)
	Michael Benjamin (R-FR)	26,028	(16%)	($121,422)

NINTH DISTRICT

Brooklyn. The single word used to arouse laughter in a comedian's monologue, applause when someone said they were from there. It evoked an accent that twisted the English language almost to non-recognition, a raucous and brusque confrontational style, a sense of humor with an edge, the chip-on-the-shoulder assertiveness of those sure they will always be in second place. Brooklyn would never be more important than Manhattan; the Dodgers would always lose the world series to the Yankees or the playoffs to the Giants, and when they finally did win, in 1955, they moved to Los Angeles two years later. Brooklyn, as its Dutch name testifies, was a separate community from the 17th Century on, one of the largest cities in the country in the 19th Century, with its own celebrities (Henry Ward Beecher, Walt Whitman, John Roebling). By 1898, when the five boroughs were welded into Greater New York, one million people lived in Brooklyn, but the Brooklyn of the comedians really came into being as the subways were built in the early 20th Century. Suddenly workers in all the little Manhattan factories no longer had to live in Lower East Side tenements. They moved out the subway lines, into neighborhoods of three- to five-story apartments and four-family houses. Brooklyn grew from 1.1 million in 1900 to 1.6 million in 1910 to 2 million in 1920 and 2.6 million in 1930. The old Brooklynites were mostly Protestant—Dutch, Yankee, German—plus some Catholic Irish. The new Brooklynites were heavily Italian and Jewish, and peopled the sports and entertainment businesses for a long generation, making their home town and its impenetrable accent nationally famous. In 1940, as the nation was about to go to war, Brooklyn had 2.7 million people: one in every 49 Americans lived in this one borough.

Today, 2.3 million people—one in every 108 Americans—live in Brooklyn, and it is no longer a staple of national comedy. Some of its old neighborhoods—Jewish Brownsville, Italian East New York—have been ravaged by crime and stand empty and toothless. But there is great vitality in much of Brooklyn, among upwardly mobile Hispanic and Asian and Russian and Jewish immigrants and a hard-working black middle class, and in neighborhoods of the grand-children of earlier Jews and Italians. The farther reaches of Ocean Parkway and the expanse of Flatlands and Canarsie, the quiet corners of Sheepshead Bay and Gerritsen are such places. Here young Orthodox Jews raise families within walking distance of school, and neighbors patrol the streets at night to keep down the crime which has wrecked neighborhoods just a few miles away.

The 9th Congressional District includes many such neighborhoods in Brooklyn and in the borough of Queens as well. Its geography is grotesque, its demography more comprehensible. This is where descendants of the 1890–1924 migrants live. In Brooklyn it extends from Prospect Park south along Ocean Parkway to Coney Island and Sheepshead Bay: still one of the most Jewish areas in the United States. It extends east over Flatlands and much of Canarsie and then across Jamaica Bay south to the Rockaway Peninsula and north to a collection of Queens neighborhoods: Howard Beach, next to Kennedy Airport; the old German neighborhoods of Glendale and Ridgewood, still orderly and spotlessly clean; Italian Woodhaven and Tudor-trimmed Forest Hills; much of the heavily Jewish high-rise area along Queens Boulevard. After the 1997 redistricting, the Queens portion has been enlarged and the Brooklyn portion reduced, and the vote is now almost evenly balanced between the two. This remains a solidly Democratic district, though there are significant Republican neighborhoods in Queens and some Orthodox neighborhoods are very conservative.

The congressman from the 9th District is Anthony Weiner, a Democrat elected in 1998 at age 34. Weiner grew up in Brooklyn, went to a SUNY college Upstate, then returned to work for Congressman Charles Schumer, the energetic and effervescent incumbent first elected to Congress in 1980, at 29, and elected senator in 1998. In 1991 Weiner was elected to the City Council, at 27, the youngest age ever; he was re-elected in 1993 and 1997. There he worked on issues from federal airport regulations to fire alarm boxes and the Fire Department-EMS merger; he worked to redevelop the Sheepshead Bay waterfront and the shopping strips on Kings Highway, Avenue U and Sheepshead Bay Road. On consumer affairs, he investigated abuses in modeling agencies and dating services. In 1997, as Schumer prepared to run for the Senate, he began running for Congress.

Naturally there was competition. Assemblywoman Melinda Katz, based in Forest Hills, ran with the support of the Queens Democratic organization, the Robert F. Kennedy Democratic Club and City Controller Alan Hevesi. Assemblyman Daniel Feldman, based in Sheepshead Bay, had the endorsement of the Brooklyn Democratic organization and Congressman Jerrold Nadler. Councilman Noach Dear, based in Borough Park, ran with the endorsement of Orthodox leaders; he raised $1.5 million and spent half of it on TV ads and much of the rest on videotapes sent out to 20,000 registered Democrats. Dear had a sharply more conservative record than the others; he is opposed to abortion, for example. Otherwise the differences were in emphasis: Weiner talked about public safety, Katz about health care, Feldman his sponsorship of Megan's law. This was mainly a battle of organizations and endorsements. In the last weeks, as he was sailing far ahead in the Senate primary, Schumer endorsed Weiner. That may have made the difference, though others thought it was his endorsement by a Canarsie club. The September 15 primary was so close that the results weren't certified for two weeks. In a turnout of 45,000—not enormous in such a heavily Democratic district—Weiner won with 28.1%, to 27.5% for Katz, and 22% each for Dear and Feldman.

Weiner won the general election easily. He is likely to have a mostly liberal voting record in the House, though he, like Schumer, will probably trumpet anti-crime stands. Weiner says he doesn't want to get too attached to Washington and hasn't looked for an apartment; instead, he sleeps on his Aunt Lois's sofa in Arlington, Virginia.

Cook's Call. *Safe.* Weiner's narrow win in the Democratic primary has encouraged at least one Democrat to take a look at challenging him in a primary. Democrats have no fear of losing this Brooklyn-based district in November.

The People: Pop. 1990: 579,876; 20.3% age 65 + ; 75.6% White, 3% Black, 8.7% Asian, 0.1% Amer. Indian, 0.2% Other; 12.5% Hispanic Origin. Households: 50.6% married couple families; 20.4% married couple fams. w. children; 43.7% college educ.; median household income: $34,758; per capita income: $17,918; median house value: $212,300; median gross rent: $490.

1996 Presidential Vote

Clinton (D)	107,835	(67%)
Dole (R)	46,400	(29%)
Perot (I)	7,884	(5%)

1992 Presidential Vote

Clinton (D)	112,182	(58%)
Bush (R)	63,874	(33%)
Perot (I)	16,603	(9%)

Rep. Anthony Weiner (D)

Elected 1998; b. Sept. 4, 1964, Brooklyn; home, Brooklyn; S.U.N.Y. Plattsburgh, B.A. 1985; Jewish; single.

Elected Office: NY City Cncl., 1991–98.

Professional Career: Aide, U.S. Rep. Charles Schumer, 1985–91.

DC Office: 501CHOB 20515, 202-225-6616; Fax: 202-226-7253; Web site: www.house.gov/weiner.

District Offices: Brooklyn, 718-332-9001; Forest Hills, 718-261-7170; Rockaway, 718-318-9255.

Committees: *Judiciary* (16th of 16 D): Commercial & Administrative Law; Crime. *Science* (18th of 23 D): Space & Aeronautics; Technology.

Group Ratings and Key Votes: Newly Elected

Election Results

1998 general	Anthony Weiner (D-Ind)	69,439	(66%)	($401,197)
	Louis Telano (R)	24,486	(23%)	($8,788)
	Melinda Katz (L)	5,698	(5%)	($741,921)
	Arthur J. Smith (C)	4,899	(5%)	
1998 primary	Anthony Weiner (D)	12,569	(28%)	
	Melinda Katz (D)	12,284	(28%)	
	Noach Dear (D)	10,041	(22%)	
	Daniel Feldman (D)	9,783	(22%)	
1996 general	Charles E. Schumer (D-L)	107,107	(75%)	($487,841)
	Robert J. Verga (R-Ind-FR)	30,488	(21%)	($36,351)
	Others	5,618	(4%)	

TENTH DISTRICT

Bedford, a century ago one of Brooklyn's fashionable neighborhoods, has given its name to half of what is Brooklyn's best known—and not most downtrodden—black neighborhood. If Bedford's and Stuyvesant's brownstones looked bedraggled even before modern urban decay, they also remain solid and, on many streets, well-tended. The black community settled here well before World War II, but they were then one of the smaller of dozens of Brooklyn ethnic enclaves. It grew in the years after World War II as crime and crowding moved people out of Harlem and busloads of blacks came north from the Carolinas in the 1950s and early 1960s. Sluggish job growth has meant less migration, but Brooklyn's black community, with some of New York's highest birth rates, has grown rapidly and far beyond the original bounds of Bedford-Stuyvesant.

The 10th Congressional District is centered on Bedford-Stuyvesant and is entirely contained within Brooklyn; there, regularity ends. It's irregular shape includes parts of gentrified Brooklyn Heights at the west end and extends east to Jamaica Bay, including much of East New York and Canarsie and Brownsville. The landscape varies widely, from utterly bombed-out blocks to secure and hardy blocks of rowhouses or high-rise rent-supplemented apartments. The district is 56% black and 18% Hispanic, with some blocks of Italians and Hasidic Jews; 1997 redistricting reduced the black percentage by only one point. Politically, it is overwhelmingly Democratic; in 1996 it gave Bill Clinton his third highest vote percentage in the country, 89%.

The congressman from the 10th is Ed Towns, elected in 1982. He is a black Democrat from East New York who is as experienced in government as in politics. Towns has been a teacher, social worker and hospital administrator, and he is active in the civic affairs of this racially changing community. He served as Brooklyn's deputy borough president for six years and became widely popular. Towns's two best known legislative initiatives are the Student Athlete Right-to-Know Act, which requires colleges to report the graduation rates of student athletes, and strengthening the National Health Service Corps and the Minority Health Initiative, especially for Native Americans (not too many of them in Brooklyn). In 1990 he got a seat on the Commerce Committee, where he has quickly moved up in seniority. There he was a mainstay of support for securities litigation reform, backed by Silicon Valley and other entrepreneurs, opposed by trial lawyers, vetoed by Clinton and passed over his veto in 1995—the only veto override of his first term. In 1997 Towns backed uniform federal standards on such suits—another measure vigorously opposed by trial lawyers. Towns has protested treatment of medical test subjects, the UPN program on Abraham Lincoln with its disparaging portrayals of blacks and India's treatment of human rights activists. He has worked on some local projects, notably a $152 million federal courthouse for Brooklyn included in the October 1998 omnibus budget.

For years Towns was re-elected without difficulty; but not in 1998. In 1997 he startled many longtime allies, notably Brooklyn Democratic Chairman Clarence Norman, by supporting Rudolph Giuliani for mayor. This took some courage; Giuliani got only 15% in two Bedford-

Stuyvesant assembly districts, his worst showing in the city. In 1998 he worked with Assemblyman Tony Genovesi in backing judicial slates against Norman's; they lost (and Genovesi died in a car crash in August 1998). Norman moved to recruit primary opposition for Towns. He approached agitator Al Sharpton, who decided not to run in March 1998. But there was opposition from Barry Ford, a Harvard-educated Wall Street lawyer and Democratic contributor. He was endorsed by leftish labor unions and Democratic clubs, by City Advocate Mark Green and former Mayor David Dinkins. Towns's reply: "Most people who are mayor and serve their term then become statesmen. David seems to be very bitter, and that's unfortunate. I was very supportive of him when he was mayor."

Towns's critics concentrated on the tobacco issue. Towns's father was a tobacco sharecropper in North Carolina, and he opposed much anti-tobacco legislation on the ground it would hurt farmers. "Tobacco is bad. So is starvation. Both will kill you." The Campaign for Tobacco-Free Kids put up billboards reading, "Representative Towns: Big Tobacco or Kids?" Others called him "the Marlboro man" and attacked him for accepting $54,000 from tobacco interests over 10 years. "Tobacco money is not illegal. I don't see any problem," Towns said at first. Later he added, "I've gotten most of my money from the health care community. If you're talking about dollars to influence, then I would have to be called the health-care congressman." Towns was helped when Giuliani, in August 1998, approved an application for a Brooklyn empowerment zone—because of Towns, he said. Towns finally beat Ford, but by only 52%–36%, not impressive for a 16-year incumbent. That means he may have serious opposition again, though it is not clear whether Towns will have such opposition—Norman, Dinkins, even the *New York Times*—arrayed against him.

Cook's Call. *Safe.* Like so many New York City-based Democratic members, Towns's only challenge here will come in a primary. He almost had a serious challenge from Reverand Al Sharpton, who in 1998 threatened to run in retaliation for Towns's support of Mayor Rudolph Giuliani. No Democrat will have to fear losing this seat, one of the most Democratic in the entire country.

The People: Pop. 1990: 581,311; 10.3% age 65 + ; 24.3% White, 55.5% Black, 1.9% Asian, 0.3% Amer. Indian, 0.3% Other; 17.8% Hispanic Origin. Households: 32.5% married couple families; 17.1% married couple fams. w. children; 35.5% college educ.; median household income: $23,164; per capita income: $11,479; median house value: $167,900; median gross rent: $396.

1996 Presidential Vote			1992 Presidential Vote		
Clinton (D)	134,677	(91%)	Clinton (D)	125,550	(81%)
Dole (R)	10,199	(7%)	Bush (R)	22,512	(15%)
Perot (I)	2,718	(2%)	Perot (I)	6,330	(4%)

Rep. Edolphus Towns (D)

Elected 1982; b. July 21, 1934, Chadbourn, NC; home, Brooklyn; NC A&T, B.S. 1956, Adelphi U., M.S.W. 1973; Presbyterian; married (Gwendolyn).

Military Career: Army, 1956–58.

Professional Career: Baptist Minister; Social Worker; Prof., Medgar Evers Col.; NY public schl. teacher; Dpty. Hospital Admin., 1965–71; Brooklyn Dpty. Borough Pres., 1976–82.

DC Office: 2232 RHOB 20515, 202-225-5936; Fax: 202-225-1018; Web site: www.house.gov/towns.

District Offices: Brooklyn, 718-855-8018; Brooklyn, 718-272-1175; Brooklyn, 718-774-5682.

Committees: *Commerce* (6th of 24 D): Finance & Hazardous Materials (RMM); Health and Environment. *Government Reform* (5th of 19 D): Criminal Justice, Drug Policy & Human Resources; District of Columbia; National Security, Veterans' Affairs & Intl. Relations.

Group Ratings

	ADA	ACLU	AFS	LCV	CON	NTU	NFIB	COC	ACU	NTLC	CHC
1998	95	86	100	100	67	14	0	31	9	3	0
1997	85	—	100	—	5	20	—	33	9	—	—

National Journal Ratings

	1997 LIB — 1997 CONS		1998 LIB — 1998 CONS	
Economic	78% —	21%	79% —	0%
Social	73% —	27%	84% —	16%
Foreign	92% —	7%	77% —	23%

Key Votes of the 105th Congress

1. Clinton Budget Deal	N	5. Puerto Rico Sthood. Ref.	N	9. Cut $ for B-2 Bombers	Y
2. Education IRAs	N	6. End Highway Set-asides	N	10. Human Rights in China	Y
3. Req. 2/3 to Raise Taxes	N	7. School Prayer Amend.	N	11. Withdraw Bosnia Troops	N
4. Fast-track Trade	N	8. Ovrd. Part. Birth Veto	N	12. End Cuban TV-Marti	*

Election Results

1998 general	Edolphus Towns (D-L)	83,528	(92%)	($736,179)
	Ernestine M. Brown (R)	5,577	(6%)	
	Others	1,396	(2%)	
1998 primary	Edolphus Towns (D)	17,990	(52%)	
	Barry Ford (D)	12,610	(36%)	
	Kenneth Diamondstone (D)	4,141	(12%)	
1996 general	Edolphus Towns (D-L)	99,889	(91%)	($533,824)
	Amelia Smith-Parker (R-C-FR)	8,660	(8%)	

ELEVENTH DISTRICT

When Jackie Robinson suited up for the Brooklyn Dodgers in 1947, becoming the first black major league baseball player, the borough didn't have many blacks. Manhattan's Harlem was the center of black life and entertainment in New York, though Brooklyn's Bedford-Stuyvesant, not far from Ebbets Field, had a scattering of blacks in modest apartments. Then a subway line, built to replace the El, connected Bed-Stuy with Harlem, and inspired Duke Ellington's "Take the A Train."

Since then, Harlem has lost population and dozens of blocks have been emptied out, their brownstone townhouses vacant or vanished. But Brooklyn's black neighborhoods have grown and to a certain degree have prospered. Many of New York's black families came from the south, but large numbers, particularly in Flatbush, the area south of the Hasidic Jewish outposts in Crown Heights, come from what New Yorkers call "the Islands"—Jamaica, Haiti, the Dominican Republic, Barbados, Trinidad and Tobago. Speaking deeply accented English, French, Spanish or various forms of Creole, they bring spiced bread, peanut punch, Matouk's Special Hot Calypso Sauce, reggae and calypso music. These Caribbean immigrants tend to stay in family units more often than low-income American-born blacks; they work hard and are commercially and civically inclined. Coming from places where life and property are not always respected by governments, they are working, like so many other immigrants to America, to build new communities.

The 11th Congressional District extends from the edge of downtown Brooklyn, across Crown Heights—the scene of violent clashes between blacks and Hasidic Jews—and centers on Flatbush; it also picks up most of Brownsville and parts of East Flatbush. This area had the largest concentration of Jews in America from the 1920s to the 1960s. For the 1990s it was one of the highest black percentage districts in the country, with probably as many blacks with roots in the Islands as in the American South. Like depopulated Brownsville, some neighborhoods here are in dreadful shape, while others, like much of Flatbush, seem to have considerable vitality.

The congressman from the 11th is Major Owens, a Democrat first elected in 1982, who claims to be the first librarian elected to Congress. Owens grew up in Memphis, TN, went to Morehouse College and Atlanta University and became a librarian. He worked in the Brownsville Community Council and with CORE, and served in Mayor John Lindsay's Administration from 1968–73 as commissioner of the city's Community Development Agency; critic Charles Morris called Owens "the most capable and canny" of New York's anti-poverty program directors. It was a high-pressure job with few guidelines, and Owens may have been relieved when he was elected to serve in the antique chamber of the New York Senate in 1974. When Congresswoman Shirley Chisholm, an immigrant from Barbados and presidential candidate in 1972, announced her retirement in 1982, Owens entered the primary to succeed her and beat Chisholm's choice. Since then Owens has had no serious electoral competition; in November 1998, he won 90% of the vote.

Owens has one of the most liberal voting records in the House. During the last Democratic Congress, he chaired Education's Subcommittee on Select Education and Civil Rights. He worked on the Americans With Disabilities Act and, fittingly for a librarian, the Literacy Corps and library funding in the child care bill. He has been outspokenly critical of the Republican majority in the House, and of the Clinton Administration as well; he is often seen making long, vigorous floor speeches after the House has finished work for the day. On the Education and the Workforce Committee he has been a strong opponent of the Republicans' plan to give employees the option of taking compensatory time rather than overtime pay; he spoke out in mistrust when Republicans took a new look at the 1977 Mining Safety Act. But he supported the Republicans in their opposition to national education testing. Owens speaks passionately of the need to support libraries, important institutions in the immigrant communities of New York's outer boroughs. He opposed increasing the number of H-1B visas for high-skill workers, saying that might take jobs from Americans. His skill at writing rap lyrics led the *New York Observer* to name him "class bard" of the city's delegation.

In June 1997 Owens supported Tony Hall's resolution apologizing for slavery. "We think so much more is needed than an apology, but it's a good place to begin. We've been asking for much more for a long time." That same month he wrote state Controller Carl McCall and Speaker Sheldon Silver, attacking Democrats for not backing Ruth Messinger for mayor. "Male Democrats who are egotistical, smug, cynical or too lazy to fight are succumbing to their worst sexist instinct as they abandon the New York City mayoral race. The party leadership must speak up." They said they weren't going to take sides in a primary. In February 1998 Owens was rated lowest in clout in the New York delegation—not necessarily a bad thing since standing on principle can have its political costs. "I just had a big battle with the White House [over education]. . . . Among Republicans, I'm the guy who gives them problems . . . who's viewed as least likely to compromise. If you talk with lobbyists from the carpenters, education, Teamsters, . . . I don't see how a lobbyist would see I'm ineffective."

Cook's Call. *Safe.* Owens will never have problems in a district that gave Clinton 90% of the vote in 1996.

The People: Pop. 1990: 582,332; 9% age 65 +; 18% White, 67% Black, 2.9% Asian, 0.3% Amer. Indian, 0.2% Other; 11.6% Hispanic Origin. Households: 34.5% married couple families; 19.7% married couple fams. w. children; 39.6% college educ.; median household income: $26,148; per capita income: $11,706; median house value: $183,900; median gross rent: $431.

1996 Presidential Vote

Clinton (D)	116,439	(92%)
Dole (R)	8,926	(7%)
Perot (I)	1,878	(1%)

1992 Presidential Vote

Clinton (D)	105,705	(86%)
Bush (R)	13,153	(11%)
Perot (I)	4,347	(4%)

Rep. Major R. Owens (D)

Elected 1982; b. June 28, 1936, Memphis, TN; home, Brooklyn; Morehouse Col., B.A. 1956, Atlanta U., M.L.S. 1957; Baptist; married (Maria).

Elected Office: NY Senate, 1974–82.

Professional Career: Librarian; Brooklyn Public Library, 1958–65; Community Coord., 1964–65; V.P., Metro. Cncl. of Housing, 1964; Chmn., Brooklyn Congress on Racial Equality; Exec. Dir., Brownsville Community Cncl., 1966–68; NYC Community Devel. Agency, Comm., 1968–73, Dpty. Admin., 1972–74; Dir., Community Media Library Program, Columbia U., 1973–74.

DC Office: 2305 RHOB 20515, 202-225-6231; Fax: 202-226-0112; Web site: www.house.gov/owens.

District Offices: Brooklyn, 718-940-3213; Brooklyn, 718-773-3100.

Committees: *Education & the Workforce* (5th of 22 D): Postsecondary Education, Training & Life-Long Learning; Workforce Protections (RMM). *Government Reform* (4th of 19 D): Government Management, Information & Technology; Postal Service.

Group Ratings

	ADA	ACLU	AFS	LCV	CON	NTU	NFIB	COC	ACU	NTLC	CHC
1998	100	94	100	100	68	20	7	22	0	0	0
1997	95	—	100	—	12	25	—	20	8	—	—

National Journal Ratings

	1997 LIB — 1997 CONS			1998 LIB — 1998 CONS		
Economic	85%	—	10%	79%	—	0%
Social	85%	—	0%	93%	—	0%
Foreign	88%	—	12%	90%	—	10%

Key Votes of the 105th Congress

1. Clinton Budget Deal	N	5. Puerto Rico Sthood. Ref.	Y	9. Cut $ for B-2 Bombers	Y
2. Education IRAs	N	6. End Highway Set-asides	N	10. Human Rights in China	Y
3. Req. 2/3 to Raise Taxes	N	7. School Prayer Amend.	N	11. Withdraw Bosnia Troops	N
4. Fast-track Trade	N	8. Ovrd. Part. Birth Veto	N	12. End Cuban TV-Marti	Y

Election Results

1998 general	Major R. Owens (D-L)	75,773	(90%)	($120,197)
	David Greene (R-C)	7,284	(9%)	
	Others	1,144	(1%)	
1998 primary	Major R. Owens (D) .... unopposed			
1996 general	Major R. Owens (D-L)	89,905	(92%)	($129,983)
	Claudette Hayle (R-C-Ind-FR)	7,866	(8%)	

TWELFTH DISTRICT

Amid a vast wave of migration that seemed destined to make Puerto Ricans the majority in New York, Leonard Bernstein in 1957 wrote his musical, *West Side Story*, with Romeo as an Italian-American and Juliet as a Manhattan Puerto Rican. While the inflow and outflow of Puerto Ricans balanced out by the early 1960s, New York has had ever since the 1965 Immigration Act a vast influx of Hispanics from places not under the U.S. flag. The largest group is the Dominicans, quite possibly more of them now than Puerto Ricans, and there are many Colombians, Mexicans, Panamanians and Peruvians.

The 12th Congressional District was designed to join these diverse people together. As drawn for the 1992, 1994 and 1996 elections it was a serpentine-shaped entity called by many the "Bullwinkle" district, because of its alleged resemblance to the cartoon character. Stitched together, often by the thinnest of threads, were the heavily Puerto Rican Sunset Park neighborhood in Brooklyn and on the other side of the borough, Bushwick, with a mixture of Latinos and a political machine run by Assemblyman Vito Lopez, who is of Spanish and Italian descent. The Dominican neighborhood of East Elmhurst and Corona, Queens were put in the 12th, as were the Colombian areas several blocks west in Jackson Heights, plus some black neighborhoods in East New York. It also jumped across the Manhattan Bridge to include Puerto Rican parts of the Lower East Side. The district is connected by cemeteries or parks in at least three places. About one-half its voters are in Brooklyn, about one-quarter each in Manhattan and Queens.

Not too surprisingly, after two Supreme Court rulings overturning district lines drawn using race as the predominant factor, a lawsuit was brought challenging the 12th District. In February 1997 a federal court ordered redrawing of the "Bullwinkle" district, because race was the predominant factor; it added that there was no need for New York to create a seventh "majority-minority" district, especially one with such erose lines. But the legislature complied and passed a new plan, drawn by Democrats, in August 1997. The new 12th, in effect for the 1998 and 2000 elections, dropped the farther Queens portions of the district and added the Williamsburg neighborhood in Brooklyn, with many Hasidic and Polish voters. Otherwise the lines were smoothed out a bit in Brooklyn and Manhattan. The Hispanic percentage dropped from 58% to 48%, the Asian percentage dropped from 19% to 14% and the black percentage stayed at about 12%. About 30% of the district was new.

The congresswoman from the 12th is Nydia Velazquez, chosen by a narrow margin in the 1992 primary and re-elected ever since; but she might not have won the district at all if the 1992 election was conducted within the 1997 lines. Velazquez was born in Puerto Rico, taught at the University of Puerto Rico in the 1970s and at Hunter College in the 1980s, worked for Congressman Ed Towns in 1983 and served on the New York City Council in 1984. Then she worked for Puerto Rico's government offices in New York. She was one of three major contenders when the district was created in 1992. One was liberal Elisabeth Colon and another was incumbent Stephen Solarz, chairman of the Asia Subcommittee and a major force on foreign policy; he decided to run here rather than in the Manhattan-dominated 8th or in the 9th District in which Charles Schumer had a heavy advantage. Velazquez got the endorsements of then-Mayor David Dinkins and of Jesse Jackson, and in a light turnout beat Solarz 34%–28%, with 26% for Colon. Williamsburg would probably have swung the race to Solarz.

After the primary, confidential hospital records were leaked to a New York tabloid showing that in September 1991, Velazquez had attempted suicide, was hospitalized and later underwent counseling. Evidently, that was of little concern to voters: she won in November with 77%. In the House she has a solidly liberal voting record. She used her seat on the Banking Committee to try to require credit bureaus to let people talk with live operators and to provide consumers with a free copy of their credit report after information is corrected. In 1996 she got $5 million to investigate and enforce labor law violations in the garment industry, in which many of her constituents work. In 1997 she complained about the lack of Hispanic appointees in the Clinton Administration. She tried to give the INS the discretion to make exceptions to the draconian requirement that all immigrants must be deported for any crimes, no matter how trivial or how long ago they were committed. She got a Bronze Star belatedly awarded to a 78-year-old Brooklyn veteran by "a very passionate plea to President Clinton himself." She backs a tunnel to replace the elevated Gowanus Expressway, built in 1941 and slated to be torn down; that would cost $6 billion, 10 times the amount for the overhaul favored by the state.

Velazquez has been one of the major voices in debates on the status of Puerto Rico. She used to favor independence; by 1997 she favored continuation of the current commonwealth status (more accurately described in the Spanish term, *estado liberado asociado*, free associated state). In the debate on the House bill passed by one vote in March 1998, she opposed her usual ally, Jose Serrano of the Bronx, who favors statehood or independence. She attacked the bill sponsored by Resources Chairman Don Young as "a one-sided bill that is biased in favor of Puerto Rican statehood" that shows "a lack of respect for the people of Puerto Rico." She said its definition of commonwealth was biased, because it did not guarantee U.S. citizenship to future generations of Puerto Ricans (citizenship is now based not on the Fourteenth Amendment, but on a law passed by Congress in 1917, which could be repealed). In any case, the Senate never took up the bill; the pro-statehood government of Puerto Rico held a referendum in December 1998 in which statehood lost narrowly to "none of the above."

Velazquez called the ruling overturning the old 12th District lines "a sad day for equal justice for communities of color." But it did not turn out to be a sad political day for her. Brooklyn Democratic Chairman Clarence Norman sought candidates to run against her, but failed. Lopez said, "She's alienated just about every part of her constituency. She has challenged people in every part of her district and that has made many people unhappy with her." But he decided not to risk his assembly seat and did not run. Councilman Martin Malave-Dilan started a campaign, but withdrew in July 1998, saying he couldn't raise enough money; he ran instead against Assemblyman Darryl Towns, son of 11th District Congressman Ed Towns, but lost. The Republican nominee was a woman temporarily paralyzed by an accident and diagnosed with breast cancer; she spent $1,620, and Velazquez won 84%–12%.

In February 1998, after John LaFalce became ranking Democrat on Banking, Velazquez became ranking Democrat on the Small Business Committee. This is a body with little jurisdiction on which many members like to serve because it sounds good at election time; Republicans wanted to abolish it after they won their majority in 1994, but refrained because it was the only committee that would be headed by a woman, Jan Meyers of Kansas. Meyers retired in 1996; now, if Democrats win in 2000 and Velazquez is re-elected, she will be the House's first woman Puerto Rican committee chairman. Thus is history made.

Cook's Call. *Safe.* Even some minor line changes had little impact on Velazquez as she again scored a huge victory in 1998.

The People: Pop. 1990: 577,757; 8.9% age 65 + ; 25.5% White, 11.6% Black, 13.7% Asian, 0.3% Amer. Indian, 0.4% Other; 48.5% Hispanic Origin. Households: 40.5% married couple families; 23.4% married couple fams. w. children; 24.6% college educ.; median household income: $20,444; per capita income: $8,534; median house value: $176,300; median gross rent: $408.

1996 Presidential Vote

Clinton (D)	89,535	(85%)
Dole (R)	12,874	(12%)
Perot (I)	3,161	(3%)

1992 Presidential Vote

Clinton (D)	80,449	(68%)
Bush (R)	30,295	(26%)
Perot (I)	6,897	(6%)

Rep. Nydia M. Velazquez (D)

Elected 1992; b. Mar. 28, 1953, Yabucoa, PR; home, Brooklyn; U. of PR, B.A. 1974, N.Y.U., M.A. 1976; Catholic; divorced.

Elected Office: NY City Cncl., 1984–86.

Professional Career: Instructor, U. of PR, 1976–81; Adjunct prof., Hunter Col., 1981–83; Special Asst., U.S. Rep. Edolphus Towns, 1983; Migration Dir., PR Dept. of Labor & Human Resources, 1986–89; Secy., PR Dept. of Community Affairs in the U.S., 1989–92.

DC Office: 2241 RHOB 20515, 202-225-2361; Fax: 202-226-0327; Web site: www.house.gov/velazquez.

District Offices: Brooklyn, 718-599-3658; Brooklyn, 718-222-5819; Manhattan, 212-673-3997.

Committees: *Banking & Financial Services* (8th of 27 D): Capital Markets, Securities & Government Sponsored Enterprises; Housing & Community Opportunity. *Small Business* (RMM of 17 D).

Group Ratings

	ADA	ACLU	AFS	LCV	CON	NTU	NFIB	COC	ACU	NTLC	CHC
1998	95	94	100	92	55	19	0	33	8	3	0
1997	95	—	100	—	7	25	—	20	4	—	—

National Journal Ratings

	1997 LIB — 1997 CONS			1998 LIB — 1998 CONS		
Economic	82%	—	18%	79%	—	0%
Social	85%	—	0%	84%	—	16%
Foreign	97%	—	0%	96%	—	2%

Key Votes of the 105th Congress

1. Clinton Budget Deal	N	5. Puerto Rico Sthood. Ref.	N	9. Cut $ for B-2 Bombers	Y
2. Education IRAs	N	6. End Highway Set-asides	N	10. Human Rights in China	Y
3. Req. 2/3 to Raise Taxes	N	7. School Prayer Amend.	N	11. Withdraw Bosnia Troops	N
4. Fast-track Trade	N	8. Ovrd. Part. Birth Veto	N	12. End Cuban TV-Marti	Y

Election Results

1998 general	Nydia M. Velazquez (D)	53,269	(84%)	($359,402)
	Rosemarie Markgraf (R)	7,405	(12%)	($1,620)
	Others	3,032	(5%)	
1998 primary	Nydia M. Velazquez (D)	unopposed		
1996 general	Nydia M. Velazquez (D-L)	61,913	(85%)	($236,564)
	Miguel I. Prado (R-C-RTL)	9,978	(14%)	($23,991)
	Others	1,283	(2%)	

THIRTEENTH DISTRICT

Staten Island is part of New York City, yet a land apart; it is closer geographically to New Jersey, separated only by narrow Arthur Kill and Kill van Kull, than to Brooklyn, over the 5-

mile-long span of the Verrazano Narrows Bridge. Its inclusion in Greater New York in 1898 was something of an afterthought, and for two-thirds of a century it was connected to the rest of the City only by ferry or through Bayonne, New Jersey, until the Verrazano was opened in 1965. It is far less densely populated than the rest of New York: with about as much acreage as Brooklyn has for 2.3 million people, Staten Island has some 400,000—and that's after recent robust population growth. Ethnically, Staten Island is one of the most heavily Italian parts of the United States; the signs on coffee shops here read *Caffe* and on delicatessens *Salumeria.*

Not so long ago you could still find some cows on Staten Island, and there still is much empty space. It has the highest point on the eastern seaboard, Todt Hill, and the vast Fresh Kills dump. Culturally, Staten Islanders are deeply conservative—more so than in most of New York's suburbs—quite a contrast from Manhattan at the other end of the ferry. New York City income taxes, the highest in the nation, pay for many programs opposed by most Staten Islanders; in November 1993, Staten Island voted for secession, but the legislature never acted; that same year Staten Islanders provided the margin of victory for Mayor Rudolph Giuliani whose records—cutting crime in half, cutting welfare by 26%—have made them less interested in seceding.

The 13th Congressional District of New York is made up of Staten Island plus a couple of adjacent neighborhoods over the Verrazano Narrows Bridge in Brooklyn. The largest of these is Bay Ridge, heavily Catholic and Italian, mostly middle-class, with thick New York accents and resentment of high New York taxes and welfare payments: large single-family houses and small apartment buildings by the looming towers of the Bridge. The 13th also includes most of heavily Italian Bensonhurst, where you can still see old men playing bocci. This district may have more Italian-Americans and may also be home to more police officers than any other district in America.

The congressman from the 13th District is Vito Fossella, a Republican elected in November 1997. Fossella comes from a political, and Democratic, Staten Island family: his great-grand-father, James O'Leary was a New Deal congressman from 1936–44, elected from Staten Island and the Wall Street tip of Manhattan; his father, Vito Fossella Sr., chaired the city's Board of Standards under Mayor Edward Koch; his uncle, Frank Fossella, was elected to the City Council in 1981; in 1985 he was beaten by Republican Susan Molinari, Vito Fossella Jr.'s predecessor in Congress. Despite the party difference, the families became close: Guy Molinari, elected to Congress in 1980 and Borough President in 1989, refers to Vito Fossella as "my son." Vito Fossella graduated from Penn and Fordham Law School and became a Republican in 1990, at 25, because of his conservative philosophy; he switched from pro-choice to pro-life in 1995, after the birth of his son. He worked on the campaigns of Susan Molinari, who succeeded her father in the House in a special election in March 1990. In April 1994, Fossella, less than a year after finishing law school, was elected to the City Council to fill a vacancy, winning 47% in a six-candidate nonpartisan election, with the help of the Molinaris. On the council he worked for increased school and transportation funding for Staten Island and, most important, passed a bill mandating the closing of the Fresh Kills dump by 2001.

Fossella was elected to Congress after the surprise resignation of Susan Molinari. With good political instincts and a cheerful big city manner, she had been part of the Republican leadership and was keynote speaker at the 1996 national convention. She was married to Congressman Bill Paxon, part of the leadership until he was part of the unsuccessful coup against Newt Gingrich in July 1997, and announced he wasn't seeking re-election in February 1998. Molinari announced in May 1997 that she was leaving to anchor a CBS Saturday morning news show and to spend more time with their child. She didn't lose her political touch, however: she timed her resignation for August, which meant that the Republican nomination would go to the party committeemen, dominated by her father; they rejected the pleas of two other contenders and chose Fossella.

This turned out to be a high visibility contest. Democrats picked a strong candidate in Eric Vitaliano, 15-year assemblyman from the conservative mid-Island district, an abortion opponent and sponsor of New York's death penalty. Vitaliano criticized Fossella as inexperienced and constantly tried to link Fossella with Gingrich. Fossella hit Vitaliano for supporting higher taxes and needle exchanges, and for not taking Americans for Tax Reform's anti-tax-raise pledge. "Eric Vitaliano: Talks like us but votes like an Albany liberal." The spending was about even— $1.1 million for Fossella and $900,000 for Vitaliano, and sufficient to get messages across in a district where most media is local: the newspaper here is the *Staten Island Advance*, the TV buy is on Staten Island cable; the campaigns relied on leafleting and the like in the quarter of the district in Brooklyn.

Two other factors helped Fossella. One was a $750,000 independent expenditure by the national Republican Party, attacking Vitaliano for supporting tax increases, and a group Victory 97, who paid for posters depicting Vitaliano's silly spending programs: snow-making equipment in Ulster County, a state Museum of Cheese. The other factor was the re-election campaign of Mayor Rudolph Giuliani, in a district where few local Democrats would admit they supported their liberal nominee Ruth Messinger. Guy Molinari took no chances: he brought in George Bush and Bob Dole on the same night, plus Jack Kemp, John McCain and of course, Giuliani and Governor George Pataki.

On election day Giuliani carried the district 3–1 and Fossella won 61%–39%—not much below Susan Molinari's 62%–35% in 1996. He won 59% in Staten Island and 67% in Brooklyn. "The message is that the government works for the people and not the other way around," he said, and in the House had a more conservative voting record than Molinari, perhaps the most conservative in the entire New York delegation. He got a seat on the Transportation and Infrastructure Committee and promised to work on interstate waste issues; he moved to Commerce in 1999. He pushed for rerouting Newark Airport flights away from Staten Island. He amended the Shays-Meehan campaign finance bill to ban contributions from foreigners, even if they reside in the U.S., in July 1998. He was not lobbied heavily on impeachment; everyone assumed he would vote for it, and he did. He was re-elected easily in November 1998.

Cook's Call. *Safe.* Fossella's solid win in the hotly contested 1997 special election helped to keep him off Democratic target lists in 1998. Don't look for Democrats to post a serious challenge here in 2000 either.

The People: Pop. 1990: 579,521; 14.6% age 65 + ; 86.6% White, 5.6% Black, 5.5% Asian, 0.1% Amer. Indian, 2.1% Other; 7.2% Hispanic Origin. Households: 55.5% married couple families; 26.6% married couple fams. w. children; 40.1% college educ.; median household income: $38,437; per capita income: $17,143; median house value: $190,700; median gross rent: $497.

1996 Presidential Vote			1992 Presidential Vote		
Clinton (D)	92,612	(52%)	Bush (R)	98,792	(48%)
Dole (R)	72,228	(41%)	Clinton (D)	81,047	(39%)
Perot (I)	12,093	(7%)	Perot (I)	25,798	(13%)

Rep. Vito Fossella (R)

Elected Nov. 1997; b. Mar. 9, 1965, Staten Island; home, Staten Island; U. of PA., B.S. 1993, Fordham U., J.D. 1994; Catholic; married (Mary Pat).

Elected Office: NY City Cncl., 1994–97.

Professional Career: Practicing atty., 1994.

DC Office: 431 CHOB 20515, 202-225-3371; Fax: 202-226-1272; Web site: www.house.gov/fossella.

District Offices: Brooklyn, 718-630-5277; Staten Island, 718-987-8400.

Committees: *Commerce* (26th of 29 R): Energy & Power; Finance & Hazardous Materials; Telecommunications, Trade & Consumer Protection.

Group Ratings (Only Served Partial Term)

	ADA	ACLU	AFS	LCV	CON	NTU	NFIB	COC	ACU	NTLC	CHC
1998	0	8	0	31	26	50	100	100	96	90	100
1997	*	—	*	—	*	*	—	*	*	—	—

National Journal Ratings (Only Served Partial Term)

	1997 LIB — 1997 CONS		1998 LIB — 1998 CONS	
Economic	*	— *	30%	— 70%
Social	*	— *	0%	— 97%
Foreign	*	— *	0%	— 93%

Key Votes of the 105th Congress (Only Served Partial Term)

1. Clinton Budget Deal	*	5. Puerto Rico Sthood. Ref. N	9. Cut $ for B-2 Bombers *
2. Education IRAs	*	6. End Highway Set-asides Y	10. Human Rights in China *
3. Req. 2/3 to Raise Taxes	Y	7. School Prayer Amend. Y	11. Withdraw Bosnia Troops Y
4. Fast-track Trade	Y	8. Ovrd. Part. Birth Veto Y	12. End Cuban TV-Marti N

Election Results

1998 general	Vito Fossella (R-C-RTL)	76,138	(65%)	($1,591,057)
	Eugene V. Prisco (D-L)	40,167	(34%)	($14,858)
	Others	1,245	(1%)	
1998 primary	Vito Fossella (R)	unopposed		
1997 special	Vito Fossella (R)	79,838	(61%)	($1,059,978)
	Eric N. Vitaliano (D)	50,373	(39%)	($896,036)
1996 general	Susan Molinari (R-C-FR)	94,660	(62%)	($557,586)
	Tyrone G. Butler (D-L)	53,376	(35%)	($53,459)
	Others	5,733	(4%)	

FOURTEENTH DISTRICT

Hardly any remnant can be found of early 19th Century New York, the city that diarists Philip Hone and George Templeton Strong said was continually being torn down and rebuilt, its earlier structures expendable after a generation or so on the high-priced real estate of this small, compact island. Yet the mayor of this quintessentially 20th Century city lives and works in two buildings of early 19th Century scale: City Hall, built in 1803–11, where his ground floor office, dwarfed by the Municipal and Woolworth Buildings, overlooks City Hall Park; and Gracie Mansion, built in 1799, which looks across East End Avenue to high-rise apartments and over the East River to the Triborough Bridge. In contrast are the gleaming postmodern skyscrapers in midtown and downtown Manhattan and the high-priced storefronts of the 1990s. But most of Manhattan has an early or mid-20th century look; its enduring landmarks—the Empire State Building, the Woolworth Building, Rockefeller Center—are the product of the first half of the century, and its infrastructure—up-to-date and gleaming when New York's last World's Fair closed in 1965—is now dilapidated and crumbling, despite recent fixups during the administration of Mayor Rudolph Giuliani.

The 14th Congressional District covers most of the East Side of Manhattan, running irregularly from 14th Street north to 96th street, and also includes small salients on the Lower East Side and Upper West Side of Manhattan; it also includes parts of the Queens neighborhoods of Astoria and Long Island City. This is the direct descendant of the famous Silk Stocking District, originally created in 1918, then consisting of the few blocks east of Fifth Avenue along Central Park. In the years since, rich and articulate Manhattan, with its securities, publishing, advertising, entertainment, broadcasting and communications industries, has spread from this narrow enclave and taken over the greater part of the island, with robust population increases in the 1990s. Meanwhile, the political leanings of this larger upper class—defined partly by income, but also by tastes in the arts, fashion, letters, all the things in which New York remains clearly the nation's capital—have changed, from elite Republican to culturally liberal.

Historically, the Silk Stocking tradition was elite Republican, cosmopolitan and international-minded, confident in its duty to lead and mistrustful of the (usually Democratic) immigrant masses—the politics of Theodore Roosevelt and the old *New York Herald Tribune* and Henry Luce's *Time* magazine. While it did not trust union leaders and Democratic Party politicians, it accepted much of the New Deal. This district believed the nation should be led by the well-educated Protestant gentlemen one saw strolling down Madison Avenue to their clubs, who for years held high government posts from Theodore Roosevelt's day and past Franklin's. But the district changed during the tenure of John Lindsay, congressman from 1958–65 and mayor from 1965–73. Lindsay changed from being a liberal Republican to a leftish Democrat. While mayor, he ran up the huge debts that led the city to the brink of bankruptcy in 1975, while neighborhoods deteriorated and the city lost one million people in the 1970s. He was succeeded as congressman and ultimately as mayor by Edward Koch, whose political travels were the reverse: Koch started as a liberal reform Democrat and became more conservative, and in the process lost the support of Manhattan by backing capital punishment, opposing racial quotas and questioning poverty programs. Now Manhattan ardently backs Giuliani, after his successes in cutting crime and welfare and making New York's streets safe and even civil; but it has nothing but loathing for the Republican Party of Newt Gingrich and Trent Lott, George Bush and Bob Dole.

The Silk Stocking district proves that economics is not necessarily the basis of American politics. Its residents have the highest average household income in America, $74,780, but they also are solidly Democratic: 70% for Bill Clinton and 23% for Dole in 1996. While the district is affluent, it also is full of gays, singles and others who consider anything past the canyons of Manhattan's east-west grid streets and the Hudson hostile country.

The congresswoman here is Carolyn Maloney, a liberal Democrat. Born and educated in North Carolina, she visited New York in 1970 at the age of 22, loved it and "just stayed." She worked on welfare education programs during the 1970s, and from 1977–82 she was a legislative staffer in Albany. She was elected to the New York City Council in 1982; one observer of her time there described her as "a little spacey" until she found a cause, but then she became "a pit bull." For 1992, redistricting created a Silk Stocking district even more Democratic than its predecessor and Maloney ran against liberal Republican Bill Green, who had held the district since winning a special election in 1977. Green was a thoughtful legislator who shared Manhattan's cultural liberalism, but he could not compete with the enthusiasm of a Democratic Party dominated by the feminist left for a woman candidate. And he was poorly positioned to appeal to voters in Astoria and (then in the district, but removed by redistricting in 1997) the

Greenpoint neighborhood of Brooklyn, who liked Republicans conservative on cultural issues and liberal on economics. Green won the Manhattan part of the district, but only by 50%–44%, below his previous showings; Maloney carried the outer borough portions with 62%, for a 50%–48% upset victory.

Maloney started off in the House with a certain naivete and has stayed to make serious contributions on important issues. In her first term she said she had no second choice for committees after Appropriations. She got Banking and Government Reform instead. She had helped to write New York City's campaign finance law, and has supported the various Shays-Meehan bills recently. With John Dingell she sponsored a campaign finance commission, whose result would have to be approved or rejected as a whole by Congress. But when Republican leaders allowed a vote on that in 1998, she backtracked, lest it get more votes than Shays-Meehan and under the rule supersede it. In 1998 she got full funding for the Federal Election Commission and blocked Republican attempts to get rid of the FEC general counsel Lawrence Noble; Democrats contended that Republicans wanted Noble out because of his aggressive investigations into Republican fundraising groups. She and Republican Stephen Horn sponsored a 1995 law requiring government agencies holding six-month-due debts to turn them over to Treasury for collection. In 1997 she was disappointed that only $2.5 million of some $50 million of debts had been collected. "It's embarrassing," she said. "We passed a law and the agencies ignored it." On Banking, she has worked to keep banks from controlling other businesses, has proposed regulation of hedge funds with assets over $1 billion, and has sought more oversight of the Federal Reserve. With Republican Richard Baker, she sponsored a "Kiddie Mac" bill for mortgage guarantees to lenders who financed child-care centers.

Maloney has weighed in on other issues as well. With an eye to Astoria, she helped found the Congressional Caucus on Hellenic Issues; with an eye to Manhattan radicals, she protested Peru's imprisonment of Lori Berenson for participating in the Tupac Amaru revolutionary groups. She opposes the Arab boycott of Israel and worked on a 1998 law to help victims of Nazi war crimes. She complained in 1997 when the Postal Service unaccountably refused to issue a stamp commemorating the 1848 Seneca Falls women's convention, and criticized Defense Secretary William Cohen's 1997 refusal to discharge General Joseph Ralston for adultery; but she defended President Clinton against impeachment in 1998. She opposed separating men and women in basic training. She put a provision for annual Medicare mammograms in the October 1998 omnibus budget. That year she also introduced a measure to give women the right to breast feed or express milk on the job.

In November 1997 she became the ranking Democrat on the new Census Subcommittee. She was a solid backer of Census sampling; the 1990 undercount in New York City, she said, was 244,000, and the city was being deprived of needed federal funds. She backed the Clinton Administration plan to present one Census result, from sampling; after the Supreme Court ruled in January 1999 that the Constitution required an actual enumeration for apportionment of House seats among the states, she backed the administration's plan to produce two figures, one from an enumeration for reapportionment and another from sampling to be used for redistricting and funding formulas. Occasionally she showed a certain imprecision, sending out a letter saying that since the original 13 states formed the Union, 39 have been added. California Republican Dana Rohrabacher quipped, "Ms. Maloney must have used the statistical sampling scheme to estimate the two extra states." A Maloney aide said it was just a typographical error: "There's no possible way we're going to create two more states by using sampling."

Maloney has shown great strength at the polls. In 1994 Manhattan Councilman Charles Millard spent almost $1 million against her; but the 14th District was voting 78% for Mario Cuomo and Maloney won 64%–35%. Against low-spending opponents, Maloney has done even better—72%–24% in 1996 and 77%–23% in 1998. Her opponent the latter year was the daughter of Theodore Kupferman, a liberal Republican who represented the Silk Stocking district in 1966–69; the breed is pretty scarce in Manhattan today.

Cook's Call. *Safe.* Like most New York City members, Maloney's greatest threat comes not from a Republican challenge but a 2002 redistricting map. New York City is likely to lose one seat, which means some serious shuffling. Until then, Maloney is safely situated in this East Side district.

The People: Pop. 1990: 578,639; 16.4% age 65 +; 78% White, 4.7% Black, 6% Asian, 0.1% Amer. Indian, 0.2% Other; 11.1% Hispanic Origin. Households: 29.6% married couple families; 9.4% married couple fams. w. children; 69.4% college educ.; median household income: $42,184; per capita income: $41,151; median house value: $235,700; median gross rent: $639.

1996 Presidential Vote

Clinton (D)	146,811	(73%)
Dole (R)	47,084	(23%)
Perot (I)	6,593	(3%)

1992 Presidential Vote

Clinton (D)	160,801	(70%)
Bush (R)	52,793	(23%)
Perot (I)	16,312	(7%)

Rep. Carolyn B. Maloney (D)

Elected 1992; b. Feb. 19, 1948, Greensboro, NC; home, Manhattan; Greensboro Col, A.B. 1968; Presbyterian; married (Clifton).

Elected Office: NY City Cncl., 1982–92.

Professional Career: NYC Bd. of Ed., 1970–77; Legis. aide, NY Assembly & NY Senate, 1977–82.

DC Office: 2430 RHOB 20515, 202-225-7944; Fax: 202-225-4709; Web site: www.house.gov/maloney.

District Offices: Manhattan, 212-860-0606; Queens, 718-932-1804.

Committees: *Banking & Financial Services* (6th of 27 D): Capital Markets, Securities & Government Sponsored Enterprises; Financial Institutions & Consumer Credit. *Government Reform* (8th of 19 D): Census (RMM); District of Columbia; Government Management, Information & Technology. *Joint Economic Committee* (9th of 10 Reps.).

Group Ratings

	ADA	ACLU	AFS	LCV	CON	NTU	NFIB	COC	ACU	NTLC	CHC
1998	100	81	100	92	82	21	14	33	8	8	0
1997	95	—	88	—	80	31	—	50	8	—	—

National Journal Ratings

	1997 LIB	—	1997 CONS	1998 LIB	—	1998 CONS
Economic	85%	—	10%	79%	—	0%
Social	82%	—	15%	81%	—	16%
Foreign	72%	—	28%	64%	—	31%

Key Votes of the 105th Congress

1. Clinton Budget Deal	N	5. Puerto Rico Sthood. Ref.	Y	9. Cut $ for B-2 Bombers	*
2. Education IRAs	N	6. End Highway Set-asides	N	10. Human Rights in China	Y
3. Req. 2/3 to Raise Taxes	N	7. School Prayer Amend.	N	11. Withdraw Bosnia Troops	N
4. Fast-track Trade	N	8. Ovrd. Part. Birth Veto	N	12. End Cuban TV-Marti	Y

Election Results

1998 general	Carolyn B. Maloney (D-Ind-L) 111,072	(77%)	($592,788)
	Stephanie E. Kupferman (R) 32,458	(23%)	($96,902)
1998 primary	Carolyn B. Maloney (D) .... unopposed		
1996 general	Carolyn B. Maloney (D-L) 130,175	(72%)	($599,406)
	Jeffrey E. Livingston (R) 42,641	(24%)	($152,503)
	Others 6,921	(4%)	

FIFTEENTH DISTRICT

Harlem, for many years America's most famous black ghetto, is now starting to recover from three decades of grim times. For a long moment Harlem was a center of writers and professionals and entertainers; the rosters of the Apollo Theater on 125th Street in the 1920s and 1930s were filled with the names of great artists still remembered today. This Harlem was a wondrous place: "To whites seeking amusement," the *WPA Guide* wrote in the late 1930s, Harlem "is an exuberant, original and unconventional entertainment center; to Negro college graduates, it is an opportunity to practice a profession among their own people; to those aspiring to racial leadership, it is a domain where they may advocate their theories unmolested; to the mass of Negro people, it is the spiritual capital of Black America." Harlem was almost new then: it was one of the last parts of Manhattan to be developed; early critics of Central Park questioned the necessity of setting aside open land when picnickers could always go to Harlem. The five-story tenements of solid brownstone were built about 100 years ago for working-class whites: Black Harlem expanded from its nucleus around Lenox Avenue and 125 Street in the years that followed even as the Italian neighborhood, later "Spanish Harlem," expanded from a nucleus at 116th Street and Pleasant Avenue.

Starting with the 1964 summer riot, Harlem had three decades of deterioration and population loss. Hundreds of brownstones were abandoned, many pulled down; as successful black families moved outward, to Springfield Gardens in Queens or Williamsbridge in the Bronx or to Jersey suburbs, Harlem was increasingly left with welfare mothers and criminal gangs; its population today is 200,000 less than in the 1940s. Drugs, crime, AIDS infection and infant mortality rose to horrifying levels. The near-disappearance of manufacturing jobs in New York City and the poor quality of the area's public schools meant that public payrolls were the only way up. Antipoverty money was channeled to a tight group of successful politicians, with few results except for the enrichment of the well-connected.

But in the 1990s there has been some upturn. The huge drop in crime under Mayor Rudolph Giuliani has made Harlem real estate now worth something again. Brownstones have been renovated, neighborhood schools upgraded (notably in East Harlem's District 4), commercial frontage repaired. The Empowerment Zone headed by Deborah Wright, an appointee of Governor George Pataki, has produced private as well as public sector growth: the state office building on 125th Street has been joined by Disney, Cineplex Odeon and Old Navy. A private developer has plans to build a shopping center, with a Home Depot and Costco and 2,000 jobs, at the old Washburn Wire factory at 116th Street and East River Drive, and Starbucks had its grand opening on 125th Street in May 1999. The heavily Dominican neighborhood in Washington Heights, northwest of central Harlem, hit hard by the crack epidemic in the late 1980s and early 1990s, once again has the vitality typical of immigrant centers, with dozens of bodegas and vastly reduced crime.

Politically, Harlem has been heavily Democratic since blacks shifted from the Republican Party of Abraham Lincoln to the Democratic Party of Franklin Roosevelt in the 1930s. Oddly, Harlem did not get its own congressional district until 1944; the lines, previously drawn in 1918, were based on the 1910 Census, when Harlem had far fewer people. The new congressman was Adam Clayton Powell Jr. minister at the Abyssinian Baptist Church, a brilliant orator who became the most famous (and infamous) black politician of his time: chairman of the

Education and Labor Committee when it passed the Great Society programs in 1965, excluded from Congress (illegally, the Supreme Court ruled) in 1967 for refusing to honor a New York decree in a libel case brought by a woman he called a "bag woman."

The current 15th Congressional District includes all of Harlem, indeed almost all of northern Manhattan, from approximately East 96th Street and West 91st Street on up. It includes some of the white-liberal Upper West Side and the precincts around Columbia University; the once Jewish and now Dominican Washington Heights and the once Irish and now Dominican Inwood to the north; East Harlem, Italian in the days of Fiorello LaGuardia, now Puerto Rican and Latino. Overall the district is 47% black and 45% Hispanic—figures testifying to black flight from Harlem and the continuing inrush of Western Hemisphere immigrants.

The congressman from the 15th is Charles Rangel, first elected in 1970 when he narrowly beat Adam Clayton Powell Jr. in the Democratic primary. Rangel is now the senior member of the New York delegation and ranking Democrat on Ways and Means. He served in the Army in Korea, then went to college and law school, served as legal counsel in several government agencies and was elected to the Assembly in 1966; in 1970 he challenged Powell and won. Like most Harlem politicians, he has long argued that government aid and racial preferences are needed to solve Harlem's problems, and with more vehemence than ever since the Republicans won control of Congress. Yet much in his own career suggests otherwise. Rangel's main emphasis for a decade was denunciation of the drug trade. From 1983 until it was abolished in 1993 with the other House select committees, Rangel chaired the Select Committee on Narcotics Abuse and Control, and seldom missed a chance to relate other problems to drugs; after all, he has seen how they can destroy a community. Rangel wants money spent on rehabilitation programs as much as interdiction and police work, but he also worked with the Bush Justice Department to create the Weed and Seed program, combining intensive law enforcement with social services. And he takes sharp issue with those who call for legalization of marijuana or provision of free needles to curtail AIDS, or giving heroin to terminal cancer patients.

On Ways and Means Rangel worked, with success, to protect state and local tax deductibility in the 1986 tax reform and for years was a prime defender of Section 936, the tax exemption that has created many jobs in Puerto Rico, now being phased out. He is an author of the Federal Empowerment Zone demonstration, the Low Income Housing tax credit (which he says financed 90% of affordable housing from 1984–94) and the Targeted Jobs tax credit: those programs have helped Harlem turn around. Rangel's own involvement with Harlem development has been more controversial. The Harlem Urban Development Corporation, on which Rangel has had a major voice, if not control, for years did not disclose its records; in May 1997 Rangel called for them to be made public, but said defensively, as they were described in the *Daily News* as "piles of documentation of ugly management": "I don't see this as any goddam thing my community has to explain! They haven't identified one son of a bitch who has done anything wrong!" And he continued to back the Apollo Theater Foundation's TV contract with a firm controlled by former Borough President Percy Sutton. Rangel can often provide counsel for restraint, as he did before the anti-semitic Khalil Muhammad's "Million Youth March" in September 1998, though he criticized the police afterward for moving to disperse it immediately at the 4 p.m. deadline.

Similarly, Rangel combines political shrewdness with an occasional tendency toward extravagant rhetoric, when it suits his purposes. When a bipartisan majority voted to end racial preferences in broadcasting in 1995, Rangel lashed out in a letter to Ways and Means Chairman Bill Archer: "Mr. Chairman, in America we cannot afford to be colorblind. Just like under Hitler, people say they don't mean to blame any particular individuals and groups, but in the U.S. those groups always turn out to be minorities and immigrants." This of course was inaccurate—Hitler did single out Jews and other groups for persecution—but it also coarsened political discourse, as Archer noted. When the House debated impeachment while U.S. planes bombed Iraq, Rangel said, "In times of war, anyone who conspires against the commander-in-chief . . . comes a lot closer to high crimes and misdemeanors than where the president's hands were at any given time in the Oval Office." But he has not always gotten along with Bill Clinton or his administration. He opposed the president's tax credit for college students as not germane to Harlem. He criticized as "a waste of my time" Clinton's call for task forces to reach common ground on budget issues between the White House and Congress. He was furious when Clinton, without notification, line-item vetoed a New York Medicaid subsidy in August 1997. He resented it when the administration negotiated directly with Republicans, leaving congressional Democrats out of the loop. He criticized the Clinton Administration for using wealth rather than income to make beneficiaries of tax cuts look richer than they are in July 1997. And he was one of the few to criticize the $300,000 "fee" imposed on Newt Gingrich for his ethics violations in January 1997.

Since January 1997 Rangel has been ranking Democrat on Ways and Means; if Democrats win in 2000, he would be the first New York City chairman since Fernando Wood in 1877–81. "Congress has always been perceived by New Yorkers as a step to go some place to run for mayor, to run for governor or to become a federal judge," he said. "We never really had seniority here. We never stuck around long enough to enjoy chairmanships. I did." Republicans argue that he would seek tax increases; that seems unlikely, at least in the short run, but it is fair to say he does not look kindly on tax cuts or on tax-free IRA-type accounts.

For years Rangel had no serious competition at home and was in the majority in Washington. In the 1994 primary he was opposed by the son of his predecessor, the Puerto Rican-raised Adam Clayton Powell IV (Adam Clayton Powell III, another son, is a respected media expert). Rangel spent $1.4 million and won 61%–33%. After the 1996 election, he became a co-chairman of the Democratic Congressional Campaign Committee, in effect a major fundraiser. Over the cycle he raised more than $1.3 million for Democratic candidates, drawing on successful black entrepreneurs like Robert Johnson of Black Entertainment Television and on many business interests eager to help out a possible chairman of Ways and Means.

Cook's Call. *Safe.* Rangel has been the congressman for this Harlem-based district for almost 30 years, and he can keep this seat for as long as he likes.

The People: Pop. 1990: 580,354; 12.4% age 65 +; 27.7% White, 46.9% Black, 2.3% Asian, 0.6% Amer. Indian, 22.5% Other; 45.2% Hispanic Origin. Households: 25% married couple families; 12.3% married couple fams. w. children; 34.7% college educ.; median household income: $19,238; per capita income: $10,367; median house value: $186,600; median gross rent: $354.

1996 Presidential Vote			1992 Presidential Vote		
Clinton (D)	135,845	(93%)	Clinton (D)	123,274	(86%)
Dole (R)	7,658	(5%)	Bush (R)	15,410	(11%)
Perot (I)	2,377	(2%)	Perot (I)	4,670	(3%)

Rep. Charles B. Rangel (D)

Elected 1970; b. June 11, 1930, New York City; home, Manhattan; N.Y.U., B.S. 1957, St. John's U., LL.B. 1960; Catholic; married (Alma).

Military Career: Army, 1948–52 (Korea).

Elected Office: NY Assembly, 1966–70.

Professional Career: Asst. U.S. Atty., S. Dist. of NY, 1961; Legal Cnsl., NYC Housing & Redevel. Bd., Neighborhood Conservation Bureau, 1963–68; Gen. Cnsl., Natl. Advisory Comm. on Selective Svc., 1966.

DC Office: 2354 RHOB 20515, 202-225-4365; Fax: 202-225-0816; Web site: www.house.gov/rangel.

District Offices: Manhattan, 212-348-9630; Manhattan, 212-663-3900.

Committees: *Ways & Means* (RMM of 16 D): Trade. *Joint Committee on Taxation* (4th of 5 Reps.).

Group Ratings

	ADA	ACLU	AFS	LCV	CON	NTU	NFIB	COC	ACU	NTLC	CHC
1998	90	94	100	69	81	18	9	29	9	3	0
1997	95	—	100	—	4	21	—	30	16	—	—

National Journal Ratings

	1997 LIB — 1997 CONS			1998 LIB — 1998 CONS		
Economic	82%	—	15%	79%	—	0%
Social	85%	—	0%	93%	—	0%
Foreign	97%	—	0%	77%	—	22%

Key Votes of the 105th Congress

1. Clinton Budget Deal	N	5. Puerto Rico Sthood. Ref.	Y	9. Cut $ for B-2 Bombers	Y
2. Education IRAs	N	6. End Highway Set-asides	*	10. Human Rights in China	Y
3. Req. 2/3 to Raise Taxes	N	7. School Prayer Amend.	N	11. Withdraw Bosnia Troops	N
4. Fast-track Trade	N	8. Ovrd. Part. Birth Veto	N	12. End Cuban TV-Marti	Y

Election Results

1998 general	Charles B. Rangel (D-L)	90,424	(93%)	($1,051,333)
	David E. Cunningham (R)	5,633	(6%)	
	Others	1,082	(1%)	
1998 primary	Charles B. Rangel (D)	unopposed		
1996 general	Charles B. Rangel (D-L)	113,898	(91%)	($1,086,065)
	Edward R. Adams (R)	5,951	(5%)	
	Others	4,885	(4%)	

SIXTEENTH DISTRICT

It may not quite be "the beautiful Bronx," as borough historian Lloyd Utlan calls it, but the Bronx seems to be coming back. The beautiful days were in the 1930s and 1940s, when Presidents Roosevelt and Truman rode down 138th Street, when Babe Ruth and Lou Gehrig and Joe DiMaggio hit home runs in Yankee Stadium, when Art Deco apartment buildings went up along the Grand Concourse, when shoppers thronged Tremont Avenue stores and New Yorkers from all over flocked to the Bronx Zoo. This Bronx was built in a trice, starting in

1906 when the first subway came in, bringing the children of immigrants from dimly lit Lower East Side tenements to more spacious apartments flooded with light. The Bronx's population grew from 200,000 in 1900 to 430,000 in 1910, 732,000 in 1920, and 1.3 million in 1930—more than the 1.2 million of 1990.

The Bronx fell rapidly in the dozen years after John Lindsay was elected mayor in 1965. One reason was rent control, insisted on by tenants, which guarantees that owners of low-rent property won't maintain it: The result is empty vandalized shells and venues for drug deals. Another was the drop in low-income, low-skill jobs in Manhattan and the Bronx, abetted by high union and minimum wages, restrictive work rules and the tolls exacted by organized crime. A third reason was the disintegration of family structure: Stable, law-abiding males became scarce in these parts. But most important was crime. With no community institutions and little parental supervision, poor teenagers here committed an alarming number of crimes, with seeming impunity. Arson became increasingly common, perpetrated by kids for kicks or on behalf of landlords who wanted to get insurance money for rent-controlled buildings. A vicious cycle was created: Crime drove away jobs, which drove away fathers, which produced more crime. A section of the South Bronx with 476,000 people in 1960 and 460,000 in 1970 dropped to 233,000 in 1980, a stunning change. As people left, presidents and presidential candidates came in—Jimmy Carter in 1977, Ronald Reagan in 1980—promising help.

Now the South Bronx seems to have turned around. It is still one of the lowest-income parts of America, but it is beginning to be possible for low-income families here to work their way up. Government has helped, particularly former Democratic Mayor Edward Koch's housing subsidies and current Republican Mayor Rudolph Giuliani's police tactics. Rent control was phased out, criminals were held in prison longer, pocket parks were built, graffiti painted over, crime vastly reduced. But citizens here did much of the work, forming community groups called Banana Kelly or Mid-Bronx Desperadoes (now MBD Housing) to build single-family pastel bungalows and small-scale apartment projects for the elderly, single-parent families and former homeless. Local institutions, notably Bronx-Lebanon Hospital, remained in operation, employing area residents and becoming a strong force for neighborhood stability; warehousing and truck terminals opened up as the streets became safer. Population rose in the South Bronx in the latter 1980s more than almost anywhere else in New York City. Charlotte Street, which Carter and Reagan once visited as the worst of the slums, is now Charlotte Gardens, with $180,000 owner-occupied homes.

The 16th Congressional District includes most of the Bronx south of the Bronx Zoo. It includes the Art Deco apartments of the Grand Concourse and the narrow commercial strips of Westchester Avenue, Boston Road and the Hub. It includes the industrial flatlands of Bruckner Boulevard and Hunts Point and the hard-rock ridges through which the original subways bore. This is still a low-income district, with more residents below the poverty line than any other in the nation in 1990, with the lowest median family income, the second lowest per capita income and the third lowest median household income of any congressional district. The people here are 59% Hispanic—though not all are Puerto Rican, the district has New York City's largest Puerto Rican community—and 43% black (the categories aren't mutually exclusive). Politically, this was the most Democratic district in the country in 1996, 95% for Bill Clinton and 4% for Bob Dole.

The congressman from the 16th is Jose Serrano, chosen in a March 1990 special election. A native of Mayaguez, Puerto Rico who grew up in the Millbrook project in the South Bronx, Serrano moved up while other Bronx politicians have fallen by the wayside due to corruption. He was elected to the New York Assembly in 1974 and chaired its Education Committee beginning in 1983; in 1985, he ran for Bronx borough president, bucking the Bronx Democratic organization, and nearly won. Two years later the winner was forced out because of scandal. Then in January 1990, South Bronx Congressman Robert Garcia was convicted for accepting money from the minority contractor Wedtech; his resignation (his conviction was later reversed) opened up the way to Serrano's election to the House, and he has held the seat without difficulty.

Serrano has one of the most liberal voting records in the House. In 1993 he got a seat on Appropriations; he was bumped off after Democrats lost control in 1994 but regained the seat in March 1996 and is now ranking Democrat on the Subcommittee on Commerce, Justice, State and the Judiciary. In January 1997, when Bill Richardson resigned from the House to become U.N. Ambassador, Minority Leader Dick Gephardt passed over Serrano for the less senior Robert Menendez of New Jersey—a better fundraiser, with his Cuban-American connections— to be chief deputy whip. In 1998 Serrano ran for Democratic Caucus vice-chairman as "the candidate who refuses to raise money to buy your vote for leadership." But in October he withdrew in favor of Menendez. Serrano is known as Fidel Castro's greatest champion in the House. He says he admires Castro and has sought repeal of economic sanctions and the Helms-Burton Act; he argued for admitting Cuban baseball players without requiring they renounce the Castro regime. He calls Puerto Rico an American "colony," and strongly backs statehood. He supported Don Young's bill authorizing a statehood referendum, which passed the House by one vote in March 1998. Serrano's own amendment to allow the 2.7 million Puerto Ricans on the mainland to vote as well as the 3.7 million Puerto Ricans on the island was defeated; but he was pleased that Gerald Solomon's amendment requiring English to be used in government and schools of a state of Puerto Rico failed as well. In December 1998, the pro-statehood Puerto Rico government conducted its own referendum, in which statehood won 46.5%, the same as in the 1993 referendum, and "none of the above," supported by backers of the current commonwealth status and of independence, got 50.3%. "You can't reject statehood without presenting an alternative," Serrano grumbled. But the move toward statehood stalled.

In New York politics, Serrano takes stubbornly liberal positions. He is at political odds with Borough President Fernando Ferrer and Bronx Democratic Chairman Roberto Ramirez. He backed Al Sharpton for mayor in 1997 and Mark Green for senator in 1998; both lost. In November 1997 he told colleagues he would run for mayor in 2001, but later said he was not interested. The statement was seen as a poke at Ferrer, who ran for a while in 1997 and then withdrew. Meanwhile, Serrano was alert to affronts from other quarters. He called an amendment to channel bilingual education money to programs which teach English in two years an attempt "to beat up on immigrants and gain votes from the far right." He attacked the Census undercount, allegedly larger here than in any other congressional district. When owner George Steinbrenner threatened to move his team out of the South Bronx's Yankee Stadium, he called on Clinton to declare it a national landmark, but as Steinbrenner's spokesman pointed out, landmark status would prevent the changes needed to make the stadium profitable and structurally sound. Serrano achieved one goal when he persuaded the House in April 1997 to award a Congressional Gold Medal to Frank Sinatra, whose work he has long admired; he presented it to Nancy Sinatra in June 1998.

Cook's Call. *Safe.* A district that gave Dole less than 5,000 votes in 1996 is not a place where Democrats should have any troubles. Serrano should be safe for 2000.

The People: Pop. 1990: 581,053; 7.3% age 65 +; 20% White, 42.7% Black, 1.9% Asian, 0.5% Amer. Indian, 34.9% Other; 59% Hispanic Origin. Households: 27.9% married couple families; 16.6% married couple fams. w. children; 22% college educ.; median household income: $15,060; per capita income: $7,102; median house value: $144,300; median gross rent: $342.

1996 Presidential Vote		
Clinton (D)	117,624	(95%)
Dole (R)	4,825	(4%)
Perot (I)	1,862	(1%)

1992 Presidential Vote		
Clinton (D)	99,357	(81%)
Bush (R)	18,692	(15%)
Perot (I)	4,025	(3%)

Rep. Jose Serrano (D)

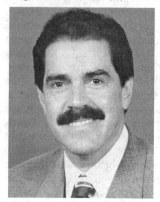

Elected Mar. 1990; b. Oct. 24, 1943, Mayaguez, PR; home, Bronx; Lehman Col.; Catholic; married (Mary).

Military Career: Army Medical Corps, 1964–66.

Elected Office: Dist. 7 Schl. Bd., 1969–74; NY Assembly, 1974–90.

Professional Career: Banker, 1961–69.

DC Office: 2342 RHOB 20515, 202-225-4361; Fax: 202-225-6001; Web site: www.house.gov/serrano.

District Office: Bronx, 718-538-5400.

Committees: *Appropriations* (12th of 27 D): Commerce, Justice, State & the Judiciary (RMM); Transportation.

Group Ratings

	ADA	ACLU	AFS	LCV	CON	NTU	NFIB	COC	ACU	NTLC	CHC
1998	90	93	100	69	55	13	0	25	0	0	0
1997	95	—	100	—	5	20	—	30	8	—	—

National Journal Ratings

	1997 LIB	—	1997 CONS	1998 LIB	—	1998 CONS
Economic	85%	—	10%	79%	—	0%
Social	85%	—	0%	93%	—	0%
Foreign	85%	—	13%	89%	—	10%

Key Votes of the 105th Congress

1. Clinton Budget Deal	N	5. Puerto Rico Sthood. Ref.	Y	9. Cut $ for B-2 Bombers	Y
2. Education IRAs	N	6. End Highway Set-asides	N	10. Human Rights in China	Y
3. Req. 2/3 to Raise Taxes	N	7. School Prayer Amend.	N	11. Withdraw Bosnia Troops	N
4. Fast-track Trade	N	8. Ovrd. Part. Birth Veto	*	12. End Cuban TV-Marti	Y

Election Results

1998 general	Jose Serrano (D-L)	67,367	(95%)	($71,281)
	Others	3,213	(5%)	
1998 primary	Jose Serrano (D)	unopposed		
1996 general	Jose Serrano (D-L)	95,568	(96%)	($149,752)
	Others	3,665	(4%)	

SEVENTEENTH DISTRICT

The Bronx, a product almost entirely of the first half of the 20th Century, was originally a collection of middle-class neighborhoods clustered around subway stops, a borough where children of immigrants left gloomy Manhattan for the sunlight of wide avenues and the vistas of a city where the street grid bent to adapt to nature's ridges and hills. Different ethnic groups were clustered here and there: Irish in Kingsbridge, in the valley between Riverdale and the Grand Concourse; Italians in Bedford Park, north of Fordham University and Bronx Park; well-to-do WASPs and Jews in Riverdale, on the palisades above the Hudson River; Jews with less education and advantages originally in the Art Deco apartments on the Grand Concourse, then in a rush to Co-op City, the giant union-built apartment complex, with 35 35-story buildings, built in 1965 on marshland between the Hutchinson River Parkway and I-95.

The 17th Congressional District includes much of these Bronx neighborhoods plus several in the Westchester County suburbs just to the north. Co-op City is one anchor, and perhaps the largest political bloc in the district. Just to the west is the heavily black, middle-income neighborhood of Williamsbridge. The 17th's portions of Yonkers, Mount Vernon and New Rochelle in Westchester are carefully drawn to include most blacks there. The district also dips south along the Harlem River to take in some housing projects in the South Bronx. The 17th is, in Voting Rights Act argot, a minority-influence district, 42% black and 29% Hispanic in 1990.

Eliot Engel, the congressman from the 17th District, is a son of the Bronx and long a resident of Co-op City (though now he lives in Riverdale), a political junkie who memorized the names of the 100 senators when he was a boy. He was a teacher and guidance counselor who has won office (like Jose Serrano in the next-door 16th District) when incumbents have been struck by scandal. He was elected to the New York Assembly in a special election in March 1977, at 30, to replace a convicted incumbent, and to the House in 1988 to replace Democrat Mario Biaggi, once the most decorated member of the New York Police Department, after he was convicted in two tawdry bribery cases. Engel beat Biaggi in the Democratic primary 48%–26% and in the general, in which Biaggi was the Republican nominee, by 56%–27%.

Engel has one of the most liberal voting records in the House. On the Education and the Workforce Committee he backed the public sector programs that are part of the fabric of New York life—public housing, education spending, mental health services. He is currently on leave from his seat on International Relations, where made his name as the backer of one ethnic cause after another—members of just about any ethnic group can be found in the Bronx. He was the prime sponsor of the 1990 resolution to recognize Jerusalem as the capital of Israel. He has met with Sinn Fein leader Gerry Adams, proposed legislation to oppose the British in Northern Ireland, and supported the Clinton involvement in seeking peace there. He has sponsored designation of October as Italian American Culture and Heritage Month and, with Rick Lazio and Alfonse D'Amato, called for investigation of the internment of Italian nationals and other harsh restrictions in 1941 and 1942. With his aide John Calvelli and his organization Fieri (Pride) he protested the inane movie *Mafia!* "I was just outraged because I feel that this has perpetuated the unfair stereotypes of the Italian-American community."

Engel is not a 1970s-style dove: he supported the Gulf war resolution in 1991 and the bombing of Serbia to get a settlement in Bosnia in 1995. He heads the Congressional Albanian Issues Caucus and in March 1997, after failure of a pyramid scheme, helped persuade President Sali Berisha to hold new elections, which he lost. He also keeps an eye on Albanian rights in the Former Yugoslav Republic of Macedonia. In March 1997 he served as the U.S. member of a delegation to Albania and sponsored House resolutions urging full human and political rights to ethnic Albanians in the Kosovo region of Serbia. He called for air strikes after the 1998 Yugoslav crackdown and got a U.S. Information Office set up in Pristina. In June 1998 he denounced Russian involvement in the Kosovo negotiations.

At home, Engel is a relentless constituency service congressman, with five district offices in this geographically tiny district. In June 1996 *The Wall Street Journal* profiled him as "Revenge of a Nerd," telling how he is known as "the mayor" in the north Bronx because of his persistent attention to local problems from broken traffic lights to congested subway trains. When stories broke about alleged arson of southern black churches, Engel held an arson protection conference for local churches and synagogues.

The major political threat to Engel is the rising percentages of blacks and Hispanics in the district; the electorate is now 42% black and 29% Hispanic. In 1994 he was opposed by salsa singer Willie Colon, who was supported by Al Sharpton and Assemblyman Larry Seabrook. Engel won 61%–39%, not an entirely reassuring margin. But he has forestalled serious primary opposition since. In 1996 Colon withdrew from the race before the primary. In 1998 Seabrook, who is black and is now a state senator, made no secret he was running, after bowing out of races for city controller and city public advocate in 1997. Engel was endorsed unanimously by Democrats in heavily black Mount Vernon; in May he got a 69% endorsement vote from the

Black Democrats of Westchester County. "The congressman says he likes primaries—they keep you sharp," one aide says. But he likes even more not having serious opposition. In June 1998 Democratic County Chairman Roberto Ramirez spoke to Seabrook, making vague promises about working on voter registration, and Seabrook bowed out of the 1998 race, saying he would run in 2000. Some said the district was staked out for a black candidate that year, but the betting here is that Eliot Engel will win again. Engel won with 80% against a man accused of date rape a month before the primary (a grand jury found insufficient evidence for indictment a month after).

One other Engel tradition: Since 1989 he has staked out an aisle seat hours before each State of the Union speech, so that he can shake the president's hand.

Cook's Call. *Safe.* Engel's only threat in this solidly Democratic district will come from another Democrat; he has been consistently challenged in the primary since he was elected in 1988.

The People: Pop. 1990: 578,424; 15% age 65 + ; 40.4% White, 41.9% Black, 3.7% Asian, 0.4% Amer. Indian, 13.7% Other; 28.5% Hispanic Origin. Households: 37.4% married couple families; 17.8% married couple fams. w. children; 37.5% college educ.; median household income: $27,227; per capita income: $13,155; median house value: $176,400; median gross rent: $437.

1996 Presidential Vote			1992 Presidential Vote		
Clinton (D)	126,787	(86%)	Clinton (D)	118,799	(76%)
Dole (R)	16,238	(11%)	Bush (R)	29,945	(19%)
Perot (I)	3,844	(3%)	Perot (I)	7,883	(5%)

Rep. Eliot L. Engel (D)

Elected 1988; b. Feb. 18, 1947, Bronx; home, Bronx; Hunter-Lehman Col., B.A. 1969, C.U.N.Y., Lehman Col., M.A. 1973, NY Law Schl., J.D. 1987; Jewish; married (Patricia).

Elected Office: NY Assembly, 1977–88.

Professional Career: Teacher, guidance counselor, NYC public schl., 1969–77.

DC Office: 2303 RHOB 20515, 202-225-2464; Web site: www.house.gov/engel.

District Offices: Bronx, 718-796-9700; Bronx, 718-652-0400; Bronx, 718-320-2314; Mt. Vernon, 914-699-4100; Yonkers, 914-423-0700.

Committees: *Commerce* (15th of 24 D): Finance & Hazardous Materials; Telecommunications, Trade & Consumer Protection.

Group Ratings

	ADA	ACLU	AFS	LCV	CON	NTU	NFIB	COC	ACU	NTLC	CHC
1998	95	81	100	100	48	15	8	24	4	3	0
1997	100	—	100	—	5	22	—	30	8	—	—

National Journal Ratings

	1997 LIB — 1997 CONS			1998 LIB — 1998 CONS		
Economic	91%	—	7%	79%	—	0%
Social	82%	—	15%	88%	—	12%
Foreign	79%	—	21%	63%	—	36%

Key Votes of the 105th Congress

1. Clinton Budget Deal	N	5. Puerto Rico Sthood. Ref.	Y	9. Cut $ for B-2 Bombers	Y
2. Education IRAs	N	6. End Highway Set-asides	N	10. Human Rights in China	Y
3. Req. 2/3 to Raise Taxes	N	7. School Prayer Amend.	N	11. Withdraw Bosnia Troops	N
4. Fast-track Trade	N	8. Ovrd. Part. Birth Veto	N	12. End Cuban TV-Marti	N

Election Results

1998 general	Eliot L. Engel (D-L)	80,947	(88%)	($364,459)
	Peter Fiumefreddo (R-C-Ind)	11,037	(12%)	($16,043)
1998 primary	Eliot L. Engel (D)	22,405	(80%)	
	Herbert Moreira-Brown (D)	5,649	(20%)	
1996 general	Eliot L. Engel (D-L)	101,287	(85%)	($374,074)
	Denis McCarthy (R-C-RTL)	15,892	(13%)	
	Others	2,008	(2%)	

EIGHTEENTH DISTRICT

The great granite ridges that form the spine of Manhattan and the Bronx move north into the thin peninsula of land between Long Island Sound and the Hudson River that is lower Westchester County. Blessed with some of America's loveliest scenery, easily accessible to Manhattan by train since the mid-19th Century, this became some of the country's first suburban terrain, with grand estates built by great millionaires, like Jay Gould's Gothic revival Lyndhurst or John D. Rockefeller's spectacular Kykuit, with villages for retainers clustered around the railroad stations.

Today, Westchester still looks suburban, perhaps more than ever now that it has a nice patina of age. It has little commuter railroad stations across from faux Tudor drugstores, soda fountains and cobblestone post offices; it also has shopping malls and galleries and corporate headquarters. The county does have its share of homeless and racial ghettos, its seedy neighborhoods if not slums. Intensive development has not proceeded too far north of White Plains, for just to the north Westchester is crossed by the first of several mountain ridges—the closest the Appalachians come to the ocean. Historically Republican, Westchester is now intensely marginal political territory. More than Nassau or Suffolk counties or northern New Jersey, it has attracted liberal-minded professionals, often Jewish, who have made very high-income places like Scarsdale Democratic strongholds. In addition, blue-collar voters and blacks in southern Westchester make this a mixed constituency. Westchester votes a lot like the comfortable central city neighborhoods it physically resembles—Cambridge's Brattle Street, Philadelphia's Chestnut Hill, Washington's Cleveland Park.

The 18th Congressional District contains the heart of suburban Westchester County but actually has less than half the county's population; it also includes a little territory in the Bronx and widely scattered areas in Queens. Politics, as one might expect, is at work here; this is a district designed for Congresswoman Nita Lowey, a Democrat first elected in 1988 and a favorite of then-Governor Mario Cuomo. The 18th includes most of southern Westchester, but not the black neighborhoods of Yonkers, Mount Vernon and New Rochelle, which are in the minority-influence 17th District. It includes the rich, Catholic and conservative suburbs of Pelham, Eastchester and Bronxville, and the more Jewish and liberal Scarsdale, plus some of the Long Island Sound towns. The 18th also contains the southern half of White Plains, the county seat-corporate headquarters-shopping mall center. From there the 18th goes on its odyssey, picking up a few thousand people in Bronx communities facing the Sound and the urban resort of City Island. Then it crosses the Throgs Neck Bridge and is connected by a block-wide land-bridge through Flushing to two distinct areas of Queens. One is Lefrak City and other high-rise apartments in Rego Park, along Queens Boulevard, where the first condominium conversion in New York took place in 1966; this area is heavily Jewish and very Democratic.

The other is the heavily Italian neighborhoods around St. John's University, including the longtime home of its most famous alumnus, Mario Cuomo, in the pleasant winding streets of Holliswood, a more politically mixed area.

Nita Lowey was born in the Bronx, raised her family in Queens, and now lives in upper-crust Harrison in Westchester. She went to work for Cuomo in 1975, after he was appointed secretary of state by Governor Hugh Carey; she was an assistant secretary of state when she decided to run for Congress in 1988. In the primary, she faced Hamilton Fish III, son and grandson of Republican Hudson River congressmen, and as a former publisher of *The Nation* considerably more liberal than Lowey; she won 44%–36%. Her opponent in the general was Joseph DioGuardi, a two-term incumbent who trumpeted his experience as a CPA but was dogged by charges of illicit contributions; she won 50%–47%. Each spent over $1 million, with Lowey spending $657,000 in personal funds.

In the House, Lowey has a fairly solid liberal record. She has been a Clinton Administration loyalist when it was tough to be so, voting for the 1993 budget and tax package in this high-income district, splitting with most New York Democrats and organized labor to support NAFTA after lobbying from Bill Clinton and an ad barrage against it from the AFL-CIO, she voted against fast track. She helped to originate the plan for federal aid for school construction; it was dropped from the budget agreement in July 1997, and revived by Clinton in his 1998 and 1999 State of the Union addresses as a major Democratic initiative. She was one of the leaders against the peanut quota and for standardized milk dating in 1997.

Much of Lowey's legislative work has been done in Appropriations, and much has been connected with feminist issues and what might be called lifestyle choices. In 1994 she organized 72 members, mostly Democrats, who pledged not to vote for a health care plan that did not cover abortions. When Hillary Rodham Clinton refused to rule out dropping abortion coverage, Lowey replied, "For those who'll say there'll be a fight if you put it in, I'm saying there'll be a fight if you take it out." She was a leading backer of funds for international family planning including abortion. She has been a leading speaker against the "partial-birth" abortion ban. In 1997 she blocked expansion of the Hyde amendment against Medicaid abortions. She achieved a rare feminist victory in Congress by getting into the October 1998 omnibus bill a provision requiring federal employee health plans that cover prescriptions to cover contraceptives; reluctantly she agreed to an exclusion for plans and physicians with religious objections. Working with Hyde, she expanded coverage of the Children's Health Insurance Program for prenatal benefits. With Rosa DeLauro and Nancy Pelosi, she worked for increased funding for breast and cervical cancer screening. She attacked Defense Secretary William Cohen's decision not to discharge General Joseph Ralston because of adultery and said the military should adjust their standards.

Lowey has been a strong supporter of the National Endowment for the Arts and was named to its board in December 1997. She opposed a 15% cap on state NEA grants: "Artistic excellence is not spread evenly around the country. Other states produce corn and soybeans; our tremendous contribution to the United States is our artistic areas, among other things." She led the fight in 1998 to reduce the legal blood alcohol level from .10% to .08%; it was not voted on in the House and rejected in conference. She has proposed a federal tobacco licensing system for stores, with revocation after the third offense of selling to minors. On local matters, she got money for restoration of Beaver Swamp Brook in Westchester and Willow Lake in Queens, dredging of Mamaroneck Harbor and cleanup of the Long Island Sound watershed. With Henry Hyde, she blocked an attempt to open new slots in four restricted airports (New York's LaGuardia and Kennedy, Chicago's O'Hare and Washington's Reagan National). She called for the Kennedy-LaGuardia rail line to be built underground instead of overhead. She sponsored a resolution condemning England's attempt to remove the original *Winnie the Pooh* from the New York Public Library.

Since Lowey first won, the 18th District has been moving left, and she has proved a prodigious fundraiser, never spending less than $878,000 on a campaign. In 1992, DioGuardi came back for a rematch; she won 71% in the Queens portion just added to the district and won overall 56%–44%. In 1994, against a lawyer who put $247,000 of his own money into the race, she won 57%–41%. In 1996 she won 64%–32%. Lowey was mentioned as a Senate candidate in 1998, but she bowed out in early 1997, apparently deferring to Geraldine Ferraro. In November 1998, when Senator Daniel Patrick Moynihan announced he would retire in 2000, Lowey was mentioned as one of several Democrats interested in the seat; several others dropped out and Lowey stayed in. When rumors of a Hillary Rodham Clinton candidacy began, Lowey said she would step aside and support the First Lady.

Cook's Call. *Safe.* There was an audible sigh of relief from national Democrats in early June when Lowey announced that she was running for re-election instead of running for the seat of retiring Senator Daniel Moynihan. Though Lowey has had little trouble in recent years holding on to this seat, it is still rather marginal and would have been hotly contested as an open seat. For the 2000 election, however, Lowey should be considered safe.

The People: Pop. 1990: 581,021; 17.7% age 65 +; 81.3% White, 7.4% Black, 8.2% Asian, 0.1% Amer. Indian, 3% Other; 10.2% Hispanic Origin. Households: 54.7% married couple families; 23.2% married couple fams. w. children; 53.7% college educ.; median household income: $43,754; per capita income: $24,392; median house value: $288,500; median gross rent: $540.

1996 Presidential Vote

Clinton (D)	121,501	(59%)
Dole (R)	73,399	(36%)
Perot (I)	10,215	(5%)

1992 Presidential Vote

Clinton (D)	117,393	(50%)
Bush (R)	94,377	(40%)
Perot (I)	21,914	(9%)

Rep. Nita M. Lowey (D)

Elected 1988; b. July 5, 1937, Bronx; home, Harrison; Mt. Holyoke Col., B.A. 1959; Jewish; married (Stephen).

Professional Career: Asst. for Econ. Devel. & Neighborhood Preservation, NY Secy. of State; Dep. Dir., Division of Econ. Opportunity, 1975–85; NY Asst. Secy. of St., 1985–87.

DC Office: 2421 RHOB 20515, 202-225-6506; Fax: 202-225-0546; Web site: www.house.gov/lowey.

District Offices: Rego Park, 718-897-3602; White Plains, 914-428-1707.

Committees: *Appropriations* (11th of 27 D): Foreign Operations & Export Financing; Labor, HHS & Education.

Group Ratings

	ADA	ACLU	AFS	LCV	CON	NTU	NFIB	COC	ACU	NTLC	CHC
1998	100	81	100	100	48	18	15	35	8	5	0
1997	95	—	88	—	52	36	—	40	8	—	—

National Journal Ratings

	1997 LIB — 1997 CONS			1998 LIB — 1998 CONS		
Economic	82%	—	15%	79%	—	0%
Social	76%	—	23%	81%	—	19%
Foreign	90%	—	10%	64%	—	31%

Key Votes of the 105th Congress

1. Clinton Budget Deal	N	5. Puerto Rico Sthood. Ref.	Y	9. Cut $ for B-2 Bombers	Y
2. Education IRAs	N	6. End Highway Set-asides	N	10. Human Rights in China	Y
3. Req. 2/3 to Raise Taxes	N	7. School Prayer Amend.	N	11. Withdraw Bosnia Troops	N
4. Fast-track Trade	N	8. Ovrd. Part. Birth Veto	N	12. End Cuban TV-Marti	Y

Election Results

1998 general	Nita M. Lowey (D) 91,623	(83%)	($932,342)
	Daniel McMahon (C) 12,594	(11%)	
	Others 6,485	(6%)	
1998 primary	Nita M. Lowey (D) .... unopposed		
1996 general	Nita M. Lowey (D) 118,194	(64%)	($1,138,456)
	Kerry J. Katsorhis (R-C) 59,487	(32%)	($238,826)
	Others 8,041	(4%)	

NINETEENTH DISTRICT

The great interior of America can be said to begin where the Hudson River squeezes through the chain of Appalachian ridges at the Hudson Highlands. This choke point was the barrier to British military power during the Revolutionary War, when American forces built a chain across the river to keep the British from sailing north. It was over control of this part of the Hudson that Benedict Arnold betrayed his country, and it was here that the new nation built its Military Academy high on the cliffs at West Point. The Hudson was the impetus for the builders of the Erie Canal and the water-level New York Central Railroad, the great projects that made New York City the port of the American interior, as well as the builders of the Croton Aqueduct not far away, which provided the water without which New York could not grow—and also provided a way for the first cockroaches to reach the city.

The lower Hudson was Dutch territory, with Washington Irving country in Tarrytown and ancient estates like the now-restored Philipsburg Manor. In the late 19th Century, the ridges east of the Lower Hudson were first the site of great estates of New York's very rich and then became high-income suburbs: colonial-style Bedford, woodsy Chappaqua, John Cheever's Ossining. And in the mid-20th Century, these hills became home to some of America's leading corporations. *Reader's Digest* had built its colonial-style campus north of Pleasantville as early as the 1930s; General Foods moved to the north side of White Plains in the 1950s; soon after, not far from the Cross-Westchester Expressway, IBM, Pepsico, and Texaco built headquarters. Yet as woods have grown over what used to be farmland, this country has also become wilder: overpopulating deer have been eating gardens in northern Westchester and in May 1997 a black bear was captured running loose in White Plains.

The 19th Congressional District covers much of the lower Hudson. It reaches south to take in part of White Plains and the corporate territory nearby, and includes northern Westchester County—now, for all its rural look, with almost as many people as the population-losing suburbs nearer New York City. The 19th runs north across towns filling up with middle-income public and corporate employees seeking reasonably priced housing in safe areas, up through Putnam County to Dutchess County and the old city of Poughkeepsie on the Hudson and the valleys of Millbrook and Amenia and the Innisfree gardens. It crosses the Hudson where the rebels' chain did, by West Point and the Storm King Highway, and runs inland in Orange County. IBM, with its headquarters in Armonk and research center in Yorktown Heights, has been a major area employer, and its longtime policy of lifetime employment was a mainstay here; IBM's big layoffs in the mid-1990s came as an unnerving shock. Politically, sentiments here run counter to what might be expected. The older communities, with their well-educated and liberally inclined residents, have been historically Republican but now lean more to the Democrats. The newer communities, with upwardly striving people often disgusted by the crime and cultural disorder of New York City, may be filled with ancestral Democrats but are trending Republican.

The congresswoman from this district is Sue Kelly, a Republican elected in 1994. Kelly is not a Hudson Valley aristocrat but the daughter of a Lima, Ohio, doctor. She met her husband while she was a botany researcher at Harvard; they raised their family in Katonah, where she volunteered in many organizations, worked as a patient advocate, rape crisis counselor and educator, and sang in a church choir. She had a business renovating buildings and owned and ran a florist shop. She also had political experience as campaign manager for Assemblyman Jon Fossel in the 1970s. In March 1994, Congressman Hamilton Fish, a Hudson County aristocrat, son of another Congressman Hamilton Fish and descendant of Ulysses S. Grant's Secretary of State Hamilton Fish, decided to retire, and Kelly decided to use the $150,000 she had saved to buy a new business to help finance a campaign for Congress instead.

It was a crowded field, in which Kelly emerged as the only candidate who was both for lower taxes and "huge" budget cuts, and pro-choice on abortion. Her chief opponent in the primary was Joseph DioGuardi, elected in 1984 and 1986 in the Westchester district to the south and defeated there by Nita Lowey in 1988 and 1992. He said Kelly was a "Democrat in disguise," but he had to dodge charges of district-shopping. Kelly won with 23% to DioGuardi's 20%, with two other candidates at 19% and 18%. The Democratic nominee was Hamilton Fish Jr., son of the retiring congressman but as publisher of the leftish and anti-Israel *The Nation*, with quite different politics; he was known as Hamilton Fish III until the death of his grandfather, Franklin Roosevelt's least favorite congressman, in January 1991 at age 102. This was expected to be a close race but with good margins in the northern counties Kelly beat Fish 52%–37%, with 10% for DioGuardi on the Conservative and Right-to-Life lines. It helped perhaps that this district includes Peekskill and Garrison, the home bases of Republican Governor George Pataki.

Having won the seat in a three-way race, Kelly, with her middle-of-the-House voting record, has been whipsawed by criticism from both right and left. She supported the Contract with America, which earned her howls from the left. On environmental issues, she sponsored the 1996 Hudson River Habitat Restoration Act, supported $17.5 million for land acquisition in Sterling Forest and pushed EPA to authorize a Superfund cleanup to reduce PCBs on the Hudson. But environmental groups were still furious when she supported Republican bills promoting cost-benefit analyses. On abortion, she irritated many conservatives by being one of the few Republicans to vote against the partial-birth abortion ban in 1996. But in March 1997, when the executive director of the National Coalition of Abortion Providers admitted he lied about the frequency of partial-birth abortions, she changed her mind and came out for the ban. "When you get into doing it on a healthy woman, with a healthy fetus, very late term, what are we talking about here?" she said. "Because I can't get a clear reading from either side of the fence, I changed my vote." And in March 1998 she joined other Republican women to ask why feminist Democrats were not outraged against the charges brought against Bill Clinton. So when in February 1999 she was chosen as the Republican co-chair of the Congressional Caucus for Women's Issues, feminists yelped in rage. She boasted of Republicans' accomplishments in balancing the budget, then took the Democrats' side of saying the surplus should mostly be reserved for saving Social Security, while supporting tax reform. She voted to keep the National Endowment for the Arts alive when it lost by one vote in July 1997. When she sponsored a $6 million redesign of New York City's West Side Highway widely supported by New York officials, she was criticized by Manhattan's Jerrold Nadler for doing the bidding of her contributor ($1,500) Donald Trump. Occasionally she did something uncontroversial, like sponsoring a private immigration bill for marathoner Khalid Khannouchi, a Moroccan living in Ossining, so he could represent the United States in the 2000 Olympics.

In elections she was challenged on all sides. Not even a plea from Speaker Newt Gingrich's office could keep Joseph DioGuardi from challenging Kelly in the 1996 Republican primary; when abortion opponents Chris Smith of New Jersey and Robert Dornan of California came in to oppose her, Gingrich disciplined them by knocking them off congressional travel delegations. Kelly won the primary, but by a narrow 53%–42%. In the general, Kelly beat the Democrat by only 46%–39%, with 12% for DioGuardi. In 1998 Democrats tried to recruit actor Christopher Reeve, who was not interested; after the filing deadline Democrats challenged her petitions because they were not (as New York's baroque petition laws require) numbered by page. The courts threw that out and Kelly won, for the first time by a convincing margin, 62%–34%. Her prospects for 2000 look good, but redistricting after the 2000 Census could change this district at the chokepoint of New York, with unpredictable results.

Cook's Call. *Safe.* The moderate Kelly's biggest problems here have come from conservative Republicans, not from Democrats. But, after overcoming a serious challenge from a Right to Life-Conservative candidate in 1994 and 1996, Kelly looks like she has settled in to this marginally Republican district.

The People: Pop. 1990: 580,386; 30.1% rural; 11.6% age 65 + ; 89.1% White, 7.2% Black, 2.3% Asian, 0.2% Amer. Indian, 1.2% Other; 5.1% Hispanic Origin. Households: 62.7% married couple families; 31% married couple fams. w. children; 56.7% college educ.; median household income: $50,239; per capita income: $22,458; median house value: $199,200; median gross rent: $587.

1996 Presidential Vote

Clinton (D)	116,697	(49%)
Dole (R)	98,597	(42%)
Perot (I)	20,803	(9%)

1992 Presidential Vote

Bush (R)	110,076	(42%)
Clinton (D)	105,142	(40%)
Perot (I)	45,126	(17%)

Rep. Sue W. Kelly (R)

Elected 1994; b. Sept. 26, 1936, Lima, OH; home, Katonah; Denison U., B.A. 1958, Sarah Lawrence Col., M.A. 1985; Presbyterian; married (Edward).

Professional Career: Owner/Mgr., Kelly & Assoc. bldg. rehab.; Researcher, Harvard U., 1958–60; Owner/Mgr., Kelly Florist, 1980–83; Prof., Sarah Lawrence Col., 1988–91.

DC Office: 1122 LHOB 20515, 202-225-5441; Fax: 202-225-3289; Web site: www.house.gov/suekelly.

District Offices: Fishkill, 914-897-5200; Mt. Kisco, 914-241-6340.

Committees: *Banking & Financial Services* (16th of 32 R): Financial Institutions & Consumer Credit; Housing & Community Opportunity. *Small Business* (7th of 19 R): Regulatory Reform & Paperwork Reduction (Chmn.). *Transportation & Infrastructure* (18th of 41 R): Ground Transportation; Water Resources & Environment.

Group Ratings

	ADA	ACLU	AFS	LCV	CON	NTU	NFIB	COC	ACU	NTLC	CHC
1998	45	38	56	85	6	43	71	83	48	49	58
1997	40	—	13	—	49	50	—	70	64	—	—

National Journal Ratings

	1997 LIB — 1997 CONS		1998 LIB — 1998 CONS	
Economic	50% —	50%	39% —	59%
Social	53% —	46%	62% —	38%
Foreign	38% —	60%	39% —	58%

Key Votes of the 105th Congress

1. Clinton Budget Deal	Y	5. Puerto Rico Sthood. Ref.	Y	9. Cut $ for B-2 Bombers	N
2. Education IRAs	Y	6. End Highway Set-asides	N	10. Human Rights in China	N
3. Req. 2/3 to Raise Taxes	Y	7. School Prayer Amend.	N	11. Withdraw Bosnia Troops	Y
4. Fast-track Trade	N	8. Ovrd. Part. Birth Veto	Y	12. End Cuban TV-Marti	Y

Election Results

1998 general	Sue W. Kelly (R-C) 104,467	(62%)	($595,985)
	Dick Collins (D) 56,378	(34%)	($8,461)
	Others 6,987	(4%)	
1998 primary	Sue W. Kelly (R) .... unopposed		
1996 general	Sue W. Kelly (R-FR) 102,142	(46%)	($906,904)
	Richard S. Klein (D-L) 86,926	(39%)	($630,471)
	Joseph J. DioGuardi (C-RTL) 27,424	(12%)	($387,759)
	Others 4,104	(2%)	

TWENTIETH DISTRICT

From Sunnyside, the whimsical house that Washington Irving built in Tarrytown near the country he immortalized as Sleepy Hollow, you can see across the waters of the Tappan Zee, the widest point of the Hudson, and get a sense of how the land looked when first settled by Dutchmen. All around is Irving country—the old towns of Tarrytown, Irvington, Dobbs Ferry and Hastings-on-Hudson, now comfortably affluent suburbs. On the other side of the Tappan Zee is Rockland County, a stretch of suburbs between the Hudson and the Ramapos, the first Appalachian chain west of New York. First settled by Dutchmen, Rockland then was studded by little towns that grew up as if 1,000 miles from Gotham, but they have thrived on the actual proximity: the town of Nyack here was the home of actress Helen Hayes; and James A. Farley, Franklin Roosevelt's chief political major domo and Democratic National Committee chairman, was from Stony Point, just below the Hudson Highlands.

The 20th Congressional District spans the Tappan Zee, connecting most of the Irving suburbs with Rockland County and stepping over the Ramapos 120 miles inland to the Pennsylvania border. Past the Ramapos is most of Orange County, New York's second-fastest-growing county since 1980, where old villages between mountains and farms on the nation's biggest deposit of muck soil outside the Everglades have been flanked with new modest-income subdivisions. Farther out, past the Shawangunk Mountains, is Sullivan County and the Catskills Borscht Belt district, a Jewish resort area with huge kosher hotels since the late 19th Century that are now fallen on hard times. Politically, this area has been trending Republican, as old Upstate-minded residents are joined by newcomers fleeing the city.

The 20th's congressman, Republican Benjamin Gilman, is chairman of the International Relations Committee. He grew up in Middletown; he traveled with his father to Nazi Germany in 1933, at 10, and remembers Hitler's storm troopers. After service in World War II, he became a lawyer, working for the state and bringing *habeas corpus* cases for mental hospital patients. In 1966 he was elected to the Assembly, and in 1972 to the U.S. House; he is tied for fifth in seniority among Republicans today. Gilman is moderate on economics and cultural issues, but more conservative on foreign policy; he is pleasant and ordinarily arouses little animosity. In the 1970s he worked, often with East German lawyer Wolfgang Vogel, to arrange spy swaps. He visited Buenos Aires newspaper editor Jacobo Timmerman in jail in Argentina and helped secure his release; he championed the human rights of Pentecostals, Ukrainians, Poles and Jews in the Soviet Union. He has long been a supporter of Israel, and he strongly backed the Gulf war resolution.

Gilman became ranking Republican on International Relations in 1993 and chairman in 1995. Under his leadership the committee has pushed and prodded the Clinton Administration, clucking disapproval helplessly sometimes, steering the course of policy at others. Gilman favored NATO expansion and air strikes against the Bosnian Serbs before Clinton; he opposed changing the mission of U.S. troops in Somalia. He wanted to delay full recognition of Vietnam pending a full accounting of American POWs. As he said just after the November 1994 election, "Instead of a strong, steady signal on foreign policy coming from Washington, regrettably the world has heard a series of wavering notes sounded by an uncertain trumpet, leaving our allies concerned and our adversaries confused." But he noted that "one-half of the Congress has less than four years of institutional memory and little experience in foreign affairs." He has urged increases in the foreign aid budget and continuation of aid to family planning programs despite the objections of most Republicans.

One of Gilman's major concerns has been drugs. For 12 years he was ranking Republican on the Select Committee on Narcotics, abolished at the urging of junior Republicans along with other select committees in 1993. "The most immediate and serious security threat to the United States today is international narcotics trafficking—because of its destructive effect on the fabric of American society and, in particular, America's youth," he wrote in May 1997. In March 1997 he led the committee in opposing certification of Mexico for its lax anti-drug program. In April 1997 he held up shipment of helicopters to Mexico, saying that the Colombian national police could make better use of them; he opposed the administration's refusal to certify that Colombia was "cooperating" even as it insisted that Mexico was "fully cooperating." In April 1998 he predicted that Bill Clinton would propose a new drug policy, with no requirement of certification, at the Santiago Summit of the Americas. That year he also tried to overturn the certification of Mexico, and in 1999 continued to oppose Clinton's decision, calling for hearings on the issue. In October 1998 he proposed to give free trade status to Panama if it allowed U.S. troops to remain there after the turnover of the Panama Canal in 2000.

On the Middle East, Gilman has been a supporter of Israel, even when the Clinton Administration has been pressing for concessions, and has backed aggressive stances against Iraq and Iran. In 1997 and 1998 he pressed the administration to stop Chinese sales of naval cruise missiles and other weapons to Iran. He was the sponsor of the October 1998 Iraq Liberation Act, which called for policies to oust Saddam Hussein. He has supported troop deployment in Bosnia and opposed resolutions intended to force troop withdrawal absent a congressional vote favoring it. He has favored Radio Free Asia broadcasts to China and listing of Chinese military firms, and is wary of the transfer of high-tech systems and weapons to China. He opposed a 1998 State Department effort to fund a peacekeeping mission in the Central African Republic. Of the Kyoto climate treaty, he said, "The rest of the world ganged up on the United States" and "the administration effectively joined the gang." On other issues, Gilman supported the Shays-Meehan campaign finance bill and the lowering of the blood alcohol level to .08% in DWI cases. He joined with Charles Rangel, his longtime colleague on the Narcotics committee, to oppose Clinton's line-item veto of a New York Medicaid provision. He tartly opposed the exemption of the Makah Indians in Washington from the international whaling ban, saying, "No living Makah knows how to whale."

Gilman still works his district hard, sometimes spending Saturdays riding around in his mobile home-office. He won the seat fairly easily in 1972 against ultra-liberal John Dow, and he has had only one difficult re-election race since, in 1982 after redistricting, when he faced Republican-turned-Democrat Peter Peyser and won 53%–42%. In 1996 and 1998 his margins came down. His 1998 opponent was the Town of Greenburgh supervisor, who set up a town matchmaking service and got the Bronx River Parkway closed Sundays for bicyclists. He beat Gilman almost 2–1 on his own turf in Westchester; Gilman won by about 2–1 west of the Hudson. On impeachment, he was listed as undecided until almost the last day. He voted for impeachment, but with four other Republicans urged senators to consider censure instead. Will he run again in 2000, at 77? It may depend on whether he can keep the International Relations chair despite the Republicans' three-term-limit. Gilman opposes the limit and said, "I am not planning to be chairman of Oversight," the committee on which he is second-ranking.

Cook's Call. *Probably Safe.* There is speculation that the 77-year-old Gilman may decide to retire in 2000. If Gilman does leave, expect a hotly contested race for this marginal district. If Gilman stays, don't expect a close race; he is well-entrenched here.

The People: Pop. 1990: 580,025; 22.5% rural; 11.5% age 65 + ; 86.6% White, 8.2% Black, 3.4% Asian, 0.2% Amer. Indian, 1.6% Other; 6.1% Hispanic Origin. Households: 64.2% married couple families; 32.7% married couple fams. w. children; 53.7% college educ.; median household income: $47,107; per capita income: $19,680; median house value: $193,600; median gross rent: $577.

1996 Presidential Vote

Clinton (D) 130,550 (55%)
Dole (R) 89,214 (37%)
Perot (I) 18,216 (8%)

1992 Presidential Vote

Clinton (D) 116,473 (45%)
Bush (R) 106,855 (41%)
Perot (I) 36,929 (14%)

Rep. Benjamin A. Gilman (R)

Elected 1972; b. Dec. 6, 1922, Poughkeepsie; home, Middletown; U. of PA, B.S. 1946, NY Law Schl., LL.B. 1950; Jewish; married (Georgia).

Military Career: Army Air Corps, 1942–45 (WWII); NY State Guard, 1981-present.

Elected Office: NY Assembly, 1966–72.

Professional Career: Practicing atty., 1950–72; NY Asst. Atty. Gen., 1953–55; Atty., NY Temporary Comm. on the Courts.

DC Office: 2449 RHOB 20515, 202-225-3776; Fax: 202-225-2541; Web site: www.house.gov/gilman.

District Offices: Middletown, 914-343-6666; Monsey, 914-357-9000.

Committees: *Government Reform* (2d of 24 R): Criminal Justice, Drug Policy & Human Resources; Postal Service. *International Relations* (Chmn. of 26 R).

Group Ratings

	ADA	ACLU	AFS	LCV	CON	NTU	NFIB	COC	ACU	NTLC	CHC
1998	45	56	63	77	2	42	69	71	38	47	50
1997	50	—	50	—	37	44	—	60	40	—	—

National Journal Ratings

	1997 LIB — 1997 CONS		1998 LIB — 1998 CONS	
Economic	53%	— 46%	49%	— 51%
Social	62%	— 37%	66%	— 34%
Foreign	49%	— 49%	49%	— 48%

Key Votes of the 105th Congress

1. Clinton Budget Deal	Y	5. Puerto Rico Sthood. Ref.	Y
2. Education IRAs	Y	6. End Highway Set-asides	N
3. Req. 2/3 to Raise Taxes	Y	7. School Prayer Amend.	N
4. Fast-track Trade	N	8. Ovrd. Part. Birth Veto	N

9. Cut $ for B-2 Bombers	N
10. Human Rights in China	Y
11. Withdraw Bosnia Troops	N
12. End Cuban TV-Marti	N

Election Results

1998 general	Benjamin A. Gilman (R)	98,546	(58%)	($942,146)
	Paul J. Feiner (D-Ind-L)	61,753	(37%)	($258,717)
	Others	8,605	(5%)	
1998 primary	Benjamin A. Gilman (R)	unopposed		
1996 general	Benjamin A. Gilman (R)	122,479	(57%)	($682,959)
	Yash P. Aggarwal (D-L)	80,761	(38%)	($210,670)
	Others	11,372	(5%)	

TWENTY-FIRST DISTRICT

Albany, as readers of its novelist laureate William Kennedy know, is within living memory an antique city. Its solid rowhouses show its 19th Century prosperity; its once teeming lumberyards and railroad car shops, old restaurants and hotels, have the patina of age and the accumulated grime of decades of coal smoke burned during six-month-long winters. Its history is traceable to 1624, when the Dutch built Fort Orange on the banks of the Hudson so seagoing ships could dock at the edge of the great gloomy forests near the confluence of the Hudson and the Mo-hawk—the natural crossroads of Upstate New York even before the building of the Erie Canal and the New York Central Railroad. This was one of America's early industrial centers. Troy, a few miles upriver, was a steel town rivaling Pittsburgh in the 1840s, and later the leading producer of detachable collars; Cohoes, at the junction of the Hudson and the Mohawk, became a leading textile producer; Schenectady, a few miles up the Mohawk, was the site of Charles Steinmetz's fabled General Electric laboratories and has been a big GE town ever since. Albany was one of America's biggest lumber towns as well as the state capital.

Albany continues to have one of the nation's most famed Democratic political machines, dating back to 1921, when Daniel O'Connell and his brothers and local aristocrat Edwin Corn-ing took control of City Hall. They never really relinquished it: O'Connell died in 1977 at age 91, still boss after 56 years, and his early partner's son, Erastus Corning II, was mayor from 1942 until his death in 1983. The machine was sustained by legions of city and county em-ployees, by a certain creativity when it came to counting votes, and by the raffish atmosphere that was found in the speakeasies of so many cities during Prohibition and lingered in Albany for decades after: read Kennedy and you are there. Curiously, the machine made possible the transformation of antique Albany into the shiny metropolis it is today. Mayor Corning provided financing for Nelson Rockefeller's monumental South Mall, expressways were built, the old Union Station was spruced up, and yuppies began buying and renovating old townhouses. These days, the Albany machine is bettered in some elections and can't always control the suburbs as it once could Albany; but it clings to power in the H.H. Richardson City Hall facing the gaudy state house.

The 21st Congressional District includes all of Albany and Schenectady Counties, plus Troy on the Hudson's east bank, and the depressed factory town of Amsterdam on the Mohawk. More than half its votes are cast in Albany County, and it is a solidly Democratic district—under a solid Democratic machine.

The congressman from the 21st District is Michael McNulty, a Democrat first elected in 1988. McNulty's roots in Albany politics go back to his grandfather, who served as Albany County sheriff, as did his father, who was also a mayor. Michael McNulty was first elected to office in 1969, at 22, and served 13 years as town supervisor and mayor in the industrial suburb of Green Island; he was elected to the Assembly in 1982, at 35. The opening to Congress came without much warning. In 1988, four days after the July filing deadline and on the last day for withdrawal, 30-year incumbent Democrat Samuel Stratton announced he was retiring for health reasons, giving the Democratic machine a chance to name a replacement, which turned out to be McNulty. Serving in Congress was a fulfillment of his family's and his own ambition. McNulty won the 1988 general election by 62%–38% against a venture capital specialist who attacked him for avoiding the issues and for having been chosen by party bosses rather than primary voters. He has not had trouble in the general election since.

McNulty is hard-working, serious, abstemious, pleasant and a conscientious campaigner. His voting record is very liberal on economics, moderate on cultural and foreign issues; he is one of a handful of New York Democrats endorsed by the Conservative, not the Liberal, Party. He is anti-abortion and for the amendment allowing penalties for desecration of the flag. He strongly opposed the 1996 welfare reform and wants to increase payments to unemployed adults, legal immigrants and families with high shelter costs. He was one of three Democrats to vote against a bipartisan Medicare bill in Ways and Means in June 1997 and one of the few against the five-year budget in July 1997. He voted for much of the Contract with America in 1995, except for tax cuts and welfare reforms. In 1996 he had primary opposition from Lee Wasserman, head of Environmental Advocates, and won by only 57%–43%, not a huge margin for an incumbent.

In 1997 McNulty endorsed the EPA's new emissions standards for ozone and particulates and criticized General Electric for not being willing to dredge the Hudson for PCBs deposited years before. He called GE "brutally impersonal" when it cut hundreds of jobs at its power systems division in Schenectady in December 1997. He criticized the Army in 1997 and 1998 when it cut the number of jobs at the Watervliet Arsenal, and wondered whether further cuts would require closure and require dependence on foreign producers. On the 1998 transportation bill he got $11 million for the Amtrak station in Rensselaer, across the Hudson from Albany, and $8.7 million for an I-90 connector near Hudson Valley Community College. He had also worked for Thruway Exit 26 and the new Albany airport, and got funds for noise abatement and the purchase of houses near Albany airport. However, he has complained about high air fares on Albany flights; Upstate New York, economically ailing, has not done well by airline deregulation.

McNulty accompanied Bill Clinton to Northern Ireland in 1995 and in July 1998 brought Hillary Rodham Clinton to Troy to commemorate Kate Mullaney, who organized the all-female Collar Laundry Union in 1864; he is seeking to make her home a labor museum. On Ways and Means, McNulty and Amo Houghton sponsored a bill to relieve David Kaczynski of taxes on the reward money he earned for turning in his brother, the Unabomber, and which he said he would distribute to his victims; it never came up for a vote. In February 1999, McNulty boycotted a prayer breakfast in D.C. because Yasir Arafat was invited.

McNulty did not have primary opposition in 1998 and in that pro-incumbent year won his highest percentage ever.

Cook's Call. *Safe.* The conservative McNulty is not entirely safe from a challenge from the left, but the solid Democratic underpinnings of this Albany-district make it hard to defeat him in a general election.

The People: Pop. 1990: 580,320; 15% rural; 16.2% age 65 +; 91.2% White, 6.3% Black, 1.6% Asian, 0.2% Amer. Indian, 0.7% Other; 2% Hispanic Origin. Households: 49% married couple families; 22.1% married couple fams. w. children; 47.9% college educ.; median household income: $31,489; per capita income: $15,304; median house value: $99,200; median gross rent: $372.

1996 Presidential Vote			1992 Presidential Vote		
Clinton (D)	151,701	(59%)	Clinton (D)	140,246	(48%)
Dole (R)	79,880	(31%)	Bush (R)	99,089	(34%)
Perot (I)	26,840	(10%)	Perot (I)	51,091	(18%)

Rep. Michael R. McNulty (D)

Elected 1988; b. Sept. 16, 1947, Troy; home, Green Island; Holy Cross Col., B.A. 1969; Catholic; married (Nancy Ann).

Elected Office: Green Island Town Supervisor, 1969–77; Green Island Mayor, 1977–82; NY Assembly, 1982–88.

DC Office: 2161 RHOB 20515, 202-225-5076; Fax: 202-225-5077; Web site: www.house.gov/mcnulty.

District Offices: Albany, 518-465-0700; Amsterdam, 518-843-3400; Schenectady, 518-374-4547; Troy, 518-271-0822.

Committees: *Ways & Means* (11th of 16 D): Oversight; Trade.

Group Ratings

	ADA	ACLU	AFS	LCV	CON	NTU	NFIB	COC	ACU	NTLC	CHC
1998	75	58	100	62	48	19	22	23	21	11	27
1997	80	—	100	—	12	24	—	30	26	—	—

National Journal Ratings

	1997 LIB — 1997 CONS		1998 LIB — 1998 CONS	
Economic	93%	0%	79%	0%
Social	57%	42%	58%	42%
Foreign	60%	40%	52%	48%

Key Votes of the 105th Congress

1. Clinton Budget Deal	N	5. Puerto Rico Sthood. Ref.	Y	9. Cut $ for B-2 Bombers	Y
2. Education IRAs	N	6. End Highway Set-asides	N	10. Human Rights in China	Y
3. Req. 2/3 to Raise Taxes	N	7. School Prayer Amend.	N	11. Withdraw Bosnia Troops	N
4. Fast-track Trade	N	8. Ovrd. Part. Birth Veto	Y	12. End Cuban TV-Marti	N

Election Results

1998 general	Michael R. McNulty (D-C-Ind)	146,639	(74%)	($243,107)
	Lauren Ayers (R)	50,931	(26%)	
1998 primary	Michael R. McNulty (D)	unopposed		
1996 general	Michael R. McNulty (D-C-Ind)	158,491	(66%)	($628,000)
	Nancy Norman (R-FR)	64,471	(27%)	($6,953)
	Lee H. Wasserman (L)	16,794	(7%)	($392,588)

TWENTY-SECOND DISTRICT

The Hudson River, an avenue of commerce in colonial days, an inspiration to artists past and present, is still one of America's great sights, though it is no longer central, as it was not so long ago, in the nation's consciousness and politics. The classic mansions overlooking the river, like Clermont, whose builder Robert Livingston financed Robert Fulton's first steamboat, and Montgomery Place, built by Janet Livingston Montgomery, widow of the general who captured Quebec in 1775, are reminders of the cool serenity of the 18th Century mind and the daring nature of its spirit. Robert Livingston (whose descendants include Eleanor Roosevelt, Tom Keane of New Jersey and Bob Livingston of Louisiana) administered the first oath of office to George Washington in 1789 and helped negotiate the Louisiana Purchase in 1803. It was on a visit to his lands in the 1790s that James Madison and Aaron Burr welded the Virginia-New York alliance that set the course of American political history. The Hudson was also a center of America during the Romantic Era: From Frederick Church's Moorish mansion, Olana, you can see the still unspoiled river landscape that inspired his art and that of others of the Hudson River school of painters.

The Hudson gave birth to our passionate party politics: Nearby is Kinderhook, home of Martin Van Buren, the innkeeper's son who in alliance with Andrew Jackson invented the torchlight parade, the national party convention and, some argue, the Democratic Party itself. Later in the 19th Century, the Hudson was lined with the palaces of the nation's first great millionaires and the comfortable country houses of New York's gentry. In one of the latter, Springwood in Hyde Park, Franklin Roosevelt was born and lived; this politician, who expanded government at home and was the victorious commander-in-chief of American military forces throughout the world, was most comfortable looking out over his sloping lawn down to the river on which he remembered iceboating during the winters of the 1880s.

The 22d Congressional District includes much of the Hudson Valley, the grand river south of Albany and the smaller river, freshly fed by the Adirondacks, to the north. It extends north to include most of Essex County and Lake Placid in the Adirondacks. Much of the district, just outside the old manufacturing city of Troy and the grand 19th Century harness racing center of Saratoga Springs (which has lost 75% of its fan base in the last 30 years), is essentially suburban Albany. Despite Van Buren and Roosevelt, this has been a Republican area since the birth of the Republican Party; indeed, Roosevelt never carried his home territory except when he ran for state Senate in 1910.

The congressman from the 22d is John Sweeney, a Republican elected in 1998. Sweeney grew up in Troy, the son of a shirt factory worker active in the Amalgamated Shirt Cutters Union; he lived for a time in a housing project. He worked his way through college, then worked for the Rensselaer County government, heading a DWI project. He went to law school part time and practiced law. He caught the eye of Republican State Chairman William Powers, an ally of then-Senator Alfonse D'Amato, who made Sweeney executive director of the party in 1992. After Pataki was elected governor in 1994, he appointed Sweeney as Labor commissioner, then in 1997 as deputy secretary to the state Executive Chamber, one of his top aides.

In April 1998, Gerald Solomon, congressman from the 22d District for 20 years and chairman of the House Rules Committee, announced he was retiring. In this heavily Republican district there was naturally a contest for the party's nomination. But it was effectively settled in a few days in May. Assemblyman John Faso, probably the best-known possibility, declined to run because he had been elected minority leader in March. Solomon had backed Roy McDonald, a township supervisor in Saratoga County, the district's largest; he said that of nine candidates running, only Sweeney was unacceptable. Facing pressure from Powers, Saratoga County Republican Chairman Jasper Nolan on May 7 announced he was not supporting McDonald, and McDonald, suddenly with no chance in the nine-county endorsement convention, withdrew from the race. Powers's message, though not public, was obvious: Pataki wanted Sweeney, and there would be rewards for those who went along and penalties for those who went the other way. Solomon understood Nolan's position: "He was between a real rock and a hard shell. Even though the governor told me he did not have a candidate, it was obvious Bill Powers wanted John Sweeney." Sweeney had yet to officially announce, but as Solomon said, "John Sweeney is going to be the candidate."

There was still a primary: Sweeney was attacked for not living in the district; he moved over the line to Spiegeltown, and now resides in Troy. It was pointed out he had never won elective office, and lost a race for council; but he refused to join debates, and won the September primary with 50%, to 28% for the nearest contender. In the general, Sweeney vastly outspent the Democratic nominee, Jean Bordewich, a writer, owner of a computer publishing company, one-time press secretary to Florida Senator Richard Stone (1975–81) and one-term council member in Red Hook in Dutchess County. She called for campaign finance reform and limiting spending in this race. Sweeney would have none of that and agreed to three debates, and no more. Like Solomon, he opposed requiring General Electric to clean up PCBs in the Hudson— a hot local issue. He said he opposed banning abortion but backed the partial-birth abortion ban. He opposed NAFTA and GATT and said he felt strongly about the Second Amendment. Bordewich struck a conciliatory note; she said she hoped GE and EPA could somehow get together on the PCBs problem. "Jean Bordewich for Congress: the closest you can get to voting for yourself." That struck a note that would have been successful in many districts. But Solomon's testimonial ad for Sweeney had greater influence. Pataki also appeared in Sweeney ads, and the Civil Service Employees Union endorsed the Republican.

Sweeney won 55%–42% and was chosen the freshman representative on the Republican Steering Committee. In Washington he said, "I'm telling them I'll take the worst office you can find but give me a good committee seat." His wishes were granted. He took the lowest number in the office lottery and got stuck with 437 Cannon, a two-room suite divided by a public bathroom. But he also got a seat on the Transportation and Infrastructure Committee, a good post from which to push Hudson Valley projects.

Cook's Call. *Safe.* While Sweeney's 55% win here in 1998 does not measure up to the Gerald Solomon-esque margins of lore, Sweeney's well-hewn political skills and the Republican nature of this district should help keep him safely settled in this Upstate district.

The People: Pop. 1990: 580,522; 66.7% rural; 13.3% age 65 +; 96.6% White, 2.2% Black, 0.6% Asian, 0.2% Amer. Indian, 0.4% Other; 1.5% Hispanic Origin. Households: 60.5% married couple families; 29.6% married couple fams. w. children; 45.6% college educ.; median household income: $33,306; per capita income: $14,646; median house value: $99,600; median gross rent: $377.

1996 Presidential Vote			1992 Presidential Vote		
Clinton (D)	117,831	(46%)	Bush (R)	116,283	(42%)
Dole (R)	105,106	(41%)	Clinton (D)	99,984	(36%)
Perot (I)	34,415	(13%)	Perot (I)	62,533	(22%)

Rep. John Sweeney (R)

Elected 1998; b. Aug. 9, 1955, Troy; home, Clifton Park; Russell Sage Col., B.A. 1981, W. New England Law Schl., J.D. 1990; Catholic; separated.

Professional Career: Practicing atty., 1990–92; Exec. Dir. & Chief Cnsl., NY State Repub. Cmte., 1992–95; NY Comm. of Labor, 1995–97; Dpty. Secy., Gov. George Pataki, 1997–98.

DC Office: 437 CHOB 20515, 202-225-5614; Fax: 202-225-6234; Web site: www.house.gov/sweeney.

District Offices: Glens Falls, 518-792-3031; Hudson, 518-828-0181; Saratoga Springs, 518-587-9800.

Committees: *Banking & Financial Services* (28th of 32 R): Capital Markets, Securities & Government Sponsored Enterprises; Housing & Community Opportunity. *Small Business* (14th of 19 R): Regulatory Reform & Paperwork Reduction; Rural Enterprise, Business Opportunities & Special Small Business Problems. *Transportation & Infrastructure* (36th of 41 R): Aviation (Vice Chmn.); Ground Transportation.

Group Ratings and Key Votes: Newly Elected

Election Results

1998 general	John Sweeney (R-C-Ind) 106,919	(55%)	($818,624)
	Jean P. Bordewich (D) 81,296	(42%)	($322,748)
	Others 5,051	(3%)	
1998 primary	John Sweeney (R) 14,443	(52%)	
	Nicholas A. Caimano Jr. (R) 7,447	(27%)	
	Maynard D. Baker (R) 3,452	(12%)	
	Francis A. Giroux (R) 2,334	(8%)	
1996 general	Gerald B. H. Solomon (R-C-RTL-FR) 144,125	(60%)	($640,080)
	Steve James (D) 94,192	(40%)	($273,887)

TWENTY-THIRD DISTRICT

One of the first American frontiers was the Mohawk River Valley of Upstate New York—a frontier that remained static for 150 years. From the establishment of Fort Orange in 1624 in what now is Albany until the Revolutionary War, white settlers did not dare move west along the Mohawk. The British used their Iroquois allies as a buffer against the French and in return kept New England Yankees from moving westward. Only after the French were driven from the colonies in 1759 did the pressures for westward settlement prevail; the British tried to keep their word to the Indians, but once the Revolutionary War started, the Iroquois dominion ended.

This is the background of *Drums Along the Mohawk* and of James Fenimore Cooper's *Leatherstocking Tales*. But there is little in these rolling hills today to evoke the bloody violence whose conclusion made possible the digging of the Erie Canal and the building of the New York Central Railroad. As migration slowed and trade increased, the Mohawk Valley became one of the nation's early industrial centers. The little Oneida County hamlets of Utica and Rome, where the canal builders had to dig through the route's highest ground, became sizable factory towns. Even the utopian Oneida Community, with its believers in plural marriage and communal ownership, operated a stainless steel factory. First settled by New England Yankees, these towns attracted a new wave of immigration from the Atlantic coast in the early 20th Century. Today they are the most heavily Italian and Polish-American communities between Albany and Buffalo; politically, they are usually marginally Republican, but Bill Clinton carried most of them in 1996.

The 23d Congressional District, in the Mohawk Valley, is centered on Utica and Rome in Oneida County and includes a row of more sparsely settled counties to the south. Here the hilly land has an early 19th Century cast, in places like Cooperstown, certainly one of the best-preserved small towns in America and home to the Baseball Hall of Fame, and Pindars Corners, the crossroads where Senator Daniel Patrick Moynihan has a farm and a 19th Century schoolhouse office. Madison County here was one of the hotbeds of abolitionism in the 1850s. But this is also an area that feels bypassed by more recent economic growth and in need of government assistance and sustenance.

The congressman from the 23d is Sherwood Boehlert, a Republican elected in 1982. He grew up and went to college in Utica, served in the Army, worked briefly in industry. For 14 years he was chief of staff for his two predecessors in Congress, then was elected Oneida County executive in 1978 and won the House seat in 1982. He has worked in government as much as politics, and does not share the free market economists' disdain for its works. He is a Republican partisan, but can dissent from much of the Republican program. He signed the Contract With America, but voted against more of it than any other Republican except Connie Morella of Maryland. Some of Boehlert's votes have a local angle: he supports dairy subsidies (the 23d is part of New York City's milkshed), he favors baseball's antitrust exemption (Cooperstown is where baseball was supposedly invented in 1839 and Boehlert is part owner of a minor league team); he sponsored Pledge of Allegiance Day (the Pledge was written by Francis

Bellamy in Rome in 1892). His great success in the Democratic 103d Congress was leading the fight against the superconducting Supercollider, a giant atom smasher that was to be built in Texas; he said it was "simply not affordable science," and in October 1993 the House voted 280–150 to kill it.

Since Republicans took control in 1994, Boehlert has taken a modulating role, defeating what he considers extreme party positions, especially on environmental issues, opposing the party on some motions, while maintaining party loyalty on many other matters and trying to forge bipartisan consensus on some issues. He was an early backer of the 1996 minimum wage (and is one of the top Republicans receiving labor money), opposed the partial-birth abortion ban and supported the National Endowment for the Arts. In 1995 Boehlert blocked Republican EPA riders and attempts to limit wetlands regulations. Then he was named by Speaker Newt Gingrich—to whom he gave crucial support when Gingrich won the whip's post by two votes in 1989—to head, with conservative Richard Pombo, a task force on environmental issues. This produced some results: Republicans agreed on the bipartisan Safe Drinking Water Act of 1996 and the environmental provisions of the 1996 Freedom to Farm Act. But in mid-1997 the truce broke down; after Boehlert rallied votes to water down an attempt by Western Republicans to exempt flood control projects from the Endangered Species Act, they complained bitterly to Gingrich that Boehlert had too much influence over Republican environmental policy. He stripped the 1997 property rights bill of the right to appeal directly to federal courts.

On the Water Resources and Environment Subcommittee he chairs, Boehlert has tried to reach bipartisan agreement on Superfund reform, so far without success. He wrote a bill in 1997 focusing on exempting small businesses and de minims parties from liability and setting explicit objectives for returning contaminated land and water to beneficial uses. It was marked up in subcommittee, but attracted little support, and was not acted on by the full Transportation Committee, which was preoccupied by the transportation bill (which Boehlert supported and which earmarked $75 million for his district, tied for the second highest in the House). He worked also for revision of the Clean Water Act and for the wetlands mitigation banking legislation sponsored by Republican Walter Jones. He produced a successful compromise on grazing laws with Republican Bob Smith. Boehlert took the lead in opposing the Resources Committee's national parks bill, which he characterized as "90% penicillin laced with 10% arsenic"; it was humiliatingly defeated 302–123 in October 1998.

Western Republicans continue to rail at Boehlert, but his record is not identical with that of Democrats or liberal environmentalists. If he favored the EPA's tougher emissions standards on ozone and particulate matter, he also opposed a ban on elephant hunting and the ivory trade and opposed the TVA's refinancing plan. He formed the TR Fund, named for the great New York Republican environmentalist Theodore Roosevelt, with John Chafee, and argued that Republicans were passing more environmental laws than Democrats had, saying Democrats "feel they own the environment as an issue, but there is a sizable and growing segment of Republicans that are proving day in and day out that they are environmentally friendly." In February 1999 he opposed the Mandates Information Act, which would have allowed members to object to bills that would impose costs of more than $100 million on private companies, concerns that it could be used to impede environmental legislation; Boehlert's amendment failed and the bill passed the House that month.

Like many successful politicians, Boehlert seems to have an optimistic streak. He embraced the October 1998 omnibus budget and proclaimed, "The moderates have really come into their own, and this package reflects it. We've ended up on center ground." But on impeachment he could not find the center ground he sought. Long on the list of undecideds, he voted for impeachment. Boehlert has not had serious competition in his district in many years. Against two primary opponents he won 65% of the vote in 1996. In 1998, potential primary challenger David Vickers was knocked off the ballot in August when the Board of Elections threw out his petitions for violations. Vickers ran on the Conservative and Right-to-Life lines; with no Democratic candidate, Boehlert won 81% of the vote. He continues to push for bipartisanship: As co-head of the Republicans' "incumbent retention" fund, he encouraged well-off incumbents to contribute to embattled incumbents and challengers regardless of ideology.

Cook's Call. *Safe.* As one of the more out-front voices of Republican moderates, Boehlert has raised the ire of some of the more conservative members of the House. But he has no such problems in his home district where he has won easily since his first re-election in 1984.

The People: Pop. 1990: 580,259; 54.8% rural; 15.6% age 65 + ; 95.8% White, 2.8% Black, 0.6% Asian, 0.3% Amer. Indian, 0.5% Other; 1.5% Hispanic Origin. Households: 56.9% married couple families; 26.9% married couple fams. w. children; 40.4% college educ.; median household income: $26,155; per capita income: $11,792; median house value: $67,900; median gross rent: $291.

1996 Presidential Vote		
Clinton (D)	102,854	(47%)
Dole (R)	88,120	(40%)
Perot (I)	29,172	(13%)

1992 Presidential Vote		
Bush (R)	99,495	(40%)
Clinton (D)	92,554	(37%)
Perot (I)	55,887	(23%)

Rep. Sherwood L. Boehlert (R)

Elected 1982; b. Sept. 28, 1936, Utica; home, New Hartford; Utica Col., B.A. 1961; Catholic; married (Marianne).

Military Career: Army, 1956–58.

Elected Office: Oneida Cnty. Exec., 1978–82.

Professional Career: P.R. Mgr., Wyandotte Chemicals Corp., 1961–64; A.A., U.S. Rep. Alexander Pirnie, 1964–72; A.A., U.S. Rep. Donald Mitchell, 1973–79.

DC Office: 2246 RHOB 20515, 202-225-3665; Fax: 202-225-1891; Web site: www.house.gov/boehlert.

District Office: Utica, 315-793-8146.

Committees: *Permanent Select Committee on Intelligence* (5th of 9 R): Technical & Tactical Intelligence (Vice Chmn.). *Science* (2d of 25 R): Basic Research. *Transportation & Infrastructure* (4th of 41 R): Ground Transportation; Water Resources & Environment (Chmn.).

Group Ratings

	ADA	ACLU	AFS	LCV	CON	NTU	NFIB	COC	ACU	NTLC	CHC
1998	60	69	78	92	33	28	50	61	24	39	25
1997	55	—	50	—	67	40	—	67	32	—	—

National Journal Ratings

	1997 LIB	—	1997 CONS	1998 LIB	—	1998 CONS
Economic	53%	—	46%	54%	—	46%
Social	62%	—	37%	69%	—	31%
Foreign	56%	—	42%	49%	—	48%

Key Votes of the 105th Congress

1. Clinton Budget Deal	Y	5. Puerto Rico Sthood. Ref.	Y	9. Cut $ for B-2 Bombers	Y
2. Education IRAs	N	6. End Highway Set-asides	N	10. Human Rights in China	N
3. Req. 2/3 to Raise Taxes	N	7. School Prayer Amend.	N	11. Withdraw Bosnia Troops	N
4. Fast-track Trade	N	8. Ovrd. Part. Birth Veto	N	12. End Cuban TV-Marti	Y

Election Results

1998 general	Sherwood L. Boehlert (R) 111,242	(81%)	($551,012)
	David Vickers (C-RTL) 26,493	(19%)	($7,894)
1998 primary	Sherwood L. Boehlert (R) .... unopposed		
1996 general	Sherwood L. Boehlert (R-FR) 124,626	(64%)	($610,166)
	Bruce W. Hapanowicz (D) 50,436	(26%)	
	Thomas E. Loughlin Jr. (Ind) 10,835	(6%)	
	William Tapley (RTL) 7,790	(4%)	

TWENTY-FOURTH DISTRICT

The North Country of Upstate New York, some early 19th Century visionaries thought, was the land of the future. Financier Gouverneur Morris, French slave trader James Leray, and Dutch silver speculator David Parish bought up thousands of acres between the Adirondacks and the St. Lawrence River and tried to unload them on farmers unaware of the shortness of the growing season and the unnavigability of the river. They left behind grand mansions, but their hopes for huge profits were frustrated when the Erie Canal turned the stream of settlement westward, and Canadians built their new capital far north of the river and away from the Americans. But northern New York was not without its business successes: It was in Watertown in 1878 that 26-year-old Frank Woolworth put a sign over a table of odds and ends that read "Any Article 5 Cents," starting America's first retail chain and inventing the concept of discount stores.

More recently, the North Country has looked to government for help. The St. Lawrence Seaway proved too small for most ocean-going freighters and remains frozen three months of the year; the locks are slow and icebreakers would wreck the shoreline. The state government has built prisons in Ogdensburg and Cape Vincent, and private developers have built big malls in Watertown and Massena (attracting Canadians, as even New York has lower taxes than Ontario). But the biggest initiative has been the enlargement of Fort Drum, near Watertown, where despite the Army's preference for warm weather training sites, a 10,000-person light infantry division was stationed in 1985; surrounding Jefferson County's population has increased in percentage more than any other New York county since 1980.

The 24th Congressional District covers most of the North Country, from Plattsburgh on Lake Champlain along the St. Lawrence Seaway and over the Adirondacks Forest Preserve to Watertown and Oswego on Lake Ontario, is geographically one of the largest districts in the East. It is ancestrally Republican country, though enough in tune with New York that it voted for Bill Clinton in 1996.

The congressman from the 24th is John McHugh, a Republican chosen in 1992. McHugh has long been in government: he worked for the Watertown city manager in 1971; for eight years he was a staffer for state Senator Douglas Barclay; in 1984 he was elected to succeed Barclay in Albany. McHugh specialized in dairy issues (New York has long price-fixed dairy products to help farmers) and military bases—both part of the North Country's economic lifeblood. When incumbent David Martin announced his retirement in June 1992, just when the district lines were redrawn, McHugh ran, with plenty of financing plus Martin's endorsement. He won the Republican primary with 70%, then won the general 61%–24%.

McHugh combines a moderate voting record with a concern about local economic needs, not surprising given his district's dependence on federal largess. In 1993 he got a seat on Armed Services and hired none other than Martin to monitor the Defense Base Closure and Realignment Commission. In that year's base closure round, McHugh found himself pitted in a fierce lobbying battle against his colleague to the south, Republican Sherwood Boehlert. Griffiss Air Force Base, a major employer in Boehlert's district, and Plattsburgh Air Force Base, in McHugh's, were competing for a similar mission. In the end, the commission voted to close both bases.

The 1994 Republican victory brought McHugh chairmanship of the Government Reform subcommittee with jurisdiction over the Postal Service, a somewhat dubious honor since it gives him responsibility for one of Congress' perennial headaches. McHugh has been working for some time on what would be the biggest reform of Postal Service law since the 1970s. His version passed his subcommittee in 1998 and he reintroduced it in early 1999. McHugh would give the Postal Service more flexibility in setting prices, and would allow volume discounts; this pleases big advertising mailers but displeases newspapers, who fear they would lose ads. It would also reduce the limits on first-class mail that others, like FedEx and UPS, could carry. The Postal Service would have to set up a separate corporation to peddle long-distance phone cards and knickknacks. This is a heavily lobbied measure, in which most members have little interest; it may be a while before it, or some alternative, passes.

In July 1997, the leadership persuaded McHugh to change his vote at the last minute, to pass by 217–216 a bill that would allow block-granting of the National Endowment for the Arts. He argued afterwards that Newt Gingrich assured him the subcommittee report would contain the detailed language he wanted on formulas for block grants; New York gets a large portion of the nation's NEA funds. On impeachment, McHugh was one of the last members to announce a position and was part of nearly a dozen Republicans who came out for impeachment on December 15, four days before the vote, thus determining the outcome.

McHugh has been re-elected with more than 70% of the vote against token opposition each election since 1992.

Cook's Call. *Safe.* Democrats haven't put up a whole lot of competition against McHugh, and it is unlikely that they ever will. His moderate voting record and attention to district needs makes him a tough target.

The People: Pop. 1990: 580,376; 64.7% rural; 12.4% age 65 + ; 95.4% White, 2.6% Black, 0.6% Asian, 0.8% Amer. Indian, 0.6% Other; 1.5% Hispanic Origin. Households: 58.8% married couple families; 30.6% married couple fams. w. children; 35.7% college educ.; median household income: $25,687; per capita income: $11,060; median house value: $56,700; median gross rent: $291.

1996 Presidential Vote

Clinton (D)	102,007	(50%)
Dole (R)	72,301	(35%)
Perot (I)	30,047	(15%)

1992 Presidential Vote

Bush (R)	86,311	(38%)
Clinton (D)	85,078	(38%)
Perot (I)	54,537	(24%)

Rep. John M. McHugh (R)

Elected 1992; b. Sept. 29, 1948, Watertown; home, Pierrepont Manor; Utica Col., B.A. 1970, S.U.N.Y. Albany, M.P.A. 1977; Catholic; divorced.

Elected Office: NY Senate, 1984–92.

Professional Career: Confidential Asst., Watertown City Mgr., 1971–76; Research & Liaison Chief, NY Sen. Douglas Barclay, 1976–84.

DC Office: 2441 RHOB 20515, 202-225-4611; Fax: 202-226-0621; Web site: www.house.gov/mchugh.

District Office: Watertown, 315-782-3150.

Committees: *Armed Services* (12th of 32 R): Military Installations & Facilities; Military Research & Development; Special Oversight Panel on Morale, Welfare and Recreation (Chmn.). *Government Reform* (6th of 24 R): National Security, Veterans' Affairs & Intl. Relations; Postal Service (Chmn.). *International Relations* (20th of 26 R): Asia & the Pacific.

Group Ratings

	ADA	ACLU	AFS	LCV	CON	NTU	NFIB	COC	ACU	NTLC	CHC
1998	25	13	44	31	13	42	86	89	68	74	80
1997	15	—	50	—	56	48	—	80	60	—	—

National Journal Ratings

	1997 LIB — 1997 CONS			1998 LIB — 1998 CONS		
Economic	50%	—	49%	52%	—	47%
Social	44%	—	56%	34%	—	64%
Foreign	48%	—	51%	38%	—	61%

Key Votes of the 105th Congress

1. Clinton Budget Deal	Y	5. Puerto Rico Sthood. Ref.	N	9. Cut $ for B-2 Bombers	N
2. Education IRAs	N	6. End Highway Set-asides	Y	10. Human Rights in China	Y
3. Req. 2/3 to Raise Taxes	Y	7. School Prayer Amend.	Y	11. Withdraw Bosnia Troops	Y
4. Fast-track Trade	N	8. Ovrd. Part. Birth Veto	Y	12. End Cuban TV-Marti	N

Election Results

1998 general	John M. McHugh (R-C) 116,682	(79%)	($293,655)
	Neil P. Tallon (D) 31,011	(21%)	
1998 primary	John M. McHugh (R) .... unopposed		
1996 general	John M. McHugh (R-C) 124,240	(71%)	($172,883)
	Donald Ravenscoft (D) 43,692	(25%)	
	Others 6,750	(4%)	

TWENTY-FIFTH DISTRICT

Syracuse is a middle American city in the middle of Upstate New York, halfway between Albany and Buffalo on the Erie Canal and the old New York Central Railroad, for years the nation's major east-west transportation routes. Built on a swamp that was a salt spring, Syracuse is the home of many inventions: the dental chair, Stickley mission furniture, the drive-in bank teller, the foot measuring devices used in shoe stores. It was one of the first big manufacturers of typewriters and is the site of the New York State Fair. Its agricultural hinterland is rich with specialty crops like wine grapes, and its industrial jobs are mostly high-skill. Syracuse has spread out slowly across the countryside, but there is redevelopment of the Erie Canal waterfront where the city got its start.

The 25th Congressional District includes all of Syracuse and Onondaga County. It goes west to include part of Auburn, the home town of Governor, Senator and Secretary of State William Seward, and south to Cortland County and almost to Binghamton. Seward was the first great Republican politician of Upstate New York, and historically Syracuse is heavily Republican, partly out of antipathy to New York City. But it is also one of the most heavily Catholic cities in the United States and very ethnic, and has elected Democratic mayors and voted for Bill Clinton in 1992 and 1996.

The congressman from the 25th District is James Walsh, a Republican elected in 1988. He grew up in Syracuse, the son of a Syracuse mayor and former (1973–79) Congressman William Walsh. He came to the House as almost a professional civic activist: He was a volunteer in the Peace Corps in Nepal, a social worker, then worked for New York Telephone and NYNEX, which detailed him to a local university. He was elected five times to the Syracuse Common Council, then ran for Congress in 1988 when a Republican incumbent nearly beaten two years earlier decided to retire. He won by a solid 57%–42%. Like other Republicans from economically sluggish Upstate areas, he is open to government intervention in the economy; he voted for the Clinton stimulus package in March 1993, for the Americans with Disabilities Act and to maintain many food programs. But he also voted for the balanced budget amendment and the line-item veto.

Walsh has a seat on the Appropriations Committee, and has now been chairman of three subcommittees in three Congresses—part of the "college of cardinals," in House lingo. In 1995 and 1996 he chaired the District of Columbia Subcommittee, just as Marion Barry was returned to the mayor's office after serving time in prison. He worked with Northern Virginia Republican Tom Davis, chairman of the D.C. Subcommittee of Government Reform, and District Delegate Eleanor Holmes Norton to create the financial control board to monitor District spending and to make the accountings and file the financial reports the D.C. government chronically failed to produce. Walsh also sponsored a limited school-choice experiment, to allow some small number of poor children options other than the wretched and mismanaged D.C. public schools. This aroused furious opposition from teachers' unions, and though it passed the House it was killed in the Senate.

In 1997 and 1998 Walsh chaired the Legislative Branch Subcommittee, which sets Congress's own budget. He suffered the embarrassment in spring 1997 of seeing his appropriation defeated because of defections by 11 Republicans, who were determined to uphold promises to cut Congress's budget (as it had been in 1995 and 1996). Trouble was averted by placing the $33 million for rebuilding the dilapidated Botanic Garden in the 1997 disaster relief supplemental. In July, Walsh came in with another bill, which froze spending at 1997 levels; it passed, despite opposition from Democrats furious that the challenge to Loretta Sanchez's election was not dealt with more speedily. Walsh is a sponsor of the Hunger Has a Cure Act, and a sponsor of the measure to restore food stamps for legal immigrants; he is a strong supporter of WIC and temporary food assistance. As chairman of Friends of Ireland and co-chairman of the U.S.-Irish Interparliamentary Group, he accompanied Bill Clinton on his 1995 trip to Ireland. In 1998 he sponsored and got into the October omnibus bill 50,000 "Walsh Visas" to allow citizens of Northern Ireland and the Irish border counties to live and work in the United States for five years.

Walsh has mostly won re-election without difficulty. After he sponsored school vouchers in Washington, D.C., the AFL-CIO, 42% of whose members are public employees, targeted Walsh's district, ran an estimated $500,000 in TV ads against Walsh and a vigorous organizing campaign for Democrat Marty Mack, former mayor of Cortland. By mid-October 1996, alarms suddenly sounded in Republican headquarters that Walsh's seat was in jeopardy. With a late-spending and organizational surge, Walsh won 55%–45%. In pro-incumbent 1998, he was re-elected 69%–31%. On returning to Washington, he became chairman of the VA, HUD and Independent Agencies Subcommittee.

Cook's Call. *Safe.* The marginal nature of this district makes it an intriguing target for Democrats who want to make some inroads into the almost all-Republican Upstate delegation. But, after surviving an all-out assault in 1996 by a healthy 10-point margin, even as Clinton was cleaning up here, it is hard to see how Democrats can knock Walsh out in 2000.

The People: Pop. 1990: 580,233; 25.7% rural; 13.5% age 65 + ; 91% White, 6.6% Black, 1.2% Asian, 0.7% Amer. Indian, 0.5% Other; 1.3% Hispanic Origin. Households: 52.9% married couple families; 25.5% married couple fams. w. children; 48.5% college educ.; median household income: $31,080; per capita income: $14,148; median house value: $78,100; median gross rent: $366.

1996 Presidential Vote

Clinton (D)	121,304	(51%)
Dole (R)	90,774	(39%)
Perot (I)	23,516	(10%)

1992 Presidential Vote

Clinton (D)	108,335	(41%)
Bush (R)	95,476	(36%)
Perot (I)	58,232	(22%)

Rep. James T. Walsh (R)

Elected 1988; b. June 19, 1947, Syracuse; home, Syracuse; St. Bonaventure U., B.A. 1970; Catholic; married (Diane).

Elected Office: Syracuse Common Cncl., 1978–88, Pres. 1986–88.

Professional Career: Peace Corps, Nepal, 1970–72; Social worker, Onondaga Cnty. Social Svcs. Dept., 1972–74; Marketing exec., NYNEX, 1974–88.

DC Office: 2351 RHOB 20515, 202-225-3701; Fax: 202-225-4042; Web site: www.house.gov/walsh.

District Offices: Auburn, 315-255-0649; Cortland, 607-758-3918; Syracuse, 315-423-5657.

Committees: *Appropriations* (12th of 34 R): Agriculture, Rural Development, & FDA; Military Construction; VA, HUD & Independent Agencies (Chmn.).

Group Ratings

	ADA	ACLU	AFS	LCV	CON	NTU	NFIB	COC	ACU	NTLC	CHC
1998	30	13	33	69	26	30	79	89	44	53	83
1997	35	—	25	—	86	41	—	80	75	—	—

National Journal Ratings

	1997 LIB	—	1997 CONS	1998 LIB	—	1998 CONS
Economic	48%	—	51%	50%	—	50%
Social	30%	—	64%	43%	—	56%
Foreign	41%	—	59%	43%	—	53%

Key Votes of the 105th Congress

1. Clinton Budget Deal	Y	5. Puerto Rico Sthood. Ref.	Y	9. Cut $ for B-2 Bombers	N
2. Education IRAs	Y	6. End Highway Set-asides	N	10. Human Rights in China	N
3. Req. 2/3 to Raise Taxes	N	7. School Prayer Amend.	Y	11. Withdraw Bosnia Troops	Y
4. Fast-track Trade	N	8. Ovrd. Part. Birth Veto	Y	12. End Cuban TV-Marti	Y

Election Results

1998 general	James T. Walsh (R-C)	121,204	(69%)	($311,345)
	Yvonne Rothenberg (D-L-Green)	53,461	(31%)	($143,309)
1998 primary	Jamse T. Walsh (R)	unopposed		
1996 general	James T. Walsh (R-C-Ind-FR)	126,691	(55%)	($698,021)
	Marty Mack (D)	103,199	(45%)	($326,595)

TWENTY-SIXTH DISTRICT

New York's Southern Tier is territory not often explored by today's Americans. In colonial days, the Catskills looming over the Hudson were a great barrier, a mysterious zone in which phantom Dutchmen played nine pins and Indians lurked in the days of James Fenimore Cooper. The area then became part of a great pathway west, along the Erie Lackawanna and Delaware & Hudson Railroad lines, with engines steaming over giant viaducts and along narrow river valleys through these hills and mountains. But today, this quarter of Upstate New York has little passenger rail service and is bypassed by major air travel networks. Its interstates are lightly traveled, particularly as the once-famous kosher resorts in the "Borscht Belt" of the Catskills have lost their popularity in the past quarter century.

The sprawling 26th Congressional District includes much of the Southern Tier. The district stretches from the city of Beacon on the east side of the Hudson—where commuters board the train daily for jobs in New York City—west and north across the still-mysterious Catskills, past Bethel, site of the misnamed 1969 Woodstock music festival, to the industrial city of Binghamton in Broome County on the upper Susquehanna River, and finally to the university town of Ithaca, with Cornell University looming high above Cayuga Lake's waters. Along the west bank of the Hudson in Ulster County lies Kingston, settled by Dutchmen more than 300 years ago. This was Rip van Winkle country, and in the 19th Century was the political base of Governor and Vice President George Clinton. There are two population centers, widely separated: Binghamton-Ithaca in the west has about half the district's votes, and the Hudson Valley has about one-third. Politically, the heritage is Republican, but the Ithaca area, like so many university communities, is heavily Democratic, and population-losing Binghamton sometimes trends that way as well.

The congressman from the 26th is Maurice Hinchey, a liberal Democrat elected in 1992. Hinchey grew up in a humble background, enlisted in the Navy at 18, labored in a cement factory for five years, then worked his way through college as a New York State Thruway toll collector. He was an analyst for the state education department, then in the Democratic year of 1974, at 36, Hinchey was elected from Ulster County to the Assembly. He served for nine terms; he was proud of the more than 600 bills he passed—on, among other things, acid rain, toxic waste, illegal dumping (and organized crime's influence over it), groundwater and wetlands protection. When he ran for Congress in 1992, Hinchey called for national health insurance, a repeal of Reagan-Bush tax cuts for the rich and corporations, and "reindustrializating America." He put forth a plan to eliminate 2.6 million military and defense jobs and create 3.4 million civilian jobs. His Republican opponent Bob Moppert, a Binghamton moving company owner elected as a Broome County legislator in 1986, called for less government spending and bureaucracy. In a contest that was not only partisan but geographic, Hinchey beat Moppert 50%–47%. Hinchey carried Ulster and Moppert carried the Binghamton area; Ithaca and Tompkins County decided it, with a big margin for Hinchey.

Hinchey has one of the most liberal voting records in the House. In 1997 he was rated ninth in Democratic Party loyalty by *Congressional Quarterly* ("In my case, at least, it's a meaningless statistic, because I have no concerns how the leaders are voting") and eighth in contributions from labor unions ("I think it's a tribute to how I fight hard for working families"). One issue that caused Hinchey both political and personal discomfort was gun control. He backed the Brady Bill on handguns. But, facing a tough re-election campaign in a heavily nonmetropolitan district, he agonized over the assault weapons ban, deciding at the last minute to vote against it, despite a call from Bill Clinton. Just weeks after his 1994 re-election victory, Hinchey was boarding a plane at Washington's National Airport when his carry-on bag was found to contain a loaded handgun. Hinchey had a license to carry a gun in New York and said he was the subject of death threats while conducting probes of organized crime in the 1980s. He told a local court he had forgotten the gun was in his luggage; he pleaded no contest and was given a suspended sentence.

Hinchey, as part of the majority in the New York Assembly, was able to pass laws; as part of the minority in the House, he has mostly taken on lost causes, lost at least for the moment. He has called for creation of Empowerment Zones in rural areas, a ban on checks for unsolicited loans, a patient's safety bill, a stop on shifting of Veteran funds to the Sun Belt and for making one-tenth of Utah a wilderness area. He was pleased when the Hudson was named a National Heritage river but has not been able to get General Electric ordered to dredge PCBs from its bed. He opposed Governor George Pataki's popular welfare reform package and called for a New York constitutional convention to provide for a one-house legislature, a guarantee of protections for gender and sexual orientation, and penalties for late budgets. He supports the designation of the Southern Tier Expressway as Interstate 86, passed by Daniel Patrick Moynihan in the Senate. He wants a statue of Franklin Roosevelt in a wheelchair. With socialist Bernie Sanders of Vermont, he came out against "privatization" of Social Security.

Not surprisingly, Hinchey has attracted strenuous Republican opposition—perhaps too strenuous, at least in 1998, for the Republicans' own good. His 1992 opponent Moppert ran again in 1994, and sought to nationalize the election; Hinchey sought to localize it and, more important, vastly outspent the challenger. Hinchey won 49%–48%, in one of the nation's closest races, with the outcome uncertain until almost two weeks after the election. This time Hinchey's base was Ithaca and Binghamton. In 1996 Hinchey was again a Republican target, but Bill Clinton carried the district with 51%, and Hinchey spent nearly $1 million, labeling his opponent "a self-proclaimed foot soldier in the army of Newt Gingrich" and an extremist; it would be more accurate to say both were at the extremes of the not terribly broad spectrum of American electoral politicians. Hinchey won 55%–42%, carrying all parts of the district.

For the 1998 cycle, Hinchey at first seemed to have problems. In 1997 a North American subsidiary of an Italian power plant construction company pleaded guilty in federal court of making $40,000 in illegal contributions to his 1992 campaign, and his 1992 finance director pleaded guilty to illegally funneling $27,000 from a company he controlled: The amounts together were about one-fifth of what he spent that year. But Hinchey was not implicated in either of these cases. In September 1997 he said he was considering running for governor; in October he decided not to. In 1998 the focus shifted to his opposition. The favored Republican candidate was William "Bud" Walker, a radio station owner. But he was overshadowed by Randall Terry, the Binghamton talk radio host who founded Operation Rescue in 1987 and staged anti-abortion rallies ever since. Terry raised and spent $1.2 million, most of it from abortion opponents across the country, and said he was campaigning against "oppressive federal taxation" as well as abortion. Terry's campaign unearthed court documents in which Walker's former wife accused him of hitting their children and failing to give them medicine. A Washington-based Republican group ran ads against Terry, quoting his words to a 1993 rally: "Let a wave of intolerance wash over you. I want to let a wave of hatred wash over you. Yes, hate is good." Upstate Congressman Gerald Solomon chimed in with an ad saying, "I will continue to fight for conservative principles and against the Randall Terrys and David Dukes of this world." Walker won the Republican primary by an unimpressive 53%–35%, and Terry kept campaigning as the Right-to-Life nominee (Walker won the Conservative nomination by 50 votes). Hinchey, meanwhile, spent $991,000 as the Republicans sputtered at each other. Hinchey won with a solid 62% to 31% for Walker and 7% for Terry; he peaked at 10% and 12% in the two Binghamton area counties.

Hinchey could have a serious challenge again in 2000, and might face redistricting problems in 2002; this is a district whose geographic shape makes it easy to slice up among its neighbors. But he has shown impressive staying power for a member whose first victory seemed something of a fluke.

Cook's Call. *Potentially Competitive.* Hinchey's liberal voting record is always going to make him a target in this Democratic-leaning but still marginal district. But, bumbling on the part of Republican candidates over the last two cycles has helped Hinchey the most. A strong, well-funded Republican candidate who avoids a contentious primary can still give Hinchey a run. He has survived three close elections and may have finally caught his stride.

The People: Pop. 1990: 580,540; 42.9% rural; 13.8% age 65 +; 90.8% White, 5.5% Black, 2% Asian, 0.2% Amer. Indian, 1.5% Other; 4.1% Hispanic Origin. Households: 53% married couple families; 24.8% married couple fams. w. children; 46.7% college educ.; median household income: $30,335; per capita income: $13,786; median house value: $94,500; median gross rent: $384.

1996 Presidential Vote			1992 Presidential Vote		
Clinton (D)	120,755	(53%)	Clinton (D)	116,450	(45%)
Dole (R)	82,044	(36%)	Bush (R)	91,462	(35%)
Perot (I)	25,237	(11%)	Perot (I)	53,675	(21%)

Rep. Maurice D. Hinchey (D)

Elected 1992; b. Oct. 27, 1938, New York, NY; home, Saugerties; S.U.N.Y. New Paltz, B.S. 1968, M.A. 1969; Catholic; married (Ilene).

Military Career: Navy, 1956–59.

Elected Office: NY Assembly, 1974–92.

Professional Career: Cement plant worker, 1959–64; NY St. Thruway toll collector, 1959–68; Analyst, NY St. Dept. of Educ., 1971–74.

DC Office: 2431 RHOB 20515, 202-225-6335; Fax: 202-226-0774; Web site: www.house.gov/hinchey.

District Offices: Binghamton, 607-773-2768; Ithaca, 607-273-1388; Kingston, 914-331-4466; Monticello, 914-791-7116.

Committees: *Appropriations* (22d of 27 D): Agriculture, Rural Development, & FDA; Interior. *Joint Economic Committee* (8th of 10 Reps.).

Group Ratings

	ADA	ACLU	AFS	LCV	CON	NTU	NFIB	COC	ACU	NTLC	CHC
1998	100	87	100	100	38	16	7	22	4	5	0
1997	95	—	100	—	17	27	—	20	8	—	—

National Journal Ratings

	1997 LIB — 1997 CONS		1998 LIB — 1998 CONS	
Economic	93%	— 0%	79%	— 0%
Social	85%	— 0%	88%	— 11%
Foreign	76%	— 22%	90%	— 5%

Key Votes of the 105th Congress

1. Clinton Budget Deal	N	5. Puerto Rico Sthood. Ref.	Y	9. Cut $ for B-2 Bombers	N
2. Education IRAs	N	6. End Highway Set-asides	N	10. Human Rights in China	Y
3. Req. 2/3 to Raise Taxes	N	7. School Prayer Amend.	N	11. Withdraw Bosnia Troops	N
4. Fast-track Trade	N	8. Ovrd. Part. Birth Veto	N	12. End Cuban TV-Marti	Y

Election Results

1998 general	Maurice D. Hinchey (D-Ind-L)	108,204	(62%)	($1,007,554)
	William H. (Bud) Walker (R-C)	54,776	(31%)	($770,134)
	Randall Terry (RTL)	12,160	(7%)	($1,214,416)
1998 primary	Maurice D. Hinchey (D)	unopposed		
1996 general	Maurice D. Hinchey (D-L)	122,850	(55%)	($994,042)
	Sue Wittig (R-C-RTL-FR)	94,125	(42%)	($586,078)
	Others	5,531	(2%)	

TWENTY-SEVENTH DISTRICT

Across the Finger Lakes of New York, the long, thin, deep-blue lakes in glacier-carved folds between rolling hillsides thick with grapevines, ran one of the first paths of westward migration. Originally cut off from white settlement by the British and the Iroquois, Upstate New York opened up after the Revolution, and streams of New England Yankees moved west. They followed the Mohawk River and the Erie Canal, dug by hand labor and finished in 1825, connecting the Hudson River and Lake Erie, the East Coast and the vast interior of America. The Finger Lakes region became one of the fastest-growing and most dynamic parts of America.

Town squares here today have monuments to the enthusiasms of the 1830s and 1840s, when these new communities were full of young families on the rise, and religious revivals were so fervent that the area was known as the Burnt-Over district. Here in the village of Palmyra, near the Erie Canal, Joseph Smith had his vision of the angel Moroni and saw the golden tablets that led him to found the Mormon Church. Preachers fanned enthusiasm for abolition of slavery, greater here than anywhere else in the country. This was the birthplace of the women's movement: in Seneca Falls in 1848, Elizabeth Cady Stanton and Lucretia Mott produced a Declaration of Sentiments that started the women's suffrage movement. Upstate was also the birthplace of the temperance movement, another women's cause in those days.

The 27th Congressional District covers much of this territory, now economically less dynamic and politically calmer than in its heyday. The district starts at Aurelius, one of the many Upstate towns with classical names, and includes Seneca Falls and Palmyra, then passes south of Rochester and through Batavia and Attica to the Buffalo suburb of Amherst. Most of this is part of America's Republican heartland, though Erie County around Buffalo, with its historic industrial base, has leaned Democratic.

The congressman from the 27th is Thomas Reynolds, a Republican elected in 1998. Reynolds grew up in Springville, in southern Erie County, and became an insurance and real estate broker there. He got into politics early: in 1973 he was aide to an assemblyman and that same year, at 23, he was elected to the Town of Concord council. In 1982 he was named to a vacant seat in the Erie County Legislature. In 1988 he was elected to the Assembly and also helped run the congressional campaign of Bill Paxon, who was elected to succeed Jack Kemp. From 1990–96 he was Erie County Republican Chairman, from 1995–98 the Assembly minority leader. He chaired Dennis Vacco's successful campaign for attorney general in 1994. In early 1998 it seemed sure that he would stay in Albany, though perhaps under a cloud; the *New York Post*'s Frederick U. Dicker reported that Governor Pataki was furious with Reynolds because Assembly Republicans did not applaud loudly enough Pataki's State of the State address.

Then suddenly the 27th House seat fell open. For 10 years Paxon had been one of the rising stars in the House. In 1993 he became chairman of the House Republicans' campaign committee, and helped them gain 52 seats and control of the House in 1994 and hold control in 1996. Newt Gingrich told intimates that Paxon was the most talented Republican in the House, and in 1997 created a position in the leadership for him. But in July 1997 Paxon played a key part in the unsuccessful coup against Gingrich; he resigned his leadership post, saying someone would have to take the blame. In early 1998 he still seemed to have leadership ambitions, but on February 25, 1998, a week after Bob Livingston said he would stay in the House and run for speaker when Gingrich stepped down, Paxon announced he would retire from Congress at the end of his term, and never run for office again.

At his side in Erie County was Reynolds, who announced he was running for the House the next morning. No serious Republican opposition appeared. Democrats spent most of March and April looking for a candidate, but Erie County Clerk David Swarts, Amherst Town Democratic Chairman Dennis Ward and businessman George Hasiotis all declined to run. At that point the party reaffirmed the endorsement it made, before Reynolds's announced, of Bill Cook, a professor at SUNY-Geneseo. It was not a suspenseful or eventful campaign. The biggest fuss came in August when Pataki signed a bill promoting Reynolds from Tier 2 to Tier 1 in the state pension system; his service as an Assembly staffer had started five days too late for Tier 1, and it was worth about $91,000 to Reynolds, who said he was employed for the appropriate amount of time but simply failed to fill out his paperwork in a timely fashion. But the pension issue didn't seem to trouble voters: Reynolds won 57%–43% and by 51%–49% in Erie County. Two days after the election, Reynolds said he wouldn't take the pension upgrade.

In the House, Reynolds was the only freshman Republican to win a seat on the Rules Committee—an indication he was in good repute with the Republican leadership.

Cook's Call. *Safe.* This district is one of the most Republican in the state, and there is little reason for Democrats to target Reynolds.

The People: Pop. 1990: 580,317; 55.5% rural; 13.4% age 65 + ; 95.6% White, 2.5% Black, 1.1% Asian, 0.4% Amer. Indian, 0.4% Other; 1.2% Hispanic Origin. Households: 62.3% married couple families; 30.1% married couple fams. w. children; 47.9% college educ.; median household income: $34,573; per capita income: $14,934; median house value: $81,300; median gross rent: $350.

1996 Presidential Vote			
Clinton (D)	111,804	(44%)	
Dole (R)	111,371	(44%)	
Perot (I)	28,980	(11%)	

1992 Presidential Vote			
Bush (R)	115,432	(42%)	
Clinton (D)	90,194	(33%)	
Perot (I)	67,721	(25%)	

Rep. Thomas Reynolds (R)

Elected 1998; b. Sept. 3, 1950, Belfonte, PA; home, Springville; Springville-Griffith Inst., Kent St. U.; Presbyterian; married (Donna).

Military Career: NY Air Natl. Guard, 1970–76.

Elected Office: Concord Town Bd., 1974–82; Erie Cnty. Legislature, 1982–88; NY Assembly, 1988–98, Min. Ldr., 1995–98.

Professional Career: Real estate & insurance broker; Erie Cty. Repub. Chmn., 1990–96.

DC Office: 413 CHOB 20515, 202-225-5265; Fax: 202-225-5910; Web site: www.house.gov/reynolds.

District Offices: Victor, 716-742-1600; Williamsville, 716-634-2324.

Committees: *Rules* (9th of 9 R): Rules & Organization of the House.

Group Ratings and Key Votes: Newly Elected

Election Results

1998 general	Thomas Reynolds (R-C)	102,042	(57%)	($851,862)
	Bill Cook (D-Ind-RTL)	75,978	(43%)	($60,622)
1998 primary	Thomas Reynolds (R)	unopposed		
1996 general	Bill Paxon (R-C-RTL-FR)	142,568	(60%)	($1,553,754)
	Thomas M. Fricano (D-SM)	95,503	(40%)	($656,490)

TWENTY-EIGHTH DISTRICT

Rochester, with a metro area of just over one million, is one of the major cities of Upstate New York. Located where the Erie Canal, the backbone of Upstate, crosses the Genesee River, Rochester became a major industrial city, the "Flour City" in the 1830s, as it milled the wheat produced by western New York farmers, and then a high-tech city, when a bank clerk named George Eastman began making photographic dry plates and marketed the first still camera and film for Thomas Edison's motion picture camera in 1888 and 1889. Later, Bausch & Lomb developed its lens business here. Rochester, the home of Susan B. Anthony and Frederick Douglass, has lived on high-tech versions of the eye. Its great industries—Bausch & Lomb, Eastman Kodak, and Xerox, which started here as Haloid—have thrived on technical innovation, precision workmanship, high reliability and customer service, giving Rochester an affluent and well-educated population that maintains fine civic institutions and traditions. This was the city that in 1918 invented the Community Chest and still has the nation's highest United Way contributions; it is also the home of Wegman's, quite possibly the nation's best supermarket chain. A *Washington Post* 1996 profile of Rochester concluded that the city's growth proves "the economic future of cities and states depends less on where the biggest companies chose to locate than where the best people chose to locate." Unhappily, Rochester's big businesses have fallen on hard times: Xerox moved many jobs out of here a decade ago, and in the late 1980s and the late 1990s Kodak has been hard pressed. Unemployment here is not as high in some parts of Upstate New York, but Rochester has not grown much either.

The 28th Congressional District includes Rochester and most of its Monroe County suburbs—a compact district in a state where redistricting produced a dozen grotesqueries. In the 1990s, for the first time in 50 years, the heart of Monroe County wasn't separated into two districts. Traditionally Republican, the Rochester area moved toward Democrats in the 1970s and 1980s.

The congresswoman from the 28th District is Louise Slaughter, a Democrat first elected in 1986. She grew up in Kentucky, and still speaks with the accent and pungent phraseology of the mountains. She is one of several notable women—Secretary of State Madeleine Albright is another—who came into public life after raising a family. Slaughter worked as a local staffer for Mario Cuomo when he was lieutenant governor in the 1970s and won a seat on the Monroe County Legislature in 1976; she was elected to the New York Assembly in 1982 and 1984. In 1986, she beat a one-term conservative Republican congressman 51%–49%, by charging that he did nothing to free reporter Terry Anderson, a hostage in Lebanon and Rochester native. She held the seat by tending carefully to local problems, by winning the support of area businessmen and the local *Democrat & Chronicle* newspaper—ironically, the flagship of Gannett, a chain founded by a diehard Upstate Republican. Because Rochester has moved left and her district includes all the central city, her solidly liberal voting record is not a liability.

When Democrats were in the majority, Slaughter became a member of the Rules Committee, a proponent of her party's House reforms (and a disparager of the Republicans'). She worked to get funding for the Rochester International Airport and the harbor, for the Center for Integrated Manufacturing Studies, and for a high-tech business incubator. She took the side of organized labor and voted against NAFTA in 1993 and fast track in 1997. Another grievance is airline deregulation. It has hurt slow-growing areas like Upstate New York; Rochester in 1998 had the fourth-highest air fares in the nation. So far Slaughter's efforts at reregulation— requiring hub airlines to service smaller airports, banning temporary price cuts to drive out competition—have not prevailed. She is a prime supporter of the National Endowment for the Arts. She has sponsored bills for free broadcast time for candidates. And she had a bill providing $1.25 billion in matching grants for local after-school crime prevention programs. She sometimes sounds sterner notes: The House has approved her proposal for federal life-without-parole sentences for serial rapists.

Slaughter strongly backs feminist causes and is active on health issues. In 1991 she was one of the seven women House members who marched on the Senate to protest its treatment of Anita Hill, in 1994 she sponsored the law to ban blockades of abortion clinics and in 1995 she spoke out loudly for surgeon general nominee Henry Foster. She worked for more funding for breast cancer research in 1996 and in 1997 she sponsored a bill to require insurance companies to cover reconstructive surgery for breast cancer victims, and in 1998 pushed for national screening for colon cancer. In 1998 she sought a report on genital mutilation of women, a common practice among certain Africans; she sponsored a 1996 law that made this a federal crime. Slaughter also wants to bar insurance companies from using genetic tests to deny or limit coverage to healthy people.

The Lewinsky scandal and impeachment obviously left Slaughter uncomfortable. In March 1998 she said defensively, "I have not changed a bit from my days with Anita Hill. Sexual harassment in the workplace is a terrible thing and should not be tolerated." Long resentful of Clinton's moderation and changeability on issues, and of his penchant for negotiating directly with House Republicans and leaving House Democrats out of the loop, she said in December, "I don't think you'd find a whole lot of loyalty to Bill Clinton around here. He's not the best Democrat any of us have seen." She said she was ready to call for resignation in August but backed away when she saw the videotape of his testimony in which she thought his rights were abridged; she voted Clinton's way when the time came.

Slaughter has been frustrated in seeking higher positions. Republican control of the House cost Slaughter her seat on Rules, though she regained it two years later. In December 1994 she lost the race for vice chairman of the Democratic Caucus to Barbara Kennelly by a 93–90 margin. And she lost the December 1996 race for ranking Democrat on the Budget Committee to the more moderate John Spratt by 106–83. In May 1998 she complained that House Democrats have done little to elevate women to positions of power: "There's not been an inch of progress made that I can determine."

In 1998 Slaughter had her most impressive electoral victory. She faced a Republican businessman who spent $408,000 of his own money and had a program called CARING, an acronym for Cash Allocations to Remediate Inequities, Nurture and Give. To explain it he self-published a book and a 100-page abridged version. Slaughter won 65%–31%, her first time over 60%.

Cook's Call. *Probably Safe.* Slaughter's marginal district and less-than-overpowering wins have made her an intriguing target over the years. But it will be interesting to see if Republicans target this district in 2000, since Slaughter garnered a 14-point win over a well-funded Republican opponent in 1996 and had another strong win in 1998.

The People: Pop. 1990: 580,347; 3.7% rural; 13.7% age 65 +; 81.7% White, 13.9% Black, 1.8% Asian, 0.3% Amer. Indian, 2.2% Other; 3.9% Hispanic Origin. Households: 48.9% married couple families; 22.5% married couple fams. w. children; 52.5% college educ.; median household income: $33,899; per capita income: $16,205; median house value: $90,700; median gross rent: $417.

1996 Presidential Vote			1992 Presidential Vote		
Clinton (D)	136,424	(56%)	Clinton (D)	119,055	(44%)
Dole (R)	88,279	(36%)	Bush (R)	103,544	(38%)
Perot (I)	17,841	(7%)	Perot (I)	48,467	(18%)

Rep. Louise M. Slaughter (D)

Elected 1986; b. Aug. 14, 1929, Harlan Cnty., KY; home, Fairport; U. of KY, B.S. 1951, M.S. 1953; Episcopalian; married (Robert).

Elected Office: Monroe Cnty. Legislature, 1976–79; NY Assembly, 1982–86.

Professional Career: Regional Coord., Lt. Gov. Mario Cuomo, 1976–79.

DC Office: 2347 RHOB 20515, 202-225-3615; Fax: 202-225-7822; Web site: www.house.gov/slaughter.

District Office: Rochester, 716-232-4850.

Committees: *Rules* (4th of 4 D): Rules & Organization of the House.

Group Ratings

	ADA	ACLU	AFS	LCV	CON	NTU	NFIB	COC	ACU	NTLC	CHC
1998	100	88	100	100	41	15	7	39	8	3	0
1997	85	—	100	—	16	25	—	30	9	—	—

National Journal Ratings

	1997 LIB — 1997 CONS			1998 LIB — 1998 CONS		
Economic	93%	—	0%	79%	—	0%
Social	85%	—	0%	80%	—	20%
Foreign	76%	—	22%	78%	—	19%

Key Votes of the 105th Congress

1. Clinton Budget Deal	N	5. Puerto Rico Sthood. Ref.	Y	9. Cut $ for B-2 Bombers	Y
2. Education IRAs	N	6. End Highway Set-asides	N	10. Human Rights in China	Y
3. Req. 2/3 to Raise Taxes	N	7. School Prayer Amend.	N	11. Withdraw Bosnia Troops	N
4. Fast-track Trade	N	8. Ovrd. Part. Birth Veto	N	12. End Cuban TV-Marti	Y

Election Results

1998 general	Louise M. Slaughter (D) 118,856	(65%)	($456,930)
	Richard A. Kaplan (R-Ind) 56,443	(31%)	($511,083)
	Others 8,159	(4%)	
1998 primary	Louise M. Slaughter (D) .... unopposed		
1996 general	Louise M. Slaughter (D) 133,084	(57%)	($868,969)
	Geoff H. Rosenberger (R-C-FR) 99,366	(43%)	($663,441)

TWENTY-NINTH DISTRICT

The Niagara Frontier is the romantic name for the Buffalo metropolitan area and the northwest corner of Upstate New York facing Lake Ontario. This really was the frontier once, between the United States and British-held Upper Canada, when American troops crossed the raging Niagara River in the War of 1812 to fight the Battle of Lundys Lane. Not many years later, Niagara Falls became a prime vacation spot, a must-see sight for European tourists and American honeymooners. By the mid-20th Century, Niagara Falls vacations had become routine, and few tourists took notice of the huge water intakes farther up the river, the hydroelectric power lines strung out on giant pylons fanning out in every direction, providing cheap public power for the chemical and steel factories that made the Niagara Frontier one of the heavy industry capitals of America. The city of Niagara Falls itself has fallen on hard times. It has lost 70% of its manufacturing since the 1960s and had the nation's third lowest rate of job growth in 1997. Its population has fallen from a peak of more than 100,000 to less than 60,000 today. Urban renewal leveled most of the downtown, but redevelopment has remained an elusive dream. In the latest scheme, Manhattan developer Howard Milstein hopes his proposed casino will build on the region's tourism industry, a strategy that has been successful on the Canadian side of the border. But political hurdles remain: Gambling is not legal in New York.

The 29th Congressional District includes the heart of the Niagara Frontier: the Falls; the Buffalo suburbs of Tonawanda and Kenmore; and the northwest one-third of Buffalo itself, with the city's downtown and its fine but financially beleaguered cultural institutions. The 29th also runs east to include towns and farm country along the southern shore of Lake Ontario to the Rochester suburb of Gates. Like most of Upstate New York, this was once Republican territory; as heavy industries declined, it trended Democratic. Its most famous congressman was William Miller, the Republican National Committee chairman from 1961–64 and Barry Goldwater's 1964 vice presidential nominee. But it hasn't elected a Republican since 1972.

The congressman from the 29th is John LaFalce, a son of Buffalo who attended Canisius College and was elected to the New York Senate in 1970, at 31, and to the Assembly in 1972. In 1974, when the Republican incumbent retired, he was elected to the House. His record is very liberal on economics, but moderate on cultural and foreign issues. Much of his work has been to get government to spur development of industrial areas. In the 1980s, LaFalce took up the banner of promoting competitiveness. He strongly backed the U.S.-Canada Free Trade Agreement, which enabled the Niagara Frontier, with its low land costs and rents, to partake of the prosperity of Ontario's Toronto-based Golden Horseshoe, but he voted against NAFTA. As chairman of the Small Business Committee from 1987–95, he superintended the various Small Business Administration loan programs, which represent only a minuscule percentage of total lending to small business. LaFalce's small business interests led him to draw up his own family and medical leave, disabilities and civil rights bills, and he was a leader in the fight to repeal the Section 89 employee-benefits tax provisions that small business owners detested.

After the 1996 election, LaFalce decided to seek the ranking position on Banking by trying to oust the often autocratic and distracted 80-year-old Henry Gonzalez. Also in the race was Bruce Vento, a longtime Gonzalez adversary. In November 1996 the Democratic Steering Committee voted 29–12 to oust Gonzalez, and Banking Committee members voted 22–19 for LaFalce over Vento. But the next day Gonzalez made an emotional plea to the Democratic Caucus for just one more two-year term. When he won only 82 votes on the first ballot, against 109 for LaFalce and Vento, it seemed likely Vento would drop out and LaFalce would prevail. But LaFalce unexpectedly dropped his challenge. "With Henry having that much support and having served so honorably, I didn't want it to end that way," he explained. It was a brilliant stroke: He won over Gonzalez's friends, including many Hispanics and blacks. In 1997 Gonzalez stopped coming to Washington, and LaFalce was named acting ranking member; in February 1998, with Gonzalez's consent, he was unanimously elected ranking member.

In 1990, 1992 and 1994, LaFalce won with just 55%—not impressive for a longtime incumbent. As part of the minority, he has spent time on measures to help the economically ailing Niagara Frontier. He helped persuade Fannie Mae to commit money, $2 billion was his estimate, to the Buffalo area over five years and worked for $120 million in improvements to the Rainbow Bridge and the Niagara Falls Air Reserve Base. With Louise Slaughter of Rochester, he sponsored measures to reregulate airlines, taking slots away from major carriers and auctioning them off; western New York has some of the nation's highest air fares. He urged regulators to guarantee competition between CSX and Norfolk Southern when they bought Conrail's lines. He called for renegotiating limits on Canadian wool imports; Rochester's Hickey-Freeman is a leading manufacturer of fine men's clothes. He sought emergency aid for western New York farmers to recover from 1998 storms. He called for dropping fees on small pleasure craft crossing the border and tried to change the new immigration law requirement that all aliens fill out visa forms when entering or leaving the U.S.—a surefire recipe for gridlock at Niagara Frontier bridges. On national issues, he has had qualms about financial services deregulation and strongly supported the $18 billion IMF bailout.

In 1996 LaFalce won re-election by his best margin since 1988. In 1998 he had stronger opposition. Republican Chris Collins had just sold a gear-making company and spent $565,000 of his own money on the race, enabling him to match LaFalce's nearly $1 million. Collins tried to benefit from dissatisfaction with the local economy. LaFalce won 57%–41%, with a big 62%–36% margin in Erie County. Collins said he might run again, but probably not in 2000; redistricting after that could significantly change any or all of the western New York seats.

Cook's Call. *Probably Safe.* LaFalce's less than impressive wins over underfunded candidates and the marginal nature of this district made him an intriguing target in 1998. But LaFalce still ended up with 57% of the vote over a well-funded candidate. The 13-term incumbent will not be easy to defeat.

The People: Pop. 1990: 579,831; 22.9% rural; 15.4% age 65 + ; 92.6% White, 4.4% Black, 0.7% Asian, 0.8% Amer. Indian, 1.5% Other; 2.8% Hispanic Origin. Households: 52.8% married couple families; 24% married couple fams. w. children; 43.1% college educ.; median household income: $28,951; per capita income: $13,350; median house value: $71,600; median gross rent: $304.

1996 Presidential Vote			1992 Presidential Vote		
Clinton (D)	120,777	(52%)	Clinton (D)	103,528	(40%)
Dole (R)	82,737	(36%)	Bush (R)	86,730	(33%)
Perot (I)	28,015	(12%)	Perot (I)	70,231	(27%)

Rep. John J. LaFalce (D)

Elected 1974; b. Oct. 6, 1939, Buffalo; home, Tonawanda; Canisius Col., B.S. 1961, Villanova U., J.D. 1964; Catholic; married (Patricia).

Military Career: Army, 1965–67.

Elected Office: NY Senate, 1970–72; NY Assembly, 1972–74.

Professional Career: Law Clerk, U.S. Navy Gen. Cnsl., 1963; Lecturer, George Washington U., 1965–66; Practicing atty., 1967–74.

DC Office: 2310 RHOB 20515, 202-225-3231; Web site: www.house.gov/lafalce.

District Offices: Buffalo, 716-846-4056; Niagara Falls, 716-284-9976; Spencerport, 716-352-4777.

Committees: *Banking & Financial Services* (RMM of 27 D).

Group Ratings

	ADA	ACLU	AFS	LCV	CON	NTU	NFIB	COC	ACU	NTLC	CHC
1998	85	63	100	92	84	23	21	41	8	5	33
1997	85	—	88	—	66	30	—	40	16	—	—

National Journal Ratings

	1997 LIB	—	1997 CONS		1998 LIB	—	1998 CONS
Economic	93%	—	0%		77%	—	22%
Social	58%	—	42%		54%	—	45%
Foreign	85%	—	13%		89%	—	10%

Key Votes of the 105th Congress

1. Clinton Budget Deal	N	5. Puerto Rico Sthood. Ref.	Y	9. Cut $ for B-2 Bombers	Y
2. Education IRAs	N	6. End Highway Set-asides	*	10. Human Rights in China	Y
3. Req. 2/3 to Raise Taxes	N	7. School Prayer Amend.	N	11. Withdraw Bosnia Troops	N
4. Fast-track Trade	N	8. Ovrd. Part. Birth Veto	Y	12. End Cuban TV-Marti	Y

Election Results

1998 general	John J. LaFalce (D-Ind-L)	97,235	(57%)	($1,026,355)
	Chris Collins (R-C)	69,481	(41%)	($963,479)
	Others	3,813	(2%)	
1998 primary	John J. LaFalce (D) .... unopposed			
1996 general	John J. LaFalce (D-L)	132,317	(62%)	($443,052)
	David B. Callard (R-C-RTL-FR)	81,135	(38%)	($123,958)

THIRTIETH DISTRICT

Buffalo, New York's second city, with its massive 1920s skyscraper City Hall overlooking the Niagara River and Lake Erie, has been going through rough times. The butt of many jokes about the snow that piles up at the eastern end of Lake Erie and that supposedly keeps it immobilized half the year, Buffalo also should be credited with building a heavy industrial base in the late 19th and early 20th Centuries, as America's number one grain milling center, and as a major steel producer. Today, the Lackawanna steel mills are cold, and grain milling waned after the St. Lawrence Seaway opened in the 1950s. Buffalo is eclipsed economically by the bigger Great Lakes industrial cities of Cleveland, Detroit and Chicago, and its architecturally bold downtown skyscrapers are far overshadowed by the high-rise horizon of Toronto, not many miles away. Though it is still one of the nation's 50 largest municipalities, the Buffalo area's population has been falling for the past three decades.

This is despite its considerable assets: a high-skill labor force and inexpensive real estate, including a gentrified and handsome waterfront on a now-clean Lake Erie. In the early 1990s Buffalo pinned its hopes for resurgence on its proximity to Canada, and on the U.S.-Canada Free Trade Agreement signed in late 1988. Right across Buffalo's Peace Bridge is the richest part of Canada, the golden horseshoe from Niagara Falls through Hamilton to Toronto. In the early 1990s, Toronto's wages, real estate prices and taxes were much higher than Buffalo's, its labor market much tighter and its unions more militant, and Canadian investment flowed into Buffalo. But as the Canadian dollar weakened and Ontario cut its sky-high taxes, Buffalo's comparative advantage declined.

The 30th Congressional District consists of the eastern and southern two-thirds of Buffalo, plus most of the Erie County suburbs east and south of the city, from working-class Cheekto-waga and the steel-mill town of Lackawanna to higher-income Hamburg on Lake Erie. This is a solidly Democratic district, by any measure the most Democratic in Upstate New York, although some of the suburbs are Republican. But in the early 1990s, as Buffalo struggled to grow, it was politically volatile. In 1992 Buffalo gave Ross Perot 28%, his best showing in a central city anywhere, and in 1994 Mario Cuomo, who had always run well in Buffalo, lost Erie County to George Pataki.

The congressman from the 30th District is Jack Quinn, a Republican elected in 1992. He is an authentic product of Buffalo, the son of a union railroad engineer, a union member himself as a steelworker and teacher, a graduate of Siena College who became a teacher and coach at Orchard Park Central High School, the Town of Hamburg supervisor (a full-time job) from 1983–92. When incumbent Democrat Henry Nowak retired in 1992, Quinn saw his chance to run as a reformer; he created his own Change Congress Party so his name would appear under this as well as the Republican Party label; he ran on an 11-point program of congressional reform, including term limits and a reduction in House staff. In a stunning upset, Quinn beat Erie County Executive Dennis Gorski by 52%–46%; in effect, Quinn got the Perot vote while Gorski ran basically even with Bill Clinton's 45% plurality.

Quinn, sometimes compared with Ronald Reagan, is known on Capitol Hill as well as in Buffalo for his affable personality and, like Reagan, has shown that he is politically shrewd. Tagged almost immediately by Democrats as their number one target in 1994, Quinn worked to reach out to organized labor, voting against NAFTA in November 1993. He was one of the few Republicans to support the defeated striker replacement law and supported family and medical leave. He favored the Clinton crime bill in August 1994, proposing changes that helped attract support for the measure—meeting with Clinton once and talking with him twice on the phone. Meanwhile, local Democrats were split among several contenders, and in November 1994 Quinn rolled over his opponent, 67%–33%.

In the Republican Congress, Quinn did even more to demonstrate his independence of the Republican leadership. He was the lead Republican pushing in 1996 for an increase in the minimum wage, and in March 1999 he was one of only two Republicans to vote against the Republican budget (the other was Maryland's Connie Morella). He supported summer youth employment and winter home heating laws, the hate crime law, the NEA, and lobby reform. He opposed fast track in 1997 and sought aid for the import-battered steel industry in 1998. He was the chief Republican sponsor of the measure to ban U.S. land mines after January 2000. He was a big booster of the 1997 bipartisan civility meeting, and in July 1998 he led 22 other Republicans to a meeting with AFL-CIO president John Sweeney. Challenged once on the floor for wearing bermuda shorts and a polo shirt with his coat and tie, he promised, "From now on I'm going to take my cue from [Ohio's James] Traficant."

On local issues, Quinn worked on the Transportation and Infrastructure Committee to save Amtrak and build a new station in Memorial Auditorium. He worked to assure local competition after CSX and Norfolk Southern bought Conrail. In the 1998 transportation bill, he got projects ranging from $40 million seed money for U.S. 219 south of Buffalo to $300,000 for a traffic calming study on Route 5 in Hamburg. He called for lifting restrictions on imports of Canadian softwood lumber to help local home builders and lumber dealers. He helped get a 30-month delay, to April 2001, of Section 110 of the new immigration law which would require aliens to get visas on entering and exiting the United States—a daffy law that would tie up traffic for hours at the Peace Bridge and in Niagara Falls.

This record has helped Quinn hold this basically Democratic seat. In 1996 the AFL-CIO endorsed Democratic Assemblyman Frank Pordum and Bill Clinton carried the 30th District 57%–29%. But Quinn won 55%–45%—in a straight-ticket year, one of the outstanding examples of ticket-splitting in the country. In 1998, against a low-spending opponent, Quinn won 68%–32%, and had $250,000 left over.

Then came the issue of impeachment. Quinn's good relations with Clinton—he watched the 1997 Super Bowl at the White House—and the Democratic leanings of the 30th District led everyone to assume he would vote against impeachment, and as late as November 23 he said he would do so. On December 9, Clinton called Quinn from *Air Force One* and Quinn gave no sign of wavering. But as he listened to the arguments of the Judiciary Committee Republicans, he did. On December 15, four days before the vote, he announced he would vote for impeachment, and eight other Republicans followed that day, deciding the issue. What changed his mind? As he told Michael Grunwald of *The Washington Post*, "It wasn't a single event; it was a gradual process. It was just a very difficult decision to make. My friendship with the president made it doubly difficult."

Much local reaction was furious. The head of the Buffalo AFL-CIO Council said, "We thought he was a friend of ours. We really, really did. Let me tell you something . . . We won't forget this in two years." Labor held an anti-Quinn rally on the day of voting; Clinton refused to shake Quinn's hand after the State of the Union in January; Clinton journeyed to Buffalo for a rally the day after. Hillary Rodham Clinton, not yet contemplating a New York Senate race herself, promised to campaign for Quinn's 2000 opponent. Evidently the Clintons and local Democrats and labor officials thought that Quinn's vote made the difference, as it may have. Quinn said he was puzzled why labor leaders were so angry, since Clinton had deserted them on important issues like NAFTA and fast track and he had held fast. "It just defies logic. I'm fighting my leadership all the time. I'm with the unions on every labor vote. But this had absolutely nothing to do with labor issues."

Cook's Call. *Probably Safe.* Local Democrats are hoping that Quinn will feel a heavy backlash for his vote for impeachment in this Democratic leaning Buffalo-based district. But, Quinn, who survived a heavily funded challenge in 1996, an excellent Democratic year in New York, will be hard to knock out of office. His moderate record and pro-labor stances insulate him from charges that he is out of step with voters here.

The People: Pop. 1990: 580,818; 13.1% rural; 15.7% age 65+; 81.4% White, 16.8% Black, 0.6% Asian, 0.5% Amer. Indian, 0.7% Other; 1.4% Hispanic Origin. Households: 50.1% married couple families; 22.3% married couple fams. w. children; 38.7% college educ.; median household income: $26,263; per capita income: $12,176; median house value: $68,300; median gross rent: $274.

1996 Presidential Vote			1992 Presidential Vote		
Clinton (D)	137,557	(59%)	Clinton (D)	119,115	(46%)
Dole (R)	69,341	(29%)	Perot (I)	73,333	(28%)
Perot (I)	28,166	(12%)	Bush (R)	68,174	(26%)

Rep. Jack Quinn (R)

Elected 1992; b. Apr. 13, 1951, Buffalo; home, Hamburg; Siena Col., B.A. 1973, S.U.N.Y. Buffalo, M.A. 1978; Catholic; married (Mary Beth).

Elected Office: Hamburg Town Supervisor, 1983–92.

Professional Career: Teacher & coach, Orchard Park Central Schl., 1973–83.

DC Office: 229 CHOB 20515, 202-225-3306; Fax: 202-226-0347; Web site: www.house.gov/quinn.

District Office: Buffalo, 716-845-5257.

Committees: *Transportation & Infrastructure* (13th of 41 R): Aviation; Ground Transportation; Water Resources & Environment. *Veterans' Affairs* (7th of 17 R): Benefits (Chmn.).

Group Ratings

	ADA	ACLU	AFS	LCV	CON	NTU	NFIB	COC	ACU	NTLC	CHC
1998	30	6	56	62	23	41	86	76	48	57	75
1997	30	—	43	—	59	46	—	78	58	—	—

National Journal Ratings

	1997 LIB	—	1997 CONS	1998 LIB	—	1998 CONS
Economic	52%	—	47%	46%	—	53%
Social	30%	—	64%	43%	—	56%
Foreign	47%	—	52%	49%	—	51%

Key Votes of the 105th Congress

1. Clinton Budget Deal	Y	5. Puerto Rico Sthood. Ref.	Y	9. Cut $ for B-2 Bombers	Y
2. Education IRAs	Y	6. End Highway Set-asides	N	10. Human Rights in China	Y
3. Req. 2/3 to Raise Taxes	Y	7. School Prayer Amend.	Y	11. Withdraw Bosnia Troops	N
4. Fast-track Trade	N	8. Ovrd. Part. Birth Veto	Y	12. End Cuban TV-Marti	Y

Election Results

1998 general	Jack Quinn (R-C-Ind)	116,093	(68%)	($405,825)
	Crystal D. Peoples (D)	55,199	(32%)	($48,613)
1998 primary	Jack Quinn (R)	unopposed		
1996 general	Jack Quinn (R-C-Ind-FR)	121,369	(55%)	($752,713)
	Francis J. Pordum (D-PS)	100,040	(45%)	($520,826)

THIRTY-FIRST DISTRICT

The Southern Tier of New York is one of the nation's forgotten stretches of territory, yet it has an interesting and distinctive history. Elmira was the hometown of Mark Twain's beloved wife, Olivia, and where Twain is buried. On Lake Chautauqua, not far from Lake Erie, a training camp for Methodist Sunday school teachers was founded in 1874, where in summers, on wide green lawns and on porches and in gazebos decorated with Victorian gingerbread, some 25,000 people heard educational talks and inspirational lectures from the likes of Ralph Waldo Emerson and William Jennings Bryan; Chautauqua lecture programs still thrive today. Corning is the headquarters of Corning Glass Works, one of America's long-successful and also artistically distinguished manufacturing companies, now specializing in high-tech products. In between are two small Indian reservations, miles and miles of dairy farms, and much of New York's wine country. Sheltered by hills, the lands at the edge of Upstate's deep lakes are the nation's largest grape-growing area outside California, and the leader in Concord grapes, with headquarters of prime New York State wineries and Welch's grape juice.

The Southern Tier's western half forms the 31st Congressional District. Politically, this has been Republican country since the party's founding. The towns and countryside are no longer homogeneously Protestant, but they remain solidly Republican in most elections—though occasionally willing to consider a Democrat (Bill Clinton increased his percentage here by 10% over 1992).

The 31st District's congressman carries his familiar name with considerable grace: He is Amory Houghton, scion of the very rich family that owns the Corning Glass Works, founded in 1851. He was a top executive at Corning for 25 years and had considered retiring to be a missionary in Africa, but instead ran for Congress. The Houghtons are not just rich folks in a small town, they are charter members of the American establishment: Houghton's father was ambassador to France; his grandfather, a congressman in the 1920s, built one of the biggest mansions on Washington's Embassy Row; his family endowed the rare books library at Harvard; and this latest Houghton sat on boards of companies like IBM, Citicorp, and Procter and Gamble. Cheerful, articulate, used to being in comfortable command, Amo Houghton ran a chipper and well-financed campaign in 1986; he chatted with voters, competed with a serious Democratic opponent and won 60% of the vote. Houghton is not just a leader. He joined the Marine Corps in 1945, at 18, and in his campaigns did "work days" as a disc jockey at an Elmira radio station, as a cook at the Texas Hots restaurant in Wellsville, and as a man-on-the-street reporter for the *Olean Times-Herald*. He has been re-elected by wide margins.

Houghton is the only former CEO of a Fortune 500 company in Congress, and he brings that perspective to government—he generally finds it wasteful and foolish, but also wants to preserve some programs with little public support. He dislikes adversariness (most CEOs hear little but praise) but is ready to listen to complaints (the up-to-date CEO had better know if the organization is not working). If he was not a typical freshman congressman in the 1980s, he may be more what the Founding Fathers had in mind than the politically adept youngsters who win in so many districts. By one estimate, he is the second richest member of Congress, with $350 million; but he says that includes the wealth of many members of his rather large family. Anyway, he is the only member of Congress who pays for his foreign travel out of personal funds. He seems to have the unassuming nature of one to whom much is given, who has been living up to his responsibilities and has mostly enjoyed himself in the process.

Houghton's moderate attitude stands in contrast to most other Republicans on many issues. He was an early Republican supporter of the Shays-Meehan campaign finance bill; he delivered a passionate speech against the school prayer amendment in June 1998 though he had written the Christian Coalition in 1996, "I support voluntary prayer in schools" (he apologized for causing confusion). In early 1997 he organized the Mainstreet Coalition, which he sees as a counterpart to the Democratic Leadership Council, a think tank for Republican moderates though it has yet to produce work of the volume or rigor as the DLC. It hired as chief staffer former Congressman Steve Gunderson, who is gay; when that choice was criticized, he said, "We went with the best person. That might bother some people, but I don't know why it should. This never bothered people who went to a Cole Porter musical." A contributor to the arts for many years, he is a staunch advocate of the National Endowment for the Arts, though not a total defender; when a Buffalo area arts group wanted to fund a proposal by two women who had created a video called, "We're Talking Vulva," he responded sensibly, "Why should they fund that? It doesn't have anything to do with elevating the spirit." He balks at declaring he will oppose new taxes and in early 1995 was demanding that his party leaders reduce to $95,000 the ceiling for families who could take advantage of the $500 per-child tax credit in the Contract with America. He was a lead sponsor of the bipartisan congressional summit.

Houghton sits on the Ways and Means and International Relations Committees. He cosponsored, with Philip Crane and Charles Rangel, the African Growth and Opportunity Act, which would authorize free trade agreements with African countries, a $150 million privately managed equity fund and $500 million in an infrastructure fund for leveraged private investment. He was chief sponsor of the bill to award Nelson Mandela a Congressional Gold Medal. With Charles Rangel, he sponsored a trial jobs program called Work Opportunity Tax Credit in the 1997 minimum wage bill. On local issues, he got a change in the Medicare reimbursement formula for the Southern Tier and a $1 million grant to start a business development center near Salamanca. He was one of four Republicans to vote against all four articles of impeachment.

For all his consensus-mindedness, Houghton had opposition from both left and right in 1998. Jim Pierce, a minister who belongs to the Patrick Henry Men group led by Operation Rescue founder Randall Terry, filed to run in the Republican primary. But local Republicans challenged his petitions and (thanks to New York's tough petition laws) got him off the ballot; he won 7% as nominee of the Right-to-Life Party. In the general, Houghton faced Caleb Rossiter, son of the famed Cornell political scientist and author of an autobiography telling about his heavy drug use, petty crimes and vehement opposition to the Vietnam war. Rossiter promised to create 6,000 new jobs locally and criticized Houghton for only lukewarmly supporting the designation of Route 17 as Interstate 86 and the finishing of U.S. 219. He raised the not inconsiderable sum of $240,000. But Houghton argued that the number of jobs had risen in the Southern Tier during his dozen years of service and, without spending more than $5,000 of his own money, outraised him 3–1. Houghton won 68%–25%; the only threat to his tenure is redistricting.

Cook's Call. *Safe.* Houghton's moderate voting record and personal wealth make him a very tough target for Democrats. His greatest concern likely will be redistricting as it is widely assumed that upstate New York will lose at least one district.

The People: Pop. 1990: 580,400; 60.3% rural; 15.1% age 65 + ; 95.9% White, 2.3% Black, 0.6% Asian, 0.5% Amer. Indian, 0.7% Other; 1.4% Hispanic Origin. Households: 57.1% married couple families; 27.2% married couple fams. w. children; 38.6% college educ.; median household income: $25,124; per capita income: $11,382; median house value: $48,500; median gross rent: $262.

1996 Presidential Vote

Clinton (D)	98,244	(45%)
Dole (R)	91,208	(42%)
Perot (I)	30,268	(14%)

1992 Presidential Vote

Bush (R)	97,447	(40%)
Clinton (D)	82,671	(34%)
Perot (I)	62,325	(26%)

Rep. Amo Houghton (R)

Elected 1986; b. Aug. 7, 1926, Corning; home, Corning; Harvard U., B.A. 1950, M.B.A. 1952; Episcopalian; married (Priscilla).

Military Career: Marine Corps, 1945–46 (WWII).

Professional Career: Exec., Corning Glass Works, 1951–86, Chmn. & CEO, 1964–86.

DC Office: 1110 LHOB 20515, 202-225-3161; Fax: 202-225-5574; Web site: www.house.gov/houghton.

District Offices: Auburn, 800-562-7431; Corning, 607-937-3333; Jamestown, 716-484-0252.

Committees: *International Relations* (18th of 26 R): Africa. *Ways & Means* (6th of 23 R): Oversight (Chmn.); Trade.

Group Ratings

	ADA	ACLU	AFS	LCV	CON	NTU	NFIB	COC	ACU	NTLC	CHC
1998	30	56	50	15	26	29	82	100	29	40	27
1997	45	—	25	—	84	39	—	90	33	—	—

National Journal Ratings

	1997 LIB — 1997 CONS	1998 LIB — 1998 CONS
Economic	49% — 50%	50% — 49%
Social	55% — 44%	64% — 35%
Foreign	58% — 41%	90% — 5%

Key Votes of the 105th Congress

1. Clinton Budget Deal	Y	5. Puerto Rico Sthood. Ref.	N	9. Cut $ for B-2 Bombers	Y
2. Education IRAs	*	6. End Highway Set-asides	N	10. Human Rights in China	N
3. Req. 2/3 to Raise Taxes	N	7. School Prayer Amend.	N	11. Withdraw Bosnia Troops	N
4. Fast-track Trade	Y	8. Ovrd. Part. Birth Veto	Y	12. End Cuban TV-Marti	Y

Election Results

1998 general	Amo Houghton (R-C)	107,615	(68%)	($820,921)
	Caleb Rossiter (D)	40,091	(25%)	($244,317)
	James R. Pierce (RTL)	10,546	(7%)	($78,217)
1998 primary	Amo Houghton (R)	unopposed		
1996 general	Amo Houghton (R-C-FR)	139,734	(72%)	($699,270)
	Bruce D. MacBain (D)	49,502	(25%)	($1,849)
	Others	6,031	(3%)	

NORTH CAROLINA

North Carolina in the 1990s, in its third century as a state, has become one of the leading-edge parts of the nation, a state whose growing economy, booming demography and vibrant culture are in many ways typical of the way the nation is going—or would like to go. This was mostly unanticipated. Few people 20 years ago picked North Carolina as a state that would chart a path to the future. It had no great central city, no Atlanta primed to become another Chicago or Los Angeles, but rather a series of small metropolitan areas spaced out over thickly-settled countryside. It did not have what seemed to be cutting-edge industries: the biggest employer was textiles, typically an underdeveloped nation's first industry, and the other two were stolid furniture and soon-to-be-disfavored tobacco. Geographically, it seemed to be off the nation's main lines of commerce—too steamy to be businesslike in the summer, too cold to be a resort in the winter. It did not seem socially advanced, with a population made up almost entirely of native-born Anglo-Saxons and African-Americans and with an attachment to traditional and sometimes fundamentalist religion.

Yet North Carolina has emerged as one of America's leading growth states. Its population grew by 28% from 1980–98 to 7,546,000 in 1998, and it vies with Georgia for the title of 10th largest state. Its economy has diversified and grown steadily. The number of textile and tobacco jobs is down, but Research Triangle Park, between Raleigh, Durham and Chapel Hill, has become one of the world's leading pharmaceutical and high-tech research centers. NationsBank, which merged with San Francisco's colossal BankAmerica in 1998, is headquarted in Charlotte as the new Bank of America, and is now the country's largest bank. First Union down the street in Charlotte and Wachovia based in Winston-Salem are behemoths as well. Charlotte-head-quartered Nucor became the nation's leading minimill steelmaker in the 1980s, even as Charlotte and Raleigh-Durham became major airport hubs.

Not all of North Carolina is upscale: The state is a big chicken producer, and has some of the nation's largest hog lots. But the overall picture is flexible, adaptive growth. While Carolina politicians were seeking protection for textiles, this more advanced economy has emerged so quietly and quickly that in many places the main economic problem is a labor shortage. But growth has not concentrated North Carolina's population in a few cities. This has always been thickly-settled rural land, and if one is never out of sight of others there is also plenty of green space and reminders of rural roots, from barbecue stands to country Baptist churches. Tarheels can live surrounded by forests or farms and yet be within an hour's drive of huge shopping centers and thousands of workplaces: more than any other big state, North Carolina has had decentralized growth.

Change has not been directed from any single establishment; the forces that have produced it are diverse and sometimes hostile. North Carolina does have a small and articulate elite, which looks for guidance to the University of North Carolina at Chapel Hill and the historically progressive editors of the state's newspapers, most prominently the Raleigh *News & Observer* and the *Charlotte Observer*. Quite different attitudes are nurtured by tradition-minded churches in a state where churchgoing is deeply ingrained, endorsed for years through Sunday blue laws and strengthened periodically by religious revivals. North Carolina's Billy Graham remains a strong voice for revealed religion, appearing in Bill Clinton's inaugurations as he had in Dwight Eisenhower's 40 years before. In the economically backward state North Carolina was when infant mortality was common and indoor plumbing was not, religion was a fountain of hope and a source of discipline; and it is still, perhaps even more, in this now bustling air-conditioned, cable- and computer-wired commonwealth, a place whose governor in 1999 declared eliminating outhouses one of his top priorities.

North Carolina has grown with the aid of both its progressive and tradition-minded citizens, and in spite of, sometimes because of, the polarized politics that has developed between the two sides. Tradition-minded religion has provided a discipline for many churchgoers that has made them steady workers and community leaders. Liberal progressivism has provided an impetus toward building good schools and universities and highways and amenities like the nation's first state-funded symphony and the state high schools for science and mathematics and the arts. North Carolina's professionals tend to share progressive values; its businessmen and conservative Protestants tend to share tradition-minded values. Both groups have contributed to the state's economic dynamism and cultural energy.

From these two strands of North Carolina tradition developed a polarized, increasingly party-line politics that is pretty evenly balanced, waged partly on economic issues but even more on cultural attitudes. It is a politics in which Democrats and Republicans have been distinctive, sometimes bitter in their rivalries, for years not overlapping in their ideas but by the mid-1990s converging on at least some issues. This politics has built on historic partisan patterns: coastal North Carolina settlers tended to be British Anglicans who became Methodists, slaveholders who supported the Confederacy and voted Democratic; Piedmont settlers tended to be Scots-Irish Presbyterians with a scattering of Germans sects, Union men in 1861 and Republicans ever after.

Today the two sides are differently but evenly balanced. The most effective paladins of both traditions, Republican Senator Jesse Helms and Democratic Governor Jim Hunt, have each been elected to statewide office five times over 25 years, and in 1984 waged what was then the most expensive Senate race in U.S. history; once bitter rivals, they have since reconciled, and work together on some issues. From the 1970s through the mid-1990s, North Carolina has had more seriously contested House races than any other state, with results tending along straight party lines, and sharp reversals of fortune: Democrats controlled the delegation 8–4

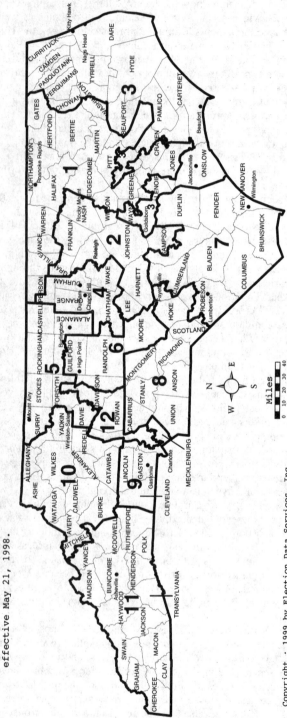

Congressional district boundaries
effective May 21, 1998.

after 1992, Republicans 8–4 after 1994, 6–6 after 1996, and Republicans 7–5 after 1998. This convergence of national and state politics came earlier than elsewhere in the South.

The results of major elections here in the late 1990s have been decided within narrow margins. This is one state where Bill Clinton's fortunes declined in 1996, partly because of the tobacco issue, partly perhaps out of cultural conservatives' distaste: he lost North Carolina by only 43.5%–42.7% in 1992, but by 49%–44% in 1996. Jesse Helms, re-elected to the Senate by 53%–47% over Harvey Gantt in 1990, beat the same opponent by 53%–46% in 1996. Republicans that year won the vote for U.S. House 53%–45%; Democrats' two gains came in races where flukish factors were at work. In 1994 Republicans took control of the North Carolina House for the first time in the 20th Century. Hunt, who had worked cooperatively with the Republican legislature and initiated welfare reform even before Congress and Clinton acted in 1996, won re-election by a solid 56%–43% in what was more a personal than a party triumph. In 1998 the balance tipped just a bit to the Democrats. Senator Lauch Faircloth, elected by 50%–46% in 1992, this time lost 51%–47% to Democrat John Edwards. Republicans won the U.S. House vote 53%–43% and picked up the open 8th District seat, but lost control of the North Carolina House by 66–54.

North Carolina's electorate breaks along cultural, not economic lines. In the 1996 exit poll blacks were overwhelmingly Democratic (91% for Bill Clinton) while religious-right whites were heavily Republican (68% for Bob Dole). High school and college graduates, the middle of the education spectrum, leaned Republican in 1996 and split evenly in 1998, but those with post-graduate degrees provided bigger Democratic majorities than those who never graduated from high school. Geographically, this means the centers of the Piedmont urban areas, filling up with professionals and with significant black populations, have trended Democratic: the counties farther out, filling up with middle-income families spreading out and working in decentralized businesses, have switched from historic Democratic preferences to solid Republican. Coastal east Carolina, once overwhelmingly Democratic, is now mixed. The result is a close balance between two cultural and political blocs which have contributed to North Carolina's unanticipated growth—though neither is inclined to give the other much credit.

Governor. Jim Hunt today is America's most experienced governor. He grew up in Wilson County, graduated from North Carolina State and UNC Law School, worked for the Ford Foundation in Nepal in the 1960s, returned to practice law in Wilson County and helped keep the peace on the awful night when Martin Luther King Jr. was murdered. He was elected lieutenant governor in 1972, at 35, when a Republican was elected governor, and pushed for universal kindergarten, making it available to every North Carolina child. He was elected governor in 1976 and, after repeal of the one-term limit, re-elected in 1980. He pushed education programs: primary reading, reduced class sizes, student and teacher competency tests, dropout prevention, the North Carolina School of Science and Mathematics. Then in 1984 he lost the hard-fought Senate race to Helms. Forceful, articulate, disciplined and well-organized, Hunt seems by nature an executive; he might not have found the Senate congenial. He became governor here two years before Bill Clinton did in Arkansas, and had successes much sooner than Clinton; had he beaten Helms, Hunt might have been the moderate Democrat elected president in the 1990s.

In 1992, after Republican Jim Martin served eight years, Hunt ran for governor again, easily beating Attorney General Lacy Thornburg in the primary and prevailing 53%–43% over Republican businessman Jim Gardner in the general. In 1993–94, Hunt pushed through tougher crime sentences, started an SOS volunteer drive for after-school activities for at-risk children, and initiated "Smart Start" to provide day care and health care to 10,000 children in 33 counties. After Republicans won the state House in 1994, he proposed a $483 million tax cut; the legislature passed $240 million. When the legislature declined to act on welfare, Hunt used his executive order privilege to start a Work First welfare reform, allowing flexibility for counties and moving 17,000 families from welfare to work. He began "Crackdown for Children," seeking overdue child support. He made it a felony to bring a gun to school; he required prisoners to work. He angered many Democrats in the legislature when he supported the Republican "conceal and carry" law which allows legal gun owners to carry concealed firearms in public.

In 1996 Hunt ran for re-election promising "Smart Start" in all 100 counties and a teacher pay raise to the national average. His opponent was state House Majority Whip Robin Hayes, who, with support from the Christian Coalition and National Rifle Association, won the Republican nomination 50%–46% over former Charlotte Mayor Richard Vinroot. Hayes called for repeal of the sales tax on food, for the death penalty for major drug dealers and for forcing people off welfare rolls. Hunt attacked him for opposing his teacher pay raise proposal and the law prohibiting guns in schools. Hunt won 56%–43%, a solid margin as Bob Dole was carrying the state and Jesse Helms was being re-elected senator and Republicans carried the vote for the U.S. and North Carolina House. At the same time voters overwhelmingly approved a proposition giving the governor a veto for the first time since the Revolutionary War.

In 1997 Hunt got bipartisan support for his Excellent Schools Act, which included raising teachers' salaries and establishing tough accountability standards for teachers; Smart Start was extended to all 100 counties. Results started coming in: North Carolina became one of the few states to show significantly improved test scores. Hunt chaired the National Commission on Teaching and America's Future and the National Education Goals Panel and is still involved at the ground level: Hunt and his wife volunteer every week as mentors in Wake County schools.

Behind the scenes, he took a lead role in the negotiations for a settlement between state attorneys general and the major tobacco companies in April 1997. He has been criticized in the liberal Raleigh *News & Observer* for not doing enough to clean the environment, especially from hog lot runoff (North Carolina had 2.6 million hogs in 1990 and 9.8 million in 1997) and by some conservatives for spending too much. Hunt's desire to attract a major league baseball team to the Greensboro-Winston-Salem area died in May 1998 when voters defeated a referendum to fund the stadium. But on balance, this forceful man has made a major difference over an extended period. While there has been much talk of New Democrats in Washington, Hunt has for many years now been a working New Democrat, setting a course for activist government informed by strong moral values in a state that often sets an example for America.

Hunt is not eligible to run again in 2000 and says that he has fought his last election. White House Chief of Staff Erskine Bowles, whose father was the Democratic nominee for governor in 1972, pondered the race but decided not to run; the Democratic nomination is wide open. Republican Chuck Neely, who resigned from the state House to make the race, began statewide TV ads in May, a full year before the primary.

Cook's Call. *Highly Competitive.* After serving as governor for 16 out of the last 24 years, Hunt is term-limited and finally willing to join the private sector. A number of candidates have already declared for the race, which will be very competitive. On the Democratic side, Attorney General Mike Easley and Lieutenant Governor Dennis Wicker are considered the frontrunners. Former Charlotte Mayor Richard Vinroot, state House Republican leader Leo Daughtry, and state Representative Chuck Neely are all officially seeking the Republican nod. Daughtry and Vinroot are considered the most serious candidates for the nomination.

Senior Senator. No American politician is more controversial, beloved in some quarters and hated in others, than Jesse Helms, now in his fifth term in the Senate and chairman of the Foreign Relations Committee. Helms grew up the son of the police chief of Monroe, North Carolina, 15 miles from the birthplace of Andrew Jackson—a breeding ground, it seems, for true-believing, contentious leaders. With Jacksonian tenacity he has stuck to his early convictions—respect for elders and law and order, traditional religious faith and moral principles, patriotism, the order imposed by racial segregation—with the exception of the last, and his abandonment of it has often seemed grudging and halfhearted. Helms has always seemed more an advocate than a doer, yet he has had a considerable effect on events over the years, and if he has not restored America to the state of the Monroe of his youth, he has succeeded in moving the country in a different direction from what his liberal critics optimistically and he pessimistically believed was inevitable 30 years ago. And he has done so with little or no surrender of principle; as Fred Barnes wrote in *The Weekly Standard*, "Helms follows a simple formula: Implacability equals strength. It works. He can't be buffaloed—or ignored. . . . The point here is Helms has gained strange, new respect not as many conservatives have—by moving left. Helms has earned it the hard way—by not moving at all."

Helms attended Wingate College and Wake Forest but did not graduate. He served in the Navy in World War II and became a journalist in Raleigh, worked for two U.S. senators from 1951–53, headed the state Banker's Association, served on the Raleigh Council and from 1960–72 was a commentator on Raleigh TV and the Tobacco Radio Network. So he was a familiar voice and a seasoned political operator when he ran for the Senate in 1972, and upset a moderate Democrat 54%–46%. Helms made then and makes now no attempt to win over everyone; he has a solidly conservative voting record, and can state his views pungently. He has had vigorous opposition every time he has run for re-election and his percentages have been in a narrow range—54%, 55%, 52%, 53%, 53%.

In his first 20 years in the Senate, Helms—nicknamed Senator No—was mostly in the posture of opposition; in the mid-1990s he has been pursuing his own reform policies, with some success. He has long served on the Agriculture Committee, and chaired it in the 1980s; he supported tobacco programs there, but had to be bailed out of difficulties managing farm bills in the 1980s by Bob Dole. Helms was happier obtaining roll call votes on cultural issues— abortion and the fetal tissue research ban, school busing, Japanese American redress, AIDS funding, and the National Endowment for the Arts. He has been an adamant supporter of the flag-burning and school prayer amendments.

Helms has used his seat on Foreign Relations to conduct something like his own foreign policy. In the Reagan and Bush years he and aides James Lucier, Christopher Manion and Deborah DeMoss developed their own sources and influenced State Department appointments to help the contras in Nicaragua and rightists in El Salvador. Helms's great cause in the 1970s was to defeat the Panama Canal treaties—a cause which helped defeat a dozen liberal senators and kept alive Ronald Reagan's candidacy when it threatened to die in the North Carolina primary in 1976. Helms brushed aside Richard Lugar to become the ranking Republican on Foreign Relations in 1987 (he had promised not to take the chairmanship in the 1984 campaign, but did not feel bound when Republicans lost the majority in 1986) and chairman in 1995. From that post he exerted influence adeptly. He favored lifting the arms embargo on Bosnia; he opposed the U.S. military intervention in Haiti; he opposed the use of U.S. troops as peace-keeping forces in the Golan Heights; he was leery of the U.S. agreement with North Korea. He promised not to obstruct most nominations. But when the White House rejected Secretary of State Warren Christopher's proposal to reorganize foreign policy agencies in 1995, Helms presented a similar plan of his own, holding up 18 ambassador nominations and approval of the START II and Chemical Weapons treaties; he ultimately passed $1.7 billion in spending cuts from State Department agencies over five years. Clinton vetoed Helms's reorganization, but he persevered. He held up the Chemical Weapons Treaty, then let it come to the floor in April 1997 at the same time Clinton announced his support for State Department reorganization. Working with Joseph Biden, who became ranking Democrat on Foreign Relations in 1997, he ultimately prevailed and in October 1998 the ACDA and USIA were abolished and their functions were folded into the State Department. Under the reorganization plan, the USAID remained an independent agency, but it's administrator started reporting to the secretary of State.

Helms also succeeded in passing the Helms-Burton Act after Fidel Castro's air force shot down the Brothers to the Rescue planes in February 1996; it codified the U.S. trade embargo against Cuba and allowed lawsuits against foreign companies who benefited by property expropriated from Americans by Castro's Communist dictatorship. Helms was pleased to see Madeleine Albright, then ambassador to the United Nations, denounce the plane attack as "cowardice" and, later in the year, maneuver to block Boutros Boutros-Ghali from a second term as UN Secretary General. Helms welcomed her appointment as secretary of State and on a trip to North Carolina in March 1997—in the midst of the State Department reorganization battles, she presented him with a T-shirt ("Someone in the State Department Loves Me") and he gave her some barbecue for the flight home. Their cooperation was productive in working towards getting the U.S. to pay its arrears in United Nations dues and producing a bill for State Department reorganization.

Cooperation with the administration continued—with exceptions. Helms balked at the nomination of Massachusetts Governor William Weld to be ambassador to Mexico in June 1997. He complained that Weld supported medical marijuana and had a poor record of drug prosecutions as U.S. Attorney in the 1980s. He may also have minded that Weld, during his unsuccessful campaign for the Senate in 1996, declined to say he would vote for Helms for Foreign Relations chairman. Lugar and other Republican conservatives tried to move the nomination forward, but Helms refused to allow the issue to be brought up for hearings, and in September Weld, who had resigned as governor, dropped out. But Albright had been conspicuously silent on Weld, a White House choice, and he and Albright continued to work together. He praised Clinton's decision against endorsing the land mines treaty in September 1997; he proposed in May 1998 a $100 million aid package to Cuba, with food to be distributed through the Catholic Church and independent relief agencies, not the Castro apparatus.

Differences of opinion came out more by mid-1998. In June 1998 Helms charged that the administration was shielding China and U.S. satellite vendors from the effects of U.S. sanctions against China for proliferating weapons. He opposed the International Criminal Court and warned that it would produce other interventions into policy like the arrest in Britain of General Pinochet at the behest of what Helms called a "rogue Spanish judge." In December 1998 Helms supported the air strikes Clinton launched against Iraq as the House was considering impeachment, but Helms added that the ouster of Saddam Hussein "must become the centerpiece of U.S. policy" toward Iraq—advice the administration seemed to ignore. He reacted similarly on Kosovo: the day after Clinton began the bombing campaign against Serbia in March 1999, Helms wrote, "Our Yugoslav policy has failed. If we are to prevent further genocide and preclude American forces from being dragged further into the Balkans, our objective must change from appeasing Milosevic to sponsoring democratic change in Serbia and Milosevic's removal from power." He sponsored a Serbia Democratization Act, with Lugar, Gordon Smith, Joseph Lieberman and Frank Lautenberg.

"I'm not in politics," he claims. "If I was in politics, they would have kicked me out a long time ago. . . . I am what I am, as Popeye says. I get a lot of flak, but I get a lot of people who say, 'Amen.' " More amens than flak in North Carolina anyway, though not by much. No one noticed particularly when Helms was re-elected in 1978, but his contest against Governor Jim Hunt in 1984 was, up to then, the most expensive Senate campaign in history, and one of the bitterest—though Helms and Hunt later came to an amicable relationship. In 1990 and 1996 Helms's opponent was Harvey Gantt, former mayor of Charlotte and who in his youth had, amid much publicity and no little danger, desegregated Clemson University. The 1990 race was especially closely fought and closely watched. Gantt did a fine job of framing the issues, dismissing Helms's preoccupation with the NEA and abortion as unimportant. But Helms, armed with money raised by a nationwide direct mail campaign, seized the initiative in mid-October. He ran ads attacking racial quotas and accusing Gantt of taking financial advantage of a law providing for racial preference in broadcast licenses, a law that when brought into light of day, most Democrats joined Republicans in repealing in 1995. Gantt fell in the polls and Helms won 53%–47%.

By 1996 Helms was visibly older and had split with his old campaign organizers. During the primary campaign, Helms ran ads attacking both Gantt and his primary opponent Charles Sanders for backing "racial preferences in hiring" and "extending health insurance to homosexual partners." In the general Helms refused Gantt's challenge to debate (they have met only once, at a 1980s reception) and refused to let the press know his schedule. Gantt attacked Helms for voting to "cut" Social Security, and called for more student loans, a higher minimum wage, tax credits and deductions for day care and college tuition; Gantt said he supported the 1996 Welfare Reform Act. Helms won 53%–46%, in a near carbon copy of the 1990 results; Gantt—an interesting note for those who insist that large numbers of whites won't vote for blacks—ran ahead of Clinton.

Will Helms retire in 2002, when he turns 81? He has suggested he might, but few are willing to bet heavily that he will or that he would lose if he runs again.

Junior Senator. John Edwards, a Democrat elected in 1998, holds North Carolina's other Senate seat, which has been under a kind of jinx: No one has been re-elected to it since 1968, and it has switched back and forth from party to party in each election since 1974. Edwards was born in South Carolina and grew up there and in Robbins, in Moore County, where his father was a supervisor in a textile mill and his mother ran a furniture refinishing business. He was the first in his family to go to college, at North Carolina State, then went to University of North Carolina Law School. He started off defending recording companies accused of pirating Elvis Presley records, then moved to Raleigh in 1981 and became a plaintiff's personal injury lawyer, working hard to prepare cases (he was one of the first trial lawyers here to use focus groups) and fluently and persuasively presenting them in down-home style to juries. He was good at it, winning verdicts of $152 million; with 30% or more going to the lawyer, this enabled him to amass a fortune variously estimated at $20 million to $50 million. One case in particular got a lot of publicity: he represented a nine-year-old girl from Cary horribly injured by a faulty swimming pool drain; he showed that 13 other children had been similarly injured, and in January 1997 won $25 million in compensatory damages, the largest personal-injury verdict in North Carolina history.

At about this time Edwards began thinking about running for the Senate. He had not run for office before, had not even voted in every election, and said he could not remember whether he had first registered as a Democrat or Republican. But he did have strong views on some issues, and he proved to have acute judgment in spotting the political weakness of incumbent Republican Senator Lauch Faircloth. In the years since his surprise victory in 1992, Faircloth, a wealthy hog farmer and long-time insider in Democratic politics, had a voting record as conservative as Jesse Helms's and had been a strong critic of the Clintons in various investigations. He was far less well known than Helms, and running at age 70. Some better-known Democrats dropped out of the race, and Edwards's main rival in the May 1998 Democratic primary was D.G. Martin, former lobbyist for the University of North Carolina and a nearly-successful House candidate in Charlotte in 1984 and 1986. "I am prepared to raise and spend whatever is necessary," Edwards said in February 1997, and spent $3.2 million of his own money and ran ads about his background and views. He promised to be a "people's senator, someone who speaks for all the people of North Carolina, not the special interests," and he refused to take money from PACs or Washington lobbyists. The ads were criticized for suggesting that he was born in North Carolina and that he worked his way through college loading UPS trucks (he worked there six months). But Edwards outspent Martin 4–1 and, needing 40% to avoid a runoff, won 51% of the vote to Martin's 28%.

The contrast between Edwards and Faircloth was vivid. Edwards was articulate, charming, young (45 and a three-time marathon finisher); Faircloth was wrinkled with age, the embodiment of an older, rural, conservative North Carolina that many natives and newcomers wanted to leave behind. Faircloth, recognizing the threat, ran ads against Edwards in the primary, saying that he was a trial lawyer who earned millions suing doctors and driving up health care costs. He continued the negative approach, despite the voters' contented, pro-incumbent mood, throughout the campaign. Edwards proposed they pool their money and, instead of running ads, buy time for televised debates; Faircloth, less than eager for debates with a highly competent trial lawyer, would have none of it, and would not even allow photographs one of the few times their paths crossed on the campaign trail. Edwards ran positive ads, and called for hiring teachers, building schools, an HMO patients' bill of rights, fixing Social Security. Occasionally his inexperience showed. He said credit unions should be taxed like banks, then backed off; he refused to say how he'd vote on tobacco bill, then later said he would have voted to kill it. But, as former political consultant and *Hotline* founder Doug Bailey said, "Edwards is an extremely effective television-age communicator. This is a guy who has very gifted communications skills and a mind behind the skills."

Faircloth seized on Edwards's role in trial lawyer clinics, and asked, "Who teaches other lawyers how to stretch the truth? Meet personal injury lawyer John Edwards." "He said he wouldn't take special interest money, but now we learn he did," another ad said, based on the $579,000 Edwards raised from lawyers, most of them presumably part of the tight and politically sophisticated network of plaintiff's trial lawyers across the country. And he attacked Edwards for having Clinton come in to Raleigh and raise $400,000. But Edwards claimed that he opposed Clinton on the tobacco bill and on trade. Faircloth struck a few positive notes as well. He touted the breast cancer stamp he co-sponsored with Dianne Feinstein, and the work he had done to preserve the beaches of the Outer Banks.

To Faircloth's attacks on trial lawyers, Edward replied, "If Faircloth wants to take the side of the big insurance companies, I'll take the side of those regular people all day long." This was a big-spending race: Edwards spent $8.3 million, nearly three-quarters of it his own money; Faircloth spent nearly $9.4 million, including $1.7 million of his own. Faircloth started to slip in the polls and even changed pollsters in October; Edwards edged to a lead, and won 51%–47%. In this race, as in Helms's, the Democrat carried younger voters, the Republican the elderly; Edwards carried the poor, Faircloth the rich, and they ran about evenly among the two-thirds in the middle; those with graduate degrees and those with no high school diploma were both heavily for Edwards. Compared to 1992, Faircloth lost the most ground in the farthest eastern counties and in a few textile mill counties in the west; Faircloth held his own in fast-growing Wake County (Raleigh).

In the Senate Edwards lobbied hard and successfully for a seat on the Banking Committee, saying he wanted to limit banks' ability to sell personal financial information; interestingly, several of the nation's biggest banks are headquartered in North Carolina. On impeachment, Edwards carefully withheld judgment and then gave what many regarded as an effective speech during the closed debate; Minority Leader Tom Daschle chose him to represent Democrats at the depositions of witnesses.

Presidential politics. North Carolina has been the South's most straight-ticket state, which left it very much in play in 1992. But Bill Clinton's campaign against tobacco put it out of his reach in 1996, and makes it less likely to be seriously contested in the future.

North Carolina, which switched its primary to Super Tuesday in 1988, switched it back to May in 1992. It has been crucial only once: in 1976, when after five straight losses, Ronald Reagan started denouncing the Panama Canal Treaty and won his first victory over Gerald Ford. In 1988 Al Gore won here, after citing his credentials as a tobacco grower; his speech against tobacco at the 1996 convention may make it hard for him to win here in 2000, at least in the same way. One possible candidate with great strength here: North Carolina native Elizabeth Dole.

Congressional districting. North Carolina has had a raging controversy over districting ever since the 1990 Census gave it a 12th House seat, its first new seat in 60 years. The Justice Department, under the prevailing interpretation of the Voting Rights Act, required the state to create two black-majority districts—difficult because North Carolina has no concentrations of blacks as large as those in Georgia or Texas. So the Democratic legislature drew a plan with a jagged-boundaried 1st District in east Carolina and a 12th extending, sometimes just along the median strip of I-85, from Gastonia through Charlotte, Winston-Salem and Greensboro.

In June 1993 the Supreme Court in *Shaw v. Reno*, focusing on the 12th, ordered the plan re-examined. On remand a three-judge federal court upheld the plan in August 1994. But in June 1996 the Supreme Court declared the 12th unconstitutional and sent it back to the three-judge panel, which ruled it had to be redrawn by April 1997. In March 1997 the legislature agreed to a new plan which smoothed out the lines but, in a spirit of bipartisan compromise, left the districts much as they were. The 1st and 12th districts, both formerly 57% black, were now 50% and 47% black, respectively (measuring by the 1990 Census). That plan was thrown out by a different three-judge court in April 1998, and never used.

In May 1998 the legislature passed a third plan which further reduced the size of the 12th district: In the first plan it stretched from Gastonia to Durham, in the second from Charlotte to Greensboro, in the third from Charlotte to Winston-Salem. The state appealed to the Supreme Court and in January 1999 argued for adoption of the 1997 plan; the result, though it will affect North Carolina for only one election, and is unlikely to change the outcome of any race, nonetheless could have great significance for the redistrictings in many states following the 2000 Census. The key issue is whether states must maximize the number of majority-minority districts (the interpretation of the Bush Justice Department in 1991–92) or must avoid drawing grotesquely-shaped districts along lines of race.

The People: Est. Pop. 1998: 7,546,493; Pop. 1990: 6,628,637, up 13.8% 1990–1998. 2.8% of U.S. total, 11th largest; 49.7% rural. Median age: 34.7 years. 12.7% 65 years and over. 75.6% White, 22% Black, 0.8% Asian, 1.2% Amer. Indian, 0.4% Other; 1% Hispanic Origin. Households: 56.6% married couple families; 26.5% married couple fams. w. children; 41% college educ.; median household income: $26,647; per capita income: $12,885; 68% owner occupied housing; median house value: $65,800; median monthly rent: $284. 3.5% Unemployment. 1998 Voting age pop.: 5,685,000. 1998 Turnout: 2,012,149; 35% of VAP. Registered voters (1998): 4,764,036; 2,504,964 D (53%), 1,598,901 R (34%), 668,064 unaffiliated and minor parties (14%).

Political Lineup: Governor, James B. Hunt Jr. (D); Lt. Gov., Dennis A. Wicker (D); Secy. of State, Elaine Marshall (D); Atty. Gen., Michael F. Easley (D); Treasurer, Harlan E. Boyles (D); State Senate, 50 (35 D, 15 R); Majority Leader, Roy A. Cooper III (D); State House, 120 (66 D, 54 R); House Speaker, James B. Black (D). Senators, Jesse Helms (R) and John Edwards (D). Representatives, 12 (5 D, 7 R).

Elections Division: 919-733-7173; **Filing Deadline for U.S. Congress:** February 7, 2000.

1996 Presidential Vote

Dole (R)	1,213,819	(49%)
Clinton (D)	1,098,297	(44%)
Perot (I)	167,465	(7%)

1996 Republican Presidential Primary

Dole (R)	202,863	(71%)
Buchanan (R)	37,126	(13%)
Keyes (R)	11,759	(4%)
Forbes (R)	11,588	(4%)
Others	20,876	(8%)

1992 Presidential Vote

Bush (R)	1,131,103	(44%)
Clinton (D)	1,109,953	(43%)
Perot (I)	357,000	(14%)

GOVERNOR

Gov. James B. Hunt, Jr. (D)

Elected 1992, term expires Jan. 2001; b. May 16, 1937, Greensboro; home, Rock Ridge; NC St., B.S. 1959, M.S. 1962, U. of NC at Chapel Hill, J.D. 1964; Presbyterian; married (Carolyn).

Elected Office: NC Lt. Gov., 1972–76; NC Gov., 1976–84.

Professional Career: Cattle rancher; Ford Foundation Econ. Advisor to Nepal, 1964–66; Practicing atty., 1966–92.

Office: State Capitol, Raleigh, 27603, 919-733-4240; Fax: 919-733-5166; Web site: www.state.nc.us.

Election Results

1996 gen.	James B. Hunt Jr. (D)	1,436,638	(56%)
	Robin Hayes (R)	1,097,053	(43%)
1996 prim.	James B. Hunt Jr. (D)	unopposed	
1992 gen.	James B. Hunt Jr. (D)	1,368,246	(53%)
	Jim Gardner (R)	1,121,955	(43%)
	Scott McLaughlin (Lib)	104,983	(4%)

SENATORS

Sen. Jesse Helms (R)

Elected 1972, seat up 2002; b. Oct. 18, 1921, Monroe; home, Raleigh; Wingate Col., Wake Forest U.; Baptist; married (Dorothy).

Military Career: Navy, 1942–45 (World War II).

Elected Office: Raleigh City Cncl., 1957–61.

Professional Career: City Editor, *Raleigh Times*; A.A., U.S. Sen. Willis Smith, 1951–53; A.A., U.S. Sen. Alton Lennon, 1953; Exec. Dir., NC Bankers Assn., 1953–60; Exec. V.P., WRAL-TV & Tobacco Radio Network, 1960–72.

DC Office: 403 DSOB, 20510, 202-224-6342; Fax: 202-228-1339; Web site: www.senate.gov/~helms.

State Offices: Hickory, 828-322-5170; Raleigh, 919-856-4630.

Committees: *Agriculture, Nutrition & Forestry* (2d of 10 R): Marketing, Inspection & Product Promotion; Production & Price Competitiveness. *Foreign Relations* (Chmn. of 10 R): East Asian & Pacific Affairs; International Operations; Western Hemisphere, Peace Corps, Narcotics & Terrorism. *Rules & Administration* (2d of 9 R).

Group Ratings

	ADA	ACLU	AFS	LCV	CON	NTU	NFIB	COC	ACU	NTLC	CHC
1998	0	20	0	0	34	71	88	88	100	93	100
1997	0	—	22	—	14	76	—	70	100	—	—

National Journal Ratings

	1997 LIB	—	1997 CONS	1998 LIB	—	1998 CONS
Economic	11%	—	76%	0%	—	88%
Social	0%	—	83%	22%	—	77%
Foreign	0%	—	77%	0%	—	88%

Key Votes of the 105th Congress

1. Bal. Budget Amend.	Y	5. Satcher for Surgeon Gen.	N	9. Chem. Weapons Treaty	N
2. Clinton Budget Deal	N	6. Highway Set-asides	*	10. Cuban Humanitarian Aid	N
3. Cloture on Tobacco	N	7. Table Child Gun locks	Y	11. Table Bosnia Troops	N
4. Education IRAs	Y	8. Ovrd. Part. Birth Veto	Y	12. $ for Test-ban Treaty	*

Election Results

1996 general	Jesse Helms (R) 1,345,833	(53%)	($14,589,266)
	Harvey B. Gantt (D) 1,173,875	(46%)	($7,992,980)
1996 primary	Jesse Helms (R) .... unopposed		
1990 general	Jesse Helms (R) 1,088,331	(53%)	($17,761,579)
	Harvey B. Gantt (D) 981,573	(47%)	($7,811,520)

Sen. John Edwards (D)

Elected 1998, seat up 2004; b. June 10, 1953, Seneca, SC; home, Raleigh; NC St. U., B.S. 1974, U. of NC at Chapel Hill, J.D. 1977; Methodist; married (Elizabeth).

Professional Career: Practicing atty., 1978–98.

DC Office: 825 HSOB, 20510, 202-224-3154; Fax: 202-228-1374; Web site: www.senate.gov/~edwards.

State Office: Raleigh, 919-856-4245.

Committees: *Banking, Housing & Urban Affairs* (9th of 9 D): Financial Institutions; Housing & Transportation; Securities. *Governmental Affairs* (7th of 7 D): International Security, Proliferation & Federal Services; Investigations (Permanent). *Small Business* (8th of 8 D).

Group Ratings and Key Votes: Newly Elected

Election Results

1998 general	John Edwards (D) 1,029,237	(51%)	($8,331,382)
	Lauch Faircloth (R) 945,943	(47%)	($9,375,771)
	Others 36,963	(2%)	
1998 primary	John Edwards (D) 277,468	(51%)	
	D. G. Martin (D) 149,049	(28%)	
	Ella Scarborough (D) 55,486	(10%)	
	Robert Ayers Jr. (D) 22,477	(4%)	
	Others 35,551	(7%)	
1992 general	Lauch Faircloth (R) 1,297,892	(50%)	($2,952,102)
	Terry Sanford (D) 1,194,015	(46%)	($2,486,380)
	Others 85,984	(3%)	

FIRST DISTRICT

Eastern North Carolina in colonial days was a smaller version of the Chesapeake Bay colonies of Virginia and Maryland—a fertile land laced by dozens of rivers and inlets, with tobacco plantations and farms with docks on the water accessible to the ocean and so to London. North Carolina was settled later than the Chesapeake colonies, and was poorer, with smaller landholdings. But vestiges of its 18th Century past can still be seen in New Bern with its Tryon Palace, the governor's house when this was the capital, and the tiny well-preserved town of Edenton on Albemarle Sound. Today, east Carolina is still tobacco country, indeed the major tobacco-producing land in the United States. It is inhabited almost entirely by the descendants of the original white settlers and black slaves of 250 years ago. They live in small towns and cities and in some of the most thickly-settled rural land in the United States. Tobacco is a labor-intensive crop which can produce yields of $4,000 an acre. A family can make a living off 40 acres of tobacco land and, with a tobacco allotment, many here do. But fewer than in the past. No-smoking laws and anti-smoking campaigns have cut cigarette sales, and many old east Carolina tobacco fields are planted with cucumbers, sweet potatoes and blueberries.

The 1st Congressional District, as redrawn in May 1998, covers much of the tobacco country of inland east Carolina. It touches Albemarle and Pamlico Sounds in the east and juts inland to reach black neighborhoods in Greenville and Goldsboro. Although the court that ordered the lines did not rule that the 1st District was unconstitutional, the lines of every district were changed, and about 30% of the residents of the 1st were new to the district. The new lines are less irregular than those of 1992–96, and the district's percentage of blacks was reduced from 57% to 50%. Politically, this has long been Democratic country; some white voters here have been attracted to the Republicanism of Jesse Helms, but overall this remains a solid Democratic district.

The congresswoman from the 1st District is Eva Clayton, a Democrat first elected in 1992. She grew up in Savannah, Georgia, and has lived for many years in North Carolina. In the mid-1970s, she was director of the Soul City Foundation, civil rights leader Floyd McKissick's attempt to form a black "new town." That foundered, but Clayton backed Jim Hunt in 1976 and became an assistant secretary for community development in his first term as governor. She was elected to, and served as chairman of, the Warren County Board of Commissioners from 1982–90. She also ran her own consulting firm and in 1992 ran for the 1st District seat when the boundaries were drawn. The incumbent, 78-year-old Walter Jones Sr., chairman of the Merchant Marine and Fisheries Committee since 1980 and chairman of the Peanuts and Tobacco Subcommittee before that, was retiring, and died in September 1992. His son, state legislator Walter Jones Jr., ran and won 38% in the first Democratic primary, just 2% less than the 40% which under North Carolina law would have given him the nomination; Clayton was second with 31%. Clayton won the runoff 55%–45%, and she won in November with 67%. (One of Jesse Jackson's crusades in the 1980s was to abolish runoffs; if he had succeeded, Clayton would have lost.) Thus she and 12th District Congressman Mel Watt became the first blacks elected to Congress from North Carolina since George White in 1898.

Clayton is part of the black middle class who have worked their way up in or close to government. In her 1992 campaign, she backed more public investment and job training and lower defense spending to cut the deficit; in office she earned one of the most liberal voting records in the House. Freshman Democrats elected her to chair their class. She was proud of working for WIC and food stamps extension, for crop disaster assistance, for the Section 515 affordable housing program. She amended the food stamps proposal in 1996 to reduce the 20-hour work requirement for those who receive food stamps worth less than what they would earn working 20 hours at the minimum wage. To urban Black Caucus members seeking her support for bills, she responds, "Does it include rural areas?" In 1998 she successfully moved to lift the statute of limitations to allow farmers to sue the Agriculture Department for racial discrimination; in January 1999 Agriculture settled with hundreds of black farmers with claims of racial discrimination in the past distribution of loans. She also pressed for amendments for relief to farmers unable to get credit after the 1996 Freedom to Farm Act. Her bills to reimburse Greenville National Guard troops for expenses the Army could not pay and to require colleges to provide voter registration forms for young people registering for classes passed.

Clayton has bucked the Clinton Administration on welfare and trade; she voted against the Africa trade bill, saying it would take jobs from her district. She said she would support a tobacco bill if it was balanced and included protection for tobacco farmers. She has been alert to district interests, including defense contracts and bases outside district lines which employ many district residents, like the Newport News shipyard. In 1998 she announced a $17.5 million grant for the Global Transpark at Kinston Regional Jetport.

Clayton disagreed with the court decision which set the lines for 1998, and she had opposition, for the first time since 1992, in the primary scheduled for September 1998. State Representative Linwood Mercer ran as a conservative Democrat. But Clayton raised far more money and Tipper Gore came in to campaign for her 12 days before the election. Clayton won the primary 67%–33% and won 62%–37% in November against pharmaceutical salesman Ted Tyler, who has faced Clayton in every election since 1992.

Cook's Call. *Safe.* Clayton's only worries in this overwhelmingly Democratic district will be a primary challenge. Still, even a well-funded Democratic challenger only took 33% of the vote against her in 1998.

The People: Pop. 1990: 553,426; 58.1% rural; 14.4% age 65 + ; 48.6% White, 50.3% Black, 0.2% Asian, 0.6% Amer. Indian, 0.3% Other; 0.6% Hispanic Origin. Households: 47.4% married couple families; 22.8% married couple fams. w. children; 27.7% college educ.; median household income: $18,226; per capita income: $8,918; median house value: $46,100; median gross rent: $183.

1996 Presidential Vote			1992 Presidential Vote		
Clinton (D)	100,650	(57%)	Clinton (D)	101,721	(55%)
Dole (R)	66,342	(38%)	Bush (R)	63,738	(34%)
Perot (I)	8,295	(5%)	Perot (I)	20,083	(11%)

Rep. Eva M. Clayton (D)

Elected 1992; b. Sept. 16, 1934, Savannah, GA; home, Littleton; Johnson C. Smith U., B.S. 1955, NC Central U., M.S. 1962, U. of NC Law Schl., 1967–68; Presbyterian; married (Theaoseus).

Elected Office: Chmn., Warren Cnty. Comm., 1982–90.

Professional Career: Exec. Dir., Soul City Foundation, 1974–76; NC Asst. Secy., Community Development, 1977–81; Pres. & Owner, Technical Resources Intl. Inc., 1981–92.

DC Office: 2440 RHOB 20515, 202-225-3101; Fax: 202-225-3354; Web site: www.house.gov/clayton.

District Offices: Greenville, 252-758-8800; Norlina, 252-456-4800.

Committees: *Agriculture* (6th of 24 D): Department Operations, Oversight, Nutrition & Forestry (RMM); General Farm Commodities, Resource Conservation & Credit. *Budget* (9th of 19 D).

Group Ratings

	ADA	ACLU	AFS	LCV	CON	NTU	NFIB	COC	ACU	NTLC	CHC
1998	100	87	100	85	82	14	29	39	0	11	0
1997	100	—	88	—	62	22	—	40	4	—	—

National Journal Ratings

	1997 LIB — 1997 CONS			1998 LIB — 1998 CONS		
Economic	75%	—	22%	68%	—	30%
Social	85%	—	0%	87%	—	13%
Foreign	92%	—	8%	96%	—	2%

Key Votes of the 105th Congress

1. Clinton Budget Deal	N	5. Puerto Rico Sthood. Ref.	Y	9. Cut $ for B-2 Bombers	Y
2. Education IRAs	N	6. End Highway Set-asides	N	10. Human Rights in China	Y
3. Req. 2/3 to Raise Taxes	N	7. School Prayer Amend.	N	11. Withdraw Bosnia Troops	N
4. Fast-track Trade	N	8. Ovrd. Part. Birth Veto	N	12. End Cuban TV-Marti	Y

Election Results

1998 general	Eva M. Clayton (D) 85,125	(62%)	($644,157)
	Ted Tyler (R) 50,578	(37%)	($27,880)
	Others 1,044	(1%)	
1998 general	Eva M. Clayton (D) 44,789	(67%)	
	Linwood E. Mercer (D) 22,299	(33%)	
1996 general	Eva M. Clayton (D) 108,759	(66%)	($300,049)
	Ted Tyler (R) 54,666	(33%)	($26,248)

SECOND DISTRICT

The coastal plain of North Carolina was long bypassed by history. It was settled after Virginia and South Carolina, and only filled in with English settlers as Scots-Irish families were streaming down the valley of Virginia to the western Piedmont. This has always been tobacco country, with life organized around a crop high-yield enough that a 40-acre plot of land can support a family (if it has a tobacco allotment). Tobacco was an important colonial crop, even more so after James B. Duke, a farmer from Durham County, created Bull Durham tobacco and Lucky Strike cigarettes. Cigarette factories grew up in Durham and eventually, from Duke's fortune, so did the Gothic buildings of Duke University. But otherwise this was a backward area. Its small farms and little cities were homes mainly to tenant farmers and mill hands, people raising families in thin-walled frame houses often with no electricity or running water.

Today, life is much better in the coastal plain. Not just because incomes are up, but because this is now one of America's fastest-growing metropolitan areas; Raleigh-Durham, with a dynamic economy, has generated tens of thousands of jobs, and subdivisions have sprouted up all over Wake County and in the once rural counties beyond. Textile mills have closed and tobacco plots have become just supplementary income sources. To the west of Raleigh, around Durham and the Research Triangle, pharmaceuticals, high-tech and universities have become the biggest employers; this area has more Ph.D.s than almost any other part of the nation, and has been moving left politically despite rising incomes. The counties, east, south and north of Raleigh, in contrast, are not quite as upscale, and have filled up with people with family roots and church affiliations in east Carolina. That is true of once-rural Wake County as well, and in the 1990s these have been the fastest-growing counties in North Carolina, except for the small coastal area around Wilmington. Politically these counties have trended Republican, with rising turnout; this was one of the few areas where defeated Senator Lauch Faircloth improved his percentage between 1992 and 1998.

The 2d Congressional District, as redrawn by the legislature in April 1998, covers much of the coastal plain in a semi-circle around Raleigh. It stretches as far east as Rocky Mount, goes south into hog-producing Sampson County, spreads west to Sanford. This is a fast-growing area: from 1990 to 1998, Wake County's population rose 34%, Johnston County 31% and Harnett County 22%. Up through the 1996 election, the 2d included Durham, which is heavily Democratic; that is now removed, but added was about half of Raleigh's Wake County including many black precincts in Raleigh. As a result, the district's black percentage rose from about 22% to 28%.

The congressman from the 2d District is Bob Etheridge, a Democrat elected in 1996. His biography seems tailored to the district: He was born in Sampson County (in the hamlet of Turkey), grew up in Johnston County, went to Campbell University in Harnett County and owned a hardware store in Lillington, the county seat. He is a tobacco farmer, the only one currently in Congress, a pillar of his community and member of many boards; he served four years on the Harnett County Commission in the 1970s, was elected to the North Carolina House in 1978 and served 10 years, eventually chairing the Appropriations Committee. In 1988 and 1992 he was elected state superintendent of Public Instruction. In the mid-1990s Governor Jim Hunt called for abolishing the superintendent post and transferred 300 employees to the State Board of Education. Etheridge, spying an opportunity, decided to run for the House.

The opportunity was to run against 1994 freshman David Funderburk, a longtime ally of Jesse Helms. Funderburk had a solid conservative voting record and the district seemed politically favorable; in 1996 under the old district lines it voted 52%–42% for Bob Dole. But in 1995, Funderburk was involved in an auto accident: His car forced another off the road, injuring three; witnesses said Funderburk was driving; the car went around the block, then appeared with Mrs. Funderburk at the wheel. The Funderburks contended she had been driving at the time of the accident, but he pleaded no-contest to crossing the center line. Funderburk tried to tie Etheridge to Bill Clinton's approval of FDA Commissioner David Kessler's announcement that tobacco could be regulated as a drug. Etheridge responded by citing his own tobacco credentials: "I'd be happy to match tobacco allotments with Mr. Funderburk. I own tobacco allotments and have for years. I'd like to know how many days Mr. Funderburk spent priming tobacco, setting tobacco, and how many days he spent under the hot sun in the tobacco fields." Then toward the end of the campaign, Etheridge ran an ad on the car accident, with the tag: "Congressman David Funderburk. Why won't he take responsibility?" This issue probably made the difference. Etheridge won 53%–46%, losing Johnston County only narrowly and carrying Harnett, both of which Funderburk swept in 1994.

In the House, Etheridge got seats on the Agriculture and Science committees, and compiled a moderate record, just a bit to the left of center. Etheridge bellowed his opposition to all attempts to regulate tobacco: he voted against the 1997 budget because it included a cigarette tax increase; he opposed eliminating crop insurance for tobacco farmers in July 1997; he was the first House member to denounce the McCain tobacco bill in 1998; he called for opening China's market to tobacco products in September 1998. He also came to the defense of another area crop, peanuts; when the Transportation Department proposed peanut-free rows on airlines to protect those with allergies to peanuts, Etheridge said, "This nutty rule is clearly an over-reaction to a serious, but limited, problem faced by a fraction of the population." He voted for fast track, successfully pushed through a provision of the Higher Education Reorganization Act to teach values in public schools, supported the flag burning amendment and partial-birth abortion ban. A special cause was school construction, especially in growing areas like those around Raleigh. When the Republicans' education bill in September 1998 called for giving states flexibility, Etheridge said, "This is just another way to cut the money for the public schools."

Republicans hoped to regain this seat in 1998, and their candidate was 32-year-old Dan Page, who had won a state Senate seat by four votes in 1994 and who distinguished himself by sponsoring the partial-birth abortion ban and inviting Senator Jesse Helms to address the legislature. He supported a flat tax and school vouchers and opposed Etheridge's education stand. But he was far behind Etheridge in fundraising, and on August 10, 1998, a week before Clinton admitted he lied about Monica Lewinsky, Page ran the nation's first ad trying to link a Democratic candidate with the Clinton scandals. It said, "His is the most corrupt administration in American history. Dishonoring our heritage. And who stands with Bill Clinton, even now? Liberal Bob Etheridge. Applauding Clinton's values, not ours. . . . " Etheridge replied, "Mr. Page is confused. He's running against me, not Bill Clinton. Last time I checked, my name was on the ballot." It may have made some difference in the month between Clinton's speech and the release of the Starr transcripts. But after that it was plain that Etheridge was still well ahead. He professed disgust for Clinton's actions and voted for the Republicans' impeachment inquiry resolution in October 1998. But he also appeared with Clinton at a Rose Garden ceremony that month.

Finances also helped Etheridge; he outspent Page by $1.1 million to $350,000. Etheridge won 57%–42%, not an overwhelming margin, but an impressive one in this district; he ran 10% to 13% ahead of Senator John Edwards in Harnett, Johnston, and Wake counties.

Cook's Call. *Potentially Competitive.* Etheridge's big win here in 1998 belies the marginal nature of this district, and a downturn in Democratic fortunes could certainly be felt here. Still, Etheridge's moderate voting record and strong fundraising ability make him a difficult Democrat to unseat.

The People: Pop. 1990: 552,529; 58.2% rural; 13.6% age 65+; 70.3% White, 27.9% Black, 0.8% Asian, 0.4% Amer. Indian, 0.6% Other; 1.3% Hispanic Origin. Households: 57.1% married couple families; 26.5% married couple fams. w. children; 40.7% college educ.; median household income: $27,271; per capita income: $13,172; median house value: $67,600; median gross rent: $266.

1996 Presidential Vote			1992 Presidential Vote		
Dole (R)	104,762	(49%)	Clinton (D)	95,609	(44%)
Clinton (D)	97,055	(45%)	Bush (R)	93,498	(43%)
Perot (I)	12,215	(6%)	Perot (I)	30,263	(14%)

Rep. Bob Etheridge (D)

Elected 1996; b. Aug. 7, 1941, Sampson County; home, Lillington; Campbell U., B.S. 1965; Presbyterian; married (Faye).

Military Career: Army, 1965–67.

Elected Office: Harnett Cnty. Comm., 1973–76, Chmn., 1975–76; NC House of Reps., 1978–88; NC Superintendent of Public Instruction, 1988–96.

Professional Career: Farmer, 1965–present; Vice Pres. Sales, Sorensen Industries, 1968–87; Owner, Layton Hardware, 1973–90; Co-owner, WLLN Radio, 1979–91.

DC Office: 1641 LHOB 20515, 202-225-4531; Fax: 202-225-5662; Web site: www.house.gov/etheridge.

District Offices: Lillington, 910-814-0335; Raleigh, 919-829-9122.

Committees: *Agriculture* (18th of 24 D): Livestock & Horticulture; Risk Management, Research & Specialty Crops. *Science* (13th of 23 D): Basic Research; Space & Aeronautics.

Group Ratings

	ADA	ACLU	AFS	LCV	CON	NTU	NFIB	COC	ACU	NTLC	CHC
1998	80	44	89	77	78	21	43	65	28	26	25
1997	65	—	75	—	11	26	—	70	32	—	—

National Journal Ratings

	1997 LIB — 1997 CONS		1998 LIB — 1998 CONS	
Economic	62% —	37%	63% —	37%
Social	58% —	40%	60% —	38%
Foreign	68% —	31%	56% —	42%

Key Votes of the 105th Congress

1. Clinton Budget Deal	N	5. Puerto Rico Sthood. Ref.	Y	9. Cut $ for B-2 Bombers	N
2. Education IRAs	N	6. End Highway Set-asides	N	10. Human Rights in China	Y
3. Req. 2/3 to Raise Taxes	Y	7. School Prayer Amend.	N	11. Withdraw Bosnia Troops	N
4. Fast-track Trade	Y	8. Ovrd. Part. Birth Veto	Y	12. End Cuban TV-Marti	Y

Election Results

1998 general	Bob Etheridge (D)	100,550	(57%)	($1,106,220)
	Dan Page (R)	72,997	(42%)	($349,939)
	Others	1,647	(1%)	
1998 general	Bob Etheridge (D)	unopposed		
1996 general	Bob Etheridge (D)	113,820	(53%)	($730,969)
	David Funderburk (R)	98,951	(46%)	($1,037,080)
	Others	3,858	(2%)	

THIRD DISTRICT

Nearly 500 years ago, Giovanni da Verrazano sailed past the Gulf Stream and landed on a sandspit island he thought was the outer edge of China. He was wrong. It was the Outer Banks of North Carolina. These are probably America's most unstable barrier islands, constantly changing shape and cut by new inlets as they are battered by the ocean currents and storm winds. They were settled early by Europeans: Sir Walter Raleigh's Roanoke colony was founded here in 1587, then vanished shortly thereafter; Edward Teach—Blackbeard—and other pirates lurked in Pamlico and Albemarle sounds behind the islets. History is still much with the Outer Banks: an antique form of English is spoken on Ocracoke Island, reachable only by ferry; the 208-foot lighthouse on Cape Hatteras, America's tallest, looks out on some of the most treacherous currents in the Atlantic which have claimed hundreds of ships; the sands along Kitty Hawk, with their constant winds, are where the Wright Brothers made mankind's first heavier-than-air flight in December 1903.

Today, the Outer Banks have become vacation and retirement country, with affluent beach-front communities around Kitty Hawk, Nags Head and Duck and, much farther south, around Beaufort (*BOWfort*, not *BEWfort* as in South Carolina) and Morehead City. Inland, amid swamps, are some of America's biggest military bases, the Marine Corps's Camp Lejeune, the Army's Fort Bragg and Seymour Johnson Air Force Base. The flat lands of east Carolina have long been tobacco- and peanut-growing country, and now also hog-raising land.

The 3d Congressional District covers the Outer Banks and much of the coastal plain. Even after the May 1998 redistricting this remains an irregularly shaped district, with fingers of land going inland to include mostly white voters around Greenville and Goldsboro while leaving black majority areas in the 50% black 1st District. Before redistricting, the boundaries here were even more bizarre; but in both cases the district was about 20% black.

The congressman from the 3rd District is Walter Jones, a Republican elected in 1994. He grew up in eastern North Carolina, attended North Carolina State and Atlantic Christian College, and served in the National Guard. His father, Walter Jones Sr., was a Democratic congressman from the 1st District, which included most of northeast North Carolina, from February 1966 until his death in September 1992, and chairman of the Merchant Marine and Fisheries Committee for a dozen years. The younger Jones was elected in 1982 to the state legislature, where he voted to oust the Democratic speaker and often broke with Democratic leaders. In 1992, he ran as a Democrat in the new black-majority 1st District after his father decided to retire, winning 38% in the first primary, just 2% shy of the 40% needed to avoid a runoff in North Carolina, then losing the runoff to Eva Clayton 55%–45%.

In April 1993, Jones switched to the Republican Party, and in May 1994, announced he was running for Congress in the 3d District: "My old party has changed and so has the world. Sadly, in my opinion, both are not for the best in far too many circumstances." This pitted Jones against four-term Congressman Martin Lancaster, a Democrat who had worked hard on local projects. But Lancaster had voted for the Clinton budget and tax package in 1993 and the crime bill in 1994, and hadn't been able to persuade the Clintons to drop the cigarette tax from their health care package. Jones ran an ad showing Lancaster jogging with Bill Clinton: "How'd Martin Lancaster get so out of touch? Well, look who he's running around with in Washington."

In a district which Clinton would lose 53%–40% in 1996, when he was more popular, Jones won 53%–47%. Jones ran especially strong in Greenville and Kinston and carried the areas around Camp Lejeune and Morehead City.

In the House, Jones got seats on Armed Services and on Resources, which absorbed his father's old Merchant Marine and Fisheries panel. His voting record has been among the most conservative in the House. In his first term one of his bills became law, the War Crimes Act of 1996, which authorizes future American prisoners of war to bring lawsuits against those who commit war crimes; this provides an enforcement mechanism for the Geneva Convention, which as a ratified treaty is the law of the land. In 1997 he sponsored an Expanded War Crimes Act, which also passed. Jones opposes gays and lesbians in the military and favors more defense spending; he sponsored a bill for a $500 tax credit for military personnel on food stamps. He has argued for sending U.S. troops abroad only when "there is a clear mission and an achievable goal," and "only under the flag and command of the United States"; in October 1998 he said, "Now is not the time to reduce our military further or to misuse it on missions that have little or no direct bearing on our national security."

With his seat on the Resources Committee, Jones has pursued environmental issues of local import. In his second term he passed laws protecting a herd of wild horses on Shackelford Banks and providing for a coin and commemorative ceremonies honoring the Wright brothers' first flight at Kitty Hawk. He opposes oil drilling on the North Carolina coast (an oil company wants to drill where the Gulf Stream and Labrador Current meet). To protect the Cape Hatteras lighthouse, which was built 1,500 feet from the sea and is now only 120 feet away, he wanted to build a barrier groin; former Senator Lauch Faircloth favored moving the lighthouse a quarter-mile inland, and was able to secure $9.8 million in funding; the relocation is expected to be completed by September 1999. He helped to get $3 million to combat *pfiesteria piscicida* outbreaks on the Neuse River. With Democrat Bob Clement, he is sponsoring a new wetlands protection act.

In 1996 Jones was opposed by one of his former staffers in Raleigh, who called him a "hypocrite." Jones refused to speak his name and won 63%–37%. In 1998 Jones had more serious opposition from a young Goldsboro trial lawyer. Jones ran ads showing him walking on the beach and showing the wild ponies of Shackelford Banks, and won 62%–37%.

Cook's Call. *Probably Safe.* Though it was represented by a Democrat as recently as 1994, the 3d District, like so many Southern districts, has trended more Republican over the years. While there is still a Democratic base here, Jones has avoided a top-tier challenger in his two re-election bids. His popular name and the conservative nature of this district will also continue to insulate him from defeat.

The People: Pop. 1990: 551,918; 62.2% rural; 12.2% age 65 +; 77.7% White, 19.8% Black, 1% Asian, 0.4% Amer. Indian, 1.1% Other; 2.3% Hispanic Origin. Households: 59.5% married couple families; 28.7% married couple fams. w. children; 40.4% college educ.; median household income: $24,553; per capita income: $11,567; median house value: $63,100; median gross rent: $258.

1996 Presidential Vote

Dole (R)	86,289	(54%)
Clinton (D)	62,941	(39%)
Perot (I)	11,550	(7%)

1992 Presidential Vote

Bush (R)	76,714	(47%)
Clinton (D)	61,183	(37%)
Perot (I)	26,048	(16%)

Rep. Walter B. Jones (R)

Elected 1994; b. Feb. 10, 1943, Farmville; home, Farmville; NC St. U., 1962–65, Atlantic Christian Col., B.A. 1967; Catholic; married (Joe Anne).

Military Career: NC Natl. Guard, 1967–71.

Elected Office: NC House of Reps., 1982–92.

Professional Career: Mgr., Walter B. Jones Office Supply Co., 1967–73; Salesman, Dunn Assoc., 1973–82; Pres., Benefit Reserves Inc., 1989–94; Pres., Judson Co., 1990–94.

DC Office: 422 CHOB 20515, 202-225-3415; Fax: 202-225-3286; Web site: www.house.gov/jones.

District Offices: Goldsboro, 919-735-5382; Greenville, 252-931-1003.

Committees: *Armed Services* (23d of 32 R): Military Readiness (Vice Chmn.); Military Research & Development; Special Oversight Panel on Morale, Welfare and Recreation; Special Oversight Panel on the Merchant Marine. *Banking & Financial Services* (25th of 32 R): Capital Markets, Securities & Government Sponsored Enterprises; Housing & Community Opportunity. *Resources* (15th of 28 R): Fisheries Conservation, Wildlife & Oceans; National Parks & Public Lands.

Group Ratings

	ADA	ACLU	AFS	LCV	CON	NTU	NFIB	COC	ACU	NTLC	CHC
1998	5	6	11	8	81	77	100	72	100	100	100
1997	5	—	13	—	17	67	—	80	100	—	—

National Journal Ratings

	1997 LIB — 1997 CONS	1998 LIB — 1998 CONS
Economic	0% — 90%	12% — 85%
Social	20% — 71%	14% — 81%
Foreign	12% — 81%	0% — 93%

Key Votes of the 105th Congress

1. Clinton Budget Deal	Y	5. Puerto Rico Sthood. Ref.	N	9. Cut $ for B-2 Bombers	N
2. Education IRAs	Y	6. End Highway Set-asides	Y	10. Human Rights in China	Y
3. Req. 2/3 to Raise Taxes	Y	7. School Prayer Amend.	Y	11. Withdraw Bosnia Troops	Y
4. Fast-track Trade	N	8. Ovrd. Part. Birth Veto	Y	12. End Cuban TV-Marti	N

Election Results

1998 general	Walter B. Jones (R)	83,529	(62%)	($626,255)
	Jon Williams (D)	50,041	(37%)	($303,883)
	Others	1,342	(1%)	
1998 general	Walter B. Jones (R)	unopposed		
1996 general	Walter B. Jones (R)	118,159	(63%)	($593,793)
	George Parrott (D)	68,887	(37%)	($37,255)

FOURTH DISTRICT

Back in the 1950s, few people would have predicted that the countryside around Raleigh and Durham, North Carolina, would be one of America's high-tech boom areas. But Governor Luther Hodges did, when he started Research Triangle Park as an R&D industrial park between the musty state capital of Raleigh, the Lucky Strike-manufacturing city of Durham and the tiny university town of Chapel Hill. With the drawing power of three universities (North Carolina

State in Raleigh, Duke in Durham and the University of North Carolina in Chapel Hill), Research Triangle Park slowly began attracting big research outfits like Glaxo-Wellcome, IBM, Northern Telecom and the Environmental Protection Agency; today it has almost 42,000 people working for more than 100 major companies, stimulating hundreds of small startups and service businesses. Raleigh-Durham airport, which had four gates in the early 1970s, became a major national hub. Its metro area grew by nearly 20% from 1990–96, to more than one million, the fastest metropolitan growth north and east of Atlanta, and for years has had one of the lowest unemployment rates in the nation.

The 4th Congressional District includes most of the Research Triangle. In the 1992, 1994 and 1996 elections it included all of Raleigh's Wake County and Chapel Hill's Orange County, plus rural Chatham County; the May 1998 redistricting removed the eastern half of Wake County and added Durham and the Research Triangle Park itself. Politics here revolves around cultural issues; economic issues play little role in this booming environment where both tradition-minded and liberal-minded cultural views are vividly articulated by Jesse Helms, and university liberals and progressives like Jim Hunt. The two Democratic bases here are the black community and whites with post-graduate degrees. The big Republican base is whites with traditional religious beliefs. The balance in the 4th District, unlike that in North Carolina as a whole, has usually gone the Democrats' way, even though it is only 21% black; the post-graduate liberals tend to outvote tradition-minded whites. But the balance is closer, and the Democrats' margins narrower, than in high-tech districts in northern California or New England.

The congressman from the 4th District now, just as before 1994, is David Price, a Democrat first elected in 1986, who lost in 1994 and came back to win again in 1996 and 1998. Price grew up in east Tennessee, the son of a school principal and an English teacher. He came to North Carolina to go to college at Chapel Hill, earned a degree in divinity and a Ph.D. in political science at Yale and taught there for four years, then became a political science professor at Duke in 1973. He was executive director of the North Carolina Democratic Party in the 1980 election cycle and chairman from 1983–84—both in effect appointments of Governor Jim Hunt; he helped develop North Carolina's robust straight-ticket two-party politics. In 1986 he ran for the House and beat a Republican who had been swept in in 1984. In the House, Price helped pass laws increasing the percentage of a home's value the FHA can insure, aiding technical education at community colleges, funding the EPA Research Triangle lab and raising the Falls Lake dam to ensure Raleigh's water supply. He is an interesting blend of political scientist and practical politician, and a lay Baptist preacher as well. He has written several books, including one on his experience in Congress.

In 1994 Price lost 50.4%–49.6% to Fred Heineman, a former New York City cop and Raleigh police chief in the 1970s. But Heineman made some unforced errors and was outspent by Price, and Price regained the seat by 54%–44% in 1996. Price returned to the Appropriations Committee on which, had he not lost in 1994, he would have had enough seniority to be ranking minority member of a subcommittee. His Education Affordability Act, "my personal centerpiece," on which he had been working for a dozen years, was folded into the 1997 Balanced Budget Act; it makes interest on student loans tax deductible and allows penalty-free withdrawals from IRAs for education expenses. His next priority on education is for building more classrooms; he has a bill with the 2d District's Bob Etheridge to fund $7.2 billion of bonds for classrooms, targeted in fast-growing areas like Wake County. Price also worked successfully for a program to increase housing loans to low-wealth buyers. In the appropriations process he has nurtured local projects: $126 million for a new EPA complex in Research Triangle Park, $35 million for Raleigh's Outer Loop, $22 million over two years for the Triangle Transit Authority to plan a regional rail line in Wake, Durham and Orange counties, $30 million for a high-tech state criminal tracking system, $15 million for research on *pfiesteria piscicida,* which has broken out in North Carolina's Neuse River. In early 1998 Price got a seat on Budget in addition to his Appropriations slot. Unfinished Price projects include putting Congressional

Research Service reports on the Web and the "Stand By Your Ad" bill, co-sponsored by Steve Horn and first suggested by Lieutenant Governor Dennis Wicker. It would require candidates to appear in the full frame of TV ads reading their disclaimers on the air, so they would more likely be held responsible for negative ads.

Impeachment became an issue in Price's campaign for re-election in 1998. He was opposed by former Wake County Republican Chairman Tom Roberg, an IBM executive who escaped from Germany during World War II with his parents at 18 months old. Price's attitude toward impeachment was queasy: "This is the last thing I would want to be dealing with as a member of Congress. I think the president's behavior has been appalling, and I do think that Congress has a responsibility to hold him accountable." Roberg's was more forthright. In September 1998 he ran an ad saying, "I remember an America where character, honesty and integrity were the rule and not the exception, and when our president was a role model for our children. Now our president has admitted lying to us." When Price voted against the Republican impeachment inquiry in October 1998, Roberg said he "stood with Bill Clinton and voted against the values and beliefs of the citizens of the 4th Congressional District." All this tended to overshadow Roberg's advocacy of a flat tax and claims that Price talked like a moderate at home and voted like a liberal in Washington, as well as Price's pitches for more spending on classrooms and campaign finance reform.

Price spent more than twice as much as Roberg, and in parts of the district Roberg's policies were repugnant: Price carried Durham County 68%–31% and Orange County 70%–28%. But redistricting had removed many black neighborhoods from Wake County, and its 4th District portion was only 11% black; moreover, the fast growth here has brought many cultural conservatives into this part of the Research Triangle. Roberg carried Wake County 51%–48%, holding Price to a solid but not overwhelming 57%–42% victory. That means that Price's prospects for continued tenure are good, but depend somewhat on redistricting. Currently Democrats control the process, but that could conceivably change in the 2000 elections, and this fast-growing district will have to be trimmed and reshaped by 2002.

Cook's Call. *Probably Safe.* Price's solid win in 1998 should deter a top-tier Republican challenge in 2000. This district is the most Democratic in the state, but not exactly rock-solid.

The People: Pop. 1990: 552,441; 30.8% rural; 8.9% age 65 + ; 76.3% White, 21% Black, 2% Asian, 0.3% Amer. Indian, 0.4% Other; 1.3% Hispanic Origin. Households: 52.6% married couple families; 25.5% married couple fams. w. children; 62.5% college educ.; median household income: $34,569; per capita income: $16,708; median house value: $96,000; median gross rent: $389.

1996 Presidential Vote		
Clinton (D)	142,650	(51%)
Dole (R)	121,839	(44%)
Perot (I)	13,356	(5%)

1992 Presidential Vote		
Clinton (D)	130,489	(48%)
Bush (R)	102,945	(38%)
Perot (I)	35,758	(13%)

Rep. David Price (D)

Elected 1996; b. Aug. 17, 1940, Erwin, TN; home, Chapel Hill; U. of NC, B.A. 1961, Yale U., B.D. 1964, Ph.D. 1969; Baptist; married (Lisa).

Elected Office: U.S. House of Reps., 1986–94.

Professional Career: Legis. Aide, U.S. Sen. Bartlett, 1963–67; Prof., Yale U., 1969–73, Duke U., 1973–present; Exec. Dir., NC Dem. Party, 1979–80, Chmn., 1983–84; Staff Dir., DNC Comm. on Pres. Nominations, 1981–82.

DC Office: 2162 RHOB 20515, 202-225-1784; Fax: 202-225-2014; Web site: www.house.gov/price.

District Offices: Chapel Hill, 919-967-7924; Durham, 919-688-3004; Raleigh, 919-789-8771.

Committees: *Appropriations* (18th of 27 D): Treasury, Postal Service & General Government; VA, HUD & Independent Agencies. *Budget* (10th of 19 D).

Group Ratings

	ADA	ACLU	AFS	LCV	CON	NTU	NFIB	COC	ACU	NTLC	CHC
1998	95	75	89	85	82	18	36	61	8	13	0
1997	95	—	88	—	62	25	—	50	8	—	—

National Journal Ratings

	1997 LIB — 1997 CONS		1998 LIB — 1998 CONS	
Economic	75%	— 22%	63%	— 36%
Social	73%	— 24%	70%	— 28%
Foreign	81%	— 18%	64%	— 31%

Key Votes of the 105th Congress

1. Clinton Budget Deal	N	5. Puerto Rico Sthood. Ref.	Y	9. Cut $ for B-2 Bombers	Y
2. Education IRAs	N	6. End Highway Set-asides	N	10. Human Rights in China	Y
3. Req. 2/3 to Raise Taxes	N	7. School Prayer Amend.	N	11. Withdraw Bosnia Troops	N
4. Fast-track Trade	Y	8. Ovrd. Part. Birth Veto	N	12. End Cuban TV-Marti	Y

Election Results

1998 general	David Price (D)	129,157	(57%)	($1,229,519)
	Tom Roberg (R)	93,469	(42%)	($452,724)
	Others	2,284	(1%)	
1998 general	David Price (D)	17,282	(87%)	
	Ralph M. McKinney Jr. (D)	2,675	(13%)	
1996 general	David Price (D)	157,194	(54%)	($1,168,542)
	Fred Heineman (R)	126,466	(44%)	($980,249)
	Others	5,333	(2%)	

FIFTH DISTRICT

From the coastal plain of North Carolina, the terrain rises slowly through modest hills cut by rivers in the Piedmont, until finally the first mountain ridges appear, their mysterious blue haze filling the crevasse valleys or clinging to the steep hillsides. The Piedmont, in between the plain and the mountains, was first settled by independent-minded Scots-Irish farmers and by followers of British and German sects like the Moravians. This was hardscrabble farm country at the time of the Civil War, with few slaves. By the late 19th Century, it was becoming industrialized, with textile mills alongside streams, furniture factories not far from hardwood forests and the R. J. Reynolds cigarette factories in Winston-Salem (the only city to be honored by the name of two cigarette brands). This Piedmont economy was hailed as the basis of a progressive New South, although textile mills paid low wages and tobacco employed few workers. In fact, North Carolina's present day affluence owes more to pharmaceuticals and banking and to high-skill Piedmont factories like the country's most advanced tire recycling plant in Winston-Salem, and a custom furniture-making operation in Kernersville.

All these are within the boundaries of the 5th Congressional District, which sweeps along the northern edge of North Carolina across the Piedmont to the Blue Ridge, stopping along the way to include the northern fringe of Greensboro and most of the Winston-Salem area. About half the district's votes are cast in and around Winston-Salem; the rest are sprinkled across the countryside and in small industrial cities like Reidsville, Eden and Mt. Airy (the setting for the fictional town of Mayberry in the "Andy Griffith Show"). The legislature's May 1998 redistricting excised the 5th's eastern and western extremities, making it somewhat more compact but not changing the political balance; most of the black sections of Winston-Salem remain in the 12th District.

The congressman from the 5th District is Richard Burr, a Republican elected in 1994. Burr grew up in Winston-Salem, was a star football player at Reynolds High and Wake Forest, then worked for a wholesaling firm. In 1992, Burr ran against Congressman Steve Neal, a Democrat first elected in 1974, who usually won by close margins; Burr was outspent 3–1 and lost 53%–46%. Neal retired in 1994 and Burr ran again, with no opposition in the primary. His Democratic opponent was state Senator Sandy Sands, a rural trial lawyer who attacked Burr for using Jerry Falwell's Liberty University studios to produce his 1992 ads. Burr supported the Contract with America, promised to make defense of tobacco his number one issue, and worked hard to tie Sands to the Clinton Administration. Burr won a solid 57%, carrying all but two counties and carrying the Winston-Salem area by nearly 2–1.

In the House he has a mostly conservative voting record, was treasurer of the freshman class and, with help from Greensboro's Howard Coble, won a seat on the Commerce Committee. His main cause there has been streamlining the FDA drug and medical device approval process, which he claims keeps valuable and life-saving products from patients; in March 1996 he introduced an FDA reform bill and held hearings, but no vote was taken in the full committee. He also attacked the FDA's move to regulate tobacco as a drug as a "witch hunt." "The tobacco industry currently spends millions of dollars to educate kids that smoking is an adult choice," he said. He helped defeat an amendment to an agriculture appropriations bill that would have cut funding for crop insurance for tobacco; the vote was 212–210. On other issues, he worked to change the Medicaid formula, which got $900 million more for North Carolina over seven years, and he sought a crackdown on illegal textile imports, routed by China through other countries to evade quotas.

His major achievement has been the FDA Modernization Act signed in November 1997. By the mid-1990s the FDA was moving so slowly that it took more than 10 years and $350 million to move a prescription drug from idea to market, and 773 days to approve a medical device. Burr at first took a radical approach that aroused much opposition, but then for over two years worked with the agency, doctors, patients, consumer groups and the pharmaceutical industry to come up with a consensus approach. The new law requires the FDA to establish protocol guidelines before extensive research is begun, to review applications in a more timely manner, to use due process to determine scientific disputes and to create a scientific advisory panel; it was criticized by some on the left but praised by HHS Secretary Donna Shalala and signed by Bill Clinton. As a bonus, that same month the FDA approved the Sensor Pad, a device to help breast self-examination, which had been a Burr crusade.

Burr's next big cause is electricity deregulation. He has been sponsoring a bill to give states the ability to design deregulation if they want; it bars mandatory power purchases but continues current contracts, and allows rural cooperatives to compete wherever investor-owned utilities can. He has also sponsored a bill to allow satellite TV providers to include local network stations. He has sponsored a bill to delay for five years EPA's new air-quality standards. He was named vice chairman of Commerce's famed Oversight Subcommittee. Burr strongly opposed tobacco legislation and when Clinton in January 1999 called for the Justice Department to sue the tobacco companies, Burr said, "He played the card of fear again. . . . This is an administration whose policy is to drive the industry out."

Burr has worked the district hard, holding women's health and electricity summits in Winston-Salem, and employing a 30-cup rule: he buys a cup of coffee everywhere he stops to talk to constituents and says he has bought as many as 30 in a day. In 1996 he was re-elected 62%–35%; he had underfunded opposition and the only county he didn't carry was removed by redistricting. In 1998 he almost avoided any Democratic opposition at all; only after the primary was delayed until September did he draw a challenger, a man who had won 3% in the Senate primary in May. Burr gave $80,000 to the Republicans' House campaign committee and ran statewide ads about the importance of voting. He won easily, and there was talk he would run for statewide office. After Raleigh Mayor Tom Fetzer, a longtime friend, dropped out of the gubernatorial race in January 1999, Burr considered running but decided in February he didn't have "the fire in my belly." But he added that his sights were set on running for the Senate in 2002 or 2004; that would be in line with his 1994 promise to serve no more than five terms in the House.

Cook's Call. *Safe.* After taking himself out of the 2000 governor's race, Burr is reportedly looking at running for Senate in 2002 should Jesse Helms retire. Burr is a solid fit for this conservative district and will have no problems here in 2000. Even if this seat opens up in 2002, Republicans would still have the edge here.

The People: Pop. 1990: 552,337; 60.4% rural; 14.5% age 65 +; 85.2% White, 13.9% Black, 0.4% Asian, 0.2% Amer. Indian, 0.3% Other; 0.8% Hispanic Origin. Households: 56.4% married couple families; 25.2% married couple fams. w. children; 35.9% college educ.; median household income: $25,543; per capita income: $12,716; median house value: $59,500; median gross rent: $264.

1996 Presidential Vote

Dole (R)	134,379	(57%)
Clinton (D)	86,437	(36%)
Perot (I)	16,203	(7%)

1992 Presidential Vote

Bush (R)	118,496	(48%)
Clinton (D)	92,933	(38%)
Perot (I)	34,517	(14%)

Rep. Richard Burr (R)

Elected 1994; b. Nov. 30, 1955, Charlottesville, VA; home, Winston-Salem; Wake Forest U., B.A. 1978; Methodist; married (Brooke).

Professional Career: Natl. Sales Mgr., Carswell Distributing, 1978–94; NC Taxpayers United, Co-Chmn., 1993–present.

DC Office: 1513 LHOB 20515, 202-225-2071; Fax: 202-225-2995; Web site: www.house.gov/burr.

District Office: Winston-Salem, 336-631-5125.

Committees: *Commerce* (13th of 29 R): Energy & Power; Health and Environment; Oversight & Investigations (Vice Chmn.). *International Relations* (22d of 26 R): Asia & the Pacific; International Economic Policy & Trade.

Group Ratings

	ADA	ACLU	AFS	LCV	CON	NTU	NFIB	COC	ACU	NTLC	CHC
1998	5	13	11	8	86	75	100	82	92	92	92
1997	10	—	25	—	31	59	—	90	92	—	—

National Journal Ratings

	1997 LIB — 1997 CONS		1998 LIB — 1998 CONS	
Economic	0%	— 90%	15%	— 81%
Social	30%	— 64%	21%	— 76%
Foreign	24%	— 72%	18%	— 81%

Key Votes of the 105th Congress

1. Clinton Budget Deal	Y	5. Puerto Rico Sthood. Ref.	N	9. Cut $ for B-2 Bombers	Y
2. Education IRAs	Y	6. End Highway Set-asides	Y	10. Human Rights in China	Y
3. Req. 2/3 to Raise Taxes	Y	7. School Prayer Amend.	Y	11. Withdraw Bosnia Troops	Y
4. Fast-track Trade	Y	8. Ovrd. Part. Birth Veto	Y	12. End Cuban TV-Marti	N

Election Results

1998 general	Richard Burr (R)	119,103	(68%)	($575,327)
	Mike Robinson (D)	55,806	(32%)	($9,702)
	Others	1,382	(1%)	
1998 general	Richard Burr (R)	unopposed		
1996 general	Richard Burr (R)	130,177	(62%)	($697,067)
	Neil Grist Cashion Jr. (D)	74,320	(35%)	($185,998)
	Others	5,201	(2%)	

SIXTH DISTRICT

For more than half a century, furniture store managers and owners from all over the country twice a year have converged on the huge Furniture Mart in High Point, the center of the U.S. furniture business, for the giant trade show put on by manufacturers. High Point sits amidst rolling farmland originally settled by Quakers, the site of the Battle of Guilford Courthouse in the Revolutionary War, then slaveholding country in the years before the Civil War. The furniture business grew here early in the 20th Century because of the hardwoods in the mountains not far west and the abundance of low-wage labor in the flatlands not far east. Soon it was said of High Point that there were so many factories, "only a wise man knows his own factory whistle." Today, employment in furniture continues to grow, unlike in textiles and tobacco, and wages have risen. Race relations are now outwardly pleasant in the city where in 1960 black students at North Carolina A&T started the first lunch counter sit-in at a local Greensboro five-and-dime.

The 6th Congressional District covers most of Greensboro and High Point, Quaker-settled Randolph County and golf-course-sprinkled Moore County to the south and part of furniture-manufacturing Davidson County to the west. The May 1998 redistricting took black precincts in Guilford County away from the 12th District and placed them back in the 6th; the result is that the 6th's black percentage increased from 7% to 21%, the biggest increase in any North Carolina district.

The congressman from the 6th District is Howard Coble, a Republican first elected in 1984. He grew up in Guilford County, went to Guilford College, then after wrecking his father's car joined the Coast Guard, in which he started off collecting garbage and served five years. He was an insurance claims representative, went to law school and became an assistant U.S. attorney, state revenue commissioner and was elected to the state House in 1968 and 1978–82.

In 1984 he was elected to Congress in what was then a swing district; it was the third time the 6th had changed parties in three elections, and Coble won re-election in 1986 by just 79 votes. But his personal popularity and the 1992–96 redistricting made this a safe seat.

Coble is a friendly man who asks visitors if they mind if he smokes his cheap cigars; he likes bluegrass music and eats pork brains and eggs for breakfast. He is solidly conservative, with interesting twists. He is tightfisted, and since his first term he has tried to pass legislation to abolish congressional pensions; he boycotts the pension program himself, but hasn't found many co-sponsors. He was proud he didn't have a single overdraft on the House bank. Like many of his constituents, he is leery of free trade. He opposed fast-track for NAFTA, but finally voted for it in 1993 (without visiting the White House or selling his vote, he said); but he opposed GATT. Naturally, he opposes FDA regulation of tobacco.

"I see my role more as one of keeping bad legislation off the books," he once said. But now as a subcommittee chairman he has become legislatively productive. In 1995 and 1996 he chaired the panel with jurisdiction over the Coast Guard, and steered to passage in the House bills replacing the maritime cartel with free markets and closing down Coast Guard stations; but they went nowhere in the Senate. In January 1997 he became chairman of the Courts and Intellectual Property Subcommittee of Judiciary. Suddenly this cigar-chomping Tarheel found himself sought out by Hollywood and Nashville stars: he dined with Billy Joel and had office visits from Johnny and June Carter Cash, Michael J. Fox and Paul Reiser. "It's been fun," he said. "And very demanding because I never practiced intellectual property law. So I've learned it from the ground up." Coble argues that copyright industries produce more GDP than manufacturing and that patent protection is essential to technological progress, and he tends to support greater protection for intellectual property. He passed a bill to extend the term of copyright by 20 years. (Otherwise Mickey Mouse would have gone out of copyright by 2004.) In July 1997 he introduced measures to make it illegal to circumvent encryption technology used to protect copyrighted material and to remove digital author codes from copyrighted material, to protect creative work transmitted over the Internet. This law was signed in October 1998, and conforms U.S. law to two World Intellectual Property Organization treaties. The Senate forced him to drop from that law a provision for legal protection of computer databases and other information collections; he promised to seek it again in 1999.

Coble also sponsored the law to set up a commission to consider realignment of the federal appeals courts, especially the cumbersomely large and often-reversed 9th Circuit. In March 1998 he sponsored two bills to maintain the reach of credit unions which the Supreme Court ruled had exceeded their charters; in April 1998 he proposed cutting the fees which finance the Patent and Trademark office, whose surplus the Clinton Administration had been raiding for deficit reduction or to finance other programs. On impeachment, Coble said, "I think most of the time we need to give additional weight to judgment and conscience even if it means conflicting with polling numbers." When former Congressman Robert Drinan said Republicans were seeking "vengeance" against Clinton, Coble replied, "We're going about our business, and if anybody thinks that vengeance is involved, I'll meet 'em in the parking lot later on tonight." No such meetings took place; Coble voted for impeachment but declined to become a House manager, because of his father's illness.

Coble was the only North Carolinian on the Transportation and Infrastructure Committee as it put together the huge highway bill in spring 1998. The highway formula was shifted very much to the state's advantage, and Coble brought home some bacon—$22 million for the Greensboro Outer Loop, $22 million to build the U.S. 311 expressway in High Point, $6.6 million for a Greensboro Intermodal Center at the old train station and $3.3 million for new Greensboro buses and vans.

Coble had no Democratic opponent in 1994 or 1998 and won easily when he did in 1996. But this district will likely be seriously contested if he retires.

Cook's Call. *Safe.* Coble has had little competition here since 1986 and he is not likely to see any action in 2000 either.

The People: Pop. 1990: 552,663; 52.9% rural; 12.9% age 65 +; 78% White, 20.5% Black, 0.8% Asian, 0.5% Amer. Indian, 0.3% Other; 0.8% Hispanic Origin. Households: 61.1% married couple families; 27.3% married couple fams. w. children; 42% college educ.; median household income: $30,628; per capita income: $14,942; median house value: $73,300; median gross rent: $307.

1996 Presidential Vote

Dole (R)	105,779	(50%)
Clinton (D)	88,812	(42%)
Perot (I)	15,484	(7%)

1992 Presidential Vote

Bush (R)	98,088	(45%)
Clinton (D)	89,441	(41%)
Perot (I)	32,498	(15%)

Rep. Howard Coble (R)

Elected 1984; b. Mar. 18, 1931, Greensboro; home, Greensboro; Appalachian St. U., 1949–50, Guilford Col., A.B. 1958, U. of NC, J.D. 1962; Presbyterian; single.

Military Career: Coast Guard, 1952–56, 1977–78, Coast Guard Reserves, 1960–81.

Elected Office: NC House of Reps., 1968–70, 1978–84.

Professional Career: Asst. U.S. Atty., NC Middle Dist., 1969–73; Commissioner, NC Dept. of Revenue, 1973–77; Practicing atty., 1979–83.

DC Office: 2468 RHOB 20515, 202-225-3065; Fax: 202-225-8611; Web site: www.house.gov/coble.

District Offices: Asheboro, 336-626-3060; Greensboro, 336-333-5005; High Point, 336-886-5106.

Committees: *Judiciary* (5th of 21 R): Courts & Intellectual Property (Chmn.); Crime. *Transportation & Infrastructure* (6th of 41 R): Coast Guard & Maritime Transportation; Ground Transportation.

Group Ratings

	ADA	ACLU	AFS	LCV	CON	NTU	NFIB	COC	ACU	NTLC	CHC
1998	10	6	13	0	65	62	86	89	96	97	100
1997	5	—	13	—	31	66	—	90	88	—	—

National Journal Ratings

	1997 LIB — 1997 CONS			1998 LIB — 1998 CONS		
Economic	0%	—	90%	15%	—	85%
Social	0%	—	90%	3%	—	90%
Foreign	32%	—	65%	33%	—	66%

Key Votes of the 105th Congress

1. Clinton Budget Deal	Y	5. Puerto Rico Sthood. Ref.	N	9. Cut $ for B-2 Bombers	Y
2. Education IRAs	Y	6. End Highway Set-asides	Y	10. Human Rights in China	N
3. Req. 2/3 to Raise Taxes	Y	7. School Prayer Amend.	Y	11. Withdraw Bosnia Troops	Y
4. Fast-track Trade	N	8. Ovrd. Part. Birth Veto	Y	12. End Cuban TV-Marti	Y

Election Results

1998 general	Howard Coble (R)	112,740	(89%)	($401,604)
	Jeffrey Bentley (Lib)	14,454	(11%)	
1998 general	Howard Coble (R)	unopposed		
1996 general	Howard Coble (R)	167,828	(73%)	($498,224)
	Mark Costley (D)	58,022	(25%)	($32,829)

SEVENTH DISTRICT

Southernmost North Carolina, where the state boundary dips down along the Atlantic coast, has been economically dependent on tobacco for more than 200 years. Tobacco can be cultivated profitably in only a few places in the world; it is labor-intensive, requiring close tending and serial picking (one leaf on a stalk matures before the one above it); and it is valuable enough that North Carolina farmers today, if they have one of the tobacco allotments handed out in the 1930s or have bought the rights to one, can make a living off 40 acres. Tobacco produces more voters per federally assisted acre than any other crop. This tobacco country, it should be added, is racially diverse, the home of many blacks as well as the Lumbee Indians, whose origins have been lost in antiquity, but who were treated by state segregation laws—and still are treated by continuing custom—as a race distinct from whites and blacks; each race makes up about one-third of the population of Robeson County around Lumberton.

Southernmost North Carolina is also military country. The port city of Wilmington is home of the World War II battleship *U.S.S. North Carolina*. Wilmington and the nearby beach towns have been the fastest-growing part of North Carolina in the 1990s. Eastward, in swampland, is Camp Lejeune, home base of one-fifth of the Marine Corps. Inland, near Fayetteville, is the huge complex of Fort Bragg and Pope Air Force Base, whence 39,000 troops left for the Persian Gulf in 1990. As the site of one of the biggest bases in the country, Fayetteville has developed the strip highway to an art form, with strip joints, fast food galore and the world's first Putt-Putt golf course.

North Carolina's 7th Congressional District covers much of this territory. For the 1992, 1994 and 1996 elections it had astonishingly jagged boundaries, and took in Camp Lejeune and Fort Bragg; the May 1998 redistricting removed the two bases, but retained Fayetteville which is so dependent on them. Politically, the 7th consists of three areas: The coastal area around Wilmington, with hundreds of affluent condo-dwellers, now trending Republican; the area around Fayetteville, pretty evenly divided between the parties; and the Lumbee Indian country in and around Robeson County, very heavily Democratic. This was for many years a solidly Democratic district, but is now more marginal.

The congressman from the 7th District is Mike McIntyre, a Democrat elected in 1996. McIntyre grew up in Lumberton, in Robeson County, graduated from college and law school at Chapel Hill and practiced law in Lumberton, where his family has been prominent for 200 years. In 1974 he was an intern in the office of Congressman Charlie Rose, then in his first term, and whispered to his father he would like one day to run for his seat. McIntyre was active in civic affairs and in his church and was often asked to run for office. In 1995, four months before Rose announced his retirement, McIntyre decided to run. He was not alone: seven Democrats and four Republicans filed. McIntyre's chief opposition in the primary was Rose Marie Lowry-Townsend, a Lumbee and a liberal, who had support from the National Education Association, labor PACs and national women's groups; nearly half of her contributions came from outside North Carolina. Lowry-Townsend led McIntyre 30%–23% in the first contest, in which most of his support came from Robeson County. McIntyre called for smaller government and cited his close ties to the district and involvement in community activities. He won the runoff 52%–48%, carrying the Lumbee country and Fayetteville and trailing on the coast.

The Republican nominee was Bill Caster, a retired Coast Guard officer and New Hanover County commissioner. McIntyre's platform was almost as conservative as Caster's—on some things, more so. McIntyre favored the balanced budget amendment, term limits, eliminating federal departments, and school prayer. He said he would vote for but would not campaign with Bill Clinton. He was moved by state labor leaders to withdraw his support for a national right-to-work law, but continued to favor right-to-work in North Carolina. He attacked Caster for backing two county tax increases, and signed the Americans for Tax Reform's anti-tax pledge months before Caster did. Caster ridiculed McIntyre's emphasis on his community ties: "While it's all well and good to coach Little League, that doesn't mean you're ready to go to

Congress." As in the primaries, there was a split between the coast and the interior. Caster carried the coastal counties 59%–39%; McIntyre carried the Fayetteville area 53%–46% and had a huge 81%–18% majority in Robeson County. Overall, he carried the district 53%–46%, even as Clinton was losing it 48%–44%.

McIntyre immediately joined the conservative Blue Dog Democrats and got seats on Armed Services and Agriculture—and the subcommittee that oversees the peanut and tobacco programs. His voting record stands at the middle of the House. He voted for the flag burning amendment, the partial-birth abortion ban and the bill to sunset the tax code in 2003. He moved to exempt small pre-1987 polluters from Superfund liability. But he supported racial quotas and preferences and opposed school vouchers. He fought the proposal to end crop insurance for tobacco farmers and prevailed. "It would punish small farmers, the ones who could least afford to lose it," he said. He was one of 31 Democrats to vote for the Republicans' impeachment inquiry

"I firmly believe that the people who elected you are first and foremost the people to whom you owe your allegiance," McIntyre said. "Projects in the district are of paramount importance to us." He got money for hurricane relief and a new postal processing center in Wilmington, and promoted projects for the Wilmington port and local highways. He pushed to reopen the Lockwood Folly River's original outlet to the sea and partially block the man-made inlet with a dike—a Rose project. He sought to impose a higher tariff on new imports of Caribbean Basin footware; Converse's plant west of Lumberton is the largest shoe factory left in the United States.

McIntyre was endorsed in March 1998 by the U.S. Chamber of Commerce and by Republican Gary Bauer's Campaign for Working Families. A spokesman for the North Carolina Republican Party said, "I wish Mike McIntyre would make it official and switch over to the Republican Party. . . . He's voted with the Republicans quite a bit and is one of their most conservative members in Congress." But McIntyre was not interested in party-switching. "There have been some individual Republicans who have talked to me in Washington. . . . But I am committed to the Democratic Party. It's not something I would consider." He was re-elected with 94% in the primary and 91% in the general. In January 1999 he became co-chair of the Rural Healthcare Coalition.

Cook's Call. *Safe.* As an open seat, this rural district will be tough for Democrats to defend, but the conservative McIntyre is well-suited for this district. Republicans were unable to recruit a top-tier challenge against him in 1998 and may pass in 2000.

The People: Pop. 1990: 552,037; 41.3% rural; 9.4% age 65 + ; 67.3% White, 24.3% Black, 0.5% Asian, 7.4% Amer. Indian, 0.6% Other; 1.4% Hispanic Origin. Households: 60.4% married couple families; 31.4% married couple fams. w. children; 43.3% college educ.; median household income: $24,708; per capita income: $11,663; median house value: $64,000; median gross rent: $308.

1996 Presidential Vote

Clinton (D) 93,133 (47%)
Dole (R) 90,785 (46%)
Perot (I) 13,699 (7%)

1992 Presidential Vote

Clinton (D) 94,597 (47%)
Bush (R) 80,214 (40%)
Perot (I) 24,970 (12%)

Rep. Mike McIntyre (D)

Elected 1996; b. Aug. 6, 1956, Lumberton; home, Lumberton; U. of NC, B.A. 1978, J.D. 1981; Presbyterian; married (Dee).

Professional Career: Practicing atty., 1982–96.

DC Office: 1605 LHOB 20515, 202-225-2731; Fax: 202-225-5773; Web site: www.house.gov/mcintyre.

District Offices: Fayetteville, 910-323-0260; Lumberton, 910-671-6223; Wilmington, 910-815-4959.

Committees: *Agriculture* (16th of 24 D): Livestock & Horticulture; Risk Management, Research & Specialty Crops. *Armed Services* (20th of 28 D): Military Procurement; Military Readiness.

Group Ratings

	ADA	ACLU	AFS	LCV	CON	NTU	NFIB	COC	ACU	NTLC	CHC
1998	60	25	78	46	48	25	79	72	52	47	50
1997	40	—	38	—	20	38	—	80	60	—	—

National Journal Ratings

	1997 LIB — 1997 CONS	1998 LIB — 1998 CONS
Economic	55% — 45%	56% — 44%
Social	47% — 52%	47% — 53%
Foreign	45% — 54%	49% — 48%

Key Votes of the 105th Congress

1. Clinton Budget Deal	Y	5. Puerto Rico Sthood. Ref.	N	9. Cut $ for B-2 Bombers	N
2. Education IRAs	N	6. End Highway Set-asides	N	10. Human Rights in China	Y
3. Req. 2/3 to Raise Taxes	Y	7. School Prayer Amend.	Y	11. Withdraw Bosnia Troops	N
4. Fast-track Trade	N	8. Ovrd. Part. Birth Veto	Y	12. End Cuban TV-Marti	Y

Election Results

1998 general	Mike McIntyre (D)	124,366	(91%)	($392,316)
	Paul Meadows (Lib)	11,924	(9%)	
1998 general	Mike McIntyre (D)	18,865	(94%)	
	Randy Crow (D)	1,139	(6%)	
1996 general	Mike McIntyre (D)	87,487	(53%)	($490,063)
	Bill Caster (R)	75,811	(46%)	($332,746)

EIGHTH DISTRICT

From Atlanta to Durham in the Carolina Piedmont, along Interstate 85, is the thickest concentration of America's textile industry—so thick you can almost see the lint. Within North Carolina, I-85 passes past Salisbury, Concord and Kannapolis—named for its founding company, Cannon Mills. East Carolina was settled by Englishmen from the coast. This Piedmont land was settled primarily by Scots and diverse groups like Quakers and Moravian sects, coming down the Blue Ridge from Pennsylvania through Virginia. These migratory patterns were reflected in Civil War divisions and continue in current voting habits. The coastal counties all the way up through the Sand Hills were Confederate and are now Democratic. The textile mill towns along I-85 were anti-secession and are now Republican.

The 8th Congressional District of North Carolina, as redistricted, combines the area around Kannapolis and Concord with Sand Hill counties extending east to Fayetteville. In the district lines in effect for 1992, nearly two-thirds of the population was in the textile country or the expanding Charlotte suburbs in fast-growing Union County. Under the May 1998 redistricting plan, the textile counties of Rowan and Iredell were removed, as was Moore County, and heavily Democratic precincts in the east were added. This raised the black percentage from 23% to 28% and the Democratic registration to over 68%—a significant political shift in a closely balanced constituency.

The congressman from the 8th District is Robin Hayes, a Republican elected in 1998. He grew up in Concord, the grandson of Cannon Mills founder Charles Cannon; he graduated from Duke and returned to Concord, where he ran several businesses—selling Mack trucks, building highways, running the Mt. Pleasant Hosiery Mills. He coached football at a local college and worked in the Prison Fellowship movement. He was elected a Concord alderman, and in 1991 he switched to the Republican Party. In 1992 he was elected to the North Carolina House, and became majority whip; there he sponsored the 1995 bill requiring schools to teach abstinence as the primary method of birth control and supported parental consent for abortion, caps on punitive damages and a big income tax cut. In 1996 he ran for governor, won the Republican primary, but lost the general to Jim Hunt 56%–43%. In November 1997 he announced he was running against 8th District Congressman Bill Hefner, a singer elected to the House in 1974 and the winner in many close races since. In January 1998 Hefner surprised just about everyone by announcing that he would retire.

But that did not trigger the usual influx of candidates to the campaign. No Republican moved to oppose Hayes, and Democrats had a hard time coming up with a candidate. Former Lieutenant Governor Bob Jordan said no in January 1998; in March former state Senator Glenn Jernigan, who had run third in the 1996 7th District primary, missing the runoff and trailing Mike McIntyre by just 2,407 votes, bowed out because of his wife's illness. That left as the sole Democratic candidate Mike Taylor, a Stanly County lawyer with an attractive biography but little name recognition. He was the grandson of a Baptist preacher who lived to 106 and son of Baptist missionaries to Africa; he served in the Navy in Vietnam's Mekong Delta; he had a Harvard Ph.D. in classical archaeology.

Hayes campaigned on a standard conservative platform, stressing the issues he had pushed in the legislature and calling for "top-to-bottom comprehensive tax reform." "I want to be part of a Congress that puts faith in God and people—not government programs," he said. His personal wealth made his candidacy appear formidable to political insiders, but he spent only $127,000 of his own money and instead spent much time on fundraising, ultimately spending $1.22 million. He was the recipient of many visits from Republican luminaries—Bob Dole, Charlton Heston, Jesse Helms, Oliver North, Dan Quayle, Dick Armey. Taylor soldiered on. "We don't need new taxes. But there are terrible problems across the 8th Congressional District," he said. He called for building more classrooms, more discipline in schools, mastering of skills before promotion, zero tolerance of violence and drugs. He referred to "Robin '$82 million' Hayes" in his press releases and said, "Hayes is very wealthy, and that's fortunate for him. But it means he doesn't have to worry about health care, a job or retirement. If voters want to send someone to Washington to talk about Social Security, they better send someone who's going to use it, like me." His military record helped him win the endorsement of the VFW, and he spent $367,000.

For all his advantages, Hayes did not make much of a dent on central North Carolina's ancestral political loyalties. He carried the textile counties 61%–38%, but after redistricting they cast only 36% of the votes in the district. He carried Union County even more heavily, 65%–34%. But the counties to the east voted in some cases more than 2–1 Democratic, and cast 43% of the district's votes; Taylor carried them overall 64%–35%. Hayes won by a close 51%–48%.

Cook's Call. *Highly Competitive.* Hayes had one of the most unexpectedly close races in the country in 1998 and Democrat Mike Taylor is likely to challenge him again in 2000. This time around, Taylor will have hard-won credibility and access to money, but Hayes will have the power of incumbency, a personal fortune, and a Republican trending district on his side. Look for a tight race.

The People: Pop. 1990: 552,039; 54.9% rural; 12.2% age 65 + ; 67.5% White, 27.7% Black, 1% Asian, 2.6% Amer. Indian, 1.2% Other; 2.3% Hispanic Origin. Households: 60.2% married couple families; 30% married couple fams. w. children; 34.3% college educ.; median household income: $26,180; per capita income: $11,462; median house value: $57,100; median gross rent: $250.

1996 Presidential Vote			1992 Presidential Vote		
Dole (R)	77,564	(46%)	Clinton (D)	77,838	(45%)
Clinton (D)	77,269	(46%)	Bush (R)	72,958	(42%)
Perot (I)	12,729	(8%)	Perot (I)	22,931	(13%)

Rep. Robin Hayes (R)

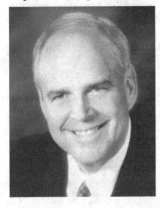

Elected 1998; b. Aug. 14, 1945, Concord; home, Concord; Duke U., B.A. 1967; Presbyterian; married (Barbara).

Elected Office: Concord Bd. of Alderman, 1978–81; NC House of Reps., 1992–96, Majority Whip, 1995–96.

Professional Career: Businessman, 1967-present; Owner, Mt. Pleasant Hosiery Mill, 1988-present.

DC Office: 130 CHOB 20515, 202-225-3715; Fax: 202-225-4036; Web site: www.house.gov/hayes.

District Offices: Concord, 704-786-1612; Rockingham, 910-997-2070.

Committees: *Agriculture* (26th of 27 R): General Farm Commodities, Resource Conservation & Credit; Risk Management, Research & Specialty Crops. *Armed Services* (30th of 32 R): Military Personnel; Military Procurement; Special Oversight Panel on Morale, Welfare and Recreation. *Resources* (26th of 28 R): Fisheries Conservation, Wildlife & Oceans; Forests & Forest Health.

Group Ratings and Key Votes: Newly Elected

Election Results

1998 general	Robin Hayes (R)	67,505	(51%)	($1,224,344)
	Mike Taylor (D)	64,127	(48%)	($366,624)
	Others	1,492	(1%)	
1998 general	Robin Hayes (R)	unopposed		
1996 general	W. G. (Bill) Hefner (D)	103,129	(55%)	($555,614)
	Curtis Blackwood (R)	81,676	(44%)	($151,081)

NINTH DISTRICT

"An agreeable village but in a damn rebellious country," recorded General Cornwallis when, before the unpleasantness at Yorktown, he visited Charlotte, North Carolina. "A veritable nest of hornets." This town, settled by Scots-Irish and German colonists who came down the Blue Ridge from Pennsylvania now has 1.3 million people. Before the California gold rush, Charlotte was the gold mining capital of the country. Now, it is the headquarters of two of the nation's biggest banks: Bank of America, formed from the September 1998 merger of NationsBank and

San Francisco's Bank America, and First Union; with over $840 billion in assets, Charlotte is the second-largest financial center in the nation, behind only New York. It is the center of the nation's biggest textile manufacturing region and an airline hub for USAirways. It has become home to the NBA Hornets and NFL Panthers. Across from Bank of America's 60-story tower is a $50 million performing arts center. The rebelliousness Cornwallis noted can still be seen in this home of one of the nation's biggest stock car race tracks. But Charlotte has also built a boosterish pride in its capacity for accommodation. It is proud that it responded amicably to a busing order approved in a landmark Supreme Court case in 1971; that it uncovered the she-nanigans of its nearby South Carolina neighbors Jim and Tammy Faye Bakker; that it elected Harvey Gantt, who is black, mayor two times and then replaced him with Sue Myrick, a Republican woman whose grievance wasn't race but traffic.

The 9th Congressional District includes about half of Charlotte and Mecklenburg County—the central and northern parts are in the 12th District—and extends west to Gaston, Cleveland and Lincoln Counties, with their many textile mills. Mecklenburg County is politically mar-ginal, but the 9th has the more Republican part: It includes 61% of the county's whites but only 10% of its blacks. So this is a heavily Republican district, though one which sometimes votes out of sync with the rest of North Carolina; people in Charlotte think the state's politics is dominated by politicians from eastern North Carolina—Jesse Helms, Jim Hunt—and that not enough respect is paid to the state's largest metropolis.

The congresswoman from the 9th District is Sue Myrick, a Republican first elected in 1994. Myrick grew up and went to college in Ohio, raised her family in Charlotte, owned an adver-tising agency and Amway distributorship. In 1981 she ran for the Charlotte Council and lost. She ran again and won in 1983, ran for mayor and lost in 1985, then beat Harvey Gantt in 1987. Despite nasty personal charges, she was re-elected in 1989; she is proud of making infrastructure improvements, bringing the NFL Carolina Panthers to Charlotte and preventing property tax increases for four years. Myrick ran for the Senate in 1992, but was beaten by Lauch Faircloth in the primary 48%–30%. In 1994 Charlotte Congressman Alex McMillan, passed over for the ranking position on Budget, retired. In the 1994 primary, against State House Minority Leader David Balmer, a 31-year-old ambitious politician, Myrick led in the first primary by just 34%–28%. But before the runoff three weeks later, it was revealed that Balmer had falsely claimed on his resume to have graduated in the top 20% of his law school class and to have played varsity soccer. Myrick won 68%–32%, then easily won the general.

Myrick was one of the proud leaders of the 1994 Republican freshman class. She served on Newt Gingrich's transition team and was first freshman- and then sophomore-class liaison to the leadership. But she was in touch with the unsuccessful coup against Gingrich in July 1997, and later that month lost the post of Conference secretary by 110–65 to Deborah Pryce, whom Gingrich backed. (Gingrich said later this wasn't in retaliation.) Myrick got a seat on the Budget Committee in 1995, and stood fast after the Republican budget was vetoed by Bill Clinton. She co-chaired a task force on privatizing HUD functions, supported a flat-rate income tax and sponsored a bill for civil monetary penalties for making false statements in political ads. She has been a strong backer of Republicans' flex-time bill to give workers a choice between overtime pay or time off. After the 1996 election, which she won easily, she was named to the Rules Committee; she took "on-leave" status on Banking, where she cannot vote but can build seniority to watch over her district's banking needs.

Myrick has taken a lead role on many Republican initiatives. She backed the ban on partial-birth abortion: "It has no place in a civilized society. . . . This shouldn't be divisive—the issue we're talking about is killing; we're talking about killing babies." And she sponsored the 1998 bill to outlaw taking a child out of state to get an abortion to avoid a state parental notification law. She sponsored the law passed in October 1998 to impose mandatory additional sentences for criminals convicted of using a firearm to commit a crime of violence or drug trafficking, and, inspired by a hideous crime in Charlotte, proposed making it a federal crime to take an officer's firearm and kill him with it. She sponsored a bill in 1997 to stop the IRS from imposing the 2.9% Medicare payroll tax on the retained earnings of limited partnerships as well as their incomes. And she turned down the Transportation Committee's offer of $15 million for Charlotte's outerbelt because she felt the transportation bill would bust the budget. "I said when I ran for this job, 'If you want somebody to bring home the bacon, don't send me.' We get a balanced budget agreement for the first time in 30 years, and now they do this?"

Myrick was easily re-elected in 1998 against an opponent who spent much of his $29,000 on an incomprehensible radio ad ("led by Amway executive Sue Myrick, congressional Republicans are trying to make a nuclear mountain out of a multi-marketing level molehill"). After the election she ran for vice chairman of the Republican Conference, the fifth-ranking leadership position, but on the first ballot her 38 votes were far behind Tillie Fowler's 90 and just behind Anne Northup's 43 and Pete Hoekstra's 39. On impeachment, she used the same kind of homey arguments Clinton Democrats like. "Just before the November election, my five-year-old grandson, Jake, asked his mother if a new president was being elected. Upon being told we already have a president, Jake replied, 'No, we don't. He lied.' Such principles from the mouths of babes."

Cook's Call. *Safe.* Even though she lost some parts of her Charlotte-based district in the 1998 remap, Myrick still represents a strongly Republican district. Redistricting in 2001 could be interesting here, however, as this area is one of the fastest growing in the state and could once again be reconfigured.

The People: Pop. 1990: 552,490; 24.3% rural; 10.7% age 65 + ; 88% White, 10.6% Black, 1% Asian, 0.3% Amer. Indian, 0.2% Other; 0.8% Hispanic Origin. Households: 59.3% married couple families; 28.2% married couple fams. w. children; 55% college educ.; median household income: $35,346; per capita income: $17,234; median house value: $83,600; median gross rent: $393.

1996 Presidential Vote		
Dole (R)	124,907	(57%)
Clinton (D)	81,994	(37%)
Perot (I)	13,839	(6%)

1992 Presidential Vote		
Bush (R)	125,214	(53%)
Clinton (D)	77,088	(33%)
Perot (I)	33,986	(14%)

Rep. Sue Myrick (R)

Elected 1994; b. Aug. 1, 1941, Tiffin, OH; home, Charlotte; Heidelberg Col., 1959–60; Methodist; married (Ed).

Elected Office: Charlotte City Cncl., 1983–85; Charlotte Mayor, 1987–91.

Professional Career: Pres. & CEO, Myrick Advertising, 1985–94; Pres. & CEO, Myrick Enterprises, 1992–94.

DC Office: 230 CHOB 20515, 202-225-1976; Fax: 202-225-3389; Web site: www.house.gov/myrick.

District Offices: Charlotte, 704-362-1060; Gastonia, 704-861-1976.

Committees: *Rules* (7th of 9 R): The Legislative & Budget Process.

Group Ratings

	ADA	ACLU	AFS	LCV	CON	NTU	NFIB	COC	ACU	NTLC	CHC
1998	5	13	11	8	70	73	100	83	88	95	100
1997	5	—	13	—	67	66	—	90	100	—	—

National Journal Ratings

	1997 LIB	—	1997 CONS	1998 LIB	—	1998 CONS
Economic	14%	—	85%	0%	—	88%
Social	20%	—	71%	26%	—	72%
Foreign	0%	—	88%	17%	—	83%

Key Votes of the 105th Congress

1. Clinton Budget Deal	Y	5. Puerto Rico Sthood. Ref.	N	9. Cut $ for B-2 Bombers	N
2. Education IRAs	Y	6. End Highway Set-asides	Y	10. Human Rights in China	N
3. Req. 2/3 to Raise Taxes	Y	7. School Prayer Amend.	Y	11. Withdraw Bosnia Troops	Y
4. Fast-track Trade	Y	8. Ovrd. Part. Birth Veto	Y	12. End Cuban TV-Marti	N

Election Results

1998 general	Sue Myrick (R)	120,570	(69%)	($721,459)
	Rory Blake (D)	51,345	(29%)	($29,048)
	Others	2,167	(1%)	.
1998 general	Sue Myrick (R)	unopposed		
1996 general	Sue Myrick (R)	147,755	(63%)	($547,194)
	Michel C. Daisley (D)	83,078	(35%)	($63,598)
	Others	3,877	(2%)	

TENTH DISTRICT

Wreathed in the haze that gave them the name "Smoky," the heavily wooded mountains of North Carolina seem placid and ancient. Geologically, they are some of the oldest ranges in the world; economically, they are churning with activity. The North Carolina counties where the hills of the Appalachians rise from the Piedmont are not just countryside. Nestled in their valleys is perhaps the largest concentration of furniture factories in the world, where skilled craftsmen create, from the hardwoods of Carolina forests, both high quality and mass market furniture. Other industries are here as well—textiles, though not as much as in the I-85 corridor in the Piedmont, and chickens in the Holly Farms complex (acquired by Tyson) in Wilkes County. And high-tech as well: The Catawba Valley is home to three large fiber-optic cable manufacturers, Comm-Scope, Alcatel and Siecor.

The 10th Congressional District covers much of this hill and mountain country, roughly west of I-77 and north of Hickory and Morganton. The district lines for 1992, 1994 and 1996 were very irregular; the May 1998 redistricting smooths out the lines and leaves the district more compact. Politically, this is a very Republican area, though the Republicans here tend not to be Jesse Helms fans, but rough-hewn hill Republicans, unsympathetic to government regulators, from factory inspectors to revenuers on the lookout for illegal stills.

The congressman from this district is Cass Ballenger, a Republican elected in 1986. Ballenger grew up in Hickory, enlisted in the Navy at 18, went to school in the East and headed a paper box company; in 1957 he founded Plastic Packaging Inc., to make plastic wrappings for J.C. Penney underwear. He served on the Catawba County Board of Commissioners for eight years and in the state legislature for 12. In 1986, after Congressman James Broyhill was appointed to the Senate (he lost in November), Ballenger ran for the House. He promised to be a "Broyhill Republican" and beat a primary opponent backed by Helms. Ballenger has won general elections by large margins.

Ballenger combines a solidly conservative voting record with a sense of civic responsibility. He and his wife have organized humanitarian trips to Central and South America, delivering donated medical supplies and second-hand fire engines; Plastic Packaging sent a half-million plastic bags to Haiti to be used to grow eucalyptus seedlings to reforest the barren hills. When Democrats were in control of Congress, he opposed the Clinton health care plan, family and medical leave and striker replacement; he amended an OSHA law by exempting employers when violations are caused by employees breaking company work rules. When Republicans gained control, Ballenger became chairman of the Workforce Protections Subcommittee. He sees his job as updating labor laws that are out of line with today's flexible management and family-conscious employees. One response was the comp-time (or flex-time) bill, which would allow employees who work overtime to choose whether to receive overtime pay or compensatory time within the next year; federal employees have had this option since 1985. "Working parents need more flexibility as they try to deal with family needs and the demands of the job," Ballenger said. Comp-time passed the House in July 1996 but was fiercely opposed by the AFL-CIO, which argues that employers will coerce employees to take leave time. It passed the House again, 222–210, in March 1997, but was not acted on in the Senate. Ballenger promises to try again.

Another major initiative has been OSHA reform. Ballenger started off pressed between subcommittee Republicans who would like to abolish the agency altogether and Democrats and labor leaders resisting any change. In 1997 he introduced a package of eight OSHA reforms; one feature was an increase from 16% to 50% of OSHA funds which must be spent on assisting businesses in complying with OSHA standards. "We ought to change the attitude of OSHA from being a Gestapo to being a teacher." Two of his proposals were enacted into law and signed in July 1998, the first free-standing changes in OSHA since it was established in 1970. One codified OSHA's own consultation program operated by the states; businesses could get advice without inviting adversarial proceedings. The second bars enforcement quotas and using enforcement activities as performance measures. Unpassed were bills that would immunize from citations employers who provide alternate protections which are equally or more protective (the AFL-CIO says this would gut the law) and keeping confidential the results of safety and health audits which are not required by specific OSHA standards. Ballenger has also proposed merging the Mine Safety and Health Administraton into another enforcement agency and repealing the Davis-Bacon Act, which requires contractors on federal construction sites to pay workers "local prevailing wages," and in practice strengthens the building trades unions.

Ballenger overall has a moderate-conservative voting record and is wary of spending measures. He opposed the big 1998 transportation bill because he thought it would break the budget: "This bill contains more pork than a North Carolina barbecue." And he voted against the October 1998 omnibus budget. "There was some good stuff in there, I don't deny that. But we blew the caps off the budget." Ballenger eschews the traditional protectionism of textile areas, now that western North Carolina is developing other strong industries. He wants to extend NAFTA to Central and South America and supported fast track in November 1997. For some years he voted to defund the National Endowment for the Arts. In February 1998 Gingrich appointed him to the National Council on the Arts, which oversees the NEA; he said that new practices adopted by the NEA or mandated by Congress were working well, and "we should give the NEA a chance to work under the new guidelines and mandates of law that now govern this agency."

Ballenger was re-elected over a Libertarian candidate in 1998 with 86% of the vote.

Cook's Call. *Safe.* Court-ordered redistricting of the majority-black 12th District had an impact on the lines of this district, but certainly not enough to make it any more competitive. Ballenger will have no problems winning here in 2000.

The People: Pop. 1990: 552,303; 70.6% rural; 12.8% age 65 + ; 92.3% White, 6.8% Black, 0.4% Asian, 0.2% Amer. Indian, 0.3% Other; 0.7% Hispanic Origin. Households: 64.4% married couple families; 29.5% married couple fams. w. children; 35.2% college educ.; median household income: $28,511; per capita income: $13,434; median house value: $64,000; median gross rent: $261.

1996 Presidential Vote			1992 Presidential Vote		
Dole (R)	120,378	(56%)	Bush (R)	116,435	(50%)
Clinton (D)	74,648	(35%)	Clinton (D)	82,515	(35%)
Perot (I)	18,365	(9%)	Perot (I)	34,183	(15%)

Rep. Cass Ballenger (R)

Elected 1986; b. Dec. 6, 1926, Hickory; home, Hickory; U. of NC, Amherst Col., B.A. 1948; Episcopalian; married (Donna).

Military Career: Naval Air Corps, 1944–45.

Elected Office: Catawba Cnty. Bd. of Commissioners, 1966–74, Chmn. 1970–74; NC House of Reps., 1974–76; NC Senate, 1976–86.

Professional Career: Businessman; Pres., Hickory Paper Box Co., 1948–70; Founder & Pres., Plastic Packaging Inc., 1957–present.

DC Office: 2182 RHOB 20515, 202-225-2576; Fax: 202-225-0316; Web site: www.house.gov/ballenger.

District Office: Hickory, 828-327-6100.

Committees: *Education & the Workforce* (4th of 27 R): Employer-Employee Relations; Workforce Protections (Chmn.). *International Relations* (10th of 26 R): International Operations and Human Rights; Western Hemisphere.

Group Ratings

	ADA	ACLU	AFS	LCV	CON	NTU	NFIB	COC	ACU	NTLC	CHC
1998	5	6	0	8	86	69	100	82	91	95	100
1997	10	—	0	—	58	58	—	100	83	—	—

National Journal Ratings

	1997 LIB	—	1997 CONS	1998 LIB	—	1998 CONS
Economic	10%	—	86%	21%	—	78%
Social	30%	—	64%	28%	—	71%
Foreign	38%	—	62%	34%	—	62%

Key Votes of the 105th Congress

1. Clinton Budget Deal	Y	5. Puerto Rico Sthood. Ref.	N	9. Cut $ for B-2 Bombers	Y
2. Education IRAs	Y	6. End Highway Set-asides	Y	10. Human Rights in China	N
3. Req. 2/3 to Raise Taxes	Y	7. School Prayer Amend.	Y	11. Withdraw Bosnia Troops	Y
4. Fast-track Trade	Y	8. Ovrd. Part. Birth Veto	Y	12. End Cuban TV-Marti	N

Election Results

1998 general	Cass Ballenger (R)	118,541	(86%)	($201,489)
	Deborah Garrett Eddins (Lib)	19,970	(14%)	
1998 general	Cass Ballenger (R)	unopposed		
1996 general	Cass Ballenger (R)	158,585	(70%)	($244,447)
	Ben Neill (D)	65,103	(29%)	($17,993)

ELEVENTH DISTRICT

Western North Carolina, the protrusion of the Tarheel state deep into the fastness of the eastern United States' highest and oldest mountains, is a land of long and ornery traditions. First settled by whites not long after the Revolutionary War, it still has tiny Indian communities and hollows where people are descended from the first white settlers. Its biggest city, Asheville, is memorialized in Thomas Wolfe's novels and was a retreat for lung patients in the early 20th Century. It was also the home of the brilliant eccentric George Vanderbilt, who built the chateau-like Biltmore mansion, and its vast forests, on which he pioneered scientific forestry. Over a ridge is the Great Smoky Mountains National Park, one of the nation's most heavily visited, 20 degrees cooler in the summer than the lowland towns an hour or so away. The climate and the forested, green, fog-wisped mountains have attracted millions of tourists and thousands of retirees to this area.

The 11th Congressional District is made up of the western end of North Carolina; its jagged boundaries in effect in 1992, 1994 and 1996 were smoothed out by the May 1998 redistricting plan. The orneriness of the mountain country has come out in its politics. This part of the state was reluctant to secede in the Civil War. There were few slaves and many small farmers loyal to the Union, and those who took up the Confederate cause did so out of loyalty to Governor Zebulon Vance, an Asheville native and reluctant secessionist himself. Ancestral party loyalties remain strong; local notables, like the Ponder family of Madison County, held power for years; the retirees in the mountains south of Asheville haven't tipped things much. The partisan balance here has been close, and for a dozen years the 11th was one of the nation's most closely contested districts, throwing out incumbents in five of six elections between 1980 and 1990.

The congressman from the 11th District is Charles Taylor, a Republican elected in 1990. He grew up in Brevard, where he has been a tree farmer and one of the biggest private land-holders in the area; his net worth was estimated by *Roll Call* at $12 million in 1999. He served in the legislature from 1966–74, and ran for Congress in 1988 and narrowly lost. In 1990 he ran again and won. Taylor has a very conservative voting record and has spent much energy on district projects. He worked to delay draw-downs of area lakes each year by the TVA until August 1, and later until October 1, to keep waters high for tourist season. He worked to get the Asheville veterans' hospital refurbished and obtained funding for the I-26 highway. He has worked for years on what he calls the Magnet Triangle economic development plan, to build three federal facilities which he says will double tourism in the area: the Blue Ridge Parkway headquarters, the Cradle of Forestry interpretive center near Brevard and the Oconaluftee museum and visitors' center. He ran a western North Carolina workforce consortium, to encourage training in skills needed in high-tech jobs.

Taylor has also been active on national issues. He was one of the members of 1991's Gang of Seven, Republican freshmen who pushed for full disclosure of overdrafts on the House bank and other congressional reforms. In the 104th Congress the House passed his property-rights protection amendments to the National Biological Survey and the Montana Wilderness Act. He sponsored the bills that greatly increased the timber salvage harvesting in national forests. Also passed was his amendment to stop EEOC guidelines he believed would promote religious harassment in workplaces; in 1996 he sought to protect religious radio stations from unfair FCC licensing practices. He sponsored the Congressional Gold Medal for Ruth and Billy Graham, residents of western North Carolina, which was awarded in May 1996.

Taylor got a seat on Appropriations in 1993, and in 1997 became chairman of the District of Columbia Subcommittee. He started off with the conviction that District spending was out of control, and tried to take more city functions away from Mayor Marion Barry and give them to the Congress-created Control Board. Speaker Newt Gingrich felt that Taylor was too abrasive and inclined to micromanagement, and gave the D.C. portfolio to northern Virginia's Tom Davis; he worked more smoothly, but in the end almost all of Barry's powers were given to the Control Board.

Taylor's confrontation-mindedness has angered some constituents. He argues that forestry policy should be made on the basis of sound science: "Forest policy is not bumper sticker simple, and protecting and furthering the values we cherish requires tough decisions, not 'feel-good responses.'" He vetoed local officials' application of the French Broad River to be one of Bill Clinton's American Heritage Rivers, which he considered a boondoggle that might intrude on property rights; when some constituents kept pestering him to talk about the issue, he said, "I don't know what part of no they don't understand." He proposed his own Western North Carolina Rivers Initiative instead. He irked them more by sponsoring a law to prohibit further designations of United Nations Biosphere Reserves in the United States; again his opponents argued that the designation wouldn't change anything but certainly must be maintained. It is not clear whether they were assuaged by his securing $20 million for tourist-clogged U.S. 19 near the Great Smoky Mountains National Park.

In August 1997 Taylor had what his doctors described as a "very minor" stroke which slurred his speech for a while, but seems to have fully recovered. He had underfunded opposition in 1998 from David Young, a travel agency owner and Buncombe County Commissioner who took conservative stands on partial-birth abortions and gun control. Despite much criticism from local activists, Taylor won 57%–42%, carrying all but one county.

Cook's Call. *Probably Safe.* Once one of the most highly competitive seats in the state (no incumbent won here with more than 53% of the vote from 1980–90), the 11th has been relatively quiet in the 1990s as Taylor has been re-elected here by wide margins. Taylor can expect a repeat challenge from 1998 nominee David Young, but this conservative and Republican trending district is still tough territory for a Democrat.

The People: Pop. 1990: 552,497; 68.7% rural; 18.4% age 65 + ; 92.8% White, 5.3% Black, 0.3% Asian, 1.4% Amer. Indian, 0.2% Other; 0.7% Hispanic Origin. Households: 59.3% married couple families; 24.1% married couple fams. w. children; 37.6% college educ.; median household income: $23,564; per capita income: $11,923; median house value: $59,700; median gross rent: $242.

1996 Presidential Vote			1992 Presidential Vote		
Dole (R)	109,629	(48%)	Bush (R)	106,119	(43%)
Clinton (D)	95,273	(42%)	Clinton (D)	102,905	(42%)
Perot (I)	21,255	(9%)	Perot (I)	35,325	(14%)

Rep. Charles H. Taylor (R)

Elected 1990; b. Jan. 23, 1941, Brevard; home, Brevard; Wake Forest U., B.A. 1963, J.D. 1966; Baptist; married (Elizabeth).

Elected Office: NC House of Reps., 1966–72, Minority Ldr., 1968–72; NC Senate, 1972–74, Minority Ldr., 1972–74.

Professional Career: Tree farmer.

DC Office: 231 CHOB 20515, 202-225-6401; Web site: www.house.gov/charlestaylor.

District Offices: Asheville, 828-251-1988; Hendersonville, 828-697-8539; Murphy, 828-837-3249; Rutherfordton, 828-286-8750.

Committees: *Appropriations* (13th of 34 R): Commerce, Justice, State & the Judiciary; Interior; The Legislative Branch (Chmn.).

Group Ratings

	ADA	ACLU	AFS	LCV	CON	NTU	NFIB	COC	ACU	NTLC	CHC
1998	5	6	22	0	4	62	100	88	96	97	100
1997	0	—	13	—	82	61	—	100	91	—	—

National Journal Ratings

	1997 LIB — 1997 CONS			1998 LIB — 1998 CONS		
Economic	10%	—	86%	12%	—	85%
Social	0%	—	90%	14%	—	81%
Foreign	32%	—	68%	32%	—	67%

Key Votes of the 105th Congress

1. Clinton Budget Deal	Y	5. Puerto Rico Sthood. Ref.	N	9. Cut $ for B-2 Bombers	N
2. Education IRAs	Y	6. End Highway Set-asides	Y	10. Human Rights in China	N
3. Req. 2/3 to Raise Taxes	Y	7. School Prayer Amend.	Y	11. Withdraw Bosnia Troops	Y
4. Fast-track Trade	N	8. Ovrd. Part. Birth Veto	Y	12. End Cuban TV-Marti	N

Election Results

1998 general	Charles H. Taylor (R)	112,908	(57%)	($826,274)
	David Young (D)	84,256	(42%)	($344,066)
	Others	2,259	(1%)	
1998 general	Charles H. Taylor (R)	unopposed		
1996 general	Charles H. Taylor (R)	132,860	(58%)	($481,658)
	James Mark Ferguson (D)	91,257	(40%)	($46,884)
	Others	3,908	(2%)	

TWELFTH DISTRICT

"This is perhaps the Negro's temporary farewell to Congress," said George White, a Tarboro, North Carolina lawyer and Republican, in his last days in the House of Representatives in 1901. Segregation was being imposed by law, and blacks informally but effectively were being stricken from the voting rolls in the rural South. It was 28 years until another black was elected to Congress and 70 years until another black won in the South. In North Carolina, although blacks have been politically influential since the Voting Rights Act of 1965, White's prophecy was not overturned until 1992, when two blacks were elected. One, Eva Clayton, was from the mostly rural and small-town 1st District—the kind of country where most blacks lived in White's day. The other, Melvin Watt, represents the new 12th District, whose original boundaries connected blacks in several different cities, and which were ruled unconstitutional by the Supreme Court.

The 12th District has been the most litigated district in the country during the 1990s. The boundaries in effect for the 1992, 1994 and 1996 elections were the most egregious example in the nation of the interpretation, urged by blacks and Republicans, that the 1982 revisions of the Voting Rights Act require the maximization of black percentages in congressional districts. It was called the I-85 district, because it consists of a series of urban black areas connected by a narrow line in some places no wider than I-85, splitting adjacent districts in two. It stretched from Gastonia, west of Charlotte, through Winston-Salem and Greensboro all the way to Durham. A lawsuit was brought, and in June 1993 the Supreme Court in *Shaw v. Reno*, focusing on the 12th, ordered the plan re-examined. On remand a three-judge federal court upheld the plan in August 1994. But in June 1996 the Supreme Court declared the 12th unconstitutional. The court allowed the 1996 election to be conducted under disapproved lines, but gave the legislature until April 1997 to come up with new ones. In March 1997 the legislature drew new lines, cutting off the Durham and Gastonia extremes but leaving the district much the same. That plan was overturned by a different three-judge court, and the legislature came up with a third plan in May 1998; this was used in 1998, with the primary delayed until September. This current 12th included the central and northern section of Charlotte and Mecklenburg County (45% black) and black neighborhoods in Winston-Salem and Forsyth County (61% black), connected by textile mill territory in Iredell, Rowan and Davidson counties (14% black). Overall the original 12th District was 57% black; the never-used April 1997 district was 37% black and the May 1998 district was 36% black. In May 1999, the Supreme Court unanimously reversed a three-judge court's 1998 conclusion that the 12th District was unlawfully drawn. That conclusion was made before a trial occurred, and the Supreme Court's decision will throw it back to the three-judge court for trial.

The congressman from the 12th District since it was created in 1992 has been Mel Watt, a Democrat. Watt grew up in a place called Dixie outside Charlotte, now overgrown with woods, in a tin-roofed house with no electricity or running water. His dream was to attend the University of North Carolina, and he was one of the first black students there; he made a fine academic record, went on to Yale Law School, and then to a civil rights law practice in Charlotte. Today he owns an elderly care facility and is part owner of McDonald's Cafeteria and Hotel in Charlotte—and has been starting pitcher on the House Democrats' baseball team. He served one term in the state Senate, then decided not to seek office again until his sons completed high school. He managed Harvey Gantt's campaigns for city council and mayor in the 1980s and for U.S. Senate in 1990. In 1992 Watt decided to run in the 12th District. The contest turned out to be the kind of friends-and-neighbors Democratic primary common in the old segregated South. Watt took 47% of all votes in a four-way race, well over the 40% necessary for victory without a runoff in North Carolina; his base in Charlotte was bigger than those of his rivals, and he made inroads in other counties as well. He won the general election easily, and on election night said he was "saddened that it took 92 years" to elect another black member to the state, "and I'm disappointed, because I know that thousands and thousands of people, but for the color of their skin, would have been just as qualified to fill this office."

In the House Watt has a very liberal voting record, the most liberal in the House in 1998. On one issue after another he has risked unpopular stands to defend principle. He refused to oppose the tobacco tax in the Clinton health care plan and backed a Canadian-style single-payer system. He has voted against crime bills because of their death penalty provisions, against increased penalties for hate crimes, against gun bans in urban housing projects, against increased prison sentences for crimes against children because he said it would interfere with the U.S. Sentencing Commission's autonomy. He voted against the 1996 terrorism bill, saying, "We can't sacrifice our constitutional principles because we're angry at people for bombing." He opposed the fence along the California-Mexico border. He attacked the 1996 juvenile justice bill as "the most extreme piece of legislation this committee will have considered during this term of Congress." He vehemently opposed the 1996 Welfare Reform Act, and on the "partial-birth" abortion ban, he wanted to put the burden of proving a woman's life in danger on the state. In 1996 he cast the only vote in the House against Megan's Law requiring registration of convicted sex offenders.

In 1998 the new boundaries of the district not only reduced the black percentage from 57% to 36%, they also reduced the Democratic registration from 77% to 65%; moreover, Watt had not previously represented 55% of the voters. Several Republicans clamored to run against him, and there was even a primary opponent. Watt won his primary 84%–16%, carrying 165 of 176 precincts: his support among white Democrats was solid. The Republican primary turned out to be a surprise. The winner was Scott Keadle, a Rowan County dentist and property developer, who had lost a race for county commissioner in 1996. But he had the support of popular Davidson County Sheriff Gerald Hege. Charlotte Councilman Mike Jackson, Mecklenburg County Commission Chairman Tom Bush and former Rowan County Commissioner Jim Cohen split the vote in Mecklenburg County, which cast almost one-third of the district's votes. Keadle nearly tied Cohen in Rowan County, but in Hege's Davidson County he won 47% in a six-candidate field. In this primary, North Carolina's usual requirement of 40% to win a first primary did not apply, and Keadle won with 28%, to 26% for Cohen, 19% for Jackson and 16% for Bush.

The numbers favored Watt in the general election, and he ran on standard Democratic issues—minimum wage increase, universal health care, setting aside the Social Security surplus. He cited his experience in Congress and his work in securing public housing money and various projects for the district. But Keadle, spending $91,000 of his own money and fortified by national Republican contributions, attacked Watt as an "extreme liberal" and called for major tax cuts. Then Keadle concentrated on Watt's vote against Megan's Law. A Keadle TV ad showed a little girl skipping down a sidewalk, then a sinister looking man coming out from behind a tree. "Mel Watt—the only vote against our children," it said. In their third and final debate Watt defended his vote by saying, "Would the next step be to register everyone who commits a murder?" But later he conceded that his vote had been wrong and said that he twice voted for funding for state compliance with the law. In some ways Watt even appealed to the establishment, citing his position on the Banking Committee—of great importance to Charlotte—and holding a fundraiser sponsored by the CEO of Food Lion.

Watt won 56%–42%, a decisive margin though far below what he had received in the old district. He ran well ahead of racial lines, winning 75% in Forsyth County, 69% in Mecklenburg County and 36% in the other three counties, which usually vote Republican. After the *Shaw v. Reno* decision was announced in 1993, Watt had been outraged. "You go down into North Carolina and you take a poll and 30% to 35% of the population will tell you under no circumstances, regardless of how qualified, would [they] vote for a black candidate. So there is a need for something that will equalize the playing field." But Watt had won 66% to 71% in a 57%-black district, and in this 36% black district he won 56%, and said shortly afterward, "I'd like to think it's an indication that race is becoming less of a factor as we go along." The argument made by many that Southern blacks cannot win in anything but black-majority districts seems refuted; indeed, Watt's margin was big enough to suggest that he would have won within these boundaries back in 1992 without the benefit of incumbency, although it's possible he might not have chosen to run.

In the House Judiciary Committee impeachment hearings Watt strongly opposed impeachment and peppered Chairman Henry Hyde with objections and dissents. His prospects for reelection in these boundaries or under the April 1997 plan are excellent. His future chances depend heavily on redistricting. The plaintiffs in the court cases against the old 12th say they want a district that includes most of Mecklenburg County; that would pit Watt against Republican Sue Myrick in a county whose total vote in 1998 went 54%–45% Republican. But if the Democrats retain the governorship and the legislature in 2000—a good possibility but not a sure thing—Watt is likely to get a new district with lines at least as favorable as this one.

Cook's Call. *Potentially Competitive.* In 1998, Watt had to contend with a dramatically altered district and an all-out Republican assault, but he still won by a significant margin. While it can be argued that Watt needs to work to solidify himself here, he has proven to be a tough contender.

The People: Pop. 1990: 551,957; 13.6% rural; 12.2% age 65 +; 62.7% White, 35.6% Black, 1% Asian, 0.3% Amer. Indian, 0.4% Other; 1% Hispanic Origin. Households: 41.5% married couple families; 19.8% married couple fams. w. children; 37.1% college educ.; median household income: $23,068; per capita income: $10,878; median house value: $58,400; median gross rent: $280.

1996 Presidential Vote			1992 Presidential Vote		
Clinton (D)	97,435	(54%)	Clinton (D)	103,634	(50%)
Dole (R)	71,166	(40%)	Bush (R)	76,684	(37%)
Perot (I)	10,475	(6%)	Perot (I)	26,438	(13%)

Rep. Melvin Watt (D)

Elected 1992; b. Aug. 26, 1945, Mecklenburg; home, Charlotte; U. of NC at Chapel Hill, B.S. 1967, Yale U., J.D. 1970; Presbyterian; married (Eulada).

Elected Office: NC Senate, 1984–86.

Professional Career: Practicing atty., 1971–92; Co-owner, East Town Manor nursing home, 1989–present; Campaign Mgr., Harvey Gantt Senate Campaign, 1990.

DC Office: 1230 LHOB 20515, 202-225-1510; Fax: 202-225-1512; Web site: www.house.gov/watt.

District Offices: Charlotte, 704-344-9950; Salisbury, 704-797-9950; Winston-Salem, 336-721-9950.

Committees: *Banking & Financial Services* (9th of 27 D): Domestic & International Monetary Policy; Financial Institutions & Consumer Credit. *Judiciary* (7th of 16 D): Commercial & Administrative Law; The Constitution (RMM). *Joint Economic Committee* (10th of 10 Reps.).

Group Ratings

	ADA	ACLU	AFS	LCV	CON	NTU	NFIB	COC	ACU	NTLC	CHC
1998	100	94	100	85	80	17	0	28	4	3	0
1997	100	—	100	—	4	21	—	30	4	—	—

National Journal Ratings

	1997 LIB — 1997 CONS			1998 LIB — 1998 CONS		
Economic	79%	—	18%	79%	—	0%
Social	85%	—	0%	93%	—	0%
Foreign	97%	—	0%	98%	—	0%

Key Votes of the 105th Congress

1. Clinton Budget Deal	N	5. Puerto Rico Sthood. Ref.	Y	9. Cut $ for B-2 Bombers	Y
2. Education IRAs	N	6. End Highway Set-asides	N	10. Human Rights in China	Y
3. Req. 2/3 to Raise Taxes	N	7. School Prayer Amend.	N	11. Withdraw Bosnia Troops	N
4. Fast-track Trade	N	8. Ovrd. Part. Birth Veto	N	12. End Cuban TV-Marti	Y

Election Results

1998 general	Melvin Watt (D)	82,305	(56%)	($641,416)
	John "Scott" Keadle (R)	62,070	(42%)	($381,065)
	Others	2,713	(2%)	
1998 general	Melvin Watt (D)	12,160	(84%)	
	Ronnie Adcock (D)	2,275	(16%)	
1996 general	Melvin Watt (D)	124,675	(71%)	($148,001)
	Joseph A. Martino Jr. (R)	46,581	(27%)	($6,902)
	Others	3,143	(2%)	

NORTH DAKOTA

For more than a century after statehood, North Dakota remained as close to its roots as any other state. Yet in its second century there are signs of change ahead. North Dakota was settled and its farm economy developed in a short generation. There are North Dakotans alive today who knew the men and women that settled this land and saw the state enter the Union in 1889. As children, they walked in the ruts left by the early settlers' wagon trains; they saw the Indians, recently defeated, herded onto reservations; they saw still shining new the rails that brought the world's commerce to these desolate prairies. This was the frontier to which Teddy Roosevelt came in 1884, determined to shoot one of the fast-disappearing buffalo, a place where settlers were only then breaking the sod and plowing under the natural prairies that are still preserved in a few places. This was some of the best wheat land in the world, empty by then of Indians and buffalo, connected to markets by rail, ready to become a cog in the industrial world being created by entrepreneurs and to raise its living standards to unparalleled heights.

And so, in a sudden rush of settlement during the 20 years before World War I, North Dakota filled up to pretty much its present population. There were 632,000 people here in 1920 and in counts since, the number has fluctuated between 617,000 and 680,000. In 1997 it was 641,000, and cumulatively it was the state with the lowest growth rate since 1950. Wheat is not the only crop here, there are also pinto beans, and as the plains become more arid to the west, ranching and livestock grazing—along with strip mining and oil and natural gas production—are important, and hardy root crops like potatoes and sugar beets grow as well. But wheat is still number one. Typically the state produces about one-tenth of the U.S. crop, and a fair percentage of the world's; its durum wheat is the main ingredient of American pasta.

This dependence on agriculture shaped North Dakota's politics. Farmers, as much as they like to extol their way of life, are seldom content with the workings of the market. When prices are high, it may be due to low production; when they are low they seek protection. The boosterish optimism of the first settlers was soon followed by cries reverberating with varying intensity for government protection against market forces. Since commodity prices tend to fall during periods of economic growth, there has been a countercyclical element in North Dakota politics, a tendency to vote against the national trends, and a radical strain going back to the 1910s and still lively in recent years. That radical strain also owes much to the immigrant origins of so many of North Dakota's early settlers: Norwegians in the eastern part of the state, Canadians along the northern border, Volga Germans (descendants of early 19th Century German migrants to Russia who kept their German language and customs) in the west, colonies of Poles and Czechs and Icelanders, and native Germans throughout the state.

These immigrants produced orderly small towns and grain and other cooperatives; they also provided support for the Non-Partisan League, which flourished from its founding in 1915 to its alliance with the Democratic Party around 1960. It appealed to marginal farmers, cut off in many cases from the wider American culture by language barriers and seemingly at the mercy of the grain millers in Minneapolis, the railroads of St. Paul, the banks of New York and the commodity traders of Chicago. The NPL's program was socialist—government ownership of railroads and grain elevators—and, like most North Dakota ethnics, it opposed going to war with Germany. The NPL often determined the outcome of the usually decisive Republican primary and sometimes swung its support to the otherwise heavily outnumbered Democrats, instituting reforms and creating a state-owned bank. By 1960, the NPL had more or less merged into the Democratic Party, a merger symbolized by the election of the late Democratic Senator Quentin Burdick, whose father, Usher Burdick, served 20 years in the House as an NPL-endorsed Republican. "Young Burdick," as he was long known, continued NPL tradition, supporting wheat subsidies and pork barrel projects and avoiding controversial cultural issues until his death in September 1992. North Dakota's leading Democrats of recent decades, Senators Kent Conrad and Byron Dorgan, have championed a politics clearly of NPL lineage: for government farm programs, wary if not hostile to American military involvement abroad, and cheerfully championing the little guy from North Dakota against out-of-state corporations.

This is a place where everyone knows everyone else—a fact much in evidence during the disastrous flooding in 1997. Some 70,000 people—10% of the state's population—were evacuated from the town and area surrounding Grand Forks when the accumulation of eight winter blizzards melted and raised the Red River 26 feet above flood stage. In late May 1997, a state rally, "Bigger, Better & Stronger," was held to help benefit the townspeople of Grand Forks and aid in their rebuilding efforts. This type of community spirit and heritage has also produced an innate conservatism in North Dakota. Divorce is as uncommon here as anywhere in the United States, the two-parent family is still very much the norm and abortions are available in only two clinics in the whole state. For years there was no voter registration because people would obviously spot anyone not eligible. North Dakota is proud that its students achieve some of the nation's highest math scores, even though its teacher pay is among the lowest in the country. The state also has among the lowest rates of student loan defaults and strikes. Politics is personal, too, in a state where every politician is known to many voters. North Dakota is one of only four states with an all-Democratic congressional delegation (Massachusetts, West Virginia and Hawaii are the others). The two senators and congressman are all allies who have worked together for years, at least since the 1974 campaign when Byron Dorgan, now junior senator, ran for the House, and lost; his campaign manager was Kent Conrad, now senior senator, and their driver was Earl Pomeroy, now congressman-at-large. The secret of their success was the office of state Tax commissioner, which Dorgan held from 1969 until his election to Congress in 1980, which was then held by Conrad until his election to the Senate

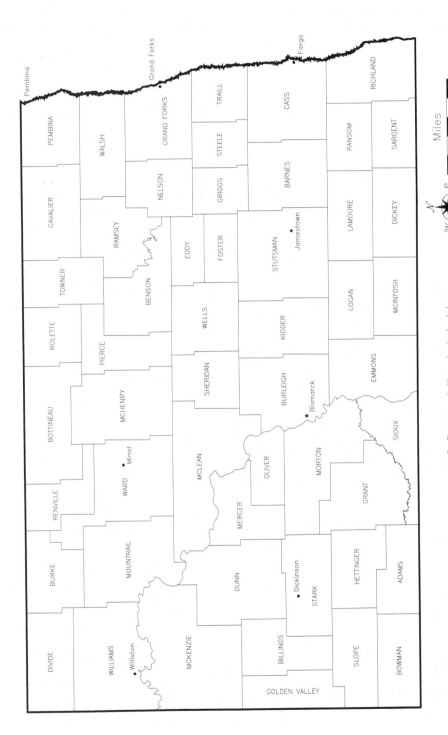

U.S. Representative elected at large.

Miles

in 1986; Pomeroy was elected Insurance commissioner in 1984. Dorgan pioneered and Conrad followed attempts to attribute out-of-state corporations' earnings to North Dakota operations and then tax them—very small potatoes to most big companies, but very helpful for thrift-minded, suspicious-of-big-corporations, farm-subsidy-hungry traditional North Dakota voters. Their interconnectedness and friendship continues: Lucy Calautti, Conrad's wife since 1986, has been a top staffer for Dorgan since 1974. And there are bipartisan connections as well: Conrad and Governor Ed Schafer were formerly brothers-in-law.

Yet there are signs of change even in this settled commonwealth. Increasing agricultural productivity has meant fewer farmers living directly off the land, and more people living in towns and off other industries. North Dakota's four biggest counties, containing Fargo, Grand Forks, Bismarck and Minot, grew from 134,000 in 1930 to 310,000 in 1996, while the state's other 48 counties dropped from 546,000 to 333,000. The diversification touted by Governor Ed Schafer has come along just as Congress passed the Freedom to Farm Act, phasing out wheat subsidies over seven years by 2002. Falling wheat prices in 1998 triggered demands for more federal aid and blockades of wheat on the Canadian border; but Congress agreed only to accelerate the 1999 Freedom to Farm transition payments, and the number of farmers dipped below 30,000. Unemployment in late 1997 was down to 1.9%, the lowest in the nation, and if wages tended to be low and home ownership dropped, these were still not the prerequisites to the old style of farm rebellion. Schafer led a delegation to Winnipeg to study the Canadian Wheat Board, which buys all of western Canada's wheat and markets it in large quantities; but North Dakotans were interested in this only as a voluntary option, not a mandatory requirement as it is north of the border. Politicians still pay homage to family farmers, but as their numbers decline, they no longer seem to have the critical mass to drive politics. Instead the movement is toward what some academics call "the Buffalo Commons." Bison have been reintroduced on Indian reservations and ranches, and North Dakota has the nation's only meatpacking plant specializing in buffalo.

On balance these developments tend to undermine the state's radical tradition and remove the advantage that farm subsidies have long given Democrats. If the typical elderly North Dakotan is a hard-working retired farmer, with fond memories of NPL agitation and a belief in government programs, the typical young North Dakotan is a family person with a college education (49% of the state's households have college graduates) more trusting of markets and the private sector. They may have noticed that nearby South Dakota has attracted white-collar jobs with low tax rates and that North Dakota, with its higher taxes and pro-government traditions, is the one Great Plains state that lost population in the first years of the 1990s—but now has lower taxes and hopes for increased economic growth. This was one state where George Bush and Bob Dole fairly easily beat Bill Clinton in 1992 and 1996, and the trend is for older North Dakotans to vote heavily Democratic and younger North Dakotans Republican. It's too soon to say that North Dakota has moved away from its radical political roots, but a conservative strain in its heritage is asserting itself as well.

Governor. North Dakota's skyscraper Capitol, towering over neatly-kept Bismarck and the rolling plains beyond, now houses more Republicans in high office than at any time since the NPL allied with the Democrats, starting with Governor Ed Schafer, who in 1996 became the first Republican governor re-elected since 1958. Schafer grew up in Bismarck, where his father founded Gold Seal, makers of Gold Seal glass wax, Snowy Bleach and Mr. Bubble. Schafer worked for the firm, in New Jersey and North Dakota, then headed a classic car dealership, Dakota Classics, and in 1991 started an aquaculture fish farm, Fish 'N Dakota. He ran for Congress in 1990 against Byron Dorgan and won 35% of the vote. In 1992 he ran for governor and did not seem the favorite. But popular Governor George Sinner retired, Democrats had a primary fight, and Schafer's call for more local and private sector development evidently appealed more than Democrat Nick Spaeth's "Growing North Dakota" plan. Schafer won by a solid 58%–41%, carrying all the major towns and all but seven counties, winning over 60% with voters under 60, while Spaeth got 55% from those 60 and over.

Schafer says his goal is to constantly scale back the reach of the state: "Today, when what people require of government is more efficiency and less cost, a vision of a smaller government is every bit as visionary as adding a whole bunch of new programs or vanity projects." In his first term he lowered taxes and "rightsized government." He called for economic diversification: "I think we'll look back on the 1990s and say North Dakota broadened its perspective beyond straight production, agriculture and energy." He claims credit for a 10% increase in jobs and for the fact that 1996 Census estimates showed North Dakota gaining population for the first time in more than a decade. He boasts that the number of state employees is down and state government's share of personal income has declined after years of increases.

That record has brought more success to Republicans, who won control of the state Senate in 1994. In 1996 Schafer won a smashing 66%–34% victory over Democrat Lee Kaldor, carrying all but three counties, and Republicans gained a seat in the Senate. In 1997 Schafer called for streamlining North Dakota's road system (it has more state roads per capita than any other state), working on international marketing of North Dakota products, and setting higher standards for public schools. In 1999 he called for continuing increases in public school and higher education spending, with $17 million set aside for salary increases for outstanding professors, and sought to increase vehicle fees and maintain the 20 cent gas tax to fund highway spending; state legislators from both parties questioned his sudden $20 million increase for prisons in a state that has the lowest per capita prison population in America. Meanwhile, Schafer was dogged through 1998 by demands that he pay back taxes on the Fish 'N Dakota property; this tilapia farm under a white bubble in North Dakota's coal country turned out to lose money. He paid the 1994–97 taxes, and avoided a foreclosure sale; in January 1999 he walked into the Mercer County courthouse and paid the debt off with a check for $198,000.

In 1997 Republican activists tried to get Schafer to run against Senator Byron Dorgan; he was not interested. In early 1999, he said, "At this point in time, it's unlikely that I'll run for a third term, but I'll leave the door open." Republicans did not seem to have other strong candidates for 2000, and Schafer said that if a "formidable" Democrat like Congressman Earl Pomeroy or Attorney General Heidi Heitkamp ran, he might be more inclined to do so. Pomeroy, who has been winning statewide elective office since 1984, is widely considered likely to run.

Cook's Call. *Probably Safe.* Schafer is very likely to win re-election in this solidly Republican state. Attorney General Heidi Heitkamp would be the dream Democratic candidate and would present a serious challenge to Schafer, but most do not believe that she will challenge the governor.

Senior Senator. Kent Conrad, North Dakota's senior senator, was first elected in 1986. He grew up in North Dakota; his parents were killed in an auto accident when he was five, and he was raised by his grandparents. He went to college at Stanford, then returned in 1974 to work on Byron Dorgan's unsuccessful House campaign. When Dorgan ran for Congress again in 1980, Conrad ran for tax commissioner and won; when Dorgan declined the opportunity again, in 1986 Conrad ran against Senator Mark Andrews, and won 50%–49%. In 1986 Conrad earnestly promised not to run again unless "the federal deficit, the trade deficit and real interest rates will be brought under control." By 1992 the latter two arguably were, and he could argue that he had worked to cut the budget deficit, calling for crackdowns on tax cheats, higher taxes on the top income brackets, and across-the-board freezes in some discretionary spending. He supported Most Favored Nation status for China, a major buyer of North Dakota wheat; he backed coal and alternative fuels research to help North Dakota's lignite deposits. Early 1992 polls showed Conrad well ahead, but in April 1992, after ruminating on the issue and after his wife had been mugged and dragged down the street near their Capitol Hill home, Conrad announced he was retiring because he had not kept his pledge.

Then in September 1992, the elderly Senator Quentin Burdick, no ally of Dorgan and Conrad, died. State law said a special election had to be held after November but before January, so Conrad ran for this seat while serving his last month in the other. This was awkward, but

Conrad's earnestness, on display in more than 1,000 town meetings over six years, helped. He was nominated unanimously at the Democratic state convention. His Republican opponent called for an absurdly expensive $5 per bushel wheat program, and an anti-abortion independent lambasted Conrad; but he had far more money and won easily, 63%–34%. For a few hours in December 1992, Conrad held both Senate seats: he was sworn in December 14 to fill Burdick's term, and a few hours later Dorgan was sworn in to fill his. In 1994 this seat came up again. Republican Ben Clayburgh, 70-year-old former head of the state medical association, accused Conrad of voting most of the time with Bill Clinton; Conrad responded with an ad saying he voted with Bob Dole more than 50% of the time. Dole endorsed Clayburgh, but Conrad won by a reduced margin of 58%–42%.

As on his pledge to serve a second term, Conrad has often taken popular positions on issues that are in tension with each other, then agonizingly resolving them when they come into conflict. Foremost among them is the balanced budget amendment. Conrad voted for it in 1994, but when Dorgan pushed an amendment taking Social Security out of deficit calculations, Conrad negotiated first in the Republican and then in the Democratic cloakroom, emerging to cast the decisive vote against the amendment in March 1995; he voted against it again in February 1997. On the specifics of the budget, he backed both the Senate Democrats' and the bipartisan Chafee-Breaux budgets in late 1995; his own proposal was rejected 60–39 in May 1996. On the 1996 Welfare Reform Act, he supported block grants to states for welfare programs, but successfully passed an amendment to keep food aid a federal program.

For years North Dakota senators tended closely to the details of farm bills, especially wheat subsidies, and then often voted against the every-four-year farm bills as insufficiently generous. But in 1995 Republicans proposed to phase out farm subsidies over seven years. Conrad naturally opposed this, as he opposed NAFTA on farm issues. He argued that this Freedom to Farm Act would reduce the number of farmers in North Dakota and attacked the transition payments, which compensated farmers who had relied on the subsidies, for being unbased on need or market prices. But Freedom to Farm passed anyway. In 1997, as North Dakota was battered by floods and by thunderstorms in calving season, Conrad pushed successfully for $500 million in flood relief and various farm relief measures—indemnity relief for those affected by freakish bad weather and speedier availability of crop insurance. But Conrad and other Great Plains Democrats had to give up their attempts to overturn Freedom to Farm and their attempts to somehow insulate North Dakota farmers from the long-term trend, observable for all basic commodities in market economies, for wheat prices to fall.

Another Conrad issue was tobacco. In 1997 Minority Leader Tom Daschle named him head of a Democratic task force on tobacco. For months he worked to forge a party position. In February 1998 he announced it: a $1.50 per pack cigarette tax, FDA authority to regulate tobacco, resolution of pending legal claims and money for Clinton Administration tobacco initiatives. The Clinton Administration promptly endorsed it. But it was overtaken by the bill John McCain got near-unanimous support for in the Commerce Committee, and by the tobacco companies' refusal to cooperate once their liability was left open. Conrad replied contemptuously: "Poor babies. We don't need their blessing to pass tough tobacco legislation. In many ways this is liberating—do it right, and not try to dance around their approval. They weren't going to approve of anything that was any good anyway." But Conrad's approach was abandoned and McCain's failed to prevail.

On other issues, Conrad has used his seat on Armed Services to keep Grand Forks and Minot Air Force Bases operational. North Dakota is the nation's one missile defense site authorized by the Anti-Ballistic Missile treaty; Conrad opposed Republican efforts to increase missile defense programs, insisting that the ABM treaty should not be weakened and opposing any missile defense deployment in space, at sea or from multiple ground sites (i.e., from anywhere else but North Dakota). He supports the e-rate telephone tax to pay for wiring schools for the Internet; he sponsored a Healthy Kids Web Site Contest in which more than 65 North Dakota high-schoolers constructed Web sites on the perils of tobacco use. He supports the J-1 visa waiver to allow foreign medical school graduates to remain in the United States. He opposed fast track, the only Finance Committee member to do so in October 1997. When Republicans attempted to bring other measures up in the 1997 flood relief bill, Conrad said truculently, "There is a tradition of people taking advantage of our states. We're going to fight back. We're not going to take it lying down."

Conrad comes up for re-election in 2000. In early 1999 it was not clear whether he would run, but it would be a stunning surprise if he doesn't.

Cook's Call. *Safe.* Conrad does not appear vulnerable and most political strategists agree that about the only candidate who could give him a competitive race is Governor Edward Schafer. Schafer is eligible to seek re-election and seems more interested in that than in challenging Conrad.

Junior Senator. Byron Dorgan, who first held statewide office in 1969 and has often had the highest popularity ratings in North Dakota, was finally elected to the Senate in 1992. Dorgan grew up in Regent, North Dakota, where his family had a farm equipment and petroleum business and raised cattle and horses. After college and business school he worked for a Denver aerospace firm, then in 1969, at 26, was appointed tax commissioner. His politics are very much out of the NPL tradition: he has a strong mistrust of economic markets, a deep belief that government should intervene to protect the family farmer and small businessman, and a capacity to frame issues in a popular and unthreatening way. His first big issue, as tax commissioner, was taxing out-of-state corporations, which struck a chord in a state always hostile to big out-of-state money. To his work Dorgan brought the zest and cornball good humor that New Deal enthusiasts liked to summon up when liberals thought they represented the ordinary, inarticulate little guy, in contrast to the conservatives seen as old stuffed shirts. On the House Ways and Means Committee, he called for more tax audits, opposed intangibles write-offs for corporate takeovers, and opposed the use of high-yield bonds for corporate takeovers. He has always fought for farm subsidies, especially payments to farmers when prices are low; he vigorously attacked the 1996 Freedom to Farm Act and promised to revisit the issue when Democrats have more votes.

Dorgan was vastly popular as tax commissioner and congressman-at-large; his lowest percentage was in 1990, 65% against now-Governor Ed Schafer. But, having lost a House race to Mark Andrews in 1974, he declined to challenge Andrews for the Senate in 1986 or 80-year-old fellow-Democrat Quentin Burdick in 1988. Only with Conrad's surprise decision not to run for re-election in 1992 did he finally run for the Senate. He and his Republican opponent both backed Most Favored Nation trade status for China (a major buyer of North Dakota wheat), but remained wary of free trade otherwise and opposed the regulations which have classified hundreds of seasonal puddles in North Dakota as protected wetlands. Dorgan won by a solid but not overwhelming 59%–39% margin—similar to Conrad's in 1994.

In the Senate, Dorgan's voting record has been almost exactly the same as Conrad's; this is one case where senators of the same party from the same state have worked harmoniously together. Dorgan strongly backed fellow Dakotan Tom Daschle for Senate Democratic leader in 1994, and became an assistant floor leader; in December 1998 he became co-chairman of the Democratic Policy Committee. Dorgan continues to be a champion of family farms, even as their numbers fall: "This isn't just about dollars and cents. The country will lose something very important. Family values roll from family farms to small towns to big cities." He worked with Conrad for the $500 million package of relief for farmers suffering losses from scab disease, floods and drought in 1998; but they were not successful in overturning the 1996 Freedom to Farm Act. He deplored the Cargill-Continental merger that produced one firm with control of one-third of the country's grain exports and one-third of its port facilities, but was unable to stop it. He sought a ban on Canadian wheat shipments, then a requirement that they all come through one border crossing; both in vain. He and Conrad tried to get Bill Clinton to intervene in the Northwest Airlines strike in September 1998. In 1997 he promised to "use every parliamentary procedure that is available and any that I can think of" to stop fast track;

but he was beaten by 69–31 and fast track had a clear majority in the Senate, although it was ultimately shelved for lack of House votes.

On taxes, he was the initial promoter of the move not to count Social Security revenues or outlays in the balanced budget amendment; this defeated the amendment in March 1995 and February 1997. He has not succeeded in changing the budget procedure, but did increase awareness of the current surplus position of payroll tax funds. In December 1997 he came forward with a tax plan which would give under-$100,000 taxpayers the option of a 15% flat tax, plus the home mortgage interest deduction, to be withheld from paychecks, so that no tax return need be filed. Uncomfortable with the capital gains tax reduction, he proposed a $1 million lifetime cap on taxpayers and sought to sunset the rate cut in 2002 unless the budget was balanced then. With a career based on taxing out-of-staters, he proposed a tax on foreign airline overflights and got Ron Wyden to agree to grandfather existing Internet taxes in his bill to prohibit them for five years. He sought to eliminate tax deductions for companies that build plants abroad, to limit deregulation in the 1996 Telecommunications Act, and to reduce the coverage of the product liability bill.

Republicans had a difficult time finding someone to oppose Dorgan in 1998. Attempts to draft Governor Ed Schafer went nowhere. In early 1998 Fargo nudist rights advocate Crystal Dueker said she would run "if no one else wants it. I'll be the sacrificial virgin. I just want to be there for the party." She added, "I fight to win. I know how to kick a man where it hurts." But she bowed out in March after Fargo police had her hospitalized for psychiatric evaluation. The eventual Republican nominee, state Senator Donna Nalewaja, peppered Dorgan with press releases and called on him to observe the limits of the McCain-Feingold campaign finance bill he supported. No go: she spent only $152,000; he had $200,000 on hand after the campaign compared to her $800. Dorgan won 63%–35%, carrying every county but one; the vote in Sheridan County was 423–423. His vote was highest among elderly North Dakotans, but he carried every demographic group by wide margins.

Representative-At-Large. Earl Pomeroy, North Dakota's single House member, is a Democrat first elected in 1992. Pomeroy grew up in Valley City, and after college served as Byron Dorgan's driver during the 1974 campaign, then went to law school and practiced law in Valley City. In 1980, when Dorgan and Conrad won statewide elections, Pomeroy at 28 won a seat in the legislature; in 1984 and 1988 he was elected insurance commissioner (his brother Glenn Pomeroy is insurance commissioner now). In 1992, he was planning to retire from politics and serve in the Peace Corps in Russia; then Dorgan ran for Conrad's seat in the Senate and Pomeroy ran for Dorgan's seat in the House. Articulate, cheerful and sincere, a critic of insurance companies yet unabrasive, he was the obvious choice for the House seat and was nominated unanimously by the Democratic convention. He won the general 57%–39%, almost exactly Dorgan's margin in the Senate race.

Pomeroy has compiled a moderate to liberal voting record, defending North Dakota interests and working with Republicans as well as Democrats on many issues. He served on the Budget Committee in his first term, and voted for both the Clinton budget and the Penny-Kasich spending cuts in 1993 and opposed the Clinton health care plan. In the Republican Congress he supported the Blue Dog budget and backed a $5,000 tax deduction for college tuition and job training. He strongly supported the adoption tax credit and brought his two-year-old daughter, adopted from Korea, onto the floor for the vote. He formed a bipartisan, bicameral committee to seek consensus on retirement and pension issues; Pomeroy, with his experience as insurance commissioner, wants to help people with their lifelong project of accumulation of wealth. He has sponsored bills to help small businesses set up pension plans and to allow employees moving from non-profit to for-profit employers to shift money from 403(b)s to 401(k)s. In the 105th Congress he became co-chair of the House Democrats' task force on Social Security. He supported the program the Clinton Administration sketched out in March 1999: investing 15% of the Social Security trust fund in private equities. He argues that such government investment would amount to only 4% of the entire stock market and that it would be insulated from political manipulation by an independent oversight board and by competition between private fund managers, who would invest in broad market index funds. He argues that individual retirement accounts would have high administrative costs and would not provide survivor benefits for women or disability coverage. But this is not a plan likely to pass in a Republican, or probably even a Democratic, Congress.

Though not averse to all change in farm programs, Pomeroy opposed the Freedom to Farm Act. "I think Freedom to Farm is essentially a bait-and-switch proposition," he said. "By the year 2003, you've got nothing—no check, no protection against price collapse." He criticized the cutoff of farm loans after the 1996 bill passed; he authored the wetlands reform provisions of the act. He wants to transform crop insurance into "almost a revenue-protection system." Like other North Dakotans, he has decried what he calls Canadian wheat "dumping" and has sought government action against it. On trade, Pomeroy broke with the state's two Democratic senators and supported fast track in November 1997. But after Canada blocked an audit of the Canadian Wheat Board which Trade Representative Charlene Barshefsky promised, he opposed fast track in October 1997 and accused Republicans of political maneuvering for bringing it up again. He worked to support the administration position in the balanced budget negotiations in May 1997 and worked on the children's health insurance bill that year. He and the two North Dakota senators expressed doubts about the global warming treaty in December 1997. He switched his vote at the last minute to pass the Puerto Rico status bill in March 1998 by a 209–208 vote: "I had no business sinking that vote and I had to make it right. I have terrific respect for the delegate from Puerto Rico and he deserved better treatment than that."

During the devastating Grand Forks flooding in April 1997, he helped man the dikes and slept in a nearby Air Force shelter in order to help residents deal with the disaster; later he worked and got nearly $500 million in flood relief, and has worked for a $300 million system of levees and walls to prevent future floods. On other local issues, he got funds for flood relief and an outlet for Devils Lake, which has tripled its size in recent years, and got the Appropriations Committee to restore funding for the USDA's Northern Great Plains Research Center in Mandan.

Pomeroy has had serious challenges every two years. In 1994 businessman Gary Porter used his own money to match the incumbent's spending, attacking Pomeroy for supporting the 1994 crime bill with its gun control provisions. Pomeroy won 52%–45%, carrying the four largest counties by only 50%–48%. In 1996 and 1998 he was opposed by state Economic Development and Finance Director Kevin Cramer. In 1996, with $604,000 in PAC contributions, Pomeroy outspent him by more than 2–1 and increased his margin to 55%–43%, carrying the four largest counties 53%–45%. In 1998 Cramer peppered Pomeroy with negative ads, charging he hadn't done enough for farmers, criticizing his pro-choice position and for flip-flopping on fast track. He also attacked him for seeking to invest Social Security funds in the stock market. In a pro-incumbent year, Pomeroy increased his percentage to 56%–41%, and 54%–44% in the four largest counties, which cast 43% of the state's votes. Pomeroy and his family moved from the Washington suburbs to Bismarck in early 1997, and he is widely expected to run for governor in 2000. If he does leave the seat open, it will probably be seriously contested, and Republicans would have their best chance of winning it since 1978.

Cook's Call. *Probably Safe.* No Democrat can feel entirely safe in this conservative leaning state, but, despite a couple of close calls, Pomeroy has won here rather handily. Pomeroy has publicly flirted with retiring in the past, and if he does, this seat will be up for grabs. Until then, Pomeroy has the edge.

Presidential politics. Massachusetts, West Virginia and Hawaii, the other states with all-Democratic congressional delegations, are heavily Democratic in presidential elections; North Dakota is Republican. In 1996 Bob Dole carried the state by a respectable though not dazzling 47%–40%. North Dakota has been one of Ross Perot's strongest states; he got 23% here in 1992 and 12% in 1996. An echo of the Non-Partisan League?

With a tiny delegation, an out-of-the-way location and frigid weather in the early primary season, North Dakota does not loom large in choosing presidential nominees. The Democrats hold a caucus, the Republicans a primary, which was switched in 1996 from the latest in the country to February, just a week after New Hampshire. Fellow prairie man Dole beat Steve Forbes 42%–20%.

The People: Est. Pop. 1998: 638,244; Pop. 1990: 638,800, down 0.1% 1990–1998. 0.2% of U.S. total, 47th largest; 46.7% rural. Median age: 34.9 years. 14.9% 65 years and over. 94.7% White, 0.6% Black, 0.5% Asian, 4% Amer. Indian, 0.3% Other; 0.7% Hispanic Origin. Households: 59.1% married couple families; 29.8% married couple fams. w. children; 48.6% college educ.; median household income: $23,213; per capita income: $11,051; 65.6% owner occupied housing; median house value: $50,800; median monthly rent: $266. 3.2% Unemployment. 1998 Voting age pop.: 476,000. 1998 Turnout: 217,584; 46% of VAP. No state voter registration.

Political Lineup: Governor, Edward T. Schafer (R); Lt. Gov., Rosemarie Myrdal (R); Secy. of State, Alvin Jaeger (R); Atty. Gen., Heidi Heitkamp (D); Treasurer, Kathi Gilmore (D); State Senate, 49 (19 D, 30 R); Majority Leader, Gary Nelson (R); State House, 98 (34 D, 64 R); House Speaker, Francis Wald (R). Senators, Kent Conrad (D) and Byron Dorgan (D). Representative, 1 D at large.

Elections Division: 701-328-4146; **Filing Deadline for U.S. Congress:** April 14, 2000.

1996 Presidential Vote

Dole (R)	125,050	(47%)
Clinton (D)	106,905	(40%)
Perot (I)	32,515	(12%)

1992 Presidential Vote

Bush (R)	136,244	(44%)
Clinton (D)	99,168	(32%)
Perot (I)	71,084	(23%)

1996 Republican Presidential Primary

Dole (R)	26,832	(42%)
Forbes (R)	12,455	(20%)
Buchanan (R)	11,653	(18%)
Gramm (R)	5,997	(9%)
Alexander (R)	4,008	(6%)
Others	2,789	(4%)

GOVERNOR
Gov. Edward T. Schafer (R)

Elected 1992, term expires Jan. 2000; b. Aug. 8, 1946, Bismarck; home, Bismarck; U. of ND, B.A. 1969, U. of Denver, M.B.A. 1970; Episcopalian; married (Nancy).

Professional Career: Gold Seal Co., 1971–86, Pres., 1978–86; Founder & Secy-Treas., American Eagle beverage distributorship, 1976–present; Pres. & owner, Dakota Classics auto dealership, and TRIESCO Properties real estate, 1986–present; Pres. & owner, Fish 'N Dakota aquaculture, 1990–94.

Office: State Capitol, 600 E. Boulevard, Bismarck, 58505, 701-328-2200; Fax: 701-328-2205; Web site: www.state.nd.us.

Election Results

1996 gen.	Edward T. Schafer (R)	174,937	(66%)
	Lee Kaldor (D)	89,349	(34%)
1996 prim.	Edward T. Schafer (R)	unopposed	
1992 gen.	Edward T. Schafer (R)	176,398	(58%)
	Nicholas Spaeth (D)	123,845	(41%)

SENATORS

Sen. Kent Conrad (D)

Elected 1986, seat up 2000; b. Mar. 12, 1948, Bismarck; home, Bismarck; Stanford U., B.A. 1971, George Washington U., M.B.A. 1975; Unitarian; married (Lucy Calautti).

Elected Office: ND Tax Commissioner, 1981–86.

Professional Career: Asst., ND Tax Commissioner, 1974–80; Dir., Mgmt. Planning & Personnel, ND Tax Dept., 1980.

DC Office: 530 HSOB, 20510, 202-224-2043; Fax: 202-224-7776; Web site: www.senate.gov/~conrad.

State Offices: Bismarck, 701-258-4648; Fargo, 701-232-8030; Grand Forks, 701-775-9601; Minot, 701-852-0703.

Committees: *Agriculture, Nutrition & Forestry* (3d of 8 D): Forestry, Conservation & Rural Revitalization (RMM); Marketing, Inspection & Product Promotion. *Budget* (3d of 10 D). *Ethics (Select)* (2d of 3 D). *Finance* (5th of 9 D): Health Care; International Trade; Taxation & IRS Oversight. *Indian Affairs* (2d of 6 D).

Group Ratings

	ADA	ACLU	AFS	LCV	CON	NTU	NFIB	COC	ACU	NTLC	CHC
1998	90	57	100	63	30	10	33	61	16	7	9
1997	65	—	67	—	57	31	—	50	16	—	—

National Journal Ratings

	1997 LIB	—	1997 CONS	1998 LIB	—	1998 CONS
Economic	71%	—	25%	75%	—	20%
Social	51%	—	45%	54%	—	45%
Foreign	73%	—	19%	79%	—	15%

Key Votes of the 105th Congress

1. Bal. Budget Amend.	N	5. Satcher for Surgeon Gen.	Y	9. Chem. Weapons Treaty	Y
2. Clinton Budget Deal	Y	6. Highway Set-asides	Y	10. Cuban Humanitarian Aid	Y
3. Cloture on Tobacco	Y	7. Table Child Gun locks	Y	11. Table Bosnia Troops	Y
4. Education IRAs	N	8. Ovrd. Part. Birth Veto	Y	12. $ for Test-ban Treaty	Y

Election Results

1994 general	Kent Conrad (D)	137,157	(58%)	($1,927,866)
	Ben Clayburgh (R)	99,390	(42%)	($941,192)
1994 primary	Kent Conrad (D)	unopposed		
1992 special	Kent Conrad (D)	103,246	(63%)	($2,479,021)
	Jack Dalrymple (R)	55,194	(34%)	($282,104)

Sen. Byron Dorgan (D)

Elected 1992, seat up 2004; b. May 14, 1942, Dickinson; home, Bismarck; U. of ND, B.S. 1965, U. of Denver, M.B.A. 1966; Lutheran; married (Kimberly).

Elected Office: ND Tax Commissioner, 1969–80; U.S. House of Reps., 1980–92.

Professional Career: Martin-Marietta Exec. Develop. Prog., 1966–68; ND Dpty. Tax Commissioner, 1968–69.

DC Office: 713 HSOB, 20510, 202-224-2551; Fax: 202-224-1193; Web site: www.senate.gov/~dorgan.

State Offices: Bismarck, 701-250-4618; Fargo, 701-239-5389; Minot, 701-852-0703.

Committees: *Appropriations* (11th of 13 D): Agriculture & Rural Development; Defense; Energy & Water Development; Interior; Treasury & General Government (RMM). *Commerce, Science & Transportation* (7th of 9 D): Aviation; Communications; Manufacturing & Competitiveness (RMM); Science, Technology & Space; Surface Transportation & Merchant Marine. *Energy & Natural Resources* (3d of 9 D): Energy, Research, Development, Production & Regulation; Water & Power (RMM). *Indian Affairs* (6th of 6 D).

Group Ratings

	ADA	ACLU	AFS	LCV	CON	NTU	NFIB	COC	ACU	NTLC	CHC
1998	90	71	100	63	30	12	33	61	12	7	9
1997	80	—	89	—	6	17	—	50	16	—	—

National Journal Ratings

	1997 LIB — 1997 CONS			1998 LIB — 1998 CONS		
Economic	88%	—	10%	75%	—	20%
Social	51%	—	45%	55%	—	43%
Foreign	73%	—	19%	79%	—	15%

Key Votes of the 105th Congress

1. Bal. Budget Amend.	N	5. Satcher for Surgeon Gen.	Y
2. Clinton Budget Deal	N	6. Highway Set-asides	Y
3. Cloture on Tobacco	Y	7. Table Child Gun locks	Y
4. Education IRAs	N	8. Ovrd. Part. Birth Veto	Y

9. Chem. Weapons Treaty	Y
10. Cuban Humanitarian Aid	Y
11. Table Bosnia Troops	Y
12. $ for Test-ban Treaty	Y

Election Results

1998 general	Byron Dorgan (D)	134,747	(63%)	($1,681,842)
	Donna Nalewaja (R)	75,013	(35%)	($152,183)
	Others	3,598	(2%)	
1998 primary	Byron Dorgan (D)	unopposed		
1992 general	Byron Dorgan (D)	179,347	(59%)	($1,124,512)
	Steve Sydness (R)	118,162	(39%)	($498,107)
	Others	6,448	(2%)	

REPRESENTATIVE

Rep. Earl Pomeroy (D)

Elected 1992; b. Sept. 2, 1952, Valley City; home, Valley City; U. of ND, B.A. 1974, J.D., 1979; Presbyterian; married (Laurie Kirby).

Elected Office: ND House of Reps., 1980–84; ND Insurance Commissioner, 1984–92.

Professional Career: Practicing atty., 1979–84; Natl. Assn. of Insurance Commissioners., Vice Pres. 1989, Pres. 1990.

DC Office: 1533 LHOB, 20515, 202-225-2611; Fax: 202-226-0893; e-mail epomeroy@hr.house.gov.

District Offices: Bismarck, 701-224-0355; Fargo, 701-235-9760.

Committees: *Agriculture* (9th of 24 D): General Farm Commodities, Resource Conservation & Credit; Risk Management, Research & Specialty Crops. *International Relations* (18th of 23 D): Asia & the Pacific; Western Hemisphere.

Group Ratings

	ADA	ACLU	AFS	LCV	CON	NTU	NFIB	COC	ACU	NTLC	CHC
1998	90	53	84	38	89	25	43	50	21	27	9
1997	70	—	75	—	67	30	—	60	38	—	—

National Journal Ratings

	1997 LIB — 1997 CONS	1998 LIB — 1998 CONS
Economic	60% — 40%	68% — 30%
Social	64% — 36%	60% — 38%
Foreign	79% — 21%	56% — 42%

Key Votes of the 105th Congress

1. Clinton Budget Deal	N	5. Puerto Rico Sthood. Ref.	Y	9. Cut $ for B-2 Bombers	Y
2. Education IRAs	N	6. End Highway Set-asides	N	10. Human Rights in China	Y
3. Req. 2/3 to Raise Taxes	N	7. School Prayer Amend.	N	11. Withdraw Bosnia Troops	N
4. Fast-track Trade	N	8. Ovrd. Part. Birth Veto	Y	12. End Cuban TV-Marti	Y

Election Results

1998 general	Earl Pomeroy (D)	119,668	(56%)	($775,948)
	Kevin Cramer (R)	87,511	(41%)	($321,242)
	Others	5,709	(3%)	
1998 primary	Earl Pomeroy (D)	unopposed		
1996 general	Earl Pomeroy (D)	144,833	(55%)	($971,332)
	Kevin Cramer (R)	113,684	(43%)	($434,082)
	Others	4,493	(2%)	

OHIO

Ohio was the first entirely American state, and one which ever since has seemed an epitome of American normalcy. The original 13 states started as British colonies, and the next three, Vermont, Kentucky and Tennessee, were spun off from them. But Ohio sprung Athena-like from the head of Congress, as the first state formed from the Northwest Territory of 1787. The Northwest Ordinance established 6 by 6 mile square townships, which imposed geometric order on diverse American landscapes west to the Pacific; it set aside one square mile per township for public schools, and the landscape was soon peppered with schoolhouses and small colleges, the foundation stones of a literate republic. The Ordinance prohibited slavery, opening the way for free labor to clear fields, raise crops, build mills and factories, and, in less than half a century, make this wilderness one of the most productive parts of western civilization. Ohio, in the years after the Civil War, became one of the great industrial states, the longtime head-quarters of John D. Rockefeller's Standard Oil, the site of major steel mills along the narrow and languidly flowing Cuyahoga and Mahoning Rivers, and home of the biggest soap com-panies, machine tool makers, tire manufacturers and producers of safety glass. Settled by Vir-ginians in the southwest around Cincinnati, by New Englanders in the northeast in the Western Reserve around Cleveland, Ohio has always been split between cultures: between the Southern-accented counties south of the National Road and U.S. 40 and the Northern-accented cities and towns to the north; between Butternut and Copperhead territory that didn't want to fight the Civil War and Yankee territory that fiercely prosecuted the War and Reconstruction afterwards.

This split heritage made Ohio politically a closely divided state—and a nationally pivotal one. A century ago Ohio produced the candidate and campaign manager—Governor and former Ways and Means Chairman William McKinley and iron and coal industrialist Mark Hanna; McKinley won the presidency in 1896 and 1900 and inaugurated a 34-year period of Republican national majorities. McKinley's Republicans were for high tariffs and hard money, had a friendly regard for workers and even some unions, but no patience with large union combi-nations and nascent socialism. They preached a nationalist Americanism tempered by a wari-ness about making major commitments abroad. Republicans were the majority in this increas-ingly industrial Ohio, losing rural Butternut counties but carrying the big industrial cities of the north.

Then came the Depression of the 1930s, and Ohio became the scene of something like class warfare, with sitdown strikes and victories for the CIO industrial unions in autos, steel and tires. CIO cities—Cleveland, Akron, Youngstown, Toledo—moved sharply toward the Dem-ocrats, while places with few CIO members—Cincinnati, Columbus, the dozens of small factory towns dotting the flat limestone plains of northern Ohio—stayed Republican. The political fighting was fierce and the stakes seemed high. CIO leaders hoped to organize the entire work force and build a Scandinavian-style welfare state; Republican leaders like Ohio's Senator Robert Taft feared union control of business would imperil freedoms and throttle the economy. In the 1930s and 1940s the unions made great gains. But Taft held them off, reducing union power with the Taft-Hartley Act of 1947, his own re-election to the Senate in 1950, and—his eventual rival—Dwight Eisenhower's presidential election in 1952.

In the years since, Ohio has oscillated and been courted by national campaigns. In the 1970s it seemed to swing toward the Democrats. Jimmy Carter won crucial electoral votes by carrying Ohio by 11,000 votes and Democrats controlled the state House throughout the 1970s and 1980s. Now in the 1990s Ohio has veered Republican. Bill Clinton did carry the state twice, but by the narrowest of his margins in any megastate—40%–38% in 1992, 47%–41% in 1996. Ohio Republicans won smashing victories in 1994 and 1998 and held their own in 1996. The

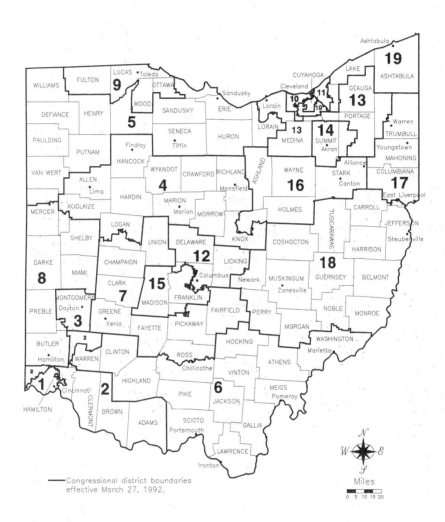

Congressional district boundaries
effective March 27, 1992.

Miles

0 5 10 15 20

leading figure has been George Voinovich, elected governor in 1990 by 56%–44%, re-elected in 1994 by 72%–25%—by far the biggest margin since 1826, when neither Republican nor Democratic parties existed—and elected senator by 56%–44% in 1998. But this has not just been a personal victory. From 1976–94 Ohio was represented by two Democrats in the Senate, but when they retired they were replaced by Republicans: Mike DeWine, who won 53%–39% in 1994, and Voinovich, both of whom had run unsuccessfully for the Senate before. And in 1998 Republican Bob Taft, bearer of a great Ohio name, was elected governor over a highly competent Democrat, Lee Fisher, by 50%–45%. Until Taft's victory, Ohio's governorship had been passed back and forth between the two parties, neither of which has held it for more than eight years, since George K. Nash won in 1899. Republicans hold every downballot statewide office, most of which were held by Democrats between 1970–94, and they have large and seemingly impervious margins in both houses of the legislature. Republicans have an 11–8 edge in the U.S. House delegation, a 21–12 margin in the state Senate and 59–40 in the state House.

The interesting question is whether this is a short-term blip or a long-run trend, a return to a McKinley-type Republican majority or a momentary interruption of New Deal voting patterns. It is a question of national significance, for in income levels, urban-rural balance, and ethnic mix, as well as presidential percentages, Ohio is not very far from the national average. One place to look for answers is in north-and-east Ohio, the traditionally Democratic area along Lake Erie and reaching south to the coal-mining counties across the Ohio River from West Virginia. This was the heartland of the CIO unions, the United Steelworkers in Youngstown and Cleveland, United Rubber Workers in Akron, United Mine Workers in the coal country, and United Auto Workers in Toledo and the Cleveland area. It is heavily ethnic, with hundreds of thousands of Poles, Hungarians, Slovaks, Serbs and Croatians streaming in throughout the early 20th Century. When its auto, steel, rubber and glass factories lost hundreds of thousands of jobs in the five years after the oil shock of 1979, north-and-east Ohio was one of the most Democratic parts of the country; as a separate state, it would have come as close to voting against Ronald Reagan in 1980 and 1984 as Massachusetts or New York. It voted solidly for Michael Dukakis in 1988 (54%–46%) and Clinton in 1992 (47%–31%). But as the shock of the early 1980s wore off, and it became clear that CIO industries' high-wage, low-skill jobs were gone for good, attitudes began changing. Voters gave up on trying to recreate the old factory economy and began building a new, more supple and adaptable manufacturing economy, with smaller factories, less rigid management and fewer union members, fewer low-skill jobs with high wages and more medium-skill, high-flexibility jobs with chances for advancement. They mostly gave up on restricting trade, as steel and auto import quotas lapsed and NAFTA was approved, and began manufacturing goods for export markets. And so Ohio began to grow again. Cleveland's new downtown is gleaming, Akron is proud of the polymer technologies which have replaced tire manufacturing, the Cuyahoga River is clean, and the valleys carved by rivers in the limestone are a source of pride.

Voinovich, long familiar to the Cleveland TV market, carried north-and-east Ohio by a small margin when he was elected governor in 1990; in 1994, against a little-known opponent, he won 69%–29%, the kind of Republican margin not seen in this area of Ohio since the 1920s; in 1998, running for the Senate, he lost the area by only 51%–49%. Even more startlingly, DeWine carried the area over Democrat Joel Hyatt 47%–45% in the 1994 Senate race; Taft lost it by 53%–42%, not a devastating margin, in the 1998 gubernatorial race. In 1996 Clinton carried north-and-east Ohio 54%–33%. But his percentage was no higher than Dukakis's, and not enough for a statewide majority. The politics of union-management struggle, class warfare and economic redistribution seems less than vigorous, perhaps dying, in one of its American heartlands.

The rest of Ohio has long been a Republican area, a stronghold for James Rhodes, governor for 16 of the 20 years between 1962 and 1982, who favored low taxes in order to attract jobs. In the 1980s and 1990s, this larger part of Ohio's cultural conservatism and patriotic nationalism, plus faith in a growing economy, made it heavily Republican: In their losing races, George Bush carried it 44%–35% in 1992 and Bob Dole carried it 47%–42% in 1996; and winning Republicans have won big majorities here—in 1998, Voinovich won here 61%–39% and Taft 55%–39%. There are only a few pockets of Democratic strength in this rest-of-Ohio, in the central cities of Cincinnati, Columbus and Dayton and in a few lightly populated Butternut counties south of U.S. 40.

The economy in both parts of Ohio has proved to be surprisingly robust in the 1990s. The unemployment rate, long high, fell below the national average; household incomes are up sharply; more than half a million jobs were created since 1991. Ohioans' high-skill manufacturing is booming, and small entrepreneurs have created thousands of jobs in the shadows of huge steel mills long since shut down. Politically, this economic growth has benefited incumbents—Clinton in 1996, Voinovich in 1994 and 1998. But Clinton's coattails have been limited—Democrats picked up two U.S. House seats in 1996, but not much else—while Voinovich's victories have been accompanied by Republican success up and down the line. Organized labor has become more active in Democratic politics, but has yet to achieve the success it wants; most of the institutional leaders in the state seem pleased with Republican dominance. The 1998 election posed a test of where Ohio stands in history. Is it New Deal Ohio, with ethnic factory workers ranged against small town businessmen, ethnic Catholics versus rural Protestants, all engaged in a contest to see how far and in what ways government should be enlarged? Or is it McKinley's Ohio, with mechanical tinkerers and can-do manufacturers, adaptive businessmen and employees, striving to work hard, raise families and serve communities that feel little class conflict or economic envy? The answer, by a decisive but not overwhelming margin, is that it is McKinley's Ohio, but it is not clear whether this consensus and political dominance can be sustained for a long generation as it was by McKinley and Hanna and their political heirs.

Governor. Bob Taft, elected governor in 1998, is from a famed Ohio family. His great-grandfather William Howard Taft was elected president in 1908 and appointed chief justice in 1921. His grandfather, Robert A. Taft, was elected senator in 1938, 1944 and 1950; a strong and principled conservative known as "Mr. Republican," he ran for president and lost the Republican nomination in 1940 and 1952, and was senate majority leader when he died in 1953. His father, Robert Taft Jr., was elected to the House in 1962, 1966 and 1968 and to the Senate in 1970, then lost to Howard Metzenbaum in 1976. The increasing informality of 20th Century politics can be gauged by the style of the Tafts' names: President Taft used three full names, the first Senator Taft an initial, the second Senator Taft a Jr. and this latest Taft calls himself simply Bob—and didn't make reference to his illustrious family in his ads. He grew up in Cincinnati, graduated from Yale, served two years in the Peace Corps in East Africa, got a masters degree at Princeton and worked four years as a budget officer in Illinois state government. Then he returned to Cincinnati, graduated from the University of Cincinnati law school, and was elected to the state House in 1976. In 1981 he was elected Hamilton County Commissioner. In 1990 he started to run for governor, then was persuaded by Republican National Chairman Lee Atwater in one of his last political acts to step aside for George Voinovich and run for secretary of State instead; he was elected to that office, critical for redistricting the state legislature, in November.

The common expectation was that Taft would run for governor in 1998, when Voinovich would be ineligible for a third term. At first he looked to have primary opposition from Treasurer Kenneth Blackwell, but Blackwell agreed in January 1998 to run for secretary of State instead (he won, too). But Taft had strong Democratic opposition: Lee Fisher, elected attorney general in 1990, defeated by a narrow margin in heavily Republican 1994, who from his base in the Cleveland suburbs raised nearly as much money as the Republican. Fisher too had primary opposition for a while, from self-financed businessman Bruce Douglas; but Douglas dropped out three weeks before the May primary and, under a campaign finance law rewritten by the Republican legislature, Fisher had to refund $1.2 million in contributions (he was allowed to exceed the $2,500 individual contribution limit, because of Douglas's self-financing, but had to return the surplus after Douglas dropped out). On primary day, voters rejected Issue 2, a one-cent sales tax for schools and property tax relief, written in response to a court decision requiring more school funding. Both Taft and Fisher supported it, and had to scramble to come up with new ways to address the number one issue, education, without a tax increase.

Fisher promised to cut property taxes by 15% over two years; Taft said this was impossible, and proposed much smaller tax cuts, a homestead exemption and a $2,500 college tuition deduction for families with incomes under $50,000. Fisher also came out for a state earned income tax credit and medical deductions. Much of the ruckus of the campaign came over attacks for backing previous tax increases: Fisher attacked Taft for backing 11 tax increases in Hamilton County; Taft attacked Fisher for backing 27 tax increases in Columbus. The newspapers made much of supposed Taft gaffes (one ad just read "Bob Taft Governor") and Fisher accused Taft of dodging debates (Taft insisted on having the two minor candidates participate). There was the obvious difference in background. As Fisher put it, "My great-grandfather was an immigrant sheet-metal worker from Russia, and I am running against a man whose great-grandfather was president of the United States. But the wonderful thing about America is that if you speak to the concerns of everyday people, you can even the playing field." He might have added that Taft's great-grandfather vetoed a bill to restrict immigration.

Taft led in polls, but not by dazzling margins; the election turned out the same. Taft won 50%–45%, losing 53%–42% in north-and-east Ohio and winning 55%–39% in the rest of the state. Taft carried all income groups over $30,000 and got about 57% among both Catholics and white Protestants, and Fisher's lead in union households was only 54%–40%: the old bright lines between Ohioans have become blurred. In office Taft worked with the Republican legislature to put into effect his campaign proposals—requiring students to take reading tests in the fourth grade to be academically promoted, creating School Safety Zones, the college tuition deduction, the homestead tax cut, tougher penalties for juvenile criminals and cheats who exploit the elderly, deregulating utilities, streamlining state jobs programs. He also promised to work for workmen's compensation reform and privatized prisons. Taft is opposed to abortion except in cases of rape, incest or saving the mother's life; in February 1999 Ohio had its first execution in 36 years. It is far too soon to predict how Taft will fare in 2002, or who will some day succeed him; Republicans now have an abundance, perhaps overabundance, of well-known state officials—Lieutenant Governor Maureen O'Connor, Attorney General Betty Montgomery, Secretary of State Kenneth Blackwell.

Senior Senator. Michael DeWine is a Republican elected in 1994. Less than formidable in appearance—he is short, gap-toothed, bespectacled, youthful looking, but he is also a seasoned political veteran and holder of public office for more than 20 years. DeWine grew up in Yellow Springs, Ohio, the home of liberal Antioch College, where his family owned a successful seed business; after finishing school, DeWine and his wife moved to nearby Cedarville, in a part of the state with rolling hills, winding creeks and covered bridges, where they now host an annual ice cream social. There DeWine was elected Greene County prosecutor at 29, where he resisted plea bargaining, and, in order to nail a drug dealer, once put up the collateral to get $50,000 cash to stage a buy. In 1980, at 33, he was elected to the Ohio Senate; two years later, he won a six-candidate Republican primary with 69% of the vote and was elected to a U.S. House seat. He worked for tougher drunk driving penalties, mandatory sentencing, and aid to child crime victims, with more success in Republican Columbus than on Democratic Capitol Hill. Elected lieutenant governor in 1990, he sought better and more responsive teenage offender facilities and an Ohio DNA analysis lab.

In 1992 he ran against Senator John Glenn. It was a hard-hitting campaign: He attacked Glenn for his part in the Keating Five case and asked the question, "What on earth has John Glenn done?" In September 1992 Glenn was below 50% in the polls. But Democrats brought up DeWine's 31 overdrafts on the House bank and the time he fell asleep at the Iran-Contra hearings. Glenn won 51%–42%, his closest general election margin ever; he needed his

58%–35% margin in north-and-east Ohio, because DeWine carried the rest of the state 47%–45%.

In 1994 DeWine decided to run for the Senate again. This time the incumbent, Howard Metzenbaum, was retiring, and hoped to be succeeded by his son-in-law, Joel Hyatt, founder of the storefront Hyatt Legal Services chain. But in the May primary, Hyatt defeated Cuyahoga County Commissioner Mary Boyle by only a 47%–43% margin, while DeWine won by 53%–32% over Dr. Bernadine Healy, former director of the National Institutes of Health. From then on, DeWine had solid leads in most polls. He spent much time in the Cleveland area, cutting into the Democrats' base. Two incidents from his past hurt Hyatt with core Democratic constituencies. A Hyatt Legal Services office in Philadelphia in 1987 fired a lawyer with AIDS, and was one of the cases that inspired the movie *Philadelphia*, which premiered the spring of the primary. And while a student at Dartmouth, Hyatt had opposed admitting women to the college. DeWine's anti-crime planks, his backing of term limits and the line-item veto helped him. Also, DeWine's support of NAFTA did not hurt; in an exit poll voters thought it was good for Ohio by a 26%–23% margin, and in fact Ohio exports to Mexico and Latin America have boomed since NAFTA was ratified. Nor did it hurt that former Operation Rescue leader Joseph Slovenec ran as an independent; Slovenec's highest percentages were in counties across from West Virginia, where he took Democratic votes. The 23% of voters in union households split evenly, while the 29% who were gun owners voted 58%–31% for the almost always plaid-shirt-clad DeWine. DeWine won statewide 53%–39%, by 47%–45% in north-and-east Ohio and 58%–35% in the rest of the state.

The common motif that runs through DeWine's career is a concern for children and the championing of legislation often prompted by tragedy striking a particular child, including his own: His daughter Becky died in an auto accident in 1993, at 22, and he and his wife decided to donate her organs; DeWine spends much effort on organ donor programs and awareness. With Jay Rockefeller, he sponsored a law to change the family preservation emphasis in social work, and helped pass a law requiring the best interest of the child as paramount in custody cases involving abusive or drug-problem parents. Before Bill Clinton, he came out for banning hospitals from discharging mothers in the 48 hours after delivery. Prompted by the death of a 13-year-old Greene County girl, he has crusaded for school bus safety and put incentives for the states to promote it in a 1996 appropriations bill. With Herb Kohl, he pushed through a law making it a felony to cross state lines to avoid paying child support in cases after one year or more than $5,000 in arrears. In 1990, while in the House, he wrote and helped pass the Child Victims Protection Act. He worked on foster care and has supported the Ricky Ray Hemophilia Relief Fund, for hemophiliacs infected with AIDS. In the recesses of the Senate's impeachment trial, he made calls to try to get medical benefits for a Middletown five-year-old with xeroderma pigmentosum, a disease so rare it is not on the Social Security Administration's list of covered treatments.

On most of these issues DeWine was careful to work with Democrats and seek bipartisan support. Similarly, as chairman of the Employment and Training Subcommittee, he assembled bipartisan support for a sweeping rewriting of job training laws, with more flexibility for cities and counties; it passed in 1998. He worked with Democrats Tony Hall of Dayton and Maryland's Paul Sarbanes to pass the Africa Seeds of Hope Act. To the Higher Education Act, he added provisions helping to repay college loans of those who work in early childhood education or day care, encouraging alternative certification of teachers, and creating public-private partnerships to train teachers. He successfully sponsored a Nazi War Crimes Disclosure Act, to make public the response of the U.S. government to the Holocaust. On the 1996 immigration bill he opposed cutting legal immigration, opposed raising the income requirement for relatives of U.S. citizens and opposed limiting family unification visas for siblings and adult children.

DeWine also worked on the Western Hemisphere Drug Elimination Act, pushing for tougher interdiction of drugs; he favors drug courts and making powdered cocaine penalties as severe as those for crack. He got a Cleveland federal courthouse named after the late Mayor Carl

Stokes, brother of retired Congressman Louis Stokes, and passed a law naming the Cleveland area NASA research center after his onetime opponent and retired colleague John Glenn. As chairman of the Antitrust Subcommittee, he called for opposition to all telephone mergers unless they clearly benefited consumers in September 1998, and urged the FTC to hold off approval of the BP-Amoco merger in December 1998. In May 1999 he voted with Democrats in supporting background checks on purchases at gun shows.

DeWine played a visible role in impeachment. Trent Lott put him, with Fred Thompson and Orrin Hatch, in charge of screening senators' questions for Chief Justice William Rehnquist; he was also asked to monitor the testimony of Monica Lewinsky. Democrats chortled at what state Chairman David Leland called "his whole embarrassing activities during the Monica Lewinsky episode" and argued that voters knew little about what he had done in the Senate. But as University of Akron political scientist John Green argued, "Mike DeWine has carved out a niche for which there is a great consensus in Ohio. I think he has tended to stay away from divisive issues—because Ohio itself is divided on those issues." A March 1999 poll showed that many could not rate his performance, but that those who could were almost entirely favorable and that in heats against possible Democratic opponents he was winning 55% to 58% of the vote. Congressman Sherrod Brown opted out of the race in March 1999; Congressman Ted Strickland and Congresswoman Marcy Kaptur opted out in April 1999; 1998 gubernatorial candidate Lee Fisher ruled himself out and former Democratic Representative Dennis Eckhart ruled out a run in May 1999. Possible opponents include former Cuyahoga County Commissioner Timothy Hagan, and 1994 and 1998 Senate nominees Joel Hyatt and Mary Boyle, but DeWine seems a clear favorite.

Cook's Call. *Potentially Competitive.* Democrats argue that DeWine is highly vulnerable, but they are having trouble coming up with a candidate. With its diverse population and numerous media markets, Ohio is not an easy place to seek a Senate seat. In fact, there is an unspoken rule that a candidate must run statewide once and lose before winning a Senate seat. DeWine may be vulnerable, but Democrats have a long way to go before they can capitalize on it.

Junior Senator. George Voinovich, elected to the Senate in 1998, is now the junior colleague of the man elected as his first lieutenant governor in 1990, Mike DeWine. Voinovich is a pleasant and unassuming man who can show temper—he was fined $1,500 for ordering his state plane to take off when the Secret Service shut down the Columbus airport for a Clinton visit—and has known tragedy—his young daughter was killed in an auto accident when he was running for mayor in 1979. He has been in government and politics most of his life. He grew up in Cleveland, of ethnic ancestry (Serbian and Slovenian descent) in an ethnic industrial metropolis; he practiced law, then was elected to the legislature in 1966, at 30. He was elected county auditor in 1971, county commissioner in 1977, and lieutenant governor in 1978. In 1979, after Mayor Dennis Kucinich bankrupted Cleveland, Voinovich was elected mayor. In 10 years in office, he fixed the budget and sparked the city's renaissance. His one defeat came in 1988, when he lost 57%–43% to Senator Howard Metzenbaum.

In 1990 he ran for governor and beat Attorney General Anthony Celebrezze Jr., 56%–44%; in 1994 he was re-elected by the spectacular margin of 72%–25%. Voinovich got the state government's fiscal house in order, with the help of a tax increase in 1992; he helped to encourage the growth of small businesses, which got Ohio's economy humming by the middle 1990s; he cut welfare rolls and helped welfare recipients get jobs. He increased school funding and wiring of schools for the Internet and spent much of his last years grappling with court decisions attacking the state's education funding formula. He sponsored a managed health care plan, OhioCare, for Medicaid recipients and the uninsured, and continued Democratic Governor Richard Celeste's program for state investment in businesses. He is opposed to abortion but recognizes *Roe v. Wade* as the law and says, "Let's deal in the real world." Voinovich also worked with Bob Dole and Newt Gingrich in early 1995 on the successful Republican move to limit unfunded mandates on the states, and at the same time urged a balanced budget amendment. He was the first governor to endorse Dole for president; he was mentioned for the vice presidential nomination, but took himself out of the running. About the same time, in July 1996, his chief of staff, Paul Mifsud, resigned while the target of a state contract-steering investigation. (Mifsud pleaded guilty in September 1997 and was sentenced to six months in prison and two years probation. Voinovich was accused of illegally transferring campaign funds to his brother and a lobbyist; he said he knew nothing about the payments; a long investigation was extended three months in April 1999, and he could be fined $10,000.)

In February 1997 Senator John Glenn announced he would retire in 1998. He will always be known as the first American to orbit the earth, in February 1962, and as the first 77-year-old astronaut, in October 1998; he was also a Marine pilot in World War II and Korea (where his wingman was a ballplayer named Ted Williams). He was elected to the Senate in 1974, after two unsuccessful tries. In the Senate he labored for years on nuclear proliferation, and delayed the Indian and Pakistani nuclear tests for perhaps 20 years; over the years his voting record became more liberal and in his last term he was Clinton's vociferous champion in the 1997 hearings on illegal campaign contributions.

After Glenn's announcement, Voinovich, who was not eligible to run for re-election, was the obvious favorite, and he led in polls for nearly two years. His Democratic opponent was another Clevelander (as a boy Voinovich delivered newspapers to her family's house), Cuyahoga County Commissioner Mary Boyle, who lost the 1994 Senate primary but this time had no competition. Boyle campaigned on education, blaming Voinovich for allowing Ohio schools to decline; she called for HMO regulation and a minimum wage increase. She also attacked him for supporting the tax increase which voters rejected in the May primary. Voinovich mostly ignored her attacks and outspent her by almost 3–1, running ads that highlighted his record as governor. He was endorsed by the National Education Association, and proclaimed, "If I get into the Senate, I will probably know more about domestic policy that any member of the Senate." Even Boyle's luck was bad: October visits by Edward Kennedy and Tipper Gore had to be canceled, and the big headlines on the charges against the 1994 Voinovich campaign appeared only a couple of days before the election. The results showed Voinovich a bit weaker than he had seemed when Glenn announced his retirement. An unknown won 28% against him in the May primary, and in November his margin over Boyle was a decisive but not overwhelming 56%–44%. He lost his home turf in north-and-east Ohio by 51%–49%, though he had won it in 1990, but he had a solid 61%–39% in the rest of Ohio. He won 30% among blacks—a fine showing for a Republican—and carried all income groups above $30,000 and lost by only 56%–42% in union households—not much class warfare there. He won more than 60% among Catholics and white Protestants—no trace of religious wars, either. Voters most concerned about education preferred Voinovich to Boyle.

In the Senate Voinovich quietly voted with other Republicans on impeachment. In March 1999 this Republican who had come out for a number of state tax increases infuriated Republican colleagues when he offered an amendment to bar any tax cut for the year; but its defeat and the leadership's imprecations made little dent on him. "This is my 33d year in government," he said. "I'm 63. I'm going to do what is right. Let the chips fall where they may. In my political career, I've been out of step all the way." Voinovich is the only Serbian-American in the Senate, and as a college freshman wrote a paper on how the United States sold out Yugoslavia at the February 1945 Yalta conference; in 1991 his Serbian relatives were forced out of their homes in the newly independent Croatia. In March 1999 he opposed the bombing of Serbia, but he has called Slobodan Milosevic a "war criminal" and tried to convince the State Department to support forces who could depose him. In May 1999 he voted with Democrats in supporting background checks for purchases at gun shows.

Presidential politics. With 21 electoral votes and a tradition of close partisan competition, Ohio is a crucial state in presidential politics. It matched the national average in 1984 and 1988 and came close to doing so in 1996. It cast the narrowest margins for Bill Clinton of any megastate in both 1992 and 1996. No Republican has ever been elected president without

1248 OHIO

carrying Ohio; no Democrat, in the electoral vote arithmetic of the 1990s, can be sure of winning without it. Richard Nixon advised Reagan and Bush managers Ed Rollins and Lee Atwater to put extra money and special ads into Ohio, to make it a roadblock for Walter Mondale and Michael Dukakis. In 1992 and 1996 that strategy was reversed, since the West Coast was lost to Bush and the South was in jeopardy; then James Carville made Ohio a roadblock. But in less one-sided races, Ohio seems likely to be not a roadblock but a battleground, and in 2000 Ohio—and the kindred industrial states of Pennsylvania and Michigan—could be the decisive battleground of the campaign.

In 1996 Ohio switched its presidential primary from May to March 19, and voted on the same day as Illinois, Michigan and Wisconsin. But even then, just four weeks after New Hampshire, the race was already over. George Voinovich was the first governor to endorse Bob Dole, and eventually the whole Republican leadership followed; Dole beat Pat Buchanan here 66%–22%. In May 1999, the state legislature voted to move the date to March 7, and Taft was expected to sign it into law.

Congressional districting. Ohio lost two districts in the 1990 Census and is likely to lose another one in 2000; this state that elected 24 congressmen in 1970 will likely elect 18 in 2002. The current contorted district lines, with at least three grotesque barbell-shaped districts, are the product of a late bipartisan compromise in 1992. But already six contests have been won by the party that redistricters thought would lose. Control after the 2000 Census will, barring big Democratic gains in legislative elections, belong to the Republicans. They are likely to redraw the lines in Cincinnati and east central Ohio to protect Republican incumbents and to redraw lines in northeast Ohio to help Republican chances. One obvious candidate for extinction is the barbell-shaped 13th District now represented by Democrat Sherrod Brown, who has had statewide ambitions and by 2002 may seek to realize them; another is the 6th District in southern Ohio.

The People: Est. Pop. 1998: 11,209,493; Pop. 1990: 10,847,115, up 3.3% 1990–1998. 4.1% of U.S. total, 7th largest; 25.9% rural. Median age: 35.3 years. 13.5% 65 years and over. 87.8% White, 10.6% Black, 0.8% Asian, 0.2% Amer. Indian, 0.5% Other; 1.2% Hispanic Origin. Households: 56.1% married couple families; 26.9% married couple fams. w. children; 39.3% college educ.; median household income: $28,706; per capita income: $13,461; 67.5% owner occupied housing; median house value: $63,500; median monthly rent: $296. 4.3% Unemployment. 1998 Voting age pop.: 8,401,000. 1998 Turnout: 3,534,782; 42% of VAP. Registered voters (1998): 7,096,423; 1,239,934 D (17%), 1,250,454 R (18%), 4,634,337 unaffiliated and minor parties (65%).

Political Lineup: Governor, Bob Taft (R); Lt. Gov., Maureen O'Connor (R); Secy. of State, J. Kenneth Blackwell (R); Atty. Gen., Betty D. Montgomery (R); Treasurer, Joseph Deters (R); State Senate, 33 (12 D, 21 R); Senate President, Richard Finan (R); State House, 99 (40 D, 59 R); House Speaker, Jo Ann Davidson (R). Senators, Mike DeWine (R) and George Voinovich (R). Representatives, 19 (8 D, 11 R).

Elections Division: 614-466-2585; **Filing Deadline for U.S. Congress:** January 7, 2000.

1996 Presidential Vote

Clinton (D) 2,148,309 (47%)
Dole (R) 1,860,768 (41%)
Perot (I) 483,277 (11%)

1992 Presidential Vote

Clinton (D) 1,984,942 (40%)
Bush (R) 1,894,310 (38%)
Perot (I) 1,036,426 (21%)

1996 Republican Presidential Primary

Dole (R) 631,192 (66%)
Buchanan (R) 204,875 (22%)
Forbes (R) 57,358 (6%)
Others 55,823 (6%)

GOVERNOR

Gov. Bob Taft (R)

Elected 1998, term expires Jan. 2003; b. Jan. 8, 1942, Boston, MA; home, Cincinnati; Yale U., B.A. 1963, Princeton U., M.A. 1967, U. of Cincinnati, J.D. 1976; Protestant; married (Hope).

Elected Office: OH House of Reps., 1976–81; Hamilton Cnty. Commissioner, 1981–90; OH Secy. of State, 1991–98.

Professional Career: Peace Corps, East Africa, 1963–65; State Dept., Vietnam, 1967–69; Budget Officer & Asst. Dir., IL Budget Bureau, 1969–73.

Office: Office of the Governor, 77 S. High St., 30th Fl.,, 43215, 614-466-3555; Fax: 614-644-0951; Web site: www.state.oh.us.

Election Results

1998 gen.	Bob Taft (R)	1,678,721	(50%)
	Lee Fisher (D)	1,498,956	(45%)
	Others	176,536	(5%)
1998 prim.	Bob Taft (R)	unopposed	
1994 gen.	George Voinovich (R)	2,401,572	(72%)
	Robert L. Burch, Jr. (D)	835,849	(25%)
	Others	108,817	(3%)

SENATORS

Sen. Mike DeWine (R)

Elected 1994, seat up 2000; b. Jan. 5. 1947, Springfield; home, Cedarville; Miami U. of OH, B.S. 1969, OH Northern U., J.D. 1972; Catholic; married (Frances).

Elected Office: Greene Cnty. Prosecuting atty., 1977–81; OH Senate, 1980–82; U.S. House of Reps., 1982–90; OH Lt. Gov., 1990–94.

Professional Career: Practicing atty; Greene Cnty. Asst. Prosecuting atty., 1973–75, .

DC Office: 140 RSOB, 20510, 202-224-2315; Fax: 202-224-6519; Web site: www.senate.gov/~dewine.

State Offices: Cincinnati, 513-763-8260; Columbus, 614-469-6774; Marietta, 740-373-2317; Toledo, 419-259-7535; Xenia, 937-376-3080.

Committees: *Health, Education, Labor & Pensions* (4th of 10 R): Aging (Chmn.); Children & Families. *Intelligence* (4th of 9 R). *Judiciary* (6th of 10 R): Antitrust, Business Rights & Competition (Chmn.); Criminal Justice Oversight; Technology, Terrorism & Government Information.

Group Ratings

	ADA	ACLU	AFS	LCV	CON	NTU	NFIB	COC	ACU	NTLC	CHC
1998	10	14	1	0	75	49	100	89	64	68	91
1997	15	—	0	—	64	67	—	80	68	—	—

National Journal Ratings

	1997 LIB — 1997 CONS		1998 LIB — 1998 CONS	
Economic	37% —	57%	46% —	52%
Social	28% —	62%	36% —	63%
Foreign	34% —	57%	29% —	58%

Key Votes of the 105th Congress

1. Bal. Budget Amend.	Y	5. Satcher for Surgeon Gen.	N	9. Chem. Weapons Treaty	Y
2. Clinton Budget Deal	Y	6. Highway Set-asides	N	10. Cuban Humanitarian Aid	N
3. Cloture on Tobacco	Y	7. Table Child Gun locks	N	11. Table Bosnia Troops	Y
4. Education IRAs	Y	8. Ovrd. Part. Birth Veto	Y	12. $ for Test-ban Treaty	N

Election Results

1994 general	Mike DeWine (R) 1,836,556	(53%)	($6,084,663)
	Joel Hyatt (D) 1,348,213	(39%)	($4,921,223)
	Joseph J. Slovenec (I) 252,031	(7%)	($192,867)
1994 primary	Mike DeWine (R) 422,366	(52%)	
	Bernadine Healy (R) 263,559	(32%)	
	Eugene J. Watts (R) 83,103	(10%)	
	George H. Rhodes (R) 42,633	(5%)	
1988 general	Howard M. Metzenbaum (D) 2,480,038	(57%)	($8,547,545)
	George Voinovich (R) 1,872,716	(43%)	($8,233,859)

Sen. George Voinovich (R)

Elected 1998, seat up 2004; b. July 15, 1936, Cleveland; home, Columbus; Ohio U., B.A. 1958, Ohio St. U., J.D. 1961; Catholic; married (Janet).

Elected Office: OH House of Reps., 1966–71; Cuyahoga Cnty. Auditor, 1971–76; Cuyahoga Cnty. Commissioner, 1977–78; OH Lt. Gov., 1978–79; Cleveland Mayor, 1979–89; OH Gov., 1990–98.

Professional Career: OH Asst. Atty. Gen., 1963–64.

DC Office: 317 HSOB, 20510, 202-224-3353; Fax: 202-228-1382; Web site: www.senate.gov/~voinovich.

State Offices: Cleveland, 216-522-7095; Columbus, 614-469-6697.

Committees: *Environment & Public Works* (7th of 10 R): Clean Air, Wetlands, Private Property & Nuclear Safety; Transportation & Infrastructure (Chmn.). *Ethics (Select)* (3d of 3 R). *Governmental Affairs* (5th of 9 R): Government Management, Restructuring and the District of Columbia (Chmn.); Investigations (Permanent). *Small Business* (9th of 10 R).

Group Ratings and Key Votes: Newly Elected

Election Results

1998 general	George Voinovich (R) 1,922,087	(56%)	($6,756,712)
	Mary O. Boyle (D) 1,482,054	(44%)	($2,236,137)
1998 primary	George Voinovich (R) 539,424	(72%)	
	David McCollough (R) 207,135	(28%)	
1992 general	John H. Glenn, Jr. (D) 2,444,419	(51%)	($4,974,109)
	Mike DeWine (R) 2,028,300	(42%)	($3,053,156)
	Martha Kathryn Grevatt (I) 321,670	(7%)	

FIRST DISTRICT

From its seven hills, Cincinnati, dubbed the Queen City of the West in the 19th Century, looks down on the curves of the Ohio River. Ohio's first major metropolis, this was the nation's fourth largest city at the outbreak of the Civil War, a heavily German beehive of riverboats and sausage factories, known as Porkopolis. Cincinnati has long given off an air of the recent past; Mark Twain said he'd like to be there for the apocalypse because everything in Cincinnati is 20 years behind. Today the city seems to be stepping, stylishly and gracefully, into the early 1980s. Growing slowly over many decades, Cincinnati has long-settled good looks and an urbanity somehow consistent with its natural terrain: the bottomlands along the river, the hills and rolling terrain above. In the middle of Cincinnati is Mill Creek, lined with factories; on the hills to the west, above the restored Union Terminal with the children's, historic, and natural history museums, are the modest streetcar suburbs of the last century and the early years of this one. On Mount Adams and toward the northeast are set a string of affluent neighborhoods, with stately mansions like the William Howard Taft house, and the comfortable Tudors and colonials of the 20th Century bourgeoisie—Reform Jewish as well as WASP and German.

Cincinnati was the site of great innovations: the first iron suspension bridge, in 1867, connecting Cincinnati to northern Kentucky and designed by John Roebling who later built the Brooklyn Bridge; the first baseball team, the Red Stockings, in 1869; the country's leading Reform Jewish seminary, Hebrew Union College, in 1875. And if over the past century Cincinnati has not had the growth spurts of cities like Cleveland or Houston, neither has it had their sharp contractions. It has spawned not flashy but solid industries, like the Procter & Gamble soap business, now headquartered in a striking two-towered office complex at the edge of downtown, and it has America's biggest concentration of machine tool makers. Downtown Cincinnati's spruced-up Fountain Square shows off the well-maintained skyscrapers of the past, and its first class restaurants still attract a dressy clientele. Old ethnic neighborhoods, crowded with brick row houses on steep hills, keep their thick local accents and special local foods, from German sauerbrauten to Cincinnati chili (try it "four way," served with spaghetti, onions and grated cheese).

The 1st Congressional District includes almost all of Cincinnati, except for its affluent eastern edge, plus the middle-class suburbs that cling to the woody hills north and west, all the way to North Bend, the home of President William Henry Harrison, and the Indiana border. Ancestrally Republican, Cincinnati was a German anti-slavery island in a Southern-stock pro-Confederate sea. City elections here have long been competitive between the old line Republicans and a combination of Democrats and Charterites (the latter started by Charles Taft, liberal brother of Senator Robert Taft Sr.). Council members here become celebrities throughout the entire media market. One or both Cincinnati-area congressional districts have been seriously contested in almost every election since 1964, and for 44 years were represented by nothing but former Cincinnati council members with the understandable exception of Robert Taft Jr. (One former council member and mayor, Jerry Springer, has even become a national talk show host; he resigned as mayor after it was revealed that he had hired a northern Kentucky prostitute.) Traditionally, Cincinnati has been a Republican stronghold, and culturally conservative, though the suburbs now are much more Republican than the city: This is a city that tried to ban the works of Larry Flynt and Robert Mapplethorpe, and passed a charter amendment (upheld in federal court) that banned special protection gays.

The congressman from the 1st District is Steve Chabot, a Republican first elected in 1994. Like so many other congressmen here, he grew up in Cincinnati and served on the council. After college he taught elementary school for a year, then went to law school and had a small law practice; he was elected to the council in 1985, at 32, and to the Hamilton County Commission in 1990. Chabot stepped forward to run in 1994 amid an odd set of circumstances. In 1992, first-termer Charles Luken (son of longtime incumbent Tom) retired suddenly after the June primary. In the special primary to replace him, moderate council member David Mann defeated liberal state Senator William Bowen, 33%–32%, by 416 votes. In the general, Mann beat 51%–43% a Republican who ran as an independent because no Republican had gotten on the ballot. In the House, Mann voted against the Clinton tax package and for NAFTA, and infuriated local unions; Bowen ran again in 1994 and this time Mann won 49%–48%, by 667 votes. In the fall, Chabot backed the balanced budget amendment, strongly opposed abortion, and attacked Mann's support of Bill Clinton. Chabot won comfortably, 56%–44%.

Chabot has a conservative voting record in the House. He has shown himself willing to take political risks for principle. He voted against the Appalachian Regional Commission, which gives money to southern Ohio, and he opposed a $2 million study of light-rail in the Cincinnati area. Chabot believes Cincinnati should look for ways to solve problems with local resources and not depend on Washington. He opposed farm subsidies, and co-sponsored with Democrat Charles Schumer of New York a losing amendment to end the Agriculture Department's Market Access Program that promotes food products overseas, which he terms "a massive taxpayer rip-off." He opposed the October 1998 omnibus budget, objecting that it neither cut taxes nor saved Social Security. But he worked with Democrat Zoe Lofgren of California to allow counties as well as cities to apply for federal anti-crime aid. On the Judiciary Immigration Subcommittee and on the floor, Chabot played a major role on the 1996 immigration bill. He opposed chairman Lamar Smith's procedure for employers to verify all employees' immigration status. "The goal of the scheme's backers is to prohibit any employee from holding his or her job unless the federal government has signed off on the arrangement," which he called "1–800-Big-Brother"; it lost 159–260. Chabot also was one of several Republican freshmen who worked hard to separate the legal and illegal immigration sections of the bill, frustrating others' attempts to reduce legal immigration. Chabot also surprised some by attacking parts of the antiterrorism bill as violations of civil liberties. As a House manager during the Clinton impeachment trial, Chabot pressed Judiciary Chairman Henry Hyde's futile demand for witnesses in the Senate. Chabot had no regrets about his role. "It didn't turn out the way we wanted, but I'm satisfied," he told *The Cincinnati Enquirer*. "I did my best. We were fair."

Back home, he has been a prime Democratic re-election target. In 1996 the AFL-CIO spent over $1 million, running nearly 2,000 television ads against him. They attacked him for Medicare "cuts" and for supporting Speaker Newt Gingrich. A light moment came in October when Democratic challenger Mark Longabaugh, a top aide in House Minority Leader Dick Gephardt's 1988 presidential campaign, ran an ad showing Chabot's yellow pages listing and noting that he took clients in DUI cases; Chabot responded with an ad showing the white pages and asking, "Where's Mark Longabaugh been listed for 15 years? Not here!" Chabot won 54%–43%.

In 1998 Chabot was opposed by Cincinnati Mayor (and Council member) Roxanne Qualls. This was one of the hardest fought races in the country, and one of the most expensive: Chabot spent $1.5 million, Qualls $1.2 million. Qualls argued that Chabot's views were too conservative for the district, citing votes against Head Start and student loans. She said the budget surplus should be saved until Congress agreed on a Social Security rescue plan. Chabot called for broad-based tax cuts, and cuts in pork barrel projects and corporate welfare. They disagreed on the partial-birth abortion ban and school vouchers. With Chabot on the Judiciary Committee, impeachment became an issue. After Clinton's August 1998 grand jury testimony, Qualls hemmed and hawed about attending a dinner for Clinton; later she escorted him on a tour of the city. Qualls made an effort at courting the black vote: She brought in Maxine Waters and Jesse Jackson Jr., who also cut ads for her. But the coolness toward Clinton still may have been a tactical mistake: The district is about 30% black, which means that about half the votes of any likely Democratic majority are cast by blacks; but turnout in black Cincinnati precincts was significantly lower than in the suburbs. Chabot won 53%–47%, just a bit closer than his earlier elections. This could easily be a seriously contested district again in 2000. If, as seems likely, Republicans control redistricting, they will probably redraw the lines, taking out some central city precincts and adding suburban territory, to make the seat safely Republican.

Cook's Call. *Competitive.* Chabot's conservative voting record and the competitive nature of this Cincinnati-based district have made him an attractive target for the past two election cycles. But, Chabot has proven to be an impressive campaigner. His solid win over Cincinnati

Mayor Roxanne Qualls in 1998, long considered to be the best candidate Democrats could offer, makes the odds of Democrats beating him in 2000 rather daunting.

The People: Pop. 1990: 571,052; 1.3% rural; 14% age 65+; 68.5% White, 30.1% Black, 1% Asian, 0.2% Amer. Indian, 0.2% Other; 0.6% Hispanic Origin. Households: 43.3% married couple families; 21% married couple fams. w. children; 43% college educ.; median household income: $25,405; per capita income: $12,616; median house value: $65,100; median gross rent: $288.

1996 Presidential Vote			1992 Presidential Vote		
Clinton (D)	110,166	(50%)	Clinton (D)	104,494	(43%)
Dole (R)	96,103	(43%)	Bush (R)	104,339	(43%)
Perot (I)	12,842	(6%)	Perot (I)	34,531	(14%)

Rep. Steve Chabot (R)

Elected 1994; b. Jan. 22, 1953, Cincinnati; home, Cincinnati; William & Mary Col., B.A. 1975, N. KY U., J.D. 1978; Catholic; married (Donna).

Elected Office: Cincinnati City Cncl., 1985–90; Hamilton Cnty. Comm., 1990–94.

Professional Career: Elem. Schl. teacher, 1975–76; Practicing atty., 1978–94.

DC Office: 129 CHOB 20515, 202-225-2216; Fax: 202-225-3012; Web site: www.house.gov/chabot.

District Office: Cincinnati, 513-684-2723.

Committees: *International Relations* (15th of 26 R): Africa; International Economic Policy & Trade. *Judiciary* (11th of 21 R): Commercial & Administrative Law; Crime. *Small Business* (8th of 19 R): Tax, Finance & Exports.

Group Ratings

	ADA	ACLU	AFS	LCV	CON	NTU	NFIB	COC	ACU	NTLC	CHC
1998	0	13	0	38	92	82	100	83	96	92	100
1997	20	—	13	—	93	74	—	100	96	—	—

National Journal Ratings

	1997 LIB — 1997 CONS		1998 LIB — 1998 CONS	
Economic	16% —	82%	15% —	81%
Social	29% —	71%	3% —	90%
Foreign	36% —	63%	19% —	75%

Key Votes of the 105th Congress

1. Clinton Budget Deal	Y	5. Puerto Rico Sthood. Ref.	N	9. Cut $ for B-2 Bombers	Y
2. Education IRAs	Y	6. End Highway Set-asides	Y	10. Human Rights in China	N
3. Req. 2/3 to Raise Taxes	Y	7. School Prayer Amend.	Y	11. Withdraw Bosnia Troops	Y
4. Fast-track Trade	Y	8. Ovrd. Part. Birth Veto	Y	12. End Cuban TV-Marti	N

Election Results

1998 general	Steve Chabot (R)	92,421	(53%)	($1,623,706)
	Roxanne Qualls (D)	82,003	(47%)	($1,229,276)
1998 primary	Steve Chabot (R)	unopposed		
1996 general	Steve Chabot (R)	118,324	(54%)	($983,163)
	Mark P. Longabaugh (D)	94,719	(43%)	($544,875)
	Others	5,381	(2%)	

SECOND DISTRICT

The most Republican major metro area in the nation over the longest time span has been Cincinnati. Back in the 1850s, when Harriet Beecher Stowe wrote *Uncle Tom's Cabin* here, Cincinnati was an island of German, pro-Union, Republican sentiment in a Southern, Democratic, pro-slavery sea. Later Cincinnati attracted fewer southern and eastern European immigrants than Great Lakes industrial cities like Cleveland, Detroit and Chicago; its ethnic character (like its physical appearance) and its political preference have remained pretty well fixed. Even many of the Appalachians here are Republicans, from Civil War Republican counties in the hills. Democratic constituencies here never got very large: economically, it was never a strong CIO town; culturally, it is home to a strong anti-pornography movement that, among other things, was the site of obscenity charges filed against *Hustler* publisher Larry Flynt. Cincinnati's Republican record remains intact in the 1990s: it was the only million-plus metro area that George Bush and Bob Dole carried by more than 50% in 1992 and 1996; in 1998 metro Cincinnati voted 61%–35% for Governor Bob Taft, holder of a great Cincinnati name.

For 140 years after 1852, Cincinnati and surrounding Hamilton County were divided by a north-south line into two congressional districts. After the 1990 Census, redistricters created one mostly urban district that leaned a bit to the Democrats and a mostly suburban district that spread out into the countryside and was heavily Republican. Ohio's 2d Congressional District includes the affluent eastern suburbs around elite Indian Hill and newer Montgomery, plus a few affluent precincts of Cincinnati itself; it includes recent growth areas like northeastern Hamilton County and Anderson Township south of the Little Miami River, plus the far west part of Hamilton County, all heavily Republican; it heads east along the Ohio River to include Clermont County, a fast-growth area for 20 years, plus two rural counties and an oddly-shaped sliver of Warren County between Cincinnati and Dayton.

The congressman from the 2d District is Rob Portman, a Republican first elected in May 1993, who quickly became one of the most important legislators in the House. Portman has good connections both in Cincinnati and Washington. He grew up in Cincinnati, campaigned for his predecessor Bill Gradison before turning 21, went to work after law school for Patton Boggs & Blow in Washington and then for a Cincinnati law firm. In 1989 he went to work in the Bush White House, first in the counsel's office and then in legislative affairs; in 1992 he was U.S. representative to the United Nations Human Rights Council. He was back in Cincinnati in January 1993 when Gradison unexpectedly resigned from Congress to become head of the Health Insurance Association of America. Portman ran for the seat with Gradison's endorsement and impressive financial backing from the Cincinnati establishment, starting with mega-financier Carl Lindner. In the special primary he faced former Congressman Bob McEwen, who had represented the 6th District to the east for 12 years and then lost it after a contentious primary in 1992, and businessman Jay Buhert, president of the National Association of Home Builders, who ran a vitriolic campaign against both Portman and McEwen. Portman won with 36% of the vote, to 30% for McEwen, who carried counties he had once represented, and 25% for Buchert. Portman won the general with 70%.

In the House, Portman made himself an expert on unfunded federal mandates. As part of the Contract with America, he helped floor-manage in early 1995 the unfunded mandates bill— a large responsibility for one who hadn't even been a member two years. This measure, signed by Bill Clinton, requires unfunded mandates over $50 million for local governments to be subject to a point of order in the House or Senate, which can be overridden only by majority vote; it does not go as far as some would like, but much farther than a Democratic House would likely have gone. With a seat on Ways and Means, Portman became active on several causes. In the 105th Congress, he authored or co-authored nine bills that were signed by Clinton, including the Drug Demand Reduction Act to streamline the federal anti-drug bureaucracy; the Tropical Forest Conservation Act to write off part of the debt to the United States from less-developed countries in exchange for them committing to protect their forests; the National

Underground Railroad Network to Freedom Act to preserve those sites within the National Park Service; and a measure protecting state and local employee pension plans from raids by local governments.

Portman's biggest accomplishment was to shepherd, as co-chairman with Senator Bob Kerrey of the National Commission on Restructuring the Internal Revenue Service, a bipartisan package to define taxpayer rights and make the 100,000-plus employee agency more user friendly. For the future, Portman wants to protect and expand pensions for small-business workers. With Democrat Ben Cardin of Maryland, he filed a bill to make pensions more portable, permit increased savings, and relax federal restrictions. He focused again on unfunded mandates by winning House passage in early 1999 of a bill—backed by 67 Democrats—requiring more disclosure of mandates on businesses and consumers.

At home Portman sponsored a community-based anti-drug effort, urging schools, businesses, churches, and local media to discourage drug abuse; he boasts that it takes no federal money. None of his re-elections has been seriously contested. He takes no contributions from political action committees.

Cook's Call. *Safe.* Drawn to be the more Republican of the Cincinnati-based districts, the 2d District is the most Republican in the state. Portman has had no trouble racking up big margins here in the past and is a cinch for 2000.

The People: Pop. 1990: 570,779; 29.2% rural; 12% age 65 + ; 96.8% White, 2.2% Black, 0.8% Asian, 0.2% Amer. Indian, 0.1% Other; 0.4% Hispanic Origin. Households: 62.1% married couple families; 31.5% married couple fams. w. children; 46.4% college educ.; median household income: $34,688; per capita income: $16,813; median house value: $79,400; median gross rent: $345.

1996 Presidential Vote			1992 Presidential Vote		
Dole (R)	153,627	(58%)	Bush (R)	143,964	(52%)
Clinton (D)	90,571	(34%)	Clinton (D)	78,117	(28%)
Perot (I)	19,894	(7%)	Perot (I)	51,356	(19%)

Rep. Rob Portman (R)

Elected May 1993; b. Dec. 19, 1955, Cincinatti; home, Terrace Park; Dartmouth Col., B.A. 1979, U. of MI, J.D. 1984; Methodist; married (Jane).

Professional Career: Practicing atty., 1984–88; Assoc. Cnsl., White House, 1989; Dpty. Asst. & White House Legis. Affairs Dir., 1990–91; Alternate U.S. Rep. to UN Human Rights Comm., 1992.

DC Office: 238 CHOB 20515, 202-225-3164; Fax: 202-225-1992; Web site: www.house.gov/portman.

District Offices: Batavia, 513-732-2948; Cincinnati, 513-791-0381.

Committees: *Standards of Official Conduct* (5th of 5 R). *Ways & Means* (15th of 23 R): Oversight; Social Security.

Group Ratings

	ADA	ACLU	AFS	LCV	CON	NTU	NFIB	COC	ACU	NTLC	CHC
1998	5	6	0	31	94	73	100	78	88	84	100
1997	20	—	13	—	88	56	—	90	92	—	—

National Journal Ratings

	1997 LIB — 1997 CONS			1998 LIB — 1998 CONS		
Economic	34%	—	66%	0%	—	88%
Social	30%	—	64%	26%	—	72%
Foreign	32%	—	65%	43%	—	53%

Key Votes of the 105th Congress

1. Clinton Budget Deal	Y	5. Puerto Rico Sthood. Ref.	N	9. Cut $ for B-2 Bombers	Y
2. Education IRAs	Y	6. End Highway Set-asides	Y	10. Human Rights in China	N
3. Req. 2/3 to Raise Taxes	Y	7. School Prayer Amend.	Y	11. Withdraw Bosnia Troops	N
4. Fast-track Trade	Y	8. Ovrd. Part. Birth Veto	Y	12. End Cuban TV-Marti	N

Election Results

1998 general	Rob Portman (R)	154,344	(76%)	($359,922)
	Charles W. Sanders (D)	49,293	(24%)	($9,174)
1998 primary	Rob Portman (R)	unopposed		
1996 general	Rob Portman (R)	186,853	(72%)	($256,544)
	Thomas R. Chandler (D)	58,715	(23%)	
	Kathleen M. McKnight (NL)	13,905	(5%)	

THIRD DISTRICT

Dayton, once a medium-sized city known as the home of the typical American voter, is now the name of the international peace agreement reached in November 1995 that temporarily stopped the slaughter in former Yugoslavia. The 21 days of negotiating took place at Wright-Patterson Air Force Base, outside the city limits but the people of Dayton played a role. "From the time we landed at the airport," wrote U.S. negotiator Richard Holbrooke, "until the time we left, we felt that we were in a community that was literally praying for us. People were lighting candles in their windows, there were signs all over the airport and on the byways. That would never have happened in New York or in Washington. And it made a tremendous impression on people."

Dayton has made a difference in people's lives in America and around the world for many years. Here, just south of the old National Road that spans the Midwest, was the home of James Ritty, who in 1879 invented the cash register—that indispensable instrument of mass retail trade—and of John Henry Patterson, who bought it from Ritty for $6,500 in 1884 and established the National Cash Register company (NCR). It was home of a former Patterson subordinate, Tom Watson Sr., who feuded with him and went off to found IBM. It was in Dayton in the 1890s that Wilbur and Orville Wright, tinkering in their bicycle shop and observing the horseless carriages driven through Dayton's streets, experimented with kites and gliders and constructed the first wind tunnel in the world and the first heavier-than-air flying machine, which they took to ever-windy Kitty Hawk, North Carolina, to fly in December 1903. A few years later, Dayton's Charles Kettering invented the automatic starter for cars. In the 1970s and 1980s, Dayton's economy seemed to be sputtering. General Motors, the area's largest employer, was in trouble; NCR was overtaken by others in a merger. But by the mid-1990s Dayton's unemployment rate was below the national average and its economic growth faster. There are now more scientists, engineers, computer specialists and technicians here than GM workers. The area's small manufacturers and suppliers have shown that Dayton's spirit of tinkering and innovation, practical organization and mechanical dreaming, are still thriving, as much as its neighborliness and compassion.

Politically, the Dayton area has been known as a bellwether since Richard Scammon and Ben Wattenberg's *The Real Majority* of 1970 profiled the Dayton housewife. In the 1980s and 1990s the area has mostly voted for statewide and national winners, leaning just a bit more

Democratic than Ohio as a whole. This is true as well of Ohio's 3d Congressional District, which includes Dayton and all but a small corner of surrounding Montgomery County.

The congressman from Dayton is Tony Hall, a Democrat first elected in 1978. Hall grew up in Dayton, where his father was once mayor; in 1966 and 1967 he served in the Peace Corps in Thailand, while the Vietnam war was raging not far away. He returned home and in 1968, at 26, was elected to the state legislature, where he served for a decade. When the 3d District came open in 1978, he was the obvious candidate, and easily won in a generally Republican year. In the early 1980s Hall became a born-again Christian. He opposes abortion, but his number one cause has been to alleviate world hunger. When Texas Congressman Mickey Leland died in a plane crash in Ethiopia, Hall succeeded him as chairman of the Select Committee on Hunger, and decried the civil wars and infrastructural deficiencies that obstructed food delivery throughout much of Africa (he talks less about how African socialism has reduced food supplies). He has traveled to Somalia, Haiti, Uganda, Rwanda, North Korea and the former Yugoslavia, and obviously has been deeply moved by those suffering from hunger. He called for a 100-day cease-fire to immunize children of the former Yugoslavia, in August 1995 and said he would support the U.S. peacekeeping force after the Dayton agreements later that year. At home he has started "gleaning" programs to use leftover hotel and restaurant food to feed the poor; he also applied these programs elsewhere—most notably at the Atlanta Olympics and both parties' 1996 convention cities. He set up the first 800 telephone number for food emergency assistance in 1995.

In the House, Hall has suffered setbacks, but he has been effective in getting results. In April 1993 the House responded to freshmen pressure to trim the institution and voted not to reauthorize the Select Committee on Hunger, and Hall embarked on a 22-day fast. Then in early 1995 the Republican House voted to eliminate all funded caucuses, including his Hunger Caucus. But Hall's dedication, hard work, and obvious sincerity have probably made more difference than a staff structure. His 15-year-old son died of leukemia in July 1996, after a bone marrow transplant. But Hall worked on, urging the Democratic National Convention to adopt "tolerance language" recognizing and welcoming those Democrats like Hall who oppose abortion. He is among the few American officials to visit North Korea, where he nearly moved doctors to tears when he carried 10 boxes of medicine to a hospital that conducts surgery without adequate anesthesia and no antibiotics. He opposed the 1996 welfare bill and called for banning "indecent material" on cable TV. In 1997 Hall introduced a resolution apologizing for slavery and said that he was "stunned" by the controversy it aroused; some criticized it as unnecessary, since the three constitutional amendments abolishing slavery and guaranteeing full rights to former slaves were passed in 1865–70, while some Black Caucus members criticized the proposal as cheap tokenism. In 1998, he sponsored passage of Seeds of Hope, to direct foreign-aid dollars to more cost-effective food distribution and economic development in Africa.

In his district, Hall fights hard to maintain Wright-Pat as the center for Air Force research and development and has saved the Dayton Aviation Heritage National Historic Park. He made sure the federal government took responsibility for cleaning up the Energy Department's former Mound Nuclear Weapons Plant, which is being converted to a high-tech industrial park. For more than 20 years, Hall has easily won re-election.

Cook's Call. *Safe.* Although this district can be rather competitive on the presidential level (Clinton eked out a narrow win in 1992 and Bush won here in 1988), Hall has had little trouble holding onto this Dayton-based district for the past 20 years. When Hall does step aside, this district could be a problem for Democrats.

The People: Pop. 1990: 570,913; 4.6% rural; 13.2% age 65 + ; 80.8% White, 17.8% Black, 0.9% Asian, 0.2% Amer. Indian, 0.3% Other; 0.7% Hispanic Origin. Households: 51.9% married couple families; 23.7% married couple fams. w. children; 47% college educ.; median household income: $30,083; per capita income: $14,500; median house value: $65,000; median gross rent: $316.

1258 OHIO

1996 Presidential Vote

Clinton (D) 115,168 (50%)
Dole (R) 95,003 (41%)
Perot (I) 18,194 (8%)

1992 Presidential Vote

Clinton (D) 107,659 (41%)
Bush (R) 104,215 (40%)
Perot (I) 47,465 (18%)

Rep. Tony P. Hall (D)

Elected 1978; b. Jan. 16, 1942, Dayton; home, Dayton; Denison U., A.B. 1964; Presbyterian; married (Janet).

Elected Office: OH House of Reps., 1968–72; OH Senate, 1972–78.

Professional Career: Peace Corps, Thailand, 1966–67; Real estate broker, 1968–78.

DC Office: 1432 LHOB 20515, 202-225-6465; Web site: www.house.gov/tonyhall.

District Office: Dayton, 937-225-2843.

Committees: *Rules* (3d of 4 D): Rules & Organization of the House (RMM).

Group Ratings

	ADA	ACLU	AFS	LCV	CON	NTU	NFIB	COC	ACU	NTLC	CHC
1998	75	31	78	62	61	17	29	44	21	29	50
1997	70	—	75	—	84	31	—	50	21	—	—

National Journal Ratings

	1997 LIB	—	1997 CONS	1998 LIB	—	1998 CONS
Economic	63%	—	37%	64%	—	36%
Social	55%	—	45%	48%	—	51%
Foreign	59%	—	40%	63%	—	36%

Key Votes of the 105th Congress

1. Clinton Budget Deal	N	5. Puerto Rico Sthood. Ref.	Y	9. Cut $ for B-2 Bombers	Y
2. Education IRAs	Y	6. End Highway Set-asides	N	10. Human Rights in China	Y
3. Req. 2/3 to Raise Taxes	N	7. School Prayer Amend.	N	11. Withdraw Bosnia Troops	N
4. Fast-track Trade	N	8. Ovrd. Part. Birth Veto	Y	12. End Cuban TV-Marti	*

Election Results

1998 general	Tony P. Hall (D) 114,198	(69%)	($122,866)
	John S. Shondel (R) 50,544	(31%)	($20,726)
1998 primary	Tony P. Hall (D) .... unopposed		
1996 general	Tony P. Hall (D) 144,583	(64%)	($247,426)
	David A. Westbrock (R) 75,732	(33%)	($403,972)
	Others 6,888	(3%)	

FOURTH DISTRICT

Central Ohio looks mostly like farmland to the traveler. Yet this is manufacturing country, indeed one of America's premier manufacturing areas, where most people make their living in factories in small towns and on rural highways. These places seem far from anywhere important, yet are on one of the great east-west routes—the old rail lines and newer highways—that cross the country. They seem old-fashioned and rooted in an older technological time, yet here, in Wapakoneta, a typically Ohioan-Indian name, is the home town of Neil Armstrong, first man on the moon. Politically, this crossroads on the flat limestone plains of northern Ohio is one of the Republican heartlands of the United States. On the B&O tracks from Dayton to Toledo that intersect the east-west rail lines used by Richard Nixon in 1968, Ronald Reagan in 1984, George Bush in 1992 and Bill Clinton in 1996 to make whistle-stop campaign tours, one can summon up memories of past campaign styles and loyalties.

Much of central Ohio makes up the 4th Congressional District, oddly regular in shape for an Ohio district. It includes Wapakoneta; Lima, whose name was pulled from a hat; Findlay, where a museum holds the captain's bathtub from the *U.S.S. Maine*, sunk in the Havana harbor in 1898; Marion, where young Socialist-to-be Norman Thomas delivered newspapers edited by President-to-be Warren Harding; and Mansfield, home of John Sherman, one of Ohio's great 19th Century Republican statesmen, and his brother General William Tecumseh Sherman, who marched his troops through Georgia for the Union and refused to be considered for president. This has been a Republican stronghold since the Civil War, industrial since the late 19th Century, quietly prosperous most of the years since World War II, though shaken by the collapse of the auto-steel-coal industries after the oil shock of 1979. It gave solid margins to George Bush in 1992 and Bob Dole in 1996.

The congressman here is Mike Oxley, first elected in June 1981, now holder of one of the most important subcommittee chairmanships in the House. Oxley is from Findlay, worked for his Republican congressman, served three years in the FBI after law school, then came home and was elected to the legislature in 1972, at 28. After the incumbent died, he ran for the House and won the special during the heyday of Reagan popularity by the surprisingly narrow margin of 378 votes.

Oxley serves on the Commerce Committee, where for years he was a minority voice on Chairman John Dingell's panel and a market-oriented conservative and critic of government regulation. Now he is in a position to call the shots. These are complex issues, which often lap across party lines, and he has shown ingenuity and had successes in the minority as well as in the majority. Oxley was a major player on the 1990 Clean Air Act, working with Ohioans of both parties to protect that state's high-sulfur power plants and big factories from being saddled with high costs. He successfully pushed his "auction" proposal, a market approach to pollution reduction, which, by allowing firms to sell polluting rights, lets supple and adaptive firms rather than rule-bound federal bureaucrats figure out how to best deal with pollution. On the Commerce Telecommunications Subcommittee, over opposition from Democrats, he required new frequencies of the radio spectrum to be allocated not by lottery but by auction; the resulting auctions for personal communications systems, cell phones, and pagers have been the largest in history and have supplied the Treasury with billions in revenue.

Oxley took a major part in the 1996 Telecommunications Act, when he helped break through deadlock to craft the first rewrite of communications law since 1934. As he earlier proposed, the act permits regional Bell companies to enter long distance and manufacturing services, and allows long distance carriers into local phone service; when a federal court overturned its ban of indecency on the Internet, he crafted a new provision that was inserted in the omnibus 1998 spending bill to restrict minors' access to adult material. Oxley has also worked to open foreign markets to U.S. telecom manufacturers and to let foreigners own U.S. telephone and broadcasting companies. He is a supporter of the Resource Conservation and Recovery Act (RCRA), regulating interstate transport of solid waste, and has worked to give states more power to ban the import of out-of-state garbage (much New York garbage is trucked to Ohio). Oxley also worked on the Storage Tank Trust Fund, and battery recycling legislation, achieving a bipartisan bill that, with voluntary recycling efforts from consumers, keeps nickel and cadmium from going into waste sites. He sponsored a bill regulating the sport of boxing, and a crime victim's restitution proposal that made it into the anti-terrorism bill. He vowed his subcommittee in

1999 would break the lengthy deadlock on Superfund reform, which has been one of his frustrations. "I'm a recovering lawyer myself, but I don't think the Superfund program should be a scholarship program for lawyers' kids," he told an industry gathering.

In late 1996 Oxley fought with Louisiana's Billy Tauzin for the chairmanship of the Commerce Telecommunications and Finance Subcommittee. Speaker Newt Gingrich promised the spot to Tauzin when he switched parties in August 1995 and Tauzin, who was first elected in May 1980, has 13 months' more seniority. The solution was to split the subcommittee, whose jurisdiction was perhaps greater than that of any other in Congress. Tauzin got first choice and took Telecommunications, Trade and Consumer Protection; Oxley got Finance and Hazardous Materials. The House's six-year limit on committee chairmanships offers an opportunity for Oxley in 2001 when Tom Bliley of Virginia must step down as Commerce Committee chairman; even if Tauzin wins the top Republican slot, Oxley likely will gain additional influence.

Oxley has been re-elected without difficulty.

Cook's Call. *Safe.* Oxley has had little trouble winning in this solidly Republican district. This north central district is about as safe as they come for Republicans in Ohio.

The People: Pop. 1990: 570,917; 45.6% rural; 13.8% age 65 + ; 94.5% White, 4.5% Black, 0.4% Asian, 0.2% Amer. Indian, 0.3% Other; 0.8% Hispanic Origin. Households: 61.6% married couple families; 29.7% married couple fams. w. children; 31.3% college educ.; median household income: $27,312; per capita income: $12,009; median house value: $50,600; median gross rent: $246.

1996 Presidential Vote

Dole (R)	118,298	(50%)
Clinton (D)	88,758	(37%)
Perot (I)	28,248	(12%)

1992 Presidential Vote

Bush (R)	118,142	(46%)
Clinton (D)	77,975	(30%)
Perot (I)	58,900	(23%)

Rep. Michael G. Oxley (R)

Elected June 1981; b. Feb. 11, 1944, Findlay; home, Findlay; Miami U. (OH), B.A. 1966, OH St. U., J.D. 1969; Lutheran; married (Patricia).

Elected Office: OH House of Reps., 1972–81.

Professional Career: FBI Spec. Agent, 1969–71; Practicing atty., 1972–1981.

DC Office: 2233 RHOB 20515, 202-225-2676; Web site: www.house.gov/oxley.

District Offices: Findlay, 419-423-3210; Lima, 419-999-6455; Mansfield, 419-522-5757.

Committees: *Commerce* (3d of 29 R): Finance & Hazardous Materials (Chmn.); Telecommunications, Trade & Consumer Protection (Vice Chmn.).

Group Ratings

	ADA	ACLU	AFS	LCV	CON	NTU	NFIB	COC	ACU	NTLC	CHC
1998	5	20	11	8	13	48	100	100	96	95	92
1997	10	—	25	—	49	46	—	100	68	—	—

National Journal Ratings

	1997 LIB — 1997 CONS			1998 LIB — 1998 CONS		
Economic	35%	—	63%	15%	—	81%
Social	36%	—	63%	40%	—	60%
Foreign	49%	—	49%	43%	—	53%

Key Votes of the 105th Congress

1. Clinton Budget Deal	Y	5. Puerto Rico Sthood. Ref.	N	9. Cut $ for B-2 Bombers	N
2. Education IRAs	Y	6. End Highway Set-asides	Y	10. Human Rights in China	N
3. Req. 2/3 to Raise Taxes	Y	7. School Prayer Amend.	Y	11. Withdraw Bosnia Troops	N
4. Fast-track Trade	Y	8. Ovrd. Part. Birth Veto	Y	12. End Cuban TV-Marti	N

Election Results

1998 general	Michael G. Oxley (R) 112,011	(64%)	($616,196)
	Paul McClain (D) 63,529	(36%)	($33,824)
1998 primary	Michael G. Oxley (R) .... unopposed		
1996 general	Michael G. Oxley (R) 147,608	(65%)	($639,496)
	Paul McClain (D) 69,096	(30%)	($27,230)
	Michael McCaffery (I) 11,057	(5%)	

FIFTH DISTRICT

Undergirded by limestone, as flat and fertile as any place in America, northwest Ohio sits astride the land routes in parts of the country that were economically the most productive in the years they were settled. Here were the "Firelands," reserved for Connecticut Yankees whose farms were burned in the Revolution, and the neat and substantial small towns built by German Protestants in the mid-19th Century. Northwest Ohio is the beginning of the great corn and hog belt that stretches through Indiana and Illinois into Iowa, and was long a heartland of the Republican Party. Fremont, settled by abstemious Yankees, was the home of President Rutherford B. Hayes, whose wife Lucy served only lemonade in the White House; nearby Sandusky, settled by Germans who built big wineries and breweries, now has its own Merry-Go-Round Museum; Port Clinton, on Lake Erie, bills itself as the "Walleye Capital of the World" and drops a walleye on New Year's Eve to rival Times Square. Not far away is Milan, birthplace of the great inventor and capitalist Thomas Edison.

This is prime industrial country: its limestone, rail connections and location near the Great Lakes have spurred the growth of a factory economy that in dollar terms is far more important than agriculture. After the first settlement, northwest Ohio grew steadily for many decades, surging ahead in the 1950s and 1960s as its small factories supplied the big auto plants in Detroit and Ohio cities. Growth lagged noticeably in the early 1980s, when the domestic auto industry collapsed, but returned in the 1990s as small firms sold not only to the Big Three but to foreign customers.

The 5th Congressional District sweeps across northwest Ohio, from Grafton, just beyond the westward expansion of metropolitan Cleveland, across the limestone plains through Sandusky, its harbor on Lake Erie, and home of the giant Cedar Point amusement park—home of the world's tallest and fastest wooden roller coaster. It continues through Milan and Fremont, past part of the university town of Bowling Green and the Toledo suburb of Perrysburg, to the western Ohio towns of Defiance and Napoleon (wonderful names!). Its factories include the world's largest ketchup plant in Fremont and the largest washing machine plant in Clyde, both in Sandusky County, plus the largest baking soda plant in Old Fort. It avoids Toledo and its suburbs directly east and west. Historically, this was a solidly Republican district from the Civil War through the New Deal and up through the 1970s. Recently it has become more competitive: its eastern counties voted for Bill Clinton in 1996, the western counties for Bob Dole.

The congressman from the 5th is Paul Gillmor, a Republican first elected in 1988. He grew up in northern Ohio, practiced law, and was elected, at 27, to the state Senate in 1966, where he later became president. He is a professional, though not especially provocative, politician. For years Gillmor eyed this seat and waited for incumbent Delbert Latta to retire; he even passed a state law blocking the party from designating Latta's son as nominee if Latta resigned. In the 1988 primary Gillmor beat the junior Latta by exactly 27 votes out of 63,000 cast. Now

Gillmor may be creating a family dynasty of his own. In 1992 his wife Karen was elected to the state Senate from the 26th District, which overlaps the 5th Congressional District in Sandusky and Seneca Counties. All the more strikingly, she had a baby (Paul Michael, known as Little P.M.) just before the primary. In June 1996, Karen Gillmor, then 48, gave birth to twin boys. Gillmor's Democratic opponent attacked him for taking a leave of absence for the occasion; *The Hill*, a Washington, D.C., newspaper, called it "one of the most ill-conceived campaign attacks in 1996."

Gillmor focused on internal reform in his first years in the House, working to freeze committee funding, and on local issues, repealing the Coast Guard recreational boating user fees. On the Commerce Committee, he backed limits on out-of-state solid waste and greater competition for cable TV and telephone companies. He has called for amending the Public Utility Holding Company Act to allow utilities to offer telecom services and wants to require corporations to disclose charitable contributions. He favors cost-benefit analysis and risk assessment and has a solidly conservative record on economics. He is comfortable with Republican moderates on cultural and foreign issues, and is a member of both the Tuesday Group and the Leadership's Whip Team.

On local issues, he saved the National Rifle Matches at Camp Perry by creating a private non-profit corporation to conduct them; they were imperiled by liberals in the appropriations process. He got the National Weather Service to keep a radar facility in Fort Wayne so that tornado-prone northwest Ohio would not have to rely on Cleveland. And he won funds to renovate the Rutherford B. Hayes home in Fremont. Gillmor has been re-elected easily.

Cook's Call. *Safe.* Gillmor is well-entrenched in this Republican-leaning district. Don't look for a competitive race here in 2000.

The People: Pop. 1990: 570,946; 54.1% rural; 13.5% age 65 + ; 95.9% White, 2.1% Black, 0.4% Asian, 0.2% Amer. Indian, 1.5% Other; 2.9% Hispanic Origin. Households: 63.9% married couple families; 32.1% married couple fams. w. children; 32.4% college educ.; median household income: $30,117; per capita income: $12,755; median house value: $58,000; median gross rent: $260.

1996 Presidential Vote		1992 Presidential Vote	
Dole (R)	108,255 (44%)	Bush (R)	108,421 (41%)
Clinton (D)	102,862 (42%)	Clinton (D)	88,773 (34%)
Perot (I)	32,365 (13%)	Perot (I)	66,051 (25%)

Rep. Paul E. Gillmor (R)

Elected 1988; b. Feb. 1, 1939, Tiffin; home, Old Fort; Ohio Wesleyan U., B.A. 1961, U. of MI, J.D. 1964; Methodist; married (Karen).

Military Career: Air Force, 1965–66.

Elected Office: OH Senate, 1966–88.

Professional Career: Practicing atty., 1965–88.

DC Office: 1203 LHOB 20515, 202-225-6405; Fax: 202-225-1985; Web site: www.house.gov/gillmor.

District Offices: Defiance, 419-782-1996; Norwalk, 419-668-0206; Port Clinton, 800-541-6446.

Committees: *Commerce* (Vice Chmn. of 29 R): Finance & Hazardous Materials; Telecommunications, Trade & Consumer Protection. *International Relations* (23d of 26 R): Asia & the Pacific; Western Hemisphere.

Group Ratings

	ADA	ACLU	AFS	LCV	CON	NTU	NFIB	COC	ACU	NTLC	CHC
1998	5	0	0	15	45	42	93	100	68	81	92
1997	10	—	25	—	82	51	—	89	84	—	—

National Journal Ratings

	1997 LIB — 1997 CONS	1998 LIB — 1998 CONS
Economic	38% — 61%	39% — 61%
Social	30% — 64%	32% — 67%
Foreign	42% — 57%	49% — 48%

Key Votes of the 105th Congress

1. Clinton Budget Deal	Y	5. Puerto Rico Sthood. Ref.	N	9. Cut $ for B-2 Bombers	N
2. Education IRAs	Y	6. End Highway Set-asides	Y	10. Human Rights in China	N
3. Req. 2/3 to Raise Taxes	N	7. School Prayer Amend.	Y	11. Withdraw Bosnia Troops	N
4. Fast-track Trade	Y	8. Ovrd. Part. Birth Veto	Y	12. End Cuban TV-Marti	N

Election Results

1998 general	Paul E. Gillmor (R)	123,979	(67%)	($264,320)
	Susan Davenport Darrow (D)	61,926	(33%)	($8,532)
1998 primary	Paul E. Gillmor (R)	unopposed		
1996 general	Paul E. Gillmor (R)	145,692	(61%)	($327,472)
	Annie Saunders (D)	81,170	(34%)	($23,710)
	David J. Schaffer (NL)	11,461	(5%)	($6,170)

SIXTH DISTRICT

Early settlers of Ohio came from the south, where the Ohio River was a superhighway through the forest. Yankees traveled down the Ohio from Pittsburgh and founded Marietta in 1788 as Ohio's first town. About the same time, George Washington procured bounty lands for Revolutionary War veterans in the Virginia Military District of Ohio between the Scioto and Miami rivers, centered on Chillicothe. In Marietta the Yankees built New England-style churches; in Chillicothe the young Virginian Thomas Worthington, who became governor of Ohio, built his home, Adena, designed by architect Benjamin Latrobe. Virginians soon outnumbered New Englanders, and their traces remain on the landscape, which is laid out in irregular-shaped parcels as in Virginia, unlike the Northwest Ordinance's checkerboard grid imposed on most of the Midwest. There have been lasting political effects too. These rolling lands south of U.S. 40 have never attracted much industry; most people here speak with an accent that sounds Southern to northern Ohioans; they retain, with conservative cultural attitudes, a Democratic heritage that manifests itself on occasion. One sign of Bill Clinton's shrewd campaign instincts was that the 1992 Clinton-Gore bus trip out of the New York convention went through this part of Ohio, and that Clinton returned in 1996, carrying Ohio both times in part because of margins he won in many southern Ohio counties.

The 6th Congressional District covers most of southern Ohio, from Marietta down the Ohio River to the gritty industrial towns of Ironton and Portsmouth; it runs across the hilly landscape to include part of Chillicothe and all of Piketon, and west over to the Warren County suburbs of Dayton and Cincinnati. It has no large central cities and mostly avoids metropolitan areas. Politically, this has been not just a battlefield but a killing ground: In the four elections this decade held in the current boundaries of the 6th District, four incumbent congressmen have been defeated. The first two were Republicans, who were thrown together in 1992 by redistricting, Clarence Miller and Bob McEwen; the third was a Democrat elected in the wake of the Clinton bus tour, Ted Strickland; the fourth was a Republican elected in 1994, Frank Cremeans, who lost to Strickland in 1996 and lost the Republican primary in 1998.

Settled in as the congressman is Ted Strickland, who ran unsuccessfully for this seat in 1976, 1978 and 1980, won in 1992, lost in 1994, and won again in 1996 (all of the last three were 51%–49% races) and 1998. Strickland, son of a steelworker and eighth of nine children, is a Methodist minister, was director of a children's home, and then a prison psychologist (at Lucasville, site of an April 1993 riot) and psychology professor at Shawnee State College. He and his wife have both made their way up as counseling professionals. He once described his goal as "building communities where children are nurtured and educated and protected and cared for."

In his first term, Strickland voted for the Clinton budget and tax package, but against the 1994 crime bill because of its gun control provisions and against NAFTA. In the 1994 campaign he was on the defensive, under attack for supporting the tax increase. As the election neared, Strickland suggested there might be a need to increase taxes to pay for health care reform; Cremeans seized on this and ran a last-minute ad that may have made the difference in his win. Cremeans compiled a conservative voting record; he was the first member of Congress to support Steve Forbes for president. In the 1996 campaign, Strickland attacked Cremeans for Medicare "cuts" and scaling down the Earned Income Tax Credit, which he called a tax increase on the poor. Strickland won by the seemingly obligatory margin of 51%–49%, with crucial votes in the counties around Gallipolis. Back on Capitol Hill, Strickland got a seat on the Commerce Committee, where he sought a moratorium on implementation of Clean Air Act regulations that affect industries in his region. He worked with Republican Tom Coburn of Oklahoma on legislation to ensure that doctors, not insurance companies, decide how long a patient should remain in the hospital. Local observers claimed that he moderated his views and distanced himself from Clinton after his 1994 defeat.

In 1998, Strickland faced what appeared likely to be another tough challenge. State Republicans recruited Lieutenant Governor Nancy Hollister to run, as a moderate concerned about funding local projects; she beat Cremeans in the primary, 39%–35%, (with 21% for political newcomer Michael Azinger, another conservative). Hollister favored a tax cut and called for a national debate on junking the tax code; Strickland warned that a tax cut could jeopardize Social Security. They also differed on fast track and federal grants for school construction. Hollister benefited from more than $400,000 in advertising from the National Republican Congressional Committee, but was hurt by opposition from local conservatives unhappy with her support of abortion rights and resentful that party bosses pushed her candidacy. And Strickland benefited from unions' on-the-ground campaign. These were both well-financed campaigns: each candidate spent just more than $1 million. Hollister carried rapidly growing Warren County in the west end of the district by 2–1 and carried Clinton County next door (America's Clinton counties are almost all heavily Republican), but she lost her home area around Marietta as well as every other county in the district in this pro-incumbent year. Strickland won overall by the huge (for this district) margin of 57%–43%: This was the first time a 6th District incumbent has been re-elected since 1990.

In April 1999 Strickland considered running against Senator Mike DeWine in 2000, but later decided against it, creating a huge sigh of relief among House Democrats worried about their ability to retain the seat—though some dismay among Senate Democrats. Michael Azinger moved early to run for the Republican nomination in 2000 and Cremeans may try to regain the seat; this could be a seriously contested district again.

Cook's Call. *Competitive.* Strickland's 57% victory in 1998 was impressive in this district that has become a Bermuda triangle for incumbents: This is the first time since 1990 that an incumbent had been re-elected here. But, it is far too early to call Strickland a safe incumbent. This rural, sprawling district has a Republican lean and, as in past elections, can sway heavily with the national tide.

The People: Pop. 1990: 570,804; 59.6% rural; 13.7% age 65 + ; 97% White, 2.1% Black, 0.5% Asian, 0.3% Amer. Indian, 0.1% Other; 0.4% Hispanic Origin. Households: 60.1% married couple families; 29.9% married couple fams. w. children; 29.6% college educ.; median household income: $21,761; per capita income: $10,349; median house value: $46,600; median gross rent: $225.

1996 Presidential Vote			1992 Presidential Vote		
Clinton (D)	106,479	(44%)	Bush (R)	102,481	(40%)
Dole (R)	101,991	(43%)	Clinton (D)	99,761	(39%)
Perot (I)	28,942	(12%)	Perot (I)	50,532	(20%)

Rep. Ted Strickland (D)

Elected 1996; b. Aug. 4, 1941, Lucasville; home, Lucasville; Asbury Col., B.A. 1963, M.A., 1967, U. of KY, Ph.D. 1980; Methodist; married (Frances).

Elected Office: U.S. House of Reps., 1992–94.

Professional Career: Assoc. Minister, Trinity Methodist Church, 1967–68; Dir. of Soc. Svcs., KY Methodist Home, 1968–70; Consulting psychologist, Southern OH Correctional Facility, 1985–92, 1995–96; Prof., Shawnee St. U., 1988–92, 1994–96.

DC Office: 336 CHOB 20515, 202-225-5705; Fax: 202-225-5907; Web site: www.house.gov/strickland.

District Offices: Jackson, 740-286-5199; Marietta, 614-376-0868; Portsmouth, 614-353-5171; Wilmington, 937-382-4585.

Committees: *Commerce* (20th of 24 D): Energy & Power; Health and Environment; Oversight & Investigations.

Group Ratings

	ADA	ACLU	AFS	LCV	CON	NTU	NFIB	COC	ACU	NTLC	CHC
1998	85	60	100	85	48	21	43	33	32	14	25
1997	75	—	88	—	84	31	—	44	24	—	—

National Journal Ratings

	1997 LIB — 1997 CONS			1998 LIB — 1998 CONS		
Economic	61%	—	38%	61%	—	37%
Social	67%	—	32%	64%	—	36%
Foreign	79%	—	19%	49%	—	48%

Key Votes of the 105th Congress

1. Clinton Budget Deal	N	5. Puerto Rico Sthood. Ref.	N	9. Cut $ for B-2 Bombers	Y
2. Education IRAs	N	6. End Highway Set-asides	N	10. Human Rights in China	Y
3. Req. 2/3 to Raise Taxes	N	7. School Prayer Amend.	N	11. Withdraw Bosnia Troops	N
4. Fast-track Trade	N	8. Ovrd. Part. Birth Veto	Y	12. End Cuban TV-Marti	Y

Election Results

1998 general	Ted Strickland (D)	102,852	(57%)	($1,050,157)
	Nancy P. Hollister (R)	77,711	(43%)	($1,008,844)
1998 primary	Ted Strickland (D)	unopposed		
1996 general	Ted Strickland (D)	118,003	(51%)	($714,172)
	Frank A. Cremeans (R)	111,907	(49%)	($1,786,582)

SEVENTH DISTRICT

The hills and plains of central Ohio are dotted with towns and small cities that have been manufacturing centers almost since they were settled in the early 19th Century, when the dominant technologies were the waterwheel and the open forge. In the decades since, they have been replaced by one new technology after another, and the local manufacturing economy, sometimes with uncomfortable fits and starts, has adjusted and advanced. There were painful job losses here in the early 1980s, but small business has grown in the years since. As old factories shut down, new ones open that are more productive; the results are higher incomes and, though not often remembered, far less of the backbreaking hard work and drudgery that were almost everyone's lot in supposedly better times.

The 7th Congressional District is made up of a G-shaped slice of the central part of the state. Its largest city is Springfield, where the truck plant of Navistar, formerly International Harvester, has long been the biggest employer. To the south are the eastern suburbs of Dayton around Wright-Patterson Air Force Base, whose name recalls the Dayton-based fathers of the airplane and the cash register. In the northern end of the 7th District are Bellefontaine, site of the first concrete street in America, and, a few miles away, Marysville, the site of Honda's first U.S. plant, where American workers assemble Honda Accords. The district has always been Republican territory. It backed the policies of Ohio Republican President William McKinley— tariff protection, railroad regulation, antitrust suits against monopolies, discouragement of labor unions—and Governor James Rhodes—low taxes, promotion of new businesses and jobs. It is culturally conservative and economically mostly satisfied with free markets. It gave good margins to George Bush in 1992 and Bob Dole in 1996.

The 7th District's congressman is David Hobson, a Republican from Springfield first elected in 1990 after eight years in the state Senate. Hobson sold real estate for many years and retains properties in the area. (Selling real estate is a useful background to politics, he says: "Always leave something on the table for the other guy.") He has a moderate to conservative voting record. After a 13-year-old Ohio girl was killed when her coat drawstring was caught in a school bus door, he got clothing manufacturers to voluntarily remove drawstrings longer than three inches. He works on local issues, from advocating Wright-Patterson Air Force Base as home for the Joint Strike Force research center to improving the U.S. 33 bypass. He worked with Dayton Democrat Tony Hall to secure a federal waiver for the Dayton Area Health Plan and to establish Dayton's National Aviation Historic Park.

Hobson is a key member of the Appropriations Committee, where he became chairman in the 106th Congress of the Military Construction Subcommittee—a useful slot for a representative concerned about a local Air Force base. He said that his top priority would be to ensure that military families have the quality housing and secure work facilities they deserve; following an early 1999 trip to bases in Germany and Italy, he criticized the troops' "substandard" housing there. Responding to reports of inadequate military health care, he won 1998 passage of a requirement that all military doctors hold unrestricted state medical licenses and complete education requirements. He also serves on the Appropriations Defense Subcommittee. Hobson was a force for moderation among Republicans in January 1996 after Bill Clinton's budget vetoes and the federal shutdown when he said, "We wanted to prove to the country that we are reasonable people." He seemed more at home with the bipartisan cooperation on budget, health care, and welfare reform that later prevailed. Hobson worked on the Republican proposal for Medicare reform and sought support from the Blue Dogs.

His steady demeanor and backroom skills have made Hobson a resource for House Republican leaders—advising them on budget issues, protecting Speaker Newt Gingrich's interests at the ethics committee and during the aborted 1997 coup, and working with Denny Hastert on health care legislation even before his Illinois friend became speaker. And he is a close ally of Budget Committee chairman and presidential candidate John Kasich, who represents the adjacent 12th District. But Hobson does not seek the spotlight on Capitol Hill: when leadership meetings break up and many head for the ever-present microphones and television cameras, Hobson typically passes them by. "That isn't my style," says Hobson. "I'm not doing this to build Dave Hobson into a national name."

Cook's Call. *Safe.* Hobson has been easily re-elected to this Republican district since 1990. There is no reason to believe that he would have trouble winning in 2000.

The People: Pop. 1990: 570,939; 42.6% rural; 12.3% age 65 + ; 93.5% White, 5.4% Black, 0.7% Asian, 0.2% Amer. Indian, 0.2% Other; 0.6% Hispanic Origin. Households: 63% married couple families; 30.9% married couple fams. w. children; 37% college educ.; median household income: $30,364; per capita income: $12,919; median house value: $62,900; median gross rent: $278.

1996 Presidential Vote			1992 Presidential Vote		
Dole (R)	115,393	(47%)	Bush (R)	112,701	(45%)
Clinton (D)	100,509	(41%)	Clinton (D)	84,098	(33%)
Perot (I)	25,373	(10%)	Perot (I)	54,307	(22%)

Rep. David Hobson (R)

Elected 1990; b. Oct. 17, 1936, Cincinnati; home, Springfield; OH Wesleyan U., B.A. 1958, OH St. U., J.D. 1963; Methodist; married (Carolyn).

Military Career: OH Air Natl. Guard, 1958–63.

Elected Office: OH Senate, 1982–90, Majority Whip, 1986–88, Pres. Pro-Tem, 1988–90.

Professional Career: Real estate agent, 1969–90; Restaurant owner, 1977–93.

DC Office: 1514 LHOB 20515, 202-225-4324; Fax: 202-225-1984; Web site: www.house.gov/hobson.

District Offices: Lancaster, 614-654-5149; Springfield, 937-325-0474.

Committees: *Appropriations* (14th of 34 R): Defense; Military Construction (Chmn.); VA, HUD & Independent Agencies.

Group Ratings

	ADA	ACLU	AFS	LCV	CON	NTU	NFIB	COC	ACU	NTLC	CHC
1998	5	31	22	23	70	65	100	82	88	89	83
1997	5	—	25	—	34	49	—	90	80	—	—

National Journal Ratings

	1997 LIB — 1997 CONS			1998 LIB — 1998 CONS		
Economic	28%	—	67%	34%	—	64%
Social	45%	—	54%	44%	—	56%
Foreign	24%	—	72%	27%	—	68%

Key Votes of the 105th Congress

1. Clinton Budget Deal	Y	5. Puerto Rico Sthood. Ref.	N	9. Cut $ for B-2 Bombers	N
2. Education IRAs	Y	6. End Highway Set-asides	Y	10. Human Rights in China	N
3. Req. 2/3 to Raise Taxes	Y	7. School Prayer Amend.	Y	11. Withdraw Bosnia Troops	Y
4. Fast-track Trade	Y	8. Ovrd. Part. Birth Veto	Y	12. End Cuban TV-Marti	N

Election Results

1998 general	David Hobson (R)	120,765	(67%)	($662,103)
	Donald E. Minor (D)	49,780	(28%)	
	James A. Schrader (Lib)	9,146	(5%)	($13,221)
1998 primary	David Hobson (R)	47,348	(86%)	
	Richard Herron (R)	7,956	(14%)	
1996 general	David Hobson (R)	158,087	(68%)	($620,093)
	Richard K. Blain (D)	61,419	(26%)	($9,824)
	Dawn Marie Johnson (NL)	13,478	(6%)	

EIGHTH DISTRICT

The far west end of Ohio—where U.S. 40, the old National Road, heads straight as an arrow in its last miles across Ohio to Indiana, and the rail lines criss-cross the land from Cincinnati to Dayton—has since the early 20th Century housed some of the nation's prime industrial country. Here the Great and Little Miami rivers drain south into the Ohio; U.S. 40 jogs southward twice to go over the Miami and Stillwater River dams, built after the great flood of 1913 that killed 361 people in Dayton and caused $1 billion in damage. Around Dayton and Cincinnati, in large factory towns like Middletown and Hamilton and smaller factory towns like Troy and Piqua, Ohioans, after the recession of the early 1980s, adapted to new conditions and began to produce exports to Europe, Latin America and Asia as well as for the American market. And as city centers slowly emptied out, comfortable suburban tracts were growing in what were once open fields.

The 8th Congressional District covers much of this territory, including most of four counties north of Dayton and U.S. 40, Preble County west of Dayton, and Butler County between Dayton and Cincinnati. About half its people live in Butler, around Hamilton and Middletown and in suburbs north of Cincinnati—now a single metropolitan strip from northern Kentucky to U.S. 40 north of Dayton. Politically, this is solidly Republican territory, which Bob Dole carried with over 50%.

The congressman from the 8th District, John Boehner (pronounced *bayner*), was first elected in 1990 and quickly became one of the Republican leaders in the House. He grew up in Cincinnati, one of 12 children, and after college moved just beyond the line to Butler County; he started a packaging company, served on the Union Township Board of Trustees, and in 1984, at 34, was elected to the Ohio House. He won the congressional seat in the 1990 primary, by beating not one but two of his predecessors—incumbent Buz Lukens, who inexplicably ran after he was convicted of having sex with a 16-year-old girl, and Tom Kindness, who gave up the seat to run against Senator John Glenn in 1986 and then, as Boehner put it, deserted the district to become a Washington lobbyist. Boehner won 49%, to 32% for Kindness and 17% for Lukens.

In the House, Boehner joined the Gang of Seven, young freshman Republicans who insisted on revealing the names of all 355 members who had overdrafts at the House bank, and then went on to assail Democratic leaders and Republican go-alongers on the pay raise and the House Post Office scandal. They also argued that members of Congress should be subject to the regulatory laws they impose on other citizens; in 1992 Boehner invited OSHA inspectors to his office, where they found what would have been 15 violations if Congress were subject to its regulations. That same month Boehner took the lead in the formal adoption of the 27th Amendment to the Constitution, proposed by James Madison with the original Bill of Rights in 1789, to prohibit Congress from varying its pay during its current term. Boehner's Gang of Seven infuriated House veterans, but they struck a chord around the nation. In the process Boehner became a top lieutenant of then-Minority Whip Newt Gingrich, raising money for Republican candidates, pressuring the U.S. Chamber of Commerce to oppose the Clinton health care plan, and managing Gingrich's campaign for Republican leader after Robert Michel announced his retirement. He was a major player in drafting and championing the 10-point Contract With America. After the 1994 election, he ran for chairman of the Republican Conference and, with Gingrich's backing, beat California's Duncan Hunter 122–102.

That made Boehner number four in the Republican leadership, with informal responsibility for encouraging political action committee contributions to Republicans. At one point Boehner was handing out tobacco PAC checks on the floor, as Democrats had sometimes done; this practice was widely condemned and subsequently banned. Boehner worked hard to prepare the party message and to enforce discipline on issues from repealing the assault weapons ban to fielding ethics charges against Gingrich. By any recent historic standard, Republicans held together quite well during their first term in the majority, despite some disarray in 1996. Boehner also pushed for the Freedom to Farm bill, which phased out most subsidies—the most important farm legislation since 1933, and one that deprives farm-state Democrats of an issue on which they have long won.

The next two years were a turbulent time for Boehner. The ethics discussions on Gingrich placed Boehner in the middle of a legal altercation after a Florida couple taped Boehner's cellular telephone conversation with Republican leaders while he was driving through the state. The couple gave the tape to Jim McDermott of Washington, the senior Democrat on the House ethics committee, who then made the contents available to *The New York Times*. After Boehner sued McDermott in federal court for invasion of privacy, the Justice Department took the unusual step of intervening on his behalf when Boehner appealed a district judge's dismissal of the complaint. In July 1997, Boehner played a disputed role in the unusual coup attempt against Gingrich. What is clear is that he attended meetings where malcontents and other Republican leaders discussed their mutual dissatisfaction with the speaker; Boehner allies said that he did not back ouster efforts, while his foes contended that he was disloyal and ought to have alerted Gingrich. The incident soured their relationship and led to complaints that Boehner was failing to effectively deliver the party's message. Boehner later conceded that he underestimated the rebels' threats, which at the time "only struck me as slightly more than average."

Meanwhile, he played a key role in coordinating the House's one-vote passage of major reform of federal banking regulations and he took the lead for Republicans in debating what to do with the federal surplus (he argued for tax cuts and debt reduction); he unsuccessfully opposed Transportation Committee Chairman Bud Shuster's budget-busting highway bill. The year came to a bitter end for Boehner when the House Republican Conference voted to oust him as chairman after the 1998 election and Gingrich's resignation. A shocked Boehner said after the 121–93 victory of J.C. Watts of Oklahoma that he thought he "had the votes" to win. His fate was probably sealed when Dick Armey was re-elected majority leader over Jennifer Dunn; many Republican members thought there needed to be at least one other change in the leadership and were dismayed at the prospect of having no highly visible woman or ethnic minority in their top ranks. In May 1999, the FEC subpoenaed Boehner in a probe of whether some business lobbyists improperly coordinated a political ad campaign when he was Conference chairman. Boehner said he would fight the subpoenas, which were also issued to Watts and Boehner's Chief of Staff Barry Jackson, challenging them on procedural grounds because they were issued by an independent executive branch agency—House rules and precedents treat subpoenas from agencies with less deference than those from judges.

Assuming he remains in the House, Boehner has many future options. Despite his relatively brief tenure, he is a senior member of three committees and could be a major beneficiary in 2001 of the three-term limit on chairmanships if Republicans retain their majority. As the new chairman of Education and the Workforce's Employer-Employee Relations Subcommittee, he moved eagerly to address health care and pension issues. And, although he has downplayed speculation, it is possible that he will seek a leadership position again. Some congressional insiders speculate that he will move to a more lucrative position in the private sector. Whichever direction he takes, Boehner has played a major role in reshaping American politics. If he misstepped and misjudged on occasion, he also showed great skill and demonstrated how in the American political system a minority party legislator in one state can quickly transform government on the national stage.

Cook's Call. *Safe.* Boehner's seat is about as safe as they come. He will easily win a 6th term in 2000.

The People: Pop. 1990: 570,837; 38% rural; 12% age 65 +; 96.3% White, 2.8% Black, 0.6% Asian, 0.2% Amer. Indian, 0.2% Other; 0.5% Hispanic Origin. Households: 63.9% married couple families; 32.2% married couple fams. w. children; 36.1% college educ.; median household income: $31,171; per capita income: $13,355; median house value: $66,300; median gross rent: $295.

1996 Presidential Vote		
Dole (R)	125,577	(52%)
Clinton (D)	89,331	(37%)
Perot (I)	26,111	(11%)

1992 Presidential Vote		
Bush (R)	121,174	(47%)
Clinton (D)	75,375	(29%)
Perot (I)	60,172	(23%)

Rep. John A. Boehner (R)

Elected 1990; b. Nov. 17, 1949, Cincinnati; home, West Chester; Xavier U., B.S. 1977; Catholic; married (Debbie).

Military Career: Navy, 1969.

Elected Office: Union Township Bd. of Trustees, 1981–85, Pres., 1984; OH House of Reps., 1984–90.

Professional Career: Pres., Nucite Sales Inc., 1976–90.

DC Office: 1011 LHOB 20515, 202-225-6205; Fax: 202-225-0704; Web site: www.house.gov/boehner.

District Offices: Hamilton, 513-870-0300; Troy, 513-339-1524.

Committees: *Agriculture* (3d of 27 R): General Farm Commodities, Resource Conservation & Credit; Livestock & Horticulture. *Education & the Workforce* (6th of 27 R): Early Childhood, Youth & Families; Employer-Employee Relations (Chmn.); Workforce Protections. *House Administration* (Vice Chmn. of 6 R). *Joint Committee on Printing* (2d of 5 Reps.). *Joint Committee on the Library of Congress* (2d of 6 Reps.).

Group Ratings

	ADA	ACLU	AFS	LCV	CON	NTU	NFIB	COC	ACU	NTLC	CHC
1998	0	7	0	8	50	66	100	89	96	100	100
1997	0	—	13	—	46	55	—	100	87	—	—

National Journal Ratings

	1997 LIB — 1997 CONS			1998 LIB — 1998 CONS		
Economic	0%	—	90%	0%	—	88%
Social	0%	—	90%	3%	—	90%
Foreign	21%	—	79%	47%	—	51%

Key Votes of the 105th Congress

1. Clinton Budget Deal	Y	5. Puerto Rico Sthood. Ref.	N	9. Cut $ for B-2 Bombers	N
2. Education IRAs	Y	6. End Highway Set-asides	Y	10. Human Rights in China	N
3. Req. 2/3 to Raise Taxes	Y	7. School Prayer Amend.	Y	11. Withdraw Bosnia Troops	N
4. Fast-track Trade	Y	8. Ovrd. Part. Birth Veto	Y	12. End Cuban TV-Marti	N

Election Results

1998 general	John A. Boehner (R)	127,979	(71%)	($1,165,947)
	John W. Griffin (D)	52,912	(29%)	
1998 primary	John A. Boehner (R)	unopposed		
1996 general	John A. Boehner (R)	165,815	(70%)	($1,312,440)
	Jeffrey D. Kitchen (D)	61,515	(26%)	($20,853)
	Others	8,613	(4%)	

NINTH DISTRICT

In the 1920s Toledo was one of America's boom towns. This was "a decade of fabulous figures," Harlan Hatcher wrote: The Willys-Overland plant employed 25,000 workers and turned out an automobile every 30 seconds; the city built $20 million coal and iron ore docks; the Libbey-Owens-Ford merger made Toledo, with local supplies of natural gas and sand, the nation's largest glass manufacturer; the city built a new museum and transcontinental airport. Toledo had long been well-situated, where the Maumee River empties into Lake Erie, where two dozen rail lines connected it with the East Coast and Chicago and the coal fields of Kentucky and West Virginia. It was also well-positioned to be a center of the brash rising auto industry, a national leader when it first produced the Jeep in the 1940s. But by the late 1970s and early 1980s, auto company management had allowed the unions to bid wages and benefits too high while watching quality decline, to the point that consumers would not buy enough American-made cars for the industry to survive without vast subsidy or major shrinkage. Subsidy, beyond the temporary Chrysler loan and a few small trade barriers, was not forthcoming; so, Toledo and other auto-dependent cities went through tough times. But revival was on its way. Toledo in the 1990s produced one of America's hottest vehicles, the Jeep Cherokee; the old plant was set to close, but the city offered Chrysler $300 million in incentives to stay—the old plant will be refurbished and a new one will be built along I-75. Toledo's small manufacturers in search of markets here and abroad show the energy and ingenuity lacking in the big auto and glass companies 20 years prior.

Ohio's 9th Congressional District is centered on Toledo, spreading east to the flatlands of Ottawa County, south to Bowling Green State University, and west to rural Fulton County. Toledo has been heavily Democratic since CIO unions organized the plants in the late 1930s; the collapse of the auto industry so unnerved the district that in 1980 it voted for Ronald Reagan and elected a Republican congressman. But in 1982, it became solidly Democratic again, and has been ever since.

The congresswoman from the 9th District is Marcy Kaptur, a Democrat elected in 1982. Kaptur is fervent and principled, hard-working and dedicated, always a loyal daughter of Toledo. She grew up there in a blue-collar neighborhood, where her parents worked at local auto plants, and has spent almost her entire career in the public sector. After eight years as an urban planner in Toledo, she got a job in the Carter White House; she was shrewd enough to return to Toledo in 1982 when no other Democrat would run for the House seat and won although outspent by 3–1. She saw Toledo's economy nosedive, and feels intensely the pain of ordinary people who played by the rules but ended up losing because of larger economic forces. Kaptur's great cause is trade. She has long been convinced that Toledo and places like it have lost jobs and industry because of unfair trade practices by the Japanese and low-wage competition in countries like Mexico. America must use its global trading power to advance democracy and the rule of law and to raise all peoples' living standards, she says. If "capitalism laughs at boundaries," as the historian Fernand Braudel wrote, Kaptur, with her faith in the public sector, has worked hard to make those boundaries stronger, and not something to be snickered at. She pressured the Japanese to buy more American auto parts, but is leery of Japanese investment in the United States. She has proposed to prohibit top government officials from representing foreign corporations for five years and foreign governments forever after they leave office; she also would ban campaign contributions by foreign individuals or corporations—a provision she got attached to the Shays-Meehan campaign finance reform bill that passed the House but languished in the Senate. She favors a constitutional amendment to permit campaign spending limits.

Kaptur was probably Congress's most vocal and dedicated opponent of the NAFTA. She visited the Mexican border in spring 1993, and returned home with soil and water samples to demonstrate the pollution there. She argued that 100,000 jobs had been transferred from Ohio to Mexico, and cited the 1993 shutdown of a Toledo auto parts plant followed by the transfer of some of its jobs to Matamoros, Mexico. She criticized President Clinton for doing nothing for sagging U.S. industries and for ignoring her and other Democrats opposed to NAFTA. She brought to this issue a commitment that was genuinely moving, and did not drop trade issues even after NAFTA passed in November 1993. In early 1995, she argued forcefully against Clinton's proposal to bail out the Mexican peso with $40 billion of U.S. loan guarantees; the president was forced to abandon the legislation and proceed with an administrative rescue. Even as the two nations' economic ties boomed, Kaptur complained in 1997 that the trade has been one-sided toward Mexico.

Kaptur weighs in on other issues as well. She opposes funding for abortion and favors the partial-birth abortion ban. She works on local projects, like restoring Toledo's Farmers' Market and the Central Union Terminal, and she has called for more portraits and statues of women in the Capitol. She has set up the Golden Eagle Awards for exemplary companies and the Vulture Awards for poor corporate citizens. On the Appropriations Agriculture Subcommittee, where she is ranking minority member, Kaptur passed an amendment requiring farmers to plant or conserve land in order to receive transition payments. She votes more often against the Clinton Administration position that almost any other Democrat, and has been willing to take on the president in meetings; perhaps that explains why he line-item vetoed two of her projects in 1998—agricultural research studies of pesticide-free tomatoes and chromosomes of certain bacteria. In early September she expressed "sadness, anger and disgust" about the Clinton scandal and urged him to "choose an honorable course and do what is right for our nation. High office should not shield one from restoring what is due to the public when one has violated the moral code of conduct from which springs the public's confidence in any elected official." She added, "If he resigned tomorrow, it wouldn't be enough in my judgment," and suggested he might perform community service.

Kaptur is exceedingly popular in Toledo, and has run far ahead of party lines in the 9th District. She has also become something of a national political figure. In August 1995 she appeared before Ross Perot's United We Stand and made a rousing speech, mostly on trade, that had delegates cheering. Perot praised her and offered his vice presidential nomination in August 1996; she turned it down. She also has also declined opportunities to run for statewide office. In April 1999 she announced she would not run against Senator Mike DeWine in 2000. But she has published a book on women in Congress, has hosted a weekly radio show on nearly 100 stations, and shows no signs of discouragement in representing the workers of Toledo.

Cook's Call. *Safe.* Kaptur should have little trouble winning a tenth term in this reliably Democratic, heavily blue-collar district.

The People: Pop. 1990: 570,911; 13.5% rural; 13.2% age 65+; 85.1% White, 12.2% Black, 1% Asian, 0.2% Amer. Indian, 1.6% Other; 3.1% Hispanic Origin. Households: 52.1% married couple families; 25.6% married couple fams. w. children; 41.9% college educ.; median household income: $28,856; per capita income: $13,477; median house value: $58,700; median gross rent: $298.

1996 Presidential Vote			1992 Presidential Vote		
Clinton (D)	125,971	(55%)	Clinton (D)	118,713	(47%)
Dole (R)	76,613	(34%)	Bush (R)	81,784	(32%)
Perot (I)	22,960	(10%)	Perot (I)	50,151	(20%)

Rep. Marcy Kaptur (D)

Elected 1982; b. June 17, 1946, Toledo; home, Toledo; U. of WI, B.A. 1968, U. of MI, M.A. 1974, M.I.T., 1981–82; Catholic; single.

Professional Career: Urban planner, Lucas Cnty. Planning Comm., 1969–75; Urban planning consultant, 1975–77; White House Asst. Dir. for Urban Affairs, 1977–80; Dpty. Secy., Natl. Consumer Coop. Bank, 1980–81; Author.

DC Office: 2366 RHOB 20515, 202-225-4146; Fax: 202-225-7711; Web site: www.house.gov/kaptur.

District Office: Toledo, 419-259-7500.

Committees: *Appropriations* (8th of 27 D): Agriculture, Rural Development, & FDA (RMM); VA, HUD & Independent Agencies.

Group Ratings

	ADA	ACLU	AFS	LCV	CON	NTU	NFIB	COC	ACU	NTLC	CHC
1998	80	63	100	92	72	18	8	17	28	11	33
1997	75	—	100	—	0	16	—	22	32	—	—

National Journal Ratings

	1997 LIB — 1997 CONS		1998 LIB — 1998 CONS	
Economic	74% —	25%	71% —	28%
Social	70% —	30%	58% —	41%
Foreign	49% —	49%	52% —	47%

Key Votes of the 105th Congress

1. Clinton Budget Deal	N	5. Puerto Rico Sthood. Ref.	N	9. Cut $ for B-2 Bombers	Y
2. Education IRAs	N	6. End Highway Set-asides	N	10. Human Rights in China	Y
3. Req. 2/3 to Raise Taxes	N	7. School Prayer Amend.	N	11. Withdraw Bosnia Troops	N
4. Fast-track Trade	N	8. Ovrd. Part. Birth Veto	Y	12. End Cuban TV-Marti	N

Election Results

1998 general	Marcy Kaptur (D)	130,793	(81%)	($148,561)
	Edward S. Emery (R)	30,312	(19%)	($5,869)
1998 primary	Marcy Kaptur (D)	unopposed		
1996 general	Marcy Kaptur (D)	170,617	(77%)	($253,432)
	Randy Whitman (R)	46,040	(21%)	($44,641)
	Others	4,677	(2%)	

TENTH DISTRICT

Cleveland, one of America's great cities at the beginning of the 20th Century, faced some hardships in the latter half of this century, but is on its way back as the century ends. It grew early in this century as a center of heavy industry: This was the original home base of John D. Rockefeller's Standard Oil; the city's twisting and deep Cuyahoga River was the site of several of the nation's largest steel mills; great industrial fortunes here built civic institutions like the museums in Wade Park, Case Western University and the Cleveland Symphony, and financed the campaigns of northeast Ohio Republican Presidents James Garfield and William McKinley. On the old Public Square, designed like a New England town green by the Yankees who settled this Western Reserve (the northeast corner of Ohio) in the early 19th Century, the two eccentric

Van Sweringen brothers, trolley magnates of the early 20th Century, built the Terminal Tower, for many years the highest skyscraper in interior America. This yeasty, ethnic city, with more than 40 nationalities—Hungarians, Czechs, Serbs, Croatians, Poles, Italians, Germans (the Hapsburg Empire and more)—and many distinct ethnic neighborhoods, produced a robust two-party politics. In the 1930s, after CIO unions organized the steel factories and auto assembly plants, Cleveland became solidly Democratic, though with some affluent Republican suburbs.

But Cleveland never led the nation as it hoped: America's fourth largest city in 1910, it was overtaken in size first by Detroit, eventually by the likes of Houston and Dallas; today, it's the center of the nation's 14th largest metropolitan area. The central city declined from 914,000 in 1950 to 498,000 in 1996, as the children who grew up in the tightly-packed neighborhoods made more money and moved to the suburbs. Movement was especially great in wards east of the Cuyahoga River, which were almost entirely ethnic in 1950 and almost entirely black by 1970. The 1970s were a bad decade for Cleveland, which became an object of ridicule by national sophisticates. Its heavy industries were fast declining, Lake Erie and the Cuyahoga River were badly polluted (the river caught fire in June 1969). City politics became racially polarized with the election of black Mayor Carl Stokes in 1967 and 1969, and in December 1978 the city defaulted on bank loans under Mayor Dennis Kucinich.

The city government was rescued by George Voinovich, elected mayor in 1979 and later governor and senator. And the current mayor, Michael White, who is black, broke down racial polarization and first won the mayor's office in 1989 by carrying white wards west of the Cuyahoga while losing the black wards east of the river to black machine politician George Forbes. Downtown Cleveland revived, with the fourth-largest performing arts center in the nation at Playhouse Square, the new Jacobs Field baseball stadium, a new basketball arena, and the Rock and Roll Hall of Fame. Following the departure of the city's beloved Browns to Baltimore, a new football stadium has been constructed with an NFL payment, $9 million in damages from Browns' owner Art Modell for breaking his lease, and public money from a sin tax voters approved in November 1995. The city has gained an expansion team for 1999, retaining the Browns name and colors. People swim in now-clean Lake Erie; restaurants and pleasure boat docks line the Cuyahoga where diners can sip Burning River pale ale. Cleveland continues to be headquarters of several of the nation's largest law firms, and some businesses, like iron-ore giant Cleveland-Cliffs, have sharply revived; the city's number one employer is now health services, and the Cleveland Clinic may be its best-known firm. The city's revival became national news in 1995, when the Cleveland Indians went to the World Series for the first time since 1954.

The 10th Congressional District includes most of the west side of Cleveland and the western suburbs in Cuyahoga County. Excluded is one salient of mostly black Cleveland precincts attached to the 11th District across the Cuyahoga; also several western suburbs—Brook Park, Middleburg Heights—are in the convoluted suburban 19th District. Suburbs in the 10th include Lakewood, well-established by the 1920s and still comfortable middle-class territory, plus Rocky River and Bay Village, growing more affluent westward along the lake. Inland is Parma, a creation of the 1950s, when second- and third-generation ethnics moved out to subdivision houses set amid what was once America's densest concentration of bowling alleys. The political tradition is almost entirely Democratic, though Voinovich has won a majorities from grateful voters here.

The congressman from the 10th District is Dennis Kucinich, elected in 1996, now 52, still unrepentant about the day he plunged the city into default. Kucinich grew up as the oldest of seven children whose father was a truckdriver and family moved 21 times in different parts of Cleveland. He was a political prodigy who was elected to the City Council in 1969, at 23; he saw himself as the champion of the working man, eager for confrontations with Cleveland's business establishment. In 1977, he was elected mayor; one of his planks was maintaining municipal control of Muny Light, the electric utility for part of the city. But city government was in terrible financial straits, and Kucinich was unwilling or unable to balance the budget and meet obligations. When bankers demanded he sell Muny Light, as other city-owned properties had been sold by the previous mayor, he refused, and they called their loans. "The city went into default on midnight of December 15, 1978, and I began my journey in the political wilderness," he said. The public verdict was negative: Kucinich lost in 1979. He taught at Cleveland State and Case Western Reserve, hosted a radio talk show, and was a TV reporter.

In 1994 he staged a political comeback, arguing that he had saved utility ratepayers money, and was elected to the state Senate, defeating an incumbent Republican. In 1996 he ran for the House, celebrating his defense of Muny Light with the slogan "Light Up Congress." The incumbent Martin Hoke, a Republican who made millions in business, was elected twice against Democrats with serious ethical problems. The Hoke-Kucinich race was a rollicking one. Hoke charged that Kucinich "would do to Medicare exactly what he did to Cleveland: he would throw it into default." Organized labor spent huge amounts—the AFL-CIO said $475,000, Hoke said $1.6 million—on ads claiming that Hoke voted to "cut" Medicare. Kucinich campaigned against NAFTA and GATT (though Ohio businesses have made money on exports to Mexico) and defended his ties with labor. Democrats, many of them former Kucinich critics, rallied around him: The Cleveland council named a public power plant for him on the same day Bill Clinton came in to campaign for him in Parma. Hoke was not helped when 19th District Republican Steve LaTourette was quoted in the Cleveland *Plain Dealer* saying he didn't think Hoke would win. Actually, given the Democratic leanings of the district, Hoke did very well. Kucinich won, but by only a 49%–46% margin.

Kucinich wants to expand job training programs for skilled workers and has been a vocal foe of international trade deals. He bars his staff from parking foreign cars in congressional lots—he drives a Mercury Sable. He effectively voiced local sentiments on issues as disparate as a new telephone area code and noise control at Hopkins Airport, saying that industry should be more efficient. In contrast to some Rustbelt Democrats, he backed the EPA's new air-quality standards. Kucinich has a grandfather who was born in Croatia and his ancestral village was destroyed in the 1990 war with Yugoslavia. Kucinich led a group of 25 Democrats to join the 187 Republicans in the House to oppose the bombing of Kosovo and has been called the "leading Democratic dove."

Kucinich easily won re-election in 1998, without advertising or polling, against Joe Slovenec, a former leader of the militantly anti-abortion Operation Rescue. The Republican Congress is unlikely to satisfy his dreams of an ever-larger public sector. But Kucinich's flair for publicity, zest for confrontation, and persistence should not be underestimated.

Cook's Call. *Safe.* Even though he is only a sophomore, Kucinich is already rather established in this Democratic-leaning district. But Kucinich's biggest threat could come during redistricting. Ohio is likely to lose a district and there is talk that this district, as well as other northeast Ohio districts, may be affected.

The People: Pop. 1990: 570,530; 0.3% rural; 15.9% age 65 + ; 94.2% White, 2.1% Black, 1.4% Asian, 0.2% Amer. Indian, 2.2% Other; 3.9% Hispanic Origin. Households: 51.4% married couple families; 23.3% married couple fams. w. children; 42.7% college educ.; median household income: $30,323; per capita income: $14,813; median house value: $73,700; median gross rent: $318.

1996 Presidential Vote			1992 Presidential Vote		
Clinton (D)	117,878	(51%)	Clinton (D)	107,465	(41%)
Dole (R)	83,055	(36%)	Bush (R)	92,846	(36%)
Perot (I)	26,952	(12%)	Perot (I)	58,092	(22%)

Rep. Dennis Kucinich (D)

Elected 1996; b. Oct. 6, 1946, Cleveland; home, Cleveland; Cleveland St. U., 1967–70, Case Western Reserve U., B.A., M.A., 1973; Catholic; single.

Elected Office: Cleveland City Cncl., 1970–75, 1983–85; Cleveland Mayor, 1977–79; OH Senate, 1994–96.

Professional Career: Clerk, Municipal Courts, 1976–77; Radio Talk Show Host, 1979, 1989; Lecturer, 1980–83; Consultant, 1986–94; TV Reporter, Channel 8, 1989–92.

DC Office: 1730 LHOB 20515, 202-225-5871; Fax: 202-225-5745.

District Office: Lakewood, 216-228-6465.

Committees: *Education & the Workforce* (20th of 22 D): Early Childhood, Youth & Families; Workforce Protections. *Government Reform* (12th of 19 D): Criminal Justice, Drug Policy & Human Resources; National Economic Growth, Natural Resources & Regulatory Affairs (RMM).

Group Ratings

	ADA	ACLU	AFS	LCV	CON	NTU	NFIB	COC	ACU	NTLC	CHC
1998	90	56	100	92	68	22	7	22	20	5	25
1997	90	—	100	—	6	32	—	20	16	—	—

National Journal Ratings

	1997 LIB — 1997 CONS	1998 LIB — 1998 CONS
Economic	85% — 10%	72% — 23%
Social	55% — 44%	59% — 41%
Foreign	79% — 19%	55% — 44%

Key Votes of the 105th Congress

1. Clinton Budget Deal	N	5. Puerto Rico Sthood. Ref.	Y	9. Cut $ for B-2 Bombers	Y
2. Education IRAs	N	6. End Highway Set-asides	N	10. Human Rights in China	Y
3. Req. 2/3 to Raise Taxes	N	7. School Prayer Amend.	N	11. Withdraw Bosnia Troops	N
4. Fast-track Trade	N	8. Ovrd. Part. Birth Veto	Y	12. End Cuban TV-Marti	N

Election Results

1998 general	Dennis Kucinich (D)	110,552	(67%)	($580,626)
	Joe Slovenec (R)	55,015	(33%)	($204,276)
1998 primary	Dennis Kucinich (D)	51,109	(88%)	
	C. River Smith (D)	6,849	(12%)	
1996 general	Dennis Kucinich (D)	110,723	(49%)	($690,367)
	Martin R. Hoke (R)	104,546	(46%)	($1,480,181)
	Robert B. Iverson (NL)	10,415	(5%)	

ELEVENTH DISTRICT

Like most great American cities, Cleveland grew in great bursts of migration, when capitalists' investments suddenly were paying off beyond their wildest dreams and low-wage workers were attracted from ready corners of the country and the world. Cleveland's greatest surge of growth started in the 1890s and lasted through the 1920s, as tens of thousands of immigrants from central and southern Europe arrived here, looking for jobs in steel, auto and other factories. Bohemians came to the tightly-packed neighborhoods along Broadway, Hungarians a bit to the northeast, Jews north of University Circle along East 105th Street, and Italians to Little Italy along Mayfield Road.

As the nation's heavy industries geared up for World War II and enjoyed years of prosperous growth afterward, a second surge of immigrants came, this time blacks from the American South. From Cleveland's old ghetto, south of Carnegie Avenue downtown to East 105th, the rapidly increasing number of blacks covered most of the east side by the middle 1960s, with only a few Bohemian and Italian enclaves left east of the Cuyahoga. Migration stopped around 1965, but blacks have continued to move out beyond the city limits to the east side suburbs, including modest East Cleveland and Warrensville Heights and upper-income Shaker Heights, laid out in 1905 on broad boulevards by streetcar magnates, the Van Sweringen brothers. These surges of migration led to political changes. A string of ethnic mayors—Frank Lausche, Anthony Celebrezze, Ralph Locher—was followed by the election in 1967 and 1969 of Carl Stokes, the nation's first black big-city mayor, and Cleveland had racially polarized politics for much of the 1970s. Ironically, the city has never had a black majority (because blacks have been moving to the eastern suburbs) and elected its second black mayor, Michael White, in 1989, because white voters preferred his accommodating politics to the more polarizing ways of longtime City Council Chairman George Forbes.

The 11th Congressional District includes most of the east side of Cleveland, plus the suburbs just to the east, which together have about as many people as the city now. Some of these—East Cleveland, Warrensville Heights—are mostly black; some, notably Shaker Heights, have stable black percentages in carefully maintained neighborhoods. Others are the destination of blacks seeking low-crime neighborhoods and middle-class schools not often found on the city side among Cleveland's impressive museums and medical centers. This is a heavily Democratic district, with a solid black majority, and it was represented for 30 years by Louis Stokes, Carl Stokes's brother, the first black member of Appropriations, chairman of the Select Committee on Presidential Assassinations in 1977 and later chairman of the ethics committee and the Intelligence Committee, who decided to retire in 1998.

The new congresswoman from the 11th District is Stephanie Tubbs Jones, for all practical purposes chosen in the May 1998 primary. She grew up in Cleveland, graduated from college and law school at Case Western and served her entire legal career as a federal or local-government attorney. She served eight years as judge on the Court of Common Pleas of Cuyahoga County and in 1990 narrowly lost as the Democratic nominee for Ohio Supreme Court. In 1991 she was appointed by the county's Democratic party as the first woman and black prosecutor in Cuyahoga County; she easily won election with 79%.

When Stokes announced his retirement Tubbs Jones decided to run for the House. Her chief opponents in the primary were state Senator Jeffrey Johnson and Reverend Marvin McMickle, minister of the Antioch Baptist Church, one of the city's largest black congregations. Tubbs Jones, the early favorite in the contest, campaigned in both black and white neighborhoods—unlike her opponents. "People don't think about the color of my skin," she said. Johnson, who served seven years on the city council before he was elected to the state Senate in 1990, was indicted on federal corruption charges during the campaign; he adamantly denied that he had accepted earlier campaign contributions in exchange for using his influence to help grocers get state licenses. Tubbs Jones faced second-guessing of her refusal to re-open the criminal investigation of Dr. Samuel Sheppard, who was convicted in a celebrated 1954 case of murdering his wife, but was later acquitted and died in 1970. Sheppard's family claimed that new DNA evidence exonerated him; Tubbs Jones said that she could not prove there had been no tampering with the evidence. Stokes was officially neutral in the campaign, but he helped Tubbs Jones raise money in Washington. Tubbs Jones won 51% of the primary vote, with Johnson and McMickle each receiving 20%.

The general election was just a formality, and Tubbs Jones has the prospect of a long congressional career before her. On Capitol Hill, she quickly showed her political skills by winning appointment as the freshman on the Democratic steering committee, which makes committee assignments. She is likely to have a strong liberal voting record.

Cook's Call. *Safe.* This is the most Democratic district in the state. Tubbs Jones will have no re-election worries in 2000.

The People: Pop. 1990: 571,295; 15.5% age 65+; 39.7% White, 58.5% Black, 1% Asian, 0.2% Amer. Indian, 0.6% Other; 1.1% Hispanic Origin. Households: 37.2% married couple families; 16.4% married couple fams. w. children; 40.6% college educ.; median household income: $22,459; per capita income: $12,629; median house value: $58,800; median gross rent: $289.

1996 Presidential Vote			1992 Presidential Vote		
Clinton (D)	155,895	(79%)	Clinton (D)	169,870	(73%)
Dole (R)	28,938	(15%)	Bush (R)	37,886	(16%)
Perot (I)	9,553	(5%)	Perot (I)	23,428	(10%)

Rep. Stephanie Tubbs Jones (D)

Elected 1998; b. Sept. 10, 1949, Cleveland; home, Cleveland; Case Western Reserve U., B.A. 1971, J.D. 1974.; Baptist; married (Mervyn Jones).

Elected Office: Cleveland Municipal Court Judge, 1982–83; Cuyahoga Cnty. Court of Common Pleas Judge, 1983–91.

Professional Career: Asst. Gen. Cnsl. & EEO Admin., NE OH Regional Sewer Dist., 1974–76; Asst. Cuyahoga Cnty. Prosecutor, 1976–79; Equal Employment Opportunity Comm., 1979–81; Cuyahoga Cnty. Prosecutor, 1991–98.

DC Office: 1516 LHOB 20515, 202-225-7032; Fax: 202-225-1339; Web site: www.house.gov/tubbsjones.

District Office: Shaker Heights, 216-522-4900.

Committees: *Banking & Financial Services* (26th of 27 D): Capital Markets, Securities & Government Sponsored Enterprises; Housing & Community Opportunity. *Small Business* (11th of 17 D): Empowerment.

Group Ratings and Key Votes: Newly Elected

Election Results

1998 general	Stephanie Tubbs Jones (D)	115,226	(80%)	($425,151)
	James D. Hereford (R)	18,592	(13%)	($4,550)
	Jean Murrell Capers (Ind)	9,477	(7%)	
1998 primary	Stephanie Tubbs Jones (D)	37,821	(51%)	
	Marvin A. McMickle (D)	14,942	(20%)	
	Jeffrey Johnson (D)	14,864	(20%)	
	William L. DeMora (D)	5,923	(8%)	
	Others	678	(1%)	
1996 general	Louis Stokes (D)	153,546	(81%)	($361,175)
	James J. Sykora (R)	28,821	(15%)	
	Others	6,672	(4%)	

TWELFTH DISTRICT

Columbus is on the verge of becoming a major metropolis. With city limits stretching toward farmland at each point of the compass, Columbus is geographically the largest city in Ohio; its metropolitan area, though far less populous than Cleveland and a bit smaller than Cincinnati, is growing more rapidly and is approaching the 1.5 million mark. Columbus has the advantages of being a state capital, the home of Ohio State University, and a major white-collar employment town: It is the home base of The Limited's Leslie Wexner and Wendy's Dave Thomas, of Nationwide Insurance and multistate giant BancOne. Columbus likes to brag of its airfreight operations at Port Columbus, the airport, among the best in the country, and about the $43 million Wexner Center for the Visual Arts, a post-post-modern structure by architect Peter Eisenman that has evoked vast controversy. This economic base and civic infrastructure has attracted the kind of upscale, enterprising people who have produced most of America's growth in recent years.

Politically, Columbus has always been a Republican city, with an even more Republican hinterland. It had few of the Eastern European immigrants and CIO unions that made Cleveland so Democratic; for most of the last 30 years, its mayor has been a Republican with support from a machine redolent of the era of William McKinley (whose statue sits in front of the flat-domed Capitol). Recently, Republicans have had spirited competition from Democrats in the city, but the suburbs are heavily Republican and the countryside even more so. The Columbus area dominates two of Ohio's congressional districts. The 12th extends east to the small industrial town of Newark and north to bucolic Delaware County, and includes black areas and the affluent east side of the city around Bexley; the 15th includes most of the territory within the city limits and extends south and west to include Madison County.

The congressman from the 12th District is John Kasich, a Republican first elected in 1982 and a familiar figure nationally as chairman of the House Budget Committee. Boyish-looking but hard-working, aggressive but ingratiating, with a command of fact and argument that can only come from perseverance and a competitive drive colleagues see on the basketball court, Kasich puts a cheerful yet earnest face on Republican policies and priorities. Kasich has been in politics just about all his adult life. He grew up the son of a mail carrier in working-class McKees Rocks, Pennsylvania, with Hungarian, Czech and Croatian ancestry; after graduating from Ohio State, he worked for a state legislator. In 1978, at 26, Kasich ran a strenuous door-to-door campaign and beat a Democratic state senator. In 1982, he ran for the House and, with the help of a favorable redistricting plan, beat a Democrat who had upset an incumbent in 1980. In the House he made his first commotion on Armed Services, where he was the leading Republican opponent of the B-2 bomber and teamed with Democrat Ron Dellums in drastically reducing its production. He offended some conservatives by supporting Clinton's assault-weapons ban and 1994 crime bill. He became a devout Christian after his parents were killed by a drunk driver and has written a book, *Courage is Contagious*, profiling everyday Americans who have done extraordinary things to improve their communities or the lives of others.

Kasich got a seat on the Budget Committee in 1989 and won the ranking Republican spot in 1993 against a more senior member with the help of Newt Gingrich. In that Democratic Congress he led the Republicans' charge to "cut spending first," which laid the groundwork for defeat of Clinton's 1993 economic stimulus package. He advanced a Republican budget alternative with no tax increases or Social Security cuts, but means-testing of Medicare and serious cuts in discretionary spending: a preview of 1995. In October 1993 and April 1994, he and Democrat Tim Penny put together spending-cut packages, which the House narrowly defeated. Kasich had a few modest wins, like zeroing out the Interstate Commerce Commission. But the serious and detailed work he did then was an indispensable ingredient of his successes in 1995–96.

Kasich took the Budget chair determined to reduce the size and scale of government, and achieved partial success. He scotched the "current services" concept, which assumed that every agency was entitled to past appropriations plus more to serve larger populations plus inflation—a concept that ensured that government would always grow faster than the economy. He was determined to start with Republican rather than Clinton Administration proposals and present a plan that would plausibly balance the budget in seven years, by 2002. He and other Republicans assumed that Clinton would eventually accept their budgets if they proved stubborn enough, but they underestimated how Clinton would attack them for "shutting the government down" for four weeks, including during Christmas (technically, of course, it was the president's veto that shut the government down; Congress had passed appropriations to keep it going). Clinton won the public relations battle in the winter of 1995–96, but Republicans won much on substance. The final budget for 1996 reduced domestic appropriations 9%, cutting some $53 billion from domestic discretionary spending over two years. It reduced the deficit to about $100 billion.

Having done that, and with their popularity lower, Kasich and the Republicans concentrated on holding ground in 1996. He wanted to avoid another budget showdown and at the same time had no faith that Clinton was negotiating in good faith for a seven-year balanced budget. But Senate insistence on some $5 billion in spending increases meant that the fiscal 1997 budget Kasich presented to the House had both spending and deficit increases; conservatives balked, and only with party leaders' intense lobbying were they able to prevail 216–211. Kasich initially insisted on a bigger devolution of federal authority: he wanted to link Medicaid cuts and welfare reform, but other leaders, worried about Bob Dole's weakness in the polls, wanted to pass welfare reform alone. They prevailed in July 1996, and Clinton, to the surprise of many, signed it in August. Other budget steps included small business tax cuts and raising the Social Security earnings limit.

"Our budget efforts in Congress have been about sending your power and your money back to you in every city and town across America," Kasich said during the budget wars. They continued into the 105th Congress, when Republican steadfastness led to the less dramatic budget deal with Clinton in July 1997 (which featured the no-longer controversial Medicaid changes) and the budget surplus in 1998—a stunning four years ahead of the Republicans' optimistic schedule. Kasich is keenly aware that Republicans have been pummeled for cutting programs for the poor and leaving in place subsidies for the rich. And he has fought efforts like those of pork-barreling Transportation Chairman Bud Shuster to bust spending caps and take large expenditures off-budget. But in important ways, as *National Review* wrote in 1997, Kasich "defined the thrust of the Republican Party." Responding to criticism that Republicans had run out of ideas, he advocated a 10% across-the-board income tax cut plus a shift in power and responsibility from Washington, allowing non-profit organizations to develop local solutions to social problems.

Kasich has been re-elected by wide margins in the 12th District; Democrats took some comfort when they held him below 70% in the past two elections. He has turned down chances to run for statewide office and disavowed interest in the vice presidential nomination. But he evidently has thought for some time about running for president, and on Presidents' Day 1999 he formally announced his presidential campaign. "A mailman's kid can change the world," he said ebulliently as he issued his anti-establishment call to return power to the people. Kasich faced huge obstacles, including fundraising, his often undisciplined personality, association with Newt Gingrich, and the not inconsequential fact that no House member—including John Anderson, Dick Gephardt or Jack Kemp—has won a major-party presidential nomination since James Garfield in 1880, while several—John Anderson, Dick Gephardt, Jack Kemp—have tried. Even if the odds against his success were long, Kasich's ideas and personality will be difficult to ignore. "I'm in this to fix my country," he said earlier. Back home, two Republicans, state Senator Eugene Watts and state House Majority Leader Pat Tiberi, have began maneuvering to succeed Kasich, but friends left the door open for him to run for re-election if his presidential bid falters.

Cook's Call. *Probably Safe.* It's uncertain whether Kasich will file for re-election to the House in 2000 or instead concentrate on his White House bid; the Republican secretary of State argues that he can run for both. The fact that this district has been closely contested on the presidential level in 1992 and 1996 and has a 23% black population certainly makes it look somewhat marginal. But Kasich has won rather easily over the past 14 years, and there is a solid Republican base here.

The People: Pop. 1990: 571,341; 14.7% rural; 9.8% age 65 + ; 74.9% White, 23.2% Black, 1.3% Asian, 0.2% Amer. Indian, 0.4% Other; 0.8% Hispanic Origin. Households: 51.1% married couple families; 25.9% married couple fams. w. children; 48.9% college educ.; median household income: $30,859; per capita income: $14,723; median house value: $75,800; median gross rent: $336.

1996 Presidential Vote

Clinton (D)	118,228	(47%)
Dole (R)	114,405	(46%)
Perot (I)	16,426	(7%)

1992 Presidential Vote

Bush (R)	108,359	(41%)
Clinton (D)	105,852	(40%)
Perot (I)	47,080	(18%)

Rep. John R. Kasich (R)

Elected 1982; b. May 13, 1952, McKees Rocks, PA; home, Westerville; OH St. U., B.A. 1974; Christian; married (Karen).

Elected Office: OH Senate, 1978–82.

Professional Career: Admin. Asst., OH Sen. Donald Lukens, 1975–77.

DC Office: 1111 LHOB 20515, 202-225-5355; Web site: www.house.gov/kasich.

District Office: Columbus, 614-523-2555.

Committees: *Armed Services* (4th of 32 R): Military Research & Development. *Budget* (Chmn. of 24 R).

Group Ratings

	ADA	ACLU	AFS	LCV	CON	NTU	NFIB	COC	ACU	NTLC	CHC
1998	0	6	0	23	70	69	100	82	96	92	100
1997	20	—	13	—	80	58	—	80	88	—	—

National Journal Ratings

	1997 LIB — 1997 CONS			1998 LIB — 1998 CONS		
Economic	33%	—	67%	19%	—	79%
Social	37%	—	61%	3%	—	90%
Foreign	36%	—	63%	38%	—	61%

Key Votes of the 105th Congress

1. Clinton Budget Deal	Y	5. Puerto Rico Sthood. Ref.	N	9. Cut $ for B-2 Bombers	Y
2. Education IRAs	Y	6. End Highway Set-asides	Y	10. Human Rights in China	N
3. Req. 2/3 to Raise Taxes	Y	7. School Prayer Amend.	Y	11. Withdraw Bosnia Troops	Y
4. Fast-track Trade	Y	8. Ovrd. Part. Birth Veto	Y	12. End Cuban TV-Marti	N

Election Results

1998 general	John R. Kasich (R)	124,197	(67%)	($769,107)
	Edward S. Brown (D)	60,694	(33%)	($8,545)
1998 primary	John R. Kasich (R)	44,113	(91%)	
	Ramona Whisler (R)	4,585	(9%)	
1996 general	John R. Kasich (R)	151,667	(64%)	($1,578,812)
	Cynthia L. Ruccia (D)	78,762	(33%)	($273,184)
	Others	7,005	(3%)	

THIRTEENTH DISTRICT

The imprint of the westward track of New England Yankee migration is still apparent today on the shores of Lake Erie in northern Ohio. The Yankees, cooped up in New England for 200 years, shot across the country through upstate New York, west across Ohio and Michigan to Chicago, and on to Kansas and southern California in just two or three generations, providing inspiration, manpower and technical might for the Union victory in the Civil War, and leaving their imprint along the way. One place they stopped was the Western Reserve, the northeast corner of Ohio, created for the excess population of Connecticut; its towns, colleges and cultural institutions were established by Yankees mostly. A prime example of Western Reserve Yankee-ism is Oberlin College, founded in 1832 as the first co-educational college in America, though no women dared apply until 1837; it accepted black students a few years later, and the town of Oberlin became a center of the Underground Railroad. Or consider Hiram, home of another college and of James Garfield, who once represented the area in Congress when it was the most Republican part of Ohio, and who was the only president elected directly from the House, in 1880.

Politically, the lands of the Yankee diaspora, with their reformist ideas and dislike of slavery and the South, were naturally Republican territory. But the great masses of immigrants lured to Cleveland and the smaller industrial cities built by Yankee capital provided a base for labor unions and Progressive politics. After the New Deal and the bloody CIO organizing drives of the late 1930s, the Western Reserve had something like class-warfare politics for 30 years, with the Democrats usually winning. Northern Ohio, like New England, moved away from the Republicans and toward the Democrats. Now the Western Reserve, like Connecticut and Mas-sachusetts, may be moving toward a post-industrial economy. Factory employment has dropped, but total jobs are rising again; small, adaptive business units with highly skilled workers are the growth sectors. That leaves the Western Reserve, like New England, leaning Democratic—but not reliably so. Bill Clinton carried it in 1992 and 1996; but so did George Voinovich for governor in 1990 and 1994 and Senator Mike DeWine in 1994.

The 13th Congressional District is grotesquely shaped—something like a barbell—with two large segments of Western Reserve lands connected by a sort of land bridge between Cleveland and Akron. The western end includes the factory towns of Lorain and Elyria, plus Oberlin and Medina County, once rural and now filling up with migrants from Cleveland along I-71. The eastern, less heavily populated area includes all of Geauga County, high-income hilly townships with many reminders of New England origins, and rural parts of Trumbull and Portage counties. This end of the district tends to vote Republican, while on the west end Lorain County is Democratic and Medina County Republican. This was an ungainly product of redistricting, with two Democratic incumbents, Don Pease of Oberlin and Dennis Eckart of suburban Cleve-land, both of whom retired in 1992.

The congressman now is Sherrod Brown, one of the Ohio Democrats' few remaining suc-cessful career politicians, who ran and won a seat in the state House the year he graduated from Yale, in 1974 (a state employee, mistaking him for an intern, gave the young man a $1 to get her a cup of coffee), and has never stopped running. In 1982 he was elected secretary of State at 30 (while his brother, Charlie Brown, was elected attorney general of West Virginia) and worked hard to increase voter registration and turnout. In 1990 he lost that office to Bob Taft, who is now governor, and Republican redistricters took care to keep Brown's home town of Mansfield outside the 13th. But in 1992 Brown moved into a rented lake cottage in Medina County and faced Republican Margaret Mueller, a millionaire social worker from Geauga County, who had lost three times to Eckart. Brown showed great flair in the campaign, taking a 200-mile bicycle tour around the district; with solid labor support, he campaigned loud and hard against NAFTA and championed universal health care. He won 53%–35%, with 61% in Lorain County.

In the House, Brown showed his usual political adeptness, winning a seat on the Commerce

Committee. He supported the Clinton economic plan and a single-pay health care plan like Canada's, across the Lake, but he did not sign onto the Clinton plan. On trade he was one of the most voluble liberal-labor members from the Great Lakes area attacking NAFTA and GATT. But he did support the balanced budget amendment and line-item veto. For two decades until 1994, Brown was part of the majority, making public policy and benefiting from the perquisites of power. Now, in the minority party, he has worked less on national issues than on local projects—a veterans' cemetery in Medina, an Export Assistance Center for Cleveland, opposition to foreign companies' selling water from Lake Superior. Even his position as ranking Democrat on the Commerce Health and the Environment Subcommittee has given him little influence because Republicans have crafted their health care proposals mostly in party task forces. But should Democrats win a majority in 2000, Brown would be chairman of one of the most important subcommittees in the House, with the power of drawing national attention (as former subcommittee Chairman Henry Waxman did by summoning tobacco company executives to testify in 1994) and framing the debate on important health issues.

Brown had a serious Republican challenge in 1994 from Lorain County Prosecutor Gregory White, who attacked him for raising taxes, opposing NAFTA and supporting the crime bill, and, as a Vietnam war hero, criticized Brown for attending Yale and studying in Russia during the conflict. Brown won 49%–46%, a liberal-labor Democrat who survived because of business and labor PAC money. Since then he has won easily. He has been mentioned as a candidate for statewide office, but decided not to run for the Senate in 1998 and 2000. Despite reports of his interest, he was bypassed for the chairmanship of the Democratic Congressional Campaign Committee. He faces a big challenge in surviving Republican redistricting after the 2000 Census if, as seems likely, Republicans draw the lines; they could attach the heavily Democratic parts of Lorain County to Dennis Kucinich's Cleveland-dominated 10th District and then draw a new 13th District in between Cleveland and Akron, which would be much more suburban. In that case Brown may consider a statewide race, perhaps against Governor Bob Taft, in the hope that voters may be tiring of Republican governors; the last time any party held the Ohio governorship for 12 straight years was between 1892 and 1906.

Cook's Call. *Probably Safe.* After two rather shaky elections, Brown has solidified himself in this marginal district, winning by big margins in 1996 and 1998. But, with Ohio likely to lose one district in 2002, there is speculation that Brown's seat could be heavily impacted.

The People: Pop. 1990: 570,838; 35.9% rural; 11.2% age 65 + ; 93.7% White, 4.5% Black, 0.5% Asian, 0.2% Amer. Indian, 1.1% Other; 2.9% Hispanic Origin. Households: 65.5% married couple families; 33.2% married couple fams. w. children; 41.1% college educ.; median household income: $34,725; per capita income: $14,307; median house value: $77,000; median gross rent: $318.

1996 Presidential Vote			1992 Presidential Vote		
Clinton (D)	116,720	(46%)	Clinton (D)	101,854	(38%)
Dole (R)	98,349	(39%)	Bush (R)	96,037	(35%)
Perot (I)	35,527	(14%)	Perot (I)	72,038	(27%)

Rep. Sherrod Brown (D)

Elected 1992; b. Nov. 9, 1952, Mansfield; home, Lorain; Yale U., B.A. 1974, OH St. U., M.A. 1979, M.A. 1981; Lutheran; divorced.

Elected Office: OH House of Reps. 1974–82; OH Secy. of State, 1982–90.

Professional Career: Prof., OH St. U. at Mansfield, 1979–81.

DC Office: 201 CHOB 20515, 202-225-3401; Fax: 202-225-2266; Web site: www.house.gov/sherrodbrown.

District Offices: Elyria, 440-934-5100; Medina, 330-722-9262.

Committees: *Commerce* (8th of 24 D): Energy & Power; Health and Environment (RMM). *International Relations* (9th of 23 D): Asia & the Pacific.

Group Ratings

	ADA	ACLU	AFS	LCV	CON	NTU	NFIB	COC	ACU	NTLC	CHC
1998	100	75	100	100	95	34	7	17	4	11	0
1997	100	—	100	—	78	21	—	22	12	—	—

National Journal Ratings

	1997 LIB — 1997 CONS		1998 LIB — 1998 CONS	
Economic	85%	— 10%	79%	— 0%
Social	73%	— 24%	80%	— 19%
Foreign	94%	— 6%	75%	— 23%

Key Votes of the 105th Congress

1. Clinton Budget Deal	N	5. Puerto Rico Sthood. Ref.	Y	9. Cut $ for B-2 Bombers	Y
2. Education IRAs	N	6. End Highway Set-asides	N	10. Human Rights in China	Y
3. Req. 2/3 to Raise Taxes	N	7. School Prayer Amend.	N	11. Withdraw Bosnia Troops	N
4. Fast-track Trade	N	8. Ovrd. Part. Birth Veto	N	12. End Cuban TV-Marti	Y

Election Results

1998 general	Sherrod Brown (D)	116,309	(62%)	($682,041)
	Grace L. Drake (R)	72,666	(38%)	($162,341)
1998 primary	Sherrod Brown (D)	unopposed		
1996 general	Sherrod Brown (D)	146,690	(60%)	($607,543)
	Kenneth C. Blair Jr. (R)	87,108	(36%)	($54,064)
	Others	8,707	(4%)	

FOURTEENTH DISTRICT

Akron, the center of what some Ohioans today call the Polymer Center of the Americas, formerly was known as Rubber Town. (Akron is named from the Greek word for high, the same root for Acropolis, because it sits on a ridge between the Great Lakes and Mississippi watersheds.) Twenty years ago, the city was as synonymous with tires as Detroit was with cars: Firestone, Goodyear, General Tire, and B.F. Goodrich all had their headquarters and big tire factories here; the United Rubber Workers had been the big union since the 1930s. But after the oil shocks of the 1970s, Akron's antiquated auto tire plants closed, and the last truck and airplane tire plants closed in 1984 and 1985; several big firms were sold to out-of-town companies, though Goodyear remains a leading employer. Akron began specializing in polymers, plastics and other hydrocarbons that can be formed or shaped like rubber into useful industrial products. The first polymer, polyvinyl chloride (PVC), was invented in 1926 when B.F. Goodrich chemist Waldo Semon, looking to make synthetic rubber, found a mysterious goo in the bottom of his test tube; the company did not bother to patent it until 1933, but now PVC is everywhere, in pipes and siding, shoes and toys, car tops and stadium covers. The region had a net increase of 36,000 jobs this decade, the Akron Regional Development Board reported in 1997, and exported $2.3 billion in goods that year. Ohio ships more plastic resins than any other state but Texas and employs more people in the field than all states except California.

This change in the local economy has had political effects. Akron's population is largely descended from migrants from Eastern Europe and, especially, West Virginia, who thronged here in the 1910s and 1920s to snap up jobs in the tire factories for 10 or 12 hours a day at the price of smelling burning rubber for 24. In the 1930s, these people joined the new United Rubber Workers union and started voting Democratic; they were courted in turn by Republicans with blue-collar backgrounds fielded by local Republican Chairman Ray Bliss, who was also Republican National Committee chairman in the 1950s and 1960s. But as the smell of rubber vanished from Akron's air, the language of class conflict has mostly passed from its politics. Now Akron has more flexible businesses and a more upscale work force. While greater Akron sometimes votes heavily Democratic, it can vote Republican as well.

Ohio's 14th Congressional District has long been made up of Akron and surrounding Summit County; currently it also includes the area around Kent (and Kent State University) just to the east. The current congressman, Tom Sawyer, has spent most of his adult life in public office: He was elected to the state House in 1976, at 31, became Akron mayor in 1984, and was elected in the 14th District when the incumbent retired in 1986. In that election and again in 1994, he survived tough competition from Summit County prosecutor Lynn Slaby.

Sawyer has a mostly liberal voting record and has supported Bill Clinton on some tough votes. He has loudly denounced Republicans but also has taken on some bipartisan initiatives. With Republican David Hobson, he sponsored a common standard for electronic transmission of health care billing information, which passed in 1996. But he failed on a so-called CAREERS bipartisan reorganization of job training programs. On welfare reform he supported the bipartisan approach of Republican Mike Castle and Democrat John Tanner. He joined The Coalition, a group of moderate Democrats, but not the Blue Dogs. Representing a district where organized labor was historically strong, Sawyer sometimes spurns the union line. After much public agonizing, he supported NAFTA in November 1993; as a result, he had opposition in the 1994 primary from plumber Kenneth Mack, whom he beat 69%–31%. In 1996 he did not oppose the Republicans' Teamwork for Employees and Management bill outright, as unions did, but proposed an amendment asserting workers' rights to independent representation. In 1997 Sawyer gave up seniority on the Education and the Workforce Committee—something no Akron Democrat would have done in the days when unions were strong—to get a seat on Commerce, where he focused on telecommunications issues and utility services. In something of a curiosity, the only bill he introduced in the 105th Congress called for development of policies for the United States to voluntarily stabilize its population growth. In 1999, he was the Democratic organizer of the House's bipartisan "civility" retreat in Hershey, Pennsylvania.

In 1996 Republicans again targeted the seat and touted their candidate, former Judge Joyce George. Sawyer's closeness to Clinton may have paid off. Clinton carried the 14th by a wide margin, and Sawyer won 54%–42%. In 1998 Sawyer easily beat a Republican who called Clinton a "sexual predator."

Cook's Call. *Probably Safe.* A couple of tough, well-funded challengers kept Sawyer under 55% in 1994 and 1996, but Sawyer has never come all that close to losing this Akron-based district. But Republicans have been eyeing this seat and the neighboring 13th for years and could play havoc here in 2002 redistricting.

The People: Pop. 1990: 570,987; 8.2% rural; 14% age 65 + ; 87.7% White, 10.9% Black, 1% Asian, 0.2% Amer. Indian, 0.2% Other; 0.6% Hispanic Origin. Households: 53.7% married couple families; 24.2% married couple fams. w. children; 43.8% college educ.; median household income: $28,184; per capita income: $13,931; median house value: $60,600; median gross rent: $314.

1996 Presidential Vote			1992 Presidential Vote		
Clinton (D)	121,635	(53%)	Clinton (D)	118,715	(45%)
Dole (R)	76,083	(33%)	Bush (R)	81,232	(31%)
Perot (I)	30,312	(13%)	Perot (I)	60,000	(23%)

Rep. Tom Sawyer (D)

Elected 1986; b. Aug. 15, 1945, Akron; home, Akron; U. of Akron, B.A., 1968; M.A., 1970; Presbyterian; married (Joyce).

Elected Office: OH House of Reps., 1976–82; Akron Mayor, 1984–86.

DC Office: 1414 LHOB 20515, 202-225-5231; Fax: 202-225-5278.

District Office: Akron, 330-375-5710.

Committees: *Commerce* (16th of 24 D): Energy & Power; Telecommunications, Trade & Consumer Protection.

Group Ratings

	ADA	ACLU	AFS	LCV	CON	NTU	NFIB	COC	ACU	NTLC	CHC
1998	95	88	89	100	82	17	29	44	0	11	0
1997	95	—	88	—	56	27	—	50	8	—	—

National Journal Ratings

	1997 LIB — 1997 CONS			1998 LIB — 1998 CONS		
Economic	91%	—	7%	79%	—	21%
Social	85%	—	0%	81%	—	16%
Foreign	82%	—	16%	90%	—	5%

Key Votes of the 105th Congress

1. Clinton Budget Deal	N	5. Puerto Rico Sthood. Ref.	Y	9. Cut $ for B-2 Bombers	Y
2. Education IRAs	N	6. End Highway Set-asides	N	10. Human Rights in China	Y
3. Req. 2/3 to Raise Taxes	N	7. School Prayer Amend.	N	11. Withdraw Bosnia Troops	N
4. Fast-track Trade	Y	8. Ovrd. Part. Birth Veto	N	12. End Cuban TV-Marti	Y

Election Results

1998 general	Tom Sawyer (D)	106,046	(63%)	($504,893)
	Tom Watkins (R)	63,027	(37%)	($93,311)
1998 primary	Tom Sawyer (D)	unopposed		
1996 general	Tom Sawyer (D)	124,136	(54%)	($523,412)
	Joyce George (R)	95,307	(42%)	($279,210)
	Others	8,992	(4%)	

FIFTEENTH DISTRICT

Columbus, smack in the center of Ohio, was founded in 1812 to be the state capital. By the early 20th century it became a regional mid-sized city. In the past couple of decades, it has become the center of a major metropolitan area, and headquarters to major research centers such as the Batelle Memorial Institute and Ohio State University, financial powers Nationwide Insurance and BancOne, The Limited retailer, and Wendy's fast food chain. Its flat-domed Capitol at Broad and High, with the statue of William McKinley out front, is surrounded by high-rises, public and private, while the city grows in all directions into the countryside.

Ohio's 15th Congressional District is made up of most of Columbus, all but the east side, plus southern and western Franklin County and rural Madison County directly to the west. The 15th includes some of Columbus's black population, white working-class areas on the south side of the city and in nearby Grove City, and the Ohio State University campus. Politically, these Democratic areas are more than balanced by the heavily Republican suburb of Upper Arlington, across the Olentangy River from Ohio State, and by Republican subdivisions sprouting up in rural land between the old villages.

The 15th District is represented in the House by Deborah Pryce, a Republican first elected in 1992. Pryce graduated from law school in Columbus in 1976, worked in state government and as a city prosecutor, and was elected municipal court judge in 1985. In 1992, when incumbent Chalmers Wylie retired after 26 years, Pryce ran for the office. She was unopposed in the primary but had tough competition in the general, from Democrat Richard Cordray and from pro-life independent Linda Reidelbach, who became angry when Pryce announced after the primary she would support a Freedom of Choice Act that would restrict states' power to limit abortions. Pryce talked much about congressional reform—term limits, rotating chairmanships, line-item veto—and called for limiting annual spending increases to 3%. She won with 44% of the vote to Cordray's 38% and Reidelbach's 18%.

In the House, Pryce has been mostly conservative on economic and foreign issues, sometimes liberal on cultural matters. In her first term, she was elected interim president of her Republican class and helped to craft the Contract with America. "Half of our job was teaching all our members to speak from the same text. We had to make sure that it was understood that the contract was not another renegade attempt, that it had leadership authority," she said. When Republicans won the majority in 1994, Newt Gingrich tapped her to chair a committee to examine legal ramifications of the transition, including severance pay for thousands of aides who lost their jobs. Pryce has been a leadership loyalist on the Rules Committee since 1995 and headed the House Republican task force on tobacco.

One of Pryce's causes has been reform of the Indian Child Welfare Act governing extratribe adoptions. She was prompted by the case of a Columbus couple whose adoption of twins was challenged after four years because the biological father had, despite his earlier assurance otherwise, Indian blood; the children, he later said, were 3/32 Indian and must be returned to him. Under the ICWA, other adoptions have been voided and children sent back to the tribe to live in foster care. Pryce would exempt from the ICWA children whose parents had no significant affiliation with tribes. In May 1996 she prevailed 212–195 against an Indian-backed amendment sponsored by Don Young of Alaska; but her version was changed in the Senate by Indian Affairs Committee Chairman John McCain, and the two measures were not reconciled. In June 1997, she and Todd Tiahrt reintroduced similar legislation that never made it out of committee.

Her priorities for the 106th Congress include legislation to focus resources on the prevention and treatment of child abuse, tax incentives to employers for on-site child-care services, tax relief for victims of employment discrimination and the EdFlex bill to give states more flexibility in managing federal education programs, which passed Congress in March 1999.

In July 1997, Pryce was elected Republican Conference secretary when leadership positions opened up following the retirement of Conference Vice Chair Susan Molinari. Running as the moderate among the four candidates, Pryce won 110 votes on the second ballot to 65 for Sue Myrick and 42 for Duke Cunningham. In her campaign, she called for opening the leaders' decision-making process and reflecting a greater diversity of views in the party's message.

Pryce took an extended leave from the House in 1998 while her 8-year-old daughter underwent treatment for bone cancer at the National Institutes of Health.

Pryce has won re-election easily. One of her local priorities has been securing funding for the $16 million West Columbus floodwall project along the Scioto River, $14 million of which came from the federal government.

Cook's Call. *Safe.* Since first winning this seat in 1992, Pryce has never dipped below 66% of the vote. Don't expect a close race here in 2000.

The People: Pop. 1990: 570,740; 9.7% rural; 10.7% age 65 + ; 92.3% White, 4.9% Black, 2.2% Asian, 0.3% Amer. Indian, 0.3% Other; 0.8% Hispanic Origin. Households: 50.6% married couple families; 24.1% married couple fams. w. children; 51.2% college educ.; median household income: $31,020; per capita income: $15,076; median house value: $73,200; median gross rent: $365.

1996 Presidential Vote

Dole (R)	114,183	(48%)
Clinton (D)	105,947	(44%)
Perot (I)	17,324	(7%)

1992 Presidential Vote

Bush (R)	119,588	(45%)
Clinton (D)	94,232	(35%)
Perot (I)	52,316	(20%)

Rep. Deborah Pryce (R)

Elected 1992; b. July 29, 1951, Warren; home, Columbus; OH St. U., B.A. 1973, Capital U. Law Schl., J.D. 1976; Presbyterian; married (Randy Walker).

Elected Office: Franklin Cnty. Municipal Court Judge, 1985–92.

Professional Career: Admin. Law Judge, OH Dept. of Insurance, 1976; Columbus City Asst. Prosecutor & Asst. City Atty., 1978–85; Practicing atty., 1992.

DC Office: 221 CHOB 20515, 202-225-2015; Web site: www.house.gov/pryce.

District Office: Columbus, 614-469-5614.

Committees: *Republican Conference Secretary. Rules* (4th of 9 R): The Legislative & Budget Process (Vice Chmn.).

Group Ratings

	ADA	ACLU	AFS	LCV	CON	NTU	NFIB	COC	ACU	NTLC	CHC
1998	5	31	29	15	46	54	100	100	83	84	73
1997	15	—	13	—	67	51	—	100	72	—	—

National Journal Ratings

	1997 LIB — 1997 CONS		1998 LIB — 1998 CONS	
Economic	40% —	59%	33% —	67%
Social	48% —	51%	50% —	50%
Foreign	38% —	60%	34% —	62%

Key Votes of the 105th Congress

1. Clinton Budget Deal	Y	5. Puerto Rico Sthood. Ref.	N	9. Cut $ for B-2 Bombers	Y
2. Education IRAs	Y	6. End Highway Set-asides	Y	10. Human Rights in China	N
3. Req. 2/3 to Raise Taxes	Y	7. School Prayer Amend.	Y	11. Withdraw Bosnia Troops	Y
4. Fast-track Trade	*	8. Ovrd. Part. Birth Veto	Y	12. End Cuban TV-Marti	N

Election Results

1998 general	Deborah Pryce (R)	113,846	(66%)	($368,958)
	Adam Clay Miller (D)	49,334	(28%)	($86,036)
	Kevin Nestor (I)	9,996	(6%)	($18,849)
1998 primary	Deborah Pryce (R)	unopposed		
1996 general	Deborah Pryce (R)	156,776	(71%)	($384,780)
	Cliff Arnebeck (D)	64,665	(29%)	($9,629)

SIXTEENTH DISTRICT

A century ago, Canton, Ohio, was at the center of American politics. Canton was already an industrial city then, though not with the huge steel factories built in Youngstown or Cleveland. Its high-skill workers were fashioning new kinds of plows and reapers, making watches and, beginning in 1899, roller bearings. Canton did not attract masses of immigrants. Its factories did not run on harsh stopwatch discipline; there were not the class-warfare politics here that would be seen later in other northern Ohio industrial cities. Instead, Canton was united then in admiring its first citizen, William McKinley, who rose to the rank of major at 22 in the Civil War, was elected congressman and governor, and chaired the House Ways and Means Committee. As Republican nominee for president in 1896, McKinley campaigned from his front porch in Canton, meeting with delegations brought in by train from all over the country. This spectacle, with its display of technological virtuosity and personal modesty, sounds an appealing and reverberating note in American politics, as does the McKinley platform—the "full dinner pail," the gold standard, the enforcement of law and order in labor relations—which has long been viewed as antiquated but still provides useful instruction.

The 16th Congressional District includes all of Stark County, plus three-and-a-half more Republican counties to the west: Wayne, site of the College of Wooster and the headquarters of Rubbermaid; Holmes, with its Amish communities; and Ashland and part of Knox. The district has been mostly Republican since McKinley's time, and has elected only Republican congressmen since 1950. Though no longer at the center of American politics, Canton and surrounding Stark County, which have voted much like the nation as a whole for the last 30 years, were the subject of a year-long series of stories by Michael Winerip in *The New York Times*. What he found in 1996 was a community still based on manufacturing—mostly high-skill, with companies like Timken, Diebold, Republic Engineered Steels, and Hoover—economically prosperous but uneasy because of downsizing and decisions by some local companies to build new plants elsewhere, politically ambivalent about both major party candidates, worried about the young House Republicans but mostly opposed to old liberal Democrats. Stark County turned out to be not quite a bellwether: Bill Clinton's 46%-38%-15% margin in 1992 was nearly the same as nationally, but in 1996 Clinton and Bob Dole each ran 3% behind and Ross Perot 6% ahead of their national percentages.

The congressman from the 16th is Ralph Regula, first elected in 1972 and one of the senior Republicans in the House. He grew up in outer Stark County, the son of a farmer and coal mine operator; he served in the Navy in World War II, worked his way through the William McKinley School of Law while teaching school, and was elected to the Ohio legislature in 1964, just before turning 40. When the incumbent retired in 1972, Regula ran for the House and was easily elected. He is a senior member of Appropriations, and since 1994 has chaired the Interior Subcommittee. That subcommittee serves as a counterweight to the Resources Committee, chaired by Don Young of Alaska and with many western Republicans who resent federal management and restrictions on their lands; Regula, with a centrist voting record, is more supportive of environmental regulations. He has long sought to reform the Mining Act of 1872 and advocates higher grazing fees—positions that infuriate Westerners—though he is dubious about some Clean Air provisions and bans on offshore oil drilling. In 1995, he was one of 51 Republicans who voted against Contract With America restrictions on EPA enforcement powers. After the 1994 election, when some conservatives wanted to deprive Regula of the sub-committee chairmanship, Newt Gingrich saw that he got the job; he was, however, passed over for full committee chairman for the more junior and partisan Bob Livingston. With Livingston's 1999 resignation, Regula gained the mostly ceremonial title of committee vice-chairman.

The Interior Appropriations bills typically stir much controversy. It generates conservative amendments to cut the National Endowment for the Arts—a source of principled controversy far out of proportion to the dollars it spends—and liberal restrictions on the Tongass National Forest in Alaska and the Mojave desert in California. After lengthy debate, these attempts have been abandoned. Spending caps have forced Regula to cut deeply into energy research and land acquisition; he believes it is more important to properly fund current parks rather than to designate new ones. But he makes some exceptions: One was for Everglades restoration, another for the 87-mile Ohio and Erie Canal Heritage Corridor, which he finally succeeded in authorizing in the omnibus parks bill in 1996. Nor does Regula forget McKinley: every Congress he introduces a bill to formally name Alaska's highest peak Mount McKinley, despite efforts to rename it Denali, the Indian-inspired name of the surrounding park. In the 106th Congress, he hopes to implement the recreation-fee program that allows facilities to keep entrance fees for their own maintenance. "These reforms will ensure that taxpayers will no longer be asked to pay outrageous costs for park service projects such as $785,000 outhouses," he said. He criticized Clinton's budget for cutting the hours when national parks are open to visitors, but adding 1,600 employees at the Interior Department. Outside of his committee work, Regula has actively backed steel industry efforts to restrict imports.

Cook's Call. *Safe.* An incumbent without a re-election woe in the world for 2000 is 14-term incumbent Regula. He is about as safely entrenched as they come.

The People: Pop. 1990: 570,705; 36.7% rural; 14.3% age 65 + ; 94.5% White, 4.8% Black, 0.4% Asian, 0.2% Amer. Indian, 0.1% Other; 0.6% Hispanic Origin. Households: 60.9% married couple families; 29% married couple fams. w. children; 33% college educ.; median household income: $27,524; per capita income: $12,413; median house value: $58,200; median gross rent: $268.

1996 Presidential Vote				1992 Presidential Vote			
Clinton (D)	100,293	(43%)		Bush (R)	98,824	(39%)
Dole (R)	98,786	(42%)		Clinton (D)	95,157	(37%)
Perot (I)	33,255	(14%)		Perot (I)	60,639	(24%)

Rep. Ralph Regula (R)

Elected 1972; b. Dec. 3, 1924, Beach City; home, Navarre; Mt. Union Col., B.A. 1948, William McKinley Law Schl., LL.B. 1952; Episcopalian; married (Mary).

Military Career: Navy, 1944–46 (WWII).

Elected Office: OH House of Reps., 1964–66; OH Senate, 1966–72.

Professional Career: Teacher & schl. principal, 1948–52; Practicing atty., 1952–73; OH Bd. of Educ., 1960–64.

DC Office: 2309 RHOB 20515, 202-225-3876; Fax: 202-225-3059; Web site: www.house.gov/regula.

District Office: Canton, 330-489-4414.

Committees: *Appropriations* (2d of 34 R): Commerce, Justice, State & the Judiciary; Interior (Chmn.); Transportation.

Group Ratings

	ADA	ACLU	AFS	LCV	CON	NTU	NFIB	COC	ACU	NTLC	CHC
1998	20	13	44	23	2	42	100	89	64	66	67
1997	30	—	25	—	76	47	—	90	56	—	—

National Journal Ratings

	1997 LIB — 1997 CONS		1998 LIB — 1998 CONS	
Economic	43% —	56%	39% —	59%
Social	41% —	57%	38% —	60%
Foreign	54% —	46%	39% —	58%

Key Votes of the 105th Congress

1. Clinton Budget Deal	Y	5. Puerto Rico Sthood. Ref.	N	9. Cut $ for B-2 Bombers	Y
2. Education IRAs	Y	6. End Highway Set-asides	Y	10. Human Rights in China	N
3. Req. 2/3 to Raise Taxes	Y	7. School Prayer Amend.	Y	11. Withdraw Bosnia Troops	Y
4. Fast-track Trade	N	8. Ovrd. Part. Birth Veto	Y	12. End Cuban TV-Marti	Y

Election Results

1998 general	Ralph Regula (R)	117,426	(64%)	($178,180)
	Peter D. Ferguson (D)	66,047	(36%)	($156,385)
1998 primary	Ralph Regula (R)	42,903	(84%)	
	Vince Yambrovich (R)	7,947	(16%)	
1996 general	Ralph Regula (R)	159,314	(69%)	($154,379)
	Thomas E. Buckhart (D)	64,902	(28%)	($3,552)
	Others	7,611	(3%)	

SEVENTEENTH DISTRICT

On a relief map the Mahoning River is just a thin line in the lowlands of eastern Ohio. But on an economic map it is, or was, one of the major waterways of the United States. For the Mahoning was one of America's prime steel valleys. The first coal mine here opened in 1826, canals followed, and in 1892 the first steel mill was built in Youngstown. "Soon," writes historian Harlan Hatcher, "the banks of the river were lined with Bessemer converters, open-hearth furnaces, strip and rolling mills, pipe plants, and manufacturers of steel accessories and products." For nearly a century, the Mahoning Valley, between the Lake Erie docks that unload iron ore from Great Lakes freighters and the coalfields of western Pennsylvania and West Virginia, was a steel capital of the United States. Now, in the late 20th Century, the steel mills stand empty, smokeless and silent—except those that have been dynamited and torn down. Big steel management allowed foreign producers to gain a technological edge in the 1950s and 1960s; worldwide overcapacity in steel grew as almost every developing country decided it needed its own steel mill, while cooperation between the United Steelworkers and management after the 119-day strike in 1959 boosted wages and fringe benefits to price domestic steel out of the market. Import restrictions kept the furnaces hot for a while, but the oil shock of 1979 produced sharply higher energy prices and a collapse in the U.S. auto and steel markets. Every plant in Youngstown and the Mahoning Valley closed and in the early 1980s metro Youngstown—Mahoning and Trumbull Counties—had one of the nation's highest unemployment rates.

Steel has since revived, but elsewhere: in decentralized minimills or in huge new rolling plants in northern Indiana. The biggest business headquartered in Youngstown is not steel, but the shopping center empire of Edward DeBartolo Jr., owner of the San Francisco '49ers, who encountered legal problems promoting gambling in Louisiana. The high-wage living standard of the 1970s has vanished; young people looking for opportunities routinely leave; population has declined. Politically, the Mahoning Valley writhed in anger. Republican in the 1920s, solidly Democratic for years after the United Steelworkers organized the plants following sometimes bloody skirmishes in the late 1930s, the area wobbled toward Republicans in the Carter 1970s, then veered back to the Democrats in the Reagan 1980s; now it is one of the most Democratic parts of the country.

The 17th Congressional District includes all of the Mahoning Valley, running south from Youngstown to the Ohio River across from West Virginia and north past Warren halfway to Lake Erie. The congressman from the 17th is a Democrat who speaks in the authentic demotic accents of the Mahoning Valley. James Traficant is loud, angry and earthy—and, in his own way, creative, consistent and compassionate. Traficant grew up in Mahoning County, directed a drug program from 1971–81, and was elected Mahoning County Sheriff in 1980, where he met controversy. He admitted taking large bribes from mobsters to overlook local gambling, loan-sharking, drug trafficking and prostitution and argued, when presented with tapes of some of these transactions, that this was his own sting operation. Tried on criminal charges in 1983 and acting as his own lawyer, he persuaded the jury to find him not guilty; but he owed more than $100,000 after the U.S. Tax Court ruled that he owed back taxes for the bribes. In 1984 he ran against a Republican incumbent and won 53%–46%.

Traficant has a middle-of-the-House voting record, but a distinctive one. Like Youngstown Republicans of the 1920s, he is protectionist and isolationist: He is vitriolically opposed for aid to Israel and for NAFTA and GATT; he has been a harsh critic of "lying, thieving, stealing CIA nincompoops." He is familiar to C-SPAN viewers for his loud speeches—tirades, some say—against foreign aid, free trade, the Federal Reserve and the oppression visited on citizens by the Internal Revenue Service. But he has some accomplishments. His "Made in America" amendments, which he offers to many spending bills, often pass. He has advanced his Taxpayer Bill of Rights measures by such tactics as standing on the floor for 10 hours and raising points of order against every section of the Treasury bill. He amended a crime bill to require a net gain in street cops, amended an immigration bill to require monitoring of federal efforts to stop illegal immigration, and amended the Taxpayer Bill of Rights to impose penalties of up to $1 million for IRS agent misconduct. Many of his other proposals remain unenacted, and perhaps always will be—a bill to study the effects of a flat tax coupled with a consumption tax, an 800 number for information on American-made products, a ban on bareheaded boxing, public meetings of the Federal Reserve Open Market Committee. Loud and abrasive on the floor, he is one of the kindest and most thoughtful members to House employees and pages. In 1998, he harshly criticized Bill Clinton: "Sex, violence, corruption, bribery, deceit. . . . It's in the White House. The whole place is out of control."

Traficant survived redistricting nicely in 1992 when his district could have been carved up, but evidently no one wanted to take him on. Now, he is something of a folk hero at home. He has secured a raft of local projects: $31 million for an air cargo facility, restoring Amtrak service to Youngstown. But his unpredictability has reached the point that he campaigned in 1998 for the re-election of Republican Steve Chabot in Cincinnati; "he's my friend," said Traficant, with his arm draped around Chabot. He has denied rumors that he will switch parties.

Cook's Call. *Safe.* While this district is one of the most Democratic in the state, you would never guess that by looking at the voting record of Jim Traficant, one of the more conservative Democrats in the House. But Traficant's populist mantra has helped to make him very popular in this working-class district.

The People: Pop. 1990: 570,963; 25.8% rural; 16.5% age 65 +; 89.2% White, 9.7% Black, 0.4% Asian, 0.2% Amer. Indian, 0.6% Other; 1.3% Hispanic Origin. Households: 57.2% married couple families; 25.6% married couple fams. w. children; 32.5% college educ.; median household income: $25,220; per capita income: $11,938; median house value: $48,600; median gross rent: $255.

1996 Presidential Vote			1992 Presidential Vote		
Clinton (D)	142,121	(58%)	Clinton (D)	131,983	(50%)
Dole (R)	67,705	(28%)	Bush (R)	67,858	(26%)
Perot (I)	31,494	(13%)	Perot (I)	64,339	(24%)

Rep. James A. Traficant, Jr. (D)

Elected 1984; b. May 8, 1941, Youngstown; home, Poland; U. of Pittsburgh, B.S. 1963, Youngstown St. U., M.S. 1973, M.S. 1976; Catholic; married (Patricia).

Elected Office: Mahoning Cnty. Sheriff, 1980–85.

Professional Career: Dir., Mahoning Cnty. Drug Program, 1971–81.

DC Office: 2446 RHOB 20515, 202-225-5261; Fax: 202-225-3719; Web site: www.house.gov/traficant.

District Offices: E. Liverpool, 330-385-5921; Niles, 330-652-5649; Youngstown, 330-743-1914.

Committees: *Transportation & Infrastructure* (6th of 34 D): Aviation; Oversight, Investigations & Emergency Management (RMM).

Group Ratings

	ADA	ACLU	AFS	LCV	CON	NTU	NFIB	COC	ACU	NTLC	CHC
1998	45	31	100	15	44	29	64	61	64	66	58
1997	25	—	50	—	11	43	—	60	76	—	—

National Journal Ratings

	1997 LIB	—	1997 CONS	1998 LIB	—	1998 CONS
Economic	55%	—	45%	53%	—	47%
Social	52%	—	47%	42%	—	58%
Foreign	22%	—	77%	7%	—	83%

Key Votes of the 105th Congress

1. Clinton Budget Deal	Y	5. Puerto Rico Sthood. Ref.	N	9. Cut $ for B-2 Bombers	N
2. Education IRAs	N	6. End Highway Set-asides	N	10. Human Rights in China	Y
3. Req. 2/3 to Raise Taxes	Y	7. School Prayer Amend.	Y	11. Withdraw Bosnia Troops	Y
4. Fast-track Trade	N	8. Ovrd. Part. Birth Veto	Y	12. End Cuban TV-Marti	N

Election Results

1998 general	James A. Traficant Jr. (D)	123,718	(68%)	($155,897)
	Paul H. Alberty (R)	57,703	(32%)	($26,013)
1998 primary	James A. Traficant Jr. (D)	unopposed		
1996 general	James A. Traficant Jr. (D)	218,283	(91%)	($156,597)
	James M. Cahaney (NL)	21,685	(9%)	

EIGHTEENTH DISTRICT

From their earliest settlement in the 1790s, the hills of east central Ohio have been industrial country. The local clay was used to make pottery, the coal that lies near the surface was dug up, a green vitriol works was built, and a nail factory went into operation, all before 1814. For more than 100 years, this area has been part of the great coal and steel belt that centers on Pittsburgh and Cleveland and stretches from the coal mines of West Virginia to Lake Erie, the destination of freighters filled with iron ore from Minnesota's Mesabi Range. This area is filled with small cities, each with its little steel mill or factory, most of them old towns whose storefronts and wooden, working-class houses bear the unmistakable imprint of the early 20th Century. For a time the pay was good, but after the oil shock of 1979, the coal and steel economy collapsed; the impact here was cushioned by continuing demand for coal from electric utilities, but that threatens to be reduced by the 1990 Clean Air Act amendments. Wage levels have sagged and the hopes many had of getting ahead have been disappointed.

The 18th Congressional District covers much of this land along the Ohio River, just west of West Virginia, and spreads west over hilly farmland pockmarked by strip mines, from Steubenville on the Ohio, which used to have the nation's worst air quality, to New Rumley, the birthplace of General Custer, and Zanesville, the birthplace of writer Zane Grey and architect Cass Gilbert and home of a famous Y-shaped bridge. As one goes west, the territory is less industrial, but overall the 18th is, sociologically and politically, a kind of ethnic working-class neighborhood. Since the New Deal, it has leaned Democratic in most elections, though it voted for Republican Governor Bob Taft and Senator George Voinovich in 1998.

The congressman from the 18th District is Bob Ney, a Republican elected in 1994 in this Democratic territory. Ney grew up in Bellaire, just across the Ohio from Wheeling, West Virginia, worked as a teacher and safety director for the city of Bellaire. A former teacher in Iran when the Shah ruled there, he is the only House member who speaks fluent Farsi and has called for closer ties with that nation. He was elected to the state House in 1980, at 26, in quite an upset, beating Wayne Hays, the longtime (1948–76) congressman from the 18th and power in the House who lost his seat due to scandal and then won a state House seat. Ney lost that seat in the Democratic year of 1982, but in 1984 was elected to the state Senate. There, he backed bills encouraging electric power plants to install scrubbers so they could use high-sulfur Ohio coal still meet air-quality standards, and sponsored measures helping people get and keep health insurance. When Democrat Douglas Applegate announced his retirement in 1994, Ney gave up his Finance Committee chair in Columbus. Democrats had a serious primary, in which state Representative Greg DiDonato beat Applegate aide James Hart 49%–36%. DiDonato criticized Ney for accepting honoraria from lobbyists; Ney criticized DiDonato for sharing an apartment with a cable TV lobbyist. Most unions backed DiDonato, except for teachers' unions who backed ex-teacher Ney. His Belmont County home base turned out to be the key; only 35% for Republican Senate candidate Mike DeWine, it voted 67% for Ney, enough to clinch a 54%–46% victory.

In the House, Ney's record is often at odds with the Republican leadership and clearly aimed at the folks back home. His first legislative action came on the House Administration Committee, where he moved to cut each member's mail allowance by one-third. He worked successfully to prevent the zeroing out of the Appalachian Regional Commission and the Development Disabilities Councils. He removed language eliminating provisions of the Coal Industry Retiree Health Benefits Act that make former employers pay for retirees' health care. He helped organized labor by amending the Transportation appropriations to protect the bargaining rights of unionized bus drivers, and he opposed Republican leaders' anti-union bills. He worked for construction of the Pike Island Project hydroelectric dam on the Ohio River, and he took pride in $40,000 that he won for four flush toilets at a rest stop on Route 78. He fought against what he called EPA's "overregulation" under the Clean Air Act, and voted to cut its budget by one-third and to stop EPA from making policy by rule-making. With Joe Kennedy, he barred from elderly public housing "disabled" persons whose only disability is alcohol or drug abuse. With John Kasich, he toughened work requirements for able-bodied food stamp recipients under 50. With other Steel Belt members, he backed quotas on foreign steel and he said the Clinton Administration was "dead wrong" to put international interests ahead of "working families who have been brutalized by a flood" of imports. He has bolstered his Republican credentials by backing tax cuts and opposing abortion rights.

Ney has twice won re-election against former state Senator Robert Burch, a favorite of organized labor and the 1994 Democratic nominee who won 25% against Governor George Voinovich. Burch tried to make the campaigns a referendum on Newt Gingrich. Ney's pro-labor record got him the NEA endorsement. In 1996, Ney did not run so well in Belmont County, but he gained ground elsewhere, enough for a 50%–46% win, even as Bob Dole was losing badly in the district. In 1998 he carried every county except for a tiny sliver of Columbiana, and won by an impressive 60%–40%. "I have defied the odds for years," Ney proclaimed, and so he has; after his impressive 1998 win, he may not even be targeted in 2000. As for redistricting, it is likely to be controlled by Republicans, and almost all the adjacent territory that could be added is more Republican than Ney's home turf.

Cook's Call. *Probably Safe.* Ney has been a top target of Democrats since he won this blue-collar, Democratic leaning district in 1994. But, Ney's moderate record on labor issues and his political savvy makes him a tough target. After a solid win in 1998, it will be interesting to see if Democrats target him in 2000.

The People: Pop. 1990: 570,784; 59.9% rural; 15.7% age 65 +; 97.1% White, 2.3% Black, 0.2% Asian, 0.2% Amer. Indian, 0.1% Other; 0.3% Hispanic Origin. Households: 60.3% married couple families; 28.6% married couple fams. w. children; 25.4% college educ.; median household income: $22,808; per capita income: $10,531; median house value: $44,400; median gross rent: $216.

1996 Presidential Vote			1992 Presidential Vote		
Clinton (D)	112,851	(47%)	Clinton (D)	110,491	(43%)
Dole (R)	86,305	(36%)	Bush (R)	87,512	(34%)
Perot (I)	36,143	(15%)	Perot (I)	58,605	(23%)

Rep. Bob Ney (R)

Elected 1994; b. July 5, 1954, Wheeling, WV; home, St. Clairsville; OH St. U., B.S. 1976; Catholic; divorced.

Elected Office: OH House of Reps., 1980–82; OH Senate, 1984–94.

Professional Career: Teacher, Iran, 1978; Program Mgr., OH Office of Appalachia, 1979; Bellaire Safety Dir., 1980.

DC Office: 1024 LHOB 20515, 202-225-6265; Fax: 202-225-3394; Web site: www.house.gov/ney.

District Offices: Bellaire, 740-676-1960; New Philadelphia, 330-364-6380; Zanesville, 740-452-7023.

Committees: *Banking & Financial Services* (14th of 32 R): Domestic & International Monetary Policy; General Oversight & Investigations; Housing & Community Opportunity (Vice Chmn.). *House Administration* (4th of 6 R). *Transportation & Infrastructure* (22d of 41 R): Ground Transportation; Water Resources & Environment. *Joint Committee on Printing* (3d of 5 Reps.).

Group Ratings

	ADA	ACLU	AFS	LCV	CON	NTU	NFIB	COC	ACU	NTLC	CHC
1998	15	13	33	8	31	47	100	83	80	68	75
1997	20	—	38	—	53	49	—	80	71	—	—

National Journal Ratings

	1997 LIB — 1997 CONS			1998 LIB — 1998 CONS		
Economic	44%	—	55%	46%	—	53%
Social	36%	—	63%	21%	—	76%
Foreign	28%	—	71%	27%	—	68%

Key Votes of the 105th Congress

1. Clinton Budget Deal	Y	5. Puerto Rico Sthood. Ref.	N	9. Cut $ for B-2 Bombers	Y
2. Education IRAs	Y	6. End Highway Set-asides	Y	10. Human Rights in China	Y
3. Req. 2/3 to Raise Taxes	Y	7. School Prayer Amend.	Y	11. Withdraw Bosnia Troops	Y
4. Fast-track Trade	N	8. Ovrd. Part. Birth Veto	Y	12. End Cuban TV-Marti	N

1296   OHIO

Election Results

1998 general	Bob Ney (R)	113,119	(60%)	($928,302)
	Robert L. Burch (D)	74,571	(40%)	($405,010)
1998 primary	Bob Ney (R)	unopposed		
1996 general	Bob Ney (R)	117,365	(50%)	($879,110)
	Robert L. Burch (D)	108,332	(46%)	($263,417)
	Others	8,146	(3%)	

NINETEENTH DISTRICT

The Western Reserve—the northeast corner of Ohio that belonged to Connecticut until 1800—still bears a distinctive New England Yankee imprint. This land was on the westward trail of Yankee settlement in the years before the Civil War; here, amid the low hills that produced the steel streams of the Cuyahoga and the Mahoning, they established New England-style townships, churches and schools. This area produced some of the strongest opposition to slavery and support of the Union armies and Republican Party in the nation. Its thrifty, hard-working, well-educated citizens built communities with fine schools and, with their accumulated savings, invested in what became some of the nation's leading industries. That brought great masses of immigrants to Cleveland and the other cities of northeast Ohio, which remained solidly Republican until the Great Depression and the bloody CIO organizing drives of the late 1930s; then, for 30 years, the Western Reserve was Democratic during Ohio's class-warfare politics. In the early 1980s, when the auto and steel industries lost thousands of jobs, northeast Ohio went heavily Democratic; in the 1990s, as the economy diversified and recovered, it hovered between the parties.

The 19th Congressional District takes in an irregularly-shaped hunk—a very irregularly-shaped hunk—of northeast Ohio and the old Western Reserve. It includes all of Lake County, with mixed middling-to-affluent suburbs and industrial Ashtabula County in the northeast corner of the state. It also includes a motley collection of the Cuyahoga County suburbs of Cleveland—"both polo fields and bingo halls," says its congressman. East of Cleveland are affluent Italian, Jewish and WASP suburbs, Beachwood, Pepper Pike and Chagrin Falls. Directly south of Cleveland are more working-class suburbs on either side of the Cuyahoga River gorge and west to Brook Park around the convention center and airport. The district has the highest per-capita income and the highest per-pupil spending of any district in Ohio.

The congressman from the 19th District is Steve LaTourette, a Republican elected in 1994. LaTourette grew up in the Cleveland area and went to law school at Cleveland State University; in the 1980s he worked as a public defender and a private lawyer in Lake County, and became Lake County District Attorney in 1988, at 34. Well-known and well-liked, he won a three-candidate 1994 Republican primary with 54%. In the general he faced Eric Fingerhut, a 35-year-old political prodigy who in 1992 was elected to replace not one but two retiring Democratic incumbents who were prodigies themselves: Dennis Eckart, who at 42 had served 12 years, and Ed Feighan, who at 45 had served 10. Fingerhut had come to Capitol Hill as an aggressive reformer, but was unable to produce a promised lobby reform and gift ban. LaTourette attacked Fingerhut for backing the Clinton budget and tax increase, for being soft on crime, and for hypocritically using his franking privileges. Fingerhut attacked LaTourette for opposing gun control and said, "Washington will never change me." But evidently some voters thought it already had. LaTourette won 48%–43%, even though he did not raise nearly as much PAC money as Fingerhut, carrying Lake County 58%–33%; Fingerhut now represents a solidly Democratic district in the Ohio Senate.

In the House, LaTourette has a moderate voting record, and shows more irreverence than one might expect from a former prosecutor or a Republican. The only bearded freshman, in his first weeks, he invited humorist Dave Barry to spend several days on his press staff, with predictably funny results. Later he was quoted as saying that being a congressman "sucks."

He backs up his independence with his votes. He was one of 10 Republicans to vote against the party's seven-year balanced budget plan in October 1995. He is among a handful of Republicans who bucked his party on the patients' bill of rights proposal, which won LaTourette praise from the AFL-CIO. He worked with Democrat Sherrod Brown to keep Coast Guard stations open on Lake Erie and secured funds for environmental dredging on the lake. On the Banking Committee, he sponsored the 1998 credit-union membership reform bill that overturned a Supreme Court decision jeopardizing many existing credit unions.

In 1996 the AFL-CIO ran ads against LaTourette for several months but quit in June to concentrate on Martin Hoke, the Republican representing the more Democratic 10th. LaTourette did Hoke no favors: In early October, when asked why he should be re-elected, he told the Cleveland *Plain Dealer*, "With all due respect to my colleague Martin Hoke, I don't think he's going to win this race. I don't think the Democrats will take control of the House, and I think it's important for northeast Ohio to have a member of the majority party in power." Such a characteristically candid answer rather than the usual ritual dishonesty naturally angered Hoke and didn't especially help LaTourette. But his base in Lake County again came through, 63%–32%, for a 55%–41% margin overall.

In 1998 Republican governor candidate Bob Taft offered LaTourette the lieutenant governor nomination; evidently unwilling to risk his career on Taft's less-than-certain chances (he ended up winning 50%–45%), and perhaps not eager for the enforced idleness of the office, he declined. Democrats did not target the district, and LaTourette won 66%–34%, carrying Lake County with 75%. If, as seems likely, Republicans control redistricting after the 2000 Census, LaTourette could end up with a more favorable district, particularly if heavily Republican Geauga County is added and some of the more Democratic Cleveland suburbs are sheared off.

Cook's Call. *Safe.* Despite the fact that this district is one of the most competitive in the state, LaTourette has won each of his two re-election contests rather easily. With three solid wins under his belt, it is hard to see how Democrats would target LaTourette in 2000.

The People: Pop. 1990: 570,834; 12.2% rural; 16% age 65 +; 96.9% White, 1.7% Black, 1% Asian, 0.1% Amer. Indian, 0.2% Other; 0.9% Hispanic Origin. Households: 60.8% married couple families; 26.6% married couple fams. w. children; 43.5% college educ.; median household income: $34,385; per capita income: $16,609; median house value: $77,900; median gross rent: $402.

1996 Presidential Vote

Clinton (D) 126,926 (48%)
Dole (R) 102,099 (39%)
Perot (I) 31,362 (12%)

1992 Presidential Vote

Clinton (D) 114,358 (40%)
Bush (R) 106,947 (37%)
Perot (I) 66,424 (23%)

Rep. Steven C. LaTourette (R)

Elected 1994; b. July 22, 1954, Cleveland; home, Madison Village; U. of MI, B.A. 1976, Cleveland St. U., J.D. 1979; Methodist; married (Susan).

Professional Career: Lake Cnty. Asst. Public Defender, 1980–83; Practicing atty., 1983–88; Lake Cnty. Prosecuting atty., 1988–94.

DC Office: 1224 LHOB 20515, 202-225-5731; Fax: 202-225-3307; Web site: www.house.gov/latourette.

District Offices: Painesville, 440-352-3939; Parma Heights, 440-887-3900.

Committees: *Banking & Financial Services* (23d of 32 R): Financial Institutions & Consumer Credit; General Oversight & Investigations (Vice Chmn.). *Government Reform* (Vice Chmn. of 24 R): Criminal Justice, Drug Policy & Human Resources; Postal Service. *Transportation & Infrastructure* (17th of 41 R): Economic Development, Public Buildings, Hazardous Materials & Pipeline Transportation; Ground Transportation; Water Resources & Environment.

Group Ratings

	ADA	ACLU	AFS	LCV	CON	NTU	NFIB	COC	ACU	NTLC	CHC
1998	40	27	67	46	33	42	86	78	52	58	83
1997	30	—	25	—	31	43	—	90	71	—	—

National Journal Ratings

	1997 LIB — 1997 CONS	1998 LIB — 1998 CONS
Economic	46% — 53%	45% — 55%
Social	39% — 59%	50% — 50%
Foreign	46% — 53%	53% — 45%

Key Votes of the 105th Congress

1. Clinton Budget Deal	Y	5. Puerto Rico Sthood. Ref.	N
2. Education IRAs	Y	6. End Highway Set-asides	N
3. Req. 2/3 to Raise Taxes	Y	7. School Prayer Amend.	N
4. Fast-track Trade	N	8. Ovrd. Part. Birth Veto	Y

9. Cut $ for B-2 Bombers	Y
10. Human Rights in China	Y
11. Withdraw Bosnia Troops	N
12. End Cuban TV-Marti	N

Election Results

1998 general	Steven C. LaTourette (R)	126,786	(66%)	($798,114)
	Elizabeth Kelley (D)	64,090	(34%)	($128,265)
1998 primary	Steven C. LaTourette (R)	unopposed		
1996 general	Steven C. LaTourette (R)	135,012	(55%)	($1,025,247)
	Thomas J. Coyne, Jr. (D)	101,152	(41%)	($568,352)
	Thomas A. Martin (NL)	10,655	(4%)	

OKLAHOMA

Oklahoma, proud of its history of rising from humble beginnings, enjoying the surging prosperity of the 1990s but uneasy about whether it is keeping pace in education and high-skill employment, is in the middle of America geographically and perhaps spiritually as well. Oklahoma was in the national spotlight when the Oklahoma City federal building was bombed in April 1995, and all Americans marveled at the grace and determination with which Oklahomans went about rescuing the wounded and honoring the dead. And in early May 1999 dozens of tornadoes tore through the Oklahoma City area, killing close to 40 people and causing about $1 billion in damage. But these are not the only catastrophes from which Oklahoma has rebounded. It has had exhilarating highs and sickening lows several times in its improbable history. Oklahoma was settled in a rush, first by the Five Civilized Tribes driven west by Andrew Jackson's troops over the Cherokees' Trail of Tears in the 1830s. Then came white settlers one morning in April 1889 when, in the great land rush memorialized in an Edna Ferber novel, the Rodgers and Hammerstein musical, and half a dozen Hollywood movies, thousands of would-be homesteaders drove their wagons across the territorial line at the sound of a gunshot, the most adventurous or unscrupulous of them literally jumping the gun—the Sooners.

The heritage of these rushes remains. Oklahoma has the second-largest Indian population in the country, after California, 253,000 in the 1990 Census, though there is just one reservation and the status of many other tribal entities is often disputed. Some Indian tribes here have unsuccessfully sought a return of native lands and face high unemployment rates. But there has been much intermarriage over the years, and many Oklahomans proudly claim some Indian blood; assimilation into everyday life plus commemoration of historic traditions and efforts to keep the Cherokee, Choctaw, Chickasaw and Seminole languages from dying out seem to have provided a better life for most Native Americans here than it approaches elsewhere.

Statehood came to Oklahoma late, in 1907, at which point it filled up with farmers, rising from 1.5 million people in 1907 to 2.4 million in 1930. Oil helped: the first well was drilled here in 1897 and by 1920 Tulsa was an oil boom town. Then came a decade of bust—or dust— as soil loosened by erosion was whipped into giant swirling clouds: the Dust Bowl. "On a single day, I heard, 50 million tons of soil were blown away," John Gunther reported later. "People sat in Oklahoma City, with the sky invisible for three days in a row, holding dust masks over their faces and wet towels to protect their mouths at night, while the farms blew by." Okies headed in droves west on U.S. 66 to the green land of California, and Oklahoma's population sank to 2.3 million in 1940 and 2.2 million in 1950, not to reach its 1930 level again until 1970.

Eventually, oil brought another boom: As the oil shocks of 1973 and 1979 sent oil prices up, Oklahoma's population rose from 2.5 million in 1970 to 3 million in 1980 and 3.3 million in 1983. Then, with the collapse of oil prices and of Oklahoma's farm economy as well, it was bust again. A giddy rise was followed by a giddier fall: The rig count fell from 882 in January 1982 to 232 in February 1983, and was just 54 in February 1999; Oklahoma's oil production in 1999 fell to its lowest point in 80 years. Just as the dust cloud symbolized Oklahoma's 1930s bust, so the auction of oil drilling equipment was a symbol of the 1980s calamity. The 1990 Census reported just 3.1 million Oklahomans. In the 1990s, Oklahoma has been building a more diversified economy, with high-tech employers like WorldCom, Lucent and Williams. Population is up 5.4% from 1990–97. Its tax breaks for any business located on current or "former" Indian reservation land—nearly the entire state—have brought in new jobs. But incomes have not risen much, if at all, and thousands of Indians in Oklahoma have filed a massive class-action suit against the government charging that officials have grossly misman-

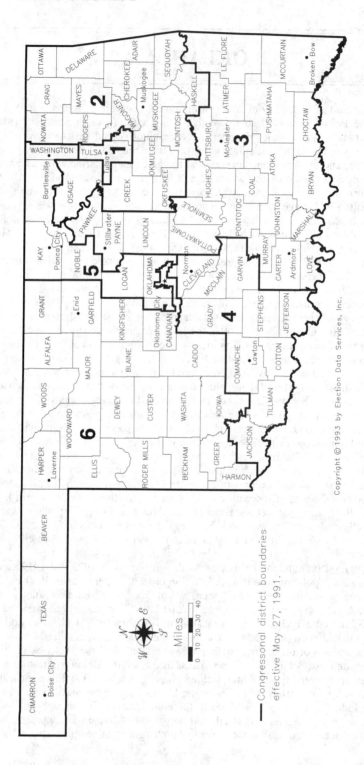

Copyright © 1993 by Election Data Services, Inc.

— Congressonal district boundaries
effective May 27, 1991.

aged Indian trust funds. Oklahoma continues to have above-average rates of divorce, teenage pregnancy and crime, and a low rate of college graduates. Oklahoma knows it has risen far but still has some distance to go.

Oklahoma is split between a Democratic heritage, reflected by its still heavily Democratic legislature and county courthouses, and a strong Republican surge in the 1990s, reflected by Governor Frank Keating and an all-Republican congressional delegation. The historical political patterns were set in the early years: most of the first settlers were Southerners and so Oklahoma leaned to the Democrats. They were especially strong in Little Dixie in the south, while the wheat counties of the northwest leaned Republican; Tulsa, originally Republican, and Oklahoma City, originally Democratic, are both now Republican. The 1990s Republican surge was sparked by a scandal-tarred Democratic governor and reaction to the first years of the Clinton Administration. In 1994 Keating was elected governor, and Tulsa Congressman Jim Inhofe was elected to the Senate over 4th District Congressman Dave McCurdy, who once harbored presidential ambitions. The House delegation was transformed in just three years from 4–2 Democratic to 6–0 Republican. Republicans won a special election in 1994, captured two Democratic seats that fall and won the Little Dixie seat in 1996.

Governor. Frank Keating, elected governor in 1994 and re-elected in 1998, grew up in Tulsa in comfortable circumstances. He went to Georgetown—where he overlapped with Bill Clinton—and the University of Oklahoma Law School, then in 1969 became an FBI agent, investigating new-left terrorists on the West Coast. Keating worked as a prosecutor in Tulsa and was elected to the Oklahoma House in 1972, at 28, and the state Senate in 1974. In 1981 he became U.S. attorney in Tulsa: During Reagan's second term Keating served as assistant secretary of the Treasury and then as associate attorney general under Bush; he was general counsel of HUD when Jack Kemp was its secretary. After Senate Democrats refused to act on his nomination for a federal judgeship, Keating returned to Oklahoma in 1993 and began running for governor. He was clearly the party leaders' choice and won the 1994 Republican primary 57%–29%.

He presented an image of competent conservatism while the Democrats were in disarray. Incumbent David Walters, after pleading guilty of campaign finance violations, hesitated before dropping out of the race. Lieutenant Governor Jack Mildren, with 49% in the August primary, was forced into a September runoff. Former Democratic Congressman Wes Watkins, from Little Dixie, who had lost the 1990 runoff to Walters 51%–49%, ran as an independent. Keating campaigned for business and other tax cuts and won with 47% of the vote, to 30% for Mildren and 23% for Watkins. Keating had wide margins in the metropolitan areas—58% in Oklahoma City, 60% in Tulsa.

In office Keating encountered vehement opposition from Democratic legislators, but was nevertheless able to pass much of his program. "Our goal is a basic one: It's time to make Oklahoma rich," he said. Among his successes were the largest tax cut in the state's history, a property tax cap, tort reform, a 58% cut in welfare rolls and workmen's compensation reform. He spent more money on higher education, as the University of Oklahoma blossomed under the leadership of former Governor and Senator David Boren, and Keating passed a $1 billion program to build highways and beef up Oklahoma's turnpikes.

Keating performed with aplomb after the April 1995 Oklahoma City bombing, supervising the search for survivors and comforting victims and their families; his wife helped raise $7 million for them and compiled a commemorative book which made the bestseller lists. In April 1998 he pushed through a partial-birth abortion ban by prodding legislators on TV. In June 1998 he signed a law regulating hog lots and another providing for technology transfer between state universities and private businesses. Democrats raised an ethics complaint, charging that he used his state car and airplane for campaign fundraising; the state Supreme Court ruled that state law required they be provided to him at all times, but Keating said it is unlikely he will use state vehicles again for campaign purposes.

In 1998 several prominent moderate Democrats declined to run, and the nominee was liberal state Representative Laura Boyd. She campaigned gamely, starting with an ad showing her riding a horse named Keating through a barrel race and saying that by the time the campaign is over Keating will "look like he's been rode hard and put up wet." But Keating vastly outspent her and won easily, 58%–41%. He was only the second Oklahoma governor to win two consecutive terms. His margin was up in metro Oklahoma City (66%–33%) but down in Tulsa (55%–43%); he carried ancestrally Democratic counties in south central and southwest Oklahoma, but lost most counties in eastern Little Dixie and in the heavily Indian northeast; he ran only even among voters under 30. Keating was unable to help Republicans make major gains in the legislature; Democrats have a veto-proof margin in the Senate but only a 61–40 majority in the House. He continues to insist that "Oklahoma is too wonderful to be poor." To cure the state's economy he called for a right-to-work law, and for cuts in personal and corporate income taxes; Oklahoma's great competitor, Texas—known hereabouts as Baja Oklahoma—has neither. He also called for public school choice and teacher performance awards.

Keating has been mentioned as a candidate for national office and in October 1998 said he would accept a vice presidential nomination; but in early 1999 he had made no move to run for president.

Senior Senator. Don Nickles, the Senate majority whip, was first elected in 1980. He grew up in Ponca City, and, after his father died when he was 13, worked his way through Oklahoma State as a janitor making the minimum wage; he then returned to Ponca City and helped run the family machine business. In 1978, at 29, he was elected to the Oklahoma Senate; two years later, he ran for the U.S. Senate seat being vacated by Republican Henry Bellmon. With support from Christian conservatives, he won 35% in a multi-candidate primary and 65% in the runoff; in the general he won 53%–44%, and at 31 became the youngest Republican ever elected to the Senate. It was a signal that conservative Republicanism was the prevailing current of opinion in Oklahoma, just as Nickles's rise to a Senate leadership post is a signal of conservative Republican strength there.

In the Senate Nickles has been a stalwart for conservative principles and, without being well known nationally, has risen to the number two position in the Republican leadership. He chaired the Republican Senate campaign committee during the 1990 cycle and, as an opponent of the 1990 budget summit tax increase, he beat the more senior Pete Domenici for Republican Conference chairman in December 1990 by 23–20. When Bob Dole resigned in June 1998, Nickles considered running for majority leader, but didn't challenge Trent Lott; both got their posts unopposed. After the November 1998 election, Nickles was urged to run against Lott, but decided not to. He said a race against Lott "would probably end one of our political careers"

Nickles and Lott took different courses on the tobacco bill, on HMO regulation, and on the October 1998 omnibus budget bill. After the June 1997 settlement between tobacco companies and state attorneys general, Lott gave Nickles the task of putting together a bill enforcing it. But Nickles disliked the tax-raising bills introduced by Edward Kennedy and Orrin Hatch. Then Lott assigned the issue to the Commerce Committee and its chairman, John McCain, who ended with a package Nickles opposed as "one of the worst pieces of legislation I've ever seen." In summer 1998 he coordinated a three-week filibuster which killed the bill; his own proposal is for a $1 billion program to discourage teen smoking and drug use. On HMO regulation, Lott in 1997 made Nickles head of a health care task force. In summer 1998 Nickles came up with his own HMO bill with 49 co-sponsors, and Democrats did not bring up their bill after a version of it passed the House. Nickles stoutly opposed the omnibus budget bill of October 1998, which was supported strongly by Lott and other members of the Republican leadership in both houses. "I think the best vote I ever cast was that one," said Nickles of his nay vote, after the election.

While taking such implacable stands, Nickles remains approachable and personable. He ascribes his views to his experience running a small business. "I'm a strong proponent and believer in the free enterprise system. . . . I built up a business that was almost bankrupt. If I see government causing problems or doing things that interfere with personal freedom or economic freedom or religious freedom, I feel very strongly that we should get involved and try to change it." Nickles has strongly opposed energy taxes and regulations; in the 1980s he backed the successful fights to deregulate oil and natural gas prices, to repeal the windfall profits tax, and to repeal the 55-mile-per-hour speed limit. He opposed the Clinton Btu and gasoline taxes in 1993, and in 1998 sponsored an electricity deregulation law which would prohibit the states from granting electric utilities exclusive service territories. On health issues, he led opposition to surgeon general nominees Joycelyn Elders and Henry Foster and to ambassador to Luxemburg nominee James Hormel. He got the Senate to go on record 76–23 in 1993 against allowing HIV-positive immigrants into the country. He sponsored the Defense of Marriage Act in 1996. He got a ban on federal funding for physician assisted suicides; his ban on the use of controlled substances in assisted suicides passed both houses but was dropped in conference. In 1998 he held up the nomination of Jane Henney to head the FDA until HHS Secretary Donna Shalala agreed not to seek a manufacturer for RU-486 or finance more abortions under Medicaid or Kiddiecare.

Nickles has had legislative successes. He sponsored the Religious Freedom Act, which passed unanimously in 1998, though without the automatic sanctions some sought. He helped to pass the Digitial Millennium Copyright Act and to ratify the World Intellectual Property Organization. He sponsored the payroll protection amendment to the McCain-Feingold campaign finance bill, against the charges it was a "poison pill." He favors more efforts on missile defense, requiring 95% of federal education aid to go directly to local schools, tax deductibility of health insurance by the self-employed, a lower federal estate tax, and the auto choice bill allowing drivers to relinquish pain and suffering damages to get lower premiums. With Nevada's Harry Reid, he won Senate passage of a bipartisan regulatory reform bill in March 1995—a more realistic and effective version of the moratorium on new regulations in the House's Contract With America. Nickles was also the chief sponsor of the Republican $500-per-child tax credit included in the 1995 budget reconciliation bill vetoed by President Clinton; the tax credit was part of the FY98 budget resolution endorsed by the White House.

Nickles has been politically controversial. In August 1997 Clinton detective Terry Lenzner, on behalf of Oklahoma's Cheyenne-Arapaho tribes, who had been rejected for a gambling license, offered to investigate Nickles and his wife for allegedly accepting money from gas and oil interests that oppose federal return of tribal lands; this reflected badly on Lenzner and his friends in the White House, not on Nickles. Democrats also criticized Nickles for allowing a promotional video for Triad Management, a conservative campaign group, to be shot in Nickles's office; he admitted this was a mistake. He was an aggressive questioner at the Governmental Affairs 1997 investigation of Clinton-Gore campaign finances; criticized by Henry Waxman for having invited contributors to the vice president's residence in 1990, Nickles left the committee after the 1998 election.

Nickles has been very popular in Oklahoma. His one tough re-election came in 1986, when he faced Tulsa Congressman Jim Jones, a Ways and Means member and Budget chairman in the first Reagan term. But Jones's ad campaign misfired and Nickles showed greater strength than many in Washington expected, winning 55%–45% in a year several other Southern Republicans elected in 1980 lost. In 1992 Nickles won easily, 59%–38%. In 1998 he had no big-name opponents. The Democratic nomination was won by Tahlequah air-conditioning contractor Don Carroll in the September runoff when he beat a woman who had died a week after filing for office by 75%–25%. Nickles carried all but one county and won 66%–31%. Does he wish to stay in the Senate as long as Strom Thurmond? Nickles professed himself "surprised I'm running for my fourth term" and suggested he might retire from office after that. But he said the possibility of a Republican president could get him to stay on: "I could be a majority leader while we have a Republican president and we're rewriting the tax code."

Junior Senator. James Inhofe, Oklahoma's junior senator, was elected to a short term in 1994 and a full term in 1996. Inhofe grew up in Tulsa, served in the Army, worked in real estate, insurance and aviation, has for years regularly flown planes and is one of Congress's few certified commercial pilots; he flew around the world following Wiley Post's route and on short notice flew into Texas military bases to check on readiness. He was elected to the Oklahoma House in 1966, at 31, and to the Oklahoma Senate in 1969; he ran for governor in 1974 and lost to David Boren, 64%–36%. In 1976, Inhofe ran for the U.S. House against Jim Jones and lost; from 1979–84 Inhofe was mayor of Tulsa. He won the heavily Republican 1st District House seat in 1986, but held it with uninspiring margins. He was hurt by negative publicity about a family business lawsuit (he eventually was awarded $3.6 million) and charges of campaign finance irregularities, leveled often by the liberal-leaning *Tulsa World*. Inhofe's great achievement in the House was reforming the arcane discharge petition rule. For years House rules kept secret the names of signers of petitions to discharge bills stuck in committees; members could lie and claim they had worked to bring legislation to the floor when they hadn't. That was changed September 28, 1993, and one of the first bills to benefit from the new rules was the aviation liability reform bill, co-sponsored by Inhofe, which limited the liability of small airplane manufacturers in lawsuits resulting from crashes.

Inhofe jumped into the 1994 Senate race when David Boren, a conservative Democrat who carried not only every county but every precinct in 1990, announced he was retiring to become president of the University of Oklahoma. The Democratic nominee was Dave McCurdy, congressman since 1980 from southwest Oklahoma, chairman of the moderate Democratic Leadership Council. An extrapolation from their past electoral showings would put Inhofe far behind: He had won by small margins in a heavily Republican district, while McCurdy had won by large margins in a district that gave Bill Clinton only one-third of its votes in 1992. But in Oklahoma in 1994 the Clinton burden was too heavy for even McCurdy to carry. McCurdy had voted for the 1993 Clinton budget and tax package with its original Btu tax and for the 1994 crime bill with its assault weapons ban. "Dave McClinton," as Republicans called him, was beaten, one Democrat said, by "God, guns and gays." Inhofe won by a solid 55%–40%, carrying the Tulsa area by a higher percentage that ever before (60%–37%) and Oklahoma City by even more (61%–35%); he also bested McCurdy in the rest of Oklahoma (52%–42%). In the Senate Inhofe was president of the conservative 11-member freshman class. He had the satisfaction of seeing the Congressional Medal of Honor awarded to seven black soldiers for their service in World War II; since 1990 he had been championing the cause of Ruben Rivers, a Hotulka, Oklahoma soldier who after being gravely wounded refused evacuation and was killed trying to save his unit. Inhofe in the House and the Senate pushed to see that the Army reviewed the cases and sponsored legislation authorizing the medals. He was elected to a full six-year term in 1996 over James Boren, David Boren's cousin, by 57%–40%.

Inhofe has a very conservative voting record and is chairman of subcommittees with jurisdiction over military readiness and the Clean Air Act. Inhofe argued in early 1998 that the military was in a poor state of readiness. Military leaders disagreed, but in September 1998 hearings Joint Chiefs Chairman Henry Shelton vindicated Inhofe's concerns. Inhofe called for a massive buildup like that of the 1980s. He has also been a strong supporter of missile defense, and attacked General Shelton's August 1998 statement, made just before North Korea launched a three-stage missile over Japan, that there was no short-term threat from hostile missiles. He opposed the proposal to ban the use of land mines in South Korea and elsewhere. He has constantly criticized the "no-end" American commitment in Bosnia; in November 1998 he said the U.S. should "pull out of the area entirely." Inhofe attacked the Clinton Administration's handling of base closings as dishonest, especially the "privatization" of depot bases in electoral-vote-rich California and Texas rather than transfer of work to bases in Oklahoma, Utah and Georgia. He passed an amendment in June 1998 to bar the closing of small bases and delay the base-closing rounds sought for 2001 and 2005. He has also sought to bar state-owned companies from leasing former military bases; the target here is the lease of part of Long Beach Harbor to a Chinese-owned company.

Inhofe has also been critical of the Clinton Administration's clean air policy. He charged EPA with dishonesty on the rationale for stricter air-quality standards; he called for delaying their issuance until scientific studies can be made and passed an amendment on that subject late one night in 1997, which was rescinded when Democrats protested they did not have proper notice. He has said that the conclusion that global warming is occurring is "based largely on selective science, alarmist rhetoric and political calculations." He sought in March 1998 to delay the air-quality standards until ISTEA was reauthorized, and in November 1998 demanded that Clinton submit the Kyoto treaty to the Senate for ratification (which it would deny). In preparation for reauthorization of the Clean Air Act in 1999 and 2000 he promised to focus on the use of science and cost-benefit analyses and to prevent major decisions from being made by citizen lawsuits.

On other issues Inhofe has taken strong conservative positions. He opposed the May 1997 budget deal and the October 1998 budget deal. He and Tim Hutchinson put holds on the nomination of the openly gay James Hormel to be ambassador to Luxemburg. He called for Bill Clinton's resignation in September 1998.

Presidential politics. Oklahoma has been a solidly Republican state in presidential elections since the 1950s. There are no large blocs of voters here who back national Democrats and almost everyone finds national Republicans acceptable. Oklahoma is thus not on anyone's list of target states in October, nor is it the subject of much attention as one of the southern Super Tuesday primaries. In recent primaries, it voted in 1996 for Bob Dole, in 1992 for George Bush and Bill Clinton, and in 1988 for Al Gore (a distant relation of onetime Oklahoma Senator Thomas Gore, grandfather of writer Gore Vidal).

Congressional districting. For the 1990s, Oklahoma narrowly missed losing a seat. State Democrats drew up an "incumbent protection plan," to strengthen the four Democratic incumbents by concentrating Republican votes in the other two districts. But retirements and anti-Clinton animus made all six districts Republican by 1996. That may not hold: Tom Coburn of the 2d District has promised to retire in 2000 and Wes Watkins of the 3d District tried to retire in 1998; Democrats would have an excellent chance in open-seat contests in both districts. If Oklahoma loses a district in the 2000 Census, it is possible Republicans could lose another seat.

The People: Est. Pop. 1998: 3,346,713; Pop. 1990: 3,145,585, up 6.4% 1990–1998. 1.2% of U.S. total, 27th largest; 32.3% rural. Median age: 34.9 years. 14% 65 years and over. 82.3% White, 7.4% Black, 1% Asian, 8% Amer. Indian, 1.3% Other; 2.7% Hispanic Origin. Households: 57.7% married couple families; 27.9% married couple fams. w. children; 44.1% college educ.; median household income: $23,577; per capita income: $11,893; 68.1% owner occupied housing; median house value: $48,100; median monthly rent: $259. 4.5% Unemployment. 1998 Voting age pop.: 2,463,000. 1998 Turnout: 873,585; 35% of VAP. Registered voters (1998): 2,059,817; 1,183,523 D (57%), 718,534 R (35%), 157,760 unaffiliated and minor parties (8%).

Political Lineup: Governor, Frank Keating (R); Lt. Gov., Mary Fallin (R); Secy. of State, Mike Hunter (R); Atty. Gen., Drew Edmondson (D); Treasurer, Robert Butkin (D); State Senate, 48 (33 D, 15 R); Majority Leader, Billy Mickle (D); State House, 101 (61 D, 40 R); House Speaker, Loyd Benson (D). Senators, Don Nickles (R) and James M. Inhofe (R). Representatives, 6 (6 R).

Elections Division: 405-521-2391; **Filing Deadline for U.S. Congress:** July 12, 2000.

1996 Presidential Vote			1992 Presidential Vote		
Dole (R)	582,315	(48%)	Bush (R)	592,929	(43%)
Clinton (D)	488,105	(40%)	Clinton (D)	473,066	(34%)
Perot (I)	130,788	(11%)	Perot (I)	319,878	(23%)

1996 Republican Presidential Primary

Dole (R)	156,829	(59%)
Buchanan (R)	56,949	(22%)
Forbes (R)	37,213	(14%)
Others	13,551	(5%)

GOVERNOR

Gov. Frank Keating (R)

Elected 1994, term expires Jan. 2003; b. Feb. 10, 1944, St. Louis, MO; home, Oklahoma City; Georgetown U., B.A. 1966, U. of OK, J.D. 1969; Catholic; married (Catherine).

Elected Office: OK House of Reps., 1972–74; OK Senate, 1974–81.

Professional Career: FBI Agent, 1969–71; Asst. Dist. Atty., Tulsa Cnty., 1971–72; U.S. Atty., N. OK Dist., 1981–84; U.S. Asst. Secy. of Treasury, 1986–88; U.S. Assoc. Atty. Gen., 1988–89; Gen. Cnsl. & Acting Dpty. Secy. of HUD, 1989–93; Practicing atty., 1993–95; Chmn., Repub. Govs. Assn., 1999-present.

Office: 212 State Capitol Bldg., Oklahoma City, 73105, 405-521-2342; Fax: 405-521-3353; Web site: www.state.ok.us.

Election Results

1998 gen.	Frank Keating (R)	505,498	(58%)
	Laura Boyd (D)	357,552	(41%)
	Others	10,535	(1%)
1998 prim.	Frank Keating (R)	unopposed	
1994 gen.	Frank Keating (R)	466,740	(47%)
	Jack Mildren (D)	294,936	(30%)
	Wes Watkins (I)	233,336	(23%)

SENATORS

Sen. Don Nickles (R)

Elected 1980, seat up 2004; b. Dec. 6, 1948, Ponca City; home, Ponca City; OK St. U., B.A. 1971; Catholic; married (Linda).

Military Career: OK Natl. Guard, 1970–76.

Elected Office: OK Senate, 1978–80.

Professional Career: V. P. & Gen. Mgr., Nickles Machine Co., 1976–80.

DC Office: 133 HSOB, 20510, 202-224-5754; Fax: 202-224-6008; Web site: www.senate.gov/~nickles.

State Offices: Lawton, 580-357-9878; Oklahoma City, 405-231-4941; Ponca City, 580-767-1270; Tulsa, 918-581-7651.

Committees: *Majority Whip. Budget* (3d of 12 R). *Energy & Natural Resources* (3d of 11 R): Energy, Research, Development, Production & Regulation (Chmn.); National Parks, Historic Preservation & Recreation. *Finance* (6th of 11 R): Health Care; Social Security & Family Policy (Chmn.); Taxation & IRS Oversight. *Rules & Administration* (7th of 9 R). *Joint Committee on Printing* (3d of 5 Sens.).

Group Ratings

	ADA	ACLU	AFS	LCV	CON	NTU	NFIB	COC	ACU	NTLC	CHC
1998	0	14	0	0	81	80	100	83	96	96	100
1997	0	—	0	—	96	85	—	100	96	—	—

National Journal Ratings

	1997 LIB — 1997 CONS		1998 LIB — 1998 CONS	
Economic	11% — 76%		0% — 88%	
Social	0% — 83%		12% — 79%	
Foreign	29% — 70%		0% — 88%	

Key Votes of the 105th Congress

1. Bal. Budget Amend.	Y	5. Satcher for Surgeon Gen.	N	9. Chem. Weapons Treaty	N
2. Clinton Budget Deal	Y	6. Highway Set-asides	N	10. Cuban Humanitarian Aid	N
3. Cloture on Tobacco	N	7. Table Child Gun locks	Y	11. Table Bosnia Troops	N
4. Education IRAs	Y	8. Ovrd. Part. Birth Veto	Y	12. $ for Test-ban Treaty	N

Election Results

1998 general	Don Nickles (R)	570,682	(66%)	($2,415,565)
	Don E. Carroll (D)	268,898	(31%)	($8,618)
	Others	20,133	(2%)	
1998 primary	Don Nickles (R)	unopposed		
1992 general	Don Nickles (R)	757,876	(59%)	($3,492,603)
	Steve Lewis (D)	494,350	(38%)	($1,455,848)
	Others	42,197	(3%)	

Sen. James M. Inhofe (R)

Elected 1994, seat up 2002; b. Nov. 17, 1934, Des Moines, IA; home, Tulsa; U. of Tulsa, B.A. 1973; Presbyterian; married (Kay).

Military Career: Army, 1957–58.

Elected Office: OK House of Reps., 1966–69; OK Senate, 1969–77, Repub. Ldr., 1975–77; Repub. gubernatorial nominee, 1974; Tulsa Mayor, 1978–84; U.S. House of Reps., 1986–94.

Professional Career: Businessman, land developer, 1962–86.

DC Office: 453 RSOB, 20510, 202-224-4721; Fax: 202-228-0380; Web site: www.senate.gov/~inhofe.

State Offices: Oklahoma City, 405-231-4381; Tulsa, 918-748-5111.

Committees: *Armed Services* (5th of 11 R): Airland Forces; Readiness & Management Support (Chmn.); Strategic Forces. *Environment & Public Works* (4th of 10 R): Clean Air, Wetlands, Private Property & Nuclear Safety (Chmn.); Superfund, Waste Control & Risk Assessment; Transportation & Infrastructure. *Indian Affairs* (8th of 8 R). *Intelligence* (6th of 9 R).

Group Ratings

	ADA	ACLU	AFS	LCV	CON	NTU	NFIB	COC	ACU	NTLC	CHC
1998	5	14	0	0	71	74	89	76	100	100	100
1997	5	—	0	—	14	81	—	50	100	—	—

National Journal Ratings

	1997 LIB — 1997 CONS		1998 LIB — 1998 CONS	
Economic	0% — 89%		0% — 88%	
Social	17% — 72%		0% — 88%	
Foreign	0% — 77%		0% — 88%	

Key Votes of the 105th Congress

1. Bal. Budget Amend.	Y	5. Satcher for Surgeon Gen.	N	9. Chem. Weapons Treaty	N
2. Clinton Budget Deal	Y	6. Highway Set-asides	N	10. Cuban Humanitarian Aid	N
3. Cloture on Tobacco	N	7. Table Child Gun locks	Y	11. Table Bosnia Troops	N
4. Education IRAs	Y	8. Ovrd. Part. Birth Veto	Y	12. $ for Test-ban Treaty	N

Election Results

1996 general	James M. Inhofe (R)	670,610	(57%)	($2,510,946)
	James Boren (D)	474,162	(40%)	($301,621)
	Others	38,378	(3%)	
1996 primary	James M. Inhofe (R)	116,241	(75%)	
	Dan Lowe (R)	38,044	(25%)	
1994 general	James M. Inhofe (R)	542,390	(55%)	($1,920,227)
	Dave McCurdy (D)	392,488	(40%)	($1,872,160)
	Danny Corn (I)	47,552	(5%)	

FIRST DISTRICT

Tulsa was one of America's oil boom towns in the early 20th Century, settled not just by people from the immediate hinterland but by Midwesterners and New Englanders of Yankee stock. In the 1920s, as its skyscrapers rose in downtown on heights above the Arkansas River, it was a raw town, but intent on culture. It was optimistic and ready to seek economic change, yet culturally and politically conservative, with a Yankee elite and an Indian heritage recalled today in the Gilcrease Museum—left by one-eighth Creek Indian oil millionaire Thomas Gilcrease—and an ethnic variety suggested by the Gershon & Rebecca Fenster Museum of Jewish Art. In the decades since, Tulsa has boomed and occasionally busted; it has remained cosmopolitan and conservative; it is one of America's leading petroleum centers, and also the headquarters of Oral Roberts and his university and 60-story City of Faith hospital.

The 1st Congressional District includes all of Tulsa County plus a bit of Wagoner County to the southeast: essentially metropolitan Tulsa. The political tradition here is heavily Republican, accentuated in recent decades by national Democrats' cultural liberalism and penchant for petroleum taxes. Even during the collapse of oil prices in the 1980s, Tulsa remained full of a contagious enthusiasm for new business enterprises and innovations. Ordinary people here do not resent the oil companies or the new rich; they identify with them. They see not class conflict, but a coincidence of economic interests. They see government as interfering with efforts to produce desired goods and services—although Tulsans are pleased that the federal government built the McClellan-Kerr Waterway that has made the Catoosa suburb a seaport.

The congressman from the 1st District is Steve Largent, a Republican elected in 1994, one of four freshmen and two football players elected from Oklahoma that year. Largent grew up in Oklahoma City and Tulsa, the son of a divorced mother and an abusive stepfather. He played football for the University of Tulsa in the mid-1970s, then went on to become a record-setting wide receiver with the Seattle Seahawks, retiring in 1989. Back in Tulsa he started an advertising and consulting firm. When Tulsa Congressman Jim Inhofe ran for the Senate, Senator Don Nickles asked Largent to run for the House. He won the Republican nomination with an impressive 51% in the six-candidate primary. His Democratic opponent spent almost as much money, but Largent won 63%–37%.

Largent is a strong Christian conservative who is used to overcoming great obstacles; when he retired he had caught more passes than anyone in pro football history though he is only 5'11", 190 pounds and not especially fleet-footed. In early 1995 he was not only sworn in as a member of Congress but also inducted into the National Football Hall of Fame. There he said: "I thank my Lord and Savior, Jesus Christ. Football is what He gave me the physical gifts to do for a time. But my faith really defines who I am, as a husband, a father and a man."

Abandoned by a father he saw only twice in his childhood, he wants to strengthen the family and enforce child support. He was the lead sponsor of the 1996 Defense of Marriage Act and of the Parental Rights and Responsibilities Act, which would give parents more control at a time when schools distribute condoms and conduct psychological tests. He opposes abortion and gay rights measures, which he sees as validating an unhealthy life style; he sponsored a 1998 House-passed amendment to bar adoptions by gay couples in the District of Columbia, and campaigned against a 1997 gay rights referendum in Washington state. He opposes federal funding for the National Endowment for the Arts and one of his early splits with Speaker Newt Gingrich occurred in summer 1995, when Gingrich included some NEA funding in a compromise bill. "Every piece of legislation legislates morality, whether it's a library fine or something else," Largent said.

In pursuing his goals, Largent has not been afraid of going against his own party's leadership. He opposed the continuing resolution to re-open the government in January 1996. After the 1996 election he said it would be a "good idea" for Gingrich to step aside as speaker pending settlement of his ethics problems. He was one of 11 members summoned by Gingrich in March 1997 to explain their votes against a routine appropriation. "I've been in smaller rooms with bigger people, and I can't be intimidated," Largent said. "I've had linebackers who wanted to kill me." He was a leading force in the coup against Gingrich in July 1997. All this, despite receiving the plum committee assignment of Commerce. Nor is he interested in pork barrel projects: in March 1997 he charged that a staffer for Transportation Chairman Bud Shuster offered him $15 million for highway projects in his district; he spoke against the big spending increases in the 1998 transportation bill.

What Largent does want is a flat tax and an eventual end to the current Social Security system, moving toward private investment accounts instead. In June 1998 his Tax Code Termination Act passed the House 219–209; it would end the current tax code by December 31, 2002, with the intent of forcing Congress to pass a new, flatter tax system. It lost in the Senate on a procedural vote after being opposed by Finance Chairman William Roth.

But Largent is not simply a critic; he is also a competitor. He lives in a bipartisan rooming house with several other House members, and has gathered a group of members for "accountability sessions" on Tuesday nights; his 4th floor Cannon Office Building corridor is known as the "hard core floor." In November 1998 he challenged Dick Armey for the majority leader post, banking on mistrust of Armey from the July 1997 coup and calling for a more "family-friendly" schedule and more principled leadership. Largent finished ahead of Jennifer Dunn by 58–45 in the first round. But in the third round, Armey, with his vote-counting apparatus intact and the support of the later-to-be-Speaker Dennis Hastert won 127–95. After his defeat Largent said, "I'm not accustomed to losing. I don't like to lose."

Early in his House career Largent said he wanted his tenure in office to be "brilliant but brief" and said he wanted to serve no more than 12 years. He was re-elected easily in 1996 and 1998. He is considered by some a potential gubernatorial candidate in 2002.

Cook's Call. *Safe.* Largent, who sits in one of the most Republican districts in the state, should not have a re-election woe in the world in 2000.

The People: Pop. 1990: 524,135; 5.8% rural; 11.9% age 65 + ; 83.2% White, 9.5% Black, 1.2% Asian, 5.2% Amer. Indian, 0.9% Other; 2.3% Hispanic Origin. Households: 53.7% married couple families; 26.2% married couple fams. w. children; 53.9% college educ.; median household income: $27,472; per capita income: $14,695; median house value: $61,100; median gross rent: $296.

1996 Presidential Vote			1992 Presidential Vote		
Dole (R)	115,997	(54%)	Bush (R)	122,137	(49%)
Clinton (D)	79,518	(37%)	Clinton (D)	73,509	(30%)
Perot (I)	19,087	(9%)	Perot (I)	52,077	(21%)

Rep. Steve Largent (R)

Elected 1994; b. Sept. 28, 1954, Tulsa; home, Tulsa; Tulsa U., B.S. 1976; Protestant; married (Terry).

Professional Career: Pro football player, Seattle Seahawks, 1976–89; Owner, adv. & mktg. co., 1989–present;.

DC Office: 426 CHOB 20515, 202-225-2211; Fax: 202-225-9187; Web site: www.house.gov/largent.

District Office: Tulsa, 918-749-0014.

Committees: *Commerce* (12th of 29 R): Energy & Power; Finance & Hazardous Materials; Telecommunications, Trade & Consumer Protection.

Group Ratings

	ADA	ACLU	AFS	LCV	CON	NTU	NFIB	COC	ACU	NTLC	CHC
1998	10	13	11	15	87	79	93	82	92	97	100
1997	5	—	13	—	16	71	—	90	96	—	—

National Journal Ratings

	1997 LIB — 1997 CONS	1998 LIB — 1998 CONS
Economic	0% — 90%	26% — 72%
Social	0% — 90%	14% — 81%
Foreign	29% — 70%	34% — 62%

Key Votes of the 105th Congress

1. Clinton Budget Deal	Y	5. Puerto Rico Sthood. Ref.	N	9. Cut $ for B-2 Bombers	Y
2. Education IRAs	Y	6. End Highway Set-asides	Y	10. Human Rights in China	Y
3. Req. 2/3 to Raise Taxes	Y	7. School Prayer Amend.	Y	11. Withdraw Bosnia Troops	N
4. Fast-track Trade	Y	8. Ovrd. Part. Birth Veto	Y	12. End Cuban TV-Marti	N

Election Results

1998 general	Steve Largent (R)	91,031	(62%)	($507,161)
	Howard Plowman (D)	56,309	(38%)	($119,690)
1998 primary	Steve Largent (R)	unopposed		
1996 general	Steve Largent (R)	143,415	(68%)	($345,612)
	Randolph John Amen (D)	57,996	(28%)	($9,377)
	Karla Condray (I)	8,996	(4%)	

SECOND DISTRICT

The land that is now northeast Oklahoma a century ago was the Indian Territory, the place where in the 1830s the Five Civilized Tribes were driven from Georgia and Alabama over the Trail of Tears. More than one in six people here report their race as American Indian, and in some counties more than 40% claim they are at least partly of Native American descent. The Indian percentage is highest in the hilly counties just west of the Ozarks of Arkansas, where county names—Cherokee, Delaware, Sequoyah—recall the Civilized Tribes; the street signs in Tahlequah, once the Cherokee capital, are written in the Cherokee script as well as English. This pleasant land of gentle hills and man-made lakes has been growing at a healthy pace in the 1990s, from overspill from Tulsa and also from retirees and young families moving into the land that became the home of the Civilized Tribes more than 150 years ago.

The 2d Congressional District is made up of the northeast corner of the state, minus Tulsa County. Its geographic enter is Muskogee, subject of Merle Haggard's song, "Okie from Muskogee"; it includes Will Rogers's home town of Claremore in Rogers County. It reaches far northeast where the TV signal is from Joplin, Missouri and spreads west of Tulsa to include Osage County, still an Indian reservation and site of a revived tallgrass prairie where buffalo again roam. Most of this area is ancestrally Democratic, but trended Republican on cultural issues in the 1980s and early 1990s; in 1998 it trended toward the Democrats once again.

The congressman from the 2d District is Tom Coburn, a Republican elected in 1994. Coburn grew up in Muskogee, graduated from Oklahoma State; in the 1970s he managed the Virginia branch of the family business, Coburn Optical Industries, which grew to 35% of the U.S. lens manufacturing market; when the firm was sold, he went to University of Oklahoma Medical School and graduated in 1983, at 35. He returned to Muskogee, practicing family medicine and obstetrics, delivering more than 3,000 babies and embarking on medical missionary trips to Haiti and Iraq. He is a deacon in the Southern Baptist Church, anti-abortion and a strong conservative on most issues. In 1994 he decided to run against Congressman Mike Synar, a liberal Democrat first elected in 1978, at 28, and a battler for gun control and higher grazing fees, for public financing of campaigns and against the Gulf war resolution—not popular stands here. Synar lost the Democratic runoff 51%–49%; he died in January 1996 of a brain tumor. In the 1994 general election, Coburn faced the conservative who beat Synar, 71-year-old retired principal Virgil Cooper. Coburn vastly outspent the Democrat, but Cooper's folksy humor and Little Dixie's Democratic heritage held the Republican's margin to 52%–48%. Coburn ran strong in the northeast part of the district and his local popularity enabled him to carry Muskogee County with 58%, the key to his victory.

Coburn has had a conservative voting record but has also bucked the Republican leadership—and just about everyone else—on certain issues. As a practicing physician (he has delivered 250 babies since he was first elected) and as a member of the Commerce Subcommittee on Health, he has specialized in medical issues. His first achievement here was a bill, signed into law, requiring testing of infants for HIV if their mothers had not been tested. He opposed the Republicans' veterans health care budget as inadequate and passed 351–73 an amendment to transfer $304 million to veterans' medical care from non-overhead administrative expenses. He passed an amendment requiring parental notification for reproductive services to minors in federally funded clinics; it was dropped from the final omnibus bill. With Gary Ackerman of New York he has a bill to require names-based HIV reporting; this Coburn says is his priority for 1999 and 2000. He favored the 1996 Republican Medicare plan for giving seniors more choices. He got amendments through the House to deny punitive damages on makers of products approved by the FDA, and to encourage use of debit cards rather than coupons in the food stamp program.

He passed a 1997 amendment, with Democrat Sherrod Brown, for basic health care rights for Medicare beneficiaries, and with Democrats James McGovern and Robert Weygand sponsored an amendment to guarantee access to home health care for the elderly; Coburn argues that the balanced budget amendment cut the program too much. With Democrats Dianne Feinstein and Ted Strickland, Coburn sponsored a 1998 bill to let doctors and patients, not insurers, determine the length of hospital stays. He opposed physician-assisted suicide in 1997 and came out against mandating medical schools to include instruction on pain management and end-of-life issues, as he had opposed in 1995, and requiring them to teach abortion. He favors the partial-birth abortion ban, parental notification and a prohibition on the development of abortifacients like RU-486. He favors Medical Savings Accounts, full deductibility of health care costs and health insurance vouchers. Every year he conducts slide shows for members of Congress and staffers on the effects of sexually transmitted diseases. Coburn founded the Congressional Family Caucus and opposed the V-Chip on grounds that it required government ratings; he favored technologies allowing families to make their own decisions.

In February 1998 Coburn protested an ethics committee ruling that he said would have stopped him from practicing medicine by barring him from using his name on his group practice and from accepting fees above expenses. Pointing out that he earned only $8,000 from medicine, and has declined his government pension and health benefits and donated his congressional pay raise to charity; he said such a ruling applied standards perhaps appropriate to the House's 163 lawyers but not to its seven physicians, and would discourage citizen-legislators. "If I have to choose between being a doctor or a congressman, I'll choose medicine." The committee changed its mind in March, and Coburn announced that he would seek a third and, as he promised in 1994, final term.

Coburn won re-election in 1996 by 55%–45%, despite opposition ads by the AFL-CIO and the candidacy of Oklahoma Speaker Glen Johnson. This was an expensive race: Coburn spent $1.3 million, with $622,000 raised from PACs, to $1 million for Johnson, plus there was heavy spending by the AFL-CIO and, later, from business groups for Coburn. In 1998 Coburn had a much lighter-spending opponent. But there was a Democratic trend here: Liberal governor nominee Laura Boyd carried the district 53%–46%, the only district she carried in the state. Coburn still won by a larger margin, 58%–40%, carrying all but three small counties. But if he retires as promised in 2000, Democrats will be favored to regain this seat.

Cook's Call. *Highly Competitive.* Coburn's decision to retire puts Republican control of this district in great danger. This traditionally Democratic district had not elected a Republican for over 70 years until 1994 when Democratic Representative Mike Synar was defeated in the primary and Coburn rolled-over the underfunded Democrat. There are a number of candidates looking at the race, but both parties must be wary of the fact that a late primary/run-off means that a bruising process could leave their eventual nominee battered and penniless with only six weeks until Election Day.

The People: Pop. 1990: 524,389; 62.6% rural; 15.5% age 65+; 77.2% White, 5% Black, 0.2% Asian, 17.2% Amer. Indian, 0.3% Other; 1.1% Hispanic Origin. Households: 61.9% married couple families; 29.3% married couple fams. w. children; 34.8% college educ.; median household income: $20,633; per capita income: $9,914; median house value: $41,300; median gross rent: $202.

1996 Presidential Vote			1992 Presidential Vote		
Clinton (D)	97,284	(47%)	Clinton (D)	96,486	(42%)
Dole (R)	81,558	(40%)	Bush (R)	81,432	(36%)
Perot (I)	25,928	(13%)	Perot (I)	49,124	(22%)

Rep. Tom Coburn (R)

Elected 1994; b. Mar. 14, 1948, Casper, WY; home, Muskogee; OK St. U., B.S. 1970, OK U., M.D. 1983; Southern Baptist; married (Carolyn).

Professional Career: Mgr., Coburn Optical Industries, 1970–78; Practicing physician, 1983–present.

DC Office: 429 CHOB 20515, 202-225-2701; Fax: 202-225-3038; Web site: www.house.gov/coburn.

District Offices: Claremore, 918-341-9336; Miami, 918-542-5337; Muskogee, 918-687-2533.

Committees: *Commerce* (18th of 29 R): Energy & Power; Health and Environment (Vice Chmn.).

Group Ratings

	ADA	ACLU	AFS	LCV	CON	NTU	NFIB	COC	ACU	NTLC	CHC
1998	5	6	25	0	93	78	92	71	100	97	100
1997	5	—	14	—	14	69	—	78	95	—	—

National Journal Ratings

	1997 LIB — 1997 CONS			1998 LIB — 1998 CONS		
Economic	27%	—	73%	26%	—	72%
Social	20%	—	71%	0%	—	97%
Foreign	40%	—	59%	0%	—	93%

Key Votes of the 105th Congress

1. Clinton Budget Deal	Y	5. Puerto Rico Sthood. Ref.	N	9. Cut $ for B-2 Bombers	Y
2. Education IRAs	Y	6. End Highway Set-asides	Y	10. Human Rights in China	Y
3. Req. 2/3 to Raise Taxes	Y	7. School Prayer Amend.	Y	11. Withdraw Bosnia Troops	Y
4. Fast-track Trade	N	8. Ovrd. Part. Birth Veto	Y	12. End Cuban TV-Marti	N

Election Results

1998 general	Tom Coburn (R)	85,581	(58%)	($496,552)
	Kent Pharaoh (D)	59,042	(40%)	($123,733)
	Others	3,641	(2%)	
1998 primary	Tom Coburn (R)	unopposed		
1996 general	Tom Coburn (R)	112,273	(55%)	($1,354,299)
	Glen D. Johnson (D)	90,120	(45%)	($1,053,616)

THIRD DISTRICT

West of Arkansas and just north of Texas, Little Dixie is the most recognizably southern part of Oklahoma. It was settled between 1889 and 1907 by white Southerners, most of them poor; some county names (Leflore, Pontotoc) were taken directly from Mississippi. It remains mostly rural today but no longer poor. A private economy that has produced jobs is one reason; another is government, which built interstate highways and turnpikes connecting many people to jobs in more vibrant metropolitan areas. Dam-made lakes have spurred the creation of resort and retirement communities. But traditional cultural attitudes are still strong here: people listen to religious radio and read the Bible twice as frequently as the average American, they serve more often in the military, they stay married longer and raise larger families.

The 3d Congressional District includes most of the Little Dixie counties, and juts up into the center of the state into the old university town of Stillwater, which is Republican territory, to include enough people to meet the population standard. It has long been solidly Democratic and voted for Bill Clinton in the 1990s. For 30 years, from 1946–76, it was represented by Carl Albert, speaker of the House his last six years and majority leader during the Kennedy-Johnson years. Until 1996 it had never elected a Republican congressman, but its conservative cultural attitudes have been helping Republicans in other races.

But the congressman today is Wes Watkins, elected as a Republican in 1996 and 1998, after serving for 14 years as a Democrat and spending six out of office. Watkins grew up in a family that moved around, from Arkansas to California and back again. He graduated from Oklahoma State, worked for the university and for a local development agency, then ran his own real estate and homebuilding firm for nine years. In 1974, at 36, he was elected to the state Senate. In 1976, when Albert retired, he ran for Congress and won the Democratic nomination by beating Albert aide Charles Ward. In the House he served on Appropriations for 10 years and concentrated on encouraging rural development, including advanced technology and international trade centers at Oklahoma State. He had a middle-of-the-House voting record and headed the House Rural Caucus and the Congressional Prayer Breakfast Group. In 1990 he ran for governor and lost the Democratic runoff to David Walters, 51%–49%. He went into private business and campaigned for Ross Perot in 1992. In 1994 he ran for governor as an Independent, finishing third with a respectable 23% of the vote and carrying the 3d District.

In December 1995, when conservative Democratic Congressman Bill Brewster announced his retirement, Watkins plunged into the race as a Republican because he was for a balanced budget amendment and against gun control. "I'm the same Wes Watkins," he said, adding that he had been promised a seat on Ways and Means (which he received) and would work hard for local projects again. The Democratic nominee, state Senator Darryl Roberts, a former Carter County district attorney and Vietnam veteran, attacked Watkins for party disloyalty, flipflopping on issues and avoiding debates. Roberts stressed his own work for education and law enforcement and accused Watkins of switching from pro-choice to anti-abortion. Watkins replied that he had "quite a transition in my life" after the birth of a premature grandson. Watkins said that Roberts had voted 50 times to raise taxes and fees, and a Watkins ad showed Roberts letting criminals out on the street, a reference to his support of a Specialized Supervision Program to relieve overcrowding in prisons. Watkins raised and spent more money and won 51%–45%. with large margins in the northern counties around Stillwater, but also carrying Little Dixie.

He entered office with the kind of commemoration veteran incumbents enjoy: Wes Watkins Lake in Pottawatomie County, stocked with fish and ramps for boaters; the Wes Watkins New Product and Process Fair in McAlester; the Wes Watkins Distinguished Leadership Series at Oklahoma State University; and Rural Enterprises Inc., which he helped found in 1984. On Ways and Means he worked to support two major tax advantages for the area. One was a 1993 law giving faster depreciation to businesses on Indian reservations and former reservations. When an Oklahoma lawyer claimed that almost all of Oklahoma was a former reservation, the IRS balked and Texas members moved to change the law. But Watkins kept it in the Code and pushed the agency to apply it to Oklahoma. The other was tax incentives for stripper and low-production wells still pumping out oil and gas in Oklahoma. Both these provisions were secured by June 1997. Watkins said, "If I never serve another day, I feel like I was able to put something together to help Oklahoma."

In April 1998 Watkins announced he was having spinal surgery and said he would not run again. No Republican replacement was apparent, and Democrats counted the seat as one reason they had a good chance to regain a majority in the House. But by mid-June then-Speaker Newt Gingrich persuaded Watkins to reconsider, promising help with fundraising and on Oklahoma issues (like ditching Ernest Istook's attempt to raise cigarette taxes for Indians). Watkins postponed a second surgery until after the election. This decision, plus Heather Wilson's narrow victory in New Mexico the next week, persuaded most observers that Republicans would hold the House.

There was nonetheless a spirited race for the Democratic nomination. Former legislator Walt Roberts, a rancher, auctioneer, fiddle player and Western artist, had entered the race before April, with support from Carl Albert, McAlester state Senator Gene Stipe, Attorney General Drew Edmondson, former Governor David Walters and Democratic Chairman Robert Kerr III, who called Watkins "a bought and paid-for puppet of Newt Gingrich." Also running was 1996 nominee Darryl Roberts, who had the support of teachers' unions. A third candidate was Chickasaw Nation Governor Bill Anoatubby. They finished in that order in the August 15 primary: Walt Roberts 38%, Darryl Roberts 32%, Anoatubby 26%. In the runoff campaign, Walt Roberts came under attack for refusing to disclose the origins of a $67,500 loan that he turned over to his campaign; he said it came from an unnamed friend in a handshake deal for cattle, and was paid off by $150,000 he made auctioning off art objects. Walt Roberts survived the charge and won the September 15 runoff by 53%–47%, with two-thirds of his margin coming from his and Albert's home Pittsburg County.

Walt Roberts lent $180,000 altogether to his campaign, but couldn't explain the origins of the money to the satisfaction of the *Tulsa World*, while Watkins had a huge money advantage.

Watkins won big, 62%–38%, carrying even Pittsburg County. Moreover, while much of the district remains Democratic, overall the 3d favored Republican Governor Frank Keating over Democrat Laura Boyd, which makes the 2d rather than the 3d the most Democratic district in the state. This may discourage tough Democratic competition in 2000, and leave the district open to major reshaping for 2002 if Oklahoma loses a seat in the 2000 Census.

Cook's Call. *Probably Safe.* The fact that Wes Watkins was easily re-elected to this Democratic leaning district in 1998 is a source of disappointment for Democrats. A strong Democratic nominee could make this race interesting, but Watkins' personal popularity is tough for even the best Democratic candidate to overcome.

The People: Pop. 1990: 524,287; 56.5% rural; 16.7% age 65 + ; 83.6% White, 4% Black, 0.6% Asian, 11.4% Amer. Indian, 0.5% Other; 1.4% Hispanic Origin. Households: 58.7% married couple families; 27.5% married couple fams. w. children; 35.1% college educ.; median household income: $18,394; per capita income: $9,635; median house value: $36,100; median gross rent: $204.

1996 Presidential Vote			1992 Presidential Vote		
Clinton (D)	92,007	(47%)	Clinton (D)	94,753	(41%)
Dole (R)	77,287	(40%)	Bush (R)	77,040	(34%)
Perot (I)	24,580	(13%)	Perot (I)	55,973	(24%)

Rep. Wes Watkins (R)

Elected 1996; b. Dec. 15, 1938, DeQueen, AR; home, Stillwater; OK St. U., B.S. 1960, M.S. 1961; Presbyterian; married (Lou).

Military Career: OK Natl. Guard, 1960–67.

Elected Office: OK Senate, 1974–76; U.S. House of Reps., 1976–90.

Professional Career: Dir., High School Relations, OK St. U., 1963–66; Exec. Dir., Kiamichi Econ. Devel. Dist., 1966–67; Residential construction, 1967–77; Pres. & CEO, World Export Services, 1990–96.

DC Office: 1401 LHOB 20515, 202-225-4565; Fax: 202-225-5966; Web site: www.house.gov/watkins.

District Offices: Ada, 580-436-1980; McAlester, 918-423-5951; Stillwater, 405-743-1400.

Committees: *Ways & Means* (17th of 23 R): Human Resources; Oversight.

Group Ratings

	ADA	ACLU	AFS	LCV	CON	NTU	NFIB	COC	ACU	NTLC	CHC
1998	5	13	11	8	21	54	100	100	92	91	100
1997	0	—	13	—	59	53	—	89	96	—	—

National Journal Ratings

	1997 LIB — 1997 CONS			1998 LIB — 1998 CONS		
Economic	24%	—	73%	23%	—	74%
Social	37%	—	61%	21%	—	76%
Foreign	0%	—	88%	7%	—	83%

Key Votes of the 105th Congress

1. Clinton Budget Deal	Y	5. Puerto Rico Sthood. Ref.	N	9. Cut $ for B-2 Bombers	N
2. Education IRAs	Y	6. End Highway Set-asides	Y	10. Human Rights in China	N
3. Req. 2/3 to Raise Taxes	Y	7. School Prayer Amend.	Y	11. Withdraw Bosnia Troops	Y
4. Fast-track Trade	Y	8. Ovrd. Part. Birth Veto	Y	12. End Cuban TV-Marti	N

Election Results

1998 general	Wes Watkins (R)	89,832	(62%)	($1,220,356)
	Walt Roberts (D)	55,163	(38%)	($808,385)
1998 primary	Wes Watkins (R)	unopposed		
1996 general	Wes Watkins (R)	98,526	(51%)	($1,106,300)
	Darryl Roberts (D)	86,647	(45%)	($542,286)
	Others	6,335	(3%)	

FOURTH DISTRICT

In the years just after 1900, the brown hills west of Oklahoma City and north of the Red River suddenly filled up with farmers riding north from Texas, past the well-watered green lands of the east toward the bare pasturelands of the west. These were young people with large families, and in the years since, this land has emptied out, as children have grown up and moved elsewhere and fewer hands are needed for farming. People in southwest Oklahoma instead have accumulated around major government institutions: the state capital of Oklahoma City; Norman, home of the University of Oklahoma; Lawton, to the southwest, home of the Army's Fort Sill.

These are major landmarks for the 4th Congressional District, which begins a few miles from the oil-derrick-surrounded state Capitol in Oklahoma City, smack dab in the middle of the state, and proceeds south and west to cover half of Oklahoma's Red River Valley. Demographically, this district is becoming more suburban, but the cultural tone remains country. That is true even in the Oklahoma City suburbs, which stretch out over the mile-grid roads, where in new subdivisions dust still gets tracked indoors and people still prefer chicken-fried steak to stir-fried chicken (though they eat both). Ancestrally, this is Democratic country, but Norman, Lawton and the Oklahoma City fringe now tend to vote Republican, and the 4th District has voted twice against Bill Clinton.

The congressman from the 4th District is J.C. Watts, a Republican, former college and professional football player, conservative Christian and African-American. Watts grew up in Eufaula, Oklahoma (named after the largest town in the Alabama county where George Wallace grew up), son of a Baptist minister who was also a policeman and cattle trader; he was one of two children who integrated his elementary school and the first black quarterback on the high school football team. "My thinking was formed in Eufaula, Oklahoma, under the roof of Buddy and Helen Watts, where you were going to work and be responsible. We were in church on Sunday morning for Bible study. In that home you understood the meaning of sacrifice, commitment, sticking with it. I didn't know growing up if this was conservative or liberal." Watts was a quarterback at the University of Oklahoma and led the team to Big Eight championships and Orange Bowl wins in 1980 and 1981. From 1981–86, he played in the Canadian Football League. In Oklahoma, Watts owned real estate and petroleum marketing companies and was a youth minister at the Sunnylane Southern Baptist Church in Del City. In 1980 he heard a debate between Senate candidates and decided that he agreed more with the young Republican, Don Nickles, but he still voted for Democrats as late as Michael Dukakis in 1988. He became a Republican in 1989, "because I think the Democratic Party leadership—not the Democrats but their party leadership—has totally deserted the values of Buddy and Helen Watts." In 1990 he ran for corporation commissioner, a statewide office, and won.

In 1994, when 4th District Congressman Dave McCurdy, head of the Democratic Leadership Council and an expert on defense policy, ran for the Senate and lost to Republican Jim Inhofe, Watts decided to run for Congress. He had plenty of competition. He led in the Republican primary, 49%–35%, but was forced into a runoff in which he was accused of bad debts and tardy taxes. Watts won by just 757 votes. In October, Democrat David Perryman ran an ad opening with a picture of Watts in high school with an Afro haircut, followed by Perryman as a Future Farmer of America holding a pig. Watts won by a comfortable 52%–43%; though he lost most of the rural counties, he won 60% in Norman's Cleveland County and 58% in Oklahoma County.

Watts inevitably attracted attention as one of two black Republicans in the House. Newt Gingrich asked him to respond to Bill Clinton's Saturday radio address right after the election, and Watts declined to join the Congressional Black Caucus ("I didn't come to Congress to be a black leader or a white leader, but a leader"). In the House his voting record was conservative, with some exceptions; he supported more spending on veterans health than other Republicans and counseled going slow on repealing racial quotas and preferences. On the National Security Committee he worked successfully to keep jobs at Tinker Air Force Base and opposed "privatization in place" of military depots. He has favored large pay increases for the military and wrote language on capital market development in Africa contained in the foreign aid bill.

His chief legislative project, co-sponsored with Jim Talent, has been the Community Renewal Act, the contents of which have changed as some parts have been enacted and others dropped to gain more support. The idea is to target low-income urban and rural areas, to reduce taxes and regulations and to encourage local and faith-based problem solving. Some of its tax, regulatory and brownfields provisions were incorporated in the 1998 tax bill and some of its housing provisions were included in a 1998 housing bill; in 1998, school choice provisions were dropped and Democrat Danny Davis became a co-sponsor.

Watts showed his self-assured and fluent speaking skills at the 1996 Republican National Convention ("character is simply doing right when nobody is looking") and in the response to Bill Clinton's 1997 State of the Union speech. But the old-line networks, which have run every minute of convention speeches by Jesse Jackson, covered little of Watts's 1996 speech and his 1997 effort was undercut by the verdict in the O.J. Simpson trial and undermined by a *Washington Post* article that spliced together an interview with Watts in a way that suggested he made derogatory remarks against Jackson and Washington, D.C., Mayor Marion Barry. He disagrees with the liberal premise that government programs help blacks. "Historically, black people believe in family, church and community. It is only when they . . . allowed government to control their lives that they encountered deepening poverty, decaying families and a sick welfare system that penalizes women for wanting to marry the father of their child and mothers for saving money." But he refused to join other Republicans in opposing racial quotas and preferences. In May 1998 he and John Lewis wrote a letter opposing Frank Riggs's attempt to bar quotas in colleges and universities. "This is not the time to eliminate the one tool we have—imperfect though it may be—to help level the field for many minority youth."

In a short time Watts has become a national leader. At the Southern Republican Leadership Conference in March 1998 he was first in straw poll for vice president with 26%, to Elizabeth Dole's 16%. In November 1998 he ran against John Boehner for House Republican Conference chairman, the number four position in the leadership, and won 121–93. Watts seems to have overstepped charges of scandal. His 1996 opponent attacked him for fathering a child out of wedlock in 1976; Watts admitted it, and said the child was adopted by an uncle and that he was "proud of the fact that I took a bad situation and made a very, very positive situation out of it." He also admitted small business debts in the early 1980s oil price downturn, and said he paid them off. Another charge came from a taped conversation in 1991 in which he agreed to pick up a campaign contribution from a lobbyist; the wiretap came from an investigation aimed at others in the corporation commission's office and after an FBI investigation, no charges were filed against Watts.

After his narrow victories in 1994, Watts has been re-elected by wide margins twice. But he has not converted his father to Republicanism: J.C. Watts Sr. ran for labor commissioner in 1998 as a Democrat, and lost 68%–32%. In 1996, Watts told voters he would not serve more than six years, but in 1999 he indicted he may break that pledge.

Cook's Call. *Safe.* Despite the fact that the head of U.S. Term Limits says he didn't, Watts claims that he limited himself to three terms in the House. Watts says that he is still deciding whether he will stand by his pledge. Regardless of Watts' ultimate decision, this seat retains a Republican advantage.

The People: Pop. 1990: 524,407; 25.8% rural; 11.4% age 65 + ; 84.4% White, 7.1% Black, 1.7% Asian, 4.8% Amer. Indian, 2.1% Other; 3.9% Hispanic Origin. Households: 60.8% married couple families; 31.3% married couple fams. w. children; 46.8% college educ.; median household income: $25,391; per capita income: $11,554; median house value: $51,200; median gross rent: $282.

1996 Presidential Vote			1992 Presidential Vote		
Dole (R)	92,011	(49%)	Bush (R)	90,975	(42%)
Clinton (D)	75,291	(40%)	Clinton (D)	72,551	(33%)
Perot (I)	20,376	(11%)	Perot (I)	53,894	(25%)

Rep. J.C. Watts (R)

Elected 1994; b. Nov. 18, 1957, Eufaula; home, Norman; U. of OK, B.A. 1981; Baptist; married (Frankie).

Elected Office: OK St. Corp. Comm., 1990–94, Chmn., 1992–94.

Professional Career: Pro football player, Canadian Football League, 1981–86; Businessman, 1986–94.

DC Office: 1210 LHOB 20515, 202-225-6165; Fax: 202-225-3512; Web site: www.house.gov/watts.

District Offices: Lawton, 580-357-2131; Norman, 405-329-6500.

Committees: *Republican Conference Chairman. Armed Services* (17th of 32 R): Military Personnel; Military Procurement; Special Oversight Panel on Morale, Welfare and Recreation. *Transportation & Infrastructure* (30th of 41 R): Aviation; Economic Development, Public Buildings, Hazardous Materials & Pipeline Transportation.

Group Ratings

	ADA	ACLU	AFS	LCV	CON	NTU	NFIB	COC	ACU	NTLC	CHC
1998	10	13	11	0	21	50	100	94	84	97	100
1997	0	—	13	—	70	61	—	89	100	—	—

National Journal Ratings

	1997 LIB — 1997 CONS			1998 LIB — 1998 CONS		
Economic	38%	—	61%	34%	—	64%
Social	10%	—	82%	38%	—	60%
Foreign	12%	—	81%	0%	—	93%

Key Votes of the 105th Congress

1. Clinton Budget Deal	Y	5. Puerto Rico Sthood. Ref.	N	9. Cut $ for B-2 Bombers	N
2. Education IRAs	Y	6. End Highway Set-asides	N	10. Human Rights in China	N
3. Req. 2/3 to Raise Taxes	Y	7. School Prayer Amend.	Y	11. Withdraw Bosnia Troops	Y
4. Fast-track Trade	Y	8. Ovrd. Part. Birth Veto	Y	12. End Cuban TV-Marti	N

Election Results

1998 general	J.C. Watts (R)	83,272	(62%)	($1,463,694)
	Ben Odom (D)	52,107	(38%)	($356,373)
1998 primary	J.C. Watts (R)	unopposed		
1996 general	J.C. Watts (R)	106,923	(58%)	($1,363,291)
	Ed Crocker (D)	73,950	(40%)	($350,073)
	Others	4,500	(2%)	

FIFTH DISTRICT

Oklahoma City, suddenly the center of the nation's attention in April 1995 when a bomb destroyed the Alfred P. Murrah federal building, killing 168 and injuring more than 500, has for a century been the center of Oklahoma. Oklahoma City, like many state capitals, was not the spontaneous creation of commerce but the deliberate creation of government, sited in the geographic center of the state, on what turned out to be oil lands; oil rigs were pumping crude on the grounds of the domeless Capitol until 1989. The land here is browner and more eroded by creeks than the greener, rolling Oklahoma farmland farther east. From its center Oklahoma City has grown far out into the countryside, followed, as in so many southwestern cities, by expanding city limits so that it extends into five counties and four congressional districts and covers 624 square miles.

The 5th Congressional District includes most of Oklahoma City, but it is a carefully chosen part: the most Democratic sections of the city, including its black areas, were chopped off and put in the 6th District. This is a solidly Republican area as a result. The 5th proceeds north through wheat country, to the one-time state capital of Guthrie and the market town of Ponca City, areas as Republican as any similar place in nearby Kansas. Connected by a strip of mostly uninhabited Osage County is Bartlesville, headquarters of Phillips Petroleum, solidly conservative in the Oil Patch manner.

The congressman from the 5th District is Ernest Istook, first elected in 1992, in his views and attitudes a forerunner of the Republican freshmen of 1994. With heavy turnover he became in just two terms the most senior of the state's House Republicans. Istook is the grandson of Hungarian immigrants; after graduating from Baylor, he was a radio reporter in Oklahoma City and went to law school at night. He attracted attention as head of Governor David Boren's alcohol control board when he refused to stop an investigation of liquor distributors; the state Senate denied Istook confirmation to complete his term. He practiced law and was elected to the Oklahoma House in 1986. In 1992 he ran for the House, taking on 16-year incumbent Republican Mickey Edwards, who had 386 overdrafts on the House bank. Edwards finished third in the primary, with 26% to 32% for Istook and 37% for 1990 gubernatorial nominee Bill Price, who harshly criticized Edwards. Istook ran on conservative issues and won the runoff 56%–44%. He won the general election by only 53%–47% over oil and gas lawyer Laurie Williams, who attacked Istook for his anti-abortion stance. He has been easily re-elected since.

Istook has a very conservative voting record and has used his seat on Appropriations to press for various controversial amendments. One was his 1995 effort to ban organizations that receive federal funds from using more than 5% of their money for lobbying: welfare reform for lobbyists. This was fought vociferously by nonprofits eager to use taxpayers' dollars as somehow an infringement on their freedom of speech. Different forms of the Istook amendment were passed by both houses, but no limit was passed. Another amendment would have allowed states to refuse to use federal funds to pay for abortions in cases of rape and incest; again his side lost. A third Istook amendment, requiring parental notification for dispensing birth control devices to minors (as it is required for dispensing aspirin), passed 224–200 in October 1998, but was dropped in conference; Istook promised to try again. In 1998 Istook pushed to require businesses on Indian-owned land to pay state gas, liquor and tobacco taxes; that was dropped to accommodate Wes Watkins, who did not want a vote on the issue, but the leadership promised to support it in 1999. Istook's moratorium on designation of new Indian lands was defeated 216–208 after Interior Secretary Bruce Babbitt threatened to recommend a veto.

Istook was the chief sponsor of the Religious Freedom amendment, which came to a vote in a revised form in June 1998; it stated, "The people's right to pray and to recognize their religious belief, heritage or tradition on public property, including schools, shall not be infringed. The government shall not require any person to join in prayer, initiate or designate school prayers, discriminate against religion, or deny equal access to a benefit on account of religion." It got 224 votes, well short of the required two-thirds, and short of the 240 a school prayer amendment got the last time it reached the floor, in 1971. But Istook has had some successes. A proposal to require schools and libraries to use softwear to screen Internet pornography was voted into an appropriation in 1998. So was an amendment to bar a regulation requiring hospitals to inform a deceased's family about the option of organ donation ("another Clinton effort to nationalize the health care system"). He was successful in limiting direct lending to 40% of all student loans, banning Centers for Disease Control research on gunshot wounds, and (after bringing the issue to the Supreme Court) stopping the Clinton Administration's imposition of a striker replacement law that failed to pass even in the Democratic Congress.

Istook denounced the bipartisan May 1997 budget agreement as "Washington at its worst." He singlehandedly stopped a $10 million light-rail project for Oklahoma City, supporting instead a $1.5 million trolley-style bus system. After the 1998 election he became chairman of the Appropriations D.C. Subcommittee, and thus a member of the "College of Cardinals."

Cook's Call. *Safe.* This is the most Republican district in Oklahoma. Istook should have nothing to fear in 2000 election.

The People: Pop. 1990: 523,729; 13.2% rural; 13.3% age 65 +; 86.7% White, 5.5% Black, 1.5% Asian, 4.6% Amer. Indian, 1.6% Other; 3.1% Hispanic Origin. Households: 55.8% married couple families; 26.7% married couple fams. w. children; 55.8% college educ.; median household income: $28,348; per capita income: $15,024; median house value: $58,700; median gross rent: $287.

1996 Presidential Vote				1992 Presidential Vote		
Dole (R)	128,792	(59%)		Bush (R)	129,379	(51%)
Clinton (D)	68,222	(31%)		Clinton (D)	62,251	(25%)
Perot (I)	20,668	(9%)		Perot (I)	59,542	(24%)

Rep. Ernest J. Istook, Jr. (R)

Elected 1992; b. Feb. 11, 1950, Ft. Worth, TX; home, Warr Acres; Baylor U., B.A. 1971, OK City U. Law Schl., J.D. 1976; Mormon; married (Judy).

Elected Office: OK House of Reps., 1986–92.

Professional Career: Political reporter, Oklahoma City KOMA Radio, 1972–73, WKY Radio, 1973–76; Dir., OK Alcohol Beverage Control Bd., 1977; Practicing atty., 1977–92.

DC Office: 2404 RHOB 20515, 202-225-2132; Fax: 202-226-1463; Web site: www.house.gov/istook.

District Offices: Bartlesville, 918-336-5546; Oklahoma City, 405-942-3636; Ponca City, 580-762-6778.

Committees: *Appropriations* (15th of 34 R): Defense; District of Columbia (Chmn.); Labor, HHS & Education.

Group Ratings

	ADA	ACLU	AFS	LCV	CON	NTU	NFIB	COC	ACU	NTLC	CHC
1998	0	0	0	8	59	64	93	94	95	97	100
1997	5	—	25	—	10	60	—	89	100	—	—

National Journal Ratings

	1997 LIB — 1997 CONS			1998 LIB — 1998 CONS		
Economic	0%	—	90%	0%	—	88%
Social	20%	—	71%	19%	—	81%
Foreign	0%	—	88%	18%	—	82%

Key Votes of the 105th Congress

1. Clinton Budget Deal	Y	5. Puerto Rico Sthood. Ref.	N	9. Cut $ for B-2 Bombers	N
2. Education IRAs	Y	6. End Highway Set-asides	Y	10. Human Rights in China	N
3. Req. 2/3 to Raise Taxes	*	7. School Prayer Amend.	Y	11. Withdraw Bosnia Troops	Y
4. Fast-track Trade	Y	8. Ovrd. Part. Birth Veto	Y	12. End Cuban TV-Marti	N

Election Results

1998 general	Ernest J. Istook Jr. (R) 103,217	(68%)	($403,434)
	Mary C. Smothermon (D) 48,182	(32%)	($146,983)
1998 primary	Ernest J. Istook Jr. (R) .... unopposed		
1996 general	Ernest J. Istook Jr. (R) 148,362	(70%)	($306,411)
	James L. Forsythe (D) 57,594	(27%)	($40,483)
	Others 6,835	(3%)	

SIXTH DISTRICT

First settled just a century ago, western Oklahoma is a fertile land forever at the mercy of the elements. The western plains are scorching hot under the summer sun and snow-blown in winter; this is one of the windiest parts of America. The rural counties here have far fewer people than before the dust bowl of the 1930s, and fewer than during the Anadarko basin oil and natural gas boom of the 1970s.

The 6th Congressional District is made up of the western plains of Oklahoma, plus blue-collar and black neighborhoods in Oklahoma City. A few of its counties in the south, settled by farmers crossing the Red River from Texas, have been heavily Democratic ever since. But most of these plains were settled by farmers coming south from Kansas, and these have long been heavily Republican. These divisions are as permanent as if Oklahoma had been split down the middle during the Civil War, even though there were no whites in the state at the time. The bigger fact here is depopulation: Counties wholly within the 6th Congressional District had 423,000 people in 1930 and 282,000 in 1990. Four in 10 votes in the district are cast in metropolitan Oklahoma City.

The congressman from the 6th District is Frank Lucas, a Republican chosen in a May 1994 special election. Lucas's roots are in western Oklahoma; he owns a farm and cattle ranch in Roger Mills County and was elected to the Oklahoma House in 1988, at 28. The seat came up because Glenn English, a 19-year conservative Democrat, resigned to head the National Rural Electric Cooperative Association—in effect, to lobby the subcommittee he chaired for years—one step ahead of the Republican majority, as it turned out. Lucas had serious competition in both the primary and general elections. In the primary he trailed 36%–34% state Senator Brooks Douglass and was campaigning from his Oklahoma City base with a Western accent. In the runoff Lucas ridiculed "some Johnny-come-lately dressed up like a drugstore cowboy" and carried all the rural areas to win 56%–44%. In the general he faced Dan Webber, 27-year-old press secretary to outgoing Senator David Boren. Lucas ran an ad showing the U.S. Capitol ("this is where Dan Webber has worked his entire adult life") and Oklahoma farmland ("this is where Frank Lucas has worked his entire adult life") and benefited from Oklahoma Taxpayers Union ads and Christian Coalition voting guides, winning 54%–46%. It was the first step in the three-year transformation of the Oklahoma House delegation from 4–2 Democratic to 6–0 Republican.

Lucas has a conservative voting record and a practical bent. Representing the site of the Oklahoma City bombing, he introduced the resolution condemning it, the bill for relief spending and the bill to authorize the bombing monument and make it part of the national parks system. He supported the anti-terrorism bill and, after the Oklahoma City trial was moved to Denver, sponsored the amendments to allow closed-circuit broadcasting of out-of-town trials and to allow bombing victims, survivors and relatives to watch the trial and still testify in the sentencing hearing. He hailed the base-closing commission's decision to close two other maintenance depots and keep open Oklahoma City's Tinker Air Force Base. He supported an SBA loan program, citing how his family got an Small Business Administration loan in the 1970s. He sponsored $610 million for repairing dams after viewing an old dam near Cordell. In 1997 he got the site of Custer's massacre of Chief Black Kettle's people, near Cheyenne, declared Black Kettle National Park.

The most important legislation Lucas worked on was the 1996 Freedom to Farm Act, which he backed. "We have to get Uncle Sam out of the farm business and give farmers the ability to produce for markets. This bill will help farmers, by breaking the bonds of the old and ringing in a market-oriented program which will guide us into the next century." In response to the heat wave of 1998 he supported the $4.2 billion relief package that accelerated payments but did not abandon the 1996 law.

Lucas has been re-elected by wide margins. His 1996 and 1998 opponent Paul Barby showed courage and commitment by announcing before running that he is gay, and by spending over $500,000 of his own money. But he was not able to make much of a dent. Lucas won 65%–33% in 1998, carrying Oklahoma County by only 49%–48% but the rest of the district 72%–26%. The only apparent threat to Lucas's tenure is if Oklahoma should lose a district in the 2000 Census and the Democratic legislature carves up the 6th District.

Cook's Call. *Safe.* Don't look for Democrats to target Lucas in 2000. He is safely ensconced in this conservative district.

The People: Pop. 1990: 524,638; 29.7% rural; 15.3% age 65 + ; 78.4% White, 13.2% Black, 1% Asian, 5% Amer. Indian, 2.4% Other; 4.2% Hispanic Origin. Households: 55.8% married couple families; 26.4% married couple fams. w. children; 38.4% college educ.; median household income: $21,797; per capita income: $10,540; median house value: $40,000; median gross rent: $232.

1996 Presidential Vote			1992 Presidential Vote		
Dole (R)	86,670	(47%)	Bush (R)	91,966	(43%)
Clinton (D)	75,783	(41%)	Clinton (D)	73,516	(34%)
Perot (I)	20,149	(11%)	Perot (I)	49,268	(23%)

Rep. Frank Lucas (R)

Elected May 1994; b. Jan. 6, 1960, Cheyenne; home, Cheyenne; OK St. U., B.S. 1982; Baptist; married (Lynda).

Elected Office: OK House of Reps., 1988–94.

Professional Career: Farmer & rancher.

DC Office: 438 CHOB 20515, 202-225-5565; Fax: 202-225-8698; Web site: www.house.gov/lucas.

District Offices: Clinton, 580-323-6232; Enid, 580-233-9224; Oklahoma City, 405-235-5311; Woodward, 580-256-5752.

Committees: *Agriculture* (10th of 27 R): General Farm Commodities, Resource Conservation & Credit; Livestock & Horticulture; Risk Management, Research & Specialty Crops. *Banking & Financial Services* (12th of 32 R): Capital Markets, Securities & Government Sponsored Enterprises (Vice Chmn.); Domestic & International Monetary Policy. *Science* (19th of 25 R): Basic Research; Space & Aeronautics.

Group Ratings

	ADA	ACLU	AFS	LCV	CON	NTU	NFIB	COC	ACU	NTLC	CHC
1998	0	6	0	0	21	55	100	100	100	97	100
1997	0	—	13	—	42	52	—	90	92	—	—

National Journal Ratings

	1997 LIB — 1997 CONS			1998 LIB — 1998 CONS		
Economic	28%	—	67%	0%	—	88%
Social	10%	—	82%	3%	—	90%
Foreign	0%	—	88%	7%	—	83%

Key Votes of the 105th Congress

1. Clinton Budget Deal	Y	5. Puerto Rico Sthood. Ref.	N	9. Cut $ for B-2 Bombers	N
2. Education IRAs	Y	6. End Highway Set-asides	Y	10. Human Rights in China	N
3. Req. 2/3 to Raise Taxes	Y	7. School Prayer Amend.	Y	11. Withdraw Bosnia Troops	Y
4. Fast-track Trade	Y	8. Ovrd. Part. Birth Veto	Y	12. End Cuban TV-Marti	N

Election Results

1998 general	Frank Lucas (R)	85,261	(65%)	($344,338)
	Paul M. Barby (D)	43,555	(33%)	($268,307)
	Others	2,455	(2%)	
1998 primary	Frank Lucas (R)	unopposed		
1996 general	Frank Lucas (R)	113,499	(64%)	($439,969)
	Paul M. Barby (D)	64,173	(36%)	($476,471)

OREGON

Oregon is an experimental commonwealth and laboratory of reform on the Pacific Rim, a maker of national trends. It is far removed from where most Americans live, but closer in touch with the rest of America than sometimes appears: within minutes after a tree branch brushed a power line in Oregon in August 1996, the entire western power grid—"the largest machine man has ever made," in one expert's words—shut down all the way from the Canadian border to San Diego, where the Republican National Convention was opening two days later. Oregon has led the nation with bike trails and Nike sneakers, light rail trams and Pendleton shirts, with assisted suicide and mail-in ballots. Oregon is an affluent high-tech civilization where one can still see much the same land and water—and rain—that Lewis and Clark saw in 1805 when they came down the Columbia River gorge, past what is now Portland, to the vast Pacific Ocean.

This Oregon was settled by Americans when John Jacob Astor set up his fur trading post at Astoria in 1811 and when New England Yankees in the 1840s rode the Oregon Trail and floated down the Columbia to the well-watered Willamette Valley. In this remote land, nearly 2,000 miles from the Mississippi River frontier and 700 miles from the small settlements of California, an orderly, productive society—a kind of western New England—was built. It grew steadily over the years, with a few booms—when timber, always its first industry, surged in 1900–10, during the war and after in the 1940s, and in the 1970s when home building sky-rocketed and Oregon's natural environment began to be widely appreciated. Too widely for some, like Governor Tom McCall (1966–74), who used to urge people to visit Oregon, "but for heaven's sake don't come to live here."

Today's Oregon is more confident it can live comfortably with growth. In the 1990s it has been the nation's 10th fastest growing state, adding more than 400,000 new residents. The newcomers are highly educated, sparkplugs of the economic growth that leaves employers begging for workers, the reason half of Oregon households have personal computers. The newcomers fill Portland's postmodern skyscrapers and high-tech offices in Silicon Forest to the west, and they prosper and invent in the smaller cities and towns of the green Willamette Valley and the sere lands of eastern Oregon as well.

They come to a state which has a distinctive culture. Founded by New England churchmen, Oregon today is America's most unchurched state, with the lowest rate of church membership, with large numbers of believers in astrology, New Age lore and the like. To the innovations of this cultural left the public voices of Oregon's big institutions, like those of New England, have been friendly. Oregon a generation ago produced one of the first bottle-deposit laws, decriminalized marijuana, legalized most abortions before *Roe v. Wade*, and backed limits on development and use of property. More recently, it has produced an Oregon Health Plan which rations medical care, denying specified low-priority treatments to Medicaid recipients. It has legalized assisted suicide, in referenda in 1994 and 1997, to the point that doctors can give lethal injections to disabled persons unable to take drugs by themselves; in 1998 15 terminally ill people in the state ended their lives with lethal injections. A gun control law passed banning semi-automatic weapons, and weekly betting on professional sports games was legalized. The Portland area has limited development and set aside green space, to the point that metropolitan area housing prices have risen to the fourth highest in the nation. Sometimes there are cross-currents: Voters in 1996 rejected an expansion of the bottle bill and bonds for Portland's light rail, and while Democrats hold most high offices here, Republicans control both houses of the state legislature. But in 1998 Oregon voters were on the move again, approving medical marijuana, mail-in ballots and the unsealing of adoption records, and the state granted health care and other benefits to employees' domestic partners. But voters rejected a ban on clearcut logging and required notice to property owners of proposed zoning changes.

The common threads seem to be a regard for personal autonomy and a readiness to discard traditional rules and ways of doing things. Voting on most of these measures has followed similar patterns, with Portland and the university towns of Eugene and Corvallis taking liberal positions and counties east of the Cascades and outside the metro reach taking more conservative stands. But in daily life, each region goes its own way. Portland is as proud of its Metropolitan Greenspaces and light rail lines as it is of its Rose Festival, and Mayor Vera Katz is an innovative and politically shrewd liberal.

These cultural differences have been reflected increasingly in Oregon's partisan politics. Back in the 1960s this state showed only the mildest of regional variations in partisan preference, disposed to support articulate moderate Republicans, like its two long-term senators, Mark Hatfield (1966–96) and Bob Packwood (1968–95). But in the 1980s and 1990s, cultural splits have sometimes favored first Portland-oriented Democrats and sometimes conservative Republicans. Oregon has voted Democratic in the last three presidential elections, but Bill Clinton's margin narrowed slightly in 1996. In gubernatorial elections in the 1990s Oregon has elected two Portland-backed Democrats in a row. Barbara Roberts, elected 46%–40% in 1990 as an Oregon Citizens' Alliance (OCA)-backed candidate, split the Republican vote, had low job ratings and did not seek a second term. John Kitzhaber, elected 51%–42% in 1994, a physician and the author of the Oregon Health Plan, has worked with the Republican legislature which came in with him, but his health program has not worked out entirely as hoped.

In 1996 Oregon had two open-seat Senate contests, one in January to replace Bob Packwood after his fall 1995 resignation, the other in November to replace Mark Hatfield, who retired after 30 years. Both were decided by narrow margins. In the January election, the nation's first election conducted by mail-in ballots, Democrat Ron Wyden beat Republican Gordon Smith 48%–47%. In November Smith ran again, and beat Democrat Tom Bruggere 50%–46%. Though the Wyden-Smith contest was full of negative campaigning and rancor, the two senators have taken to working closely together in Washington and holding joint meetings all over Oregon—another Oregon innovation, it seems. In the process they have worked for legislative consensus in the Senate and seem to be promoting a spirit of comity and mutual regard in a state that has been split sharply on cultural lines.

Consensus has also been promoted by an evening out of the demographic balance. In the 1980s growth in Oregon was concentrated in metro Portland, which tended to attract bright young people of a liberal bent. But metro Portland's restrictions on development have slowed

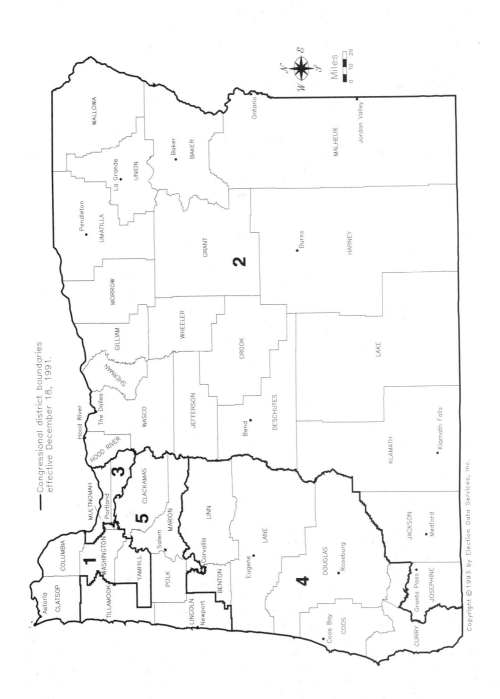

—Congressional district boundaries
effective December 18, 1991.

Miles
0   10   20

Copyright © 1993 by Election Data Services, Inc.

its population growth, at least relatively, and in the 1990s the culturally conservative areas have been growing faster. Voter turnout from 1990–98 was down almost 15% in Portland's strongly liberal Multnomah County, and it was up most sharply around medium-sized towns like Bend, Grants Pass and Newport and in counties just beyond the development limits of metropolitan Portland.

Governor. John Kitzhaber is a Democrat elected governor in 1994 and 1998. He grew up in Eugene, graduated from Dartmouth and the University of Oregon medical school and practiced emergency medicine in Roseburg from 1974–88. In 1978 he was elected to the state House, in 1980 to the state Senate; he was Senate president from 1985–93. His great achievement there was the Oregon Health Plan (the other physician-governor, Vermont Democrat Howard Dean, is a health care reformer too). Its strategy is to increase Medicaid coverage by rationing treatments. Blocked by the Bush Administration, it went into effect in February 1994. Cigarette taxes were increased 10 cents per pack to pay for the plan, under which state officials drew up a list of 696 (now 745) medical treatments and ranked them by effectiveness and importance to basic health. Then based on cost estimates, the state decides how many treatments it can afford, and draws a line—originally it was at 606, in 1998 it was 574 and Kitzhaber has proposed 564. Above the line, the state will pay; below, it won't. Among the uncovered treatments are aggressive cancer therapies for which the five-year survival rate is under 50% and treatments for the final stages of AIDS. At first the plan attracted more than twice as many new enrollees as expected, and the percentage of uninsured fell from 15% to 11%. But overall spending rose by nearly one-quarter from 1995–97 to 1997–99, and 350,000 people were still uninsured. There is much evidence that physicians ignore the limits on treatments and federal Medicaid officials have resisted efforts to deny more treatments.

The Oregon Health Plan gave Kitzhaber a solid platform, and his personal manner—he usually wears blue jeans, he loves river rafting and fly fishing—made him attractive to many voters beyond the Democratic core in 1994. Incumbent Governor Barbara Roberts was unpopular; her "Conversation with Oregon," attempt to get voters to suggest spending cuts and tax increases fizzled when the legislature rejected tax increases and economic growth surged and made them seem unnecessary. In January 1994 she withdrew from the race. Meanwhile, Republicans had a primary between former Congressman Denny Smith, son of a former governor and head of a family newspaper chain, and Craig Berkman, former state party chairman and critic of the Oregon Citizens' Alliance; Smith rallied conservatives and won 50%–41%. In the general, Kitzhaber won statewide 51%–42%; he carried the Portland area and the university towns handsomely, but carried only a handful of counties in the rest of the state.

The Oregon Health Plan has been characteristic of Kitzhaber's initiatives as governor—its cool rationality, its faith in the judgment of centralized experts, its taste for complexity, its willingness to use the power of the state to make decisions for others, its secular disregard for tradition. He supports assisted suicide (Oregon Medicaid pays for lethal injections) and distanced himself from the medical marijuana initiative. His welfare reform plan used money from food stamps and cash benefits to subsidize employment for nine months, with employers contributing $1 an hour to education accounts. He called for a statewide teacher salary schedule in 1997, has sought performance-based incentives for school districts to meet a 1991 standards law (he asked educators how much it would cost to meet standards), he opposes school vouchers and any charter schools not controlled by school districts. (In the 1920s Oregon outlawed private schools altogether; the Supreme Court ruled the law unconstitutional.) He has spent much time on concocting a program of incentives for private landowners to preserve the habitat of coastal coho and steelhead salmon; despite his efforts, the federal government stepped in and listed coho as a threatened species. He sought a new bottle tax for the salmon plan and state parks; the state House nixed that. His biggest failure was a transportation plan, with a tax based on cars' size and mileage, to cut down auto travel. Senate Republicans rejected the tax in 1997, arguing that the transportation department spent too much on administration and bicycle paths, and in 1999 sought to raise the gas tax instead.

Kitzhaber went into the 1998 election cycle with high job ratings and hoped to help Democrats win control of the state House. His Republican opponent was Bill Sizemore, head of Oregon Taxpayers United, a group pushing conservative ballot propositions. His Measure 47 cut property taxes and limited increases to 3% a year. In response, Kitzhaber (Sizemore called him "Taxhaber") tried to send a $383 million surplus to schools, but Republicans pressed for a tax rebate instead. For 1998 Sizemore's big project was Measure 59, to prohibit unions from using members' dues money for political purposes without written authorization. In April 1998 the Portland *Oregonian* ran a long story on Sizemore's financial reverses: in 1987 he was discharged from $358,000 of debts in bankruptcy court from a carpet business; in the early 1990s a toy company he owned left behind $795,000 in unpaid loans and debts. Sizemore won the May 1998 primary, but with only 50% of the vote against three weak opponents; his unfavorable rating was over 50%, and the unions opposing Measure 59 ran ads featuring him. There were rumors he was quitting the race in July 1998; he said he was concentrating on Measure 59 and "only doing the things I have to do in the governor's race." In November both Measure 59 and Sizemore lost, the latter by a wider margin, 64%–30%; Kitzhaber carried all but one county.

Kitzhaber was the first Democratic governor re-elected since 1906, indeed the first Oregon governor re-elected since 1982. There seemed to be a consensus on spending more on education to meet standards, and Kitzhaber called for a $30 million juvenile crime prevention program and even greater efforts, building on Oregon's 1973 land-use law, to cut down on commercial sprawl.

Senior Senator. Ron Wyden grew up in California, graduated from Stanford, and came to Oregon to attend the University of Oregon Law School. After graduating in 1974 he founded the Gray Panthers, an advocacy group for the elderly; his first foray into electoral politics was sponsoring a successful referendum reducing the price of dentures. In 1980, at 31, he challenged an incumbent in the heavily Democratic 3d District, which covers most of Portland, and won the primary 60%–40%. In his first term in the House, he got a seat on Commerce Committee and became an ally of both Chairman John Dingell and Health Subcommittee Chairman Henry Waxman. Wyden has a genius for coming up with sensible-sounding ideas no one else has thought of and a knack for making the counter-intuitive political alliances which are so helpful in passing unfamiliar measures through the House. His achievements include a law, co-sponsored with Connecticut Republican Nancy Johnson, reducing federally funded community health clinics' malpractice insurance premiums by requiring the Justice Department to defend them in malpractice cases. He worked hard to get a waiver for John Kitzhaber's Oregon Health Plan and salmon recovery plan, and to bring the abortifacient RU-486 to the United States. Wyden did not respond confrontationally when Republicans won the House majority in November 1994, voting for their unfunded mandates bill and for the line-item veto.

When the Senate Ethics Committee recommended the expulsion of Bob Packwood in September 1995, Wyden, who had long been eyeing the seat, decided to run in the January 1996 special election to replace him—the first election Oregon conducted by mail-in ballot. With his home base in Portland, whose TV stations cover most of the state, he had greater name identification than any competitor. But he had spirited opposition in the primary, for which voting ended December 5, from Eugene-based Congressman Peter DeFazio. They differed on some issues—DeFazio opposed NAFTA, GATT and gun control—and DeFazio was helped when Wyden, taking a quiz on KOIN-TV, could not name the prime minister of Canada or locate Bosnia on a globe. DeFazio carried his own district overwhelmingly, holding Wyden to a 50%–44% win. Meanwhile, the Republican nominee was state Senate President Gordon Smith, a frozen vegetable tycoon from eastern Oregon who ultimately spent $2 million of his own money to beat longtime statewide official Norma Paulus 63%–25% in the primary.

Most polls had the race in a dead heat as Smith adroitly avoided identification with House Republicans' intransigent stands on the budget and won the support of Senator Mark Hatfield. But organized labor and environmental groups ran heavy flights of ads against him, including a Sierra Club spot that charged spills from his plant had polluted a local creek. Early in January, after balloting started, Wyden said he would stop all negative campaigning; Smith, noting the Sierra Club ad was continuing, refused to join him. Wyden seemed to pick up strength the week before the January 30 deadline and won 48%–47%. This was hailed as a rejection of Newt Gingrich and a victory for abortion rights, but most voters deciding on abortion picked Smith, and Wyden, with his considerable strengths, had just barely managed to win in a state carried by Bill Clinton and Michael Dukakis.

In the Senate Wyden continued some of his crusades from the House. In April 1997 he and Republican Charles Grassley called for disclosure of the names of senators who place "holds" on legislation—a cause Wyden started working on in 1992 when a bill he backed was killed by anonymous holds. Wyden was not averse to holds as such—he held up the confirmation of Joint Chiefs Chairman Henry Shelton to force the Pentagon to give an explanation of a C-130 crash in which 10 Oregon reservists died—but to the lack of accountability in secret holds. Wyden and Grassley got their provision in a D.C. appropriation in 1997 and a defense appropriation in 1998, but both were eliminated in conference. Wyden persevered, and in March 1999 Majority Leader Trent Lott and Minority Leader Tom Daschle unveiled a new procedure: a senator putting a hold on a bill must inform the sponsor, the committee chairman and the two party leaders. "The fog of secrecy is starting to lift from the U.S. Senate," Wyden said.

Another Wyden cause was the Internet. In summer 1996 he worked with California Congressman Christopher Cox to push their amendment prohibiting government censorship of the Internet and urging online providers to offer technologies to help parents control their children's access to Internet materials. He and Cox also sponsored a two-year ban on state and local taxes on Internet transactions or content providers that passed in October 1998. A cross-country traveler, Wyden is interested in airlines: a call for disclosure of airline safety records resulted in FAA action to put that information on the Internet in January 1997. With Commerce Chairman John McCain, he co-sponsored an airline passenger bill of rights in February 1999, to inform passengers when flights are oversold and why planes are late or flights cancelled, and to legalize back-to-back ticketing and hidden cities (means of taking advantage of low air fares). The two also worked closely on the 1998 tobacco bill. In McCain's words, "He's very active, in fact, to the point of being a pain in the ass. I say that in a complimentary fashion. He's very tenacious about the things he believes in."

Wyden continues to be interested in health issues. He has worked on HMO regulation, to bar restrictions on physicians from mentioning alternative treatments to allowing lawsuits; he wants to bar higher insurance rates for victims of domestic abuse. He worked to stop federal repeal of Oregon's assisted suicide law. Aware of the crunch coming around 2010, he has tried to find middle ground between the Clinton Administration and Republicans on Medicare reform. On Oregon issues, he has opposed the sale of the Bonneville Power Administration, opposed a restart of the experimental reactor on the Hanford Reservation, and has sought to ban logging in the Little Sandy Watershed, a potential site for Portland's drinking water—he has pushed for closing of many logging roads nationally. He and Conrad Burns of Montana want to let states use Clean Water Act money to lay irrigation pipe, line canals and improve irrigation systems. He worked on the new highway funding formula and Medicare reimbursement formula. In April 1997 Wyden was blocked from bringing a blind staffer's guide dog to the floor of the Senate when Robert Byrd objected; Trent Lott quickly scurried to change the rules, and all three appeared on the floor the next day.

When Bob Packwood resigned in 1995 and Mark Hatfield retired in 1996, Oregon lost 57 years of seniority in the Senate; the election of Ron Wyden in January 1996 and Gordon Smith in November 1996 was the first time two senators were elected who had run against each other in the same year. Surprisingly, considering the negative character of their campaign, they became friends (and found they had attended the same elementary school in the late 1950s). They started holding town meetings in every congressional district together. Wyden explains it was a kind of "penance" for the 1995–96 campaign: "Both of us by the end of it said we can hardly recognize ourselves with all the muck and charges and countercharges and the like. And so we said, on our watch, Oregon is not going to have a food fight in the United States Senate." After the shooting deaths in a Springfield school, they sponsored jointly a bill to require pupils who bring guns to school to be held for 72 hours and undergo psychological evaluation. They collaborated on a bill, passed by the Senate in August 1998 but killed in conference, to handle migrant farm workers. It would allow farmers to hire aliens, through Labor Department exchanges, reduce application time from 60 to 21 days, would guarantee workers wages 5% above Davis-Bacon levels, on-site housing or a housing allowance, repayment of transportation costs and full workplace protections.

This bipartisan collaboration seemed to suit the mood of voters in the late 1990s and was certainly sounded in Wyden's election to a full term in November 1998. His opponent, state Senator John Lim, who is of Korean descent, raised much less money than he hoped, and Wyden was so far ahead he had $500,000 left over after the campaign. He won 61%–34%, carrying all but one county, and improved his January 1996 showing by 10% in metro Portland, 14% in the Willamette Valley and 18% in the rest of the state.

Junior Senator. Republican Gordon Smith was born in Pendleton and grew up, after his father sold his food processing business to serve as an aide to Eisenhower Agriculture Secretary Ezra Taft Benson, in the Washington suburbs. He is a cousin of former Congressmen Morris and Stewart Udall and therefore of their sons, freshmen Congressmen Mark Udall and Tom Udall. Smith served two years as a Mormon missionary in New Zealand, then graduated from Brigham Young and from law school in Los Angeles, was a law clerk in New Mexico and practiced law in Arizona. Then he bought a frozen vegetable processing company in Pendleton, and guided it out of debt to profitability; Smith Frozen Foods is now one of largest private label packers of frozen vegetables in the country. In 1992 he was elected to the state Senate and in 1995 became Senate president and ran for Bob Packwood's U.S. Senate seat, losing after a battle of negative ads to Ron Wyden 48%–47% in January 1996. The month before, Mark Hatfield had announced his retirement after 30 years in the Senate. At first Smith was reluctant to run again—indeed, he is the first person to run in two Senate races in the same year—but Republicans urged him to run even after he insisted he would not spend $2 million of his own money as he did in the earlier race. Another difference was that he positioned himself closer to the center. Attacked during the Wyden race for being endorsed by the conservative Oregon Citizens' Alliance, he turned down the OCA endorsement this time; when OCA head Lon Mabon ran against him in the primary, Smith beat him 78%–8%.

Smith's opponent in the general was Tom Bruggere, another self-made millionaire, who started Mentor Graphics near Portland and, like Smith, owned a Ferrari. Bruggere had not run for office before, but won his primary 50%–25% over Harry Lonsdale, Hatfield's opponent in 1990. In an ad shot in soft focus, Smith said he continued to oppose abortion, but promised not to back a constitutional amendment banning it and at the end of the campaign said he would vote for Medicaid to cover abortions in cases of rape, incest or threat to life of the mother; he promised to work for a balance of environmental protection, economic development and job creation. He ran an ad in which Hatfield praised his work in the legislature for education, the Oregon Health Plan and Portland's light rail. Bruggere ran positive ads, touting his firm's day care care program and contribution of 1% of profits to charity; he attacked Smith on abortion and the environment and charged that his plant polluted the water. Smith responded with an ad attacking Bruggere for taking $2.5 million in stock options while laying off 500 employees in 1991 and 1992. And he called Bruggere "your classic, extremist Democratic liberal" supported by "extreme preservationist organizations." The result was apparent only when Oregon's large number of absentee ballots were counted: Smith won 50%–46%, carrying every county but Portland, two university towns and two northwest counties; he lost metro Portland by 53%–43%, far less than in January, and carried the Willamette Valley 50%–45% and the rest of the state 58%–37%. Bruggere's vote closely tracked Bill Clinton's 47%, but that was not enough to win a two-way race.

In the Senate Smith has a moderate voting record. He got $3.2 million to buy out mining claims and preserve the wilderness on the Chetco River in the Siskiyou National Forest in October 1998. But he also went against environmental groups by objecting to a proposed ban on logging in roadless parts of national forests and by opposing the designation of the Canadian lynx as a threatened species: "We're talking here about listing an animal that has not been seen [in Oregon] in over 30 years. If we're going to do that, we might as well list Sasquatch." He became chairman of the Water and Power Subcommittee in January 1999, with jurisdiction over the Bonneville Power Administration (he has said he will not allow it to be sold). This also gave him influence over decisions on whether to breach Snake River dams. With Massachusetts Democrat John Kerry, he proposed an education plan in December 1998 with $5 billion for raising teacher pay, tightening discipline and improving student health, with minimal federal regulation. He joined Orrin Hatch in April 1997 in calling for higher tobacco taxes to pay for health insurance for children.

Smith serves on Foreign Relations and chairs the subcommittee on Europe. Again he has steered something of a middle course; while his voting record on foreign issues has been quite conservative, he joined former Chairman Richard Lugar in calling on current Chairman Jesse Helms to hold hearings on the nomination of William Weld to be ambassador to Mexico in September 1997. He traveled to Russia in April 1998 to investigate charges of persecution of religious minorities. On impeachment, he approached the case in an unruffled manner, insisting on a trial before any consideration of censure. "We may be proving that the president has been an aggressive philanderer and an adulterer, but you don't remove him on that. But if it's proven that he is a serial perjurer and an obstructor of justice and civil rights, then we must remove him," he said, and so voted for removal.

The election of Wyden in January 1996 and Smith in November 1996 was the first time two senators were elected who had run against each other in the same year. Surprisingly, considering the negative character of their campaign, they became friends. They started holding town meetings in every congressional district together and took to issuing joint press releases on transportation projects, the Medicare reimbursement formula, deepening the Columbia River channel to 43 feet. This bipartisan collaboration seemed to suit the mood of voters in the late 1990s. Smith said, "Frankly, our colleagues look at Senator Wyden and myself and they scratch their heads and they wonder, what is in the water out there that they're drinking. Well, we hope it's contagious."

That spirit may serve Smith well when his seat comes up in 2002.

Presidential politics. Oregon was once the most Republican state in the West, voting for Thomas Dewey over Harry Truman in 1948; more recently it has been one of the most Democratic, voting for Michael Dukakis over George Bush in 1988 and twice for Bill Clinton by solid margins. But Clinton's margin went down from 1992's 43%–33% to 1996's 47%–39%. One reason was that Ralph Nader won 4% here, his best showing in any state; another was the conservative trend apparent in Republican strength in the state legislature. Oregon now stacks up as less Republican than Washington State, the opposite of 1988, and it could easily be a seriously contested state in 2000.

Oregon once had an important presidential primary, scheduled in May. In 1948 Oregon ended Harold Stassen's serious presidential prospects, when he lost 52%–48% to Dewey; in 1968 Oregon gave Robert Kennedy his only defeat when it voted 44%–38% for Eugene McCarthy. Oregon in those days was part of a West Coast campaign swing, just before the California primary; at a time when campaigners were not used to flying all over the country they, like National Football League teams in the 1950s, scheduled West Coast contests together to minimize travel time. For 1992 and 1996, Oregon scheduled its primary for Super Tuesday in March, but it was overshadowed by bigger contests in the South. Thanks to a 1998 referendum, all elections here are conducted by mail-in ballots; the Democratic National Committee says that violates its rules (though Democrats were the big backers of the change in Oregon), because ballots will be mailed out in late February so Oregonians can vote before New Hampshire. In early 1999 it was not clear how or whether this objection could be overcome.

Congressional districting. Congressional politics in Oregon has a certain volatility, because distance and the sparsity of nonstop flights make it hard for even the most conscientious congressman to get back to the district very often. The 1990s redistricting plan created two safe Democratic seats, the 3d in Portland and the 4th centered on Eugene, and one safe Republican, the eastern 2d. The 1st and 5th, centered on Portland suburbs, are marginal; both are now held by Democrats.

The People: Est. Pop. 1998: 3,281,974; Pop. 1990: 2,842,321, up 15.5% 1990–1998. 1.2% of U.S. total, 28th largest; 29.5% rural. Median age: 36.3 years. 14.3% 65 years and over. 92.8% White, 1.6% Black, 2.4% Asian, 1.5% Amer. Indian, 1.8% Other; 3.9% Hispanic Origin. Households: 55.6% married couple families; 25.2% married couple fams. w. children; 52.6% college educ.; median household income: $27,250; per capita income: $13,418; 63.1% owner occupied housing; median house value: $67,100; median monthly rent: $344. 5.6% Unemployment. 1998 Voting age pop.: 2,484,000. 1998 Turnout: 1,160,400; 47% of VAP. Registered voters (1998): 1,965,981; 791,970 D (40%), 704,593 R (36%), 469,418 unaffiliated and minor parties (24%).

Political Lineup: Governor, John Kitzhaber (D); Secy. of State, Phil Keisling (D); Atty. Gen., Hardy Myers (D); Treasurer, Jim Hill (D); State Senate, 30 (13 D, 17 R); Majority Leader, Gene Derfler (R); State House, 60 (25 D, 34 R, 1 I); House Speaker, Lynn Snodgrass (R). Senators, Ron Wyden (D) and Gordon H. Smith (R). Representatives, 5 (4 D, 1 R).

Elections Division: 503-986-1518; **Filing Deadline for U.S. Congress:** March 7, 2000.

1996 Presidential Vote

Clinton (D)	649,631	(47%)
Dole (R)	538,155	(39%)
Perot (I)	121,218	(9%)
Others	68,746	(5%)

1996 Republican Presidential Primary

Dole (R)	206,938	(51%)
Buchanan (R)	86,987	(21%)
Forbes (R)	54,121	(13%)
Alexander (R)	28,332	(7%)
Keyes (R)	14,340	(4%)
Others	16,796	(4%)

1992 Presidential Vote

Clinton (D)	621,314	(43%)
Bush (R)	475,757	(33%)
Perot (I)	354,091	(24%)

GOVERNOR
Gov. John Kitzhaber (D)

Elected 1994, term expires Jan. 2003; b. Mar. 5, 1947, Colfax, WA; home, Eugene; Dartmouth Col., B.S. 1969; U. of OR Med. Schl., M.D. 1973; no religious affiliation; married (Sharon).

Elected Office: OR House of Reps., 1978–80; OR Senate, 1980–94, Pres., 1985–93.

Professional Career: Practicing physician, 1974–88; Health & environment consultant, 1988–93.

Office: State Capitol, #254, Salem, 97310, 503-378-3111; Fax: 503-378-6827; Web site: www.state.or.us.

Election Results

1998 gen.	John Kitzhaber (D)	717,061	(64%)
	Bill Sizemore (R)	334,001	(30%)
	Others	62,036	(6%)
1998 prim.	John Kitzhaber (D)	271,781	(88%)
	Dave Foley (D)	23,870	(8%)
	Others	14,094	(5%)
1994 gen.	John Kitzhaber (D)	622,083	(51%)
	Denny Smith (R)	517,874	(42%)
	Ed Hickman (American)	58,449	(5%)
	Others	22,604	(2%)

SENATORS
Sen. Ron Wyden (D)

Elected Jan. 1996, seat up 2004; b. May 3, 1949, Wichita, KS; home, Portland; Stanford U., B.A. 1971, U. of OR, J.D. 1974; Jewish; married (Laurie).

Elected Office: U.S. House of Reps., 1980–96.

Professional Career: Co-Dir. & Co-Founder, OR Gray Panthers, 1974–80; Dir., OR Legal Svcs. for the Elderly, 1977–79; Prof. of Gerontology, U. of OR, 1976, Portland St. U., 1979, U. of Portland, 1980.

DC Office: 516 HSOB, 20510, 202-224-5244; Fax: 202-228-2717; Web site: www.senate.gov/~wyden.

State Offices: Bend, 541-330-9142; Eugene, 541-431-0229; La-Grande, 541-962-7691; Medford, 541-858-5122; Portland, 503-326-7525; Salem, 503-589-4555.

Committees: *Aging (Special)* (5th of 9 D). *Budget* (7th of 10 D). *Commerce, Science & Transportation* (8th of 9 D): Aviation; Communications; Surface Transportation & Merchant Marine. *Energy & Natural Resources* (5th of 9 D): Forests & Public Land Management (RMM); Water & Power. *Environment & Public Works* (8th of 8 D): Fisheries, Wildlife & Drinking Water.

Group Ratings

	ADA	ACLU	AFS	LCV	CON	NTU	NFIB	COC	ACU	NTLC	CHC
1998	100	86	100	100	52	21	33	56	4	11	0
1997	80	—	78	—	38	34	—	70	8	—	—

National Journal Ratings

	1997 LIB — 1997 CONS			1998 LIB — 1998 CONS		
Economic	71%	—	25%	69%	—	28%
Social	71%	—	0%	63%	—	26%
Foreign	83%	—	14%	85%	—	14%

Key Votes of the 105th Congress

1. Bal. Budget Amend.	N	5. Satcher for Surgeon Gen.	Y	9. Chem. Weapons Treaty	Y
2. Clinton Budget Deal	Y	6. Highway Set-asides	Y	10. Cuban Humanitarian Aid	Y
3. Cloture on Tobacco	Y	7. Table Child Gun locks	N	11. Table Bosnia Troops	Y
4. Education IRAs	N	8. Ovrd. Part. Birth Veto	N	12. $ for Test-ban Treaty	Y

Election Results

1998 general	Ron Wyden (D)	682,425	(61%)	($2,866,368)
	John Lim (R)	377,739	(34%)	($413,187)
	Others	57,583	(5%)	
1998 primary	Ron Wyden (D)	283,654	(92%)	
	John Sweeney (D)	25,456	(8%)	
	Others	853	(0%)	
1996 special	Ron Wyden (D)	571,739	(48%)	($4,237,134)
	Gordon H. Smith (R)	553,519	(47%)	($5,542,482)
	Others	56,392	(5%)	
1992 general	Bob Packwood (R)	717,455	(52%)	($8,034,249)
	Les AuCoin (D)	639,851	(47%)	($2,629,397)

Sen. Gordon H. Smith (R)

Elected 1996, seat up 2002; b. May 25, 1952, Pendleton; home, Pendleton; Brigham Young U., B.A. 1976, Southwestern U., J.D. 1979; Mormon; married (Sharon).

Elected Office: OR Senate, 1992–96, Pres., 1994–96.

Professional Career: Law Clerk, NM Supreme Court, 1979–80; Practicing atty., 1980–81; Pres., Smith Frozen Foods, 1980–96.

DC Office: 404 RSOB, 20510, 202-224-3753; Fax: 202-228-3997; Web site: www.senate.gov/~gsmith.

State Offices: Bend, 541-318-1298; Eugene, 541-465-6750; Medford, 541-608-9102; Pendleton, 541-278-1129; Portland, 503-326-3386.

Committees: *Budget* (12th of 12 R). *Energy & Natural Resources* (7th of 11 R): Energy, Research, Development, Production & Regulation; Forests & Public Land Management; Water & Power (Chmn.). *Foreign Relations* (5th of 10 R): East Asian & Pacific Affairs; European Affairs (Chmn.); Near Eastern & South Asian Affairs.

Group Ratings

	ADA	ACLU	AFS	LCV	CON	NTU	NFIB	COC	ACU	NTLC	CHC
1998	5	29	22	13	38	54	100	94	72	68	82
1997	25	—	0	—	71	68	—	100	72	—	—

National Journal Ratings

	1997 LIB — 1997 CONS			1998 LIB — 1998 CONS		
Economic	37%	—	57%	38%	—	57%
Social	45%	—	50%	39%	—	58%
Foreign	34%	—	57%	12%	—	75%

Key Votes of the 105th Congress

1. Bal. Budget Amend.	Y	5. Satcher for Surgeon Gen.	N	9. Chem. Weapons Treaty	Y
2. Clinton Budget Deal	Y	6. Highway Set-asides	N	10. Cuban Humanitarian Aid	N
3. Cloture on Tobacco	Y	7. Table Child Gun locks	Y	11. Table Bosnia Troops	N
4. Education IRAs	Y	8. Ovrd. Part. Birth Veto	Y	12. $ for Test-ban Treaty	N

Election Results

1996 general	Gordon H. Smith (R)	677,336	(50%)	($3,527,252)
	Tom Bruggere (D)	624,370	(46%)	($3,301,736)
	Others	58,524	(4%)	
1996 primary	Gordon H. Smith (R)	224,428	(78%)	
	Lon Mabon (R)	23,479	(8%)	
	Kirby Brumfield (R)	15,744	(5%)	
	Jeff Lewis (R)	13,359	(5%)	
	Others	10,490	(4%)	
1990 general	Mark O. Hatfield (R)	590,095	(54%)	($2,714,661)
	Harry Lonsdale (D)	507,743	(46%)	($1,479,099)

FIRST DISTRICT

Postmodern skyscrapers rising above the riverfront and below a range of hills: This is downtown Portland. The city—which would have been named Boston if a coin toss had gone the other way—started here, along the Willamette River just before it flows into the Columbia, and downtown was built on the narrow margin of land west of the river and below the hills, not on the flat expanse that stretches east towards the snow-capped peak of Mount Hood. Downtown Portland was once a dowdy place, proper in a New Englandish way, with a few formal buildings above the warehouses and factories. But in the last 20 years there has been an explosion of creativity here, symbolized by handsome high-rises—the pyramid-crested brick KOIN Tower, the wedge-shaped Justice Center—restored Victorian storefronts, a downtown transit trolley and a new light rail line know as MAX (Metropolitan Area Express), and just across the river the new Oregon Museum of Science and Industry. The affluent neighborhoods in the hills overlooking downtown are full of old lumber barons' mansions with splendid views, and snazzy new houses with hot tubs.

Just over the hills are the valleys and interstices between green mountains of suburban Washington County. Not so long ago, this was farm country, with 39,000 people in 1940; now it has about 400,000 and is an integral part of metro Portland. This is an affluent area, with clusters of towns and protected forest areas that feature a high-tech, healthy-lifestyle aura; major employers here are Tektronix, Intel, Nike and Sequent Computer Systems. Like Silicon Valley, the Silicon Forest has an environment—at the foot of mountains, woodsy and even rustic but outfitted with all the comforts and services of modern civilization—that appeals to a highly skilled work force.

The 1st Congressional District includes downtown Portland and its western hills, plus a bit of the residential areas east of the Willamette, and all of Washington County. The 1st also proceeds northwest along the Columbia to Astoria and the Pacific Coast, and southwest to Yamhill County, where metro growth is spreading. Like Oregon, the 1st District is historically New England Republican, electing only Republican congressmen from 1892 to 1972; like New England, it then trended sharply left on cultural issues, even as its high-tech economy brought new affluence, and since 1974 it has elected liberal Democrats. But the political balance is close here: Washington County has become increasingly Republican, and no one has won more than 52% of the vote in the 1st District since 1990.

The congressman from the 1st District is David Wu, a Democrat elected in 1998, the third Chinese-American to have served in Congress. He was born in Taiwan in 1955 and came to the U.S. with the rest of his family to join his father, studying at Rensselaer Polytechnic Institute in 1961, after restrictions on non-European immigration were softened. He grew up mostly in Orange County, California, went to college at Stanford, started medical school at Harvard, then switched to law school at Yale. He clerked for a federal judge in Portland and settled there; he also worked on Jimmy Carter's campaign in 1980 and Gary Hart's in 1984. He started his own law firm in 1988 and served on the Portland Planning Commission.

In June 1997, three-term Congresswoman Elizabeth Furse, a liberal Democrat and supporter of term limits, announced she would not run again, and Wu entered a seriously contested race. The Democratic frontrunner was Linda Peters, who was well known as Washington County Board chairwoman and had the backing of EMILY's List. Wu spent $100,000 of his own money and left his law practice; he got a big break when Peters missed the deadline for getting her picture in a voters' guide. Then he started attacking Peters in ads, for taking a personal loan from a developer and for misspending tax dollars while traveling on county business. This drew cries of protest from Furse, the League of Women Voters and state party leaders, but Wu won the primary 52%–43%. Republicans also had a primary, in which Molly Bordonaro, who had lost the 1996 primary 32%–22%, ran against Metro board member John Kvistad, who pitched himself as an establishment moderate. The 29-year-old Bordonaro, whose father is a prominent real estate man in Portland, won 66%–34%. Coming out of the primary, she had more money than Wu, a more united party behind her and was running even in the polls.

Yet Wu won. One reason was that, with help from national Democrats and labor unions, he caught up in fundraising. Another was that Wu established himself early as a moderate. He talked of a balanced approach to the environment, smaller government, less business regulation. He attacked the House's huge new transportation bill, saying he wanted to put the money into Head Start. He used his own life story to extol America's system of education and to call for more spending on Head Start (his wife is a Head Start teacher) and aid to college students: "Education was my way up in the world. To me, this is not the issue *du jour*. This is my life." He favored more immigration and broke with many businessmen in this export-conscious district by opposing normal trade status for China because of its human rights abuses. But he also opposed restrictions on exports of encryption technology—a hot issue in Silicon Forest.

A third reason for Wu's victory was that Bordonaro's strategy misfired. Her campaign was run by veterans of Senator Gordon Smith's 1996 campaigns and, just as Smith had repositioned himself between his January 1996 loss and November 1996 win, she started to position herself as more moderate than two years before. She backed off supporting an anti-abortion constitutional amendment, abandoned her support of school vouchers and elimination of the Education Department, came out for government aid to the arts, said she would not repeal the assault weapons ban. She attributed her switches to having talked and listened to voters over two years. But her changes antagonized some supporters: the National Rifle Association canceled a $105,000 radio ad campaign. In October, *Willamette Week*, an alternative weekly, released a tape of a 1996 Christian radio interview with Bordonaro in which she came across as a staunch social conservative. Wu seized on that and ran ads attacking her both for being too conservative for the district and for having sought to conceal from voters her 1996 views on gun control, abortion and education. Bordonaro, taking the advice of many good-hearted critics of political campaigns, declined to respond with negative ads.

This was a high-spending campaign—each nominee spent about $1.5 million. A mid-October poll showed the race even; in November Wu won 50%–47%. All of his margin and much more came from the Multnomah County part of the district, which he carried 67%–30%; Bordonaro carried Washington County 51%–47%, but that was not enough. In the House, Wu has seats on the Education Committee, where he can pitch support of Head Start, and on Science. With his narrow margin, he could easily have serious competition in 2000. And if he survives that, he could face more trouble from redistricting in 2002 if the Multnomah County portion of the district is removed.

Cook's Call. *Competitive.* As a moderate Democrat, Wu may have an easier time than his liberal predecessor, Elizabeth Furse, in holding onto this Democratic-leaning, but increasingly suburbanized district.

The People: Pop. 1990: 568,501; 18.5% rural; 12.2% age 65+; 93.3% White, 0.8% Black, 3.3% Asian, 0.8% Amer. Indian, 1.9% Other; 4% Hispanic Origin. Households: 54.8% married couple families; 26.2% married couple fams. w. children; 64.1% college educ.; median household income: $33,227; per capita income: $17,120; median house value: $84,800; median gross rent: $397.

1996 Presidential Vote			1992 Presidential Vote		
Clinton (D)	145,540	(50%)	Clinton (D)	136,630	(44%)
Dole (R)	112,152	(38%)	Bush (R)	99,304	(32%)
Perot (I)	21,304	(7%)	Perot (I)	73,134	(24%)
Others	14,310	(5%)			

Rep. David Wu (D)

Elected 1998; b. Apr. 8, 1955, Taiwan; home, Portland; Stanford U., B.S. 1977; Harvard Med. Schl., 1978; Yale Law Schl., J.D. 1982; Presbyterian; married (Michelle).

Professional Career: Law clerk, 9th Circuit Court of Appeals, 1982–83; Campaign staff, Gary Hart for President, 1984; Practicing atty., 1984–98.

DC Office: 510 CHOB 20515, 202-225-0855; Fax: 202-225-9497; Web site: www.house.gov/wu.

District Office: Portland, 503-326-2901.

Committees: *Education & the Workforce* (21st of 22 D): Early Childhood, Youth & Families; Employer-Employee Relations. *Science* (17th of 23 D): Space & Aeronautics; Technology.

Group Ratings and Key Votes: Newly Elected

Election Results

1998 general	David Wu (D)	119,993	(50%)	($1,602,063)
	Molly Bordonaro (R)	112,827	(47%)	($1,367,154)
	Others	6,676	(3%)	
1998 primary	David Wu (D)	29,100	(52%)	
	Linda Peters (D)	23,863	(43%)	
	Harold H. Sigurdson (D)	2,663	(5%)	
1996 general	Elizabeth Furse (D)	144,588	(52%)	($1,370,710)
	Bill Witt (R)	126,146	(45%)	($874,271)
	Others	7,870	(3%)	

SECOND DISTRICT

The Cascade Mountains that wall eastern Oregon off from the rest of the state are a magnificent chain of once (and quite possibly still) active volcanic mountains that drain almost every drop of moisture out of the air coming in from the Pacific, and thus separate green, wet western Oregon from the brown, parched east. Eastern Oregon has 70% of the state's land, but less than 400,000 of its 3.2 million people, most of whom still make their living off the land: beef and dairy cattle, timber and lumber, fish from the Columbia River and wheat from the irrigated plains. The effect of the Cascades can be felt in the one place they are breached—by the Columbia River Gorge. There, surrounded by brown hills on both sides, funneled winds pound in steadily from the west, making the confluence of the Columbia and Hood rivers the best windsurfing site in the United States.

The 2d Congressional District covers all of the state east of the Cascades and the southern-most valley between the Cascades and the Coast Range. Much of this land is empty: Harney County, with a land area larger than that of nine states, has a population of 7,000. Population concentrations here are far apart: Pendleton, a genuine rodeo town amid the northeastern wheat fields; La Grande in the rich Grande Ronde Valley; The Dalles where the Columbia River Gorge begins; Bend in the center of the state, near Crook County, which until it voted for George Bush in 1992 was the only county in the country to have voted for the winning pres-idential candidate in every election (it went for Bob Dole in 1996). In the southwestern corner, separated from other areas by the Cascades and the once huge volcano whose blown-off cone is now 2,000-foot deep Crater Lake, is the lumber and pear orchard country around Medford, Ashland, Klamath Falls and Grants Pass.

Politically, the 2d District has grown very Republican and often suspicious of the federal government. A few government pursuits here are considered acceptable; the Army's Umatilla Chemical Depot, near Hermiston, with 3,700 tons of chemical weapons, generated no contro-versy for 50 years until the Army announced it would destroy the weapons by incineration. But the federal government is more often viewed here as the owner of three-quarters of the district's land and the protector of the endangered spotted owl, which has forced timber com-panies increasingly onto Oregon's limited expanses of state and private land. When Interior Secretary Bruce Babbitt came to Medford in 1998 to take a ceremonial whack out of a soon-to-be-demolished dam, he was heckled mercilessly; though the dam-removal project was un-controversial locally, the removal of the nearby Elk Creek Dam, sought by environmentalists and the Army Corps of Engineers, continues to be fought by locals. The cultural liberalism of Portland and the East Coast isn't particularly welcomed, either; this is more a part of the leave-us-alone Rocky Mountain basin than of the culturally hip West Coast.

The congressman from the 2d District is Greg Walden, a Republican elected in 1998. He grew up on a cherry orchard near The Dalles in the Columbia gorge; his father served in the state House. Walden served as press secretary and chief of staff to Congressman Denny Smith from 1981–87, then returned to Hood River as a radio station owner. In 1988 he was elected to the state House, and in his second term became majority leader. In 1993 he started running for governor; he left the race when he and his wife learned their unborn son had a life-threat-ening heart problem. In the legislature Walden was known for cobbling together consensus on issues that divided the state, working to expand the lottery and write rules for the Oregon Health Plan, putting together a $750 million transportation package (later rejected by voters) that included a light rail for Portland and roads for rural counties. He is conservative on economic issues but more moderate on social issues; he is pro-choice but opposes federal funding.

Walden succeeds Bob Smith, co-chairman of the Congressional Beef Caucus and a quiet, solid conservative within a noisy Democratic chamber, who first retired in November 1993, long before a Republican House seemed likely. Wes Cooley, owner of a nutritional supplements firm and two-year state senator, won the seven-candidate Republican primary for Smith's House seat with 23% of the vote. He won the general 57%–39% and quickly established a conservative voting record. Then, in April 1996, the *Medford Mail Tribune* revealed that Cooley had lied about his military service and that his wife had received benefits as a Marine widow until 1994, but in a 1985 bank loan they claimed to be married—which would have made her ineligible for the benefits. He was also accused of paying an employee illegally low wages and then claiming the man as a dependent on his income tax form. Cooley was unrepentant; he easily won the May primary against nuisance candidates, but trailed the Democrat in summer polls by 30%. Republicans called for him to withdraw, but he refused. Walden, then a state senator who had been appointed to fill Cooley's seat there, got the signatures for a third-party candidacy.

Smith rebuffed pleas to run until House Republican leaders promised him the chairmanship of the Agriculture Committee. Cooley quit, Smith relented, became the Republican nominee and won 62%–37% in the general, carrying every county. Cooley was indicted for making a false statement on the voter guide and was convicted in March 1997; Smith fought what he called the Clinton Administration's "war on the West" for one more term.

In December 1997 Smith again announced he would retire, and this time endorsed Walden. He was opposed in the Republican primary by familiar faces—astonishingly, one was Cooley, who argued, "In the state of Oregon, who has higher name recognition than Wes Cooley? A lot of it is negative—but who does have higher name recognition?" But more substantial opposition came from outside the district, in the form of $130,000 in ads by Americans for Limited Terms and $50,000 in ads by Gary Bauer's Family Research Council. There was lots of grumbling about outside interference. Walden, the target, was miffed: "It's such an irony to have developed such a broad base of support, and then these groups can come in from back East and nail you." But Walden's wide support and the $500,000 he raised enabled him to win fairly easily: he won 55% of the vote (83% in his home county) to 33% for religious braodcaster Perry Atkinson (Walden carried his home county) and 9% for the unembarrassable Cooley.

The general election was anticlimactic. Democrat Kevin Campbell ran as a conservative but carried only his home county; Walden won 61%–35%. He sounded the consensus-minded note so many Republicans failed to produce in that consensus-minded year: "I just hope we're able to build the coalitions necessary to resolve some of these extraordinary battles over water and our land and our timber." Just four days after the election, Majority Leader Dick Armey gave him the assignment of delivering the Republican response to Bill Clinton's Saturday radio message. Walden received his top committee assignments—Resources and Agriculture—as well as Government Relations. Cooley in January petitioned the House to postpone Walden's swearing-in because he was challenging the Oregon law that barred him from getting another party's nomination once he had run in a major party primary; in April a federal judge recommended that Cooley's challenge be thrown out.

Cook's Call. *Safe.* Don't look for a competitive race in this district, the most Republican in the state. Walden may have to put up with yet another challenge from disgraced former Representative Wes Cooley, but Walden should prevail easily.

The People: Pop. 1990: 568,437; 50% rural; 16.2% age 65 + ; 93.7% White, 0.3% Black, 0.9% Asian, 2.5% Amer. Indian, 2.7% Other; 5.3% Hispanic Origin. Households: 59.5% married couple families; 26% married couple fams. w. children; 44.3% college educ.; median household income: $23,949; per capita income: $11,704; median house value: $62,600; median gross rent: $291.

1996 Presidential Vote

Dole (R)	130,408	(48%)
Clinton (D)	103,116	(38%)
Perot (I)	30,093	(11%)
Others	10,362	(4%)

1992 Presidential Vote

Bush (R)	106,696	(38%)
Clinton (D)	97,458	(35%)
Perot (I)	74,346	(27%)

Rep. Greg Walden (R)

Elected 1998; b. Jan. 10, 1957, The Dalles; home, Hood River; U. of OR, B.S. 1981; Episcopalian; married (Mylene).

Elected Office: OR House of Reps., 1988–94, Majority Ldr., 1991–93; OR Senate, 1994–96.

Professional Career: Press secy., U.S. Rep. Denny Smith, 1981–84, Chief of staff, 1984–86; Owner, Columbia Gorge Broadcasters Inc., 1986-present.

DC Office: 1404 LHOB 20515, 202-225-6730; Fax: 202-225-5774; Web site: www.house.gov/walden.

District Office: Medford, 503-326-2901.

Committees: *Agriculture* (23d of 27 R): Department Operations, Oversight, Nutrition & Forestry; Risk Management, Research & Specialty Crops. *Government Reform* (20th of 24 R): Government Management, Information & Technology; National Economic Growth, Natural Resources & Regulatory Affairs. *Resources* (24th of 28 R): Energy & Mineral Resources; Water & Power.

Group Ratings and Key Votes: Newly Elected

Election Results

1998 general	Greg Walden (R)	132,316	(61%)	($879,010)
	Kevin M. Campbell (D)	74,924	(35%)	($86,931)
	Others	7,976	(4%)	
1998 primary	Greg Walden (R)	36,909	(55%)	
	Perry A. Atkinson (R)	22,162	(33%)	
	Wes Cooley (R)	6,156	(9%)	
	Others	2,299	(3%)	
1996 general	Robert F. (Bob) Smith (R)	164,062	(62%)	($412,394)
	Mike Dugan (D)	97,195	(37%)	($264,902)
	Others	4,799	(2%)	

THIRD DISTRICT

Postmodern Portland, the Rose City set between Mount Hood to the east and the Tualatin Mountains to the west, spanning the Willamette River with its airport and industrial back to the Columbia, is still one of America's least known major cities—and one of its most distinctive. This was not always so. For most of its history Portland was a prosaic city in a magic setting; it was in many ways a muscular, blue-collar town, which piled Oregon lumber and Oregon pears into freight cars or unloaded machines from back East or autos from Japan on its docks. But in the past three decades Portland has been transformed. Out on the Pacific Rim, it increasingly makes its living on foreign trade, seeing East Asians as customers more than competitors. It has become a home of high-tech industries, particularly in the Washington County suburbs to the west—Silicon Alley. Government has also produced change. Oregon's land-use act, passed in 1974, required local governments to set geographic limits on growth; Metro, the regional government established in 1992 just as growth was accelerating, has created something of a counterweight against the endless spread outward of population into former farmland. Portland opened its first light-rail line in 1986 and has encouraged the development of high-density commercial space and housing around transit stops; it has opened bicycle paths throughout the metropolitan area; its downtown, west of the Willamette River, has sprouted postmodern structures public and private amid classic masonry buildings.

In the process, the central city of Portland, like San Francisco and Seattle, has come to

1340 OREGON

attract political and cultural liberals. But this "livable community" comes at a price. The Portland area was recently rated the fourth-least affordable place in the nation to purchase a new home. Portland's policies guarantee greater traffic congestion; even optimistic planners acknowledge that its population growth will be much larger than the number of people who can be persuaded to use mass transit. Greater population densities produce more intense pollution and, probably, higher property taxes. Income disparities are already growing. And environmental laws that have heretofore imposed burdens on rural areas may now impose them on Portland. But Portlanders seem willing to pay the price.

The 3d Congressional District takes in most of Portland and Multnomah County east of the Willamette River, extending over suburban plains and hills to the splendid scenery of the Bonneville Dam in the Columbia River Gorge and Mount Hood high in the Cascades. Politically, it is dominated by a cultural liberalism which sets Portland apart even from its suburbs and the rest of Oregon. In 1996 Portland's Multnomah County voted 59%–26% for Bill Clinton, and gave Ralph Nader more votes (7%) than Ross Perot (6%); while the rest of Oregon gave Clinton a bare 44%–42% margin, with 9% for Perot and 3% for Nader.

The congressman from the 3d District is Earl Blumenauer, elected in May 1996 to replace Ron Wyden, who was elected to the Senate in January. Blumenauer grew up in Portland, graduated from Lewis and Clark College and its Northwestern Law School. He was inspired by the civil rights and anti-Vietnam war movements while in his teens; in 1969, in college, he headed a statewide campaign to lower Oregon's voting age. He has held public office almost all his adult life. In 1972, at 23, he was elected to the Oregon House; in 1978 he was elected to the Multnomah County Board of Commissioners; in 1986 he was elected to the Portland City Council. In these offices he has championed many of the policies which have made Portland distinctive—regional light rail transit, curbside recycling, land use planning. He successfully fought the Mount Hood Freeway and neighborhood school closures. He initiated a law taking away the cars of repeat drunk driving offenders. He encouraged bike riding and Regional Rail Summits, which try to bring neighborhood residents into the process of planning for higher densities at transit nodes.

Blumenauer has had his name on the ballot 26 times and has had some setbacks, notably when he lost the 1992 mayoral race to Vera Katz. But when Wyden was elected to the Senate, Blumenauer was the obvious candidate. He was supported by prominent Democrats including former Governors Neil Goldschmidt and Barbara Roberts and even by Republican Senator Mark Hatfield (Blumenauer headed "Democrats for Hatfield" in 1990). He won the mail-in primary 72%–24% over a labor stalwart, and won the May special election 68%–25%; he won the May primary for the full term 78%–21% and the general in November 67%–26%; he had no Republican opposition in 1998.

In the House Blumenauer has a very liberal voting record and a distinctive agenda. He rides his bicycle everywhere and formed a 26-member Bicycle Caucus; he fought for showers for bike commuters and boasts that he has never driven a car in Washington. He was astonished to find that the House subsidized parking for employees, but not mass transit; now employees can get $21 a month toward transit fares. He started a Livable Communities Task Force, and sought out Republicans as well as Democrats. He hails the 1991 ISTEA transportation act that allows communities to choose to use money for mass transit and bike paths as well as highways, and he notes that 30% of the project requests addressed to Transportation Chairman Bud Shuster as he was concocting TEA-21 in 1998 were for transit projects. He supported the 1997 law exempting capital gains up to $500,000 on sales of homes from tax; he sees that as encouraging suburban empty nesters to become city neighborhood pioneers. He is interested in what seem like quixotic projects now, but may not in a few years: an interstate highway system for bicycle paths, development of "livable communities" on the sites of Denver's closed Stapleton Airport and closed military bases.

In Portland, Blumenauer saw how old post offices can anchor walking neighborhoods; he wants to require the Postal Service to comply with local zoning laws and give the community more say in renovation and relocation plans. Pointing to the Green Bay Packers, he has sponsored what he calls the Give Fans a Chance Act, to encourage public ownership of sports teams by revoking the antitrust broadcast exemption for any league that prohibits public ownership. He wants a federal law echoing Portland to require all gun sellers to offer a locking gun-storing device, and another authorizing vehicle forfeiture for repeat drunk drivers; the latter was put into the transportation bill as one way for states to qualify for federal traffic safety money. To those who say that Portland-style zoning restrictions and the intentional buildup of density are an elitist limit on the choices most people prefer, he argues that he is encouraging options and flexibility, and removing old laws which encouraged freeways and low-density subdivisions to the exclusion of all else. He was encouraged when Vice President Al Gore gave a speech praising "livable communities" in September 1998. How popular those issues become nationally, and how well their unintended consequences can be ironed out, remains to be seen. Either way, Blumenauer's seat seems safe.

Cook's Call. *Safe.* Blumenauer is sitting in a solidly Democratic district and will have no trouble winning re-election in 2000.

The People: Pop. 1990: 568,276; 5.8% rural; 14% age 65+; 87.4% White, 5.9% Black, 4.4% Asian, 1.3% Amer. Indian, 1% Other; 3% Hispanic Origin. Households: 47.9% married couple families; 22.2% married couple fams. w. children; 52.8% college educ.; median household income: $27,150; per capita income: $13,167; median house value: $59,800; median gross rent: $349.

1996 Presidential Vote

Clinton (D)	147,056	(58%)
Dole (R)	72,124	(28%)
Perot (I)	18,553	(7%)
Others	17,884	(7%)

1992 Presidential Vote

Clinton (D)	146,835	(53%)
Bush (R)	72,338	(26%)
Perot (I)	58,900	(21%)

Rep. Earl Blumenauer (D)

Elected May 1996; b. Aug. 16, 1948, Portland; home, Portland; Lewis & Clark Col., B.A. 1970, J.D. 1976; no religious affiliation; divorced.

Elected Office: OR House of Reps., 1972–78; Multnomah Cnty. Comm., 1978–86; Portland City Cncl., 1986–96.

Professional Career: Asst. to Pres., Portland St. U., 1970–77.

DC Office: 1406 LHOB 20515, 202-225-4811; Fax: 202-225-8941; Web site: www.house.gov/blumenauer.

District Office: Portland, 503-231-2300.

Committees: *Transportation & Infrastructure* (22d of 34 D): Ground Transportation; Water Resources & Environment.

Group Ratings

	ADA	ACLU	AFS	LCV	CON	NTU	NFIB	COC	ACU	NTLC	CHC
1998	95	94	100	100	80	23	14	41	4	8	0
1997	95	—	88	—	18	28	—	40	4	—	—

National Journal Ratings

	1997 LIB	—	1997 CONS	1998 LIB	—	1998 CONS
Economic	75%	—	25%	79%	—	0%
Social	85%	—	0%	93%	—	0%
Foreign	94%	—	3%	90%	—	5%

Key Votes of the 105th Congress

1. Clinton Budget Deal	N	5. Puerto Rico Sthood. Ref.	Y	9. Cut $ for B-2 Bombers	Y
2. Education IRAs	N	6. End Highway Set-asides	N	10. Human Rights in China	Y
3. Req. 2/3 to Raise Taxes	N	7. School Prayer Amend.	N	11. Withdraw Bosnia Troops	N
4. Fast-track Trade	*	8. Ovrd. Part. Birth Veto	N	12. End Cuban TV-Marti	Y

Election Results

1998 general	Earl Blumenauer (D)	153,889	(84%)	($237,571)
	Bruce Alexander Knight (Lib)	16,930	(9%)	
	Walter F. Brown (Soc)	10,199	(6%)	
	Others	2,333	(1%)	
1998 primary	Earl Blumenauer (D)	59,830	(98%)	
	Others	978	(2%)	
1996 general	Earl Blumenauer (D)	165,922	(67%)	($196,703)
	Scott Bruun (R)	65,259	(26%)	($11,823)
	Others	16,728	(7%)	

FOURTH DISTRICT

Eugene is nestled in the southernmost bit of lowland at the end of Oregon's Willamette Valley, surrounded by mountains on three sides. It is a farming center, a lumber metropolis and, most notably, a leafy university town. Settlers first arrived here in 1846, farming in the valley and cutting timber in the hills. In 1876, the University of Oregon was established, a symbol of Oregon's strong Yankee cultural ethic and sparse settlement; its first graduating class had just five students. Thousands of miles from most Americans, Eugene and next-door Springfield, once a lumber town and now with computer chip factories, have grown steadily into the comfortable middle-sized towns in which many Americans would like to live. Eugene has bicycle paths along the river banks and on main streets and likes to bill itself as the Running Capital of the Universe; it is where Phil Knight and his former University of Oregon track coach, Bill Bowerman, started Nike—the first soles formed on a waffle iron. But there is also tragedy here. Springfield was the place where in May 1998 a 15-year-old, after killing his parents, opened fire in a school, killing two students and injuring 22 others.

Beyond Eugene and Springfield, southwestern Oregon is surrounded by green-clad mountains and for years cut more timber than any other place in the country. But demand for wood is volatile, dependent on the vagaries of interest rates; East Asia increasingly wants unprocessed logs rather than milled lumber, which means fewer jobs for Oregon. The early 1980s, when recession reduced the demand for housing, were tough on southern Oregon; the late 1980s, when cutting of old-growth forests was banned to protect the endangered spotted owl, were even worse. In between, many big lumber companies switched their major operations to the pinelands of the Southeastern U.S., while sawmills ran short of work because of log exports to the Far East. In the early 1990s, it seemed federal restrictions on logging would destroy the area's economy. But an otherwise robust local economy and active job retraining has resulted in local job gains and far less unemployment than forecast.

The 4th Congressional District of Oregon includes Eugene and Springfield and surrounding Lane County; it goes south to include Roseburg in Douglas County, once perhaps the premier logging county in the United States; it extends north to Albany and part of Corvallis, home of Oregon State University; and includes the entire southern half of Oregon's stunning Pacific coastline, whose craggy seastacks and surging whitecaps were stained by oil as the cargo ship New Carissa was wrecked in Coos Bay in February 1999 and later washed up 60 miles north. Eugene is now heavily Democratic, and so is Corvallis. Roseburg and Albany tend to be Republican, but the overall balance here is toward the cultural left.

The congressman from the 4th District is Peter DeFazio, a Democrat first elected in 1986.

He grew up in Massachusetts, came to Oregon for graduate school, and in 1977 went to work for 4th District Congressman Jim Weaver; in 1982, he moved to Springfield and won a seat on the county commission. When Weaver retired in 1986, DeFazio won the House seat in a three-way race. In the House, DeFazio has compiled a record that seems to satisfy both Eugene and the rest of the district—liberal on most issues, moderate or even conservative on others. He voted against the October 1998 omnibus budget: "They always say the devil is in the details, and this bill is full of devils." He has opposed NAFTA, GATT and fast track and strongly criticized the Mexican financial bailout; he wants to require congressional approval for international loans over $250 million. He offered a bill, with interesting support from right and left, to allow patients greater access to alternative medical treatments and, with Republican Jack Metcalf, vigorously opposed Agriculture Department regulations on organic foods for failing to adequately protect consumers. He called for a moratorium on airline alliances in May 1998, wants mental illness covered by health insurers and wants military and Energy Department installations covered by the Clean Water Act.

Within 72 hours after the Springfield shooting, DeFazio introduced nine bills aimed at school violence, including a 72-hour hold for juveniles who bring guns to school, mandatory trigger locks, background checks of buyers at gun shows and identification of troubled dropouts. In July 1998 he moved to repeal new recreation fees on federal lands imposed by the 1996 budget act, including parking lot fees at Oregon Dunes National Recreation Area and Forest Service trail fees; he would replace the revenue with royalties on gold and other minerals on federal lands. He serves on the Transportation Committee and has obtained funds for district projects, including $10 million for the Albany Rail Station, $10 million to renovate the Gold Beach Bridge and $5.5 million to rebuild the Coos Bay rail bridge.

DeFazio has won re-election by impressive margins in a district which before him was often marginal. After Senator Bob Packwood resigned in 1995, DeFazio ran to succeed him. He had far less money than Portland Congressman Ron Wyden, whom he attacked for receiving money from Packwood contributors; in an ad, DeFazio made the best of this: "[DeFazio's] '63 Dodge tells the lobbyists and special interests he's not for sale." His opposition to gun control, NAFTA and GATT provided clear contrasts with Wyden. He ran strongly in the 4th District and the two counties just to the south, leading Wyden 72%–22% there. But Wyden ran ahead 61%–32% in the rest of the state, for a 50%–44% victory, and went on to win the seat in January. In February DeFazio, daunted by the financial prowess of millionaire candidates Gordon Smith and Tom Bruggere, decided not to run for the Senate seat Mark Hatfield was vacating; since then, he has called for public financing of campaigns.

Cook's Call. *Safe.* Though the 4th District is not as safely Democratic as the two Portland-based districts, DeFazio has had little trouble winning here by large margins since his first re-election campaign in 1988. Once this seat opens up, it is likely to be heavily contested. Until then, DeFazio is safe.

The People: Pop. 1990: 568,395; 38.9% rural; 15.1% age 65 + ; 95.9% White, 0.5% Black, 1.4% Asian, 1.5% Amer. Indian, 0.7% Other; 2.3% Hispanic Origin. Households: 57.4% married couple families; 24.9% married couple fams. w. children; 48.5% college educ.; median household income: $24,593; per capita income: $11,919; median house value: $60,600; median gross rent: $324.

1996 Presidential Vote			1992 Presidential Vote		
Clinton (D)	122,392	(45%)	Clinton (D)	123,593	(42%)
Dole (R)	108,780	(40%)	Bush (R)	94,032	(32%)
Perot (I)	26,826	(10%)	Perot (I)	74,640	(25%)

Rep. Peter DeFazio (D)

Elected 1986; b. May 27, 1947, Needham, MA; home, Springfield; Tufts U., B.A. 1969, U. of OR, M.S. 1977; Catholic; married (Myrnie).

Military Career: Air Force, 1967–71.

Elected Office: Lane Cnty. Bd. of Commissioners, 1982–86.

Professional Career: Dist. Dir., U.S. Rep. James Weaver, 1977–82.

DC Office: 2134 RHOB 20515, 202-225-6416; Fax: 202-225-0032; Web site: www.house.gov/defazio.

District Offices: Coos Bay, 541-269-2609; Eugene, 541-465-6732; Roseburg, 541-440-3523.

Committees: *Resources* (5th of 24 D): Fisheries Conservation, Wildlife & Oceans; Water & Power. *Transportation & Infrastructure* (7th of 34 D): Aviation; Coast Guard & Maritime Transportation (RMM).

Group Ratings

	ADA	ACLU	AFS	LCV	CON	NTU	NFIB	COC	ACU	NTLC	CHC
1998	95	88	100	100	88	31	0	12	16	5	8
1997	85	—	88	—	22	40	—	20	28	—	—

National Journal Ratings

	1997 LIB	—	1997 CONS	1998 LIB	—	1998 CONS
Economic	73%	—	27%	67%	—	32%
Social	85%	—	0%	85%	—	14%
Foreign	60%	—	38%	53%	—	45%

Key Votes of the 105th Congress

1. Clinton Budget Deal	N	5. Puerto Rico Sthood. Ref.	Y
2. Education IRAs	N	6. End Highway Set-asides	N
3. Req. 2/3 to Raise Taxes	N	7. School Prayer Amend.	N
4. Fast-track Trade	N	8. Ovrd. Part. Birth Veto	N

9. Cut $ for B-2 Bombers	Y
10. Human Rights in China	Y
11. Withdraw Bosnia Troops	Y
12. End Cuban TV-Marti	Y

Election Results

1998 general	Peter DeFazio (D)	157,524	(70%)	($262,098)
	Steve J. Webb (R)	64,143	(29%)	
	Others	2,970	(1%)	
1998 primary	Peter DeFazio (D)	unopposed		
1996 general	Peter DeFazio (D)	177,270	(66%)	($301,211)
	John D. Newkirk (R)	76,649	(28%)	($10,609)
	Others	15,937	(6%)	

FIFTH DISTRICT

The Willamette Valley was the great promised land at the end of the Oregon Trail, shielded by the Coast Range from the cold storms of the Pacific but squeezing most of the moisture out of the clouds in the form of rain, fog and persistent mist. Here, New England Yankees planted small towns they called Salem and Albany and Oregon City, founded schools and colleges, built high-spired churches and eventually Salem's cylindrical-domed Art Deco state Capitol. This was one of the few valleys in the West which settlers found readily suitable for agriculture.

The Willamette Valley's soil is fertile, the plain created by the waters of the Willamette sweeping down from the mountains is broad, and the rains everyone hears about in Oregon are dependable. Today metro Portland is spreading south, with young people leapfrogging over the lands protected from development by and into counties to the south.

The 5th Congressional District includes much of the northern Willamette Valley. Near Portland it has the old pioneer town of Oregon City, and spreads south to the state capital of Salem (rather conservative) and Corvallis (home of Oregon State University and quite liberal). Then the district hops over the Coast Range to take in Lincoln and Tillamook counties, fishing and logging and cheesemaking communities (strongly Democratic) and also includes all of Polk County. Historically, the Willamette Valley was Republican, like the New England whence most of its settlers came, but, also like New England, it has been trending Democratic, and now is prime marginal territory.

The congresswoman from the 5th District is Darlene Hooley, a Democrat elected in 1996. Born in North Dakota, Hooley moved with her family to Salem at age 8. She worked as a reading and physical education teacher in rural Woodburn Gervais and raised her family in West Linn, on the Willamette north of Oregon City. Angry when council members wouldn't replace the rugged asphalt after her son fell off a playground swing and cut his head, she served on the Park District board and then was elected to the City Council in 1976, at 37. In 1980 she was elected to the Oregon House, where she worked on recycling, land use and equal pay laws. In 1987 she was appointed to the Clackamas County Board of Supervisors, where she worked on roads, welfare reform and crime and claimed credit for creating 10,000 private-sector jobs.

Rather late in the 1996 campaign cycle, Hooley decided to run for Congress. Incumbent Republican Jim Bunn, elected 50%–47% in 1994 after Democrat Mike Kopetski abruptly retired, combined religious conservatism with a moderate record on issues and support of the Oregon Health Plan and Portland light rail. Hooley had two Democratic primary opponents, but with help from EMILY's List had far more money—ultimately she spent $1.1 million, twice as much as the incumbent. She won the three-way primary with 51% and launched into attacks on Bunn for supporting Newt Gingrich and Medicare "cuts." Working most strongly against Bunn was his divorce and subsequent marriage to his 31-year-old chief of staff, whom he was paying $97,500—more than any other staffer in the Oregon House delegation. She quit, but the issue may well have kept Bunn from being re-elected. Hooley won 51%–46%, carrying all but one county, though most by narrow margins.

In the House Hooley has a mostly liberal record. She did not get the seat on Appropriations she wanted and served on the Banking and Science Committees instead; in 1999 she got a seat on Budget and left Science. Hooley supported the Shays-Meehan campaign finance bill, sought to expand health insurance coverage for children, pushed federal spending for education and light-rail, while also crossing party lines to urge cutting the estate tax. She got funding for a highway interchange at Sunnyside, Portland area light rail and local after-school programs. In 1998 she called for review of Forest Service approval of a Windy Canyon timber sale, for fear it would foul Salem's water.

In this marginal seat, which has been represented by two Republicans and two Democrats over the last decade, Hooley was opposed by state Senator Marylin Shannon, a conservative who was against same-sex marriage and attacked inefficiency in Oregon's Transportation Department; Shannon first got involved in politics when she was shocked by her daughter's vulgar textbooks. Hooley spent more than $1 million to Shannon's $290,000, and won 55%–41%, the first time this district has returned the incumbent since 1992. A sad note: Hooley's husband filed for divorce in 1997, making her the fourth representative from this district in a row to go through divorce; evidently the arduous commute exacts a toll on members' personal lives.

Cook's Call. *Competitive.* Hooley dodged a bullet in 1998 when Republicans failed to recruit a top-tier challenger against her. But, Hooley is not out of the woods yet. This district is the most marginal in the state, and as a sophomore with only one re-election under her belt, Hooley has not yet established a solid foothold here.

The People: Pop. 1990: 568,712; 34.6% rural; 14.1% age 65 +; 93.7% White, 0.6% Black, 2% Asian, 1.3% Amer. Indian, 2.5% Other; 4.8% Hispanic Origin. Households: 58.8% married couple families; 27.1% married couple fams. w. children; 53.1% college educ.; median household income: $28,608; per capita income: $13,180; median house value: $69,200; median gross rent: $338.

1996 Presidential Vote

Clinton (D)	131,527	(47%)
Dole (R)	114,691	(41%)
Perot (I)	24,442	(9%)
Others	11,103	(5%)

1992 Presidential Vote

Clinton (D)	116,798	(40%)
Bush (R)	103,387	(35%)
Perot (I)	73,071	(25%)

Rep. Darlene Hooley (D)

Elected 1996; b. Apr. 4, 1939, Williston, ND; home, West Linn; OR St. U., B.S. 1961; Lutheran; divorced.

Elected Office: West Linn City Cncl., 1977–80; OR House of Reps., 1980–86; Clackamas Cnty. Comm., 1987–96.

Professional Career: Teacher, 1961–75.

DC Office: 1130 LHOB 20515, 202-225-5711; Fax: 202-225-5699; Web site: www.house.gov/hooley.

District Offices: Oregon City, 503-557-1324; Salem, 503-588-9100.

Committees: *Banking & Financial Services* (13th of 27 D): Capital Markets, Securities & Government Sponsored Enterprises; Housing & Community Opportunity. *Budget* (15th of 19 D).

Group Ratings

	ADA	ACLU	AFS	LCV	CON	NTU	NFIB	COC	ACU	NTLC	CHC
1998	95	75	78	92	42	22	43	59	12	5	0
1997	90	—	75	—	80	37	—	50	16	—	—

National Journal Ratings

	1997 LIB	—	1997 CONS	1998 LIB	—	1998 CONS
Economic	67%	—	32%	67%	—	32%
Social	73%	—	24%	81%	—	16%
Foreign	88%	—	10%	84%	—	11%

Key Votes of the 105th Congress

1. Clinton Budget Deal	N	5. Puerto Rico Sthood. Ref.	Y	9. Cut $ for B-2 Bombers	Y
2. Education IRAs	N	6. End Highway Set-asides	N	10. Human Rights in China	Y
3. Req. 2/3 to Raise Taxes	N	7. School Prayer Amend.	N	11. Withdraw Bosnia Troops	N
4. Fast-track Trade	Y	8. Ovrd. Part. Birth Veto	N	12. End Cuban TV-Marti	Y

Election Results

1998 general	Darlene Hooley (D)	124,916	(55%)	($1,005,353)
	Marylin Shannon (R)	92,215	(41%)	($289,053)
	Others	10,526	(5%)	
1998 primary	Darlene Hooley (D)	52,952	(99%)	
	Others	386	(1%)	
1996 general	Darlene Hooley (D)	139,521	(51%)	($1,109,312)
	Jim Bunn (R)	125,409	(46%)	($553,726)
	Others	7,706	(3%)	

PENNSYLVANIA

Pennsylvania started off as the center of America: Philadelphia was the 13 colonies' largest city when it hosted the Continental Congress in 1776 and the Constitutional Convention in 1787. This was one of the newer colonies, founded 50 years after Massachusetts and 70 years after Virginia. Under the benevolent rule of the early Penns and with its Quaker traditions, Pennsylvania soon became the major settlement in the Middle Colonies: Its tolerance attracted Englishmen of all religious sects and thousands of Germans as well. The rich green farmlands west to the first Appalachian chain filled rapidly. Bordermen from Scotland, Yorkshire and Northern Ireland crossed the corduroy-like ridges and settled the mountainous interior where General Braddock had been beaten by the French and Indians not long before, and where a decade later George Washington would again lead troops when the Whiskey Rebellion flared up. On the banks of a wide estuary, with its thriving commerce and rich hinterland, Philadelphia was, after London and Dublin, the largest Georgian city in the late 18th Century. It seemed destined to be the London of America, the metropolis of government and commerce and culture.

But Philadelphia—and Pennsylvania—failed to hold the central position the Founders had expected. The nation's capital was put on the Potomac rather than the Delaware as part of a political deal, and the Erie Canal and the water-level railroad from the Hudson to Lake Erie channeled trade away from Philadelphia to New York. Philadelphia lost its chance to be the nation's financial capital when Andrew Jackson in righteous rage vetoed the rechartering of the Second Bank of the United States. Philadelphia's Quaker tradition, tolerant of diversity and indifferent to others' behavior, was overshadowed in intellectual life by New England's Puritan tradition, angrily intolerant and ready to use the state to impose cultural values from abolition to prohibition. In antebellum America, Philadelphia was eclipsed by Washington in government, New York in commerce, and Boston in education and literature.

Instead, Pennsylvania became America's energy and heavy industry capital. The key was coal. Northeast Pennsylvania was the nation's primary source of anthracite, the hard coal used for home heating, and western Pennsylvania was laced with bituminous coal, the soft coal used in steel production. Connected with Philadelphia by the Pennsylvania Railroad, Pittsburgh, where the Allegheny and Monongahela rivers join to become the Ohio, was the center of the nation's steel industry by 1890. Immigrants poured in from Europe and from the surrounding hills to work in western Pennsylvania's mines and factories. Pittsburgh became synonymous with industrial prosperity, the inspiration behind the civic pride that celebrated huffing smokestacks. In 1900, Pennsylvania was the nation's second-largest state and growing rapidly. But the boom ended conclusively with the Depression of the 1930s, and in parts of Pennsylvania it has never returned. After World War II, both home heating and industry switched away from coal. John L. Lewis's United Mine Workers traded higher pay and benefits for payroll cuts. Even when coal prices boomed in the 1970s, strip mining created relatively few new jobs. Similarly, Pennsylvania steel began its decline three decades ago, when management decided not to keep up with new technology and agreed to big wage and benefit increases with the mistaken confidence they could pass the costs along. Big steel got import quotas in 1969— Pennsylvania has been the nation's most protectionist state since the first Bessemer converter furnaces were lit—but they didn't create jobs. By the time quotas lapsed in the 1990s, the industry had modernized, but mostly in huge new Indiana mills and small mini-mills scattered far from the factories that once lined the Monongahela; in 1998 they were again hit by low-price competition—dumping from Japan, Russia and Brazil.

The result has been the slowest population growth in the nation: There were 9.5 million Pennsylvanians in 1930, 12.0 million in 1996. Pennsylvania cast 36 electoral votes for Franklin

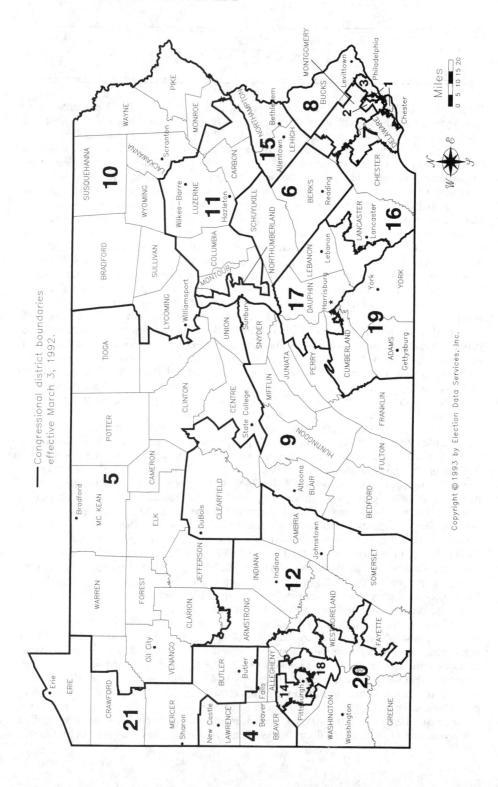

Congressional district boundaries effective March 3, 1992.

Roosevelt in 1940 and 23 for Bill Clinton in 1996; it had as many congressmen (30) as California in 1960, but now has 21 while California has 52. People growing up here are as likely to leave the state as stay, and few out-of-staters move in. Pennsylvania looks and sounds today more like it did in the 1940s than any other major state. The 1980s and 1990s booms have produced some new Pennsylvania growth in southeast Pennsylvania, around Philadelphia, which partook of the upscale boom that was more spectacular up and down the East Coast. Center City Philadelphia sprouted new office towers and will host the Republican National Convention in 2000, the edge city around King of Prussia blossomed, and pharmaceutical and biotech jobs replaced those of the Fairless steel plant. Outlet stores proliferated around Reading and Lancaster, and new jobs sprung up in the Pennsylvania Dutch country. In the 1990s there has been some growth in the west, radiating outward from Pittsburgh, with the growth of a high-tech, research-oriented economy.

Although Pennsylvania started off as our center of government, government has not been central to Pennsylvania for most of its history. During the Civil War, Pennsylvania was the site of the northernmost advance of the Confederate Army—Carlisle, just north of Gettysburg; for generations after it was the most Republican of the large states—for Lincoln and the Union, for the steel industry and the high tariff. Its malodorous Republican machines built parties which were not representative of one ethnic segment but had a place for just about everyone: in Philadelphia's huge City Hall, a knockoff of Paris' Hotel de Ville; in Pittsburgh's massive, Roman-columned City-County Building; in Harrisburg's grandiose Capitol with its rotunda modeled after St. Peter's in Rome and staircase modeled after the Paris Opera. In 1932, Pennsylvania was the only big state that stuck with Herbert Hoover and voted against Franklin Roosevelt. But the New Deal, John L. Lewis's United Mine Workers and the CIO industrial union movement, and a series of bloody strikes made industrial Pennsylvania almost as Democratic in the 1930s and 1940s as it had been Republican from the 1860s to the 1920s. Even then, parts of Pennsylvania not heavy with big steel factories and coal mines—the northern tier of counties along the New York border, the central part of the state around the Welsh railroad town of Altoona, and the Pennsylvania Dutch country around Lancaster, an area referred to by political consultants as the T—remained the strongest Republican voting bloc in the East. Philadelphia became a mostly Democratic city, but in the suburban counties the antique Republican machines stayed in control. The result was a key marginal state in presidential elections from the 1950s to the 1990s, and not always a state that moved in one direction.

In the 1980s, prosperous eastern Pennsylvania trended Republican and ailing western Pennsylvania trended Democratic. The east gave decisive margins to Ronald Reagan and George Bush while greater Pittsburgh produced some of the nation's highest percentages for Walter Mondale and Michael Dukakis. Both regions reversed direction in the 1990s. The fall in suburban real estate values in the early 1990s helped produce an upset Senate win for Democrat Harris Wofford in 1991, when he ran even in the usually Republican Philadelphia suburbs; it was Wofford's campaign which put the health care issue on the national agenda. Metro Philadelphia, which voted only 50%–49% for Dukakis in 1988, gave Bill Clinton a 51%–33% margin in 1992 and an even more impressive 58%–33% win in 1996. Western Pennsylvania meanwhile dabbled with Perot populism and was repelled by Clinton's cultural liberalism. This was the Pennsylvania which supported Democratic Governor (1986–94) Bob Casey's abortion restrictions. In 1988 Dukakis carried metro Pittsburgh 59%–40%, and Pennsylvania west of the first mountain ridge 51%–48%. Clinton carried this western region only 45%–35% in 1992, with 20% for Ross Perot, and by only 51%–39% in 1996.

Who is coming out ahead from these changes? The Republicans—but not always by much. Pennsylvania has two very different Republican senators, who won in 1992 and 1994 with just 49%; Arlen Specter was re-elected 61%–35% in 1998. Governor Tom Ridge was elected in 1994 with even less, 45%, because an anti-abortion candidate took 13% of the vote; he was re-elected 57%–31% in 1998, again against weak opposition. Republicans hold three of the four downballot statewide offices (a fifth office is non-partisan), the exception being Auditor

Bob Casey Jr., son of the former governor. Republicans have held majorities in both houses of the state legislature since 1994, but only by paper-thin margins, 102–101 after 1994, 104–99 after 1996, 103–100 in 1999. In the 1996 presidential race, Pennsylvania's percentages for each candidate were very close to the national average. But Democrats here tend to be culturally more conservative than those in most states and Republicans sometimes economically more liberal; the balance is more like the America of the 1950s than the America of the 1990s, and strategies that work nationally can be counterproductive in Pennsylvania. The 2000 Republican National Convention will bring the political spotlight on Philadelphia, rejuvenated after eight years of Democrat Ed Rendell as mayor, and Pennsylvania will again for a moment be the center of the nation's politics.

Governor. Tom Ridge, elected governor in 1994, grew up in Erie, off in the far northwestern corner of the state. His father was a salesman, of Slavic descent, his mother Irish; they lived modestly, in a veterans' housing project and then in the bungalow where Ridge's mother lives today—she appears in his campaign ads to remind him to wear his hat. He went to Harvard, spent a year at Dickinson Law School, then served in the Army as a staff sergeant in Vietnam, serving in combat and winning the Bronze Star. He finished law school, returned to Erie and practiced law, and was an assistant district attorney for a couple of years. He did a bit of work for George Bush's presidential campaign in 1980. In 1982 he ran for the open House seat in the closely divided 21st District (now the 19th) and in a Democratic year in western Pennsylvania beat state legislator Buzz Andrezeski by 729 votes, 50.2%–49.8%. He became the first enlisted man who saw combat in Vietnam to be elected to the House. In the House he had a mixed voting record by the lights of almost every rating group—not always market-oriented on economics, sometimes dovish on defense and foreign policy, liberal on some cultural issues and tradition-minded on others. He worked on banking and home finance legislation; he favored more spending for homeless veterans and treatment of post traumatic stress disorder.

· In February 1993, 21 months before the election, he announced he would run for governor. Outside his district he was hardly known, though the addition of a new county in 1992 gave him an excuse to run ads on Pittsburgh TV. This was a crowded race. Ridge's best known Republican primary opponent was Attorney General Ernie Preate, a statewide winner in 1990 who was hurt when, a month before the primary, the Crime Commission said he had taken money from illegal video poker operators. Ridge, with backing from party leaders, won the May primary with 35% to 29% for Preate, 16% for Philadelphia businessman Sam Katz, campaigning as tough on crime and for school vouchers, and 14% for Pittsburgh legislator Mike Fisher, an opponent of abortion and gun control; Katz was the Republican candidate for mayor of Philadelphia in 1999 and Fisher was elected state attorney general in 1996. Democrats had an even more crowded primary; Lieutenant Governor Mark Singel, who was acting governor for six months while Governor Bob Casey recovered from a heart and liver transplant, won with 31%.

In the general, Ridge campaigned for tough crime measures, citizens rights' to statewide initiatives and referenda, less-strict environmental regulation and a lower corporate tax. Both Ridge and Singel were pro-choice on abortion, which probably hurt them: Singel, because Casey was lukewarm to him; Ridge, because of the independent candidacy of anti-abortion Peg Luksik, who won 13% of the vote, with more than 20% in heavily Republican counties in central and western Pennsylvania. But the defining issue was probably crime. Ridge attacked Singel for his votes as chairman of the Pardons Board recommending the release of 55 prisoners serving life sentences. Casey approved only eight releases, but one of them kidnapped, raped and robbed a woman in New York, and Ridge made that a major issue. Singel apologized, but Ridge won 45%–40%, continuing Pennsylvania's 40-year practice of alternating the two parties in the governorship every eight years.

Ridge's hallmark as governor has been cutting taxes: He pushed tax cuts in each of his first five years in office, and claims that altogether they cut taxes by $2.6 billion. In the process he cut state spending growth in half and increased the Rainy Day fund from $30 million to $700 million. His first two budgets increased spending at less than the rate of inflation and he got the legislature to abolish the state tax on computer services and give a tax credit for research and development. In 1997 and 1998 he moved to cut the state income tax on lower-income families; there is now no state income tax on families of four with income under $25,000. In 1999 he pushed a package of $273 million in cuts in corporate taxes, the capital stock and franchise tax, the natural gas tax and the personal income tax. He even proposed a 60% legislative supermajority for raising taxes. In addition, a Ridge reform of workmen's compensation cut insurance rates by an average of one-quarter. But the gas tax was increased to provide for more road building. He set up an opportunity zones program for distressed areas and set up a program that cleaned up 350 polluted industrial sites, by limiting landowners' liability after certain conditions were met; in contrast, the federal government's Superfund program, which relies on lawyers seeking big judgment from landowners, had cleaned up only 13 of 111 sites in Pennsylvania in nearly 20 years. A pilot electricity deregulation program was passed in 1997. His chief goal was to make Pennsylvania more welcoming to business, and since he took office the state gained some 250,000 jobs, despite well-publicized layoffs by some big employers.

At the same time Ridge pushed for welfare, education and criminal justice reforms. His 1996 welfare reform required able-bodied recipients to work at least 100 hours a month or, if they are school-age, remain in schools; money was added for job readiness and child care, and more than 148,000 welfare recipients left the rolls. On education, Ridge got $132 million to spend on computers in schools in 1995. In 1996 he got reform of teacher tenure and sabbaticals. In 1997 he got the legislature to create more charter schools. He set up an advisory commission to produce rigorous standards that were so comprehensible that "parents can hang them on the refrigerator door and discuss them with their children. No jargon, no buzz words, no educational fads." By a narrow margin, Ridge's proposal for school choice failed in the legislature in his first term; he pressed again for choice in May 1999. On crime, Ridge got the legislature to pass Megan's Law, a tougher rape law and a victims' rights measure in 1995, and he has restored capital punishment by signing more than 100 death warrants; executions have followed. His most conspicuous failure came when he tried to get a German shipbuilding firm to set up shop in the closed Philadelphia Navy Yard; later a Norwegian shipbuilding company agreed to use some of the facility.

Re-election was not a serious problem for Ridge: He was one of several big-state Republican governors who won in a pro-incumbent year by standing for a mostly conservative consensus that seemed to be producing good results. He raised more than $15 million, while Democrats had a difficult time fielding a candidate. When longtime Pittsburgh legislator (and nuclear engineer) Ivan Itkin announced, Singel, then Democratic state chairman, said he had no chance to win. Itkin did capture the Democratic primary, by 49%–39% over former two-term Congressman and one-term Auditor Don Bailey. But his liberal record was anathema to many traditional Democrats, and Ridge was not even hurt as Luksik ran again and won 10% of the vote. Ridge beat Itkin 57%–31%; the Democrat carried Philadelphia and the Republican the other 66 counties. Traditional economic divisions all but vanished: Ridge won by large margins in all income groups over $15,000, and union households were split evenly.

In early 1999 Ridge pressed for more tax cuts, school choice, a freeze on garbage landfills (Pennsylvania is the nation's largest waste importing state); he beamed when the legislature passed a bill to help pay for new stadiums for Pennsylvania's two baseball and two football franchises, and proudly unveiled the state's new license plates, the first to include a Website address. Ridge was mentioned as a possible nominee for vice president in 1996, but some conservatives complained about his pro-choice views on abortion, and he asked not to be considered. He may well be mentioned again in 2000, and possibly chosen: As a Northeasterner well known in Pennsylvania and with a resume (ethnic, Harvard, Vietnam) especially attractive in the industrial states Ohio, Michigan and Illinois, he would bring some assets to a ticket headed by George W. Bush or most of his rivals; he can run as a governor with experience in reform, but he has also served in Congress; he has a relationship with Bush that goes back to 1980.

Senior Senator. Arlen Specter, one of the nation's most durable career politicians, has held public office and has been an important national figure off and on for most of four decades. Specter grew up in Russell, Kansas—also the home town of Bob Dole—and came to Philadelphia at 17 to attend the University of Pennsylvania. After college he served in the Air Force, went to Yale Law School and practiced law in Philadelphia. In 1964 he was a top staffer for the Warren Commission investigating the Kennedy assassination, where he helped develop the single-bullet theory. After the Warren Commission, he returned to his law practice, switched to the Republican Party, and was elected district attorney in Democratic Philadelphia in 1965 and again in 1969. He lost the race for D.A. in 1973, for the Senate in 1976, and for governor in 1978, before narrowly (36%–33%) edging a former state Republican chairman in the 1980 primary and beating a low-spending Democrat 50%–48% in the general for his Senate seat. In 1986, he won re-election by a 56%–43% margin against a low-profile House Democrat; in 1992 he was re-elected 49%–46% after he became a target of feminists for his questioning of Anita Hill during the confirmation hearings of Clarence Thomas. He ran for president in 1995, but withdrew before the first caucus or primary.

Throughout this career of narrow victories and numerous defeats, Specter's assets have been brains and hard work. He is respected by colleagues and constituents, though not always well-liked. He sides with conservatives on some divisive issues, with liberals on others, building up no permanent credit with either. He is aggressive and prosecutorial, well-prepared and persuasive once he takes a stand. These traits are both his strengths and weaknesses; they explain why he was vulnerable in 1992, and why he won; why he ran for president, and why his campaign foundered. His voting record is almost precisely at the midpoint of the Senate, and he has played key roles on a variety of issues. Though he switched and voted to override President Clinton's "partial-birth" abortion veto, he is generally pro-choice on abortion—an issue he featured in his presidential campaign, infuriating many Republican activists. He pushes tough penalties for crime and supports capital punishment. He argued persuasively for the Gulf war resolution. On a closely divided and rancorous Judiciary Committee, he played a key role on several Supreme Court nominations. More than anyone else, he defeated Robert Bork in 1987 and, more than anyone but John Danforth, he confirmed Clarence Thomas in 1991.

In the latter case he caught the nation's attention. When Anita Hill came before the committee with serious and unsubstantiated charges against Thomas, he questioned her with rigor. But this evoked a firestorm of criticism from the feminist left and its allies in the press; hard as it may be to believe after Clinton's impeachment trial, they then believed that charges of sexual misconduct against an employer should be accepted without demur. Specter accused Hill of committing perjury, and was attacked for this in the 1992 campaign; by fall 1994 he was declining to defend his entirely defensible questioning, saying simply that the hearings enabled him to learn a lot about sexual harassment. In June 1994, he attended an Iowa straw poll and confrontationally attacked the religious right. His presidential campaign was never going anywhere and it consisted mostly of denunciations of religious conservatism; he dropped out in November 1995.

On other issues Specter showed he was just as capable of confronting the left. His devastatingly complex chart describing the Clinton health care plan played no small part in defeating it. He has worked aggressively to expedite death penalty appeals. He called for a 20% flat tax in 1995. He called the FBI raid on Ruby Ridge "bizarre." But he also took some liberal stands, voting for the minimum wage increase and to ban discrimination against gays, and fighting against the immigration amendment allowing states to deny public schooling to children of illegal immigrants. He was chairman of the Intelligence Committee from 1995–96, but failed in his attempt to reorganize the intelligence agencies and to make theft of "proprietary economic information" a crime. In December 1996 he questioned whether CIA nominee Anthony Lake was sensitive to the need to keep Congress informed, given his approval of the decision to let Iran secretly arm the Bosnian Muslims; Lake withdrew his nomination in March 1997.

As the 1998 election approached, Specter increasingly emphasized his work on Pennsylvania causes, from the Philadelphia Navy Yard to cleaning up Lake Erie. He is the third-ranking Republican on Appropriations, and chairman of the Labor-HHS-Education Subcommittee, in which capacity he has worked to sharply increase funding for medical research; he declined to switch to the Foreign Operations Subcommittee in December 1998. He supported changes in federal organ transplant policy in 1998 (Pittsburgh has a big organ transplant hospital) and called in 1999 for research on stem cells from human embryos. No project is too small for him: In March 1998 alone he backed $400,000 for Saw Mill Run flood control and $800,000 for the anthracite coal historical library in Montgomery County; in April 1998 he sought $8.8 million for projects in Pittsburgh's airport, and he backs a high-speed train between Pittsburgh and Philadelphia. When Citizens Against Government Waste listed him in the "Pig Book," Specter said, "If they left me out, I'd be worried." He opposed the highway bill in March 1998 and the omnibus budget in October 1998: both infringements on the turf of appropriators.

But Specter has not neglected national issues. With Edward Kennedy, he sponsored hate crimes legislation in November 1997. He and Ernest Hollings sponsored a constitutional amendment to allow Congress to set limits on political contributions and expenditures; it was beaten 61–38 in March 1997. As chairman of the Veterans' Affairs Committee in 1997, he called for doing more to investigate whether there is a Gulf war syndrome and what was known about chemical hazards in the region. In early 1999 he supported tariffs and revisions in dumping laws to protect Pennsylvania steelmakers against Russian and East Asian imports. With Congressman Frank Wolf, he introduced in May 1997 a religious persecution bill to retaliate against countries that engage in that practice; in 1998 he revised it to try to meet the objections of the Clinton Administration. In March 1998, Specter, ever the prosecutor, said that Saddam Hussein should be tried as a war criminal. In August 1998 he questioned whether President Clinton's order of cruise missile strikes in Afghanistan and Sudan had a "diversionary motive"; after Republican leaders declined to follow his lead, he backtracked. In July 1998 he urged the appointment of an independent counsel to investigate Clinton-Gore campaign fundraising and threatened to take Janet Reno to court if she didn't. Specter's May 1999 amendment to the defense authorization bill, invoking the War Powers Act to prevent the deployment of ground troops in the former Yugoslavia, failed 52–48.

On impeachment, Specter took his own course. In November 1998, he said, "I propose abandoning impeachment and, after the president leaves office, holding him accountable in the same way any other person would be: through indictment and prosecution for any federal cirmes established by the evidence. . . . My experience as district attorney of Philadelphia convinces me that the issues of character, lying to the American people and putting the country through hell for months would weigh heavily in the sentencing phase after any conviction." But in February 1999, in a decision he called "a lot ambiguous, maybe even a little amorphous," Specter said he would vote "not proven," citing Scottish criminal law. "I think it is important to make a distinction that I do not believe that the president is not guilty," he said. "It's a trial on which you can't really come to a verdict because of the absence of witnesses and the absence of relevant evidence."

In 1992 Specter was challenged by an anti-abortion legislator in the Republican primary and by feminist Democrat Lynn Yeakel in the general election. Specter won the primary 65%–35%. He attacked Yeakel's ethics problems, proceeded to out-debate her and won 49%–46%, running about even in metro Philadelphia and Pittsburgh, far ahead of usual Republican showings, and carried most smaller areas. He overcame serious health problems—he had brain tumor surgery in June 1993, underwent a radiation procedure in October 1996 and had double heart-bypass surgery in June 1998, returning to the Senate in early July—and continued to work hard getting around the state and raising money. Pennsylvania Democrats have shown little adeptness at winning Senate elections: they have won only one, the 1991 special after the death of John Heinz, since 1962. In 1997, well-known Democrats one after the other declined to run against a candidate who had won only 49% five years before. Specter's 1998 opponent was former state Representative William Lloyd, who ran third in the 1996 Democratic primary for auditor. He spent only $187,000 and put up no TV spots. Specter spent $4.5 million and ran spots showing him being praised by Philadelphia Mayor Ed Rendell, the state's most prominent Democrat. The Pennsylvania AFL-CIO endorsed Specter in July, the United Steelworkers in October. So confident was Specter that he had more than $2.6 million in cash left over. Specter won 61%–35%, carrying every county but Philadelphia and Somerset. He became the first Pennsylvania senator to be popularly elected to four terms, and if he finishes out the term he will be only nine months behind the record tenure for a Pennsylvania senator, held by Boies Penrose (1897–1921).

Junior Senator. Rick Santorum, a Republican elected in 1994, is the third youngest senator (Peter Fitzgerald and Blanche Lincoln are younger), elected from one of the oldest states, a strong conservative elected in a state that still has many New Deal voters. Santorum is the son of an Italian immigrant who was a clinical psychologist for the Veterans' Administration; he was born in Virginia and moved to Butler, Pennsylvania, at age 7. He started in politics working for John Heinz's first Senate campaign in 1976; he went to Penn State and Pitt business school and worked his way through Dickinson law school as a staffer for state Senate Republicans in Harrisburg; he worked for a blue chip law firm in Pittsburgh for four years. In 1990, at 32, he challenged seven-term incumbent Congressman Doug Walgren, who outspent him $717,000 to $251,000. But Santorum knocked on 25,000 doors, amassed an army of volunteers including many right-to-lifers, attacked Walgren for voting for a pay raise seven times and for living in the Washington suburbs. Santorum opposed the congressional pay raise, backed the line-item veto and came out for limits on PAC contributions. He won 51%–49%.

In the House he had a solid conservative voting record and was one of the "Gang of Seven" freshman Republicans who helped expose the House bank scandal. Redistricting gave him a seat shorn of many Republican suburbs and centered on the industrial Monongahela Valley, historically very Democratic. George Bush got only 30% in this new district, but Santorum beat a state senator 61%–38%—an astonishing victory. Brash and confident, Santorum immediately started running for the Senate. His opponent was Harris Wofford, elected in November 1991 to replace John Heinz, who died in a plane crash. Wofford was a civil rights activist in the 1960s, the adviser who persuaded John Kennedy to phone Coretta Scott King when her husband was jailed during the 1960 campaign, one of Sargent Shriver's top aides at the Peace Corps. Appointed to the Senate by Governor Bob Casey in May 1991, he upset former Governor Dick Thornburgh 55%–45% by emphasizing health care: "If criminals have the right to a lawyer, I think working Americans should have a right to a doctor." In the Senate Wofford sponsored the AmeriCorps bill. But he was politically hurt when the Clinton health care bill failed to pass.

This was a race of sharp contrasts in issues and style: Santorum, brashly eager to chop government, backing medical savings accounts and opposing gun control; Wofford, earnestly working for government health care financing, backing the 1994 crime bill and gun control. Wofford appealed to a long liberal tradition; Santorum scoffed at him for championing 1960s ideas in the 1990s. Wofford was helped in the last week of the campaign by Teresa Heinz, widow of John Heinz, who called Santorum part of a "worrisome breed" of politicians who "mock, belittle and vilify those who disagree with them"; in 1995 she married Democratic Senator John Kerry. But with home town appeal, Santorum ran behind only 50%–47% in metro Pittsburgh, where Wofford had won 61% in 1991. Santorum did not go over so well in metro Philadelphia, which Wofford carried 54%–42%. But in the rest of the state—where half the votes are cast and where gun control hurt Wofford—Santorum won 55%–41%, for a statewide victory of 49%–47%.

Santorum was not cowed by the traditions of the Senate. In his first full month there he argued about the balanced budget amendment with Robert Byrd, who was elected to the Senate the year Santorum was born. Then, when senior Republican Mark Hatfield cast a decisive vote against the amendment, Santorum called on Hatfield to be removed as Appropriations chairman. Senior senators and Washington insiders tut-tutted. Hatfield wasn't removed, but Senate Republicans changed the rules, limiting chairmen to six years and calling for secret ballot elections of chairmen starting in 1997. That will tend to produce more party discipline and cohesion, as secret ballot elections by House Democrats have done since they were instituted by Phillip Burton in 1974. Later in 1995 Santorum took to the floor a dozen times with a "Where's Bill?" sign, asking where the President's balanced budget was; Democrats were furious. On the Agriculture Committee and on the floor he conducted a campaign against the peanut and sugar subsidies—a sop to Hershey, cynics suggested—which threatened to undercut the Republicans' farm bill, and got the sugar subsidy cut a bit and the peanut program limited to five years. Santorum's reply to those who call him brash: "I don't run around looking for a fight. I just stand up for what I'm elected to do."

Santorum has a mostly, but not entirely, conservative voting record: He voted to increase the minimum wage and opposed NAFTA in the House. But he took the lead on important conservative legislation. With Bob Packwood busy with ethics charges, Santorum floor-managed the welfare reform bill in 1995; he was calm rather than brash when the bill passed, recognizing that many people's lives would be affected, though he was convinced it was better than the status quo. Later, noting the difficulty of commuting from inner cities to suburban jobs, he sponsored reverse commuting initiatives which made it into the 1998 transportation act. Santorum also took the lead on the partial birth abortion ban, which passed the Senate 64–36 in May 1997—a big gain from 54–44 in 1995—and was vetoed by Bill Clinton. This was not just a theoretical issue for him: In 1996 he and his wife had to decide what to do when their unborn child had a fatal defect; the baby was born in October 1996 and died two hours later. Santorum is part of the Renewal Alliance: conservative Republicans who want to encourage private sector, especially faith-based, organizations to care for the poor and helpless, even as they repeal government programs originally intended to help them. And he sponsored a bill to reduce the liability for charitable donations of equipment by private companies.

On the Agriculture Committee, Santorum got into the 1996 farm bill an amendment helping states' farmland protection programs, which in Pennsylvania covers more than 100,000 acres. On the Armed Services Committee, he moved to stop wasteful Pentagon purchasing practices and to preserve the Army Regional Support Command near Pittsburgh. Santorum voted against the Senate version of the transportation bill in March 1998, because the funding formula hurt Pennsylvania; he later criticized the administration for not including the $20 million authorized for development of a high-speed elevated train. He attacked Democrats' education bills to provide more classrooms: "They believe that if we had better looking schools or nicely appointed schools or better equipment, that somehow the problem would go away. . . . It's not brick and mortar. It's not the number of teachers." His brashness is still in evidence: He backed down when senior Republicans objected to his bill to force the sale of Soldier's Home land in Washington to the Catholic Church in 1998; he attacked the Senate's barber facility in 1999. On impeachment he was uncharacteristically quiet. In January 1999 he said he was undecided; ultimately, he voted for removal.

Perhaps Santorum's greatest gamble has been to propose Social Security reform; Pennsylvania has a high percentage of elderly. In 1999 he came forward with a plan to allow personal retirement accounts, with 4% of earnings up to $18,000 and then 2% up to the Social Security wage limit, to be invested, with limitations, in the stock market; benefits similar to the current system would be guaranteed. Santorum argues that this would enable low- and middle-income workers to accumulate wealth as upper-income workers do already. He argues that having the government invest the funds in the markets, as some Democrats have proposed, would mean that stock market increases would go to other government programs rather than individuals. Far from quailing at this issue, Santorum became co-chairman of Trent Lott's Social Security task force and spoke forcefully for his plan at the December 1998 White House conference on Social Security.

As the election for Arlen Specter's seat approached, prominent Democrats dropped out one after the other from the race. As the election for Santorum's seat nears, Democrats have dropped into the race—by March 1999, there were five Democrats with some credentials running. The first was state Senator Allyson Schwartz, from the Philadelphia area; she netted support from Louisiana Senator Mary Landrieu, whom she knew from state legislators' conferences. Another was former Congresswoman Marjorie Margolies-Mezvinsky, also from the Philadelphia suburbs, who switched and cast the deciding vote for the Clinton budget and tax increase in August 1993 after promising not to; she lost in 1994 and later headed the Women's Campaign Fund, and is likely to get support and money from national feminist groups. Also running was former Congressman Peter Kostmayer, who represented Bucks and Montgomery Counties, just outside Philadelphia, for 14 years from 1976–80 and 1982–92, when he lost to Republican Jim Greenwood; he was Washington head of Zero Population Growth but took a leave of absence to run. A fourth candidate was former state Labor Secretary Tom Foley, from Hershey, who ran unsuccessfully for lieutenant governor in 1994 and auditor general in 1996; he might count on labor support. Another candidate was Congressman Ron Klink, from suburban Pittsburgh and a former anchor on KDKA-TV, who called Santorum an "absolute embarrassment." Unlike the other Democrats, Klink opposes abortion, which could help with the many cultural conservatives in the Democratic primary. Klink also has a geographic advantage: He is the only candidate from western Pennsylvania, and the Pittsburgh region cast 44% of the votes in the 1998 Democratic Senate primary, while three of the others have a base in the Philadelphia suburbs, which cast only 8% of the votes in that contest (although Philadelphia casts another 12%). National Democratic strategies in early 1999 were looking fondly at Klink's candidacy, hoping that he could cut Santorum's margin in his home base; by April 1999 Klink was already leading the pack in money from labor unions. But Santorum's positions may not appear as extremist to many Pennsylvania voters as they do to fundraisers and strategists, and Santorum has won some big bets against long odds before.

Cook's Call. *Competitive.* There is a long line of Democrats vying for the right to challenge Santorum. Representative Ron Klink, former Labor Commissioner Tom Foley, state Senator Allyson Schwartz, and former Representatives Marjorie Margolies-Mezvinsky and Peter Kostmayer have all announced their intention to seek the Democratic nomination. It is unclear whether all five will actually file in February of 2000, but for now Klink and Foley are considered the frontrunners. If one of the two women drop out of the race, the remaining one could become a real contender. Santorum may not be as vulnerable as Democrats believe, but this is certain to be a hard-fought contest.

Presidential politics. Pennsylvania, with its 23 electoral votes, has been a swing state in every close presidential election, and even some that were not close; it voted near the national average in 1996. However, it is not typical of the country. With its older, deeply-rooted population, it tends to be culturally conservative; with its long-dying, blue-collar communities, it tends to be economically more liberal—though both tendencies are being muted with time.

Pennsylvania's late April presidential primary has not been crucial since 1976, when Jimmy Carter clinched the Democratic nomination here by beating Henry Jackson and Morris Udall. Bill Clinton and Bob Dole easily won the unremarkable 1996 primaries.

Congressional districting. Pennsylvania lost three congressional districts in the 1950 Census and two in each of the following four decades, reducing its delegation to 21. It seems likely to lose two more in the 2000 Census. Control of redistricting after the 1990 Census was split between the parties, and the plan seemed to hurt Republicans, but they now have an 11–10 advantage. Control of redistricting next time will be in the hands of the Republicans if—a fairly big if—they hold onto their 103–100 margin in the state House in 2000; their control of the Senate is secure, and Governor Tom Ridge was re-elected to a four-year term in 1998.

Demographics suggest that the two significantly population-losing parts of the state in the

1990s—the city of Philadelphia and metro Pittsburgh—will each lose a seat; that would certainly be the Republicans' impulse, since all seats in both areas are held by Democrats. In addition, Republicans might try to lean one of the remaining Pittsburgh area seats toward their party or make the 13th District outside Philadelphia, where Democrat Joe Hoeffel beat Republican incumbent Jon Fox in 1998, more Republican. That could give Pennsylvania a 12–7 Republican margin—one of the bigger changes in the country.

The People: Est. Pop. 1998: 12,001,451; Pop. 1990: 11,881,643, up 1% 1990–1998. 4.4% of U.S. total, 6th largest; 31.1% rural. Median age: 36.9 years. 16.1% 65 years and over. 88.6% White, 9.2% Black, 1.1% Asian, 0.1% Amer. Indian, 1% Other; 1.9% Hispanic Origin. Households: 55.7% married couple families; 25.2% married couple fams. w. children; 36.1% college educ.; median household income: $29,069; per capita income: $14,068; 70.7% owner occupied housing; median house value: $69,700; median monthly rent: $322. 4.6% Unemployment. 1998 Voting age pop.: 9,118,000. 1998 Turnout: 3,024,941; 33% of VAP. Registered voters (1998): 7,258,822; 3,514,970 D (48%), 3,072,299 R (42%), 671,553 unaffiliated and minor parties (9%).

Political Lineup: Governor, Tom Ridge (R); Lt. Gov., Mark Schweiker (R); Secy. of Commonwealth, Kim Pizzingrilli; Atty. Gen., D. Michael Fisher (R); Treasurer, Barbara Hafer (R); State Senate, 50 (20 D, 30 R); Majority Leader, F. Joseph Loeper (R); State House, 203 (100 D, 103 R); House Speaker, Matthew J. Ryan (R). Senators, Arlen Specter (R) and Rick Santorum (R). Representatives, 21 (11 D, 10 R).

Elections Division: 717-787-5280; **Filing Deadline for U.S. Congress:** February 15, 2000.

1996 Presidential Vote

Clinton (D)	2,215,819	(49%)
Dole (R)	1,801,169	(40%)
Perot (I)	430,984	(10%)

1996 Republican Presidential Primary

Dole (R)	435,031	(64%)
Buchanan (R)	123,011	(18%)
Forbes (R)	55,018	(8%)
Keyes (R)	40,025	(6%)
Lugar (R)	31,119	(5%)

1992 Presidential Vote

Clinton (D)	2,239,164	(45%)
Bush (R)	1,791,841	(36%)
Perot (I)	902,667	(18%)

GOVERNOR

Gov. Tom Ridge (R)

Elected 1994, term expires Jan. 2003; b. Aug. 26, 1945, Munhall; home, Erie; Harvard U., B.A. 1967, Dickinson Law Schl., J.D. 1972; Catholic; married (Michele).

Military Career: Army, 1968–70 (Vietnam).

Elected Office: U.S. House of Reps., 1982–94.

Professional Career: Practicing atty., 1972–82; Erie Cnty. Asst. Dist. Atty., 1979–81.

Office: 225 Capitol Bldg., Harrisburg, 17120, 717-787-2500; Fax: 717-772-8284; Web site: www.state.pa.us.

Election Results

1998 gen.	Tom Ridge (R)	....	1,736,844	(57%)
	Ivan Itkin (D)	....	938,745	(31%)
	Peg Luksik (Const)	....	315,761	(10%)
	Others	....	33,802	(1%)
1998 prim.	Tom Ridge (R)	....	unopposed	
1994 gen.	Tom Ridge (R)	....	1,627,976	(45%)
	Mark S. Singel (D)	....	1,430,099	(40%)
	Peg Luksik (Const)	....	460,269	(13%)
	Others	....	67,182	(2%)

SENATORS

Sen. Arlen Specter (R)

Elected 1980, seat up 2004; b. Feb. 12, 1930, Wichita, KS; home, Philadelphia; U. of PA, B.A. 1951, Yale U., LL.B. 1956; Jewish; married (Joan).

Military Career: Air Force, 1951–53.

Elected Office: Philadelphia Dist. Atty., 1965–73.

Professional Career: Practicing atty., 1955–56, 1974–80; Asst. Cnsl., Warren Comm., 1964; PA Asst. Atty. Gen., 1964–65.

DC Office: 711 HSOB, 20510, 202-224-4254; Fax: 202-228-1229; Web site: www.senate.gov/~specter.

State Offices: Allentown, 610-434-1444; Erie, 814-453-3010; Harrisburg, 717-782-3951; Philadelphia, 215-597-7200; Pittsburgh, 412-644-3400; Scranton, 717-346-2006.

Committees: *Appropriations* (3d of 15 R): Agriculture & Rural Development; Defense; Foreign Operations & Export Financing; Labor & HHS (Chmn.); Transportation. *Governmental Affairs* (8th of 9 R): International Security, Proliferation & Federal Services; Investigations (Permanent). *Judiciary* (4th of 10 R): Antitrust, Business Rights & Competition; Immigration; The Constitution, Federalism & Property Rights. *Veterans' Affairs* (Chmn. of 7 R).

Group Ratings

	ADA	ACLU	AFS	LCV	CON	NTU	NFIB	COC	ACU	NTLC	CHC
1998	45	50	80	50	58	44	63	60	33	48	20
1997	70	—	56	—	5	51	—	50	32	—	—

National Journal Ratings

	1997 LIB — 1997 CONS			1998 LIB — 1998 CONS	
Economic	52%	—	46%	52%	—	47%
Social	55%	—	37%	59%	—	40%
Foreign	51%	—	46%	50%	—	49%

Key Votes of the 105th Congress

1. Bal. Budget Amend.	Y	5. Satcher for Surgeon Gen.	Y	9. Chem. Weapons Treaty	Y
2. Clinton Budget Deal	Y	6. Highway Set-asides	Y	10. Cuban Humanitarian Aid	N
3. Cloture on Tobacco	*	7. Table Child Gun locks	Y	11. Table Bosnia Troops	*
4. Education IRAs	*	8. Ovrd. Part. Birth Veto	Y	12. $ for Test-ban Treaty	Y

Election Results

1998 general	Arlen Spector (R)	1,814,180	(61%)	($4,535,887)
	Bill Lloyd (D)	1,028,839	(35%)	($187,157)
	Others	114,753	(4%)	
1998 primary	Arlen Spector (R)	376,322	(67%)	
	Larry Murphy (R)	101,120	(18%)	
	Tom Lingenfelter (R)	82,168	(15%)	
1992 general	Arlen Specter (R)	2,358,125	(49%)	($10,454,793)
	Lynn Yeakel (D)	2,224,966	(46%)	($5,028,669)
	John F. Perry (Lib)	219,319	(5%)	($53,690)

Sen. Rick Santorum (R)

Elected 1994, seat up 2000; b. May 10, 1958, Winchester, VA; home, Penn Hills; PA St. U., B.A. 1980, U. of Pittsburgh, M.B.A. 1981, Dickinson Law Schl., J.D. 1986; Catholic; married (Karen).

Elected Office: U.S. House of Reps., 1990–94.

Professional Career: A.A., PA Sen. J. Doyle 1981–86; Exec. Dir., PA Senate Local Govt. Cmte., 1981–84; Exec. Dir., PA Senate Transportation Cmte., 1984–86; Practicing atty., 1986–90.

DC Office: 120 RSOB, 20510, 202-224-6324; Fax: 202-228-0604; Web site: www.senate.gov/~santorum.

State Offices: Allentown, 610-770-0142; Altoona, 814-946-7023; Erie, 814-454-7114; Harrisburg, 717-231-7540; Philadelphia, 215-864-6900; Pittsburgh, 412-562-0533; Scranton, 717-344-8799.

Committees: *Aging (Special)* (6th of 11 R). *Agriculture, Nutrition & Forestry* (10th of 10 R): Forestry, Conservation & Rural Revitalization; Research, Nutrition & General Legislation. *Armed Services* (6th of 11 R): Airland Forces (Chmn.); Emerging Threats & Capabilities; Readiness & Management Support. *Banking, Housing & Urban Affairs* (9th of 11 R): Financial Institutions; Housing & Transportation (Vice Chmn.); Securities. *Rules & Administration* (6th of 9 R).

Group Ratings

	ADA	ACLU	AFS	LCV	CON	NTU	NFIB	COC	ACU	NTLC	CHC
1998	0	14	0	0	71	69	100	89	84	89	91
1997	15	—	0	—	89	83	—	90	84	—	—

National Journal Ratings

	1997 LIB — 1997 CONS			1998 LIB — 1998 CONS	
Economic	0%	—	89%	18%	—	72%
Social	28%	—	62%	24%	—	73%
Foreign	30%	—	66%	12%	—	75%

Key Votes of the 105th Congress

1. Bal. Budget Amend.	Y	5. Satcher for Surgeon Gen.	N	9. Chem. Weapons Treaty	Y
2. Clinton Budget Deal	Y	6. Highway Set-asides	N	10. Cuban Humanitarian Aid	N
3. Cloture on Tobacco	N	7. Table Child Gun locks	Y	11. Table Bosnia Troops	N
4. Education IRAs	Y	8. Ovrd. Part. Birth Veto	Y	12. $ for Test-ban Treaty	N

Election Results

1994 general	Rick Santorum (R)	1,735,691	(49%)	($6,732,849)
	Harris Wofford (D)	1,648,481	(47%)	($6,300,560)
	Others	129,189	(4%)	
1994 primary	Rick Santorum (R)	667,115	(82%)	
	Joe Watkins (R)	150,969	(18%)	
1991 special	Harris Wofford (D)	1,860,760	(55%)	($3,241,556)
	Dick Thornburgh (R)	1,521,986	(45%)	($3,993,070)

FIRST DISTRICT

In Center City Philadelphia, the 1680s look out on the 1780s, 1880s and 1980s. The statue of William Penn, who founded the city in 1682, stands 37 feet high atop the 548-foot tower of the 1880s Second Empire-style City Hall at Market and Broad; east, is Independence Hall, where Americans in the 1780s drew up the nation's Constitution; west, is the tower of One Liberty Place, with its "romantic modernist" spire, the 1980s building that broke tradition to rise above City Hall. Philadelphia is built on a certain order. Earlier American colonies were settled by practical men, out to make money or replicate a farm settlement back home. But Penn was a Quaker, a member of one of those rationalizing sects of the 17th Century, who intended to impose order on his new environment, and did: no cowpath street patterns here, like those in Boston or Charleston, but a grid of numbered and named streets, with precisely spaced open squares.

Penn's city of brotherly love has turned out to be a commercial and industrial metropolis that has grown steadily over the years, spreading out over the countryside. Yet there are still places in which you can see the distant past: in the restored townhouses of Society Hill and the tree-shaded public buildings around Independence Hall and, on the way to the ornate City Hall, the Federal and Greek Revival buildings and the temples of commerce, built when Philadelphia was the nation's largest city. Interspersed are I.M. Pei's modernist Society Hill Towers (though the rich in Philadelphia, unlike New York or Chicago, don't much like apartments) and the 1920s masonry-faced skyscrapers and 1970s glass-and-steel towers built around City Hall and in Center City farther west.

For all the grandness of City Hall, Philadelphia has seldom had a city government of which to be proud. Corruption has reigned here off and on for more than a century, and so has incompetence. While the city's private economy grew robustly in the 1980s, the city government—swollen with overpaid employees, committed to a costly, union-run health plan and mismanaged with ferocious ineptitude—lurched unknowingly toward bankruptcy under Mayor Wilson Goode. Then in 1991 Democrat Ed Rendell was elected mayor. Ebullient and energetic, he immediately set to work, literally scrubbing City Hall's grimy steps. He cut spending sharply, privatized government functions and faced down unions in a strike threat. At the same time, he improved performance and sponsored innovative new programs, took over the closed-down Philadelphia Navy Yard and found new employers to save at least half the jobs there. Overwhelmingly re-elected in 1995, Rendell showed national Democrats the viable future for their politics: not increasing spending and defending public employees against constituents, but cutting spending and producing more and better services for less money. That progress will be on display when Republicans hold their national convention here in the summer of 2000.

City Hall lies at the geographic center of Pennsylvania's 1st Congressional District. The 1st runs north on both sides of the Broad Street corridor to include much of black North Philadelphia and south through most of heavily Italian South Philadelphia, where Italian families and their grocery stores and restaurants have been pressed tightly into narrow streets under a tangle of overhead wires; this is the neighborhood where the various *Rockys* were filmed and the original Philadelphia cheesesteaks are sold. The district also includes the oil tank farms where the Schuylkill River flows into the Delaware River, the Navy Yard, the Philadelphia airport, and the swath of industrial suburbs along the river to the black-majority city of Chester. This was created as a black-majority district, in the argot of the Voting Rights Act, but also includes many Hispanics, and is overwhelmingly Democratic.

The 1st is represented by Bob Brady, a Democrat elected in May 1998. Though he was the House's junior member when first elected, he symbolizes the nation's old-fashioned urban politics. He grew up in Overbrook Park in West Philadelphia, with an Irish father and Italian mother, he depicts himself as a roll-up-your-sleeves guy who represents working-class voters. After high school he went to work as a carpenter and quickly rose up the ranks of the carpenter's union leadership. He entered politics in 1967, at 22, when the local ward leader wouldn't replace a burnt-out streetlight; Brady was elected to the 34th Ward Democratic Executive Committee; in 1980 he was elected Ward leader. In 1975 he became assistant Sergeant-at-Arms of the city council; he was a consultant to the state Senate and member of the Pennsylvania Turnpike Commission and on the board of the city's Redevelopment Authority. In 1986 he became chairman of the Philadelphia Democratic Party, where he has been a close ally of talented politicians like former state Senator Buddy Cianfrani and state Senator Vincent Fumo.

In November 1997, Thomas Foglietta, 1st District congressman since 1980 and a veteran of South Philly politics, who started off as a Republican and who beat black primary opponents, resigned after being confirmed in October 1997 as ambassador to Italy, and Brady moved to run for the seat. In other cities, this might have led to a primary fight between black politicians; in Philadelphia the Democratic nomination for the special election, held on the same day as the regular primary, was determined by the Democratic ward leaders in the district. That gave Brady a great advantage, for he seemed sure to win the committeemen's vote; former 2d District Congressman Lucien Blackwell, probably his strongest opponent, dropped out of the race in January 1998, even before Brady officially declared; former Common Pleas Judge John Braxton, who got 27% against Foglietta in April 1996, pondered a race but did not run; radio station owner Cody Anderson was knocked off the ballot when his petitions were challenged. Brady won the endorsement of many black leaders and built a strong election day organization. He won the special election with 74% of the vote and the Democratic nomination for November, against three little-known opponents, with 64%. In November 1998 he won 81%–17%. This was the triumph of a politician known for making "accommodations" with others—"they're always accommodations, never deals," he insists—whose positions on national issues were not always set in stone—he decided that he was in favor of abortion rights after asking his mother.

Even after he was elected to the House, his attention focused back home. In July 1998, local officials credited him with mediating an end to the 41-day strike that had shut down parts of the SEPTA transit system. His ties to City Hall and to the local unions gave him credibility with both sides. He was elected easily to a full term in November 1998. Brady has said that he dreamed as a boy of becoming a U.S. senator. But it is unlikely that his machine-style politics will play well in a statewide campaign. Nor is it clear that he will have a long career in the House. Philadelphia has been losing population, and redistricting after the 2000 Census seems likely to be controlled by Republicans, who could put the current 1st and 3d Districts together, with a faceoff between Brady and the 3d's Robert Borski.

Cook's Call. *Safe.* Brady's biggest threat to re-election in this heavily Democratic district will come not from Republicans but from the remapping that will take place here in 2002. There is strong speculation that Pennsylvania will lose two seats, one of which will likely be a Philadelphia-based district.

The People: Pop. 1990: 566,133; 13.5% age 65 +; 37.8% White, 52.4% Black, 2.4% Asian, 0.2% Amer. Indian, 7.2% Other; 9.4% Hispanic Origin. Households: 33.3% married couple families; 16.1% married couple fams. w. children; 25.2% college educ.; median household income: $20,372; per capita income: $9,703; median house value: $37,600; median gross rent: $301.

1996 Presidential Vote

Clinton (D)	148,850	(83%)
Dole (R)	21,845	(12%)
Perot (I)	7,519	(4%)

1992 Presidential Vote

Clinton (D)	150,091	(72%)
Bush (R)	39,086	(19%)
Perot (I)	17,052	(8%)

Rep. Robert Brady (D)

Elected May 1998; b. April 7, 1945, Philadelphia; home, Philadelphia; Catholic; married (Debra).

Elected Office: 34th Ward Dem. Exec. Cmte. Mbr., 1967–present, Ward Ldr., 1980.

Professional Career: Carpenter; Real estate salesman; Philadelphia Dpty. Mayor for Labor, 1984–87; Chmn., Philadelphia Dem. Party, 1986; Legis. Rep., Metro. Regional Cncl. of Carpenters & Joiners, 1987–98; Lecturer, U. of PA, 1997-present.

DC Office: 216 CHOB 20515, 202-225-4731; Fax: 202-225-0088; Web site: www.house.gov/robertbrady

District Offices: Chester, 610-874-7094; Philadelphia, 215-236-5430; Philadelphia, 215-389-4627.

Committees: *Armed Services* (24th of 28 D): Military Installations & Facilities; Military Procurement. *Small Business* (8th of 17 D): Regulatory Reform & Paperwork Reduction.

Group Ratings (Only Served Partial Term)

	ADA	ACLU	AFS	LCV	CON	NTU	NFIB	COC	ACU	NTLC	CHC
1998	50	89	100	17	90	20	0	25	0	6	10
1997	*	—	—	—	*	*	—	*	*	—	—

National Journal Ratings (Only Served Partial Term)

	1997 LIB — 1997 CONS			1998 LIB — 1998 CONS		
Economic	*	—	*	79%	—	0%
Social	*	—	*	79%	—	21%
Foreign	*	—	*	90%	—	10%

Key Votes of the 105th Congress (Only Served Partial Term)

1. Clinton Budget Deal	*	5. Puerto Rico Sthood. Ref.	*	9. Cut $ for B-2 Bombers	*
2. Education IRAs	*	6. End Highway Set-asides	*	10. Human Rights in China	*
3. Req. 2/3 to Raise Taxes	*	7. School Prayer Amend.	N	11. Withdraw Bosnia Troops	*
4. Fast-track Trade	N	8. Ovrd. Part. Birth Veto	*	12. End Cuban TV-Marti	Y

Election Results

1998 general	Robert A. Brady (D) 77,788	(81%)	($333,055)
	William M. Harrison (R) 15,898	(17%)	
	Others 2,162	(2%)	
1998 primary	Robert A. Brady (D) 23,181	(64%)	
	Andrew J. Carn (D) 8,061	(22%)	
	Dennis Morrison-Wesley (D) 4,052	(11%)	
	Others 986	(3%)	
1998 special	Robert A. Brady (D) 13,923	(74%)	($186,846)
	William M. Harrison (R) 2,436	(13%)	
	Juanita Norwood (Ref) 1,993	(11%)	
	Others 558	(3%)	
1996 general	Thomas M. Foglietta (D) 145,210	(88%)	($485,748)
	James Cella (R) 20,734	(12%)	($4,603)

SECOND DISTRICT

Looking out over the Schuylkill River north of Center City Philadelphia, you can still see the landscape painted 100 years ago by Philadelphia artist Thomas Eakins—the tightly-packed but formidable rowhouses, the old fieldstone houses of Germantown, the gray-blue water flowing past boat houses below the small Greek temples of the Water Works and the larger temple of the Museum of Art and the skyscraper towers looming behind. On both sides of this romantic scene are some of Philadelphia's long-established black neighborhoods—West Philadelphia, across the Schuylkill on either side of Market Street; North Philadelphia, on either side of Broad Street; to the northwest, off the narrow diagonal of Germantown Avenue that ran through open fields in Benjamin Franklin's time.

The 2d Congressional District is centered on this part of Philadelphia, following the Schuyl-kill north and south. It includes Center City skyscrapers, affluent Chestnut Hill, upper-class Rittenhouse Square, and the University of Pennsylvania. Pennsylvania never had slavery—thanks to William Penn's Quaker legacy—and Philadelphia had a large black community even before the Civil War. As redistricted for the 1990s, the 2d District is 62% black, and over-whelmingly Democratic.

The congressman from the 2d District is Chaka Fattah, first elected in 1994. Fattah grew up in Philadelphia, and in 1982, at 25, was elected to the state House—the youngest member ever. In 1988 he was elected to the state Senate, where he worked to fend off bankruptcy for Phila-delphia. In 1991, much to everyone's surprise, 2d District Congressman William Gray resigned to become head of the United Negro College Fund. Gray was a shining star in the political firmament, chairman of the Budget Committee from 1984–88, majority whip since 1989. Local ward leaders nominated Councilman Lucien Blackwell, a former longshoreman, boxer and labor union stalwart; he attended to parochial neighborhood concerns while leaders like Gray were concerned about the world beyond. Fattah ran under the Consumer Party label and state Welfare Secretary John White ran as an independent. Blackwell won the special election with 39% to 28% for Fattah and 27% for White. In 1994 Fattah ran again. Blackwell was endorsed by Mayor Ed Rendell and City Council President John Street, but relied mostly on ward pol-iticians. Fattah was endorsed by the Black Clergy of Philadelphia and Vicinity and by state Senator Hardy Williams and produced position papers on several urban issues. In this rematch Fattah won, 58%–42%.

Fattah annually is rated among the most liberal voting records in the House and he voted against Contract with America measures more often than all but one other member. He has a checklist of legislative initiatives—guaranteed Pell grants for students in poverty areas who stay in high school and maintain the necessary grades, a federal law to get states to equalize school district funding, expanded HUD lending to community development. In 1998, he won

$120 million in funding for the new High Hopes 21st Century Scholarship Initiative, which gives certificates for college scholarships to students starting as early as sixth grade; the program, which Fattah originally included in the 1998 Higher Education Act, is designed to encourage partnerships between colleges and public schools with at least 50% low-income students.

Since entering the House, Fattah has had no serious primary or general election challenge. He criticized Speaker Newt Gingrich in 1997 for dismissing as a "dead-end" gesture a resolution for a federal apology for slavery. He strongly defended President Clinton against impeachment charges, pointing to the benefits that he has brought the black community. "Like any group, African-Americans operate from self-interest," Fattah said. He suffered a setback at the start of the 106th Congress when Pennsylvania's senior Democrat John Murtha was unable to win him a seat on the Appropriations Committee. Fattah is articulate and telegenic, and could be an attractive candidate for higher office, though his liberal stands on some issues would be a handicap in a statewide race. Redistricting after 2000 is likely to create another black-majority Philadelphia seat which Fattah can win easily.

Cook's Call. *Safe.* Fattah is safely settled in this solidly Democratic district. He does have to be wary of redistricting in 2002 which is expected to alter the Philadelphia-based districts the most, though the Voting Rights Act should preserve a minority district here.

The People: Pop. 1990: 565,242; 15.8% age 65 + ; 34.7% White, 62.3% Black, 2.1% Asian, 0.3% Amer. Indian, 0.6% Other; 1.4% Hispanic Origin. Households: 30.8% married couple families; 13.2% married couple fams. w. children; 39.9% college educ.; median household income: $24,880; per capita income: $13,121; median house value: $42,800; median gross rent: $388.

1996 Presidential Vote		
Clinton (D)	173,723	(86%)
Dole (R)	20,675	(10%)
Perot (I)	5,981	(3%)

1992 Presidential Vote		
Clinton (D)	183,758	(79%)
Bush (R)	31,878	(14%)
Perot (I)	14,514	(6%)

Rep. Chaka Fattah (D)

Elected 1994; b. Nov. 21, 1956, Philadelphia; home, Philadelphia; Community Col. of Philadelphia, U. of PA, M.A. 1986, Harvard U. Kennedy Schl. of Gov., 1984.; Baptist; divorced.

Elected Office: PA House of Reps., 1982–88; PA Senate, 1988–94.

Professional Career: Asst. Dir., House of Umoja, 1977–79; City of Philadelphia, Spec. Asst. to Dir. of Housing & Community Dev., 1980, Spec. Asst. to Managing Director, 1981.

DC Office: 1205 LHOB 20515, 202-225-4001; Fax: 202-225-5392; Web site: www.house.gov/fattah.

District Offices: Philadelphia, 215-848-9386; Philadelphia, 215-387-6404.

Committees: *Education & the Workforce* (13th of 22 D): Early Childhood, Youth & Families; Postsecondary Education, Training & Life-Long Learning. *Government Reform* (10th of 19 D): Postal Service (RMM). *House Administration* (2d of 3 D). *Standards of Official Conduct* (4th of 5 D). *Joint Committee on Printing* (5th of 5 Reps.).

Group Ratings

	ADA	ACLU	AFS	LCV	CON	NTU	NFIB	COC	ACU	NTLC	CHC
1998	95	93	100	69	68	16	17	25	0	8	0
1997	100	—	88	—	49	31	—	50	0	—	—

National Journal Ratings

	1997 LIB — 1997 CONS			1998 LIB — 1998 CONS		
Economic	91%	—	7%	79%	—	0%
Social	85%	—	0%	85%	—	15%
Foreign	94%	—	6%	98%	—	0%

Key Votes of the 105th Congress

1. Clinton Budget Deal	N	5. Puerto Rico Sthood. Ref.	Y	9. Cut $ for B-2 Bombers	Y
2. Education IRAs	N	6. End Highway Set-asides	N	10. Human Rights in China	Y
3. Req. 2/3 to Raise Taxes	N	7. School Prayer Amend.	N	11. Withdraw Bosnia Troops	N
4. Fast-track Trade	N	8. Ovrd. Part. Birth Veto	N	12. End Cuban TV-Marti	Y

Election Results

1998 general	Chaka Fattah (D) 102,763	(87%)	($327,896)
	Anne Marie Mulligan (R) 16,001	(13%)	
1998 primary	Chaka Fattah (D) .... unopposed		
1996 general	Chaka Fattah (D) 168,887	(88%)	($412,478)
	Larry G. Murphy (R) 23,047	(12%)	

THIRD DISTRICT

North and east of Center City Philadelphia, stretching more than a dozen miles along the Delaware River and back along the parklands by Frankford, Tacony and Pennypacker Creeks, are most of the white residential neighborhoods of Philadelphia. They start off in the closely packed 19th Century homes of Kensington, where descendants of Irish and Italian immigrants live in inelegant frame houses and often earn less than the residents in many black neighborhoods. Farther out is Northeast Philadelphia, a more suburban area itself the size of a major city. Here, when the alley-wide streets of North and South Philadelphia and the river wards were already teeming and the Main Line suburbs were already well-settled, the workers of Philadelphia's docks, factories and Center City offices were just starting to fill up vacant land. They settled in neighborhoods like the one near Pennypack Park, where local hero Sylvester Stallone grew up. Unlike much of the city, with its high crime and struggling government, Northeast Philadelphia remains new urban territory, with more than half of its dwellings built after 1950, and still growing.

Politically the district appears to be a throwback to an earlier era, when you would expect to see ward heelers walking through the neighborhoods of Kensington and Frankford, distributing coal for the winter. Most people here are Catholic, and there are also many Jews. The houses are pleasant, but modest. Many residents are part of the hard-pressed lower middle class and are Democrats, but also are conservative on cultural issues, and there is a Republican tradition in some wards. Northeast Philadelphia voted for Mayor Frank Rizzo when he was running as a Republican in the 1980s; now it seems to have returned to its Democratic roots.

The congressman from the 3d District is Robert Borski, a Democrat first elected in 1982. He grew up in Northeast Philadelphia, and first distinguished himself as an athlete: He was captain of the Frankford High basketball and baseball teams in 1966 and became a coach after graduating from college with an athletic scholarship. Contacts made as an athlete helped him get a job as a floor manager at the Philadelphia Stock Exchange, and in 1976 he was elected to the state House of Representatives, where he served until his election to Congress. In 1982 Borski defeated Republican Charlie Dougherty, who had won in 1978 over a Democrat who had been indicted. He has won easily ever since.

Borski is a party loyalist, favorable to organized labor, with a voting record a bit to the conservative side on cultural issues. But most of all, he is concerned about Philadelphia, and about using his seat on the Transportation and Infrastructure Committee to help it. In December

1996 he served unhappily on the ethics committee, painstakingly and soberly judging the case against Speaker Newt Gingrich, at the eye of the Washington political hurricane. But his thoughts were of home: "I do need to be talking to the people in Philadelphia. I normally spend this time talking to the airport folks and the port people about what their legislative wishes are." He does work on national legislation, like his bills to ban backhauling of toxic chemicals and to ban triple-trailer trucks. He objects to Republican Superfund changes as reimbursing polluters. He sponsored an amendment, partially drafted by the National Governors' Association, to protect wetlands, and has also sponsored a brownfields law.

But Philadelphia seems to come first. On the Transportation Committee, he beat a provision in the Amtrak privatization law which would have required the local SEPTA transit authority to pay Amtrak higher fees for use of its tracks. He has superintended the Superfund toxic waste cleanup at the Metal Bank property in Tacony. His accomplishments in the 1998 highway bill included about $90 million in local improvements for I-95, a new transportation center for SEPTA and refurbishing of the Philadelphia Airport. He considers one of his greatest achievements the reversal of a base-closing commission plan to close the Aviation Supply Office in Northeast Philadelphia, which would have cost 8,000 jobs. He wants a new visitors center at Independence Park.

In 1998, he easily prevailed in his second rematch with Dougherty, who had settled in as a senior vice president in Washington with Cassidy and Associates, a large lobbying firm where he specializes in education funding. Dougherty claimed that Borski's views had shown that he had lost touch with the district, but didn't get much traction with that argument. The chief threat to Borski's tenure is redistricting. Pennsylvania stands to lose two congressional districts after the 2000 Census. Republicans will control the process if they hold onto their legislative majorities, and they will probably collapse the three Philadelphia districts into two, putting Borski and the 1st District's Bob Brady in the same district.

Cook's Call. *Safe.* Although this district is not as solidly Democratic as the other two Philadelphia districts, Borski has kept a good hold of this seat for 16 years and has beat back twice the Republican whom he defeated to win the seat in the first place. Like his Philadelphia-based neighbors in Congress, Borski's biggest concern will come from redistricting in 2002 as it is widely assumed that the city will lose one district.

The People: Pop. 1990: 565,884; 18.5% age 65 + ; 89.2% White, 4.8% Black, 3.2% Asian, 0.2% Amer. Indian, 2.6% Other; 4.5% Hispanic Origin. Households: 49.9% married couple families; 22.3% married couple fams. w. children; 28.9% college educ.; median household income: $29,157; per capita income: $13,429; median house value: $65,800; median gross rent: $388.

1996 Presidential Vote

Clinton (D)	114,680	(61%)
Dole (R)	51,781	(28%)
Perot (I)	18,878	(10%)
Others	2,870	(2%)

1992 Presidential Vote

Clinton (D)	125,078	(52%)
Bush (R)	75,388	(31%)
Perot (I)	39,582	(16%)

Rep. Robert A. Borski (D)

Elected 1982; b. Oct. 20, 1948, Philadelphia; home, Philadelphia; U. of Baltimore, B.A. 1971; Catholic; married (Karen).

Elected Office: PA House of Reps., 1976–82.

Professional Career: Asst. Coach, U. of Baltimore, 1971–72; Stockbroker, 1972–76.

DC Office: 2267 RHOB 20515, 202-225-8251; Fax: 202-225-4628; Web site: www.house.gov/borski.

District Offices: Philadelphia, 215-426-4616; Philadelphia, 215-335-3355.

Committees: *Transportation & Infrastructure* (3d of 34 D): Ground Transportation; Water Resources & Environment (RMM).

Group Ratings

	ADA	ACLU	AFS	LCV	CON	NTU	NFIB	COC	ACU	NTLC	CHC
1998	90	63	100	92	68	13	7	22	12	11	27
1997	75	—	100	—	2	15	—	30	17	—	—

National Journal Ratings

	1997 LIB	—	1997 CONS		1998 LIB	—	1998 CONS
Economic	91%	—	7%		72%	—	23%
Social	60%	—	39%		60%	—	38%
Foreign	69%	—	28%		84%	—	11%

Key Votes of the 105th Congress

1. Clinton Budget Deal	N	5. Puerto Rico Sthood. Ref.	Y	9. Cut $ for B-2 Bombers	N
2. Education IRAs	N	6. End Highway Set-asides	N	10. Human Rights in China	Y
3. Req. 2/3 to Raise Taxes	N	7. School Prayer Amend.	N	11. Withdraw Bosnia Troops	N
4. Fast-track Trade	N	8. Ovrd. Part. Birth Veto	Y	12. End Cuban TV-Marti	Y

Election Results

1998 general	Robert A. Borski (D)	66,270	(59%)	($514,639)
	Charles F. Dougherty (R)	45,390	(41%)	($226,280)
1998 primary	Robert A. Borski (D)	20,989	(87%)	
	John R. Kates (D)	3,157	(13%)	
1996 general	Robert A. Borski (D)	121,120	(69%)	($317,799)
	Joseph M. McColgan (R)	54,681	(31%)	($95,008)

FOURTH DISTRICT

For a century, one of America's great industrial zones was along the banks of the Beaver and Ohio Rivers, near where they join in westernmost Pennsylvania. This was steel country, with mills rising black and brooding from the bottomlands and filling the narrow river valleys with smoke. The sinewy sons of immigrant families worked hard in the hot mills. Looking down on riverscapes lined with piles of iron ore, limestone and coal, and littered with cranes, stocks and furnaces, families lived in small frame houses on the hillsides. Although not an environmentalist's idea of perfection, this was a land of opportunity for thousands whose lives were far worse before moving to steel country. For a few heady years, the high union wages and early retirement plans seemed to make working in the mills the way to affluence. But the industry crashed after the oil shock of 1979, when mills were closed and jobs vanished. Today, thousands of workers who long ago exhausted their unemployment benefits have given up and left the Beaver and Ohio valleys. Forty years ago, the western Pennsylvania steel country had 11 House Members; it now has six and will probably have five after the redistricting following the 2000 Census.

The congressman from the 4th District is Ron Klink, a Democrat first elected in 1992. Klink grew up in Myersdale, Pennsylvania, and has been a jack of many trades. In his 20s he was a restaurant owner; in 1978 he became a reporter and anchor for Pittsburgh's KDKA-TV. In 1992, he decided to run for the House. The incumbent, Democrat Joe Kolter, was lightly regarded and drew no fewer than three primary opponents; after years of supporting union positions, he missed a key vote on unemployment benefits and in March lost the AFL-CIO endorsement, which went to another Democrat. But Klink, from his years on the air, was much better known, and his "Ron Klink Plan for Jobs" struck a chord in an area long suffering from high unemployment. Klink won the primary with a rousing 35%, two state legislators got 22% and 13%, and the hapless Kolter 20%. Klink won the general election handily.

In the House, Klink has a liberal, pro-labor voting record on economics and has been more moderate on cultural and foreign issues. He supported the Clinton budget and tax plan (though only after Democrats dropped the Btu tax on energy consumption) but vigorously opposed NAFTA in 1993. Unlike most Democrats, he favors restrictions on abortion and proposed that no health care plan should require insurers to cover abortions. He co-sponsored the Uniform Adoption Act, to make adoption more secure. Switching to the Commerce Committee in his second term, he worked to get FDA approval of home drug-testing kits. As ranking Democrat on Commerce's Oversight and Investigations Subcommittee, once a John Dingell power base, Klink has sought to impede hearings where he thought Republicans were harassing the Clinton Administration. But Klink also has opposed the president, especially on environmental initiatives that could impact his region's heavy industry. With Democrat Rick Boucher and Republican Fred Upton, he filed legislation in 1997 to delay implementation of the EPA's new air-quality standards. He led opposition to the Kyoto agreement to control global warming, a pact that Klink said would be the first major step toward the deindustrialization of this country. And he pressed the steel industry's agenda to reduce steel imports. Klink's work to bolster the 4th District's economy also includes promoting the domestic and international growth of USAirways, whose Pittsburgh hub is nearby, and obtaining a moratorium on zinc sales from the strategic stockpile to save 700 jobs at Zinc Corporation of America's Monaca plant.

Klink won re-election handily in 1998, despite facing his best-financed opponent. Republican Mike Turzai, a former Allegheny County prosecutor and former Democrat who was elected to the Bradford Woods Borough Council, ran an aggressive campaign that included a confrontation by Turzai aides accusing Klink of having an affair with a staff member, plus a helicopter taping shots while hovering over Klink's suburban home. The latter incident created a furor that forced Turzai to apologize. Klink won by nearly 2–1 in November 1998 and in early 1999 announced that he would challenge Senator Rick Santorum in 2000. It seemed likely he would be the only candidate from western Pennsylvania facing two or three candidates from the Philadelphia area; in the 1998 Democratic Senate primary, 44% of the votes were cast in the Pittsburgh region. Klink's pro-life, anti-gun control positions would probably help in the heavily blue-collar Democratic primary and would neutralize Santorum's advantage on those issues. With Klink not running, Republicans have a chance of carrying this district; one possible Republican is suburban Pittsburgh state Senator Melissa Hart.

Cook's Call. *Competitive.* Klink's announcement that he will challenge Senator Rick Santorum puts Democrats in the unenviable position of defending this Democratic leaning, but rather marginal Western Pennsylvania district. Plus, Republicans argue that they have a top-notch potential nominee in state Senator Melissa Hart. The underlying blue-collar base here does help Democrats, but there is some concern that this district may be redrawn in 2002 (when Pennsylvania is scheduled to lose two seats) to the detriment of Democrats.

The People: Pop. 1990: 565,809; 32.7% rural; 17% age 65 +; 96.3% White, 3.2% Black, 0.3% Asian, 0.1% Amer. Indian, 0.1% Other; 0.4% Hispanic Origin. Households: 61.6% married couple families; 27.1% married couple fams. w. children; 35.8% college educ.; median household income: $26,792; per capita income: $12,684; median house value: $55,700; median gross rent: $244.

1996 Presidential Vote			1992 Presidential Vote		
Clinton (D)	107,017	(47%)	Clinton (D)	118,701	(48%)
Dole (R)	96,511	(42%)	Bush (R)	76,291	(31%)
Perot (I)	23,375	(10%)	Perot (I)	50,654	(21%)

Rep. Ron Klink (D)

Elected 1992; b. Sept. 23, 1951, Canton, OH; home, Murrysville; United Church of Christ; married (Linda).

Professional Career: Businessman; Restaurant owner; Reporter & Anchor, KDKA-TV, Pittsburgh, 1978–92.

DC Office: 2448 RHOB 20515, 202-225-2565; Fax: 202-226-2274; Web site: www.house.gov/klink.

District Offices: Beaver, 724-728-3005; Cranberry Township, 724-772-6080; Lower Burrell, 724-335-4518; N. Huntingdon, 724-864-8681; New Castle, 724-654-9036.

Committees: *Commerce* (13th of 24 D): Energy & Power; Oversight & Investigations (RMM); Telecommunications, Trade & Consumer Protection.

Group Ratings

	ADA	ACLU	AFS	LCV	CON	NTU	NFIB	COC	ACU	NTLC	CHC
1998	80	63	100	69	91	20	29	22	13	18	36
1997	65	—	88	—	56	25	—	33	32	—	—

National Journal Ratings

	1997 LIB — 1997 CONS			1998 LIB — 1998 CONS		
Economic	66%	—	34%	66%	—	33%
Social	58%	—	40%	56%	—	43%
Foreign	76%	—	22%	61%	—	37%

Key Votes of the 105th Congress

1. Clinton Budget Deal	N	5. Puerto Rico Sthood. Ref.	Y	9. Cut $ for B-2 Bombers	Y
2. Education IRAs	N	6. End Highway Set-asides	N	10. Human Rights in China	Y
3. Req. 2/3 to Raise Taxes	N	7. School Prayer Amend.	N	11. Withdraw Bosnia Troops	N
4. Fast-track Trade	N	8. Ovrd. Part. Birth Veto	Y	12. End Cuban TV-Marti	Y

Election Results

1998 general	Ron Klink (D)	103,763	(64%)	($861,377)
	Mike Turzai (R)	58,485	(36%)	($555,368)
1998 primary	Ron Klink (D)	unopposed		
1996 general	Ron Klink (D)	142,621	(64%)	($506,560)
	Paul T. Adametz (R)	79,448	(36%)	($17,028)

FIFTH DISTRICT

North central Pennsylvania—isolated from the rest of the country by chains of mountains, off the main east-west rail and highway lines until the 1970s—is one of those empty spaces that make even the northeastern states seem lightly populated to someone used to the densely packed terrain of Western Europe or East Asia. In narrow valleys, pressed tightly by mountains and fast-flowing rivers, connected by roads that switch back and wind precariously over mountains, there are few population concentrations. The largest is in the Nittany Valley, home of Pennsylvania State University, long known for its powerful football teams coached by Joe Paterno. To the west are Titusville, where Colonel Edwin Drake sank the first successful oil well in 1859, and Oil City, headquarters of Quaker State Oil from 1931 until it left for Texas in 1995. To the east, near the Susquehanna River, is Lewisburg, home of Bucknell University and the federal penitentiary. The solidly built courthouses and banks in the center of each county seat testify to the long history of hard work and thrift in this part of the country. Yet today, even with the main east-west truck line, Interstate 80, it is a low-wage area.

The 5th Congressional District includes a very wide swath of north central Pennsylvania, and has somewhat irregular boundaries. Its largest city is State College. The small towns include Punxsutawney, home of legendary groundhog Phil, who predicts the arrival of spring based on whether he sees his shadow on Groundhog Day each year. The political heritage here is Republican, with few exceptions, from the Civil War through the New Deal and Great Society, in Ronald Reagan's 1980s and Bill Clinton's 1990s.

The congressman from the 5th District is John Peterson, a Republican elected in 1996. Peterson grew up in Titusville, the son of a steelworker; he went to Penn State, served in the Army as a cook, then opened a grocery store that eventually became Peterson's Golden Dawn Supermarket chain. He served on the Pleasantville Borough Council for eight years, then in 1977, at 39, was elected to the state House. In 1984 he was elected to the state Senate, where he chaired the Public Health and Welfare Committee, concentrating on rural health issues, and working on Pennsylvania's welfare reform. Then in 1996 Congressman Bill Clinger announced his retirement after 18 years in the House. Peterson was an obvious candidate; his state Senate district included eight of the 5th's 17 counties. Three other Republicans ran. The one who attracted the most attention was Bob Shuster, the 31-year-old son of 9th District Congressman Bud Shuster, chairman of the Transportation and Infrastructure Committee and an unashamed builder of roads in his home district. "What a one-two punch we could be for central Pennsylvania," Bud Shuster said on announcement day, and his son had controversial fundraising help from Ann Eppard, a lobbyist and former Shuster aide who was later indicted on charges of fraud. But Peterson's chief competition was Daniel Gordeuk, a Centre County surgeon with strong local roots. Peterson won with 38%, to 28% for Gordeuk, and 18% for Shuster. In the general, Peterson attacked the nominee, state Representative Ruth Rudy as "an old-fashioned liberal" and touted his work in the legislature, his support for a "flatter tax" and his opposition to abortion and gun control. Peterson won 60%–40%.

In his first term, Peterson usually was a Republican loyalist, helping to enact renewal of higher education and vocational education measures. He favors 12-year term limits and tax cuts. He emerged as a critic of environmentalists, complaining about their "push for world government" in the Kyoto treaty and opposing a proposed moratorium on roadbuilding in national forests. Peterson was rewarded with an Appropriations Committee seat in the 106th Congress, beating at least two other Pennsylvania Republicans for the position. He had no Democratic opponent in November 1998.

Cook's Call. *Safe.* Though not as heavily Republican as other parts of the state, the 5th District still has a serious Republican lean to it. While only a sophomore, Peterson is already well-entrenched in this district, garnering the second highest winning percentage of the delegation (not including, of course, unopposed members).

The People: Pop. 1990: 565,736; 66% rural; 14.6% age 65 + ; 97.7% White, 1% Black, 1% Asian, 0.2% Amer. Indian, 0.2% Other; 0.6% Hispanic Origin. Households: 59.5% married couple families; 27.6% married couple fams. w. children; 31.3% college educ.; median household income: $23,934; per capita income: $10,946; median house value: $47,900; median gross rent: $251.

1996 Presidential Vote

Dole (R)	91,619	(46%)
Clinton (D)	80,003	(40%)
Perot (I)	25,687	(13%)

1992 Presidential Vote

Bush (R)	89,385	(41%)
Clinton (D)	78,057	(36%)
Perot (I)	48,100	(22%)

Rep. John E. Peterson (R)

Elected 1996; b. Dec. 25, 1938, Titusville; home, Pleasantville; PA St. U., 1974–76; Methodist; married (Sandy).

Military Career: Army, 1958–64.

Elected Office: Pleasantville Borough Cncl., 1969–77; PA House of Reps., 1977–84; PA Senate, 1984–96.

Professional Career: Owner, Peterson's Golden Dawn Food Market, 1958–84.

DC Office: 307 CHOB 20515, 202-225-5121; Fax: 202-225-5796; Web site: www.house.gov/johnpeterson.

District Offices: State College, 814-238-1776; Titusville, 814-827-3985; Warren, 814-726-3910.

Committees: *Appropriations* (34th of 34 R): Interior; The Legislative Branch; Treasury, Postal Service & General Government. *Resources* (19th of 28 R): Forests & Forest Health.

Group Ratings

	ADA	ACLU	AFS	LCV	CON	NTU	NFIB	COC	ACU	NTLC	CHC
1998	0	6	0	0	13	51	100	100	96	97	100
1997	5	—	13	—	29	53	—	100	96	—	—

National Journal Ratings

	1997 LIB — 1997 CONS			1998 LIB — 1998 CONS		
Economic	10%	—	86%	0%	—	88%
Social	30%	—	64%	29%	—	71%
Foreign	0%	—	88%	0%	—	93%

Key Votes of the 105th Congress

1. Clinton Budget Deal	Y	5. Puerto Rico Sthood. Ref.	Y	9. Cut $ for B-2 Bombers	N
2. Education IRAs	Y	6. End Highway Set-asides	Y	10. Human Rights in China	N
3. Req. 2/3 to Raise Taxes	Y	7. School Prayer Amend.	Y	11. Withdraw Bosnia Troops	Y
4. Fast-track Trade	Y	8. Ovrd. Part. Birth Veto	Y	12. End Cuban TV-Marti	N

Election Results

1998 general	John E. Peterson (R)	99,502	(85%)	($245,311)
	William M. Belitskus (Green)	17,734	(15%)	
1998 primary	John E. Peterson (R)	unopposed		
1996 general	John E. Peterson (R)	116,303	(60%)	($858,637)
	Ruth C. Rudy (D)	76,627	(40%)	($446,613)

SIXTH DISTRICT

The gentle hills of southeastern Pennsylvania, settled in the 18th Century by Quaker townsmen, Welsh farmers, German peasants, and members of pietistic sects who became known as the Pennsylvania Dutch, were America's first polyglot interior. A diverse lot looking for tolerance in the area above Philadelphia and the Delaware River and below the first chains of the Appalachians, they found a land that yielded riches, first in crops, then in ironworking and other industry. This was the Pennsylvania John Updike described in his 1960 novel *Rabbit, Run* and its sequels. In time this civilization poured over the mountain chains, where the farmers were rough-hewn and more violence-prone, and where the towns existed solely to mine rich veins of anthracite and bituminous coal, the primary energy source of late 19th and early 20th Century America. These mountain towns were less orderly, filled with tough-talking miners and factory workers who stayed menacingly in the background unless a character stumbled into the wrong roadhouse at night or the wrong diner at dawn: This was the Pennsylvania John O'Hara grew up in and described in his 1930s and 1940s novels and stories.

These two areas were linked by the Reading Railroad in 1842 and became one of America's prime industrial sites for a century after. The anthracite country around Pottsville, nestled amid mountains, has never rebounded from the switch from coal to oil and natural gas for home heating: Schuylkill County around Pottsville had 228,000 people in 1940 and 148,000 in 1998. But Reading has come back, starting in 1970, when a company called Vanity Fair began selling seconds and overruns of stockings and lingerie at wholesale prices in what had been the Berkshire Knitting Mills; this was the first of the factory outlets. Reading was home to more than 300 outlets by the late-1990s, selling deeply-discounted goods on the polished wood floors of converted brick mills, bringing in more than half a billion dollars a year, generating thousands of jobs and spawning 2,200 motel and hotel rooms.

The 6th Congressional District includes Berks and Schuylkill Counties centered on Reading and Pottsville, plus an almost unconnected sliver of Northumberland County, an industrial area between mountains and the upper Susquehanna River. It is politically divided between the rough mining tradition of the anthracite country and the quietism of the Pennsylvania Dutch, between Democratic Schuylkill County and Republican Berks County.

The congressman from the 6th District is Tim Holden, a Democrat first elected in 1992. Holden comes from a political family from the coal mining hamlet of St. Clair; his great-grandfather was a coal miner who founded the forerunner to the United Mine Workers, and his father served four terms as Schuylkill County commissioner. Holden gained fame as a local football player, although tuberculosis cut short his college career. In 1985, at age 28, after selling insurance and real estate for five years, he was elected Schuylkill County sheriff, and re-elected with 75%. Holden's opponent in the 1992 Congressional race was John Jones III, a lawyer who ran a family business operating golf courses: two characters out of Updike and O'Hara. Jones called Holden "clueless" and called for term limits and congressional salary cuts; Holden said he represented "the hardworking men and women" of the district. In culturally conservative but economically polarized Schuylkill County, this appeal sold, and Holden won 52%–48%.

Holden has a moderate voting record: He has consistently been near the middle of the House on economic, cultural and foreign issues. He is one of the centrist Blue Dog Democrats. "The problems our country is facing need to be solved in a bipartisan manner," he says. "There's about 70 liberals and 70 ultraconservatives still in the House. They need to be left behind." He opposed NAFTA and the Clinton health care plan, but backed welfare reform and health care portability. He opposes any tax cut or spending increase from the budget surplus until the Treasury fully reimburses the social security trust fund. On the Agriculture Committee, Holden looks after dairy programs; he wants the government to buy more cheese, increase the flow of dairy products in international food aid and resume a dairy export subsidy program. He seeks new roads in Schuylkill County and wants to increase black lung benefits for miners. Most of all, he works the district hard, talking issues and solving constituents' problems. As the Pottsville *Republican & Evening Herald* wrote, "It would be hard to imagine a legislator more precisely in tune with his county on virtually any and every issue that has come before Congress in the past four years."

Although the district continues to vote Republican for president and statewide offices,

Holden's re-election victory margin has increased steadily since his first election; he won with 61% in 1998.

Cook's Call. *Safe.* This conservative district is not friendly Democratic territory. But Holden's deep local roots and conservative voting record make him a difficult target for Republicans. Once this seat opens up, (or is reshaped in 2002 redistricting), this will be a tough seat for Democrats to keep.

The People: Pop. 1990: 565,923; 43.8% rural; 17.6% age 65 + ; 95.3% White, 2.4% Black, 0.6% Asian, 0.1% Amer. Indian, 1.6% Other; 3.1% Hispanic Origin. Households: 58% married couple families; 25.4% married couple fams. w. children; 27.5% college educ.; median household income: $28,766; per capita income: $13,349; median house value: $66,500; median gross rent: $294.

1996 Presidential Vote

Dole (R)	89,695	(45%)
Clinton (D)	83,779	(42%)
Perot (I)	25,139	(13%)

1992 Presidential Vote

Bush (R)	90,140	(41%)
Clinton (D)	78,776	(36%)
Perot (I)	50,333	(23%)

Rep. Tim Holden (D)

Elected 1992; b. Mar. 5, 1957, Pottsville; home, St. Clair; U. of Richmond, 1976–78, Bloomsburg St. U., B.A. 1980; Catholic; married (Gwen).

Elected Office: Schuylkill Cnty. Sheriff, 1985–92.

Professional Career: Real estate agent; Insurance broker, Holden Insurance Agency, 1980–85; Probation Officer, 1980–85.

DC Office: 1421 LHOB 20515, 202-225-5546; Fax: 202-226-0996; Web site: www.house.gov/holden.

District Offices: Pottsville, 570-622-4212; Reading, 610-371-9931; Sunbury, 570-988-1902.

Committees: *Agriculture* (10th of 24 D): General Farm Commodities, Resource Conservation & Credit; Livestock & Horticulture. *Transportation & Infrastructure* (28th of 34 D): Aviation; Ground Transportation.

Group Ratings

	ADA	ACLU	AFS	LCV	CON	NTU	NFIB	COC	ACU	NTLC	CHC
1998	70	31	100	62	80	20	36	56	24	27	55
1997	50	—	71	—	62	29	—	70	54	—	—

National Journal Ratings

	1997 LIB — 1997 CONS			1998 LIB — 1998 CONS		
Economic	58%	—	42%	61%	—	37%
Social	50%	—	48%	51%	—	48%
Foreign	54%	—	45%	61%	—	37%

Key Votes of the 105th Congress

1. Clinton Budget Deal	N	5. Puerto Rico Sthood. Ref.	Y	9. Cut $ for B-2 Bombers	N
2. Education IRAs	N	6. End Highway Set-asides	N	10. Human Rights in China	Y
3. Req. 2/3 to Raise Taxes	N	7. School Prayer Amend.	N	11. Withdraw Bosnia Troops	N
4. Fast-track Trade	N	8. Ovrd. Part. Birth Veto	Y	12. End Cuban TV-Marti	Y

Election Results

1998 general	Tim Holden (D) 85,374	(61%)	($602,163)	
	John Meckley (R) 54,579	(39%)	($175,568)	
1998 primary	Tim Holden (D) .... unopposed			
1996 general	Tim Holden (D) 115,193	(59%)	($609,346)	
	Christian Y. Leinbach (R) 80,061	(41%)	($419,013)	

SEVENTH DISTRICT

The close-in suburbs of the great eastern cities are homes to some of the most curious and long-lasting political machines in America. They are Republican; they conduct business in the accents of ordinary people, ethnic as well as WASP; they have a tolerance for patronage, and for what city reform liberals would call corruption, that is sharply at odds with their embodiment of middle-class morality; they are old, going back to the days when political machines were as much a part of the urban landscape as trolley lines or overhead electrical wires; and, unlike most big-city Democratic machines, they are still in business. One such machine is the War Board of Pennsylvania's Delaware County. This is a diverse area, mostly but not entirely white, predominantly Catholic where it was predominantly Protestant two generations ago. Its housing is aging but well-maintained; its population is above average in income but differs from the affluent Main Line commuter towns. People here treasure traditional cultural values but also feel pinched by family obligations and worry about retirement; they have deep roots in greater Philadelphia, but also deep fears about crime in nearby city neighborhoods.

The 7th Congressional District includes almost all of Delaware County, except for a few towns appended to Philadelphia districts, and extends north to include Main Line suburbs and King of Prussia, the edge city where the Schuylkill Expressway intersects the Pennsylvania Turnpike. This remains a solidly Republican district in most elections, although it gave a narrow margin to Bill Clinton in 1996.

The congressman from the 7th is Curt Weldon, a Republican backed by the War Board and with anything but an aristocratic pedigree. A teacher and personnel trainer, he first came to public attention as mayor of Marcus Hook, Pennsylvania's southernmost town on the Delaware River, the home of oil tank farms and a rusty-looking steel mill. Weldon was elected to the county council, ran for the House in 1984 against liberal Democrat Bob Edgar (who got to Congress when the War Board split 10 years earlier), lost by 412 votes, then ran successfully in 1986 when Edgar ran unsuccessfully for the Senate.

Weldon is a local congressman first: attending every Eagle Scout induction in the district, seeking out work for the closed Philadelphia Navy Yard, and promoting the V-22 Osprey tilt-rotor aircraft—components of it are made at Boeing's helicopter plant in nearby Ridley Park. But he also works hard on national issues. As chairman of the Armed Services Subcommittee on Military Research and Development, he favors missile defense and attacked the Clinton Administration for slowing down its development by fudging intelligence estimates and ignoring congressional dictates. A Russian studies major in college, he has initiated a U.S. Congress-Duma Study Group and meets regularly with senior Russian officials, both in Moscow and Washington; he wants to do the same with China's People's Congress. But Weldon has remained vigilant about problems in each of those nations. He worries that crime, corruption and internal disintegration are so rampant in Russia that nuclear-weapons theft "seems entirely plausible." He is concerned about ocean dumping, especially dumping of nuclear waste by Russia. And he harshly criticized reports of the Clinton Administration's approval of export licenses for commercial satellite sales to China that likely revealed vital weapons technology. He also has criticized the Clinton Administration for weakening national defense by over-extending military forces and equipment with a record number of deployments. In April 1999 he led an 11-member congressional delegation to Vienna to discuss a possible peace plan for

Kosovo with Russian officials and a key ally of Yugoslav President Slobodan Milosevic, but canceled plans to visit Serbia at the Clinton Administration's request; he claimed his efforts helped lead to the release of three U.S. POWs.

Weldon is usually a partisan Republican but not always a free-market enthusiast; like Pennsylvanian Republicans of yore, he supports trade restrictions and voted against NAFTA and fast-track legislation. Although he has supported unions on some issues, including family-leave legislation, he is a co-sponsor of Davis-Bacon reform and favors the flextime law which would let workers take compensatory time off rather than overtime pay. Nor is he as thorough a budget-cutter as some Republicans. In the 104th Congress, he urged Speaker Newt Gingrich to back $3.5 billion in education block grants to the states, and they were included in the final budget deal. He strongly backs the partial-birth abortion ban. As a former volunteer fireman, he founded the Congressional Fire Services Caucus (Weldon once put out a fire in Speaker Jim Wright's office). Although he voted for Clinton's impeachment, he said that he preferred a Senate censure.

Weldon has been re-elected by robust margins—72%–28% against a little-known challenger in 1998. His one moment of political peril came when redistricting put him and 18-year veteran Richard Schulze in the same district in 1992, but Schulze retired.

Cook's Call. *Safe.* While this suburban district is not as conservative or Republican as other parts of the state, it still has a healthy Republican lean to it. Weldon has won easily here for 12 years and is about as safe as can be.

The People: Pop. 1990: 565,815; 4.7% rural; 15.8% age 65 + ; 93.9% White, 3.8% Black, 2% Asian, 0.1% Amer. Indian, 0.3% Other; 1% Hispanic Origin. Households: 58.6% married couple families; 26% married couple fams. w. children; 52.7% college educ.; median household income: $41,710; per capita income: $20,175; median house value: $134,500; median gross rent: $491.

1996 Presidential Vote

Clinton (D)	116,654	(45%)
Dole (R)	112,429	(44%)
Perot (I)	23,647	(9%)
Others	4,338	(2%)

1992 Presidential Vote

Bush (R)	124,751	(43%)
Clinton (D)	111,511	(39%)
Perot (I)	49,798	(17%)

Rep. Curt Weldon (R)

Elected 1986; b. July 22, 1947, Marcus Hook; home, Aston; West Chester St. Col., B.A. 1969; Protestant; married (Mary).

Elected Office: Marcus Hook Mayor, 1977–82; Delaware Cnty. Cncl., 1982–86, Chmn. 1985–86.

Professional Career: Elem. schl. teacher & Vice principal, 1969–76; Dir., Training & Manpower Devel., CIGNA Corp., 1976–81.

DC Office: 2452 RHOB 20515, 202-225-2011; Fax: 202-225-8137; Web site: www.house.gov/curtweldon.

District Offices: Paoli, 610-640-9064; Upper Darby, 610-259-0700.

Committees: *Armed Services* (7th of 32 R): Military Readiness; Military Research & Development (Chmn.); Special Oversight Panel on the Merchant Marine. *Science* (5th of 25 R): Energy & Environment; Technology.

Group Ratings

	ADA	ACLU	AFS	LCV	CON	NTU	NFIB	COC	ACU	NTLC	CHC
1998	25	0	44	69	35	51	93	78	60	66	92
1997	30	—	25	—	58	47	—	89	60	—	—

National Journal Ratings

	1997 LIB	—	1997 CONS		1998 LIB	—	1998 CONS
Economic	50%	—	50%		45%	—	55%
Social	30%	—	64%		36%	—	63%
Foreign	46%	—	53%		34%	—	62%

Key Votes of the 105th Congress

1. Clinton Budget Deal	Y	5. Puerto Rico Sthood. Ref.	N	9. Cut $ for B-2 Bombers	Y
2. Education IRAs	Y	6. End Highway Set-asides	Y	10. Human Rights in China	N
3. Req. 2/3 to Raise Taxes	Y	7. School Prayer Amend.	Y	11. Withdraw Bosnia Troops	Y
4. Fast-track Trade	N	8. Ovrd. Part. Birth Veto	Y	12. End Cuban TV-Marti	N

Election Results

1998 general	Curt Weldon (R)	119,491	(72%)	($493,502)
	Martin J. D'Urso (D)	46,920	(28%)	($6,677)
1998 primary	Curt Weldon (R)	unopposed		
1996 general	Curt Weldon (R)	165,087	(67%)	($362,252)
	John F. Innelli (D)	79,875	(32%)	($50,252)

EIGHTH DISTRICT

One of William Penn's three original settlements, Bucks County had a split personality from the start. It was a paradise of bucolic hills and creeks running into the Delaware River and, after Penn's secretary James Logan built the Durham Furnace iron works in 1727, one of the nation's major industrial sites. In the 1920s, Bucks County's well-settled farmland, old field-stone houses and covered bridges in its northern parts captured the imagination of writers and artists, attracting the New York theatrical crowd—Oscar Hammerstein, Moss Hart, Dorothy Parker, S. J. Perelman. After World War II, its location between Philadelphia and industrial Trenton, New Jersey, brought industrial Bucks to the forefront. The ocean-navigable Delaware River and several rail lines resulted in huge new developments: U.S. Steel's Fairless Works, one of the few big postwar steel plants, down by the river, and the Levitt organization's second Levittown, in what had been farmland and swamp between U.S. 13 and U.S. 1. But with the steel mill closed, Bucks County's economy now depends more on modern technologies: the biggest new operation here came when Lockheed Martin bought 52 acres from Holy Name College in Newtown and built a communications center with 1,200 jobs in 1997.

Bucks County's political tradition was heavily Republican and protectionist; more recently it has been marginally Republican and environmentalist. This was the home of Senator Joseph Grundy, longtime head of the Pennsylvania Manufacturers Association, who opposed the 1930 Smoot-Hawley tariff as not protectionist enough. Development in Bucks came after the New Deal, unlike other suburban Philadelphia counties where most blue-collar immigration occurred years earlier, when county political organizations were ready to enroll new residents in their party. So Lower Bucks, around the Fairless Works and Levittown, with its tightly-packed homes filled with blue collar workers, became Democratic. And Upper Bucks, faster-growing and still attracting trendy New Yorkers, is Republican but environment-conscious.

The 8th Congressional District includes all of Bucks County plus Horsham Township in Montgomery County. One of the few districts in the country with boundaries almost entirely unchanged for the last two decades, it was marginal in congressional elections between 1976 and 1992, and narrowly voted for Bill Clinton in 1992 and 1996. But it has gone back to its Republican roots in House races.

The congressman from the 8th is Jim Greenwood, a Republican elected in 1992. Greenwood grew up in Newtown, on the margin between Lower Bucks and Upper Bucks. After college he worked for a state legislator, then was a social worker in Langhorne. He was elected to the state House in 1980 and the state Senate in 1986. In 1992 he ran against Peter Kostmayer, an environment-minded, defense-cutting liberal, who first won the seat in 1976, lost it in 1980 but won it back in 1982, by spotlighting environmental issues at home and raising large sums nationally from admirers of his leftish foreign and environmental stands. But Kostmayer had 50 overdrafts on the House bank and other financial problems, and Greenwood won 52%–46%.

In the House, Greenwood's voting record has been conservative on economic issues and moderate-to-liberal on cultural issues. He has worked closely with Republican leaders and has headed the moderate Tuesday Group's representative at Republican leadership meetings; in August 1997 Speaker Newt Gingrich appointed him to head the House Republican long-term planning team after Bill Paxon resigned the post following a botched "coup attempt" against Gingrich. When Dennis Hastert prepared to take over as speaker in 1999, Greenwood sought assurances that moderates would have a voice in the leadership. Unlike most of the leadership's Southern conservatives, Greenwood supported the 1994 crime bill and was one of 24 Republicans to oppose increased spending for missile defense. He sought a bipartisan health care alternative, in vain. One of his big causes has been to maintain funding of international family planning; he prevailed in the House in February 1997, insisting the issue wasn't abortion. "The whole planet is too fragile to support a runaway population," he said. Domestically, he wants to ensure that all private health insurance cover contraceptives. He has been among the handful of House Republicans opposing the ban on partial-birth abortions.

Greenwood is an active legislator on an array of consumer issues. He worked with Commerce Chairman Thomas Bliley on legislation enacted in 1997 to speed up FDA approval of drugs. He wants to give state and local governments power to control the disposal of out-of-state solid waste, and in March 1999 was lead sponsor of a bill that would allow states to freeze trash imports to 1993 levels. He is dismayed that Superfund's liability clauses make brownfield sites in older cities unmarketable and has held hearings on how this could be changed. On another Commerce issue, he helped to write legislation restricting Internet pornography's availability to kids. He wants an I-95 southbound exit at Bristol and an interchange between I-95 and the Pennsylvania Turnpike (astonishingly, there isn't one).

Greenwood's political formula seems to suit the 8th District well. He has been re-elected comfortably. His bigger problem may be conservative Republicans: In both 1996 and 1998 he had competitive primary challenges, and won 60%–40% and 67%–33%. On impeachment, he was undecided until nearly the vote and displayed his balancing act by voting for House charges but urging Senate Majority Leader Trent Lott to quickly end the trial with a bipartisan rebuke of Clinton. A largely party-line vote in the Senate would leave the nation "confused as to why we had gone through all of this for nothing," Greenwood said after the House vote. He has said he might be interested in running for the Senate if Arlen Specter retires in 2004.

Cook's Call. *Safe.* Though this district is quite competitive on the national level, Jim Greenwood is difficult to beat. His moderate voting record, especially on social issues, mirrors this district and has insulated him from tough challenges. Once this seat opens however, this district could be quite competitive.

The People: Pop. 1990: 565,820; 18.2% rural; 11.2% age 65 +; 95% White, 2.8% Black, 1.5% Asian, 0.1% Amer. Indian, 0.5% Other; 1.5% Hispanic Origin. Households: 65% married couple families; 32.6% married couple fams. w. children; 49.1% college educ.; median household income: $43,483; per capita income: $18,374; median house value: $140,700; median gross rent: $527.

1996 Presidential Vote			1992 Presidential Vote		
Clinton (D)	107,500	(45%)	Clinton (D)	101,630	(39%)
Dole (R)	99,458	(42%)	Bush (R)	99,269	(38%)
Perot (I)	25,570	(11%)	Perot (I)	56,261	(22%)
Others	4,771	(2%)			

Rep. Jim Greenwood (R)

Elected 1992; b. May 4, 1951, Philadelphia; home, Erwinna; Dickinson Col., B.A. 1973; Protestant; married (Christina).

Elected Office: PA House of Reps., 1980–86; PA Senate, 1986–93.

Professional Career: Legis. Asst., PA Rep. John Renninger, 1972–76; Social worker, Woods Schools, 1974–76; Caseworker, Bucks Cnty. Children & Youth Social Svc. Agency, 1977–80.

DC Office: 2436 RHOB 20515, 202-225-4276; Fax: 202-225-9511; Web site: www.house.gov/greenwood.

District Offices: Doylestown, 215-348-7511; Langhorne, 215-752-7711.

Committees: *Commerce* (9th of 29 R): Finance & Hazardous Materials; Health and Environment. *Education & the Workforce* (12th of 27 R): Early Childhood, Youth & Families; Postsecondary Education, Training & Life-Long Learning.

Group Ratings

	ADA	ACLU	AFS	LCV	CON	NTU	NFIB	COC	ACU	NTLC	CHC
1998	25	53	22	69	26	47	100	94	48	58	50
1997	55	—	13	—	62	49	—	90	50	—	—

National Journal Ratings

	1997 LIB — 1997 CONS		1998 LIB — 1998 CONS	
Economic	40%	60%	42%	57%
Social	61%	39%	67%	33%
Foreign	49%	51%	47%	51%

Key Votes of the 105th Congress

1. Clinton Budget Deal	Y	5. Puerto Rico Sthood. Ref.	N	9. Cut $ for B-2 Bombers	Y
2. Education IRAs	Y	6. End Highway Set-asides	Y	10. Human Rights in China	N
3. Req. 2/3 to Raise Taxes	Y	7. School Prayer Amend.	N	11. Withdraw Bosnia Troops	Y
4. Fast-track Trade	Y	8. Ovrd. Part. Birth Veto	N	12. End Cuban TV-Marti	N

Election Results

1998 general	Jim Greenwood (R)	93,697	(63%)	($915,287)
	Bill Tuthill (D)	48,320	(33%)	($22,681)
	Others	6,183	(4%)	
1998 primary	Jim Greenwood (R)	21,347	(67%)	
	Joseph P. Schiaffino (R)	10,305	(33%)	
1996 general	Jim Greenwood (R)	133,749	(59%)	($614,221)
	John P. Murray (D)	79,856	(35%)	($67,321)
	Others	12,717	(6%)	

NINTH DISTRICT

Like a series of vertebrae through central Pennsylvania, the Appalachian mountain chain has been a formidable barrier throughout most of the state's history. Up close the mountains look tantalizingly low: you imagine that you could hike over them in an hour or so. But they are much more daunting than they seem. The colonials and British regulars (led by General Braddock to defeat near Pittsburgh in 1754) found it hard going, despite guidance from George Washington; 19th Century pioneers in Conestoga wagons found it not much easier, for there are few gaps in the ridges and, unless you build a tunnel, you have to climb over the top.

During the 18th Century, the mountains provided Quaker Pennsylvania with a rampart against Indian attacks and allowed the commonwealth to become the richest and most populous of the colonies. But in the 19th Century, when people wanted to open up and trade with the vast interior, the mountains proved to be a barrier, and at first people traveled via New York's Erie Canal and New York Central Railroad instead. It took the aggressive capitalists who built the Pennsylvania Railroad to get trains over these ridges, and a nation facing war in 1940 to build the first highway, the Pennsylvania Turnpike, that could dependably get trucks over them. Today, the old towns look much as they did 60 years ago; the farmhouses and red barns still sit on rolling hills in the shadow of the ridges, seemingly isolated and out of touch with the pulsing rhythms of 1990s America.

Pennsylvania's 9th Congressional District lies wholly within these mountains. This part of the Alleghenies (the term is often used interchangeably with Appalachians in Pennsylvania) was settled by poor Scottish and Ulster Irish farmers just after the Revolutionary War. They were fiercely independent and proud, as the Whiskey Rebellion demonstrated—corn was not an article of commerce out here unless distilled into easily portable, if not very potable, alcohol. The settlers worked their hardscrabble farms and built little towns. Most of the 9th is not coal country and was thus spared the boom-bust cycles of northeastern Pennsylvania and West Virginia. This was an important area for the Pennsylvania Railroad, however. Near Altoona was the railroad's famous Horseshoe Curve, and in Altoona the nation's largest car yards were built. As rail transportation became less important and the prosperous Pennsylvania Railroad became the bankrupt Penn Central, Altoona's population fell from 82,000 in 1930 to 52,000 in 1990; it is 99% white, the highest percentage of any metro area. This part of Pennsylvania has been solidly Republican since 1860 and has not come close to electing a Democrat to Congress for decades.

The congressman from the 9th District is Bud Shuster, a Republican first elected in 1972 and now chairman of the House Transportation and Infrastructure Committee. Shuster grew up in western Pennsylvania, made a fortune building a computer business, then settled in the southern Pennsylvania mountains. He became interested in local affairs, ran for Congress and beat the favorite, a local state senator, in the 1972 Republican primary. In the 1970s, Shuster was a hard-driving partisan and conservative firebrand, the House's most vociferous opponent of the automobile air bag, and chairman of the Republican Policy Committee until 1980. Then he ran for minority whip against Trent Lott and lost. He abruptly shifted course and spent most of his time on Public Works, as the committee was then called, working to craft bipartisan highway and water project bills with national scope—and with plenty of pork for the 9th District. In the 1990s he has had a solidly conservative voting record but has concentrated on committee work. Shuster has obviously taken a long journey from market conservatism, although his work is arguably in line with the 19th Century Republican tradition of subsidizing canals and railroads and the World War II subsidies for the Pennsylvania Turnpike—transportation arteries that made most commerce possible in these mountains. Like Robert Byrd in West Virginia, Shuster already has plenty of local monuments in central Pennsylvania, from the 53-mile interstate christened the Bud Shuster Highway by Democratic Governor Bob Casey that winds along hills from the turnpike through Altoona and on to State College, to the nation's first federally funded bus testing center, in Blair County.

Shuster is not just a generous local benefactor but a serious national policymaker. Even before he was chairman, he was instrumental in passing the 1991 Intermodal Surface Transportation Efficiency Act (ISTEA), the revolutionary bill giving states much more leeway in transportation projects, in deregulating interstate trucking and abolishing the Interstate Commerce Commission. To his work Shuster brings energy and efficiency: "I'm a very competitive guy," he said. "It gets your adrenaline pumping." He is not afraid to stand up for his views, even at the risk of alienating other powerful lawmakers. "Bud just puts his head down and charges forward," said Jim Oberstar, the senior Democrat on the Transportation Committee.

Shuster was the dominant force in enacting in 1998 the Transportation Efficiency Act for the 21st Century (TEA-21), arguably the most important accomplishment of the 105th Congress. Although he clashed with many of the House's most powerful chairmen—including Bill Archer of Ways and Means, Bob Livingston of Appropriations, and John Kasich of Budget—he achieved virtually all of his goals. Shuster forced Republican leaders to abandon the spending limits in the balanced-budget deal that they reached with President Clinton in 1997. "He is legendary for his pugnacious way of protecting funding for transportation programs," *National Journal* wrote. In crafting the formula for divvying up the funds across the country, he rewarded allies—especially on his 75-member committee, the largest in House history—and punished opponents. Members who went along with him got $15 million in projects for their districts, more in the case of committee members; those who didn't go along got little or nothing. And he insisted all gas-tax revenues be allocated directly to the transportation programs, jettisoning the arrangement in which some revenue went to the Treasury. He argued that appropriators have held back the money and cheated users of their fair spending, that in effect the trust funds were being raided to balance the budget. Following his success on the highway program, Shuster turned his attention in 1999 to the aviation trust fund, where he set the goal of assuring that all user-tax revenues go to airport and airways projects, not to general budget needs.

In the midst of all this success Shuster has been plagued with ethics charges. In April 1998, federal prosecutors in Boston indicted his former aide and current campaign fundraiser Ann Eppard for alleged embezzlement and taking illegal payments to influence the "Big Dig" highway-construction project in that city. She is a transportation lobbyist who has earned more than $1 million a year, largely for her contacts with Shuster's committee, and has raised money both for Shuster and for his son Bob, who finished third in 1996 for the Republican nomination in the neighboring 5th District. Shuster and his family also have been frequent overnight guests at Eppard's northern Virginia home. Shuster's lawyer said that he was told that his client is no longer under investigation. Still, the Eppard trial could prove embarrassing for him.

None of this seems to have hurt Shuster within driving distance of the Bud Shuster Highway. He had no opposition in primary or general elections between 1988 and 1994. In 1998, it came as something of a surprise locally that he faced a Republican primary—against the candidate who challenged him as a Democrat in 1996. Shuster won 81%–19%. To protect himself, Shuster in 1998 also won the Democratic nomination with write-in stickers. But Shuster faced a new problem on Capitol Hill as it became increasingly apparent in 1999 that House Republicans will stick by their six-year limit for committee chairmen, assuming they retain the majority after 2000. After Newt Gingrich's exit as speaker, Denny Hastert dismissed demands from chairmen for a relaxation of the rule. Hastert also turned down Shuster's plea to waive the limit for years served on the Intelligence Committee; Shuster was hoping to use that panel as a way-station for his chairman's gavel if he is forced to abandon the Transportation chairmanship.

Cook's Call. *Safe.* Despite his ethics woes, Shuster remains deeply entrenched in this solidly Republican district. Even as an open seat, this district will be very difficult to rip from Republican hands.

The People: Pop. 1990: 565,858; 70.3% rural; 15.9% age 65 + ; 98.2% White, 1.1% Black, 0.3% Asian, 0.1% Amer. Indian, 0.2% Other; 0.4% Hispanic Origin. Households: 61.8% married couple families; 28.7% married couple fams. w. children; 23.4% college educ.; median household income: $24,309; per capita income: $11,229; median house value: $49,700; median gross rent: $225.

1996 Presidential Vote			1992 Presidential Vote		
Dole (R)	102,847	(53%)	Bush (R)	97,764	(48%)
Clinton (D)	70,206	(36%)	Clinton (D)	66,923	(33%)
Perot (I)	21,239	(11%)	Perot (I)	40,200	(20%)

Rep. Bud Shuster (R)

Elected 1972; b. Jan. 23, 1932, Glassport; home, Everett; U. of Pittsburgh, B.S. 1954, Duquesne U., M.B.A. 1960, American U., Ph.D. 1967; United Church of Christ; married (Patricia).

Military Career: Army, 1954–56.

Professional Career: V.P., Electronic Computer Div., RCA, 1965–68; Founder & Chmn., computer software co., 1968–72.

DC Office: 2188 RHOB 20515, 202-225-2431; Fax: 202-225-2486; Web site: www.house.gov/shuster.

District Offices: Altoona, 814-946-1653; Chambersburg, 717-264-8308; Clearfield, 814-765-9106.

Committees: *Transportation & Infrastructure* (Chmn. of 41 R).

Group Ratings

	ADA	ACLU	AFS	LCV	CON	NTU	NFIB	COC	ACU	NTLC	CHC
1998	10	7	13	8	26	52	92	94	96	97	92
1997	15	—	25	—	8	53	—	90	84	—	—

National Journal Ratings

	1997 LIB — 1997 CONS		1998 LIB — 1998 CONS	
Economic	28%	— 67%	26%	— 74%
Social	20%	— 71%	31%	— 69%
Foreign	35%	— 64%	27%	— 68%

Key Votes of the 105th Congress

1. Clinton Budget Deal	Y	5. Puerto Rico Sthood. Ref.	N	9. Cut $ for B-2 Bombers	Y
2. Education IRAs	Y	6. End Highway Set-asides	N	10. Human Rights in China	Y
3. Req. 2/3 to Raise Taxes	Y	7. School Prayer Amend.	Y	11. Withdraw Bosnia Troops	Y
4. Fast-track Trade	N	8. Ovrd. Part. Birth Veto	Y	12. End Cuban TV-Marti	Y

Election Results

1998 general	Bud Shuster (R)	.... unopposed		($1,487,872)
1998 primary	Bud Shuster (R)	 24,768	(81%)	
	Monte Kemmler (R)	 5,830	(19%)	
1996 general	Bud Shuster (R)	 142,105	(74%)	($1,213,304)
	Monte Kemmler (D)	 50,650	(26%)	($113,294)

TENTH DISTRICT

"Coal is the theme song of this city in the hills," the *WPA Guide* said of Scranton in the middle of this century. But as those words were written, the anthracite kingdom was dying. Demand for hard coal as a home heating fuel started falling in the 1920s and plummeted in the 1940s; the three major anthracite counties in Pennsylvania had 991,000 people in 1930 and 699,000 in 1990; Scranton's Lackawanna County fell from 310,000 to 219,000. In the process, the coal dust and air pollution vanished, the ethnic groups—Irish and Poles, Ukrainians and Welsh—became less distinctive, and what had been boom towns full of young families became time-worn communities of senior citizens. In the 1960s and 1970s, there was an influx of textile and apparel mills, bringing low-wage, non-union jobs to what had once been a high-wage, unionized area. But the anthracite kingdom, created by unbridled free enterprise, was looking to government for sustenance.

The 10th Congressional District is centered on Scranton and includes most of the northeast corner of Pennsylvania—green hills with little towns in crevassed river valleys, criss-crossed by giant viaducts built for the railroads linking coal and iron mines with great cities' factories, the outer-borough New Yorkers' resorts of the Poconos and, in the three counties closest to New York and New Jersey, new subdivisions for refugees from high taxes. In the early part of the century all this territory was heavily Republican; since the 1930s Scranton and Lackawanna County have been strongly Democratic and the rest of the district strongly Republican. But for years congressional politics depended less on party than on pork. Congressman Joseph McDade, a Republican first elected in 1962, rose to become top-ranking Republican on the Appropriations Committee and worked with members of both parties, often Pennsylvania Democrat John Murtha, to bring home the bacon on projects ranging from the $66 million Steamtown train historic site to securing Pentagon contracts for the Chamberlain Manufacturing Corporation's production of howitzer shells. But McDade did not become chairman when the Republicans gained their majority because he had been indicted on charges that he received campaign contributions and speaking fees from officials of a local company for which he helped get a Defense Department minority set-aside contract. He was eventually acquitted in August 1996 but by that time Bob Livingston was firmly ensconced as chairman, and McDade became chairman of the Appropriations Energy and Water Development Subcommittee.

The new congressman from the 10th District is Don Sherwood, a Republican elected in 1998. He has deep roots in Tunkhannock in Wyoming County, 40 winding miles northwest of Scranton. Sherwood became a Chevrolet dealer in 1967—at age 26 the youngest Chevy dealer in the East—and he also served on the Tunkhannock school board since 1975. He raises Belgian horses, which he shows throughout the state. When McDade announced his retirement, Sherwood ran for the seat, assembling a grass-roots organization of 1,800 volunteers and propounding an agenda that combined small business goals to cut taxes and "eliminate the IRS as we know it" with calls for a minimum wage increase and HMO reform. With a personable style and an open wallet—he ultimately spent $795,000 of his own money on the campaign—he won 43% in the eight-candidate Republican primary, well ahead of the 23% for Scranton Mayor James Connors in second place.

The general election was a tougher challenge. The Democratic nominee was 32-year-old Pat Casey, son of former Governor Robert Casey; another son, Robert Casey Jr., is state auditor. Governor Casey, a strong opponent of abortion and advocate of government programs to help children, still lives in Scranton and is highly popular there; he has been a tough critic of Bill Clinton and, while still governor, was barred from speaking at the 1992 Democratic National Convention. Pat Casey, whose political views are similar, started off with a big advantage in name identification. One ad showed a photo of him as a toddler holding his father's hand that morphed into another with him holding the hand of his son Bobby: "He's the product of a strong family and strong faith." Casey appealed to the pork tradition of northeast Pennsylvania, arguing that by entering Congress at a young age he could aid the district for many years to come, and said that Sherwood's ideas on Social Security and education are "walking in lockstep with Dick Armey and Newt Gingrich." Sherwood argued that he was "a proven job creator" and that his support of a higher minimum wage showed he was alert to the district's needs. He outspent Casey $1.9 million to $1.3 million, and benefited from the Republican strength at the top of the ticket: Governor Tom Ridge and Senator Arlen Specter were obviously heading to big wins over obscure Democratic nominees. Sherwood got a big boost in the closing days when Speaker Newt Gingrich came in and pledged to assign him to fill McDade's seat on the Appropriations, but when Gingrich resigned the offer was not honored and the seat was given to John Peterson.

This turned out to be one of the closest races in the nation. Sherwood won by just 515 votes, 49%–48%. Casey carried Lackawanna County by 62%–36%, but it cast only 42% of the total votes—compared to over 50% a generation ago. Sherwood carried the other counties 58%–39%. His margin was only 51%–46%, however, in the two fast-growing counties at the eastern edge of the district, Monroe and Pike, suggesting that newcomers are a fluid part of the electorate here, less moored to old partisan preferences than Scranton or the other rural areas. They could be a critical voting bloc in 2000 if, as seems likely, this district is seriously contested again; Casey has declared he is running again.

Cook's Call. *Highly Competitive.* One of the more exciting races of 1998 will play out again in 2000 when Sherwood and Casey have a re-match. Sherwood will have incumbency on his side, but Casey is hoping that having his brother, Auditor Bobby Casey Jr., on top of the ticket will help turn-out in Democratic-leaning Scranton.

The People: Pop. 1990: 565,777; 53.6% rural; 17.5% age 65 +; 98.2% White, 1% Black, 0.5% Asian, 0.2% Amer. Indian, 0.2% Other; 0.7% Hispanic Origin. Households: 58.5% married couple families; 26.8% married couple fams. w. children; 32.7% college educ.; median household income: $25,648; per capita income: $12,005; median house value: $70,600; median gross rent: $263.

1996 Presidential Vote			1992 Presidential Vote		
Clinton (D)	95,712	(45%)	Bush (R)	95,803	(41%)
Dole (R)	91,629	(43%)	Clinton (D)	88,193	(38%)
Perot (I)	24,303	(11%)	Perot (I)	46,881	(20%)

Rep. Don Sherwood (R)

Elected 1998; b. Mar. 5, 1941, Nicholson; home, Tunkhannock; Dartmouth Col., B.A. 1963; Methodist; married (Carol).

Military Career: Army, 1964–66.

Elected Office: Tunkhannock Area Schl. Bd., 1975–98, Pres., 1992–98.

Professional Career: Businessman; Auto dealer, 1967-present.

DC Office: 1223 LHOB 20515, 202-225-3731; Fax: 202-225-9594; Web site: www.house.gov/sherwood.

District Offices: Scranton, 570-346-3834; Williamsport, 570-327-8161.

Committees: *Armed Services* (32d of 32 R): Military Readiness; Military Research & Development. *Resources* (25th of 28 R): Forests & Forest Health; National Parks & Public Lands. *Transportation & Infrastructure* (34th of 41 R): Aviation; Water Resources & Environment (Vice Chmn.).

Group Ratings and Key Votes: Newly Elected

Election Results

1998 general	Don Sherwood (R)	84,275	(49%)	($1,921,129)
	Patrick Casey (D)	83,760	(48%)	($1,287,027)
	Others	5,021	(3%)	
1998 primary	Don Sherwood (R)	21,252	(44%)	
	James P. Connors (R)	11,554	(24%)	
	Errol Flynn (R)	7,714	(16%)	
	Jerry Donahue (R)	4,797	(10%)	
	Others	3,301	(7%)	
1996 general	Joseph M. McDade (R)	124,670	(60%)	($724,776)
	Joe Cullen (D)	75,536	(36%)	($204,185)
	Others	8,334	(4%)	

ELEVENTH DISTRICT

One of the major industrial centers of America grew up in the 19th Century, nestled in the valley of the East Branch of the Susquehanna River, surrounded by mountain ridges. The mountains were laced with anthracite coal, the main home-heating fuel of the time. Thousands of immigrants, attracted by the high wages paid to scrape out the coal, flocked to this valley, in the chain of little cities north and south of Wilkes-Barre, named for two backers of the American revolution. While the supply was endless—the area produced 40% of the world's hard coal—the demand was not. The peak year of anthracite production was 1917, and long strikes in 1922 and 1925 quickened the conversion to oil and gas. By the 1930s, the valley around Wilkes-Barre was in decline; surrounding Luzerne County's population, 445,000 in 1930, was 328,000 in 1990.

This is Pennsylvania's 11th Congressional District, including all of Luzerne County and similar land east to the town of Jim Thorpe and the Poconos, and west almost to the Susquehanna. A large Democratic voting bloc, the miners, has been here since the 1930s, but there also were a lot of white-collar and rural Republicans. In presidential politics this was a Republican district in the 1980s, Democratic in the 1990s. It is a district which long has hungered for federal aid and subsidy, much of which was delivered by longtime Congressman Daniel Flood, a theatrical Democrat who used his seat on Appropriations to bring millions of dollars into the anthracite country; but in 1980 he resigned amid scandal and in six years the 11th had three different congressmen.

The congressman from the 11th District now is Paul Kanjorski, first elected in 1984. Kanjorski grew up in Nanticoke, near Wilkes-Barre. As a 16-year-old page in 1954, he witnessed the shooting of five congressmen by Puerto Rican terrorists in the House gallery and he was sprayed by dust from the gunfire. After college, Army Reserves and law school, he returned home to practice law; he was a workmen's compensation administrative law judge for nine years and Nanticoke city solicitor for 12. In 1984 he ran for Congress and won the May Democratic primary by pointing out the incumbent was in Central America while flood-soaked Wilkes-Barre area residents had to boil tap water because of contamination. Kanjorski has retained the seat easily ever since.

In the House, Kanjorski's voting record has been liberal on economics and moderate on cultural issues. He is anti-abortion but voted for international family planning aid in 1997. He is skeptical about foreign commitments and Washington lobbyists. He is also a tough partisan. While chairing a subcommittee with jurisdiction over White House operations, he sharply attacked the Bush White House for lavish spending; Bush once apologized at a breakfast meeting for the skimpy meal, blaming Kanjorski's investigations. But with Bill Clinton in the White House, Kanjorski vociferously attacked fellow Pennsylvanian Bill Clinger's investigation of the White House travel office firings, delaying issuance of the report and saying, "Like horses, we should take it out and shoot it." When Dan Burton led the Government Reform Committee's review of campaign finance abuses, Kanjorski said the panel "should be holding its meeting in a chamber with padded walls." When the House considered impeachment options in October 1998, he was one of five House Democrats who voted against all impeachment inquiry resolutions. Legislatively, Kanjorski helped to enact in 1998 credit-union reforms, featuring expanded access to membership. That measure, which he termed "a victory of David over Goliath," was a setback for banks by overturning a Supreme Court ruling that limited credit union membership to one occupational group.

Most important to Kanjorski is helping his economically ailing district. *The New York Times* called him "a master of earmarking" for capturing millions of dollars for the Earth Conservancy Applied Research Center, a public-private project for developing new technologies to reclaim mine-ravaged northeastern Pennsylvania. Other Kanjorski projects include a Social Security claims processing center in Plains Township, renovation of a VA hospital, and the Stegmaier Brewery project. When President Clinton called for 10 more National Historic Rivers in his

1997 State of the Union address, Kanjorski set the designation of the Susquehanna as his main district project. Although the river was not included on the list of 10 rivers, Kanjorski's active intervention led Clinton to expand the list to 14—including the Susquehanna. Referring to the White House, he boasted to his local newspaper, "They know I'm a nag."

Cook's Call. *Safe.* This culturally conservative district has trended more Republican over the past decade, but that has not threatened Kanjorski's tenure here. Kanjorski's pro-labor but socially conservative record is well-suited for this old coal mining district.

The People: Pop. 1990: 565,802; 39.6% rural; 19.4% age 65 + ; 98.4% White, 0.9% Black, 0.4% Asian, 0.1% Amer. Indian, 0.2% Other; 0.8% Hispanic Origin. Households: 55.9% married couple families; 24.5% married couple fams. w. children; 29.3% college educ.; median household income: $24,310; per capita income: $11,937; median house value: $58,000; median gross rent: $247.

1996 Presidential Vote			1992 Presidential Vote		
Clinton (D)	97,393	(48%)	Clinton (D)	91,616	(42%)
Dole (R)	76,969	(38%)	Bush (R)	84,199	(38%)
Perot (I)	25,597	(13%)	Perot (I)	42,950	(20%)

Rep. Paul E. Kanjorski (D)

Elected 1984; b. Apr. 2, 1937, Nanticoke; home, Nanticoke; Temple U., B.A. 1957–61, Dickinson Law Schl., J.D. 1962–65; Catholic; married (Nancy).

Military Career: Army Reserves, 1960–61.

Professional Career: Practicing atty., 1966–85; Nanticoke City Solicitor, 1969–81; Admin. Law Judge, 1971–80.

DC Office: 2353 RHOB 20515, 202-225-6511; Web site: www.house.gov/kanjorski.

District Offices: Kulpmont, 570-373-1540; Wilkes-Barre, 570-825-2200.

Committees: *Banking & Financial Services* (4th of 27 D): Capital Markets, Securities & Government Sponsored Enterprises (RMM); Domestic & International Monetary Policy. *Government Reform* (6th of 19 D): Government Management, Information & Technology; National Economic Growth, Natural Resources & Regulatory Affairs.

Group Ratings

	ADA	ACLU	AFS	LCV	CON	NTU	NFIB	COC	ACU	NTLC	CHC
1998	85	63	100	85	85	20	21	22	12	11	25
1997	90	—	100	—	20	26	—	40	12	—	—

National Journal Ratings

	1997 LIB — 1997 CONS			1998 LIB — 1998 CONS		
Economic	75%	—	22%	79%	—	0%
Social	60%	—	40%	56%	—	44%
Foreign	97%	—	0%	90%	—	5%

Key Votes of the 105th Congress

1. Clinton Budget Deal	N	5. Puerto Rico Sthood. Ref.	Y	9. Cut $ for B-2 Bombers	Y
2. Education IRAs	N	6. End Highway Set-asides	N	10. Human Rights in China	Y
3. Req. 2/3 to Raise Taxes	N	7. School Prayer Amend.	N	11. Withdraw Bosnia Troops	N
4. Fast-track Trade	N	8. Ovrd. Part. Birth Veto	Y	12. End Cuban TV-Marti	Y

Election Results

1998 general	Paul E. Kanjorski (D) 88,933	(67%)	($273,588)
	Stephen A. Urban (R) 44,123	(33%)	($24,412)
1998 primary	Paul E. Kanjorski (D) .... unopposed		
1996 general	Paul E. Kanjorski (D) 128,258	(68%)	($342,141)
	Stephen A. Urban (R) 60,339	(32%)	($43,761)

TWELFTH DISTRICT

The mountains and valley within a 100-mile radius of Pittsburgh are one of America's most beautiful areas—and have also been one of the most economically troubled. This has been tough, hard-working country ever since Scots-Irish farmers settled here in the 1790s. Their first big product was whiskey—this was the site of the Whiskey Rebellion of 1794—but historically the most important product was bituminous coal. Discovered in the 19th Century, it was the basic energy source for the production of iron and steel, and in the 19th Century, local farmers were joined by thousands of immigrants to work the mines and blast furnaces. Politically, this was one of the most Republican parts of America from the Civil War up to the Depression of the 1930s. Republican policies, including high tariffs and discouragement of labor unions, were seen as protecting jobs and increasing growth in the steel economy centered on Pittsburgh. But with the coming of the New Deal, and the successes of the United Mine Workers and the United Steelworkers, people here began voting mostly Democratic. But they have not followed the national Democratic Party on all issues. As employment in coal collapsed in the 1950s and employment in steel collapsed in the 1980s, people here sought trade restrictions to protect the remaining jobs, even as Democrats elsewhere favored free trade. And people here maintained their conservative views on cultural issues and foreign policy, even as Democrats elsewhere embraced various forms of liberation. Today those traditions continue in muted form, as un-employment has dropped and the area has perked up. First Pittsburgh and now the mountain areas all around are fighting to develop a more diverse and supple economy.

The 12th Congressional District includes much of this coal and steel country. Its best known community is Johnstown, the steel town that was ravaged by the disastrous flood of May 31, 1889, when a dam broke and a 75-foot wall of water half a mile wide swept through the town killing more than 2,200 people. Johnstown had 67,000 people in 1920, and about 27,000 in 1996. From Johnstown, the 12th reaches south to the West Virginia border and west to take in Armstrong and Indiana Counties northeast of Pittsburgh. It also includes the hills around Li-gonier, green with prosperity, where Mellons and others of Pittsburgh's elite have vast estates. On balance this is a Democratic district, though one troubled by some of the party's tendencies.

The congressman from the 12th District is John Murtha, a Democrat first elected in one of those 1974 special elections that signalled the political weakness of Richard Nixon. Murtha grew up in this area, served in the Marine Corps, then graduated from the University of Pitts-burgh and re-enlisted in the Marines in 1966, at 34; he was the first Vietnam veteran to serve in Congress. He is a member of the Appropriations Committee and the ranking Democrat on the Defense Subcommittee, his party's key man on the defense budget. His voting record—hawkish and patriotic on foreign policy, interventionist on economics and usually tradition-minded on cultural issues—seems perfectly suited to the steel and coal country. Murtha is also one of those old-time politicians who operate best in secret, standing at the back of the House chamber and trading gossip and votes, speaking for attribution to few national or local reporters and appearing on television only when he presided over the Democrat-majority chamber. He works on many back-room issues dear to his colleagues, including pay raises, committee as-signments and a 1997 provision requiring the Justice Department to reimburse the expenses of members of Congress who are indicted but subsequently acquitted.

On foreign issues, Murtha voted for the Gulf war resolution but opposed intervention in

Bosnia and deployment in Somalia, arguing that U.N. officials lacked the know-how to command U.S. troops. He was embarrassed when the House voted not to support air strikes against Kosovo, and supported a $13 billion supplemental spending bill for increased military readiness. He also pushed a proposal that would have barred funds for U.N. peacekeeping missions unless the president gave Congress 15 days advance notice of deployment; it was added as non-binding language to a defense appropriations bill. He calls for "more clear rules on when the United States will intervene on humanitarian missions in other countries." He argues that we need to have a "clear national interest, achievable goals and a clear timetable and plan for getting out—before we get into any troop deployment." He has supported the Nunn-Lugar program to decommission former Soviet nuclear weapons. He favors technology that provides "force multipliers" and has focused on quality-of-life improvements for service men and women, recognizing it's harder for the military to attract and retain good volunteers when the economy is humming along. He is caught sometimes between Democratic demands for lower defense spending to make more money available for domestic programs and Republican desires to spend even more on defense, but he seeks to come up with appropriations that will be sustained on a bipartisan basis in the House. Murtha might have become chairman of Appropriations in March 1994, after William Natcher died. Instead he supported the senior Democrat, Neal Smith of Iowa, who lost in the Democratic Caucus to the less senior David Obey, who is now ranking minority member.

In 1990 Murtha had an uncomfortably close primary race, and since then his interests in the district have taken interesting turns. He hired a press secretary who concentrated on local press, and he traveled around the district, staying days in communities. From these visits has come a conviction that environmental cleanup and amenities could be the key to the area's economic growth in the post-steel era. He has pushed for passive treatment systems to clean up creeks, inspired river improvement projects, urged groups to develop processes to extract minerals from mine draining so that restoring the environment will become a business itself. Interestingly, he seems to be relying less on providing federal dollars, though he does some of that, than in stimulating imaginative commercial ideas and community action. Like most other steel-district members, he has aggressively backed that industry's push for federal relief from claims of subsidized imports.

Cook's Call. *Safe.* The dean of the Pennsylvania Democrats, Murtha has been safely re-elected to this central Pennsylvania district for 22 years. He is a sure bet for 2000.

The People: Pop. 1990: 565,760; 70% rural; 17.7% age 65 + ; 98.3% White, 1.3% Black, 0.2% Asian, 0.1% Amer. Indian, 0.1% Other; 0.4% Hispanic Origin. Households: 60.2% married couple families; 27.6% married couple fams. w. children; 25.3% college educ.; median household income: $22,024; per capita income: $10,586; median house value: $44,400; median gross rent: $209.

1996 Presidential Vote

Clinton (D)	93,532	(46%)
Dole (R)	81,122	(40%)
Perot (I)	25,755	(13%)

1992 Presidential Vote

Clinton (D)	102,768	(47%)
Bush (R)	72,664	(33%)
Perot (I)	44,846	(20%)

Rep. John P. Murtha (D)

Elected Feb. 1974; b. June 17, 1932, New Martinsville, WV; home, Johnstown; U. of Pittsburgh, B.A. 1962, Indiana U. of PA, 1963–64; Catholic; married (Joyce).

Military Career: Marine Corps, 1952–55, 1966–67 (Vietnam); Marine Corps Reserves, 1955–66, 1967–90.

Elected Office: PA House of Reps., 1969–74.

Professional Career: Owner, Johnstown Minute Car Wash.

DC Office: 2423 RHOB 20515, 202-225-2065; Fax: 202-225-5709; Web site: www.house.gov/murtha.

District Office: Johnstown, 814-535-2642.

Committees: *Appropriations* (2d of 27 D): Defense (RMM); Interior; The Legislative Branch.

Group Ratings

	ADA	ACLU	AFS	LCV	CON	NTU	NFIB	COC	ACU	NTLC	CHC
1998	75	56	100	54	55	14	36	47	21	24	42
1997	50	—	88	—	42	27	—	56	32	—	—

National Journal Ratings

	1997 LIB — 1997 CONS		1998 LIB — 1998 CONS	
Economic	61%	— 39%	61%	— 37%
Social	55%	— 45%	52%	— 48%
Foreign	64%	— 36%	64%	— 36%

Key Votes of the 105th Congress

1. Clinton Budget Deal	N	5. Puerto Rico Sthood. Ref.	Y	9. Cut $ for B-2 Bombers	N
2. Education IRAs	N	6. End Highway Set-asides	N	10. Human Rights in China	Y
3. Req. 2/3 to Raise Taxes	N	7. School Prayer Amend.	N	11. Withdraw Bosnia Troops	N
4. Fast-track Trade	N	8. Ovrd. Part. Birth Veto	Y	12. End Cuban TV-Marti	N

Election Results

1998 general	John P. Murtha (D)	100,528	(68%)	($742,261)
	Timothy E. Holloway (R)	46,239	(32%)	($75,395)
1998 primary	John P. Murtha (D)	unopposed		
1996 general	John P. Murtha (D)	136,815	(70%)	($785,486)
	Bill Choby (R)	58,643	(30%)	($22,867)

THIRTEENTH DISTRICT

Montgomery County, Pennsylvania, is the hinterland of Philadelphia: rolling hills cut on one side by the Schuylkill River and at intervals by the Pennsylvania and Reading Railroad lines radiating outward from Center City. Older suburbs, the rich Main Line towns and more modest places like Glenside and Ambler, grew up around rail stations, with comfortable houses within walking distance for commuters. Here and there are the old Schuylkill River factory towns, Conshohocken and Norristown and towns established 200 years ago by German sects; near the big shopping malls around King of Prussia is Valley Forge, where George Washington wintered in 1778 and Ross Perot was nominated by the Reform Party in 1996. Farther out are 18th and 19th Century villages, once surrounded by farm fields, now encroached on by subdivisions where people depend on cars, not rail lines, to get to work, and office complexes in places like

Blue Bell, the headquarters of Unisys. Statistically, Montgomery County is the most affluent part of metro Philadelphia, but as in most suburban counties there is much variety here—economically, with high income enclaves like Gladwyne, and ethnically, with Jewish suburbs out York Road.

The 13th Congressional District is made up of most of Montgomery County, but parts of the county are nibbled off by four other districts. Historically it was a quintessentially Republican seat, where the style of politics was set for years by Ivy-educated Republican men, and where Republicans with more modest and sometimes ethnic backgrounds manned the local precincts and staffed local offices. But now the suburbs are as multi-ethnic as the central city, if not more so, and with varied cultural attitudes. The suburbs were a land of discontent in the recession of the early 1990s, which hit harder at residential real estate and other forms of wealth than incomes, and which saw more permanent layoffs of white-collar and professional workers than temporary layoffs of blue-collar and factory workers. This remained a land of discontent in the mid-1990s economic recovery as well, as taxes seemed to increase and government provided services poorly and in ways that seemed to undercut hard work and traditional values. Montgomery County cast huge margins for Ronald Reagan and George Bush in the 1980s but voted for Bill Clinton in the 1990s.

The congressman from the 13th District is Joseph Hoeffel, a Democrat elected in 1998. Hoeffel grew up in the Philadelphia area and has spent most of his adult life in politics and public office. He was elected to the state House in 1976, at 26, and re-elected three times. In 1984 he challenged Republican Congressman Lawrence Coughlin and was beaten 56%–44%—a respectable showing in the year of the Reagan landslide. Two years later he ran again and lost 59%–41% to the incumbent. After five years in law practice, he was elected a Montgomery County commissioner in 1991. There he forged an alliance with a Democrat to keep Jon Fox, his predecessor in the House, from being elected commission chairman. That may have helped propel Fox into running for Congress. In 1992 Fox won the Republican nomination, but lost by 1,373 votes to Marjorie Margolies-Mezvinsky; in 1994 he beat her by 8,000 votes after her embarrassing last-minute shift provided the one-vote margin for the Clinton budget and tax increase in August 1993. In 1996 Hoeffel ran against Fox and lost by 84 votes, 48.91%–48.87%. In 1998 Hoeffel ran again, and won the Democratic nomination without opposition, while Fox was peppered by primary opponents from both left and right, and won only 49% of the votes—an obvious trouble sign for an incumbent.

In both his campaigns against Fox, Hoeffel linked him to Newt Gingrich and said such a political profile does not fit the district's "moderate, progressive community." But Fox's greater problem may have been, as one primary opponent put it, "You don't know where Fox stands on the issues." A congenial politician well known for his constituency service, Fox seemed to try to please everyone. He said he favored both the Clinton and the Republican approaches to HMO reform, for example, even as the American Medical Association spent $450,000 on independent advertising to promote his position that patients should choose their own doctors. His anti-abortion stance, while probably popular, attracted $70,000 in negative advertising from Planned Parenthood as well as opposition from pro-lifers in the primary. Impeachment may have had an impact on this contest. Hoeffel said he initially feared that the Lewinsky scandal would harm other Democrats, but later he argued Republicans overplayed their hand and produced a voter backlash by October. But Hoeffel did not invite Clinton to make a campaign appearance in Montgomery County, nor did he join the president's October Democratic fundraiser in Philadelphia. Instead, Hillary Rodham Clinton made an appearance for Hoeffel, as did Minority Leader Dick Gephardt.

Hoeffel won 52%–47%, not an overwhelming margin, but a significant defeat for a Republican incumbent who never managed to win 50% of the vote in a historically Republican district. Several Republicans, including Fox, quickly lined up to run against Hoeffel in 2000. But national Republican officials showed less interest in Fox, whose percentage has declined each time he has run, than in moderate state Senator Stewart Greenleaf.

Cook's Call. *Highly Competitive.* There is little doubt that Hoeffel will be a top Republican target in 2000. Though this suburban Philadelphia district has been trending Democratic over the past 10 years, the district still has a serious Republican base. Plus, for the first time since 1990, Republicans look likely to nominate someone other than the perennially underachieving Fox.

The People: Pop. 1990: 565,663; 7.6% rural; 16.1% age 65 + ; 91.1% White, 6.1% Black, 2.5% Asian, 0.1% Amer. Indian, 0.3% Other; 1.2% Hispanic Origin. Households: 60.3% married couple families; 27% married couple fams. w. children; 55.4% college educ.; median household income: $44,764; per capita income: $22,786; median house value: $147,500; median gross rent: $528.

1996 Presidential Vote				1992 Presidential Vote			
Clinton (D)	125,364	(50%)		Clinton (D)	118,579	(44%)	
Dole (R)	103,461	(41%)		Bush (R)	107,439	(39%)	
Perot (I)	19,922	(8%)		Perot (I)	44,148	(16%)	
Others	4,179	(2%)					

Rep. Joseph M. Hoeffel (D)

Elected 1998; b. Sept. 3, 1950, Philadelphia; home, Abington; Boston U., B.A. 1972, Temple U. Law Schl., J.D. 1986; Protestant; married (Francesca).

Military Career: Army Reserves, 1970–76.

Elected Office: PA House of Reps., 1976–84; Montgomery Cnty. Comm., 1991–98.

Professional Career: Practicing atty., 1986–91.

DC Office: 1229 LHOB 20515, 202-225-6111; Fax: 202-226-0611; Web site: www.house.gov/hoeffel.

District Office: Norristown, 610-272-8400.

Committees: *Budget* (18th of 19 D). *International Relations* (23d of 23 D): International Economic Policy & Trade.

Group Ratings and Key Votes: Newly Elected

Election Results

1998 general	Joseph M. Hoeffel (D)	95,105	(52%)	($1,259,326)
	Jon D. Fox (R)	85,915	(47%)	($1,921,005)
	Others	3,470	(2%)	
1998 primary	Joseph M. Hoeffel (D)	unopposed		
1996 general	Jon D. Fox (R)	120,304	(49%)	($1,659,723)
	Joseph M. Hoeffel (D)	120,220	(49%)	($697,490)
	Others	5,455	(2%)	

FOURTEENTH DISTRICT

The Golden Triangle is the inevitable focus of Pittsburgh, the tip of land where the Allegheny and Monongahela Rivers come together to form the Ohio, and has been a strategic site for more than 200 years. It was there, to Fort Duquesne in the French and Indian War, that Braddock's army was headed (with George Washington helping lead the way) when it was ambushed and defeated in 1754. A few years later, the first American city west of the Appalachian chain was carved out of the wilderness here and named after the English statesman William Pitt. Pittsburgh grew rapidly in those days when most of the nation's commerce moved over water. When traffic switched to railroads, Pittsburgh still did nicely, since rail lines run at riverside rather than scale the mountains. Then came Andrew Carnegie—and steel. A Scottish immigrant working as a telegrapher for the Pennsylvania Railroad, he saw that steel would replace iron for railroad bridges and built a steel factory in Pittsburgh—then a rail junction with large deposits of coal nearby and ready access to iron ore from the Great Lakes. With associates like Henry Clay Frick and Henry Phipps, Carnegie built his capacity to the point that when he sold out in 1901, the resulting U.S. Steel Corporation had a near-monopoly of the business.

The Pittsburgh that Carnegie and his steel men built is one of giant mills in the bottomlands along the rivers and massive buildings downtown, like the classic City-County Building next to the Richardsonian jail. There were 12 cable cars going up the Duquesne Incline and other routes, connecting mills with neighborhoods above, and the ever-present grime of coal smoke in the air. The Pittsburgh smog—a word used here before it was in Los Angeles—was so bad that street lights stayed on all day downtown; a 1947 photograph shows a midnight-like darkness at nine in the morning. In the years after World War II, Pittsburgh's business leaders and Mayor David Lawrence were determined to clean up the smog and succeeded: Pittsburgh is one of our cleaner-air cities today. They also cleaned up the riverfront and created a grand park at the junction of the three rivers. Pittsburgh ranks high, though not as high as it used to, as a headquarters of major corporations (USX, Heinz, Alcoa, Koppers, PPG) and has fine cultural institutions, from Carnegie-Mellon University and the University of Pittsburgh with its "cathedral of learning" to its public television station (home of *Mr. Rogers' Neighborhood*) and the Andy Warhol museum. In the early 1980s, Pittsburgh formed a high-tech council to encourage start-up businesses. By the early 1990s, it had a robust high-tech, white-collar sector, replacing the manufacturing jobs which had declined in the metropolitan area from 265,000 in the mid-1970s to 140,000 in 1999. The old millworker towns in the outer metro ring continued to lose population and jobs, but much of the central city is vital, with yuppie-like growth in Mount Washington and Manchester and fine homes still maintained in Shadyside and Squirrel Hill. Vacant lots with abandoned steel mills have been converted into industrial parks and residential developments.

The 14th Congressional District includes all of the city of Pittsburgh plus suburban territory to the west and north. It takes in the city's black neighborhoods and Shadyside and its depopulated white working-class areas. To the west it goes out along a new expressway up to the airport, which is USAir's major hub; to the north, through middle-income townships and northeast along the Ohio River to some of the hilly high-income precincts of Sewickley. The 14th has its Republican neighborhoods but its Republican heritage has not been very lively since the New Deal, and this is a solidly Democratic district today. Though unhappy with the Democrats' cultural liberalism in the 1970s, it became more Democratic during the steel industry's collapse in the 1980s.

The congressman from the 14th District is William Coyne, a Democrat first elected in 1980. He grew up in an Irish-American family in Pittsburgh, served in the Army, worked as an accountant, graduated from Robert Morris College. With a characteristic Irish-American knack for politics, he went to the legislature in 1970, at 34, then to the city council in 1973, to the chairmanship of the Democratic Party in Pittsburgh in 1978, and then to Congress when he beat his predecessor's son in the Democratic primary by a 65%–35% margin. After the 1984 election, he won a seat on the Ways and Means Committee, where he was the kind of reliable Democrat with whom then-Chairman Dan Rostenkowski was comfortable; he is now the fourth-ranking Democrat there and ranking Democrat on the Oversight Subcommittee.

Coyne's voting record is one of the most liberal in the House. He wants the government to spend more on transportation, education and energy conservation, which he believes will produce economic growth. He was the only western Pennsylvanian to oppose the partial-birth abortion ban. He worked to make the earned income tax credit payable monthly rather than yearly. He has secured funding for many local projects—the Software Engineering Institute, Children's Hospital, restructuring the former Hays Ammunition Plant. In the minority, he has been less successful in seeking incentives to clean up urban brownfields, expanding workers' rights in trade agreements and seeking federal monitoring of fatal medication errors. In 1997 he worked to reorganize the IRS and in 1999 to simplify the capital gains tax.

For years Coyne worked quietly, not seeking publicity as most congressmen do. "I am a quiet person by nature," he told a local reporter, and he said that he has never held a press conference. That modesty changed a bit in 1996, when he was challenged in the primary by 38-year-old Pittsburgh Councilman Dan Cohen, a graduate of Yale and Stanford Law. Coyne, who had never spent more than $323,000, spent $1 million this time. "Results. Not Talk," was his slogan, making his taciturnity an asset, and he worked to knock on 25,000 doors by the April primary. He was endorsed by the local Democratic Party, the AFL-CIO, and the Sierra Club; District Attorney Bob Colville cut an ad praising Coyne's record against crime. The result was a thumping 66%–34% victory for Coyne. He was re-elected easily that fall and, with no primary opposition, in 1998.

His biggest problem for the future may be redistricting. Pennsylvania will likely lose two districts, one of them most likely in metropolitan Pittsburgh. If Republicans continue to hold the legislature in 2000, they will probably draw a plan that combines the four Democratic Pittsburgh-area districts into three, which means that Coyne could find himself in the same district with another incumbent Democrat.

Cook's Call. *Safe.* Though his winning percentage over the past three cycles is down significantly from his 1982–92 margins, Coyne remains a safe bet in this Pittsburgh-based district.

The People: Pop. 1990: 565,838; 0.4% rural; 18.3% age 65 + ; 80.5% White, 17.8% Black, 1.3% Asian, 0.1% Amer. Indian, 0.2% Other; 0.8% Hispanic Origin. Households: 43.1% married couple families; 17.7% married couple fams. w. children; 41.8% college educ.; median household income: $24,751; per capita income: $14,255; median house value: $52,000; median gross rent: $309.

1996 Presidential Vote

Clinton (D)	126,704	(59%)
Dole (R)	70,466	(33%)
Perot (I)	15,417	(7%)
Others	3,690	(2%)

1992 Presidential Vote

Clinton (D)	145,419	(58%)
Bush (R)	66,016	(26%)
Perot (I)	38,460	(15%)

Rep. William J. Coyne (D)

Elected 1980; b. Aug. 24, 1936, Pittsburgh; home, Pittsburgh; Robert Morris Col., B.S. 1965; Catholic; single.

Military Career: Army, 1955–57.

Elected Office: PA House of Reps., 1970–72; Pittsburgh City Cncl., 1973–80.

Professional Career: Accountant, 1957–70; Chmn., Pittsburg Dem. Party, 1978–84.

DC Office: 2455 RHOB 20515, 202-225-2301; Fax: 202-225-1844; Web site: www.house.gov/coyne.

District Office: Pittsburgh, 412-644-2870.

Committees: *Ways & Means* (4th of 16 D): Human Resources; Oversight (RMM).

Group Ratings

	ADA	ACLU	AFS	LCV	CON	NTU	NFIB	COC	ACU	NTLC	CHC
1998	100	88	100	92	68	17	21	22	4	5	0
1997	100	—	100	—	20	26	—	20	0	—	—

National Journal Ratings

	1997 LIB	—	1997 CONS	1998 LIB	—	1998 CONS
Economic	93%	—	0%	79%	—	0%
Social	85%	—	0%	90%	—	7%
Foreign	88%	—	10%	75%	—	23%

Key Votes of the 105th Congress

1. Clinton Budget Deal	N	5. Puerto Rico Sthood. Ref.	Y	9. Cut $ for B-2 Bombers	Y
2. Education IRAs	N	6. End Highway Set-asides	N	10. Human Rights in China	Y
3. Req. 2/3 to Raise Taxes	N	7. School Prayer Amend.	N	11. Withdraw Bosnia Troops	N
4. Fast-track Trade	N	8. Ovrd. Part. Birth Veto	N	12. End Cuban TV-Marti	N

Election Results

1998 general	William J. Coyne (D)	83,355	(61%)	($526,781)
	Bill Ravotti (R)	52,745	(38%)	($450,349)
	Others	1,636	(1%)	
1998 primary	William J. Coyne (D)	unopposed		
1996 general	William J. Coyne (D)	122,922	(61%)	($1,027,674)
	Bill Ravotti (R)	78,921	(39%)	($212,284)

FIFTEENTH DISTRICT

Allentown, Pennsylvania, has long been derided by show biz songwriters, from "42nd Street" back in 1933, in which it is scorned as nowhere, the polar opposite of Broadway, to Billy Joel's "Allentown" in 1982, with its grim picture of closed factories and unemployment. Neither is an entirely fair portrait of Allentown, the largest city in Pennsylvania's Lehigh Valley, though both have nuggets of truth. Allentown and next-door Bethlehem are off the Metroliner corridor that is the big population center of the Northeast, and both have suffered from industrial shut-downs—Allentown, when Mack Truck moved one of its main assembly plants to non-union South Carolina, and Bethlehem, when Bethlehem Steel announced it was shutting down its last blast furnace in its headquarters city since 1857. But the rolling hills of the Lehigh Valley today are economically productive and creative, with big new installations from AT&T and Nestle, long-surviving businesses like Crayola Crayons and Dixie cups, and dozens of small startups which never get the visibility of the big closedowns but together have produced more new jobs than have been lost. If the Lehigh Valley is off the main lines of traffic, it is connected by I-78 to New York and by the Turnpike Extension to Philadelphia, and its lower living costs and taxes make it attractive to people from both big metro areas.

The 15th Congressional District consists of the Lehigh Valley plus a small adjacent portion of Montgomery County. This has been a marginal political area for years, the intersection of heavily Democratic industrial precincts with the Republican farmlands of the Pennsylvania Dutch Country. Yet it had only four congressmen from 1933 to 1992—two Democrats and a Republican—each of whom lasted at least 14 years.

The congressman from the 15th today is businessman Pat Toomey, a Republican elected in 1998. Toomey grew up in a blue-collar Rhode Island family, got enough scholarship aid to attend Harvard as an undergraduate, then turned to a career in investment banking. After getting wealthy by creating an international financial services consulting firm, he moved to Allentown in 1990, where he invested in Rookies' Restaurants, which he helped to organize with his brothers. He entered government in 1994 as an elected member of the Allentown Government

Study Commission, where he helped to author tax-limitation plans, including the requirement of a super-majority for the city council to raise taxes. In November 1997, three-term Democratic Congressman Paul McHale announced he was retiring; McHale opposed Clinton's first-term health care plan and, as a Gulf war veteran, criticized Pentagon plans that he believed would reduce combat readiness; he became the first House Democrat to call for Clinton's resignation in August 1998 and one of five Democrats to vote for impeachment.

Toomey started to run for the House right after McHale's announcement. The six-candidate Republican primary included two state legislators, but Toomey was helped by the fact that he was one of only two candidates from Lehigh County. Toomey called for Social Security reform and a simple 17% flat tax; he pledged to serve no more than six years and promised never to vote to raise taxes. He spent heavily and won the Republican primary with 27% to 24% for realtor and Christian conservative Bob Kilbanks (who lost to McHale 55%–41% in 1996) and 23% for state Senator Joseph Uliana.

The Democratic nominee was Allentown state Senator Roy Afflerbach. Toomey put him on the defensive early with an ad that highlighted Afflerbach's support of tax increases in the legislature, calling him "the tax man" and attacking him for voting against repeal of a tax on toothpaste and dental floss. Afflerbach criticized Toomey's tax plan as a threat to Social Security and the budget surplus. Afflerbach tried to appeal to conservative, blue-collar voters by calling Toomey an outsider: "Pat has only been in Pennsylvania for seven years and prior to that he was all over the world doing private business, while I was here doing public business." But Toomey won by the surprisingly large margin of 55%–45%. One reason was that he spent $1.1 million, $203,000 of it his own money, to Afflerbach's $559,000. McHale's support of impeachment may have cast a pall over Democratic efforts here. Toomey's win demonstrated the growing strength of suburbs over the declining Democratic strongholds of Allentown and Bethlehem, where Afflerbach had only single-digit margins.

After his election, Toomey quickly went to work on national economic issues. Budget Committee Chairman John Kasich named him to a bipartisan Social Security task force that held hearings on possible reforms. He likely will face a competitive re-election again in 2000 and, if he wins, may be helped by redistricting after the 2000 Census.

Cook's Call. *Competitive.* Toomey's strong win here last cycle gives him some serious momentum heading into 2000. But he still has to prove that he can win re-election in this swing district that has strong Democratic undertones. To make this a real race, Democrats will need to put forth a better candidate than they did in 1998.

The People: Pop. 1990: 565,818; 25.9% rural; 15.7% age 65 + ; 93.9% White, 2.2% Black, 1.1% Asian, 0.1% Amer. Indian, 2.6% Other; 4.7% Hispanic Origin. Households: 59.8% married couple families; 26.7% married couple fams. w. children; 37.3% college educ.; median household income: $33,049; per capita income: $15,073; median house value: $102,100; median gross rent: $393.

1996 Presidential Vote

Clinton (D)	96,380	(46%)
Dole (R)	85,736	(41%)
Perot (I)	22,125	(11%)
Others	3,130	(2%)

1992 Presidential Vote

Clinton (D)	92,363	(41%)
Bush (R)	81,349	(37%)
Perot (I)	47,740	(21%)

Rep. Patrick Toomey (R)

Elected 1998; b. Nov. 17, 1961, Providence, RI; home, Allentown; Harvard U., B.S. 1984; Catholic; married (Kris).

Elected Office: Allentown Govt. Study Comm., 1994.

Professional Career: Investment Banker, 1984–89; Financial Consultant, 1990; Restaurateur, 1990-present.

DC Office: 511 CHOB 20515, 202-225-6411; Fax: 202-226-0778; Web site: www.house.gov/toomey.

District Office: Allentown, 610-439-8861.

Committees: *Banking & Financial Services* (32d of 32 R): Capital Markets, Securities & Government Sponsored Enterprises; Domestic & International Monetary Policy. *Budget* (24th of 24 R). *Small Business* (15th of 19 R): Government Programs & Oversight; Tax, Finance & Exports.

Group Ratings and Key Votes: Newly Elected

Election Results

1998 general	Patrick Toomey (R)	81,755	(55%)	($1,039,189)
	Roy C. Afflerbach (D)	66,930	(45%)	($562,251)
1998 primary	Patrick Toomey (R)	7,981	(27%)	
	Bob Kilbanks (R)	7,266	(25%)	
	Joseph M. Uliana (R)	6,912	(23%)	
	Joe Pascuzzo (R)	3,518	(12%)	
	Nick Sabatine (R)	3,219	(11%)	
	Others	525	(2%)	
1996 general	Paul McHale (D)	109,812	(55%)	($366,847)
	Bob Kilbanks (R)	82,803	(41%)	($263,747)
	Others	7,748	(4%)	

SIXTEENTH DISTRICT

The Pennsylvania Dutch Country, settled by Germans in the 18th Century when it was Pennsylvania's frontier, remains a distinctive part of America. These Germans were Amish and Mennonite, pietistic sects seeking religious liberty and determined to farm rich lands in the same intensive way they had in Germany. Today, many of their descendants—the Eisenhower family is the most famous example—have blended into mainstream America, but in the Dutch area around Lancaster, many "Plain People" still live. Tourists can still see Amish families clad in black, clattering over the back roads in horse-drawn carriages, with scrupulously tended farms set amid rolling hills, the barns decorated with hex signs. Farmers here continue to produce some of the highest per-acre yields on earth, with simple equipment and limited use of chemicals. But efficient farming is not all that is happening here economically. Lancaster is the headquarters of Armstrong, and nearby Hershey is where Milton Hershey built his chocolate firm back in 1903; this was the site of the bipartisan House of Representatives "civility retreats" in 1997 and 1999. The Dutch area also has many small firms and new outlet malls; new startups prosper, profiting from the skills and work habits of the labor force. Lancaster County has had solid growth in recent years, and so has western Chester County, technically part of metro Philadelphia, but with its own Pennsylvania Dutch communities. Local business groups claim that Lancaster ranks first nationally in farm receipts for non-irrigated counties and in the number of egg-laying hens.

The 16th District includes most of Lancaster County and part of Chester County, ranging east from the Dutch Country through the small towns and spreading suburbs of greater Philadelphia, including America's leading mushroom-growing center around Kennett Square (fragrant with the compost needed for the crop) and on to the Wyeth country around Chadds Ford. By most measures this is the most Republican district in Pennsylvania and perhaps the whole Northeast. It has favored the party of Lincoln since it abandoned the party of Pennsylvania's only president, Lancaster resident James Buchanan, in the years just before the Civil War.

The congressman from the 16th District is Joe Pitts, a Republican elected in 1996. Pitts grew up in Kentucky, joined the Air Force after college, served three tours of duty and flew 116 B-52 combat missions in Vietnam. He returned to become a math and science teacher in Malvern, in Chester County, and later owned a nursery near Kennett Square. In 1972, at 33, he was elected to the Pennsylvania House. Pitts became a leader in Harrisburg, a "champion of traditional values," in his words, and staunchly anti-abortion. In 1989 he became chairman of the Appropriations Committee, and was proud of balancing budgets and starting a program in which low-income neighborhood leaders met regularly with legislators to discuss how government could "support and not hinder" their organizations. He also oversaw the restoration of the Pennsylvania Capitol. In December 1995, when Congressman Bob Walker, one of the conservative reformers close to Newt Gingrich who helped revolutionize the House, cited the "Pennsylvania Dutch tradition" of not serving over 20 years and said he was retiring, Pitts plunged into the primary. He spoke favorably of home-schooling and unfavorably of gambling, and ran as a "true conservative." He raised the most money and won the most votes in the five-candidate race. In the general, Pitts easily defeated newspaper publisher James Blaine, a descendant of James G. Blaine, the "Plumed Knight" of late 19th Century politics and Republican presidential nominee in 1884.

In the House, Pitts sought to abolish the estate tax, which he says breaks up family businesses and produces little net revenue, and he won House passage of an "Amish bill" to permit Amish youth to work with adult supervision at sites with heavy machinery. He co-chairs the Renewal Alliance, seeking ways to encourage local and faith-based groups in low-income neighborhoods to work on the needs of the poor. He also headed the House Republicans' "values action team" that worked with the Christian Coalition and other family groups to promote a pro-family agenda. And he founded the religious prisoners' congressional task force to plead for human rights around the world. He became a member of Tom DeLay's whip organization. Unlike Walker, Pitts focused on earmarking local highway projects and won major improvements on U.S. 30 in Lancaster County and Route 41 in Chester County.

Pitts was re-elected easily in 1998, against the 1996 Reform Party candidate who won the Democratic nomination with write-in votes. After the 1998 election Pitts made an unsuccessful bid for a seat on the House Appropriations Committee, losing out to fellow Pennsylvanian John Peterson, who had the support of top party leaders.

Cook's Call. *Safe.* Though he is only a sophomore, Pitts is already safely settled in this heavily Republican seat. This seat is never going to show up on Democratic target lists.

The People: Pop. 1990: 565,908; 43.8% rural; 12.5% age 65 +; 91.5% White, 5.2% Black, 1.1% Asian, 0.1% Amer. Indian, 2.1% Other; 3.6% Hispanic Origin. Households: 63.1% married couple families; 31.1% married couple fams. w. children; 42.3% college educ.; median household income: $37,553; per capita income: $16,321; median house value: $115,800; median gross rent: $417.

1996 Presidential Vote		1992 Presidential Vote	
Dole (R)	114,164 (53%)	Bush (R)	109,019 (48%)
Clinton (D)	80,476 (37%)	Clinton (D)	72,724 (32%)
Perot (I)	18,010 (8%)	Perot (I)	43,271 (19%)

Rep. Joseph R. Pitts (R)

Elected 1996; b. Oct. 10, 1939, Lexington, KY; home, Kennett Square; Asbury Col., B.A. 1961, West Chester U., M.Ed. 1972; Protestant; married (Virginia).

Military Career: Air Force, 1963–69 (Vietnam).

Professional Career: High schl. teacher, 1969–72; PA House of Reps., 1972–96; Owner, Landscape & Nursery Co., 1974–90.

DC Office: 504 CHOB 20515, 202-225-2411; Web site: www.house.gov/pitts.

District Offices: Kennett Square, 610-444-4581; Lancaster, 717-393-0667.

Committees: *Armed Services* (29th of 32 R): Military Personnel; Military Procurement. *Budget* (14th of 24 R). *Small Business* (12th of 19 R): Empowerment (Chmn.). *Joint Economic Committee* (5th of 10 Reps.).

Group Ratings

	ADA	ACLU	AFS	LCV	CON	NTU	NFIB	COC	ACU	NTLC	CHC
1998	0	6	0	15	13	54	100	100	96	92	100
1997	5	—	13	—	37	57	—	100	96	—	—

National Journal Ratings

	1997 LIB — 1997 CONS		1998 LIB — 1998 CONS	
Economic	28%	67%	15%	81%
Social	30%	64%	14%	81%
Foreign	24%	72%	7%	83%

Key Votes of the 105th Congress

1. Clinton Budget Deal	Y	5. Puerto Rico Sthood. Ref.	N	9. Cut $ for B-2 Bombers	N
2. Education IRAs	Y	6. End Highway Set-asides	Y	10. Human Rights in China	Y
3. Req. 2/3 to Raise Taxes	Y	7. School Prayer Amend.	Y	11. Withdraw Bosnia Troops	Y
4. Fast-track Trade	Y	8. Ovrd. Part. Birth Veto	Y	12. End Cuban TV-Marti	N

Election Results

1998 general	Joseph R. Pitts (R)	95,979	(71%)	($372,699)
	Robert S. Yorczyk (D)	40,092	(29%)	($3,686)
1998 primary	Joseph R. Pitts (R)	unopposed		
1996 general	Joseph R. Pitts (R)	124,511	(59%)	($616,874)
	James G. Blaine (D)	78,598	(38%)	($405,264)
	Others	6,493	(3%)	

SEVENTEENTH DISTRICT

Through the center of Pennsylvania flows the Susquehanna, the longest river in the East if you include the Chesapeake Bay, which is actually the flooded lower Susquehanna Valley. Starting in Cooperstown, New York, emptying into the Chesapeake next to the antique town of Havre de Grace, Maryland, the Susquehanna is the one river strong enough to break through the Appalachian chains of central Pennsylvania. But few songs are written to celebrate the Susquehanna; it has not given a name to a fever (Potomac), a school of painting (Hudson) or economics (Charles), or to a state (Delaware, Connecticut, Ohio, Mississippi, Alabama, Illinois, Missouri, Colorado).

The 17th Congressional District covers much of the lower Susquehanna Valley, where the river drains the fertile plains of the Pennsylvania Dutch Country, one of colonial America's great frontiers. Its population center is Harrisburg, the central city huddled around the marvelous restored Capitol building—its dome is modeled after St. Peter's in Rome, its stairway on the Paris Opera—with the metro area spreading over various valleys, not far upstream from the Three Mile Island nuclear power plant. From there the district spreads east to the Pennsylvania Dutch Country, including Lebanon County and part of Lancaster County. Here the black buggies of the "Plain People" click-clack over the roads of some of the most fertile farmland in the world. This is a solidly Republican area. Harrisburg has been a Republican town from the days when the party seemed to conquer all in Pennsylvania; Republicans held the governorship for all but eight years from 1860 to 1934 and filled the ornate halls of the Capitol with Republican patronage hacks. The Pennsylvania Dutch Country is even more Republican.

The congressman from the 17th District is George Gekas, who as state senator from Harrisburg helped draw the district boundaries and won the seat easily in 1982. Gekas grew up in Harrisburg, went to Dickinson College in nearby Carlisle, served in the Army, graduated from Dickinson Law. Within two years he was in the public sector as Dauphin County assistant district attorney. He was elected to the Pennsylvania House in 1966, at 36, to the Pennsylvania Senate in 1976, and to the U.S. House in 1982: an example of a conservative who has spent most of his life in government.

Gekas is fourth-ranking Republican on the Judiciary Committee, an active and sometimes creative legislator, with a solidly conservative voting record leavened by some moderate votes on cultural issues. For years he has sponsored the death penalty for various heinous crimes. Prompted by constituents' experiences, he enacted a proposal preventing international kidnapping of children and another preventing evictions of the elderly. He sponsored the law, which took effect in 1992, that bars congressmen from converting leftover campaign funds for personal use. He has worked to keep Legal Services Corporation lawyers from taking abortion cases and, more recently, has proposed block-granting legal aid funds to the states and abolishing the Legal Services Corporation—a solution not entirely satisfactory to House conservatives or liberals; in 1996 he went along with House Republicans' small cuts but promises to phase out LSC.

Gekas also parted company with Judiciary Committee conservatives when he helped to sink in 1997 their attempt to end most federal affirmative action programs; he said that the Supreme Court was fixing past problems and feared that a national debate would be "divisive." Gekas sponsored the International Child Adoption Act signed by President Clinton. He is interested in biomedical research, calling for increases in funding for the National Institutes of Health. He seeks limited protection from lawsuits for suppliers of raw materials for biomedical implantation devices. He sponsored a law punishing animal rights "terrorism." He authored the House-passed Government Shutdown Protection Act, providing enough funds if appropriations bills aren't signed to "keep the government's lights on," but the proposal died as part of a supplemental-spending bill that Clinton vetoed. In 1998, he also won House passage of a bankruptcy-reform bill, which would make it more difficult for individuals to file for bankruptcy to erase their debts; "people use it as a tool for financial management rather than a last resort," he complained of the current law. The bill got bogged down in a dispute with the Senate during the session's closing days but Gekas moved an identical one in 1999.

Gekas gained his place in the national spotlight as one of the House managers during the impeachment trial during which he spoke without notes as a home-spun defender of common-sense values against Clinton's "falsehoods uttered under oath." He subsequently refused to join the managers in a political action committee to support Republican candidates on the ground it would be presumptuous to try to turn the impeachment proceedings into a fund-raising effort. On local issues, Gekas has worked to save Fort Indiantown Gap military base and to clean up the Harrisburg Airport Superfund site. Gekas has been re-elected with large majorities every two years; he was unopposed in 1998.

Cook's Call. *Safe.* Although he was one of the famed House impeachment managers, Gekas is not going to show up on any Democratic hit lists in 2000. This heavily Republican district has re-elected Gekas with solid margins since 1982.

The People: Pop. 1990: 565,702; 39.2% rural; 14.1% age 65 +; 91.3% White, 6.6% Black, 1% Asian, 0.2% Amer. Indian, 0.9% Other; 1.7% Hispanic Origin. Households: 58.2% married couple families; 27% married couple fams. w. children; 33.5% college educ.; median household income: $31,841; per capita income: $14,434; median house value: $76,700; median gross rent: $341.

1996 Presidential Vote			1992 Presidential Vote		
Dole (R)	116,473	(54%)	Bush (R)	114,245	(50%)
Clinton (D)	81,205	(37%)	Clinton (D)	72,594	(32%)
Perot (I)	17,997	(8%)	Perot (I)	40,495	(18%)

Rep. George W. Gekas (R)

Elected 1982; b. Apr. 14, 1930, Harrisburg; home, Harrisburg; Dickinson Col., B.A. 1952, Dickinson Law Schl., J.D. 1958; Greek Orthodox; married (Evangeline).

Military Career: Army, 1953–55.

Elected Office: PA House of Reps., 1966–74; PA Senate, 1976–82.

Professional Career: Asst. Dist. Atty., Dauphin Cnty., 1960–66.

DC Office: 2410 RHOB 20515, 202-225-4315; Fax: 202-225-8440; Web site: www.house.gov/gekas.

District Offices: Elizabethtown, 717-367-6731; Harrisburg, 717-541-5507; Lebanon, 717-273-1451.

Committees: *Judiciary* (4th of 21 R): Commercial & Administrative Law (Chmn.); Crime.

Group Ratings

	ADA	ACLU	AFS	LCV	CON	NTU	NFIB	COC	ACU	NTLC	CHC
1998	10	13	0	8	13	46	100	100	84	92	92
1997	15	—	13	—	70	56	—	100	88	—	—

National Journal Ratings

	1997 LIB — 1997 CONS			1998 LIB — 1998 CONS		
Economic	10%	—	86%	37%	—	61%
Social	39%	—	59%	34%	—	64%
Foreign	30%	—	68%	0%	—	93%

Key Votes of the 105th Congress

1. Clinton Budget Deal	Y	5. Puerto Rico Sthood. Ref.	Y	9. Cut $ for B-2 Bombers	N
2. Education IRAs	Y	6. End Highway Set-asides	Y	10. Human Rights in China	N
3. Req. 2/3 to Raise Taxes	Y	7. School Prayer Amend.	Y	11. Withdraw Bosnia Troops	Y
4. Fast-track Trade	Y	8. Ovrd. Part. Birth Veto	Y	12. End Cuban TV-Marti	N

Election Results

1998 general	George W. Gekas (R)	unopposed		($92,690)
1998 primary	George W. Gekas (R)	unopposed		
1996 general	George W. Gekas (R)	150,678	(72%)	($110,578)
	Paul Kettl (D)	57,911	(28%)	($1,476)

EIGHTEENTH DISTRICT

Pittsburgh is surely the hilliest of the large metropolitan areas of the United States—indicative of the nerve of its founders that they were willing to build on such steep terrain. In its years of great growth, from the mid-1800s to the early 1900s, with the steel mills lining the riverbanks, Pittsburgh and its suburbs spread up and down hills, through the interstices of river valleys and over gaps to the next nearly level spot. Then, as growth resumed in the mid-20th Century, the spreading-out process continued. One result is that there are no clusters of rich and poor suburbs, no one middle-class zone: they are spread out around the irregular terrain. The richest Pitts-burghers, for example, live in Fox Chapel and Sewickley to the northeast and northwest; there are upper-middle-income suburbs like Mount Lebanon south of the Golden Triangle, but also some north of the Allegheny; working-class enclaves, now greatly depopulated, are strung along the Monongahela River near the mostly cold steel mills, but are found in other pockets as well. Pittsburgh does not yet have an edge city, though there are new housing and a few office developments to the north and to the west around the airport, now a major hub for USAirways.

When John Kennedy was elected president, there were four congressional districts in Pitts-burgh's Allegheny County, numbered 27 through 30; now all of Pennsylvania has only 21 districts, and there are only two fully in Allegheny County. One, the 14th, is made up primarily of the city of Pittsburgh; the other, the 18th, includes suburbs to the north, south and east, plus most of the industrial Mon Valley to the southeast. This is the creation of 1990s redistricting, containing much of the old Republican-leaning suburban 18th and some of the heavily Dem-ocratic Mon Valley 20th. It was expected to be a Democratic district, but has been seriously contested.

The congressman from the 18th is Mike Doyle, a Democrat who won in 1994 when the 18th District's Republican incumbent, 36-year-old brash conservative Rick Santorum, was elected to the U.S. Senate. Of Irish and Italian descent, Doyle grew up in the Mon Valley town of Swissvale, returned there after Penn State, worked as an insurance agent and for a nonprofit agency and was elected to the Swissvale Borough Council in 1977, at 24. In 1978 he became chief of staff to state Senator Frank Pecora, a Republican who had switched parties and had run in the 18th District against Santorum in 1992, and lost 61%–38%. When Santorum ran for the Senate, Doyle was one of seven Democrats and four Republicans to seek the open seat. The Democrats were close to evenly matched: all won between 10% and 20% of the vote. Doyle, who had switched to the Democratic Party only recently, was helped by endorsements from unions and community leaders; he, like Santorum in his first campaign, knocked on 40,000 doors. In the general, he faced John McCarty, a former aide to the late Senator John Heinz; interestingly, McCarty was pro-choice and Doyle anti-abortion. Doyle campaigned for sweep-ing health care reform, against the new General Agreement on Tariffs and Trade, and for rebuilding the Mon Valley's industrial base, and won 55%–45%.

In the House, Doyle has a mixed voting record, toward the right on cultural issues, toward the left on economics. He did support the Blue Dog budget, welfare and regulatory reform, and he voted with most Republicans in opposing Clinton Administration plans for national student testing. He opposed tax cuts and called for higher Medicare co-payments for high-income recipients. He worked to funnel federal dollars to the Pittsburgh Supercomputing Cen-ter, the Pittsburgh Energy Technology Center and the Oakland veterans hospital. As a Steel Caucus member—and the third-generation Doyle to work in the steel mills—he cosponsored the industry's legislation to reduce foreign imports. He opposed the EPA's new air-quality standards for fear of further local job losses. And he helped win a brownfields provision in the 1997 tax package to give tax incentives for cleaning up contaminated industrial sites.

Since his 1994 election, Doyle has cemented his own switch and that of his district to Democratic ranks. In the 1998 primary, he easily defeated 65%–35% Mary Beth Hacke, who ran seeking to break "this vicious cycle of violence" after her 1-year-old son was killed by a stray bullet fired at a gas station. In the general, Doyle won 68%–32%, against an investment banker who called for abolition of the Education Department and criticized Doyle as "a Clinton guy." Doyle now calls his earlier party switches "ancient history." He is part of the shrinking number of House members who drive their car back home after each week's final vote.

The major threat to Doyle's tenure is redistricting. Pittsburgh and Allegheny County have been losing population in the 1990s, and Pennsylvania is likely to lose seats. If Republicans hold the legislature in 2000, they will control the drawing of the lines, and are likely to collapse the four Democratic Pittsburgh-area districts into three. That could put Doyle in a primary against another Democratic incumbent.

Cook's Call. *Safe.* With three solid wins under his belt, Doyle has established a good foothold in this Democratic-leaning, but marginal district. Redistricting in 2002, however, may be Doyle's worst enemy. It is widely assumed that Pennsylvania will lose two seats, with one of those seats coming from the west.

The People: Pop. 1990: 565,771; 2% rural; 19.2% age 65 + ; 91.4% White, 7.7% Black, 0.7% Asian, 0.1% Amer. Indian, 0.2% Other; 0.4% Hispanic Origin. Households: 54% married couple families; 21.6% married couple fams. w. children; 42.7% college educ.; median household income: $29,003; per capita income: $15,251; median house value: $55,800; median gross rent: $316.

1996 Presidential Vote			1992 Presidential Vote		
Clinton (D)	119,943	(52%)	Clinton (D)	137,507	(52%)
Dole (R)	89,580	(39%)	Bush (R)	80,795	(30%)
Perot (I)	19,689	(8%)	Perot (I)	46,754	(18%)

Rep. Mike Doyle (D)

Elected 1994; b. Aug. 5, 1953, Pittsburgh; home, Swissvale; PA St. U., B.S. 1975; Catholic; married (Susan).

Elected Office: Swissvale Borough Cncl., 1977–81.

Professional Career: Insurance agent, 1975–77; Exec. Dir., Turtle Creek Valley Citizens Union, 1977–79; Chief of Staff, PA Sen. Frank Pecora, 1978–94; Co-Founder/Owner, Eastgate Insurance Agency, 1983–present.

DC Office: 133 CHOB 20515, 202-225-2135; Fax: 202-225-3084; Web site: www.house.gov/doyle.

District Offices: McKeesport, 412-664-4049; Penn Hills, 412-241-6055.

Committees: *Science* (10th of 23 D): Basic Research; Energy & Environment. *Veterans' Affairs* (5th of 14 D): Health.

Group Ratings

	ADA	ACLU	AFS	LCV	CON	NTU	NFIB	COC	ACU	NTLC	CHC
1998	80	53	100	38	61	15	36	50	25	26	50
1997	65	—	50	—	91	40	—	70	36	—	—

National Journal Ratings

	1997 LIB — 1997 CONS			1998 LIB — 1998 CONS		
Economic	58%	—	42%	61%	—	37%
Social	53%	—	47%	53%	—	47%
Foreign	79%	—	19%	58%	—	42%

Key Votes of the 105th Congress

1. Clinton Budget Deal	N	5. Puerto Rico Sthood. Ref.	Y	9. Cut $ for B-2 Bombers	Y
2. Education IRAs	N	6. End Highway Set-asides	N	10. Human Rights in China	Y
3. Req. 2/3 to Raise Taxes	N	7. School Prayer Amend.	N	11. Withdraw Bosnia Troops	N
4. Fast-track Trade	N	8. Ovrd. Part. Birth Veto	Y	12. End Cuban TV-Marti	Y

Election Results

1998 general	Mike Doyle (D)	98,363	(68%)	($400,293)
	Dick Walker (R)	46,945	(32%)	($81,999)
1998 primary	Mike Doyle (D)	42,288	(65%)	
	Mary Beth Hacke (D)	22,672	(35%)	
1996 general	Mike Doyle (D)	120,410	(56%)	($528,291)
	David B. Fawcett (R)	86,829	(40%)	($343,898)
	Others	7,751	(4%)	

NINETEENTH DISTRICT

The Mason-Dixon Line, the historic boundary between Maryland and Pennsylvania, runs through some of the country's most pleasant rolling farmlands, west of the Susquehanna River up through the first of the Appalachian chains. It was over this invisible line that Robert E. Lee's confederate troops crossed and were then repulsed in the Battle of Gettysburg in July 1863. Nearby was the westernmost capital of the United States during the Revolutionary War, the small city of York, capital from September 1777 to June 1778. This is where the Continental Congress passed the Articles of Confederation, received word from Benjamin Franklin in Paris that the French would help the colonies with money and ships, and issued the first proclamation calling for a national day of thanksgiving. Little today recalls it was once frontier and later fiercely fought over: The green farmland looks peaceful, prosperous and mostly undisturbed by the commercial trappings and stylistic excesses of the late 20th Century.

Some 50 miles of the Mason-Dixon Line is the southern boundary of the 19th Congressional District, which is centered on York, including the suburbs of Harrisburg across the Susquehanna, the old town of Carlisle with Dickinson College, the Carlisle Barracks, the U.S. Army War College, and President Eisenhower's retirement home near Gettysburg. Eisenhower was of Pennsylvania Dutch stock himself; his father migrated in the late 19th Century, with a group of Mennonite brethren, to Kansas and Texas. The district has the look of deeply contented land and has been, with occasional exceptions, heavily Republican.

The congressman from the 19th District is Bill Goodling, chairman of the Education and the Workforce Committee, a Republican first elected in 1974. Goodling was a public school teacher, coach and principal in a small town in York County for 22 years; his father was 19th District congressman for 12 years, elected every two years from 1960–72 except in 1964. When George Goodling retired, his son Bill won the primary and general in 1974 by rather narrow margins. His toughest re-election came in 1992, after it was revealed he had 430 overdrafts on the House bank totalling $188,000. Goodling won with 45% to 34% for the Democrat and 20% for a former Jack Kemp aide running as an independent—almost the same percentages as in the presidential race that year.

Goodling has labored long and hard over the years on the baroque edifice of federal education laws, until 1994 as a minority member with limited influence on the Education and Labor Committee, then as chairman of the now twice renamed committee. After the 1950s, when a bipartisan coalition wanted to limit union power, organized labor saw to it the committee had a majority of pro-labor members, including Republicans; as the focus shifted to education programs in the 1970s and 1980s, the committee strove to boost the federal role in education—on the order of 8% of all government spending in America—to steer school systems and other social agencies in liberal directions. Now Goodling and the Republicans are attempting to move things back towards state and local government, up until 1998 with limited success. In 1997, Goodling led Republican opposition that halted the administration's plan for increased testing of elementary school pupils, which Goodling termed a waste of taxpayers' money and increased federal control of local schools; but he worked with the White House on a compromise to study the usefulness of state tests. Goodling was more successful in molding his Individuals with Disabilities Education Act (IDEA); it contained some provisions to make it easier to discipline and remove disruptive pupils and at the same time contained provisions supported by disability advocates. In the 105th Congress, Goodling and his Senate counterpart, Vermont's Jim Jeffords, also worked out a compromise measure that gave states slightly more flexibility to discipline students but left most protections intact; it passed by near-unanimous margins.

The Higher Education Act was reauthorized in September 1998 with less than revolutionary change. But more change may be forthcoming with the reauthorization of the Elementary and Secondary Education Act in 1999. Goodling and other Republicans are seeking to give states and localities more flexibility, and at the same time to hold them more accountable for results. The widespread perception that public schools have not been performing as well as other public and private sector institutions has moved the fulcrum point of debate toward change. In March 1999, Goodling and the Republicans passed an EdFlex bill, to allow more flexibility and waive regulatory requirements on certain education programs; it attracted support from many Democrats. The next step, Republicans hope, is what an approach to ESEA reauthorization they call Super EdFlex. The Clinton Administration stepped back from a posture of total opposition, and it is possible that a major change in policy may be made—starting in Goodling's committee.

Goodling and the Republicans have already approached the complex gaggle of job training programs in a similar way. In 1995 they voted to give states block grants and let them decide how to use them. But repeal of Clinton's school-to-work law and the de-earmarking of aid to workers affected by trade agreements, a favorite of organized labor, meant that the measure languished in conference committee. In 1997 Goodling proposed a different approach that received significant bipartisan support and would consolidate over 60 job training and adult education programs into three block grants, including one aiding dislocated workers.

In the 104th Congress, Republicans made limited progress on labor issues, but they did come up with some interesting initiatives. One was the Teamwork for Employees and Managers (TEAM) Act, to encourage worker-management teams in non-union companies, but this was furiously opposed by Democrats and Clinton vetoed it. The other initiative was the flextime bill pushed by North Carolina Republican Cass Ballenger, to allow non-union workers to agree to take compensatory time rather than work overtime at higher rates. Again, unions were solidly against, but the bill passed the House, after union workers (only 10% of the private sector work force) were exempted. Goodling has grappled with the minimum wage increase, a policy whose economic arguments are so weak it was not advanced when Democrats had a majority in 1993 and 1994, but which they revived in 1995 as an attractive issue with which to batter and divide Republicans. That is what happened in 1996; a key Goodling amendment exempting employers with annual sales under $500,000 from any minimum wage was defeated in May, and the bill passed in the summer. It was not much mentioned in the fall campaign, but Democrats moved for further increases in 1999.

In April 1996 Goodling faced tough primary competition from Charles Gerow, head of the state Citizens Against Government Waste. After a campaign in which Gerow called him an insider, attacked him on term limits and ran as a cultural conservative, Goodling was renominated by only 55%–45%, losing one of the 19th's three counties. In a rematch in the 1998 primary, Goodling ran a better-organized and financed campaign, which included local appearances from Newt Gingrich and other top Republicans plus support from some conservative leaders, including Phyllis Schlafly and the National Rifle Association. Although Gerow was the beneficiary of about $300,000 in independent-expenditure advertising from the Wisconsin-based Americans for Limited Terms, whom Goodling criticized for demanding Republicans "commit suicide as a party," he won easily, 68%–32%.

Goodling announced during the 1998 campaign that he would not run again in 2000—in part because of the House Republicans' rule limiting committee chairmen's terms to six years. With his retirement, local Republicans promised a lively primary to succeed Goodling, with Gerow likely to face competition from state Representatives Albert Masland and Todd Platts, and possibly others. Whoever wins the primary will be favored strongly in the general election.

Cook's Call. *Safe.* This solidly Republican district is highly likely to stay in Republican hands even though long-time incumbent Goodling will retire from this seat in 2000. Expect a crowded and contentious Republican primary but little other action here in 2000.

The People: Pop. 1990: 565,789; 50.2% rural; 13.9% age 65 + ; 95.9% White, 2.6% Black, 0.7% Asian, 0.1% Amer. Indian, 0.7% Other; 1.3% Hispanic Origin. Households: 62% married couple families; 28.3% married couple fams. w. children; 33.5% college educ.; median household income: $32,424; per capita income: $14,539; median house value: $80,600; median gross rent: $336.

1996 Presidential Vote			1992 Presidential Vote		
Dole (R)	112,221	(52%)	Bush (R)	105,647	(47%)
Clinton (D)	81,319	(38%)	Clinton (D)	75,515	(33%)
Perot (I)	18,972	(9%)	Perot (I)	44,373	(20%)

Rep. William F. Goodling (R)

Elected 1974; b. Dec. 5, 1927, Loganville; home, Jacobus; U. of MD, B.S. 1953, Western MD Col., M.Ed. 1957; Methodist; married (Hilda).

Military Career: Army, 1946–48.

Elected Office: Pres., Dallastown School Bd., 1966–67.

Professional Career: Public schl. teacher & admin., 1952–74.

DC Office: 2107 RHOB 20515, 202-225-5836; Fax: 202-226-1000; Web site: www.house.gov/goodling.

District Offices: Camp Hill, 717-763-1988; Carlisle, 717-243-5432; Gettysburg, 717-334-3430; Hanover, 717-632-7855; York, 717-843-8887.

Committees: *Education & the Workforce* (Chmn. of 27 R): Early Childhood, Youth & Families; Employer-Employee Relations; Postsecondary Education, Training & Life-Long Learning. *International Relations* (2d of 26 R): International Operations and Human Rights.

Group Ratings

	ADA	ACLU	AFS	LCV	CON	NTU	NFIB	COC	ACU	NTLC	CHC
1998	5	7	13	15	13	52	100	88	92	92	100
1997	10	—	0	—	62	57	—	90	88	—	—

National Journal Ratings

	1997 LIB — 1997 CONS			1998 LIB — 1998 CONS		
Economic	19%	—	76%	36%	—	64%
Social	20%	—	71%	25%	—	75%
Foreign	24%	—	72%	7%	—	83%

Key Votes of the 105th Congress

1. Clinton Budget Deal	Y	5. Puerto Rico Sthood. Ref.	N	9. Cut $ for B-2 Bombers	Y
2. Education IRAs	Y	6. End Highway Set-asides	Y	10. Human Rights in China	Y
3. Req. 2/3 to Raise Taxes	Y	7. School Prayer Amend.	Y	11. Withdraw Bosnia Troops	Y
4. Fast-track Trade	N	8. Ovrd. Part. Birth Veto	Y	12. End Cuban TV-Marti	N

Election Results

1998 general	William F. Goodling (R)	96,284	(68%)	($458,976)
	Linda G. Ropp (D)	40,674	(29%)	($6,905)
	Others	5,531	(4%)	
1998 primary	William F. Goodling (R)	36,054	(68%)	
	Charlie Gerow (R)	17,247	(32%)	
1996 general	William F. Goodling (R)	130,716	(63%)	($305,541)
	Scott L. Chronister (D)	74,944	(36%)	($63,803)
	Others	3,303	(2%)	

TWENTIETH DISTRICT

The area south of Pittsburgh and next to the deceptively straight-edged West Virginia state line is one of the industrial backlands of America. The Scots and Irish bordermen who came here 200 years ago were wild settlers who were never tamed by townsmen in their native countries or here; this was the land of the Whiskey Rebellion of 1794. In the 19th Century, more or less continuous seams of bituminous coal were discovered under these never-ending ridges. The offspring of the original settlers were joined by immigrants from Italy, Poland and Czechoslovakia, living in little frame houses packed into the towns on interstices between hills and rivers, within walking distance of steel factories, foundries and coal mine shafts. Life was never easy here; after some prosperous years in the 1960s and 1970s, the coal country was hit hard by the recession that followed the 1979 oil shock. Young people have been leaving the area for years, and it has a disproportionate elderly population. Only in recent years has the revived high-tech economy of greater Pittsburgh radiated outward into these hills, so far with limited effect.

The 20th Congressional District consists of most of this southwest corner of Pennsylvania. It includes Washington, Fayette, and Greene Counties, which have been heavily Democratic since the United Mine Workers backed the New Deal and established the United Steelworkers as the bargaining agent in the steel mills. But there is political balance: The 20th also includes some high- and middle-income suburbs of Pittsburgh in Allegheny County and a corner of Westmoreland County.

The congressman from the 20th District is Frank Mascara, a Democrat who won the seat in 1994 after coming close in 1992. Mascara grew up in this rough industrial country and knows its risks personally: His father was injured and suffered for years from the aftermath of a steel mill accident in Monessen and his grandfather was killed in a mining accident in Fayette County. Frank Mascara served in the Army as a teenager and was an accountant and small businessman before being elected Washington County controller in 1973; he was elected chairman of the county board of commissioners in 1980 and held that post through 1994. There he helped create Southpointe industrial park, a magnet for business development and new communities. In 1992 he ran for Congress and lost to scandal-tarred incumbent Austin Murphy in the Democratic primary by only 36%–34%. In 1994, after Murphy retired, Mascara ran again, winning a three-candidate primary with 54%, and in the general beating financial consultant Mike McCormick by 53%–47%.

In the House Mascara has on balance a moderate voting record. He vociferously attacked the Contract with America, but he also voted for many of its provisions—the line-item veto, the unfunded mandates bill, welfare reform. He calls himself "pro-life and pro-gun." He voted to override President Clinton's veto of the ban on partial-birth abortion. One of the few congressmen with vivid memories of the hardships of the 1930s, when his injured father supported a family of seven as a WPA worker, he called the Republican labor plans "class warfare" and proclaimed, "I believe in workplace safety and do not want it diluted!" Mascara also worked on local issues, keeping the 911th Air Wing at Pittsburgh Airport and Charles E. Kelly Army Support facility off the base-closing list and seeking funding for the proposed Mon-Fayette Freeway. He helped to authorize the coin commemorating General George C. Marshall, a native of Fayette County, and sought flexibility for meeting air quality standards. On the highway bill, Mascara won $20 million for the Mon-Fayette Freeway.

After winning a bitterly-contested 1996 re-election against McCormick, Mascara enjoyed the leisure of running without opposition in 1998.

Cook's Call. *Safe.* Given his rather tight elections in 1994 and 1996, the fact that Republicans were unable to recruit a candidate to run against Mascara in 1998 makes it less likely that they will find a top-notch candidate to run in 2000. But, like so many of his Democratic colleagues in western Pennsylvania, Mascara could find himself in a very difficult situation after 2002 redistricting, as it is widely assumed that western Pennsylvania will lose one district.

The People: Pop. 1990: 565,789; 40.5% rural; 17.6% age 65 + ; 96.1% White, 3.2% Black, 0.5% Asian, 0.1% Amer. Indian, 0.1% Other; 0.5% Hispanic Origin. Households: 59.8% married couple families; 26.3% married couple fams. w. children; 35.5% college educ.; median household income: $26,294; per capita income: $13,349; median house value: $56,900; median gross rent: $250.

1996 Presidential Vote			1992 Presidential Vote		
Clinton (D)	109,299	(50%)	Clinton (D)	121,823	(51%)
Dole (R)	85,040	(39%)	Bush (R)	69,811	(29%)
Perot (I)	23,652	(11%)	Perot (I)	48,251	(20%)

Rep. Frank R. Mascara (D)

Elected 1994; b. Jan. 19, 1930, Belle Vernon; home, Charleroi; CA U. of PA., B.S. 1972; Catholic; married (Delores).

Military Career: Army, 1946–47.

Elected Office: Washington Cnty. Controller, 1973–80; Chmn., Bd. of Cnty. Commissioners, 1980–94.

Professional Career: Businessman & Accountant, 1956–74.

DC Office: 314 CHOB 20515, 202-225-4665; Fax: 202-225-3377; Web site: www.house.gov/mascara.

District Offices: Greensburg, 724-834-6441; N. Charleroi, 724-483-9016; Uniontown, 724-437-5078; Washington, 724-228-4326; Waynesburg, 724-852-2182.

Committees: *Banking & Financial Services* (21st of 27 D): Capital Markets, Securities & Government Sponsored Enterprises; Financial Institutions & Consumer Credit. *Transportation & Infrastructure* (18th of 34 D): Ground Transportation; Water Resources & Environment.

Group Ratings

	ADA	ACLU	AFS	LCV	CON	NTU	NFIB	COC	ACU	NTLC	CHC
1998	85	44	100	62	68	14	29	33	20	21	33
1997	65	—	88	—	70	30	—	50	32	—	—

National Journal Ratings

	1997 LIB — 1997 CONS			1998 LIB — 1998 CONS		
Economic	71%	—	28%	72%	—	23%
Social	54%	—	46%	51%	—	48%
Foreign	69%	—	28%	71%	—	27%

Key Votes of the 105th Congress

1. Clinton Budget Deal	N	5. Puerto Rico Sthood. Ref.	Y	9. Cut $ for B-2 Bombers	Y
2. Education IRAs	N	6. End Highway Set-asides	N	10. Human Rights in China	Y
3. Req. 2/3 to Raise Taxes	N	7. School Prayer Amend.	N	11. Withdraw Bosnia Troops	N
4. Fast-track Trade	N	8. Ovrd. Part. Birth Veto	Y	12. End Cuban TV-Marti	Y

Election Results

1998 general	Frank R. Mascara (D) .... unopposed			($424,974)
1998 primary	Frank R. Mascara (D) .... unopposed			
1996 general	Frank R. Mascara (D) 113,394	(54%)	($577,217)
	Mike McCormick (R) 97,004	(46%)	($381,404)

TWENTY-FIRST DISTRICT

The best natural harbor on Lake Erie is in a state that few think of as a Great Lakes state. This is Erie, protected by the Presque Isle peninsula, up in the remotest corner of Pennsylvania, 428 miles from Center City Philadelphia. This is heavy industry country: There is farmland here, and even some woods, but this land between the Great Lakes and the basin of the Ohio River has been prime heavy industry territory for more than 100 years.

The 21st Congressional District occupies this corner of Pennsylvania. About half its people are in Erie County. To the south are the farming areas of Crawford County, the steel-producing town of Sharon in Mercer County—on the Ohio border and part of the Youngstown-Warren area—and Butler County, a suburban area directly north of Pittsburgh. Politically this is closely balanced territory: Erie and Mercer counties usually vote Democratic, and Butler and Crawford counties usually vote Republican. The result was one of the classic marginal seats in the nation from 1964–82 and again in the middle 1990s. In between came the tenure of Tom Ridge, a Republican from a Catholic working class family in Erie, a Harvard graduate and Vietnam veteran, first elected here by a narrow margin in 1982, who then won easily until he was elected governor in 1994.

The congressman from the 21st now is Phil English, a Republican elected in 1994. English grew up in Erie and has worked at little else but politics and government. At 20, he was an alternate to the 1976 Republican National Convention, and he worked during the early 1980s as a Republican staffer in Harrisburg. In 1985 he became Erie controller; in 1988, he was the Republican nominee for state treasurer, losing to Democrat Catherine Baker Knoll. In 1990 he helped produce Rick Santorum's upset win in the Pittsburgh-area 18th District, the first step on Santorum's path to the Senate, and went on to other Republican staff jobs. In 1994, when Ridge ran for governor, English ran for the House and won 66% in the Republican primary—which attracted almost as many voters (61,000) as the Democratic primary (62,000). In the general, English promised to reform welfare, cut wasteful spending and create jobs for northwestern Pennsylvania with an 18-point plan for revitalizing small business and manufacturing. Three of the four counties voted on party lines. But Erie, English's home—and probably more important, Ridge's—voted for the Republican, giving him a 49%–47% victory.

In the House, the obviously vulnerable English became one of the first freshman Republicans since George Bush to win a seat on Ways and Means, an excellent spot from which to both legislate and raise money. Early on, English made a record on local issues, getting the Army Corps of Engineers to dredge and replenish the beach at Presque Isle, co-sponsoring a Rural Telemedicine Act, working to stop Korea's dumping of pipe and tubing (the Shenango Valley is the leading U.S. producer), preserving spending on low-income heating, saving an Erie bus project, and protecting Erie Forge & Steel from the IRS. While he supported the Contract with America and the Republican leadership on most votes, he has a moderate record on economic and foreign issues and has dissented prominently on occasion. He was one of three Republicans who publicly supported the minimum wage increase early on and voted against the budget resolution in 1996. He sponsored the "Lockbox Amendment," purporting to guarantee that Medicare savings are not spent on anything else.

His policy goals include fundamental tax reform to replace the individual and corporate income taxes with a consumption tax to promote savings and level the playing field for U.S. businesses and workers. (He did suffer a minor setback, though, when he held a press conference to cut the tax code in half with a chainsaw: Despite repeated efforts, English was only able to nick it and he finally gave up.) With Democrat Richard Neal, English formed the Congressional Real Estate Caucus. He won enactment in October 1998 of his innovative proposal to grant a tax break to donors to groups such as the Make-A-Wish Foundation. "No child with a severe illness should have to be careful of what they wish for," English said. English was out front on behalf of the steel industry's efforts to impose quotas on steel imports—a campaign to warn the international community that "Congress is not willing to roll over and be a patsy." But when the Kosovo crisis erupted, English conceded that he was uncertain what direction U.S. policy should head and that his international interest has not spread much beyond economic issues. "Foreign policy is not really my thing," he told *The Washington Post*. "My constituents don't get too fired up about it either. They focus more on things like health care, and so do I."

The 21st District was the scene of one of 1996's most fiercely fought battles. English was one the of the top targets in the AFL-CIO's negative TV campaigns. He in turn spent $1.3 million and attacked Democratic candidate Ron DiNicola for having practiced law in Los Angeles before he returned to Erie to run: "California office. California driver's license. And a great tan." "Independent voice. Pennsylvania values," English's campaign proclaimed, emphasizing his support for the minimum wage. English won 51%–49%, winning 48% in Erie County, carrying Butler and Crawford counties solidly and taking 47% in Mercer County.

English had a much easier time in 1998. His Democratic opponent was a vocational school principal with little political experience; in a pro-incumbent year he criticized English as a career politician. English was also helped by the strong re-election campaign of Governor Ridge, who carried Erie County 64%–22%; he mollified labor with his opposition to fast track and support for Amtrak unions. English reiterated his support for term limits, though he did not define how many for himself. But English is not guaranteed an easy ride in 2000; DiNicola, presumably less tan, has said he might run again, and the state ticket may be headed by western Pennsylvania's Ron Klink running for the Senate. Redistricting after the 2000 Census probably does not hold peril for English. Republicans, unless they lose one house of the legislature in 2000, will control the process and any new territory is likely to be Republican.

Cook's Call. *Probably Safe.* While this Erie-based district is quite marginal, Democrats were not able to recruit a strong challenger against English in 1998. 1996 Democratic nominee DiNicola is reportedly looking to run again, but English, who beat him by two points even as Clinton won the district by nine points, would still be considered the favorite.

The People: Pop. 1990: 565,806; 43.7% rural; 15.4% age 65 + ; 95.3% White, 3.8% Black, 0.4% Asian, 0.1% Amer. Indian, 0.3% Other; 0.7% Hispanic Origin. Households: 57.7% married couple families; 26.7% married couple fams. w. children; 33.1% college educ.; median household income: $25,845; per capita income: $11,884; median house value: $50,600; median gross rent: $240.

1996 Presidential Vote			1992 Presidential Vote		
Clinton (D)	106,080	(49%)	Clinton (D)	105,538	(45%)
Dole (R)	87,448	(40%)	Bush (R)	80,902	(34%)
Perot (I)	22,510	(10%)	Perot (I)	48,004	(20%)

Rep. Phil English (R)

Elected 1994; b. June 20, 1956, Erie; home, Erie; U. of PA., B.A. 1978; Catholic; married (Christiane).

Elected Office: Erie City Controller, 1985–89.

Professional Career: Staff aide, PA Senate; 1980–84; Chief of Staff, PA Sen. Melissa Hart 1990–92; Exec. Dir., PA Senate Finance Cmte., 1990–94.

DC Office: 1410 LHOB 20515, 202-225-5406; Fax: 202-225-3103; Web site: www.house.gov/english.

District Offices: Butler, 724-285-7005; Erie, 814-456-2038; Hermitage, 724-342-6132; Meadville, 814-724-8414.

Committees: *Small Business* (9th of 19 R): Empowerment; Tax, Finance & Exports. *Ways & Means* (16th of 23 R): Health; Human Resources.

Group Ratings

	ADA	ACLU	AFS	LCV	CON	NTU	NFIB	COC	ACU	NTLC	CHC
1998	35	33	44	31	6	46	93	89	68	58	92
1997	20	—	50	—	49	55	—	70	76	—	—

National Journal Ratings

	1997 LIB — 1997 CONS			1998 LIB — 1998 CONS		
Economic	47%	—	52%	47%	—	53%
Social	18%	—	81%	46%	—	53%
Foreign	30%	—	68%	27%	—	68%

Key Votes of the 105th Congress

1. Clinton Budget Deal	Y	5. Puerto Rico Sthood. Ref.	Y	9. Cut $ for B-2 Bombers	N
2. Education IRAs	Y	6. End Highway Set-asides	N	10. Human Rights in China	N
3. Req. 2/3 to Raise Taxes	Y	7. School Prayer Amend.	Y	11. Withdraw Bosnia Troops	Y
4. Fast-track Trade	N	8. Ovrd. Part. Birth Veto	Y	12. End Cuban TV-Marti	N

Election Results

1998 general	Phil English (R)	94,518	(63%)	($1,140,104)
	Larry Klemens (D)	54,591	(37%)	($19,228)
1998 primary	Phil English (R)	unopposed		
1996 general	Phil English (R)	106,875	(51%)	($1,262,645)
	Ronald A. DiNicola (D)	104,004	(49%)	($478,871)

RHODE ISLAND

The tiny little city-state with a mouthful of an official name, Rhode Island and Providence Plantations, has as turbulent a political history as any state in the Union. A successful trading community since the 1600s, a leader in manufacturing since Samuel Slater replicated from memory an English water-powered cotton textile mill in Pawtucket in 1791, Rhode Island also had its beginning as an upstart community, a refuge for religious dissenters, "the sewer of New England," as the orthodox Cotton Mather put it. Rhode Island profited from slavery (two-thirds of America's slaves arrived on ships owned by Rhode Islanders) and war (the state boomed during the Civil War), and carried its tradition of tolerating just about anything into its politics. Rhode Island refused to pay its share for the Revolutionary War, declined to send delegates to the 1787 Constitutional Convention, and delayed joining the Union until the other 12 states had, prompting George Washington to say, "Rhode Island still perseveres in that impolitic, unjust—and one might add without much impropriety—scandalous conduct, which seems to have marked all her public counsels of late." The new nation's first bank failure occurred here in 1809, when a bank capitalized at $45 issued $800,000 in bank notes. In the 1840s, conflict between hard money merchants and soft money farmers resulted in two state governments and a conflict known as Dorr's War, with the outcome determined when merchant Dorr's two ancient cannons failed to fire.

Then, in the 1930s, Rhode Island had something resembling a political revolution. Thousands of immigrants from French Canada, Ireland and Italy came to Rhode Island to work in the textile mills and this colony of dissident Protestants became the most heavily Catholic state in the nation. Yankee Republicans tried to appeal to Catholics by running French-Canadians for office. But national events—Al Smith's candidacy in 1928, when he carried Rhode Island, and Franklin Roosevelt's New Deal—moved the Catholics toward the Democrats. Then came the revolution: in 1935, the Democrats under Governor Theodore Green, although they had won only 20 of the 42 state Senate seats, refused to seat two Republicans. With the lieutenant governor's tie-breaker, they voted Democrats into the seats, and proceeded in 14 minutes to declare the state Supreme Court seats vacant, abolish state boards that controlled Democratic cities, strengthen the power of the governor and reorganize state government to purge Republicans. This ended the direct political control of Rhode Island's "Five Families"—the Browns, Metcalfs, Goddards, Lippitts and Chafees—who owned or ran many of the textile mills, the Rhode Island Hospital Trust (long the largest bank), the Providence *Journal-Bulletin*, Brown University, the Rhode Island School of Design and the state Republican Party; they ultimately lost the leadership of Rhode Island politics to the heirs of the 1935 Green revolution. The Democrats have won most elections with the lion's share of votes from Rhode Island's 64% Catholic majority, starting with Green's election in 1936, at age 69, to the first of his four terms as U.S. senator. From 1940–80, Democrats won every election for U.S. House seats; its Democratic percentages in presidential elections from 1968–96 are rivalled only by Massachusetts. Republicans have won when they've been able to capitalize on scandal or Democratic disarray, as Governor Lincoln Almond did in 1994. But the only really durable Republican politician has been John Chafee, elected governor in 1962, 1964 and 1966, senator in 1976, 1982, 1988 and 1994; and even he has lost twice statewide, in 1968 and 1972.

But if Rhode Island's national politics are mostly stable and Democratic, its state politics have been bipartisan and antic. The state's economy was transformed, not without some distress, from blue collar to white collar, from textiles to high tech. The recession of the early 1990s hit hard here, and Rhode Island has lost population in the 1990s, slipping below the million mark in 1996. The submarine factory and Navy base at Quonset Point lost thousands of jobs; em-

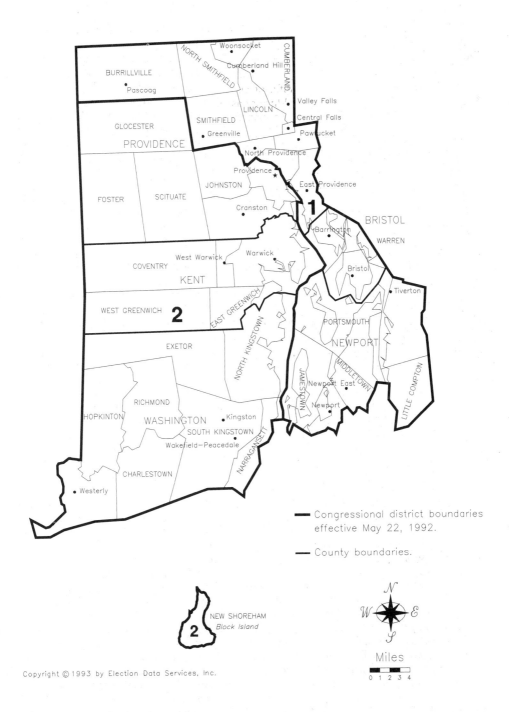

- Congressional district boundaries effective May 22, 1992.
- County boundaries.

NEW SHOREHAM
Block Island

Miles
0 1 2 3 4

ployment in costume jewelry, Rhode Island's major manufacture, fell from 32,500 in 1977 to 12,600 in 1998; overfishing has cut the lobster and winter flounder stocks sharply. One reason for the economic troubles is that wages and taxes are high by national standards. Unions remained politically powerful, though they lost many members, and the legislature remains the most Democratic in the nation: 42–8 in the Senate, 86–13 in the House (with one independent). But by the late 1990s Rhode Island's economy was once again generating jobs. Taxes were cut, Governor Lincoln Almond proposed a huge container port at Quonset Point/Davisville, and drug store giant CVS decided to keep its headquarters in Woonsocket.

Policy debacles and scandals have resulted in wild oscillations in gubernatorial races. In 1984, voters rejected 80%–20% Democratic Governor Joseph Garrahy's Greenhouse Compact, an industrial policy concocted by Ira Magaziner, later the author of the Clinton health care plan. Garrahy retired and Republican Edward DiPrete was elected governor that year, promising to encourage private sector growth. But personal scandal helped oust him (he went to jail in December 1998) and elect Democrat Bruce Sundlun, who after two unsuccessful runs finally won with 74% in 1990. In 1991 Sundlun closed 45 state-backed credit unions and banks because of the collapse of the Rhode Island Share and Deposit Indemnity Corporation, triggered by the disappearance of one mob-connected bank executive with $13 million. Scandal was rampant: Chief Justice Thomas Fay was forced from the bench in 1993 and pled guilty to crimes; DiPrete pled guilty to steering contracts in return for campaign contributions. Meanwhile it was come-back time for Providence Mayor Buddy Cianci, convicted in 1984 of assaulting and burning a man he accused of having an affair with his wife; Cianci hosted a talk radio show and was re-elected mayor in 1990 and 1994, the latter year Sundlun lost the Democratic primary to Myrth York, and Republican Lincoln Almond won Rhode Island's first four-year term in the fall. Politics is even exotic on Block Island, 10 miles out in the Atlantic Ocean: the mayor was beaten by a write-in candidate after he was accused of participating in a gang rape.

Governor. Lincoln Almond grew up in the mill town of Central Falls, not the usual venue for a Republican, and got involved in local government in Lincoln in 1963, at 26. He ran for Congress in 1968 and lost, then served as U.S. attorney from 1969–78, ran for governor in 1978 and lost, and was U.S. attorney again from 1981–93. He ran for governor again in 1994, and this time won. It was an upset not only in the general but also in the primary. The favorite was 1st District Congressman Ron Machtley, a career military veteran who in 1988 beat Banking Chairman Fernand St Germain, the man whose lax savings and loan laws led to the collapse of the industry and hundreds of billions in losses to taxpayers. But Almond rallied more party support and won the primary 58%–42%. Meanwhile, incumbent Democrat Bruce Sundlun, who had been unpopular since his first-term tax increases, lost to liberal state Senator Myrth York by a humiliating 57%–27% margin. In the general, Almond and York disputed over casino gambling: Almond was totally opposed, York said it was up to the people; the Mashantucket Pequot's Foxwoods casino in Connecticut has become a major employer of Rhode Islanders. Ultimately, Almond won by the narrow margin of 47%–44%, with 9% for Robert Healey, the bearded and long-haired candidate of the Cool Moose Party.

Almond seems oddly unpolitical; the Providence *Journal-Bulletin* called him "a man with no instinctive grasp of politics," who refuses to adjust his off-hours schedule to walk in parades, attend christenings or wakes or even fundraisers. He jousted much of the time with the over-whelmingly Democratic legislature. Yet he made progress on some fronts. His veto of the budget in July 1996 was overridden by the legislature, but he managed to reduce the number of state employees. He signed a welfare reform bill requiring recipients to work after two years, a bill to deregulate electric utilities and a bill banning discrimination against gays. He reorganized the Department of Economic Development and claimed credit when Fidelity announced it was bringing 2,500 jobs to Smithfield, though he had to settle disputes with unions. He pushed for passage of a $72 million bond issue to finance rail construction to Quonset Point/Davisville. He hailed the 500 jobs at the new Navy Underseas Lab in Newport. He pushed through a 9% income tax cut over five years, a R&D investment tax credit, and a new formula for distributing state educational aid. In January 1997 Democrats angered Almond when they rejected state Supreme Court nominee Margaret Curran, and they argued that he had no right to appoint a new lieutenant governor when incumbent Robert Weygand retired to serve in Congress; Almond appointed Bernard Jackvony anyway and the state Supreme Court upheld him. Almond remained a staunch opponent of casino gambling, despite the importunings of the Narragansett Indians.

In 1998 Almond was again opposed by York, who won the Democratic nomination easily after state Senate Majority Leader Paul Kelly dropped out of the race in November 1997. York actually raised more money than Almond up through August, put ads up on the air first and led in many polls up through October. She argued that Almond's education spending hadn't produced any increase in test scores and called for building more classrooms and reducing class sizes in early grades. Almond claimed credit for the booming economy and increase in jobs. He promised to keep pushing for the Quonset Point/Davisville container port, despite criticism by environmentalists; York said it needed more study, though a campaign e-mail sent out without her authority in October said she was against it. York brought in EPA Administrator Carol Browner, who criticized Almond surprisingly harshly for a person in her position. Almond was careful to propitiate the unions, ordering new state construction to be done by unionized firms only; in September, just after the primaries, the AFL-CIO announced its neutrality. Almond backed a $43 million basketball arena and convocation center for the University of Rhode Island (he is the first URI graduate to become governor); York opposed the project. Both sought the support of Providence Mayor Buddy Cianci, a Republican in the 1970s and an independent in the 1990s; he stayed coolly neutral. Healey, the Cool Moose candidate, ran again, with the slogan, "Healey for governor. Why not? You've done worse before."

Waiting to raise money and run ads apparently did not hurt Almond; he did well among those who made up their minds in the last month, and in a pro-incumbent year won 51%–42%, with 6% for Healey. Turnout in Providence was low and stumping by Hillary Rodham Clinton and Congressman Patrick Kennedy did not prevent Almond from carrying Woonsocket, his wife's home town. But Lieutenant Governor Bernard Jackvony lost 50%–44% to Democrat Charles Fogarty, whom Jackvony called an insider who "never had a job he didn't get from political patronage."

In 1999 Almond continued to push for the container port and worked with Cianci to sell Pfizer on a waterfront site for a research facility. He encouraged Massachusetts software firms to move to the state. He also wants to get rid of Providence's and Pawtucket's residency requirements for teachers, to require teacher applicants to pass a state exam and to offer full-day kindergarten.

Senior Senator. John Chafee was first elected to the Senate in 1976, but had a long career in public life before that. He grew up a scion of one of Rhode Island's "Five Families," left Yale to enlist in the Marine Corps and served at Guadalcanal, was recalled to active duty in 1951 and commanded a rifle company in Korea. He was elected to the legislature as a young lawyer, in 1956; at that time, he says, "the state was in a shambles" under a "rock-hard Democratic leadership, with every giveaway program known to man, leading the country in unemployment and with labor completely dominant." Chafee ran for governor in 1962 and beat a Democratic incumbent by 398 votes, and was re-elected by wide margins in 1964 and 1966. For all his popularity, this Republican has had electoral setbacks in this Democratic state: He was defeated for a fourth term as governor in 1968 and, after three years as Richard Nixon's secretary of the Navy, he lost the 1972 Senate race to incumbent Claiborne Pell. But he won an open Senate seat in 1976, was re-elected with just 51% in the recession year of 1982, won with 55% in 1988 over Lieutenant Governor Richard Licht, whose uncle had defeated him 20 years before, and was re-elected with 65% in 1994, carrying every city and town.

Chafee's voting record is roughly at midpoint in the Senate, a bit more liberal on cultural issues, a bit more conservative on foreign and defense policy. But he can also be a tough and stubborn Republican partisan. He is knowledgeable, thoughtful, widely respected, an unassuming hard worker not given to political cheap shots. He backed the 1996 Welfare Reform Act after working to preserve federal child welfare and adoption assistance programs. He supported the 1995 Republican Medicaid reform, but pushed to continue it as an entitlement for pregnant women, children and the disabled.

Chafee's impulse, in a Senate increasingly populated by conservative Republicans and liberal Democrats, is toward bipartisan compromise. He and John Breaux have assembled a group of about 20 senators of both parties who meet in Chafee's office to explore opportunities for bipartisan initiatives. One such was the Chafee-Breaux compromise budget, which was defeated in May 1996 by only a 53–46 margin, winning the support of 22 Republicans and 24 Democrats; it had a smaller tax cut than the Republican package and included an adjustment of the Consumer Price Index. On health care, it was widely assumed that Chafee would be at the center of a bipartisan compromise in 1994, and he might have been except that the Clintons held fast to their own plan until the summer, when it was too late to work out a compromise on such a complex issue. In 1996 Chafee worked to pass the Kassebaum-Kennedy Health Care Portability Act, and in 1997, with Jay Rockefeller, Chafee sponsored the law to expand children's health insurance through Medicaid. Another example is the Chafee-Graham managed care bill, which was introduced in summer 1998 and again in January 1999. It allows lawsuits against HMOs, but none of the "pain and suffering" awards which enrich trial lawyers. Still another is the 1997 law, co-sponsored by Jay Rockefeller, to make a child's health and safety, not family preservation, the prime consideration in order to speed the adoption of children in foster care. He passed bills to modify copyright requirements to expand the availability of books for the blind and for a memorial on the Mall to African-American Revolutionary War patriots.

On the environment, Chafee is a Republican in the conservationist tradition that goes back to Theodore Roosevelt; he and Congressman Sherwood Boehlert formed a TR Fund, which in 1998 gave $75,000 to Republican candidates who share their views. As chairman of the Environment and Public Works Committee since 1994 and ranking Republican for eight years before that, Chafee supported the 1987 water projects bill passed over Ronald Reagan's veto, the 1988 ocean dumping law, the 1989 oil spill law and, especially, the 1990 Clean Air Act. He has been a major force for protection of wetlands and barrier islands. He has also backed billboard control, commercial fishing safety, state partnerships for wildlife preservation and the Rio treaties on global climate change and biodiversity. He took the lead on reforming the Safe Drinking Water Act in 1995 and 1996, requiring cost-benefit analysis for EPA regulations and revoking its authority to set water contaminant standards every three years. This was passed with strong bipartisan support, as were the 1998 amendments to combat the water-borne parasite cryptosporidium with more filtering and disinfection.

But he is not a down-the-line supporter of liberal environmental groups. He surprised some in late 1996 and early 1997 when he circulated letters critical of the EPA's air-quality standards. He said that costs should be taken into account, and questioned the science behind the EPA's conclusions. He warned that regulations requiring extremely expensive steps to meet dangers not clearly visible might provoke a "revolt" against the Clean Air Act. "You overload the horse . . . and you get the whole program in jeopardy," he said. On the Endangered Species Act, he favored incentives for property owners who comply with regulations, but contrary to many other Republicans he opposed compensation for landowners whose property value decreases as a result of regulations; he and Dirk Kempthorne tried to get an ESA rewrite with bipartisan support in the Senate into the October 1998 omnibus budget, but House Republicans prevented it.

Chafee believes that emissions of the gases alleged to cause global warming should be reduced, but he responded sharply to the December 1997 Kyoto treaty: "While the intentions, efforts and goals of the participants were worthwhile, the fact that there is no binding, meaningful participation by developing nations is a major shortcoming. I am deeply skeptical about the chances for approval by the U.S. Senate of the treaty in its present form." That pretty much killed the treaty, for without Chafee's support it could never come close to the two-thirds needed for ratification. In March 1999 he produced a bill, co-sponsored by Connie Mack and Joseph Lieberman, to give credits in a kind of escrow account for businesses which reduce emissions voluntarily; otherwise, he argues, the possibility that Kyoto might be ratified is a disincentive to spending on reductions now because businesses might have to spend much more later.

Chafee's biggest bill in the 105th Congress was also bipartisan: the May 1998 reauthorization of the giant transportation act. The strategy was to satisfy demands for changes in the funding formula by increasing total spending substantially; Chafee, however, has opposed efforts by House Chairman Bud Shuster to take transportation spending off-budget. Chafee also continued and enriched options for non-highway spending by states, including air pollution reduction, transit improvements, shared ride services, alternative fuels and vehicle exhaust inspections; his one major loss was his failure to get a requirement of .08% blood alcohol level for DUIs. Rhode Island got $155 million for earmarked projects and $2.18 for every dollar it pays in gas taxes, the most favorable return after Alaska and the District of Columbia. He has helped get money for a commuter rail line to Theodore F. Green Airport, $1.3 million to preserve the William Viall farm and its wetlands in North Kingstown, and $6.75 million for wildlife refuges on the south shore; when the Clinton Administration cut funding of the Blackstone River Valley National Heritage Corridor to $500,000, Chafee got it raised to $1.5 million.

On another local issue, Chafee has long opposed Indian gambling. He secured passage of the Rhode Island Indian Claims Settlement in 1978, requiring state voter approval for Indian gambling; after that seemed threatened by a state law, he passed another such bill in 1996. On that, and many other issues, he received sharp criticism from Congressman Patrick Kennedy. Kennedy at one point accused Chafee of "masquerading as a Republican moderate who does deals with the right wing in order to maintain his leadership status." Chafee told a Rhode Island reporter, "I have no interest in what he has to say. I find those remarks ill-tempered and juvenile." Kennedy was obviously eyeing Chafee's seat, and in early 1997 a poll showed Kennedy with a higher job approval rating. But through 1997 and into 1998 Chafee stepped up his activities in the state; his numbers went up and Kennedy's went down. In November 1998 Kennedy was named chairman of the Democratic Congressional Campaign Committee; soon after he announced he would not run for the Senate whether or not Chafee ran. Chafee voted against impeachment in February 1999, but he had supported Republican positions on procedure and drafted a six-point plan that was used to depose the witnesses quickly. In March 1999 Chafee announced he would not run again. "I want to make it clear that I'm not going away mad or disillusioned or upset with the Senate," he said. "I think it's a great place." He regretted leaving fellow moderates "high and dry," but had faith "others will come along."

The race for Chafee's seat will be a hard-fought one. Senate seats don't come up often here: Chafee will have held his 24 years, Claiborne Pell held his for 36, John Pastore for 26, Theodore Green for 24—they, plus Jack Reed, are the only senators from Rhode Island this half-century. The likely Republican candidate is Lincoln Chafee, John Chafee's son and mayor of Warwick, the state's second largest city, since 1992. Lincoln Chafee worked as a farrier, shoeing horses, for seven years, then returned to Rhode Island and worked in business and ran for office; he announced in April 1999, and his father was quickly asking Governor Lincoln Almond for his support. Former Congressman Ron Machtley had already announced he would not run. Other Republicans mentioned as candidates—former Lieutenant Governor Bernard Jackvony, 1998 Treasurer nominee James Bennett and former Treasurer Nancy Mayer—all lost statewide races in 1996 or 1998. Some Democrats were dismissive of Chafee's chances. But it will be an uphill race for any Republican in heavily Democratic Rhode Island.

Democrats are likely to have a lively primary. Soon after Chafee's announcement, 2d District Congressman Robert Weygand got into the race and said he would campaign on early childhood programs, home health care and support for small business; he has good ties to unions and is anti-abortion. Also quickly in the running was former Lieutenant Governor Richard Licht, who lost 55%–45% to Chafee in 1988. Kennedy said he would support Speaker John Harwood, his mentor in the state House. Other possible candidates include Secretary of State Jim Langevin,

1416   RHODE ISLAND

1994 and 1998 governor candidate Myrth York, Attorney General Sheldon Whitehouse and former Providence Mayor and Ambassador to Malta Joseph Paolino. Rhode Island has a September primary; Democrats hope their primary will produce a winner with momentum; Republicans hope it will be a bloodbath with a weakened nominee.

Cook's Call. *Highly Competitive.* There is likely to be a hotly contested race to replace Chafee. On the Republican side, Lincoln Chafee, the senator's son and the mayor of Warwick, is likely to be the nominee. For Democrats, Representative Bob Weygand and former Lieutenant Governor and 1988 Senate nominee Richard Licht have said they are running. Given the state's Democratic leanings, they should have an edge here, but Republicans are poised to fight for the seat.

Junior Senator. Jack Reed is a Democrat elected in 1996 after six years in the House. Reed grew up in working-class Cranston, the son of a school custodian; he graduated from West Point, served in the 82d Airborne, then taught at West Point. In 1979 he retired from the Army and went to Harvard Law School. In 1984, at 35, he beat an incumbent in the primary for state Senate, where he served for six years, was close to the party leadership, and built a good reputation. When Republican Claudine Schneider left the House to run against Senator Claiborne Pell in 1990, Reed ran for the House seat, overcoming several better known candidates in the primary, and winning with 59% over Save the Bay Executive Director Trudy Coxe in the general.

Reed compiled a substantially, though not quite totally, liberal record in the House. In 1991 he worked successfully for a $180 million loan guarantee package for Rhode Island during its banking crisis. On the Education and the Workforce Committee he worked for the Goals 2000 Act, insisting on a requirement that states show gradual progress in meeting educational standards; on reauthorization of the Elementary and Secondary Education Act, he backed the "opportunity to learn" standards—spending requirements— backed by teachers' unions. He tried to amend the 1996 Welfare Reform Act to have block grants increase when national unemployment is more than 6%. Using his military experience, he criticized U.N. efforts in the Balkans as trying to be "all things to all people" and, before American Rangers were killed, said the Somalia mission was hampered by "poor intelligence" and "an awkward command structure." In summer 1994, after a trip to Haiti, he called for tougher economic sanctions and no military involvement; in March 1995 he said he was "pleasantly surprised" about Aristide's "apparent commitment to democratic reform." On local issues, Reed worked for the freight rail connection at the Quonset Point/Davisville port and introduced legislation to require indelible country-of-origin markings on foreign-made jewelry and jewelry boxes; Rhode Island's jewelry industry, which produces about a third of the costume jewelry in the United States, has been in decline for the past 20 years as it increasingly competes with foreign imports.

When Senator Claiborne Pell announced his retirement after 36 years in the Senate, Reed almost immediately started running. His most formidable Democratic opponent, former Providence Mayor Joseph Paolino, ran for the House instead and lost his primary. Reed was easily nominated and faced state Treasurer Nancy Mayer in the general. National Republicans spent nearly $1 million on ads attacking Reed as a liberal for opposing workfare and for supporting labor unions; in liberal, unionized Rhode Island these did not hurt him and may have helped. Mayer's support for campaign finance reform and opposition to soft money were parried when Reed in debate asked her why she didn't call off the Republican soft money campaign against him. She attacked him as a supporter of "pension giveaways" when he was a legislator and for being too close to teacher unions. But Mayer's campaign was overshadowed by Reed's: She spent $773,000 and he spent $2.7 million. His biography was his message: Reed launched his campaign in a school conference room named after his late father; he stressed how he came up from humble beginnings by hard work and called for education spending to help others rise as he had. That message, and his own pleasant, unassuming demeanor evidently touched a chord. He won 63%–35%, an impressive first Senate victory.

In the Senate, Reed has a mostly liberal voting record. He serves on the Labor Committee and has sought to amend major bills. With Paul Wellstone, he called for raising the maximum Pell grants from $3,000 to $5,800. He restored a $35 million program cut by Appropriations which gives federal money to state programs aiding low-income college students. The 1998 Higher Education law included his TEACH program, grants to teacher colleges for partnerships with K-12 schools. He has sponsored bills to limit cardholders' liability on debit cards to $50 and to prohibit banks from canceling credit cards of holders who pay their bills in full. With Congressmen John Spratt and Amo Houghton, he filed a brief with the Supreme Court against the 8th Circuit decision outlawing Missouri's campaign contribution limits.

Reed is one of the few senators of his generation with military experience. He was appointed to the governing board of West Point in 1998 and got a seat on the Armed Services Committee in January 1999. He wants to consolidate the Naval War College and the Naval Undersea Warfare Center, two of the remaining Rhode Island military facilities; defense jobs in the state declined from 44,000 in 1970 to 14,000 in 1996. In January 1998 he called for extending the June 1998 deadline for withdrawal of U.S. troops from Bosnia, but with clear "milestones" for withdrawal. In June 1998 he and John McCain led the fight against cutting off funds for the Bosnia deployment. In February 1999 he expressed "deep skepticism" about U.S. involvement in Yugoslavia, but he supported the air war over Serbia and Kosovo.

In Rhode Island politics, Reed has always been his own man, unentangled with the various machine politicians who come and go. He picked a non-political prosecutor to be U.S. attorney in 1998. On local projects, he and Robert Weygand got a $15 million grant for a job training center at the former Ladd Center; he obtained a planning grant to protect Conanicut Battery, a Revolutionary War gun emplacement. He sponsored a bill to extend the stay of 200 Liberians allowed into Rhode Island as refugees seven years before.

This is a Senate seat whose members have had long tenures. Theodore Green, elected at 69, served 24 years; Claiborne Pell, elected at 41, served 36 years. Reed, elected just before turning 47, has the prospect of long service before him; there is no reason to believe he will have trouble winning re-election in 2002.

Presidential politics. Rhode Island is always among the most Democratic states in presidential elections—over the last generation, the most Democratic on average: It voted 60%–27% for Bill Clinton in 1996. Rhode Island's Catholic majority is heavily Democratic and, interestingly, pro-choice on abortion: In states where Catholics are beleaguered minorities they may stand together and strongly oppose abortion; here, where they're the strong majority and where the mostly Mediterranean Catholics don't always pay strict attention to the mostly Irish priests, they come out against the church position.

Rhode Island holds a presidential primary the same day as Massachusetts, usually with the lowest turnout rate in the nation. It has not won much attention. In 1992 only 66,000 of the one million Rhode Islanders voted in both parties' primaries; in 1996 only 14,000 voted in the Republican primary.

Congressional districting. The boundaries of Rhode Island's two congressional districts were altered only slightly for 1992. Providence is split and both districts are overwhelmingly Democratic.

The People: Est. Pop. 1998: 988,480; Pop. 1990: 1,003,464, down 1.5% 1990–1998. 0.4% of U.S. total, 43d largest; 14% rural. Median age: 35.8 years. 15.8% 65 years and over. 91.6% White, 3.8% Black, 1.8% Asian, 0.4% Amer. Indian, 2.4% Other; 4.4% Hispanic Origin. Households: 53.5% married couple families; 24.4% married couple fams. w. children; 42.6% college educ.; median household income: $32,181; per capita income: $14,981; 59.5% owner occupied housing; median house value: $133,500; median monthly rent: $416. 4.9% Unemployment. 1998 Voting age pop.: 751,000. 1998 Turnout: 309,835; 41% of VAP. Registered voters (1998): 632,955; no party registration.

1418   RHODE ISLAND

Political Lineup: Governor, Lincoln Almond (R); Lt. Gov., Charles J. Fogarty (D); Secy. of State, James Langevin (D); Atty. Gen., Sheldon Whitehouse (D); General Treasurer, Paul Tavares (D); State Senate, 50 (42 D, 8 R); Majority Leader, Paul S. Kelly (D); State House, 100 (86 D, 13 R, 1 I); House Speaker, John Harwood (D). Senators, John H. Chafee (R) and Jack Reed (D). Representatives, 2 (2 D).

Elections Division: 401-222-2340; **Filing Deadline for U.S. Congress:** June 28, 2000.

1996 Presidential Vote
Clinton (D)	233,050	(60%)
Dole (R)	104,683	(27%)
Perot (I)	43,723	(11%)
Others	8,674	(2%)

1996 Republican Presidential Primary
Dole (R)	9,664	(64%)
Alexander (R)	2,859	(19%)
Others	2,486	(17%)

1992 Presidential Vote
Clinton (D)	213,299	(47%)
Bush (R)	131,601	(29%)
Perot (I)	105,045	(23%)

GOVERNOR

Gov. Lincoln Almond (R)

Elected 1994, term expires Jan. 2003; b. June 16, 1936, Pawtucket; home, Lincoln; U. of RI, B.S. 1958, Boston U., J.D. 1961; Episcopalian; married (Marilyn).

Military Career: Naval Reserves, 1953–61.

Elected Office: Lincoln Town Admin., 1963–68; Repub. nominee for U.S. House, 1968; Repub. nominee for Gov., 1978.

Professional Career: Practicing atty., 1962–94; U.S. Atty. for RI, 1969–78, 1981–93; Pres., Blackstone Valley Land Develop. Foundation, 1982–94.

Office: The State House, Providence, 02903, 401-222-2080; Fax: 401-861-5894; Web site: www.state.ri.us.

Election Results

1998 gen.	Lincoln Almond (R)		156,180	(51%)
	Myrth York (D)		129,105	(42%)
	Robert J. Healey (Cool Moose)		19,250	(6%)
	Others		1,910	(1%)
1998 prim.	Lincoln Almond (R)		unopposed	
1994 gen.	Lincoln Almond (R)		171,194	(47%)
	Myrth York (D)		157,361	(44%)
	Robert J. Healey (Cool Moose)		32,822	(9%)

SENATORS

Sen. John H. Chafee (R)

Elected 1976, seat up 2000; b. Oct. 22, 1922, Providence; home, Warwick; Yale U., B.A. 1947, Harvard U., LL.B. 1950; Episcopalian; married (Virginia).

Military Career: Marine Corps, 1942–45 (WWII), 1951–53 (Korea).

Elected Office: RI House of Reps., 1956–62, Minority Ldr., 1959–62; RI Gov., 1962–69; Repub. nominee for U.S. Senate, 1972.

Professional Career: Practicing atty., 1952–63, 1973–75; U.S. Navy Secy., 1969–72.

DC Office: 505 DSOB, 20510, 202-224-2921; Web site: www.senate.gov/~chafee.

State Office: Providence, 401-453-5294.

Committees: *Environment & Public Works* (Chmn. of 10 R). *Finance* (2d of 11 R): Health Care (Chmn.); International Trade; Long-Term Growth & Debt Reduction; Social Security & Family Policy. *Intelligence* (2d of 9 R). *Joint Committee on Taxation* (2d of 5 Sens.).

Group Ratings

	ADA	ACLU	AFS	LCV	CON	NTU	NFIB	COC	ACU	NTLC	CHC
1998	45	86	56	50	75	36	89	89	32	46	20
1997	55	—	22	—	85	59	—	100	24	—	—

National Journal Ratings

	1997 LIB — 1997 CONS		1998 LIB — 1998 CONS	
Economic	50%	— 49%	51%	— 48%
Social	71%	— 0%	63%	— 26%
Foreign	73%	— 19%	51%	— 36%

Key Votes of the 105th Congress

1. Bal. Budget Amend.	Y	5. Satcher for Surgeon Gen.	Y	9. Chem. Weapons Treaty	Y
2. Clinton Budget Deal	Y	6. Highway Set-asides	Y	10. Cuban Humanitarian Aid	Y
3. Cloture on Tobacco	Y	7. Table Child Gun locks	N	11. Table Bosnia Troops	Y
4. Education IRAs	N	8. Ovrd. Part. Birth Veto	N	12. $ for Test-ban Treaty	Y

Election Results

1994 general	John H. Chafee (R)	222,856	(65%)	($2,086,236)
	Linda J. Kushner (D)	122,532	(35%)	($805,867)
1994 primary	John H. Chafee (R)	27,906	(69%)	
	Thomas Post (R)	12,517	(31%)	
1988 general	John H. Chafee (R)	217,273	(55%)	($2,841,985)
	Richard A. Licht (D)	180,717	(45%)	($2,735,917)

1420   RHODE ISLAND

Sen. Jack Reed (D)

Elected 1996, seat up 2002; b. Nov. 12, 1949, Cranston; home, Cranston; U.S. Military Acad., West Point, B.S. 1971, Harvard U., M.P.P. 1973, J.D. 1982; Catholic; single.

Military Career: Army, 1967–79; Army Reserves, 1979–91.

Elected Office: RI Senate, 1984–90; U.S. House of Reps., 1990–96.

Professional Career: Assoc. Prof., U.S. Military Acad. at West Point, 1978–79; Practicing atty., 1982–90.

DC Office: 320 HSOB, 20510, 202-224-4642; Fax: 202-224-4680; Web site: www.senate.gov/~reed.

State Offices: Cranston, 401-943-3100; Providence, 401-528-5200.

Committees: *Aging (Special)* (6th of 9 D). *Armed Services* (9th of 9 D): Airland Forces; Personnel; Seapower. *Banking, Housing & Urban Affairs* (6th of 9 D): Economic Policy (RMM); Financial Institutions; Securities. *Health, Education, Labor & Pensions* (8th of 8 D): Children & Families; Public Health.

Group Ratings

	ADA	ACLU	AFS	LCV	CON	NTU	NFIB	COC	ACU	NTLC	CHC
1998	95	86	100	100	62	10	22	56	0	0	0
1997	100	—	100	—	8	12	—	44	0	—	—

National Journal Ratings

	1997 LIB — 1997 CONS		1998 LIB — 1998 CONS	
Economic	95% —	4%	83% —	10%
Social	71% —	0%	74% —	0%
Foreign	87% —	8%	65% —	27%

Key Votes of the 105th Congress

1. Bal. Budget Amend.	N	5. Satcher for Surgeon Gen.	Y
2. Clinton Budget Deal	N	6. Highway Set-asides	Y
3. Cloture on Tobacco	Y	7. Table Child Gun locks	N
4. Education IRAs	N	8. Ovrd. Part. Birth Veto	N

9. Chem. Weapons Treaty	Y
10. Cuban Humanitarian Aid	Y
11. Table Bosnia Troops	Y
12. $ for Test-ban Treaty	Y

Election Results

1996 general	Jack Reed (D)	230,676	(63%)	($2,732,011)
	Nancy J. Mayer (R)	127,368	(35%)	($773,789)
1996 primary	Jack Reed (D)	59,336	(86%)	
	Don Gil (D)	9,554	(14%)	
1990 general	Claiborne Pell (D)	225,105	(62%)	($2,363,904)
	Claudine Schneider (R)	138,947	(38%)	($2,056,923)

FIRST DISTRICT

The 1st Congressional District is the eastern half of Rhode Island, east of Narragansett Bay, a line that cuts through Providence and then proceeds west and north to the Massachusetts-Connecticut-Rhode Island border. It includes much of Providence (including elite College Hill around Brown University) and all of next-door Pawtucket whose Slater Mill is known as the birthplace of the American Industrial Revolution. The onetime textile mill towns of the Black-stone Valley, Woonsocket and Central Falls are also in the 1st, along with high-income Barrington and Bristol and, south on the ocean, the old city of Newport, with its restored 18th Century houses and the summer "cottages" that are really palaces. Newport was once home to the America's Cup races and now hosts a famous jazz festival. It is also the site of the oldest synagogue in North America. Ethnically, this district is the more French-Canadian and the less Italian of the two Rhode Island districts; politically, it is strongly Democratic in most elections.

The congressman from the 1st District is Patrick Kennedy, a Democrat elected in 1994. Patrick Kennedy was born in 1967, his father Edward Kennedy's fifth year in the Senate; a week after his second birthday came the terrible accident at Chappaquiddick. He grew up in McLean, Virginia, and had a somewhat troubled youth, spending time in a drug rehabilitation clinic in 1986 before enrolling at Providence College, at 20, in 1987. Almost immediately, in 1988, he ran for a seat in the state House and beat the longtime incumbent as the tiny (population 9,800) district was inundated with visits by Kennedy family members and funds raised by the Kennedy national fundraising network. He became chairman of the Rules Committee in 1992, a year after spending the now-infamous Easter weekend in Palm Beach with his father and cousin William Kennedy Smith. In 1994, when the 1st District's Congressman Ron Machtley ran for governor, Kennedy decided to run for Congress. Kennedy had an attractive and energetic Republican opponent, Kevin Vigilante, a doctor who worked with handicapped orphans in Romania and with female prison inmates infected with HIV. Vigilante was a moderate on issues and raised enough to spend $803,000. But Kennedy had the advantages of money and his family name, and won 54%–46% in a Republican year.

In the House Kennedy has a liberal voting record and has proven an excitable if not always eloquent debater. He started off by avoiding national media and working on local issues, from the Naval Undersea Warfare Center in Newport to visas for Portuguese immigrants. He was co-founder of the Portuguese-American Caucus and brought the president of Portugal to Rhode Island and visited the former Portuguese colony of East Timor. He worked to save funding for Meals on Wheels and sought tax deductibility for interest on student loans. He sponsored a bill to fund public-private partnerships on ocean research. He supported the law to make it easier to evict unruly tenants from public housing. He voted for the Helms-Burton Act and was strongly anti-Castro, and he strongly supported gun control: two issues with family reverberations. He raised vast sums of money, including $5,000 which was funneled from the Hsi Lai Buddhist temple where Al Gore made his famous appearance; Kennedy had no reason to know that and returned the funds promptly when this came out in September 1997.

After winning re-election by 69%–28% in 1996, he took on a more combative role. He criticized Governor Lincoln Almond sharply for vetoing a bill to make it harder for non-profit hospitals to take over for-profits. He criticized Senator John Chafee sharply for voting for the Defense of Marriage Act and for his bill, passed in 1996, blocking the Narragansett Indians from building a casino without a referendum. He did conventional work on local projects—for a maritime research center at the Naval War College and for two new labs at the Naval Undersea Warfare Center—and less conventionally joined the sometimes violent Teamster picket line during the UPS strike. It seemed obvious that Kennedy was eyeing Chafee's Senate seat in 2000, whether or not Chafee sought re-election. But Chafee fought back gamely, returning often to the state, working hard on local projects, and his standing in the polls, never weak, slowly rose. Meanwhile, the harshness of Kennedy's attacks evidently grated; his job approval fell from 62% to 44% during the year. Former Republican state Chairman John Holmes argued that Kennedy's attacks made him seem an "uncontrollable young man who is trying to grab as many headlines as possible. Rhode Islanders do not forgive you for immaturely attacking 60- and 70-year old people who have passed the test of time."

In April 1998 Kennedy said he wanted a seat on Appropriations—not a likely goal if he intended to seek only one more term in the House. He struck up a friendship with Minority Leader Dick Gephardt, even forming a joint PAC with him to help finance their political travels;

Kennedy let it be known that he would support Gephardt for president over Al Gore. Kennedy bristled in November 1997 when the Clinton Administration threatened to put some of the Blackstone Valley National Heritage Corridor on the line-item veto list a day before fast track, which he and Gephardt opposed; Kennedy bristled again when he was not invited to be at a Rhode Island Social Security forum featuring Al Gore, though Chafee and 2d District Congressman Robert Weygand were. His relations with Weygand were edgy; they disagreed on abortion, and Weygand's wife, known locally as "Hurricane Fran," said of Kennedy in *Rhode Island Monthly*, "He's a very nice young man. But I don't think he has a heck of a lot going for him. I think he feels very intimidated by Bob. Bob has worked hard to get where he is. Bob knows the issues." Kennedy harshly criticized Weygand when he voted for the Republican version of the impeachment inquiry in October 1998. "I think he's trying to cover his backside. I don't know where he went to learn, you know, Politics 101," Kennedy said—a curious analysis since Rhode Island was perhaps the most anti-impeachment state.

What Kennedy excels in is raising money. He is probably the biggest single draw at fundraisers around the country of any Democratic House member, except perhaps Gephardt, and in the 1998 cycle he went to dozens. The draw, of course, is that he is a Kennedy: "It does give me a big leg-up in raising money. It's one of the advantages that I have, coming from the family that I come from." He also contributed $50,000 to the Democratic Congressional Campaign Committee, contributed $170,000 more to colleagues from his leadership PAC. He spent little time that fall in Rhode Island, avoiding joint appearances and spending $1 million. He was re-elected 67%–28%, a margin a bit smaller than Weygand's, and was plainly elated by the results, and convinced that Democrats would capture the House in 2000.

In November 1998 Gephardt named Kennedy DCCC chairman (it is one of the few leadership positions in either party that is appointive rather than elective). A few days later Kennedy announced what was already pretty plain, that he would not run for the Senate, whatever Chafee's decision. He said he thought he was better suited to the "hurlyburly" of the House than the comity of the Senate; those who decry the partisanship of the House could easily, but usually do not, have Kennedy in mind when they make their plaints. Some doubted Kennedy's ability to make the political judgments required of a DCCC chairman. But he gamely worked at memorizing political statistics, and Gephardt installed some of his top staffers in the office. Some moderate Democrats noted that the new executive director was also a political director of the feminist EMILY's List, and wondered whether Kennedy, however attractive to Democratic contributors, would be a millstone to the party in Southern and other conservatively inclined districts. In December 1998 he went to Puerto Rico to urge voters to support statehood in a referendum—something few other mainland politicians would think of doing.

The likely long-term career path for Patrick Kennedy seems fairly clear. He got a seat on Appropriations in December 1998, but took a leave of absence; once he rotates off the DCCC chairmanship (as most chairmen have after a few terms), he can take a middling-seniority position there or run for another leadership spot. This dynast, who seemed in early 1997 to have a strong chance for a lifetime career in the Senate, and from there to become the kind of visible national leader his father has been, seemed by early 1999 to be unlikely to serve there at all. Senator Jack Reed turns 51 in 2000 and most of the contenders for the Chafee seat are about the same age; Reed is politically safe and seems to have no national ambitions and that is likely to be true for the senator elected in 2000 as well. So Kennedy, an elected official since age 21, may not find an open Senate seat to run for until he is 60 or so. His likely future is as a noisy, energetic, fiercely partisan leader of the House, ambitious for a leadership position— but for the first time needing to convince colleagues voting in secret ballot that he has the necessary skills and judgment, not just the fund of boyish energy and the famous name that have taken him to where he is now.

Cook's Call. *Safe.* Patrick Kennedy can keep this House seat for as long as he wants it. And from his decision to turn down a run for the open Senate seat of John Chafee, it looks like he plans to stay put for quite a while.

The People: Pop. 1990: 501,696; 8.6% rural; 16.5% age 65 +; 93% White, 3.2% Black, 1.2% Asian, 0.2% Amer. Indian, 2.4% Other; 3.7% Hispanic Origin. Households: 52.9% married couple families; 23.8% married couple fams. w. children; 42% college educ.; median household income: $31,675; per capita income: $15,224; median house value: $137,300; median gross rent: $413.

1996 Presidential Vote

Clinton (D)	114,858	(61%)
Dole (R)	48,964	(26%)
Perot (I)	20,287	(11%)
Others	4,304	(2%)

1992 Presidential Vote

Clinton (D)	107,141	(48%)
Bush (R)	62,758	(28%)
Perot (I)	50,842	(23%)

Rep. Patrick J. Kennedy (D)

Elected 1994; b. July 14, 1967, Brighton, MA; home, Providence; Providence Col., B.A. 1991; Catholic; single.

Elected Office: RI House of Reps., 1988–94.

DC Office: 312 CHOB 20515, 202-225-4911; Fax: 202-225-3290; Web site: www.house.gov/patrickkennedy.

District Office: Pawtucket, 401-729-5600.

Committees: *DCCC Chairman. Armed Services* (11th of 28 D): Military Personnel; Military Research & Development. *Resources* (14th of 24 D): Energy & Mineral Resources; Forests & Forest Health (RMM).

Group Ratings

	ADA	ACLU	AFS	LCV	CON	NTU	NFIB	COC	ACU	NTLC	CHC
1998	95	88	100	100	89	19	0	33	12	11	8
1997	80	—	100	—	12	28	—	20	17	—	—

National Journal Ratings

	1997 LIB	—	1997 CONS	1998 LIB	—	1998 CONS
Economic	93%	—	0%	72%	—	23%
Social	77%	—	22%	81%	—	16%
Foreign	63%	—	36%	61%	—	37%

Key Votes of the 105th Congress

1. Clinton Budget Deal	N	5. Puerto Rico Sthood. Ref.	Y	9. Cut $ for B-2 Bombers	Y
2. Education IRAs	N	6. End Highway Set-asides	N	10. Human Rights in China	Y
3. Req. 2/3 to Raise Taxes	N	7. School Prayer Amend.	N	11. Withdraw Bosnia Troops	N
4. Fast-track Trade	N	8. Ovrd. Part. Birth Veto	Y	12. End Cuban TV-Marti	N

Election Results

1998 general	Patrick J. Kennedy (D)	92,788	(67%)	($1,023,152)
	Ronald G. Santa (R)	38,460	(28%)	($26,044)
	James C. Sheehan (Ref)	6,202	(4%)	($22,577)
1998 primary	Patrick J. Kennedy (D)	unopposed		
1996 general	Patrick J. Kennedy (D)	121,781	(69%)	($1,051,719)
	Giovanni D. Cicione (R)	49,199	(28%)	($23,237)
	Others	4,445	(3%)	

SECOND DISTRICT

The 2d Congressional District is the western half of Rhode Island. While the 1st includes many mill towns, the 2d has most of its population in working- and middle-class towns like Cranston and Warwick which, despite their British names, are inhabited mostly by people with Irish, Italian, French and Portuguese surnames. The 2d also has the affluent suburbs to the south along Narragansett Bay and the area around Westerly, where many residents work at the Electric Boat shipyards in Groton, Connecticut.

The congressman from the 2d District is Robert Weygand, a Democrat elected in 1996. Weygand grew up in Rhode Island, received arts and engineering degrees at the University of Rhode Island, became a landscape architect and started his own architectural firm. He served on the East Providence Planning Board in 1978, at 30, and in 1984 was elected to the state House, where he chaired the Corporations Committee and worked on land use, lead poisoning and nursing home legislation. In 1992 and 1994 he was elected lieutenant governor, where he worked on small business and elderly care programs. But he made his political name in 1991 as a state representative, when he was offered a city architectural contract for a $1,750 kickback by Pawtucket Mayor Brian Sarault; Weygand immediately went to the FBI, was fitted with a listening device, and went back to Sarault's office where the offer was repeated—FBI agents stormed in and arrested the mayor, who was sent to prison.

In 1996 Weygand looked to have an easy run of it, in the usually decisive Democratic primary, until Joseph Paolino, former Providence mayor and recently resigned ambassador to Malta, withdrew from the Senate race and ran in the 2d District. Paolino called for a crackdown on illegal immigration, a phasing out of bilingual education and making English the official language. He outmaneuvered Weygand to get the party endorsement at the state convention, partly because of Weygand's opposition to abortion, and was backed by Providence Mayor Buddy Cianci, Congressman and Senate candidate Jack Reed, Congressman Patrick Kennedy and 1994 gubernatorial nominee Myrth York. Paolino spent liberally of his own money and seemed well ahead. But Weygand had resources of his own. He was supported by Rhode Island's usually outnumbered right-to-lifers and by many labor unions. He ran an ad in which actors portraying figures in *The Maltese Falcon* made fun of Paolino for giving up his ambassadorship. He accused Paolino of hiring relatives in his last days as mayor. In something of a shocker, Weygand won the primary 48%–38%. Paolino carried Providence and next-door Johnston, plus heavily Italian-American Westerly, but Weygand carried everything else. The general was easier: In this Democratic district Weygand won 64%–32%, carrying every city and town.

In the House Weygand has a moderate to liberal voting record. He has fought cuts in Medicare home health care programs; with Republican Tom Coburn and fellow Democrat Jim McGovern, he argued that the 1997 anti-fraud provisions had gone too far and forced many providers out of business; in early 1999 he called on the Clinton Administration to hold off further changes in Medicare until the impact of earlier adjustments could be assessed. He serves on the Budget Committee and in February 1998 called for using two-thirds of any surplus for retiring the national debt and one-third for new spending. He criticized Governor Lincoln Almond sharply for using tobacco lawsuit revenue for general spending and not devoting it to health programs. He often seems to relate issues to his personal experiences: On the Lewinsky scandal, he referred to his own 25-year-old daughter; he opposed a wetlands proposal, remembering how hard it was as a small businessman to comply with all the forms; he supports property rights, remembering the effect of a zoning downgrade he considered unfair on his property in Charlestown. He has called for a national child abuse law as tough as Rhode Island's and proposed his own version of a child-care tax credit. He sought $80 million above what Almond budgeted for an access road to the Quonset Point/Davisville industrial park.

Weygand has had several clashes with his Rhode Island colleague Patrick Kennedy. For two years Kennedy had been attacking 1978 and 1996 laws, pushed by Senator John Chafee, barring the Narragansett Indians from building a casino in Charlestown without local or state referenda.

With much invective, Kennedy tried to move a bill to undo this in 1998. Weygand responded, "This [is] being proposed by Patrick, who doesn't represent the district, while the person who represents it is vehemently opposed to it." Kennedy made progress in the Resources Committee, but Weygand went to Rules Committee Chairman Gerald Solomon, who declared himself opposed, and the bill was dead. Kennedy was miffed when Weygand was asked to speak, and he was not, at a July 1998 Rhode Island Social Security forum featuring Al Gore; Kennedy was backing Dick Gephardt for president, while Weygand was expected to back Gore. The acrimony was even greater when Weygand cast what he called a "gut-wrenching" vote for the Republican impeachment inquiry resolution in October 1998; Kennedy questioned his political acumen.

Weygand was re-elected 72%–25%—a bigger margin than Kennedy's—against a Republican who campaigned under the banner "A Carpenter for Congress." In March 1999, Senator John Chafee announced he would not run for re-election in 2000. Weygand jumped into the race. Kennedy, now chairman of the Democratic Congressional Campaign Committee, said he was "disheartened" because of the danger of losing the House seat, though the district voted 59%–28% for Clinton in 1996. Weygand replied, "My point to Patrick is, I'd love to have your support and I think we need to stand behind one candidate formally, because if we do not we stand to lose this seat." But Kennedy was expected to endorse his mentor in the state House, Speaker John Harwood. Cranston City Council President Kevin McAllister quickly announced for the 2nd District seat, but the best-known possible candidate is Secretary of State Jim Langevin. Other possible Democratic candidates include Kate Coyne-McCoy, director of the National Association of State Workers, and Paolino, Weygand's 1996 primary opponent. Possible Republicans include state House Minority Leader Bob Watson, former Lieutenant Governor Bernard Jackvony and 1998 Treasurer candidate James Bennett.

Cook's Call. *Probably Safe.* Weygand's decision to run for the open Senate seat of John Chafee opens up this west Providence/Warwick seat to a great deal of competition. Democrats have an automatic advantage in this Democratic leaning district and will likely have a crowded primary. But, this district also has a history of supporting moderate Republicans, and the right Republican nominee could make this a race in November.

The People: Pop. 1990: 501,768; 19.3% rural; 15.1% age 65 + ; 90.2% White, 4.4% Black, 2.3% Asian, 0.6% Amer. Indian, 2.5% Other; 5.1% Hispanic Origin. Households: 54.1% married couple families; 25% married couple fams. w. children; 43.1% college educ.; median household income: $32,729; per capita income: $14,739; median house value: $130,200; median gross rent: $419.

1996 Presidential Vote

Clinton (D) 118,192 (59%)
Dole (R) 55,719 (28%)
Perot (I) 23,436 (12%)
Others 4,370 (2%)

1992 Presidential Vote

Clinton (D) 106,158 (46%)
Bush (R) 68,843 (30%)
Perot (I) 54,203 (23%)

Rep. Robert A. Weygand (D)

Elected 1996; b. May 10, 1948, Attelboro, MA; home, N. Kingstown; U. of RI, B.A. 1971, B.S. 1976; Catholic; married (Frances).

Elected Office: RI House of Reps., 1984–92; RI Lt. Gov., 1992–96.

Professional Career: Landscape Architect, 1973–93; East Providence Planning Board, 1978.

DC Office: 215 CHOB 20515, 202-225-2735; Fax: 202-225-5876; Web site: www.house.gov/weygand.

District Office: Warwick, 401-732-9400.

Committees: *Banking & Financial Services* (15th of 27 D): Capital Markets, Securities & Government Sponsored Enterprises; Housing & Community Opportunity. *Budget* (8th of 19 D).

Group Ratings

	ADA	ACLU	AFS	LCV	CON	NTU	NFIB	COC	ACU	NTLC	CHC
1998	90	75	100	77	82	15	29	56	20	18	25
1997	70	—	100	—	52	23	—	30	25	—	—

National Journal Ratings

	1997 LIB — 1997 CONS		1998 LIB — 1998 CONS	
Economic	79% —	18%	64% —	34%
Social	62% —	37%	62% —	37%
Foreign	74% —	25%	84% —	11%

Key Votes of the 105th Congress

1. Clinton Budget Deal	N	5. Puerto Rico Sthood. Ref.	Y	9. Cut $ for B-2 Bombers	Y
2. Education IRAs	N	6. End Highway Set-asides	N	10. Human Rights in China	Y
3. Req. 2/3 to Raise Taxes	N	7. School Prayer Amend.	N	11. Withdraw Bosnia Troops	N
4. Fast-track Trade	N	8. Ovrd. Part. Birth Veto	Y	12. End Cuban TV-Marti	Y

Election Results

1998 general	Robert A. Weygand (D)	110,917	(72%)	($566,499)
	John O. Matson (R)	38,170	(25%)	($39,945)
	Others	4,966	(3%)	
1998 primary	Robert A. Weygand (D)	unopposed		
1996 general	Robert A. Weygand (D)	118,827	(64%)	($785,547)
	Rick Wild (R)	58,458	(32%)	($416,771)
	Others	7,033	(4%)	

SOUTH CAROLINA

South Carolina, at times beleaguered and under attack, stands proud but not untroubled, a state that has made much progress but still feels it has some distance to go. Within living memory this state looked like an underdeveloped country: beneath a thin veneer of rich people, it was among the poorest of states, with income levels less than half the national average and with high levels of illiteracy and disease. South Carolina was founded by planters from Barbados and even today there are reminders of the West Indies—the semitropical climate, the lush foliage and trademark palmettos, and the billions of damage from hurricanes. But economically and culturally, South Carolina is now clearly part of the booming South Atlantic region from Maryland to Florida, filling up with new retirement condominiums, factories and office buildings, giant shopping centers, and leading the nation's economic growth in the 1990s.

In South Carolina, growth occurs atop the plantation economy built on the swampy Low Country below the Fall Line, where the great 18th and 19th Century planters built rice paddies and cultivated exotic crops like indigo in the days before cotton was king. The great wealth of these Low Country planters was destroyed by the Civil War which they, more than any other Southerners, provoked. But their pride and way of life continued as did that of former slaves. As late as 1940, 43% of South Carolinians were black, most living in conditions inconceivable today. South Carolina's economic growth started only in the 1920s, with that lowest-wage of industries, textiles. Mills were built in the Up Country above Columbia, hiring poor whites (never blacks) from the hardscrabble farms in the area. Politics remained a rough business, with harsh appeals to racial fear and economic envy, and with limited participation: in 1940, just 99,000 South Carolinians voted for president, 96% of them Democratic—the highest Democratic percentage in the nation. In the 1946 Democratic primary, the year Strom Thurmond ran for governor, only 271,000 people voted in this state of more than two million.

Now this once underdeveloped country has joined the First World. Personal incomes are up toward national levels; health standards are as good as those in the rest of the nation; educational achievement still lags, though not nearly so much as before. South Carolina was helped for some years by the military bases clustered around Charleston, by the big textile mills around Greenville and Spartanburg, and by the outmigration of Low Country blacks to big cities of the Northeast. Then, starting in the 1970s, South Carolina became the most aggressive state in the South in attracting new industry. It advertised its business climate (one of the lowest rates of unionization), its taxes (low), and its willingness to meet local employers' needs (very high). It enticed French and German firms to set up major operations in the Piedmont and the Low Country, a process capped when BMW in 1992 built its first U.S. assembly plant off I-85 in Spartanburg. But even more typical are the decisions of hundreds of small employers to open plants, rent offices and create jobs in what has become one of America's more vibrant economic environments. This has happened even as federal support has diminished: the Navy pretty much pulled out of the port of Charleston in the 1980s; the Savannah River nuclear plant, including the only tritium plant in the country, closed down in 1993, but could become a plutonium treatment facility for the DOE.

All this progress has happened even as South Carolina has been overcoming its heritage of slavery and racial segregation. Starting in the 1950s, fewer people were kept from voting by the poll tax, and turnout surged as South Carolina became competitive in the presidential elections of 1952, 1956 and 1960. Then the Civil Rights Act of 1964 and the Voting Rights Act of 1965 ended legal segregation of public accommodations and workplaces and brought blacks suddenly into the electorate. This naturally shook up South Carolina politics, though not in the way widely expected: Democrats hoped to build biracial majorities, and sometimes did,

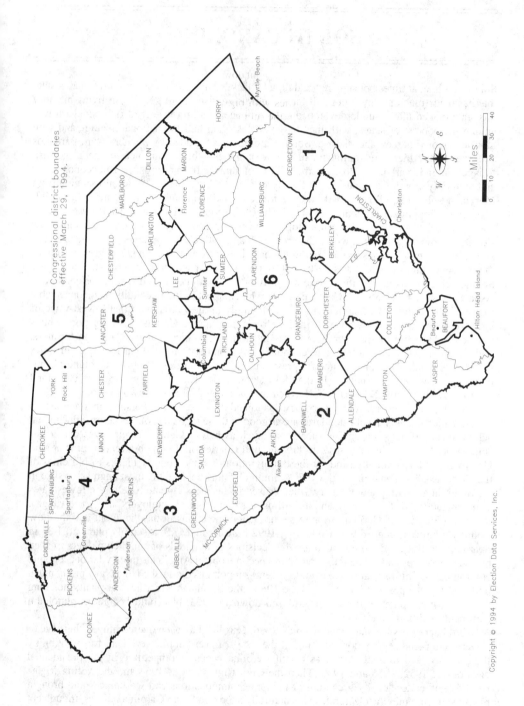

Congressional district boundaries
effective March 29, 1994.

but overall South Carolina moved, more than any other state in the South, toward the Republicanism exemplified by its native son, the late Republican National Chairman Lee Atwater. During the governorship of Carroll Campbell, elected in 1986 and 1990, Republicans came close to achieving a kind of hegemony here: They held the governorship and one Senate seat and came close to unseating Senator Ernest Holling in 1992; they held four of six House seats and threatened a fifth in 1994; they won six of eight downballot state offices in 1994 and elected a Republican speaker of the House in 1995.

But Americans dislike hegemony. Parties with big majorities become complacent and fissiparous, while parties seemingly stuck in the minority find new leaders, develop new issues and build new coalitions. That is what happened in South Carolina in 1998. House Minority Leader Jim Hodges upset Governor David Beasley by a decisive margin, and Hollings was reelected to a sixth term with a margin bigger than six years before. Democrats recaptured three downballot offices and narrowed Republicans' margin in the state House. Campbell's Republican organization, which produced nomination-winning victories for George Bush in 1988 and Bob Dole in 1996 in South Carolina's Saturday-before-Super-Tuesday primary, and which had narrowly nominated and elected Beasley in 1994, lay in ruins; and the chances of Campbell, now the $1 million a year head of the American Council of Life Insurance, to succeed to one of the state's Senate seats seemed seriously diminished. Democrats had finally built the black-and-white majority coalition they had dreamed of a long generation before, and now have the opportunity—and burdens—of governing.

The issue that split the Republican majority and produced the Democratic victories was gambling. When Campbell was elected in 1986, it seemed inconceivable that gambling could be a winning issue; casino gambling was allowed in only two states, Nevada and New Jersey, and religious leaders in this very religious state were sternly opposed. But in 1991 Georgia Governor Zell Miller pushed through a lottery, with proceeds to be used for college scholarships, and that same year the South Carolina Supreme Court ruled that video poker did not run afoul of the state Constitution's prohibition of gambling because it was a game of skill, not chance. In 1994 there was a county-by-county referendum on video poker; it passed in 34 counties and was rejected in 12. The business mushroomed, with 60% more machines in four years, to a $2.4 billion industry, the third biggest video poker operation in any state. Video poker operators wanted to expand into the 12 other counties; Beasley opposed them, as well calls from Democrats for a Georgia-style lottery.

All this energized the candidacy of Hodges, even though he had opposed both video poker and the lottery in the state legislature. He argued that the voters should decide on both, and the governor should seek the two-thirds margin in the legislature which would put them on the 2000 ballot; he added a charge that Beasley had not properly regulated video poker. Video poker money rushed into Hodge's campaign, to the point that he almost equaled Beasley's fundraising by October, and video poker operators bought their own independent "Ban Beasley" ads. The lottery proved popular enough that Beasley switched in October and backed a lottery referendum.

That switch was harmful, for it reminded voters of how Beasley had switched on another controversial issue, which aroused strong feelings about South Carolina's past. This was whether the Confederate battle flag should fly over the state Capitol, as it has since 1962. In 1994 he called for keeping it there and that position was supported 3–1 by Republican primary voters in a referendum that same year. But in November 1996 Beasley went on TV and called for moving the battle flag to a separate Confederate memorial on the Capitol grounds, a compromise which had passed the state Senate in 1994. Beasley said his mind had been changed by reflecting in prayer on church arsons, the drive-by shooting of three black teenagers and KKK scrawls on walls, and he denounced "hate-filled cowards" who dishonored the heritage the flag commemorates. Beasley's move united Democrats and blacks and split Republicans and whites; the legislature took no action, and the flag was still flying when the renovated Capitol was reopened in August 1998. When black protestors marched on the Capitol in December 1998, Hodges, then governor-elect, said, "The reality is that there was an effort made a few years ago to try to bring that about and it didn't succeed. . . . Realistically, I don't think it's going to happen any time soon."

But South Carolina's past is not all burden, and its present is alive with great possibilities. Charleston has been restored and revived by the efforts of Joe Riley Jr., mayor since 1976; its Spoleto Festival every June attracts music-lovers from around the world. South Carolina is host every year to Renaissance Weekend at Hilton Head, where Bill and Hillary Rodham Clinton spend New Year's Eve with hundreds of friends in gatherings hosted by Phil Lader, now ambassador to Britain, and to the Southern 500 stock car race in Darlington, which attracts a different but no less vibrant crowd. If South Carolina has not had the spectacular growth of metropolitan Atlanta or the Piedmont of North Carolina, it is not the backwater that it seemed fated to be for many years but a state that has transformed its fighting spirit into an engine of innovation and growth.

Governor. Jim Hodges, the first Democrat elected governor of South Carolina since 1982, grew up in rural Lancaster County, near the North Carolina border. After graduating from college and law school at the University of South Carolina, he returned to Lancaster to practice law. In short order he became county attorney, and in 1986, at 29, was elected to the state House. In 1994 he became House minority leader; he had a conservative enough record to be supported by the National Federation of Independent Businesses and National Rifle Association. Meanwhile (South Carolina has a part-time legislature) he became general counsel at Springs Company, a major textile and financial services firm, whose CEO is Crandall Bowles, wife of former White House Chief of Staff Erskine Bowles.

Hodges was not Democrats' first choice to run for governor in 1998, but others were daunted by Beasley's lead in the polls and the might of Carroll Campbell's Republican organization. He started off attacking Beasley on education, citing the state's low ranking on SAT scores, and presented detailed critiques of Beasley's record, including his opposition to all-day kindergarten; Hodges got the legislature to vote for that in 1996, and Beasley switched to support further study into it. He charged that Beasley's plan to use the Savannah River Site in Barnwell County for a nuclear waste depository was not bringing in the money Beasley promised for his need-based and Palmetto merit-based college scholarships. Hodges's solution was an adaptation of Georgia Governor Zell Miller's lottery and HOPE scholarships; Hodges called them COPE scholarships for college tuition and added that he would spend lottery proceeds on all-day kindergarten and school construction as well. One TV ad showed a Georgian "Bubba" sitting behind a cash register thanking South Carolinians for buying lottery tickets and educating Georgia youngsters.

Beasley had won by only 50%–48% in 1994, and had suffered from his much-publicized switches on the Confederate battle flag and his party switch as well: he was elected as a Democrat to the legislature in 1978 at age 20, served as majority leader and only switched parties shortly before running for governor. In 1998 he highlighted his record of welfare reform, two-strikes-you're-out sentences for violent criminals, college scholarships, education accountability law and encouraging economic growth and new jobs—all winning issues in South Carolina in the past. But Beasley's opposition to video poker gave Hodges the campaign contributions he needed to get his message across, and Beasley's September switch on the lottery referendum provided yet another example of flip-flopping, undermining his base without attracting the opposition. In spring 1998 Sheriff Jimmy Metts of heavily Republican Lexington County announced he was running as an independent and dredged up rumors that Beasley had had an extramarital affair. Metts later withdrew from the race, but the rumors lingered; in September 1998 Beasley held a press conference with his former press secretary and their two spouses in which they all denied any extramarital affair.

Turnout in November rose sharply, up 15% from 1994: it was up more than that in heavily black counties in central South Carolina, but also along the coast, in the edges of metropolitan areas and in Republican-leaning Greenville and Spartanburg. Some 25% of voters were black, more than in past elections but not out of line with population. Hodges won by the solid margin of 53%–45%, carrying almost every rural county and wide margins in Charleston County and Columbia's Richland County as well. Beasley carried only affluent Lexington and Aiken Counties, outside Columbia, the upcountry counties along I-85 from Rock Hill through Greenville to Clemson and Anderson, and Beaufort County, where newcomers to Hilton Head have made this once black-majority county now solidly Republican. Hodges won 21% of self-identified Republicans, an unusually higher percentage; Democrats won back the offices of treasurer, comptroller and education superintendent. Hodges won 92% from blacks and cut Beasley's margin among whites almost in half.

In early 1999 both the state House and Senate approved the referendum on the lottery but squabbled more about video poker. Hodges said he would accept a referendum on whether to abolish video poker, but added, "As long as it's legal, I will lead the fight to make sure video poker is tightly regulated and fairly taxed." In the legislature, Republicans complained that Hodges had produced only guidelines, and not detailed regulations. Hodges may also put his stamp on national politics. He is actuarially more likely than any other governor to have to appoint a senator in his four-year term, for South Carolina has the oldest Senate delegation in history: Strom Thurmond was elected in 1996 to a term which ends in January 2003, a month after he turns 100; Ernest Hollings was re-elected in 1998 to a sixth term at age 77. But both men are hardy and fit and neither has shown any inclination to retire early.

Senior Senator. The most enduring figure in American politics today is Strom Thurmond. The man who was elected to his eighth term in the Senate in 1996 as a Republican was elected to the South Carolina House as a Democrat in 1932. Thurmond grew up in the small town of Edgefield, was a teacher, coach and school superintendent, studied law under his father and was elected to the legislature at 31. In his youth he knew "Pitchfork Ben" Tillman, South Carolina governor and senator, who was born in 1847. On June 6, 1944, Thurmond parachuted into Normandy on D-Day only after getting an exemption because he was over age. He attended the Democratic National Convention in 1932 and voted for Franklin D. Roosevelt, and he attended the Republican National Convention in 1996 and voted for Bob Dole—64 years later. Thurmond was elected governor in 1946, ran for president in 1948 as a "States' Rights Democrat" and won 39 electoral votes. He was elected senator as a write-in candidate in 1954, resigned and ran for the seat again in 1956. In March 1996, at 93, he became the oldest person ever to serve in Congress; in May 1997 he became the longest-serving senator in history. In early 1999 he was still exercising 50 minutes a day and was still giving his powerful handshake known as "the Grip."

Thurmond switched to the Republican Party to support Barry Goldwater in 1964, which means that by 1996 he had been a Democrat 32 years and a Republican 32 years in his political career. His party switch seemed unwise at the time but proved sentient about the direction of opinion; in 1968, Thurmond provided key backing to hold the South for Richard Nixon at the Republican National Convention. Thurmond has combined a reputation for steadfastness with a flexibility and adroitness that have enabled this onetime symbol of racial segregation to prosper politically in an era of integration. In 1957, he set a record, filibustering for over 24 hours against a fair housing bill. But when South Carolina blacks started voting in large numbers after the Voting Rights Act of 1965, Thurmond shifted gears and became the first Southern senator to hire black staffers and appoint blacks to high positions (including a federal judgeship). He voted for renewal of the Voting Rights Act and the Martin Luther King Jr. Holiday. He gets more votes from blacks than most Republicans.

Thurmond has been a proud teetotaler and physical fitness buff all his life, and still seems in amazingly good physical health. His first wife was 23 years his junior; after she died, he married a South Carolina beauty queen 44 years younger; the first of his four children was born when he was 68. He volunteered to become an organ donor after his oldest daughter was killed by a drunk driver in a traffic accident in 1993. He worked for years and finally got warning labels on alcoholic beverages in 1988; in February 1999 he moved swiftly to stop educational labeling of wine that would promote its health benefits. He has backed fetal tissue research and moved to oppose a ban on human cloning and cloning tissue, because his daughter has a medical condition for which such tissue is needed in research. In hearings and on the Senate floor, as well as on the campaign trail, Thurmond usually reads from notes and has slowed some physically, but he recognizes many South Carolina constituents and responds aptly to arguments and interjections and is polite and courtly. When asked his opinion of the band Hootie and the Blowfish, he said he was unfamiliar with their music but knew they must be good because they are from South Carolina. In any case, he has never been much for subtlety or nuance; his mind is simple and strong, and if he increasingly relies on staff he does so with confidence that they understand where he wants to go.

As the senior Republican in the Senate, Thurmond is president pro tempore, which puts him third in line for the presidency. In January 1999 he stepped forward in full view of the country to administer the oath to Chief Justice William Rehnquist to preside over the impeachment trial of Bill Clinton. For the entire trial he sat upright in his chair and listened carefully, but bellowed out "Noooo!" when the House managers sought to have Monica Lewinsky testify on the floor of the Senate. From 1981–86 he was chairman of the Judiciary Committee; from 1995–99 he was chairman of Armed Services. He announced in December 1997 that he would step down from the chairmanship in January 1999. "I've been up there a long time and I've seen some . . . get in the position of chairman and serve as long as they can. . . . I think that's selfish." He believes that it is important to maintain high defense spending, quality of life for members of the military and speedy development of missile defense. He has sponsored many bills to extend the death penalty and reduce federal courts' jurisdiction over collateral attacks on state criminal convictions. He has supported some gun control measures endorsed by police, such as bans on cop-killer bullets and plastic guns. He is a stickler for ethics, supporting outside income limits for senators, bans on lobbying for federal projects on a contingent fee basis and lobbying for foreign countries by former federal officials.

Thurmond's popularity remained high in South Carolina as he sought re-election in 1996 at age 93, but polls also showed that a majority thought it was time for him to retire. His last tough challenge was from businessman Charles Ravenel in 1978, when he got 56%; Thurmond won with 67% in 1984 and 64% and 1990. In the 1996 primary he had opposition from Harold Worley, a state legislator and developer from the Grand Stand along Myrtle Beach. Worley spent $600,000 of his own money and said that Thurmond was "simply too old." Thurmond won 61%–30%, carrying everything but Worley's home base of Horry County. In the general, Thurmond faced Elliott Close, 43-year-old scion of the Springs Mills textile family. Thurmond campaigned actively, shaking hands and speaking from note cards; he has refused to debate since 1950. He got a bit tough with Close. "It might have been more in order for him to run for the town council of Fort Mill," he said. "It would take my opponent 60 years to catch up with what I can do in the next six years." Close spent $944,000 of his own money on a stumbling campaign that had three different managers. He boasted that his family's mill never laid off workers during the Depression, just one week before it closed three mills and laid off 850 workers. Close focused on Thurmond's age and alleged infirmity: "Is Strom Thurmond still up to the job? . . . Vote for our future, not for our past." Thurmond supporters like Carroll Campbell bellowed in rage, but the attacks on age didn't seem to have a huge impact. During the fall Thurmond was running in the low 50s in polls, and on election day he won 53%–44%. He carried all the bigger metropolitan areas and lost mainly low-income rural counties.

In December 1998 *National Review* and the *Wall Street Journal* called on him to resign so that Republican Governor David Beasley, defeated for re-election, could appoint a Republican successor. Thurmond would have none of it. He has said often that he will not run again in 2002, and if he serves out his term he will turn 100 one month and 29 days before he retires.

Junior Senator. Ernest Hollings has served more than 30 years in the Senate and is still the junior senator from South Carolina—the longest-serving junior senator in history. Hollings grew up in Charleston, in moderate but not aristocratic circumstances, graduated from The Citadel and served in the Army in World War II. Returning home, he worked as a trial lawyer and was elected to the legislature in 1948, at 26, and was a member of the leadership two years later; he was elected governor in 1958, at 36, serving as South Carolina first faced school desegregation, which thanks to his efforts proceeded in an orderly fashion—a considerable achievement at the time. Hollings then spent four years out of office until he beat another former governor in the 1966 special election Senate race. Hollings has one of the quickest and sharpest tongues in the Senate and his instinct for zeroing in on others' weaknesses can be directed at the strong as well as the weak. When twitted by ABC's Sam Donaldson for wearing imported suits when he supported trade restrictions, and asked by Donaldson where he got his suit, he replied, "The same place you bought your wig, Sam."

In the 1980s Hollings concentrated on budget issues, arguing for a budget freeze in the early 1980s. In 1983 and 1984 he ran for president; his candidacy did not get far, but when Congress after a long struggle with Bill Clinton did freeze spending for a year in 1996, balance followed not long after. In 1985 he co-sponsored the Gramm-Rudman-Hollings deficit-cutting bill, which did in fact lead to lower deficits. He strongly backed the line-item veto and was one of 19 Senate Democrats to vote for it in 1995. In 1993 he argued for a value-added tax as an alternative to the Clinton tax increases. Overall, Hollings believes in an activist but disciplined government, disagreeing with Republicans on the former and Democrats on the latter. In the Democratic Senate, his voting record was usually middle-of-the-road; in the Republican Senate, it is somewhat left of center.

In the 1990s Hollings has concentrated on telecommunications issues, as chairman or ranking minority member on the Commerce Committee and its Communications Subcommittee. Telecom issues were probably the most intellectually demanding and certainly the most heavily lobbied issues in Congress during those years, and Hollings managed to keep an even keel—and to get legislation passed. Hollings's instinct is to regulate at the federal level, which puts him at odds with many trends of the times. He was the major opponent of deregulating broadcasting and a major proponent of the 1992 Cable Reregulation Act, the one law on which Congress overrode President Bush's veto. But he has also been the most persistent backer of telecommunications reform, for more competition between long distance companies and the regional Bells. He first raised the issue in the early 1990s, then worked hard as a bill passed the House in 1994; but it died in the Senate because Hollings insisted that regional Bell companies get actual competition in local service before they were permitted to enter the long distance or cable markets. In 1995 and 1996, Hollings worked with new Chairman Larry Pressler to produce a bipartisan bill, which was signed into law in February 1996; he had to mend ties frayed with Republicans after Al Gore stepped forward to claim credit for the bill as it was being negotiated, but prevailed in the end.

Hollings has worked since then to superintend the deregulatory process. He pushed against Al Gore's choice as chairman of the FCC; neither man's first choice got the job, but the ultimate choice, William Kennard, was closer to Gore. He opposed Joel Klein as head of the Antitrust Division after Klein refused to oppose the Bell Atlantic-Nynex merger. He continued to insist on FCC rather than state regulation of the rates regional Bells could charge long distance companies for interconnecting their wires, but at the same time criticized the FCC for its enforcement, or non-enforcement, of the act.

Hollings's relations with John McCain, Commerce chairman since 1997, have not always been warm. In May 1998 Hollings vigorously opposed the tobacco bill that McCain passed through the committee 19–1 after it was changed to phase out tobacco price supports; there are many tobacco farmers in the corner of South Carolina around Marlboro and Chesterfield counties. In early 1999 he seemed to mistrust McCain for his presidential candidacy, though he did join with him in sponsoring a bill to require software to block inappropriate material from the Internet wired up to schools under a Gore-backed FCC measure.

Other Hollings causes include education funding, on which he has sharply opposed Republicans, and trade, on which he proclaims himself a "hawk." He shepherded a textile bill to passage in 1990, only to see it vetoed; he opposed NAFTA and caused GATT to be postponed until after the 1994 elections over the objections of then-Majority Leader George Mitchell, and then voted against. He opposes using federal tax money for private and religious schools and opposes counting Social Security surpluses toward the budget deficit. He has passed laws on ocean dumping and climate change. Since 1987 he has called for amending the First Amendment to allow Congress to set "reasonable limits" on campaign spending; his approach was taken up in early 1997 by Minority Leaders Tom Daschle and Dick Gephardt, but was defeated 61–38 in the Senate.

In increasingly Republican South Carolina, Hollings was re-elected by only 50%–47% in 1992 over former Congressman Tommy Harnett; his January 1991 vote against the Gulf war resolution probably hurt. In a July 1997 poll former Governor Carroll Campbell led Hollings 51%–39%. But Campbell decided to remain in his job with the American Council on Life Insurance and in January 1998 bowed out of the race; it is widely thought he is waiting to run for Strom Thurmond's seat in 2002.

That left as Hollings's chief opponent 4th District Congressman Bob Inglis, who beat an incumbent Democrat in 1992 by promising to serve only three terms and to vote against pork barrel spending, even for South Carolina. He kept his word, running for the Senate in 1998 rather than for re-election to the House and voting against measures including bridge repairs for Charleston County, the Southern Connector in Greenville County and upgrading the Greenville-Spartanburg Airport. He said that if voters wanted a senator to go on "a looting misson of the federal treasury, then I don't want the job." He also vowed to serve only 12 years in Senate, promised to accept no PAC money and asked Hollings to join him in a pledge to wage a "courteous" campaign. Hollings, from a state whose two senators at that point had served a total of 74 years, scorned term limits and "courtesy," and proceeded to raise far more money than Inglis—ultimately the spending gap was $4.8 million to $2.1 million.

Hollings used his money for a saturation TV buy starting in late September, reminding voters of the dollars he had brought to the state and of his efforts on Social Security, education, the environment and HMO reform; he chided Inglis on votes "to weaken clean air and water laws" and to "put profits ahead of patient rights." Meanwhile, a national Republican ad showed a limousine approaching a business jet and accused Hollings of fighting welfare reform and voting even "to give full welfare benefits to foreign immigrants." Inglis was not on television until October, with one ad showing Hollings on election night in 1992 saying, "I don't have to do things that are politically correct. I'm free at last." Hollings placed operatives in the state Democratic Party, and organized a turnout drive which had a major effort on election day; he also benefited from the lively campaign of gubernatorial candidate Jim Hodges, financed heavily by video poker money. Inglis in contrast was stand-offish to his state party and avoided campaign professionals; his 1992 victory convinced him he had the formula for victory, though that was fought in an anti-incumbent year and this one was in a pro-incumbent atmosphere. Inglis also hoped that Bill Clinton's misdeeds would help him in a state where Clinton had long been unpopular. In the *Greenville News* he wrote, "Bill Clinton must resign. If he doesn't resign, he will put us to the test: Does the truth matter? Is power and politics constrained by principle?" But attempts to link Hollings to Clinton were unconvincing, since Hollings had made clear his contempt for Clinton many times; in 1996 he had said, "Clinton's as popular as AIDS in South Carolina," and when the president's ratings rose that same year he said, "If they reach 60%, then he can start dating again." Hollings also turned his fire against Inglis. Irritated by his courtesy and self-righteousness, Hollings described him to the *Rock Hill Herald* in mid-October thusly: "He finesses all around. He is Jack be nimble, Jack be quick. He's all around the damn clock, so oozing and goozing and such a nice little choirboy and so pleasant, and everybody's rude, and he wants to be courteous. He is a goddamn skunk." He apologized the next day, and said he was angered by "the gross distortions of my record and the callous accusations that have been leveled against me"—obviously staff-written language, without the authentic Hollings touch.

Hollings always led Inglis in polls, but in early 1998 was still running under 50% himself; it was a reasonable assumption that the undecideds might all go to the challenger. But Hollings outcampaigned Inglis, and in the first solid Democratic year in South Carolina in nearly 20 years won a sixth term 53%–46%. In January 2003, after 36 years, he is slated to become the state's senior senator. Hollings has made statements that suggest he will not run again in 2004, when he turns 82, but South Carolina has certainly shown it has no bias against elderly senators.

Presidential politics. South Carolina can be said to have led the South into the Republican Party. It was the only Deep South state to vote for Richard Nixon over George Wallace in 1968 and since then has voted Democratic only once, for Jimmy Carter in 1976. It was one of the top three Republican states in 1988 and 1992; among Southern states, only Mississippi in 1992 and Alabama in 1996 gave Republican nominees higher percentages. Traditional values and a booming, non-union private sector have reinforced the Republican trend.

South Carolina also has been pivotal in Republican nomination contests. In 1987 Lee Atwater purposefully scheduled the Republican primary here for the Saturday before Super Tuesday, and in 1988 George Bush won a smashing victory over Bob Dole and Pat Robertson, forecasting the Southern sweep that clinched his nomination. In 1992 Bush won with two-thirds of the vote, squashing Pat Buchanan's claims to represent the South. And in 1996 former Governor Carroll Campbell and Governor David Beasley led a grass-roots campaign that gave Bob Dole, after his disappointing showings elsewhere, an impressive 45%–29% victory over Buchanan March 9.

But past rules may not govern in South Carolina in 2000. The Republican organization which delivered victories to Bush and Dole is now in tatters after the defeat of Governor David Beasley; in early 1999 George W. Bush had strong backers here, but so did John McCain, and Campbell was reported to be leaning toward Dan Quayle. In June 1999, the Republican Party voted to move its primary up to February 19; South Carolina Democrats soon after followed suit, but national Demcratic party rules prevent any state from holding a presidential primary before the first Tuesday in March other than Iowa and New Hampshire. As for the general election, Republicans are still the favorites, but the Democrats' big victories and big boost in turnout in 1998 make this a state the Republican nominee can no longer take for granted.

Congressional districting. The Voting Rights Act amendments of 1982 were interpreted to require creation of a black-majority district in South Carolina, and the plan adopted in May 1992 stitches together black majority areas in the Low Country (but not the condominium-glutted coast) and in Columbia and Charleston to create the 6th District. The plan made the 1st, 2d, 3d and 5th Districts more Republican. After the Supreme Court's *Shaw v. Reno* case, that plan was overturned by a federal court in July 1993; the legislature passed a plan the following March with only minor changes for 1994. That version was challenged in a lawsuit in which local Republicans sued state authorities. But in August 1997 the plaintiffs and Governor David Beasley settled the case and agreed not to seek a redrawing of the lines: a case of Republicans maintaining a black-majority district, presumably because it gathered heavily Democratic precincts into one district and left the surrounding four districts more Republican.

The People: Est. Pop. 1998: 3,835,962; Pop. 1990: 3,486,703, up 10% 1990–1998. 1.4% of U.S. total, 26th largest; 45.3% rural. Median age: 34.4 years. 11.9% 65 years and over. 69.1% White, 29.8% Black, 0.6% Asian, 0.3% Amer. Indian, 0.3% Other; 0.8% Hispanic Origin. Households: 56.4% married couple families; 28.1% married couple fams. w. children; 38.8% college educ.; median household income: $26,256; per capita income: $11,897; 69.9% owner occupied housing; median house value: $61,100; median monthly rent: $276. 3.8% Unemployment. 1998 Voting age pop.: 2,886,000. 1998 Turnout: 1,098,484; 38% of VAP. Registered voters (1998): 2,021,763; no party registration.

1436   SOUTH CAROLINA

Political Lineup: Governor, Jim Hodges (D); Lt. Gov., Bob Peeler (R); Secy. of State, Jim Miles (R); Atty. Gen., Charles M. Condon (R); Treasurer, Grady Patterson Jr. (D); State Senate, 46 (24 D, 22 R); Majority Leader, John C. Land III (D); State House, 124 (57 D, 65 R, 2 vacancies); House Speaker, David Wilkins (R). Senators, Strom Thurmond (R) and Ernest F. Hollings (D). Representatives, 6 (2 D, 4 R).

Elections Division: 803-734-9060; **Filing Deadline for U.S. Congress:** March 30, 2000.

1996 Presidential Vote

Dole (R)	573,458	(50%)
Clinton (D)	506,283	(44%)
Perot (I)	64,386	(6%)

1992 Presidential Vote

Bush (R)	577,508	(48%)
Clinton (D)	479,514	(40%)
Perot (I)	138,782	(12%)

1996 Republican Presidential Primary

Dole (R)	124,904	(45%)
Buchanan (R)	80,824	(29%)
Forbes (R)	35,039	(13%)
Alexander (R)	28,647	(10%)
Others	7,327	(3%)

GOVERNOR

Gov. Jim Hodges (D)

Elected 1998, term expires Jan. 2003; b. Nov. 19, 1956, Lancaster; home, Lancaster; U. of SC, B.S. 1979, J.D. 1982; Methodist; married (Rachel).

Elected Office: SC House of Reps., 1986–97, Minority Ldr. 1994–97.

Professional Career: Practicing atty., 1983–90; Lancaster Cnty. Atty., 1983–86; Gen. Cnsl., Springs Co., 1990–98.

Office: P.O. Box 11829, The State House, Columbia, 29211, 803-734-9818; Fax: 803-734-1598; Web site: www.state.sc.us.

Election Results

1998 gen.		Jim Hodges (D)	574,035	(53%)
		David Beasley (R)	486,342	(45%)
		Others	16,758	(2%)
1998 prim.		Jim Hodges (D)	unopposed	
1994 gen.		David Beasley (R)	470,756	(50%)
		Nick A. Theodore (D)	447,002	(48%)
		Others	17,128	(2%)

SENATORS

Sen. Strom Thurmond (R)

Elected 1956, seat up 2002; b. Dec. 5, 1902, Edgefield; home, Aiken; Clemson U., B.S. 1923; Baptist; separated.

Military Career: Army, 1942–46 (WWII), Army Reserves, 1923–59.

Elected Office: SC Senate, 1933–38; Circuit Judge, 1938–42; SC Gov., 1947–51; States' Rights candidate for U.S. Pres., 1948; US Senate, 1954–56.

Professional Career: Teacher & coach, 1923–29; Edgefield Cnty. Supervisor of Ed., 1929–33; Practicing atty., 1930–38, 1951–55.

DC Office: 217 RSOB, 20510, 202-224-5972; Fax: 202-224-1300; Web site: www.senate.gov/~thurmond.

State Offices: Aiken, 803-649-2591; Charleston, 843-727-4282; Columbia, 803-765-5494; Florence, 843-662-8873.

Committees: *President Pro-Tempore. Armed Services* (2d of 11 R): Personnel; Readiness & Management Support; Strategic Forces. *Judiciary* (2d of 10 R): Administrative Oversight & the Courts; Antitrust, Business Rights & Competition; Criminal Justice Oversight (Chmn.); The Constitution, Federalism & Property Rights. *Veterans' Affairs* (3d of 7 R).

Group Ratings

	ADA	ACLU	AFS	LCV	CON	NTU	NFIB	COC	ACU	NTLC	CHC
1998	0	29	0	0	14	62	100	94	76	93	82
1997	5	—	0	—	74	79	—	80	96	—	—

National Journal Ratings

	1997 LIB — 1997 CONS			1998 LIB — 1998 CONS		
Economic	0%	—	89%	15%	—	84%
Social	0%	—	83%	31%	—	64%
Foreign	0%	—	77%	26%	—	71%

Key Votes of the 105th Congress

1. Bal. Budget Amend.	Y	5. Satcher for Surgeon Gen.	Y	9. Chem. Weapons Treaty	N
2. Clinton Budget Deal	Y	6. Highway Set-asides	N	10. Cuban Humanitarian Aid	N
3. Cloture on Tobacco	N	7. Table Child Gun locks	Y	11. Table Bosnia Troops	Y
4. Education IRAs	Y	8. Ovrd. Part. Birth Veto	Y	12. $ for Test-ban Treaty	N

Election Results

1996 general	Strom Thurmond (R)	619,739	(53%)	($2,632,682)
	Elliott Close (D)	510,810	(44%)	($1,913,574)
	Others	30,419	(3%)	
1996 primary	Strom Thurmond (R)	132,157	(61%)	
	Harold Worley (R)	65,670	(30%)	
	Charlie Thompson (R)	20,188	(9%)	
1990 general	Strom Thurmond (R)	482,032	(64%)	($2,333,689)
	Robert H. Cunningham (D)	244,112	(33%)	($6,232)

Sen. Ernest F. Hollings (D)

Elected 1966, seat up 2004; b. Jan. 1, 1922, Charleston; home, Charleston; The Citadel, B.A. 1942, U. of SC, LL.B. 1947; Lutheran; married (Peatsy).

Military Career: Army, 1942–45 (WWII).

Elected Office: SC House of Reps., 1948–54, Speaker Pro-Tem, 1951–54; SC Lt. Gov., 1954–58; SC Gov., 1958–62.

Professional Career: Practicing atty., 1947–55, 1963–66.

DC Office: 125 RSOB, 20510, 202-224-6121; Fax: 202-224-4293; Web site: www.senate.gov/~hollings.

State Offices: Charleston, 843-727-4525; Columbia, 803-765-5731; Greenville, 864-233-5366.

Committees: *Appropriations* (3d of 13 D): Commerce, Justice, State & the Judiciary (RMM); Defense; Energy & Water Development; Interior; Labor & HHS. *Budget* (2d of 10 D). *Commerce, Science & Transportation* (RMM of 9 D): Aviation; Communications (RMM); Manufacturing & Competitiveness.

Group Ratings

	ADA	ACLU	AFS	LCV	CON	NTU	NFIB	COC	ACU	NTLC	CHC
1998	55	29	75	75	57	17	25	71	33	23	9
1997	75	—	88	—	3	23	—	20	8	—	—

National Journal Ratings

	1997 LIB — 1997 CONS		1998 LIB — 1998 CONS	
Economic	70%	— 29%	61%	— 36%
Social	64%	— 29%	37%	— 62%
Foreign	55%	— 41%	51%	— 36%

Key Votes of the 105th Congress

1. Bal. Budget Amend.	N	5. Satcher for Surgeon Gen.	Y	9. Chem. Weapons Treaty	Y
2. Clinton Budget Deal	N	6. Highway Set-asides	N	10. Cuban Humanitarian Aid	N
3. Cloture on Tobacco	Y	7. Table Child Gun locks	Y	11. Table Bosnia Troops	Y
4. Education IRAs	N	8. Ovrd. Part. Birth Veto	Y	12. $ for Test-ban Treaty	Y

Election Results

1998 general	Ernest F. Hollings (D)	563,296	(53%)	($4,968,456)
	Bob Inglis (R)	488,217	(46%)	($2,143,278)
	Others	17,444	(2%)	
1998 primary	Ernest F. Hollings (D)	unopposed		
1992 general	Ernest F. Hollings (D)	591,030	(50%)	($4,188,829)
	Tommy Hartnett (R)	554,175	(47%)	($886,816)
	Others	35,233	(3%)	

FIRST DISTRICT

Looking out across the harbor to Fort Sumter are the glorious mansions of the Battery, gazing on the same view that the hot-blooded young swells of Charleston saw in April 1861 when they fired the shots that began the Civil War. Today there are few more beautiful urban scenes in America than the pastel "single houses" of Charleston, built flush with the sidewalk, turning their shoulders to the streets, with open piazzas inside their gateways facing south to catch the breeze, lovingly restored and maintained. Charleston, founded in 1670, was blessed with one of the finest harbors on the Atlantic, at the point where, Charlestonians say, the Ashley and Cooper rivers meet to form the Atlantic Ocean. It was one of the South's two leading cities through the Civil War. Across its docks went cargoes of rice, indigo and cotton—all cultivated by black slaves, enriching the white planters and merchants who dominated the state's economic and political life. In the years following the Civil War, Charleston became an economic backwater, enabling the old buildings to survive; now the prosperity of recent years has financed their restoration.

This old society, descended from Barbados planters and French Huguenots, Sephardic Jews and English gentry second sons, was once a leading force in American political life. The hotheads in the gallery disrupted the 1860 Democratic National Convention here so boisterously that it was adjourned and reconvened in Baltimore, while Southern Democrats split off and nominated their own candidate, enabling Abraham Lincoln to win with 38% of the popular vote. South Carolina's blacks also have a lively history. There were free blacks here before the Civil War (some even owned slaves themselves), and Charleston's historic black culture was memorialized in George Gershwin's *Porgy and Bess*. The local accent, which seems to outsiders to have a touch of New Jersey and which can be incomprehensible when rapidly spoken, is best appreciated in the speech of Charlestonian Senator Ernest Hollings.

Some 25 years ago, the Charleston area depended heavily on its Navy and Air Force bases, which accounted for 20% of regional payrolls. In the years since, Charleston has lost most of the bases, but far from languishing it has built a vibrant private economy with lots of small companies. Joe Riley Jr., mayor since 1976, has cut crime along with Reuben Greenberg, the only black Jewish police chief in the United States (or perhaps anywhere), and has sponsored new parks and commercial projects that respect and amplify Charleston's historic heritage, and have made it a major tourist destination. Also prime tourist destinations are the South Carolina beaches from the high rises of the Grand Strand around Myrtle Beach through the eponymous hammocks of Pawleys Island south to Hilton Head with its tasteful condos. Low Country South Carolina, once a backwater dependent on the military, is now one of the most gracefully growing parts of the United States.

The 1st Congressional District includes most of the Charleston area and much of the Low Country. Its lines were drawn to maximize the black population of the next-door 6th; but, given the plantation heritage here, it is still 20% black. It includes the old houses of the Battery of Charleston and the beachfront and affluent suburbs strung out on high ground in all directions. It proceeds north past Pawleys Island to the Grand Strand; it runs south to Kiawah Island, but stops short of Hilton Head. About two-thirds of the voters are in metropolitan Charleston. Politically, it is solidly Republican, the more so as more newcomers move to the Charleston area and the Grand Strand.

The congressman from the 1st District is Mark Sanford, a Republican who was a surprise winner in 1994. Sanford grew up on a family farm in Beaufort County, went to Furman and the University of Virginia business school, then worked in real estate finance and investment in New York City and Charleston. When 1st District incumbent Arthur Ravenel ran for governor in 1994, Sanford, with no political experience, decided at 34 to run for Congress. Sanford gave his own campaign $100,000 and ran as an outsider. He called for term limits and cutting the deficit; he said citizen-legislators needed to replace career politicians; he pledged to serve only three terms, to take no PAC money, to vote for no tax increases and to refuse any salary increase until the budget was balanced. In the first primary he trailed former Pentagon official and state Republican chairman Van Hipp 31%–19%. In the runoff Sanford held conference calls each week with Bob Inglis, elected in the 4th District in 1992, and 3d District nominee Lindsey Graham. He emphasized his outsider status and won 52%–48%, and won the general with 66%.

In the House, Sanford voted for the Contract with America but has been a party maverick, with a moderate record on many issues and a willingness to buck the Republican leadership. He criticized leadership tactics in handling the votes on Newt Gingrich's ethics problems. He strongly advocated term limits and made a point of sleeping in his office and returning to his family in Charleston as often as possible. He has been one of the few members voting against measures passed with near-unanimity: the resolution against the bombing of Iraq in December 1998, a bill to preserve sites significant to the Underground Railroad in June 1998, a defense appropriation in September 1997 that included funds for Charleston harbor. He opposed pork barrel spending, including demonstration projects for Charleston's Cooper River bridges; he opposed (as did Mayor Riley) building I-73 to Charleston and said less populous Myrtle Beach would be a better terminus. His attempts to freeze spending for the National Science Foundation and to cut the sugar subsidy failed by wide margins in summer 1998.

But Sanford's willingness to challenge conventional political wisdom may turn out to make a bigger difference than all those spending bills put together. From his election in 1994 he has advocated replacing part of Social Security with individual retirement accounts; his latest bill would dedicate two-thirds of the payroll tax to them. At first he and Michigan's Nick Smith were the only members willing—even eager—to discuss these proposals. Sanford wants to give ordinary people the ability to accumulate wealth in investments. "The biggest flaw in Social Security is it doesn't take advantage of the power of compounding interest," he said. Soon other members began talking about such plans, and by spring 1998, Democrats like Daniel Patrick Moynihan and Bob Kerrey were proposing their version of individual retirement accounts. The decision of Bill Clinton, apparently in aid of the Gore campaign, to squelch such reform in 1999 may have delayed reform, but it is likely to come eventually, as younger voters figure out that a payroll-tax retirement system cannot deliver promised benefits and an investment-based system can yield far more. In July 1998 Sanford said, "There's really been a remarkable change. I really thought this would be a more slow-moving debate."

Sanford did not have Republican opponents in 1996 or 1998; in the latter year he was reelected over a Natural Law party candidate who sells shirts and perfumes in Isle of Palms. Sanford seems highly popular, and voters in the 1st District seem not at all displeased with his spurning of seniority, his disdain for pork barrel projects and his support of term limits, about which in early 1999 he said he was writing a book based on the journal he keeps: "Sometimes, it's a pleasure to know that what I'm doing just might make a positive difference in someone's life. Other times, it's a rank and ugly business, where, too often, expediency overrules principle and the nation is left poorer as a result." But he may not be succeeded by a similarly daring reformer. He seems so determined to keep his word and not run again in 2000 that others started talking about running within weeks after the November 1998 election. One likely candidate is state Representative Henry Brown, chairman of the Ways and Means Committee, who says he won't limit his terms; he is an in-law of South Carolina Christian Coalition head Roberta Combs and reliably has her support. Another candidate is state Senator Larry Grooms, who said he wouldn't limit his terms either. Tommy Hartnett, who held this seat before losing a challenge to Senator Ernest Hollings in 1992, is also a possibility. Charleston County Democratic Chairman Andy Brack said in early 1999 that he was interested in the race, and that it would take $1 million for a Democrat to win. More than that, one might think, in this district carried solidly by Bob Dole; but Democratic Governor Jim Hodges in 1998 raised plenty of money from video poker operators and scored an impressive victory.

Cook's Call. *Safe.* Sanford's retirement from this seat will not change the fact that it will most assuredly remain in Republican hands. Expect a crowded Republican primary, but don't look for a competitive general election.

The People: Pop. 1990: 581,195; 25.1% rural; 9.8% age 65 +; 78.1% White, 20% Black, 1.1% Asian, 0.4% Amer. Indian, 0.4% Other; 1.2% Hispanic Origin. Households: 59.4% married couple families; 30.3% married couple fams. w. children; 47.9% college educ.; median household income: $28,765; per capita income: $13,112; median house value: $75,600; median gross rent: $362.

1996 Presidential Vote

Dole (R) 107,221 (55%)
Clinton (D) 74,150 (38%)
Perot (I) 11,491 (6%)

1992 Presidential Vote

Bush (R) 101,830 (53%)
Clinton (D) 63,318 (33%)
Perot (I) 26,620 (14%)

Rep. Mark Sanford (R)

Elected 1994; b. May 28, 1960, Ft. Lauderdale, FL; home, Charleston; Furman U., B.A. 1983; U. of VA, M.B.A. 1988; Episcopalian; married (Jenny).

Professional Career: Real estate investor, 1988–92; Owner, Norton & Sanford real estate investment firm, 1992–present.

DC Office: 1233 LHOB 20515, 202-225-3176; Fax: 202-225-3407; Web site: www.house.gov/sanford.

District Offices: Charleston, 803-727-4175; Conway, 843-248-2660; Georgetown, 843-527-6868.

Committees: *Government Reform* (14th of 24 R): National Security, Veterans' Affairs & Intl. Relations; Postal Service (Vice Chmn.). *International Relations* (16th of 26 R): Asia & the Pacific; Western Hemisphere. *Science* (24th of 25 R): Space & Aeronautics. *Joint Economic Committee* (2d of 10 Reps.).

Group Ratings

	ADA	ACLU	AFS	LCV	CON	NTU	NFIB	COC	ACU	NTLC	CHC
1998	20	19	22	38	100	90	86	71	72	76	100
1997	20	—	13	—	34	78	—	60	88	—	—

National Journal Ratings

	1997 LIB — 1997 CONS	1998 LIB — 1998 CONS
Economic	28% — 67%	43% — 56%
Social	30% — 64%	29% — 69%
Foreign	38% — 60%	34% — 62%

Key Votes of the 105th Congress

1. Clinton Budget Deal	Y	5. Puerto Rico Sthood. Ref.	N	9. Cut $ for B-2 Bombers	Y
2. Education IRAs	Y	6. End Highway Set-asides	Y	10. Human Rights in China	Y
3. Req. 2/3 to Raise Taxes	Y	7. School Prayer Amend.	Y	11. Withdraw Bosnia Troops	Y
4. Fast-track Trade	Y	8. Ovrd. Part. Birth Veto	Y	12. End Cuban TV-Marti	N

Election Results

1998 general	Mark Sanford (R) 118,414	(91%)	($49,458)
	Joe Innella (NL) 11,586	(9%)	
1998 primary	Mark Sanford (R) .... unopposed		
1996 general	Mark Sanford (R) 138,467	(96%)	($97,231)
	Others 5,226	(4%)	

SECOND DISTRICT

Soon after the Revolutionary War, in 1786, the South Carolina legislature decided to move the state's capital away from the Charleston aristocracy and into the Up Country interior, away from a city named after a king to a new city named after a discoverer of America: so began Columbia. The State House was built on high ground above the Congaree River in a town of one-and-a-half story houses with first floor porticoes, dormers and raised brick basements—"Columbia cottages." In 1865, General William Tecumseh Sherman's army burned everything here but the State House. In the post-Sherman years, Columbia grew slowly, with state government and the university, the Army's Fort Jackson and local insurance companies proving steady employers. In the 1970s and 1980s, it started to boom, attracting plants such as Michelin, Allied Chemical, United Technologies, FN of Belgium, DuPont and Square D. Approaching half a million in metro area population in the 1990s, Columbia is becoming a true city and not just a village-capital.

The Columbia to which Jimmy Byrnes, after years in top posts in Democratic Washington, returned as governor to lament the *Brown v. Board of Education* decision in 1954, has trended Republican in the years since. Upwardly mobile South Carolinians, transplanted from underdeveloped rural areas to comfortable subdivisions with two-car garages, preferred Republicans first in national and then in state and local elections. Columbia voted for Eisenhower in the 1950s; in the late 1960s and 1970s, blacks were usually outnumbered by increasingly Republican whites in Columbia's Richland County and fast-growing Lexington County across the river. In the 1990s, as Columbia has spread out over adjacent counties, Richland County, with a higher black percentage, has been voting Democratic, and in 1998 even generated a large enough margin to overcome Lexington's Republican majority.

The 2d Congressional District includes most of metropolitan Columbia, except for black neighborhoods lopped off in 1992 to create a black-majority 6th District. It contains the city's affluent white neighborhoods and the spread-out towns of Richland and Lexington counties, with their shopping centers and many churches and the Army's huge training center, Fort Jackson. The district extends south through the horse-farm area around Aiken and several lightly populated black-majority rural counties, and then includes Beaufort and Hilton Head on the coast—the former is an old town, with wonderful mansions and a history intertwined with slave plantations and the Marine Corps's Parris Island training base; the latter, made famous by Pat Conroy's novel, *The Prince of Tides*, has been developed with much meticulous attention to its natural environment, a model now for Atlantic coast condominium and vacation communities. This is a solidly Republican district, though Democrats, with relatively big turnouts in black areas, were able to whittle down its Republican majority in 1998.

The congressman from the 2d District is Floyd Spence, a Republican first elected in 1970, now chairman of the Armed Services Committee. Spence was a star football player and student body president at the University of South Carolina; he served as an officer in the Navy and was in the Naval Reserve until 1988. When he graduated from law school in 1956, he was elected to the state House; he switched parties and became a Republican in 1962, two years before Strom Thurmond. He narrowly lost a House race that year to a Democrat who later switched parties; then Spence was elected to the state Senate as a Republican in 1966. When the incumbent ran for governor in 1970, Spence ran again for the House seat and won. He is now tied for second in seniority among House Republicans, trailing only Philip Crane and tied with Bill Archer and Bill Young.

Spence has a solidly conservative voting record. He was the first House member to sponsor the balanced budget constitutional amendment, in 1971; he served for 13 years as ranking Republican on the ethics committee. But his greatest energy has been devoted to military issues. He supported the defense buildup of the 1980s and called for "responsible downsizing of defense expenditures rather than drastic cuts" in the 1990s. But the downsizing has gone much farther than he considers wise. As chairman, Spence has peppered the Clinton Administration with criticism even as he has managed the complex and lengthy defense authorization bills. He argues that defense cuts have been too deep, twice as deep as Clinton promised in 1992. He is worried about the erosion of the nuclear stockpile. He argues that cuts have jeopardized the technological superiority so apparent in the Gulf war. "Our national strategy is to be able to [simultaneously] fight and win two major regional contingencies. But we've cut back so much since Desert Storm that I don't think we could do even one," he said in May 1998.

Spence was particularly concerned when retention rates declined and standards for enlistment were cut in 1998. "The decline in military quality of life is approaching a state of crisis," he said, and in November 1998 said he would support a military draft if retention rates and readiness did not improve. In 1996 he criticized the administration for not withdrawing from Bosnia after the promised period of one year and issued a tough report on the June 1996 bombing of the Khobar Towers troop facility in Saudi Arabia. He has decried the administration policy of selling high-tech devices to China. He seized on CIA Director John Deutch's September 1996 statement that Clinton's bombings in northern Iraq left Saddam Hussein stronger than before. He secured funding to support the troops in Iraq and Bosnia despite voicing his disapproval of the way NATO was conducting the operation of the latter.

Spence has been urging the United States to build a system of missile defense even before he was chairman. "We don't have a defense against weapons of mass destruction, and the president has blocked all our efforts to increase national security," he said in 1998. Efforts to declare missile defense a national priority were frustrated by a Democratic filibuster in September 1998 (South Carolina's Ernest Hollings was one of four Democrats to vote to cut off the filibuster), but in late May 1999 the House passed legislation that would commit the U.S. to building a missile defense system as soon as it is technologically possible, and Clinton seemed likely to sign the bill.

One change Spence has stoutly resisted is a new round of base closures. South Carolina suffered heavily from base closures in the 1980s and 1990s, but has recovered economically with little damage; the greater problem for Spence is that President Clinton changed his position in 1995 to keep politically sensitive bases operating, and a large majority of the House doesn't trust him to administer the process fairly. Spence charges that more base closures won't save money for several years anyway: "The reality of ongoing base closures is that the upfront costs, including huge bills for environmental cleanup, are enormous." Indeed, the largest South Carolina project by far in the defense appropriation passed in 1998 was $1.3 billion for cleanup of the closed Savannah River nuclear site.

Spence received a double lung transplant in 1988, but has seemed in fine health in the years since. From 1990 to 1996 he did not have a Democratic opponent. In 1998 he was opposed by Beaufort County architect Jane Frederick, a self-styled "feminist" who attacked his "archaic, insensitive and unacceptable view toward women" and his stands on abortion, family leave and the minimum wage. Spence campaigned robustly around the district, but his campaign organization was rusty after years of little opposition, and Democrats—fed by video poker money—made their best South Carolina showing in years. Spence won 58%–41%, a solid but not overwhelming margin. He ran ahead of the state ticket but, despite years of helping local black officials, lost in three black-majority counties. Under Republican rules, Spence will have to give up the Armed Services chairmanship after the 2000 election, which may raise questions in the minds of some whether, at 72, he will run for another term.

Cook's Call. *Probably Safe.* Though Spence's 1998 margin of victory was the narrowest it had been in 10 years, he is still solidly settled in this Republican leaning district. Even if this seat were to open up (there is speculation that Spence may not run in 2000 since he has to give up his chairmanship of the Armed Services Committee in 2001), it will be hard to wrest it from Republican control.

The People: Pop. 1990: 580,636; 39.3% rural; 10.6% age 65 + ; 73.2% White, 25.1% Black, 0.9% Asian, 0.2% Amer. Indian, 0.6% Other; 1.4% Hispanic Origin. Households: 57.5% married couple families; 28.9% married couple fams. w. children; 50.5% college educ.; median household income: $30,693; per capita income: $13,913; median house value: $74,000; median gross rent: $355.

1996 Presidential Vote			1992 Presidential Vote		
Dole (R)	117,261	(53%)	Bush (R)	119,658	(52%)
Clinton (D)	90,871	(41%)	Clinton (D)	82,652	(36%)
Perot (I)	10,827	(5%)	Perot (I)	25,853	(11%)

Rep. Floyd Spence (R)

Elected 1970; b. Apr. 9, 1928, Columbia; home, Lexington; U. of SC, A.B. 1952, LL.B. 1956; Lutheran; married (Deborah).

Military Career: Naval Reserves, 1947–88 (Korea).

Elected Office: SC House of Reps., 1956–62; SC Senate, 1966–70, Minority Ldr., 1966–70.

Professional Career: Practicing atty., 1956–70.

DC Office: 2405 RHOB 20515, 202-225-2452; Fax: 202-225-2455.

District Offices: Beaufort, 843-521-2530; Columbia, 803-254-5120; Estill, 803-625-3177; Orangeburg, 803-536-4641.

Committees: *Armed Services* (Chmn. of 32 R): Military Procurement. *Veterans' Affairs* (4th of 17 R): Oversight & Investigations.

Group Ratings

	ADA	ACLU	AFS	LCV	CON	NTU	NFIB	COC	ACU	NTLC	CHC
1998	5	6	11	8	13	53	100	78	100	97	100
1997	0	—	13	—	26	47	—	90	88	—	—

National Journal Ratings

	1997 LIB — 1997 CONS		1998 LIB — 1998 CONS	
Economic	28%	67%	23%	74%
Social	10%	82%	14%	81%
Foreign	0%	88%	7%	83%

Key Votes of the 105th Congress

1. Clinton Budget Deal	Y	5. Puerto Rico Sthood. Ref.	N	9. Cut $ for B-2 Bombers	N
2. Education IRAs	Y	6. End Highway Set-asides	Y	10. Human Rights in China	N
3. Req. 2/3 to Raise Taxes	Y	7. School Prayer Amend.	Y	11. Withdraw Bosnia Troops	Y
4. Fast-track Trade	N	8. Ovrd. Part. Birth Veto	Y	12. End Cuban TV-Marti	N

Election Results

1998 general	Floyd Spence (R)	119,583	(58%)	($537,752)
	Jane Frederick (D)	84,864	(41%)	($202,584)
1998 primary	Floyd Spence (R)	unopposed		
1996 general	Floyd Spence (R)	158,229	(90%)	($303,421)
	Maurice T. Raidford (NL)	17,713	(10%)	

THIRD DISTRICT

The South Carolina Up Country, many days' travel by wagon from the Low Country plantations, was first settled by Scots-Irish farmers, like the family of John C. Calhoun in the years around the Revolutionary War. The pioneers wanted to make big plantations of these forests, but the land did not always cooperate; it was often too hilly for the labor-intensive rice crop grown in the Low Country and sometimes too cold for cotton. So relatively few slaves were brought here, and the land was mostly small farms owned by whites. Today, the racial and cultural tone of Up Country South Carolina shows traces of these roots. This is a mostly white part of the South, with a hell-of-a-fella tone to daily life, an economically growing and culturally tradition-minded slice of Middle America.

The 3d Congressional District covers much of this territory, following the Georgia border from the government's troubled Savannah River Site all the way north to mountains on the North Carolina border. In the southern part of the 3d are a few heavily black communities, like Edgefield, where Strom Thurmond grew up and first won public office in the 1930s. But the major population center here is the increasingly affluent suburban strip linking Aiken and Augusta, Georgia. In the northern part of this district, Calhoun had his mansion and his son-in-law founded Clemson University nearby. Here today, the Savannah River intersects Interstate 85, the main street of what was once America's textile belt and now of the booming Southeast from Raleigh-Durham to Atlanta, one of the nation's prime economic growth areas.

The politics of this area, ancestrally Democratic, has been trending Republican for years. Yankified Aiken started voting Republican for Dwight Eisenhower in the 1950s, well before Thurmond switched parties in 1964; Anderson skittered around, supporting Jimmy Carter for a while but then veering Republican again; Pickens and Oconee counties around Clemson and the mountains are heavily Republican. This is a fervently religious part of America, and the increasing secularism and hostility to religious values of many leading Democrats moved it away from its ancestral party. In presidential elections the 3d has been solidly Republican in the 1980s and 1990s, and it voted Republican even as Democrats swept the state in 1998.

The congressman from the 3d District is Lindsey Graham, a Republican first elected in 1994. Graham grew up in Oconee County, where his parents owned a "beer joint"; he was the first in his family to graduate from college and law school, then served in the Air Force as a prosecutor; in 1988 he returned home and practiced law, also serving as judge advocate at McEntire Air National Guard base. He was called up to active duty and served stateside in the Gulf war. In 1992 he was elected state representative. In 1994, with the retirement of 20-year Congressman Butler Derrick, a member of the Democratic leadership who came under tough criticism in South Carolina, Graham ran for Congress. Both parties here had contested primaries, but the Republican contest attracted more voters—41,000 versus 35,000—and Graham emerged as a clear winner, with 52% of the vote. In the general he faced state Senator Jim Bryan, who won the Democratic runoff against Deborah Dorn, daughter of Derrick's predecessor in the House. Graham called for term limits, supported more defense spending and was against gays in the military. His attitude toward the Clinton Administration and the House Democratic leadership was unequivocal: "I'm one less vote for an agenda that makes you want to throw up." Bryan also campaigned as a conservative—pro-life, anti-gays in the military, against employer mandates in health care, against defense cuts, and boasted of his experience in the legislature. But Graham modeled his campaign after Bob Inglis's successful 1992 race in the next-door 4th District and won 60%–40%—a smashing victory in a district represented only by Democrats since Reconstruction. In 1996 he was opposed by Dorn, and won by 60%–39%. In 1998 he was unopposed.

In the House Graham has a strong though not entirely conservative voting record. He supported the Contract with America and called for lifting the tax burden on individuals and removing onerous regulations on business. He continued to be an enthusiast for term limits. He opposed the May 1997 budget deal because it included a children's health insurance plan financed by higher tobacco taxes, but he bucked the leadership in 1998 on HMO reform, arguing that patients should have the right to sue. Much of his legislative work has been devoted to the Savannah River Site (SRS). This huge installation was once used to manufacture tritium for nuclear weapons; with as many as 35,000 jobs, it was among the largest employers in South Carolina. Now the nuclear plant is shut down and SRS is used as a holding site for foreign nuclear waste while the government works on developing a long-term disposal. Graham has worked to make SRS a waste processing site for surplus weapons-grade plutonium and highly-enriched uranium, to keep reprocessing canyons fully used to process nuclear waste and to place a linear accelerator there; with nuclear power foe Edward Markey he sponsored an amendment to block any commercial tritium reactor that would be built elsewhere.

Graham is the kind of politician who often follows his own piper. In January 1996 he was one of 15 Republicans who voted against settling the budget fight. He came to see Newt

Gingrich as just another deal-making career politician: "The Contract with America was a political event for him; it was sort of my reason for being." In July 1997 Graham helped organize a group of Republican leaders to plot the toppling of Gingrich, and Tom DeLay said he would vote to oust the speaker. This coup quickly foundered—it could have given Democrats control of the House—and in a Republican conference meeting when Dick Armey said no Republican leader was involved, Graham lunged to the microphone to contradict him.

As a member of the Judiciary Committee, Graham played a major role in impeachment. At first he noted that his district strongly favored removal, but insisted that he started off undecided. But when Clinton defenders quibbled about the meanings of words and insisted that Clinton's deposition testimony was "legally accurate," Graham exploded in opposition. In December 1998, he said, "If people in America follow Bill Clintonspeak, we're going to ruin the rule of law, and he's not worth that. No one person in America is worth trashing out the rule of law and creating a situation where you can't rely on your common sense." He was especially upset with the way Clinton used the official powers of the White House to discredit Monica Lewinsky: "The way he treated Monica Lewinsky, his political interests were more important than the truth or welfare of the person he was involved in a sexual relationship with. He was using the office in a most sinister way. The country is in trouble when you let politicians use the resources of their office to crush a citizen who may get in their way." Yet Graham voted against impeaching Clinton for lying in the Paula Jones deposition, on the ground that it was later ruled immaterial by the judge (although after Congress voted the judge held him in contempt of court for it). In the Senate trial, Graham's folksy manner and clear description of Clinton's offenses— "Where I come from, a man who calls someone up at 2:30 in the morning is up to no good"— made him one of the most effective managers. Yet he conceded a major political point when he agreed that a reasonable person could disagree on whether Clinton should be removed.

When Graham was elected in 1994, he imposed a six-term limit on himself, but he may well run for the Senate before that comes up in 2006. In December 1998 he said, "If I can live long enough to see Senator Thurmond retire—and I have no doubt about him, but I have some doubts about me—it would be an honor to serve in the Senate." He should be considered a strong candidate for Thurmond's seat in 2002 or Ernest Hollings's in 2004.

Cook's Call. *Safe.* Despite his high-profile role as a House impeachment manager, Graham is not going to feel a serious fall-out in this very conservative district that has never given Clinton more than 39% of the vote.

The People: Pop. 1990: 580,861; 58.5% rural; 13.6% age 65 + ; 78.3% White, 21% Black, 0.4% Asian, 0.2% Amer. Indian, 0.1% Other; 0.5% Hispanic Origin. Households: 58.8% married couple families; 28% married couple fams. w. children; 33.3% college educ.; median household income: $25,693; per capita income: $11,707; median house value: $53,900; median gross rent: $222.

1996 Presidential Vote			1992 Presidential Vote		
Dole (R)	100,390	(54%)	Bush (R)	101,962	(51%)
Clinton (D)	71,755	(39%)	Clinton (D)	69,161	(35%)
Perot (I)	13,220	(7%)	Perot (I)	26,424	(13%)

Rep. Lindsey Graham (R)

Elected 1994; b. July 9, 1955, Central; home, Seneca; U. of SC, B.A. 1977, J.D. 1981; Baptist; single.

Military Career: Air Force, 1982–88; Air Force Reserves, 1988–present (Persian Gulf), Air Natl. Guard, 1989–present.

Elected Office: SC House of Reps., 1992–94.

Professional Career: Air Force Chief Prosecutor, 1984–88; Asst. Oconee Cnty. Atty., 1988–92; Practicing atty., 1988–94; Judge Advocate, McEntire Air Natl. Guard Base, 1989–94; Central SC City Atty., 1990–94.

DC Office: 1429 LHOB 20515, 202-225-5301; Fax: 202-225-3216; Web site: www.house.gov/graham.

District Offices: Aiken, 803-649-5571; Anderson, 864-224-7401; Greenwood, 864-223-8251.

Committees: *Armed Services* (24th of 32 R): Military Personnel (Vice Chmn.); Military Procurement. *Education & the Workforce* (13th of 27 R): Early Childhood, Youth & Families; Postsecondary Education, Training & Life-Long Learning (Vice Chmn.); Workforce Protections. *Judiciary* (18th of 21 R): Commercial & Administrative Law; The Constitution.

Group Ratings

	ADA	ACLU	AFS	LCV	CON	NTU	NFIB	COC	ACU	NTLC	CHC
1998	15	0	11	8	86	72	100	76	88	97	100
1997	5	—	0	—	27	65	—	90	92	—	—

National Journal Ratings

	1997 LIB — 1997 CONS	1998 LIB — 1998 CONS
Economic	0% — 90%	12% — 85%
Social	0% — 90%	14% — 81%
Foreign	38% — 60%	7% — 83%

Key Votes of the 105th Congress

1. Clinton Budget Deal	Y	5. Puerto Rico Sthood. Ref.	N	9. Cut $ for B-2 Bombers	N
2. Education IRAs	Y	6. End Highway Set-asides	Y	10. Human Rights in China	N
3. Req. 2/3 to Raise Taxes	Y	7. School Prayer Amend.	Y	11. Withdraw Bosnia Troops	Y
4. Fast-track Trade	N	8. Ovrd. Part. Birth Veto	Y	12. End Cuban TV-Marti	N

Election Results

1998 general	Lindsey Graham (R) .... unopposed			($321,502)
1998 primary	Lindsey Graham (R) .... unopposed			
1996 general	Lindsey Graham (R) 114,273	(60%)		($644,451)
	Deborah Dorn (D) 73,417	(39%)		($128,230)

FOURTH DISTRICT

A century ago, Northern investors looking for sites for textile mills, looked at the Up Country of South Carolina and "were attracted by the mild climate, abundant water power, proximity to the cotton fields and plenty of native [white] labor already accustomed to a low standard of living." As mills fled New England, the textile industry became concentrated along the Southern Railway and Seaboard Coast Line tracks between Charlotte and Atlanta, especially in the Piedmont of South Carolina. The textile country might look bucolic, but Greenville, Spartanburg and the dozens of mill towns thick in the surrounding countryside were as industrial as Lancashire or the Ruhr, with mills rising up on what were once twisting woodland paths.

Today, this same stretch of land along Interstate 85, which parallels the Southern Railway, remains the number one textile-producing area in the United States. But it is much more than that. The number of textile and apparel jobs declined in the early 1970s but many more jobs were created in the 1990s by big and small companies to the extent that the South Carolina Manufacturers Alliance dropped the word "textiles" from its name. Michelin's North American headquarters is near Greenville and BMW's one American plant is next to the regional airport in Spartanburg County just off I-85. What attracts these businesses? Sometimes big tax concessions do, as with BMW. More importantly, overall tax levels are low, with good state-built infrastructure—the airport, the interstate highways, the port of Charleston, now one of the busiest on the East Coast. Unions are almost nonexistent. Culturally this area ranges from conservative to very conservative, with a strong influence by Greenville's Bob Jones University and many evangelical and fundamentalist churches. But the culture of mainstream churches and civic boosters has a certain bedrock conservatism to it as well.

The 4th Congressional District fits almost perfectly around the Greenville-Spartanburg area. It has voted Republican in national elections for many years now, and Republican voting habits have spread to downballot races as well. Often the real contest here is between evangelical and economic conservatives.

The congressman from the 4th District is Jim DeMint, a Republican elected in 1998. DeMint grew up in Greenville, graduated from the University of Tennessee and Clemson Business School, returned to Greenville to work as a paper salesman and in the advertising business. In 1983 he founded DeMint Marketing, with businesses, schools, colleges and hospitals as clients. In 1992 he went to work for 33-year-old lawyer Bob Inglis's House campaign. As he explains, "I became increasingly concerned that the freedoms we take for granted in America are under attack in such a subtle way that no one is noticing it. I developed the feeling that I had a burden to try to change things." Inglis pledged to serve only three terms, to take no PAC money, to oppose pork barrel projects even in South Carolina; DeMint honed his message using focus groups and advertising expertise. Inglis upset an incumbent Democrat by 50%–48%, and proceeded to keep his promises. He was re-elected twice and in 1998 ran against Senator Ernest Hollings, and lost 53%–46%.

DeMint proceeded to run, with Inglis's support, for the open seat. Like Inglis, he pledged to serve only three terms and take no PAC money; on pork, he was more practical, saying that if bills were going to pass he would make sure some of the money went to South Carolina. He called for a national sales tax or flat tax, for individual retirement accounts in Social Security, for the right-to-life amendment, for the English rule (loser pays winner's attorney fees) in tort cases. Four other Republicans ran, and the favorite was Mike Fair, former University of South Carolina quarterback, 10-year state representative and first term state senator, "arguably the state's most conservative politician," according to the Columbia *State*. He opposed co-ed dorms at the state university, criticized sex education that advocated condom use, backed covenant marriage and fought for a ban on all abortion. He was endorsed by Gary Bauer, Steve Forbes, Oliver North, Ralph Reed and Phyllis Schlafly. Also running were hospital executive Howell Clyborne and Spartanburg lawyer Jim Ritchie. In the June 9 primary Fair led with 32%; DeMint came in second with 23%, 699 votes ahead of Clyborne, who had 22%; Ritchie was fourth with 20%. The order was the same in Greenville County; but Spartanburg County, which cast 36% of the vote, went 42% to Ritchie, with 17% to 21% for each of the other contenders.

It seemed obvious that Spartanburg would determine the outcome of the June 23 runoff. DeMint campaigned heavily on the affluent east side of Spartanburg, while Fair concentrated on energizing his religious conservative base. Fair bragged about his experience, DeMint called him a "career politician." The result was a 53%–47% upset win for DeMint. He trailed in Greenville County 51%–49%, but carried Spartanburg County by 60%–40%. DeMint's verdict on the result: "There is a distinction with us as Christians as we go into the political arena believing that our purpose is to use government to push our ideas on people. I don't think that was Mike Fair's objective, but the problem is the message we're sending is that we want to get involved in social engineering ourselves, but from our point of view." Democrat Glenn Reese, a state Senator since 1991 and owner of a Krispy Kreme franchise, made a game effort. But DeMint heavily outspent him and Inglis, while losing statewide, carried the district, as did Republican Governor David Beasley. This time heavily Republican Greenville County was DeMint's charm; he carried it 64%–34%, while carrying Spartanburg County 50%–48%. Overall he won 58%–40%.

In Washington, DeMint's speech to incoming Republicans impressed then-Speaker-designate Bob Livingston, who named him to the Republican Marketing Task Force; he was also elected president of the freshman class.

Cook's Call. *Safe.* Arguably the most Republican district in the state, this deeply conservative district is also one of the most Republican in the South. The only thing preventing DeMint from planting himself here for a good long time is the fact that he limited himself to three terms and has pledged to leave the House in 2004.

The People: Pop. 1990: 581,385; 35.6% rural; 12.9% age 65 + ; 79.3% White, 19.7% Black, 0.6% Asian, 0.1% Amer. Indian, 0.2% Other; 0.8% Hispanic Origin. Households: 57% married couple families; 26.9% married couple fams. w. children; 39.4% college educ.; median household income: $27,703; per capita income: $13,011; median house value: $59,500; median gross rent: $272.

1996 Presidential Vote		
Dole (R)	111,699	(56%)
Clinton (D)	74,208	(37%)
Perot (I)	11,496	(6%)

1992 Presidential Vote		
Bush (R)	107,970	(54%)
Clinton (D)	65,106	(33%)
Perot (I)	24,131	(12%)

Rep. Jim DeMint (R)

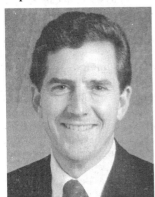

Elected 1998; b. Sept. 2, 1951, Greenville; home, Greenville; U. of TN, B.S. 1973, Clemson U., M.B.A. 1981; Presbyterian; married (Debbie).

Professional Career: Sales Rep., Scott Paper, 1973–75; Acct. Rep., Henderson Advertising, 1975–81; V.P., Leslie Advertising, 1981–84; Pres., DeMint Marketing, 1983-present.

DC Office: 507 CHOB 20515, 202-225-6030; Fax: 202-226-1177; Web site: www.demint.house.gov.

District Offices: Greenville, 864-232-1141; Spartanburg, 864-582-6422; Union, 864-427-2205.

Committees: *Education & the Workforce* (26th of 27 R): Early Childhood, Youth & Families; Employer-Employee Relations. *Small Business* (16th of 19 R): Empowerment (Vice Chmn.); Rural Enterprise, Business Opportunities & Special Small Business Problems. *Transportation & Infrastructure* (37th of 41 R): Aviation; Ground Transportation.

Group Ratings and Key Votes: Newly Elected

Election Results

1998 general	Jim DeMint (R)	105,264	(58%)	($453,336)
	Glenn Reese (D)	73,314	(40%)	($112,995)
	Others	3,972	(2%)	
1998 runoff	Jim DeMint (R)	18,445	(53%)	
	Mike Fair (R)	16,413	(47%)	
1998 primary	Mike Fair (R)	12,924	(32%)	
	Jim DeMint (R)	9,300	(23%)	
	Howell Clyborne (R)	8,601	(22%)	
	Jim Ritchie (R)	7,788	(20%)	
	Others	1,232	(3%)	
1996 general	Bob Inglis (R)	138,165	(71%)	($143,966)
	Darrell E. Curry (D)	54,126	(28%)	($15,643)

FIFTH DISTRICT

Some of the fiercest battles of the Revolutionary War were fought in South Carolina's Up Country, on hilly lands just being settled by Scots-Irish farmers moving up from the Low Country or down the Virginia Piedmont valley. This was a country of violent passions and unclear lines; Carolinians have long argued over which side of the North and South Carolina boundary Andrew Jackson was born in 1767. Ever since, the fighting spirit and Calvinist faith of Up Country Carolinians have never wavered. This "Olde English District" remains intensely religious and pro-military. But it is no longer impoverished. For many years, the dominant industry here was textiles, traditionally the first factory enterprise of industrializing countries, with low pay and poor working conditions. But in the 1980s and 1990s the number of textile jobs declined, and small-business prosperity more recently has been barreling out the interstates from Greenville-Spartanburg and Columbia and Charlotte, to transform counties once dependent on tobacco fields and textile mills.

The 5th Congressional District consists of all or part of 13 counties, mostly in the Up Country. It includes none of the state's three large metropolitan centers, but much of their growing fringe. In the east, the 5th includes Darlington, site of the Southern 500 stock car race every Labor Day, and verges on lowland tobacco country, including Marlboro and Chesterfield counties. In the west, it includes Fort Mill and Rock Hill in York County, just south of Charlotte, ready for fast development now that a land settlement with the Catawba Indians has been reached. Politically, this homeland of Andrew Jackson is ancestrally Democratic. But in the 1990s Republicans have become competitive here.

The congressman from the 5th District is John Spratt, one of the leading Democrats in the House, first elected in 1982. He comes from a prominent York County family and has degrees from Davidson, Yale Law and Oxford; he first got involved in politics in Charles Ravenel's unsuccessful 1974 campaign for governor. In 1982 the 5th District incumbent announced his retirement a week before the filing deadline; Spratt put a campaign together fast and won 38% in the primary, 55% in the runoff against a high-spending candidate, and 68% in the general. For 10 years he was re-elected easily; then in 1994 and 1996 he had tough races, winning by 52%–48% and 54%–45%, carrying the rural counties and running even in York County. It is a measure of the strength of the Republican tide of the mid-1990s that a Democrat with so many political assets could be so hard pressed. But the Democrats came back in South Carolina, winning the governorship and holding Hollings's senate seat, and Spratt won 58%–40%.

Spratt's two specialties are military issues and the budget; he is ranking Democrat on the Budget Committee and third-ranking Democrat on Armed Services. In the 1980s, he worked with then-Chairman Les Aspin and, in his thick Carolina accent and with impressive knowledge of details, stitched together compromises on the MX missile, binary nerve gas weapons, the Strategic Defense Initiative, and the Savannah River Site and other nuclear plants—keeping military projects flowing through the House, many of whose members were constantly looking to cut military spending. In the 1990s he has worked on the details of defense budgets, concentrating on maintaining troop levels and equipment in good condition. He has conceded for some time that the ABM Treaty will have to be abandoned some day, but has been cautious about rapid development and deployment of missile defense. His amendment on the subject prevailed in February 1995 by 218–212, the first significant defeat of a Contract with America promise in the Republican House. In August 1998, a month after the Rumsfeld Commission report on missile defense, he joined Curt Weldon and other Republicans in support of a one-sentence bill declaring "the policy of the United States to deploy a national missile defense." This passed the House, but Senate Democrats (except for Hollings and three others) filibustered against any missile defense measure in September 1998. In late May 1999 the House passed a bill that would make the construction of a national missile defense a top priority.

Spratt supported the 1990 budget deal and tax increase, and in 1991 got a seat on the Budget Committee. His moderate voting record made him a natural point of contact between the parties, but Democrats did not see him as their leader: in their November 1992 caucus he was beaten for Budget chairman by the more liberal Martin Sabo by 149–112. He rotated off the committee in 1992, then ran for the ranking Democrat position on Budget again in December 1996, proclaiming his "determination" to balance the budget. Democrats, now in the minority, were more ready for his leadership; he was nominated by Appropriations ranking Democrat David Obey and beat the more liberal Louise Slaughter by 106–83; he actually had fewer votes than four years before.

He started off with a good relationship with Budget Chairman John Kasich; as he noted in February 1997, when Kasich announced his engagement, "If John Kasich can find someone to marry him, then surely we can find some way to balance the budget." He played a major role in putting together the May 1997 agreement to reach a balanced budget, holding together Democrats who disliked the concessions to wealthy tax payers and staying in touch with Republicans who wanted more spending cuts. In the process, he got support from Bill Archer and Al Gore against a proposed Medicaid funding cut which would have hurt South Carolina, and came up with an alternative Republican Governor David Beasley praised. Spratt continued to work with the White House, House Republicans and House Democrats in establishing the specific details of the balanced budget package, which finally were agreed on in August 1997. "My party was no longer calling the shots, but I was in the middle of the biggest game going on," he said. Minority Leader Dick Gephardt and 51 other Democrats and 32 Republicans voted against this, but it passed by a wide margin. Spratt gave much credit to the 1990 budget deal and noted that Newt Gingrich and most of the current Republican leadership voted against it. In June 1998, unsatisfied with the House Republicans' budget, Spratt introduced a Democratic budget with $30 billion in tax cuts and $30 billion for new Clinton spending programs.

On other issues, Spratt has a moderate record, somewhat to the left of the middle of the House. He voted for the line-item veto in 1995, though he thought its particular form was unconstitutional; the Supreme Court agreed. He co-sponsored the Democratic welfare alternative with Georgia's Nathan Deal in March 1995, which came close to passing; but it was overtaken by the welfare reform act Clinton signed in August 1996, for which Spratt voted. He has been co-chair of the Textile Caucus, and pressed in various ways to get the Clinton Administration to enforce rules against illegal textile imports. He criticized the FDA's attempts to regulate tobacco as unjustified by law, and sponsored a bill to prohibit FDA regulation. He sponsored the V-chip legislation adopted in 1996. He has worked to keep Shaw Air Force Base near Sumter off the base-closing list, and he settled a 15-year controversy just before a 1992 deadline which would have triggered a lawsuit by Catawba Indians against 62,000 landowners. With Edward Markey he opposed building a civilian nuclear plant for tritium production; South Carolina wants the work at the Savannah River Site, and Spratt argued that a civilian plant would undermine U.S. anti-nuclear proliferation efforts.

In 1994 and 1996 Spratt was opposed by Republican Larry Bigham, who denounced government mandates and pledged, "I will work to get government out of our lives, out of our schools, out of our homes, out of our businesses" and argued that "a vote for John Spratt is a vote for Bill Clinton." As opinion continued to move away from Republicans, Spratt received a rousing reception at a Democratic forum in Rock Hill in January 1998 for balancing the budget. In 1998 Spratt was opposed by a 29-year-old food company owner and York County town official who pledged to serve only three terms. This gave Spratt an opportunity to argue that no term-limited member could accomplish the things he had. This was one of the three districts where the House Republicans' campaign committee ran their most virulent anti-Clinton ads in the last week of the campaign—ads that received national publicity all out of proportion to the actual buy. Here they seem to have made little difference. Spratt won 58%–40%, carrying every county but York, which newcomers flooding over the state line from Charlotte have made more Republican; York County has been the fourth fastest-growing in the state since 1990, behind only Beaufort (Hilton Head), Lexington (Columbia suburbs) and Horry (Myrtle Beach and the Grand Strand). Speaking of his own victory and those of other South Carolina Democrats, Spratt said, "You could feel the river rising. This exceeds my wildest expectations." This highly competent and productive member seems once again to have a safe seat.

   Cook's Call. *Probably Safe.* This is one of those Republican trending districts that Democrats will have an excruciatingly difficult time holding on to once the popular Democrat retires. Until then, Spratt, who survived the 1994 anti-Democratic tidal wave that swept through the South as well as aggressive Republican challengers over the past two cycles, will be very tough to beat.

The People: Pop. 1990: 581,174; 62.7% rural; 12.3% age 65+; 68.3% White, 30.8% Black, 0.4% Asian, 0.5% Amer. Indian, 0.1% Other; 0.5% Hispanic Origin. Households: 57.7% married couple families; 29.3% married couple fams. w. children; 31.9% college educ.; median household income: $25,215; per capita income: $11,009; median house value: $53,300; median gross rent: $216.

1996 Presidential Vote			1992 Presidential Vote		
Dole (R)	83,273	(47%)	Bush (R)	86,118	(45%)
Clinton (D)	82,203	(46%)	Clinton (D)	81,192	(42%)
Perot (I)	11,827	(7%)	Perot (I)	23,462	(12%)

Rep. John M. Spratt, Jr. (D)

Elected 1982; b. Nov. 1, 1942, Charlotte, NC; home, York; Davidson Col., A.B. 1964, Oxford U., M.A. 1966, Yale U., LL.B. 1969; Presbyterian; married (Jane Stacy).

Military Career: Army Operations, U.S. Dept. of Defense, 1969–71.

Professional Career: Practicing atty., 1971–82; Pres., Bank of Ft. Mill, 1973–82; Pres., Spratt Insurance Agcy., 1973–82.

DC Office: 1536 LHOB 20515, 202-225-5501; Fax: 202-225-0464; Web site: www.house.gov/spratt.

District Offices: Darlington, 803-393-3998; Rock Hill, 803-327-1114; Sumter, 803-773-3362.

Committees: *Armed Services* (3d of 28 D): Military Procurement; Military Readiness. *Budget* (RMM of 19 D).

Group Ratings

	ADA	ACLU	AFS	LCV	CON	NTU	NFIB	COC	ACU	NTLC	CHC
1998	85	44	100	85	89	18	36	50	17	19	17
1997	70	—	75	—	80	29	—	50	17	—	—

National Journal Ratings

	1997 LIB — 1997 CONS			1998 LIB — 1998 CONS	
Economic	66%	—	34%	64%	—	34%
Social	61%	—	39%	60%	—	40%
Foreign	55%	—	45%	69%	—	30%

Key Votes of the 105th Congress

1. Clinton Budget Deal	N	5. Puerto Rico Sthood. Ref.	Y	9. Cut $ for B-2 Bombers	Y
2. Education IRAs	N	6. End Highway Set-asides	N	10. Human Rights in China	Y
3. Req. 2/3 to Raise Taxes	N	7. School Prayer Amend.	N	11. Withdraw Bosnia Troops	N
4. Fast-track Trade	N	8. Ovrd. Part. Birth Veto	Y	12. End Cuban TV-Marti	N

Election Results

1998 general	John M. Spratt Jr. (D)	95,696	(58%)	($869,632)
	Mike Burkhold (R)	66,367	(40%)	($494,042)
	Others	2,868	(2%)	
1998 primary	John M. Spratt Jr. (D) .... unopposed			
1996 general	John M. Spratt Jr. (D)	97,174	(54%)	($855,622)
	Larry L. Bigham (R)	81,360	(45%)	($373,117)

SIXTH DISTRICT

South Carolina was first settled by planters from Barbados, bringing with them a tropical plantation economy, which they transferred to the not quite tropical climate of the Carolina coastal lowlands. Here the flat Low Country and many islands are laced with sluggish-flowing rivers and swamps, and here the planters brought thousands of slaves directly from Africa. Colonial South Carolina was one of the richest parts of North America, with dazzling Georgian architecture in Charleston and classic plantation gardens; the planters built great irrigation systems and grew rice and cotton and the dye-plant indigo, all heavily in demand in Britain and elsewhere. And of course all this wealth was built on the slave labor of thousands of African-Americans, many of them still speaking their ancestral languages, or a patois mixing them with English. A majority of colonial South Carolinians were black slaves; so were most residents of the lowlands when the Civil War started with the bombardment of Fort Sumter in Charleston Harbor, although by that time there were also many free blacks in Charleston, some of whom owned slaves themselves.

South Carolina's black heritage has left an imprint on American culture, and is still apparent in the lowlands today. The special accents and dialects of lowland blacks were long retained: Traces of Gullah and other accents still can be found on lowland islands and in the Charleston accent, which to outsiders seems often incomprehensible (how many C-SPAN watchers click on closed-caption text when Senator Hollings speaks?). The poverty that was the almost universal lot of lowland blacks after the Civil War has only in the last generation been alleviated, as development comes to the coast and the long cultural isolation of people here is dissipated. But many blacks who grew up here have long since left, leaving after high school graduation on the bus for New York, nicknamed "the chicken-bone special" because of the fried chicken their families packed for the journey.

The 6th Congressional District, created for 1992 to have a black majority, and modified slightly for 1994, includes very little of the coast, now mostly lined with affluent condominium communities; but it does include most of the geographic expanse of Low Country South Carolina. Its erose boundaries are designed to include the black central city neighborhoods of Charleston and Columbia but leave in the adjacent 1st and 2d districts their affluent white city and suburban areas. The 6th District includes much of Orangeburg, home of the historically black South Carolina State University, and Florence, at the center of the Pee Dee tobacco-growing country in eastern South Carolina.

The congressman from the 6th is James Clyburn, a Democrat elected in 1992. Clyburn grew up in Sumter, the son of a minister. In 1960 he was one of seven who organized the state's first sit-ins, at a five-and-dime store in the Orangeburg town square. He worked as a teacher, in government antipoverty programs, and on the staff of Governor John West. In 1974 he became state Human Affairs Commissioner, serving 18 years under Republican and Democratic governors; criticized for working for Republican Carroll Campbell, he got him to back the state's first fair housing act. Twice he ran for secretary of State, losing narrowly. Clyburn effectively won the 6th District seat in the 1992 Democratic primary, with 56% of the vote against four black opponents, all with serious claims for the nomination; the white incumbent in the old 6th District, Robin Tallon, at the last minute decided not to run. Each of the others had regional strengths. But Clyburn, well known statewide, ran first or second in each major center and piled up huge margins in others (88% in his home county of Sumter).

Clyburn is the first black to represent South Carolina in Congress since 1897. He has good working relationships with leading businessmen and Republicans. He has a generally liberal voting record, but supported the balanced budget amendment and term limits; he joined the moderate New Democrat Coalition at its inception in March 1997, the only black to do so. With a seat on the Transportation Committee, he has worked on local projects like airport funding and the South Carolina Heritage Corridor and has pushed for funds for restoring buildings at historically black colleges and universities. He won a fight with Strom Thurmond to get the new courthouse in Columbia named after Matthew Perry, South Carolina's first black federal judge. He sponsored a bill, before the ValuJet crash, to protect whistleblowers in the aviation industry. Against reformers in his own party, he has defended PACs as the voice of the little guy. When cigarette tax increases have been proposed, he has urged safeguards for tobacco farmers.

In the 105th Congress, Clyburn worked on the transportation bill, which increased South Carolina's share of federal monies from 71% of gas tax proceeds to at least 90%, a projected $175 million extra per year. In addition, he and Senator Ernest Hollings worked to insure funding for a new Cooper River bridge in Charleston. In the 1998 election he urged Democrats not to register voters, but to energize voters: good advice, since an active Democratic organization effort resulted in the election of Governor Jim Hodges and the re-election of the once seemingly endangered Hollings. In November 1998 Clyburn was unanimously chosen chairman of the Congressional Black Caucus; while he has a reputation for being conciliatory and non-confrontational, he says, "When I need to be, I can be articulate. When I need to, I can get in your face. I have no problem doing that." In December 1998, he won a seat on the Appropriations Committee. His subcommittees are Energy and Water and Transportation; there he can secure funding for South Carolina projects authorized by the transportation bill he worked on in spring 1998.

Clyburn has been re-elected by increasing margins against the same opponent in 1994, 1996 and 1998. The district lines were challenged once again as racially gerrymandered, but the lawsuit was settled by Republicans unwilling to change the status quo in August 1997. In January 1999, Clyburn said, "I've often given thought to serving in the U.S. Senate," then added, "I like to manage things. I certainly wouldn't rule it out, if I thought it possible, running for governor."

Cook's Call. *Safe.* Clyburn sits in the only safe Democratic seat left in the state. He will be able to hold onto this seat for as long as he wants to.

The People: Pop. 1990: 581,452; 50.8% rural; 12.3% age 65+; 37.1% White, 62.3% Black, 0.3% Asian, 0.2% Amer. Indian, 0.1% Other; 0.5% Hispanic Origin. Households: 47.5% married couple families; 25.3% married couple fams. w. children; 29.7% college educ.; median household income: $19,189; per capita income: $8,631; median house value: $48,500; median gross rent: $202.

1996 Presidential Vote

Clinton (D)	113,096	(65%)
Dole (R)	53,614	(31%)
Perot (I)	5,525	(3%)

1992 Presidential Vote

Clinton (D)	118,085	(62%)
Bush (R)	59,970	(31%)
Perot (I)	12,292	(6%)

Rep. James E. Clyburn (D)

Elected 1992; b. July 21, 1940, Sumter; home, Columbia; SC St. U., B.A. 1962; African Methodist Episcopal; married (Emily).

Professional Career: Teacher, 1962–66; Dir., Charleston Neighborhood Youth Corps, 1966–68; Exec. Dir., SC Comm. for Farm Workers, 1968–71; Asst., SC Gov. West, 1971–74; SC Human Affairs Comm., 1974–92.

DC Office: 319 CHOB 20515, 202-225-3315; Fax: 202-225-2313; Web site: www.house.gov/clyburn.

District Offices: Columbia, 803-799-1100; Florence, 803-622-1212; N. Charleston, 803-965-5578.

Committees: *Appropriations* (21st of 27 D): Energy & Water Development; Transportation.

Group Ratings

	ADA	ACLU	AFS	LCV	CON	NTU	NFIB	COC	ACU	NTLC	CHC
1998	95	81	100	92	55	13	21	28	4	13	0
1997	90	—	100	—	20	19	—	30	16	—	—

National Journal Ratings

	1997 LIB	—	1997 CONS		1998 LIB	—	1998 CONS
Economic	66%	—	33%		79%	—	0%
Social	73%	—	24%		84%	—	15%
Foreign	72%	—	26%		84%	—	11%

Key Votes of the 105th Congress

1. Clinton Budget Deal	N	5. Puerto Rico Sthood. Ref.	Y	9. Cut $ for B-2 Bombers	N
2. Education IRAs	N	6. End Highway Set-asides	N	10. Human Rights in China	Y
3. Req. 2/3 to Raise Taxes	N	7. School Prayer Amend.	N	11. Withdraw Bosnia Troops	N
4. Fast-track Trade	N	8. Ovrd. Part. Birth Veto	N	12. End Cuban TV-Marti	Y

Election Results

1998 general	James E. Clyburn (D)	116,446	(73%)	($294,243)
	Gary McLeod (R)	41,385	(26%)	($25,108)
	Others	2,646	(2%)	
1998 primary	James E. Clyburn (D)	32,652	(83%)	
	Mike Wilson (D)	6,655	(17%)	
1996 general	James E. Clyburn (D)	120,132	(69%)	($196,440)
	Gary McLeod (R)	51,974	(30%)	($39,395)

SOUTH DAKOTA

When the Census Bureau proclaimed the closing of the American frontier in 1890, one of the last places to close was the southern part of the Dakota Territory, just admitted to the Union in 1889 as the state of South Dakota. For years this land had been the home of the Oglala Sioux, one of the largest Native American tribes, who had built a buffalo hunting civilization by becoming masters of the horses the Spaniards had imported to North America 350 years earlier. It was the Sioux warrior chief Sitting Bull, now buried on a bluff above the Missouri River, who destroyed Custer at Little Big Horn in 1876; it was Oglala Sioux who were the victims at the massacre of Wounded Knee in 1890. After half a century of horrifying disease and a decade of defeat, the Sioux were a traumatized people, and still are today, living on reservations with proud traditions but in terrible poverty. They are isolated far from the mainstream economic marketplace, beset by high rates of alcoholism and suicide, with life expectancy and disease rates like those of sub-Saharan Africa, which may be the after-effects of the traumas of 100 years ago. There have been clashes between the civilizations in recent memory—the killings of government agents by Indian rebels at Wounded Knee in 1975—but also moves in the other direction, as when Governor George Mickelson declared 1990 a Year of Reconciliation. And the Indians are in the process of getting a great monument, the late Korczak Ziolkowski's Crazy Horse sculpture, which—when and if finished—will dwarf Mount Rushmore (which was left unfinished itself at the start of World War II); by the late 1990s the chief's full mouth and cleft chin have begun to emerge.

Less tragic and more successful, though not without its moments of violence, has been the whites' settlement of South Dakota. It was a rapid process: the first gold strikes in the Black Hills came in 1876, and soon the mountains swarmed with settlers; Deadwood became a city of 20,000 where Calamity Jane ruled the saloons and Wild Bill Hickok was shot in the back while holding two pair—aces and eights. Ranchers, knowing that the buffalo could not be contained by barbed wire fences, massacred them so thoroughly that when Teddy Roosevelt got to the Dakota Territory in 1884, he had a hard time finding one to shoot. It was not long before the railroad came through, and then settlers, many of them German and Scandinavian immigrants recruited by the railroads, had built sodhouses, broken the land and set down enough roots to justify making both the two Dakota states.

Geographically, South Dakota has never entirely filled up. In the 25 years between statehood and World War I, the eastern third of the state, sectioned off Midwestern style into 640 acre square miles, was settled by farmers. But moving westward, before a traveler reaches the Missouri River in the middle of the state, green turns to brown, cultivation grows sparse and then stops; the plains are open grazing land, scarcely touched by the white men who were so eager to establish dominion over them a century ago. The land is punctuated, not by roads meeting every mile at precise angles, but by buttes, gullies and grasslands sweeping to the horizon with no sign of human habitation except the occasional missile silos which once were pointed at the Soviet Union, and which by 1994 were all empty.

South Dakota's political patterns were fairly well set by the early 1900s. Its early settlers were mostly Midwesterners who brought their Republicanism with them. Voters here never had much use for the Non-Partisan League, which caught on in the more Scandinavian soil of North Dakota, and there was never anything here comparable to the Farmer-Labor Party of Minnesota. But the nature of the farm economy—its dependence on the great railroads and milling companies, and on the vagaries of international markets—meant that South Dakota was subject to periodic farm revolts. It voted for Populists and William Jennings Bryan in the 1890s; it supported the early New Deal; it revolted against the Eisenhower Administration in the 1950s by

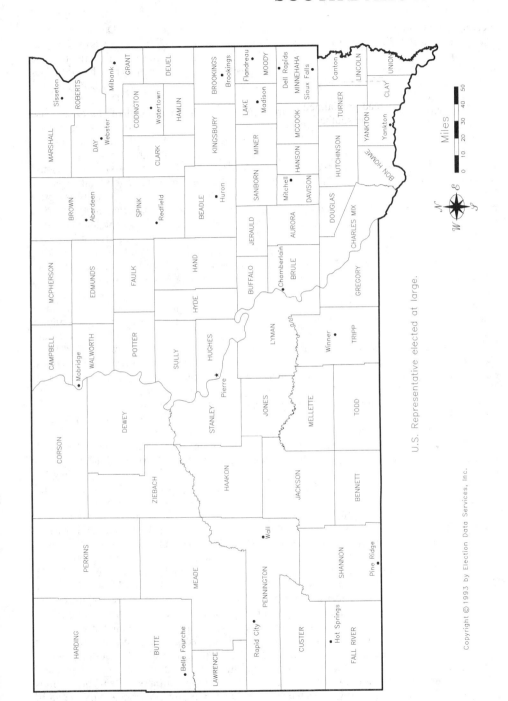

Miles

0 10 20 30 40 50

U.S. Representative elected at large.

electing a young congressman named George McGovern, then a professor at Dakota Wesleyan University in Mitchell, home also of the Corn Palace, built in 1892 and decorated every year with 13 murals using 275,000 ears of corn. South Dakota also shared the isolationist impulse of much of the Great Plains, and McGovern's opposition to the Vietnam war in the late 1960s was not a liability here. In the early 1970s, Democrats seemed on the verge of becoming the majority party.

Instead, South Dakota moved sharply to the Republicans. This began with the angry response to Wounded Knee in 1975. And it was perpetuated by the policies of Republican Governor William Janklow, elected in 1978 and 1982 and then again in 1994 and 1998. It was Janklow who changed the usury laws and invited Citicorp to move its credit card operations to Sioux Falls, where they could charge market interest rates and which had no state corporate or personal income taxes, and a literate low-wage work force. As Gateway computer's Ted Waitt says, "A lot of it has to do with the people. It basically gets back to Midwest values . . . honesty, integrity and loyalty." The Citibank operation here grew from 50 employees to more than 3,000 in 1999, replacing the meatpacker John Morrell as the biggest employer; other banks and telemarketing followed, and new firms started up, like NordicTrak and Gateway (their executive offices have moved to San Diego but most employees are still in North Sioux City). Some meatpacking plants have closed, but others are manned now by a largely Hispanic work force, recruited from the Southwest and beyond; 40 languages are spoken on the floor of the John Morrell plant in Sioux City.

Metro Sioux Falls grew 13% in the 1980s and another 10% by 1997—amazing growth in a state which had often lost population between censuses—and Lincoln County, just south of Sioux Falls, in 1997 was the nation's second-fastest growing county in the 1990s. South Dakota has also had the nation's lowest unemployment rate, down to 1.4% in Sioux Falls in 1999; Rapid City, with a similar economic boost plus tourism, grew 16%; Watertown and Brookings, mid-sized freeway towns, grew as well, even as most small counties lost population. By March 1999 there were 32,500 farms in South Dakota, but population patterns here on the Plains now look more like those in the Rockies, with most people concentrated around a few cities and towns, while vast acreage remains vacant, punctuated with infrequent ranches and resort areas—a landscape that would not have been totally alien to Sitting Bull.

South Dakota also works hard to court tourists. The lure of natural attractions in the Black Hills and the huge and varyingly unfinished sculptures of Mount Rushmore and the Crazy Horse Memorial are augmented by such enterprises as gold-panning creeks and gambling casinos in Deadwood and on Indian reservations. And Wall Drug, the 46,000-square foot emporium between the Badlands and Rapid City, snares three-quarters of the freeway traffic.

Politically, this economic success has helped to re-establish South Dakota's Republican heritage. True, the state has two Democratic Senators—Tim Johnson, elected by a narrow margin in 1996, and Senate Minority Leader Tom Daschle, who won his first race for the House in 1978 by just 139 votes. (This is a fine example of a few votes making a big difference: If just 70 votes in one obscure Senate race more than 20 years ago had gone the other way, South Dakota today would probably have two Republican senators.) But the Democrats' hold may be weakened in the long run, because the phasing out of farm subsidies by the 1996 Freedom to Farm Act removes what has long been the Democrats' number one issue in Senate and House races. Republicans have won almost everything else—the governorship and the legislature, the state's lone House seat and the presidential race, for both George Bush and Bob Dole. And conservative stands are popular: South Dakota passed a law (overturned by the courts) requiring parental consent for abortions, and an initiative requiring a two-thirds majority vote to increase taxes; in a gesture to old times, it also passed a law prohibiting non-family farm corporations to buy farms and ranches, but it is expected to be challenged in court. After a century as a farm state, South Dakota is turning into something else. The 2000 Census is likely to show more South Dakotans in cities and towns than in rural areas.

Governor. Bill Janklow has had more impact on state government and the South Dakota economy than any other South Dakota governor. He grew up in Chicago, then after the death of his father, a prosecutor at the Nuremburg war crimes trial, the family moved to his mother's home town, Flandreau, South Dakota. Janklow dropped out of high school and joined the Marines; he returned in 1960, married, and without a high school diploma talked his way into the University of South Dakota. After law school, he worked in the legal aid program at the Rosebud Indian Reservation. But he did not sympathize with the Indian rebels of the 1970s. He was elected state attorney general in 1974, with 67% of the vote, getting tough on Indian violence and compiling a high conviction record. In 1978 he was elected governor with 56%; in 1982, re-elected with 71%. During this time, he attracted Citicorp to the state, reduced agricultural and residential property taxes, cut state payrolls, stimulated new business, and converted a state college into a prison. Term-limited in 1986 Janklow ran against incumbent Republican Senator Jim Abdnor and lost 55%–45% in the primary; it is a tantalyzing question whether Janklow would have beaten Tom Daschle in the fall.

Janklow's successor, Republican George Mickelson, took a different course, with a revolving economic development fund financed by a temporary one-cent sales tax increase. He died in a plane crash in April 1993, and was succeeded by 67-year-old Walter Dale Miller, a rancher from near Rapid City who served 20 years in the legislature and six as lieutenant governor. Janklow challenged him in the 1994 Republican primary and won by a 54%–46% margin, carrying most of eastern South Dakota and losing much of the west. In the general election he won easily, 55%–41%, over Jim Beddow, the former president of George McGovern's alma mater, Dakota Wesleyan University.

Janklow ran promising to cut homeowners' property taxes by 30%; by the 1998 election they were down 25%, and he promised to seek the last 5% in 2000. He cut the state payroll, and even cut total spending in 1996; he worked to establish state standards for student learning and give school districts the leeway to achieve them. He welcomed more new businesses including the headquarters of IBP meatpackers to South Dakota, and reduced EPA hazardous waste reporting forms from 155 pages to four. He has reduced foster care by encouraging adoption and has worked to increase child immunizations. He changed the name "correctional facility" to "prison" and "client" to "inmate." And he set up a program to use inmates for public labor, building small houses for the elderly and disabled, and day care centers, as well as wiring schools, public libraries, colleges and hospitals to the Internet; all but two schools were connected by June 1999.

In March 1998 Janklow was in the hospital for 22 days for intestinal surgery. When he returned he announced he was running for an unprecedented fourth term. He continued to make unusual headlines. After the town of Spencer was destroyed by a May 1998 tornado he camped out there and superintended evacuation and recovery plans. In September 1998, in protest of what he considered unfair Canadian trade practices, he ordered state troopers to stop and inspect trucks carrying Canadian livestock and grain; they were to be searched and not allowed in the state if the livestock was not proved free of drugs legal in Canada but not in the U.S., and if the grain was not certified as free of disease and wild oats. The searches continued from September 16 to October 5, when Agriculture Secretary Dan Glickman promised to raise the issues with Canadian officials.

Janklow paid little attention to his 1998 Democratic opponent, state Senate Minority Leader Bernie Hunhoff. Hunhoff called for higher wages, fairer taxes, more protection of the environment and increased agricultural processing. He attracted some attention when he charged Janklow with using state planes to inspect a personal investment; Janklow replied by displaying checks he wrote to reimburse the state. Janklow paid even less attention to Republican Senate candidate Ron Schmidt; instead Janklow continued to lavish praise on Senator Tom Daschle for using his position as minority leader on South Dakota issues. Their friendship went back to 1994, when Daschle was accused of exerting undue influence with the FAA; Janklow wrote a letter to the *New York Times* affirming his integrity, and Daschle responded with a handwritten letter. Said Janklow, "He and I philosophically are different. I jokingly say we go to different churches together. When I ask him to help us with something for South Dakota, he always says yes. He has never let us down." One example was shifting control of boat ramps and the Missouri River shoreline from the Army Corps of Engineers to the state government and the Cheyenne River and Lower Brule Sioux tribes, which Daschle put in the October 1998 omnibus budget. Janklow was re-elected 64%–33%, and Daschle was re-elected 62%–36%. According to the VNS exit poll, 62% of Daschle voters voted for Janklow, and 60% of Janklow voters voted for Daschle.

Janklow promised that his fourth term would be devoted to education; he called for public preschool, more reading and music programs, classes in parenting skills. Noting South Dakota's high percentage of working mothers, he hired a former Democratic legislator to work on day care. He got the legislature to address another controversial issue, the Dakota, Minnesota and Eastern Railroad's proposal for a rail line from Wyoming's Powder River coal basin to Winona, Minnesota, on the Mississippi River. The new law cut the DM&E's tax breaks and required it to meet certain criteria and get the approval of the governor before it could exercise the power of eminent domain. Janklow continued to be enthusiastic about his job: "I'm good at it. If you want to know the truth, I know how to be governor. I flat know how to be a governor." But he said he will never run for office again.

Senior Senator. Tom Daschle, first elected to the Senate in 1986, is the Senate minority leader. He grew up in Aberdeen, graduated from South Dakota State, served in the Air Force in the years George McGovern was running for president. In 1973 he became a Washington staffer for Senator James Abourezk. In 1978, as Abourezk was about to retire, Daschle returned to South Dakota, ran for the eastern House district that Larry Pressler was vacating to run for the Senate, and won by exactly 139 votes over former P.O.W. Leo Thorsness, who had come close to beating George McGovern in 1974. Daschle was a generally faithful follower of the Democratic leadership in the House, trapped far behind others in seniority; his political highlight came in 1982, when South Dakota lost one of its two House seats and he ran against incumbent Republican Cliff Roberts and won 52%–48%.

Already representing the entire state, it was natural for Daschle to run in 1986 for the Senate seat held by Republican Jim Abdnor. Daschle had the additional good luck that Governor Bill Janklow was opposing Abdnor in the primary, putting Abdnor on the defensive and forcing him to use much of his money. Daschle again won 52%–48%, in one of the key victories that returned control of the Senate to the Democrats for eight years. Two years later, in January 1989, new Senate Majority Leader George Mitchell named Daschle co-chairman of the Senate Democratic Policy Committee—in effect, though not in title, the number two man in the Senate leadership. When Mitchell announced his retirement in March 1994, Daschle immediately started running for majority leader—too soon to suit some traditionalists. His opponent Jim Sasser seemed to have enough votes to win, but Sasser lost to Republican Bill Frist in Tennessee in November. That was the good news for Daschle; the bad news was that Democrats had lost enough seats that the race was for minority rather than majority leader. Connecticut's Christopher Dodd immediately entered the race, with encouragement from some older committee chairmen; but Daschle relinquished his seat on the Finance Committee to Carol Moseley-Braun of Illinois, whose vote gave him a 24–23 victory—one that brings to mind his first election to the House.

Daschle's capacity for dogged hard work, his seemingly mild manner and ability to stay unruffled, his efforts at building consensus and fellow feeling have made the Democratic Caucus more united than in many years—maybe ever—and more effective legislatively than almost anyone expected. Senator Robert Byrd, nominating him for re-election in 1996, recalled that he had opposed him in 1994 because he thought him not tough enough to deal with Bob Dole: "I am here today to tell you that I was totally wrong about this young man. He has steel in his spine, despite his reasonable and modest demeanor." Or as Republican journalist William Kristol admitted, "Daschle has been tougher than expected, and Democrats have been more united than Republicans hoped." His first big test was on the balanced budget amendment.

Daschle segued smoothly from his former support of the amendment to opposition, with the argument that any such amendment should exclude Social Security. That provided cover for him and five other Democrats who had previously supported balanced budget amendments to switch and defeat the amendment by one vote in March 1995. To this achievement he added other successes in 1996: passage of the minimum wage hike and the bipartisan health care portability bill. Congress also passed a law declaring children born with spina bifida to Vietnam veterans exposed to Agent Orange to be entitled to VA benefits—the first entitlement ever for children of veterans, and a follow-up to Daschle's long advocacy of compensation for Agent Orange victims.

Probably Daschle's greatest disappointment in the 104th Congress came on Agriculture. For years he was a "prairie populist," resisting cuts in farm subsidies, which were nonetheless cut in the farm bills of 1985 and 1990—big losses, compared to his gains in getting reformulated gas included in the 1990 Clean Air Act and subsidizing ethanol. But in 1996 he was not able to stop the Republicans and Democrats, including ranking Agriculture Committee Democrat Patrick Leahy, from supporting the Freedom to Farm Act, which phases out farm subsidies for most crops over seven years. In 1998, as farm prices sagged, he helped put together a $6 billion package of emergency aid, and in 1999 he introduced an agricultural package including making crop insurance more accessible, labeling country of origin of imported meat and (the South Dakota legislature already passed this) a requirement that meat packers report the prices they are paying for livestock. But maintaining price supports—the number one issue for South Dakota Democrats for years—seems beyond the powers of even the minority leader.

Through all this, Daschle's soft-spoken style, about which many Democrats had qualms, proved effective on television. He maintained his generally liberal voting record; a strong backer of the Clinton health care plan in 1994, he pushed health coverage for uninsured children. Once rather skeptical of American foreign involvements, and an opponent of the Gulf war resolution, he has steadily supported the Clinton Administration on Bosnia and Kosovo and on normal trade relations for China. After Republicans gained two seats in the 1996 election, Daschle advanced his own priorities. One was campaign finance: he backs a constitutional amendment to limit spending by candidates, parties and independent groups. He backed the 1997 budget deal, and hailed the inclusion of children's health insurance and college tax credits. He came up with an alternative to the partial-birth abortion ban, which he had voted against and whose backers were running ads in South Dakota. But Daschle's version, which would have limited late-term abortions but allow the exception for health, was beaten 64–36; Daschle switched and voted for the ban, which passed 64–36 but fell short of a veto-proof two-thirds.

Daschle worked to stuff a few favored programs into the humongous October 1998 omnibus budget, including compensation to Gulf war veterans for unexplained illnesses, money to combat Fetal Alcohol Syndrome, and $7.5 million for the Nationwide Differential Global Positioning System. He used his leadership position to win results on several state issues in close cooperation with Republican Governor Bill Janklow, who had run for the same Senate seat in 1986. And despite his general support for unions, in September 1998 Daschle urged Bill Clinton to look at all options to settle the Northwest strike.

In his first 12 years as senator, Daschle has traveled to all 66 of South Dakota's counties every year; he sometimes just drives by himself, dressed casually, and over coffee or at gas stations asks voters about their concerns. That—and a whole lot of money—have paid off at the polls. In 1992 he was re-elected 65%–33% over Republican Charlene Haar; he ignored Republican calls for turning down out-of-state money since the large majority of funds for Democrats here come from outside South Dakota. In 1997 he was attacked in a TV ad for selling "special access to Mount Rushmore for $5,000"; what he had done was to invite previous contributors to climb a Rushmore trail with him. In 1998 his opponent was Ron Schmidt, lawyer and Republican national committeeman; the Libertarian nominee did no campaiging since he was in jail. Daschle ignored the opposition and outspent Schmidt by more than $4.8 million to $492,000. Daschle argued that his leadership position had helped the state.

"I think it clearly has made a difference in the last four years. . . . I've always said that my major responsibility in the Senate is to put South Dakota's agenda on the national agenda." Janklow frequently chimed in to agree: "Senator Daschle is in the position he is in and the cooperative spirit that he has, has been terribly beneficial in terms of Bill Janklow and his administration's ability to work with him." Daschle won 62%–36%, while Janklow was winning 64%–33%. According to the VNS exit poll, 60% of Janklow voters voted for Daschle, and 62% of Daschle voters voted for Janklow.

On impeachment, Daschle pretty steadily defended the president and advanced partisan positions in a pleasant but steely manner. But as Clinton's lawyers kept trying to insist that he had not lied under oath in August 1998 about lying under oath in January 1998, Daschle called on Clinton to stop "hairsplitting" in September. "There is a basic understanding of the standard of truthfulness that the president failed to meet," he said. During the impeachment trial, as on other issues, he stayed in close and constant touch with Majority Leader Trent Lott, which led to the 100-senator caucus in the Old Senate Chamber and a much more harmonious proceeding than had been expected. His top agenda items in early 1999 included a patients' bill of rights, more teachers, a cut in the marriage tax penalty, raising the minimum wage and Medicare for certain people under 65. In February 1999, after several years of declining, he formed a leadership PAC. There are fewer Democratic senators now than when Daschle became minority leader, but that is not his fault; in the 1996 and 1998 cycles more Democratic than Republican seats were vulnerable. In early 1999, the opposite appeared to be true for 2000, and Daschle had reason to hope for Democratic gains—just possibly enough to make him majority leader in January 2001.

Junior Senator. Tim Johnson, a Democrat elected in 1996, grew up in southeast South Dakota, went to the University of South Dakota and served briefly in the Army (he was discharged because of a hearing problem). He went to graduate school in Michigan, then returned to South Dakota to law school and a law practice. He was elected to the legislature in 1978, at 31, and served in the House and Senate until he ran for South Dakota's single House seat in 1986, when incumbent Tom Daschle ran for the Senate. Like Daschle, Johnson won his House seat by a narrow margin; he edged a fellow state senator in the primary 48%–45%, with big margins in his southeastern home area and in Sioux Falls and Rapid City. He won the general by 59%–41%, and ran even better every two years thereafter.

In the House, he compiled a generally liberal voting record, though he voted for the balanced budget amendment and was the only Democrat to switch his vote to support lifting the Bosnia arms embargo. He worked on South Dakota water and public works projects and tried to maintain farm subsidies. He successfully managed reauthorization of crop insurance as a subcommittee chairman in the 103d Congress and, in the 104th, helped relax the "swampbuster" provisions penalizing farmers who violated wetlands regulations in the 1996 Freedom to Farm Act; but he warned that the phasing out of farm supports would hurt in drought years. Johnson opposed any cuts in or taxes on Social Security benefits and favored penalties for drug companies that charge seniors high prices for medication.

Johnson's race against Republican Senator Larry Pressler had been a long time contemplated. Pressler won election to the House in 1974 and the Senate in 1978 as a constituency-service, ear-to-the-ground Republican, in tune with South Dakota opinion; in the late 1980s, and after 1994 when he became chairman of the Commerce Committee, he became consistently more conservative. This was a high-spending, high-stakes race: Pressler spent $5.1 million, with over $1.7 million from PACs; Johnson spent almost $3 million, with $850,000 from PACs. TV ads began in August 1995, when the race was about even, and it stayed that way for 15 months. Since South Dakota TV is cheap, that meant one barrage of ads after another—plus seven debates. Pressler attacked Johnson as too liberal, going back to a 1981 vote in the legislature against workfare. Johnson attacked Pressler as a Newt-oid Medicare cutter and charged that he switched from opposition to support of maritime subsidies after receiving $29,000 from maritime PACs. Johnson was assisted by collateral attacks from others: the Sioux

Falls *Argus Leader* charged that Pressler didn't properly itemize some campaign expenses. But the key role may have been played by national issues. Pressler spent much time in 1995 and 1996 on the telecommunications bill, the most-lobbied and arguably most complex bill before the 104th Congress. In negotiations he held out for deregulation, and to South Dakotans he promised lower telephone and cable TV rates. Pressler succeeded in passing the bill, the first major rewrite of communications law in 63 years, but back home Johnson was charging that phone and cable rates were going up.

The final result was a 51%–49% Johnson victory, narrower than final month's polls suggested, but nonetheless decisive. The state split almost precisely along the 100th meridian that is often taken as the dividing line between farm land and grazing land. Johnson carried almost every county east of the 100th, except for a couple of ethnic Republican counties; Pressler carried almost everything west of the 100th, except for a few Indian counties.

In the Senate Johnson got seats on the Agriculture, Banking, Budget and Energy committees, presumably a gift from his South Dakota colleague, the minority leader. His voting record has been generally liberal, except on some cultural issues—he opposes abortion and supported the partial-birth abortion ban. On farm issues, long the staple of South Dakota Democrats, he has been displeased that low crop prices have not led the Senate to revisit the Freedom to Farm Act. "Five years of declining transition payments and a pat on the back and a 'Good luck' isn't much of a farm policy, but that's what we've got right now," he said in August 1998. He pushed hard for country-of-origin labeling of imported meat; that passed the Senate, but was killed in conference; he has said it is a top priority for the 106th Congress. He also got extension of farmers' Chapter 12 of the Bankruptcy Act into the October 1998 omnibus budget. He worked on rail grain issues and the bill granting $6 billion in emergency relief for farmers; he worked to promote biodiesel and wants to make permanent the tax treatment of ethanol.

Johnson supported the transportation bill, which raised South Dakota's take from $120 million to $180 million. He secured earmarks for completing the first phase of the Heartland Expressway and the Vermillion bridge. He and Republican Craig Thomas worked to increase spending on rural transit by $500 million over five years. He has promoted a bill, similar to one passed in South Dakota, requiring prisoners to pay health care costs if they have the money. He backs Tom Daschle's proposal to amend the First Amendment to allow limits on campaign spending and contributions. Some of his work was prompted by the terrible winter weather and floods of 1997–98 and the Spencer tornado of May 1998: $7.5 million for the National Differential Global Positioning System, $10 million for the James River Water Development District, regulatory relief for banks so they can respond quickly to disasters, expanding weather radio, funding for a tornado pilot preparedness program. He pushed through a rural water system for Fall River County, and preservation of Spirit Mound in Clay County (one of the few sights in South Dakota unchanged since Lewis and Clark saw it). He passed through the Senate a Minuteman Missile National Historic Site (much of South Dakota is laced with missile sites), worked to build Indian schools and housing, sponsored a ban on Internet gambling, and worked to maintain Great Lakes air service to Brookings and Yankton. His older son served in the Army in Bosnia in the late 1990s.

Johnson comes up for re-election in 2002. Naturally he is overshadowed by Daschle, and his poll ratings have not been overpowering. Republicans were heartened when a poll showed Republican Congressman-at-Large John Thune leading him 49%–37% in March 1999. But the sample was small and it was a partisan poll: such numbers should not be regarded as etched in stone. Certainly Daschle will do everything he can to help him win a second term.

Representative-At-Large. South Dakota has had only one seat in the House since 1982. The congressman-at-large is John Thune, a Republican elected in 1996. He grew up in Murdo, on the dusty plains west of the Missouri River, went to college and business school. As a high school freshman he met then Congressman Jim Abdnor, when Abdnor spotted him at a grocery checkout counter and recalled that he had missed one of six free throws in the basketball game the previous night. They kept in touch and Thune got a job on by-then Senator Abdnor's staff in Washington in 1985; he stayed with Abdnor after he lost to Tom Daschle and was appointed to the Small Business Administration. He returned to South Dakota in 1989, at 28, to become executive director of the state Republican Party. In 1991 he became state railroad director under Governor George Mickelson and in 1993 director of the state Municipal League. In his early 30s he had many contacts in Pierre, the nation's smallest state capital, and around the state.

Thune nevertheless entered the 1996 race as very much an underdog. The favorite in the Republican primary was Lieutenant Governor Carole Hillard, who seemed to have Governor Bill Janklow on her side and was endorsed by the 1994 Republican nominee. A poll released in May 1996 showed her ahead of Thune 69%–15%. But Thune was escorted around main streets by Abdnor, he attracted the support of religious conservatives and presidential campaign leaders, fresh from organizing for the February 27 presidential primary. Hillard lent her campaign $140,000 but didn't raise much money, and Janklow eventually announced he was neutral. It turned out to be no contest. Thune carried 54 counties, Hillard 12; Thune won 59%–41%; it would have been more except that Hillard carried Rapid City. The Democratic nominee was Rick Weiland, a former state director for Senator Daschle, who carried 46 counties and led television executive Jim Abbott 42%–28%, well above the 35% needed in South Dakota to avoid a runoff.

After the primary the Sioux Falls *Argus Leader* summarized the race: "November's option is crystal clear: choose a liberal or a conservative." Thune was for term limits, against all tax increases (and against Bob Dole's tax cut pending a balanced budget), and pledged to refuse the congressional pension; he promised to serve only three terms; he had the support of Christian conservatives and cattlemen's organizations. Weiland attacked Newt Gingrich and Medicare "cuts" and called for an "impact fee" on big hog producers to build a loan fund for small hog producers. On agriculture, Thune called not for farm subsidies, but for increasing exports and promoting value-added goods: "market solutions that can help keep prices high." The two raised similar amounts, but from different sources: Thune raised more from individuals, $580,000 to $500,000, while Weiland, with strong labor support, led in PAC money, $346,000 to $176,000. In response to which Thune attacked him for taking contributions from a union (the Laborers) connected with organized crime.

Weiland carried only six counties (his home, a university county, and four Indian counties), and Thune won 58%–37%. On election night Thune promised, "I won't forget that the tax dollars you pay to the government isn't their money. It's your money." In the House he has had a very conservative voting record and serves on the Agriculture and Transportation committees; he was chosen the freshman class representative to the Republican leadership. In May 1997 he criticized the House leadership for attaching other issues to the bill for relief of floods that had devastated much of North Dakota and Minnesota and damaged much of South Dakota that spring. When Dakota Democrats criticized Speaker Gingrich and Appropriations Chairman Bob Livingston for refusing cash payments to local communities, Gingrich asked Thune to come up with a way to do so; ultimately the House passed a $500 million amendment. In June 1998 he proposed to make it easier for the government to buy property in flood prone areas.

As farm prices started plunging in 1998, Thune proposed to increase price supports, but admitted, "This is a tough pull even in the Agriculture Committee itself, not only among Republicans, but among Democrats as well." Instead he proposed a bill to allow farmers to receive the present value of Freedom to Farm Act transition payments due up to 2002. He said he was pleased with the ultimate $6 billion emergency aid package, which allowed farmers to claim 1999 payments early. He sponsored a bill to require labeling of imported meat and supported renewal of the ethanol tax incentive.

On Transportation and Infrastructure, Thune worked on the May 1998 transportation bill, which raised South Dakota's payments from roughly $120 million to $180 million. As a committee member, he got $60 million worth of earmarked projects, and put some into the Heartland Expressway Phase 1 and Eastern Dakota Expressway, and bridges in Hell Canyon, Yankton and Vermillion. Thune also proposed raising to $70,000 for married couples the 15% income tax rate, and for making the office of U.S. attorney general elective. On impeachment, he did not mince words; in December 1998 he said, "Either he has a reckless contempt for the truth, or he can't discern the truth from lies. . . . In either case, that's a miserable commentary on the elected leader of the free world."

Despite entreaties, Thune declined to run for governor or senator in 1998. He outspent his Democratic opponent $621,000 to $56,000 and won 75%–25%—a record-breaking showing for a statewide candidate for Congress or governor. But he lost a bid for a seat on Ways and Means because of his term-limits pledge. Thune called for encouraging farm exports and for using the budget surplus to save Social Security and only then for a tax cut. He reintroduced his meat labeling bill and called for taking the airport building program off-budget—a prime goal of Transportation Chairman Bud Shuster. It is widely expected in South Dakota that Thune will run against Senator Tim Johnson in 2002. He would have to violate his term-limit pledge to run for the House, and a March 1999 Republican poll showed him leading Johnson 49%–37%. But Johnson and his close ally Daschle seem determined to stop him. In 1998 they criticized Thune for not seeking even higher transportation spending in South Dakota, and when he supported the B-2 bomber, they accused him of undercutting the B-1, which is flown out of Ellsworth Air Force Base, near Rapid City. Thune's response seemed bemusement: "It's all pretty clear. I think I am the object of the obsession." In the meantime it's not clear that the Democrats will be able to field a stronger House candidate in 2000 than they did in 1998.

Cook's Call. *Safe.* Though only a sophomore, Thune has two solid wins under his belt and has established a solid foothold here. He is well-positioned to win a third term in 2000.

Presidential politics. South Dakota has voted Democratic for president just four times, since 1892 (1896, 1932, 1936 and 1964). Still, it has been reasonably close in five of the last seven elections, tilting against the party in power in countercyclical Farm Belt fashion. But with only three electoral votes, it is not high on anyone's target list.

South Dakota's presidential primary for years was held on the same day as California's, and eclipsed by it. Since 1988 it has been held in February, just one week after New Hampshire. So far it has been not a trendsetter, but a booster of Great Plains candidates who do not fare well elsewhere: Bob Dole and Dick Gephardt in 1988, Bob Kerrey and Tom Harkin in 1992. In 1996 Dole beat Pat Buchanan here 45%–29%. For 2000 the primary is scheduled June 6, but there has been some movement to join a Midwestern primary on April 4.

The People: Est. Pop. 1998: 738,171; Pop. 1990: 696,004, up 6.1% 1990–1998. 0.3% of U.S. total, 46th largest; 50% rural. Median age: 34.5 years. 15.3% 65 years and over. 91.5% White, 0.5% Black, 0.5% Asian, 7.2% Amer. Indian, 0.3% Other; 0.8% Hispanic Origin. Households: 58.9% married couple families; 29.3% married couple fams. w. children; 43.4% college educ.; median household income: $22,503; per capita income: $10,661; 66.1% owner occupied housing; median house value: $45,200; median monthly rent: $242. 2.9% Unemployment. 1998 Voting age pop.: 538,000. 1998 Turnout: 266,355; 50% of VAP. Registered voters (1998): 452,901; 179,195 D (40%), 219,624 R (48%), 54,082 unaffiliated and minor parties (12%).

Political Lineup: Governor, William J. Janklow (R); Lt. Gov., Carole Hillard (R); Secy. of State, Joyce Hazeltine (R); Atty. Gen., Mark Barnett (R); Treasurer, Richard Butler (D); State Senate, 35 (13 D, 22 R); Majority Leader, M. Michael Rounds (R); State House, 70 (19 D, 51 R); House Speaker, Roger Hunt (R). Senators, Thomas A. Daschle (D) and Timothy P. Johnson (D). Representative, 1 R at large.

Elections Division: 605-773-3537; **Filing Deadline for U.S. Congress:** April 4, 2000.

1996 Presidential Vote

Dole (R)	150,543	(46%)
Clinton (D)	139,333	(43%)
Perot (I)	31,250	(10%)

1996 Republican Presidential Primary

Dole (R)	30,918	(45%)
Buchanan (R)	19,780	(29%)
Forbes (R)	8,831	(13%)
Alexander (R)	6,037	(9%)
Others	3,604	(5%)

1992 Presidential Vote

Bush (R)	136,718	(41%)
Clinton (D)	124,888	(37%)
Perot (I)	73,295	(22%)

GOVERNOR

Gov. William J. Janklow (R)

Elected 1994, term expires Jan. 2003; b. Sept. 13, 1939, Chicago, IL; home, Brandon; U. of SD, B.S. 1964, LL.B 1966; Lutheran; married (Mary Dean).

Military Career: Marine Corps, 1956–59.

Elected Office: SD Atty. Gen., 1974–78; SD Gov., 1978–86.

Professional Career: Legal Aid, Rosebud Indian Reservation, 1966–73; SD Special Prosecutor, 1973–75; Practicing atty., 1987–94.

Office: Executive Office, State Capitol, Pierre, 57501, 605-773-3212; Fax: 605-773-5844; Web site: www.state.sd.us.

Election Results

1998 gen.	William J. Janklow (R)	166,621	(64%)
	Bernie Hunhoff (D)	85,473	(33%)
	Others	8,093	(3%)
1998 prim.	William J. Janklow (R)	unopposed	
1994 gen.	William J. Janklow (R)	172,515	(55%)
	Jim Beddow (D)	126,273	(41%)
	Nathan A. Barton (Lib)	12,825	(4%)

SENATORS

Sen. Thomas A. Daschle (D)

Elected 1986, seat up 2004; b. Dec. 9, 1947, Aberdeen; home, Aberdeen; SD St. U., B.A. 1969; Catholic; married (Linda).

Military Career: Air Force, 1969–72, Air Force Reserves, 1975–78.

Elected Office: U.S. House of Reps., 1978–86.

Professional Career: Legis. Asst., U.S. Sen. James Abourezk, 1973–77.

DC Office: 509 HSOB, 20510, 202-224-2321; Fax: 202-224-7895; Web site: www.senate.gov/~daschle.

State Offices: Aberdeen, 605-225-8823; Rapid City, 605-348-7551; Sioux Falls, 605-334-9596.

Committees: *Minority Leader. Agriculture, Nutrition & Forestry* (4th of 8 D): Forestry, Conservation & Rural Revitalization; Production & Price Competitiveness.

Group Ratings

	ADA	ACLU	AFS	LCV	CON	NTU	NFIB	COC	ACU	NTLC	CHC
1998	90	71	100	75	42	12	33	61	4	0	9
1997	80	—	89	—	25	17	—	60	4	—	—

National Journal Ratings

	1997 LIB	—	1997 CONS	1998 LIB	—	1998 CONS
Economic	82%	—	12%	83%	—	10%
Social	64%	—	29%	63%	—	26%
Foreign	86%	—	13%	79%	—	15%

Key Votes of the 105th Congress

1. Bal. Budget Amend.	N	5. Satcher for Surgeon Gen.	Y	9. Chem. Weapons Treaty	Y
2. Clinton Budget Deal	N	6. Highway Set-asides	Y	10. Cuban Humanitarian Aid	Y
3. Cloture on Tobacco	Y	7. Table Child Gun locks	N	11. Table Bosnia Troops	Y
4. Education IRAs	N	8. Ovrd. Part. Birth Veto	Y	12. $ for Test-ban Treaty	Y

Election Results

1998 general	Thomas A. Daschle (D)	162,884	(62%)	($4,861,541)
	Ron Schmidt (R)	95,431	(36%)	($492,854)
	Others	3,796	(1%)	
1998 primary	Thomas A. Daschle (D)	unopposed		
1992 general	Thomas A. Daschle (D)	217,095	(65%)	($3,981,548)
	Charlene Haar (R)	108,733	(33%)	($478,421)
	Others	8,667	(3%)	

Sen. Timothy P. Johnson (D)

Elected 1996, seat up 2002; b. Dec. 28, 1946, Canton; home, Vermillion; U. of SD, B.A. 1969, M.A. 1970, J.D. 1975, MI St. U., 1970–71; Lutheran; married (Barbara).

Military Career: Army, 1969.

Elected Office: SD House of Reps., 1978–82; SD Senate, 1982–86; U.S. House of Reps., 1986–96.

Professional Career: Budget Analyst, MI Senate, 1971–72; Practicing atty., 1975–85; Clay Cnty. Dpty. Atty., 1985.

DC Office: 324 HSOB, 20510, 202-224-5842; Fax: 202-228-5765; Web site: www.senate.gov/~johnson.

State Offices: Aberdeen, 605-226-3440; Rapid City, 605-341-3990; Sioux Falls, 605-332-8896.

Committees: *Agriculture, Nutrition & Forestry* (7th of 8 D): Production & Price Competitiveness; Research, Nutrition & General Legislation. *Banking, Housing & Urban Affairs* (5th of 9 D): Financial Institutions; International Trade & Finance (RMM); Securities. *Budget* (9th of 10 D). *Energy & Natural Resources* (6th of 9 D): Energy, Research, Development, Production & Regulation; Forests & Public Land Management.

Group Ratings

	ADA	ACLU	AFS	LCV	CON	NTU	NFIB	COC	ACU	NTLC	CHC
1998	90	71	100	88	62	12	33	56	4	0	9
1997	80	—	89	—	19	19	—	70	12	—	—

National Journal Ratings

	1997 LIB — 1997 CONS		1998 LIB — 1998 CONS	
Economic	82% —	12%	90% —	0%
Social	55% —	37%	63% —	26%
Foreign	81% —	18%	95% —	0%

Key Votes of the 105th Congress

1. Bal. Budget Amend.	N	5. Satcher for Surgeon Gen.	Y	9. Chem. Weapons Treaty	Y
2. Clinton Budget Deal	N	6. Highway Set-asides	Y	10. Cuban Humanitarian Aid	Y
3. Cloture on Tobacco	Y	7. Table Child Gun locks	N	11. Table Bosnia Troops	Y
4. Education IRAs	N	8. Ovrd. Part. Birth Veto	Y	12. $ for Test-ban Treaty	Y

Election Results

1996 general	Timothy P. Johnson (D) 166,533	(51%)	($2,990,554)
	Larry Pressler (R) 157,954	(49%)	($5,138,298)
1996 primary	Timothy P. Johnson (D) .... unopposed		
1990 general	Larry Pressler (R) 135,682	(52%)	($2,124,359)
	Ted Muenster (D) 116,727	(45%)	($1,323,770)

REPRESENTATIVE

Rep. John Thune (R)

Elected 1996; b. Jan. 7, 1961, Pierre; home, Pierre; Biola U., B.A. 1983, U. of SD, M.B.A. 1984; Protestant; married (Kimberley).

Professional Career: Legis. Asst., U.S. Sen. James Abdnor, 1985–87; Special Asst., U.S. Small Business Admin., 1987–89; Exec. Dir., SD Republican Party, 1989–91; SD Railroad Dir., 1991–93; Exec. Dir., SD Municipal League, 1993–96.

DC Office: 1005 LHOB, 20515, 202-225-2801; Fax: 202-225-5823; Web site: www.house.gov/thune.

District Offices: Aberdeen, 605-622-7988; Rapid City, 605-342-5135; Sioux Falls, 605-331-1010.

Committees: *Agriculture* (17th of 27 R): General Farm Commodities, Resource Conservation & Credit; Risk Management, Research & Specialty Crops. *Small Business* (18th of 19 R): Regulatory Reform & Paperwork Reduction (Vice Chmn.); Rural Enterprise, Business Opportunities & Special Small Business Problems. *Transportation & Infrastructure* (28th of 41 R): Aviation; Ground Transportation.

Group Ratings

	ADA	ACLU	AFS	LCV	CON	NTU	NFIB	COC	ACU	NTLC	CHC
1998	5	6	0	23	13	48	100	100	92	89	92
1997	5	—	25	—	37	54	—	90	88	—	—

National Journal Ratings

	1997 LIB — 1997 CONS		1998 LIB — 1998 CONS	
Economic	0% —	90%	0% —	88%
Social	0% —	90%	3% —	90%
Foreign	12% —	81%	7% —	83%

Key Votes of the 105th Congress

1. Clinton Budget Deal	Y	5. Puerto Rico Sthood. Ref.	N	9. Cut $ for B-2 Bombers	N
2. Education IRAs	Y	6. End Highway Set-asides	Y	10. Human Rights in China	Y
3. Req. 2/3 to Raise Taxes	Y	7. School Prayer Amend.	Y	11. Withdraw Bosnia Troops	Y
4. Fast-track Trade	Y	8. Ovrd. Part. Birth Veto	Y	12. End Cuban TV-Marti	N

Election Results

1998 general	John Thune (R)	194,157	(75%)	($621,024)
	Jeff Moser (D)	64,433	(25%)	($56,266)
1998 primary	John Thune (R)	unopposed		
1996 general	John Thune (R)	186,393	(58%)	($773,125)
	Rick Weiland (D)	119,547	(37%)	($890,708)
	Others	17,263	(5%)	

TENNESSEE

Tennessee is a battleground state, with a fighting temperament since it was settled 200 years ago by the likes of Andrew Jackson and went on to produce so many soldiers it came to be known as the Volunteer State. This was a frontier battleground in the 1790s, from which Jackson launched his wars on the Indians and the British. It was a military battleground in the 1860s, when Yankee troops swept down the Tennessee and Cumberland rivers on their way to Mississippi and through Chattanooga's Lookout Mountain on their way to Atlanta and the sea. It has been a cultural battleground for much of this century. On one side were the Fugitives, writers like John Crowe Ransom and Allen Tate, who contributed to "I'll Take My Stand," a manifesto calling for retaining the South's rural economy and heritage. On the other side have been business leaders and politicians who have made Tennessee the fastest-growing state of the interior South: Tennessee has given birth to the first supermarket, the Holiday Inn, Federal Express and Goo-Goo Clusters.

This state has also been a marshaling ground for the music traditions which have vied for a large place in Americans' lives. East Tennessee is one of the homes of bluegrass music and mountain fiddling, with string bands and vocal harmony; Knoxville's Tennessee Barn Dance has been broadcast since 1942. Gospel music has long been centered in Nashville, which is also the nation's leading center of religious publishing. Country music got its commercial start in Nashville, with broadcasts of the Grand Ole Opry from Ryman Auditorium starting in 1925 and then the Opryland U.S.A. theme park; and Nashville remains indisputably the capital of this ever-popular music form. The Mississippi lowlands around Memphis, economically and culturally the metropolis of the Mississippi Delta, gave birth to the blues in the years from the 1890s to 1920; and the blues were in turn the inspiration for the jazz musicians of Beale Street in the 1920s and Elvis Presley, whose Graceland mansion is now a major tourist destination, in the 1950s and 1960s.

Tennessee is and has long been a political battleground. Its political divisions have their roots in the Civil War, and most counties today still vote their 1860s loyalties: the Union counties, mainly in the east but with a scattering to the west, vote solidly Republican, while the Confederate counties in middle and west Tennessee have long been heavily Democratic. Within the limits of these enduring party loyalties, political entrepreneurs have set the tone for the state. From the 1920s to 1948, Edward Crump, longtime mayor of Memphis, used his total control of Democratic primary votes there to elect governors and senators. The Tennessee Valley Authority and the cheap electric power it generated provided an institutional base for reform liberal Democrats Estes Kefauver and Albert Gore Sr., elected to the Senate in 1948 and 1952. They were soon national figures, with reliable enough backing from Tennessee's yellow-dog Democratic majority to vote for civil rights bills and to refuse to sign the segregationist Southern Manifesto, and still thrive electorally. Kefauver died in 1963 and Gore was defeated in 1970, but lived on to see his son twice elected vice president, before dying in December 1998. Tennessee has never had a large black population—about 16% in the 1990s, half of whom live in and around Memphis—and the state was not riven by the racial animosity that seared so much of the South in the 1950s and 1960s, thanks in large part to the actions of its leading politicians, but also to the continuing hold of ancestral partisan preferences.

Eventually, the Democrats' cultural liberalism on issues other than race moved west Tennessee voters away from their ancestral party, and moderate east Tennessee Republicans Howard Baker and Bill Brock, elected to the Senate in 1966 and 1970, set the state's tone; Baker protege and 1996 and 2000 Republican presidential candidate Lamar Alexander, elected governor in 1978, instituted education reforms and attracted Japanese investment that have changed and strengthened the state over the last dozen or so years. But Jimmy Carter carried Tennessee solidly, and Democrats were elected to both Senate seats—Jim Sasser in 1976 and Albert Gore Jr. in 1984. Tennessee voted 47%–42% for the Clinton-Gore ticket in 1992. But by 1994 it turned against the Clinton Administration and produced a kind of political revolution. Republican Fred Thompson, famous as a Watergate investigator and movie actor, won the remainder of Gore's Senate term by a landslide, surgeon Bill Frist beat Sasser, and Republican Don Sundquist was elected governor. Republicans won a majority of the vote for the U.S. House, gaining two seats and coming close in a third. In 1996, as the Clinton-Gore ticket was sweeping nationally, Republicans remained strong in Tennessee. The Clinton-Gore campaign poured money into Tennessee, and Gore made 16 campaign appearances in the state; Clinton made six, Bob Dole nine and Jack Kemp four. Clinton-Gore won, but by just 48%–46%, and Republicans maintained their 5–4 majority in the House. Young voters here did not embrace Clinton as they did nationally; the exit poll shows the vote almost even among voters under 45, with Democrats winning their biggest margin among the elderly—not a good augury for the future. In 1998 Republicans continued to dominate: Governor Don Sundquist was re-elected in a landslide and House incumbents held their seats by impressive margins. The great confrontation may come in the presidential election of 2000, when Tennessee is likely to be a target state for both parties.

Tennessee's swing toward Republicans in the early 1970s resulted mainly from switches in west Tennessee; its apparent swing toward Republicans in the middle 1990s was centered in middle Tennessee. This has been the most rapidly growing and changing part of the state. It grew first in manufacturing: in the 1980s Nissan built a huge plant in Smyrna, in Rutherford County, and General Motors put its Saturn plant in Spring Hill, in Maury County, both within an hour's drive of Nashville; both have specialized in the new style of team cooperation between workers and management. Nashville has also become "the Silicon Valley" of health care, in the words of Thomas F. Frist Jr.—Senator Bill Frist's brother and the boss at Columbia/HCA, the Nashville-headquartered hospital company. Politically, the core of Nashville-Davidson remains Democratic, but the counties all around have grown faster and most are now Republican. One result: the two districts (6th and 7th) that contain many of the counties Al Gore once represented in the House voted for the Dole-Kemp ticket over Clinton-Gore in 1996. The Nashville establishment traditionally supported Democrats in Tennessee politics. But now Nashville money has become heavily Republican: the presidential campaign of Nashville's Lamar Alexander raised so much money locally that 37205 and 37215 have become two of the Republicans' top five fundraising zip codes.

There seems to be economic change in east Tennessee as well. For years east Tennessee Republicans vied with middle Tennessee Democrats in supporting the TVA. But in 1997 TVA Chairman Craven Crowell Jr., a Clinton appointee, proposed eliminating the authority's $106 million in federal funding by 1999, so that TVA could concentrate on electricity sales in the

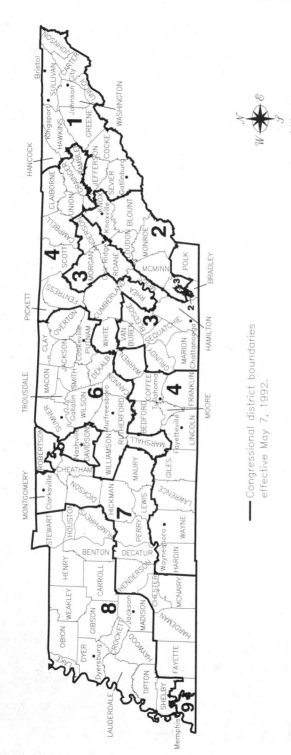

Congressional district boundaries
effective May 7, 1992.

1472 TENNESSEE

increasingly competitive market and spin off its navigation and flood control functions to state or federal agencies. Tennessee has grown, attracting and spawning new businesses, in part because its institutions were mostly untouched by the labor union strife of the 1930s and the civil rights strife of the 1960s. The lack of strong unions and racial divisions attracted the many Japanese companies here, which in turn attracted General Motors. If Tennessee's economy lagged behind the nation's through much of the 20th Century, its respect for hard work and its open climate for entrepreneurism have enabled it to grow mightily in its last decades.

Tennessee in the late 1990s seemed to be a hotbed of political candidates. The most prominent of course is Vice President Gore, whose poll ratings held up well even after the Republican sweep and the revelations that he was present at a Buddhist temple fundraiser where legally questionable contributions appear to have been made, and that he made improper fundraising phone calls from the White House. Like all vice presidents since Walter Mondale, he has been a working and influential part of the administration, running the Reinventing Government program, superintending the space program, often announcing Clinton Administration environmental initiatives, regularly conducting sensitive foreign policy talks with leaders like Russia's Viktor Chernomyrdin and being involved in most of Bill Clinton's important policy and political decisions. Another Tennessee presidential candidate is Alexander, elected governor in 1978 and 1982, and Education secretary under George Bush. Alexander instituted merit pay for teachers and teacher competency tests in Tennessee, and later endorsed school choice. His 1996 campaign was disciplined and well-organized, raised large amounts of money and was based on a coherent theme of devolving power from the federal government, expecting "less from Washington and more from ourselves." It came closer than is generally thought to winning; Alexander finished just behind Bob Dole in New Hampshire, and if 7,600 votes had switched and he had come out ahead, he might have replaced Dole as Pat Buchanan's main competitor and the Republican nominee. Clinton pollster Dick Morris has said that Alexander was the only Republican candidate Clinton and especially Gore feared. The Republican trend suggests that if this were not Gore's home state, he would run well behind here; indeed Clinton-Gore lost next-door Kentucky in 1996. But Democrats will not want to abandon in the long run the surging South any more than Republicans want to abandon trend-setting California.

Governor. Don Sundquist is a Republican elected governor in 1994 and 1998. Unusually for a Tennessee politician, he grew up elsewhere, in Illinois, the son of a welder, was the first in his family to go to college and served in the Navy. He worked for Jostens, a college and high school ring maker, in Shelbyville, Tennessee, for 10 years; in 1972, he started his own graphics and printing firm in Memphis. He volunteered for Howard Baker as early as 1964, when Baker lost a Senate race, and became active in the national Young Republicans organization. In 1982, Sundquist ran for Congress from the 7th District, which stretched from Memphis all the way to Nashville; he won 51%–49% over current 5th District Congressman Bob Clement, carrying the white Memphis suburbs but losing the rural counties. Sundquist served on the Ways and Means Committee and opposed tax increases; he worked his rural counties with 100 "community days" a year. He was re-elected easily.

In 1994 Sundquist ran for governor. The Democratic nominee was Nashville Mayor Phil Bredesen, also a migrant from the North, who made a fortune in health care. Bredesen was popular in Nashville, center of the state's largest media market, and rich enough to self-finance his campaign generously. Moreover, the record of Democratic incumbent Ned McWherter was impressive: the passage of TennCare; 21st Century Schools, with teacher salary raises and more leeway for superintendents and principals in choosing teachers; no income tax (Tennessee is one of nine states without one). Sundquist was boosted by Alexander, Baker and east Tennessee Congressman Jimmy Quillen, and won by a solid 54%–45% margin, losing Nashville but carrying the other big metro areas handily.

Sundquist worked on a bipartisan basis with the state legislature to pass a 20-bill crime package and Families First, a plan to move welfare recipients to work in 18 months; by October 1998 the rolls were down 60%. He put all children's programs in one department and eliminated the Public Service Commission. In early 1997 he promised to make TennCare coverage available to all uninsured children. His main negative publicity came when he questioned high spending at the University of Tennessee, and gave substantial raises to members of his staff. Tennessee became the first state to connect every school and library to the Internet. He successfully opposed a vote on a lottery and telephone reregulation but was frustrated when the Democratic legislature rejected private prisons and charter schools.

With this record Sundquist had no serious opposition for re-election in 1998. Bredesen, Clement and developer Doug Horne declined to run. State Senator Steve Cohen dropped out of the race in January 1998. Then into the race strode John Jay Hooker, "a half-comic caricature from the past," in the words of *The Tennessean*'s Larry Daughtrey. Hooker had run for governor twice before, losing to Buford Ellington in 1966 and Republican Winfield Dunn in 1970; he headed Minnie Pearl Chicken (renamed Performance Systems), which went bust; STP Corp. and UPI; he ran for the Senate unsuccessfully in 1976, 1994 and 1996; in his one success, he urged Ross Perot to run for president in 1992. He challenged the constitutionality of Tennessee's campaign finance practices in 1997, and ran for governor in 1998, saying his two issues would be judicial selection and campaign reform, especially contributions, or "bribes" as he called them. He raised no money, ran no ads, seldom ventured from Nashville and sued Sundquist twice, for libel and for not letting him use the governor's mansion for a rally. So weak was the competition that Hooker won the Democratic primary with 41% of the vote (Tennessee has no runoff). At the end of October Sundquist said, "Don't take me for granted unless you want John Jay Hooker as your governor. . . . Now that's a scary thought on Halloween." Not to worry. Sundquist won 69%–29%, carrying all but two counties—an astonishing feat given rural Tennessee's Civil War loyalties—and had $3 million in unspent funds. Republicans made minor gains in the state House.

In the months that followed Sundquist reversed some of the stands that had brought him such success. In November he said that Tennesseans should have a chance to vote on a lottery, though maybe not till 2002. In his February 1999 budget proposal, looking to a future revenue crunch, he called for revision of Tennessee's business taxes. He called for repealing the grocery tax and removing the 6% franchise and excise tax and imposing a 2.5% tax on business profits and compensation paid, and to include previously untaxed limited liability companies and partnerships. Democratic legislators protested that a tax on compensation was an income tax, which Sundquist had always said he opposed. Sharp increases in TennCare were evidently one reason for Sundquist's proposal; he also proposed closing TennCare to new enrollment. But the legislature adjourned in May 1999 after passing a budget that included more than $190 million for TennCare but without the tax reforms Sundquist called for. He said it was likely to call the legislature back in November to try again.

Senior Senator. Fred Thompson, first elected in 1994, grew up in Lawrenceburg, Tennessee, the son of a used car dealer, and worked his way through school rearing a young family. After law school at Vanderbilt, he became an assistant U.S. attorney in Nashville, handling moonshine and stolen car cases. In 1973, Howard Baker made Thompson chief Republican counsel to the Senate Watergate Committee, where he helped uncover the scandal that drove a Republican president from office. Back in Tennessee, incoming Governor Lamar Alexander appointed Thompson special counsel to investigate clemency-selling by outgoing Governor Ray Blanton, who went to jail. In the process, Thompson defended parole board chairman Marie Ragghianti, whose plight was the subject of the movie *Marie*, Thompson's first movie role. He took a couple more special counsel assignments in Washington and acted in 18 movies, including box office hits like *The Hunt for Red October*. His roles included a CIA chief, FBI director, a White House chief of staff and a senator, as well as some explicit villains. But he spent most of his time practicing law and lobbying, and for years made no move to run for office

Then Al Gore resigned his Senate seat to become vice president, and Governor Ned McWherter passed over the Democrat who seemed the most likely candidate—Congressman Jim Cooper—to appoint his own aide Harlan Mathews, who did not run in the election to fill the last two years of Gore's term in 1994. Thompson and Cooper did. Cooper seemed well positioned for the race. The son of a former governor, he had represented the elongated 4th District for 12 years and was conspicuously a New Democrat and chief sponsor of a managed care health bill, which was vigorously opposed by the Clinton White House. With a seat on Commerce, he raised plenty of money and ultimately spent slightly more than Thompson.

But Thompson stressed some issues which caught voters' attention and found a device to symbolize his message. One of his issues has long been advocated by Baker and was featured by Alexander in his first presidential campaign: limiting congressional sessions to half the year and allowing lawmakers to make their livings in their home communities. To this he coupled strong advocacy of term limits. The symbol—gimmick, Democrats said—for this was the red pickup truck which Thompson leased in August 1994 and drove all around Tennessee, speaking to small groups over coffee or fried chicken. Ads also captured a personal contrast between the candidates: the six-foot-five Thompson appeared in workshirts, speaking confidently to the camera while walking up porch stairs (not so easy to do: his acting experience helped); the much shorter and youthful-looking Cooper appeared before a church in starched white shirt and tie. In early October, Thompson zoomed to a lead. Cooper responded by citing his opposition to the Clinton health care plan. But Cooper got squeezed out of the middle ground he had long worked to occupy. Tennesseans decided to vote against the Clinton Administration and career politicians, and Thompson won 60%–39%.

He quickly became a political star in Washington. Bob Dole named him to respond on television to Clinton's 1994 speech urging a tax cut. Thompson's strong words and delivery made him seem the more presidential: "We welcome the president to help us lead America in a new direction, but if he will not, we will welcome the president to follow—because we are moving ahead." Thompson voted for most of the Contract with America provisions. He soft-pedaled issues like abortion, but emphasized campaign finance reform, sponsoring a measure to save the current presidential checkoff system. He brought the term limit amendment to the floor in 1995 and sponsored the 1996 amendment to freeze congressional pay. He had objections to the Republicans' tort reform proposals. He sponsored a two-year budget and a bipartisan juvenile justice bill giving more flexibility to the states.

Thompson then became chairman of the Governmental Affairs Committee, and was assigned the duty of investigating the Clinton scandals by Majority Leader Trent Lott. He started off uncertainly, asking for a $6.5 million budget without consulting Lott or the Democrats, then irritating Republicans when he promised a broad investigation of congressional and Republican campaigns as well as the Clinton-Gore operation. Ultimately, Thompson got $4.35 million and the broader mandate he had originally sought. He started the hearings in July 1997 by asserting that "high-level Chinese government officials crafted a plan to increase China's influence over the U.S. political process" by allocating "substantial sums of money" to congressional and the 1996 presidential elections. Democrats responded with outrage and obstruction. "There wasn't five minutes," Thompson reflected later, "where the many times I reached out to them in trying to be fair with them and give them more than the rules give them entitlement to, that they reached back toward me." Thompson could not produce direct evidence of the Chinese efforts as key witnesses declined to testify or fled the country—though plenty of evidence came out by 1999. Then he focused on Clinton's and Gore's fundraising on federal property—a clear violation of the letter of the law—and called their raising and spending of vast sums of soft money a "ruse." But Democrats raised hairsplitting objections and Attorney General Janet Reno refused to call for an independent counsel. Facing an end-of-the-year deadline Democrats had insisted on, Thompson shifted his focus to the campaign finance bill, to Lott's disgust.

Perhaps because he was miffed by some of Thompson's moves, Lott assigned the Y2K problem to Bob Bennett and appointed Richard Shelby to chair a task force on technology transfers to China, on which Thompson served. But Thompson found other work to do. With Carl Levin and Gore, he helped develop a regulatory reform package that found its way into the October 1998 omnibus budget; it set up a framework for cost-benefit analysis and risk assessment of major government regulations. With Pete Domenici, he proposed biennial budgets. Decrying the status quo—"We don't have a campaign finance system any more. . . . The loopholes are bigger than the laws"—he was one of the few Republicans actively backing the McCain-Feingold campaign finance bill. He bristled when Levin gathered information from independent counsels; during 1998 he expressed doubts about the independent counsel statute and in March 1999 he came out against reauthorization. He passed a vacancy reform act in October 1998, limiting acting officers to 120 days in office unless the president has submitted a permanent nomination.

Thompson has expressed frustrations with the pace of the Senate: "I'm not 30 years old. I don't want to spend the rest of my life up here. . . . I don't like spending 14- and 16-hour days voting on 'sense of the Senate' resolutions on irrelevant matters." He has been willing to cast lonely votes against popular measures because on federalism grounds he believes they should be left to the states: the .08% blood alcohol level for DWI, the school gun law, limiting tort liability of volunteers. He drew on his prosecutorial experience to question the victim's rights amendment. He came out against the tobacco bill in May 1998 and supported an amendment to pay tobacco farmers $18 billion if they would get out of the business.

Thompson worked very often with junior colleague Bill Frist on Tennessee-related issues. He passed a bill to protect 2,000 civilians working at Fort Campbell from paying Kentucky taxes. In May 1998 he formed the Great Smoky Mountains National Park Congressional Caucus, and pushed to allow the park to retain 100% rather than 80% of fees. He got funding for the $1 billion Spallation Neutron Source at the Oak Ridge National Laboratory. He backed copyright extensions and opposed exempting small restaurants from paying royalties to songwriters: matters of interest in Nashville. He pushed for language in 1997 to require the building of the World Runway at Memphis airport and called for a 60-day cooling-off period in the Northwest Airlines (Memphis is one of its hubs) strike in September 1998. He got the Senate to vote 60–33 to bar a nuclear waste storage facility in Oak Ridge. Thompson and Frist have said that proposals for TVA to spin off non-power functions need more study. In 1998 they came up with a plan to save TVA $100 million a year by refinancing its $3.2 billion debt (much of it run up by uneconomic nuclear power plants) plus a $50 million direct appropriation for non-power activities; this went into the October 1998 omnibus budget and was praised by TVA's Craven Crowell.

Thompson was named to the six-senator committee working on procedure for impeachment; he oversaw the deposition of Vernon Jordan. He voted not guilty on perjury but guilty on obstruction of justice. In January 1999 he got a seat on Finance; he has backed Social Security reform which would put 15% of payroll taxes in individual investment accounts, but has said that any reform must be bipartisan.

When Thompson's seat came up in 1996, he ran an ad saying, "I want you to meet my number one adviser on Social Security and Medicare," and introduced his mother. Thompson won 61%–37%, winning nearly 1.1 million votes, more than anyone ever has in Tennessee. In March 1999 Thompson announced that he wouldn't run for president and that he would support Alexander, who was set to launch his campaign. His pledge to serve two full terms leaves him free to run again in 2002.

Junior Senator. Bill Frist, first elected in 1994, grew up in Nashville, in an old Tennessee family; his father practiced medicine for 55 years and was the physician for six Tennessee governors. Frist graduated from Princeton and Harvard Medical School, studied at Mass General, in England and at Stanford, and became a heart and lung transplant surgeon, setting up the transplant program at Vanderbilt. He performed 250 transplants and wrote a book, *Transplant*, on the social and ethical issues of these surgeries; he has written more than 100 peer-reviewed articles. In 1968 his father and brother, Thomas Frist Jr., set up HCA, which through a 1994 merger became Columbia/HCA, the world's largest hospital company; the new firm was hit with charges of Medicare violations in 1997, and Thomas Frist Jr. came back from semi-retirement to run it; he owns hundreds of millions of dollars of the stock and Bill Frist has some $9 million, put into blind trust. Frist also pilots his own airplane and runs marathons (51 seconds faster than Al Gore in 1998), and regularly does volunteer medical work in Washington, Tennessee and Sudan. For years he was unpolitical: he never voted until age 36, after he moved back to Nashville. He was appointed by Democratic Governor Ned Ray McWherter to head a task force on Medicaid in 1992.

In 1994 Frist decided to run against Senator Jim Sasser, then Budget Committee Chairman and a candidate for majority leader. He had tough primary opposition from east Tennessee businessman Bob Corker, who attacked him for not voting and for obtaining cats from animal shelters for experiments as a medical student. But Frist, spending liberally, carried the Nashville and Memphis media markets and beat Corker 44%–32% (Tennessee is the one former Confederate state without a runoff). In the general, Frist said he wanted to "give communities and individuals the freedom to solve problems and return to our basic conservative values," and backed welfare reform, federal spending cuts, school prayer and term limits; he follows Howard Baker in calling for citizen-politicians and pledged to serve just two terms—"Term limits for career politicians and the death penalty for career criminals," one ad said. Sasser emphasized school prayer, the balanced budget amendment and cracking down on illegal immigrants, and he ridiculed Frist as a bored, rich surgeon. Frist charged that Sasser "never met a tax he didn't like" and as majority leader would be "the official water boy to Bill Clinton." Frist outspent Sasser, with $7 million total, $3.7 million of it his own money to $5 million for Sasser. Sasser led in polls up through October, but in November Frist won 56%–42%, carrying all the large metro areas and losing only scattered traditionally Democratic rural counties.

Frist is the first physician to serve in the Senate for 50 years; he points out that there were many more in the days of the citizen-politician. In September 1995 he resuscitated a constituent outside the Dirksen Office Building, and in July 1998 he ran over to the House and tended to those wounded in the shooting that killed two Capitol police officers. Frist was credited with saving the life of the shooter, Russell Weston Jr.; "From a physician's point of view, you are not a judge, you are not a jury, you are a physician." Naturally he got involved in health issues; the Senate Ethics Committee said his Columbia/HCA stock did not pose a conflict. He played a key role on the 1996 health care bill on portability and pre-existing conditions, working to include Medical Savings Accounts. He also helped to write the provision guaranteeing insurance coverage for 48-hour hospital maternity stays. He worked to reauthorize the Ryan White CARE Act for the treatment and support of AIDS patients. He put on the income tax form a box to check off for information on organ donor cards. He worked to make sure Tennessee was not penalized for extending TennCare to uninsured children.

In 1997 Frist became chairman of two subcommittees with medical and research jurisdiction—Public Health and Safety, and Science, Technology and Space. He has worked on many health insurance reforms, advocating the use of market based principles first, "and if it doesn't work, then we'll have to step in and give it a guiding hand." With Jay Rockefeller, he sponsored a law to allow physicians and hospitals to establish service provider organizations to contract directly with Medicare. "The mother-may-I mentality that has emerged has frustrated both parties and providers and led them to question who is in charge," said Frist. He worked on putting together the Republican HMO reform in July 1998, but he points out that 70% of employees and 86% of Medicare recipients are not in managed care; he thinks a greater problem is the time it takes to put into practice new scientific discoveries, and called for creating an Agency for Health Care Quality. He served on the Medicare Commission and was part of the bipartisan majority that supported John Breaux's March 1999 premium support proposal.

On several medical issues he broke with most of his fellow Republicans. He wrote the FDA sections of John McCain's tobacco bill and supported it at first, but voted to kill it in June 1998, saying he feared the money for tobacco farmers would be stripped. He supports doubling NIH funding over five years. He supported Surgeon General nominees Henry Foster and David Satcher. He backed the 1997 Clinton bill to ban discrimination by insurers by genetic traits and to assure privacy of genetic information.

On other health issues, Frist sponsored a congressional medal for organ donors and their families with Democrat Pete Stark. He passed a law with incentives for primary care physicians in rural and inner city areas, and worked to reauthorize the bone marrow registry, with recruitment of minorities. He helped get both houses to pass a 1998 law for research on women's health problems. Frist sponsored the ban on human cloning and supported the partial-birth abortion ban, "because it is needlessly risky to the woman, because it is an unnecessary procedure, because it is inhumane to the fetus, and because it is medically unacceptable and offends the very basic civil sensibilities of people all across this country." Looking ahead, Frist wants to examine the rise in infectious diseases and the threat of drug-resistant microbes. He amended the HMO bill in March 1999 to increase access to specialists, strengthen independent external review, study patient access to clinical trials and coverage of routine costs and improve data collection from rural areas.

On the Science Subcommittee Frist led passage of a law encouraging commercial space travel in July 1998. With Democrat Ron Wyden, he was the lead sponsor of the Ed-Flex bill which passed by a wide margin in March 1999; it would give school systems greater flexibility in return for holding them to greater accountability. He favors individual retirement accounts as part of Social Security. After a trip to Sudan, he said in 1998 that the Clinton Administration's acquiescence to Sudanese government manipulation of humanitarian relief "may be a contributing factor in the horrendous prospect of widespread starvation." He voted for both articles of impeachment and said, "Acquittal regrettably will inject a slow-acting moral poison into the American consciousness."

Senators of the same party from the same state often have acrimonious relationships (see New Jersey), but Frist and Fred Thompson, elected the same year, seem to get on unusually well, although they disagree on about 20% of roll call votes—many of the disagreements are what you might expect between a doctor and a lawyer. They have worked in tandem on many Tennessee issues, including the 1998 TVA bill which refinanced its debt, saving $100 million, and added $50 million for its non-power activities, like the Land Between the Lakes park. They obtained funding for the Spallation Neutron Source at Oak Ridge, a ban on a nuclear waste depository there, and an investigation of unexplained illnesses in one Oak Ridge neighborhood. They sought a cooling-off period in the Northwest Airlines strike in September 1998. Frist obtained $970,000 for trail repair in the Great Smoky Mountains National Park and $2 million to repair erosion damage at Shiloh National Military Park. He sponsored bills to ban low overflights over the Smokies and to keep 100% rather than 80% of fees at the park.

Frist comes up for re-election in 2000, and this will be the only statewide race in Tennessee, which Al Gore dearly wants to carry; and so recruiting a good candidate has been a goal of Democrats. But as of early 1999 it was hard slogging. Frist had more than $2 million by the end of 1998, and his capacity to raise money from Nashville's giant network of Republican contributors is very high. Nashville Mayor Phil Bredesen, the Democrat strongest in the polls, is "strongly inclined not to run." Two days after winning 29% in the 1998 gubernatorial campaign, John Jay Hooker announced he was running; it is not clear if he could exceed that percentage against Frist. There have been stories that Gore's campaign has encouraged Memphis Congressman Harold Ford Jr. to run; Ford won his father's seat in 1996, at 26, and has had a conspicuously more moderate voting record and has shown interest in running statewide some day. One interesting possibility is John Lowery, a onetime aide to Harold Ford Sr., and founder of Revelation Corporation, a company affiliated with large black churches; Lowery has said he is willing to spend $1 million of his own money, but would step aside for Harold Ford Jr.

Cook's Call. *Safe.* Democrats have taken a drubbing here in recent statewide elections, and no one seems particularly anxious to take on Frist. The potential candidate making the most noise is 29-year-old, second-term Representative Harold Ford Jr., but he is unlikely to draw much support outside of the black community. Democrats dream of convincing Nashville Mayor Phil Bredesen of running but that seems highly unlikely. Unless Democrats can tempt someone of Bredesen's caliber and fundraising potential, Frist should have little trouble winning a second term.

Presidential politics. The existence of two strong partisan traditions, with the Democrats' base somewhat larger over the years, has made for unusual stability in Tennessee presidential politics. While other Southern states went Republican, Tennessee stayed about evenly divided— in the Eisenhower 1950s and the Carter-Reagan race of 1980—with similar percentages in almost every county. When southern Democrats have run strong races, they have carried Tennessee, as in 1964, 1976 and 1992. When Republicans are strong, they have won similarly: Ronald Reagan and George Bush both won 58% here in 1984 and 1988, and the Republican percentages in the three major statewide races in 1994 ranged between 54% and 60%. In 1996 Tennessee was almost dead even. Tennessee should be sharply contested in 2000: Al Gore has a strong local base here, but the state trend, as prosperity has ballooned the population of once-rural counties, has been strongly Republican.

Tennessee's presidential primary is held on Super Tuesday (though Tennessee holds its state primaries on Thursdays, the only state to do so). The easy winners in 1992 were those two Southern moderates, Bill Clinton and George Bush. Native son Lamar Alexander had already withdrawn from the race and endorsed and campaigned with Bob Dole by the time the Super Tuesday Republican contest rolled around in 1996; Dole won handily.

Congressional districting. Tennessee needed only minor changes to get its districts back to equal population after the 1990 Census. Democrats controlled the process, and tried to help their prospects marginally, but the 1994 Republican revolution swept most of their advantage away. Control of the process after the 2000 Census is likely to be split between the parties, which suggests a compromise which helps most or all incumbents.

The People: Est. Pop. 1998: 5,430,621; Pop. 1990: 4,877,185, up 11.3% 1990–1998. 2% of U.S. total, 17th largest; 39.1% rural. Median age: 35.3 years. 13.3% 65 years and over. 83% White, 15.9% Black, 0.6% Asian, 0.3% Amer. Indian, 0.2% Other; 0.6% Hispanic Origin. Households: 57.2% married couple families; 27.1% married couple fams. w. children; 37% college educ.; median household income: $24,807; per capita income: $12,255; 68% owner occupied housing; median house value: $58,400; median monthly rent: $273. 4.2% Unemployment. 1998 Voting age pop.: 4,120,000. 1998 Turnout: 1,026,017; 25% of VAP. Registered voters (1998): 3,154,487; no party registration.

Political Lineup: Governor, Don Sundquist (R); Lt. Gov., John Wilder (D); Secy. of State, Riley C. Darnell (D); Atty. Gen., Paul Summers; Treasurer, Steve Adams (D); State Senate, 33 (18 D, 15 R); Majority Leader, Ward Crutchfield (D); State House, 99 (59 D, 40 R); House Speaker, Jimmy Naifeh (D). Senators, Fred D. Thompson (R) and Bill Frist (R). Representatives, 9 (4 D, 5 R).

Elections Division: 615-741-7956; **Filing Deadline for U.S. Congress:** May 18, 2000.

1996 Presidential Vote

Clinton (D)	909,146	(48%)
Dole (R)	863,530	(46%)
Perot (I)	105,918	(6%)

1992 Presidential Vote

Clinton (D)	933,521	(47%)
Bush (R)	841,300	(42%)
Perot (I)	199,968	(10%)

1996 Republican Presidential Primary

Dole (R)	148,063	(51%)
Buchanan (R)	72,929	(25%)
Alexander (R)	32,742	(11%)
Forbes (R)	22,171	(8%)
Others	13,138	(5%)

GOVERNOR

Gov. Don Sundquist (R)

Elected 1994, term expires Jan. 2003; b. Mar. 15, 1936, Moline, IL; home, Memphis; Augustana Col., B.A. 1957; Lutheran; married (Martha).

Military Career: Navy, 1957–59.

Elected Office: U.S. House of Reps., 1982–94.

Professional Career: Jostens, Inc., 1962–72; Pres. & Partner, Graphic Sales of Amer., 1972–82; Shelby Cnty. Repub. Chmn., 1976–78; Campaign Mgr., Howard Baker for President, 1979; Cofounder, Red, Hot & Blue Restaurant.

Office: State Capitol, 7th Ave. & Charlotte, Nashville, 37243, 615-741-2001; Fax: 615-741-1416; Web site: www.state.tn.us.

Election Results

1998 gen.	Don Sundquist (R)	669,973	(69%)
	John Jay Hooker (D)	287,750	(29%)
	Others	18,513	(2%)
1998 prim.	Don Sundquist (R)	358,014	(93%)
	Shirley Beck-Vosse (R)	28,912	(7%)
1994 gen.	Don Sundquist (R)	807,104	(54%)
	Phil Bredesen (D)	664,252	(45%)

SENATORS

Sen. Fred D. Thompson (R)

Elected 1994, seat up 2002; b. Aug. 19, 1942, Sheffield, AL; home, Nashville; Memphis St. U., B.S. 1964, Vanderbilt U. Law Schl., J.D. 1967; Protestant; divorced.

Professional Career: Practicing Atty,. 1967–94; Asst. US Atty., Middle TN Dist., 1969–72; Minority Cnsl., U.S. Sen. Watergate Cmte., 1973–74; Special Cnsl., TN Gov. Lamar Alexander, 1980; Special Cnsl., U.S. Sen. Foreign Relations Cmte., 1980–81; Special Cnsl., U.S. Sen. Intelligence Cmte., 1982; TN Appellate Court Nom. Comm., 1985–87; Author; Actor.

DC Office: 523 DSOB, 20515, 202-224-4944; Fax: 202-228-3679; Web site: www.senate.gov/~thompson.

State Offices: Chattanooga, 423-752-5337; Jackson, 901-423-9344; Knoxville, 423-545-4253; Memphis, 901-544-4224; Nashville, 615-736-5129; Tri-Cities, 423-325-6217.

Committees: *Finance* (11th of 11 R): Health Care; International Trade; Social Security & Family Policy; Taxation & IRS Oversight. *Governmental Affairs* (Chmn. of 9 R).

Group Ratings

	ADA	ACLU	AFS	LCV	CON	NTU	NFIB	COC	ACU	NTLC	CHC
1998	10	0	11	0	52	70	89	89	84	89	82
1997	0	—	0	—	25	78	—	60	88	—	—

National Journal Ratings

	1997 LIB — 1997 CONS		1998 LIB — 1998 CONS	
Economic	11% —	76%	0% —	88%
Social	17% —	72%	28% —	71%
Foreign	0% —	77%	12% —	75%

Key Votes of the 105th Congress

1. Bal. Budget Amend.	Y	5. Satcher for Surgeon Gen.	Y	9. Chem. Weapons Treaty	N
2. Clinton Budget Deal	Y	6. Highway Set-asides	N	10. Cuban Humanitarian Aid	N
3. Cloture on Tobacco	N	7. Table Child Gun locks	Y	11. Table Bosnia Troops	N
4. Education IRAs	Y	8. Ovrd. Part. Birth Veto	Y	12. $ for Test-ban Treaty	N

Election Results

1996 general	Fred D. Thompson (R) 1,091,554	(61%)	($3,469,369)
	Houston Gordon (D) 654,937	(37%)	($795,969)
	Others 32,173	(2%)	
1996 primary	Fred D. Thompson (R) 266,549	(94%)	
	Jim F. Counts (R) 16,715	(6%)	
1994 general	Fred D. Thompson (R) 885,998	(60%)	($3,793,813)
	Jim Cooper (D) 565,930	(39%)	($3,979,425)

Sen. Bill Frist (R)

Elected 1994, seat up 2000; b. Feb. 22, 1952, Nashville; home, Nashville; Princeton U., A.B. 1974, Harvard Med. Schl., M.D. 1978; Presbyterian; married (Karyn).

Professional Career: Practicing surgeon, 1978–94; Dir., Vanderbilt Medical Ctr. Heart-Lung Transplant Program, 1986–93.

DC Office: 416 RSOB, 20510, 202-224-3344; Fax: 202-228-1264; Web site: www.senate.gov/~frist.

State Offices: Chattanooga, 423-894-2203; Jackson, 901-424-9655; Kingsport, 423-323-1252; Knoxville, 423-602-7977; Memphis, 901-683-1910; Nashville, 615-352-9411.

Committees: *Budget* (10th of 12 R). *Commerce, Science & Transportation* (9th of 11 R): Aviation; Communications; Manufacturing & Competitiveness; Science, Technology & Space (Chmn.); Surface Transportation & Merchant Marine. *Foreign Relations* (10th of 10 R): African Affairs (Chmn.); International Economic Policy, Export & Trade Promotion; International Operations. *Health, Education, Labor & Pensions* (3d of 10 R): Children & Families; Public Health (Chmn.).

Group Ratings

	ADA	ACLU	AFS	LCV	CON	NTU	NFIB	COC	ACU	NTLC	CHC
1998	5	14	11	13	14	59	100	94	80	81	82
1997	10	—	0	—	85	77	—	100	72	—	—

National Journal Ratings

	1997 LIB — 1997 CONS		1998 LIB — 1998 CONS	
Economic	25% —	67%	37% —	62%
Social	17% —	72%	31% —	64%
Foreign	43% —	50%	12% —	75%

Key Votes of the 105th Congress

1. Bal. Budget Amend.	Y	5. Satcher for Surgeon Gen.	Y	9. Chem. Weapons Treaty	Y
2. Clinton Budget Deal	Y	6. Highway Set-asides	N	10. Cuban Humanitarian Aid	N
3. Cloture on Tobacco	Y	7. Table Child Gun locks	Y	11. Table Bosnia Troops	N
4. Education IRAs	Y	8. Ovrd. Part. Birth Veto	Y	12. $ for Test-ban Treaty	N

Election Results

1994 general	Bill Frist (R)	834,226	(56%)	($7,017,424)
	James R. (Jim) Sasser (D)	623,164	(42%)	($5,020,515)
	Others	23,001	(2%)	
1994 primary	Bill Frist (R)	197,734	(44%)	
	Bob Corker (R)	143,808	(32%)	
	Steve Wilson (R)	50,274	(11%)	
	Harold Sterling (R)	28,425	(6%)	
	Others	25,410	(6%)	
1988 general	James R. (Jim) Sasser (D)	1,020,061	(65%)	($3,069,615)
	Bill Andersen (R)	541,033	(35%)	($612,421)

FIRST DISTRICT

Between the corduroy-like ridges of the Appalachian chains, as they bend west and then south, the valley of Virginia extends far into northeastern Tennessee. The communities of this region—a hilly patchwork of industrial centers, small farms and federal land—were largely shaped by the building of railroads in the 1850s. The land rush immediately after the Revolutionary War populated the area; here in tiny Jonesborough the early settlers established the free state of Franklin in 1784, and many pioneer cabins, federal mansions and Greek Revival churches are lovingly preserved. It was the railroads, however, that determined the winners and losers. Other Appalachian areas were cut off from the rest of America, with tracks running only to the coal mines, but the small industrial cities that had grown up here—Johnson City, Kingsport, Bristol—were on the main lines of national commerce even before the Civil War. The War had a different political effect here than in most of the South: northeast Tennessee, the home of wartime Governor and then Vice President Andrew Johnson, had few slaves and with its connection to northern industry was Union territory. It remains heavily Republican to this day.

The political continuity is all the more surprising because this area has had continuous economic growth and has developed the sort of industrial economy which produced unions and Democrats in the North. Its growth has been helped by modest wage levels, a skilled and hard-working labor force, low electric power rates because of the Tennessee Valley Authority and good transportation routes (rail lines and now Interstate 81). Its small cities boast major paper and printing plants, and have the look of comfortable, clean, 1920s factory towns. Growth has been rapid only around Sevier County, where Gatlinburg and Pigeon Forge (home of Dolly Parton's Dollywood theme park) are the main tourist centers—more than 14,000 motel and hotel rooms and numerous attractions—for travelers to the Great Smoky Mountains National Park. And even there, the small-town flavor lingers: Pigeon Forge's big scandal of 1994 was the mysterious killing of some 80 rabbits at Bunnyland Mini Golf.

The far northeastern end of Tennessee forms the 1st Congressional District, a district so heavily Republican that it has not elected a Democrat to the House for more than 100 years. Nonetheless, it has had turbulent politics on occasion. For almost 40 years (1921–61, with one four-year and one two-year hiatus), the seat was held by B. Carroll Reece, a fierce mountain politician who was once Republican National Chairman. After Reece died in 1961, and his widow was elected to fill out his term, there was a hotly contested primary here. The winner, Jimmy Quillen, a bread-and-butter politician and former owner of the *Johnson City Times*, represented the 1st for the next 34 years. His crowning achievements were the building of the James H. Quillen College of Medicine at East Tennessee State University and the James H. and Cecile C. Quillen Center for Rehabilitative Medicine, both in Johnson City. In 1995, Quillen was named the first-ever House committee chairman emeritus—of Rules—but he announced his retirement in April 1996, saying, "Let's face it. Younger people are emerging as leaders in Washington and those with long records of service are stepping aside."

The congressman from the 1st District now is Bill Jenkins, elected in 1996. Jenkins is a lawyer from Rogersville in Hawkins County, and a farmer who raises beef cattle and grows burley tobacco. He was elected to the state House in 1962, at 25. In 1969, the state House was evenly split between Democrats and Republicans, and Jenkins was elected speaker, the only Republican to serve in that position in the 20th Century. In 1971 he was named to the TVA Board of Directors; he served as commissioner of the state Department of Conservation; in 1990 he was elected Circuit Court Judge. In May 1996 he resigned to run for Congress.

Jenkins was just one of 11 Republicans—the Quillen 11—filed to run in the August 1996 primary. Tennessee has no runoff, and this was what political scientist V.O. Key called a "friends and neighbors" primary: there were few perceptible differences on issues, and candidates struggled to get enough votes out in their home areas to win. Jenkins won with just 18% of the votes, including 74% in Hawkins County. In second, just 331 votes behind, was state Senator Jim Holcomb, who had conservative Christian activist support, with 18%, including 37% in Sullivan County, the highest-voting county in the district. Sevierville District Attorney Al Schmutzer was third with 15%; medical supply millionaire David Davis won 13%. Quillen's second cousin, state Representative Richard Venable, whom Quillen endorsed late in the race, won 13%; David Crockett, who ran an ad saying race driver Richard Petty was supporting him, but which Petty promptly denied, won 12%; and Kingsport businesswoman Anne Pope won 10%. The general election was anticlimactic; Jenkins won 65%–32%.

In the House, Jenkins serves on the Judiciary and Agriculture committees and has a strong conservative voting record. He began tending to local needs in early 1997, pressing the EPA to deny a wastewater discharge permit and variance to Champion International's Canton, North Carolina, paper mill just across the Pigeon River from the 1st District, and closely watched a proposal to spin off some of EPA's functions. He promised to look out for tobacco farmers when the tobacco bill came up. Like Quillen, he had no press secretary but, unlike Quillen, he seldom returned Tennessee reporters' phone calls; "the P.R. aspects of it are not that essential for him," a district staffer explained. But he did hold many open-door sessions in the district. He was perhaps the quietest member of the Judiciary Committee in its impeachment sessions, but firmly supported impeachment.

It was obvious that the key obstacle to a second term for Jenkins would be the August 1998 Republican primary. Many of his 1996 opponents did not regard the result as final and itched to run, but one after another dropped out. But Holcomb, the second-place finisher in 1996, sharply attacked Jenkins's vote for normal trade relations with China on his radio show "There Ought to Be a Law," and announced his candidacy in March 1998. The chairman of the Sullivan County Republican party resigned to support him. But others rallied to the incumbent: Majority Leader Dick Armey attended a Jenkins fundraiser in April, and later that month Jimmy Quillen appeared at Jenkins's re-election announcement. By May, Schmutzer, Venable and Pope were supporting him along with Speaker Newt Gingrich and Governor Don Sundquist. Jenkins pointed out that he had 100% voting records from National Right to Life, the National Federation of Independent Businesses and the National Association of Manufacturers and had been praised by the National Rifle Association and the Christian Coalition. Holcomb dropped out of the race in May; he had not been able to raise much money. Jenkins was unopposed in August and won easily in November.

Cook's Call. *Safe.* The only thing that Jenkins has to worry about in this solidly Republican district is a serious primary challenge. But, as an incumbent with two good wins under his belt, it is hard to see why he would be contested.

The People: Pop. 1990: 541,978; 52.7% rural; 14.6% age 65 + ; 97.5% White, 1.8% Black, 0.2% Asian, 0.3% Amer. Indian, 0.1% Other; 0.4% Hispanic Origin. Households: 61.6% married couple families; 27.5% married couple fams. w. children; 30.6% college educ.; median household income: $21,952; per capita income: $11,024; median house value: $51,200; median gross rent: $219.

1996 Presidential Vote

Dole (R)	107,668	(54%)
Clinton (D)	73,681	(37%)
Perot (I)	14,532	(7%)

1992 Presidential Vote

Bush (R)	107,515	(51%)
Clinton (D)	76,113	(36%)
Perot (I)	24,358	(12%)

Rep. Bill Jenkins (R)

Elected 1996; b. Nov. 29, 1936, Detroit, MI; home, Rogersville; TN Tech., B.B.A. 1957, U. of TN, J.D. 1961; Baptist; married (Kathryn).

Military Career: Army, 1960–62.

Elected Office: TN Assembly, 1962–71, Speaker, 1969–71; TN Circuit Court Judge, 1990–96.

Professional Career: Farmer, 1961–present; Practicing atty., 1961–90; Commissioner, TN Dept. of Conservation, 1971–72; Dir., TN Valley Authority, 1971–78.

DC Office: 1708 LHOB 20515, 202-225-6356; Fax: 202-225-5714; Web site: www.house.gov/jenkins.

District Office: Kingsport, 423-247-8161.

Committees: *Agriculture* (18th of 27 R): General Farm Commodities, Resource Conservation & Credit; Risk Management, Research & Specialty Crops. *Judiciary* (13th of 21 R): Courts & Intellectual Property; The Constitution.

Group Ratings

	ADA	ACLU	AFS	LCV	CON	NTU	NFIB	COC	ACU	NTLC	CHC
1998	5	6	11	0	13	50	93	89	100	92	92
1997	5	—	25	—	42	48	—	100	88	—	—

National Journal Ratings

	1997 LIB	—	1997 CONS	1998 LIB	—	1998 CONS
Economic	19%	—	76%	12%	—	85%
Social	10%	—	82%	14%	—	81%
Foreign	12%	—	81%	0%	—	93%

Key Votes of the 105th Congress

1. Clinton Budget Deal	Y	5. Puerto Rico Sthood. Ref.	N	9. Cut $ for B-2 Bombers	N
2. Education IRAs	Y	6. End Highway Set-asides	Y	10. Human Rights in China	Y
3. Req. 2/3 to Raise Taxes	Y	7. School Prayer Amend.	Y	11. Withdraw Bosnia Troops	Y
4. Fast-track Trade	N	8. Ovrd. Part. Birth Veto	Y	12. End Cuban TV-Marti	N

Election Results

1998 general	Bill Jenkins (R)	68,904	(69%)	($336,612)
	Kay C. White (D)	30,710	(31%)	($39,296)
1998 primary	Bill Jenkins (R)	unopposed		
1996 general	Bill Jenkins (R)	117,676	(65%)	($457,975)
	Kay C. Smith (D)	58,657	(32%)	($32,296)
	Others	5,375	(3%)	

SECOND DISTRICT

Knoxville, the largest city in east Tennessee, is nestled between mountain ridges where the Holston and French Broad rivers join to form the Tennessee River. It was established not long after the first wave of pioneers came through the gaps and down between the mountains of the Appalachian chain. During the Civil War it was Union territory, and has remained Republican in allegiance ever since: the ancestral tug of Tennessee politics. But its Republican heritage is tempered by another tradition, that of the Tennessee Valley Authority. A venturesome program when created in the 1930s, it is now part of the fabric of life in east Tennessee, sometimes criticized as its cheap hydroelectric power capacity was filled and more of its production came from expensive and sometimes poorly functioning nuclear plants.

But both TVA and the region have been undergoing turbulent changes in recent years. TVA has cut its payroll sharply and held down rates; in a newly competitive electricity market, its director has proposed abandoning federal subsidies and spinning off navigation and flood control functions to state or federal agencies; but TVA is laboring under a $3.2 billion debt mostly incurred in building uneconomic nuclear power plants. In other ways Knoxville has been down on its luck. The banking empire of 1982 World's Fair promoter (and 1978 Democratic governor nominee) Jake Butcher collapsed in scandal in 1983. Then education entrepreneur Christopher Whittle's projects fell short of financial goals, leaving his Harvard-style campus in downtown Knoxville to be sold to the federal government for a courthouse complex. The remains of the 1982 World's Fair remain an embarrassment; local officials have proposed more than a dozen redevelopment plans, none of them implemented.

The 2d Congressional District, which includes Knoxville and several mountainous counties to the south (including Blount County and Lamar Alexander's home town of Maryville), is one of the nation's most reliably Republican districts and one of the more practical-minded.

The congressman from the district is Jimmy Duncan, a Republican first elected in 1988; his father represented the 2nd from 1964 until his death in May 1988. Duncan studied in Knoxville and Washington, practiced law and was a trial judge in the 1980s. When his father died, he won the seat despite a spirited challenge from Democrat Dudley Taylor, also a scion of a prominent east Tennessee political family. Taylor attacked Duncan for signing up with the National Guard in 1970 and for his ties to Butcher, but Duncan won with 57% in the special and 56% in November. He has been re-elected easily in the 1990s.

Duncan is now chairman of the Aviation Subcommittee of Transportation and Infrastructure, dealing with issues like airline ticket taxes, aviation safety and unruly airplane passengers. He has sponsored bills to encourage lower air fares for small airports like ones in Knoxville and Chattanooga, including federal loan guarantees for regional jets and allotting new slots at LaGuardia, Kennedy, Reagan and O'Hare for airlines that provide new service to underserved airports. He has a conservative voting record and likes to point out questionable projects like NASA's $12 million to search for extraterrestrial intelligence. Duncan opposed the U.S. troop deployment to Bosnia, questioned the Mexico bailout in 1995, and criticized Alan Greenspan for actions to prop up Japanese banks. He showed independence from party lines when he voted against term limits in 1997 and for the Shays-Meehan campaign finance bill in 1998.

In 1997, Duncan voted to end subsidies for sugar, peanuts and tobacco—not an obvious vote-winner back home. Still, Duncan hasn't been shy about seeking funding for other local projects: resurfacing the Foothills Parkway in the Great Smoky Mountains National Park, a $1.25 million grant to help Kimberly-Clark expand its Loudon County operations, a $1 million grant to help put local public TV Channel 15 on the air, $1.5 million for a rail and trolley system for downtown Knoxville, and $500,000 to enable the U.S. Forest Service to buy parcels of mountain property in McMinn County. Duncan is chief sponsor of a National Parks check off on the income tax form, which would provide more funding for U.S. parks, including the Great Smoky Mountains National Park.

Cook's Call. *Safe.* Over the last eight years, Duncan has had little competition for this solidly Republican seat. There is no reason to think he will be challenged seriously in 2000.

The People: Pop. 1990: 541,780; 36% rural; 13.6% age 65 + ; 92.4% White, 6.5% Black, 0.7% Asian, 0.3% Amer. Indian, 0.2% Other; 0.5% Hispanic Origin. Households: 57.5% married couple families; 26.1% married couple fams. w. children; 41.2% college educ.; median household income: $25,267; per capita income: $13,118; median house value: $59,700; median gross rent: $257.

1996 Presidential Vote			1992 Presidential Vote		
Dole (R)	117,248	(51%)	Bush (R)	107,920	(48%)
Clinton (D)	95,810	(42%)	Clinton (D)	92,752	(41%)
Perot (I)	12,522	(5%)	Perot (I)	25,157	(11%)

Rep. John J. Duncan, Jr. (R)

Elected 1988; b. July 21, 1947, Lebanon; home, Knoxville; U. of TN, B.S. 1969, George Washington U., J.D. 1973; Presbyterian; married (Lynn).

Military Career: Army Natl. Guard & Army Reserves, 1970–87.

Professional Career: Practicing atty., 1973–81; TN St. Trial Judge, 1981–88.

DC Office: 2400 RHOB 20515, 202-225-5435; Fax: 202-225-6440; Web site: www.house.gov/duncan.

District Offices: Athens, 615-745-4671; Knoxville, 615-523-3772; Maryville, 615-984-5464.

Committees: *Resources* (6th of 28 R): Forests & Forest Health; National Parks & Public Lands. *Transportation & Infrastructure* (7th of 41 R): Aviation (Chmn.); Ground Transportation.

Group Ratings

	ADA	ACLU	AFS	LCV	CON	NTU	NFIB	COC	ACU	NTLC	CHC
1998	15	0	11	8	65	65	100	78	84	92	92
1997	10	—	0	—	95	75	—	80	88	—	—

National Journal Ratings

	1997 LIB — 1997 CONS			1998 LIB — 1998 CONS		
Economic	10%	—	86%	28%	—	70%
Social	0%	—	90%	3%	—	90%
Foreign	38%	—	60%	7%	—	83%

Key Votes of the 105th Congress

1. Clinton Budget Deal	Y	5. Puerto Rico Sthood. Ref.	N	9. Cut $ for B-2 Bombers	Y
2. Education IRAs	Y	6. End Highway Set-asides	Y	10. Human Rights in China	Y
3. Req. 2/3 to Raise Taxes	Y	7. School Prayer Amend.	Y	11. Withdraw Bosnia Troops	Y
4. Fast-track Trade	N	8. Ovrd. Part. Birth Veto	Y	12. End Cuban TV-Marti	N

Election Results

1998 general	John J. Duncan Jr. (R)	90,860	(89%)	($288,566)
	Robert O. Watson (I)	4,372	(4%)	
	Greg Samples (I)	4,332	(4%)	
	Others	2,938	(3%)	
1998 primary	John J. Duncan Jr. (R)	unopposed		
1996 general	John J. Duncan Jr. (R)	150,953	(71%)	($260,818)
	Stephen Smith (D)	61,020	(29%)	($53,820)

THIRD DISTRICT

Through some of the most vivid scenery of the Appalachian chain, etching its way through the serrated ridges of east Tennessee, is the river that gave Tennessee its name. From Knoxville, the river cuts through a ridge and then plunges down a long valley to the city of Chattanooga at the Georgia line. There it switches course again, winding around the table-top Lookout Mountain and then moving into northern Alabama. Chattanooga, the city at the base of Lookout Mountain, was just a village when it was a Civil War battlefield; after the war, it became the industrial "dynamo of Dixie." A quarter-century ago it was labeled America's most polluted city. But regional political leaders, prodded by the influential and civically minded remnants of its Industrial Age aristocracy, used creative measures, such as a locally built electric shuttle bus, to reduce pollution and spruce up the city's scenic river banks. Chattanooga is now the proud home of the 12-story-high Tennessee Aquarium, the world's largest fresh water aquarium, with an exhibit in which you can follow the course of a drop of rain from the headwaters of the Tennessee until it flows out the Mississippi River into the ocean.

The 3d Congressional District of Tennessee is centered on Chattanooga, with an irregular outline that has a political provenance. It reaches far north to take in Oak Ridge, a highly educated enclave that is still shaped by the can-do ideals of the New Deal pioneers who secretly constructed it from virgin Appalachian forest during World War II in order to house the key nuclear facility that is now called the Oak Ridge National Laboratory. From there, the district avoids heavily Republican counties as it reaches east to the North Carolina line and west to the Cumberland Plateau. In recent years, the region has pinned its hopes for growth more on the private sector and less on the public sector institutions that had heretofore shaped it. The Tennessee Valley Authority, buffeted by a changing energy market and pro-competition moves in Congress, has slashed its workforce from its 1980 peak of more than 50,000 to less than 13,500 in 1999; the Oak Ridge National Laboratory, faced with shifting priorities in the post-Cold War era, has also cut its staff. Oak Ridge officials now take pains to sponsor entrepreneurial efforts to market the lab's discoveries; further south, outside Chattanooga, the Army's enormous Volunteer TNT plant, which had been dormant since 1977, now pitches itself as a place where private businesses can set up shop. Downtown Chattanooga's revival was accomplished with a 4–1 ratio of private money to government cash.

The congressman from the 3d District is Zach Wamp, a Republican elected in 1994. Wamp left college before graduating to become a real estate developer in Chattanooga, selling $22 million in real estate in five years. In 1992 he ran a high-voltage race for Congress against 20-year Democratic incumbent Marilyn Lloyd. At the start, Wamp revealed he had used cocaine and received treatment for it 10 years earlier. Wamp carried Chattanooga and Hamilton County 51%–44%. Overall, Lloyd won by just 49%–47%, the closest margin of her career; with that, she decided to retire in 1994.

In 1994, Wamp ran again as a strong conservative; one proposal was to pay members of Congress the same as a lieutenant colonel and billet them in officer housing. Democrat Randy Button, winner of a close primary, attacked Wamp's character, resurrecting the cocaine issue and accusing him of lying about his level of security clearance at Oak Ridge. Wamp accused Button of flip-flopping on issues, attacked him for taking PAC money, and, like many Republicans, ran an ad showing his opponent's face morphing into Bill Clinton's. Wamp trailed the statewide Republican ticket, but still won, carrying Hamilton County 54%–43% and losing the Oak Ridge area only narrowly, for an overall win of 52%–46%.

In the House, Wamp was elected the freshman representative on the Republican Steering Committee and was made the number two Republican on the subcommittee overseeing the Tennessee Valley Authority. He has a conservative record laced with locally appealing stands. He got $25 million for flood control in East Ridge, funding for a NEXRAD weather radar station that would serve southeast Tennessee, and funding for natural gas lines to Meigs County. He supported study of a Chattanooga-to-Atlanta high-speed rail route, secured funding for replacing the Chickamauga Lock, and sought to convince the National Park Service to absorb 956 acres of Moccasin Bend, a scenic portion of the Tennessee River. He successfully pushed for direct flights from Chattanooga to Chicago and in May 1999 proposed legislation to improve access for flights from Chattanooga-sized cities to four of the nation's largest airports. He got a seat on the Appropriations Committee in 1997, though not yet on the subcommittee he sought, Energy and Water Development.

Despite his generally conservative record, Wamp has taken some maverick stances. His support for TVA—he chaired the TVA Caucus in the 105th Congress—annoyed many conservatives. He has never accepted PAC money and he supported the McCain-Feingold campaign finance bill vocally, a stance that irritated the Republican leadership and prompted the National Right to Life Committee to run radio ads against him, even though he is opposed to abortion; it feared that the bill would prevent them from running issue-advocacy ads at campaign time. Wamp also called for reforming managed health care to ensure that patients "get the treatment they need," showed little zeal to abolish racial quotas and preferences and placed the preservation of Social Security above tax cuts. "My attitude toward the Congress has changed," Wamp told *The New York Times Magazine*. "We must realize public service is a great way of life. I came in with the attitude there were a bunch of thieves here. That's not true."

In 1996 Wamp faced a spirited challenge from Chuck Jolly, the second-place finisher in the 1994 Democratic primary; Marilyn Lloyd endorsed Wamp for re-election in late 1995. Wamp won 56%–43%, an improvement on 1994 and nearly 10 points ahead of Bob Dole. In 1998, Wamp beat former state Senator Jim Lewis, 66%–33%, the biggest margin for any Republican in the district since Reconstruction. Wamp has been mentioned as a possible candidate for governor in 2002.

Cook's Call. *Safe.* Despite the fact that this district has a deep Democratic heritage and has been quite competitive at the presidential level for the last two cycles, Wamp remains a difficult target for Democrats. Since his initital 52% win in 1994, Wamp has increased his margin of victory every year and looks to have found the right formula to keep a hold of the 3d District.

The People: Pop. 1990: 542,065; 35.4% rural; 14.2% age 65 + ; 87.4% White, 11.6% Black, 0.6% Asian, 0.3% Amer. Indian, 0.2% Other; 0.6% Hispanic Origin. Households: 57.7% married couple families; 26.7% married couple fams. w. children; 38.2% college educ.; median household income: $24,687; per capita income: $12,338; median house value: $55,200; median gross rent: $261.

1996 Presidential Vote			**1992 Presidential Vote**		
Dole (R)	93,799	(47%)	Clinton (D)	97,112	(44%)
Clinton (D)	92,780	(46%)	Bush (R)	97,073	(44%)
Perot (I)	13,284	(7%)	Perot (I)	25,719	(12%)

Rep. Zach Wamp (R)

Elected 1994; b. Oct. 28, 1957, Fort Benning, GA; home, Chattanooga; U. of NC, 1976–77, 1979–80, U. of TN, 1978–79; Baptist; married (Kim).

Professional Career: Regional Sales Super., 1981–82, Partner, Wamp Alliance Architectural Devel. Co., 1983–89; Real Estate broker, 1989–94.

DC Office: 423 CHOB 20515, 202-225-3271; Fax: 202-225-3494; Web site: www.house.gov/wamp.

District Offices: Chattanooga, 423-894-7400; Oak Ridge, 423-576-1976.

Committees: *Appropriations* (27th of 34 R): Commerce, Justice, State & the Judiciary; Interior; The Legislative Branch. *Budget* (19th of 24 R).

Group Ratings

	ADA	ACLU	AFS	LCV	CON	NTU	NFIB	COC	ACU	NTLC	CHC
1998	15	0	11	8	66	71	93	76	84	92	100
1997	5	—	0	—	88	66	—	80	92	—	—

National Journal Ratings

	1997 LIB	—	1997 CONS		1998 LIB	—	1998 CONS
Economic	33%	—	67%		23%	—	74%
Social	10%	—	82%		21%	—	76%
Foreign	24%	—	72%		0%	—	93%

Key Votes of the 105th Congress

1. Clinton Budget Deal	Y	5. Puerto Rico Sthood. Ref.	N	9. Cut $ for B-2 Bombers	Y
2. Education IRAs	Y	6. End Highway Set-asides	Y	10. Human Rights in China	Y
3. Req. 2/3 to Raise Taxes	Y	7. School Prayer Amend.	Y	11. Withdraw Bosnia Troops	Y
4. Fast-track Trade	N	8. Ovrd. Part. Birth Veto	Y	12. End Cuban TV-Marti	N

Election Results

1998 general	Zach Wamp (R)	75,100	(66%)	($384,227)
	James M. Lewis Jr. (D)	37,144	(33%)	($27,074)
1998 primary	Zach Wamp (R)	48,217	(93%)	
	John L. Brooks (R)	3,764	(7%)	
1996 general	Zach Wamp (R)	113,408	(56%)	($942,237)
	Charles N. Jolly (D)	85,714	(43%)	($420,390)

FOURTH DISTRICT

The invisible line between Civil War Republican and Civil War Democratic territory runs along the Cumberland Plateau, the westernmost upswelling of the Appalachians, west of the valley where the Tennessee River runs south from Knoxville to Chattanooga. It separates the Tennessee valley, which had few slaves and whose economic ties were with the North, from the rolling farmlands of middle Tennessee, first settled by Andrew Jackson in the 1790s and resolutely Democratic from the time he became the first president to call himself a Democrat in the 1830s. And not only is this line invisible, it is also irregular: some counties in west Tennessee, where the Tennessee River runs north from Alabama to Kentucky, are Union Republican.

The 4th Congressional District runs across this line and crosses Tennessee northeast to southwest, from Lee County, Virginia, all the way to Tishomingo County, Mississippi. It is some 300 miles long, yet seldom more than one county wide. The district includes Sewanee, the pleasant home of the University of the South, and Dayton, where in 1925 John Scopes was prosecuted by William Jennings Bryan and defended by Clarence Darrow for teaching Darwin's theory of evolution. Jack Daniels whiskey has been made for generations in Lynchburg, which appears every bit the idealized small town that the distillery's folksy, black-and-white advertisements make it out to be.

The congressman from the 4th District is Van Hilleary, a Republican elected in 1994. Hilleary grew up in Spring City, where he helped start the family textile company; after college he served in the Air Force, went to law school and volunteered for duty in the Persian Gulf, where he flew 24 missions on a C-130. In 1992, at 33, he ran for the state Senate against 18-year incumbent Anna Belle Clement O'Brien, sister of former Governor Frank Clement, and lost by only 52%–48% despite her much greater fame and financing. In 1994, when 4th District incumbent Democrat Jim Cooper ran for the Senate, Hilleary easily won a three-way primary with 58%, arguing for term limits, welfare reform, tougher sentencing and PAC-donation limits. In the general, Hilleary faced Democrat Jeff Whorley, at 34 a veteran of campaigns since he was 18 and a onetime aide to 6th District Democrat Bart Gordon. Whorley favored the death penalty, school vouchers, school prayer and gun control—mostly a conservative platform— and spent $225,000 more than Hilleary, who took no PAC money. Hilleary carried the eastern Republican counties by wide margins, and he carried the far western counties, where Whorley was hurt by the harsh primary campaign. These offset his losses in the middle Tennessee counties; overall, Hilleary won 57%–42%.

In his second full month in the House, Hilleary was in the spotlight for sponsoring a term-limit constitutional amendment—the first freshman to put an amendment to a vote since 1897. Hilleary's version, which would have limited members to 12 years or less if required by state law, was caught between advocates of six- and 12-year term limits and failed, 164–265. Hilleary was more successful on a quieter issue: an amendment to kill a $1,000 docking fee imposed by the Tennessee Valley Authority's Shoreline Management Initiative on anyone who builds or improves a dock on the TVA's lakes. Hilleary's amendment passed, but was killed in conference by pro-TVA Republican Jimmy Quillen. However, Hilleary snuck his dock deposit ban into the October 1996 continuing resolution and it became law. Writer Linda Killian focused on Hilleary as "the perfect everyman of the freshman class" in her 1998 book *The Freshmen: What Happened to the Republican Revolution?*

In 1996 Hilleary faced spirited opposition from Democrat Mark Stewart, whose grandfather, A. Tom Stewart, had been a U.S. senator from 1939–49. A Stewart ad said "Van Hilleary and Newt Gingrich have hurt Tennessee families" and "taken food away from the elderly," citing a $23 million cut in Meals on Wheels which Hilleary said was just a cut in bureaucracy. A Hilleary ad countered, "Fact is, Van Hilleary's been in Congress fighting for senior citizens and working families. What's Mark Stewart been doing? He's a trial lawyer. Defended criminals convicted of child abuse. He defended child molesters, drunk drivers, even a man accused of attempted murder." Although Bill Clinton carried the district 46%–45%, Hilleary outspent his opponent 2–1 and won 58%–41%, carrying every county but two.

In the 105th Congress Hilleary got a seat on the Budget Committee and was named a deputy whip. But he still showed independence of the leadership. He refused to back reinstatement of the airline ticket tax without an offsetting tax cut; later he became involved with a group of dissident Republicans concerned about the party's "leadership vacuum"; Hilleary later said that the group did not initiate or support the coup against Speaker Newt Gingrich, as some reports had indicated. Hilleary passed an amendment switching $10 million from housing for people with AIDS to extended care facilities for veterans, and in February 1999 introduced legislation to block an FDIC regulation which would require banks to notify the government of large deposits or withdrawals. He pushed unsuccessfully to end the U.S. troop deployment in Bosnia by December 1997 and opposed military actions in Serbia and Kosovo in 1999.

In the 1998 general election, Hilleary faced lumber company owner and 14-year state Senator Jerry Cooper, who had the support of key Democrats, including Vice President Gore and former Governor Ned McWherter. Hilleary, despite a continued rejection of PAC money, outspent Cooper more than 2–1 and won 60%–40%, his best margin yet. Cooper carried his home county and only two other middle Tennessee counties, by narrow margins; Hilleary won by better than 2–1 in the eastern counties. Hilleary has been mentioned as a possible candidate for governor in 2002.

Cook's Call. *Safe.* Though the Clinton-Gore ticket has won this district twice, the 4th remains difficult territory for Democrats running for Congress. Van Hilleary has racked up solid wins here since 1994 and the sheer enormity of this district makes it very difficult for any challenger to get known here.

The People: Pop. 1990: 541,650; 74% rural; 15% age 65 + ; 95.7% White, 3.6% Black, 0.2% Asian, 0.3% Amer. Indian, 0.1% Other; 0.4% Hispanic Origin. Households: 63.5% married couple families; 30% married couple fams. w. children; 24.1% college educ.; median household income: $20,685; per capita income: $9,886; median house value: $44,600; median gross rent: $196.

1996 Presidential Vote

Clinton (D)	92,106	(46%)
Dole (R)	90,135	(45%)
Perot (I)	14,816	(7%)

1992 Presidential Vote

Clinton (D)	100,292	(48%)
Bush (R)	83,923	(40%)
Perot (I)	23,838	(11%)

Rep. Van Hilleary (R)

Elected 1994; b. June 20, 1959, Dayton; home, Spring City; U. of TN, B.S. 1981, Samford U. Law Schl., J.D. 1990; Presbyterian; single.

Military Career: Air Force, 1982, Air Force Reserves, 1982-present (Persian Gulf).

Professional Career: Dir., Planning & Business Devel., SSM Industries Inc., 1984–86, 1992–94.

DC Office: 114 CHOB 20515, 202-225-6831; Fax: 202-225-3272; Web site: www.house.gov/hilleary.

District Offices: Crossville, 931-484-1114; Morristown, 423-587-0396; Tullahoma, 931-393-4764.

Committees: *Armed Services* (21st of 32 R): Military Installations & Facilities (Vice Chmn.); Military Research & Development. *Budget* (12th of 24 R). *Education & the Workforce* (21st of 27 R): Early Childhood, Youth & Families; Oversight & Investigations.

Group Ratings

	ADA	ACLU	AFS	LCV	CON	NTU	NFIB	COC	ACU	NTLC	CHC
1998	5	6	11	8	21	61	93	83	96	95	100
1997	5	—	13	—	20	68	—	90	100	—	—

National Journal Ratings

	1997 LIB — 1997 CONS			1998 LIB — 1998 CONS		
Economic	0%	—	90%	12%	—	85%
Social	20%	—	71%	14%	—	81%
Foreign	0%	—	88%	0%	—	93%

Key Votes of the 105th Congress

1. Clinton Budget Deal	Y	5. Puerto Rico Sthood. Ref.	N	9. Cut $ for B-2 Bombers	N
2. Education IRAs	Y	6. End Highway Set-asides	Y	10. Human Rights in China	N
3. Req. 2/3 to Raise Taxes	Y	7. School Prayer Amend.	Y	11. Withdraw Bosnia Troops	Y
4. Fast-track Trade	N	8. Ovrd. Part. Birth Veto	Y	12. End Cuban TV-Marti	N

Election Results

1998 general	Van Hilleary (R)	62,829	(60%)	($1,084,001)
	Jerry W. Cooper (D)	42,627	(40%)	($487,914)
1998 primary	Van Hilleary (R)	unopposed		
1996 general	Van Hilleary (R)	103,091	(58%)	($1,183,570)
	Mark Stewart (D)	73,331	(41%)	($586,987)

FIFTH DISTRICT

Nashville is the home of country music, the buckle of the Bible Belt, and in almost every way the heart of Tennessee. This was one of the first American cities established west of the Appalachians; Andrew Jackson built his Hermitage nearby above the banks of the Cumberland

River, and his political home base has remained Democratic ever since. It was the capital of Tennessee early on, just as it was, and still is, the center of the state's political life and discourse: home to *The Tennessean* (the *Nashville Banner* closed in 1998) and the state's biggest television market. Nashville is proud of its universities and of its columned Capitol and its Parthenon; this is perhaps the greatest center of Greek Revival architecture in America. Nashville is also firmly established as the religious publishing center of the country, producing more bibles than probably any other city in the world.

Country music, an art form that emerged from the hardscrabble, mountainous counties of eastern Tennessee, now constitutes a $2 billion-a-year business and is the nation's dominant radio format. The industry, run from a series of deceptively modest homes-turned-offices on what's called Music Row, congregated in Nashville because local radio station WSM possessed a clear channel from which to beam its weekly "barn dances" throughout the South in the 1920s; these later became known as the Grand Ole Opry, a venerable institution that survived its 1970s move from a downtown tabernacle to Opryland, a giant theme park on the banks of the Cumberland, closed the last day of 1997 to be re-opened as a mall in 2000.

For years, both the city's Parthenon-building elite and its religious leadership resented the growing local influence of country music; the former looked down on the music's uneducated practitioners, while the latter cringed at the musicians' unwholesome travails and occasional indecorous deaths. But all three groups made their peace in the 1970s, and since then, Nashville has become one of the South's boom cities—the fastest growing metropolitan area between Atlanta and Dallas-Fort Worth. New-generation industry moved in, with Nissan building a big plant in nearby Smyrna and General Motors setting up its Saturn plant in nearby Spring Hill. There were commercial and apartment real estate booms as well, though naturally followed by some busts. In the 1990s, Nashville and Tennessee got their first major-league sports teams, the NFL's Titans and the NHL's Predators. An agreeable quality of life, plenty of medium-wage, high-skill labor, a central location, and absence of urban strife and militant unions have all helped Nashville grow.

The 5th District of Tennessee includes all but one precinct of Nashville and Davidson County plus the bulk of increasingly suburban Robertson County to the north—but this is not all of metropolitan Nashville, now that development has spread into once-rural areas. The 5th is usually reliably Democratic in statewide elections, and to Congress it has long elected rather liberal Democrats: this is, after all, the home of the first Democratic president. It was also for several years the home of Al Gore, when he was a divinity student at Vanderbilt and reporter for *The Tennessean*, and is as much his home base as is his ancestral home near Carthage in Smith County.

The congressman from the 5th District is Bob Clement, a Democrat first elected in 1988. His father Frank Clement served three terms as governor of Tennessee. In 1972, at 29, Bob Clement was elected to the Public Service Commission; he served six years, went into private business, sat on the Tennessee Valley Authority board from 1979–81, and in 1982 lost a House race in the 7th District to Don Sundquist, the current governor, by 51%–49%. He then went into real estate and became president of Cumberland University. In 1987, after incumbent Bill Boner resigned one step ahead of an ethics investigation, Clement ran in a special election in the 5th, winning the Democratic primary with 40% (Tennessee has no runoff) and easily winning the January 1988 special election.

In the House, Clement has compiled a moderate voting record, voting for welfare reform and English as the official language, and taking leading roles in backing the 1997 balanced budget amendment and the International Freedom from Religious Persecution Act. He was a key sponsor of the law to criminalize the theft of another person's identity. He has supported music and arts education and has won funding for the restoration of buildings at historically black colleges and universities. He helped form the House Education Caucus, made up of former teachers and administrators in schools and colleges, and served as its co-chairman. He has proposed to eliminate soft money, saying he's "weary of the negative politics."

Clement has been re-elected by wide margins in the 5th District. He considered running for governor in 1994, but decided not to do so, and was not interested in running in 1998. He has been mentioned as a candidate in 2002.

Cook's Call. *Safe.* Clement has run up big margins of victory over the past 10 years and there is no reason to believe that he won't win easily in this Democratic-leaning district in 2000.

The People: Pop. 1990: 541,878; 4.8% rural; 12.2% age 65 + ; 75.5% White, 22.8% Black, 1.2% Asian, 0.3% Amer. Indian, 0.2% Other; 0.8% Hispanic Origin. Households: 47.1% married couple families; 21.3% married couple fams. w. children; 47.5% college educ.; median household income: $28,208; per capita income: $14,874; median house value: $74,500; median gross rent: $356.

1996 Presidential Vote			1992 Presidential Vote		
Clinton (D)	116,987	(55%)	Clinton (D)	112,795	(53%)
Dole (R)	82,053	(39%)	Bush (R)	79,398	(37%)
Perot (I)	9,727	(5%)	Perot (I)	21,531	(10%)

Rep. Bob Clement (D)

Elected Jan. 1988; b. Sept. 23, 1943, Nashville; home, Nashville; U. of TN, B.S. 1967, Memphis St. U., M.B.A. 1968; Christ Church; married (Mary).

Military Career: Army, 1969–71, Army Natl. Guard, 1971–present.

Elected Office: TN Public Svc. Comm., 1972–78.

Professional Career: Bd. of Dir., TN Valley Authority, 1979–81; Founder & owner, Bob Clement & Assoc., 1981–83; Owner, Charter Equities real estate, 1981–83; Pres., Cumberland U., 1983–87.

DC Office: 2229 RHOB 20515, 202-225-4311; Fax: 202-226-1035; Web site: www.house.gov/clement.

District Offices: N. Nashville, 615-320-1363; Nashville, 615-736-5295; Springfield, 615-384-6600.

Committees: *Budget* (13th of 19 D). *Transportation & Infrastructure* (8th of 34 D): Ground Transportation; Water Resources & Environment.

Group Ratings

	ADA	ACLU	AFS	LCV	CON	NTU	NFIB	COC	ACU	NTLC	CHC
1998	85	33	78	62	55	14	29	72	24	29	27
1997	55	—	63	—	65	31	—	80	25	—	—

National Journal Ratings

	1997 LIB — 1997 CONS			1998 LIB — 1998 CONS		
Economic	57%	—	43%	59%	—	41%
Social	56%	—	43%	57%	—	43%
Foreign	56%	—	42%	61%	—	37%

Key Votes of the 105th Congress

1. Clinton Budget Deal	Y	5. Puerto Rico Sthood. Ref.	Y	9. Cut $ for B-2 Bombers	Y
2. Education IRAs	Y	6. End Highway Set-asides	N	10. Human Rights in China	Y
3. Req. 2/3 to Raise Taxes	N	7. School Prayer Amend.	Y	11. Withdraw Bosnia Troops	N
4. Fast-track Trade	Y	8. Ovrd. Part. Birth Veto	Y	12. End Cuban TV-Marti	Y

Election Results

1998 general	Bob Clement (D)	....	74,611	(83%)	($282,219)
	William M. Lancaster (I)	....	6,162	(7%)	
	Al Borgman (I)	....	4,983	(6%)	
	Gary I. Wordon (I)	....	4,345	(5%)	
1998 primary	Bob Clement (D)	....	unopposed		
1996 general	Bob Clement (D)	....	140,264	(72%)	($299,403)
	Steven L. Edmondson (R)	....	46,201	(24%)	
	Others	....	7,318	(4%)	

SIXTH DISTRICT

The rolling countryside of middle Tennessee, west of the Cumberland Plateau and the last chain of Appalachians, has been called "the dimple of the universe." This is hilly and fertile land, cut by deep rivers ambling along in S-curves. The terrain here was never much suited for plantation crops; this has long been a land of small farmers and small county seat towns, nestled amid what people here regard as some of the loveliest scenery on earth. Middle Tennessee has also been one of the heartlands of the Democratic Party. It was the political home base of Andrew Jackson and supported him nearly unanimously; during the Civil War, though it had very few slaves, it resisted the invading Union armies. For 140 years after Jackson, it voted solidly Democratic and elected as its congressmen some of the luminaries of the national Democratic Party: James K. Polk (1825–39), speaker of the House and later president; Cordell Hull (1907–21, 1923–31), later senator and secretary of State; Albert Gore Sr., (1939–53), later senator; and Albert Gore Jr., (1977–85), later senator and now vice president.

The 6th Congressional District of Tennessee includes 14 middle Tennessee counties east and south of Nashville, plus one precinct of Nashville itself. The heritage here is old and rural, but economic growth has fanned out into the farmland from Nashville, evident in thousands of jobs created by Japanese companies and American startups, firms fleeing the North and entrepreneurs fleeing Texas. Many new voters here are Republican, not only in the affluent suburbs of Williamson County just south of Nashville, but in the more modest suburbs spreading to the east. The 6th District voted for the Clinton-Gore ticket by 47%–40% in 1992, a margin that was decisive but which would not have impressed Andrew Jackson. In 1996, however, it voted for the Dole-Kemp ticket 47%–45%.

The congressman from the 6th District is Bart Gordon, a Democrat first elected in 1984 when Al Gore gave up his House seat to run for the Senate. Gordon grew up in Murfreesboro in Rutherford County and went to college there. He practiced law and became Tennessee Democratic chairman in 1981: politics has been most of his life. In 1984, he ran a computerized fund-raising operation and voter contact system—then a novelty in this district where a personal handshake from a candidate was the norm. He won a multi-candidate primary with 28% of the vote—there is no runoff in Tennessee—and won the general election 63%–37%.

In the House, Gordon has used his insider skills to build a close relationship with the Democratic leadership, and got a seat on the Rules Committee in 1987. He went after trade schools with high student loan default rates, even posing in 1991 as a student (though he was 42 at the time) with an NBC investigative unit. He passed new accountability provisions for the federal financial aid system in 1992 and claims that defaults have dropped from 22% of loans in 1990 to 12% in 1993—a significant saving for taxpayers. He also helped pass a proposal to ban Pell grants to prison inmates, which amazingly enough has saved between $70 million and $200 million a year. Gordon, who lost his seat on Rules and moved to Commerce when the Republicans took control of Congress, has consistently worked to limit children's access to adult material, by phone, on television, and on the Internet. With a similar ear for constituents' complaints, he has opposed construction of a temporary nuclear waste dump in middle Tennessee. He has also opposed Republican proposals to sell the Southeastern Power Administration, which he says will put the dam-created lakes on the Tennessee and Cumberland rivers up for auction.

Still, Gordon's moderate-to-liberal voting record and his ties to the Democratic leadership in this Republican-trending district have caused him trouble in the 1990s. In 1992, after winning four races with over 60% of the vote, Gordon won by only 57%–41%. In 1994 he faced Steve Gill, a lawyer from Williamson County and a veteran of a championship basketball team at the University of Tennessee. In a good Republican year, Gill voiced an anti-Clinton message—balanced budget amendment, tougher sentences, term limits. Gordon spent $1,386,000, with $608,000 of it from PACs—more than Gill spent altogether. Gill ran ahead, 52%–48%, in the fringes of Nashville, where most of the votes are cast. But Gordon carried the smaller rural counties 58%–42%, for a slim overall margin of 51%–49%.

After the election, Gill never stopped running, and for that matter neither did Gordon. Much of the dialogue stayed the same. Traveling the district in an 18-wheel tractor-trailer, Gill hit Gordon as a liberal who voted 40 times for tax increases in 12 years and voted himself a $45,000 pay increase. Gordon ran an ad charging that Gill used campaign money to get his personal car back after it had been repossessed and that he failed to pay property taxes on time, though Gordon later offered to pull his ad in order to "take the high road." Gordon courted local tobacco farmers, even as former local farmer Al Gore was pummeling the tobacco industry at the Chicago convention. Gill spent $1.1 million, but Gordon spent $1.6 million, raising—despite Republican control of the House—$743,000 from PACs. Gordon ended up winning, 54%–42%, with 51% in the counties outside Nashville and 64% in the rural counties.

Gordon faced another serious challenge in 1998. Walt Massey, an engineer and Persian Gulf war veteran who had polled only 8% in the 1996 Republican primary, beat three opponents in the 1998 primary—insurance executive Porter Stark (who outspent Massey 2–1), attorney Dennis Nordhoff and Putnam County Property Assessor Byron "Low Tax" Looper. (Looper would later be arrested and charged with the October 1998 murder of state Senator Tommy Burks, whom he was running against; Burks's wife won as a write-in candidate.) Massey, citing "Tennessee common sense and strong Christian values," made an issue of the Clinton scandals in the primary and in the general. He sent several thousand likely Republican voters direct mail with the word "SCANDAL" partly obscuring images of Clinton and the White House. "We'd rather talk about defense or tax policy, but this is the thing people want to talk about," Massey's campaign manager David Allison told *The Washington Post*. In a pro-incumbent year Gordon won 55%–45%; he won 63% in the rural counties but only 46% in the Nashville area. Whether Gordon can continue to hold this seat may depend on redistricting after the 2000 Census: the suburban counties around Nashville are the fastest-growing parts of Tennessee, and if the 6th District loses the small rural counties it will be very tempting for Republican challengers.

Cook's Call. *Potentially Competitive.* There's not much doubt that the 6th district is marginal, but it's pretty unlikely that Gordon will be upset. Aside from his close-call in the 1994 Republican tidal wave, when he won with just 51%, Gordon has managed to consistently pull between 54%–77%, typically better in presidential years.

The People: Pop. 1990: 542,002; 53.9% rural; 11.4% age 65 +; 93.3% White, 5.7% Black, 0.6% Asian, 0.2% Amer. Indian, 0.2% Other; 0.6% Hispanic Origin. Households: 65.2% married couple families; 33.5% married couple fams. w. children; 37.8% college educ.; median household income: $29,234; per capita income: $13,286; median house value: $71,400; median gross rent: $301.

1996 Presidential Vote			1992 Presidential Vote		
Dole (R)	112,827	(47%)	Clinton (D)	109,895	(47%)
Clinton (D)	107,821	(45%)	Bush (R)	93,036	(40%)
Perot (I)	15,375	(6%)	Perot (I)	28,151	(12%)

Rep. Bart Gordon (D)

Elected 1984; b. Jan. 24, 1949, Murfreesboro; home, Murfreesboro; Middle TN St. U., B.S. 1971, U. of TN, J.D. 1973; United Methodist; married (Leslie).

Military Career: Army Reserves, 1971–72.

Professional Career: Practicing atty., 1974–84; Chmn., TN Dem. Party, 1981–83.

DC Office: 2368 RHOB 20515, 202-225-4231; Fax: 202-225-6887; Web site: www.house.gov/gordon.

District Offices: Cookeville, 615-528-5907; Murfreesboro, 615-896-1986.

Committees: *Commerce* (9th of 24 D): Energy & Power; Telecommunications, Trade & Consumer Protection. *Science* (3d of 23 D): Space & Aeronautics (RMM); Technology.

Group Ratings

	ADA	ACLU	AFS	LCV	CON	NTU	NFIB	COC	ACU	NTLC	CHC
1998	90	38	89	62	2	22	50	72	36	39	25
1997	60	—	63	—	42	41	—	70	36	—	—

National Journal Ratings

	1997 LIB — 1997 CONS		1998 LIB — 1998 CONS	
Economic	56%	— 43%	58%	— 42%
Social	58%	— 40%	51%	— 49%
Foreign	51%	— 49%	56%	— 42%

Key Votes of the 105th Congress

1. Clinton Budget Deal	Y	5. Puerto Rico Sthood. Ref.	N	9. Cut $ for B-2 Bombers	*
2. Education IRAs	N	6. End Highway Set-asides	N	10. Human Rights in China	N
3. Req. 2/3 to Raise Taxes	Y	7. School Prayer Amend.	Y	11. Withdraw Bosnia Troops	N
4. Fast-track Trade	N	8. Ovrd. Part. Birth Veto	Y	12. End Cuban TV-Marti	N

Election Results

1998 general	Bart Gordon (D)	75,055	(55%)	($981,306)
	Walt Massey (R)	62,277	(45%)	($417,743)
1998 primary	Bart Gordon (D)	unopposed		
1996 general	Bart Gordon (D)	123,846	(54%)	($1,609,419)
	Steve Gill (R)	94,599	(42%)	($1,107,850)
	Jim Coffer (I)	9,125	(4%)	($1,113)

SEVENTH DISTRICT

Rural Tennessee north of Mississippi is one of the most sparsely settled areas in the state. Along each side of the Tennessee River, as it flows north and widens out into Kentucky Lake amid heavy forests, are small rural communities with colorful names like Spot, Only and Bucksnort; many go back to pre-Civil War days and have not grown much since. Farther west the land is flatter and more open, a northward extension economically and demographically of the northern Mississippi farmlands, with cotton fields and a large black rural population. This mostly empty land is bounded on two sides by large metropolitan areas, Nashville to the east and Memphis to the west.

The 7th Congressional District spans this territory, from the Cheatham County suburban fringe of Nashville, west across the Tennessee River and south to the Mississippi border and finally to the white neighborhoods on the east side of Memphis and Shelby County. It is a mixed district politically. Most of the rural counties are traditionally Democratic, with a few Republican exceptions, while the fringe of Nashville is mixed and the 7th District's portion of Memphis is, like all white parts of Memphis, heavily Republican. The balance has usually tipped toward Republicans, though the lines in Memphis and Shelby County were altered by 1990s redistricting to help the Democrats.

The congressman from the 7th District is Ed Bryant, a Republican elected in 1994 to replace Republican Don Sundquist, who was elected governor. Bryant is from Jackson in west Tennessee, went to school at Ole Miss, served in the Army, taught law at West Point and practiced law in Tennessee starting in 1978. In 1991, President Bush, on the recommendation of Don Sundquist, made him U.S. attorney in West Tennessee; Bryant left that post in 1993 in a dispute over jury selection in the bank fraud trial of then-Memphis Democratic Congressman Harold Ford Sr. The case was hugely visible and controversial, which gave Bryant wide celebrity.

In the 1994 Republican primary, Bryant lost Shelby County to Germantown Mayor Charles Salvaggio. But he won in all but one of the rural counties by enough votes to win overall 35%–33% (Tennessee has no runoff). The Democratic nomination went to Harold Byrd, a former state legislator and former aide to Senator Jim Sasser. Bryant called for term limits, congressional staff cuts and the conversion of closed military bases into prisons; he proposed that half of all congressional campaign contributions must be from in-state. Byrd called for market-oriented health care reform, a balanced budget amendment and the line-item veto: a pretty conservative platform. Outside Shelby County the race was close—51%–48% for Bryant. But Bryant carried Shelby County with 72% for a solid overall win, 60%–39%.

In the House, Bryant was a visible co-sponsor of the Contract With America crime bills, and also sponsored bills that doubled the penalty for prison escapes from five to 10 years, for a life-without-parole sentence in military law, and for trying federal judges in different circuits from where they served. He was especially strong for *habeas corpus* reform, but he also argued that measures like midnight basketball were useful when properly administered. In response to a bill that was blocking the move of the Houston Oilers to Tennessee, Bryant proposed the Sports Relocation Reform Act. In 1998 he helped open a new veterans' clinic in Clarkville. After struggling with the issue, Bryant supported normal trade relations status with China in June 1997. He successfully sponsored legislation to repeal taxes that Tennessee residents working in Kentucky's Fort Campbell had to pay the state of Kentucky.

Bryant's 1996 race was still close in the rural areas; Bryant lost seven counties, including the area around Clarksville and Fort Campbell. But he carried the Shelby County portion of the district 81%–17%, for a 65%–33% victory. After a relatively quiet two terms, Bryant leapt onto the national stage as one of the managers of President Clinton's Senate impeachment trial. "He has lost his moral leadership, his moral authority that all of us expect the president to have," Bryant said in September 1998. Bryant was the House manager picked to interview former White House intern Monica Lewinsky; Bryant explained his selection by citing the rumor that his subdued style had made him the manager Lewinsky "disliked the least."

Bryant was unopposed in 1998. But Democrats were trying to recruit candidates in early 1999, including state Senator Pete Springer and state Representative Kim McMillan.

Cook's Call. *Safe.* While there has been much talk about the potential backlash against House managers, Bryant has little to worry about in this heavily Republican district that has never given Clinton more than 41% of the vote.

The People: Pop. 1990: 542,270; 42.8% rural; 10.6% age 65+; 86.2% White, 12.3% Black, 0.9% Asian, 0.2% Amer. Indian, 0.3% Other; 1% Hispanic Origin. Households: 63.7% married couple families; 33% married couple fams. w. children; 42.5% college educ.; median household income: $29,242; per capita income: $13,758; median house value: $69,600; median gross rent: $337.

1996 Presidential Vote

Dole (R)	122,177	(54%)
Clinton (D)	92,802	(41%)
Perot (I)	10,965	(5%)

1992 Presidential Vote

Bush (R)	114,544	(50%)
Clinton (D)	91,644	(40%)
Perot (I)	22,486	(10%)

Rep. Ed Bryant (R)

Elected 1994; b. Sept. 7, 1948, Jackson; home, Henderson; U. of MS, B.A. 1970, J.D. 1972; Protestant; married (Cyndi).

Military Career: Army, Judge Advocate General Corps, 1970–78; Instructor, West Point Military Acad., 1977–78.

Professional Career: Practicing atty., 1978–90; US Atty. for W. TN, 1991–93.

DC Office: 408 CHOB 20515, 202-225-2811; Fax: 202-225-2989; Web site: www.house.gov/bryant.

District Offices: Clarksville, 931-503-0391; Columbia, 931-381-8100; Memphis, 901-382-5811.

Committees: *Commerce* (28th of 29 R): Energy & Power; Health and Environment; Oversight & Investigations. *Judiciary* (10th of 21 R): Commercial & Administrative Law.

Group Ratings

	ADA	ACLU	AFS	LCV	CON	NTU	NFIB	COC	ACU	NTLC	CHC
1998	0	6	0	8	13	50	93	100	100	100	100
1997	5	—	13	—	27	62	—	100	100	—	—

National Journal Ratings

	1997 LIB — 1997 CONS			1998 LIB — 1998 CONS		
Economic	0%	—	90%	0%	—	88%
Social	20%	—	71%	14%	—	81%
Foreign	21%	—	79%	7%	—	83%

Key Votes of the 105th Congress

1. Clinton Budget Deal	Y	5. Puerto Rico Sthood. Ref.	N	9. Cut $ for B-2 Bombers	N
2. Education IRAs	Y	6. End Highway Set-asides	Y	10. Human Rights in China	Y
3. Req. 2/3 to Raise Taxes	Y	7. School Prayer Amend.	Y	11. Withdraw Bosnia Troops	Y
4. Fast-track Trade	Y	8. Ovrd. Part. Birth Veto	Y	12. End Cuban TV-Marti	N

Election Results

1998 general	Ed Bryant (R)	unopposed		($392,944)
1998 primary	Ed Bryant (R)	unopposed		
1996 general	Ed Bryant (R)	126,737	(65%)	($649,783)
	Don Trotter (D)	64,512	(33%)	($315,501)

EIGHTH DISTRICT

West of Nashville and the lakes along the Tennessee River and north of Memphis, the rivers roll lazily through flat or gently rolling land that almost could be the northern end of Mississippi. Cotton and soybeans are the main crops; more blacks remain in rural areas here than in any other part of Tennessee, a reminder of its old plantation economy. The towns here are small, edged in by farm fields; the river bottoms, often flooded, are heavily forested. Here is Henning, the home town of Alex Haley, where he used to sit on his porch and listen to his aunts tell him stories about slave ships and the Civil War that in time became *Roots*.

The 8th Congressional District includes much of this west Tennessee farmland, from the lakes west to the Mississippi; its largest city is Jackson, but it includes the northern fringe of Memphis. Historically, this is Democratic country; Republicans haven't represented most of the counties that make up the 8th since the end of Reconstruction. The region trended Republican in national races in the 1960s and 1970s, then turned back toward the Democrats with the help of some smart local politicians. One of them is Ned McWherter, first elected to the legislature from Weakley County in 1968, speaker from 1973–86, then governor until 1994; another was Congressman Ed Jones, elected in a 1969 special election over a Republican and a George Wallace-supported independent in a race which presaged the survival of conservative Democrats in rural Southern districts for another quarter century.

The congressman from the 8th District is John Tanner, a Democrat elected in 1988. Tanner grew up in Obion County, went to college and law school at the University of Tennessee, served four years in the Navy, then practiced law in Union City. In 1976, at 32, he successfully ran for the Tennessee House, where he served 12 years. In 1988, when Jones retired, he ran for Congress and won with a whopping 66% in a four-candidate primary and 62% in the general.

Tanner's voting record put him solidly in the middle of the Democratic House, a little to the left of midpoint in the Republican House. He has worked on local issues, promoting the City of Millington and then getting a grant to redevelop its Naval Air Station's surplus property. He successfully opposed a 1995 move to end federal payments to the Tennessee Valley Authority, which would have cut funding for the Land Between the Lakes park; in 1997 the TVA director called for an end to federal payments and spinning off of such functions to state governments and federal agencies, but $50 million in funding of non-power operations, like the Land Between the Lakes park, was voted in 1998. Tanner has sponsored research on the New Madrid Fault, which produced three great earthquakes in 1811–12. He wants to eliminate estate taxes on family-owned farms and small businesses and in early 1997 opposed the IRS's current-year taxation of farmers' income from deferred payment contracts. In 1999 he joined Jennifer Dunn in sponsoring legislation to eliminate the death tax. Tanner has long supported the balanced budget amendment and line-item veto, though he has opposed some Republican versions.

In 1992, Tanner could have been a senator for the asking. Governor McWherter was ready to appoint him to succeed Al Gore, but Tanner refused the post and chose instead to stay in the House. If he had accepted he might have become a more nationally prominent figure, but he would also have had to defend the seat against Fred Thompson in what turned out to be the very Republican year of 1994. Instead, Tanner has become a major force in the House. He is one of the founders of a group of conservative Democrats called the Blue Dogs who advanced their own proposals for balancing the budget and instituting welfare reform. Tanner co-sponsored the Blue Dogs' welfare reform proposal, which, he claims with some legitimacy, was "the genesis for the broad welfare reform plan that the President signed" in August 1996. When House Republicans revived the welfare issue in July 1996, Tanner passed amendments allowing states to provide non-cash assistance such as baby formula and diapers and providing that no one loses Medicaid because of federally-imposed time limits; he also grandfathered in time limits of the states' currently approved reform plans, like Tennessee's bipartisan Families First. These provisions helped win the support of half the House's Democrats and went into the final Welfare Reform Act. In 1998, Tanner voted against funding for the National Endowment for the Arts. He supported fast-track trade authority in November 1997.

In the 8th District Tanner has held more than 1,000 town hall meetings and has been re-elected by wide margins. In 1996 he carried the Shelby County (Memphis) portion of the district by only 51%–43%, but carried the rest of the district 71%–27%, for a 67%–30% victory. After the election he was named to the Ways and Means Committee; his 8th District predecessor Jere

Cooper served there from 1932–57, the last three years as chairman. In 1998, Tanner was unopposed, and has been mentioned as a possible candidate for governor in 2002.

Cook's Call. *Safe.* Tanner's Blue Dog voting record and down-home style have helped to safely insulate him in this Democratic-leaning district.

The People: Pop. 1990: 541,852; 52.4% rural; 14.7% age 65+; 79.5% White, 19.6% Black, 0.4% Asian, 0.2% Amer. Indian, 0.2% Other; 0.7% Hispanic Origin. Households: 59.3% married couple families; 28.3% married couple fams. w. children; 29.7% college educ.; median household income: $22,622; per capita income: $10,712; median house value: $47,400; median gross rent: $219.

1996 Presidential Vote			1992 Presidential Vote		
Clinton (D)	98,925	(50%)	Clinton (D)	101,328	(48%)
Dole (R)	85,856	(44%)	Bush (R)	89,533	(42%)
Perot (I)	10,835	(6%)	Perot (I)	19,328	(9%)

Rep. John S. Tanner (D)

Elected 1988; b. Sept. 22, 1944, Halls; home, Union City; U. of TN, B.S. 1966, J.D. 1968; Disciples of Christ; married (Betty Ann).

Military Career: Navy, 1968–72; TN Natl. Guard, 1974–present.

Elected Office: TN House of Reps., 1976–88.

Professional Career: Practicing atty., 1973–88.

DC Office: 1127 LHOB 20515, 202-225-4714; Fax: 202-225-1765; Web site: www.house.gov/tanner.

District Offices: Jackson, 901-423-4848; Millington, 901-873-5690; Union City, 901-885-7070.

Committees: *Ways & Means* (13th of 16 D): Social Security.

Group Ratings

	ADA	ACLU	AFS	LCV	CON	NTU	NFIB	COC	ACU	NTLC	CHC
1998	60	31	63	38	76	21	43	88	41	43	25
1997	40	—	38	—	86	33	—	80	40	—	—

National Journal Ratings

	1997 LIB — 1997 CONS			1998 LIB — 1998 CONS		
Economic	55%	—	45%	56%	—	43%
Social	58%	—	40%	47%	—	52%
Foreign	55%	—	44%	55%	—	45%

Key Votes of the 105th Congress

1. Clinton Budget Deal	N	5. Puerto Rico Sthood. Ref.	N	9. Cut $ for B-2 Bombers	Y
2. Education IRAs	Y	6. End Highway Set-asides	N	10. Human Rights in China	N
3. Req. 2/3 to Raise Taxes	*	7. School Prayer Amend.	Y	11. Withdraw Bosnia Troops	N
4. Fast-track Trade	Y	8. Ovrd. Part. Birth Veto	Y	12. End Cuban TV-Marti	Y

Election Results

1998 general	John S. Tanner (D)	unopposed		($369,763)
1998 primary	John S. Tanner (D)	unopposed		
1996 general	John S. Tanner (D)	123,681	(67%)	($395,726)
	Tom Watson (R)	55,024	(30%)	($14,478)
	Others	5,193	(3%)	

NINTH DISTRICT

Memphis, the largest city in Tennessee, is in the state's far southwestern corner, 500 miles from the Appalachian border with Virginia but only 20 miles from Mississippi's cotton fields. Some 41% of metropolitan Memphis's residents are black—one of the highest percentages in the country and evidence of the city's economic heritage as a capital of the Cotton Kingdom. Big Mississippi planters used to come north to sell their crop in the courtyard of the Peabody Hotel, then make financial arrangements for the next growing season.

Such facts have shaped the city's most celebrated tradition, the blues—a musical form worlds apart from Nashville's country music. Whereas country music emerged from mountainous, mainly white eastern Tennessee, the Memphis sound originated from the self-taught musical stylings of poor, rural blacks in the Mississippi Delta. Throughout the first half of the twentieth century, the most talented black musicians migrated north to Memphis and congregated downtown on Beale Street. The blues sound was later adapted by Elvis Presley, a poor white from rural Mississippi, in pivotal sessions in July 1954 at Sam Phillips' Sun Studio in Memphis—the birth of rock 'n' roll, and the beginnings of an Elvis cult that long outlived the man. In the early 1960s, Memphis once again became the crucible of a new sound, soul music, which emerged as a counterpoint to rock, its increasingly white-dominated cousin. For some years Memphis tried to live down all this musical heritage; much of Beale Street was razed and set on a misguided path towards urban renewal. But more recently, the city has come to recognize its history as an asset, nowhere more so than Graceland, Presley's garishly decorated mansion, which attracts hordes of musical pilgrims from all over the world.

Music is not the city's only asset. Geographically central in the U.S., Memphis is the home of the first supermarket chain (the Piggly Wiggly, founded in 1916; its symbol, Mr. Pig, was slimmed down in 1998) and the first Holiday Inn. Home of the world's busiest cargo airport, Memphis calls itself "America's distribution center": by far its biggest employer is FedEx, which ships all of its domestic packages in and out of Memphis Airport every night. Despite such enterprises, racial discord has scarred the political life of Memphis. It is the city where Martin Luther King Jr. was assassinated in 1968; the site of the murder, the Lorraine Motel, was recently converted into a civil rights museum. Even today, the resurgent Beale Street is one of the few racially integrated spaces in the city, a division that holds equally true in voting. Blacks vote almost unanimously Democratic; whites vote Republican by percentages almost as high. The 9th Congressional District consists of most of the city of Memphis and a bit of its suburban fringe; in 1992, 54% of its residents were black.

The congressman from the 9th District is Harold Ford Jr., who was elected in 1996 at the age of 26; his father, Harold Ford Sr., had been elected at 29 and represented the 9th for 22 years. Harold Ford Jr. grew up in Memphis until 1979, when the family moved to Washington. He graduated from the elite St. Albans School, a classmate of Jesse Jackson's son Yusef, then graduated from the University of Pennsylvania in 1992. He worked on his father's 1992 and 1994 campaigns and on the Clinton transition team and as a special assistant in the Economic Development Administration (and thus technically worked for Commerce Secretary Ron Brown, whom he has praised as a "profound influence"). In 1993 he went off to the University of Michigan Law School.

The Ford family had long been prominent as morticians; Harold Ford Sr. was elected to the state legislature in 1970, at 25, and moved up to the House by beating a white Republican incumbent in 1974. He became chairman of the Ways and Means subcommittee handling welfare in 1981, but lost the post when he was indicted in April 1987 for receiving allegedly illegal loans from political backers; a Memphis jury hung 8–4 along racial lines for acquittal in April 1990, and a jury of 11 whites and 1 black acquitted him in April 1993, at which point he became chairman again. All the while he remained active in Memphis politics. In April 1996, Ford Sr. announced his retirement and Ford Jr. announced his candidacy. Willie Herenton, Memphis's first black mayor and a Ford rival, looked for a candidate who would challenge the younger Ford, but only liberal state Senator Steve Cohen jumped in the race. Cohen's effort faltered when he lost the endorsement of public employee unions that he had always supported, and Ford rolled on to a 60%–34% primary win. In the general, "Jr."—as Ford's campaign buttons read—won 61%–37%, slightly better than the 58% his father had won during his last three general elections.

In the House, Harold Ford Jr. formed a Congressional Children's Caucus and said that his goal was to give every child access to a high-quality education. He sought additional funding for school construction, but he also backed efforts to end "social promotion" and opposes the teaching of Ebonics, and he favored the introduction of "competition, competency and accountability" into public schools. He acknowledges that he comes from a different political generation than his father, and that his views are less liberal. Upon entering the House, Ford joined the moderate New Democrat Coalition; when the centrist Democratic Leadership Council launched *Blueprint*, a policy journal, in 1998, it spotlighted Ford as one of the party's up-and-coming moderates. Ford angered some liberals at home by supporting an amendment to ban flag burning. Ford even took a shot at House Minority Leader Richard Gephardt—in no less a forum than a *New York Times Magazine* profile of himself—by rejecting Gephardt's assertion that "New Democrats . . . too often market a political strategy masquerading as policy."

Ford easily won re-election in 1998, with 79% of the vote, which means that he won a solid majority from whites as well as blacks. Tennessee Democrats, eager for a strong challenger to Senator Bill Frist in 2000, have urged him to run; he reaches the constitutionally required age of 30 in May 2000. In early 1999, he seemed disinclined to make that race, but he started making appearances around the state. He could be a strong candidate in the open-seat race for governor in 2002, or for the Senate seats Frist and Fred Thompson have promised not to run for in 2006 and 2008, when Ford will still be in his 30s.

Cook's Call. *Safe.* There are rumors that Ford is contemplating a run against Republican Senator Bill Frist in 2000. Whether or not he ultimately decides to do so, this solidly Democratic seat will remain in Democratic hands.

The People: Pop. 1990: 541,710; 0.2% rural; 13% age 65 + ; 39.5% White, 59.4% Black, 0.7% Asian, 0.2% Amer. Indian, 0.2% Other; 0.6% Hispanic Origin. Households: 39.7% married couple families; 18.7% married couple fams. w. children; 42.1% college educ.; median household income: $22,117; per capita income: $11,296; median house value: $55,700; median gross rent: $272.

1996 Presidential Vote

Clinton (D) 138,234 (71%)
Dole (R) 51,767 (27%)
Perot (I) 3,862 (2%)

1992 Presidential Vote

Clinton (D) 151,590 (66%)
Bush (R) 68,358 (30%)
Perot (I) 9,400 (4%)

1502   TENNESSEE

Rep. Harold E. Ford, Jr. (D)

Elected 1996; b. May 11, 1970, Memphis; home, Memphis; U. of PA, B.A. 1992, U. of MI, J.D. 1996; Baptist; single.

Professional Career: Staff Aide, U.S. Senate Budget Cmte., 1992; Spec. Asst., Clinton/Gore Transition Team, 1992; Spec. Asst., DNC Chairs Ron Brown & Alexis Herman, 1993; Spec. Asst., U.S. Dept. of Commerce, 1993.

DC Office: 325 CHOB 20515, 202-225-3265; Fax: 202-225-5663; Web site: www.house.gov/ford.

District Office: Memphis, 901-544-4131.

Committees: *Education & the Workforce* (19th of 22 D): Early Childhood, Youth & Families; Oversight & Investigations. *Government Reform* (18th of 19 D): Census; National Economic Growth, Natural Resources & Regulatory Affairs.

Group Ratings

	ADA	ACLU	AFS	LCV	CON	NTU	NFIB	COC	ACU	NTLC	CHC
1998	80	64	86	23	55	14	30	62	14	13	0
1997	85	—	88	—	62	26	—	60	8	—	—

National Journal Ratings

	1997 LIB — 1997 CONS			1998 LIB — 1998 CONS		
Economic	64%	—	35%	70%	—	30%
Social	73%	—	24%	66%	—	33%
Foreign	72%	—	26%	84%	—	11%

Key Votes of the 105th Congress

1. Clinton Budget Deal	N	5. Puerto Rico Sthood. Ref.	Y
2. Education IRAs	N	6. End Highway Set-asides	N
3. Req. 2/3 to Raise Taxes	N	7. School Prayer Amend.	Y
4. Fast-track Trade	Y	8. Ovrd. Part. Birth Veto	*

9. Cut $ for B-2 Bombers	Y
10. Human Rights in China	Y
11. Withdraw Bosnia Troops	N
12. End Cuban TV-Marti	Y

Election Results

1998 general	Harold E. Ford Jr. (D)	75,428	(79%)	($521,544)
	Claude Burdikoff (R)	18,078	(19%)	
	Others	2,276	(2%)	
1998 primary	Harold E. Ford Jr. (D)	unopposed		
1996 general	Harold E. Ford Jr. (D)	116,345	(61%)	($679,843)
	Rod DeBerry (R)	70,951	(37%)	($95,687)
	Others	3,118	(2%)	

TEXAS

Texas is a country-sized state, one of four (the others are California, Vermont and Hawaii) to have been an independent republic, but the only one to have had national ambitions throughout its history. Texas has been the second largest state in area since Alaska was admitted to the Union in 1959; it became the second largest in population in 1994, when it passed New York. The key to Texas's history is that this is a society with no aristocratic past, a state not formed by plantation owners or plutocrats but by dirt farmers. Texas was founded by Southerners, mainly Tennesseans, who wanted to establish their own republic in what were empty spaces within the borders of Mexico, a republic with Anglo-Saxon freedoms and black slavery. They defended their dream to the death at the Alamo and to a bloody victory at San Jacinto; they entered the Union willingly in 1845 and left it enthusiastically in 1861. The Texas that emerged from the Civil War was still young and poor; it was only in 1901 that oil was discovered at Spindletop, and the Texas wildcatters made their first fortunes.

Without the underpinnings and burdens of tradition, 20th Century Texas has produced fabulous wealth, generously rewarding success while unforgiving of error. It has respect for learning and style—think of its great universities, or of Neiman Marcus—but it revels in rough manners and western wear. Texans are prone to wild swings in fortune—think of Sam Houston, or the great wildcatters, or Lyndon Johnson. And in the late 20th Century, Texans, for all their history of slavery and segregation, have proved open to immigrants and friendly with their neighbors in Mexico. NAFTA, the opening up of the border and the coming together of these two countries which are at such different economic levels and have such different cultures, is a project mainly of Texans of both political parties, of President George Bush and Treasury Secretary Lloyd Bentsen, Governors Ann Richards and George W. Bush. At the same time, Texas has become a high-tech powerhouse, a country with some of the nation's most creative businesses. But its success is not just economic. There are large elements of heroism—some mythical, some genuine—in the Texas history that every high school student here learns. "What Texans dream, Texans can do," George W. Bush likes to say.

Their dreams, sometimes seemingly unrealistic, have taken them far. Texas started off as a marchland on the border of the Third World, with an economy based on commodities, mainly cotton, whose prices were in long-term decline. Its farmers felt like part of a colonial economy controlled by bankers and Wall Street financiers. After Spindletop, Texas became the nation's— and for a time the world's—leading producer of oil. But oil prices, too, fell in free markets, and were propped up by politicians—the 1936 "hot oil" act that Sam Rayburn, as chairman of the Commerce Committee, pushed through and the oil depletion allowance maintained for years by Rayburn when he was speaker, Senate Majority Leader Johnson, Senate Finance Committee Chairman Bentsen and others. These politicians also got subsidies for cotton growers and defense plants and space facilities in World War II and through the long years of the Cold War. Most Texas voters stayed Democratic up to 1970 because of Confederate memories, New Deal affections, and the clout and competence of Texas's Democratic politicians.

But as Texas's economy became complex and creative, Texas's politics changed from a mostly Democratic effort to prop up the price of commodities to an increasingly Republican push to open up markets. By the 1970s Texas's economy was no longer dependent on raw commodities. The "awl bidness" here is less a matter of extracting oil from Texas; instead, Texas has the greatest concentration of high-skill specialists in extracting oil and natural gas in any part of the world. Also, beginning in the 1960s Texas has become a center for high tech, with the critical mass of knowledge and finances needed to produce firms like Texas Instruments and Ross Perot's Electronic Data Systems, and a university infrastructure in the University of

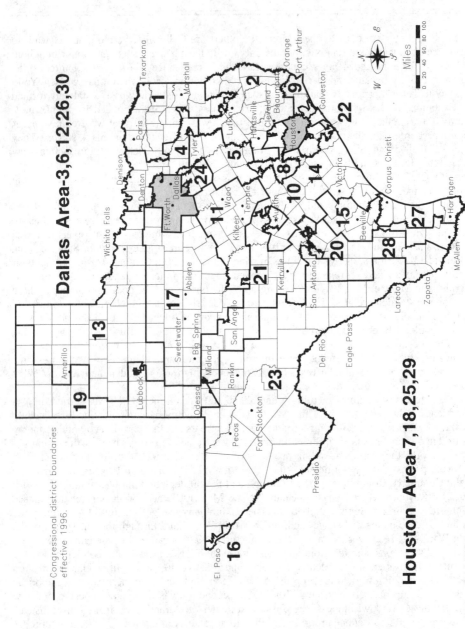

Dallas Area-3,6,12,26,30

Houston Area-7,18,25,29

Congressional district boundaries effective 1996.

Copyright ©1997 by Election Data Services, Inc.

Texas and Texas A&M to match the highway system that ties the state together. The Dallas-Fort Worth Metroplex is rich with defense contractors, big and small, and small firms that have become large with exports to Mexico. Houston is home to firms like Compaq, the sudden computer giant, to many of the high-tech spinoffs from the space program, and to the enormous Texas Medical Center. San Antonio, with the Air Force's prime hospital, has big medical technology and biotech industries. Austin, as UT doubled its number of engineering professors, is a high-tech center vying for second place after Silicon Valley in California. Texas's low taxes (and lack of a state income tax) helped attract corporate headquarters like American Airlines, GTE, J.C. Penney and Exxon. The result has been to put Dallas-Fort Worth and Houston solidly on the list of the top ten metro areas, ahead of old industrial centers like Cleveland, Pittsburgh and St. Louis, and threatening to overtake Detroit, Boston and Philadelphia.

The early and middle 1980s were rough in Texas, when oil prices crashed and the commercial real estate market collapsed and banks failed in the wake of the politically-created savings and loan crisis (Speaker Jim Wright was trying to give the S&Ls the protection Rayburn and Johnson used to give cotton farmers and oil drillers, but it could not be sustained). Defense spending cuts in the early 1990s hurt as well. But Texas has stormed ahead nevertheless. It has created more jobs in the 1990s than any other state. The Resolution Trust Corporation disposed of failed S&L assets, and Texas real estate prices are booming once again. Oil is just a small part of the Texas economy now; as *The Wall Street Journal* put it, "The new wildcatters are striking it big in personal computers, telecommunications, plastics, home building and airlines."

Texas has also surged ahead because it, in vivid contrast to that other onetime republic, California, has nurtured and profited from its relationship with its southern neighbor, Mexico. California, for all the proud liberalism of its articulate elite, has shown its scorn, disgust and, worst of all, indifference to Mexico; it has portrayed its southern neighbor as generating illegal aliens and criminals California taxpayers must pay for; for most of the 1990s both its right and its left did little to assimilate Mexican-Americans and other Latinos into a united America. Texas has taken a different course. Its border with Mexico is longer, and more often crossed; southern Texas along the Rio Grande is a kind of transition zone, and Monterrey, 140 miles from Laredo, is perhaps Mexico's most America-friendly city; despite a history of racial segregation, Texas has shown a friendly face to Mexicans, while Mexican immigrants have shown they wanted to become Texans and Americans. As *Mexico Business* magazine wrote, "Texas has embraced Mexico while California has given it the cold shoulder." Fewer Latinos have crossed the border here to take advantage of welfare programs, which are much less generous in Texas than in California. Political leadership has made a difference. California's former Governor Pete Wilson had little contact with Mexico and strongly championed Proposition 187 against services for illegal immigrants in 1994 and Proposition 209 banning racial quotas and preferences in 1996; strong arguments can be made for both propositions, and Mexican officials in Baja California Norte for years were egregiously corrupt: but a chilly tone was set, which has only begun to be dissipated by Wilson's successor Gray Davis. George W. Bush, like Governor Ann Richards before him, has journeyed often to Mexico and has invited Mexican leaders to Texas, emphasizing the positive in public and leaving any negative details to private negotiations. "You cannot wall off Mexico," says Bush. "Our cultures are completely intertwined." So increasingly are their economies. Nearly half of U.S. merchandise exports to Mexico are from Texas, significantly more than California; 70% of U.S. exports to Mexico go through Texas. The NAFTA secretariat of labor is in Dallas, the North American Development Bank is headquartered in San Antonio and the Border Environmental Cooperation Commission is in Juarez, across the Rio Grande from El Paso.

Texas stands as a model for the American future, a model admired by many and disparaged by others. It is an open society, unpretentious, delivered from its heritage of racial and ethnic discrimination. But it also has vast income disparities, between struggling and population-losing rural counties and the surging cities, and between the gleaming affluent neighborhoods spreading out into the countryside and the poor and crime-ridden neighborhoods of rickety frame houses not far from the urban cores. Texas presents a contrast with and a challenge to the traditions of other megastates—New York which pioneered the American welfare state, California which used high taxes to build highways and schools, the Great Lakes industrial states with their big labor unions. For Texas has some of the lowest taxes in the country and some of the lowest welfare levels; it has few union members and a relatively small public sector; it has resisted court-ordered moves to equalize spending among school districts; it continues to be a violent state, with a high crime rate and the nation's most executions. For years, out-of-state elites and liberals in Texas have called on the state to become more like New York or California or Michigan. But most Texans prefer their own model. Indeed, in important respects New York and California and Michigan are choosing to become more like Texas; so is Mexico: the last 25 years can be seen as—at least the beginnings of—the Texafication of North America. Low taxes and high tech, few barriers to opportunity but a less elaborate safety net, moving away from reliance on agriculture and oil, bypassing the era of big factories and big unions of the Great Lakes and eschewing the liberal cultural values of the two coasts: this is Texas's way, and increasingly North America's.

Politically, Texas is now an indisputably Republican state. This was not always so: Its three major officeholders, George W. Bush, Phil Gramm and Kay Bailey Hutchison each lost an election before they started winning, though now each seems unbeatable. One-party Democratic dominance ended in the 1960s, and for two decades Democratic victories were largely the product of Lloyd Bentsen, when he was on the ballot in 1970, 1976, 1982 and 1988 and when he exerted his influence for Ann Richards for governor in 1990. The old Democratic strength in the Texas countryside is gone—in 1994 George W. Bush carried 189 of 254 counties and in 1998 he carried 239—and the Republican hold on the big cities is solid. Bush carried 55% of the Dallas-Forth Worth Metroplex in 1994 and 70% in 1998, and 56% of greater Houston in 1994 and 66% in 1998: together those two areas cast 45% of Texas's votes. Democrats still have a majority in the U.S. House delegation, but that is only because of the cleverest Democratic redistricting plan of the 1990s: in 1994 Republicans won the House vote 56%–42% but took only 11 of 30 seats; in 1996, after the plan was slightly revised, Republicans won the House votes 54%–44%, winning 13 of 30 seats; in 1998 they also won 13 of 30 seats while winning the popular vote 52%–44%. In races sharply contested by trial lawyers and their adversaries, Republicans have taken over the state Supreme Court and in 1998 elected Attorney General John Cornyn, who sharply criticized his predecessor's huge fees to trial lawyers in the tobacco case. Republicans won three of seven downballot offices in 1994 and all seven in 1998, thanks in part to George W. Bush's 68%–31% re-election victory but also due to a basic Republican preference. Republicans have rolled toward majorities in the state legislature. The state Senate was 18–13 Democratic after 1992, 17–14 Democratic after 1994, 17–14 Republican after 1996; Democrats gained a seat in 1998, but it was still 16–15 Republican, with leadership powers in the new Republican Lieutenant Governor Rick Perry. The state House was 92–58 Democratic after 1992, 81–69 after 1994, 82–68 after 1996, 78–72 after 1998. The Democratic primary electorate has shrunk, from 1.8 million in 1978 to 890,000 in 1996, a more liberal, minority-dominated constituency. The Republican primary electorate has grown, from 158,000 in 1978 to just over one million in 1996: more Republicans than Democrats for the first time in history. In 1998, perhaps not a good year for comparison since neither party's gubernatorial contest was seriously contested, 596,000 Republicans voted compared to 492,000 Democrats. Bob Dole carried Texas 49%–44%, his best showing in a large state.

Pockets of Democratic strength in Texas are increasingly isolated. Their best vote is in the Border counties, which cast 7% of the state's votes; they voted 61%–38% for Richards in 1994, 65%–29% for Clinton in 1996. But George W. Bush has made huge inroads among Latinos, and carried the Border counties 51%–49% in 1998. Another traditionally Democratic area is the urban strip from San Antonio to Austin. But the cultural liberals who hang out on Austin's Sixth Street are now being joined by high-tech engineers and hard-charging entrepreneurs in the new subdivisions and office centers running north of the pink marble Capitol and the UT campus; this area voted only 48%–45% for Clinton in 1996, and went for Bush in 1998, 66%–33%. Rural Texas, more heavily Democratic than the rest of the state in the heyday of Lyndon Johnson and Lloyd Bentsen, voted 52%–40% for Dole in 1996 and 72%–28% for George W. Bush in 1998. Cultural attitudes are conservative here, and there is little of the economic populism of Sam Rayburn's day.

Nearly half of Texas's votes are cast in the two big metro areas. Dallas-Fort Worth, with an increasingly Democratic core city but burgeoning heavily Republican edge cities, has been volatile, supplying the votes that elected Richards in 1990 and giving native son Ross Perot 28% of its votes in 1992, nearly as many as Clinton. But Bush won in DFW 55%–45% in 1994 and Dole beat Clinton there 51%–41%, with only 7% for Perot in 1996; in 1998 Bush carried the Metroplex 70%–29%. Metro Houston, slightly less Republican, voted 56%–44% for Bush in 1994, 50%–43% for Dole in 1996, 66%–32% for Bush in 1998.

The prospect for Texas Democrats is bleak. They have their enclaves of control, but few statewide prospects. Their two large political figures, capable of rallying statewide majorities and governing ably, are absent from the scene: Lloyd Bentsen spends much of his time in San Diego and Ann Richards much of hers in Washington. Bob Bullock, lieutenant governor during most of the 1990s, retired in 1998 and endorsed Bush for re-election—even though he was godfather to one of the children of Democratic nominee Garry Mauro; Bullock died in June 1999. Texas's national political figures are almost all Republicans—Senators Gramm and Hutchison, House Majority Leader Dick Armey, House Majority Whip Tom DeLay, House Ways and Means Committee Chairman Bill Archer. On the major issues, and on the overriding question of whether to continue Texas's traditions of cultural conservatism and minimalist government, Bush and the Republicans seem very much on the majority side. The future in Texas appears to be theirs and, if this state is as attractive a model as it thinks, perhaps in the nation as well.

Governor. George W. Bush is governor of the nation's second largest state, arguably the most popular governor of any big state, and by mid-1999 was far ahead in national polls for the Republican presidential nomination and for the presidency itself. Yet outside Texas he was still known primarily as the son of President George Bush and as a big state governor who won re-election with 68% of the vote. Born when his father was an undergraduate at Yale, Bush grew up in a modest ranch house in Midland, when it was a fast-growing, rough and tumble Permian Basin oil boom town. Soon after his parents moved to Houston in 1960, Bush went east to school, where he was uncomfortable with the radicalism of late 1960s Yale College and the trendy leftism of mid-1970s Harvard Business School. He returned to Texas, became a fighter pilot in the Air National Guard, got into the oil business in Midland and ran for Congress in 1978. He lost that race 53%–47% to Kent Hance, then a Democrat from Lubbock: rural West Texas wasn't yet ready for a Midland Republican. Bush's business career wasn't spectacularly successful. He did better as a political adviser to his father in 1988 and after, and as the 2% owner and managing director of the Texas Rangers baseball team. He supervised the building of the attractive Ballpark at Arlington and, when the team was sold in June 1998, his original $600,000 investment was, with the help of a bonus for his work as managing director, turned into some $15 million.

After his father's defeat in 1992, Bush decided to run for governor. He brought his nervous intensity to the race and a determination to discuss specifics of state issues in a way that illustrated sensitivity to the texture of everyday life—just the opposite of his father's perceived uninterest in domestic issues and distance from ordinary life. In heavy personal campaigning he consistently called for tougher sentences for criminals, adult prison for violent offenders as young as 14, limiting welfare benefits to two years and requiring job training, and limiting punitive damages in lawsuits. He did not pick an easy opponent. Ann Richards, first known nationally for her keynote speech attacking George Bush in 1988 ("born with a silver foot in his mouth"), had been elected in 1990 after a grueling campaign and had proved popular in office. Richards pushed through a state lottery and a corporate income tax, but stoutly opposed any income tax; she got increased minimum sentences for murder and a new school finance formula to respond to court orders. She hosted Mexico's President Carlos Salinas and campaigned for NAFTA. Yet Richards unaccountably failed to sound the positive, triumphalist note she might have. In public she called George W. Bush "shrub" and referred to him as "some jerk who's running for public office," while he was careful always to refer to her as Governor Richards. While Richards launched late attacks on Bush and was endorsed by Ross Perot, Bush stuck with his message, "Take a stand for Texas values." The opinion polls were close from spring on, so it was a bit of a surprise when Bush won 53%–46%.

Texas's legislature meets for 140 days every two years, with key roles being played by the speaker, Democrat Pete Laney, and lieutenant governor, Democrat Bob Bullock, who remained leader of the Senate even after Republicans won a majority there in 1996. In his session, Bush, working closely with Bullock and Laney, was exceedingly successful in enacting his programs. Bush got the legislature to pass tort reform, limiting punitive damages and changing some rules, though not imposing loser-pays. He passed a bill giving much more autonomy to local school districts, though initially none took advantage of it; he endorsed a 1994 commission's recommendation for tough accountability standards and regular testing, and over the next few years Texas's TAAS tests showed noticeable improvement in scores. He got welfare reform limiting benefits and requiring job training, though it did include his proposal for a cutoff after two children, and the Clinton Administration denied a waiver in May 1997 to allow welfare services to be provided by faith-based charities. The legislature also passed a law enabling law-abiding citizens to get a permit to carry concealed weapons. In his second session, in 1997, Bush was not so successful. He started off with an ambitious plan to cut property taxes by 40% and to raise the sales tax and business taxes. Court rulings have been threatening Texas, like many other states, with drastic action because of school districts' widely varying property tax bases. But Bush could not put the different sides together, and in May 1997 settled for a $1 billion property tax cut funded by budget savings. He signed a health care bill providing easier payment for emergency care, direct access to obstetricians and gynecologists, 48-hour hospital stays after childbirth, and a ban on retaliation by HMOs against physicians who file complaints.

Going into the 1998 campaign cycle, Bush's poll ratings were exceedingly high; for a while Democrats thought about running no candidate at all against him. The eventual Democratic nominee was Land Commissioner Garry Mauro, an old friend of Bill Clinton best known for his high-profile environmental campaigns, including the "Adopt-a-Beach" program. But despite numerous appearances by the Clintons, Mauro lagged far behind in money (in early August Bush had $14.5 million on hand and Mauro $220,000) and polls (the July Texas Poll had Bush ahead 67%–20%). Bullock, a veteran Democrat and godfather to one of Mauro's children, endorsed Bush; as he said later, "I've served under seven governors, and Bush is the best I've served under. It just does not make sense to retire a responsive and proven leader."

Much of the campaign concentrated on the 3.9 million voters who are Hispanics. The 1994 exit poll showed Bush with 24% of Hispanic votes; he said he hoped to win 40% in 1998. He traveled frequently to heavily Hispanic areas, including faraway El Paso and the Lower Rio Grande Valley; he kept in touch with and hosted Mexico's President Ernesto Zedillo and the governors of the four adjoining Mexican states; he spoke Spanish serviceably enough to engage in repartee with voters and to conduct a press conference outside the Foreign Ministry in Mexico City. He opposed national Republicans' policy of eliminating aid to legal immigrants, opposed use of military troops to patrol the border and took a characteristically consensus-minded stand on bilingual education. "There is a great debate about bilingualism. Remember, the goal is to teach children how to read and write and add and subtract in English. And here is my position loud and clear. We are going to measure it, and if the bilingual program serves to teach our children English, then we ought to say thank you very much and leave it in place. And if the bilingual program does not achieve state objectives, we must say change the program, eliminate the program because what we want is for every single child to get the gateway to freedom and that is called English." A portion of his ad budget was devoted to Spanish language radio and television, some of it featuring a song, "Juntos con Bush (Together with Bush)," written and sung by Tejano star Emilio Nivaria.

Less prominently, he worked to make sure that Republicans won up and down the ballot. Bush has refused to campaign against Democratic legislators who supported his program, but he did exert himself for Republican candidates in open legislative seats. Behind the scenes, he worked hard for the Republican lieutenant governor candidate, Agriculture Commissioner Rick Perry, who was running against the Democrats' strongest candidate, Comptroller John Sharp; they overlapped at Texas A&M, where Sharp was student body president and Perry a cheerleader. A Sharp victory would have made a Bush presidential candidacy awkward (as a Democratic lieutenant governor did for California Governor Pete Wilson in 1996). Perry's fundraisers included one other potential Republican national candidate (John McCain) but also featured George H.W. Bush and Barbara Bush; he beat Sharp 50%–48%. In the race for attorney general—important for its significance for tort reform—Bush forces backed former Supreme Court Justice John Cornyn who ultimately beat Barry Williamson, former railroad commissioner, in the runoff. Cornyn then beat former Congressman and Attorney General Jim Mattox, a loud populist, 54%–44%.

Bush's victory margin was in line with the polls, 68%–31%; he is the first Texas governor to win a second consecutive four-year term. He won almost across the board, carrying 239 counties and losing 15. The VNS exit poll showed him trailing among Hispanics by the statistically insignificant margin of 50%–49%; polls by the Willie Velasquez Institute showed him winning 39% of Hispanics statewide and by a UT-El Paso professor 37% in El Paso County. In any case it was an impressive showing: Texas Hispanics have been heavily Democratic for years. The VNS exit poll also showed Bush winning 27% of votes from blacks—unusually high for a Republican. He carried men and women, all income and age and education groups by wide margins. Republicans won all seven statewide offices, for the first time. But Bush did not necessarily have coattails: Perry and Cornyn won only about 30% of Hispanic votes, for instance, and Republicans gained only three seats in the state House and lost one in the state Senate. The state's basic Republican preference is closer to Cornyn's 54% than Bush's 68%. But Bush's performance was certainly enough to recommend him as a candidate for president.

In his disciplined manner, Bush tried not to let his looming presidential candidacy overshadow the 1999 session of the legislature. "We can either view it as a distraction, or seize it as an opportunity to show the world what limited and constructive government looks like," he said. He took few out-of-state trips, although at the Washington National Governors Association meeting, Montana's Marc Racicot, Massachusetts's Paul Cellucci, and Michigan's John Engler led a move that got a majority of Republican governors endorsing him for president; and he formed an exploratory committee in March, which raked in huge contributions. His 1999 budget program included a $2 billion property tax cut; the legislature cut that back, as state revenue estimates slipped, but it was mostly enacted. He also cut the franchise tax on small businesses, pointing out that most new small businesses in Texas are owned by Hispanics, and eliminated the sales tax on disposable diapers, children's over-the-counter medicine and, for two weeks in August, children's clothes. He called for a research and development tax credit. Democratic legislators blocked his call for a pilot program of school vouchers for poor students, but he had more success on his call for blocking social promotion and holding back children who consistently fail TAAS exams. He also got parental notification for abortions of minors.

After the legislature adjourned on May 31, Bush planned mid-June trips to Iowa and New Hampshire. In 1998 he was already talking about "compassionate conservatism," and in March 1999 he said: "It is conservative to cut taxes and compassionate to give people more money to spend. It is conservative to insist upon local control of schools and high standards and results. It is compassionate to make sure every single child learns to read and no one is left behind." His hostility to what he regards as the culture of the 1960s came out in a 1998 campaign ad: "Whether for government or individuals, I believe in accountability and responsibility. For too long, we've encouraged a culture that says if it feels good, do it, and blame somebody else if you've got a problem. We've got to change our culture to one based on responsibility." Bush is plainly uncomfortable with winging it on issues, as Bill Clinton does so often and with so much flair. In 1998 and 1999 he quietly brought to Austin experts in foreign and domestic policy for what amounted to tutorials—foreign policy experts like George Shultz, Paul Wolfowitz, Robert Zoellick, Richard Perle, Condoleezza Rice and domestic policy experts like Larry Lindsay, Stephen Goldsmith, James Q. Wilson, John DiIulio, Michael Boskin. But in early 1999 he only started to enunciate his own stands on these matters. He quickly supported the bombing of Serbia and Kosovo in March 1999, but seemed uncomfortable going farther; a week later he said the need for a stable Europe and the refugee crisis made it imperative to win the war. He continued to oppose abortion, but said that abolishing it was an unrealistic goal, and backed the partial-birth abortion ban and parental consent. In June 1999 he took the Americans for Tax Reform pledge against tax increases. Bush's positions on many national issues were not known in May 1999, but his record in Texas has been open to public view and he has not been shy about declaring general principles. As for his character—perhaps the most important consideration in a post-Clinton election—voters may feel they know more about him than they do about his contenders, since they already know his family.

Senior Senator. Phil Gramm is a Republican first elected to the House in 1978 and the Senate in 1984. He is the product of adverse circumstances who makes his own considerable success sound like a hard grind. His father was an Army sergeant who died young; his mother, as he remembered in a grim-looking 1996 presidential campaign ad, sat him and his brother around the kitchen table and decided which bills they would pay. He flunked third, seventh and ninth grades, but his mother made him work hard and he went on to earn his Ph.D. from the University of Georgia. His field was economics, the one discipline that has moved to the right since the 1960s, with the growing belief in the efficacy of free markets; and Gramm certainly is a believer in free markets. He moved to Texas in 1967 to teach economics at Texas A&M. There he met and married his second wife, Wendy Lee, granddaughter of Korean immigrants and also an economics Ph.D. In the Texas of Lyndon Johnson's time, where Democrats held almost all offices and while preaching conservatism concentrated on funneling federal money into what was then considered an underdeveloped economy, Gramm conceived political ambitions, though he had no local connections, no personal money and little to none of the good ol' boy charm which was long an ingredient of political success in the state.

Seething with energy and conviction, he started giving speeches around the state, boosting free market economics and decrying the grasping hand of government. One of his first fans was Dicky Flatt, a print shop owner in Mexia who became a staple in Gramm speeches as the hard-working American whose money the government was taking away to spend on someone else. In 1976, at 34, Gramm ran as a Democrat in the primary against Senator Lloyd Bentsen and lost 64%–28%. Undaunted, Gramm ran for an open House seat in 1978, making the runoff by 115 votes over current 11th District Congressman Chet Edwards, and then winning the primary runoff 53%–47% and easily beating the Republican in the general. One sign of future races: He spent the then very considerable sum of $480,000. Within three years, Gramm was a major national figure. He got a seat on the Budget Committee, promising Majority Leader Jim Wright to be a team player. But, while he kept attending Democratic strategy meetings, he became co-sponsor of the Gramm-Latta budget resolution, the 1981 Reagan budget cuts, which passed the House over the opposition of the Democratic leadership.

For that apostasy and because Democrats decided that they could not trust him with confidential information, Speaker Tip O'Neill kicked Gramm off the Budget Committee in 1983. But Gramm turned that to his advantage by switching parties, resigning and triumphantly running in a special election campaign that gave him exposure in both the Houston and Dallas-Fort Worth media markets. "I had to choose between Tip O'Neill and y'all," he said, showing his capacity for attractively framing issues, "and I decided to stand with y'all." He won with 55% and in 1984 easily won the Republican Senate nomination when John Tower announced his retirement from Congress. The Democratic winner in an epic three-way primary was Lloyd

Doggett, then a liberal state senator from Austin and now congressman from the 10th District, whom Gramm attacked for holding a fundraiser at a gay male strip joint in San Antonio. Gramm won 59%–41%.

In his first year in the Senate Gramm had two major initiatives. First, he engineered a vacancy in the east Texas 1st District seat by securing a federal judgeship for the incumbent Democrat and, with the aid of a young operative named Lee Atwater, came close to having his Republican candidate win in that yellow dog Democratic territory. His idea was to encourage Republicans to run in rural southern districts. If he had succeeded, they might have captured the House in 1988 or 1990, rather than 1994. Gramm's second initiative, advanced immediately after his first, was the Gramm-Rudman deficit reduction law requiring automatic budget cuts if the deficit was not reduced to specific levels. Politically, Gramm-Rudman swept all before it and passed both houses. Fiscally, under the lead of OMB Director James Miller (who earned his economics Ph.D. from the University of Georgia at the same time as Gramm), it did in fact result in lowering the deficit.

Gramm was one of the Republican negotiators at the 1990 budget summit, but did not resist a tax increase, as some conservatives had hoped. After George Bush caved in on the issue, Gramm ended up negotiating the final package of budget cuts, spending caps and tax increases. Texas loyalty, perhaps: Gramm gave the nominating speech for Bush in New Orleans in 1988 and the keynote speech in Houston in 1992. Texas loyalty works other ways too: Critics on both sides of the aisle also noted that he has worked hard to keep money for big government projects flowing into Texas—Houston's space program, Austin's Sematech research center, Ingleside's Navy base. But Gramm's government-cutting initiatives kept coming. In 1991, he joined with Newt Gingrich to propose a series of tax cuts; in 1992, he held up Senate business to press for the balanced budget amendment; in 1995, he saw abolition of "baseline" and "current services" budgeting which he had long opposed.

Gramm was also all business at politics. In 1991, he was elected chairman of the National Republican Senatorial Committee by 26–17; Democrats hoped initially to gain seats, but despite the Clinton victory and the press ballyhoo about "the year of the woman" (there were no such articles when most women candidates were Republicans in 1990) Republicans picked up one seat on election day and then another weeks later in the Georgia runoff. Gramm sought an unusual second term as campaign chairman, and beat Mitch McConnell (who now holds the job) by 20–19. Gramm ended up with a splendid record: Republicans gained seven seats on November 8, 1994, and an eighth a day later when Richard Shelby of Alabama switched parties, and won control of the Senate.

Gramm was also running for president, and was not shy about it. "I love raising money," he said, and put out the theory that any candidate would have to spend $20 million to win the 1996 Republican nomination. That kept several candidates out of the field. He also tried to define the terms of the debate. "I have always felt on budget issues the party that defines the parameters of the debate almost always wins the debate," he once said, and he is as good as anyone in American politics at tightly defining issues to steer the public his way. Gramm preached root-and-branch opposition to the Clinton health care plan in 1993 and 1994; he supported the House Republicans' tough line on the budget in 1995. A strong free trader, he took on Pat Buchanan on trade issues when others counseled quiet. To his presidential campaign Gramm brought a bullish aggressiveness, a strong and well-disciplined mind, a gift for pungent phrase, the ability to frame issues favorably for his cause. But he also insisted on doing things his way, even when it did not help him. His commercials and his stump speech projected an angry, even pessimistic tone; there was nothing of the geniality and uplift of his fellow party-switcher Ronald Reagan. Gramm raised vast sums of money, but also spent vast sums on staff and in contests like the August 1995 Iowa straw poll in which he tied Bob Dole. He angered James Dobson of Focus on the Family by insisting that he would not stress cultural issues, even though his stands were almost identical to Dobson's. He tried to engineer contests earlier than the Iowa caucuses and New Hampshire primary, in order to get a lead on others with lesser resources. But that infuriated the governors of Iowa and New Hampshire, and cast a pall over his campaigns in those states. Then Buchanan took up his challenge in a Gramm-engineered firehouse primary in Louisiana February 6. Gramm, confident that his party backers would triumph, spent little time there, while Buchanan criss-crossed the state, calling talk radio hosts on his cell phone and getting interviewed by country editors. Gramm predicted he would win all 21 delegates; instead Buchanan won 13, and Gramm's campaign was effectively over. He finished fifth eight days later in Iowa, and pulled out of the race two days later, when it was obvious he would get nowhere in New Hampshire. In contrast to his high visibility in 1988 and 1992, he was quiet the rest of the year; "when you lose, you sit down," he said.

Gramm was also running for re-election in Texas and, under a law written by Democrats for Lyndon Johnson and used also by Lloyd Bentsen, he was allowed to run for both offices. Two Democratic congressmen ran against him, John Bryant of Dallas and Jim Chapman of east Texas, but the lead in the March 1996 primary went to Victor Morales (with the same last name as state Attorney General Dan Morales), a civics teacher at Poteet High School in Mesquite, who campaigned driving his pickup truck around the state. Bryant carried the Dallas-Fort Worth area with 62% of the vote, but it cast only 10% of primary votes; in rural Texas Chapman had a lead of only 38%–28% over Morales; in the border counties, which cast 19% of the vote, far more than their share of population, Morales won 60% of the vote. Statewide he had 36% to 30% for Bryant and 27% for Chapman. In the runoff Morales's ingenuous stands on issues and his Hispanic name got him past Bryant 51%–49%. Gramm, re-elected six years before with 60%, now seemed beleaguered. But Morales was hurt by the fact that his wife had not repaid delinquent student loans and by his stands against the balanced budget amendment and welfare reform and for affirmative action and same-sex marriage. Gramm won 55%–44%, losing the border counties which he had carried in 1990 but winning 60% again in rural Texas.

For a few months Gramm was quiet, but he vociferously opposed the April 1997 budget deal, charging it would "open the floodgates for new spending"—to the dismay of House Majority Leader Dick Armey, who remembered when Gramm flailed at him for opposing the 1990 budget agreement with its tax increase. Gramm also got involved in Texas projects. He passed a demonstration project in August 1997 to let military retirees in San Antonio and Wichita Falls use Medicare at base hospitals and clinics. He got $350 million more for Texas border guards and exemption from Social Security for college students in Texas, as in 47 other states. With Robert Byrd, he passed an amendment requiring all gas tax proceeds to be used for highways and transportation; this was part of the May 1998 BESTEA bill that brought $2 billion more to Texas. With Christopher Dodd he sponsored the securities litigation act passed in May 1998. And he sponsored successful amendments to IRS reform, shifting the burden of proof to the IRS and giving the commissioner authority to fire abusive agents. He worked to end the marriage penalty and for full voting rights for military personnel (in the 1940s this was a Democratic cause; now it seems a Republican cause). With Joseph Lieberman he sponsored an October 1998 law to double federal research and development spending over 10 years.

Gramm is now chairman of the Banking Committee. In October 1998, he carried off parliamentary manuevers on the financial services deregulation bill for which then-Chairman Alfonse D'Amato had assembled bipartisan support and which had already passed the House. Gramm opposed much of the Community Reinvestment Act, which he regarded as a "vehicle for fraud and extortion," encouraging "crony capitalism" because it requires bankers to provide loans to low and moderate income areas. As a result, the bill was killed. He also had a confrontation with SEC Chairman Arthur Levitt, charging that he was pressuring people not to testify against the Financial Accounting Standards Board's change in treatment of derivatives, one opposed by large banks and Federal Reserve Chairman Alan Greenspan. Gramm proceeded to mark up his own version of financial services deregulation, but he reopened some issues considered settled in 1998, notably by allowing banks to cross over into insurance, real estate and securities industries. He also insisted on exempting small banks from the Community Reinvestment Act. His bill passed by an 11–9 party-line vote, but ranking Democrat Paul

Sarbanes strongly opposed it, and Treasury Secretary Robert Rubin threatened a presidential veto. Another problem was that it provided for regulation of banks which merge with other financial service companies by the Federal Reserve, while the House committee bill provided for regulation by the Treasury. This difference, plus the CRA provisions, seemed to doom any chance of a financial services bill in the 106th Congress. But Gramm held fast, in line with the reputation for stubbornness which prompted Joseph Biden to once refer to him on the floor as "Barbed-wire Gramm." Biden apologized, but Gramm said he liked the nickname: "That helps me back home."

Gramm is not always confrontation-minded. In the 100-member Senate closed meeting on impeachment in January 1999, Gramm steered the way to compromise by pointing out that any decision at that time on whether to call witnesses could, under Senate rules, be overturned by 51 senators later; Edward Kennedy picked up the theme, and they agreed to postpone the decision on witnesses until later, and the senators emerged in a glow of consensus. It did not last forever, of course; and Gramm took the lead in objecting to resolutions of censure.

Gramm comes up for re-election in 2002. He seems politically safe in Texas, although he has mused about the possibility of doing something else, but odds are he will run again. As he said in April 1999, "I think maybe one of the things—running for president and losing—you relax a little bit, you understand. One thing is it makes you appreciate the job you got."

Junior Senator. Kay Bailey Hutchison is a Republican who won her seat in a June 1993 special election. She is of old Texas stock, the great-great-granddaughter of Charles S. Taylor, a signer of the Texas Declaration of Independence, who was a friend and business partner of Senator Thomas Jefferson Rusk, the first person to hold this seat. She grew up in LaMarque, near the refinery town of Texas City, a prom queen who went to college and then law school at the University of Texas and then, unable to get a law job, in 1967 worked for a Houston TV station as a reporter. In 1972, she won a seat in the legislature, its first Republican woman. In 1976 she went to Washington to fill the number two position at the National Transportation Safety Board. She married, moved to Dallas and went into banking and became a small business owner in 1978. In 1982, she lost a House race to Steve Bartlett, later mayor of Dallas. But she stayed active in Republican politics and in 1990 was elected state treasurer, a breakthrough race for state Republicans. Hutchison has been mocked by liberals for her tight-lipped good manners, but she remembers when being a woman was much more of a career handicap than today's younger generation has ever encountered, and she has passed through political ordeals as searing as those endured by her predecessor as treasurer—and political non-friend—former Governor Ann Richards.

In January 1993 Lloyd Bentsen resigned his Senate seat after 22 years to become secretary of the Treasury. To replace him Richards appointed Bob Krueger, a two-term congressman in the 1970s who nearly beat Senator John Tower in 1978, then ran third in a three-way Senate primary in 1984 and was elected Railroad commissioner (actually, oil regulator) in 1990. Running against him in the May 1993 all-party primary were three Republicans, Hutchison and Congressmen Joe Barton and Jack Fields. Krueger opposed the Clinton budget and tax plan, but Democrats were so unpopular in Texas then—Clinton had a 73% negative job rating—that Krueger won only 29% of the total vote, just behind Hutchison, also with 29%; Barton and Fields won 14% each. Krueger's cause was obviously doomed, and his campaign flailed around, running absurd ads in which Krueger, dressed in an Arnold Schwarzenegger *Terminator* outfit, claimed to be a lousy politician. Meanwhile, Hutchison weathered charges she had hit a Treasury employee (the daughter of former Governor John Connally), and kept the focus on Clinton. Hutchison won the June runoff by an astonishing 67%–33%, ahead of any Senate candidate here since the 1950s, when Republicans did not put up serious candidates. She won the Dallas-Fort Worth Metroplex 71%–29% and greater Houston 70%–30%, carried the usually Democratic San Antonio-Austin corridor and the Border counties; rural Texas, once heavily Democratic, went for Hutchison 70%–30%: totals very much like George W. Bush's in 1998. Yellow dog Democratic counties went Republican in droves: Krueger carried 15 counties, Hutchison

239. Her victory echoed with greater resonance the defeat of the last Texas senator appointed by a Democratic governor to replace a Texan taking a high position in Washington: the 1961 loss of conservative Democrat "Dollar Bill" Blakeley to Republican John Tower, replacing then-Vice President Lyndon Johnson. Tower's victory was a sign that Republicans could be competitive in Texas; Hutchison's victory was a sign that they were the majority.

Hutchison started her Senate career articulate and pleasant but willing to be partisan; pro-choice on abortion but opposing taxpayer funding and a Freedom of Choice Act that would wipe out state parental consent laws; opposing the Clinton tax increase and supporting NAFTA; and voting with two other women senators to deny Admiral Frank Kelso retirement with his four-star rank. But immediately after her win in 1993, Austin District Attorney Ronnie Earle, a liberal Democrat, worked to indict Hutchison for using office employees for political purposes and for destroying some records. It was a rotten prosecution from the beginning: the law imposes limits on state elected officials which at times seem absurd, and the destroyed records were mailing lists Hutchison had purged from her Texas computer on the advice of the Democratic attorney general. Then, in February 1994, Earle dropped the charges when the trial judge refused to rule on the admissibility of evidence seized in a June 1993 raid on Hutchison's office, in effect admitting he had no case.

Hutchison's job rating had declined, but not disastrously, and she avoided any serious Republican primary opposition in the race for the full term in 1994. Three serious Democrats were running. The potentially strongest candidate, moderate Houston Congressman Mike Andrews, was eliminated in the March primary. In the April runoff, former Attorney General and bitter Richards enemy Jim Mattox lost 54%–46% to Richard Fisher, a free-spending moderate who campaigned extensively in the Border counties in Spanish. Fisher's credentials seemed a bit fishy—he claimed to have been an adviser to former British Prime Minister Margaret Thatcher, though Thatcher said their acquaintance was minor—and Hutchison cruised to a solid 61%–38% victory. This time she lost the Border, but won the San Antonio-Austin corridor and took over 60% in the big metro areas and the rural counties.

In the Senate she worked on welfare reform, helping to write a funding formula helpful to Texas and getting funding for colonias and other border infrastructure. She supported the partial-birth abortion ban but was still the target of conservatives who wanted to keep her off the delegation to the Republican National Convention in San Diego. But as a delegate there she presented the toughest criticism of Bill Clinton, mocking his changing schedule for balancing the federal budget. She sponsored a federal anti-stalking bill and homemakers' IRAs. In a time of falling prices, she has worked to keep Texas's oil industry pumping. In May 1998 she put into the disaster relief bill an amendment to stop the government from increasing the fees oil companies pay for pumping oil on federal land. In 1999, she called for tax credits to keep marginal wells operating and a tax exemption for restarting plugged up wells; she applauded Energy Secretary Bill Richardson for diverting 100,000 barrels a day into the Strategic Petroleum Reserve when prices were low. When Al Gore said on a hot summer day that anyone who wanted proof of global warming should just step outside, Hutchison consulted the statistics and said, "We're in a cooling period. It's not a cool, cooling period, but for the last 20 years we have been coming into a cooling period from the high in the '40s, when it really was from natural causes."

Hutchison has also staked out positions on foreign policy. Most notably, she has been wary of U.S. involvement in the former Yugoslavia, calling for an eventual pullout from Bosnia, and decrying Clinton's policy in Kosovo. With Christopher Dodd, she tried in 1997 to get Germany to pay pensions to Jewish survivors of Nazi concentration camps in eastern Europe and the former Soviet Union. On impeachment, Hutchison, who unlike many feminist Democrats showed genuine concern over sexual harrassment, favored opening Senate deliberations to the public and opposed live testimony by Monica Lewinsky. In 1999 she became chairman of the D.C. Appropriations Subcommittee, and said she was looking forward to working with the new administration of Mayor Anthony Williams.

Hutchison's seat comes up in 2000 and there has been no doubt she is running; by February 1999 she had $5 million in her campaign treasury. Her job approval has been high and Democrats have no prominent officials to run against her. Possible opponents include Austin Mayor Kirk Watson and Victor Morales, who lost races for the Senate in 1996 and the 5th District House seat in 1998. Any national ambitions Hutchison has have been subordinated to the presidential candidacies of Phil Gramm in 1996 and George W. Bush in 2000, however, she looks to be a potential candidate.

Cook's Call. *Safe.* With all the attention on Governor George W. Bush and his presidential race, the fact that Hutchison is up for re-election has gone unnoticed by most. This is a very expensive and difficult state in which to run a statewide campaign, and Democrats do not currently have any first-tier potential candidates on the horizon. Hutchison may get something close to a free ride.

Presidential politics. Texas can hardly be ignored in presidential politics: it is too big, with 32 electoral votes; it has too many leading politicians, too many fundraisers. But there is little suspense about the outcome here. Texas voted Republican 56%–43% in 1988, when Lloyd Bentsen was on the Democratic ticket; it voted 41%–37% Republican in 1992, when Bill Clinton was sweeping to victory over George Bush; it voted 49%–44% for Bob Dole in 1996, when Sun Belt states like Florida and California went Democratic. Texas is a sort of counterpoint to New York, which it surpassed in size in 1993 but which still has one more electoral vote: just as New York is safely Democratic and has generated dozens of major Democratic national politicians, so Texas is safely Republican and is generating dozens of major national politicians. The campaign of Senator Phil Gramm, its Republican presidential candidate in 1996, fizzled early; the campaign of George W. Bush, when it formally started after the Texas legislature adjourned at the end of May 1999, seemed to be headed toward the nomination.

Texas's presidential primary, originally in May, was moved to March for Super Tuesday in 1988; attempts to move it back to May for 2000 failed in 1997. Its results have mostly been unsurprising; Clinton and Bush both won twice, easily; Dole won easily in 1996; George W. Bush seems sure to win in 2000. It is interesting to look back on the 1988 Democratic primary here, with an eye on 2000. The winner then was Michael Dukakis, with 33%, who did well with Hispanics; Jesse Jackson had 25%; Al Gore trailed with 20%; and Dick Gephardt had 14%. But that was with a turnout of 1.7 million, nearly twice the 900,000 Democrats who turned out in the 1996 primary. A smaller Democratic turnout means that Hispanic voters and committed liberals will be a larger percentage of the total; Texas could be important, though scarcely typical.

Congressional districting. Texas's congressional districting plan was the shrewdest gerrymader of the 1990s. The original 1991 redistricting plan was the product of Bob Mansker, aide to Democratic Congressman Martin Frost, put into law when Democrats controlled the legislature and held the governorship. While modified in 1996 by court ruling, it is still in effect for 17 of the 30 districts, and has not been much changed for the others. The lines were smoothed out for the heavily black 30th District in Dallas and 18th District in Houston and the heavily Latino 29th District in Houston, and accordingly in adjacent districts. This Democratic gerrymander has not been entirely availing against the clear Republican trend in Texans' voting. In 1992 Democrats carried the popular vote for House by only 50%–48% but won 21 of 30 seats. In 1994 they lost the popular vote 56%–42%, but won 19 seats. In 1996 and 1998 they lost the popular vote 54%–44% and 52%–44% and still won 17 seats.

The prospect is for a very different plan after the 2000 Census, which is likely to increase the Texas delegation from 30 to 32. Republicans will hold the governorship, thanks to George W. Bush's smashing victory and the narrow margin for Republican Lieutenant Governor Rick Perry in 1998. Control of the legislature is less clear: after the 1998 election Republicans had a 16–15 margin in the state Senate and Democrats a 78–72 margin in the state House. But Texas's legislature is far less partisan than, say, New York's or California's; minority party members are routinely given chairmanships, and few votes are on party lines; and Bush has nurtured bipartisan consensus on most major issues, made easier by the fact that many Democratic legislators are conservative on many issues. In that setting, the likelihood is for a districting plan with regularly-shaped districts—a vivid contrast to Mansker's 1991 masterpiece. This could spell trouble for Democratic incumbents in East Texas, who will get new territory, for Mansker's boss Martin Frost in the 24th District and Ken Bentsen in the 25th, whose metropolitan area districts were very carefully drawn to avoid the Republican precincts all around. Demographics work for the Republicans too: the fastest growth has been in outer counties of the Metroplex, the Houston area and greater Austin, which are very heavily Republican indeed. Even a not very partisan plan could shift the balance of the Texas delegation from 17–13 Democratic to something like 18–14 Republican—a shift with national significance in a very closely divided House.

The People: Est. Pop. 1998: 19,759,614; Pop. 1990: 16,986,510, up 16.3% 1990–1998. 7.3% of U.S. total, 2d largest; 19.7% rural. Median age: 32.6 years. 10.5% 65 years and over. 75.3% White, 11.9% Black, 1.9% Asian, 0.4% Amer. Indian, 10.6% Other; 25.3% Hispanic Origin. Households: 56.6% married couple families; 30.4% married couple fams. w. children; 46.5% college educ.; median household income: $27,016; per capita income: $12,904; 60.9% owner occupied housing; median house value: $59,600; median monthly rent: $328. 4.8% Unemployment. 1998 Voting age pop.: 14,299,000. 1998 Turnout: 3,738,078; 26% of VAP. Registered voters (1998): 11,538,235; no party registration.

Political Lineup: Governor, George W. Bush (R); Lt. Gov., Rick Perry (R); Secy. of State, Elton Bomer (R); Atty. Gen., John Cornyn (R); Comptroller, Carole Keeton Rylander (R); State Senate, 31 (15 D, 16 R); Senate President, Rick Perry (R); State House, 150 (78 D, 72 R); House Speaker, Pete Laney (D). Senators, Phil Gramm (R) and Kay Bailey Hutchison (R). Representatives, 30 (17 D, 13 R).

Elections Division: 512-463-5650; **Filing Deadline for U.S. Congress:** January 3, 2000.

1996 Presidential Vote

Dole (R)	2,730,085	(49%)
Clinton (D)	2,455,853	(44%)
Perot (I)	378,117	(7%)

1996 Republican Presidential Primary

Dole (R)	567,164	(56%)
Buchanan (R)	217,974	(21%)
Forbes (R)	130,938	(13%)
Others	103,727	(10%)

1992 Presidential Vote

Bush (R)	2,495,608	(41%)
Clinton (D)	2,281,735	(37%)
Perot (I)	1,354,676	(22%)

GOVERNOR
Gov. George W. Bush (R)

Elected 1994, term expires Jan. 2003; b. July 6, 1946, New Haven, CT; home, Austin; Yale U., B.A. 1968, Harvard U., M.B.A. 1975; Methodist; married (Laura).

Military Career: TX Air Natl. Guard, 1968–73.

Professional Career: Founder & CEO, Bush Exploration Oil & Gas Co., 1975–87; Sr. Advisor, Bush Presidential Camp., 1988; Managing Gen. Partner, Texas Rangers baseball org., 1989–98.

Office: State Capitol, P.O. Box 12428, Austin, 78711, 512-463-2000; Fax: 512-463-1849; Web site: www.state.tx.us.

Election Results

1998 gen.	George W. Bush (R)	2,550,821	(68%)
	Garry Mauro (D)	1,165,592	(31%)
	Others	21,665	(1%)
1998 prim.	George W. Bush (R)	576,528	(97%)
	Others	20,311	(3%)
1994 gen.	George W. Bush (R)	2,350,994	(53%)
	Ann Richards (D)	2,016,928	(46%)

SENATORS
Sen. Phil Gramm (R)

Elected 1984, seat up 2002; b. July 8, 1942, Ft. Benning, GA; home, College Station; U. of GA, B.A. 1964, Ph.D. 1967; Episcopalian; married (Wendy).

Elected Office: U.S. House of Reps., 1978–84.

Professional Career: Prof., TX A&M U., 1967–78.

DC Office: 370 RSOB, 20510, 202-224-2934; Fax: 202-228-2856; Web site: www.senate.gov/~gramm.

State Offices: Dallas, 214-767-3000; El Paso, 915-534-6896; Harlingen, 210-423-6118; Houston, 713-718-4000; Lubbock, 806-472-7533; San Antonio, 210-366-9494; Tyler, 903-593-0902.

Committees: *Banking, Housing & Urban Affairs* (Chmn. of 11 R): Housing & Transportation. *Budget* (4th of 12 R). *Finance* (7th of 11 R): Health Care; International Trade; Social Security & Family Policy.

Group Ratings

	ADA	ACLU	AFS	LCV	CON	NTU	NFIB	COC	ACU	NTLC	CHC
1998	0	14	0	0	90	73	89	94	96	96	100
1997	0	—	11	—	42	83	—	80	100	—	—

National Journal Ratings

	1997 LIB — 1997 CONS			1998 LIB — 1998 CONS		
Economic	0%	—	89%	0%	—	88%
Social	0%	—	83%	0%	—	88%
Foreign	0%	—	77%	25%	—	74%

Key Votes of the 105th Congress

1. Bal. Budget Amend.	Y	5. Satcher for Surgeon Gen.	N	9. Chem. Weapons Treaty	N
2. Clinton Budget Deal	Y	6. Highway Set-asides	N	10. Cuban Humanitarian Aid	N
3. Cloture on Tobacco	N	7. Table Child Gun locks	Y	11. Table Bosnia Troops	N
4. Education IRAs	Y	8. Ovrd. Part. Birth Veto	Y	12. $ for Test-ban Treaty	*

Election Results

1996 general	Phil Gramm (R) 3,027,680	(55%)	($14,078,131)
	Victor M. Morales (D) 2,428,776	(44%)	($978,862)
1996 primary	Phil Gramm (R) 838,339	(85%)	
	David Young (R) 75,463	(8%)	
	Henry C. Grover (R) 72,400	(7%)	
1990 general	Phil Gramm (R) 2,302,357	(60%)	($12,349,397)
	Hugh Parmer (D) 1,429,986	(37%)	($1,677,087)
	Others 89,814	(2%)	

Sen. Kay Bailey Hutchison (R)

Elected June 1993, seat up 2000; b. July 22, 1943, Galveston; home, Dallas; U. of TX, B.A. 1992, J.D. 1967; Episcopalian; married (Ray).

Elected Office: TX House of Reps., 1972–76; TX Treasurer, 1990–93.

Professional Career: Political & legal corresp., KPRC-TV, 1967–70; Vice Chmn., Natl. Transp. Safety Bd., 1976–78; V.P. & Gen. Cnsl., RepublicBank Corp., 1978–82; Owner, McCraw Candies, 1984–88.

DC Office: 284 RSOB, 20510, 202-224-5922; Fax: 202-224-0776; Web site: www.senate.gov/~hutchison.

State Offices: Abilene, 915-676-2839; Austin, 512-916-5834; Dallas, 214-361-3500; Houston, 713-653-3456; San Antonio, 210-340-2885.

Committees: *Appropriations* (14th of 15 R): Commerce, Justice, State & the Judiciary; Defense; District of Columbia (Chmn.); Labor & HHS; Military Construction; VA, HUD & Independent Agencies. *Commerce, Science & Transportation* (6th of 11 R): Aviation; Communications; Oceans & Fisheries; Science, Technology & Space; Surface Transportation & Merchant Marine (Chmn.). *Environment & Public Works* (10th of 10 R): Clean Air, Wetlands, Private Property & Nuclear Safety; Fisheries, Wildlife & Drinking Water. *Rules & Administration* (9th of 9 R).

Group Ratings

	ADA	ACLU	AFS	LCV	CON	NTU	NFIB	COC	ACU	NTLC	CHC
1998	0	17	11	0	14	64	100	100	88	93	91
1997	5	—	0	—	89	84	—	100	92	—	—

National Journal Ratings

	1997 LIB — 1997 CONS			1998 LIB — 1998 CONS		
Economic	25%	—	67%	17%	—	82%
Social	28%	—	62%	21%	—	78%
Foreign	0%	—	77%	0%	—	88%

Key Votes of the 105th Congress

1. Bal. Budget Amend.	Y	5. Satcher for Surgeon Gen.	N	9. Chem. Weapons Treaty	N
2. Clinton Budget Deal	Y	6. Highway Set-asides	*	10. Cuban Humanitarian Aid	N
3. Cloture on Tobacco	N	7. Table Child Gun locks	Y	11. Table Bosnia Troops	N
4. Education IRAs	Y	8. Ovrd. Part. Birth Veto	Y	12. $ for Test-ban Treaty	N

Election Results

1994 general	Kay Bailey Hutchison (R) 2,604,218	(61%)	($6,114,755)
	Richard Fisher (D) 1,639,615	(38%)	($3,360,850)
1994 primary	Kay Bailey Hutchison (R) 467,975	(84%)	
	Stephen Hopkins (R) 34,703	(6%)	
	Others 52,660	(9%)	
1993 runoff	Kay Bailey Hutchison (R) 1,188,716	(67%)	($6,255,765)
	Bob Krueger (D) 576,538	(33%)	($4,582,323)

FIRST DISTRICT

Texarkana, with a population of 50,000 and a rural and small town hinterland somewhat larger, for years was noteworthy mainly because its neat grid streets cross the Texas-Arkansas state line. The downtown post office straddles the boundary, with the west wing serving Texarkana, Texas 75501 and the east wing Texarkana, Arkansas 75502; Texarkana, Arkansas, is exempted from the state income tax because Texas has none. Yet this small city and its hinterland produced not one but two 1990s presidential candidates: Ross Perot grew up in Texarkana, Texas, while Bill Clinton's boyhood home of Hope, Arkansas, is only 30 miles east on Interstate 30. Both grew up in comfortable but not lavish circumstances: Perot's father was a cotton broker, Clinton's stepfather a Buick dealer. Both lived in town, where most people had electricity and indoor plumbing—a vivid contrast with those living in the countryside when Perot was growing up in the 1930s and even when Clinton was young in the late 1940s.

Did the particular atmosphere of the Texarkana area have an effect on these men's politics? Maybe. Both were taught that they had obligations to those less fortunate, even while they were obliged themselves to work hard to get ahead. Texarkana was populist country then, a place where farmers producing crops felt themselves at the mercy of Dallas cotton brokers, Wall Street financiers and railroad magnates who were grabbing all the gains of their hard work. Outside Texarkana, in landscape littered with small houses amid lazily winding rivers, there was little protection from the sun and wind, and precious little ornament. The politics here has always been Democratic: Clinton, who remembers his grandfather as an FDR fan, has never been anything else, while Perot seems more at ease with moderate Democrats Lloyd Bentsen and Ann Richards than with Republicans. And in Texarkana this politics was surely affected by Wright Patman, congressman from the 1st District from 1929 until his death in 1976, a populist who began his career in the House by moving to impeach Treasury Secretary Andrew Mellon, punctuated it by calling constantly for low interest rates, and ended it after 12 years as Banking Committee chairman. But culture here was always traditional: this is an area of heavy churchgoing and proud patriotism. Traces of that can be seen in Perot's military bearing and Clinton's religious cadences.

The 1st Congressional District includes most of the northeastern corner of the Texas—from Texarkana west to within two counties of Dallas and south almost to Lufkin. Politically, it is traditionally Democratic but has trended toward Republicans since the 1980s. In 1985 it was the scene of an epic special election, contrived by Phil Gramm, opposed by Jim Wright and Tony Coelho; the result was a narrow 51%–49% win for Democrat Jim Chapman and a halt to Gramm's plans to take control of rural Southern seats.

The congressman from the 1st District is Max Sandlin, a Democrat elected in 1996 to replace Chapman. Sandlin grew up in East Texas, went to Baylor, practiced law in Marshall and got involved in oil and gas exploration. He was Harrison County judge, an elected administrative position, when he ran for the House in a campaign far less dramatic and politically meaningful than the 1985 contest. Despite the district's Republican strength in statewide races, the Democratic primary attracted four times as many voters—a vestige of tradition—and Sandlin led attorney Jo Ann Howard, wife of a longtime Chapman opponent, 42%–34%. In the runoff, Sandlin, spending his own money and using his oil business connections to raise more, beat

Howard 56%–44%. Sandlin pointed to his local tax-cutting experience and promised to find "common sense" solutions to Medicare and education. He attacked Republican Ed Merritt, an insurance attorney with no political experience, for backing Medicare "cuts." Merritt attacked him for appearing with Clinton. Overall Sandlin spent $1.7 million, including $784,000 of his own money—a campaign budget almost four times Merritt's. Sandlin won 52%–47%, losing counties only in the periphery of the district, perhaps out of range of his media buy.

In the House Sandlin failed to get a seat on the coveted Commerce Committee, but on the Transportation and Infrastructure Committee he worked for a funding formula to bring more highway money to Texas in the May 1998 transportation bill. He carefully straddles Democratic wings, joining the centrist Blue Dogs but also taking on populist causes like the right to sue HMOs. Feeling local pain from low energy prices and a record-low oil rig count, Sandlin wants to increase tax credits for marginal wells, fill the Strategic Petroleum Reserve, and take other steps to bolster domestic production.

Over a poorly-financed Republican he was re-elected 59%–41% in pro-incumbent 1998, again losing three counties; the National Republican Congressional Committee is targeting Sandlin's seat for 2000.

Cook's Call. *Potentially Competitive.* Sophomore Sandlin ducked a bullet in 1998 when Republicans were unable to recruit a strong candidate against him and breezed to re-election. But, this marginal district is by no means safe territory for Democrats and Sandlin must be on his toes in 2000.

The People: Pop. 1990: 565,594; 56.1% rural; 16.6% age 65 + ; 79.5% White, 18.1% Black, 0.3% Asian, 0.5% Amer. Indian, 1.6% Other; 3.1% Hispanic Origin. Households: 58.7% married couple families; 27.8% married couple fams. w. children; 37.1% college educ.; median household income: $21,697; per capita income: $10,785; median house value: $44,100; median gross rent: $246.

1996 Presidential Vote			1992 Presidential Vote		
Dole (R)	94,433	(46%)	Clinton (D)	85,771	(39%)
Clinton (D)	91,721	(45%)	Bush (R)	84,545	(38%)
Perot (I)	17,237	(8%)	Perot (I)	50,567	(23%)

Rep. Max Sandlin (D)

Elected 1996; b. Sept. 29, 1952, Texarkana; home, Marshall; Baylor U., B.A. 1975, J.D. 1978; Baptist; married (Leslie).

Elected Office: Harrison Cnty. Judge, 1986–89; Judge, Harrison Cnty. Court at Law, 1989–96.

Professional Career: Practicing atty., 1978–96; V.P., Howell & Sandlin Inc., 1989–96; Pres., E. TX Fuels, Inc., 1992–96.

DC Office: 214 CHOB 20515, 202-225-3035; Fax: 202-225-5866; Web site: www.house.gov/sandlin.

District Offices: Marshall, 903-938-8386; New Boston, 903-628-5594; Sulphur Springs, 903-885-8682.

Committees: *Banking & Financial Services* (17th of 27 D): Capital Markets, Securities & Government Sponsored Enterprises; Financial Institutions & Consumer Credit. *Transportation & Infrastructure* (23d of 34 D): Aviation; Ground Transportation.

Group Ratings

	ADA	ACLU	AFS	LCV	CON	NTU	NFIB	COC	ACU	NTLC	CHC
1998	80	20	78	23	2	29	79	61	40	42	25
1997	60	—	75	—	29	31	—	70	36	—	—

National Journal Ratings

	1997 LIB	—	1997 CONS	1998 LIB	—	1998 CONS
Economic	60%	—	40%	57%	—	43%
Social	64%	—	35%	57%	—	42%
Foreign	68%	—	31%	56%	—	42%

Key Votes of the 105th Congress

1. Clinton Budget Deal	Y	5. Puerto Rico Sthood. Ref.	Y	9. Cut $ for B-2 Bombers	N
2. Education IRAs	N	6. End Highway Set-asides	N	10. Human Rights in China	Y
3. Req. 2/3 to Raise Taxes	Y	7. School Prayer Amend.	Y	11. Withdraw Bosnia Troops	N
4. Fast-track Trade	N	8. Ovrd. Part. Birth Veto	Y	12. End Cuban TV-Marti	Y

Election Results

1998 general	Max Sandlin (D)	80,788	(59%)	($814,434)
	Dennis Boerner (R)	55,191	(41%)	($72,992)
1998 primary	Max Sandlin (D)	unopposed		
1996 general	Max Sandlin (D)	102,697	(52%)	($1,691,255)
	Ed Merritt (R)	93,105	(47%)	($467,750)
	Others	3,368	(2%)	

SECOND DISTRICT

East Texas is thick with landmarks of Lone Star history. There's still an Indian reservation in Polk County, and the Big Thicket National Preserve reminds you of what this land once looked like. Near Beaumont is Spindletop, where the world's first gusher spewed out in 1901 and started the Texas oil boom. Not far away is the huge oil field that wildcatter H. L. Hunt found in 1931, the foundation of a billion-dollar fortune. Much of East Texas looks little different from the wildcat days of 50 years ago: the town squares with courthouses and churches; the stands of cheap, quick-growing pine; the rough farmland. Yet much has changed. Real incomes have tripled over 50 years, endemic diseases have been wiped out, and racial segregation has mostly been abolished. When three white men in Jasper dragged James Byrd, an African American, behind their truck to his death in June 1998, a local jury quickly returned with guilty verdicts and the death sentence. Small-town isolation has been ended by television, interstate highways and regional shopping malls; metropolitan growth, sprinting outward from Houston's loop freeways, is spreading between the pine forests and reservoirs.

The 2d Congressional District includes all or part of 19 East Texas counties, most of them still seemingly rural; it runs from the oil port of Orange past Lufkin and Nacogodoches to Jacksonville. Political tradition here is Democratic and populist, devoted to traditional values but with a taste for military posture and a certain Texas rowdiness. This is the kind of district Democrats must carry to win Texas: Ann Richards won it in 1990 and Bill Clinton in 1992; but he carried it only narrowly in 1996, and it voted for George W. Bush in his narrow 1994 win and even more strongly in 1998.

The congressman from the 2d District is Jim Turner, a Democrat elected in 1996. He grew up in East Texas, went to college and law school in Austin, served in the Army, then returned to Crockett in Houston County, practiced law and was active in church and community organizations. In 1980 he was elected to the Texas House and served four years; he was mayor of Crockett for two years; in 1990 he returned to Austin in the state Senate.

His opportunity to run for the House came when Congressman Charlie Wilson decided to retire after 24 years. Turner's legislative work against crime and for patient protection against HMOs, plus Wilson's support, helped him win a three-candidate Democratic primary with 59%, carrying everything but his opponents' home counties. The Republican primary was something of a surprise. Running again was Donna Peterson, a West Point graduate who was Wilson's opponent in 1990, 1992 and 1994. She led in the five-candidate primary, but with only 35% to

31% for dentist Brian Babin, who was supported by Christian conservatives. Babin took the runoff with a motivated constituency 67%–33%, although he won fewer votes than before. Babin charged that Turner was an "elitist liberal," who voted for an income tax on small businesses and tried to weaken the law permitting concealed weapons. Turner charged that Babin backed the Republican budget and Medicare "cuts," and he called for more police and college tuition deductions. Turner outspent Babin by nearly 2–1 and won 52%–46%. Babin carried three counties closest to Houston and ran about even in several nearby. But Turner carried more rural counties, some by 2–1.

In the House Turner joined the conservative-leaning New Democrat Coalition and Blue Dog Democrats. When Clinton announced the bipartisan deal on the budget in May 1997, Turner was there beaming right behind him in the photograph. After the murder of James Byrd, Turner spoke eloquently about "this terrible act" and joined Congressional Black Caucus members in calling for federal prosecution. Like other skillful Texas Democrats over the years, he took on legislative tasks in the House, like promoting the Shays-Meehan campaign finance bill by filing a discharge petition in early 1999. He was a leader in backing legislation to reduce prescription drug costs under Medicare and to assure that members of the armed services will not suffer a loss of benefits.

Turner had an easier time in the 1998 rematch. Babin was plagued by a hefty 1996 campaign-finance violation, the well-publicized resignation of a top campaign aide who was homosexual and who quit because of Babin's position's on gay rights, and raised only half the money he had in 1996. Opposition to Turner by national term-limits advocates had little impact. Turner won 58%–41%. His biggest long-term threat is redistricting: a seat with more population in metro Houston would be much more Republican.

Cook's Call. *Potentially Competitive.* Jim Turner's 58% win over a flawed candidate in 1998 belies the marginal nature of this district. But Turner's moderate-to-conservative voting record can help to insulate him against charges that he is too liberal for this Republican trending, conservative district.

The People: Pop. 1990: 565,906; 61.1% rural; 14.8% age 65+; 79.3% White, 16.7% Black, 0.4% Asian, 0.4% Amer. Indian, 3.1% Other; 5.4% Hispanic Origin. Households: 60.4% married couple families; 29.2% married couple fams. w. children; 31.6% college educ.; median household income: $21,216; per capita income: $10,113; median house value: $42,200; median gross rent: $238.

1996 Presidential Vote

Clinton (D) 90,379 (45%)
Dole (R) 89,817 (45%)
Perot (I) 19,136 (10%)

1992 Presidential Vote

Clinton (D) 91,731 (43%)
Bush (R) 76,365 (35%)
Perot (I) 47,157 (22%)

Rep. Jim Turner (D)

Elected 1996; b. Feb. 6, 1946, Ft. Lewis, WA; home, Crockett; U. of TX, B.B.A. 1968, M.B.A. 1971, J.D. 1971; Baptist; married (Ginny).

Military Career: Army, 1970–78.

Elected Office: TX House of Reps., 1981–84; Crockett Mayor, 1989–91; TX Senate, 1991–96.

Professional Career: Practicing atty., 1978–96; Exec. Asst., Gov. Mark White, 1984–86; Practicing atty., 1986–96; Chmn., TX Comm. on Children & Youth, 1993–94.

DC Office: 208 CHOB 20515, 202-225-2401; Fax: 202-225-5955; Web site: www.house.gov/turner.

District Offices: Crockett, 409-544-8414; Lufkin, 409-637-1770; Orange, 409-883-4990.

Committees: *Armed Services* (16th of 28 D): Military Procurement; Military Research & Development. *Government Reform* (16th of 19 D): Criminal Justice, Drug Policy & Human Resources; Government Management, Information & Technology (RMM).

Group Ratings

	ADA	ACLU	AFS	LCV	CON	NTU	NFIB	COC	ACU	NTLC	CHC
1998	65	19	78	23	30	19	64	72	48	50	25
1997	50	—	50	—	76	32	—	80	48	—	—

National Journal Ratings

	1997 LIB — 1997 CONS	1998 LIB — 1998 CONS
Economic	55% — 44%	55% — 45%
Social	58% — 40%	48% — 51%
Foreign	60% — 38%	55% — 44%

Key Votes of the 105th Congress

1. Clinton Budget Deal	Y	5. Puerto Rico Sthood. Ref.	Y	9. Cut $ for B-2 Bombers	N
2. Education IRAs	N	6. End Highway Set-asides	N	10. Human Rights in China	Y
3. Req. 2/3 to Raise Taxes	N	7. School Prayer Amend.	Y	11. Withdraw Bosnia Troops	N
4. Fast-track Trade	N	8. Ovrd. Part. Birth Veto	Y	12. End Cuban TV-Marti	Y

Election Results

1998 general	Jim Turner (D)	81,556	(58%)	($575,117)
	Brian Babin (R)	56,891	(41%)	($287,322)
1998 primary	Jim Turner (D)	unopposed		
1996 general	Jim Turner (D)	102,908	(52%)	($919,505)
	Brian Babin (R)	89,838	(46%)	($595,410)
	Others	4,225	(2%)	

THIRD DISTRICT

North Dallas today is one of America's most affluent, educated and Republican areas, famed as the locus of the most successful television program of the 1980s and the eponymous football novel of the 1970s. But in its youth, it was one of the poorest, least educated and most Democratic parts of the nation. Named for the Philadelphia lawyer who was James K. Polk's vice president, Dallas got its commercial start as the place where the first railroad in Texas stopped at the three forks of the Trinity River, surrounded by dirt-poor farm country. "Its wealth originally came from cotton," John Gunther wrote in 1946, "but primarily it is a banking and jobbing and distributing center, the headquarters of railroads and utilities." Since then Dallas has become one of the nation's leading high-tech cities, the home of Texas Instruments and EDS (founded by Ross Perot), and one of the nation's major defense centers. As Dallas's private sector has demanded and rewarded expertise, it has attracted high-skill people from all over the world, and those who can afford it tend to move to the north side.

On rolling, scrub-covered hills north of downtown Dallas, this growth has built a vast affluent metropolis, extending 30 miles into the countryside, far from the mansion-lined streets of Highland Park and Southern Methodist University's larger-than-life copy of Thomas Jefferson's University of Virginia. Less known than these landmarks are more modest neighborhoods: a *new* North Dallas *north* of North Dallas. Outside the LBJ Freeway have grown up middle-income Mesquite east of Dallas, higher-income Garland and Richardson to the northeast, and the almost entirely new city of Plano in Collin County, now a corporate headquarters as well as bedroom community and the highest-income section of the Dallas-Fort Worth Metroplex.

The 3d Congressional District, with lines redrawn by a federal court for the 1996 election, no longer includes the Park Cities and North Park Center—the heart of historic North Dallas. Instead, inside much more regular boundaries, it includes most of Mesquite, and all of Garland, Richardson and Plano. This is a very Republican district, 60% for Bob Dole in 1996, though not as Republican as in its 1992 boundaries.

The congressman from the 3d District is Republican Sam Johnson, first elected in 1991, a former Air Force fighter pilot and prisoner of war in Vietnam for almost seven years, including nearly three years in solitary confinement. Johnson grew up in Dallas, graduated from SMU and George Washington University. In the Air Force, he fought in both Korea and Vietnam; after his F-4 was shot down over North Vietnam during his 25th mission, he was imprisoned from 1966–73 and was left with a slight stoop in his walk and a disfigured hand. On his return, Johnson started a home-building company and was elected to the Texas House in 1984. He won the 3d District seat in a 1991 special election after incumbent Steve Bartlett, frustrated with being in the minority, became mayor of Dallas. Johnson ran second in the primary to former Peace Corps head Tom Pauken. In the runoff Johnson emphasized his war record and, although he showed limited knowledge of issues in debate, won by a 53%–47% margin over Pauken, later the Texas Republican chairman and a sharp critic of Governor George W. Bush.

In the House, Johnson has a strong conservative record, opposing pork barrel projects of all kinds, voting for more IRAs and against extending unemployment benefits. He was a founder and chaired the Conservative Action Team, which presses Republicans leaders to stick with goals from budget targets to shutting down the National Endowment for the Arts. He criticized Newt Gingrich's handling of the 1997 disaster-relief bill, and his support, for Majority Leader Dick Armey to take over as speaker, helped lead the July 1997 abortive coup. Every Congress he offers a constitutional amendment to repeal the 16th Amendment, which authorized the federal income tax. As a Ways and Means Committee member, he staunchly supports chairman Bill Archer and shares his goal of replacing the income tax with some form of consumption tax and abolishing the IRS. In 1998, he worked with moderate Nancy Johnson of Connecticut to produce the Republicans' "Johnson and Johnson" tax-cut plan. For months he led opposition to the *Enola Gay* exhibit at the National Air and Space Museum; after he was appointed to the Board of Regents, he led the move to replace the exhibit and get rid of the museum director. Unlike some other former POWs in Congress, Johnson strongly opposed the Clinton decision to give diplomatic recognition to Vietnam. On the 25th anniversary of his release as a POW, House colleagues paid tribute to him as "an American hero."

Redistricting gave Johnson his first Democratic foe in 1996, but he had no major-party opposition in 1998. In early 1999, he denied rumors he was planning to retire.

Cook's Call. *Safe.* Johnson is sitting in one of the safest Republican seats in the state (if not the country). He will win re-election easily.

The People: Pop. 1990: 567,383; 2.5% rural; 5% age 65 +; 83.5% White, 7.4% Black, 4.5% Asian, 0.5% Amer. Indian, 4.2% Other; 8% Hispanic Origin. Households: 60.3% married couple families; 34.5% married couple fams. w. children; 68% college educ.; median household income: $41,683; per capita income: $18,858; median house value: $92,400; median gross rent: $432.

1996 Presidential Vote			1992 Presidential Vote		
Dole (R)	103,465	(61%)	Bush (R)	81,730	(46%)
Clinton (D)	53,832	(32%)	Perot (I)	59,491	(33%)
Perot (I)	13,402	(8%)	Clinton (D)	37,499	(21%)

Rep. Sam Johnson (R)

Elected May 1991; b. Oct. 11, 1930, San Antonio; home, Dallas; S. Methodist U., B.B.A. 1951, George Washington U., M.S. 1974; Methodist; married (Shirley).

Military Career: Air Force, 1950–79 (Korea & Vietnam).

Elected Office: TX House of Reps., 1984–91.

Professional Career: Home builder.

DC Office: 1030 LHOB 20515, 202-225-4201; Fax: 202-225-1485; Web site: www.house.gov/samjohnson.

District Office: Richardson, 972-470-0892.

Committees: *Education & the Workforce* (10th of 27 R): Early Childhood, Youth & Families; Workforce Protections. *Ways & Means* (12th of 23 R): Health; Social Security.

Group Ratings

	ADA	ACLU	AFS	LCV	CON	NTU	NFIB	COC	ACU	NTLC	CHC
1998	0	6	0	0	43	78	100	88	100	100	100
1997	10	—	13	—	9	65	—	100	96	—	—

National Journal Ratings

	1997 LIB — 1997 CONS			1998 LIB — 1998 CONS		
Economic	0%	—	90%	0%	—	88%
Social	29%	—	71%	11%	—	88%
Foreign	0%	—	88%	0%	—	93%

Key Votes of the 105th Congress

1. Clinton Budget Deal	Y	5. Puerto Rico Sthood. Ref.	N	9. Cut $ for B-2 Bombers	N
2. Education IRAs	Y	6. End Highway Set-asides	Y	10. Human Rights in China	N
3. Req. 2/3 to Raise Taxes	Y	7. School Prayer Amend.	Y	11. Withdraw Bosnia Troops	Y
4. Fast-track Trade	Y	8. Ovrd. Part. Birth Veto	Y	12. End Cuban TV-Marti	N

Election Results

1998 general	Sam Johnson (R)	106,690	(91%)	($601,473)
	Ken Ashby (Lib)	10,288	(9%)	
1998 primary	Sam Johnson (R)	unopposed		
1996 spec. prim.	Sam Johnson (R)	142,325	(73%)	($625,107)
	Lee Cole (D)	47,654	(24%)	($7,968)
	Others	5,047	(3%)	

FOURTH DISTRICT

The Red River Valley is just one of the hearts of Texas. It is hardscrabble farm country along an unnavigable river. First settled in the 1830s, in the days of the Texas Republic, many counties here reached their population peak around 1900, when every 160 acres was worked by a large extended farm family. This was the part of Texas that first sent Speaker Sam Rayburn to Congress in 1912. The Red River then was one of the strongest Democratic parts of the country, with a sentimental regard for Confederate veterans and a seething hatred of Wall Street bankers. Today, that economic populism is muted, but traditional religious values remain strong, even as people head for work on the interstate, listen to country music on their Walkmans and shop at Wal-Marts.

The 4th Congressional District is the lineal descendant of the seat that Rayburn held for 49 years, and still includes his home town of Bonham in Fannin County, which houses a Rayburn museum. But almost one-third of the district's voters now live in the Dallas-Fort Worth Metroplex, with another third in the small oil cities of Tyler (famous for its annual Texas Rose Festival) and Longview. These are the homes of upwardly mobile families, still conservative in their cultural values, far more trusting of free markets than of government regulation. Politics here has changed as well. In 1940, when Rayburn first became speaker, his district voted 90% for Franklin Roosevelt. In 1992, Bill Clinton finished third here, with 28%, behind George Bush and Ross Perot, and in 1996 Clinton lost to Bob Dole 56%–35%.

The congressman from the 4th is Ralph Hall, a conservative Democrat of the old Tory mold, one of the few left in the House. He was first elected in 1980 after a 30-year career in local politics and business; he was a county judge as long ago as 1950 and from 1962–72 was in the Texas Senate. He often has the most conservative voting record of any House Democrat and usually does not back the leadership except on purely party matters, and not always on these: He once declined to vote for Tip O'Neill for speaker. He opposed the Clinton budget and tax package in 1993 and supported just about everything in the Contract with America in 1995. He continues as a prime sponsor of the constitutional amendment to require two-thirds House and Senate votes to raise taxes. He took over in 1998 as chairman of Paul Weyrich's Free Congress Foundation, a conservative Washington think tank. And he was one of five House Democrats to vote to impeach President Clinton. Clinton's lying under oath "was perjury and perjury is a felony and it's impeachable," Hall said. "I'm not a big fan of his." But Hall is not a pure free marketeer: He voted against NAFTA. On the Commerce Committee he was skeptical about allowing the regional Bells into long distance and favored cable reregulation.

Those views are perhaps one reason why Hall, unlike five other Democrats—some with voting records actually less conservative than his—did not switch parties after Republicans won the House majority. "I think it's my duty to stay [a Democrat] and try to pull them back toward the middle," he said. Hall is a hunting pal of Commerce's ranking Democrat John Dingell, and he is the ranking Democrat himself on the Energy and Power Subcommittee, a convenient slot for a booster of the oil and gas industry; the panel handles electric utility deregulation, a heavily lobbied issue in the 105th and 106th Congresses. Previously, he chaired a space subcommittee and emphasized the use of space for biomedical research: "I fully and firmly believe that we're going to find some cures for the dreaded diseases, cancer and diabetes, there, because we can't find them on Earth." He authored a 1997 law banning federal funding for physician-assisted suicide.

Despite continuing speculation about his retirement, Hall continues to win handily. But he faced better-financed opposition than usual in 1998 from Tyler physician Jim Lohmeyer, who said government is "too intrusive" and wanted to privatize Social Security; this was the only 1998 House contest in which National Rifle Association President Charlton Heston campaigned for the Democrat. Hall endorsed Republican Senator Phil Gramm for re-election in 1996 and he has spoken favorably about Governor George W. Bush as president. Most political observers agree that the 4th will elect a Republican when Hall retires. But it's also possible that this rather ungainly-shaped district will be altered beyond recognition after the 2000 Census, thus sparing "Mister Sam" the pain of seeing his former district in Republican hands.

Cook's Call. *Probably Safe.* When nine-term Representative Hall decides to retire, this

Republican-leaning seat will almost certainly fall into Republican hands. Until then, the popular and conservative Hall remains a tough target.

The People: Pop. 1990: 567,231; 48.9% rural; 14.1% age 65 + ; 88.3% White, 8.3% Black, 0.5% Asian, 0.7% Amer. Indian, 2.2% Other; 4.3% Hispanic Origin. Households: 61.9% married couple families; 30.5% married couple fams. w. children; 44.8% college educ.; median household income: $26,974; per capita income: $12,724; median house value: $57,500; median gross rent: $299.

1996 Presidential Vote			1992 Presidential Vote		
Dole (R)	114,787	(56%)	Bush (R)	92,865	(41%)
Clinton (D)	71,784	(35%)	Perot (I)	67,184	(30%)
Perot (I)	18,021	(9%)	Clinton (D)	64,068	(29%)

Rep. Ralph M. Hall (D)

Elected 1980; b. May 3, 1923, Fate; home, Rockwall; U. of TX, TX Christian U., S. Methodist U., LL.B. 1951; United Methodist; married (Mary Ellen).

Military Career: Navy, 1942–45 (WWII).

Elected Office: Rockwall Cnty. Judge, 1950–62; TX Senate, 1962–72.

Professional Career: Practicing atty., 1951–80; Pres. & CEO, TX Aluminum Corp., 1967–68; Spec. Cnsl., Howmet Corp., 1970–74.

DC Office: 2221 RHOB 20515, 202-225-6673; Fax: 202-225-3332; Web site: www.house.gov/ralphhall.

District Offices: Rockwall, 214-771-9118; Sherman, 903-892-1112; Tyler, 903-597-3729.

Committees: *Commerce* (4th of 24 D): Energy & Power (RMM); Finance & Hazardous Materials; Health and Environment. *Science* (2d of 23 D): Energy & Environment; Space & Aeronautics.

Group Ratings

	ADA	ACLU	AFS	LCV	CON	NTU	NFIB	COC	ACU	NTLC	CHC
1998	15	7	22	15	74	63	86	76	96	82	92
1997	10	—	13	—	37	53	—	80	96	—	—

National Journal Ratings

	1997 LIB	—	1997 CONS	1998 LIB	—	1998 CONS
Economic	43%	—	56%	41%	—	58%
Social	30%	—	64%	3%	—	90%
Foreign	22%	—	77%	7%	—	83%

Key Votes of the 105th Congress

1. Clinton Budget Deal	Y	5. Puerto Rico Sthood. Ref.	N	9. Cut $ for B-2 Bombers	N
2. Education IRAs	Y	6. End Highway Set-asides	Y	10. Human Rights in China	N
3. Req. 2/3 to Raise Taxes	Y	7. School Prayer Amend.	Y	11. Withdraw Bosnia Troops	Y
4. Fast-track Trade	Y	8. Ovrd. Part. Birth Veto	Y	12. End Cuban TV-Marti	N

1998 general	Ralph M. Hall (D)	82,989	(58%)	($597,793)
	Jim Lohmeyer (R)	58,954	(41%)	($246,101)
	Others	2,137	(1%)	
1998 primary	Ralph M. Hall (D)	unopposed		
1996 general	Ralph M. Hall (D)	132,126	(64%)	($527,260)
	Jerry Ray Hall (R)	71,065	(34%)	($30,156)
	Others	3,986	(2%)	

FIFTH DISTRICT

Not all of Dallas is glitz and postmodern marble. From each side of downtown, on one of the three street grids that run skew to each other, is an older Dallas, with neighborhoods of high-ceilinged old mansions, modest bungalows and shotgun houses running out toward the old airport at Love Field or the State Fair Grounds and the Cotton Bowl in east Dallas, or south to the desolate treeless parks along the cement-lined Trinity River. Some of this older Dallas is being renovated and rebuilt, with chic cafes and trendy stores serving those who make their livings catering to the rich farther north. Other once middle-class neighborhoods are filling up with immigrants from Mexico and other parts of Latin America, once again noisy with children as they were in the 1950s when people moved here not from Mexico or Central America but from the almost all-Anglo counties of north and central Texas.

Texas's 5th Congressional District, as redistricted in 1996, includes such neighborhoods just south and east of downtown Dallas. Added in the redistricting were the affluent Lakewood and Lake Highlands areas around and beyond White Rock Lake, out to the LBJ Freeway. Then, following the same lines used in the Democrats' creative 1991 redistricting, the 5th proceeds in a narrow corridor through the suburbs to combine this part of Dallas County with seven rural and small town counties about halfway between Dallas and Houston, plus black neighborhoods in Tyler and Bryan. But the political balance in 1996 was a bit different than before redistricting. The affluent precincts added are heavily Republican and mostly white, reducing the 5th's black and Hispanic percentages, and changing a district Bill Clinton carried in 1992 by 40%–34% to one that he lost 39%–34% that year and lost 48%–44% in 1996.

The congressman from the 5th District is Pete Sessions, a Republican elected in 1996. Sessions grew up in Waco, graduated from Southwestern University, then worked at Southwestern Bell in Dallas for 16 years; his father William Sessions, a federal judge, served as FBI director from 1987–93. Pete Sessions ran in the 1991 special election in the 3d District and finished sixth. In 1993 he resigned his job to run against 5th District Democrat John Bryant. A liberal and an active legislator, Bryant was a prime beneficiary of Texas's Democratic districting plan, and he won easily in 1992. But in 1994, Sessions ran a vigorous campaign, making a two-day, 12-city tour of the district's rural portions with a livestock trailer full of horse manure and a sign saying "the Clinton health care plan stinks worse than this trailer." "A vulgar thing," Bryant sniffed. Although he outspent Sessions 2–1, Bryant was closely pressed and won by just 50%–47%. In 1996, even before redistricting, Bryant decided to run for the Senate against Phil Gramm; Bryant was the surprise loser in the Democratic primary to the pickup truck campaign of high school teacher Victor Morales, who lost 55%–44% to Gramm.

Sessions ran again in 1996 and won the March primary. That result was thrown out in the redistricting case in the summer, but only Sessions and the winner of the Democratic primary, John Pouland, a former regional GSA administrator, ran in November. Sessions was pleased that his home area in east Dallas was now included in the district. He charged that Pouland was a big government liberal and would abandon U.S. military bases overseas; Pouland criticized subsidizing the foreign bases while pursuing Medicare "cuts." Pouland charged that Sessions had changed to an anti-abortion stance after his 1991 race; Sessions sent out brochures graphically describing partial-birth abortions. This was a seriously contested race: Sessions spent $1 million, Pouland $600,000. Redistricting probably made the difference. Sessions won 56%–44% in Dallas County, 10% ahead of his 1994 showing there. Pouland carried the rest of the district by 507 votes, nearly a carbon copy of Bryant's showing there. Overall Sessions won 53%–47%.

In 1998, his opponent was none other than Morales, who again ran a shoestring campaign, criticizing Sessions for taking special-interest contributions. Sessions backed school vouchers, tax cuts and removing troops from Bosnia. Sessions again won 56%–44%; most of his margin came from the 51% who cast their vote in Dallas County, but he also carried seven of the 11 other counties.

In the House Sessions has a solidly conservative voting record. Majority Leader Dick Armey named him to chair the Results Caucus, which oversees progress toward targets for government reform. In November 1998 he won a seat on the Rules Committee, a sure sign that he is a leadership loyalist. In early 1999 he launched the House bandwagon for the presidential candidacy of Governor George W. Bush.

Cook's Call. *Probably Safe.* Sessions has never won here by big margins, but it is still hard for Democrats to wrest this district away from its Republican trend.

The People: Pop. 1990: 566,887; 25% rural; 13.2% age 65 + ; 74.6% White, 15.8% Black, 1.2% Asian, 0.4% Amer. Indian, 8% Other; 14.1% Hispanic Origin. Households: 50.3% married couple families; 24.4% married couple fams. w. children; 44.3% college educ.; median household income: $25,817; per capita income: $13,045; median house value: $62,400; median gross rent: $357.

1996 Presidential Vote

Dole (R)	97,057	(48%)
Clinton (D)	87,987	(44%)
Perot (I)	16,045	(8%)

1992 Presidential Vote

Bush (R)	91,136	(39%)
Clinton (D)	80,051	(34%)
Perot (I)	62,708	(27%)

Rep. Pete Sessions (R)

Elected 1996; b. Mar. 22, 1955, Waco; home, Dallas; SW U., B.A. 1978; Methodist; married (Juanita).

Professional Career: District Mgr., SW Bell Telephone Co., 1978–93; V.P., Public Policy, Natl. Center for Policy Analysis, 1994–95.

DC Office: 1318 LHOB 20515, 202-225-2231; Fax: 202-225-5878; Web site: www.house.gov/sessions.

District Offices: Athens, 903-675-8288; Dallas, 214-349-9996.

Committees: *Rules* (8th of 9 R): Rules & Organization of the House.

Group Ratings

	ADA	ACLU	AFS	LCV	CON	NTU	NFIB	COC	ACU	NTLC	CHC
1998	0	6	0	0	60	70	100	89	100	97	100
1997	0	—	13	—	70	62	—	90	100	—	—

National Journal Ratings

	1997 LIB — 1997 CONS		1998 LIB — 1998 CONS	
Economic	0% —	90%	0% —	88%
Social	0% —	90%	0% —	97%
Foreign	0% —	88%	0% —	93%

Key Votes of the 105th Congress

1. Clinton Budget Deal	Y	5. Puerto Rico Sthood. Ref.	N	9. Cut $ for B-2 Bombers	N
2. Education IRAs	Y	6. End Highway Set-asides	Y	10. Human Rights in China	*
3. Req. 2/3 to Raise Taxes	Y	7. School Prayer Amend.	Y	11. Withdraw Bosnia Troops	Y
4. Fast-track Trade	Y	8. Ovrd. Part. Birth Veto	Y	12. End Cuban TV-Marti	N

Election Results

1998 general	Pete Sessions (R)	61,714	(56%)	($747,685)
	Victor M. Morales (D)	48,073	(43%)	($107,870)
1998 primary	Pete Sessions (R)	unopposed		
1996 spec. prim.	Pete Sessions (R)	80,196	(53%)	($1,091,122)
	John Pouland (D)	70,922	(47%)	($602,884)

SIXTH DISTRICT

The Dallas-Fort Worth Metroplex—yes, the name is part of everyday speech there—has spread outward from its historic nodes in downtown Dallas and Fort Worth. Although Dallas is the larger population center, much of the development has moved west, across the dusty plains where one crosses the barely perceptible Balcones Escarpment, the geologist's boundary between green and grassy East Texas and the brown and barren West. This was empty territory a few decades ago; now it has mostly been filled in, with subdivisions and shopping centers that leave some feeling of the shape of this land under the enormous Texas sky.

The 6th Congressional District takes in much of this territory. It is the descendant of a more-rural district that stretched from Dallas-Fort Worth to Houston and was represented from 1978–84 by Phil Gramm. Now the 6th is entirely within the Metroplex. It includes much of Dallas/Fort Worth International Airport and cargo-servicing Alliance Airport, developed by Ross Perot Jr. In between are rapidly growing and increasingly affluent suburbs—Colleyville, Grapevine, Euless, Bedford—and to the south is Arlington, home of the Texas Rangers' new Ballpark and of Six Flags Over Texas. Essentially the 6th is a ring of suburban territory around Fort Worth, wrapping around the 12th District and part of the 24th. The boundaries were only slightly smoothed out by a federal court in 1996. The original Democratic redistricters were trying to concentrate Republican votes in this heavily Republican district; asked the court's motivation, 6th District Congressman Joe Barton responded, "I'd like to be able to talk to the federal judges and ask what the heck they were trying to accomplish."

Barton grew up in rural Ennis, graduated from Texas A&M and Purdue, worked in business and was a White House Fellow. When Gramm ran for the Senate in 1984, Barton ran for the House, and won the Republican runoff by only 10 votes and the general with 57%. Barton has had two great causes, one defunct, the other hanging fire. The first was the Superconductor Supercollider, an enormous scientific laboratory that was to have been built in Waxahachie, south of Dallas, part of which is in the district. In retrospect this was a Texas project, alive only so long as George Bush was president; despite Barton's efforts, the House voted 282–143 to zero it out in October 1993.

Barton's other great cause has been the balanced budget amendment. He has been the chief House sponsor of the version requiring a two-thirds vote to raise taxes. When the House took up the issue in early 1995, many freshmen complained that party leaders were not doing enough to support Barton's version, while leaders whispered there was no way the tax-limitation measure could win the needed 290 votes. In fact it got 253. Barton played a vital role in getting all but two Republicans to vote for it, and in return Newt Gingrich promised to schedule the two-thirds amendment for a vote on subsequent April 15ths until it passed. It got 243 votes in 1996, 233 in 1997, 238 in 1998, 229 in 1999—not an encouraging trajectory. But Barton claims he is making progress across the country; 14 states have approved tax-limitation plans, and he is campaigning for support elsewhere. And he got the House to vote a rule requiring a two-thirds vote for a tax increase. He also has sponsored a bill to overhaul the budget process, by creating a biennial budget plan that the president must sign into law.

In the 104th and 105th Congresses, Barton chaired the Commerce Oversight and Investigation Subcommittee and conducted extensive hearings on food and drug laws. These resulted in the 1997 enactment, with bipartisan support, of major FDA modernization, encouraging the agency to more quickly review innovative drugs and medical devices. Barton was an official observer to the November 1997 global warming talks in Kyoto, and said the treaty was overly stringent and would have adverse economic consequences. But he supported legislation to encourage companies to reduce greenhouse emissions on their own. He also gained attention with hearings that explored millions of dollars in travel expenses by Energy Secretary Hazel O'Leary and examined Clinton's 1996 campaign fundraising practices. In January 1999 Barton became chairman of the Commerce Energy and Power Subcommittee. Early priorities include electricity deregulation—which Barton said is "doable" and needed because of inconsistent state plans—and nuclear-waste disposal. With conservative Texan Ralph Hall as ranking Democrat, the subcommittee is sympathetic to the oil and gas industry.

Barton can be stubborn and original. He has voted against compromise budgets backed by the Republican leadership and has pressed for mandatory random drug testing for the House. Back home, he has assisted Dallas/Forth Worth International Airport—which he predicts will soon become the world's busiest—with new radar consoles and computer software for its air-traffic system. He has passed a relaxation of the Wright Amendment, named for former House Speaker Jim Wright, restricting flights to Dallas's Love Field; his 1998 primary and general election foes criticized Barton's action as harmful to DFW, but the issue had little impact.

Barton has had some political disappointments. He ran for the Senate in 1993 after Lloyd Bentsen resigned to be Treasury secretary. Despite the support of former Governor Bill Clements, he finished third with just 14% of the vote in the May all-party primary. In June 1994 he was outgoing Republican state Chairman Fred Meyer's choice to succeed him. But Clements (in a move he has since regretted) opposed his candidacy, and Barton lost at the convention to Tom Pauken. And in 1995 he was the House chairman of Phil Gramm's hapless presidential campaign. He has been more fortunate in his own House races: In 1998 he was re-elected with 73% of the vote.

Cook's Call. *Safe.* This conservative Republican district is not going to make it onto any Democratic target lists anytime soon. Barton is in solid standing for 2000.

The People: Pop. 1990: 565,504; 9% rural; 6.1% age 65 + ; 90% White, 5.1% Black, 2.2% Asian, 0.4% Amer. Indian, 2.2% Other; 5.6% Hispanic Origin. Households: 62.5% married couple families; 33.6% married couple fams. w. children; 67.3% college educ.; median household income: $40,930; per capita income: $18,573; median house value: $90,900; median gross rent: $394.

1996 Presidential Vote

Dole (R)	143,067	(60%)
Clinton (D)	77,542	(33%)
Perot (I)	17,234	(7%)

1992 Presidential Vote

Bush (R)	122,176	(46%)
Perot (I)	80,372	(30%)
Clinton (D)	65,514	(24%)

Rep. Joe Barton (R)

Elected 1984; b. Sept. 15, 1949, Waco; home, Ennis; Texas A&M U., B.S. 1972, Purdue U., M.S. 1973; United Methodist; married (Janet).

Professional Career: Asst. to V.P., Ennis Business Forms, 1973–81; White House Fellow, U.S. Dept. of Energy, 1981–82; Consultant, Atlantic Richfield Co., 1982–84.

DC Office: 2264 RHOB 20515, 202-225-2002; Fax: 202-225-3052; Web site: www.house.gov/barton.

District Offices: Arlington, 817-543-1000; Ennis, 972-875-8488.

Committees: *Commerce* (5th of 29 R): Energy & Power (Chmn.); Oversight & Investigations. *Science* (7th of 25 R): Energy & Environment; Space & Aeronautics.

Group Ratings

	ADA	ACLU	AFS	LCV	CON	NTU	NFIB	COC	ACU	NTLC	CHC
1998	5	6	0	8	81	75	93	78	100	100	100
1997	10	—	13	—	18	61	—	78	92	—	—

National Journal Ratings

	1997 LIB — 1997 CONS	1998 LIB — 1998 CONS
Economic	27% — 73%	0% — 88%
Social	41% — 57%	11% — 88%
Foreign	24% — 72%	7% — 83%

Key Votes of the 105th Congress

1. Clinton Budget Deal	Y	5. Puerto Rico Sthood. Ref.	N	9. Cut $ for B-2 Bombers	Y
2. Education IRAs	Y	6. End Highway Set-asides	Y	10. Human Rights in China	N
3. Req. 2/3 to Raise Taxes	Y	7. School Prayer Amend.	Y	11. Withdraw Bosnia Troops	Y
4. Fast-track Trade	Y	8. Ovrd. Part. Birth Veto	Y	12. End Cuban TV-Marti	N

Election Results

1998 general	Joe Barton (R)	112,957	(73%)	($1,117,657)
	Ben B. Boothe (D)	40,112	(26%)	($61,462)
1998 primary	Joe Barton (R)	21,480	(73%)	
	Greg Mullanax (R)	7,965	(27%)	
1996 spec. prim.	Joe Barton (R)	160,800	(77%)	($890,468)
	Janet Carroll Richardson (I)	26,713	(13%)	($123,291)
	Catherine A. Anderson (Lib)	14,456	(7%)	
	Others	6,547	(3%)	

SEVENTH DISTRICT

When George Bush moved from Midland in West Texas to Houston in 1960, he bought a house in Briarwood, in what was then the western edge of the fast-growing city, beyond Memorial Park and Loop 610, long before the Galleria and high-rises went up around the intersection of Post Oak and Westheimer. Bush returned to Houston in 1993 and built a new house a mile from his old one, just west of Memorial Park, the largest in Houston. Bush's favorite shopping mall is nearby on Sage and San Felipe and his favorite barbecue joint a mile east on Memorial; his new office is atop the Park Laureate building at 10000 Memorial. But now all these landmarks are not at the edge of the vastly bigger—and in the 1990s increasingly economically vibrant—Houston metropolitan area, but near its epicenter, certainly its retail center and not far from its commercial center, though the industrial center of gravity remains far to the east, near the Ship Channel.

The 7th Congressional District is the lineal descendant of the district that elected George Bush its first member of the House in 1966 and 1968. It occupied far more territory then, and its boundaries have been pared back as the population of the west side of Houston has sky-rocketed. There are more than 1.5 million people today in the area that had 350,000 when Bush was first elected. Indeed, in 1990 the then-7th District had 784,000 people, the second most in Texas. The district was pared back in 1992, and it was not much changed by the 1996 court redistricting, so that it now starts just outside Memorial Park and extends west on Westheimer and the Katy Freeway and occupies most of Harris County west of Hillcroft and Bingle. It remains hyper-Republican, arguably the most Republican district in the nation.

The congressman from the 7th District is Bill Archer, chairman of the House Ways and Means Committee, who was elected to the House in 1970 when Bush ran for the Senate. Archer grew up in Houston, graduated from the University of Texas and after service in the Air Force ran a feed business and participated in civic affairs. He was elected to the state House in 1966 as a Democrat, a very conservative one; in 1968 he switched parties and in 1970 was easily elected to the House as a Republican. His devotion to free market economics, cultural conser-vatism and an assertive foreign policy give him one of the most conservative voting records in the House. He joined Ways and Means in 1973, when Chairman Wilbur Mills let Republicans participate as much as Democrats. From 1975–94, when Al Ullman and Dan Rostenkowski were chairmen, Archer was given little say on most issues. Sometimes he was even a minority within his party. He opposed the 1983 Social Security bailout and was one of the Republicans who nearly scuttled the 1986 tax reform in December 1985. He opposed the budget summit agreement of 1990. He is a scrupulous man, who insists on preparing his own income tax every year because he wants to understand the burdens it imposes—in 1998 it took him "two full weekend days"; he refuses to take PAC contributions and has never held a Washington fun-draiser, though he could easily raise millions, and he stays punctiliously loyal to his convictions.

As chairman, Archer has behaved courteously and worked hard, has cooperated with the Republican leadership on many major issues but has also moved strategically to put his own imprint on long-term policy. Through much of the 104th Congress, Archer's leeway on issues was sharply circumscribed by the Republican leadership. The Contract with America specified what tax cuts Republicans would seek, and Budget Chairman John Kasich pressed other tasks on Archer and his committee, including what Kasich considers cuts in corporate welfare and what Archer considers tax increases on business. On two other major issues in which Ways and Means passed major reforms—welfare and Medicare—subcommittee chairmen, Clay Shaw on welfare and Bill Thomas on Medicare, did much of the detail work, and Republican gov-ernors made large contributions as well. But Archer also showed a mastery of specifics and strategy. He played a major role in keeping Medical Savings Accounts in the health care bill passed in August 1996. Archer managed to do all this while leaving committee meetings and legislative drafting much more open than they had been under Rostenkowski, though Democrats still complained.

The May 1997 balanced budget agreement gave Archer the task of coming up with a package of tax cuts that had been vaguely defined and limited to specific sums. Archer's package included a significant cut in the capital gains tax—a longtime goal—raising the threshold for the inheritance tax from $600,000 to $1 million, expanding IRAs and the $150 per child tax credit. Archer's leeway was narrow, since the total cuts were limited to $95 billion; since computers allow rapid calculations of tax impacts, the process produced exceptions and income limits which complicated the Code far more than Archer desired. This was not the only issue on which Archer was frustrated by the Republican leadership. He opposed extending the ethanol subsidies; but Newt Gingrich, concerned about Republican incumbents in farm states, insisted on an extension to 2007 in the June 1998 transportation bill. Archer produced a bill in September 1998 which included ending the marriage penalty, 100% deductibility for health insurance for the self-employed, and a speed-up of raising the threshold for the inheritance tax. But it was abandoned in October. As Mark McGwire and Sammy Sosa were hitting record numbers of home runs, Archer said he would introduce a bill to prevent fans who caught home run balls and donated them from having to pay a gift tax. In October 1998 he barred the move to exempt from tax the reward money for David Kaczynski, brother of the Unabomber, although he promised to donate it all to his brothers' victims.

Archer took up Bill Clinton's January 1999 challenge to reserve 62% of the surplus for Social Security, though he wanted much of the rest to go to tax cuts. In December 1998 he called on Clinton to introduce his own Social Security reform before Ways and Means would act on the issue; although Clinton presented only a sketchy outline, in April 1999 Archer and subcommittee Chairman Clay Shaw introduced their own bill. It would give workers tax credits amounting to 2% of income and require them to put it into one of several private investment funds; on retirement, they would have to turn the funds over to the government, which would pay them an annuity based on the amount, with a minimum of what they would have gotten through the Social Security payroll tax. A Clinton spokesman said it "could be the basis for bipartisan consensus," but it was criticized both on left and right, and in June 1999 it seemed unlikely to be passed by either house.

Republican rules impose a three-term limit on chairmanships; Archer announced before the 1998 election that he would not run for re-election in 2000. How much will he have achieved as chairman of his goals? His greatest long-term goal has been to replace the income tax with a broad-based consumption tax. That never became party policy, partly because Majority Leader Dick Armey called for a flat tax and partly because after Clinton's re-election in 1996 the House has not had the stomach to do all the work needed to enact a major reform when it seemed to face a sure veto and much demagoguery. But Archer has made some progress, within the limits set by budget negotiations, on cutting taxes. And if in the process he has had to make the tax code more rather than less complicated, that may in fact build more pressure over the long-run for abandonment of the income tax for a less complex tax system. The issue has been put on the table and, whatever the prospects of the Archer-Shaw Social Security bill, so has the issue of Social Security reform. And it is hard to imagine even a Democratic Congress and president increasing taxes again after the experience of 1994. In either case Archer, who before 1994 seemed to be a backer of lost causes, has reason to feel some satisfaction as well as frustration.

Archer was always re-elected easily; in 1998 he won with 93% of the vote. The next congressman from the 7th District seems sure to be chosen in the March 2000 Republican primary. The leading candidate in mid-1999 seemed to be state Representative John Culberson, a 14-year legislator who worked on tort reform, tax cuts and an end of federal control of the Texas prison system. Running more as a cultural conservative was Harris County Republican Vice-Chairman Cathy McConn. Other possible candidates include businessman Peter Wareing, son-in-law of Texas oilman Jack Blanton, and attorney Mark Brewer. This is likely to be a million-dollar battle for what could be a lifetime seat.

Cook's Call. *Safe.* Though Archer is retiring at the end of this—his 15th—term, Republicans will have no trouble keeping this seat in their column. Expect a crowded Republican primary, but little other action here in 2000.

The People: Pop. 1990: 565,007; 3.5% rural; 6.1% age 65+; 80.5% White, 6% Black, 5.4% Asian, 0.3% Amer. Indian, 7.8% Other; 16.1% Hispanic Origin. Households: 54% married couple families; 29.9% married couple fams. w. children; 69.8% college educ.; median household income: $40,331; per capita income: $22,666; median house value: $92,100; median gross rent: $394.

1996 Presidential Vote			1992 Presidential Vote		
Dole (R)	146,923	(66%)	Bush (R)	133,180	(57%)
Clinton (D)	63,853	(29%)	Clinton (D)	52,718	(23%)
Perot (I)	10,569	(5%)	Perot (I)	46,912	(20%)

Rep. Bill Archer (R)

Elected 1970; b. Mar. 22, 1928, Houston; home, Houston; Rice U., 1945–46, U. of TX, B.B.A. 1949, LL.B. 1951; Catholic; married (Sharon).

Military Career: Air Force, 1951–53.

Elected Office: Hunters Creek Village Cncl., Mayor Pro-Tem, 1955–62; TX House of Reps., 1966–70.

Professional Career: Pres., Uncle Johnny Mills Inc., 1953–61; Dir., Heights State Bank, Houston, 1967–70; Practicing atty., 1968–70.

DC Office: 1236 LHOB 20515, 202-225-2571; Fax: 202-225-4381; Web site: www.house.gov/archer.

District Office: Houston, 713-682-8828.

Committees: *Ways & Means* (Chmn. of 23 R). *Joint Committee on Taxation* (Chmn. of 5 Reps.).

Group Ratings

	ADA	ACLU	AFS	LCV	CON	NTU	NFIB	COC	ACU	NTLC	CHC
1998	0	7	0	15	31	65	100	100	92	95	100
1997	5	—	13	—	62	55	—	100	80	—	—

National Journal Ratings

	1997 LIB — 1997 CONS			1998 LIB — 1998 CONS		
Economic	19%	—	76%	0%	—	88%
Social	0%	—	90%	10%	—	89%
Foreign	12%	—	81%	34%	—	62%

Key Votes of the 105th Congress

1. Clinton Budget Deal	Y	5. Puerto Rico Sthood. Ref.	N
2. Education IRAs	Y	6. End Highway Set-asides	Y
3. Req. 2/3 to Raise Taxes	Y	7. School Prayer Amend.	Y
4. Fast-track Trade	Y	8. Ovrd. Part. Birth Veto	Y

9. Cut $ for B-2 Bombers	Y
10. Human Rights in China	N
11. Withdraw Bosnia Troops	Y
12. End Cuban TV-Marti	N

Election Results

1998 general	Bill Archer (R)	111,010	(93%)	($346,064)
	Drew Parks (Lib)	7,889	(7%)	
1998 primary	Bill Archer (R)	28,625	(97%)	
	Others	961	(3%)	
1996 spec. prim.	Bill Archer (R)	152,024	(81%)	($298,951)
	Al J.K. Siegmind (D)	28,187	(15%)	
	Others	6,620	(4%)	

EIGHTH DISTRICT

When Houston Intercontinental Airport opened in 1969, it was located far north of the city, in vacant ground near the small town of Humble (named for the oil company that was the predecessor of Exxon)—far from downtown Houston or from just about any other concentration of population. Today, Intercontinental is still a long way from downtown Houston, but it is no longer in the middle of nowhere. It's in the middle of a zone of rapid metropolitan expansion and growth, of commercial office space and upscale residential subdivisions rising on land that once held roadside stands and barbecues and unpainted farmhouses with water pooling on low swampy fields. Greater Houston has spread far out into the countryside, past Loop 610 in the inner city, past the Sam Houston Tollway, past the now mislabeled Farm-Market 1960, out past Conroe and Woodbranch Village in once rural Montgomery County.

The 8th Congressional District occupies most of this territory. A district that once covered the docks along the Houston Ship Channel has moved out with the people, so that its southern boundary runs roughly along FM 1960, sometimes dipping south to the Sam Houston Tollway. In its current boundaries, with minor changes made by the court-ordered redistricting in 1996, the 8th includes almost all of Montgomery County and two still mostly rural counties to the west and takes in College Station, home of Texas A&M University. This institution deserves more notice than it usually gets: It is one of Texas's two major state universities, with quite a different atmosphere from the University of Texas at Austin. A&M has an agricultural and military tradition and is the site of the George Bush Presidential Library; its students' test scores are similar to those at UT, but their political attitudes are far more conservative. College Station and almost all the rest of the 8th District are staunchly Republican: defiantly free market on economics, respectful of tradition on cultural issues, firmly hawkish on military policy.

The congressman from the 8th District is Kevin Brady, a Republican who grew up and went to college in South Dakota. Then he moved to Montgomery County and worked as a Chamber of Commerce executive for 18 years. In 1990 he was elected to the Texas House. When 8th District Congressman Jack Fields announced in 1995 he was retiring, Brady's main rival in this Republican district was Eugene Fontenot, a physician who wanted "to restore America to its Christian heritage." Fontenot spent $4.7 million, a good portion of it his own money, running in the open 25th District seat in 1994, but lost to Ken Bentsen 52%–45%. In 1996 Fontenot moved his campaign operation to the north side 8th District; he and Brady ran against each other no less than four times that year. Brady had the support of Fields, Governor George W. Bush, and Senators Phil Gramm and Kay Bailey Hutchison; Fontenot was endorsed by Patrick Buchanan, Pat Robertson and Phyllis Schlafly. Brady touted the sunset law he had passed in the legislature. Fontenot attacked him for being one of two Republicans to vote against the carrying-concealed-weapons law. Brady opposed most gun control bills, but not this; when he was 12 his father was shot and killed while trying a case in a South Dakota courtroom.

In the March 1996 primary, Fontenot beat Brady 36%–22% in a six-candidate field. Then in the April runoff Brady won 53%–47%. But as part of a Supreme Court order in August that redrew the boundaries of three invalid congressional districts and 10 of those adjoining, the court mandated an all-party primary November 5. Fontenot started spending liberally again, though less than in 1994—$1.3 million in all—and Brady nearly matched him, with $1.1 million. While the district seemed sure to remain Republican, suddenly Brady's victory was in doubt. In November Brady led 41%–39%. This was due to his big margin in Montgomery County; Fontenot carried College Station and the Harris County part of the district. In the December runoff, turnout was sharply down. This evidently helped party-regular Brady, who won 59%–41%, carrying every county.

On the International Relations Committee, Brady called for renegotiating extradition treaties to deny safe harbors overseas to fugitives accused of heinous crimes in the U.S. The murder of his father also has made Brady an advocate of victims' rights and the death penalty. He pushed for sunset reform of ineffective government agencies. In a man-bites-dog tale, he refused to support a company's application for a $9.5 million grant for a riverwalk at The Woodlands: "I think projects that aren't essential can't be supported, even if they're in a congressman's district or hometown," he said.

Brady had no Democratic opponent in 1998 and won easily. Redistricting could change his district boundaries again, but this fast-growing area will surely remain a heavily Republican. He has said he will seek Bill Archer's seat on Ways and Means when Archer retires as he has promised to do in 2000.

Cook's Call. *Safe.* In a district that gave Clinton only 26% of the vote in 1996, it's not hard to see why Brady is a sure bet for re-election in 2000.

The People: Pop. 1990: 565,315; 35.6% rural; 7.4% age 65 + ; 89.8% White, 5.1% Black, 1.9% Asian, 0.3% Amer. Indian, 2.9% Other; 7% Hispanic Origin. Households: 63.5% married couple families; 35.5% married couple fams. w. children; 58% college educ.; median household income: $35,809; per capita income: $16,006; median house value: $79,200; median gross rent: $360.

1996 Presidential Vote

Dole (R) 149,402 (67%)
Clinton (D) 59,045 (26%)
Perot (I) 14,589 (7%)

1992 Presidential Vote

Bush (R) 135,048 (55%)
Clinton (D) 55,847 (23%)
Perot (I) 55,373 (22%)

Rep. Kevin Brady (R)

Elected 1996; b. Apr. 11, 1955, Vermillion, SD; home, The Woodlands, TX; U. of SD, B.S. 1990; Catholic; married (Kathy).

Elected Office: TX House of Reps., 1990–96.

Professional Career: Exec., Woodlands Chamber of Commerce, 1978–96.

DC Office: 1531 LHOB 20515, 202-225-4901; Fax: 202-225-5524; Web site: www.house.gov/brady.

District Offices: College Station, 409-846-6068; Conroe, 409-441-5700; Houston, 281-895-8892.

Committees: *International Relations* (21st of 26 R): International Economic Policy & Trade; Western Hemisphere. *Resources* (18th of 28 R): Energy & Mineral Resources. *Science* (16th of 25 R): Space & Aeronautics; Technology.

Group Ratings

	ADA	ACLU	AFS	LCV	CON	NTU	NFIB	COC	ACU	NTLC	CHC
1998	0	6	0	0	45	60	100	94	96	95	100
1997	5	—	0	—	86	64	—	100	100	—	—

National Journal Ratings

	1997 LIB — 1997 CONS		1998 LIB — 1998 CONS	
Economic	0% —	90%	23% —	74%
Social	20% —	71%	20% —	80%
Foreign	19% —	80%	27% —	68%

Key Votes of the 105th Congress

1. Clinton Budget Deal	Y	5. Puerto Rico Sthood. Ref. N	9. Cut $ for B-2 Bombers N
2. Education IRAs	Y	6. End Highway Set-asides Y	10. Human Rights in China N
3. Req. 2/3 to Raise Taxes	Y	7. School Prayer Amend. Y	11. Withdraw Bosnia Troops Y
4. Fast-track Trade	Y	8. Ovrd. Part. Birth Veto Y	12. End Cuban TV-Marti N

Election Results

1998 general	Kevin Brady (R)	123,372	(93%)	($496,717)
	Don L. Richards (Lib)	9,576	(7%)	
1998 primary	Kevin Brady (R)	34,841	(89%)	
	Andre Dean (R)	4,452	(11%)	
1996 spec. runoff	Kevin Brady (R)	30,366	(59%)	($1,094,498)
	Gene Fontenot (R)	21,004	(41%)	($1,379,749)
1996 spec. prim.	Kevin Brady (R)	80,325	(41%)	
	Gene Fontenot (R)	75,399	(39%)	
	Cynthia Newman (D)	26,246	(14%)	
	Robert Musemeche (D)	11,689	(6%)	

NINTH DISTRICT

The spongy land of the Texas Gulf Coast, where the French explorer LaSalle and the Spanish colonizer Galvez dreamed of thriving settlements, remained mostly unsettled until well into the 20th Century. The elements here are not gentle, as Galveston learned when a hurricane in 1900 destroyed this city on a sandspit. The summer heat is ferocious and the rains torrential; few crops grow well here. But this is a land of oil. Ever since the Spindletop strike in Beaumont in 1901, the coastal area has grown. First oil exploration, then petroleum refining, then petrochemicals: The straight-edged metal of oil rigs and the intricate curving metalwork of refineries shine through the swampy landscape of southeast Texas. And the rig workers and mechanical engineers they brought here have given a kind of permanent roughneck air to the region.

The 9th Congressional District occupies much of this territory. About half its people live in and around Beaumont and Port Arthur, still very much oil country and among the few places in Texas where labor unions have had any strength. The other half live south of Houston—in Galveston, now restoring its grand historic buildings (and the unlikely site of a Dickensian Christmas celebration every year); the refinery town of Texas City, where more than 500 died in a huge liquefied natural gas tanker explosion in 1947; and the Lyndon B. Johnson Space Center, where America's space missions are planned, brought here originally by then-Vice President Johnson and longtime Houston Congressman Albert Thomas.

The congressman from the 9th District is Nick Lampson, a Democrat elected in December 1996. Lampson grew up in Beaumont; he got his first job at age 12 when his father died. After graduating from Lamar University, he taught science in Beaumont schools, leading the first local Earth Day celebration in 1969, and then a real estate management course at Lamar; he also headed a home health care company. In 1977, at 32, he was elected Jefferson County tax assessor. He claims to have cut the cost of tax collections during 18 years on the job. In 1996 Lampson ran against Steve Stockman: one of the most controversial Republican freshmen elected in 1994. Stockman won the seat by upsetting 42-year incumbent and Judiciary Committee Chairman Jack Brooks. Stockman stirred controversy for writing a letter to Attorney General Janet Reno expressing concern about raids allegedly planned on militias and for a garbled report about a threatening fax from a militia group his office received the day of the 1995 Oklahoma City bombing. Even so, he was in trouble in the 9th, if only because of the district's Democratic leanings.

Lampson had solid backing for the Democratic nomination. But when the Supreme Court ruled three Texas districts unconstitutional, and the redistricting plan adopted by a three-judge federal court marginally shifted the 9th's boundaries and required a whole new election, the going got nasty. Stockman said Lampson's home health care company had been accused of defrauding Medicare, while Lampson accused Stockman of failing to repay his college loans on time. Democrats cried foul when one of the losing primary candidates, Geraldine Sam, ran in the open November 5 election; the Democratic vote was split, and Stockman led Lampson 46%–44%. Then Sam endorsed Stockman: more screams from Democrats. Labor unions worked Beaumont hard to get Lampson votes in the December runoff, and its county turnout fell only 29% compared to 50% in the rest of the district. Lampson won 53%–47%, winning more than his entire margin in the Beaumont area.

In the House, Lampson promoted the Johnson Space Center from his Science Committee assignment and on the Transportation and Infrastructure Committee worked for improvement of the hurricane evacuation route on U.S. 69 and deepening of the Sabine-Neches Ship Channel. Following several local slayings, in particular the abduction and murder of a 12-year-old girl, he became a national advocate for missing and exploited children and formed a Congressional Missing and Exploited Children's Caucus. On impeachment, Lampson was one of 31 Democrats to vote for the Republican impeachment inquiry in October 1998.

Back home, following new allegations of Medicare irregularities and declining business, his wife sold their home health care business. Lampson was re-elected by the impressive margin of 64%–36% in November 1998. Redistricting will probably not hurt him, given his strong base in Beaumont.

Cook's Call. *Probably Safe.* Lampson's 64% victory here in 1998 belies the underlying competitiveness of this district. Though the district still has a Democratic lean to it, Lampson should not feel entirely safe here, especially in a down year for Democrats. But, if Republicans once again fail to recruit a top-tier candidate, Lampson could find himself pretty well-settled by 2002.

The People: Pop. 1990: 564,287; 12.8% rural; 11.6% age 65 + ; 72.5% White, 21.7% Black, 2% Asian, 0.4% Amer. Indian, 3.5% Other; 9.2% Hispanic Origin. Households: 55.1% married couple families; 27.7% married couple fams. w. children; 47% college educ.; median household income: $29,406; per capita income: $13,759; median house value: $53,400; median gross rent: $313.

1996 Presidential Vote

Clinton (D)	97,268	(48%)
Dole (R)	89,942	(45%)
Perot (I)	14,144	(7%)

1992 Presidential Vote

Clinton (D)	98,959	(44%)
Bush (R)	80,813	(36%)
Perot (I)	47,418	(21%)

Rep. Nick Lampson (D)

Elected 1996; b. Feb. 14, 1945, Beaumont; home, Beaumont; Lamar U., B.S. 1968, M.Ed. 1971; Catholic; married (Susan).

Elected Office: Jefferson Cnty. Assessor, 1977–95.

Professional Career: Public schl. teacher, 1968–71; Instructor, Lamar U., 1971–76; Pres., Jefferson Cnty. Home Health Care, 1993–95.

DC Office: 417 CHOB 20515, 202-225-6565; Fax: 202-225-5547; Web site: www.house.gov/lampson.

District Offices: Beaumont, 409-838-0061; Galveston, 409-762-5877.

Committees: *Science* (14th of 23 D): Space & Aeronautics. *Transportation & Infrastructure* (29th of 34 D): Aviation; Water Resources & Environment.

Group Ratings

	ADA	ACLU	AFS	LCV	CON	NTU	NFIB	COC	ACU	NTLC	CHC
1998	90	63	100	92	38	8	14	33	16	11	8
1997	75	—	75	—	70	31	—	50	24	—	—

National Journal Ratings

	1997 LIB — 1997 CONS		1998 LIB — 1998 CONS	
Economic	67% —	32%	79% —	0%
Social	62% —	37%	65% —	34%
Foreign	76% —	22%	64% —	31%

Key Votes of the 105th Congress

1. Clinton Budget Deal	N	5. Puerto Rico Sthood. Ref.	Y	9. Cut $ for B-2 Bombers	Y
2. Education IRAs	N	6. End Highway Set-asides	N	10. Human Rights in China	Y
3. Req. 2/3 to Raise Taxes	N	7. School Prayer Amend.	N	11. Withdraw Bosnia Troops	N
4. Fast-track Trade	N	8. Ovrd. Part. Birth Veto	Y	12. End Cuban TV-Marti	N

Election Results

1998 general	Nick Lampson (D) 86,055	(64%)	($945,497)
	Tom Cottar (R) 49,107	(36%)	($57,990)
1998 primary	Nick Lampson (D) .... unopposed		
1996 spec. runoff	Nick Lampson (D) 59,225	(53%)	($1,379,749)
	Steve Stockman (R) 52,870	(47%)	($1,898,778)
1996 spec. prim.	Steve Stockman (R) 88,171	(46%)	
	Nick Lampson (D) 83,782	(44%)	
	Geraldine Sam (D) 17,887	(9%)	

TENTH DISTRICT

Austin, the capital of the second-largest state in the United States and site of its largest Capitol building, is also the southernmost capital in the continental 48 states. It is one of many capitals with a first-rate university, the University of Texas, but one of the few (Nashville is the obvious other) with its own musical tradition, symbolized by Willie Nelson. Not so long ago Austin seemed as laid-back and countrified as Nelson himself. There has never been much commerce here, and for much of the year the Capitol basked in a sun that seemed to ban gainful employment. Its skies were untainted with the smoke of industry, its ground unpocked with pumping oil rigs, its downtown streets lined not with business offices but with buildings holding a few lobbyists and the antique Driskill Hotel.

Today Austin is quite different. If not bustling, it is busy; if it is still laid-back, it is everywhere air-conditioned. The Driskill still stands, but glass high-rises also have popped up all over downtown, to the south and far to the north in what was once lonely hill country. Sparking the change is the University of Texas. Endowed with thousands of west Texas acres that turned out to sit on top of oil, the nation's largest single university campus is in Austin. With some 50,000 students, it has a tower at its symbolic center that looms high over the campus, and houses the exemplary LBJ Presidential Library with its 35 million documents. The University has spawned a community of liberal intellectuals since the 1950s and a high-tech industry that started booming in the 1980s. Austin is now one of America's four or five leading high-tech centers, with the headquarters of Dell, big Motorola and Advanced Micro Devices facilities, vast growth in high-tech manufacturing. In the 1990s, the Austin metro area had some of the nation's fastest population growth, up 33% between 1990–99 to 1,127,000, and its job growth skyrocketed 60% between 1989–98. City limits have expanded, with vast new tracts of houses built north of the old town, far beyond the Capitol and the University, and south of the Colorado River. Bergstrom Air Force Base—after the Pentagon shut it down—was converted to a much-needed commercial airport.

Historically Democratic, Austin moved toward the Republicans in the 1980s, but not all the way. The new subdivisions in the high-tech north and south are Republican, though less so than similar places in Houston or Dallas. The University area is still heavily Democratic. In 1992, Austin's Travis County voted for Bill Clinton over George Bush by a 44%–34% margin, and voted Clinton over Bob Dole by a reduced 48%–43% margin in 1996. Other high-tech areas, like California's Silicon Valley and North Carolina's Research Triangle, have trended Democratic in the 1990s, out of revulsion to Republicans' cultural conservatism; Austin-area techies evidently do not share this discomfort, and the Austin area is trending Republican.

The 10th District, which once spread over the Hill Country to the west and south, now is entirely within Travis County: essentially Austin and its inner suburban fringe. It is the descendant of the 10th District that in April 1937 elected a gangly-looking 29-year-old New Dealer named Lyndon Johnson, who established a kind of dynasty here. When Johnson gave up the seat to make his second, and successful, run for the Senate in 1948, his friend Homer Thornberry won the seat and held it until he became a federal judge in December 1963; another

LBJ backer, Jake Pickle, was elected that month and served until he retired in 1994—57 years of representation by three political allies, all born between 1908 and 1913.

Today the congressman from the 10th is Lloyd Doggett, first elected in 1994. He is a liberal Democrat with a dream resume and an up-and-down political career. Doggett grew up in Austin, finished first in his class and was president of UT's student body in 1967. In 1972, he was elected to the state Senate at 26; he is the same age as Clinton, who spent that fall in Austin as the Texas McGovern coordinator. Doggett was part of a surprisingly large liberal bloc in the state Senate in the 1970s; he pushed laws against job discrimination and cop-killer bullets and for generic drugs. He had a certain flair. He was one of the "killer bees" who hid out to prevent a quorum on changing the rules in the Democratic primary and filibustered—wearing sneakers—against what he called anti-consumer bills. In 1984 he ran for the U.S. Senate, narrowly edging out future Senator Bob Krueger in the primary and conservative Congressman Kent Hance in the runoff. Then, despite the campaign help of James Carville, Doggett lost the general by a resounding 59%–41% to party-switching Congressman Phil Gramm, who sharply attacked him for holding a fund raiser at a San Antonio gay strip bar. Doggett came back and, with strong support from trial lawyers, was elected to the Texas Supreme Court in 1988. When Pickle retired, Doggett left that position and ran for Congress. He won the Democratic primary with token opposition and in the general outpolled black Republican Jo Baylor. In November he won by the solid, but not quite overwhelming, margin of 56%–40%.

This made Doggett one of the 13 House Democratic freshman of 1994, vastly outnumbered by the 73 Republican freshmen. Doggett's voting record was mostly but not totally liberal; he voted for the final version of welfare reform and voted to bring the Blue Dog budget to the floor (but not for it). With Tom Davis of Virginia he formed an Information Technology Working Group. He soon emerged as a vocal critic of Newt Gingrich and as a close ally of Minority Whip David Bonior. "He's like a first-round draft choice," Bonior told *National Journal*. Doggett showed his legislative dexterity when he worked with Senator Paul Wellstone of Minnesota to limit nuclear waste dumping at Sierra Blanca, a poor Latino community near the Rio Grande.

In 1996 his Republican opponent was Teresa Doggett, small business owner and unsuccessful candidate for state controller in 1994. Lloyd Doggett won 56%–41%, spending less money than he took in and leaving $972,000 in his treasury afterwards, which miffed some Democrats who would have liked contributions elsewhere. But he overcame that lingering unhappiness in 1998 when he outmaneuvered other aspirants to become the first Texas Democrat in four years assigned to the Ways and Means Committee.

Cook's Call. *Safe.* The fact that Doggett has consistently won this district by significant margins, even as state and national trends were going against Democrats, shows just how Democratic this district is. Doggett should not have any problems winning re-election in 2000.

The People: Pop. 1990: 566,357; 7.9% rural; 7.5% age 65 + ; 73.1% White, 11.1% Black, 2.9% Asian, 0.4% Amer. Indian, 12.6% Other; 21.1% Hispanic Origin. Households: 43.9% married couple families; 22.7% married couple fams. w. children; 63.8% college educ.; median household income: $27,280; per capita income: $14,978; median house value: $77,400; median gross rent: $349.

1996 Presidential Vote

Clinton (D) 126,855 (54%)
Dole (R) 93,219 (40%)
Perot (I) 13,453   (6%)

1992 Presidential Vote

Clinton (D) 128,813 (48%)
Bush (R) 84,560 (32%)
Perot (I) 54,304 (20%)

Rep. Lloyd Doggett (D)

Elected 1994; b. Oct. 6, 1946, Austin; home, Austin; U. of TX, B.B.A. 1967, J.D. 1970; Methodist; married (Libby).

Elected Office: TX Senate, 1973–85; TX Supreme Ct. Justice, 1989–94.

Professional Career: Practicing atty., 1970–89; Adjunct Prof., U. of TX Law Schl., 1989–94.

DC Office: 328 CHOB 20515, 202-225-4865; Fax: 202-225-3073; Web site: www.house.gov/doggett.

District Office: Austin, 512-916-5921.

Committees: *Ways & Means* (16th of 16 D): Social Security.

Group Ratings

	ADA	ACLU	AFS	LCV	CON	NTU	NFIB	COC	ACU	NTLC	CHC
1998	100	88	100	100	99	28	14	39	8	8	0
1997	95	—	75	—	98	42	—	40	16	—	—

National Journal Ratings

	1997 LIB — 1997 CONS		1998 LIB — 1998 CONS	
Economic	67%	— 32%	67%	— 32%
Social	80%	— 19%	81%	— 16%
Foreign	76%	— 22%	75%	— 23%

Key Votes of the 105th Congress

1. Clinton Budget Deal	N	5. Puerto Rico Sthood. Ref.	Y	9. Cut $ for B-2 Bombers	Y
2. Education IRAs	N	6. End Highway Set-asides	N	10. Human Rights in China	Y
3. Req. 2/3 to Raise Taxes	N	7. School Prayer Amend.	N	11. Withdraw Bosnia Troops	Y
4. Fast-track Trade	N	8. Ovrd. Part. Birth Veto	N	12. End Cuban TV-Marti	Y

Election Results

1998 general	Lloyd Doggett (D)	116,127	(85%)	($111,248)
	Vincent J. May (Lib)	20,155	(15%)	
1998 primary	Lloyd Doggett (D)	unopposed		
1996 general	Lloyd Doggett (D)	132,066	(56%)	($410,302)
	Teresa Doggett (R)	97,204	(41%)	($402,904)
	Others	5,721	(2%)	

ELEVENTH DISTRICT

Waco, at the intersection of lines from Dallas to Austin and Houston to Amarillo, is arguably the geographic and cultural heart of Texas. The accent here may be the purest Texas accent around: listen to former Governor Ann Richards, a Waco native. Waco is now a city of over 100,000, but the farm fields and small towns all around recall the state as it was years ago, before the oil industry transformed Texas from a rural backwater into one of the centers of Western capitalism, while the latest extravagances of affluent metropolitan Texas can be sampled at galleries of the Dallas-Fort Worth Metroplex, a little more than an hour away on I-35. Some of Texas's characteristic institutions cluster around Waco: Baylor University, the oldest college in Texas and the largest Baptist university in the world, and Fort Hood, the Army's second largest installation, which occupies much of next-door Bell and Coryell counties and employs just under 50,000 military personnel and civilians. The violence that is also part of Texas's history flared here in February 1993 when, in a dreadful misuse of government power, agents of the Bureau of Alcohol, Tobacco and Firearms moved in on David Koresh's Branch Davidian compound, Ranch Apocalypse, near Waco, until agents stormed the compound and Koresh and his followers immolated themselves.

The 11th Congressional District is centered on Waco and the Fort Hood area. It includes all or most of 12 counties, most of them still quite rural, all of them ancestrally Democratic. But that loyalty has slowly waned. Ann Richards carried the 11th with 51% in 1990, but it voted for 52% for George W. Bush in 1994 and 71% in 1998.

The congressman from the 11th is Chet Edwards, a Democrat elected in 1990, and only the third congressman from this district since 1936. Edwards is one of those highly skilled and motivated Democrats who has made politics his life—and who made the House Democratic until 1994. He graduated from Texas A&M, where he studied economics under Phil Gramm, then a conservative Democrat; from there, Edwards went to work as district director for 6th District Congressman Olin Teague. In 1978, at 27, Edwards ran for the 6th District seat when Teague retired. In the first Democratic primary, Edwards wound up in third place, just 115 votes behind Gramm, who went on to win the seat; if Edwards had won just 116 more votes, a lot of Texas and national political history would be different. Edwards went off to Harvard to get an M.B.A., returned and moved to Duncanville in southwest Dallas County, and at age 31 ran for the state Senate in 1982 and won. There he had a moderate-to-liberal record, helping to incorporate Texas into the Super Tuesday primary and working to attract the Supercollider, bucking the unions and trial lawyers on workmen's compensation reform.

In 1990 when 11th District Congressman Marvin Leath retired, Edwards moved his residence to Waco (the state Senate district overlapped), and ran for the 11th District seat unopposed in the Democratic primary. With a promise of an Armed Services Committee slot from Speaker Thomas Foley and strong support from Leath, Edwards got 56% in Waco's McLennan County and carried all the rural counties for a 53%–47% victory. In the House, Edwards worked for Fort Hood and claims credit for nearly a quarter-billion dollars in construction there. He bucked the Democratic leadership quickly on the Gulf war resolution and the balanced budget amendment and he voted against the Clinton tax increase. He worked successfully to stop the designation of 33 Texas counties as a critical habitat for the allegedly endangered golden-cheeked warbler and supported the Private Property Owners Bill of Rights. He voted against the Brady bill but for the assault weapons ban and the 1994 crime bill.

In previous decades he might have become part of the majority party leadership in the House; instead, after Democrats lost their majority, Dick Gephardt asked him to serve as one of four chief deputy whips. Edwards accepted, adding, "I did not ask for this job and I will not change my political independence to keep it." He promptly voted for the Contract with America's balanced budget amendment and line-item veto. Also in 1995, he moved from Armed Services to Appropriations, where he continues to look after Fort Hood. In his leadership position, Edwards has served as a bridge-builder among Democrats. He sometimes takes the lead in pointing out the harder ideological edges of the Republican majority. Although he was targeted by Christian Coalition lobbying, he led opposition in 1998 to the school-prayer constitutional amendment, citing the freedom that the Bill of Rights has "protected extraordinarily well for over two centuries."

Edwards has managed to win re-election by comfortable margins. He survived in 1996 his toughest re-election challenge 57%–42% from an opponent who raised over $500,000 and cited Edwards's "liberal vote of the day" each day during the campaign. In 1998, the expected Republican candidate decided at the last minute not to run; House Republican campaign leaders conceded that this district was one of their major recruiting failures, and vowed to make an early start in 1999. Edwards beat a Libertarian 83%–17%, but evidently many Republicans did not cast a ballot in this contest; Edwards's votes as a percentage of those voting for governor was a still impressive but not unanimous 62%.

Cook's Call. *Probably Safe.* Considering that Clinton only took 42% of the vote here in 1996, the fact that Edwards won re-election that year with 57% of the vote against a well-funded opponent is a testament to Edward's popularity and a signal of just how tough it will be for Republicans to knock him out of office. This district is definitely trending away from Democrats, but Republicans may have to wait until Edwards leaves office before they pick this seat up.

The People: Pop. 1990: 566,280; 28.6% rural; 13.3% age 65+; 76.2% White, 15.9% Black, 1.6% Asian, 0.4% Amer. Indian, 5.9% Other; 11.9% Hispanic Origin. Households: 59% married couple families; 30.2% married couple fams. w. children; 42.5% college educ.; median household income: $22,283; per capita income: $10,630; median house value: $50,400; median gross rent: $283.

1996 Presidential Vote

Dole (R)	88,429	(50%)
Clinton (D)	74,063	(42%)
Perot (I)	14,671	(8%)

1992 Presidential Vote

Bush (R)	75,545	(41%)
Clinton (D)	66,440	(36%)
Perot (I)	42,305	(23%)

Rep. Chet Edwards (D)

Elected 1990; b. Nov. 24, 1951, Corpus Christi; home, Waco; TX A&M U., B.A. 1974, Harvard U., M.B.A. 1981; Methodist; married (Lea Ann).

Elected Office: TX Senate, 1982–90.

Professional Career: Legis. & Dist. Dir., U.S. Rep. Olin Teague, 1975–77; Marketing Rep., Trammell Crow Co., 1981–85; Pres., Edwards Communications, 1985–90.

DC Office: 2459 RHOB 20515, 202-225-6105; Fax: 202-225-0350; Web site: www.house.gov/edwards.

District Offices: Belton, 254-933-2904; Waco, 254-752-9600.

Committees: *Chief Deputy Minority Whip. Appropriations* (19th of 27 D): Energy & Water Development; Military Construction.

Group Ratings

	ADA	ACLU	AFS	LCV	CON	NTU	NFIB	COC	ACU	NTLC	CHC
1998	90	75	89	38	89	31	43	44	8	30	9
1997	60	—	75	—	56	30	—	70	28	—	—

National Journal Ratings

	1997 LIB — 1997 CONS		1998 LIB — 1998 CONS	
Economic	59% —	40%	72% —	23%
Social	66% —	33%	67% —	32%
Foreign	56% —	44%	84% —	11%

Key Votes of the 105th Congress

1. Clinton Budget Deal	N	5. Puerto Rico Sthood. Ref.	Y	9. Cut $ for B-2 Bombers	Y
2. Education IRAs	N	6. End Highway Set-asides	N	10. Human Rights in China	Y
3. Req. 2/3 to Raise Taxes	N	7. School Prayer Amend.	N	11. Withdraw Bosnia Troops	N
4. Fast-track Trade	Y	8. Ovrd. Part. Birth Veto	N	12. End Cuban TV-Marti	Y

Election Results

1998 general	Chet Edwards (D)	71,142	(82%)	($255,608)
	Vince Hanke (Lib)	15,161	(18%)	($8,215)
1998 primary	Chet Edwards (D)	unopposed		
1996 general	Chet Edwards (D)	99,990	(57%)	($844,126)
	Jay Mathis (R)	74,549	(42%)	($565,402)

TWELFTH DISTRICT

Fort Worth, Texas, has a fair claim to being the quintessential mid-American city: halfway across the continent, just west of the Balcones Escarpment that divides the dry treeless grazing lands of West Texas from the humid green croplands of East Texas. It is Southern in heritage and Northern in its advanced post-industrial economy. It has the nation's longest row of Western wear shops and one of the nation's richest families, the Basses, whose steel-sheen skyscrapers, outlined at night by lights, dominate the skyline. This is where the West begins, Fort Worth boosters say, adding, as Will Rogers said, that Dallas is "where the East peters out."

But this is not a primitive West. Fort Worth has a high-tech economy, though one hard hit by defense cuts. The big General Dynamics plant that produced so many U.S. bombers was sold to Lockheed Martin, which produces the fuselage of the F-22 fighter there; next-door Carswell Air Force Base, the home of B-52s for years, was slated for closure in 1993 but was turned into a Joint Reserve Base in late 1994. The assembly lines at Bell Helicopter Textron's nearby plant were kept going only when the Texas delegation and others overruled the cancellation of the V-22 Osprey. Fort Worth also has some of the nation's premier small museums, the Amon Carter Museum of Western Art, Louis Kahn's gem, the Kimbell Museum, and the Will Rogers Coliseum with exhibits of Texas history. The 1998 opening of the $67 million downtown Bass Performance Hall, which has been acclaimed for its superb architectual design, was a major civic event. Other cities have their claims, but the visitor from abroad who wants to see what is quintessentially American would be well advised to fly to Dallas/Forth Worth International Airport and head west.

The 12th District is centered on Fort Worth. Its highly convoluted boundaries drawn in 1991 (and not changed in the 1996 redistricting case) include much of the city, though not the poor black southeast or rich white southwest areas, which are in the 24th and 6th districts. It also extends south and west in a whirl around Fort Worth, taking in much of rural Johnson and Parker counties, including Weatherford, where former House Speaker Jim Wright got his start in politics. Fort Worth's political heritage is Democratic, but lately it has been trending Republican and has become more diverse, with extensive rich as well as poor neighborhoods. Tarrant County, with a population boom in Arlington between Fort Worth and Dallas and in the north around DFW airport and Ross Perot Jr.'s Alliance cargo airport, has become more Republican than Dallas County: 70% for George W. Bush in 1998, compared to 65% in Dallas.

The congresswoman from the 12th District is Republican Kay Granger, elected in 1996. Granger went to college at Texas Wesleyan in Fort Worth, raised three children and started her own insurance agency. In 1989 she was elected to the Fort Worth Council, and two years later was elected as the non-partisan mayor. She became very popular for her "Code: Blue" anti-crime initiatives and encouragement of citizen patrols, as violent crime dropped 49%. She also formed the Vision Coalition, a community-wide consensus-building organization, and attracted new business facilities from Motorola, Intel, FedEx and the Texas Motor Speedway. In late 1995 Congressman Pete Geren, a conservative Democrat elected to replace Wright in 1989, announced his retirement, and both Republican and Democratic leaders tried to recruit Granger. After being elected to the U.S. Conference of Mayors board of trustees, she said she was a Republican, and ran in the March 1996 Republican primary. Attacked as a liberal, partly for her pro-choice stand on abortion, she won 69% in a three-candidate race. In the general, Granger ran against Hugh Parmer, also a former Fort Worth mayor and the Democratic nominee against Senator Phil Gramm in 1990. That turned out to be a liability when it was revealed that he had large unpaid debts left over from that campaign. He attacked Republican Medicare plans and Newt Gingrich. She called for a balanced budget and tax cuts for business and ran on her record as mayor. Granger won 58%–41%, a stunning victory in a district carried twice by Bill Clinton and represented a decade before by a Democratic speaker of the House.

On opening day in the 105th Congress, to highlight her bipartisanship, Granger held a press conference with California Democrat Gary Condit to trumpet their balanced budget proposal. But she soon became a favorite of Republican leaders, winning enactment of tax-free savings accounts for higher education expenses and serving as the only freshman on Denny Hastert's health care task force. One setback was the Republican leadership's support of legislation that diluted the Wright Amendment's protection of Dallas/Fort Worth International Airport from competition from Dallas's Love Field; following that effort, Granger worked locally to create a regional airport authority that would encourage cooperation between the two. In 1999, she became the third Texas Republican on the Appropriations Committee.

Granger had an unexpectedly easy re-election in 1998, when Democratic challenger Tom Hall, who had said he would spend as much as $1 million of his own money on the campaign, withdrew in September after suffering a heart ailment, though his name remained on the ballot. Democratic Caucus Chairman Martin Frost, who represents the adjacent 24th district, said that if Granger is not defeated in 2000, she'll be there "as long as she wants to be." With Pete Sessions, she was one of the first members from Texas on the early 1999 committee of current and former lawmakers urging Governor George W. Bush to run for president.

Cook's Call. *Safe.* Granger's big win in her first re-election campaign may help insulate her from a serious challenge in 2000. But, while this formerly Democratic district has continued to trend toward Republicans, it is still somewhat marginal political territory. Still, Granger looks well-positioned for re-election in 2000.

The People: Pop. 1990: 565,988; 13% rural; 12.2% age 65+; 80.3% White, 8% Black, 1.8% Asian, 0.5% Amer. Indian, 9.4% Other; 15.9% Hispanic Origin. Households: 55.9% married couple families; 28.7% married couple fams. w. children; 42.7% college educ.; median household income: $27,366; per capita income: $12,641; median house value: $57,800; median gross rent: $335.

1996 Presidential Vote			1992 Presidential Vote		
Clinton (D)	80,709	(46%)	Clinton (D)	76,637	(38%)
Dole (R)	79,299	(46%)	Bush (R)	70,522	(35%)
Perot (I)	14,187	(8%)	Perot (I)	55,951	(28%)

Rep. Kay Granger (R)

Elected 1996; b. Jan. 18, 1943, Greenville; home, Ft. Worth; TX Wesleyan U., B.S. 1965; Methodist; divorced.

Elected Office: Ft. Worth City Cncl., 1989–91; Ft. Worth Mayor, 1991–96.

Professional Career: Teacher, 1965–78; Life Insurance Agent, 1978–85; Chmn., Ft. Worth Zoning Comm., 1981–88; Founder & Pres., Kay Granger Insurance Co., Inc., 1985–present.

DC Office: 435 CHOB 20515, 202-225-5071; Fax: 202-225-5683; Web site: www.house.gov/granger.

District Office: Ft. Worth, 817-338-0909.

Committees: *Appropriations* (33d of 34 R): Military Construction; The Legislative Branch; Transportation.

Group Ratings

	ADA	ACLU	AFS	LCV	CON	NTU	NFIB	COC	ACU	NTLC	CHC
1998	5	19	11	8	13	49	100	100	84	89	100
1997	0	—	13	—	49·	51	—	100	92	—	—

National Journal Ratings

	1997 LIB — 1997 CONS			1998 LIB — 1998 CONS		
Economic	19%	—	76%	0%	—	88%
Social	30%	—	64%	45%	—	55%
Foreign	22%	—	77%	34%	—	62%

Key Votes of the 105th Congress

1. Clinton Budget Deal	Y	5. Puerto Rico Sthood. Ref.	Y	9. Cut $ for B-2 Bombers	N
2. Education IRAs	Y	6. End Highway Set-asides	Y	10. Human Rights in China	N
3. Req. 2/3 to Raise Taxes	Y	7. School Prayer Amend.	Y	11. Withdraw Bosnia Troops	Y
4. Fast-track Trade	Y	8. Ovrd. Part. Birth Veto	Y	12. End Cuban TV-Marti	N

Election Results

1998 general	Kay Granger (R)	66,740	(62%)	($883,397)
	Tom Hall (D)	39,084	(36%)	($622,443)
	Others	1,917	(2%)	
1998 primary	Kay Granger (R)	unopposed		
1996 general	Kay Granger (R)	98,349	(58%)	($1,001,836)
	Hugh Parmer (D)	69,859	(41%)	($455,703)

THIRTEENTH DISTRICT

Heading west in Texas, the population thins out, the land becomes browner until you can travel through a whole county containing only a few hundred people—plus quite a few more head of cattle. And then the land rises nearly 1,000 feet in elevation, up steep hillsides from the gullies that surround the rivers which for most of the year are just tiny trickles, to the tilted tableland that is the High Plains of West Texas. The winds here sweep down from the Rockies, the land is barren except where irrigated, often with the now dangerously depleted waters of the Ogallala Aquifer. But here and there in this demanding environment—sticky-hot in the summer, swept by north winds from Canada in winter, always threatened in "Tornado Alley"— comfortable cities have been built to house the people and businesses that bring forth some of the nation's most abundant oil, natural gas, helium and other elements from the earth.

The 13th Congressional District spans more than 30,000 square miles and 38 counties of this territory. Population declined here in the 1980s, in some rural counties by as much as 30%, with only small gains in and around two of the three biggest cities, Wichita Falls and Amarillo. Around Wichita Falls, in the eastern part of the district, is the agricultural land of the Red River Valley—dusty land with empty skylines, like Archer City, the boyhood home of novelist Larry McMurtry, chronicled in *The Last Picture Show* and *Texasville* and where he lives now and maintains an enormous used-book store. The area claims to produce more cotton than any other congressional district. This is white Anglo Texas: Few blacks got this far west and few Mexican-Americans go this far north. Up on the High Plains, the economy is different: It is based on natural resources. The largest city here is Amarillo, once the helium capital of North America (before Congress shut down production) and still—not Chicago—the windiest city in the United States. Just outside town is the Pantex Plant that made thousands of nuclear warheads—the epicenter of American defense in the Cold War; its 16,000 acres have been used to dismantle some disarmed weapons and now maintains the remainder of the arsenal.

Political traditions here differ. The Red River Valley, settled by Confederate veterans, was until recently Democratic. The High Plains, settled overland from Kansas wheatlands, is more

Republican. District lines were changed for the 1990s: not all of Amarillo is in the 13th any more, and black portions of Lubbock have been added in an effort to help Democrats, though it turned out to be not enough. By 1998 ancestral Democratic ties had withered to the point that George W. Bush lost just one Red River Valley county here, by one vote, and overall won 75% of the vote.

The congressman from the 13th District is Mac Thornberry, a Republican elected in 1994. His great-great-grandfather Amos Thornberry, a Union Army veteran and staunch Republican, moved to Clay County, just east of Wichita Falls, in the 1880s; a year after Amos died in 1925, his son bought the cattle ranch which Mac Thornberry, his brothers and father now run. From the window of his ranch house, writes *The Texas Techsan*, "as far as the eye can see is the Golden Spread of Texas for which this part of the state is named. There are no buildings, no roadways, no signs of life. Gaze out long enough and you begin to think you can actually see the curvature of the earth." And, as the writer goes on, you can get a sense of why Thornberry is so unhappy with federal government intrusion into people's lives. But Thornberry is not just a local farmer: After college and law school in Texas he worked for Congressmen Tom Loeffler and Larry Combest and at the State Department in Washington. Then he returned to practice law in West Texas.

In 1994 the well-connected Thornberry decided to take on Democratic Congressman Bill Sarpalius. He attacked Sarpalius for voting for the Clinton budget and tax package. He also profited from a series of stories about how Sarpalius did not pay a moving company that shipped his furniture to Washington, then accepted a fee for speaking at the company's convention in Las Vegas. The FBI investigated in October 1994: not helpful for Sarpalius's campaign. Thornberry won a solid 55%–45% victory, carrying the northern panhandle by wide margins and carrying Wichita Falls as well, trailing only in sparsely populated ranching counties.

In the House Thornberry has an almost perfectly conservative voting record. He pressed hard for estate tax repeal and tax credits for energy production to encourage production in marginal wells. Responding to the punishing dip in oil prices, he pushed to fill the Strategic Petroleum Reserve to its 750 million barrel capacity and urged a cutoff of the oil-for-food program that permitted Saddam Hussein's Iraq to flood the oil market. He was not loath to seek drought assistance for parched West Texas. As a member, he got Armed Services to pass his proposal barring transfer of Pantex Plant explosives work elsewhere. He wants to reform the Endangered Species Act and to allow state-inspected meat to be sold in other states the same as foreign-inspected meat, which does not need USDA approval.

Thornberry has been easily re-elected twice in what seems to now be a safe Republican seat.

Cook's Call. *Safe.* Though this district elected a Democrat to Congress as recently as 1992, it will be very difficult for Democrats to wrest this Republican leaning district back from three-term Thornberry. Thornberry has had little trouble crushing his opposition in his two re-election contests and looks very tough to beat in 2000.

The People: Pop. 1990: 566,682; 27.3% rural; 15% age 65 +; 79% White, 7.9% Black, 1.2% Asian, 0.7% Amer. Indian, 11.2% Other; 19.2% Hispanic Origin. Households: 56.9% married couple families; 28.2% married couple fams. w. children; 37.3% college educ.; median household income: $20,907; per capita income: $10,344; median house value: $38,600; median gross rent: $265.

1996 Presidential Vote

Dole (R)	92,815	(53%)
Clinton (D)	69,149	(39%)
Perot (I)	14,030	(8%)

1992 Presidential Vote

Bush (R)	87,492	(43%)
Clinton (D)	73,454	(36%)
Perot (I)	41,187	(20%)

Rep. Mac Thornberry (R)

Elected 1994; b. July 15, 1958, Clarendon; home, Clarendon; TX Tech. U., B.A. 1980, U. of TX Law Schl., J.D. 1983; Presbyterian; married (Sally).

Professional Career: Legis. Cnsl., U.S. Rep. Tom Loeffler, 1983–85; Chief of Staff, U.S. Rep. Larry Combest, 1985–88; Dpty. Asst. Secy. of State for Legis. Affairs, 1988–89; Practicing atty., 1989–94.

DC Office: 131 CHOB 20515, 202-225-3706; Fax: 202-225-3486; Web site: www.house.gov/thornberry.

District Offices: Amarillo, 806-371-8844; Wichita Falls, 940-692-1700.

Committees: *Armed Services* (18th of 32 R): Military Personnel; Military Procurement (Vice Chmn.). *Budget* (16th of 24 R). *Resources* (16th of 28 R): Energy & Mineral Resources; Water & Power.

Group Ratings

	ADA	ACLU	AFS	LCV	CON	NTU	NFIB	COC	ACU	NTLC	CHC
1998	5	6	0	0	60	69	100	89	100	100	92
1997	5	—	13	—	49	64	—	100	96	—	—

National Journal Ratings

	1997 LIB — 1997 CONS	1998 LIB — 1998 CONS
Economic	10% — 86%	0% — 88%
Social	37% — 61%	21% — 76%
Foreign	30% — 68%	19% — 75%

Key Votes of the 105th Congress

1. Clinton Budget Deal	Y	5. Puerto Rico Sthood. Ref.	N	9. Cut $ for B-2 Bombers	N
2. Education IRAs	Y	6. End Highway Set-asides	Y	10. Human Rights in China	N
3. Req. 2/3 to Raise Taxes	Y	7. School Prayer Amend.	Y	11. Withdraw Bosnia Troops	N
4. Fast-track Trade	Y	8. Ovrd. Part. Birth Veto	Y	12. End Cuban TV-Marti	N

Election Results

1998 general	Mac Thornberry (R)	81,141	(68%)	($448,727)
	Mark Harmon (D)	37,027	(31%)	($16,243)
1998 primary	Mac Thornberry (R)	19,827	(94%)	
	Richard Amon (R)	1,345	(6%)	
1996 general	Mac Thornberry (R)	116,098	(67%)	($565,578)
	Samuel Brown Silverman (D)	56,066	(32%)	($16,126)

FOURTEENTH DISTRICT

Retreating east from the Alamo, the ragtag army led by Sam Houston passed over what would become, after their bloody and conclusive victory at San Jacinto, some of the prime cropland in the new Republic and later the state of Texas. The hilly and river-crossed land between Houston and Austin, both named after Texas' first leaders, was settled early. The flat coastal plains, steamy and humid so much of the year, were settled later when the railroads came in. The Gulf of Mexico coastline, though it has plenty of inlets, never had any important ports in the stretch between Houston and Corpus Christi until the discovery of oil here made it worthwhile to build channels to ship the oil out.

This is the land of the 14th Congressional District. Made up of rural countrysides, small towns and a couple of small cities, it runs along the Gulf Coast and inland toward the old Texas German country. Its eastern and northern edges bring it within metropolitan range of Houston, Austin and San Antonio; more than one-third of its people live in these areas. Redistricting in 1991 changed its shape somewhat, adding Blanco County in the Hill Country west of Austin, the birthplace and first political base of Lyndon B. Johnson. This country is ancestrally Democratic except for a couple of counties settled by Texas Germans, who were pro-Union in the Civil War and have remained Republican ever since. But it voted Republican in the 1980s and twice rejected the candidacy of Bill Clinton.

The congressman from the 14th District is Ron Paul, a Republican elected in 1996, but also once a Libertarian candidate for president. Paul grew up in Pennsylvania, went to Duke medical school, served as a Air Force flight surgeon, then moved to Texas to practice obstetrics and gynecology in Brazoria County, just southwest of Houston. Paul was dismayed when Richard Nixon cut the connection between the dollar and gold in August 1971 and became interested in politics. After winning House elections four times since 1976, he ran for the Senate in 1984 and lost the primary to Phil Gramm 73%–16%. In 1988, as the Libertarian candidate for president, he ran third with 432,000 votes, 0.47% of the total. In Congress, Paul advanced some ideas that have now become more mainstream—term limits, which a majority of House members have voted for, and abolition of the income tax, a project of the chairman of the Ways and Means Committee. Other Paul ideas remain outside the political pale—endorsing a group that wants to end all government funding of education and compulsory attendance laws, cutting $150 billion from the defense budget and returning to the gold standard. Paul practices what he preaches. He will not accept payment by Medicare or Medicaid, he wouldn't let his children accept federal student loans and he refuses his congressional pension.

Paul re-entered congressional politics after one-time Democratic Congressman Greg Laughlin switched parties in June 1995. Laughlin had a moderate voting record, but by no means the most conservative of Texas Democrats. In spring 1995 Republicans offered him a seat on Ways and Means if he switched, and he did. "I tried to be part of the Democratic team, but I was miserable on some of the votes I cast," he said later. "Since I've been a Republican, I haven't cast one hard vote. I'm really comfortable where I am." But others weren't so comfortable. Paul decided to run again as—well, as Ron Paul, raising money from his nationwide network of Libertarians, gold bugs and subscribers to the *Ron Paul Political Report*. He may not have always been a Republican, but his convictions came through. "The [federal] government perpetually takes our money, lies to us and makes our lives worse," he said. After Laughlin finished first in the primary with 43%, Paul won the runoff 54%–46%.

This set up an excruciating situation for Republican leaders. They did not want to lose the seat to Democrat Charles "Lefty" Morris, who ran as a "conservative Democrat" but omitted from his resume the fact that he had been president of the state trial lawyers' association. But they didn't want to get associated with Paul's wackier-seeming views either. Morris ("Lefty is right") hit Paul for favoring abolition of the minimum wage, repealing federal anti-drug laws (Paul said that would leave states to ban drugs, but he opposed that too) and anti-prostitution laws. Researchers reported that Paul's newsletter in 1992 said that 95% of black men in Washington, D.C. are "semi-criminal or entirely criminal" and that black teenagers are "unbelievably fleet of foot." "Ron Paul wants to abandon the federal government. I want to fix it," said Morris. Paul ran 1% ahead of Bob Dole and won 51%–48% in a close race.

In Washington Paul made a bit of a sensation, not through his work on committees, but by saying on C-SPAN, "I fear there's a lot of people in the country who fear that they may be bombed by the federal government at another Waco." Democrat Chet Edwards, who represents Waco, on the floor called Paul's comments "sheer lunacy at best." Republican Whip Tom DeLay, who represents the 22d District, rebuked Edwards for not having the "courtesy" to alert Paul about his intended remarks so Paul could reply on the floor. With his Libertarian views opposed to strong defense and support for business, Paul's voting record was anything but rock-solid Republican. Frequently, his insistence on limited government made Paul the

House's lonely dissenter—against bills to require states to computerize child-support records, to punish China if it restricts freedom in Hong Kong, and to award Rosa Parks with the Congressional Gold Medal. He also opposed regulations to require banks to gather data on customer transactions.

Although Paul was at the top of Democrats' re-election target lists, he comfortably survived in 1998 against rice-farmer Loy Sneary, the winner of a three-candidate party, who attacked Paul's votes "against Texas family farmers and ranchers" and his defense of medical marijuana. Paul criticized Sneary for raising his own pay and trying to raise taxes as county judge, and he won 55%–44%, winning all but four of 22 counties. But Paul is sufficiently offbeat to attract serious opposition in the future.

Cook's Call. *Competitive.* Paul's quirky nature and unconventional voting record helped to land him on the Democratic target list in 1998. But what keeps Paul in Congress is his tremendous fundraising ability (crucial in a district this size) and the conservative and Republican nature of this rural district. A good challenger may be able to keep Paul under 60% in 2000, but he is tough to beat.

The People: Pop. 1990: 566,008; 51.3% rural; 14% age 65 + ; 77.8% White, 10.6% Black, 0.6% Asian, 0.3% Amer. Indian, 10.7% Other; 23.3% Hispanic Origin. Households: 59.9% married couple families; 30.4% married couple fams. w. children; 36.6% college educ.; median household income: $23,812; per capita income: $11,127; median house value: $52,800; median gross rent: $263.

1996 Presidential Vote

Dole (R)	100,319	(50%)
Clinton (D)	84,317	(42%)
Perot (I)	15,696	(8%)

1992 Presidential Vote

Bush (R)	86,225	(41%)
Clinton (D)	78,706	(37%)
Perot (I)	47,119	(22%)

Rep. Ron Paul (R)

Elected 1996; b. Aug. 20, 1935, Pittsburgh, PA; home, Surfside; Gettysburg Col., B.A. 1957, Duke U., M.D. 1961; Protestant; married (Carol).

Military Career: Flight Surgeon, Air Force, 1963–68.

Elected Office: U.S. House of Reps., 1976, 1978–84.

Professional Career: Practicing physician, 1968–96.

DC Office: 203 CHOB 20515, 202-225-2831; Fax: 202-226-4871; Web site: www.house.gov/paul.

District Offices: Freeport, 409-230-0000; San Marcos, 512-396-1400; Victoria, 512-576-1231.

Committees: *Banking & Financial Services* (17th of 32 R): Capital Markets, Securities & Government Sponsored Enterprises; Domestic & International Monetary Policy (Vice Chmn.); General Oversight & Investigations. *Education & the Workforce* (17th of 27 R): Early Childhood, Youth & Families; Workforce Protections.

Group Ratings

	ADA	ACLU	AFS	LCV	CON	NTU	NFIB	COC	ACU	NTLC	CHC
1998	20	40	38	23	97	88	79	65	88	71	91
1997	30	—	38	—	14	78	—	60	80	—	—

National Journal Ratings

	1997 LIB — 1997 CONS		1998 LIB — 1998 CONS	
Economic	43% —	56%	49% —	50%
Social	45% —	54%	43% —	56%
Foreign	51% —	46%	43% —	53%

Key Votes of the 105th Congress

1. Clinton Budget Deal	Y	5. Puerto Rico Sthood. Ref.	N	9. Cut $ for B-2 Bombers	Y
2. Education IRAs	N	6. End Highway Set-asides	Y	10. Human Rights in China	Y
3. Req. 2/3 to Raise Taxes	Y	7. School Prayer Amend.	N	11. Withdraw Bosnia Troops	Y
4. Fast-track Trade	N	8. Ovrd. Part. Birth Veto	Y	12. End Cuban TV-Marti	Y

Election Results

1998 general	Ron Paul (R)	84,459	(55%)	($1,987,457)
	Loy Sneary (D)	68,014	(44%)	($1,119,087)
1998 primary	Ron Paul (R)	unopposed		
1996 general	Ron Paul (R)	99,961	(51%)	($1,927,756)
	Charles (Lefty) Morris (D)	93,200	(48%)	($977,888)

FIFTEENTH DISTRICT

The Lower Rio Grande Valley of south Texas is one of America's 20th Century frontiers. A century ago, there was little here but desert wilderness. Only a handful of people lived anywhere near the shallow, sluggish Rio Grande; there was no Border Patrol because in this desert land no one bothered to cross it. Then in the early days of this century came pioneers like Lloyd Bentsen Sr., father of the former senator and Treasury secretary, who arrived after World War I with $5 in his pocket and became one of the biggest Valley landowners, remaining active in his business until he died in an auto accident in 1989 at age 95. Bentsen and others cleared the land and dug canals, hired Mexican and Mexican-American workers, planted citrus groves, cornfields and palm windbreaks, ran cattle and drilled for oil and gas. Along U.S. 83 north of the Rio Grande these pioneers built a string of towns with Anglo names and storefronts. But most of the people here were Latino in culture and language. Wage levels higher than in Mexico (though low by U.S. standards) brought more Mexicans over the border. But if wages are low, so is the cost of living—which makes this a haven for low-income "winter Texan" retirees coming down from the North in their RVs. The days are past when ranchers and oil men wielded absolute political power here. There is instead a robust, mostly Hispanic politics, with results not always what you would expect from the rhetoric of some of the foundation-financed Hispanic organizations in Washington.

The 15th Congressional District is one of three districts dividing up the Lower Rio Grande Valley. Some two-thirds of its residents and about 55% of its voters live in Hidalgo County, in or near the string of towns from Mercedes through McAllen to Los Ebanos, just north of the river. The 15th then moves north through a narrow corridor of land between Corpus Christi and San Antonio to include Goliad, where 352 captured Texans were massacred by Santa Ana's troops in 1836, and Bee County, where President George Bush goes to hunt quail at each year's end. The 15th's population is 75% Hispanic and mostly Democratic. This is the descendant of a district that three times elected Lloyd Bentsen Jr. to the House, before he went to Houston to make his fortune and then on to national office.

The congressman from the 15th District is Ruben Hinojosa, a Democrat elected in 1996. His background is not in politics but in business and civic affairs. He grew up in Mercedes, between McAllen and Harlingen, where his family owns H&H Foods, which produces Mexican foods and beef patties and is one of the largest employers in the Valley. Hinojosa graduated from the University of Texas, then went into the family business and was active in civic affairs, primarily in education and regional development. He served on the state Board of Education and led an effort to create three regional magnet schools, including the South Texas School for Health Professions, a high school.

After former Agriculture Committee Chairman Kika de la Garza announced he would not seek re-election in 1996, Hinojosa ran in the Democratic primary; his main political assets were his civic activities and cash—he spent $431,000 of his own money. In the primary he won 34%

to 33% for lawyer Jim Selman. An Anglo lawyer who ran as a reformer, Selman promised to fight corruption; he questioned Hinojosa's Democratic credentials and profiting from government contracts. Hinojosa emphasized his interest in improving educational opportunities in the Lower Rio Grande Valley and extending I-69 to the Valley; he called for reducing the capital gains tax and giving investment tax credits to those making capital improvements. The runoff between Hinojosa and Selman was close to the end, but Hinojosa won 52%–48%. He carried Hidalgo County 51%–49% and the rest of the district 55%–45%. In effect, the more conservative of the two candidates won; only one of the three Lower Valley districts is represented by the sort of liberals who lead most national and Texas Hispanic organizations. Hinojosa won the general election over Mennonite minister Tom Haughey 62%–37%.

Hinojosa's top priority in the House is increasing educational opportunities. He chairs the Hispanic Caucus's education task force, and has pushed for a $500 million spending increase in President Clinton's Hispanic education action plan to decrease drop-out rates and boost educational attainment. He has sought to protect benefits for legal immigrants and to promote NAFTA. He claimed credit for progress on I-69 in the 1998 highway bill. He has enthusiastically supported the House's bipartisan "civility" retreats.

The 1998 election saw a downtick in Hinojosa's support despite the pro-incumbent tenor of the year and his opponent's weak finances. Overall Hinojosa won 59%–41%, but he ran behind 52%–48% in the northern six counties. This may have reflected the undertow of the top of the ticket, for George W. Bush carried this heavily Latino district with 57% of the vote.

Cook's Call. *Safe.* Hinojosa should have no re-election problems in this solidly Democratic district that gave Clinton 60% of the vote in 1996.

The People: Pop. 1990: 566,805; 29.4% rural; 11.4% age 65 +; 75.5% White, 1.1% Black, 0.3% Asian, 0.2% Amer. Indian, 22.8% Other; 74.5% Hispanic Origin. Households: 64.5% married couple families; 39.8% married couple fams. w. children; 29.3% college educ.; median household income: $17,866; per capita income: $7,407; median house value: $37,200; median gross rent: $223.

1996 Presidential Vote

Clinton (D)	86,707	(60%)
Dole (R)	49,595	(35%)
Perot (I)	7,093	(5%)

1992 Presidential Vote

Clinton (D)	80,135	(53%)
Bush (R)	52,102	(34%)
Perot (I)	19,995	(13%)

Rep. Ruben Hinojosa (D)

Elected 1996; b. Aug. 20, 1940, Mercedes; home, Mercedes; U. of TX, B.B.A. 1962, M.B.A. 1980; Catholic; married (Marty).

Elected Office: TX Bd. of Educ., 1974–84.

Professional Career: Pres. & CEO, H&H Foods Inc., 1962–present.

DC Office: 1032 LHOB 20515, 202-225-2531; Fax: 202-225-5688; Web site: www.house.gov/hinojosa.

District Offices: Beeville, 512-358-8400; McAllen, 210-682-5545.

Committees: *Education & the Workforce* (14th of 22 D): Early Childhood, Youth & Families; Postsecondary Education, Training & Life-Long Learning. *Small Business* (6th of 17 D): Government Programs & Oversight; Tax, Finance & Exports.

Group Ratings

	ADA	ACLU	AFS	LCV	CON	NTU	NFIB	COC	ACU	NTLC	CHC
1998	95	63	100	69	55	10	38	59	16	19	17
1997	75	—	88	—	62	25	—	60	29	—	—

National Journal Ratings

	1997 LIB — 1997 CONS			1998 LIB — 1998 CONS	
Economic	67%	—	33%	68%	—	30%
Social	64%	—	35%	70%	—	28%
Foreign	67%	—	32%	75%	—	23%

Key Votes of the 105th Congress

1. Clinton Budget Deal	N	5. Puerto Rico Sthood. Ref.	Y	9. Cut $ for B-2 Bombers	N
2. Education IRAs	N	6. End Highway Set-asides	N	10. Human Rights in China	Y
3. Req. 2/3 to Raise Taxes	N	7. School Prayer Amend.	N	11. Withdraw Bosnia Troops	N
4. Fast-track Trade	N	8. Ovrd. Part. Birth Veto	Y	12. End Cuban TV-Marti	Y

Election Results

1998 general	Ruben Hinojosa (D)	47,957	(58%)	($795,235)
	Tom Haughey (R)	34,221	(42%)	($15,009)
1998 primary	Ruben Hinojosa (D)	unopposed		
1996 general	Ruben Hinojosa (D)	86,347	(62%)	($715,391)
	Tom Haughey (R)	50,914	(37%)	($39,345)

SIXTEENTH DISTRICT

El Paso, Texas, and Juarez, Mexico, sit across from each other on the narrow Rio Grande, their tree-shaded streets spread out below the rough brown face of Comanche Peak, two border cities surrounded by hundreds of miles of some of the country's most desolate landscape—400 miles from Phoenix and 600 from Dallas-Fort Worth. There is much history here: Texas claims the first Thanksgiving took place in San Elizario near El Paso in 1598. Fifty years ago, there were still only 140,000 people in both cities; now there are more than 700,000 in El Paso, and more than 1 million in Juarez. This is a bilingual, bicultural pair of cities, where most people have a Mexican heritage; the thrust of growth is from Spanish-speaking people and an English-speaking economy. El Paso is one of the lowest-wage cities in the U.S., Juarez one of the highest-wage in Mexico; *maquiladora* plants pioneered a cross-border economy and the NAFTA has strengthened it.

But free trade doesn't necessarily mean porous borders. In September 1993, El Paso Immigration and Naturalization Service leader Silvestre Reyes started Operation Hold the Line, positioning 400 officers on the border instead of trying to intercept illegals after they had already crossed into El Paso (amazingly enough, this was firmly-rooted INS policy). Prior to this, 8,000 illegals crossed the border each day; but under Reyes' plan that was drastically reduced by more than half. Mexico complained about threats to its sovereignty, merchants worried about loss of sales, a few homeowners fretted about finding domestic help. But auto thefts were down 30%, burglaries and robberies were down, beggars were absent from the streets, fewer Mexicans were having babies in El Paso hospitals; the move was almost universally popular. The law finally was being enforced by an agency that had long said it was impossible; Californians began asking why the INS couldn't hold the line in their state.

The 16th Congressional District of Texas is made up of most of the city of El Paso, small communities along the Rio Grande, and giant Fort Bliss to the north. A full 70% of the people here are Latino. For many years politics divided people on ethnic lines, with most Anglos Republican and Latinos Democratic. El Paso feels distant from the rest of Texas; it is even in a different time zone. But during his first four years as governor, George W. Bush paid close attention to El Paso, and in November 1998 he carried El Paso County 50%–49%.

The congressman from the 16th District is Silvestre Reyes, a Democrat elected in 1996. He grew up on a farm in Canutillo, just five miles north of El Paso, the oldest of 10 children; he went to college in El Paso and Austin. He served in the Army in Vietnam, then "took as many civil service tests as I could, and the Border Patrol called" in 1969. He worked for the INS in four cities in Texas and Glynco, Georgia, and returned to El Paso in 1993 as chief patrol agent. When he got there he found that "people could basically cross the border at any time, wherever they wanted to." More than 40 boatmen ran "what were essentially international ferries" across the Rio Grande. So he instituted Operation Hold the Line almost immediately, circumventing INS standard procedures against the wishes of many border agents eager to get credit for apprehending aliens, which would be impossible if they never got across the border at all. By November 1995 Reyes's name recognition was 65%, higher than most elected officials; he resigned from the INS and started running for Congress as a Democrat.

Reyes talked of the need for integrity and common sense. His target was Ron Coleman, a Democrat first elected in 1982, around whom scandals lurked: He had 673 overdrafts at the House bank, he was accused by Texas Attorney General Dan Morales on *60 Minutes* of trying to block prosecution of a local developer; a local businessman reportedly had assumed $65,000 of Coleman's debts. "My message is one of change," said Reyes. "I'm giving voters an option to change what they've had for a decade and a half." In December 1995 Coleman announced he was retiring, but his legislative assistant for 13 years, Jose Luis Sanchez, ran with backing from Coleman and labor unions. Sanchez attacked Reyes harshly as a crypto-Republican, pointing out that his campaign treasurer had worked for Republicans in the past and that he had the support of Republican former Mayor Jonathan Rogers, and criticizing Reyes for backing a capital gains tax cut. One Sanchez mailing read, "Two of a kind: Gingrich and Reyes." Reyes hewed to his moderate platform, calling for water conservation research, a capital gains tax cut (but not entitlement cuts, as Sanchez charged), promoting high-tech jobs, developing more highways and border crossings. He waffled on abortion. He came out for repeal of the assault weapons ban and was endorsed by the National Rifle Association. After Reyes led the primary 42%–28%, Sanchez and the unions pressed hard in the runoff, but Reyes won 51%–49%. He won the general election 71%–28%. In surmounting political stereotypes, Reyes told *George* magazine, "The one thing I find curious is that people are amazed that Hispanics react like other groups. We're concerned about crime, taxes, education."

He admits that Operation Hold the Line is "not a permanent solution. The permanent solution is the economic stabilization of Mexico." He says a border fence is unnecessary, because electronic monitoring can work for most of the border, and he opposes a national identification card. In the meantime, he objected when President Clinton failed to respond to a Congressional mandate for 1,000 additional Border Patrol agents in the 2000 budget. He spoke out against the resolution to decertify Mexico for its drug enforcement record, saying it would upset the Mexican economy. He backs retraining for workers displaced by NAFTA, though he says that overall it is a great success. But he was one of the late-deciding Democrats whose opposition helped doom fast track in November 1997. He has also worked on border environmental problems and water conservation, and to promote high-tech jobs and Fort Bliss.

Cook's Call. *Safe.* This heavily Democratic district is a safe haven for Reyes. Don't look for an interesting Election Day here in 2000.

The People: Pop. 1990: 566,238; 1.7% rural; 8.7% age 65 + ; 76.5% White, 3.6% Black, 1.1% Asian, 0.4% Amer. Indian, 18.4% Other; 70.3% Hispanic Origin. Households: 60.2% married couple families; 37.5% married couple fams. w. children; 40.6% college educ.; median household income: $22,632; per capita income: $9,195; median house value: $57,600; median gross rent: $299.

1996 Presidential Vote

Clinton (D)	80,475	(63%)
Dole (R)	40,983	(32%)
Perot (I)	5,902	(5%)

1992 Presidential Vote

Clinton (D)	65,614	(51%)
Bush (R)	45,367	(35%)
Perot (I)	18,779	(14%)

Rep. Silvestre Reyes (D)

Elected 1996; b. Nov. 10, 1944, Canutillo; home, El Paso; El Paso Commun. Col., A.A. 1977; Catholic; married (Carolina).

Military Career: Army, 1966–68 (Vietnam).

Elected Office: Canutillo Schl. Board, 1968–70.

Professional Career: Border Patrol Agent, 1969–95.

DC Office: 514 CHOB 20515, 202-225-4831; Fax: 202-225-2016; Web site: www.house.gov/reyes.

District Office: El Paso, 915-534-4400.

Committees: *Armed Services* (13th of 28 D): Military Installations & Facilities; Military Research & Development; Special Oversight Panel on Morale, Welfare and Recreation. *Veterans' Affairs* (8th of 14 D): Benefits.

Group Ratings

	ADA	ACLU	AFS	LCV	CON	NTU	NFIB	COC	ACU	NTLC	CHC
1998	80	47	100	54	43	10	36	47	13	16	17
1997	65	—	88	—	36	24	—	40	38	—	—

National Journal Ratings

	1997 LIB — 1997 CONS		1998 LIB — 1998 CONS	
Economic	70% —	29%	77% —	22%
Social	62% —	38%	63% —	37%
Foreign	58% —	41%	74% —	25%

Key Votes of the 105th Congress

1. Clinton Budget Deal	N	5. Puerto Rico Sthood. Ref.	Y	9. Cut $ for B-2 Bombers	N
2. Education IRAs	N	6. End Highway Set-asides	N	10. Human Rights in China	Y
3. Req. 2/3 to Raise Taxes	N	7. School Prayer Amend.	*	11. Withdraw Bosnia Troops	N
4. Fast-track Trade	N	8. Ovrd. Part. Birth Veto	Y	12. End Cuban TV-Marti	N

Election Results

1998 general	Silvestre Reyes (D)	67,486	(88%)	($340,427)
	Stu Nance (Lib)	5,329	(7%)	
	Lorenzo Morales (I)	3,952	(5%)	
1998 primary	Silvestre Reyes (D)	unopposed		
1996 general	Silvestre Reyes (D)	90,260	(71%)	($587,193)
	Rick Ledesma (R)	35,271	(28%)	($110,765)
	Others	2,253	(2%)	

SEVENTEENTH DISTRICT

West from Fort Worth, the West Texas plains stretch miles beyond the horizon, thousands and thousands of acres of rolling grazing land punctuated occasionally by oases of irrigated farmland (often in circles that show the reach of the sprinklers). This is primarily cattle country, although there is some oil here, and cotton and grain. On the interstate going west from Fort Worth, settlements start thinning out quickly. Before long, you are on open plains, with enormous skies and no people in sight. Then in the distance is a good-sized town, an oasis of activity. The largest town here is Abilene, with a high concentration of bankers, lawyers and professionals. Settled by Confederate veterans suspicious of Eastern bankers and Yankee businessmen, this was one of the Democratic heartlands of America up through the 1970s; now it is voting Republican in top-of-the-ticket races. In the sparsely populated counties that seem utterly left behind, the few hundred voters may tilt crazily left or resoundingly right.

The 17th Congressional District takes up much of this "God's country," starting a few miles from Fort Worth and including most of three tiers of counties westward almost to New Mexico. This ancestrally Democratic region voted 51%–39% for Bob Dole over Bill Clinton in 1996.

The congressman from the 17th District is Charles Stenholm, one of several conservative Texas Democrats elected in 1978, but the only one still in the House. Stenholm is a farmer from a small town settled by Swedes near Abilene, a natural politician who went to Congress after leading the Rolling Plains Cotton Growers Association and the Stamford Electric Cooperative (Stamford is the home town also of Democratic super-lobbyist Robert Strauss). Stenholm became a Democrat because in the 1970 Senate race Lloyd Bentsen was interested in his issues but George Bush wasn't. In 1978, when 32-year incumbent Omar Burleson retired, Stenholm ran for the seat and easily won.

In the House, Stenholm and Phil Gramm were leaders of the "Boll Weevils," backing the 1981 Reagan budget and tax cuts. He threatened momentarily to run against Speaker Tip O'Neill in 1985, but desisted when conservatives were promised more attention. His voting record is conservative, especially on cultural issues, but not always market-oriented. On the Agriculture Committee, where he is now ranking minority member, he says his goals are expanding world trade, streamlining the bureaucracy, boosting research and promoting the needs of producers and consumers. He favors relaxing environmental restrictions and opposes caps on subsidies. He favored a "better safety net" than that provided in the Republicans' Freedom to Farm Act and a government insurance program to protect farmers against price risk in "the volatile global marketplace."

Stenholm used to be the lead conservative Democrat on budget issues, as head of the Conservative Democratic Forum and on the Budget Committee. But that role faded as Republican leaders started viewing Stenholm as a conservative talker but a partisan Democratic doer, and the spotlight passed to other members of the Democratic Blue Dogs. "I think maybe people felt I was getting too much attention," he told *National Journal*. "I needed to step back and let others take some credit." In the Democratic House, Stenholm was a crucial vote for Republicans; in the Republican House, he is less often. But he was co-author of the balanced budget amendment, which the House passed in 1995. And he has worked closely with Budget Committee Democrats on preparing a budget both Blue Dogs and liberals could back.

On welfare reform, he pushed to allow school to be counted as work for people over 20 and voted for the final reform measure. He worked to save the Legal Services Corporation but voted against increasing the minimum wage. He worked to fund construction at Dyess Air Force Base and to bring more Border Patrol officers to San Angelo. Working with Republican Jim Kolbe of Arizona, he turned his quest for bipartisanship to Social Security, endorsing steps such as directing all of the budget surplus to Social Security, improving the safety net for low-income retirees, increasing the retirement age, introducing individual investment accounts and not raising withholding taxes. Despite the lukewarm response from both parties' leaders, Stenholm has demonstrated his persistence. On impeachment, Stenholm harshly criticized Clinton for lying under oath, and—after lengthy reflection, and despite a final plea from the president—was one of five House Democrats to vote for impeachment.

Unlike some other Democrats with similar voting records, Stenholm did not switch parties. Instead, in December 1994 he ran for minority whip, predictably losing to David Bonior 145–60. He has plenty of seniority, and the ranking position on Agriculture; Republicans have never been ready to offer him anything comparable. Plus, when he was starting out, it was politically safer to be a Democrat: Democratic incumbents were never beaten by Republicans in central Texas, and seldom lost in primaries, while Republicans were guaranteed an opponent every time, often a seasoned and popular local officeholder. But that is no longer the case in the 17th District. Stenholm was unopposed in general elections from 1980–90 and won in 1992 with 66% of the vote. But in 1994 Republican Phil Boone, though vastly outspent, carried Abilene and seven other counties and held Stenholm to a 54%–46% win. In 1996, Republican Rudy Izzard, a dentist and former San Angelo councilman, carried Abilene and eight other counties and held Stenholm to a 52%–47% win. Again, Stenholm raised and spent far more money than his opponent.

Izzard ran again in 1998 and Republicans hoped that the coattails of George W. Bush would provide the margin of difference for their side. Izzard also was helped by support from Christian conservatives unhappy with Stenholm's support for campaign-finance legislation that they feared would limit political speech. Turning his foes to his advantage, Stenholm said that Newt Gingrich and Dick Armey wanted to defeat him because they opposed the needs of agriculture. And Stenholm turned the tables by winning business endorsements, including the local Chamber of Commerce. Stenholm carried 28 of 32 counties, but 11 of them with less than 55%. Overall he won 54%–45%. If he retires, Republicans must be favored to win this district; if he doesn't, he could face redistricting problems.

Cook's Call. *Competitive.* Since 1992, Stenholm has had to fight like crazy to keep hold of this conservative, Republican trending district. He has survived just about everything that Republicans have thrown at him, and remains a difficult target in 2000.

The People: Pop. 1990: 566,255; 38.4% rural; 16.5% age 65 +; 85.9% White, 3.5% Black, 0.5% Asian, 0.4% Amer. Indian, 9.7% Other; 16.8% Hispanic Origin. Households: 61.3% married couple families; 29.5% married couple fams. w. children; 36.3% college educ.; median household income: $21,532; per capita income: $10,642; median house value: $38,900; median gross rent: $245.

1996 Presidential Vote			1992 Presidential Vote		
Dole (R)	98,804	(51%)	Bush (R)	86,490	(40%)
Clinton (D)	76,057	(39%)	Clinton (D)	73,388	(34%)
Perot (I)	19,182	(10%)	Perot (I)	55,834	(26%)

Rep. Charles W. Stenholm (D)

Elected 1978; b. Oct. 26, 1938, Stamford; home, Avoca; TX Tech. U., B.S. 1961, M.S. 1962; Lutheran; married (Cynthia).

Professional Career: Farmer; Vocational educ. teacher, 1962–65; Exec. V.P., Rolling Plains Cotton Growers, 1965–68; Mgr., Stamford Electric Co-op., 1968–76.

DC Office: 1211 LHOB 20515, 202-225-6605; Fax: 202-225-2234; Web site: www.house.gov/stenholm.

District Offices: Abilene, 915-673-7221; San Angelo, 915-655-7994; Stamford, 915-773-3623.

Committees: *Agriculture* (RMM of 24 D).

Group Ratings

	ADA	ACLU	AFS	LCV	CON	NTU	NFIB	COC	ACU	NTLC	CHC
1998	40	19	67	15	97	37	57	76	48	63	58
1997	40	—	38	—	91	41	—	90	58	—	—

National Journal Ratings

	1997 LIB	—	1997 CONS	1998 LIB	—	1998 CONS
Economic	51%	—	48%	55%	—	45%
Social	49%	—	50%	36%	—	63%
Foreign	42%	—	57%	53%	—	45%

Key Votes of the 105th Congress

1. Clinton Budget Deal	N	5. Puerto Rico Sthood. Ref.	Y	9. Cut $ for B-2 Bombers	Y
2. Education IRAs	N	6. End Highway Set-asides	Y	10. Human Rights in China	N
3. Req. 2/3 to Raise Taxes	N	7. School Prayer Amend.	Y	11. Withdraw Bosnia Troops	N
4. Fast-track Trade	Y	8. Ovrd. Part. Birth Veto	Y	12. End Cuban TV-Marti	N

Election Results

1998 general	Charles W. Stenholm (D) 75,367	(54%)	($1,529,708)
	Rudy Izzard (R) 63,700	(45%)	($572,253)
1998 primary	Charles W. Stenholm (D) .... unopposed		
1996 general	Charles W. Stenholm (D) 99,678	(52%)	($804,936)
	Rudy Izzard (R) 91,429	(47%)	($192,082)

EIGHTEENTH DISTRICT

Houston contains, within its vast bounds, disparities of income and wealth as striking as any city in the United States. This is what one must expect in an expanding city with dynamic economic growth, vast immigration, absence of centralized planning and openness to cultural diversity. The contrast is most glaringly apparent at the edge of Houston's gleaming downtown with its keynote Pennzoil, Heritage Plaza and NationsBank buildings; only a few blocks away are the slums where blacks and Mexican-Americans live in unpainted frame houses full of cracks wide enough to let in Houston's humid, smoggy air. But the contrasts are less obvious as one moves out from Houston's historic center. Half a century ago, when Houston pioneers like Jesse Jones, millionaire cotton broker and newspaper publisher, started building downtown skyscrapers, they were operating in a town with a Third World economy, a low-skill producer of basic commodities, where a few got rich and many lived near subsistence level. Today, Houston has a high-tech advanced economy offering a myriad of opportunities and wide range of economic outcomes. One result is that as Houston's blacks and Hispanics have moved outward from the city, increasingly they are living in comfortable middle-class neighborhoods.

The 18th Congressional District contains central Houston and many of these outlying neighborhoods, to the northeast, the south and especially the northwest. Its boundaries were redrawn by a three-judge federal court in August 1996, after the Supreme Court ruled the previous boundaries as unconstitutional because they were racially motivated. Those 1991 boundaries were convoluted, perhaps the most irregular in American history. The aim was to maximize the black percentage in the 18th and the Hispanic percentage in the interlocking 29th District. But was it worth all the trouble? Within the 1991 boundaries the 18th District was 50% black and 15% Hispanic; in the 1996 boundaries it was 45% black and 23% Hispanic: not really much difference in the overall balance. The 1996 redistricting added the Heights, just north of downtown Houston, and dropped Pleasantville and North Forest. The new district can be thought of as having three spokes running out from Loop 610, a northeast spoke along the Eastex Freeway, a southern spoke between the South Freeway and Telegraph Road, and a long northwest spoke between the Northwest Freeway and Route 249.

The congresswoman from the 18th District is Sheila Jackson Lee, a Democrat first elected in 1994. A native of Queens, New York, she was educated at Yale and Virginia Law School, worked on Capitol Hill and practiced law in Houston, served as a local judge and won two terms in an at-large seat on the Houston Council. After a local term limits law took effect in January 1994, she ran for Congress in the March Democratic primary. The incumbent was Craig Washington, a talented but storm-tossed legislator, elected after Mickey Leland was killed in a 1989 plane crash in Ethiopia. Washington often was an iconoclast: he voted against thanking U.S. military personnel for serving in Operation Desert Storm, and against the Space Station and NAFTA, both of which are big pluses for the Houston-area economy. Jackson Lee supported NAFTA and raised lots of money from business interests who favored it. Jackson Lee

1560 TEXAS

won unambiguously, 63%–37%. She was re-elected with 77% in the 1996 all-party primary and had no major-party opposition in 1998.

In the House she has been prolific in offering amendments on the floor. More often than not, her liberal proposals—on NASA funding and abortion—were defeated, though she has won funds for science research at minority colleges. She voted "present" on the Defense of Marriage Act, the only Texan not to vote for it. As chairman of the Children's Caucus, Jackson Lee has focused on the need for improved child-care centers. Prompted by a Virginia case, she has backed criminal penalties for anyone who switches a baby's identity and, prompted by stories about the "date rape" drug Rohypnol, she sponsored a law making it a crime to give an unconsenting person a drug with the intention of harming them later. On the Judiciary Committee during bankruptcy reform, she unsuccessfully sought to give child-support payments priority over everything except taxes. She is known for her high staff turnover; after her first term she fired half her staff.

But she emerged into national prominence as an outspoken—and sometimes querulous— defender of President Clinton during impeachment. She called for censure as "right, punitive and just" and called impeachment a "preposterous" trampling of the Constitution. She perhaps contrasted herself to Barbara Jordan, the first representative elected by the predominantly black 18th District and an eloquent advocate of the impeachment of Richard Nixon in the Judiciary Committee in 1974. Jackson Lee interposed comments often during the Judiciary hearings, spoke frequently on the debate on the floor, and in January and February 1999 was the only House member to sit on the Senate floor, silently at the back making copious notes. She "has become Congress's resident noodge, an endlessly loquacious presence here, there and everywhere," wrote *The New York Times*, perhaps unfairly, for her comments were often to the point and as defensible as those of many other members.

In January 1999, Jackson Lee became ranking Democrat on the Immigration Subcommittee, whose chairman, Lamar Smith from San Antonio, has opposed increased immigration. Jackson Lee may face conflicting desires among her constituents: Latinos tend to favor greater immigration and more generous treatment of immigrants, but some African-Americans and union leaders see immigrants as dangerous competition for jobs. Evidently she comes out on the pro-immigrant side: "We can't accept the goodness of immigration and what the immigrants have been able to do and at the same time characterize immigrants for all of the ailments and problems of America," she has said, and she criticized the different treatment of Nicaraguans and Cubans admitted as political refugees and Guatemalans and Salvadorans who are usually treated as seeking economic benefits rather than protection against political persecution.

Cook's Call. *Safe.* There is little reason to believe that Jackson Lee's high-profile role on the Judiciary Committee during the impeachment hearings will hurt her at all in this solidly Democratic district that gave Clinton 73% of the vote in 1996. She is safe for 2000.

The People: Pop. 1990: 568,146; 10% age 65 +; 40% White, 44.7% Black, 2.8% Asian, 0.2% Amer. Indian, 12.3% Other; 23% Hispanic Origin. Households: 40.5% married couple families; 21.6% married couple fams. w. children; 37.2% college educ.; median household income: $22,240; per capita income: $10,744; median house value: $47,600; median gross rent: $290.

1996 Presidential Vote

Clinton (D) 116,661 (73%)
Dole (R) 38,192 (24%)
Perot (I) 5,699 (4%)

1992 Presidential Vote

Clinton (D) 120,000 (65%)
Bush (R) 41,543 (23%)
Perot (I) 22,225 (12%)

Rep. Sheila Jackson Lee (D)

Elected 1994; b. Jan. 12, 1950, Queens, NY; home, Houston; Yale U., B.A. 1972, U. of VA Law Schl., J.D. 1975; Seventh Day Adventist; married (Elwyn).

Elected Office: Houston City Cncl., 1990–94.

Professional Career: Practicing atty., 1975–77, 1978–87; Staff Cnsl., U.S. House Select Assassinations Cmte., 1977–78; Houston Assoc. Municipal Judge, 1987–90.

DC Office: 410 CHOB 20515, 202-225-3816; Fax: 202-225-3317; Web site: www.house.gov/jacksonlee.

District Offices: Houston, 713-691-4882; Houston, 713-861-4070; Houston, 713-655-0050.

Committees: *Judiciary* (9th of 16 D): Crime; Immigration & Claims (RMM). *Science* (11th of 23 D): Space & Aeronautics.

Group Ratings

	ADA	ACLU	AFS	LCV	CON	NTU	NFIB	COC	ACU	NTLC	CHC
1998	95	88	100	62	38	14	9	44	4	11	0
1997	80	—	100	—	20	24	—	44	13	—	—

National Journal Ratings

	1997 LIB — 1997 CONS		1998 LIB — 1998 CONS	
Economic	79%	— 21%	79%	— 0%
Social	85%	— 0%	90%	— 7%
Foreign	74%	— 25%	75%	— 23%

Key Votes of the 105th Congress

1. Clinton Budget Deal	N	5. Puerto Rico Sthood. Ref.	Y	9. Cut $ for B-2 Bombers	N
2. Education IRAs	N	6. End Highway Set-asides	N	10. Human Rights in China	Y
3. Req. 2/3 to Raise Taxes	N	7. School Prayer Amend.	N	11. Withdraw Bosnia Troops	N
4. Fast-track Trade	N	8. Ovrd. Part. Birth Veto	N	12. End Cuban TV-Marti	N

Election Results

1998 general	Sheila Jackson Lee (D)	82,091	(90%)	($254,445)
	James Galvan (Lib)	9,176	(10%)	
1998 primary	Sheila Jackson Lee (D)	unopposed		
1996 spec. prim.	Sheila Jackson Lee (D)	106,111	(77%)	($477,866)
	Larry White (R)	13,956	(10%)	($124,166)
	Jerry Burley (R)	7,877	(6%)	($29,151)
	Others	9,744	(7%)	

NINETEENTH DISTRICT

On the High Plains of Texas, separated from the dusty cattlelands further east by rising gullies astride wide river courses, is some of the most productive cotton and wheat land in the United States, centered around the city of Lubbock. This is irrigated land, which gets its water from the giant Ogallala Aquifer that undergirds so much of the western Great Plains, making this part of Texas a sort of green island in a vast brown sea of arid grazing land. The area was settled relatively late, with most growth after World War II. Lubbock grew from 31,000 in 1940 to 128,000 in 1960 and 197,000 in 1998, with an economy that includes Texas Tech University as well as agribusiness. But the 1980s and 1990s were tough on the High Plains. The aquifer seemed to be going dry, populations declined in almost every rural county, hospitals were closed in small towns.

Politically this was once Democratic territory: Lubbock elected George Mahon, chairman of the House Appropriations Committee from 1964–79. And when Mahon retired in 1978, the 19th preferred a conservative Democrat to a young oil man named George W. Bush. Now the area around Lubbock is heavily Republican, so much so that President George Bush always liked to refer to it as a bellwether of public opinion. Lubbock County, which voted against George W. Bush for Congress in 1978, voted for him for governor over Ann Richards 63%–37% in 1994 and 82%–18% against Garry Mauro in 1998.

The 19th Congressional District runs roughly 400 miles along the western edge of the High Plains of Texas, from the northern edge of the Panhandle south to the Permian Basin. Tantalizingly, it includes only part of each of its four major cities. In 1992, the Democratic legislature took the black area of Lubbock and the lower-income areas of Amarillo and put them in the 13th District to help the incumbent Democrat there; the Permian Basin oil towns of Midland and Odessa, where George and Barbara Bush moved in the pre-air-conditioning days of 1948, were split to help the incumbent Democrat in the 23rd District. Now both Democrats are gone, beaten in 1994 and 1992, but the lines remain, helping to make the 19th Texas's most Republican district in 1996, when it gave Bob Dole a 67%–26% margin over Bill Clinton.

The congressman from the 19th District is Larry Combest, a Republican first elected in 1984. He graduated from West Texas State University, worked as a teacher, farmer and for the Soil Conservation Service; from 1971–78 he specialized on farm issues on Senator John Tower's staff. He then returned to Lubbock, where he owned an electronics company. In 1984, when conservative Democratic Congressman Kent Hance ran for the Senate, Combest ran for the House. After a tough primary, runoff and general election that year, he has since won easily.

In the House, Combest has a solidly conservative record. Much of his work has been on farm issues, and he became Agriculture Committee chairman in 1999. He has not been as hostile to farm subsidies as most other Republicans. He opposed cutting target prices and ending subsidies in the 1990 farm bill. In 1995, he and three other Southern Republicans killed the Republicans' original Freedom to Farm Act in committee, because of its changes in the cotton marketing program. He argued that cotton farmers need protection because Third World governments manipulate world prices much more than commodities like wheat and corn. Chairman Pat Roberts was forced to concede to the "cottonmouth moccasins," as he called them, and left cotton pretty much as is. Immediately after passage of the bill, Combest softened its farm credit terms when farmers in the 19th District were unable to get crop loans. He supports the Conservation Reserve Program to retain topsoil in areas exposed to wind erosion. When Clinton during a State of the Union message took a swipe at the work of the Plant Stress Laboratory at Texas Tech, Combest said the result of Clinton's comments was positive because the criticism was seen as shortsighted. He insists that the prime farm issue is protecting property rights against government intervention to enforce environmental laws. He has resisted Clinton Administration efforts to remove millions of acres from farm production. When he took over as committee chairman, he said he expected no major policy reversals, though he discussed crop insurance reforms to protect against low prices. He passed in March 1999 a bill with a $500 million farm-credit increase.

Combest's elevation to the committee chairmanship followed his disappointment when Republican leaders in 1997 awarded the post to Bob Smith of Oregon, who was promised the chairmanship in exchange for returning from retirement to run for a House seat that Democrats might otherwise have captured. At the same time, Combest was forced to give up his Intelligence Committee chairmanship because of committee term limits. Combest was generally favorable to the enterprise of intelligence, but he criticized CIA handling of the Aldrich Ames case and "the compartmented culture of the intelligence community." He worries about the effects of secret budget cuts and laments that secret successes cannot be known: He said that budget cuts forced the withdrawal of American intelligence from Somalia six months before

Marines hit the beach, while intelligence agencies foiled a plan after the World Trade Center bombing in New York to set off five simultaneous bombs elsewhere. In 1996 he unveiled "fairly radical" CIA reforms—combining the CIA's Directorate of Operations with the Defense Department's Clandestine Service, with the new agency separate from both CIA and Defense, and melding the National Security Agency into a new Technical Collection Agency also embodying non-Directorate of Operations parts of the CIA. But this was vastly scaled back in committee, and the bill that passed made only modest changes.

Combest has been active on two other diverse projects. He was vice chairman of the Commission on Protecting and Reducing Government Secrecy, which produced a unanimous report in 1997 calling for both more and less secrecy. "The government must be made to discharge its superfluous secrets and behave in a more open manner," he said. "Government officials must be more subject to limits on what they can classify. But in our rush to widen access, we must not compromise vital secrets, nor betray those who have risked their lives and fortunes to confide in us." Combest also has sought to increase the availability of two-way tele-medicine treatment between a doctor's office and a patient's home—of special interest to rural citizens.

Cook's Call. *Safe.* Here's a district that won't ever show up on a Democratic target list. Combest represents one of the most Republican districts in Texas and the nation.

The People: Pop. 1990: 565,925; 18.4% rural; 10.6% age 65 + ; 86.3% White, 2.5% Black, 0.8% Asian, 0.5% Amer. Indian, 9.9% Other; 19.3% Hispanic Origin. Households: 61.5% married couple families; 32.3% married couple fams. w. children; 49.8% college educ.; median household income: $27,267; per capita income: $13,184; median house value: $55,400; median gross rent: $296.

1996 Presidential Vote

Dole (R)	133,397	(67%)
Clinton (D)	51,996	(26%)
Perot (I)	12,323	(6%)

1992 Presidential Vote

Bush (R)	130,639	(60%)
Clinton (D)	50,815	(23%)
Perot (I)	36,068	(17%)

Rep. Larry Combest (R)

Elected 1984; b. Mar. 20, 1945, Memphis; home, Lubbock; W. TX St. U., B.B.A. 1969; United Methodist; married (Sharon).

Professional Career: Farmer; Teacher, 1970–71; Dir., U.S. Agric. Stabilization & Conservation Svc., Graham TX, 1971; Aide, U.S. Sen. John Tower, 1971–78; Founder & Pres., Combest Distrib. Co., 1978–85.

DC Office: 1026 LHOB 20515, 202-225-4005; Fax: 202-225-9615; Web site: www.house.gov/combest.

District Offices: Amarillo, 806-353-3945; Lubbock, 806-763-1611; Odessa, 915-550-0743.

Committees: *Agriculture* (Chmn. of 27 R). *Small Business* (2d of 19 R): Regulatory Reform & Paperwork Reduction.

Group Ratings

	ADA	ACLU	AFS	LCV	CON	NTU	NFIB	COC	ACU	NTLC	CHC
1998	0	6	0	0	33	52	100	94	100	97	100
1997	10	—	0	—	56	63	—	100	92	—	—

National Journal Ratings

	1997 LIB — 1997 CONS			1998 LIB — 1998 CONS		
Economic	0%	—	90%	0%	—	88%
Social	20%	—	71%	14%	—	81%
Foreign	12%	—	81%	7%	—	83%

1564   TEXAS

Key Votes of the 105th Congress

1. Clinton Budget Deal	Y	5. Puerto Rico Sthood. Ref.	N	9. Cut $ for B-2 Bombers	Y
2. Education IRAs	Y	6. End Highway Set-asides	Y	10. Human Rights in China	N
3. Req. 2/3 to Raise Taxes	Y	7. School Prayer Amend.	Y	11. Withdraw Bosnia Troops	Y
4. Fast-track Trade	Y	8. Ovrd. Part. Birth Veto	Y	12. End Cuban TV-Marti	N

Election Results

1998 general	Larry Combest (R)	108,266	(84%)	($459,193)
	Sidney Blankenship (D)	21,162	(16%)	($8,937)
1998 primary	Larry Combest (R)	unopposed		
1996 general	Larry Combest (R)	156,910	(80%)	($440,379)
	John W. Sawyer (D)	38,316	(20%)	($46,000)

TWENTIETH DISTRICT

San Antonio, with its antique past and theme-park future, its Hispanic heritage, its military superstructure and its high-tech hopes, is unlike any other city in the United States. Here on a plaza is the Alamo, preserved by the Daughters of the Republic of Texas, where Davy Crockett, Jim Bowie and 184 others were wiped out in 1836 (Crockett was a Tennessee congressman for three terms; if he had not lost his re-election in 1834, he presumably would not have left Tennessee for Texas). The Spanish architecture recalls San Antonio's days as the most important town in Texas, when the state was part of Mexico, and contrasts with the 31-story Tower Life Building, which contrasts with the armadillo-like Alamodome; the stark terrain contrasts with the lushness of the Paseo, the 1970s-redeveloped Riverwalk along the tiny San Antonio River. The city includes old neighborhoods redolent of the Texas Germans who were its chief Anglo citizens for many years.

For most of this century, San Antonio's economy has been built on the military: This is the home of three Air Force bases and the Brooks Army Medical Center at Fort Sam Houston, contributing some $3 billion to the local economy. In July 1995 Bill Clinton bent the rules of the base closing process to keep in San Antonio the thousands of depot jobs at Kelly Air Force Base, a move so resented that Congress has blocked new rounds of base closings; weeks later then-San Antonio Congressman Henry B. Gonzalez, as ranking Democrat, defended Clinton like a tiger at the Banking Committee hearings on Whitewater. Behind the bases as a local employer is the medical complex centered on the Health Science Center. San Antonio also has 45,500 military retirees, the highest in the country. And it is becoming a tourist center: For generations Texas schoolchildren have made pilgrimages to the Alamo, and in recent decades, they stop at the nearby HemisFair, preserved from the 1968 World's Fair, and the Riverwalk.

With almost a million people, San Antonio is the third-largest city in Texas, though its metro area is barely more than one-third the size of metro Houston or the Dallas-Fort Worth Metroplex. Notable as the only Hispanic-majority major city in the country, San Antonio has the low education and income levels one might expect from a city whose economy is affected by the proximity of the Mexican border. Yet it has mostly avoided the polarized politics and ethnic anger that were manifested in the urban black-white tensions of the 1960s, and it has made progress as a low-wage, high-tech center, making some linkage with nearby Austin. In 1998, the metro area added 24,000 jobs, chiefly in construction and services—mostly for tourism. Kelly is scheduled to be closed in 2001, but some jobs will be retained by Clinton's "privatization in place" scheme.

The 20th Congressional District includes most of central San Antonio and its west side. Its boundaries on the north are irregular, since affluent Anglo neighborhoods are set off and placed in the 21st District. On the west it extends beyond I-410 to Loop 1604 and in some places past that highway. This is one of Texas's six Hispanic-majority districts, and the first to elect a Hispanic congressman. It is solidly Democratic.

The congressman from the 20th District is Charlie Gonzalez, a Democrat elected in 1998. He is one of eight children of Henry B. Gonzales, who held the seat since a 1961 special election and was for six years chairman of the Banking Committee. Charlie Gonzalez grew up in San Antonio, and was 16 when his father was elected to the House. He graduated from the University of Texas and St. Mary's University School of Law and served in the Texas Air National Guard. He was an elementary school teacher, practiced law and served as a judge from 1982–97. As a judge, he considered himself a reformer who created a statewide model for mediation to accelerate the justice system and protect children from broken families. He obviously benefited from his father's renown as the patron saint of Texas liberalism for many years; throughout his career, the elder Gonzalez brought a determination to do right and an indifference to what others may think. In September 1997, at 81 and in poor health, Gonzalez announced he would resign from the House at the end of the year. Later, he changed his mind but was absent from the House for most of 1998, returning only to vote against impeachment in December; critics charged that he wanted to prevent a special election for fear it would hurt his son's chances to succeed him.

Charlie Gonzalez was the frontrunner for the seat but the contest was more competitive than many had expected. With six other Democrats in the March primary, Gonzalez campaigned as a consensus-builder, emphasizing his background in negotiation and compromise. Symbolizing the economic transformation of San Antonio, he said he would work for the entire district, not simply the low-income groups, and would promote San Antonio's future by stressing education. Taking a more feisty tone was Maria Berriozabal, a former city council member and the daughter of Mexican immigrants, who called for more outspoken leadership and had a picture of farmworkers-leader Cesar Chavez on her campaign walls. In a brash move, she used a picture of Henry B. in her campaign literature and claimed that she was more his model than was Charlie. Just before the primary, his father issued a brief statement endorsing his son. Gonzalez led the first balloting with 44% to 22% for Berriozabal, 13% for state Representative Christine Hernandez, 10% for outgoing Bexar County Democratic Chairman Walter Martinez, and 7% for former Gonzalez staffer Armando Falcon. In the April runoff, Berriozabal assembled a formidable grass-roots organization and questioned Gonzalez's political experience. But the former judge benefited from a fundraising advantage of more than 2–1 that reinforced his connection to his father—"Gonzalez Congress" read his campaign posters—and mostly ignored his opponent. He won 62%–38%. He won the general election with 63% of the vote.

In the House, Gonzalez took his father's seat on the Banking Committee and became a lead man on census issues for both the Democratic Caucus and the Hispanic Caucus.

Cook's Call. *Safe.* For 37 years, Henry B. Gonzalez represented this San Antonio based district in Congress. His son Charlie Gonzalez can probably hold onto it for as long as he would like as well.

The People: Pop. 1990: 564,865; 2.7% rural; 10% age 65 + ; 71.9% White, 5.7% Black, 1.3% Asian, 0.4% Amer. Indian, 20.7% Other; 60.4% Hispanic Origin. Households: 50.5% married couple families; 29% married couple fams. w. children; 43.7% college educ.; median household income: $22,372; per capita income: $9,672; median house value: $48,900; median gross rent: $305.

1996 Presidential Vote			1992 Presidential Vote		
Clinton (D)	82,892	(60%)	Clinton (D)	81,381	(48%)
Dole (R)	48,488	(35%)	Bush (R)	57,977	(34%)
Perot (I)	7,285	(5%)	Perot (I)	28,968	(17%)

Rep. Charles Gonzalez (D)

Elected 1998; b. May 5, 1945, San Antonio; home, San Antonio; U. of TX, B. A. 1969; St. Mary's Law Schl., J. D. 1972.; Catholic; married (Becky Whetstone).

Military Career: TX Air Natl. Guard, 1969–75.

Elected Office: Judge, San Antonio Municipal Court; Judge, Bexar Cnty. Court at Law, 1983–87; Judge, 57th State Judicial Dist. Court, 1988–97.

Professional Career: Elem. schl. teacher, 1969–71; Practicing atty., 1972–82.

DC Office: 327 CHOB 20515, 202-225-3236; Fax: 202-225-1915; Web site: www.house.gov/gonzalez.

District Office: San Antonio, 210-472-6195.

Committees: *Banking & Financial Services* (25th of 27 D): Financial Institutions & Consumer Credit; General Oversight & Investigations. *Small Business* (12th of 17 D): Government Programs & Oversight; Tax, Finance & Exports.

Group Ratings and Key Votes: Newly Elected

Election Results

1998 general	Charles Gonzalez (D)	50,356	(63%)	($657,280)
	James Walker (R)	28,347	(36%)	($89,200)
1998 runoff	Charles Gonzalez (D)	13,439	(62%)	
	Maria Antonietta Berriozabal (D)	8,189	(38%)	
1998 primary	Charles Gonzalez (D)	9,482	(44%)	
	Maria Antonietta Berriozabal (D)	4,809	(22%)	
	Christine Hernandez (D)	2,731	(13%)	
	Walter Martinez (D)	2,109	(10%)	
	Armando Falcon (D)	1,572	(7%)	
	Others	873	(4%)	
1996 general	Henry B. Gonzalez (D)	88,190	(64%)	($86,231)
	James Walker (R)	47,616	(34%)	($138,735)
	Others	2,603	(2%)	

TWENTY-FIRST DISTRICT

The Texas German country, on the gently rolling plains between San Antonio and Austin and west into the Hill Country, is one of America's lesser known ethnic enclaves. First settled by refugees from the failed democratic revolutions of 1848, the German country has always been a set of orderly communities in riproaring Texas, economically prosperous in a state that considered itself poor until it struck oil. It has been anti-slavery and politically Republican in a state whose enthusiasm for the Democratic Party had roots in Confederate loyalties and populist rebellions. The Texas Germans are entwined with the career of Lyndon Johnson: The death of Republican Congressman Harry Wurzbach of Guadalupe County gave Democrats the majority and enabled them to elect John Nance Garner of Uvalde as speaker in 1931, while Wurzbach's replacement in the House, Democrat Richard Kleberg (of the King Ranch family) hired the then 23-year-old Johnson to his first Washington job. And, though Johnson never emphasized this, his LBJ Ranch was neither in Blanco County nor poor Johnson City, where he grew up, but west in Gillespie County near the prosperous town of Fredericksburg, historically Texas German, heavily Republican (87% for George W. Bush in 1998), and now the home of the nation's largest working wildflower seed farm.

The 21st Congressional District has its demographic center in the old Texas German country, where the San Antonio and Austin metropolitan areas are now growing together. As with so many Texas districts under the 1991 redistricting, its boundaries are quite complex. About 40% is on the north side of San Antonio and Bexar County (pronounced like a drawn-out *bear*), mostly Anglo neighborhoods around Alamo Heights and out I-35, and in Guadalupe and Comal Counties just beyond—Texas German country now classified as part of metro San Antonio. Another 20% is in Williamson County, just north of Austin—one of the state's fastest-growing counties, with suburban overspill subdivisions full of high-tech and white-collar workers who are much more Republican than the liberals who live in older neighborhoods near downtown Austin and UT. These two areas are connected by sparsely populated Hill Country and Texas German counties, including Fredericksburg and the LBJ Ranch, the almost mountainous country around Kerrville, sheep and goat ranching country reaching northwest to San Angelo—America's wool and mohair capital—and all the way to Midland, headquarters of the high-income, oil-rich Permian Basin, where George Bush and George W. Bush lived from 1949–60. All this is heavily Republican and has become a mecca for retirees, especially from adjacent military bases.

The congressman from the 21st District is Lamar Smith, a Republican first elected in 1986, now chairman of both the Judiciary Committee's Immigration Subcommittee and the ethics committee. Smith is from an old San Antonio and south Texas ranching family; he went to Yale and SMU Law School, worked as a reporter and a lawyer, was elected to the Texas House in 1980 and the Bexar County Commission in 1982. In 1986, when Congressman Tom Loeffler ran for governor, Smith ran for the House; at that time the 21st ranged even wider and had more acreage than Ohio. Smith won by beating two other San Antonio-based candidates in the primary and then winning the runoff, with help from Senator Phil Gramm, against a religious conservative. He has been re-elected easily since, without major-party opposition in 1998.

When Democrats held the majority, Smith compiled a conservative record and pursued original initiatives. One bill added 100,000 acres to Big Bend National Park along the Rio Grande; another sponsored the Bush Administration's government-wide ethics act. By 1991, Smith was proposing cuts in every appropriations bill, with emphasis on cutting government overhead costs, especially travel; often Democrats prevented them from coming to a vote. In April 1993 he was appointed head of the Republicans' "theme team," organizing more than 800 one-minute speeches by members. Meanwhile, he pursued other interests: stopping designation of part of Texas as "critical habitat" for the golden-cheeked warbler, funding programs to promote teen abstinence, stopping HIV-positive foreigners from attending the Gay Games.

When he became chairman of the Immigration Subcommittee in 1995, Smith had long believed in stronger action to stop illegal immigration and to reduce legal immigration. "While we welcome immigrants who see America as a land of opportunity to make good through their own efforts, we should not subsidize immigration through the welfare system," he said. He steered his bill through committee largely unchanged, although he did make telephone verification of immigrant status by employers a pilot project rather than a national requirement and dropped a provision preventing businesses from sponsoring foreign workers with specific skills. On the House floor, several provisions were challenged. A bipartisan group including liberal Democrats and freshmen Republicans successfully moved to strip almost all provisions on legal immigration. Other moves to cut the verification pilot project and to require a tamper-proof identification card were beaten. The bill passed by a wide margin, but more negotiations were ahead. House-Senate conferees removed almost all aid for illegals, even as the welfare bill barred states from aiding legal immigrants. The final version had harsher deportation proceedings, including for legals on welfare; it doubled the number of Border Patrol agents and mandated a 14-mile fence on the California-Mexico border. In the midst of his re-election campaign, Bill Clinton signed it. Since enactment of the 1996 law, Smith has focused on what he calls "the unintended consequences" of the increased number of low-skilled legal immigrants; he presided over a compromise bill to increase H-1B visas for high-skilled foreign workers, though he was less enthusiastic about the idea than many other Republicans, including his Senate counterpart, Spencer Abraham of Michigan.

Smith's appointment in 1999 to chair the ethics committee (official name: Standards of Official Conduct Committee) was announced by Speaker Dennis Hastert: "A strong ethics committee is essential to the integrity of the House and Lamar Smith is well-qualified to serve as chairman." The committee had been reconstituted after settlement of the acrimonious battle over the charges against Newt Gingrich; the new chairman, James Hansen of Utah, had been on the committee years before and had agreed to serve only one term. Smith started serving on the committee after Jim Bunning resigned in January 1997; Smith found the charges against Gingrich largely without merit and the bipartisan call for a reprimand to be excessive. He became the only committee member to vote against the penalties, and he led the debate against the measure on the House floor. Smith, like all other members, left the committee after the Gingrich case, but was persuaded to return in September 1997. He served as the subcommittee chairman investigating Jay Kim; Kim was not punished by the House because he had already lost his June 1998 primary. As chairman, Smith has said that he wants to emphasize the panel's "advice and education" rather than its investigative duties.

Cook's Call. *Safe.* Lamar Smith is safely entrenched in this heavily Republican district.

The People: Pop. 1990: 566,105; 29% rural; 13.9% age 65 +; 91.4% White, 2.5% Black, 1% Asian, 0.4% Amer. Indian, 4.8% Other; 14% Hispanic Origin. Households: 62% married couple families; 29.4% married couple fams. w. children; 58.5% college educ.; median household income: $32,103; per capita income: $16,086; median house value: $79,400; median gross rent: $359.

1996 Presidential Vote			1992 Presidential Vote		
Dole (R)	174,072	(63%)	Bush (R)	144,073	(52%)
Clinton (D)	81,940	(30%)	Clinton (D)	70,677	(25%)
Perot (I)	18,474	(7%)	Perot (I)	63,454	(23%)

Rep. Lamar S. Smith (R)

Elected 1986; b. Nov. 19, 1947, San Antonio; home, San Antonio; Yale U., B.A. 1969, S. Methodist U., J.D. 1975; Christian Scientist; married (Beth).

Elected Office: TX House of Reps., 1981–82; Bexar Cnty. Comm., 1982–85.

Professional Career: U.S. Small Business Admin., 1969–70; Business writer, *Christian Science Monitor*, 1970–72; Practicing atty., 1975–76.

DC Office: 2231 RHOB 20515, 202-225-4236; Fax: 202-225-8628; Web site: www.house.gov/lamarsmith.

District Offices: Kerrville, 210-895-1414; Midland, 915-687-5232; Round Rock, 512-218-4221; San Angelo, 915-653-3971; San Antonio, 210-821-5024.

Committees: *Judiciary* (6th of 21 R): Crime; Immigration & Claims (Chmn.). *Science* (3d of 25 R): Basic Research; Space & Aeronautics. *Standards of Official Conduct* (Chmn. of 5 R).

Group Ratings

	ADA	ACLU	AFS	LCV	CON	NTU	NFIB	COC	ACU	NTLC	CHC
1998	0	7	0	8	13	50	100	100	92	97	100
1997	0	—	0	—	76	55	—	100	88	—	—

National Journal Ratings

	1997 LIB — 1997 CONS			1998 LIB — 1998 CONS		
Economic	10%	—	86%	0%	—	88%
Social	10%	—	82%	14%	—	81%
Foreign	21%	—	79%	27%	—	68%

Key Votes of the 105th Congress

1. Clinton Budget Deal	Y	5. Puerto Rico Sthood. Ref.	N	9. Cut $ for B-2 Bombers	N
2. Education IRAs	Y	6. End Highway Set-asides	Y	10. Human Rights in China	N
3. Req. 2/3 to Raise Taxes	Y	7. School Prayer Amend.	Y	11. Withdraw Bosnia Troops	Y
4. Fast-track Trade	Y	8. Ovrd. Part. Birth Veto	Y	12. End Cuban TV-Marti	N

Election Results

1998 general	Lamar S. Smith (R)	165,047	(91%)	($531,538)
	Jeffrey Charles Blunt (Lib)	15,561	(9%)	
1998 primary	Lamar S. Smith (R)	unopposed		
1996 general	Lamar S. Smith (R)	205,830	(76%)	($443,571)
	Gordon H. Wharton (D)	60,338	(22%)	($18,844)

TWENTY-SECOND DISTRICT

Spreading out in all directions from its historic center at Allen's Landing on Buffalo Bayou, Houston has become one of the great metropolises of North America. A half-century ago, the steaming flatlands south of Houston running down to the Gulf of Mexico did not seem a likely site for one of the world's most advanced civilizations. But they are today. It was Houston where most of the scientific work was done that put the first man on the moon—the first word spoken on the moon was "Houston." Houston is the undisputed center of expertise in the oil business, where the greatest concentration of experts in the world are within a few miles of each other. Houston has also become one of the great medical centers of the world, with the giant Texas Medical Center looming as impressively massive as any great office skyscraper. And Houston has become one of the great surprise growth cities of the 1990s, creating thousands of small businesses, with special growth among immigrants. All this success and sophistication are testimony to human—and Texan—creativity, and to the triumph of air conditioning. For who supposed that all these people would move here if they had to sweat through Houston's steamy five-month summer?

The 22d Congressional District is made up of the southwest quadrant of metropolitan Houston, starting near Loop 610 and heading out into Fort Bend and Brazoria Counties. It also has a spur heading westward to a point near the Johnson Space Center and Galveston Bay. Much of the district's shape derives from the 1991 redistricting, but its lines in Houston and Harris County were very much smoothed out by the court-ordered redistricting plan of August 1996, adopted after the Supreme Court ruled the 18th and 29th Districts unconstitutional because they were racially motivated. The new lines raised the 22d's black percentage from 8% to 13%; not much changed were its Hispanic and Asian percentages, the latter the highest in Texas. The 22d is a heavily Republican district. There are not many national Democrats among the people who have come from other parts of Texas and the nation to live in these new, mostly affluent subdivisions. Even in local elections the historic Democratic leanings of the rural areas are usually overwhelmed by the strong Republican allegiance of the newcomers.

The congressman from the 22d District is Tom DeLay, the House majority whip and number three member of the House Republican leadership—an aggressive political operator, strong ideological conservative and, in the view of some critics as well as admirers, the most powerful member of the House. DeLay was born in the border town of Laredo and spent much of his childhood in Venezuela, where his father drilled oil wells. After graduating from the University of Houston, he settled in Sugar Land, in Fort Bend County southwest of Houston, where he built a pest control business and was elected to the state legislature in 1978, the first Republican legislator from Fort Bend County this century. When 22d District Congressman Ron Paul (now congressman from the 14th District) ran for the Senate in 1984, DeLay ran for the House.

DeLay's voting record in the House has been very conservative; he has combined a strong ideological motivation and a knack for practical politics. In his first term, he was the freshman representative on the Republican Committee on Committees. In his second term he got a seat on the Appropriations Committee, where he has been known to seek money for his district, like grants for a bus system to ease traffic on the choked Southwest Freeway. But he opposed a $1.2 billion monorail, a sure clunker in this auto town. More recently he has pushed the designation of a new I-69 heading southwest from Houston and backed the May 1998 transportation bill, with its formula giving millions more to Texas. DeLay is an ardent booster of the space program and has worked mightily to save the Space Station from demise. Partly through his efforts, this venture survived in 1994, winning 278–155 in the House, while the scientifically much more interesting Supercollider was killed in October 1993.

DeLay has been interested in leadership positions since the 1980s—and in the process became a master vote-counter. In March 1989, only in his third term, he managed the campaign of moderate Edward Madigan to replace Dick Cheney as minority whip; Madigan had the backing of his Illinois neighbor, Minority Leader Robert Michel, but he lost 87–85 to Newt Gingrich—a result that made a revolutionary change in the House. Madigan's loss didn't stop DeLay from running in December 1992 against incumbent Bill Gradison for the post of Republican Conference secretary; DeLay won 95–71. It was clear that Michel would retire in 1994, and Gingrich would run for Republican leader. DeLay started running for whip, presumed to be the second-highest leadership post at a time when almost no one thought Republicans would win a majority in the 1994 elections; that meant that DeLay was leapfrogging Dick Armey, who had described him as his best friend, on the leadership ladder. Then Republicans won their majority in 1994, after which Gingrich was easily elected speaker and Armey majority leader. DeLay had serious opposition from Robert Walker, Gingrich's best friend in the House, and Bill McCollum. But he had done much more to prepare, campaigning in 25 states and contributing $2 million to Republican candidates, many of them incoming freshmen as well as incumbents. DeLay showed his vote-counting acumen by proclaiming that he was not interested in the second-ballot votes he would need if no one had a majority: "We are locked into winning this outright." He won with 119 votes to 80 for Walker and 28 for McCollum.

"I'm very aggressive. I'm a hard-working, aggressive, persistent whip. That's why I'm whip," says DeLay, and not many would disagree. He spent much of 1995 and 1996 pursuing his great policy interest, regulatory reform. In early 1995, working with committee leaders on Capitol Hill and with lobbyists from downtown, he led to passage bills and appropriations riders designed to halt and reverse the steady growth and power of the federal bureaucracy. Through increased use of risk assessment and cost-benefit analyses and a moratorium on new regulations, DeLay's goal has been to change the culture of federal regulatory agencies—a tall order—and the way they treat small businesses. In doing that, he also has sought to make the downtown lobbyists more sympathetic to what he considers their natural allies among Republicans and to end their alliance of convenience with Democrats. But much of his legislative product was vetoed by Bill Clinton, and his attempts to cut back environmental regulations spurred protests from many, including Republicans in parts of the country unfamiliar with the regulatory excess DeLay likes to chronicle. Moderate Republicans, led by Sherwood Boehlert, took to opposing DeLay's EPA riders, and by summer 1995 DeLay was having more trouble winning majorities. And his aggressive courting of K Street lobbyists has made for embarrassments. Many squawked in early 1999 when he attacked the Electronics Industries Alliance for hiring former Democratic Congressman Dave McCurdy as president; the ethics committee privately rebuked him for badgering. DeLay has changed the culture of K Street—but not nearly as much as he wants.

Between other House leaders and DeLay there has been a gulf, of varying width. He is admired for the efficiency of his whip organization and the accuracy of its counts. But he is no one's subordinate. In December 1996 and January 1997, when Newt Gingrich was scrambling to win re-election as speaker, DeLay was his most ardent supporter. He was one of 28 members who voted against the Gingrich reprimand and $300,000 fine recommended by the ethics committee, claiming that he was defending not Gingrich but "the speaker and his office and this institution." But in July 1997 DeLeay met with disgruntled fellow Republicans, telling them the leadership would support a floor vote to oust Gingrich as speaker. What is not clear is what DeLay expected to happen—how he supposed the speaker's chair could be vacated without a Democratic takeover and whom he thought would take Gingrich's place. But at a Republican Conference meeting afterward, DeLay came dramatically forward and admitted his participation in the coup attempt, while Dick Armey seemed to deny his. From that point forward, it was clear DeLay had much more support in the conference than Armey.

On impeachment DeLay also took the lead. Many Republicans wanted to avoid a vote or reach some compromise like censure. DeLay, convinced that Clinton violated the law and should be impeached, kept the issue clearly framed and squelched all talk of censure. He claims that he did not lobby members to vote one way or the other, but through his whip organization he was more closely in touch with Republican members than anyone else. In the days after the November 1998 election, when Gingrich announced his retirement, it was widely assumed that impeachment would fail. But DeLay, even as his pledge of loyalty and phone calls clinched the choice of Bob Livingston as speaker-designate, pressed forward. The morning of the impeachment vote, Livingston shocked everyone by announcing that he would resign. Members began hovering around DeLay at the back of the chamber. Armey clearly did not have the support to win the speakership; DeLay, presumably aware of his polarizing reputation among Democrats, made no move to run. Instead he threw his support to his chief deputy whip, Denny Hastert, little known outside the House, but respected by Republican members as a hard worker, consensus builder and party loyalist. Within hours it would be clear that Hastert would be the next speaker. DeLay may have lost when he tried to put an Illinois Republican on the road to being Republican leader in 1989; he finally won with Hastert in 1998.

Democrats and the press shouted that Hastert would be DeLay's puppet and that DeLay would run the House. That is unrealistic: Hastert, like any serious person in his position, is not likely to take orders, and DeLay, like anyone nominating a leader, was surely acting out of confidence based on his close working knowlege of what Hastert would do rather than out of confidence that he could be manipulated. But DeLay remains a powerful force in the House. Hastert, Armey and other Republican leaders, with their 11-vote majority, must rely more than ever on his whip organization. And he has established close ties with Texas Governor George W. Bush, who in early 1999 seemed the likely Republican presidential nominee; in March 1999 DeLay's new chief deputy whip, Roy Blunt of Missouri, was named liaison between House Republicans and the Bush operation.

Cook's Call. *Safe.* Though Delay's district is not as Republican as some other districts in the state, there is little chance that a Democrat could ever win here. Delay is a sure bet for 2000.

The People: Pop. 1990: 569,350; 13.8% rural; 5.9% age 65 +; 71.6% White, 12.6% Black, 7% Asian, 0.3% Amer. Indian, 8.4% Other; 16.7% Hispanic Origin. Households: 63% married couple families; 37% married couple fams. w. children; 60.4% college educ.; median household income: $40,160; per capita income: $16,291; median house value: $70,900; median gross rent: $378.

1996 Presidential Vote			1992 Presidential Vote		
Dole (R)	119,770	(56%)	Bush (R)	106,306	(48%)
Clinton (D)	80,280	(38%)	Clinton (D)	67,360	(30%)
Perot (I)	12,278	(6%)	Perot (I)	47,991	(22%)

Rep. Tom DeLay (R)

Elected 1984; b. Apr. 8, 1947, Laredo; home, Sugar Land; U. of Houston, B.S. 1970; Baptist; married (Christine).

Elected Office: TX House of Reps., 1978–84.

Professional Career: Owner, Albo Pest Control, 1973–84.

DC Office: 341 CHOB 20515, 202-225-5951; Fax: 202-225-5241; Web site: tomdelay.house.gov.

District Office: Stafford, 281-240-3700.

Committees: *Majority Whip. Appropriations* (8th of 34 R): Transportation; VA, HUD & Independent Agencies.

Group Ratings

	ADA	ACLU	AFS	LCV	CON	NTU	NFIB	COC	ACU	NTLC	CHC
1998	0	6	0	0	26	57	100	100	96	95	100
1997	0	—	13	—	76	55	—	100	88	—	—

National Journal Ratings

	1997 LIB	—	1997 CONS	1998 LIB	—	1998 CONS
Economic	18%	—	81%	0%	—	88%
Social	0%	—	90%	24%	—	75%
Foreign	0%	—	88%	0%	—	93%

Key Votes of the 105th Congress

1. Clinton Budget Deal	Y	5. Puerto Rico Sthood. Ref.	Y	9. Cut $ for B-2 Bombers	N
2. Education IRAs	Y	6. End Highway Set-asides	Y	10. Human Rights in China	N
3. Req. 2/3 to Raise Taxes	Y	7. School Prayer Amend.	Y	11. Withdraw Bosnia Troops	Y
4. Fast-track Trade	Y	8. Ovrd. Part. Birth Veto	Y	12. End Cuban TV-Marti	N

Election Results

1998 general	Tom DeLay (R)	87,840	(65%)	($1,170,867)
	Hill Kemp (D)	45,386	(34%)	($75,849)
1998 primary	Tom DeLay (R)	unopposed		
1996 spec. prim.	Tom DeLay (R)	126,056	(68%)	($1,621,708)
	Scott Douglas Cunningham (D)	59,030	(32%)	($28,383)

TWENTY-THIRD DISTRICT

The border country of Texas is a zone all its own. It is part of the United States but its culture and economy are not entirely Yanqui or Latino—a fluid mixture captured with great subtlety by John Sayles's 1996 movie *Lone Star*, which was filmed in and around the border town of Eagle Pass. The local economy fluctuates depending on, among other things, the strength of the peso and the aggressiveness of INS patrols. Years ago, movements like La Raza Unida—which got its beginnings here in 1969 when Hispanic youngsters wanted to elect high school cheerleaders in Crystal City—wanted the border country to become more like Mexico, with its union and party apparatchiks. More recently, with its economic reforms and NAFTA, Mexico has been trying to become more like the United States, and particularly like Texas, with open markets and privatized companies, less controlled by political or labor bosses. Border towns like Laredo have seen great booms as Mexico grows rapidly, and then great busts when, as in 1982 and 1994, Mexico devalues the peso. In the first half of the 1990s, Laredo was the second fastest-growing U.S. metro area, with one of the largest Wal-Marts and the busiest railroad crossing on the border; trucks are often backed up for miles waiting to cross. Then came devaluation and things slowed down for a while. Bustling also, but on a more even keel, have been San Antonio and the smaller cities 100 miles or so from the border. In between is quiet ranching and oil country; the town of Sierra Blanca near El Paso, where a Texas commission denied permission for a nuclear waste dump; not to mention the nation's prime repository of peyote, a cactus with mind-altering properties that is gathered and sold, with the consent of federal and state regulators, only to members of the Native American Church.

The 23d Congressional District—geographically the largest by far in Texas—includes the longest portion of the 2,500-mile U.S.-Mexico border, following the Rio Grande almost from El Paso south past Laredo. The district includes Anglo neighborhoods on the north side of San Antonio and goes all the way to the Big Bend territory, where 7,000-foot peaks tower over stony desert. It covers miles of arid hills and rugged desert, of cattle grazing, sheep ranching and oil wells. Loving County, located halfway between El Paso and San Angelo, is the least-populated U.S. county, with only 141 residents in 1990 and 108 voters in 1998. Most of the 23d's people live in a few widely scattered metropolitan areas—about one-third in or near San Antonio, with others in Laredo, parts of Midland and Odessa, and on the fringes of El Paso. Overall the population was 63% Hispanic in 1990. Politically, the border counties around Laredo and Eagle Pass are heavily Democratic, while many of the grazing counties inland are Republican. But in 1998 the district delivered a solid majority for Republican Governor George W. Bush.

The congressman from the 23d is Henry Bonilla, a Republican first elected in 1992, when he beat a scandal-tarred incumbent, and has been re-elected impressively ever since. He was raised in a Latino neighborhood in San Antonio. His grandmother worked as a maid, and his father held down two jobs. Bonilla went to the University of Texas and then worked as a TV reporter, producer and executive in San Antonio, New York, Philadelphia and, by 1986, San Antonio again. In 1991, Bexar County Republican leaders recruited Bonilla to run for Congress against incumbent Democrat Albert Bustamante, who reportedly was being investigated by the FBI for racketeering, who had 30 overdrafts on the House bank and who, after the election, was convicted of two counts of misuse of office for racketeering and bribery. Bonilla backed standard conservative planks but he crafted his own issues as well. He opposed two new hazardous waste dumps near Del Rio, backed tax and environmental policies more favorable to the oil industry, and sided with water-users over the allegedly endangered fountain darter fish in a dispute over Comal Springs. Bustamante called Bonilla "a eunuch for the plantation owners" for opposing a minimum wage bill, but Bonilla won by a large 59%–38%, with most of his margin in San Antonio's Bexar County, which he won 81%–16%.

Republicans gave Bonilla a seat on Appropriations, where he has displayed a talent for placing deregulatory riders on appropriations bills—to eliminate funding for enforcing a rule on cardboard balers and to block the Labor Department from developing ergonomic standards. Bonilla voted enthusiastically for NAFTA and against gun control, but he also bragged of getting $800 million for health centers and attacked the Clinton Administration for diverting funds from bilingual education to school administration. Though Bonilla refuses to join the Hispanic Caucus, lamenting that it lacks a bipartisan agenda, he is cautious about banning racial quotas and preferences.

In 1994, voting rights attorney Rolando Rios attacked Bonilla for opposing the Clinton budget, the earned income tax credit and gun control. But Bonilla won 63%–37%, with 76% in Bexar County but, more important for the long run, carrying most of the border counties. In 1996 he nearly duplicated this showing, winning 62%–36% while Bob Dole was losing the district 50%–44%; the *San Antonio Express-News* headlined that Bonilla was "strong as [an] acre of garlic." In 1998, he won again, 64%–35%.

Texas and national Republicans have been happy to give Bonilla plenty of visibility. He gave a seconding speech for Dole at the 1996 Republican National Convention, and he surely will be featured in the presidential campaign of George W. Bush. His position in the 23d District seems solid, and the post-2000 Census redistricting, likely to be controlled or heavily influenced by Republicans, will probably be kind to Bonilla.

Cook's Call. *Safe.* This district is more marginal than Bonilla's solid victories would suggest. But, the fact that Bonilla has never been seriously challenged since his first win in 1992 has helped him become well-entrenched here.

The People: Pop. 1990: 566,736; 24.9% rural; 9.3% age 65+; 74% White, 2.9% Black, 0.6% Asian, 0.4% Amer. Indian, 22% Other; 62.4% Hispanic Origin. Households: 64.6% married couple families; 40% married couple fams. w. children; 38.7% college educ.; median household income: $21,555; per capita income: $9,764; median house value: $48,200; median gross rent: $252.

1996 Presidential Vote			1992 Presidential Vote		
Clinton (D)	83,965	(50%)	Clinton (D)	72,452	(42%)
Dole (R)	73,282	(44%)	Bush (R)	70,576	(41%)
Perot (I)	9,372	(6%)	Perot (I)	28,846	(17%)

Rep. Henry Bonilla (R)

Elected 1992; b. Jan. 2, 1954, San Antonio; home, San Antonio; U. of TX, B.A. 1976; Baptist; married (Deborah).

Professional Career: TV Reporter, 1976–80; Asst. Press Secy., PA Gov. Thornburgh, 1981; Writer/producer, WABC, New York, 1982–85; Asst. News Dir., WATF-TV, Philadelphia, 1985–86; KENS-TV, San Antonio, Exec. News Producer, 1986–89, Public Affairs, 1989–92.

DC Office: 1427 LHOB 20515, 202-225-4511; Fax: 202-225-2237; Web site: www.house.gov/bonilla.

District Offices: Del Rio, 830-774-6547; Laredo, 956-726-4682; Midland, 915-686-8833; San Antonio, 210-697-9055.

Committees: *Appropriations* (16th of 34 R): Agriculture, Rural Development, & FDA; Defense; Labor, HHS & Education.

Group Ratings

	ADA	ACLU	AFS	LCV	CON	NTU	NFIB	COC	ACU	NTLC	CHC
1998	10	25	13	0	35	66	100	88	92	94	100
1997	5	—	25	—	15	52	—	90	95	—	—

National Journal Ratings

	1997 LIB — 1997 CONS			1998 LIB — 1998 CONS		
Economic	19%	—	81%	28%	—	72%
Social	37%	—	63%	41%	—	58%
Foreign	38%	—	62%	19%	—	75%

Key Votes of the 105th Congress

1. Clinton Budget Deal	Y	5. Puerto Rico Sthood. Ref.	Y	9. Cut $ for B-2 Bombers	N		
2. Education IRAs	Y	6. End Highway Set-asides	Y	10. Human Rights in China	N		
3. Req. 2/3 to Raise Taxes	Y	7. School Prayer Amend.	Y	11. Withdraw Bosnia Troops	Y		
4. Fast-track Trade	Y	8. Ovrd. Part. Birth Veto	Y	12. End Cuban TV-Marti	N		

Election Results

1998 general	Henry Bonilla (R)	73,177	(64%)	($820,842)
	Charlie Jones (D)	40,281	(35%)	($30,958)
1998 primary	Henry Bonilla (R)	unopposed		
1996 general	Henry Bonilla (R)	101,332	(62%)	($779,893)
	Charlie Jones (D)	59,596	(36%)	($74,755)
	Others	2,911	(2%)	

TWENTY-FOURTH DISTRICT

The geographical heart of the Dallas-Fort Worth Metroplex was open country as late as the 1950s, when the Dallas-Fort Worth Turnpike was built over open land to link the two downtowns. Then, over the next three decades, the bottomlands of the West Fork of the Trinity River and the barren hills overlooking them filled up. Whole new Dallases and Fort Worths, with as many people as the central cities had in the 1940s—Grand Prairie and Arlington and Irving—grew up in these once impoverished lands and became central to one of America's richest and most productive metropolitan areas. Major landmarks have arisen here as well, from Six Flags Over Texas to The Ballpark in Arlington, the new old-style baseball stadium for the Texas Rangers that replaced the old modern-looking Turnpike Stadium. New subdivisions continue to grow here, but one can still see barren hills above the Metroplex. These new towns are taking on a graceful aging air, as trees grow, houses are renovated or expanded, and commercial buildings are adapted to new and unexpected uses. Not that all of the oldest areas are left behind: There are slums in the Metroplex, but large parts of neighborhoods like Oak Cliff, across the Trinity River south of Dallas, are being redeveloped by Texans appreciating their prairie architectural heritage.

When the Mid-Cities area, as some call it, started filling up in the 1950s, Dallas was Republican and Fort Worth Democratic; since then, the white Anglo majority in the Metroplex has tilted heavily Republican, and most Democratic votes have come from blacks and Hispanics. But there are a few pockets of blue-collar whites who give Democrats sizable support, in lower-income areas of Grand Prairie or around Arlington's General Motors assembly plant.

The 24th Congressional District contains much of this area. Since it was first established in 1972, the 24th's boundaries have changed several times, most recently in August 1996, following a Supreme Court decision declaring the adjacent 30th District unconstitutional. The lines used in the 1996 election are much more regular, though the districts' basic outline and character is similar. The 24th now includes Grand Prairie and the eastern half of Arlington, the older part of Oak Cliff and Duncanville and the south suburban fringe of Dallas County, the heavily black southeast side of Fort Worth and, to connect these areas, parts of rural Ellis and Navarro Counties south of Dallas. The 24th is 20% black and 26% Hispanic. It is solidly Democratic, 54%–39% for Bill Clinton in 1996.

The congressman from the 24th District is Martin Frost, a Democrat first elected in 1978; the 1991 redistricting, the work of Frost and his staffer Bob Mansker, managed to create a majority-black 30th District in Dallas for Eddie Bernice Johnson, while compensating Frost for his loss of blacks in Dallas by annexing blacks in Fort Worth. Frost grew up in Fort Worth, went to the University of Missouri and Georgetown Law School, was a commentator on public TV and practiced law. But politics has been most of his professional life. He first ran in the 24th in 1974, at 32, and lost the primary 3–2; he ran again in 1978 and reversed the result, ousting a conservative Democrat. As a freshman he got a seat on the Rules Committee, thanks to then-Majority Leader Jim Wright of Fort Worth. Frost was a stalwart supporter of Wright to the end and has been a Democratic leadership man ever since. He worked in tandem with Wright to kill measures that would have tightened lending and investment requirements for S&Ls and would have increased capital requirements. He lost two leadership bids in the 1980s, backing off a bid to chair the Budget Committee in 1984 and losing the race for caucus vice chairman to Vic Fazio in 1989 by 147–74. But he came back to chair the IMPAC 2000 redistricting panel from 1991–94 and was appointed chairman of the Democratic Congressional Campaign Committee after the debacle of 1994. His efforts to restore optimism to his downtrodden party include coining the widely-cited depiction of Speaker Newt Gingrich as a "crybaby" following his complaints about his *Air Force One* treatment during the 1995 return trip from Yitzhak Rabin's funeral. In November 1998, despite many Democrats' desire to spotlight women in leadership positions, he defeated Rosa DeLauro 108–97 to replace Fazio as Democratic caucus chairman; a rare case of the moderate defeating the more liberal Democrat. When some complained that the result left women without a leadership position in the party, Frost responded that he is the first Jew ever elected to the House leadership. Frost is also the second-ranking Democrat on the Rules Committee; he combines great political acuity with impressive legislative skills.

Frost has worked on local causes, including funding the V-22 Osprey at Bell Helicopter Textron in Fort Worth, expanding Dallas/Forth Worth International Airport, building a Dallas-area light rail; he helped to keep open the GM plant in Arlington. He is proud of having sponsored the Amber Hagerman Child Protection Act, tacked onto an appropriation bill in October 1996 and named for an Arlington nine-year-old who was kidnapped and murdered; it mandates life in prison for anyone twice convicted of a sex offense against a child. In 1997 he switched his vote and voted for the partial-birth abortion ban.

Despite all his strengths, Frost has had some tough competition this past decade. He raised and spent $1.5 million in 1992 and 1994, nearly $2 million in 1996 and again in 1998. In 1994 home builder Ed Harrison attacked Frost for voting with Bill Clinton 91% of the time. Frost scampered on the crime issue (switching to oppose the assault weapons ban, then voting for the crime bill rule) and had the chutzpah, after years of loyalty to party leadership, to accuse Harrison of kowtowing to Gingrich. Frost ended up losing Dallas County 54%–46% but carried Tarrant County 62%–38%, for a 53%–47% victory—his lowest general election percentage ever. When Harrison ran again in 1996, Frost went on the attack, hitting him as a clone of the now unpopular Gingrich and for backing Medicare "cuts" and tax breaks for the wealthy: the same tactics he was counseling for Democrats across the country. Frost won 56%–39%, in a vote that came close to echoing the presidential result; this time Frost carried Dallas as well as Tarrant. In 1998, against business consultant and political newcomer Shawn Terry, Frost won 57%–41%.

In 1996 and 1998, Frost led Democrats to House gains, though he was disappointed that they fell short of the majority. He has succeeded in holding down the number of Democratic retirees and, despite Republican Tom DeLay's efforts, has maintained the flow of PAC money to Democratic incumbents and even many open-seat candidates. As *The New York Times* wrote, Frost was "a master at raising cash, through persistence, mostly, and with an attention to detail" at a time when Democratic National Committee fundraising was under intense questioning. He also kept money flowing into Texas: As much as 30% of DCCC soft money in 1996 was sent by Frost to Texas, much of it to Tarrant and Dallas counties, where it could help his campaign; but Frost could reply that Texas had many open seats that year and that his own race was a legitimate target for Democratic spending.

Frost obviously hopes that Democrats regain their majority in 2000; it is certainly within the realm of possibility that as caucus chairman or (if Joe Moakley retires) Rules chairman, he will be working with a Democratic administration. But he may be pressed again in the 24th District, though he would still be a heavy favorite, and after that Frost faces redistricting. A decade ago, with a cooperative Democratic legislature and governor, Frost and Mansker drew the lines, carefully putting together a Democratic-leaning district in the heavily Republican Dallas-Fort Worth Metroplex. But Texas now has a Republican governor and a Republican lieutenant governor to succeed him if he is elected president; it has a state Senate with a one-seat Republican majority and a narrow Democratic margin in the state House, which could be overturned; and many Texas Democrats are moderates used to bipartisan cooperation. The prospect is for a districting plan with much neater lines and more regularly-shaped districts, much like California's plan in the 1990s—which could mean a very tough race for Frost.

Cook's Call. *Probably Safe.* Although Frost's winning margins have dipped in the last few elections, he remains a difficult target for Republicans. A good challenger can keep him under 60%, but knocking out the heavily funded Frost is tough.

The People: Pop. 1990: 567,791; 8.9% rural; 9.5% age 65+; 64.1% White, 20.4% Black, 2% Asian, 0.6% Amer. Indian, 12.9% Other; 20.6% Hispanic Origin. Households: 55% married couple families; 31.4% married couple fams. w. children; 40.6% college educ.; median household income: $27,091; per capita income: $11,371; median house value: $58,800; median gross rent: $346.

1996 Presidential Vote

Clinton (D)	86,529	(53%)
Dole (R)	66,106	(40%)
Perot (I)	11,937	(7%)

1992 Presidential Vote

Clinton (D)	79,001	(41%)
Bush (R)	64,979	(33%)
Perot (I)	50,465	(26%)

Rep. Martin Frost (D)

Elected 1978; b. Jan. 1, 1942, Glendale, CA; home, Dallas; U. of MO, B.A., B.J., 1964, Georgetown U., J.D. 1970; Jewish; married (Kathy).

Military Career: Army Reserves, 1966–72.

Professional Career: Legal commentator, KERA-TV, Dallas, 1971–72; Practicing atty., 1972–78.

DC Office: 2256 RHOB 20515, 202-225-3605; Fax: 202-225-4951; Web site: www.house.gov/frost.

District Offices: Corsicana, 903-874-0760; Dallas, 214-948-3401; Ft. Worth, 817-293-9231.

Committees: *Democratic Caucus Chairman. Rules* (2d of 4 D): The Legislative & Budget Process (RMM).

Group Ratings

	ADA	ACLU	AFS	LCV	CON	NTU	NFIB	COC	ACU	NTLC	CHC
1998	95	75	100	46	55	14	29	56	8	24	0
1997	80	—	88	—	49	23	—	60	20	—	—

National Journal Ratings

	1997 LIB	—	1997 CONS	1998 LIB	—	1998 CONS
Economic	63%	—	36%	68%	—	32%
Social	76%	—	24%	69%	—	30%
Foreign	60%	—	38%	74%	—	25%

Key Votes of the 105th Congress

1. Clinton Budget Deal	N	5. Puerto Rico Sthood. Ref.	Y	9. Cut $ for B-2 Bombers	N
2. Education IRAs	N	6. End Highway Set-asides	N	10. Human Rights in China	Y
3. Req. 2/3 to Raise Taxes	N	7. School Prayer Amend.	N	11. Withdraw Bosnia Troops	N
4. Fast-track Trade	N	8. Ovrd. Part. Birth Veto	N	12. End Cuban TV-Marti	Y

Election Results

1998 general	Martin Frost (D)	56,321	(57%)	($1,790,674)
	Shawn Terry (R)	40,105	(41%)	($789,196)
	Others	1,566	(2%)	
1998 primary	Martin Frost (D)	unopposed		
1996 spec. prim.	Martin Frost (D)	77,847	(56%)	($1,963,529)
	Ed Harrison (R)	54,551	(39%)	($868,345)
	Others	7,239	(5%)	

TWENTY-FIFTH DISTRICT

Houston is, among other things, a blue-collar city. The Ship Channel, which made it the nation's second-largest port, is lined with petrochemical plants and refineries and surrounded by factories, truck terminals and railroad-offloading platforms. Although some neighborhoods long have been close-knit places, others have sprouted up in and around Houston's wide city limits in the past three decades, with their plain, contemporary houses and commercial strip highways. After all, physical mobility is easy in spread-out Houston and many people keep in touch through churches though they are miles apart.

The 25th District includes many such neighborhoods on the east and south sides of Houston. Its boundaries, now that they have been smoothed out by the August 1996 federal court redistricting, can be described more easily. On the east it includes Baytown and the industrial corridor to the north, Deer Park and Pasadena south of the Ship Channel, Highlands on the north. It includes the southern edge of Houston from Hobby Airport west to the Southwest Freeway. It includes Bellaire and the affluent neighborhoods just west of the Texas Medical Center and Rice University. The 1996 redistricting removed some black precincts; black percentage dropped from 27% to 23% but Hispanics increased from 16% to 19%. The political complexion was changed more than any other Texas district. The district under the old lines voted 47%–36% for Bill Clinton in 1992; the district under the new lines was 42%–39% for Clinton.

The congressman from the 25th District is Ken Bentsen, a Democrat elected in 1994. He grew up in Houston, where his father is an architect; his grandfather was the fabled Rio Grande Valley pioneer Lloyd Bentsen Sr., and his uncle is former Senator and Treasury Secretary Lloyd Bentsen Jr. After college in Houston, Ken Bentsen worked four years as a Capitol Hill staffer for Ron Coleman, spending much of his time at the Appropriations Committee; then he joined an investment banking firm in Houston and was elected Harris County Democratic chairman in 1990 and 1992. In 1994, when incumbent Democrat Mike Andrews ran for the Senate (he finished third in the primary), Bentsen ran for the House. In a light-turnout Democratic primary, Bentsen had only 26% to 37% for Beverley Clark, a black, former Houston Council member, anti-abortion and supported by the Christian right, 23% for former legislator Paul Colbert and 13% for high-spending Carrin Patman, the daughter and granddaughter of a Texas congressmen. In the runoff, Bentsen, pro-choice on abortion, concentrated on crime issues, supporting boot camps and more death penalties, and won 64%–36%. Meanwhile, the Republican nomination was won by Dr. Eugene Fontenot, a Christian conservative, who spent more than any other candidate in the country that year, $4.7 million. Bentsen, spending a comparatively modest $973,000, attacked Fontenot as "radical right," and called for a budget freeze with a pledge of universal health care coverage. Bentsen won 52%–45%, getting only 50% in Harris County but adding nearly 6,000 votes to his margin from the heavily black portion of Fort Bend County then in the district.

Bentsen's voting record has been just to the left of the midpoint of the House. He supported the moderate Blue Dog budget; he sought more money for medical research, space exploration, education—Houston priorities. In the 1997 balanced-budget deal, he included a requirement that Medicare managed-care plans contribute to medical-education costs in the same way as traditional Medicare—help for Houston's training hospitals. He called for ending the ethanol subsidy (not popular in oil-producing territory) and for indexing capital gains.

The August 1996 court-ordered redistricting threw Bentsen for a loop, and reintroduced a cast of familiar characters—though not Fontenot, who managed to lose the heavily Republican 8th in the December runoff. The chances of avoiding a December runoff became nil when Democrat Beverley Clark and 1992 Republican nominee Dolly Madison McKenna entered the race—two women at odds with most of their fellow party members on abortion. Bentsen led in November, but won just 34%; Clark and McKenna had 17% each, with McKenna ahead by 199 votes. Clark challenged the results, citing ballot irregularities; after a court dismissed her challenge, she endorsed McKenna two days before the runoff. Meanwhile, McKenna had been spending much time and energy trying to mollify abortion opponents. It failed to work. "The last thing Republicans need is a high-profile woman parading around Congress, being the darling of the pro-abortion forces," Al Clements of the Texas Right to Life Committee told the *Houston Chronicle*. Democrats had only a 51%–49% lead in total votes in the November primary. But Bentsen won the December runoff 57%–43%. In 1998 Bentsen had a less challenging campaign. The Republican nominee was John Sanchez, a physician who defeated Beverley Clark 61%–39% in the Republican runoff. Interestingly, he opposed impeachment, at least until the national party urged that he review the evidence. Bentsen distanced himself from the Clinton scandal and won 58%–41%.

Bentsen has taken an important Democratic leadership post as federal chairman of IMPAC 2000, the national party's redistricting project; presumably he will work closely with Texas's Martin Frost, who headed the organization during the 1990 redistricting cycle. The organization faces the daunting task of preparing House Democrats for 2001 redistricting, when they face grim prospects in many key states. As a Democrat who has had to deal with the consequences of redistricting—and indeed who stands to be affected by it himself, since the Houston area can be divided up many ways—he seems well prepared for the project.

Cook's Call. *Probably Safe.* The fact that Bentsen has survived just about everything thrown at him over the last three cycles, including one very bad political climate (1994) and one drastic remapping of the seat in 1996 shows that he will be pretty tough to beat in 2000.

The People: Pop. 1990: 563,510; 0.7% rural; 8% age 65 + ; 63.4% White, 23% Black, 3.7% Asian, 0.3% Amer. Indian, 9.6% Other; 18.2% Hispanic Origin. Households: 48.2% married couple families; 26.1% married couple fams. w. children; 53.9% college educ.; median household income: $29,611; per capita income: $15,056; median house value: $63,300; median gross rent: $337.

1996 Presidential Vote			1992 Presidential Vote		
Clinton (D)	80,283	(51%)	Clinton (D)	76,191	(43%)
Dole (R)	69,165	(44%)	Bush (R)	70,161	(39%)
Perot (I)	8,199	(5%)	Perot (I)	32,543	(18%)

Rep. Ken Bentsen (D)

Elected 1994; b. June 3, 1959, Houston; home, Houston; U. of St. Thomas., B.A. 1982, American U., M.P.A., 1985; Presbyterian; married (Tamra).

Elected Office: Chair, Harris Cnty. Dem. Cmte., 1990–94.

Professional Career: Legis. Asst., U.S. Rep. Ronald Coleman, 1983–87; Staff Assoc., U.S. House Approprations Cmte., 1985–87; Investment Banker, 1987–94.

DC Office: 326 CHOB 20515, 202-225-7508; Fax: 202-225-2947; Web site: www.house.gov/bentsen.

District Offices: Baytown, 281-837-8225; Bellaire, 713-667-3554; Houston, 713-718-4100; Pasadena, 713-473-4334.

Committees: *Banking & Financial Services* (11th of 27 D): Capital Markets, Securities & Government Sponsored Enterprises; Financial Institutions & Consumer Credit. *Budget* (6th of 19 D).

Group Ratings

	ADA	ACLU	AFS	LCV	CON	NTU	NFIB	COC	ACU	NTLC	CHC
1998	95	75	89	85	89	27	36	50	4	16	8
1997	75	—	75	—	80	29	—	60	13	—	—

National Journal Ratings

	1997 LIB — 1997 CONS		1998 LIB — 1998 CONS	
Economic	69%	— 30%	67%	— 32%
Social	69%	— 31%	70%	— 28%
Foreign	63%	— 36%	84%	— 11%

Key Votes of the 105th Congress

1. Clinton Budget Deal	N	5. Puerto Rico Sthood. Ref.	Y	9. Cut $ for B-2 Bombers	N
2. Education IRAs	N	6. End Highway Set-asides	N	10. Human Rights in China	N
3. Req. 2/3 to Raise Taxes	N	7. School Prayer Amend.	N	11. Withdraw Bosnia Troops	N
4. Fast-track Trade	Y	8. Ovrd. Part. Birth Veto	N	12. End Cuban TV-Marti	Y

Election Results

1998 general	Ken Bentsen (D)	58,591	(58%)	($892,840)
	John M. Sanchez (R)	41,848	(41%)	($274,895)
1998 primary	Ken Bentsen (D)	unopposed		
1996 spec. runoff	Ken Bentsen (D)	29,396	(57%)	($1,654,345)
	Dolly Madison McKenna (R)	21,892	(43%)	($649,716)
1996 spec. prim.	Ken Bentsen (D)	43,701	(34%)	
	Dolly Madison McKenna (R)	21,898	(17%)	
	Beverley Clark (D)	21,699	(17%)	
	Brent Perry (R)	16,737	(13%)	
	John Devine (R)	9,070	(7%)	
	John M. Sanchez (R)	8,984	(7%)	
	Others	6,304	(5%)	

TWENTY-SIXTH DISTRICT

On the northern edge of the Dallas-Fort Worth Metroplex, one of America's most affluent and fastest-growing metropolitan areas heads out into hardscrabble countryside. Here is a clash of cultures, the advance of one set of values and beliefs with another. On one side are the values of North Dallas, of the entrepreneurs who have created fortunes, starting from scratch with a good idea, a willingness to work, a determination to find good luck. They work in the dozens of high-rises that line the freeways of north Dallas or in smaller offices in industrial areas, they live in the affluent areas, starting with the super-wealthy Park Cities area not far north of downtown Dallas or in any one of dozens of comfortable neighborhoods running dozens of miles north. They believe in free markets, in personal responsibility, in traditional values, in the Republican Party: This is one of the most heavily Republican areas in the nation. And it is advancing into what used to be one of the most Democratic.

The tiers of Texas counties south of the Red River were the home of Sam Rayburn, speaker of the House and author of New Deal regulations, always suspicious of bankers and big corporations and eager to have government weigh in on the side of the little guy. Rayburn and his colleagues were sometimes infected with the pessimism of the farmer, for whom there is always something that can go wrong and not much protection against it and whose spirit was held down by the sheer physical effort needed to scratch a living from these hills. They believed in economic redistribution, regulations and usury ceilings, and the Democratic Party. It is fairly clear which of these views is winning in North Texas. Forty years ago the Republican vote here was limited to affluent neighborhoods within a few miles of the Park Cities. Now it has spread out far into the countryside, into counties which once voted near-unanimously for Mr. Sam's Democrats.

The 26th Congressional District covers much of the northern part of the Dallas-Fort Worth Metroplex. Its boundaries were substantially changed by the August 1996 court-ordered redistricting which followed the June 1996 Supreme Court decision declaring the boundaries of the adjacent 30th District unconstitutional because of racial gerrymandering. It now includes the Park Cities and the affluent quadrant of North Dallas between the Central Expressway and the Stemmons Freeway. It includes Carrollton and Farmers Branch to the northwest and the wonderfully named Grapevine just north of the Dallas/Fort Worth International Airport. It also includes half of Denton County, once rural and Democratic, now suburban and affluent and very heavily Republican. Overall, this is a very Republican district, with little partisan effect from the boundary changes. A little more than half its voters are in Dallas County and about one-third in Denton County.

The congressman from the 26th District is Dick Armey, first elected in 1984, now the House majority leader. He is a free market economist who once was such a political nonentity that he did not even attend the 1984 Republican National Convention in nearby Dallas where Ronald Reagan was renominated. His political career could never have happened before the 1980s. He grew up on a farm in Cando, North Dakota—pronounced affirmatively as *can do*. At 18, working atop an electric pole at night when it was 30 below zero, he decided to become the first in his family to go to college. By 1984, Armey was an economics professor at the University of North Texas in Denton, a Northern-accented academic in the Red River Valley of Texas: not a likely candidate for anything. But as he was watching the House sessions on C-SPAN, it occurred to him that he could do as well as or better than the people he was watching on the screen. He got the Republican nomination in the 26th in 1984 unopposed, because no one thought incumbent Tom Vandergriff, the long-time mayor of Arlington, then the largest city in the 26th, could be unseated. But Armey won 51%–49%.

Armey arrived in Washington in modest circumstances—"When I came to Washington, the only congressman I'd known or spent much time with was the man I beat"—and he saved money by sleeping first in the House gym and, when forced to stop, on his office couch—a practice that has since been abandoned by Armey but was okayed for others by Speaker Newt Gingrich in 1995. Armey brought to the House a sometimes impolitic bluntness, but also fine political instincts and an appreciation of how to sell his principles to his colleagues. His first major achievement was the military base closing bill. In 1987, Armey proposed a base closing commission operating outside of politics, but neither Congress nor then-Defense Secretary Caspar Weinberger were ready to delegate such power. After a long debate, Armey worked with the Pentagon, the Joint Chiefs of Staff and then-Armed Services Chairman Les Aspin to create an independent commission that would draw up a list of base closings which Congress would have to approve or reject in its entirety. The result: In 1988 Congress approved the first base closings in 12 years. The 1990 round of closings was rejected, but in 1993 the second round of base closings was approved. In 1995, a more modest third round was proposed by the Clinton Administration and subsequently was approved. Armey's bill had changed political incentives so that they ratcheted government spending down, not up.

Armey has had less immediate success with his next target, farm subsidies. He argued persuasively that subsidies are no more needed to maintain supplies of the six large subsidized crops than they are for the hundreds of crops which manage to be produced without subsidies and that farmers no more deserve subsidies than any other small businessmen. He forged an alliance on the issue with Brooklyn Democrat Charles Schumer, but was never able to prevail on the floor. But in 1996 the Republican Congress passed the Freedom to Farm Act, phasing out most of the subsidies over seven years.

Armey had little success in his first decade as a minority back-bencher on the Economic and Educational Opportunities or Budget Committees, where he was outvoted by committed partisans of expanded domestic programs, which he attacked. But he found more sympathizers in the Republican Conference. He strongly opposed President Bush's budget summit tax increase and determined to get "a seat at the table." So after the 1992 election, Armey ran for Republican Conference chairman against incumbent Jerry Lewis, who had supported the budget summit. Armey won the number-three leadership position 88–84, winning the lion's share of the 47 freshmen Republicans and gaining crucial support from Lewis's California delegation as well. This put Armey into leadership meetings at the White House, at one of the first of which he told President Clinton that passage of his budget and tax plan would make him a "one-term president"—not the first or last Armey breach of Washington's collegial etiquette. He is capable of bitter riposte: During the 1994 crime bill debate, when Democrats talked of the need to support Clinton, Armey said, "Your president is just not that important for us"— he soon apologized, and Minority Leader Bob Michel took him to task.

When Gingrich came up with the idea of having all Republican incumbents and candidates sign a pledge on the steps of the Capitol in September 1994, Armey spearheaded the effort to draw up and then sell—including to some doubters within his own party, let alone other parts of Washington's political class—many of the specifics of the Contract with America. Along with Gingrich, he then traveled virtually non-stop across the nation in the month before the election to raise money and enthusiasm for Republican candidates. After Republicans won control in November, Armey gained his just reward of being elected majority leader without opposition. And he then surprised many with his legislative skill in commanding the 100-day schedule that delivered on the Republicans' campaign promise to debate each item of the Contract, with the House passing everything except term limits. Later scheduling got more ragged, and members complained about votes scheduled at odd hours or business put off until inconvenient times. Some of these were due to the inevitable inefficiency of a process never designed to be efficient. In fact, the Republicans, with Gingrich plotting long-range strategy in his office overlooking the Washington Monument and Armey operating more on the floor as "the chief operating officer," performed more competently than their utter lack of experience managing a legislative majority gave warrant to imagine. During the 1996–97 controversy over the Gingrich ethics complaint, Armey was careful to stay supportive in public but presumably made some preparation in private to succeed Gingrich should that have been necessary.

There was some tension between Armey's personal stands and his leadership responsibilities. He would have liked to see all farm subsidies cut, but realized that Southern Republicans from cotton districts would block such a bill. He said that he would oppose a minimum wage increase "with every fiber of my being," but became reconciled when Gingrich and others realized they had to let it go through. And he acquiesced in the 1997 budget deal, with its complicated tax incentives, which were entirely contrary to the thrust of his current favorite proposal, a flat tax of 20% for two years, then 17%, with generous personal allowances and no taxes on capital gains, dividends, interest or inheritances. But the flat tax had competition from Ways and Means Committee Chairman Bill Archer's consumption-based tax, and neither was likely to be pushed forward as long as Clinton was president—although Armey and Billy Tauzin conducted a series of "scrap the code" debates across the country on the merits of the flat tax versus the consumption tax.

By mid-1997 there was tension between Gingrich and Armey, who felt the speaker had undercut him. As he said later, "I had his responsibilities while he retained the authority, and it turned out to be a difficult thing." Asked by reporters on June 17 whether he had faith in Gingrich's leadership, Armey pointedly said, "Y'all have a good day, now." Then in July came the attempted coup. Armey met with the aggrieved conservative junior members who wanted to get rid of Gingrich and listened to their case. He also met with fellow leadership members Tom DeLay, John Boehner and Bill Paxon; all said they had the impression he supported the coup, and said he had said he would run for speaker if Gingrich was ousted. But when DeLay met with the coup leaders, Tom Coburn said they wanted Paxon to replace Gingrich. The leaders had agreed to inform Gingrich of the coup, but Armey arrived first and told him. The coup collapsed and recriminations began. At a mid-July meeting of the Republican Conference, Armey insisted that he had never supported the coup, at which point Lindsey Graham knocked down a chair and tried to rush to the microphone. The belief was widespread that Armey supported the coup until he learned its leaders supported Paxon over him for speaker. But it was Paxon, not Armey, who resigned his leadership position. This episode pretty well killed Armey's chances of moving up the leadership ladder. Bob Livingston, persuaded by Gingrich to stay in Congress in early 1998, began to organize an aggressive campaign for speaker should Gingrich step down; Paxon was rumored to be running for majority leader until his sudden resignation in February 1998.

It was plain that Armey would be challenged for the majority leadership post at the November 1998 Republican Conference. When Gingrich announced his retirement as speaker, Armey did not run for it; it soon became clear that Livingston had the votes, and he reportedly decided to strip Armey of his power over the House schedule. Running against Armey were Steve Largent, with the support of many coup leaders and strong conservatives, and Jennifer Dunn. Chief Deputy Whip Denny Hastert was urged to run by Mike Castle and Thomas Ewing, and Hastert asked Armey to be relieved of his commitment to vote for him; Armey refused, and Hastert declined to run, though his name was put in nomination. On the first round of voting, Armey led with 100 votes to 58 for Largent, 45 for Dunn and 18 for Hastert. On the second round, Armey led with 99 to 73 for Largent and 49 for Dunn. Finally Armey beat Largent on the third round, 127–95, a decisive margin but scarcely an inspiring one for an incumbent.

As majority leader, Armey has sponsored few pieces of legislation himself. One exception is the auto choice bill, which would encourage states to allow car owners to agree to give up "pain and suffering" damages, most of which go directly to trial lawyers, in return for lower insurance premiums; it has an interesting set of co-sponsors, including Senators Daniel Patrick Moynihan and Mitch McConnell. He also sponsored the voucher amendment to provide as much as $3,200 for tuition for poor children at private schools in the District of Columbia. He strongly opposed Clinton's $18 billion IMF funding package, and in discussing the subject, mentioned that he had not been out of the U.S. since 1986: "I've been to Europe once. I don't have to go again." But he did travel to the Balkans to visit troops in May 1999.

Out on the stump he was one of the most caustic critics of Clinton's conduct in 1998. In April 1998 he said, "If it were me that had documented personal conduct along the line of the president's, I would be so filled with shame that I would resign. This president won't do that. His basic credo in life is, 'I will do whatever I can get away with.' " More jokingly, when asked what his wife would do if he had done what Clinton did, he said, "I would be looking up from a pool of blood and hearing, 'How do I reload this thing?' " In August 1998, he told an audience of Texas fundraisers, "The more you look into this business of the transfer of advanced, sophisticated technology to the Chinese military, which seems to be clearly for campaign contributions, the harder it is to stay away from words like treason."

Armey still has a rough and ready style. He drives a pickup, wears cowboy boots, quotes country music lyrics and loves to go fishing, often with Justice Clarence Thomas (whose wife Virginia was an Armey staffer from 1993–98). He said that he has never tried to bring home pork, and in fact his base-closing law closed Carswell Air Force Base in Fort Worth. He has been re-elected by overwhelming margins, with 88% against a Libertarian in 1998.

Cook's Call. *Safe.* Armey has consistently been re-elected by huge margins in this very Republican, suburban Dallas district. He will win easily in 2000.

The People: Pop. 1990: 564,764; 4.7% rural; 7.9% age 65 + ; 86.7% White, 5.4% Black, 2.8% Asian, 0.5% Amer. Indian, 4.5% Other; 9.3% Hispanic Origin. Households: 51.7% married couple families; 25.6% married couple fams. w. children; 71.1% college educ.; median household income: $40,269; per capita income: $23,770; median house value: $117,800; median gross rent: $430.

1996 Presidential Vote			1992 Presidential Vote		
Dole (R)	160,684	(62%)	Bush (R)	134,061	(47%)
Clinton (D)	79,441	(31%)	Perot (I)	85,898	(30%)
Perot (I)	19,194	(7%)	Clinton (D)	62,537	(22%)

Rep. Dick Armey (R)

Elected 1984; b. July 7, 1940, Cando, ND; home, Cooper Canyon; Jamestown Col., B.A. 1963, U. of ND, M.A. 1964, U. of OK, Ph.D. 1969; Presbyterian; married (Susan).

Professional Career: Prof., West TX St. U., 1967–68, Austin Col., 1968–72, U. of N. TX, 1972–77, Chmn., Dept. of Economics, 1977–83.

DC Office: 301 CHOB 20515, 202-225-7772; Web site: armey.house.gov.

District Office: Irving, 972-556-2500.

Committees: *Majority Leader.*

Group Ratings

	ADA	ACLU	AFS	LCV	CON	NTU	NFIB	COC	ACU	NTLC	CHC
1998	0	6	0	8	28	55	100	100	100	97	100
1997	0	—	13	—	80	60	—	100	88	—	—

National Journal Ratings

	1997 LIB — 1997 CONS			1998 LIB — 1998 CONS		
Economic	16%	—	82%	0%	—	88%
Social	0%	—	90%	3%	—	90%
Foreign	12%	—	81%	26%	—	73%

Key Votes of the 105th Congress

1. Clinton Budget Deal	Y	5. Puerto Rico Sthood. Ref.	N	9. Cut $ for B-2 Bombers	N
2. Education IRAs	Y	6. End Highway Set-asides	Y	10. Human Rights in China	N
3. Req. 2/3 to Raise Taxes	Y	7. School Prayer Amend.	Y	11. Withdraw Bosnia Troops	Y
4. Fast-track Trade	Y	8. Ovrd. Part. Birth Veto	Y	12. End Cuban TV-Marti	N

Election Results

1998 general	Dick Armey (R)	120,332	(88%)	($2,125,437)
	Joe Turner (Lib)	16,182	(12%)	($257)
1998 primary	Dick Armey (R)	unopposed		
1996 spec. prim.	Dick Armey (R)	163,708	(74%)	($1,673,388)
	Jerry Frankel (D)	58,623	(26%)	($56,094)

TWENTY-SEVENTH DISTRICT

South from Corpus Christi, the southernmost natural port on Texas's Gulf Coast and the nation's fourth-largest in trading volume with big petrochemical plants, to the Rio Grande and the Mexican border, are two Texan versions of dreamland. One, fronting the Gulf of Mexico, is the sandspit of Padre Island, for most of its length a national seashore, at the southern tip of which is a high-rise resort to which college students throng for spring break. Remains of a 1554 Spanish shipwreck have been found offshore, and Portuguese settlers began cattle ranching here. The other, inland from the Laguna Madre, are the vast grazing and oil lands of the 825,000-acre (that's 1,289 square miles, partner) King Ranch. This still seemingly vacant land between the Nueces and the Rio Grande was the territory in contention in the Mexican-American War. The United States won that war and established its sovereignty. But today most people here are of Mexican ancestry: If their culture and economy, ultimately, are thoroughly *Norteamericano*, they also have a pronounced Mexican accent.

The 27th Congressional District includes this land from Corpus Christi south to the Rio Grande. More than half of the 27th's voters live in and around Corpus (as it is called locally). Most of the remainder live some 150 miles south in the Lower Rio Grande Valley around Brownsville and Harlingen. With a 66% Hispanic majority, the 27th is a Democratic district, though not quite as Democratic as some may suspect; in 1998 it cast a comfortable 60%–40% majority for Republican Governor George W. Bush.

The congressman from the 27th, since its creation following the 1982 redistricting, has been Solomon Ortiz. He grew up in the Canta Ranas (singing frogs) neighborhood of Robstown, inland from Corpus. His father died when he was 14, leaving him the eldest of four children who scratched out a living as migrant farm workers, sometimes working as far away as Colorado and Michigan. "I know what it is being poor, going home and nothing to eat," he says. When his father died, his employer at the local newspaper raised his wage, and then urged him to join the Army. Ortiz worked as an Army investigator and translator, using his Spanish to learn French, then took a correspondence course in police work and returned home to run for constable. "If it wasn't for the military, I wouldn't be here today," he has said. In 1976 he was elected Nueces County sheriff. In 1982 he ran for Congress; after receiving 26% in the primary, he made a propitious alliance with party leaders in the Brownsville area and won the runoff with 52% and the general with 64%.

Ortiz's voting record has been moderate; he was "probably the only Democrat who did not have to sit down in horror" when Republicans won their majority in 1994, according to an aide. Ortiz is now the fourth-ranking Democrat on the Armed Services Committee. He watches out for the four military installations in the Coastal Bend, as he calls the area; they emerged from the 1995 base-closing review with more jobs than before. Looking after the Corpus Christi Army Depot, he authored the provision requiring 60% of military maintenance to be performed at military depots rather than by private contractors; noting that privatization has been sought by the Clinton White House, the Pentagon, major defense contractors and important senators (especially from California), he said, after the 60–40 formula survived in 1996, "I often felt like David going up against Goliath. In both cases, the Philistines went down." Ortiz is proud also of the public-private Navy housing being built in Portland and Kingsville. Not surprisingly, he adamantly opposes additional rounds of base closings.

Ortiz is a sturdy internationalist: an enthusiastic supporter of NAFTA, and one of the few Democrats to back Clinton's request for fast-track trade negotiating authority. He made a rare floor speech against decertification of Mexico as a partner in good standing in the drug war. He fought successfully to get the proposed I-69 corridor ("the free trade highway") dedicated from Houston to the Lower Rio Grande Valley, and he arranged for the transfer of two Army surplus tugboats to south Texas. He is proud of the Birth Defects Prevention Act of 1998, which he initiated after a rare outbreak in Brownsville of infants born lacking most of their brains.

Ortiz has generally won re-election without difficulty. In 1996 he had primary opposition from Mary Helen Berlanga, whose husband is a state senator representing part of the district (Texas Senate districts are just slightly smaller than congressional districts), his first primary opposition since 1982. He won 70%–30%

Cook's Call. *Safe.* Solomon Ortiz has run in this district eight times and the closest he came to losing was in 1992 when he took 56% of the vote. He is a sure bet in 2000.

The People: Pop. 1990: 565,992; 13.8% rural; 10.6% age 65 +; 78.8% White, 2.4% Black, 0.6% Asian, 0.3% Amer. Indian, 17.9% Other; 65.9% Hispanic Origin. Households: 59.5% married couple families; 35.2% married couple fams. w. children; 38.1% college educ.; median household income: $21,552; per capita income: $9,366; median house value: $47,700; median gross rent: $279.

1996 Presidential Vote			1992 Presidential Vote		
Clinton (D)	87,511	(57%)	Clinton (D)	78,441	(48%)
Dole (R)	57,533	(38%)	Bush (R)	58,780	(36%)
Perot (I)	8,094	(5%)	Perot (I)	27,468	(17%)

Rep. Solomon P. Ortiz (D)

Elected 1982; b. June 3, 1937, Robstown; home, Corpus Christi; Del Mar Col., Natl. Sheriffs Training Inst., 1977; Methodist; divorced.

Military Career: Army, 1960–62.

Elected Office: Nueces Cnty. Constable, 1965–68, Commissioner, 1969–76, Sheriff, 1976–82.

DC Office: 2136 RHOB 20515, 202-225-7742; Fax: 202-226-1134; Web site: www.house.gov/ortiz.

District Offices: Brownsville, 956-541-1242; Corpus Christi, 361-883-5868.

Committees: *Armed Services* (4th of 28 D): Military Installations & Facilities; Military Readiness (RMM); Special Oversight Panel on Morale, Welfare and Recreation. *Resources* (8th of 24 D): Energy & Mineral Resources; Fisheries Conservation, Wildlife & Oceans.

Group Ratings

	ADA	ACLU	AFS	LCV	CON	NTU	NFIB	COC	ACU	NTLC	CHC
1998	70	29	89	38	55	13	21	56	17	21	42
1997	60	—	88	—	49	22	—	60	35	—	—

National Journal Ratings

	1997 LIB	—	1997 CONS	1998 LIB	—	1998 CONS
Economic	65%	—	34%	70%	—	29%
Social	48%	—	51%	50%	—	49%
Foreign	55%	—	45%	64%	—	31%

Key Votes of the 105th Congress

1. Clinton Budget Deal	N	5. Puerto Rico Sthood. Ref.	Y	9. Cut $ for B-2 Bombers	N
2. Education IRAs	N	6. End Highway Set-asides	N	10. Human Rights in China	Y
3. Req. 2/3 to Raise Taxes	N	7. School Prayer Amend.	Y	11. Withdraw Bosnia Troops	N
4. Fast-track Trade	Y	8. Ovrd. Part. Birth Veto	Y	12. End Cuban TV-Marti	N

Election Results

1998 general	Solomon P. Ortiz (D)	61,638	(63%)	($316,095)
	Erol A. Stone (R)	34,284	(35%)	($21,115)
	Others	1,476	(2%)	
1998 primary	Solomon P. Ortiz (D) .... unopposed			
1996 general	Solomon P. Ortiz (D)	97,350	(65%)	($407,316)
	Joe Gardner (R)	50,964	(34%)	($96,900)
	Others	2,286	(2%)	

TWENTY-EIGHTH DISTRICT

The Mexican-American tradition in the part of south Texas radiating from San Antonio is anchored in two culturally conservative but adaptive institutions, the Catholic Church and the United States military. They are a major presence in San Antonio, which for many years had the largest Mexican-American population of any American city, a place just 150 miles north of the border, where Spanish was widely spoken and political refugees from Mexico's revolution could be sure of freedom. The church in San Antonio was led for years by liberal bishops who also ran St. Mary's University, which educated many Hispanic politicians and leaders, including two longtime House committee chairmen, Henry B. Gonzalez and Kika de la Garza. Just as visible a presence in San Antonio are the Army and Air Force, with huge Fort Sam Houston, Lackland Air Force Base, Randolph Air Force Base, and the Brooks Army Medical Center, all in or near the city limits. Mexican-Americans have long volunteered for military service in numbers higher than most ethnic groups, and for many years Mexican-Americans in San Antonio worked in civilian jobs for the military service—Uncle Sam has long been an equal opportunity employer. San Antonio's Mexican-American community has produced many politicians who are liberal on economic issues, civil rights and civil liberties. But it has not produced many who are hostile to the military or to traditional religious and cultural values.

The 28th Congressional District stretches from the southern half of San Antonio to the Mexican border. Some 63% of its people are in San Antonio and Bexar County, on the south and east sides of the city. It has a salient north to Hispanic precincts in Guadalupe County and also heads south, through thinly settled ranch and oil well country, to the Lower Rio Grande. There it includes Starr County, home of many blatant and wealthy drug smugglers, and, not far north, Duval County, often the most Democratic county in the United States, whose then-boss George Parr provided the key votes Lyndon Johnson needed for his disputed 87-vote victory in the 1948 Democratic Senate runoff; in 1998 it voted 77%–22% for Democrat Gary Mauro over Governor George W. Bush. This was a new district for 1992, it is now 66% Hispanic and solidly Democratic.

The congressman from the 28th District is Ciro Rodriguez, a Democrat chosen in the special election in April 1997 to replace Frank Tejeda, who died of a brain tumor in January. Tejeda helped design the 28th District and won the 1992 Democratic primary without opposition. After his death, many prominent local politicians decided not to run, but Ciro Rodriguez was soon up and running (too soon, some opponents charged). He grew up in San Antonio, worked as a social worker, teacher and educational consultant, and spent 12 years on the Harlandale school board. In 1986 he was elected to the Texas House, where he had a liberal record, working on equalizing education funding and private development of Kelly Air Force Base. Critical in the campaign was his endorsement by the San Antonio Central Labor Council; he raised $280,000 from PACs, mostly union PACs, more than half of his $505,000 total.

The only serious competition came from San Antonio Councilman Juan Solis, who was supported by Robert Tejeda and Justice of the Peace Edmund Zaragoza. Solis, like Tejeda, was pro-life on abortion and against gun control; he backed term limits and school vouchers; he called Rodriguez "more of a wild-eyed liberal, and that's not what we need in Congress." Rodriguez was backed by more prominent politicians and Congress members Ruben Hinojosa, Lloyd Doggett, Sheila Jackson Lee, Chet Edwards and Gene Green, and was promised Tejeda's seat on the Armed Services Committee by House Democratic leaders. Even more important, Rodriguez had the money to go on television and Solis didn't. In the March all-party primary, Rodriguez led Solis 46%–27%, leaving little doubt about the outcome; with only a 9% voter turnout, Rodriguez won the April runoff 67%–33%.

Rodriguez got Tejeda's seat on Armed Services and successfully fought to preserve the loan rate for the federal peanut program as set in the 1996 Freedom to Farm Act (the district produced $46 million worth of peanuts in 1996). He was disappointed when the House voted against allowing public and private competition for depot maintenance at Kelly Air Force Base, which is scheduled to be closed in 2001. He wants to designate the 2,580-mile El Camino Real de los Tejas, the Spanish "Royal Road," from Laredo to Natchitoches, Louisiana, as a National Historic Trail, which he said would symbolize the immigration and trade route's critical link between Mexico and the new American frontier.

Rodriguez won 76% of the vote in the three-candidate March 1998 Democratic primary— his third election in 12 months—and won 91% against a Libertarian in the 1998 general.

Cook's Call. *Safe.* This is about as safe as it gets for a Democrat in Texas. Rodriguez is a favorite in 2000.

The People: Pop. 1990: 566,447; 21.3% rural; 11% age 65 +; 68.6% White, 8.6% Black, 0.7% Asian, 0.3% Amer. Indian, 21.9% Other; 60.2% Hispanic Origin. Households: 59.6% married couple families; 35.4% married couple fams. w. children; 30% college educ.; median household income: $20,276; per capita income: $8,050; median house value: $40,400; median gross rent: $251.

1996 Presidential Vote			1992 Presidential Vote		
Clinton (D)	93,147	(63%)	Clinton (D)	94,113	(55%)
Dole (R)	47,338	(32%)	Bush (R)	51,292	(30%)
Perot (I)	8,211	(6%)	Perot (I)	27,202	(16%)

Rep. Ciro Rodriguez (D)

Elected April 1997; b. Dec. 9, 1946, Piedras Negras, Coah., Mexico; home, San Antonio; St. Mary's U., B.A. 1973, Our Lady of the Lake U., M.S.W., 1978; Catholic; married (Carolina).

Elected Office: Harlandale Schl. Bd., 1975–87; TX House of Reps., 1986–97.

Professional Career: Substance Abuse Counselor, 1971–74, 1978–80; Educ. Consultant, 1980–87; Faculty, Our Lady of the Lake U., 1987–97.

DC Office: 323 CHOB 20515, 202-225-1640; Fax: 202-225-1641.

District Offices: Roma, 956-847-1111; San Antonio, 210-924-7383; San Diego, 512-279-3907.

Committees: *Armed Services* (21st of 28 D): Military Readiness; Military Research & Development. *Veterans' Affairs* (10th of 14 D): Health.

Group Ratings

	ADA	ACLU	AFS	LCV	CON	NTU	NFIB	COC	ACU	NTLC	CHC
1998	100	73	100	85	38	12	42	39	4	16	9
1997	75	—	86	—	26	27	—	56	26	—	—

National Journal Ratings

	1997 LIB — 1997 CONS			1998 LIB — 1998 CONS		
Economic	78%	—	22%	77%	—	23%
Social	68%	—	32%	73%	—	27%
Foreign	75%	—	25%	90%	—	5%

Key Votes of the 105th Congress

1. Clinton Budget Deal	N	5. Puerto Rico Sthood. Ref.	Y	9. Cut $ for B-2 Bombers	N
2. Education IRAs	N	6. End Highway Set-asides	N	10. Human Rights in China	Y
3. Req. 2/3 to Raise Taxes	N	7. School Prayer Amend.	N	11. Withdraw Bosnia Troops	N
4. Fast-track Trade	N	8. Ovrd. Part. Birth Veto	N	12. End Cuban TV-Marti	Y

Election Results

1998 general	Ciro Rodriguez (D)	71,849	(91%)	($762,187)
	Edward Elmer (Lib)	7,504	(9%)	
1998 primary	Ciro Rodriguez (D)	28,420	(76%)	
	Lauro A. Bustamante (D)	4,780	(13%)	
	Oscar H. Flores (D)	4,227	(11%)	
1997 runoff	Ciro Rodriguez (D)	19,992	(67%)	($504,945)
	Juan Solis (D)	9,990	(33%)	($91,552)
1997 special	Ciro Rodriguez (D)	14,018	(46%)	
	Juan Solis (D)	8,056	(27%)	
	Mark L. Cude (R)	2,452	(8%)	
	Carlos Uresti (D)	1,345	(4%)	
	John Kelly (R)	1,229	(4%)	
	Others	3,294	(11%)	
1996 general	Frank M. Tejeda (D)	110,148	(75%)	($222,182)
	Mark L. Cude (R)	34,191	(23%)	($9,476)

TWENTY-NINTH DISTRICT

"What built Houston," wrote John Gunther in *Inside U.S.A.*, "was a combination of cotton, oil, and the ship canal." The cotton and oil were gifts of nature, though they required much human effort and ingenuity to produce in commercial quantities; the Houston Ship Channel, by contrast, was almost totally man's creation. After the sand-spit port of Galveston was destroyed by a hurricane and tidal wave in 1900, Houston's elders decided to dredge out Buffalo Bayou and make their inland city a seaport. And so a sluggish, 6-foot-deep creek became a 40-foot-deep channel (45 feet by 2005, following a $500 million expansion) and Houston turned into the nation's busiest port for foreign trade, generating 200,000 jobs and $5.5 billion a year for the local economy. On the west side of town, Houston—a world-class metropolis of 3.5 million people—seems entirely a white-collar, office-bound city. But on the east and north, around the turning basin in the port and through the maze of refinery towers and tubing, Houston is plainly blue collar, with blacks, Mexican-Americans and large numbers of whites from the rural South and even Michigan and California, who came here to move up in the world.

The 29th Congressional District covers much of the Ship Channel area and working-class Houston. It is one of three Texas districts declared unconstitutional by the Supreme Court as racially gerrymandered (the other two are the 18th and 30th); it was created in 1991 to be the Houston area's Hispanic-majority district, but has not elected a Hispanic congressman. Its boundaries in effect for the 1992 and 1994 elections were well described by Paul Burka in *Texas Monthly*: "The 29th District looks like a sacred Mayan bird, with its body running eastward along the Ship Channel from downtown Houston until the tail terminates in Baytown. Spindly legs reach south to Hobby Airport, while the plumed head rises northward almost to Intercontinental Airport. In the western extremity of the district, an open beak appears to be searching for worms in Spring Branch. Here and there, ruffled feathers jut out at odd angles." The district lines for 1996, drawn by a three-judge federal court in August 1996 are much more regular. Removed from the 29th are Baytown, Spring Branch and the Heights neighborhood in Houston. Added is much area on Houston's Northside, between the Eastex and North Freeways all the way out to Houston Intercontinental Airport and FM 1960, and blue-collar neighborhoods in northeast Houston. The old district was 55% Hispanic and 10% black; the new 29th is about 45% Hispanic and 15% black: not an enormous change.

The congressman from the 29th District is Gene Green, a Democrat elected since the district was created in 1992. Green grew up in Houston, worked as a printer's apprentice and was admitted to the bar at age 30; he was elected to the state House in 1972, at 25, and to the state Senate in a special election in 1985. He has been a faithful union and trial-lawyer man in Austin and Washington, and also an opponent of gun control—a politician whose natural base is Texas's small union, blue-collar class. He is a compulsive campaigner who goes door to door, with lawn signs and a hammer in his trunk; and a good thing, for him anyway, since otherwise he never would have won in the 29th. In the 1992 Democratic primary he faced Ben Reyes, a tempestuous Houston councilman who once protested official inaction by demolishing a crack house. In the March primary, Reyes led 34%–28% over Green. For the April runoff, Green came out ahead by 180 votes out of 31,508 cast. Then Reyes went to court and charged that Republican voters had illegally crossed over and voted in the runoff. That got him a July re-runoff, but to no avail. This time Green won with 52%, by 1,132 votes out of 36,722 cast. Green won the general election with 65%.

In the House, Green cast two controversial votes: against NAFTA and against the Brady bill. That got him strong support from unions and the National Rifle Association. Reyes ran again in 1994, pro-NAFTA and pro-gun control, supported by downtown business money and most Latino politicians. Green won 55%–45%, winning 80% of Anglos and 30% of Latinos. In 1996, after the lines were redrawn, no other Democrat ran and Green won with 68%.

Green has worked with other local officials on the Houston Ship Channel widening and deepening project, which is intended to keep the port viable in an era of bigger cargo ships. After a spirited fight with other Texas Democrats, he won a seat in 1997 on the Commerce Committee. But his most satisfying victory, among his many local efforts, may have been an agreement that wrested the bulk of Harris County's grant money away from the county's long-standing Head Start contractor. Always sensitive to his Hispanic constituents, Green complained to the Health and Human Services Department that Latinos in his district were being shut out of Head Start by the contractor's isolated and dysfunctional bureaucracy. This was "awkward," Green explained to *National Journal*, because the bureaucracy in question was run by African-Americans and supported, at least tacitly, by virtually all of the city's black leadership, including Green's House colleague Sheila Jackson Lee. After careful negotiations, a deal was struck to open three-quarters of the contract to bidding—a constructive agreement for a city that prides itself on easing racial discord rather than letting hostility into the open.

Such attention to constituent service appears to be paying off. Green was unopposed in the 1998 Democratic primary and faced only token opposition in the general.

Cook's Call. *Safe.* Gene Green is sitting in a solidly Democratic district. Don't look for a competitive race here in 2000.

The People: Pop. 1990: 568,250; 1.2% rural; 7.1% age 65 + ; 57.6% White, 15.3% Black, 2% Asian, 0.3% Amer. Indian, 24.8% Other; 44.6% Hispanic Origin. Households: 54% married couple families; 33.7% married couple fams. w. children; 28.7% college educ.; median household income: $23,808; per capita income: $9,314; median house value: $40,900; median gross rent: $289.

1996 Presidential Vote			1992 Presidential Vote		
Clinton (D)	63,624	(61%)	Clinton (D)	57,904	(49%)
Dole (R)	34,497	(33%)	Bush (R)	39,374	(33%)
Perot (I)	5,994	(6%)	Perot (I)	21,613	(18%)

Rep. Gene Green (D)

Elected 1992; b. Oct. 17, 1947, Houston; home, Houston; U. of Houston, B.A., 1971, Bates Col. of Law at U. of Houston, 1973–77; Methodist; married (Helen).

Elected Office: TX House of Reps., 1972–84; TX Senate, 1985–92.

Professional Career: Practicing atty., 1977–92.

DC Office: 2429 RHOB 20515, 202-225-1688; Fax: 202-225-9903; Web site: www.house.gov/green.

District Office: Houston, 713-330-0807.

Committees: *Commerce* (18th of 24 D): Health and Environment; Oversight & Investigations; Telecommunications, Trade & Consumer Protection.

Group Ratings

	ADA	ACLU	AFS	LCV	CON	NTU	NFIB	COC	ACU	NTLC	CHC
1998	95	60	100	62	35	24	43	47	16	32	17
1997	75	—	88	—	34	28	—	60	42	—	—

National Journal Ratings

	1997 LIB — 1997 CONS			1998 LIB — 1998 CONS		
Economic	63%	—	36%	64%	—	36%
Social	65%	—	34%	70%	—	28%
Foreign	56%	—	42%	61%	—	37%

Key Votes of the 105th Congress

1. Clinton Budget Deal	N	5. Puerto Rico Sthood. Ref.	Y	9. Cut $ for B-2 Bombers	N
2. Education IRAs	N	6. End Highway Set-asides	N	10. Human Rights in China	Y
3. Req. 2/3 to Raise Taxes	Y	7. School Prayer Amend.	N	11. Withdraw Bosnia Troops	N
4. Fast-track Trade	N	8. Ovrd. Part. Birth Veto	N	12. End Cuban TV-Marti	N

Election Results

1998 general	Gene Green (D)	44,179	(93%)	($392,122)
	Lea Sherman (I)	2,013	(4%)	
	Others	1,439	(3%)	
1998 primary	Gene Green (D)	unopposed		
1996 spec. prim.	Gene Green (D)	61,751	(68%)	($552,655)
	Jack Rodriguez (R)	28,381	(31%)	($58,181)

THIRTIETH DISTRICT

Dallas is, among other things, the westernmost city of the Deep South. Cotton was originally the major crop in this part of Texas, and many of Dallas's first enterprising businessmen, when the railroad reached the Trinity River here in the 1870s, were cotton brokers. Geographically, Dallas is directly west of the Black Belt of Alabama and the Mississippi Delta, both heavy cotton-producing areas in the days before the boll weevil. Many blacks and whites came west on U.S. 80—and now Interstate 20—to this metropolis, which is now the largest metro area in the South. The south side of Dallas, not much visited by tourists or conventioneers, is predominately black.

The 30th Congressional District, originally designed to be the Dallas-Fort Worth Metroplex's black-majority district, includes most of Dallas's predominantly black neighborhoods. Its creation in 1991 was insisted on by Eddie Bernice Johnson, then chairwoman of the Texas Senate's committee on redistricting, and the precise lines were drawn by Bob Mansker, aide to 24th District Congressman Martin Frost, who made them exceedingly complex in order to create safe districts for Frost and 5th District Democrat (now retired) John Bryant. The result was one of the most grotesquely-shaped districts in the country: Attached to the central body in south and east Dallas, were tentacles that appeared as complex and attenuated as a series of DNA molecules. A lawsuit was filed, claiming racial gerrymandering; Democrats contended the lawsuit was politically motivated. The Supreme Court in June 1996 ruled the 30th and two other Texas districts (both in Houston) unconstitutional. In August 1996 a three-judge federal court drew new lines for the 1996 election, and ordered an all-party primary to be held November 5, with a runoff in December if no candidate got 50%. The new 30th consists of two compact geographic units, connected by downtown Dallas. One consists of the south side of Dallas; the other runs northwest out Stemmons Freeway and includes most of Irving. The old 30th was 50% black and 17% Hispanic; the new 30th is 49% black and 22% Hispanic. The new boundaries reduced the 1992 Clinton percentage by 3%—not an earthshaking change in a heavily Democratic district.

The congresswoman from the 30th District is its creator, Eddie Bernice Johnson. She grew up in Texas and graduated from college as a registered nurse—one of only three professional nurses in Congress. She worked at St. Paul Hospital and was chief psychiatric nurse at the VA Hospital in Dallas. In 1972 she was elected to the Texas House—the first black woman elected to anything in Dallas. She became a regional HEW director in the Carter Administration and then was elected to the state Senate in 1986. She has never had effective opposition in the 30th District; she won the 1992 Democratic primary with 92% of the vote. That made her the first—and, still, the only—African-American to represent Dallas in the House. After the 1996 redistricting, she won comfortably with 55% against seven opponents in the November special election, thus avoiding a December runoff. In 1998, she won 72%–27% against Republican Carrie Kelleher, a 27-year-old newcomer who carried a sign that said, "I will work for votes."

In the House, Johnson has a mostly liberal voting record, but she has been attentive to business interests in Dallas. Though she once pledged to unions to oppose NAFTA, she changed her mind and voted for it; Dallas probably exports more to Mexico than any other American city, and many jobs depend on exports to Mexico. She has worked to get NAFTA Superhighway status for I-35. Johnson also strongly favors normal trade relations with China. She is concerned that "in too many high school classrooms, the world of work is distant and removed," and praises school-to-work programs for involving industry in education. She helped to enact in 1998 the Next Generation Internet Research Act, to support research on networking technologies, and promises additional initiatives to help improve the students' science and math skills while encouraging them to pursue technical careers. Serving on the Transportation and Infrastructure Committee, she got a seat in 1997 on the Aviation Subcommittee, of great importance here: The 30th District includes half of Dallas/Fort Worth International Airport and three others, Love Field, Red Bird Airport and Lancaster Airport. During the Clinton impeachment trial, Johnson strongly rallied the black community on his behalf: "He's been the best president on our issues."

Cook's Call. *Safe.* A court-ordered remapping of this once black majority district in 1996 has had little impact on Johnson's ability to rack up large victories here. She is safe in 2000.

The People: Pop. 1990: 564,902; 8.4% age 65 +; 42% White, 44.6% Black, 2% Asian, 0.5% Amer. Indian, 10.9% Other; 17.8% Hispanic Origin. Households: 44.9% married couple families; 24.8% married couple fams. w. children; 38.7% college educ.; median household income: $24,775; per capita income: $11,015; median house value: $60,200; median gross rent: $357.

1996 Presidential Vote			1992 Presidential Vote		
Clinton (D)	95,841	(70%)	Clinton (D)	95,518	(58%)
Dole (R)	35,205	(26%)	Bush (R)	39,686	(24%)
Perot (I)	6,466	(5%)	Perot (I)	29,279	(18%)

Rep. Eddie Bernice Johnson (D)

Elected 1992; b. Dec. 3, 1935, Waco; home, Dallas; St. Mary's at Notre Dame, B.A. 1955, TX Christian U., B.S. 1967, S. Methodist U., M.B.A. 1976; Baptist; divorced.

Elected Office: TX House of Reps., 1972–1977; TX Senate, 1986–92.

Professional Career: Registered nurse; Regional Dir., U.S. Dept. of HEW, 1977–80; Mgmt. consultant, Sammons Corp., 1979–81; Owner, Eddie Bernice Johnson & Assoc., 1981–present.

DC Office: 1511 LHOB 20515, 202-225-8885; Fax: 202-226-1477; Web site: www.house.gov/ebjohnson.

District Office: Dallas, 972-253-8885.

Committees: *Science* (6th of 23 D): Basic Research (RMM); Energy & Environment. *Transportation & Infrastructure* (17th of 34 D): Aviation; Ground Transportation.

Group Ratings

	ADA	ACLU	AFS	LCV	CON	NTU	NFIB	COC	ACU	NTLC	CHC
1998	90	88	86	69	35	15	9	47	4	11	0
1997	85	—	100	—	66	18	—	40	16	—	—

National Journal Ratings

	1997 LIB — 1997 CONS			1998 LIB — 1998 CONS		
Economic	79%	—	18%	78%	—	21%
Social	82%	—	15%	93%	—	0%
Foreign	67%	—	32%	75%	—	23%

Key Votes of the 105th Congress

1. Clinton Budget Deal	N	5. Puerto Rico Sthood. Ref.	Y	9. Cut $ for B-2 Bombers	N
2. Education IRAs	N	6. End Highway Set-asides	N	10. Human Rights in China	Y
3. Req. 2/3 to Raise Taxes	N	7. School Prayer Amend.	N	11. Withdraw Bosnia Troops	N
4. Fast-track Trade	Y	8. Ovrd. Part. Birth Veto	N	12. End Cuban TV-Marti	Y

Election Results

1998 general	Eddie Bernice Johnson (D)	57,603	(72%)	($241,756)
	Carrie Kelleher (R)	21,338	(27%)	($57,988)
1998 primary	Eddie Bernice Johnson (D)	unopposed		
1996 spec. prim.	Eddie Bernice Johnson (D)	61,723	(55%)	($416,694)
	John Hendry (R)	20,664	(18%)	($101,948)
	James L. Sweatt (D)	9,909	(9%)	($112,343)
	Marvin E. Crenshaw (D)	7,765	(7%)	
	Lisa Kitterman (R)	7,761	(7%)	($18,467)
	Others	5,250	(5%)	

UTAH

Utah is a triumph of man over nature, the creation of a productive and orderly civilization in a remote expanse of desert and mountain, arrayed around a desolate salt sea. Today's Utah and Mormonism have their roots in a very different landscape of more than 150 years ago, when a wave of religious enthusiasm, prophecy and utopianism swept across the "burnt-over district" of Upstate New York in the 1820s and 1830s. There Joseph Smith, a 14-year-old farmer, experienced a vision in which the angel Moroni appeared and told him where to unearth several golden tablets inscribed with hieroglyphic writings. With the aid of special spectacles, Smith translated the tablets and published them as the Book of Mormon in 1831. He later declared himself a prophet and founded the Church of Jesus Christ of Latter-day Saints.

The Mormons, as they were called, attracted thousands of converts and created their own communities; persecuted for their beliefs, they moved west to Ohio, Missouri and then Illinois. In 1844, the Mormon colony at Nauvoo, Illinois, had some 15,000 members living under the theocratic rule of Smith. It was here that Smith received a revelation sanctioning the practice of polygamy, which led to his death at the hands of a mob in 1844. After the murder, the new church president, Brigham Young, decided to move the faithful, "the saints," farther west into territory that was still part of Mexico and far beyond white settlement. In 1847 Young led a well-organized march across the Great Plains and into the Rocky Mountains on a path where Mormons re-enacted the march 150 years later in 1997. In 1847, they stopped on the western slope of the Wasatch Range and, as Young gazed over the valley of the Great Salt Lake spread out below, he uttered the now famous words, "This is the place."

The place was Utah. Young was governor of the territory for many years, and it is the only state that largely continues to live by the teachings of a church. The early pioneers laid out towns foursquare to the points of the compass with huge city blocks, built sturdy houses and planted dozens of trees. Young's home still stands a block away from Temple Square, where the Temple, closed to non-Mormons, stands in gleaming marble, topped by the golden angel Moroni, across from the oval Mormon Tabernacle where its great choir sings. For 150 years this "Zion" has attracted thousands of converts from the Midwest, the north of England and Scandinavia. The object of religious fear and prejudice, Utah was not granted statehood until 1896, after the church renounced polygamy. Utah has grown steadily since then, and remains heavily Mormon, its basic character is stamped on the desert, mountain-shadowed, often surrealistic landscape that without the Mormons would probably have remained as unpopulated as Nevada without gambling.

The Mormon church remains distinctive in many ways. It cares deeply about its past: in caves in the mountains of Utah, the Church preserves America's most complete genealogical records in its Family History Library, which is also being put on the Internet. It tries to spread the faith: young Mormons spend missionary years abroad, and their experiences in turn give Utah the biggest inventory of people with knowledge of obscure foreign languages of any state in the union, a nice commercial advantage. The church prohibits the consumption of tobacco, alcohol and caffeine; it encourages hard work and large families, and Utah has by far the nation's highest birth rate and lowest median age; Mormons are healthier than the average American; better educated, they work longer hours and earn more money. In an individualist country, it fosters communitarian attitudes: the LDS Church has no clergy, but members serve in positions for which they are chosen, conducting religious services but also keeping in touch with members and counseling them when they need help. The church also maintains its own social service organizations. It evidently works: while American mainline denominations are losing members, the Mormon Church is growing, with more members than either the Presby-

UTAH   1595

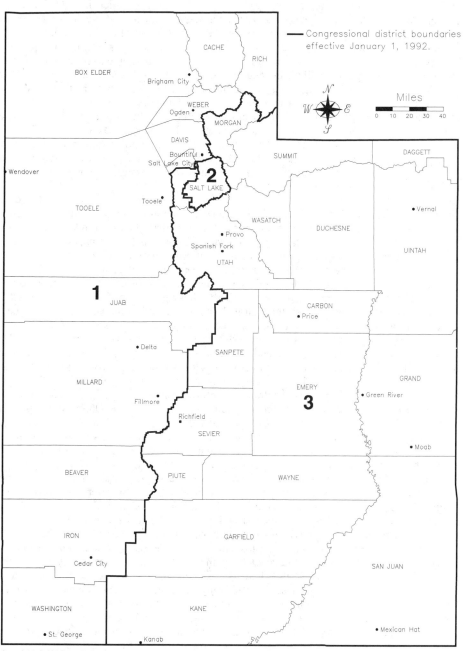

Congressional district boundaries effective January 1, 1992.

Miles

0 10 20 30 40

CACHE

RICH

BOX ELDER

Brigham City

WEBER

Ogden

MORGAN

DAVIS

Bountiful

Salt Lake City

SUMMIT

DAGGETT

Wendover

2

SALT LAKE

Tooele

Tooele

WASATCH

DUCHESNE

Vernal

Provo

Spanish Fork

UTAH

UINTAH

1

JUAB

CARBON

Price

Delta

SANPETE

MILLARD

EMERY

GRAND

Green River

Fillmore

3

Richfield

SEVIER

BEAVER

PIUTE

WAYNE

Moab

IRON

GARFIELD

Cedar City

SAN JUAN

WASHINGTON

KANE

St. George

Kanab

Mexican Hat

terian or Episcopalian churches. There were 2.9 million Mormons in 1970 and 10 million by 1997, with more than half outside the United States.

The church's influence in Utah is great—it owns one of the two leading Salt Lake City newspapers and a TV station, it has holdings in an insurance company, several banks, real estate and owns ZCMI, the largest department store in Salt Lake City—and it is sometimes resented. The conservative hold that the church has over the state can appear in political issues. In 1991 Utah passed the strictest abortion law of any state, banning abortion except in cases of rape and incest, or if the mother's life is endangered. Also in 1990, it became the first state to ban the sale of vending machine cigarettes, although earlier in the year it became the last state to abolish the provision that stated hard liquor could not be served in public. And the church itself, financed by the tradition of tithing, runs its own high-quality welfare programs. This is a society that favors market economics and free enterprise, but also has a lively tradition of communal effort and responsibility. Utah's state workfare program, started in 1983, requires one adult in a welfare family to spend 32 hours a week in community service or training, plus job search, and benefits are paid only after performance; social workers here seem to strengthen middle-class values rather than rebel against them.

If the moral underpinnings of life in Utah have not changed in 50 years, Utah's view of its place in the nation has. Before World War II, Utah saw itself as a colonial victim of East Coast bankers and financiers and Mormons saw themselves as suffering religious discrimination and bigotry—all with some cause. Utah's income levels were well below the national average, its cost of living higher, the prices paid for the things it produced seemed to be controlled else-where. Politically, this perspective translated into a Democratic allegiance: in 1940 Utah was represented by staunch New Dealers in Congress and cast 62% of its votes for Franklin Roo-sevelt. Today, Utah is more likely to see itself as a busy generator of wealth, with a raft of successful businesses and a knack for high-tech innovation. It has the youngest and highest-productivity work force of any in the nation, second in job creation (Nevada was first), with more than 5% job growth every year since 1992. Its population has grown almost 20% in the 1990s, the fourth highest rate in the nation. Work weeks average 48 hours here, more than Japan and far more than anywhere else in America. It has fast-rising incomes and in the mid-1990s America's fastest-rising house prices as thousands of people migrated from California. And Utah has the second largest concentration of information technology firms, after California. WordPerfect, long a favorite word processing software, was invented in Orem; Novell is head-quartered in Provo; the University of Utah in Salt Lake City and Brigham Young University in Provo are producing hundreds of computer engineers. Utah has over 42,000 jobs in infor-mation technology; the state government has a Centers of Excellence program to fund small high-tech startups; it has the highest proportion of households with personal computers. In 1997 the Salt Lake City-Provo area was rated the number one entrepreneurial hot spot, with lots of "baby gazelles"—small companies with the potential to be the Intels or Microsofts of the future. Utah is also a place with community spirit: it rejoiced when it won the 2002 Winter Olympics, and started a $1.6 billion reconstruction of I-15, an airport expansion, a downtown light rail system and building a winter sports park, new stadium space and an athlete's village.

Politically, this perspective now translates into a strong Republican preference; Utah was pretty solidly Republican by the middle 1960s. In the last 20 years, as traditional values thriving in Utah have come under attack elsewhere, it has become arguably the most Republican of states—standing out in national statistics politically just as it does demographically. In 1960, Richard Nixon carried Utah with 55% of the vote; by 1972, he won with 72%. Ronald Reagan won 73% here in 1980 and 75% in 1984; George Bush won 66% here in 1988. In five of the last six presidential elections, Utah has been the nation's most Republican state, and in the other, 1992, it was the least Democratic: Ross Perot finished ahead of Bill Clinton, 27% to 25%. Utah is so Republican now that church leaders have been at pains to affirm that there is nothing contradictory about being a Mormon and voting Democratic. Interestingly, the Salt Lake City neighborhoods close to the church headquarters, with gracious old houses and a smaller street grid that attract academic and professional newcomers, have become the most heavily "gentile" and politically liberal part of the state: as Yankee Republican Boston filled up with Irish Catholic Democrats in the 1890s, so Salt Lake City is getting more than its share of secular liberal Democrats in the 1990s. But for the most part, Democrats are competitive only if they seem consistent with Utah values and attitudes, and even then are in jeopardy.

Not quite everything is rosy in Utah. Scandal appeared in late 1998 when it was revealed that members of the International Olympics Committee had received gifts—$400,000 for college scholarships, $28,000 in medical care, airline tickets, guns and skis—from Salt Lake Olympics organizers. Six members of the IOC resigned in January 1999, as did the president and executive vice president of the Salt Lake Organizing Committee. The Olympics were not canceled, and Utah stands to gain $2.8 billion in spending and 20,000 man-years of employment. But as former Mayor Ted Wilson said, "Utahns are very ashamed of what they are seeing. We felt we had earned the Games and now we find out we probably bought them."

There are disputes as well about environmental protection, over the vast expanses of mostly empty land beyond the Wasatch Front from Ogden to Provo where 77% of Utahns live. There are still "downwinders," including Governor Mike Leavitt, who remember living downwind from the 1950s nuclear tests in Nevada, and some are uneasy about the new chemical weapons incinerator southwest of Tooele. Leavitt objected strongly to the Goshute Indians' contract to store nuclear waste in Skull Valley, between the Dugway Proving Grounds and the Tooele Army Depot; he worked to swap property with the federal government to build a "moat" around the Goshutes' "island" and bar nuclear waste shipments there. Some accommodation was also made on another rankling issue. Utahns were furious in September 1996 when Bill Clinton, campaigning for re-election in Arizona with the Grand Canyon as a backdrop, announced that he was creating a 1.7 million acre new Grand Staircase-Escalante National Monument in southern Utah, which would bar coal mining and mineral exploration—without notification to Utah officials, although a planned coal mine would bring over $1 billion in royalties to Utah schools. This obvious electioneering gimmick (which helped Clinton carry Arizona) led to the defeat of Utah's lone Democratic congressman, Bill Orton, and to passage in the House of a bill sponsored by Utah's James Hansen to limit the president's ability to create national monuments. But within a year tourism picked up in the area and Clinton acted to allow oil drilling there. In spring 1998 the state and the Interior Department agreed on a land swap: the federal government would take 377,000 acres of state school trust land parcels, about half in the national monument, and would pay the state $50 million in cash and $13 million in future coal revenues, plus turn over 153,000 acres of exploitable lands elsewhere. And in May 1999 Leavitt and the federal government agreed to an even larger land swap involving more than 1 million acres. Utah still feels victimized by the federal government, but it knows how to adapt and fight back.

Governor. Mike Leavitt is from the southwest corner of Utah, far from Salt Lake. He grew up in Cedar City, graduated from Southern Utah University, worked for and in the 1980s ran the family businesses, including an insurance company that has spread all over the West and land holdings in southern Utah and Nevada. In between, he managed the campaigns of Governor Norman Bangerter and Senator Jake Garn. In 1992, when Bangerter retired after two terms, Leavitt ran himself. He won the Republican primary 56%–44% over Richard Eyre, who backed a $1,200 school choice voucher; Leavitt had his own Strategic Plan for Education and opposed vouchers. In the general, liberal Democrat Stewart Hanson ran third, with only 23%; second was anti-tax crusader and now 2nd District Congressman Merrill Cook, with 34%; Leavitt won with 42%.

In office, Leavitt cut taxes in 1994, 1995 and 1996, as the state's economy surged, and pushed activist programs with catchy labels. One was the 1994 Healthprint insurance reforms; he boasted that Utah had lower health care costs than all but one other state. Another was a $120 million, seven-year Technology 2000 initiative. In 1995 he convened a Growth Summit, which came up with a 10-year, $2.6 billion highway-building program, with half the money to make I-15 in Salt Lake County a 10-lane highway by 2001, in time for the 2002 Winter Olympics; for that he raised gas taxes while cutting the sales tax. In 1996 he proposed a Legacy project, to build a north-south highway west of I-15; this has been stoutly attacked by Democrats. He has sponsored a Centennial Charter schools program and Highly Impacted Schools program for disadvantaged children; in 1998 he called for reading testing in early grades with summer school for those who fall short, and for competency testing in high school, with diplomas denied those who fail. He has worked to start, with other Western states, a Western Virtual University, and is completing UtahLINK, giving Internet access to all Utah schools.

On environmental issues, he backed a quality growth initiative, with incentives to local communities to preserve valuable open space, but no mandates. After discussions with Oregon's Democratic Governor John Kitzhaber, he advanced what he called Enlibra, "a symbol of balance and stewardship," based on collabortion, local decision-making and free market incentives rather than government command and control, "not to eliminate conflict but to shorten the conflict so as to increase the velocity of environmental problem-solving." There was conflict here with the Clinton approach, including the election-year creation of the Grand Staircase-Escalante National Monument and EPA's rejection of the plan Leavitt developed while vice chairman of the Grand Canyon Visibility Transport Commission, which would allow sale of clean-air credits by those who exceed standards. But he was ready to use state powers to prevent the Goshute Indians from opening a nuclear waste depository.

In his 1999 State of the State address, Leavitt talked of the Olympic scandal then breaking: "We do not excuse our contribution to this problem; we accept responsibility and pledge its correction. What we hunger for the world to understand—and for history to record—is that the dishonorable actions of a few do not represent the collective aspirations of the many." He called for expulsion of IOC members, restructured the Salt Lake Organizing Committee and called in Mitt Romney, Massachusetts entrepreneur and 1994 Republican Senate candidate, to run it. Leavitt sought more business tax cuts, called for every family to fill out Envision Utah's citizen questionnaire, and proposed charter schools. Not all of Leavitt's initiatives have been successful. His attempt to create a Western states presidential primary seemed in early 1999 to involve only four rather than the originally intended eight states. He had to retract some statements he made when a controversy over polygamy broke in summer 1998; he handed off enforcement to Attorney General Jan Graham, who handed them to county prosecutors. Disputes with Graham, a Democrat, over tobacco suit money led Republican legislators in 1999 to seek to end her power to make decisions on civil lawsuits. Leavitt has been active in the National Governors Association and is slated to become chairman in summer 1999; his seatmate (in alphabetical order by state) is George W. Bush, with whom he traveled to Israel after the November 1998 election.

In 1996 Democrats had to scrounge to find a candidate to run against Leavitt; he was reelected 75%–23%. In 1998 his job approval was hovering around 80%, and if he seeks a third term in 2000 he is the overwhelming favorite to win. His name also seems to be on the short list for a top administration position should Bush win the White House.

Cook's Call. *Safe.* Leavitt is a lock to win re-election in this overwhelmingly Republican state.

Senior Senator. Orrin Hatch, who never planned a political career, is now in his third decade in the United States Senate. Hatch grew up in Pittsburgh, where his father was a metal lather; he worked his way through Brigham Young University, then Pittsburgh law school, practiced law there and then moved to Salt Lake City. He got into the 1976 Senate race late, filing the last day; an endorsement from Ronald Reagan helped him win the Republican nomination, and in the general he upset three-term Democrat Frank Moss 54%–45%. His toughest re-election fight came in 1982, when he was opposed by popular Salt Lake City Mayor Ted Wilson; Hatch won 58%–41%.

Hatch's Senate career has been shaped by two impulses which are sometimes in tension with each other: a strong conservative philosophy and a sense of responsibility for the superintendency of legislation. He first attracted attention in a Senate dominated by Democrats when he successfully filibustered the AFL-CIO's labor law reform, which had been expected to pass. Then, after just four years, he became chairman of the Labor Committee after Republicans won a Senate majority in 1980. He worked to convert federal programs to block grants to states, but became a fan of some programs, like the Job Corps. He worked for bipartisan compromise on child care, family and medical leave, immunizations, the WIC program and AIDS babies. He backed the Americans With Disabilities Act. But he remained a strong opponent of the striker replacement law sought by unions and eventually passed a subminimum wage for teens. On the Judiciary Committee, he fought abortion and a civil rights bill that produced racial quotas and preferences, and staunchly defended Supreme Court nominees Robert Bork and Clarence Thomas. He also worked on less politically divisive issues—railway labor disputes, bankruptcy reform, sovereign immunity of states for patents and trademarks, patent protection for pharmaceuticals under GATT and compensation for people exposed to radiation during nuclear tests (which affects southern Utah).

In 1993 Hatch switched from ranking Republican on Labor to the same post on Judiciary, when it was vacated by Strom Thurmond, and took a seat on Finance; in 1995 he became chairman of Judiciary and left Labor altogether. On Judiciary he worked on tort reform and regulatory reform and managed the balanced budget amendment to one-vote defeats in 1995 and 1997. He worked also on the flag amendment, the anti-terrorism law and the Religious Freedom Restoration Act. In early 1996 he criticized the administration on drugs, saying that Bill Clinton "has abandoned the bully pulpit, overemphasized treatment of hard-core users and—most importantly—de-emphasized core law enforcement and interdiction activities." On judicial appointments, Hatch promised in 1995 to cooperate with the Clinton Administration; by early 1997 some Democrats were charging that he was stalling approval of nominees, while some Republicans were complaining that he was allowing too many liberal, activist judges on the bench. When Chief Justice William Rehnquist complained of the slow response to nominations, Hatch replied that many vacancies existed because Clinton was slow to appoint judges. He also criticized Clinton for holding Assistant Attorney General for Civil Rights Bill Lann Lee, whose confirmation the committee refused to consider, in office past the 120 days specified in the Vacancies Act.

In 1997 and 1998 Hatch passionately defended Independent Counsel Kenneth Starr against attacks by Clinton advisors. In March 1997 he revealed that the FBI had warned some members of Congress that China was planning to make illegal campaign contributions, and over the next two years criticized Attorney General Janet Reno for not seeking an independent counsel to investigate these and other allegations of misconduct. Watching Clinton's speech August 17, 1998, Hatch said he was ready to "blow my cork"; off-camera, he called Clinton a "jerk" and said his speech was "pathetic."

In 1997 Hatch again surprised some on both sides of the aisle when he joined Ted Kennedy in sponsoring a $24 billion program to get states to provide health insurance for children of low-income working parents who don't qualify for Medicaid; for Hatch, a tobacco opponent, one attraction must have been that the money would come from increasing the cigarette tax from 24 to 67 cents a pack. Hatch also sponsored his own tobacco bill, with Dianne Feinstein, which would have tobacco companies pay $428 billion over 25 years and insulate them against class-action suits; it was overtaken by John McCain's bill, which then died. Hatch praised the Microsoft antitrust suit in May 1998; one of Microsoft's major competitors is Utah-based Novell. In 1997 he sponsored a patent law revision, championed also by Al Gore, which would require disclosure of patent applications after 18 months and allow informal challenges and prior use by companies that developed technology but failed to apply for a patent; it would also corporatize the Patent Office; this was criticized by some as weakening patent protection. Hatch's bill to expand the jurisdiction of the Court of Federal Claims to assess property rights failed to get past a filibuster, but he did pass an end to the labor component of the 76-year antitrust exemption for baseball. Hatch has worked to prevent specious suits on Y2K problems, to allow homeowners to claim capital losses on sales of homes, to bar the federal government from using racial or gender quotas, to stop operation of Oregon's assisted suicide law, and to ban stalking of celebrities by paparazzi. In 1997 Hatch revealed that he has been writing songs, which have been recorded by a Utah firm; they are religious and titles include "At the Foot of the Cross" and "Jesus, Lord, I Think of Thee."

Hatch has been re-elected three times and comes before voters again in 2000. The greatest threat to his tenure was removed in November 1993 when the Ethics Committee cleared him of charges of involvement with scandal-plagued BCCI. In November 1994 he beat, by 69%–28%, Pat Shea, former Democratic state chairman and later Clinton's nominee to head the Bureau of Land Management. In June 1999 Hatch was reported to be planning to run for president; a recently passed state law allows him to concurrently seek both offices.

Cook's Call. *Safe.* In his five Senate elections, Hatch has averaged 62%, and the 2000 race is not likely to change things. It appears that Democrats may pass on this one, focusing their efforts on unseating second-term Representative Merrill Cook in the 2d District.

Junior Senator. Bob Bennett was first elected in 1992, but was no stranger to the Senate. He grew up in Salt Lake City, and was 17 when his father Wallace Bennett was elected in 1950 to the first of four terms in the Senate. Bob Bennett worked as a congressional staffer and was the Transportation Department's chief lobbyist during the Nixon Administration. He also headed the public relations firm (and CIA front) that employed Watergate burglar Howard Hunt, but was involved in no wrongdoing himself; some Watergate buffs believe that Bennett was Bob Woodward's "Deep Throat," but both Bennett and Woodward have denied it. After that, Bennett headed Microsonics Corporation, which makes audio discs for talking toys, for three years, then became head of Franklin Quest, which produces the Franklin day planners and organizers; he increased it from four to 700 employees and brought in sales of $80 million; he sold his interest in 1991 for a reported $25 million. He headed a commission that produced Utah's Strategic Plan for Education and wrote *Gaining Control*, a book on the forces that control daily life.

In 1992, when Jake Garn retired from the Senate, Bennett decided to run for the seat his father once held. He was not the only millionaire in the race. The initial favorite was Republican Joseph Cannon, who had taken over the old Geneva Steel plant and made it profitable, and who spent $5 million of his own money. But Bennett spent $1.4 million of his own and effectively attacked Geneva's environmental record, and won 51%–49%. The Democratic nominee, Congressman Wayne Owens, was a familiar face; he was elected to the House from Salt Lake City in 1972 and ran for the Senate in 1974, then after Mormon missionary work in Canada was elected to the House again in 1986. His record in Washington was moderate, but perhaps too liberal for Utah; Bennett won 55%–40%, with exit polls showing Owens carrying only the elderly—not a good omen for Utah Democrats.

Bennett has a moderate to conservative voting record. Bob Dole appointed Bennett head of a task force on health care in August 1994; he worked on the health insurance portability law that passed in 1996. He has worked for several years on a bill to protect the confidentiality of medical records, with uniform rules for access by researchers and law enforcement personnel. He sponsored a bill to limit liability on debit cards as it is on credit cards, and one to establish a uniform "minimalist" framework for digital signatures and electronic verification over the Internet. He traveled to Moscow to lobby against the Russian religious bill, which would have limited the number of churches with official recognition. He has strongly opposed campaign finance bills, which he says would prescribe "ways in which the government itself will inject federal power into the process of determining who can speak, when they can speak, how they will speak." He was fined $55,000 by the FEC for alleged late disclosures and donations beyond the contribution limit in his 1992 campaign; his own solution would be to require immediate computer-accessible disclosure of contributions and otherwise let free expression prevail. Bennett gave a long speech in March 1998 to "connect the dots" on the Clinton-Gore Chinese fundraising. He was among the first senators to suggest censure of Bill Clinton in August 1998;

in January and February he worked with Democrat Dianne Feinstein to work out censure language, but the censure move foundered after the Senate voted for acquittal.

In 1997, before most other senators were thinking about the problem, Bennett sponsored a bill to require businesses to disclose what they were doing to fix the Y2K problem. In April 1998 Trent Lott made him chairman of a Select Committee on the Year 2000 Technology Problem. His first priorities were public utilities, telecommunications and transportation; later he spotlighted the unpreparedness of health care providers, and got the SEC to require disclosure of business spending on the problem. By October 1998 he said he was confident about electric power grids and domestic flying, but added that he plans to stockpile water in a 55-gallon drum just to be safe.

On Utah issues, Bennett has worked on land exchanges to help the Olympics and, after Clinton without consultation created the Grand Staircase-Escalante National Monument, pressed for land exchanges. He co-sponsored the Utah Land Exchanges Act of 1998, noting that the idea was pushed by his father 40 years ago and by Democratic Governor Scott Matheson 20 years ago; the law enabled Utah to give up lands in the national monument and gain lands which could produce income for its schools. On the Appropriations Committee, he has worked to fund the improvements on I-15, to be ready for the 2002 Winter Olympics. When Clinton refused to close down military depots in California and Texas as required by the 1995 base closings act, Bennett worked to make sure Hill Air Force Base's depot would not lose work.

Democrats had a hard time finding a candidate against Bennett in 1998, and he was renominated at the party convention in May with more than the 70% required to avoid a primary. His Democratic opponent was a surgeon with an interest in the microloans program in Bangladesh; he called for a $500,000 limit on campaign spending, but raised only about half as much. Bennett won 64%–33%, losing tiny Carbon County and running 10% behind his statewide level in Salt Lake County. In 1992 he said he would run for only two terms, but in 1998 Bennett said he would not rule out running again in 2004. Longevity runs in the family: his father lived to be 95, and his grandfather Heber Grant, was president of the LDS Church, a job that goes to the longest serving member of the Quorum of the Twelve Disciples.

Presidential politics. Utah has been the most Republican state in five of the last six presidential elections. It sees few candidates in presidential years; Bill Clinton's 1996 announcement that he was establishing a national monument in southern Utah was made in Arizona. Utah's relatively few delegates to national conventions are chosen in caucuses; in the last serious contest, in 1992, Democrats preferred Paul Tsongas and Jerry Brown to Clinton.

Governor Mike Leavitt proposed a Western states regional primary, and Utah passed a March 10 primary date in March 1999. Besides Utah, only Colorado, Wyoming, and possibly Nevada seemed ready to jump on board.

Congressional districting. The Republican legislature drew new lines for Utah's three congressional districts for 1992. Salt Lake County, the most Democratic part of the state now, had to be split between districts, and the legislature gave some of the less Republican portions to the 1st and 3d Districts. Utah is likely to gain a seat for 2002.

The People: Est. Pop. 1998: 2,099,758; Pop. 1990: 1,722,850, up 21.9% 1990–1998. 0.8% of U.S. total, 34th largest; 13% rural. Median age: 26.8 years. 9.1% 65 years and over. 93.9% White, 0.6% Black, 1.9% Asian, 1.4% Amer. Indian, 2.1% Other; 4.8% Hispanic Origin. Households: 64.8% married couple families; 38.6% married couple fams. w. children; 57.9% college educ.; median household income: $29,470; per capita income: $11,029; 68.1% owner occupied housing; median house value: $68,900; median monthly rent: $300. 3.8% Unemployment. 1998 Voting age pop.: 1,432,000. 1998 Turnout: 506,553; 35% of VAP. Registered voters (1998): 1,115,821; no party registration.

1602 UTAH

Political Lineup: Governor, Michael O. Leavitt (R); Lt. Gov., Olene S. Walker (R); Atty. Gen., Jan Graham (D); Treasurer, Edward T. Alter (R); State Senate, 29 (11 D, 18 R); Majority Leader, Lyle W. Hillyard (R); State House, 75 (21 D, 54 R); House Speaker, Martin Stephens (R). Senators, Orrin G. Hatch (R) and Robert Bennett (R). Representatives, 3 (3 R).

Elections Division: 801-538-1041; **Filing Deadline for U.S. Congress:** March 17, 2000.

1996 Presidential Vote			1992 Presidential Vote		
Dole (R)	361,911	(54%)	Bush (R)	322,632	(43%)
Clinton (D)	221,633	(33%)	Perot (I)	203,400	(27%)
Perot (I)	66,461	(10%)	Clinton (D)	183,429	(25%)
Others	15,623	(2%)	Others	34,607	(5%)

GOVERNOR
Gov. Michael O. Leavitt (R)

Elected 1992, term expires Jan. 2001; b. Feb. 11, 1951, Cedar City; home, Salt Lake City; S. UT U., B.A. 1976; Mormon; married (Jacalyn).

Military Career: Army Natl. Guard, 1969–78.

Professional Career: Pres. & CEO, Leavitt Group Insurance Co., 1984–92; Chmn., S. UT U. Bd. of Trustees, 1985–89; UT Board of Regents, 1989–92.

Office: 210 State Capitol, Salt Lake City, 84114, 801-538-1000; Web site: www.state.ut.us.

Election Results

1996 gen.	Michael O. Leavitt (R)	503,693	(75%)
	Jim Bradley (D)	156,616	(23%)
	Others	11,570	(2%)
1996 prim.	Michael O. Leavitt (R)	unopposed	
1992 gen.	Michael O. Leavitt (R)	321,713	(42%)
	Merrill Cook (I)	255,733	(34%)
	Stewart Hanson (D)	177,181	(23%)

SENATORS
Sen. Orrin G. Hatch (R)

Elected 1976, seat up 2000; b. Mar. 22, 1934, Pittsburgh, PA; home, Salt Lake City; Brigham Young U., B.S. 1959; U. of Pittsburgh, J.D. 1962; Mormon; married (Elaine).

Professional Career: Practicing atty., 1962–76.

DC Office: 131 RSOB, 20510, 202-224-5251; Fax: 202-224-6331; Web site: www.senate.gov/~hatch.

State Offices: Cedar City, 801-586-8435; Ogden, 801-625-5672; Provo, 801-375-7881; Salt Lake City, 801-524-4380; St. George, 801-634-1795.

Committees: *Finance* (4th of 11 R): Health Care; International Trade; Taxation & IRS Oversight (Chmn.). *Indian Affairs* (7th of 8 R). *Intelligence* (7th of 9 R). *Judiciary* (Chmn. of 10 R): Antitrust, Business Rights & Competition; Technology, Terrorism & Government Information; The Constitution, Federalism & Property Rights.

Group Ratings

	ADA	ACLU	AFS	LCV	CON	NTU	NFIB	COC	ACU	NTLC	CHC
1998	5	14	11	13	14	57	100	94	80	75	82
1997	15	—	0	—	49	70	—	100	68	—	—

National Journal Ratings

	1997 LIB — 1997 CONS			1998 LIB — 1998 CONS		
Economic	37%	—	57%	31%	—	63%
Social	39%	—	55%	43%	—	55%
Foreign	34%	—	57%	12%	—	75%

Key Votes of the 105th Congress

1. Bal. Budget Amend.	Y	5. Satcher for Surgeon Gen.	Y	9. Chem. Weapons Treaty	Y
2. Clinton Budget Deal	Y	6. Highway Set-asides	N	10. Cuban Humanitarian Aid	N
3. Cloture on Tobacco	N	7. Table Child Gun locks	Y	11. Table Bosnia Troops	N
4. Education IRAs	Y	8. Ovrd. Part. Birth Veto	Y	12. $ for Test-ban Treaty	N

Election Results

1994 general	Orrin G. Hatch (R)	357,297	(69%)	($4,209,993)
	Pat Shea (D)	146,938	(28%)	($311,491)
	Others	15,088	(3%)	
1994 primary	Orrin G. Hatch (R)	unopposed		
1988 general	Orrin G. Hatch (R)	430,089	(67%)	($3,706,381)
	Brian H. Moss (D)	203,364	(32%)	($153,475)

Sen. Robert Bennett (R)

Elected 1992, seat up 2004; b. Sept. 18, 1933, Salt Lake City; home, Salt Lake City; U. of UT, B.S. 1957; Mormon; married (Joyce).

Military Career: Chaplain, Army Natl. Guard, 1957–60.

Professional Career: Staff Aide, U.S. Rep. Sherm Lloyd, 1962; Staff Aide, U.S. Sen. Wallace F. Bennett, 1963; Cong. Liaison, U.S. Dept. of Transp., 1969–70; Pres., Robert Mullen P.R., 1970–74; P.R. Dir., Summa Corp., 1974–78; Pres., Osmond Communications, 1978–79; Chmn., American Computers Corp., 1979–81; Pres., Microsonics Corp., 1981–84; CEO, Franklin Quest Co., 1984–91; Chmn., UT Educ. Strategic Plng. Comm., 1988.

DC Office: 818 HSOB, 20510, 202-224-5444; Fax: 202-228-1168; Web site: www.senate.gov/~bennett.

State Offices: Cedar City, 801-865-1335; Ogden, 801-625-5676; Provo, 801-379-2525; Salt Lake City, 801-524-5933; St. George, 801-628-5514.

Committees: *Appropriations* (11th of 15 R): Energy & Water Development; Foreign Operations & Export Financing; Interior; Legislative Branch (Chmn.); Transportation. *Banking, Housing & Urban Affairs* (4th of 11 R): Economic Policy (Vice Chmn.); Financial Institutions (Chmn.); Securities. *Environment & Public Works* (9th of 10 R): Clean Air, Wetlands, Private Property & Nuclear Safety; Fisheries, Wildlife & Drinking Water. *Small Business* (4th of 10 R). *Joint Economic Committee* (3d of 10 Sens.).

Group Ratings

	ADA	ACLU	AFS	LCV	CON	NTU	NFIB	COC	ACU	NTLC	CHC
1998	10	33	22	13	2	50	100	89	64	74	82
1997	10	—	0	—	66	69	—	100	68	—	—

National Journal Ratings

	1997 LIB — 1997 CONS			1998 LIB — 1998 CONS		
Economic	34%	—	65%	38%	—	57%
Social	39%	—	55%	46%	—	53%
Foreign	0%	—	77%	51%	—	36%

Key Votes of the 105th Congress

1. Bal. Budget Amend.	Y	5. Satcher for Surgeon Gen.	Y	9. Chem. Weapons Treaty	N
2. Clinton Budget Deal	Y	6. Highway Set-asides	*	10. Cuban Humanitarian Aid	N
3. Cloture on Tobacco	Y	7. Table Child Gun locks	Y	11. Table Bosnia Troops	Y
4. Education IRAs	Y	8. Ovrd. Part. Birth Veto	Y	12. $ for Test-ban Treaty	Y

Election Results

1998 general	Robert Bennett (R) 316,652	(64%)	($1,546,219)
	Scott Leckman (D) 163,172	(33%)	($265,494)
	Others 15,085	(3%)	
1998 primary	Robert Bennett (R) .... unopposed		
1992 general	Robert Bennett (R) 420,069	(55%)	($3,339,325)
	Wayne Owens (D) 301,228	(40%)	($1,904,750)
	Others 37,182	(5%)	

FIRST DISTRICT

In May 1869, a motley crowd of Irish and Chinese laborers, teamsters, engineers, train crews, officials and guests from California and Salt Lake City gathered in Promontory Point, Utah, to watch the opening of the transcontinental railroad. The Union Pacific train was late and Leland Stanford raised his hammer and totally missed the golden spike, but an alert telegrapher mimicked the sound over the wire and a photographer recorded the scene for posterity: United at last were the civilized East and the mostly untamed West. Here, beyond sight of the snow-capped mountains crossed by the Mormon pioneers, the salt flats still stretch out endlessly; the rail lines now pass north of here, and Promontory Point lies on uninhabited flat land beside the Great Salt Lake. Back in the middle 1980s the lake was rising and threatened to cover the historic site; the state legislature passed a law forbidding it to rise above a certain level and the local county commissioners called for a day of prayer for drought in May 1986; finally, for whatever reason, the lake level fell and the state didn't have to pump water through canals that would have formed a vast new lake in the salt flats to the west.

The 1st Congressional District includes the western half of Utah, from Promontory Point down to the Arizona and Nevada borders near Las Vegas, where the Colorado River flows south through Glen Canyon into Arizona; Zion National Park is in the south, there is mining country in the center and the desert lies west of the lake. But 75% of the people in this district live along the Wasatch Front, a thin strip of land on the east side of the Lake between the salt flats and the Wasatch Mountains. It takes in Brigham City and Logan near the Idaho border, goes south through Ogden, an old working-class town on the Union Pacific line and the nearest station stop to Promontory Point, and then proceeds through a strip of suburbs to the salt flats northwest of downtown Salt Lake City near the airport. The rest of the 1st's voters live in small communities, many entirely Mormon, in central and southern Utah.

The congressman from this district is James Hansen, a Republican first elected in 1980. Hansen grew up in Farmington, Utah, served in the Navy, worked as an insurance agent and head of a land development company. He was elected to the City Council in Farmington, just north of Salt Lake City, and then to the Utah House in 1972, at 40; he was speaker in 1979 and 1980. In 1980 he ran against incumbent Democratic Congressman Gunn McKay and won 52%–48%; except in 1986 and 1990, he has won by wide margins ever since. Hansen, who describes himself as a "common kid from Utah," holds important positions in the House. He is third ranking Republican on the Resources Committee and chairman of the National Parks and Public Lands Subcommittee. He was chairman of the ethics committee in 1997 and 1998, but in 1999 got his wish to be removed. He is on the Armed Services Committee as well.

Hansen has often decried what he considers extremist environmental groups; he called a Sierra Club plan to drain Lake Powell "ridiculous." He worked to complete the Central Utah Project to bring Colorado River water to the Wasatch Front in 1992, and helped crack down on cheap water rates in the Central Valley of California. He favors "multiple uses" of public land, including mining, timber, ranching and grazing. He was outraged when Bill Clinton created the Grand Staircase-Escalante National Monument in September 1996: "Without any public input, without any consideration under the National Environmental Policy Act and any consultation with Utah's elected officials, President Clinton with one stroke of the pen made a decision that will steal over $1 billion from Utah's school children and end up costing the state of Utah over $6.5 billion." In response, he sponsored bills to limit the president's power to create national monuments and to allow the Bureau of Land Management to turn over lands to state governments to manage; he also obtained and made public White House e-mails that showed the administration's dishonesty and campaign gimmickry. The end result was the Utah Land Exchange Act of 1998, which turned over federal lands and cash to Utah in compensation for about half of the national monument lands.

Hansen also worked to produce the national parks law of 1998. His first version was beaten badly, as Clinton threatened a veto and many Republicans opposed it at the behest of environmental groups. Hansen dropped some pet provisions, including the set-aside of the San Rafael Swell canyonlands, and a week later it passed with bipartisan support. The law set up a competitive bidding process for park concessions and kept 80% of concessionaire fees in the local site; it also required a study of whether proposed national parks are worthy of the designation. Other Hansen bills in the 105th Congress included a study of lands east of the 100th parallel for wilderness designation—the same Easterners who support wilderness in the West objected loudly—and a bill to cede to the state of Utah lands surrounding the Goshute Indians' proposed nuclear waste depository so the state could stop shipments. He hammered the National Park Service for leaving Ronald Reagan's name off the George Washington Parkway signs leading to Ronald Reagan Washington National Airport. He called for revision of the 1969 law setting up the EPA, which he charged "simply serves as a tool of the bureaucrats to achieve desired results and predetermined decisions regardless of the public's input." The Clinton Administration, he said, uses EPA requirements to block projects it opposes but ignores them when they would block projects, like Grand Staircase-Escalante, it favors.

On the Armed Services Committee, he fought successfully to save Hill Air Force Base, Utah's number two employer, from the base closing commission in 1995. He has opposed the Clinton "privatization in place" plan designed to keep politically sensitive depot bases open in California and Texas, and has attacked the Pentagon for setting criteria that undercut Hill. "Hill Air Force Base wouldn't be there if it weren't for me and my staff," he said on election night 1998. Hansen is co-chairman of the House Anti-Smoking Caucus. In May 1998 he proposed a tobacco bill with a $1.50 per pack cigarette tax, the provisions sought by former Surgeon General Everett Koop, and with 55% of revenues devoted to lowering the deficit; it did not pass. In July 1998 he came within seven votes of getting the House to eliminate tobacco subsidies. Another Hansen cause: disclosure of the terms of private mortgage insurance, which is required on low-down-payment mortgages but which, as Hansen found out with his Crystal City, Virginia, condominium, is very hard to cancel when the borrower has built up the required equity. Hansen's bill to require disclosure of how to cancel passed the House 421–7 in April 1997; he persuaded Alfonse D'Amato to pilot a similar measure through the Senate, and it became law. "They picked on the wrong guy," Hansen said about his insurers.

In January 1997 Hansen was tapped to be chairman of the House Committee on Standards of Official Conduct. "I've lost out," he said. He had already spent 12 years as a member of the committee (from 1980–92) and refers to its basement meeting room as "the dungeon." But he and ranking Democrat Howard Berman, for months the committee's only members, turned it around from the partisan circus it had been in 1996. After a nine-month moratorium on new complaints, Hansen and Berman came forward with recommendations for reforms. The House accepted this revision in December 1997, including a ban on complaints from non-members. In January 1999 Speaker Dennis Hastert asked Hansen to serve another term. "I told him I served on the committee 12 years before plus the last two years as its chairman. I've paid my debt to society, and it's time to be paroled." His last effort was to repeal the near-total gift ban passed by his former Utah colleague Enid Greene Waldholtz; instead the House voted Senate rules, banning gifts worth more than $50 and more than $100 a year from a single source.

Hansen's energetic Democratic opponent in 1998 spent $178,000 of his own money and, in total, exactly $250 more than the incumbent. It didn't change the result much. Hansen won by the same 68%–30% margin as in 1996.

Cook's Call. *Safe.* In his 19-year tenure, Hansen has had only a handful of close races and is safely settled in this heavily Republican district.

The People: Pop. 1990: 574,205; 15.7% rural; 9.8% age 65 + ; 94.4% White, 0.9% Black, 1.6% Asian, 0.9% Amer. Indian, 2.2% Other; 4.6% Hispanic Origin. Households: 68.2% married couple families; 40.1% married couple fams. w. children; 57.1% college educ.; median household income: $30,563; per capita income: $10,856; median house value: $69,000; median gross rent: $293.

1996 Presidential Vote			1992 Presidential Vote		
Dole (R)	129,273	(59%)	Bush (R)	115,627	(47%)
Clinton (D)	64,104	(29%)	Perot (I)	68,884	(28%)
Perot (I)	22,893	(10%)	Clinton (D)	50,622	(20%)
Others	4,548	(2%)	Others	12,989	(5%)

Rep. James V. Hansen (R)

Elected 1980; b. Aug. 14, 1932, Salt Lake City; home, Farmington; U. of UT, B.A. 1960; Mormon; married (Ann).

Military Career: Navy, 1951–55.

Elected Office: Farmington City Cncl., 1962–72; UT House of Reps., 1972–80, Speaker, 1978–80.

Professional Career: Insurance agent, 1961–80; Land developer, 1970–80.

DC Office: 242 CHOB 20515, 202-225-0453; Fax: 202-225-5857; Web site: www.house.gov/hansen.

District Offices: Ogden, 801-393-8362; St. George, 801-628-1071.

Committees: *Armed Services* (6th of 32 R): Military Procurement; Military Readiness. *Resources* (3d of 28 R): Fisheries Conservation, Wildlife & Oceans; National Parks & Public Lands (Chmn.). *Veterans' Affairs* (13th of 17 R): Benefits.

Group Ratings

	ADA	ACLU	AFS	LCV	CON	NTU	NFIB	COC	ACU	NTLC	CHC
1998	5	7	0	0	23	56	93	100	100	94	100
1997	0	—	13	—	53	54	—	90	91	—	—

National Journal Ratings

	1997 LIB — 1997 CONS			1998 LIB — 1998 CONS		
Economic	14%	—	85%	0%	—	88%
Social	0%	—	90%	12%	—	87%
Foreign	0%	—	88%	0%	—	93%

Key Votes of the 105th Congress

1. Clinton Budget Deal	Y	5. Puerto Rico Sthood. Ref.	N	9. Cut $ for B-2 Bombers	N
2. Education IRAs	Y	6. End Highway Set-asides	Y	10. Human Rights in China	N
3. Req. 2/3 to Raise Taxes	Y	7. School Prayer Amend.	Y	11. Withdraw Bosnia Troops	Y
4. Fast-track Trade	Y	8. Ovrd. Part. Birth Veto	Y	12. End Cuban TV-Marti	N

Election Results

1998 general	James V. Hansen (R)	109,708	(68%)	($291,891)
	Steve Beierlein (D)	49,307	(30%)	($284,627)
	Others	3,070	(2%)	
1998 primary	James V. Hansen (R)	unopposed		
1996 general	James V. Hansen (R)	150,126	(68%)	($274,156)
	Gregory J. Sanders (D)	65,866	(30%)	($72,989)
	Others	3,787	(2%)	

SECOND DISTRICT

The center of Utah and of the Mormon Church is Temple Square, illuminated by 300,000 lights during Christmas week, and nestled beneath the towering, snow-capped mountains that flank Salt Lake City. Here you can find the Mormon Tabernacle, home of the famous choir, and the Temple itself, crowned with the golden angel Moroni. Two long blocks north is the state Capitol, four blocks south is City Hall, and all around are Salt Lake City's impressive skyscrapers. Ironically, Salt Lake City is the least Mormon and most cosmopolitan part of Utah, with the state university and businesses bringing in outsiders. Some think it now has a non-Mormon majority, but most likely it doesn't; it has grown by more than 25% since 1980, and the metro area has 1.2 million people now, but much of that growth is internally generated by Utah's large Mormon families.

Utah's 2d Congressional District, which includes most of Salt Lake County, has somewhat fewer families and children than the other two Utah districts. Its boundaries exclude the western suburbs on the flats out toward the Great Salt Lake, which lean toward the Democrats—an attempt by the Republican legislature to help Republican chances. The 2d has most of Utah's affluent people, living in Salt Lake City and suburbs like East Millcreek, Holladay and Cottonwood, right next to the Wasatch Mountains, which rise at that point to 11,000 feet. It's just a 20-minute drive—well, 30—from offices to ski slopes, as Utah boosters like to tell prospective new residents. The district also includes a string of suburbs south of Salt Lake City—West Jordan, South Jordan, Murray, Sandy, Draper, Riverton, Bluffdale. By national standards, this is a Republican district, but it is the most Democratic of Utah's three House seats, and in fact has been seriously contested in 13 of the last 15 elections.

The congressman from the 2d District is Merrill Cook, a Republican elected in 1996. Cook grew up in Salt Lake City, served as a missionary in Britain, graduated from the University of Utah and Harvard Business School, then worked two years in Cambridge. He returned to Salt Lake City in 1973 and founded Cook Slurry Company, and made millions developing mining explosives. A conservative Republican, Cook was angered when Republican Governor Norman Bangerter raised taxes; in 1988 he put a tax rollback and property tax freeze proposition on the ballot and that same year ran against Bangerter as an independent, finishing third with 21% of the vote. He put two more propositions on the ballot, a removal of the sales tax on food in 1990 and term limits in 1994; the latter was defeated after the legislature passed 12-year limits for state officials. He also ran for governor again in 1992, finishing second to Republican Mike Leavitt with 34% of the vote. In between he ran unsuccessfully for school board, mayor of Salt Lake City and Salt Lake County commissioner. In 1994 he ran as an independent in the 2d District, coming in third with 18%, behind incumbent Democrat Karen Shepherd (36%) and Republican Enid Greene Waldholtz (46%). By early 1995 it seemed Cook's running days were over: he had said he would not run again if he lost, Leavitt had become an exceedingly popular governor, and there seemed no way to oust an attractive Republican like Waldholtz from the 2d District seat.

But Waldholtz turned out to have problems—to say the least. She had run (as Enid Greene) and lost in 1992, spending $446,000; in August 1993 she married Joe Waldholtz, reportedly a rich political operative from Pennsylvania, and in 1994 she spent nearly $2 million, some $1.6 million of it supposedly her own money. She made news in Congress when she got a seat on the Rules Committee and when she announced in March 1995 that she was pregnant. But she could not answer questions about her personal finances and how she had paid for the campaign, and in November 1995 Joe Waldholtz disappeared for several days before turning himself over to the police; she announced she was seeking a divorce. It became clear that he had embezzled the money from her father; she said he had passed it off as his own. Enid Greene—she changed her name back—held a five-hour televised press conference to apologize and answer questions. In March 1996, she finally bowed to pressure from Utah and Washington and announced she would not seek re-election. Joe Waldholtz was charged with bank fraud and falsifying campaign spending reports in May 1996 and pled guilty in June.

Given this opening, Cook ran again despite his pledge. Many Republicans resented Cook's previous independent candidacy, and he got just barely enough votes at the May 1996 party convention to make it onto the primary ballot. His primary opponent, Todd Neilson, a forensic accountant who worked on the case against savings and loan magnate Charles Keating, charged that Cook would cut Social Security; Cook had written his Harvard Business School thesis on how to make Social Security fiscally sound and favored restructuring and portable private pensions. Cook, spending liberally of his own money, just barely beat Neilson, 52%–48%. "To anybody who ever flunked a test or got fired from a job or lost a political race—lost six races— my message is try once more," he said. The Democratic primary winner was Ross Anderson, who opposed the death penalty and said he would vote against the Defense of Marriage Act— a sign of how liberal the Democratic core constituency is in Salt Lake City. In the general election Cook again peppered the district with TV ads and mailings, spending $1 million altogether, $866,000 of it his own. Cook emphasized taxes, Social Security, and the death penalty. He ran ads charging that Anderson once referred to Utahns as murderers for executing a black man and said that Anderson backed same-sex marriage. In the last week Anderson ran a defensive ad, saying he wouldn't go to Congress advocating same-sex marriages; Cook was running ads showing Senator Bob Bennett and former Senator Jake Garn speaking highly of him. Cook won 55%–42%.

In the House Cook has a conservative voting record and almost as stormy a tenure as in his previous stints as a candidate. He got a seat on the Transportation Committee, the only Utahn in either body, and claimed some credit for the transportation bill which increased Utah's funding from $130 million to $205 million. He placed an amendment which gave priority for $1 billion in discretionary funds for Olympics-related projects: Utah is scrambling to widen I-15 before the crowds arrive in 2002. He even supported Salt Lake's light rail, which he used to crusade against: "My job is to get the money. It's the locals' job to decide how to spend it." He worked with others on the Utah delegation to ban the transport of nuclear waste to the Goshute reservation and to amend the IMF funding bill to prohibit aid to Korean semiconductor companies. But he opposed the bill sponsored by Bennett and Chris Cannon to set aside the San Rafael Swell in southern Utah. He predicted Newt Gingrich would not be re-elected speaker (then said he'd vote for him) and voted for the Shays-Meehan campaign finance bill. He voted against fast track and sought rescission of cuts in Medicare home health care. He introduced bills for electronic filing of campaign finance reports and low airline fares for patients flying to federally funded clinical health trials.

Cook prided himself on never missing votes and seldom missing committee hearings: "For 10 years, I fought so hard to get the opportunity to serve. I think I appreciate this office more than most. I love it more than I ever thought I would." He campaigned vigorously for re-election, perhaps too vigorously. The Democratic candidate in 1998 was Lily Eskelsen, a sixth-grade teacher and National Education Association board member, with strong union support. She sounded a note of consensus—"I can give a perspective that's truly missing from politics today, a perspective that you really can sit down with people, bring them together and find real solutions"—but was also a capable negative campaigner: her ads ran pictures of Cook with hair disheveled and face contorted. Cook did not spend his own money on this campaign, and Eskelsen raised and spent almost as much; she was the beneficiary of ads by US Term Limits and the target of ads from the National Rifle Association. September and October polls showed the race within the margin of error. In the last week of the campaign, Cook, enraged that the Republican Party was running ads mentioning Bennett (who was in no trouble) and not him, stormed into Republican headquarters and yelled, "[expletive] the Republican Party! [expletive] Senator Bennett!"

Cook ended up winning by 53%–43%, not quite a landslide, but not as close as expected either; Cook was the first candidate re-elected in this district since 1990. Later in November, Cook's chief of staff and district director were fired—for poor performance and to seek better jobs, Cook said. But one of the staffers sent an e-mail saying, "Merrill has taken up permanent residence in wackoland and we are all in serious jeopardy," and the other told the *Salt Lake Tribune*, "The guy has a grenade in his mouth and is going to pull the pin." Then Cook accused two former chiefs of staff of forging his signature on pay raise forms in May 1997. Then in January 1999 he hired a former Democratic candidate for lieutenant governor who the previous March charged she had been wiretapped; two aides of Congressman Chris Cannon were interviewed by the FBI, but no charges were brought. Cook also has twice been accused of ramming his car into other vehicles (one time into his daughter's boyfriend's car), though no criminal charges were ever filed.

None of this helped Cook's standing with the voters; at the least, he was guilty of poor choice of staff. By March 1999 his job rating was solidly negative, and Jim Matheson, son of the late Democratic Governor Scott Matheson, filed papers to run in the 2d District in 2000. It looks like this district will have another strongly contested race.

Cook's Call. *Competitive.* Cook's well-publicized run-ins, with staff, campaign workers and even a daughter's former boyfriend, have helped to make him a top target. There are rumors that Cook may be challenged in the primary, and it is likely that he will face attorney Jim Matheson, the son of former Democratic Governor Scott Matheson, in November. But Cook still has a couple of advantages. This district, while not overly Republican, has a conservative, Republican edge. And Cook's role on the Transportation Committee has helped him to bring needed federal dollars to this booming city.

The People: Pop. 1990: 574,412; 0.4% rural; 9.4% age 65+; 94.5% White, 0.6% Black, 2.2% Asian, 0.7% Amer. Indian, 1.9% Other; 4.9% Hispanic Origin. Households: 59.3% married couple families; 34.5% married couple fams. w. children; 62.5% college educ.; median household income: $30,960; per capita income: $12,971; median house value: $76,900; median gross rent: $319.

1996 Presidential Vote

Dole (R)	111,166	(47%)
Clinton (D)	96,037	(41%)
Perot (I)	22,143	(9%)
Others	6,619	(3%)

1992 Presidential Vote

Bush (R)	101,169	(38%)
Clinton (D)	81,233	(31%)
Perot (I)	75,921	(29%)

Rep. Merrill Cook (R)

Elected 1996; b. May 6, 1946, Philadelphia, PA; home, Salt Lake City; U. of UT, B.A. 1969, Harvard U., M.B.A. 1971; Mormon; married (Camille).

Professional Career: Mgmt. Consultant & Budget Analyst, Arthur D. Little Inc., 1971–73; Pres. & Founder, Cook Slurry Co., 1973–96.

DC Office: 1431 LHOB 20515, 202-225-3011; Fax: 202-225-5638; Web site: www.house.gov/cook.

District Office: Salt Lake City, 801-524-4394.

Committees: *Banking & Financial Services* (20th of 32 R): Capital Markets, Securities & Government Sponsored Enterprises; Financial Institutions & Consumer Credit. *Science* (17th of 25 R): Space & Aeronautics; Technology. *Transportation & Infrastructure* (26th of 41 R): Aviation; Ground Transportation.

Group Ratings

	ADA	ACLU	AFS	LCV	CON	NTU	NFIB	COC	ACU	NTLC	CHC
1998	15	6	11	8	13	48	100	89	84	84	92
1997	5	—	13	—	37	50	—	80	88	—	—

National Journal Ratings

	1997 LIB — 1997 CONS		1998 LIB — 1998 CONS	
Economic	19%	— 76%	12%	— 85%
Social	10%	— 82%	40%	— 59%
Foreign	0%	— 88%	7%	— 83%

Key Votes of the 105th Congress

1. Clinton Budget Deal	Y	5. Puerto Rico Sthood. Ref.	N	9. Cut $ for B-2 Bombers	N
2. Education IRAs	Y	6. End Highway Set-asides	Y	10. Human Rights in China	N
3. Req. 2/3 to Raise Taxes	Y	7. School Prayer Amend.	Y	11. Withdraw Bosnia Troops	Y
4. Fast-track Trade	N	8. Ovrd. Part. Birth Veto	Y	12. End Cuban TV-Marti	N

Election Results

1998 general	Merrill Cook (R)	93,718	(53%)	($647,249)
	Lily Eskelsen (D)	77,198	(43%)	($677,327)
	Others	6,725	(4%)	
1998 primary	Merrill Cook (R)	unopposed		
1996 general	Merrill Cook (R)	129,963	(55%)	($1,061,793)
	Ross Anderson (D)	100,283	(42%)	($491,738)
	Others	6,075	(3%)	

THIRD DISTRICT

The heartland of the Mormon Church in America is in a geographically isolated valley between 11,000-foot peaks of the Wasatch Range and the shores of Utah Lake. Here is Provo, the home of Brigham Young University, an institution long known for the rigorously conservative views of its faculty, the old-fashioned moral standards it encourages, and its welcoming of technological innovation. The Mormon commonwealth, after all, started off with a terrific shortage of both labor and water and was eager to use technology to make up for this and prosper in this fearsome terrain. Today this is one of America's high-tech centers, the home of WordPerfect and Novell and hundreds of other firms, some fleeing California's high taxes and cultural liberalism.

The 3d Congressional District includes Provo and Utah County and most of the west side of Salt Lake City and its suburb of West Valley. These two urban areas cast more than two-thirds of the district's votes; the rest are cast in towns scattered amid huge mountains, florid rock formations and deep canyons from Wyoming down to the Arizona border. Its northernmost point is in the Wasatch Range, and it includes the depressed uranium country in eastern Utah around Moab and the surreal rock formations of Canyonlands and Capitol Reef National Parks, described by John Wesley Powell in the 19th Century: "Wherever we look there is but a wilderness of rock. Deep gorges, where the rivers are lost below the cliffs and towers and pinnacles; and ten thousand strangely carved forms in every direction; and beyond them, mountains blending with the clouds." Today the area around Moab has one of the nation's premier stretches of whitewater, the famed Slickrock Trail for mountain bikes, dozens of unclimbed cliff faces, tree-lined back-country ski runs and a spidery maze of treacherous Jeep tracks. Politically, Utah County is one of the most heavily Republican areas in the United States, and the 3d District is one of the most Republican districts in the country in presidential elections; Bill Clinton finished a poor third here in 1992 with 22% of the vote in 1992 and lost 58%–29% to Bob Dole in 1996. Republican redistricters for 1992, however, added the Democratic west side of Salt Lake County to make the 2d District more Republican, which strengthened Democrats marginally in the 3d.

The congressman from the 3d District is Chris Cannon, a Republican elected in 1996. Cannon is a great-grandson of Utah's first territorial delegate and counselor to Church President Brigham Young, George Q. Cannon, who had five wives and a lot of progeny. Chris Cannon grew up in Salt Lake City, practiced law, and from 1983–86 worked, sometimes controversially, in the Reagan Interior and Commerce departments, on coal surface mining and other issues. In 1987, with his brother Joe, he purchased and reopened the Geneva Steel plant near Provo, restoring 2,500 jobs. In 1988 they had a dispute about modernizing the plant. In 1990 Chris Cannon was bought out and set up his own venture capital investment firm, which invested in Onyx Graphics (imaging software), Unibase (data processing, data entry, software), Kyzen (environmentally sensitive high-tech cleaning chemicals), Premium Beef of Nebraska (slaughterhouse). He was active in Republican politics, as was Joe, who ran for the Senate in 1992 and lost the primary 51%–49% to Bob Bennett.

In 1996 Chris Cannon ran for the 3d District seat held by Democrat Bill Orton, a conservative Democrat who first won it in 1990 after a fractious Republican primary. In the Republican primary, Cannon faced Tom Draschil, who called Cannon (a backer of Lamar Alexander for president) too moderate; Cannon said that Draschil was an extremist and had a lawn sign backing militia favorite Bo Gritz for president in 1992. Cannon won by only 56%–44%—a sign of how conservative the Republican core vote is here. In the general election, Cannon spent $1.8 million, $1.5 million of it his own money, against Orton's $709,000. He was helped also when in September 1996, speaking in Arizona without consultation with Utah officials (including Orton), Bill Clinton announced that he was establishing a 1.7 million-acre Grand Staircase-Escalante National Monument in southern Utah. This was heartily opposed in the area: much of the land is owned by a state school fund, which wanted to lease it for coal mining, and now would not get the revenue; and locals were busy turning trails into roads which federal officials legally couldn't close. Cannon ran an ad showing himself denim-clad, leading a horse, attacking Clinton, "I feel like I'm back in the 1850s again with the federal government encamped all around us." Orton responded, "It doesn't facilitate working toward solutions to use the rhetoric of a war on government." But he said the designation was "a monumental blunder—pun intended." Polls showed Orton ahead, but the downdraft of the Clinton candidacy was powerful. Orton said that he had never voted a straight-party ticket in his life, but many of his constituents did. Orton carried the Salt Lake County portion, but Cannon won solidly in the Provo area and carried most of the rural counties, winning 51%–47%.

In the House, Cannon got seats on the Resources, Judiciary and Science committees and has a conservative voting record. He continued to attack the national monument, deftly, backing

1612   UTAH

James Hansen's bill to reduce the president's power to make such decisions unilaterally, gaining a consensus for a bill altering its boundaries to exclude a school site and include all of Lost Spring Canyon, suggesting that Clinton had established the monument to benefit his longtime contributors, the Riadys (he said their Indonesia coal mine was the second largest source of "supercompliance" clean coal and the Utah site the first).

Cannon brought together all parties and achieved consensus support for expanding Arches National Park by 3,140 acres; he supported what became the Utah Land Exchange Act of 1998. Cannon got less consensus on his bill to set aside the San Rafael Swell; it was opposed by the Clinton Administration and the 2d District's Merrill Cook. Cook and Cannon also exchanged nasty letters after they were on opposite sides of a transportation bill. Cannon sought to have uranium tailings removed from Moab, not capped as the Nuclear Regulatory Commission proposed. On Judiciary he introduced a bill to ban willful distribution of copyrighted material on the Internet. He got some bad publicity when his chief of staff was sued by another employee for sexual harassment; the man resigned and the case was settled.

Re-election was only a minor problem. Democrats gave up on running a candidate in March 1998. Cannon's only hitch was at the Republican state convention in May, when he narrowly failed to win the 70% needed to avoid a primary. The convention was tilted heavily to the right. "Many of the people who are discontented have taken the Bo Gritz position," Cannon said. His opponent, Jeremy Friedbaum, was a Provo harp maker whose grandfather was a rabbi and who had converted to the LDS Church: "I was bred to be a religious fanatic like a racehorse is bred to run." Friedbaum patterned his campaign after King Benjamin, a Book of Mormon prophet who says he took neither silver nor gold from no man; Cannon won 77%–16%. In the general he faced an Independent American Party candidate who headed the Provo chapter of the John Birch Society, and a Libertarian who in an earlier campaign was arrested for handing out anti-tax leaflets without a permit in front of the Salt Lake City IRS office. Cannon won with 77% of the vote.

Cannon's moment in the spotlight came after the election, in the Judiciary Committee hearings and House floor debate on impeachment, and in the Senate where he was one of the 13 House managers prosecuting the case against the president. As it became clear that the Senate would not vote for removal, Cannon reflected that it was a mistake to release the salacious material in the Starr report. But he argued that it was Clinton who inserted such matters into public discussion, not only in his personal misconduct but in his official acts: "You look at what this president's policy has been from day one. The first thing he did was create a debate about homosexuality, by talking about homosexuals in the military. One of the first things he did was to hire Joycelyn Elders as his surgeon general. The whole point was to have an advocate for weird alternative lifestyles. This administration has had as a policy goal the public discussion of weird sex."

Cook's Call. *Safe.* Although this seat was held by conservative Democrat Bill Orton for six years, it is highly unlikely that this district, one of the most Republican in the nation, will again fall into Democratic hands.

The People: Pop. 1990: 574,233; 22.9% rural; 8.2% age 65 +; 92.7% White, 0.4% Black, 1.9% Asian, 2.6% Amer. Indian, 2.3% Other; 5% Hispanic Origin. Households: 67.5% married couple families; 41.7% married couple fams. w. children; 53.7% college educ.; median household income: $26,570; per capita income: $9,259; median house value: $60,100; median gross rent: $287.

1996 Presidential Vote

Dole (R)	121,472	(58%)
Clinton (D)	61,492	(29%)
Perot (I)	21,425	(10%)
Others	4,456	(2%)

1992 Presidential Vote

Bush (R)	105,836	(46%)
Perot (I)	58,595	(25%)
Clinton (D)	51,574	(22%)
Others	14,245	(6%)

Rep. Chris Cannon (R)

Elected 1996; b. Oct. 20, 1950, Salt Lake City; home, Mapleton; Brigham Young U., B.S. 1974, J.D. 1980; Mormon; married (Claudia).

Professional Career: Practicing atty., 1980–83; Dpty. Assoc. Solicitor, Dept. of Interior, 1983–84, Assoc. Solicitor, 1984–86; Co-owner, Geneva Steel, 1987–90; Founder, Cannon Industries Inc., 1990–96.

DC Office: 118 CHOB 20515, 202-225-7751; Fax: 202-225-5629; Web site: www.house.gov/cannon.

District Office: Provo, 801-379-2500.

Committees: *Judiciary* (16th of 21 R): Courts & Intellectual Property; Immigration & Claims. *Resources* (17th of 28 R): Energy & Mineral Resources; National Parks & Public Lands. *Science* (15th of 25 R): Space & Aeronautics; Technology.

Group Ratings

	ADA	ACLU	AFS	LCV	CON	NTU	NFIB	COC	ACU	NTLC	CHC
1998	5	13	0	8	7	62	100	100	95	91	91
1997	10	—	29	—	70	63	—	90	96	—	—

National Journal Ratings

	1997 LIB — 1997 CONS		1998 LIB — 1998 CONS	
Economic	0%	— 90%	0%	— 88%
Social	39%	— 59%	20%	— 79%
Foreign	12%	— 81%	7%	— 83%

Key Votes of the 105th Congress

1. Clinton Budget Deal	Y	5. Puerto Rico Sthood. Ref.	Y	9. Cut $ for B-2 Bombers	N
2. Education IRAs	Y	6. End Highway Set-asides	*	10. Human Rights in China	N
3. Req. 2/3 to Raise Taxes	Y	7. School Prayer Amend.	Y	11. Withdraw Bosnia Troops	Y
4. Fast-track Trade	Y	8. Ovrd. Part. Birth Veto	Y	12. End Cuban TV-Marti	N

Election Results

1998 general	Chris Cannon (R)	100,830	(77%)	($571,999)
	Will Christensen (AI)	20,720	(16%)	($6,197)
	Kitty K. Burton (Lib)	9,553	(7%)	
1998 primary	Chris Cannon (R)	41,592	(76%)	
	Jeremy Friedbaum (R)	13,283	(24%)	
1996 general	Chris Cannon (R)	106,220	(51%)	($1,826,849)
	Bill Orton (D)	98,178	(47%)	($708,778)
	Others	3,317	(2%)	

VERMONT

Maple syrup, snowy tracks through the woods, tiny clapboard villages, mountains seemingly carpeted in green: this is the image of Vermont. This is an antique state, almost as carefully preserved as its Shelburne Museum, with a barn and jail, railroad station and blacksmith shop, and covered bridge and 37 buildings of folk art. Vermont, wrote native Dorothy Canfield Fisher half a century ago, "represents the past, is a piece of the past in the midst of the present and future." Today, reverence for that past has made Vermont, for many Americans approaching the 21st Century, a guide to a congenial future. Vermont's closeness to nature, the intimacy of its small communities, its 114 covered bridges, its lack of unattractive accoutrements of early 20th Century industrialism, its carefully controlled zoning and abhorrence of glaring advertising and gimcrack commercial structures have all made it a kind of promised land for urban expatriates: The state that missed out on U.S. Steel now produces Ben & Jerry's Ice Cream. By the 1980s, for the first time in nearly 200 years, Vermont became a growth area: in an era when Americans are increasingly ill-served by the rigidities of big organizations and repelled by big-city congestion, small businesses and computers enable more and more Americans to make their livings where they want, which often means Vermont.

Vermont was first settled by flinty Yankees from Connecticut, and showed an independent streak from the beginning. After Ethan Allen's Green Mountain Boys repulsed the British in 1777, this was an independent republic for 14 years, claimed by New York and New Hampshire without avail, their argument settled when Vermont was admitted as the 14th state in 1791. The economy at first was agricultural, as second sons and daughters from small New England farms struggled to scratch out livings from the rocky soil. In time they quit struggling and raised dairy cows instead, producing milk for the masses of New York City. But Vermont developed commerce as well. With its legendary thriftiness, it accumulated capital that, invested wisely, was used to build the solid stone office buildings and courthouses, the thick-timbered houses and gold-topped state Capitol that have remained long after ramshackle wooden buildings of the 19th Century have crumbled into dust. But Vermont never developed labor-intensive industry, and so over the years it exported people, and aged. Today, millions of Americans have Vermont blood—far more than the 600,000 who live here now, many of whom have no Vermont roots at all. Two presidents were born here, but both made their careers elsewhere—Chester Arthur in New York, Calvin Coolidge in Massachusetts—while Vermont made no visible impression on two great writers who lived here for years—Rudyard Kipling and Aleksander Solzhenitsyn. From 1850 to the 1960s, as a result of continuous outmigration, Vermont's population hovered between 300,000 and 400,000.

Since then—perhaps the key date was 1963, when people started outnumbering cows—Vermont has changed rapidly. Its economy has boomed, led by leisure-time industries—ski resorts, summer homes—and IBM, with several big high-tech facilities around the Burlington area on the mostly undeveloped shores of glorious Lake Champlain. Vermont's tradition of cottage industries continues, with knitters seeking to overturn union-inspired federal bans on home production. Home-grown firms started by erstwhile Baby Boom rebels—Ben & Jerry's Ice Cream is the archetype—have flourished. The population rose from 390,000 in 1960 to 444,000 in 1970, 511,000 in 1980 and 591,000 in 1998, and it hasn't been random settlement. While next-door New Hampshire, trumpeting its low taxes and aversion to government, has attracted right-leaning migrants from Massachusetts happy to live in spanking-new developments and ravenous for low taxes, Vermont, proclaiming its desire to preserve the environment and the past, has attracted left-leaning migrants from New York and elsewhere, willing to pay higher taxes and higher prices for the privilege of living in a seemingly pristine setting where

VERMONT   1615

GRAND ISLE

FRANKLIN
• St. Albans

• Newport

ORLEANS

ESSEX

LAMOILLE
• Morrisville

CALEDONIA
• St. Johnsbury

Burlington
•
CHITTENDEN

WASHINGTON ★ Montpelier
• Barre

• Vergennes

ADDISON

• Middlebury

ORANGE

• White River Junction

• Rutland

WINDSOR

• Fair Haven

RUTLAND

U.S. Representative elected at large.

• Springfield

• Bellows Falls

BENNINGTON

WINDHAM

• Bennington

• Brattleboro

N
W ✦ E
S

Miles
0   5   10   15   20

the governor tries to confine Wal-Marts to the existing tiny downtowns. The result has been growth, not as lusty as New Hampshire's but also without as big a recession in the early 1990s. There is high-tech growth around Burlington but also a high dependence on tourism; as Vermont Preservation Trust Director Paul Bruhn says, "At least 30% of our economy is based upon Vermont being Vermont." People throng not only to ski resorts but to the free Bread and Puppet Theater in Glover, near the Canadian border. Vermont's latest celebrity is retired dairy farmer Fred Tuttle, who as a Senate candidate in 1998 at 77 played someone very much like himself in the 1996 independent film *Man With a Plan*.

Public policy has helped keep Vermont Vermont. Back in 1970, Republican Governor Deane Davis, facing a primary challenge, pushed through a sweeping land use law (Act 250) that helped give Vermont its environmental reputation. Housing developments and new ski resorts were required to meet 10 environmental criteria and get the approval of a state commission. Davis also raised more money for education, authorized higher fines for water polluters and liberalized divorce laws. Since then, Vermont has passed its own Clean Air Act that levies a tax on new cars that get less than 20 miles per gallon. With its Yankee heritage, it was the most Republican state in the nation in the 19th Century; in 1936, Vermont and Maine were the only states to resist Franklin Roosevelt's landslide. For three decades thereafter Vermont's Yankee Protestant Republicans outnumbered its French Canadian and Irish Catholic Democrats. But now, with more growth in the last 30 years than in the preceding 110, Vermont is a liberal state, especially on cultural issues. Its legislature was the only one to reject the flag burning amendment, its Supreme Court in November 1998 heard a case arguing for gay marriage, it has a campaign finance law that limits contributions and total spending—the liberal position evidently being that the First Amendment protects obscenity and advocacy of violent overthrow of the government but not ordinary political speech. In 1992 and 1996 Vermont gave Bill Clinton his fifth biggest percentage margin in the country and handily re-elected its Democratic governor and Socialist congressman; its one Republican member of Congress is probably the most liberal Republican in the Senate. Vermont, valuing tradition, has become one of the leaders of America's left.

Governor. Howard Dean grew up in East Hampton, Long Island, and came to Vermont after medical school for his residency; he and his wife started a medical practice in Shelburne in 1981. He was elected to the state legislature in 1982 and lieutenant governor in 1986; when Republican Governor Richard Snelling died suddenly in August 1991, Dean was given the news (while he was treating a patient) that he had become governor. Pleasant and articulate, he is probably one of the four or five most liberal governors on cultural issues, though he likes to say that he is the most fiscally conservative Vermont governor in 40 years.

The major issue in Dean's early tenure was health care. In 1992 he signed a bill to negotiate with insurance companies for universal coverage; but in 1993 his legislation was rejected by the legislature, foreshadowing the fate of the Clinton health care plan in Washington. He moved to promote early childhood development, and pushed a Success By Six prevention program, offering home visits to babies, and claimed that as a result child abuse was down 30%, teen pregnancies down 20% and the child immunization rate was the highest in the country. He worked to subsidize health insurance for children. But Dean is not a believer in giveaway programs: his medical plans all include co-payments, and he sponsored a welfare reform which time-limits and imposes work requirements on recipients and has reduced the caseload.

Dean also shepherded Vermont's June 1997 campaign finance law, which took effect after the November 1998 election. It imposes sliding-scale spending limits on all state candidates, from $2,000 for a state representative from a small district to $16,500 for state senator with the largest, and $2,000 contribution limits; Vermont acted even though the Supreme Court ruled spending limits unconstitutional in 1976 and declined to review that decision in November 1998. Said Dean, "This is one of the areas where the Supreme Court is out of step with what the average person on the street wants." In an effort not to tilt the system too much against challengers, incumbents are allowed to spend only 85% as much. But however much he supports the limits, Dean maneuvered to get around them; in the nine days before the law took effect, he contributed $150,000 from his campaign treasury to the state Democratic Party.

Dean's biggest issue in the late 1990s was education funding. In February 1997 the state Supreme Court declared the state school funding formula unconstitutional. In response Dean and the Democratic legislature passed Act 60, with a statewide property tax providing school districts with $5,010 per student; taxes would be limited to 2% of income for those earning under $75,000. Half the districts would pay more property tax, half less. Districts wishing to raise money beyond that are required to donate a percentage of revenues to the state sharing pool—the shark pool, to Act 60 opponents—which ladels it out to other districts. Said Dean, "Under Act 60, one penny on the property tax raises exactly the same amount of money per child. I think that's fair. Everybody has to play by the same rules." But many strongly opposed the measure, some because it raised taxes, some because of fear of loss of local control; some, like author John Irving, set up private schools.

Act 60 became a major issue in the 1998 election. Vermont along with New Hampshire is the last state to elect its governors every two years, and Dean previously had won with huge percentages—75% in 1992, 69% in 1994, 71% in 1996. His Republican opponent in 1998 was Ruth Dwyer, two-term state legislator from Thetford, who said she was on the side of the "forgotten Vermonter" and wanted to get government out of people's lives. She attacked Act 60, and argued that people earning below $47,000 were doing worse because of it, since they lost state rebates of property taxes. She opposed Dean's proposal to expand child care subsidies to higher-income families: it was against flinty self-reliance. She called for taking money from social programs to build more bridges. She attacked the Act 250 board for squelching development where economically ailing local communities wanted it. She opposed, while Dean favored, teacher tests before certification. It was a frontal attack on Vermont's governance over the past 30 years, and it struck something of a chord. Little known, poorly financed, Dwyer held Dean to a 56%–41% margin—by no means a defeat but far below his previous showings—and Democrats lost 12 seats in the state House, bringing their margin to 77–67–6. Dean ran strongly around Burlington, where middle-income suburbs were big gainers under Act 60; he ran well behind in the Northeast Kingdom, geographically and attitudinally closer to New Hampshire.

In January 1999 Dean proposed only a 3% increase in spending; "What I am trying to do is get the state ready for the next recession." He had become convinced the sharing pool wouldn't work, and asked, "Are there other ways to do equity? I think that's the question." He called for generating higher-paying jobs and cutting the state income tax. He said U.S. House Republicans were "unfit to govern" because they supported impeachment. Earlier in the decade, Dean traveled around the country and was even mentioned as a presidential candidate; in January 1998 he said he would not run because his children were still in school and a poll showed most Vermonters were against the idea. Dwyer announced in February 1999 that she would run again, and said she would raise more money; will she challenge the campaign finance law? Dean said he would decide whether to run again in January 2000. Other possible Democratic candidates include Lieutenant Governor Douglas Racine and legislative leaders Michael Obuchowski and Peter Shumlin. Dean seems unlikely to run against Senator Jim Jeffords in 2000; in 1999 he said, "I certainly am going to encourage Democrats to run for the seat. But Jim and I are very good friends, and I think he's done a great job for the state."

Cook's Call. *Safe.* Although Dean is up every two years, he has won re-election easily since he assumed office in 1991. It is unlikely that Republicans will be able to field a competitive candidate here.

Senior Senator. Patrick Leahy has held public office for most of his adult life. He grew up in Burlington, went to Georgetown Law School, then returned home to Burlington to practice law. He was elected Chittenden County state's attorney in 1966, at 26, and, after eight years in that post—and few public officials are scrutinized as closely as a local prosecutor—he was elected to the U.S. Senate at 34, the only Democratic senator elected in Vermont history. Now he is in his third decade in the Senate and his second stint in the minority party.

Leahy is ranking Democrat on the Judiciary Committee and was formerly chairman of Agriculture; he also serves on Appropriations. A gadgeteer and fine amateur photographer, he was one of the first senators to go online and use the Internet; early on he conducted town meetings over the Internet and is known in some quarters as a "cyber-Senator." He was named the number one "net-friendly" member of Congress by *Yahoo! Internet Life* magazine and commended for one of the 12 best Capitol Hill Websites by the Congressional Management Foundation. He has co-sponsored bills to remove export controls on encryption and has opposed the Clinton Administration proposal to provide law enforcement agencies with encryption codes. He was the Senate's lead opponent of the Communications Decency Act, which was later declared unconstitutional. He sponsored a 1996 law to update the Freedom of Information Act to provide online access to government documents. He has been concerned about medical privacy for some time, and led the fight to repeal portions of the 1996 health care law assigning medical identification numbers, and has sponsored a bill to allow individual access to and control of medical records, and to require law enforcement officials to get search warrants to inspect them. He co-sponsored with Orrin Hatch the Digital Millennium Copyright law, passed to comply with the WIPO treaty; with Jon Kyl the law making the theft of personal identification information a crime; and with Mike DeWine a Crime Identification Technology Act. He and Hatch also pushed through a Y2K bill in October 1998 and sponsored a satellite TV bill which would allow satellite services to transmit local stations' broadcasts.

Another Leahy cause has been the elimination of land mines. Since 1989, he has been crusading against the export and use of landmines, which are easy and cheap to implant yet difficult and expensive to remove, and which injure thousands of civilians long after hostilities have ended. In 1992 he got a one-year moratorium on U.S. export of landmines, since renewed; in 1994 he got the United Nations to approve unanimously their eventual elimination. In 1997 he and Chuck Hagel moved to support the treaty ban worked out in Ottawa; but the Clinton Administration, worried especially about U.S. forces in Korea, refused to support a total ban. Still, Leahy kept working to aid land mine victims, to deactivate the thousands of land mines still active in many parts of the world and to find alternatives for them, and he got a commitment from the White House and Pentagon to support the Ottawa treaty by 2006. He helped pass 1996 and 1998 laws banning loans and gifts to police forces that have records of human rights violations. He sponsored a $50 million program to control global transmission of communicable diseases. On foreign issues he tends to stand to the left of the Senate: he was one of three senators to vote against authorization of missile defense in March 1999 and has called for an end to the travel ban that prevents Americans from spending dollars in Cuba.

Leahy did yeoman work on the Agriculture Committee in the enactment of the Freedom to Farm Act in 1996. Working with Republican Richard Lugar—whose Indiana like Leahy's Vermont has not been a major beneficiary of farm subsidies—Leahy supported phasing them out over seven years. In return, he worked hard shaping the bill's conservation provisions and also got the Northeast Dairy Compact, allowing a commission to set milk prices in the six New England states. Separately the Senate passed Leahy's Northern Forests bill, to protect privately owned New England and Upstate New York forests; as a result privately owned forests have been set aside for preservation in a belt from Maine to Upstate New York. He got approval of a compact allowing nuclear waste from Vermont and Maine to be sent to Sierra Blanca, Texas, near the Rio Grande. He has worked to clean up Lake Champlain. In February 1998 he slipped into the Sea Grant College program a provision declaring Champlain one of the Great Lakes; the Michigan delegation squawked, and a bill passed in March revoked the designation but continued the Champlain research funds.

Leahy's overall voting record is quite liberal, except on some cultural issues. On the Judiciary Committee he has led the move to confirm Clinton's judicial appointments; he made some progress in 1998, but not in early 1999. He successfully moved to get rid of the $1 per-person border crossing fee in the 1996 Immigration Act and with Spencer Abraham of Michigan got a postponement of the requirement for increased documentation of travelers coming in over the Canadian border. His motion in May 1998 to eliminate the cap on tobacco companies' liability passed 61–37, but effectively killed John McCain's tobacco bill, since the cap was the linchpin for tobacco companies' support and Republicans were opposed to the amendment's tax increases. He sponsored the 1998 Curt Flood Act eliminating the exemption from antitrust laws of major league baseball, but not the minors. On impeachment he was a vocal defender of Bill Clinton and derider of the House managers' charges, and was the Democratic senator presiding over Monica Lewinsky's testimony.

To all this Leahy brings a quiet, thoughtful temperament and a puckish sense of humor, part of the Yankee heritage of Vermont, though his Irish and Italian ethnic origin is certainly not standard Yankee. He is a fine amateur photographer, who has taken pictures of presidents and land mine victims, foreign countries and Vermont; he is a big fan of the Grateful Dead and a Batman buff who had a bit part in the movie *Batman and Robin*. His standing in Vermont has been strong over the years: he narrowly survived the Republican sweep in 1980 and beat popular Governor Richard Snelling 63%–35% in 1986. In 1992, against Republican state Treasurer Jim Douglas, who attacked him for voting for the congressional pay raise and for the loss of dairy jobs, he won 54%–43%—a decisive margin, but no landslide.

In 1998 his re-election campaign took another turn. Running for the Republican nomination was Massachusetts businessman Jack McMullen, who a year earlier established residence in his Bennington County second home and spent $475,000 on his primary race. But John O'Brien, filmmaker, Democrat, who was seeking publicity for his 1996 film *A Man with a Plan*, in which then 77-year-old dairy farmer Fred Tuttle runs for Congress, decided life would imitate art. "I spend all my time in the barn. I'd just like to spend a little time in the House," said Tuttle in his barely comprehensible accent. O'Brien got Tuttle to run in the Republican primary; he promised to spend $16 on his campaign and called McMullen a "flatlander." With generous free publicity Tuttle won the primary 55%–45%. Tuttle was not the kind of candidate likely to be funded by the national Republican party. Of Leahy, he said, "I like Pat. He's a smart man, and he's done a good job." His wife said, "I hope they have more sense than to vote for him." In October 1998, when *A Man With a Plan* was aired on PBS, Leahy had dinner at the Tuttles' home and contrasted this contest with the negative campaigns being waged elsewhere. "I had expected an opponent with deep pockets, not someone with holes in their pockets," Leahy said. Leahy won 72%–22%, after having spent less than in 1992 or 1986.

Junior Senator. Jim Jeffords was elected to the House in 1974 and to the Senate in 1988, and over those years has compiled one of the most liberal voting records of any Republican. He grew up in Rutland, son of a Vermont chief justice, went to Yale, served in the Navy, went to Harvard Law School and then returned to Shrewsbury in the Green Mountains to practice law. He was elected state senator in 1966, at 32, and then state attorney general in 1968 and 1970. In 1974, he was elected to the House and in 1988, when Senator Robert Stafford retired, to the Senate. There he has a record somewhat to the left of midpoint of the Senate, especially on cultural issues, and has usually voted more often with Democrats than any other Republican senator. In the Clinton years he voted for family and medical leave, motor voter, national service, the Brady bill and the 1994 crime package, despite Vermont's anti-gun control senti-ment; in July 1993 he announced he was supporting the not-yet-written Clinton health care plan—the only Republican member of Congress who ever did. He pushed for more funding for the National Endowment for the Arts and raising the minimum wage; he supports abortion rights, favors banning discrimination against gays and lesbians. As chairman of the D.C. Sub-committee on Appropriations in the 104th Congress, Jeffords opposed the Republican plan for a limited number of school vouchers for students in the District, thus sentencing them to continue in the dreadful D.C. public schools, which with he must be familiar—he volunteers in the Everyone Wins! program in Capitol Hill schools to encourage kids to read.

In 1997 Jeffords became chairman of the Labor and Human Resources Committee. Some conservatives wanted to substitute the less senior and more conservative Dan Coats; but Majority Leader Trent Lott, desirous of party unity and part of a singing quartet with Jeffords, Larry Craig and John Ashcroft, persuaded Coats not to run. Of his approach, Jeffords said, "The country demands that we be bipartisan. They're more involved in solving difficult situations we have for individuals, more than they are with political posturing and all. So, that's me. I'm independent, these are all well-known facts." But he also was careful not to block Republican initiatives: "I have told the members if we disagree, I won't hold up legislation that all Republicans except me want." His own stated policy goals seem almost quixotic: raising dollar limits on health insurance policies (he tried and failed to do that in the 1996 health care portability law), increasing the percentage of the nation's workforce covered by company pensions, getting more people health insurance.

But as chairman he took the lead on the Republican-backed Teamwork for Employees and Managers Act to allow worker-management consultation, vehemently opposed by labor unions. On health care he promised "to go slow" on regulating managed care and said that micromanagement, such as the 48-hour maternity stay he backed in 1996, should be approached with caution. He promised to move ahead on OSHA reform, a Republican goal. He worked on re-authorization of the bipartisan IDEA special education bill, which passed in May 1997, and worked on re-authorizing the Higher Education Act in 1998, plus updates of laws on vocational education, rehabilitation services, workforce investment, reading excellence, charter schools and Jeffords's community learning centers. He sponsored the bipartisan FDA reform to speed up approvals of drugs and medical devices. He supported the Kennedy-Hatch child health insurance bill. In 1999 he said he would seek an overhaul of the Elementary and Secondary Education Act, a bipartisan HMO bill (he said, "You cannot simply sue your way to better health,") and a tobacco bill giving the FDA the authority to regulate tobacco. He worked with Edward Kennedy on a bill that would allow disabled individuals to return to work without losing their Medicaid or Medicare benefits, which unanimously passed the Senate in June 1999.

Jeffords was obviously uncomfortable with impeachment, and went back and forth on some procedural issues. In the end, he voted to acquit on both counts. Later that month, when Juanita Broaddrick charged Clinton with sexual assault, Jeffords said on Vermont radio, "I think that the kind of things like that are supposedly private matters and should stay that way. I don't know why it wouldn't be a private matter." The next day he apologized and said, "Juanita Broaddrick's statements are disturbing and should be taken seriously, as any claim of rape should be."

Jeffords also tends to Vermont issues and his own special causes. In 1996 he maintained support for Vermont wind and solar energy projects, and he passed an amendment to increase food stamp eligibility for recipients of federal heating assistance. A history buff, he had a bill to catalogue and study unprotected Civil War sites, has sponsored a Revolutionary War and War of 1812 historic preservation act, and backs an historic corridor along the New York-Vermont border. He saw that the May 1998 transportation bill included money for the Missisquoi Bay Bridge and his National Historic Covered Bridge Preservation Act.

Jeffords's toughest hurdle in winning the seat in 1988 was the Republican primary, in which a conservative opponent attacked him on gun control, abortion, and church and family issues; Jeffords won 61%–39%. In 1994 his serious competition was in the general. State Senator Jan Backus clearly benefited from being a woman in this culturally liberal state and, though little known and not well financed, held Jeffords to a 50%–41% win. Jeffords's seat comes up in 2000, and the question in early 1999 was whether he would be opposed by Congressman-at-Large Bernie Sanders, a socialist who runs as an independent. Among the names mentioned for Democratic challengers, were Backus and state Senators Peter Shumlin and Elizabeth Ready. Auditor Ed Flanagan, who is openly gay and said he hoped to raise money from "gay and Irish friends," announced in March 1999 that he was running against Jeffords, but said he would drop out if Sanders runs. In a February 1999 poll, Jeffords led Sanders 42%–37%, not a statistically significant margin. Sanders has said he will not run unless he is treated like a Democrat in seniority in the Senate, as he has been in the House; Democratic Senatorial Campaign Committee Chairman Bob Torricelli said this would not be a problem.

Cook's Call. *Potentially Competitive.* If Jeffords gets a competitive contest it will be at the hands of Representative Bernie Sanders. But, if Sanders decides to stay in the House, Jeffords should not have too much trouble winning another term.

Representative-At-Large. Vermont's single House member is Bernie Sanders, a Socialist elected as an independent since 1990 but treated as a Democrat in the House. Sanders grew up in Flatbush, Brooklyn, the son of a paint salesman, became involved in radical politics at the University of Chicago, then came to Vermont as part of the hippie invasion of 1968. His rumpled, tieless, sincere persona helped him win election as mayor of Burlington in 1981 by 10 votes, after losing four statewide races. There he governed ably for eight years, using the city's prosperity to start a municipal day-care center, expand low- and moderate-income housing, put a pollution control facility on Lake Champlain and switch the tax base from property to hotel and restaurant fees and a utility tax on companies using certain public facilities. In 1988, when Congressman Jim Jeffords ran for the Senate, Sanders ran for the House and lost to Republican Peter Smith. Two years later he ran again and reversed the result by capitalizing on Smith's support of the 1990 budget summit agreement and his vote for the ban on semi-automatic weapons. The National Rifle Association came out against Smith, and Sanders' opposition to gun control—Vermont is the only state with no limits on gun ownership at all— helped this urban-based Socialist carry 227 of Vermont's 251 cities and towns, and three gores and one grant. Sanders became only the third Socialist elected to the House, after Victor Berger of Milwaukee (1911–13, 1923–29) and Meyer London of Manhattan's Lower East Side (1915–23), and the only Socialist elected by an entire state.

Sanders's Socialist label doesn't matter much in the House. Initially Democrats balked at accepting him in their caucus, but they have granted him seniority as a Democrat since 1991; when a Democrat had the effrontery to run against him in 1996, none less than George Stephanopoulos came to Burlington to speak at a Sanders fundraiser. House Democrats gave him the ranking minority position on a Government Reform subcommittee in 1997 over the objections of Elijah Cummings and, when a Banking subcommittee ranking position opened up in November 1997, he got that over the claims of Carolyn Maloney. Sanders adds to a heavily liberal voting record his own particular stamp. He formed a Progressive Caucus, with 58 members in the 104th Congress, with what is for the moment a quixotic agenda: progressive tax reform, a Canadian-style single-payer health care system, a 50% cut in military spending over five years, a national energy policy and—here Vermont speaks—support for family farms (including opposition to bovine growth hormone). He decries the tumbling of the barriers to international capital movement, and says the world economy is growing more slowly than at any time in the last 30 years; he joined conservative Republicans in voting against IMF funding. Why has he not become a Democrat? "Here is the Democratic Party, a party which prided itself for 60 years on defending the interests of working people and the poor, making a radical shift to the right, and accepting policy which Richard Nixon would have summarily rejected," writes Sanders in his biography, *Outsider in the House.*

But Sanders has also been a practical and sometimes successful legislator, gaining Republican allies in targeting what they consider corporate welfare. With Chris Smith of New Jersey, for example, he passed an amendment barring Defense spending for defense contractor mergers ("payoffs for layoffs"), and he passed another barring defense spending on bonuses for defense contractor executives. With Budget Chairman John Kasich, he got the House to pass a three-year phaseout of OPIC, which provides risk insurance for foreign investments. With Gerald Solomon, whose Upstate New York district borders Vermont, he battled Wisconsin's Steven Gunderson who was trying to end the milk marketing system; and he was the House's leading backer of the Northeast Dairy Compact, which Senator Patrick Leahy got into the 1996 Freedom to Farm Act; he backed the Vermont-Maine-Texas compact to send nuclear waste to Sierra Blanca, Texas. He got Majority Leader Dick Armey to agree to a vote in the 105th Congress

1622 VERMONT

banning "gag rules," HMO directives to doctors not to mention procedures not covered by insurance. He has passed amendments requiring U.S. representatives on the IMF to insist on workers' rights (but none ever has voted against a loan for this reason, he notes) and banning import of goods made by indentured child labor. He co-sponsored the 1998 law criminalizing identity fraud. He has called for a "Manhattan-type project on Gulf war illness," and for satellite TV subscribers to receive local stations.

Sanders was re-elected 58%–31% in 1992, and considered running against Republican Senator Jim Jeffords in 1994, but decided not to. In 1994, after voting for the assault weapons ban and the crime bill with its gun control provisions, Sanders was opposed by the National Rifle Association-backed Vermont Sportsmen's Coalition. Sanders outspent state Senator John Carroll, but won by only 50%–47%. His gun control stand evidently hurt in rural areas; Sanders carried only 136 cities and towns. In 1996 Republican state Senator Susan Sweetser was expected to be a strong challenger. But the candidacy of moderate Democrat Jack Long, an attorney and former state commissioner of environmental conservation, may have hurt her more than Sanders; Sanders spent $942,000 and beat Sweetser 55%–33%. In pro-incumbent 1998, against a low-spending Republican and with no Democratic nominee, Sanders did better than ever, 63%–33%.

Sanders has promised to work for a higher minimum wage and to double Pell grants, to oppose "bloated" weapons spending and corporate welfare. He fiercely opposed Social Security privatization and the Medicare commission's recommended co-payments for home health care. In early 1999 Sanders was giving thought to running against Jeffords. He said that he would have to be given assurances that he would be treated like a Democrat in seniority and chairmanships, as he has been in the House; Democratic Senatorial Campaign Committee Chairman Bob Torricelli said he thought that would be no problem.

Cook's Call. *Safe.* There is strong speculation that Sanders will challenge Republican Senator Jim Jeffords in 2000. If so, this At-large District will be heavily contested. The Democratic nature of the state gives Democrats an early advantage in an open seat situation, but a moderate Republican like Jeffords (who held this seat from 1975 to 1989) could have a solid shot here. If Sanders stays put, he is unlikely to face a serious challenge.

Presidential politics. James A. Farley had a good laugh on Vermont in 1936 when he updated an adage to say "As goes Maine, so goes Vermont." But today's Vermont, liberal on cultural and foreign issues, not tremendously conservative on economics, has little use for conservative Republicans and seems solidly Democratic. Back in 1980, Ronald Reagan got his seventh lowest percentage here and John Anderson his best, 15%; in 1984 and 1988 Vermont was more Democratic than the nation, and in 1992 and 1996 it gave Bill Clinton his fifth largest percentage margins.

The Vermont presidential primary, abolished for 1992, reappeared in 1996. Richard Lugar made this state his last stand, hoping that Vermont's traditions of thoughtful town meeting discourse would enable him to deliver his message. Not enough, it seems: Bob Dole won with 40%, Pat Buchanan had 17%, Steve Forbes had 16%, and Lugar 14%, ahead of Lamar Alexander with 11%.

The People: Est. Pop. 1998: 590,883; Pop. 1990: 562,758, up 5% 1990–1998. 0.2% of U.S. total, 49th largest; 67.9% rural. Median age: 35.7 years. 12.3% 65 years and over. 98.5% White, 0.4% Black, 0.5% Asian, 0.4% Amer. Indian, 0.1% Other; 0.7% Hispanic Origin. Households: 56.4% married couple families; 28.1% married couple fams. w. children; 46.2% college educ.; median household income: $29,792; per capita income: $13,527; 69% owner occupied housing; median house value: $95,500; median monthly rent: $378. 3.4% Unemployment. 1998 Voting age pop.: 448,000. 1998 Turnout: 220,991; 49% of VAP. Registered voters (1998): 402,603; no party registration.

Political Lineup: Governor, Howard Dean (D); Lt. Gov., Douglas A. Racine (D); Secy. of State, James Milne (R); Atty. Gen., William H. Sorrell (D); Treasurer, James H. Douglas (R); State Senate, 30 (17 D, 13 R); Majority Leader, Dick McCormack (D); State House, 150 (77 D, 67 R, 2 I, 4 Progressive); House Speaker, Michael Obuchowski (D). Senators, Patrick Leahy (D) and James M. Jeffords (R). Representative, 1 I at large.

Elections Division: 802-828-2464; **Filing Deadline for U.S. Congress:** July 17, 2000.

1996 Presidential Vote

Clinton (D)	137,894	(53%)
Dole (R)	80,352	(31%)
Perot (I)	31,024	(12%)
Others	9,179	(4%)

1992 Presidential Vote

Clinton (D)	133,592	(46%)
Bush (R)	88,122	(30%)
Perot (I)	65,991	(23%)

1996 Republican Presidential Primary

Dole (R)	23,419	(40%)
Buchanan (R)	9,730	(17%)
Forbes (R)	9,066	(16%)
Lugar (R)	7,881	(14%)
Alexander (R)	6,145	(11%)
Others	1,872	(3%)

GOVERNOR

Gov. Howard Dean (D)

Assumed office, Aug. 1991, term expires Jan. 2001; b. Nov. 17, 1948, New York, NY; home, Burlington; Yale U., B.A. 1977, Albert Einstein Col. of Medicine, M.D. 1978; Congregationalist; married (Judith).

Elected Office: VT House of Reps, 1982–86; VT Lt. Gov., 1986–91.

Professional Career: Practicing physician, 1981–91; Chmn., Natl. Govs. Assn., 1994–95; Chmn., Dem. Govs. Assn., 1997.

Office: Pavilion State Office Bldg., 109 State St., Montpelier, 05609, 802-828-3333; Web site: www.state.vt.us.

Election Results

1998 gen.	Howard Dean (D)	121,425	(56%)
	Ruth Dwyer (R)	89,726	(41%)
	Others	6,969	(3%)
1998 prim.	Howard Dean (D)	16,798	(94%)
	Other	1,150	(6%)
1996 gen.	Howard Dean (D)	179,544	(71%)
	John L. Gropper (R)	57,161	(22%)
	Others	17,943	(7%)

1624 VERMONT

SENATORS

Sen. Patrick Leahy (D)

Elected 1974, seat up 2004; b. Mar. 31, 1940, Montpelier; home, Burlington; St. Michael's Col., B.A. 1961, Georgetown U., J.D. 1964; Catholic; married (Marcelle).

Elected Office: VT St. Atty., Chittenden Cnty., 1966–74.

Professional Career: Practicing atty., 1964–74.

DC Office: 433 RSOB, 20510, 202-224-4242; Web site: www.senate.gov/~leahy.

State Offices: Burlington, 802-863-2525; Montpelier, 802-229-0569.

Committees: *Agriculture, Nutrition & Forestry* (2d of 8 D): Forestry, Conservation & Rural Revitalization; Research, Nutrition & General Legislation (RMM). *Appropriations* (4th of 13 D): Commerce, Justice, State & the Judiciary; Defense; Foreign Operations & Export Financing (RMM); Interior; VA, HUD & Independent Agencies. *Judiciary* (RMM of 8 D): Antitrust, Business Rights & Competition; Criminal Justice Oversight; The Constitution, Federalism & Property Rights.

Group Ratings

	ADA	ACLU	AFS	LCV	CON	NTU	NFIB	COC	ACU	NTLC	CHC
1998	90	67	100	100	30	14	33	56	12	7	9
1997	80	—	78	—	25	26	—	60	13	—	—

National Journal Ratings

	1997 LIB	—	1997 CONS		1998 LIB	—	1998 CONS
Economic	71%	—	25%		83%	—	10%
Social	63%	—	36%		60%	—	38%
Foreign	92%	—	0%		95%	—	0%

Key Votes of the 105th Congress

1. Bal. Budget Amend.	N	5. Satcher for Surgeon Gen.	Y	9. Chem. Weapons Treaty	Y
2. Clinton Budget Deal	Y	6. Highway Set-asides	Y	10. Cuban Humanitarian Aid	Y
3. Cloture on Tobacco	Y	7. Table Child Gun locks	Y	11. Table Bosnia Troops	Y
4. Education IRAs	N	8. Ovrd. Part. Birth Veto	Y	12. $ for Test-ban Treaty	Y

Election Results

1998 general	Patrick Leahy (D)	154,567	(72%)	($1,014,751)
	Fred H. Tuttle (R)	48,051	(22%)	
	Others	11,418	(5%)	
1998 primary	Patrick Leahy (D)	18,643	(97%)	
	Others	647	(3%)	
1992 general	Patrick Leahy (D)	154,762	(54%)	($1,202,445)
	James H. Douglas (R)	123,854	(43%)	($195,737)
	Others	7,123	(2%)	

Sen. James M. Jeffords (R)

Elected 1988, seat up 2000; b. May 11, 1934, Rutland; home, Shrewsbury; Yale U., B.S. 1956, Harvard U., LL.B. 1962; Congregationalist; married (Elizabeth).

Military Career: Navy, 1956–59, Naval Reserves, 1959–90.

Elected Office: VT Senate, 1966–68; VT Atty. Gen., 1968–72; U.S. House of Reps. 1974–88.

Professional Career: Law clerk, 1962–63; Practicing atty., 1963–69, 1973–75; Shrewsbury Repub. Party Chmn., 1963–74; Town Agent, Grand Juror, 1964.

DC Office: 728 HSOB, 20515, 202-224-5141; Web site: www.senate.gov/~jeffords.

State Offices: Burlington, 802-658-6001; Montpelier, 802-223-5273; Rutland, 802-773-3875.

Committees: *Aging (Special)* (2d of 11 R). *Finance* (9th of 11 R): Health Care; International Trade; Social Security & Family Policy. *Health, Education, Labor & Pensions* (Chmn. of 10 R): Aging; Employment, Safety & Training. *Veterans' Affairs* (4th of 7 R).

Group Ratings

	ADA	ACLU	AFS	LCV	CON	NTU	NFIB	COC	ACU	NTLC	CHC
1998	55	57	44	50	36	32	89	89	24	32	9
1997	45	—	25	—	61	57	—	100	21	—	—

National Journal Ratings

	1997 LIB — 1997 CONS			1998 LIB — 1998 CONS		
Economic	49%	—	50%	55%	—	43%
Social	64%	—	29%	60%	—	38%
Foreign	73%	—	19%	88%	—	11%

Key Votes of the 105th Congress

1. Bal. Budget Amend.	Y	5. Satcher for Surgeon Gen.	Y	9. Chem. Weapons Treaty	Y
2. Clinton Budget Deal	Y	6. Highway Set-asides	Y	10. Cuban Humanitarian Aid	Y
3. Cloture on Tobacco	Y	7. Table Child Gun locks	Y	11. Table Bosnia Troops	Y
4. Education IRAs	N	8. Ovrd. Part. Birth Veto	N	12. $ for Test-ban Treaty	Y

Election Results

1994 general	James M. Jeffords (R) 106,505	(50%)	($1,174,973)	
	Jan Backus (D) 85,868	(41%)	($308,069)	
	Gavin T. Mills (I) 12,465	(6%)		
	Others 6,834	(3%)		
1994 primary	James M. Jeffords (R) .... unopposed			
1988 general	James M. Jeffords (R) 163,183	(70%)	($876,877)	
	Bill Gray (D) 71,460	(30%)	($549,908)	

REPRESENTATIVE

Rep. Bernard Sanders (I)

Elected 1990; b. Sept. 8, 1941, New York, NY; home, Burlington; U. of Chicago, B.A. 1964; Jewish; married (Jane).

Elected Office: Burlington Mayor, 1981–89.

Professional Career: Writer; Dir., Amer. People's History Soc.; Lecturer, Harvard U., 1989; Prof., Hamilton Col., 1989–90.

DC Office: 2202 RHOB, 20515, 202-225-4115; Fax: 202-225-6790; Web site: www.house.gov/bernie.

District Office: Burlington, 802-862-0697.

Committees: *Banking & Financial Services* (1st of 1 I): Domestic & International Monetary Policy; General Oversight & Investigations. *Government Reform* (1st of 1 I): National Economic Growth, Natural Resources & Regulatory Affairs; National Security, Veterans' Affairs & Intl. Relations.

Group Ratings

	ADA	ACLU	AFS	LCV	CON	NTU	NFIB	COC	ACU	NTLC	CHC
1998	100	94	100	100	48	21	0	18	8	3	0
1997	100	—	100	—	8	29	—	20	12	—	—

National Journal Ratings

	1997 LIB — 1997 CONS			1998 LIB — 1998 CONS		
Economic	93%	—	0%	72%	—	23%
Social	85%	—	0%	93%	—	0%
Foreign	64%	—	33%	64%	—	31%

Key Votes of the 105th Congress

1. Clinton Budget Deal	N	5. Puerto Rico Sthood. Ref.	Y	9. Cut $ for B-2 Bombers	Y
2. Education IRAs	N	6. End Highway Set-asides	N	10. Human Rights in China	Y
3. Req. 2/3 to Raise Taxes	N	7. School Prayer Amend.	N	11. Withdraw Bosnia Troops	N
4. Fast-track Trade	N	8. Ovrd. Part. Birth Veto	N	12. End Cuban TV-Marti	Y

Election Results

1998 general	Bernard Sanders (I)	136,403	(63%)	($529,499)
	Mark Candon (R)	70,740	(33%)	($103,631)
	Others	7,990	(4%)	
1998 primary	Bernard Sanders (I)	unopposed		
1996 general	Bernard Sanders (I)	140,678	(55%)	($942,438)
	Susan W. Sweetser (R)	83,021	(33%)	($572,021)
	Jack Long (D)	23,830	(9%)	($8,504)
	Others	7,177	(3%)	

VIRGINIA

In Virginia traditions endure. Through nearly 400 years of history, Virginians have honored, and sometimes been fixated by, traditions going back to the Revolution and before. For half a century Virginia has been growing lustily, but the first state in the nation to elect a black governor still hews to a course close to its roots. In the first years after World War II, Virginia's growth came mainly from an expanding government, but in recent decades it has come more from a vibrant private sector. The first Virginia was a commonwealth ruled by a landed gentry which was, in the words of historian David Hackett Fischer, "elitist and libertarian." From the tobacco-growing counties emerged in the 1770s a group of leaders—George Washington, Patrick Henry, Thomas Jefferson, Richard Henry Lee, James Madison, James Monroe—who in learning, wisdom and strength of character, equal any such group from any similarly sized polity since Periclean Athens or republican Rome. They were slaveholders who insisted on liberty, armed men living on the marches of civilization who insisted on the rule of law, believers in racial inequality who set forth principles of equality to form the basis of a non-racist society. The Virginia they led into the American Revolution was not only the most populous and richest of the 13 colonies, it also was the indispensable creator of the Republic and the Constitution that has held together the world's greatest democracy.

After the Revolutionary War, gentry control continued even as Virginia was eclipsed in population and wealth by Pennsylvania and New York and, its tobacco fields all but exhausted, became a breeding ground for slaves. But Virginia had two more great heroes, Robert E. Lee and Stonewall Jackson, both of whom reluctantly and brilliantly fought for their state rather than their country. The state's leadership class was impoverished and embittered by the Civil War, so much of which was fought on Virginia soil. Industrialization was haphazard: Railroads were constructed to ship cotton up from the South and coal east to the seaports; textile mills were built in Southside towns and tobacco factories in Richmond; the giant Newport News Shipbuilding & Drydock Company was built by railroad magnate Collis Huntington.

But most of Virginia remained agricultural, sunk in a low-wage economy and ruled by a local gentry who had become a small class of landowners, bankers and lawyers worshipping their Revolutionary past and their Lost Cause. They were pessimists, looking not for economic growth but for stability, bent on maintaining Virginia's segregation and content with its second-class economy, determined that the poor masses not use government to pillage the rich as Yankee troops once had done. County courthouse organizations became the political machine of Harry Byrd, who ran Virginia politics from 1925, when he was elected governor, until 1965, when he retired from the Senate. In national politics, this machine lost battles more often than Lee lost on the battlefield, and less gallantly. But the machine succeeded in keeping most vestiges of the welfare state and racial equality out of Virginia, to the point of closing public schools in the 1950s rather than obeying federal court desegregation orders. This "massive resistance," however, collapsed in the late 1950s, and Governor Mills Godwin, though a Byrd loyalist, accepted integration and reformed state government in the late 1960s.

Meanwhile, demographics changed the Old Dominion. As the 20th Century progressed, the peripheral parts of the state grew: the coal-mining counties of the southwest, the Tidewater area around the Navy bases in Norfolk and the shipbuilding yards in Newport News, and the government employee-filled suburbs across the Potomac from Washington, D.C. Courthouse politicians no longer carried the vote for the Byrd machine by the middle 1960s: Harry Byrd Jr., appointed to his father's Senate seat, was nearly beaten in the 1966 Senate primary, and 20-year Senate veteran A. Willis Robertson—father of 1988 presidential candidate and televangelist Pat Robertson—was beaten in the Democratic primary. There began a quarter-century

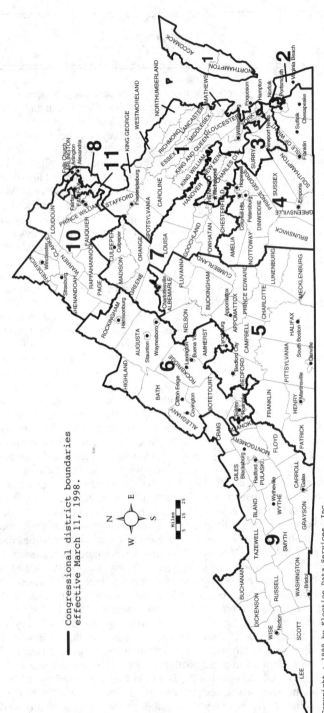

Congressional district boundaries
effective March 11, 1998.

N
W E
S

Miles
5 15 25

Copyright · 1999 by Election Data Services, Inc.

of political flux. The Byrd Democrats were beaten in primaries and ran as independents (Senator Harry Byrd Jr. in 1976) or became Republicans (Mills Godwin in 1973). In the 1970s conservative Republicans won most statewide races, while Democrats still held the legislature. In the 1980s three moderate Democrats were elected governor—Charles Robb in 1981, Gerald Baliles in 1985, Douglas Wilder in 1989—because they no longer represented an attempt to impose a labor-liberal agenda on an unwilling Virginia, and because they argued they could use government effectively to improve education and build Virginia's economy. Wilder's election was a national breakthrough, a successful attempt by a black politician to campaign and govern on equal terms; he won largely because of his margins in the Tidewater and Northern Virginia, where his pro-choice stand on abortion clearly helped, but he also ran solidly across the state. His fiscal conservatism, which resulted in sharp spending cuts in the early 1990s, like his elegant manners and thick Richmond accent, echoed Virginia's elitist and libertarian tradition.

Now Virginia seems to have developed ideological politics along party lines, where Republicans have made historic strides by winning majorities with traditional party platforms. George Allen was elected governor by a wide margin in 1993 as a Republican who believed in lower taxes, traditional cultural values, longer prison terms, and teaching basic skills, combining crunchy issue positions with a sunny temperament. He succeeded in passing most of his programs through a Democratic legislature, which traditionally favored more spending over discipline in the areas of education, welfare and crime. But Democrats blocked his tax cuts in 1995, and his efforts to win legislative majorities that fall fell just short. Republicans won a 20–20 tie in the state Senate, but the tie-breaking vote belonged to Democratic Lieutenant Governor Donald Beyer, and Democrats won a 53–46–1 majority in the House of Delegates.

The 1997 contest to succeed Allen (Virginia is the last state which limits its governors to one term) was a race between Lieutenant Governor Beyer of Northern Virginia and Republican Attorney General James Gilmore from the Richmond suburbs. The suburban origin of the two candidates was no accident: six of Virginia's heaviest voting jurisdictions in the 1998 election were suburban counties, and the seventh, Virginia Beach, is so in all but name. Beyer's election would have been a repudiation of much of Allen's politics; Gilmore's was a confirmation. Gilmore's politics is less confrontational than Allen's, but he had one powerful issue, phasing out the property tax on automobiles, and carried it to a 56%–43% victory. Republicans for the first time swept the top three statewide offices including attorney general, won by Christian conservative Mark Earley. Virginia today has more faith in growth through market economics than the Byrd machine did, more commitment to racial equality than the Founders imagined possible and more confidence that it can be a national leader than it has had since Appomattox.

Governor. James Gilmore, a Republican, was elected governor of Virginia in 1997. Gilmore grew up in the Fan neighborhood of Richmond and the Richmond suburbs, the son of a supermarket meat-cutter and a church secretary; despite the "III" in his name, he is not part of Virginia's ancestral elite. He graduated from University of Virginia; between college and law school he served in the Army. For 10 years he practiced law in the Richmond suburbs, and in 1987 was elected Henrico County commonwealth's attorney. In 1993, after starting out no better than even, he was elected attorney general with 56% of the vote. Gilmore supported Allen's achievements: abolition of parole, parental notification for abortions, welfare reform, strict education standards. The race between Gilmore and Beyer, owner of a well-known Volvo dealership in Northern Virginia, began about even; both candidates had familiar names but neither was known in depth.

Gilmore concentrated on one major pledge: to cut the car tax. The property tax on automobiles was unusually high in Virginia—some Northern Virginians paid more than $1,000 a year, and Gilmore pledged to cut it to zero on up to $20,000 of value by 2002. Beyer was initially opposed, then came up with a plan for smaller cuts of his own. His platform emphasized bringing Virginia teachers' salaries up to the national average by 2002; at one point he declined to rule out a tax increase to do so. Beyer attacked Gilmore for being soft on polluters while he was attorney general and for supporting state funded school vouchers which could be used for private schools. Gilmore criticized Beyer for negative campaigning and for flip-flopping on the car tax. "The people . . . will not be fooled by pretending to be for one thing and then speaking out for another," Gilmore said. Beyer charged that Gilmore was "out of step with Virginia's mainstream" for backing parental consent in teenage abortion cases—a correct analysis perhaps for his home area of Northern Virginia but hardly for the state as a whole. Gilmore called for prohibiting state employees from accessing pornography on state computers; Beyer, a supporter of public employee unions, made a point of opposing that in debate. Former Governor Douglas Wilder refused to endorse Beyer, who some accused of taking the minority vote for granted.

Gilmore won by the solid margin of 56%–43%. He carried Northern Virginia, which casts about 30% of the state's votes, 52%–46%; the area has the state's highest car taxes, and would surely have gone for Beyer absent that issue. He also carried the Norfolk-Newport News area, which casts about 20% of the state's votes, by 53%–44%. As expected, he carried the Richmond area 58%–40% and the rest of the state 59%–39%, piling up margins that would have been hard to overcome in Northern Virginia and Norfolk in any case, and running far ahead there of the showings of Bob Dole and Senator John Warner the year before.

Virginia has brief (less than 50 day) legislative sessions every even-numbered year. Despite the Democratic majority in the House, Gilmore succeeded in pushing through the first phase of the car tax cut in 1998. He implemented the Standards of Learning tests and created Best Practice Centers for schools and teachers. School systems were required to pay for the cost of remedial education for their graduates in the first two years of college—a form of accountability about which administrators and unions loudly squawked. He paid close attention to the high-tech industry in Northern Virginia (which initially backed Beyer) by appointing a secretary of Technology (the country's first cabinet-level technology post), taking the lead in opposing Internet taxes and passing the Internet Policy Act, with criminal penalties for spamming. He opposed state laws which limited growth but was against interference with county governments that tried to do so. In a special election in January 1998 Republicans won a majority in the state Senate 21–19; in special elections to replace Democratic legislators in Republican-leaning districts whom Gilmore appointed to state posts, Republicans cut the Democratic edge in the House of Delegates to 50–49–1. Democrats elected a speaker before the special election winners could take their oaths but, to the fury of Democratic leaders accustomed to ironclad control of the schedule, Republicans insisted on a power-sharing agreement in which they would have equal representation on committees.

Despite his considerable attempts to make common cause with blacks and his courting of the high-tech community, Gilmore has a temper and has taken sharp stands on issues he could have avoided. In fall 1998 he went to court to stop the wife of brain-damaged Hugh Finn from removing his feeding tube; he lost in court, the man died, and after some resistance Gilmore signed a bill reimbursing her $48,000 for legal expenses. When in February 1999 complaints arose about leakage from barges taking New York garbage to a landfill in Charles City County, a poor black-majority area down the James River from Richmond, Gilmore protested such arrangements that have made Virginia the number two recipient of garbage (Pennsylvania is number one). New York Mayor Rudolph Giuliani, always ready to take and give offense, replied, "People in Virginia like to utilize New York because we're a cultural center, because we're a business center. This is a reciprocal relationship." Gilmore replied that New York's cultural achievements do not "obligate Virginia and other states to take your garbage" and "we are very much on the rise and we don't want anyone to get the impression that Virginia is good only as a garbage depository." In March 1999 he got the legislature to ban garbage barges, restrict the construction of new landfills and cap the amount of garbage dumped in seven "megafills" to 1998 levels. When Democrats called for eliminating the food tax, Gilmore agreed to cut it from 4.5% to 2.5%, and when he called for distributing an extra $245 million in lottery funds to schools, Democrats could not help but cheer. Gilmore also moved to require teachers to show they could prepare students for Standards for Learning tests and to require schools to teach patriotism, the Pledge of Allegiance, economic self-reliance, non-discrimination and consequences for bad behavior. He pushed through competition in electricity, to begin on a limited basis in 2002.

In mid-1999 Republicans were vowing they would win a majority in the state House in the fall elections to go with their majority in the state Senate; Democrats vowed that they would roll them back. Gilmore will not run for the Senate in 2000—George Allen declared in that race in early 1999—but could be a candidate for John Warner's seat if he retires in 2002. The two major Republican candidates for governor in 2001 are Lieutenant Governor John Hager, a former tobacco executive who is wheelchair-bound by polio, and Attorney General Mark Earley, who has strong support from Christian conservatives, including blacks, and served as a missionary for two years in the Philippines. The best-known potential candidate for Democrats is Mark Warner, a telecommunications millionaire, who won 47% of the vote in his 1996 Senate race against (no relation) John Warner.

Senior Senator. John Warner, a Republican first elected in 1978, is now chairman of the Armed Services Committee. He grew up in Washington, D.C., with Virginia roots; his grandparents lived in Amherst County, Virginia. His father was a field surgeon in World War I; a great-uncle served in the Confederate Army and lost his arm in the Battle of the Wilderness. Warner volunteered for both the Army and Navy in 1944, at 17; the Navy snapped him up first. (There are only 11 World War II veterans left in the Senate: Ted Stevens, William Roth, Daniel Inouye, Daniel Akaka, Frank Lautenberg, Daniel Patrick Moynihan, Jesse Helms, John Chafee, Strom Thurmond, Ernest Hollings, John Warner; in contrast 29 senators were not born until after World War II.) He went to college at Washington & Lee and then interrupted his years at the University of Virginia Law School to serve in the Marine Corps in Korea. He worked as an assistant U.S. attorney and then practiced law in Washington and had a house in the horse country in Middleburg, Virginia. During the Nixon Administration he was secretary of the Navy. He ran for the Senate in 1978 with few political assets other than his then-wife, Elizabeth Taylor. Finishing second at the huge Republican state convention, he graciously supported winner Richard Obenshain; then, when Obenshain died in a plane crash, Republican leaders reluctantly named Warner to fill his place. Warner won the general over Democrat Andrew Miller by a 4,721-vote margin. For many years he made few enemies, and was easily re-elected over a liberal Democrat in 1984 and had no serious opposition in 1990.

Warner can be grandiloquent and showy, yet he works hard on important issues and has shown steadfastness in his beliefs. His voting record is moderate on economics and cultural issues, conservative on foreign policy and defense. He has voted for government funding of abortions in some cases, but favors parental consent laws and the partial-birth abortion ban. He cast a critical vote against the Supreme Court nomination of Judge Robert Bork in 1987. He voted for the Brady gun control bill and in May 1999 to control gun sales by non-licensed dealers at gun shows. He opposes term limits but would back sending a constitutional amendment to the states for a "national referendum." Representing a state which still has a large number of public employees (though the proportion is dropping), he favors higher federal pay and supported repeal of the Hatch Act.

Warner waited a long time to become chairman of Armed Services. He was the ranking Republican on the committee from 1987–93, when he was bumped by the more senior Strom Thurmond; when both were re-elected in 1996 Warner expressed the hope he might be chairman some time within six years. In December 1997, on the day before his 95th birthday, Thurmond announced he would step down in January 1999 to give the younger generation a chance; he kept his word and Warner became chairman at 71. For years on the committee he had worked closely with Democratic Chairman Sam Nunn; but he opposed Nunn and led the fight in 1991 for the Gulf war resolution, which passed by only 52–47. He has long backed a strong missile defense and has said that the continuing controversy over the Tailhook incident is "debilitating to the morale of naval aviation."

A month before he took over as chairman he spent hours on Pentagon briefings; he spent the first night of the December 1998 air attacks on Iraq with the Joint Chiefs in the situation room examining damage-assessment reports. He has weekly breakfasts with his former Armed Services colleague and Senate classmate, Defense Secretary William Cohen. He summarized his attitude: "I'd like to be in the camp that constructively comments and, if necessary, criticizes the administration, taking out the political element." He showed he was willing to go against the administration when he opposed NATO expansion in March 1998.

Warner moved fast in January 1999. In the first major bill of the 106th Congress, he hammered through the big military pay and pension increases in nearly 20 years. He called for a January 1999 hearing with the Joint Chiefs on the needs of the military; perhaps prodded by the prospect of adverse publicity, the Clinton Administration switched and called for $110 billion in increased spending over six years. He created a new Emerging Threats Subcommittee to focus on terrorism, chemical and biological warfare and cyberwarfare; he is concerned about what might happen if the military's high-tech computers fail or are somehow jammed by low-tech countermeasures. "The entire history of the military," he warned, is "you craft the sword and [the enemy] devises the shield." He added, "If we have to build one or two less F-22s to get adequate money to deal with the threat of chemical and biological warfare being brought to the shores of the United States, you're looking at a senator who's going to make it happen." As he has in the past, he stressed spending on readiness and missile defense. He has supported previous rounds of base closings, but after Bill Clinton's politically-motivated tampering with the 1995 round of closings, he voted against another round in May 1999, saying, "The sticky fingerprints of politics got in there." Over the years he has looked out for Virginia's defense installations; with the Pentagon and the Norfolk Navy Base, Virginia is the number one state in defense spending per capita.

Warner's willingness to go his own way despite rains of criticism and amid some political peril has been apparent on a number of occasions. In 1993, he refused to endorse lieutenant governor candidate Michael Farris, who was seen by some in the party as too conservative and who years later still blamed Warner for his loss. In 1994 Warner announced he could not support Senate nominee Oliver North, whose conviction on Iran-Contra charges was overturned on the grounds of inadmissibility of some critical evidence. Instead Warner backed independent (and twice Republican gubernatorial candidate) Marshall Coleman, and many blamed Warner for North's loss. Many Farris and North backers hoped to deny Warner renomination in 1996 at the gigantic (up to 10,000 delegates) Virginia Republican state conventions. But Warner invoked a Virginia law that entitled him to insist on a primary. Running against him there was James Miller, budget director under President Ronald Reagan who lost narrowly to North at the 1994 convention and then supported him. But Miller raised little money, while Warner ran ads trumpeting his record. Turnout was high, and Warner won 66%–34%.

The Democratic nominee was Alexandria businessman Mark Warner, former state party chairman, a native of Connecticut who was criticized by John Warner for using his Democratic connections to win cellular phone licenses, amassing a personal fortune of over $100 million. Mark Warner crushed former Congresswoman Leslie Byrne at the party convention and proceeded to spend liberally—$11.6 million in all, $10.3 million of it his own money, far more per capita than what Michael Huffington spent in California in 1994, though the Democratic Warner was never attacked in the press as the Republican Huffington was. Mark Warner argued that John Warner "talks like Mr. Independent but votes like Mr. Gingrich." Mark Warner called for cautious reductions in Medicare spending, the federal Goals 2000 education program, federal regulation of wetlands, and was pro-choice on abortion. John Warner called himself a "common sense conservative" and, citing seniority, said, "Virginia's got an investment in me."

John Warner led in public polls, but still hovered around 50%—a danger sign for an incumbent. And he was placed on the defensive in October 1996 when his media consultant ran an ad superimposing Mark Warner's face on a picture of Charles Robb shaking hands with Douglas Wilder, as President Clinton looked on. John Warner fired the consultant and apologized for the deception, but did not repudiate the ad's quotation of a *Richmond Times-Dispatch* editorial calling Mark Warner "dirty, stupid, reckless, dangerous." John Warner won, but only narrowly,

52%–47%. He carried by narrow 51%–49% margins the usually Republican Richmond areas and non-metropolitan Virginia: evidence that some Farris and North enthusiasts hurt him. He carried the Norfolk area by only 52%–47%: he was not yet Armed Services chairman. He ran best, 55%–45%, in Northern Virginia, where his highly visible opposition to Farris and North was probably an asset.

Warner showed his willingness to anger colleagues in his investigation of the 1996 Louisiana Senate election, in which the 5,788-vote loser, Republican Woody Jenkins, charged large-scale fraud. In June 1997, Democrats walked out on the hearings, calling them a "witch hunt," and promised to shut down the Senate. Said Warner, "The Senate is my client. We [the Rules Committee] have a constitutional obligation to be the sole judge of the election of those in the Senate. Until we have looked at everything reasonable, this investigation will not conclude." Republicans gave Warner subpoena power in July 1997 and he held hearings in New Orleans. In October 1997 the committee voted unanimously to end the inquiry; though "isolated instances" of voter fraud did occur, Warner said, there was no evidence to prove a "widespread effort to illegally affect the outcome of the election."

In 1998, as chairman of the Subcommittee on Transportation, Warner worked on the giant transportation bill and conducted extensive negotiations to get a funding formula that would satisfy just about everyone. He largely succeeded, and in the process increased Virginia's annual transportation funding by $150 million, provided funding for replacing the deteriorating Woodrow Wilson Bridge on the Capital Beltway and preserved spending for the much-criticized "smart road" in the hills about Virginia Tech University. On impeachment he kept his own counsel, apparently unconcerned about fretful conservatives hoping for removal or the majority of voters who seemed against; he voted for acquittal on perjury and removal on obstruction of justice. His seat comes up in 2002. No Democrat seemed actively running in mid-1999; among Republicans, Congressman Tom Davis and Governor James Gilmore might be interested in running if Warner chooses to retire.

Junior Senator. Senator Charles Robb, first elected in 1988, is one of only four Virginians to serve as governor and senator (the others were James Monroe, Claude Swanson and Harry Byrd Sr.). He has had a roller coaster of a career in the public spotlight for more than 30 years by proving himself on the military battlefield and on the political battleground. He grew up in various parts of the country, went to high school in Mount Vernon, Virginia, college in Wisconsin, then served in the Marines. He became one of the Marine Guards in the White House, and there met Lynda Byrd Johnson, whom he married in 1967. Then he went off to command an infantry company in Vietnam and was awarded the Bronze Star. He later retired from the military and graduated from University of Virginia Law School.

Robb began his political career in 1977 when, working in Washington and living across the river in McLean, he ran for lieutenant governor and won, while Republicans were carrying other offices. In 1981, he ran for governor and beat Republican Marshall Coleman 54%–46%. As governor, he was widely popular and was given credit for much of Virginia's dynamic growth; he added $1 billion to the education budget, worked to boost Virginia's coal export industry and appointed blacks and women to top posts in large numbers. Out of office, he was the second chairman of the Democratic Leadership Council. He was easily elected to the Senate in 1988: Incumbent Paul Trible decided to retire at age 42, and Robb's only opponent was a hapless Republican black minister, whom he beat 71%–29%.

Robb's voting record is just a bit to the left of the center of the Senate. In his first years he often voted with Republicans, supporting the Gulf war resolution and the nomination of Clarence Thomas, even while chairing the Democratic Senatorial Campaign Committee in 1991 and 1992. Then Robb gave the Clinton Administration much-needed support on gays in the military, and voted for the 1993 budget and tax package and the 1994 crime bill. But he had other troubles. In August 1988, newspaper stories reported that, while governor, he was present at parties in Virginia Beach where cocaine was used. Charges of a sexual encounter with a former Miss Virginia were aired by NBC in April 1991. That same month, Robb aides played for reporters a tape of Governor Douglas Wilder in a car phone conversation gloating over Robb's problems; Robb was the object of a grand jury investigation related to the phone incident, but the grand jury voted in January 1993 not to indict him.

All of which left him vulnerable to almost any Republican in 1994, except the eventual nominee, Oliver North. North stirred more emotions, pro and con, than any other candidate in the 1994 cycle: His believers saw him as a man who struggled to save the West from effete liberals, his detractors saw him as a man who lied to even his own associates in government as well as to Congress and broke the law. Scorn for inside-the-Beltway elites annealed his support in far-beyond-the-Beltway hinterlands in Virginia, which produced the votes enabling him to beat conservative James Miller 55%–45% at the state convention; in remote zip codes all over the country, direct mail helped North raise and spend over $20 million. Robb was fortunate that the sharp-tongued Wilder did not run against him, and in the primary he beat conservative Delegate (and now congressman) Virgil Goode 58%–34%. Marshall Coleman, who narrowly lost the 1981 and 1989 governor races, ran as an independent and got 11% of the vote, including Senator John Warner's. In the end, Robb won 46%–43%. He carried Northern Virginia and the Norfolk area 50%–38%, and did not run too far behind in the Richmond area (41%–49%) and the rest of the state (41%–47%). North wisely retired from electoral politics and became a talk radio host; Robb went back to the Senate, chastened but politically alive.

In his second term Robb has staked out a position independent of either party. He was the only Democrat to vote for all six of the Republicans' major initiatives in early 1995; he supported the Republican budget resolution in 1995, but in May 1996 opposed it and was one of 46 senators of both parties who backed the Chafee-Breaux budget compromise. He supported the balanced budget amendment and opposed tax cuts. He voted against the Defense of Marriage Act and for a ban on job discrimination against gays in September 1996. Robb became the first senator in history to serve on the Armed Services, Foreign Relations and Intelligence committees. He has a genuine zest for military issues and did much of his work behind the scenes: intelligence deals mostly with secret material, and much of Armed Service's work is bipartisan and is done out of the public eye. To those who questioned whether he was not publicly visible enough he said in May 1998, "I've had more than my share of visibility in life." He did say in 1997 that "defense spending has fallen to a level that will not meet the national military strategy for fighting and winning in two major regional conflicts." He sponsored the bill for another round of military base closings which was defeated 60–40 in May 1999. Some of his work is clearly aimed at rural Virginia. On the 1998 tobacco bill, he concentrated on getting $3.5 billion for tobacco growers. In February 1999 the Senate passed a Robb bill to re-establish the Agriculture Department's civil rights investigative unit. Another Robb project was wiring all Virginia schools for the Internet: In 1996 he announced a public-private partnership, Net Day East, to do so by 2000, and he and his staff volunteered Saturdays to wire individual schools.

After the 1994 election many in Virginia assumed Robb would not run again. In August 1997 he criticized both James Gilmore's and Donald Beyer's plans to cut the car tax; Robb, who refused to rule out a tax increase in his 1981 campaign for governor, has never been an enthusiast for tax cuts. But by 1998 it seemed apparent that Robb was running again. The identity of his opponent was no surprise. In April 1999 former Governor George Allen entered the race. Like Robb, he grew up outside the state, the son of former Washington Redskins head coach George Allen; he was elected to the House of Delegates in 1981 and won a special election for a seat in the U.S. House in 1991. The Democratic legislators districted the seat out of existence, and Allen ran for governor in 1993 and beat Democrat Mary Sue Terry 58%–41%. Allen takes confrontational stands on issues, but his poll ratings seem more affected by his sunny temperament and country demeanor. A January 1999 poll showed Allen leading Robb 47%–38% and a June 1999 poll showed him leading 49%–38%. It is unusual for an incumbent to trail a challenger, but Allen's margins here are no larger than many that have been turned around in the course of a Senate campaign. Republican Senator John Warner, who opposed North's candidacy in 1994, said in 1999 that he would support Allen. Former Governor Douglas Wilder, who declined to endorse Beyer in the 1997 gubernatorial race but who was helpful to Robb in 1994, by mid-1999 had not made it clear what he would do in this race, which is likely to be one of the most seriously contested Senate campaigns in 2000.

Cook's Call. *Highly Competitive.* Robb is the most vulnerable Democratic incumbent seeking re-election in 2000, and former Governor George Allen is perhaps the best candidate Republicans could have recruited to run against him. Both parties agree that Allen is leading in early polling, but the race is expected to be extremely competitive.

Presidential politics. Virginia remains one of the most Republican states in presidential races, though it came close to voting for Bill Clinton in 1996. Virginia's national convention delegates are chosen at state conventions. Virginia, so near the White House and the Capitol, sees relatively little presidential politicking.

Congressional districting. Virginia's districting plans for the 1990s have been monstrosities. The plan in effect for 1992 and modified slightly for 1994 and 1996 was a partisan Democratic contraption, with an odd-shaped black-majority 3d District and an even more grotesque 7th District designed to end the brief House career of Republican George Allen. It did, but Allen had the revenge of being elected governor and led in 1999 polls for the Senate in 2000.

In early 1998 the legislature, under court order, redrew the boundaries to reduce the black percentage in the 3d District from 64% to 53%. But it made no difference: the 3d District's Bobby Scott and six of the state's other 10 incumbents had no major-party opposition. Democrats currently hold a 6–5 edge in the delegation of this Republican-leaning state, but that is due less to redistricting than to the personal popularity of incumbents. Republicans hope to control the redistricting process in 2001, and if they do they will likely draw a very different plan, with a more compact but still heavily Democratic 3d District in the Tidewater and a more Richmond-based 7th.

The People: Est. Pop. 1998: 6,791,345; Pop. 1990: 6,187,358, up 9.7% 1990–1998. 2.5% of U.S. total, 12th largest; 30.6% rural. Median age: 34.5 years. 11.3% 65 years and over. 77.5% White, 18.8% Black, 2.6% Asian, 0.3% Amer. Indian, 0.9% Other; 2.5% Hispanic Origin. Households: 56.8% married couple families; 27.9% married couple fams. w. children; 48.5% college educ.; median household income: $33,328; per capita income: $15,713; 66.3% owner occupied housing; median house value: $91,000; median monthly rent: $411. 2.9% Unemployment. 1998 Voting age pop.: 5,165,000. 1998 Turnout: 1,229,139; 24% of VAP. Registered voters (1998): 3,725,921; no party registration.

Political Lineup: Governor, James S. Gilmore III (R); Lt. Gov., John H. Hager (R); Secy. of Commonwealth, Anne P. Petera (R); Atty. Gen., Mark L. Earley (R); Treasurer, Susan Dewey (R); State Senate, 40 (19 D, 21 R); Majority Leader, Walter A. Stosch (R); House of Delegates, 100 (50 D, 49 R, 1 I); House Speaker, Thomas W. Moss Jr. (D). Senators, John W. Warner (R) and Charles S. Robb (D). Representatives, 11 (6 D, 5 R).

Elections Division: 804-786-6551; **Filing Deadline for U.S. Congress:** April 14, 2000.

1996 Presidential Vote			1992 Presidential Vote		
Dole (R)	1,137,171	(48%)	Bush (R)	1,153,296	(45%)
Clinton (D)	1,090,219	(46%)	Clinton (D)	1,040,993	(41%)
Perot (I)	159,795	(7%)	Perot (I)	349,400	(14%)

1636 VIRGINIA

GOVERNOR

Gov. James S. Gilmore, III (R)

Elected 1997, term expires Jan. 2002; b. Oct. 6, 1949, Richmond; home, Richmond; U. of VA, B.A. 1971, J.D. 1977; Methodist; married (Roxane Gatling).

Military Career: Army, 1971–74.

Elected Office: Henrico Cnty. Commonwealth's Atty., 1988–93; VA Atty. Gen., 1994–97..

Professional Career: Practicing atty., 1977–87, 1997.

Office: State Capitol, Richmond, 23219, 804-786-2211; Fax: 804-371-6351; Web site: www.state.va.us.

Election Results

1997 gen.	James S. Gilmore III (R)	969,062	(56%)
	Don Beyer (D)	738,971	(43%)
	Sue Harris DeBauche (I)	25,777	(2%)
1997 prim.	James S. Gilmore III (R)	nominated	
1993 gen.	George F. Allen (R)	1,045,319	(58%)
	Mary Sue Terry (D)	733,527	(41%)

SENATORS

Sen. John W. Warner (R)

Elected 1978, seat up 2002; b. Feb. 18, 1927, Washington, D.C.; home, Middleburg; Washington & Lee U., B.S., 1949, U. of VA, LL.B. 1953; Episcopalian; divorced.

Military Career: Navy, 1944–46 (WWII), Marine Corps, 1950–52 (Korea).

Professional Career: Law Clerk, U.S. Court of Appeals, Chief Judge Barrett Prettyman, 1953–54; Practicing atty., 1954–56, 1960–69; Asst. U.S. Atty., 1956–60; U.S. Navy, Undersecy., 1969–72, U.S. Navy, Secy., 1972–74; Dir., Amer. Rev. Bicentennial Comm., 1974–76.

DC Office: 225 RSOB, 20510, 202-224-2023; Fax: 202-224-6295; Web site: www.senate.gov/~warner.

State Offices: Abingdon, 540-628-8158; Norfolk, 757-441-3079; Richmond, 804-771-2579; Roanoke, 540-857-2676.

Committees: *Armed Services* (Chmn. of 11 R). *Environment & Public Works* (2d of 10 R): Fisheries, Wildlife & Drinking Water; Superfund, Waste Control & Risk Assessment; Transportation & Infrastructure. *Rules & Administration* (4th of 9 R).

Group Ratings

	ADA	ACLU	AFS	LCV	CON	NTU	NFIB	COC	ACU	NTLC	CHC
1998	20	29	11	13	38	63	100	100	79	86	80
1997	10	—	0	—	82	79	—	100	80	—	—

National Journal Ratings

	1997 LIB — 1997 CONS			1998 LIB — 1998 CONS		
Economic	60%	—	36%	38%	—	57%
Social	71%	—	0%	42%	—	57%
Foreign	55%	—	41%	12%	—	75%

Key Votes of the 105th Congress

1. Bal. Budget Amend.	Y	5. Satcher for Surgeon Gen.	*	9. Chem. Weapons Treaty	Y
2. Clinton Budget Deal	Y	6. Highway Set-asides	Y	10. Cuban Humanitarian Aid	N
3. Cloture on Tobacco	N	7. Table Child Gun locks	N	11. Table Bosnia Troops	N
4. Education IRAs	Y	8. Ovrd. Part. Birth Veto	Y	12. $ for Test-ban Treaty	N

Election Results

1996 general	John W. Warner (R) 1,235,744	(52%)	($5,819,157)
	Mark R. Warner (D) 1,115,982	(47%)	($11,600,424)
1996 primary	John W. Warner (R) 323,520	(66%)	
	James C. (Jim) Miller (R) 170,015	(34%)	
1990 general	John W. Warner (R) 876,782	(81%)	($1,219,726)
	Nancy B. Spannaus (I) 196,755	(18%)	

Sen. Charles S. Robb (D)

Elected 1988, seat up 2000; b. June 26, 1939, Phoenix, AZ; home, McLean; U. of WI, B.B.A. 1961, U. of VA, J.D. 1973; Episcopalian; married (Lynda).

Military Career: Marine Corps, 1961–70 (Vietnam), Marine Corps Reserves, 1970–91.

Elected Office: VA Lt. Gov., 1977–81; VA Gov., 1981–86.

Professional Career: Law Clerk, U.S. Court of Appeals Judge John Butzner, 1973–74; Practicing atty., 1974–77, 1986–88.

DC Office: 154 RSOB, 20510, 202-224-4024; Fax: 202-224-8689; Web site: www.senate.gov/~robb.

State Offices: Clintwood, 540-926-4104; Danville, 804-791-0330; Norfolk, 757-441-3124; Richmond, 804-771-2221; Roanoke, 540-985-0103.

Committees: *Armed Services* (5th of 9 D): Readiness & Management Support (RMM); Seapower; Strategic Forces. *Finance* (9th of 9 D): International Trade; Social Security & Family Policy; Taxation & IRS Oversight. *Intelligence* (6th of 8 D). *Joint Economic Committee* (10th of 10 Sens.).

Group Ratings

	ADA	ACLU	AFS	LCV	CON	NTU	NFIB	COC	ACU	NTLC	CHC
1998	80	86	78	88	97	26	33	72	12	25	9
1997	60	—	56	—	100	51	—	70	4	—	—

National Journal Ratings

	1997 LIB — 1997 CONS			1998 LIB — 1998 CONS		
Economic	11%	—	76%	59%	—	39%
Social	45%	—	50%	63%	—	26%
Foreign	34%	—	57%	51%	—	36%

Key Votes of the 105th Congress

1. Bal. Budget Amend.	Y	5. Satcher for Surgeon Gen.	Y	9. Chem. Weapons Treaty	Y
2. Clinton Budget Deal	Y	6. Highway Set-asides	Y	10. Cuban Humanitarian Aid	N
3. Cloture on Tobacco	N	7. Table Child Gun locks	Y	11. Table Bosnia Troops	Y
4. Education IRAs	N	8. Ovrd. Part. Birth Veto	N	12. $ for Test-ban Treaty	Y

Election Results

1994 general	Charles S. Robb (D)	938,376	(46%)	($5,501,697)
	Oliver L. (Ollie) North (R)	882,213	(43%)	($20,607,367)
	J. Marshall Coleman (I)	235,324	(11%)	($813,409)
1994 primary	Charles S. Robb (D)	154,561	(58%)	
	Virgil H. Goode Jr. (D)	90,547	(34%)	
	Sylvia L. Clute (D)	17,329	(6%)	
	Others	4,507	(2%)	
1988 general	Charles S. Robb (D)	1,474,086	(71%)	($2,881,666)
	Maurice A. Dawkins (R)	593,652	(29%)	($282,229)

FIRST DISTRICT

When the first British settlers sailed up the estuaries that flow into the Chesapeake Bay, they were searching for gold, hoping to sail back soon with fortunes. But they couldn't help noticing that the spot where the James River feeds into the bay, now Hampton Roads, was a fine natural harbor, with calm, deep water and good anchorages. There they established a civilization whose elegance is recalled in the craftsmanship of restored Williamsburg and whose coarseness and brutality is brought to life by the story of Jamestown and the other beleaguered settlements. Tidewater Virginia brought slavery to America and tobacco to the world, and slave-raised tobacco was the center of its economy in the colonial era and in the years afterward, when its most talented sons left its depleted soil for better opportunities elsewhere.

Now the economy and tone of life in Tidewater Virginia are set by the American military. Sixty years ago, as America was on the brink of world war, the Navy base at Norfolk and the shipbuilding centers in Newport News across Hampton Roads became the center of American naval might in the Atlantic. There were less than 370,000 people living then on both sides of Hampton Roads. Today there are 1.5 million—a population collected from all over the country, making this a metropolitan area that is not so much Southern in atmosphere as it is, in the manner of military bases abroad, national. But you can still see this area's origins in the Newport News Shipbuilding and Drydock Company that lies over the flat neighborhoods lining the baysides, with ships looming larger than life, their turrets and superstructures bristling with armored might. This is the biggest private employer in Virginia. At the height of 1980s naval expansion, 30,000 people worked here, and defense spending here has topped $1 billion a year.

Virginia's 1st Congressional District—America's First District, Congressman Herb Bateman calls it—contains much of this territory. Its boundaries are convoluted in order to accommodate the black-majority 3d District, although they were smoothed out in 1998 in response to a February 1997 federal court decision that ruled the 3d unconstitutional. Nearly half the district's residents live on the Peninsula, in and around Newport News, Williamsburg and other Hampton Roads area towns. It also includes the southern tip of the Delmarva Peninsula—Virginia's Eastern Shore, site of the annual roundup of wild Chincoteague ponies—and much of the Northern Neck between the Rappahannock and Potomac Rivers, where Robert "King" Carter, one of the great landowners of colonial Virginia, reigned, and where George Washington and Robert E. Lee were born; the Northern Neck is now growing robustly again for the first time in two centuries. Ancestrally, most of this area is Democratic, but with black precincts shorn away, the 1st now is reliably Republican in most elections.

The congressman from the 1st District is Herb Bateman, a Republican first elected in 1982. He grew up in Newport News, went to William and Mary, enlisted in the Air Force during the Korean war, practiced law and was elected to the Virginia Senate as a Democrat in 1967. He switched parties in 1976, and was outmaneuvered for the congressional nomination that year. But when the district became open again in 1982, he easily won the nomination and then won the general. Bateman has a moderate voting record; he opposed term limits and voted for the Brady bill and the assault weapons ban.

Most of Bateman's work has been on the Armed Services Committee, where he now chairs the Readiness Subcommittee. He has been warning that military readiness is deteriorating, charging in May 1999 that Marines were forward-deployed 250 days a year, sailors were "cross-decking" (getting off one ship and immediately being placed on another) and helicopters and planes were being cannibalized for parts. "Too few people are trying to do too much work with too few resources." Over the past decade he led the effort to build three Nimitz-class aircraft carriers at Newport News—the *U.S.S. John C. Stennis*, *Harry S Truman* and, still under construction in 1999, *Ronald Reagan*—that together cost more than $10 billion. In 1995 and 1996 he worked to reverse a Pentagon decision to build all future nuclear submarines at the Electric Boat plant in Connecticut; instead, two subs will be built there and two at Newport News, and the yards will compete again in 2003. In 1999 he opposed General Dynamics' bid to buy Newport News, since GD already owns Electric Boat. He played a role in building the Thomas Jefferson National Accelerator Facility in Newport News. He is chairman of the House Merchant Marine Panel, which reports to Armed Services, and helped pass a 1993 law to encourage commercial ship construction in the U.S.; Newport News got a contract for four double-hulled tankers for a Greek company. Bateman also sponsored the 1995 law granting subsidies to U.S. shipping lines, which suffer higher taxes and operating costs than foreign ships, in return for a commitment to make all their ships available to the Defense Department in case of war. Bateman brags no military base has been closed in this area during the four rounds of closings since the 1980s; he worked hard to save Fort Monroe, Fort Eustis and Fort A.P. Hill.

On the Transportation and Infrastructure Committee, he helped secure $14 million for widening the Coleman Bridge over the James River and working to secure funding for an I-95 interchange in Stafford County and extension of HOV lanes on I-95 to the Rappahannock River. He worked to fund the Chesapeake Bay cleanup at $21 million a year, to fund a $10 million program to protect oysters and crabs and to impose a ban on tributyltin-based paints to save oyster beds, and to have George Washington's childhood home, Ferry Farm in Stafford County, included in the Washington Birthplace National Monument.

In 1994 Bateman promised to retire in 1996, but when Republicans won control of the House he reconsidered. In the past he had some tough challenges from Democrats: Bobby Scott, now congressman from the 3d District, held him to 56% in 1986, and former TV anchorman Andy Fox held him to 51% in 1990. More recently, Bateman has been opposed by conservatives angry at his votes for gun control. In 1996, when he was opposed by a former housing director for Governor George Allen, he opted for a primary, rather than a convention where conservative activists might dominate; he won the primary 80%–20%. Bateman had no Democratic opponent in 1996 or 1998; in 1998 independent Bradford Phillips, based in Northern Virginia, campaigned on the Internet and won 13% of the vote.

Cook's Call. *Safe.* Since winning election here in 1982, Bateman has had only one really close re-election contest. He is safely ensconced in this Republican district.

The People: Pop. 1990: 563,486; 45.4% rural; 12.2% age 65 + ; 79.4% White, 18.6% Black, 2% Other. Households: 62% married couple families; 30.4% married couple fams. w. children; 47.1% college educ.; median household income: $33,743; per capita income: $14,872; median house value: $93,600; median gross rent: $406.

1996 Presidential Vote

Dole (R)	120,429	(51%)
Clinton (D)	96,475	(41%)
Perot (I)	17,195	(7%)

1992 Presidential Vote

Bush (R)	121,134	(49%)
Clinton (D)	86,115	(35%)
Perot (I)	39,343	(16%)

Rep. Herbert H. Bateman (R)

Elected 1982; b. Aug. 7, 1928, Elizabeth City, NC; home, Newport News; William & Mary, B.A. 1949, Georgetown U., LL.B. 1956; Protestant; married (Laura).

Military Career: Air Force, 1951–53.

Elected Office: VA Senate, 1967–82.

Professional Career: Teacher, Hampton Schl., 1949–51; Law Clerk, Judge Bastian, 1956–57; Practicing atty., 1957–82.

DC Office: 2211 RHOB 20515, 202-225-4261; Fax: 202-225-4382; Web site: www.house.gov/bateman.

District Offices: Accomac, 757-787-7836; Fredericksburg, 540-898-2975; Newport News, 757-873-1132.

Committees: *Armed Services* (5th of 32 R): Military Readiness (Chmn.); Military Research & Development; Special Oversight Panel on Morale, Welfare and Recreation; Special Oversight Panel on the Merchant Marine (Chmn.). *Transportation & Infrastructure* (5th of 41 R): Ground Transportation; Water Resources & Environment.

Group Ratings

	ADA	ACLU	AFS	LCV	CON	NTU	NFIB	COC	ACU	NTLC	CHC
1998	5	15	25	15	5	43	83	100	86	84	83
1997	15	—	25	—	42	39	—	100	64	—	—

National Journal Ratings

	1997 LIB	—	1997 CONS	1998 LIB	—	1998 CONS
Economic	45%	—	54%	39%	—	61%
Social	10%	—	82%	25%	—	74%
Foreign	51%	—	46%	58%	—	42%

Key Votes of the 105th Congress

1. Clinton Budget Deal	Y	5. Puerto Rico Sthood. Ref.	N	9. Cut $ for B-2 Bombers	N
2. Education IRAs	N	6. End Highway Set-asides	Y	10. Human Rights in China	N
3. Req. 2/3 to Raise Taxes	*	7. School Prayer Amend.	Y	11. Withdraw Bosnia Troops	N
4. Fast-track Trade	Y	8. Ovrd. Part. Birth Veto	Y	12. End Cuban TV-Marti	N

Election Results

1998 general	Herbert H. Bateman (R)	76,474	(76%)	($304,245)
	Bradford L. Phillips (I)	13,235	(13%)	($53,862)
	Josh Billings (I)	9,492	(9%)	
1998 primary	Herbert H. Bateman (R) ... nominated by convention			
1996 general	Herbert H. Bateman (R) .... unopposed			($534,156)

SECOND DISTRICT

The United States Navy Atlantic fleet berthed in its home port of Norfolk is one of the great awe-inspiring sights in America, or anywhere. The aggregation of destructive power in the line of towering gray ships is probably greater than in any other single port in history—over 100 ships are based here, with some 100,000 sailors and Marines, some $2 billion in annual spending. Norfolk has been a Navy port since 1801, and has long been recognized as one of the best natural harbors on the East Coast, one that never freezes, has a channel 50 feet deep and is within 750 miles of three-quarters of U.S. manufacturing capacity.

Norfolk, once a small city, is now the center of a metropolitan area on both sides of Hampton Roads with over 1.5 million people. Nearly one-third of the total workforce here is employed by the military, but with its skilled labor force and lack of unions the Hampton Roads area has also attracted a lot of private employment; the port has taken a great deal of business away from the labor-torn piers of Baltimore. To the Hampton Roads area, this growth over the last 45 years has brought a wider cross-section of people than usually found in the South. There is no heavy accent here: the brothy Tidewater accent is heard more often farther up the rivers toward Richmond. And Norfolk preserves its antique past more carefully now, developing cultural institutions and commercial amenities appropriate to a major metro area. Older parts of Norfolk have the look and feel of a working-class town, with shipyard workers and many blacks (39% in the city of Norfolk), but most of it is white middle-class suburbia, plus Virginia Beach's string of oceanfront motels.

The 2d Congressional District is made up of most of Norfolk and Virginia Beach, with boundaries that put most of Norfolk's heavily black neighborhoods in the black-majority 3d District. The politics here has changed as the area has become more heavily suburban, and the Democrats more associated with defense policy critics. In 1968, the 2d voted for Hubert Humphrey, as Norfolk cast 65,000 votes and Virginia Beach 37,000. In 1996, it voted 48%–45% for Bob Dole, as its portion of Norfolk cast 40,000 votes and Virginia Beach 123,000. In the light-turnout 1998 election, with slightly revised boundaries, Norfolk cast 13,000 votes and Virginia Beach 59,000.

The congressman from the 2d District is Owen Pickett, a Democrat first elected in 1986. With old Virginia roots, he became an accountant and lawyer, was elected to the Virginia House of Delegates in 1971, at 41, where he was known as a fiscal conservative and for his hard work restructuring the state retirement system. He was state Democratic chairman in 1981, when Charles Robb won the governorship, beginning a string of Democratic victories. In 1982, he was Robb's choice for the Senate but withdrew after Douglas Wilder, then state senator and later governor, threatened to run as an independent. But by the time he ran for Congress in 1986, the quiet and methodical Pickett had Wilder's support and that of Jesse Jackson's Norfolk coordinator. Pickett carried Norfolk heavily, and won 49%–42%.

In the House, Pickett showed his political acumen by getting a new seat created for him on the Armed Services Committee and getting a seat on the old Merchant Marine Committee as well—two crucial spots for any Norfolk congressman. His voting record is a bit to the left of the House as a whole. He is a member of the Blue Dogs, who have proposed their own budget with no tax cuts until the budget is balanced and faster spending cuts than either Democratic or Republican versions.

Pickett is ranking Democrat on the Military Research and Development Subcommittee and a strong backer of missile defense. Much of Pickett's work has been in supporting Hampton Roads military bases and defense contractors, and revitalizing the shipbuilding industry and merchant marine. That work has mostly been successful. Newport News Shipbuilding and Drydock across the bay has been building three Nimitz-class aircraft carriers in the 1990s, at a cost over $10 billion, and has kept Electric Boat Company in Connecticut from getting a monopoly on building nuclear submarines. With subsidies for operating costs and new contract terms, U.S.-flag shipping firms have thrived and Newport News is building commercial ships too. The Norfolk Navy Shipyard has survived four rounds of base-closings and calls for privatization. His reponse to proposals for another round of base closings in May 1997 was, "Not just no, hell no!" By October 1998 he said one final round might be all right, if it came in 2001, when Bill Clinton is no longer president. Pickett opposed General Dynamics's bid to buy Newport News Shipbuilding in February 1999 (it already owns Electric Boat), sponsored a bill to move the battleship *Wisconsin* next to the Nauticus maritime center in downtown Norfolk, opposed proposals to make Camp Pendleton in Virginia Beach a public park. He helped get the Navy to move the Military Sealift Command from Bayonne, New Jersey, to Virginia Beach; when the Navy moved from Florida 10 F/A-18 Hornet Squads to Virginia Beach and two to

Beaufort, South Carolina, he loudly protested that all should have gone to Virginia. In August 1998 he objected to the awarding of a military health care contract for 418,000 military personnel and dependents in Hampton Roads to Anthem Alliance, which seems to have been woefully unprepared to process claims; a month later the Pentagon reopened negotiations and requested new bids.

Pickett was one of 31 Democrats to vote for the Republican impeachment inquiry in October 1998; he waited till the last minute to announce his vote against impeachment and submitted his remarks in writing. To a *Richmond Times-Dispatch* reporter he sounded a note of weariness. "There's a certain feeling that once you're in it, you want to conclude some of the things that you've worked on or that you got in to do," he said of his service, adding, "If I knew what I know now . . . I would have devoted my energies to some other, perhaps community type of activity, and not have become so involved in political matters." In 1992 and 1994 Pickett beat a vocal conservative with 56% and 59% of the vote; he won 65% in 1996, running 21% ahead of Clinton, and had no opposition in 1998.

Cook's Call. *Safe.* In six re-election contests, Pickett has never dropped below 56% and the fact that he was unopposed in 1998 is a good sign that he will not have a serious challenge in 2000. But, this Republican leaning district will be trouble for Democrats to hold onto once this seat does open up.

The People: Pop. 1990: 562,789; 0.6% rural; 7.8% age 65+; 76.2% White, 18.5% Black, 5.4% Other. Households: 58.5% married couple families; 31.9% married couple fams. w. children; 55.3% college educ.; median household income: $32,576; per capita income: $14,492; median house value: $93,100; median gross rent: $450.

1996 Presidential Vote		
Dole (R)	77,936	(48%)
Clinton (D)	73,367	(45%)
Perot (I)	11,637	(7%)

1992 Presidential Vote		
Bush (R)	86,263	(47%)
Clinton (D)	65,787	(36%)
Perot (I)	30,298	(17%)

Rep. Owen Pickett (D)

Elected 1986; b. Aug. 31, 1930, Richmond; home, Virginia Beach; VA Polytechnic Inst., B.S. 1952, U. of Richmond, LL.B. 1955; Baptist; married (Sybil).

Elected Office: VA House of Delegates, 1971–86.

Professional Career: Accountant; Practicing atty., 1955–86; Chmn., VA Dem. Party, 1980–82.

DC Office: 2133 RHOB 20515, 202-225-4215; Fax: 202-225-4218; Web site: www.house.gov/pickett.

District Offices: Norfolk, 757-583-5892; Virginia Beach, 757-486-3710.

Committees: *Armed Services* (5th of 28 D): Military Readiness; Military Research & Development (RMM); Special Oversight Panel on Morale, Welfare and Recreation. *Resources* (9th of 24 D): Forests & Forest Health; Water & Power.

Group Ratings

	ADA	ACLU	AFS	LCV	CON	NTU	NFIB	COC	ACU	NTLC	CHC
1998	55	50	89	8	62	17	57	78	16	37	8
1997	65	—	63	—	76	29	—	80	20	—	—

National Journal Ratings

	1997 LIB — 1997 CONS			1998 LIB — 1998 CONS		
Economic	55%	—	44%	55%	—	44%
Social	71%	—	27%	59%	—	40%
Foreign	64%	—	33%	78%	—	19%

Key Votes of the 105th Congress

1. Clinton Budget Deal	Y	5. Puerto Rico Sthood. Ref.	N	9. Cut $ for B-2 Bombers	Y
2. Education IRAs	N	6. End Highway Set-asides	N	10. Human Rights in China	N
3. Req. 2/3 to Raise Taxes	N	7. School Prayer Amend.	N	11. Withdraw Bosnia Troops	N
4. Fast-track Trade	Y	8. Ovrd. Part. Birth Veto	N	12. End Cuban TV-Marti	Y

Election Results

1998 general	Owen Pickett (D) .... unopposed			($129,837)
1998 primary	Owen Pickett (D) .... nominated by convention			
1996 general	Owen Pickett (D) 106,215	(65%)		($266,059)
	John F. Tate (R) 57,586	(35%)		($194,912)

THIRD DISTRICT

The history of African-American slavery literally began along the tidal expanse of the James River. In 1607, the first English colonists chose one of the marshiest, least healthy spots along the broad river as the site of their settlement at Jamestown. Only a dozen years later, the first slave ship sailed up the James and offloaded its human cargo, giving birth to the biracial society of the American South. In the 20th Century, the great plantation houses of the Tidewater, entire communities once adorned by the most impressive architecture of the day and attended by hundreds of slaves, still dot the banks of the James. Charles City County, the site of William Byrd II's Westover, Benjamin Harrison III's Berkeley, and John Carter's Shirley, also was the birthplace of two successive presidents, William Henry Harrison and John Tyler. The county's population continues to be heavily black—the demography of the plantation remains.

The 3d Congressional District is the descendant of a black-majority district formed in 1992, slightly redrawn in 1993 and then redrawn once again in 1998 after it was ruled unconstitutional by a federal court in February 1997. The 1998 plan, agreed to by the five congressmen affected, smoothed out the boundaries and consolidated eight localities formerly split between districts, but the basic character of the district is the same. It strings together black precincts and communities along the James River from Norfolk and Newport News upriver on the Peninsula past Jamestown and Charles City County all the way to Richmond and suburban Henrico County. Politically, the 3d is by far the most Democratic in Virginia. But it also is sensitive to the needs of the businesses that supply its economic base—notably Newport News Shipbuilding and Drydock Company, the state's largest private employer.

The congressman from the 3d District is Bobby Scott, a Democrat elected when the district was created in 1992. He grew up in Newport News, the son of a doctor, went to Harvard, where he was a classmate of Al Gore, and then to Boston College Law School. He served in the National Guard and Army Reserves and returned home to practice law in 1973. In 1977, he was elected to the Virginia House of Delegates and in 1983 to the state Senate, representing a multi-racial district in a community where, because of the military tradition of integration, biracial politics comes more naturally than in other places. In 1986 he ran a creditable race for Congress in the 1st District and lost to Republican Herb Bateman, 56%–44%. In 1992 he ran in the 3d. With his base in the Peninsula, and against two Richmond-based candidates, Scott won the crucial Democratic primary with 67% of the vote. The general election made him the first black member of Congress to be elected from Virginia since Reconstruction.

Scott has had a solidly liberal voting record, except on some foreign and defense issues. On the Education and the Workforce Committee, he jumped into the health care debate: remembering how his father had been denied staff privileges in a Newport News hospital, he vowed that any health care bill would prohibit racial discrimination against patients and health care providers. He opposes the death penalty and supports a requirement that it not be applied disproportionately by race; he has voted against many bills that contain capital punishment, from the Democrats' 1994 crime bill, when they desperately needed the votes, to the noncontroversial adoption of the Geneva Conventions in July 1996. He opposed Megan's Law, requiring public disclosure of released sexual predators, and he opposed expelling problematic special needs students in the IDEA debate: "the child still needs an education," he said.

In the 105th Congress he had an investigative workload greater than any other member of Congress. He served on the Education and Workforce subcommittee investigating the Teamsters, where Democrats strongly opposed the Republican majority. On the Judiciary Committee he was an outspoken defender of Bill Clinton against impeachment. He spoke out often against what he considered an unfair and partisan proceeding. Scott was the only Democrat to vote against Rick Boucher's motion to censure Clinton. On the complaints he received from some constituents, he said, "Every time you speak up for the Constitution, it hurts you politically." At the same time, Scott was engaging in partisan warfare in the highly publicized impeachment hearings, he was also taking an active role in the highly technical and carefully bipartisan proceedings in the special committee on China chaired by Christopher Cox, to which he was appointed in June 1998. Amazingly, there were no leaks from this committee (until its draft report went to the Clinton White House in January 1999) and by all accounts Scott participated actively and helped build consensus for a unanimous report on an intellectually difficult and politically sensitive issue. On the ethics committee, reconstituted after the Newt Gingrich case was settled, Scott also contributed to a nonpartisan approach, notably in the case of Republican Congressman Jay Kim. On Judiciary, Scott co-authored a juvenile crime bill which passed with broad bipartisan support.

Through all these travails, Scott retained his composure over redistricting. In late 1997 he and the other four congressmen reached agreement on new boundaries; the three Republicans were happy to see Scott retain heavily black precincts, and evidently moderate Democrat Owen Pickett did not mind. Newport News Shipbuilding was pleased to see all the incumbents protected; three are on Armed Services and Scott adds a pro-defense voice to the Congressional Black Caucus. The districts were not finally approved until just weeks before the filing deadline. As Scott noted in August 1997, "Whatever uncertainty I face, what about the uncertainty for someone who is challenging me? They wouldn't even know where to live." Just so: none of the five members had major party opposition. Scott was re-elected with 76% of the vote against an independent. If Republicans control redistricting after the 2000 Census, they may try to remove the Richmond area from the 3d and substitute other parts of the Tidewater area. But these all have large black percentages, and such a district should be safe for Scott.

Cook's Call. *Safe.* Although this district was altered slightly due to a court order in 1998, Scott has shown no signs of vulnerability. He is heavily favored to hold onto this solidly Democratic district.

The People: Pop. 1990: 560,280; 9.1% rural; 12% age 65 + ; 44.1% White, 53.6% Black, 2.4% Other. Households: 40.3% married couple families; 19.5% married couple fams. w. children; 35.6% college educ.; median household income: $22,351; per capita income: $10,357; median house value: $62,100; median gross rent: $315.

1996 Presidential Vote			1992 Presidential Vote		
Clinton (D)	111,918	(66%)	Clinton (D)	118,652	(58%)
Dole (R)	48,955	(29%)	Bush (R)	62,924	(31%)
Perot (I)	9,389	(6%)	Perot (I)	21,855	(11%)

Rep. Bobby Scott (D)

Elected 1992; b. Apr. 30, 1947, Washington, D.C.; home, Newport News; Harvard U., B.A. 1969, Boston Col. Law Schl., J.D. 1973; Episcopalian; single.

Military Career: Army Natl. Guard, 1970–73; Army Reserves, 1973–76.

Elected Office: VA House of Delegates, 1977–82; VA Senate, 1983–92.

Professional Career: Practicing atty., 1973–91.

DC Office: 2464 RHOB 20515, 202-225-8351; Fax: 202-225-8354; Web site: www.house.gov/scott.

District Offices: Newport News, 757-380-1000; Richmond, 804-644-4845.

Committees: *Education & the Workforce* (10th of 22 D): Early Childhood, Youth & Families; Oversight & Investigations. *Judiciary* (6th of 16 D): Crime (RMM).

Group Ratings

	ADA	ACLU	AFS	LCV	CON	NTU	NFIB	COC	ACU	NTLC	CHC
1998	95	100	100	92	82	14	14	28	20	16	0
1997	90	—	100	—	27	14	—	40	8	—	—

National Journal Ratings

	1997 LIB	—	1997 CONS	1998 LIB	—	1998 CONS
Economic	71%	—	28%	79%	—	0%
Social	85%	—	0%	93%	—	0%
Foreign	72%	—	26%	75%	—	23%

Key Votes of the 105th Congress

1. Clinton Budget Deal	N	5. Puerto Rico Sthood. Ref.	Y	9. Cut $ for B-2 Bombers	Y
2. Education IRAs	N	6. End Highway Set-asides	N	10. Human Rights in China	Y
3. Req. 2/3 to Raise Taxes	N	7. School Prayer Amend.	N	11. Withdraw Bosnia Troops	N
4. Fast-track Trade	N	8. Ovrd. Part. Birth Veto	N	12. End Cuban TV-Marti	Y

Election Results

1998 general	Bobby Scott (D)	48,129	(76%)	($182,679)
	Robert S. (Bob) Barnett (I)	14,453	(23%)	
1998 primary	Bobby Scott (D) .... nominated by convention			
1996 general	Bobby Scott (D)	118,603	(82%)	($176,104)
	Elsie Goodwyn Holland (R)	25,781	(18%)	($1,856)

FOURTH DISTRICT

The clash of arms resounds through much of the history of Tidewater Virginia. This was the scene of the first permanent English settlement in North America, at Jamestown, and of its first revolution, Bacon's Rebellion, in 1676. In 1781, George Washington's tattered and exhausted army finally pushed General Cornwallis to the sea, where the French Navy waited at Yorktown: the final victory of the Revolutionary War. The Tidewater also was the scene of bitter fighting more than 80 years later in the Civil War, as Union troops invested the battlements of the small industrial city of Petersburg, 25 miles south of Richmond. Today, the Tidewater region boasts one of the densest concentrations of military power in the world: the Hampton Roads area has the United States' largest accumulation of Navy bases, while Fort Lee, the big Army base near Petersburg, provides an estimated 17,000 local jobs.

The 4th Congressional District includes much of the Tidewater. More than half its people are in the Hampton Roads area, in Portsmouth—a Navy port and industrial town with a charming old section—and in the suburban expanse of Chesapeake and Suffolk. The district also takes in the flat lands of Southside Virginia fanning south from the James River. These were tobacco lands when the English first settled them in the 17th Century; today they also produce Virginia's peanut crop and its Smithfield hams. The district includes Petersburg and Hopewell, with its Allied Chemical plant facing 18th Century plantations. Historically, this was a Democratic area, and the 4th's Democratic percentages are buoyed up by the fact that about one-third of its residents are black. But in national and increasingly in state elections, this area has been trending Republican: It voted for Governors George Allen and James Gilmore in the 1990s.

The congressman from the 4th District is Norman Sisisky, a Democrat elected in 1982. Sisisky grew up in Richmond and enlisted in the Navy as a teenager during World War II; after the war he transformed a small Pepsi bottling company in Petersburg into one of the largest soft drink bottling operations in the South. In 1973, when he had owned his firm 24 years, Sisisky was elected to the Virginia House of Delegates. He ran for Congress in 1982, financing a solid campaign with his own money; he donates his congressional salary to charity. Once in the House, he immediately got a seat on the Armed Services Committee and compiled a moderate voting record. He is a member of the Blue Dogs, moderate Democrats whose budget has no tax cuts until it reaches balance, and cuts spending more quickly than other plans. In 1993 he joined six colleagues calling themselves "Democrats for a Strong Defense" who mobilized against defense cuts. He drafted the Federal Acquisition Streamlining Act passed in 1994 and sponsored the Paperwork Reduction Act, passed in 1995 with broad bipartisan support.

Sisisky became ranking Democrat on the Military Procurement Subcommittee in February 1998. He brings his experience as a businessman and an entrepreneurial drive to military issues. He pushed hard to build the $4.5 billion Nimitz-class aircraft carrier, the *U.S.S. Ronald Reagan*, now under construction in Newport News; he has called for building another Nimitz-class carrier (the 10th and last planned to be built) before developing the new CVX carrier design. He has worked to speed up production of ships and has called for multiyear procurement of the F/A-18E/F carrier-based fighter. He worries that military spending is not enough: "The biggest problem with the fleet right now is that it's not going to be big enough. The Navy has shrunk, but I don't believe the seas have shrunk. [They're] budgeting for a 200-ship Navy to carry out what is probably a 400-ship strategy." In May 1999 he said, "We have ratcheted down the defense budget to the point where key, critical shortages—in procurement, operations and maintenance and personnel accounts—threaten to put our ability to protect the national security at risk." He said that it might be necessary to revive the draft.

Sisisky was one of 31 Democrats who voted for the Republicans' impeachment inquiry, but he voted against impeachment in December. On local issues, he has worked to preserve the peanut and tobacco programs and got funding for the Great Bridge Locks Bridge. Another favorite Sisisky project: promoting Medicare coverage for colon cancer screening; he had surgery in 1995 and underwent 52 weeks of chemotherapy.

Sisisky's moderate views and work for local bases have made him highly popular in a marginal district. Against the minister of a Baptist church, Sisisky spent $290,000 of his own money and won 62%–38% in 1994. In 1996 he won 79%–21%; in 1998 he was unopposed.

Cook's Call. *Safe.* Though this district has been consistently trending away from Democrats at the statewide and presidential level, Sisisky has consistently racked up big margins here since his first win in 1982. Sisisky should have little trouble in 2000, but Democrats could have a hard time holding onto this seat when it eventually opens.

The People: Pop. 1990: 563,206; 36.8% rural; 12% age 65 + ; 59.9% White, 38.6% Black, 1.5% Other. Households: 59.8% married couple families; 30.2% married couple fams. w. children; 38.4% college educ.; median household income: $30,425; per capita income: $12,887; median house value: $73,200; median gross rent: $327.

1996 Presidential Vote			1992 Presidential Vote		
Clinton (D)	107,109	(50%)	Clinton (D)	97,728	(44%)
Dole (R)	91,241	(43%)	Bush (R)	96,983	(43%)
Perot (I)	14,581	(7%)	Perot (I)	28,662	(13%)

Rep. Norman Sisisky (D)

Elected 1982; b. June 9, 1927, Baltimore, MD; home, Petersburg; VA Commonwealth U., B.A. 1949; Jewish; married (Rhoda).

Military Career: Navy, 1945–46.

Elected Office: VA House of Delegates, 1973–82.

Professional Career: Pres., Pepsi-Cola Bottling Co. of Petersburg, 1949–82.

DC Office: 2371 RHOB 20515, 202-225-6365; Fax: 202-226-1170; Web site: www.house.gov/sisisky.

District Offices: Emporia, 804-634-5575; Petersburg, 804-732-2544; Portsmouth, 757-393-2068.

Committees: *Armed Services* (2d of 28 D): Military Procurement (RMM); Military Readiness; Special Oversight Panel on Morale, Welfare and Recreation. *Permanent Select Committee on Intelligence* (4th of 7 D): Human Intelligence, Analysis & Counterintelligence; Technical & Tactical Intelligence.

Group Ratings

	ADA	ACLU	AFS	LCV	CON	NTU	NFIB	COC	ACU	NTLC	CHC
1998	65	56	100	8	72	19	50	61	28	37	25
1997	55	—	50	—	91	34	—	70	28	—	—

National Journal Ratings

	1997 LIB — 1997 CONS			1998 LIB — 1998 CONS		
Economic	55%	—	44%	59%	—	40%
Social	64%	—	35%	59%	—	41%
Foreign	60%	—	38%	59%	—	40%

Key Votes of the 105th Congress

1. Clinton Budget Deal	Y	5. Puerto Rico Sthood. Ref.	N	9. Cut $ for B-2 Bombers	Y
2. Education IRAs	N	6. End Highway Set-asides	N	10. Human Rights in China	Y
3. Req. 2/3 to Raise Taxes	N	7. School Prayer Amend.	N	11. Withdraw Bosnia Troops	N
4. Fast-track Trade	N	8. Ovrd. Part. Birth Veto	Y	12. End Cuban TV-Marti	N

Election Results

1998 general	Norman Sisisky (D)	unopposed		($75,130)
1998 primary	Norman Sisisky (D)	nominated by convention		
1996 general	Norman Sisisky (D)	160,100	(79%)	($223,771)
	Anthony J. Zevgolis (R)	43,516	(21%)	($2,878)

FIFTH DISTRICT

Southside Virginia is a geographic name which for years was shorthand for a state of mind. Here is Appomattox Court House, in the serene little hamlet where Robert E. Lee surrendered to his onetime subordinate Ulysses S. Grant; here is Danville, where the tobacco auction originated in 1858; here also is Prince Edward County, where Harry Byrd's massive resistance shut down public schools in 1957 rather than obey a federal court desegregation order. This land north of the dividing line Colonel William Byrd surveyed in 1728 has some variety. Its eastern counties are flat and humid—frontier in the late colonial period, plantation country by 1800, now peanut fields and pine forests. To the west, into the Piedmont, the land gradually gets hillier. Here are textile mill towns and furniture manufacturing centers—Danville, Martinsville and a dozen smaller towns. Westward, nearer to the mountains, is more livestock and less tobacco, and the thick syrupy tones of the Southside Virginia accent turn to mountain twangs.

The 5th Congressional District consists of much of Southside Virginia, west of metropolitan Richmond and at some points up to the Blue Ridge. It includes Charlottesville and much of surrounding Albemarle County, but skirts around Lynchburg. Historically, politics here were Democratic, segregationist and conservative, run by chain-smoking local bankers and courthouse lawyers. Such Democrats are a rare breed these days, but not entirely extinct. Much of Southside Virginia is still represented by Democratic legislators in Richmond and the 5th District is represented by a conservative Democrat in Congress.

The congressman from the 5th District is Virgil Goode (rhymes with mood), a Democrat from Rocky Mount elected in 1996. He grew up in Franklin County, where his father was a prominent enough figure that part of U.S. 220 was named after him. He attended the University of Richmond and the University of Virginia law school. In 1973, the same year he graduated from law school, he was elected to the Virginia Senate, at 27. In 1994, Goode ran against scandal-beleaguered Senator Charles Robb in the Democratic primary; he lost 58%–34%, but showed local strength. In 1995, his re-election in a Republican-leaning state Senate district enabled Democrats to hold control of the Senate with a 20–20 tie that could be broken by Democratic Lieutenant Governor Donald Beyer.

In 1996, when conservative Democratic Congressman L.F. Payne retired, Goode seemed the only Democrat with a strong chance to win the district. He ran emphasizing bipartisan cooperation with the slogan on the pencils and emery boards he handed out to voters: "Work together in Congress." Republicans had a convention in which Delegate Frank Ruff, recruited by 7th District Congressman Tom Bliley, lost to George Landrith, a former Albemarle County school board member who lost 53%–47% to Payne in 1994. This time it was no contest. Goode carried Franklin County 87%–10%; Landrith carried only two counties, one by a single vote. Overall, Goode won by the impressive margin of 61%–36%.

In the House, Goode has a moderate voting record on economic and cultural issues and a very conservative one on defense and foreign policy. He joined the Blue Dogs and supported the Shays-Meehan campaign finance bill. He had one of the most conservative voting records of any House Democrat; "I think a representative should look at what's best for his district and not what the party line is," he said. Overall his voting record was closer to that of Republican neighbor Bob Goodlatte than Democratic neighbor Rick Boucher. He passionately opposed one of the Clinton White House's favorite projects, the tobacco bill: "I'm not going to support legislation that bankrupts the companies, destroys the family farm and relegates land to a place where hope is a stranger and mercy will never reach!" In Washington, he runs a low-budget operation that defies the sometimes opulent culture of Capitol Hill; lobbyists who visit must sit on a oak stump he has had since his days as a state senator, and during off-hours, he answers his own phone and takes messages for his aides.

Goode was closely watched on impeachment. He was one of 31 Democrats to vote for the Republicans' impeachment inquiry in October 1998. In December 1998 he voted for impeachment, and evidently it was not a close issue for him. "The party line says that lying under oath in a court proceeding is not an impeachable offense. I disagree with that." Even in Southside Virginia local Democrats reacted angrily to Goode. In January 1999 the district Democratic Party decided not to invite him to a February fundraising dinner. His chief of staff, who had told friends he would leave if Goode switched parties, quit that month. Cooler heads prevailed among the more senior Democrats, who understood that without Goode they were unlikely to carry this district, and who probably feared he would switch parties. "I think Virgil voted his conscience, and I think everybody needs to understand that," said House of Delegates Democratic leader Richard Cranwell. Former Governor Douglas Wilder announced he would be happy to vote for Goode next time. State Democratic Chairman Kenneth Plum refrained from criticism.

In the past, when asked about switching parties, Goode had said his father was a Democrat and his uncle was a Democrat and his grandfather was a Democrat and he was a Democrat too. The House Republican leadership assigned Bob Goodlatte to see if he wanted to switch. Goode continued to flaunt the party line—in March 1999 he was the only Democrat to vote with Republicans on the legislative appropriations—but as of June had not switched parties. He probably could be re-elected either way, or as an independent; in 1998 he was unopposed.

Cook's Call. *Probably Safe.* Goode's biggest threat in this conservative, Republican leaning district comes not from Republicans but from disgruntled members of his own party, angry at his vote to impeach President Clinton. In a general election, however, Goode's conservative record and down-home style make him tough to defeat.

The People: Pop. 1990: 562,273; 67.4% rural; 14.9% age 65+; 74.3% White, 24.8% Black, 0.6% Asian, 0.1% Amer. Indian, 0.1% Other; 0.5% Hispanic Origin. Households: 57.4% married couple families; 25.6% married couple fams. w. children; 31.7% college educ.; median household income: $24,807; per capita income: $11,675; median house value: $56,000; median gross rent: $243.

1996 Presidential Vote

Dole (R)	103,796	(49%)
Clinton (D)	92,656	(43%)
Perot (I)	16,867	(8%)

1992 Presidential Vote

Bush (R)	104,783	(47%)
Clinton (D)	91,363	(41%)
Perot (I)	27,105	(12%)

Rep. Virgil H. Goode (D)

Elected 1996; b. Oct. 17, 1946, Richmond; home, Rocky Mount; U. of Richmond, B.A. 1969, U. of VA, J.D. 1973; Baptist; married (Lucy).

Military Career: VA Natl. Guard, 1969–75.

Elected Office: VA Senate, 1973–96.

Professional Career: Practicing atty., 1973–96.

DC Office: 1520 LHOB 20515, 202-225-4711; Fax: 202-225-5681; Web site: www.house.gov/goode.

District Offices: Charlottesville, 804-295-6372; Danville, 804-792-1280; Formville, 804-392-8331; Rocky Mount, 540-484-1254.

Committees: *Agriculture* (15th of 24 D): Department Operations, Oversight, Nutrition & Forestry; Risk Management, Research & Specialty Crops. *Banking & Financial Services* (20th of 27 D): General Oversight & Investigations; Housing & Community Opportunity.

Group Ratings

	ADA	ACLU	AFS	LCV	CON	NTU	NFIB	COC	ACU	NTLC	CHC
1998	30	13	33	15	30	53	93	72	83	81	75
1997	25	—	13	—	24	53	—	80	84	—	—

National Journal Ratings

	1997 LIB	—	1997 CONS	1998 LIB	—	1998 CONS
Economic	35%	—	63%	30%	—	70%
Social	41%	—	57%	38%	—	60%
Foreign	35%	—	64%	7%	—	83%

Key Votes of the 105th Congress

1. Clinton Budget Deal	Y	5. Puerto Rico Sthood. Ref.	N	9. Cut $ for B-2 Bombers	Y
2. Education IRAs	Y	6. End Highway Set-asides	N	10. Human Rights in China	Y
3. Req. 2/3 to Raise Taxes	Y	7. School Prayer Amend.	Y	11. Withdraw Bosnia Troops	Y
4. Fast-track Trade	N	8. Ovrd. Part. Birth Veto	Y	12. End Cuban TV-Marti	N

Election Results

1998 general	Virgil H. Goode (D) .... unopposed			($129,066)
1998 primary	Virgil H. Goode (D) .... nominated by convention			
1996 general	Virgil H. Goode (D) 120,323	(61%)		($4,851,194)
	George C. Landrith III (R) 70,869	(36%)		($392,152)
	Others 6,731	(3%)		

SIXTH DISTRICT

The sturdy men and women who settled the Valley of Virginia west of the Blue Ridge could hardly have differed more from the "second sons" of the European aristocracy who cleared the marshy forests of the Tidewater and built grand plantations there. Even before the Revolutionary War, Englishmen and Scots, German Protestants and Mennonites and Moravians—members of religious communities and fiercely independent farmers—poured down the great Wagon Road from Pennsylvania to the Valley. They were looking not for the flat, mahogany-brown land that eastern tobacco growers sought, but for fields which could support wheat, corn and hay, crops which could be rotated and which an individual farmer and his family could handle. That same independent spirit nurtured the growth of higher education here. In Lexington alone are Washington and Lee University, which Robert E. Lee headed, and the Virginia Military Institute, where Stonewall Jackson taught philosophy and artillery tactics, and which began admitting women in 1996 under order from the U.S. Supreme Court. A quartet of the South's most distinguished women's private colleges are only a short drive away: Mary Baldwin College at Staunton, Randolph-Macon Woman's College at Lynchburg, Sweet Briar College at Sweet Briar, and Hollins College at Roanoke, farther south in the Valley. Industry flourished here more than in most of Virginia east of the Blue Ridge. In the 19th Century the Norfolk and Southern Railroad established its chief junction at Roanoke; as the years passed the city became the railroad's headquarters, and many major companies have plants here.

The 6th Congressional District covers the heart of the Valley of Virginia, from Harrisonburg south to Roanoke, and crosses over the Blue Ridge to take in Lynchburg. Politically, this area has a Republican tradition hospitable to economic assistance for the little guy, and fiercely opposed to Harry Byrd Democrats. But in more recent years, the ancestral conservatism of Byrd Democrats and the feisty politics of the mountain rebels have melded into a single conservative Republicanism, more populist than elite in tone, as concerned with moral values as economic freedom, prickly about interference from Washington or even Richmond.

The congressman from the 6th District is Bob Goodlatte, a Republican first elected in 1992. Goodlatte grew up in Massachusetts, attended college in Maine and then law school at W&L, and went to work in Congressman Caldwell Butler's office in Roanoke. Goodlatte then practiced law and stayed active in politics; in 1992, when Democratic Congressman Jim Olin retired, Goodlatte was nominated by convention and won the general 60%–40%.

Goodlatte has compiled a mostly conservative voting record. Early in his first term, he was one of the Republican freshmen who pushed successfully for term limits on committees' ranking minority members—which now applies to committee chairmen. When Republicans took control in the 104th Congress, Goodlatte rushed to confront OMB Director Alice Rivlin on the administration's unbalanced budget and was floor leader for the "loser pays" provision in Contract with America litigation reform legislation. He chairs an Agriculture subcommittee, on which he has sought to prevent families from receiving food stamps benefits for members in prison and to stop food stamps being sent out to those the USDA delicately labels "deceased individuals." He favors scrapping the current tax code and replacing it with a much simpler tax. He has proposed limited campaign finance measures including requiring candidates' supporters to identify themselves on polls of more than 1,200 respondents, repealing voter registration by mail, banning fundraising in the White House and requiring disclosure of contributions and expenditures by computer.

Goodlatte is an enthusiast for the Internet, co-chairman with Virginia neighbor Rick Boucher of the Internet Caucus and chairman of Speaker Denny Hastert's High-Tech Working Group. "I view the Internet as a way to put rural areas and small cities like Roanoke on a par with major cities," he said. "We can have the best jobs here that used to be done in major cities because you don't have to be in the major cities any more to do them." He has been chief sponsor, with Silicon Valley Democrat Zoe Lofgren, of bills to liberalize export controls on encryption technology. These have been opposed by the NSA and FBI, which want law enforcement and intelligence agencies to possess keys to encryption. Goodlatte argues that Internet commerce will thrive only if users can be confident of confidentiality. Goodlatte also sponsored the Communications Decency Act, allowing censorship of obscene material on the Internet, which was overturned by the Supreme Court. He sponsored a law imposing tougher penalties on commercial counterfeiters, especially important in the software industry; he sought tougher penalties for telemarketing fraud. He amended the Telecommunications Act to give local governments more say over the location of cellular phone towers. He has co-sponsored with Frank LoBiondo a ban on Internet gambling. Goodlatte has embarked on tours of Silicon Valley as an ambassador of House Republicans, distrusted there for their cultural conservatism. In an April 1999 interview with *National Journal's Technology Daily* he argued, "It was the Republican Congress that passed a litany of bills—securities litigation reform, H1-B visas— that Al Gore was on the wrong side of."

Goodlatte appears to have a solid hold on the 6th District. In 1998 he was opposed by David Bowers, mayor of Roanoke since 1992. Goodlatte was confident enough to leave $460,000 cash on hand after the campaign, which he won 69%–31%, carrying every city and county and winning in Roanoke 58%–42%.

Cook's Call. *Safe.* Since winning this formerly Democratic seat in 1992, Goodlatte has had no trouble racking up big re-election margins. Don't expect a competitive race here in 2000.

The People: Pop. 1990: 562,426; 34% rural; 15.3% age 65 + ; 87.6% White, 11.5% Black, 0.6% Asian, 0.1% Amer. Indian, 0.2% Other; 0.7% Hispanic Origin. Households: 56.1% married couple families; 24.8% married couple fams. w. children; 39.1% college educ.; median household income: $27,155; per capita income: $13,017; median house value: $65,100; median gross rent: $287.

1996 Presidential Vote

Dole (R)	108,757	(51%)
Clinton (D)	87,883	(41%)
Perot (I)	16,116	(8%)

1992 Presidential Vote

Bush (R)	111,405	(50%)
Clinton (D)	84,037	(37%)
Perot (I)	29,207	(13%)

Rep. Bob Goodlatte (R)

Elected 1992; b. Sept. 22, 1952, Holyoke, MA; home, Roanoke; Bates Col., B.A. 1974, Washington & Lee Law Schl., J.D. 1977; Christian Scientist; married (Maryellen).

Professional Career: Dist. Dir., U.S. Rep. Caldwell Butler, 1977–79; Practicing atty., 1979–92.

DC Office: 2240 RHOB 20515, 202-225-5431; Fax: 202-225-9681; Web site: www.house.gov/goodlatte.

District Offices: Harrisonburg, 540-432-2391; Lynchburg, 804-845-8306; Roanoke, 540-857-2672; Staunton, 540-885-3861.

Committees: *Agriculture* (5th of 27 R): Department Operations, Oversight, Nutrition & Forestry (Chmn.); Livestock & Horticulture. *Judiciary* (9th of 21 R): Courts & Intellectual Property; Immigration & Claims; The Constitution.

Group Ratings

	ADA	ACLU	AFS	LCV	CON	NTU	NFIB	COC	ACU	NTLC	CHC
1998	0	6	0	8	21	61	93	100	100	95	92
1997	10	—	25	—	56	61	—	100	80	—	—

National Journal Ratings

	1997 LIB — 1997 CONS		1998 LIB — 1998 CONS	
Economic	10%	— 86%	23%	— 74%
Social	0%	— 90%	14%	— 81%
Foreign	24%	— 72%	19%	— 75%

Key Votes of the 105th Congress

1. Clinton Budget Deal	Y	5. Puerto Rico Sthood. Ref.	N	9. Cut $ for B-2 Bombers	Y
2. Education IRAs	Y	6. End Highway Set-asides	Y	10. Human Rights in China	N
3. Req. 2/3 to Raise Taxes	Y	7. School Prayer Amend.	Y	11. Withdraw Bosnia Troops	Y
4. Fast-track Trade	Y	8. Ovrd. Part. Birth Veto	Y	12. End Cuban TV-Marti	N

Election Results

1998 general	Bob Goodlatte (R)	89,177	(69%)	($824,510)
	David A. Bowers (D)	39,487	(31%)	($83,760)
1998 primary	Bob Goodlatte (R) .... nominated by convention			
1996 general	Bob Goodlatte (R)	133,576	(67%)	($566,763)
	Jeffrey W. Grey (D)	61,485	(31%)	($92,744)
	Others	4,300	(2%)	

SEVENTH DISTRICT

In the center of Virginia, on a hill in downtown Richmond above the James River, is Thomas Jefferson's Capitol, one of the first classical-style buildings in North America, chaste and simple in the Jefferson style. A mile or so west is Monument Avenue, Richmond's grand 140-foot-wide boulevard, punctuated by circles, each with a statue of a Confederate hero—Robert E. Lee (62 feet tall, dedicated Memorial Day 1890), Jeb Stuart, Jefferson Davis, Stonewall Jackson, Matthew Fountain Maury, "the Pathfinder of the Sea." Richmond is a monument to Jefferson and to the Confederacy; its metro area is only the third largest in the state, but it still sets the tone for Virginia, and is the home of many of the state's great institutions—Virginia Power, the big Main Street banks, big law firms, and the Richmond newspapers. Richmond has long since grown out past its city borders, covering almost all of suburban Henrico and Chesterfield counties and spreading out into what was until recently countryside. For many years Richmond was riven by sharp racial differences; it was from here that Virginia's leaders called for massive resistance to desegregation in the 1950s, and when Richmond elected its first black-majority council in the 1970s, the outgoing council deeded the statue of Lee to the state for fear it would be torn down.

Now Richmond has come to a better place. Blacks have been a majority in the city for two decades now, and in 1989 Virginia elected a black governor, Douglas Wilder, who grew up on Church Hill, in a segregated neighborhood overlooking the Capitol. The state's Martin Luther King Jr. Holiday pays homage to Confederate heroes and to the civil rights leader, and a statue of Richmond-born African-American tennis champion Arthur Ashe has been added to Monument Avenue. Politically there remain differences. Black-majority Richmond is solidly Democratic; Henrico and Chesterfield and the counties beyond are heavily Republican.

The 7th Congressional District includes most of the Richmond area, but many black precincts in the city and Henrico County are in the black-majority 3d District, which extends downriver along the James to Newport News and Norfolk. The 1992 and 1993 districting plans were overturned by federal court decisions, and replaced with a 1998 plan which smooths out the lines and which adds three counties upriver from Richmond; the district also has an extension that runs north past James Madison's home at Montpelier to Culpeper County and the Blue Ridge Mountains. But nearly 80% of the 7th's population is in metro Richmond. This is the most heavily Republican district in Virginia.

The congressman from the 7th District is Tom Bliley, elected in 1980, now chairman of the Commerce Committee. Bliley grew up in Richmond, where his family owned a funeral home; he graduated from Georgetown, served in the Navy, then returned to the family business. He started off in politics as a conservative Democrat and was elected to the Richmond Council in 1968; he was mayor of Richmond from 1970–77. In 1980, he was elected to the House as a Republican by a 53%–33% margin, and has been re-elected easily. The Democrats' 1992 redistricting put one-year incumbent George Allen in the same district, but Allen decided to leave the House and had the last laugh when he was elected governor in 1993. Bliley got on Commerce in his first term, became ranking Republican on John Dingell's Oversight Committee in 1989, then in 1993 became ranking Republican on Henry Waxman's Health and Environment Subcommittee. Bliley early on showed legislative skill dealing with issues from the electric utility grid and Medicaid formulas to home medical services and drug discounts for veterans. He showed he could stand up to tough partisans like Dingell and Waxman and also work for bipartisan solutions.

When Republicans won their House majority, Speaker Newt Gingrich, impressed by Bliley's skills, passed over more senior Republican Carlos Moorhead of California to make Bliley chairman of Commerce. The press initially focused on tobacco: Waxman had hauled tobacco company executives before TV cameras in 1994 and Bliley, representing a city that has been a tobacco center for 250 years and one of whose largest employers is Philip Morris, had decried the spectacle. But Bliley proved himself to be more than the creature of the companies. In February 1998, angry about the companies' concealment of documents on marketing strategies and scientific research, Bliley subpoenaed 39,000 pages of documents. He was not involved in the companies' $368 billion settlement with state attorneys general in June 1997, and in April 1998 quietly opposed John McCain's Senate bill; "I hope Congress will ultimately agree on a tough bipartisan plan to reduce teen smoking. We have lacked strong leadership from the president. Now we don't have the cooperation of the tobacco industry. That is unfortunate, but not a reason for inaction." But the collapse of the McCain bill in June 1998 ended the prospect of legislation.

He has in fact been a chairman who keeps tight rein on subcommittee chairmen and has moved a lot of legislation to passage. In 1995 and 1996 he moved securities litigation reform, a top priority for Silicon Valley; it was vetoed by Bill Clinton, and then both houses overrode the veto—the first and, as of this writing, only veto override of the Clinton presidency. Bipartisan agreement was hammered out on many important bills, including some where it initially seemed improbable. For all his strong conservative views, Bliley understands that on complex regulatory bills, compromise is usually necessary for passage: "You can stand like the oak or you can bend like the pine. If you choose to stand like the oak, you'll probably fall like the oak. If you stand like the pine and bend a little bit, you'll usually come out of the storm in pretty good shape." One striking example of bipartisan agreement came on the pesticide bill in July 1996. Republicans wanted to repeal the Delaney clause, which bans any substance with any provable carcinogenic effect; modern instruments are so sensitive that many harmless substances would have to be banned. Bliley and Waxman hammered out a bill which replaced Delaney and limited stricter state regulations, but which would make safety rules for certain foods more stringent and established a "no reasonable risk of harm" standard. Similarly, the Safe Drinking Water Act, after some tussles, was signed by President Clinton in August 1996.

Another example of bipartisan cooperation is the Telecommunications Act of 1996. A law speeding up the FDA approval process for drugs and medical devices was passed. So was a three-year moratorium on Internet taxes and a bill strengthening protection for copyrighted material on the Internet by penalizing evasion of safeguard devices and setting a two-year trial period for allowing libraries to make fair use of Internet copyrighted material. Also reauthorized was the Mammography Quality Standards Act. Bliley and subcommittee Chairman Joe Barton were preparing in early 1999 to move a comprehensive electricity deregulation bill, though Senator Frank Murkowski favored only a minimalist approach letting the states go ahead as they wished. Bliley has called for allowing satellite TV systems to transmit local broadcast stations: "People deserve more, not fewer choices." In May 1999 Bliley sponsored a bill to insure that stock prices are in the public domain, not owned by stock exchange; but that has strong opposition from the stock exchanges and, on the Judiciary Committee, from Bliley's frequent ally Howard Coble. Despite Governor James Gilmore's denunciations of New York's shipping of garbage to Virginia, Bliley seemed dubious about bans of interstate shipment of trash: "I don't think that I was sent to Washington to be a zoning commissioner for the counties of Virginia." Bliley also worked on local issues, getting some $25 million for renovating Richmond's Main Street train station, encouraging public-private efforts to preserve Civil War battlefields, rehousing the National Ground Intelligence Center in Charlottesville and obtaining $531,000 for the Dutch Gap Conservation Area in Chesterfield County.

House Republicans' six-year limits on committee chairmanships means that Bliley must relinquish the Commerce chair after the 2000 elections. In December 1998 he said that he wanted to stay in Congress at least four more years; perhaps he will become chairman (or ranking member) of one of the Commerce subcommittees.

Cook's Call. *Safe.* Bliley is safely entrenched in this solidly Republican district. When he does move on, Republicans should have little to worry about.

The People: Pop. 1990: 562,729; 26.5% rural; 11.4% age 65+; 86.5% White, 11.5% Black, 2.1% Other. Households: 58.8% married couple families; 29.3% married couple fams. w. children; 56.5% college educ.; median household income: $38,865; per capita income: $18,360; median house value: $91,800; median gross rent: $446.

1996 Presidential Vote			1992 Presidential Vote		
Dole (R)	158,918	(60%)	Bush (R)	148,430	(56%)
Clinton (D)	90,351	(34%)	Clinton (D)	77,119	(29%)
Perot (I)	16,647	(6%)	Perot (I)	40,798	(15%)

Rep. Tom Bliley (R)

Elected 1980; b. Jan. 28, 1932, Chesterfield Cnty.; home, Richmond; Georgetown U., B.A. 1952; Catholic; married (Mary Virginia).

Military Career: Navy, 1952–55.

Elected Office: Richmond City Cncl. 1968–77, Vice Mayor 1968–70, Mayor, 1970–77.

Professional Career: Dir., Funeral home, 1955–80.

DC Office: 2409 RHOB 20515, 202-225-2815; Fax: 202-225-0011; Web site: www.house.gov/bliley.

District Offices: Culpeper, 540-825-8960; Richmond, 804-771-2809.

Committees: *Commerce* (Chmn. of 29 R).

Group Ratings

	ADA	ACLU	AFS	LCV	CON	NTU	NFIB	COC	ACU	NTLC	CHC
1998	0	13	13	8	13	50	93	100	100	95	100
1997	5	—	0	—	84	51	—	100	75	—	—

National Journal Ratings

	1997 LIB — 1997 CONS		1998 LIB — 1998 CONS	
Economic	19%	— 76%	30%	— 67%
Social	30%	— 64%	29%	— 69%
Foreign	45%	— 55%	34%	— 62%

Key Votes of the 105th Congress

1. Clinton Budget Deal	Y	5. Puerto Rico Sthood. Ref.	N	9. Cut $ for B-2 Bombers	N
2. Education IRAs	Y	6. End Highway Set-asides	Y	10. Human Rights in China	N
3. Req. 2/3 to Raise Taxes	Y	7. School Prayer Amend.	Y	11. Withdraw Bosnia Troops	N
4. Fast-track Trade	Y	8. Ovrd. Part. Birth Veto	Y	12. End Cuban TV-Marti	N

Election Results

1998 general	Tom Bliley (R)	77,044	(79%)	($817,037)
	Bradley E. Evans (I)	20,293	(21%)	($564)
1998 primary	Tom Bliley (R) .... nominated by convention			
1996 general	Tom Bliley (R)	189,644	(75%)	($1,092,570)
	Roderic H. Slayton (D)	51,206	(20%)	($28,328)
	Bradley E. Evans (I)	11,527	(5%)	($195)

EIGHTH DISTRICT

Some two hundred years ago, when George Washington trod the brick sidewalks of Alexandria, Virginia, on his way to market or court or church, this was the largest city in northern Virginia, and dwarfed Georgetown, Maryland, just up the Potomac River; what is now Capitol Hill and downtown Washington were hills above the river's mud flats. As Washington grew, Northern Virginia seemed left behind. The District of Columbia retroceded its land south of the Potomac—now Alexandria and Arlington—to Virginia in 1846 because it seemed obvious that the federal government would never need it, and it was 97 years before the first federal building was built on the Virginia side—the Pentagon; Franklin Roosevelt wondered out loud what they would do with all that space after the war. When the Pentagon was built, Alexandria and the rural countryside of Northern Virginia were represented in Congress by Judge Howard W. Smith, a Harry Byrd Democrat, who saw as his mission the maintenance of the standards of George Washington, Thomas Jefferson and Robert E. Lee. Yet by the 1960s, even as Judge Smith kept his law offices in Old Town, Alexandria, the area was changing around him. New subdivision dwellers with white-collar jobs and lots of children wanted schools with good academic programs—not the segregated schoolhouses Judge Smith's friends were willing to finance. The new generation wanted freeways and traffic lights, planning instituted to regulate development, parks and recreation facilities. Smith's district was moved farther out into the countryside, two-party politics came to the suburbs, and local governments got to work. The congressional seat here, though often bitterly contested, was held from 1952–74 by Republican Joel Broyhill, a real estate developer who ran a fine constituency service operation in a district more than one-third of whose residents were federal employees. Democrats still held many legislative and local offices.

Now the onetime suburbs of Arlington and Alexandria have become central cities of a sort—"edge cities," using Joel Garreau's term—themselves. Giant office developments sprang up from rail yards in Crystal City and from used car lots in Rosslyn. Vietnamese and Salvadorans, immigrants from Asia and Latin America have moved into these neighborhoods, and one of America's biggest Vietnamese commercial districts is in Clarendon, about a mile from Arlington National Cemetery and Fort Myer. Politically, Alexandria and Arlington, once hotly contested, are now solidly Democratic.

The 8th Congressional District consists of Arlington County and the cities of Alexandria and Falls Church. It also takes in two separate parts of Fairfax County: the portion of high-income McLean inside the Capital Beltway and several areas south of Alexandria's Old Town—the gentle landscapes of Mount Vernon, lower-income Groveton along the old U.S. 1, suburban Springfield and the more rural areas around Lorton and Fort Belvoir. This district was designed for the 1990s by a Democratic legislature and governor to be solidly Democratic. Where formerly there had been two marginal Northern Virginia districts, now there is the safely Democratic 8th, the safely Republican 10th and the toss-up 11th (Democratic in 1992, Republican in 1994, 1996 and 1998).

The congressman from the 8th District is Jim Moran, an oft-embattled Alexandria politician with traces in his accent of his Massachusetts roots. He graduated from Holy Cross and got a master's degree, worked in Washington for HEW, the Library of Congress and the Senate Appropriations Committee. He was elected to the Alexandria City Council in 1979 and vice mayor in 1982; in 1984 he pleaded no contest to a conflict of interest charge and resigned from the Council. The charges were eventually dropped (the law he supposedly violated was even changed), and in 1985 Moran was elected mayor. In 1990, he ran for Congress in what had become one of the most populous districts in the country, stretching from Alexandria south almost to Fredericksburg, against Republican incumbent Stanford Parris. It was a nasty race: Parris said Moran was a supporter of Saddam Hussein; Moran said he wanted to "break [Parris's] nose," and called him "a deceitful, fatuous jerk." The major substantive issue was abortion, on which Moran ran a pro-choice ad portraying Lady Liberty behind bars. With a big margin in Alexandria, Moran won 52%–45%.

In the House, Moran was freshman class whip, but flip-flopped on his first big vote, the Gulf war resolution, which he ultimately voted against. He has engaged in a long and mostly unsuccessful fight to stop 11,000 Navy employees from being relocated out of Crystal City but he successfully fought Redskins owner Jack Kent Cooke's plan to build a football stadium at Potomac Yards in Alexandria. In 1993 he voted for the Clinton budget and tax package, despite its one-year pay freeze on federal employees—a tough vote in a district where 21% of workers are federal employees, the second highest in the country. He switched his vote at the last minute in June 1994 to save NASA's space station. He balked at the Clinton health care reform because it threatened federal employees' plan, and he blasted as "politically expedient" and based on "sound bites" the reinventing government plan as threatening the most talented federal employees.

Moran, with Calvin Dooley and Tim Roemer, was one of the founders in March 1997 of the New Democrat Coalition, made up of moderate Democrats mostly from suburban districts to work for alternatives to "traditional Democratic policies." He was the only Democrat to vote for a Republican program to allow local governments to consolidate federal grants into more flexible spending plans: his Alexandria experience counted. He jousted with Chairman John Mica of the subcommittee handling civil service, concerned that strengthening veterans' preferences would give them too much of an advantage over other workers. Moran also worried about streamlining the civil service appeals process with language that would have excluded the EEOC. He jousted—literally—with other Republicans, shoving Californian Randy Cunningham off the floor and out the House chamber doors in November 1995 after Cunningham said that Moran had "turned his back on Desert Storm." Moran later apologized and said, "I would prefer to be known as a statesman rather than a fighter in the literal way."

Since 1993 he has been on the Appropriations Committee; from his seat on the District of Columbia Subcommittee he has put in much bipartisan labor on straightening out the District's finances—and in the process helped force the District to close Lorton prison. He strongly opposed the February 1998 Republican initiative to rename Washington National Airport after Ronald Reagan. Moran was a strong supporter of fast track and struggled in vain to get enough Democratic votes to pass it in November 1997. His interests range widely: He has worked to get more foreign "information technology professionals" admitted under H-1B visas and called for a logging moratorium to protect roadless sections of the southern Appalachian national forests. He was strongly critical of Bill Clinton's conduct in the Lewinsky scandal and in September 1998 suggested the president should resign. In October 1998 he was one of 31 Democrats who voted for the Republicans' impeachment inquiry, but he voted against impeachment in December.

The 1992 redistricting gave Moran a solidly Democratic district, but he has had serious competition anyway; perhaps combativeness invites combativeness. He won 56% of the vote in 1992 and 59% in 1994 against Kyle McSlarrow, later a top aide to Bob Dole and Trent Lott and manager of Dan Quayle's presidential campaign. In 1998 he was opposed by psychologist Demaris Miller, wife of Reagan OMB Director James Miller. Miller spent the impressive sum of $643,000, almost as much as Moran's $559,000. But the race evidently never got very close; Moran had $703,000 cash on hand after he won 67%–33%.

Cook's Call. *Safe.* This Northern Virginia district has seen some competition in the past, but Moran has established a pretty solid hold of this Democratic leaning district. He is safe for 2000.

The People: Pop. 1990: 562,808; 0.3% rural; 9.9% age 65 + ; 76.1% White, 13.4% Black, 6.6% Asian, 0.3% Amer. Indian, 3.6% Other; 8.6% Hispanic Origin. Households: 46.5% married couple families; 20.6% married couple fams. w. children; 71.3% college educ.; median household income: $48,839; per capita income: $24,799; median house value: $209,900; median gross rent: $687.

1996 Presidential Vote

Clinton (D)	130,177	(55%)
Dole (R)	95,839	(41%)
Perot (I)	9,439	(4%)

1992 Presidential Vote

Clinton (D)	144,092	(51%)
Bush (R)	107,196	(38%)
Perot (I)	31,757	(11%)

Rep. James P. Moran (D)

Elected 1990; b. May 16, 1945, Buffalo, NY; home, Alexandria; Col. of Holy Cross, B.A. 1967, City U. of NY, 1968, U. of Pittsburgh; M.P.A. 1970; Catholic; separated.

Elected Office: Alexandria City Cncl., 1979–82; Alexandria Vice Mayor, 1982–84, Alexandria Mayor, 1985–90.

Professional Career: Budget analyst & auditor, U.S. Dept. of H.E.W., 1968–74; Fiscal policy spec., Library of Congress, 1974–76; Staff, U.S. Senate Approp. Cmte., 1976–80; Investment broker, 1980–88.

DC Office: 2239 RHOB 20515, 202-225-4376; Fax: 202-225-0017; Web site: www.house.gov/moran.

District Office: Alexandria, 703-971-4700.

Committees: *Appropriations* (14th of 27 D): Defense; District of Columbia (RMM); Interior. *Budget* (14th of 19 D).

Group Ratings

	ADA	ACLU	AFS	LCV	CON	NTU	NFIB	COC	ACU	NTLC	CHC
1998	75	50	78	77	91	32	36	61	8	16	17
1997	65	—	75	—	62	34	—	50	13	—	—

National Journal Ratings

	1997 LIB — 1997 CONS	1998 LIB — 1998 CONS
Economic	63% — 36%	58% — 42%
Social	65% — 34%	73% — 27%
Foreign	82% — 16%	82% — 16%

Key Votes of the 105th Congress

1. Clinton Budget Deal	N	5. Puerto Rico Sthood. Ref.	Y
2. Education IRAs	Y	6. End Highway Set-asides	N
3. Req. 2/3 to Raise Taxes	N	7. School Prayer Amend.	N
4. Fast-track Trade	Y	8. Ovrd. Part. Birth Veto	Y

9. Cut $ for B-2 Bombers	Y
10. Human Rights in China	Y
11. Withdraw Bosnia Troops	N
12. End Cuban TV-Marti	Y

Election Results

1998 general	James P. Moran (D)	97,545	(67%)	($559,357)
	Demaris H. Miller (R)	48,352	(33%)	($643,434)
1998 primary	James P. Moran (D) .... nominated by convention			
1996 general	James P. Moran (D)	152,334	(66%)	($319,334)
	John E. Otey (R)	64,562	(28%)	($71,267)
	Others	12,525	(5%)	

NINTH DISTRICT

One of the first areas to be settled from the seacoast to the great American interior was what is now southwest Virginia. As early as 1765, settlements were carved out in the great Valley of Virginia, which bends westward and south toward Tennessee and the Cumberland Gap. Most settlers were of Scots-Irish lineage, and the mountainous area where they moved developed almost apart from the rest of Virginia. The fiercely independent settlers were first farmers, later often coal miners, as in West Virginia, which wasn't a separate state until 1863. Politically, this virtually all-white area opposed slavery and was skeptical if not hostile to the Confederacy. Out of the crucible of struggle between secessionists and unionists, southwest Virginia developed a robust two-party politics after the Civil War, with both parties resembling their national counterparts more closely than in the rest of Virginia.

The 9th Congressional District covers all of southwest Virginia west of Roanoke. Over the years, the district became known as the "Fighting Ninth," because of its taste for raucous politics, culturally conservative and economically populist. It is becoming somewhat more like the rest of Virginia, as development has moved down Interstate 81 to, and even past, Blacksburg, home of Virginia Tech. But mountain counties farther west have lost population and have not changed much. The Fighting Ninth voted for Republican Governors George Allen and James Gilmore and for 1994 Republican Senate candidate Oliver North; it voted for Bill Clinton in 1992 and 1996 and for 1996 Democratic Senate candidate Mark Warner. No other Virginia district voted for that combination.

The congressman from the 9th is Rick Boucher, a Democrat first elected in 1982. Boucher grew up in the antique town of Abingdon, went to Roanoke College and then the University of Virginia for law school; he practiced law in Abingdon and was elected to the Virginia Senate in 1975, at 29. Politics runs in the family: his father was the Republican commonwealth's attorney in Washington County, while his mother was county Democratic chairwoman; his grandfather and great-grandfather were Democratic members of the House of Delegates. In 1982 Boucher ran for the U.S. House against veteran incumbent William Wampler and won with big margins in the coal counties on the Kentucky border. Boucher, like other "Fighting Ninth" Democrats, tends to vote with House Democrats most but not all of the time.

Much of Boucher's work has been done on the Commerce Committee's Telecommunications Subcommittee. Back in 1988 he co-sponsored with Al Gore a bill to allow phone companies to offer cable TV and sponsored the 1988 Satellite Home Viewers Act, so viewers without over-the-air network reception could subscribe to satellite services carrying network channels: the beginning of the now booming satellite TV business. Cable TV had its start in mountainous areas where network TV signals were weak, and Boucher sees new technologies, from satellite TV to the Internet, as a means for out-of-the-way places like the 9th to compete on an equal commercial basis with urban areas. On the 1996 Telecommunications Act Boucher helped write provisions intended to open up competition in the local telephone and cable TV markets.

Boucher was a co-founder of the House Internet Caucus in April 1996 with Rick White of Washington; he is now co-chair with Bob Godlatte of the next-door 6th District. He worked on the Judiciary Subcommittee on Courts and Intellectual Property with Goodlatte to update copyright laws for the digital age and for a consensus on a National Information Infrastructure. He had sponsored the 1993 law which permitted messages with commercial content to traverse the Internet backbone. He has gotten Appalachian Regional Commission grant money to create an electronic classroom in Floyd County which will allow communication and instruction in all the schools in southwest Virginia. He has set up "electronic villages" in Blacksburg and Abingdon, with entire communities online. He has worked for binding arbitration to settle Superfund suits, for allowing state and local governments to an interstate shipment of municipal waste and for electricity deregulation, which he hopes will benefit the coal industry and stimulate investment in mine facilities.

Boucher has set up various organizations to spur economic development in the 9th. In 1993 he set up a Commission on the Future of Southwest Virginia, which has called for a venture capital fund, a joint state legislative agenda and winterizing state parks. Boucher has promoted projects from a museum at an excavated Indian site in Bland County to a gold course on national forest lands. In 1998 he announced a $500,000 TVA grant to set up a Nature Conservancy Timber Bank, to which landholders can sell their timber rights. He conducts an active constituency service operation in an area where many people have problems with Social Security, veterans' benefits and black lung payments.

Boucher came into the national spotlight in the Judiciary Committee hearings on impeachment. Far less strident than most other Judiciary Democrats, speaking with old-fashioned formality in a businesslike manner, he pressed Kenneth Starr on whether a president can be prosecuted after leaving office. He was the author of the Democratic resolution to conduct a limited impeachment inquiry in October 1998. In December 1998 he was the author of the Democrats' censure resolution.

In this usually partisan district, Boucher has become highly popular. His Commerce Committee seat helps him to raise large sums of money; in 1998 he spent $795,000 and had $390,000 cash on hand afterwards. He had competition that year from folksy ophthalmologist Joe Barta, who spent $292,000 of his own money on the race. Boucher won 61%–39%, carrying all but two counties. Redistricting is unlikely to change the shape of this corner-of-the-state district.

Cook's Call. *Safe.* Though this conservative district has been quite competitive on the presidential level, Boucher has continued to post impressive margins of victory since his first re-election contest in 1984. His strong win over a well-funded challenger in 1998 is a sign that Boucher is well-positioned for re-election in 2000.

The People: Pop. 1990: 562,508; 71.3% rural; 14.1% age 65 + ; 96.6% White, 2.4% Black, 0.8% Asian, 0.1% Amer. Indian, 0.1% Other; 0.4% Hispanic Origin. Households: 61.1% married couple families; 29% married couple fams. w. children; 29.7% college educ.; median household income: $20,857; per capita income: $10,097; median house value: $49,100; median gross rent: $235.

1996 Presidential Vote			1992 Presidential Vote		
Clinton (D)	91,469	(46%)	Clinton (D)	99,099	(45%)
Dole (R)	85,531	(43%)	Bush (R)	93,673	(43%)
Perot (I)	20,603	(10%)	Perot (I)	26,676	(12%)

Rep. Rick Boucher (D)

Elected 1982; b. Aug. 1, 1946, Abingdon; home, Abingdon; Roanoke Col., B.A. 1968, U. of VA, J.D. 1971; United Methodist; single.

Elected Office: VA Senate, 1975–1983.

Professional Career: Practicing atty., 1971–83.

DC Office: 2329 RHOB 20515, 202-225-3861; Fax: 202-225-0442; Web site: www.house.gov/boucher.

District Offices: Abingdon, 540-628-1145; Big Stone Gap, 540-523-5450; Pulaski, 540-980-4310.

Committees: *Commerce* (5th of 24 D): Energy & Power; Telecommunications, Trade & Consumer Protection. *Judiciary* (4th of 16 D): Courts & Intellectual Property.

Group Ratings

	ADA	ACLU	AFS	LCV	CON	NTU	NFIB	COC	ACU	NTLC	CHC
1998	95	75	100	85	43	13	14	35	4	6	0
1997	85	—	100	—	3	15	—	40	8	—	—

National Journal Ratings

	1997 LIB — 1997 CONS			1998 LIB — 1998 CONS		
Economic	71%	—	28%	64%	—	34%
Social	70%	—	29%	73%	—	27%
Foreign	69%	—	28%	78%	—	19%

Key Votes of the 105th Congress

1. Clinton Budget Deal	N	5. Puerto Rico Sthood. Ref.	Y	9. Cut $ for B-2 Bombers	Y
2. Education IRAs	N	6. End Highway Set-asides	N	10. Human Rights in China	Y
3. Req. 2/3 to Raise Taxes	N	7. School Prayer Amend.	N	11. Withdraw Bosnia Troops	N
4. Fast-track Trade	N	8. Ovrd. Part. Birth Veto	N	12. End Cuban TV-Marti	Y

Election Results

1998 general	Rick Boucher (D) 87,163	(61%)	($795,457)
	J. A. (Joe) Barta (R) 55,918	(39%)	($443,938)
1998 primary	Rick Boucher (D) .... nominated by convention		
1996 general	Rick Boucher (D) 122,908	(65%)	($576,709)
	Patrick C. Muldoon (R) 58,055	(31%)	($71,662)
	Thomas I. Roberts (Ref) 8,080	(4%)	($5,110)

TENTH DISTRICT

Even as the Constitution was being hammered out in Philadelphia, the rolling green Piedmont of northern Virginia and the fertile mountain-bound lands of the Shenandoah Valley were buzzing with new settlers. They came up the rivers that flow into the Chesapeake, into the Valley from the great Wagon Road south from Pennsylvania, moving onto lands speculated on by George Washington and his peers. During the Civil War, this was some of the most heavily contested land on the continent; afterwards, the surge of movement having propelled new settlers much farther west, this part of Virginia was well-settled and became prime fox hunting country. Now subdivisions have sprouted up on fields, and the horse farms of the Piedmont, long first or second homes of some of the richest people in America, are attracting a growing population of Washington, D.C., commuters and weekend residents. What looked like marginal farmlands to the settlers of the early 19th Century now looks like heaven for city-dwellers: bucolic green hills with views of the Blue Ridge and other mountains, antique houses and tiny crossroads communities. There is still an old-fashioned air in the narrow streets of the old county seat towns, but a McDonald's culture has developed on the bypass roads on their out-skirts.

The 10th Congressional District covers much of this territory. The district has expanded as people have moved outward; today it is entirely, in the familiar phrase, outside the Beltway. About one-third of its people live in suburban Fairfax County, by many measures the most affluent county in the United States: 61% of its households had incomes over $50,000 in 1989, number one in the country, though it was only number seven in percentage of over $100,000 households. Also, 49% of its adults over 25 were college graduates, more than double the national figure. Fairfax, and especially the 10th's portion of it—affluent and woodsy Great Falls and parts of McLean, the new subdivisions around the old crossroads of Centreville and the upscale Fair Oaks shopping mall area—is full of high-salaried, two-earner families, young and well-educated, employed more often by the private sector than by government, frazzled by commuting on clogged roads. Beyond Fairfax, another one-third of district residents live in Loudoun County and parts of Prince William County, once rural—the Manassas battlefield is here—but one of the most rapidly growing parts of the nation in the 1990s, with subdivisions sprouting in all directions and huge new tollways and parkways full of traffic in and out of edge cities from Tysons Corner to Dulles Airport and beyond. These new areas are not quite as high-income as Fairfax, and culturally considerably more conservative. The last third of the 10th's residents are in smaller, still rural-appearing Fauquier and Rappahannock counties, and west of the Blue Ridge in the Shenandoah Valley. Politically, this is a very Republican district. The Shenandoah tradition of Harry Byrd Democrats switched seamlessly to Republicanism, as indeed many local politicians switched parties themselves; the new suburbanites are if anything more determinedly Republican.

The congressman from the 10th District is Frank Wolf, first elected in 1980 in a district most of whose residents were inside the Beltway. Wolf grew up in Philadelphia, went to law school at Georgetown, worked as a staffer on Capitol Hill and as an Interior Department ap-pointee in the Nixon and Ford administrations and practiced law. In 1978 he ran for Congress against Joseph Fisher, a liberal who had won the district in 1974, and lost 53%–47%; in 1980 he ran again and won 51%–49%. He worked hard on federal employee and transportation issues and, as the district moved outward, became unbeatable. His overall voting record is moderately conservative. He has long maintained a crackerjack constituency service operation and has been key in promoting federal employee causes. He has promoted on-site child care centers at federal workplaces, flextime and flexplace arrangements, leave-sharing and telecommuting (the first center was in Winchester). He opposed Hatch Act repeal, saying it would politicize the federal workforce. He opposed the Clinton health care reform in 1994 because it would have gutted the federal employee health plan, and he opposed the Contract with America tax cut in 1995 because it would have required higher pension payments by federal employees; he and Tom Davis and Maryland's Connie Morella were three of only 11 Republicans to vote against the tax cut.

Wolf has used his seat on the Transporation Appropriations Subcommittee to work on projects in trafffic-choked Northern Virginia more than to set national transportation policy. He got full funding for the 103-mile Metro subway system, for widening I-66 from the Beltway to Gainesville, for the Route 234 interchange in Manassas, for express buses in the Dulles Airport corridor and for improvements in the Virginia commuter rail system. He led the move to put Reagan National and Dulles airports under a regional authority, which built a new terminal for Reagan National and has vastly expanded Dulles, and pushed to get the National Air and Space Museum annex located at Dulles. Wolf has consistently opposed earmarking funds for members' pet transportation projects in appropriations bills as "immoral"; Transportation Committee Chairman Bud Shuster has no such scruples, and systematically offered members $15 million for earmarked projects in return for their votes for the giant transportation bill passed in May 1998. To these negotiations Wolf was mainly a spectator, calling at one point for repealing 4.3 cents of the per gallon federal gas tax and letting states collect and spend their own money. Wolf has been concerned about truck safety and charges that the Office of Motor Carriers' enforcement has been deteriorating; in February 1999 he proposed to move the bureau from the Federal Highway Administration to safety-conscious NHTSA, and he has called for separate Interstate lanes for trucks on I-81. In October 1998 he moved to overturn the DOT order for peanut-free zones in every plane to accommodate those with peanut allergies. He passed a 1996 law creating the Shenandoah National Battlefields Historic District.

On some issues Wolf has been motivated by deep moral concerns. One is gambling, to which he is strongly opposed. He first proposed the National Gambling Impact Study Commission, passed in 1997, but was not pleased by the appointees, many of whom are pro-gambling; while awaiting the commission report promised for June 1999, he called for a GAO study of the influence of the gambling industry in national and state politics—a "witch hunt," said gambling lobbyist and former Republican National Chairman Frank Fahrenkopf.

Wolf has also worked diligently to protect human rights abroad, on the Foreign Operations Subcommittee and on many trips abroad. He met with Li Peng in China and went to Beijing Prison No. 1 where Tiananmen Square protesters have been held; he visited the Perm Camp 35 in the Soviet gulag and a Serb-run prison camp in Bosnia. With California's Nancy Pelosi, he has led the annual moves to withdraw normal trade status for China because of human right violations. He was the chief sponsor of the Freedom from Religious Persecution Act, which passed the House 375–41 in May 1998. It would set up a monitoring bureau in the State Department, target the most serious violators and could cut off foreign aid of Export-Import Bank loans; although it would let the president issue waivers, it was opposed by the Clinton Administration.

Wolf is offended by what he considers political wrongdoing, from whatever quarter. In 1994 he worked doggedly to find out how many non-employees had White House passes and to get campaign consultants with passes to make financial disclosures. In 1997, when the embattled Newt Gingrich needed every vote he could get to be re-elected speaker, Wolf voted "present."

Wolf was re-elected by the identical margin, 72%–25%, in 1996 and 1998.

Cook's Call. *Safe.* Wolf does a good job of balancing the needs of a district that has a conservative lean but is heavily populated by federal workers. He is well-entrenched in this district.

The People: Pop. 1990: 562,257; 43.6% rural; 7.8% age 65 + ; 90.7% White, 5.7% Black, 2.7% Asian, 0.2% Amer. Indian, 0.7% Other; 2.2% Hispanic Origin. Households: 66.3% married couple families; 35.5% married couple fams. w. children; 55.4% college educ.; median household income: $46,205; per capita income: $20,065; median house value: $155,400; median gross rent: $556.

1996 Presidential Vote

Dole (R)	140,684	(55%)
Clinton (D)	99,510	(39%)
Perot (I)	16,476	(6%)

1992 Presidential Vote

Bush (R)	124,783	(50%)
Clinton (D)	83,214	(33%)
Perot (I)	41,228	(17%)

Rep. Frank R. Wolf (R)

Elected 1980; b. Jan. 30, 1939, Philadelphia, PA; home, Vienna; PA St. U., B.A. 1961, Georgetown U., LL.B. 1965; Presbyterian; married (Carolyn).

Military Career: Army, 1962–63, Army Reserves 1963–67.

Professional Career: Legis. Asst., U.S. Rep. Edward Biester, 1968–71; Asst., U.S. Interior Secy. Rogers Morton, 1971–74; Dep. Asst. Secy., U.S. Dept. of Interior, 1974–75; Practicing atty., 1975–80.

DC Office: 241 CHOB 20515, 202-225-5136; Fax: 202-225-0437; Web site: www.house.gov/wolf.

District Offices: Herndon, 703-709-5800; Winchester, 540-667-0990.

Committees: *Appropriations* (7th of 34 R): Foreign Operations & Export Financing; Transportation (Chmn.); Treasury, Postal Service & General Government.

Group Ratings

	ADA	ACLU	AFS	LCV	CON	NTU	NFIB	COC	ACU	NTLC	CHC
1998	10	13	22	15	81	66	93	72	80	89	100
1997	15	—	25	—	70	49	—	90	84	—	—

National Journal Ratings

	1997 LIB — 1997 CONS			1998 LIB — 1998 CONS		
Economic	40%	—	59%	39%	—	59%
Social	19%	—	80%	29%	—	69%
Foreign	32%	—	65%	43%	—	57%

Key Votes of the 105th Congress

1. Clinton Budget Deal	Y	5. Puerto Rico Sthood. Ref.	N	9. Cut $ for B-2 Bombers	N
2. Education IRAs	Y	6. End Highway Set-asides	Y	10. Human Rights in China	Y
3. Req. 2/3 to Raise Taxes	Y	7. School Prayer Amend.	Y	11. Withdraw Bosnia Troops	N
4. Fast-track Trade	N	8. Ovrd. Part. Birth Veto	Y	12. End Cuban TV-Marti	*

Election Results

1998 general	Frank R. Wolf (R) 103,648	(72%)	($465,350)
	Cornell W. Brooks (D) 36,476	(25%)	($116,526)
	Others 4,631	(3%)	
1998 primary	Frank R. Wolf (R) .... nominated by convention		
1996 general	Frank R. Wolf (R) 169,266	(72%)	($251,763)
	Robert L. Weinberg (D) 59,145	(25%)	($61,881)
	Others 6,602	(3%)	

ELEVENTH DISTRICT

When author and *Washington Post* reporter Joel Garreau coined the term "edge city" to describe the autonomous urban centers developing on the rims of some of the nation's oldest municipalities, his prime example was Tysons Corner, Virginia. Rising on a hill west of Washington, Tysons Corner was a back-country intersection 50 years ago and a junction of several suburban roads 25 years ago; today it is home to the largest concentration of office space to be found anywhere between Washington and Atlanta, with a modern skyline and busy multi-lane avenues that serve as arteries to the nearby Capital Beltway. Fairfax County, which includes all of Tysons Corner, has changed just as dramatically since the end of World War II. At first only a few District of Columbia residents seeking breathing room in the suburbs trickled into Northern Virginia; initially they went to Arlington and Alexandria. But that trickle became a rush as young marrieds with large families and whites avoiding the increasingly high-crime District pushed farther out into Fairfax. Now Fairfax County is no longer Washington's country cousin. By July 1998 it was estimated to have 929,000 residents, nearly twice the District's 523,000. It had in 1990 the nation's highest median household income ($59,284), almost half its residents have a bachelor's degree or more and nearly 70% of its households have two or more vehicles. Fairfax has been transformed from a suburban county where people commute to government jobs in Washington, to a 21st Century urban county where people work somewhere around the Beltway and mostly for private sector employers.

The 11th Congressional District, the seat Virginia gained in the 1990 Census, went to fast-growing Fairfax County and its neighbor just to the south, Prince William County. The 11th straddles the Beltway; its inner portion includes older comfortable areas like Annandale, which has increasing Korean and Vietnamese populations, while the outer portion spans Tysons Corner and the office corridor out the Dulles Toll Road, to the airport. The 11th runs south through comfortable subdivision areas like Burke and covers the somewhat lower-income Woodbridge and Dale City areas of Prince William. This is a cosmopolitan district: 8% black, 7% Hispanic, 8% Asian; 19% of residents speak a language other than English at home. The district is made up largely of two-income families, many with at least one spouse employed in one of the many divisions of high-tech companies that dot Fairfax County. Politically, the 11th's educated, mobile electorate produces a robust two-party politics. In the 1980s, it would have voted Republican for president, with both Democratic and Republican state legislators; in the 1990s it voted 43%–42% for George Bush in 1992 and 49%–47% for Bill Clinton in 1996.

The congressman from the 11th District is Tom Davis, a Republican elected in 1994. Davis grew up in northern Virginia, was president of his class at the Capitol Page School, was a friend of David Eisenhower at Amherst College, and served on active duty in the Army before earning a law degree. He was first elected to the Fairfax County Board of Supervisors, a high visibility position here, in 1979. Over the years, he gained a reputation for financial savvy in municipal matters and for seeking compromise over confrontation; in 1991 he was elected board chairman, something in the nature of a mayor.

In 1994 Davis ran for the 11th District seat against Democrat Leslie Byrne, who had won 50%–45% in 1992. Byrne had voted solidly for Clinton Administration positions and called for discipline against members of the Democratic Caucus who did not; she had strong support from labor and feminist groups, and spent $1.1 million. But Davis was able to raise and spend even more, $1.4 million. He won 53%–45%, even as Republican Oliver North fell to Democratic Senator Charles Robb in the 11th by 51%–36%.

As soon as he arrived on Capitol Hill, Davis was handed by Speaker Newt Gingrich one of the hottest potatoes of the new Congress: dealing with the affairs of the troubled District of Columbia government and its then-mayor, Marion Barry. As chairman of the House Government Reform and Oversight Committee's D. C. Subcommittee, Davis first rejected Barry's request for massive federal aid, working closely with Gingrich and District Delegate Eleanor Holmes Norton to cut District spending. Together they passed in April 1995 a law establishing a five-member control board to oversee the D.C. government. Davis's years in local government, including many dealings with Barry, gave him a reputation as "Mr. Conciliation," and he tried not to be confrontational with the District, playing "good cop" to the "bad cop" of successive D.C. Appropriations Subcommittee Chairmen James Walsh and Charles Taylor. Davis tended to oppose the appropriators' detailed policy prescription as micromanagement. He went along with the 1997 law taking power over nine agencies from Barry and giving it to the control board. In the process Congress ordered the closing of D.C.'s Lorton Prison in Fairfax County, long a goal of Northern Virginia politicians; the last inmates were transferred to a new Sussex County, Virginia, prison in August 1998. In 1998 Barry did not run for re-election; in his place voters elected Anthony Williams, chief financial officer of the controlboard. In February 1999 Davis and District Delegate Eleanor Holmes Norton sponsored a bill restoring full management powers to the District; it was speedily passed. Davis and Norton also sponsored a bill suggested by *Washington Post* publisher Donald Graham to enable District students to attend public colleges at in-state tuition rates. When this was criticized as undercutting the University of the District of Columbia, they added funds for it; they also included private colleges in the District, Maryland and Virginia to help District students stay close to home.

On other issues, Davis has a moderate voting record, near the midpoint of the House. He opposed the Contract with America tax cut in 1995 because it would have required higher pension payments by federal employees; he and suburban Washington's Frank Wolf and Connie Morella were three of only 11 Republicans who voted against the tax cut. He supported the Democratic Blue Dogs' budget as well as the Republicans'. He also worked on unfunded mandate reform, federal acquisition policy and the securities litigation reform which was passed over Clinton's veto. He has looked out for the interests of federal employees and contractors and was one of four co-chairmen of the Information Technology Working Group. In May 1999 he sponsored the Y2K litigation bill which passed the House 236–190. It would give sued firms a 90-day window to solve problems, would limit punitive damages to $250,000 or three times compensatory damages and would take cases out of state courts and into federal court. Opposed by most Democrats, it would force the Clinton-Gore team to choose between trial lawyers and Silicon Valley.

Davis is a political buff with a detailed knowledge of political statistics across the country. In Virginia's 1997 elections, he criss-crossed the state and created a PAC which gave at least $150,000 to state legislative candidates. When challenged as partisan, he said, "I don't think it's being overly partisan to say we need two-party competition. I just got tired of seeing a lot of institutional money going to Democrats in legislative races and then having these people vote against business." He is said to be interested in running for the Senate if John Warner retires in 2002. In September 1997, National Republican Congressional Committee Chairman John Linder named Davis to be his chief recruiter. After the November 1998 election, Newt Gingrich changed the rules and made the NRCC chairmanship elective rather than appointive, and Davis ran against Linder for the post. Many members blamed Linder for the disappointing 1998 results, which were far out of line with his predictions, and Tom DeLay put his whip organization to work for Davis. Davis won 130–77. He insists that he will help conservatives as well as his fellow moderates; he could hardly protect or enlarge the Republican majority without doing so. Even so, he was criticized by the Family Research Council for meeting with the Log Cabin Republicans of Northern Virginia in February 1999 (his response: "These are constituents of mine. As you know, I have a longstanding policy of meeting with everybody") and he risked further wrath by meeting with AFL-CIO leaders in March 1999. At the Williamsburg Republican retreat in February 1999, he shocked members with a video showing a delighted Dick Gephardt celebrating the Democratic takeover of the House and distributed polls with ominous analysis; but the poll showed Republicans only 3% behind Democrats in the generic vote—a result at least as favorable to Republicans as poll results before their victories in 1994, 1996 and 1998.

At home Davis is so strong in the 11th District that the local Democrats canceled their June 1998 nominating convention. In November Davis won 82% of the vote against an independent.

Cook's Call. *Safe.* Though this district has been a battleground for presidential contests in recent years, Davis has won re-election rather easily. His moderate image and ability to remain highly visible in the hard to break through D.C. media market, make him a very tough target.

The People: Pop. 1990: 562,596; 1.7% rural; 6.2% age 65+; 80.8% White, 8.2% Black, 8.1% Asian, 0.3% Amer. Indian, 2.6% Other; 7.2% Hispanic Origin. Households: 60.3% married couple families; 32.5% married couple fams. w. children; 71.4% college educ.; median household income: $54,369; per capita income: $22,202; median house value: $191,000; median gross rent: $718.

1996 Presidential Vote			1992 Presidential Vote		
Clinton (D)	109,304	(49%)	Bush (R)	95,722	(43%)
Dole (R)	105,085	(47%)	Clinton (D)	93,787	(42%)
Perot (I)	10,845	(5%)	Perot (I)	32,471	(15%)

Rep. Tom Davis (R)

Elected 1994; b. Jan. 5, 1949, Minot, ND; home, Falls Church; Amherst Col. B.A. 1971, U. of VA, J.D. 1975; Christian Scientist; married (Peggy).

Military Career: Army, 1971–72; Army Reserves, 1972–79.

Elected Office: Fairfax Cnty. Bd. of Supervisors, 1979–94, Chmn., 1991–94.

Professional Career: Vice Pres. & Gen. Cnsl., PRC Inc., 1977–94.

DC Office: 224 CHOB 20515, 202-225-1492; Fax: 202-225-3071; Web site: www.house.gov/tomdavis.

District Offices: Annandale, 703-916-9610; Herndon, 703-437-1726; Woodbridge, 703-590-4599.

Committees: *NRCC Chairman. Government Reform* (9th of 24 R): Census; District of Columbia (Chmn.); Government Management, Information & Technology.

Group Ratings

	ADA	ACLU	AFS	LCV	CON	NTU	NFIB	COC	ACU	NTLC	CHC
1998	15	69	33	38	42	41	86	100	64	67	75
1997	25	—	38	—	37	46	—	100	72	—	—

National Journal Ratings

	1997 LIB — 1997 CONS			1998 LIB — 1998 CONS		
Economic	39%	—	60%	39%	—	59%
Social	41%	—	57%	53%	—	47%
Foreign	43%	—	55%	49%	—	48%

Key Votes of the 105th Congress

1. Clinton Budget Deal	Y	5. Puerto Rico Sthood. Ref.	Y	9. Cut $ for B-2 Bombers	N
2. Education IRAs	Y	6. End Highway Set-asides	N	10. Human Rights in China	N
3. Req. 2/3 to Raise Taxes	Y	7. School Prayer Amend.	Y	11. Withdraw Bosnia Troops	N
4. Fast-track Trade	Y	8. Ovrd. Part. Birth Veto	Y	12. End Cuban TV-Marti	N

Election Results

1998 general	Tom Davis (R)	91,603	(82%)	($917,158)
	C. W. (Levi) Levy (I)	18,807	(17%)	
	Others	1,701	(2%)	
1998 primary	Tom Davis (R)	nominated by convention		
1996 general	Tom Davis (R)	138,758	(64%)	($1,333,607)
	Thomas J. Horton (D)	74,701	(35%)	($290,492)

WASHINGTON

From Starbucks coffee to grunge music, from America's leading exporter Boeing to America's leading software maker Microsoft, Washington—the state at the far northwest corner of the continental United States—became a national trend-setter in the 1990s. An unusual environment and human creativity have combined to produce these achievements: Seattle's cold misty air and 225 overcast days a year stimulate the appetite for strong aromatic coffee, and the shapeless blue jeans and sweatshirts worn year-round in this moist climate by professionals and teenagers alike created a trend made famous by Nirvana and Soundgarden and other grunge artists. Boeing's airframe business took off during World War II because the Pacific Northwest's abundant hydroelectric power made cheap aluminum possible, and through booms and despite busts Boeing has mostly kept growing. Microsoft, founded by the usually tieless and tousle-haired Bill Gates and based in Redmond, east of Lake Washington, became one of America's great success stories as its computer software business boomed, while the computer hardware business faced increasing problems. With flannel shirts and umbrellas, blue-collar types working off hangovers as if in a Raymond Carver story, and professionals relaxing on woodsy acreage, Washington set a tone for the 1990s, a style plainly Middle American but with attitude, an ordinariness so apt it is no longer ordinary.

All this comes to a state barely a century old, which in the two decades after statehood in 1889 built a new civilization, as transcontinental railroads reached the great ports of Puget Sound, the wheat-processing city of Spokane inland, orchard towns and fishing ports and lumber settlements. Shielded from the heavy rains and storms of the Pacific by the Olympic Mountains and the Sound, Seattle quickly became a serious American city, a lusty town full of lumbermen and railroad workers. When gold was struck in the Klondike and Alaska, Seattle became a metropolis of miners, prospectors and get-rich-quick operators, the site of the original "Skid Road" (skid row is a corruption propagated by a 1937 magazine article), where logs were rolled downhill to the port; today it's the focus of the restored Pioneer Square area. Booming, young Seattle had a turbulent class-warfare politics in the years before World War I, pitting the Industrial Workers of the World (the IWW, or Wobblies) against city business and civic leaders; the businessmen, after some violence, prevailed. Adding to the area's distinctiveness was its large numbers of Scandinavian immigrants, with their favorable views of cooperative enterprises and government ownership.

Over time, Washington was transformed by a series of national decisions which set its course for decades. One was government development of hydroelectric power. The Columbia River and its tributary, the Snake, falling thousands of feet in a relatively short distance, had far greater hydroelectric potential than any other American river system, and Franklin Roosevelt was always interested in these river valley projects. In 1937, Bonneville Dam was completed on the lower Columbia; in 1940, Grand Coulee Dam, the largest man-made structure in the world at the time, was opened where the Columbia cuts through the arid, surrealistically contoured plains of eastern Washington. Washington proved hospitable to the industrial union movement of the 1930s and became one of the nation's most heavily unionized states. When war came, Washington's hydroelectric power—the cheapest electricity in the country—made it the natural site for huge aluminum production plants, which require vast amounts of electricity, and the Seattle area became the home not only of shipbuilders, but of what became the biggest aircraft manufacturer in the country, Boeing. After the war, the Hanford plant on the Columbia was one of the government's main nuclear weapons manufacturing sites. Cheap power, aluminum, aircraft, nuclear weapons and high unionized wages: These became Washington's economic foundations in the post-World War II years.

Today, Washington is a commonwealth of 5.7 million, economically booming though not as much as in the mid-1990s, pleased to the point of smugness with its physical environment. It now lives less off the brawn of hydroelectric power and rail and ship tonnage and more off the brains that have made Boeing the world leader in aircraft and Microsoft the world leader in software. There are some problems: Boeing, which added 15,000 to its payroll in 1996, ran into headwinds in 1998 as east Asian countries canceled orders, forcing Boeing to cut its workforce 20% in December 1998; the aircraft business is cyclical and chancy, and newcomers are told how Boeing cut its payroll from 100,000 in 1967 to 38,000 in 1971. Similarly, Microsoft in 1998 was sued by the Justice Department's antitrust division and a number of states and is aware that it cannot afford to rest on yesterday's products and business practices; even as Bill Gates built his huge high-tech mansion on the shore of Lake Washington, his wealth, mostly in the form of Microsoft stock, is subject to diminishment as well as astonishing growth. Even as Gates squirmed while giving Senate testimony in March 1998 and in videotaped testimony in November 1998 in the antitrust trial, Microsoft stepped up its lobbying activity and political contributions—much of them to Republicans, though Gates in 1993 declared himself a Democrat.

The Columbia basin's hydroelectric power is no longer at capacity, and the dams have reduced the salmon population so much that the Seattle region is the first big metropolitan area subject to the stringent regulations of the Endangered Species Act. The Hanford Nuclear Reservation, which produced plutonium for the military, for years leaked radioactive waste, which must now be cleaned up at the cost of billions, while new underground storage procedures have been criticized as unsafe. Washington's apples, half the nation's production, have long been barred from obvious markets in East Asia, and face stiff competition from China, while wheat sales can be cut off (as they nearly were for Pakistan in 1998) by U.S. foreign policy sanctions. Jobs in logging are always at risk, as became apparent a decade ago when a federal judge in Seattle ruled that old-growth forests must be left uncut to protect the seldom-seen spotted owl.

Yet these are footnotes to what is mainly a story of success. Look at a map that shows elevation of mountains and density of population. On both sides of the Pacific, vast numbers of people are squeezed into small margins of level land between steeply rising volcanic mountains and the sea, or tucked into valleys. These islands of settlement are surrounded by vast wildernesses—desert and mountains, open sea and Arctic lands. Yet the inhabitants of these pockets of the Pacific Rim in the last three decades have produced more economic growth than anywhere else in the world and, if there are occasional slumps, the Pacific Rim has always come surging back, as East Asia and maybe Japan seemed to be doing in 1999. This has happened despite occasional tension between widely diverse ethnic groups: the Japanese and Koreans, the Chinese of Taiwan, Hong Kong and Singapore, the Malays and Filipinos; and Washington's ethnic mix of Scandinavians, Yankees and new migrants.

Politically, Washington, with its Scandinavian and labor union heritage, was once one of

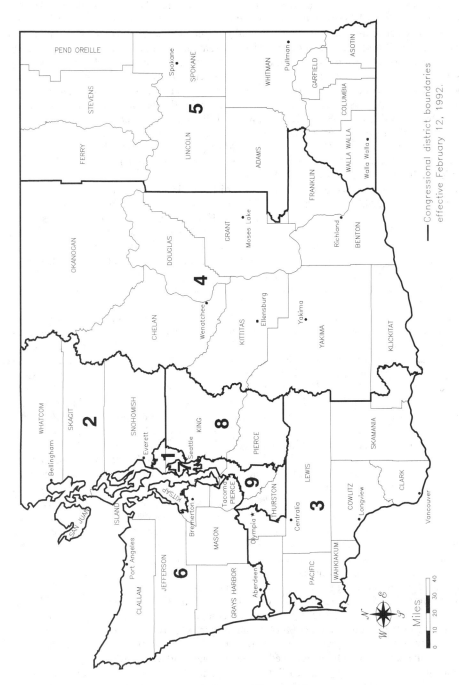

—Congressional district boundaries effective February 12, 1992.

the most Democratic states: Franklin Roosevelt's campaign manager James Farley used to refer to "the 47 states and the Soviet of Washington." Its mainstream Democrats—notably Warren Magnuson and Henry Jackson, who represented the state in Congress for a total of 87 years—believed in an active and compassionate federal government that built dams, aluminum plants and the Hanford Works at home, and pursued an internationalist, anti-Communist foreign policy abroad. Their political strength was built on a blue-collar base, augmented by the respect big businesses had for their political clout. Today, the fulcrum of the electorate has moved from blue collar to white collar, from economic class warfare to cultural wars. The balance is fairly close. Presidentially, Washington leans Democratic: big Seattle-area margins delivered the state for Michael Dukakis in 1988 and Bill Clinton in 1992 and 1996. Democrats have also won most downballot races in presidential years. Three different Democrats have held the governorship since 1984, and in 1992 Democrat Patty Murray was elected to the Senate. Republicans have done better in off-years: Senator Slade Gorton was re-elected handily in 1994, and that year Republicans won seven of nine U.S. House seats.

But farther down the ballot the trend is toward Republicans—and then a bit back toward the Democrats. In 1992 Democrats won the House vote 56%–41% and won eight of nine seats. But in 1994 Republicans won the House vote 51%–49% and carried seven of nine seats, in the process beating House Speaker Thomas Foley. In 1996 Democrats won back one House seat and in 1998 two; several of both parties' seats may be in play in 2000. Republicans in 1994 also won control of both houses of the legislature, a reaction against unpopular liberal Governor Mike Lowry. Lowry retired in 1996, and was succeeded by Democrat Gary Locke. He has proved more popular, and in 1998 Democrats recaptured the state Senate and got a 49–49 tie in the state House.

The political lines are fairly clear. The central city of Seattle is increasingly the liberal bastion, while old blue-collar lumber country strongholds have soured on many Democrats. Republicans run best in the arid country east of the Cascades, a marchland between the culturally liberal Pacific Rim and the culturally conservative Rocky Mountains. Culture wars also are fought out in referenda. Washington rejected a "death with dignity" physician assisted suicide measure in 1991 by 54%–46%. It voted for term limits, opposed by most liberals, 52%–48% in 1992; Tom Foley had filed a lawsuit against the application of this measure to congressmen—he won in the Supreme Court but was defeated at the polls. One unanticipated result of term limits: with the churning of membership, 41% of Washington state legislators are women, the highest percentage in the country.

In 1996 voters rejected bear baiting 63%–37% and rejected video poker on Indian reservations 56%–44%—a victory each for cultural liberals and conservatives. In 1997 voters rejected easing penalties for marijuana use and a ban on discrimination against (or for) gays; a gun control measure, requiring trigger locks for guns and safety tests for handgun owners, was rejected 71%–29%. These were all victories for cultural conservatives. In 1998 the results were mixed. Despite opposition from almost all editorial pages, all Democratic and some Republican politicians, Boeing, Starbucks, Microsoft and Eddie Bauer, voters approved by 58%–42% a ban on racial and gender quotas and preferences in state government. But they also approved a higher and indexed minimum wage by 2–1, rejected a variation of the partial-birth abortion ban, and approved allowing the use of medical marijuana.

Governor. Gary Locke, a Democrat elected in 1996, is the first governor of Chinese descent elected in American history. Locke grew up in Seattle, the son of immigrants from Guandong and Hong Kong; he lived six years in a housing project and worked in his father's restaurant and grocery store. He graduated from Yale (a beneficiary of affirmative action, he says) and Boston University Law School, returned to Seattle and worked as a deputy prosecutor and community relations manager for US West. In 1982, at 32, he was elected to the state House and rose to chair the Appropriations Committee; he supported the 1993 tax increases that helped to make Democratic Governor Mike Lowry unpopular. That same year, Locke was elected

King County executive where he cut the budget, established a savings incentive program and produced a growth management plan.

In February 1996 Lowry, a liberal and former congressman who was staggering under charges of sexual harassment, announced his retirement, and Locke decided to run for governor. It was a crowded field in Washington's all-party primary. Locke's main opponent, Seattle Mayor Norm Rice, shared the same base; they also faced former Congressman Jay Inslee from east of the mountains (he has since moved to the Seattle area and is now congressman from the 1st District). Locke won with 24% of the total vote to 18% for Rice and 10% for Inslee. The Republican field was more fragmented, and the nomination was won by former state Senator Ellen Craswell, who emphasized her religious faith. Altogether Democrats won 52% of votes, Republicans 48%, indicating a close race in November. Republicans had lost some good campaign issues by repealing much of Lowry's tax increases, employer health care mandates and insurance premium caps, though the mandates for portability and increased coverage of the poor that were not repealed resulted in steep increases in health insurance premiums. Craswell, however, emphasized what she called "God's plan" to cut state taxes 30% (later modified to 15%) and to privatize state universities, which evidently struck many voters as bizarre. Republican ads accusing Locke of supporting prostitution (a county prostitute-counseling service may have added to that impression). Locke, despite his liberal record in the legislature, took a moderate tack, abjuring tax increases and calling for more spending on education, with higher standards and accountability. Although some polls showed a close race, Locke won 58%–42%, fortified by a 62%–38% lead in the Seattle area; Craswell just barely carried the east.

Locke cultivated an image of moderation and compromise even as he vetoed more bills than any previous governor in his first months. But he and the legislature operate under the constraints of Initiative 601, passed in 1994, which limits spending increases to a formula based on population and inflation; that has forced the state into smart decisions, according to Syracuse University's Government Performance Project, which in February 1999 rated Washington one of the four best-managed state governments. Locke vetoed some changes in welfare reform but approved a business tax cut. He vetoed a bill banning gay marriage in February 1998; that was overridden in five hours as Democrats scampered to keep the issue off the November 1998 ballot. Left on was Referendum 49, a proposal to cut the auto tax at the expense of education funding and place the revenue, plus money from a huge bond issue, into a fund devoted to transportation; that passed 57%–43%. Locke campaigned hard against Initiative 200, to ban state racial and gender quotas and preferences, which passed; he had better luck campaigning for Democratic legislative candidates.

In 1998, Democrats won a 27–22 margin in the Senate and a 49–49 tie in the House, which left Locke to, in the words of the *Seattle Times*'s David Postman, "stick to the middle ground, think bite-sized reform, press hard for results and focus on the direct delivery of state services." His proposed two-year spending plan balanced the budget with the help of tobacco suit money, and called for paying for 1,000 new teachers with welfare savings and spending $40 million over 10 years on farm migrant worker housing; he pushed a salmon recovery plan which also amounted to a water conservation plan. He called for two years of unemployment benefits for laid-off Boeing employees, like the benefits displaced workers in the timber and fishing industries already receive.

Hanging over Locke is some controversy about his 1996 campaign finances. He was given $5,000 in cash at a Buddhist temple in Redmond, promptly returned the money, then later was given $10,000 in apparently legal checks. Locke gave back $1,000 from the mother-in-law of Pauline Kanchanalak 10 days after she was named as an unindicted co-conspirator in a foreign money laundering scheme for which her Pauline was indicted; Locke gave two hours of secret testimony in Congress about Ted Sioeng, whose family gave him $5,400; he also got $1,000 from John Huang. There was an investigation of a purportedly independent expenditure by a group that produced a brochure suggesting that Senators Slade Gorton and Patty Murray endorsed Locke; the only contributors to the group were the father of an aide to Locke's fundraising consultant, the owner of a Bellevue site Locke recommended King County buy for a prison, and the father of a top volunteer fundraiser (Locke has stayed in the family's Hawaii condominium).

Locke is considered a strong candidate for re-election in 2000; he was moving smoothly to raise money in early 1999. Locke seems to have no interest in running for the Senate; with two young children born just before he turned 50, he said in 1999, "I don't see any life in Washington, D.C., in the cards."

Cook's Call. *Safe.* Locke faced a competitive race to win this seat in 1996, but 2000 looks like it will be a much smoother ride.

Senior Senator. Slade Gorton is a Republican first elected in 1980, defeated in 1986, then elected again in 1988 and 1994. Gorton grew up in Chicago, served in the Army as a teenager, went to school in the east, and moved to Seattle in 1953, where he also served in the Air Force. He was elected to the state House in 1958, at 30, and was elected attorney general for 12 years starting in 1968. In 1980 he challenged and beat 75-year-old Senator Warren Magnuson. In 1986 Gorton was upset for re-election by Democrat Brock Adams, who ended up retiring in 1992 after a charge of sexual harassment. In 1988, when Republican Senator Daniel Evans retired, Gorton came back and beat Democrat Mike Lowry, then a Seattle congressman and later governor.

Gorton is a cerebral man and a long-distance runner, one of the few state attorneys general capable of arguing before the Supreme Court with the skill of a top-rank lawyer, and is a determined, hard-working political fighter. In the 1970s his acuity gained him the reputation as a liberal Republican, with a political base in then middle-of-the-road Seattle. Seattle has changed over the years and so, his political enemies charge, has Gorton. He took umbrage at being pummeled by environmentalists in the 1986 and 1988 elections even though he had often supported their positions (the fight against fishing rights was, after all, also a fight to save salmon), and broke off relations with them. Meanwhile, Seattle was moving sharply to the left, with new litmus test issues ever farther from the positions taken by ordinary voters in other parts of the state. Gorton's stands on issues, he could argue, have not moved very far, but his political stance shifted; he has emphasized conservative stands on high-visibility local issues like timber harvesting and Indian fishing rights, and his political base has shifted to eastern Washington and western Washington counties outside the Seattle area.

On Indian issues, Gorton argued as attorney general in the 1970s unsuccessfully for state regulation of Indian fishing rights and won a Supreme Court decision that Indians must collect state cigarette taxes. In 1995, as Appropriations' Interior Subcommittee chairman, he passed a bill that cut funding to tribes that violated the property rights of non-Indians living on their reservations. In September 1997, he inserted into the appropriations bill language that would waive tribes' sovereign immunity from civil litigation and means-test tribes that receive federal assistance; after much controversy over such a major change in Indian law, this did not go through. Native American leaders were happy when he allowed himself to be passed over for the chair of the Indian Affairs Committee in favor of Colorado's Ben Nighthorse Campbell.

On environmental issues, Gorton opposed the court decision outlawing cutting of old-growth timber to save spotted owl habitat, and in 1995 passed a law allowing clear-cutting in some old-growth forests. He opposed reintroducing wolves in the Olympic Peninsula and the Forest Service proposal to ban rock climbers' use of fixed anchors in wilderness areas; he even went rock-climbing to publicize his stand. He has sought funding for cleanup of the Hanford Nuclear Reservation (which he had tried to keep in operation), opposes privatization of the Bonneville Power Administration, and tried to overturn the Clinton Administration's disapproval of a gold mine on Buckhorn Mountain in Okanogan County. As chairman of Appropriations's Interior Subcommittee, Gorton tried to link funding for the removal of the Elwha Dam with protections against removing or breaching any other dams on the Columbia and Snake rivers. He worked hard for the Plum Creek Timber Company's 100,000-acre land swap in the Cascades in 1998, under which the federal government got more old-growth forests and land for the Mountains-to-Sound hiking trail near I-90. Taking a more conciliatory note than he often has, he praised the Clinton Administration's 1999 plan to increase salmon populations, in light of the pending EPA endangered species designation in an area covering metropolitan Seattle. After opposing National Endowment of the Arts funding of obscene and sacrilegious "art" in 1989, he worked for NEA funding in 1998. After working to revise IDEA to allow violent children to be removed from school in 1995, Gorton supported research on autism in 1998 (he has an autistic grandson).

Gorton has unsurprisingly been an advocate for Washington's major businesses. He defended the Market Promotion Program and opposed Airbus's unfair trading practices (a concern of Boeing). But he did not join Boeing in urging normal trade relations with China to become permanent status, arguing instead for annual renewals to pressure China into fair trading practices. He and colleague Patty Murray accompanied Bill Gates to the March 1998 Judiciary Committee hearings on Microsoft and criticized the grillings by Chairman Orrin Hatch of Utah, home of Microsoft competitor Novell. "Much of what Microsoft stands for—innovation, leadership and opportunity—was at risk of being destroyed by a growing resentment in Washington, D.C," he said in March 1998, and pointed out that Microsoft has only 4% of worldwide software industry revenues—some monopoly! He also saw a political motive: "As a Washingtonian, I am incensed at the blatant attempt by Al Gore's wannabe administration to court my state's electoral votes even as his current administration's Justice Department orchestrates the destruction of Washington's superb economic engine in favor of Silicon Valley's greater financial and electoral prize."

Gorton is a hardliner on crime, and worked to get a *habeas corpus* reform amendment in the 1996 anti-terrorism bill and to get grants for projects to monitor sexual predators. He has worked to get more moderate judges on the left-leaning Ninth Circuit Court of Appeals, asserting senatorial prerogative to insist on his own appointees in return for supporting Democratic choices. With Jay Rockefeller, he has been the lead sponsor of the product liability reform bill, which passed both houses but was vetoed by Bill Clinton in May 1996 and was busy trying to reach a compromise in 1997 and 1998. He supported the V-chip provision of the Telecommunications Reform Act and criticized the broadcasters' program rating code as insufficient. He co-sponsored the farm worker immigration bill worked out in 1998 by Oregon Senators Ron Wyden and Gordon Smith and passed 68–31.

Gorton's close ties to Majority Leader Trent Lott were on national view in January 1999 as Lott encouraged his and Joseph Lieberman's plan to limit the impeachment trial to a few days of testimony, argument and voting. That fell through, and Gorton voted to acquit Clinton on perjury and convict on obstruction of justice. That sparked a threat of a separate candidacy by Washington's conservative American Heritage Party, whose candidate contributed to the defeat of Republican Congressman Rick White in the 1st District in 1998. Gorton is clearly a top target for Democrats; after all, he is the only Republican candidate for senator or governor who has carried Washington since 1983. He did win re-election in 1994 by a solid 56%–44% margin, against King County Councilman Ron Sims, who campaigned as a budget-balancer and New Democrat. But that was in a strong Republican year, and turnout was higher in Republican east Washington and lower in the Democratic Seattle area than it has been since: apply Gorton's regional percentages in 1994 to 1998 turnout, and his margin slips to 55%–45%. Gorton's more conciliatory stands on salmon recovery and environmental issues are presumably a recognition that Washington has been moving a bit to the left.

Nevertheless, Gorton's chances in 2000 should not be too deeply discounted. His strategy again will be to build up large margins in the east (he carried it 66%–34% in 1994) and to win also in the west outside the Seattle area (57%–43%). In the Seattle area, he has conceded big Democratic margins in the city but will try to build a "boa constrictor" around it in the suburbs; he carried the Seattle area as a whole 51%–49% in 1994. But those suburbs were where Democrats made their legislative gains in 1998, and Indian tribes, long anti-Gorton, now have the resources to play a major role; the Muckleshoots have a casino in Auburn that rakes in $45 million a year. State Insurance Commissioner Deborah Senn, skilled at gaining publicity and not well-liked by fellow Democrats, announced she was running. Another possibility is Congressman Jim McDermott who was incensed by Gorton's vote on gun control in May 1999. But the Seattle-based McDermott is farther to the left than Gorton is to the right and lost gubernatorial races in 1972, 1980 and 1984. Then there is Bill Marler, a trial lawyer from Pullman who won $40 million in a case for children who got sick from *E. coli* bacteria in Jack-in-the-Box hamburgers; he might try to duplicate trial lawyer John Edwards's 1998 victory in North Carolina.

Cook's Call. *Potentially Competitive.* Democrats lost their strongest potential candidate when state Attorney General Christine Gregoire announced that she would not challenge Gorton. State Insurance Commissioner Deborah Senn is running, but the party has not united behind her and there is talk of other candidates getting in the race. Gorton has always had difficult re-election campaigns, and this year may be no different.

Junior Senator. Patty Murray is one of the Democrats whose election made 1992 "the year of the woman." Murray grew up in Bothell, the daughter of a disabled veteran, graduated from Washington State University in 1972, married and stayed home to raise her children. "Our culture needs to value parents who stay at home much more than they do," she said in 1996. In 1980, when she was in Olympia trying to save a parent education class she was teaching at Shoreline Community College from being cut from the budget, a state legislator told her gruffly, "You're just a mom in tennis shoes; you can't make a difference." But, like many committed public employees, she won her fight; then she ran for the Shoreline School District board, lost, was appointed and then elected, and served as president. In 1988, she challenged a Republican state senator, knocked on 17,000 doors, and won the seat. Her first great cause there was extending a family leave bill to include leave for a parent whose child is sick or dying; she threatened to put the proposal on the ballot, and won the issue; she worked on school bus safety, "negative option" mail orders, accidental pesticide exposure—the warp and woof of everyday life. Then in late 1991, she decided to run against U.S. Senator Brock Adams, who was then under a cloud from charges of sexual harassment and later decided not to seek re-election.

Amid a crowd of better-known conventional male politicians, Murray, with her flat accent and "mom in tennis shoes" line, attracted most of the attention and most of the votes. In the all-party primary, her main Democratic opponent was former Congressman Don Bonker, who had narrowly lost a Senate nomination in 1988. But Murray won 28% to Bonker's 19% of the total vote. Meanwhile, three well-known Republicans vied: Congressman Rod Chandler won 20% to 16% for state Senator (and former opponent of George McGovern in South Dakota) Leo Thorsness and 11% for King County Executive Tim Hill. The two nominees were quite a contrast: Murray is short with a squeaky voice, Chandler tall with the booming voice of a former TV reporter. Murray sprinted to a big lead in polls, and in November won 54%–46%, carrying 60% in King County and winning Puget Sound and the west. Her margins over Chandler were similar to Bill Clinton's over George Bush, except in eastern Washington, which Clinton nearly carried but where Murray ran 10% behind.

In the Senate Murray has a liberal voting record and an unconventional approach. In her first years, she refused to see Washington industry lobbyists; in a scathing *Seattle Times* profile in 1996, Robert Nelson wrote of Murray, "Colleagues, lobbyists and former staff members view her as indifferent to issues that can't be explained through anecdotes about her family and neighbors." When Democrats were in control, she did not stake out areas of expertise, though she did get a seat on Appropriations. She attracted attention instead by demanding that the Senate Ethics Committee subpoena Oregon Senator Bob Packwood's diaries (he later resigned under threat of expulsion). In time she worked on Washington issues: seeking funding for cleanup of the Hanford Nuclear Reservation, trying to preserve the undammed Hanford Reach of the Columbia as a Wild and Scenic River, delaying with Slade Gorton the Alaska fisheries bill until a provision hurting Washington fishermen was removed. She opposed Gorton and Oregon's Mark Hatfield on timber cutting issues; their measure to allow some clear-cutting of old-growth forests passed in March 1995, and her plan to allow environmentalists to challenge timber sales in court failed.

Several years into her term, Murray developed more legislative expertise and established a focus on certain issues; she also worked closely with Washington's economic interests and, on some issues, with Gorton. She pledges a "Commitment to Children," with money for children's health care, child care, and technology in the classroom. She formed the Senate Advisory Youth Involvement Team (SAY IT!) to meet with kids via her computer. She backed Clinton's commitment to 100,000 new teachers and tried to push it into an education bill without providing financing; that was beaten 50–49 in April 1998, with Gorton leading the opposition. But she got a down payment on the goal into the October 1998 omnibus budget. She worked with Gorton on the Plum Creek Timber land swap, and he gave her credit for the key move of squelching White House environmental policy adviser Katie McGinty's opposition to a ban on lawsuits. But she did not heed environmentalists' demands that she oppose the restart of Hanford's Fast Flux Test nuclear reactor. Blocked in an attempt to name the Strait of Juan De Fuca as a federal marine sanctuary, she worked with Congressman Jack Metcalf to create a Northwest Straits Advisory Commission to search for ways to replenish fish stocks. She and Metcalf also worked to insist on tug escorts for oil tankers in the Strait. She voted for the Defense of Marriage Act and advised Governor Gary Locke that Democrats should help override his veto of a ban on gay marriage to keep the issue off the 1998 ballot.

Murray is one of the Senate's strongest proponents of permanent normal trade relations status with China—a position strongly backed by Boeing; "The best way we can affect human rights in China is to have a good conversation going with them," she said in 1996. She also favors relaxing export restrictions on encryption technology. She appeared with Bill Gates at the March 1998 Judiciary Committee hearing where he was grilled by Orrin Hatch and lambasted the Justice Department in May 1998 for "putting America's technological leader on trial in the press." On IRS reform she narrowly was beaten, 50–48, on an attempt to restore veterans' health benefits for smoking-related illnesses. On impeachment, Murray moved to allow transcripts of testimony without videos, and lost 73–27. She asked a question seeking to establish that Monica Lewinsky had never claimed sexual harassment and argued that those saying she had been harassed had not been much interested in the issue in the past. Of course, feminists used to insist that a sexual relationship between a boss and a subordinate was inherently coercive and involuntary.

Republicans entered 1998 with some hope of beating Murray, but those they considered their ideal candidates—House members George Nethercutt, Rick White and Jennifer Dunn—declined to run. Out running hard was Congresswoman Linda Smith, an articulate conservative, a strong opponent of abortion and backer of campaign finance reform, never a reliable member of anyone's caucus. Smith won the Democratic-inclined 3d District in 1994 and 1996 with strong support from "Linda's Army"—thousands of families volunteering to help her—and promised not to take PAC contributions. Her opposition to free trade—NAFTA, GATT, fast track—made her a heroine to Ross Perot and anathema to Washington's corporate leaders, who searched for another Republican candidate. They finally found one in Christopher Bayley, King County prosecutor 20 years before, now an affluent retired businessman. He spent $750,000 of his own money and ran ads attacking Smith for opposing free trade and the IRS reform bill (which she voted against because of the veterans' health issue). Smith signed up 35,000 families in Linda's Army and said Bayley was soft on crime and tax increases. Meanwhile, Murray was raking in PAC money from business as well as from liberal groups.

The September all-party primary set up what was only the third Senate race between two women. Smith won the Republican primary with 32% of all votes, to 15% for Bayley, beating him in every county. Murray won 46% of all votes, with 2% for nuisance Democrats. Since Washington's all-party primary results have often been a good forecast of the general election, notably in 1994, Murray seemed to be in a not entirely strong position; Republicans outpolled Democrats 50%–48%. But the primary was September 15, during the period when Bill Clinton's numbers were lowest in 1998; with the release of the Starr Report his numbers went up again, and Washington is one state where there was a perceptible move of opinion toward Democrats between September and October. Murray campaigned not so much as a "mom in tennis shoes" but as a public official who had addressed issues of importance to Washington voters—"apples to aerospace, high-tech to Hanford, saving salmon to educating kids." She far outraised Smith, much of whose money was spent on direct mail solicitations rather than TV ads. National Republican Senatorial Committee Chairman Mitch McConnell, the party's leading opponent of campaign finance bills, sent only about $100,000 to Smith; he argued that polls showed the race to be unpromising, which the results suggest may have been true. On election day and before (about one-third of Washington's votes are cast by absentee ballot) Murray won 58%–42%, winning 63% in the Seattle area and 55% in west Washington; Smith carried the east by only 51%–49%. Murray carried men as well as women and all age groups; her support of Washington economic interests helped her win 58% of those with incomes over $75,000, 56% of college graduates and 67% of those with graduate school degrees. After the election, she was named vice chairman of the Democratic Senatorial Campaign Committee; among her responsibilities is raising money to defeat Gorton.

Presidential politics. For three decades Washington was one of the most contrarian states in presidential politics, voting for Richard Nixon in 1960, Hubert Humphrey in 1968, Gerald Ford in 1976 and Michael Dukakis in 1988. In the 1990s it has been in sync with the nation, voting for Bill Clinton twice, but there has been an increasing divergence between coastal and interior voting patterns. In 1996 Clinton carried the state 50%–37%, winning by solid margins in the Seattle area (54%–34%) and the west (47%–39%). In the eastern part of Washington, which Clinton carried narrowly in 1992, Bob Dole won 45%–42%.

Washington switched from a caucus system to primaries in 1992, when Pat Robertson won among Republicans and Jesse Jackson finished a solid second among Democrats: not much precedent for November there. Dole easily beat Pat Buchanan here in March 1996. In April 1999 Washington, which has never seen much of presidential primary candidates, set its primary for leap year day, February 29, 2000. To gauge how much later presidential campaigns used to begin, in 1956 Dwight Eisenhower announced he was running for a second term on leap year day.

Congressional districting. Washington gained a seat in each of the last two censuses, and both new districts went to fast-growing suburban areas east and south of Seattle. A nonpartisan commission drew the district lines for the 1990s and most districts are evenly balanced—Democrats won eight of nine districts in 1992 and Republicans seven of nine in 1994, six of nine in 1996, four of nine in 1998: in 36 contests in four elections, each party has won 18 times. All but the heavily Democratic 6th and 7th and the heavily Republican 8th have been in play at some point in the 1990s; another commission plan will probably result in a similarly large number of contestable seats.

The People: Est. Pop. 1998: 5,689,263; Pop. 1990: 4,866,692, up 16.9% 1990–1998. 2.1% of U.S. total, 15th largest; 23.6% rural. Median age: 34.9 years. 12.3% 65 years and over. 88.6% White, 3% Black, 4.3% Asian, 1.7% Amer. Indian, 2.3% Other; 4.2% Hispanic Origin. Households: 55% married couple families; 26.2% married couple fams. w. children; 55.9% college educ.; median household income: $31,183; per capita income: $14,923; 62.6% owner occupied housing; median house value: $93,400; median monthly rent: $383. 4.8% Unemployment. 1998 Voting age pop.: 4,257,000. 1998 Turnout: 1,939,421; 46% of VAP. Registered voters (1998): 3,119,562; no party registration.

Political Lineup: Governor, Gary Locke (D); Lt. Gov., Brad Owen (D); Secy. of State, Ralph Munro (R); Atty. Gen., Christine Gregoire (D); Treasurer, Mike Murphy (D); State Senate, 49 (27 D, 22 R); Majority Leader, Sid Snyder (D); State House, 98 (49 D, 49 R); House Co-Speaker, Clyde Ballard (R); House Co-Speaker, Frank Chopp (D). Senators, Slade Gorton (R) and Patty Murray (D). Representatives, 9 (5 D, 4 R).

Elections Division: 360-902-4151; **Filing Deadline for U.S. Congress:** July 28, 2000.

1996 Presidential Vote

Clinton (D)	1,123,323	(50%)
Dole (R)	840,712	(37%)
Perot (I)	201,003	(9%)
Others	90,465	(4%)

1996 Republican Presidential Primary

Dole (R)	76,155	(63%)
Buchanan (R)	25,247	(21%)
Forbes (R)	10,339	(9%)
Keyes (R)	5,610	(5%)
Others	3,333	(3%)

1992 Presidential Vote

Clinton (D)	993,037	(43%)
Bush (R)	731,234	(32%)
Perot (I)	541,780	(24%)

GOVERNOR

Gov. Gary Locke (D)

Elected 1996, term expires Jan. 2001; b. Jan. 21, 1950, Seattle; home, Olympia; Yale U., B.A. 1972, Boston U., J.D. 1975; Protestant; married (Mona).

Elected Office: WA House of Reps., 1982–93; King Cnty. Chief Exec., 1994–97.

Professional Career: Dpty. King Cnty. Prosecuting atty., 1976–80; Staff atty., WA Senate, 1981; Legal Advisor, Seattle Human Rights Dept., 1981–82; Community Relations Mgr., U.S. West, 1988–92.

Office: Office of the Governor, P.O. Box 40002, Olympia, 98504, 360-753-6780; Fax: 360-753-4110; Web site: www.wa.gov.us.

Election Results

1996 gen.	Gary Locke (D)	1,296,492	(58%)
	Ellen Craswell (R)	940,538	(42%)
1996 prim.	Gary Locke (D)	287,762	(24%)
	Norm Rice (D)	212,888	(18%)
	Ellen Craswell (R)	185,680	(15%)
	Dale Foreman (R)	162,615	(13%)
	Jay Inslee (D)	118,571	(10%)
	Norm Maleng (R)	109,088	(9%)
	Jim Waldo (R)	63,854	(5%)
	Others	76,219	(6%)
1992 gen.	Michael Lowry (D)	1,184,315	(52%)
	Ken Eikenberry (R)	1,086,216	(48%)

SENATORS

Sen. Slade Gorton (R)

Elected 1988, seat up 2000; b. Jan. 8, 1928, Chicago, IL; home, Bellevue; Dartmouth Col., A.B. 1950, Columbia U., LL.B. 1953; Episcopalian; married (Sally).

Military Career: Army, 1946–47, Air Force, 1953–56, Air Force Reserves, 1956–81.

Elected Office: WA House of Reps., 1958–68, Majority Ldr., 1966–68; WA Atty. Gen., 1968–80; U.S. Senate, 1980–86.

Professional Career: Pres., Natl. Assn. of Attys. Gen., 1976–78.

DC Office: 730 HSOB, 20510, 202-224-3441; Fax: 202-224-9393; Web site: www.senate.gov/~gorton.

State Offices: Bellevue, 425-451-0103; Kennewick, 509-783-0640; Lakewood, 253-581-1646; Spokane, 509-353-2507; Vancouver, 360-696-7838; Wenatchee, 509-884-3447; Yakima, 509-248-8084.

Committees: *Appropriations* (6th of 15 R): Agriculture & Rural Development; Energy & Water Development; Interior (Chmn.); Labor & HHS; Transportation. *Budget* (6th of 12 R). *Commerce, Science & Transportation* (4th of 11 R): Aviation (Chmn.); Communications; Consumer Affairs, Foreign Commerce & Tourism; Oceans & Fisheries. *Energy & Natural Resources* (10th of 11 R): Energy, Research, Development, Production & Regulation; National Parks, Historic Preservation & Recreation; Water & Power (Vice Chmn.). *Indian Affairs* (4th of 8 R).

Group Ratings

	ADA	ACLU	AFS	LCV	CON	NTU	NFIB	COC	ACU	NTLC	CHC
1998	0	14	0	0	45	56	100	89	72	64	82
1997	20	—	0	—	77	66	—	100	60	—	—

National Journal Ratings

	1997 LIB — 1997 CONS	1998 LIB — 1998 CONS
Economic	44% — 52%	31% — 63%
Social	45% — 50%	45% — 54%
Foreign	34% — 57%	29% — 58%

Key Votes of the 105th Congress

1. Bal. Budget Amend.	Y	5. Satcher for Surgeon Gen.	Y	9. Chem. Weapons Treaty	Y
2. Clinton Budget Deal	Y	6. Highway Set-asides	N	10. Cuban Humanitarian Aid	N
3. Cloture on Tobacco	N	7. Table Child Gun locks	Y	11. Table Bosnia Troops	Y
4. Education IRAs	Y	8. Ovrd. Part. Birth Veto	Y	12. $ for Test-ban Treaty	N

Election Results

1994 general	Slade Gorton (R)	947,821	(56%)	($4,792,764)
	Ron Sims (D)	752,352	(44%)	($1,228,098)
1994 primary	Slade Gorton (R)	492,251	(53%)	
	Ron Sims (D)	162,382	(17%)	
	Mike James (D)	138,005	(15%)	
	Others	136,965	(15%)	
1988 general	Slade Gorton (R)	944,359	(51%)	($2,851,591)
	Michael Lowry (D)	904,183	(49%)	($2,191,187)

Sen. Patty Murray (D)

Elected 1992, seat up 2004; b. Oct. 11, 1950, Seattle; home, Seattle; WA St. U., B.A. 1972; no religious affiliation; married (Rob).

Elected Office: Shoreline Schl. Bd., 1985–89, Pres., 1985–86; WA Senate, 1988–92.

DC Office: 173 RSOB, 20510, 202-224-2621; Fax: 202-224-0238; Web site: www.senate.gov/~murray.

State Offices: Everett, 425-259-6515; Seattle, 206-553-5545; Spokane, 509-624-9515; Vancouver, 360-696-7797; Yakima, 509-453-7462.

Committees: *DSCC Vice Chairman. Appropriations* (10th of 13 D): Energy & Water Development; Foreign Operations & Export Financing; Labor & HHS; Military Construction (RMM); Transportation. *Budget* (6th of 10 D). *Health, Education, Labor & Pensions* (7th of 8 D): Aging; Children & Families. *Veterans' Affairs* (5th of 5 D).

Group Ratings

	ADA	ACLU	AFS	LCV	CON	NTU	NFIB	COC	ACU	NTLC	CHC
1998	90	86	100	100	30	13	33	56	4	0	0
1997	90	—	89	—	18	14	—	70	0	—	—

National Journal Ratings

	1997 LIB — 1997 CONS			1998 LIB — 1998 CONS		
Economic	90%	—	6%	72%	—	25%
Social	71%	—	0%	74%	—	0%
Foreign	73%	—	19%	73%	—	21%

Key Votes of the 105th Congress

1. Bal. Budget Amend.	N	5. Satcher for Surgeon Gen.	Y	9. Chem. Weapons Treaty	Y
2. Clinton Budget Deal	N	6. Highway Set-asides	Y	10. Cuban Humanitarian Aid	Y
3. Cloture on Tobacco	Y	7. Table Child Gun locks	N	11. Table Bosnia Troops	Y
4. Education IRAs	N	8. Ovrd. Part. Birth Veto	N	12. $ for Test-ban Treaty	Y

Election Results

1998 general	Patty Murray (D)	1,103,184	(58%)	($5,600,592)
	Linda Smith (R)	785,377	(42%)	($5,159,527)
1998 primary	Patty Murray (D)	479,009	(46%)	
	Linda Smith (R)	337,407	(32%)	
	Chris Bayley (R)	155,864	(15%)	
	Others	72,109	(7%)	
1992 general	Patty Murray (D)	1,197,973	(54%)	($1,342,038)
	Rod Chandler (R)	1,020,829	(46%)	($2,504,777)

FIRST DISTRICT

In the last 20 years metropolitan Seattle has spread out to the north and the east, as a tidal wave of newcomers have arrived seeking this area's distinctive blend of natural environmental beauty, free-wheeling culture and briskly expanding economy. With growth, Seattle has lost a bit of its distinctiveness: The fishy odor of its docks does not permeate the new subdivisions built on what were once vegetable fields or vineyards; the Scandinavian heritage of old neighborhoods like Ballard has been mixed into a Pacific Northwest blend; the hoboes who used to hang around Yesler Way, the original "Skid Road," with its cast iron buildings and its street clocks, aren't allowed in the shopping malls off I-5 or I-405.

The heart of the new Seattle is east of Lake Washington, in Redmond, where the turquoise, pine-shaded low-rise buildings of the Microsoft campus house one of America's most innovative and successful corporations, the creator of the standard for computer software, still working hard to stay ahead of the technological and economic curve. Not far away, in Medina on the eastern shore of Lake Washington, is the $60 million mansion Microsoft founder Bill Gates began building in 1991 and completed in 1997—a 37,000-square-foot complex with a trampoline room with vaulted ceilings, video walls that can be electronically programmed with art from the world's great museums and a garage large enough to hold 30 cars: from across the lake you can see it rising, Seattle's Xanadu.

The 1st Congressional District includes Redmond, Medina and a small part of Seattle, then stretches north to take in much of the northern and eastern suburbs of Seattle in Snohomish and King counties. It also runs west across Puget Sound, to Kitsap County, and gathers in Bainbridge Island, where you can commute by ferry to downtown Seattle each day and return home to what looks like the perfect American small town in the evening. Politically, this is an area torn by forces of roughly equal strength between the two parties. Most Seattle-area residents appreciate, and want to preserve, the region's unique natural aura: the evergreen smell of a well-watered land; the subtle cultural patterns that are plainly American yet geographically distant from most of the nation. But it is impossible not to recognize the spectacular success of market economics in the 1st District—and to predict which way the district will lean if that success goes sour, as recent events indicate it could.

The congressman from the 1st District is Jay Inslee, a Democrat elected in 1998. Inslee grew up in north Seattle, the son of a school athletic administrator, graduated from the University of Washington and Willamette School of Law. He moved to Selah, in Yakima County east of the Cascades, to practice law and served on the State Trial Lawyers board of directors. In 1988, at 37, he was elected to the state House over a former Yakima mayor; in 1990 he beat a well-known businessman who outspent him, with 62% of the vote. In 1992, when 4th District Congressman Sid Morrison ran for governor (and lost the primary), Inslee entered the race for Congress in April. In the primary Inslee beat a Democratic legislator who outspent him, and in the general he won 51%–49% over Doc Hastings, a conservative supported by the Christian Coalition. In the House Inslee voted for the Clinton budget and tax increase and for the crime bill with the assault weapons ban, despite promising to vote against gun control bills. In 1994 Hastings ran again and in the September primary, usually a good forecast of November, led Inslee 50%–41%. The lead held in November: Inslee lost 53%–47%.

After his defeat Inslee moved to Bainbridge Island and practiced law in Seattle. In 1996 he ran for governor, attacking the Seattle Seahawks stadium deal. He finished fifth, with 10% of all votes, in the primary. Briefly he was a regional director of HHS. Then in April 1998 he decided to run for Congress in the 1st District against Republican Congressman Rick White; another Democrat already running left the race. White was first elected in 1994, upsetting one-term Democrat Maria Cantwell; a lawyer at a big Seattle law firm active in Republican politics, he actually raised more money and ran ads against the single Cantwell featuring his wife and four children. He won 52%–48%. In the House, White was an economic conservative with liberal votes on some cultural issues. He won re-election in 1996 by 54%–46%, but White also had problems. In April 1998 he was divorced—though in both campaigns he had portrayed himself as a family man. And in July 1998 Bruce Craswell, whose wife Ellen Craswell lost 58%–42% to Governor Gary Locke in 1996, decided to run against him on the line of the conservative American Heritage Party.

Inslee attacked White for voting to reduce spending on Head Start and education and for supporting electricity deregulation, claiming that White was "willing to sell our reasonably priced electricity to California." White tried to paint Inslee as an opportunist. To the carpet-bagger issue, Inslee replied that he had grown up in the 1st District and had lived there more years than White. In the September all-party primary White led 50%–44%; Craswell got 7%. That primary is ordinarily a good forecast of the November vote. But two issues intervened to change the balance. One was White's divorce: An Inslee ad claimed that White intended to spend 10 years in the House and then be a lobbyist—a reference to a statement by his wife in the divorce papers. The second issue was impeachment: After White voted for the impeachment inquiry, and despite the fact that all but five members of the House voted for some form of impeachment inquiry, Inslee ran an ad for five days saying, "Rick White and Newt Gingrich shouldn't be dragging us through this. Enough is enough." As in the Senate race, opinion—or turnout—seemed to be moving toward Democrats in October. The campaign became acrimonious; after a debate that went 45 minutes over the time limit, White and Inslee refused to shake hands. Inslee won with 49.8% of the vote, to 44% for White, while Craswell won 6%; the White and Craswell vote added up to 50.2%.

Inslee got seats on the Banking and Resources committees. White said that it "isn't likely" he would run in the 1st in 2000, though he might run for governor or attorney general.

Cook's Call. *Highly Competitive.* Given the fact that this marginal district has hosted highly competitive races since 1992, and that freshman Inslee won here in 1998 with only 50% of the vote, it is very likely that there will be a spirited contest for this district in 2000.

The People: Pop. 1990: 540,315; 9.7% rural; 9.8% age 65 + ; 91.8% White, 1.3% Black, 5.3% Asian, 1% Amer. Indian, 0.6% Other; 2.1% Hispanic Origin. Households: 59.3% married couple families; 29.5% married couple fams. w. children; 67.3% college educ.; median household income: $40,390; per capita income: $18,687; median house value: $148,200; median gross rent: $522.

1996 Presidential Vote

Clinton (D)	140,182	(51%)
Dole (R)	103,002	(37%)
Perot (I)	21,352	(8%)
Others	10,527	(4%)

1992 Presidential Vote

Clinton (D)	118,386	(42%)
Bush (R)	90,537	(32%)
Perot (I)	70,340	(25%)

Rep. Jay Inslee (D)

Elected 1998; b. Feb. 9, 1951, Seattle; home, Bainbridge Island; Stanford U., 1969–70, U. of WA, B.A. 1973, Willamette U., J.D. 1976.; Protestant; married (Trudi).

Elected Office: WA House of Reps., 1988–92; U.S. House of Reps., 1992–94.

Professional Career: Practicing atty., 1976–92, 1995–96; Regional Dir., U.S. Dept. of H.H.S., 1997–98.

DC Office: 308 CHOB 20515, 202-225-6311; Fax: 202-226-1606; Web site: www.house.gov/inslee.

District Offices: Mountlake Terrace, 425-640-0233; Poulsbo, 360-598-2342.

Committees: *Banking & Financial Services* (22d of 27 D): Domestic & International Monetary Policy; Financial Institutions & Consumer Credit. *Resources* (19th of 24 D): Energy & Mineral Resources; National Parks & Public Lands.

Group Ratings and Key Votes: Newly Elected

Election Results

1998 general	Jay Inslee (D)	112,726	(50%)	($1,254,460)
	Rick White (R)	99,910	(44%)	($1,655,274)
	Bruce Craswell (AHP)	13,837	(6%)	($35,063)
1998 primary	Rick White (R)	59,636	(50%)	
	Jay Inslee (D)	52,602	(44%)	
	Bruce Craswell (AHP)	8,051	(7%)	
1996 general	Rick White (R)	141,948	(54%)	($1,671,909)
	Jeff Coopersmith (D)	122,187	(46%)	($1,079,648)

SECOND DISTRICT

The 172 San Juan Islands, in the waters of Puget Sound at the far northwest corner of Washington, were the last part of the continental United States to be turned over to this country; these waters were great whaling ground, and not until 1860 did the British relinquish the islands. Today, ferry boats ply the waters of the Sound, connecting the islands to mainland Washington, and to British Columbia directly to the west. This is some of the most beautiful land and water of North America, the steely blue Sound with green forested hills rising behind; it is wet country, shielded from the full force of Pacific rains by the Olympic Mountains, but still seldom dry. The little towns, on bits of level land between the water and mountains, have the look of pristine New England villages or Midwestern historic towns, but are better preserved than the originals; the stores are full of fresh produce and local seafood. Here the Seattle metropolitan area has marched north along the shore of Puget Sound, to and beyond the old lumber port and railroad terminus of Everett, with the huge Boeing plant—the largest building in the world—where 747s, 767s and 777s are built. Far to the north is the small city of Bellingham and the town of Blaine on the 49th parallel, with America's most attractively landscaped border crossing and International Peace Arch, just south of British Columbia.

The 2d Congressional District includes the San Juan Islands, Whidbey Island and most of Puget Sound from Everett north, plus the margin of mainland along the Sound and the huge mountains, topped by snow-capped Mount Baker. The political tradition in most of the lumbering and fishing areas here is Democratic, while the rich agricultural areas, like the flower-bulb-growing Skagit Valley, are more Republican. Overall, this is a pretty evenly balanced district which tends to vote as the state does.

The congressman from the 2d District is Jack Metcalf, a Republican elected in 1994, successful at last in getting elected to Congress 26 years after his first attempt. Metcalf grew up in this part of Washington, where his father worked as a fisherman; he served in the Army just after World War II and was a high school history teacher in Everett for 29 years. He was first elected to the state House in 1960, at 33. He lost his seat in the anti-Goldwater landslide of 1964, was elected to a four-year term to the Washington Senate in 1966, then was the Republican candidate against Senator Warren Magnuson in 1968 and 1974. Metcalf was again elected to the state Senate in 1980, and after his retirement from teaching, Metcalf and his wife started the Log Castle Bed and Breakfast on Whidbey Island. He was known for his opposition to court decisions curbing limits on Indian fishing rights, and to the money-creating powers of the Federal Reserve. In 1992 he ran for Congress again and lost 52%–42% to incumbent Democrat Al Swift, the last in a line of Democrats who represented the district for 52 of 54 years going back to the election of 28-year-old Henry Jackson in 1940.

In 1994 Swift retired and Metcalf ran again. His attacks on congressional corruption, his promise to serve no more than three terms, and his opposition to gun control and Indian fishing rights resonated with the Republican themes of that year; he easily beat a state legislator in the primary. His Democratic opponent, state Senator Harriet Spanel, sounded Clintonesque notes, calling for "a more holistic approach to these needs, recognizing that our country's problems cannot be overcome by repairing just one link in a chain." Metcalf won 55%–45%.

Metcalf was the oldest member of the freshman class, and by no means typical. His voting record was more moderate than expected, but not predictable on standard lines. He supported Linda Smith's campaign finance bill in 1996 and pressed for the Shays-Meehan bill in 1998. He sponsored the 1996 amendment barring automatic pay increases for members of Congress and other federal officials. He tried to get a congressional vote on the deployment of U.S. troops to Bosnia and pushed for further investigation of Gulf war syndrome. He fought Newt Gingrich to get Boeing's 747 considered as a supplemental cargo plane to McDonnell Douglas's C-17. He spent much time on local issues, in 1995 killing a Forest Service project to spend $37,000 to paint rocks along US-2, which the Forest Service claimed was necessary "because it could take up to five years for the rock to weather naturally," and opposing a plan to tax northern border crossings. He lobbied the FCC to lower licensing fees for VHF radios used by Puget Sound boat owners and protected the Magnuson Act's Northwest halibut and sablefish quota program from revision. He worked with Joe Kennedy to extend aid to homeless veterans and supported a greater low-income-housing tax credit. His bill allowing interest on business checking accounts passed the House in October 1998; despite his views on the Federal Reserve, he got the support of Chairman Alan Greenspan.

Metcalf has lived within sight of Puget Sound much of his life and despite the area's conservatism he has worked to protect the waters and creatures of the sea. He opposed the move to make part of Puget Sound and the Straits of Juan De Fuca a marine sanctuary but, working with Senator Patty Murray in 1998, got Congress to set up a Northwest Straits Advisory Commission, with local members, to seek over five years ways to renew fishing stocks. Again working with Murray, he sought to require escort tugs on oil tankers in Puget Sound and the Straits of Juan De Fuca. He supported the "debt for nature" swap that passed the House in March 1998; this would authorize the U.S. to forgive foreign countries' debts in return for their protection of tropical rain forests. He worked strenuously to get the Clinton Administration to oppose the WTO when it tried to overturn the U.S. ban on shrimp from countries that don't require turtle excluder devices; failure to use them kills 150,000 sea turtles, he said. He got $1 million to preserve native habitat in the Lopez Islands.

Starting in 1996, Metcalf worked with liberal Californian George Miller and the Canadian Sea Shepherd Conservation Society to fight a Clinton Administration plan to allow the Makah Indians to kill only five gray whales a year in the waters off Neah Bay at the far northwest tip of the Olympic Peninsula. Metcalf remembered as a boy of eight seeing 100 orcas swimming in the waters off Whidbey Island, and they are still seen sometimes from his bed and breakfast. "I don't see how anyone could not want to protect those wonderful creatures," he said. Metcalf went at his own expense to the International Whaling Organization meeting in Monaco in October 1997 to oppose the administration, which argued that killing whales was part of subsistence for the Makahs. The fact is that they have not killed any whales for more than 70 years, and Metcalf noted that the administration's extension of the definition of subsistence from nutritional necessity to cultural preservation was inspiring similar claims for more whale-killing from Japan and Russia. He also noted that administration negotiators in a back-door deal got the five-whale quota from the Russians' quota. Metcalf introduced a resolution to prevent the extension of whaling in May 1998 and later sued the Coast Guard for not allowing any vessels within 1,500 feet of the Makah hunt. But in May 1999 the Makah boats went out and killed a female whale, for the first time in 75 years, using traditional harpoons but finishing the kill with high-caliber rifles; then they had to figure out how to carve the meat and distribute it to the tribe, many members of which did not care for it.

This is a marginal district and Metcalf, who pledged in 1994 to serve no more than three terms, had tough competition in 1996 and 1998. In 1996 he faced state Senator Kevin Quigley, a Harvard Law graduate with deep roots in the district; he lived in the log house built in Lake Stevens, near Everett, by his grandfather, who as a physician delivered Scoop Jackson back in 1912. He took some moderate positions—for the 1996 welfare reform and the balanced budget amendment—and called Metcalf an extremist. But Quigley had been reprimanded by an ethics

1684   WASHINGTON

board for writing a memo to his former law firm offering to introduce clients to state legislators; a Metcalf ad asked, "Is this the kind of person we want to represent us in Congress?" Metcalf got 52% in the September all-party primary, a good sign for victory; but Quigley's campaigning cut into his margin. Quigley came out of election night 2,200 votes ahead, and exuberant news media proclaimed Metcalf the loser. But there were 40,000 absentee votes still uncounted, and Quigley's lead disappeared. Metcalf finally won 49%–48%.

In 1998 Metcalf had an opponent who won much more national publicity but a smaller share of the votes: Margarethe Cammermeyer, a childhood immigrant from Norway, and six-foot-plus mother of four. Cammermeyer was a nurse who served many years in the Army, won a Bronze Star in Vietnam and rose to the rank of colonel. In 1992 she told an inspecting officer that she was a lesbian; she was discharged, sued for reinstatement, and won in federal court; she finally retired from the Army National Guard in 1997 and, from her home near Metcalf's bed and breakfast on Whidbey Island, started running for Congress. Her story had been made into a TV movie, produced by Barbra Streisand and starring Glenn Close; from their friends and showbiz associates, and from many supporters of gay and lesbian rights nationally, Cammermeyer began raising large sums, ultimately spending $1,051,000. Metcalf in a May 1998 fundraising letter criticized the "lesbian lifestyle" and referred to her as "the controversial lesbian Army National Guard colonel."

Cammermeyer easily beat a Whidbey Island small business owner in the September primary, by 28% to 14% of the total vote; but Metcalf won 51%. Usually that is a pretty good indicator of an incumbent's November percentage, but in Washington in 1998 there was noticeable movement toward Democrats in several races; but not in Cammermeyer's. She hired a large staff and spent much money on travel; only in the last six days of the campaign did she put ads up on TV. Meanwhile, Metcalf, a strong opponent of free trade, was endorsed by the Machinists Union for the work he had done for Boeing. Cammermeyer sent out envelopes reading "Please open immediately. Notification regarding denial of your health care coverage." The letter inside criticized Metcalf for voting against the right to sue HMOs, but Metcalf, his office flooded with tearful calls from elderly women, decided that the campaign honor code the two had agreed on in September was out the window. Metcalf carried every county but San Juan, in the farther island, and won 61% in their common home of Whidbey Island; overall Metcalf won 55%–45%. In a speech after the campaign Cammermeyer profanely attacked national Democrats for not putting money into her campaign; many other Democratic challengers would have loved the chance to show that they could make $1 million go farther.

Metcalf reaffirmed his term-limits promise after the campaign, and by December one candidate had announced, outgoing state Representative Barry Sehlin, a self-described moderate Republican, who once was commander of the Whidbey Island Naval Air Station. Another likely Republican is conservative state Representative John Koster. Possible Democratic candidates include Snohomish County Council President Rick Larsen, supported by Snohomish County Executive Bob Drewel; and state Representative Jeff Morris, who for six years was former Congressman Al Swift's political director.

Cook's Call. *Highly Competitive.* Metcalf's decision to retire at the end of this term has put control of this marginal northwestern district up in the air. While there are a number of candidates from both parties already taking a serious look at this seat, neither party can afford a contentious primary that will ultimately leave their eventual nominee bruised and penniless with only a few weeks until Election Day.

The People: Pop. 1990: 540,861; 41.5% rural; 12.9% age 65 + ; 93.7% White, 0.9% Black, 2.1% Asian, 2% Amer. Indian, 1.2% Other; 2.8% Hispanic Origin. Households: 58.9% married couple families; 28.3% married couple fams. w. children; 52.1% college educ.; median household income: $31,305; per capita income: $14,419; median house value: $100,500; median gross rent: $396.

1996 Presidential Vote

Clinton (D)	123,729	(47%)
Dole (R)	103,901	(39%)
Perot (I)	27,177	(10%)
Others	11,055	(4%)

1992 Presidential Vote

Clinton (D)	103,405	(39%)
Bush (R)	85,876	(33%)
Perot (I)	71,794	(27%)

Rep. Jack Metcalf (R)

Elected 1994; b. Nov. 30, 1927, Marysville; home, Marysville; Pacific Lutheran U., B.A. 1951, U. of WA, M.A. 1966; Protestant; married (Norma).

Military Career: Army, 1946–47.

Elected Office: WA House of Reps., 1960–64; Repub. nominee for U.S. Senate, 1968, 1974; WA Senate, 1966–74, 1980–92.

Professional Career: U.S. Marshal Patrol Boat Skipper, 1947–48; High schl. teacher, 1951–81; Owner, Log Castle Bed & Breakfast, 1978–present.

DC Office: 1510 LHOB 20515, 202-225-2605; Fax: 202-225-4420; Web site: www.house.gov/metcalf.

District Offices: Bellingham, 360-733-4500; Everett, 425-252-3188.

Committees: *Banking & Financial Services* (13th of 32 R): Domestic & International Monetary Policy; Financial Institutions & Consumer Credit; Housing & Community Opportunity. *Science* (25th of 25 R): Energy & Environment. *Transportation & Infrastructure* (23d of 41 R): Aviation; Ground Transportation.

Group Ratings

	ADA	ACLU	AFS	LCV	CON	NTU	NFIB	COC	ACU	NTLC	CHC
1998	20	0	33	23	2	49	86	83	80	71	100
1997	15	—	50	—	49	49	—	60	88	—	—

National Journal Ratings

	1997 LIB — 1997 CONS			1998 LIB — 1998 CONS		
Economic	49%	—	51%	39%	—	59%
Social	10%	—	82%	14%	—	81%
Foreign	24%	—	72%	19%	—	75%

Key Votes of the 105th Congress

1. Clinton Budget Deal	Y	5. Puerto Rico Sthood. Ref.	N	9. Cut $ for B-2 Bombers	N
2. Education IRAs	Y	6. End Highway Set-asides	Y	10. Human Rights in China	N
3. Req. 2/3 to Raise Taxes	Y	7. School Prayer Amend.	Y	11. Withdraw Bosnia Troops	Y
4. Fast-track Trade	N	8. Ovrd. Part. Birth Veto	Y	12. End Cuban TV-Marti	N

Election Results

1998 general	Jack Metcalf (R)	124,125	(55%)	($1,063,851)
	Margarethe Cammermeyer (D)	100,776	(45%)	($1,050,926)
1998 primary	Jack Metcalf (R)	62,121	(51%)	
	Margarethe Cammermeyer (D)	33,720	(28%)	
	Fran Einterz (D)	17,020	(14%)	
	Robert Imhof (R)	8,778	(7%)	
1996 general	Jack Metcalf (R)	124,655	(49%)	($797,442)
	Kevin Quigley (D)	122,728	(48%)	($447,812)
	Others	9,561	(4%)	

THIRD DISTRICT

From the Pacific Ocean to the majestic row of active and inactive volcanoes from Mount Rainier to Mount St. Helens to Oregon's Mount Hood, southwest Washington is one of America's most productive lumber areas. The moist air and almost constant rains blown in from the Pacific keep the trees on the coast growing rapidly; in the valleys just past the Coast Range, there is still plenty of precipitation and fast-growing forest. Then come the high mountains: The Cascades are a genuine divide, wrenching almost all precipitation out of the air so the climate eastward for a thousand miles is arid. Americans were reminded of the force of the volcanoes when Mount St. Helens, dormant for 123 years, erupted in 1980, killing 65 people and ruining the land in its path. But nature has repaired itself, as it must have done many times before.

Lewis and Clark came here in 1805, down the Columbia River to a rainy and foggy winter by the ocean, and for many years this part of Washington was sparsely settled, with lumber mill- and fishing boat-towns interspersed between mountains and water. It was flannel shirt country, Democratic since the New Deal days. In recent years, its resource-based economy was threatened by the environmental movement, which restricted fishing practices and got a court decision shutting down old-growth forest logging to save spotted owl habitat. This roiled local politics, and gave Republicans an opening.

More important recently has been the spread of the Pacific Northwest's great metropolitan areas into these valleys. Clark County across the Columbia from Portland, Oregon, has filled up with new residents, eager to avoid Oregon's income tax; the Seattle-Tacoma metro area has been moving down from the north past the small state capital of Olympia. This is one of America's great international trading areas, with big exports of logs and timber and vast imports on the docks of Portland and the Puget Sound.

The 3d Congressional District covers the land between the ocean and the Cascades, from Olympia on an inlet of Puget Sound, south to Vancouver in Clark County, site of the Hudson Bay Company headquarters in the 19th Century. Politically, this was long a solidly Democratic district, indeed sometimes the most Democratic district in Washington. But economic growth and diversification and the coming of many new residents with no roots in the old industries have made the 3d now a politically marginal district.

The congressman from the 3d District is Brian Baird, a Democrat elected in 1998. Baird grew up in northern New Mexico and western Colorado. He got a Ph.D. in clinical psychology from the University of Wyoming, and worked with veterans and families dealing with cancer, with juvenile delinquents in prison, and families of murder victims. He also wrote a book called *Are We Having Fun Yet?* for couples on vacation. He moved to Washington in 1980 and was a professor at Pacific Lutheran University in Tacoma and living in Olympia when he ran for the House in 1996 against Republican incumbent Linda Smith. Smith was one of the most revolutionary of the 1994 Republican freshmen, an opponent of free trade and a backer of campaign finance reform, strongly supported by Christian conservatives. She got into the 1994 race in August, when a high-spending Republican dropped out, won the Republican nomination on write-in votes and beat incumbent Democrat Jolene Unsoeld 52%–45%. Democrats did not target Smith until well into the 1996 cycle, after she led Baird by just 52%–48% in the September all-party primary, which is often a good forecast of the general election. On election night Baird was ahead by 2,400 votes and was pronounced the winner by an overeager media; Baird spent five days in Washington, D.C., at freshman orientation. But when the more than 40,000 absentee votes outstanding were counted, Smith won by 887 votes, 50.2%–49.8%.

Baird returned to southwest Washington and, taking a leave from his job, never stopped running, while Smith decided to challenge Senator Patty Murray; she won the Republican nomination but lost the general election 58%–42%, running behind in the 3d District as well. Campaigning constantly, Baird picked up the consensus-minded inclination of voters and emphasized how confrontation-minded the Republicans were. "People really want to focus on a positive agenda. People are tired of candidates who just want to tear down government and tear down their opposition," he said. He called for applying 100% of the budget surplus to Social Security, opposed school vouchers, favored campaign finance reform, opposed breaching the Columbia River dams and said Washington taxpayers should be able to deduct their sales tax payments, as they could before the tax reform act of 1986.

The two leading Republicans started far behind Baird in fundraising and both took confrontational, crunchy stands on issues. State Senator Don Benton called for a flat tax and respect for gun rights and property rights. Former legislator and 1992 nominee Pat Fiske, who was Smith's chief of staff, took similar positions in a similar tone. In the September 1998 all-party primary, Benton won 22% of all votes and Fiske 16%; Republican candidates altogether won 52%, while Baird, unopposed by other Democrats, won 48%.

This suggested another very close result in November. But opinion in several Washington races shifted perceptibly toward the Democrats in the seven weeks of the general election campaign. This was accentuated by the tone of the campaign. Independent expenditure ads were run by Americans for Limited Terms (against Baird), the Sierra Club (against Benton) and the Republican Party. The last seized on the fact that on a Project Vote Smart questionnaire, Baird left blank the question whether he would prosecute as adults youths accused of murder and violent crimes. "Brian Baird wouldn't support trying even the most violent juveniles as adults," the ad said. Baird replied that "to make it a black-or-white blanket judgment and eliminate any judicial discretion is, I think, a big mistake. Voters are fed up with this kind of deception." It was unclear why, if Baird felt that way on the issue, he had not checked the yes box. But he managed to frame the issue as one of positive versus negative campaigning and the media, very unsympathetic to conservatives here (the *Olympian* called Benton "an arrogant divisive blowhard"), accepted his argument that the ad was inaccurate. One Portland station pulled the ad and the issue probably worked for Baird. Baird also spent twice as much money, $1,602,000, an impressive amount for an open seat, which Democrats wisely targeted. Baird won 55%–45%, winning more than 60% in the Olympia area and the coast and running barely ahead in the area around Vancouver, Benton's home base.

In the months after the election Baird performed well. He was elected Democratic freshman president for the first six months of 1999 and got a seat on the Transportation and Infrastructure Committee. He sought aid for victims of the landslide that slowly enveloped most of the houses in the Aldercrest neighborhood of Kelso. But he also got some bad publicity. During his two campaigns Baird had featured pictures of him and his wife embracing and holding hands by a river bank; he talked of how, with her two children in college, they avoided the "peace of an empty nest" by becoming hosts to an injured Bosnian teenager. But two days after the election the Bairds were divorced. Mary Baird said that her husband told her in April that he wanted a divorce but did not want to announce it until after the election for fear it would hurt his campaign. She stopped attending his rallies and asked that her pictures be dropped from his brochures and Website; most but not all were. Reporters recalled how Baird said during the campaign things like, "Voters demand and deserve honesty and integrity from their public officials," and "All the time we hear about how people are disgusted with negative and deceptive advertising." *The Seattle Times*, which endorsed Baird, wrote, "Baird squanders his potential when he puts short-term personal gain over long-term public trust." Baird replied, "It has never been my intention to deceive the public, only to protect my family's privacy in this painful time." But it escaped no one's notice in Washington that 1st District Congressman Rick White, who had featured his wife and four children in his 1994 and 1996 campaign ads, was divorced in April 1998 and defeated in November 1998, not so much because voters abhor divorce but because they dislike hypocrisy.

Baird has shown the skills and perseverance to make this once-safe Democratic district safely Democratic again. But he may face serious competition again in 2000.

Cook's Call. *Competitive.* Baird's convincing win here in 1998 belies the underlying competitiveness of this district. But, to be competitive here in 2000, Republicans need to find a stronger and less controversial candidate than their 1998 nominee.

The People: Pop. 1990: 540,658; 37.5% rural; 13.2% age 65 +; 94.8% White, 0.9% Black, 2.2% Asian, 1.4% Amer. Indian, 0.8% Other; 2.3% Hispanic Origin. Households: 57.8% married couple families; 27.5% married couple fams. w. children; 50.5% college educ.; median household income: $29,154; per capita income: $13,328; median house value: $70,400; median gross rent: $346.

1996 Presidential Vote

Clinton (D)	124,864	(49%)
Dole (R)	97,985	(38%)
Perot (I)	24,407	(9%)
Others	9,895	(4%)

1992 Presidential Vote

Clinton (D)	104,682	(42%)
Bush (R)	82,648	(33%)
Perot (I)	61,609	(25%)

Rep. Brian Baird (D)

Elected 1998; b. Mar. 7, 1956, Chama, NM; home, Olympia; U. of UT, B.A. 1977, U. of WY, M.S. 1980, Ph.D. 1984; Protestant; divorced.

Elected Office: Dem. nominee for U.S. House of Reps., 1996.

Professional Career: Prof., Pacific Lutheran U., 1986–98.

DC Office: 1721 LHOB 20515, 202-225-3536; Fax: 202-225-3478; Web site: www.house.gov/baird.

District Offices: Olympia, 360-352-9768; Vancouver, 360-695-6292.

Committees: *Science* (21st of 23 D). *Small Business* (15th of 17 D): Rural Enterprise, Business Opportunities & Special Small Business Problems. *Transportation & Infrastructure* (33d of 34 D): Coast Guard & Maritime Transportation; Water Resources & Environment.

Group Ratings and Key Votes: Newly Elected

Election Results

1998 general	Brian Baird (D)	120,364	(55%)	($1,602,437)
	Don Benton (R)	99,855	(45%)	($755,022)
1998 primary	Brian Baird (D)	63,979	(48%)	
	Don Benton (R)	29,153	(22%)	
	Pat Fiske (R)	21,564	(16%)	
	Rick Jackson (R)	12,970	(10%)	
	Paul Phillips (R)	5,755	(4%)	
1996 general	Linda Smith (R)	123,117	(50%)	($1,216,368)
	Brian Baird (D)	122,230	(50%)	($718,322)

FOURTH DISTRICT

The rugged peaks of the Cascade Mountains divide Washington State into two starkly different climate zones and two almost as starkly different political cultures. West of the Cascades, Washington is moist, green, full of watery inlets; to the east, it is barren and brown, except where irrigation ditches feed the waters of the Columbia River into thirsty valleys, or where mountaintop waters fall east, as they do to water the apple orchards in the Yakima Valley. The federal government has been a presence in the East-of-the-Cascades since the 1930s, when it began to build dams that provided cheap power and boosted economic development in this forbidding, often surreal, landscape: A giant bust of Franklin Roosevelt gazes from a bluff on the Columbia out over 550-foot-high Grand Coulee Dam, which Roosevelt initiated and which was one of his favorite projects. Other dams are strung along downriver, like beads on the necklace of the Columbia, along most of the way to Bonneville Dam near Portland, where the river breaks through the Cascades.

The one exception is the Hanford Reach, the last undammed, undeveloped stretch of the upper Columbia River, near the 560-square mile Hanford Nuclear Reservation, north of the Tri-Cities of Richland, Kennewick and Pasco. Hanford was built by the Army to manufacture plutonium for the Manhattan Project and was where the Nagasaki bomb was constructed. After the war the Hanford Works became the primary producer of materials for America's nuclear weapons and eastern Washington's largest employer. Then in 1988 Hanford's plutonium plant was shut down because of hazardous leaks and contaminated waste. There is a proposal to restart the Fast Flux Test Facility reactor, closed in 1993, to produce plutonium for space batteries and medical isotopes; it costs $30 million a year to keep on standby and would cost $371 million to restart and $120 million a year to operate. Another proposal is to begin converting the waste to glass starting in 2006; cleanup costs now run about $1 billion a year.

The 4th Congressional District covers the western half of Washington east of the Cascades, running from the Canadian border past Grand Coulee and through the Hanford Works down to the Dalles Dam. Sentiment toward the federal government has soured in other parts of the district almost as much as around the Tri-Cities. The Yakima Valley, which produces more than half of the nation's apples, was angry that the apparently groundless Alar scare in 1989 hurt sales. Lumber towns in the Cascades are furious that those who want to preserve the spotted owl may shut down logging businesses. In an area once pretty evenly divided between the parties, opinion has shifted away from Democrats and toward Republicans; the cultural liberalism of Seattle seems very far away here. Said Rick Locke, the 1996 Democratic nominee here, when he looked at a party poll in spring 1998, "I don't know what Democrats did to these people, but it sure must have been bad."

The congressman from the 4th District is Doc Hastings, a Republican elected in 1994. Hastings grew up in the Tri-Cities, went to college in Ellensburg, served in the Army Reserves and for 27 years ran the Columbia Basin Paper and Supply Company in Pasco. In 1979 he was elected to the state House, served as a Republican leader, then retired after eight years in 1987. In 1992 he ran for Congress, won the Republican nomination, but was beaten 51%–49% by moderate Democrat Jay Inslee. But Inslee voted for the Clinton budget and tax package in 1993 and the crime bill with its gun control provisions in 1994—big liabilities when Hastings ran again in 1994. Hastings led with 50% in the September all-party primary, to only 41% for Inslee. Hastings campaigned heavily in three counties in the north of the district where Inslee had eked out his victory margin in 1992. This time Hastings carried all three, swept the Tri-Cities and, despite losing Yakima, won overall 53%–47%.

In the House Hastings has a solidly conservative voting record, even opposing a $24 million remodeling of the Richland federal building. Much of his time was spent on Hanford. With Senator Slade Gorton, he sponsored a bill in 1995 to make the state of Washington responsible for the cleanup, allowing privatization of cleanup work and avoiding the plethora of often impractical and duplicative federal regulations; this was supported also by Democratic Congressman Norman Dicks and Senator Patty Murray. Hastings also worked closely with Dicks, a high-ranking and politically savvy member of Appropriations, to stop a proposal by Lloyd Doggett of Texas to zero out the nearly-completed $230 million Environmental and Molecular Sciences Laboratory at Hanford; they even enlisted support from scientists in Austin, Doggett's home town. On another local issue, Hastings and Gorton in January 1998 urged the Army Corps of Engineers not to bury the site where the prehistoric Kennewick Man skeleton was found in January 1996.

Hastings has opposed Senator Patty Murray's proposal, supported by Dicks, to designate the 51-mile Hanford Reach of the Columbia a Wild and Scenic River; it has been kept free from development by the Hanford Reservation and as a result is the closest thing to a free-flowing part of the river, producing most of its wild salmon run, which is higher than in 1964–84 but lower than 1985–96. Hastings has argued for a county-state-federal management panel, with a quarter-mile on each side of the river kept free from development. "Nobody would argue that Hanford Reach is something that ought to be preserved and protected, but it ought to be accessible," he said. "There needs to be local decision making. It's an important part of any final decision on the Hanford Reach. Local control can work." White House Counsel on Environmental Quality Chair Katie McGinty said in 1998 that Clinton would veto a bill with combined management. Interior Secretary Bruce Babbitt has said that he would like to tear down one of the major hydroelectric dams in Washington. Hastings opposes that, along with the rest of the Washington delegation; they and Democratic Governor Gary Locke oppose even the breaching of dams proposed by some environmentalists and Indian leaders.

Hastings has won re-election twice. Inslee, his 1992 and 1994 opponent, was returned to the House by beating 1st District incumbent Rick White in 1998. Hastings had a serious opponent in 1996 in Rick Locke. Locke ran an ad in which a menacing voice said Hastings's votes were controlled by "someone back East named Newtie." Hastings retaliated with an ad with a Robin Leach-like voice saying: "Today we'll meet political candidate Rick Locke, the Seattle millionaire who just moved to central Washington to buy a seat in Congress. Of course, buying things comes naturally to Rick Locke. He still maintains several luxurious homes in Seattle and a 38-foot sailing yacht on nearby Puget Sound. Rick also likes to unwind at his exclusive resort home hideaway in the chic San Juan Islands." Hastings won 55% of the total vote in the September all-party primary and 53% in the general; Locke carried Yakima and Kittitas counties narrowly and Hastings carried everything else. In 1998 Hastings had easier going. His Democratic opponent had served six days in jail for assault in 1996, which he said would give him a unique perspective in the House; he spent $450 on his campaign. Hastings won with 69% of the vote.

Cook's Call. *Safe.* It is unlikely that three-term Hastings will be a top target in 2000. Though his first two wins here were not overwhelming, his 69% win in 1998 and the overall Republican nature of this district should help to insulate him from a serious challenge in 2000.

The People: Pop. 1990: 540,701; 38.6% rural; 13% age 65 +; 83.3% White, 0.9% Black, 1.3% Asian, 2.8% Amer. Indian, 11.7% Other; 15.7% Hispanic Origin. Households: 58.3% married couple families; 28.7% married couple fams. w. children; 44.5% college educ.; median household income: $25,055; per capita income: $11,578; median house value: $60,300; median gross rent: $270.

1996 Presidential Vote		
Dole (R)	101,963	(48%)
Clinton (D)	84,157	(40%)
Perot (I)	20,516	(10%)
Others	4,868	(2%)

1992 Presidential Vote		
Bush (R)	87,995	(42%)
Clinton (D)	71,914	(35%)
Perot (I)	45,256	(22%)

Rep. Doc Hastings (R)

Elected 1994; b. Feb. 7, 1941, Spokane; home, Pasco; Columbia Basin Col., 1959–61, Central Washington U., 1963–64; Catholic; married (Claire).

Military Career: Army Reserves, 1964–69.

Elected Office: WA House of Reps., 1979–87; Repub. nominee for U.S. House of Reps., 1992.

Professional Career: Pres., Columbia Basin Paper & Supply, 1967–94.

DC Office: 1323 LHOB 20515, 202-225-5816; Fax: 202-225-3251; Web site: www.house.gov/hastings.

District Offices: Tri-Cities, 509-543-9396; Yakima, 509-452-3243.

Committees: *Rules* (6th of 9 R): The Legislative & Budget Process.

Group Ratings

	ADA	ACLU	AFS	LCV	CON	NTU	NFIB	COC	ACU	NTLC	CHC
1998	0	7	0	8	21	59	100	94	100	100	100
1997	0	—	13	—	49	57	—	100	92	—	—

National Journal Ratings

	1997 LIB — 1997 CONS		1998 LIB — 1998 CONS	
Economic	14%	— 85%	15%	— 81%
Social	0%	— 90%	3%	— 90%
Foreign	0%	— 88%	34%	— 62%

Key Votes of the 105th Congress

1. Clinton Budget Deal	Y	5. Puerto Rico Sthood. Ref.	N	9. Cut $ for B-2 Bombers	N
2. Education IRAs	Y	6. End Highway Set-asides	Y	10. Human Rights in China	N
3. Req. 2/3 to Raise Taxes	Y	7. School Prayer Amend.	Y	11. Withdraw Bosnia Troops	N
4. Fast-track Trade	Y	8. Ovrd. Part. Birth Veto	Y	12. End Cuban TV-Marti	N

Election Results

1998 general	Doc Hastings (R)	121,684	(69%)	($468,365)
	Gordon Allen Pross (D)	43,043	(24%)	
	Peggy McKerlie (Ref)	11,363	(6%)	($11,538)
1998 primary	Doc Hastings (R)	71,557	(69%)	
	Gordon Allen Pross (D)	25,670	(25%)	
	Peggy McKerlie (Ref)	4,209	(4%)	
	Others	1,871	(2%)	
1996 general	Doc Hastings (R)	108,647	(53%)	($734,640)
	Rick Locke (D)	96,502	(47%)	($408,772)

FIFTH DISTRICT

Eastern Washington is a land of great rivers and bare parched land, where the Columbia, Spokane and Snake Rivers wind among vast plateaus, bringing water from the Rockies to the desert. Spokane grew up at the falls of the Spokane River when the railroads first came through, and became a major wheat, mining, electrical and railroad center early in this century, the center of the so-called "Inland Empire"; it celebrated with the 1974 World's Exposition on the downtown riverfront. Nearby are some of the most fascinating landscapes in the United States:

surreally undulating yellow wheatfields, the ridges of the Palouse where the topsoil is 200 feet deep, the bare-rock coulees rising above dammed-up lakes and barren desert. This is remote and inhospitable land: The summers can be blazing hot and winters bitter cold; many rivers run wildly. But it has been tamed by man, and the water from the Grand Coulee and other dams irrigates some of the richest farmland in the country.

The 5th Congressional District covers the easternmost part of Washington. About two-thirds of the people here live in greater Spokane, a city whose voting habits are a fairly good proxy of the nation's. Its heritage leans toward the Republicans, but it is not as Republican as most of the nearby Rocky Mountain states, though it veers toward them angrily at times; it is open also to Democrats, and Spokane County voted for Bill Clinton in 1992 and 1996.

The congressman from the 5th District is George Nethercutt, a Republican elected in 1994 when he defeated Speaker of the House Thomas Foley—the first time a speaker of the House has been defeated in his home district since Galusha Grow lost in Pennsylvania in 1862. Nethercutt grew up in Spokane, graduated from Washington State University in Pullman and Gonzaga Law School in Spokane, served four years on the staff of Alaska Senator Ted Stevens in the 1970s, then returned home and practiced law. He was involved in civic work, representing clients in adoptions, heading the local Diabetes Foundation (his daughter was diagnosed with the disease), and starting a crisis nursery for abused children. In 1994 he decided to run for Congress. Foley had served the district for 30 years and had wide personal popularity. But in 1992 his margin was not much larger than that of Clinton's, whose popularity had plummeted since, and many in the state were angry at Foley for filing a lawsuit against congressional term limits imposed by the voters in 1992. Nethercutt announced his candidacy in April 1994; in May two former Foley opponents also announced—Duane Alton, owner of a chain of tire stores who ran in 1976 and 1978, and John Sonneland, a physician who ran in 1980, 1982 and 1992, when he spent $400,000 of his own money and won 45% of the vote. For a time the contest among Republicans seemed more intense than the race against Foley; Nethercutt won the primary with 29% of the total vote, to 20% for Alton and 15% for Sonneland.

But the big news was that in the all-party primary, which often forecasts the November results, Foley took only 35% of the votes. Immediately Foley began spending heavily, emphasizing the work he had done for the district and what he could do in the future. However, he had to buck not only Nethercutt's ads but campaigns by the National Rifle Association (furious that Foley, a longtime gun control opponent, backed the 1994 crime bill) and the National Taxpayers Union. Nethercutt in an ad promised never to sue the people of Washington—a swipe at Foley's lawsuit against the term limits initiative—and pledged to serve only three terms himself. When attacked for his conservatism and support for the Kasich budget cuts, Nethercutt responded with sensitive ads showing him walking out of a crisis nursery holding a baby, and with his family walking in a park; he was helped also by a November 4th campaign appearance by Ross Perot. This was one of the most expensive House races in the nation: Foley spent $2.1 million; Nethercutt, $1.1 million. Foley did carry Spokane County, but not by much, and lost all but one of the smaller counties; that gave Nethercutt a 51%–49% win.

In the House, Nethercutt got a seat on Appropriations and supported most of the Contract with America. Initially noncommittal, he supported the Freedom to Farm Act, including the fixed payments to formerly subsidized farmers in its seven-year phaseout. He opposed the Interior Columbia Basin Ecosystem Management Project, which he feared might lead to restrictions on logging, mining and grazing on private lands; he pushed a measure to authorize a scientific survey of forests, but bar any environmental impact statement that could impose broad restrictions on land use.

In 1996 three Democrats vied to run against Nethercutt. The winner, with 25% of the total in the September all-party primary, was Judy Olson, former president of the National Association of Wheat Growers. She accused him of supporting Medicare "cuts" and said, "His priority was marching in the Republican revolution." She criticized him for buying a $400,000 house in the Washington, D.C., suburbs; Nethercutt replied that he had two mortgages and added, "Don't criticize my kids for wanting a stable home." Nethercutt attacked Olson for getting most of her contributions from unions. In response to the Medicare charges, he featured his mother in ads and said, "I resent people thinking I would do anything to hurt my own mother." Nethercutt spent $1.1 million, compared to Olson's $616,000. He won 51% in the all-party primary, suggesting a very close general election, and won 56%–44% in the general, carrying Spokane County smartly and every smaller county. After the election, Nethercutt called for a truth-in-advertising law.

Nethercutt continued his moderate voting record but cast some surprising votes, notably in 1997 voting to take the United States out of the United Nations. He joined the Clinton Administration in trying to keep the Conservation Reserve Program at 19 million acres, but Appropriations voted to trim it to 14 million acres in April 1997. In July 1998 he helped put together the repeal of sanctions against Pakistan, the single largest buyer of winter wheat, in time for Washington grain sellers to qualify for a $35 million purchase; he pushed a bill in October to lift sanctions on farm products except in cases where the president exercises a national security waiver. He grilled Interior Secretary Bruce Babbitt about whether he would dismantle or breach the Columbia River dams; Babbitt said he had authority to do so, but could not act unless Congress provided money. Nethercutt strongly opposes getting rid of the dams and attacked Babbitt's "green sledge hammer." He has pushed hard for increased diabetes research, working with others, from Speaker Newt Gingrich to liberal Democrat Elizabeth Furse and White House Chief of Staff Erskine Bowles. He sponsored a bill to rename the Spokane federal courthouse after Foley, and the plaza outside after Foley's predecessor, Walt Horan; together they represented the district for 52 years. He expressed regret in October 1998 for voting to release the Starr Report; but he called for Clinton to resign, defended the independent counsel and voted for impeachment. Locally, he worked to build a $16 million dorm at Fairchild Air Force Base and backed a HUD loan to Spokane for downtown redevelopment opposed by the owner of NorthTown Mall.

Nethercutt considered running for senator in 1998 and governor in 2000, but in October 1997 announced for a third term instead. This was a less eventful campaign. Nethercutt beat his Republican opponent 57%–38% in 1998. His self-imposed term limit looming, he said in February 1999, "I meant it when I said six years is enough." But, he went on to say, he had found the issues so complicated that six years "is probably not enough," and he talked occasionally about becoming a member of the college of cardinals—the 13 Appropriations subcommittee chairmen—though 10 other Republicans with more seniority would presumably get those posts before he would. In February 1999 U.S. Term Limits put up a billboard thanking Nethercutt for keeping his pledge; in March 1999, after he made no move to retire, they launched a $100,000 ad campaign that started with an ad showing Richard Nixon, George Bush and Bill Clinton making promises they were not to keep, then posing the question "Will George Nethercutt be next?" Another ad suggested that Nethercutt might favor dismantling Columbia River dams because he had voted for the Endangered Species Act 12 times. Nethercutt got two Spokane TV stations to pull the ads as inaccurate. He said he would decide whether to run "after extended conversations with the people of Washington." A pro-Nethercutt group formed in March 1999 sought 60,000 signatures on a petition urging him to run again; another group formed to persuade him to retire.

"I've changed my mind," Nethercutt said in June 1999 when he announced he would run. "I made a mistake when I chose to set a limit on my service." His prospects must be regarded as uncertain. A March U.S. Term Limits poll showed that only 32% wanted him to run for re-election and 57% said he should leave Congress. It also showed him leading Democrat John Allison, but by a less than overwhelming 43%–33% margin. U.S. Term Limits has pledged to spend up to $1 million to defeat Nethercutt; this could be a furiously contested district in 2000, and on some of the same terms as in 1994.

Cook's Call. *Potentially Competitive.* Though he has been the prime target of thousands of dollars of negative advertising by the national term limits movement, Nethercutt still remains a difficult target. First, this formerly Democratic district has been steadily trending toward Republicans. Second, it is unclear if voters here will be moved by the term limit message. But a serious Democratic challenger and the continual negative attacks by the term limits group make this a race worth watching.

The People: Pop. 1990: 540,865; 28.7% rural; 14% age 65 + ; 93.4% White, 1.2% Black, 1.8% Asian, 1.7% Amer. Indian, 1.9% Other; 3.2% Hispanic Origin. Households: 54.1% married couple families; 25.3% married couple fams. w. children; 54.5% college educ.; median household income: $25,107; per capita income: $12,177; median house value: $57,700; median gross rent: $280.

1996 Presidential Vote

Clinton (D)	104,052	(44%)
Dole (R)	102,384	(43%)
Perot (I)	25,250	(11%)
Others	6,826	(3%)

1992 Presidential Vote

Clinton (D)	99,676	(40%)
Bush (R)	90,294	(36%)
Perot (I)	56,472	(23%)

Rep. George Nethercutt (R)

Elected 1994; b. Oct. 7, 1944, Spokane; home, Spokane; WA St. U., B.A. 1967, Gonzaga U. Law Schl., J.D. 1971; Presbyterian; married (Mary Beth).

Professional Career: Law Clerk, Fed. Judge Ralph Plumer, 1971–72; Chief of Staff & Cnsl., U.S. Sen. Ted Stevens, 1972–76; Practicing atty., 1976–94.

DC Office: 1527 LHOB 20515, 202-225-2006; Fax: 202-225-3392; Web site: www.house.gov/nethercutt.

District Offices: Colville, 509-684-3481; Spokane, 509-353-2374; Walla Walla, 509-529-9358.

Committees: *Appropriations* (24th of 34 R): Agriculture, Rural Development, & FDA; Defense; Interior. *Science* (18th of 25 R): Space & Aeronautics.

Group Ratings

	ADA	ACLU	AFS	LCV	CON	NTU	NFIB	COC	ACU	NTLC	CHC
1998	0	13	0	8	60	64	100	89	96	95	92
1997	5	—	13	—	42	53	—	100	92	—	—

National Journal Ratings

	1997 LIB — 1997 CONS			1998 LIB — 1998 CONS		
Economic	28%	—	67%	34%	—	64%
Social	41%	—	59%	26%	—	72%
Foreign	0%	—	88%	38%	—	61%

Key Votes of the 105th Congress

1. Clinton Budget Deal	Y	5. Puerto Rico Sthood. Ref.	N	9. Cut $ for B-2 Bombers	N
2. Education IRAs	Y	6. End Highway Set-asides	Y	10. Human Rights in China	N
3. Req. 2/3 to Raise Taxes	Y	7. School Prayer Amend.	Y	11. Withdraw Bosnia Troops	Y
4. Fast-track Trade	Y	8. Ovrd. Part. Birth Veto	Y	12. End Cuban TV-Marti	Y

Election Results

1998 general	George Nethercutt (R)	110,040	(57%)	($762,004)
	Brad Lyons (D)	73,545	(38%)	($187,781)
	John Beal (AHP)	9,673	(5%)	($37,866)
1998 primary	George Nethercutt (R)	60,955	(58%)	
	Brad Lyons (D)	38,095	(36%)	
	John Beal (AHP)	5,889	(6%)	
1996 general	George Nethercutt (R)	131,618	(56%)	($1,071,823)
	Judy Olson (D)	105,166	(44%)	($615,636)

SIXTH DISTRICT

The rainiest part of the continental United States is at its far northwest corner, where the Olympic Mountains of Washington thrust into the Pacific Ocean. The waters of the Pacific evaporate, condense and then mist or rain down on the hills and mountains that jut up from the ocean and Puget Sound. The mountains here are always green, the trees that line the inlets towering, and during heavy rainfalls the rivers can rise six feet a day. This has long been lumbering and fishing country, where men go out to work at 6 a.m. in air cold enough to see your breath year round, and where dependence on the vagaries of nature and harsh environmental laws—like the ban on old-growth logging to protect the habitat of the spotted owl—have strengthened a traditional surly independence and suspicion of authority.

The inlets of Puget Sound, winding sinuously through the mountains, are among America's most picturesque waterways and strategically among its most important. Here during World War II, shipyards built and sheltered much of the U.S. Navy's Pacific fleet, and here during the Cold War much of the nuclear submarine fleet anchored at the giant Bremerton Navy base. To the south is the Tacoma Straits Bridge, the replacement of the narrow span that, in a scene preserved on newsreel (and still viewed by civil engineering students), started vibrating on the wrong harmonic in high winds and collapsed in 1940. On the other side is Tacoma, long the second-ranking city on Puget Sound, with its impressive massive docks and pleasant hilly residential neighborhoods.

The 6th Congressional District contains the Olympic Peninsula, Bremerton and most of surrounding Kitsap County amid various inlets of Puget Sound and about half of Tacoma. Politically, the Olympic Peninsula and Bremerton are working-class Democratic. Tacoma also is traditionally Democratic, though the 6th's portion of it is the more white-collar side of town. On balance the 6th is, after the central Seattle 7th, Washington's most Democratic district.

The congressman from the 6th District is Norman Dicks, a onetime University of Washington football player who was on Senator Warren Magnuson's staff when it was one of the best on Capitol Hill. Dicks returned home to Kitsap County to run for Congress in 1976, when the 6th District incumbent got the judgeship for which he had been hankering for 12 years. Dicks was elected easily that year, and in every year since except 1980, when Magnuson lost. He has passed up several chances to run for the Senate, and seems firmly committed to the House.

Dicks has brought to the House the aggressiveness and political shrewdness that were the hallmarks of the Magnuson staff in its golden days—"the word 'can't' leaves your vocabulary when you go to work for Norm," one former aide said—plus an interest in defense and intelligence reminiscent of Magnuson's colleague for 40 years, Henry Jackson. These talents would be deployed, he long assumed, from a place in the majority; in 1995 he said: "In 27 years I never once thought about being in the minority. It never, ever occurred to me until about noon on election day" in November 1994. But he has adapted smoothly to being part of the minority party, helped by the fact that on some issues, though not all, his goals are more congenial to many Republicans than Democrats. "I still feel it's worth doing," he said. "And with Speaker Foley gone now, we've got to have a couple of people who know how to operate. I've got to be the person who takes the lessons of 27 years and puts them to use."

Dicks has a seat on the Appropriations Committee and on the Defense Subcommittee—a vital post for Kitsap County, where most workers depend on Pentagon payrolls, and for Washington generally, because of Boeing. In these posts Dicks, even in the minority, has exerted pivotal influence on important policies, usually operating quietly and behind the scenes. For example, in the early 1980s, Dicks took the lead on restoring Export-Import Bank loan authority—Boeing is America's biggest exporter and user of the loans—when the Reagan Administration wanted to cut it, and led a campaign that switched 80 House votes overnight. In the middle 1980s, he helped keep the MX missile alive in return for arms control commitments from the Reagan Administration. During the post-Cold War downsizing of the Pentagon, he has looked out for the F-117 Stealth aircraft and especially for the B-2 Stealth bomber, for which he has been an enthusiast since Defense Secretary Harold Brown proposed the plane in 1980. In the 105th Congress, he led the fight for more B-2s than the administration requested, arguing that their stealth capability might have deterred Saddam Hussein from invading Kuwait and prevented Scott O'Grady from being shot down over Bosnia. Dicks lobbied colleagues persistently at Camden Yards Stadium in September 1995, on the day Cal Ripken was setting his consecutive-games-played record, pausing only for the long fifth-inning ovation. The next day the B-2s were authorized, over the opposition of many Democrats and Budget Chairman John Kasich, by a 213–210 vote; Dicks told Kasich he had six or seven votes in reserve. In 1996 and 1997 he won four straight votes on the B-2: "We are undefeated, untied, unscored on. That's the way I like it." Dicks complained when B-2s weren't used in 1998 air attacks on Iraq; he was vindicated when the B-2 was used in the bombing of Serbia and Kosovo in 1999, flying nonstop from Whiteman Air Force Base in Missouri and being refueled in-air, delivering weapons with pinpoint accuracy, with the pilots returning to sleep in their own beds.

Dicks has also used his Appropriations seat to help Washington communities, funneling money to lumber mill towns when logging in old-growth forests was banned, passing timber salvage riders to keep mills going, dealing with the cost of maintaining salmon runs in dammed rivers. He worked to maintain Washington's military bases during two rounds of base closings. In 1997 he called for reintroducing grey wolves into Olympic National Park after traveling to Canada's Algonquin Province Park and hearing them howl in response to his simulated howls; he pushed to tear down the Elwha River Dam to help salmon runs; he obtained a full-time tug boat for Neah Bay to help oil tankers through the Straits of Juan De Fuca. Naturally he looks after the interests of the Bremerton waterfront and has pushed for funding of a Tacoma waterfront development from which visitors can gaze upon Mount Rainier and see I-705, the last of the original interstate routes to be built. He was not able to keep *U.S.S. Missouri* in Bremerton, but in the 1999 defense budget the largest construction project was for dredging the Bremerton shipyard and building a new pier for the carrier *U.S.S. Carl Vinson*. Over several years, $100 million was earmarked for improvements at Tacoma's McChord Air Force Base, and the Todd Pacific Shipyards in Seattle got contracts for another $100 million to repair three carriers. Dicks worked for five years to settle the Puyallup Indian land claims and advanced the claim that Lewis and Clark ended their journey on the Washington, not the Oregon, side of the Columbia River. In 1999, he became ranking Democrat on the Interior Subcommittee, replacing 89-year-old Sidney Yates.

Dicks served as ranking Democrat on the Intelligence Committee in the 104th and 105th Congresses, operating quietly, knowledgeably and in a bipartisan manner—quite an accomplishment in the House of the mid-1990s. In time that came to mix with his role on China. He has been a strong supporter of normal trade relations status for China; Washington accounts for one-quarter of U.S. exports to China, and Boeing foresees a great market there. In October 1998 he worked to get Boeing an exemption so it could sell $120 billion in high-tech airplanes to China over the next 20 years. But Dicks knows there are problems: "We're trying to have a constructive engagement with China, and they just get worse and worse," he said in March 1996. How much worse began to be apparent in 1998, when Speaker Newt Gingrich set up a special committee to study technology transfers and, it turned out, espionage losses to China.

Democratic Leader Dick Gephart wanted to give the ranking minority post on the panel to Bob Menendez, a strong partisan, but in June 1998 was prevailed on to appoint Dicks instead. Dicks found panel Chairman Christopher Cox and Republican leaders willing to take his suggestions seriously, determined to proceed in a factual, bipartisan manner. He took the same approach. Over the fall, during the impeachment controversy and campaign period, until the committee's report was delivered to the White House, there were no leaks of any kind, no hint of partisan wrangling. The committee held 22 hearings, took 200 hours of testimony from 75 witnesses, conducted another 700 hours of interviews with 150 more people and issued 21 subpoenas. Dicks went over the draft report with Cox until they reached agreement. "We were surprised at how ineffective our counterespionage has been," Dicks said later. Optimistically, Dicks predicted the White House would declassify the report within a few weeks; in fact, they took until May 1999, obviously delaying for political advantage. But Dicks and Cox were ready with 38 specific recommendations for improving security and regulating technology transfers.

Cook's Call. *Safe.* Dicks has established a solid hold on this Democratic leaning, though not solidly partisan district. He is unlikely to face stiff competition in 2000.

The People: Pop. 1990: 540,836; 25.9% rural; 14.9% age 65 + ; 87.4% White, 5.3% Black, 3.9% Asian, 2.3% Amer. Indian, 1% Other; 3% Hispanic Origin. Households: 53.9% married couple families; 23.9% married couple fams. w. children; 50.7% college educ.; median household income: $27,882; per capita income: $13,403; median house value: $74,700; median gross rent: $351.

1996 Presidential Vote		
Clinton (D)	122,342	(50%)
Dole (R)	87,961	(36%)
Perot (I)	23,830	(10%)
Others	8,968	(4%)

1992 Presidential Vote		
Clinton (D)	106,370	(43%)
Bush (R)	77,539	(31%)
Perot (I)	60,582	(25%)

Rep. Norman Dicks (D)

Elected 1976; b. Dec. 16, 1940, Bremerton; home, Bremerton; U. of WA, B.A. 1963, J.D. 1968; Lutheran; married (Suzanne).

Professional Career: Legis. Asst., U.S. Sen. Warren Magnuson, 1968–73, A.A., 1973–76.

DC Office: 2467 RHOB 20515, 202-225-5916; Fax: 202-226-1176; Web site: www.house.gov/dicks.

District Offices: Bremerton, 360-479-4011; Tacoma, 453-593-6536.

Committees: *Appropriations* (3d of 27 D): Defense; Interior (RMM); Military Construction.

Group Ratings

	ADA	ACLU	AFS	LCV	CON	NTU	NFIB	COC	ACU	NTLC	CHC
1998	95	87	89	77	72	14	36	39	0	16	0
1997	70	—	75	—	42	27	—	60	17	—	—

National Journal Ratings

	1997 LIB — 1997 CONS			1998 LIB — 1998 CONS		
Economic	66%	—	33%	79%	—	21%
Social	82%	—	15%	72%	—	28%
Foreign	58%	—	41%	90%	—	5%

Key Votes of the 105th Congress

1. Clinton Budget Deal	Y	5. Puerto Rico Sthood. Ref.	Y	9. Cut $ for B-2 Bombers	N
2. Education IRAs	N	6. End Highway Set-asides	N	10. Human Rights in China	N
3. Req. 2/3 to Raise Taxes	N	7. School Prayer Amend.	N	11. Withdraw Bosnia Troops	N
4. Fast-track Trade	Y	8. Ovrd. Part. Birth Veto	N	12. End Cuban TV-Marti	Y

Election Results

1998 general	Norman Dicks (D)	143,308	(68%)	($495,257)
	Bob Lawrence (R)	66,291	(32%)	($30,031)
1998 primary	Norman Dicks (D)	91,906	(71%)	
	Bob Lawrence (R)	19,755	(15%)	
	William L. Worthington (R)	9,379	(7%)	
	Donald L. Bilderback (R)	8,226	(6%)	
1996 general	Norman Dicks (D)	155,467	(66%)	($477,269)
	Bill Tinsley (R)	71,337	(30%)	($16,384)
	Others	9,106	(4%)	

SEVENTH DISTRICT

Seattle is America's hot city of the 1990s. It first zoomed into the national consciousness with the 1897 Klondike gold strike, has been a major American city since around 1910, and hosted its own World's Fair in 1962. But only in the last decade has its combination of economic growth and creativity and its physical beauty and distinctive style made it a national leader. Seattle rises from the Puget Sound harbor of Elliott Bay on steep hills, once covered with 300-foot-high Douglas firs; behind the hills and buildings you can see on a clear day, from almost anywhere, the nimbus of Mount Rainier. On the waterfront, below gleaming high-rises, is the Pike Place market, where you can get fresh salmon and Dungeness crabs; nearby is Pioneer Square, where stores and warehouses from the turn of the century have been restored and renovated; and Yesler Way, America's original "Skid Road," now has upscale shops but still some homeless people too. Seattle's upper class, like San Francisco's, continues to be anchored downtown, with its upscale stores and busy sidewalks; but the most remarkable growth has come east of Lake Washington, where Microsoft has dominated the computer software business from its turquoise-building campus.

Seattle still has its old ethnic neighborhoods, like Scandinavian Ballard, and comfortable working-class frame houses on steep hillsides. But it also has a new ethnic mix, with thousands of Asian immigrants, and the Capitol Hill neighborhood with shoppers jamming busy stores and clubs. Yet the downtown office district and the affluent quarter along Lake Washington and Queen Anne overlooking Puget Sound have a certain formality. Generally, blue-collar workers live on the south side of the city and in valleys, or midway between Puget Sound and Lake Washington; the factories, warehouses and railroad yards are concentrated in a flat plain near Puget Sound and south of downtown. The big Boeing factories are located farther south, and younger blue-collar workers have followed them into the suburban areas directly south of the city: Burien, Tukwila, Kent and Renton, which lie at the southern end of Lake Washington.

All this is knit together by infrastructure that was high-tech for its time: the pontoon bridge across Lake Washington, the Lake Washington Ship Canal, connecting the Sound and the Lake, whose Chittenden Locks are the second-largest locks in this hemisphere, behind the Panama Canal. Seattle has been booming, and exporting its own institutions—Boeing airplanes have been the world's best sellers for many years; Nordstrom department stores with their famously polite service (even in the New York area); Seattle espresso bars—especially Starbucks, named after the coffee-crazed first mate in Herman Melville's *Moby Dick*—have brought caffe latte across America.

The 7th Congressional District includes almost all the city of Seattle, a little industrial suburban fringe to the south, plus rural-looking Vashon Island in Puget Sound. This is the Seattle area's minority district, 11% black and 14% Asian. The 7th has the highest education levels of any Washington district (37% of adults are college grads), but not the highest household income; it has the oldest housing and by far the highest percentage of householders living alone (41%) and the fewest households with families (48%). Central Seattle, in other words, shares more with central San Francisco than hills and scenery: it is heavily populated by singles and gays, young professionals and elderly pensioners. A generation ago, the city of Seattle was roughly split between the parties; today, it is heavily Democratic and liberal, ready to support minority candidates like former Mayor Norm Rice and former King County Executive and now Governor Gary Locke.

The congressman from the 7th District is Jim McDermott, one of the most liberal members of the House and its only (credentialed) psychiatrist. McDermott was the first in his family to attend college, and went to conservative religious Wheaton College; after service in the Navy and stints in New York and Illinois hospitals, he came to the University of Washington Hospital in Seattle. Almost immediately, he was elected to the state House in 1970, ran for governor in 1972 and finished third in the Republican primary, and was elected to the state Senate in 1974, where he worked on issues from clean water to health care. He ran for governor again in 1980, beat incumbent Dixy Lee Ray in the primary, then lost to Republican John Spellman; in 1984 he ran for governor a third time, and lost the primary to Booth Gardner. In 1987 he retired from the legislature and went to Zaire (now Congo) as a medical officer in the Foreign Service. But when Congressman Mike Lowry ran for the Senate in 1988 (he lost, but in 1992 was elected governor), McDermott returned home and ran for the 7th District seat and easily won, beating Norm Rice 38%–29% in the primary and winning 76% in the general. He has been re-elected without difficulty.

In the House, McDermott's great cause has been health care and his greatest publicity has come from ethics investigations; he has had some frustrations on both. He passed an AIDS Housing Opportunity Act in 1990, in his first term, and remains head of the Congressional Task Force on International HIV/AIDS. He has long backed a single-payer, Canadian-style national health insurance program and had a bill, with some 90 co-sponsors in 1993, financed by a $2 cigarette tax and 50-cent handgun and ammunition excise. But he deferred to the Clinton health care plan, even while making the point that his was simpler to administer and more comprehensible to voters. Then in August 1994, as the Clinton plan was failing and Democratic leaders George Mitchell and Richard Gephardt were scrambling to come up with an alternative, McDermott urged Congress to abandon all health care bills for the year. He evidently expected a more favorable political environment after the 1994 elections, and, like many, was surprised by the result. After Republicans took control, he said: "A lot of people around here have never been in the minority. I have. I know what to do: attack." He criticized Republicans for abandoning the refundability of their $500 per-child tax credit, so that those with low income tax liabilities or receiving the Earned Income Tax Credit didn't get a payment. He put together a bill in 1997 for a 30% tax credit for health insurance costs for families without insurance from their employers. He served on the Medicare commission co-chaired by John Breaux, and opposed Breaux's plan for premium support or, as McDermott termed it, vouchers; he refused to support Breaux's plan which had a 10-vote bipartisan majority but not the 11-vote supermajority required by statute to become official. Later McDermott argued that cost-control mechanisms were excluding people from Medigap insurance. He sponsored an Indian health equity plan, to provide the usual measure of federal assistance to urban-area Indians treated through the Indian Health Service.

Another measure, which seemed quixotic when McDermott first pushed it, by early 1999 seemed to be moving toward passage. This was the African Growth and Opportunity Act, which would eliminate import quotas and tariffs on African goods for 10 years and includes $600 million in investment funds. McDermott is co-sponsor with free-market Republican Philip

Crane and Harlem Democrat Charles Rangel; as large parts of Africa move toward free markets and political democracy, it may prove an idea whose time has come.

McDermott joined the ethics committee in 1991 and was made chairman in 1993 by Speaker Thomas Foley; for some time McDermott called for nonpartisan investigations and got along with his successor in the chair, Nancy Johnson. But that changed during the long hearings on charges against Speaker Newt Gingrich. McDermott was frustrated with what he considered Republican dilatoriness and successfully pressed for the appointment of special counsel James Cole, a former prosecutor, rather than a tax lawyer who might conduct a more limited review. McDermott was angry that Johnson would not make public Cole's report before the House voted for speaker on January 7, 1997, and he attacked Johnson for canceling a series of committee hearings after a meeting with Majority Leader Dick Armey. During the public hearing on January 17, the full committee approved the proposed sanctions of a House reprimand and a $300,000 penalty, which the House approved a few days later.

Amidst all this, on January 10, *The New York Times* printed an excerpt of a tape made by Florida Democratic activists John and Alice Martin of a December 1996 phone conversation between Gingrich and Republican leaders and advisers. It was presented as evidence that Gingrich was violating an agreement not to orchestrate a response to the committee's action, but much of it was taken up by discussions as to how to comply with the agreement. In any case it quickly became apparent that taping the call was a felony. The Martins said they ultimately gave the tape to McDermott, and it was widely assumed he was the *Times'* source; McDermott denied he ever possessed or knew anything about the tape. On January 14 the FBI announced it was investigating, and McDermott announced he was conditionally excusing himself from the case against Gingrich, blasting the Republicans in the process. In ensuing days McDermott, long known as intellectually honest and candid, said he wouldn't give an explanation of the incident and said of the investigation, "Nobody has come out pure." The Martins eventually pleaded guilty to intercepting the call and were given a small fine; no action was taken against McDermott. More than a year later, in March 1998, John Boehner, one of the Republican leaders taped, sued McDermott for infringing his privacy and property rights by disseminating the tape. McDermott refused to deny or admit that he passed the tape on, and argued that he was protected by the First Amendment. In July 1998 a federal judge dismissed the case, but the three-judge court which heard the appeal in May 1999 seemed to be leaning the other way.

McDermott had no Republican opponent in 1998 and was re-elected with 88% of the vote. Mentioned as a possible candidate against Senator Slade Gorton in 2000, he seemed uninterested in the race until Gorton voted against a Democratic gun control measure in May 1999. Suddenly he said he might run. "Slade Gorton has fought against every legislative initiative that I have supported since I became a congressman. He is anti-environment, pro-gun and constantly divisive at a time when we need to bring people together." Some Republicans were gleeful, looking forward to running against this "liberal psychiatrist from Seattle" who had lost three statewide races. But McDermott argued that now that Washington Republicans have seen how unpalatable conservative Republicans are, he will have a better chance.

Cook's Call. *Safe.* This Seattle-based district is the most solidly Democratic seat in the state. McDermott will have no problem winning a 7th term.

The People: Pop. 1990: 541,202; 1.5% rural; 15.6% age 65 +; 75.6% White, 9.9% Black, 11.7% Asian, 1.4% Amer. Indian, 1.3% Other; 3.3% Hispanic Origin. Households: 36.8% married couple families; 14.2% married couple fams. w. children; 66.1% college educ.; median household income: $29,707; per capita income: $18,021; median house value: $133,300; median gross rent: $423.

1996 Presidential Vote			1992 Presidential Vote		
Clinton (D)	182,671	(67%)	Clinton (D)	191,781	(65%)
Dole (R)	53,437	(20%)	Bush (R)	54,478	(18%)
Perot (I)	13,671	(5%)	Perot (I)	45,167	(15%)
Others	23,267	(9%)			

Rep. Jim McDermott (D)

Elected 1988; b. Dec. 28, 1936, Chicago, IL; home, Seattle; Wheaton Col., B.S. 1958, U. of IL, M.D. 1963; Episcopalian; married (Therese Hansen).

Military Career: U.S. Navy Medical Corps., 1968–70.

Elected Office: WA House of Reps., 1970–72; WA Senate, 1974–87; Dem. gubernatorial nominee, 1980.

Professional Career: Asst. Prof., U. of WA, Practicing psychiatrist, 1970–83; Medical Officer, U.S. Foreign Svc., Zaire, 1987–88.

DC Office: 1035 LHOB 20515, 202-225-3106; Web site: www.house.gov/mcdermott.

District Office: Seattle, 206-553-7170.

Committees: *Budget* (2d of 19 D). *Ways & Means* (7th of 16 D): Health; Oversight.

Group Ratings

	ADA	ACLU	AFS	LCV	CON	NTU	NFIB	COC	ACU	NTLC	CHC
1998	90	94	88	77	89	25	0	38	0	11	0
1997	90	—	100	—	6	23	—	20	4	—	—

National Journal Ratings

	1997 LIB — 1997 CONS		1998 LIB — 1998 CONS	
Economic	85%	10%	79%	21%
Social	85%	0%	90%	7%
Foreign	90%	8%	98%	0%

Key Votes of the 105th Congress

1. Clinton Budget Deal	N	5. Puerto Rico Sthood. Ref.	Y	9. Cut $ for B-2 Bombers	Y
2. Education IRAs	N	6. End Highway Set-asides	N	10. Human Rights in China	N
3. Req. 2/3 to Raise Taxes	N	7. School Prayer Amend.	N	11. Withdraw Bosnia Troops	N
4. Fast-track Trade	Y	8. Ovrd. Part. Birth Veto	N	12. End Cuban TV-Marti	Y

Election Results

1998 general	Jim McDermott (D)	183,076	(88%)	($332,241)
	Stan Lippmann (Ref)	19,545	(9%)	
	Others	4,921	(2%)	
1998 primary	Jim McDermott (D)	80,149	(84%)	
	Stan Lippmann (Ref)	12,423	(13%)	
	Others	2,411	(3%)	
1996 general	Jim McDermott (D)	209,753	(81%)	($190,250)
	Frank Kleschen (R)	49,341	(19%)	($6,680)

EIGHTH DISTRICT

The land east of Seattle's Lake Washington half a century ago was quiet countryside. Orchards and vineyards flourished in the rich, moist soil just below the rise of the Cascades Mountains, while farms and broad pasturelands spread toward 14,410-foot Mount Rainier like a living green quilt. But as Seattle has grown over the years, people have crossed the pontoon bridge across Mercer Island to Bellevue and have made this Overlake area, sometimes called the Eastside, one of the most vibrant parts of metropolitan Seattle. Bellevue now has more than 100,000 people and enough office space to make it an edge city. While downtown Seattle specialized in banks and law firms and trading companies, Bellevue and other communities in Overlake specialized in high-tech startups. Redmond, just to the north, is the headquarters of Microsoft, and there are dozens of other firms here that make this one of America's leading high-tech centers.

The 8th Congressional District includes most of the eastern edge of metro Seattle, plus the scarcely inhabited territory of the Cascades. It includes most of Bellevue and all of Mercer Island, Issaquah at the edge of the Cascades and Renton at the south edge of Lake Washington. It spreads south along Kent, Auburn and Puyallup to include the countryside and suburban fringe east of Tacoma, and includes Mount Rainier itself. This is the most affluent district in Washington, rivaled only by the 1st; politically it is market-oriented on economics, more liberal on the environment, mixed on cultural issues. In partisan terms, it is also one of the two most Republican districts in the state.

The congresswoman from the 8th District is Jennifer Dunn, a Republican elected in 1992. Dunn grew up in Bellevue, went to Stanford, worked as a systems engineer for IBM in the 1960s, then stayed home to raise her children (her younger son is named Reagan, after the then-California governor, whom she supported over Gerald Ford in 1976). She is a distant cousin of Senator Slade Gorton. In 1981 she became Washington Republican Party chairwoman and served for 12 years. She is a peppery partisan, vigorous and knowledgeable about issues, persevering through bad times for her party and working to make them better. In 1992, when Congressman Rod Chandler ran for the Senate, she ran for the House and won in a walkaway. In the House she was a vocal deficit hawk, backing the Penny-Kasich budget cuts and the A-to-Z spending cut procedure. With Georgia's Nathan Deal, she passed a Dunn-Deal bill to allow local communities to track convicted sex offenders. She served as the only freshman on the Joint Committee on the Organization of Congress. Her voting record has been conservative on economic and foreign policy, moderate on cultural issues.

When Republicans won the majority in 1994, Dunn was put on the transition team and Speaker Newt Gingrich's task force on committee review, and given a seat on Ways and Means. She was appointed to the three-member task force on the contested Connecticut 2d District race. On Ways and Means, she worked on the child support provisions of the welfare reform bill and pushed for medical savings accounts in the 1996 health care bill. She sponsored an IRAs for homemakers amendment, which was vetoed, a small business tax relief package, a rise in the earning limits for seniors, and estate tax reductions. She backed a pension plan for employees of small companies with no plans of their own. She worked on the Medicaid formula for Washington state and on the preventive medicine provisions of Medicare reform. She worked to allow software firms to lower their taxes by setting up foreign sales corporations as other businesses can. She got an extra $850,000 for Mount Rainier National Park to repair storm damage and $8 million for a Puyallup-area levee repair. She worked against privatization of the Bonneville Power Administration and sought lower power rates.

Dunn, as one might expect of a longtime state party chairman, took political initiatives as well. She was a loyal supporter of Gingrich through his travails. Dunn spent much of her third term climbing—or trying to climb—up the leadership ladder. In November 1996 she was elected secretary of the Republican Conference. In May 1997, when Susan Molinari announced her resignation from the House, Dunn ran for her post of Conference vice chair. Running in July 1997, just as the coup against Newt Gingrich was disintegrating, Dunn had leadership support and won over Jim Nussle of Iowa, who had been going off the reservation, by 129–85. Having won that position, she spurned running against Senator Patty Murray in 1998.

Dunn has strongly supported tax cuts—in income tax rates, in the death tax (she called for reducing it 5% every year, to zero in 2009), in capital gains and through Education Savings Accounts. She has worked on addressing the gender gap for Republicans, urging candidates to relate their policies to women's lives—she talks often about how she coped as a divorced working mom, and of how two-thirds of new small businesses are being formed by women. As she explains, "We are developing speech-modules that are women-friendly." To help businesses, she called for a three-point (instead of the IRS's current 20-point) test of who is a subcontractor and who an employee; she has a bill to make it easier for start-up companies to offer stock options. She is a strong backer of free trade and normal trade relations status for China. She objected to American Heritage River designation for the Puyallup and in July 1998 got the House to earmark $18 million for Sound Transit on the Eastside; she asked for an environmental review of the Muckleshoot Indians' proposed amphitheater near Auburn. She strongly opposed the Shays-Meehan campaign finance bill, and raised $100,000 for her federal and $54,000 for her Washington leadership PACs, as well as $1.5 million for her own 1998 campaign. Despite all this—or perhaps because she campaigned all over the country and identified herself with partisan rather than consensus policies—she saw her share of the vote drop from 76% in 1994 to 65% in 1996 to a still safe but lower 60% in 1998, as Democrat Heidi Behrens-Benedict, who entered the race in June 1998 after the Springfield, Oregon, school shooting, denounced her on gun control and social issues.

Dunn's real fight came in the leadership races two weeks after the 1998 election. She had already moved to challenge Majority Leader Dick Armey, who was in low regard after the collapse of the anti-Gingrich coup. But the Tuesday Group and liberal Republicans did not all endorse her, her longtime supporter Gingrich had announced his retirement, and Steve Largent, one of the most principle-bound of the 1994 freshmen—and well-known in the Seattle area as a pass receiver for the Seattle Seahawks—was running as well. Dunn stressed the importance of having a woman in the Republican leadership. But other women were running for other leadership positions. In the first round of voting, Armey led with 100 votes to 58 for Largent, 45 for Dunn and 18 for Denny Hastert, whose name was advanced by others as he stuck by a commitment to support Armey. At that point Largent asked Dunn to withdraw, in return for appointment to a new position as assistant majority leader should he win; Dunn refused and stayed in the race. On the second ballot, Armey got 99 votes, Largent 73 and Dunn 49—which meant that Dunn was eliminated; Armey won on the third ballot, 127–95. Shortly afterward, Tillie Fowler was elected Republican Conference vice chair. "I have no regrets," said Dunn.

Dunn and Largent were the Republicans' responders to Bill Clinton's State of the Union address in January 1999. It fell to Dunn to allude to the impeachment proceedings. "A couple of weeks ago, I heard a network anchor say, 'The capital is in chaos.' Another proclaimed that we were in the midst of a constitutional crisis. Ladies and gentlemen, our country is not in crisis. There are no tanks in the streets. No matter what the outcome of the president's situation, life in America will go on. Our lives will continue to be filled with practical matters, not constitutional ones."

In the meantime, Dunn endorsed George W. Bush for president in March 1999. She seems certain to run again in 2000; as she said in 1997, "I really love the House. I hate to think of anything that would cause me to leave the House."

Cook's Call. *Safe.* The fact that Dunn won this seat in 1992 with 60% of the vote even as Democrats were elected to every other district in the state shows just how tough it is for a Democrat to win here. Dunn is solidly positioned for 2000.

The People: Pop. 1990: 540,735; 20.6% rural; 8.2% age 65 + ; 92.1% White, 1.5% Black, 4.6% Asian, 1% Amer. Indian, 0.7% Other; 2.1% Hispanic Origin. Households: 64.2% married couple families; 33.3% married couple fams. w. children; 63.1% college educ.; median household income: $42,379; per capita income: $18,432; median house value: $142,200; median gross rent: $479.

1996 Presidential Vote			1992 Presidential Vote		
Clinton (D)	130,472	(47%)	Clinton (D)	102,859	(38%)
Dole (R)	112,463	(41%)	Bush (R)	92,274	(34%)
Perot (I)	23,994	(9%)	Perot (I)	72,523	(27%)
Others	8,593	(3%)			

Rep. Jennifer Dunn (R)

Elected 1992; b. July 29, 1941, Seattle; home, Bellevue; U. of WA, 1960–62, Stanford U., B.A. 1963; Episcopalian; divorced.

Professional Career: Systems Engineer, IBM, 1964–69; P.R., King Cnty. Assessors Office, 1978–80; Chmn., WA Repub. Party, 1981–92; Delegate, U.N. Comm. on Status of Women, 1984 & 1990.

DC Office: 432 CHOB 20515, 202-225-7761; Fax: 202-225-8673; Web site: www.house.gov/dunn.

District Office: Mercer Island, 206-275-3438.

Committees: *Ways & Means* (13th of 23 R): Oversight; Trade.

Group Ratings

	ADA	ACLU	AFS	LCV	CON	NTU	NFIB	COC	ACU	NTLC	CHC
1998	0	13	0	8	13	51	100	100	96	100	83
1997	0	—	13	—	56	55	—	100	92	—	—

National Journal Ratings

	1997 LIB — 1997 CONS			1998 LIB — 1998 CONS		
Economic	10%	—	86%	19%	—	79%
Social	45%	—	54%	26%	—	72%
Foreign	12%	—	81%	43%	—	53%

Key Votes of the 105th Congress

1. Clinton Budget Deal	Y	5. Puerto Rico Sthood. Ref.	N	9. Cut $ for B-2 Bombers	N
2. Education IRAs	Y	6. End Highway Set-asides	Y	10. Human Rights in China	N
3. Req. 2/3 to Raise Taxes	Y	7. School Prayer Amend.	Y	11. Withdraw Bosnia Troops	N
4. Fast-track Trade	Y	8. Ovrd. Part. Birth Veto	Y	12. End Cuban TV-Marti	N

Election Results

1998 general	Jennifer Dunn (R)	135,539	(60%)	($1,490,563)
	Heidi Behrens-Benedict (D)	91,371	(40%)	($172,349)
1998 primary	Jennifer Dunn (R)	77,063	(66%)	
	Heidi Behrens-Benedict (D)	40,363	(34%)	
1996 general	Jennifer Dunn (R)	170,691	(65%)	($1,146,933)
	Dave Little (D)	90,340	(35%)	($6,838)

NINTH DISTRICT

The misty shores of Puget Sound have seen some of America's most vibrant economic growth over the last two decades. It has spread south from Seattle, over the mixed suburban territory, south and west to the once industrial city of Tacoma. The subdivisions along the Sound, which have some of the loveliest views in America, tend to be high-income. But much of greater Seattle's prime industrial territory lies between the ridges that run north and south inland. Weyerhaeuser, the world's largest private owner of softwood timber, has its headquarters here in Federal Way. Boeing is also a major presence in Renton, on the south end of Lake Washington; its aircraft and electronic components plants and its business services division, employing more than 11,000 people, have helped make the company America's number one exporter. A host of smaller factories cluster near the rail lines that run from Minneapolis-St. Paul across the Great Plains to Puget Sound. The military has influenced this area too. Fort Lewis is just west of Tacoma and active-duty and retired military personnel and their families make up perhaps one-fifth of the population.

The 9th Congressional District covers much of this area. It is a new seat created after the 1990 Census and confirmed by a June 1992 Supreme Court decision that upheld the counting of servicemen abroad in their state of residence (otherwise, this seat would have gone to Massachusetts). The 9th District's northern end wraps around Sea-Tac International Airport and Renton, then winds south past Kent, Auburn and Federal Way, and reaches the shipyards and docks of Tacoma. It covers half of Tacoma, including McChord Air Force Base, and proceeds west, taking in the Army's vast Fort Lewis in Pierce County and stopping just shy of the boundaries of the state capital of Olympia. It is not heavily Democratic or Republican; as the district director for its first congressman once said, "Everybody was happy to unload this district. It's sort of a mutt in a way." For three elections the 9th district was balanced at equipoise: it went Democratic in 1992, Republican in 1994, Democratic in 1996.

The congressman from the 9th District is Adam Smith, a Democrat elected in 1996 and re-elected in 1998. He grew up in the Sea-Tac area; his father, a baggage handler for United Airlines and active in the Machinists' Union, died when Smith was 17. The family went on welfare; Smith worked his way through Fordham driving trucks for UPS, then went to the University of Washington Law School. He worked as a lawyer, then as a Seattle prosecutor, handling drunk driving and domestic abuse cases. In 1990, at 25, he was elected to the state Senate, beating an incumbent Republican by doorbelling the district twice. He was re-elected in 1994 and in July 1995 decided to run against Congressman Randy Tate.

In many ways Smith and Tate were similar: born the same year to families of modest backgrounds, first elected to office at young ages (in Tate's case at 22), firm believers in doorbelling. In 1994 Tate ran against Democrat Congressman Mike Kreidler, and beat him 52%–48%, becoming at 28 the youngest member of the 1994 Republican freshman class. A religious conservative and strong supporter of Speaker Newt Gingrich, he was an immediate target of the AFL-CIO in 1996, which spent somewhere between $500,000 and $1 million on ads against him; he spent $1.6 million on his re-election campaign. Smith spent $711,000—a large share from unions—and campaigned as a moderate Democrat, a supporter of the death penalty and three strikes legislation—a believer in a more efficient and responsive government. The brunt of Smith's campaign consisted of attacks on Tate for supporting Gingrich on 96% of House votes and for backing Medicare "cuts." Tate attacked Smith for opposing a bill giving homeowners additional rights to defend themselves against intruders, for opposing channeling youthful offenders to adult courts and prisons, and for voting for Governor Mike Lowry's $1.2 billion tax increase in 1993. This was one of the closest races in the country. In the September all-party primary, usually a good indicator of the final result in Washington, Smith led 49%–48%. The result in November was not as close: 50%–47% for Smith. Tate went on to become head of the Christian Coalition from 1997 to May 1999.

In the House, Smith showed political acumen, winning good committee assignments—Resources and Armed Services—and stationing his top staffers in the district. He announced he would not accept contributions from PACs or individuals outside Washington state in his first year, and kept doorbelling constituents. He has had a mostly liberal voting record, but with interesting exceptions. He voted for the balanced budget and for charter schools (but against school vouchers); he supported term limits and voted to allow concealed weapons permits to be transferred from state to state. Despite the pleas of Norm Dicks from the next-door 6th District, he voted against additional B-2 stealth bombers and against fast track—going against Boeing both times. But there are an estimated 54,000 union members in the 9th District, and the fast track vote did please his labor backers. Interestingly, Smith did not introduce a single bill in the 105th Congress. "If I see a situation where introducing a piece of legislation would help, I will do it. If not, I will just help other people in a quiet way." He finally introduced a bill for budgeting honesty in February 1999. He did pass an amendment to the defense authorization in May 1998 to cap overhead spending on cleanup at the Hanford Nuclear Reservation to 33% of the total cleanup budget, saying, "Too much money is going to management, and not enough is going to cleanup."

His criticism of Bill Clinton was harsh. In early September he said, "I am just incredibly repulsed by what I've seen the president do over the last year. It goes beyond betrayal. Anybody who knew about this had blackmail power. He jeopardized his ability to do his job. He has done serious damage to his ability to lead our country and our party. It disgusted me on a level I can't describe." Criticized by some fellow Democrats, he said a few days later, "If we let it go, we send the message that you should judge your politicians on how the economy is doing and how good his policies are. I wouldn't follow Clinton across the street. He looked into the camera and lied to us. He wasn't trying to obstruct justice. He was just trying to save his butt." He rejected offers from the White House to help him raise money, and was pointedly absent when Al Gore came to a grade school in the 9th District to praise a reading program.

Smith promised not to take PAC money during 1997, but did collect significant amounts in 1998. He held no community meetings, but continued doorbelling around the district—on 10,000 doors, he estimates. In January 1998, he made a point of ringing the doorbell of Robert Seipel, president of World Vision, a Republican who was contemplating running against him. Seipel was watching a sports game on TV, and having seen what Smith's job was like, decided in February 1998 not to run. The Republican nominee was Ron Taber, a businessman who spent more than $1 million on a race for state superintendent of public instruction in 1996; he was a provocative campaigner, answering a question about bilingual education by saying that Spanish "is the language of dishwashers, fruit pickers and doormen." Taber spent only $68,000 of his own money this time and, spurned by the Republican Party, raised little else. Smith won 58% in the September all-party primary, usually a good indicator of an incumbent's performance in November; then he won 65%–35% in the general, an impressive performance in a district which had never re-elected an incumbent before.

Smith was mentioned as a candidate against Senator Slade Gorton in 2000, but in May 1999 announced he would not run. Perhaps the prospect of doorbelling the entire state was daunting. But Smith seems determined to go his own way; to a February 1999 local Democratic gathering where officeholders were telling jokes about Republicans, Smith said, "I think we should work with Republicans where possible. We should be the ones to show that we can be bipartisan because the country right now doesn't just hate Republicans; they more or less hate government." Meanwhile, Republican King County Councilman Chris Vance announced he would run in the 9th District. Vance is a conservative who was first elected to the state legislature in 1990, at 28, and if Smith is known as the doorbelling king of Puget Sound politics, Vance calls himself "Mr. Cul-de-sac." Despite Smith's impressive re-election, the 9th District could once again be seriously contested in 2000.

Cook's Call. *Potentially Competitive.* Smith's 65% win here in 1998 belies the competitiveness of this district. This newly created district was drawn to be competitive, and a good, well-funded Republican could give Smith a race. Still, Smith's moderate image and don't-rock-the-boat style helps to insulate him from charges that he is too liberal for this marginal district.

The People: Pop. 1990: 540,519; 8.5% rural; 9.6% age 65 + ; 85.6% White, 5.4% Black, 6.1% Asian, 1.5% Amer. Indian, 1.4% Other; 3.6% Hispanic Origin. Households: 55.5% married couple families; 27.7% married couple fams. w. children; 52.3% college educ.; median household income: $32,194; per capita income: $14,264; median house value: $93,300; median gross rent: $415.

1996 Presidential Vote			1992 Presidential Vote		
Clinton (D)	110,854	(51%)	Clinton (D)	93,964	(42%)
Dole (R)	77,616	(36%)	Bush (R)	69,593	(31%)
Perot (I)	20,806	(10%)	Perot (I)	58,037	(26%)
Others	6,466	(3%)			

Rep. Adam Smith (D)

Elected 1996; b. June 15, 1965, Washington, DC; home, Kent; Fordham U. B.A. 1987, U. of WA, J.D. 1990; Christian; married (Sara).

Elected Office: WA Senate, 1990–96.

Professional Career: Practicing atty., 1991–92; Seattle Prosecutor, 1992–95.

DC Office: 116 CHOB 20515, 202-225-8901; Fax: 202-225-5893; Web site: www.house.gov/adamsmith.

District Office: Tacoma, 253-926-6683.

Committees: *Armed Services* (17th of 28 D): Military Procurement; Military Readiness. *Resources* (15th of 24 D): Fisheries Conservation, Wildlife & Oceans; Water & Power.

Group Ratings

	ADA	ACLU	AFS	LCV	CON	NTU	NFIB	COC	ACU	NTLC	CHC
1998	100	75	100	85	62	29	36	39	0	18	0
1997	80	—	75	—	17	32	—	50	20	—	—

National Journal Ratings

	1997 LIB — 1997 CONS	1998 LIB — 1998 CONS
Economic	64% — 35%	64% — 34%
Social	76% — 23%	70% — 28%
Foreign	60% — 38%	90% — 5%

Key Votes of the 105th Congress

1. Clinton Budget Deal	N	5. Puerto Rico Sthood. Ref.	Y	9. Cut $ for B-2 Bombers	Y
2. Education IRAs	N	6. End Highway Set-asides	N	10. Human Rights in China	N
3. Req. 2/3 to Raise Taxes	N	7. School Prayer Amend.	N	11. Withdraw Bosnia Troops	N
4. Fast-track Trade	N	8. Ovrd. Part. Birth Veto	N	12. End Cuban TV-Marti	Y

Election Results

1998 general	Adam Smith (D)	111,948	(65%)	($814,303)
	Ron Taber (R)	61,108	(35%)	($84,964)
1998 primary	Adam Smith (D)	53,899	(58%)	
	Ron Taber (R)	23,304	(25%)	
	Randy Bell (R)	8,232	(9%)	
	Keith Peterson (R)	7,689	(8%)	
1996 general	Adam Smith (D)	105,236	(50%)	($711,722)
	Randy Tate (R)	99,199	(47%)	($1,578,748)
	Others	5,432	(3%)	

WEST VIRGINIA

Things are finally looking up for West Virginia. It's about time: this is a state that has had more than its share of tragedy and heartbreak, but whose people have never lost their sense of hope or their affection for the hills and mountains that make this the most unhorizontal state in the nation. West Virginia was born out of the tragedy of the Civil War, when 55 mountain counties with few slaves seceded from Virginia, and made its living most of the years since on that cruelest of commodities, coal. Coal kept the sons of large mountaineer families here for much of the 20th Century, men who would otherwise have left for big cities; coal brought immigrants in, a few from odd corners of Europe, but more from adjacent areas of the South where the local farming economies were stagnant when West Virginia's coal economy was booming. Coal and local rock salt and brines brought the large concentration of chemical plants 50 years ago to the Kanawha Valley around Charleston; it built steel mills and glass factories in the panhandle and the Monongahela River valley, not far south of Pittsburgh.

Coal did not build a self-sustaining economy. When America was beleaguered abroad, demand for coal increased and energy prices rose, and West Virginia boomed, during World War II (the state reached its all-time population peak of 2 million in 1950) and the oil shocks of the 1970s. Coal changed West Virginia's politics too. West Virginia's heritage from the Civil War days was Republican, though some counties tilted toward the Confederacy and the Democrats. But after John L. Lewis's United Mine Workers organized most of the West Virginia mines, the coal country shifted toward the New Deal Democrats, and West Virginia for half a century has been one of the most Democratic states, deserting the ticket only in Republican landslide years (1956, 1972, 1984); its legislature has been controlled by Democrats since 1930.

But neither Democratic administrations nor the pensions and medical benefits the UMW negotiated for retired miners have been able to provide the economic growth to keep thousands of West Virginians from leaving their mountains to find work elsewhere—now more often south on I-77 to the booming Carolinas than north to the Great Lakes' industrial cities. As underground miners were replaced by strip-mining machines, coal tonnage went way up but coal mine employment dropped from 22% of the state's work force in 1950 to 10% in 1980 and 5% in 1990, and was only 3.9% in March 1997. The state's population, 1.95 million in 1980, fell to about 1.8 million in 1990—the largest decrease, absolutely and in percentage terms, of any state. But West Virginians have a strong attachment to this unique state, where the accent sounds Southern and the early 20th Century factories and houses look Northern, where the landscape is rural and the economy industrial.

Now West Virginia is on the rebound, and not because of upward spikes of energy prices. Population showed a slight up-tick from 1990–98, and the number of jobs rose 6%; unemployment was down to 6.6% in 1998, the lowest since 1978. In 1998 this long job-losing state created 10,000 jobs. All this despite a continuing drop in coal mining jobs, as machines replace men and the Clean Air Act of 1990 reduces demand for West Virginia's high-sulfur coal. Government has played a role. Senator Robert Byrd, chairman for six years and now ranking Democrat on the Appropriations Committee, achieved his career goal of channeling $1 billion of federal projects into West Virginia, and more: over $1.5 billion. They include offices for the FBI, Fish and Wildlife Service, NASA and the National Institute of Occupational Safety; federal jobs in West Virginia have grown 20% since 1988. State tax breaks promoted by Governor Gaston Caperton (1988–96) attracted investments from Georgia Pacific, Swearingen Aircraft, NGK Sparkplugs and Toyota. West Virginia's plastics and chemicals industries have been expanding, forest products are replacing coal in rural counties, health care is growing as everywhere and telemarketing is growing as well. Even the number of farms is increasing.

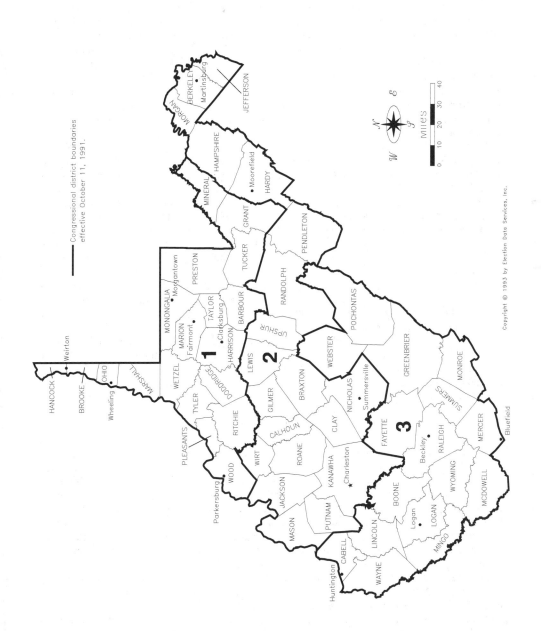

Congressional district boundaries
effective October 11, 1991.

Copyright © 1993 by Election Data Services, Inc.

West Virginia has finally completed its interstate highway network and in a computer age it is no longer isolated; with low wages, good work habits, low land costs, West Virginia has even developed a software industry in the corridor between Morgantown and Clarksburg. Governor Cecil Underwood, elected in 1956 and then again in 1996, notes that he started building the interstate highway system 40 years ago and now is building a "technology superhighway system"—the West Virginia State Unified Network, capable of carrying data, voice and video. In Caperton's two terms, the state moved from 46th to 33d in teachers' salaries and the legislature approved more than $60 million to put a computer in every school classroom. In 1996, his last year in office, Caperton sponsored a Homecoming '96 program, with 300 communities scheduling street fairs, parades, motorcycle rallies and other commemorative events, celebrating West Virginia. An estimated 40% of West Virginians who leave the state come back, very often to retire. Now for the first time in 50 years West Virginia has reason to be hopeful about its economic future and its young people have reason to stay.

Governor. Cecil Underwood was the nation's youngest governor when he was first elected in 1956 at 34 and its oldest governor when he was elected in 1996 at 74: surely the longest-spanning gubernatorial career in American history. In between terms, he ran for office unsuccessfully (for senator in 1960 and governor in 1964 and 1976), ran businesses and was president of Bethany College in the 1970s. He is a Republican, but in many ways he represents continuity with his Democratic predecessor, Gaston Caperton. Caperton, elected in 1988 and 1992, immediately raised taxes and cut spending to fill a budget gap; but he also used tax incentives to attract jobs, raised teacher pay, started a $500 million school construction plan, began a program to put computers in every classroom, and passed brownfields legislation to redevelop cleaned up industrial sites.

Underwood was elected in 1996 largely because of fears that his Democratic opponent, state Senator Charlotte Pritt, was too liberal. A coal miner's daughter and favorite of the United Mine Workers and other unions, she held Caperton to a 43%–35% victory in the 1992 primary and won the 1996 primary against state Senator Joe Manchin by 40%–33%. The specter of a Pritt victory in 1996 had prompted business leaders to urge Underwood to run, and he won the Republican primary 41%–33%–26% over ex-astronaut Jon McBride and former West Virginia Republican Chairman David McKinley. Pritt called for collective bargaining for state employees and no cuts in the state work force and opposed managed care; while she had strong support from labor, others worried that she would cut off the state's economic recovery. Caperton and Senator Robert Byrd shunned her, though Senator Jay Rockefeller endorsed her warmly; former top Caperton staffers endorsed Underwood. Underwood calmed concerns about his age by campaigning vigorously and promising to govern much as Caperton had. Underwood won 52%–46%, losing heavily in coal mining counties but winning just about everywhere else.

In office, Underwood decried "ancient conflicts pitting one group against another, one region against another and one value system against another," and said, "We see obsolete government all about us." Working with state Treasurer John Perdue, he started a program of fixed-price tuition contracts for state colleges. He pushed through tough welfare reform which cut the rolls by more than 60%; a provision counting Supplemental Security Income payments as income was overturned by a court in February 1999. He created Mission West Virginia to work against illiteracy. He signed into law legislation codifying the practice of mountaintop mining and formed a task force to study how this type of mining might impact the environment. It risks scarring the land and fouling streams and rivers, but mountaintop mining is far safer than mining underground. Despite a general aversion to tax increases, Underwood proposed a smokeless tobacco tax and an increased cigarette tax in 1999.

Underwood's Republicans had a dreadful year in 1998. They lost some of their few seats in the legislature, a Supreme Court justice nominated by Underwood was beaten by a Democrat, and the tax-financing amendment Underwood campaigned for was rejected by the voters. But Underwood's job approval remained up toward 60%, and by mid-1999 he had amassed some $700,000 for his re-election campaign. The array of candidates showing interest in running in

2000 was large. Caperton gave it some thought, then bowed out in December 1998. Pritt, Manchin and House Speaker Robert Kiss showed interest. Congressman Bob Wise announced in May 1999. Caperton's banking commissioner and tax secretary Jim Paige switched to the Republican Party and said he might run against Underwood in the primary. Meanwhile, Underwood, who turns 78 in election week 2000, seemed to be running vigorously; he is, after all, five years younger than Senator Robert Byrd.

Cook's Call. *Competitive.* Underwood's status as the only Republican statewide elected official in this overwhelmingly Democratic state makes him potentially vulnerable in 2000. He will likely face a primary challenge and a well-funded Democrat in the general. Representative Bob Wise is considered the frontrunner for the Democratic nod, although he will face credible primary opposition. Underwood has built a strong record as governor but will need all of his political wiles to win another term in 2000.

Senior Senator. Robert Byrd, former chairman of and now ranking Democrat on the Appropriations Committee, may come closer to the kind of senator the Founding Fathers had in mind than any other. He comes from the humblest of beginnings, and when first elected to the Senate, as part of the large and talented Democratic class of 1958, he was scarcely noticed. Now he is the last member of that class still in the Senate, and even in the minority an authentic power. From a background as grindingly poor as that of any American politician, he has continually moved up with awesome persistence. Son of a coal miner, he was a welder in wartime shipyards and a meat cutter in a coal company town when he won his seat in the House of Delegates in 1946; he campaigned in every hollow in the county, playing his fiddle and even going to the length of joining the Ku Klux Klan (which he quickly quit and has ever since regretted joining). He worked hard in the legislature, and won a U.S. House seat when the incumbent retired in 1952; he made such a name for himself in West Virginia that by 1958, when he was 40, he was elected to the Senate even though the United Mine Workers initially opposed him and the coal companies never supported him.

In the Senate, he became a supporter of Majority Leader Lyndon Johnson and in return got a seat on Appropriations his first year. He backed Hubert Humphrey against John Kennedy in the 1960 West Virginia presidential primary not because he shared Humphrey's liberal politics—his voting record then was as conservative as any Southerner's and he opposed civil rights—but because Johnson wanted to stop Kennedy. Then, in the 1960s, Byrd's career took what in retrospect was a helpful detour. He became assistant majority whip, an unimportant position in 1965; in 1971, when Edward Kennedy neglected his duties as whip after Chappaquiddick, Byrd quietly lined up support and, with Richard Russell's deathbed vote, ousted Kennedy. There Byrd performed ably, managing Senate business and accommodating colleagues' needs, and when Majority Leader Mike Mansfield retired in 1976, Byrd easily won the job, and not because of any close personal ties; he shuns Washington social events and says he has never had another senator to his house. All the while Byrd was working hard to keep in touch with West Virginians, to the point that he won 78% of the vote in 1970, becoming the first West Virginian in history to carry all 55 counties.

Byrd did not like being majority leader. Contrary to most people's assumptions, the post carries little power, because Senate rules requiring unanimous consent or supermajorities allow individual senators to block action; the office gained its reputation in the six years Lyndon Johnson held it, when his extraordinary abilities and compulsive personality, applied in a closely divided Senate, enabled him temporarily to become a national leader. No majority leader has since, and Byrd was aware that his power came from meeting other senators' needs and did not have a national issues agenda of his own, though his voting record became notably less conservative. His formal manner did not project well on television, and when Democrats were in the minority, Byrd was challenged in 1984 for the minority leader post by then-Florida Senator (later Governor) Lawton Chiles. In 1987, with Democrats back in the majority after six years out of power, Byrd established some legislative priorities and then announced he would leave the post after the 1988 election.

In 1989 Byrd got the position he had been aiming for all along, chairman of the Appropriations Committee. "I want to be West Virginia's billion dollar industry," he announced in 1990, and in six years as chairman succeeded handsomely. An FBI office went to Clarksburg, Treasury and IRS offices to Parkersburg, the Fish and Wildlife Training Center in Harper's Ferry, a Bureau of Alcohol, Tobacco and Firearms in Martinsburg, a NASA Research center in Wheeling. "All roads, they say, lead to Rome," he said in 1994 in Logan, West Virginia. "They haven't seen anything yet. All roads lead to Logan." Byrd does not always deliver: a GAO report helped defeat his attempt to build a $1.2 billion CIA facility in Jefferson County; and he lost by one vote, despite personally lobbying every senator, his amendment to compensate coal miners who lose their jobs because of the Clean Air Act. But he has continued the fight for West Virginia's coal industry, opposing the Kyoto Protocol on Climate Change and EPA's new air-quality standards. Though he occasionally loses, Byrd usually wins. And, while he insists that he does not retaliate against those who oppose his projects, no one doubts he remembers how every senator voted: "You might as well slap my wife as take the highway money from West Virginia."

It should be added that Byrd's positions are not just parochial but are the product of serious study of the Constitution and of history. He always carries a copy of the Constitution in his left breast pocket. With the assistance of Senate historian Richard Baker, he wrote *The Senate 1789–1989*, a two-volume history, plus two volumes of classic speeches and statistics; based on impressive research, gracefully written, full of arresting anecdotes and sound insights, it surpasses any previous work on the subject. In 1995 he published *The Senate of the Roman Republic: Addresses on the History of Roman Constitutionalism*. Byrd earned his law degree while in the Senate and had his diploma presented to him by President Kennedy at the 1963 American University commencement where Kennedy delivered his most important foreign policy speech; in 1994 he was awarded his B.A. summa cum laude by Marshall University, which he had attended for one semester 43 years before and could not afford to continue, and where he earned As in all eight courses he took. Byrd has been educating himself as well, systematically reading the classics, and takes to quoting Shakespeare, Thucydides or Cato the Younger in debates on the balanced budget amendment and the line-item veto. In December 1995, in the budget crisis, he decried "insolence" and "harsh and severe" speeches, referring to the partisan climate on Capitol Hill. "Little did I know when I came here that I would live to see pygmies stride like Colossus while marveling, like Aesop's fly, sitting on the axle of a chariot, 'My, what a dust I do raise.' " He said the balanced budget amendment "would rudely disrupt the carefully balanced powers of the three branches so assiduously planned by the Framers." He said passage of the line-item veto in 1996 was "one of the darkest moments in the history of the republic," and with five other members of Congress brought suit against it; the Supreme Court rejected their challenge in July 1997; it was ruled unconstitutional in June 1998. He objected as well to the October 1998 omnibus budget: "Only God knows what's in this monstrosity." In 1998 he objected to the Clinton Administration's recess appointments as an undermining of the prerogatives of the Senate. "After 200 years," he wrote in his history, the Senate "is still the anchor of the Republic, the morning and evening star in the American constitutional constellation."

Byrd's insistence on Senate prerogatives have not always worked well. His practice of earmarking West Virginia projects in appropriations bills has come under attack. He is a stickler for Senate rules. When a blind aide to freshman Ron Wyden wanted to bring her leader dog onto the floor in 1997, Byrd raised an objection. "Matters such as this ought to go to the Committee on Rules and Administration for any change in regulations or rules deemed necessary. Senator Wyden's resolution may pass with flying colors, but the proper procedure should be followed." It was and it did. He objected in 1997 to laptop computers on the Senate floor, and the Senate agreed; the inkwells remain. Byrd may not be easy to deal with, but he is open to persuasion. He switched and voted for the partial-birth abortion ban in May 1997 after an abortion clinic lobbyist admitted he lied in arguing against the ban in 1995 and after the American Medical Association endorsed the bill.

As might be expected, Byrd played a leading role on impeachment. In October 1998, when the White House sought to forestall a House vote by getting 34 Democratic senators to sign a letter saying they would never vote to remove Clinton, Byrd responded, "Don't tamper with this jury." The tampering stopped. After Clinton and most Democratic House members held a campaign-style rally at the White House after the House voted for impeachment, Byrd called it, "an egregious display of shameless arrogance the likes of which I don't think I have seen." "I started out to vote to convict," Byrd said later. But he also wanted the Senate to avoid the partisanship of the House proceedings. To the senators-only meeting in the old Senate Chamber in January 1999 he delivered a 20-minute speech, saying, "The House has fallen into the black pit of partisan self-indulgence. The Senate is teetering on the brink of that same black pit." Later in January, he introduced a resolution to dismiss the charges, but that was defeated 56–44. In February 1999, he sounded ambivalent: "It would be very difficult to stand and say not guilty, very difficult. . . . Who's kidding whom here? I have to live with myself. I have to live with my conscience." But, though he evidently continued to believe that Clinton committed high crimes, he decided that a vote to remove would abet partisanship.

In 1994 Byrd was re-elected with 69% of the vote, repeating his 1970 victory of carrying all 55 counties. He became the third senator to be elected to seven six-year terms (the others were Carl Hayden of Arizona and Strom Thurmond of South Carolina); he has served longer than any senator but those two and John Stennis, whose tenure he will surpass in March 2000. In 1997 a spokesman said he was "adamant" about running again and, while some other Democrats might like to run for the Senate, there was not a murmur of opposition from anywhere in the West Virginia political firmament.

Cook's Call. *Safe.* Byrd's low point in the polls was in 1958, when he won his first Senate election with 59% of the vote. His high mark came in 1976, when he was unopposed. Don't look for any excitement in this race.

Junior Senator. Jay Rockefeller's full name, John D. Rockefeller IV, has a familiar ring to most older voters, who remember his great-grandfather as the oil billionaire who was America's richest man, and his grandfather as the heir who had more than enough money to build New York's Rockefeller Center, restore Colonial Williamsburg, and found the Museum of Modern Art during the Depression. Jay Rockefeller's father and uncles were men of impressive achievement in different fields, in two cases in politics. His uncle Winthrop Rockefeller moved to an impoverished state in the southern hills—in his case Arkansas—ran for governor and lost, ran again and won two terms and ran an honest and reforming administration: the same could be said of Jay Rockefeller's career in West Virginia. There are interesting comparisons between the careers of Jay Rockefeller and his other governor-uncle: Nelson Rockefeller, in his 30s, became head of Franklin Roosevelt's Latin American policy program; Jay Rockefeller, in his 20s, studied for three years in Japan. Nelson Rockefeller became governor of the nation's then-biggest state and spent money expansively on generous welfare and gigantic monuments; Jay Rockefeller became governor of what turned out to be America's number one population-losing state of the 1980s, leaving behind a network of roads and highways and a progressive tax structure. Nelson Rockefeller was a Republican at a time when the party's Ivy League establishment believed it was in the minority and had to move left to win votes. Jay Rockefeller broke family tradition and became a Democrat at a time when the party's Ivy League ideologues believed it would always remain the majority party even as it was losing that status. Both Rockefellers were mentioned early on as presidential candidates: Nelson, never very shy about running, finally did so in 1964 at 56, and again in 1968 (he ultimately served briefly as vice president under Gerald Ford); Jay for years avoided projecting his name forward, then almost decided to run in the summer of 1991 at 54, but now as an ally of Bill Clinton and Al Gore seems unlikely ever to run.

The parallels stop here, for Jay Rockefeller lacks the aloof, imperial bearing of his Uncle

Nelson; he is affable, full of self-deprecating humor, tall enough so that he stoops to get through doorways and uses hearing aids because of noise damage from frequent helicopter travel. He was careful to work his way up the political ladder. He first came to West Virginia as a VISTA volunteer, was elected to the House of Delegates in Kanawha County in 1966 and as secretary of State in 1968, and then had the chastening experience of losing the gubernatorial race to Arch Moore in 1972. He served three years as president of West Virginia Wesleyan College in Buckhannon, and became more practical, dropping his opposition to strip mining. He was not shy about spending his own millions and was elected governor in 1976 and, against Moore, in 1980, after which the state was plunged into deep recession. In 1984, he ran for the U.S. Senate and beat Republican businessman John Raese by just 52%–48% after spending $12 million. Every penny helped, especially the huge sums needed to air ads on Washington and Pittsburgh TV. In most counties in the state, Rockefeller ran between 1% and 7% ahead of Walter Mondale's 45% showing; in all but one of the dozen or so panhandle counties in these hugely expensive media markets, he ran 12% to 18% ahead of Mondale.

Initially in the Senate Rockefeller deferred to Robert Byrd, compiled a conventional liberal voting record, somewhat more inclined to free trade because of his experience in East Asia. Then he began his concentration on health care. With a seat on the Finance Committee, he got a place on the Pepper Commission on long-term health care and became chairman when Claude Pepper died in June 1989. He got majorities on the commission to back long-term care for all Americans regardless of age and, by 8–7, universal medical insurance coverage. But getting others to agree was harder. Rockefeller talked mostly about health care financing when he was mulling a presidential race; but he warmly endorsed Clinton and applauded his emphasis on health care. He was motivated in part by anger at his mother's treatment during a long terminal illness—an experience that would be much worse for people of ordinary incomes, he thought—and he worked to increase the number of general practitioners, especially in states like West Virginia and Arkansas, at the risk of harming the major teaching hospitals. He resisted efforts at any compromise. "We're going to push through healthcare reform regardless of the views of the American people," he said at one point. Poor political judgment: efforts at compromise came far too late, after voters had turned against a government takeover of health care, and the health care bill crashed and burned in September 1994.

Rockefeller has worked on other health care issues since. Perhaps his biggest legislative achievement was his 1992 law, passed over furious opposition from Western coal states, which forced union and non-union coal companies and "reachback" companies that had gone out of the coal business to pay for the exploding cost of the United Mine Workers' health care trust funds; he successfully defended it against Republican attacks in 1995. He also opposed the Republicans' Medicare reform, worked to save Medicaid for pregnant women, children and the disabled, and backed compensation for veterans suffering from the vaguely-defined Gulf war syndrome. He is lead sponsor of a bipartisan Medigap bill, which would require insurers to issue policies to people with pre-existing conditions who don't qualify for Medicaid. He pushed through the children's health insurance bill passed in 1997, which requires state matching funds. With Bill Frist, he passed a law with incentives for primary care physicians in rural and inner city areas. With Susan Collins of Maine, he has sponsored a bill to improve treatment at the end of life. Again with Frist, he sponsored a law to all physicians and hospitals to establish health provider organizations to contract directly with Medicare.

Rockefeller's voting record is mostly but not entirely liberal. He was one of 14 Democrats, along with Robert Byrd, who voted for the flag burning amendment. He supported the 1996 Welfare Reform Act, working to maintain programs for abused and neglected children. For a dozen frustrating years one of his major causes has been a uniform federal product liability law, to reduce the burden of expensive lawsuit settlements on manufacturers. A product liability bill passed the House in March 1995; a similar bill was filibustered in the Senate, but Rockefeller scaled it down, dropping controversial medical malpractice provisions, to get 61 votes for passage in May 1995. After a nearly year-long conference, it was vetoed by Clinton in May

1996. In summer 1998 a milder product liability reform, tailored to Clinton's specifications, seemed set to pass the Senate. The House Judiciary Committee passed a similar measure in September; the same day it received the impeachment referral of Independent Counsel Kenneth Starr, and the chance for action in the 105th Congress was gone. Rockefeller was a key supporter of the adoption tax credit, raising it to $6,000 for special needs children. He was also chief sponsor for the 1998 law making the interest of the child, rather than the theory of family preservation, the chief criterion for decisions on adoption.

For the 106th Congress Rockefeller is said to be more interested in working on Medicare and Social Security reform. On telecommunications reform, Rockefeller and Olympia Snowe of Maine passed an amendment to connect every school and library to the Internet, to connect their sometimes isolated states to the world. Rockefeller has left funding local West Virginia projects mostly in the capable hands of Byrd. Rockefeller specializes in attracting industry to the state. He has led two Project Harvest trade missions to Japan and Taiwan, and has brokered negotiations for the Wheeling-Nisshin Steel, NGK Sparkplugs, and Sino-Swearingen Aircraft plants in the state and the $900 million Toyota engine plant in Buffalo in Putnam County. He has followed that up by encouraging West Virginia exports. In 1999 he worked on a bill for steel quotas. "A quota bill is like a nuclear bomb in the trade industry," he said, arguing that passage would ensure "that there is no more explosion of imported steel."

Rockefeller is in strong shape politically, strong enough that he no longer spends any of his own money and wins handsomely. In 1990 he won 68%–32%; in 1996, against a nurse's aide who didn't like to see the ballot space empty, he won 77%–23%, duplicating Byrd's feat of winning all 55 counties.

Presidential politics. West Virginia is one of the nation's most Democratic states in presidential elections; it has voted Republican only three times in the last 65 years. West Virginia's presidential primary, held in May, has not attracted much attention in years. But in 1960 it was the focus of the nation's attention when John Kennedy, reportedly fortified with large injections of cash from his father, took on Hubert Humphrey and beat him, proving that a Catholic could carry a virtually all-Protestant state.

Congressional districting. West Virginia lost one of its four House seats for 1992, and so one of its four Democratic congressmen had to go. This game of musical chairs was played out lustily in the legislature, and the loser turned out to be Harley Staggers, whose 2d District was divided up among the other three; he ran against Alan Mollohan in the 1st District primary and lost. West Virginia has had an all-Democratic congressional delegation since 1982.

The People: Est. Pop. 1998: 1,811,156; Pop. 1990: 1,793,477, up 1% 1990–1998. 0.7% of U.S. total, 35th largest; 63.9% rural. Median age: 37.7 years. 15.6% 65 years and over. 96.2% White, 3.1% Black, 0.4% Asian, 0.2% Amer. Indian, 0.1% Other; 0.4% Hispanic Origin. Households: 59% married couple families; 28.3% married couple fams. w. children; 29.4% college educ.; median household income: $20,795; per capita income: $10,520; 74.1% owner occupied housing; median house value: $47,900; median monthly rent: $221. 6.6% Unemployment. 1998 Voting age pop.: 1,406,000. 1998 Turnout: 405,139; 29% of VAP. Registered voters (1998): 1,007,811; 632,288 D (63%), 295,825 R (29%), 79,698 unaffiliated and minor parties (8%).

Political Lineup: Governor, Cecil H. Underwood (R); Secy. of State, Ken Hechler (D); Atty. Gen., Darrell V. McGraw Jr. (D); Treasurer, John Perdue (D); State Senate, 34 (29 D, 5 R); Senate President, Earl Ray Tomblin (D); State House, 100 (75 D, 25 R); House Speaker, Robert Kiss (D). Senators, Robert C. Byrd (D) and John D. Rockefeller IV (D). Representatives, 3 D.

Elections Division: 304-558-6000; **Filing Deadline for U.S. Congress:** January 29, 2000.

1716   WEST VIRGINIA

GOVERNOR

Gov. Cecil H. Underwood (R)

Elected 1996, term expires Jan. 2001; b. Nov. 5, 1922, Joseph's Mills; home, Huntington; Salem Col., A.B. 1943, WV U., M.A. 1952; Methodist; married (Hovah).

Military Career: Army Reserves, 1942–43.

Elected Office: WV House of Delegates, 1944–56; WV Gov., 1956–61; Repub. nominee for U.S. Senate, 1960; Repub. gubernatorial nominee, 1964, 1976.

Professional Career: Teacher, 1943–46; Faculty, Marietta Col., 1946–50; Vice Pres., Salem Col., 1950–56; Vice Pres., Island Creek Coal Co., 1961–64; Vice Pres., Gov. & Civic Affairs, Monsanto Co., 1965–68; Pres., Bethany Col., 1972–75; Pres., Princess Coals, Inc., 1978–81, Chmn., 1981–83; Pres., Morgantown Industrial Research Park, 1983–89, Chmn., 1989–96; Pres., Software Valley, 1989–93; Pres., Mon View Heights of WV, 1993–96.

Office: State Capitol, Charleston, 25305, 304-558-2000; Fax: 304-558-2722; Web site: www.state.wv.us.

Election Results

1996 gen.	Cecil H. Underwood (R)	324,518	(52%)
	Charlotte Pritt (D)	287,870	(46%)
	Others	16,171	(3%)
1996 prim.	Cecil H. Underwood (R)	54,628	(41%)
	Jon McBride (R)	44,255	(33%)
	David McKinley (R)	35,089	(26%)
1992 gen.	Gaston Caperton (D)	368,302	(56%)
	Cleve Benedict (R)	240,390	(37%)
	Charlotte Pritt (I)	48,501	(7%)

SENATORS

Sen. Robert C. Byrd (D)

Elected 1958, seat up 2000; b. Nov. 20, 1917, North Wilkesboro, NC; home, Sophia; American U., J.D. 1963; Baptist; married (Erma).

Elected Office: WV House of Delegates, 1946–50; WV Senate, 1950–52; U.S. House of Reps., 1952–58; U.S. Senate Majority Whip, 1971–76, Majority Ldr., 1977–80, Minority Ldr., 1981–86, Pres. Pro-tem, 1989–94.

DC Office: 311 HSOB, 20510, 202-224-3954; Fax: 202-228-0002; Web site: www.senate.gov/~byrd.

State Office: Charleston, 304-342-5855.

Committees: *Appropriations* (RMM of 13 D): Defense; Energy & Water Development; Interior (RMM); Transportation; VA, HUD & Independent Agencies. *Armed Services* (4th of 9 D): Emerging Threats & Capabilities; Readiness & Management Support; Strategic Forces. *Rules & Administration* (2d of 7 D).

Group Ratings

	ADA	ACLU	AFS	LCV	CON	NTU	NFIB	COC	ACU	NTLC	CHC
1998	80	43	89	63	62	27	22	44	16	14	18
1997	70	—	100	—	37	20	—	40	16	—	—

National Journal Ratings

	1997 LIB	—	1997 CONS	1998 LIB	—	1998 CONS
Economic	69%	—	30%	68%	—	31%
Social	55%	—	37%	55%	—	43%
Foreign	68%	—	27%	89%	—	9%

Key Votes of the 105th Congress

1. Bal. Budget Amend.	N	5. Satcher for Surgeon Gen.	Y	9. Chem. Weapons Treaty	Y
2. Clinton Budget Deal	N	6. Highway Set-asides	Y	10. Cuban Humanitarian Aid	Y
3. Cloture on Tobacco	Y	7. Table Child Gun locks	N	11. Table Bosnia Troops	Y
4. Education IRAs	Y	8. Ovrd. Part. Birth Veto	Y	12. $ for Test-ban Treaty	Y

Election Results

1994 general	Robert C. Byrd (D)	290,495	(69%)	($1,550,354)
	Stan Klos (R)	130,441	(31%)	($267,165)
1994 primary	Robert C. Byrd (D)	190,061	(85%)	
	John M. Fuller (D)	20,057	(9%)	
	Paul Nuchims (D)	12,381	(6%)	
1988 general	Robert C. Byrd (D)	410,983	(65%)	($1,282,746)
	M. Jay Wolfe (R)	223,564	(35%)	($115,284)

Sen. John D. Rockefeller, IV (D)

Elected 1984, seat up 2002; b. June 18, 1937, New York, NY; home, Charleston; Harvard U., B.A. 1961, Intl. Christian U., Tokyo, Japan, 1957–60; Presbyterian; married (Sharon).

Elected Office: WV House of Delegates, 1966–68; WV Secy. of State, 1968–72; Dem. gubernatorial nominee, 1972; WV Gov., 1976–84.

Professional Career: Natl. Advisory Cncl., Peace Corps, 1961; Asst., Peace Corps Dir. Sargent Shriver, 1962–63; VISTA worker, 1964–66; Pres., WV Wesleyan Col., 1973–75.

DC Office: 531 HSOB, 20510, 202-224-6472; Fax: 202-224-7665; Web site: www.senate.gov/~rockefeller.

State Offices: Beckley, 304-253-9704; Charleston, 304-347-5372; Fairmont, 304-367-0122; Martinsburg, 304-262-9285.

Committees: *Commerce, Science & Transportation* (3d of 9 D): Aviation (RMM); Communications; Manufacturing & Competitiveness; Science, Technology & Space. *Finance* (3d of 9 D): Health Care (RMM); International Trade; Social Security & Family Policy. *Veterans' Affairs* (RMM of 5 D).

Group Ratings

	ADA	ACLU	AFS	LCV	CON	NTU	NFIB	COC	ACU	NTLC	CHC
1998	90	83	100	88	49	6	33	56	0	11	0
1997	70	—	78	—	22	26	—	67	8	—	—

National Journal Ratings

	1997 LIB — 1997 CONS		1998 LIB — 1998 CONS	
Economic	78%	21%	81%	17%
Social	71%	0%	74%	0%
Foreign	68%	27%	65%	27%

Key Votes of the 105th Congress

1. Bal. Budget Amend.	N	5. Satcher for Surgeon Gen.	Y	9. Chem. Weapons Treaty	Y
2. Clinton Budget Deal	Y	6. Highway Set-asides	Y	10. Cuban Humanitarian Aid	N
3. Cloture on Tobacco	Y	7. Table Child Gun locks	N	11. Table Bosnia Troops	*
4. Education IRAs	*	8. Ovrd. Part. Birth Veto	N	12. $ for Test-ban Treaty	Y

Election Results

1996 general	John D. Rockefeller IV (D)	456,526	(77%)	($5,819,157)
	Betty A. Burks (R)	139,088	(23%)	
1996 primary	John D. Rockefeller IV (D)	280,303	(88%)	
	Bruce Barilla (D)	36,637	(12%)	
1990 general	John D. Rockefeller IV (D)	276,234	(68%)	($2,709,665)
	John Yoder (R)	128,071	(32%)	($22,904)

FIRST DISTRICT

The northern part of West Virginia is in many ways an extension of the Pittsburgh metropolitan area. People here are Steelers and Pirates fans, they drink Iron City and Rolling Rock beer, they watch Pittsburgh TV, they live in the crevasses between hills cut by the Monongahela and Ohio rivers, on terrain that seems forbidding to industrial and urban development. Yet this has been one of America's prime industrial areas; northern West Virginia is part of the same coal-

and-steel economy that made Pittsburgh one of the nation's largest cities and filled the narrow bottomlands along the rivers with steel and glass factories, foundries and coal yards. In the 1980s and 1990s these have been declining industries, or rather industries becoming far less labor-intensive. Replacing them are Japanese factories and high-tech startups, as well as federal office complexes obtained by Senator Robert Byrd.

The 1st Congressional District includes the northern third of West Virginia. On the panhandle along the Ohio River are Victorian Wheeling, once one of the richest cities in the country with its steel and glass company investors and executives, and where the radio show "Jamboree U.S.A." has been broadcast every Saturday night for more than 50 years, and Weirton, a steel company town and site of one of the most visible experiments in employee ownership, where steelworkers decided to cut their own pay in order to produce profits, but were still threatened with the loss of jobs in 1998. South of Pittsburgh on the Monongahela are Morgantown, site of West Virginia University, and Clarksburg and Fairmont. Far to the west, the district includes Parkersburg and the surrounding hills on the Ohio River. To the east, it extends to the upper Potomac River opposite Cumberland, Maryland. Politically, most of this territory is solidly Democratic, except for some mountain counties never heavily industrialized which have remained Republican since the Civil War.

The congressman from the 1st District is Alan Mollohan, a Democrat first elected in 1982. His father Robert Mollohan was elected congressman in 1952 and 1954, ran for governor and lost in 1956, and then won the House seat again when Arch Moore was elected governor in 1968 and kept it until he retired in 1982. Alan Mollohan, a Washington lawyer for Consolidation Coal, among other clients, returned home in 1982 and won the seat. His one major challenge came in the 1992 primary, after he was redistricted in with another congressman who was also the son of a congressman, Harley Staggers Jr. The younger staggers Staggers made his name as chief sponsor of the National Rifle Association-supported substitute for the Brady bill seven-day handgun purchase waiting period, to establish a computerized list of felons which gun sellers could check before sales. The younger Mollohan made his name as a member of the Appropriations Committee who hustled to bring jobs to northern West Virginia. But the key was that only 20% of the Democratic primary vote here was cast in Staggers's old district. He carried that part with 73%, but Mollohan won 70% in his old district and won overall, 62%–38%.

Mollohan has compiled a moderately liberal voting record and concentrated on bringing projects to the district, working often with Senator Byrd. He claims credit for a First District Federal Procurement Team and a West Virginia High-Technology Consortium, headquartered in the Alan B. Mollohan Innovation Center, and spurring a computer software testing center in Fairmont. Mollohan secured $5 million for the Consortium to manage a national weather project. He sponsored an Institute for Software Research and an E-Commerce Connection. He has worked to fund waterways, education projects, a flight simulator for Fairmont State College and a defense procurement center in Parkersburg, historic sites, a law enforcement training system at the closed Moundsville prison, the Orbital Science Corporation's satellite tracking station, the Mid-Atlantic Aerospace Complex at Harrison County's Benedum airport. In April 1994 Mollohan moved up to the "college of cardinals" when he became chairman of the Commerce, Justice, State, and Judiciary Appropriations Subcommittee; he is now the ranking member on the VA-HUD and Independent Agencies Subcommittee. Even in the minority, Mollohan got an SBA Business Information Center in Fairmont, $750,000 to combat acid mine drainage problems in the Tygart River valley, favorable language on the use of high-sulfur coal for the Kammer power plant in Marshall County. He helped form the Canaan Valley Institute, to work with local watershed groups in West Virginia and adjoining states. He helped get an expansion of Morgantown's federal prison and community-based outpatient clinics in Wood and Tucker counties.

On national issues, Mollohan sponsored the Democrats' attempt to get full-year funding for the Census in August 1998, and he has worked to prevent what he considers unfair competition from foreign steelmakers. In June 1999 he voted to loosen restrictions on gun control regulations.

Mollohan was re-elected without Republican opposition in 1996 and 1998.

Cook's Call. *Safe.* Mollohan is safely entrenched in this Democratic leaning district. Don't look for a competitive race here.

The People: Pop. 1990: 598,056; 55.1% rural; 16.2% age 65 + ; 97.6% White, 1.6% Black, 0.5% Asian, 0.2% Amer. Indian, 0.1% Other; 0.6% Hispanic Origin. Households: 58.2% married couple families; 27% married couple fams. w. children; 32.1% college educ.; median household income: $21,903; per capita income: $10,920; median house value: $46,700; median gross rent: $221.

1996 Presidential Vote			1992 Presidential Vote		
Clinton (D)	107,835	(49%)	Clinton (D)	113,756	(46%)
Dole (R)	83,306	(38%)	Bush (R)	86,131	(35%)
Perot (I)	28,900	(13%)	Perot (I)	45,856	(19%)

Rep. Alan Mollohan (D)

Elected 1982; b. May 14, 1943, Fairmont; home, Fairmont; Col. of William & Mary, A.B. 1966, WV U., J.D. 1970; Baptist; married (Barbara).

Military Career: Army, 1970, Army Reserves, 1970–83.

Professional Career: Practicing atty., 1970–82.

DC Office: 2346 RHOB 20515, 202-225-4172; Fax: 202-225-7564.

District Offices: Clarksburg, 304-623-4422; Morgantown, 304-292-3019; Parkersburg, 304-428-9032; Wheeling, 304-232-5390.

Committees: *Appropriations* (7th of 27 D): Commerce, Justice, State & the Judiciary; District of Columbia; VA, HUD & Independent Agencies (RMM).

Group Ratings

	ADA	ACLU	AFS	LCV	CON	NTU	NFIB	COC	ACU	NTLC	CHC
1998	70	53	100	46	40	14	14	27	32	9	50
1997	70	—	100	—	1	14	—	30	33	—	—

National Journal Ratings

	1997 LIB — 1997 CONS			1998 LIB — 1998 CONS		
Economic	73%	—	27%	63%	—	37%
Social	52%	—	48%	52%	—	47%
Foreign	68%	—	31%	69%	—	31%

Key Votes of the 105th Congress

1. Clinton Budget Deal	N	5. Puerto Rico Sthood. Ref.	Y	9. Cut $ for B-2 Bombers	N
2. Education IRAs	N	6. End Highway Set-asides	N	10. Human Rights in China	Y
3. Req. 2/3 to Raise Taxes	N	7. School Prayer Amend.	*	11. Withdraw Bosnia Troops	N
4. Fast-track Trade	N	8. Ovrd. Part. Birth Veto	Y	12. End Cuban TV-Marti	Y

Election Results

1998 general	Alan Mollohan (D)	105,101	(85%)	($284,832)
	Richard Kerr (Lib)	19,013	(15%)	($21,232)
1998 primary	Alan Mollohan (D)	57,425	(87%)	
	W. E. (Bill) Ruehl (D)	8,706	(13%)	
1996 general	Alan Mollohan (D)	unopposed		($195,128)

SECOND DISTRICT

Not all of West Virginia is coal country, not all of its valleys are industrial hollows choked with workingmen's homes and small factories, not all of its hills are scarred with strip mining wounds or piled with tailings. For miles you can see gentle hills and rugged mountains, stands of green trees and vistas stretching to far horizons. Yet over another hill you may find, amid scenery primeval and rural, sudden evidence of industrialization: a pulp mill or charcoal factory in a clearing scraped out of the forest; a small factory town, built close to a river in a cleft bordered with hills, its houses built in the same 1910s style as in the factory suburbs of Pittsburgh; the entrance to an underground coal mine or the exposed brown earth of a strip mine scar. Large parts of this naturally beautiful state look as verdant and unchanged as they must have when George Washington was speculating in land here or taking the waters in Berkeley Springs, or when John Brown launched his assault at the federal arsenal at Harper's Ferry, or when the Civil War pitted brother against brother.

The 2d Congressional District is the central part of West Virginia, a belt of land from Berkeley Springs and Harper's Ferry all the way west to the Ohio River town of Point Pleasant, where the Kanawha River (pronounced *kaNAW*) flows into the Ohio. It could easily take a full day to drive through this district which, if ironed out, would probably spread across the country. The 2d District includes Putnam County, where Toyota opened its new $400 million engine plant in 1998. The major urban center here is Charleston, where on the banks of the Kanawha rises West Virginia's Capitol, built in 1932 and designed by Cass Gilbert with a dome higher than the U.S. Capitol and a chandelier with 10,000 pieces of cut glass. Charleston, with its two partisan newspapers, the Democratic *Gazette* and the Republican *Daily Mail*, is the state capital and the center of the state's political culture. Charleston is a major industrial center, with coal in the hills all around and, downriver from the Capitol, huge petrochemical plants that convert coal tar into everyday products. This was a center of American high tech in the 1940s, when it produced all the nation's lucite, polyethylenes and nylon, as well as much of its artificial rubber and antifreeze. More recently, these factories are seen as heavy polluters in a valley that has well above average rates of cancer. Charleston is also West Virginia's white-collar and professional center, with a few downtown skyscrapers and some pleasant affluent residential districts. Politically, the 2d has some mountain Republican counties, and Charleston's Kanawha County sometimes goes Republican too; but in national terms this is a solidly Democratic seat.

The congressman from the 2d District is Bob Wise, a Democrat first elected in 1982. He grew up in Charleston in an affluent family and returned home after law school to start a law practice geared to low- and middle-income clients, and led a movement to force coal companies to pay higher taxes. A strong advocate of West Virginia culture—he is renowned for his clog dancing—he urges West Virginia students to make their careers, as he did, in their home state. But he is not a total traditionalist. In a state where past politicians got ahead by relying on ancestral loyalties and smoothing relations with big economic institutions, he made his way by emphasizing issues on which he opposes the big interests. Wise, elected to the state Senate in 1980, was shrewd and popular enough to beat the state House majority leader and a former Kanawha County sheriff in the 1982 primary for the 2d District House seat, and then to beat a Republican incumbent soundly in November. He has been re-elected easily ever since.

In the House Wise is an enthusiastic and articulate partisan Democrat. He is a booster of alternative fuels and has championed compressed natural gas as an auto fuel; he got the Postal Service to use it for their fleet of vehicles and has had two CNG-powered cars himself (though one broke down on I-64 with transmission problems). His biggest legislative success was his 1990 amendment, adopted 274–146, to provide benefits for workers displaced by compliance with the Clean Air Act, with a $250 million cap. In 1995, he took to the floor with Barney Frank to oppose Republican initiatives. But he has supported some conservative policies— repeal of the assault weapons ban, the flag amendment, the Welfare Reform Act of 1996. Moreover, unlike most Democrats, he did not automatically defend the Clinton White House against any scandal charge; in June 1996 he backed hearings on the White House's wrongful acquisition of 400 FBI files and in March 1997 he called for an independent counsel to investigate Clinton campaign finance improprieties. After Clinton acknowledged lying about his relationship with Monica Lewinsky, Wise said, "I think this calls more for a preacher than a prosecutor."

Many of Wise's initiatives relate to West Virginia. He sponsored the 1986 Community Right to Know Act, requiring disclosure by chemical companies of discharges of hazardous chemicals. He leads "Project Europe" trade missions, to Germany, Spain and Norway, to attract jobs to West Virginia. He questioned the Clean Air guidelines of EPA in 1998 which would require reductions of nitrogen oxide in West Virginia to 44% below 1990 levels, the biggest drop in the nation, and sponsored a bill to delay the guidelines until September 1999. Arguing that EPA's own scientific advisors said they would do little good, he said, "My greatest fear of this particular set of proposals from the EPA is after all is said and done you will have significantly affected West Virginia and yet not gotten the kind of results that you set out to get in New England." In August 1998 he called for a temporary moratorium on mountaintop mining. In late 1998 he attacked foreign dumping of apple juice concentrate; apples are West Virginia's major cash crop.

In December 1998 Wise filed pre-candidacy papers for a race for governor in 2000. "A lot of power has shifted from Washington to the statehouses in the last 10 years. . . . I have loved my Congressional service, but I have learned that it's not a place where you have an immediate cause and effect. At some point, you want to run something." Looking back to the 1996 primary between labor-backed Charlotte Pritt and business-backed Joe Manchin, he said, "I want to stop this division between business and labor. It's a false division. I believe I'm the one to bring business and labor together." In May 1999 he announced for governor, to a crowd that included the representatives of West Virginia's teacher unions and AFL-CIO. Wise said he would support a patient protection act and backed the 1999 PROMISE scholarship law and called for "making sure the 30,000 gray-market video poker machines in this state pay their fair share."

Who will run for the 2d District House seat in 2000? An easier question might be: who won't run? Former state Senator and asbestos lawyer Jim Humphreys announced and put $600,000 of his own money into a candidate account. Two former congressmen expressed interest: Harley Staggers Jr., who after 10 years in the House lost the 1992 primary when he was redistricted in with Alan Mollohan, and Secretary of State Ken Hechler, who was elected in the 4th District from 1958–76, when he ran unsuccessfully for governor. Hechler, born in 1914 and a speechwriter for Adlai Stevenson in 1956, in 1998 walked 200 miles in support of campaign finance reform. Other possible Democrats in early 1999 included state Senator Martha Walker, and Delegates John Amores and Mark Hunt. Republicans are enthusiastic about Delegate Shelley Moore Capito, daughter of longtime Congressman (1956–68) and Governor (1968–76) Arch Moore.

Cook's Call. *Potentially Competitive.* With the announcement by nine-term incumbent Wise that he will run for governor, a scramble has ensued to replace him. Democrats should have an edge in this Charleston-based district that has a Democratic lean. But the 2d District is the least Democratic of the three West Virginia districts and the right Republican candidate could make this an interesting race.

The People: Pop. 1990: 597,921; 62.1% rural; 14.9% age 65 + ; 96.1% White, 3.3% Black, 0.4% Asian, 0.1% Amer. Indian, 0.1% Other; 0.4% Hispanic Origin. Households: 59.7% married couple families; 28.5% married couple fams. w. children; 30% college educ.; median household income: $22,253; per capita income: $11,083; median house value: $55,600; median gross rent: $239.

1996 Presidential Vote			1992 Presidential Vote		
Clinton (D)	108,503	(49%)	Clinton (D)	104,257	(45%)
Dole (R)	88,930	(40%)	Bush (R)	90,375	(39%)
Perot (I)	23,238	(10%)	Perot (I)	36,813	(16%)

Rep. Robert E. Wise, Jr. (D)

Elected 1982; b. Jan. 6, 1948, Washington, D.C.; home, Clendenin; Duke U., B.A. 1970, Tulane U., J.D. 1975; Episcopalian; married (Sandy).

Elected Office: WV Senate, 1980–82.

Professional Career: Practicing atty., 1975–80; Dir., WV for Fair & Equitable Assessment of Taxes, 1977–80.

DC Office: 2367 RHOB 20515, 202-225-2711; Fax: 202-225-7856; Web site: www.house.gov/wise.

District Offices: Charleston, 304-965-0865; Martinsburg, 304-264-8810.

Committees: *Government Reform* (3d of 19 D): National Security, Veterans' Affairs & Intl. Relations. *Transportation & Infrastructure* (5th of 34 D): Economic Development, Public Buildings, Hazardous Materials & Pipeline Transportation (RMM); Ground Transportation.

Group Ratings

	ADA	ACLU	AFS	LCV	CON	NTU	NFIB	COC	ACU	NTLC	CHC
1998	80	73	100	69	55	11	23	33	4	6	8
1997	80	—	88	—	34	20	—	40	17	—	—

National Journal Ratings

	1997 LIB	—	1997 CONS	1998 LIB	—	1998 CONS
Economic	85%	—	10%	79%	—	0%
Social	70%	—	30%	77%	—	22%
Foreign	74%	—	26%	73%	—	26%

Key Votes of the 105th Congress

1. Clinton Budget Deal	N	5. Puerto Rico Sthood. Ref.	Y	9. Cut $ for B-2 Bombers	Y
2. Education IRAs	N	6. End Highway Set-asides	N	10. Human Rights in China	Y
3. Req. 2/3 to Raise Taxes	N	7. School Prayer Amend.	N	11. Withdraw Bosnia Troops	N
4. Fast-track Trade	N	8. Ovrd. Part. Birth Veto	N	12. End Cuban TV-Marti	N

Election Results

1998 general	Robert E. Wise Jr. (D)	99,357	(73%)	($433,816)
	Sally Anne Kay (R)	29,136	(21%)	
	John Brown (Lib)	7,660	(6%)	($5,105)
1998 primary	Robert E. Wise Jr. (D)	52,059	(86%)	
	Beth Taylor (D)	4,539	(8%)	
	Wendel Blair Turner (D)	3,795	(6%)	
1996 general	Robert E. Wise Jr. (D)	141,551	(69%)	($376,555)
	Greg Morris (R)	63,933	(31%)	($49,732)

THIRD DISTRICT

Early in this century, the coalfields of southern West Virginia were one of America's boom areas. Into rural farmland and hollows, inhabited by the same families since they first arrived at these mountains 100 years before, came coal company lawyers with mineral rights' leases to sign, coal company engineers to design and sink the mineshafts, and men from other mountain counties, as well as Europe, to work the mines. Company houses were built, company stores stocked with goods as the company dictated and company paymasters kept close tabs on the finances of every employee. These conditions bred dull discontent, ignited into the fire of industrial unionism by the tongue of John L. Lewis, president of the United Mine Workers, who organized most of the mines in the 1930s. Lewis was not only a militant unionist, but an isolationist, and during and after World War II he called out his coal miners on strikes, to the fury of Franklin Roosevelt and Harry Truman. The entire national war effort and postwar economic recovery seemed gravely threatened by these labor stoppages involving perhaps 300,000 workers, centered in back corners of the country like southern West Virginia.

All that is history now. Coal is no longer central to the U.S. economy and there are only a few thousand coal miners left in southern West Virginia—and many are not UMW members anymore. In 1950, when coal area population peaked, there were 579,000 people in the eight counties that made up the heart of southern West Virginia's coal country. Their population fell to 437,000 in 1970, then spurted up after energy prices were raised by the two oil shocks of the 1970s to 487,000 in 1980, but went down to 421,000 in 1990. Most of the old underground mines have been abandoned, leaving behind mineshafts and piles of tailings—and lives that were snuffed out by cave-ins or simple carelessness in America's deadliest industry.

The 3d Congressional District includes most of the coal country in the southern part of West Virginia, the mountainous counties directly south of Charleston that are among America's most heavily Democratic—and in some cases most politically corrupt—jurisdictions: Mingo County, where in the 1980s a sheriff bought his job for $100,000 and other politicos bought votes for $2 or a half-pint of bourbon. But the coal mining counties are no longer populous enough for a full congressional district and now make up about half the 3d District. About one-quarter is in and around the industrial city of Huntington on the Ohio River, and another quarter is to the east, in the farming uplands around the resort of White Sulphur Springs, where President John Tyler honeymooned in 1844, and the interstate junction at Beckley, which has become a popular whitewater rafting area. These two areas as a whole are much less Democratic than the coal counties.

The congressman here is Nick Joe Rahall, a Democrat first elected in 1976, at 27; he was the youngest member of the 95th Congress. He comes from the thin economic upper crust of the coal country; his family owned radio and TV stations in Beckley and in St. Petersburg, Florida. Rahall has concentrated on bringing public works projects and jobs to his district. He got seats on Transportation and Infrastructure, and Resources early on, and is now high-ranking on both; he is ranking Democrat on the Ground Transportation Subcommittee. He was the chief sponsor in the House of the 1992 law requiring union and non-union coal operators to bail out the United Mine Workers health care funds. He has worked for flood control in the Greenbrier River basin, for $25 million for southern West Virginia water and wastewater systems, a Lower Mud River flood control project in Milton, and the Hatfield-McCoy Trail System. He was a lead House sponsor of a bill establishing a new National Highway System comprised of Interstate Highways, leading arterial roads and other corridors designated by Congress. In West Virginia they include the I-73 Corridor (Route 52 replacement), Route 2, Appalachian Corridors G and L, the Coalfields Expressway and the proposed Shawnee Parkway, all of which became eligible for federal highway trust funds when the bill was signed into law in November 1995. But when local residents opposed making U.S. 219 a four-lane highway, Rahall opposed it too, and he opposed the building of the north-south highway, Continental One. He has sought to improve airport service in West Virginia, using his Avaiation Subcommittee seat on Transportation to host a March 1999 hearing in Huntington.

In May 1998, Rahall criticized West Virginia regulators for improperly permitting mountaintop mining operations. This is a contentious issue in the Mountain State: 61 of the 81 active mountaintop removal mines approved by state regulators since 1978 did not receive variances for flattening the land after mining is complete, according to a 1998 investigation by the Charleston *Gazette*. Rahall helped obtain $21 million in abandoned mine reclamation funds for 1999. He also passed laws creating a National Coal Heritage Area and expanding the boundaries of the New River Gorge National River.

On national issues, Rahall was successful in opposing Cass Ballenger's revisions of the 1969 Coal Mine Health and Safety Act and Barbara Cubin's move to make enforcement of the Surface Mining Control and Reclamation Act a state rather than federal and state responsibility. With Scott Klug, he got the House to vote to continue a moratorium on mining claim patents under the Mining Act of 1872; Western mining interests have prevented repeal of this law, which allows minerals to be mined for $2.50 an acre, but the amendment prevents the law from operating. In a 1995 bill which terminated the Interstate Commerce Commission, Rahall succeeded in retaining rail pricing protections (or captive coal provisions) for coal shippers. In June 1999 he voted to loosen restrictions on gun control regulations.

Rahall has mostly won re-election easily. In 1990, after negative publicity for gambling debts and a drunk driving arrest, he had close calls. His predecessor, then 75-year-old Secretary of State Ken Hechler, won 43% of the vote in the primary; an underfinanced Republican in the general won 48%. But Rahall worked hard on district projects and recovered politically. He is criticized sometimes for taking lavish lobbyist-paid trips, but in 1996 his Republican opponent withdrew for medical reasons and in 1998 no Republican ran.

Cook's Call. *Safe.* For the past 20 years, Rahall has had little trouble holding onto this solidly Democratic district. He is about as safe as an incumbent can be.

The People: Pop. 1990: 597,500; 74.4% rural; 15.5% age 65 + ; 95% White, 4.4% Black, 0.3% Asian, 0.2% Amer. Indian, 0.1% Other; 0.3% Hispanic Origin. Households: 59% married couple families; 29.4% married couple fams. w. children; 25.9% college educ.; median household income: $18,166; per capita income: $9,557; median house value: $41,900; median gross rent: $205.

1996 Presidential Vote			1992 Presidential Vote		
Clinton (D)	111,474	(58%)	Clinton (D)	112,988	(55%)
Dole (R)	61,710	(32%)	Bush (R)	65,468	(32%)
Perot (I)	19,501	(10%)	Perot (I)	26,160	(13%)

Rep. Nick J. Rahall, II (D)

Elected 1976; b. May 20, 1949, Beckley; home, Beckley; Duke U., B.A. 1971; Presbyterian; divorced.

Professional Career: Civil Air Patrol, 1977–88; Staff Asst., U.S. Sen. Robert Byrd, 1971–74; Bd. of Dir., Rahall Communications Corp. 1974–76; Pres., Mountaineer Tour & Travel Agency, 1974–76; Pres., WV Broadcasting Corp. 1980–present.

DC Office: 2307 RHOB 20515, 202-225-3452; Fax: 202-225-9061.

District Offices: Beckley, 304-252-5000; Bluefield, 304-325-6222; Huntington, 304-522-6425; Lewisburg, 304-647-3228; Logan, 304-752-4934.

Committees: *Resources* (2d of 24 D): Energy & Mineral Resources; National Parks & Public Lands. *Transportation & Infrastructure* (2d of 34 D): Aviation; Ground Transportation (RMM).

Group Ratings

	ADA	ACLU	AFS	LCV	CON	NTU	NFIB	COC	ACU	NTLC	CHC
1998	85	60	100	77	55	14	7	28	24	5	33
1997	80	—	100	—	3	16	—	20	21	—	—

National Journal Ratings

	1997 LIB — 1997 CONS			1998 LIB — 1998 CONS		
Economic	93%	—	0%	71%	—	28%
Social	54%	—	45%	55%	—	45%
Foreign	87%	—	12%	64%	—	36%

Key Votes of the 105th Congress

1. Clinton Budget Deal	N	5. Puerto Rico Sthood. Ref.	Y	9. Cut $ for B-2 Bombers	Y
2. Education IRAs	N	6. End Highway Set-asides	N	10. Human Rights in China	Y
3. Req. 2/3 to Raise Taxes	N	7. School Prayer Amend.	Y	11. Withdraw Bosnia Troops	N
4. Fast-track Trade	N	8. Ovrd. Part. Birth Veto	Y	12. End Cuban TV-Marti	Y

Election Results

1998 general	Nick J. Rahall II (D)	78,814	(87%)	($377,311)
	Joe Whelan (Lib)	12,196	(13%)	($22,647)
1998 primary	Nick J. Rahall II (D)	69,434	(82%)	
	James J. MacCallum (D)	15,438	(18%)	
1996 general	Nick J. Rahall II (D)	unopposed		($145,980)

WISCONSIN

Wisconsin, tucked off north of the main east-west routes across the country and squeezed between Lake Michigan and the Mississippi River, was a century ago one of America's premier "laboratories of reform," in Justice Louis Brandeis's phrase—and is still today: a state originating new public policies, seeing how they work, serving as an example for others. Wisconsin's first fame as a laboratory came during the Progressive era that began around 1900, and its primacy was due to an extraordinary governor, Robert LaFollette Sr., and to the state's unique history and German heritage. Wisconsin is the first state of the Old Northwest, that vast stretch of the United States reaching all the way to the Pacific, settled first by New England Yankees but even more by immigrants from Germany and Scandinavia. The German language is seldom heard now, the once plainly German beer brands now seem quintessentially American and few ties remain with the old country after two world wars. But in the late 19th and early 20th Centuries, Germans were among America's most numerous immigrants and until the 1890s probably the most distinct. They established, on the rolling dairyland of Wisconsin and the orderly streets of Milwaukee, their separate religions, often retaining their language and maintaining old customs, from country weddings to drinking beer—a source of friction in temperance-minded America—to eating bratwurst.

Politically, the Germans were not monolithic. Their origins were diverse and they were spread too widely across the nation. But where they were concentrated, there was a distinctive politics, basically American, but with echoes of progressive ideas current in German-speaking countries in Europe. Nowhere was the politics of German-Americans more apparent than in Wisconsin. This is one of the two states that gave birth to the Republican Party in 1854 (the other is Michigan), and Germans, then arriving in America in vast numbers, heavily favored it. They abhorred slavery and welcomed the free lands Republicans advocated in the Homestead Act, the free education promised by setting up land grant colleges, and the transportation routes constructed by subsidizing railroad builders. Then came the Progressive movement of Robert LaFollette, elected governor of Wisconsin in 1900. Up to that time a conventional Republican politician, LaFollette completely revamped the state government before going to the Senate in 1906. At a time when Germany was Europe's leader in graduate education and the application of science to government, LaFollette had professors from the University of Wisconsin, just across town in Madison, help develop the state workmen's compensation system and income tax. The Progressive movement favored rational use of government to improve the lot of the ordinary citizen—an idea borrowed partly from German liberals and adopted by the New Dealers a generation later. All these programs were an attempt to bring bureaucratic rationality—Germanic systematization—to the seemingly disordered America of free markets and multiple cultures, gigantic fortunes and vast open spaces.

LaFollette became a national figure. He tried to run for president in 1912 as a Progressive, but was shoved aside by Theodore Roosevelt. He did run in 1924 on his Progressive ticket and won 18% of the vote, the best third-candidate showing between 1912 and 1992. He was strongest in the northern tier of states from Wisconsin west and along the West Coast—the same area of strength of later liberals George McGovern, Walter Mondale and Michael Dukakis. After LaFollette died in 1925, his sons carried on his tradition, progressive at home and isolationist abroad: Robert LaFollette Jr., for 22 years in the Senate; Philip, elected governor in 1930, 1934 and 1936. Philip created his own Progressive Party in 1934, with ominous overtones: a "Cross in Circle" symbol his critics called a circumcised swastika, huge rally-like parades reminiscent of some in Europe at the time and a call for the governor to propose all legislation. But Philip lost in 1938 and did not run again, and Robert Jr. decided to run for reelection in 1946 as a Republican but lost the primary to Joseph McCarthy. McCarthy's charges that Communists were influencing American foreign policy fed on the inarticulate convictions of many in Wisconsin and elsewhere that the U.S. should have been fighting Russia as well as Germany in World War II.

McCarthy's national prominence made Wisconsin seem like a Republican state. But he won by narrow margins and the LaFollette Progressive tradition was taken up by liberal Democrats like Senators William Proxmire and Gaylord Nelson, and Governor Patrick Lucey. Like most liberals of their era, these progressives saw Washington rather than Madison as the main site of their laboratory of reform. Wisconsin, a mostly Republican state in the mostly Democratic years from 1944–64, became a mostly Democratic state in the mostly Republican years from 1968–88. It was one of the most dovish states, as if many Wisconsin voters were hit by the same impulse that led so many West German voters in the early 1980s to fear the presence of nuclear weapons and to favor disarmament.

In the 1990s Wisconsin moved in another direction, and was a laboratory for different reforms, for which the state's economy provided a favorable environment. Wisconsin's high-skill, precision manufacturing economy—its biggest companies include Allen Bradley, Johnson Controls, Harnischfeger, Briggs & Stratton, Harley-Davidson—jumped into gear in the late 1980s, and led the nation's export boom of the 1990s. The labor force is highly skilled and famously productive, with fewer hours lost to health, weather or strikes than average; unemployment fell to 3.4% in 1998, entry level-wages were $2 over the legal minimum wage, and Wisconsin's major economic problem was a shortage of workers. Population has been rising robustly, particularly in the ring of counties around Milwaukee, around Madison and in the Fox River Valley from Oshkosh to Green Bay, and in the once rural counties within commuting range of greater Minneapolis-St. Paul.

The motivating force for reform in the 1990s has been, as in the early 1900s, a Republican governor, in this case Tommy Thompson, who beat a liberal Democrat in 1986 and has had some of the nation's highest job approval ratings. He has cut taxes, sponsored a school choice program championed by Milwaukee black activist Polly Williams, and passed a series of wel-

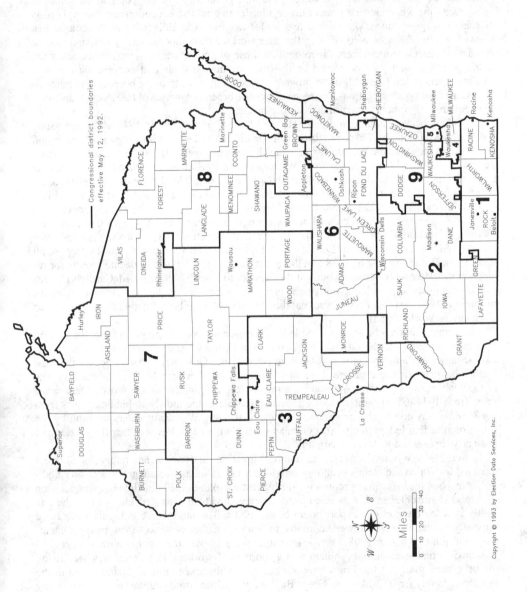

Congressional district boundaries effective May 12, 1992.

Copyright © 1993 by Election Data Services, Inc.

fare reforms—the nation's most thoroughgoing—which since 1987 has cut caseloads by 91%. Thompson also provided yeoman support for Milwaukee's experiment with school vouchers, stifled by state bureaucrats and teachers' unions for several years, but backed by Milwaukee's Democratic Mayor John Norquist. The movement triumphed in 1998 when the Wisconsin Supreme Court ruled that vouchers could go to parochial schools and in 1999 when Milwaukee voters swept anti-voucher members off the school board despite heavy spending by the teachers' unions.

Thompson has not carried all before him. Wisconsin has two Democratic U.S. senators. It voted for Bill Clinton in 1992 and 1996 and its House delegation is 5–4 Democratic. Thompson's Republicans lost control of the state Senate in June 1996, because of a tax increase Thompson supported for a new Milwaukee stadium; but they won their majority back in April 1998 and Thompson remains overwhelmingly popular. Milwaukee Mayor Norquist, a Democrat, echoes some though not all of Thompson's themes. Norquist prides himself on lowering taxes while providing better services, and argues that central cities should see themselves not as hovels full of victims but as shining examples of excellence. Across the nation other governors and leaders of the Republican Congress have looked to learn from Wisconsin's experiments: it's a fair question whether the 1996 federal Welfare Reform Act would have passed without Wisconsin's example to give its backers confidence. Thompson and Wisconsin seem to have decided that the bureaucratic, supposedly rational state that the LaFollettes championed is now dysfunctional, and that individuals making their own choices, in the framework of a fair and orderly society, can achieve more than planners can ever conceive. Milwaukee's last of three Socialist mayors, Frank Zeidler, who served from 1948–60, in 1999 said mournfully, "What you're seeing in Wisconsin is a deconstruction of the progress we made in the first decades of the 20th Century." But most Wisconsin—and perhaps most American—voters apparently see the state's reforms as the construction of progress heading into the 21st.

Governor. Tommy Thompson, Wisconsin's Republican governor, was first elected in 1986. He grew up in Elroy, 85 miles north of Madison, where his father ran a gas station and general store and his mother taught school. For most of his life he has been commuting from Elroy to Madison, first as a student at the University of Wisconsin, where he was a Goldwater Republican on a campus full of liberal Democrats, then to the legislature when he was elected in 1966 just after finishing law school, and since 1986 as governor. For years he was part of the minority party in Madison, assistant minority leader in 1973 and minority leader in 1981; "Dr. No," his liberal critics called him. Now he is the dominant political figure in the state. He has used Wisconsin's extraordinary "partial veto" more than 1,600 times on spending. He can strike not only lines from the budget, but words and numbers, enabling him to cut a program by 90% by dropping one zero. He cut income and capital gains taxes and repealed the gift and inheritance taxes; he funded a property tax cut with spending cuts; he improved the business climate. He boasts that he has cut taxes 87 times and reduced them by more than $8 billion, and says that Wisconsin now has one of the smallest state bureaucracies. And he has kept going: in 1999 he proposed a $300 million income tax cut. He pushed for tough crime bills and an Information Technology Fund which will make government services more efficient and cost effective through expanded technology. He sponsored a Stewardship Fund to spend $250 million over 10 years on buying environmentally sensitive land; he worked to reintroduce elk and wolves to northern Wisconsin and to protect the state's bald eagles. He is an enthusiast for mass transit and rail transportation, and was appointed to the Amtrak Board of Directors by George Bush and Bill Clinton; in 1998 he became chairman.

Thompson is best known, however, for having instituted the nation's most thoroughgoing welfare reform. This was not a single piece of legislation, but an ongoing process in which Thompson sought not only new laws from the legislature but worked to reshuffle agencies and create new incentives for government agencies and employers to change the culture of the caregiving institutions—from one favoring continual dependence to one favoring work and independence. Thompson started with "learnfare" in 1987, tying grants to children's school attendance; then "bridefare" in 1992, with incentives for marriage and against more children; "work not welfare" in 1995, requiring work and scouting for jobs for recipients. His "Wisconsin Works," (known as W-2) ending welfare grants altogether and requiring recipients to either work or perform community service, went into effect in stages around the state in 1997 and 1998, with government agencies and nonprofits bidding for the chance to run county or Milwaukee-area programs, and welfare rolls plunged down from 100,000 families a decade ago to 9,000. This is not necessarily a cheap program; W-2 provides generous child care for new workers, provides job skills counseling, and has created public sector jobs—at lower than private-sector wages—to employ every former recipient. Initial results suggest that 80% have found jobs, most at or above the minimum wage.

Thompson has strongly supported Milwaukee's school voucher program and has pushed through statewide charter schools. He started a youth apprenticeship program, based on a German model, in 1992, and has put together School-to-Work programs. In 1999 he proposed a Family Care program, with options for seniors and the disabled.

The secrets of Thompson's success have been hard work, good political instincts and a common touch. He refers constantly to his home town of Elroy, and refers to the rest of the state as "greater metropolitan Elroy." "Let's face it," he likes to say, "It's hard to be humble when you're from Wisconsin." He has had some disappointments: he lost the primary for a vacant congressional seat to Tom Petri in 1979, and he has not always been taken as seriously at the national level as he thinks he deserves. He has been mentioned as a presidential candidate, and has a record that would entitle him to serious attention; but in March 1999 he concluded that he had little chance and said he would not run, instead endorsing George W. Bush.

Thompson was first elected governor with 53% of the vote; he was re-elected with 58% in 1990 and 67% in 1994. He said in 1994 he would not run again, then changed his mind, saying many of his initiatives needed more work. In 1998 there was talk that Senator Herb Kohl would run for governor, but in January 1998 he took himself out of the race. The Democratic nominee was Ed Garvey, once head of the National Football League Players' Association and a Senate candidate in 1986 (he lost to Republican Bob Kasten 51%–47%) and 1988 (he finished third in the primary). Garvey promised to accept no contribution over $100; Thompson outspent him by about 8–1, and won 60%–39%, carrying all but four counties: two in the far north, one an Indian reservation and the other the county containing Madison. He has said he will not run for another term as governor. But he could run for senator some day, or serve in a Republican Cabinet in Washington, or perhaps as vice president.

Senior Senator. Herb Kohl, a Democrat first elected in 1988, is one of the richest members of Congress, and one of the least flamboyant, a mild-mannered but persistent and successful politician. His parents immigrated to Milwaukee from Russia and Poland in the 1920s and opened a food store. Kohl's ultimately became a Wisconsin supermarket chain and was sold in 1979, for great profit; Kohl's fortune has been estimated at $250 million. In 1985 he became a local celebrity, in a city smarting from sports franchises with lousy records and eager to move elsewhere, when he bought the Milwaukee Bucks basketball team to keep it from moving out of the city. When Senator William Proxmire retired in 1988, Kohl decided to run. He spent his own money liberally, running an extensive ad campaign with the theme, "Nobody's senator but yours." He won 47% in the primary to 38% for former Governor Tony Earl. In the general, against moderate Republican Susan Engeleiter, Kohl stressed his support of defense cuts—popular in dovish Wisconsin—and for requiring businesses to provide medical insurance; Engeleiter stressed her environmental stands, her legislative experience and her status as a wife and mother—in contrast to Kohl, a bachelor. This turned out to be one of the closest Senate races in the country, with Kohl winning 52%–48% after spending $7 million of his own money.

Kohl is a pleasant, shy, almost painfully earnest man, of transparent good will and seemingly little guile. He has a liberal record on cultural and foreign issues and is more moderate on economics; he dislikes the clash of partisan fighting. He favors the balanced budget amendment and voted for the Chafee-Breaux bipartisan budget in May 1996. He exerted great leverage when Democrats had a narrow majority in 1993 by insisting on paying for the Clinton stimulus package with spending cuts and by refusing to support a gas tax increase over 4.3 cents. He opposed the Supercollider, the space station, and Trident II missiles, and has tried to keep defense spending increases down to Clinton budget levels. In 1994, prompted by Governor Tommy Thompson's welfare reforms, he sponsored a welfare-to-work bill, one of the predecessors of 1996's welfare reform. He has sponsored a tax credit for businesses and institutions that build child care facilities at or near worksites and has supported child care tax credits.

Kohl has been active on crime and gun issues. He was a sponsor of the Brady bill, and wrote the 1990 law banning guns in schools; when that was overturned by the Supreme Court in 1995 (on the ground it had nothing to do with interstate commerce), he wrote another bill prohibiting guns within 1,000 feet of schools; it passed in 1996. He has sponsored an amendment to require child safety locks on guns; it was rejected 61–39 in July 1998, but after the Littleton, Colorado, massacre it passed 78–20 in May 1999. He voted against the partial-birth abortion ban in May 1997, which led to a statewide recall effort, sponsored by a Milwaukee-based organization called First Breath Alliance, that fell just 50,000 signatures short. In response to a 1997 Milwaukee *Journal Sentinel* series, he sponsored in September 1998 a bill to require criminal background checks of health care workers and to maintain a national registry of workers guilty of abuse. In 1998 he called for a bipartisan campaign finance commission, modeled on the base-closing commission, to present Congress with a reform bill that would have to be voted on in toto.

Kohl also supports Wisconsin causes. As a subcommittee chairman, he stood stoutly against adjustment of the 1990 Census figures—a worthy stand against a measure that, as it happens, would have cost Wisconsin a congressional seat. He has worked on Great Lakes issues, from farm commodity shipping to the zebra mussel. On the 1996 Freedom to Farm Act, he got the Senate to vote 50–46 against the Northeast Dairy Compact, intended to cartelize New England dairy markets; but it was slipped in during conference and passed. In July 1998 he and Russ Feingold moved to block a six-month extension of the Compact to October 1999, in hope of reaching a more market-oriented system sooner. In July 1998 he moved to give Milwaukee Mayor John Norquist and Milwaukee County Executive Thomas Ament control of some $241 million in transportation funds; Governor Tommy Thompson, who opposes their light rail projects and wants to spend money on the Marquette Interchange instead, objected, as did 6th District Congressman Thomas Petri, number two Republican on the House Transportation Committee. Kohl personally funds the Herb Kohl Educational Foundation, which has given $1.8 million in scholarships and grants to Wisconsin students, teachers and schools, and he has donated $25 million to the University of Wisconsin for the Kohl Center sports complex, opened in early 1998.

In his 1994 re-election campaign, Kohl stressed his work against spending and crime and also his own sincere, unprepossessing demeanor. He was able to get his message across: with far less press criticism than in 1988, he spent $6.5 million of his own money on the campaign (far more per voter, incidentally, than the much-ridiculed Michael Huffington was spending in California). His Republican opponent, Robert Welch, a land surveyor and a young conservative firebrand in the state legislature, raised many of the issues Republicans were winning on elsewhere, but did not have the funds to get much attention. Meanwhile, Kohl joked with voters by asking them to contribute to meet basketball player Glenn Robinson's demands for the Bucks to give him a $100 million contract. Kohl won 58%–41%.

Kohl's job approval has continued to be high and he ran far better in polls against Governor Tommy Thompson than any other Democrat (trailing 48%–40% in one), but in January 1998 he said he would not run for governor. In October 1998 state Republicans ran an ad calling Kohl "our moderate senator" in contrast to Russ Feingold, with his allegedly "weird liberal theories." In response Kohl cut a spot for Feingold. Kohl was spared opposition from Mark Neumann, who lost 50%–48% to Feingold in 1998. In 1994 Neumann had asked both senators to nominate his son for the Air Force Academy; Feingold declined, but Kohl agreed to do so, and Neumann said he would never run against him. Possible Republican opponents include 1994 nominee Robert Welch and Waukesha County Executive Dan Finley. Kohl brings two great advantages to the 2000 contest, his money and his unassuming personality; as state Democratic Chairwoman Terri Spring says, "People go beyond the party label with Herb, they feel this personal connection with him. He's just so unassuming, he's retained that no matter how successful he is in business. He's always been just a nice guy, and he doesn't travel with an entourage."

Cook's Call. *Safe.* Kohl's personal wealth and willingness to spend it intimidates most first-tier challengers, and his 2000 re-election bid will be no different. Former Representative Mark Neumann said he wouldn't take a shot at Kohl's seat, and Republicans do not have any hot prospects waiting in the wings.

Junior Senator. Russ Feingold is a Democrat first elected in 1992. He was raised in Janesville, and said he wanted to be a senator while growing up there. He nurtured his ambition at the University of Wisconsin, as a Rhodes Scholar, and at Harvard Law School; he moved to Middleton, a not-so-academic suburb of Madison, and beat an incumbent state senator in 1982, at 29. Feingold has a flair for publicity, and for political reform issues and novel arguments. His great goal in the legislature was to ban bovine growth hormone, a luddite measure aimed at keeping in business Wisconsin's numerous and long-subsidized dairy farmers, whose chief problem is that Americans drink less milk today than in the 1950s. Feingold also opposed Governor Tommy Thompson's welfare reforms and tax cuts and opposed capital punishment. Feingold's goal for 1992 was the Senate seat held by Bob Kasten, a free-market conservative who pushed tort reform and capital gains tax cuts, and had won by narrow margins in 1980 and 1986. In the Democratic primary, while Milwaukee businessman Joseph Checota and Congressman Jim Moody battered each other with negative ads, Feingold ran clever, humorous spots: one showing Elvis, alive and endorsing Feingold; another showing Feingold at home, opening up a closet and saying, "No skeletons." He also had detailed position papers, including an 82-point plan for reducing the deficit. Near primary day, Checota apologized for his ads and asked voters to vote for Feingold if they didn't vote for him. Feingold, already ahead in polls, zoomed to an astonishing 70% win in this three-way primary. Feingold also bounced way ahead of Kasten, who ran his own Elvis ads attacking Feingold on issues; Feingold attacked Kasten's negativity and avoided engaging on specifics. The race narrowed, but Feingold won 53%–46%.

In the Senate, Feingold built a very liberal record on cultural and foreign issues, more moderate on economics. He attacked spending virtually wherever he could find it: the Pentagon's medical school, helium subsidies and the Supercollider; he moved to eliminate the Extremely Low Frequency radio system—"a Cold War relic" in his words—embedded in northern Wisconsin. He has opposed the F/A-18E/F Super Hornet fighter-bomber, arguing that the F/A-18C/D Hornet is superior in some respects and that any improvements are not worth the doubled cost; his amendments to require the Pentagon to eliminate either the Super Hornet, the F-22 Raptor stealth plane or the Joint Strike Fighter were beaten by 4–1 margins. He worked against the CVN-76 aircraft carrier, Western water subsidies, TVA overheads and tax breaks for asbestos, lead, mercury and uranium mining. He was one of the crusaders against lobbyists' gifts to lawmakers.

Feingold's most widely publicized reform has been the McCain-Feingold campaign finance bill, which would (in its most recent forms) ban soft money, regulate issue advertising and increase disclosure requirements. The measure was filibustered to death in July 1996 and again in February 1998; House Republican leaders agreed under pressure to bring up the House version (Shays-Meehan), and it passed 252–179 in August 1998. But Feingold's efforts to end a filibuster failed again in September 1998. Despite near-fanatical support on news pages as well as editorial pages in *The New York Times*, McCain-Feingold has never been able to come up with more than 52 or 53 votes in the Senate, far short of the 60 required to shut off debate; but Feingold promises to keep on trying. In April 1999, Feingold and McCain received the John F. Kennedy Profile in Courage Award for their effort; a month later Feingold announced he would publicly read the "bankroll" of special interests' contributions as related bills come to the floor until Congress passes his reform measure.

Feingold has taken original and interesting positions on many issues. He voted against the 1996 anti-terrorism bill because it included the death penalty. He voted against the 1997 budget agreement because it included tax cuts. He sponsored a bill to prevent surpluses in Social Security from counting toward the overall budget surplus. With Orrin Hatch he sponsored a measure that passed in June 1997 that punishes crimes of sexual abuse and exploitation of children over the Internet. He opposed interim storage of nuclear waste in February 1998, arguing it should be moved only once. He called for special duty pay for National Guard and Reserves personnel called to active duty. In March 1999 he was one of three Democratic senators to vote against air strikes in Serbia and Kosovo. He opposed the Communications Decency Act and with Michigan's Spencer Abraham opposed the cumbersome worker verification provisions of the immigration bill. He wants to prohibit members of Congress from using for personal gain frequent flyer miles earned on business trips and to establish a long-term health care program like Wisconsin's Community Options. Feingold has not always gone along lockstep with other Democrats in responding to the Clinton scandals. In Febuary 1997 he called for an independent counsel on the Clinton-Gore fundraising operations. In January 1999 he was the only Democrat to vote against Robert Byrd's motion to dismiss the charges against Clinton. "I simply cannot say that the House managers cannot prevail," he said. He voted against removal in February. In March 1999 he called for changes in Senate procedures on impeachment, including a ban on party caucuses while a case is pending.

Feingold promised in 1992 to hold listening sessions in every county every year. He proceeded to do so, speaking for five minutes and then taking all questions, for 432 sessions in his first term. He attacked the national milk-marketing system as anti-Midwest and opposed the Northeast Dairy Compact, though it got through on conference committee; he has beaten attempts to extend its life. Feingold has opposed what he calls merger mania in the dairy industry. He has pushed amendments to base Medicare home health payments on the national average rather than on regional cost variations (orderly Wisconsin is penalized for its efficiency, he says) and to create an Office of the Small Farms Advocate in the Department of Agriculture.

Going into the 1998 campaign cycle, Feingold's poll ratings were good but not overwhelming. Congressman Mark Neumann announced for the seat in October 1997. They had similar records in some ways. Neumann proposed to reserve all the budget surplus for paying down the national debt and retain money for Social Security—similar though not identical to Feingold's views—and touted his independence by saying he had been thrown off an Appropriations subcommittee for voting against the leadership. But they differed sharply on others. Neumann urged Feingold to vote for the partial-birth abortion ban in May 1997, to no avail, which led Neumann to encourage a recall effort, sponsored by the Milwaukee-based First Breath Alliance, that failed by just 50,000 signatures. After some negotiation, Feingold and Neumann agreed to limit their campaign spending, Feingold to $3.8 million, Neumann to $4.7 million (he actually spent $4.4 million), and to limit PAC money to 10% of donations and out-of-state contributions to 25% and to impose a $2,000 limit on candidate contributions (less of a limit on Feingold, who has one of the lowest net worths in the Senate, than on Neumann, a self-made homebuilder millionaire, who spent $700,000 of his own money on a losing race in 1992). Feingold sought to limit himself to what his campaign finance bill would allow—an idealistic move in that it reduced his chances at a time when his poll numbers did not top the 50% level, but also with a view toward framing the issues his way; as he said in October 1998, "The issue is my issue now. We're on my playing field. Is Wisconsin going to become another state where money rules?"

The National Republican Senatorial Committee, headed by Mitch McConnell, who led the fight against Feingold's campaign finance bill, spent heavily on this race, running anti-Feingold ads. But when the Democratic Senate Campaign Committee starting running anti-Neumann ads, Feingold said, "Get the hell out of my state with those things"; the ads continued until the buy was finished. But Neumann argued that Feingold's stand was hypocritical, since the Sierra Club, League of Conservation Voters and AFL-CIO all spent heavily on ads against Neumann. Republican attacks dominated the TV screens in August and into September; Feingold's leads of 10% or so melted away and the race became pretty much even in the polls. Feingold started out with positive ads: "Promises made, promises kept," they proclaimed, showing his van on his journeys to the state's 72 counties. But he also ran negative spots on Neumann's stands on HMOs and Social Security. Neumann traveled around the state with an overhead slide projector explaining his positions on Social Security and paying down the national debt; he stressed that both Bill Clinton and Newt Gingrich opposed his stands. He ran humorous ads attacking Feingold for sending dollars to Russia to study monkeys in space and for voting for a study of cow flatulence (the ad showed smock-clad scientists out in a field trying to isolate samples of cow gas). He was one of the few Republicans in 1998 to run an ad on partial-birth abortion: "In a ninth-month partial-birth abortion, the baby is delivered feet first, up to the head. The delivery is halted. And the young child's life is ended. Senator Feingold voted to keep partial-birth abortions legal. You see, it's not about Republicans or Democrats—it's about doing what's right for America." Although Eastern media scoffed at these, the VNS exit poll showed that of the 20% of voters who voted on abortion, 82% voted for Neumann—an even larger percentage than on taxes.

This was one of the nation's closest Senate races. Feingold won 50%–48%. This was not a big-city victory: metro Milwaukee voted for Feingold by only 50%–49%. His biggest margin came in Madison's Dane County, and he carried and ran ahead of Democratic norms in most counties in the Madison media market and along the Mississippi River as well as in the Democratic Lake Superior counties. Neumann ran only about even in his own 1st District, but ran well ahead in the prosperous Fox River Valley and the Lake Michigan counties. There was little difference along lines of income; Feingold carried those without high school diplomas and with graduate degrees by solid margins; there was very little gender gap.

Presidential politics. For all the distinctiveness of its history, Wisconsin has come pretty close to voting the national average for president in the last two elections, a little light for Bill Clinton in 1992 and a little light for Bob Dole in 1996. It has been seriously contested in five of the last six elections, and may well be again. There are not huge regional differences in Wisconsin. Dole, who never targeted Wisconsin, carried only one of the state's nine congressional districts, and Clinton carried only two with more than 50%; the other six voted pretty much all alike.

Wisconsin once had one of the nation's most influential presidential primaries. It knocked Wendell Willkie out of the race in 1944, helped John Kennedy establish his lead over Hubert Humphrey in 1960, and prompted Lyndon Johnson to withdraw as Eugene McCarthy was about to beat him here in 1968. But now Wisconsin's primary, even moved from April to March, tends to get lost. The national Democrats, incidentally, have allowed Wisconsin to continue its open primary (that is, there is no party registration), one of Bob LaFollette's reforms.

Congressional districting. Wisconsin did not lose a congressional district in the 1990 Census, and its population grew evenly enough that no major changes were needed in the current district lines to meet the equal-population standard. The legislature's plan shifted a few dozen townships between districts. It is possible that Wisconsin will lose a district after the 2000 Census, and Republicans could try to eliminate one of the Democratic seats if they hold onto their legislative majorities in 2000.

The People: Est. Pop. 1998: 5,223,500; Pop. 1990: 4,891,769, up 6.8% 1990–1998. 1.9% of U.S. total, 18th largest; 34.3% rural. Median age: 35.1 years. 13.9% 65 years and over. 92.3% White, 5% Black, 1.1% Asian, 0.8% Amer. Indian, 0.8% Other; 1.8% Hispanic Origin. Households: 57.5% married couple families; 27.7% married couple fams. w. children; 41.5% college educ.; median household income: $29,442; per capita income: $13,276; 66.7% owner occupied housing; median house value: $62,500; median monthly rent: $331. 3.4% Unemployment. 1998 Voting age pop.: 3,877,000. 1998 Turnout: 1,760,836; 45% of VAP. No state voter registration.

Political Lineup: Governor, Tommy G. Thompson (R); Lt. Gov., Scott McCallum (R); Secy. of State, Douglas LaFollette (D); Atty. Gen., James E. Doyle (D); Treasurer, Jack C. Voight (R); State Senate, 33 (17 D, 16 R); Majority Leader, Chuck Chvala (D); State Assembly, 99 (45 D and 54 R); Assembly Speaker, Scott Jensen (R). Senators, Herb Kohl (D) and Russell Feingold (D). Representatives, 9 (5 D, 4 R).

Elections Division: 608-266-8005; **Filing Deadline for U.S. Congress:** July 11, 2000.

1996 Presidential Vote

Clinton (D)	1,071,970	(49%)
Dole (R)	845,028	(38%)
Perot (I)	227,310	(10%)
Others	51,881	(2%)

1992 Presidential Vote

Clinton (D)	1,041,066	(41%)
Bush (R)	930,855	(37%)
Perot (I)	544,479	(22%)

1996 Republican Presidential Primary

Dole (R)	301,628	(53%)
Buchanan (R)	194,733	(34%)
Forbes (R)	32,205	(6%)
Others	45,203	(8%)

GOVERNOR

Gov. Tommy G. Thompson (R)

Elected 1986, term expires Jan. 2003; b. Nov. 19, 1941, Elroy; home, Elroy; U. of WI, B.A. 1963, J.D. 1966; Catholic; married (Sue Ann).

Elected Office: WI Assembly, 1966–86, Asst. Minority Ldr., 1973–81, Floor Ldr., 1981–86.

Professional Career: Practicing atty, 1966-present; Chmn., Repub. Govs. Assn., 1991–92; Chmn., Natl. Govs. Assn., 1995–96.

Office: State Capitol, 115 E. State Capitol, Madison, 53707, 608-266-1212; Web site: www.state.wi.us.

Election Results

1998 gen.	Tommy G.Thompson (R)	1,047,716	(60%)
	Ed Garvey (D)	679,553	(39%)
	Others	28,745	(2%)
1998 prim.	Tommy G. Thompson (R)	229,916	(83%)
	Jeffrey A. Hyslop (R)	45,252	(16%)
1994 gen.	Tommy G. Thompson (R)	1,051,326	(67%)
	Chuck Chvala (D)	482,850	(31%)
	Others	29,659	(2%)

SENATORS

Sen. Herb Kohl (D)

Elected 1988, seat up 2000; b. Feb. 7, 1935, Milwaukee; home, Milwaukee; U. of WI, B.A. 1956, Harvard U., M.B.A. 1958; Jewish; single.

Military Career: Army Reserves, 1958–64.

Professional Career: Businessman; Pres., Kohl Corp., 1970–79; Chmn., WI Dem. Party, 1975–77; Pres., Herbert Kohl Investments, 1979–88; Owner, Milwaukee Bucks pro basketball team, 1985–present.

DC Office: 330 HSOB, 20510, 202-224-5653; Fax: 202-224-9787; Web site: www.senate.gov/~kohl.

State Offices: Appleton, 920-738-1640; Eau Claire, 715-832-8424; Madison, 608-264-5338; Milwaukee, 414-297-4451.

Committees: *Aging (Special)* (3d of 9 D). *Appropriations* (9th of 13 D): Agriculture & Rural Development (RMM); Energy & Water Development; Interior; Labor & HHS; Transportation. *Judiciary* (4th of 8 D): Antitrust, Business Rights & Competition (RMM); Technology, Terrorism & Government Information; Youth Violence.

Group Ratings

	ADA	ACLU	AFS	LCV	CON	NTU	NFIB	COC	ACU	NTLC	CHC
1998	85	86	89	100	94	28	44	44	4	21	18
1997	70	—	44	—	99	56	—	80	20	—	—

National Journal Ratings

	1997 LIB — 1997 CONS		1998 LIB — 1998 CONS	
Economic	57%	— 40%	58%	— 41%
Social	64%	— 29%	74%	— 0%
Foreign	68%	— 27%	91%	— 5%

Key Votes of the 105th Congress

1. Bal. Budget Amend.	Y	5. Satcher for Surgeon Gen.	Y	9. Chem. Weapons Treaty	Y
2. Clinton Budget Deal	Y	6. Highway Set-asides	Y	10. Cuban Humanitarian Aid	N
3. Cloture on Tobacco	Y	7. Table Child Gun locks	N	11. Table Bosnia Troops	Y
4. Education IRAs	Y	8. Ovrd. Part. Birth Veto	N	12. $ for Test-ban Treaty	Y

Election Results

1994 general	Herb Kohl (D)	912,662	(58%)	($8,249,531)
	Robert T. Welch (R)	636,989	(41%)	($1,180,382)
1994 primary	Herb Kohl (D)	135,982	(90%)	
	Edmond Galileo Hou-Seye (D)	15,579	(10%)	
1988 general	Herb Kohl (D)	1,128,625	(52%)	($7,491,600)
	Susan Engeleiter (R)	1,030,440	(48%)	($2,853,842)

Sen. Russell Feingold (D)

Elected 1992, seat up 2004; b. Mar. 2, 1953, Janesville; home, Middleton; U. of WI, B.A. 1975, Rhodes Scholar, Oxford U., 1977, Harvard Law Schl., J.D. 1979; Jewish; married (Mary).

Elected Office: WI Senate, 1982–92.

Professional Career: Practicing atty., 1979–83; Prof., Beloit Col., 1985–93.

DC Office: 716 HSOB, 20510, 202-224-5323; Fax: 202-224-2725; Web site: www.senate.gov/~feingold.

State Offices: Green Bay, 920-465-7508; LaCrosse, 608-782-5585; Middleton, 608-828-1200; Milwaukee, 414-276-7282; Wausau, 715-848-5660.

Committees: *Aging (Special)* (4th of 9 D). *Budget* (8th of 10 D). *Foreign Relations* (5th of 8 D): African Affairs (RMM); East Asian & Pacific Affairs; International Operations. *Judiciary* (6th of 8 D): Administrative Oversight & the Courts; The Constitution, Federalism & Property Rights (RMM).

Group Ratings

	ADA	ACLU	AFS	LCV	CON	NTU	NFIB	COC	ACU	NTLC	CHC
1998	90	86	100	100	99	35	22	28	12	11	9
1997	95	—	78	—	85	30	—	20	8	—	—

National Journal Ratings

	1997 LIB	—	1997 CONS	1998 LIB	—	1998 CONS
Economic	82%	—	12%	61%	—	36%
Social	71%	—	0%	74%	—	0%
Foreign	92%	—	0%	73%	—	21%

Key Votes of the 105th Congress

1. Bal. Budget Amend.	N	5. Satcher for Surgeon Gen.	Y	9. Chem. Weapons Treaty	Y
2. Clinton Budget Deal	Y	6. Highway Set-asides	Y	10. Cuban Humanitarian Aid	Y
3. Cloture on Tobacco	Y	7. Table Child Gun locks	Y	11. Table Bosnia Troops	N
4. Education IRAs	N	8. Ovrd. Part. Birth Veto	N	12. $ for Test-ban Treaty	Y

Election Results

1998 general	Russell Feingold (D)	890,059	(51%)	($3,846,089)
	Mark W. Neumann (R)	852,272	(48%)	($4,373,953)
1998 primary	Russell Feingold (D)	unopposed		
1992 general	Russell Feingold (D)	1,290,662	(53%)	($2,056,079)
	Robert W. Kasten Jr. (R)	1,129,599	(46%)	($5,427,163)

FIRST DISTRICT

Rolling dairy country, blanketed by snow during most of the winter, gloriously green under sunny blue skies in summer, the southern tier of Wisconsin from Lake Michigan inland to the Rock River Valley, is some of America's prime industrial country. Settled by Yankee and German farmers 150 years ago, it was once primarily dairyland. By the early 20th Century, the steady habits and high skills of the local dairy farmers provided a good labor pool for factories. Today there are still major plants here: the operations center for Johnson Wax (and its Frank Lloyd Wright-designed tower and Wingspread Center) in Racine, and the Parker Pen operation in Janesville. In between are lake resorts, most notably Lake Geneva, a favorite of wealthy

Chicagoans. To the untrained eye, this part of southern Wisconsin looks much the same as nearby northern Illinois; but politically there is a vast difference. The dotted line on the map is the boundary between the corruption-prone machine politics of Illinois and squeaky-clean progressive politics of Wisconsin.

This is the land of the 1st District, from Lake Michigan west to the Rock River and beyond, a politically marginal area in Wisconsin politics and a marginal district in congressional politics from 1958–70 and then again since 1993. In between, it was the district represented by the late Les Aspin, chairman of the House Armed Services Committee from 1985–93 and secretary of Defense from 1993–94.

The congressman from the 1st District is Paul Ryan, a Republican elected in 1998. He grew up in Janesville, in Rock County, where in 1884 his great-grandfather started a family construction firm now run by his cousins. Ryan got started in politics early, as a staffer for Senator Bob Kasten during college; then he worked as a speechwriter for Jack Kemp and William Bennett at Empower America and was legislative director to Kansas Senator Sam Brownback. Ryan returned to the 1st District in anticipation of the Senate candidacy of Congressman Mark Neumann, a homebuilder who lost to Aspin in 1992 and to Democrat Peter Barca in May 1993 and then beat Barca 49.4%–48.8% in 1994 and Kenosha Council President Lydia Spottswood 51%–49% in 1996. Neumann was one of the most obstreperous of the 1994 Republican freshmen; he was thrown off an Appropriations subcommittee by Bob Livingston and Newt Gingrich, and undercut Republican tax cuts by arguing that any budget surplus should be used to pay down the national debt. Ryan's first test was to dispose of Republican primary opponents. One was state Senator George Petak, the only Wisconsin legislator to be recalled by voters, in June 1995, for voting for a tax increase for a new Milwaukee stadium; Ryan made it known he would make an issue of that, and Petak withdrew in March 1998. A month later beer distributor Brian Morello also withdrew. Ryan won 81% against an unknown in the September 1998 primary.

The Democratic primary was more closely contested. Spottswood was running again, and was expected to win easily. Her overall margin of 66%–34% was impressive, but in her home county, Kenosha, usually the most Democratic part of the district, she won by only 53%–47% over an unknown. One old controversy revolved around her vote in 1990 for a Kenosha redevelopment project that boosted the value of an apartment partly owned by her husband, a successful physician. Another revolved around her vote to put on the ballot in 1994 a ban on handguns; her statements on the issue at the time were ambiguous, but she did say that as a nurse she had seen the devastating results of handgun violence, and many regarded her as an advocate of handgun bans; this didn't fly in a city where the General Motors factory closes on the opening day of deer-hunting season.

Against this candidate with weaknesses greater than her 1996 showing suggested, Ryan campaigned on the kind of overall theme that House Republican leaders in 1998 failed to provide. He called it his "Paycheck Protection Plan": he was for local control, against tax increases, in favor of gun ownership rights. He finessed the Social Security issue: "From day one, my Paycheck Protection Plan has advocated using Social Security surpluses to save Social Security and preserve the trust fund. I will not support any tax cuts unless they are paid for with cuts in government spending or non-Social Security surpluses, should they ever materialize." Spottswood in September dared him to sign a pledge to use the budget surplus to guarantee the solvency of Social Security; he said her pledge was too vague, and that he was going farther, even if it meant opposing House Republican leaders. He seized on her statement that she would consider removing the cap on the Social Security payroll tax, and accused her in ads, recalling her support of tax increases in Kenosha, of wanting to increase taxes by "a trillion dollars." Ryan also called for the Ed-Flex bill that would lift federal restrictions on how education funds could be spent at the local level. A Spottswood ad accused him of wanting to cut funding for computers in classrooms, after-school learning programs and school-to-work programs—the kind of mini-initiatives the Clinton Administration is so fond of. He said he would cut nothing, but leave local school officials with the same amount of money, to be spent as they wished.

The candidates' personal backgrounds came into play. Spottswood campaigned on her "life experiences" as a nurse, a mother and a local official; at one appearance she said she was old enough to be Ryan's mother (a teenage mother, actually; she was 18 when he was born). Ryan, at age 28, proclaimed that he was old enough. "My five o'clock shadow shows up every day at four," he said, even while running ads about the five generations of Ryans in southern Wisconsin. They also argued about partial-birth abortion, an issue Neumann ran ads on in his race against Senator Russ Feingold. In September 1998 Spottwood said she opposed partial-birth abortion except when the mother's life was threatened or the child had an abnormality incompatible with life. Ryan accused her of an "election-year conversion"; she said she was following the change of position made by the state Medical Society.

This was a strenuously and expensively contested election, one of the Democrats' top 10 priorities in the nation. Spottswood spent $1.28 million, Ryan $1.19 million. But the final result was not that close. Ryan won 58%–42%, carrying Kenosha County by that margin and Racine County by just one point less. Curiously his weakest area was his home county of Rock, which he carried 52%–48%; he carried heavily Republican Walworth County 67%–33%. That made him the second youngest congressman, after Harold Ford Jr. of the Tennessee 9th District. This could easily be a seriously contested district in 2000, although Ryan's strong showing might prove daunting to local Democrats. His high percentage, and his success at defining issues and setting an overall conceptual framework, suggests he might, if he holds the district, be a strong statewide candidate some day.

Cook's Call. *Potentially Competitive.* Ryan's huge win here in 1998 belies this district's marginal status. But Ryan, who showed great political savvy and fundraising skills in his 1998 win, has avoided political trouble thus far. Barring any self-inflicted political wounds, he will be tough to beat in 2000.

The People: Pop. 1990: 543,380; 28.6% rural; 13% age 65 + ; 92% White, 5.4% Black, 0.7% Asian, 0.3% Amer. Indian, 1.6% Other; 3.3% Hispanic Origin. Households: 58.5% married couple families; 28.3% married couple fams. w. children; 39.1% college educ.; median household income: $31,431; per capita income: $13,567; median house value: $61,700; median gross rent: $327.

1996 Presidential Vote

Clinton (D)	117,308	(50%)
Dole (R)	88,599	(38%)
Perot (I)	25,957	(11%)
Others	4,353	(2%)

1992 Presidential Vote

Clinton (D)	109,790	(41%)
Bush (R)	94,712	(35%)
Perot (I)	62,465	(23%)

Rep. Paul Ryan (R)

Elected 1998; b. Jan. 29, 1970, Janesville; home, Janesville; Miami U. of OH, B.A., 1992; Catholic; single.

Professional Career: Aide, U.S. Sen. Bob Kasten, 1992; Advisor & speechwriter, Empower America, 1993–95; Legis. Dir., U.S. Sen. Sam Brownback, 1995–97; Mktg. consultant., Ryan Inc. Central, 1997–98.

DC Office: 1217 LHOB 20515, 202-225-3031; Fax: 202-225-3393; Web site: www.house.gov/ryan.

District Offices: Janesville, 608-752-4050; Kenosha, 414-654-1901; Racine, 414-637-0510.

Committees: *Banking & Financial Services* (26th of 32 R): Capital Markets, Securities & Government Sponsored Enterprises; Domestic & International Monetary Policy. *Budget* (23d of 24 R). *Government Reform* (22d of 24 R): Census; Government Management, Information & Technology; National Economic Growth, Natural Resources & Regulatory Affairs (Vice Chmn.). *Joint Economic Committee* (6th of 10 Reps.).

Group Ratings and Key Votes: Newly Elected

Election Results

1998 general	Paul Ryan (R)	....	108,475 (57%)	($1,245,568)
	Lydia Spottswood (D)	....	81,164 (43%)	($1,339,361)
1998 primary	Paul Ryan (R)	....	15,858 (81%)	
	Michael J. Logan (R)	....	3,784 (19%)	
1996 general	Mark W. Neumann (R)	....	118,408 (51%)	($1,211,134)
	Lydia Spottswood (D)	....	114,148 (49%)	($708,825)

SECOND DISTRICT

On a narrow isthmus between Lakes Mendota and Monona is the center of Madison and, in many ways, the center of Wisconsin. Here the state Capitol rises at the one end of State Street; at the other end of several commercial blocks is the main campus of the University of Wisconsin, on a beautiful, parklike, sometimes windswept setting above Lake Mendota. For most of this century, Wisconsin politics was dominated by the Madison-based LaFollettes and their liberal Democratic successors. And the traffic on State Street was two-way, with university faculty devoted to Bob LaFollette's "Wisconsin idea" of an apolitical bureaucracy, his Wisconsin Tax Commission and workmen's compensation law—both firsts in the nation. Now there is more division, with the liberal campus at odds with the welfare and school choice reforms of Governor Tommy Thompson. But there is a steady debate carried on here between the liberal Madison *Capital-Times* and its conservative rival, the *Wisconsin State Journal*, with a much larger circulation; the two newspapers practice the kind of partisan journalism still seen in only a few major cities and state capitals (Detroit, Boston, Sacramento). Meanwhile, Madison's varied economy is thriving, with unemployment in January 1999 at about 1.4%, but down to as low as 1.2% in recent years.

Madison is the center of Wisconsin's 2d Congressional District and, with surrounding Dane County, casts some 70% of the district's votes. The rest are in several rural dairy counties which are more Republican and conservative; they include such picturesque Wisconsin scenes as Frank Lloyd Wright's home, Taliesin, the Swiss-settled town of New Glarus, and the headquarters of Lands' End in Dodgeville. Madison was LaFollette country for the first half of the century, and very liberal and Democratic for most of the second, enough so that, despite the Republican leanings of the rural counties, the 2d District voted for George McGovern in 1972 and Walter Mondale in 1984. It also spawned an activist and sometimes violent student movement (during the Vietnam war, a graduate student was killed in a laboratory by a bomb set off by a protester) and a permanent postgraduate proletariat. But there has been some mellowing out. Grad students stuck in the 1960s have left, and there are now Republicans as well as Democrats among undergraduates. And Madison has even been known to vote Republican, for Governor Tommy Thompson in 1994 and in 2d Congressional District races in the 1990s. But overall this is a mostly Democratic district; it voted 55%–33% for Bill Clinton in 1996.

The congresswoman from the 2d District is Tammy Baldwin, a Democrat elected in 1998. She grew up in Madison, where she was raised by her mother (a University of Wisconsin student when she was born) and her maternal grandparents, a UW biochemist and the theater department's head costume designer. She graduated first in her class at Madison West High School and went on to Smith College and UW Law School. In 1986, at 24, while still in law school, she was elected to the Dane County Board of Commissioners; in 1992 she was elected to the Wisconsin Assembly from a heavily Democratic Madison seat; in her first term she chaired the Elections Committee. She was proud of a law requiring campaigns to file disclosure reports electronically; her greatest disappointment was passage of a 24-hour waiting period for abortions.

In 1998 the 2d District seat opened up when Republican Congressman Scott Klug honored his promise to serve only four terms. Klug, a TV anchor, had a moderate record which helped him win re-election by wide margins three times. But when Klug announced his retirement in February 1997, the 2d District seemed the Democrats' best chance for an open-seat pickup. The 1998 contest eventually attracted 10 candidates, all but one of whom proved serious contenders—four Democrats and six Republicans. Entering the Democratic race early were Rick Phelps, Dane County executive for nine years, and state Senator Joe Wineke, a legislator for 15 years, and Baldwin. The three took similar liberal stands on issues, and had worked together on some matters; Phelps's wife, Hannah Rosenthal, was one of Baldwin's mentors in Democratic politics. But Baldwin had special advantages. As a woman with great political skills, she was supported by EMILY's List, which helped raised about one-quarter of her $1.5 million. And as a self-proclaimed lesbian, she had support from national gay and lesbian organizations, and raised money from a large and affluent national constituency. With almost all (86%) of Democratic votes cast in Dane County, this was mostly a Madison contest. Baldwin won with 37% of the votes, to 35% for Phelps and 27% for Wineke, who carried the small-county vote.

Baldwin in some ways was the focus of the Republican primary as much as the Democratic. Most of the Republicans ran as pro-choice fiscal conservatives: former state Insurance Commissioner Jo Musser, UW history professor John Sharpless, beer distributor Don Carrig, chiropractor Meredith Bakke. To their right was former congressional aide and Dane County Republican Chairman Nick Fuhrman. But most prominent in the spotlight was Ron Greer, a black minister and Madison firefighter who was suspended from the force for distributing what many considered anti-gay literature. Greer relished the prospect of running against Baldwin, saying that she had a right to live as she wished, but that he opposed her allegedly radical gay rights agenda. He got vocal support from Green Bay Packer and preacher Reggie White and presidential candidate Alan Keyes, and from national Christian conservatives Gary Bauer and Dr. James Dobson. One bumper sticker read: "Annoy the liberals in Madison, vote for Ron Greer." This was a race almost anybody could have won; the counties beyond Dane County cast 41% of the votes and made the difference. Musser ran first there, ahead of Carrig; she ran third in Dane County, behind Sharpless and Greer. Overall, Musser had 21% of the vote, Greer 20%, Sharpless 18%, Carrig 17%, Fuhrman 14% and Bakke 10%. Musser led Greer by only 394 votes, and for a time Greer considered a recount. He was encouraged to run as a write-in, but said that he would "stay out of it" and support Governor Tommy Thompson and Senate nominee Mark Neumann.

The primary results guaranteed that Wisconsin would elect its first woman member to Congress (the other states that have not are an odd bunch: Alaska, Delaware, Iowa, Mississippi,

New Hampshire and Vermont). But Baldwin's candidacy seemed to rouse the enthusiasm of Madison liberals in a way not seen in years. Baldwin called for a single-payer health insurance system, and suggested that Musser was dominated by cash from insurance companies; Musser, a nurse who founded the Madison Employers Health Care Alliance, argued that single-payer would reduce choices and create long waiting periods for elective surgery. Musser did not attack Baldwin for her support of same-sex marriage or public financing of campaigns—unpopular positions in most districts—but campaigned as a friend of small business and burdened taxpayers. Both sides were well-financed: Baldwin, fortified with contributions from national liberals, spent almost $1.5 million; Musser, fortified by nearly $300,000 of her own money, spent $872,000. The difference may have been due to high turnout in Madison and Dane County, higher than in any off-year election in years. Some precincts ran out of ballots and had to photocopy more; Governor Tommy Thompson, with some hyperbole, later credited the Madison turnout with reducing his own percentage, defeating Mark Neumann and re-electing Senator Russ Feingold, and allowing Democrats to win a seat that gave them control of the state Senate (their nominee was Feingold's brother-in-law) Dane County, which cast 73% of the district's votes, went 57%–42% for Baldwin; Musser's 59%–40% margin in the smaller counties was not enough to overcome that margin, and Baldwin won 53%–47%.

Baldwin thus became the first openly homosexual candidate to win election to Congress; the two other openly gay members of the House, Barney Frank and Jim Kolbe, divulged their sexual orientation after they had served several terms. Baldwin said that she did not want to be seen primarily as a lesbian congresswoman: "I have frequently said I will do more to advance gay and lesbian civil rights in this country if I become the congressperson associated with health care for everyone—who just happens to be lesbian." And she expressed confidence her constituents would approve her work. "They'll be able to watch what I do. I feel very comfortably they'll find I represent a broad cross-section of values."

Cook's Call. *Potentially Competitive.* Baldwin's tremendous fundraising skills and the underlying Democratic and liberal nature of this district make beating Baldwin a tall order for Republicans. But, like every other freshman member, Baldwin does have to be careful in her first term and avoid political miscues that could give a Republican an opening for attack.

The People: Pop. 1990: 543,625; 36.5% rural; 11.9% age 65 +; 95.5% White, 2% Black, 1.6% Asian, 0.3% Amer. Indian, 0.5% Other; 1.1% Hispanic Origin. Households: 54.3% married couple families; 26.2% married couple fams. w. children; 52.6% college educ.; median household income: $30,625; per capita income: $14,319; median house value: $70,000; median gross rent: $396.

1996 Presidential Vote		
Clinton (D)	146,819	(55%)
Dole (R)	88,072	(33%)
Perot (I)	21,682	(8%)
Others	12,743	(5%)

1992 Presidential Vote		
Clinton (D)	149,340	(50%)
Bush (R)	94,368	(32%)
Perot (I)	52,552	(18%)

Rep. Tammy Baldwin (D)

Elected 1998; b. Feb. 11, 1962, Madison; home, Madison; Smith Col., A.B. 1984; U. of WI Law Schl., J.D. 1989; No religious affiliation; single.

Elected Office: Dane Cnty. Bd. of Supervisors, 1986–94; WI Assembly, 1992–98.

Professional Career: Practicing atty, 1989–92.

DC Office: 1020 LHOB 20515, 202-225-2906; Fax: 202-225-6942; Web site: www.house.gov/baldwin.

District Office: Madison, 608-258-9800.

Committees: *Budget* (19th of 19 D). *Judiciary* (15th of 16 D): Commercial & Administrative Law.

Group Ratings and Key Votes: Newly Elected

Election Results

1998 general	Tammy Baldwin (D)	116,377	(52%)	($1,469,905)
	Josephine W. Musser (R)	103,528	(47%)	($872,778)
1998 primary	Tammy Baldwin (D)	24,227	(37%)	
	Rick Phelps (D)	22,610	(35%)	
	Joseph S. Wineke (D)	17,444	(27%)	
	Others	1,055	(2%)	
1996 general	Scott Klug (R)	154,557	(57%)	($1,261,546)
	Paul R. Soglin (D)	110,467	(41%)	($506,513)
	Others	4,350	(2%)	

THIRD DISTRICT

On the rolling land of western Wisconsin, in the knobby hills just east of the Mississippi River, is some of the most beautiful river landscape in the country. This is where Laura Ingalls Wilder's family built the "little house in the big woods" in the 1870s, before the first railroad came steaming up the narrow floodplain alongside the Mississippi River. Today, it is hard to imagine the big woods: The trees have long since been cut and the hillsides are covered with grass grazed by placid dairy cattle. Where pioneers tried to scratch out diversified crops, farmers soon created America's premier dairy region, producing milk, butter and especially cheese. Today the dairy industry is in trouble. Cows are more productive, while demand for milk has decreased because there are fewer children in America now than in the 1950s, and fewer Americans are descended exclusively from the northern European stock that carries the genes for the enzymes adults need to effectively digest milk. And Wisconsin has trouble competing against the European Common Market's hugely subsidized cheese and butter. In the 1980s many communities here lost population, but in the 1990s there has been slow but steady growth—a result perhaps of a decreasing tax burden and disappearing welfare rolls—which has been more rapid in the northern counties within commuting distance of Minneapolis-St. Paul; unemployment is at a record low.

The 3d Congressional District follows the Mississippi and St. Croix River counties from the southern border of the state almost to Lake Superior, and here and there reaches east a county or two. This is probably the nation's number one dairy district, with more cows than people. It was settled largely by German and Scandinavian immigrants (Laura's Yankee family moved away as Swedes were moving into the area), and it once voted for LaFollette Progressives. More recently, it has been fairly closely divided between Democrats and Republicans.

The congressman from the 3d District is Ron Kind, a Democrat elected in 1996. He grew up in a large family in La Crosse, the son of a telephone repairman and a secretary. He went to Harvard on scholarship and played quarterback, and worked as a summer intern for Senator William Proxmire, doing research for his Golden Fleece awards. He attended the London School of Economics and University of Minnesota Law School, practiced law in a big firm in Milwaukee, then returned home to La Crosse to work as an assistant prosecutor on rape and sexual abuse cases.

Kind started running for Congress soon after Congressman Steve Gunderson announced during the 1994 campaign that he would not run again in 1996. Gunderson was known nationally as the Republican revealed to be gay in an October 1994 *New York Times Magazine* article; in the district he was known as a hard-working young politician, first elected at 29 in 1980, who was the top Republican on the Agriculture subcommittee handling dairy programs. Early in the race to succeed him was Republican former state Senator Jim Harsdorf, from the northern part of the district up near Minneapolis-St. Paul. Kind was one of five Democrats running. He set a tone for the primary election by renting the Hollywood Theater in La Crosse for a special showing of *Mr. Smith Goes to Washington*. Kind's leading opponent, Lee Rasch, president of a La Crosse technical college, had run before and called for farmers to wean themselves from federal price supports. Kind talked of cutting corporate welfare and aiding the poor, and won the September primary 46%–29%.

There was much commotion on the Republican side. Gunderson was third-ranking Republican on Agriculture; Chairman Pat Roberts was running for the Senate, and in June 1996 second-ranking Republican Bill Emerson died. That put Gunderson in line for the chairmanship, and many Wisconsin dairy people urged him to run for re-election. He said in June that he would only if he had no primary opponent, but Harsdorf refused to leave the race, and Gunderson did not file. In July a Gunderson write-in movement was launched. In late July Newt Gingrich called Gunderson and told him that conservative activist (and Wisconsin native) Paul Weyrich was planning an independent expenditure effort against him and that four of the five other Wisconsin Republicans were against the write-in. On July 31 in Eau Claire, Gunderson asked the write-in organizers "to not go forward" and added, "It has been explained to me bluntly that if you, as an openly gay person, became chairman of the Agriculture Committee, you would legitimatize homosexuality."

In the general election, Harsdorf took hard-edged, well-defined stands, for the balanced budget and Governor Tommy Thompson's "Wisconsin Works" welfare reform (known as W-2). Kind complained the ads were misleading and called for an end to such campaigning, though the ads accurately set out the candidates' differences on two important issues: Kind said he was concerned whether W-2 provided enough job training and child care and wanted to see how Congress tackled the budget in 1997 before considering an amendment. He talked instead of campaign finance reform and presented his own balanced budget proposal. On November 1 Gunderson announced he was neutral on the candidates because he didn't agree with Harsdorf's views on civil and human rights and thought him too close to the Christian Coalition. In a district that Bill Clinton carried 50%–34%, Kind won 52%–48%. Harsdorf won over some Clinton voters in his northwest base and in southern Grant County, but Kind ran 8% ahead of Clinton in his base of La Crosse and 6% ahead in Eau Claire.

In the House, Kind joined the New Democrat Coalition and compiled a moderate record on economics and cultural issues, and a more liberal one on foreign and defense issues. He did not get a seat on the Agriculture Committee, but stayed in touch with Agriculture Secretary Dan Glickman and with Gunderson on dairy issues. Like other Wisconsin members, he wants to reform the Federal Milk Marketing Order System, instituted in 1937, which pays higher prices the farther the farmer is from Eau Claire, Wisconsin; he opposed the Northeast Dairy Compact, which was set up under the 1996 farm bill to allow New England and Upstate New York to set prices for their products; he was wary of the move of the National Cheese Exchange from Green Bay to the Chicago Mercantile Exchange, and argued that the basic price formula for cheese is not accurately determined by the market. He opposed delays in the end date of the Northeast Dairy Compact and predicted there might be new compacts in the Southeast and California under current policy. In June 1997 the president of the Upper Midwest Milk Producers said, "Ron doesn't have any pull anywhere, but he seems to understand what's going on. He just doesn't have the power to do anything." Kind said he was "disappointed" with the milk marketing system Glickman proposed in April 1999, which produced tiny price increases for Wisconsin but didn't level the national playing field.

Kind is founder and co-chair of the Upper Mississippi River Congressional Task Force. He worked on the bipartisan task force on campaign finance, and made speeches for campaign finance changes on 98 consecutive days in 1997, in imitation of Proxmire's daily speeches urging ratification of the genocide treaty (it finally was ratified in 1986, his 30th year in the Senate). After strong lobbying by union leaders and dairy interests, he opposed fast track in October 1997, even declining an invitation to play golf with President Clinton for fear he'd be lobbied. He was not a sycophantic follower of White House talking points during the Clinton scandals. When Clinton made his first trip out of Washington after the Lewinsky scandal broke to La Crosse, Kind said, "Obviously, it's going to cast a shadow on what he's doing. Everything he does now is going to be seen within that context." Kind was one of 31 Democrats in October 1998 to vote for the Republicans' impeachment inquiry, but he later voted against all four counts of impeachment. He sponsored a bill to relax the English language requirement for citizenship for Hmong immigrants, some of whom fought for the United States in Vietnam and would lose their welfare benefits under the 1996 Immigration Act.

Kind tends to strike a positive tone. "There's a lot of cynicism about politics, but I see a lot of positive things get done," he says, and points out that civility is greater now than in the 19th Century when members of Congress beat each other on the floor and fought duels. After a tumultuous and heavily contested campaign in 1996, Kind had opposition in 1998 only from a Republican who spent $7,500 on the race. Kind won 72%–28%. He could conceivably be a candidate for statewide office some year.

Cook's Call. *Probably Safe.* Though only a sophomore, Kind has established himself pretty well in this Democratic leaning district. Republicans were unable to find a top-tier challenger in 1998 to take on Kind; his subsequent drubbing of the opponent may be enough to scare off other high caliber Republicans in 2000.

The People: Pop. 1990: 543,447; 55.9% rural; 14.6% age 65+; 97.9% White, 0.3% Black, 1.2% Asian, 0.5% Amer. Indian, 0.1% Other; 0.4% Hispanic Origin. Households: 59.3% married couple families; 29.6% married couple fams. w. children; 39.4% college educ.; median household income: $25,758; per capita income: $11,505; median house value: $52,600; median gross rent: $267.

1996 Presidential Vote

Clinton (D)	120,717	(50%)
Dole (R)	82,678	(34%)
Perot (I)	33,325	(14%)
Others	5,274	(2%)

1992 Presidential Vote

Clinton (D)	119,721	(43%)
Bush (R)	90,813	(33%)
Perot (I)	67,134	(24%)

Rep. Ron Kind (D)

Elected 1996; b. Mar. 16, 1963, La Crosse; home, La Crosse; Harvard U., B.A. 1985, London Schl. of Econ., 1986, U. of MN, J.D. 1990; Lutheran; married (Tawni).

Professional Career: Practicing atty., 1990–92; Asst. St. Prosecutor, La Crosse Cnty., 1992–96.

DC Office: 1713 LHOB 20515, 202-225-5506; Fax: 202-225-5739; Web site: www.house.gov/kind.

District Offices: Eau Claire, 715-831-9214; La Crosse, 608-782-2558.

Committees: *Education & the Workforce* (17th of 22 D): Oversight & Investigations; Postsecondary Education, Training & Life-Long Learning. *Resources* (18th of 24 D): Forests & Forest Health; National Parks & Public Lands.

Group Ratings

	ADA	ACLU	AFS	LCV	CON	NTU	NFIB	COC	ACU	NTLC	CHC
1998	85	75	100	77	99	40	36	56	20	16	8
1997	85	—	63	—	99	42	—	50	28	—	—

National Journal Ratings

	1997 LIB	—	1997 CONS	1998 LIB	—	1998 CONS
Economic	71%	—	28%	61%	—	37%
Social	69%	—	30%	67%	—	32%
Foreign	88%	—	10%	84%	—	11%

Key Votes of the 105th Congress

1. Clinton Budget Deal	N	5. Puerto Rico Sthood. Ref.	N	9. Cut $ for B-2 Bombers	Y
2. Education IRAs	N	6. End Highway Set-asides	N	10. Human Rights in China	Y
3. Req. 2/3 to Raise Taxes	N	7. School Prayer Amend.	N	11. Withdraw Bosnia Troops	N
4. Fast-track Trade	N	8. Ovrd. Part. Birth Veto	Y	12. End Cuban TV-Marti	Y

Election Results

1998 general	Ron Kind (D)	128,256	(71%)	($457,273)
	Troy A. Brechler (R)	51,001	(28%)	($7,507)
1998 primary	Ron Kind (D)	unopposed		
1996 general	Ron Kind (D)	121,967	(52%)	($497,919)
	James E. Harsdorf (R)	112,146	(48%)	($507,175)

FOURTH DISTRICT

The world's largest four-sided clock faces outward from all sides of the tower on the Allen-Bradley factory, looking out over the manufacturing city of Milwaukee. It is an apt symbol, a piece of precision engineering, in this high-skill manufacturing town, with its skyline of smoke-stacks and church steeples, the closest thing in America to the factory cities of the Germany whence so many Milwaukeans' ancestors came. Chicago, just 90 miles away, provides much of the banking, advertising, insurance, accounting and legal services Milwaukee businesses need, and the retail and entertainment base as well, and Madison has the big research university. But Milwaukee leads the nation in industrial control equipment, mining gear, cranes and in-dependent foundries. The work force, with German, Polish, Mitteleuropean work habits, is highly skilled and hard-working. German-Americans made Milwaukee the nation's major beer brewer for years, though brewing employs fewer than 4,000 here today. Milwaukee lost 60,000 manufacturing jobs in the 1979–82 recession years, but it stuck to its high-skill manufacturing strength and eventually prospered. Since that recession, Allen-Bradley has spent millions on improvements and new facilities, Rockwell International doubled sales to $1.5 billion, and Harnischfeger has recovered nicely to regain its status as a leader in mining equipment and papermaking machinery, after nearly going bankrupt in 1983.

Prospering quietly from this growth, for this is still a union, high-wage town, are the residents of Milwaukee's traditionally blue-collar south side. Here, in neighborhoods with sturdy houses that withstand northern winters and streets lined with bars emblazoned with beer signs, are Milwaukee's prototypical Polish neighborhoods and its even larger number of German-Americans; here also in old immigrant neighborhoods are the largest numbers of Wisconsin's Hispanics and Hmongs.

The 4th Congressional District, which has been the south-side Milwaukee district since 1892, has spread out with the population into the suburbs. Now only one-third of its voters are in Milwaukee, another 40% in the Milwaukee County suburbs, and one-quarter farther west in suburban Waukesha County. Historically this was the only securely Democratic part of Wisconsin. But Waukesha County is solidly Republican, and the 4th District is now far less Democratic than the north side 5th. In 1996 it went for Bill Clinton by only 49%–40%, less than some rural Wisconsin districts.

The congressman from the 4th District is Jerry Kleczka, a Democrat elected in April 1984. Kleczka is a product of the south side, the sort of man who has remodeled his house from top to bottom and maintains the best lawn in the neighborhood. He was elected to the Wisconsin Assembly in 1968 at 24, to the state Senate in 1974 where he chaired several committees, and to the U.S. House in April 1984, after the death of Clement Zablocki, who represented the district for 35 years and chaired the Foreign Affairs Committee.

In the House Kleczka has a moderate-to-liberal voting record. He supported both family and medical leave in 1993 and welfare reform in 1996; he opposed the October 1998 omnibus budget because it cut $20 billion from the surplus. He has criticized Supplemental Security Income for providing benefits for children who are not in any serious way disabled and for drug addicts and alcoholics. He favors tax-free withdrawals from IRAs for first-time home-buying, college education, medical expenses, and during long-term unemployment. Inspired by the Pabst Brewery Company closure in early 1997, he has sponsored a CARE Act to require employers to give six months' notice before changing health benefits; inspired by the Louis Allis Company bankruptcy, he wants to protect employee contributions to pension funds from being seized by banks and other creditors in bankruptcy proceeding. On the Ways and Means' Health Subcommittee, he has stood strongly against allowing private contracts between Medicare beneficiaries and doctors; that would create a two-tier system, he argues. He wants to end the marriage penalty and to eliminate split-dollar insurance arrangements to avoid taxes. He has sponsored a Personal Information and Privacy Act, to halt the sale and dissemination of Social Security numbers and other personal information, and wants to take other steps to stop identity fraud. He has sponsored bills to require school buses to be equipped with seat belts and to extend the ban on dog and cat fur in domestic clothing to imported clothing.

In the last three elections Kleczka has been opposed by Republican Tom Reynolds, a Christian conservative printer whose backyard print shop churned out anti-abortion as well as campaign literature. In 1994 Reynolds held Kleczka to a 54%–45% victory. In May 1995, after a second drunk driving arrest, Kleczka gave up drinking. In 1998 Kleczka was furious when Reynolds charged him with supporting tax-funded abortions and tax-funded pornography (the latter a reference to the National Endowment for the Arts). Kleczka won convincingly, 58%–42%, in 1996, and by an almost identical 57%–43% in 1998. But the presence of a Republican base in Waukesha County means that this could someday be a seriously contested district, especially if redistricting shifts it farther out into the suburbs in 2002.

Cook's Call. *Safe.* Eight-term Kleczka's is safely entrenched in this blue-collar Milwaukee district. Kleczka's biggest threat may come in 2002 redistricting. Wisconsin is expected to lose one district and there has been some speculation that the two Milwaukee districts could be heavily impacted and potentially melded into one district.

The People: Pop. 1990: 543,482; 2.3% rural; 13.9% age 65 + ; 94% White, 0.8% Black, 1.2% Asian, 0.9% Amer. Indian, 3.1% Other; 6.2% Hispanic Origin. Households: 54.7% married couple families; 25.4% married couple fams. w. children; 42.9% college educ.; median household income: $32,260; per capita income: $14,177; median house value: $71,800; median gross rent: $385.

1996 Presidential Vote			1992 Presidential Vote		
Clinton (D)	115,466	(49%)	Clinton (D)	116,048	(41%)
Dole (R)	94,003	(40%)	Bush (R)	108,761	(38%)
Perot (I)	21,373	(9%)	Perot (I)	59,263	(21%)
Others	5,032	(2%)			

Rep. Gerald D. Kleczka (D)

Elected Apr. 1984; b. Nov. 26, 1943, Milwaukee; home, Milwaukee; Catholic; married (Bonnie).

Military Career: Air Natl. Guard, 1963–69.

Elected Office: Milwaukee Cnty. Cncl., 1965–68; WI Assembly, 1968–74; WI Senate, 1974–84, Asst. Majority Ldr., 1977–82.

Professional Career: Accountant, 1982–84.

DC Office: 2301 RHOB 20515, 202-225-4572; Fax: 202-225-8135; Web site: www.house.gov/kleczka.

District Offices: Milwaukee, 414-297-1140; Waukesha, 414-549-6360.

Committees: *Budget* (12th of 19 D). *Ways & Means* (8th of 16 D): Health.

Group Ratings

	ADA	ACLU	AFS	LCV	CON	NTU	NFIB	COC	ACU	NTLC	CHC
1998	90	75	100	92	89	27	25	39	20	13	33
1997	70	—	63	—	88	38	—	50	25	—	—

National Journal Ratings

	1997 LIB — 1997 CONS		1998 LIB — 1998 CONS	
Economic	67% —	33%	64% —	34%
Social	60% —	40%	60% —	38%
Foreign	82% —	16%	84% —	11%

Key Votes of the 105th Congress

1. Clinton Budget Deal	N	5. Puerto Rico Sthood. Ref.	N	9. Cut $ for B-2 Bombers	Y
2. Education IRAs	N	6. End Highway Set-asides	N	10. Human Rights in China	Y
3. Req. 2/3 to Raise Taxes	N	7. School Prayer Amend.	N	11. Withdraw Bosnia Troops	N
4. Fast-track Trade	N	8. Ovrd. Part. Birth Veto	Y	12. End Cuban TV-Marti	Y

Election Results

1998 general	Gerald D. Kleczka (D)	105,841	(58%)	($631,856)
	Tom Reynolds (R)	76,666	(42%)	($195,318)
1998 primary	Gerald D. Kleczka (D)	19,114	(89%)	
	Roman R. Blenski (D)	2,384	(11%)	
1996 general	Gerald D. Kleczka (D)	134,470	(58%)	($862,686)
	Tom Reynolds (R)	98,438	(42%)	($253,357)

FIFTH DISTRICT

Milwaukee is America's most German city, with an ethnic heritage noticeable not just in the names of its beers and its old German restaurants but in the solidness of its houses and the orderliness of its streets. Until the World Wars made this German character seem un-American, German was spoken on the streets and read in newspapers, German beer was produced in dozens of breweries and German cultural traditions breathed in churches, union halls and parlors. There was a German-type politics, with a Socialist mayor and an efficient, honest city government. Wisconsin's 5th Congressional District, which since 1892 has included the north side of Milwaukee, elected Socialist Victor Berger to Congress in 1910 and again from 1918–20 and 1922–26, even though he was denied his House seat after the 1918 election because of his opposition to World War I; in 1919, he was sentenced to 20 years in prison for writing anti-war articles, but that was later reversed by the Supreme Court.

Though some ghetto neighborhoods here are beset by crime and drug use, most of Milwaukee is solid and upstanding, and some of it—Brewers Hill near the old Schlitz brewery—is gentrifying. There is an Oktoberfest (as well as an Irish Fest, summerfest, etc.), and there are large and efficiently run factories that pay high wages to highly-skilled and well-disciplined workers. This is also the place where state legislator Polly Williams, a Jesse Jackson backer in 1988, joined forces with Republican Governor Tommy Thompson to oppose the Democratic education bureaucracy and enact a school choice program, bitterly attacked by teachers' unions but now upheld by the Wisconsin Supreme Court and perceptibly raising the testing scores of disadvantaged students.

The 5th Congressional District includes the northern half of Milwaukee and Milwaukee County, including its black neighborhoods and the high-income suburbs on Lake Michigan. Overall, its tone is sturdily blue and white collar. Once Socialist and LaFollette Progressive, the 5th is now the most heavily Democratic district in Wisconsin.

The congressman from the 5th District is Tom Barrett, first elected in 1992. He grew up in Milwaukee, went to college and law school in Madison, practiced law and has spent most of his adult life in politics. He was elected to the state Assembly in 1984, at 30; in 1988 he was overwhelmingly elected to the state Senate in a district that conveniently was one of only two entirely within the 5th District. His legislation included bringing 911 emergency call service to Milwaukee and passing a state version of the Brady bill. Running for the House in 1992 when the 5th District's Jim Moody ran for the Senate, Barrett presented detailed position papers on the economy and health care reform. He also called for large defense cutbacks, a national police corps and federal encouragement of direct investment in "microenterprises" in depressed city neighborhoods. He won his primary with 41% over a black county supervisor, a former circuit judge who spent $200,000 of his own money, and a former Marquette basketball star; the general election was easy.

Barrett has a moderate-to-liberal voting record; he calls himself a "deficit hawk and military dove." He was a strong supporter of lobbying reform and the gift ban; he has a bill to prohibit congressmen from using frequent flier miles from official travel for personal vacations. In response to local concerns, he worked to require HUD to give owner-occupants preference in resales of HUD-owned houses and to allow public housing residents to ban firearms. His provision to prohibit Community Development Block Grants from being used to attract business from one part of the country to another was incorporated into the Republican housing bill in early 1997. Inspired by the Pabst Brewery closure in early 1997, he sponsored a bill to require companies that wish to terminate retiree benefits to notify employees and face a court hearing within 14 days if someone objects. From the state with the highest response rate, Barrett is one of the few Democrats to oppose Census sampling. He has supported the adoption tax credit, health insurance deductibility for the self-employed, trigger locks on guns, and a ban on the manufacture of cop-killer bullets. With David Obey and Jerry Kleczka, he tried to stop Mark Neumann's bill for waivers for Governor Tommy Thompson's W-2 welfare reform. That became moot when national welfare reform passed in July 1996; Barrett was one of two Wisconsin votes against it (David Obey was the other), arguing that there isn't enough child care capacity in Milwaukee County.

For his first three terms, Barrett served on the Government Reform and Oversight Committee, where he was witness to the partisan clashes over the investigation of Bill Clinton. In September 1998 he was assigned to Judiciary to fill a vacancy, just in time for Independent Counsel Kenneth Starr's referral of the Clinton case. "If you are going to go to a prize fight, you might as well sit in the front row," Barrett said, but with his transparently good-hearted attempt to find common ground, he was soon frustrated at the impeachment hearings. "It was like watching concrete dry, watching both sides get farther and farther apart," he said. From early on, Barrett thought censure was the appropriate response, and in December 1998 he co-sponsored with Rick Boucher and William Delahunt a censure resolution which did not pass. Barrett then voted against impeachment. In January 1999 he finally got the seat he had been seeking on the Commerce Committee, and rotated off Government Reform and Judiciary.

Cook's Call. *Safe.* Barrett should have little trouble winning a fifth election to this heavily Democratic district. Barrett's biggest threat may come in 2002 redistricting. Wisconsin is expected to lose one district and there has been some speculation that this district and the neighboring Milwaukee-based 4th could potentially be melded into one seat or otherwise heavily impacted.

The People: Pop. 1990: 543,607; 13.4% age 65 + ; 61.3% White, 35.2% Black, 1.7% Asian, 0.5% Amer. Indian, 1.2% Other; 2.3% Hispanic Origin. Households: 39.9% married couple families; 18.2% married couple fams. w. children; 49.1% college educ.; median household income: $26,267; per capita income: $13,277; median house value: $63,200; median gross rent: $358.

1996 Presidential Vote		
Clinton (D)	126,179	(63%)
Dole (R)	58,560	(29%)
Perot (I)	10,182	(5%)
Others	5,603	(3%)

1992 Presidential Vote		
Clinton (D)	142,047	(56%)
Bush (R)	76,935	(30%)
Perot (I)	32,138	(13%)

Rep. Tom Barrett (D)

Elected 1992; b. Dec. 8, 1953, Milwaukee; home, Milwaukee; U. of WI, B.A. 1976, J.D., 1980; Catholic; married (Kristine).

Elected Office: WI Assembly, 1984–88; WI Senate, 1988–92.

Professional Career: FDIC bank examiner, 1977; Law Clerk, Fed. Dist. Judge Robert Warren 1980–82; Practicing atty., 1982–84.

DC Office: 1214 LHOB 20515, 202-225-3571; Fax: 202-225-2185; Web site: www.house.gov/barrett.

District Office: Milwaukee, 414-297-1331.

Committees: *Commerce* (22d of 24 D): Finance & Hazardous Materials; Health and Environment.

Group Ratings

	ADA	ACLU	AFS	LCV	CON	NTU	NFIB	COC	ACU	NTLC	CHC
1998	95	81	100	100	99	42	29	17	4	8	8
1997	90	—	63	—	100	47	—	40	20	—	—

National Journal Ratings

	1997 LIB — 1997 CONS			1998 LIB — 1998 CONS		
Economic	75%	—	22%	79%	—	0%
Social	69%	—	31%	76%	—	23%
Foreign	88%	—	10%	98%	—	0%

Key Votes of the 105th Congress

1. Clinton Budget Deal	N	5. Puerto Rico Sthood. Ref.	Y	9. Cut $ for B-2 Bombers	Y
2. Education IRAs	N	6. End Highway Set-asides	N	10. Human Rights in China	Y
3. Req. 2/3 to Raise Taxes	N	7. School Prayer Amend.	N	11. Withdraw Bosnia Troops	N
4. Fast-track Trade	N	8. Ovrd. Part. Birth Veto	Y	12. End Cuban TV-Marti	Y

Election Results

1998 general	Tom Barrett (D)	121,129	(78%)	($139,501)
	Jack Melvin (R)	33,506	(22%)	
1998 primary	Tom Barrett (D)	unopposed		
1996 general	Tom Barrett (D)	141,179	(73%)	($153,139)
	Paul D. Melotik (R)	47,384	(25%)	($13,315)
	Others	4,006	(2%)	

SIXTH DISTRICT

Central Wisconsin is solid country, a producer of basic commodities—milk, butter and cheese, paper products, Mirro pots and pans, Mercury outboard motors and Kleenex. Settled first by Yankee Protestants, it was one of the birthplaces of the Republican Party in February 1854, when a group of Whigs, Free Soilers and Democrats met in a small white schoolhouse in Ripon, Wisconsin, and proclaimed themselves Republicans; Jackson, Michigan, also claims to be the birthplace of the party. Whichever, the party grew rapidly, winning a near-majority in the House in the 1854 elections. But Republican roots here are not just Yankee. The 1850s brought the first surge of German migration into the United States, and central Wisconsin was a favorite destination. Here they built the dairy farms and factory towns that seemed steadfastly prosperous 50 years ago, and are now part of a manufacturing boom. Here also is the testing ground, in Fond du Lac County, of Governor Tommy Thompson's W-2 welfare reform; the welfare rolls there, never high, have fallen to almost zero since the program began in early 1997.

The 6th Congressional District, which cuts a swath across Wisconsin from Manitowoc on Lake Michigan through Oshkosh and Ripon west almost to the Mississippi River, includes country that has voted Republican almost without interruption since that first meeting in Ripon. It has also elected Republican congressmen who have come up with thoughtful and original solutions to problems. One was William Steiger, first elected in 1966, whose chief monuments are the all-volunteer military and the 1978 Steiger amendment cutting capital gains tax rates—considerable accomplishments for a member of the minority party, and for one who died at age 40 in 1978.

The congressman from the 6th District is Tom Petri, a Republican first elected in the April 1979 contest to succeed Steiger. Petri grew up in Fond du Lac, went to Harvard, was a Peace Corps volunteer in Somalia and was elected to the state Senate in 1972, at 32. In 1974 he was the Republican nominee against Senator Gaylord Nelson; he walked across the state campaigning but in that Democratic year lost 62%–36%. In 1979 Petri ran for the House, beating Tommy Thompson in the primary 35%–19% and then winning the special with 50.4%.

Some of Petri's ideas have been adopted. He long boosted the Earned Income Tax Credit, which results in payments to low-income people who work, targeting aid to families much better than the minimum wage; the Clinton Administration agreed and increased the EITC when Democrats were in control, then dragged out the tattered arguments for the minimum wage when they wanted an issue to bash Republicans with in 1996. Petri called for expanding the EITC concept with a $1,000 tax credit per child, in place of the current deduction; Congress and Clinton agreed on a $500 per-child credit, leaving the deduction in place. Petri favors making college loans repayable in amounts regulated by post-college earnings; this was adopted in the Clinton direct student loan program, which Petri supports. In the 1998 Higher Education Act reauthorization, he worked to lock in current loan rates, to preserve the direct loan program and to increase Pell grants from $3,000 to $5,300 by 2004. Other Petri successes has been stopping the Auburn Dam near Sacramento and slowing down the Animas-Las Palata water project in southwest Colorado—"dinosaurs," he calls them.

Some Petri reforms have been pretty much ignored. He would withdraw health care deductibility and substitute "Multicare," a fixed subsidy for catastrophic coverage, allowing people or employers to buy more insurance if they like. His campaign finance reform bill would include a 50% tax credit for up to $200 in contributions. He would privatize deposit insurance, on the theory that private insurers are better at spotting risks than government regulators. To supplement Social Security, he would provide every newborn with $1,000 in a tax-free retirement savings account; the miracle of compound interest over 67 years would pay for most of today's promised Social Security benefits, he says. He wants to maintain the Census by actual enumeration, as provided in the Constitution, not by sampling, which could be politically manipulated; he also wants to give people the option of saying they are multi-racial. Petri is definitely not a fan of "the outdated relic of Soviet-style central planning that is our federal dairy program." He is dismayed by the Northeast Dairy Compact's cartel and the exclusion of Wisconsin milk from other markets by the Eau Claire pricing system.

Petri is third ranking Republican on the Transportation Committee and chairman of the Surface Transportation Subcommittee, and played a major role in shaping the May 1998 transportation bill. He strongly supported Chairman Bud Shuster's move to require all gas tax revenues to be taken off-budget and used for transportation; he passed an amendment raising Wisconsin's return on its gas tax dollars to about $1, which means a $533 million increase for the state. He brokered a compromise in the dispute between the city of Milwaukee—whose Mayor John Norquist has long opposed freeways and wants to spend money on a light rail system—and the state of Wisconsin, whose Governor Tommy Thompson wants to rebuild the Marquette Interchange. He also supports Shuster's 1999 move to take airport spending off-budget and to devote all revenues from the air ticket tax to it. On his subcommittee he has promised to work on natural gas and oil pipeline safety and safer transportation of hazardous materials.

Petri's Website was rated one of the 12 best congressional Websites by the Congressional Management Foundation in May 1999. He is usually re-elected easily, though in the anti-incumbent atmosphere of 1992 he beat Democratic District Attorney Peggy Lautenschlager by only 53%–47%. In 1994 and 1998 he had no Democratic opponent; in 1996 he was re-elected with 73% of the vote. Petri has a good chance to become chairman (or ranking minority member, if Democrats win a majority) of two House committees, thanks to Republicans' six-year term limit on chairmanships: he is number two ranking Republican on Education and the Workforce and number three on Transportation and Infrastructure, behind Shuster and Don Young of Alaska, who is serving his third term as chairman of Resources.

Cook's Call. *Safe.* But for one close call in 1992, 10-term Petri has easily won re-election to this central Wisconsin district. He should have little trouble in 2000.

The People: Pop. 1990: 543,531; 47.1% rural; 15.4% age 65 + ; 98.2% White, 0.3% Black, 0.7% Asian, 0.5% Amer. Indian, 0.3% Other; 0.9% Hispanic Origin. Households: 62% married couple families; 29.4% married couple fams. w. children; 33.8% college educ.; median household income: $28,038; per capita income: $12,400; median house value: $55,000; median gross rent: $279.

1996 Presidential Vote		
Clinton (D)	108,004	(45%)
Dole (R)	99,650	(41%)
Perot (I)	28,459	(12%)
Others	4,280	(2%)

1992 Presidential Vote		
Bush (R)	114,517	(41%)
Clinton (D)	97,121	(34%)
Perot (I)	69,339	(25%)

Rep. Thomas E. Petri (R)

Elected Apr. 1979; b. May 28, 1940, Marinette; home, Fond du Lac; Harvard U., B.A. 1962, J.D. 1965; Lutheran; married (Anne).

Elected Office: WI Senate, 1972–79.

Professional Career: Peace Corps, Somalia, 1966–67; Law Clerk, Fed. Judge James Doyle, 1965–66; White House aide, 1969; Practicing atty., 1970–79.

DC Office: 2462 RHOB 20515, 202-225-2476; Fax: 202-225-2356; Web site: www.house.gov/petri.

District Offices: Fond du Lac, 920-922-1180; Oshkosh, 920-231-6333.

Committees: *Education & the Workforce* (Vice Chmn. of 27 R): Early Childhood, Youth & Families; Employer-Employee Relations; Postsecondary Education, Training & Life-Long Learning. *Transportation & Infrastructure* (3d of 41 R): Aviation; Ground Transportation (Chmn.).

Group Ratings

	ADA	ACLU	AFS	LCV	CON	NTU	NFIB	COC	ACU	NTLC	CHC
1998	15	13	11	46	65	70	100	94	88	84	100
1997	25	—	13	—	93	76	—	80	80	—	—

National Journal Ratings

	1997 LIB — 1997 CONS			1998 LIB — 1998 CONS		
Economic	19%	—	76%	30%	—	67%
Social	20%	—	71%	29%	—	71%
Foreign	55%	—	44%	27%	—	68%

1754 WISCONSIN

Key Votes of the 105th Congress

1. Clinton Budget Deal	Y	5. Puerto Rico Sthood. Ref.	N	9. Cut $ for B-2 Bombers	Y
2. Education IRAs	Y	6. End Highway Set-asides	N	10. Human Rights in China	Y
3. Req. 2/3 to Raise Taxes	Y	7. School Prayer Amend.	Y	11. Withdraw Bosnia Troops	Y
4. Fast-track Trade	Y	8. Ovrd. Part. Birth Veto	Y	12. End Cuban TV-Marti	N

Election Results

1998 general	Thomas E. Petri (R) 144,144	(93%)	($279,748)
	Timothy J. Farness (TXP) 11,267	(7%)	
1998 primary	Thomas E. Petri (R) .... unopposed		
1996 general	Thomas E. Petri (R) 169,213	(73%)	($364,660)
	Al Lindskoog (D) 55,377	(24%)	
	Others 7,129	(3%)	

SEVENTH DISTRICT

In the late 19th Century, on the rail lines radiating northwest from Chicago and Milwaukee, came thousands of migrants whose descendants have made the northern reaches of Wisconsin the most thickly settled land this far north in the United States east of the Mississippi. What brought people up so far was not cropland—there are no industrial-sized wheat farms as in the Red River Valley of North Dakota—but trees, iron and cows. This was one of America's largest virgin timberlands, and the river towns are still dotted with paper mills. Farther north, iron brought Finns and Italians to the port of Superior, Wisconsin, right next to Duluth, Minnesota, and to smaller towns on the chilly lake. Then on the cleared forestlands came dairy farms. Dairy cattle, properly cared for, thrive in these northern uplands, and the sons of Wisconsin dairymen, many of them immigrants from Germany and Norway, moved their dairy herds even farther north. On this base small cities grew, some with big enterprises. Wausau has paper mills and Wausau Insurance, Wisconsin Rapids has Georgia-Pacific, and Stevens Point has Sentry Insurance.

All these places are in Wisconsin's 7th Congressional District, which stretches from a point not far from Green Bay and Madison in the south up to Lake Superior in the north. The politics of northern Wisconsin and the 7th District has a rough-hewn quality, a certain lumberjack populist flavor. Ancestrally Republican, this area favored the progressivism of the LaFollettes. Today, Superior and Stevens Point are heavily Democratic, while much of the country in between leans Republican.

The congressman from the 7th District is David Obey, a Democrat first elected in April 1969. Chairman of the Appropriations Committee from March 1994 to January 1995, and since then ranking minority member, he is one of the most capable and strongly motivated legislators on either side of the aisle. He grew up in Wausau, where his father worked in a roofing factory; he started off as a Republican, but was influenced by history teacher Arthur Henderson—who assigned papers on the politics of the 1920s and was attacked by McCarthyites—and between 1952 and 1956 Obey switched from supporting Dwight Eisenhower and Joe McCarthy to Adlai Stevenson and William Proxmire. By 1962, when he was 24, Obey was elected to the Wisconsin Assembly even before he got his master's degree. When Melvin Laird resigned his House seat to become Richard Nixon's Defense secretary, Obey won an upset in the April 1969 special election.

In the state legislature, Obey was inspired by older New Deal Democrats who fought hard for the little guy; when he entered the House, the driving energy came from liberal Democrats opposed to the Vietnam war. Obey preserves something of the force of each group. He is not a sentimental liberal: He has a prickly personality and a vigorous temper and does not suffer gladly those he considers fools or knaves. Even as he has moved to the top of the seniority ladder, Obey has retained his sense of outrage and his eagerness to fight for what he believes in—a quality that even some Democrats complain has been too intense. But he continues to display abundant energy and leadership on a host of fronts. In the mid-1970s he chaired a special committee on ethics, pushing through a code requiring detailed disclosure of personal finances and limiting outside income: this was not forgiven by some of the oldtimers. From 1979 well into the 1980s he was the chief sponsor of campaign finance bills to limit PAC contributions, reduce individual donations and provide public financing. In 1991 the office of House administrator was created—something Obey proposed 16 years before, and a recommendation that might have saved a lot of House Democrats and some House Republicans much trouble if it had been followed earlier. He had his disappointments. He lost the Budget Committee chairmanship to Oklahoma's Jim Jones in 1980 by 121–116. In 1984 he wanted to become Caucus chairman, but demurred when it became clear that Dick Gephardt had the votes. Even so, informally Obey became a key leader of liberal Democrats, in 1989 pushing Gephardt for majority leader when Jim Wright and Tony Coelho were resigning, and in 1990 pushing a rules change requiring Ways and Means subcommittee chairmen to be elected by the whole Caucus.

Obey remains a true believer in traditional liberalism, in Keynesian economics and economic redistribution. He thinks that government should provide economic security, create jobs and build infrastructure through public investment, that it should control health care costs and guarantee coverage and a choice of providers. In 1994 he wanted to give the president power to lower taxes to counterbalance Federal Reserve interest rate increases and stood ready to back middle-class tax cuts even as the economy by some measures was growing smartly. In two stints as chairman of the Joint Economic Committee, he prepared studies arguing that Reagan-Bush policies enriched the rich and hurt the middle class. He has bucked the Democratic leadership on behalf of principle, leading the opposition to the 1990 budget summit package. He also has bucked the Clinton Administration, vocally opposing NAFTA and, when Clinton seemed to be backing away from universal health care coverage in July 1994, said "then I will walk away from the Clinton health care plan" and supported his real preference, a single-payer system. In June 1995, when Clinton accepted the Republicans' goal of a budget balanced in seven years, Obey immediately issued a written statement reading, "I think most of us learned some time ago that if you don't like the president's position on a particular issue you simply need to wait a few weeks." Or months—Obey was pleased when Clinton started vetoing Republican appropriations bills in the fall. Obey also opposes some administration positions from the right. He has long opposed abortion, and backs the partial-birth abortion ban; he opposes gun control, and pointed out that one of the guns singled out in the assault weapons ban is owned by 23,000 residents of the 7th District, including two sheriffs.

Obey is above all an appropriator, and takes some justifiable pride in his skill at this work. He first got his seat on Appropriations in August 1969, when he was just 30; when he became chairman, in March 1994, he was the youngest person to hold the post since James Good of Iowa in 1919. Obey has shown great skill, plus a determination to get things done on time—which is not always how appropriating works. Much of his work came on the Foreign Operations Subcommittee, which he chaired from 1985–95. This subcommittee handles rather small sums of money but deals with some very sensitive issues, and it was often rocked in disputes about aid to the Nicaraguan Contras, the pace of negotiations in the Middle East, the treatment of the liberated nations of Eastern Europe. Obey was inclined to think the Camp David agreements committed too much aid to Egypt and Israel and wanted to see more spent on humanitarian assistance. Obey has not always gotten his way, but in each case he worked to move appropriations bills forward in an orderly manner. He passed separate foreign operations appropriation bills nine out of 10 years, something that had only been accomplished twice in 10 years by his predecessors. Similarly, when Obey became chairman of the full committee, all 13 appropriations bills were signed into law prior to the beginning of the new fiscal year for the first time in 47 years.

Obey's climb to the chairmanship was sudden. In January 1993 Jamie Whitten, whose health was impaired, was voted out after 14 years as chairman. William Natcher, holder of the record for consecutive roll call votes, performed ably for a year, but then his health visibly failed in January 1994. When he died in March 1994, Obey challenged the next Democrat in line, 74-year-old Neal Smith of Iowa. Smith had the support of other "cardinals," but Obey had more from non-committee liberals and less senior members, and won in the Democratic Caucus 152–106. But Obey was not as partisan as some may have hoped. "Our mission has been fairly well defined by circumstances," he said. "We've been trying to dig out of the Reagan-era deficits and manage the downsizing of programs while freeing up a tiny bit for the president's programs, and I want to do that in the most collegial and bipartisan way."

Looking back on the first two Clinton years, it was obvious that the president foundered when he failed to unite Democrats on issues with no possible bipartisan strategy—on tax increases, gun control, the health care proposal. Obey, in fashioning party positions, took care not just to express his own views but to take stands that could unify Democrats and put them in a position to prevail if they could win just a few Republican votes—as they did on occasions that became more numerous in 1996 than in 1995. This approach was exemplified by Obey's support for South Carolina's John Spratt for ranking Democrat on the Budget Committee in late 1996. And despite some loud arguments—both men are known for their tempers—Obey and Chairman Bob Livingston managed to work together on numerous occasions, sometimes to reach agreement, often to frame disagreement in orderly choices for other members. Along the way Obey has worked successfully for some favorite causes—funding supplemental payments for dairy farmers when prices fell in 1999, promoting the National Endowment for the Arts, opposing nine new B-2 stealth bombers. He fought the May 1998 transportation bill, even though it increased funds for Wisconsin, because it took transportation spending off-budget, and beyond the reach of appropriators. He has opposed holding up appropriations on what he considers extraneous issues, as when conservatives attempted to tie a ban on abortion funding to the IMF funding bill, or when Republicans in his view reneged on a compromise on national testing on the education appropriation.

The 7th is a pretty solidly Democratic district—it voted for Michael Dukakis in the 1980s as well as Clinton in the 1990s—and for years Obey won with little difficulty. But in Republican 1994 his opponent, Scott West, a 32-year-old admissions counselor at UW-Stevens Point, though outspent by a wide margin, held him to a 54%–46% victory—a bit too close for comfort. Obey even lost the southern part of the district, his home base, by 52%–48%. That created some interest in the 1996 race and Eau Claire state Senator David Zien was touted as the strongest Republican. But he lost the primary to West, who was again vastly outspent. West said Obey was aloof and out of touch and that he had a bad temper. Obey said that he certainly was angry at the way working families were being treated by Republican policies and continually pounded away at Newt Gingrich. "A new direction or a Newt direction?" he asked. Obey won 57%–43%. In 1998 West ran again, and was allowed on the ballot though he filed his papers three minutes late; in that incumbent-inclined year Obey won 60%–40%.

Cook's Call. *Safe.* In 15 re-election contests, Obey has had but one close one; he took 54% in the terrible Democratic year of 1994. Though this is not an overwhelmingly Democratic district, Obey is well entrenched here and looks to be in good shape for 2000.

The People: Pop. 1990: 543,569; 58.8% rural; 15.7% age 65 +; 97.3% White, 0.1% Black, 0.9% Asian, 1.6% Amer. Indian, 0.1% Other; 0.4% Hispanic Origin. Households: 61% married couple families; 29.6% married couple fams. w. children; 34.4% college educ.; median household income: $25,277; per capita income: $11,427; median house value: $48,600; median gross rent: $258.

1996 Presidential Vote

Clinton (D)	119,984	(49%)
Dole (R)	86,374	(35%)
Perot (I)	34,328	(14%)
Others	5,257	(2%)

1992 Presidential Vote

Clinton (D)	117,203	(42%)
Bush (R)	93,156	(33%)
Perot (I)	67,558	(24%)

Rep. David R. Obey (D)

Elected Apr. 1969; b. Oct. 3, 1938, Okmulgee, OK; home, Wausau; U. of WI, B.S. 1960, M.A., 1962; Catholic; married (Joan).

Elected Office: WI Assembly, 1962–69.

Professional Career: Asst., family-run supper club & motel, 1962–68.

DC Office: 2314 RHOB 20515, 202-225-3365.

District Office: Wausau, 715-842-5606.

Committees: *Appropriations* (RMM of 27 D): Labor, HHS & Education (RMM).

Group Ratings

	ADA	ACLU	AFS	LCV	CON	NTU	NFIB	COC	ACU	NTLC	CHC
1998	95	75	100	100	89	35	7	11	16	11	8
1997	80	—	88	—	10	28	—	30	21	—	—

National Journal Ratings

	1997 LIB — 1997 CONS		1998 LIB — 1998 CONS	
Economic	75% —	22%	79% —	0%
Social	63% —	36%	68% —	31%
Foreign	94% —	3%	78% —	19%

Key Votes of the 105th Congress

1. Clinton Budget Deal	N	5. Puerto Rico Sthood. Ref.	N	9. Cut $ for B-2 Bombers	Y
2. Education IRAs	N	6. End Highway Set-asides	N	10. Human Rights in China	Y
3. Req. 2/3 to Raise Taxes	N	7. School Prayer Amend.	N	11. Withdraw Bosnia Troops	N
4. Fast-track Trade	N	8. Ovrd. Part. Birth Veto	Y	12. End Cuban TV-Marti	Y

Election Results

1998 general	David R. Obey (D) 115,613	(61%)	($848,023)
	Scott West (R) 75,049	(39%)	($71,534)
1998 primary	David R. Obey (D) .... unopposed		
1996 general	David R. Obey (D) 137,428	(57%)	($862,370)
	Scott West (R) 103,365	(43%)	($161,402)

EIGHTH DISTRICT

In 1673, the French explorer and priest Father Marquette sailed from the open waters of Lake Michigan into what is now Green Bay. He had hoped to find the Northwest Passage to the Pacific. He actually found the Fox River, which leads to Lake Winnebago and, after a not-too-difficult portage, the Wisconsin River, which flows into the Mississippi. Green Bay and the Fox River Valley remained mostly wilderness and Indian country for more than 150 years. But once settled by Europeans, they became, as Father Marquette would have liked, one of the most heavily Catholic parts of the United States, though Indians still remain a presence; there was a long dispute over Chippewa Indian spearfishing rights and Green Bay's best hotel is now next to the Oneida Indian casino. This is a thriving area economically, with traditional paper mills joined by high-skill manufacturing in Green Bay and the Fox River Valley. And it was thriving even more psychically, after the January 1997 Super Bowl victory of the Green Bay Packers, the only community-owned franchise in the National Football League.

The 8th Congressional District includes Green Bay and the Fox River Valley south to Appleton. It also includes several north woods and dairy counties inland, plus the Door County peninsula that juts out into Lake Michigan, a favorite summer vacation spot for Chicago and Milwaukee families. Politically, this has often been malleable country. Democrats, especially Catholics, can win here: John Kennedy carried the Fox River Valley in the primary and general election in 1960, and Bill Clinton carried it in 1996. But the 8th District can turn almost ferociously Republican: Appleton was the home of Senator Joseph McCarthy, who did much to tar the good names of politics, Congress, conservatism and the Republican Party in the early 1950s.

The congressman from the 8th District is Mark Green, a Republican elected in 1998, the only Republican to beat a Democratic incumbent that year. Green grew up in the Green Bay area; his father was from South Africa and his mother from Britain. In high school and college he was a champion swimmer; after graduating from the University of Wisconsin at Eau Claire and UW Law School in Madison, he and his wife spent a year in Kenya, working in a WorldTeach program. He practiced law and in 1992, at 32, was elected to the Wisconsin Assembly, where he became Republican Caucus chairman. In 1998 he decided to run against freshman Democratic Congressman Jay Johnson, a former TV news anchor, who had upset state House Speaker David Prosser in the open seat race caused by the retirement of Republican Congressman Toby Roth in 1996. Green faced the same primary opponent, businessman Chuck Dettman, who had spent $200,000 and raised Prosser's negatives in 1996. But this time Dettman initiated a fair campaign pledge and Green a party unity pledge; and Dettman decided to use shoe leather rather than his own money to make his case. Green, already campaigning on general election themes, won the primary 80%–20%.

Green brought a conceptual framework to his campaign. He listed 55 issues on which he would vote differently from Johnson, one for each day between the primary and general election; they ranged from taxes and spending to education to abortion and defense. It was a solidly conservative platform, in opposition to Johnson's moderate-to-liberal voting record. Green called for "restoration of American values," an end to partial-birth abortions, scrapping the tax code, increasing local control of education, and tougher crime laws. He carefully avoided any reference to the Clinton-Lewinsky scandal or to impeachment, saying that he had called for Clinton's resignation only to get the issue out of the way. He called for limits on out-of-state political contributions, bringing troops home from Bosnia and the English-as-official-language bill Roth had long backed. He squarely opposed some of the small-issue initiatives the Clinton White House thought were popular, like national education standards and gun control. He ran an ad showing himself with a halo (he checked with a minister on the propriety of this) saying that he was willing to scrap "the temple of big government's" holy book, the Internal Revenue Code.

Johnson made patients' HMO rights a major issue and responded to the halo ad with an ad attacking Green for backing a $350,000 cap on jury awards in medical malpractice cases: "Green's a politician who took thousands in campaign cash from insurance companies, and voted to protect doctors who commit malpractice—even if they were drunk or on drugs. . . . Mark Green has a tarnished halo and can't be trusted." To that Green responded with an ad showing people watching TV in a diner, with a waitress disgustedly turning off the TV as Johnson's anti-halo ad was playing, saying he wasn't the "nice guy" she had thought and adding, with references universally recognized in these parts to the Green Bay Packers, "Lindy Infante was wrong about Tony Mandarich, and I was wrong on Jay Johnson."

Even before the primary, Green was leading Johnson in Republican polls—a real trouble sign for an incumbent. Johnson tried to stress the accomplishments of the 105th Congress—the first balanced budget in 30 years, tax cuts, the IRS reform. But other Democrats called his campaign unfocused. Nor did he have the incumbent's usual financial advantage. Johnson spent

$830,000, Green $823,000. Some 70% of Johnson's money was from PACs, mostly from unions—indeed no other House candidate in the country relied as heavily on PACs as he did in the first 18 months of the cycle—which undercut his claim to be for campaign finance reform. Johnson was also thrown on the defensive by August 1998 independent ads run by Americans for Job Security suggesting he received contributions from Indian tribes and lobbied to prevent Indian casinos from paying taxes—ads which Green and Dettman as well as Johnson attacked.

But Johnson's greatest problem was that the 8th is not a very Democratic district: It had previously elected only three Democratic congressmen in the 20th century, two of whom were defeated for re-election and another who lost a race for a third term. In November 1998 the 8th District went heavily for Governor Tommy Thompson and voted 55%–44% for Republican Mark Neumann over Senator Russ Feingold. Green won 54%–46%.

In the House, Green was the only freshman appointed to the Republican Policy Committee and, with fellow Wisconsin Republican freshman Paul Ryan, got seats on the Budget and Banking Committees.

Cook's Call. *Probably Safe.* Green defeated a Democratic incumbent in 1998 to win this seat. But, don't look for Democrats to heavily target this Republican-leaning district in 2000. This district has only elected three Democrats to Congress in this century and barring any big mistakes by Green, they have little hope of winning here at the start of the next century either.

The People: Pop. 1990: 543,526; 44.4% rural; 14.4% age 65 + ; 96.1% White, 0.3% Black, 0.9% Asian, 2.6% Amer. Indian, 0.2% Other; 0.6% Hispanic Origin. Households: 61.3% married couple families; 29.8% married couple fams. w. children; 36.8% college educ.; median household income: $28,169; per capita income: $12,628; median house value: $58,100; median gross rent: $297.

1996 Presidential Vote

Clinton (D)	116,073	(46%)
Dole (R)	105,131	(41%)
Perot (I)	28,567	(11%)
Others	3,862	(2%)

1992 Presidential Vote

Bush (R)	115,128	(40%)
Clinton (D)	101,493	(35%)
Perot (I)	69,373	(24%)

Rep. Mark Green (R)

Elected 1998; b. June 1, 1960, Boston, MA; home, Green Bay; U. of WI, B.A. 1983, J.D. 1987; Catholic; married (Sue).

Elected Office: WI Assembly, 1992–98.

Professional Career: Teacher, Africa, 1988–89; Practicing atty., 1988–92.

DC Office: 1218 LHOB 20515, 202-225-5665; Fax: 225-5729; Web site: www.house.gov/markgreen.

District Offices: Antigo, 715-627-1511; Appleton, 920-380-0061; Green Bay, 920-437-1954.

Committees: *Banking & Financial Services* (31st of 32 R): Domestic & International Monetary Policy; Housing & Community Opportunity. *Budget* (20th of 24 R). *Science* (20th of 25 R): Space & Aeronautics; Technology.

Group Ratings and Key Votes: Newly Elected

Election Results

1998 general	Mark Green (R)	112,418	(55%)	($847,692)
	Jay Johnson (D)	93,441	(45%)	($850,577)
1998 primary	Mark Green (R)	32,265	(80%)	
	Chuck Dettman (R)	8,228	(20%)	
1996 general	Jay Johnson (D)	129,551	(52%)	($289,624)
	David Prosser (R)	119,398	(48%)	($556,074)

NINTH DISTRICT

For decades, the orderly, heavily German-American factory city of Milwaukee has been spreading slowly, mostly west and north, into Wisconsin dairy country. There are high-income enclaves here, like close-in Elm Grove and Oconomowoc spread out around its lakes. There is office development in Brookfield; subdivisions spread out in Mequon and Menomonee Falls and farther, to reach small towns with roots deep in the 19th Century. This is comfortable but not fancy territory, and the economy here is still based heavily on skilled manufacturing. Not far from Milwaukee are Sheboygan, home of Kohler plumbing fixtures; Port Washington, with Allen-Edmonds shoes; West Bend, with West Bend kitchen appliances; Pewaukee, with Quad/Graphics printing.

The 9th Congressional District includes most of the western, northwestern and northern suburbs of Milwaukee and spreads out into rich dairy farm country and to these factory towns. The large majority of precincts here vote Republican, and this is usually the most Republican district in the state—the only Wisconsin district for Bob Dole in 1996.

The congressman from the 9th District, James Sensenbrenner, first elected in 1978, is one of the most senior Republicans in the House. His Wisconsin roots are strong—his great-grandfather was a founder of Kimberly-Clark—and Sensenbrenner is among the richest members of Congress, and one of the few who lists his net worth ($10.2 million in 1999) and investments with meticulous detail every year. In December 1997 he won $250,000 in the District of Columbia lottery after buying two tickets at a Capitol Hill liquor store. "It was an impulse purchase. I was purchasing Wisconsin beer for my office's Christmas party, and I paid $2 for two Quick Cash tickets," Sensenbrenner explained. When he turned in the ticket and found he had won considerably more than the $10 he expected, he splurged and bought an $85 bottle of champagne.

Sensenbrenner grew up in the Milwaukee area, graduated from Stanford and the University of Wisconsin Law School and has spent most of his adult life in politics, briefly as a U.S. House staffer, and then serving 10 years in the Wisconsin legislature from 1968–78. For almost all that time, Sensenbrenner has been in the minority, gamely undertaking the Sisyphean task of moving amendments certain to lose. But he has persevered out of a dogged sense of principle. His voting record is mostly conservative, but not entirely: He supported the Brady bill, but led the fight against the assault weapons ban. He was an original co-sponsor and floor manager of the Defense of Marriage Act, to let states refuse to recognize same-sex marriage if courts rule them legal in other states.

Sensenbrenner is the second ranking Republican on the Judiciary Committee and looks forward to becoming chairman, thanks to House Republicans' six-year term limits on chairmen, after the 2000 election. "It is my intention when Henry Hyde is term-limited to seek the Republican leadership's support for me to become chairman of Judiciary," he said in March 1998, though he prudently added, "If we go into the minority, none of us are going to be chairman of anything." One of his major efforts there has been to exempt from royalty fees small restaurants and bars that play recorded music; this issue aroused him when auditors from the American Society of Composers, Authors and Publishers converged on Pewaukee Lake bars and demanded payments. Persevering, he negotiated in October 1998 an exemption for small businesses under 2,000 square feet and restaurants and bars under 3,750 square feet. "It was Main Street versus Hollywood and Nashvillle. And Main Street won," he said.

Sensenbrenner played a major role on Bill Clinton's impeachment. He has long been a stickler for ethics, and was one of the first to urge that Congress apply to itself the laws it imposes on the rest of the country. He served on the ethics committee in the early 1980s, when in the Abscam case the committee recommended and secured the first expulsions from the House since the Civil War era. In 1989 he helped to prosecute Judge Walter Nixon for perjury; in 1995 he sought to expel Congressman Walter Tucker for tax evasion and extortion, who resigned before the House could act. In 1994 he prepared motions to censure or expel Dan Rostenkowski if he pleaded guilty to any crimes—one reason, perhaps, why he did not. "I have a rather low tolerance for official misconduct. I've been extremely consistent on that," he noted drily in 1998. Sensenbrenner seemed clearly inclined to vote for impeachment beginning in September 1998. He was one of the 13 House managers and was chosen by Hyde to lead off the managers' presentation to the Senate in January 1999. "We are here today because President William Jefferson Clinton decided to put himself above the law not once, not twice, but repeatedly," he said. Clinton "has not owned up to the false testimony, the stonewalling and legal hairsplitting and obstructing the courts from finding the truth. In doing so, he has turned his affair into a public wrong."

Sensenbrenner is chairman of the House Science Committee, after serving a term as chairman of its Space Subcommittee. On those bodies he has worked in a bipartisan manner with ranking Democrat George Brown. He supports the Space Station, which survived by a one-vote margin in 1993 and by larger margins since. He has generally supported manned space flight, but was persistently critical of the U.S.-Russia space agreement, particularly of the condition of the Russian Mir. In September 1997 he told NASA Administrator Daniel Goldin that he "put his reputation on the line" by ordering U.S. astronauts to take extended flights on the decrepit Mir, because "the risks have increased and the science dropped off." He has called for more privatization of the U.S. space program, and hailed the Pathfinder mission to Mars: "Our ecology is very fragile, and the earth is a unique place. If there ever was life on Mars, and Mars became a dead planet, finding out why that happened will be very useful in preventing something like that from happening on earth some time in the future." He also supports increasing federal research and development programs.

Sensenbrenner has been a leading critic of the December 1997 Kyoto Protocol on Climate Change. At the time he said "it would be a welcome development" if the U.S. walked out until developing nations agreed to reduce emissions. He has pointed to studies that show implementation of Kyoto would cut Wisconsin economic output by $4 billion and cut real incomes 15%; he warned the administration against signing the Kyoto text in Buenos Aires in November 1998, and has said it is dishonest not to have submitted it to the Senate, where 95 senators have agreed to oppose it unless developing countries are subject to its limits.

On other issues, Sensenbrenner has spoken out strongly for Milwaukee's school choice experiment; he favors educational savings accounts and wants to replace federal K-12 regulations with block grants. He has long opposed racial quotas and preferences. He seeks repeal of the Northeast Dairy Compact, which he argues suffuses the national market with unfairly priced milk, butter and cheese.

Sensenbrenner's only tough race was the 1978 primary. He had no Democratic opponent in 1994 and 1998 and was re-elected with 74% of the vote in 1996.

Cook's Call. *Safe.* Sensenbrenner has never come close to losing this heavily Republican district in 10 re-election contests. There is no reason to believe he is in any danger in 2000.

The People: Pop. 1990: 543,602; 35.5% rural; 12.7% age 65 + ; 98.1% White, 0.4% Black, 0.9% Asian, 0.2% Amer. Indian, 0.4% Other; 1% Hispanic Origin. Households: 67.9% married couple families; 33.6% married couple fams. w. children; 45.9% college educ.; median household income: $37,579; per capita income: $16,187; median house value: $82,800; median gross rent: $361.

1762 WISCONSIN

Rep. F. James Sensenbrenner, Jr. (R)

Elected 1978; b. June 14, 1943, Chicago, IL; home, Menomonee Falls; Stanford U., A.B. 1965, U. of WI, J.D. 1968; Episcopalian; married (Cheryl).

Elected Office: WI Assembly, 1968–74; WI Senate, 1974–78.

Professional Career: Practicing atty., 1968–69; Staff asst., U.S. Rep. Arthur Younger, 1965.

DC Office: 2332 RHOB 20515, 202-225-5101; Fax: 202-225-3190; Web site: www.house.gov/sensenbrenner.

District Office: Brookfield, 414-784-1111.

Committees: *Judiciary* (2d of 21 R): Courts & Intellectual Property. *Science* (Chmn. of 25 R).

Group Ratings

	ADA	ACLU	AFS	LCV	CON	NTU	NFIB	COC	ACU	NTLC	CHC
1998	5	6	0	38	77	87	100	78	92	92	100
1997	20	—	0	—	97	84	—	80	88	—	—

National Journal Ratings

	1997 LIB — 1997 CONS		1998 LIB — 1998 CONS	
Economic	0% —	90%	30% —	67%
Social	0% —	90%	14% —	81%
Foreign	43% —	55%	39% —	58%

Key Votes of the 105th Congress

1. Clinton Budget Deal	Y	5. Puerto Rico Sthood. Ref.	N	9. Cut $ for B-2 Bombers	Y
2. Education IRAs	Y	6. End Highway Set-asides	Y	10. Human Rights in China	N
3. Req. 2/3 to Raise Taxes	Y	7. School Prayer Amend.	Y	11. Withdraw Bosnia Troops	Y
4. Fast-track Trade	Y	8. Ovrd. Part. Birth Veto	Y	12. End Cuban TV-Marti	Y

Election Results

1998 general	F. James Sensenbrenner Jr. (R)	175,533	(91%)	($290,913)
	Jeffrey M. Gonyo (Ind)	16,419	(9%)	
1998 primary	F. James Sensenbrenner Jr. (R)	unopposed		
1996 general	F. James Sensenbrenner Jr. (R)	197,910	(74%)	($261,644)
	Floyd Brenholt (D)	67,740	(25%)	($13,781)

WYOMING

"The land of the cowboy," the *WPA Guide* called Wyoming 60 years ago. "Its mountains, plains, and valleys are essentially livestock country. A cowboy astride a bucking bronco greets the visitor from enameled license plates, from newspapers, magazines and painted signs." The cowboy is still on the license plates, and Wyoming remains the most western of states in spirit—largely unsettled, the least populous state, a thin veneer of civilization stretched over a forbidding and beautiful land. Wyoming "has a 'lean-to' look," writes Gretel Ehrlich. "Instead of big, roomy barns and Victorian houses, there are dugouts, low sheds, log cabins, sheep camps and fence lines that look like driftwood blown haphazardly into place. People here still feel pride because they live in such a harsh place, part of the glamorous cowboy past." "What you see now in Wyoming is the promotion of things we used to apologize for," says the state Commerce Department director. "Wide open spaces, a huge expansive sky with no pollution, uncluttered clean rivers with maybe a lone fly fisherman, a cowboy and his dog and a herd of cattle."

But Wyoming's economy now depends not on cowboys and cattle but, precariously, on mining and minerals. Wyoming boomed with oil prospectors during the energy price surge of the 1970s, but was hit hard by drops in oil prices in the early 1980s and again in the late 1990s. The result was population losses in both decades. As the exploration for oil slumped, the production of other minerals has surged. The Clean Air Act put a premium on Wyoming's low-sulfur coal, and this is now the number one coal producing state; the strip mines of the Powder River Basin produce 30% of the nation's coal and a private company is preparing to build a new $1.4 billion rail line from there to the Mississippi River—the biggest U.S. rail construction project in a century. Wyoming is also the number four oil and number six natural gas producer, and the nation's top producer of the mineral bentonite (used in oil drilling and cosmetics) and has the world's largest reserve of trona (used in glass and baking soda). But these are all capital-intensive industries, with few jobs for young people: the number of young families here fell 20% in the 1980s and Wyoming ranked 50th in states on creating jobs that add value. Wage levels, above the national average during the oil boom, are now well below. But Governor Jim Geringer, starting a new $23 million Wyoming Business Council, insists that, "Wyoming is going to grow."

Wyoming's second industry is now tourism. Yellowstone National Park continues to draw millions, and Jackson Hole just to the south has become one of America's elite resort areas year-round; its airport is Wyoming's busiest, and Teton County is now trying to restore the Upper Snake River to its pre-levee condition with new islands and braiding. There has been growth as well in the scenic and pastoral country on the eastern slope of the Big Horn mountains around Buffalo and Sheridan. The third industry is agriculture: Wyoming is second in the nation in wool production, third in sheep inventory and also produces sugar beets, barley, pinto beans and beef cattle.

Reliance on high-tech mineral extraction and high-end tourism may seem a contradiction of Wyoming's Old West heritage. But Wyoming has always depended on new technology to tame age-old nature. Cattle ranches after the open-range era were made possible only by the barbed wire that could fence in roaming herds, and the steam locomotives that could carry cattle to markets back east. This 19th Century high tech was brought to Wyoming by large capitalist operators, some of them onetime Texas cowhands or second sons of English landed gentry, who started the first big operations after the Civil War. And of course mining depends on high-tech machinery and responsiveness to markets that reward innovation and penalize

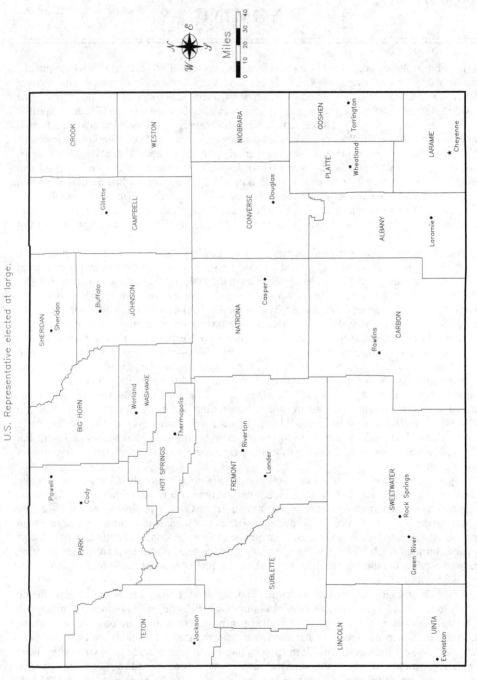

U.S. Representative elected at large.

stasis. Oil prices have gone down partly because sophisticated, computer-based techniques for locating it are much more efficient than even a few years ago.

At the same time the old Wyoming is coming back. In the 1990s grey wolves were returned to the Yellowstone area, despite local ranchers' objections—nature edging man back just a little bit. Then in 1997 a federal judge ruled the wolf introduction illegal—an intrusion of the modern world—but stayed the order pending appeal. The International Rocky Mountain Stage Stop Sled Race, run in daily stages over a 400-mile course, keeps Wyoming in touch with the past while promoting it for visitors. Coyote hunting contests are held to rid the range of predators, while vandal-environmentalists cut barbed wire fences. Lakota Indians want to change the name of Devils Tower to Bear Lodge, the original name, they say. Wyoming still is a kind of frontier: it was until recently one of the few states with more men than women—one reason it was the first part of the United States, when it was a territory in 1869, to give women the vote.

There is a settled part of Wyoming as well, in the medium-sized towns that are the state's largest cities, and among sheep and cattle ranches, sugar beet and malting barley farms and denizens of tiny settlements. This is a small state, a single community really, where people remember who played what position, when and how well, for what high-school football team; where because all locals know who your father's cousins married, you mostly live on the straight and narrow. The locals set the tone of life in Wyoming, and they were shocked and outraged in October, 1998, when Matthew Shepard, a gay student at the University of Wyoming, was gruesomely murdered.

There was once a sharp economic and regional split traditionally reflected in partisan politics. The big economic interests—cattle ranchers, organized in the Wyoming Stock Growers' Association, and the Union Pacific Railroad management always favored the Republicans, as did the wildcatters, independent producers and oil company geologists. The main Democratic constituency had been the Union Pacific Railroad workers who built the first transcontinental line across southern Wyoming in the 1860s; the southern tier of counties, from Cheyenne through Laramie to Evanston, once voted Democratic, but Laramie and surrounding Albany County are about the only solidly Democratic areas left. So the population balance clearly favors the Republicans, and Wyoming has been one of the most Republican states since the 1970s; it hasn't elected a Democrat to the Senate since 1970 or the House since 1976, but has had mostly Democratic governors over that time. In presidential elections it is safely Republican, but with a large Perot vote—the nation's fourth highest in 1996.

Wyoming's Republican strength has been tested in the 1990s, and has prevailed. The Clinton Administration's environmental policies, from proposed grazing fee increases to reintroduction of grey wolves into Yellowstone—have not been popular here, indeed are sometimes referred to as the "war on the West." That has hobbled even Democrats who have won state office and do well in the personal campaigning which has always remained important here: there aren't many people—not even half a million, less than the size of an average congressional district—and Wyoming voters expect to talk person-to-person with their governors, senators and congressmen every few years. Democrat Mike Sullivan was elected governor twice and had high job ratings. But nonetheless in 1994 he lost the Senate race 59%–39% to Congressman-at-Large Craig Thomas. Democrat Kathy Karpan became popular as secretary of State. But she lost the governorship to Jim Geringer in 1994 59%–40% and a Senate race to Mike Enzi in 1996 54%–42%. In 1998 Republicans continued to win: Geringer was re-elected 56%–40% and Congresswoman-at-Large Barbara Cubin 58%–39%.

Governor. Jim Geringer, the governor of Wyoming, grew up in Wheatland, where his father, a Volga German, had emigrated early in the century. That was his Old West background; his high-tech experience came from service in the Air Force, where he worked on Air Force and NASA space boosters for 10 years. In 1977, Geringer returned to Wyoming, started from scratch and bought his own farm. He was elected to the state legislature in 1982. In 1994, when incumbent Mike Sullivan ran for the Senate, Geringer ran for governor. He won the four-way

Republican primary with 43%, then beat Secretary of State Kathy Karpan by 59%–40%, carrying all but one county.

Geringer says his goal is to use Wyoming's mineral resources and low taxes to build a more diversified, high-tech economy. But state government is highly dependent on volatile mineral revenues, and oil production and exports to Asia are declining sharply. Geringer's answer in 1998 was to put the state Commerce Department and other agencies into a Wyoming Business Council, to be run by a business with a 15-member board of directors and an economic development specialist as chief executive. He emphasizes that Wyoming is the cheapest state to do business in, with low taxes, low wages, low energy costs and little state government regulation. But he does not want explosive growth like Colorado's. "Are we growing as fast as our neighbors? No. Do we want to? I'm not sure that we do."

On other issues, Wyoming has cut its welfare rolls by 74% in the 1990s. Geringer signed a contract with USWest to connect all the state's schools by internet and the legislature passed a law to end a school finance suit. He criticized the legislature when it appropriated only $400,000 for his $7.6 million campaign against methamphetamines. He supported a gas tax increase and expanded the scope of the line-item veto. He criticized AOL for allowing a web site run by a serial killer that described his crimes, including one in Wyoming; Geringer debated the subject with pornographer Larry Flynt on *Larry King Live*.

In 1998 Geringer had articulate opposition in both the primary and general election. In the primary sheep rancher Bill Taliaferro charged that Geringer had been ineffective in stimulating the Wyoming economy. He got 33% of the vote—more than challengers of sitting governors usually do. In the general he faced John Vinich, 24-year state legislator, and candidate for the U.S. Senate in 1988 and for the U.S. House in the spring 1989 special election. Vinich attacked Geringer for hiring a Colorado expert to head the Wyoming Business Council and proposed to revive the state's link program—using state funds to generate low-interest business loans from banks. Geringer said that link lost money, and held out the hope that more jobs would mean that fewer kids would have to leave Wyoming to find jobs elsewhere. He won 56%–40%, a decisive but not overwhelming margin. The legislature continues to be heavily Republican.

Senior Senator. Craig Thomas grew up in Cody, where he knew his later Senate colleague Alan Simpson, graduated from the University of Wyoming and served in the Marines. He worked for the Wyoming Farm Bureau and the Wyoming Rural Electric Association, organizations with conservative political leanings that kept him in touch with hundreds of people active in their communities. In 1984 he was elected to the Wyoming House. In March 1989, when Congressman-at-Large Dick Cheney was appointed secretary of Defense, Thomas ran in a contest which turned out to be close, as is often the case in special elections early in a president's term. Democrat John Vinich, just a few months after nearly beating Malcolm Wallop, noted that national Republicans were helping Thomas and sounded a powerful Wyoming theme—don't let outsiders make decisions for Wyoming. But Thomas rallied and won with 53% of the vote; Vinich was the Democratic candidate for governor in 1998, and lost again.

Thomas had a solid conservative voting record and concentrated on Wyoming issues in the House. He opposed the reintroduction of wolves into Yellowstone Park (it was done anyway) and proposed giving states the option of acquiring all federal Bureau of Land Management lands (a nonstarter). He won re-election with 55% in 1990 and 58% in 1992. When Wallop retired in 1994, Thomas was the obvious Republican candidate and had no primary opposition. In the general, he faced Governor Mike Sullivan, personally popular and with a conservative record, but handicapped by his association with Bill Clinton at governors' conferences; Clinton personally asked him to run for the Senate. Thomas relentlessly attacked Sullivan as a "Friend of Bill" and ally of Interior Secretary Bruce Babbitt, whose policies were highly unpopular here. Thomas won 59%–39%, losing only one southern tier county, and that by only six votes.

Thomas is chairman of two subcommittees. One covers the national parks, and despite his disagreements with Babbitt he steered the 1998 national parks reauthorization bill to passage. This renewed the parks' higher fees, which did not seem to cut visits, overhauled the rules for concessions and established a new system to decide on new parks. He has opposed Babbitt's higher grazing fees on federal lands; locally, his law allows ranchers three more years of grazing rights in the Grand Teton National Park until the Park Service figures out how to protect their property from unrestrained development.

Thomas also chairs the East Asian and Pacific Affairs Subcommittee of Foreign Affairs. There he has spent most of his time on China. He favors normal trade relations with China and has not pushed the use of force. He has worked closely with the Clinton Administration on China issues and has held many hearings. He has charged that the Clinton Administration is too focused on the Korea Energy Development Organization and not focused enough on making sure that North Korea complies with the agreement. Other Thomas causes include higher Medicare reimbursement rates for rural areas, stopping an immediate cut in the tariff on imported wool and giving states the lead in electricity deregulation. Thomas casts some quixotic votes, against the October 1998 budget, for example. But he has also hammered out laws passed with bipartisan support, like the Freedom from Government Competition Act, which opens to public bids activities agencies don't have to do themselves, and another which overturned a court ruling that separated ownership of methane in coal veins from that of the coal itself.

Cook's Call. *Safe.* In 1994, Democrats thought they had the perfect candidate in Governor Mike Sullivan to take the seat being vacated by Malcolm Wallop. The Republican tidal wave and Sullivan's close relationship with President Clinton, however, proved to be a damaging combination, and Thomas was elected easily. Democrats are not harboring any serious hope of knocking Thomas off this time.

Junior Senator. Wyoming's junior senator is Mike Enzi, elected in 1996. Enzi grew up in Thermopolis and Sheridan, the son of a shoe salesman, got degrees in accounting and marketing, moved to Gillette and became an oil company accountant and founded NZ Shoes. He served eight years as mayor of Gillette, the center of Wyoming's coal belt and its fastest-growing town. In 1986 he was elected to the legislature, where he served for 10 years.

In December 1995 Senator Alan Simpson announced he was retiring from the Senate after 18 years, taking his Wyoming-brand sense of humor and common sense to Harvard, which is always in need of them. Enzi was one of nine Republicans and two Democrats to run. With support from a grass roots network of conservatives, Enzi finished first in a straw poll at the May 1996 Republican state convention; in second place was John Barrasso, an orthopedic surgeon from Casper who had appeared on statewide TV discussing health issues for 12 years; his chief difference on issues was his support of abortion rights. Barrasso had more money, but Enzi won 32%–30%, with a big majority in his home area in northeast Wyoming and narrow margins in the Casper and Cheyenne areas.

The Democratic nominee was Kathy Karpan, secretary of State from 1986–94, gubernatorial candidate in 1994, who beat a man who called for construction of a 22,000-mile-high tower into space to promote world peace. Karpan had an appealing story—she helped raise her siblings when her mother died, she worked her way through school and then was a prosecutor—and moderate stances on many issues: she called herself "a DLC Democrat." Her opposition to gun control led the National Rifle Association to stay neutral; her opposition to federally funded abortions kept her off EMILY's List. But she had the liabilities of having supported the presidential candidacies of Bill Clinton in 1992 and Bruce Babbitt in 1988. She appeared in one ad in hunting gear, toting a shotgun. "She's all in camouflage, but you can see right through her," was Enzi's reply. She opposed the balanced budget amendment and Senator Craig Thomas's bill to turn over BLM lands to state governments; Enzi favored both. It was a game effort by Karpan, but Enzi led in polls all the way and won 54%–42%. She carried the southern counties and ran nearly even in Cheyenne and Casper; he won big just about everywhere else.

Enzi started off in the Senate by presiding for 100 hours in the chair by July and seeking permission to bring his laptop on the floor (the Rules Committee said no). Enzi has sponsored a bill to modernize OSHA and he succesfully pushed a home-based business fairness bill, providing deductibility for home offices and health insurance for the self-employed and clarifying the status of independent contractors: an accountant at work. He voted against the budget agreement in October 1998 and opposed the Kyoto treaty at the Buenos Aires conference in November 1998. He sought to bar EPA from blocking state efforts to develop environmental self-audits and to prevent the Interior Department from bypassing state governments on Indian gambling. He cast a lone vote in committee against FDA Administrator Jane Henney because of her support for the abortifacient RU-486.

Representative-At-Large. Wyoming, the nation's least populous state, has elected one congressman-at-large since it was admitted to the Union in 1890. The current incumbent is Barbara Cubin, a Republican elected in 1994. The great-great-granddaughter of one of Wyoming's original homesteaders, she grew up in Casper, where she worked as a teacher, social worker, chemist and realtor; for 19 years she managed her husband's medical practice. She was divorced after an early first marriage, worked as a single mother, was subjected to sexual harassment, but insists: "I am not a feminist. I am not gender sensitive." She worked in Casper charities and was elected to the legislature in 1986, where she was prime sponsor of a 1994 ballot measure authorizing life without parole sentences.

In 1994, when Congressman Craig Thomas ran for the Senate, Cubin was one of five Republicans and two Democrats to run for the House. She sharply attacked "the Clinton-Babbitt war on the West," though she said she would accept an increase in some grazing fees and slightly higher mining royalties. In the Republican primary, she won 39% to 25% for House staffer Rob Wallace, 18% for sheep rancher Jim Magagna and 17% for state House Speaker Doug Chamberlain. The Democratic nominee was Bob Schuster, a law partner of high-profile Wyoming trial lawyer Gerry Spence, who spent $2.4 million, most of it his own money, on what was the third-highest spending campaign in the country. Schuster's big issue was abortion; she called him a "a slick trial-lawyer Clinton Democrat." Them was fightin' words in Wyoming in 1994: Schuster carried only four counties, three in the southern tier and the other in Jackson Hole, and Cubin won 53%–41%.

In the House Cubin has had a solidly conservative voting record and quickly became chairman of the Energy and Mineral Resources Subcommittee. She continued to oppose many Interior policies and took some interesting initiatives. She worked with others in the delegation to overturn a court decision that delinked ownership of methane from the coalbeds in which it is found. She sought to overturn the Forest Service's ban on fixed climbing anchors for mountain and rock climbers. She got $10 million for a National Historic Trails Interpretive Center (the Oregon Trail goes right through Wyoming). "My point to everyone was that in the East we have preserved our history very well, but in the West we haven't done that." She was one of four members to switch their votes at the last minute and pass the budget resolution in June 1996. She spearheaded the effort to obtain Medicare coverage for the breast cancer treatment Xeloda. She co-sponsored a resolution condemning the killing of Matthew Shepard, whom two of her sons knew. She wants to require the federal government to take oil and other mineral royalties in-kind rather than in money.

In 1998 Cubin was re-elected 58%–39% in a campaign in which both candidates mostly avoided the negative themes prevalent elsewhere.

Cook's Call. *Safe.* Democrats have little hope of ousting Cubin in this increasingly Republican trending state.

Presidential politics. Wyoming is one of the least likely states in the nation to be seriously contested in presidential general elections: it is too Republican, too remote and has only three electoral votes. But with a high Perot vote, Wyoming looked close enough that Bill Clinton vacationed here in August 1996 at the prompting of pollster Dick Morris. He still lost the state, and got his best support from older voters—not a good augury for Wyoming Democrats.

Wyoming has held presidential caucuses in early March, which attract some attention; it will be part of the Mountain States primary March 10 in 2000. This was one of the few non-southern states where Al Gore won in the 1988 presidential primary.

The People: Est. Pop. 1998: 480,907; Pop. 1990: 453,588, up 6% 1990–1998. 0.2% of U.S. total, 51st largest; 35.1% rural. Median age: 34.9 years. 10.7% 65 years and over. 94.2% White, 0.7% Black, 0.6% Asian, 2.2% Amer. Indian, 2.3% Other; 5.5% Hispanic Origin. Households: 59.7% married couple families; 31.5% married couple fams. w. children; 49.9% college educ.; median household income: $27,096; per capita income: $12,311; 67.8% owner occupied housing; median house value: $61,600; median monthly rent: $270. 4.8% Unemployment. 1998 Voting age pop.: 354,000. 1998 Turnout: 178,401; 50% of VAP. Registered voters (1998): 239,539; 70,926 D (30%), 142,447 R (59%), 26,166 unaffiliated and minor parties (11%).

Political Lineup: Governor, Jim Geringer (R); Secy. of State, Joe Meyer (R); Atty. Gen., Gay Woodhouse (R); Treasurer, Cynthia M. Lummis (R); State Senate, 30 (10 D, 20 R); Majority Leader, Henry H. R. Coe (R); State House, 60 (17 D, 43 R); House Speaker, Eli Bebout (R). Senators, Craig Thomas (R) and Michael Enzi (R). Representative, 1 R at large.

Elections Division: 307-777-7186; **Filing Deadline for U.S. Congress:** June 2, 2000.

1996 Presidential Vote

Dole (R)	105,388	(50%)
Clinton (D)	77,934	(37%)
Perot (I)	25,928	(12%)

1992 Presidential Vote

Bush (R)	79,347	(40%)
Clinton (D)	68,160	(34%)
Perot (I)	51,263	(26%)

GOVERNOR

Gov. Jim Geringer (R)

Elected 1994, term expires Jan. 2003; b. Apr. 24, 1944, Wheatland; home, Wheatland; KS St. U., B.S. 1967; Lutheran; married (Sherri).

Military Career: Air Force, 1967–77, Air Force Reserves, 1977–91.

Elected Office: WY House of Reps., 1982–88; WY Senate, 1988–94.

Professional Career: Farmer, Rancher; Contract Admin., Missouri Basin Power Project, 1977–79.

Office: State Capitol Bldg., No. 124, Cheyenne, 82002, 307-777-7434; Fax: 307-632-3909; Web site: www.state.wy.us.

Election Results

1998 gen.	Jim Geringer (R)	97,235	(56%)
	John P. Vinich (D)	70,754	(40%)
	Others	6,899	(4%)
1998 prim.	Jim Geringer (R)	56,015	(67%)
	Bill Taliaferro (R)	28,164	(33%)
1994 gen.	Jim Geringer (R)	118,016	(59%)
	Kathy Karpan (D)	80,747	(40%)

SENATORS

Sen. Craig Thomas (R)

Elected 1994, seat up 2000; b. Feb. 17, 1933, Cody; home, Casper; U. of WY, B.S. 1954, LaSalle U., LL.B. 1968; Methodist; married (Susan).

Military Career: Marine Corps, 1955–59.

Elected Office: WY House of Reps., 1984–89; U.S. House of Reps., 1989–94.

Professional Career: V.P., WY Farm Bureau, 1960–66; Legis. staff, Amer. Farm Bureau, 1966–75; Gen. Mgr., WY Rural Electric Assn., 1975–89.

DC Office: 109 HSOB, 20515, 202-224-6441; Fax: 202-224-1724; Web site: www.senate.gov/~thomas.

State Offices: Casper, 307-261-6413; Cheyenne, 307-772-2451; Riverton, 307-856-6642; Rock Springs, 307-362-5012; Sheridan, 307-672-6456.

Committees: *Energy & Natural Resources* (6th of 11 R): Forests & Public Land Management; National Parks, Historic Preservation & Recreation (Chmn.). *Environment & Public Works* (5th of 10 R): Fisheries, Wildlife & Drinking Water; Transportation & Infrastructure. *Foreign Relations* (8th of 10 R): East Asian & Pacific Affairs (Chmn.); International Economic Policy, Export & Trade Promotion; Near Eastern & South Asian Affairs. *Indian Affairs* (6th of 8 R).

Group Ratings

	ADA	ACLU	AFS	LCV	CON	NTU	NFIB	COC	ACU	NTLC	CHC
1998	5	29	0	0	71	72	89	89	84	86	91
1997	10	—	0	—	66	83	—	90	84	—	—

National Journal Ratings

	1997 LIB — 1997 CONS		1998 LIB — 1998 CONS	
Economic	0%	— 89%	18%	— 72%
Social	28%	— 62%	24%	— 73%
Foreign	24%	— 72%	26%	— 71%

Key Votes of the 105th Congress

1. Bal. Budget Amend.	Y	5. Satcher for Surgeon Gen.	N	9. Chem. Weapons Treaty	Y
2. Clinton Budget Deal	Y	6. Highway Set-asides	N	10. Cuban Humanitarian Aid	N
3. Cloture on Tobacco	N	7. Table Child Gun locks	Y	11. Table Bosnia Troops	N
4. Education IRAs	Y	8. Ovrd. Part. Birth Veto	Y	12. $ for Test-ban Treaty	N

Election Results

1994 general	Craig Thomas (R)	118,754	(59%)	($1,068,335)
	Mike Sullivan (D)	79,287	(39%)	($712,991)
	Others	3,669	(2%)	
1994 primary	Craig Thomas (R)	unopposed		
1988 general	Malcolm Wallop (R)	91,143	(50%)	($1,344,185)
	John P. Vinich (D)	89,821	(50%)	($490,230)

Sen. Michael Enzi (R)

Elected 1996, seat up 2002; b. Feb. 1, 1944, Bremerton, WA; home, Gillette; George Washington U., B.S. 1966, Denver U., M.B.A. 1968; Presbyterian; married (Diana).

Military Career: WY Natl. Guard, 1967–73.

Elected Office: Gillette Mayor, 1975–82; WY House of Reps., 1986–90; WY Senate, 1990–96.

Professional Career: Owner, NZ Shoes, 1969–95; Dir. & Chmn., First WY Bank of Gillette, 1978–88; Accounting Mgr. & Computer Programmer, Dunbar Well Service, 1985–97; Educ. Comm. of States, 1989–93; Dir., Black Hills Corp., 1992–96; Western Interstate Comm. for Higher Educ., 1995–96.

DC Office: 290 RSOB, 20510, 202-224-3424; Fax: 202-228-0359; Web site: www.senate.gov/~enzi.

State Offices: Casper, 307-261-6572; Cheyenne, 307-772-2477; Cody, 307-527-9444; Gillette, 307-682-6268; Jackson, 307-739-9507.

Committees: *Aging (Special)* (9th of 11 R). *Banking, Housing & Urban Affairs* (7th of 11 R): Economic Policy; Financial Institutions; International Trade & Finance (Chmn.). *Health, Education, Labor & Pensions* (5th of 10 R): Employment, Safety & Training (Chmn.); Public Health. *Small Business* (6th of 10 R).

Group Ratings

	ADA	ACLU	AFS	LCV	CON	NTU	NFIB	COC	ACU	NTLC	CHC
1998	0	14	0	0	84	70	89	94	92	93	100
1997	10	—	0	—	34	81	—	70	88	—	—

National Journal Ratings

	1997 LIB — 1997 CONS	1998 LIB — 1998 CONS
Economic	11% — 76%	0% — 88%
Social	0% — 83%	12% — 79%
Foreign	28% — 71%	45% — 52%

Key Votes of the 105th Congress

1. Bal. Budget Amend.	Y	5. Satcher for Surgeon Gen.	N	9. Chem. Weapons Treaty	Y
2. Clinton Budget Deal	Y	6. Highway Set-asides	N	10. Cuban Humanitarian Aid	N
3. Cloture on Tobacco	N	7. Table Child Gun locks	Y	11. Table Bosnia Troops	Y
4. Education IRAs	Y	8. Ovrd. Part. Birth Veto	Y	12. $ for Test-ban Treaty	N

Election Results

1996 general	Michael Enzi (R)	114,116	(54%)	($953,572)
	Kathy Karpan (D)	89,103	(42%)	($814,258)
	Others	7,858	(4%)	
1996 primary	Michael Enzi (R)	27,056	(32%)	
	John Barrasso (R)	24,918	(30%)	
	Curt Meier (R)	14,739	(18%)	
	Nimi McConigley (R)	6,005	(7%)	
	Kevin P. Meenan (R)	6,000	(7%)	
	Others	4,610	(6%)	
1990 general	Alan K. Simpson (R)	100,784	(64%)	($1,435,814)
	Kathy Helling (D)	56,848	(36%)	($6,243)

REPRESENTATIVE

Rep. Barbara Cubin (R)

Elected 1994; b. Nov. 30, 1946, Salinas, CA; home, Casper; Creighton U., B.S. 1969; Episcopalian; married (Frederick).

Elected Office: WY House of Reps., 1986–92; WY Senate, 1992–94.

Professional Career: Office Mgr., Dr. Frederick Cubin, 1975–94.

DC Office: 1114 LHOB, 20515, 202-225-2311; Fax: 202-225-3057; Web site: www.house.gov/cubin.

District Offices: Casper, 307-261-6595; Cheyenne, 307-772-2595; Rock Springs, 307-362-4095.

Committees: *Commerce* (20th of 29 R): Health and Environment; Telecommunications, Trade & Consumer Protection. *Resources* (12th of 28 R): Energy & Mineral Resources (Chmn.).

Group Ratings

	ADA	ACLU	AFS	LCV	CON	NTU	NFIB	COC	ACU	NTLC	CHC
1998	5	13	0	0	42	63	93	94	100	97	100
1997	0	—	29	—	13	60	—	71	100	—	—

National Journal Ratings

	1997 LIB — 1997 CONS		1998 LIB — 1998 CONS	
Economic	16% —	84%	15% —	81%
Social	0% —	90%	10% —	89%
Foreign	0% —	88%	0% —	93%

Key Votes of the 105th Congress

1. Clinton Budget Deal	Y	5. Puerto Rico Sthood. Ref.	N	9. Cut $ for B-2 Bombers	N
2. Education IRAs	*	6. End Highway Set-asides	Y	10. Human Rights in China	N
3. Req. 2/3 to Raise Taxes	Y	7. School Prayer Amend.	Y	11. Withdraw Bosnia Troops	Y
4. Fast-track Trade	Y	8. Ovrd. Part. Birth Veto	Y	12. End Cuban TV-Marti	N

Election Results

1998 general	Barbara Cubin (R)	100,687	(58%)	($569,704)
	Scott Farris (D)	67,399	(39%)	($134,427)
	Others	6,133	(4%)	
1998 primary	Barbara Cubin (R)	unopposed		
1996 general	Barbara Cubin (R)	116,004	(55%)	($679,599)
	Pete Maxfield (D)	85,724	(41%)	($273,881)
	Others	8,255	(4%)	

PUERTO RICO, VIRGIN ISLANDS, GUAM, AMERICAN SAMOA

Four American insular territories—Puerto Rico, Virgin Islands, Guam, American Samoa—are represented in Congress by elected delegates who, like the District of Columbia's delegate, have floor privileges and votes on committees but not votes on the floor; House Democrats let them vote in committee of the whole proceedings in 1993 and 1994; but Republicans changed that rule back in 1995. Each territory's status—its relationship to the United States—is different, governed by a separate law, and status is often the pivot around which territorial politics turn.

PUERTO RICO

Puerto Rico has a unique history. For four centuries, from Columbus's landing here in 1493 until the Spanish-American War of 1898, Puerto Rico was a Spanish colony, and the port of San Juan was the gathering place for its annual convoy of gold and silver from the Americas to Spain. Today, with 3.8 million people, it is the largest American territory—about the same population as Kentucky; also, some 3 million people of Puerto Rican descent live on the mainland. Fifty years ago, it was "the poorhouse of the Caribbean," heavily populated, devoted almost entirely to sugar and coffee cultivation.

Puerto Rico has elected a resident commissioner to Congress since 1900 and its residents have been American citizens since 1917, but it didn't elect its own governor until 1948. In the 1940s, 1950s and early 1960s, Puerto Rico was transformed by Governor Luis Munoz Marin and his Popular Democratic Party. Munoz initiated "Operation Bootstrap" (called "Operation Hands to Work" by Puerto Ricans) to lure businesses to Puerto Rico with promises of low-wage labor and government-built factories and tax exemptions. Munoz also developed Puerto Rico's commonwealth form of government—better understood in Spanish, Estado Libre Asociado (ELA): Free Associated State—approved by plebiscite in 1952. As a commonwealth, Puerto Rico is part of the United States for purposes of international trade, foreign policy and war, but has its own separate laws, taxes and representative government; it is not subject to federal income taxes and is not eligible for federal benefits (though some have been approved). Puerto Rico has also developed its own political parties: Munoz's Popular Democrats, the New Progressives who favor statehood, and two Independence parties.

But the commonwealth solution, by its own terms, was open to amendment; ever since Munoz's voluntary retirement in 1964, the central issue in Puerto Rico's politics has been status: should this island continue or modify ELA, should it seek statehood, or should it seek independence? Over time there clearly has been gradual movement toward statehood. In the July 1967 referendum, conducted when the Popular Democrats were in power, Puerto Ricans voted for ELA over statehood by 60%–39%; in the November 1993 referendum, conducted with New Progressive Governor Pedro Rossello in office, the vote was 48% for ELA, 46% for statehood; in the December 1998 referendum, ordered by Rossello, 46.5% voted for statehood and 50.3% for "none of the above," the option favored by the Popular Democrats. Independence has negligible support—4% in 1993, 2.5% in 1998—primarily from university students; nor are there many pro-independence abstentions, for voter turnout in the enthusiastic politics of Puerto Rico is the highest under the American flag, higher than in even the most affluent, long-settled suburbs of the mainland.

But if Puerto Rico's legal status remains unsettled in the 1990s, the island's economy and government have been undergoing important changes. One was Congress's decision in 1996 to phase out through 2005 Section 936, the provision that shelters earnings of some Puerto Rico manufacturers from federal taxes and allows their products into the U.S. duty-free. Pharmaceutical companies in particular have set up highly visible plants in Puerto Rico—half of U.S. prescription drugs are manufactured in Puerto Rico—and ELA supporters have claimed that the island's economy depends on the tax exemptions. But if the number of manufacturing jobs has declined slightly, Puerto Rico's overall economy has kept pace with the mainland's pace, growing about 3% a year; unemployment in 1998 was 13%, but that is far less than in the 1980s. Puerto Rico has long since lost low-wage garment jobs to lower-wage countries in the Caribbean and Latin America, and is developing new jobs in services, tourism, trading and exports. Rossello and Resident Commissioner Carlos Romero-Barcelo both supported the phaseout of 936, confident that Puerto Rico would grow without it.

Their views prevailed in the 1996 election, in which status and the 936 phaseout were the chief issues. Rossello, opposed by Popular Democrat San Juan Mayor Hector Luis Acevedo, won 51%–44%, a slight improvement on his 50%–46% victory in 1992, and the biggest margin since 1964; Romero-Barcelo was re-elected over Celeste Benitez 50%–46%. The New Progressives also maintained control of the legislature and most municipios, though Popular Democrat Sila Calderon was elected mayor of San Juan. Rossello was also helped by his *mano dura* stand against crime; he has fought the drug trade by sending National Guard troops into 76 housing projects, arresting drug dealers, then putting fences around projects, enabling police to control who enters and leaves. He made English Puerto Rico's second official language again (as it was during the first half of the century) and took steps to increase teaching in English in schools.

Rossello made even more important policy changes in his second term. To compensate for the phaseout of 936 benefits, he reduced the corporate tax from 14.5% to 7%, with credits for job creation and investment reducing it to as low as 2%. Taxes on distributed dividends were eliminated and a 200% deduction allowed for research and development and job training. He started massive public works—a $300 million Superaqueduct, a $1.5 billion *Tren Urbano* (mass transit) in San Juan, and other major road projects. Puerto Rico provides health insurance to the poor via la tarjetita (the little card) and Rossello instituted school vouchers and five minutes of daily reflection in schools.

Under Rossello, Puerto Rico has followed the trend in many Latin American countries toward privatization of state-owned companies and state-run services. He has privatized the Aqueduct and Sewer Authority's 1,600 facilities; private companies are building and will administer 3,000 prison cells; the government has sold two hotels, seven hospitals and 78 health clinics. It sold the longtime money-losing Navieras shipping company and the Lotus pineapple processing plant. Most controversially, in April 1998 Rossello announced he was selling the Puerto Rican Telephone Company. The unions representing its 6,400 workers went on strike in June, blocking major highways from the airport; a group called the Boricua Popular Army claimed credit for bombings; there was a two-day general strike that ended in July 1998. At the end of the month, the purchaser, GTE, guaranteed more jobs and protections than in its original offer and the strike was called off. Romero-Barcelo called the strike Rossello's "worst moment"; Rossello responded in English, "Frankly, my dear, I don't give a damn." In February 1999 GTE raised a $1.5 billion credit on Wall Street, and the acquisition went through.

Next came Hurricane Georges in September 1998, the worst storm to hit Puerto Rico in 70 years. Fifty thousand homes were damaged or destroyed and damages totaled $3 billion. But Puerto Rico showed the energy and resilience of an advanced economy in its response. Insurance payments and federal government aid rolled in, the construction industry boomed, appliance sales skyrocketed and virtually all the island's hotels were open for the Christmas season. Much focus was on damage to farms, but agriculture today accounts for only 1% of Puerto Rico's domestic product; manufacturing provides 40%, but that is declining as the economy becomes more service-centered. And with the solid dollar, U.S. interest rates and the U.S. bond market, Puerto Rico has kept growing. Its per-capita income is still among the highest in Latin

America, but only about half that of Mississippi. But it is a perceptibly American economy, with the world's largest J. C. Penney and the highest density of Burger Kings in the world.

Rossello sees statehood as the obvious goal: "That has been my vision since I became governor. I want Puerto Rico to be the link among all cultures in our hemisphere. Having in mind that by the year 2005 there will be a common market in all Americas, Puerto Rico can position itself as the cultural and linguistic bridge, because for 100 years in Puerto Rico two cultures and two languages have been living together." For much of 1998 he and Romero-Barcelo hoped Congress would require a referendum. The House Republican leadership, eager to win some credit with Hispanic voters, and Resources Committee Chairman Don Young, an Alaskan who remembers the days when he was petitioning for statehood, put together a yeoman effort to pass such a bill in the House. They finessed the amendment offered by Rules Chairman Gerald Solomon requiring English to be the official language of a state; the revision would have applied mainland official language requirements and sought to increase English proficiency in schools. It also provided that if statehood or independence won in a referendum, the president would have to submit a transition plan to Congress for approval; to many it looked like a fast track to statehood. Romero-Barcelo strongly supported the bill, but only one other ethnic Puerto Rican congressman did, Jose Serrano of the Bronx; Luis Gutierrez of Chicago and Nydia Velazquez of Brooklyn, commonwealth backers, peppered it with amendments. In March 1998 Newt Gingrich and Young had to pull out all the stops to pass the Young bill by 209–208; only 43 of the 226 Republicans voted for it. There was little enthusiasm for it in the Senate: Majority Leader Trent Lott said it would not get on the floor, and while Energy Committee Chairman Frank Murkowski introduced a bill, it did not get far. In late July, Rossello announced there would be a referendum in December.

Familiar arguments were made yet again. Statehood backers said they wanted full citizenship, contending that if Puerto Ricans can be drafted and serve in the U.S. military, they should be able to vote for president and members of Congress, and that Puerto Rico would grow more as a state. ELA backers vowed to keep Puerto Rico's flag, the Spanish language, the Olympic team and Miss Universe contestant. Unhappy with Rossello's definitions, the Popular Democrats called for statehood opponents to vote for "none of the above." That was the option that prevailed with 50.3% of a typically large Puerto Rico turnout; statehood got 46.5%, only microscopically more than in 1993. Rossello, wearing his 51st star lapel pin, gamely tried to claim victory, but persuaded few. Independence Party leader Ruben Berrios Martinez argued that Congress's reluctance to admit Puerto Rico as a state would shift opinion toward independence. Certainly it is not at all clear that either a Democratic or a Republican Congress would vote statehood if only a small majority favored it; statehood was voted for Alaska and Hawaii only after more than 80% of voters approved it in referenda. The Republican Party has long endorsed statehood, dating back to the time when Puerto Rico's New Progressives identified with mainland Republicans; but none of the party's leaders do now, and even though Puerto Rico has voted for some conservative policies, it seems likely it would elect mostly Democrats to the two Senate and five or six House seats it would have if it were a state. As for the mainland, few have a strong commitment to Puerto Rican statehood, long opposed by the Popular Democrats who have always identified with mainland Democrats, and many sense it could be a political liability at home. But the issue will surely arise again; and there is the danger of a rupture between most Americans and the 3 million of their fellow citizens who live in Puerto Rico.

Presidential politics. Puerto Rico does not vote for president, but it does choose delegates to the parties' national conventions. It elects only a few Republicans, but its Democratic delegation is larger than that of 25 other states and, since it is usually made up of backers of a single leader, it casts a bigger margin for its candidate than all but a few large states.

Governor. Pedro Rossello is the son of a psychiatrist, educated at Notre Dame and Yale Medical School, trained at Harvard and Boston teaching hospitals; he returned to Puerto Rico in 1976, specialized in pediatric surgery, wrote scholarly articles, and played championship tennis. In 1988 he ran for resident commissioner and lost 49%–47%; in 1992 he ran for governor against commonwealth Senator Victoria "Melo" Munoz, the daughter of Luis Munoz Marin, and won 50%–46%. Puerto Rico's straight-ticket voting swept his party to large majorities in the legislature.

Rossello's considerable successes on many programs have been counterbalanced by his failure to win a majority for statehood in the 1993 and 1998 referendums, and by some scandals in the spending of FEMA and AIDS' patient funds. When the island's highest-circulation newspaper, *El Nuevo Dia*, attacked Rossello's administration for corruption in April 1997, the following day 16 government agencies canceled advertising amounting to $4.5 million annually. Just a more efficient allocation of advertising, Rossello argued unconvincingly; in December 1997 *El Nuevo Dia* sued, claiming a "systematic campaign of harassment and punishment." Interestingly, Rossello's privatization plan would remove most of that advertising from control of any future governor.

In June 1999 Rossello surprised most Puerto Ricans by declaring that he would not run for a third term in 2000. A strong Clinton supporter, he has been mentioned as a possible candidate in a Gore administration. He is likely to name the New Progressive candidate to succeed him. That candidate will face San Juan Mayor Sila Calderon, who became the official Popular Democratic candidate in May 1999.

Resident Commissioner. Carlos Romero-Barcelo, a two-term governor, was elected resident commissioner in 1992 in a party-line vote; he is the only member of Congress with a four-year term. He was educated at Exeter and Yale and earned a law degree in Puerto Rico; he was elected mayor of San Juan in 1968 and 1972 and governor in 1976 and 1980; he lost to his longtime rival Rafael Hernandez Colon in 1984.

Romero-Barcelo has worked to get federal funding for Puerto Rico projects: nutritional programs, Medicaid, *Tren Urbano*, drug-fighting projects, El Portal de El Yunque tropical research center at the Caribbean National Forest. He was chastised by some Democrats for endorsing, with Governor Pedro Rossello, Senator Alfonse D'Amato in 1998; he has had a lively rivalry with Governor Pedro Rossello. He is now ranking minority member of a Resources subcommittee, the first Puerto Rico representative to reach such a position.

He won in 1992 by 49%–47% and in 1996 by 50%–46%; he is thought likely to run for a third term in 2000.

Del. Carlos A. Romero-Barcelo (D)

Elected 1992; b. Sept. 4, 1932, San Juan; home, San Juan; Yale U., B.A. 1951, U. of PR Law Schl., LL.B. 1956; Catholic; married (Kathleen).

Elected Office: San Juan Mayor, 1968–76; PR Gov., 1976–84.

Professional Career: Practicing atty., 1956–68, 1985–92; Pres., New Progressive Party, 1989–91.

DC Office: 2443 RHOB, 20515, 202-225-2615; Fax: 202-225-2154; Web site: www.house.gov/romero-barcelo.

District Offices: Ponce, 787-841-3300; San Juan, 787-723-6333.

Committees: *Education & the Workforce* (12th of 22 D): Early Childhood, Youth & Families; Employer-Employee Relations. *Resources* (12th of 24 D): Fisheries Conservation, Wildlife & Oceans; National Parks & Public Lands (RMM).

VIRGIN ISLANDS

The United States' other insular territory in the Caribbean is the Virgin Islands, a very different sort of place than Puerto Rico. It is much smaller, with a resident population of only 110,000, mainly on the three islands of St. Thomas, St. John and St. Croix; 50 acres of the federal government's Water Island officially became part of the Virgin Islands in December 1996. Puerto Rico is multiracial and not self-conscious about it, but most Virgin Islanders are black, and resent the clear divide between the races. While Puerto Rico has attracted all kinds of light industry, the Virgin Islands live off tourism and refineries, industries that have produced higher income levels for its few citizens but have not provided the basis for a mature economy.

But tourism is hostage to the weather, which can be treacherous. Hurricane Hugo in September 1989 destroyed 90% of the buildings on St. Croix, and tourism has never recovered; Hurricanes Luis and Marilyn in September 1995 caused terrible damage on St. Thomas; Hurricane Georges in September 1998 was not as bad, but still slowed down recovery. Some 75% of tourists arrive on cruise ships, but they spend only about one-quarter as much time on shore as those who arrive by plane. St. Croix is trying to stimulate tourism by building gambling casinos, with the first scheduled to open in fall 1999; St. Thomas has rejected gambling, and counts heavily on cruise ships; St. John remains mostly a natural paradise, with a few very high-end hotels.

Politics in the Virgin Islands is a personal thing, with big rivalries between St. Thomas and St. Croix; candidates for the highest offices tend to be physicians. There was a sort of political revolution here in 1994, with the replacement by independents of two longtime Democratic officeholders—Governor Alexander Farrelly, first elected in 1986, and Congressional Delegate Ron de Lugo, first elected in 1968 and in office since, except for one two-year interval. Roy Schneider, an oncologist, is a Virgin Island native who worked at Howard Medical School and Sloan-Kettering Institute, then came back to be Governor Cyril King's health director in 1977. In the 1994 gubernatorial race Schneider called for smaller government and getting tough on drugs, and beat Lieutenant Governor Derek Hodge. In office Schneider, who was an independent, said the deficit was far worse than he thought, and called for spending cuts, a war against drugs and an enterprise zone in St. Croix. But his program evidently proved unpopular, and in 1998 he was beaten 59%–41% by Education Commissioner Charles Turnbull.

Governor. Charles Turnbull was born in St. Thomas, the son of immigrants from the British Virgin Islands. He earned undergraduate and graduate degrees from Hampton University and a doctorate in education from the University of Minnesota, then returned home to teach. As Virgin Island's Education commissioner, Turnbull upgraded the curriculum, established a cultural education division to promote greater understanding and appreciation of the history and culture of the Caribbean region, and built enough new schools to eliminate double school-day sessions. Promising a "grander vision" than offered by independent Governor Roy Schneider—who focused on downsizing government, reducing spending and fighting drugs—Turnbull in 1998 defeated the one-term incumbent 59%–41%.

In April 1999, Turnbull said the government would be unable to pay 10,000 workers because of $1 billion in debt from the previous administration. Turnbull said he would seek legislative approval for short-term borrowing, but he is also considering a bailout from controversial businessman Jeffrey Prosser, who offered to give government employees some of his own property in lieu of paychecks and build community projects in return for tax exemptions for himself.

Delegate. The delegate from the Virgin Islands is Donna Christian-Christensen (Christian-Green until early 1999), elected in 1996, when she beat Victor Frazer, an independent and the upset winner in 1994. Christian-Christensen is from an old St. Croix family; her father was Virgin Islands Chief District Court Judge Almeric Christian. She graduated from St. Mary's College and George Washington Medical School; she practiced medicine for more than 20 years in the Virgin Islands, in a family practice and in several public positions. She was elected a Democratic National committeewoman in 1984 and ran one losing race for delegate in 1994. In 1996 she attacked Frazer, who after some hesitation caucused with the Democrats, for foreign travel (11 trips to four continents), and for inaction in opposing the welfare reform bill. Frazer, who spent far less money, said, "What they don't realize is, these things are not possible," in reference to Christian-Christensen's promise that she would get the floor vote back for delegates. Christian-Christensen led Frazer 38%–34% on November 5; in the runoff two weeks later she won 52%–48%. It was a regional race: Christian-Christensen won 69% on St. Croix, Frazer 64% on St. Thomas and St. John.

In the House, Christian-Christensen has tried to forge alliances with the Congressional Black Caucus and the Clinton Administration to achieve her goals. She defended Clinton during the impeachment debate. She fought for the Virgin Islands to retain its share of the rum tax ($11.30 of the $13.50 per proof gallon tax); the Ways and Means bill did not include this but the White House budget did. She got the support of Resources Chairman Don Young, who can remember when his Alaska was a territory and subject to the whims of Congress. She supported Virgin Islands Senator Adlah "Foncie" Donastorg's proposal to reduce the V.I. Senate from 15 to nine members. (Some of the names remind us that the Virgin Islands are the one American possession that was once a colony of Denmark.) She wanted the territories' children's health care programs to be funded at the same level as states, which would increase funding for the Virgin Island's from $300,000 to $1.2 million, and sought to provide tax credits for wages paid by watch manufacturers to their employees—a direct subsidy to an industry evidently in trouble. She boasted of getting $10 million for restoring damaged coral reefs. She spoke out against the case the United States brought in the WTO challenging European Union trade preferences for EU members' Caribbean colonies, arguing that removing the preferences would cause devastating economic losses in the Caribbean.

In 1998 Christian-Christensen was re-elected by the impressive margin of 88%–12%

Del. Donna M. Christian-Christensen (D)

Elected 1996; b. Sept. 19, 1945, Teaneck, NJ; home, St. Croix; St. Mary's Col., B.S. 1966, George Washington U., M.D. 1970; Moravian; married (Christian).

Professional Career: Practicing physician, 1975–97; Territorial Asst., Commissioner of Health, 1988–94; Acting Commissioner of Health, 1994–95.

DC Office: 1711 LHOB, 20515, 202-225-1790; Fax: 202-225-5517; Web site: www.house.gov/christian-christensen.

District Offices: St. Croix, 340-778-5900; St. Thomas, 340-774-4408.

Committees: *Resources* (17th of 24 D): National Parks & Public Lands; Water & Power. *Small Business* (7th of 17 D): Rural Enterprise, Business Opportunities & Special Small Business Problems (RMM).

GUAM

Some 3,500 miles west of Hawaii, 19 hours of flying time from Washington, D.C., is Guam, the place where America's day begins. Guam lies just west of the International Date Line, and it is in the early hours of Tuesday there when the rest of us are just trying to get through Monday afternoon. Geographically in the center of the Mariana Islands, Guam is legally separate: the Northern Marianas were administered by the U.S. as a United Nations trust territory until they became a commonwealth in 1978. Guam was ruled by Navy captains from 1898 to 1950, except for 32 months of Japanese occupation during World War II; in 1950 the Guam Organic Act made Guamanians U.S. citizens and allowed them to elect a local government, but Congress still retained final power over the territory; it started electing a delegate to Congress in 1972.

Guam is 36 miles long by four to nine miles wide, with 150,000 people; in 1990, 47% were Chamorro (descendants of the original islanders), 25% Filipino, 18% other Asian and 10% Caucasian; almost everyone is Catholic. (In 1990 Guam passed a law barring almost all abortions; it was overturned by a federal court in 1992, as clearly contrary to *Roe v. Wade*, and the Supreme Court dodged a direct challenge to that decision by refusing to hear the case.) There are about 4,000 U.S. military personnel here, on bases which occupy one-third of the island; they have room for refugees, including 6,000 Kurds after the Gulf; in April 1999 U.S. officials said they could put up to 20,000 Kosovars here, but that never came about. Guam is tropical, but not an easy environment: in August 1993 it lived through an earthquake rated at 8.2 on the Richter scale, comparable to San Francisco in 1906; in December 1997 Typhoon Paka raged through with winds of 236 miles per hour. Guam has feral water buffalo, descendants of those imported from Asia hundreds of years ago; it has the brown tree snake, an import from somewhere in the Pacific, which has rid the island of native birds and many bats and has been known to try to eat sleeping babies; the island's coral reefs are being destroyed by erosion.

Economically, Guam depended for years on American military bases; now it is diversifying, with 1.5 million tourists a year, mostly from Japan. Guamanian entrepreneurs want to build garment and other low-wage factories here, to be staffed by guest workers from the Philippines and China, like those in the Commonwealth of the Northern Marianas, where as Henry Hurt reported in *Reader's Digest* in 1997, many have been abused by employers. But Guam, unlike the CNMI, is covered by U.S. immigration laws. In the late 1990s guest workers from the CNMI entered Guam and claimed political asylum; in 1998 "snakehead" Chinese smugglers started bringing in Chinese from Fujian province for a reputed $20,000 to $30,000 a head. In Guam they could claim asylum and seek an INS hearing in Seattle; the Clinton Administration in April 1999 started shipping them to the CNMI instead. Guam is indeed "America in Asia," as its leaders like to proclaim, but that causes problems as much as it brings opportunity.

The major political issue in Guam is status. In a 1982 plebiscite, Guamanians voted for commonwealth status and a Commission on Self-Determination drafted a bill, which has been introduced in every Congress since 1988, proposing a commonwealth with two major provisions. One is immigration control. Chamorros say they want to block others from coming in, establishing citizenship and making them more of a minority. But more important, this would also allow Guamanians to bring in guest workers as the CNMI has done, and the commonwealth bill would allow local enforcement of labor laws. The other provision is "mutual consent," which would bar Congress from changing laws and treaties that affect Guam without Guam's consent; Guam's governor has even called for a five-member commission to review legislation for its effects on Guam before it is passed "perfunctorily" by Congress: Guamanians remembered that its just-created watch and garment industries were destroyed by congressional action in the 1970s and 1980s.

Commonwealth status has been strongly supported by Republican Governor Joe Ada, elected in 1986 and 1990, and Democratic Governor Carl Gutierrez, elected in 1994 and (the election is under challenge) 1998; it has been pushed in Congress by Guam's Delegate Robert Underwood, a Democrat first elected in 1992. The Bush Administration rejected the bill as inconsistent with the constitutional provision giving Congress full powers over territories. The Clinton Interior Department started off more sympathetic. Its first negotiator, former University of California Chancellor Michael Heyman, agreed with Ada in 1994 on "mutual consent," and prepared a bill that, as Underwood pointed out, would establish a relation similar to that of New Zealand and the Cook Islands. But the election of the Republican Congress abruptly changed the provision's prospects. The Resources Native American and Insular Affairs Chairman at that time, Elton Gallegly of California, announced in January 1995 that he would block any mutual consent bill that seeks to bind future congresses; in February 1995 Heyman was appointed head of the Smithsonian Institution and resigned his negotiating post.

It did not soothe feelings when in November 1994 Clinton top advisers Anthony Lake and Robert Rubin laughed out loud (they later apologized) when they heard a suggestion that Guam take part in the APEC summit. But when seeking re-election funds, Clintonites were much more sympathetic. In August 1996 Democratic National Committee Chairman Donald Fowler wrote to Guam Governor Carl Gutierrez requesting $250,000 in donations. Fifteen days later Hillary Rodham Clinton stopped in Guam on her way to the UN women's conference in Beijing and attended a buffet hosted by Gutierrez. Three weeks later Guamanians arrived in Washington with more than $250,000 in contributions for President Clinton and the Democratic Party; within six months Guamanians had given the Clinton-Gore campaign and the DNC $892,000— the largest amount per capita anywhere under the U.S. flag. Gutierrez said, "Only when we showed Washington that there were people who could write a $1,000 check, a $5,000 check, a $25,000 check, did people begin to sit up and take notice."

In December 1996 the new Interior negotiator, John Garamendi, circulated a report supporting key provisions of the Guam commonwealth bill, including giving Guam a right to take over lands relinquished by the military. But after the political contributions made news, the administration seemed to step back. At an August 1998 reception for Gutierrez, Clinton promised Guam $585,000 in special non-matching welfare-to-work funds. Then in October 1997 Garamendi said, "We have been unable to find constitutional and otherwise appropriate ways of bridging the gap between the full extent of what Guam has originally proposed and what the executive branch is able to support under the American flag." He said the administration could not support mutual consent and could not support a referendum in which "only the indigenous Chamorro people" could vote. It would not transfer control over labor and immigration policy nor a joint commission which could bind future congresses. Guam leaders responded in the tones of those who thought they had made an under-the-table deal only to find the table removed and nothing there. "We have been betrayed. We must continue to fight," said Ada. Underwood said the U.S.-Guam relationship was supposed to be a marriage but was more like a "kept woman." Garamendi resigned in April 1998, and negotiations seemed to founder. In 1998 Guam, the CNMI and Hawaii sued the federal government to overturn a law that allowed citizens of freely associated states in Micronesia (other former U.S. trust territories) to immigrate to Guam, the CNMI and Hawaii. As a Guam official said, "In an island, having limits on migration is really about self-government; it's about controlling demography."

There things stood until Bill Clinton stopped at Guam in November 1998 on his way back from an Asian trip. Clinton, then threatened with impeachment at home, was warmly cheered in Guam. He continued to reject commonwealth status but said he had "tried to offer viable alternatives." Gutierrez and Underwood met in February 1999 with White House officials and others in a so-called interagency working group. But it is hard to see how any administration or any Congress is going to concede what the Guamanians want. Meanwhile, the Guamanians struggle on: they have announced a December 1999 Chamorro-only vote on status.

Governor. Carl Gutierrez is a Democrat elected in 1994. He went to high school in California, served in the Air Force, then set up the first data processing center in Guam and started a construction business; he was elected to the Guam Senate for all but four years since 1972. He campaigned for commonwealth status, for return of federal lands to Guam, and for exemption from the Jones Act requirement that goods from the U.S. be shipped in U.S.-registered ships; only two lines serve Guam, and Gutierrez wants foreign competition.

After the 1994 election Gutierrez attacked, Republican-style, the high-handedness of federal bureaucrats: "Guam has to survive with minor federal luminaries who operate with no apparent adult supervision," he said, and complained that the Fish and Wildlife Service seized 20% of Guam's land for a wildlife refuge. And when California Republican Dana Rohrabacher called Guam and other territories "economic basket cases" that are "backward and economically depressed," Gutierrez attacked "this ignorance and lack of sensitivity which run counter to our country's democratic traditions and which ensures the continuation of our status as second-class citizens in the American family." He is a vigorous presence in Guam and rushed to the scene when KAL 801 crashed on the island in August 1997 and even rescued an 11-year-old girl from the wreckage.

The 1998 election was a close contest between two familiar figures, Gutierrez and former Governor Joe Ada. Gutierrez raised the astonishing sum of $2.8 million, Ada $358,000—sums one thinks might have been enough to communicate with some 48,000 voters spread over an area three times the size of Washington, D.C. Initially the result was reported as a 51%–44% victory for Gutierrez, with 7% write-ins or defective ballots. But Republicans, who won most of the seats in the 15-member legislature, argued that 1,313 blank ballots should be counted as well, which would make the results 49.8%–43.58%, giving neither candidate the "majority of votes cast" required by the Guam Organic Act. The election commission certified Gutierrez's victory anyway by a quick 4–2 vote. It was reported that the FBI was conducting a criminal investigation. In December 1998 a federal judge ordered a runoff election; the order was suspended pending appeal. A week before that decision, Ada filed suit in Guam Superior Court, arguing that non-citizens and non-Guam residents and dead or underage people had voted; this was dismissed although earlier the Superior Court had found 571 non-citizens registered and that 151 voters shared the same Social Security number. The fraud case was dismissed in February 1999, after 45 witnesses testified at trial.

In April 1999 a three-judge federal appeals court upheld the trial court ruling requiring a runoff and, after taking a month to deny a rehearing and a full-court appeal, sent the case back to the federal district court, presumably to order a runoff. By June 1999 it was not clear when or if a runoff would be held, much less who would win.

Delegate. Robert Underwood was educated in California. He started teaching at the University of Guam in 1976 and was known for his efforts promoting and preserving Chamorro language and culture; he was appointed to the Chamorro Language Commission in 1977 and served as its chairman for 12 years, until 1991. By 1990 he had become the university's academic vice president, and he ran against Republican Delegate Ben Blaz, a former Marine general. Personal connections are often more important than party in Guam, and Underwood explained his victory thus: "I have a lot of relatives. His grandfather and my great-grandfather are first cousins. So I cut into his action when I ran—more of the relatives are closer to me." He was re-elected in 1994 and 1996 without opposition; evidently no one has more relatives. In 1998 he was re-elected by 70%–22%.

Underwood strongly backs the Guam Commonwealth Act but has not actively tried to push it forward in the House, where its chances are obviously dimmer than with the Clinton Administration. Instead he has concentrated on achieving solutions to practical problems. In January 1994 he pushed through the House a bill transferring 3,200 acres from federal to GovGuam (as the government here is called) control; he called for a land summit, not the Interior Department, to parcel out the territory. He has made some progress in getting reparations for Guamanians harmed by Japanese during their occupation in World War II. He has passed amendments providing for car rental reimbursement when Defense Department personnel's vehicles are shipped late, commissary and PX privileges for National Guard troops called up for disaster relief, and a $65 million reserve for Guam businesses on A-76 outsourcing contracts. He seeks help in eradicating, not just containing, the brown tree snake; he wants the Endangered Species Act amended to allow Guamanians to bring in predators for the snakes, and he criticized a $1.6 million appropriation in 1996 for eradication programs because he said the designated funds, which come from the Department of Interior's Office of Insular Affairs, will mean less money available for other territorial programs. "The way it's been handled, it sounds like we need St. Patrick more than $1.6 million," he said.

Underwood has used his seats on the Armed Services and Resources committees to achieve his goals; he is now ranking Democrat on Armed Service's Special Oversight Panel on the Merchant Marine and became chairman of the Asian Pacific American Caucus in January 1999. In protest of France's nuclear tests in the Pacific, he boycotted French President Jacques Chirac's speech in Washington, D.C. in 1996. He got Guam included in the State Commemorative Coin Act and the World War II memorial. He has closely monitored re-engineering troop assignments to Guam. In October 1998 he got the House to pass an amendment to the Guam Organic Act, allowing the legislature to create an elective office of attorney general, to redefine a quorum as a majority of those present (it has been 11 of 15), and to make laws over "rightful" subjects, not just local subjects. He has been pushing for years for a non-voting congressional representative for the CNMI. He had a bill signed into law eliminating the requirement for a separate ballot for Guam delegate elections (no one can remember why it was required) and persuaded the U.S. Board of Geographic Names to rename Agana Hagatna. In March 1999 he introduced a bill to prevent aliens in Guam from claiming political asylum and requiring their cases to be decided within 30 days—an obvious response to the "snakehead" Chinese smugglers. He hailed the increases in the Clinton budget for funds to preserve the coral reefs and kill the tree snakes and was pleaded when federal impact aid for Guam was doubled to $10 million.

Del. Robert Underwood (D)

Elected 1992; b. July 13, 1948, Tamuning; home, Yona; CA St. U., B.A. 1969, M.A. 1971, U. of S. CA, Ph.D. 1988; Catholic; married (Lorraine).

Professional Career: Teacher, Admin., Guam Public Schls., 1972–76; Prof., U. of Guam, 1976–88, Dean, 1988–90, Academic Vice Pres., 1990–92.

DC Office: 2418 RHOB, 20515, 202-225-1188; Fax: 202-226-0341; Web site: www.house.gov/underwood.

District Offices: Hagatna, 671-477-4272.

Committees: *Armed Services* (10th of 28 D): Military Installations & Facilities; Military Readiness; Special Oversight Panel on Morale, Welfare and Recreation; Special Oversight Panel on the Merchant Marine (RMM). *Resources* (13th of 24 D): Energy & Mineral Resources (RMM).

AMERICAN SAMOA

American Samoa, the only American territory south of the Equator, has been little influenced by Western settlers and remains almost as Polynesian today as it was when the United States took possession in 1900. These seven islands are 2,300 miles southwest of Hawaii, 1,600 miles northeast of New Zealand. American Samoa has 61,000 people, 89% of them Polynesian, mostly Christian (50% Congregationalist, 20% Catholic); it is an unincorporated territory administered by the Interior Department since 1951. Its islands of Ofu, Tau and Tutuila are the site the National Park of American Samoa, opened in April 1997, preserving fruit bat habitat, tropical forests and coral reefs.

The market economy has not made much progress here: American Samoa lives on the federal government, which spends some $23 million annually here, plus varying amounts for construction, and two big tuna canneries. Residents are eligible for U.S. food stamps and welfare; local agriculture is minimal and efforts to attract investment have brought in just one garment factory. Tourism is also minimal; when the South Pacific Mini Games were held here in 1997, the 2,000 athletes were, in the dry words of an uncharmed non-islander, "hosted—with some difficulty—by the territory."

A cause celebre here is the renaming of nearby Samoa, formerly British Samoa and Western Samoa; the single name suggests to many in American Samoa that they are regarded as not full Samoans, and the legislature threatened not to recognize Samoan passports—a problem, since most of the cannery work force is from Samoa. But the governor, a nephew of the Samoan prime minister, promise to veto any such bill. But if American Samoans are proud Samoans, they are also proud Americans: on April 17, 2000, they will celebrate the 100th anniversary of the American takeover, at Fagatogo Malae where the American flag was first raised; there will be traditional singing and dancing at Veterans Stadium and a long boat race in Pago Pago Harbor.

American Samoa staged a Democratic presidential primary in 1988, but only 36 people voted. None of the candidates campaigned in person.

Governor. Tauese Sunia, the son of Congregationalist ministers, taught high school in Nebraska and in American Samoa, and was the first Samoan television teacher. Tauese (it is Somoan tradition to refer to chieftans by their first names) headed the local department of education and the bar association and is the father of 10 children. He was elected lieutenant governor in 1992, serving under then-Governor A. P. Lutali, then was elected governor in 1996 as a Democrat; Lutali finished third in the first election, and in the runoff Tauese won by a 51%–49% margin over Lealaifuaneva Peter Reid.

In office Tauese had to struggle with American Samoa's $60 million debt, its difficulty in paying bills and in collecting taxes and fees—perhaps a natural development in a society where many live outside the market economy. His solution, for the U.S. government to station an aircraft carrier here, seems unrealistic. With apparent regret, he set aside an American Samoa law giving local preference to contractors on projects financed with federal money. He strived to stamp out video poker and to prevent other forms of gambling. In May 1999, Tauese was poised to sign into law a bill that would prevent non-"full-blooded" Samoans from owning land; a sponsor said the legislation was not an attempt at discrimination but a move to prevent foreign ownership of the island.

Tauese's term is for four years, but opponents in September 1998 sought to impeach him. They charged him with using $18,000 in school repair funds to build a sauna in the governor's mansion, using $10,000 in public funds to pay off a personal credit card, and selling government vehicles and spare parts without notice or competitive bidding. The High Court of American Samoa also ruled that he could not spend revenues from a government-owned oil tank farm without the legislature's approval. But impeachment and removal require a two-thirds vote first in the American Samoan House of Representatives and then in the Senate; in the 1998 election several anti-Tauese legislators were defeated and he seems likely to serve out his term.

Delegate. American Samoa has elected a delegate to Congress since 1980. Delegate Eni F. H. Faleomavaega is a Democrat first elected in 1988. He went to high school in Hawaii, to Brigham Young University, then to law school in Houston and Berkeley; he served in Vietnam in the Army. In the 1970s he worked on the Natural Resources Insular subcommittee staff and for former Utah Democrat Gunn McKay. In 1981 he became deputy attorney general of American Samoa, and in 1985 lieutenant governor.

Faleomavaega serves on the Resources Committee, where he has been ranking Democrat on three subcommittees—Native Americans and Insular Affairs in January 1995; National Parks and Public Lands in January 1998; Fisheries, Conservation, Wildlife and Oceans in January 1999. He is also a member of International Affairs and on its Asian and the Pacific Affairs Subcommittee. Faleomavaega worked to improve conditions at the StarKist tuna plant and to get the British Ceramic Tile Company to make the largest investment there since the canneries were built decades ago. He worked to warm up the frosty relations between the United States and New Zealand. He led the congressional protest against the French nuclear tests in the Pacific, and was stopped by the French for approaching the French nuclear testing site at Mururoa Atoll and imprisoned in Tahiti in 1996; he boycotted French President Jacques Chirac's speech in Washington, D.C. and tried to bring the issue of French nuclear waste shipments in the Pacific before the UN Security Council. In June 1998 he said it was difficult to believe the International Atomic Energy Agency study which found little or no effect on plants or animals by French nuclear tests from 1966 to 1996; in June 1998 he went back to

Mururoa as a guest on Autonomy Day. Faleomavaega has also kept an eye on Indonesia, criticizing the Suharto government for the murder or "disappearance" of perhaps 300,000 Malanesians in West Papua New Guinea (the Indonesians call it Irian Jaya), which he says the U.S. has ignored. In March 1999 he and four other members called on Indonesia President B.J. Habibie to engage in dialogue with Irian Jaya.

On domestic matters, Faleomavaega brings a perspective unique in the House. When others proposed more research on the Kennewick man skeleton found in Washington state in 1996, he urged reburial: "This is not just a clash between science and religion, it's about human rights." He tends to oppose exemptions from environmental laws: he weighed in against the proposed Ivanpah Valley airport near Las Vegas and resisted exceptions to the ban on horse slaughtering. He resisted New Mexico Republican Bill Redmond's proposal to honor Spanish land claims in New Mexico. But, perhaps because he had worked for a Utah congressman, he strongly backed the land swap proposed by Utah Republican Jim Hansen to compensate the state for the seizure of its school lands when Bill Clinton created the Escalante-Giant Staircase National Monument. On impeachment, he passionately supported Clinton.

Faleomavaega has expressed fears that American Samoa will be threatened by an "invasion" of Asian small businessmen, comparing it to Fiji, where Indian-origin immigrants have sparked its economy and have become a near-majority. He and Hawaii Senator Daniel Inouye got $2 million to repair and certify the *Ataata o Samoa*, a vessel to provide transportation for people in Manu'a. With help from Inouye and Pennsylvania Democrat John Murtha, Faleomavaega got into the October 1998 omnibus budget free transportation on military aircraft for veterans approved for VA health care in Hawaii. He got $34 million over six years in earmarks in the May 1998 transportation bill, and an amendment requiring the General Services Administration to study the need for a federal building in American Samoa; a 1988 study said there was none. In January 1998 he had the pleasure of congratulating two Samoans who played in the Super Bowl, Maa Tanuvasa of the Denver Broncos and Esera Tuaolo of the Atlanta Falcons.

Faleomavaega won re-election in 1994 with 63% of the vote. In 1996 he fell just short of winning re-election on November 5, with 49.6%, to 26% for independent Gus Hanneman and 24% for Republican Aumua Amata Coleman, daughter of the late Governor Peter Coleman. But Faleomavaega won the November 19 runoff 56%–44%. In 1998 he won 86%–14% over Seigafolava Pene; Coleman got perhaps 400 votes as a write-in, but they were voided since local law doesn't authorize write-ins. American Samoa has the lowest number of votes cast in any congressional race, fewer than 10,000 in 1998.

Del. Eni F. H. Faleomavaega (D)

Elected 1988; b. Aug. 15, 1943, Vailoatai; home, Pago Pago; Brigham Young U., B.A. 1972, U. of CA, LL.M. 1973; Mormon; married (Hinanui).

Military Career: Army, 1966–69 (Vietnam).

Elected Office: AS Lt. Gov., 1984–89.

Professional Career: A.A., U.S. Del. from AS, 1973–75; Cnsl., U.S. House Interior Cmte., 1975–81; AS Dpty. Atty. Gen., 1981–84.

DC Office: 2422 RHOB, 20515, 202-225-8577; Fax: 202-225-8757; Web site: www.house.gov/faleomavaega.

District Offices: Pago Pago, 684-633-1372.

Committees: *International Relations* (5th of 23 D): Asia & the Pacific; International Operations and Human Rights. *Resources* (6th of 24 D): Energy & Mineral Resources; Fisheries Conservation, Wildlife & Oceans (RMM).

GUBERNATORIAL ELECTION CYCLE

1999, 3 States

Kentucky (D)   **Mississippi (R)**
Louisiana (R)

2000, 11 States

Delaware (D)   North Dakota (R)
Indiana (D)   Utah (R)
Missouri (D)   Vermont (D)
Montana (R)   Washington (D)
New Hampshire (D)   West Virginia (R)
North Carolina (D)

2001, 2 States

New Jersey (R)   **Virginia (R)**

2002, 36 States

Alabama (D)   Minnesota (Ref)
Alaska (D)   Nebraska (R)
Arizona (R)   Nevada (R)
Arkansas (R)   New Hampshire
California (D)   **New Mexico (R)**
Colorado (R)   New York (R)
Connecticut (R)   Ohio (R)
Florida (R)   **Oklahoma (R)**
Georgia (D)   **Oregon (D)**
Hawaii (D)   **Pennsylvania (R)**
Idaho (R)   **Rhode Island (R)**
Illinois (R)   South Carolina (D)
Iowa (D)   **South Dakota (R)**
Kansas (R)   **Tennessee (R)**
Maine (I)   Texas (R)
Maryland (D)   Vermont
Massachusetts (R)   Wisconsin (R)
Michigan (R)   **Wyoming (R)**

31 Republicans, 17 Democrats, 1 Independent, 1 Reform

New Hampshire and Vermont have two year terms. All others are four year.
Boldface indicates governors who may not succeed themselves in the election that year.

SENATE SEATS

2000 ELECTION CYCLE

Republicans (19)

Spencer Abraham (MI)
John Ashcroft (MO)
Conrad Burns (MT)
John H. Chafee (RI)*
Mike DeWine (OH)
Bill Frist (TN)
Slade Gorton (WA)
Rod Grams (MN)
Orrin G. Hatch (UT)
Kay Bailey Hutchison (TX)
James M. Jeffords (VT)
Jon Kyl (AZ)
Trent Lott (MS)
Richard G. Lugar (IN)
Connie Mack (FL)*
William V. Roth Jr. (DE)
Rick Santorum (PA)
Olympia Snowe (ME)
Craig Thomas (WY)

Democrats (14)

Daniel K. Akaka (HI)
Jeff Bingaman (NM)
Richard H. Bryan (NV)*
Robert C. Byrd (WV)
Kent Conrad (ND)
Dianne Feinstein (CA)
Edward Kennedy (MA)
Bob Kerrey (NE)
Herb Kohl (WI)
Frank Lautenberg (NJ)*
Joseph I. Lieberman (CT)
Daniel Patrick Moynihan (NY)*
Charles S. Robb (VA)
Paul S. Sarbanes (MD)

will not seek re-election in 2000

2002 ELECTION CYCLE

Republicans (20)

Wayne Allard (CO)
Thad Cochran (MS)
Susan Collins (ME)
Larry Craig (ID)
Pete V. Dominici (NM)
Michael Enzi (WY)
Phil Gramm (TX)
Chuck Hagel (NE)
Jesse Helms (NC)
Tim Hutchinson (AR)
James M. Inhofe (OK)
Mitch McConnell (KY)
Pat Roberts (KS)
Jeff Sessions (AL)
Bob Smith (NH)
Gordon H. Smith (OR)
Ted Stevens (AK)
Fred D. Thompson (TN)
Strom Thurmond (SC)*
John W. Warner (VA)

Democrats (13)

Max Baucus (MT)
Joseph R. Biden Jr. (DE)
Max Cleland (GA)
Richard J. Durbin (IL)
Tom Harkin (IA)
Timothy P. Johnson (SD)
John F. Kerry (MA)
Mary L. Landrieu (LA)
Carl Levin (MI)
Jack Reed (RI)
John D. Rockefeller IV (WV)
Robert G. Torricelli (NJ)
Paul Wellstone (MN)

will not seek re-election in 2002

CONGRESSIONAL LEADERSHIP

U.S. SENATE

Republicans

Majority Leader	Trent Lott (MS)
Majority Whip	Don Nickles (OK)
President Pro Tempore	Strom Thurmond (SC)
Republican Conference Chairman	Connie Mack (FL)
Republican Conference Secretary	Paul Coverdell (GA)
Republican Policy Committee Chairman	Larry Craig (ID)
NRSC Chairman	Mitch McConnell (KY)

Democrats

Minority Leader	Thomas A. Daschle (SD)
Minority Whip	Harry Reid (NV)
Democratic Policy Committee Chairman	Thomas A. Daschle (SD)
DSCC Chairman	Robert G. Torricelli (NJ)
DSCC Vice Chairman	Patty Murray (WA)

U.S. HOUSE OF REPRESENTATIVES

Republicans

Speaker of the House	J. Dennis Hastert (IL-14)
Majority Leader	Dick Armey (TX-26)
Majority Whip	Tom DeLay (TX-22)
Chief Deputy Majority Whip	Roy Blunt (MO-7)
Republican Conference Chairman	J.C. Watts (OK-4)
Republican Conference Vice Chairman	Tillie K. Fowler (FL-4)
Republican Conference Secretary	Deborah Pryce (OH-15)
Republican Policy Committee Chairman	Christopher Cox (CA-47)
NRCC Chairman	Tom Davis (VA-11)

Democrats

Minority Leader	Richard A. Gephardt (MO-3)
Minority Whip	David E. Bonior (MI-10)
Chief Deputy Minority Whip	Chet Edwards (TX-11)
Chief Deputy Minority Whip	John Lewis (GA-5)
Chief Deputy Minority Whip	Ed Pastor (AZ-2)
Chief Deputy Minority Whip	Maxine Waters (CA-35)
Democratic Caucus Chairman	Martin Frost (TX-24)
Democratic Caucus Vice Chairman	Robert Menendez (NJ-13)
Democratic Policy Committee Chairman	Richard A. Gephardt (MO-3)
DCCC Chairman	Patrick J. Kennedy (RI-1)

COMMITTEE CHAIRMEN

COMMITTEE CHAIRMEN

Senate Committees	Chairman	Ranking Member
Aging (Special)	Charles Grassley (IA)	John Breaux (LA)
Agriculture, Nutrition & Forestry	Richard G. Lugar (IN)	Tom Harkin (IA)
Appropriations	Ted Stevens (AK)	Robert C. Byrd (WV)
Armed Services	John Warner (VA)	Carl Levin (MI)
Banking, Housing & Urban Affairs	Phil Gramm (TX)	Paul S. Sarbanes (MD)
Budget	Pete V. Domenici (NM)	Frank Lautenberg (NJ)
Commerce, Science & Transportation	John McCain (AZ)	Ernest F. Hollings (SC)
Energy & Natural Resources	Frank Murkowski (AK)	Jeff Bingaman (NM)
Environment & Public Works	John H. Chafee (R)	Max Baucus (MT)
Ethics (Select)	Bob Smith (NH)	Harry Reid (NV)
Finance	William V. Roth Jr. (DE)	Daniel Patrick Moynihan (NY)
Foreign Relations	Jesse Helms (NC)	Joseph R. Biden Jr. (DE)
Governmental Affairs	Fred D. Thompson (TN)	Joseph I. Lieberman (CT)
Health, Education, Labor, and Pensions	James M. Jeffords (VT)	Edward Kennedy (MA)
Indian Affairs	Ben Nighthorse Campbell (CO)	Daniel K. Inouye (HI)
Intelligence (Select)	Richard C. Shelby (AL)	Bob Kerrey (NE)
Judiciary	Orrin G. Hatch (UT)	Patrick Leahy (VT)
Rules & Administration	Mitch McConnell (KY)	Christopher J. Dodd (CT)
Small Business	Christopher S. Bond (MO)	John F. Kerry (MA)
Veterans' Affairs	Arlen Specter (PA)	John D. Rockefeller IV (WV)

House Committees	Chairman	Ranking Member
Agriculture	Larry Combest (TX-19)	Charles W. Stenholm (TX-17)
Appropriations	C.W. (Bill) Young (FL-10)	David R. Obey (WI-7)
Armed Services	Floyd Spence (SC-2)	Ike Skelton (MO-4)
Banking & Financial Services	Jim Leach (IA-1)	John J. LaFalce (NY-29)
Budget	John R. Kasich (OH-12)	John M. Spratt Jr.(SC-5)
Commerce	Tom Bliley (VA-7)	John D. Dingell (MI-16)
Education & The Workforce	William F. Goodling (PA-19)	William (Bill) Clay (MO-1)
Government Reform	Dan Burton (IN-6)	Henry A. Waxman (CA-29)
House Administration	Bill Thomas (CA-21)	Steny H. Hoyer (MD-5)
Intelligence (Select)	Porter J. Goss (FL-14)	Julian C. Dixon (CA-32)
International Relations	Benjamin A. Gilman (NY-20)	Samuel Gejdenson (CT-2)
Judiciary	Henry J. Hyde (IL-6)	John Conyers Jr. (MI-14)
Resources	Don Young (AK-AL)	George Miller (CA-7)
Rules	David Dreier (CA-28)	Joe Moakley (MA-9)
Science	F. James Sensenbrenner Jr. (WI-9)	George Brown (CA-42)
Small Business	James M. Talent (MO-2)	Nydia M. Velazquez (NY-12)
Standards of Official Conduct	Lamar S. Smith (TX-21)	Howard L. Berman (CA-26)
Transportation & Infrastructure	Bud Shuster (PA-9)	James L. Oberstar (MN-8)
Veterans' Affairs	Bob Stump (AZ-3)	Lane Evans (IL-17)
Ways & Means	Bill Archer (TX-7)	Charles B. Rangel (NY-15)

SENATE COMMITTEES

AGING (Special)
www.senate.gov/~aging

G-31 Dirksen
202-224-5364

Majority (R 11): Grassley (IA), Chmn.; Jeffords (VT), Craig (ID), Burns (MT), Shelby (AL), Santorum (PA), Hagel (NE), Collins (ME), Enzi (WY), Bunning (KY), Hutchinson (AR)
Minority (D 9): Breaux (LA), RMM; Reid (NV), Kohl (WI), Feingold (WI), Wyden (OR), Reed (RI), Bryan (NV), Bayh (IN), Lincoln (AR)

NO SUBCOMMITTEES

AGRICULTURE, NUTRITION & FORESTRY
www.senate.gov/~agriculture

328-A Russell
202-224-2035

Majority (R 10): Lugar (IN), Chmn.; Helms (NC), Cochran (MS), McConnell (KY), Coverdell (GA), Roberts (KS), Fitzgerald (IL), Grassley (IA), Craig (ID), Santorum (PA)
Minority (D 8): Harkin (IA), RMM; Leahy (VT), Conrad (ND), Daschle (SD), Baucus (MT), Kerrey (NE), Johnson (SD), Lincoln (AR)

SUBCOMMITTEES

FORESTRY, CONSERVATION & RURAL REVITALIZATION

Majority (R 5): Craig, Chmn.; Santorum, Coverdell, Fitzgerald, Grassley
Minority (D 4): Conrad, RMM; Leahy, Daschle, Baucus

MARKETING, INSPECTION & PRODUCT PROMOTION

Majority (R 4): Coverdell, Chmn.; Helms, Cochran, McConnell
Minority (D 3): Baucus, RMM; Conrad, Kerrey

PRODUCTION & PRICE COMPETITIVENESS

Majority (R 5): Roberts, Chmn.; Helms, Cochran, Grassley, Craig
Minority (D 4): Kerrey, RMM; Daschle, Johnson, Lincoln

RESEARCH, NUTRITION & GENERAL LEGISLATION

Majority (R 4): Fitzgerald, Chmn.; McConnell, Roberts, Santorum
Minority (D 3): Leahy, RMM; Johnson, Lincoln

APPROPRIATIONS
www.senate.gov/~appropriations

S-128 The Capitol
202-224-3471

Majority (R 15): Stevens (AK), Chmn.; Cochran (MS), Specter (PA), Domenici (NM), Bond (MO), Gorton (WA), McConnell (KY), Burns (MT), Shelby (AL), Gregg (NH), Bennett (UT), Campbell (CO), Craig (ID), Hutchison (TX), Kyl (AZ)
Minority (D 13): Byrd (WV), RMM; Inouye (HI), Hollings (SC), Leahy (VT), Lautenberg (NJ), Harkin (IA), Mikulski (MD), Reid (NV), Kohl (WI), Murray (WA), Dorgan (ND), Feinstein (CA), Durbin (IL)

SUBCOMMITTEES

AGRICULTURE & RURAL DEVELOPMENT

Majority (R 6): Cochran, Chmn.; Specter, Bond, Gorton, McConnell, Burns
Minority (D 5): Kohl, RMM; Harkin, Dorgan, Feinstein, Durbin

COMMERCE, JUSTICE, STATE & THE JUDICIARY

Majority (R 6): Gregg, Chmn.; Stevens, Domenici, McConnell, Hutchison, Campbell
Minority (D 5): Hollings, RMM; Inouye, Lautenberg, Mikulski, Leahy

DEFENSE

Majority (R 9): Stevens, Chmn.; Cochran, Specter, Domenici, Bond, McConnell, Shelby, Gregg, Hutchison
Minority (D 8): Inouye, RMM; Hollings, Byrd, Leahy, Lautenberg, Harkin, Dorgan, Durbin

DISTRICT OF COLUMBIA

Majority (R 2): Hutchison, Chmn.; Kyl
Minority (D 1): Durbin, RMM;

ENERGY & WATER DEVELOPMENT

Majority (R 7): Domenici, Chmn.; Cochran, Gorton, McConnell, Bennett, Burns, Craig
Minority (D 6): Reid, RMM; Byrd, Hollings, Murray, Kohl, Dorgan

FOREIGN OPERATIONS & EXPORT FINANCING

Majority (R 7): McConnell, Chmn.; Specter, Gregg, Shelby, Bennett, Campbell, Bond
Minority (D 6): Leahy, RMM; Inouye, Lautenberg, Harkin, Mikulski, Murray

INTERIOR

Majority (R 8): Gorton, Chmn.; Stevens, Cochran, Domenici, Burns, Bennett, Gregg, Campbell
Minority (D 7): Byrd, RMM; Leahy, Hollings, Reid, Dorgan, Kohl, Feinstein

LABOR & HHS

Majority (R 8): Specter, Chmn.; Cochran, Gorton, Gregg, Craig, Hutchison, Stevens, Kyl
Minority (D 7): Harkin, RMM; Hollings, Inouye, Reid, Kohl, Murray, Feinstein

LEGISLATIVE BRANCH

Majority (R 3): Bennett, Chmn.; Stevens, Craig
Minority (D 2): Feinstein, RMM; Durbin

MILITARY CONSTRUCTION

Majority (R 4): Burns, Chmn.; Hutchison, Craig, Kyl
Minority (D 3): Murray, RMM; Reid, Inouye

TRANSPORTATION

Majority (R 7): Shelby, Chmn.; Domenici, Specter, Bond, Gorton, Bennett, Campbell
Minority (D 6): Lautenberg, RMM; Byrd, Mikulski, Reid, Kohl, Murray

TREASURY & GENERAL GOVERNMENT

Majority (R 3): Campbell, Chmn.; Shelby, Kyl
Minority (D 2): Dorgan, RMM; Mikulski

VA, HUD & INDEPENDENT AGENCIES

Majority (R 6): Bond, Chmn.; Burns, Shelby, Craig, Hutchison, Kyl
Minority (D 5): Mikulski, RMM; Leahy, Lautenberg, Harkin, Byrd

ARMED SERVICES
www.senate.gov/~armed-services

228 Russell
202-224-3871

Majority (R 11): Warner (VA), Chmn.; Thurmond (SC), McCain (AZ), Smith (NH), Inhofe (OK), Santorum (PA), Snowe (ME), Roberts (KS), Allard (CO), Hutchinson (AR), Sessions (AL)

Minority (D 9): Levin (MI), RMM; Kennedy (MA), Bingaman (NM), Byrd (WV), Robb (VA), Lieberman (CT), Cleland (GA), Landrieu (LA), Reed (RI)

SUBCOMMITTEES

AIRLAND FORCES

Majority (R 5): Santorum, Chmn.; Inhofe, Roberts, Allard, Hutchinson
Minority (D 4): Lieberman, RMM; Cleland, Landrieu, Reed

EMERGING THREATS & CAPABILITIES

Majority (R 5): Roberts, Chmn.; Smith, Santorum, Snowe, Sessions
Minority (D 4): Bingaman, RMM; Kennedy, Byrd, Lieberman

PERSONNEL

Majority (R 4): Allard, Chmn.; Thurmond, McCain, Snowe
Minority (D 3): Cleland, RMM; Kennedy, Reed

READINESS & MANAGEMENT SUPPORT

Majority (R 6): Inhofe, Chmn.; Thurmond, McCain, Santorum, Roberts, Hutchinson
Minority (D 5): Robb, RMM; Bingaman, Byrd, Cleland, Landrieu

SEAPOWER

Majority (R 4): Snowe, Chmn.; McCain, Smith, Sessions
Minority (D 3): Kennedy, RMM; Robb, Reed

STRATEGIC FORCES

Majority (R 6): Smith, Chmn.; Thurmond, Inhofe, Allard, Hutchinson, Sessions
Minority (D 5): Landrieu, RMM; Bingaman, Byrd, Robb, Lieberman

BANKING, HOUSING & URBAN AFFAIRS
www.senate.gov/~banking

534 Dirksen
202-224-7391

Majority (R 11): Gramm (TX), Chmn.; Shelby (AL), Mack (FL), Bennett (UT), Grams (MN), Allard (CO), Enzi (WY), Hagel (NE), Santorum (PA), Bunning (KY), Crapo (ID)

Minority (D 9): Sarbanes (MD), RMM; Dodd (CT), Kerry (MA), Bryan (NV), Johnson (SD), Reed (RI), Schumer (NY), Bayh (IN), Edwards (NC)

SUBCOMMITTEES

ECONOMIC POLICY

Majority (R 4): Mack, Chmn.; Bennett, Vice Chmn.; Enzi, Bunning
Minority (D 3): Reed, RMM; Dodd, Kerry

FINANCIAL INSTITUTIONS

Majority (R 9): Bennett, Chmn.; Hagel, Vice Chmn.; Mack, Enzi, Santorum, Bunning, Crapo, Shelby, Allard
Minority (D 7): Bryan, RMM; Reed, Schumer, Edwards, Johnson, Bayh, Sarbanes

HOUSING & TRANSPORTATION

Majority (R 5): Allard, Chmn.; Santorum, Vice Chmn.; Grams, Shelby, Gramm
Minority (D 4): Kerry, RMM; Edwards, Dodd, Bryan

INTERNATIONAL TRADE & FINANCE

Majority (R 5): Enzi, Chmn.; Crapo, Vice Chmn.; Grams, Hagel, Mack
Minority (D 4): Johnson, RMM; Kerry, Bayh, Schumer

SECURITIES

Majority (R 8): Grams, Chmn.; Bunning, Vice Chmn.; Shelby, Allard, Bennett, Hagel, Santorum, Crapo
Minority (D 7): Dodd, RMM; Schumer, Bayh, Johnson, Bryan, Reed, Edwards

BUDGET
www.senate.gov/~budget

621 Dirksen
202-224-0642

Majority (R 12): Domenici (NM), Chmn.; Grassley (IA), Nickles (OK), Gramm (TX), Bond (MO), Gorton (WA), Gregg (NH), Snowe (ME), Abraham (MI), Frist (TN), Grams (MN), Smith (OR)
Minority (D 10): Lautenberg (NJ), RMM; Hollings (SC), Conrad (ND), Sarbanes (MD), Boxer (CA), Murray (WA), Wyden (OR), Feingold (WI), Johnson (SD), Durbin (IL)

NO SUBCOMMITTEES

COMMERCE, SCIENCE & TRANSPORTATION
www.senate.gov/~commerce

508 Dirksen
202-224-5115

Majority (R 11): McCain (AZ), Chmn.; Stevens (AK), Burns (MT), Gorton (WA), Lott (MS), Hutchison (TX), Snowe (ME), Ashcroft (MO), Frist (TN), Abraham (MI), Brownback (KS)
Minority (D 9): Hollings (SC), RMM; Inouye (HI), Rockefeller (WV), Kerry (MA), Breaux (LA), Bryan (NV), Dorgan (ND), Wyden (OR), Cleland (GA)

SUBCOMMITTEES

AVIATION

Majority (R 10): Gorton, Chmn.; Stevens, Burns, Lott, Hutchison, Ashcroft, Frist, Snowe, Brownback, Abraham
Minority (D 8): Rockefeller, RMM; Hollings, Inouye, Bryan, Breaux, Dorgan, Wyden, Cleland

COMMUNICATIONS

Majority (R 9): Burns, Chmn.; Stevens, Gorton, Lott, Ashcroft, Hutchison, Abraham, Frist, Brownback
Minority (D 8): Hollings, RMM; Inouye, Kerry, Breaux, Rockefeller, Dorgan, Wyden, Cleland

CONSUMER AFFAIRS, FOREIGN COMMERCE & TOURISM

Majority (R 5): Ashcroft, Chmn.; Gorton, Abraham, Burns, Brownback
Minority (D 2): Bryan, RMM; Breaux

MANUFACTURING & COMPETITIVENESS

Majority (R 5): Abraham, Chmn.; Snowe, Ashcroft, Frist, Brownback
Minority (D 4): Dorgan, RMM; Bryan, Hollings, Rockefeller

OCEANS & FISHERIES

Majority (R 4): Snowe, Chmn.; Stevens, Gorton, Hutchison
Minority (D 3): Kerry, RMM; Inouye, Breaux

SCIENCE, TECHNOLOGY & SPACE

Majority (R 5): Frist, Chmn.; Burns, Hutchison, Stevens, Abraham
Minority (D 4): Breaux, RMM; Rockefeller, Kerry, Dorgan

SURFACE TRANSPORTATION & MERCHANT MARINE

Majority (R 8): Hutchison, Chmn.; Stevens, Burns, Snowe, Frist, Abraham, Ashcroft, Brownback
Minority (D 6): Inouye, RMM; Breaux, Dorgan, Bryan, Wyden, Cleland

ENERGY & NATURAL RESOURCES   364 Dirksen
www.senate.gov/~energy   202-224-4971

Majority (R 11): Murkowski (AK), Chmn.; Domenici (NM), Nickles (OK), Craig (ID), Campbell (CO), Thomas (WY), Smith (OR), Bunning (KY), Fitzgerald (IL), Gorton (WA), Burns (MT)
Minority (D 9): Bingaman (NM), RMM; Akaka (HI), Dorgan (ND), Graham (FL), Wyden (OR), Johnson (SD), Landrieu (LA), Bayh (IN), Lincoln (AR)

SUBCOMMITTEES

ENERGY, RESEARCH, DEVELOPMENT, PRODUCTION & REGULATION

Majority (R 7): Nickles, Chmn.; Domenici, Vice Chmn.; Bunning, Gorton, Craig, Fitzgerald, Smith
Minority (D 6): Graham, RMM; Akaka, Dorgan, Johnson, Landrieu, Bayh

FORESTS & PUBLIC LAND MANAGEMENT

Majority (R 7): Craig, Chmn.; Burns, Vice Chmn.; Fitzgerald, Campbell, Domenici, Thomas, Smith
Minority (D 6): Wyden, RMM; Akaka, Johnson, Landrieu, Bayh, Lincoln

NATIONAL PARKS, HISTORIC PRESERVATION & RECREATION

Majority (R 6): Thomas, Chmn.; Campbell, Vice Chmn.; Burns, Nickles, Bunning, Gorton
Minority (D 5): Akaka, RMM; Graham, Landrieu, Bayh, Lincoln

WATER & POWER

Majority (R 5): Smith, Chmn.; Gorton, Vice Chmn.; Bunning, Craig, Campbell
Minority (D 4): Dorgan, RMM; Graham, Wyden, Lincoln

ENVIRONMENT & PUBLIC WORKS   410 Dirksen
www.senate.gov/~epw   202-224-6176

Majority (R 10): Chafee (RI), Chmn.; Warner (VA), Smith (NH), Inhofe (OK), Thomas (WY), Bond (MO), Voinovich (OH), Crapo (ID), Bennett (UT), Hutchison (TX)
Minority (D 8): Baucus (MT), RMM; Moynihan (NY), Lautenberg (NJ), Reid (NV), Graham (FL), Lieberman (CT), Boxer (CA), Wyden (OR)

SUBCOMMITTEES

CLEAN AIR, WETLANDS, PRIVATE PROPERTY & NUCLEAR SAFETY
Majority (R 4): Inhofe, Chmn.; Voinovich, Bennett, Hutchison
Minority (D 3): Graham, RMM; Lieberman, Boxer

FISHERIES, WILDLIFE & DRINKING WATER
Majority (R 6): Crapo, Chmn.; Thomas, Bond, Warner, Bennett, Hutchison
Minority (D 5): Reid, RMM; Lautenberg, Wyden, Graham, Boxer

SUPERFUND, WASTE CONTROL & RISK ASSESSMENT
Majority (R 4): Smith, Chmn.; Warner, Inhofe, Crapo
Minority (D 3): Lautenberg, RMM; Moynihan, Boxer

TRANSPORTATION & INFRASTRUCTURE
Majority (R 6): Voinovich, Chmn.; Warner, Smith, Bond, Inhofe, Thomas
Minority (D 5): Baucus, RMM; Moynihan, Reid, Graham, Lieberman

ETHICS (Select)   220 Hart
www.senate.gov/~committees   **202-224-2981**

Majority (R 3): Smith (NH), Chmn.; Roberts (KS), Voinovich (OH)
Minority (D 3): Reid (NV), Vice Chmn.; Conrad (ND), Durbin (IL)

NO SUBCOMMITTEES

FINANCE   219 Dirksen
www.senate.gov/~finance   **202-224-4515**

Majority (R 11): Roth (DE), Chmn.; Chafee (RI), Grassley (IA), Hatch (UT), Murkowski (AK), Nickles (OK), Gramm (TX), Lott (MS), Jeffords (VT), Mack (FL), Thompson (TN)
Minority (D 9): Moynihan (NY), RMM; Baucus (MT), Rockefeller (WV), Breaux (LA), Conrad (ND), Graham (FL), Bryan (NV), Kerrey (NE), Robb (VA)

SUBCOMMITTEES

HEALTH CARE
Majority (R 8): Chafee, Chmn.; Roth, Jeffords, Grassley, Gramm, Nickles, Hatch, Thompson
Minority (D 7): Rockefeller, RMM; Baucus, Breaux, Conrad, Graham, Bryan, Kerrey

INTERNATIONAL TRADE
Majority (R 9): Grassley, Chmn.; Thompson, Murkowski, Roth, Lott, Gramm, Hatch, Chafee, Jeffords
Minority (D 8): Moynihan, RMM; Baucus, Rockefeller, Breaux, Conrad, Graham, Kerrey, Robb

LONG-TERM GROWTH & DEBT REDUCTION
Majority (R 3): Murkowski, Chmn.; Mack, Chafee
Minority (D 2): Graham, RMM; Bryan

SOCIAL SECURITY & FAMILY POLICY
Majority (R 6): Nickles, Chmn.; Gramm, Lott, Jeffords, Chafee, Thompson
Minority (D 5): Breaux, RMM; Moynihan, Rockefeller, Kerrey, Robb

TAXATION & IRS OVERSIGHT

Majority (R 7): Hatch, Chmn.; Lott, Nickles, Mack, Murkowski, Grassley, Thompson
Minority (D 5): Baucus, RMM; Moynihan, Conrad, Bryan, Robb

FOREIGN RELATIONS
www.senate.gov/~foreign

450 Dirksen
202-224-4651

Majority (R 10): Helms (NC), Chmn.; Lugar (IN), Coverdell (GA), Hagel (NE), Smith (OR),
  Grams (MN), Brownback (KS), Thomas (WY), Ashcroft (MO), Frist (TN)
Minority (D 8): Biden (DE), RMM; Sarbanes (MD), Dodd (CT), Kerry (MA), Feingold (WI),
  Wellstone (MN), Boxer (CA), Torricelli (NJ)

SUBCOMMITTEES

AFRICAN AFFAIRS

Majority (R 3): Frist, Chmn.; Grams, Brownback
Minority (D 2): Feingold, RMM; Sarbanes

EAST ASIAN & PACIFIC AFFAIRS

Majority (R 5): Thomas, Chmn.; Helms, Coverdell, Hagel, Smith
Minority (D 4): Kerry, RMM; Feingold, Wellstone, Torricelli

EUROPEAN AFFAIRS

Majority (R 5): Smith, Chmn.; Lugar, Ashcroft, Coverdell, Hagel
Minority (D 4): Biden, RMM; Sarbanes, Dodd, Wellstone

INTERNATIONAL ECONOMIC POLICY, EXPORT & TRADE PROMOTION

Majority (R 4): Hagel, Chmn.; Thomas, Frist, Lugar
Minority (D 3): Sarbanes, RMM; Kerry, Boxer

INTERNATIONAL OPERATIONS

Majority (R 4): Grams, Chmn.; Helms, Brownback, Frist
Minority (D 3): Boxer, RMM; Kerry, Feingold

NEAR EASTERN & SOUTH ASIAN AFFAIRS

Majority (R 5): Brownback, Chmn.; Ashcroft, Smith, Grams, Thomas
Minority (D 4): Wellstone, RMM; Torricelli, Sarbanes, Dodd

WESTERN HEMISPHERE, PEACE CORPS, NARCOTICS & TERRORISM

Majority (R 4): Coverdell, Chmn.; Helms, Lugar, Ashcroft
Minority (D 3): Dodd, RMM; Boxer, Torricelli

GOVERNMENTAL AFFAIRS
www.senate.gov/~gov_affairs

340 Dirksen
202-224-4751

Majority (R 9): Thompson (TN), Chmn.; Roth (DE), Stevens (AK), Collins (ME), Voinovich
  (OH), Domenici (NM), Cochran (MS), Specter (PA), Gregg (NH)
Minority (D 7): Lieberman (CT), RMM; Levin (MI), Akaka (HI), Durbin (IL), Torricelli (NJ),
  Cleland (GA), Edwards (NC)

SUBCOMMITTEES

GOVERNMENT MANAGEMENT, RESTRUCTURING AND THE DISTRICT OF
  COLUMBIA
Majority (R 3): Voinovich, Chmn.; Roth, Gregg
Minority (D 2): Durbin, RMM; Torricelli
INTERNATIONAL SECURITY, PROLIFERATION & FEDERAL SERVICES
Majority (R 6): Cochran, Chmn.; Stevens, Collins, Domenici, Specter, Gregg
Minority (D 5): Akaka, RMM; Levin, Torricelli, Cleland, Edwards
INVESTIGATIONS (Permanent)
Majority (R 7): Collins, Chmn.; Roth, Stevens, Voinovich, Domenici, Cochran, Specter
Minority (D 5): Levin, RMM; Akaka, Durbin, Cleland, Edwards

HEALTH, EDUCATION, LABOR & PENSIONS   428 Dirksen
www.senate.gov/~labor   202-224-5375

Majority (R 10): Jeffords (VT), Chmn.; Gregg (NH), Frist (TN), DeWine (OH), Enzi (WY),
  Hutchinson (AR), Collins (ME), Brownback (KS), Hagel (NE), Sessions (AL)
Minority (D 8): Kennedy (MA), RMM; Dodd (CT), Harkin (IA), Mikulski (MD), Bingaman
  (NM), Wellstone (MN), Murray (WA), Reed (RI)

SUBCOMMITTEES

AGING
Majority (R 4): DeWine, Chmn.; Jeffords, Hutchinson, Gregg
Minority (D 3): Mikulski, RMM; Murray, Dodd
CHILDREN & FAMILIES
Majority (R 6): Gregg, Chmn.; Frist, DeWine, Collins, Brownback, Hagel
Minority (D 5): Dodd, RMM; Bingaman, Wellstone, Murray, Reed
EMPLOYMENT, SAFETY & TRAINING
Majority (R 5): Enzi, Chmn.; Jeffords, Hutchinson, Hagel, Sessions
Minority (D 4): Wellstone, RMM; Kennedy, Harkin, Dodd
PUBLIC HEALTH
Majority (R 6): Frist, Chmn.; Gregg, Enzi, Collins, Brownback, Sessions
Minority (D 5): Kennedy, RMM; Harkin, Mikulski, Bingaman, Reed

INDIAN AFFAIRS   838 Hart
indian.senate.gov   202-224-2251

Majority (R 8): Campbell (CO), Chmn.; Murkowski (AK), McCain (AZ), Gorton (WA), Do-
  menici (NM), Thomas (WY), Hatch (UT), Inhofe (OK)
Minority (D 6): Inouye (HI), RMM; Conrad (ND), Reid (NV), Akaka (HI), Wellstone (MN),
  Dorgan (ND)

NO SUBCOMMITTEES

INTELLIGENCE   211 Hart
www.senate.gov/committees   202-224-1700

Majority (R 9): Shelby (AL), Chmn.; Chafee (RI), Lugar (IN), DeWine (OH), Kyl (AZ), Inhofe
  (OK), Hatch (UT), Roberts (KS), Allard (CO)
Minority (D 8): Kerrey (NE), RMM; Bryan (NV), Graham (FL), Kerry (MA), Baucus (MT),
  Robb (VA), Lautenberg (NJ), Levin (MI)

NO SUBCOMMITTEES

JUDICIARY
www.senate.gov/~judiciary

Majority (R 10): Hatch (UT), Chmn.; Thurmond (SC), Grassley (IA), Specter (PA), Kyl (AZ), DeWine (OH), Ashcroft (MO), Abraham (MI), Sessions (AL), Smith (NH)
Minority (D 8): Leahy (VT), RMM; Kennedy (MA), Biden (DE), Kohl (WI), Feinstein (CA), Feingold (WI), Torricelli (NJ), Schumer (NY)

SUBCOMMITTEES

ADMINISTRATIVE OVERSIGHT & THE COURTS

Majority (R 4): Grassley, Chmn.; Sessions, Thurmond, Abraham
Minority (D 3): Torricelli, RMM; Feingold, Schumer

ANTITRUST, BUSINESS RIGHTS & COMPETITION

Majority (R 4): DeWine, Chmn.; Hatch, Specter, Thurmond
Minority (D 3): Kohl, RMM; Torricelli, Leahy

CRIMINAL JUSTICE OVERSIGHT

Majority (R 5): Thurmond, Chmn.; DeWine, Ashcroft, Abraham, Sessions
Minority (D 4): Schumer, RMM; Biden, Torricelli, Leahy

IMMIGRATION

Majority (R 4): Abraham, Chmn.; Specter, Grassley, Kyl
Minority (D 3): Kennedy, RMM; Feinstein, Schumer

TECHNOLOGY, TERRORISM & GOVERNMENT INFORMATION

Majority (R 4): Kyl, Chmn.; Hatch, Grassley, DeWine
Minority (D 3): Feinstein, RMM; Biden, Kohl

THE CONSTITUTION, FEDERALISM & PROPERTY RIGHTS

Majority (R 5): Ashcroft, Chmn.; Hatch, Smith, Specter, Thurmond
Minority (D 3): Feingold, RMM; Kennedy, Leahy

YOUTH VIOLENCE

Majority (R 4): Sessions, Chmn.; Smith, Kyl, Ashcroft
Minority (D 3): Biden, RMM; Feinstein, Kohl

RULES & ADMINISTRATION
www.senate.gov/~rules

305 Russell
202-224-6352

Majority (R 9): McConnell (KY), Chmn.; Helms (NC), Stevens (AK), Warner (VA), Cochran (MS), Santorum (PA), Nickles (OK), Lott (MS), Hutchison (TX)
Minority (D 7): Dodd (CT), RMM; Byrd (WV), Inouye (HI), Moynihan (NY), Feinstein (CA), Torricelli (NJ), Schumer (NY)

NO SUBCOMMITTEES

SMALL BUSINESS
sbc.senate.gov

428A Russell
202-224-5175

Majority (R 10): Bond (MO), Chmn.; Burns (MT), Coverdell (GA), Bennett (UT), Snowe (ME), Enzi (WY), Fitzgerald (IL), Crapo (ID), Voinovich (OH), Abraham (MI)
Minority (D 8): Kerry (MA), RMM; Levin (MI), Harkin (IA), Lieberman (CT), Wellstone (MN), Cleland (GA), Landrieu (LA), Edwards (NC)

NO SUBCOMMITTEES

VETERANS' AFFAIRS
www.senate.gov/~veterans

412 Russell
202-224-9126

Majority (R 7): Specter (PA), Chmn.; Murkowski (AK), Thurmond (SC), Jeffords (VT), Campbell (CO), Craig (ID), Hutchinson (AR)

Minority (D 5): Rockefeller (WV), RMM; Graham (FL), Akaka (HI), Wellstone (MN), Murray (WA)

NO SUBCOMMITTEES

HOUSE COMMITTEES

AGRICULTURE
www.house.gov/agriculture

1301 Longworth
202-225-2171

Majority (R 27): Combest (TX), Chmn.; Barrett (NE), Vice Chmn.; Boehner (OH), Ewing (IL), Goodlatte (VA), Pombo (CA), Canady (FL), Smith (MI), Everett (AL), Lucas (OK), Chenoweth (ID), Hostettler (IN), Chambliss (GA), LaHood (IL), Moran (KS), Schaffer (CO), Thune (SD), Jenkins (TN), Cooksey (LA), Calvert (CA), Gutknecht (MN), Riley (AL), Walden (OR), Simpson (ID), Ose (CA), Hayes (NC), Fletcher (KY)

Minority (D 24): Stenholm (TX), RMM; Brown (CA), Condit (CA), Peterson (MN), Dooley (CA), Clayton (NC), Minge (MN), Hilliard (AL), Pomeroy (ND), Holden (PA), Bishop (GA), Thompson (MS), Baldacci (ME), Berry (AR), Goode (VA), McIntyre (NC), Stabenow (MI), Etheridge (NC), John (LA), Boswell (IA), Phelps (IL), Lucas (KY), Thompson (CA), Hill (IN)

SUBCOMMITTEES

DEPARTMENT OPERATIONS, OVERSIGHT, NUTRITION & FORESTRY

Majority (R 10): Goodlatte, Chmn.; Ewing, Pombo, Canady, Hostettler, Chambliss, LaHood, Moran, Cooksey, Walden

Minority (D 9): Clayton, RMM; Berry, Thompson, Goode, Phelps, Hill, Thompson, Brown, Minge

GENERAL FARM COMMODITIES, RESOURCE CONSERVATION & CREDIT

Majority (R 10): Barrett, Chmn.; Boehner, Smith, Lucas, Chambliss, Moran, Thune, Jenkins, Ose, Hayes

Minority (D 9): Minge, RMM; Thompson, Phelps, Hill, Clayton, Pomeroy, Holden, Bishop, Baldacci

LIVESTOCK & HORTICULTURE

Majority (R 11): Pombo, Chmn.; Boehner, Goodlatte, Everett, Lucas, Chenoweth, Hostettler, Schaffer, Calvert, Gutknecht, Riley

Minority (D 10): Peterson, RMM; Holden, Condit, Dooley, Berry, McIntyre, Stabenow, Etheridge, Boswell, Lucas

RISK MANAGEMENT, RESEARCH & SPECIALTY CROPS

Majority (R 17): Ewing, Chmn.; Barrett, Smith, Everett, Lucas, Chambliss, LaHood, Moran, Thune, Jenkins, Gutknecht, Riley, Walden, Simpson, Ose, Hayes, Fletcher

Minority (D 15): Condit, RMM; Brown, Dooley, Hilliard, Pomeroy, Bishop, Baldacci, Goode, McIntyre, Stabenow, Etheridge, John, Boswell, Lucas, Thompson

APPROPRIATIONS
www.house.gov/appropriations

H-218 The Capitol
202-225-2771

Majority (R 34): Young (FL), Chmn.; Regula (OH), Lewis (CA), Porter (IL), Rogers (KY), Skeen (NM), Wolf (VA), DeLay (TX), Kolbe (AZ), Packard (CA), Callahan (AL), Walsh (NY), Taylor (NC), Hobson (OH), Istook (OK), Bonilla (TX), Knollenberg (MI), Miller (FL), Dickey (AR), Kingston (GA), Frelinghuysen (NJ), Wicker (MS), Forbes (NY), Nethercutt (WA), Cunningham (CA), Tiahrt (KS), Wamp (TN), Latham (IA), Northup (KY), Aderholt (AL), Emerson (MO), Sununu (NH), Granger (TX), Peterson (PA)

Minority (D 27): Obey (WI), RMM; Murtha (PA), Dicks (WA), Sabo (MN), Dixon (CA), Hoyer (MD), Mollohan (WV), Kaptur (OH), Pelosi (CA), Visclosky (IN), Lowey (NY), Serrano (NY), DeLauro (CT), Moran (VA), Olver (MA), Pastor (AZ), Meek (FL), Price (NC), Edwards (TX), Cramer (AL), Clyburn (SC), Hinchey (NY), Roybal-Allard (CA), Farr (CA), Jackson (IL), Kilpatrick (MI), Boyd (FL)

SUBCOMMITTEES

AGRICULTURE, RURAL DEVELOPMENT, & FDA

Majority (R 8): Skeen, Chmn.; Walsh, Dickey, Kingston, Nethercutt, Bonilla, Latham, Emerson
Minority (D 5): Kaptur, RMM; DeLauro, Hinchey, Farr, Boyd

COMMERCE, JUSTICE, STATE & THE JUDICIARY

Majority (R 7): Rogers, Chmn.; Kolbe, Taylor, Regula, Latham, Miller, Wamp
Minority (D 4): Serrano, RMM; Dixon, Mollohan, Roybal-Allard

DEFENSE

Majority (R 10): Lewis, Chmn.; Young, Skeen, Hobson, Bonilla, Nethercutt, Istook, Cunningham, Dickey, Frelinghuysen
Minority (D 6): Murtha, RMM; Dicks, Sabo, Dixon, Visclosky, Moran

DISTRICT OF COLUMBIA

Majority (R 6): Istook, Chmn.; Cunningham, Tiahrt, Aderholt, Emerson, Sununu
Minority (D 3): Moran, RMM; Dixon, Mollohan

ENERGY & WATER DEVELOPMENT

Majority (R 7): Packard, Chmn.; Rogers, Knollenberg, Forbes, Frelinghuysen, Callahan, Latham
Minority (D 4): Visclosky, RMM; Edwards, Pastor, Clyburn

FOREIGN OPERATIONS & EXPORT FINANCING

Majority (R 8): Callahan, Chmn.; Porter, Wolf, Packard, Knollenberg, Forbes, Kingston, Lewis
Minority (D 5): Pelosi, RMM; Lowey, Jackson, Kilpatrick, Sabo

INTERIOR

Majority (R 8): Regula, Chmn.; Kolbe, Skeen, Taylor, Nethercutt, Wamp, Kingston, Peterson
Minority (D 5): Dicks, RMM; Murtha, Moran, Cramer, Hinchey

LABOR, HHS & EDUCATION

Majority (R 9): Porter, Chmn.; Young, Bonilla, Istook, Miller, Dickey, Wicker, Northup, Cunningham

Minority (D 6): Obey, RMM; Hoyer, Pelosi, Lowey, DeLauro, Jackson

MILITARY CONSTRUCTION

Majority (R 8): Hobson, Chmn.; Porter, Wicker, Tiahrt, Walsh, Miller, Aderholt, Granger

Minority (D 5): Olver, RMM; Edwards, Farr, Boyd, Dicks

THE LEGISLATIVE BRANCH

Majority (R 5): Taylor, Chmn.; Wamp, Lewis, Granger, Peterson

Minority (D 3): Pastor, RMM; Murtha, Hoyer

TRANSPORTATION

Majority (R 9): Wolf, Chmn.; DeLay, Regula, Rogers, Packard, Callahan, Tiahrt, Aderholt, Granger

Minority (D 5): Sabo, RMM; Olver, Pastor, Kilpatrick, Serrano, Clyburn

TREASURY, POSTAL SERVICE & GENERAL GOVERNMENT

Majority (R 7): Kolbe, Chmn.; Wolf, Forbes, Northup, Emerson, Sununu, Peterson

Minority (D 4): Hoyer, RMM; Meek, Price, Roybal-Allard

VA, HUD & INDEPENDENT AGENCIES

Majority (R 8): Walsh, Chmn.; DeLay, Hobson, Knollenberg, Frelinghuysen, Wicker, Northup, Sununu

Minority (D 5): Mollohan, RMM; Kaptur, Meek, Price, Cramer

ARMED SERVICES   2120 Rayburn
www.house.gov/hasc   202-225-4151

Majority (R 32): Spence (SC), Chmn.; Stump (AZ), Vice Chmn.; Hunter (CA), Kasich (OH), Bateman (VA), Hansen (UT), Weldon (PA), Hefley (CO), Saxton (NJ), Buyer (IN), Fowler (FL), McHugh (NY), Talent (MO), Everett (AL), Bartlett (MD), McKeon (CA), Watts (OK), Thornberry (TX), Hostettler (IN), Chambliss (GA), Hilleary (TN), Scarborough (FL), Jones (NC), Graham (SC), Ryun (KS), Riley (AL), Gibbons (NV), Bono (CA), Pitts (PA), Hayes (NC), Kuykendall (CA), Sherwood (PA)

Minority (D 28): Skelton (MO), RMM; Sisisky (VA), Spratt (SC), Ortiz (TX), Pickett (VA), Evans (IL), Taylor (MS), Abercrombie (HI), Meehan (MA), Underwood (GU), Kennedy (RI), Blagojevich (IL), Reyes (TX), Allen (ME), Snyder (AR), Turner (TX), Smith (WA), Sanchez (CA), Maloney (CT), McIntyre (NC), Rodriguez (TX), McKinney (GA), Tauscher (CA), Brady (PA), Andrews (NJ), Hill (IN), Thompson (CA), Larson (CT)

SUBCOMMITTEES

MILITARY INSTALLATIONS & FACILITIES

Majority (R 10): Hefley, Chmn.; Fowler, McHugh, McKeon, Hostettler, Hilleary, Vice Chmn.; Scarborough, Stump, Saxton, Buyer

Minority (D 8): Taylor, RMM; Ortiz, Abercrombie, Underwood, Reyes, Snyder, Brady, Thompson

MILITARY PERSONNEL

Majority (R 10): Buyer, Chmn.; Bartlett, Watts, Thornberry, Graham, Vice Chmn.; Ryun, Bono, Pitts, Hayes, Kuykendall

Minority (D 8): Abercrombie, RMM; Meehan, Kennedy, Sanchez, McKinney, Tauscher, Thompson, Larson

MILITARY PROCUREMENT

Majority (R 15): Hunter, Chmn.; Spence, Stump, Hansen, Saxton, Talent, Everett, Watts, Thornberry, Vice Chmn.; Graham, Ryun, Gibbons, Bono, Pitts, Hayes
Minority (D 13): Sisisky, RMM; Skelton, Spratt, Evans, Blagojevich, Allen, Turner, Smith, Maloney, McIntyre, McKinney, Tauscher, Brady

MILITARY READINESS

Majority (R 12): Bateman, Chmn.; Chambliss, Jones, Vice Chmn.; Riley, Hunter, Hansen, Weldon, Fowler, Talent, Everett, Gibbons, Sherwood
Minority (D 10): Ortiz, RMM; Sisisky, Spratt, Pickett, Underwood, Blagojevich, Smith, Maloney, McIntyre, Rodriguez

MILITARY RESEARCH & DEVELOPMENT

Majority (R 15): Weldon, Chmn.; Bartlett, Kuykendall, Sherwood, Kasich, Bateman, Hefley, McHugh, McKeon, Hostettler, Vice Chmn.; Chambliss, Hilleary, Scarborough, Jones, Riley
Minority (D 13): Pickett, RMM; Taylor, Meehan, Kennedy, Reyes, Allen, Snyder, Turner, Sanchez, Rodriguez, Andrews, Hill, Larson

SPECIAL OVERSIGHT PANEL ON MORALE, WELFARE AND RECREATION

Majority (R 10): McHugh, Chmn.; Stump, Bateman, Bartlett, Watts, Chambliss, Scarborough, Jones, Riley, Vice Chmn.; Hayes
Minority (D 8): Meehan, RMM; Sisisky, Ortiz, Pickett, Underwood, Reyes, Andrews

SPECIAL OVERSIGHT PANEL ON THE MERCHANT MARINE

Majority (R 7): Bateman, Chmn.; Hunter, Weldon, Saxton, Scarborough, Jones, Kuykendall, Vice Chmn.
Minority (D 5): Underwood, RMM; Taylor, Abercrombie, Allen, Maloney

BANKING & FINANCIAL SERVICES

www.house.gov/banking

2129 Rayburn
202-225-7502

Majority (R 32): Leach (IA), Chmn.; McCollum (FL), Vice Chmn.; Roukema (NJ), Bereuter (NE), Baker (LA), Lazio (NY), Bachus (AL), Castle (DE), King (NY), Campbell (CA), Royce (CA), Lucas (OK), Metcalf (WA), Ney (OH), Barr (GA), Kelly (NY), Paul (TX), Weldon (FL), Ryun (KS), Cook (UT), Riley (AL), Hill (MT), LaTourette (OH), Manzullo (IL), Jones (NC), Ryan (WI), Ose (CA), Sweeney (NY), Biggert (IL), Terry (NE), Green (WI), Toomey (PA)
Minority (D 27): LaFalce (NY), RMM; Vento (MN), Frank (MA), Kanjorski (PA), Waters (CA), Maloney (NY), Gutierrez (IL), Velazquez (NY), Watt (NC), Ackerman (NY), Bentsen (TX), Maloney (CT), Hooley (OR), Carson (IN), Weygand (RI), Sherman (CA), Sandlin (TX), Meeks (NY), Lee (CA), Goode (VA), Mascara (PA), Inslee (WA), Schakowsky (IL), Moore (KS), Gonzalez (TX), Tubbs Jones (OH), Capuano (MA)
Independent (1): Sanders (I-VT)

SUBCOMMITTEES

CAPITAL MARKETS, SECURITIES & GOVERNMENT SPONSORED ENTERPRISES

Majority (R 15): Baker, Chmn.; Lucas, Vice Chmn.; Manzullo, Jones, Ryan, Sweeney, Biggert, Terry, Toomey, Roukema, King, Royce, Paul, Cook, Riley
Minority (D 13): Kanjorski, RMM; Ackerman, Velazquez, Bentsen, Weygand, Sandlin, Waters, Maloney, Maloney, Hooley, Mascara, Tubbs Jones, Capuano

1802   HOUSE COMMITTEES

DOMESTIC & INTERNATIONAL MONETARY POLICY

Majority (R 14): Bachus, Chmn.; Paul, Vice Chmn.; Ose, McCollum, Castle, Lucas, Metcalf, Ney, Weldon, Ryun, Ryan, Biggert, Green, Toomey
Minority (D 12): Waters, RMM; Frank, Watt, Carson, Meeks, Lee, Kanjorski, Sanders, Sherman, Inslee, Schakowsky, Moore

FINANCIAL INSTITUTIONS & CONSUMER CREDIT

Majority (R 15): Roukema, Chmn.; McCollum, Vice Chmn.; Bereuter, Castle, Campbell, Royce, Metcalf, Barr, Kelly, Weldon, Ryun, Cook, Riley, Hill, LaTourette
Minority (D 13): Vento, RMM; Maloney, Watt, Ackerman, Bentsen, Sherman, Sandlin, Meeks, Gutierrez, Mascara, Inslee, Moore, Gonzalez

GENERAL OVERSIGHT & INVESTIGATIONS

Majority (R 6): King, Chmn.; LaTourette, Vice Chmn.; Bachus, Ney, Barr, Paul
Minority (D 4): Sanders, Gutierrez, Goode, Gonzalez

HOUSING & COMMUNITY OPPORTUNITY

Majority (R 14): Lazio, Chmn.; Ney, Vice Chmn.; Green, Bereuter, Baker, Campbell, Barr, Kelly, Hill, Jones, Ose, Sweeney, Terry, Metcalf
Minority (D 12): Frank, RMM; Velazquez, Maloney, Hooley, Carson, Weygand, Vento, Lee, Goode, Schakowsky, Tubbs Jones, Capuano

BUDGET
www.house.gov/budget

309 Cannon
202-226-7270

Majority (R 24): Kasich (OH), Chmn.; Chambliss (GA), Shays (CT), Herger (CA), Franks (NJ), Smith (MI), Nussle (IA), Hoekstra (MI), Radanovich (CA), Bass (NH), Gutknecht (MN), Hilleary (TN), Sununu (NH), Pitts (PA), Knollenberg (MI), Thornberry (TX), Ryun (KS), Collins (GA), Wamp (TN), Green (WI), Fletcher (KY), Miller (CA), Ryan (WI), Toomey (PA)
Minority (D 19): Spratt (SC), RMM; McDermott (WA), Rivers (MI), Thompson (MS), Minge (MN), Bentsen (TX), Davis (FL), Weygand (RI), Clayton (NC), Price (NC), Markey (MA), Kleczka (WI), Clement (TN), Moran (VA), Hooley (OR), Lucas (KY), Holt (NJ), Hoeffel (PA), Baldwin (WI)

NO SUBCOMMITTEES

COMMERCE
www.house.gov/commerce

2125 Rayburn
202-225-2927

Majority (R 29): Bliley (VA), Chmn.; Tauzin (LA), Oxley (OH), Bilirakis (FL), Barton (TX), Upton (MI), Stearns (FL), Gillmor (OH), Vice Chmn.; Greenwood (PA), Cox (CA), Deal (GA), Largent (OK), Burr (NC), Bilbray (CA), Whitfield (KY), Ganske (IA), Norwood (GA), Coburn (OK), Lazio (NY), Cubin (WY), Rogan (CA), Shimkus (IL), Wilson (NM), Shadegg (AZ), Pickering (MS), Fossella (NY), Blunt (MO), Bryant (TN), Ehrlich (MD)
Minority (D 24): Dingell (MI), RMM; Waxman (CA), Markey (MA), Hall (TX), Boucher (VA), Towns (NY), Pallone (NJ), Brown (OH), Gordon (TN), Deutsch (FL), Rush (IL), Eshoo (CA), Klink (PA), Stupak (MI), Engel (NY), Sawyer (OH), Wynn (MD), Green (TX), McCarthy (MO), Strickland (OH), DeGette (CO), Barrett (WI), Luther (MN), Capps (CA)

ENERGY & POWER

Majority (R 16): Barton, Chmn.; Bilirakis, Stearns, Vice Chmn.; Largent, Burr, Whitfield, Norwood, Coburn, Rogan, Shimkus, Wilson, Shadegg, Pickering, Fossella, Bryant, Ehrlich
Minority (D 13): Hall, RMM; McCarthy, Sawyer, Markey, Boucher, Pallone, Brown, Gordon, Rush, Wynn, Strickland, Deutsch, Klink

FINANCE & HAZARDOUS MATERIALS

Majority (R 15): Oxley, Chmn.; Tauzin, Vice Chmn.; Gillmor, Greenwood, Cox, Largent, Bilbray, Ganske, Lazio, Shimkus, Wilson, Shadegg, Fossella, Blunt, Ehrlich
Minority (D 12): Towns, RMM; Deutsch, Stupak, Engel, DeGette, Barrett, Luther, Capps, Markey, Hall, Pallone, Rush

HEALTH AND ENVIRONMENT

Majority (R 16): Bilirakis, Chmn.; Upton, Stearns, Greenwood, Deal, Burr, Bilbray, Whitfield, Ganske, Norwood, Coburn, Vice Chmn.; Lazio, Cubin, Shadegg, Pickering, Bryant
Minority (D 13): Brown, RMM; Waxman, Pallone, Deutsch, Stupak, Green, Strickland, DeGette, Barrett, Capps, Hall, Towns, Eshoo

OVERSIGHT & INVESTIGATIONS

Majority (R 9): Upton, Chmn.; Barton, Cox, Burr, Vice Chmn.; Bilbray, Whitfield, Ganske, Blunt, Bryant
Minority (D 7): Klink, RMM; Waxman, Stupak, Green, McCarthy, Strickland, DeGette

TELECOMMUNICATIONS, TRADE & CONSUMER PROTECTION

Majority (R 15): Tauzin, Chmn.; Oxley, Vice Chmn.; Stearns, Gillmor, Cox, Deal, Largent, Cubin, Rogan, Shimkus, Wilson, Pickering, Fossella, Blunt, Ehrlich
Minority (D 12): Markey, RMM; Boucher, Gordon, Rush, Eshoo, Engel, Wynn, Luther, Klink, Sawyer, Green, McCarthy

EDUCATION & THE WORKFORCE
www.house.gov/eeo

2181 Rayburn
202-225-4527

Majority (R 27): Goodling (PA), Chmn.; Petri (WI), Vice Chmn.; Roukema (NJ), Ballenger (NC), Barrett (NE), Boehner (OH), Hoekstra (MI), McKeon (CA), Castle (DE), Johnson (TX), Talent (MO), Greenwood (PA), Graham (SC), Souder (IN), McIntosh (IN), Norwood (GA), Paul (TX), Schaffer (CO), Upton (MI), Deal (GA), Hilleary (TN), Ehlers (MI), Salmon (AZ), Tancredo (CO), Fletcher (KY), DeMint (SC), Isakson (GA)
Minority (D 22): Clay (MO), RMM; Miller (CA), Kildee (MI), Martinez (CA), Owens (NY), Payne (NJ), Mink (HI), Andrews (NJ), Roemer (IN), Scott (VA), Woolsey (CA), Romero-Barcelo (PR), Fattah (PA), Hinojosa (TX), McCarthy (NY), Tierney (MA), Kind (WI), Sanchez (CA), Ford (TN), Kucinich (OH), Wu (OR), Holt (NJ)

EARLY CHILDHOOD, YOUTH & FAMILIES

Majority (R 17): Castle, Chmn.; Johnson, Souder, Paul, Goodling, Greenwood, McIntosh, Upton, Hilleary, Petri, Roukema, Boehner, Graham, Schaffer, Vice Chmn.; Salmon, Tancredo, DeMint
Minority (D 14): Kildee, RMM; Miller, Payne, Mink, Scott, Kucinich, Woolsey, Romero-Barcelo, Fattah, Hinojosa, McCarthy, Sanchez, Ford, Wu

1804 HOUSE COMMITTEES

EMPLOYER-EMPLOYEE RELATIONS

Majority (R 7): Boehner, Chmn.; Talent, Petri, Roukema, Ballenger, Goodling, McKeon, Hoekstra, Salmon, Fletcher, Vice Chmn.; DeMint
Minority (D 8): Andrews, RMM; Kildee, Payne, Romero-Barcelo, McCarthy, Tierney, Wu, Holt

OVERSIGHT & INVESTIGATIONS

Majority (R 6): Hoekstra, Chmn.; Norwood, Vice Chmn.; Hilleary, Schaffer, Tancredo, Fletcher
Minority (D 4): Roemer, RMM; Scott, Kind, Ford

POSTSECONDARY EDUCATION, TRAINING & LIFE-LONG LEARNING

Majority (R 12): McKeon, Chmn.; Goodling, Petri, Barrett, Greenwood, Graham, Vice Chmn.; McIntosh, Castle, Souder, Deal, Ehlers, Isakson
Minority (D 10): Martinez, RMM; Tierney, Kind, Holt, Owens, Mink, Andrews, Roemer, Fattah, Hinojosa

WORKFORCE PROTECTIONS

Majority (R 8): Ballenger, Chmn.; Barrett, Vice Chmn.; Hoekstra, Graham, Paul, Johnson, Boehner, Isakson
Minority (D 6): Owens, RMM; Miller, Martinez, Woolsey, Sanchez, Kucinich

GOVERNMENT REFORM
www.house.gov/reform

2157 Rayburn
202-225-5074

Majority (R 24): Burton (IN), Chmn.; Gilman (NY), Morella (MD), Shays (CT), Ros-Lehtinen (FL), McHugh (NY), Horn (CA), Mica (FL), Davis (VA), McIntosh (IN), Souder (IN), Scarborough (FL), LaTourette (OH), Vice Chmn.; Sanford (SC), Barr (GA), Miller (FL), Hutchinson (AR), Terry (NE), Biggert (IL), Walden (OR), Ose (CA), Ryan (WI), Chenoweth (ID), Vitter (LA)
Minority (D 19): Waxman (CA), RMM; Lantos (CA), Wise (WV), Owens (NY), Towns (NY), Kanjorski (PA), Mink (HI), Maloney (NY), Norton (DC), Fattah (PA), Cummings (MD), Kucinich (OH), Blagojevich (IL), Davis (IL), Tierney (MA), Turner (TX), Allen (ME), Ford (TN), Schakowsky (IL)
Independent (1): Sanders (I-VT)

SUBCOMMITTEES

CENSUS

Majority (R 5): Miller, Chmn.; Davis, Ryan, Souder
Minority (D 3): Maloney, RMM; Davis, Ford

CIVIL SERVICE

Majority (R 5): Scarborough, Chmn.; Hutchinson, Vice Chmn.; Morella, Mica, Miller
Minority (D 3): Cummings, RMM; Norton, Allen

CRIMINAL JUSTICE, DRUG POLICY & HUMAN RESOURCES

Majority (R 9): Mica, Chmn.; Barr, Vice Chmn.; Gilman, Shays, Ros-Lehtinen, Souder, LaTourette, Hutchinson, Ose
Minority (D 7): Mink, RMM; Towns, Cummings, Kucinich, Blagojevich, Tierney, Turner

DISTRICT OF COLUMBIA

Majority (R 4): Davis, Chmn.; Morella, Vice Chmn.; Horn, Scarborough
Minority (D 3): Norton, RMM; Maloney, Towns

GOVERNMENT MANAGEMENT, INFORMATION & TECHNOLOGY
Majority (R 6): Horn, Chmn.; Biggert, Vice Chmn.; Davis, Walden, Ose, Ryan
Minority (D 5): Turner, RMM; Kanjorski, Owens, Mink, Maloney

NATIONAL ECONOMIC GROWTH, NATURAL RESOURCES & REGULATORY AFFAIRS
Majority (R 7): McIntosh, Chmn.; Ryan, Vice Chmn.; Barr, Terry, Walden, Chenoweth, Doolittle
Minority (D 5): Kucinich, RMM; Lantos, Kanjorski, Sanders, Ford

NATIONAL SECURITY, VETERANS' AFFAIRS & INTL. RELATIONS
Majority (R 10): Shays, Chmn.; Souder, Vice Chmn.; Ros-Lehtinen, McHugh, Mica, McIntosh, Sanford, Terry, Biggert, Chenoweth
Minority (D 8): Blagojevich, RMM; Lantos, Wise, Tierney, Allen, Towns, Sanders, Schakowsky

POSTAL SERVICE
Majority (R 5): McHugh, Chmn.; Sanford, Vice Chmn.; Gilman, LaTourette, Miller
Minority (D 3): Fattah, RMM; Owens, Davis

HOUSE ADMINISTRATION
www.house.gov/cha

1309 Longworth
202-225-8281

Majority (R 6): Thomas (CA), Chmn.; Boehner (OH), Vice Chmn.; Ehlers (MI), Ney (OH), Mica (FL), Ewing (IL)
Minority (D 3): Hoyer (MD), RMM; Fattah (PA), Davis (FL)

NO SUBCOMMITTEES

INTERNATIONAL RELATIONS
www.house.gov/international-relations

2170 Rayburn
202-225-5021

Majority (R 26): Gilman (NY), Chmn.; Goodling (PA), Leach (IA), Hyde (IL), Bereuter (NE), Smith (NJ), Burton (IN), Gallegly (CA), Ros-Lehtinen (FL), Ballenger (NC), Rohrabacher (CA), Manzullo (IL), Royce (CA), King (NY), Chabot (OH), Sanford (SC), Salmon (AZ), Houghton (NY), Campbell (CA), McHugh (NY), Brady (TX), Burr (NC), Gillmor (OH), Radanovich (CA), Cooksey (LA), Tancredo (CO)
Minority (D 23): Gejdenson (CT), RMM; Lantos (CA), Berman (CA), Ackerman (NY), Faleomavaega (AS), Martinez (CA), Payne (NJ), Menendez (NJ), Brown (OH), McKinney (GA), Hastings (FL), Danner (MO), Hilliard (AL), Sherman (CA), Wexler (FL), Rothman (NJ), Davis (FL), Pomeroy (ND), Delahunt (MA), Meeks (NY), Lee (CA), Crowley (NY), Hoeffel (PA)

SUBCOMMITTEES

AFRICA
Majority (R 6): Royce, Chmn.; Houghton, Campbell, Chabot, Tancredo, Radanovich
Minority (D 4): Payne, RMM; Hastings, Meeks, Lee

ASIA & THE PACIFIC
Majority (R 12): Bereuter, Chmn.; Leach, Rohrabacher, King, Sanford, Salmon, McHugh, Burr, Gillmor, Manzullo, Royce, Cooksey
Minority (D 10): Lantos, RMM; Berman, Faleomavaega, Martinez, Brown, Wexler, Davis, Pomeroy, Ackerman, Hastings

INTERNATIONAL ECONOMIC POLICY & TRADE

Majority (R 10): Ros-Lehtinen, Chmn.; Manzullo, Chabot, Brady, Radanovich, Cooksey, Bereuter, Rohrabacher, Campbell, Burr
Minority (D 8): Menendez, RMM; Danner, Hilliard, Sherman, Rothman, Delahunt, Crowley, Hoeffel

INTERNATIONAL OPERATIONS AND HUMAN RIGHTS

Majority (R 8): Smith, Chmn.; Goodling, Hyde, Tancredo, Burton, Ballenger, King, Salmon
Minority (D 6): McKinney, RMM; Faleomavaega, Hilliard, Sherman, Delahunt, Meeks

WESTERN HEMISPHERE

Majority (R 9): Gallegly, Chmn.; Burton, Ballenger, Smith, Ros-Lehtinen, Sanford, Brady, Gillmor
Minority (D 7): Ackerman, RMM; Martinez, Menendez, Wexler, Rothman, Davis, Pomeroy

JUDICIARY
www.house.gov/judiciary

2138 Rayburn
202-225-3951

Majority (R 21): Hyde (IL), Chmn.; Sensenbrenner (WI), McCollum (FL), Gekas (PA), Coble (NC), Smith (TX), Gallegly (CA), Canady (FL), Goodlatte (VA), Chabot (OH), Barr (GA), Jenkins (TN), Hutchinson (AR), Pease (IN), Cannon (UT), Rogan (CA), Graham (SC), Bono (CA), Bachus (AL), Scarborough (FL), Vitter (LA)
Minority (D 16): Conyers (MI), RMM; Frank (MA), Berman (CA), Boucher (VA), Nadler (NY), Scott (VA), Watt (NC), Lofgren (CA), Jackson Lee (TX), Waters (CA), Meehan (MA), Delahunt (MA), Wexler (FL), Rothman (NJ), Baldwin (WI), Weiner (NY)

SUBCOMMITTEES

COMMERCIAL & ADMINISTRATIVE LAW

Majority (R 7): Gekas, Chmn.; Graham, Chabot, Bachus, Bono, Scarborough
Minority (D 5): Nadler, RMM; Baldwin, Watt, Weiner, Delahunt

COURTS & INTELLECTUAL PROPERTY

Majority (R 9): Coble, Chmn.; Sensenbrenner, Gallegly, Goodlatte, Jenkins, Pease, Cannon, Rogan, Bono
Minority (D 6): Berman, RMM; Conyers, Boucher, Lofgren, Delahunt, Wexler

CRIME

Majority (R 8): McCollum, Chmn.; Chabot, Barr, Gekas, Coble, Smith, Canady, Hutchinson
Minority (D 5): Scott, RMM; Meehan, Rothman, Weiner, Jackson Lee

IMMIGRATION & CLAIMS

Majority (R 8): Smith, Chmn.; McCollum, Gallegly, Pease, Cannon, Canady, Goodlatte, Scarborough
Minority (D 5): Jackson Lee, RMM; Berman, Lofgren, Frank, Meehan

THE CONSTITUTION

Majority (R 8): Canady, Chmn.; Hyde, Hutchinson, Bachus, Goodlatte, Barr, Jenkins, Graham
Minority (D 5): Watt, RMM; Waters, Frank, Conyers, Nadler

PERMANENT SELECT COMMITTEE ON INTELLIGENCE

H-405 The Capitol
202-225-4121

Majority (R 9): Goss (FL), Chmn.; Lewis (CA), Vice Chmn.; McCollum (FL), Castle (DE), Boehlert (NY), Bass (NH), Gibbons (NV), LaHood (IL), Wilson (NM)
Minority (D 7): Dixon (CA), RMM; Pelosi (CA), Bishop (GA), Sisisky (VA), Condit (CA), Roemer (IN), Hastings (FL)

SUBCOMMITTEES

HUMAN INTELLIGENCE, ANALYSIS & COUNTERINTELLIGENCE

Majority (R 6): McCollum, Chmn.; Bass, Vice Chmn.; Lewis, Gibbons, LaHood, Wilson
Minority (D 4): Hastings, RMM; Pelosi, Sisisky, Condit

TECHNICAL & TACTICAL INTELLIGENCE

Majority (R 6): Castle, Chmn.; Boehlert, Vice Chmn.; Bass, Gibbons, LaHood, Wilson
Minority (D 4): Bishop, RMM; Roemer, Condit, Sisisky

RESOURCES
www.house.gov/resources

1324 Longworth
202-225-2761

Majority (R 28): Young (AK), Chmn.; Tauzin (LA), Hansen (UT), Saxton (NJ), Gallegly (CA), Duncan (TN), Hefley (CO), Doolittle (CA), Gilchrest (MD), Calvert (CA), Pombo (CA), Cubin (WY), Chenoweth (ID), Radanovich (CA), Jones (NC), Thornberry (TX), Cannon (UT), Brady (TX), Peterson (PA), Hill (MT), Schaffer (CO), Gibbons (NV), Souder (IN), Walden (OR), Sherwood (PA), Hayes (NC), Simpson (ID), Tancredo (CO)
Minority (D 24): Miller (CA), RMM; Rahall (WV), Vento (MN), Kildee (MI), DeFazio (OR), Faleomavaega (AS), Abercrombie (HI), Ortiz (TX), Pickett (VA), Pallone (NJ), Dooley (CA), Romero-Barcelo (PR), Underwood (GU), Kennedy (RI), Smith (WA), John (LA), Christian-Christensen (VI), Kind (WI), Inslee (WA), Napolitano (CA), Udall (NM), Udall (CO), Crowley (NY), Holt (NJ)

SUBCOMMITTEES

ENERGY & MINERAL RESOURCES

Majority (R 9): Cubin, Chmn.; Tauzin, Thornberry, Cannon, Brady, Schaffer, Gibbons, Walden, Tancredo
Minority (D 8): Underwood, RMM; Rahall, Faleomavaega, Ortiz, Dooley, Kennedy, John, Inslee

FISHERIES CONSERVATION, WILDLIFE & OCEANS

Majority (R 9): Saxton, Chmn.; Tauzin, Hansen, Gilchrest, Pombo, Jones, Souder, Hayes, Simpson
Minority (D 8): Faleomavaega, RMM; Vento, DeFazio, Abercrombie, Ortiz, Pallone, Romero-Barcelo, Smith

FORESTS & FOREST HEALTH

Majority (R 9): Chenoweth, Chmn.; Duncan, Doolittle, Gilchrest, Peterson, Hill, Schaffer, Sherwood, Hayes
Minority (D 8): Kennedy, RMM; Kildee, Pickett, Kind, Napolitano, Udall (NM), Udall (CO), Crowley

NATIONAL PARKS & PUBLIC LANDS

Majority (R 12): Hansen, Chmn.; Gallegly, Duncan, Hefley, Pombo, Radanovich, Jones, Cannon, Hill, Gibbons, Souder, Sherwood
Minority (D 10): Romero-Barcelo, RMM; Rahall, Vento, Kildee, Christian-Christensen, Kind, Inslee, Udall (NM), Udall (CO), Crowley

WATER & POWER

Majority (R 8): Doolittle, Chmn.; Calvert, Pombo, Chenoweth, Radanovich, Thornberry, Walden, Simpson
Minority (D 7): Dooley, RMM; Miller, DeFazio, Pickett, Smith, Christian-Christensen, Napolitano

RULES   H-312 The Capitol
www.house.gov/rules   202-225-9191

Majority (R 9): Dreier (CA), Chmn.; Goss (FL), Linder (GA), Pryce (OH), Diaz-Balart (FL), Hastings (WA), Myrick (NC), Sessions (TX), Reynolds (NY)
Minority (D 4): Moakley (MA), RMM; Frost (TX), Hall (OH), Slaughter (NY)

SUBCOMMITTEES

RULES & ORGANIZATION OF THE HOUSE

Majority (R 5): Linder, Chmn.; Diaz-Balart, Vice Chmn.; Sessions, Reynolds, Dreier
Minority (D 2): Hall, RMM; Slaughter

THE LEGISLATIVE & BUDGET PROCESS

Majority (R 5): Goss, Chmn.; Pryce, Vice Chmn.; Hastings, Myrick, Dreier
Minority (D 2): Frost, RMM; Moakley

SCIENCE   2320 Rayburn
www.house.gov/science   202-225-6371

Majority (R 25): Sensenbrenner (WI), Chmn.; Boehlert (NY), Smith (TX), Morella (MD), Weldon (PA), Rohrabacher (CA), Barton (TX), Calvert (CA), Smith (MI), Bartlett (MD), Ehlers (MI), Vice Chmn.; Weldon (FL), Gutknecht (MN), Ewing (IL), Cannon (UT), Brady (TX), Cook (UT), Nethercutt (WA), Lucas (OK), Green (WI), Kuykendall (CA), Miller (CA), Biggert (IL), Sanford (SC), Metcalf (WA)
Minority (D 23): Brown (CA), RMM; Hall (TX), Gordon (TN), Costello (IL), Barcia (MI), Johnson (TX), Woolsey (CA), Rivers (MI), Lofgren (CA), Doyle (PA), Jackson Lee (TX), Stabenow (MI), Etheridge (NC), Lampson (TX), Larson (CT), Udall (CO), Wu (OR), Weiner (NY), Capuano (MA), Baird (WA), Hoeffel (PA), Moore (KS)

SUBCOMMITTEES

BASIC RESEARCH

Majority (R 8): Smith (MI), Chmn.; Boehlert, Smith (TX), Morella, Gutknecht, Ewing, Lucas, Biggert, Vice Chmn.
Minority (D 6): Johnson, RMM; Etheridge, Woolsey, Larson, Rivers, Doyle

ENERGY & ENVIRONMENT

Majority (R 9): Calvert, Chmn.; Weldon, Barton, Rohrabacher, Ehlers, Weldon, Miller, Vice Chmn.; Biggert, Metcalf
Minority (D 7): Costello, RMM; Doyle, Hall, Barcia, Johnson, Lofgren

HOUSE COMMITTEES 1809

SPACE & AERONAUTICS

Majority (R 15): Rohrabacher, Chmn.; Smith, Barton, Calvert, Bartlett, Ehlers, Weldon, Vice Chmn.; Cannon, Brady, Cook, Nethercutt, Lucas, Green, Kuykendall, Sanford

Minority (D 13): Gordon, RMM; Hall, Lofgren, Jackson Lee, Lampson, Stabenow, Etheridge, Larson, Udall, Wu, Weiner

TECHNOLOGY

Majority (R 11): Morella, Chmn.; Weldon, Bartlett, Gutknecht, Vice Chmn.; Ewing, Cannon, Brady, Cook, Green, Kuykendall, Miller

Minority (D 9): Barcia, RMM; Rivers, Stabenow, Udall, Wu, Weiner, Capuano, Gordon

SMALL BUSINESS
www.house.gov/smbiz

2361 Rayburn
202-225-5821

Majority (R 19): Talent (MO), Chmn.; Combest (TX), Hefley (CO), Manzullo (IL), Bartlett (MD), LoBiondo (NJ), Kelly (NY), Chabot (OH), English (PA), McIntosh (IN), Hill (MT), Pitts (PA), Forbes (NY), Sweeney (NY), Toomey (PA), DeMint (SC), Pease (IN), Thune (SD), Bono (CA)

Minority (D 17): Velazquez (NY), RMM; Millender-McDonald (CA), Davis (IL), McCarthy (NY), Pascrell (NJ), Hinojosa (TX), Christian-Christensen (VI), Brady (PA), Udall (NM), Moore (KS), Tubbs Jones (OH), Gonzalez (TX), Phelps (IL), Napolitano (CA), Baird (WA), Udall (CO), Berkley (NV)

SUBCOMMITTEES

EMPOWERMENT

Majority (R 5): Pitts, Chmn.; English, DeMint, Vice Chmn.; LoBiondo, Pease
Minority (D 5): Millender-McDonald, RMM; Moore, Tubbs Jones, Udall

GOVERNMENT PROGRAMS & OVERSIGHT

Majority (R 5): Bartlett, Chmn.; Bono, Vice Chmn.; Forbes, Toomey, Hill
Minority (D 4): Davis, RMM; Hinojosa, Gonzalez

REGULATORY REFORM & PAPERWORK REDUCTION

Majority (R 5): Kelly, Chmn.; McIntosh, Combest, Sweeney, Thune, Vice Chmn.
Minority (D 4): Pascrell, RMM; Brady, Moore

RURAL ENTERPRISE, BUSINESS OPPORTUNITIES & SPECIAL SMALL BUSINESS PROBLEMS

Majority (R 5): LoBiondo, Chmn.; Hill, Vice Chmn.; DeMint, Thune, Sweeney
Minority (D 4): Christian-Christensen, RMM; Phelps, Udall, Baird

TAX, FINANCE & EXPORTS

Majority (R 5): Manzullo, Chmn.; Chabot, English, Forbes, Toomey
Minority (D 4): McCarthy, RMM; Hinojosa, Gonzalez, Napolitano

STANDARDS OF OFFICIAL CONDUCT
www.house.gov/ethics

HT-2 The Capitol
202-225-7103

Majority (R 5): Smith (TX), Chmn.; Hefley (CO), Knollenberg (MI), Camp (MI), Portman (OH)
Minority (D 5): Berman (CA), RMM; Sabo (MN), Pastor (AZ), Fattah (PA), Lofgren (CA)

NO SUBCOMMITTEES

TRANSPORTATION & INFRASTRUCTURE
www.house.gov/transportation

2165 Rayburn
202-225-9446

Majority (R 41): Shuster (PA), Chmn.; Young (AK), Petri (WI), Boehlert (NY), Bateman (VA), Coble (NC), Duncan (TN), Ewing (IL), Gilchrest (MD), Horn (CA), Franks (NJ), Mica (FL), Quinn (NY), Fowler (FL), Ehlers (MI), Bachus (AL), LaTourette (OH), Kelly (NY), LaHood (IL), Baker (LA), Bass (NH), Ney (OH), Metcalf (WA), Pease (IN), Hutchinson (AR), Cook (UT), Cooksey (LA), Thune (SD), LoBiondo (NJ), Moran (KS), Doolittle (CA), Terry (NE), Sherwood (PA), Miller (CA), Sweeney (NY), DeMint (SC), Bereuter (NE), Kuykendall (CA), Simpson (ID), Isakson (GA), Vitter (LA)

Minority (D 34): Oberstar (MN), RMM; Rahall (WV), Borski (PA), Lipinski (IL), Wise (WV), Traficant (OH), DeFazio (OR), Clement (TN), Costello (IL), Norton (DC), Nadler (NY), Danner (MO), Menendez (NJ), Brown (FL), Barcia (MI), Filner (CA), Johnson (TX), Mascara (PA), Taylor (MS), Millender-McDonald (CA), Cummings (MD), Blumenauer (OR), Sandlin (TX), Tauscher (CA), Pascrell (NJ), Boswell (IA), McGovern (MA), Holden (PA), Lampson (TX), Baldacci (ME), Berry (AR), Shows (MS), Baird (WA), Berkley (NV)

SUBCOMMITTEES

AVIATION

Majority (R 27): Duncan, Chmn.; Sweeney, Vice Chmn.; Young, Petri, Ewing, Mica, Quinn, Ehlers, Bachus, LaHood, Bass, Metcalf, Pease, Hutchinson, Cook, Cooksey, Thune, LoBiondo, Moran, Doolittle, Sherwood, Miller, DeMint, Kuykendall, Simpson, Isakson

Minority (D 21): Lipinski, RMM; Costello, Brown, Johnson, Millender-McDonald, Cummings, Boswell, Baldacci, Berry, Norton, Menendez, Tauscher, McGovern, Lampson, Rahall, Traficant, DeFazio, Danner, Filner, Sandlin, Holden

COAST GUARD & MARITIME TRANSPORTATION

Majority (R 4): Gilchrest, Chmn.; LoBiondo, Vice Chmn.; Young, Coble
Minority (D 3): DeFazio, RMM; Taylor, Baird

ECONOMIC DEVELOPMENT, PUBLIC BUILDINGS, HAZARDOUS MATERIALS & PIPELINE TRANSPORTATION

Majority (R 5): Franks, Chmn.; Cooksey, Vice Chmn.; Ewing, LaTourette
Minority (D 3): Wise, RMM; Norton, Shows

GROUND TRANSPORTATION

Majority (R 27): Petri, Chmn.; Franks, Vice Chmn.; Boehlert, Bateman, Coble, Duncan, Horn, Mica, Quinn, Fowler, Bachus, LaTourette, Kelly, LaHood, Baker, Bass, Ney, Metcalf, Pease, Cook, Thune, Moran, Terry, Miller, Sweeney, DeMint, Bereuter

Minority (D 21): Rahall, RMM; Clement, Nadler, Danner, Barcia, Filner, Mascara, Sandlin, Pascrell, Holden, Shows, Berkley, Borski, Lipinski, Wise, Brown, Johnson, Millender-McDonald, Cummings, Blumenauer, Berry

OVERSIGHT, INVESTIGATIONS & EMERGENCY MANAGEMENT

Majority (R 4): Fowler, Chmn.; Terry, Vice Chmn.; Doolittle, Isakson
Minority (D 3): Traficant, RMM; Nadler, Berkley

WATER RESOURCES & ENVIRONMENT

Majority (R 19): Boehlert, Chmn.; Sherwood, Vice Chmn.; Young, Bateman, Gilchrest, Horn, Franks, Quinn, Ehlers, LaTourette, Kelly, Baker, Ney, Hutchinson, LoBiondo, Doolittle, Bereuter, Kuykendall, Simpson

Minority (D 15): Borski, RMM; Taylor, Blumenauer, Baird, Clement, Costello, Menendez, Barcia, Mascara, Tauscher, Pascrell, Boswell, McGovern, Lampson, Baldacci

VETERANS' AFFAIRS
www.house.gov/va

335 Cannon
202-225-3527

Majority (R 17): Stump (AZ), Chmn.; Smith (NJ), Vice Chmn.; Bilirakis (FL), Spence (SC), Everett (AL), Buyer (IN), Quinn (NY), Stearns (FL), Moran (KS), Hayworth (AZ), Chenoweth (ID), LaHood (IL), Hansen (UT), McKeon (CA), Gibbons (NV), Simpson (ID), Baker (LA)

Minority (D 14): Evans (IL), RMM; Filner (CA), Gutierrez (IL), Brown (FL), Doyle (PA), Peterson (MN), Carson (IN), Reyes (TX), Snyder (AR), Rodriguez (TX), Shows (MS), Berkley (NV), Hill (IN), Udall (NM)

SUBCOMMITTEES

BENEFITS

Majority (R 5): Quinn, Chmn.; Hayworth, Vice Chmn.; LaHood, Hansen, Gibbons
Minority (D 4): Filner, RMM; Reyes, Berkley

HEALTH

Majority (R 9): Stearns, Chmn.; Smith, Vice Chmn.; Bilirakis, Moran, Chenoweth, McKeon, Simpson
Minority (D 7): Gutierrez, RMM; Doyle, Peterson, Carson, Snyder, Rodriguez, Shows

OVERSIGHT & INVESTIGATIONS

Majority (R 4): Everett, Chmn.; Stump, Spence, Buyer
Minority (D 3): Brown, RMM; Hill

WAYS & MEANS
www.house.gov/ways-means

1102 Longworth
202-225-3625

Majority (R 23): Archer (TX), Chmn.; Crane (IL), Thomas (CA), Shaw (FL), Johnson (CT), Houghton (NY), Herger (CA), McCrery (LA), Camp (MI), Ramstad (MN), Nussle (IA), Johnson (TX), Dunn (WA), Collins (GA), Portman (OH), English (PA), Watkins (OK), Hayworth (AZ), Weller (IL), Hulshof (MO), McInnis (CO), Lewis (KY), Foley (FL)

Minority (D 16): Rangel (NY), RMM; Stark (CA), Matsui (CA), Coyne (PA), Levin (MI), Cardin (MD), McDermott (WA), Kleczka (WI), Lewis (GA), Neal (MA), McNulty (NY), Jefferson (LA), Tanner (TN), Becerra (CA), Thurman (FL), Doggett (TX)

SUBCOMMITTEES

HEALTH

Majority (R 8): Thomas, Chmn.; Johnson, McCrery, Crane, Johnson, Camp, Ramstad, English
Minority (D 5): Stark, RMM; Kleczka, Lewis, McDermott, Thurman

HUMAN RESOURCES

Majority (R 8): Johnson, Chmn.; English, Watkins, Lewis, Foley, McInnis, McCrery, Camp
Minority (D 5): Cardin, RMM; Stark, Matsui, Coyne, Jefferson

OVERSIGHT

Majority (R 8): Houghton, Chmn.; Portman, Dunn, Watkins, Weller, Hulshof, Hayworth, McInnis
Minority (D 5): Coyne, RMM; McNulty, McDermott, Lewis, Neal

SOCIAL SECURITY

Majority (R 8): Shaw, Chmn.; Johnson, Collins, Portman, Hayworth, Weller, Hulshof, McCrery
Minority (D 5): Matsui, RMM; Levin, Tanner, Doggett, Cardin

TRADE
Majority (R 9): Crane, Chmn.; Thomas, Shaw, Houghton, Camp, Ramstad, Dunn, Herger, Nussle
Minority (D 6): Levin, RMM; Rangel, Neal, McNulty, Jefferson, Becerra

JOINT COMMITTEES

JOINT COMMITTEE ON PRINTING

1309 Longworth
202-225-8281

House (5): Thomas (CA), Boehner (OH), Ney (OH), Hoyer (MD), Fattah (PA)
Senate (5): McConnell (KY), Cochran (MS), Nickles (OK), Feinstein (CA), Inouye (HI)

JOINT COMMITTEE ON TAXATION
www.house.gov/jct

1015 Longworth
202-225-3621

House (5): Archer (TX), Chmn.; Crane (IL), Thomas (CA), Rangel (NY), Stark (CA)
Senate (5): Roth (DE), Vice Chmn.; Chafee (RI), Grassley (IA), Moynihan (NY), Baucus (MT)

JOINT COMMITTEE ON THE LIBRARY OF CONGRESS

S-128 The Capitol
202-224-8921

House (6): Thomas (CA), Vice Chmn.; Boehner (OH), Ehlers (MI), Hoyer (MD), Davis (FL)
Senate (5): Stevens (AK), Chmn.; McConnell (KY), Cochran (MS), Moynihan (NY), Dodd (CT)

JOINT ECONOMIC COMMITTEE
www.house.gov/jec

G-01 Dirksen
202-224-5171

House (10): Saxton (NJ), Vice Chmn.; Sanford (SC), Doolittle (CA), Campbell (CA), Pitts (PA), Ryan (WI), Stark (CA), Hinchey (NY), Maloney (NY), Watt (NC)
Senate (10): Mack (FL), Chmn.; Roth (DE), Bennett (UT), Grams (MN), Brownback (KS), Sessions (AL), Bingaman (NM), Sarbanes (MD), Kennedy (MA), Robb (VA)

CAMPAIGN FINANCE

All data are derived from candidate and party reports as well as other official studies available from the Federal Election Commission (FEC) located at 999 E Street, N.W., Washington, DC 20463. Telephone (202) 694-1100 (or toll-free 800-424-9530). Individuals listed in italics were losing candidates in that election.

U.S. SENATE

The following charts show the top 15 1998 Senate candidates in terms of the highest total net receipts, net expenditures, political action committee (PAC) contributions, individual contributions, cash on hand and debts owed during the 1997–98 election cycle.

1998 Senate: Top Raisers

1.	Peter G. Fitzgerald (R-IL)	$17,898,456
2.	*Alfonse M. D'Amato (R-NY)*	17,760,311
3.	Charles E. Schumer (D-NY)	16,825,671
4.	*Darrell Edward Issa (R-CA)*	13,582,767
5.	Barbara Boxer (D-CA)	12,837,493
6.	*Matthew K. Fong (R-CA)*	10,818,417
7.	*Lauch Faircloth (R-NC)*	9,370,462
8.	John Edwards (D-NC)	8,420,983
9.	*Carol Moseley-Braun (D-IL)*	7,222,013
10.	*Charles Owen (D-KY)*	6,823,911
11.	Arlen Specter (R-PA)	6,264,387
12.	George Voinovich (R-OH)	6,098,620
13.	Paul Coverdell (R-GA)	5,944,031
14.	Christopher S. Bond (R-MO)	5,848,137
15.	Thomas A. Daschle (D-SD)	5,614,668

1998 Senate: Top Spenders

1.	*Alfonse M. D'Amato (R-NY)*	$24,195,287
2.	Peter G. Fitzgerald (R-IL)	17,678,198
3.	Charles E. Schumer (D-NY)	16,671,877
4.	Barbara Boxer (D-CA)	13,738,578
5.	*Darrell Edward Issa (R-CA)*	13,549,659
6.	*Matthew K. Fong (R-CA)*	10,764,892
7.	*Lauch Faircloth (R-NC)*	9,367,671
8.	John Edwards (D-NC)	8,331,382
9.	*Carol Moseley-Braun (D-IL)*	7,200,895
10.	Paul Coverdell(R-GA)	6,936,745
11.	*Charles Owen (D-KY)*	6,823,911
12.	George Voinovich (R-OH)	6,756,712
13.	Christopher S. Bond (R-MO)	6,229,649
14.	Patty Murray (D-WA)	5,600,592
15.	*Michael J. Coles (D-GA)*	5,275,419

1998 Senate: Top PAC Recipients

1.	*Lauch Faircloth (R-NC)*	$2,047,711
2.	Christopher S. Bond (R-MO)	2,026,360
3.	*Alfonse M. D'Amato (R-NY)*	1,928,372
4.	Thomas A. Daschle (D-SD)	1,849,856
5.	Paul Coverdell (R-GA)	1,693,422
6.	John Breaux (D-LA)	1,570,133
7.	*Matthew K. Fong (R-CA)*	1,481,702
8.	Barbara Boxer (D-CA)	1,457,179
9.	Arlen Specter (R-PA)	1,423,963
10.	Charles Grassley (R-IA)	1,406,561
11.	Jim Bunning (R-KY)	1,357,474
12.	*John Ensign (R-NV)*	1,289,495
13.	George Voinovich (R-OH)	1,260,740
14.	Richard Shelby (R-AL)	1,243,751
15.	Don Nickles (R-OK)	1,241,238

1998 Senate: Top Individual Contributions

1.	*Alfonse M. D'Amato (R-NY)*	$14,511,521
2.	Charles E. Schumer (D-NY)	10,410,255
3.	Barbara Boxer (D-CA)	10,052,111
4.	*Matthew K. Fong (R-CA)*	9,153,332
5.	*Carol Moseley-Braun (D-IL)*	5,649,261
6.	*Linda Smith (R-WA)*	5,153,918
7.	*Lauch Faircloth (R-NC)*	5,087,388
8.	Arlen Specter (R-PA)	4,501,241
9.	George Voinovich (R-OH)	4,242,059
10.	Patty Murray (D-WA)	4,113,966
11.	Paul Coverdell (R-GA)	3,984,212
12.	*Mark W. Neumann (R-WI)*	3,676,865
13.	Christopher S. Bond (R-MO)	3,639,858
14.	Russell Feingold (D-WI)	3,611,000
15.	Thomas A. Daschle (D-SD)	3,435,189

1998 Senate: Top Cash-on-Hand

1. Richard C. Shelby (R-AL) — $4,559,425
2. Arlen Specter (R-PA) — 2,661,115
3. John McCain (R-AZ) — 2,017,327
4. Evan Bayh (D-IN) — 1,839,609
5. Charles Grassley (R-IA) — 1,589,560
6. John Breaux (D-LA) — 1,544,260
7. Thomas A. Daschle (D-SD) — 1,049,992
8. Don Nickles (R-OK) — 945,916
9. Christopher J. Dodd (D-CT) — 916,658
10. Russell Feingold (D-WI) — 723,722
11. Judd Gregg (R-NH) — 645,825
12. George Voinovich (R-OH) — 638,703
13. Frank Murkowski (R-AK) — 617,168
14. Barbara A. Mikulski (D-MD) — 455,624
15. Ron Wyden (D-OR) — 446,227

1998 Senate: Top Debts Owed

1. Peter G. Fitzgerald (R-IL) — $11,769,121
2. *Darrell Edward Issa (R-CA)* — 9,469,564
3. John R. Edwards (D-NC) — 6,150,000
4. *Michael J. Coles (D-GA)* — 3,644,700
5. *Lauch Faircloth (R-NC)* — 1,700,000
6. Robert Bennett (R-UT) — 1,673,000
7. *Christopher T. Bayley (R-WA)* — 1,320,000
8. *Geraldine A. Ferraro (D-NY)* — 932,287
9. *Alfonse M. D'Amato (R-NY)* — 638,734
10. *Stephen Lewis Henry (D-KY)* — 537,333
11. *Matthew K. Fong (R-CA)* — 396,688
12. Charles E. Schumer (D-NY) — 337,115
13. *David Grier Martin Jr. (D-NC)* — 315,000
14. *John A. McMullen (R-VT)* — 277,000
15. *Edgar Scott Ferguson (D-AR)* — 262,500

U.S. HOUSE OF REPRESENTATIVES

The following charts show the top 25 1998 House candidates in terms of the highest total net receipts, net expenditures, political action committee (PAC) contributions, individual contributions, cash on hand and debts owed during the 1997-98 election cycle.

1998 House: Top Raisers

1. Newt Gingrich (R-GA)[†] — $6,831,829
2. *Phillip Maloof (D-NM)* — 5,475,052
3. *Christopher Gabrieli (D-MA)* — 5,289,033
4. Richard A. Gephardt (D-MO) — 4,978,701
5. *Robert Dornan (R-CA)* — 3,765,673
6. Loretta Sanchez (D-CA) — 3,372,283
7. *John T. O'Connor (D-MA)* — 3,356,471
8. *Phillip Maloof (D-NM)** — 2,649,637
9. Doug Ose (R-CA) — 2,257,397
10. Ron Paul (R-TX) — 2,098,777
11. Dick Armey (R-TX) — 2,061,340
12. Bob Riley (R-AL) — 1,986,617
13. *Jon D. Fox (R-PA)* — 1,935,548
14. J. D. Hayworth (R-AZ) — 1,926,630
15. Don Sherwood (R-PA) — 1,924,165
16. *Jay Robert Pritzker (D-IL)* — 1,902,224
17. *Robert D. Greenlee (R-CO)* — 1,879,012
18. Anne Northup (R-KY) — 1,856,830
19. Rick A. Lazio (R-NY) — 1,813,900
20. John R. Kasich (R-OH) — 1,801,762
21. Nancy L. Johnson (R-CT) — 1,791,391
22. Martin Frost (D-TX) — 1,775,137
23. Lois Capps (D-CA) — 1,734,261
24. *Noach Dear (D-NY)* — 1,729,016
25. Brian Baird (D-WA) — 1,671,658

Money raised for June 1998 special election.

1998 House: Top Spenders

1. Newt Gingrich (R-GA)[†] — $7,578,716
2. *Phillip Maloof (D-NM)* — 5,379,249
3. *Christophe Gabrieli (D-MA)* — 5,283,156
4. *Robert Dornan (R-CA)* — 3,864,920
5. *John T. O'Connor (D-MA)* — 3,347,128
6. Richard A. Gephardt (D-MO) — 3,340,959
7. *Phillip Maloof (D-NM)** — 2,641,394
8. Loretta Sanchez (D-CA) — 2,535,243
9. Doug Ose (R-CA) — 2,373,133
10. Dick Armey (R-TX) — 2,125,437
11. Ron Paul (R-TX) — 1,987,457
12. Bob Riley (R-AL) — 1,985,984
13. Don Sherwood (R-PA) — 1,921,129
14. *Jon D. Fox (R-PA)* — 1,921,005
15. *Jay Robert Pritzker (D-IL)* — 1,904,070
16. *Robert D. Greenlee (R-CO)* — 1,879,887
17. J. D. Hayworth (R-AZ) — 1,839,460
18. Martin Frost (D-TX) — 1,790,674
19. Anne Northup (R-KY) — 1,772,613
20. Nancy L. Johnson (R-CT) — 1,768,957
21. *Rick White (R-WA)* — 1,655,274
22. Sander M. Levin (D-MI) — 1,638,901
23. Steve Chabot (R-OH) — 1,636,614
24. Robert Aderholt (R-AL) — 1,605,092
25. Lois Capps (D-CA) — 1,602,656

Money spent for June 1998 special election.

1998 House: Top PAC Recipients

1.	Richard A. Gephardt (D-MO)	$1,168,446
2.	Nancy L. Johnson (R-CT)	1,025,016
3.	Martin Frost (D-TX)	987,673
4.	Newt Gingrich (R-GA)[†]	986,268
5.	*Rick White (R-WA)*	887,971
6.	Tom Delay (R-TX)	863,808
7.	John D. Dingell (D-MI)	855,891
8.	David E. Bonior (D-MI)	850,526
9.	Charles W. Stenholm (D-TX)	834,748
10.	J. D. Hayworth (R-AZ)	806,540
11.	Tom Bliley (R-VA)	735,307
12.	Bob Livingston (R-LA)[‡]	723,813
13.	Bart Gordon (D-TN)	717,745
14.	Bill Thomas (R-CA)	717,066
15.	Rick A. Lazio (R-NY)	712,907
16.	Richard H. Baker (R-LA)	696,222
17.	Steny H. Hoyer (D-MD)	695,600
18.	*Jon D. Fox (R-PA)*	688,512
19.	Anne Northup (R-KY)	686,286
20.	Gerald C. (Jerry) Weller (R-IL)	680,013
21.	Sander M. Levin (D-MI)	669,158
22.	Joe Barton (R-TX)	666,325
23.	James E. Rogan (R-CA)	660,110
24.	Loretta Sanchez (D-CA)	656,138
25.	Robert Aderholt (R-AL)	656,043

1998 House: Top Individual Contributions

1.	Newt Gingrich (R-GA)[†]	$5,780,780
2.	*Robert Dornan (R-CA)*	3,354,397
3.	Richard A. Gephardt (D-MO)	2,651,714
4.	Loretta Sanchez, (D-CA)	2,635,562
5.	Ron Paul (R-TX)	1,944,158
6.	*Noach Dear (D-NY)*	1,694,930
7.	Dick Armey (R-TX)	1,424,748
8.	Bob Barr (R-GA)	1,273,106
9.	John R. Kasich (R-OH)	1,219,910
10.	Jan Schakowsky (D-IL)	1,214,630
11.	Tammy Baldwin (D-WI)	1,208,850
12.	*Randall A. Terry (RTL-NY)*	1,203,761
13.	Tom Udall (D-NM)	1,155,964
14.	J. C. Watts Jr (R-OK)	1,142,878
15.	Brian Baird (D-WA)	1,138,040
16.	*Jon D. Fox (R-PA)*	1,129,810
17.	Nita M. Lowey (D-NY)	1,099,104
18.	Anne Northup (R-KY)	1,091,001
19.	J. D. Hayworth (R-AZ)	1,039,072
20.	Lois Capps (D-CA)	1,035,684
21.	David Wu (D-OR)	1,022,578
22.	*Molly H. Bordonaro (R-OR)*	1,001,924
23.	Tom Campbell (R-CA)	971,601
24.	Rick A. Lazio (R-NY)	963,648
25.	Jim Greenwood (R-PA)	962,718

1998 House: Top Cash-on-Hand

1.	David Dreier, (R-CA)	$2,643,806
2.	Rick A. Lazio (R-NY)	1,853,834
3.	Richard A. Gephardt (D-MO)	1,838,821
4.	Peter R. Deutsch (D-FL)	1,545,673
5.	John R. Kasich (R-OH)	1,436,537
6.	Lloyd Doggett (D-TX)	1,337,173
7.	William P. (Bill) Luther (D-MN)	1,250,774
8.	Robert Menendez (D-NJ)	1,207,328
9.	Nick J. Rahall II (D-WV)	1,112,575
10.	Martin T. Meehan (D-MA)	1,063,975
11.	Jerry Lewis (R-CA)	1,032,214
12.	Ileana Ros-Lehtinen (R-FL)	1,009,067
13.	Dan Burton (R-IN)	955,310
14.	David McIntosh (R-IN)	908,231
15.	Cliff Stearns (R-FL)	857,116
16.	Loretta Sanchez (D-CA)	848,201
17.	Nita M. Lowey (D-NY)	842,645
18.	Scott McInnis (R-CO)	839,324
19.	W. J. (Billy) Tauzin (R-LA)	829,775
20.	Michael N. Castle (R-DE)	823,642
21.	Jim Saxton (R-NJ)	803,453
22.	Bill McCollum (R-FL)	775,585
23.	Sherrod Brown (D-OH)	769,015
24.	Joe Barton (R-TX)	766,490
25.	Edward J. Markey, (D-MA)	754,053

1998 House: Debts Owed

1.	*Christopher Gabrieli (D-MA)*	$5,090,000
2.	*John T. O'Connor (D-MA)*	3,210,528
3.	Chris Cannon (R-UT)	1,662,530
4.	Doug Ose (R-CA)	1,458,666
5.	*Jonathan H. Newman (R-PA)*	1,197,371
6.	*Jay R. Pritzker (D-IL)*	1,193,000
7.	*Robert D. Greenlee (R-CO)*	1,164,100
8.	*Randy D. Hoffman (R-CA)*	811,328
9.	*Carl J. Mayer (I-NJ)*	802,589
10.	*Christopher Collins (R-NY)*	791,550
11.	Max Sandlin (D-TX)	738,025
12.	Brad Sherman (D-CA)	717,610
13.	R. Terry Everett (R-AL)	649,373
14.	Norman Sisisky (D-VA)	639,183
15.	Don Sherwood (R-PA)	578,373
16.	*Paul M. Barby (D-OK)*	577,000
17.	*Robert T. (Bob) Wilson (D-AL)*	539,233
18.	*Jay C. Kim (R-CA)*	519,639
19.	*Lydia Spottswood (D-WI)*	497,700
20.	*David Mcsweeney (R-IL)*	489,420
21.	Rodney Frelinghuysen (R-NJ)	441,079
22.	*Ralph Waite (D-CA)*	409,239
23.	*Ralph Waite (D-CA)**	404,048
24.	*Charles H. Dettman (R-WI)*	401,844
25.	*Robert S. Guzman (R-CA)*	396,973

Debts incurred for June 1998 special election.
[†]*Retired January 1999.*
[‡]*Retired February 1999.*

DEMOGRAPHICS

Population. All population figures are from the Bureau of the Census, U.S. Department of Commerce, Washington, D.C. 20233, 301-457-3030. Figures for 1970, 1980 and 1990 are final Census Bureau population counts as of April 1 of those years. Figures for 1998 are estimates as of July 1. (The District of Columbia is included as a state in all the following charts.)

Voting Age Population. This figure indicates all persons at least 18 years of age who are eligible to vote, including the Armed Forces, aliens and institutional members.

Chart I shows the total U.S. population and total U.S. voting age population for 1998, 1990, 1980 and 1970.

Chart I

Total U.S. Population		Total U.S. Voting Age Population	
July 1, 1998 (est.)	270,298,524	Nov. 1, 1998 (est.)	200,927,000
April 1, 1990	248,709,873	April 1, 1990	185,105,441
April 1, 1980	226,545,805	April 1, 1980	163,997,000
April 1, 1970	203,302,031	April 1, 1970	135,290,000

Chart II indicates the range of highest and lowest state population changes in percentage growth and absolute change for 1980–90.

Chart II

1980–90 Population Change
(National Avg.: up 9.8%)

State	Highest		State	Lowest	
Nevada	50.1%	401,340	West Virginia	−8.0%	−156,167
Alaska	36.9	148,192	District of Columbia	−4.9	−31,433
Arizona	34.8	947,013	Iowa	−4.7	−137,053
Florida	32.7	3,191,602	Wyoming	−3.4	−15,969
California	25.7	6,092,119	North Dakota	−2.1	−13,917

Chart III shows the ten highest and the ten lowest state populations.

Chart III

1998 (Est.) U.S. Population: Ten Highest and Lowest States

State	Highest	State	Lowest
California	32,666,550	Wyoming	480,907
Texas	19,759,614	District of Columbia	523,124
New York	18,175,301	Vermont	590,883
Florida	14,915,980	Alaska	614,010
Illinois	12,045,326	North Dakota	638,244
Pennsylvania	12,001,451	South Dakota	738,171
Ohio	11,209,493	Delaware	743,603
Michigan	9,817,242	Montana	880,453
New Jersey	8,115,011	Rhode Island	988,480
Georgia	7,642,207	New Hampshire	1,185,048

Chart IV lists the states with the highest and lowest median age.

Chart IV

1990 Median Age
(National Avg.: 34.6 years)

State	Highest	State	Lowest
West Virginia	37.7 years	Utah	26.8 years
Florida	37.6	Alaska	31.9
Pennsylvania	36.9	Texas	32.6
Maine	36.6	California	32.7
Montana	36.5	Mississippi	32.9

Chart V illustrates the states with the highest and lowest average percentages of married-couple family households.

Chart V

1990 Married-Couple Family Households
(National Avg.: 55.9%)

State	Highest	State	Lowest
Utah	64.8%	District of Columbia	25.3%
Idaho	62.2	New York	49.9
Wyoming, New Hampshire	59.7	Nevada	51.4
Arkansas, Iowa, Kentucky	59.2	Massachusetts	52.1
North Dakota	59.1	California	52.7

Chart VI illustrates the states with the highest and lowest average percentages of population over 65 years of age.

Chart VI

1990 Population Over 65 Years of Age
(National Avg.: 12.8%)

State	Highest	State	Lowest
Florida	18.5%	Alaska	5.2%
Pennsylvania	15.9	Utah	8.8
Rhode Island	15.8	Georgia	9.9
West Virginia, Iowa	15.2	Colorado	10.1
North Dakota	14.5	Texas	10.2

Chart VII illustrates the states with the highest and lowest average percentages of Owner Occupied Housing.

Chart VII

1990 Owner Occupied Housing
(National Avg.: 65.4%)

State	Highest	State	Lowest
West Virginia	74.1%	District of Columbia	38.9%
Minnesota	71.8	New York	52.2
Mississippi	71.5	Hawaii	53.9
Michigan	71.0	Nevada	54.8
Pennsylvania	70.6	California	55.6

Chart VIII illustrates the states with the highest and lowest median house value.

Chart VIII

1990 Median House Value
(National Avg.: $84,209)

State	Highest	State	Lowest
Hawaii	$245,300	South Dakota	$45,200
California	195,500	Mississippi	45,600
Connecticut	177,800	Iowa	45,900
Massachusetts	162,800	Arkansas	46,300
New Jersey	162,300	West Virginia	47,900

Chart IX illustrates the states with the highest and lowest median monthly rent.

Chart IX

1990 Median Monthly Rent
(National Avg.: $350)

State	Highest	State	Lowest
Hawaii	$599	Mississippi	$215
California	561	West Virginia	221
New Jersey	521	Alabama	229
Connecticut	510	Arkansas	230
Massachusetts	506	South Dakota	242

Chart X shows the states with the highest and lowest per capita income.

Chart X

1990 Per Capita Income
(National Avg.: $18,685)

State	Highest	State	Lowest
Connecticut	$25,358	Mississippi	$12,735
New Jersey	24,968	West Virginia	13,747
District of Columbia	23,491	Utah	14,083
Massachusetts	22,642	Arkansas	14,218
New York	21,975	New Mexico	14,228
Maryland	21,864	Louisiana	14,391
Alaska	21,761	Alabama	14,826
California	20,795	Kentucky	14,929
New Hampshire	20,789	South Carolina	15,099
Illinois	20,303	Montana	15,110

Chart XI shows the states with the highest and lowest average unemployment rates for 1998. These figures are from the U.S. Department of Labor, Bureau of Labor Statistics, and were compiled independently of the Census Bureau figures.

Chart XI

1998 Average Unemployment Rate
(National Avg: 4.5%)

Highest		Lowest	
District of Columbia	8.8%	Minnesota	2.5%
West Virginia	6.6	Nebraska	2.7
Hawaii	6.2	Iowa	2.8
New Mexico	6.2	New Hampshire	2.9
California	5.9	South Dakota	2.9
Alaska	5.8	Virginia	2.9
Louisiana	5.7	Indiana	3.1
Oregon	5.6	North Dakota	3.2
Montana	5.6	Massachusetts	3.3
New York	5.6	Connecticut	3.4
		Wisconsin	3.4
		Vermont	3.4

1820   DEMOGRAPHICS

Ethnic Breakdown. The racial and ethnic breakdowns illustrate the potential ethnic vote as opposed to the overall population. The concepts of race and ethnicity as defined by the Census Bureau reflect self-identification and not clear-cut biological definitions.

Chart XII lists voting age and total state population figures for the fourteen states with black populations above the national average of 12.1% in 1990. Black ethnic classification refers to those persons who indicated their race as Black on the Census questionnaire.

Chart XII

1990 Black Population: Total State Population

State	% of voting age pop.	% of total state pop.	State	% of voting age pop.	% of total state pop.
District of Columbia	62.4%	65.8%	North Carolina	20.1%	22.0%
Mississippi	31.6	35.6	Virginia	17.6	18.8
Louisiana	27.9	30.8	Delaware	15.3	16.9
South Carolina	26.9	29.8	Tennessee	14.4	16.0
Georgia	24.6	27.0	New York	14.7	15.9
Alabama	22.7	25.3	Arkansas	13.7	15.9
Maryland	23.5	24.9	Illinois	13.4	14.8

Chart XIII illustrates the voting age and total population figures for the fourteen states with American Indian concentrations above the national average of 0.8% in 1990. The American Indian classification includes persons who classified themselves as American Indian, Eskimo, or Aleut.

Chart XIII

1990 American Indian: Total State and Voting Age Population

State	% of voting age pop.	% of total state pop.	State	% of voting age pop.	% of total state pop.
Alaska	13.5%	15.6%	Wyoming	1.8%	2.1%
New Mexico	7.5	8.9	Washington	1.4	1.7
Oklahoma	6.9	8.0	Nevada	1.5	1.6
South Dakota	5.4	7.3	Utah	1.2	1.4
Montana	4.8	6.0	Oregon	1.2	1.4
Arizona	4.4	5.6	Idaho	1.2	1.4
North Dakota	3.1	4.1	North Carolina	1.1	1.2

Chart XIV illustrates the voting age and total state population figures for the eight states with Asian concentrations at or above the national average of 2.9% in 1990. The Asian classification includes persons who classified themselves as Asian or Pacific Islander.

Chart XIV

1990 Asian Origin: Total State and Voting Age Population

State	% of voting age pop.	% of total state pop.	State	% of voting age pop.	% of total state pop.
Hawaii	61.3%	61.8%	Alaska	3.6%	3.6%
California	9.2	9.6	New Jersey	3.2	3.5
Washington	4.1	4.3	Nevada	3.1	3.2
New York	3.8	3.9	Maryland	2.8	2.9

Chart XV illustrates voting age and total state population figures for the eight states with Hispanic origin concentrations above the national average of 9.0% in 1990. The Hispanic origin classification includes three specific categories—Mexican, Puerto Rican and Cuban—as well as those who indicated that they were of other Spanish or Hispanic origin (origin can be viewed as ancestry, nationality group, lineage or country of birth of the person or the person's parents or ancestors prior to their arrival in the United States). Persons of Hispanic origin may be of any race.

Chart XV

1990 Hispanic Origin: Total State and Voting Age Population

State	% of voting age pop.	% of total state pop.	State	% of voting age pop.	% of total state pop.
New Mexico	33.0%	38.2%	Colorado	11.2%	12.9%
California	22.5	25.8	New York	11.2	12.3
Texas	22.4	25.5	Florida	11.7	12.2
Arizona	15.8	18.8	Nevada	9.1	10.4

INDEX

The 50 States and the names of all the Governors, Senators and Representatives appear in boldface type. The number of the page that includes Members' corresponding biographical, voting and campaign finance information also appears in bold.

1836   INDEX

1852 INDEX